CASES AND MATERIALS

FOOD AND DRUG LAW

THIRD EDITION

by

PETER BARTON HUTT
Senior Counsel, Covington & Burling LLP, Washington, D.C.
Lecturer on Food and Drug Law, Harvard Law School

RICHARD A. MERRILL
Daniel Caplin Professor of Law, University of Virginia
Senior Of Counsel, Covington & Burling LLP

LEWIS A. GROSSMAN
Professor of Law
Washington College of Law, American University

FOUNDATION PRESS

2007

THOMSON
WEST

© 1980, 1991 FOUNDATION PRESS
© 2007 By FOUNDATION PRESS
     395 Hudson Street
     New York, NY 10014
     Phone Toll Free 1–877–888–1330
     Fax (212) 367–6799
     foundation–press.com
Printed in the United States of America
ISBN 978–1–58778–068–4

TEXT IS PRINTED ON 10% POST CONSUMER RECYCLED PAPER

Dedicated to
Louise Fraser Hutt
Elizabeth D. Merrill
and
Lisa M. Rabin

And to the thousands of dedicated women and men who have worked at the
Food and Drug Administration since its creation

*

PREFACE

Food and Drug Law is the oldest field of consumer protection legislation in the United States. City, county, and state food and drug laws originated in colonial times. The Federal Food and Drugs Act of 1906, and the Federal Meat Inspection Act of the same year, were Congress's first major efforts to protect consumers on a national level. Lawyers have thus been involved in advising and representing private clients and government officials on federal food and drug law matters for more than a century. The 1906 Act predated the creation of the Federal Trade Commission by nearly a decade and the establishment of other agencies with a consumer protection role—such as the Environmental Protection Agency and the Consumer Product Safety Commission—by a full half-century.

Notwithstanding this long history, food and drug law did not command the attention of a large number of lawyers until the 1970s. The still relatively small size of the community of private practitioners specializing in this area can be attributed to the concentration of the practice in Washington, D.C., and to the modest resources of the Food and Drug Administration. Prior to the 1980s, food and drug law was taught in only a few law schools and generated little serious scholarship. The inattention of legal academia was, we suspect, a function not only of the limited number of practitioners, but also of professors' failure to recognize the richness of the issues presented by FDA regulation.

Food and drug law deals primarily with government protection of public health and safety with regard to the marketing of food, drugs, cosmetics, medical devices, and biological products. The scope of these commercial markets is impressive. On any day, few Americans escape exposure to drugs, devices, or cosmetics, and all of us require food. By a rough estimate, 25 cents of every consumer dollar is spent for products that fall within the categories of products regulated by FDA. The personal and economic importance of these products alone justifies serious study of food and drug regulation. Moreover, the subject merits, and now receives, the attention of students and scholars for additional reasons.

First, an examination of FDA's continuing efforts to come to grips with its regulatory responsibilities provides a mini-history of American administrative law. Many judicial decisions that are accepted as part of the corpus of administrative law have involved FDA. The agency has devised numerous major innovations in administrative procedure, and in the agency's experience one can discern the intimate interrelationship between administrative procedure and regulatory substance.

Second, over the past five decades the regulation of food, drugs, and related products has presented some of the most vivid illustrations of the tense interplay between law and science. FDA has been at the forefront of government efforts to identify, evaluate, and control the risks of potentially harmful substances. This responsibility has forced it to determine the reliability of animal test results, explore the limits of techniques for chemical analysis, evaluate modern biostatistical methods for estimating human risk, and confront the dangers of both new pathogens and lifesaving drugs. FDA has also been involved in some of the most controversial issues of preventive medicine, in every significant nutrition trend, and in the development of advanced medical technology. And as government has assumed an increasing share of the cost of medical care, FDA has become a quality control expert for public health care programs.

Third, because of the growing complexity of its responsibilities and the potential clash among competing public objectives, FDA has been forced to develop a wide variety of novel administrative procedures for resolving controversial law-science issues. It was the first federal agency to experiment with a "science court" model for decisionmaking. It has successfully exploited the scientific expertise of advisors from the academic community—and in the process grappled with the constraints of federal conflict-of-interest legislation. And FDA has employed various types of trade-off analysis, ranging across the spectrum of cost-effectiveness, cost-benefit, and risk-benefit formulations.

Finally, and not unimportantly, we find the story of federal efforts to regulate the marketing of food and drugs fascinating as history. The experience of any regulatory agency undoubtedly mirrors strong political and economic currents, but few other agencies regulate products or activities that play so intimate a role in the daily lives of citizens. The visibility of food and drugs, the concern of individuals for their health, and the expectations citizens have for those officials charged with protecting them have made FDA a resonant amplifier of American social history.

No single volume can capture all of these facets of FDA regulation. We do not pretend to have compiled either a text on administrative law or a history of the American market for consumer goods. This is a coursebook on food and drug law, intended primarily for law students. The materials included, the organization used, and the issues dealt with reflect this focus. In addition, we hope that the book will prove useful in teaching students and professionals in other fields, such as nutrition, medicine, and public administration.

We also believe that the book will be helpful to practitioners of food and drug law. In most instances, the statutory provisions referred to and the cases reproduced reflect legal requirements prevailing in 2006. The changes in this field, however, are so rapid that practitioners should not rely on the book to the exclusion of other, more current sources. Our organization of materials and bibliographic information should help frame the pertinent questions and identify many of the relevant sources, but no careful lawyer should fail to consult standard legal publications that can provide the most recent legal and policy developments.

Changes from the Second Edition

The revised substance of this third edition reflects the dramatic changes in law, science, and the regulated industries that have occurred since the release of the second edition. The legal developments are manifold. Congress has made numerous significant modifications to the Federal Food, Drug, and Cosmetic Act. Important amendatory statutes include the Prescription Drug User Fee Act of 1992 (reauthorized in 1997 and 2002), the Animal Medicinal Drug Use Clarification Act of 1994, the Dietary Supplement Health and Education Act of 1994, the Food and Drug Administration Modernization Act of 1997, and the Bioterrorism Act of 2002—to name just a few. FDA has also taken important steps to implement various statutory regimes that were still in their youth at the time of the second edition, most notably the Medical Device Amendments of 1976 and the Nutrition Labeling and Education Act of 1990.

The courts have also influenced the field of food and drug law in important ways during the past decade. Judges have held, in a variety of contexts, that the First Amendment limits FDA's authority to regulate labeling and advertising. Shortly before the completion of this book, a panel of the D.C. Circuit found that terminally ill patients have a substantive due process right to purchase unapproved drugs—a development that, if upheld, promises to revolutionize pharmaceutical regulation. And in an historic legal battle resolved by the United States Supreme Court, FDA attempted but failed to assert regulatory control over tobacco products.

Since the early 1990s, FDA has faced new challenges to health and safety, ranging from mad cow disease to antibiotic resistance to terrorism. The agency has also confronted a variety of new technologies, including bioengineering, gene therapy, stem cell research, and pharmacogenomics. The problem of escalating health care costs has increasingly shaped debate and policy surrounding various aspects of drug regulation, including importation of unapproved drugs, direct-to-consumer advertising, and generic drug market entry. Various dietary fads have come and gone, the dietary supplement and organic food industries have exploded, and claims have proliferated on food packages. The advent of user fees has increased FDA's resources in the drug and medical device areas and also effectively compelled the agency to accept more rigorous performance goals with regard to the review of these products. The new edition addresses all of these developments.

Finally, we have made several changes in the structure of the book for pedagogical reasons. The text contains two entirely new chapters, one addressing the definitions of product categories regulated by FDA and the other considering the relationship between federal regulation and civil liability. The chapter on drugs has been reorganized to present a comprehensive, ground-level portrait of the new drug development process. We have eliminated the separate chapter on biotechnology and instead dealt with these issues, which now suffuse all food and drug regulation, at relevant points throughout the text. Finally, to reflect the growing importance of international trade in FDA-regulated products, we have presented the import-export materials in a separate chapter.

Selection of Materials

Various considerations have influenced our selection of primary materials, which consist mainly of five types: judicial opinions; documents published in the Federal Register, including notices, proposed regulations, final regulations, and other final orders; articles from law reviews and other academic and professional journals; congressional sources, including reports of the General Accounting Office (GAO) and the Office of Technology Assessment (OTA); and articles from the popular press. Obviously, economy of space is one important criterion in the choice of materials. A major problem for the editors of a coursebook in any regulatory field is the sheer volume of printed pages available. Demands that administrative agencies explicitly explain their decisions, and that they analyze the environmental, economic, and other effects of their actions, have generated challenges for scholars and practitioners alike. Not only are there more words to evaluate, but it is increasingly difficult to capture the reality of the regulatory process in a single book. Authentic course materials in food and drug law would consist of the contents of a four-drawer file cabinet or a shelf of looseleaf binders.

Judicial opinions, too often maligned as teaching materials, provide one way of responding to this problem. The opinions of conscientious judges engaged in reviewing administrative action are often the best summaries of the labyrinthine proceedings and complex factual and legal issues underlying regulators' decisions. In many opinions concerning FDA, the court must condense the entire history of a regulatory question to determine how the case should be decided. Furthermore, because most manufacturers of food and drugs strive to avoid adverse publicity, judicial decisions elicit a high degree of voluntary compliance. Still another reason to feature judicial decisions is that from the earliest days of federal regulation until the 1970s, most substantive food and drug law was reflected in court rulings. FDA relied mainly on judicial enforcement of loosely defined statutory standards to make new law.

Starting about 1970, FDA's regulatory approach changed. Faced with increasingly complex substantive issues and a growing number of firms making regulated products, FDA turned toward rulemaking as the principal technique for defining legal requirements. The agency attempted to resolve most of the major issues it confronted through administrative, rather than court, action. The Federal Register thus became the primary vehicle for official resolution of food and drug problems. Accordingly, we have included numerous excerpts from this source, now the principal "library" of both regulators and private practitioners. More recently, FDA has increasingly relied on the promulgation of informal guidance, particularly with respect to pharmaceutical products. We have thus also included examples of this substitute for notice-and-comment rulemaking.

Our use of congressional materials cannot be explained in terms of economy, for committee reports and hearing records tend to be prolix and unfocused. But they can provide useful summaries of problems and, more important, they reflect legislative perceptions that significantly influence FDA officials, and thus the firms whose products the agency regulates. This influence, if anything, increased during the 1970s. One seeking to understand the focus and intensity of FDA regulation during this period must appreciate the impact of Congress's consideration of new legislation and its oversight of the enforcement of existing law.

FDA began to attract broad public interest and scrutiny in the 1960s, largely as the result of increasing congressional explorations of food and drug issues. Today it is almost impossible to read any newspaper without encountering an article that deals with an FDA matter. Although this book cannot convey the true extent and impact of press coverage, we have included such materials to remind students that research in food and drug law extends far beyond traditional legal sources.

Throughout the book, in addition to primary original sources, we have included extensive Comments and Notes. These have multiple objectives. Our Comments contain substantive information and analysis we have chosen to relate in our own voices. Our Notes have diverse goals. First, they attempt to bring the reader up to date on a subject and supply historical background missing from primary sources. Second, they raise questions about the policies reflected in agency decisions or judicial rulings. Third, they provide bibliographic assistance to the reader who wishes to pursue a subject in depth. Our listings of secondary sources, though often lengthy, are only illustrative. Our listings of Federal Register documents are intended to permit the reader to trace the development of regulatory policy from its inception.

The full text of the Federal Food, Drug, and Cosmetic Act of 1938, 21 U.S.C. 301 et seq. (the Act or FD&C Act) and other statutes referred to in the book are reproduced separately in a paperback supplement. The FD&C Act is also available online on the FDA website.

Citation Format

Though our citation forms generally follow the current, 18th edition of *The Blue Book: A Uniform System of Citation*, we have adopted some distinctive practices of our own, sometimes to save space that would be wasted if we endlessly repeated the prescribed form.

Our statutory references are generally not to the United States Code, but rather to sections of the FD&C Act of 1938, as amended, or to sections of other laws as enacted, such as the Public Health Service Act. We have not, however, substituted FD&C Act references for U.S. Code citations in original sources, such as judicial opinions. Determining the proper U.S. Code citation for most sections of the FD&C Act is straightforward. By dropping the middle digit and inserting a "3" in front of the two digits remaining, one can usually derive the U.S. Code section. For example, section 402 of the Act is codified as 21 U.S.C. 342.

We have again used short forms for agencies and organizations that are mentioned frequently. For example, "OTA" is our routine description for the Office of Technology Assessment of Congress, "GAO" is our colloquial, as well as official, reference to the Government Accounting Office, and "NAS" usually substitutes for the National Academy of Sciences.

In quoted original sources, we have routinely omitted citations and footnotes without any notation in the text. Footnotes included retain their original numbering. We have also omitted, again without notation, most organizational designations, such as headings and paragraph numbers. All omissions of text are disclosed by ellipses appearing at the beginning, in the middle, or at the end of sentences or paragraphs, with the exception of omissions of paragraphs from the beginning of an excerpted source, which are not always indicated in this manner. A three-dot ellipsis at the end of a paragraph denotes the omission of the balance of that paragraph and perhaps of additional paragraphs. A stand-alone four-dot ellipsis denotes the omission of at least one full paragraph. Errors in spelling or grammar in original Federal Register documents are frequently corrected without notation because they are routinely corrected by the Office of the Federal Register in subsequent issues or when published in the Code of Federal Regulations. Errors in other original sources are denoted by [sic], in the conventional fashion.

Internet Sources and Citations

FDA operates one of the most comprehensive websites in the federal government. Most information available from FDA under the Freedom of Information Act is now routinely posted on its website. We refer throughout this book simply to the "FDA website." It can be accessed at www.fda.gov.

The Electronic Book

Since 1994, Mr. Hutt has taught a full course on Food and Drug Law each year during Winter Term at Harvard Law School. *See* Peter Barton Hutt, *Food and Drug Law: Journal of an Academic Adventure*, 46 J. OF LEGAL EDUC. 1 (1996). Each student prepares a course paper, and most combine it with Harvard's third-year written work requirement. Virtually all of these papers—more than 700—have been compiled in an "Electronic Book of Harvard Law School Student Papers on Food and Drug Law," which can be accessed online at http://www.law.harvard.edu/faculty/hutt. Throughout the coursebook, we refer to this resource as the "Electronic Book."

Disclosure of Interests

Two of us have served as Chief Counsel to the Food and Drug Administration. Mr. Hutt occupied that position from 1971 to 1975, when he was succeeded by Mr. Merrill, who served until 1977. With the exception of his period of government service, Mr. Hutt has been engaged in the private practice of food and drug law with Covington & Burling since 1962. Professor Merrill was an associate at Covington & Burling from 1965 to 1969. He rejoined the firm as Senior Of Counsel in 1991. Professor Grossman was an associate at Covington & Burling from 1993 to 1997 and has been Of Counsel to the firm since 2004.

Appreciation

Two Covington & Burling paralegals, Marilynn Whitney, who assisted with all three editions, and Katherine MacRae, who worked on the edition prior to this one, retrieved and helped organize materials that cannot be found in conventional libraries. The founding librarian of the Covington & Burling Food and Drug Law Library, Meg Gleason, and her successors, Dorothy Donahoe and Jennifer Korpacz, have facilitated our work by maintaining the country's most comprehensive collection of food and drug legal materials. Portions of the manuscript of all three editions were prepared by Beth Vida at Covington & Burling, and portions of the current manuscript were prepared by Deborah Shong at the University of Virginia School of Law.

We owe a major debt to the libraries at the University of Virginia and to many students at Virginia and at American University's Washington College of Law. From Charlottesville, these include Michael Beverly, Jim Czaban, Catherine DeRover, Mary Dunbar, Charles Durant, Jeff Gansey, Josh Grubaugh, Christine Kim, Tony Lim, John Palmer, Gregg Macy, John Palmer, and Karen Rosenthal. At American University, invaluable research assistance was provided by Derek Howard, Jaime Tohave, Amy Swift, Kasey Podzius, Megan Michiels, Erin Overturf, and Claire Boisen. Special thanks are due to American University law student Gwendolyn McKee, who, over the past two years, has spent countless hours skillfully researching, critiquing, and editing this edition.

Eugene Lambert of Covington & Burling helped us prepare the chapter on food and drugs for animals. Dean Claudio Grossman of the Washington College of Law has generously supported Professor Grossman's work on this project.

PETER BARTON HUTT
Washington, D.C.

RICHARD A. MERRILL
Charlottesville, Virginia

LEWIS A. GROSSMAN
Washington, D.C.

*

ACKNOWLEDGEMENTS

We acknowledge the courtesy of the following publishers, journals, law reviews and authors who have permitted us to reprint excerpts from their publications:

1.   Food Drug Cosmetic Law Journal, Food and Drug Law Journal, and the Food and Drug Law Institute, which gave us blanket permission to reproduce or quote from articles appearing in the Journal, and to whom we owe a special debt of thanks.

2.   "The Choice Between Formal and Informal Modes of Administrative Regulation" by Todd Rakoff, published in Administrative Law Review, Volume 52, No. 1, Winter 2000. © 2000 by the American Bar Association. Reprinted with permission.

3.   American Academy of Dermatology: Bergfeld et al., *Safety of Ingredients Used in Cosmetics*, 52 J. Am. Acad. of Dermatology 125 (2005).

4.   Associated Press: Brasher, *When is a Catfish not a Catfish? When it Comes from Vietnam and Cuts into U.S. Sales, Hill Says*, Washington Post, December 27, 2001, at A 21.

5.   BMJ Books: Hutt, *The Regulation of Drug Products by the United States Food and Drug Administration*, in John P. Griffin & John O'Grady, the Textbook of Pharmaceutical Medicine (5th edition 2006).

6.   BioCentury Publications: Usdin, *Diminishing Returns*, BioCentury February 13, 2006, at A1.

7.   Biotechnology Law Report: Glidden, *The Generic Industry Going Biologic*, 20 Biotechnology Law Report 172 (2001).

8.   A. Larry Branen: Hutt, *Regulation of Food Additives in the United States*, in Food Additives (2d ed. 2001).

9.   Bulletin of the Association of Food & Drug Officials of U.S.: Austern, *Federalism in Consumer Protection: Conflict or Coordination?*, No. 4 (1965).

10. Business Lawyer: Goodrich, *The Coming Struggle Over Vitamin-Mineral Pills*, 20 Bus.Law. 145 (1964).

11. Columbia Law Review: Merrill and Collier, *"Like Mother Used to Make": An Analysis of FDA Food Standards of Identity*, 74 Colum.L.Rev. 561 (1974).

12. Marcel Dekker: Hutt, *A History of Government Regulation of Adulteration and Misbranding of Cosmetics,* in Norman F. Estrin & James M. Akerson, eds., Cosmetic Regulation in a Competitive Environment (2000).

13. Peter Elsner & Howard I. Maibach: Hutt, *The Legal Distinction in the United States Between a Cosmetic and a Drug*, in Cosmeceuticals (2000).

14. Environmental Lawyer: Carpenter, *Impact of the Food Quality Protection Act of 1996*, 3 Environmental Lawyer 479 (1997).

15. FDC Reports: *FDA Examples of Acceptable and Unacceptable Dietary Supplement Claims*, 8 The Tan Sheet, No. 3, at 12-13 (January 17, 2000).

16. Florida Law Review: Noah, *Assisted Reproductive Technologies and the Pitfalls of Unregulated Biomedical Innovation, 55 Fla.L.Rev. 603 (2003).*

17. Food Technology: Hutt, *Regulating the Misbranding of Food*, 43 Food Technology 288 (Sept., 1989).

18. George Washington Law Review: Merrill, *Risk-Benefit Decisionmaking by the Food and Drug Administration,* 45 Geo.Washington L.Rev. 994 (1977).

19. Ethan Gilsdorf: *Backstory: Is It Really Just A Bunch Of Fluff?*, Christian Sci. Monitor, July 12, 2006, at 20.

20. Malcolm Gladwell: *High Prices*, The New Yorker, October 25, 2004, at 86.

21. Harvard Law Review: Merrill & Watts, *Agency Rules with the Force of Law: The Original Convention*, 116 Harv.L.Rev. 467 (2002).

22. Health Scan: Hutt, *Landmark Pharmaceutical Law Enacted*, 1 Health Scan, No. 3, p. 11 (1984).

23. Houston Journal of Health Law & Policy: Merrill, *Human Tissues and Reproductive Cloning: New Technologies Challenge FDA*, 3 Houston J. of Health Law & Policy 1 (2002).

24. Institute of Medicine: Financing Vaccines in the 21st Century: Assuring Access and Availability (2003); Food and Drug Administration Advisory Committees (1992).

25. International Association for Food Protection: Todd, *Preliminary Estimates of Costs of Foodbourne Disease in the United States*, 52 J. Food Protection 595 (1989).

26. Journal of Health Care Law & Policy: Greenberger, *The 800 Pound Gorilla Sleeps: The Federal Government's Lackadaisical Liability and Compensation Policies in the Context of Pre-Event Vaccine Immunization Programs*, 8 J. of Health Care Law & Policy 7 (2005).

27. Journal of Law and Economics: Temin, *The Origin of Compulsory Drug Prescriptions*, 22 J. of Law & Econ. 91 (1979).

28. Journal of the Association of Analytical Chemists: Hutt, *The Importance of Analytical Chemistry to Food and Drug Regulation*, 68 J.A. of Analytical Chemists 147 (1985).

29. Journal of the Association of Food and Drug Officials: Hutt, *Regulation of the Practice of Medicine Under the Pure Food and Drug Laws*, 33 J.A. of Food and Drug Officials 3 (1969); Miller, *The Saga of Chicken Little and Rambo*, 51 J.A. of Food and Drug Officials 196 (1987).

30. Kellogg Nutrition Foundation: Hutt, *Health Claims For Foods – An American Perspective*, Symposium 1986.

31. Law & Contemporary Problems: Cavers, *The Food, Drug and Cosmetic Act of 1938: Its Legislative History and Its Substantive Provisions*, 6 Law & Contemp. Probs. 2 (1939).

32. Legal Times of Washington: Hutt, *Laetrile Decision Ignores Constitutional Questions*, July 2, 1979.

33. National Academy Press: Committee on the Biological and Biomedical Applications of Stem Cell Research, Stem Cells and the Future of Regenerative Medicine (2001); Olson, Biotechnology: An Industry Comes of Age (1986).

34. New England Journal of Medicine: Acheson & Fiore, *Preventing Foodborne Disease -- What Clinicians Can Do*, 350 New Eng. J. Med. 437 (2004); Haffner, *Adopting Orphan Drugs – Two Dozen Years of Treating Rare Diseases,* 354 New England J. of Medicine 445 (2006); Sloan, et al., *The Fragility of the U.S. Vaccine Supply*, 351 New England J. of Medicine 23 (2004); Steinbrook, *Financial Conflicts of Interest and the Food and Drug Administration's Advisory Committees*, 353 New England J. of Medicine 126 (2005).

35. New York Sun: Gottlieb, *The Price of Too Much Caution*, December 22, 2004, at 8.

36. New York Times: Kolata, *An Angry Response to Actions on AIDS Spurs F.D.A. Shift*, June 26, 1988.

37. Nutrition Policy Issues: Hutt & Sloan, FDA *Regulation of Vegetable Protein Products,* Nutrition Policy Issues, No. 3 (Jan. 1979).

38. Owen, Products Liability Law (2000).

39. Pharmacogenomics Journal: Lesko & Woodcock, *Pharmacogenomic-Guided Drug Development: Regulatory Perspective*, 2 The Pharmacogenomics Journal 20 (2002).

40. Quarterly Bulletin of the Association of Food and Drug Officials: Hutt, *Public Information and Public Participation in the Food and Drug Administration,* 36 Quarterly Bulletin of the Ass'n of Food and Drug Officials 212 (1972).

41. Mary K. Schmidl & Theodore P. Labuza: Hutt, *U.S. Government Regulation of Food with Claims for Special Physiological Value*, in Essentials of Functional Foods (2000).

42. Science, copyright by the American Association for the Advancement of Science: Editorial, *Food Additives and Hyperactivity*, 199 Science 516 (1978); Mortimer, *Immunization Against Infectious Disease*, 200 Science 902 (1978); Wade, *Division of Biologics Standards: In the Matter of J. Anthony Morris*, 175 Science 861 (1972); Wade, *Division of Biologics Standards: Scientific Managements Questioned*, 175 Science 966 (1972); Wade, *Division of Biologics Standards: The Boat That Never Rocked*, 175 Science 1225 (1972); Wade, *DBS: Agency Contravenes Its Own Regulations*, 176 Science 34 (1972); Wade, *Ice Cream: Dairymen Imperiled by FDA's Recipe*, 197 Science 844 (1977).

43. Semet, Toward National Uniformity for FDA-Regulated Products (2000).

44. Stanford Environmental Law Journal: Smart, *All the Stars in the Heavens Were in the Right Places: The Passage of the Food Quality Protection Act of 1996*, 17 Stanford Environmental L.J. 273 (1998).

45. Taylor & Francis Group LLC: Hutt, *A Brief History of FDA Regulation Relating to the Nutrient Content of Food*, in Ralph Shapiro, ed., *Nutrition Labeling Handbook* (1995).

46. U.S. News & World Report: Healy, *Food with a Purpose*, February 13, 2006, at 60, and *What is a "Safe" Drug?*, December 13, 2004, at 37.

47. Virginia Law Review: Merrill, *The Architecture of Government Regulation of Medical Products*, 82 Va.L.Rev. 753 (1996.)

48. Wall Street Journal: Burton, *Risk v. Benefit*: *FDA Weighs Antipsychotic*, October 14, 1996, at B1; Davis P. Hamilton, *Dose of Reality -- Biotech's Dismal Bottom Line: More than $40 Billion Losses*, May 20, 2004, at A1.

49. Washington Post: Carlson, *Hey, Don't Say They Didn't Warn You ...*, September 1, 2006; Ross, *Remember That Vichyssoise?*, June 25, 1972.

50. Yale Journal on Regulation: Noah, *The Imperative to Warn: Disentangling the "Right to Know" from the "Need to Know" about Consumer Product Hazards*, 11 Yale J. on Regul. 293 (1994).

*

SUMMARY OF CONTENTS

TABLE OF CONTENTS

TABLE OF CASES

Principal cases are in bold type. Non-principal cases are in roman type. References are to Pages.

FOOD AND DRUG LAW

*

CHAPTER I

HISTORICAL BACKGROUND

A. EARLY REGULATION OF FOOD AND DRUGS

Peter Barton Hutt, *Government Regulation of the Integrity of the Food Supply*

4 ANNUAL REVIEW OF NUTRITION 1 (1984).

For centuries, government has had an essential role in assuring the integrity of the food supply. The focus of the regulatory function has, of course, evolved over the years. It originated essentially as a means to protect against fraud in the marketplace. Very quickly, it expanded into a mechanism for preventing the sale of unsafe food. As the science of nutrition has developed, it has assumed the role of protecting the nutritional integrity of the food supply as well....

Ancient Times....

The first great botanical treatise on plants as a source of food and medicine, the *Enquiry Into Plants* written by Theophrastus (370–285 BC), reported on the use of artificial preservatives and flavors in the food supply even at that early date. Theophrastus noted that "even uncompounded substances have certain odors which men endeavor to assist by artificial means even as they assist nature in producing palatable tastes." He reported that items of commerce, such as balsam gum, were mixed with adulterants for economic reasons. The treatise *On Agriculture* by Cato (234–149 BC) recommended the addition to wine of boiled-down must, salt, marble dust, and resin, and included a method "to determine whether wine has been watered."

Pliny the Elder (23–79 AD) found widespread adulteration throughout the food supply. He described, for example, the adulteration of bread with chalk, vegetable meals, and even cattle fodder. He pointed out that pepper was commonly adulterated with juniper berries. Indeed, his *Natural History* is replete with so many references to adulteration of the natural food and drug supply that he observed: "So many poisons are employed to force wine to suit our taste—and we are surprised that it is not wholesome!" Pliny, describing "the remedies that are in the control of a man's will," stated that "the greatest aid to health is moderation in food." He urged the value of a kitchen garden for "harmless" market supplies. Galen (131–201 AD), a renowned Roman physician who followed the philosophical tradition of the School of Hippocrates, similarly warned against the adulteration of common food products, such as pepper....

1

The Roman civil law reflected the concern expressed by these early writers about preserving the integrity of the food supply. Fraud in the sale of merchandise not only gave rise to a private right of action, but also constituted the offense of *stellionatus*, which included the adulteration of food: "And, where anyone has substituted some article for another; or has put aside goods which he was obliged to deliver, or has spoiled them, he is also liable for this offense." Although *stellionatus* was technically not a crime, it was comparable to a civil offense under present law, subject to government prosecution, and resulted in such punishment as condemnation to the mines or temporary exile.

The English Experience, 1200–1875

... At the end of the Dark Ages ... concern about the food supply once again emerged. Nowhere is this more evident than in the experience reflected in the laws of England at that time.

Initial governmental concern came in the form of regulating the price of bread, and perhaps other staple food products as well. It did not take long for the English government to realize that the price of food could be regulated only in relation to the quality of that food. Accordingly, the early English regulatory statutes prohibited the adulteration of any staple food that was also subject to price controls.

These regulatory enactments, called assizes, were codified by Parliament in 1266. The 1266 statutes prohibited the sale of any "corrupted wine" or of any meat, fish, bread, or water that was "not wholesome for Man's body" or that was kept so long "that it loseth its natural wholesomeness." These laws, with periodic amendments, continued in effect throughout England until 1844. They were supplemented, from time to time, with additional statutes directed at other food commodities that became a source of commerce, such as butter, cheese, and spices.

In addition to the statutes enacted by Parliament, local cities enacted their own ordinances to prevent food adulteration. The judicially-created common law, reflecting the principles underlying the statutes and ordinances, created both a civil cause of action for damages for any aggrieved party, and a criminal offense as well. Numerous examples of early enforcement actions against the purveyors of adulterated food may be found in the records of the City of London.

Finally, the trade guilds ... also performed a major regulatory function. These guilds covered every important food category, including the bakers, butchers, cooks, grocers, fruiters, poulters, and salters. Using their power to search all premises and to seize all unwholesome products, the guilds exercised a relatively strong regulatory power in policing the marketing of food to the public.

The Development of Chemistry and the Accum Treatise

As the Renaissance emerged out of the Middle Ages, a few pioneers in the newly developing discipline of "chymistry" broke away from the philosophic mysticism of alchemy and initiated modern scientific inquiry. While earlier analyses of food adulteration depended almost completely upon taste and sight, the new science of chemistry, led particularly by Boyle, slowly began to develop chemical methods of analysis....

By the beginning of the 19th century ... chemical analysis had advanced to the point where at least qualitative methods had become available for detecting many common food adulterants. In 1820, a German-born chemist, Frederick Accum, working in England, published his landmark *Treatise on Adulterations of Food and Culinary Poisons*.... Accum undertook to describe both the numerous kinds of adulteration practiced at that time and the various methods available to detect them. His treatise was an immediate and worldwide success.... The treatise spawned a generation of books on food adulteration in England, the United States, and Europe. Ultimately, it resulted in the modern era of food regulatory statutes.

... [T]he English Parliament enacted statutes in 1860, 1872, and 1875, replacing the assizes that had been repealed in 1844, to assure strong regulatory authority to protect the integrity of the food supply.

As would be expected, these English statutes reflect only the state of scientific, medical, and nutritional knowledge at that time. There is no specific mention in those statutes of nutrition. Instead, they broadly prohibited any form of food adulteration, thus assuring that food would reach the marketplace and the consumer in its natural and most nutritious state. Indeed, the prohibitions against adulteration contained in these statutes encompass the same prohibitions contained in our most modern food regulatory statutes, and were in fact the models for the 1906 and 1938 legislation enacted in the United States.

NOTE

For additional discussion of early food and drug laws, *see, e.g.*, Frederick A. Filby, A HISTORY OF FOOD ADULTERATION AND ANALYSIS (1934); F. Leslie Hart, *A History of the Adulteration of Food Before 1906*, 7 FOOD DRUG COSM. L.J. 5 (1952); Peter Barton Hutt, *Criminal Prosecution for Adulteration and Misbranding of Food at Common Law*, 15 FOOD DRUG COSM. L.J. 382 (1960); Wallace F. Janssen, *America's First Food and Drug Laws*, 30 FOOD DRUG COSM. L.J. 665 (1975); Peter Barton Hutt and Peter Barton Hutt II, *A History of Government Regulation of Adulteration and Misbranding of Food*, 39 FOOD DRUG COSM. L.J. 2 (1984). The origins of Jewish regulation of food are discussed in Daniel J. Silber, *The Jewish Dietary Laws and Their Foundation* (1994), and Wendy Ann Wilkenfeld, *Food Regulation in Biblical Law* (1998), in Chapter I(A) of the Electronic Book.

B.   STATUTORY AND INSTITUTIONAL HISTORY

1.   THE FOOD AND DRUG ADMINISTRATION

The history of food and drug regulation in the United States is chronicled both in congressional enactments and in the establishment and growth of an institution, the Food and Drug Administration (FDA).

Peter Barton Hutt, *A Historical Introduction*

45 FOOD DRUG COSMETIC LAW JOURNAL 17 (1990).

In his 1837 annual report, Patent Commissioner Henry L. Ellsworth recommended a national agency for the encouragement of agriculture. Congress responded in 1839 by an appropriation of $1000 to the Commissioner of Patents for "the collection of agricultural statistics, and for other agricultural purposes." From then on, the Patent Office collected and reported agricultural statistics, sponsored or conducted chemical investigations on agricultural matters, monitored agricultural developments, and reported on all of these in its annual reports. Beginning in 1849, a separate report was made by the Patent Commissioner to Congress on agricultural matters. An Agricultural Division was established in the Patent Office and a chemical laboratory was created in that Division.

In 1846, Professor Lewis C. Beck, M.D., of Rutgers College and Albany Medical College, published the first American treatise on adulteration of food and drugs. Two years later, at the request of Patent Commissioner Edmund Burke, Congress appropriated $1000 for the Commissioner of Patents to conduct chemical analyses of "vegetable substances produced and used for the food of man and animals in the United States." Commissioner Burke recruited Dr. Beck to do this work for the Patent Office. Dr. Beck submitted his *Report on the Breadstuffs of the United States* in 1849 and a second report in 1850.

When the United States Department of Agriculture (USDA) was created by Congress in 1862, it included authorization to employ chemists. The Agricultural Division of the Patent Office, including its chemical laboratory, was transferred to the new department and the USDA occupied the office space in the basement of the Patent Office that previously had belonged to that Division. The first Commissioner of Agriculture, Isaac Newton, immediately established the Chemical Division from the former Patent Office chemical laboratory, which became the Division of Chemistry in 1890; the Bureau of Chemistry in 1901; the Food, Drug, and Insecticide Administration in 1927; and the Food and Drug Administration (FDA) in 1930. The FDA was transferred from the USDA to the Federal Security Agency in 1940 and to the Department of Health, Education, and Welfare in 1953, which became the Department of Health and Human Services in 1979. . . .

———

The organization that is now FDA has been a functioning regulatory agency for almost 150 years. Its birth occurred when the Patent Office created a chemical laboratory and hired the first analytical chemist sometime during 1858–1860. It grew in size as the federal government grew, assuming larger responsibilities as private ordering gave way to regulation in many areas and Washington supplanted the states as the primary locus of regulatory activity. The organic statute that FDA administers and enforces, the Federal Food, Drug, and Cosmetic Act (FD&C Act) of 1938, has been amended more than a hundred times. The current version dwarfs the law Congress passed in 1938.

Throughout its history FDA has had essentially the same assignment: to assure that the products it regulates are safe and truthfully labeled. This statement, however, oversimplifies the agency's current responsibilities, which encompass a much larger role in the development, testing, introduction, and marketing of these products. By Washington, D.C., standards, FDA is a venerable institution, whose employees have long memories and a tradition of dedicated, often single-minded public service—in sum, a strong commitment to the job of regulation. As science has advanced, and as the FD&C Act has been amended to transfer the burden of proof from FDA to the regulated industry by requiring premarket approval of products, the agency's activities have changed from court enforcement of clear-cut statutory prohibitions to approval of products based upon an administrative choice among closely balanced alternatives in controlling advanced technologies.

Richard A. Merrill, *The Architecture of Government Regulation of Medical Products*

82 VIRGINIA LAW REVIEW 753 (1996).

... Under the 1906 law, FDA had relatively little influence over the therapeutic claims made for drugs. Its authority was exerted, if at all, after a drug was on the market and evidence had accumulated that it might not work. The 1938 Act gave the agency a gatekeeper role, which permitted officials to examine and sometimes question a drug's clinical utility. The 1962 Amendments completed the law's reversal of the burden of proof. Since the passage of the Amendments, FDA has been responsible for judging, on the basis of evidence that it prescribed and makers supplied, whether new drugs worked. This shift in responsibility transformed the way in which drugs are developed, tested and marketed.

With this shift came a more subtle change in FDA's own view of its consumer protection role. Citizens may complain when local police fail to curtail unlawful or violent activity, but few believe that even the best functioning police force can solve, much less prevent, all crimes. FDA is believed to have a different role, a responsibility to prevent harm before it occurs. The law makes it unlawful, without proof of intent or demonstration of actual injury or deception, to market drugs that the agency has not approved. In some sense, the agency becomes a warrantor of manufacturer compliance with the rules that govern drug development and marketing. This responsibility is implicitly acknowledged in the agency's own publications, is frequently referred to in press accounts of its performance, and historically has permeated the dialogue between the agency and congressional oversight committees. FDA is repeatedly reminded, and often reminds us, that it shares responsibility for any drug that causes harm. Many observers claim that this perception of FDA's role has made agency officials responsible for allowing drugs to reach the market exceptionally, and inappropriately, cautious....

Over FDA's long history of evaluation and approval of drugs and devices the familiar artifacts of law have often been hard to detect. With the notable exception of Congress's decision to require premarket proof of safety and effectiveness for virtually all new drugs and many medical devices, legal rules have not been a dominant determinant of FDA behavior. The FD&C Act provides formal procedures for challenging agency decisions, but these administrative safeguards are almost never invoked. Nor are FDA's decisions—to grant, withhold, or delay approval—commonly challenged in court. Statutory directives do not materially affect the conduct or pace of agency review, nor do they control its evolving requirements for the data product sponsors must submit to gain marketing approval. The FDA product approval system is, in short, remarkably free from conventional legal constraint. . . .

———

Accompanying this change has been the replacement of court enforcement by reliance on regulations, guidance documents, and other less formal mechanisms of communication not explicitly enumerated in the FD&C Act.

This is not a book about FDA as an institution. Our focus is on the requirements of the FD&C Act and related laws and their impact on consumers, medical professionals, and producers and distributors of regulated products. One cannot fully understand contemporary regulation, however, without some appreciation of the history of the agency responsible for the law's administration.

NOTES

1. *Patent Office Origin.* The origin of FDA in the Patent Office is described in John V. Donnelly III, *Genesis: The Birth of the FDA in the Patent Office* (1999), in Chapter I(A) of the Electronic Book.

2. *FDA Annual Reports.* FDA and its predecessor agencies issued formal annual reports from 1862 through 1974. The FDA reports from 1862 through 1906 were published as parts of the USDA annual reports for those years. The FDA annual reports from 1907 through 1974 are reprinted in Food Law Institute, FEDERAL FOOD, DRUG, AND COSMETIC LAW: ADMINISTRATIVE REPORTS 1907–1949 (1951), and in Food and Drug Administration, FOOD AND DRUG ADMINISTRATION ANNUAL REPORTS 1950–1974 (1976). From 1975 through 1995, the agency's activities were chronicled by the FDA Office of Planning and Evaluation in the FDA QUARTERLY ACTIVITIES REPORT. Since 1995 there have been no agency-wide annual reports but some FDA Centers have issued their own reports.

3. *Organizational Growth.* The organizational history of FDA since 1906 is traced in Michael Brannon, *Organizing and Reorganizing FDA*, in Food and Drug Law Institute, SEVENTY-FIFTH ANNIVERSARY COMMEMORATIVE VOLUME OF FOOD AND DRUG LAW 135 (1984).

4. *Historical Sources.* Useful general histories of FDA include GUSTAVUS A. WEBER, THE FOOD, DRUG, AND INSECTICIDE ADMINISTRATION (1928); STEPHEN WILSON, FOOD AND DRUG REGULATION (1942); Peter Barton Hutt, *The Transformation of United States Food and Drug Law*, 60 J. ASS'N FOOD & DRUG OFFICIALS 1 (1996); FDA: A CENTURY OF CONSUMER PROTECTION (Wayne L. Pines, ed., 2006); Philip J. Hilts, PROTECTING AMERICA'S HEALTH: THE FDA, BUSINESS, AND ONE HUNDRED YEARS OF REGULATION (2003). Numerous articles chronicling the agency's history may be found in the FOOD DRUG COSMETIC LAW JOURNAL (now the FOOD AND DRUG LAW JOURNAL), which has been published since 1946. *See, e.g.,* the five-part series by

Fred B. Linton, *Leaders in Food and Drug Law*, 4 FOOD DRUG COSM. L.J. 451 (1949), 5 FOOD DRUG COSM. L.J. 103, 326, 479, 771 (1950); Paul B. Dunbar, *Memories of Early Days of Federal Food and Drug Law Enforcement*, 14 FOOD DRUG COSM. L.J. 87 (1959); Francis E. McKay, *Lawyers of the FDA—Yesterday and Today*, 30 FOOD DRUG COSM. L.J. 621 (1975); James R. Dean, *The FDA at War: Securing the Food that Secured Victory*, 53 FOOD & DRUG L.J. 453 (1998). *See also* THE IMPACT OF THE FOOD AND DRUG ADMINISTRATION ON OUR SOCIETY (Henry Welch & Felix Marti–Ibanez, eds., 1956).

5. *Popular Culture*. For articles on the portrayal of food and drug law in books, movies, and other forms of popular culture, *see* Chapter I(I) of the Electronic Book.

2.   THE EVOLUTION OF FEDERAL FOOD AND DRUG LEGISLATION

A single statute, the 1938 FD&C Act, as amended, provides the basic legal framework controlling the activities of producers of food, drugs, cosmetics, and medical devices. The 1938 Act replaced an earlier law, the Federal Food and Drugs Act of 1906, 34 Stat. 768. FDA has also been delegated responsibility for administering other important regulatory laws applicable to these four categories of products. Thus, FDA's current statutory armamentarium is an ensemble of laws enacted by Congress over a hundred years in more than a hundred statutes.

a.   STATE AND LOCAL LAWS IN THE 19TH CENTURY

Colonial America was an agrarian society. People consumed the food and herbal drugs they produced at home. Even those who lived in small towns kept livestock and maintained their own gardens. As urban centers grew, local food markets were established to serve them. In a classic study published in 1862, T. F. De Voe traced the history of the public markets of the City of New York from the establishment of the West India Company's store in the 1630s through the 1840s. THE MARKET BOOK: A HISTORY OF THE PUBLIC MARKETS OF THE CITY OF NEW YORK (1862). As these markets were established, the City of New York adopted various requirements to regulate them. These requirements largely reflected the English common and statutory law.

Although many of these early laws were aimed at specific commodities or narrow problems, a number were directed more generally at preventing any form of adulteration. As cities grew larger, concern about public health expanded. Lemuel Shattuck's landmark report on public health in 1850 documented the decrease in average life expectancy in America's large urban centers and identified the adulteration of food and drugs as a matter of public health concern. REPORT OF THE SANITARY COMMISSION OF MASSACHUSETTS (1850). Shattuck recommended the establishment of local boards of health which would "endeavor to prevent the sale and use of unwholesome, spurious, and adulterated articles, dangerous to the public health, designed for food, drink, or medicine." *Id.* at 220.

In 1867, De Voe published another study in which he noted the great expansion in public trade and the need for increased regulation to protect both the producer and the consumer:

The producer is often hundreds of miles in one direction, while the consumer may be as many hundred in another, from the *mart* at which the productions were sold and purchased. . . .

A great trade has imperceptibly grown upon us (particularly in New York), which I have sometimes thought, would have been more profitable to both producer and consumer, if proper laws, and practical, honest heads, had been placed over these vast interests, which so much affect the general health and comfort, as well as the pockets of our over-taxed citizens. . . .

THE MARKET ASSISTANT 9 (1867). Following Shattuck's report and this expansion in trade, boards of health were established in cities, counties, and states throughout the country. Congress initially enacted food and drug legislation for the District of Columbia in 1888 and substantially strengthened it in 1898.

b.   THE FEDERAL FOOD AND DRUGS ACT OF 1906

Congress enacted a short-lived statute during the early 1800s to assure a safe and effective supply of smallpox vaccine. 2 Stat. 806 (1813), repealed 3 Stat. 677 (1822). During the nineteenth century, Congress also passed several statutes to regulate foreign commerce in food and drugs. *E.g.*, 9 Stat. 237 (1848) (imported drugs); 22 Stat. 451 (1883) and 29 Stat. 604 (1897) (imported tea); 26 Stat. 414 (1890), 26 Stat. 1089 (1891), 30 Stat. 151, 210 (1897), and 30 Stat. 947, 951 (1899) (imported and exported food). However, no pre-1900 federal law dealt generally with the safety or utility of domestically marketed food and drugs.

At the same time that De Voe was documenting the growth of public food markets, the English and American authors who followed Accum were warning the public about adulteration of food and drugs.

Peter Barton Hutt & Peter Barton Hutt II, *A History of Government Regulation of Adulteration and Misbranding of Food*

39 FOOD DRUG COSMETIC L.J. 2 (1984).

. . . Campaigns were mounted by *Frank Leslie's Illustrated Newspaper*, beginning in 1858 and by the *New York World*, beginning in 1868, to publicize this problem. By 1879, there was a full-fledged public outcry against adulteration of food and drugs in the United States. Dr. E.R. Squibb, in an address to the Medical Society of the State of New York, proposed the enactment of a national statute patterned after the English law of 1875.

In December 1879, the National Board of Trade adopted a resolution establishing a "$1000 Competition for the Draft of a Food Adulteration Act." . . .

In October 1880, the award committee announced the top three submissions, which were printed in full in a special supplement to the December 1880 issue of *The Sanitary Engineer* . . . .

The prize-winning essay was submitted by G.W. Wigner, a public analyst in England. . . .

Only 10 days after Dr. Squibb's January 1879 address to the Medical Society of the State of New York, urging enactment of a national food and drug law, Congressman Wright introduced the first comprehensive federal food legislation in Congress. It was to take 27 years before such a law ultimately would be enacted by Congress as the Pure Food and Drugs Act of 1906.

———

The appeal of uniform national regulation of food and drugs was an important argument in favor of federal legislation. The Director of the Bureau of Chemistry of the New York State Department of Health argued for uniform national regulation of food and drugs in 1903:

> . . . [I]t is very certain that the widely differing statutes relating to our food supply in the different States have worked much mischief, been the cause of much confusion, and seriously embarrassed some useful industries. I think all who have studied the matter will be inclined to admit that uniformity in our food laws is much to be desired. . . .

W. TUCKER, FOOD ADULTERATION: ITS NATURE AND EXTENT, AND HOW TO DEAL WITH IT 21 (1903).

However, because of strong sentiment that food and drug regulation was properly a matter for state and local regulation, federal legislation languished in Congress until 1906. As has often been repeated in the history of food and drug regulation, a tragedy intervened to spur the enactment of the first national statute. The Biologics Act of 1902, 32 Stat. 728, was enacted in response to the distribution in St. Louis of a tetanus-infected diphtheria antitoxin, which resulted in the death of several children. The 1902 law required that biological drugs sold in interstate commerce be produced in licensed establishments. Administration of this statutory scheme was the responsibility of the National Institutes of Health (and its predecessors) before being transferred to FDA in 1972.

The USDA Division of Chemistry played an important role in the investigation of food adulteration that ultimately led to enactment of the Federal Food and Drugs Act of 1906. When Peter Collier became Chief Chemist in 1879, the Division began a major investigation of food and drug adulteration. Collier was succeeded by Dr. Harvey W. Wiley, who served from 1883 to 1912. In 1883, the Division of Chemistry began to publish bulletins containing the results of its investigations. Bulletin 13, issued in 10 parts and 1417 pages from 1887 to 1902, dealt extensively with adulteration of common food products. After the Department of Agriculture was given Cabinet status in 1889, Congress appropriated funds "to enable the Secretary of Agriculture to extend and continue the investigation of the adulteration of food, drugs, and liquors." The appropriations continued through enactment of the 1906 Act and permitted USDA to conduct extensive work in this area.

Perhaps the most dramatic work of the Division of Chemistry involved food preservatives. Congress specifically appropriated funds in 1900 "to investigate the character of proposed food preservatives and coloring matters; to determine their relation to digestion and health; and to establish the principles which should guide their use." A "poison squad" of twelve USDA employees acted as human volunteers to test the safety of boric acid and borax, salicylic acid and salicylates, sulfurous acid and sulfites, benzoic acid and benzoates, and formaldehyde, during 1902–1904. Each member of the squad complied with a strict, carefully recorded dietary regimen and was subject to extensive examination respecting the effects of the preservatives included in the diet. The results, published in five parts during 1904–1908, drew interest throughout the country.

But the event that finally precipitated enactment of the Food and Drugs Act of 1906 was publication that year of Upton Sinclair's THE JUNGLE, the first work by a twenty-seven-year-old author who hoped to convert America to socialism and had no interest in legislation to regulate food and drugs. His description of the Chicago meat industry captured nationwide attention and inexorably carried to enactment both the Federal Meat Inspection Act of 1906 and the Federal Food and Drugs Act of the same year. Upton Sinclair claimed to have been bitterly disappointed that "I aimed at the public's heart and by accident I hit it in the stomach," but he will forever be remembered as the person who galvanized Congress and the country to bring federal food and drug legislation to fruition after 27 years of consideration.

Lauffer Hayes & Frank Ruff, *The Administration of the Federal Food and Drugs Act*

1 LAW & CONTEMPORARY PROBLEMS 16 (1933).

The [1906] Act forbids interstate commerce in adulterated and misbranded food and drugs. It provides criminal penalties for violation and also authorizes the seizure of offending products. In the case of standard drugs, the United States Pharmacopoeia and the National Formulary were resorted to by Congress for the purpose of establishing standards of purity and quality which the drug manufacturers were enjoined to follow—unless they declared standards of their own on the labels of their products.... In the case of foods, standards were not available, and in their stead, the draftsmen of the Act resorted to generalities proscribing the intermixture or substitution of substances reducing quality, the abstraction of valuable constituents, the concealment of damage or inferiority, the addition of deleterious ingredients, and the use of spoiled animal or vegetable products. Misbranding was confined chiefly to the making of false or misleading statements regarding a food or drug on the package or label thereof. The sale of an imitation was forbidden, but this was accompanied by provisos which relieved mixtures or compounds not in themselves harmful when sold under "their own distinctive names" or when labeled with the word "compound," "imitation" or "blend," from the operation of both the misbranding and adulteration provisions of the Act. Aside from the latter, the only affirmative labeling requirements were the disclosure of the presence and quantity of enumerated narcotic drugs and the declaration of the net weight of foods when sold in package form.

NOTES

1. *1906 Act's History.* The legislative and administrative histories of the 1906 Act are chronicled in ARTHUR P. GREELEY, THE FOOD AND DRUGS ACT (1907); GUSTAVUS A. WEBER, THE FOOD, DRUG, AND INSECTICIDE ADMINISTRATION: ITS HISTORY, ACTIVITIES, AND ORGANIZATION (1928); HARVEY W. WILEY, THE HISTORY OF A CRIME AGAINST THE FOOD LAW (1929); HARVEY W. WILEY, AN AUTOBIOGRAPHY (1930); *Legislation: The Consumer's Protection Under the Federal Pure Food and Drugs Act*, 32 COLUM. L. REV. 720 (1932); Symposium, *The Protection of the Consumer of Food and Drugs*, 1 LAW & CONTEMP. PROBS. 1 (1933); Symposium, *The Fortieth Anniversary of the Original Federal Food and Drugs Act of 1906*, 1 FOOD DRUG COSM. L.Q. 285 (1946); OSCAR E. ANDERSON, *THE HEALTH OF A NATION: HARVEY W. WILEY AND THE FIGHT FOR PURE FOOD* (1958); Oscar E. Anderson, *Pioneer Statute: The Pure Food and Drugs Act of 1906*, 13 J. PUB. L. 189 (1964); James Harvey Young, *From Oysters to After-Dinner Mints: The Role of the Early Food and Drug Inspector*, 42 J. HIST. MED. & ALLIED SCI. 30 (1987); JAMES HARVEY YOUNG, PURE FOOD: SECURING THE FEDERAL FOOD AND DRUGS ACT OF 1906 (1989); Wallace F. Jannsen, *Crawford*, Parts I—IV, 54 & 55 J. ASS'N OF FOOD & DRUG OFFICIALS (1990–1991); Kathleen May Ryan, *The Meaning of Meat in Industrial Social Protest Novels, Upton Sinclair's "The Jungle" and Yuri Olesha's "Envy"* (1996), Jenny Ann Diamond, *Who Shall Meet the Foe if Not She?: Women's Participation in the Movement Leading Up to the Federal Food and Drug Act of 1906, As Seen Through the Pages of Good Housekeeping* (2002), and Anthony Gaughan, *Harvey Wiley, Theodore Roosevelt, and the Federal Regulation of Food and Drugs* (2004), in Chapter I(B) of the Electronic Book; CLAYTON A. COPPIN & JACK C. HIGH, THE POLITICS OF PURITY: HARVEY WASHINGTON WILEY AND THE ORIGINS OF FEDERAL FOOD POLICY (1999); LORINE S. GOODWIN, *THE PURE FOOD, DRINK, AND DRUG CRUSADERS, 1879–1914* (1999); Jason Pickavance, *Gastronomic Realism: Upton Sinclair's "The Jungle," the Fight for Pure Food, and the Magic of Mastication*, 11 FOOD & FOODWAYS 87 (2003); John P. Swann, *The Formation and Early Work of the Drug Laboratory, USDA Bureau of Chemistry*, AM. INST. HIST. PHARMACY, APOTHECARY'S CABINET, No. 9 (Fall 2005).

2. *Decisions Under the 1906 Act.* FDA's administrative decisions under the 1906 Act were issued by FDA in periodic regulations, Food Inspection Decisions, and Service and Regulatory Announcements, which were compiled through mid–1914 in C. A. GWINN, FOOD AND DRUGS ACT (1914). Court decisions under the 1906 Act were compiled through mid–1934 in MASTIN G. WHITE & OTIS H. GATES, DECISIONS OF COURTS IN CASES UNDER THE FEDERAL FOOD AND DRUGS ACT (1934).

c. LIMITATIONS OF THE FEDERAL FOOD AND DRUGS ACT OF 1906

After a decade of implementing the 1906 Act, FDA talked openly about the statute's weaknesses as well as its strengths.

1917 Report of the USDA Bureau of Chemistry

It is perhaps impossible for any one correctly to estimate the general effect of the Food and Drugs Act. To state that more than six thousand cases have been terminated in the courts during the first decade since the enactment of the act; that manufacturers have been cited to hearing more than forty thousand times, that many thousands of factory inspections have been made, that more than seven hundred and fifty thousand shipments of food and drugs, both domestic and imported, have been examined, gives but an imperfect indication of results. . . .

The Food and Drugs Act was among the first of that group of laws which today would be classed as laws for the prevention of unfair competition. The suppression of fraud upon the consumer and of unfair competition among business rivals are but the two faces of the same coin. In consequence the food industries are sincerely and effectively supporting and helping the Bureau of Chemistry to enforce the law. Indeed, the Bureau is not infrequently appealed to by the industries to compel the cessation of unfair practices and to encourage the standardization of products when the industry is incapable by itself of bringing about these results. . . .

The Food and Drugs Act's chief contributions to the safeguarding of the peoples' health have been its effect upon the drug and patent medicine industry, upon the control of the traffic in polluted, decomposed or filthy foods and upon the elimination from foodstuffs of contamination with poisons such as lead and arsenic which entered the product because of the use of impure reagents in the process of manufacture, or of utensils constructed of improper materials.

While the accomplishments of the Food and Drugs Act have been considerable, it must be admitted that it has its serious limitations. Especially conspicuous ones are the lack of legal standards for foods, of authority to inspect warehouses, and of any restriction whatever upon the use of many of the most virulent poisons in drugs; the limitations placed upon the term "drug" by definition which render it difficult to control injurious cosmetics, fraudulent mechanical devices used for therapeutic purposes, as well as fraudulent remedies for obesity and leanness; the limitation of dangerous adulterants to those that are added so that the interstate shipment of a food that naturally contains a virulent poison is unrestricted. Furthermore, the law fails to take cognizance of fraudulent statements covering foods or drugs which are not in or upon the food or drug package. Greater flexibility to prescribe the disposition of imports is also desirable. The Secretary of Agriculture has at one time or another recommended legislation to fill most of these gaps in the law. It should also be noted that at present there is no Federal law which prohibits unregistered or unlicensed persons from sending into interstate commerce medicinal agents, poisons, and the like, although they can not be sold locally by them nor indiscriminately even by registered or licensed pharmacists or physicians.

d. THE FEDERAL FOOD, DRUG, AND COSMETIC ACT OF 1938

In the early days of the New Deal, FDA convinced the new Roosevelt Administration to sponsor a complete revision of the 1906 Act.

1933 Report of the Food and Drug Administration

Demand for a complete overhauling of the outworn mechanism of 1906 received a new impetus during the year through the interest of the

President of the United States and the sympathy and cooperation of the Secretary and Assistant Secretary of Agriculture. A bill to supplant the present measure was drafted in the Department, reviewed and approved by the Department of Justice, and introduced in the Senate on June 12, by Senator Royal S. Copeland, of New York, as S. 1944.

The new draft preserves all of the worthy features of the present law. Its principal additional features are as follows:

1. Cosmetics are brought within the scope of the statute.

2. Mechanical devices intended for curative purposes, and devices and preparations intended to bring about changes in the structure of the body are also included within the purview of the law.

3. False advertising of foods, drugs, and cosmetics is prohibited.

4. Definitely informative labeling is required.

5. A drug which is, or may be, dangerous to health under the conditions of use prescribed in its labeling is classed as adulterated.

6. The promulgation of definitions and standards for foods, which will have the force and effect of law, is authorized.

7. The prohibition of added poisons in foods or the establishment of safe tolerances therefor is provided for.

8. The operation of factories under Federal permit is prescribed where protection of the public health cannot be otherwise effected.

9. More effective methods for the control of false labeling and advertising of drug products are provided.

10. More severe penalties, as well as injunctions in the case of repeated offenses, are prescribed.

———

Five years of hearings and debate elapsed before Congress enacted and President Roosevelt, on June 25, 1938, signed the FD&C Act. In structure, the 1938 Act is a catalogue of definitions elaborating two basic concepts: "adulteration" and "misbranding." Most of the Act's operative provisions describe circumstances under which a food, drug, device, or cosmetic will be considered adulterated or misbranded under the law and thus subject to FDA enforcement action. For example, section 402(a) of the Act does not forthrightly forbid the marketing of food that is decomposed or filthy. It specifies that food that is decomposed or filthy shall be "deemed adulterated." Then Section 301 enumerates a series of "prohibited acts," among them the shipment, distribution, or sale of any adulterated food. In short, much of the statute is devoted to ascribing the labels "adulterated" or "misbranded" to products whose composition, production, or labeling fails to meet substantive requirements that are the real focus of the law. In this respect, the Act's basic format has not changed since 1906. Rather, changes in the scope of FDA's responsibilities have generally been reflected in the addition of new definitions of adulteration and misbranding.

We examine the enforcement remedies available to FDA in Chapter X. The principal statutorily authorized sanctions remain those Congress provided in 1938: criminal prosecution of individuals and firms guilty of prohibited acts, injunction against such acts, and seizure of adulterated or misbranded goods. More recently, Congress has authorized civil penalties for some violations of the FD&C Act. From the beginning, however, FDA has also relied on informal remedies not explicitly provided in the Act, such as publicity, recalls, and warning letters, which now comprise the primary routine enforcement tools of the agency.

NOTE

On the history of the 1938 Act, see Symposium, *The New Food, Drug, and Cosmetic Legislation*, 6 LAW & CONTEMP. PROBS. 1 (1939); Vincent A. Kleinfeld, *Legislative History of the Federal Food, Drug, and Cosmetic Act*, 1 FOOD DRUG COSM. L.Q. 532 (1946); CHARLES O. JACKSON, FOOD AND DRUG LEGISLATION IN THE NEW DEAL (1970); Gwen Kay, *Healthy Public Relations: The FDA's 1930s Legislative Campaign*, 75 BULL. OF THE HIST. OF MED. 446 (2001); Catherine N. Karuga, *The Expansion of FDA's Enforcement Powers from 1906 to 2003* (2003), in Chapter I(B) of the Electronic Book. The documents comprising the statutory history are collected in part in CHARLES WESLEY DUNN, FEDERAL FOOD, DRUG, AND COSMETIC ACT (1938), and in full in FDA, A LEGISLATIVE HISTORY OF THE FEDERAL FOOD, DRUG, AND COSMETIC ACT AND ITS AMENDMENTS, Vols. 1–24 and Apps. A–J (1979).

e.   POST-1938 AMENDMENTS

The FD&C Act has been amended more than a hundred times since its original passage. Some of the changes made by Congress can fairly be described as technical or remedial. The more noteworthy amendments have extended the coverage of the Act or, more commonly, enlarged FDA's substantive authority over products already within its jurisdiction. Examples of such legislation include the Miller Pesticides Amendment of 1954, which empowered FDA to establish tolerances for pesticides on agricultural commodities; the Food Additives Amendment of 1958, which required premarket approval of new food ingredients and many food contact articles; and the Color Additive Amendments of 1960, which established a premarket approval system for colors used in food, drugs, and cosmetics.

Two major amendments to the basic Act were enacted in 1962 and 1976. The Drug Amendments of 1962 fundamentally restructured the way in which FDA regulated new medicines, transforming a system of premarket notification into one that requires individual premarket approval of the safety and effectiveness of every new drug. The 1962 Amendments also thrust FDA into significant roles in regulating prescription drug promotion and clinical testing of new agents. With the passage of this legislation, the regulation of drugs became the single most controversial, and probably the most important, of FDA's activities.

In 1976 Congress made fundamental changes in the way that medical devices are regulated under the FD&C Act. The Medical Device Amendments were the culmination of fifteen years of careful study and debate, not only within Congress and the agency, but also among representatives of clinical medicine, biomedical engineering, device manufacturers, and consumer groups. While the 1976 Amendments did not significantly enlarge FDA's jurisdiction, they transformed its approach to regulation of these products and substantially enlarged the array of regulatory tools available to it.

The 1980s were punctuated by additional but more narrowly focused amendments, including the Infant Formula Amendments of 1980, the Orphan Drug Act of 1983, the Drug Price Competition and Patent Term Restoration Act of 1984, the Drug Export Amendments of 1986, the Prescription Drug Marketing Act of 1987, and the Generic Animal Drug and Patent Term Restoration Act of 1988. In 1988, Congress created FDA by statute.

The 1990s produced a plethora of important amendments to the FD&C Act, some narrow and others very broad. In 1990, Congress passed the Nutrition Labeling and Education Act and the Safe Medical Devices Act, as well as a statute to control food transportation. To finance FDA's ever-increasing responsibilities for premarket approval, Congress enacted user fee authority for prescription drugs in 1992, 1997, and 2002; for medical devices in 2002, 2004, and 2005; and for animal drugs in 2003. Legislation regarding pediatric testing of new drugs was enacted in 1997, 2002, and 2003. As part of the 1990 medical device legislation, Congress incorporated the 1967 Radiation Control for Health and Safety Act into the FD&C Act. Narrowly drawn statutes in 1994, 1996, and 2004 also amended animal drug provisions of the Act relating, respectively, to the limitations imposed on unapproved uses of prescription animal drugs, the new animal drug approval process, and animal drugs for minor species. The drug export provisions enacted in 1986 were replaced by more lenient provisions in the FDA Export Reform and Enhancement Act of 1996, and new drug import provisions were enacted in 2000, 2003, and 2006. Following the September 11, 2001 terrorist attack, Congress passed the Public Health Security and Bioterrorism Preparedness and Response Act of 2002 to strengthen food security and to promote the development of drug and device products to counter bioterrorism.

FDA has inherited entire programs from other agencies. The seafood, milk, and food service sanitation programs were transferred from the Public Health Service in 1968. The National Center for Toxicological Research was made part of FDA in 1971. Responsibility for the Radiation Control for Health and Safety Act of 1968 was transferred to FDA in 1971 and the Biologics Act of 1902 came to FDA in 1972.

The history of federal food and drug legislation has not, however, been an unbroken succession of enlargements of regulatory power. Congress transferred primary jurisdiction over poultry to USDA in 1957, over pesticides to the Environmental Protection Agency in 1970, over controlled substances to the Drug Enforcement Agency in 1970, and over hazardous household products to the Consumer Product Safety Commission in 1972. In 1976, FDA also saw the first of a series of enactments intended to curtail its authority under the FD&C Act, perhaps reflecting growing congressional skepticism of regulation generally as well as specific solicitude for the targets of FDA attention. The Vitamin–Mineral Amendments of 1976 limited FDA's authority to regulate the composition and promotion of dietary supplements—marking a rejection of the agency's decade-long efforts to control high-potency nutritional products and health foods. A year later, Congress passed the first of a series of laws forestalling any FDA action to ban the use of saccharin in food. In 1977, it also adopted a rider to unrelated legislation that directed FDA to refrain from implementing a proposed system for controlling the sanitation of shellfish harvested in U.S. waters until the Department of Commerce had completed what was expected to be an alarming assessment of the economic impact. In 1994, Congress enacted the Dietary Supplement Health and Education Act to prevent FDA from taking stringent regulatory action against dietary supplements. And in 1997, Congress enacted the Food and Drug Administration Modernization Act, which reformed several facets of FDA regulation.

While these and other expressions of congressional disagreement on specific issues depart from the general trajectory of federal food and drug legislation, they do not appear to represent a fundamental shift in legislative policy. Over the past several decades, both parties in both houses of Congress have generally displayed support for vigorous regulation of food, drugs, and other medical products.

3.   OTHER LAWS ENFORCED BY FDA

While the much-amended FD&C Act forms the agency's basic legal framework, FDA also administers several other statutes applicable to one or more categories of products within its jurisdiction. It has been delegated authority to enforce the Biologics Act, originally enacted in 1902 and now codified in Section 351 of the Public Health Service Act, 42 U.S.C. 262. The Biologics Act provides the agency's primary authority to regulate biological products, such as vaccines, products derived from human blood, and drugs produced by the recent advances in biotechnology. FDA relies on section 361 of the Public Health Service Act, 42 U.S.C. 264 ("Regulations to control communicable diseases"), to regulate sanitation in food service establishments and on interstate carriers and to prevent the transmission of disease by blood, human tissue, and more unusual products such as pet turtles. Specific aspects of food packaging and labeling are regulated by FDA under the Fair Packaging and Labeling Act of 1966. FDA enforces pesticide tolerances for food as required by the Environmental Protection Agency and child resistant packaging as required by the Consumer Product Safety Commission under the Poison Prevention Packaging Act of 1970. Another important law delegated to FDA is the Radiation Control for Health and Safety Act of 1968, now recodified by the Safe Medical Devices Act of 1990 as Section 531 *et seq.* of the FD&C Act, under which it regulates X-ray machines, microwave ovens, ultrasound equipment, and other products capable of emitting potentially harmful radiation.

NOTES

1. *Authorities Delegated to FDA.* The statutory functions performed by FDA are formally delegated to the Secretary of Health and Human Services, who then delegates them to the Commissioner of Food and Drugs. The latter delegations used

to be listed in 21 C.F.R. 5.10, but they are now found on the FDA website. *See* 64 Fed. Reg. 17285 (Apr. 2, 2004).

2. *Attempted Recodification.* In 1950, the House Committee on the Judiciary introduced a revision of the FD&C Act designed simply to codify the existing provisions in clearer language. After four years of consideration, the bill ultimately passed both houses of Congress. President Eisenhower withheld his approval, however, because the bill did not appear to achieve its objective of avoiding substantive change in the current law. H.R. Rep. No. 906, 84th Cong., 1st Sess. (1955). Although the legislation was subsequently revised, it was never able to overcome presidential disapproval, and it subsequently died. There has been no subsequent attempt at general recodification.

3. *Attempted Revisions.* Revision of the new drug provisions was attempted in 1977–1980, and revision of the food safety provisions was attempted in the early 1980s, but neither effort produced legislation. Proponents of statutory change since then have focused primarily on amendments that target limited issues.

C. FDA's Structure and Organization

While FDA's legal authority is outlined in the FD&C Act and related laws, the agency's structure is described in regulations, which are subject to change. 21 C.F.R. 5.1100. In fact, although it has a long institutional history, FDA was a creature of administrative action until it was recognized in legislation in 1988. 102 Stat. 3048, 3120–3122 (1988). Similarly, the agency's top official, the Commissioner of Food and Drugs, was not recognized by statute until that year. Formal legal responsibility for implementing the FD&C Act and the other statutes that the agency administers continues to lie with the Secretary of Health and Human Services (HHS).

Every FDA Commissioner who took office before 1988, though perhaps approved by the White House, was appointed by the Secretary of HHS or its predecessor departments and thus was not subject to Senate confirmation. Under Section 903(b)(1) of the FD&C Act, added in 1988, the Commissioner must now be appointed by the President with the advice and consent of the Senate. In formal organizational terms, the Commissioner ranks in the third tier of the Department, below the Assistant Secretaries of HHS. In fact, the job is more prominent than many ostensibly higher-ranking HHS offices, and it attracts individuals of national reputation. Because of the agency's visibility and the potential sensitivity of its decisions, FDA Commissioners have always had a direct line to the Secretary of HHS and sometimes to the White House as well.

Ironically, the avowed purpose of the 1988 statute making the Commissioner a political appointee was to insulate the Commissioner from political influence. It has had the opposite effect. During President George W. Bush's first six years in office (2001–2006), there was a confirmed FDA Commissioner in office for a total of only 18 months. Two of the individuals Bush nominated were subject to lengthy delays, imposed by both Democrats and Republicans. *See generally* Alex S. Gordon, *The Delicate Dance of Immersion and Insulation: The Politicization of the FDA Commissioner* (2003), in Chapter I(C) of the Electronic Book. For discussion of the politicization of FDA under President Clinton, see Kathryn R. Cook, *The*

Presidential FDA: Politics Meet Science (2001), in Chapter I(E) of the Electronic Book.

As the FDA organizational location reveals, the agency does not have the same independence from presidential control that independent regulatory commissions like the Federal Trade Commission (FTC), Securities and Exchange Commission (SEC), and Consumer Product Safety Commission (CPSC) ostensibly enjoy. A Commissioner of Food and Drugs is subject to direction and may be removed by the Secretary (now by the President) for any or no reason. The agency is headed by a single administrator. Its decisions represent collegial judgments only to the extent that the Commissioner has collegial support. Deliberative meetings among agency officials are frequent, informal, unannounced, and closed to the public. The Government in the Sunshine Act, 90 Stat. 1241 (1976), has no application to FDA's internal major deliberations. However, the agency's numerous expert advisory committees hold open meetings as required by the Federal Advisory Committee Act, 86 Stat. 770 (1972).

FDA's location in the Department of HHS might suggest that the agency is subject to pervasive political influence. For several reasons, however, this has not been the historical pattern. First, the evident scientific basis for most of FDA's decisions has helped insulate it from many of the customary forms of political pressure. Second, the visibility of FDA's programs has given the agency a public standing that often blunts pressure from within any administration. Finally, the agency's relatively low rank in the bureaucratic hierarchy means that few other jobs within it are subject to political appointment. As a technical matter, only two positions in FDA—the Commissioner and the Deputy Commissioner—have been formally subjected to Secretarial or Presidential appointment. Other top positions, such as the Chief Counsel and his Deputy and the Associate Commissioners are now also usually regarded as political appointees. But the Directors of the Centers for Food, Drugs, Biologics, Devices, and Veterinary Medicine are not political appointees. A change in administration therefore does not result in resignations or reassignments among the agency's middle and upper level managers, even though it may abruptly terminate the service of a Commissioner and some Associate Commissioners. Accordingly, for most of its existence, FDA has operated with considerable decisional independence and enjoyed continuity in the service of employees who hold managerial positions and staff its several field offices. When FDA abruptly changes its position or delays a decision on a controversial issue—as has happened under both Democratic and Republican Administrations—it is unclear whether this reflects policy changes or political considerations, if indeed there is a difference.

FDA's total full-time workforce numbered 10,668 in 2005 and now undoubtedly exceeds 11,000, a majority of whom are located in the Washington, D.C. area. Most of the remainder—inspectors, compliance officers, and laboratory scientists—work in one of five Regional Offices, 24 District Offices, or 144 Resident Posts around the country. FDA's headquarters personnel are dispersed among about three dozen different buildings in and around Washington. They are divided among eight primary components. First, there is the Commissioner's office and central administrative staff, which includes several Associate Commissioners, budget officers, and personnel experts. Second, there are the field operations, which consist of regional, district, and local offices throughout the country that carry on FDA's inspectional and enforcement activities, all of which are coordinated by the Associate Commissioner for Regulatory Affairs. Third, there is the National Center for Toxicological Research, established in 1971 in the converted facilities of the former biological warfare project in Jefferson, Arkansas. Finally, there are five Centers (formerly "Bureaus") responsible for one or more categories of products within FDA's jurisdiction: the Center for Drug Evaluation and Research (CDER), the Center for Biologics Evaluation and Research (CBER), the Center for Food Safety and Applied Nutrition (CFSAN), the Center for Devices and Radiological Health (CDRH), and the Center for Veterinary Medicine (CVM). The heads of each of these entities—Center directors—report to the Commissioner.

A key organization in FDA's regulatory operations, but not formally a part of the agency, is the Chief Counsel's office—officially the Food and Drug Division of the Office of the General Counsel of the Department of Health and Human Services. FDA's Chief Counsel is thus an employee of the Secretary of HHS, not of the Commissioner of Food and Drugs. In practice, however, the office generally functions more as an active component of the agency than as a representative of the Department. The FDA Chief Counsel essentially functions as the Commissioner's lawyer.

One other important organizational development deserves attention. Throughout the first 70–80 years of FDA's history, regulatory policy was made by the Office of the Commissioner and the Office of the Chief Counsel and carried out through the lower levels of the headquarters staff and the field force. Within the past generation, this dynamic has changed dramatically. Today, policy is largely made at the lowest levels of FDA rather than at the top. There are a number of interrelated reasons for this development. First, the vast bulk of FDA's daily decisions now come in the form of action taken with respect to applications for FDA approval of drugs, biologics, devices, and other products that require FDA approval prior to marketing. The Office of the Commissioner almost never reviews these decisions and may not even know about them. It is these decisions that determine FDA policy, not the FD&C Act or the implementing regulations. Second, the Office of the Commissioner and the Office of Chief Counsel are occupied with establishing very broad policy, overseeing the operations of the agency, and managing relations with HHS, OMB, other government agencies, Congress, the media, trade associations, professional societies, and a host of other interested domestic and international organizations and individuals. To the extent that they consider specific regulatory issues, it is almost always in the context of a crisis or emotionally-charged matter that commands national interest, such as a major recall; the approval of a controversial product like RU–486, Plan B, or breast implants; or another question that demands prompt and complete attention at a high level. Third, the agency has now grown so large that the Office of the Commissioner could not oversee all of the agency's activities even if it had the resources and desire to do so. For example, more than 2000 informal guidances have been issued in the past decade governing in minute detail thousands of issues relating to new drug regulation alone. It is doubtful that the Office of the Commissioner has the expertise, much less the staff, to review, understand, and comment on even a small fraction of them. Accordingly, the actions of low-level FDA employees almost always prevail within the agency and thus constitute the true agency policy with regard to the matters involved.

During the 1970s, the Office of the Commissioner conducted a comprehensive review of all agency actions through weekly three-hour meetings with each Center (then called Bureaus). Few important issues took longer than seven days to be considered and resolved under this intensive scrutiny. But this approach was abandoned by the 1990s, and it would be difficult to revive it today. One former Center Director famously confided that he had not met with the Commissioner in over a year and had not even been in his presence in more than six months. Today the Center Directors, rather than the Commissioner, largely run the agency.

Even at the Centers, however, review and supervision of the working level is attenuated, and in many situations nonexistent. An issue that rises to the level of the Center Director is inherently a very difficult one, and it is only under extraordinary circumstances that the top management of the Center will overrule a decision made below. Thus, again, low level agency employees frequently make the most important decisions, with major impact on the country's health and economy.

FDA's 10,000 employees are responsible for regulating the products of several large and diverse industries. FDA fared relatively well in maintaining its budget during the general reductions of the 1980s and 1990s. For FY 2005, the agency budget was $1.777 billion (including user fees), compared with $567 million in 1990 and $313 million in 1980. But even this figure is dwarfed by the amount of economic activity represented by the sale of products FDA regulates. Approximately 20–25 cents of every consumer retail sales dollar is spent for products within the agency's jurisdiction. As the following chapters reveal, the scope of FDA's authority over this heterogeneous universe of products varies widely, ranging from comprehensive premarket approval responsibility for new drugs, food additives, and life-supporting medical devices, to the policing activities applicable to most food products, nonprescription drugs, and cosmetics. Within the several industries over which FDA has some measure of regulatory control, there is enormous diversity among individual firms. They range in size from giant nationwide food processors and distributors to small warehousemen, from multinational chemical companies to small partnerships of biomedical engineers engaged in the development of a single type of device, and from the nation's largest cattle feed lots to contract laboratories engaged in preclinical testing of new food ingredients.

The structure and location of FDA within the executive branch have been the subject of continuous study and debate. In the 1950s, the Hoover Commission initially concluded that FDA should be split in two, with the responsibility for food regulation transferred to USDA and the responsibility for drug regulation transferred to a new Union Medical Administration. A Hoover Commission Task Force then, without referring to the earlier proposal, recommended that the pesticide regulatory functions of the Department of Agriculture be transferred to FDA and the animal biologics regulatory functions of the Department of Agriculture be combined with the human biologics regulatory functions of the National Institutes of Health. The 1955 Hoover Commission Report concluded that the matter should be decided by administrative determination and took no action on it.

In January 1971, the President's Advisory Council on Executive Reorganization recommended that consideration be given to transferring FDA to a new Federal Trade Practices Agency. The Ash Council Report, also in January 1971, proposed that FDA be made part of a new Department of Human Resources. In 1975, Senator Edward Kennedy introduced legislation to divide FDA into two separate agencies (drug and devices, and food and cosmetics), but the National Academy of Sciences issued a report in 1976 concluding that the problems faced by FDA were not primarily organizational, and the legislation was not reported out of committee. President Carter's Office of Management and Budget conducted a study in 1978 that was never released but that reportedly recommended transfer of FDA's food regulation to USDA. However, both agencies testified in a 1979 Senate hearing that their food programs would remain unchanged. A 1977 report by the Senate Committee on Governmental Affairs recommended transfer of USDA food regulatory functions to FDA.

A 1984 Office of Technology Assessment (OTA) study recommended that regulation of animal vaccines be transferred from USDA to FDA. Senator Albert Gore pursued legislation in 1987 to make FDA a virtually independent agency within HHS, but the final legislation required only that the Commissioner be confirmed by the Senate. The Government Accounting Office has recommended consolidation of all food regulation under a single agency in reports and testimony in 1992, 1994, 2004, and 2005. As Vice President, Gore recommended in 1993 that USDA food regulatory functions be transferred to FDA. Senator Howard Metzenbaum advocated transferring all food regulatory functions to the Consumer Product Safety Commission. Legislation was introduced in the House and Senate in 1997 to consolidate all food regulation in a new independent agency. A 1998 Institute of Medicine study recommended a single food regulatory entity and gave four options with regard to placement. Hearings were held in the Senate in 1999 and in the House in 2004 on legislation to consolidate all food regulation, but no legislation was reported out of committee. "Overlap and Duplication in the Federal Food Safety System," Hearing before the Oversight of Government Management, Restructuring and the District of Columbia Subcomm. of the Senate Comm. on Governmental Affairs, 106th Cong., 1st Sess. (1999); "A System Rued: Inspecting Food," Hearing before the Subcomm. on Civil Service and Agency Organization of the House Comm. on Government Reform, 108th Cong., 2d Sess. (2004). GAO recently produced two reports on consolidation of food regulation. FOOD SAFETY: EXPERIENCES OF SEVEN COUNTRIES IN CONSOLIDATING THEIR FOOD SAFETY SYSTEMS, No. GAO–05–213 (Feb. 2005); FEDERAL AGENCIES SHOULD PURSUE OPPORTUNITIES TO REDUCE OVERLAP AND BETTER LEVERAGE RESOURCES (Mar. 2005). These GAO reports were the subject of a congressional hearing in May 2005. "Question: What is More Scrambled Than an Egg? Answer: The Federal Food Inspection System," Hearing before the Subcomm. on the Federal Workforce and Agency Organization of the House Comm. on Government Reform, 109th Cong., 1st Sess. (2005).

NOTE

See Edward Brown Williams, *The Proposed Division of Functions of the Food and Drug Administration*, 4 FOOD DRUG COSM. L.Q. 163 (1949); Richard A. Merrill & Jeffrey K. Francer, *Organizing Federal Food Safety Regulation*, 31 SETON HALL L. REV. 64 (2000); Richard J. Durbin, *Food Safety Oversight for the 21st Century: The Creation of a Single, Independent Federal Food Safety Agency*, 59 FOOD & DRUG L.J. 383 (2004).

D.   THE REGULATORY ENVIRONMENT

Experienced practitioners in any regulatory field appreciate the need to understand the background and motives of the agency with which they are dealing, and sophisticated observers of federal regulation have commented on the influence of history, personality, and style on the regulatory process. Though it is not possible to describe the style or atmosphere of a century-old agency in a few pages, our account of FDA's formulation and enforcement of substantive legal requirements in this book attempts to convey a sense of the forces that drive FDA and the political and scientific environment in which it functions. It is therefore appropriate at the outset to identify some features of the FDA landscape that cast long shadows over its administration of the law.

While many federal agencies come under close public and journalistic scrutiny, FDA has been watched intensely even by Washington standards. It is unlikely that any other agency has been the subject of more study during the last four decades. A partial catalogue of external and internal studies of the agency's performance appears in Peter Barton Hutt, *Investigations and Reports on the Food and Drug Administration, in* FOOD AND DRUG LAW INSTITUTE, TWENTY-FIFTH ANNIVERSARY COMMEMORATIVE VOLUME OF FOOD AND DRUG LAW 27 (1984). In the late 1980s, two national committees began to study FDA: the National Committee to Review Current Procedures for Approval of New Drugs for Cancer and AIDS, established in 53 Fed. Reg. 46942 (Nov. 21, 1988) at the request of President Bush, and the Advisory Committee on the Food and Drug Administration, established in 54 Fed. Reg. 51236 (Dec. 13, 1989) at the request of HHS Secretary Louis Sullivan.

The intensity of scrutiny has not abated since then. The number of studies of FDA's performance is certainly evidence of the high degree of public interest in its work, but it also betrays the persistence of a belief in some quarters that the agency is not doing its job well enough or fast enough. This skepticism contributes to the self-doubt that periodically besets FDA employees. The public at large does not generally share this skepticism, however; according to repeated surveys, it ranks FDA among the federal agencies in which it has the greatest confidence.

FDA's attraction as a subject of study mirrors congressional interest in its work. Beginning in the late 1950s, FDA has been the subject of a degree of congressional attention unmatched by the amount focused on any other regulatory agency. Between September 1971 and July 1977, for example, FDA officials were called to testify before congressional committees a total of 198 times. The inauguration of a Democratic President in 1977 and the appointment of a new Commissioner did not diminish congressional interest in overseeing FDA's performance. The arrival of a Republican President in 1981, combined with Republican control of the Senate, did reduce congressional oversight, but pressure resumed following the Senate elections in 1986. The Republican sweep of the House and Senate in 1994 only intensified critical congressional oversight. Both Republican and Democratic members of Congress interrogate the agency regardless of which party holds the White House.

The sheer number of congressional hearings involving FDA tells only part of the story. Fewer than 20 percent of its appearances deal with legislation affecting the agency, and in most years, no more than two appearances concern the agency's budget. The remainder of hearings, almost thirty a year, are "oversight" hearings in the conventional sense. Our purpose is not to argue that FDA *should* be left alone to do its work, but simply to document that it *is not* left alone. The agency is controversial. Its decisions affect every citizen and are closely watched. Many congressional committees are interested in its performance, frequently concluding that it has been either reckless or tardy in approving new products or insufficiently vigorous in acting against old ones. The message conveyed by both the intensity and frequency of congressional oversight has substantially influenced both the content of FDA's requirements and the thrust of the agency's enforcement efforts.

Richard A. Merrill, *Risk–Benefit Decisionmaking by the Food and Drug Administration*

45 GEORGE WASHINGTON LAW REVIEW 994 (1977).

... Historically, the agency devoted its primary energies to combatting unsanitary food production and preventing the marketing of deficient drugs, principally through instituted product recalls and court enforcement actions halting or punishing distribution of adulterated and misbranded products. FDA rarely had difficulty determining whether a process was deficient or a product mislabeled; the agency's major problems were the detection and prevention of individual violations.

Although policing activities still comprise a major part of FDA's work, the agency's regulatory agenda has expanded and shifted. Both the passage of legislation regulating food additives, color additives, and human and veterinary drugs and mounting public concern about environmental hazards have broadened the nature of FDA decision-making. The agency increasingly is required to determine the level of risk acceptable in products that are properly manufactured and used as intended. Rather than measuring the practices of individual manufacturers against well-established standards of conduct, FDA now must prescribe the standards of safety and, in some instances, the standards of performance particular products must meet before they reach the public....

Only since 1970 has FDA functioned like a modern "regulatory agency"—a body routinely monitoring the operations of several industries and exercising comprehensive authority to prescribe how they must make and market their products. However, FDA brings to this modern responsibility a history and experience that continue to influence the attitudes of agency officials about the appropriate role of a health regulatory agency. Many FDA employees have devoted their lives to gathering evidence of statutory violations in preparation for court enforcement proceedings, and this adversary responsibility has engendered suspicion of regulated firms.

But FDA's modern duties have forced the agency to become less suspicious and more inventive. As we discuss more fully in Chapters X and XIV, *infra*, the agency has shifted its emphasis from court enforcement against individual violators to the establishment of generic requirements through rulemaking, guidance, and other informal processes. In the process, FDA has assumed a larger role in determining the content of regulatory policy. Whenever Congress establishes a regulatory program, it necessarily must allow the responsible agency discretion to fashion the precise requirements applicable to regulated firms. But while administrative discretion is inherent in the regulatory process, FDA has enjoyed unusual freedom to adopt and revise regulatory approaches. Other health regulatory agencies are creatures of modern organic statutes, which typically express more explicit legislative choices among available regulatory techniques. The FD&C Act, by contrast, is comparatively old-fashioned. Though it is quite lengthy, many of its most important provisions are couched in general language, which FDA has had the responsibility and opportunity to adapt to contemporary problems.

NOTE

For discussions of the effects of congressional oversight of FDA, see H. Thomas Austern, *Drug Regulation and the Public Health: Side Effects and Contraindications of Congressional Committee Post Hoc Medical Judgments*, 19 Food Drug Cosm. L.J. 259 (1964); Peter Barton Hutt, *Balanced Government Regulation of Consumer Products*, 31 Food Drug Cosm. L.J. 592 (1976).

E.   FDA'S MISSION AND RESOURCES

1.   FDA'S MISSION

The FD&C Act, like its 1906 predecessor, consists of statutory prohibitions against adulterated and misbranded products. From the time of its origin, FDA—reflecting the constant pressure from Congress and the media—has regarded its mission as protecting the public against unsafe and mislabeled products. In the past two decades, however, advocates for seriously ill patients have argued that FDA has a corresponding responsibility to promote health by rapid review and approval of new medical products. This issue was directly addressed in the Food and Drug Administration Modernization Act of 1997, which added Section 903(b) to the FD&C Act:

(b) MISSION.—The [Food and Drug] Administration shall—

(1) promote the public health by promptly and efficiently review-ing clinical research and taking appropriate action on the market-ing of regulated products in a timely manner;

(2) with respect to such products, protect the public health by assuring that [they are not adulterated or misbranded].

Notwithstanding the clear decision by Congress to put health pro-motion first and health protection second, FDA, reflecting its heritage, has reversed this order in the mission statement that appears on the agency's website.

Congress describes the agency in the following terms:

Agriculture, Rural Development, Food and Drug Administration, and Related Agencies Appropriations Bill, 2006

Senate Report No. 109–92, 109th Congress, 1st Session (2005).

The Food and Drug Administration [FDA] is a scientific regulatory agency whose mission is to promote and protect the public health and safety of Americans. FDA's work is a blending of science and law. The Food and Drug Administration Modernization Act of 1997 [FDAMA] (Public Law 105–115) reaffirmed the responsibilities of the FDA; to ensure safe and effective products reach the market to a timely way, and to monitor products for continued safety after they are in use. In addition, FDA is entrusted with two critical functions in the Nation's war on terrorism; preventing willful contamination of all regulated products, including food, and improving the availability of medications to prevent or treat injuries caused by biological, chemical or nuclear agents.

The FDA Foods program has the primary responsibility for assuring that the food supply, quality of foods, food ingredients and dietary supple-ments are safe, sanitary, nutritious, wholesome, and honestly labeled, and that cosmetic products are safe and properly labeled. The variety and complexity of the food supply has grown dramatically while new and more complex safety issues, such as emerging microbial pathogens, natural toxins, and technological innovations in production and processing, have developed. This program plays a major role in keeping the United States food supply among the safest in the world.

The FDA Drugs programs are comprised of three separate areas, Human Drugs, Animal Drugs and Biologics. FDA is responsible for the life cycle of the product, including premarket review and postmarket surveil-lance of human, animal and biological products to ensure their safety and efficacy. For Human Drugs this includes assuring that all drug products used for the prevention, diagnosis and treatment of disease are safe and effective. Additional procedures include the review of investigational new drug applications; evaluation of market applications for new and generic drugs, labeling and composition of prescription and over-the-counter drugs; monitoring the quality and safety of products manufactured in, or imported into, the United States; and, regulating the advertising and promotion of prescription drugs. The Animal Drugs and Feeds Program ensures only safe and beneficial veterinary drugs, intended for the treatment and/or prevention of diseases in animals and the improved production of food-producing animals, are approved for marketing.

The FDA Biologics program assures that blood and blood products, blood test kits, vaccines, and therapeutics are pure, potent safe, effective, and properly labeled. The program inspects blood banks and blood processors, licenses and inspects firms collecting human source plasma, evaluates and licenses biologics manufacturing firms and products; lot releases licensed products; and monitors adverse events associated with vaccine immunization.

The FDA Devices and Radiological program ensures the safety and effectiveness of medical devices and eliminates unnecessary human exposure to manmade radiation from medical, occupational and consumer products. In addition, the program enforces quality standards under the Mammography Quality Standards Act (Public Law 108–365). Medical devices include thousands of products from thermometers and contact lenses to heart pacemakers, hearing aids, MRIs, microwave ovens, and video display terminals.

FDA's National Center for Toxicological Research in Jefferson, Arkansas, serves as a specialized resource, conducting peer-reviewed scientific research that provides the basis for FDA to make sound science-based regulatory decisions through its premarket review and postmarket surveillance. The research is designed to define and understand the biological mechanisms of action underlying the toxicity of products and developing methods to improve assessment of human exposure, susceptibility and risk of those products regulated by FDA.

2.   FDA RESOURCES

There is at present no validated historical statistical series reflecting the resources and work of FDA throughout its history. The following table represents the best available data on the growth of the agency budget (including user fees) from 1862 to the present.

YEAR	APPROPRIATION	EMPLOYEES
1862		
1870		
1880		
1890	12,000	
1900	17,100	
1910	880,560	70
1920	1,391,571	374
1930	1,537,300	
1940	2,741,000	719
1950	4,802,500	955
1960	13,800,000	1660

YEAR	APPROPRIATION	EMPLOYEES
1970	72,352,000	4363
1980	312,796,000	7517
1990	567,079,000	7692
1995	897,104,000	9264
2000	1,183,095,000	8857
2005	1,776,784,000	10,668

In the years prior to 1906, there was increasing investigation of food and drug adulteration but no direct regulatory functions. From 1906 to 1927, FDA combined regulatory work with continuing research on agricultural chemistry. Since 1927, the entire FDA budget has been devoted, directly or indirectly, to regulation.

NOTES

1. *Commentary.* For an analysis of the difficulty of determining the yearly FDA appropriation, and the failure of appropriations to keep pace with program needs, see Margaret McGlinch, *Hollow Government: Resource Constraints and Workload Expansion at the Food and Drug Administration* (2001), in Chapter I(D) of the Electronic Book.

2. *Citizens Committees.* On three occasions, the Secretary of HEW/HHS has appointed a Citizens Committee to review the FDA mission, resources, and programs. See REPORT OF THE CITIZENS ADVISORY COMMITTEE ON THE FOOD AND DRUG ADMINISTRATION TO THE SECRETARY OF HEALTH, EDUCATION, AND WELFARE (June 1955); REPORT OF THE CITIZENS ADVISORY COMMITTEE TO THE SECRETARY OF HEALTH, EDUCATION, AND WELFARE ON THE FOOD AND DRUG ADMINISTRATION (Oct. 1962); FINAL REPORT OF THE ADVISORY COMMITTEE ON THE FOOD AND DRUG ADMINISTRATION (May 1991). *See also* "Food and Drug Administration Oversight," Hearings before the Subcomm. on Health and the Environment of the House Comm. on Energy and Commerce, 102d Cong., 1st Sess. (1991). On each occasion the report has resulted in a substantial increase in FDA appropriations.

CHAPTER II

FDA JURISDICTION: A MATTER OF DEFINITIONS

A. INTRODUCTION

The 1938 Act gave FDA authority over four broad categories of products, all of which the agency still regulates: food, drugs, cosmetics, and medical devices. In the ensuing decades, the agency assumed or was given responsibility for additional classes of products, some of which (human biological products, electronic radiation-emitting products) it continues to regulate today, while others (toys, pesticides) it later ceded to other agencies. In addition, Congress has repeatedly tweaked the FD&C Act definitions, in some instances establishing entire subcategories with their own definitions, such as "food additives" and "dietary supplements" (both subcategories of "food").

The scope of FDA's power is defined almost entirely by the list of product categories over which it has jurisdiction.* The statutory definitions of these categories thus delineate the outer boundaries of the arena within which the agency operates. The definitions are also important for another reason. FDA has different degrees of power over different categories of products. In general, the agency has greater authority over drugs, devices, and biological products than over food and cosmetics. The category to which FDA—or Congress—assigns an article thus largely controls the shape of the regulatory regime the agency will impose on it.

As the materials in this chapter show, the product definitions are strikingly broad and thus confer jurisdiction over a vast range of goods. Furthermore, the definitions which are not mutually exclusive, are remarkably plastic, providing the agency with great flexibility to decide whether and how to regulate products. Sometimes FDA has interpreted the definitions expansively, so as to expand its power. On other occasions, the agency has construed the definitions narrowly, so as to avoid taking responsibility for products it does not want to regulate or to minimize the burdensomeness of the requirements it does impose.

Occasionally, when FDA interprets the definitions flexibly so as to achieve particular policy objectives, the courts will rein in the agency, as the Supreme Court did with respect to FDA's attempts in the 1990s to regulate cigarettes as medical devices. *FDA v. Brown & Williamson*, 529

---

* [The most important exception to this principle is the power FDA shares with the Centers for Disease Control under Section 361 of the Public Health Service Act (42 U.S.C. 264) to take measures to control the spread of communicable diseases.

U.S. 120 (2000), *infra* p. 82. In general, however, as the next case illustrates, courts have granted the agency considerable latitude in applying the product definitions.

United States v. An Article of Drug ... Bacto–Unidisk

394 U.S. 784 (1969).

■ MR. CHIEF JUSTICE WARREN delivered the opinion of the court.

At issue here is the scope of the statutory definition of drug contained in the Federal Food, Drug, and Cosmetic Act and the extent of the Secretary of Health, Education, and Welfare's regulatory authority under that definition. The specific item involved in this definitional controversy is a laboratory aid known as an antibiotic sensitivity disc, used as a screening test for help in determining the proper antibiotic drug to administer to patients. If the article is a "drug" ... then the Secretary can subject it to pre-market clearance regulations promulgated pursuant to § 507 of the Act.... If, on the other hand, the article is merely a "device" under the Act, it is subject only to the misbranding and adulteration proscriptions of the Act and does not have to be pretested before marketing; and, of course, if the disc does not fall under either definition, the Act itself is totally inapplicable....

At the outset, it is clear from § 201 that the word "drug" is a term of art for the purposes of the Act, encompassing far more than the strict medical definition of that word....

The historical expansion of the definition of drug, and the creation of a parallel concept of devices, clearly show, we think, that Congress fully intended that the Act's coverage be as broad as its literal language indicates and equally clearly, broader than any strict medical definition might otherwise allow. Strong indications from legislative history that Congress intended the broad coverage the District Court thought "ridiculous" should satisfy us that the lower courts erred in refusing to apply the Act's language as written. But we are all the more convinced that we must give effect to congressional intent in view of the well-accepted principle that remedial legislation such as the Food, Drug, and Cosmetic Act is to be given a liberal construction consistent with the Act's overriding purpose to protect the public health, and specifically, § 507's purpose to ensure that antibiotic products marketed serve the public with "efficacy" and "safety."

Respondent's alternative contention, that even if its product does fall within the purview of the Act, it is plainly a "device" and therefore by definition necessarily not a "drug," must also be rejected, we believe, in light of the foregoing analysis. At the outset, it must be conceded that the language of the statute is of little assistance in determining precisely what differentiates a "drug" from a "device": to the extent that both are intended for use in the treatment, mitigation and cure of disease, the former is an "article" and the latter includes "instruments," "apparatus," and "contrivances." Despite the obvious areas of overlap in definition, we are not entirely without guidance in determining the propriety of the

Secretary's decision below, given the overall goals of the Act and its legislative history.

More specifically, . . . the "natural way" to draw the line "is in light of the statutory purpose." Since the patient will tend to derive less benefit and perhaps some harm from a particular antibiotic if, though the drug itself was properly batch-tested, it was not the proper antibiotic to use, it was entirely reasonable for the Secretary to determine that the discs, like the antibiotics they serve, are drugs and similarly subject to pre-clearance certification under § 507. An opposite conclusion might undercut the value of testing the antibiotics themselves, for such testing would be a useless exercise if the wrong drug were ultimately administered, even partially as the result of an unreliable disc. . . .

Reversed.

B. FOOD

Section 201(f) of the FD&C Act defines "food" as follows: "The term 'food' means (1) articles used for food and drink for man or other animals, (2) chewing gum, and (3) articles used for components of any such article." Not surprisingly, this tautological definition ("food" means "food") leaves many open questions. The issue of the definition's precise meaning has sometimes arisen in disputes over whether a particular product is a food or falls outside FDA's authority altogether. On other occasions, as in the case excerpted below, the question has come up when FDA has tried to regulate as a drug a product that the manufacturer claims is only a food. Because new drugs are subject to premarket approval by the agency for safety and effectiveness, whereas foods are not, the resolution of such a dispute over application of the food definition frequently determines the fate of the product.

Nutrilab, Inc. v. Schweiker

713 F.2d 335 (7th Cir. 1983).

■ CUMMINGS, CHIEF JUDGE.

Plaintiffs manufacture and market a product known as "starch blockers" which "block" the human body's digestion of starch as an aid in controlling weight. On July 1, 1982, the Food and Drug Administration ("FDA") classified starch blockers as "drugs" and requested that all such products be removed from the market until FDA approval was received. . . .

The only issue on appeal is whether starch blockers are foods or drugs under the Federal Food, Drug, and Cosmetic Act. Starch blocker tablets and capsules consist of a protein which is extracted from a certain type of raw kidney bean. That particular protein functions as an alpha-amylase inhibitor; alpha-amylase is an enzyme produced by the body which is utilized in digesting starch. When starch blockers are ingested during a meal, the protein acts to prevent the alpha-amylase enzyme from acting, thus allowing the undigested starch to pass through the body and avoiding the calories that would be realized from its digestion.

Kidney beans, from which alpha-amylase inhibitor is derived, are dangerous if eaten raw. By August 1982, FDA had received seventy-five reports of adverse effects on people who had taken starch blockers, including complaints of gastro-intestinal distress such as bloating, nausea, abdominal pain, constipation and vomiting. Because plaintiffs consider starch blockers to be food, no testing as required to obtain FDA approval as a new drug has taken place. If starch blockers were drugs, the manufacturers would be required to file a new drug application pursuant to 21 U.S.C. § 355 and remove the product from the marketplace until approved as a drug by the FDA.

The statutory scheme under the Food, Drug, and Cosmetic Act is a complicated one. Section 321(g)(1) provides that the term "drug" means

> ... (B) articles intended for use in the diagnosis, cure, mitigation, treatment, or prevention of disease in man or other animals; and (C) articles (other than food) intended to affect the structure or any function of the body of man or other animals; and (D) articles intended for use as a component of any article specified in clauses (A), (B), or (C) of this paragraph; but does not include devices or their components, parts, or accessories.

The term "food" as defined in Section 321(f) means

> (1) articles used for food or drink for man or other animals, (2) chewing gum, and (3) articles used for components of any such article.

Section 321(g)(1)(C) was added to the statute in 1938 to expand the definition of "drug." The amendment was necessary because certain articles intended by manufacturers to be used as drugs did not fit within the "disease" requirement of Section 321(g)(1)(B). Obesity in particular was not considered a disease. Thus "anti-fat remedies" marketed with claims of "slenderizing effects" had escaped regulation under the prior definition....

It is well established that the definitions of food and drug are normally not mutually exclusive; an article that happens to be a food but is intended for use in the treatment of disease fits squarely within the drug definition in part B of Section 321(g)(1) and may be regulated as such. Under part C of the statutory drug definition, however, "articles (other than food)" are expressly excluded from the drug definition (as are devices) in Section 321(g)(1).* In order to decide if starch blockers are drugs under Section 321(g)(1)(C), therefore, we must decide if they are foods within the meaning of the part C "other than food" parenthetical exception to Section 321(g)(1)(C). And in order to decide the meaning of "food" in that parenthetical exception, we must first decide the meaning of "food" in Section 321(f).

---

* [Authors' Note: the definition of "drug" at 21 U.S.C. § 321(g)(1) no longer explicitly excludes devices.]

Congress defined "food" in Section 321(f) as "articles used as food." This definition is not too helpful, but it does emphasize that "food" is to be defined in terms of its function as food, rather than in terms of its source, biochemical composition or ingestibility. Plaintiffs' argument that starch blockers are food because they are derived from food—kidney beans—is not convincing; if Congress intended food to mean articles derived from food it would have so specified. Indeed some articles that are derived from food are indisputably not food, such as caffeine and penicillin. In addition, all articles that are classed biochemically as proteins cannot be food either, because for example, insulin, botulism toxin, human hair and influenza virus are proteins that are clearly not food.

Plaintiffs argue that 21 U.S.C. § 343(j) specifying labeling requirements for food for special dietary uses indicates that Congress intended products offered for weight conditions to come within the statutory definition of "food." Plaintiffs misinterpret that statutory section. It does not define food but merely requires that if a product is a food and purports to be for special dietary uses, its label must contain certain information to avoid being misbranded. If all products intended to affect underweight or overweight conditions were *per se* foods, no diet product could be regulated as a drug under Section 321(g)(1)(C), a result clearly contrary to the intent of Congress that "anti-fat remedies" and "slenderizers" qualify as drugs under that Section.

If defining food in terms of its source or defining it in terms of its biochemical composition is clearly wrong, defining food as articles intended by the manufacturer to be used as food is problematic. When Congress meant to define a drug in terms of its intended use, it explicitly incorporated that element into its statutory definition. For example, Section 321(g)(1)(B) defines drugs as articles "intended for use" in, among other things, the treatment of disease; Section 321(g)(1)(C) defines drugs as "articles (other than food) intended to affect the structure or any function of the body of man or other animals." The definition of food in Section 321(f) omits any reference to intent.... Further, a manufacturer cannot avoid the reach of the FDA by claiming that a product which looks like food and smells like food is not food because it was not intended for consumption. In *United States v. Technical Egg Prods., Inc.*, 171 F. Supp. 326 (N.D. Ga. 1959), the defendant argued that the eggs at issue were not adulterated food under the Act because they were not intended to be eaten. The court held that there was a danger of their being diverted to food use and rejected defendant's argument.

Although it is easy to reject the proffered food definitions, it is difficult to arrive at a satisfactory one. In the absence of clearcut Congressional guidance, it is best to rely on statutory language and common sense. The statute evidently uses the word "food" in two different ways. The statutory definition of "food" in Section 321(f) is a term of art and is clearly intended to be broader than the common-sense definition of food, because the statutory definition of "food" also includes chewing gum and food additives. Food additives can be any substance the intended use of which results or may reasonably [be expected to] result in its becoming a component or otherwise affecting the characteristics of any food. *See* 21 U.S.C. § 321(s). Paper food-packaging when containing polychlorinated biphenyls

(PCB's), for example, is an adulterated food because the PCB's may migrate from the package to the food and thereby become a component of it.... Yet the statutory definition of "food" also includes in Section 321(f)(1) the common-sense definition of food. When the statute defines "food" as "articles used for food," it means that the statutory definition of "food" includes articles used by people in the ordinary way most people use food—primarily for taste, aroma, or nutritive value. To hold as did the district court that articles used as food are articles used solely for taste, aroma or nutritive value is unduly restrictive since some products such as coffee or prune juice are undoubtedly food but may be consumed on occasion for reasons other than taste, aroma, or nutritive value.

This double use of the word "food" in Section 321(f) makes it difficult to interpret the parenthetical "other than food" exclusion in the Section 321(g)(1)(C) drug definition. As shown by that exclusion, Congress obviously meant a drug to be something "other than food," but was it referring to "food" as a term of art in the statutory sense or to foods in their ordinary meaning? Because all such foods are "intended to affect the structure or any function of the body of man or other animals" and would thus come within the part C drug definition, presumably Congress meant to exclude common-sense foods. Fortunately, it is not necessary to decide this question here because starch blockers are not food in either sense.* The tablets and pills at issue are not consumed primarily for taste, aroma, or nutritive value under Section 321(f)(1); in fact, as noted earlier, they are taken for their ability to block the digestion of food and aid in weight loss. In addition, starch blockers are not chewing gum under Section 321(f)(2) and are not components of food under Section 321(f)(3). To qualify as a drug under Section 321(g)(1)(C), the articles must not only be articles "other than food," but must also be "intended to affect the structure or any function of the body of man or other animals." Starch blockers indisputably satisfy this requirement for they are intended to affect digestion in the people who take them. Therefore, starch blockers are drugs under Section 321(g)(1)(C) of the Food, Drug, and Cosmetic Act.

Affirmed.

NOTES

1. *Dual Classification.* It is indisputable that a product fitting the common sense definition of a "food" in section 201(f) is also subject to regulation as a drug

---

* The FDA urges an interpretation of the statute that would allow drug regulation of a product if, for example, an appetite suppressant were added to a recognized food. According to the FDA, addition of the drug might make it a "component" and therefore subject to regulation as a statutory "food". As such, the literal language of Section 321(g)(1)(C) would preclude regulation as a drug because the product would qualify as a statutory "food". Even if Section 321(g)(1)(C) meant only to exclude common-sense foods, an article might still be considered food unless addition of an appetite suppressant so changed its nature that it was no longer used primarily for taste, aroma or nutritional value. The FDA submits that a drug manufacturer could easily escape drug regulation by simply adding the drug to a food.

It is not necessary to resolve this problem in order to resolve this case. We merely note the possibility that the word "component" might be interpreted to exclude substances specifically added to a food to avoid bringing the substance within the drug definition, and, as noted above, a food may lose its food character if a drug is added.

under section 201(g)(1)(B) if the manufacturer makes a therapeutic claim for it. *See* Senate Rep. No. 361, 74th Cong. 1st Sess. 4 (1935). In *American Health Products Co., Inc. v. Hayes*, 574 F. Supp. 1498 (S.D.N.Y. 1983), a case brought about the same time as *Nutrilab* by a different starchblocker manufacturer, the government advanced a bolder argument. It contended that a food is subject to dual classification, even in the absence of a therapeutic claim, if there is a claim regarding a specific physiological effect (that is, a structure or function claim). The United States asserted that a product making such a claim falls outside the food exclusion from section 201(g)(1)(C)'s definition of "drug," even if it is also a common sense food under section 201(f). Although the District Court held for the government on the same grounds as the Seventh Circuit in *Nutrilab*, it rejected FDA's argument as to dual classification.

> The government's contention [in favor of dual classification] is untenable. Though most sections of the Act countenance dual classification, no other contains a parenthetical like that Congress inserted in part (C). Ignoring that parenthetical would render meaningless the distinctions Congress has attempted to delineate. Nevertheless, the government is correct in claiming that starchblocker pills are a "drug" under the Act, because the pills are not a "food" in any sense cognizable under the statute. . . .

In affirming the district court, the Second Circuit specifically stated that "we do not reach the issue whether dual classification is appropriate under section 321(g)(1)(C)." *American Health Prods. Co. v. Hayes*, 744 F.2d 912 (2d Cir. 1984) (per curiam).

2. *Caffeine.* FDA regulates over-the-counter stimulants in which caffeine is the active ingredient as drugs. 21 C.F.R. Part 340. However, when caffeine is added to food, such as a soft drink, the agency does not regulate the product as a drug even if the manufacturer promotes the food's high level of caffeine and its "energizing" qualities. Apparently, in FDA's view, such products fall within the food exception to the structure/function drug definition in section 201(g)(1)(C).

3. *The Impact of DSHEA.* The Dietary Supplement Health and Education Act of 1994 (DSHEA) amended the FD&C Act in a way that dramatically changed the categorization question for products such as starchblockers. A product that satisfies DSHEA's definition of a "dietary supplement" is now automatically classified as a food, regardless of whether it satisfies *Nutrilab*'s "common sense" test. Indeed, "starch-blocking" amylase inhibitors derived from kidney beans are currently marketed as dietary supplements, and thus as foods. Nonetheless, for products that do not qualify as dietary supplements under DSHEA, *Nutrilab*'s "common sense" definition of food still applies. DSHEA is addressed in detail below, *infra* p. 260.

4. *Structure/Function Claims Versus Disease Claims.* The line between structure/function claims and disease claims can be a maddeningly indistinct one. Nevertheless, FDA did not set forth a comprehensive analysis of the distinction until 2000. We consider the agency's assessment of the difference between the types of claims, *infra* p. 276.

COMMENT: OTHER APPLICATIONS OF THE DEFINITION OF "FOOD"

Food Additives. As explained by the *Nutrilab* court, the distinction between a food and a drug is critical because new drugs, unlike conventional foods, are subject to the requirement of premarket approval by FDA. The manufacturer of a new drug must establish to FDA that its product is safe and effective before the agency will approve it. Observe, however, that there is a subcategory of foods, called "food additives," that are subject to a premarket safety approval by the agency. The definition of food in section 201(f) includes "articles used for components" of food or drink. As set forth in section 201(s) of the FD&C Act, "The term 'food additive' means any substance the intended use of which results or may reasonably be expected to result, directly or indirectly, in its becoming a component or otherwise affecting the characteristics of any food . . . if such substance is not generally recognized, among experts qualified by scientific training and experience to evaluate its safety . . . to be safe under the conditions of its intended use." The exemption for foods that are generally recognized as safe (GRAS) frees most conventional food ingredients from the requirement of premarket approval. Section 201(s) also lists a number of specific exceptions to the definition of "food additive." This section is examined in detail *infra* Chapter III.

Migrating Food–Contact Materials. The statutory definition of food includes substances that migrate to food from food packaging and dinnerware, even before such migration takes place. *Natick Paperboard Corp. v. Weinberger*, 525 F.2d 1103 (1st Cir. 1975); *United States v. Articles of Food Consisting of Pottery . . . Labeled Cathy Rose*, 370 F. Supp. 371 (E.D. Mich. 1974).

Chewing Gum. Section 201(f)(2) of the FD&C Act specifically classifies chewing gum as food. As a result, FDA has taken the position that when snuff is included in a masticatory carrier base, which has the appearance of a piece of confectionary, it is properly regulated as a food. *See* Letter from FDA Associate Commissioner for Regulatory Affairs J.M. Taylor to S.M. Pape (Apr. 11, 1988).

No Longer "Fit" Food. A product is a food under the Act if it is generally regarded as food when sold in food form even if it is decomposed or otherwise unfit for food at the time FDA institutes legal action against it. *See, e.g., United States v. H.B. Gregory Co.*, 502 F.2d 700 (7th Cir. 1974); *Otis McAllister & Co. v. United States*, 194 F.2d 386 (5th Cir. 1952); *United States v. O.F. Bayer & Co.*, 188 F.2d 555 (2d Cir. 1951); *United States v. 52 Drums Maple Syrup*, 110 F.2d 914 (2d Cir. 1940); *United States v. Technical Egg Products, Inc.*, 171 F. Supp. 326 (N.D. Ga. 1959); *United States v. Thirteen Crates of Frozen Eggs*, 215 F. 584 (2d Cir. 1914). *See also* Annotation: *What is "Food" Within Meaning of Statute*, 17 A.L.R. 1282 (1922).

COMMENT: OTHER AGENCIES' ROLES IN REGULATING FOOD

Several categories of food products are subject to specific regulatory requirements.

Meat, Poultry, and Eggs. These products are regulated by the United States Department of Agriculture (USDA) under the Federal Meat Inspection Act (FMIA), 21 U.S.C. 601 *et seq.*, the Poultry Products Inspection Act, 21 U.S.C. 451 *et seq.*, and the Egg Products Inspection Act, 21 U.S.C. 1031 *et seq.* USDA has ceded to FDA jurisdiction over any food that is less than two percent meat or poultry. The jurisdiction of USDA and FDA over these three categories of food products is otherwise complex and uncertain. FDA has exclusive regulatory jurisdiction over live animals intended to be used for food. *United States v. Tomahara Enterprises, Ltd.*, Food Drug Cosm. L. Rep. (CCH) ¶ 38,217 (N.D.N.Y. 1983). USDA has exclusive jurisdiction over the slaughter of food animals and over the subsequent processing of meat and poultry, except that USDA and FDA have joint jurisdiction over the use of food additives in meat and poultry. After processing, USDA and FDA have joint jurisdiction over the distribution of meat and poultry up to the retail establishment where it is sold. FDA has exclusive jurisdiction over retail food establishments. *D&W Food Centers, Inc. v. Block*, 786 F.2d 751 (6th Cir. 1986), held that a central kitchen making pizza containing meat was not subject to the continuous inspection requirements of the Federal Meat Inspection Act. *See generally Food Regulation: A Case Study of USDA and FDA*, in "Study on Federal Regulation: Regulatory Organization," Senate Comm. on Governmental Affairs, 95th Cong., 1st Sess., Vol. V, at Ch. 4 (Comm. Print 1977).

The FMIA has long applied to the meat of only five named species (cattle, sheep, swine, goats, and equines), and not to meat of other species such as rabbit, venison, or bison, which remained within FDA's purview. *See, e.g.*, 21 U.S.C. 601(j) (definition of "meat food product"). In 2005, however, Congress, as part of the FY 2006 Agriculture Appropriations bill, 119 Stat. 2120, amended the FMIA to extend the USDA inspection system to all "amenable species," defined as the above species plus "any additional species of livestock that the Secretary considers appropriate." 21 U.S.C. 601(w)(2).

FDA has primary responsibility for the safety and labeling of shell eggs, although the voluntary grading of shell eggs is done under USDA supervision. Egg processing plants that wash, sort, break, and pasteurize eggs are under USDA jurisdiction, as are processed products known for their egg content.

Alcoholic Beverages. The Alcohol and Tobacco Tax and Trade Bureau (TTB) of the Department of the Treasury has jurisdiction over alcoholic beverages under the Federal Alcohol Administration Act, 49 Stat. 977 (1935), codified in 27 U.S.C. 201 *et seq.* The Bureau of Alcohol, Tobacco and Firearms in the Department of the Treasury formerly performed this function, but the Homeland Security Act of 2002 shifted certain law enforcement responsibilities of BATF to the Department of Justice and kept tax and trade regulation within a newly-named unit of the Treasury Department. TTB regulates all beer products regardless of their alcohol content. 51 Fed. Reg. 39666 (Oct. 30, 1986). In contrast, TTB regulates only those wine products that contain 7 percent alcohol or more, and FDA regulates all wine products containing less than 7 percent alcohol. FDA Compliance Policy Guide No. 7101.05 (Oct. 1, 1980). Attempts to amend the Federal Alcohol Administration Act to extend the Department of the Treasury's jurisdiction to wine products containing as little as 0.5 percent alcohol have been unsuccessful. Accordingly, wine coolers, which have an alcohol content of less than 7 percent, are regulated by FDA rather than TTB.

One court has held that the labeling of alcoholic beverages (except for wine products containing less than 7 percent alcohol) is subject only to

BATF (now TTB) jurisdiction and is exempt from the labeling requirements of the FD&C Act. *Brown–Forman Distillers Corp. v. Mathews*, 435 F. Supp. 5 (W.D. Ky. 1976). In other respects, however, alcoholic beverages are regulated as food by FDA, although the two agencies have a memorandum of understanding that confirms TTB's primary responsibility for overseeing voluntary recalls of adulterated products. *See* FDA Compliance Policy Guide No. 7155.04 (Nov. 1987); Elaine T. Byszewski, *What's in the Wine? A History of FDA's Role*, 57 Food & Drug L.J. 545 (2002); Iver P. Cooper, *The FDA, the BATF, and Liquor Labeling: A Case Study of Interagency Jurisdictional Conflict*, 34 Food Drug Cosm. L.J. 370 (1979); Mary Hancock, *Federal Jurisdictional Disputes in the Labeling and Advertising of Malt Beverages*, 34 Food Drug Cosm. L.J. 271 (1979); *Symposium on Alcoholic Beverage Control*, 7 Law & Contemp. Probs. 543 (1940). FDA has also adopted Compliance Policy Guide 7101.04, 54 Fed. Reg. 38559 (Sept. 19, 1989), governing the labeling of dealcoholized wine beverages.

Water and Ice. Under the Safe Drinking Water Act, 88 Stat. 1660 (1974), general responsibility for the purity of drinking water was placed in the Environmental Protection Agency (EPA), but section 410 was added to the FD&C Act to preserve FDA's jurisdiction over bottled drinking water. The agency also has jurisdiction over ice. *See* C.W. Felix, *Ice—the Forgotten Food*, 53 J. Ass'n Food & Drug Officials 19 (July 1989). Water used to process food or as an ingredient in food is subject to the same requirements under the FD&C Act as any other food constituent.

C. COSMETICS

Section 201(i) of the FD&C Act defines "cosmetic" as "(1) articles intended to be rubbed, poured, sprinkled, or sprayed on, introduced into, or otherwise applied to the human body or any part thereof for cleansing, beautifying, promoting attractiveness, or altering the appearance, and (2) articles intended for use as a component of any such articles; except that such term shall not include soap." Cosmetics are the least intensively regulated of all the product categories under FDA's jurisdiction. There is no premarket approval requirement for any cosmetic or cosmetic ingredient, with the exception of color additives. But, like foods, cosmetics may be simultaneously classified as drugs. Moreover, because the structure/function leg of the drug definition, section 201(g)(1)(C), does not contain an exception for cosmetics, as it does for food, a cosmetic may be dual-classified as a drug even if it is a nontherapeutic product intended only to affect the structure or any function of the body. The question of when a cosmetic is also a drug is addressed later in this chapter, *infra* p. 48.

Section 201(i)—the "cosmetic" definition itself—has raised relatively few interpretive questions. Even so, several features of this provision deserve further discussion.

NOTES

1. *Odors.* FDA considers products intended to mask or prevent body odors, such as mouthwashes and underarm deodorants, to be cosmetics.

2. *Soap Exemption.* The FD&C Act does not define "soap." FDA has defined the scope of the soap exemption by regulation. According to the agency, the exemption applies only to articles that meet the following conditions: "(1) The bulk of the nonvolatile matter in the product consists of an alkali salt of fatty acids and the detergent properties of the article are due to the alkali-fatty acid compounds; and (2) The product is labeled, sold, and represented only as soap." 23 Fed. Reg. 7483 (Sept. 26, 1958), codified at 21 C.F.R. 701.20. If a product is intended not only for cleansing but also for other cosmetic uses, such as beautifying, moisturizing, or deodorizing, FDA will regulate it as a cosmetic. The exemption is thus quite narrow, and most products on the soap shelves of stores are cosmetics. In *United States v. An Article of Cosmetic ... Beacon Castile Shampoo*, 1969–1974 FDLI Jud. Rec. 149 (N.D. Ohio 1973), the court held that the claimant had the burden of proving the product fell within the soap exemption. The court acknowledged that a shampoo made from soap would fall within that exemption, but concluded that the claimant's shampoo did not qualify because it contained a synthetic detergent.

A soap-like product may also be a drug if it is intended to cure, treat or prevent disease or to affect the structure or any function of the human body. It remains unclear whether simply calling a soap product "antibacterial" renders it a drug, *see infra* p. 57, but any explicit therapeutic claims indisputably place a soap product in the drug category.

3. *Tattoos.* FDA regulates the inks used in tattoos and permanent makeup as cosmetics and the pigments used in these inks as color additives. Office of Cosmetics & Colors Fact Sheet: *Tattoos & Permanent Makeup*, Nov. 29, 2000. FDA, however, does not regulate the actual practice of tattooing; instead, oversight is left to local laws and jurisdictions.

4. *Animal Cosmetics.* The FD&C Act's definition of "cosmetic" is limited to articles intended to be applied to the "human body." Products intended to cleanse or promote the attractiveness of animals thus fall outside FDA's control. *Cf. United States v. Articles of Drug for Veterinary Use ... Goshen Laboratories, Inc.*, Food Drug Cosm. L. Rep. (CCH) ¶ 38,174 (S.D.N.Y. 1982) (claimant argued that the veterinary products involved were "canine cosmetics" not subject to the FD&C Act, but court concluded the articles were animal drugs under FDA control). By contrast, the FD&C Act's definitions of "food," "drug," and "device" (but not the definition of "biological product" in the Public Health Service Act) refer to "man or other animals."

5. *Cosmetic Foods.* Because breath freshening is a cosmetic effect, the line between foods and cosmetics can sometimes be elusive. For example, some dissolvable "breath strips" have been labeled as foods, whereas most are now labeled as cosmetics. FDA apparently has not voiced its opinion on the proper categorization of these products.

COMMENT: ARE COSMETIC DEVICES "COSMETICS"?

Are combs, nail files, or razor blades "cosmetics"? The requirement that a cosmetic be "rubbed, poured, sprinkled, or sprayed on, introduced into, or otherwise applied to the human body" seems to exclude many common household implements from the definition, despite their cosmetic uses. Indeed, prior to the passage of the FD&C Act, a Senate report considering this language declared, "[T]he definition of the term cosmetic does not include devices...." S. Rep. No. 361, 74th Cong., 1st Sess. 3 (1935). Nevertheless, until the early 1960s, FDA, on rare occasions, took legal action against household devices such as hair brushes, stockings, and toothpicks under the cosmetic provisions of the Act. In more recent decades, although the agency has never explicitly disclaimed its authority to classify such products as cosmetics, it has declined to assert jurisdiction over them.

In 2003, FDA took regulatory action against a type of device under the cosmetics provisions of the Act, apparently for the first time in many years. FDA declared that noncorrective decorative contact lenses were not medical devices, *see infra* p. 61, but it simultaneously asserted that they qualified as cosmetics and would be regulated as such. The agency observed that "decorative contact lenses are articles intended to be introduced into the eye, which is a part of the body, to beautify the wearer, promote the attractiveness of the wearer, or alter the wearer's appearance." 68 Fed. Reg. 16520, 16521 (Apr. 4, 2003). In asserting that these products were cosmetics, the agency observed: "The fact that contact lenses are 'devices' in the colloquial sense does not preclude cosmetic status under the act. FDA has previously determined that section 201(i) of the act applies to appearance-enhancing devices such as wigs, hair brushes, stockings and toothpicks." Later that year, FDA sent a warning letter to a distributor of decorative contact lenses, asserted that the lenses were adulterated cosmetics (because they were distributed without the involvement of a qualified eye care professional) and misbranded cosmetics (because their labeling failed to include sufficient instructions or warnings). Warning Letter from Timothy Ulatowski, Director, CDRH Office of Compliance, to BWild Inc. (Sept. 16, 2003). The agency has since sent similar letters to at least two other distributors of decorative contact lenses.

D.   Drugs and Devices

In general, drugs and devices are subject to much more rigorous regulatory regimes than food or cosmetics. Most important, since 1938, "new drugs" have been subject to premarket approval, and since 1976, many medical devices have been subject to either premarket approval or to the requirement that their manufacturers demonstrate that they are substantially equivalent to products already on the market. Consequently, a determination that a product is a drug or device is often tantamount to a determination that the product cannot be sold at all until FDA approves it for marketing.

Section 201(g)(1) of the FD&C Act defines "drug" as follows:

The term "drug" means

(A) articles recognized in the official United States Pharmacopoeia, official Homeopathic Pharmacopoeia of the United States, or official National Formulary, or any supplement to any of them; and

(B) articles intended for use in the diagnosis, cure, mitigation, treatment, or prevention of disease in man or other animals; and

(C) articles (other than food) intended to affect the structure or any function of the body of man or other animals; and

(D) articles intended for use as a component of any article specified in clause (A), (B), or (C)....

Section 201(h) of the FD&C Act defines "device" as follows:

The term "device" ... means an instrument, apparatus, implement, machine, contrivance, implant, in vitro reagent, or other similar or related article, including any component, part, or accessory, which is—

(1) recognized in the official National Formulary, or the United States Pharmacopeia, or any supplement to them,

(2) intended for use in the diagnosis of disease or other conditions, or in the cure, mitigation, treatment, or prevention of disease, in man or other animals, or

(3) intended to affect the structure or any function of the body of man or other animals,

and which does not achieve its primary intended purposes through chemical action within or on the body of man or other animals and which is not dependent upon being metabolized for the achievement of its primary intended purposes.

The Act's definitions of *drug* and *device* are parallel in many respects. This chapter focuses primarily on their common elements, while the distinctions between drugs and devices are considered in Chapter VII, which examines device regulation.

1.   INCLUSION IN OFFICIAL COMPENDIA

Section 321(g)(1)(A) of the Act includes within the definition of "drug" any article "recognized in the official United States Pharmacopeia, official Homeopathic Pharmacopoeia of the United States, or official National Formulary, or any supplement to any of them." The definition of "device" contains a parallel provision. *See* FD&C Act 321(h)(1).

The *United States Pharmacopeia and National Formulary (USP–NF)* is a compendium of standards for drug strength, quality, purity, packaging, labeling, and storage, published by the United States Pharmacopeia (USP), a nongovernmental organization more than a century old. The *National Formulary* was published separately by the American Pharmaceutical Association until 1975, when USP acquired the *NF* and combined the two publications under one cover. In addition to products universally viewed as drugs, the *USP–NF* also contains standards for most vitamins and minerals. The Homeopathic Pharmacopeia contains many herbal products.

Although section 321(g)(1)(A) appears on its face to give FDA the power to treat any item listed in these compendia as a drug, the agency generally has not viewed this provision so expansively. When FDA has attempted to regulate products as drugs based solely on their inclusion in the *USP* or *NF*, courts have usually thwarted these efforts. *Compare National Nutritional Foods Assoc. v. FDA*, 504 F.2d 761, 788–89 (2d Cir. 1974) (rejecting argument that vitamins and minerals are drugs because of their recognition in the official compendia); *National Nutritional Foods Association v. Mathews*, 557 F.2d 325, 337–38 (2d Cir. 1977) (rejecting the argument with regard to high potency vitamins); *and U.S. v. An Article of Drug ... Ova II*, 414 F. Supp. 660 (D.N.J. 1975), *aff'd without op.* 535 F.2d 1248 (3d Cir. 1976) (rejecting the argument with regard to pregnancy test kit), *with U.S. v. Articles of Drug ... Beuthanasia*, Food Drug Cosm. L.

Rep. (CCH) ¶ 38,265 (D. Neb. 1979) (accepting the argument with regard to animal euthanasia drug).

In *U.S. v. Ova II*, a federal district court considering the regulatory status of a pregnancy test concluded that the official compendia provision of the drug definition "cannot be taken literally," because a literal interpretation would "run[ ] afoul of the principle that a legislative body may not lawfully delegate its functions to a private citizen or organization." Nonetheless, the court observed that the inclusion of a product in such a compendium has real, if limited, legal significance.

> [T]he first definition, *i.e.*, recognition in the U.S.P. or other named compendium must be read to mean that:
>
> (a) an article put into the stream of interstate commerce with the intention that it be used for medicinal purposes, as evidenced by the label designation "U.S.P.," "N.F.," and the like, must meet the privately designated standards for quality and strength, or else be subject to appropriate action for misbranding or adulteration;
>
> (b) the recognition of an item in the U.S.P., etc., by a monograph, coupled with a label indicating compliance with standards, constitutes evidence that the item is a "drug" as a matter of prima facie proof only, calling on the opposing party to come forward with contrary evidence or else risk an adverse ruling; ...
>
> (d) an item recognized in U.S.P., etc., such as sodium hydroxide, hydrochloric acid, or whatever, by name, is not a drug if it is put into the channels of interstate commerce without a label such as "U.S.P.," "N.F." and the like, to imply that it is intended for medicinal use.

414 F. Supp. at 665–66.

For a further analysis of the official compendia provision of the drug definition, see *National Nutritional Foods Ass'n v. Mathews, infra* p. 42.

2.   "INTENDED USE" AND THE FOOD–DRUG SPECTRUM

The most important similarity between the definitions of "drug" and "device" is their common reference to "intended" use. In most instances, if a product is "intended for use in the diagnosis, cure, mitigation, treatment, or prevention" of disease or is "intended to affect the structure or function of the body," it is either a drug or a device. Not surprisingly, there have been countless disputes over the meaning of "intent" and over the types of evidence required to establish intent.

For both drugs and devices, FDA has used the following regulatory definition of "intended use" since 1952:

> The words *intended uses* or words of similar import ... refer to the objective intent of the persons legally responsible for the labeling of drugs. The intent is determined by such persons' expressions or may be shown by the circumstances surrounding the distribution of the article. This objective intent may, for example, be shown by labeling claims, advertising matter, or oral or written statements by such persons or their representatives. It

> may be shown by the circumstances that the article is, with the knowledge of such persons or their representatives, offered and used for a purpose for which it is neither labeled nor advertised. The intended uses of an article may change after it has been introduced into interstate commerce by its manufacturer. If, for example, a packer, distributor, or seller intends an article for different uses than those intended by the person from whom he received the drug [device], such packer, distributor, or seller is required to supply adequate labeling in accordance with the new intended uses. But if a manufacturer knows, or has knowledge of facts that would give him notice, that a drug [device] introduced into interstate commerce by him is to be used for conditions, purposes, or uses other than the ones for which he offers it, he is required to provide adequate labeling for such a drug [device] which accords with such other uses to which the article is to be put.

21 C.F.R. 201.128 (drugs); 21 C.F.R. 801.4 (devices). This definition articulates an extremely broad view of the types of evidence the agency can rely upon to establish a product's intended use. However, FDA has rarely attempted to classify a product as a drug or device in the absence of relevant representations by the manufacturer or distributor. The following, seminal case concerns one of the rare instances in which the agency attempted to do so.

The case involves high-dose vitamin supplements. FDA traditionally classified vitamin and mineral products as foods unless therapeutic claims were made for them. In the early 1970s, however, the agency was confronted with reports of people experiencing toxic effects from large doses of vitamins A and D. Adelle Davis, a self-proclaimed nutritional expert who advocated a "natural" approach to good health, recommended megadoses of these vitamins in her books. Vitamins A and D are fat-soluble nutrients (which accumulate in fatty tissue), and FDA thus concluded that ingestion of excess quantities of these vitamins could lead to serious harm.

To meet this problem, FDA promulgated regulations, 37 Fed. Reg. 26618 (Dec. 14, 1972), 38 Fed. Reg. 20723 (Aug. 2, 1973), classifying preparations providing more than 10,000 international units (IU) of vitamin A or 400 IU of vitamin D per daily serving as drugs and requiring further that they be sold only on prescription. Vitamin manufacturers challenged these regulations in court. The District Court initially upheld the regulations, *National Nutritional Foods Ass'n v. Weinberger*, 376 F. Supp. 142 (S.D.N.Y. 1974), but the Court of Appeals concluded that the administrative record was incomplete. It remanded the case with instructions that the district court inquire into the FDA Commissioner's reasoning. 512 F.2d 688 (2d Cir. 1975). After conducting the mandated hearing, the District Court once again upheld the regulations, 418 F. Supp. 394 (S.D.N.Y. 1976), and the plaintiffs appealed for a second time.

National Nutritional Foods Ass'n v. Mathews

557 F.2d 325 (2d Cir. 1977).

■ ROBERT P. ANDERSON, CIRCUIT JUDGE:

... When this case was previously remanded by us to the district court, we said, "... a serious question is raised as to whether the

Commissioner, in concluding that the higher level dosage forms of Vitamins A and D are 'drugs,' acted 'in accordance with law.' " ... In the statement announcing the proposal of the Vitamins A and D regulations and in the one accompanying their adoption, the Commissioner did not rely upon the recognition of these preparations in the [official compendia] as the basis of the drug classification. Rather, the Commissioner determined that the circumstances surrounding the use of Vitamins A and D at the regulated levels indicated an intended therapeutic use under § 201(g)(1)(B). The vendors' intent in selling the product to the public is the key element in this statutory definition.

In determining whether an article is a "drug" because of an intended therapeutic use, the FDA is not bound by the manufacturer's subjective claims of intent but can find actual therapeutic intent on the basis of objective evidence. Such intent also may be derived or inferred from labeling, promotional material, advertising, and "any other relevant source." [Case citations omitted.] In remanding this case, this court expressly indicated that evidence that Vitamins A and D at the regulated levels were used "almost exclusively for therapeutic purposes" when coupled with lack of a recognized nutritional use, would be sufficient to show that high dosage Vitamins A and D products were intended for use in the treatment of disease.

In proposing the regulations, the Commissioner emphasized the potential for toxicity and the widespread promotion of the intake of high doses of Vitamins A and D to cure a variety of ills. To show objective therapeutic intent, the Commissioner's affidavit submitted on remand relied upon three factors: (1) widespread promotion to the public in the use of high potency Vitamins A and D preparations for the treatment of various ailments; (2) lack of recognized nutritional usefulness; and (3) potential for toxicity from the ingestion of large doses of these vitamins over extended periods of time....

Plaintiffs assert that toxicity is irrelevant to the issue of therapeutic intent and, although the key element in determining that a drug should be limited to prescription use under § 503(b) of the Act, it has no bearing upon whether an article is a drug. The Government argues, on the other hand, that toxicity is relevant to therapeutic intent and that the Commissioner must make the decision of whether there should be a regulation which classifies an article as a food or as a drug, for the purposes of the Act. Although an article may be recognized as a food, this does not preclude it from being regulated as a drug. The determination that an article is properly regulated as a drug, however, is not left to the Commissioner's unbridled discretion to act to protect the public health but must be in accordance with the statutory definition. Toxicity is not included as an element in the statutory definition of a drug. It is relevant as a factor supporting the Commissioner's classification under § 201(g)(1)(B), but only to the extent that it constitutes objective evidence of therapeutic intent. Toxicity is cited by the Commissioner as constituting objective evidence of "something more" than lack of nutritional usefulness.... Such evidence, however, only presents a further indication that the excessive intake of Vitamins A and D may not be nutritionally useful and does not provide the objective evidence of therapeutic intent necessary to support these regulations.

There is no evidence in the administrative record that the manufacturers and vendors of Vitamins A and D preparations, at the regulated dosages, represent through labeling, promotional materials, or advertising that these products are effective in the cure or treatment of disease. They are sold as "dietary supplements." . . .

The main issue on this appeal is whether the evidence of the extensive use of large doses of Vitamins A and D to treat or prevent diseases and the promotion of such usage by persons not associated with the manufacturers or vendors establishes such widespread therapeutic use at the regulated levels as to overcome the plaintiffs' claim of the lack of an intended use to cure or prevent disease and thus justifies the Commissioner's determination.

The Commissioner admits that below the stated levels of potency, Vitamins A and D are foods. The evidence relied upon to show therapeutic intent, therefore, must be related to the potency level chosen to differentiate between the use of Vitamins A and D as foods and the use of these vitamins as drugs. The administrative record clearly establishes that the factors involved in choosing the levels at which Vitamins A and D become drugs were solely related to the Commissioner's fear of potential toxic effect and his belief that the ingestion of vitamins at levels above the U.S. RDA is not nutritionally useful. No further record evidence has been produced on the remand to show that the 10,000 IU and 400 IU levels were chosen because at those potencies, consumption of them is almost exclusively for therapeutic purposes. A sampling of the comments submitted to the FDA after publication of the proposed regulations reveals that people believe that a wide range of doses of these vitamins are therapeutically useful. A large group of individuals indicated that they ingested these vitamins at various dosages solely to supplement their daily diet in the belief that more Vitamins A and D were needed to maintain optimal health than the upper limits in the U.S. RDA.

In remanding this case, this court suggested that proof in the record demonstrating that, at the 10,000 IU and 400 IU levels, respectively, these vitamins were taken "almost exclusively" for therapeutic purposes, would tend to show that the regulations were not arbitrary or capricious. There was no evidence, however, supporting the Commissioner's conclusion that, when sold at the regulated, *i.e.* prescription, levels, therapeutic usage of these vitamins so far outweighed their use as dietary supplements, it showed an objective intent that these products were used in the mitigation and cure of diseases. This claim furnished no contradiction to the charge that the FDA's regulations are arbitrary and capricious and not in accordance with law. . . .

The Commissioner also seeks to justify the Vitamins A and D regulations on the basis of § 201(g)(1)(A), which defines as drugs, articles "recognized" in the United States Pharmacopoeia (USP) or National Formulary (NF). . . . To construe § 201(g)(1)(A) so as to grant the Commis-

sioner the power to regulate as drugs every item mentioned in the USP and
NF solely on the basis of such inclusion would give the FDA virtually
unlimited discretion to regulate as drugs a vast range of items.... An
administrator's decision under a regulatory statute, such as the Food,
Drug, and Cosmetic Act, must be governed by an intelligible statutory
principle. If § 201(g)(1)(A) defines as drugs every item included in the USP
and NF, the FDA is not being consistent in its treatment of other items
similarly recognized. The Commissioner, therefore, has not applied the
§ 201(g)(1)(A) definition to every item in the compendia. Rather he has
singled out for drug classification items included in the USP and NF on the
basis of factors, such as toxicity in this case, that are not relevant to the
statutory criteria in § 201(g).

The Commissioner admitted in his affidavit that mere inclusion in the
USP and NF is an insufficient basis for drug classification after the
decision in *National Nutritional Foods Ass'n v. FDA* [504 F.2d 761 (2d Cir.
1974)]. He attempts to distinguish that case on the ground that Vitamins A
and D are recognized at therapeutic dosages in the compendia and are
regulated as drugs in this case only at levels in excess of the recognized
food levels in the USP. Other articles, however, are recognized in the
compendia at therapeutic levels and not regulated as drugs, for example
Vitamin C. The Commissioner must, therefore, show that the conflicting
treatment in the regulations of items similarly classified in the USP and
NF is not arbitrary under the applicable criteria. The FDA regulates
Vitamin C preparations at the USP's therapeutic level as food. To justify
the regulation of Vitamins A and D as drugs by relying on § 201(g)(1)(A)
the Commissioner would have to distinguish his treatment of Vitamin C as
food.

In proposing and adopting these regulations for Vitamins A and D, the
Commissioner did not rely upon or cite the recognition of these vitamins in
the USP and NF. He may not at this late hour on appeal rely upon them as
the basis for his drug classification because it is sheer *post hoc* rationaliza-
tion....

NOTES

1. *Subsequent Proceedings.* Following this decision, FDA revoked the challenged regulations. 43 Fed. Reg. 10551 (Mar. 14, 1978).

2. *Dual Classification.* There is no doubt that a product can be classified
simultaneously as both a therapeutic drug under section 201(g)(1)(B) and as a food.
Indeed, a product currently marketed as a food may at the same time undergo
clinical investigation for drug uses (in compliance with the FDA investigational
drug requirements, discussed *infra* p. 624). *See, e.g.*, "Nutrition Education—1973:
Phosphate Research and Dental Decay," Hearings before the Senate Select Comm.
on Nutrition and Human Needs, 93d Cong., 1st Sess. 549 (1973).

On various occasions, courts have upheld FDA's reliance on the Act's broad
definition of "drug" to regulate products that were concededly also subject to the
food provisions of the Act. In the following cases, courts held that products
ordinarily regarded as foods were properly classified as drugs because of the claims
made for them: *United States v. 250 Jars ... "Cal's Tupelo Blossom U.S. Fancy
Pure Honey"*, 344 F.2d 288 (6th Cir. 1965); *United States v. 24 Bottles ... "Sterling*

Vinegar and Honey", 338 F.2d 157 (2d Cir. 1964); *United States v. Hohensee*, 243 F.2d 367 (3d Cir. 1957) (tea); *United States v. 500 Plastic Bottles . . . "Wilfley's Bio Water,"* Food Drug Cosm. L. Rep. (CCH) ¶ 38,143 (D. Or. 1989) (water); *United States v. Kollman*, Food Drug Cosm. L. Rep. (CCH) ¶ 38,342 (D. Or. 1985 & 1986) (blue-green algae harvested from Klamath Lake, Oregon). In each instance, the agency invoked the drug definition in order to demand premarket testing and approval. As discussed *infra* p. 49, a product can also be simultaneously both a drug and a cosmetic.

3. *Once a Drug?* In *United States v. Articles of Drug . . . Neptone*, Food Drug Cosm. L. Rep. (CCH) ¶ 38,240 (N.D. Cal. 1983), FDA contended that the seized product was a drug and was granted summary judgment based on the following reasoning:

> . . . Claimant Aquaculture Corporation markets in the United States a product called Neptone, which is freeze-dried, homogenized, powdered New Zealand green mussel (Perna canaliculus) in capsule form. In 1976, claimant received from the Food and Drug Administration ("FDA") an Investigational Exemption for New Drug ("IND") for Neptone. The purpose of this exemption is to permit claimant to conduct clinical investigations into Neptone's safety and effectiveness.

> Neptone is sold in health food stores and by mail order. Claimant advertises in various health food magazines. Since 1980, claimant has also promoted Neptone through several brochures, magazine reprints, and a scientific paper. These were available on request and were sent to mail order customers. FDA Consumer Safety Officer Paul J. Sage was one such customer. In general, claimant's advertising extols the green mussel (and Neptone) as being high in mucopolysaccharides, which are claimed to help prevent diseases commonly associated with aging, such as arthritis and hardening of the arteries. . . .

> . . . The Court finds that the claimant's promotional claims clearly show that it intended Neptone to be used "in the diagnosis, cure, mitigation, treatment, or prevention of disease in man." The so-called "brown brochure" is the most flagrant example, but even the so-called "blue brochure" claims, among other things, that Neptone helps to repel infection, prevent blood clots, and maintain the elasticity of the arteries. . . .

> The Court does not view this opinion as establishing for all time that Neptone is a drug. The determination that Neptone is a drug rests entirely on the pattern of promotion used by claimant in the several years immediately preceding the instant seizure. Should Neptone again be marketed after some hiatus and a change in labelling, this order will not necessarily work an estoppel on whether that batch of Neptone is a drug.[1] The answer will turn on the relationship between the future sales and the offensive labelling. Clearly, this opinion cannot work any estoppel on the issues of misbranding and safety and effectiveness. . . .

> The Court recognizes that not applying collateral estoppel to future batches of Neptone might allow it to be marketed without its having been established as safe and effective. Fault for this lies with the drafters of this statute for conditioning the safety and effectiveness requirements on

---

1. This reasoning does not apply to any Neptone now in existence that is not currently under the *in rem* jurisdiction of this Court. The Court has found that claimant's promotions over the past few years reveal Neptone's intended use as a drug. These promotional claims presumably apply to the Neptone that was effectively seized as well as to the Neptone that was [not] effectively seized.

labelling. As noted above, claimant brought the regulatory scheme down upon itself through its labelling and promotional brochures; this Court will not take the further step of saying that now claimant can never get out from under the regulatory scheme.

See also In the Matter of Property Seized from International Nutrition, Food Drug Cosm. L. Rep. (CCH) ¶ 37, 177 (D. Nev. 1997).

4. *Commentary.* For discussion on food and drug classifications, see Roseann B. Termini, *Product Classification Under the Federal Food, Drug, & Cosmetic Act: When a Food Becomes a Drug*, 2 J. PHARMACY & L. 1 (1993). For a discussion of the regulatory boundaries between foods and drugs throughout the world, see Peter Mansell, *Battling Over the Boundaries*, SCRIP MAGAZINE, Oct. 2000, at 71.

COMMENT: "INTENDED USE" IN THE ABSENCE OF CLAIMS

Since the decision in *Mathews*, FDA has rarely asserted its drug or device jurisdiction over a product unless the manufacturer or distributor has made representations about product's disease or structure/function effects. But neither has the agency unequivocally disclaimed its authority to establish intended use based on the "circumstances surrounding the distribution of the article." 21 C.F.R. 201.128, 21 C.F.R. 801.4.

The most famous instance in which FDA attempted to declare a product to be a drug (or device) in the absence of relevant manufacturer claims was its 1996 rulemaking on cigarettes and smokeless tobacco. 61 Fed. Reg. 44396 (Aug. 28, 1996). FDA argued that tobacco products were "intended" to affect the structure/function of the body based solely on evidence concerning the foreseeable and actual use of the products for stimulation, tranquilization, weight control, and satisfaction of nicotine addiction and on internal company statements confirming the manufacturers' awareness of these uses. The Supreme Court ultimately denied FDA jurisdiction without reaching the "intended use" issue. *FDA v. Brown & Williamson Tobacco*, 529 U.S. 120 (2000), excerpted *infra* p. 82.

Throughout the *Brown & Williamson* litigation, the tobacco industry asserted that no court had ever found that a product was "intended for use" or "intended to affect" absent manufacturer claims regarding that product's use. This assertion would no longer be true if made today. In 2001, the United States brought criminal charges against a number of individuals for selling unlabeled balloons containing nitrous oxide ("laughing gas") in a parking lot outside a rock concert. The government alleged the defendants were unlawfully distributing misbranded prescription drugs, in violation of the FD&C Act. In *U.S. v. Travia*, 180 F. Supp.2d 115, 119 (D.D.C. 2001), the District Court rejected the defendants' argument that the nitrous oxide they sold was not a "drug" under the FD&C Act because they made no representations about its use. Judge Thomas Hogan stressed that intent could be determined not only by labeling, promotional claims, and advertising, but also by "any other relevant source." He observed, "This case is obviously unique in that . . . the sellers did not need to label or advertise their product, as the environment provided the necessary information between buyer and seller. In this context . . . the fact that there was no labeling may actually bolster the evidence of an intent to sell a mind-altering article without a prescription—that is, a misbranded drug."

COMMENT: DISEASE CLAIMS FOR FOOD AND STRUCTURE/FUNCTION CLAIMS FOR DIETARY SUPPLEMENTS

The definition of "drug" in section 201(g)(1) of the FD&C Act concludes with the following proviso:

> A food or dietary supplement for which a claim, subject to sections 403(r)(1)(B) and 403(r)(3) of this title or sections 403(r)(1)(B) and 403(r)(5)(D) of this title, is made in accordance with the requirements of 403(r) of this title is not a drug solely because the label or the labeling contains such a claim. A food, dietary ingredient, or dietary supplement for which a truthful and not misleading statement is made in accordance with section 403(r)(6) of this title is not a drug under clause (C) solely because the label or the labeling contains such a statement.

This language reflects dramatic changes in the relationship between food and drugs made by two important statutes passed in the 1990s: the Nutrition Labeling and Education Act of 1990 (NLEA) and the Dietary Supplement and Health Act of 1994 (DSHEA). The first sentence refers to the fact that under the NLEA, a food may, with approval by FDA (or in accordance with an authoritative statement by a federal scientific body or the National Academy of Sciences), make a claim "which expressly or by implication ... characterizes the relationship of any nutrient ... to a disease or a health-related condition." FD&C Act 403(r)(1)(B). The second sentence refers to the fact DSHEA establishes a new subcategory of food called "dietary supplements" and allows such products (many of which are not "common sense" foods) to make structure and function claims.

FDA began to permit explicit disease claims (termed "health claims" by the agency) on food labels in the 1980s, following the lead of the Federal Trade Commission, which started to allow such claims in food advertisements in the 1970s. *See infra* p. 272. By establishing the NLEA health claims regime in 1990, Congress was thus authorizing a lenient regulatory approach that FDA had, in broad terms, already embraced. By contrast, before the passage of DSHEA, FDA demonstrated a willingness to regulate dietary supplements aggressively, particularly through the imposition of the FD&C Act's premarket approval requirements for drugs and food additives. In short, DSHEA represented an effort by Congress to rein in the agency. The regulatory regimes for disease claims and dietary supplements are discussed at length, *infra* p. 284 and p. 246. At this early stage, however, it is important to recognize that the desire to subject certain classes of products to more or less regulation not only shapes FDA's interpretation of the statutory definitions, but sometimes leads Congress to revise the definitions.

3.   "INTENDED USE" AND THE COSMETIC–DRUG SPECTRUM

An article may fall under the FD&C Act's definitions of "drug" or "medical device" even if it has no therapeutic purpose, so long as it is "intended to affect the structure or any function of the body." FD&C Act 201(g)(1)(C) and 201(h). The definitions thus raise the question of how much, and in what way, a nontherapeutic product must be intended to alter the body to be considered a drug or device.

Just as an article may be both a "food" and a "drug," a product may simultaneously fall within the definitions of "cosmetic" and "drug" and be subject to the requirements of both categories. Cosmetics are the least intensively regulated of any of the products under FDA's jurisdiction. The agency thus has sometimes reached for greater authority over particular cosmetic products by trying to categorize them as new drugs subject to premarket review for safety and effectiveness.

Peter Barton Hutt, *Reconciling the Legal, Medical, and Cosmetic Chemist Approach to the Definition of a "Cosmetic"*

3 CTFA COSMETICS JOURNAL, No. 3 (1971).

The first principle is that the intended use of the product, rather than its inherent properties, control[s] its classification.... [T]he controlling representations made by the manufacturer may appear in labeling, in advertising, or in any other form of oral or written communication. And an implicit representation is as controlling as an explicit one....

The second general principle is that the representations made for a product may properly classify it in more than one product category under the Act. If a product were represented both to treat a disease and to promote attractiveness, it would properly be classified as both a drug and cosmetic, and must meet the legal requirements for both categories....

The third, and final, general principle is that it is the initial and primary responsibility of the manufacturer or distributor of a product to determine the proper classification of his product, and to make certain that it meets all applicable legal requirements....

Attempting to formulate a hard and fast rule differentiating between cosmetic claims and drug claims is virtually impossible. Some cosmetics are intended merely to color some part of the body, in order to promote attractiveness, and present no problem of proper classification. And on the other end of the scale, some products are represented to effect a physiological change in the body, and these would clearly fall into the drug category as well as the cosmetic category. But in between these two extremes is the difficult area of judgment—the cosmetics that claim to promote attractiveness through a slight, and usually temporary, physical but not physiological, effect upon the skin.

The Food and Drug Administration attempted to deal with the proper legal classification of some of these various types of products in the advisory opinions contained in its Trade Correspondence during 1938–1946. The difficulty in resolving these matters on a purely rational basis is readily demonstrated by just three of those opinions. FDA stated that mercury preparations used to bleach or remove tan are drugs because they are intended to affect the structure and function of the body. On the other hand, an article represented solely to produce an even tan is regarded by

FDA as a cosmetic. And a product intended not just to produce an even tan, but also to prevent sunburn, is a drug. . . .

A further indication of the distinction between a product that does and does not affect a bodily structure or function may be found in the area of deodorants. A product that absorbs perspiration, or masks its odor, or prevents odor by germicidal or bacteriostatic agents that act upon odor-producing bacteria, is classified by the Food and Drug Administration as a cosmetic and not a drug. A product that is designed to reduce perspiration odor by reducing the perspiration itself, through a change in the sweat glands, is considered by the Food and Drug Administration to be a drug.

A cosmetic may properly be represented for use to mask or cover up the physical manifestations of a disease, without becoming a drug. Acne and dandruff are regarded as disease conditions, and any product represented to treat those conditions is classified as a drug. But products that claim merely to cover up manifestations of acne, or to wash away loose dandruff flakes, would properly be classified solely as cosmetics.

An analogous question is presented by "hypoallergenic" cosmetic products, which claim to have "screened out" most irritants. Since hypoallergenic foods have not been regarded as drugs it would appear that hypoallergenic cosmetics would similarly not be regarded as drugs absent specific claims that certain diseases will be treated or relieved by the product. . . .

A question frequently asked is whether any inclusion of an active ingredient in a cosmetic automatically classifies it as a drug. The answer is that classification depends upon the claims made, not upon the inclusion of the ingredient itself. . . .

United States v. An Article . . . Sudden Change

409 F.2d 734 (2d Cir. 1969).

■ ANDERSON, CIRCUIT JUDGE:

This is an appeal in a seizure action from an order of the United States District Court for the Eastern District of New York . . . granting summary judgment for the claimant. The seizure concerned 216 bottles of a cosmetic product called "Sudden Change" which is a clear liquid lotion consisting primarily of two ingredients: bovine albumen (15%) and distilled water (over 84%). It is meant to be applied externally to the surface of the facial skin, and it is claimed, *inter alia*, in its labeling and advertising that it will provide a "Face Lift Without Surgery." The court below described the effects of the product as follows:

> Allowed to dry on the skin, it leaves a film which (1) masks imperfections, making the skin look smoother and (2) acts mechanically to smooth and firm the skin by tightening the surface. Both effects are temporary. There is apparently no absorption by, or changes in, skin tissue resulting from its applications; it washes off.

The central issue presented in this appeal is whether Sudden Change is, within the meaning of the Federal Food, Drug and Cosmetic Act, 21 U.S.C. § 321(g)(1), a "drug." . . . .

It is well settled that the intended use of a product may be determined from its label, accompanying labeling, promotional material, advertising and any other relevant source. Regardless of the actual physical effect of a product, it will be deemed a drug for purposes of the Act where the labeling and promotional claims show intended uses that bring it within the drug definition. . . .

The mere statement of this rule poses a crucial issue: by what standards are these claims to be evaluated? Or, to put it another way, what degree of sophistication or vulnerability is to be ascribed to the hypothetical potential consumer in order to understand how these claims are understood by the buying public? . . . . [W]e conclude that the purposes of the Act will best be effected by postulating a consuming public which includes "the ignorant, the unthinking and the credulous. . . ." . . .

While it is not altogether clear what standard the court below applied, the reasoning appears to assume something like a "reasonable woman" standard. Thus, the District Court assumes that the "constant exposure to puffing and extravagant claims" has induced "some immunity in the beautifiers' hyperbole" which is such that the court "cannot believe" that the potential consumer of Sudden Change "expects anything other than a possibility that she may look better." We agree that certain claims which arguably would bring the product within § 321(g)(1)(C) have so drenched the potential consumer that even the "ignorant, the unthinking and the credulous" must be presumed able to discount their promises as typical of cosmetic advertising puffery. We cannot agree, however, with the conclusion that such immunity or skepticism somehow transfers to the promise to "lift out puffs" or give a "face lift without surgery." The references to "face lift" and "surgery" carry distinctly physiological connotations, suggesting, at least to the vulnerable consumer that the product will "affect the structure . . . of the body . . ." in some way other than merely temporarily altering the appearance. We do not accept the concept that skepticism toward familiar claims necessarily entails skepticism toward unfamiliar claims; the theory of the legislation is that someone might take the claim literally.

In other words, with the exception of those claims which have become so associated with the familiar exaggerations of cosmetics advertising that virtually everyone can be presumed to be capable of discounting them as puffery,[10] the question of whether a product is "intended to affect the structure . . . of the body of man . . ." is to be answered by considering,

---

10. . . . We agree that the legislative history and the language of the Act require rejection of any rule which would convert all cosmetics into drugs. We believe, however, that the test which we have applied draws the necessary line while at the same time protecting the public. For example, promises that a product will "soften" or "moisturize" a woman's skin are so thoroughly familiar that constant exposure can be presumed to have induced sufficient immunity even in our hypothetical vulnerable consumer (this assumes, *arguendo*, that these promises have exactly the same degree of drug-type connotations as the "face lift without surgery" claim—an assumption which we reject).

first, how the claim might be understood by the "ignorant, unthinking or credulous" consumer, and second, whether the claim as so understood may fairly be said to constitute a representation that the product will affect the structure of the body in some medical—or drug-type fashion, *i.e.*, in some way other than merely "altering the appearance."

We hold, therefore, that so long as Sudden Change is claimed to give a "face lift without surgery" and to "lift out puffs" it is to be deemed a drug within the meaning of 21 U.S.C. § 321(g)(l)(C). It should be understood, however, that if the claimant ceases to employ these promotional claims and avoids any others which may fairly be interpreted as claiming to affect the structure of the skin in some physiological, though temporary, way, then, assuming *arguendo* that no actual physical effect exists, the product will not be deemed a drug for purposes of the Act. While there may be merit in the cause of those who seek to require pretesting of new cosmetics, it is not for the courts to legislate such a requirement; rather it must rest in the hands of Congress to decide whether such an amendment to the statute should be enacted or not. . . .

■ Mansfield, District Judge (dissenting): . . . .

In view of the existence of ample authority for regulation of cosmetics, it strikes me as unnecessary, in the absence of some imminent danger to public health—and none is suggested here—for the Court to adopt new standards of construction for the purpose of determining whether an article is intended as a "drug" rather than to follow time-proven rules. Yet that is exactly what the Court does here, with the result that it opens up a new—and in my view, unnecessary—avenue for regulation of cosmetics as drugs. If Congress believes that protection of the public requires pretesting and clearance of cosmetics by the Food and Drug Administration . . . and that their components be listed on the label, it has the power to act. I do not think the Court should do so by a process of tortuous construction. . . .

It may well be that the existence of fraud upon consumers of such products (whether drugs or cosmetics) should depend upon whether "the ignorant, the unthinking and credulous" would be deceived. The issue before us, however, is not whether consumers may be defrauded by the labelling and enclosures used in connection with the sale of "Sudden Change." The issue is whether the product must be classified as a "drug" which must be pre-tested, cleared and bear a label listing its components. Since that issue turns upon whether the article is *"intended* to affect the structure of the body" (emphasis added), it seems to me that the "gullible" woman standard is both irrelevant and unnecessary, and that the standard should be whether a reasonable person would construe the labeling and advertising as showing that the product was so intended. . . .

NOTES

1. *Parallel Cases.* In *United States v. An Article . . . "Line Away,"* 415 F.2d 369 (3d Cir. 1969), the court concluded that the promotional material for a similar product attributed drug characteristics to it:

> . . . [T]he repeated statements that Line Away is made in a "pharmaceutical laboratory" and packaged under "biologically aseptic conditions"

imply that the product itself is a pharmaceutical. Characterizing the lotion as "super-active" and "amazing," creating a "tingling sensation" when "at work," "tightening" the skin and "discouraging new wrinkles from form- ing" strongly reinforces the impression that this is a therapeutic product, the protein content of which has a tonic or otherwise wholesome physiolog- ical effect on the skin itself.

... Even the denial that Line Away is a "hormone" or a "harmful drug," read in the context of the other representations, suggests that it is a harmless drug.

Some "puffery" may not amount to representation of a cosmetic as a drug, but when "puffery" contains the strong therapeutic implications we find in the Line Away promotional material, we think the dividing line has been crossed.

But *United States v. An Article ... "Helene Curtis Magic Secret ..."*, 331 F. Supp. 912 (D. Md. 1971), held that Helene Curtis's very similar wrinkle smoother was a cosmetic and not a drug:

... The only two claims made for "Magic Secret" which even approach the magnitude of the claims made in *Line Away* and *Sudden Change* are that "Magic Secret" is a "pure protein" which causes an "astringent sensation." The promotional material does not emphasize these two claims and even the "ignorant, unthinking and credulous" consumer would not be led by these references to believe that "Magic Secret" would do other than alter their appearance. It is apparent that the promotional claims made for "Magic Secret" are less exaggerated than those reported in *Line Away* and *Sudden Change*. It cannot be said that they carry the same drug connota- tions as found by the Second and Third Circuits.

The court concluded that the product's promotional material would lead a prospec- tive purchaser only to expect that she may look better, and not that the structure of the body would be affected. *See also FTC v. Pantron I Corp.*, 33 F.3d 1088, 1105 (9th Cir. 1994) (endorsing *Magic Secret* analysis, but concluding that a baldness remedy claiming new hair growth was a drug).

2. *Subsequent FDA Actions Regarding Antiwrinkle Products.* Beginning in April 1987, FDA sent regulatory letters to dozens of cosmetic manufacturers alleging that products with "wrinkle remover" claims were illegal new drugs. " 'Antiaging' Creams Challenged," FDA Talk Paper No. T87–24 (May 14, 1987). A series of meetings and correspondence between an industry coalition and FDA on this matter was abruptly terminated on November 19, 1987 by the following statement in a letter by the FDA Associate Commissioner for Regulatory Affairs.

We consider a claim that a product will affect the body in some physiologi- cal way to be a drug claim, even if the claim is that the effect is only temporary. Such a claim constitutes a representation that the product is intended to affect the structure or function of the body and thus makes the product a drug under 21 U.S.C. 321(g)(1)(C). Therefore, we consider most of the anti-aging and skin physiology claims that you outline in your letter to be drug claims. For example, claims that a product 'counteracts,' 'retards,' or 'controls' aging or the aging process, as well as claims that a product will 'rejuvenate,' 'repair,' or 'renew' the skin, are drug claims because they can be fairly understood as claims that a function of the body, or that the structure of the body, will be affected by the product. For this reason also, all of the examples that you use to allege an effect within the epidermis as the basis for a temporary beneficial effect on wrinkles, lines, or fine lines are unacceptable. A claim such as 'molecules absorb ... and expand,' exerting upward pressure to 'lift' wrinkles 'upward' is a claim for an inner, structural change.

The Associate Commissioner did offer some guidelines for cosmetic claims:

> While we agree with your statements that wrinkles will not be reversed or removed by these products . . . we would not object to claims that products will temporarily improve the appearance of such outward signs of aging. The label of such products should state that the product is intended to cover up the signs of aging, to improve the appearance by adding color or a luster to skin, or otherwise to affect the appearance through physical means. . . .

> . . . [W]e would consider a product that claims to improve or to maintain temporarily the appearance or the feel of the skin to be a cosmetic. For example, a product that claims to moisturize or soften the skin is a cosmetic.

An attempt by one manufacturer to obtain clarification of the dividing line between cosmetic and drug claims for these products through a declaratory judgment action was thwarted when the court agreed with FDA's contention that the matter was not ripe for judicial review. *Estee Lauder, Inc. v. FDA*, 727 F. Supp. 1 (D.D.C. 1989). Individual companies eventually resolved their issues with FDA, and the agency ultimately did not bring formal action against any of these products.

After a lull, FDA has recently resumed taking action against antiwrinkle products. It issued warning letters to two manufacturers of skin creams, stating that the companies were selling unapproved drugs. *See Warning Letters Address Claims Made for Topical Skincare Preparations*, Office of Cosmetics and Colors Press Release (Mar. 1, 2005). The objectionable claims cited by FDA with respect to one of these products, Collagen5, included: "Collagen5™ is proven to reduce deep wrinkles up to . . . 70%," "Stimulates your skin's own collagen building network," "Reduces deep wrinkles from within the skin's surface," and "Visible results that won't fade away." Warning Letter from Alonza E. Cruse, Director, Los Angeles District, FDA, to University Medical Products USA, Inc. (Jan. 22, 2004). The other warning letter cited (among many other statements) the manufacturers' reference to "Pal–KTTKS solution's effectiveness at reducing the appearance of fine lines and wrinkles." Warning Letter from B. Belinda Collins, Director, Denver District Office, FDA, to Basic Research, LLC (Jan. 14, 2005). It is unclear why FDA took issue with this particular claim; perhaps it objected to the manufacturer's failure to declare that the effects were only "temporary."

3. *Thigh Creams*. The warning letters discussed above in Note 2 also informed companies that products claiming to combat cellulite, stretch marks, and breast sag and shrinkage and to reduce thigh circumference and overall weight were unapproved drugs. Warning Letter from Alonza E. Cruse, Director, Los Angeles District, FDA, to University Medical Products USA, Inc. (Jan. 22, 2004); Warning Letter from B. Belinda Collins, Director, Denver District, FDA, to Basic Research, LLC. FDA has suggested that it views all thigh creams promoted for cellulite reduction as drugs. *See Thigh Creams*, Office of Cosmetics and Colors Fact Sheet (Feb. 24, 2000) ("Thigh creams may more appropriately be classified as drugs under the Food, Drug, and Cosmetic Act since removal or reduction of cellulite affects the 'structure or function' of the body.")

4. *Hair Care Products*: In *United States v. Kasz Enterprises, Inc.*, 855 F. Supp. 534 (D.R.I. 1994), the U.S. District Court found that the distributor's two hair care products were drugs. Although the defendant stated that it never labeled or promoted its products as cures for baldness or to prevent hair loss, the court found the company was aware that its products were being offered by others to prevent

baldness. "The promotional materials accompanying Solutions 109 are replete with claims (testimonials) that hair growth has occurred and hair loss prevented with use of these products. Therefore, Solutions 109 are intended by Kasz for use in the mitigation, treatment, or prevention of hair loss and are thus drugs. . . ."

In a series of warning letters that FDA began issuing in April 2003, it reminded manufacturers that hair care products marketed with claims such as restoration of hair growth, hair loss prevention, and treatment of dandruff are considered drugs, not cosmetics. Office of Cosmetics and Colors, *Warning Letters Address Hair Care Products*, Apr. 3, 2003.

5. *FDA's Persistence.* FDA continues to challenge, as unapproved drugs, numerous products portrayed if not expressly labeled as providing health benefits. *E.g., United States v. Eighteen Units, More or Less, of "Sports Oxygen,"* Food Drug Cosm. L. Rep. (CCH) ¶ 39,025, 5 F.3d 1491 (3d Cir. 1993); *United States v. Ten Cartons, More or Less, of an Article . . . Ener–B,* Food Drug Cosm. L. Rep. (CCH) ¶ 39,518, 72 F.3d 285 (2d Cir. 1995) (nasal gel containing vitamin B12); Letter from Ronald G. Chesemore, FDA Associate Commissioner for Regulatory Affairs, to Walter E. Byerley (Dec. 26, 1990)(facial tissue impregnated with antibiotic).

COMMENT: "COSMECEUTICALS"

FDA scientists recognized very early that all cosmetics penetrate the skin and thus affect the body. As one wrote: "[T]here are few if any substances which are not absorbed through the intact skin, even though the idea is prevalent that the skin is a relatively effective barrier to its environment." H.O. Calvery, *Safeguarding Foods and Drugs in Wartime*, 32 AM. SCIENTIST No. 2, at 103, 119 (1944). There are some skin care products marketed as cosmetics, however, that clearly have more significant effects on the body than do traditional cosmetics. These products are often referred to as "cosmeceuticals." Although the FDA does not itself use the term "cosmeceutical," it recognizes that cosmetic manufacturers use this word "to refer to cosmetic products that have medicinal or drug-like benefits." Office of Cosmetics & Color Fact Sheet, (rev. Feb. 24, 2000).

When defining "cosmeceutical," the FDA remarked, "If a product has drug properties, it must be approved as a drug." *Id.* This statement is one of several instances in which the agency has suggested that the presence of an ingredient with pharmacological effects may render a product a drug, regardless of the claims made by the manufacturer. In 1996, John Bailey, the Director of FDA's Office of Cosmetics and Colors, stated, "If an active ingredient is present in a therapeutic concentration, the product is a drug, even if that product does not claim to produce the effect that will result from the action of the therapeutically effective ingredient." Anita H. Shaw, *The News in Skin Care*, SOAP-COSM.-CHEM. SPECIALTIES, Oct. 1, 1996, at 72.

The validity of Bailey's statement hinges on whether the agency must, in determining "intent," always depend at least in part on claims by the manufacturer. As will be discussed *infra* p. 81, when FDA asserted jurisdiction over tobacco products as medical devices in the 1990s, it vigorously maintained that evidence from "other relevant sources" could, on its own, establish objective intent. In the world of "cosmeceuticals," this question has been raised most frequently with regard to two types of topically applied products: cosmetics containing hormones and cosmetics containing alpha hydroxy acids.

In 1993, FDA proposed a rule declaring that any cosmetic product containing more than a specified amount of the hormones pregnenolone acetate or progesterone was an unapproved drug, regardless of manufacturer claims. The agency observed that, above these amounts, the ingredients affected the structure or function of the body. 58 Fed Reg. 47611 (Sept. 9, 1993). The agency also proposed banning "natural estrogens" from cosmetics altogether, unless manufacturers provided adequate data on the safety and exact chemical identity of such estrogens. "[T]he agency concludes at this time that any use of natural estrogens in cosmetic products makes the product an unapproved new drug. The conclusion is based on available data stating conclusively that at some levels the ingredients affect the structure or function of the body, and a concomitant lack of data establishing at what level, if any, the drug effect ceases." Finally, FDA also proposed that the use of the word "hormone" in the labeling or ingredient statement of any cosmetic product was an implied drug claim. In 2004, the agency withdrew this proposed rule but remarked that "this withdrawal neither affirms nor rejects statements contained in the preamble [to the proposed rule]." 69 Fed. Reg. 68833 (Nov. 26, 2004). Although the rule was never finalized, FDA did finalize a drug regulation, proposed simultaneously, providing that the use of the word "hormone" in the labeling or ingredient statement of any topically applied product is an implied drug claim. 58 Fed. Reg. 47610 (Sept. 9, 1993), codified at 21 C.F.R. 310.530(a).

Alpha hydroxy acids (AHAs) are chemicals that cause the skin to lose its outer layer. Manufacturers of cosmetics containing AHAs claim their products will smooth fine lines, reduce spots, and improve skin condition in general. In a 1994 speech, FDA official John Bailey stated: "In the final analysis, it is well established that AHAs exert an effect on the skin. I don't think that there is any doubt that, under some conditions of formulation and use, AHA containing products are affecting the structure and function of the body and that they should be regulated as drugs." *Quoted in* Jacqueline A. Greff, *Regulation of Cosmetics that are also Drugs*, 51 FOOD DRUG COSM. L.J. 243, 257 (1997). Nonetheless, FDA has not, to this point, charged a manufacturer with selling an unapproved drug based solely on the fact that the product contains AHAs. It has addressed safety issues raised by AHA-containing skin care products based solely on its authority over cosmetics. *See* 70 Fed. Reg. 1721 (Jan. 10, 2005) (announcing availability of final guidance advising manufacturers of AHA-containing cosmetics to label them so as to alert consumers of the need to limit sun exposure and apply sunscreen). For further discussion on AHAs, see Laura A. Heymann, *The Cosmetic/Drug Dilemma: FDA Regulation of Alpha–Hydroxy Acids*, 52 FOOD & DRUG L.J. 357 (1997).

NOTES

1. *Approved Cosmetic Drugs and Devices.* In recent years, FDA has approved new drug applications (NDAs) and device premarket approval applications (PMAs) for antiwrinkle products. Renova (tretinoin) is a prescription drug approved to reduce fine wrinkles, discoloration, and roughness on facial skin. BOTOX Cosmetic

(Botulinum Toxin Type A) is a prescription drug approved to treat frown lines between the eyebrows. The agency has approved collagen and hyaluronic acid gel, both injectable antiwrinkle products, as medical devices, as well as lasers making antiwrinkle claims.

The agency has approved NDAs for two types of hair regrowth products: Rogaine (minoxidil), a topical solution, and Propecia (finasteride), a drug in pill form.

2. *OTC Drug Review.* As discussed in Chapter IV, the Over-the-Counter (OTC) Drug Review is the primary process by which the agency has assessed the safety and effectiveness of active ingredients in OTC drug products. In this context, the relationship between the Act's definitions of "cosmetic" and "drug" has frequently been at issue. The agency has frequently evaded the question of whether a particular use of a substance is solely a cosmetic use or also a drug use by simply restricting the use of the substance in both cosmetics and drugs. *E.g.*, 21 C.F.R. 250.250(d) & (c) (limiting the use of hexacholorophene in OTC drugs and cosmetics). *Cf.* 21 C.F.R. 310.545(a)(17) (skin-bleaching OTC drug products containing ammoniated mercury are not generally recognized as safe and effective) & 700.13 (mercury-containing skin-bleaching agents are drugs as well as cosmetics and are misbranded and adulterated). For discussions of the various OTC drug monographs in which the cosmetic/drug distinction has been considered, see William E. Gilbertson, *FDA OTC Drugs Standards Versus Cosmetic Standards*, 21 DRUG INFO. J. 379 (1987); Stephen H. McNamara, *The Food and Drug Administration Over-the-Counter Drug Review—Concerns of the Cosmetic Industry*, 38 FOOD DRUG COSM. L.J. 289 (1983).

COMMENT: DEODORANT PRODUCTS

FDA's policy for products that deal with body odors seems to have evolved recently. Describing a product as a deodorant is indisputably a cosmetic claim, and deodorant products that merely mask odor with perfumes are clearly cosmetics and not drugs. But what of products that attack odors with antimicrobial ingredients? It was long assumed that a mouthwash or deodorant soap could make a claim like "kills germs that cause odor" without becoming a drug for regulatory purposes. In the early 1990s, however, the preambles to the tentative final monographs for various types of OTC antiseptic drug products firmly stated that claims of this sort would subject a product to regulation as a drug. 56 Fed. Reg. 33644, 33648–49 (July 22, 1991) (first aid antiseptics); 59 Fed. Reg. 6084, 6088–89 (Feb. 9, 1994) (oral antiseptics); 59 Fed. Reg. 31402, 31440 (health care antiseptics). Importantly, in these preambles, FDA disclaimed any intention to regulate deodorant products without such claims as drugs merely because they contained antimicrobial ingredients. 56 Fed. Reg. at 33648; 59 Fed. Reg. at 6088.

About the same time, FDA initiated a seizure action against a product called Pets Smellfree. The agency contended that the product, a pet food additive containing a subtherapeutic dose of an antibiotic, was an adulterated and misbranded animal drug. The manufacturer claimed the product "stops those awful odors associated with feces, urine, gas and BAD BREATH." One advertisement added that Pets Smellfree "will neutralize the undesirable mercaptans in the digestive tract without affecting the desirable bacterial flora." *U.S. v. Undetermined Quantities of Bottles of . . .*

"Pets Smellfree", 1991 WL 11666517 (D. Utah 1991). (Mercaptans are sulfur-containing organic compounds.) The District Court accepted the company's argument that the product was not a drug, but the court of appeals reversed. *U.S. v. Undetermined Quantities of Bottles of . . . "Pets Smellfree"*, 22 F.3d 235 (10th Cir. 1994). Interestingly, the Court of Appeals did not refer to even one instance in which the manufacturer mentioned the product's antibacterial properties. Instead, the court seemed to hold that Pets Smellfree could properly be deemed a drug simply because of common knowledge that bacterial contamination causes those odors the product claimed to stop. *Id.* 239–40. The *Pets Smellfree* analysis of the drug status of a deodorant product was thus even more expansive than the principles FDA enunciated in the human antiseptic drug monographs discussed above. *But see E.R. Squibb & Sons v. Bowen*, 870 F.2d 678, 682 (D.C. Cir. 1989) (a claim that a product suppresses the growth a fungus in the body does not implicate the drug definition's structure-function provision, in part because "it is questionable whether a drug that acts only upon non-human organisms that happen to reside within the human body can properly be understood as affecting the 'body of man.' ")

NOTES

1. *Other Products on the Cosmetic–Drug Line.* There are a variety of common claims that can turn a product with cleansing or beautifying uses into a drug in addition to, or instead of, a cosmetic. A recent article included a list of some important examples of this phenomenon, based on decades of FDA literature and practice:

A suntan product is a cosmetic but a sunscreen product is a drug.

A deodorant is a cosmetic but an antiperspirant is a drug.

A shampoo is a cosmetic but an antidandruff shampoo is a drug.

A toothpaste is a cosmetic but an anticaries toothpaste is a drug.

A skin exfoliant is a cosmetic but a skin peel is a drug.

A mouthwash is a cosmetic but an antigingivitis mouthwash is a drug.

A hair bulking product is a cosmetic but a hair growth product is a drug.

A skin product to hide acne is a cosmetic but an antiacne product is a drug.

An antibacterial deodorant soap is a cosmetic but an antibacterial anti-infective soap is a drug.

A skin moisturizer is a cosmetic but a wrinkle remover is a drug.

A lip softener is a cosmetic but a product for chapped lips is a drug.

Peter Barton Hutt, *The Legal Distinction in the United States Between a Cosmetic and a Drug, in* COSMECEUTICALS: DRUGS VS. COSMETICS 223, 228 (Peter Elsner & Howard I. Maibach, eds., 2000).

Recent developments have reinforced many of these traditional positions taken by the agency. With regard to some of these products, however, FDA has manifested an inclination to categorize articles containing pharmacologically active ingredients as drugs even when their manufacturers make only cosmetic claims. As discussed above, the agency has made some moves in this direction with regard to AHA and hormone-containing skin care products. Moreover, when issuing its tentative final monograph for sunscreen drug products, FDA stated unambiguously that "a product containing a sunscreen ingredient, even when labeled solely as a tanning aid, is both intended and understood to be a sunburn preventative. Such a product, therefore, is a drug under the act." 58 Fed. Reg. 28194, 28204 (May 12, 1993). At the same time that it issued its final sunscreen monograph, 64 Fed. Reg. 27666 (May 21, 1999), the agency revoked a 1940 official trade correspondence declaring that products promoted solely for tanning purposes (as opposed to products intended to be used as sunburn preventatives) are cosmetics and not drugs. 64 Fed. Reg. 27798 (May 21, 1999).

2. *Intercenter Agreement.* To facilitate oversight of products claiming to be cosmetics but that also fulfill the statutory definition of a drug, CDER and CFSAN entered an agreement affording either center the jurisdiction to bring regulatory actions relating to such products. *See Intercenter Agreement Between the Center for Drug Evaluation and Research and the Center for Food Safety and Applied Nutrition to Assist FDA in Implementing the Drug and Cosmetic Provisions of the Federal Food, Drug, and Cosmetic Act for Products that Purport to be Cosmetics but Meet the Statutory Definition of a Drug* (June 2002).

3. *Commentary.* For additional discussion of the cosmetic-drug spectrum, see Arlene Erlebacher, *When Is a "Cosmetic" Also a "Drug" Under the Federal Food, Drug and Cosmetic Act*, 27 FOOD DRUG COSM. L.J. 740 (1972); Jacqueline A. Greff, *Regulation of Cosmetics that are also Drugs*, 51 FOOD & DRUG L.J. 243 (1996); *The Legal Distinction in the United States Between a Cosmetic and a Drug*, Peter Barton Hutt, *in* COSMECEUTICALS: DRUGS VS. COSMETICS 223 (Peter Elsner et al., eds. 2000); Vincent A. Kleinfeld, *"Cosmetic" or "Drug"—The Minotaur's Labyrinth*, 22 FOOD DRUG COSM. L.J. 376 (1967); Bryan A. Liang and Kurt M. Hartman, *It's Only Skin Deep: FDA Regulation of Skin Care Cosmetics Claims*, 8 CORNELL J.L. & PUB. POL'Y 249 (1999); Stephen H. McNamara, *Performance Claims for Skin Care Cosmetics*, 41 FOOD DRUG COSM. L.J. 151 (1986); *Symposium on the Cosmetic–Drug Distinction*, 21 DRUG INFO. J. 377 (1987).

COMMENT: OTHER TYPES OF DRUGS WITH NONTHERAPEUTIC USES

Lethal Products. In *United States v. Beuthanasia D Regular*, Food Drug Cosm. L. Rep. (CCH) ¶ 38,265 (D. Neb. 1979), the court upheld an FDA seizure of products intended for euthanasia of animals, rejecting the company's argument that the products were not drugs and thus were outside the jurisdiction of the FD&C Act. Two years later, FDA rejected a petition to assert jurisdiction over the use of approved pharmaceuticals by state prison officials to execute prisoners sentenced to death. Letter from FDA Commissioner A.H. Hayes, Jr., to D.E. Kendall, FDA Dkt No. 80P–0513 (July 7, 1981). The Supreme Court ultimately held that the agency's refusal to take enforcement action in this instance was unreviewable. *Heckler v. Chaney*, 470 U.S. 821 (1985).

Drugs of Abuse. Prior to 1970, federal control of narcotic drugs, marijuana, and other drugs used for recreational and nonmedical purposes was shared among several agencies and rested on a haphazard cluster of laws enacted since 1900. For example, FDA was responsible for enforcement of the Drug Abuse Control Amendments of 1965, 79 Stat. 226, to prevent abuse of depressant and stimulant drugs that also have legitimate medical uses, such as amphetamines and barbiturates.

In 1970, Congress repealed the earlier statutes and enacted a new comprehensive law, the Controlled Substances Act, 84 Stat. 1236, 1242, codified in 21 U.S.C. 801 *et seq.* The CSA establishes five "schedules" of substances with strong potential for abuse, calibrated according to their degree of danger. Responsibility for enforcement of the distribution controls of the Controlled Substances Act rests with the Drug Enforcement Administration (DEA) of the Department of Justice. DEA has the obligation to consult with FDA on the scheduling of controlled substances. FDA's recommendations on scientific and medical matters are binding, and DEA may not schedule a drug if FDA recommends against it. Moreover, FDA regulates the legitimate medical uses of scheduled substances the same way it regulates other drugs. Schedule I drugs—that is, illegal drugs with no approved medical use, such as heroin, cocaine, and marijuana—are under the exclusive jurisdiction of DEA.

Street Drug Alternatives. The FDA considers products manufactured, marketed, or distributed as alternatives to illicit street drugs to be unapproved new drugs. FDA, CENTER FOR DRUG EVALUATION AND RESEARCH, GUIDANCE FOR INDUSTRY; STREET DRUG ALTERNATIVES (2000). Street drug alternatives are often labeled as dietary supplements containing botanicals, vitamins, and minerals. They are marketed with claims implying that they mimic the effects of controlled substances. In *United States v. Undetermined Quantities of Articles of Drug*, 145 F. Supp. 2d 692 (D. Md. 2001). The district court concluded that the defendants' products, comprising a variety of herbs, were not dietary supplements. Instead, it found them to be unapproved new drugs because the labeling and promotional claims, including a catalog explicitly stating the products were "for mood enhancement," showed that the manufacturers intended these products to affect the function of the mind.

Oxygen Bars. Establishments known as "oxygen bars" first became popular in the late 1990s. These businesses offer customers the opportunity to sniff purified oxygen through a plastic hose inserted into their nostrils. The oxygen is sometimes "flavored" with aromatic solutions. Oxygen bar patrons variously believe that this practice reduces stress, increases energy and alertness, reduces headaches and hangover symptoms, and generally relaxes the body. Oxygen has legitimate uses as a medical gas, of course, and FDA regulates it as a prescription drug. Although oxygen bar proprietors are careful not to make medical claims, FDA has declared that any type of oxygen administered for breathing is a prescription drug, regardless of its labeling. Nevertheless, the agency has chosen to exercise its administrative discretion and leave the regulation of oxygen intended for recreational use to the states. *See Oxygen Bars: Is a Breath of Fresh Air Worth It?*, FDA CONSUMER MAG., Nov.–Dec. 2002, at 9.

4. THE "DEVICE" DEFINITION

a. COSMETIC DEVICES

The section above on the cosmetic-drug spectrum discussed the categorization of products intended to cleanse, beautify, or promote attractiveness. Some articles intended for cosmetic use operate through physical, rather than chemical, action and thus raise similar issues with respect to the device definition. As with cosmetic drugs, the question of whether a cosmetic device is a "device" under the FD&C Act hinges on how much, and in what way, the article is "intended to affect the structure or any function of the body." FD&C Act 201(h)(3).

FDA does not consider most nonmechanical household cosmetic implements to be "devices" under the Act. The following products, for example, fall outside the device requirements unless they make medical claims: toothpicks, hair brushes, combs, nail files, nail clippers, nail scissors, razors, tweezers, and loofah sponges (used to exfoliate the skin). On the other hand, FDA regulates breast implants and chin prostheses as medical devices, regardless of whether they are intended to be used for reconstructive or cosmetic purposes. 21 C.F.R. 878.3530, 3540, 3550. In addition, the agency treats collagen used to correct wrinkles and acne scars as a medical device, defined as "dermal collagen implants for aesthetic use." *See* PMA Approval for CosmoDerm 1 Human–Based Collagen, CosmoDerm 2 Human–Based Collagen, and CosmoPlast Human–Based Collagen (Mar. 11, 2003). FDA also treats tanning lamps, epilators (used for hair removal), and tongue scrapers (used to treat bad breath) as medical devices. 21 C.F.R. 878.5350 ("needle-type epilator"); 878.5360 ("tweezer-type epilator"); 868.4635 ("ultraviolet lamp for tanning"); 872.6855 ("manual toothbrushes," which is how FDA categorizes tongue scrapers).

Decorative contact lenses are products that do not correct vision but change the apparent color of the iris, seem to add a design to it, or give the eye a nonhuman or otherwise abnormal appearance. They present the same significant risks of eye injury that corrective contact lenses do. Corrective contact lenses are regulated as prescription medical devices, and it had long been assumed that noncorrective lenses were devices, as well. In 2002, however, Daniel Troy, the FDA Chief Counsel, informed the agency's Center for Devices and Radiological Health (CDRH) that he was considering declaring that noncorrective decorative contact lenses are not medical devices. Megan Garvey, *Health Concerns Tinge Use of Cosmetic Lenses*, L.A. TIMES, Aug. 26, 2002, at 1. This information motivated California Congressman Henry Waxman, the ranking minority member of the House of Representatives Committee on Government Reform, to write the following letter to Tommy Thompson, the Secretary of Health and Human Services.

Letter from Rep. Henry A. Waxman to Tommy Thompson, Secretary of Health and Human Services

August 26, 2002.

... I am writing to alert you to a plan apparently set in motion by the Chief Counsel of the Food and Drug Administration (FDA) to reclassify colored contact lenses that do not correct vision as cosmetics instead of medical devices, essentially deregulating these products. Under current law, manufacturers of colored lenses must meet federal standards of hygiene and sterility and can sell their products only with a prescription. FDA's new plan, however, would eliminate these rules, make colored lenses available over-the-counter without adequate directions for safe use, and depend on an underfunded cosmetics enforcement division with limited safety authority to protect consumers. It would also establish a precedent that could lead to the deregulation of many more potentially hazardous prescription drugs and devices.

Because poor-quality or misused contact lenses can cause severe eye infections, painful corneal disease, and even blindness, the FDA plan virtually guarantees serious medical complications.... Ophthalmologists and optometrists find no justification to treat colored lenses differently from corrective contact lenses. I urge you to intervene personally and stop what is a legally unsound and medically dangerous policy....

Contact lenses all qualify as medical devices under the third part of the [medical device definition at section 201(h)], as a product that is "intended to affect the structure or any function of the body of man." Lenses unavoidably alter the structure of the body by profoundly altering the biology of the eye. As one leading ophthalmology textbook states:

> A contact lens may be considered to be an optical patch and bandage. As a patch it reduces the availability of oxygen to and the dissipation of carbon dioxide from the cornea. As a bandage it creates pressure on the underlying tissues and reduces wetting of the ocular surface and dissipation of material from between the contact lens and the cornea.

These effects are unavoidable and foreseeable. Any manufacturer of contact lenses that intends for users to place the products in the eye must also intend for these effects to occur.

This longstanding and fair reading of the law, however, has apparently been rejected by the Chief Counsel of FDA, Daniel Troy. Mr. Troy appears to believe that a product is only a "medical device" if it is marketed expressly as something that will affect the structure or function of the body. His argument seems to be that since colored noncorrective contact lenses are not marketed as something to correct a problem (like poor vision), these products cannot be classified as medical devices.

This reasoning is both wrong and dangerous. It is wrong because of legislative history, administrative precedent, and legal precedent, including cases in which courts have acknowledged FDA's ability to regulate products on the basis of evidence other than express marketing claims. Indeed, two such cases have expressly found that colored noncorrective contact lenses are medical devices. It is dangerous because of its logical consequence. If a medical device or a drug (which is defined using similar terms) must be expressly marketed as a treatment to fall under the FDCA, then manufacturers can simply use their marketing claims to evade regulation altogether. Breast implants and collagen injections marketed for aesthetic appeal and condoms marketed for pleasure would not be medical devices. Botox marketed for cosmetic purposes would not be a drug. A company might even attempt to market valium as "fun" to evade drug regulation....

NOTES

1. *Subsequent Events.* In April 2003, FDA officially stated that it considered noncorrective decorative contact lenses to be cosmetics, but not devices. *See* GUID-

ANCE FOR FDA STAFF ON SAMPLING OR DETENTION WITHOUT PHYSICAL EXAMINATION OF DECORATIVE CONTACT LENSES (Import Alert 86–10); 68 Fed. Reg. 16520, 16521 (Apr. 4, 2003). Subsequently, Rep. Waxman—with support from the major manufacturers of colored lenses, advocacy organizations dedicated to eye health and safety, and eye health professionals—cosponsored legislation requiring FDA to regulate decorative contact lenses as medical devices. In November 2005, Congress amended the FD&C Act by adding new subsection 520(n), "Regulation of Contact Lens [sic] as Devices." This new provision provides: "All contact lenses shall be deemed to be devices under section 201(h)." 119 Stat. 2119. It also, however, declares: "Paragraph (1) shall not be construed as bearing on or being relevant to the question of whether any product other than a contact lens is a device as defined by section 201(h) or a drug as defined by section 201(g)."

2. *Are Contact Lenses "Cosmetics"?* As discussed above, *supra* p. 39, there are valid questions as to whether contact lenses fit the definition of "cosmetic."

b. DIAGNOSTIC DEVICES

The device definition includes articles (including "in vitro reagents") "intended for use in the diagnosis of disease or other conditions." FD&C Act 201(h). This provision raises its own interpretive problems.

United States of America v. 25 Cases, More or Less, of an Article of Device ... "Sensor Pad for Breast Self–Examination"

942 F.2d 1179 (7th Cir. 1991).

■ CUDAHY, CIRCUIT JUDGE:

In this case we are called on to interpret the word "device" as used in the Federal Food, Drug and Cosmetic Act, 21 U.S.C. § 321(h)(2) (1988) (the Act). The government brought this action to seize the appellant's inventory, believing it to consist of adulterated devices in interstate commerce. The district court granted summary judgment for the government....

In the mid–1980s, Earl Wright developed a product which he believed would aid women in conducting self-examinations for the early detection of breast cancer. This product, descriptively named the "Sensor Pad," consists of a flat, circular latex bag filled with a layer of silicone lubricant. It is intended to be placed over the breast during self-examinations to improve the woman's ability to feel abnormalities beneath the skin. Wright and his associates believed the Pad was not a "device" under the Act....

According to the Act, the term device "means an instrument, apparatus, implement, machine, contrivance, implant, in vitro reagent, or other similar or related article, including any component, part, or accessory, which is ... (2) intended for use in the diagnosis of disease or other conditions, or in the cure, mitigation, treatment, or prevention of disease...." 21 U.S.C. § 321(h).... Although agreeing that its Pad aids in the detection and screening of breast cancer, Inventive Products nevertheless argues that the word diagnosis does not encompass the function of the Sensor Pad. Diagnosis, the appellant suggests, includes only examinations to "determine the nature and circumstances of a diseased condition." Because the Sensor Pad merely helps the woman in detecting abnormalities that could be symptoms of a disease, strictly speaking it is used *before* actual diagnosis.

The distinction appellant attempts to draw between screening and diagnosis is an untenable one. In its opening brief, Inventive Products appears to argue that diagnosis occurs only at the last step in the process of discovering a disease, that step which ultimately determines the nature and circumstances of a diseased condition. Thus, because the Sensor Pad only detects irregularities which may or may not be cancerous growths, it does not diagnose the disease. Indeed appellant agrees with one of its expert physicians, who averred that "biopsy is the only means of diagnosing breast cancer." By proposing that medical inquiries change from screening to diagnosis only at the final determination, the appellant's theory would apparently exclude even a mammography unit from being classified as diagnostic, because it too cannot confirm the presence of cancer. . . .

The obscurity of the line appellant would draw between diagnosis and screening . . . well illustrates the arbitrariness of the line-drawing. Pursuing this fruitless inquiry is irrelevant in any event since we believe Congress had no such screening/diagnosing distinction in mind when it wrote section 321(h).

The current description of "device" in the Act was adopted essentially in the original version of the Federal Food, Drug and Cosmetic Act, 52 Stat. 1040 (1938), the development of which is discussed in *United States v. Article of Drug . . . Bacto–Unidisk*, 394 U.S. 784, 793–98 (1969). The bill emerged from committee in the Senate with several amendments, one of which proposed broadening the definition of "device" to include tools used in diagnosis of disease. At that time one senator, with the voiced approval of the bill's sponsor, summarized the amendment on the floor of the chamber: "the word 'diagnosis' merely adds to their uses, namely, their use in looking into a situation prior to the time when the cure or mitigation shall begin." 79 Cong. Rec. 4843 (1935) (statement of Sen. Barkley). Another senator meanwhile offered the view that weight scales used during the diagnosis of a patient would come within the bill's regulation. *Id.* (statement of Sen. Clark).

Moreover, even if Congress' intentions with regard to the scope of "diagnosis" were not clear from its debate, the FDA's position in this matter would still prevail. It would be entirely plausible to suggest that Congress intended the FDA to decide for itself which devices are used for diagnosing disease. One senator opined on the floor of the Senate that "the language [of the bill] is broad enough to cover any device of which the Food and Drug Bureau of the Agricultural Department chooses to take jurisdiction." *Id.* at 4841. Such a delegation to the FDA would require a court to give considerable deference to the agency's decision. . . .

Second, even had Congress never considered the question before us, we might allow the FDA room to decide the question itself. Courts often will defer to an agency's reasonable interpretation of an ambiguous provision within the agency's own organic statute. *Chevron U.S.A., Inc. v. Natural Resources Defense Council, Inc.*, 467 U.S. 837, 843 (1984). . . .

Our approach in this case has been further reinforced by the Supreme Court, which reminded litigants that "remedial legislation such as the Food, Drug and Cosmetic Act is to be given a liberal construction consistent with the Act's overriding purpose to protect the public health...." *Bacto-Unidisk*, 394 U.S. at 798. A broad definition of "diagnosis" allows for greater authority in the agency to oversee developments in health care, and thus to better protect the public health.

For each of the above reasons, the district court was correct to grant the government's motion for summary judgment in this case....

NOTES

1. *Diagnostic Drugs.* The definition of "drug" at FD&C Act 201(g)(1) includes "articles intended for use in the diagnosis ... of disease." Unlike the definition of "device," this provision does not embrace products intended for the diagnosis of "conditions" other than diseases. Since 1976, FDA has regulated almost all diagnostic products (whether for diseases or "other conditions") as medical devices. *See infra* p. 983.

2. *"Diagnosis" for What Purpose?* FDA regulates as devices "OTC test sample collection systems for drugs of abuse testing." These products, according to the regulation, are intended to "[c]ollect biological specimens (such as hair, urine, sweat, or saliva), outside of a medical setting and not on order of a health care professional (*e.g.*, in the home, insurance, sports, or workplace setting); maintain the integrity of such specimens during storage and transport in order that the matter contained therein can be tested in a laboratory for the presence of drugs of abuse or their metabolites; and provide access to test results and counseling." 21 C.F.R. 864.3260. When it finalized this regulation, FDA rejected a comment which asserted that kits for detecting drugs of abuse in hair are not medical devices under section 201(h) of the FD&C Act because they are not for medical diagnosis and treatment. 65 Fed. Reg. 18230, 18232 (Apr. 7, 2000).

In *U.S. v. Undetermined Number of Unlabeled Cases*, 21 F.3d 1026 (10th Cir. 1994), the Tenth Circuit held that containers used to collect urine and saliva specimens for HIV testing were devices, even though the laboratory-defendant that distributed the containers performed the testing for insurance risk-assessment purposes rather than for medical treatment.

c.   LIMITS OF THE DEVICE DEFINITION

COMMENT: COMMON SENSE LIMITATIONS ON THE DEFINITION OF "DEVICE"?

FDA's 1996 tobacco rulemaking raised fascinating issues concerning the definitions of "device" and "drug," which were explored at length in the preambles to the proposed and final rules. *See* 60 Fed. Reg. 41314 (Aug. 16, 1995); 61 Fed. Reg. 44396 (Aug. 28, 1996). We have already mentioned FDA's expansive approach to establishing the "intended use" of cigarettes and smokeless tobacco in the absence of representations by the manufacturers. *Supra* p. 47. Another important interpretive issue was whether there are unstated common sense limitations on the categories of "drug" and "device" as defined by the FD&C Act.

As discussed at the beginning of this chapter, courts use a "common sense" approach in interpreting the FD&C Act's definition of "food." The circular brevity of that definition leaves them with little other choice. By contrast, the more detailed definitions of "drug" and "device" are less obvious candidates for the imposition of implied limitations. However, the plain language of these definitions encompasses an enormous range of products not traditionally viewed as being within FDA's authority. This is particularly true of the definition of "device," which embraces products that do not act primarily through chemical action or metabolization. As the tobacco manufacturers pointed out repeatedly in attacking FDA's jurisdiction over its products, the device definition, applied literally, would include guns and ammunition, thermal pajamas, air conditioners, scuba diving gear, automobile airbags, and roller coasters. The industry thus argued that a product could be treated as a device only if its intended effects on structure or function were "therapeutic," "medical," or "beneficial." *See* 61 Fed. Reg. 44619, 44674–75 (Aug. 28, 1996). FDA emphatically opposed reading such limitations into the statute. The agency also observed that, in any event, tobacco products achieve their effects pharmacologically and are thus indistinguishable from products that the agency has traditionally regulated as drugs and devices. *Id.* at 44675–85.

The federal district court hearing the challenge to the tobacco rule rejected the industry's argument that the structure/function provisions must be construed narrowly to avoid absurd implications for other types of products. The court remarked that a statute's scope "is not to be judicially narrowed . . . by envisioning extreme possible applications." *Coyne Beahm v. FDA*, 966 F. Supp. 1374, 1393 (M.D.N.C. 1997) (quoting *U.S. v. Sullivan*, 332 U.S. 689, 694 (1948)). Ultimately, however, the Supreme Court ruled for the tobacco industry without reaching the issue of the precise meaning of "affect the structure or any function of the body." *FDA v. Brown & Williamson*, 529 U.S. 120 (2000) (*infra* p. 82). Consequently, whether there are any unstated limits on the definition of "device" remains an open question. In the following 2002 letter, FDA Chief Counsel Daniel Troy—who had represented Brown & Williamson in its challenge to the agency's regulation of cigarettes—firmly embraced the notion that the device definition encompasses consumer products only if they are marketed with claims of therapeutic or medical utility. He also advanced a narrow interpretation of what types of evidence can establish "intended use."

Letter from Daniel E. Troy, FDA Chief Counsel, to Jeffrey N. Gibbs

October 17, 2002.

. . . This responds to your letters concerning Applied Digital Solutions (ADS)'s two separate written requests submitted to the Center for Devices and Radiological Health under Section 513(g) of the Federal Food, Drug, and Cosmetic Act (FD&C Act) requesting a determination that the Veri-Chip is not a medical device under the FD&C Act for the intended uses described in the requests. Your requests cover two different intended uses of the product. The first is for use of the VeriChip in health information applications ("health information VeriChip"). The second is for security, financial, and personal identification\safety applications ("personal ID\security VeriChip"). For the reasons discussed below, FDA believes that the health information VeriChip is a medical device subject to FDA's jurisdiction. FDA agrees, however, that the personal ID/security VeriChip is not covered by the FD&C Act.

Background

Since 1986, Digital Angel Corporation, which is working with VeriChip Corporation, has sold more than 20 million implantable RFID transponders for animals. . . . The transponders provide access to information necessary to identify the animal.

In January of 1984, the Center for Veterinary Medicine (CVM) within FDA issued a letter to the manufacturer of this product stating: ". . . The device does not have a medical\therapeutic function. Therefore, we have no objection to marketing of this identification device for use in animals." . . .

ADS has determined to market in the United States a version of the microminiature transponder, known by the trade name "VeriChip," for a variety of uses in human beings. We understand from ADS that the VeriChip is a microminiature transponder that is encapsulated in medical grade glass that may be inserted by hypodermic needle under the skin of the upper arm in humans. The chip\transponder stores a unique identification number only. A small, handheld introducer is used to place the chip subcutaneously. A small, handheld battery-powered scanner can read the identification number on the chip. That number enables access to a database. . . . The personal\security VeriChip would allow access, via the database, to information related to security, financial, and personal safety applications only. You have represented that it will not contain any medical information. By contrast, ADS and its representatives have explained, the health information VeriChip would allow access, via the database, to medical history and other information to assist medical personnel in diagnosing or treating an injury or illness.

Regulatory Status of the VeriChip

We believe that the health information product, which facilitates access to information for use by medical professionals in treating the individual with the VeriChip embedded in his or her arm, is "intended for use in the diagnosis of disease or other conditions, or in the cure [or] mitigation of disease." The information in the database is meant to be used by medical professionals in diagnosing a disease or other condition. Indeed, the entire purpose of this product is for a medical professional to employ when treating a stricken individual. For example, information about whether the person is allergic to a particular medicine, or has an implanted pacemaker, which is accessed in connection with the VeriChip, is intended for use in treating the person. Accordingly, FDA has determined that the health information VeriChip is a medical device within the meaning of Section 201(h)(2) of the FD&C Act.

By contrast, as CVM recognized with respect to the use of the VeriChip predecessor in animals, it does not appear that the personal ID/security

VeriChip is a medical device, even though it is an "implant." It is of course true that virtually any product that comes into contact with the body—and many that do not—could be said to have an effect on the structure or a function of the body. However ... FDA's medical device jurisdiction under Section 201(h)(2) extends only to such products that are marketed by their manufacturers or distributors with claims of effects on the structure or a function of the body. In the language of the statute itself, the product must be "intended to" affect the structure or a function of the body. It is well settled that intended use is determined with reference to marketing claims. . . .

In [its brief in] a 1994 case, FDA stated that it "does not claim that a device which has no *medical* application could 'qualify as a device under the FD&CA.' " Courts have held that Section 201(h)(3) only encompasses products claimed to affect the body "in some *medical*—or drug-type fashion, *i.e.*, in some way other than merely altering the appearance." *An Article . . . "Sudden Change,"* 409 F.2d at 742 (emphasis added).

The pertinent legislative history supports this interpretation. Specifically, the Senate Report accompanying the legislation that became the Federal Food, Drug, and Cosmetic Act of 1938 states:

> The use to which the product is to be put will determine the category into which it will fall. . . . The manufacturer of the article, *through his representations in connection with its sale*, can determine the use to which the article is to be put.

S. Rep. No. 74–361, at 240 (1935) (emphasis added). . . .

Accordingly, assuming that no medical claims are made for the personal ID\security VeriChip, and the product marketed for that purpose contains no health information, FDA can confirm that it is not a medical device.

It is, of course, foreseeable that any implant, such as the personal ID\security VeriChip, will have an effect on the structure and function of the body; indeed, it will be permanently embedded under a person's skin. However, as the Fourth Circuit recently held, a foreseeable effect on the structure or function of the body does not establish an intended use. If the foreseeability theory had been accepted by the courts, FDA would have won several cases that it lost. *See, e.g., National Nutritional Foods Ass'n v. Mathews*, 557 F.2d 325 (2d Cir. 1977).

Also, if foreseeability were a permissible basis for finding an intended use as that term is used in Section 201(h)(3), FDA's jurisdiction would encompass many articles having foreseeable physical effects. Yet FDA only regulates products if they are marketed with claims of medical or therapeutic utility. For example, FDA only regulates exercise equipment as a medical device when it is marketed with claims to prevent, treat, or rehabilitate injury or disability. Otherwise, it is a consumer product.

In addition, if foreseeable effects were cognizable under Section 201(h)(3), FDA's legal authority would intrude into consumer product regulation—an area of responsibility delegated by Congress to another federal agency. CPSC's jurisdiction extends to "consumer products," which means "any article, or component part thereof, produced or distributed (i) for sale to a consumer for use in or around a permanent or temporary household or residence, a school, in recreation, or otherwise, or (ii) for the personal use, consumption or enjoyment of a consumer in or around a permanent or temporary household or residence, a school, in recreation, or otherwise...." 15 U.S.C. § 2052(a)(1). The definition expressly excludes "drugs, devices, or cosmetics (as such terms are defined in sections 201(g), (h), and (i) of the Federal Food, Drug, and Cosmetic Act ...)." *Id.* § 2052(a)(1)(H).

Similarly, if Section 201(h)(3) of the FD&C Act were interpreted to give FDA jurisdiction over any product foreseeably having an effect on the structure or a function of the body, then regulatory authority would shift from the CPSC to FDA for a host of non-health-related products. Hiking boots; shirts, pants, and coats; exercise equipment; insulated gloves; airbags; and chemical sprays can be said to affect bodily structure or function. Clothing and gloves, for example, keep the body warm....

NOTES

1. *Subsequent Regulatory Treatment.* Because no product similar to the health information VeriChip was in commercial circulation prior to the 1976 enactment of the Medical Device Amendments, FDA automatically classified it into class III in 2004, when the agency received premarket notification under section 510(k). Immediately thereafter, however, FDA received a reclassification petition from Digital Angel, requesting that the device be placed in class II. FDA granted this petition in October 2004. Letter from Donna Bea–Tillman, FDA–CDER, to James Santelli (Oct. 12, 2004). Accordingly, the agency then promulgated a new classification regulation for the class II "Implantable radiofrequency transponder system for patient identification and health information." 21 C.F.R. 880.6300. The rule identifies a guidance document as the special control for the device.

2. *"Behind-the-Wall" Medical Gas Pipeline Systems.* Most hospitals and many other health care facilities have permanently installed medical gas pipeline systems as part of their architectural infrastructure. These systems deliver medical gases such as oxygen and nitrous oxide from remote tanks to wall outlets throughout the facility. Medical gases are prescription drugs, and medical gas delivery products on the patients' side of the wall (such as flowmeters, gauges, tubing, and masks) are indisputably devices. But what about the "behind-the-wall" pipes, manifolds, valves, and connectors, typically installed by plumbing contractors? FDA originally took the position that such systems were "part of the physical plant" rather than medical devices. *See* Letter from Franklin K. Coombs, P.E., Biomedical Engineering Branch, Division of Classification and Scientific Classification, FDA to Larry R. Pilot, Director of the Division of Compliance, FDA (Jan. 3, 1977); Memorandum from Pilot to Coombs (Jan. 10, 1977) (response confirming that oxygen supply systems "are not devices as that term is defined in the Act"). More recently, however, the agency has indicated that medical gas delivery distribution systems are in fact devices under the statute. Letter from Eugene M. Berk, Center for Devices and Radiological Health, FDA, to Howard Holstein (May 11, 1993). Nevertheless, FDA has said it will use its regulatory discretion to exempt such systems from the legal requirements for devices, with the exception of the general misbranding and adulteration regulations, which still apply.

3. *Leeches and Maggots.* FDA treats maggots and leeches marketed for medicinal purposes as medical devices. Maggots, or fly larvae, are normally associated with corpses and adulterated food, but they also help heal wounds and burns in living

patients' tissue by liquefying dead tissue. Leeches, the bloodsucking aquatic animals with cameo roles in the films *The African Queen* and *Stand By Me*, have been used in medicine for thousands of years. Today, doctors use them primarily to remove pooled blood in skin grafts and reattachment surgery. In 2004, FDA cleared separate 510(k) applications to market each of these products as a medical device substantially equivalent to a device sold prior to the enactment of the Medical Device Amendments in 1976. *See* FDA Talk Paper, No. T04–19 (June 28, 2004).

4. *Sterilizers*. Federal courts have held that machines used to sterilize other medical devices are themselves medical devices. *See United States v. 22 Rectangular or Cylindrical Devices . . . "The Ster–O–Lizer MD–200"*, 714 F. Supp. 1159 (D. Utah 1989) (surgical instruments); *United States v. Bowen*, 172 F.3d 682 (9th Cir. 1999) (dental handpieces).

COMMENT: DUAL USE PRODUCTS

FDA has set forth the following policy for products that have both medical and nonmedical uses.

> FDA will regulate a multi-purpose product as a medical device if it is intended for a medical purpose . . . FDA will determine the intended use of a product based upon the expressions of the person legally responsible for its labeling and by the circumstances surrounding its distribution. The most important factors the agency will consider in determining the intended use of a particular product are the labeling, advertising, and other representations accompanying the product. Products that have medical uses only are clearly intended for medical purposes, and, therefore, will be regulated as medical devices whether or not medical claims are made for them.

45 Fed. Reg. 60576, 60579 (Sept. 12, 1980).

FDA has taken the position that exercise equipment used in recreational and sporting activities will be regulated as medical devices only where those products are intended for medical purposes and thus are properly classified as "therapeutic equipment." 48 Fed. Reg. 53032, 53043–44 (Nov. 23, 1983). Similarly, the agency has concluded that "electrostatic air cleaners are not inherently medical devices," because they have other uses as well, and that the fact that FDA regulates the emission of ozone from medical devices in 21 C.F.R. § 801.415 does not mean that all products emitting ozone are medical devices. Letter from FDA Chief Counsel R.M. Cooper to CPSC Assistant General Counsel S. Lemberg (May 14, 1979).

FDA considers magnets marketed with medical claims, including treatment of cancer or arthritis, to be medical devices. CDRH Consumer Information (Mar. 1, 2000). Similarly, the FDA website states that the agency considers clothes that are labeled or promoted as providing protection against the sun or limiting exposure to the sun's UVA/UVB rays to be medical devices. FDA imposed unapproved device status on an electric gas grill igniter advertised to relieve various kinds of pain when used to send an electric current into acupressure points on the body. A federal appeals court upheld this determination. *U.S. v. Universal Management Services, Inc.*, 191 F.3d 750 (6th Cir. 1999).

d. FIRST AMENDMENT LIMITS

United States v. 23 ... Articles

192 F.2d 308 (2d Cir. 1951).

■ WOODBURY, CIRCUIT JUDGE.

The United States of America filed a libel ... seeking the seizure and condemnation of certain phonograph records, and various accompanying items of printed and graphic matter, all of which were moving or had moved in interstate commerce. The phonograph records were entitled in part "Time To Sleep," and their accompanying literature consists of (1) an album in part entitled, "De Luxe Records Presents Time To Sleep a Tested Method of Inducing Sleep Conceived and Transcribed by Ralph Slater," (2) a leaflet in part reading: "Sleep With This Amazing Record 'Time to Sleep,'" (3) a certificate entitled "Sleep Guaranteed," (4) display cards entitled "De Luxe Records Presents Time to Sleep," and (5) a poster headed "A 'Dream Girl' Shows a New Way to Dreamland." ...

Section 201(h) of the Act under consideration provides in material part that "[t]he term 'device' ... means instruments, apparatus, and contrivances, including their components, parts, and accessories, intended (1) for use in the diagnosis, cure, mitigation, treatment, or prevention of disease in man or other animals; or (2) to affect the structure or any function of the body of man or other animals."

Certainly a phonograph record, if not itself an instrument or an apparatus, is a contrivance. And moreover, it is without question a component, part or accessory of a phonograph, or like record playing machine, which in its turn is without any doubt at all an instrument, apparatus or contrivance. The real question therefore is whether the libeled records were intended for either of the uses described in (1) or (2) of § 201(h), supra. Obviously the records were intended for use in the cure, mitigation, treatment or perhaps prevention of insomnia. But the medical experts who testified at the trial were agreed that insomnia is not a disease, but is a symptom of a disease, usually although not necessarily a neurological one, or of an emotional disturbance of some kind. Thus it may be argued that the records do not fall within the coverage of (1) above.

However, all the expert witnesses who testified on the point were unanimous that sleep is a function of the body, or body and mind, of man and other animals, and this testimony brings the records within the terms of (2), supra, for their intended use was to affect that function, *i.e.* to induce sleep in those who needed it but had difficulty in obtaining enough. Without further laboring the point it will suffice to say that the records involved are "devices within the meaning of § 201(h)(2) of the Act...."

United States v. Undetermined Quantities of Article of Device

Med. Devices Rep. (CCH) ¶ 15,055 (W.D. Mich. 1982).

This is an action by the United States ... seeking the condemnation and forfeiture of thirty-two different tape recordings, marketed by the claimant, Potentials Unlimited, Inc. under various titles. These tape recordings were initially seized, pursuant to warrant, on January 6, 1981. The tapes sought to be condemned include:

1. "Relief of Back Pain" or "Back Pain"

2. "Removal of Warts"

3. "Bust Enlargement" or "Natural Bust Enlargement"

4. "Migraine Relief" or "Headaches"

.... [28 additional titles suggesting disease or structure/function effects]

Although the claimant disputes whether the labeling of the tapes is false or misleading and whether they lack adequate directions for use, it does not dispute that the tapes were manufactured in an unregistered establishment, that the tapes themselves are not registered as medical devices, or that there was no premarket notification of their manufacture and sale. It follows that if, in fact, the tapes are medical devices, they are in violation of the Act and are subject to forfeiture. Therefore, the resolution of this action turns upon one question; are these tapes medical devices within the meaning of the Act?....

In January, 1981 Potentials Unlimited marketed over 100 tape recordings. Most of these are unrelated to health or medical problems, as evidenced by the fact that only 32 of the tapes are under seizure. The catalogue distributed by Potentials identifies many different "self-hypnosis" tapes with such titles as "Memory," "Good Study Habits," "Fear of Flying," "Stop Smoking," "Freedom from Guilt," "Jealousy," "Self–Confidence," "How to be Popular," "Be a Better Bowler," and "How to be a Great Golfer." ... The tapes are divided, by the catalogue, into several different "series." Most of the seized tapes fall under the "Health Series" although a few are listed under other categories.

The Potentials Unlimited catalogue comprises the most significant and detailed promotional literature used to market the tapes.... The introduction refers to the tape recordings, at one point, as "learning"; however, read as a whole, the introduction leaves the impression that the positive suggestions contained on the tapes will act upon the "subconscious mind" to automatically bring about the changes which a person desires. Any teaching and learning aspects of the tapes are deemphasized or negated by the reference to "magic" and the implication that the tapes will work better, "without any interference from your conscious mind." Indeed, the introduction suggests that the tapes will be more beneficial if played during sleep, rather than actually being listened to and assimilated.

The catalogue distributed in 1981 contains a disclaimer on page 3, in small but easily legible print, which states:

> No therapeutic claims of any kind are made with regard to these tape programs. We believe cures or improvements are a matter of mind over matter and these tapes are not intended as a substitute for seeing your physician, or for medical treatment. Parental guidance is suggested for children's use.

An earlier version of this disclaimer was introduced into the catalogue sometime in 1980 after the FDA had begun investigating Potentials Unlimited in February of that year. In previous catalogues no such disclaimer was included.

The general introduction applies to all of the self-hypnosis tapes. The separate descriptive paragraphs contained in the catalogue refer by title and content to specific tapes and the specific problem or aspect of a person's life which that tape is designed to improve. The paragraphs are not specific regarding how the tapes work, instead they are anecdotal and conversational attempts to interest the reader in the specific tape. When combined with the general introduction, the individual descriptions generally leave the impression that the tapes will cure or treat the specific health-related problem indicated by the title of the tape.

Generally there is no dispute that the tapes purport to effect [sic] structures or functions of the body or to mitigate the effects of diseases. . . .

The tape recordings themselves are very similar in style, structure, and content. They begin with brief instructions regarding the use and purpose of the particular tape, a standard hypnotic induction, and a series of statements, descriptions of visual images, and suggestions designed to influence the listener's thinking. Many of the images are repeated in more than one tape.

All of the tapes clearly convey a number of related ideas revolving around a central theme, *i.e.* that a person's thoughts can influence their health or physical characteristics. This central theme is developed through an emphasis on the benefits of relaxation, the elimination of negative feelings such as anger, hate and jealousy, the creation of a positive self-image, and the idea that reality is a reflection of one's own perceptions. Thus, according to the tapes, if a person thinks of himself in a particular, desired way, such as thin, free of allergies or pain, or generally healthy, the person will actually take on those desired characteristics. The tapes are clearly designed to communicate both this central tenet, and a method for putting it into practice.

The court does not find that the tapes themselves are, apart from the claims made in the catalogue, designed or intended to be used in the cure or treatment of the physical and mental conditions indicated by their titles. Each tape is designed to teach a method of mental therapy which it is claimed will have beneficial effects on a particular aspect of a person's life. Any therapeutic results flow from the listener's successful implementation of the lessons contained on the tape. The purported "treatment", therefore, consists of the new thought patterns, beliefs, and behaviors which the listener has learned and adopted. The lessons contained on the tapes are communicated linguistically, and can be understood as well by reading transcripts of the tapes as by listening to the tapes. The contents of the tapes could also be transmitted directly between two individuals, using speech, without the use of tape recording devices. Therefore, the court finds that the mechanical components of these tape recordings are not part of any medical treatment and are used only as a means of communicating the verbal ideas and methods found on the tapes.

The tapes use hypnosis and hypnotic suggestion to communicate the ideas which they contain. The American Medical Association has recognized hypnosis as a useful "modality" for medical treatment, when used in conjunction with other treatments, since 1957. There are controlled studies indicating that hypnosis techniques may be useful in the removal of warts, the treatment of asthma, the mitigation of all kinds of pain, the reduction of myopia (near-sightedness), and in enlarging the female bust. In addition, there are anecdotal reports of the successful use of hypnosis to cure or treat virtually every condition encompassed by the 32 self-hypnosis tapes under seizure. Scientific research regarding the use of hypnosis in treating these other conditions has generally been negative. No research has been done, specifically, regarding the use of hypnotic tape recordings. . . .

The fundamental finding regarding hypnosis, as it impacts upon this case, is that hypnosis is an ill defined and little understood concept which it is at least possible to view as a special form of communication or as a teaching device. This finding is significant since the court has found that the tapes under seizure communicate several clearly identifiable ideas. Since hypnosis can be considered a form of communication, the fact that the tapes use hypnosis techniques, does not prevent their classification as communication or teaching devices. The court rejects Dr. Reyher's testimony that communication must be logical, rational, or objectively purposeful. His definition of communication, besides being outside his field of expertise (as he readily admitted) would exclude poetry, art, music, and drama from the area of communication. Whatever the merits of such a restricted definition for some purposes, it does not comport with the ordinary concept of communication and is irrelevant for First Amendment purposes.

There is no evidence that the self-hypnosis tapes manufactured by Potentials Unlimited can actually achieve the results which are claimed in the Potential catalogue. The tapes could be harmful if they caused someone to delay seeking adequate medical care for a disease condition. Additionally, the uncontrolled use of hypnosis could be dangerous because persons could develop anxiety reactions to some of the suggestions contained on the tapes.

This case illustrates the difficulty which inevitably arises in balancing the ideal of philosophical and economic freedom against the practical need to protect unwary and vulnerable individuals from the claims of rapacious and unethical businessmen. . . . Underlying this case, of course, is the fundamental question of whether consumers should be allowed the choice of buying Potentials Unlimited self-hypnosis tapes without the prior intervention and approval of the Federal government in the form of the Food and Drug Administration.

Representing the other side of the balancing dilemma is society's concern for the gullible or the desperate individual who is induced to forego necessary medical treatment by the fraudulent, or simply mistaken, claims of the purveyors of medical drugs and devices. Although the construction and fantastic claims made for many quack devices over the years often seem quite amusing, use of these devices can have serious health consequences. Whether sold to a consumer or a health professional, a device which does not perform as promised may pose a risk to health as well as an economic detriment to the purchaser. Reliance on unwarranted claims made for a device, recommending use in serious disease conditions, may induce the purchaser to forego seeking timely and appropriate medical treatment.

Fortunately, the court need not confront the problem presented in this case from the fundamental level of balancing the costs and benefits of the two competing perspectives suggested above. Congress has already engaged in such a balancing process and has determined that "medical devices" should be regulated by the FDA for the protection and benefit of the consuming public seeking medical treatment. In doing so, Congress has adopted a broad definition of medical device which is to be liberally construed in order to effectuate the purpose of the Act. *United States v. Bacto–Unidisk*, 394 U.S. 784 (1969).

There is no doubt that a tape recording is an implement, apparatus, or contrivance [as required by the FD&C Act definition]. However, a distinction must be made in this case between the tapes themselves, and the ideas that are contained on the tapes. Congress did not intend to regulate an article or device, the sole function of which is to serve as a means of communicating health related ideas or information. Had Congress had such an intent it would have expressly included books, the quintessential communication device, in the definition of "medical device." It did not do so.

The idea that a person can control and improve their [sic] health in general, or specific physical conditions, through the intervention of their thoughts, *i.e.* with their minds, is simply that, an idea, which anyone, including the claimant in this case, is free to believe, to disseminate, and, unless specifically prohibited, to act upon as they wish by virtue of the First Amendment. As found by the court, the tape recordings under seizure in this case are designed and intended to communicate and to teach certain ideas, beliefs, and mental processes which are claimed to have health benefits when adopted and practiced by the listener. Congress did not purport to regulate quack medical ideas or beliefs when it drafted the definition of medical device contained in the Act. By no stretch of language can an idea or a mental process be considered an instrument, apparatus, implement, machine, contrivance, implant, or in vitro reagent, or a similar or related article.

The "liberal interpretation" to be accorded the Act must yield somewhat when it comes into conflict with First Amendment freedoms.... Since ideas, beliefs and mental processes do not come within the statutory definition they are outside the jurisdiction of the FDA. Mechanical devices which do no more than communicate or expound such ideas, beliefs and mental processes are likewise outside the jurisdiction of the FDA. To include such devices within the definition would have grave First Amendment implications and would, by implication, bring health related books, magazines, and publications within the agency jurisdiction. That is a result Congress clearly did not contemplate or intend.

The fact that the tapes in issue do no more than communicate certain ideas using hypnosis as a tool in that communication does not end the inquiry into whether these tapes, as marketed by Potentials Unlimited, are subject to regulation as medical devices. Articles and devices which have no intended therapeutic qualities may be regulated if they are sold by the vendor accompanied by therapeutic claims. Thus, the seller's objective manifestation of a therapeutic intent brings otherwise medically benign articles within the purview of the Act. . . .

The therapeutic claims contained in promotional literature can convert the most innocent of articles into drugs or devices within the meaning of the Act. . . . The conduct of Potentials Unlimited in marketing these tapes as therapeutic medical devices is subject to regulation by Congress, even if the tapes themselves communicate ideas.

As stated in the court's findings of fact, the catalogue distributed by Potentials Unlimited tells the reader through its general introduction, that the self-hypnosis tapes will work "like magic," by "saturating the subconscious mind with positive suggestions." This language creates the expectation of an automatic and mechanical process by which suggestions will be implanted in the brain, much like a drug, and miraculous cures will result from the therapeutic effects of these suggestions. The whole introduction is designed to imply a therapeutic result from listening to the tapes, rather than a simple act of communication. Hypnosis is regarded, in the catalogue, as a treatment rather than a form of communication. Coupled with the titles of the seized tapes, an intended therapeutic use for the tapes is objectively manifested. This objective manifestation makes the tapes, as they are presently marketed, medical devices, to the extent they are used in treating disease or to affect body function. . . .

The petition for condemnation against the . . . tapes . . . is granted. . . .

Draft Policy Guidance for Regulation of Computer Products

52 Fed. Reg. 36104 (September 25, 1987).

FDA is making available for public comment draft policy guidance for the regulation of computer products. The draft policy guidance clarifies how FDA would apply existing statutory requirements to the regulation of computer products (*i.e.*, both hardware and software) when such products meet the definition of a medical device in the Medical Device Amendments of 1976. . . .

Under the draft policy, FDA would not regard computer products used only for traditional "library" functions such as storage, retrieval, and dissemination of information—functions traditionally carried out through textbooks and journals—to be medical devices subject to regulation by the agency. Similarly, the policy notes that FDA's device regulations and authorities also would not apply to computer products used for general accounting or communications functions or solely for instructional purposes, rather than to diagnose or treat patients.

When a computer product is a "component, part, or accessory" of a product recognized as a medical device in its own right, the computer component is regulated according to the requirements for the parent device (unless the component of the device is separately classified).

Computer products which are medical devices, and not components, parts, or accessories of other articles which are themselves medical devices, are regulated with the least degree of control necessary to provide reasonable assurance of safety and effectiveness. For example, many software products known as "expert" or "knowledge based" systems that are not used with existing medical devices and that are intended to involve competent human intervention before any impact on human health occurs (*e.g.*, where clinical judgment and experience can be used to check and interpret a system's output) are exempt from registration, listing, premarket notification, and premarket approval requirements. FDA is also not aware of any computer product that is not a component, part, or accessory of another device that would require [a] ... premarket approval (PMA) application before marketing.

The agency is cognizant of the need to safeguard First Amendment protections and recognizes that, in some cases, it may be difficult to make a clear distinction between software products that perform traditional "book" or "library" functions, and software products that fall within the definition of a medical device under the draft policy, based on their intended use in the diagnosis or management of health-related conditions. FDA believes flexible guidance is necessary for effective implementation of the medical devices law and specifically invites comments on the appropriateness of the approach taken in the draft policy.

NOTES

1. *Further Developments*. A November 13, 1989, revised draft of the Policy for the Regulation of Computer Products reiterated the basic statements of the 1987 draft. FDA has never finalized the policy. The agency has more recently announced that it is considering establishing a risk-based classification of stand-alone computer software products that fit the definition of a medical device, but it has not taken any further action. 65 Fed. Reg. 73822 (Nov. 30, 2000). *See generally* Bruce M. Fried & Jason M. Zuckerman, *FDA Regulation of Medical Software*, 33 J. Health L. 129 (2000); E. Stewart Crumpler & Harvey Rudolph, *FDA Software Policy and Regulation of Medical Device Software*, 52 Food & Drug L.J. 511 (1997); Dee Simons, *Medical Device Software Regulation; An Industry Perspective*, 52 Food & Drug L.J. 189 (1997).

2. *Specific* Case. In FDA Regulatory Letter BOS–88–10 (June 23, 1988), FDA Boston District Director E. J. McDonnell took the position that a computerized blood bank and laboratory management system that takes data directly from automated blood analyzers and uses it as the basis for labeling blood and blood components is a medical device and subject to the premarket notification requirements of section 510(k). This position was reaffirmed in 1994 in a letter from CBER Director Kathryn C. Zoon to Blood Establishment Computer Software Manufacturers (Mar. 31, 1994).

E. Implicit Limits on FDA's Jurisdiction: Tobacco

In 1995, FDA announced that it was going to assert jurisdiction over cigarettes and smokeless tobacco and regulate their manufacture, labeling, and advertising. For legal authority, the agency invoked the FD&C Act.

Contending that tobacco products were responsible for as many as 400,000 American deaths annually, the agency mounted what it considered a compelling case for government intervention. The agency's goal was to protect adolescents who had not yet begun to smoke. Its plan was designed to obstruct their access to tobacco and discourage manufacturer promotional efforts to attract new smokers. FDA's notice of proposed rulemaking immediately precipitated litigation that probed the boundaries of the agency's legal authority. The eventual failure of FDA's initiative exposed new limits of the Act's definitions as measures of its regulatory jurisdiction.

Decades before the 1995 announcement, FDA had asserted its authority over at least some tobacco products. Shortly after World War II, the agency successfully challenged the marketing of two brands of cigarettes that it claimed were illegal drugs. In *United States v. 46 Cartons . . . Fairfax Cigarettes*, 113 F. Supp. 336 (D.N.J. 1953), FDA seized a shipment of cigarettes whose labeling "represents that the article is effective in preventing respiratory disease, common cold, influenza, pneumonia" and more than a dozen other illnesses. The government charged that these express claims made Fairfax Cigarettes a "drug" under the Act, and thus that the product required FDA approval. The district court agreed and ordered the seized goods relabeled or destroyed. The manufacturer, of course, abandoned the challenged claims, effectively depriving FDA of jurisdiction. A similar result followed FDA's seizure of another brand of cigarettes making weight-loss claims. *See United States v. 354 Bulk Cartons Trim Reducing–Aid Cigarettes*, 178 F. Supp. 847 (D.N.J. 1959).

FDA thereafter appears to have lost interest in contesting the health claims made for different brands of cigarettes. Within a decade, however, Congress began to explore measures to combat the health effects of tobacco. In 1964 the Surgeon General released a ground-breaking report which documented the heavy price smokers paid for the pleasure of smoking. *See* SMOKING AND HEALTH: REPORT OF THE ADVISORY COMMITTEE OF THE SURGEON GENERAL OF THE PUBLIC HEALTH SERVICE (1964). The report inspired several proposals to regulate the manufacture, labeling, and sale of cigarettes and, later, of smokeless tobacco. During congressional hearings on these bills, FDA officials were asked what, if any, role their agency could play. Their uniform response was that FDA had no authority over cigarettes unless they bore claims that they could prevent or relieve disease.

Ultimately, suggestions that FDA be given authority to regulate cigarettes were rejected in favor of statutes passed in 1965 and 1969 curbing the labeling and, later, the advertising for cigarettes and requiring their labels to bear mild warnings about their health effects. The 1960s came to an end with no material change in the marketing of cigarettes despite mounting evidence of their adverse effects.

Advocates of tobacco control, however, never lost hope that FDA might be persuaded to acknowledge, and then exercise, jurisdiction over tobacco. In 1977, Action on Smoking and Health (ASH), a citizen action group, filed a petition urging the agency to assert jurisdiction over cigarettes under the FD&C Act and impose restrictions on their advertising and distribution. The petition cited evidence that smokers smoked to gain the physiological

effects of nicotine, and it contended that these effects were thus "intended." Once again, FDA declined to exercise jurisdiction:

> The petitioners have presented no evidence that manufacturers or
> vendors of cigarettes represent that the cigarettes are "intended to
> affect the structure or any function of the body of man. . . ." 21
> U.S.C. § 321(g)(1)(C). Statements by the petitioners and citations
> in the petition that cigarettes are used by smokers to affect the
> structure or any functions of their bodies are not evidence of such
> intent by the manufacturers or vendors of cigarettes, as required
> under the provisions of 21 U.S.C. § 321(g)(1)(C). . . .

Letter memorandum from Donald Kennedy, Commissioner, FDA, to ASH
(Dec. 5, 1977), *quoted in Action on Smoking and Health v. Harris*, 655 F.2d
236, 239 (D.C. Cir. 1980).

The D.C. Circuit upheld FDA's refusal to regulate cigarettes in the
following words:

>   . . . [B]y failing to introduce any evidence of vendors' intent—
> whether based upon subjective vendor claims or objective evidence
> such as labeling, promotional material, and advertising—ASH
> placed itself in the position of having to meet the high standard
> established in cases where the statutory "intent" is derived from
> consumer use alone. Clearly, it is well established "that the
> 'intended use' of a product, within the meaning of the Act, is
> determined from its label, accompanying labeling, promotional
> claims, advertising, and any other relevant source." Whether evi-
> dence of consumer intent is a "relevant source" for these purposes
> depends upon whether such evidence is strong enough to justify an
> inference as to the vendors' intent. This requires a substantial
> showing. . . .
>
>   In cases such as the one at hand, consumers must use the
> product predominantly—and in fact nearly exclusively—with the
> appropriate intent before the requisite statutory intent can be
> inferred. . . . ASH did not establish, and arguably cannot establish,
> the near-exclusivity of consumer use of cigarettes with the intent
> "to affect the structure or any function of the body of man. . . ."

Action on Smoking and Health v. Harris, 655 F.2d 236, 239–40 (D.C. Cir.
1980).

In separate petitions, ASH also requested FDA to assert jurisdiction
over both attached and detached cigarette filters as medical devices, based
on a recommendation by an FDA advisory committee that they be classified
as class III under the Medical Device Amendments of 1976. Following a
court order to rule on the petitions, *Action on Smoking and Health v. Food
and Drug Administration*, FDLI 1978–1980 Jud. Rec. 862 (D.D.C. 1980),
FDA denied both in a letter from Deputy Commissioner M. Novitch to J.F.
Banzhaf, III, FDA Dkt Nos. 77P–0185 & 78P–0338/CP (Nov. 25, 1980).

Both FDA and the D.C. Circuit in *ASH* left open the possibility that
the agency might be able to assert jurisdiction over cigarettes if there were
evidence that the manufacturers themselves intended their products to
"affect the structure or function of the body." Events soon reopened this

line of analysis. In the early 1990s, several states sued the major manufacturers of cigarettes to recover the costs of state-funded medical care provided to smokers suffering from tobacco-related illness. In the course of discovery in these cases, some of the defendants disgorged documents that strongly suggested, and in the view of many proved beyond question, that the companies knew their customers smoked to gain the effects of nicotine and designed their products to satisfy this desire. These disclosures provided FDA the opportunity to revisit the issue left open by the *ASH* case: Could sellers of tobacco products be said to intend the bodily effects of nicotine?

FDA faced this question shortly after the appointment of a new Commissioner, David Kessler. A series of petitions renewed demands that the agency assert jurisdiction over cigarettes as "drugs" or "devices" and take steps to curb or prohibit their sale. Kessler launched FDA's own extensive investigation into the cigarette business—how they were made and marketed, and what the manufacturers knew or intended about their effects. At the same time, agency lawyers were directed to design a plan for regulating cigarettes that would substantially dampen their appeal to younger people, without threatening an outright ban that could cause Congress to intervene.

Shortly afterwards, FDA published a notice of proposed rulemaking in which it asserted jurisdiction over cigarettes as a "device" for delivering the "drug" nicotine. 60 Fed. Reg. 41314 (Aug. 11, 1995). The agency proposed measures to make cigarettes difficult for young people to obtain and less appealing to consumers generally, including mandatory carding of youthful customers, relocation of cigarette displays, and outright bans on the industry's favorite promotions, including sponsorship of concerts, art exhibits, and sporting events. To support this proposal, FDA contended that the evidence from company files made clear that the cigarette manufacturers did "intend" their products to affect the bodily functions of their customers. In addition, the agency asserted that the FD&C Act allowed a range of remedial options short of an outright ban.

The cigarette manufacturers, along with representatives of advertising interests who saw FDA's proposed curbs on promotion as an assault on the First Amendment, did not wait for the rulemaking to conclude; they brought suit immediately, contending that FDA's lack of jurisdiction was so obvious that they need not exhaust the opportunity for comment that the agency had provided. The exhaustion question was never resolved, because the United States District Court for the Middle District of North Carolina, where the manufacturers had chosen to file their suit, did not take up the parties' cross motions for summary judgment until after publication of FDA's final rule in 61 Fed. Reg. 44396 (Aug. 28, 1996). In its preamble to the final rule, the agency made some adjustments to its defense of its jurisdiction and more significant revisions to its regulatory scheme, but its fundamental claims remained the same. The agency contended that the evidence now revealed that cigarettes were intended by their manufacturers to affect the body by delivering nicotine and that FDA could restrict their promotion and sale as "devices" without having to confront the Act's categorical ban of any "drug" that cannot be shown to be safe.

The District Court scheduled a full day of argument on the cross motions for summary judgment. Within a few weeks of the argument, Judge Osteen rendered a decision that was widely interpreted as a victory for FDA. It focused on the central issue of the agency's jurisdiction to regulate.

> The precise question presented to the court is whether Congress has evidenced its clear intent to withhold from FDA jurisdiction to regulate tobacco products as customarily marketed. The inquiry as to whether Congress has directly spoken to the issue should begin with an examination of the text of the FDCA. A product is subject to the FDCA if it meets the statute's definition of a "food," "drug," "device," or "cosmetic." Rather than itemize each product subject to regulation under the FDCA, Congress defined these categories broadly so that each encompasses a wide range of products.
>
> ... [T]he court finds that tobacco products fit within the FDCA's definitions of "drug" and "device." Therefore, Plaintiffs must prove to the court that Congress has expressed its clear intent to withhold from FDA jurisdiction to regulate tobacco products in some place other than the text of the FDCA....
>
> ... This court is convinced that neither the text nor the legislative history of the FDCA evidences clear congressional intent to withhold from FDA authority to regulate tobacco products....
>
> FDA offers that tobacco products fall within the FDCA's definitions of "drugs" and "devices" because they are "intended to affect the structure or any function of the body." FDA explains that the nicotine in tobacco products affects the structure or function of the body by causing and sustaining addiction and by acting as a stimulant, sedative, and weight regulator. FDA further argues that manufacturers intend nicotine to produce such effects....
>
> Plaintiffs claim that a product's "intended use" can be established only by manufacturer representations about the product.[30] FDA counters that it appropriately relied on evidence of foreseeability, consumer use, and internal manufacturer memoranda to establish intended use. The text, legislative history, and past judicial and agency interpretation of the structure-or-function definitions of "drug" and "device" reveal that intended use may be established by evidence other than manufacturer representations.
>
> ... Although the regulations defining "intended use" [21 C.F.R. 201.128, 801.4] clearly anticipate the establishment of intended use through evidence of promotional claims, the plain language does not prohibit the establishment of intended use by

---

30. FDA does not contend that tobacco manufacturers make any representations in connection with the sale of tobacco products. Therefore, if intended use can be established only by manufacturer representations, tobacco products would not be subject to regulation pursuant to the FDCA.

other evidence. To illustrate, the regulations specifically provide that intent may be shown by circumstances surrounding the sale of the article and that one such circumstance could be the offering and use of a product for a purpose for which it is neither advertised nor labeled with the manufacturer's knowledge. The regulations defining "intended use" do not prohibit reliance on evidence other than manufacturer representations to establish intended use.

. . . .

Plaintiffs infer that Congress intended for the structure-or-function definition of device to "apply only to products that are marketed to provide some medical or other health benefit to users." They support their argument in part by noting that Congress entitled its 1976 amendments to the FDCA's device provisions the "Medical Device Amendments" ("MDA"). The definition of device, however, expressly includes those products "intended to affect the structure or any function of the body of man or other animals" and gives no indication that it is to apply only to those devices with a medical purpose. 21 U.S.C. § 321(h). . . .

Coyne Beahm, Inc. v. U.S. Food and Drug Administration, 966 F. Supp. 1374 (M.D.N.C. 1997).

On one important issue, however, Judge Osteen's opinion disappointed FDA. He ruled that the FD&C Act did not authorize the agency—by invoking its power to "restrict" the "sale" of a device—to impose any limits on its advertising. This issue, discussed *infra* p. 1051, was briefed on appeal but was not reached by the Fourth Circuit, which, by a 2–1 vote, overturned Judge Osteen's ruling upholding FDA's assertion of jurisdiction. *Brown & Williamson Tobacco Corporation v. Food and Drug Administration*, 153 F.3d 155 (4th Cir. 1999). Predictably, the Supreme Court granted the government's Petition for Certiorari.

The opposing opinions of Justice O'Connor and Justice Breyer focused on several questions that together framed the issue of FDA's jurisdiction. Could an article's "intended" use be shown by evidence of the manufacturers' private plans? Did the evidence assembled by FDA establish that cigarettes are intended to produce drug-like effects? Did the Act's requirements permit the continued sale of a drug or device that the agency had said was unsafe? And, critically, had Congress left FDA free to invoke its authority under the FD&C Act?

Food and Drug Administration v. Brown & Williamson Tobacco Corp.

529 U.S. 120 (2000).

■ JUSTICE O'CONNOR delivered the opinion of the Court.

. . . .

The FDA's assertion of jurisdiction to regulate tobacco products is founded on its conclusions that nicotine is a "drug" and that cigarettes and smokeless tobacco are "drug delivery devices." Again, the FDA found that tobacco products are "intended" to deliver the pharmacological effects of satisfying addiction, stimulation and tranquilization, and weight control because those effects are foreseeable to any reasonable manufacturer, consumers use tobacco products to obtain those effects, and tobacco manufacturers have designed their products to produce those effects. As an initial matter, respondents take issue with the FDA's reading of "intended," arguing that it is a term of art that refers exclusively to claims made by the manufacturer or vendor about the product. That is, a product is not a drug or device under the FDCA unless the manufacturer or vendor makes some express claim concerning the product's therapeutic benefits. We need not resolve this question, however, because assuming, *arguendo*, that a product can be "intended to affect the structure or any function of the body" absent claims of therapeutic or medical benefit, the FDA's claim to jurisdiction contravenes the clear intent of Congress.

A threshold issue is the appropriate framework for analyzing the FDA's assertion of authority to regulate tobacco products. Because this case involves an administrative agency's construction of a statute that it administers, our analysis is governed by *Chevron U.S.A. Inc. v. Natural Resources Defense Council, Inc.*, 467 U.S. 837 (1984). Under *Chevron*, a reviewing court must first ask "whether Congress has directly spoken to the precise question at issue." *Id.*, at 842. If Congress has done so, the inquiry is at an end; the court "must give effect to the unambiguously expressed intent of Congress." *Id.*, at 843. But if Congress has not specifically addressed the question, a reviewing court must respect the agency's construction of the statute so long as it is permissible. . . .

In determining whether Congress has specifically addressed the question at issue, a reviewing court should not confine itself to examining a particular statutory provision in isolation. The meaning—or ambiguity—of certain words or phrases may only become evident when placed in context. A court must therefore interpret the statute "as a symmetrical and coherent regulatory scheme," *Gustafson v. Alloyd Co.*, 513 U.S. 561, 569 (1995), and "fit, if possible, all parts into an harmonious whole," *FTC v. Mandel Brothers, Inc.*, 359 U.S. 385, 389 (1959). Similarly, the meaning of one statute may be affected by other Acts, particularly where Congress has spoken subsequently and more specifically to the topic at hand. In addition, we must be guided to a degree by common sense as to the manner in which Congress is likely to delegate a policy decision of such economic and political magnitude to an administrative agency.

With these principles in mind, we find that Congress has directly spoken to the issue here and precluded the FDA's jurisdiction to regulate tobacco products.

Viewing the FDCA as a whole, it is evident that one of the Act's core objectives is to ensure that any product regulated by the FDA is "safe" and "effective" for its intended use. This essential purpose pervades the FDCA. . . . Thus, the Act generally requires the FDA to prevent the marketing of any drug or device where the "potential for inflicting death or physical injury is not offset by the possibility of therapeutic benefit." *United States v. Rutherford*, 442 U.S. 544, 556 (1979).

[margin note: cigs dangerous]

In its rulemaking proceeding, the FDA quite exhaustively documented that "tobacco products are unsafe," "dangerous," and "cause great pain and suffering from illness." It found that the consumption of tobacco products presents "extraordinary health risks," and that "tobacco use is the single leading cause of preventable death in the United States." . . .

[margin note: FDA would need to remove]

These findings logically imply that, if tobacco products were "devices" under the FDCA, the FDA would be required to remove them from the market. . . .

Second, the FDCA requires the FDA to place all devices that it regulates into one of three classifications. See § 360c(b)(1). . . . Given the FDA's findings regarding the health consequences of tobacco use, the agency would have to place cigarettes and smokeless tobacco in Class III because, even after the application of the Act's available controls, they would "present a potential unreasonable risk of illness or injury." 21 U.S.C. § 360c(a)(1)(C). As Class III devices, tobacco products would be subject to the FDCA's premarket approval process. *See* 21 U.S.C. § 360c(a)(1)(C); 21 U.S.C. § 360e. Under these provisions, the FDA would be prohibited from approving an application for premarket approval without "a showing of reasonable assurance that such device is safe under the conditions of use prescribed, recommended, or suggested on the labeling thereof." 21 U.S.C. § 360e(d)(2)(A). In view of the FDA's conclusions regarding the health effects of tobacco use, the agency would have no basis for finding any such reasonable assurance of safety. Thus, once the FDA fulfilled its statutory obligation to classify tobacco products, it could not allow them to be marketed.

In determining whether Congress has spoken directly to the FDA's authority to regulate tobacco, we must also consider in greater detail the tobacco-specific legislation that Congress has enacted over the past 35 years. . . .

Congress has enacted six separate pieces of legislation since 1965 addressing the problem of tobacco use and human health. . . .

[margin note: Congress's legis]

In adopting each statute, Congress has acted against the backdrop of the FDA's consistent and repeated statements that it lacked authority under the FDCA to regulate tobacco absent claims of therapeutic benefit by the manufacturer. In fact, on several occasions over this period, and after the health consequences of tobacco use and nicotine's pharmacological effects had become well known, Congress considered and rejected bills that would have granted the FDA such jurisdiction. Under these circumstances, it is evident that Congress' tobacco-specific statutes have effectively ratified the FDA's long-held position that it lacks jurisdiction under the FDCA to regulate tobacco products. Congress has created a distinct regulatory scheme to address the problem of tobacco and health, and that scheme, as presently constructed, precludes any role for the FDA. . . .

. . . Reading the FDCA as a whole, as well as in conjunction with Congress' subsequent tobacco-specific legislation, it is plain that Congress has not given the FDA the authority that it seeks to exercise here. For these reasons, the judgment of the Court of Appeals for the Fourth Circuit is affirmed.

It is so ordered.

■ Justice Breyer, with whom Justice Stevens, Justice Souter, and Justice Ginsburg join, dissenting.

. . . .

The Food and Drug Administration (FDA) has the authority to regulate "articles (other than food) intended to affect the structure or any function of the body...." Unlike the majority, I believe that tobacco products fit within this statutory language.

In its own interpretation, the majority nowhere denies the following two salient points. First, tobacco products (including cigarettes) fall within the scope of this statutory definition, read literally. Cigarettes achieve their mood-stabilizing effects through the interaction of the chemical nicotine and the cells of the central nervous system. Both cigarette manufacturers and smokers alike know of, and desire, that chemically induced result. Hence, cigarettes are "intended to affect" the body's "structure" and "function," in the literal sense of these words.

Second, the statute's basic purpose—the protection of public health—supports the inclusion of cigarettes within its scope.... Unregulated tobacco use causes "[m]ore than 400,000 people [to] die each year from tobacco-related illnesses, such as cancer, respiratory illnesses, and heart disease." 61 Fed. Reg. 44398 (1996). Indeed, tobacco products kill more people in this country every year "than ... AIDS ..., car accidents, alcohol, homicides, illegal drugs, suicides, and fires, *combined*." *Ibid.* (emphasis added)....

... Taken literally, [the structure/function] definition might include everything from room air conditioners to thermal pajamas. The companies argue that, to avoid such a result, the meaning of "drug" or "device" should be confined to *medical* or *therapeutic* products, narrowly defined.

The companies may well be right that the statute should not be read to cover room air conditioners and winter underwear. But I do not agree that we must accept their proposed limitation. For one thing, such a cramped reading contravenes the established purpose of the statutory language. For another, the companies' restriction would render the other two "drug" definitions superfluous. *See* 21 U.S.C. §§ 321(g)(1)(A), (g)(1)(B) (covering articles in the leading pharmacology compendia and those "intended for use in the diagnosis, cure, mitigation, treatment, or prevention of disease").

Most importantly, the statute's language itself supplies a different, more suitable, limitation: that a "drug" must be a *chemical* agent. The FDCA's "device" definition states that an article which affects the structure or function of the body is a "device" only if it "does *not* achieve its primary intended purposes through chemical action within ... the body," and "is *not* dependent upon being metabolized for the achievement of its primary intended purposes." § 321(h) (emphasis added). One can readily infer from this language that at least an article that *does* achieve its primary purpose through chemical action within the body and that *is* dependent upon being metabolized is a "drug," provided that it otherwise falls within the scope of the "drug" definition. And one need not hypothesize about air conditioners or thermal pajamas to recognize that the chemical nicotine, an important tobacco ingredient, meets this test....

The tobacco companies' principal definitional argument focuses upon the statutory word "intended." The companies say that "intended" in this context is a term of art. They assert that the statutory word "intended" means that the product's maker has made an *express claim* about the effect that its product will have on the body. Indeed, according to the companies, the FDA's inability to prove that cigarette manufacturers make such claims is precisely why that agency historically has said it lacked the statutory power to regulate tobacco.

The FDCA, however, does not use the word "claimed"; it uses the word "intended." And the FDA long ago issued regulations that say the relevant "intent" can be shown not only by a manufacturer's "expressions," *but also* "by the circumstances surrounding the distribution of the article." 21 CFR § 801.4. Thus, even in the absence of express claims, the FDA has regulated products that affect the body if the manufacturer wants, and knows, that consumers so use the product. . . .

Nor is the FDA's "objective intent" interpretation unreasonable. It falls well within the established scope of the ordinary meaning of the word "intended." And the companies acknowledge that the FDA can regulate a drug-like substance in the ordinary circumstance, *i.e.*, where the manufacturer makes an express claim, so it is not unreasonable to conclude that the agency retains such power where a product's effects on the body are so well known (say, like those of aspirin or calamine lotion), that there is no *need* for express representations because the product speaks for itself. . . .

The majority nonetheless reaches the "inescapable conclusion" that the language and structure of the FDCA as a whole "simply do not fit" the kind of public health problem that tobacco creates. That is because, in the majority's view, the FDCA requires the FDA to ban outright "dangerous" drugs or devices (such as cigarettes); yet, the FDA concedes that an immediate and total cigarette-sale ban is inappropriate. . . .

In my view, where linguistically permissible, we should interpret the FDCA in light of Congress' overall desire to protect health. That purpose requires a flexible interpretation that both permits the FDA to take into account the realities of human behavior and allows it, in appropriate cases, to choose from its arsenal of statutory remedies. . . .

NOTES

1. *Action in Congress.* In July 2004, the Senate passed legislation that would have given FDA specific statutory authority to regulate cigarettes and chewing tobacco. The legislation would not have put these products in the medical device category, but would have added a new chapter to the FD&C Act dedicated to these products. The legislation died in the House of Representatives. In March 2005, the bill was reintroduced in the House (H.R. 1376) and the Senate (S. 666), but it was not been reported out of committee.

2. *FDA Approval of Smoking Cessation Products.* In 1984, FDA approved a new drug application (NDA) for Nicorette chewing gum, which was indicated "as a temporary aid to the cigarette smoker seeking to give up his or her smoking habit while participating in a behavior modification program under medical or dental supervision." Nicorette, originally approved as a prescription drug but now sold over-the-counter, contains either 2 mg or 4 mg nicotine in each piece of chewing gum. FDA considered, but ultimately rejected, establishing an over-the-counter

monograph for smoking deterrent drug products. 58 Fed. Reg. 31236 (June 1, 1993). Consequently, any drug product that is labeled, represented, or promoted as a smoking deterrent is a new drug subject to the NDA process. 21 C.F.R. 310.544.

FDA has since approved NDAs for nicotine transdermal patches and nicotine inhalers to aid in smoking cessation. The former are now available over-the-counter, whereas the latter remain available only by prescription. In 2002, FDA found that "nicotine lollipops" and "lip balm," promoted to assist smoking cessation were intended for use as drugs. The FDA based its decision on the manufacturers' claims that these products are a "convenient, tasty way" to replace cigarettes and helped to decrease the "hand to mouth" fixation associated with smoking. FDA Talk Paper No. T02–17, *FDA Warns Sellers of Nicotine Lollipops & Lip Balm that their Products are Illegal* (Apr. 10, 2002).

3. *FDA's Regulation of Other Tobacco and Nicotine Products.* In December 2001, after the Supreme Court decided *Brown & Williamson*, a consortium of major public health organizations submitted four citizen petitions requesting that the agency regulate various tobacco and nicotine products marketed as safer than traditional cigarettes or smokeless tobacco.

Reduced–Risk Cigarettes. One type of product addressed by the petitions was reduced-risk cigarettes. Eclipse is a cigarette that primarily heats, rather than burns, the tobacco. It claims a reduced risk of cancer, respiratory inflammation, bronchitis, and emphysema as compared with other cigarettes. OMNI and Advance, which use other technologies, claim reduced carcinogenicity. (OMNI cigarettes are no longer commercially available.) The health organizations' petition urged FDA to regulate these cigarettes as drugs or medical devices, asserting that the explicit claims of risk reduction distinguished these products from the conventional cigarettes addressed in *Brown & Williamson*. FDA has not yet ruled on these petitions. FDA Docket No. 01P–0570 (Eclipse); Docket No. 01P–0571 (OMNI and Advance). Some of the comments filed by industry opposing the petitions acknowledged that a cigarette making affirmative therapeutic claims, as opposed to risk-reduction claims, would fall under FDA's jurisdiction. In other words, they acknowledged the continuing validity of the *Fairfax Cigarettes* decision, *supra* p. 78.

Nicotine Water. The manufacturer of this product attempted to market it as a dietary supplement exempt from the FD&C Act's requirements for drugs. FDA granted the health organizations' petition requesting that it regulate Nicotine Water as a drug. FDA Docket No. 01P–0573. The agency concluded that the manufacturer promoted Nicotine Water to treat or mitigate nicotine addiction. It based this conclusion on statements on the manufacturer's website describing Nicotine Water as a smoking cessation product that "contains the nicotine equivalent of 2 cigarettes" in one bottle of water and is "more effective than the Patch or Gum using Less Nicotine." Upon FDA's conclusion, the manufacturer of Nicotine Water then labeled its product a "homeopathic nicotinum formula."

Tobacco Lozenges. Ariva, a mint-flavored lozenge, contains tobacco powder compressed into tablet form. The organizations petitioned FDA to classify tobacco lozenges like Ariva as "drugs" or, alternatively, as "foods" containing a food additive. FDA disagreed, concluding in part that Ariva was a "customarily marketed" tobacco product as defined by *FDA v. Brown & Williamson Tobacco Corp. See* Docket Nos. 01P–0572 and 02P–0075.

F.   Human Biological Products

The Public Health Service Act gives FDA jurisdiction to regulate "biological products." Under the PHS Act, most biological products are subject to a regulatory regime similarly rigorous to that for drugs, including premarket review by FDA for safety and effectiveness. Section 262(i) of the PHS Act defines "biological product" as follows:

> In this section, the term "biological product" means a virus, therapeutic serum, toxin, antitoxin, vaccine, blood, blood component or derivative, allergenic product, or analogous product, or arsphenamine or derivative of arsphenamine (or any other trivalent organic arsenic compound), applicable to the prevention, treatment, or cure of a disease or condition of human beings.

This definition, with its list of examples and reference to "analogous" products, is of a different character from the FD&C Act's product definitions. It presents its own interpretive problems.

David M. Dudzinski, *Reflections on Historical, Scientific, and Legal Issues Relevant to Designing Approval Pathways for Generic Versions of Recombinant Protein–Based Therapeutics and Monoclonal Antibodies*

60 Food & Drug Law Journal 143 (2005).

... Concurrent with rising demand for treatments for the major nineteenth century diseases, private entities began to manufacture vaccine and antitoxin. Especially after the introduction of diphtheria antitoxin in 1894 from Germany, many small outfits run by pharmacies and physicians, as well as two large pharmaceutical ventures, H.K. Mulford Co. and Parke Davis, moved to produce antitoxins and supplant the government suppliers. While Mulford and Parke Davis had devoted significant resources to quality control and standardization of their antitoxin products, other smaller concerns manufacturing antitoxins did not. Instances of unscrupulous behavior by some smaller firms had previously resulted in a fake smallpox vaccine being sold in the early 1800s. Instances of contamination of commercial products also became a frequently recognized problem: large outbreaks of tetanus allegedly occurred via contamination of diphtheria antitoxin in the late 1890s and contamination of smallpox vaccine in 1901.

Though numerous investigations revealed that the tetanus outbreak in 1901 was most likely not associated with the smallpox vaccine, the "report[s] did not silence public outcry." The major manufacturers of biologics, pitted against each other by the assignment of blame for the tetanus outbreaks, found themselves under increasing scrutiny of the state governments and public. In response, the majors buried their disputes and redoubled their efforts to attack the smaller biologics manufacturers who were more likely to have "unsanitary and outmoded" facilities. Ultimately, it was deaths of thirteen children from tetanus-contaminated vaccine that "convinced Congress and the public that producing antitoxin or vaccine was not a simple matter like weighing out a dose of a drug on a scale" and provided an impetus for legislation.

Congress responded to the recent outbreaks as well as to the companies' lobbying by enacting the Biologics Act of 1902, the first enduring scheme of national regulation for any pharmaceutical product. The Biologics Act was groundbreaking in part because it set new precedents both in terms of shifting from retrospective post-market to prospective pre-market government review, and modifying the common law notion of punishing conduct only of intentional or reckless actors, in favor of moving toward pro-active safety measures for all entities.

The Biologics Act exerted jurisdiction over "viruses, therapeutic serums, toxins, antitoxins, or analogous products" as "biologics" that were intended for the "prevention, and cure of diseases of man." Each of the categories of regulated biologics represent immunologic agents, and Congress seemed to select these particular substances out of particular concern for immunologic, allergenic, and (at least what was then perceived to be) possibly contagious side effects. Viruses and toxins function to stimulate development of active immunity and antibody production when introduced into humans. Vaccines had been made for decades by exposing patients to a relatively non-pathogenic strain of bacteria or killed or inactivated pathogens. Antitoxins and therapeutic serums confer passive immunity simply by providing preformed antibodies, often developed by another animal like horse or goat in response to the toxin. All of these products—even in their final form after "manufacturing"—remained relatively crude mixtures; in fact, most of the products regulated in 1902 had a purity less than 1%. The Congressional concern for immunologic side effects was heightened especially in light of the biologics' animal origin and their parenteral, or injectable route of administration; compared to oral administration, where the digestive system provided some barriers protecting the body, injection gave the biologics direct access to the inner body....

... In 1963 *United States v. Steinschreiber* held blood plasma and other components derived from processing of blood were subject to biologics regulations as analogues to serum. 219 F. Supp. 373, 382–83 (S.D.N.Y. 1963), *aff'd*, 326 F.2d 759 (2d Cir. 1964) (*per curiam*). In contrast, in 1968 *Blank v. United States* held blood and red blood cells were drugs but exempt from biologics regulation. 400 F.2d at 305 (5th Cir. 1968). Individual adjudications are a poor means to develop any comprehensive regulatory scheme because of the lack of a guiding principle and the resultant fragmented, confusing system. Recognizing that every "[f]ederal court ... has held that blood is a drug" but diverged on the issue of blood as a biologic, Congress unified the law by amending the PHSA § 351 to include the classes of "blood, blood components or derivatives". Heart Disease, Cancer, Stroke, and Kidney Disease Amendments [to the Public Health Service Act] of 1970, 84 Stat. 1297, 1308 (Oct. 30, 1970)....

The very notion of a biologic has changed many times over the last century, and has deviated far from the root concern of grouping and regulating non-human organism (virus, bacteria, or large animal) immunogenic molecules. By statute, biological products are now "defined" as including viruses, therapeutic sera, toxins and antitoxins, vaccines, blood, blood components or derivatives, allergenic products, any analogous products, and arsphenamines used treating disease. Though several of these terms (*e.g.* therapeutic sera, antitoxin) lack crisp scientific meaning, no actual definition of "biologic" is offered in the statute or its regulations.

However, no definition is probably preferable to the alternative of scientifically invalid definition, such as for virus, which is "interpreted to be a product containing the minute living cause of an infectious disease and includes but is not limited to filterable viruses, bacteria, rickettsia, fungi, and protozoa." 21 C.F.R. § 600.3(h)(1). It is also far from clear that the earliest premise of biologics regulation was even internally consistent, as many of the first substances considered to be biologics were not really immunogenic per se, but designed to confer passive immunity. The more modern additions to the family of designated biologics are also questionable. Arsphenamines, while toxic, do no more to affect the immune process or cause immunogenic toxicities than do other well-known antibiotics and anti-microbials. Moreover the "analogous" language greatly amplifies the specter of biologics: for example, a product is analogous to 1) a virus if it is merely prepared from any "potentially infectious agent", 2) a therapeutic serum if it contains "some organic constituent" from blood (amino acids and hormones, like insulin and human growth hormone, excepted), or 3) a toxin or antitoxin if it addresses human disease "through a specific immune process." 21 C.F.R. § 600.3(h)(5)(i)–(iii). When one considers that virtually every chemical, including small molecules, can be an allergen to a certain fraction of the population, and that "products analogous to blood" has been theorized to encompass everything from the most well-characterized and well-purified serum protein all the way to whole organs, bewilderment about the definition of a biologic is understandable.

. . . .

NOTES

1. *Dual Classification.* Because the definition of "biological products" refers exclusively to articles "applicable to the prevention, treatment, or cure of a disease or condition of human beings," all biologics are simultaneously also drugs or devices. This dual classification raises many issues regarding the appropriate application of the requirements of PHS Act and the FD&C Act to biologics, as well as the division of responsibility over these products among FDA's biologics, drug, and device centers. These issues are addressed in Chapter VI.

2. *Human Cellular and Tissue–Based Products.* Human tissue products have been used by doctors for decades. Skin, tendons, bones, heart valves, and corneas that are damaged or diseased are replaced by tissues removed the body of a donor. Semen, ova, and embryos are transferred to aid reproduction. Recent years have seen an explosion of research into human cellular products for therapeutic purposes, including somatic cell therapy products and gene therapy products. FDA deems some human cellular and tissue-based products to be biologics, as well as medical devices or drugs. The agency's regulation of these products is discussed in Chapter VI, *infra*.

CHAPTER III

FOOD

A. HISTORICAL AND STATUTORY BACKGROUND

The history of food regulation, both abroad and in the United States, is discussed in Chapter I *supra*.

B. DEFINITION OF "FOOD"

The statutory definition of a "food," and its relation to the definition of a "drug," are explored in Chapter II *supra*.

COMMENT: CULTURAL INFLUENCES ON FOOD REGULATION

The authors are indebted to Lewis A. Segall for pointing out the current debate on the origin and meaning of dietary practices and the problems they create for FDA. Marshall Sahlins, CULTURAL AND PRACTICAL REASON (1976), argues that western societies eat cattle but not dogs, not because of the difference in their worth as foodstuffs, but because of the difference in the degree to which they are identified with humanity. Marvin Harris, CULTURAL MATERIALISM: THE STRUGGLE FOR A SCIENCE OF CULTURE (1979), contends that food decisions are made solely on the basis of material factors. Dogs are bred for hunting and companionship and are not used for food because many other meat sources exist. These opposing views illustrate Segall's point:

> [F]requently attitudes toward different foods may have less to do with rational instrumental reasoning than with cultural meaning. Contemporary fears of cancer are from this perspective an interesting case. On the one hand, cancer is a serious threat to health, and it is rational to want to avoid foods which may cause it. On the other hand, the public appears to have somewhat irrational attitudes toward cancer-causing food, failing to realize the greater danger from natural than from artificial substances, and generally having great difficulty in comparing levels of risk and acting accordingly. Public attitudes toward cancer and food seem neither solely material or cultural.
>
> The case of alar on apples seems a good example of how cultural meanings (in this instance the possibility of cancer in the school lunchbox) may play a significant role in shaping regulatory policy... . [O]ne of the fascinating aspects of food regulation is precisely the interaction of these two realms: a federal agency concerned with safety and health, and basing its decisions on

scientific grounds, is charged with regulating a part of society which is fraught with nonrational cultural attitudes, prejudices, and allegiances.... [F]ood regulation ... operates in a world of cultural meanings. The point is not that these cultural meanings are wrong or misguided, much less that they should determine regulatory decisions. Rather it is that accounting for culture may give a fuller account of the dynamics of regulatory policy.

Letter from Lewis A. Segall to Peter Barton Hutt (Apr. 12, 1990).

C. REGULATION OF FOOD LABELING

This part focuses on government efforts to protect the economic expectations of both consumers and food distributors. It begins with a historical overview, to place the various FDA policies that relate to food misbranding in their broader context, and then proceeds to analyze each of those policies in detail. It covers all of the FD&C Act's mandatory food labeling requirements except for the name of the food itself. Part D reviews both standards of identity for food and the requirement that every food be labeled with its own common or usual name, including the requirement that imitation food be labeled as such. Part E covers the application of the basic food labeling provisions, surveyed in Parts C and D, to the regulation of the nutrient content of food. Part F reviews specific requirements applicable to dietary supplement products. Part G covers the recent developments in the use of structure/function and disease claims for both conventional food and dietary supplements.

1. HISTORICAL OVERVIEW

Section 403 of the FD&C Act itemizes the circumstances under which a food will be considered "misbranded" and thus subject to enforcement action. Most of the forms of "misbranding" specified in section 403 relate to information included in, or omitted from, the "label" or "labeling" of food products. In various ways, these definitions of misbranding are designed to force food suppliers to tell the truth about their products. Section 403(a) thus prohibits label statements that are "false or misleading in any particular." Additional provisions prohibit other types of affirmative deceptions respecting quality, quantity, or identity. Other provisions force manufacturers to provide information that they might otherwise omit—such as the complete ingredients or the nutrient content of a product. These affirmative requirements thus make assumptions about the types of information that consumers need to make wise food choices.

Peter Barton Hutt, *Regulating the Misbranding of Food*

43 FOOD TECHNOLOGY 288 (September 1989).

The statutory provisions enacted by Congress in 1938 to regulate food misbranding have remained virtually unchanged.... This history therefore reflects evolving administrative policy implemented by FDA, not statutory changes adopted by Congress. This history is split into two eras, divided by the White House Conference on Food, Nutrition, and Health held in December 1969. The Conference report and the new FDA leadership that was committed to implementation of the regulatory policy recommended in that report profoundly changed FDA's approach to food regulation and permitted the full use of modern food technology.

1939–69

Following enactment of the FD&C Act in 1938, FDA relied primarily upon five statutory provisions to regulate food misbranding: (1) the mandatory information required by the statute to appear on all food labels, (2) mandatory standards of identity for food products, (3) the labeling of imitation food, (4) nutrition information for special dietary food, and (5) the prohibition of any false or misleading claims.

1. *Mandatory Food Labeling.* Under section 403 of the FD&C Act, every food label must bear, at the very minimum, the following four categories of information: the name of the food; a statement of the ingredients; the net quantity of contents; and the name and address of the manufacturer or distributor. Under the 1906 Act, as it was originally enacted, none of this information was required. The Gould Amendment of 1913 for the first time required that the net quantity of contents be labeled on food packages....

2. *Standards of Identity for Food.* Ancient botanists, beginning with Theophrastus (370–285 B.C.), established "standards" by describing the available food supply and warning against its adulteration with other substances. Standards of identity for bread were established in the Roman Empire and in medieval England, to assure the integrity of the food supply. The same approach has been pursued to the present.

Even before *enactment* of the 1906 Act, FDA had established some 200 informal food standards. Although Congress declined to include legal authority for mandatory food standards in the 1906 Act, FDA continued with this work until the FD&C Act was enacted in 1938. Section 401 of the FD&C Act authorized FDA to promulgate definitions and standards of identity for any food product in order to "promote honesty and fair dealing in the interest of consumers." Because of its long interest in food standards, FDA promptly moved to implement this new authority.... By 1970, it was estimated that half of the American food supply was subject to an FDA food standard.

When these *early* food standards were adopted, modern food technology was just beginning to flourish. Some functional food ingredients (*e.g.,* preservatives, emulsifiers, thickeners, and so forth) were in use, but many staple foods remained quite simple and had not yet undergone the transformation that later occurred. Moreover, at this time FDA had no independent statutory authority to require premarket testing and approval of new food additives for safety. Accordingly, FDA adopted the policy of establishing "recipe" standards of identity, under which every permitted ingredient was specifically listed in the standard. Under this policy, no new ingredient could be used until the standard was amended to include it. Accordingly, all progress in food technology for standardized foods depended upon amendment of the applicable food standards. With enactment of the Food Additives Amendment of 1958 and the Color Additive Amendments of 1960, and the rapid development of food technology, use of recipe standards was no longer warranted. FDA initially experimented with a new, broader form of standard, which permitted any "safe and suitable" functional ingredient, in the 1960s, but did not move to broaden all of the existing standards.

One particular aspect of food standards, not specifically mentioned in the statute, became a principal focus of this activity. Developing knowledge about essential vitamins and minerals during the 1930s led the American Medical Association's Council on Food and Nutrition to adopt a policy that food fortification should be reserved for exceptional cases where there is convincing evidence of a need for the vitamin or mineral and where the food to be fortified is a suitable carrier. When FDA announced public hearings in 1940 to establish a standard of identity for flour, both AMA and the National Academy of Sciences recommended that the standard establish appropriate levels for enrichment with vitamins and minerals. The enriched flour standard of identity became effective on January 1, 1942, and set a pattern for numerous subsequent standards for enriched food.

To prevent indiscriminate food fortification, FDA issued a statement in July 1943 setting forth the agency policy on addition of vitamins and minerals to food. Following World War II, however, food fortification continued to grow. By the early 1960s, FDA was convinced that a more restrictive regulatory approach was necessary to prevent overfortification of the American food supply. FDA proposed to limit fortification to eight classes of food, with 12 essential nutrients. . . .

3. *Imitation Food.* The 1906 Act had prohibited imitation food. Section 403(c) of the FD&C Act provided, however, that any imitation food must be labeled as an imitation. FDA initially sought to apply this statutory provision to control the development of new substitute food products. It argued that any imitation of a standardized product was inherently illegal, but the Supreme Court overruled the agency on this point in 1951. When a substitute ice cream was made from soybeans and marketed as "Chil-Zert," FDA brought a successful legal action to require that it be labeled as an imitation ice cream. This was, however, the high point of FDA's use of the imitation provision to inhibit the marketing of new food products. As food technology progressed, and more substitute products were marketed, the agency did not institute legal action to prevent their sale.

Nonetheless, FDA did adhere tenaciously to the position that the name of a standardized food could not be used as part of the name of a nonstandardized substitute product. The Supreme Court had ruled in 1943 that, once FDA had established a standard of identity, the standard could not be evaded by adding nonpermitted ingredients and revising the name of the food to reflect that change. . . .

. . . FDA took no administrative action to clarify its position on the imitation provision. Several states therefore brought action against new substitute food products under comparable provisions in their state laws. . . .

4. *Special Dietary Food Labeling.* Under section 403(j) of the FD&C Act, FDA was authorized to promulgate regulations to require label information concerning the vitamin, mineral, and other dietary properties of food represented for special dietary uses. In November 1941, following a public hearing, FDA promulgated regulations governing vitamin-mineral supplements, fortified food products, and such other special dietary foods as infant food, hypo-allergenic food, and food used in weight control.

[handwritten: label only]

Because these were labeling requirements and imposed no limit upon other claims or permissible formulations, the types of special dietary products marketed, and the claims made for them, proliferated. In spite of numerous court actions and educational approaches, FDA could not bring these products under control.... As a result, FDA concluded that the only reasonable approach to this matter would be through revision of the 1941 regulations. As part of the proposed regulations to restrict food fortification already discussed above, FDA proposed to limit the number of permitted formulations of dietary supplements of vitamins and minerals and to ban common labeling claims for these products that the agency regarded as false or misleading....

[handwritten: increase in claims made]

[handwritten: proposed limits]

5. *Prohibition of False or Misleading Claims.* Like the 1906 Act, section 403(a) of the FD&C Act prohibited any false or misleading statement in food labeling. Most fraudulent or outrageous food claims had long since disappeared as a result of FDA regulatory action taken under the 1906 Act. With the advent of food fortification and vitamin-mineral supplements, and the gradual unfolding of scientific evidence about the relationship of diet and health, new regulatory problems emerged.

[handwritten: new scientific evidence]

... FDA readily permitted general health claims for food products, but sought to prohibit any specific claim that a food or food component would prevent a particular disease. Following publication of a major report to the American Heart Association in August 1957 recommending a reduction in dietary cholesterol and saturated fats, labeling and advertising claims for common food products made reference to this new information. Faced with these claims, FDA sought to prohibit any reference to cholesterol or saturated fat, considering such reference as "nutritional quackery." As time wore on, however, and the scientific evidence became more compelling, increased pressure was placed on the agency to change its position. By the late 1960s, FDA continued to adhere to its policy in public, but took relatively little legal action to enforce it.

[handwritten: ex: cholesterol]

[handwritten: little enforcement]

The White House Conference on Food, Nutrition, and Health

President Nixon announced a White House Conference on Food, Nutrition, and Health in May 1969.... Although the White House Conference was convened in response to charges of hunger and malnutrition in America, and not to consider regulatory issues, its conclusions had a dramatic and unexpected impact on FDA policy in regulating food misbranding. The highly restrictive approach to food standards, imitation labeling, special dietary foods, and nutrition claims that was the subject of the formal public hearing conducted by FDA during 1968 and 1969 was thoroughly criticized and rejected. The White House Conference report emphasized the need for sound nutrition, the capability of modern food technology to provide products to fill that need, and the use of increased public information about nutrition, rather than the problems of nutrition quackery.

Release of the report coincided, moreover, with a major change in FDA personnel. Those who had determined the FDA food regulatory approach during the 1960s were gone from the agency when the administrative hearing of 1968–69 was completed and the matter was ready for a final decision in the early 1970s. Many who formed the new leadership in FDA during the early 1970s had participated in the White House Conference. Within 18 months, five individuals who had helped shape the conference policy and prepare the report had left their former positions to join FDA and were ready to implement the regulatory recommendations of the report. . . .

1969–89

The White House Conference represented the end of the restrictive approach to food regulation proposed by FDA during the 1960s. In its place emerged a number of new regulations, based largely on food labeling requirements rather than on rigid standards for product composition.

1. *Mandatory Food Labeling Information.* The same four statutory categories of mandatory information remain. In two respects, however, they have been changed to reflect the new emphasis on provision of adequate information to consumers rather than on establishing rigid standards for product composition.

Under the FD&C Act, a standardized food is not required to include on the label any mandatory ingredient in the food, and is required to include on the label only those optional ingredients that are specified as required to be labeled under the standard. Pursuant to its policy of encouraging full labeling for all food products, FDA urged food manufacturers and distributors to include in the statement of ingredients both mandatory and optional ingredients and began systematically to amend all existing food standards to make as many "mandatory" ingredients optional as possible and to require the labeling of all optional ingredients.

FDA also promulgated new regulations governing the names to be used on the labels for food products. The new regulations emphasized that a food name must accurately identify or describe the basic nature of the food or its characterizing properties or ingredients, and distinguish the food from different foods. Related regulations provided for inclusion, as part of the food name, the percentage of any characterizing ingredients, or a statement that the food does not contain ingredients that might otherwise be expected.

2. *Food Standards.* In the early 1970s, FDA began a systematic amendment of all existing food standards to eliminate the old "recipe" approach and to permit any "safe and suitable" functional ingredient. Accordingly, it is no longer necessary to amend existing food standards to permit the use of new food additives and color additives once they have been approved as safe for use.

Since 1970, FDA has not proposed or promulgated new food standards. In a number of instances where food standards had been proposed in the past, they were replaced with regulations that simply establish the name of the food, pursuant to the regulations discussed above. This approach has permitted greater flexibility in food labeling and food formulation.

As a related policy, FDA has abandoned its old position that any resemblance of a new food to a traditional standardized food, or any reference to a standardized food in the name for a new food, automatically renders the new food illegal. For example, FDA has stated that "raisin bread made with enriched flour" does not violate the raisin bread standard; "enriched macaroni products with fortified protein" does not violate the enriched macaroni standard; "tomato juice enriched with vitamin C" does not violate the tomato juice standard; and "goat's milk yogurt" does not violate the yogurt standard.

The limitation of fortification to listed foods, within specified levels, was totally abandoned. Fortification of standardized foods was permitted, where no enrichment standard already existed.

Finally, FDA adopted new regulations governing nutrition labeling for all food. Except for bread products that must be enriched under state laws, it is not mandatory that any food product either be enriched with vitamins or minerals or bear labeling relating to its nutritional value. FDA therefore promulgated a requirement that, if any nutrient is added to a food, or any nutrition claim is made for a food, the product must bear full nutrition labeling in the format established by FDA.

FDA made a conscious trade-off in adopting this new approach. It substantially reduced the restrictions on formulation and composition imposed by food standards and other regulations, and correspondingly increased the labeling requirements for all food. The food industry was thus free to pursue the benefits of modern food technology, but only at the price of providing far more information to consumers through food labeling.

3. *Imitation Food.* To eliminate the confusion and resulting barrier to innovation in the food industry caused by the lack of a clear policy relating to the imitation labeling provision, FDA in 1973 promulgated a regulation defining "imitation" solely in terms of nutritional inferiority.... FDA emphasized that a new food product, rather than being called "imitation," should bear its own descriptive name under the rules already discussed above.

4. *Special Dietary Foods.* When FDA abandoned its restrictive approach to food fortification, it retained limitations upon the composition and potency of vitamin-mineral supplements. In 1974, however, the courts remanded part of these regulations for further action, and in 1976 Congress amended the FD&C Act to add a new section 411 which significantly curtailed FDA's authority to restrict the composition of dietary supplements.

In all other areas relating to special dietary foods, however, FDA has successfully completed its modernization of the regulations. Final special dietary food regulations have now been promulgated for hypo-allergenic food, infant food, weight-control food, diabetic food, and low-sodium food.

5. *Prohibition of False or Misleading Claims.* As part of its new approach to more expansive food labeling, FDA adopted in the early 1970s a distinction between the provision of specific information relating to food composition, and the use of specific health claims based upon that composition. FDA took the position that product composition information was lawful, as permitted by nutrition labeling, but that any specific claim that the composition of a product would help prevent a particular disease was unlawful. Thus, FDA permitted cholesterol and fatty acid information as an optional part of nutrition labeling, but prohibited any claims linking that information to a potential reduction in heart disease.

In March 1985, however, FDA announced a major change in this policy. Under the new FDA policy, specific claims about prevention of disease are permitted if they are recognized as valid by qualified experts, they emphasize that good nutrition is a function of the total diet, the claims are reasonably uniform within the marketplace, and they do not result in dietary "power" races.

6. *Slack Fill and Deceptive Packaging.* Although Congress considered amending the 1906 Act to prohibit slack fill and deceptive packaging, such a provision was not enacted until the FD&C Act. In large part because FDA lost every contested case under this provision, Congress included in the Fair Packaging and Labeling Act of 1966 discretionary authority for FDA to establish regulations governing nonfunctional slack fill. After a decade of study, however, FDA concluded that slack fill did not represent a major problem, and thus no such regulations have been promulgated. . . .

COMMENT: JURISDICTION OVER FOOD ADVERTISING

The Federal Trade Commission Act, 38 Stat. 717 (1914), 15 U.S.C. 41 et seq., authorizes the Federal Trade Commission (FTC) to take regulatory action to prevent unfair methods of competition. The courts have interpreted this to include false or misleading labeling or advertising for food (and drugs, devices, and cosmetics). The Wheeler–Lea Amendments of 1938, 52 Stat. 111, 114, confirmed the authority of the FTC to regulate advertising for these products, while FDA retained primary responsibility for labeling. This division of jurisdiction was a point of sharp controversy during congressional consideration of the FD&C Act, and the FTC's retention of jurisdiction was viewed as a victory for the industries that produced and marketed these products. The bifurcation of authority has meant that considerable attention has been focused on defining the outer limits of FDA jurisdiction over "labeling." For further discussion of the FTC regulation of advertising see p. 275 *infra*; Nicole Gerhart, *The FDA and the FTC: An Alphabet Soup regulating the Misbranding of Food* (2002), in Chapter I(G)(1) of the Electronic Book.

2.   SCOPE OF "LABELING"

The cases immediately following deal with the jurisdictional reach of FDA's labeling requirements. All of them involve health food products against which FDA took action because of their therapeutic claims. The term "labeling" is defined by section 201(m) of the FD&C Act as "all labels and other written, printed, or graphic matter (1) upon any article or any of its containers or wrappers, or (2) accompanying such article." The term "label" is defined by section 201(k) as "a display of written, printed, or graphic matter upon the immediate container of any article...." These terms have the same meaning for all products covered by the Act.

Kordel v. United States

335 U.S. 345 (1948).

■ Opinion of the Court by MR. JUSTICE DOUGLAS, announced by MR. JUSTICE REED.

Kordel was charged by informations containing twenty counts of introducing or delivering for introduction into interstate commerce misbranded drugs. He was tried without a jury, found guilty, and fined two hundred dollars on each count. This judgment was affirmed on appeal.

... Since 1941 [Kordel] has been marketing his own health food products, which appear to be compounds of various vitamins, minerals and herbs. The alleged misbranding consists of statements in circulars or pamphlets distributed to consumers by the vendors of the products, relating to their efficacy. The petitioner supplies these pamphlets as well as the products to the vendors. Some of the literature was displayed in stores in which the petitioner's products were on sale. Some of it was given away with the sale of products; some sold independently of the drugs; and some mailed to customers by the vendors.

It is undisputed that petitioner shipped or caused to be shipped in interstate commerce both the drugs and the literature. Seven of the counts charged that the drugs and literature were shipped in the same cartons. The literature involved in the other counts was shipped separately from the drugs and at different times—both before and after the shipments of the drugs with which they were associated. The question whether the separate shipment of the literature saved the drugs from being misbranded within the meaning of the [FD&C] Act presents the main issue in the case.

... The term labeling is defined in § 201(m) to mean "all labels and other written, printed, or graphic matter (1) upon any article or any of its containers or wrappers, or (2) accompanying such article." ... In this case the drugs and the literature had a common origin and a common destination. The literature was used in the sale of the drugs. It explained their uses. Nowhere else was the purchaser advised how to use them. It constituted an essential supplement to the label attached to the package. Thus the products and the literature were interdependent. ...

It would, indeed, create an obviously wide loophole to hold that these drugs would be misbranded if the literature had been shipped in the same container but not misbranded if the literature left in the next or in the preceding mail. The high purpose of the Act to protect consumers who under present conditions are largely unable to protect themselves in this field would then be easily defeated. The administrative agency charged with its enforcement has not given the Act any such restricted construction.... Accordingly, we conclude that the phrase "accompanying such article" is not restricted to labels that are on or in the article or package that is transported. . . .

One article or thing is accompanied by another when it supplements or explains it, in the manner that a committee report of the Congress accompanies a bill. No physical attachment one to the other is necessary. It is the textual relationship that is significant. . . .

Petitioner points out that in the evolution of the Act the ban on false advertising was eliminated, the control over it being transferred to the Federal Trade Commission. We have searched the legislative history in vain, however, to find any indication that Congress had the purpose to eliminate from the Act advertising which performs the function of labeling. Every labeling is in a sense an advertisement. The advertising which we have here performs the same function as it would if it were on the article or on the containers or wrappers. As we have said, physical attachment or contiguity is unnecessary under § 201(m)(2). . . .

NOTE

The defendant in *Kordel* was responsible for the shipment of both the products and the descriptive pamphlets, even though the two acts were separated in time. The possibility that the Court's expansive interpretation of the Act's definition of "labeling" might have been influenced by the particular facts of the case was laid to rest the same day by its decision in *United States v. Urbuteit*, 335 U.S. 355 (1948). In *Urbuteit*, a seizure action, the Court similarly found that leaflets shipped at a different time than medical devices nonetheless accompanied the devices:

> . . . The common sense of the matter is to view the interstate transaction in its entirety—the purpose of the advertising and its actual use. In this case it is plain to us that the movements of machines and leaflets in interstate commerce were a single interrelated activity, not separate or isolated ones. The Act is not concerned with the purification of the stream of commerce in the abstract. The problem is a practical one of consumer protection, not dialectics. The fact that the false literature leaves in a separate mail does not save the article from being misbranded. Where by functional standards the two transactions are integrated, the requirements of § 304(a) are satisfied, though the mailing or shipments are at different times.

United States v. 24 Bottles "Sterling Vinegar & Honey," Etc.

338 F.2d 157 (2d Cir. 1964).

■ LUMBARD, CHIEF JUDGE.

Balanced Foods, Inc., appeals from an order of the District Court for the Southern District of New York condemning a number of bottles of Sterling Vinegar and Honey and a number of copies of two books, "Folk Medicine" and "Arthritis and Folk Medicine." Balanced Foods wholesales health foods and related products. The books and Vinegar and Honey were seized in its warehouse in New York City and condemned as misbranded drugs . . . on the ground that the books were "labeling" for the Vinegar and Honey and are misleading. . . .

Vinegar and Honey seems to have been one of the minor ephemera characteristic of the health and diet food trade. That it gained shelf space among boxes of sunflower seed, wheat germ and healing grasses can be attributed to the wide reading of Dr. D. C. Jarvis' first book, "Folk Medicine," subtitled "A Vermont Doctor's Guide to Good Health." ...

Prominent among Dr. Jarvis' remedies is a mixture of cider vinegar and honey, which is prescribed for a wide variety of maladies. Inevitably some people found it burdensome to mix the vinegar with the honey, and, true to the traditions of free enterprise, several companies responded by producing a pre-mixed product. Among them was Sterling. "Folk Medicine" and its sequel, "Arthritis and Folk Medicine," mention Sterling cider vinegar by name as suitable for medicinal use, and the two books certainly have promoted the sale of Sterling's Honey and Vinegar. In addition, Balanced Foods stocked both and sold both to a number of retailers. The question is whether the sum of these relationships constitutes labeling. We do not think that it does.

The Vinegar and Honey bottles bear a label, which claims no more than that they contain one pint of "aged in wood cider vinegar blended with finest honey." The labeling subject to the Act is not limited to this common form of label.... On the other hand, labeling does not include every writing which bears some relation to the product. There is a line to be drawn, and, if the statutory purpose is to be served, it must be drawn in terms of the function served by the writing.

... Advertising and labeling overlap; most labels advertise as well. They are not identical, however, and material which serves only as an advertisement is not covered by the Act.

The distinguishing characteristic of a label is that, in some manner or another, it is presented to the customer in immediate connection with his view and his purchase of the product. Such a connection existed at both wholesale and retail levels in Kordel: Although the pamphlets and drugs were mailed to retailers separately, they were mailed in "integrated transactions"; the vendors in turn gave the pamphlets away with the sale of the drugs in some cases....

We need not consider whether or under what circumstances integrated use of written material and a drug product by a retailer would by itself allow condemnation of the goods in the hands of the wholesaler, for there is no evidence of such use of "Folk Medicine" or "Arthritis and Folk Medicine" with Vinegar and Honey at either level. Balanced Foods sold both, and the government presented some evidence that it took special steps to promote "Folk Medicine." There was no evidence of any joint promotion of either book with Vinegar and Honey, however. It perhaps could be inferred that the officers of Balanced Foods realized that sale of the books would tend to promote sale of Vinegar and Honey. But there can be no inference that it sold the books for that purpose. It first ordered "Folk Medicine" almost two years before it began carrying Vinegar and Honey; it sold over 7,000 copies of "Folk Medicine" at $2.00 each wholesale and fewer than 2,000 pint bottles of Vinegar and Honey. There was, in sum, no basis for finding that Balanced Foods did more than carry two related products....

"Folk Medicine" ... made broad claims for a vinegar and honey mixture, which led ultimately to Sterling's marketing Vinegar and Honey. It is not disputed that these claims were misleading, but the Federal Food, Drug and Cosmetic Act was not intended to deal generally with misleading claims....

The judgment of the district court is reversed.

NOTES

1. *Books as Labeling. Compare United States v. 250 Jars ... "Cal's Tupelo Blossom U.S. Fancy Pure Honey"*, 344 F.2d 288 (6th Cir. 1965), in which the court held that a booklet was labeling because it was shown to an FDA inspector acting as a prospective purchaser of the honey. In *United States v. 8 Cartons, More or Less, Molasses*, 97 F. Supp. 313 (W.D.N.Y. 1951), the court declined to hold that a book constituted labeling for a food solely upon a showing that the book was shipped simultaneously with the food. The court stated that the determination whether the book constitutes labeling depends upon "the use to which the book was put in connection with marketing the molasses," not upon shipment. After FDA amended its complaint, however, the court held that the book did constitute labeling because it was displayed with the molasses and customers were referred to the book when purchasing the molasses. Responding to the claim that the seizure of a book violates the First Amendment, the court observed:

> The Administrator by resorting to the seizure provisions of the Act does not undertake to interfere with the publication or circulation of the publisher's book. The seizure has not interfered with the bona fide sale of the book. The publisher may continue to sell its books wherever it finds a market, even in food stores, and even in stores where "Plantation" blackstrap molasses is sold. The seizure relates not to books offered for bona fide sale but to copies of the book claimed to be offending against the Act by being associated with the article "Plantation" Blackstrap Molasses in a distribution plan in such a way as to misbrand the product.

103 F. Supp. 626, 627 (W.D.N.Y. 1951).

2. *Compliance Policy.* In 1982 FDA initiated seizure of an unapproved drug, DMSO, and copies of an accompanying book about the drug. After the author's widow challenged the seizure of the book on the ground that the Supreme Court had extended the First Amendment to commercial speech, FDA issued Compliance Policy Guide No. 7153.13 (Dec. 1, 1982) determining that, where labeling does not include books, FDA will continue to seize both the offending product and the labeling, but where the labeling is in the form of a book the agency will seize only the product and will request an injunction to halt, after a hearing, the misuse of the book. On the basis of this policy, the book was released to the author's widow and the court denied her motion to intervene. *United States v. An Article of Drug on the Premises of DMSO, Inc.*, 1983–1984 FDLI Jud. Rec. 1 (W.D.N.Y. 1983). In response to a citizen petition alleging that FDA was ordering the destruction of books, FDA Docket No. 98P–0509 (July 1, 1998), the agency issued a clarification of CPG 7153.13 in 64 Fed. Reg. 22616 (Apr. 27, 1999) stating that it does not recommend the seizure or the destruction of books that are used as illegal labeling under the FD&C Act.

3. *Dietary Supplement Labeling Exemption.* As a result of a dispute regarding FDA compliance action with respect to books associated with the promotion and sale of stevia, an herbal substance, FDA revised Compliance Policy Guide Nos. 7153.13 and 7135.130 to clarify its policy. Letter from Gary J. Dykstra, Acting

Associate Commissioner for Regulatory Affairs, FDA, to Jonathan W. Emord (Apr. 9, 1999), FDA Docket No. 98P–0509. The draft revised CPG, 64 Fed. Reg. 22616 (Apr. 27, 1999), clearly spells out the exemption from labeling for dietary supplement publications set forth in section 403B of the FD&C Act, as added by the Dietary Supplement Health and Education Act of 1994.

The Dietary Supplement Health and Education Act of 1994 (DSHEA), which applies only to products for human use, added Section 403B to the Act. Section 403B(a) exempts certain publications when used in connection with the sale of a dietary supplement to consumers from the definition of labeling, under Section 201(m) of the Act. Section 403B(a) provides that such a publication—which may include an article, a chapter in a book, or an official abstract of a peer-reviewed scientific publication that appears in an article and that was prepared by its author or the editors of the publication—is not labeling provided it is printed in its entirety and meets each of the following five criteria:

1. It may not be false and misleading;

2. it may not promote a particular manufacturer or brand of a dietary supplement;

3. it must be displayed or presented with other such items on the same subject matter, so as to present a balanced view of the available scientific information on a dietary supplement;

4. if displayed in an establishment, it must be physically separate from the dietary supplements; and

5. it may not have appended to it any information by sticker or any other method.

Under Section 403B(a), therefore, a retail store that sells dietary supplements may, in connection with those sales, use publications that meet these five conditions without the publications becoming labeling for those dietary supplements. For example, the publications may be made available in a reference section of the store.

Section 403B(a) implies that publications that fail to meet any one of these five criteria *are* labeling. However, Section 403B(b) provides that Section 403B(a) "shall not apply to or restrict a retailer or wholesaler of dietary supplements in any way whatsoever in the sale of books or other publications as a part of the business of such retailer or wholesaler." Section 403B(b) means that books or other publications that are offered for sale by a retailer or wholesaler of dietary supplements do not become labeling for those dietary supplements simply because they fail to meet one or more of the criteria of Section 403B(a). Books or other publications for sale by a retailer or wholesaler of dietary supplements become labeling for a product in the wholesaler's warehouse or the retailer's store *only* if the wholesaler or retailer uses them to promote the sale of the product.

In general, under Section 201(m) of the Act, for a dietary supplement wholesaler, a publication written and published by a party who is independent of the manufacturer or distributor of a product (a "third party") does not become labeling if the wholesaler does not promote the publication and the product together. In general, a dietary supplement retailer does not use a book or other publication that is written and published by a third party to promote a product when the publication is displayed with other books and publications and these books and publications are physically separate from the product, and there is no joint display of the publication and the product. Third party books and other publications so used would not become labeling in the retail store even if they are false or misleading, they reference a particular manufacturer or brand of dietary supplements, or they do not present a balanced view of the scientific information on a dietary supplement.

For discussion of the labeling exemption, *see* Charles J. Raubicheck, *DSHEA's Third–Party Literature Exemption: Mail Order Sales, Direct Marketing, and Internet Use*, 54 FOOD & DRUG L.J. 587 (1999).

4. *Other Authority.* For other cases construing the scope of labeling *see Seven Cases of Eckman's Alternative v. United States*, 239 U.S. 510 (1916); *United States v. Guardian Chemical Corp.*, 410 F.2d 157 (2d Cir. 1969); *United States v. Diapulse Manufacturing Corp.*, 389 F.2d 612 (2d Cir. 1968); *United States v. Article of Drug Designated B–Complex Cholinos Capsules*, 362 F.2d 923 (3d Cir. 1966); *United States v. 47 Bottles, More or Less, Jenasol RJ Formula "60"*, 320 F.2d 564 (3d Cir. 1963); *Nature Food Centers, Inc. v. United States*, 310 F.2d 67 (1st Cir. 1962); *United States v. 353 Cases Mountain Valley Mineral Water*, 247 F.2d 473 (8th Cir. 1957); *V.E. Irons, Inc. v. United States*, 244 F.2d 34 (1st Cir. 1957); *United States v. Hohensee*, 243 F.2d 367 (3d Cir. 1957); *Alberty Food Products v. United States*, 194 F.2d 463 (9th Cir. 1952); *Alberty Food Products Co. v. United States*, 185 F.2d 321 (9th Cir. 1950); *Alberty v. United States*, 159 F.2d 278 (9th Cir. 1947); *United States v. Research Laboratories, Inc.*, 126 F.2d 42 (9th Cir. 1942); *United States v. Articles of Drug . . ., Foods Plus, Inc.*, 239 F. Supp. 465 (D.N.J. 1965); *United States v. "Vitasafe Formula M,"* 226 F. Supp. 266 (D.N.J. 1964); *United States v. 40 Cases CDC Capsules*, 204 F. Supp. 280 (E.D.N.Y. 1962); *United States v. Vitamin Industries, Inc.*, 130 F. Supp. 755 (D. Neb. 1955).

5. *State–Mandated Warnings.* Do posters or other public notices bearing warnings required by state statute constitute "labeling" that is preempted under federal law? One court has held that a poster warning required by Michigan was labeling and thus was preempted. *American Meat Institute v. Ball*, 550 F. Supp. 285 (W.D. Mich. 1982), *aff'd sub. nom. American Meat Institute v. Pridgeon*, 724 F.2d 45 (6th Cir. 1984). The California Supreme Court has held that the public warning requirement of Proposition 65, California Health and Safety Code 25249.6, is preempted where FDA has explicitly determined that the warning is not warranted. *Dowhal v. SmithKline Beecham Consumer Healthcare*, 32 Cal.4th 910, 88 P.3d 1 (2004). Three other cases have held that similar public notices are not labeling and thus are not preempted. *Grocery Manufacturers of America, Inc. v. Gerace*, 755 F.2d 993 (2d Cir. 1985); *New York State Pesticide Coalition, Inc. v. Jorling*, 874 F.2d 115 (2d Cir. 1989); *D–Con v. Allenby*, 728 F. Supp. 605 (N.D. Cal. 1989).

6. *Commentary. See* George Link, Jr., *Judicial Interpretation of the Words "Accompanying Such Article" Contained in the Federal Food, Drug, and Cosmetic Act*, 2 FOOD DRUG COSM. L.Q. 207 (1947).

United States v. Articles of Drug ... Century Food Co.

32 F.R.D. 32 (S.D. Ill. 1963).

■ MERCER, DISTRICT JUDGE.

This case is a libel of information by the United States against divers [sic] vitamin and mineral compounds offered for sale by Century Food Company after shipment in interstate commerce, alleging that each such article of drug is misbranded. Misbranding is alleged to arise from the fact that various pamphlets and articles of literature accompanying the several drug products contain false and misleading representation as to medical guidance for the use of vitamins and minerals in the cure of serious diseases. One such book alleged to constitute a false labeling of the drug products is a paper back book entitled, "Eat, Live and be Merry," written by the intervenor, Carlton Fredericks. . . .

Paragraph 3 of the answer alleges, in summary, that the intervenor had no knowledge of the nature of the seized drug articles or of the operation of Century, that Century's use of intervenor's book to sell or promote the seized articles was not authorized by intervenor, that intervenor had no knowledge of the efficacy of the seized articles for the treatment of any disease, and that over 20,000 copies of intervenor's book have been sold through book stores and other outlets to the public.

Each of those averments of fact is completely irrelevant to any issue in this case. In fact, a fair reading of the libel imports the implication that intervenor was not culpable in the premises alleged. Certainly there is no allegation in the libel that intervenor had any knowledge of Century's operation, or drug products, or that intervenor's book was used as labeling for those products by his authority. If it be assumed that intervenor had no knowledge of Century's operation, and had not authorized Century's use of his book as labeling for its drug products, copies of intervenor's book would, nevertheless, be subject to seizure to the extent that they were used and are being used as false labeling for Century's products. . . .

Intervenor's second affirmative defense avers that the seizure of intervenor's book in connection with this case constitutes a prior restraint in violation of the First Amendment to the Constitution of the United States. . . .

The Act prohibits false labeling and misbranding, and authorizes the seizure of articles which are so misbranded. Certainly, the Act contemplates that a book, as well as any other type of representation, may be so used as to become a label for an article offered for sale. It was so held in *United States v. 8 Cartons, etc., Molasses*, in which the court entered a judgment of condemnation against a book to the extent that it was used as a label for the sale of a brand of black strap molasses. The same case resolved the issue of the constitutionality of that seizure, the court holding that the First Amendment does not prohibit the seizure and condemnation of a book which was being used as prohibited labeling. The court was careful there to point out that the condemnation related to the use of the book for that purpose, only, and that it could not operate as a restraint upon the sale of the book through book stores or other outlets. As the court there suggested, the condemnation did not prohibit the sale of the book in food stores, and even in stores in which the brand of molasses involved was offered for sale, so long as the book was not offered in conjunction with the product as a label for the product. . . .

NOTES

1. *Religious Tracts as Labeling.* In *Founding Church of Scientology v. United States*, 409 F.2d 1146 (D.C. Cir. 1969), p. 971 *infra*, FDA seized, as misbranded, electrical equipment used by adherents of the Scientology religion. The agency claimed that the items were "devices" under the Act for which false and misleading

claims had been made. To prove its case, the FDA cited claims contained in literature published by the church. The Court of Appeals expressed concern about the constitutionality of the government's attack on the truth of what the claimant argued were essentially assertions of religious belief.

2.   *Commercial Free Speech.* The First Amendment protection of commercial speech limits the power of government to regulate the content of labeling for food and other products covered by the FD&C Act. The content and reach of these limits are considered at p. 285 *infra.*

3.   LABELING REQUIREMENTS OF SECTION 403

Section 403 ("Misbranded Food") contains two quite different types of provisions: those that prohibit certain types of representations, and those that require disclosure of specified information.

a.   PROHIBITED REPRESENTATIONS

Section 403(a) prohibits statements in labels or labeling that are "false or misleading in any particular," repeating language of the original 1906 Act. Proponents of the 1938 Act were successful in resisting the addition of qualifying terms, such as the insertion of the word "material" before "particular," although one has difficulty finding a case in which FDA successfully attacked labeling representations to which that qualifier would not have applied. *See* David F. Cavers, *The Food, Drug, and Cosmetic Act of 1938: Its Legislative History and Its Substantive Provisions*, 6 LAW & CONTEMP. PROBS. 2 (1939).

United States v. Ninety–Five Barrels of ... Apple Cider Vinegar

265 U.S. 438 (1924).

■ MR. JUSTICE BUTLER delivered the opinion of the Court.

This case arises under the Food and Drugs Act of June 30, 1906. The United States filed information in the District Court for the Northern District of Ohio, Eastern Division, for the condemnation of 95 barrels of vinegar. Every barrel seized was labeled:

> "Douglas Packing Company
> Excelsior Brand Apple Cider Vinegar
> Made from Selected Apples
> Reduced to 4 Percentum
> Rochester, N.Y."

The information alleged ... that the vinegar was made from dried or evaporated apples, and was misbranded in violation of § 8 [of the Act], in that the statements on the label were false and misleading, and in that it was an imitation of and offered for sale under the distinctive name of another article, namely apple cider vinegar....

Section 8 provides:

> "That the term 'misbranded,' as used herein, shall apply to all ... articles of food, or articles which enter into the composition of

food, the package or label of which shall bear any statement, design, or device regarding such article, or the ingredients or substances contained therein which shall be false or misleading in any particular.... That for the purpose of this Act an article shall also be deemed to be misbranded: ... In the case of food: First. If it be an imitation of or offered for sale under the distinctive name of another article. Second. If it be labeled or branded so as to deceive or mislead the purchaser, ... Fourth. If the package containing it or its label shall bear any statement, design, or device regarding the ingredients or the substances contained therein, which statement, design, or device shall be false or misleading in any particular...."

The statute is plain and direct. Its comprehensive terms condemn every statement, design and device which may mislead or deceive. Deception may result from the use of statements not technically false or which may be literally true. The aim of the statute is to prevent that resulting from indirection and ambiguity, as well as from statements which are false. It is not difficult to choose statements, designs and devices which will not deceive. Those which are ambiguous and liable to mislead should be read favorably to the accomplishment of the purpose of the act. The statute applies to food, and the ingredients and substances contained therein. It was enacted to enable purchasers to buy food for what it really is....

If an article is not the identical thing that the brand indicates it to be, it is misbranded. The vinegar in question was not the identical thing that the statement "Excelsior Brand Apple Cider Vinegar made from selected apples," indicated it to be.... [T]he words, "apple cider vinegar made from selected apples" are misleading. Apple cider vinegar is made from apple cider. Cider is the expressed juice of apples and is so popularly and generally known. It was stipulated that the juice of unevaporated apples when subjected to alcoholic and subsequent acetous fermentation is entitled to the name "apple cider vinegar." The vinegar in question was not the same as if made from apples without dehydration. The name "apple cider vinegar" included in the brand did not represent the article to be what it really was; and, in effect, did represent it to be what it was not—vinegar made from fresh or unevaporated apples. The words "made from selected apples" indicate that the apples used were chosen with special regard to their fitness for the purpose of making apple cider vinegar. They give no hint that the vinegar was made from dried apples, or that the larger part of the moisture content of the apples was eliminated and water substituted therefor. As used on the label, they aid the misrepresentation made by the words "apple cider vinegar."

The misrepresentation was in respect of the vinegar itself, and did not relate to the method of production merely. When considered independently of the product, the method of manufacture is not material. The act requires no disclosure concerning it. And it makes no difference whether vinegar made from dried apples is or is not inferior to apple cider vinegar.

The label was misleading as to the vinegar, its substance and ingredients. The facts admitted sustain the charge of misbranding.

NOTES

1. *Misbranding and Economic Adulteration.* The several food misbranding provisions of the FD&C Act are to some extent duplicative, as the charges in the *Apple Cider Vinegar* case suggest. They also overlap the economic adulteration provisions in section 402(b). In most such cases, FDA relies only upon the basic prohibition of deception in section 403(a). The *Apple Cider Vinegar* case is one of the very few in which FDA explicitly relied on the prohibition, now found in section 403(b), against offering a food for sale "under the name of another food." Like the economic adulteration provisions, which are designed to prevent the marketing of debased foods, section 403(b) requires a court to identify a standard against which to compare the product involved, *i.e.*, the "other" food that the seized product is charged with imitating. The need for a standard of comparison is common to statutory as well as common law "passing off" offenses. The economic adulteration provisions of the Act are discussed beginning at p. 155 *infra*.

2. *Proving Product Identity.* In addition to the problem of identifying the standard for comparison in such cases, there may be technical difficulties in proving that a food product is not, in fact, what it is represented to be. *See* Charles W. Crawford, *Technical Problems in Food and Drug Law Enforcement*, 1 LAW & CONTEMP. PROBS. 36 (1933).

United States v. 432 Cartons . . . Candy Lollipops

292 F. Supp. 839 (S.D.N.Y. 1968).

■ MANSFIELD, DISTRICT JUDGE. . . .

The article of food in question consists of about 432 cartons each containing six lollipops. On the outside the carton is labeled on top "Candy . . . for one with Sophisticated Taste," on one side, "A. Freed Novelty, Inc., N.Y.C.," and on the other side, "Ingredients: Sugar, corn syrup, citric acid, natural and artificial flavors." The inside of the box contains the legend, "Liquor Flavored Lollypops," and the slogan, "Take Your Pick of a Liquor Stick." In addition the lollipops themselves are labeled, both in the box and on the cellophane in which they are individually wrapped as "Scotch," "Bourbon," and "Gin."

The Government contends that the internal labeling is false or misleading [in violation of section 403(a)] in that it implies and represents that "the article is flavored with liquor, which it is not." In response claimant does not allege that the lollipops are flavored with liquor, but by way of affirmative defenses contends that they are not misbranded because the cartons are clearly labeled "candy" and the ingredients are distinctly set forth, and that the ordinary purchaser would not read or understand it to represent that the lollipops contain any alcohol or liquor.

In approaching the question of whether the labeling here was false and misleading within the meaning of the statute, we recognize that the statute does not provide for much flexibility in interpretation, since it requires only that the labeling be false or misleading *"in any particular."* (emphasis supplied). This represents a stricter substantive standard than that applied with respect to false advertising, which in order to be prohibited must be "misleading in a *material respect*." (emphasis supplied) 15 U.S.C. § 55(a). Furthermore the statute says "false *or* misleading." . . .

The issue of whether a label is false or misleading may not be resolved by fragmentizing it, or isolating statements claimed to be false from the label in its entirety, since such statements may not be deemed misleading when read in the light of the label as a whole. However, even though the actual ingredients are stated on the outside of a carton, false or misleading statements inside the carton may lead to the conclusion that the labeling is misleading, since a true statement will not necessarily cure or neutralize a false one contained in the label. Furthermore, the fact that purchasers of a product have not been misled, while admissible on the issue of whether the label is false or misleading, would not constitute a defense.

Applying these principles here, it cannot be concluded as a matter of law that no material issue exists with respect to the alleged false and misleading character of the label here before us. Although the labeling on the inside of each box of "candy," when read alone, might be misleading, the detailed description of the contents of the box listed on the outside of the carton could convince a jury, when the labeling or literature is read as a whole, that it is not "misleading in any particular." . . .

. . . The Government's motion for a judgment on the pleadings is therefore denied.

NOTES

1. *Subsequent Resolution.* On remand, "an order for the discontinuance of the action was entered pursuant to stipulation of the parties." 5 FDA Papers, No. 3, at 42 (Apr. 1971).

2. *"All Meat" Frankfurters.* In *Federation of Homemakers v. Butz*, 466 F.2d 462 (D.C. Cir. 1972), the Court of Appeals upheld a lower court ruling invalidating a USDA regulation which permitted frankfurters containing up to 15 percent water, filler, and spices, to be labeled "All Meat." The court held that the regulation was not a legitimate exercise of the Secretary's authority to prescribe labeling for meat products that is not false or misleading to the consumer:

> Do the words "All Meat" mean to an ordinary consumer, as distinguished from an expert, that a frankfurter in a package on which these words appear contains 85 percent meat and other components, and not 81½ percent meat and other components? We think the answer to the question is plain, that the words do not convey that meaning and distinction, and that the Secretary could not reasonably conclude that they do.

USDA has explained how to differentiate between added and nonadded water in 52 Fed. Reg. 30925 (Aug. 18, 1987), 55 Fed. Reg. 7294 (Mar. 1, 1990).

3. *Oral Representations.* In *Weeks v. United States*, 245 U.S. 618 (1918), the Court held that oral misrepresentations could constitute misbranding under the 1906 Act's prohibition against offering a food for sale under the name of another article. Under the FD&C Act, only misrepresentations in a product's label or labeling constitute misbranding.

4. *Wine Labeling. Wawszkiewicz v. Department of the Treasury*, 480 F. Supp. 739 (D.D.C. 1979), invalidated regulations governing the labeling of wine on the ground that the permitted labeling would be misleading. The challenged regulations would have permitted wine labels to carry the name of a single grape variety without disclosing that other grape varieties constituted up to 25 percent of the volume; to represent that the product was made from grapes grown entirely within

one geographic region with no disclosure that up to 25 percent of the volume was grown in other regions; and to represent that a winery "produced" the product even though it fermented as little as 75 percent of the volume.

5. *Disclaimers Ineffective.* Prior to recent elaboration of commercial free speech doctrine, p. 285 *infra*, disclaimers were often held insufficient to cure otherwise misleading labeling. *E.g., United States v. 24 Unlabeled Cans ... "Compound Vegetable Butter Brand ...",* 1969–1974 FDLI Jud. Rec. 32 (E.D. Mich. 1969) ("Not a dairy product" insufficient to overcome misleading use of the word "butter").

6. *Misleading Brand Name.* While a product's brand name may be misleading, *United States v. 70 1/2 Dozen Bottles ... "666",* 1938–1964 FDLI Jud. Rec. 89 (M.D. Ga. 1944), courts are reluctant to sustain orders that would require abandonment of a brand name. *Jacob Siegel Co. v. FTC,* 327 U.S. 608 (1946); *FTC v. Algoma Lumber Co.,* 291 U.S. 67 (1934).

7. *Private Enforcement.* Although there is no private right of enforcement under the FD&C Act, p. 1464 *infra,* a company can sue a competitor for false or misleading labeling or advertising under the Lanham Act, 15 U.S.C. 1125(a). *E.g., Potato Chip Institute v. General Mills, Inc.,* 461 F.2d 1088 (8th Cir. 1972); *Abruzzi Foods, Inc. v. Pasta & Cheese, Inc.,* 986 F.2d 605 (1st Cir. 1993); *Vermont Pure Holdings, Ltd. v. Nestle Waters North America, Inc.,* 2004 WL 2030254 (D. Mass. 2004), 2006 WL 839486 (D. Mass. 2006).

United States v. An Article of Food ... "Manischewitz ... Diet Thins"

377 F. Supp. 746 (E.D.N.Y. 1974).

■ JUDD, DISTRICT JUDGE....

The government initiated this action in 1972 when 423 cases of Diet Thins were seized in Baltimore, Maryland. The government contended that the name Diet–Thins prominently displayed on the label's front panel conveyed to consumers the misleading impression that the matzos were lower in caloric content than other matzos and were useful in weight control diets. Claimant asserts that the label is not misleading because Diet–Thins have several dietary uses other than weight control and that the present label incorporates changes requested by the Food and Drug Administration (FDA) in 1963....

Originally the Diet–Thins were thinner than the regular matzos manufactured and marketed by the claimant. Sometime during the mid–60's, however, the thickness of the regular matzos were reduced, so that at the time of the seizure the Diet–Thins was identical with other matzo crackers made by claimant, except that the Diet–Thins were made with enriched flour rather than ordinary flour. The Diet–Thins furnish the same number of calories as plain matzo crackers and have no greater value in weight control diets than claimant's ordinary matzo crackers.... Although matzos contain less calories than many other crackers on the market, their caloric content is substantially the same as Melba toast, wholewheat crackers, and certain other crackers....

In order to sustain a seizure, the government need not prove that all the label representations are both false and misleading. A food is misbranded if it appears that any *one* representation is false *or* misleading.... [T]he test is not the effect of the label on a "reasonable consumer," but upon "the ignorant, the unthinking and the credulous" consumer. Even a technically accurate description of a food or drug's content may violate 21 U.S.C. § 343 if the description is misleading in other respects....

Purchasers of diet products are often "pathetically eager" to obtain a more slender figure. There can be no doubt that the weight-conscious consumer may be led to believe that Diet–Thin Matzos are lower in calories than ordinary matzo crackers....

ppl maybe considered lower cal!

Claimant may have a right to assert that ordinary matzo crackers have value in diet and weight control. If this were the issue, further discovery and cross-examination of the government's deponents might be useful. Since it is sufficient that only one label statement may be misleading in any particular, the use of the phrase "Diet–Thins" violates the statute.

This does not appear to be a case where the label reference to Diet–Thins can be clarified by an explanatory phrase as was true in *Potato Chip Institute v. General Mills, Inc.* The function of the court is merely to determine whether the existing label is misleading, not to tell the Food and Drug Administration what amendments may be appropriate in order to rectify the situation....

Calol or explanatory phrase

It is ordered that the government's motion for summary judgment be granted, and that a decree of condemnation be entered, and that defendants' motions be denied.

NOTES

1. *Analogous Case. Compare United States v. 88 Cases ... Bireley's Orange Beverage*, 187 F.2d 967 (3d Cir. 1951), p. 155 *infra*, an economic adulteration case.

2. *Consumers to be Protected.* Prior to 2002 the courts articulated a variety of standards for determining whether statements in labeling are "misleading." In *United States v. 62 Packages ... Marmola Prescription Tablets*, 48 F. Supp. 878 (W.D. Wis. 1943), the court stated that the purpose of the FD&C Act is "to protect the public, the vast multitude which includes the ignorant, the unthinking and the credulous who, when making a purchase, do not stop to analyze." By contrast the court in *United States v. Pinaud, Inc.*, 1938–1949 FDLI Jud. & Admin. Rec. 526, 529 (S.D.N.Y. 1949), stated that the proper standard was "purchasers who are of normal capacity and use that capacity in a common sense way." The standard was characterized as the "ordinary person" in *United States v. 1 Device ... Radiant Ozone Generator*, 1949–1950 FDLI Jud. & Admin. Rec. 139, 143 (W.D. Mo. 1949), and *United States v. Vrilium Products, Co.*, 1949–1950 FDLI Jud. & Admin. Rec. 210, 214 (N.D. Ill. 1950). But in *United States v. Article Consisting of 216 Cartoned Bottles ... "Sudden Change"*, 409 F.2d 734 (2d Cir. 1969), the court concluded that the law should protect "the ignorant, the unthinking and the credulous." Another court characterized the standard as the "often unthinking and gullible consumer" in *United States v. An Article of Food ... "Schmidt's Blue Ribbon"*, 1969–1974 FDLI Jud. Rec. 139 (D. Md. 1973). FDA resolved this confusion in December 2002 by announcing, "In assessing whether food labeling is misleading, FDA will use a 'reasonable consumer' standard...." 67 Fed. Reg. 78002, 78003 (Dec. 20, 2002). The FTC has used this same standard since 1984. 103 F.T.C. 100, 174, 177 (1984).

3. *Use of Nonnutritive Sweeteners.* In *Zapka v. The Coca–Cola Company*, Food Drug Cosm. L. Rep. (CCH) ¶ 38,684 (N.D. Ill. 2001), the plaintiff alleged that the defendant failed to disclose that different nonnutritive sweeteners were used in the retail and restaurant versions of Diet Coke. The court denied the defendant's motion for summary judgment.

4. *Vitamin–Mineral Products.* Until the 1970s, litigation over the "misleading" character of vitamin-mineral supplements and other health food products was commonplace. During the 1970s and 1980s, such litigation largely ended for two related reasons. First, FDA sought to reclassify these products as drugs, based on the therapeutic claims made or implied for them, and then sought to have them condemned as illegal new drugs, marketed without an approved NDA. *See* p. 249 *infra.* Second, the regulations promulgated by FDA in the early 1970s for special dietary foods reduced the potential for misleading labeling. Occasionally, however, FDA continued to bring actions against such products solely under the food misbranding provisions. In *United States v. Earthquest Oriental Ginseng*, Food Drug Cosm. L. Rep. (CCH) ¶ 38,043 (N.D. Ga. 1980), for example, FDA challenged as misleading a claim that a vitamin and mineral supplement would increase hair growth. With the enactment of the Dietary Supplement Health and Education Act of 1994 and the increased use of structure/function claims for both dietary supplements and conventional food, the potential for litigation under section 403(a) has re-emerged. *See* p. 276 *infra.*

5. *Sell or Use Dates.* Some food manufacturers voluntarily include on their labels a specific date by which it is recommended that the product be sold or consumed. FDA has considered, but never proposed, regulations governing this type of disclosure. For an analysis of the issues involved, *see* Office of Technology Assessment, OPEN SHELF-LIFE DATING OF FOOD, No. OTA–F–94 (Aug. 1979). *See also* Brian Wansink & Alan O. Wright, *"Best if Used By ...": How Freshness Dating Influences Food Acceptance*, 71 J. FOOD SCI., No. 4., at s354 (2006).

COMMENT: *SPECIAL LABELING ISSUES*

1. *USDA Food Grade Labeling.* Under the Agricultural Marketing Act of 1946, 60 Stat. 1082, 1087, codified in 7 U.S.C. 1621 *et seq.*, USDA is authorized to establish a voluntary system of food grading, inspection, and certification. The regulations governing this program appear at 7 C.F.R. Part 51 *et seq.* Producers who desire to participate must request, and pay for, the USDA inspection and grading service. The USDA quality standards, which are established by notice-and-comment rulemaking, relate to food quality and include such factors as color, size, shape, flavor, texture, maturity, and defects. The USDA grade assigned to a lot of food can then be used by the producer in labeling. Thus, the USDA grading system serves two purposes. First, it allows an independent quality determination on the basis of which wholesale buyers establish prices. Second, it provides useful information to retail consumers. *See* GAO, FOOD LABELING: GOALS, SHORTCOMINGS, AND PROPOSED CHANGES, Ch. 5, No. NWD–75–19 (Jan. 19, 1975). Although use of USDA grade labeling is subject to section 403(a) of the Act, FDA has never participated in this program or objected to inclusion of grade information in food labels.

2. *USDA Production/Marketing Claims.* In 67 Fed. Reg. 79552 (Dec. 30, 2002), USDA proposed to establish minimum requirements for several claims commonly used for livestock, including claims about the nonuse of

antibiotics and hormones and the term "free range." Final action has not yet been taken on this proposal. These and other claims are also defined on the USDA website. For example, "free range" is defined in the proposed requirement to include "Livestock that have had continuous and unconfined access to pasture throughout their life cycle" and on the website as simply "access to the outside."

3. *Kosher Labeling.* Section 403(a)'s prohibition against false or misleading labeling applies to any statement made in food labeling. FDA initially stated in 21 C.F.R. 101.29 that a food may lawfully be described as "kosher" only if it meets the applicable religious dietary requirements. The agency discouraged use of the phrase "kosher style" because it may mislead purchasers into believing that the product is in fact kosher. It explained the two label symbols used to signify compliance with Jewish dietary laws in FDA, SYMBOLS ON FOOD LABELS, DHEW Pub. No. (FDA) 76–2021 (Rev. December 1975):

> The symbol which consists of the letter "J" inside the letter "O" is one whose use is authorized by the Union of Orthodox Jewish Congregations of America, more familiarly known as the Orthodox Union, for use of foods which comply with the Jewish dietary laws. Detailed information regarding the significance and use of this symbol may be obtained from the headquarters of that organization at 116 E. 27th St., New York, New York 10016.

> The symbol which consists of the letter "K" inside the letter "O" is one whose use is authorized by "O.K." Laboratories, 105 Hudson St., New York, New York 10013, to indicate that the food is "Kosher," that is, it complies with the Jewish dietary laws, and its processing has been under the direction of a rabbi.

Because of concern about the constitutionality of its regulation of kosher labeling, however, FDA revoked 21 C.F.R. 101.29 in 61 Fed. Reg. 29708, 29710 (June 12, 1996), 62 Fed. Reg. 43071, 43072 (Aug. 12, 1997). State laws governing Kosher labeling have been struck down as an unconstitutional violation of the separation of church and state. Gerald F. Masoudi, *Kosher Food Regulation and the Religion Clauses of the First Amendment*, 60 U. CHI. L. REV. 667 (1993); Catherine Beth Sullivan, *Are Kosher Food Laws Constitutionally Kosher?*, 21 B.C. ENVIRON. AFF. L. REV. 201 (1993); Ari D. Wasserman, *Kashrut Enforcement* (1994), Joshua L. Fogel, *Kosher Food Regulation and the First Amendment: Irreconcilable Differences?* (1995), and Caren E. Gottlieb, *Can the FDA Keep Kosher? Regulation of Kosher Claims on Product Labeling* (1998), in Chapters I(F)(2) and V(B)(3) of the Electronic Book; Stephen F. Rosenthal, *Food for Thought: Kosher Fraud Laws and the Religion Clauses of the First Amendment*, 65 G.W. L. REV. 951 (1997).

4. *Geographic Designation Labeling.* For over a century federal regulatory officials have worried about false or misleading claims about the geographic origin of food products. A 1902 statute provided that no person may sell "any dairy or food product which shall be falsely labeled or branded as to the State or Territory in which they are made, produced, or grown ..." 32 Stat. 632 (1902), 21 U.S.C. 16. FDA found it unnecessary to issue regulations implementing this statute prior to the early 1970s, when

it proposed and finalized a rule regarding geographical origin labeling in response to both domestic and foreign complaints. 35 Fed. Reg. 9214 (June 12, 1970), 36 Fed. Reg. 9444 (May 25, 1971), codified at 21 C.F.R. 101.18(c). Today states continue to protect the use of their geographic designations. H. David Gold, *Legal Strategies to Address the Misrepresentation of Vermont Maple Syrup*, 58 FOOD & DRUG L.J. 93 (2004). Europe also continues to seek to prevent false or misleading use of its geographic designations. Peter J. Wied, *An Edict from the Thought Police: Reconciling American and European Approaches to Geographical Designations* (1997), Raffi Melkonian, *The History and Future of Geographical Indications in Europe and the United States* (2005), Jennifer Chu, *The Latest Development in the Transatlantic Big Stink over Cheeses and other Geographical Indications* (2006), in Chapter V(B)(1) of the Electronic Book.

5. *Mandatory Country of Origin Labeling.* The United States Customs Service has long required, under the Tariff Act of 1890, 26 Stat. 567, 613 (1891) and section 304 of the Tariff Act of 1930, 19 U.S.C. 1304, that food imported into the United States must be labeled with the country of origin pursuant to regulations established in 19 C.F.R. Part 134. *See National Juice Products Association v. United States*, 628 F. Supp. 978 (Ct. Int'l Trade 1986). The Customs Service implemented this requirement with respect to imported fruit juice products in 51 Fed. Reg. 7285 (Mar. 3, 1986), 51 Fed. Reg. 23045 (June 25, 1986), 51 Fed. Reg. 27195 (July 30, 1986), 53 Fed. Reg. 20836 & 20869 (June 7, 1988), 54 Fed. Reg. 24168 (June 6, 1989), 54 Fed. Reg. 29540 (July 13, 1989), 62 Fed. Reg. 49597 (Sept. 23, 1997). *See generally* Donna L. Bade, *Beyond Marking: Country of Origin Rules and the Decision in CPC International*, 31 J. MARSHALL L. REV. 179 (1997); "Country-of-Origin Labeling Requirements for Imported Meat and Other Food Products," Hearing before the Subcomm. on Trade of the House Comm. on Ways and Means, 100th Cong., 2d Sess. (1988) (containing discussion of extending country-of-origin labeling to all food containing an imported ingredient).

In *Norcal/Crosetti Foods, Inc. v. United States*, 963 F.2d 356 (Fed. Cir. 1992), the Court of Appeals determined that the country of origin need not appear on the principal display panel of a food. In 58 Fed. Reg. 68743 (Dec. 29, 1993) the Customs Service published a final interpretive regulation requiring country of origin marking for frozen produce on the principal display panel, but it was overturned in *American Frozen Food Institute v. United States*, 855 F. Supp. 388 (Ct. Int'l Trade 1994). Customs reproposed the regulations in 61 Fed. Reg. 38119 (July 23, 1996) but announced its withdrawal of the proposal in 67 Fed. Reg. 33570 (May 13, 2002).

In the Farm Bill of 2002, Congress included mandatory country of origin labeling by September 30, 2004 for meat, fish, and produce. 116 Stat. 134, 533 (2002). GAO and USDA released conflicting reports on the impact of the legislation. Compare FSIS, USDA, MANDATORY COUNTRY OF ORIGIN LABELING OF IMPORTED FRESH MUSCLE CUTS OF BEEF AND LAMB (Jan. 2000) with GAO, FRESH PRODUCE: POTENTIAL CONSEQUENCES OF COUNTRY-OF-ORIGIN LABELING, Rep. No. RCED–99–112 (Apr. 1999); GAO, BEEF AND LAMB: IMPLICATIONS OF LABELING BY COUNTRY OF ORIGIN, Rep. No. GAO/RCED–00–44 (Jan. 27, 2000); GAO, COUNTRY OF ORIGIN LABELING: OPPORTUNITIES FOR USDA AND

INDUSTRY TO IMPLEMENT CHALLENGING ASPECTS OF THE NEW LAW, Rep. No. GAO–03–780 (Aug. 2003). *See also* "Country-of-Origin Meat Labeling Act": Hearing before the Subcomm. on Livestock and Horticulture of the House Comm. on Agriculture, 106th Cong., 2d Sess. (2000); Elise Golan et al., *Economics of Food Labeling* 30, AGRIC. ECON. REP. No. 793 (Jan. 2001). USDA issued draft guidelines for voluntary compliance in 67 Fed. Reg. 63367 (Oct. 11, 2002) and proposed regulations in 68 Fed. Reg. 61943 (Oct. 30, 2003). As part of the FY 2004 and FY 2006 USDA appropriations, however, Congress delayed implementation of the new law until September 30, 2008 except for fish and shellfish. USDA therefore issued interim final regulations for fish and shellfish in 69 Fed. Reg. 59708 (Oct. 5, 2004) but delayed the time for comment in 69 Fed. Reg. 77609 (Dec. 28, 2004) beyond the statutory deadline of April 2005 and has taken no further action. No final regulations for meat have yet been promulgated. A report by Public Citizen, *Tabled Labels: Consumers Eat Blind While Congress Feasts on Campaign Cash* (Sept. 2005), describes food industry lobbying against mandatory country of origin labeling.

COMMENT: "NATURAL" FOOD CLAIMS

As processed food has become increasingly more prevalent, claims that a product is "natural," or contains only "natural ingredients," or contains no "preservatives" or other additives, have become common. These representations have led four federal regulatory agencies and a voluntary industry organization to establish enforcement policies in this area.

1.   *FDA.* FDA initially took the position that the only food products that could lawfully be characterized as "natural" were raw agricultural commodities that were sold in their natural state, without any processing. Faced with growing numbers of such claims, however, the agency chose not to expend the resources that would be necessary to enforce this policy or to promulgate regulations defining these terms. Beginning in the mid–1970s, FDA concluded that it would prohibit use of the term "natural" only on products containing artificial color, artificial flavor, or synthetic ingredients such as chemical additives. Later, in its proposed regulations to implement the Nutrition Labeling and Education Act, FDA stated that a food may not be represented as "natural" if it has undergone more than "minimal processing." 56 Fed. Reg. 60421, 60466–60467 (Nov. 27, 1991). In the final regulations, FDA reiterated that it would adhere to its current policy of allowing use of "natural" as meaning that "nothing artificial or synthetic (including all color additives regardless of source) has been included in, or has been added to, a food that normally would not be expected to be in the food." FDA said that it would delay a formal rulemaking to define the term. 58 Fed. Reg. 2302, 2407 (Jan. 6, 1993). FDA has stated that no decaffeinated coffee can be labeled as "natural." Letter from Nina L. Adler, CFSAN Office of Food Labeling, Division of Programs and Enforcement Policy, to Timothy P. O'Shea (Feb. 22, 1994). On February 28, 2006, the Sugar Association submitted a citizen petition requesting FDA to define the term "natural" based on the USDA definition. FDA Docket No. 2006P.0094/CPI. FDA has not taken further action to define "natural" food.

2. *FTC.* In a trade regulation rule (TRR) governing nutrition claims in food advertising proposed in 39 Fed. Reg. 39842 (Nov. 11, 1974), and debated for nearly ten years, the FTC would have prohibited use of the terms "natural" and "organic." The Commission later proposed to require advertisers to state the precise facts applicable to the food (*e.g.*, that the food contains no artificial preservatives or artificial fertilizers). The agency eventually abandoned that position and agreed to permit a food to be represented as "natural" if it had not undergone more than "minimal processing" after harvest or slaughter and contained no artificial flavor, color additive, chemical preservative, or other artificial or synthetic ingredient. Appreciating the uncertainty of the "minimal processing" standard, however, the Commission announced in 48 Fed. Reg. 23270 (May 24, 1983) that it was abandoning the entire proceeding.

3. *USDA.* For many years, USDA simply banned any claim using the term "natural" or referring to the absence of preservatives or other additives of any kind on the premise that such claims were inherently misleading. In 1980, faced with a new form of packaging (retortable pouches) that required no preservatives, USDA relented cautiously and permitted labeling statements linking the absence of preservatives to the new type of packaging. In Policy Memorandum No. 055, issued on November 22, 1982, the Department went further and provided that the term "natural" could be used if the product does not contain any artificial flavor, color, chemical preservative, or other artificial or synthetic ingredient, and the product and its ingredients are not more than minimally processed. The USDA policy memorandum defined minimal processing. It required that all products claimed to be "natural" must be accompanied by a brief statement which explains what is meant by the term "natural," *i.e.*, it contains no artificial ingredients and is only minimally processed. The agency explained that it was adopting the approach endorsed by the FTC. Although the Commission subsequently abandoned this approach in May 1983, USDA has continued to apply its November 1982 policy memorandum.

4. *BATF/TTB.* Following the FTC approach, the Bureau of Alcohol, Tobacco and Firearms (BATF), now the Alcohol and Tobacco Tax and Trade Bureau (TTB), proposed to adopt a formal definition of the term "natural" on alcoholic beverage labeling in 45 Fed. Reg. 83530 (Dec. 19, 1980). It took the position that a "natural" alcoholic beverage was one that had been minimally processed and contained no artificial additives. After the FTC abandoned this approach, however, BATF withdrew its proposal. 50 Fed. Reg. 960 (Jan. 8, 1985). BATF/TTB has also severely restricted use of the term "pure" for alcoholic beverages, but in 70 Fed. Reg. 72731 (Dec. 7, 2005) the agency published an advance notice of proposed rulemaking to request comment on whether its policy should be revised.

5. *NAD.* In 1971, the advertising industry established a system of self-regulation through the National Advertising Division (NAD) of the Council of Better Business Bureaus. In October 1984 the NAD issued a special report summarizing thirty NAD cases relating to "natural" and "no artificial ingredient" food advertising claims between June 1975 and September 1984. In general, the NAD has applied a flexible rule that allows the

advertiser to define the scope of the term "natural" or, failing that, holds the advertiser to the broadest meaning of that term. *See* Ronald H. Smithies, *Nutritional Issues in Advertising*, 31 CEREAL FOODS WORLD 464 (1986).

6. *Decision Tree.* A decision tree for determining whether a substance is "natural" has been published in Cynthia J. Mussinan and Patrick G. Hoffman, *Naturalness Decision Tree*, 53 FOOD TECH. No. 5, at 54 (May 1999).

COMMENT: "ORGANIC" FOOD CLAIMS

In the Organic Foods Production Act of 1990, 104 Stat. 3359, 3935, Congress directed USDA to establish national standards for the certification of foods as "organic." *See also* Institute of Food Technologists, *Organically Grown Foods*, 44 FOOD TECH. 26 (June 1990). The statute set forth three objectives: (1) to establish national standards for the marketing of agricultural products as organically produced products, (2) to assure consumers that such products meet a consistent standard, and (3) to facilitate improved interstate commerce in food that is organically produced. After lengthy meetings of the National Organic Standards Board, USDA proposed regulations to establish the National Organic Program in 62 Fed. Reg. 65850 (Dec. 16, 1997). Attacked as allowing excessive nonorganic content, that proposal was withdrawn and a new proposal was published in 65 Fed. Reg. 13512 (Mar. 13, 2000). Final regulations were promulgated in 65 Fed. Reg. 80548 (Dec. 21, 2000), 7 C.F.R. Part 205.

The final regulations recognize four organic product categories: (1) "100 percent organic," (2) "organic" (95–99 percent organic), (3) "made with organic ingredients" (70–90 percent organic), and (4) products for which the organic status of particular ingredients may be indicated only in the ingredients statement (below 70 percent organic). To be labeled as organic a product must be certified by an accredited certifying agent. Use of the term "organic" was further narrowed by the decision in *Harvey v. Veneman*, 396 F.3d 28 (1st Cir. 2005), which held that the statute precludes designating any food product as organic if it contains any synthetic ingredient. However, Congress overruled this aspect of *Harvey* in 119 Stat. 2120, 2153, 2165 (2005), and USDA thus did not revise its regulations to prohibit the use of synthetic ingredients in organic products. USDA implemented other aspects of the *Harvey* decision and the new statutory provisions in 70 Fed. Reg. 38090 (July 1, 2005), 71 Fed. Reg. 24820 (Apr. 27, 2006), 71 Fed. Reg. 32803 (June 7, 2006). *See generally* Elizabeth A. Dungey, *Drafting Organic Food Regulations: The Case for Incorporating Congressional Intent and Interest Group Commentary* (1999), Jessica L. Ellsworth, *The History of Organic Food Regulation* (2001), Stephanie Jillian, *Federal Regulation of Organic Food: A Research Guide for Legal Practitioners & Food Industry Professionals* (2005), in Chapter V(F) of the Electronic Book; Jean M. Rawson, *Organic Agriculture in the United States: Program and Policy Issues*, CRS Rep. No. RL 31595 (Sept. 15, 2006); Stephen R. Vina, *Harvey v. Veneman and the National Organic Program: A Legal Analysis*, CRS Rep. No. RS22318 (Sept. 26, 2006); Clark K. Winter's synopsis of IFT's Scientific

Status Summary on Organic Foods, 60 FOOD TECH., No. 10, at 44 (Oct. 2006).

COMMENT: "FRESH" FOOD CLAIMS

In Compliance Policy Guide 7120.06 (Oct. 1, 1980), FDA sought to provide general guidance with respect to designation of food as "fresh," and in 56 Fed. Reg. 5694 (Feb. 12, 1991) the agency announced its intention to issue proposed regulations to govern the use of this term. FDA proposed to define the term "fresh" in 56 Fed. Reg. 60421, 60463 (Nov. 27, 1991) and issued final regulations in 58 Fed. Reg. 2302, 2401 (Jan. 6, 1993), codified at 21 C.F.R. 101.95. Under the regulations, the term "fresh" may be used only on the label of a raw food that has not been frozen or subjected to any form of thermal processing or any other form of preservation. The regulation provides that pasteurized milk is exempt because consumers recognize that milk is nearly always pasteurized, whereas pasteurized orange juice or bakery products with preservatives are not exempt and may not be labeled as "fresh." When the baking industry protested, FDA stated that "the agency would not object to the use of terms such as 'freshly baked' or 'freshly prepared' on bread that has been preserved...." Letter from Elizabeth Campbell, Acting Director, FDA CFSAN Office of Food Labeling, to Paul C. Abenante (May 15, 1998). FDA conducted a public hearing on use of the term "fresh" for foods processed with alternative nonthermal technologies as announced in 65 Fed. Reg. 41029 (July 3, 2000) but has taken no further action on this matter.

In *Abruzzi Foods, Inc. v. Pasta & Cheese, Inc.*, 986 F.2d 605 (1st Cir. 1993), the court held that the plaintiff in a Lanham Act case failed to sustain its argument that a competitor's use of the term "fresh" for refrigerated pasta in extended shelf-life packaging is unfair or deceptive. The National Advertising Division of the Council of Better Business Bureaus has determined that the term "fresh" may describe the ingredients used to prepare a processed product if they refer to the ingredients and do not imply that the final product is unprocessed. *Del Monte Foods, Inc.*, 28 NAD Case Reports 21 (Mar. 1998).

A District Court struck down a California statute which would have required poultry labeled as "fresh" to be maintained at a temperature of 26°F or above on the ground that it unconstitutionally discriminated against out-of-state poultry. *National Broiler Council v. Voss*, 851 F. Supp. 1461 (E.D. Cal. 1994), *aff'd* 44 F.3d 740 (9th Cir. 1994). USDA conducted a hearing announced in 59 Fed. Reg. 44089 (Aug. 26, 1994) to consider use of the term "fresh" on the labeling of raw poultry products. The USDA policy of allowing chilled but unfrozen poultry to be labeled as "fresh" was severely criticized at a congressional hearing on June 16, 1994. Soon after, USDA announced public hearings on the matter in 59 Fed. Reg. 44089 (Aug. 26, 1994) and proposed a regulation in 60 Fed. Reg. 3454 (Jan. 17, 1995) to define poultry held at temperatures below 0°F as "frozen," those held between 0°F and 26°F as "previously frozen," and those above 26°F as "fresh." Final USDA regulations, which preserved the three categories but changed the term "previously frozen" to "hard chilled," were promulgated in 60 Fed. Reg. 44396 (Aug. 25, 1995). In the 1997 appropriations legislation, however, Congress ordered USDA to delete the term "hard chilled" and to reserve the term "fresh" for poultry never cooled below 26°F. Revised regulations were therefore promulgated in 61 Fed. Reg. 66198 (Dec. 17, 1996), codified at 9 C.F.R. 381.29(b)(6).

b. AFFIRMATIVE DISCLOSURES

Section 403 explicitly mandates affirmative disclosure of five types of information on every food label: the name of the food, the name and place of business of the manufacturer, a statement of ingredients, the net quantity of contents, and nutrient content. In addition, section 201(n) provides that, in determining whether labeling is misleading, "there shall be taken into account" not only the representations made about the product but also the extent to which the labeling fails to reveal material facts. Since the early 1970s, FDA has exploited this provision to prescribe, by regulation, additional requirements for affirmative disclosure of information in food labeling.

Section 403(f) mandates that information required by other provisions of the section to appear on the label or labeling be "prominently placed thereon with such conspicuousness ... and in such terms as to render it likely to be read and understood by the ordinary individual under customary conditions of use." From 1938 until 1973, FDA enforced this requirement based solely on the subjective impressions and informed judgment of agency compliance personnel. Few cases were ever litigated. One attempt to enforce section 403(f), *United States v. 46 Cases, More or Less, "Welch's Nut Caramels,"* 204 F. Supp. 321 (D.R.I. 1962), evoked the following response from the court:

> The net weight and ingredient statements are printed on the label in a distinctive silver color that is not employed for any other statements appearing on said package. Both statements are printed in the same size type which the evidence establishes as being easily readable at a distance of approximately 29 inches by the average person. The Act prescribes no minimum specific standard as to how prominent such statements should be. It would seem that the requirements of said section 403(f) are met in a particular case if such statements are prominent enough to be seen and understood by the ordinary individual who is interested in discovering and learning the information disclosed thereby, and who makes a minimum examination of the package to determine its net weight and the ingredients of the candy contained in said package.

A decade later FDA relied on section 403(f) to promulgate regulations 38 Fed. Reg. 2124 (Jan. 19, 1973), 38 Fed. Reg. 6950 (Mar. 14, 1973), codified at 21 C.F.R. 101.1 & 101.2.

Food Labeling

21 C.F.R. Part 101.

§ 101.1   Principal display panel of package form food

The term "principal display panel" as it applies to food in package form and as used in this part, means the part of a label that is most likely to be displayed, presented, shown, or examined under customary conditions of display for retail sale. The principal display panel shall be large enough to accommodate all the mandatory label information required to be placed thereon by this part with clarity and conspicuousness and without obscuring design, vignettes, or crowding. Where packages bear alternate principal display panels, information required to be placed on the principal display panel shall be duplicated on each principal display panel. . . .

§ 101.2   Information panel of package form food

(a) The term "information panel" as it applies to packaged food means that part of the label immediately contiguous and to the right of the principal display panel as observed by an individual facing the principal display panel with the following exceptions. . . .

(b) All information required to appear on the label of any package of food pursuant to . . . this chapter shall appear either on the principal display panel or on the information panel, unless otherwise specified by regulations in this chapter.

(c) All information appearing on the principal display panel or the information panel pursuant to this section shall appear prominently and conspicuously, but in no case may the letters and/or numbers be less than one-sixteenth inch in height unless an exemption pursuant to paragraph (f) of this section is established. . . .

(d)(1) All information required to appear on the principal display panel or on the information panel pursuant to this section shall appear on the same panel unless there is insufficient space. In determining the sufficiency of the available space, any vignettes, design, and other nonmandatory label information shall not be considered. . . .

(e) All information appearing on the information panel pursuant to this section shall appear in one place without other intervening material.

(f) If the label of any package of food is too small to accommodate all of the information required by . . . this chapter, the Commissioner may establish by regulation an acceptable alternative method of disseminating such information to the public, *e.g.*, a type size smaller than one-sixteenth inch in height, or labeling attached to or inserted in the package or available at the point of purchase. . . .

NOTE

For caustic commentary on this regulation, *see* H. Thomas Austern, *The Regulatory Gospel According to Saint Peter*, 29 FOOD DRUG COSM. L.J. 316 (1974). *See generally* Merrill S. Thompson, *FDA—They Mean Well, But* . . . , 28 FOOD DRUG COSM. L.J. 205 (1973).

4.   DECEPTIVE PACKAGING

Ruth Lamb, *American Chamber of Horrors* (1936)

In a recent survey by State authorities in Alabama, six samples of black pepper showed a fill of container from 82 per cent to as low as 43 per cent of what the housewife might reasonably expect. Coffee and chicory compounds ranged from 67 to 80 per cent, the average being about 70, and one sample of tea was hardly more than half full. An attractive basket of fancy sealed pecans, thanks to a false bottom, was only 77 per cent filled. Three samples of salt showed fills of 72, 75 and 80 per cent respectively....

... A candy box one of the inspectors told me about was big enough to hold a pound; but it had a false bottom occupying a quarter of the space, and such other structures that there was room actually for only six ounces. Candy boxes holding no more than fifteen ounces are common.

And Mr. W. R. M. Wharton, Chief of the Eastern District, has a story about a cheese manufacturer who, on finding competition keen, reduced the quantity of cheese in his package from the conventional eight ounces to six by putting in a false bottom. But a competitor went him one better by putting in two layers of false bottom, thus reducing the quantity to four ounces. And then came another competitor who chiseled away yet another ounce by adding a third false bottom! ...

It was in response to such practices that Congress included in the 1938 Act section 403(d), which declares a food misbranded "if its container is so made, formed, or filled as to be misleading." *See generally* Peter Barton Hutt, *Development of Federal Law Regulating Slack Fill and Deceptive Packaging of Food, Drugs, and Cosmetics*, 42 FOOD DRUG COSM. L.J. 1 (1987).

United States v. 116 Boxes ... Arden Assorted Candy Drops

80 F. Supp. 911 (D. Mass. 1948).

■ WYZANSKI, DISTRICT JUDGE....

Each box measures in inches: 3 3/4 × 2 1/2 × 1 1/4. A box is intended to sell at retail at five cents. Each bears a legend stating the name of the drop and showing the weight of the box as 1 1/2 ounces.... There is no statement as to the number of pieces of candy. Most of the boxes contain 17 pieces. Some, however, contain 18 or 19. When 17 pieces are in the box and a reasonable time has elapsed since manufacture, the candy settles so that there is an average air space in the box of 33%.

Each box in evidence was packaged by a standard packaging machine, manufactured by a third party, of the type used by a majority of leading concerns packaging candy or cough drops intended to retail at five or ten cents. Such a packaging machine is made with only slight variations necessary for each concern....

Upon the basis of the foregoing facts and for the following reasons I conclude as a matter of law that the shipment did not violate § 403(d) of the Act and that the libel should be dismissed without costs and the boxes delivered to the shipper.

... I do not go so far as to accept the argument, advanced by the Government, that the question is whether the package is so filled as to mislead an average five-year old child who might expect the box to be filled to overflowing. Infantile anticipation is not the test. Rather it is what would be expected by an ordinary person—not necessarily an adult—who had been led to expect and desire machine-packing. Such a customer knows machine-packing is more sanitary than hand-packing. He knows it results in economies of mass production and that these economies are in some measure likely to be passed on to the ultimate consumer. Moreover, from buying various types of five-cent candies, cough drops and lozenges packed by machine in standard rectangular containers, he has come to expect some slack or air space. Indeed, he recognizes that tight packing would often solidify into a mass pieces [sic] which he prefers to have separate. It is the expectations of a person who has that common degree of familiarity with our industrial civilization which furnish the standard which Congress intended to be applied. . . .

In the case at bar no evidence was introduced as to what an ordinary non-infantile purchaser would expect. But in my view he would not expect any particular number of lozenges. So long as he received ordinary lozenges not obviously so eccentric in shape as to result in peculiar packing difficulties, and so long as he received approximately as many of these lozenges as could conveniently be packed in a standard rectangular carton by machine, he would not in my opinion be misled.

United States v. 174 Cases . . . "Delson Thin Mints"

287 F.2d 246 (3d Cir. 1961).

■ BIGGS, CHIEF JUDGE. . . .

There are two ways in which a trial court may hold for the claimant in cases such as that at bar. First, the court can find as a fact that the accused package is not made, formed, or filled in such a way that it would deceive the ordinary purchaser as to the quantity of its contents. Alternatively, the court may find as a fact that even though the form or filling of the package deceives the ordinary purchaser into thinking that it contains more food than it actually does, the form and filling of the package is justified by considerations of safety and is reasonable in the light of available alternative safety features. . . .

. . . [T]he court below did not find that the Delson package did not deceive the ordinary purchaser by making him think that it contained more than it actually did contain. The court stated in respect to this issue: "The case is, in my opinion, lacking in adequate proof that the average adult, of normal intelligence, would be induced by the exterior appearance of the accused containers to buy a box of Delson mints with the expectation that it would contain any particular number of individual candies." This statement is beside the point. The question was not whether the ordinary purchaser would expect to find a particular number of individual candies in the box but whether such a purchaser would expect to find more of the Delson box filled. . . . People do not think in terms of the number of individual mints when buying them in containers.

... [E]vidence introduced by the United States tended to show that only 44% of the total volume of the accused container and that only 75% of its practical volume was filled with mints; that the remainder of the usable space was taken up with hollow cardboard dividers and hollow end pieces. The United States introduced substantial uncontradicted evidence to show that purchasers of the mints, opening the boxes, expected to find far more mints in them than were there. In view of this it is obvious, if there were nothing more in the case, that the containers might well fall within the interdiction of the statute.

But, and this is a point which we must emphasize, a showing by the United States that the ordinary purchaser, on viewing a container, will believe that it contains significantly more food than in fact it does contain, and was deceived, cannot be dispositive of the issues of such a case as that at bar. A claimant may go forward and show, as the claimant has attempted to do here, that the circumstantial deception was forced upon it by other considerations such as packaging features necessary to safeguard its product. But safety considerations, before they can be held to justify a slack package must be shown to be reasonably necessary in the light of alternative methods of safeguarding the contents....

... The court has to find that the container's efficacy outweighs its deceptive quality. Further, it has to find that the available alternative efficacious means are not less deceptive than those actually employed.

Since the court below has not made the necessary findings of fact to support the legal conclusions which it has reached, we will vacate the judgment and remand with the direction to proceed as the facts and the law require.

NOTES

1. *Subsequent Proceedings.* On remand, 195 F. Supp. 326 (D.N.J. 1961), the District Court held that the package was not deceptive, and that even if it were the available alternative means of packaging were no less deceptive and the efficacy of the present package outweighed any deception.

2. *Other Authority. See also United States v. 738 Cases ... Jiffy–Lou Vanilla Flavor Pudding,* 71 F. Supp. 279 (D. Ariz. 1946), which held 55% slack fill not to violate section 403(d), noting that "the container used ... is commonly and universally recognized as containing enough formula and ingredients to make a standard and publicly recognized recipe producing one pint of pudding," and that "the container used is sanitary, convenient to the user, and of a type reasonably necessary in packaging, handling and utilizing the product."

3. *Economic Adulteration.* Deceptive packaging practices may also be addressed under section 402(b)(2), which declares a food to be adulterated "if any substance has been substituted wholly or in part" for "any valuable constituent." See *United States v. 149 Cases ... "Silver Brand ... Dried Black Eyed Peas,"* 1938–1964 FDLI Jud. Rec. 1289 (D. Colo. 1953), in which FDA prevailed on a charge of economic adulteration under section 402(b)(2) on the ground that excess packing material had been substituted for the peas.

4. *Commentary. See* Franklin M. Depew, *The Slack–Filled Package Law,* 1 FOOD DRUG COSM. L.Q. 86 (1946); John C. Martin, *Section 403(d)—Containers So Made, Formed or Filled as to be Misleading,* 8 FOOD DRUG COSM. L.J. 663 (1953);

Wesley E. Forte, *Food and Drug Administration, Federal Trade Commission and the Deceptive Packaging of Foods*, 21 FOOD DRUG COSM. L.J. 205 (1966); Merrill S. Thompson, *Functional Slack–Fill in the Manufacture and Packaging of Confections*, 27 FOOD DRUG COSM. L.J. 779 (1972).

5. *Enforcement of Section 403(d)*. The prohibition against misleading packaging has rarely been the basis for FDA enforcement proceedings. Between 1938 and the enactment of the Fair Packaging and Labeling Act in 1966, the agency had not prevailed in a single contested case under section 403(d). One obstacle to successful enforcement was the lack of legislatively prescribed criteria of deception and FDA's failure to develop criteria by regulation. Thus, according to one court, "There is no hard and fast rule as to what would constitute slack-filling. Whether or not over 50 per cent space in a particular package of candy was slack-filling is a question of fact for the district court to decide." *United States v. Cataldo*, 157 F.2d 802, 804 (1st Cir. 1946). Furthermore, courts vacillated over whether it was incumbent upon the FDA to introduce evidence of actual consumer deception. Courts appeared reluctant to find a package misleading without such evidence, perhaps because the Act requires the net contents to be disclosed on the label.

6. *FDA Regulations*. FDA belatedly promulgated regulations establishing general principles on nonfunctional slack fill in response to the Institute of Medicine report mandated by section 6(b) of the Nutrition Labeling and Education Act, 104 Stat. 2353, 2363 (1990), in 58 Fed. Reg. 2957 (Jan. 6, 1993), 58 Fed. Reg. 27932 (May 12, 1993), 58 Fed. Reg. 64123, 64208 (Dec. 6, 1993), 59 Fed. Reg. 536 (Jan. 5, 1994), 21 C.F.R. 100.100, but it has otherwise continued to ignore section 403(d).

Harold Marquis, *Fair Packaging and Consumer Protection*

18 JOURNAL OF PUBLIC LAW 61 (1969).

One approach that would avoid the complexities of promulgating standards of fill for individual commodities would be to require a conspicuous disclosure of fill for commodities when the regulatory authorities thought consumer deception was occurring. Regulations, on a commodity-by-commodity basis, could require the disclosure when the fill was below a certain percentage of the maximum fill possible. This disclosure requirement might be satisfied by a "___% Full" statement, or a "Filled to Here" line, or by a transparent window that allows the consumer to view the content level. Less technical information would be needed to draw this type of regulation on a commodity-by-commodity basis than would be necessary to establish a standard of fill, as a manufacturer would not be forced to meet a minimum standard of fill, regardless of expense.

The disclosure approach not only circumvents the technological arguments raised by industry against fill standards, but could exert some pressure on industry to overcome major technological obstacles to full packaging. At the least, it should neutralize attempts by manufacturers to use slack fill to obtain a competitive advantage at the expense of consumers....

NOTES

1. *Fill of Container Standards*. Section 401 authorizes FDA to issue "reasonable standards of fill of container," and the agency has issued such standards for many canned foods. 21 C.F.R. Parts 145 *et seq.*

2. *FPLA*. In 1966, Congress enacted the Fair Packaging and Labeling Act, 80 Stat. 1296, 15 U.S.C. 1451–1461, a law primarily designed to facilitate price comparisons by consumers between competing products. The core of the FPLA is a requirement that packages of consumer commodities bear a legible, prominent label statement of net quantity of contents (in terms of weight, measure or numerical count). In addition, section 5(c)(4) of the FPLA authorizes FDA to adopt regulations to "prevent the nonfunctional-slack-fill of packages containing" food, drugs, devices, or cosmetics. The regulations belatedly promulgated by FDA in 1994, *supra* p. 124, Note 6, were promulgated under section 403(d) of the FD&C Act rather than under the FPLA because reliance on the latter would have required compliance with the formal rulemaking requirements of section 701(e) of the FD&C Act.

3. *California Requirements*. Although the California statutes governing slack fill and deceptive packaging are the same as the federal statutes, the state, on the basis of *Hobby Industry Association of America, Inc. v. Younger*, 161 Cal. Rptr. 601 (Cal. Ct. App. 1980), took the position that all nonfunctional slack fill is inherently illegal whether or not there is evidence of deception. California applied this standard both to the fill of the immediate container and to the fit of the immediate container in an outer package. The state subsequently adopted Slack Fill Enforcement Guidelines (Apr. 21, 1988), setting forth 14 principles for determining when exterior packaging and immediate product containers may be considered as not slack filled. The California interpretation was subsequently preempted for food by the enactment of section 403A(a)(3) of the FD&C Act in 1990.

4. *Milk Container Variations*. In *Perry v. Foremost Farms USA Cooperative*, 620 N.W.2d 482 (Wis. Ct. App. 2000), the court denied an injunction against underfilling of milk containers where evidence showed that the manufacturer overfilled its milk containers as much as it underfilled them and there was no evidence that the manufacturer failed to use good manufacturing processes.

COMMENT: FOOD TAMPERING

Although the first publicized example of tampering with a product subject to FDA jurisdiction involved a nonprescription drug, Extra Strength Tylenol, p. 812 *infra*, there have been numerous reports of tampering with food products since then. *E.g.*, "Tampering–Related Arrest," FDA Talk Paper No. T86–37 (May 30, 1986). In many cases the manufacturer has been forced to take steps to prevent distribution or consumption of a product without knowing whether a tampering threat is true or false. *E.g.*, "Sugar–Free Jello—Cyanide Threat," FDA Talk Paper No. T86–51 (July 10, 1986); "Lemon–Lime Slice—Cyanide Threat," FDA Talk Paper No. T86–52 (July 11, 1986); "Foremost Dairy Threat," FDA Talk Paper No. T86–55 (July 23, 1986); "Acme Milk Products," FDA Talk Paper No. T87–14 (Feb. 25, 1987). In at least two instances, however, ingestion of cyanide in food resulted in death. *E.g.*, "Camden, N.J., Death," FDA Talk Paper No. T89–1 (Jan. 4, 1989).

The most widely reported food tampering involved the discovery by FDA of two grapes apparently contaminated with trace amounts of cyanide in a large shipment of fruit from Chile. HHS News No. P89–10 (Mar. 6, 1989). All Chilean fruit was detained until FDA completed further inspections, which found no evidence of contamination. HHS News Nos. P89–11 (Mar. 13, 1989), P89–13 (Mar. 17, 1989), P89–15 (Mar. 21, 1989), P89–19 (Apr. 14, 1989). The temporary detention had a severe impact on the

Chilean economy. When the Chilean fruit industry sought damages under the Federal Tort Claims Act, however, the courts rejected all claims on the ground that FDA's action fell within the discretionary function exception. *Balmaceda v. United States*, 815 F. Supp. 823 (E.D. Pa. 1992), *aff'd sub nom Fisher Bros. Sales v. United States*, 46 F.3d 279 (3d Cir. 1995) (en banc).

5. WEIGHT LABELING

The requirement in section 403(e)(2) of net weight labeling originated with the Gould Amendment to the 1906 Act, 37 Stat. 732 (1913). Although straightforward in principle, implementation of the requirement has presented two difficult problems, both of which involve the moisture content of food.

a. GAIN AND LOSS OF MOISTURE

Food packaged in a dry climate will gain moisture, and thus weight, when it is stored and marketed in a moister climate. Conversely, food packaged in a moist climate will lose weight when marketed in a dry climate. Accordingly, rules must be developed to govern the gain or loss of moisture during transportation and storage. When California adopted its own rules, which differed slightly from those followed by FDA and USDA, the Supreme Court held them preempted in *Jones v. Rath Packing Co.*, 430 U.S. 519 (1977), p. 1426 *infra*. Following the *Rath* decision, FDA held public hearings, 42 Fed. Reg. 55227 (Oct. 14, 1977), to reconsider its policy, and together with USDA proposed new regulations in 45 Fed. Reg. 53002, 53023 (Aug. 8, 1980). Under these proposed regulations, the two agencies would have established maximum allowable variations below the declared net weight for categories of food products.

For many years, the National Bureau of Standards (now the National Institute of Standards and Technology, or NIST) in the Department of Commerce has published handbooks explaining how to determine the net weight of consumer products. Following the August 1980 FDA and USDA proposals, the National Conference on Weights and Measures (NCWM), an organization of state and local officials supported by NIST, became the principal forum for building a consensus on determining the net weight of food products. Based upon the work of NCWM, performed in consultation with FDA and USDA, NIST issued revised versions of its two handbooks on weights and measures, which establish acceptable maximum allowable variances for moisture loss for food products. NIST HANDBOOK 44, SPECIFICATIONS, TOLERANCES AND OTHER TECHNICAL REQUIREMENTS FOR WEIGHING AND MEASURING DEVICES; NIST HANDBOOK 133, CHECKING THE CONTENTS OF PACKAGED GOODS. USDA therefore withdrew its August 1980 proposal and adopted the NIST handbooks in 54 Fed. Reg. 9370 (Mar. 6, 1989), 55 Fed. Reg. 49826 (Nov. 30, 1990). The USDA preamble stated that FDA intended to adopt the same approach, but FDA withdrew its August 1980 proposal in 56 Fed. Reg. 67440, 67447 (Dec. 30, 1991) without formally adopting the NIST handbooks. FDA later made clear, however, that although the agency was not adopting the NIST handbooks, they are largely consistent with FDA requirements for the declaration of net contents. 58 Fed. Reg. 2462,

2463 (Jan. 6, 1993). FDA subsequently proposed comprehensive new regulations governing net quantity of contents in 62 Fed. Reg. 9826 (Mar. 4, 1997), only to withdraw them in 69 Fed. Reg. 68831 (Apr. 26, 2004). Thus the declaration of net quantity provisions in 21 C.F.R. 101.105(a) & (q) remain unchanged, and the only reference to the NIST handbooks in FDA regulations is the decades-old incorporation of Handbook 44 in 21 C.F.R. 1.24(a)(6)(i) (exemption from required label statements for frozen desserts). Nevertheless, it therefore appears that compliance with the NIST handbooks will in virtually all circumstances satisfy both federal and state requirements.

b.   DRAINED WEIGHT

Many food products naturally contain juice or moisture or are traditionally packed in some type of liquid. At the same time FDA was considering the problem of moisture loss, it also confronted the issue of proper net weight declaration for these other food products as well.

Drained Weights for Processed Fruits and Vegetables
40 Fed. Reg. 52172 (November 7, 1975).

The Food and Drug Administration is proposing to require label declarations of the drained weight of canned fruit and vegetable products....

... Containers of the same product marked with the same net weight, were found to vary considerably in drained weight from packer to packer. Furthermore, many private label as well as brand name products are obtained from contract canners who may vary the fill of fruit or vegetable as commodity prices rise. Hence, petitioner [Consumers Union] contended, the lack of drained weight labeling totally frustrates the consumer's attempt to obtain the most fruit or vegetable for his money. Consumers Union was of the opinion that the value of providing drained weight labeling would far exceed the costs such a regulation would entail....

Thirteen comments opposed drained weight labeling of processed fruits and vegetables because of the inability to determine accurately a figure for the drained weight of the processed food prior to processing and storage. This inability to predetermine a value for the drained weight of the food was reported to result from differences in maturity of the food, differences in variety, variations within a particular variety resulting from growth conditions, differences due to seasonal changes, grade, and shape and size of the individual pieces....

Comments were received from manufacturers and two trade associations regarding the added costs of drained weight declaration. All indicated that there would be cost increases and that, in most cases, the increases would be passed on to the consumer....

The Commissioner believes the wisdom of a proposal to require drained weight labeling ultimately depends on the dollar value to the consumer of any benefit of knowing drained weight, when buying food, in relation to any increase in the product cost resulting from manufacturers' costs being passed on to the consumer.... Any final decision about a drained weight labeling regulation will depend primarily on an analysis of the economic information ultimately available to the Commissioner....

Drained Weight or Solid Content Weight for Canned Fruits and Vegetables

42 Fed. Reg. 62282 (December 9, 1977).

The Commissioner of Food and Drugs is proposing to require label declaration of the drained weight or, alternatively, the solid content weight (fill weight) on most canned fruits and vegetables....

In a comment dated May 5, 1976 on the drained weight proposal, the National Canners Association (NCA) ... proposed a regulation to require the declaration of the solid content weight as an alternative to the declaration of the drained weight.... In support of its proposal ... CA stated that the costs of compliance with drained weight labeling ... [are] prohibitive....

Battelle Columbus Laboratories (Battelle), Columbus, Ohio was commissioned by FDA to review the cost information submitted in comments on the drained weight proposal and to interview canners to obtain an independent cost estimate for drained weight labeling.... They estimated the cost of compliance with drained weight labeling ... at $74 million annually with an initial capital investment of $44.3 million....

To further support solid content labeling, NCA cited a consumer survey conducted for NCA by Opinion Research Corp. (ORC), Princeton, NJ, in which more than half of the consumers polled would not be willing to support a drained weight regulation costing 1 cent per can and still fewer consumers would support a regulation at greater expense.

The Commissioner notes that consumer surveys sponsored by Consumers Union in Detroit, MI, and Denver, CO, found that more than half of consumers polled would be willing to pay increased costs for drained weight labeling. Among those willing to pay for drained weight information, a majority of consumers polled in both cities would pay as much as 1 cent per can (41 percent in Detroit v. 63 percent in Denver)....

On November 12, 1976, NCA announced that food canners would begin to declare voluntarily the solid content weight (fill weight) in addition to the net weight on labels of canned fruits and vegetables; NCA said that the new weight information would assist consumers in making food buying selection. Further, NCA contended that it would give consumers, at far less cost, information as meaningful as the drained weight....

In that announcement, NCA stated that it has recommended that individual canners keep fill weight records and make these records available on a voluntary basis to FDA upon written request, for compliance purposes.... In the past, FDA has not considered proposing a requirement for declaration of the solid content weight (fill weight) because of the lack of effective means to determine compliance with the fill weight before canning. Since the weight of the solid contents of many canned fruits and vegetables changes after processing, FDA has no means of determining the accuracy of a fill weight declaration unless an FDA inspector is present at the time of processing to check the fill weights or, alternatively, unless canners make fill weight records available. . . .

The Commissioner . . . is not fully convinced that solid content labeling, although admittedly less costly, is superior to drained weight labeling. However, he is of the opinion that the voluntary solid content labeling program announced by NCA will provide a good opportunity to test the merits of solid content labeling. He is proposing . . . to permit canners to declare either the solid content weight (fill weight) or drained weight in conjunction with the net weight before he makes a final decision on this new proposal for drained weight or solid content (fill weight) labeling and the November 7, 1975 drained weight labeling proposal. . . .

NOTES

1. *Voluntary Solid Content Labeling.* The National Canners Association (now the Grocery Manufacturers Association) implemented its voluntary solid content labeling program. FDA withdrew its November 1975 and December 1977 proposals in 56 Fed. Reg. 67440, 67446 (Dec. 30, 1991).

2. *Descriptive Weight or Size Labeling.* Section 4(b) of the FPLA prohibits the use of "qualifying words or phrases" in conjunction with the net quantity of contents statement, but permits such words to be used elsewhere in labeling. Section 5(c)(1) authorizes FDA to establish standards for characterizing the size of packages, but this authority has not been exercised. Both provisions were designed to deal with the common practice of characterizing the size of consumer product packages with such terms as "giant" or "jumbo."

3. *Package Size.* Section 5(d) of the FPLA authorizes the Secretary of Commerce to establish voluntary product standards governing the sizes of retail packages to prevent "undue proliferation" in package sizes that "impairs the reasonable ability of consumers to make value comparisons." This provision, designed to preclude odd package sizes that hinder price comparison, requires use of the voluntary product standard procedures in 15 C.F.R. Part 10. Following an opinion of the Department of Justice that permitted the private formulation of package size standards without adherence to the Department of Commerce's formal procedures, several industries voluntarily established standard package sizes.

4. *Commentary. See generally* Eric C. Wall, *A Comprehensive Look at the Fair Packaging and Labeling Act of 1966 and the FDA Regulation of Deceptive Labeling and Packaging Practices: 1906 to Today* (2002), in Chapter V(B)(4) of the Electronic Book.

c. METRIC LABELING

Following enactment of the Metric Conversion Act of 1975, 89 Stat. 1007, many anticipated that the United States would rapidly convert to use of the metric system for weights and measures. Although that expectation has been disappointed, FDA issued Compliance Policy Guide No. 7150.17, 52 Fed. Reg. 8534 (Mar. 18, 1987), to establish an acceptable approach to the use of the metric system in declaring the net contents on the labels of FDA-regulated products. The Metric Usage Act of 1988, enacted as section 5164 of the Omnibus Trade and Competitiveness Act of 1988, 102 Stat.

1107, 1451, designates the metric system as the preferred system for trade and commerce.

Prior to 1992, FDA regulations governing label declaration of the net quantity of contents required that the declaration be expressed in terms of avoirdupois (English) rather than metric units, although a separate statement of the net quantity of contents in terms of the metric system was also permitted. In early 1992, however, Congress enacted the American Technology Preeminence Act of 1991, which contained an amendment to the Fair Packaging and Labeling Act to require that consumer commodities declare the net quantity of contents using the metric system "as the primary system for measuring quantity." 106 Stat. 7, 13 (1992). This provision caught the regulated industry completely by surprise. Congress quickly enacted legislation to amend the FPLA to repeal the metric requirement of the American Technology Preeminence Act and to replace it with a requirement for dual declaration of both the avoirdupois and metric content. 106 Stat. 847 (1992). FDA subsequently proposed regulations to implement this compromise statute in 58 Fed. Reg. 29716 (May 21, 1993) (foods) and 58 Fed. Reg. 67444 (Dec. 21, 1993) (other FDA-regulated products), but withdrew both proposals in 69 Fed. Reg. 68831, 68837 (Nov. 26, 2004). FDA also published proposed regulations to establish specific procedures for checking conformance to net contents labeling requirements, 62 Fed. Reg. 9826 (Mar. 4, 1997), but withdrew the proposal in 69 Fed. Reg. 68831, 68837 (Nov. 26, 2004).

6.   INGREDIENT LABELING

FDA has issued numerous regulations to explain and amplify the requirements for ingredient labeling in sections 403(i) and 403(k) of the Act. 21 C.F.R. 101.4, 101.22–35. The basic rule can be stated simply: All of the ingredients of a food must be listed, in descending order of predominance. Listing is to be by chemical name, rather than by class or function (*e.g.*, sweeteners or emulsifiers), except that spices, flavorings, and uncertified colorings *may* be listed generically. Chemical preservatives are the only class of food ingredient that must be declared both by chemical name and by function.

In recent years, attention has focused on the consumer's ability to identity and avoid specific ingredients, but in 1938 the new requirement of ingredient declaration was also viewed as a matter of economics.

David F. Cavers, *The Food, Drug, and Cosmetic Act of 1938: Its Legislative History and Its Substantive Provisions*

6 LAW AND CONTEMPORARY PROBLEMS 2 (1939).

. . . Deception with respect to foods is most frequently effected through creating the impression that a product is a commonly-known food when it does not in fact contain the ingredients which may properly be expected of that food. The tactic may result in both adulteration and misbranding. Suppose tea-seed oil is added to olive oil and the mixture labeled "olive oil."

Here both offenses are clearly present. Yet tea-seed oil is harmless and its presence cannot easily be detected. It should be possible to market such a compound so long as the public is not deceived.

The old Act had sought to escape this difficulty by providing that harmless "mixtures or compounds" might be offered for sale under their own "distinctive names," provided that an article was not "an imitation of or offered for sale under the distinctive name of another article" and, in the case of a compound, imitation or blend of foods not sold under a distinctive name, that the word "compound," "imitation" or "blend" plainly appear on the label. This solution provided a convenient loophole for evasion of the Act. To return to the example given above, adulterated olive oil could be sold as, say, "Spanola—For Salads," in an olive-hued can resembling those used for genuine olive oil, and an undiscriminating public would purchase it without any awareness that the distinctive name meant an inferior product. . . .

[handwritten margin note: problem w/ old Act— Similar packaging?]

NOTES

1. *Color in Dairy Products.* Section 403(k) of the FD&C Act specifically exempts artificial coloring in butter, cheese, and ice cream from ingredient labeling.

2. *Ingredients of Standardized Foods.* Under section 403(g), as enacted in 1938, the label of a standardized food did not have to declare any mandatory ingredients and had to declare only those optional ingredients the standard required be declared. For many years food standards required the labeling of only a few optional ingredients. In 37 Fed. Reg. 5120 (Mar. 10, 1972), 38 Fed. Reg. 2137 (Jan. 19, 1973), FDA urged that the labels of standardized foods voluntarily be revised to declare all ingredients. At the same time the agency undertook to revise existing standards to mandate disclosure of all optional ingredients. It took the position that where a standard permitted more than one form of a mandatory ingredient the form chosen was to be considered "optional," thus requiring full ingredient disclosure. The 1990 Nutrition Labeling and Education Act amended section 403(i) to require the listing of all ingredients in standardized food.

3. *Chemical Preservatives.* In 38 Fed. Reg. 20745 (Aug. 2, 1973), 39 Fed. Reg. 5627 (Feb. 14, 1974), FDA promulgated 21 C.F.R. 101.22(j), interpreting section 403(k) to require that a preservative be declared in the statement of ingredients both by its chemical name and by a separate description of its function.

4. *Flavorings.* Section 403(i)(2) of the Act permits generic declaration of flavors in the ingredient statement. In addition, however, FDA has promulgated complex regulations in 21 C.F.R. 101.22 governing prominent label disclosure of natural and artificial flavoring. 38 Fed. Reg. 2139 (Jan. 19, 1973), 38 Fed. Reg. 20718 (Aug. 2, 1973), 38 Fed. Reg. 27622 (Oct. 5, 1973), 38 Fed. Reg. 33284 (Dec. 3, 1973). Section 403(k) mandates the declaration of the presence of artificial flavoring, and FDA requires that this declaration be placed so as to be "likely to be read by the ordinary person under customary conditions of purchase and use." 21 C.F.R. 101.22(c). See also the USDA flavor regulations for meat food products promulgated in 52 Fed. Reg. 30922 (Aug. 18, 1987), 55 Fed. Reg. 7289 (Mar. 1, 1990), 7 C.F.R. 317.2(f)(1)(i).

5. *Colors.* Section 403(i)(2), as enacted in 1938, also permitted generic declaration of all colors. On January 3, 1978, FDA Commissioner Donald Kennedy wrote to the 100 largest manufacturers and distributors of packaged foods, requesting that they voluntarily label the specific colors used in their foods:

This Agency believes that all colors added to a food product should be identified by name in the list of ingredients appearing on the product. Only through full ingredient disclosure can the consumer exercise in full measure the fundamental right to choose to be informed, and to be assured of safety. I believe that label declaration of colors, in particular, is essential to individuals who may be sensitive to certain color additives or who, for various reasons, wish to avoid products containing them. These individuals should be given the means to make an informed choice....

FDA proposed to allow the declaration of specific color additives in abbreviated form, by deleting the prefix "FD&C" in 50 Fed. Reg. 23815 (June 6, 1985), and explicitly permitted the use of abbreviated names pending publication of a final regulation, but the proposal was withdrawn in 69 Fed. Reg. 68831, 68835 (Nov. 26, 2004). The Nutrition Labeling and Education Act of 1990 (NLEA) amended section 403(i)(2) to require the declaration of all colors required to be certified under section 721(c), *i.e.*, all FD&C color additives. Under section 403(k) of the Act and 21 C.F.R. 101.22(c), the presence of artificial colors, as well as artificial flavors, must be prominently declared.

6. *Legislative Reform Proposals.* Proposals to amend section 403(i) to require specific labeling of colors, flavorings, and spices have been before Congress for many years. In 44 Fed. Reg. 75990 (Dec. 21, 1979) FDA reiterated its intention to seek legislative authority to require label declaration of the specific identity of colors and spices, but not of flavors because the number of flavors in a single processed food may exceed forty. The agency also said it would seek to repeal the proviso in section 403(k) which exempts butter, cheese, and ice cream from label declaration of added artificial color. The 1990 NLEA, however, amended section 403(i) only to require the declaration of colors required to be certified, and left section 403(k) unchanged.

7. *Percentage Ingredient Labeling.* FDA proposed a uniform method for declaration of the percentage of any ingredient in the ingredient statement, when this is done voluntarily by the manufacturer, in 39 Fed. Reg. 20885 (June 14, 1974). The proposal was withdrawn in 51 Fed. Reg. 15653 (Apr. 25, 1986).

8. *Reconditioning After Condemnation.* The requirement that all ingredients be labeled can have unforeseen consequences. After a product labeled "honey" was condemned as misbranded because it was in fact table syrup rather than honey, the court in *United States v. An Article of Food ... Pure Raw Honey,* 550 F. Supp. 15 (W.D. Okl. 1982), upheld FDA's refusal to allow the product to be relabeled because the distributor could not prove that there were no undeclared additional ingredients present in the food.

9. *Ingredient Nomenclature.* Although 21 C.F.R. 101.4(a) & (b) require that a food ingredient be declared on the label by a "specific" common or usual name, the regulations do not specify how that name is to be determined. In practice, FDA has determined the specific name for food ingredients when it has promulgated standards of identity and published food additive or GRAS regulations.

10. *Change in Ingredient Nomenclature.* Where a food manufacturer wishes to shorten or simplify the chemical name of a food ingredient, FDA has customarily permitted use of the shortened version in parentheses following the full chemical or biological name for a period of time, and eventually allowed use of the shortened version alone. For example, the agency's initial GRAS affirmation regulation for rapeseed oil with a low erucic acid content, 47 Fed. Reg. 35342 (Aug. 13, 1982), 50 Fed. Reg. 3745 (Jan. 28, 1985), specified the name "low erucic acid rapeseed oil." The petitioners requested use of the specific name "canola oil," but FDA replied that this term had no meaning in the United States and suggested that it be used in parentheses following the name the agency had designated. Several years later, FDA changed the name to "canola oil." 53 Fed. Reg. 36067 (Sept. 16, 1988); 53 Fed. Reg.

52681 (Dec. 29, 1988), codified at 21 C.F.R. 184.1555(c). See also 43 Fed. Reg. 54238 (Nov. 21, 1978) and 49 Fed. Reg. 22796 (June 1, 1984), establishing the specific name "cocoa butter substitute primarily from palm oil" for "1–palmitoy/1–2–oleoyl–3–stearin" without ever requiring that the former be used in parentheses following the latter. Because food ingredient nomenclature has a low priority at FDA, it has been suggested that the designation of specific names should be undertaken by the National Academy of Sciences (which publishes the Food Chemicals Codex) or a consortium of organizations like those responsible for designating United States Adopted Names (USAN) for drugs, *see* p. 534 Note 1 *infra*, but no action has been taken to implement this approach.

COMMENT: FOOD ALLERGENS

Many individuals are allergic to even very common food ingredients. A principal reason the FD&C Act required ingredient labeling was to enable allergic consumers to "protect themselves from the consumption of foods to which they are allergic by the information made available to them" under the ingredient labeling provisions of the new law. S. Rep. No. 493, 73d Cong. 2d Sess. 12 (1934). Based upon reports of allergic reactions to FD&C Yellow No. 5, FDA published a regulation in 42 Fed. Reg. 6835 (Feb. 4, 1977), 44 Fed. Reg. 37212 (June 26, 1979), 45 Fed. Reg. 60419 (Sept. 12, 1980), 21 C.F.R. 74.705(d)(2), requiring label disclosure of this color additive, but the agency rejected an outright ban, p. 449 *infra*. When it approved FD&C Yellow No. 6, 51 Fed. Reg. 41765 (Nov. 19, 1986), FDA also required specific label declaration of this color. The Certified Color Manufacturers Association objected on the ground that there was insufficient evidence of allergic reactions to the color additive and that FDA had failed to provide an opportunity for public comment. After the agency rejected these objections in 52 Fed. Reg. 21505 (June 8, 1987), the CCMA contested the requirement in court. Rather than litigate the issue, FDA agreed to suspend and withdraw the label declaration requirement and commence notice-and-comment rulemaking. 53 Fed. Reg. 49138 (Dec. 6, 1988). The agency later issued proposed rules, never finalized, to require label declaration of Yellow No. 6. 60 Fed. Reg. 37611 (July 21, 1995); 61 Fed. Reg. 8372 (March 4, 1996). More recently, FDA proposed to require label disclosure of the color additives cochineal extract and carmine because of severe allergic reactions, including anaphylaxis. 71 Fed. Reg. 4839 (Jan. 30, 2006).

Based upon new information indicating allergic reactions to sulfiting agents in food, FDA took action requiring label declaration of sulfites in food if they can be detected using an analytical method specified by FDA and sensitive to 10 ppm. 50 Fed. Reg. 13306 (Apr. 3, 1985); 51 Fed. Reg. 25012 (July 9, 1986), codified at 21 C.F.R. 101.100(a)(4).

As a result of its experience with allergic reactions to Yellow 6, aspartame, and sulfites, FDA established an ad hoc advisory committee in 49 Fed. Reg. 15021 (Apr. 16, 1984), initially to review hypersensitivity to sulfites and later to review all food constituents. Based upon an internal report by Linda R. Tollefson, A Computerized Monitoring System for Recording and Assessing Adverse Reactions to Food Products and Additives Regulated By the Food and Drug Administration (July 1985), FDA created

Form 2516 for reporting complaints of injury from food products. In an article published in 15 FDA DRUG BULL. 34 (Dec. 1985), physicians and other health professionals were asked to inform FDA of "any severe and well-documented non-microbiologic reactions associated with food." *See* Linda R. Tollefson, *Monitoring Adverse Reactions to Food Additives in the U.S. Food and Drug Administration*, 8 REG. TOX. & PHARMACOL. 438 (1988). For an overview of food allergy, *see* Hugh A. Sampson et al., *Food Allergy*, 258 J.A.M.A. 2886 (Nov. 27, 1987); Hugh A. Sampson and Dean D. Metcalfe, *Food Allergies*, 268 J.A.M.A. 2840 (Nov. 25, 1992); Hugh A. Sampson, *Food Allergy*, 278 J.A.M.A. 1888 (Dec. 10, 1997).

FDA has made no attempt to specify the frequency of adverse reactions that warrants declaration of an ingredient or justifies a ban. Allergic reactions to food are common. In the late 1980s, food allergies were estimated to affect up to 8 percent of children and 2 percent of adults. Dean D. Metcalfe, *Diseases of Food Hypersensitivity*, 321 NEW ENG. J. MED. 255 (July 27, 1989). Fifteen years later those estimates have doubled to 4 percent for adults.

Faced with this apparent increase in food allergy, the food industry, as well as FDA, recognized that more informative labeling was needed. For a complete history of the development of food labeling policy to address food allergen labeling, see Laura E. Derr, *When Food is Poison: The History, Consequences, and Limitations of the Food Allergen Labeling and Consumer Protection Act of 2004*, 61 FOOD & DRUG L.J. 65 (2006).

Although FDA's efforts to require complete ingredient labeling beginning in the early 1970s were inspired by concerns about allergic reactions other ingredient labeling policies made it difficult for some consumers to detect the presence of allergens. As examples, the source of some ingredients was not apparent from the common or usual name itself, incidental additives were exempt from label declaration, spices and flavorings were declared only by collective terms, and some labels declared that the food "may contain" ingredients because formulations varied from batch to batch. FDA responded by requiring specific labeling to address particular allergens, such as FD&C Yellow No. 5, sulfites, aspartame, and monosodium glutamate, but it announced no general reform of agency policy.

This changed in June 1996, when FDA issued a notice to food manufacturers directly addressing the labeling of food allergens. FDA Center for Food Safety and Applied Nutrition, Notice to Manufacturers: Label Declarations of Allergic Substances in Foods (June 10, 1996). Reversing prior policy, FDA declared that an incidental additive must be declared as an ingredient when the additive contains a "known allergen;" that ambiguous declarations such as "may contain" should not be used to deal with avoidable cross-contamination; and that allergens present in spices, flavor, and color should also be declared. A public meeting announced by the agency in 66 Fed. Reg. 38591 (July 25, 2001) was held to determine what additional action might be necessary to provide allergic consumers with adequate information on product labels. This was followed by a notice proposing a regulation to require the labeling of the eight most prevalent food allergens. 68 Fed. Reg. 72889 (Dec. 22, 2003).

In response, the food industry established voluntary guidelines for label disclosure of the so-called Big Eight allergens beginning in the early 2000s. These efforts resulted in enactment of the Food Allergen Labeling and Consumer Protection Act of 2004, 118 Stat. 891, 905. The statute added section 201(qq) to the FD&C Act, defining the term "major food allergen" to include eight foods: milk, egg, fish, crustacean shell fish, tree nuts, wheat, peanuts, and soy beans. New section 403(w) requires the label of a food that contains a major food allergen to declare the presence of the allergen unless FDA issues an exemption. A flavoring, coloring, or incidental additive that contains a major food allergen is subject to the same requirement. Moreover, under section 403(x), a spice, flavor, color, or incidental additive that contains a food allergen other than a major food allergen must also disclose its presence as determined by FDA regulations. Section 403(w) is self-executing and do not require the promulgation of regulations. In 70 Fed. Reg. 35258 (June 17, 2005), FDA published a draft report on approaches to establish thresholds for major food allergens, below which they would be exempt from label declaration under the new statute.

The Allergen Act did not deal with the issue of labeling to disclose the possible cross-contamination of a food with another food that contains a major allergen, but it did require FDA to report back to Congress on this issue. The FDA report, issued in July 2006, found that the food industry uses a variety of labeling approaches to communicate potential cross-contamination and that consumers preferred "Allergy Information: May contain _____."

In a letter from FDA CFSAN Deputy Director for Regulatory Affairs Michael M. Landa to Melanie Fairchild–Dzanis (May 11, 2006), FDA rejected a petition for a qualified disease prevention claim that use of a partially hydrolyzed whey protein infant formula represents a reduced risk of an allergic reaction as compared to whole cow's milk. FDA concluded that there was "no credible evidence" to support the requested claim.

In the early 1970s a physician concluded that the additives in food were causing an increase in hyperactivity in children.

Food Additives and Hyperactivity

199 Science 516 (1978).

For the past 5 years, many members of the public have been intrigued by a theory that food additives cause hyperactivity. This theory was put forth in 1973 by Ben F. Feingold, an allergist at the Kaiser–Permanente Medical Center in San Francisco. Feingold developed a diet in which foods containing synthetic colors, synthetic flavors, and salicylates are banned. He reported that 50 percent of hyperactive children dramatically improved their behavior when they followed his diet.

Last year, in response to the huge acclaim for the Feingold diet, J. Preston Harley and his associates at the University of Wisconsin tested the effects of the diet with a controlled clinical trial. Forty-six hyperactive boys who participated were observed for 8 weeks by parents, teachers, neurologists, and trained observers. Some of the children followed an additive-free diet and some did not, but neither the children, their parents nor the other observers knew which child followed which diet. . . .

The results of this study failed to confirm Feingold's claims. In fact, Harley and his associates report no effects of the additive-free diet on hyperactivity of school-age children. . . .

———

Unique issues arise where an allergen is both an ingredient in and of itself and a constituent of other ingredients, as is true with monosodium glutamate (MSG). Under 21 C.F.R. 101.22(h)(5) & (7), MSG must be declared in the statement of ingredients of a food when it is added as a single ingredient but not when it is added as a natural constituent of another substance. In 1994, Truth in Labeling Campaign filed a citizen petition requesting disclosure of free glutamic acid for all food and an accompanying warning to assist people who are MSG-sensitive. When FDA did not respond to the petition within 180 days, the organization brought suit contending that the present MSG regulations allowed misleading labeling. FDA subsequently published an advance notice of proposed rulemaking to obtain public comment on what action is necessary to protect consumers from inadvertently ingesting levels of MSG or other forms of free glutamate that could cause an adverse reaction, and specifically whether additional labeling requirements are necessary. 61 Fed. Reg. 48102 (Sept. 12, 1996). FDA then denied the citizen petition and suggested that the petitioner respond to the Federal Register notice. The District Court hearing the Campaign's suit reviewed the extensive history of this matter and granted summary judgment to FDA. *Truth in Labeling Campaign v. Shalala*, 999 F. Supp. 1289 (E.D. Mo. 1998).

COMMENT: INGREDIENT LABELING FOR ALCOHOLIC BEVERAGES

Alcoholic beverages have been regulated as food under both the 1906 Act and the FD&C Act. The Federal Alcohol Administration Act, 27 U.S.C. 201 *et seq.*, administered by the Alcohol and Tobacco Tax and Trade Bureau (TTB) of the Department of Treasury, formerly the Bureau of Alcohol, Tobacco, and Firearms (BATF), provides independent authority to regulate the labeling of alcoholic beverages. Regulations to implement this authority have been promulgated in 27 C.F.R. Parts 4, 5, and 7. For many years, although BATF did not require labeling of ingredients in distilled spirits, wine, or beer, FDA did not itself insist that these products' labels comply with section 403 of the FD&C Act (except for wine with less than seven percent alcohol, which is not regulated under the FAA Act). However, as FDA became convinced of the desirability of complete ingredient labeling of foods, it began to pressure BATF to require such labeling for alcoholic beverages. When BATF concluded that ingredient labeling was likely to be costly for the industry and not useful for consumers, 39 Fed.

Reg. 27812 (Aug. 1, 1974), 40 Fed. Reg. 6349 & 6354 (Feb. 11, 1975), 40 Fed. Reg. 52613 (Nov. 11, 1975), FDA announced that it was abandoning its historical posture and would require compliance by all alcoholic beverages with the labeling requirements of the FD&C Act, including section 403(i), the ingredient labeling provision. 40 Fed. Reg. 54455 (Nov. 24, 1975).

The following year, in a suit brought in Owensboro, Kentucky by producers of distilled spirits and wine, alcoholic beverages were held exempt from the labeling requirements of the FD&C Act. *Brown–Forman Distillers Corp. v. Mathews*, 435 F. Supp. 5 (W.D. Ky. 1976). The Department of Justice declined to allow FDA to appeal this ruling after BATF agreed to initiate rulemaking to require at least partial ingredient labeling of alcoholic beverages. After BATF issued this proposal, 44 Fed. Reg. 6740 (Feb. 2, 1979), the *Brown–Forman* plaintiffs unsuccessfully asked the court to hold FDA and its Commissioner in contempt of the earlier order because of their efforts to pressure BATF into requiring ingredient labeling under the FAA Act. *Brown–Forman Distillers Corp. v. Califano*, Food Drug Cosm. L. Rep. (CCH) ¶ 38,245 (W.D. Ky. 1979).

Following BATF's February 1979 proposal, the alcohol beverage industry sought unsuccessfully to obtain a directive in the Bureau's pending appropriations legislation prohibiting the use of funds to require ingredient labeling for alcoholic beverages. BATF then published final regulations requiring alcoholic beverage ingredient labeling in 45 Fed. Reg. 40538 (June 13, 1980). After review under the standards of Executive Order No. 12291, 46 Fed. Reg. 13193 (Feb. 19, 1981), however, it rescinded the regulations, 46 Fed. Reg. 24962 (May 4, 1981), 46 Fed. Reg. 55093 (Nov. 6, 1981). This action was held unlawful in *Center for Science in the Public Interest v. Department of the Treasury*, 573 F. Supp. 1168 (D.D.C. 1983), *appeal dismissed as moot*, 727 F.2d 1161 (D.C. Cir. 1984), and BATF thereupon reinstated the regulations, 48 Fed. Reg. 10309 (Mar. 11, 1983). It subsequently proposed to reconsider the entire matter in 48 Fed. Reg. 27782 (June 17, 1983). In this new rulemaking, BATF determined that the only ingredient whose labeling could be justified on health grounds was FD&C Yellow No. 5, and it therefore again revoked its ingredient labeling requirement except with respect to that allergenic color additive. 48 Fed. Reg. 45549 (Oct. 6, 1983). In a new suit by the Center for Science in the Public Interest challenging BATF's rescission of the reinstated regulations, the District Court once again held that BATF failed to provide a reasoned explanation for its refusal to mandate ingredient labeling. The Court of Appeals reversed this ruling, concluding that the BATF decision was supported by the record. *Center for Science in the Public Interest v. Department of the Treasury*, 797 F.2d 995 (D.C. Cir. 1986).

Subsequent to mandating the disclosure of FD&C Yellow No. 5, BATF required the disclosure of sulfites on alcoholic beverage labels based on a health concern. 50 Fed. Reg. 26001 (June 24, 1985), 51 Fed. Reg. 34706 (Sept. 30, 1986). BATF issued an advance notice of proposed rulemaking in 58 Fed. Reg. 42517 (Aug. 10, 1993) to determine whether FDA's nutrition labeling requirements should be adopted, but did not take further action on the matter. In *Rubin v. Coors Brewing Co.*, 514 U.S. 476 (1995), the

Supreme Court struck down as unconstitutional, in violation of the First Amendment's freedom of speech provision, a prohibition in the FAA Act against alcohol content statements on beer labels.

Recently, in response to a petition, TTB published an advance notice of proposed rulemaking soliciting public comment on the possibility of requiring alcoholic beverage labels to declare alcohol content, serving size, calories, ingredients, servings per container, macronutrient content, and advice on moderate drinking. 70 Fed. Reg. 22274 (Apr. 29, 2005). An ''Alcohol Facts'' box and a ''Serving Facts'' box were presented for comment.

The *Brown–Forman* decision, *supra*, holds that the labeling requirements of the FD&C Act are supplanted by the product-specific provisions of the FAA Act. Other cases, however, have held that the adulteration provisions of section 402(a) do apply to alcoholic beverages. *United States v. 1,800.2625 Wine Gallons of Distilled Spirits*, 121 F. Supp. 735 (W.D. Mo. 1954); *United States v. Commonwealth Brewing Corp.*, Food Drug Cosm. L. Rep. (CCH) ¶ 50,051.43 (D. Mass. 1945). *See* Iver P. Cooper, *The FDA, the BATF, and Liquor Labeling: A Case Study of Interagency Jurisdictional Conflict*, 34 FOOD DRUG COSM. L.J. 370 (1979); Elaine Moore Byszewski, *What's in the Wine?: A History of FDA's Role*, 57 FOOD & DRUG L.J. 545 (2002); articles in Chapter V(O) of the Electronic Book.

The Homeland Security Act of 2002 divided BATF into two new agencies: The Bureau of Alcohol, Tobacco, Firearms, and Explosives (now called ATF) which became part of the Department of Justice and the Alcohol and Tobacco Tax and Trade Bureau (now called TTB) which was left in the Department of the Treasury. These new Bureaus were created in 68 Fed. Reg. 3584, 3744 (Jan. 24, 2003). TTB is responsible for administration of the Federal Alcohol Administration Act and related statutes and ATF is a law enforcement agency.

———

As FDA has moved in the direction of insisting that all food ingredients be specifically labeled in order of predominance, it has been pressed to address the practical difficulties confronting manufacturers who adjust the ingredients in their products in response to changes in the price and seasonal fluctuations in the characteristics of basic ingredients.

Food Labeling: Ingredient Labeling Exemptions

42 Fed. Reg. 43095 (August 26, 1977).

In the FEDERAL REGISTER of January 6, 1976 (41 FR 1156), FDA promulgated regulations amending § 101.4 concerning the manner in which ingredients are to be declared on the labels of finished foods. One of the results of the promulgation of these regulations is that Trade Correspondence Number 94 (TC–94) was revoked in its entirety. TC–94 had provided that manufacturers of bakery products using ingredients acting as leavening, yeast nutrients and dough conditioners could declare these ingredients as such on labels of bakery products in place of the specific common or usual names of these ingredients.

In a final rule published in the FEDERAL REGISTER of February 12, 1976 (41 FR 6242), FDA issued amendments to the definitions and standards of identity for bakery products and required label declaration of all optional ingredients. . . .

rule

The American Bakers Association (ABA) . . . has submitted two petitions requesting relief. . . . One petition proposes that the Commissioner of Food and Drugs amend § 101.4 to permit all ingredients that act as leavening agents, yeast nutrients, or dough conditioners in bakery products to be listed together in order of predominance in parentheses following the appropriate collective term that describes the ingredients' function.

Baker's

petitions

The second petition requests that the Commissioner amend the definition and standard of identity for bread in § 136.110 to permit the declaration of dough conditioners (other than potassium iodate or calcium iodate) that may be added to bakery products so that the label declaration would be the same whether or not specific dough conditioners were present in the finished food, provided that such declarations are followed by the statement "used as needed." . . .

In its petition to amend the standard of identity for bread, ABA states that bakers have found it necessary to add certain safe and suitable ingredients from time to time, depending on raw material variations. For example, if a wheat crop is "weak," it may be necessary to add additional dough strengtheners to obtain a uniformly high quality product. Although bakers know that these ingredients may be needed to produce an acceptable food, they find it impossible to predict in advance what ingredients will be needed at any particular time. . . .

[T]he Commissioner is proposing an amendment to § 101.4 to provide that ingredients that act as dough conditioners, yeast nutrients, or leavening agents may be listed by their specific common or usual names in the ingredient statement in parentheses following the appropriate collective names "leavening," "yeast nutrients," or "dough conditioners." The exemption stated in this manner will apply to all foods utilizing these functional ingredients. . . .

On the assumption that the manufacturers are unable to predict in advance the specific dough conditioners, yeast nutrients, and leavening agents to be used in a particular food and they are unable to maintain a uniform quantity of these ingredients in a formulation because of raw material variation, the Commissioner is proposing that the specific dough-conditioners, yeast nutrients, and leavening agents need not be listed in descending order of predominance.

In addition, the Commissioner is proposing that ingredients that act as dough conditioners, yeast nutrients, or leavening agents in foods, but which are used intermittently in foods, may be declared in the ingredient statement even though they may not be present in the finished food, provided the ingredients are identified by words indicating that they may not be present, such as "dough conditioners (ammonium chloride and/or L-cysteine)" or "dough conditioners (one or more of the following: Ammonium chloride, L-cystgine, potassium bromate)." . . .

The Commissioner is of the opinion that the proposed exemption from ingredient labeling for foods will provide sufficient flexibility for the baking industry while retaining complete ingredient disclosure for consumers. Furthermore, because the proposed exemption is a general labeling provision applicable to both standardized and nonstandardized foods, there is no need to amend individual standards of identity. . . .

NOTES

1. *Collective Ingredient Labeling.* FDA promulgated final regulations in 43 Fed. Reg. 24518 (June 6, 1978), 21 C.F.R. 101.4(b)(16)–(18). Similarly, in 43 Fed. Reg. 16347 (Apr. 18, 1978), 48 Fed. Reg. 8053 (Feb. 25, 1983), FDA permitted the labeling of firming agents in food to be declared in an ingredient statement by the collective name "firming agents" followed in parentheses by the specific name of each firming agent used albeit not in descending order of predominance. The agency has, however, since expressed concern that consumers who are allergic to particular ingredients may not be able to protect themselves adequately if alternative ingredient declaration were permitted on a widespread basis.

2. *Order of Predominance.* In 43 Fed. Reg. 14677 (Apr. 7, 1978), FDA proposed to permit manufacturers of bakery products to list ingredients present in their products at levels of 2 percent or less by weight at the end of the ingredient statement in other than descending order of predominance. The proposal was designed to enable manufacturers to respond to seasonal variations and changes in raw materials. FDA's final regulations expanded this proposal to include all food products. 51 Fed. Reg. 2405 (Jan. 16, 1986); 55 Fed. Reg. 17431 (Apr. 25, 1990), codified at 21 C.F.R. 101.4(a)(2).

3. *Consumer Understanding.* Apparently many, perhaps most, consumers do not understand that food ingredients are listed in descending order of predominance. FDA has considered the possibility of requiring a label statement of this fact. For an economic analysis of this approach, *see* Arthur D. Little, Inc., Economic Impact Analysis of a Declaration That Ingredients are Listed in Descending Order of Predominance, Report to FDA under HHS Contract No. 223–79–8052 (May 19, 1981).

4. *Exempt Incidental Ingredients.* Incidental additives that are present in a food at insignificant levels and do not achieve any technical or functional effect in the food are exempt from label declaration under 21 C.F.R. 101.100(a)(3). In the only reported case interpreting this provision, *Sea Snack Foods, Inc. v. United States*, Food Drug Cosm. L. Rep. (CCH) ¶ 38,062 (D.D.C. 1987), the court upheld FDA's determination that the processing aid involved served a functional purpose in the finished food and thus must be declared on the label. In part to clarify that sulfites are not incidental additives when used in food, FDA promulgated regulations requiring the declaration of sulfites as part of ingredient labeling. 50 Fed. Reg. 13306 (Apr. 3, 1985); 51 Fed. Reg. 25012 (July 9, 1986), codified at 21 C.F.R. 101.100(a)(4).

7.   Label Warnings

The FD&C Act contains no specific authority for FDA to require warning statements on food labels. Until the 1970s such warnings were rare. In 38 Fed. Reg. 6191 (Mar. 7, 1973), 40 Fed. Reg. 8912 (Mar. 3, 1975),

FDA promulgated a regulation, now codified at 21 C.F.R. 101.17, establishing a framework for mandatory label warnings under section 201(n) of the FD&C Act. Since then, the number of warnings required by regulation or by statute as well as provided voluntarily by food manufacturers has increased significantly, and this trend can be expected to continue.

1. *Safe Use.* The first FDA warning statement regulation prescribed warnings against unsafe use of self-pressurized containers for food products by inhaling the propellant, spraying in eyes, or incinerating the container. 40 Fed. Reg. 8912 (Mar. 3, 1975), codified at 21 C.F.R. 101.17(a), (b).

2. *Inborn Errors of Metabolism.* Many individuals are born with natural metabolic defects that require them to avoid specific food constituents. For example, phenylketonurics must avoid the amino acid phenylalanine. Accordingly, 21 C.F.R. 172.804(e)(2) requires that any food containing the sweetener aspartame must bear the following prominent statement: "Phenylketonurics: contains phenylalanine." Similarly, a diet beverage containing a combination of nutritive and nonnutritive sweeteners was required under 21 C.F.R. 100.130(d)(3) to bear the statement: "Contains sugar(s); not for use by diabetics without advice of a physician," but section 100.130 was revoked in 61 Fed. Reg. 27771, 27778 (June 3, 1996).

3. *Saccharin.* Following the results of studies indicating that saccharin may be an animal carcinogen, FDA proposed in 42 Fed. Reg. 19996 (Apr. 15, 1977) to prohibit saccharin in food. Congress responded by enacting the Saccharin Study and Labeling Act, 91 Stat. 1451 (1977), adding Sections 403(o) and 403(p) to the FD&C Act. Section 403(o) required the following statement on the labels and labeling of food containing saccharin:

Use of This Product May Be Hazardous to Your Health.
THIS PRODUCT CONTAINS SACCHARIN WHICH HAS BEEN DETERMINED TO CAUSE CANCER IN LABORATORY ANIMALS

Section 403(p) required a notice containing the same saccharin statement at every retail establishment selling food containing saccharin for other than immediate consumption. FDA had published tentative guidelines and announced a public hearing in anticipation of the enactment of the statute in 42 Fed. Reg. 59119 (Nov. 15, 1977) and, after the public hearing and enactment of the statute, issued final guidelines in 42 Fed. Reg. 62209 (Dec. 9, 1977). The agency held a public hearing specifically to consider the retail establishment notice, announced in 42 Fed. Reg. 62160 (Dec. 9, 1977) and promulgated regulations governing the retail establishment notice in 43 Fed. Reg. 8793 (Mar. 3, 1978). Almost two decades later, Congress repealed section 403(p), 110 Stat. 882 (1996), and FDA revoked the retail establishment notice regulations in 61 Fed. Reg. 50770 (Sept. 27, 1996), 62 Fed. Reg. 3791 (Jan. 27, 1997). This is the only instance where Congress or FDA has imposed the requirement of a retail establishment warning for an FDA-regulated product.

Because the December 1977 guidelines regarding the warning statement to be included in labels and labeling proved to be sufficient, FDA never promulgated regulations to implement section 403(o) of the Act. FDA did propose to require that vending machines bear the saccharin warning in 43 Fed. Reg. 5851 (Feb. 10, 1978), but withdrew this proposal in 43 Fed. Reg. 45613 (Oct. 3, 1978) on the ground that it would not add significantly to consumer awareness of the health risks of saccharin. Based on accumulated scientific tests demonstrating that the original concern about the carcinogenicity of saccharin was unfounded, Congress repealed section 403(o) in 114 Stat. 2763, 2763A–73 (2000).

4. *Alcoholic Beverages.* In the Alcoholic Beverage Labeling Act of 1988, 102 Stat. 4181, 4518, 27 U.S.C. 213 *et seq.*, Congress required the following statement on the container of every alcoholic beverage: "GOVERNMENT WARNING: (1) According to the Surgeon General, women should not drink alcoholic beverages during pregnancy because of the risk of birth defects. (2) Consumption of alcoholic beverages impairs your ability to drive a car or operate machinery, and may cause health problems." BATF implemented this statute with regulations published in 54 Fed. Reg. 7160 (Feb. 16, 1989), 55 Fed. Reg. 5414 (Feb. 14, 1990).

5. *Protein Diet Products.* In the mid–1970s, low calorie protein-based diets were marketed for rapid weight loss. Following reports of illness and death associated with these products, FDA required label warnings. 42 Fed. Reg. 61285 (Dec. 2, 1977); 45 Fed. Reg. 22904 (Apr. 4, 1980). Two courts determined that FDA failed to justify the specific warnings. *National Nutritional Foods Association v. Goyan*, 493 F. Supp. 1044 (S.D.N.Y. 1980); *Council for Responsible Nutrition v. Goyan*, Food Drug Cosm. L. Rep. (CCH) ¶ 38,057 (D.D.C. 1980). On remand, FDA amended the regulations. 47 Fed. Reg. 25379 (June 11, 1982); 49 Fed. Reg. 13679 (Apr. 6, 1984), codified at 21 C.F.R. 101.17(d). Both the required warnings and the requirement that they appear on the principal display panel were subsequently upheld. *Council for Responsible Nutrition v. Novitch*, Food Drug Cosm. L. Rep. (CCH) ¶ 38,281 (D.D.C. 1984); *National Nutritional Foods Association v. Novitch*, 589 F. Supp. 798 (S.D.N.Y. 1984); *National Nutritional Foods Association v. Young*, 598 F. Supp. 1107 (S.D.N.Y. 1984).

6. *Side Effects.* Many food ingredients produce undesirable but temporary physiological effects in some consumers. Food labels bear warnings about many of these side effects. For example, 21 C.F.R. 184.1835(e) requires that any food whose reasonably foreseeable consumption may result in a daily ingestion of 50 grams of sorbitol shall bear the statement: "Excess consumption may have a laxative effect." When the food additive Olestra was approved by FDA in 61 Fed. Reg. 3118 (Jan. 30, 1996), 21 C.F.R. 172.867, FDA required the following label warning statement: "Olestra may cause abdominal cramping and loose stools." Following the conduct of studies which demonstrated that this warning was not supported by the evidence, FDA revoked this requirement. 68 Fed. Reg. 46364 (Aug. 5, 2003); 69 Fed. Reg. 29428 (May 24, 2004). More than 50 common food substances are also used as active ingredients in nonprescription drug products. *See, e.g.*, 50 Fed. Reg. 2124, 2132 (Jan. 15, 1985), discussing the use of fiber as both an active ingredient in OTC laxative drugs and an ingredient in high fiber food products. The labeling of food containing these ingredients can be expected to bear warnings comparable to any required when they are included in a nonprescription drug.

COMMENT: CALIFORNIA PROPOSITION 65

Proposition 65 was adopted as an Initiative Measure under Article II, section 8, of the California Constitution by the voters of California on November 4, 1986. It is codified in chapter 6.6 of the California Health and Safety Code, Sections 25249.5–25249.13. Proposition 65 requires the California Governor to publish, and periodically to revise, a list of natural and synthetic chemicals "known to the State to cause cancer or reproductive toxicity." Any listed chemical is presumed to be a health hazard, and any individual exposed to a listed chemical must be given a "clear and reasonable warning" about the exposure by the person responsible for the exposure unless it is preempted by federal law or the person responsible for the exposure can show "no significant risk" for a carcinogen or "no observable effect" for a reproductive toxicant. Proposition 65 is enforceable both by the California Attorney General and by private bounty hunters. Cases have been brought against a wide variety of food products, including alcoholic beverages, the lead content of calcium and of candy, acrylamide in a variety of food products, polycyclic aromatic hydrocarbons in broiled meat, and mercury in fish. In the only litigated case, involving mercury in fish, the California Superior Court determined both that the State failed to prove a violation of Proposition 65 and that specific FDA action regarding mercury in fish preempts State action. *California* v. *Tri-Union Seafoods*, 2006 WL 1544384 (San Francisco Super, Ct., 2006).

8. LABELING OF GENETICALLY MODIFIED FOOD

In 1953, James Watson and Francis Crick discovered and described the double-helix structure of deoxyribonucleic acid (DNA) and thus opened the field of molecular biology. In the early 1970s, scientists developed the techniques for cutting DNA molecules with a restriction enzyme, inserting foreign DNA, placing the recombined (recombinant) DNA into a host microorganism, and then replicating (cloning) the recombined DNA through fermentation of the microorganism. These remarkable technical achievements laid the foundations for commercial biotechnology.

Steve Olson, *Biotechnology: An Industry Comes of Age*

National Academy of Sciences (1986).

Human beings rely on the earth's bountiful supply of life for a wide variety of essential substances. We survive by consuming the edible portions of plants and animals.... Microorganisms are used to make bread, to convert milk into cheese, and to brew alcoholic beverages. Common substances like vinegar, vitamins, and monosodium glutamate are manufactured using microbial "factories." ...

Over the course of time, human ingenuity has gradually worked to improve these organisms. People have selected plants, animals, and microorganisms with the most useful characteristics from among those found wild in the environment. They have bred individuals from the same or closely related species to produce offspring with new, more desirable combinations of traits. Among the results of this genetic husbandry have been improved varieties of crops and livestock....

... The techniques of genetic engineering, and in particular recombinant DNA, have made it possible to manipulate genetic material on the smallest possible scale—individual genes....

But genetic engineering has done more than give researchers the ability to understand the genetic structure of living things; it has also given them the ability to change that structure. It is now possible to move genetic material in a functional form from one organism to another, creating genetic constructs that have never before existed in nature....

But biotechnology has a fundamentally different capability in agriculture. It can potentially be used to change the genetic constitution of microorganisms, plants, and animals to make them more productive, more resistant to disease or environmental stress, or more nutritious....

Probably the first application of this type will involve the genetic engineering of microorganisms. Researchers are working to produce microorganisms that will supply plants or animals with essential nutrients, protect them from insects or disease, or provide them with compounds that influence their growth. A central concern of this work is the competitiveness of the genetically engineered microorganisms in agricultural environments, since the microorganisms will generally have to survive and multiply to perform their functions.

The genetic engineering of plants and animals is a far more daunting technical task than the genetic engineering of microorganisms, but this is where the greatest potential benefits lie. Researchers have already succeeded in inserting functional genes into plant cells, in regenerating whole plants that express the gene, and in having the gene passed on to offspring. In this way, they hope to eventually be able to transfer into plants such traits as resistance to pesticides, tolerance to environmental conditions such as salinity or toxic metals, greater nutritive value or productivity, or perhaps even the ability to fix nitrogen from the atmosphere....

Genes have also been inserted into the sex cells of animals in such a way that they are reproduced in the cells of the mature animal, function in those cells, and are passed on to offspring. For instance, researchers have introduced growth hormone genes into several kinds of agriculturally important animals in an attempt to make the animals grow faster, larger, or leaner....

Food Biotechnology

A Scientific Status Summary by the Institute of Food Technologists' Expert Panel on Food Safety & Nutrition.
42 Food Technology 133 (January 1988).

. . . .

Biotechnology has been broadly defined as the utilization of biologically derived molecules, structures, cells, or organisms to carry out a specific process. This is true of many established food processes—for example, cheesemaking and brewing. The beauty of modern biotechnology lies in its specificity. The biotechnologist can target only one or two protein molecules for change in an organism containing thousands of proteins. This seemingly minor alteration can have profound effects. The amount of an important flavor, color, or enzyme may be increased manyfold. It can allow crops to grow under marginal or poor conditions. With a few exceptions, most short-term results of modern biotechnology applied to food production will be invisible to the consumer's eye. However, indirect effects on existing products, such as cost savings and product improvements, will be far-reaching.

Faced with the rapid development of recombinant DNA and other biotechnology techniques, two federal agencies took the lead in organizing a comprehensive national approach. The National Institutes of Health (NIH) adopted guidelines for scientific research in this new field. The White House Office of Science and Technology Policy (OSTP) coordinated the role and response of the federal regulatory agencies.

OSTP concluded early that existing regulatory laws are appropriate and sufficient to assure adequate regulation of the new products of biotechnology and that no new legislation is needed or desirable. In 49 Fed. Reg. 50856 (Dec. 31, 1984), 51 Fed. Reg. 23302 (June 26, 1986), OSTP published a Coordinated Framework for the Regulation of Biotechnology that described the jurisdiction and function of the various applicable statutes and regulatory agencies. Although these were relatively short and simple documents, they had the desired effect.

Parallel with the Coordinated Framework, FDA published its own policy statement for regulating biotechnology products. 43 Fed. Reg. 50878 (Dec. 31, 1984), 51 Fed. Reg. 23309 (June 26, 1986). In addressing food biotechnology, FDA firmly established the policy of applying "the relevant statutory or regulatory provisions" under the FD&C Act. The entire discussion focused on food safety, not food labeling. Within a short time, however food labeling issues were also raised.

Food and Drug Administration, Statement of Policy: Foods Derived From New Plant Varieties

57 Fed. Reg. 22984 (May 29, 1992).

. . . .

Under this policy, foods, such as fruits, vegetables, grains, and their byproducts, derived from plant varieties developed by the new methods of genetic modification are regulated within the existing framework of the act, FDA's implementing regulations, and current practice, utilizing an approach identical in principle to that applied to foods developed by traditional plant breeding. The regulatory status of a food, irrespective of the method by which it is developed, is dependent upon objective characteristics of the food and the intended use of the food (or its components)....

FDA has received several inquiries concerning labeling requirements for foods derived from new plant varieties developed by recombinant DNA techniques. Section 403(j) of the act requires that a producer of a food product describe the product by its common or usual name or in the absence thereof, an appropriately descriptive term and reveal all facts that are material in light of representations made or suggested by labeling or with respect to consequences which may result from use. Thus, consumers must be informed, by appropriate labeling, if a food derived from a new plant variety differs from its traditional counterpart such that the common or usual name no longer applies to the new food, or if a safety or usage issue exists to which consumers must be alerted.

For example, if a tomato has had a peanut protein introduced into it and there is insufficient information to demonstrate that the introduced protein could not cause an allergic reaction in a susceptible population, a label declaration would be required to alert consumers who are allergic to peanuts so they could avoid that tomato, even if its basic taste and texture remained unchanged. Such information would be a material fact whose omission may make the label of the tomato misleading under section 403(a) of the act.

FDA has also been asked whether foods developed using techniques such as recombinant DNA techniques would be required to bear special labeling to reveal that fact to consumers. To date, FDA has not considered the methods used in the development of a new plant variety (such as hybridization, chemical and radiation-induced mutagenesis, protoplast fusion, embryo rescue, somaclonal variation, or any other method) to be material information within the meaning of section 201(n) of the act. As discussed above, FDA believes that the new techniques are extensions at the molecular level of traditional methods and will be used to achieve the same goals as pursued with traditional plant breeding. The agency is not aware of any information showing that foods derived by these new methods differ from other foods in any meaningful or uniform way, or that, as a class, foods developed by the new techniques present any different or greater safety concern than foods developed by traditional plant breeding. For this reason, the agency does not believe that the method of development of a new plant variety (including the use of new techniques including recombinant DNA techniques) is normally material information within the meaning of 21 U.S.C. 321(n) and would not usually be required to be disclosed in labeling for the food. . . .

———

The first commercial genetically modified food, the Flavr Savr tomato, publicly positioned itself as a biotechnology product, and the FDA labeling policy was thus not invoked. *See* Belinda Martineau, *Food Fight: The Short, Unhappy Life of the Flavr Savr Tomato*, 41 SCIENCES, No. 2, at 24 (Spring 2001). When FDA approved the use of a recombinant bovine growth hormone (BGH) called Bovine Somatotropin (BST) to increase milk production in cows, however, the issue was clearly raised. FDA took the position that, because BST is safe and even undetectable in the milk, its use need not be labeled. The State of Vermont, however, enacted a law to require disclosure of the use of BST.

International Dairy Foods Association v. Amestoy

92 F.3d 67 (2d Cir. 1996).

■ ALTIMARI, CIRCUIT JUDGE. . . .

In 1993, the federal Food and Drug Administration ("FDA") approved the use of recombinant Bovine Somatotropin ("rBST") (also known as recombinant Bovine Growth Hormone ("rBGH")), a synthetic growth hormone that increases milk production by cows. It is undisputed that the dairy products derived from herds treated with rBST are indistinguishable from products derived from untreated herds; consequently, the FDA declined to require the labeling of products derived from cows receiving the supplemental hormone.

In April 1994, defendant-appellee the State of Vermont ("Vermont") enacted a statute requiring that "[i]f rBST has been used in the production of milk or a milk product for retail sale in this state, the retail milk or milk product shall be labeled as such." The State of Vermont's Commissioner of Agriculture ("Commissioner") subsequently promulgated regulations giving those dairy manufacturers who use rBST four labeling options, among them the posting of a sign to the following effect in any store selling dairy products:

rBST Information

THE PRODUCTS IN THIS CASE THAT CONTAIN OR MAY CONTAIN MILK FROM rBST–TREATED COWS EITHER (1) STATE ON THE PACKAGE THAT rBST HAS BEEN OR MAY HAVE BEEN USED, OR (2) ARE IDENTIFIED BY A BLUE SHELF LABEL LIKE THIS

[BLUE RECTANGLE]

OR (3) A BLUE STICKER ON THE PACKAGE LIKE THIS. [BLUE DOT]

The United States Food and Drug Administration has determined that there is no significant difference between milk from treated and untreated cows. It is the law of Vermont that products made from the milk of rBST-treated cows be labeled to help consumers make informed shopping decisions.

. . . .

Appellants filed suit in April 1994, asserting that the statute was unconstitutional. In June 1995, the dairy manufacturers moved for preliminary injunctive relief, seeking to enjoin enforcement of the statute. The dairy manufacturers alleged that the Vermont statute (1) infringed their protected rights under the First Amendment to the Constitution and (2) violated the Constitution's Commerce Clause, U.S. Const., Art. 1, § 8. Following an extensive hearing, the United States District Court for the District of Vermont (Murtha, C.J.), denied appellants' motion. *See* 898 F. Supp. at 254. The dairy manufacturers now appeal.

1st amend
only

Because we find that the dairy manufacturers are entitled to an injunction on First Amendment grounds, we do not reach their claims made pursuant to the Commerce Clause....

It is not enough for appellants to show as they have, that they were irreparably harmed by the statute; because the dairy manufacturers challenge government action taken in the public interest, they must also show a likelihood of success on the merits. We find that such success is likely.

In [*Central Hudson Gas & Elec. Corp. v. Public Serv. Comm'r*, 447 U.S. 557 (1980)], the Supreme Court articulated a four-part analysis for determining whether a government restriction on commercial speech is permissible.... We need not address the controversy concerning the nature of the speech in question—commercial or political—because we find that Vermont fails to meet the less stringent constitutional requirements applicable to compelled commercial speech.

test

Under *Central Hudson*, we must determine: (1) whether the expression concerns lawful activity and is not misleading; (2) whether the government's interest is substantial; (3) whether the labeling law directly serves the asserted interest; and (4) whether the labeling law is no more extensive than necessary.

state interest

In our view, Vermont has failed to establish the second prong of the *Central Hudson* test, namely that its interest is substantial. In making this determination, we rely only upon those interests set forth by Vermont before the district court. As the district court made clear, Vermont "does not claim that health or safety concerns prompted the passage of the Vermont Labeling Law," but instead defends the statute on the basis of "strong consumer interest and the public's 'right to know'...." These interests are insufficient to justify compromising protected constitutional rights.

no real safety issue

Vermont's failure to defend its constitutional intrusion on the ground that it negatively impacts public health is easily understood. After exhaustive studies, the FDA has "concluded that rBST has no appreciable effect on the composition of milk produced by treated cows, and that there are no human safety or health concerns associated with food products derived from cows treated with rBST." Because bovine somatotropin ("BST") appears naturally in cows, and because there are no BST receptors in a cow's mammary glands, only trace amounts of BST can be detected in milk, whether or not the cows received the supplement. Moreover, it is undisputed that neither consumers nor scientists can distinguish rBST-derived milk from milk produced by an untreated cow. Indeed, the already extensive record in this case contains no scientific evidence from which an objective observer could conclude that rBST has any impact at all on dairy products. It is thus plain that Vermont could not justify the statute on the basis of "real" harms.

We do not doubt that Vermont's asserted interest, the demand of its citizenry for such information, is genuine; reluctantly, however, we conclude that it is inadequate. We are aware of no case in which consumer interest alone was sufficient to justify requiring a product's manufacturers to publish the functional equivalent of a warning about a production method that has no discernable impact on a final product.

Although the Court is sympathetic to the Vermont consumers who wish to know which products may derive from rBST-treated herds, their desire is insufficient to permit the State of Vermont to compel the dairy manufacturers to speak against their will. Were consumer interest alone sufficient, there is no end to the information that states could require manufacturers to disclose about their production methods. For instance, with respect to cattle, consumers might reasonably evince an interest in knowing which grains herds were fed, with which medicines they were treated, or the age at which they were slaughtered. Absent, however, some indication that this information bears on a reasonable concern for human health or safety or some other sufficiently substantial governmental concern, the manufacturers cannot be compelled to disclose it. Instead, those consumers interested in such information should exercise the power of their purses by buying products from manufacturers who voluntarily reveal it.

"slippery slope"

Accordingly, we hold that consumer curiosity alone is not a strong enough state interest to sustain the compulsion of even an accurate, factual statement. Because Vermont has demonstrated no cognizable harms, its statute is likely to be held unconstitutional.

Because appellants have demonstrated both irreparable harm and a likelihood of success on the merits, the judgment of the district court is reversed, and the case is remanded for entry of an appropriate injunction.

■ LEVAL, CIRCUIT JUDGE, dissenting:

I respectfully dissent. Vermont's regulation requiring disclosure of use of rBST in milk production was based on substantial state interests, including worries about rBST's impact on human and cow health, fears for the survival of small dairy farms, and concerns about the manipulation of nature through biotechnology. The objective of the plaintiff milk producers is to conceal their use of rBST from consumers. The policy of the First Amendment, in its application to commercial speech, is to favor the flow of accurate relevant information. The majority's invocation of the First Amendment to invalidate a state law requiring disclosure of information consumers reasonably desire stands the Amendment on its ear. In my view, the district court correctly found that plaintiffs were unlikely to succeed in proving Vermont's law unconstitutional. . . .

Dissent lists several other state interest

I am comforted by two considerations: First, the precedential effect of the majority's ruling is quite limited. By its own terms, it applies only to cases where a state disclosure requirement is supported by no interest other than the gratification of consumer curiosity. In any case in which a state advanced something more, the majority's ruling would have no bearing.

Second, Vermont will have a further opportunity to defend its law. The majority's conclusion perhaps results from Vermont's failure to put forth sufficiently clear evidence of the interests it sought to advance. If so, the failure in remediable because it occurred only at the preliminary injunction stage. Trial on the merits has yet to be held. The majority has found on the basis of the evidence presented at the hearing that the plaintiffs are likely to succeed on the merits; it has of course not ruled on the ultimate issue. If Vermont succeeds at trial in putting forth clear evidence that its laws were in fact motivated by the concerns discussed above (and not merely by consumer curiosity), it will have shown a substantial interest sufficient to satisfy the requirements of the First Amendment.

NOTES

1. *On Remand.* Vermont made no attempt to show that BST is harmful, and therefore the decision of the Court of Appeals prevailed on remand.

2. *Second Case.* In *Stauber v. Shalala*, 895 F. Supp. 1178 (W.D. Wis. 1995), the District Court held that FDA did not act arbitrarily and capriciously in not requiring the labeling of dairy products derived from cows treated with BST. The District Court concluded, "In the absence of evidence of a material difference between rBST-derived milk and ordinary milk, the use of consumer demand as the rationale for labeling would violate the Food, Drug, and Cosmetic Act."

3. *Bovine Sematotropin.* The development of bovine sematotropin engendered considerable controversy. Responses included a citizen petition to FDA (promptly denied by the agency) requesting preparation of an environmental impact statement and denial of the new animal drug application (NADA), and a congressional hearing on the implications of this product for the dairy industry. *E.g.*, "Review of status and potential impact of Bovine Growth Hormone," Hearing before the Subcommittee on Livestock, Dairy, and Poultry of the House Committee on Agriculture, 99th Cong. 2d Sess. (1986); Geoffrey S. Becker & Sarah Taylor, BOVINE GROWTH HORMONE (SOMATOTROPIN): AGRICULTURAL AND REGULATORY ISSUES, CRS (Nov. 20, 1986); Jonathan Rauch, *Drug on the Market*, 19 NAT'L J. 818 (Apr. 4, 1987).

4. *Commentary.* For articles on the labeling of genetically modified food, see Chapter V(B)(2) of the Electronic Book.

Not long after the *Amestoy* decision, a coalition of consumer advocates brought suit to challenge the legality of the May 1992 FDA policy statement.

Alliance for Bio–Integrity v. Shalala

116 F. Supp. 2d 166 (D.D.C. 2000).

■ KOLLAR–KOTELLY, DISTRICT JUDGE.

Technological advances have dramatically increased our ability to manipulate our environment, including the foods we consume. One of these advances, recombinant deoxyribonucleic acid (rDNA) technology, has enabled scientists to alter the genetic composition of organisms by mixing genes on the cellular and molecular level in order to create new breeds of plants for human and animal consumption. These new breeds may be designed to repel pests, retain their freshness for a longer period of time, or contain more intense flavor and/or nutritional value. Much controversy has attended such developments in biotechnology, and in particular the production, sale, and trade of genetically modified organisms and foods. The above-captioned lawsuit represents one articulation of this controversy....

Plaintiffs have ... challenged the [FDA May 1992] Statement of Policy's failure to require labeling for genetically engineered foods, for which FDA relied on the presumption that most genetically modified food ingredients would be GRAS [generally recognized as safe]. Plaintiffs claim that FDA should have considered the widespread consumer interest in having genetically engineered foods labeled, as well as the special concerns of religious groups and persons with allergies in having these foods labeled.

The FDCA, 21 U.S.C. § 321(n), grants the FDA limited authority to require labeling. In general, foods shall be deemed misbranded if their labeling "fails to reveal facts ... material with respect to consequences which may result from the use of the article to which the labeling ... relates under the conditions of use prescribed in the labeling ... or under such conditions of use as are customary or usual." Plaintiffs challenge the FDA's interpretation of the term "material." Thus, the question is ... one of statutory interpretation. As is apparent from the statutory language, Congress has not squarely addressed whether materiality pertains only to safety concerns or whether it also includes consumer interest. Accordingly, interpretation of the § 321(n)'s broad language is left to the agency.

Because Congress has not spoken directly to the issue, this Court must determine whether the agency's interpretation of the statute is reasonable. *See Chevron, U.S.A. v. Natural Resources Defense Council*, 467 U.S. 837, 864 (1984).... Even if the agency's interpretation is not "the best or most natural by grammatical or other standards," if the interpretation is reasonable, then it is entitled to deference.

The FDA takes the position that no "material change," under § 321(n), has occurred in the rDNA derived foods at issue here. Absent unique risks to consumer health or uniform changes to food derived through rDNA technology, the FDA does not read § 321(n) to authorize an agency imposed food labeling requirement. More specifically irksome to the Plaintiffs, the FDA does not read § 321(n) to authorize labeling requirements solely because of consumer demand. The FDA's exclusion of consumer interest from the factors which determine whether a change is "material" constitutes a reasonable interpretation of the statute. Moreover, it is doubtful whether the FDA would even have the power under the FDCA to require labeling in a situation where the sole justification for such a requirement is consumer demand.

Plaintiffs fail to understand the limitation on the FDA's power to consider consumer demand when making labeling decisions because they fail to recognize that the determination that a product differs materially from the type of product it purports to be is a factual predicate to the requirement of labeling. Only once materiality has been established may the FDA consider consumer opinion to determine whether a label is required to disclose a material fact. Thus, "if there is a [material] difference, and consumers would likely want to know about the difference, then labeling is appropriate. If, however, the product does not differ in any significant way from what it purports to be, then it would be misbranding to label the product as different, even if consumers misperceived the product as different." *Stauber v. Shalala*, 895 F. Supp. 1178, 1193 (W.D.Wis. 1995). The FDA has already determined that, in general, rDNA modification does not "materially" alter foods, and as discussed, *supra*, this determination is entitled to deference. Given these facts, the FDA lacks a basis upon which it can legally mandate labeling, regardless of the level of consumer demand.

Plaintiffs also contend that the process[10] of genetic modification is a "material fact" under § 321(n) which mandates special labeling, implying that there are new risks posed to the consumer. However, the FDA has determined that foods produced through rDNA techniques do not "present any different or greater safety concern than foods developed by traditional plant breeding," and concluded that labeling was not warranted. That determination, unless irrational, is entitled to deference. Accordingly, there is little basis upon which this Court could find that the FDA's interpretation of § 321(n) is arbitrary and capricious....

NOTE

To address widespread "GMO free" claims, FDA announced a Draft Guidance in 66 Fed. Reg. 4839 (Jan. 18, 2001) that discouraged such claims:

> The guidance ... addresses the use of statements in the labeling that indicate that the food, or its ingredients, was not bioengineered. The agency is soliciting comments on the entire guidance document, but it is particularly interested in comments on how the draft guidance deals with statements like "GMO free," "GM free," "biotech free," and "no genetically engineered materials." For example, we are seeking comment on whether, and how, statements like "GM free" or "no genetically engineered material" can be made without being false or misleading. In the guidance document, FDA advises that the term "free" may be difficult to use without being false or misleading. If it implies "zero," it may be very difficult to substantiate. The adventitious presence of bioengineered material may make a "zero" claim inaccurate. Further, these terms would be misleading if they imply that the food is superior because the food is not bioengineered. We have concluded that the use, or absence of use, of bioengineering in the production of a food is not a fact that is material either with respect to consequences resulting from the use of the food or due to representations on the labeling.

This Draft Guidance has neither been made final nor withdrawn.

D.   REGULATION OF FOOD IDENTITY AND QUALITY

1.   PREMISES OF REGULATION

The Federal Filled Milk Act, 42 Stat. 1486 (1923), 21 U.S.C. 61–64, prohibits the blending of milk with any fat or oil other than milk fat.

---

10. Disclosure of the conditions or methods of manufacture has long been deemed unnecessary under the law. The Supreme Court reasoned in 1924, "When considered independently of the product, the method of manufacture is not material. The act requires no disclosure concerning it." *U.S.* v. *Ninety-Five Barrels (More or Less) Alleged Apple Cider Vinegar*, 265 U.S. 438, 445....

Carolene Products Co. v. United States

323 U.S. 18 (1944).

■ MR. JUSTICE REED delivered the opinion of the Court.

... The corporate petitioner sells the products mentioned in the indictment which are manufactured for it by another corporation from skim milk, that is, milk from which a large percentage of the butterfat has been removed. The process of manufacture consists of taking natural whole milk, extracting the butterfat content and then adding cottonseed or coconut oil and fish liver oil, which latter oil contains vitamins A and D.... The compound is sold under various trade names in cans of the same size and shape as those used for evaporated milk. The contents of the can are practically indistinguishable by the buying public from evaporated whole milk, but the cans are truthfully labeled to show the trade names and the ingredients.

The indictment charged the petitioner corporation and the individual petitioners, its president and vice president, with violation of the [Federal Filled Milk Act]....

Filled milk is defined in § 1(c) of the act as any milk, "whether or not condensed, evaporated, concentrated, powdered, dried, or desiccated, to which has been added, or which has been blended or compounded with, any fat or oil other than milk fat, so that the resulting product is in imitation or semblance of milk ..., whether or not condensed, evaporated, concentrated, powdered, dried, or desiccated." The petitioner's compounds, it is agreed, fall within this definition. But, petitioners contend, they do not fall within its spirit, since the vitamins which cause deficiency have been restored and that therefore the act is inapplicable to the enriched compounds....

Petitioners' position as to the legislative purpose of the act was not accepted by the trial or reviewing court. We agree with those courts. While, as we have stated above, the vitamin deficiency was an efficient cause in bringing about the enactment of the Filled Milk Act, it was not the sole reason for its passage. A second reason was that the compounds lend themselves readily to substitution for or confusion with milk products. Although, so far as the record shows, filled milk compounds as enriched are equally wholesome and nutritious as milk with the same content of calories and vitamins, they are artificial or manufactured foods which are cheaper to produce than similar whole milk products. When compounded and canned, whether enriched or not, they are indistinguishable by the ordinary consumer from processed natural milk. The purchaser of these compounds does not get evaporated milk. This situation has not changed since the enactment of the act. The possibility and actuality of confusion, deception and substitution was appraised by Congress. The prevention of such practices or dangers through control of shipments in interstate commerce is within the power of Congress. The manner by which Congress carries out this power, subject to constitutional objections which are considered hereinafter ... is within legislative discretion, even though the method chosen is prohibition of manufacture, sale or shipment....

If the Filled Milk Act is applicable to the compounds whose shipment was the basis of the indictment in this case, as we have just concluded, petitioners assert that the act, as thus applied, violates the due process clause of the Fifth Amendment. Their argument runs in this manner. Since these enriched compounds are admittedly wholesome and sold under trade names with proper labels without the commission of any fraud by petitioners on the public, Congress cannot prohibit their interstate shipment without denying to petitioners a right protected by the due process clause, the right to trade in innocent articles....

In the action of Congress on filled milk there is no prohibition of the shipment of an article of commerce merely because it competes with another such article which it resembles.... Here a milk product, skimmed milk, from which a valuable element—butterfat—has been removed is artificially enriched with cheaper fats and vitamins so that it is indistinguishable in the eyes of the average purchaser from whole milk products. The result is that the compound is confused with and passed off as the whole milk product in spite of proper labeling.

When Congress exercises a delegated power such as that over interstate commerce, the methods which it employs to carry out its purposes are beyond attack without a clear and convincing showing that there is no rational basis for the legislation; that it is an arbitrary fiat. This is not shown here....

Affirmed.

NOTES

1. *Related Case.* In an earlier decision, *United States v. Carolene Products Co.*, 304 U.S. 144 (1938), the Supreme Court upheld the application of the Filled Milk Act to a version of this product that was not fortified with vitamins to make it as nutritious as milk.

2. *Grounds Justifying Regulation.* The Supreme Court has upheld laws prohibiting the sale of food to prevent injury or deception but it has displayed skepticism about other grounds for regulation. In *Minnesota v. Barber*, 136 U.S. 313 (1890), the Court struck down a Minnesota statute that prohibited the importation of meat from animals slaughtered in other states, holding that no state can bar the interstate shipment of products fit for human food. In *Schollenberger v. Pennsylvania*, 171 U.S. 1 (1898), the Court also struck down a Pennsylvania statute prohibiting the importation of oleomargarine.

> This does not interfere with the acknowledged right of the State to use such means as may be necessary to prevent the introduction of an adulterated article, and for that purpose to inspect and test the article introduced, provided the state law does really inspect and does not substantially prohibit the introduction of the pure article and thereby interfere with interstate commerce. It cannot for the purpose of preventing the introduction of an impure or adulterated article absolutely prohibit the introduction of that which is pure and wholesome.

Similarly, in *Collins v. New Hampshire*, 171 U.S. 30 (1898), the Court overturned a New Hampshire statute that required all margarine to be colored pink, on the ground that the statute was ''prohibitory'' in nature and thus fell within the rule established in *Schollenberger*. The practical limits on state power, however, sometimes prove illusory. For example, in *Hebe Co. v. Shaw*, 248 U.S. 297, 302 (1919), the Court upheld a state law prohibiting a properly labeled, wholesome food, condensed skim milk, on the ground that the states have a right "to save the public from the fraudulent substitution of an inferior product that would be hard to detect."

3. *Substantive Due Process.* Since the dismantling of economic substantive due process by the Supreme Court during the 1930s and 1940s in cases like *Carolene Products*, courts' reluctance to invoke the doctrine as a limitation on state or federal economic regulation has resulted in judicial validation of a wide range of laws that impinge on the food and drug area. State restrictions on the sale of products that compete with traditional dairy foods—such as milk, cream, and butter—have long been almost routinely upheld. But *Milnot Co. v. Richardson*, 350 F. Supp. 221 (N.D. Ill. 1972), p. 176 *infra*, signaled closer judicial scrutiny of statutes designed to protect traditional food products against new products made through modern food technology. Judicial doctrines that permit wide latitude in legislative choice to aid consumers whom the market would not otherwise protect—and that allow legislative schemes whose primary effect, and perhaps purpose, is to protect established producers from competition—have not gone uncriticized. *See, e.g.* Jerry L. Mashaw, *Constitutional Deregulation: Notes Toward a Public, Public Law*, 54 TUL. L. REV. 849 (1980).

4. *Industry Use of Regulation.* In *The Theory of Economic Regulation*, 2 BELL J. OF ECON. & MGT. SCI. 3 (1971), Professor George Stigler argues:

... as a rule, regulation is acquired by the industry and is designed and operated primarily for its benefit....

The most obvious contribution that a group may seek of the government is a direct subsidy of money....

The second major public resource commonly sought by an industry is control over entry by new rivals....

We propose the general hypothesis: every industry or occupation that has enough political power to utilize the state will seek to control entry. In addition, the regulatory policy will often be so fashioned as to retard the rate of growth of new firms....

A third general set of powers of the state which will be sought by the industry are those which affect substitutes and complements. Crudely put, the butter producers wish to suppress margarine and encourage the production of bread....

2. ECONOMIC ADULTERATION

Section 402(b)(4) of the FD&C Act provides that a food is adulterated if "any substance has been added thereto or mixed or packed therewith so as to ... make it appear better or of greater value than it is."

United States v. 88 Cases ... Bireley's Orange Beverage
187 F.2d 967 (3d Cir. 1951).

■ HASTIE, CIRCUIT JUDGE.

Pursuant to its libel charging economic adulteration of certain food within the meaning of Section 402(b)(4) of the Federal Food, Drug and Cosmetic Act, the United States seized for condemnation 88 cases of an article of food labeled "Bireley's Orange Beverage." The charges thus asserted were tried to a jury in the District Court for the District of New Jersey with a resultant finding of adulteration and a decree of condemnation. . . .

In this case the United States charged and undertook to prove that the "food" in question—Bireley's Orange Beverage—was "adulterated" within the meaning of the statute in that "substances["]—particularly, yellow coal tar dyes, sugar, lactic acid, and orange oil—had been "added thereto or mixed therewith . . . so as to make it appear better or of greater value than it is." . . .

Preliminarily, we consider an argument that the types of processing and manufacture covered by Section 402(b)(4) should be limited by a strict grammatical application of the words of the statute. Such an approach suggests that the noun "food" used in the introductory line of the section, and the articles and adverbs referring back to it be applied precisely and consistently to denote either an adulterated end product or an unadulterated original food. Further, it is argued that the statutory description of adulteration in terms of substances "mixed with" or "added to" a "food" limits the application of the section to situations in which the process of manufacture has been the modification of a basic identifiable and unadulterated article of food through the introduction of some additive.

We reject this restrictive analysis. In Section 402(b)(4) we think Congress has employed a very brief text, informally phrased in non-technical language, to cover generally a very considerable and diverse, but not precisely delimited, field of processing and fabrication. We view the language of the section as a comprehensive, if not always grammatically precise and consistent, description applicable to the manufacture and processing of foods generally, whether a recognized food is altered or sundry ingredients are combined or compounded to make what is essentially a new article of manufacture. . . .

More difficult questions arise in construing and applying the requirement of the statute that admixture shall have made the food "appear better than it is." To whom must the food appear better than it is? And how is it to be determined whether the food "appears better than it is"?

With reference to the first question, the trial judge charged the jury as follows: "Your function in this case is to determine whether any part of the public, the vast multitude which includes the ignorant, the unthinking and the credulous, and those who do not stop to analyze in making a purchase would be so misled." We have found nothing else in the charge which modifies the impression created by this statement. The jury was told that deceptive appearance to "any part" of the public sufficed and the significance of "any part" was emphasized and underlined by the accompanying reference to "the ignorant, the unthinking and the credulous." This was error.

The correct standard was the reaction of the ordinary consumer under such circumstances as attended retail distribution of this product. When a statute leaves such a matter as this without specification, the normal inference is that the legislature contemplated the reaction of the ordinary person who is neither savant nor dolt, who lacks special competency with reference to the matter at hand but has and exercises a normal measure of the layman's common sense and judgment. What constitutes the norm of common sense and judgment is peculiarly the province of the jury.... Congress has indicated no extraordinary standard in this section under consideration and we find no basis for imposing one....

This formulation also disposes of an issue that has arisen whether such matters as bottling, labeling and retail price, as well as the taste and physical appearance of the food, constitute appearance under the statute. In our view, all customary circumstances of retail acquisition and consumption are relevant....

We next consider what is meant by a description of food as appearing "better than it is" and what criteria are applicable to the determination of such apparent superiority over actual quality....

The parties agree that Bireley's orange drink contains about 6% orange juice, 2% lemon juice, 87% water, and small quantities of various other harmless substances. Undoubtedly, any percentage increase in the orange juice content with a corresponding decrease in water content would represent some improvement in food value. Hence, literally the product appears better than it is if it appears to the consumer to contain more than 6% orange juice.

But here we encounter serious difficulties of vagueness. The statutory test in Section 402(b)(4) is unreasonable and unenforceable if it requires manufacturers in first instance to anticipate and the trier of fact thereafter to measure anything so speculative or even whimsical as the customer's guess whether an artificial beverage contains five, six, seven, or some other percentage of orange juice. Popular judgments as to degree of dilution, more or less than actuality, are in our view too vague and speculative for meaningful guidance or fair and practical administration of a prohibition against the introduction of otherwise unobjectionable food into commerce. The difficulty with this entire approach is that the "adulterated" food is made to serve as its own only standard.

The solution to the problem and the correct construction of the statutory language are to be found in the rationale of the legislative exclusion of products from commerce for economic adulteration where no hygienic adulteration exists. In such cases a product is recognized as wholesome but is excluded from commerce because of the danger of confusing it with something else which is defined, familiar, and superior. There is no evidence to indicate a legislative intent to bar from the market foods which are wholesome merely because they may in fact be of relatively little value. So long as they are not confused with more wholesome products, their presence does no harm. Without a finding that a marketable inferior product is likely to be confused with a specified superior counterpart, we think there can be no appearing "better than it is" within the scope of disapproval of a section patently concerned only with confusion. Thus, in the case before us, proof of violation of the statute requires first description and definition of the superior counterpart, and second, proof that the consumer is likely to mistake the inferior for the superior....

In the instant case, undiluted orange juice is the only defined and familiar food pointed out in the libel and in evidence as possibly to be confused with Bireley's Orange Beverage. We therefore agree with the claimant that the issue on this aspect of the case is squarely this: Would the ordinary consumer confuse claimant's product with undiluted orange juice?

Legislative consideration of the problem of standards under the Act gives further support to our conclusion that Section 402(b)(4) is not applicable if the allegedly adulterated food is its own only standard. The inability of the government to establish enforceable standards for fabricated foods, considerably hampered the work of enforcement of the 1906 Act. The solution to this problem suggested in the course of legislative consideration of the 1938 bill, and in due course adopted, was the enactment of provisions giving the Secretary of Agriculture power to promulgate standards of identity for foods . . . .

Questions of various permissible degrees of dilution which were regarded below as relevant and in issue are peculiarly appropriate for disposition by this administrative technique. Under the required administrative procedure, the whole industry can participate in the determination whether orange-flavored soft drinks are capable of satisfactory definition, how their composition should be restricted, and even whether such a food as orange drink, or any of its variants, should be permitted in commerce.

However, we agree with the government that it is not necessary that this channel be used. We agree that the statute does not foreclose the procedure used here. But as already indicated, we think the procedure used here permits condemnation only where there is confusion with a defined superior product. If the government would go further it must undertake the formulation of standards of identity in this area.

The trial court's instruction to the jury did not ask simply and directly whether the Bireley product could be confused with undiluted orange juice. Nor did it ask anything sufficiently close so that we can say that the issue was in effect determined. . . . In a new trial that issue should be made entirely clear to the jury. . . .

NOTES

1. *Artificial Color.* In *United States v. Two Bags Poppy Seeds*, 147 F.2d 123 (6th Cir. 1945), the product at issue was white poppy seeds which had been artificially colored with charcoal to look like naturally dark poppy seeds. The court held that the seeds were adulterated under section 402(b)(4).

2. *Concealment of Inferiority.* Section 402(b)(3) of the FD&C Act prohibits the concealment "in any manner" of a food's "damage or inferiority." In *United States v. 36 Drums of Pop'n Oil*, 164 F.2d 250 (5th Cir. 1947), the majority sustained a charge of economic adulteration under sections 402(b)(3) and (b)(4) against artificially colored and flavored mineral oil marketed, with truthful labeling, principally to movie theaters for use with popcorn. At trial the government disavowed any charge that the mineral oil was deleterious or harmful. The concurring judge, though agreeing with the dissent's assertion that "zeal for enforcement . . . is here outrunning common sense and the true intent of the law," reluctantly concluded that the product was adulterated under section 402(b)(3) because its inferiority had

been concealed by making it look like butter, and under section 402(b)(4) because mineral oil had been colored to make it appear of greater value than it was. Compare the "ordinary consumer" standard applied in the *Bireley's* case with the various standards applied in the misbranding cases cited in Note 2 at p. 111 *supra*.

3. *Ineffectiveness of Truthful Labeling.* In the *Pop'n Oil* case, the product was intended for use in a way that consumers could never know its composition, *i.e.*, on popcorn sold at movie theaters without ingredient labeling. Under the *Pop'n Oil* rationale, would all fabricated food sold at restaurants or other food service institutions without ingredient labeling violate section 402(b)? If ingredient information had been provided to consumers in this case should the result have been different? *See United States v. 55 Cases Popped Corn*, 62 F. Supp. 843 (D. Idaho 1943), posing the same issue as *Pop'n Oil* in the context of a consumer product that bore full ingredient labeling disclosing the presence of mineral oil and coloring. FDA contended the product was not popcorn because neither melted butter nor vegetable oil was used. The court rejected this contention because "there is no exact formula used in the preparation of popcorn for the market" and "the consumer was fully advised as to the contents of the various packages." *But see United States v. 716 Cases ... Del Comida Brand Tomatoes ...*, 179 F.2d 174 (10th Cir. 1950) (holding that truthful labeling cannot cure economic adulteration).

4. *Nonenforcement of Section 402(b).* Applied literally, the economic adulteration provisions of the FD&C Act would render most modern food technology problematic. Many functional ingredients—color additives, preservatives, emulsifiers—are intended to improve the appearance of the product and thus could be challenged as making food appear "better than it is." Food producers would claim that these ingredients in fact improve the food and only make it appear to be as good as it genuinely is. Without purporting to resolve this debate, FDA has virtually abandoned enforcement of section 402(b) except in cases of outright fraud, which are rare. The agency has embraced, though never publicized, the philosophy that, notwithstanding the proper legal interpretation of the statute, informative labeling can cure "economic adulteration."

5. *Vagueness of Standard.* The court in *United States v. Fabro, Inc.*, 206 F. Supp. 523 (M.D. Ga. 1962), declared section 402(b)(1), prohibiting the omission of a "valuable constituent," unconstitutionally vague as applied to a nonstandardized food. *Van Liew v. United States*, 321 F.2d 664 (5th Cir. 1963), held that an indictment charging a violation of sections 402(b)(2) and (4) was impermissibly vague because it did not specify in detail what valuable constituent was omitted from the defendants' orange drink product, what substance was substituted therefor, or how it was made to appear better or of greater value than it was.

6. *1906 Act Cases.* The central economic adulteration decision under the 1906 Act was *United States v. Ten Cases ... Bred Spred*, 49 F.2d 87 (8th Cir. 1931). There the court held that a strawberry flavored spread containing less than half the strawberries found in traditional strawberry jam was not adulterated:

> The mere fact that the product contained fewer strawberries than some other product, *e.g.*, jam, does not show that Bred Spred was inferior to jam; nor does it show that a comparison with jam was called for by the statute unless Bred Spred was being palmed off on the public as jam. No showing of this kind was made.

Other economic adulteration cases under the 1906 Act include *United States v. Seven Hundred and Seventy–Nine Cases of Molasses*, 174 Fed. 325 (8th Cir. 1909); *Libby, McNeill & Libby v. United States*, 210 Fed. 148 (4th Cir. 1913); *F.B. Washburn & Co. v. United States*, 224 Fed. 395 (1st Cir. 1915); *United States v. Schider*, 246 U.S. 519 (1918); *United States v. Krumm*, 269 Fed. 848 (E.D. Pa. 1921); *United States v. 154 Sacks of Oats*, 283 Fed. 985 (W.D. Va. 1922), 294 Fed.

340 (W.D. Va. 1923); *W.B. Wood Mfg. Co. v. United States*, 292 Fed. 133 (8th Cir. 1923); *United States v. Nesbitt Fruit Products, Inc.*, 96 F.2d 972 (5th Cir. 1938).

7. *USDA Regulation.* In *Chip Steak Co. v. Hardin*, 332 F. Supp. 1084 (N.D. Cal. 1971), a USDA ban on preservatives in cooked sausage was upheld on the ground that such additives "conceal inferiority and damage and make the product appear better than it actually is."

8. *Commentary. See* Richard C. Nelson, *What Standard for the Non-standardized Food?*, 8 FOOD DRUG COSM. L.J. 425 (1953); Allan S. Kushen, *The Significance of Section 402(b)*, 10 FOOD DRUG COSM. L.J. 829 (1955); Wesley E. Forte, *The Food and Drug Administration and the Economic Adulteration of Foods*, 21 FOOD DRUG COSM. L.J. 533 (1966).

————

In Trade Correspondence No. 381 (Jan. 23, 1942), FDA recounted that it had historically considered foods in which saccharin was substituted for sugar to be adulterated. The agency did not renounce this position though it did acknowledge that "products which contain saccharin and are for special dietary uses may be legally manufactured and sold under the restrictions laid down by the regulations under section 403(j) of the Act."

United States v. 1200 Candy Bars ... "Sta–Trim"

1965–1968 FDLI Judicial and Administrative Record 148 (N.D. Calif. 1961).

■ SWEIGERT, DISTRICT JUDGE.

On the issue of adulteration, the amended libel alleges that the Sta–Trim bars are adulterated within the meaning of 21 U.S.C. § 342(d), in that they are confectionery and contain saccharin and sodium cyclamate, which are alleged to be non-nutritive substances. This section reads in pertinent part as follows: "A food shall be deemed to be adulterated ... (d) If it is confectionery, and it bears or contains any alcohol or non-nutritive article or substance except authorized coloring, harmless flavoring...."

The ... question is therefore presented whether Section 342(d) is to be construed as prohibiting the use in confectionery of non-nutritive substances which are not harmful or inedible.

When Congress enacted the Food and Drug Act in 1906, its obvious purpose was to eliminate from confectionery certain non-nutritive substances which were poisonous or deleterious ingredients.... When Congress enacted the present law in 1938, the section was broadened to omit references of specific harmful substances and there was substituted the general phrase, "non-nutritive substance," with certain specific exceptions in regard to authorized coloring and harmless flavoring.... [But] Section 342(d), when read in light of its predecessor Section 7 of the 1906 Act, embodies a legislative purpose to prohibit non-nutritive ingredients which are either harmful or inedible....

The use of artificial sugars, such as saccharin and sodium cyclamate in the manufacture of a confection may possibly give rise to questions relating to a statutory standard of identity, Section 343(g), or problems of misbranding, Section 343. But, as far as adulteration, within the meaning of Section 342(d) is concerned, we hold that the statutory phrase, "non-nutritive substances," means only non-nutritive substances that are harmful or inedible.

If Section 342(d) were to be read to prohibit the addition of harmless non-nutritive substances, such as saccharin and sodium cyclamate, into confectionery, this section would conflict with Section 343(j) which permits the sale of special dietary foods, when properly labeled, including foods containing saccharin and sodium cyclamate. Interpretations that result in such conflicts should be avoided as far as reasonably possible. . . .

NOTES

1. *Subsequent Proceedings.* The District Court later reconsidered and reaffirmed this ruling, but ultimately held the product misbranded. Because the government prevailed on the misbranding charge, FDA's appeal of the adulteration issue was dismissed as moot, but the Court of Appeals stated, "So much of the judgment below as dealt with the issue of adulteration is vacated and set aside, and the same is and shall be without further force and effect." *United States v. 1200 Candy Bars . . . "Sta–Trim,"* 1961–1964 FDLI Judicial and Administrative Record 79 (N.D. Cal. 1961), *vacated as moot,* 313 F.2d 219 (9th Cir. 1963).

2. *Statutory Amendments.* Section 402(d)(1) and (3) were amended to their present form by 80 Stat. 231 (1966), which signaled the end of FDA's traditional opposition to the use of nonnutritive sweeteners in ordinary foods.

3. *Confectionery Containing Alcohol.* From its enactment in 1938, the provision that is now section 402(d)(2) prohibited confectionery containing any alcohol, with the exception of alcohol, not in excess of 0.5 percent in volume, derived solely from the use of flavoring extracts. This provision was amended by the Comprehensive Smokeless Tobacco Health Education Act of 1986, 100 Stat. 30, 35, to permit confectionery containing alcohol to be shipped to states where such products are lawful. By 1986, eleven states had enacted laws specifically permitting the sale of candy containing alcohol, 132 Cong. Rec. 1862 (Feb. 6, 1986). FDA has interpreted the 1986 statute to authorize the importation of candy containing alcohol if it is to be sold in a state that allows the sale of such products. Letter from Sanford A. Miller, Director, FDA, CFSAN, to R.T. O'Connell (May 27, 1986). For FDA enforcement policy in states that have not legalized candy containing alcohol, see 48 Fed. Reg. 18896 (Apr. 26, 1983), 50 Fed. Reg. 8677 (Mar. 4, 1985).

4. *Mixtures of Candy and Trinkets.* FDA initially took the position that the sale of trinkets mixed with candy and sold in vending machines violated section 402(a), which provides that food is adulterated "if it bears or contains any poisonous or deleterious substance which may render it injurious to health." After this interpretation was overruled in *Cavalier Vending Corp. v. United States,* 190 F.2d 386 (4th Cir. 1951), legislative proposals to ban the practice were unsuccessful. When section 402(d)(1) was enacted in its present form, 80 Stat. 231 (1966), it prohibited only those trinkets that are partially or completely embedded in a confectionary. Nonetheless, FDA continues to express concern about the mixing of trinkets with confectionery in vending machines and recommends that the trinkets be "physically separated from candy or gum by some form of wrapping as a safety precaution." Compliance Policy Guide No. 7105.04 (Oct. 1, 1980).

5. *Toys in Candy.* After a major confectionary manufacturer marketed a chocolate-coated plastic egg containing a toy in 1997, lawyers debated its legality under section 402(d)(1). *Cf.* John A. Eldred and Stuart M. Pape, *Toys and Confec-*

tionery—A Legally Hazardous Combination?, 53 FOOD & DRUG L.J. 1 (1998), with Fred H. Degman and Steven B. Steinborn, *Toys and Confectionery—A Legally Compatible Combination*, 53 FOOD & DRUG L.J. 9 (1998).

6. *Nonnutritive Decoration.* Under the 1906 Act, nonnutritive decorations on candy did not violate the law. *French Silver Drageè Co. v. United States*, 179 Fed. 824 (2d Cir. 1910); *United States v. R.C. Boeckel & Co.*, 221 Fed. 885 (1st Cir. 1915). The courts interpreted the 1906 Act to prohibit any amount of the nonnutritive substances specifically prohibited by name in the statute, but to prohibit only harmful amounts of other nonnutritive substances. The use of silver dragees (candy beads used to decorate baked goods) was similarly permitted by FDA under the 1938 Act. FDA Trade Correspondence No. 239 (Apr. 11, 1940).

3.   FOOD STANDARDS OF IDENTITY

a.   THE RISE OF FOOD STANDARDS: 1938–1970

Developments in the Law—The Federal Food, Drug, and Cosmetic Act

67 HARVARD LAW REVIEW 632 (1954).

One of the *greatest* weaknesses of the 1906 Act was its failure to provide for mandatory standards of identity and quality for food, which would have the force of law in prosecutions for adulteration and misbranding. The Secretary could and did establish standards for his own guidance in deciding when to proceed against a food as adulterated or misbranded, but in each prosecution he had to reestablish the validity and reasonableness of the standard from which he claimed the offending food departed.... There were individual statutes authorizing the establishment of mandatory standards for certain types of food, and the McNary–Mapes Amendment of 1930 empowered the Secretary to promulgate standards of "quality, condition and/or fill of container" for almost all canned foods, requiring foods that fell below such standards to be appropriately labeled. But in large and important areas of the food industry there was no provision for mandatory standards....

Before any standard for a food ... can be issued [under the 1938 Act] the Secretary must publish the proposal in general terms, together with notice of the hearing which is required by Section 701(e) of the Act. Any interested person may appear and offer testimony at the hearing, and all relevant and material evidence is to be accepted, without regard to common law rules of admissibility.... Every detail of the standard as finally promulgated must be supported by "substantial evidence of record," and detailed findings of fact must be set out in the order, covering not only all ingredients included in the standard, but also those not included although suggested at the hearing.

Hearings have tended to grow longer; those on the proposed bread standard spanned ten years and amassed a record of 17,000 pages. In view of the ponderousness of the procedure and time wasted in putting into the record evidence as to which there is no disagreement, it was proposed in

Congress [in 1953] that hearings be dispensed with in cases where there is no objection to the standard or amendment proposed by the Secretary....

NOTE

The original requirement of a administrative trial-type hearing under section 701(e) for every food standard was amended (1) by 68 Stat. 54 (1954) and 70 Stat. 919 (1956) to require a hearing only upon the filing of objections and (2) by 104 Stat. 2353, 2365 (1990) to remove all food standards except those for dairy products and maple syrup from section 701(e), thus permitting FDA to adopt or amend standards through notice and comment rulemaking under section 701(a) and the Administrative Procedure Act.

i.   Operation of Food Standards

Federal Security Administrator v. Quaker Oats Co.
318 U.S. 218 (1943).

■ MR. CHIEF JUSTICE STONE delivered the opinion of the Court.

The Federal Security Administrator, acting under §§ 401 and 701(e), promulgated regulations establishing "standards of identity" for various milled wheat products, excluding vitamin D from the defined standard of "farina" and permitting it only in "enriched farina," which was required to contain Vitamin B_1, riboflavin, nicotinic acid and iron. The question is whether the regulations are valid as applied to respondent. The answer turns upon (a) whether there is substantial evidence in support of the Administrator's finding that indiscriminate enrichment of farina with vitamin and mineral contents would tend to confuse and mislead consumers; (b) if so, whether, upon such a finding, the Administrator has statutory authority to adopt a standard of identity, which excludes a disclosed non-deleterious ingredient, in order to promote honesty and fair dealing in the interest of consumers; and (c) whether the Administrator's treatment, by the challenged regulations, of the use of vitamin D as an ingredient of a product sold as "farina" is within his statutory authority to prescribe "a reasonable definition and standard of identity." ...

Any food which "purports to be or is represented as a food for which a definition and standard of identity has been prescribed" pursuant to § 401 is declared by § 403(g) to be misbranded "unless (1) it conforms to such definition and standard, and (2) its label bears the name of the food specified in the definition and standard, and, insofar as may be required by such regulations, the common names of optional ingredients ... present in such food." ...

... Regulation 15.130 defined "farina" as a food prepared by grinding and bolting cleaned wheat, other than certain specified kinds, to a prescribed fineness with the bran coat and germ of the wheat berry removed to a prescribed extent. The regulation made no provision for the addition of any ingredients to "farina." Regulation 15.140 defined "enriched farina" as conforming to the regulation defining "farina," but with added prescribed minimum quantities of vitamin B1, riboflavin, nicotinic acid ... and iron. The regulation also provided that minimum quantities of vitamin D, calcium, wheat germ or disodium phosphate might be added as optional ingredients of "enriched farina," and required that ingredients so added be specified on the label. . . .

Respondent, The Quaker Oats Company, has for the past ten years manufactured and marketed a wheat product commonly used as a cereal food, consisting of farina as defined by the Administrator's regulation, but with vitamin D added. Respondent distributes this product in packages labeled "Quaker Farina Wheat Cereal Enriched with Vitamin D," or "Quaker Farina enriched by the Sunshine Vitamin." The packages also bear the label "Contents 400 U.S.P. units of Vitamin D per ounce, supplied by approximately the addition of 1/5 of 1 percent irradiated dry yeast."

Respondent asserts, and the Government agrees, that the Act as supplemented by the Administrator's standards will prevent the marketing of its product as "farina" since, by reason of the presence of vitamin D as an ingredient, it does not conform to the standard of identity prescribed for "farina," and that respondent cannot market its product as "enriched farina" unless it adds the prescribed minimum quantities of vitamin B_1, riboflavin, nicotinic acid and iron. Respondent challenges the validity of the regulations on the grounds sustained below and others so closely related to them as not to require separate consideration. . . .

In recent years millers of wheat have placed on the market flours and farinas which have been enriched by the addition of various vitamins and minerals. The composition of these enriched products varies widely. There was testimony of weight before the Administrator, principally by expert nutritionists, that such products, because of the variety and combination of added ingredients, are widely variable in nutritional value; and that consumers generally lack knowledge of the relative value of such ingredients and combinations of them.

These witnesses also testified, as did representatives of consumer organizations which had made special studies of the problems of food standardization, that the number, variety and varying combinations of the added ingredients tend to confuse the large number of consumers who desire to purchase vitamin-enriched wheat food products but who lack the knowledge essential to discriminating purchase of them; that because of this lack of knowledge and discrimination they are subject to exploitation by the sale of foods described as "enriched," but of whose inferior or unsuitable quality they are not informed. . . .

. . . Taking into account the evidence of public demand for vitamin-enriched foods, their increasing sale, their variable vitamin composition and dietary value, and the general lack of consumer knowledge of such values, there was sufficient evidence of "rational probative force" to support the Administrator's judgment that, in the absence of appropriate standards of identity, consumer confusion would ensue. . . .

Both the text and legislative history of the present statute plainly show that its purpose was not confined to a requirement of truthful and informative labeling. False and misleading labeling had been prohibited by the Pure Food and Drugs Act of 1906. But it was found that such a prohibition was inadequate to protect the consumer from "economic adulteration," by which less expensive ingredients were substituted, or the proportion of more expensive ingredients diminished, so as to make the product, although not in itself deleterious, inferior to that which the consumer expected to receive when purchasing a product with the name under which it was sold. The remedy chosen was not a requirement of informative labeling. Rather it was the purpose to authorize the Administrator to promulgate definitions and standards of identity "under which the integrity of food products can be effectively maintained," and to require informative labeling only where no such standard had been promulgated, where the food did not purport to comply with a standard, or where the regulations permitted optional ingredients and required their mention on the label.

The provisions for standards of identity thus reflect a recognition by Congress of the inability of consumers in some cases to determine, solely on the basis of informative labeling, the relative merits of a variety of products superficially resembling each other. We cannot say that such a standard of identity, designed to eliminate a source of confusion to purchasers—which otherwise would be likely to facilitate unfair dealing and make protection of the consumer difficult—will not "promote honesty and fair dealing" within the meaning of the statute.

Respondent's final and most vigorous attack on the regulations is that they fail to establish reasonable definitions and standards of identity, as § 401 requires, in that they prohibit the marketing, under the name "farina," of a wholesome and honestly labeled product consisting of farina with vitamin D added, and that they prevent the addition of vitamin D to products marketed as "enriched farina" unless accompanied by the other prescribed vitamin ingredients which do not co-act with or have any dietary relationship to vitamin D. Stated in another form, the argument is that it is unreasonable to prohibit the addition to farina of vitamin D as an optional ingredient while permitting its addition as an optional ingredient to enriched farina, to the detriment of respondent's business.

. . . We must reject at the outset the argument earnestly pressed upon us that the statute does not contemplate a regulation excluding a wholesome and beneficial ingredient from the definition and standard of identity of a food. . . .

We cannot say that the Administrator made an unreasonable choice of standards. . . . Consumers who buy farina will have no reason to believe that it is enriched. Those who buy enriched farina are assured of receiving a wheat product containing those vitamins naturally present in wheat, and, if so stated on the label, an additional vitamin D, not found in wheat. . . .

Columbia Cheese Co. v. McNutt

137 F.2d 576 (2d Cir. 1943).

■ CHASE, CIRCUIT JUDGE.

The administrative proceedings which led to the issuance of the order here under review began in August of 1939 with the object of establishing a definition and standard of identity for cream cheese; and these resulted in a proposed order which was issued on September 28, 1940, with findings of fact and a proposed regulation. But on application of the petitioners, who filed exceptions to the order, the hearing was reopened and consolidated with a hearing on proposals for standards for neufchatel, cottage and creamed cottage cheeses....

The Administrator found that there are produced and marketed various cheeses of a soft uncured nature, but that these cheeses, while they have similar characteristics, have separate and distinct identities....

Consumers, it was found, cannot readily distinguish between the cream cheese made by the older process and the lower-fat, higher-moisture cheese made by the "hot-pack" process; and since fat content is the chief item of expense in such cheeses retailers sometimes sold the cheaper product as "cream cheese".... The cheaper product being sold consumers was found by the administrator to be more closely akin to neufchatel cheese, which was found to be the common or usual name of a cheese made by the same process as cream cheese, but having a fat content of a minimum of 20% and a moisture content of a maximum of 65%. This type of cheese, prior to about 1920, was marketed in substantial quantities, but gradually the market declined until it almost vanished because of a progressive cheapening of the product in quality....

One of petitioners' chief objections to the regulations promulgated by the Administrator is that a substantial portion of the cheese manufactured by them must be designated as neufchatel cheese.... The fact that neufchatel had fallen into disrepute in the 1920's is of no particular significance so long as [the Administrator] could find, as he did, that cheese made with a fat content of below 33% and with a moisture content of above 55% was not the product cream cheese as it was traditionally known. Nor does petitioners' assertion that these standards of identity will create a monopoly for one manufacturer make the order unlawful. If they continue to make the product they now make, they can sell it as neufchatel; and if they want to make a product that they can sell as cream cheese, they need only comply with the standards of the product that the Administrator has identified as cream cheese....

■ SWAN, CIRCUIT JUDGE (dissenting in part).

For many years cheese having less than 33% of milk fat has been sold as "cream cheese." Almost every one in the industry, with the exception of the Kraft Cheese Co., objects to the requirement that such cheese hereafter be called "neufchatel." The statute authorizes the Administrator to promulgate regulations "establishing for any food, under its common or usual name so far as practicable, a reasonable definition and standard of identity," etc. There is no finding that it is impracticable to use the common name and distinguish between cheese of different milk fat content by adjectives, for example, light cream cheese or heavy cream cheese. Without at least a finding of impracticability, I think it unreasonable to deprive the bulk of the industry of their good will in the commonly used name....

NOTE

Compare *Brunetto Cheese Mfg. Corp. v. Celebrezze*, 356 F.2d 874 (2d Cir. 1966), which upheld FDA's decision to authorize the use of the name Mozzarella for two types of standardized cheese, one described as "Low Moisture Mozzarella."

Richard A. Merrill & Earl M. Collier, *"Like Mother Used to Make": An Analysis of FDA Food Standards of Identity*

74 COLUMBIA LAW REVIEW 561 (1974).

... From the very beginning, Congress conceived that standards of identity would resemble "recipes" for foods. Legislators explicitly analogized processed foods purchased in the market to their home-made counterparts.... Starting from this initial conception—that standards of identity should define foods in terms of "time-honored" home recipes—the FDA began promulgating standards that prescribed the composition of foods in detail. The first standards fixed every ingredient in a food, but gradually FDA "recipes" began not only to specify mandatory ingredients but to allow certain optional ingredients as well. Nevertheless, until the early 1960's virtually all identity standards faithfully followed the basic "recipe" concept, leaving manufacturers comparatively little choice among ingredients and affording consumers practically no information about the composition of standardized foods....

Two objectives explain the FDA's prolonged adherence to its original recipe format: (1) a desire to preclude any modifications of basic food formulas that could contribute to consumer deception, and (2) a concern to restrain the growing use in food production of chemical additives whose safety had not been demonstrated....

... Recipe standards would not have dramatically affected the availability of substitutes for traditional foods if the FDA had not simultaneously espoused an expansive reading of the "purports to be or is represented as" language in section 403(g). A broad reading obviously imperils more products than a narrow one, for any product that "purports to be or is represented as" a standardized food must meet FDA's compositional requirements.... An expansive reading thus contributes to product homogeneity in those food markets for which standards have been adopted.

The FDA has never formally announced general criteria for determining whether a new product is subject to an existing food standard, *i.e.*, whether a product does, or if marketed would, purport to be the standard food.... The few reported cases ... demonstrate an early consistency of purpose by the FDA to apply section 403(g) to reach most substitutes for standardized foods, sometimes even when there was no risk that consumers would confuse a challenged product with the standard item. Moreover, they reflect the courts' willingness to support the FDA's initial broad reading of that provision....

Even if the FDA had read "purports to be" more narrowly, however, the use of recipe standards would itself have significantly restricted the range of substitutes for standard foods. For instance, by fixing the amount of fruit that "jam" must contain, the FDA's recipe standard for that food prevents marketing as "jam" other products that contain less fruit. Of course, a relaxed construction of section 403(g) would allow a manufacturer of a low-fruit product to establish a separate market identity without altering its labeling or appearance so substantially that it could not compete with "jam." ...

NOTES

1. *Multiple Standards of Quality.* In 1938 Congress declined to give FDA authority to establish multiple standards of quality for a single food. It can be argued, however, that the agency has sometimes circumvented the limits on its authority simply by establishing individual identity standards for different "grades" of the same product, *e.g.*, for "cream cheese" and "neufchatel." Most identity standards include requirements that are designed to maintain the quality of the standardized food, such as minimum amounts of important constituents.

2. *Peanut Butter.* In *Corn Products Co. v. Department of HEW*, 427 F.2d 511 (3d Cir. 1970), the court upheld FDA's infamous standard requiring 90% peanuts in peanut butter, rejecting the claim that 87% peanuts should be sufficient. This demonstrates that a standard of identity may raise the "quality" of existing foods.

3. *Court Challenges to Food Standards.* Because of their economic impact, food standards used to be frequently challenged in court. Other notable cases include *A.E. Staley Manufacturing Co. v. Secretary of Agriculture*, 120 F.2d 258 (7th Cir. 1941); *Twin City Milk Producers Association v. McNutt*, 122 F.2d 564 (8th Cir. 1941), 123 F.2d 396 (8th Cir. 1941); *Land O'Lakes Creameries v. McNutt*, 132 F.2d 653 (8th Cir. 1943); *United States Cane Sugar Refiners' Association v. McNutt*, 138 F.2d 116 (2d Cir. 1943); *Willapoint Oysters v. Ewing*, 174 F.2d 676 (9th Cir. 1949); *Cream Wipt Food Products Co. v. Federal Security Administration*, 187 F.2d 789 (3d Cir. 1951); *Atlas Powder Co. v. Ewing*, 201 F.2d 347 (3d Cir. 1952); *Reade v. Ewing*, 205 F.2d 630 (2d Cir. 1953); *Pineapple Growers Association of Hawaii v. FDA*, 673 F.2d 1083 (9th Cir. 1982).

4. *Challenges to Nonconforming Products.* Cases involving the failure of a product to conform to a standard of identity have rarely been litigated. A rare illustration is *United States v. Articles of Food ... [Concentrated Orange Juice]*, Food Drug Cosm. L. Rep. (CCH) ¶ 38,152 (W.D. Tex. 1981) (products labeled "concentrated orange juice for manufacturing" or "orange juice" failed to comply with applicable standards). For a description of a complex fraudulent scheme to adulterate orange juice in violation of the standard of identity for orange juice from concentrate, resulting in criminal prosecution of the responsible individuals, see *United States v. Kohlbach*, 38 F.3d 832 (6th Cir. 1994). In *United States v. Dakota Cheese, Inc.*, 906 F.2d 335 (8th cir. 1990), the defendants were found guilty of illegally using calcium caseinate to fortify raw milk used to make cheese. In *Stauffer Chemical Co. v. FDA*, Food Drug Cosm. L. Rep. (CCH) ¶ 38,065 (C.D. Cal. 1980), the court declined to entertain a challenge to a letter from FDA stating that use of a processing aid for the canning of tuna would violate the standard of identity for canned tuna. The court held that the matter was not yet ripe for judicial review and the company had failed to exhaust its administrative remedies. The court indicated, however, that it agreed with FDA's position on the merits.

5. *Colors in Standardized Foods.* In promulgating standards of identity, FDA confronted decisions about the permitted composition of a food that might otherwise have gone unexamined. An example is the use of color additives, which can result in economic adulteration and in violations of section 721(b)(6) of the Act. When FDA promulgated standards of identity for egg bread and other bakery products containing eggs, the major issue, requiring a full evidentiary hearing, related to the use of ingredients capable of imparting a yellow color that could mislead consumers into believing the product had a higher egg content than it did. 39 Fed. Reg. 32753 (Sept. 11, 1974); 41 Fed. Reg. 6242 (Feb. 12, 1976); 41 Fed. Reg. 45540 (Oct. 15, 1976); 43 Fed. Reg. 22785 (May 26, 1978); Food Drug Cosm. L. Rep. (CCH) ¶ 38,240 (Apr. 4, 1979); 48 Fed. Reg. 51448 (Nov. 9, 1983); 49 Fed. Reg. 1982 (Jan. 17, 1984); 49 Fed. Reg. 13690 (Apr. 6, 1984).

6. *Revocation of Food Standards.* FDA has revoked only one food standard. The standard for soda water (soft drinks), which had been promulgated in 28 Fed. Reg. 9988 (Sept. 14, 1963), 31 Fed. Reg. 1066 (Jan. 27, 1966), 31 Fed. Reg. 5490 (Apr. 7, 1966), was revoked in 52 Fed. Reg. 18922 (May 20, 1987), 54 Fed. Reg. 398 (Jan. 6, 1989), 54 Fed. Reg. 18651 (May 2, 1989).

7. *Statutory Standards of Identity.* Congress has defined by statute three food products: butter, 42 Stat. 1500 (1923), 21 U.S.C. 321a; oleomargarine, 64 Stat. 20 (1950), 15 U.S.C. 55(f); and nonfat dry milk, 70 Stat. 486 (1956), 21 U.S.C. 321c.

8. *Commentary.* Among the most insightful analyses of FDA's early approach to food standards are two articles by H. Thomas Austern, *The F–O–R–M–U–L–A–T–I–O–N of Mandatory Food Standards*, 2 FOOD DRUG COSM. L.Q. 532 (1947), and *Food Standards: The Balance Between Certainty and Innovation*, 24 FOOD DRUG COSM. L.J. 440 (1969). *See also* Charles W. Crawford, *Ten Years of Food Standardization*, 3 FOOD DRUG COSM. L.Q. 243 (1948); L. M. Beacham, *Why and How—Standard Making*, 6 FOOD DRUG COSM. L.J. 167 (1951); Alan H. Kaplan, *Food Standard Making Procedures*, 20 FOOD DRUG COSM. L.J. 149 (1965); Eugene H. Holeman, *The Role of the States in Establishing Food Standards*, 20 FOOD DRUG COSM. L.J. 159 (1965); George M. Burditt, *The Need for New Uses of the Regulatory Power to Establish Food Standards*, 20 FOOD DRUG COSM. L.J. 165 (1965); Malcolm R. Stephens et al., *Do FDA's Present Food Standards and Standard Making Policy Best Serve the Consumer?*, 20 FOOD DRUG COSM. L.J. 180 (1965); Vincent A. Kleinfeld, *Reflections on Food Standards*, 22 FOOD DRUG COSM. L.J. 100 (1967); William W. Goodrich, *Food Standardization Past, Present and Future*, 24 FOOD DRUG COSM. L.J. 464 (1969); D. M. Hegsted, *Food Standards*, 24 FOOD DRUG COSM. L.J. 384 (1969); William F. Cody, *Food Standards and the White House Conference on Food and Nutrition*, 26 FOOD DRUG COSM. L.J. 347 (1971).

ii. Effects of Food Standards

FDA has promulgated nearly 300 standards of identity. At their broadest reach they covered nearly 45 percent of the wholesale value of food shipped in interstate commerce, excluding fresh fruits and vegetables. 44 Fed. Reg. 75990 (Dec. 21, 1979).

Label Declarations on Standardized and Nonstandardized Foods: Notice of Denial of Petition

37 FEDERAL REGISTER 5131 (March 10, 1972).

A notice of proposed rule making was published in the FEDERAL REGISTER of May 12, 1971 (36 F.R. 8738), in response to a petition filed by Label, Inc., concerning disclosure, on the label, of all ingredients contained in standardized and nonstandardized foods....

The Commissioner ... concludes that he does not have legal authority to promulgate the requested regulation and that the petition must therefore be denied ...

For standardized food, the statute requires that the label must bear only the common name of each optional ingredient (other than spices, flavoring, and coloring) included in the definition and standard of identity and specifically designated in the standard to be named on the label. Failure to comply with these labeling requirements is a misbranding violation. There is no statutory authority to require that the label bear the name of each mandatory ingredient contained in a standardized food or the name of each spice, flavoring, or coloring contained in any food. . . .

Although the Commissioner lacks legal authority to require complete ingredient disclosure, there is nothing in the act prohibiting manufacturers, packers, and distributors from voluntarily making such disclosure, and there is published elsewhere in this issue of the FEDERAL REGISTER, a notice to that effect. . . .

NOTES

1. *Court Review.* In *Label, Inc. v. Edwards*, 475 F.2d 418 (D.C. Cir. 1973), the Court of Appeals sustained the FDA order.

2. *Voluntary Ingredient Disclosure.* In 37 Fed. Reg. 5120 (Mar. 10, 1972), 38 Fed. Reg. 2137 (Jan. 19, 1973), FDA urged food manufacturers to label voluntarily all ingredients in standardized foods and announced it would amend existing standards to require the maximum ingredient disclosure permitted by law. *See* Note 2, p. 131 *supra.* For an analysis of the cost of providing this information, *see* Arthur D. Little, Inc., COST IMPACT ANALYSIS OF LISTING OF OPTIONAL INGREDIENTS IN STANDARDIZED FOOD, Report to FDA under HHS Contract No. 223–79–8052 (Dec. 19, 1981).

3. *Statutory Amendment.* The 1990 Nutrition Labeling and Education Act amended section 403(g) to require the declaration of all ingredients in standardized foods.

Robert W. Hamilton, *Rulemaking on a Record by the Food and Drug Administration*

50 TEXAS LAW REVIEW 1132 (1972).

. . . .

The following tables illustrate the delays in § 701(e) proceedings of the past decade:

	Notice to Order (Months)	Order to Notice of Hearing (Months)	Days of Hearing/ Pages of Transcript	Notice of Hearing to Proposed Findings (Months)	Proposed Findings to Final Order (Months)	Total Time Elapsed (Months)
Orange Juice I	40	9	27/3434	23	11½	83½
Orange Juice II	9½	4	8/874	15½	7	36
Breaded Shrimp I	25	7½	9/1308	12	2½	47
Cheddar Cheese I	8	5	4/490	12	9	34
Cold Pack Cheese Foods/Spreads	7½	8½	4/527	9	5	30
Fruit Jellies	2½	6½	2/234	27	19	55
Jelly	5	6½	2/399	36	10	57½
Peanut Butter	29	45½	30/7736	26½	8	109
Foods for Special Dietary Uses	48	21½	247/32,405	—	—	—

. . . .

NOTES

1. *Impact of Formal Procedures.* The advantages and disadvantages of the formal hearing requirement of section 701(e) for establishing food standards are

explored at in Chapter XIV *infra*. For a vigorous defense of the requirement, see H. Thomas Austern, *Food Standards: The Balance Between Certainty and Innovation*, 24 FOOD DRUG COSM. L.J. 440 (1969).

2. *Statutory Amendment.* The 1990 Nutrition Labeling and Education Act amended section 701(e) to exclude all standards of identity except for the amendment or repeal of standards for dairy products and maple syrup.

COMMENT: TEMPORARY MARKETING PERMITS

To facilitate the development of new foods that deviate from a standard of identity, FDA established a system of temporary permits for test marketing of such products pending amendment of the standard. 21 C.F.R. 130.17. Recognizing the difficulty of amending existing standards, the agency has increasingly liberalized this temporary permit system to allow continuous marketing during consideration of a pending amendment. 37 Fed. Reg. 26340 (Dec. 9, 1972), 40 Fed. Reg. 21721 (May 19, 1975). Yet the temporary permit system itself remains an impediment to product innovation because FDA has adopted the policy that, when the agency approves a permit, it must also approve the entire product label and not just the deviation from the standard. Many temporary permits involve trivial variations from a standard and in fact illustrate the need to amend standards to make them more flexible. *See, e.g.,* 70 Fed. Reg. 57607 (Oct. 3, 2005) (temporarily permitting the use of icebergs as a source of bottled water rather than the sources specified in 21 C.F.R. 165.110).

b.   THE DECLINE OF FOOD STANDARDS: 1970–PRESENT

Following enactment of the 1958 Food Additives Amendment and the 1960 Color Additive Amendments, FDA concluded that it could permit greater flexibility in food standards. In 30 Fed. Reg. 2860 (Mar. 5, 1965), FDA promulgated a food standard for frozen raw breaded shrimp, 21 C.F.R. 161.175, the first that permitted the use of any "safe and suitable" functional ingredients rather than specifying each functional ingredient that could be included in the food.

Report of the White House Conference on Food, Nutrition and Health

New Foods Panel (Dec. 1969).

Background.—The availability of new foods to consumers in the market is limited by present Government regulations. Wider consumer choice of foods could be made available, with the same protection against deceptive or unsafe ingredients, by emphasizing the basic purpose of food standards, to protect the reasonable expectations of consumers. This action could be taken by an immediate review and improvement of existing food standards and a policy directive, and would not require a change in the law.

Under present practice, a Government food standard usually specifies in detail the "recipe" required for the product. Improvements in any standardized food must therefore await a change in the Government standard, which may take many months or even years, before the improved food product can be made available to consumers. In addition, variations from a standardized food are usually prohibited without a change in the standard, under the interpretation that the standard is intended to encompass all similar products.

Because of this deadening effect on food technology, industry is encouraged to avoid the promulgation of standards, and to contest vigorously any proposed attempt at this form of regulation, which it might otherwise accept as reasonable and beneficial. Once promulgated, a detailed food standard of this kind impedes further research, hinders product improvement, and hence denies useful new products to the consumer.

New food technology has permitted development of new foods that are variations of traditional products or wholly new foods that resemble traditional products but are not tied to traditional ingredients. It is important that standards be sufficiently flexible to permit alternative safe ingredients within the limits of the basic nature of the food. A recent example of such a modern standard is the one for breaded shrimp, which guarantees the amount of shrimp the consumer receives but permits any safe and suitable breading ingredients with only a very few specified exceptions. It is equally important that new variations and new foods be permitted to be marketed under their own accurate and informative names and not subject to an old standard, in the way that special formula breads are marketed separate from the standard for enriched bread....

"Safe and Suitable" Food Ingredients: General Definition

39 Fed. Reg. 17304 (May 15, 1974).

In the FEDERAL REGISTER of April 26, 1973 (38 FR 10274), the Commissioner of Food and Drugs proposed a new § 10.1(d) [now § 130.3(d)] which defines the phrase "safe and suitable" as it describes food ingredients. This phrase has been variously defined in numerous food standard regulations, and it was the intent of the Commissioner in his proposal to avoid repeating the same or similar definitions in every individual food standard in the future where it might be applicable....

... *It is ordered*, that 21 CFR 10.1 be amended by adding a new paragraph (d) to read as follows:

§ 130.3   Definitions and interpretations

(d) "Safe and suitable" means that the ingredient:

(1) Performs an appropriate function in the food in which it is used.

(2) Is used at a level no higher than necessary to achieve its intended purpose in that food.

(3) Is not a food additive or color additive as defined in section 201(s) or (t) of the Federal Food, Drug, and Cosmetic Act as used in that food, or is a food additive or color additive as so defined and is used in conformity with regulations established pursuant to section 409 or 706 of the act....

NOTE

Beginning in 1972, FDA undertook to modernize all important food standards to (1) require full labeling of optional ingredients, (2) permit use of any safe and suitable functional food ingredients, and (3) adopt any appropriate aspects of the international food standards developed by the FAO/WHO Codex Alimentarius Commission. *See, e.g.,* 37 Fed. Reg. 18392 (Sept. 9, 1972), 38 Fed. Reg. 27924 (Oct. 10, 1973) (revision of the standards for milk and cream); 38 Fed. Reg. 2334 (Jan. 24, 1973), 38 Fed. Reg. 32787 (Nov. 28, 1973) (flour); 38 Fed. Reg. 10952 (May 3, 1973), 38 Fed. Reg. 25671 (Sept. 14, 1973) (margarine); 39 Fed. Reg. 32753 (Sept. 11, 1974), 41 Fed. Reg. 6242 (Feb. 12, 1976) (bakery products). This was part of the FDA policy to eliminate differences between labeling for standardized and for nonstandardized food.

COMMENT: CODEX ALIMENTARIUS FOOD STANDARDS

The Food and Agriculture Organization (FAO) and the World Health Organization (WHO) created the Codex Alimentarius Commission in 1961 with the objective of establishing food standards that will protect consumer expectations and the public health and facilitate international trade. FDA adopted a procedure for review of all Codex Alimentarius commodity food standards in 37 Fed. Reg. 21102 (Oct. 5, 1972), 38 Fed. Reg. 12396 (May 11, 1973), 21 C.F.R. 130.6. As of 1995, it had considered 83 Codex standards for adoption. 60 Fed. Reg. 67492, 67499 (Dec. 29, 1995). The Codex standards have had a larger impact on dairy products than in any other area. *See, e.g.,* 42 Fed. Reg. 37006 (July 19, 1977), 43 Fed. Reg. 19834 (May 9, 1978) (amendments to standards for nonfat dry milk and related products); 42 Fed. Reg. 37013 (July 19, 1977), 43 Fed. Reg. 21668 (May 19, 1978) (amendments to standards for evaporated milk and related products); and 42 Fed. Reg. 29919 (June 10, 1977), 46 Fed. Reg. 9924 (Jan. 30, 1981) (establishing standards for cultured and acidified dairy products). The agency has also adopted or amended standards for vegetables in response to Codex standards. 37 Fed. Reg. 21106 (Oct. 5, 1972), 39 Fed. Reg. 3541 (Jan. 28, 1974), 39 Fed. Reg. 33663 (Sept. 19, 1974) (adoption of new standard for frozen peas); 37 Fed. Reg. 21112 (Oct. 5, 1972), 39 Fed. Reg. 5760 (Feb. 15, 1974), 40 Fed. Reg. 30940 (July 24, 1975) (amending standard for canned corn); Consideration of virtually all other Codex standards has been terminated by FDA without action, but their publication in the Federal Register served the useful purpose of informing United States food producers about the existence and content of food standards that are often adopted and enforced in other countries. *See, e.g.,* 39 Fed. Reg. 35809 (Oct. 4, 1974) 43 Fed. Reg. 16991 (Apr. 21, 1978), 50 Fed. Reg. 2693 (Jan. 18, 1985) (proposal and withdrawal of new standard for frozen strawberries); 44 Fed. Reg. 10724 (Feb. 23, 1979), 44 Fed. Reg. 60314 (Oct. 19, 1979) (termination of consideration of standard for table olives); 46 Fed. Reg. 60625 (Dec. 11, 1981), 47 Fed. Reg. 41580 (Sept. 21, 1982) (termination of consideration of standard for fructose); 49 Fed. Reg. 8627 (Mar. 8, 1984), 49 Fed. Reg. 29804 (July 24, 1984) (termination of consideration of standard for quick-frozen shrimp or prawns); 53 Fed. Reg. 8512 (Mar. 15, 1988), 54 Fed. Reg. 14396 (Apr. 11, 1989) (termination of consideration of standard for dessert mousse). No Codex standard has been published by FDA in the Federal Register since 1989.

The principal international trade agreement is the General Agreement on Tariffs and Trade (GATT), which became effective on January 1, 1948. The GATT Agreement on Technical Barriers to Trade (TBT) became effective on January 1, 1980. The Uruguay Round that created the World Trade Organization, a new agreement on TBT, and the agreement on the application of sanitary and phytosantitary measures (SPS), became effective on January 1, 1995. The SPS agreement defers specifically to standards established by the Codex Alimentarius. *See* Julie D. Cromer, *Before and After the Uruguay Round: How GATT Affects the Import Policy of the FDA*, 36 HARV. INTERN'L L.J. 557 (1995); articles in Chapter II(C)(4) of the Electronic Book.

As required by the statute implementing the Uruguay Round agreements, 19 U.S.C. 2548, 108 Stat. 4809, 4970 (1994), President Clinton designated USDA as the lead agency for the Codex Alimentarius, with the obligation to publish in the Federal Register yearly reports on Codex standard-setting activities. 60 Fed. Reg. 15845 (Mar. 27, 1995). USDA has published informative reports each year since. *E.g.*, 60 Fed. Reg. 27250 (May 23, 1995); 65 Fed. Reg. 34637 (May 31, 2000); 70 Fed. Reg. 30675 (May 27, 2005); 71 Fed. Reg. 31142 (June 1, 2006); 71 Fed. Reg. 60461 (Oct. 13, 2006).

In 59 Fed. Reg. 60870 (Nov. 28, 1994) and 60 Fed. Reg. 53078 (Oct. 11, 1995), FDA published a policy statement on the development and use of standards with respect to international harmonization of regulatory requirements and guidelines. In 60 Fed. Reg. 67492, 67499 (Dec. 29, 1995), the agency specifically asked for comment on the impact of FDA domestic policy regarding food standards on international food standards. This was part of an advance notice of proposed rulemaking about the future of the agency's food standards program. *See* Joseph A. Levitt and H. Michael Wehr, *The Importance of International Activities to the Work of the Food and Drug Administration's Center for Food Safety and Applied Nutrition*, 56 FOOD & DRUG L.J. 1 (2001).

In addition to food commodity standards, Codex adopts standards regarding food additives, food contaminants, animal drug residues, food labeling, and a host of other food regulatory policies. FDA and USDA participate in these standard-setting activities as well, and they are covered in the yearly report published by USDA in the Federal Register.

For the extensive literature on the early work of the Codex Alimentarius, see L. M. Beacham, *Current Codex Alimentarius Activities*, 28 FOOD DRUG COSM. L.J. 79 (1973); Eddie F. Kimbrell, *Food Composition Regulation and Codex Standards*, 33 FOOD DRUG COSM. L.J. 145 (1978); bibliographies by Julius G. Zimmerman in 26 FOOD DRUG COSM. L.J. 303 (1971) and 31 FOOD DRUG COSM. L.J. 229 (1976).

————

When FDA applied a liberalized approach to the standard of identity for ice cream, 39 Fed. Reg. 27144 (July 25, 1974), 42 Fed. Reg. 19127 (Apr. 12, 1977), 42 Fed. Reg. 35152 (July 8, 1977), it encountered fierce and unexpected opposition.

Nicholas Wade, *Ice Cream: Dairymen Imperiled By FDA's Recipe*

197 SCIENCE 844 (1977).

The FDA's proposed standard for "America's number one fun food," as the ice cream maker's chief lobbyist touts it, would allow manufacturers to use more casein and whey in their mixes and less milk powder. Casein is the principal protein of milk, and is found mainly in milk. Whey is the even more highly nutritious product left over when milk is converted to cheese.... Where is the harm in that?

"This is a terrible, terrible thing that should happen," Pat Healy, chief lobbyist of the National Milk Producers Federation, moans about his dairy industry colleagues, the ice cream makers. "For a group of people operating on the fringes of the industry to take the chance of destroying an industry which is a valuable national asset in order to make a couple of cents extra per gallon of ice cream—I think it is a despicable act by short-sighted, quick-buck artists who have no thought for the long-range impact of their actions."

"The FDA is proposing a technologized frozen dessert product filled with chemicals and dairy waste products—the leftovers of the dairy manufacturing process. This is a matter which is seriously and radically altering one of America's favorite foods," Congressman Frederick Richmond (D–N.Y.) declaimed at a house hearing held on 2 August.

"We want ice cream to stay the real thing," stated Congressman Charles Rose (D–N.C.). "I think what we are concerned about is that America does not go the way of Hitler's Germany in World War II where ersatz became a by-word of products that were sold to its people out of economic necessity." ...

What has happened is that a new regulatory philosophy ... holds that the agency should not prevent food producers making use of new technologies as long as the nutritional standards of the products are maintained. The doctrine is perfectly in accord with the principles of the free market, but it has opened the way for head-on collision with sectors such as the milk producers, whose approach to maintaining their market share rests not on technological adaptation but on protective measures backed by political clout....

Ice cream at present may be made from milk powder (nonfat dried milk), whey, and 11 other milk-derived products including casein, but there are limits on the amounts of whey and casein that ice cream makers may use. The proposed new standards would lift the limits on whey and casein, stipulating only a minimum protein percentage and leaving manufacturers to choose whatever mix of dairy products they pleased to meet it....

Imported casein is a far cheaper product than American-protected milk powder. So too is whey, a surplus by-product of the burgeoning cheese industry. Under the FDA's proposed changes, ice cream makers would have a strong incentive to substitute as much whey and casein for milk powder as possible. Consumer preferences and other factors impose limits on the extent of this substitution.... The cost savings to manufacturers would eventually, through competition, be passed on to the consumer, amounting to a reduction of 2% in the retail price of ice cream....

Against this background, the milk producers' heated reaction to the ice cream issue becomes immediately comprehensible. The milk powder displaced by the FDA's proposed new standards would have to be bought by the government at an estimated cost of $183 million, according to USDA. Coming on top of the support program's expected doubling in cost, the extra $183 million could be a very damaging shock, not to say the final straw that breaks the program's political support in Congress....

NOTE

In 43 Fed. Reg. 4596 (Feb. 3, 1978), FDA announced that it was revoking the controversial provisions of its proposed ice cream standard:

> ... When it issued these standards, FDA did not expect that there would be measurable nutritional differences between ice cream made under the new standard and that made under the present one. But the agency's studies determined that under the new standard some ice cream formulations could have lesser amounts of some nutrients than under the current standard....

Embolded by FDA's emphasis in the early 1970s on information labeling as the preferred method of regulating food, a manufacturer of filled milk brought suit to overturn the Filled Milk Act—which had twice been upheld by the Supreme Court. *See supra* p. 153.

Milnot Co. v. Richardson

350 F. Supp. 221 (N.D. Ill. 1972).

■ MORGAN, DISTRICT JUDGE.

This is an action for declaratory judgment ... asking the court to declare that the product known as "Milnot," manufactured by the plaintiff, is not within the purview of the provisions of 21 U.S.C. §§ 61–64 [The Filled Milk Act]; or, in the alternative, to declare that Act unconstitutional on the ground that it violates the provisions of the Fifth Amendment to the Constitution of the United States....

... The substance involved in this case, Milnot, is a food product which basically is a blend of fat free milk and vegetable soya oil, to which are added vitamins A and D. In the production of this product cream is skimmed from whole fresh milk. The cream contains the butterfat content of the milk including the fat-soluble vitamins A, D and E. To the portion of the milk which remains after the skimming process, plaintiff adds, *inter alia*, soybean oil as well as vitamins A and D. This restores the liquid to a milk-like consistency and composition. The mixture is then evaporated so as to remove a portion of the water content. That Milnot is wholesome, nutritious, and useful as a food source is clear from the record.

The Filled Milk Act, promulgated by Congress in 1923, prohibits interstate shipment of filled milk products. Following enactment of that statute, plaintiff, then known as Carolene Products Company, violated it and was convicted. After much litigation, the United States Supreme Court twice upheld the validity of the statute.... At least since affirmance of its second conviction, plaintiff has limited its distribution of Milnot to intrastate commerce in the several states where it is produced....

... Plaintiff suggests, and this court agrees, that the appearance and continued existence of new products on the market and in interstate commerce which are quite similar in composition to and competitive with Milnot, and also in imitation or semblance of milk as fully as is Milnot (even though perhaps not "filled milk" in a technical sense under the statutory definition), creates a new factual situation upon which the court should reconsider the constitutionality of the Filled Milk Act as applied to Milnot....

The measuring stick to which legislative acts must conform in order to satisfy due process has been stated in the previous *Carolene* decisions. That is, regulatory legislation affecting ordinary commercial transactions is not to be pronounced unconstitutional unless, in light of the known facts, it is of such a character as to preclude the assumption that it rests upon some rational basis within the knowledge and experience of the legislators. And as previously stated, the constitutionality of a statute predicated upon the existence of a particular state of facts may be challenged by showing to the court that those facts have ceased to exist.

From the undisputed facts in the record here, it appears crystal clear that certain imitation milk and dairy products are so similar to Milnot in composition, appearance, and use that different treatment as to interstate shipment caused by application of the Filled Milk Act to Milnot violates the due process of law to which Milnot Company is constitutionally entitled. No useful purpose is served by listing such products here by name or otherwise, or by discussing the dairy market conditions and dangers of confusion which led to the passage and judicial upholding of the Filled Milk Act many years ago. Suffice it to say that this court finds that the latter have long since ceased to exist. [1]

... The possibility of confusion, or passing off, in the marketplace, which justified the statute in 1944, can no longer be used rationally as a constitutional prop to prevent interstate shipment of Milnot. There is at least as much danger in this regard with imitation milk as with filled milk, and actually no longer any such real danger with either....

NOTES

1. *Agency Response.* Following the *Milnot* decision FDA published this announcement in 38 Fed. Reg. 20748 (Aug. 2, 1973):

1. It is not insignificant in this regard that some eleven states which passed filled milk acts have since discarded them—five by repeal and six by court action. By far the majority of states now permit wholesome and properly labeled filled milk products. It is worth noting, also, that when the Federal Filled Milk Act was passed by Congress and upheld by the Supreme Court, the presently accepted dangers of "cholesterol" in animal fat were almost unknown.

The court in the *Milnot* case concluded that, since other substitute milk and dairy products may lawfully be shipped in interstate commerce, the prohibition against interstate shipment of filled milk products was an unconstitutional discrimination against these products. The White House Conference on Food, Nutrition and Health recommended in 1969 that the Filled Milk Act be repealed, and the Food and Drug Administration has concurred in that recommendation. Accordingly, it has been concluded that the decision in the *Milnot* case will not be appealed. . . .

This notice will serve to inform the public that, pursuant to the court decision in this case, the Filled Milk Act will no longer be enforced. Henceforth, filled milk products may lawfully be shipped in interstate commerce and will be regulated under the provisions of the Federal Food, Drug, and Cosmetic Act, just as any other foods.

In conjunction with this statement of enforcement policy, FDA proposed the establishment of a common or usual name for "filled milk" in 38 Fed. Reg. 20743 (Aug. 2, 1973). The agency subsequently withdrew the proposed common or usual name regulation and proposed a standard of identity for filled milk and other substitute dairy products in 43 Fed. Reg. 42118 (Sept. 19, 1978), which was withdrawn in 48 Fed. Reg. 37666 (Aug. 19, 1983).

2. *Rejection of State Filled Milk Laws.* Several state filled milk statutes have also been held invalid, principally under state constitutional provisions. *E.g., Milnot Co. v. Arkansas State Board of Health*, 388 F. Supp. 901 (E.D. Ark. 1975); *Milnot Co. v. Douglas*, 452 F. Supp. 505 (S.D.W. Va. 1978); *General Foods Corp. v. Priddle*, 569 F. Supp. 1378 (D. Kan. 1983); *Strehlow v. Kansas State Board of Agriculture*, 232 Kan. 589, 659 P.2d 785 (1983).

3. *Narrowed Application.* In *Dean Foods Co. v. Wisconsin Department. of Agriculture, Trade and Consumer Protection*, 478 F. Supp. 224 (W.D. Wis. 1979), the District Court granted a preliminary injunction against enforcement of a state statute prohibiting the sale of any food which purports to be or is represented as milk and which contains any fat or oil other than milkfat. The state proposed to prohibit the sale of "Choco–Riffic," a nondairy beverage that resembles chocolate milk. The District Court concluded that the manufacturer had a reasonably good chance to prevail on its contention that a ban of a healthy, nutritious product unduly burdens interstate commerce and thus enjoined an outright prohibition of sale while allowing the state to explore less restrictive measures. On reargument, the District Court withdrew its initial conclusion that the product "purports to be" a dairy product and stated that this determination must depend not upon mere physical resemblance but upon whether, in light of all circumstances, a substantial portion of consumers believes that the product is a dairy product. 504 F. Supp. 520 (W.D. Wis. 1980).

4. *Other Dairy Protection Statutes.* The Oleomargarine Act, 24 Stat. 209 (1886), was repealed and replaced by section 407 of the FD&C Act in 64 Stat. 20 (1950). The Filled Cheese Act, 29 Stat. 253 (1896), 68A Stat. 576 (1939), was repealed by 88 Stat. 1466 (1974). The Renovated Butter Act, 32 Stat. 193 (1902), was repealed by 90 Stat. 1520, 1814 (1976).

5. *Tea Quality Standards.* Under the Tea Importation Act of 1883, 22 Stat. 451, repealed and replaced in 1897, 29 Stat. 604, FDA established a Board of Tea Experts to establish uniform quality standards for imported tea. In *Buttfield v. Stranahan*, 192 U.S. 470 (1904), the Supreme Court upheld FDA's constitutional authority to ban import of substandard tea. Fearful of this precedent, the food industry successfully opposed FDA authority to promulgate food standards under the 1906 Act. The Tea Importation Act was repealed in 110 Stat. 1198 (1996) on the ground of regulatory reform. *See* Patricia J.B. DeWitt, *A Brief History of Tea: The*

Rise and Fall of the Tea Importation Act (2000), in Chapter I(A) of the Electronic Book.

———

In 60 Fed. Reg. 67492 (Dec. 29, 1995), FDA published an advance notice of proposed rulemaking (ANPRM) to invite public comment on whether food standards are still needed and, if so, whether they should be modified or streamlined. Ten years later, FDA and USDA jointly published proposed regulations to establish general principles for the modernization of food standards.

Food Standards; General Principles and Food Standards Modernization

70 Fed. Reg. 29214 (May 20, 2005).

. . . [T]he Work Group considered five options, as the next step in the process of food standards reform, and analyzed the advantages and disadvantages of each option. The first option the Work Group considered was not proceeding any further with the review of the food standards regulations. The advantage of this option is that, in the short run, it would require little or no increase in the agencies' use of resources.

A major disadvantage of this option is that there is very little industry or consumer support for it. As noted previously, the majority of comments supported revising the existing system of food standards to simplify them and to make them more flexible. . . .

The second option the Work Group considered was removing all food standards from the regulations and treating all foods as nonstandardized foods. One advantage of this option is that, in most cases, fewer agency resources would be required to eliminate food standards than to review and revise them. Also, under this option, we no longer would devote resources to responding to petitions requesting an amendment to an existing standard or the establishment of a new food standard.

As with the first option, however, very few comments on the ANPRMs supported eliminating food standards completely. We agree with the comments that stated that States might establish their own food standards in the absence of Federal food standards. . . .

The third option the Work Group considered was using our resources to review and revise food standards to make them internally consistent, more flexible for manufacturers and consumers, and easier to administer. . . . The disadvantage of this option is competing priorities would make it unlikely we could do this in a timely manner.

The fourth option the Work Group considered was to request external industry groups to review, revise, and administer the food standards (private certification). This option would require little or no use of the agencies' resources. In addition, the revised food standards would provide the level of flexibility that industry desires. However, for private organizations to review, revise, and administer the food standards, the [FD&C Act, the Federal Meat Inspection Act, and the Poultry Products Inspection Act] would have to be amended, so that these standards would have the force of law. . . .

The fifth option the Work Group considered was to rely on external groups—consumer, industry, commodity, or other groups—to draft recommended revisions to existing Federal food standards but retain the agencies' authority to establish the final food standards. . . .

One major advantage of this option is that it would require the use of fewer of our agencies' resources than would be required if we were to review and propose amendments to the food standards without the benefit of petitions. . . .

The disadvantage to this fifth option is that, if a consumer, industry, or commodity group does not feel strongly about revising a particular group of food standards, we might not receive a petition and would then need to commit resources to reviewing the food standards without the benefit of a petition. . . .

For the reasons discussed previously, we have tentatively determined that the fifth option is the most appropriate course of action. The Work Group preliminarily determined that we could rely on external groups to suggest new food standards, revisions to existing food standards, or elimination of certain food standards that are consistent with the proposed general principles. The general principles approach would allow us to chart the basic course of food standards review and modernization. Moreover, it would allow consumer and industry groups to participate in the development of new and revised food standards and to identify food standards that should be eliminated. In addition, it would provide an opportunity for consumer and industry groups to submit data to support any claims made in petitions relating to consumer expectations or beliefs, and hence, protect consumer interests. . . .

NOTES

1. *Stone Ground Wheat Flour.* In a letter from John M. Taylor, III, Associate Commissioner for Regulatory Affairs, FDA, to Bob Goldstein (Dec. 24, 2003), FDA declined to establish a standard of identity for stone ground wheat flour. *See* FDA Dockets Nos. OIP–0290/CP1, OIP–0290/CP2, OIP–0290/PRC1.

2. *Technological Change.* In 70 Fed. Reg. 56409 (Sept. 27, 2005), FDA published an advance notice of proposed rulemaking based on two industry petitions to bring the standards of identity for specified frozen desert and cheese products up to current technological standards.

4. "IMITATION" LABELING

Section 403(c) of the FD&C Act provides that a food that is an imitation of another food must be labeled as such. As discussed later in this chapter, *infra* p. 218, in 1973 FDA restricted the required application of the term "imitation" to substitute food that is nutritionally inferior to the food for which it is a substitute. The materials directly below address developments in FDA's approach to "imitation" labeling prior to 1973.

62 Cases of Jam v. United States

340 U.S. 593 (1951).

■ MR. JUSTICE FRANKFURTER delivered the opinion of the Court.

The proceeding before us was commenced in 1949 in the District Court for the District of New Mexico. By it the United States seeks to condemn 62 cases of "Delicious Brand Imitation Jam," manufactured in Colorado and shipped to New Mexico. The Government claims that this product "purports" to be fruit jam, a food for which the Federal Security Administrator has promulgated a "definition and standard of identity." The regulation specifies that a fruit jam must contain "not less than 45 parts by weight" of the fruit ingredient. The product in question is composed of 55% sugar, 25% fruit, 20% pectin, and small amounts of citric acid and soda. These specifications show that pectin, a gelatinized solution consisting largely of water, has been substituted for a substantial proportion of the fruit required. The Government contends that the product is therefore to be deemed "misbranded" under § 403(g)....

According to the Federal Food, Drug, and Cosmetic Act, nothing can be legally "jam" after the Administrator promulgated his regulation in 1940, unless it contains the specified ingredients in prescribed proportion. Hence the product in controversy is not "jam." It cannot lawfully be labeled "jam" and introduced into interstate commerce, for to do so would "represent" as a standardized food a product which does not meet prescribed specifications.

But the product with which we are concerned is sold as "imitation jam." Imitation foods are dealt with in § 403(c) of the Act. In that section Congress did not give an esoteric meaning to "imitation." It left it to the understanding of ordinary English speech....

In ordinary speech there can be no doubt that the product which the United States here seeks to condemn is an "imitation" jam. It looks and tastes like jam; it is unequivocally labeled "imitation jam." The Government does not argue that its label in any way falls short of the requirements of § 403(c). Its distribution in interstate commerce would therefore clearly seem to be authorized by that section. We could hold it to be "misbranded" only if we held that a practice Congress authorized by § 403(c) Congress impliedly prohibited by § 403(g).

We see no justification so to distort the ordinary meaning of the statute. Nothing in the text or history of the legislation points to such a reading of what Congress wrote. In § 403(g) Congress used the words "purport" and "represent"—terms suggesting the idea of counterfeit. But the name "imitation jam" at once connotes precisely what the product is: a different, an inferior preserve, not meeting the defined specifications.... A product so labeled is described with precise accuracy. It neither conveys any ambiguity nor emanates any untrue innuendo, as was the case with the "Bred Spred" considered by Congress in its deliberation on § 403(g). It purports and is represented to be only what it is—an imitation. It does not purport nor represent to be what it is not—the Administrator's genuine "jam." ...

■ MR. JUSTICE DOUGLAS, with whom MR. JUSTICE BLACK concurs, dissenting.

The result reached by the Court may be sound by legislative standards. But the legal standards which govern us make the process of reaching that result tortuous to say the least. We must say that petitioner's "jam" purports to be "jam" when we read § 403(g) and purports to be not "jam" but another food when we read § 403(c). Yet if petitioner's product did not purport to be "jam" petitioner would have no claim to press and the Government no objection to raise.

NOTES

1. *Imitation Margarine.* In *United States v. 856 Cases ... "Demi"*, 254 F. Supp. 57 (N.D.N.Y. 1966), the government seized as misbranded the claimant's "imitation margarine," a product that failed to conform to FDA's standard of identity for margarine. The government unsuccessfully attempted to distinguish *62 Cases of Jam* by arguing that Congress intended all products made in semblance of butter to be called "margarine," and that FDA had in effect defined the only marketable imitation of butter in its standard of identity for margarine.

2. *Chil–Zert.* In *United States v. 651 Cases ... Chocolate Chil–Zert*, 114 F. Supp. 430 (N.D.N.Y. 1953), the District Court determined that a chocolate-flavored frozen dessert, made from soy fat and protein, had to be labeled "imitation ice cream." The *Chil–Zert* case was the first FDA brought based solely under section 403(c). The agency brought no other enforcement actions based solely on section 403(c) and it failed to challenge as "imitations" a wide variety of foods made from vegetable oil marketed as substitutes for dairy products, such as whipped toppings and coffee whiteners. Compare *United States v. Schider*, 246 U.S. 519 (1918).

3. *State Enforcement.* During the 1960s several state regulatory agencies challenged vegetable oil-based substitutes for dairy products under state laws restricting "imitations." Most courts refused to suppress the marketing of such products when truthfully labeled. *See, e.g., Coffee–Rich, Inc. v. Kansas State Bd. of Health*, 388 P.2d 582 (Kan. 1964); *Coffee–Rich, Inc. v. Michigan Dept. of Agriculture*, 135 N.W.2d 594 (Mich. Ct. App. 1965); *Coffee-Rich, Inc. v. Commissioner of Public Health*, 204 N.E.2d 281 (Mass. 1965).

4. *USDA Policy.* In *In re Castleberry's Food Co.*, USDA FMIA Dkt No. 36 (Jan. 3, 1980), a Department of Agriculture Administrative Law Judge ruled that USDA had improperly required a product that varied from its standard for corned beef hash to be labeled "imitation." The ALJ's opinion documented substantial inconsistency in USDA labeling practices and endorsed the FDA approach. It found that the product was properly labeled with its own descriptive phrase and a statement of how it varied from the standard. Although the USDA Judicial Officer overruled the ALJ and determined that the product was an imitation, his decision stated that the FDA definition of imitation was used by USDA in the case-by-case approval of meat food labels. 40 Agric. Dec. 1262, 1277–78 (1981). See also *Grocery Manufacturers of America v. Gerace*, 755 F.2d at 1001–02, where USDA represented that it had adopted the FDA definition of imitation. In *Armour & Co. v. Freeman*, 304 F.2d 404 (D.C. Cir.1962), the Court of Appeals held that USDA could not lawfully require smoked ham containing added moisture of up to 10 percent to be labeled as "imitation ham," because that would be a "false or deceptive name" prohibited by the Federal Meat Inspection Act. *Swift & Co., Inc. v. Walkley*, 369 F. Supp. 1198 (S.D.N.Y. 1973), upheld application of New York's "imitation" labeling requirement—essentially identical to section 601(n)(3) of the Federal Meat Inspection Act—to "All American Fun–Links," a product made in link form from meat, isolated soybean, flavorings, water, and curing agents. The product's label had been

approved by USDA, which apparently relied on the White House Conference recommendations.

5. *Commentary.* The controversy over required and permissible "imitation" labeling inspired a large literature prior to FDA's August 1973 regulation. *See* Michael F. Markel, *The Law on Imitation Food*, 5 FOOD DRUG COSM. L.J. 145 (1950); Edward Brown Williams, *What Price Imitation*, 5 FOOD DRUG COSM. L.J. 185 (1950); H. Thomas Austern, *Ordinary English but Not Ordinary Jam*, 6 FOOD DRUG COSM. L.J. 909 (1951); Robert W. Austin, *The Jam Standard Case—Its Social Significance*, 6 FOOD DRUG COSM. L.J. 919 (1951); Robert M. Rubenstein, *The Bugaboo of Imitation Foods*, 7 FOOD DRUG COSM. L.J. 266 (1952); John L. Harvey, *Imitation Dairy Products*, 8 FOOD DRUG COSM. L.J. 527 (1953); Harvey L. Hensel, *Dietary Version of a Standardized Food—Is it an Imitation?*, 13 FOOD DRUG COSM. L.J. 172 (1958); George M. Burditt, *Imitation*, 19 FOOD DRUG COSM. L.J. 72 (1964); Kenneth R. Myers, *The Wet Ham Controversy and New Concepts in Federal Food Regulation: Armour v. Freeman*, 19 FOOD DRUG COSM. L.J. 196 (1964); Lester Hankin, *Quality Aspects of Imitation and Artificial Foods*, 24 FOOD DRUG COSM. L.J. 368 (1969); Eugene I. Lambert, *New Foods and Old Laws: Conflict or Accommodation?*, 26 FOOD DRUG COSM. L.J. 644 (1971); Philip C. Olsson, *New Foods—Another Viewpoint*, 26 FOOD DRUG COSM. L.J. 652 (1971).

5. COMMON OR USUAL FOOD NAMES

Section 403(i)(1) of the FD&C Act requires that a nonstandardized food bear on the label its "common or usual name." Perhaps no provision in the Act has engendered more controversy, and produced such disparate decisions.

a. FDA POLICY PRIOR TO 1970

FDA policy on food names during the first two decades of the FD&C Act was relatively straightforward. Staple foods were expected to bear their traditional names. To the extent that FDA felt impelled to prescribe the name of a food, it did so by promulgating a standard of identity. Products that were substitutes either for staples or for standardized food were deemed to be imitations. This framework worked relatively well until, following World War II, modern food technology emerged to transform our food supply from one based on easily-recognized staple foods to the cornucopia of fabricated food to which we are now accustomed. Beginning in the 1960s there was increasing conflict between FDA and the food industry over the proper common or usual name for these new nonstandardized foods.

b. THE WHITE HOUSE CONFERENCE ON FOOD, NUTRITION AND HEALTH

The Report of the White House Conference, issued in December 1969, directly addressed the issue of food names.

Report of the White House Conference on Food, Nutrition and Health
New Foods Panel (Dec. 1969).

. . . Every food should bear a generic name that accurately identifies or describes it, in terms readily understandable to consumers. . . .

Under existing law, Government agencies could adopt an administrative policy no longer requiring or permitting over-simplified and inaccurate words. Instead, they could require an informative and descriptive generic name for every food. The existing legal prohibitions against false or misleading labeling and advertising could be utilized to prevent the use of any terminology that could mislead consumers about the identity or characteristics of the new product. Existing law could also be used to establish, by regulation, a uniform generic name that would accurately reflect reasonable expectations of consumers.

Such a policy would better serve the public interest. It would provide more accurate and useful information for consumers about the identity of foods than is presently the situation. It would also encourage the development and marketing of variations of traditional foods and of completely new foods, that can provide consumers a greater variety of acceptable, higher quality, and more nutritious food products at lower prices....

c.   THE NEW FDA POLICY OF THE 1970s

In response to the proliferation of new foods that did not conform to an established standard of identity, FDA adopted a new policy on food names, based on the Report of the White House Conference. First, FDA officials concluded that the agency should cease adopting new standards of identity. Second, they decided to interpret the "purports to be" language in section 403(g) narrowly, thus restricting the reach of standards of identity to products labeled or otherwise clearly represented as standardized foods. The third component of this new policy was reliance on informative common or usual names. FDA established general criteria for all common or usual names for food products and established a formal procedure for adopting common or usual names by regulation.

Common or Usual Names For Nonstandardized Foods
38 Fed. Reg. 6964 (March 14, 1973).

In the FEDERAL REGISTER of June 22, 1972 (37 FR 12327), the Commissioner of Food and Drugs proposed a procedure for the establishment by regulation of common or usual names for foods. The Commissioner also proposed to establish a common or usual name for seafood cocktails, to include the percentage of the characterizing seafood ingredient(s)....

Twenty-eight requests were made that the proposal be expanded to include additional labeling requirements such as the percentage of all ingredients for all foods; the percentage of primary ingredients for all foods; the percentage of fats, carbohydrates, and proteins; the vitamin and mineral content; and the specific source of ingredients.

The Commissioner concludes that percentage labeling of ingredients should be restricted to situations where this information has a material bearing on price or consumer acceptance of the food, or where such information may prevent deception. Labeling the percentage of all ingredients would be extremely costly and would provide no proven benefits to consumers. A mechanism for establishing a regulation requiring labeling of the percentage of all "primary" ingredients that have a material bearing on the price or consumer acceptance is provided for in this regulation....

Common or usual names will not be established ... for all non-standardized foods. Such names will be established by such regulation only when it is necessary fully to inform the consumer, or where different names are used for the same product by different manufacturers.

Common or usual names for "like" or "similar" products, where none now exists, may be proposed under the provisions of this regulation and will reflect the reasonable expectations of consumers. The name itself will accurately identify or describe the basic nature or characterizing properties of the food in a way that will distinguish it from other foods.

A food that purports to be a standardized food does not cease purporting to be a standardized food merely because its label bears the percent of characterizing ingredients. The label of a food which neither purports to be nor is represented as being a standardized food must bear on the label its common or usual name, which may not be false or misleading. Nor may a manufacturer avoid a standard merely by adding an ingredient not permitted in the standard unless that ingredient substantially changes the nature or characteristics of the food.... Use of a new method or process, with or without an added artificial sweetener, to produce a substantial reduction in calories would, on the other hand, result in the new product not purporting to be the standardized food when a distinctive descriptive name is used and the food is not an "imitation" under proposed new § 1.8(e)....

————

The Federal Register document quoted above promulgated a new 21 C.F.R. Part 102, "Common or Usual Name for Nonstandardized Foods." In addition to general principles, this new part originally contained common and usual name regulations for four particular foods, all seafood products. FDA has since added to Part 102 twelve additional common and usual name regulations for particular nonstandardized foods, some of which are excerpted below, along with the general principles.

Common or Usual Name For Nonstandardized Foods

21 C.F.R. Part 102.

§ 102.5   General principles

(a) The common or usual name of a food, which may be a coined term, shall accurately identify or describe, in as simple and direct terms as possible, the basic nature of the food or its characterizing properties or ingredients. The name shall be uniform among all identical or similar products and may not be confusingly similar to the name of any other food that is not reasonably encompassed within the same name....

(b) The common or usual name of a food shall include the percentage(s) of any characterizing ingredient(s) or component(s) when the proportion of such ingredient(s) or component(s) in the food has a material bearing on price or consumer acceptance or when the labeling or the appearance of the food may otherwise create an erroneous impression that such ingredient(s) or component(s) is present in an amount greater than is actually the case....

(c) The common or usual name of a food shall include a statement of the presence or absence of any characterizing ingredient(s) or component(s) and/or the need for the user to add any characterizing ingredient(s) or component(s) when the presence or absence of such ingredient(s) or component(s) in the food has a material bearing on price or consumer acceptance or when the labeling or the appearance of the food may otherwise create an erroneous impression that such ingredient(s) or component(s) is present when it is not, and consumers may otherwise be misled about the presence or absence of the ingredient(s) or component(s) in the food....

§ 102.26   Frozen "heat and serve" dinners

(a) A frozen "heat and serve" dinner:

(1) Shall contain at least three components, one of which shall be a significant source of protein and each of which shall consist of one or more of the following: meat, poultry, fish, cheese, eggs, vegetables, fruit, potatoes, rice, or other cereal based products (other than bread or rolls).

(2) May also contain other servings of food (*e.g.*, soup, bread or rolls, beverage, dessert).

(b) The common or usual name of the food consists of all of the following:

(1) The phrase "frozen 'heat and serve' dinner," except that the name of the predominant characterizing ingredient or other appropriately descriptive term may immediately precede the word "dinner" (*e.g.*, "frozen chicken dinner" or "frozen heat and serve beef dinner"). The words "heat and serve" are optional. The word "frozen" is also optional, provided that the words "Keep Frozen" or the equivalent are prominently and conspicuously placed on the principal display panel....

(2) The phrase "containing (or contains) _____" the blank to be filled in with an accurate description of each of the three or more dish components listed in paragraph (a)(1) of this section in their order of descending predominance by weight (*e.g.*, ham, mashed potatoes, and peas), followed by any of the other servings specified in paragraph (a)(2) of this section contained in the package (*e.g.*, onion soup, enriched white bread, and artificially flavored vanilla pudding) in their order of descending predominance by weight. This part of the name shall be placed immediately following or directly below the part specified in paragraph (b)(1) of this section.... The words "contains" or "containing" are optional.

(3) If the labeling implies that the package contains other foods and these foods are not present in the package, *e.g.*, if a vignette on the package depicts a "serving suggestion" which includes any foods not present in the package, the principal display panel shall bear a statement that such foods are not present....

§ 102.41 Potato chips made from dried potatoes

(a) The common or usual name of the food product that resembles and is of the same composition as potato chips, except that it is composed of dehydrated potatoes (buds, flakes, granules, or other form), shall be "potato chips made from dried potatoes." ...

§ 102.54 Seafood cocktails

The common or usual name of a seafood cocktail in package form fabricated with one or more seafood ingredients shall be:

(a) When the cocktail contains only one seafood ingredient, the name of the seafood ingredient followed by the word "cocktail" (*e.g.*, shrimp cocktail, crabmeat cocktail) and a statement of the percentage by weight of that seafood ingredient in the product....

(b) When the cocktail contains more than one seafood ingredient, the term "seafood cocktail" and a statement of the percentage by weight of each seafood ingredient in the product....

American Frozen Food Institute v. Mathews

413 F. Supp. 548 (D.D.C. 1976).

■ Robinson, Jr., District Judge.

By this action Plaintiff American Frozen Food Institute (AFFI) challenges the innovative attempt by the Food and Drug Administration (FDA) to regulate labeling in certain areas of the food industry through establishing "common and usual names" for nonstandardized foods. AFFI contends that two recent rulings from FDA which establish common and usual names for seafood cocktails and frozen heat and serve dinners must be set aside by this Court on the grounds that they were promulgated in a manner excessive of agency authority, establish an unlawful presumption, violate the First Amendment and are arbitrary and capricious without sufficient support in the record.... [T]he Court concludes that the FDA acted within its statutory authority and that the defendants are entitled to summary judgment....

... FDA has established common and usual names for certain of these foods under its general rulemaking authority, Section 701(a) of the Act. The regulations were prompted by a concern expressed by the White House Conference on Food Nutrition and Health, regarding the lack of informative food labeling....

The Plaintiff contends that FDA lacks authority to *create* common and usual names through substantive rulemaking.... In the alternative, AFFI contends that even if FDA has authority to establish common and usual names through its general rulemaking authority, these two specific regulations exceed that authority....

... Under the general rulemaking provision of the governing statute set forth in 21 U.S.C. § 371(a) [FD&C Act 701(a)], FDA is authorized to "promulgate regulations for the efficient enforcement of [the Act]." Plaintiff contends that despite the broad mandate reflected by this provision,

FDA is restricted to two methods for establishing common and usual names. AFFI's position is that FDA can either recognize an already established common and usual name in the context of a Section 701[(e)] proceeding (establishing a definition and standard of identity) or may bring a judicial action pursuant to the sanctions set forth in 21 U.S.C. §§ 331–334 for violations of the Act, during which the Court can recognize the common and usual name of a particular food. . . .

The Court is not persuaded that the Act should be read so narrowly. Plaintiff[] . . . ignores significant case law which by analogy supports the FDA's authority to proceed by substantive lawmaking in this case. The cases are legion in which Courts have recognized the preference of substantive rulemaking by an agency over the time consuming and often unfair process of case by case adjudication. . . .

By the action challenged herein, FDA is attempting to provide consumers with relevant buying information on food labels of nonstandardized products. It is not attempting to eradicate economic adulteration nor to prescribe food composition. As stated earlier, the label of a standardized food bears only optional ingredients. The nonstandardized foods for which FDA has established common and usual names by the procedure challenged herein will bear on the label such information deemed appropriate by the agency in light of the purpose of the Act.

Although there is nothing in the legislative history which clearly indicates that FDA has the authority to provide this consumer information pursuant to its rulemaking authority by establishing common and usual names, there is nothing in the legislative history of Section 701(a) or (e) which indicates that it cannot. . . .

Next the Court must determine whether the two specific regulations challenged by this action have additional infirmities requiring this Court to set them aside. The thrust of Plaintiff's attack directed at the common and usual name for frozen heat and serve dinners is that this regulation . . . is actually a definition and standard of identity because it includes components as part of the name. Plaintiff contends that it must be set aside because it was not promulgated pursuant to a Section 701(e) proceeding. . . .

Although the Court recognizes that this name [frozen "heat and serve" dinner] appears to be more than just a name, Plaintiff's argument that it is a definition and standard of identity is not persuasive. This regulation controls use of the term "dinner" and requires an accurate description of each component in order of descending predominance. As the regulation makes clear, all the specific ingredients are optional. Only categories are mandatory. Therefore, to require a definition and standard of identity, which normally sets forth a "recipe" for a food, would be inappropriate since there *are* no specific mandatory ingredients for frozen heat and serve dinners. Therefore, it cannot be said that this particular regulation is actually a definition and standard of identity.

Lastly, Plaintiff challenges that portion of the regulation for seafood cocktails . . . which requires that the percentage of seafood ingredients be plainly stated on the label. Plaintiff argues strongly that FDA's authority to enforce such percentage of ingredient labeling requirements was specifically deleted from the statute when originally enacted. However, the Court is influenced by the subsequent inclusion of Section 201(n) which authorizes the Commissioner to consider "the extent to which the labeling fails to reveal facts material in the light of such representations" in determining whether a label is false or misleading.

FDA's reasoning for the general principle of requiring disclosure of the percentage of characterizing ingredients for certain foods is that such information may be a "material fact" which must be disclosed to prevent a food label from being misleading. . . .

The Court also notes that the record support for this regulation indicates the materiality of the percentage of characterizing ingredient in this particular product. Virtually all of the consumer responses heartily supported the general principle proposed, and several consumers indicated express approval of disclosure of percentage of ingredients for seafood cocktails as a necessary device for comparative food shopping. In light of the materiality of the information required to be disclosed by this regulation, the Court is not persuaded that the Commissioner has exceeded his statutory authority in requiring that the label of seafood cocktail reveal the percentage of seafood ingredients therein. . . .

NOTES

1. *Affirmed on Appeal.* The District Court was affirmed on appeal *sub nom. American Frozen Food Institute v. Califano*, 555 F.2d 1059 (D.C. Cir. 1977).

2. *Peanut Butter versus Peanut Spread.* Compare the standard of identity for "peanut butter" in 21 C.F.R. 164.150, which requires at least 90 percent peanuts, *see* Note 2, *supra* p. 168, with the FDA-prescribed common or usual name for "peanut spread" in 21 C.F.R. 102.23, promulgated in 40 Fed. Reg. 51052 (Nov. 3, 1975), 42 Fed. Reg. 36452 (July 15, 1977), which merely requires label declaration of the percent of peanuts in products containing between 10 percent and 90 percent.

3. *Infant Food.* In 41 Fed. Reg. 37593 and 37595 (Sept. 7, 1976), FDA proposed two regulations for infant food. One would have established a common or usual name that would have included the percent of the characterizing ingredient or ingredients. The other, based on section 403(j) of the Act, would have required the percent declaration of each ingredient present at a level of 5 percent or more by weight. Both of these proposals were withdrawn in 51 Fed. Reg. 15653 (Apr. 25, 1986), reinstated in 51 Fed. Reg. 39546 (Oct. 29, 1986), and then withdrawn again in 56 Fed. Reg. 67440, 67446 (Dec. 30, 1991).

4. *Procedures for Establishing Food Names.* The fact that FDA may establish a common or usual name through notice-and-comment rulemaking does not mean that the process is uncontroversial. Following promulgation of the regulation requiring that any diluted orange juice beverage declare the percent of orange juice, 21 C.F.R. 102.32, FDA promulgated a similar regulation for all other diluted fruit or vegetable juices. 39 Fed. Reg. 20908 (June 14, 1974), 45 Fed. Reg. 39247 (June 10, 1980), codified at 21 C.F.R. 102.33. After the agency rejected a petition for reconsideration, 45 Fed. Reg. 80497 (Dec. 5, 1980), and extended the time for compliance, 47 Fed. Reg. 13003 (Mar. 26, 1982), 48 Fed. Reg. 2735 (Jan. 21, 1983), 49 Fed. Reg. 26541 (June 27, 1984), a court upheld the rule. *Processors Council of the California–Arizona Citrus League v. FDA*, Food Drug Cosm. L. Rep. (CCH) ¶ 38,186 (C.D. Cal. 1982). Opponents of the regulation persisted, however, and FDA first proposed amendments, 49 Fed. Reg. 22831 (June 1, 1984), and then proposed its revocation, 52 Fed. Reg. 26690 (July 16, 1987). This proposal, in turn, provoked efforts to salvage the regulation. 55 Fed. Reg. 3266 (Jan. 31, 1990). Finally, the 1990 Nutrition Labeling and Education Act amended section 403(i) to require that a

beverage containing a fruit or vegetable juice must declare the percent of juice on the label. In 56 Fed. Reg. 30452 (July 2, 1991), 58 Fed. Reg. 2897 (Jan. 6, 1993), FDA revoked 21 C.F.R. 102.32, revised 102.33, and promulgated 21 C.F.R. 101.30 to implement the NLEA requirement.

5. *Other Names.* In addition to the regulations discussed above, FDA also established common or usual name regulations for protein hydrolysates, 21 C.F.R. 102.22; foods packaged for use in the preparation of "main dishes" or "dinners," 21 C.F.R. 102.28; mixtures of edible fat or oil and olive oil, 21 C.F.R. 102.37; onion rings made from diced onion, 21 C.F.R. 102.39; fish sticks or portions made from minced fish, 21 C.F.R. 102.45; pacific whiting, 21 C.F.R. 102.46; bonito, 21 C.F.R. 102.47; fried clams made from minced clams, 21 C.F.R. 102.49; crabmeat, 21 C.F.R. 102.50; nonstandardized breaded composite shrimp units, 21 C.F.R. 102.55; and Greenland turbot, 21 C.F.R. 102.57.

6. *Other Proposed Names.* FDA proposed names for main dish products, 39 Fed. Reg. 20906 (June 14, 1974); formulated meal replacements, 39 Fed. Reg. 20905 (June 14, 1974); fruit-flavored sweetened spreads, 40 Fed. Reg. 52616 (Nov. 11, 1975); and substitutes for margarine and butter, 41 Fed. Reg. 36509 (Aug. 30, 1976). But all of these proposals were withdrawn in 51 Fed. Reg. 15653 (Apr. 25, 1986), and no new common or usual names have been proposed since then.

7. *Commentary.* For discussion of the concept of a "common or usual name," *see* John L. Harvey, *"Common or Usual Name,"* 14 FOOD DRUG COSM. L.J. 555 (1959); Vincent A. Kleinfeld, *"Common or Usual Name"—Its Meaning, If Any,* 16 FOOD DRUG COSM. L.J. 513 (1961); Murray D. Sayer, *A Rose by Any Other Name,* 30 FOOD DRUG COSM. L.J. 415 (1975).

———

The naming of fish species has become controversial as federal health officials, members of Congress, and the seafood industry have sought to encourage increased consumption of fish. *E.g.,* GAO, DEVELOPING MARKETS FOR FISH NOT TRADITIONALLY HARVESTED BY THE UNITED STATES: THE PROBLEMS AND THE FEDERAL ROLE, Rep. No. CED–80–73 (May 7, 1980); GAO, SEAFOOD MARKETING: OPPORTUNITIES TO IMPROVE THE U.S. POSITION, Rep. No. RCED–87–11BR (Oct. 22, 1986). In 33 Fed. Reg. 11813 (Aug. 21, 1968), 33 Fed. Reg. 19007 (Dec. 20, 1968), now codified at 21 C.F.R. 102.57, FDA found it necessary to prohibit use of the term "halibut" as a substitute for "Greenland turbot." 21 C.F.R. Part 102 contains common or usual names for fish sticks or portions made from minced fish, Pacific Whiting, Bonito, fried clams made from minced clams, crabmeat, seafood cocktails, and nonstandardized breaded composite shrimp units. In 54 Fed. Reg. 12284 (Mar. 24, 1989), 59 Fed. Reg. 47144 (Sept. 14, 1994), FDA announced the availability of the FDA GUIDE TO ACCEPTABLE MARKET NAMES FOR FOOD FISH SOLD IN INTERSTATE COMMERCE (The Seafood List), which was developed jointly with the National Marine Fisheries Service.

Philip Brasher, *When Is a Catfish Not a Catfish? When It Comes From Vietnam and Cuts Into U.S. Sales, Hill Says*

THE WASHINGTON POST, December 27, 2001, at A21.

It has whiskers and feeds at the bottom of rivers, but can no longer be sold as a catfish if it comes from Vietnam.

Congress has barred labeling catfish from Vietnam as catfish because imports are cutting into sales of more expensive U.S. catfish grown in man-made ponds in the South. . . .

"Not only does it look like a catfish, but it acts like a catfish," Sen. Phil Gramm (R–Tex.), said of the Vietnamese version. "And the people who make a living in fisheries science call it a catfish. Why do we want to call it anything other than a catfish?". . . .

U.S. farmers say the only true catfish belong to the family with the Latin name Ictaluridae. The Vietnamese variety are in the family Pangasii-dae, which are "freshwater catfishes of Africa and southern Asia," the Food and Drug Administration said last year after reviewing American Fisheries Society terminology. The agency decided it was permissible to use names such as "basa catfish" for the Vietnamese product. . . .

NOTE

This issue was ultimately resolved by Congress, 116 Stat. 134, 526–27 (2002), which added section 403(t) to the FD&C Act to provide that catfish is the common or usual name only for fish classified within the family Ictaluridae. FDA issued an implementing guidance in 67 Fed. Reg. 72691 (Dec. 6, 2002). The same statute added section 403(u) to define ginseng as the common or usual name only for an herb classified within the genus Panax.

———

Recent decades have witnessed the growing use of "surimi," a minced fish product that can be obtained from a number of different types of fish, to make products that resemble other seafood products. FDA announced the following policy regarding this practice in 50 Fed. Reg. 30523 (July 26, 1985).

Compliance Policy Guide No. 7108.16

June 3, 1985.

Surimi is an intermediate processed seafood product used in the formulation/fabrication of a variety of finished seafood products. It is normally traded in 10 kg. frozen blocks which are individually wrapped in waxed cardboard boxes. Surimi is minced fish meat (usually pollock) which has been washed to remove fat and undesirable matters (such as blood, pigments, and odorous substances), and mixed with cryoprotectants (such as sugar and/or sorbitol for a good frozen shelflife). In formulating finished seafood products, surimi is thawed and blended with other ingredients and additives such as natural shellfish meat, and/or shellfish flavoring, salt, water, and starch and/or egg white; and processed by heat for making fibrous, flake, chunk, and composite-molded consumer products. The finished products are marketed frozen or unfrozen and may be breaded.

The following guidance is in response to inquiries FDA has received regarding the proper labeling for surimi-based seafood products.

1. If the surimi-based product purports to be or is represented as any specific type of natural seafood, including shape or form representations, but is nutritionally inferior to that seafood, it must be labeled as imitation in accordance with 21 CFR 101.3. To date FDA has not encountered any surimi-based product in which nutritional equivalency has been achieved.

2. An additional statement of product identity must appear on the principal display panel such as "A Blend of Fish with _____." The blank is to be filled in with the common or usual name of the ingredient or component, such as "snow crab." Because the fish used in the surimi-base has been decharacterized, the word "fish" is adequate for the statement of product identity....

3. The specific names of all seafoods used in the product shall appear in the ingredient statement in descending order of predominance ("pollock" must be used as opposed to "white fish"; "snow crab" rather than "crab"). All other ingredients present must also be declared in descending order of predominance....

4. Products that are not purported or represented to be a specific type of seafood or seafood body part, need not be labeled imitation, but may be marketed if the label properly reflects their composition.

5. Labeling of surimi-based products may suggest use in recipes in place of the natural seafood products by a generalized statement such as, "use like crabmeat, lobster, or shrimp in all seafood recipes," or a similar statement.

NOTE

In *Mrs. Paul's Kitchens, Inc. v. Califano*, 1978–1980 FDLI Jud. Rec. 685 (E.D. Pa. 1978), the District Court was required to confront a labeling issue posed by the requirements of high speed food processing and uniform portion sizes. The company cut uniform portions of fish from frozen blocks of fish filets in a way that there could be no assurance that the individual portion consisted of a piece of only one fish. The District Court overruled FDA's position that the proper name for the product was "fish portion" or "pieces of filet" and instead held that "fish filet" is a proper common or usual name for the product and is not false or misleading.

COMMENT: MEAT FOOD NAMES

Although USDA and FDA formally share jurisdiction over meat food labeling, *see supra* p. 35, USDA exercises primary jurisdiction in this area, and many important meat food names are established in standards of identity that it has promulgated in 9 C.F.R. Parts 317 and 319.

Armour & Co. v. Freeman, 304 F.2d 404 (D.C. Cir. 1962), held invalid a USDA regulation that required meat packers who added moisture to ham during the curing process to use the label "Imitation Ham." The Court of Appeals concluded that the required labeling was false and deceptive and thus inconsistent with USDA's own statute, the Federal Meat Inspection Act. Judge Prettyman, concurring with the Court's decision, declared: "Everybody knows that a ham made of the cured thigh of a hog and otherwise unaltered save by the addition of a bit of water is not an imitation of some product other than ham.... As a matter of plain fact, such a ham is not even an imitation ham. It is a real ham, a ham by definition and by universal common acceptance." In *American Meat Institute v. United States Dept. of Agriculture*, 646 F.2d 125 (4th Cir. 1981) (per curiam), the court, reversing the district court, upheld a USDA regulation permitting cured turkey to be labeled as "turkey ham" with the additional qualifying phrase "cured turkey thigh meat." In *National Pork Producers Council v. Bergland*, 631 F.2d 1353 (8th Cir. 1980), *cert. denied*, 450 U.S. 912 (1981), the Court of Appeals upheld a USDA regulation permitting nitrate-free and nitrite-free meat products to be sold under the product names traditionally reserved for food containing these preservatives as long as the word "uncured" appeared as part of the product name and the label stated that no nitrate or nitrite had been added and that refrigeration was required.

Even in an instance when USDA changed its mind about the proper labeling for a standardized meat food product, its ultimate decision was upheld. The agency initially determined that mechanically deboned meat could lawfully be used in processed meat food products without any special labeling. After *Community Nutrition Institute v. Butz*, 420 F. Supp. 751 (D.D.C. 1976), overturned this ruling, USDA promulgated regulations requiring that the product be identified in the ingredient statement as "mechanically processed [species] product" and that the presence of the ingredient also be emphasized by two prominent qualifying phrases next to the common or usual name of the food: "With mechanically processed [species] product" and "Contains up to _____ percent powdered bone." On the basis of an industry petition, and following the change in administration produced by the 1980 presidential election, USDA revised the regulations to require that the product be declared in the ingredient statement as "mechanically processed [species]," to repeal the requirement that the common or usual name refer to the ingredient, and to replace the powdered bone statement with a mandatory statement of the percent of the U.S. RDA of calcium in a serving. These changed requirements, 9 C.F.R. 317.2(j)(13), were upheld in *Community Nutrition Institute v. Block*, 749 F.2d 50 (D.C. Cir. 1984).

USDA's efforts to grapple with the naming of pizza products have gained widespread notoriety. Pizza without a meat component is subject to the exclusive jurisdiction of FDA. Pizza containing pepperoni or any other meat component is subject to USDA jurisdiction. FDA has established no regulations or guidelines governing pizza labeling, but USDA established a standard of identity in 9 C.F.R. 319.600. In 38 Fed. Reg. 16363 (June 22, 1973), USDA proposed to establish a minimum of 12 percent cheese for any pizza product subject to its jurisdiction. In the face of industry objections to this requirement and support for the use of substitute cheese ingredients, the agency published a request for additional comments in 44 Fed. Reg. 71417 (Dec. 11, 1979). It published another proposal in 48 Fed. Reg. 35654 (Aug. 5, 1983), requiring that any substitute for cheese in pizza be labeled as a "cheese substitute" (or, if nutritionally inferior, "imitation cheese") as part of the name of the food. Manufacturers opposed this proposal on the ground that the use of cheese substitutes is made known through the statement of ingredients. Based upon these comments, USDA withdrew the proposed regulations in 52 Fed. Reg. 11828 (Apr. 13, 1987). The same year, legislation requiring any pizza containing a substitute cheese product to be labeled as "contains imitation cheese" (rather than "substitute cheese") came close to enactment, but ultimately failed. *See* "Labeling of Meat Food Products to Reflect the Inclusion of Imitation or Alternate Cheese; The Effects of Consumption of Tropical Oils on the Soybean Program," Joint Hearing before the Subcommittee on Livestock, Dairy, and Poultry and the Subcommittee on Wheat, Soybeans, and Feed Grains of the House Committee on Agriculture, 100th Cong., 1st Sess. (1987); GAO, FOOD MARKETING: FROZEN CHEESE PIZZA—REPRESENTATIVE OF BROADER FOOD LABELING ISSUES, No. RCED–88–70 (Mar. 1988). USDA finally gave up and revoked its pizza standard in 66 Fed. Reg. 55601 (Nov. 2, 2001), 68 Fed. Reg. 44859 (July 31, 2003), 69 Fed. Reg. 28042 (May 18, 2004), and issued guidance on future labeling of these products.

NOTE

In 70 Fed. Reg. 67490 (Nov. 7, 2005), FDA and USDA announced a joint public meeting to reconsider the dividing line between FDA and USDA jurisdiction over food products containing meat and poultry.

d.   COMMON AND USUAL NAMES FOR MODIFIED STANDARDIZED FOODS

As part of its early–1970s policy on food names, FDA decided to apply the same principles for naming standardized and nonstandardized foods. The agency had previously taken the position that any new substitute for a standardized food was required to be labeled as an imitation but a substitute for a nonstandardized food was not required to be so labeled. Dressings for salad illustrate the impact of this policy on different versions of the same food. FDA had promulgated a standard for French dressing, 21 C.F.R. 169.115, but not for Italian or Russian dressing. Under the agency's traditional policy, a reduced calorie version of French dressing had to be labeled as "imitation" French dressing, but a reduced calorie version of Italian or Russian dressing could be described as "reduced calorie" Italian or Russian dressing. Under its new policy, FDA took the position that the common or usual name for a nonstandardized food could include the name of the standardized food that it copied, as long as the difference between the products was made clear.

Soon after the establishment of the new policy, however, it became apparent that there were substantial difficulties in implementing it, resulting in inconsistent FDA decisions and actions that persist to this day. Many longtime FDA employees disagreed with the new policy, and their advice to the food industry continued to reflect the old policy. Representatives of staple and standardized food products fought to prevent new foods from capitalizing on the well-recognized terminology previously reserved for their exclusive use. FDA officials recognized that the appropriateness of including a standardized name in the name of a substitute food depended upon the specific facts involved. As a result, following the establishment of the FDA new policy, one can find examples where it was ignored.

One of the most frequent reasons for modifying standardized foods has been to improve their nutritional profiles. The particular naming issues arising from such modifications are discussed in detail later in this chapter, *infra* p. 222.

NOTES

1. *Use of Standardized Name on Nonstandard Products.* During the late 1970s and 1980s, FDA vacillated on the use of standardized names for nonstandardized products. In 1979, FDA stated, "The existence of a standard of identity for a particular food does not necessarily preclude the use of the standardized name in connection with the name of a nonstandardized food, and 'in some cases it may be necessary to include a standardized name in the name of a substitute food in order to provide the consumer with accurate, descriptive, and fully informative labeling.'" 44 Fed. Reg. 3964 (Jan. 19, 1979) (citing 38 Fed. Reg. 20703 (Aug. 2, 1973)). Manufacturers of traditional standardized foods, however, strenuously objected to the incorporation of those food names in the names for new substitute foods and contended that entirely new fanciful names should be adopted for these new products. *See, e.g.,* 43 Fed. Reg. 42118 (Sept. 19, 1978), in which FDA described a National Cheese Institute petition proposing the name "Golana" ("analog" spelled backward) rather than "substitute," "alternate," or even "imitation" cheese. In 49 Fed.Reg. 22796 (June 1, 1984), FDA adopted "cocoa butter substitute primarily from palm oil" as the common or usual name for a substance it affirmed as generally recognized as safe (GRAS), rejecting the contention that it has no authority to establish a common or usual name that incorporates the name of a traditional food.

2. *Enriched Standardized Foods.* In 41 Fed. Reg. 46851 (Oct. 26, 1976), FDA issued a final standard of identity for "enriched raisin bread." The standard permitted the same quantity of nutrients required by the standard for enriched bread and the same quantity of raisins required by the standard for raisin bread, which did not provide for the use of enriched flour. Formal objections to the new standard were filed, resulting in a stay of its effective date. Rather than hold the necessary evidentiary hearing to resolve the objections, FDA concluded that the new standard could be rendered unnecessary by "providing advice" on the appropriate labeling for raisin bread made with enriched flour:

> The Commissioner ... advises that a raisin bread conforming to the requirements of § 136.160 except that it is made with enriched flour, enriched brominated flour, or a combination, as the sole farinaceous ingredient may be sold as a nonstandardized bread under a suitable name, *e.g.,* "raisin bread made with enriched flour." Many breads are sold as nonstandardized foods when they contain and are named to identify ingredients not provided for in the standard for bread that provide a distinctive flavor, color, or other feature important to consumers, *e.g.,* rye bread. If a raisin bread has been enriched to the nutrient levels in § 136.115, (with additional amounts of nutrients added to compensate for the flour displaced by the raisins), the food may be sold as "enriched raisin bread." Either raisin bread so labeled must also bear nutrition labeling in accordance with § 101.9.

43 Fed. Reg. 43456 (Sept. 26, 1978). *See also* 43 Fed. Reg. 11695 (Mar. 21, 1978) ("enriched macaroni with fortified protein" does not purport to be standardized

"enriched macaroni"); 39 Fed. Reg. 31898 (Sept. 3, 1974) ("tomato juice enriched with vitamin C" does not purport to be standardized "tomato juice").

The market for dairy products has been a major battlefield in the war over names for modifications of or substitutes for traditional foods. For decades, dairy producers sought to suppress modified or substitute products through laws such as the Filled Milk Act, *supra* p. 152. When the courts began to allow the marketing of new products bearing truthful labeling, the dairy industry sought to require coined names, or in any event to prohibit the use of dairy terms, for modified or substitute products. In 43 Fed. Reg. 42118 (Sept. 19, 1978), FDA proposed to establish standards of identity for substitutes for milk, cream, and cheese. These proposed standards of identity required that the substitute products be labeled "imitation" if they were nutritionally inferior to their dairy counterparts, and they mandated that the name of nutritionally equivalent substitutes be the name of the simulated food followed by "substitute." The resulting comments revealed a deep divergence of views, and the agency decided to abandon any effort to standardize modifications of or substitutes for traditional dairy products. Instead, FDA decided to focus on the development of guidelines for common or usual names.

Substitutes for Milk, Cream, and Cheese; Withdrawal of Proposed Standards of Identity

48 Fed. Reg. 37666 (August 19, 1983).

. . . .

In response to the proposal, FDA received 1,393 letters of comment. . . . The principal objection to the proposal was to the use of the names of traditional and standardized dairy foods in the names of the milk, cream, cheese, and cheese product substitutes. Most of these comments contended that the proposed names are confusingly similar to those of traditional dairy products and, as such, have the potential for misleading consumers, particularly when the substitute foods are packed in materials similar to those of traditional dairy products and are displayed in close proximity to dairy products in supermarkets. Some comments stated that all such foods should be labeled "imitations", whether or not they are nutritionally equivalent to the foods simulated. Others stated that substitute foods should be marketed under their own distinctive names which make no reference to the foods simulated as is done in the case of mellorine and margarine.

Comments from dairy farmers and persons or organizations representing dairy farmers contended that the proposed regulations were unfair to dairy farmers and should be withdrawn because they could have an adverse economic impact on them. One comment expressed the opinion that the use of dairy terms in the names of these foods will, over time, cloud the distinction in consumers' minds between dairy and nondairy products, resulting in economic losses to the dairy industry.

Several comments from manufacturers of substitute foods objected to the proposed compositional requirements because some of their products would have to be reformulated in order to comply and thus avoid the "imitation" designation in the name. Some also objected to the need to change the name of existing products that have had many years of consumer acceptance under their current names and requested that exemptions be granted for these products.

Several comments from manufacturers of cheese and cheese product substitutes opposed coined names such as "Golana", "Cheesana", or "Emarine" because such names are not meaningful to consumers and their adoption would require extensive advertising to establish name recognition. Some comments also stated that the term "substitute" is not meaningful to consumers, and in particular, when the term is used in conjunction with the term "imitation" as proposed for substitute products which are nutritionally inferior to the foods they simulate.

As the comments evidence, there is a lack of agreement regarding the most appropriate nomenclature for milk, cream, and cheese substitutes. Under these particular circumstances, the agency believes that honesty and fair dealing are best served by the withdrawal of the proposal and the termination of the rulemaking proceedings. Milk, cream, and cheese substitutes will continue to be governed by the regulations in 21 CFR 101.3(e) regarding the use of the term "imitation" and in 21 CFR 102.5 that set forth the general principles for common or usual names for nonstandardized foods. A food made in semblance of a milk, cream, cheese, or cheese product will be deemed to be an imitation and thus subject to the requirements of section 403(c) of the Federal Food, Drug, and Cosmetic Act if it is nutritionally inferior to the milk, cream, cheese, or cheese product simulated. If it is not nutritionally inferior, it must bear a common or usual name that complies with the provisions of 21 CFR 102.5 which is not false or misleading in any particular or, in the absence of an existing common or usual name, an appropriately descriptive name which is not false or misleading. The label may, in addition, bear a fanciful name that is not misleading.

To ensure that the name of a substitute food is not misleading, the name should ordinarily not include the name of a product subject to a standard of identity unless (1) it complies with the standard of identity, or (2) it is nutritionally inferior to the food simulated and is labeled with the term "imitation". However, in some cases, it may be reasonable and appropriate to include the name of a standardized food or other traditional food in the name of a substitute food in order to provide the consumer with an accurate description. When this is done, the name of the food must be modified such that the nature of the substitute food is clearly described and is clearly distinguished from the food which it resembles and for which it is intended to substitute. The modification of the traditional or standardized food's name must be descriptive of all differences that are not apparent to the consumer. Thus, the procedure for naming these foods will depend on the nature of the substitute food and the manner and extent to which it differs from the food it simulates. . . .

NOTES

1. *Sour Cream Dressings.* In 43 Fed. Reg. 11150 and 11226 (Mar. 17, 1978), FDA revoked a stayed standard of identity for sour cream dressing and repealed the standard of identity for sour half-and-half dressing on the ground that the use of the word "dressing" was insufficient to inform consumers of the difference between the previously standardized products and the new versions of those products.

2. *Goat's Milk Yogurt.* In 1986, FDA was asked to approve distribution of "goat's milk yogurt," a product that conformed to the standard of identity for yogurt except for the source of milk. The agency responded:

> It is our conclusion that "goat's milk yogurt" is sufficiently distinctive as an identity statement under Section 403(i)(1). It is sufficiently different from yogurt so as not to purport or represent the product as the standardized food under Section 403(g) of the Federal Food, Drug, and Cosmetic Act. We therefore agree that it can be used as a statement of identity.

Letter from L. Robert Lake, Director, FDA, CFSAN Office of Regulations and Policy, to Peter Barton Hutt (Nov. 25, 1986).

3. *Dairy Terms for Margarine.* In *Anderson, Clayton & Co. v. Washington State Department of Agriculture*, 402 F. Supp. 1253 (W.D. Wash. 1975), a Washington statute prohibiting the use of dairy terms in labeling or advertising for margarine was declared unconstitutional.

E.   REGULATION OF THE NUTRIENT CONTENT OF FOOD

FDA efforts to regulate the nutrient content of food merit separate treatment for several reasons. Good nutrition is a matter of intense individual and public concern. It is closely related to individual physical and mental development and to the avoidance of disease and has been made a priority objective by administrations from both political parties. Accordingly, FDA programs relating to the nutritional value of food comprise one of the agency's most important functions.

Until the 1970s, FDA relied largely upon the statutory provisions and policies already discussed in this chapter. The agency challenged misleading nutritional claims in food labeling under section 403(a) and promulgated standards of identity for enriched food to assure the nutritional quality of basic staples. In addition, shortly after the FD&C Act was passed FDA issued regulations governing the labeling of food promoted for "special dietary uses," as specifically authorized by section 403(j). *See* Part F, *infra* p. 246. But during the 1970s and 1980s, faced with increasing concern about the relationship between diet and health and mounting public demand for information about food and nutrition, the agency undertook new regulatory initiatives based on provisions that have been in the Act from the beginning. For an overview, see Peter Barton Hutt, *Government Regulation of Health Claims in Food Labeling and Advertising*, 41 FOOD DRUG COSM. L.J. 3 (1986) and *Regulating the Misbranding of Food*, 43 FOOD TECH. 288 (Sept. 1989).

1.   NUTRITIONAL STATUS OF AMERICANS

Through the 1950s and 1960s, FDA food policy rested on the assumptions that Americans could get proper nourishment from ordinary foods and that most people were in fact adequately nourished. These assumptions came under serious question in the late 1960s. Several events combined to undermine these assumptions, but none was more important than the investigations of the Senate Select Committee on Nutrition and Human Needs, chaired by Senator George McGovern.

The Food Gap: Poverty and Malnutrition in the United States

Staff Report of the Senate Committee on Nutrition and Human Needs.
91st Congress, 1st Session (1969).

The national nutrition survey, supported by the Department of Health, Education, and Welfare, ... is studying the extent of malnutrition in low-income census districts in 10 states.... [T]he survey has found an alarming prevalence of those characteristics that are associated with undernourished groups. More specifically, seven cases of marasmus and kwashiorkor—cases of caloric and protein starvation—were identified and clinically validated; one-third of the children under 6 years and 15 percent of the total sample population were found to be anemic, to have hemoglobin levels in the "unacceptable range"; 3.5 percent of the children X-rayed showed evidence of retarded bone growth; vitamin A, essential for the formation of cells and for normal vision, was found to be at unacceptable levels for 33 percent of the children under 6 [years of age] and 13 percent of the population; vitamin C, important for normal tooth and bone formation, wound healing, and resistance to infection was found at less than acceptable levels in 12 to 16 percent of all age groups; vitamin D, necessary for the absorption of calcium and the normal development of bones, was found to be at less than acceptable levels for 3.7 percent of all children under 6 years....

In the spring of 1965, the Department of Agriculture conducted its customary nationwide survey of food consumption, covering 7,500 households. The results of this survey tend to corroborate the preliminary results of the national nutrition survey. Half of the households surveyed had diets that failed to meet the recommended dietary allowances set by the Food and Nutrition Board of the National Academy of Sciences–National Research Council for one or more nutrients. About one-fifth of the sample had "poor" diets—their food intake provided less than two-thirds of the NRC allowance for one or more nutrients.

Of greater significance, the number of "good" diets fell 10 percent from 1955 to 1965, while the number of "poor" diets rose 6 percent in the same period. Although southern and north-central households had higher concentrations of "poor" diets, urban and rural households yielded similar proportions of diets below the allowances for one or more nutrients....

These and other surveys lead to one clear, general conclusion: Clinically validated malnutrition not only exists in the United States but is a serious problem....

————

The work of Senator McGovern's Select Committee led to the periodic publication of Dietary Guidelines for Americans. Under 21 U.S.C. 5341, enacted by the National Nutritional Monitoring and Related Research Act of 1990, FDA and USDA are required jointly to publish guidelines every five years that reflect sound nutrition and dietary habits. In past years, the Dietary Guidelines could easily be summarized with fewer than ten clear and concise rules. The 2005 edition of Dietary Guidelines for Americans, however, has expanded to 70 pages and relies to a substantial degree on a complex new food pyramid, called "MyPyramid," that provides an individualized approach to improve health by making changes in diet and incorporating regular physical activity into daily living. In nine lengthy and detailed chapters, the guidelines provide advice in the following areas:

Adequate nutrients within calorie needs

Weight management

Physical activity

Food groups to encourage

Fats

Carbohydrates

Sodium and potassium

Alcoholic beverages

Food safety

This is the first time that food safety—to avoid microbial foodborne illness—and physical activity have been included in the Dietary Guidelines. *See* Emily J. Schaffer, *Is the Fox Guarding the Hen House? Who Makes the Rules in American Nutrition Policy?*, 57 FOOD & DRUG L.J. 371 (2002); Julie Black, *There's a Government in My Soup: The 2005 Dietary Guidelines for Americans* (2005) in Chapter V(D)(2) of the Electronic Book.

NOTES

1. *Dietary Goals.* Dietary goals have often been controversial. For an instructive debate over the wisdom of implementing them, compare Alfred E. Harper, *What Are Appropriate Dietary Guidelines?*, 32 FOOD TECH., Sept. 1978, at 48, with D. Mark Hegsted, *Rationale for Change in the American Diet*, 32 FOOD TECH., Sept. 1978, at 44. *See also* National Nutrition Consortium, GUIDELINES FOR A NATIONAL NUTRITION POLICY (1974); AMA Council on Scientific Affairs, *American Medical Association Concepts of Nutrition and Health*, 242 J.A.M.A. 2335 (1979); Council for Agricultural Science and Technology, *Dietary Goals for the United States: A Commentary*, Rep. No. 71 (1977). For a discussion of changes in the food supply that would be needed to meet these dietary goals, *see* Betty B. Peterkin, *The Dietary Goals and Food on the Table*, 32 FOOD TECH., Feb. 1978, at 34. Two reports by the National Academy of Sciences, TOWARD HEALTHFUL DIETS (1980) and DIET, NUTRITION, AND CANCER (1982), which echoed many of the conclusions of the Senate Select Committee, were sufficiently controversial that eleven numbers of Congress requested a GAO review of the Academy's committee selection procedures and objectivity. *See* GAO, NATIONAL ACADEMY OF SCIENCES' REPORTS ON DIET AND HEALTH—ARE THEY CREDIBLE AND CONSISTENT?, Rep. No. RCED–84–109 (Aug. 21, 1984).

2. *Institutional Food.* For discussion of food quality in closed institutions, see Jonathan M. Wilan, *Regulation of Prison Food* (1996), Cyrus Naim, *Prison Food Law* (2005), and Carlye A. Murphy, *Over 187 Billion Served: Food Safety in the National School Lunch Program* (2005), in Chapters I(G)(6) & V(J) of the Electronic Book; "Hearing on Food Safety in the School Lunch Program," Hearing before the Subcommittee on Early Childhood, Youth and Families of the House Committee on Education and the Workforce, 105th Cong., 1st Sess. (1997); "Kids and Cafeterias: How Safe are Federal School Lunches?" Joint Hearing before the Oversight of Government Management, Restructuring, and the District of Columbia Subcommittee of the Senate Committee on Governmental Affairs and the Subcommittee on Government Efficiency, Financial Management, and Intergovernmental Relations of the House Committee on Government Reform, 107th Cong., 2d Sess. (2002).

In the 2000s it became clear that one symptom of malnutrition, obesity, was reaching epidemic levels in the United States.

Calories Count: Report of the Food and Drug Administration Working Group on Obesity

March 12, 2004.

The scope of the growing and urgent public health problem of obesity is outlined in the Surgeon General's Call to Action.... In 1999–2000, 64% of the U.S. adults were overweight, increased from 56% when surveyed in 1988–1994; 30% of adults were obese, increased from 23% in the earlier survey.... Among children age 6 through 19 years, 15% were overweight, compared with 10 to 11% in the earlier survey.... Overweight and obesity are associated with increased morbidity and mortality. It is estimated that about 400,000 deaths per year may be attributed to obesity, and overweight and obesity increase the risk for coronary heart disease, type 2 diabetes, and certain cancers.... The total economic cost of obesity in the United States is up to $117 billion per year ... including more than $50 billion in avoidable medical costs, more than 5 percent of total annual health care expenditures....

NOTES

1. *Impact of Obesity.* After one study by the Centers for Disease Control reporting that obesity contributed to 400,000 deaths per year in the United States was discredited, a more reliable CDC study found that obesity contributed to 112,000 deaths, overweight was not associated with excess mortality, and underweight contributed to 34,000 deaths per year. Compare Ali H. Mokdad et al., *Actual Causes of Death in the United States, 2000*, 291 J.A.M.A. 1238 (Mar. 10, 2004) with Katherine M. Flegal et al., *Excess Deaths Associated with Underweight, Overweight, and Obesity*, 293 J.A.M.A., 1861 (Apr. 20, 2005).

2. *FDA Responsibility.* Many nutrition programs are beyond the FDA budget or legal authority to implement. Yet the agency's regulatory policies can affect the success of other programs. *See, e.g.,* Peter Barton Hutt, *Regulatory Implementation of Dietary Recommendations*, 36 FOOD DRUG COSM. L.J. 66 (1981). A recurrent

question is whether the FDA efforts to help consumers eat wisely aid or impede efforts to combat malnutrition.

3. *Nutrition Update.* Years after Senator McGovern's investigations, reports of hunger and malnutrition among Americans have continued. *E.g.,* "Oversight on Nutritional Status of Low–Income Americans in the 1980's," Hearing before the Subcommittee on Nutrition of the Senate Committee on Agriculture, Nutrition, and Forestry, 98th Cong., 1st Sess. (1983); Physician Task Force on Hunger in America, HUNGER IN AMERICA: THE GROWTH EPIDEMIC (1985); Jon Ellison, *Hunger in America: A History of Public and Private Responses* (2004), in Chapter V(U) of the Electronic Book.

4. *FDA Response on Obesity.* FDA's principal regulatory authority applicable to obesity is its control over food labeling. The FDA report and related advance notice of proposed rulemaking in 63 Fed. Reg. 17008 (Apr. 4, 2005) focus on such matters as changing nutrition labeling to increase the emphasis on the caloric content and the serving size for packaged food. *See generally* Sarah C. Johnson, *Countering the Obesity Epidemic: Policy Proposals for a New Century* (2003); Melanie Westover, *An Evaluation of the Legal Responses to America's Obesity Epidemic* (2004), and Emily Wolf, *The Obesity Epidemic: Why and How the Government Must Act* (2004), in Chapter V(S) of the Electronic Book. Citizen Petition No. 2005P–0282/CPI (July 13, 2005) relied upon both the food additive and the food labeling provisions of the FD&C Act to request FDA to require that sweetened soft drinks bear a variety of rotating health messages to help reduce obesity and related diseases. No action has been taken by FDA on this petition. *See also* "The Supersizing of America: The Federal Government's Role in Combating Obesity and Promoting Healthy Living," Hearing before the House Committee on Government Reform, 108th Cong., 2d Sess. (2004); "Conquering Obesity: The U.S. Approach to Combating this National Health Crisis," Hearing before the Subcommittee on Human Rights and Wellness of the House Committee on Government Reform, 108th Cong. 2d Sess. (2004).

5. *HHS/FTC Report.* On May 2, 2006 the Department of HHS and the FTC issued a joint report titled MARKETING, SELF-REGULATION, AND CHILDHOOD OBESITY. *See also* INSTITUTE OF MEDICINE, FOOD MARKETING TO CHILDREN AND YOUTH: THREAT OR OPPORTUNITY? (2005). Thirty years ago, as part of a broad approach to regulation of food advertising that was ultimately abandoned, the FTC proposed to restrict television advertising to children of sugared food products. 43 Fed. Reg. 17967 (Apr. 22, 1978); Peter Barton Hutt, *Regulatory Implementation of Dietary Recommendations*, 36 FOOD DRUG COSM. L.J. 66, 77–80 (1981). This culminated in Congress enacting the Federal Trade Commission Improvements Act of 1980, 94 Stat. 374, 15 U.S.C. 57a(h), to prohibit the FTC from regulating children's advertising as an "unfair act or practice."

6. *Obesity Lawsuits.* The fact that dietary selection is a matter of personal choice and responsibility has not deterred exploration of legal remedies against the food industry. Several lawsuits have attempted to replicate the success of tort litigation against tobacco companies, thus far without success. *See, e.g.,* Jonathan Benloulou, *Pelman v. McDonalds: An In–Depth Case Study of a Fast Food Obesity Lawsuit* (2005), in Chapter V(S) of the Electronic Book; Sarah Taylor Roller et al., *Obesity, Food Marketing and Consumer Litigation: Threat or Opportunity?*, 61 FOOD & DRUG L.J. 419 (2006). Legislation to prevent such litigation has been enacted in several states and has been considered by Congress. "Personal Responsibility in Food Consumption Act," Hearing before the Subcommittee on Commercial and Administrative Law, House Committee on the Judiciary, 108th Cong., 1st Sess. (2003); H.R. Rep. No. 109–130, 109th Cong., 1st Sess. (2005); "Common Sense Consumption: Super–Sizing Versus Personal Responsibility," Hearing before the

Subcommittee on Administrative Oversight and the Courts of the Senate Committee on the Judiciary, 108th Cong., 1st Sess. (2003).

7.   *Food Disparagement Statutes*. Several states have enacted statutes prohibiting the disparagement of economically important agricultural products. *See* Daniel E. Cochran, *State Agricultural Disparagement Statutes: Suing Chicken Little* (2001), in Chapter IV(A) of the Electronic Book.

8.   *Nutrition Monitoring*. Repeated attempts since 1977 to enact legislation to establish a coordinated national nutrition monitoring and research program culminated in the passage of the National Nutrition Monitoring and Related Research Act of 1990, 104 Stat. 1034, 7 U.S.C. 5301 et seq., which establishes a comprehensive federal interagency approach to nutrition monitoring, including such programs as the National Health and Nutrition Examination Survey (NHANES) and the Nationwide Food Consumption Survey (NFCS), and requires publication at least every five years of the Dietary Guidelines for Americans.

9.   *International Strategy*. The obesity epidemic affects the entire world, not just the United States. *See* Emily Lee, *The World Health Organization's Global Strategy on Diet, Physical Activity, and Health: Turning Strategy into Action*, 60 FOOD & DRUG L.J. 569 (2005).

10.   *Hunger and Eating Disorders*. In spite of the current emphasis on obesity, hunger and eating disorders remain serious problems. *See* Jon Ellison, *Hunger in America: A History of Public and Private Responses* (2004) and Michelle C. Yau, *Food as a Means of Self–Torture: Have FDA Policies Facilitated the Growth of Eating Disorders?* (2003), in Chapters V(T) and (U) of the Electronic Book.

11.   *Marshmallow Fluff*. The debate over appropriate measures to address obesity has at times led to legislative excess:

> Either way, passions run high in Massachusetts about Marshmallow Fluff, a gooey sandwich spread little-known beyond the kitchen tables and cafeterias of New England. In the vacuum of summer, it has become a Rorschach test of what foods schools should serve to students and the state of nutrition in America.
>
> In case you missed "Fluffgate," here's a summary: A tempest in a baggie blew through the Massachusetts State House in late June, when state Sen. Jarrett Barrios (D) attempted to censor the beloved but nutritionally vapid lunchtime staple. He did so after his son came home from school eating a "Fluffernutter" sandwich: peanut butter and Marshmallow Fluff.
>
> Mr. Barrio's amendment to a food nutrition bill would have regulated how often schools could serve Fluff to his children, and anyone else's. In retaliation, state Rep. Kathi–Anne Reinstein (D) sponsored a bill making Fluffernutter the state's official sandwich. Fluff, after all, is made by a Massachusetts firm—Lynn-based Durkee–Mower.
>
> Fond of stories about oddball lawmakers, the media whipped the dispute into whitecaps, and Barrios found himself mired in a controversy that pun-happy pundits couldn't resist calling sticky.
>
> In the end, Barrios backpedaled and never filed his amendment, and Ms. Reinstein's bill went nowhere. The result: Fluffgate—an end-of-school snit made from equal parts Cambridge liberal paternalism, local pride over a homegrown product, and garish politics—deflated like a marshmallow in the noontime sun.

Ethan Gilsdorf, *Backstory: Is It Really Just A Bunch Of Fluff?*, CHRISTIAN SCI. MONITOR, July 12, 2006, at 20.

2. NUTRITION LABELING

The White House Conference on Food, Nutrition and Health, held in December 1969, was a watershed event in the history of FDA food policy. Many recommendations were made that the agency place greater emphasis on regulating the nutritional quality of food and label information about the nutritional characteristics of food. Five individuals who participated actively in the White House Conference had, within two years, assumed positions at FDA, as Deputy Commissioner, Director of the Bureau of Foods, Director of the Division of Nutrition, Deputy Director of the Division of Nutrition, and Chief Counsel. The cornerstone of the new policy was the initial version of nutrition labeling that has evolved into the label format that appears on almost all packaged food. FDA promulgated its first nutrition labeling requirements in 37 Fed. Reg. 6493 (Mar. 30, 1972), 38 Fed. Reg. 2125 (Jan. 19, 1973), 38 Fed. Reg. 6951 (Mar. 14, 1973).

Peter Barton Hutt, *A Brief History of FDA Regulation Relating to the Nutrient Content of Food*

In Ralph Shapiro, ed., NUTRITION LABELING HANDBOOK, Ch. 1 (1995).

. . . .

C. *1970–1990*

The foundation for all FDA policy regarding the nutrient content of food during this twenty-year period was nutrition labeling. Although the concept of nutrition labeling was set firmly in place with promulgation of the special dietary food regulations in November 1941, the approach taken in those regulations was inadequate to implement the White House Conference Report. The November 1941 regulations applied only where a specific claim was made about a particular nutrient, and the required label declaration related only to that nutrient. The November 1941 regulations were, moreover, directed only to special dietary food, not to general purpose food. It was therefore necessary to construct a new approach.

To construct that approach, FDA turned to Section 201(n) of the Act, which stated that, in determining whether labeling is misleading, there shall be taken into account the extent to which the labeling "fails to reveal facts material in the light of such representations" as are made elsewhere in the labeling. FDA took the position that, where the manufacturer added a nutrient to a food or made any representation about the nutrient content of the food in advertising or labeling, full nutrition labeling was required in order to present all of the facts material to that representation. Those material facts, moreover, included not just the nutrients that were added or about which claims were made, but rather extended to representative micronutrients and macronutrients that would provide a balanced nutrient profile of the food. Whereas the November 1941 regulations focused only on the positive nutrient attributes of the food, the new nutrition labeling regulations required disclosure of any negative nutrient attributes as well.

The 1973 nutrition labeling requirements included a uniform format. Under the overall heading of "Nutrition Information," data were required for specified micronutrients and macronutrients. The data on the micronutrients (vitamins and minerals) were required to be presented in terms of the percentage of the United States recommended daily allowances (U.S. RDA), a level derived by FDA from the recommended dietary allowances established periodically by the Food and Nutrition Board of the National Academy of Sciences. Thus, these values were stated in percentages, not in international units or metric weight (grams and milligrams). In contrast, the data on macronutrients were presented solely in terms of metric weight and provided no percentage information. Unlike the November 1941 regulations, which provided the percent of the minimum daily requirement of micronutrients per day, the 1973 regulations required declaration of the percent of the U.S. RDA per serving.

The initial 1973 nutrition labeling regulations did not specify either a generalized standard for determining how to calculate a serving of food for purposes of the new regulations or set particular serving sizes for specific foods. When labeling began to appear that specified differing serving sizes for identical food products, FDA proposed a regulation to standardize serving sizes. The Agency failed to carry through with that approach, however, and withdrew that proposal some years later. . . .

To make nutrition labeling work, FDA at the same time promulgated additional related labeling requirements. Nutrition labeling was required to appear in a standardized format, with a minimum type size, in a uniform place on the package. This meant that consumers could find information more readily and understand it more easily.

Other regulations were promulgated at the same time to back up the new approach to nutrition labeling. Since 1938, Section 403(c) of the FD&C Act had required that any "imitation" food be labeled as such. FDA for the first time defined the term "imitation" to mean nutritional inferiority, thus prompting food manufacturers to formulate new substitute and processed foods in a way that would assure nutritional equivalence to traditional foods and to use nutrition labeling on these foods. New foods that were specially formulated to improve their nutrition profile (*e.g.*, low fat or low sodium) were no longer regarded as illegal violations of existing food standards, but were permitted to bear their own "common or usual name" to distinguish them from the traditional product and to bear nutrition labeling. FDA began to promulgate nutrition quality guidelines and issued a general statement of fortification policy to establish criteria under which vitamins and minerals should be added to food.

In promulgating regulations for food used in weight control, following the 1968–1969 public hearing, FDA for the first time included definitions for nutrient descriptors. The new regulations defined such terms as low calorie, reduced calorie, sugar free, and related claims. This approach established the FDA policy that was later to be used for definitions of all nutrient descriptors. . . .

The 1970s ended with a series of four public hearings on food labeling conducted jointly throughout the country by FDA, the FTC, and USDA during 1978 and 1979. These hearings culminated in publication by FDA in December 1979 of a major analysis of the food labeling issues that must be addressed by the Agency in the near future. That analysis identified such

issues as expansion of nutrition labeling to include additional macronutrients, further definitions for widely-used nutrient descriptors, and permission for disease prevention claims in food labeling in order to address
emerging new information on the relation between diet and health.

Throughout the 1980s, however, FDA lagged behind congressional and
public expectations in addressing these issues. The Agency did define
nutrient descriptors for sodium, and proposed to define some nutrient
descriptors for cholesterol, but it did not address this area systemically.
Only after industry forced the issue in 1984 by beginning to use disease
prevention claims in food labeling did FDA attempt to address that area.
No consideration was given to a substantial review of the content of
nutrition labeling, to reflect new information obtained on diet and health
since nutrition labeling was developed in the early 1970s. As a result, FDA
came under increasing criticism from Congress and the public, and Congress ultimately took the matter into their own hands in 1990....

NOTES

1. *Fresh Fruits and Vegetables.* The nutrition labeling regulations promulgated by FDA in 1973 applied to fresh fruits and vegetables. When a suit was brought
to challenge this application, however, FDA exempted these products pending
further study. 38 Fed. Reg. 32786 (Nov. 28, 1973). Based upon the proviso in section
401 that no standard of identity may be established for fresh fruits or vegetables
except in limited circumstances, the court in *National Nutritional Foods Association
v. FDA*, 504 F.2d 761, 806–807 (2d Cir. 1974), p. 254 *supra*, enjoined application of
FDA's vitamin-mineral regulations to fresh fruits and vegetables. FDA subsequently
issued a new proposal respecting nutrition labeling for fresh fruits and vegetables,
40 Fed. Reg. 8214 (Feb. 26, 1975), but withdrew the proposal in 48 Fed. Reg. 27266
(June 14, 1983) on the ground that the costs outweighed the benefits.

2. *Serving Size.* A central element of nutrition labeling is the "serving size" of
the food, the basis on which the nutrient content is declared. Because of wide
variations among serving sizes used in labeling for identical food products, FDA
proposed a procedure for standardizing serving sizes in 39 Fed. Reg. 20887 (June
14, 1974) and a specific serving size for soft drinks in 40 Fed. Reg. 4315 (Jan. 29,
1975), but it withdrew both proposals in 51 Fed. Reg. 15653 (Apr. 25, 1986). An
FDA survey completed later indicated that, as a result of increased consumer
concern about problem nutrients such as sodium, fat, cholesterol, and calories, food
manufacturers had reduced the labeled serving sizes to minimize the declared
amounts of these nutrients. James T. Heimbach et al., *Declared Serving Sizes of
Packaged Foods, 1977–86*, 44 FOOD TECH., No. 6, at 82 (June 1990).

3. *Abbreviated Format.* In an effort to simplify nutrition labeling, FDA proposed in 39 Fed. Reg. 8621 (Mar. 6, 1974) to permit a short format for foods which
are not meaningful sources of nutrition by allowing statements such as "contains
no vitamins or minerals." Because the comments reflected a wide disparity of views,
the proposal was withdrawn in 42 Fed. Reg. 27261 (May 27, 1977).

4. *Coverage of Nutrition Labeling.* FDA's 1973 nutrition labeling requirements
applied only to foods to which a nutrient was added or for which a representation
about nutritional content was made. A 1978 FDA survey determined that 40
percent of the leading national brands, 25 percent of the remaining national brands,
and 44 percent of chain store private label brands used nutrition labeling for
packaged processed foods. This amounted to about 40 percent of the retail sales
value of this category of food. *See* Raymond E. Schucker, A SURVEILLANCE OF

NUTRITION LABELING IN THE RETAIL PACKAGED FOOD SUPPLY (1978). A decade later, according to FDA, "about 60 percent of FDA-regulated packaged foods bear nutrition labeling." 54 Fed. Reg. 32610, 32612 (Aug. 8, 1989).

5. *Consumer Education.* From the inception of nutrition labeling, FDA stated that use of this new information by the public would depend upon supportive educational efforts that were beyond the agency's mandate and resources. Some efforts were undertaken, *e.g.*, National Nutrition Consortium, NUTRITION LABELING: HOW IT CAN WORK FOR YOU (1975), and USDA, *Nutrition Labeling: Tools For Its Use*, AGRIC. INFO. BULL. 382 (1975), but the government never mounted a major educational campaign. One study found that the attitude of consumers towards nutrition labeling was "highly positive" but comprehension was "low" and thus more consumer education was "essential." Patricia A. Daly, *The Response of Consumers to Nutrition Labeling*, 10 J. CONSUMER AFFAIRS 170 (1976). *See also* Richard B. Smith et al., *Consumer Attitudes Toward Food Labeling and Other Shopping Aids*, USDA Agric. Econ. Rep. No. 439 (1979).

6. *Commentary. See generally* Ben H. Wells, *The Consumer Research Institute's Nutrient Labeling Research*, 27 FOOD DRUG COSM. L.J. 40 (1972); Raymond C. Stokes, *The Consumer Research Institute's Nutrient Labeling Research Program*, 27 FOOD DRUG COSM. L.J. 249 (1972); James D. Grant, *Nutrient Labeling*, 27 FOOD DRUG COSM. L.J. 271 (1972); Ira I. Somers, *Quality Control Problems in Nutritional Labeling*, 27 FOOD DRUG COSM. L.J. 287 (1972); Ogden C. Johnson, *Nutrition Labeling—A Foremost Concern*, 28 FOOD DRUG COSM. L.J. 108 (1973); Merrill S. Thompson, *FDA—They Mean Well, But ...*, 37 J. AFDO 185 (1973); D. Mark Hegsted, *Nutrition Labeling: Not All Good—Not All Bad*, 29 FOOD DRUG COSM. L.J. 412 (1974); J. Lyle Littlefield, *Nutritional Labeling Revisited—Regulatory Considerations*, 29 FOOD DRUG COSM. L.J. 331 (1974); Alexander M. Schmidt, *Nutrition Labeling and the Consumer: Feast or Famine?*, 29 FOOD DRUG COSM. L.J. 414 (1974); Howard R. Roberts, *Nutrition-Labeling Compliance*, 30 FOOD DRUG COSM. L.J. 89 (1975); Esther Peterson, *Consumer Nutrition Advocacy*, 32 FOOD DRUG COSM. L.J. 423 (1977). For a discussion of the impact of FDA's nutrition labeling on USDA and the FTC, see Harry C. Mussman, *USDA Nutritional Labeling Regulations and the Growth of Voluntary Nutritional Labeling on Meat*, 29 FOOD DRUG COSM. L.J. 425 (1974); J. Thomas Rosch, *Nutrition Information and Nutrition Advertising*, 29 FOOD DRUG COSM. L.J. 429 (1974).

7. *Labeling Format.* FDA's 1973 prescribed format never satisfied all critics. *See, e.g.*, Marlene Cimons and Michael F. Jacobson, *How to Decode a Food Label*, MOTHER JONES MAG., Mar. 1978. at 32; Michael Specter, *Food Labels Often Light on Nutrition Information*, WASH. POST, July 23, 1989, at A1.

8. *Exemptions.* In 1983, to encourage experimentation in nutrition labeling, FDA established a procedure, still in effect as amended, under which exemptions from current labeling requirements may be granted. 45 Fed. Reg. 58880 (Sept. 5, 1980), 48 Fed. Reg. 15236 (Apr. 8, 1983), codified at 21 C.F.R. 101.108.

9. *Nutrient Discovery and Analysis.* Nutrition labeling depends entirely on the extraordinary work of food scientists during the first half of the 20th century in the discovery, isolation, and ultimately the development of methods of analysis for essential nutrients. For a concise history of these events see Richard Crowley, *The History and Evolution of Food and Supplement Testing*, COVANCE FOOD SCIENCE NEWSLETTER No. 81 (Aug. 2004).

———

In the late 1980s, support emerged for new legislation to establish a firm legal basis for nutrition labeling of all food, as well as to mandate related labeling reforms.

Michael Specter, *Food Labels Often Light on Nutrition Information*

THE WASHINGTON POST, July 23, 1989, at A1.

Realizing that a walk down a supermarket aisle can be a trip into the twilight zone, consumer groups have spent years trying to force a fundamental revision of food-labeling practices.... Current nutrition labels were designed when federal health officials thought that vitamin and mineral contents were the most important aspect of food. But these days, vitamin deficiencies are rare in this country. Instead, the repeated message from doctors and public health officers is that we should increase fiber intake and cut back on eating fat, particularly saturated fat.

In the past year, two major reports, from the surgeon general and the National Academy of Sciences, said that by cutting back on fat Americans can vastly reduce the incidence of heart disease and, possibly, certain types of cancer. Marketing surveys have shown that consumers have received the message but have run into major road-blocks at the grocery store. Fat content, for example, is usually listed in grams, a measure rarely used and poorly understood in this country. Saturated fat is almost never even noted on most processed food packages. Calories are often listed per portion, but many portion sizes are misleading. A 50–cent bag of pretzels bought out of a machine, for instance, is usually listed as containing 1.65 servings although it was clearly intended as a snack for one person....

MODEL LABEL OF UNSPECIFIED FOOD

———

FDA belatedly published a notice in 54 Fed. Reg. 32610 (Aug. 8, 1989) requesting public comment on "significant new improvements in food labeling," and published proposed regulations in 55 Fed. Reg. 29476 (July 19, 1990) to reform nutrition labeling, but this was too little too late.

Peter Barton Hutt, *A Brief History of FDA Regulation Relating to the Nutrient Content of Food*

In Ralph Shapiro, ed., NUTRITION LABELING HANDBOOK, Ch. 1 (1995).

. . . The Nutrition Labeling and Education Act (NL&E Act) was signed into law by President Bush on November 9, 1990. The statute dealt with six separate matters, all of which involved, directly or indirectly, FDA regulation relating to the nutrient content of food.

First, Section 403(q) was added to the FD&C Act to require nutrition labeling for virtually all food products. This was not a controversial issue. FDA had belatedly proposed to do this by regulation in 1989 and the industry had supported it. The statute required a shift in emphasis from micronutrients to macronutrients and authorized FDA to set standards for serving sizes. Because FDA could do this under existing law however, this represented little change.

Second, FDA was required to define the nutrient descriptors commonly in use throughout the food industry—high fiber, low fat, reduced cholesterol, and so forth. FDA had begun this task in the 1970s, but had not completed it. The Agency could do this under existing law, and thus the new authority represented no additional statutory power for FDA.

Third, FDA was required to review specified disease prevention claims to determine whether they were appropriate for labeling. The Agency asserted that it could do this under existing law, and thus it represented no new statutory power. Even though FDA had twice proposed regulations to govern these matters prior to enactment of the NL&E Act, this provision was quite controversial because it reflected some of the same criteria that had been proposed by FDA and strongly criticized by the food industry. It was correctly anticipated that this provision would ultimately produce the most serious controversy.

Fourth, the NL&E Act contained several new food labeling and food standards provisions. Vegetable and fruit juice beverages were required to bear the percent of each juice on the information panel. All ingredients in standardized food products were required to be included in the label statement of ingredients. All certified color additives were required to be included by name in the label statement of ingredients. In the future, food standards (except for dairy products and maple sirup) were permitted to be promulgated, amended, and repealed using informal notice-and-comment rulemaking, rather than the formal trial-type administrative hearing procedure that prevailed in the past.

Fifth, all of the labeling requirements under the FD&C Act were explicitly made subject to national uniformity (federal preemption) except for the general prohibition against false or misleading labeling, health and safety warnings, special dietary food regulation, and such local matters as unit pricing and open date labeling. Thus, by requiring national uniformity in nutrition labeling, nutrient descriptors, disease prevention claims, food standards, and the other food labeling provisions involved, the NL&E Act effectively removed state and local government from establishing regulatory requirements relating to the nutrient content of food. This represented a major change in national food policy, one that had been sought by the food industry for a century.

Sixth, in return for national uniformity, states were for the first time explicitly authorized to enforce the food labeling provisions of the FD&C Act, with the same exceptions that apply to national uniformity, in federal courts, rather than state courts, after first informing FDA and giving FDA the opportunity to take action. Because state officials can enforce directly in state courts the identical requirements under state law, however, without any of the procedural requirements established in the NL&E Act, it is doubtful that this provision has any practical impact....

NOTES

1. *Final Format Selection.* For the story of the dramatic confrontation between FDA and USDA over the appropriate format for nutrition labeling, and how President George H.W. Bush personally chose the final version that was then incorporated in the January 1993 regulations, *see* Peter Barton Hutt, *A Brief History of FDA Regulation Relating to the Nutrient Content of Food*, in Ralph Shapiro, ed., NUTRITION LABELING HANDBOOK, Ch. 1 (1995).

2. *State Enforcement.* To date, no state has taken advantage of the opportunity to bring an enforcement action in federal court rather than in state court under new section 310(b) of the FD&C Act, as added by the NLEA.

3. *Implementing Regulations.* FDA has promulgated regulations to implement the following provisions of the NLEA.

Nutrition labeling: 56 Fed. Reg. 60366 (Nov. 27, 1991), 57 Fed. Reg. 32058 (July 20, 1992), 57 Fed. Reg. 32750 (July 23, 1992), 58 Fed. Reg. 2079 (Jan. 6, 1993), codified at 21 C.F.R. 101.9.

Nutrient descriptors: 56 Fed. Reg. 60421 (Nov. 27, 1991), 58 Fed. Reg. 2302 (Jan. 6, 1993), codified at 21 C.F.R. 101.13 & Subpart D.

Disease claims: 56 Fed. Reg. 60537 (Nov. 27, 1991), 58 Fed. Reg. 2478 (Jan. 6, 1993), codified at 21 C.F.R. 101.14 & Subpart E.

Fresh fruit and vegetable labeling: 56 Fed. Reg. 30468 (July 2, 1991), 56 Fed. Reg. 60880 (Nov. 27, 1991), codified at 21 C.F.R. Part 101, Subpart C.

Serving sizes: 56 Fed. Reg. 60394 (Nov. 27, 1991), 58 Fed. Reg. 2229 (Jan. 6, 1993), codified at 21 C.F.R. 101.8(a), 101.9(b), 101.12

State enforcement: 56 Fed. Reg. 60534 (Nov. 27, 1991), 58 Fed. Reg. 2457 (Jan. 6, 1993), codified at 21 C.F.R. 100.2.

National uniformity: 56 Fed. Reg. 60528 (Nov. 27, 1991), 58 Fed. Reg. 2462 (Jan. 6, 1993), codified at 21 C.F.R. 100.1.

Other matters: Peripheral regulations can be found in the Federal Registers of November 27, 1991 and January 6, 1993.

4. *Nutrition Labeling in Restaurants.* Under section 403(q)(5)(A)(1) of the FD&C Act, restaurants are exempt from nutrition labeling. In promulgating its regulations on nutrient descriptors and disease claims, FDA made these requirements applicable to restaurant signs, placards, and posters, but not to menus. 58 Fed. Reg. 2302, 2386–90 & 58 Fed. Reg. 2478, 2515–19 (Jan. 6, 1993). After Public Citizen brought suit to contest this exemption for restaurant menus, FDA proposed to delete the exemption. 58 Fed. Reg. 33055 (June 15, 1993). After the menu

exemption was declared unlawful in *Public Citizen, Inc. v. Shalala*, 932 F. Supp. 13 (D.D.C. 1996), FDA published a final regulation deleting the exemption. 61 Fed. Reg. 40320 (Aug. 2, 1996, codified at 21 C.F.R. 101.10. Under the regulation, nutrition labeling "shall be provided upon request for any restaurant food or meal for which" a nutrient descriptor or disease claim is made. Nutrient levels may be determined by nutrient databases rather than by analyses, and may be provided in any reasonable form. *See* Miriam P. Hechler, *Nutrition Labeling and Restaurants: Issues, Options, and the FDA, 1970–1995* (1995), Hope S. Yen, *Nutrition Labeling for Restaurants: A Proposal for Change* (1996), Melissa Fien, *The Restaurant Industry and FDA: Striving for a Safer America* (2002), in Chapter I(J) of the Electronic Book.

5. *Nutrition Facts Box.* The final nutrition labeling format, as now amended, is illustrated by the following sample label included in 21 C.F.R. 101.9. The regulations actually require a larger type size than appears below. 21 C.F.R. 101.9(d)(1)(ii).

Nutrition Facts

Serving Size 1 cup (228g)
Servings Per Container 2

Amount Per Serving

Calories 260	Calories from Fat 120

	% Daily Value*
Total Fat 13g	**20%**
Saturated Fat 5g	**25%**
Trans Fat 2g	
Cholesterol 30mg	**10%**
Sodium 660mg	**28%**
Total Carbohydrate 31g	**10%**
Dietary Fiber 0g	**0%**
Sugars 5g	
Protein 5g	

Vitamin A 4%	•	Vitamin C 2%
Calcium 15%	•	Iron 4%

* Percent Daily Values are based on a 2,000 calorie diet. Your Daily Values may be higher or lower depending on your calorie needs:

	Calories:	2,000	2,500
Total Fat	Less than	65g	80g
Sat Fat	Less than	20g	25g
Cholesterol	Less than	300mg	300mg
Sodium	Less than	2,400mg	2,400mg
Total Carbohydrate		300g	375g
Dietary Fiber		25g	30g

Calories per gram:
Fat 9   •   Carbohydrate 4   •   Protein 4

6. *Fresh Fruits and Vegetables.* As a legislative compromise, section 403(q)(4) provides that nutrition labeling for the 20 most frequently consumed raw fruits, vegetables, and fish shall be implemented voluntarily in retail food stores based on FDA guidelines. FDA has implemented this provision through 56 Fed. Reg. 60880 (Nov. 27, 1991), 59 Fed. Reg. 36379 (July 18, 1994), 61 Fed. Reg. 42742 (Aug. 16, 1996), 67 Fed. Reg. 38913 (June 6, 2002), 71 Fed. Reg. 42031 (July 25, 2006), codified at 21 C.F.R. 101.42–45 & Appendix C & D. FDA is required to issue a report on this program every two years. If there is substantial compliance, the voluntary system will remain in place. If there is not substantial compliance, the voluntary system shall become mandatory. The first FDA report, published in 58 Fed. Reg. 28985 (May 18, 1993), found substantial compliance. Subsequent reports repeated this finding, *e.g.*, 62 Fed. Reg. 25635 (May 9, 1997), but FDA has not had sufficient funds to prepare any reports since 1997. In *Arent v. Shalala*, 70 F.3d 610

(D.C. Cir. 1995), *aff'g* 866 F. Supp. 6 (D.D.C. 1994); the courts determined that the FDA implementing regulations in 21 C.F.R. 101.43, which define "substantial compliance" as 90 percent compliance in 60 percent of all stores, are not arbitrary or capricious.

7. *FDA Enforcement.* In response to requests from the House and Senate Appropriations Committees, H.R. Rep. No. 109–102 and S. Rep. No. 109–92, 109th Cong., 1st Sess. (2005), FDA issued a *Report to Congress on Compliance with Food Label Regulations Under the Food and Drug Administration's Purview* (Apr. 19, 2006).

COMMENT: CHOLESTEROL AND FAT LABELING

No aspect of nutrition labeling has occasioned more debate during the past 70 years than disclosure of cholesterol and fat composition. The issues raised in this area include the manner in which the fat in any fabricated food should be declared in the statement of ingredients; label declarations stating or characterizing the amount of cholesterol, fat, or fatty acid in food; and labeling claims relating to the potential relationship of these nutrients to heart disease and other ailments.

Shortly after enactment of the 1938 Act, FDA issued various trade correspondences (TCs) permitting the declaration of individual fats and oils in the ingredient statement of fabricated foods under generic terms such as "shortening" or "vegetable oil." *See* TC–62 (Feb. 15, 1940), TC–94 (Feb. 21, 1940), and TC–209 (Mar. 21, 1940). At that time, no nutritionally significant difference was thought to exist among the various fats and oils used in food. In the 1950s, however, some scientific research indicated that there may be a correlation between blood cholesterol levels and heart disease. Scientific research also showed that saturated fat tends to increase blood cholesterol and polyunsaturated fat tends to decrease blood cholesterol. Concerned that this preliminary information might prompt unwarranted claims in food labeling, FDA published a statement of policy stating that the role of cholesterol in heart disease had not been established, that the advisability of making extensive changes in dietary fat intake had not been demonstrated, and that any labeling claims related to heart disease would be regarded as illegal. 24 Fed. Reg. 9990 (Dec. 10, 1959). FDA interpreted this statement of policy to prohibit use of the term "cholesterol" and any related claims.

In May 1964, the agency reported the results of a consumer survey which showed that food labels referring to "polyunsaturated" or "cholesterol" misled many people to believe that the foods would reduce blood cholesterol and thus treat heart disease. It therefore reaffirmed its earlier policy statement. In response, prominent physicians requested FDA to permit labeling statements that would assist physicians in recommending a proper diet for patients and to assist patients in following that diet. Accordingly, in 30 Fed. Reg. 6984 (May 25, 1965), FDA proposed to retain its earlier policy statement but at the same time to permit factual declaration of the fatty acid content of foods—*i.e.*, the number of grams of saturated fatty acids, monounsaturated fatty acids, and polyunsaturated acids—in an ordinary serving and in 100 grams of the food. This proposal was withdrawn in 31 Fed. Reg. 3301 (Mar. 2, 1966), pending further study.

By the 1970s, interest in the dietary fat issue had intensified. In 36 Fed. Reg. 11521 (June 15, 1971), FDA published two new proposals to replace the 1965 proposal. First, the agency proposed to revoke the old TCs and to require in the statement of ingredients declaration of the specific name of each individual fat or oil ingredient in the order of predominance. Second, it offered two alternative proposals to replace its 1965 proposal respecting cholesterol/fatty acid labeling. The first alternative involved retention of the 1959 policy statement with the addition of a prohibition of any labeling use of the terms "polyunsaturated," "monounsaturated," or "saturated," except as specifically permitted by FDA regulation. The other alternative would have established a form for the voluntary declaration of the fatty acid composition of any food containing 10 percent or more fat and not less than 3 grams of fat in an average serving.

In 1973, as part of its final nutrition labeling regulations, FDA established rules governing cholesterol/fatty acid labeling. 36 Fed. Reg. 11521 (June 15, 1971), 38 Fed. Reg. 2132 (Jan. 19, 1973). The agency made cholesterol and fatty acid composition labeling an optional, rather than a mandatory, part of nutrition labeling. Where this information was provided, it was required to conform to the format specified by FDA. The principal display panel of the label could state "cholesterol (fat) information appears ___," the blank to be filled in with a phrase stating where the information was contained on the label, but only in small size type. The 1959 policy statement was revoked as obsolete. The new regulation was modified in 38 Fed. Reg. 6961 (Mar. 14, 1973) and in 38 Fed. Reg. 20071 (July 27, 1973). FDA added an additional paragraph to make it clear that no statements relating to cholesterol or fatty acid content could be made in labeling other than those specifically permitted in the regulation.

In 39 Fed. Reg. 20888 (June 14, 1974), FDA took action on its 1971 proposal respecting specific declaration of fats and oils in the ingredient statement for fabricated food. FDA adopted the approach described above, revoking the old TCs and requiring specific individual declaration of fats and oils, but permitting declaration of alternative ingredients to allow flexibility in food formulation. The final regulation was published in 41 Fed. Reg. 1156 (Jan. 6, 1976). A subsequent modification substituted the term "hydrogenated" for "saturated" in describing fats and oils. 41 Fed. Reg. 52481 (Nov. 30, 1976), 43 Fed. Reg. 12856 (Mar. 28, 1978). In 1980, FDA amended its regulations to permit dairy products to declare fat content as part of the ingredient statement without providing full nutrition information. 42 Fed. Reg. 6834 (Feb. 4, 1977), 45 Fed. Reg. 37420 (June 3, 1980).

As scientific reports during the 1980s emphasized the relationship between serum cholesterol and heart disease, consumer demand grew for information about the cholesterol and fatty acid composition of food products. FDA responded in 51 Fed. Reg. 42584 (Nov. 25, 1986) by proposing to define the terms "cholesterol free," "low cholesterol," and "cholesterol reduced," to require that both cholesterol and fatty acid composition be included as a part of nutrition labeling whenever either is declared, and to delete the provision requiring the label to state that "information on fat and cholesterol content is provided for individuals who, on the advice of a physician, are modifying their dietary intake of fat and cholesterol." The proposal stopped short of making information about cholesterol and fatty acid composition a mandatory part of nutrition labeling or of revoking the regulation that permits alternative "and/or" declaration of fats and oils in a statement of ingredients. FDA commissioned economic analyses of its policy regarding ingredient labeling of fats and oils and its policy on fat composition information as a part of nutrition labeling. Arthur D. Little, COST OF COMPLIANCE AND ECONOMIC IMPACT OF SPECIFIC SOURCE DECLARATION OF FATS AND OILS IN FOODS, Report to FDA under HHS Contract No. 223–79–8052 (May 1981); Arthur D. Little, Inc., COST IMPACT ANALYSIS OF DECLARATION OF FATTY ACID AND CHOLESTEROL CONTENT IN FOODS, Report to FDA under HHS Contract No. 223–79–8052 (Oct. 1981). FDA published a tentative final regulation in 55 Fed. Reg. 29456 (July 19, 1990), but passage of the Nutrition Labeling and Education Act in 1990 necessitated reconsideration by the agency.

Under section 403(q) of the FD&C Act, as added by the NLEA, Congress left FDA no choice. The statute explicitly required nutrition labeling to include fat, calories from fat, saturated fat, and cholesterol. Accordingly, the regulations promulgated by FDA in 56 Fed. Reg. 60366 (Nov. 27, 1991) and 58 Fed. Reg. 2079 (Jan. 6, 1993) faithfully followed these requirements. When later faced with scientific evidence showing that trans fat has the same effect on serum cholesterol as saturated fat, the agency amended the nutrition labeling regulations to require that trans fat be labeled separately as part of the nutrition labeling. 64 Fed. Reg. 62746 (Nov. 17, 1999), 67 Fed. Reg. 69171 (Nov. 15, 2002), 68 Fed. Reg. 41434 (July 11, 2003). *See generally* Stacy R. Anderson, *Regulation of Fat Content in Food: Recent History and Cultural Commentary* (2006), in Chapter V(D)(2) of the Electronic Book.

COMMENT: SODIUM LABELING

The original FDA special dietary food regulations, promulgated in November 1941, contained no provision relating to sodium labeling. In 1954, FDA promulgated a special dietary food regulation under section 403(j) requiring that a food represented as a means of regulating the intake of sodium or salt be labeled with the number of milligrams of sodium in 100 grams of the food and in an average serving of the food. 18 Fed. Reg. 7249 (Nov. 14, 1953), 19 Fed. Reg. 2767 (May 13, 1954), 19 Fed. Reg. 3999 (July 1, 1954). As part of its wholesale revision of the regulations on food for special dietary uses during the 1960s, FDA revised the sodium regulation in 27 Fed. Reg. 5515 (June 20, 1962), 31 Fed. Reg. 8521 (June 18, 1966). The agency stayed the revised regulations on food for special dietary uses when it received objections and requests for a public hearing, and it included the sodium regulation in the resulting 1969 hearing even though no specific issues had been raised about it. The final regulation, promulgated in 37 Fed. Reg. 9763 (May 17, 1972), retained the 1954 requirement and added some clarifying details. FDA's nutrition labeling regulations, adopted at the same time, specified that sodium labeling in accordance with the regulation would not trigger full nutrition labeling.

The association between sodium and hypertension was not widely accepted in 1972. Indeed, the FTC later entered consent orders prohibiting any representation for salt substitute products that there is "a causal connection between sodium intake and high blood pressure or water retention, or that a reduction in the level of sodium intake will promote or maintain good health." *Morton-Norwich Products, Inc.*, 86 F.T.C. 299 (1975); *Nagle, Spillman & Bergman, Inc.*, 88 F.T.C. 244 (1976). By the early 1980s, however, scientific opinion on this matter had changed dramatically. FDA commissioned an economic analysis of options for expanded sodium labeling. Arthur D. Little, Inc., COST OF COMPLIANCE AND ECONOMIC IMPACT OF SODIUM/POTASSIUM LABELING REGULATORY ALTERNATIVES (Dec. 1981). The agency then promulgated new regulations governing sodium labeling of food. 47 Fed. Reg. 26580 (June 18, 1982), 49 Fed. Reg. 15510 (Apr. 18, 1984). These regulations reflected three significant changes. First, although sodium labeling alone still did not trigger full nutrition labeling, sodium content became a mandatory part of nutrition labeling. Second, FDA defined the terms "sodium free," "very low sodium," "low sodium," and "reduced sodium." To be labeled as reduced sodium, a food had to achieve a 75 percent reduction. Third, the sodium provision in the special dietary food regulations was revised to state that, where a food is represented as a means of regulating the intake of sodium or salt, the label must either bear full nutrition labeling or, at the very least, a statement of the number of milligrams of sodium in a specified serving. As a practical matter, most food labels that declared the sodium content did so as part of nutrition labeling.

An attempt to enact legislation mandating sodium labeling for all food failed in the 98th Congress. *See* "Sodium in Food and High Blood Pressure," Hearing before the Subcomm. on Investigations and Oversight of the House Comm. on Science and Technology, 97th Cong., 1st Sess. (1981); "Sodium in Food and High Blood Pressure," Report Prepared by the Subcomm. on Investigations and Oversight of the House Comm. on Science and Technology, 97th Cong., 1st Sess. (Committee Print 1981). Three years later a suit to force FDA to institute a rulemaking to prescribe sodium labeling for all food products, including those not required to provide full nutrition labeling, was dismissed. *Center for Science in the Public Interest v. Novitch*, Food Drug Cosm. L. Rep. (CCH) ¶ 38,275 (D.D.C. 1984). Finally, under the Nutrition Labeling and Education Act of 1990, sodium became a mandatory part of nutrition labeling for all food. 21 C.F.R. 101.9(c)(4).

COMMENT: OTHER NUTRITION INFORMATION

As part of its complete revision of the November 1941 special dietary food regulations, *see infra* p. 251, FDA included in the June 1962 proposal and June 1966 "final" order changes in the regulations governing labeling of infant food, hypoallergenic food, low sodium food, and food for which caloric claims are made. All of these regulations were considered during the FDA 1968–1969 special dietary food hearings, although only the regulation respecting caloric claims was the subject of any significant interest.

Following those hearings, FDA published the infant food regulations. 35 Fed. Reg. 16737 (Oct. 29, 1970), 36 Fed. Reg. 23555 (Dec. 10, 1971), codified at 21 C.F.R. 105.65. The regulations for hypoallergenic food, which were not contested, were published in 37 Fed. Reg. 9763 (May 17, 1972) and codified at 21 C.F.R. 105.62. The low sodium regulation was promulgated but later revoked because it was superseded by the NLEA regulations. In 42 Fed. Reg. 37166 (July 19, 1977) and 43 Fed. Reg. 43248 (Sept.

22, 1978), FDA promulgated its final regulations respecting caloric claims for food, 21 C.F.R. 105.66. In spite of the major commercial importance of these regulations, they were not challenged in court pursuant to section 701(f), and thus became effective. They were later revised as part of the NLEA regulations.

Although the special dietary food regulations, 21 C.F.R. 105.62, provide for the labeling of hypoallergenic food, such claims are rarely made. In early 1989, however, in accordance with the requirements of the Infant Formula Act of 1980, 94 Stat. 1190, FD&C Act 412, FDA undertook a review of the labeling claims for existing infant formulas. The agency concluded that the claims for hypoallergenicity, *i.e.*, "usefulness in the management of severe food allergies, sensitivity to intact protein and galactosemia (inability to metabolize one milk sugar)," were not supported by "a convincing body of evidence." "Infant Formula Claims," FDA Talk Paper No. T89–18 (Mar. 27, 1989); "Update on Good Start Formula," FDA Talk Paper No. T89–31 (May 10, 1989).

3. NUTRIENT DESCRIPTORS

The original FDA special dietary food regulations, promulgated in November 1941 pursuant to section 403(j) of the FD&C Act, provided that any food purporting to be for special dietary use as a means of regulating calories for the purpose of controlling body weight must bear a statement of the number of available calories supplied by a specified quantity of the food. Along with all of the other special dietary food regulations, the caloric provision was subjected to the infamous FDA administrative hearings of 1968–1969. Following those hearings, FDA promulgated its final regulations respecting caloric claims for food. 42 Fed. Reg. 37166 (July 19, 1977), 43 Fed Reg. 43248 (Sept. 22, 1978). The regulations prescribed requirements for the nutrient descriptors "low calorie," "reduced calorie," and "for calorie restricted diets," as well as for related terminology such as "diet," "dietetic," and "artificially sweetened." These were the first nutrient descriptors defined by FDA by regulation, and they set a template for those that followed.

In 47 Fed. Reg. 26580 (June 18, 1982), 49 Fed. Reg. 15510 (Apr. 18, 1984), the agency defined the nutrient descriptors "sodium free," "very low sodium," "low sodium," and "reduced sodium." Following that, in 51 Fed. Reg. 42584 (Nov. 25, 1986), FDA proposed to define the nutrient descriptors "cholesterol free," "low cholesterol," and "cholesterol reduced," but it did not take final action on that matter prior to enactment of the NLEA.

In section 403(r)(1)(A) of the FD&C Act, as added by the NLEA, Congress ordered FDA to complete the job of defining nutrient descriptors. Congress identified a nutrient descriptor as a claim that "characterizes the level of any nutrient." For reasons that remain unclear, FDA has chosen in its regulations to call nutrient descriptors "nutrient content claims." It is clear from the statutory language, however, that a nutrient content claim that merely provides factual information and does not in any way characterize the level of a nutrient does not fall within section 403(r)(1)(A). Indeed, when FDA issued its nutrient descriptor regulations, it explicitly recognized in 21 C.F.R. 101.13(i)(3) that a factual statement about nutrient content is not covered by the regulations. Accordingly, we use the correct terminology of a "nutrient descriptor."

The regulations promulgated by FDA to implement the nutrient descriptor provisions of the NLEA are detailed and complex. The general principles applicable to this category of claims are found in 21 C.F.R. 101.13, and the specific nutrient descriptors that have been defined by the agency are set forth in 21 C.F.R. Part 101, Subpart D. The nutrients for which descriptors have been defined are calories; sodium; fat, fatty acid, and cholesterol; and fiber. General descriptors such as "high" and "good source" are defined for purposes of protein, vitamins, minerals, dietary fiber, and potassium. The term "high potency" is defined specifically for vitamins and minerals. Comparative claims such as "less" and "more" are also defined, as are general terms such as "light" and "healthy." This summary barely skims the surface of these regulations and does not begin to explore the details that govern how nutrient descriptors can be used in food labeling.

NOTES

1. *Carbohydrate Descriptors.* FDA has consistently declined to define nutrient descriptors for carbohydrates. 58 Fed. Reg. 2302, 2343 (Jan. 6, 1993). Even in the early 2000s, at the height of the popularity of diet programs based upon a restricted carbohydrate intake, FDA adhered to its policy of not proposing regulations to clarify the various carbohydrate claims made by the food industry. *See* Andrew D. Cooper, *Carbohydrate Nutrient Content Claims: Proposals for FDA Action and Lessons for Regulatory Response to Emerging Consumer Trends* (2006), in Chapter V(D)(3) of the Electronic Book.

2. *Whole Grains.* Now that consumer interest has shifted from carbohydrates to whole grains, FDA has again declined to propose regulations or guidance to define the descriptors for this category of food components. *E.g.*, Letter from Margaret O'K. Glavin, Associate Commissioner for Regulatory Affairs, FDA, to Stuart M. Pape (Nov. 8, 2005), FDA Docket No. 2004P–0223/CPI. Unlike carbohydrates, however, whole grains are foods rather than nutrients under the FD&C Act and therefore the industry can lawfully use descriptors without the need for an FDA regulation.

3. *Restriction on Terms.* Section 403(r)(2)(A)(i) restricts the use of nutrient descriptors to those terms defined in FDA regulations. FDA has declined to expand defined terminology other than to allow creative spelling (*e.g.*, "lo" rather than "low"). 58 Fed. Reg. 2302, 2319–2320, 2343–2344 (Jan. 6, 1993). The food industry has argued that the prohibition against using terms not defined by FDA raises constitutional questions under commercial free speech doctrine. In 60 Fed. Reg. 66206 (Dec. 21, 1995) and 69 Fed. Reg. 24541 (May 4, 2004), FDA reopened the record to reconsider additional synonyms for nutrient descriptors.

4. *Descriptor Bans.* The provisions of section 403(r) contain outright bans against the use of descriptors in specified circumstances, *e.g.*, a ban in 21 C.F.R. 101.62(d)(i)(C) and (ii)(C) on any cholesterol descriptor if the food contains more than 2 grams of saturated fat. The food industry has argued that in such circumstances, disclosure of the health risk, rather than an outright ban of the claim, is required under commercial free speech doctrine.

5. *Nutrient Descriptor Determined by Authoritative Body.* Because of concern about FDA's restrictive implementation of the nutrient descriptor provisions, Con-

gress included in the Food and Drug Administration Modernization Act of 1997 a new section 403(r)(2)(G) of the FD&C Act that permits a food manufacturer to make a nutrient descriptor claim based upon a published authoritative statement by a scientific body of the United States Government with official responsibility for public health protection or research directly relating to human nutrition or the National Academy of Sciences. This provision has been invoked on a relatively few occasions. FDA action under the provision is published on its website, not in the Federal Register. The agency has not proposed regulations to implement this provision. When FDA published interim final rules prohibiting nine disease claims based on the parallel "authoritative body" provision for disease claims in section 403(r)(3)(C), it expressed a very narrow and restrictive interpretation of what constitutes an "authoritative statement." 63 Fed. Reg. 34083 (June 22, 1998),

6. *Nutrient Descriptor in Brand Name.* Section 403(r)(4)(A)(iii) of the FD&C Act, as added by the NLEA, provides a unique procedure for a company to petition FDA for permission to use an implied nutrient descriptor in a brand name. After publishing a notice in 67 Fed. Reg. 72963 (Dec. 9, 2002) requesting comment on the use of "Carbolite" as a brand name, FDA denied the petition. Letter from L. Robert Lake, Director, FDA, CFSAN Office of Regulations and Policy, to Carbolite Foods, Inc. (Jan. 15, 2003), FDA Docket No. 02P–0462.

4. REDEFINITION OF "IMITATION"

Report of the White House Conference on Food, Nutrition and Health

New Foods Panel (December 1969).

Presently, new foods are often required by Government regulatory agencies to be called "imitation" products. The "imitation" label has been regarded as equally applicable when the new product is inferior to the old as it is when the new product is superior to the old. Thus, the use of such over simplified and inaccurate words are [sic] potentially misleading to consumers, and fail[s] to inform the public about the actual characteristics and properties of the new product....

Under existing law, Government agencies could ... require an informative and descriptive generic name for every food. The existing legal prohibitions against false or misleading labeling and advertising could be utilized to prevent the use of any terminology that could mislead consumers about the identity or characteristics of the new product.... Such a policy ... would provide more accurate and useful information for consumer[s] about the identify of foods than is presently the situation. It would also encourage the development and marketing of variations of traditional foods and of completely new foods that can provide consumers a greater variety of acceptable, higher quality, and more nutritious food products at lower prices....

Imitation Foods, Application of Term "Imitation": Proposed Rulemaking

38 Fed. Reg. 2138 (January 19, 1973).

....

Vast strides in food technology have taken place since section 403(c) of the act was enacted, and there are now on the market many new wholesome and nutritious food products, some of which resemble and are substitutes for other, traditional foods. Significantly, it is no longer the case that such products are necessarily inferior to the traditional foods for which they may be substituted.

There has been some uncertainty as to the proper scope of the term "imitation" in this modern context. The term clearly fails to inform the public of the actual characteristics and properties of a new food product. . . . To apply automatically the term "imitation" to new substitute food products which are not nutritionally inferior would be a disservice to consumers and would be contrary to the common understanding that the word "imitation" connotes inferiority. Section 403(c) of the act would then present a serious obstacle to the development and marketing of modified products with improved nutritional content. Indeed, because of the traditional connotation of inferiority, application of the term "imitation" to a substitute food product which is not inferior could be misleading to the consumer, in violation of section 403(a) of the act.

Accordingly, the Commissioner of Food and Drugs has concluded that it is in the interest of consumers and consistent with the general intent of Congress to restrict required application of the term "imitation" to a substitute food which is nutritionally inferior to the food for which it is a substitute.

The consumer, however, must be protected from unwitting purchase of a product which is different, although not inferior, from what he may reasonably expect. The Commissioner concurs with the further recommendation of the White House Conference that the "name of a food should accurately describe, in as simple and direct terms as possible, the basic nature of the food or its characterizing properties or ingredients." Accordingly, in order to avoid "imitation" status, a substitute food product which is not nutritionally inferior must also bear a label which clearly states the common or usual name of the product and which is not false or misleading. . . .

The Commissioner has considered whether there may be basis for imitation labeling other than nutritional inferiority. In reviewing this matter, it appears that nutritional inferiority is the only type of inferiority that is quantifiable on an objective basis. All other potential aspects of inferiority involve essentially subjective judgment which may vary from person to person. . . . The Commissioner has concluded that it is not the function of the Food and Drug Administration to attempt to arbitrate between the likes and dislikes of different individuals or between the different economic considerations that motivate different producers of agricultural commodities or different manufacturers and distributors of foods. The function of the Food and Drug Administration is solely to assure the safety of all foods and to prevent misleading labeling. . . .

NOTE

In promulgating the final regulation, 21 C.F.R. 101.3(e), FDA noted, "No comment was able to articulate or even suggest objective standards constituting inferiority in addition to nutritional inferiority.'' 38 Fed. Reg. 20702 (Aug. 2, 1973). Under the regulation, ''nutritional inferiority'' was defined as a reduction of 2 percent or more of the U.S. RDA of protein or any essential nutrient but not of fat or caloric content.

Federation of Homemakers v. Schmidt

539 F.2d 740 (D.C. Cir. 1976).

■ TAMM, CIRCUIT JUDGE.

The Food and Drug Administration (FDA) recently promulgated a regulation which, for the first time, attempted to define an imitation food subject to section 403(c) of the Federal Food, Drug, and Cosmetic Act. The appellants in this case challenge the new regulation as contrary to the terms of the Act and as arbitrary and capricious. We affirm the district court's finding that the regulation fulfills the objectives of the statute in question and is a reasonable exercise of the regulatory power of the FDA. . . .

The Federation of Homemakers, a national consumer group, filed suit to enjoin enforcement of the new definition by the FDA, but on cross motions for summary judgment, District Judge Joseph C. Waddy held that the regulation is consistent with the statute and Congressional intent. *Federation of Homemakers v. Schmidt*, 385 F. Supp. 362 (D.D.C. 1974). . . .

. . . Beginning with the Supreme Court's admonition in *62 Cases of Jam v. United States* [*supra* p. 181] that ''imitation'' must be ''left . . . to the understanding of ordinary English speech,'' appellants call our attention to cases in which texture, smell, taste, appearance, manufacture, packaging and marketing all contribute to a determination of whether the food in question must be labeled an imitation.[8] While it is true that these judicial definitions may be reasonable ones, we do not believe that they prevent the promulgation of an equally reasonable definition by the agency charged with administering the Act. Congress chose not to define the parameters of its imitation label requirements; our deference to the enforcing agency's interpretation limits our review to determining only whether the regulation violates the language of the statute or is arbitrary and capricious. Neither the legislative history of the companion section regarding standardized foods, 21 U.S.C. § 341 (1970), nor the undefined use of ''imitation'' in the statute leads us to conclude that a food nutritionally equivalent to the ordinary food and clearly labeled with a common name established by regulation or with a descriptive term violates Congressional objectives if it is marketed without the imitation label. Indeed, the new

---

8. In response to criticisms that the new regulation considers only nutritional equivalency, the FDA pointed out that by defining an imitation as a *substitute*, the characteristics previously noted by courts are still applicable in reaching this threshold finding.

Nutritional inferiority is not the only criterion involved in defining ''imitation'' status. An evaluation of the over-all impression conveyed by the food must first establish that the food is a substitute for and resembles another food.

Response to Comments, 38 Fed. Reg. 20202 (1973). . . .

regulation successfully reconciles the need to alert the public to inferior products with the proscription in subsection 343(a) against false or misleading labels.

As to the arbitrary and capricious issue raised by the Federation of Homemakers, we are convinced that the FDA regulation is well within the zone of reasonableness required of agency rulemaking. We note first that appellant's primary complaint with the regulation is that the FDA has not decided to issue standards of identity for all new foods, but instead has promulgated regulations which provide for developing new common names as well as for employing standards of identity and imitation labeling. . . .

This regulatory scheme satisfies prior criticisms that the imitation requirement as interpreted by courts had unduly deterred the development of new food products, desirable for consumers, because the manufacturer's product, even if superior, was subject to the disparagement intimated by the imitation label. *See, e.g.*, Report of Panel III–2; White House Conference on Food and Nutrition, *Final Report* (Dec. 24, 1969). In addition, the FDA reasonably expects this more flexible approach to encourage greater emphasis on nutritional value and consumer knowledge about purchased food products. Furthermore, the regulation provides a safety valve for specific cases arising later in which nutritional equivalency and descriptive labeling do not adequately protect consumers from food substitutes which are inferior in other ways.

This regulation, directed at the laudable aims of encouraging manufacture of nutritional food products and of better informing consumers so that they may exercise a knowledgeable choice of differing foods within general categories, lies well within the bounds of discretion which the FDA may exercise. . . .

NOTES

1. *Collateral Challenges.* In *National Milk Producers Federation v. Harris*, 653 F.2d 339 (8th Cir. 1981), the court rejected the plaintiffs' claim that FDA violated section 403(c) by failing to require cheese substitutes to be labeled as imitations and upheld the agency's definition of "imitation." In *Grocery Manufacturers of America, Inc. v. Gerace*, 755 F.2d 993 (2d Cir. 1985), Note 1, p. 1430 *infra*, a trade association challenged a New York statute requiring all food products that resemble or are intended to substitute for cheese be labeled as imitation cheese. The court of appeals held that the FDA definition of an imitation food was reasonable, that the New York statute was in direct conflict with the federal regulation and thus was preempted insofar as it applied to food labeling, but that the New York statute was not preempted insofar as it applied to signs and menus that do not constitute labeling. In *Dyson v. Miles Laboratories, Inc.*, 57 A.D.2d 197 (N.Y. 1977), the court refused to dismiss New York's complaint that Morningstar Farms Breakfast Links and similar soy-based substitutes for sausage and bacon were misbranded under local law because they failed to bear "imitation" labeling. The court acknowledged the existence of the FDA regulation sustained in the *Federation of Homemakers* case, but concluded that New York could constitutionally apply its own standard, which is based on the *Chil–Zert* decision, Note 2, p. 182 *supra*. A decade after it promulgated its regulation defining "imitation" in terms of nutritional inferiority, FDA reaffirmed that decision and rejected alternative approaches. 48 Fed. Reg. 37665 (Aug. 19, 1983).

5.   COMMON OR USUAL NAMES

In establishing names for new fabricated foods, *see supra* p. 183, FDA has been forced to devote as much attention to the nutritional quality of the new foods as to the terminology to describe them.

Peter Barton Hutt & Elizabeth Sloan, *FDA Regulation of Vegetable Protein Products*

NUTRITION POLICY ISSUES, No. 3 (Jan. 1979).

During the 1960's a substantial amount of developmental work was undertaken by the food industry on extraction of protein from numerous vegetable sources and use of that protein in the fabrication of new food products.... Many were intended to resemble and substitute for traditional foods, such as meat, seafood, poultry, eggs, and cheese, that are regarded as "major protein foods." ...

In the Federal Register of June 14, 1974 (39 Fed. Reg. 20892), FDA concluded that, because the technology of new protein sources was still in a very active stage of development and because the most important public issue involved the accurate and informative labeling of final food products made from these new vegetable proteins, the proposed standard of identity [for "Textured Protein Products" prepared from vegetable protein and other ingredients] from should be abandoned. Instead, FDA proposed to establish descriptive "common or usual names" for food products containing vegetable protein as extenders or replacements for five "major protein foods"....

... FDA issued a tentative final regulation in the Federal Register of July 14, 1978 (43 Fed. Reg. 30472). The tentative final regulation would establish both (1) common or usual names for vegetable proteins that are processed so that some portion of the nonprotein constituents of the vegetable is removed, and thus that can be made into or become part of finished food products, and (2) common or usual names for finished food products that are intended to be substitutes for the five designated major protein foods and that contain vegetable protein as a protein source....

1.   *Vegetable protein.* This portion of the regulation would establish common or usual names for three categories of vegetable protein. A vegetable protein containing less than 65 percent protein by weight would include the name of the source of the protein and the term "flour" and/or a term which describes the physical form of the product (*e.g.,* "soy flour," "soy granules," or "soy flour granules"). The word "protein" could not be included in the name of this type of product. A vegetable protein containing 65–90 percent protein by weight would be a "protein concentrate" (*e.g.,* "soy protein concentrate").... A vegetable protein containing 90 percent or more protein by weight would be a "protein isolate" or "isolated protein" (*e.g.,* "soy protein isolate" or "isolated soy protein")....

2.   *Substitutes for major protein foods (meat, seafood, poultry, eggs, and cheese) which contain vegetable protein.* This portion of the regulation would establish both nutrition and labeling requirements for any finished

food product that contains vegetable protein as a source of protein and that resembles and substitutes for one of the five major protein foods.

3. *Nutritional requirements.* In order to avoid being labeled as "imitation," a finished food product containing any vegetable protein intended for use as a source of protein must be nutritionally equivalent to the type of food for which it substitutes. . . .

4. *Labeling.* The tentative final regulation proposes two separate labeling rules depending on whether the vegetable protein is the sole source of protein or is mixed with one of the other traditional sources. If the finished food contains only vegetable protein and is intended to substitute for one of the five major protein foods, the common or usual name of that food would be required to include the term "vegetable [or 'plant'] protein product." . . .

If the finished food contains a combination of vegetable protein and one of the five major protein foods, the common or usual name of that food would be required to include the name of both constituents in descending order of predominance and in the same size type. For example, a combination of tuna and a vegetable protein product, in which the tuna was the predominant ingredient by weight, would properly be labeled as "tuna and artificial tuna-flavored vegetable protein product."

The name of a finished multicomponent food that contains a characterizing component food that is made in whole or in part of vegetable protein and that substitutes for one of the five major protein foods must be accompanied by a statement such as "contains" or "made with," the blank to be filled with the name of the component containing the substitute food. For example, a food substituting for "fish chowder" in which the fish component is wholly replaced by vegetable protein would properly be labeled as "chowder made with artificially fish-flavored vegetable protein product." Similarly, a food resembling "macaroni and cheese" in which vegetable protein substitutes for part of the cheese would properly be labeled as "macaroni casserole, made with cheese and vegetable protein product." . . .

NOTES

1. *History.* This tentative final regulation was later withdrawn in 56 Fed. Reg. 67440, 67446 (Dec. 30, 1991). The earlier history of FDA's efforts to regulate plant protein products is reflected in 32 Fed. Reg. 14237 (Oct. 13, 1967), 34 Fed. Reg. 11423 (July 10, 1969), 35 Fed. Reg. 18530 (Dec. 5, 1979).

2. *USDA Adherence.* USDA required that all vegetable protein products used in child nutrition programs conform to the FDA tentative final regulation in 48 Fed. Reg. 775 (Jan. 7, 1983), 7 C.F.R. Parts 210, 225, and 226, App. A, and did not change its regulations following withdrawal of the FDA tentative final regulation.

3. *Butter and Margarine Substitutes.* See also the nutritional considerations involved in the FDA proposal to establish common or usual names for substitutes for margarine and butter, 41 Fed. Reg. 36509 (Aug. 30, 1976), subsequently withdrawn in 51 Fed. Reg. 15653 (Apr. 25, 1986).

As discussed *supra* p. 218, in the early 1970s FDA decided to abandon its earlier policy of mandating that all substitutes for standardized foods be labeled as imitations while not imposing the same requirement on substitutes for nonstandardized foods. Instead, FDA took the new position that the common or usual name for a substitute for a standardized food could include the name of the standardized food it copied, so long as the difference was made clear. This new policy was intended to prevent standards of identity from operating as barriers to the development of new food products, especially new versions of traditional foods whose macronutrient composition was modified to meet national nutrition goals. Food producers responded by introducing new products with increased vitamin and mineral content or with a reduced content of calories, sodium, cholesterol, and fat. For example, in 52 Fed. Reg. 31667 (Aug. 21, 1987), FDA issued an advisory opinion on whether standardized orange or grapefruit juice may lawfully be fortified in a manner not provided for in the standard of identity. The agency opined that the product could lawfully be fortified as long as the labeling did not represent it as the standardized food and the addition of the nutrients was consistent with the 1980 fortification policy, p. 238 *infra*.

A decade later FDA reverted to its pre-1970 approach. Modified versions of standardized foods were required to be designated as "alternative" or "substitute" products. If a modified product had its own standard of identity, however, the "alternative" or "substitute" qualifier could be omitted. In substance, the agency substituted the terms "alternative" or "substitute" for the older "imitation" as a way of differentiating between standardized and nonstandardized versions of the same product.

Consider, for example, FDA's application of its 1983 guidelines, excerpted *supra* p. 196, for establishing the common and usual names for dairy products. In applying these guidelines, FDA treated the naming of standardized and nonstandardized substitute dairy products differently. For example, when FDA promulgated a standard of identity for yogurt, it also published standards for lowfat yogurt and nonfat yogurt. 21 C.F.R. 131.200, 131.203, and 131.206. The agency also promulgated a standard of identity for low sodium cheddar cheese in 21 C.F.R. 133.116. None of these standardized modified products was required to be labeled as a "substitute" or "alternative." When manufacturers began to market nonstandardized versions of other dairy products, however, they received the following letters from FDA:

> This replies to your letter of November 20, 1986 concerning a "sour cream product" which conforms to the standard for sour cream in 21 CFR 131.160 except that it contains 8% milkfat whereas the standard requires not less than 18% milkfat.... [O]ne of our concerns with your client's proposed product is that 8% milkfat is not significantly different from standardized sour half and half under 21 CFR 131.185. This standard requires not less than 10.5% milkfat with an absolute minimum of 8.4% milkfat if bulky ingredients are added. You indicated that your client was interested in FDA's position on a 4% milkfat substitute for sour cream.

> Our other concern has been with the word "product" as part of the identity statement. Although we understand that many dislike the word "substitute," we have decided after consideration that "product" is not fully informative in this situation....

If your client's proposed product contained only 4% milkfat and were labeled as you proposed in your letter with the change from 8% to 4% milkfat and from "product" to "alternative" the label would read:

> "Reduced milkfat sour cream alternative
> contains four percent milkfat
> regular sour cream contains 18% milkfat."

We would not object to such a label designation. We believe, however, the top line should appear in letters of equal type size and prominence.

Letter from L. Robert Lake, Director, FDA, CFSAN Office of Regulations and Policy, to Peter Barton Hutt, February 27, 1987.

... [W]e continue to maintain that the statements "Colby Reduced Fat Cheese," and "Swiss Reduced Fat Cheese", "Mild Cheddar Reduced Fat Cheese", and "Monterey Jack Reduced Fat Cheese" are inappropriate as statements of identity of your products....

As you know, the fat content, which affects taste and other characteristics, is a major component of the standards of identity for cheeses. In fact the minimum fat content is specified by most cheese standards. Consequently, we believe it is inappropriate for a nonstandardized cheese to bear a reduced fat claim on its label while still using the name of the standardized food if the fat is reduced below the minimum for the standard. This would be of particular concern if the reduction is obtained by substituting, in whole or in part, for mandatory ingredients specified in the standard of identity. This practice does not adequately inform consumers of the differences between the nonstandardized product and the standardized food. Furthermore, a product made in semblance of cheddar cheese but with lower fat than required by the standard for cheddar cheese could easily have characteristics that differ from the standardized product. Consequently the product may not bear both a reduced fat claim and the unmodified standardized name because it would no longer be cheddar cheese. In order to assure that consumers are not confused, some further modification of the name such as "substitute" or "alternative" after the standardized name is necessary.

Appropriate identity statements for [your] nonstandardized cheese products are as follows:

(1) Assuming that these cheeses are nutritionally equivalent to the products they are intended to simulate, *i.e.*, Monterey Jack cheese, Swiss cheese, Cheddar cheese, and Colby cheese, they may be identified as "Monterey Jack cheese substitute," "Swiss cheese substitute," "Cheddar cheese substitute," and "Colby cheese substitute," respectively. The word "alternative" may be used in place of "substitute". We would also be willing to consider other terms that would clearly inform consumers that these are not the standardized cheeses.

(2) On the other hand, if these cheeses are nutritionally inferior and bear the traditional names, such names shall be immediately preceded by the word "imitation" in type of uniform size and prominence....

Letter from Sanford A. Miller, Director, FDA, CFSAN, to J. E. Thompson (July 9, 1987). FDA also declared that the name "nonfat ice cream" was illegal. Letter from FDA CFSAN Director Fred R. Shank to M. S. Thompson (Mar. 13, 1990).

In each instance FDA made clear that the common or usual name it rejected for the nonstandardized product would be acceptable it if were established by a standard of identity. To underscore this policy, FDA issued temporary permits for the marketing of "light eggnog" in 54 Fed. Reg. 35725 (Aug. 29, 1989), "lite sour cream" in 54 Fed. Reg. 43989 (Oct. 30, 1989), and "light ice cream" in 55 Fed. Reg. 3772 (Feb. 5, 1990).

NOTES

1. *Reduced Calorie Butter.* In *Lever Bros. Co. v. Maurer,* 712 F. Supp. 645 (S.D. Ohio 1989), the District Court declared unconstitutional an Ohio statute that prohibited the word "butter" in labeling or advertising a reduced calorie product containing 50 percent butter. FDA objected to the specific common or usual name used for the product, however, and prepared the following affidavit for use in the event of litigation:

> . . . [M]anufacturers in the United States market margarines and other table spreads which are flavored with butter, but which do not purport to be butter and do not meet the requirements of the butter standard of identity set forth at 42 Stat. 1500. With respect to such products, FDA has not objected to statements such as "Contains ___% butter" as part of the identity statement as long as the butter in the product is present in a significant amount.

> The FDA has no objection to the use of the word "butter" as part of a descriptive name of a product that does not comply with the standard of identity, as long as that name describes how the product differs from butter in all significant respects. With respect to the Lever Brothers Company ("Lever") product currently named "Dairybrook Reduced Calorie Butter Product," the product's name does not comply with this general requirement because the name does not make clear that the product consists, to a significant degree, of something other than butter. While we do not object to the term "reduced calorie" when used in compliance with 21 CFR § 105.66, that term, as used in the current name of Lever's product, is insufficient to adequately distinguish the product from standardized butter or properly identify the product.

> Therefore, FDA has objected in writing, to Lever, to the use of the phrase "Reduced Calorie Butter Product" as part of the product's identity statement.

Rather than litigate the case, the company changed its label.

2. *Reduced Calorie Yogurt.* In 1988 the agency rejected suggestions that yogurt and ice cream-like products sweetened with aspartame could be marked as "Reduced Calorie Yogurt" and "Reduced Calorie Ice Cream."

> These products would not be yogurts because they do not comply with the yogurt standards. These are yogurt substitutes or alternatives, not yogurts. Furthermore, these are not reduced calorie products because sweeteners are optional ingredients in yogurts, not mandatory, and yogurt-type products sweetened with aspartame are not calorie reduced at all when compared to the unsweetened standardized yogurts. . . .

> Your advice on non-standardized frozen desserts is contrary to the standards of identity because you state that the standards of identity do not preclude the use of aspartame, and that frozen desserts sweetened with aspartame can use the name "ice cream", as shown in your examples of "Diet ice cream—Calorie Reduced" or "Reduced Calorie Ice Cream." We disagree because your advice is not consistent with the standard of identity for ice cream. There is a good analogy which involves a precedent set some years ago. A GRAS affirmation regulation was issued under 21 CFR

184.1835 which permitted sorbitol to be used in frozen desserts. Sorbitol is a nutritive sweetener but, like aspartame, is not an ingredient permitted by the standard. There are a number of sorbitol sweetened frozen desserts on the market, and they are labeled as "frozen desserts" or "frozen dairy desserts" but not "ice cream" because the manufacturers realize they cannot be called by any of the standardized names.

Letter from Robert Lake, Director, FDA, CFSAN Office of Regulations and Policy, to G. Witte (Aug. 10, 1988).

————

Following enactment of the Nutrition Labeling and Education Act of 1990, FDA was forced to reconcile its already weakened policy of protecting standardized food names with its new mandate to define nutrient descriptors, *supra* p. 216. The agency's nutrient descriptors responsibility prevailed, thus further undermining the stature of standardized food names. In 56 Fed. Reg. 60512 (Nov. 27, 1991) and 58 Fed. Reg. 2431 (Jan. 6, 1993), FDA promulgated 21 C.F.R. 130.10 to permit the use of any nutrient descriptor defined by FDA as part of the common or usual name of a modified version of a standardized food, *e.g.*, "low calorie ice cream," "high fiber enriched white bread," or "nonfat French dressing." In an attempt to rationalize this change in its legal and policy position, FDA described the regulations as a "general definition and standard of identity." By this action the agency abandoned the "substitute" or "alternative" approach, although it has never said so.

Requirements for Foods Named by Use of a Nutrient Content Claim and a Standardized Term

21 CFR 130.10.

(a) *Description.* The foods prescribed by this general definition and standard of identity are those foods that substitute for a standardized food defined in parts 131 through 169 of this chapter and that use the name of that standardized food in their statement of identity but that do not comply with the standard of identity because of a deviation that is described by an expressed nutrient content claim that has been defined by FDA regulation. The nutrient content claim shall comply with the requirements of § 101.13 of this chapter and with the requirements of the regulations in part 101 of this chapter that define the particular nutrient content claim that is used. The food shall comply with the relevant standard in all other respects except as provided in paragraphs (b), (c), and (d) of this section.

(b) *Nutrient addition.* Nutrients shall be added to the food to restore nutrient levels so that the product is not nutritionally inferior ... to the standardized food as defined in parts 131 through 169 of this chapter....

(c) *Performance characteristics.* Deviations from noningredient provisions of the standard of identity (*e.g.*, moisture content, food solids content requirements, or processing conditions) are permitted in order that the substitute food possesses performance characteristics similar to those of the standardized food. Deviations from ingredient and noningredient provisions of the standard must be the minimum necessary to qualify for the nutrient content claim while maintaining similar performance characteristics as the standardized food, or the food will be deemed to be adulterated under section 402(b) of the act. The performance characteristics (*e.g.*, physical properties, flavor characteristics, functional properties, shelf life) of the food shall be similar to those of the standardized food as produced under parts 131 through 169 of this chapter, except that if there is a significant difference in performance characteristics that materially limits the uses of the food compared to the uses of the standardized food, the label shall include a statement informing the consumer of such difference (*e.g.*, if appropriate, "not recommended for cooking").... The modified product shall perform at least one of the principal functions of the standardized product substantially as well as the standardized product.

(d) *Other ingredients.* (1) Ingredients used in the product shall be those ingredients provided for by the standard as defined in parts 131 through 169 of this chapter and in paragraph (b) of this section, except that safe and suitable ingredients may be used to improve texture, add flavor, prevent syneresis, extend shelf life, improve appearance, or add sweetness so that the product is not inferior in performance characteristics to the standardized food defined in parts 131 through 169 of this chapter.

(2) An ingredient or component of an ingredient that is specifically required by the standard (*i.e.*, a mandatory ingredient) as defined in parts 131 through 169 of this chapter, shall not be replaced or exchanged with a similar ingredient from another source unless the standard, as defined in parts 131 through 169 of this chapter, provides for the addition of such ingredient (*e.g.*, vegetable oil shall not replace milkfat in light sour cream).

(3) An ingredient or component of an ingredient that is specifically prohibited by the standard as defined in parts 131 through 169 of this chapter, shall not be added to a substitute food under this section.

(4) An ingredient that is specifically required by the standard as defined in parts 131 through 169 of this chapter, shall be present in the product in a significant amount. A significant amount of an ingredient or component of an ingredient is at least that amount that is required to achieve the technical effect of that ingredient in the food....

(e) *Nomenclature.* The name of a substitute food that complies with all parts of this regulation is the appropriate expressed nutrient content claim and the applicable standardized term....

NOTES

1. *Implications of the General Standard of Identity.* With the enactment of 21 CFR 130.10, FDA effectively abandoned its "substitute" and "alternative" nomenclature, at least for foods modified to satisfy a nutrient content claim regulation. Note, however, that according to 130.10(b), the general standard does not apply to nutritionally inferior substitutes for a standardized food, and FDA may thus still require that such products be labeled "imitation."

2. *Dairy Products.* Prior to the enactment of the NLEA, FDA had established numerous standards of identity for dairy products with reduced amounts of fat, such as lowfat and skim milk, lowfat and nonfat yogurt, and lowfat cottage cheese.

The amount of fat permitted by these standards did not correspond to the amount allowed by the corresponding NLEA nutrient content claim regulations. In response to a petition filed jointly by the milk industry and a public interest group, the agency revoked the standards of identity for lowfat and nonfat dairy products while preserving the standards of identity for whole-fat dairy products. 60 Fed. Reg. 56541 (Nov. 9, 1995), 61 Fed. Reg. 58991 (Nov. 20, 1996). Consequently, modified-fat dairy products are now named in accordance with 21 CFR 130.10, the general standard of identity, and the fat content descriptors have the same meaning when applied to dairy products as when applied to other foods. The application of the general standard of identity also allows producers to improve the performance characteristics of reduced fat, lowfat, and nonfat dairy products by adding ingredients that were not permitted by the now-revoked standards of identity. For example, milk processors now can add ingredients such as cellulose gel, carrageenan (a seaweed extract), and flavor to skim milk to better approximate the taste, appearance, and mouthfeel of whole milk.

6.   NUTRIENT FORTIFICATION

Food fortification began in the 1830s when a French chemist observed the need to add iodine to salt to prevent goiter. It was not until 1917, however, that this practice was adopted in the United States. During World War I, Denmark added vitamin A concentrate derived from fish liver oil to margarine to prevent vitamin A deficiency. Irradiation of milk to increase its vitamin D content began in this country about 1930.

The American Medical Association (AMA) Council on Foods and Nutrition spearheaded the early drive to fortify food products. In the early 1930s, the AMA endorsed the addition of vitamin D to milk and of iodine to table salt. Later it recommended that fortification should be reserved for exceptional cases where there was convincing evidence of a need for enhanced amounts of the vitamin or mineral in the general food supply and the foods proposed as vehicles for fortification were appropriate. 107 J.A.M.A. 39 (1936). Subsequently the AMA issued a formal statement of policy, 113 J.A.M.A. 681 (1939), which opposed indiscriminate fortification but endorsed the addition of vitamin D to milk, vitamin A to substitutes for butter, iodine to table salt, and calcium and iron to cereal products. This statement also encouraged the restoration of vitamins and minerals lost through processing, which led to experimentation with the addition of vitamins to flour and bread.

In mid–1940, the National Academy of Sciences (NAS) established a Subcommittee on Medical Nutrition, which later grew into the Food and Nutrition Board, whose recommendations had a major impact on food fortification. The Board immediately endorsed enrichment of flour and bread with thiamine, iron, and nicotinic acid, and in 1941 added iron, and then calcium and vitamin D, as optional nutrients for enrichment. The Board published its first Recommended Dietary Allowances (RDAs) in 1943, and now calls them Dietary Reference Intakes (DRIs). The most recent DRIs were published by the Board in a series of volumes beginning in 1997.

As the Food and Nutrition Board commenced its activities, FDA began to implement its new authority to promulgate food standards under the

FD&C Act. In 5 Fed. Reg. 2746 (Aug. 3, 1940), FDA announced public hearings on proposed standards of identity for flour. At the hearings, the AMA and NAS fortification recommendations were supported by industry witnesses, who urged FDA to promulgate standards for both enriched and unenriched versions of appropriate foods. Standards for both enriched and unenriched flour were promulgated in 6 Fed. Reg. 1729 (Apr. 1, 1941), 6 Fed. Reg. 2574 (May 27, 1941). This established the regulatory approach to the use of food standards for food fortification that has continued to this day.

During World War II, the War Food Administration was given authority over all food distributed in the United States. War Food Order No. 1 required the enrichment of all bread and rolls. 7 Fed. Reg. 11105 (Dec. 13, 1942). Since FDA's enriched flour standards had already become effective, and many bakers voluntarily enriched their bread, this order reinforced existing industry practice. In response to the growing interest in fortified food, FDA issued the following statement of policy.

Statement of Policy With Respect to the Addition of Nutritive Ingredients to Foods

8 Fed. Reg. 9170 (July 3, 1943).

The labeling or advertising of a food as enriched with vitamins and minerals is an implied promise to consumers that it contains, in addition to the normal constituents of the unenriched food, sufficient vitamins and minerals to make a substantial contribution to the nutritional welfare of persons eating the enriched food in customary amounts. In order to promote honesty and fair dealing by fulfilling this implied promise, it is necessary that the kinds and quantities of enriching ingredients be determined in the light of deficiencies of the various nutritional factors in the diets of the population in general and of significant population groups, the place occupied by the food in such diets, and the suitability and effectiveness of the food as a carrier of the enriching ingredients without undue separation or loss before consumption.

Honesty and fair dealing will best be promoted if such enriched foods as are available to consumers serve to correct such deficiencies and furnish a reasonable margin of safety. Enrichment above the levels required to accomplish this end is wasteful and contrary to the interest of most consumers.... Enrichment of foods with nutrients that are supplied in adequate quantities by the diets of all significant population groups is not only wasteful but tends to confuse consumers as to their nutritional needs....

Because of the lack of adequate production of a number of foods high in certain nutrients and the lack of consumer knowledge of nutrition, appropriate enrichment of a few foods widely consumed by the population in general or by significant population groups will contribute substantially to the nutritional welfare of consumers and to meeting their expectations of benefit. Enrichment of those foods which are not a substantial part of the diet of any significant group tends to confuse and mislead consumers through giving rise to conflicting claims of nutritional values and by creating an exaggerated impression of the benefits to be derived from the consumption of such foods.

If the customary process of manufacturing a staple food refines it so as to remove significant quantities of nutritive factors present in the natural product from which the food is made, and if the refined food is a suitable and efficient carrier of the factors so removed, some nutritionists advocate the restoration of such factors to the levels of the natural product as the most desirable basis of enrichment. To the extent that restoration serves to correct deficiencies of such factors, it is consistent with the promotion of honesty and fair dealing that refined foods be enriched on a restoration basis. However, when the evidence shows that the restoration levels are too low to correct deficiencies, or that deficiencies exist in other factors for which the refined food is an efficient carrier, the promotion of honesty and fair dealing may require the inclusion of corrective quantities of nutritive factors in the enriched food even though such factors are present in smaller quantities or wholly lacking in the natural product from which the food is made. Similar considerations may require the enrichment of unrefined foods....

────────

Following World War II, food fortification proliferated. Most states enacted laws making enrichment of flour and bread mandatory. The standard of identity for enriched bread, which had been postponed at the request of the War Food Administration, was promulgated. 13 Fed. Reg. 6024 (Oct. 14, 1948), 15 Fed. Reg. 5102 (Aug. 8, 1950), 17 Fed. Reg. 4453 (May 15, 1953). FDA also established standards of identity for other enriched foods such as dairy products, macaroni and noodle products, and margarine. 21 C.F.R. Parts 131, 139, 166.

In 1961, the AMA and NAS issued a joint statement on "General Policy on Addition of Specific Nutrients to Foods." 178 J.A.M.A. 1024 (1961). The statement endorsed fortification where the addition of a specific nutrient to a particular food was shown to be advantageous for a significant segment of the consumer population, the food chosen was an effective vehicle, and the nutrient addition would not prejudice the achievement of a sound diet.

By the early 1960s, FDA had become concerned about possible excessive fortification of food. The agency concluded that aggressive enforcement against misleading or blatantly false claims was insufficient. Its proposed revision of the special dietary food regulations in 27 Fed. Reg. 5815 (June 20, 1962) would have permitted fortification of food only with specific listed nutrients recognized as both essential in human nutrition and appropriate for supplementation. Comments on this proposal and the decision in the *Dextra Sugar* case, *infra* p. 233, convinced FDA that an even more restrictive approach was necessary to stem the tide of indiscriminate food fortification. Thus, the agency published regulations that included a novel standard of identity which would have drastically limited the number of foods that could lawfully be fortified. 31 Fed. Reg. 8525 (June 18, 1966), 31 Fed. Reg. 15730 (Dec. 14, 1966).

The AMA and NAS, encouraged by FDA's use of their 1961 statement to support its 1966 approach to restricting food fortification, issued another joint policy statement to clarify their position. 205 J.A.M.A. 868 (1968). This statement distinguished between modification of traditional foods and fortification of new and formulated foods. It endorsed the addition of nutrients to new and formulated foods so that their nutritional value would at least be equal to the foods they replace.

Ultimately, a political event transformed public attitudes about food fortification. The Report of the White House Conference on Food, Nutrition and Health contained several recommendations for fortification of existing and new food products which cut directly against FDA's prevailing approach of restricting fortification. A special report to the AMA Board of Trustees, agreeing with this conclusion, stated that malnutrition is probably more prevalent than hunger, although not as dramatic, and noted that half of the households studied by USDA in 1965 failed to meet the NAS recommended dietary allowances for one or more nutrients. 213 J.A.M.A. 272 (1970). By the early 1970s, the officials who had designed the restrictive strategy of the 1960s had left FDA and been succeeded by individuals who had helped prepare the Report of the White House Conference. Accordingly, FDA in its 1973 regulations explicitly abandoned its attempt to control food fortification through new restrictive standards of identity. Instead, the agency developed a new approach, based largely upon requirements for affirmative label disclosure of the nutritional value of foods.

NOTES

1. *AMA and NAS Policy.* A subsequent report of the AMA respecting food fortification appears at 242 J.A.M.A. 2335 (1979). For some of the important NAS reports on food fortification, *see* THE PROBLEM OF CHANGING FOOD HABITS, NRC Bull. No. 108 (1943); INADEQUATE DIETS AND NUTRITIONAL DEFICIENCIES IN THE UNITED STATES, NRC Bull. No. 109 (1943); ENRICHMENT OF FLOUR AND BREAD, NRC Bull. No. 110 (1944); THE FACTS ABOUT ENRICHMENT OF FLOUR AND BREAD (1944); CEREAL ENRICHMENT IN PERSPECTIVE (1958); PROPOSED FORTIFICATION POLICY FOR CEREAL-GRAIN PRODUCTS (1974); TECHNOLOGY OF FORTIFICATION OF FOODS (1975). *See also* Donald F. Miller & Leroy Vorist, *Chronologic Changes in the Recommended Dietary Allowances*, 54 J. AM. DIETETIC ASS'N 109 (1969); GAO, NATIONAL NUTRITION ISSUES, No. CED–78–7 (1977).

2. *Commentary.* See generally Norman Jolliffe, *The Enrichment Program for White Flour and Bread*, 1 FOOD DRUG COSM. L.Q. 66 (1946); Frank G. Boudreau, *The Food and Nutrition Board of the National Research Council*, 1 FOOD DRUG COSM. L.Q. 144 (1946); Russell M. Wilder, *The Nutritional Quality of Food and Standards of Identity*, 2 FOOD DRUG COSM. L.Q. 73 (1947); Fredrick J. Stare, *Nutrition, Health, and the Law*, 2 FOOD DRUG COSM. L.Q. 382 (1947); Frank L. Gunderson, *Improvement in Nutritive Value of Foods*, 7 FOOD DRUG COSM. L.J. 128 (1952); Robert R. Williams, *Modern Progress in Food Enrichment*, 8 FOOD DRUG COSM. L.J. 357 (1953); James R. Wilson, *Influence of the Council on Foods and Nutrition, American Medical Association, for Voluntary Food–Industry Standards to Protect and Improve Public Health*, 10 FOOD DRUG COSM. L.J. 140 (1955); Robert R. Williams, *The Relationship of the Work of the Food and Nutrition Board, National Research*

Council, to Food–Law Enforcement, 10 FOOD DRUG COSM. L.J. 197 (1955); Charles Glen King, *Contributions of Technology to the Nutritional Value of Food*, 16 FOOD DRUG COSM. L.J. 8 (1961); David Bashi and Ritu Nalubola, *The History of Food Fortification in the United States*, 51 ECON. DEV. & CULTURAL CHANGE, No. 1, at 37 (2002).

United States v. 119 Cases ... "New Dextra Brand Fortified Cane Sugar"

231 F. Supp. 551 (S.D. Fla. 1963).

■ CHOATE, DISTRICT JUDGE.

... [T]he Government alleges that the label of the seized article of food contains statements which represent, suggest, and imply:

(a) *That the American diet is deficient in vitamins and minerals and that Dextra Sugar will correct this implied deficiency.* There is no persuasive evidence of any kind that consumers would construe the label statements referring to the fact that the Dextra Brand product is "fortified with vitamins and minerals" to represent, suggest or imply that the "American diet," or their own diets, are significantly deficient in vitamins and minerals, and that use of this product would overcome such a deficiency....

(b) *That the nutritional content of diets generally is significantly improved by the use of the seized article.* The Government contends that the added nutrients in Dextra Brand Fortified Sugar are not nutritionally significant because adequate amounts of these nutrients are available in the average "American" diet, and that the added nutrients in the product would be excreted and of no value.... If the Government's contention were valid, any vitamin-fortified product could be singled out and challenged on the ground that the added vitamins and minerals in any particular food are of no value inasmuch as these nutrients are available elsewhere in the food supply, and the consumers' requirements are met....

(c) *That Dextra Sugar when used in the ordinary diet is significantly more nutritious than any other sugar.* The disclosures of the fact that the product is fortified do not misrepresent the product's nutritional value in comparison with ordinary sugar....

(d) *That the article under seizure is of significant value because it restores vitamins and minerals lost in the refinement of cane juice....* The process of fortifying sugar with vitamins and minerals was created by a biochemist, John Paul Bartz. Over a fifteen-year period, he developed a method of refining sugar to retain the vitamins and minerals found in natural sugar plants. He also developed a process of adding these vitamins and minerals to ordinary sugar essentially to duplicate the product obtained by use of his refining methods. Claimant uses this latter method for making fortified sugar at this time, inasmuch as the Bartz refining process requires large-scale production to be economically feasible. The implication italicized above rather than false or misleading seems to be true in all respects....

(e) Finally, the Government contends that the labels falsely imply, "That all of the vitamins and minerals in the article are present in nutritionally significant amounts for special dietary use." However, the label makes no specific therapeutic or health claims. The label states "Almost any diet can be nutritionally improved" by using the product "in place of sweetening agents containing only 'empty' calories—calories unaccompanied by nutrients." The Government has failed to show that this statement is factually in error. . . .

Although the foregoing disposes of the specific allegations of mislabeling, the Government's principal contention is that the offering of a sugar fortified with vitamins and minerals and labeled to disclose such facts is "per se" false and misleading to consumers. Specifically, the Government charges that the mere mention on the labels of such product that it is fortified with vitamins and minerals infers contrary to fact that (1) the diet available to the American consumer is vitamin deficient; (2) such product might promote the increase of sugar as a part of the American diet contrary to sound nutritional practice; and (3) sugar is not an effective or preferable vehicle of vitamin supplementation. . . .

However, the Government failed to present any valid factual support for its principal objection. It introduced no authoritative studies or other data to show that American consumers are receiving all the nutrients they need and that the added vitamins and minerals would be of no value to them. . . .

The testimony of the Government's witnesses disclosed that the real basis of the Government's objection to the sale of fortified sugar is the notion that sugar is not a preferable vehicle for distributing vitamins and minerals. Two Government witnesses expressed the belief that the fortification of sugar might lead to its increased use in place of other foods, which would be contrary to "sound nutritional teachings." Even if this were true, and no proof to the effect that such was the case was offered, it would not justify condemnation of the product. The implementation of sound nutritional principles, and the encouragement or discouragement of the consumption of particular foods in accordance with these principles, are matters for consumer education, not for legal enforcement pursuant to the seizure provisions of the Federal Food, Drug, and Cosmetic Act. . . .

The basic flaw in the Government's case against the product is that it is seeking, under the guise of misbranding charges, to prohibit the sale of a food in the marketplace simply because it is not in sympathy with its use. But the Government's position is clearly untenable. The provisions of the Federal Food, Drug, and Cosmetic Act did not vest in the Food and Drug Administration or any other federal agency the power to determine what foods should be included in the American diet; this is the function of the marketplace. . . .

The court does not undertake to constitute itself an arbiter of nutritional problems involved in determining more or less desirable agents for vending vitamin and mineral supplements to the consumer. The Congress did not provide the necessity for such determination. Neither will the Court permit a federal agency to appoint itself such an arbiter under the guise of prosecuting an action under the Act in question. Plainly, only Congress can or should regulate the use of vitamins and then only to prevent public injury. . . .

NOTE

In affirming the District Court, the Court of Appeals stated only that:

> In light of the fact that any purchaser of food products could elect to maintain his present "average" diet with sufficient nutrients in it, or, if he wished, change to a different diet and substitute dextra fortified cane sugar for some other item, we conclude that the trial court was not in error in finding as a fact that the challenged statement was not false and misleading.

United States v. 119 Cases, More or Less, 334 F.2d 238, 239 (5th Cir. 1964) (per curiam).

Improvement of Nutrient Levels of Enriched Flour, Enriched Self–Rising Flour, and Enriched Breads, Rolls or Buns

38 Fed. Reg. 28558 (October 15, 1973).

A notice of proposed rulemaking was published in the FEDERAL REGISTER of April 1, 1970 (35 FR 5412) [amending the standards of identity for enriched flour and bread to double the permitted level of iron]. . . .

Three respondents, all physicians, opposed the proposal on the grounds that increased iron in the diet, especially in the case of males, could lead to excessive iron storage and such diseases as cirrhosis of the liver and hemochromatosis or to an increased prevalence of iron storage disorders. As the 1969 White House Conference on Food, Nutrition and Health, the Food and Nutrition Board, National Academy of Sciences—National Research Council, and the Council on Foods and Nutrition, American Medical Association had all recommended increasing the iron content in the diet, the Commissioner deemed it advisable to pursue the matter further. . . .

On further consideration . . . a notice of proposed rulemaking was published in the FEDERAL REGISTER of December 3, 1971 (36 FR 23074), in which the Commissioner, on his own initiative, made an alternate proposal that the standards of identity for enriched flour, enriched self-rising flour, enriched farina, and enriched bread, rolls or buns be amended to revise the requirements, not only for iron, but also for calcium and vitamins. . . .

The only major opposition to the proposal concerned the increase in iron enrichment. The principal reasons for concern expressed by those opposing the increase in iron enrichment and the Commissioner's conclusions are as follows:

(1) *It was asserted that higher iron intakes might result in chronic iron toxicity in males, manifested by an increase in the prevalence and/or severity of iron storage disorders, particularly hemochromatosis.* On the basis of the comments received, the comprehensive report from FASEB, the AMA review statement and other information, the Commissioner concludes that the proposed increase in the iron content of enriched flours and enriched bread, rolls or buns will not jeopardize the health of normal males (or females), and that the additional iron will not increase the incidence of hemochromatosis or other hereditary iron storage disorders. . . .

(2) *Doubts were expressed as to the need for or efficacy of the iron enrichment as proposed....* The Commissioner initiated reexaminations of each of [the questions raised by letters opposing the increased iron levels] within the Food and Drug Administration to determine if the stated conclusions of such groups as the AMA Council on Foods and Nutrition, the NAS–NRC Food and Nutrition Board, and the White House Conference on Food, Nutrition, and Health remained valid. The Commissioner's conclusions are discussed below:

(a) There has been a steadily increasing number of studies on specific population groups indicating substantial prevalences of iron deficiency anemia in various sex, age, and physiologic groups....

(b) There is general agreement that severe iron deficiency anemia is debilitating and, in rare cases, that it can be extremely serious and even fatal; that sufficient dietary iron leads to a maximum hemoglobin level generally thought of as being optimal for good health; and that marked iron deficiency is harmful to both pregnant women and the newborn....

(c) ... The Commissioner concludes that there is a need to define sources of iron with reasonable bioavailability characteristics, but does not feel that it is in the public interest to delay publication of these regulations to await the outcome of evaluation of the single matter of acceptable sources of iron....

(e) Concerning the matter as to whether cereal products generally are the most suitable vehicles for iron enrichment, the Commissioner notes that cereal-based foods, particularly bread and other products made from wheat flour, continue to be the most uniformly consumed major foods in the American diet (except for meat, poultry and fish which are not amenable to enrichment)....

Accordingly, having considered the comments received and other relevant information, the Commissioner concludes that it will promote honesty and fair dealing in the interests of consumers to rule jointly on the proposals published in the FEDERAL REGISTERS of April 1, 1970 (35 FR 5412), and December 3, 1971 (36 FR 23074), by adopting the proposed amendments as modified....

Iron Fortification of Flour and Bread: Tentative Order

42 Fed. Reg. 59513 (November 18, 1977).

. . . .

Thirty objections to the [1973] final order [amending the standards of identity for flour and bread to increase the added iron content] were received, leading the Commissioner to conclude in his order published in the FEDERAL REGISTER of February 11, 1974 (39 FR 5188), that, in light of questions regarding the public health raised by members of the medical profession opposing the increase in added iron content of flour and bread, a formal evidentiary public hearing on the matter was justified.... Having considered the evidence received at the hearing, the Hearing Examiner's Recommended Decision and all the written arguments that were filed, the

Commission is issuing this tentative order to withdraw the stayed provisions of the amendments.

One respondent ... challenged the authority of the Commissioner to promulgate any identity standards whose purpose is to correct for dietary deficiencies unrelated to the standard. The basis for Dr. Crosby's argument is the contention that the only purpose of standards promulgated pursuant to section 401 is to prevent consumer fraud. Although the purpose of the present document is to withdraw the stayed augmented-iron provisions of the regulation, the Commissioner is not basing the withdrawal upon this theory. On the contrary, to read section 401 so narrowly would be counter to the purposes of the act as a whole....

The first major contested issue at the hearing was the need for additional iron in the diet. The Food and Drug Administration produced a number of witnesses and studies which, it argues, point to the conclusion of need for additional iron in the diet....

The Commissioner concludes that, whereas available data show that there is a need for additional iron for two well-defined groups (preschool infants and pregnant women), the need has not been proven to be as great or as general as the proponents of the amendments have argued.

In addition, the Commissioner concludes that there are far better ways of reaching those persons in need of additional iron than through fortification of bread.... Additional fortification of bread, which would subject the entire population, including those involuntarily exposed, to increased dietary iron, would seem to be an inefficient and—in light of unresolved safety questions—a possibly more dangerous approach to take....

Therefore, the Commissioner concludes that, before he can make a finding of efficacy, more studies will have to be done. The issue of efficacy is rendered all the more important in light of the issue of safety.

A substantial number of experts who made their views known on the record at the hearing testified that (a) in their view the augmentations are not safe or (b) have not been proven safe....

The Commissioner concludes that, on the present record, the increased iron levels should not be approved, since, among other things, the burden of proving them safe has not been satisfied. Better data must be obtained before what amounts to an uncontrolled study on the United States population is attempted. The Commissioner emphasizes that in his view the increased iron levels have not been proven unsafe either; but enough serious questions have been raised to prevent his approval of the increased levels at this time....

NOTES

1. *Further Proceedings.* In 43 Fed. Reg. 38575 (Aug. 29, 1978), FDA issued findings of fact, conclusions, and a final order. The Commissioner sought to relieve concern that his tentative order would deter further research into iron fortification:

> The Commissioner has no intention to discourage research, and no control over the research budgets of food manufacturers. If, as seems likely, this exception is intended to present the Commissioner with an opportuni-

ty to narrow the scope of his final order, he accepts the opportunity to do so. The order in this proceeding results from the finding that a proposed fortification has not been proven to be safe, effective, or needed. In another situation, if the evidence supporting the safety, effectiveness, or necessity of the fortifying ingredient is more favorable to the proposed change, the Commissioner may decide another way. . . .

The requirement of "adequate studies" in the tentative order should be seen as applying in situations where serious concern about the safety of a proposed ingredient has been voiced and where the needed amount of that ingredient is in dispute. Also, this requirement will apply especially in cases where the food in question is a widely eaten staple product. . . .

The Commissioner also rejected criticism of his suggestion that attempts should be made to "supplement" only the diets of individuals known to be at risk:

The Commissioner believes that this idea cannot be rejected until it has been tried, although he recognizes that there may be difficulties with it. Where there are safety questions of the sort set forth in the tentative order, educational programs for people at risk and the promotion of iron supplementation or the consumption of high-iron-content foods present possible alternatives to the assumption of involuntary risks by others. . . .

2. *Anemia in Women of Child–Bearing Age.* In 53 Fed. Reg. 51009 (Dec. 19, 1988), FDA announced the initiation of a study by the Federation of American Societies for Experimental Biology (FASEB) on how iron deficiency anemia in women of childbearing age can be managed without "possible harmful effects of ingestion of large amounts of iron-rich foods or dietary supplements."

3. *Poison Prevention Packaging.* In 40 Fed. Reg. 2827 (Jan. 16, 1975), 41 Fed. Reg. 22261 (June 2, 1976), 16 C.F.R. 1700.14(a)(13), the Consumer Product Safety Commission promulgated a regulation requiring poison prevention packaging for iron-containing dietary supplement products in order to protect children from ingesting dangerously high levels of iron.

———

After FDA decided in 1973 to abandon its 1966 attempt to restrict food fortification through food standards, it published proposed regulations establishing principles governing the addition of nutrients to food. 39 Fed. Reg. 20900 (June 14, 1974). The agency issued its final food fortification policy in 45 Fed. Reg. 6314 (Jan. 25, 1980), codified at 21 C.F.R. 104.20. The agency expressed concern that, in the absence of a unifying set of principles, random and arbitrary fortification of foods would be likely. This could result in overfortification with nutrients that are inexpensive and easy to add, and underfortification with others. Yet promulgation of standards of identity for fortification of all foods would be unnecessarily inflexible.

The June 1974 proposal had incorporated enforcement mechanisms to assure compliance with the fortification principles. FDA had proposed that any fortified food that did not comply with the proposed policy would be required to bear the statement that "the addition of ____ to this product has been determined by the U.S. government to be unnecessary and inappropriate and does not increase the dietary value of the food." In addition, claims that a product was fortified would have been prohibited unless the fortified food provided at least 10 percent of the U.S. RDA in a serving. The agency's final policy statement, however, eliminated these restrictions because, according to FDA, a substantive rule covering all aspects of fortification and labeling of fortified foods was not feasible at that time. Thus, the January 1980 policy statement represents only a set of guidelines that are not directly enforceable as legal requirements.

The 1980 policy acknowledges that fortification can be an effective way of maintaining and improving the nutritional quality of the food supply, but it emphasizes that FDA considers fortification of the following foods inappropriate: fresh produce; meat, poultry, and fish products; sugar; and snack foods such as candies and carbonated beverages. The agency states that neither the public nor the scientific community considers snack foods to be appropriate carriers for added nutrients. The statement then enunciates five principles for appropriate food fortification.

1. *To correct dietary insufficiency.* FDA states that any of 22 listed nutrients may appropriately be added to a food to correct a dietary insufficiency recognized by the scientific community to exist and known to result in nutritional deficiency disease.

2. *To restore lost nutrients.* FDA recognizes that it is appropriate to add any of the 22 listed nutrients to a food to restore levels representative of the food prior to storage, handling, and processing, but only if they have been lost in a "measurable amount," *i.e.*, at least 2 percent of the U.S. RDA per serving. If restoration is undertaken, all measurably depleted nutrients should be restored.

3. *To balance calories with nutrients.* In the most controversial portion of its policy, FDA states that addition of nutrients is appropriate to balance the vitamin, mineral, and protein content with the total caloric content of the food. For purposes of implementing this principle, FDA adopts a standard daily caloric intake of 2000 kilocalories as contrasted with the 2800 kilocalories reflected in the June 1974 proposal.

4. *To avoid nutritional inferiority.* Under current FDA regulations, p. 218 *supra*, a new food that resembles, and is intended to substitute for, another food must be labeled as an "imitation" if it is nutritionally inferior. This principle encourages the common practice of adding nutrients to new substitute foods in order to avoid the "imitation" label.

5. *To comply with other regulations.* This principle permits nutrient addition to comply with any requirements found in existing standards of identity, nutrition quality guidelines, and regulations establishing common or usual names for foods.

NOTES

1. *Protein–Nutrient Balance.* For an alternative proposal to permit balanced fortification on the basis of protein rather than calories, see Paul A. Lachance, *Nutrification: A Concept for Assuring Nutritional Quality by Primary Intervention in Feeding Systems*, 20 J. AGRIC. FOOD CHEM. 522 (1972); Paul A. Lachance et al., *Balanced Nutrition through Food Processor Practice of Nutrification*, 26 FOOD TECH. No. 6, at 30 (1972). *See also* Odgen C. Johnson, *Rationale for Constraints on Nutrient Additions*, 34 FOOD DRUG COSM. L.J. 426 (1979).

2. *Congressional Oversight.* The application of the FDA's 1980 food fortification policy statement to the fortification of flour and bread was explored in "Fortification of Cereal Grains with Essential Vitamins and Minerals," Hearing

Before the Subcommittee on Natural Resources, Agriculture Research, and Environment of the House Committee on Science and Technology, 97th Cong., 2d Sess. (1982).

3. *Incorporation in Other Regulations.* Although the FDA food fortification policy was published in 21 C.F.R. 104.20 as a statement of policy and not as a regulation, it was later incorporated into the FDA regulations implementing the Nutrition Labeling and Education Act as a requirement for "more" and "high potency" claims where the nutrient has been added to the food. 21 C.F.R. 101.54(e)(2)(ii) and (f)(2).

4. *Enforcement.* FDA has never initiated formal compliance action to enforce its food fortification policy.

COMMENT: FDA REGULATION OF INFANT FORMULAS

FDA's original special dietary food regulations included provisions for the labeling of infant food, including infant formulas. Proposed revisions of those regulations, 27 Fed. Reg. 5815 (June 20, 1962), 31 Fed. Reg. 8521 (June 18, 1966), were the subject of the 1968–1969 FDA hearings, and final regulations were promulgated in 35 Fed. Reg. 16737 (Oct. 29, 1970), 36 Fed. Reg. 23553 (Dec. 10, 1971), and codified at 21 C.F.R. § 105.65.

In mid–1979, Syntex Laboratories recalled three soy protein-based infant formulas that, because of an inadequate level of chlorine, resulted in a number of cases of metabolic alkalosis, an abnormal condition generally characterized in infants by a failure to thrive. "Infant Formulas Being Recalled," FDA Talk Paper No. T79–34 (Aug. 2, 1979). Following a public meeting, 45 Fed. Reg. 6702 (Jan. 29, 1980), FDA published interim guidelines for the nutrient composition of infant formulas in 45 Fed. Reg. 17206 (Mar. 18, 1980). Not satisfied with this response, Congress enacted the Infant Formula Act of 1980, 94 Stat. 1190, adding section 412 to the FD&C Act. Section 412(g) enacted the FDA interim guidelines into law, with slight modifications. The 1980 Act also enlarged FDA's regulatory authority over infant formulas.

Pursuant to the 1980 Act, FDA established reporting requirements in 45 Fed. Reg. 77136 (Nov. 21, 1980); quality control procedures in 45 Fed. Reg. 86362 (Dec. 30, 1980), 47 Fed. Reg. 17016 (Apr. 20, 1982); recall requirements in 47 Fed. Reg. 2331 (Jan. 15, 1982), 47 Fed. Reg. 18832 (Apr. 30, 1982); exemptions in 48 Fed. Reg. 31875 (July 12, 1983), 50 Fed. Reg. 48183 (Nov. 22, 1985); labeling requirements in 48 Fed. Reg. 31880 (July 12, 1983), 50 Fed. Reg. 1833 (Jan. 14, 1985); and nutrient requirements in 49 Fed. Reg. 14396 (Apr. 11, 1984), 50 Fed. Reg. 45106 (Oct. 30, 1985).

The quality control and recordkeeping requirements of these regulations were unsuccessfully challenged by a consortium of citizen organizations in *Formula v. Heckler*, 779 F.2d 743 (D.C. Cir. 1985). The organizations then sought relief from Congress. Section 4014 of the Anti–Drug Abuse Act of 1986, 100 Stat. 3207, 3207–116, amended section 412 of the FD&C Act to add additional requirements. FDA has implemented the 1986 Amendments by amending the recall regulations, 52 Fed. Reg. 30171 (Aug. 13, 1987), 54 Fed. Reg. 4006 (Jan. 27, 1989), 54 Fed. Reg. 11518 (Mar. 21, 1989), and by promulgating detailed new microbiological testing and record retention requirements, 54 Fed. Reg. 3783 (Jan. 26, 1989), 56 Fed. Reg.

66566 (Dec. 24, 1991). The agency has also proposed additional changes in its infant formula regulations. 61 Fed. Reg. 36154 (July 9, 1996), 68 Fed. Reg. 22341 (Apr. 28, 2003), 71 Fed. Reg. 43392 (Aug. 1, 2006). The infant formula regulations are codified in 21 C.F.R. Parts 106 & 107.

7. NUTRITIONAL QUALITY GUIDELINES

In 1970, FDA Commissioner Charles Edwards announced a new agency initiative in regulating the nutritional quality of foods:

> We propose to establish ... nutritional guidelines for selected classes of foods.... [T]entatively we have in mind formulated main dishes; new foods, such as analogs for meat products, dairy products and fruit juices; staples that are important in the diet of ethnic groups in which malnutrition has been found through the surveys.

> We do not plan to set formal standards of nutritional quality. If guidelines are issued, this should be accomplished within a very small number of years, in part, because it will be done on a class basis rather than an individual food basis. We would then expect that commercial pressures would cause processors to use the guidelines in formulating and designing their products. If they do so extensively, there will be no reason to consider a mandatory mechanism.

"Regulatory Policies of the FDA," Hearings Before a Subcommittee of the House Committee on Government Operations, 91st Cong., 2d Sess. 40–41 (1970). Soon thereafter, FDA promulgated regulations establishing general principles for nutritional quality guidelines and a nutrition quality guideline for frozen "heat and serve" dinners. 36 Fed. Reg. 24822 (Dec. 23, 1971), 38 Fed. Reg. 6969 (Mar. 14, 1973), codified at 21 C.F.R. Part 104.

In addition to the nutrition quality guideline for frozen convenience dinners, FDA proposed guidelines for breakfast beverage products, 39 Fed. Reg. 20895 (June 14, 1974); fortified hot breakfast cereals, 39 Fed. Reg. 20896 (June 14, 1974); fortified ready-to-eat breakfast cereals, 39 Fed. Reg. 20898 (June 14, 1974); formulated meal replacements, 39 Fed. Reg. 20905 (June 14, 1974); and main dish products, 39 Fed. Reg. 20906 (June 14, 1974). The agency initially announced that it was holding these proposals in abeyance pending publication of a final food fortification policy, which appeared at 45 Fed. Reg. 6314 (Jan. 25, 1980), but it later withdrew all of them in 51 Fed. Reg. 15653 (Apr. 25, 1986), leaving only the guideline for frozen "heat and serve" dinners.

8. MEDICAL FOOD

Peter Barton Hutt, *U.S. Government Regulation of Food With Claims for Special Physiological Value*

In Mary K. Schmidl and Theodore P. Labuza, eds., ESSENTIALS OF FUNCTIONAL FOODS, Ch. 16 (2000).

The category of medical food was initially an administrative creation without statutory authority. It was subsequently defined in the Orphan

Drug Act Amendments of 1988 and is now reflected in the FD&C Act in the form of statutory exemptions from nutrition labeling, nutrient descriptors, and disease prevention claims for food.

The statutory definition in [section 5(b) of the Orphan Drug Act, 21 U.S.C. 360ee(b),] requires only the supervision of a physician and the use of the product for specific dietary management of a disease for which distinctive nutritional requirements, based on recognized scientific principles, are established by medical evaluation. FDA has attempted to narrow this definition by regulation, however, to add five limitations not found in the statute itself: (1) a medical food is specifically formulated and processed for feeding a patient and is not a natural food, (2) the patient must have limited or impaired capacity to use ordinary food or must have other special medical needs that cannot be achieved by the modification of the normal diet alone, (3) the nutritional support must be specifically modified for the unique nutrient needs that result from the specific disease involved, (4) the product is intended for use under medical supervision, and (5) the medical supervision must be personal and active. Although these additional non-statutory requirements are of highly doubtful legality, they have served to reduce the number of medical foods that are marketed, and they indicate a very negative FDA view of these products.

For many years, FDA has considered imposing additional regulatory requirements on medical food by adopting new regulations. The agency asked for public comment on this subject in an Advance Notice of Proposed Rulemaking published in November 1996 but has taken no further action.

A Review of Foods For Medical Purposes: Specially Formulated Products For Nutritional Management of Medical Conditions

Federation of American Societies for Experimental Biology (June 1977).

Several investigators have characterized the important properties of specially formulated complete diets for use under medical supervision in terms of their nutritional and physiological impact on the patient. They included a number of properties that should be considered in effective dietary management of various diseases:

- *High Nutritional Efficacy:* Preparations can provide 3000 kcal or more daily and at least 25 percent of the water requirement for extended periods. Nutritionally complete products would supply, in addition to caloric needs, adequate amounts of essential fatty acids, minerals and vitamins, and essential and nonessential nitrogen.

- *Uniform Composition:* Use of chemically identifiable ingredients provides control of product uniformity, allowing modification or supplementation to meet special nutritional needs of individual patients as required. However, deletion, substitution, or reduction of certain nutrients is not possible with commercial preparations.

- *Low Residue:* Most products contain little or no fiber or complex carbohydrates; consequently, gastrointestinal contents and fecal volume are reduced considerably.

- *Ease of Digestibility:* Dietary components may be supplied as readily digestible low molecular weight substances. Absorption in the duodenum and jejunum occurs readily....

- *Microbial Flora Alterations:* Qualitative and quantitative changes in fecal flora suggest that gastrointestinal microbial flora may be altered by consumption of special dietary foods....

- *Alteration of Serum Lipid Levels:* While the nature and amount of carbohydrate or other components in the product may affect the rate of decrease, reduction of serum cholesterol levels has been observed.

- *Reduction of Blood Pressure:* Decreased systolic and diastolic blood pressure levels have been reported in *normal* subjects maintained several days on special dietary products. Blood pressure levels returned to baseline values after normal diets were resumed.

- *Gastric Effects:* Consumption of such diets reduces gastric acid secretions and delays gastric emptying.

- *Hypoallergenicity:* The ability to eliminate protein components or alter their composition provides a convenient method of supplying nonallergenic nutrients to patients with food allergies.

- *Water Solubility or Dispersibility:* Liquid preparations allow either tube feeding or consumption without mastication which can be important in pediatric and geriatric patients and in patients with oral, dental and other head and neck surgical problems. Some can be administered through extremely small (No. 4 French) feeding tubes.

- *Stabilization of Nutritional State:* The uniformity of types of special dietary products facilitates establishing a stable nutritional status and accurate measurements of the intake of all nutrients....

Exact definition of these types of products is difficult because of their composition and manner of use. Many currently available products and formulas include widely used foods, food ingredients, and substances that are generally recognized as safe. Similarly, a broad array of regular dietary items is useful in feeding patients with disorders amenable to dietary management. On the other hand, some nutritionally complete products were developed originally to facilitate digestion, provide less bulk and thus lower fecal volume, and at the same time, provide nutrients in amounts equivalent to the estimated requirements of a normal adult. In current practice, these latter formulations are being used in such diverse conditions as obesity and weight reduction, acute and chronic pancreatitis, preoperative preparation for intestinal surgery, enteral nutrition of cancer and terminally ill patients, extensive body burns, radiation enteropathy, and the short bowel syndrome....

While each of the terms in current usage has some advantages, for purposes of this report the term "medical foods" has been used and it is defined as follows:

> *Medical Foods* are foods that are specially formulated or prepared products consumed or administered enterally under direct or indirect medical supervision in the dietary management of individuals with specific diseases, disorders, or medical conditions in which the

existence of associated special nutritional requirements is established by medical evaluation.

Regardless of composition, medical foods are foods for use by patients who require professional medical counsel and supervision to meet special or unique nutritional requirements. Use of the term, "medical foods," should connote reference to special dietary foods intended for use solely under medical supervision to meet nutritional requirements in specific medical conditions which may be potentially life-threatening or critically disabling....

Research, clinical experience, and technical development during the past three decades have established the value of medical foods in patient nutrition and dietary management of a wide variety of diseases and disorders. Additional research and clinical experience can be expected to provide a basis for continued evolution of products that meet special nutritional requirements of a broader array of diseases and disorders. Similarly, evolving concepts in health care delivery and long-term maintenance of patients with chronic diseases suggest that applications of medical foods will expand substantially.

NOTES

1. *Orphan Medical Food.* FDA announced the availability of a report on evaluation of incentives for development of "orphan" medical foods in 55 Fed. Reg. 11439 (Mar. 28, 1990).

2. *Definition of Medical Food.* FDA has attempted to narrow the statutory definition of a medical food by letters to the manufacturers of specific products, but has stopped short of testing its position through court enforcement action. *See, e.g.,* November 1999—June 2000 correspondence between FDA and Cooke Pharma on the status of a product with the name HeartBar containing L-arginine and represented as a medical food for the dietary management of cardiovascular disease.

3. *Commentary. See generally* Peter Barton Hutt, *Government Regulation of Health Claims in Food Labeling and Advertising,* 41 FOOD DRUG COSM. L.J. 3, 68 (1986); Sanford A. Miller & F. Edward Scarbrough, *Foods as Drugs,* 21 DRUG INFO. J. 221 (1987); Symposium: *Medical Foods: Their Past, Present, and Future Regulation,* 44 FOOD DRUG COSM. L.J. 461 (1989); Institute of Food Technologists Expert Panel on Food Safety and Nutrition, *Medical Foods,* 46 FOOD TECH., No. 4, at 87 (Apr. 1992).

9.   NUTRIGENOMICS

Nutrigenomics is the emerging field that studies how an individual's unique genetic makeup determines the appropriate nutrients and food for that individual. Although this field is in its infancy, nutrigenomics will undoubtedly have a substantial impact on the labeling and formulation of personalized conventional food and dietary supplements in the future.

Bernadine Healy, M.D., *Food With a Purpose*

U.S. NEWS & WORLD REPORT, Feb. 13, 2006, at 60.

There's an old medical saying that we dig our grave with our spoon. Enter nutrigenomics, a new field that tailors your food to your genes. It just might be the answer to our epidemic of obesity and metabolic syndrome. It could even improve how we age, better our bone and brain health, and lower our risks for certain cancers. Built around the idea that one person's medicine is another's poison, nutrigenomics, and its related technologies of proteomics (the proteins that genes order up) and metabolomics (the soup of molecules that results from metabolic activity), provide a personalized dietary road map. The field is exciting and promising but is by no means ripe for the picking—despite some commercial ventures telling you otherwise. Before we turn an important new domain of nutrition into unappetizing snake oil, let's understand what it is and isn't.

Customizing one's diet to one's genes and metabolism isn't anything like the traditional, one-size-fits-all food pyramid. That approach is geared toward preventing nutritional deficiencies. The recommended daily allowances, or RDAs, printed on food labels tell you the macronutrients (carbohydrates, protein, and fat) and micronutrients (vitamins and minerals) you need. Even in the newer and booming field of functional foods, in which certain foods and supplements are singled out for health benefits beyond basic nutrition, it is assumed they'd bring value to everyone. Functional foods include megavitamins, animal extracts such as fish oils, and concentrates of the many biologically active plant chemicals that make fruits and vegetables veritable treasure troves of prevention for heart disease and cancer. . . .

. . . Nutrigenomics and metabolomics should allow us to develop eating plans based on each food's chemical profile and our individual metabolism. For example, some chemicals in food promote genetic stability in less stable genomes, or modify proteins once formed, that might regulate tumor incidence or behavior. Others can alter the level of certain proteins that control how much dietary fat is stored as body fat versus being burned up as calories.

Imagine a doctor's being able to quickly identify a patient's DNA profile for type 2 diabetes or obesity and then get a dynamic snapshot of his or her metabolic responses to a particular diet. Food shopping might be like going to the shoe store. You'd have the size and, combined with your taste and energy expenditures (yes exercise is a partner of nutrition), you'd select what fits. But this approach is several years away, as our knowledge of chronic disease susceptibility genes is limited, and metabolomics is an entirely new endeavor.

Companies are already pushing DNA diets, which concerns John Erdman, a professor of food sciences and human nutrition at the University of Illinois–Urbana–Champaign. "Identifying a handful of genes from a snippet of hair or a mouth swab and returning with a diet plan and a bill for several hundred dollars is a waste of money and is way premature," says Erdman. In a field known for fads and reckless health claims, we will have to struggle to keep nutrigenomics from being hijacked by the P. T. Barnums.

NOTE

See also "Nutrigenetic Testing," Hearing before the Senate Special Comm. on Aging, 110th Cong., 2d Sess. (2006).

F. REGULATION OF DIETARY SUPPLEMENTS

In enacting the FD&C Act in 1938, Congress authorized FDA in section 403(j) to promulgate regulations governing the labeling of the "vitamin, mineral, and other dietary properties" of food "represented for special dietary uses." In the Vitamin–Mineral Amendments of 1976, 90 Stat. 410, Congress defined "special dietary use" in section 411(c)(3) of the FD&C Act to include food "[s]upplying a vitamin, mineral, or other ingredient for use by man to supplement his diet by increasing the total dietary intake." It was not until the Dietary Supplement Health and Education Act (DSHEA) of 1994, 108 Stat. 4325, however, that Congress defined the term "dietary supplement" in section 201(ff) and enacted new provisions specifically applicable to this subcategory of food.

1. DECEPTIVE MARKETING PRACTICES

V.E. Irons, Inc. v. United States

244 F.2d 34 (1st Cir. 1957).

■ MAGRUDER, CHIEF JUDGE.

V.E. Irons, Inc. and V. Earl Irons in his individual capacity stand convicted, after a three-week trial, on a six-count information for causing the introduction into interstate commerce of misbranded food and drugs. . . .

Count II charged that the appellants caused to be introduced into interstate commerce articles of drug known as Vit–Ra–Tox 21A and Vit–Ra–Tox 21B . . . which were (a) misbranded under 21 U.S.C. § 352(a) in that their accompanying labeling—consisting of certain leaflets and various issues of a newsletter—falsely represented "when viewed in [their] entirety as well as through specific claims . . . that nearly everyone in this country is suffering from malnutrition or in danger of such suffering because of demineralization and depletion of soils and the refining and process of foods, that particularly all illnesses and diseases of mankind are due to improper nutrition, that said article[s] possessed nutritive properties superior to any other vitamin and mineral supplement, that said article[s] would be effective in the cure, treatment, and prevention of the ills and diseases of mankind," including certain specific diseases; and which were (b) misbranded under § 352(f)(1) in that their labeling failed to bear adequate directions for the use of which they were intended, namely, for treatment of the specific diseases which appellants represented that the drugs could cure or prevent. . . .

At the conclusion of the trial the jury returned a verdict of guilty against both defendants on all six counts. The court sentenced V. Earl Irons to one year of imprisonment on each of the six counts, the sentences to run concurrently; and imposed upon the defendant corporation a fine of $1,000 on each count. Appeals were duly taken by both defendants. . . .

In determining whether such labeling contained "false or misleading" statements, we must be careful not to read the literature with the eyes either of experts in nutrition or of overly skeptical buyers. What is pertinent is the effect the claims would have on those to whom they are addressed, namely, prospective purchasers and actual customers of appellants, who cannot be presumed to have special expertness or to be unduly cautious, but who are more likely than not to be persons who are pathetically eager to find some simple cure-all for the diseases with which they are afflicted or who are susceptible to luridly painted scare literature as to the prospect of being disease-ridden unless they consistently partake of the vaunted drug product. . . .

When appellants' labeling is examined in this light and in its entirety, it readily appears that the government introduced at least sufficient evidence to warrant submission to the jury of the issues whether appellants made the representations charged against them, and whether these representations were false or misleading. . . . [M]any representations are made that, fairly interpreted, provide adequate support for the government's charges. There are, first of all, numerous assertions that "all human ailments" can be traced to nutritive deficiencies and that various specific ills are caused thereby. For example, there is the statement:

"The evidence is overwhelming! That we Are what we Eat. That practically All Human ailments are traceable to our food. From the times we are conceived until we reach 150 lbs;

It's the Material Out of Which we are built that determines the structure. If that material is faulty the structure Breaks Down. If it is Not Faulty, it does Not Break Down. . . . It's our Food, that makes us sick or well.

Similarly, in one of appellants' pamphlets it is stated: 'We believe that practically all the ailments that beset our civilized world are caused by deficient foods which can lower one's resistance.' "

With respect to specific diseases, the literature quotes from the writings of one Dr. Sutherland[6] that:

At the present time many conditions are considered as essentially deficiency diseases and are associated in one's thought with the classical Beri–Beri, Pellagra, Rickets and Scurvy. Such conditions are Infantile Scorbutus, Marasmus, Dentition Difficulties and Imperfect Teeth in Children and Adults, Dyspepsias, Indigestions, Diarrhoeas and Constipation, Obesity, Inability to Nurse Children, Diabetes, Neuroses, Infantile Paralysis, Certain Myalgias or "Rheumatism," Dementia Praecox, and even Tuberculosis and Cancer. The list can be extended but it is already a formidable one. . . .

At another point appellants modestly state in an unqualified way that "It [Vit–Ra–Tox No. 21] is the One Hope for suffering humanity." And

---

6. The literature employs quotations from the writings of others. It is obvious that so long as these writings are quoted with approval, they become the representations of appellants and can be used by the government to sustain its charges.

again, that " 'This Product' *alone* of all products now on the market has *all* the vitamins, minerals, enzymes, coenzymes, mineral activators and synergists (co-workers or helpers) needed by the human body except Vitamin D."

Apart from these general representations about the value of their product, the record discloses that appellants claimed the power to cure or ameliorate specific diseases. . . .

. . . The record discloses many other illustrations of references to specific diseases cleverly coupled with boosts for or information concerning Vit–Ra–Tox. On the basis of this record it is not at all surprising that a lay jury reading the literature came to the conclusion that special curative or at least preventive powers for the diseases mentioned were claimed by appellants for their Vit–Ra–Tox line.[8] And if such was the impression made upon the jury, it seems more than likely that a prospective purchaser, hoping finally to obtain relief from a long-endured disease, would not read appellants' literature with any skeptical literalness. Bearing in mind the broadly remedial purposes of the Act in preventing deception, the Congress must be taken to have meant to strike not only at palpably false claims but also at clever indirection and ambiguity in the creation of misleading impressions. . . .

A judgment will be entered affirming the judgments of the District Court.

NOTES

1. *Double–Barrel Attack. V.E. Irons v. United States* demonstrates FDA's use of the Act's overlapping definitions of "food" and of "drug" to attack products marketed to prevent nutritional deficiencies and other diseases. In attempting to identify the criteria for determining whether a product is subject to the "drug" requirements of the Act, consider the following excerpt from *United States v. Nutrition Service, Inc.*, 227 F. Supp. 375 (W.D. Pa. 1964):

> Certain evidence was presented by the plaintiff that the defendants here claimed for Mucorhicin antibiotic qualities by reason of a relationship with penicillin. . . . While in fact it may be true that mold growth exists naturally in certain foods and that such foods are sold regularly there is essentially this difference, that such foods are sold only as foods and not for treatment, mitigation and prevention of disease. If cheese were to be sold by any processor for the cure, treatment, mitigation and prevention of

8. On its cartons and in one or two of appellants' newsletters or pamphlets, one may find disclaimers such as the following:

Important—We do not diagnose or prescribe

Neither we nor our Vit–Ra–Tox Distributors are doctors. We do not attempt to diagnose or prescribe. We do not approach our customer's health problem from the standpoint of specific ailments. We are, however, interested in teaching them how, to the extent possible through nutritional influences, we can help them. . . .

Our sales talk and theory of body building through nutritional elements are not to be interpreted as entering the field of medicine or as violating a doctor's prerogative. Since, therefore, we try only to improve the nutritional vitality of our customers, if any dangerous acute conditions exist, or are suspected, a physician should be consulted.

disease under the classification of food, within the provisions of the Food and Drug Act, it would be necessarily a drug.

. . . The real test is how was this product being sold? If as a food, was it for the furnishing of energy and body building? Or was it being sold for the treatment and mitigation of disease? . . .

2. *Enforcement History.* The *Irons* case is illustrative of literally hundreds of court actions that FDA instituted against false or misleading nutritional claims in product labeling under both the food and drug sections of the FD&C Act. At least prior to 1970, FDA and the FTC undoubtedly expended more enforcement resources in the area of nutrition than in any other single field. The failure of this case-by-case approach to stem the tide of deception explains why both agencies ultimately turned to rulemaking. *See infra* p. 251.

United States v. "Vitasafe Formula M"

226 F. Supp. 266 (D.N.J. 1964).

■ Lane, District Judge. . . .

The United States alleges that the Vitasafe capsule, *as an article of food* within the meaning of 21 U.S.C. § 321(f), is misbranded under 21 U.S.C. § 343(a) in that:

I. Its labeling, when viewed as a whole, represents, suggests and implies that the nutritional needs for men and women differ, and that the "Formula M" capsules are designed to satisfy the special needs of men as contrasted to the "Formula W" capsules which are designed to satisfy the special needs of women, which representations, suggestions, and implications are contrary to fact;

II. The listing on the label of, and references in the labeling to, certain ingredients implies and suggests that the nutritional value of Vitasafe capsules is enhanced by the presence of such ingredients, when in fact such implications and suggestions are false and misleading in that the presence of these ingredients is of no nutritional significance for dietary supplementation. . . .

IV. The overall impression suggested and implied by the statements in the labeling concerning the large amounts of common foods that must be consumed in order to furnish quantities of nutrients equal to the quantities of such nutrients present in one Vitasafe capsule is false and misleading since such large quantities of food would not be needed to supply the necessary dietary requirements for these nutrients and since the labeling does not list all the various nutrients furnished by the stated quantities of food designated in the labeling.

It is further alleged that the Vitasafe capsule, *as a drug* within the meaning of 21 U.S.C. § 321(g), is misbranded under 21 U.S.C. § 352(a) in that:

V. Its labeling contains false and misleading representations, suggestions, and implications that the article is an adequate and effective treatment for depression, tension, weakness, nervous disorders, lethargy, lack of energy, lassitude, impotence, aches and pains, aging, impaired digestion, loss of appetite . . . which representations, suggestions, and implications are false and misleading since the article is not an adequate and effective treatment of the disease conditions and symptoms as stated and implied.

VI. Its labeling contains false and misleading representations, suggestions, and implications that practically everyone in this country is suffering from or is in danger of suffering from a dietary deficiency of vitamins, minerals and proteins which is likely to result in specific deficiency diseases. . . .

A study of all the exhibits and the expert testimony . . . leads this court to the following conclusions:

1. The labeling of the seized article, when viewed as a whole, does represent, suggest and imply that a woman, because of sex alone, has different nutritional needs than a man, and "Vitasafe Formula W" will satisfy these special needs of women as contrasted to "Vitasafe Formula M" which will satisfy the special needs of men.

These representations are false and misleading since there is no difference in the nutritional requirements of non-pregnant non-lactating women as compared to men, except for iron in women of childbearing age, which need is adequately satisfied by the normal diet readily available and normally consumed. With the exception of iron, nutritional need is the same for men and women. . . .

2. The labeling of the seized *res*, when viewed in its entirety, does represent, suggest and imply that the nutritional value of Vitasafe capsules is enhanced by the presence in these capsules of the following ingredients . . .

The evidence produced at trial proves that the normal or ordinary diet supplies amounts of the above-listed ingredients greatly in excess of those necessary for good nutrition. Furthermore, with the exception of the fat soluble vitamins A and D, vitamins ingested in excess of those required are excreted and make no nutritional contribution. The evidence further proves that the following ingredients represented to be present in the Vitasafe product have no nutritional value whatever, namely rutin, lemon bioflavonoid, monopotassium glutamate, sulfur, choline bitartrate, inositol and royal jelly. Other ingredients, such as all the amino acids are in such small quantities as to be of no significant value when compared to the quantities of such ingredients which are required and which are present in the average diet. Because the ingredients here designated are either of no nutritional significance per se or are contained in the Vitasafe product in such minute quantities, these ingredients do not enhance the nutritional value of the Vitasafe capsules. Consequently, the representation and suggestion referred to in this finding is false and misleading. . . .

4. Although correct if read literally and carefully, the labeling of the seized *res* represents and suggests to the ordinary reader that it is necessary to eat enormous quantities and varieties of foods in order to obtain the variety of vitamins and minerals in the amounts provided by one Vitasafe capsule. This representation is false and misleading because the variety and quantity of foods referred to in the labeling of the seized *res* provide many times the amounts of nutrients as well as additional nutrients than are supplied by one Vitasafe capsule.

5.   The labeling of the seized *res* represents, suggests, and implies that Vitasafe capsules are an adequate and effective treatment of or preventive for the following symptoms and conditions which are referred to in this labeling:. . . .

This representation is false and misleading. The evidence produced at trial conclusively proves that the above designated symptoms or conditions are caused by and associated with a great number of serious pathological diseases. . . .

7.   The article under seizure is both a food within the meaning of 21 U.S.C. § 321(f) because its labeling recommends its use as and represents it to be of value as a dietary and nutritional supplement, and also a drug within the meaning of 21 U.S.C. § 321(g) because its labeling recommends its use as and represents it to be of value as a curative or preventive of disease conditions in man affecting the structure and function of the body of man. . . .

The Decree of Condemnation is granted.. . . .

NOTE

See also *United States v. An Article of Food . . . Nuclomin*, 482 F.2d 581 (8th Cir. 1973), which held that the labeling of a dietary supplement was misleading because it featured ingredients that "were either not needed in the human diet or . . . the amount of the ingredient was so small that it would have no value." The Court of Appeals emphasized that "the fact that no purchasers have actually been misled is not a defense under the Act." Compare *United States v. 119 Cases . . . "New Dextra Brand Fortified Cane Sugar,"* 231 F. Supp. 551 (S.D. Fla. 1963), *aff'd*, 334 F.2d 238 (5th Cir. 1964), p. 233 *supra*, where FDA unsuccessfully pursued the same legal theory against a fortified food.

2.   THE FDA VITAMIN–MINERAL REGULATIONS

Shortly after enactment of the 1938 Act, FDA established detailed labeling requirements for foods marketed for "special dietary uses" pursuant to section 403(j). 5 Fed. Reg. 3565 (Sept. 5, 1940), 6 Fed. Reg. 3304 (July 8, 1941), 6 Fed. Reg. 5921 (Nov. 22, 1941). These requirements remained unchanged until FDA undertook a general revision of its special dietary food regulations, a project begun in 1962 that was interrupted both by court challenges to the agency's policies and procedures and by congressional restrictions on its substantive authority.

The original special dietary food regulations established quantitative "minimum daily requirements" (MDR) for individual nutrients. The label for any product represented for special dietary use because of its vitamin or mineral properties was required to declare the percent of the MDR in the amount of the product consumed during one day. For nutrients for which no MDR existed, the label was required to state that "The need for _____ in human nutrition has not been established." By 1962, FDA had concluded that these requirements were insufficient to control the claims made for vitamin-mineral products. It thus published a proposal to revise the regulations completely. 27 Fed. Reg. 5815 (June 20, 1962). The "minimum daily requirements" were to be replaced with "daily requirements" for purposes of labeling. The proposal also stated that the label of a dietary supplement could declare "only those nutrients recognized by competent authorities as essential and of significant dietary-supplement value in human nutrition and that are present in amounts that are consistent with the nutritional requirements for such nutrients." FDA went on to specify the nutrients that it considered essential and the amounts believed nutritionally appropriate, as well as other nutrients not regarded as appropriate for supplementation. Within a short time, however, the agency decided that the June 1962 proposal did not go far enough.

William D. Goodrich, *The Coming Struggle Over Vitamin–Mineral Pills**

20 BUSINESS LAWYER 145 (1964).

A little over two years ago—in June 1962—FDA announced a proposed revision of the regulations for the labeling of foods for special dietary uses. . . .

What was proposed was to eliminate some of the basic causes of confusion and misrepresentation so that the unwary consumer would be spared the snares which now influence his purchase. . . .

1. Formulations of vitamin-mineral tablets which contain many times the "minimum daily requirement" of the nutrients, designed to appeal to the layman's belief that if a little is good to satisfy his "minimum" daily requirement, then much more than that minimum would be much better for his health.

2. Formulations based on no rational nutritional principles at all, for example, those which might have one-tenth of the minimum daily requirement of an expensive nutrient and ten times the minimum daily requirement of the cheaper ones.

3. So-called "shotgun" preparations, which contain not only all the vitamins and minerals which might possibly play a part in improving the nutritive well being of the customer, but also all the other nutrients so far discovered, regardless of the fact that there is no evidence whatever to support a belief that they are needed in human nutrition. . . .

4. And finally, formulations to support promotional efforts based on the four great myths of nutrition: (a) that our soils are so depleted that ordinary foods do not contain the expected nutrients; (b) that modern processing and storage of food strips them of virtually all important nutritive values; (c) that it is essentially impossible to obtain from our daily diets the nutrients we require; (d) and that as a result almost every one is now or will soon be suffering from a subclinical nutritional deficiency which may be the cause of some serious condition of ill health.

Our own out-dated regulations have contributed to the confusion by requiring that nutrients be declared in terms of percentage of the "minimum daily requirement," and that the need in human nutrition for others has not been established. The classification of vitamin-mineral pills as

---

* [Mr. Goodrich was FDA Chief Counsel.]

special dietary foods, rather than as drugs, resulted in the anomalous situation in which all the ingredients of these pills and tablets had to be declared on the label, even the inert ingredients which could not contribute anything of nutritional value. Our drug regulations specifically forbid the declaration of inert ingredients when this may mislead the consumer. To the uninitiated, all this carried the message that a product supplying ten times the "minimum daily requirement" was a superior product, even though it was a well-established scientific fact that the particular vitamins involved were water soluble, not stored in the body, and the excess would be promptly excreted as unneeded nutrients. The "not yet established" legend seemed to promise that the evidence was just around the corner—else why would the manufacturer include this nutrient as an ingredient at all. . . .

———

In 1966, FDA issued its "final" revision of the special dietary food regulations. 31 Fed. Reg. 8521, 8525 (June 18, 1966). The MDRs became "recommended dietary allowances" (RDAs). To solve the problems Goodrich described, the final regulations included four new elements: (1) a standard of identity limiting the nutrients and their levels in dietary supplements; (2) a novel standard of identity specifying the foods to which nutrients could be added; (3) a prohibition of any representation resembling Goodrich's "four great myths of nutrition;" and (4) a requirement that the main panel of every dietary supplement bear the following so-called "crepe" label statement:

> Vitamins and minerals are supplied in abundant amounts by the foods we eat. The Food and Nutrition Board of the National Research Council recommends that dietary needs be satisfied by foods. Except for persons with special medical needs, there is no scientific basis for recommending routine use of dietary supplements.

This order precipitated an avalanche of objections which automatically stayed the regulations and led to an evidentiary hearing lasting much of 1968 and 1969. As one scholar observed:

> When the hearing ground to a halt in May 1970, its tangible products had reached Brobdingnagian proportions. Testimony of Government witnesses accounted for about 25,000 pages of transcript—slightly more than two-thirds of the total. The Government and the industry participants had proffered testimony of 162 witnesses and more than 2,000 pieces of documentary evidence. . . .

Robert W. Hamilton, *Rulemaking on a Record by the Food and Drug Administration*, 50 Tex. L. Rev. 1132 (1972).

———

In the interim, the problem of "hunger in America" was publicized in the news media and by the White House Conference on Food, Nutrition and Health. The FDA drive to restrict the use of vitamin-mineral products was therefore substantially blunted. The agency's tentative order and final regulations, 38 Fed. Reg. 2143, 2152 (Jan. 19, 1973), 38 Fed. Reg. 20708, 20730 (Aug. 2, 1973), reflected a major shift in approach, but still did not escape court challenge. The regulations adopted "recommended daily allowances" (RDAs) and continued to require products to be labeled with the percent of the RDAs in a day's serving. Representations exploiting the "myths" of nutrition were banned, but the agency abandoned the crepe label statement. Of primary interest, FDA abandoned any limitations on food fortification, but it did establish standards of identity for four types of combination dietary supplements. With reference to a list of vitamins and minerals included in the regulation, these combination products were: (1) all vitamins and minerals, (2) all vitamins, (3) all minerals, and (4) all vitamins plus iron. The agency set the floor for nutrients in these standardized products at 50 percent of the RDA and the ceiling at 150 percent of the RDA. No other combinations were permitted, but each individual vitamin or mineral could be sold by itself. FDA also ruled that any product containing amounts in excess of 150 percent of the RDA would be a drug. The regulations were immediately challenged in court in 15 separate appeals

In *National Nutritional Foods Association v. FDA*, 504 F.2d 761 (2d Cir. 1994), the FDA regulations were in large part upheld but were nonetheless stayed in their entirety, pending further rulemaking by FDA, because of certain provisions that the Court of Appeals determined required further agency consideration.

1.   The Court of Appeals rejected the argument that the FDA could not proceed simultaneously under section 401, governing food standards of identity, and section 403(j), governing the labeling of foods for special dietary uses.

2.   The Court of Appeals upheld the need to limit the composition of combination vitamin and mineral products through both qualitative and quantitative standards of identity. The court concluded that FDA was justified in concluding that labeling alone would not be sufficient to eliminate consumer confusion.

3.   Nonetheless, the Court of Appeals directed FDA to permit exceptions to the limits for particular vitamins and minerals, and to deal explicitly with applications for increases in particular limits before the regulations would become effective. The regulations were stayed in their entirety until this process was completed.

4.   The Court of Appeals struck down the FDA prohibition against the use of two vitamins and six minerals that are essential to human nutrition but for which no U.S. RDA had yet been established.

5.   The Court of Appeals invalidated the FDA determination that more than 150 percent of the RDA of a nutrient constitutes a drug use, stating that the demonstrated uselessness of high amounts of nutrients for food purposes does not demonstrate a therapeutic intent.

6. The Court of Appeals upheld the FDA prohibitions against the types of claims that the agency had previously found unwarranted in court litigation.

All of the remaining provisions of the regulations were either not contested or were upheld.

———

In addition to challenging its regulations in court, FDA's critics continued their efforts to prevent any official limitations on the formulation and sale of dietary supplements through legislation. On April 22, 1976, President Ford signed the Health Research and Health Services Amendments of 1976, 90 Stat. 401. Title V of this legislation, known as the Vitamin–Mineral Amendments of 1976, 90 Stat. at 410, was a rider adopted on the Senate floor with the objective of constricting the authority on which FDA had relied in adopting its controversial vitamin and mineral regulations. The Amendments added a new section 411 to the FD&C Act which significantly curtailed FDA's authority to restrict the composition of dietary supplements under sections 201(n), 401, or 403.

Health Research and Health Services Amendments of 1976

Conference Report No. 94–1005, 94th Congress, 2d Session (1976).

... [T]hree significant restrictions would be imposed on the Secretary with regard to the regulation of products subject to the conference substitute. First, new section 411(a)(1)(A) of the Act prohibits the Secretary from using his existing authority under sections 201(n) or 403 of the Act (relating to misbranding) or under section 401 of the Act (relating to standards of identity) to impose maximum limits on the potency of safe vitamins and minerals contained in products subject to the conference substitute. This provision would not restrict the Secretary from prescribing minimum potency levels for vitamins or minerals in such products in order to prevent the addition of insignificant or useless amounts.

Second, new section 411(a)(1)(B) of the Act prohibits the Secretary from classifying as a drug a natural or synthetic vitamin or mineral, offered by itself or in combination, solely because it exceeds the level of potency that the Secretary determines is nutritionally rational or useful.

Third, new section 411(a)(1)(C) of the Act prohibits the Secretary from using his authority with respect to misbranding or establishment of standards of identity to limit the combination or number of any safe vitamin, mineral or other ingredient of food in products subject to the conference substitute....

... [T]he limitations on the Secretary, described above, do not apply with respect to a product otherwise subject to the provisions of the conference substitute where such product is represented for use by (1) individuals in the treatment or management of specific diseases or disorders, (2) children, or (3) pregnant or lactating women....

Except as specifically provided, the conference substitute does not alter the drug or food provisions of the Federal Food, Drug, and Cosmetic Act. . . .

The Secretary also has the authority to regulate the composition or potency of a product subject to the provisions of the conference substitute on the basis of safety. . . .

Similarly, if any vitamin, mineral or other food ingredient is not generally recognized as safe by qualified experts and meets the other criteria of the definition of a "food additive" under section 201(s) of the Act, it would be subject to regulation under section 409 of the Act. . . . It is on precisely this basis that the Secretary has, by regulation, restricted the potency of the vitamin folic acid that may be added to a food. . . .

The conference substitute provides that a food to which the conference substitute is applicable shall not be deemed misbranded under section 403 of the Act solely because its label bears a listing of all of the ingredients in the food, or solely because its advertising contains references to ingredients in the food that are not vitamins or minerals. Thus, for example, if a tablet or capsule of vitamin C contains rutin, a substance that the Secretary has concluded has no dietary usefulness, the list of ingredients as well as the advertising for the product may refer to rutin without causing the food to be deemed misbranded. However, because of the conferees' concern that consumers not be misled into a belief that such substances have nutritional value, the conference substitute provides that the labeling so [sic] such a product may not list ingredients that are not vitamins or minerals except as a part of a list of all the ingredients of the food, in accordance with applicable regulations promulgated by the Secretary pursuant to section 403 of the Act. . . .

––––––––

At the same time it curtailed FDA's power, the Vitamin–Mineral Amendments of 1976 gave the agency limited authority to regulate the advertising of vitamins and minerals. The pertinent changes in the FD&C Act appear in sections 201(n), 303(d), 304(a)(3), 403(a)(2), and 411. Congress added Section 303(d) to exempt such advertising from the Act's criminal sanctions. In section 304(a) it added language to restrict seizures charging misbranding based on advertising for a dietary supplement to those instances where the advertising was disseminated and paid for by the establishment where the product is seized.

The 1976 legislation added a new Section 707 to the FD&C Act which, in substance, requires FDA to defer to the FTC before seeking to enforce its new authority over vitamin and mineral advertising. This new authority was considered by some members of Congress to be compensation for the agency's loss of its more important authority over composition and labeling of dietary foods. FDA has not used this authority over advertising since it was conferred, however, and the procedural restrictions imposed by Section 707 make it likely that the authority will rarely be invoked.

Following the ruling in *National Nutritional Foods Ass'n v. FDA*, FDA reopened its vitamin-mineral rulemaking proceedings. 40 Fed. Reg. 23244

(May 28, 1975), 40 Fed. Reg. 44857 (Sept. 30, 1975). Congress enacted the Vitamin–Mineral Amendments before the agency could complete the rulemaking. In 41 Fed. Reg. 46156 (Oct. 19, 1976) and 42 Fed. Reg. 20292 (Apr. 19, 1977), FDA issued final revised regulations that it believed responded to the Court of Appeals' ruling and complied with the limitations imposed by Congress under the statutory amendments. But it did not invite further public comment on the impact of the new legislation before completing its rulemaking, concluding, pursuant to 5 U.S.C. 553(b)(B), that it had good cause for dispensing with this step.

In *National Nutritional Foods Ass'n v. Kennedy*, 572 F.2d 377 (2d Cir. 1978), excerpted below, the Court of Appeals again remanded the matter to FDA. The Court of Appeals determined that FDA incorrectly issued its revised regulations without providing public notice and opportunity for comment as required by the Administrative Procedure Act, both to respond to the earlier decision and to implement the 1976 legislation.

NOTES

1. *Subsequent Proceedings.* FDA revoked its various vitamin-mineral regulations in 44 Fed. Reg. 16005 (Mar. 16, 1979) and has taken no further action in response to *National Nutritional Foods Ass'n v. Kennedy. The agency repealed even those regulations that were upheld* in 1974 by *National Nutritional Foods Ass'n v. FDA and were not nullified by the 1976 statute.*

2. *OTC Vitamin–Mineral Products.* On the same day FDA revoked the vitamin-mineral regulations, it published the report of its advisory panel on OTC vitamin-mineral drugs. 44 Fed. Reg. 16126 (Mar. 16, 1979). This report embodied the results of a four-year review of the safety and effectiveness of vitamins and minerals sold as OTC drugs, part of the OTC Drug Review discussed *infra* at p. 788. It perhaps was not by coincidence that FDA published the proposed monograph for OTC vitamin-mineral drugs in the same issue of the Federal Register as its revocation of the vitamin-mineral food regulations. FDA was deluged with objections from individuals and organizations who concluded that the agency was renewing its offensive against vitamin-mineral products. To avoid further confrontation and to allow study of the impact of the Vitamin–Mineral Amendments of 1976 on the FDA regulation of OTC vitamin-mineral drugs, FDA withdrew the proposed monograph in 46 Fed. Reg. 57914 (Nov. 27, 1981). The agency has taken no further action on this monograph.

3.   Regulation of Hazardous Nutrients

In the regulations FDA promulgated following the first remand in the *National Nutritional Foods Association* litigation, the agency included a provision, since revoked, which asserted the power to regulate vitamins and minerals under the food safety provisions of the Act. Predictably, this provision came under sharp attack when the case went back before the Second Circuit.

National Nutritional Foods Ass'n v. Kennedy

572 F.2d 377 (2d Cir. 1978).

■ Friendly, Circuit Judge. . . .

. . . Petitioners focus on the paragraph [in FDA's regulations] that follows:

(8) Any vitamin or mineral which is included in a dietary supplement and which is not generally recognized, among experts qualified by scientific training and experience to evaluate its safety, as having been adequately shown to be safe under the conditions of its intended use is a food additive within the meaning of section 201(s) of the act; and pursuant to sections 402(a)(2)(C) and 409 of the act, such inclusion is illegal in the absence of a food additive regulation approving such inclusion. A listing of some of the vitamin and/or mineral properties which are generally recognized as safe, and which thus may lawfully be included in a dietary supplement without a food additive regulation, appears at Subpart F of Part 182 of this chapter.

Petitioners say that having been foiled by us, and by Congress, in his effort to classify high potency vitamins and minerals as drugs, the Commissioner is now seeking to reach essentially the same goal by threatening to treat added quantities as food additives. . . .

Petitioners contend that vitamins and minerals are foods within § 201(f), . . . and that in the nature of things a "food" cannot be a "food additive," especially when it is just more of the same. Recognizing that the Commissioner must have power to prevent the sale of vitamin and mineral preparations of such high potency as to be dangerous, they say the Commissioner must proceed under more general provisions relating to adulteration on a case by case basis, *see, e.g.* § 402(a)(1), (3)–(7), (b), rather than the more readily enforceable provisions relating to food additives. . . .

. . . The sole criterion for identifying a food additive is whether a substance which may become a component of or affect the characteristics of any food be not generally recognized among qualified experts as having been shown to be safe. We do not believe a substance gains immunity from this criterion merely because it also qualifies as a food. . . . Congress has vested the Commissioner with broad "authority to promulgate regulations for the efficient enforcement" of the Food, Drug and Cosmetic Act, § 701(a), and we see no reason why we cannot determine that too much of even a good thing may come within the definition of a "food additive."

Still more important, Congress, which most likely was aware of the May 1975 regulations, seems to have held that view. The Senate decided not to include in the 1976 legislation a provision prohibiting FDA from regulating safe vitamins, minerals, and associated ingredients as food additives, stating in the report on the bill:

This was not done for two reasons. First of all, it is unnecessary. It would be inappropriate and contrary to the intention of this Title for the FDA to treat vitamins, minerals, and their associated ingredients about whose safety there currently is no doubt, as food additives. There are those who considered vitamins and minerals essentially foods with a long history of safe use. The authors rejected that course of action on grounds that there was insufficient evidence to support such a course of action at this time.

Second, there are some nutrients and ingredients or natural chemicals which are tangentially a part of vitamins or minerals which currently may be considered food additives because of their potential toxicity. We did not wish to prevent the FDA from acting in these circumstances. For the agency to do so based on the policies on potency and combinations which this amendment endorses, however, would be inappropriate.

S. Rep. No. 94–509, 94th Cong., 1st Sess. 40–41 (1975). And the House Conference Report observed ... [here the court quoted the passage on FDA's food additive authority from the Conference Report, set out *supra* p. 255]. . . .

NOTES

1. *Mineral Toxicity.* In October 1975, FDA issued a 231–page analysis of the toxicity of the essential minerals. The agency has taken no action on the basis of this report.

2. *Actions Against Toxic Nutrients.* FDA has restricted the use of several nutrients because of their toxicity. *See* 21 C.F.R. 170.45 (flourine); 25 Fed. Reg. 6633 (July 14, 1960), 25 Fed. Reg. 8224 (Aug. 27, 1960), 28 Fed. Reg. 4768 (May 11, 1963), 28 Fed. Reg. 7425 (July 20, 1963), 36 Fed. Reg. 6843 (Apr. 9, 1971), 38 Fed. Reg. 20725, and 20750 (Aug. 2, 1973), codified at 21 C.F.R. 172.345 (folic acid); 37 Fed. Reg. 6938 (Apr. 6, 1972), 38 Fed. Reg. 20036 (July 26, 1973), codified at 21 C.F.R. 172.30 (amino acids). FDA denied a food additive petition for menadione (vitamin K), thus precluding its use in dietary supplements or in food. 28 Fed. Reg. 3051 (Mar. 28, 1963), 28 Fed. Reg. 7262 (July 16, 1963).

3. *L-tryptophan.* Because of its association with an outbreak of eosinophilia heyalgia syndrome (EMS), FDA announced that L-tryptophan was unsafe except when used as part of a balanced protein product. *See* HHS Press Release P89–49 (Nov. 17, 1989); "Update on L-Tryptophan," FDA Talk Paper No. T89–76 (Dec. 5, 1989); "Answers on the L–Tryptophan Recall and Warning," FDA Talk Paper No. T90–16 (Mar. 29, 1990); "L–Tryptophan Update: Company Link Suggested," FDA Talk Paper No. T90–18 (Apr. 26, 1990). *See also* "FDA's Regulation of the Dietary Supplement L–Tryptophan," Hearing before the Human Resources and Intergovernmental Relations Subcommittee of the House Committee on Government Operations, 102d Cong., 1st Sess. (1991). The cause of the EMS outbreak has never been determined, and L-tryptophan has returned to use in dietary supplements.

4. *Adverse Event Reporting.* In late 2006, Congress enacted the Dietary Supplement and Nonprescription Drug Consumer Protection Act, 120 Stat. 3469, which added sections 760 and 761 to the FD&C Act to require serious adverse event reporting to FDA for both dietary supplements and nonprescription drugs. The law provides that such a report does not constitute an admission that the product caused the adverse event, and it preempts any non-identical state law.

COMMENT: FDA REGULATION OF VITAMINS A AND D

Vitamins A and D (as well as vitamins E and K) are fat soluble and stored in the body. Because high dosages of A and D have been heavily promoted for disease prevention, for many years FDA has been concerned about their indiscriminate use. Both vitamins were included by FDA in the original list of generally recognized as safe (GRAS) food substances under the Food Additives Amendment of 1958. 24 Fed. Reg. 9368 (Nov. 20, 1959). FDA first proposed to restrict use of vitamin D as a food additive because of concern about its toxicity in 30 Fed. Reg. 11140 (Aug. 28, 1965). This proposal was later withdrawn. 33 Fed. Reg. 9783 (July 6, 1968). A few years later, based upon "widespread promotion to the laity of excessive quantities of [vitamin A and vitamin D] for prophylaxis and treatment of a variety of diseases and disorders," the agency promulgated regulations ruling that vitamin A in excess of 10,000 international units (IU) and vitamin D in excess of 400 IU per day would be restricted to prescription sale only. 37 Fed. Reg. 26618 (Dec. 14, 1972), 38 Fed. Reg. 20723 (Aug. 2, 1973). A preliminary injunction to enjoin these regulations from becoming effective was denied in *National Nutritional Foods Ass'n v. Weinberger*, 366 F. Supp. 1341 (S.D.N.Y.), *aff'd*, 491 F.2d 845 (2d Cir. 1973). The regulations were initially upheld on their merits by the District Court, but then remanded to the agency by the Court of Appeals in order to develop a more complete administrative record of the Commissioner's decision to classify vitamins A and D at the specified levels as drugs. 376 F. Supp. 142 (S.D.N.Y. 1974); 512 F.2d 688 (2d Cir. 1975). The same court, the Court of Appeals for the Second Circuit, had previously invalidated FDA's attempt to classify as a drug any product providing more than 150 percent of the upper limit of the U.S. RDA for any nutrient. *National Nutritional Foods Ass'n v. FDA, supra* p. 254.

On remand, FDA supplemented the administrative record with an affidavit documenting the decision to classify high levels of vitamin A and vitamin D as drugs. Although the District Court once more upheld the regulations, 418 F. Supp. 394 (S.D.N.Y. 1976), the Court of Appeals held the regulations invalid because FDA had failed to demonstrate an "objective intent" that high levels of vitamins A and D were intended for use as therapeutic (drug) rather than nutritional (food) purposes. *National Nutritional Foods Association v. Mathews*, 557 F.2d 325 (2d Cir. 1977), *supra* p. 42. Following this decision, FDA revoked the regulations in 43 Fed. Reg. 10551 (Mar. 14, 1978). Since then, FDA has affirmed the GRAS status of vitamin A and vitamin D for purposes of food fortification. 21 C.F.R. 184.1930, 184.1950. Both vitamins were once listed as GRAS for dietary supplement use, but these listings were deleted in 61 Fed. Reg. 27771 (June 3, 1996).

4.   THE DIETARY SUPPLEMENT HEALTH AND EDUCATION ACT OF 1994

Following the judicial rejection of FDA's 1973 vitamin-mineral regulations and the subsequent congressional rejection of restrictive vitamin-mineral regulation in the Vitamin–Mineral Amendments of 1976, FDA revoked those regulations in 43 Fed. Reg. 10551 (Mar. 14, 1978). For the next decade, FDA took relatively little regulatory action that focused on dietary supplements. When the agency began to implement the Nutrition Labeling and Education Act of 1990, however, it saw an opportunity to revive to its earlier strategy of tightening the regulatory controls over dietary supplements. This strategy backfired, and resulted in a second congressional rejection of its approach.

Peter Barton Hutt, *U.S. Government Regulation of Food With Claims For Special Physiological Value*

In Mary K. Schmidl and Theodore P. Labuza, eds., ESSENTIALS OF FUNCTIONAL FOODS, Ch. 16 (2000).

. . . When FDA promulgated its regulations implementing the provision authorizing disease prevention claims under the Nutrition Labeling Education Act of 1990, the agency ignored a congressional invitation to establish separate standards and requirements for dietary supplements, instead using the new statutory authority to deny all such claims for this category of food products, and threatening to impose stringent food additive requirements on important dietary supplement ingredients. The dietary supplement industry again displayed its formidable political power and obtained enactment of the Dietary Supplement Health and Education Act of 1994 over the strong objection of FDA. The 1994 Act was an even more overwhelming and humiliating defeat for FDA than the Vitamin–Mineral Amendments of 1976. The 1994 Act broadly defined dietary supplements; explicitly authorized structure-function claims and related nutritional support claims for dietary supplements; exempted the dietary ingredients in dietary supplement products from the food additive requirements of the FD&C Act and substituted more flexible food safety provisions that place the burden on FDA to demonstrate the lack of safety; and exempted literature reprints from the labeling provisions of the FD&C Act, thereby establishing substantial limitations on FDA authority over dietary supplements. . . .

———

The Dietary Supplement Health and Education Act (DSHEA) established a new product category called "dietary supplement" and declared that, for most purposes, "a dietary supplement shall be deemed to be a food within the meaning of this Act." FD&C Act 201(ff). There are two especially important things to note about the regulation of dietary supplements under the Act as amended by DSHEA. First, new section 201(s)(6) of the Act specifically excludes dietary supplement ingredients from the definition of "food additive," thus releasing them from the requirement of premarket approval under the food additive provisions of the Act.

Second, the Act now specifically categorizes all dietary supplements as "food" and excludes supplements that make structure/function claims (subject to certain conditions) from the definition of "drug." FD&C Act 201(ff); 201(g)(1)(D). As discussed above, the drug definition excludes common sense foods making structure/function claims. *See Nutrilab v. Schweiker, supra* p. 30. Therefore, vitamins and minerals, which are consumed primarily for their nutritive value, have always been permitted to make such claims. By contrast, before DSHEA, supplements that were not common sense foods, such as botanicals, were drugs if they made structure/function claims. DSHEA added section 403(r)(6), which allows dietary supplement manufacturers to make statements that, among other things, "describe[] the role of a nutrient or dietary ingredient intended to affect the structure or function in humans, [or] characterize[] the documented mechanism by which a nutrient or dietary ingredient acts to maintain such structure or function...." FDCA § 403(r)(6). DSHEA also amended the FDCA to exclude supplements making such statements from the definition of drug. FDCA § 201(g)(1). Consequently, today, all dietary supplements, even those that do not satisfy the common sense definition of food, can make structure/function claims without being subject to the premarket approval requirements for new drugs. It is important to note, however, that structure/function claims for dietary supplements, unlike those for conventional foods, are governed by section 403(r)(6), which requires the manufacturer to have substantiation for the claim and to include the following disclaimer: "This statement has not been evaluated by the Food and Drug Administration. This product is not intended to diagnose, treat, cure, or prevent any disease."

Because of the two aspects of DSHEA discussed above, the question of what products are properly categorized as dietary supplements has profound regulatory implications. Section 201(ff) of the FDCA defines "dietary supplement" as follows:

The term "dietary supplement"—

(1) means a product (other than tobacco) intended to supplement the diet that bears or contains one or more of the following dietary ingredients:

(A) a vitamin;

(B) a mineral;

(C) an herb or other botanical;

(D) an amino acid;

(E) a dietary substance for use by man to supplement the diet by increasing the total dietary intake; or

(F) a concentrate; metabolite, constituent, extract, or combination of any ingredient described in clause (A), (B), (C), (D), or (E);

(2) means a product that—

(A)(i) is intended for ingestion in a form described in section 411(c)(1)(B)(i) of this title; or

(ii) complies with section 411(c)(1)(B)(ii) of this title;

(B) is not represented for use as a conventional food or as a sole item of a meal or the diet; and

(C) is labeled as a dietary supplement ...

Section 411(c)(1)(B), mentioned within the definition, refers to a product "which (i) is intended for ingestion in tablet, capsule, powder, softgel, gelcap, or liquid form, or (ii) if not intended for ingestion in such a form, is not represented as conventional food and is not represented for use as a sole item of a meal or of the diet."

NOTES

1. *Scope of Definition.* The very broad definition of a dietary ingredient in section 201(ff)(1) encompasses not only vitamins, minerals, and amino acids, but also botanicals and any natural or synthetic "dietary substance for use by man to supplement the diet by increasing the total dietary intake." FDA has suggested that this may be limited to natural substances commonly used as human food or drink, but this narrow interpretation would exclude many traditional dietary ingredients and is not supported by the statutory language or the legislative history. *See* 136 CONG. REC. 33427–33428 (Oct. 24, 1990); Robert G. Pinco & Paul D. Rubin, *Ambiguities of the Dietary Supplement Health and Education Act of 1994*, 51 FOOD DRUG COSM. L. J. 383 (1996); Citizen Petition FDA Docket No. 2004P–0169 (Apr. 8, 2004).

2. *Examples of FDA Interpretations.* FDA has in some instances taken a narrow interpretation of section 201(ff)(1)(E) ("a dietary substance for use by man to supplement the diet by increasing the total dietary intake"). For example, the agency denied that products containing freeze-dried bacteria and bacterial lysates are dietary supplements. In a letter to one manufacturer, FDA stated: "These ingredients in your product . . . are not 'dietary substances' that increase the 'total dietary intake' because they cannot reasonably be viewed as part of man's usual food or drink. The substances in your product are composed of pathogenic organisms. Pathogens are not substances that are food or that are used for food." Letter from Lynn A. Larsen, Director, CFSAN Office of Special Nutritionals, Division of Programs and Enforcement Policy, to David Balzer (Nov. 15, 1999). On the other hand, FDA has concluded that fungi, algae, and plant enzymes are botanicals and that fish oil and enzymes derived from bacteria are dietary ingredients. The agency has declined opportunities to declare that melatonin—a hormone produced in the pineal gland—is not a dietary ingredient. Letter from Lynn A. Larson to R. Doug Metz (Oct. 1, 1999) (denying that the company's melatonin product was a dietary supplement, but only because it was not "intended for ingestion"). FDA has also allowed non-botanical enzymes to be marketed as dietary supplements. Letter from James Tanner, Acting Director, CFSAN Office of Special Nutritionals, Division of Programs and Enforcement Policy, to Vic Rathi (July 30, 1996) (accepting the company's position that Enzyme–Peptidase, an enzyme derived from bacteria, is a dietary supplement ingredient.)

3. *Metabolites.* It is not clear when a substance can properly be designated a "metabolite" of another dietary ingredient. An entire open meeting of the Dietary Supplements Subcommittee of FDA's Food Advisory Committee was devoted to this complex scientific question. *See* Summary Minutes, Meeting of the Dietary Supplements Subcommittee (Mar. 25, 2003).

4. *"Intended to Supplement the Diet".* FDA has stated that products marketed as alternatives to illicit street drugs are not dietary supplements, even if they are composed of botanicals, vitamins, minerals, or amino acids. In a guidance on the topic, the agency declared:

> FDA does not consider street drug alternatives to be dietary supplements. The term *dietary supplement* as defined in section 201(ff) of the Act means, inter alia, a product "intended to supplement the diet." While the Act does not elaborate on the meaning of this phrase, many congressional findings, set forth in the Dietary Supplement Health and Education Act of 1994, suggest that dietary supplements are intended to be used to augment the diet to promote health and reduce the risk of disease. FDA does not believe that street drug alternatives are intended to be used to augment the diet to promote health or reduce the risk of disease. Moreover, FDA considers the diet to be composed of usual food and drink that may be designed to meet

specific nutritional requirements. Illicit street drugs are not food or drink, and neither they, nor alternative street drugs, can be said to supplement the diet. Rather, these products are intended to be used for recreational purposes to effect psychological states (*e.g.*, to get high, to promote euphoria, or to induce hallucinations). Accordingly, street drug alternatives are not intended to supplement the diet and are not dietary supplements.

FDA CENTER FOR DRUG EVALUATION AND RESEARCH, GUIDANCE FOR INDUSTRY: STREET DRUG ALTERNATIVES (Mar. 2000). *See also* "FDA Warns Manufacturers About Illegal Steroid Products Sold as Dietary Supplements," FDA News No. P06–37 (Mar. 9, 2006).

5. *Method of Administration*. In *United States v. Ten Cartons ... Ener–B Nasal Gel*, the District Court found that Ener–B, a Vitamin B–12 gel designed to be applied to the inside of the nose and absorbed into the bloodstream, was a drug and not a dietary supplement because it was not "intended for ingestion," as required by section 201(ff)(2)(A). 888 F. Supp. 381, 395 (E.D.N.Y. 1995). The court remarked that the "ordinary and plain meaning of the term 'ingestion' means to take into the stomach and gastrointestinal tract by means of enteral administration." The Court of Appeals in *Enter–B* did not reach the method of intake question, because it determined that under the last sentence of 201(ff), a dietary supplement may also be a drug. 72 F.3d 285 (2d Cir. 1995). Citing the District Court opinion in *Ten Cartons*, FDA later denied dietary supplement status to a melatonin product in the form of "a sublingual lozenge (to be placed under the tongue) for rapid absorption" and to an herbal throat drop. Letters from Lynn A. Larson, Director, FDA CFSAN Office of Special Nutritionals Division of Programs and Enforcement Policy, to R. Doug Metz (Oct. 1, 1999) and to Bryan J. Simmons (Nov. 4, 1999). In each instance, the agency explained that the product in question was not a dietary supplement because it was intended to deliver its contents prior to introduction into the gastrointestinal tract. Similarly, a skin cream does not qualify as a dietary supplement because it is not ingested. *United States v. Lane Labs–USA, Inc.*, 324 F. Supp. 2d 547, 569 (D.N.J. 2004).

6. *Use of Previously Designated Drugs*. Section 201(ff)(3)(B) excludes from the definition of a dietary supplement a drug that was the subject of an IND, NDA or BLA prior to its marketing as a dietary supplement. Thus, red rice yeast—which has the same active ingredient, lovastatin, as the prescription drug Mevacor—was held to be a drug and not a dietary supplement. *Pharmanex, Inc. v. Shalala*, 221 F.3d 1151 (10th Cir. 2000), *rev'g* 35 F. Supp. 2d 1341 (D. Utah 1999). Following the decision in the Court of Appeals, FDA determined that the remaining inventory of the product could not be exported because Pharmanex had not shown that it was intended for export and not offered for sale in domestic commerce. Letter from Kevin M. Fain, FDA Associate Chief Counsel for Enforcement, to Daniel A. Kracov (Sept. 10, 2001). On the authority of 201(ff)(3)(B), FDA took the position that nicotine, which is found naturally in various foods, is not a dietary ingredient because it has been the subject of an NDA for investigation as a new drug beginning in 1987, before it was added to food or dietary supplements. Letter from Vasilios H. Frankos, Acting Director, CFSAN Office of Nutritional Products, Labeling and Dietary Supplements Division of Dietary Supplement Programs, to Joseph R. Knight (June 29, 2006). Following the *Pharmanex* decision, pharmaceutical companies have requested FDA to take action against other dietary ingredients used in dietary supplements on the ground that they were the subject of an investigational new drug (IND) application or a new drug application (NDA) prior to use in a dietary supplement. *E.g.*, Citizen Petition FDA Docket No. 2005P–0305 (July 29, 2005) (pyridoxamine).

7. *Combination of Drug and Dietary Supplement.* The legislative history of the 1938 Act makes it clear that a product can fall within more than one statutory category, depending on the claims made for it. *See* Senate Rep. No. 361, 74th Cong. 1st Sess. 4 (1935). Many marketed products are combination cosmetic-drugs or drug-devices. Accordingly, a combination dietary supplement-nonprescription drug is also lawful. In a letter from Melinda K. Plaisier, FDA Associate Commissioner for Legislation, to Representative Dan Burton, Chairman of the House Committee on Government Reform (Feb. 1, 2002), FDA took the position that a combination product containing a dietary supplement and an over-the-counter drug would be illegal because the added dietary ingredient becomes a drug ingredient. This position directly conflicts with the FDA position that the addition of a cosmetic ingredient to an OTC drug does not convert the cosmetic ingredient into a drug. FDA has sent warning letters stating its position but has taken no court enforcement action to implement it.

8. *Exemption from Labeling.* DSHEA added section 403B(a) to the FD&C Act to exempt from FDA regulation as labeling for a dietary supplement a "publication, including an article, a chapter in a book, or an official abstract of a peer-reviewed scientific publication that appears in an article and was prepared by the author or the editors of the publication, which is reprinted in its entirety," subject to five qualifications. Although this is often referred to as the "third party" literature exemption, in fact section 403B(a) does not require that the publication be prepared by an independent person who has no economic interest in the dietary supplement. For a case where the defendant was unsuccessful in its attempt to invoke this exemption, see *United States v. Lane Labs–USA, Inc.*, 324 F. Supp. 2d 547, 568 (D.N.J. 2004). Because health food stores often sell books and other publications that do not accompany the dietary supplements in the store and thus are not labeling even absent the Section 403B(a) exemption, section 403B(b) was added to make certain that section 403B(a) has no application to those materials.

9. *FDA's Strategic Plan.* Six years after enactment of DSHEA, FDA published a broad strategic plan for implementing the statute. 64 Fed. Reg. 32880 (June 18, 1999). *See* Joseph A. Levitt, *Regulation of Dietary Supplements: FDA's Strategic Plan*, 57 FOOD & DRUG L.J. 1 (2002). In response to the House Appropriations Committee Report for FY 2001, FDA submitted cost estimates for implementing the 10–year strategic plan. Lester M. Crawford, *Dietary Supplement Strategic Plan Cost Out, Report to Congress* (May 28, 2002).

10. *FDA Nonenforcement.* From 1994 to 2002 FDA did not enforce DSHEA, hoping that the resulting proliferation of illegal claims would convince Congress to repeal the statute. FDA Commissioner Mark McClellan reversed this strategy in 2002 and began to enforce the requirements of the 1994 Act.

11. *FTC Enforcement.* During the eight years that FDA did not enforce the 1994 statute, the Federal Trade Commission and the National Advertising Division of the Better Business Bureau stepped into the breach. *See, e.g.,* C. Lee Peeler & Susan Cohn, *The Federal Trade Commission's Regulation of Advertising Claims for Dietary Supplements*, 50 FOOD DRUG COSM. L.J. 349 (1995); Robert G. Pinco and Todd H. Halpern, *Guidelines for the Promotion of Dietary Supplements: Examining Government Regulation Five Years After Enactment of the Dietary Supplement Health and Education Act of 1994*, 54 FOOD & DRUG L.J. 567 (1999); FTC, DIETARY SUPPLEMENTS ADVERTISING GUIDE FOR INDUSTRY (1998).

12. *Commentary.* For further commentary, see the articles in Chapter V(E) of the Electronic Book.

As enacted, the Nutrition Labeling and Education Act of 1990 made no mandatory distinction in section 403(q) of the FD&C Act between the nutrition labeling required for conventional food and for dietary supplements, but it included in section 403(q)(5)(E) of the FD&C Act (later redesignated as Section 403(q)(5)(F)) discretionary authority to provide different nutrition labeling requirements for dietary supplements. When FDA ignored this discretionary authority and proposed nutrition labeling regulations for dietary supplements in 56 Fed. Reg. 60366, 60381 (Nov. 27, 1991) that were regarded as too close to those for conventional food and unduly restrictive for dietary supplements, Congress enacted the Dietary Supplement Act of 1992, 106 Stat 4491, 4500, to overrule the agency, require a new rulemaking proceeding, and grant an additional one year for compliance. After this congressional rebuke, FDA promulgated final nutritional labeling regulations for dietary supplements that were not significantly different from its November 1991 proposal. 58 Fed. Reg. 33690 (June

Supplement Facts

Serving Size 1 Packet
Servings Per Container 10

Amount Per Serving	AM Packet		PM Packet	
		% Daily Value		% Daily Value
Vitamin A	2500 IU	50%	2500 IU	50%
Vitamin C	60 mg	100%	60 mg	100%
Vitamin D	400 IU	100%		
Vitamin E	30 IU	100%		
Thiamin	1.5 mg	100%	1.5 mg	100%
Riboflavin	1.7 mg	100%	1.7 mg	100%
Niacin	20 mg	100%	20 mg	100%
Vitamin B₆	2.0 mg	100%	2.0 mg	100%
Folic Acid	200 mcg	50%	200 mcg	50%
Vitamin B₁₂	3 mcg	50%	3 mcg	50%
Biotin			30 mcg	10%
Pantothenic Acid	5 mg	50%	5 mg	50%

Ingredients: Sodium ascorbate, ascorbic acid, calcium pantothenate, niacinamide, di-alpha tocopheryl acetate, microcrystalline cellulose, artificial flavors, dextrin, starch, mono- and diglycerides, vitamin A acetate, magnesium stearate, gelatin, FD&C Blue #1, FD&C Red #3, artificial colors, thiamin mononitrate, pyridoxine hydrochloride, citric acid, lactose, sorbic acid, tricalcium phosphate, sodium benzoate, sodium caseinate, methylparaben, potassium sorbate, BHA, BHT, ergocalciferol and cyanocobalamin.

Supplement Facts

Serving Size 1 Packet

Amount Per Packet		% Daily Value	Amount Per Packet		% Daily Value
Vitamin A (from cod liver oil)	5,000 IU	100%	Zinc (as zinc oxide)	15 mg	100%
Vitamin C (as ascorbic acid)	250 mg	417%	Selenium (as sodium selenate)	25 mcg	36%
Vitamin D (as ergocalciferol)	400 IU	100%	Copper (as cupric oxide)	1 mg	50%
Vitamin E (as d-alpha tocopherol)	150 IU	500%	Manganese (as manganese sulfate)	5 mg	250%
Thiamin (as thiamin mononitrate)	75 mg	5000%	Chromium (as chromium chloride)	50 mcg	42%
Riboflavin	75 mg	4412%	Molybdenum (as sodium molybdate)	50 mcg	67%
Niacin (as niacinamide)	75 mg	375%	Potassium (as potassium chloride)	10 mg	< 1%
Vitamin B₆ (as pyridoxine hydrochloride)	75 mg	3750%			
Folic Acid	400 mcg	100%	Choline (as choline chloride)	100 mg	*
Vitamin B₁₂ (as cyanocobalamin)	100 mcg	1667%	Betaine (as betaine hydrochloride)	25 mg	*
Biotin	100 mcg	33%	Glutamic Acid (as L-glutamic acid)	25 mg	*
Pantothenic Acid (as calcium pantothenate)	75 mg	750%	Inositol (as inositol monophosphate)	75 mg	*
Calcium (from oystershell)	100 mg	10%	para-Aminobenzoic acid	30 mg	*
Iron (as ferrous fumarate)	10 mg	56%	Deoxyribonucleic acid	50 mg	*
Iodine (from kelp)	150 mcg	100%	Boron	500 mcg	*
Magnesium (as magnesium oxide)	60 mg	15%			

* Daily Value not established

Other ingredients: Cellulose, stearic acid and silica.

18, 1993), 59 Fed. Reg. 350, 354 (Jan. 4, 1994). Congress therefore over-ruled the agency a second time by including in the Dietary Supplement Health and Education Act of 1994 an amendment to Section 403(q)(5)(F) of the FD&C Act to require FDA to establish different nutrition labeling requirements for dietary supplements. FDA implemented this provision in 60 Fed. Reg. 67194 (Dec. 28, 1995), 62 Fed. Reg. 49826 (Sept. 23, 1996), 21 C.F.R. 101.36. Examples of the final form of dietary supplement nutrition labeling are found on the preceding page. The regulations require a larger type size than appears in these examples. 21 C.F.R. 101.36(e)(4).

NOTES

1. *Dietary Supplement/Conventional Food Distinction*. A product may be represented as either a dietary supplement or a conventional food depending on the labeling. A dietary supplement must be designated as such on the principal display panel and bear a Supplement Facts box. A conventional food bears a Nutrition Facts box.

2. *Form of Dietary Supplement*. Section 411(c)(1)(B)(ii) of the FD&C Act was added by the Vitamin–Mineral Amendments of 1976 to exclude dietary supplements that "simulated" or were "represented" as conventional food. The Dietary Supplement Health and Education Act deleted the "simulated" exclusion but retained the "represented" exclusion. In 1997, FDA stated that dietary supplements may be similar to conventional foods in composition and form, noting that cranberry juice cocktail may be marketed as either a conventional food or a dietary supplement. 60 Fed. Reg. 67194, 67196 (Dec. 28, 1995), 62 Fed. Reg. 49826, 49937, 49860 (Sept. 23, 1997). Subsequently, however, FDA issued warning letters asserting that use of a conventional food form—except perhaps for bars and drinks—constitutes an inherent representation that the product is a conventional food. In a 1998 letter, FDA took the position that describing a dietary supplement as a "chewing gum" would require that it be labeled as a conventional food rather than as a dietary supplement, but if the product were described as a dietary ingredient in a chewing gum base it could be marketed as a dietary supplement. Letter from James T. Tanner, Acting Director, FDA CFSAN Office of Special Nutritionals Division of Programs and Enforcement Policy, to John P. Vernardos (June 28, 1998). Similarly, FDA has objected to the use of stevia as a sugar substitute but not as a dietary ingredient. *See* Warning Letter from Tyler H. Thornberg, Acting Director, FDA Denver District Office, to D. Gary Young (Apr. 26, 2002).

3. *Benecol*. After McNeil informed FDA that it intended to market Benecol, a margarine-like spread containing plant stanol esters and labeled for use in maintaining cholesterol at a healthy level, as a dietary supplement, FDA cautioned the company not to do so. In a letter to McNeil, FDA stated: "The [prototype] label for the Benecol spread, through statements that the product replaces butter or margarine, vignettes picturing the product in common butter or margarine uses, statements promoting the flavor and texture of the product, and statements such as '. . . help(s) you manage your cholesterol naturally through foods you eat,' represents this product for use as a conventional food. Therefore, the product is not a dietary supplement." Letter from Joseph A. Levitt, Director, CFSAN, FDA, to Brian D. Perkins (Oct. 28, 1998). McNeil strongly disagreed with FDA but chose not to contest the matter. Today, McNeil markets Benecol as a conventional food with an approved disease claim.

4. *Herbs in Food*. FDA has objected to the use of herbs as dietary ingredients or even as conventional food ingredients in common food products. It has issued warning letters against such products but has not taken court enforcement action. *E.g.*, Letter from John B. Foret, Director, CFSAN Office of Food Labeling Division of Programs and Enforcement Policy, to Myron Cooper (June 21, 1999) (soups containing St. John's Wort and echinicea); Warning Letter from Charles M. Breen,

Director, FDA Seattle District Office, to Jerry L. Smith (Jan. 14, 2004) (herbal tea) and to Judd A. Pindell (Dec. 3, 2004) (juices containing herbs).

5. *Congressional Oversight. See* "Dietary Supplement Health and Education Act: Is FDA Trying to Change the Intent of Congress?," Hearing before the House Committee on Government Reform, 106th Cong., 1st Sess. (1999); "When Diets Turn Deadly: Consumer Safety and Weight Loss Supplements," Hearing before the Oversight of Government Management, Restructuring, and the District of Columbia Subcommittee of the Senate Committee on Governmental Affairs, 107th Cong., 2d Sess. (2002); "Diet, Physical Activity, Dietary Supplements, Lifestyle and Health," Hearing before the House Committee on Government Reform, 107th Cong., 2d Sess. (2002); "10 Years After the Implementation of DSHEA: The Status of Dietary Supplements in the United States" and "Dietary Supplements: Nature's Answer to Cost Effective Preventative Medicine," Hearings before the Subcommittee on Human Rights and Wellness of the House Committee on Government Reform, 108th Cong., 2d Sess. (2004).

G.   REGULATION OF STRUCTURE/FUNCTION AND DISEASE CLAIMS FOR FOOD AND DIETARY SUPPLEMENTS

1.   BACKGROUND

Since 1938, a major FDA enforcement priority has been to prevent false or misleading nutrition claims in food labeling. As illustrated at p. 249 *infra*, a key component of the agency's strategy has been to classify disease prevention claims as drug claims, thus permitting summary disposition of enforcement actions based on expert affidavits that the challenged product is not "generally recognized" as safe and effective and thus is an unapproved new drug. Where a manufacturer makes no explicit disease prevention claim, however, this gambit often does not work. And as the evidence of the important relationships between diet and disease has mounted, the agency has had to reconsider even its traditional ban on specific disease prevention claims for food.

Peter Barton Hutt, *Government Regulation of Health Claims in Food Labeling and Advertising*

41 FOOD DRUG COSMETIC LAW JOURNAL 3 (1986).

. . . In February 1964, President Johnson announced the formation of a Commission on Heart Disease, Cancer, and Stroke with the mission of recommending "steps to reduce the incidence of these diseases through new knowledge and more complete utilization of the medical knowledge we already have." Ten months later, the Commission issued its report, recommending major new research on these three diseases. The source paper on atherosclerosis stated that "diet, particularly the amount and kind of fat in it, is considered to have a major influence on atherogenesis." It noted that research suggested that "modification of the American diet can be an effective way to reduce the incidence of coronary heart disease."

Following the report of the Commission, further research and study on the relation of diet to health was stimulated throughout the country. The results became apparent with publication of the first edition of "Dietary Goals for the United States" by the Senate Select Committee on Nutrition and Human Needs in February 1977. Similar reports immediately followed:

— The Second Edition of the Senate Committee's Dietary Goals.

— The Report of the DHEW Task Force on Prevention.

— Recommendations for a Prudent Diet by the American Health Foundation.

— The DHEW Surgeon General's Report on "Healthy People."

— The DHEW Conference on Objectives for the Nation in Promoting Health and Preventing Disease.

— The National Cancer Institute's Statement on Diet, Nutrition and Cancer.

— The American Medical Association's Concepts of Nutrition and Health.

— The Department of Agriculture's (USDA) Hassle–Free Guide to a Better Diet.

— The Consensus Papers of the American Society for Clinical Nutrition.

— The Joint USDA/DHEW Dietary Guidelines for Americans.

— The National Academy of Sciences (NAS) Food and Nutrition Board's Report on Healthful Diets.

These reports in turn fostered a deeper interest in federal research on diet and health and nutrition education. The Comptroller General of the United States, through the General Accounting Office (GAO), strongly urged federal agencies to adopt and implement a coordinated national nutrition policy.

. . . This information on the relationship between diet and health had an impact on Congress as well as FDA. In 1976, Congress enacted the National Consumer Health Information and Health Promotion Act. Under this statute, the Secretary of Health and Human Services (HHS) was required to implement a wide variety of programs designed to prevent disease and promote health. Education relating to nutrition was explicitly included. In 1984, Congress established an Office of Disease Prevention and Health Promotion in the Office of the HHS Assistant Secretary for Health, to implement these requirements.

In 1978, as part of the Biomedical Research and Research Training Amendments, Congress added section 301(b)(3) to the Public Health Service Act to require research and studies on the role of human nutrition in the prevention and treatment of disease. . . .

The Assistant Secretary for Health had already delegated to FDA all functions under section 301 of the Public Health Service Act which relate to the functions of FDA, and thus FDA was equally responsible for carrying out the provisions of this statute. As part of the Health Services and Centers Amendments of 1978, Congress also required the Secretary of Health and Human Services to submit to Congress every three years a "national disease prevention data profile" which must include "the behavioral determinants of health of the population of the United States including . . . nutritional and dietary habits."

Beginning in 1946, Congress has also enacted a wide variety of statutory provisions relating to the use of food to prevent or treat disease, as part of the National School Lunch Act of 1946 and the Child Nutrition Act of 1966. Pursuant to these statutory provisions, USDA administered six major food programs, one of which (the Child Nutrition Program) includes six substantial programs. Each of these embodied a congressional determination of the importance of sound nutrition to good health. The Nutrition Education and Training Program, however, is of particular importance to the matter of health claims for food.

In 1975, Congress amended the Child Nutrition Act to authorize and direct "projects to teach schoolchildren the nutritional value of foods and the relationship of nutrition to human health." As part of the National School Lunch Act and Child Nutrition Amendments of 1977, Congress enacted a broad program for nutrition education and training. This statute established a program of nutrition education for school children, school food service personnel, parents, and teachers. The law broadly authorized education about "the relationship between food, nutrition, and health." The program was specifically defined to include information to allow individuals to "maximize their well-being through food consumption practices" and to understand "the relationship between food and human health."

That same year, as part of the Food and Agriculture Act of 1977, Congress established a national food and human nutrition research program in USDA. Congress found that:

> [T]here is increasing evidence of a relationship between diet and many of the leading causes of death in the United States; that improved nutrition is an integral component of preventive health care; that there is a serious need for research on the chronic effects of diet on degenerative diseases and related disorders.

COMMENT: FDA TERMINOLOGY REGARDING THE RELATION OF DIET TO DISEASE AND HEALTH

In its Federal Register notices published since 1987 on claims about the relation of diet to disease and health, FDA has used inconsistent and conflicting terminology that does not conform to the statutory language and congressional intent. As a result, even the agency often has difficulty articulating or understanding its policy in this area.

In its first recognition that disease claims could properly be used for food products, FDA used the terms "health messages" and "health claims" interchangeably and never once admitted that they were in fact disease claims. 52 Fed. Reg. 28843 (Aug. 4, 1987). FDA's reluctance to admit that the agency was permitting disease claims was undoubtedly because it had banned all disease claims from food labeling for the prior 80 years. By failing to address the matter directly, FDA set an unfortunate pattern that continues to plague the agency to this day.

When Congress addressed the matter in the NLEA of 1990, in contrast, it did so in plain English. Section 403(r)(1)(B) of the FD&C Act authorizes claims relating a nutrient to "a disease or health-related condition." It is only because Congress recognized them as disease claims that section 201(g)(1) had to be amended to exclude them from the definition of a drug. Rather than designate these as "disease claims," however, in its regulations FDA adhered to its terminology of "health claims." 21 C.F.R. 101.14 & 101.70 et seq. In the preamble to those regulations, FDA also introduced a new category of claims termed "dietary guidance," which the FDA characterized as general health messages. 58 Fed. Reg. 2478, 2487 (Jan. 6, 1993).

When Congress again addressed this area in enacting DSHEA in 1994, it also used plain English. Section 403(r)(6) of the FD&C Act authorizes two relevant types of claims, characterized as "nutritional support claims," for dietary supplements: (1) general health claims and (2) structure/function claims. Neither falls within the disease claims category that requires FDA approval under NLEA.

In its Task Force Report and 67 Fed. Reg. 78002 (Dec. 20, 2002), FDA reverted to its August 1987 approach and used the terms "health claims" and "health messages" interchangeably. In its notice in 68 Fed. Reg. 66040, 66041 n.9 (Nov. 25, 2003), FDA attempted to reconcile this inconsistency, but failed to address the underlying confusion in terminology. And in the same notice, the agency characterized "dietary guidance" as originating from federal agencies "with public health missions related to diet and disease."

Faced with this continuing confusion in FDA terminology, we have concluded consistently to use the following terms throughout this chapter except where quotations force use to follow whatever FDA has written. First, the unqualified or qualified claims authorized by section 403(r)(1)(B) and the First Amendment are "disease claims" or "disease prevention claims." They require FDA premarket review. Second, claims that fall outside Section 403(r)(1)(B), such as those described by FDA as "dietary guidance" or those permitted by Congress in section 403(r)(6), are "general health claims" or, when appropriate, "structure/function claims." They do not require FDA premarket review.

Peter Barton Hutt, *Health Claims For Foods—An American Perspective*

Kellogg Nutrition Symposium, Toronto, Canada. (Apr. 1986).

For purposes of analysis, it is useful to differentiate among three separate types of health claims for food products: implicit health claims, general health claims, and explicit health claims. Implicit health claims are made whenever labeling refers to the nutrient content of a food, whether that content results from nutrients that are naturally present in the food or nutrients that are added through fortification. Nutrition labelling, in short, is an inherent health claim. General health claims can, and often are, made in a wide variety of ways. Statements that a food is nutritious, or good for you, or will promote health, are examples of general health claims frequently found in labelling and advertising. Explicit health claims, in contrast, have infrequently been found in food labelling and advertising until quite recently. Explicit health claims include statements that a food will help prevent specific diseases, such as heart disease and cancer.

... FDA has long approved implicit health claims for food products in the form of accurate information about the composition of food. Such information includes not just the ingredients, but specific information about the micronutrient and macronutrient content as well. Nor has FDA sought to prevent general health claims, that a food is nutritious or healthful. But for many years, FDA drew the line at explicit health claims....

The FDA prohibition against explicit health claims in food labeling meant that the United States public received its information on diet and health from other, usually more unreliable, sources.... Beginning in the 1960s, books with false and even harmful information about nutrition flooded the market. Misinformation was disseminated through every conceivable medium except the ones over which the government does in fact have control—food labelling and advertising. Only if a specific book was used as promotional material to sell a product did the government have jurisdiction to regulate the content of that book, and even then the precise contours of that regulatory authority remained uncertain in light of the constitutional right to a free press.

Thus, FDA was faced, in the early 1980s, with two choices. First, it could continue its prohibition against explicit health claims, and thus allow books, newspapers, television, and other media to remain the sole source of information to the United States public on diet and health. Second, it could modify that position, but retain regulatory control over the type of explicit health claims that could be made, and thus assure that at least some of the explicit health claims made to the United States public are reliable, accurate, and truthful.

As often occurs in this kind of situation, the decision was made for FDA, by outside forces, and not by FDA itself. Throughout the 1970s, the FTC had sided with FDA in its continuing opposition to explicit health claims. With the change of administration in the early 1980s, however, the FTC began to change its position on this matter. Convinced that truthful advertising is not only protected under the Constitution but also is genuinely beneficial to the public, the FTC concluded that explicit health claims for food should be permitted where they are in fact accurate and truthful.

The first test of this issue in the United States occurred when Kellogg began to promote its All–Bran Cereal product to reduce the risk of cancer, in October 1984. This claim, based upon authoritative reports issued in 1982 and 1984 by two of the most respected scientific organizations in the United States—the National Academy of Sciences and the National Cancer Institute—was neither false nor misleading. It was, in fact, specifically endorsed by the National Cancer Institute. Seizing the occasion, representatives of the FTC made numerous speeches, in the fall of 1984, endorsing this approach and encouraging a wide range of explicit health claims designed to educate the United States public about the relationship between diet and health. Faced with responsible claims, specific NCI endorsement, and then FTC encouragement, FDA could do nothing. The matter had been taken out of its hands.

In March 1985, FDA announced a new policy. No longer would it oppose all forms of explicit health claims for food. The Agency was prepared to permit such claims, for the first time, as part of the disease prevention programs of the United States Public Health Service. FDA recognized that food labeling could properly be used as a means of conveying health messages to the United States public, as long as the Agency's ability to regulate health fraud was not diminished or compromised.

To implement this new policy, FDA adopted four general enforcement principles. First, explicit health claims must be based upon a consensus of medical and scientific information. Second, explicit health claims must emphasize that good nutrition is a function of total diet. Third, the wording of explicit health claims should be reasonably uniform from product to product in order to make it more understandable and less confusing to consumers. Fourth, dietary "power races" should be prevented. Within these four principles, FDA said that it was prepared to allow explicit health claims. . . .

Food Labeling; Public Health Messages on Food Labels and Labeling

52 Fed. Reg. 28843 (August 4, 1987).

ACTION: Notice of Proposed Rulemaking. . . .

FDA believes that it is worthwhile to consider new ways to inform and educate the general public or target subpopulations concerning the relationship between diet and health. The agency believes that, if proper criteria are followed, it is possible to use the food label to communicate more explicit health-related information. The agency acknowledges that in the past, foods labeled with information of this type could have been viewed as subject to action under 21 CFR 101.9(i) and the new drug provisions of the act. The agency's current view is that appropriate health messages would not be inconsistent with either of these provisions. . . .

The agency's criteria for evaluating health-related claims and information on food labeling are as follows:

1.   Information on the labeling must be truthful and not misleading to the consumer. The information should not imply that a particular food be used as part of a drug-like treatment or therapy oriented approach to health care. Information on food labeling must not over emphasize or distort the role of a food in enhancing good health. The term "health" includes specific health problems, including disease.

2.   The information should be based on and be consistent with valid, reliable, scientific evidence that is publically [sic] available (prior to any health related claim being made), including data derived from clinical and other studies performed and evaluated by persons qualified by experience and training to evaluate such studies, and should conform to generally

recognized medical and nutritional principles. Preliminary findings should be confirmed. Conclusions supported by a less-than-clear data may prove in time to be correct, but are not appropriate for use on food labeling if they do not reflect the weight of scientific evidence. . . .

3. Available information regarding the relationship between nutrition and health shows that good nutrition is a function, not of specific foods, but of total diet over time. Appropriate information on food labeling should describe the role of a specific food or a specific ingredient in terms that are consistent with generally recognized medical and nutritional principles for a sound total dietary pattern. The dietary characteristics of the food must be consistent with the message being used.

4. The use of health-related information constitutes a nutritional claim that triggers the requirements of FDA's regulations regarding nutrition labeling. Therefore, any product bearing health-related information must comply with the nutrition labeling requirements found in 21 CFR 101.9. However, the use of health-related information in conformity with the agency's criteria will not be deemed misbranding within the meaning of 21 CFR 101.9(i) and will not be deemed to invoke the new drug provisions of the act.

Manufacturers may make health-related claims on food labels that conform to these guidelines without prior approval, with the understanding that, if a manufacturer fails to adhere to the criteria, the product and the manufacturer's activity may be subject to regulatory action. FDA welcomes discussions with any manufacturer who wishes to consult with the agency on health-related claims before making changes in existing labeling.

NOTES

1. *Authoritative Reports.* Authoritative statements on the relationship of diet to health and disease include HHS & USDA, DIETARY GUIDELINES FOR AMERICANS 2005 (6th ed. 2005); National Academy of Sciences, DIET AND HEALTH: IMPLICATIONS FOR REDUCING CHRONIC DISEASE RISK (1989); PHS, SURGEON GENERAL'S REPORT ON NUTRITION AND HEALTH, DHHS Pub. No. 88–50210 (1988); PHS, PROMOTING HEALTH/PREVENTING DISEASE: OBJECTIVES FOR THE NATION (1980); PHS, THE SURGEON GENERAL'S REPORT ON HEALTH PROMOTION AND DISEASE PREVENTION (1979). HHS sets national objectives for disease prevention and health promotion every decade. *See Health Objectives for the Nation*, 38 MORBIDITY AND MORTALITY WEEKLY REP. 629 (Sept. 22, 1989); HHS, HEALTHY PEOPLE 2010 (2000); HHS, HEALTHY PEOPLE 2000 (1990); *see also* 70 Fed. Reg. 47206 (Aug. 12, 2005) (midcourse review of HEALTHY PEOPLE 2010).

2. *Congressional Action.* Following hearings at which FDA explained its new policy, "FDA Proposals to Permit the Use of Disease–Specific Health Claims on Food Labels," Hearing before a Subcommittee of the House Committee on Government Operations, 100th Cong., 1st Sess. (1987), the Subcommittee issued a critical report, "Disease–Specific Health Claims on Food Labels: An Unhealthy Idea," H.R. REP. NO. 100–561, 100th Cong., 2d Sess. (1988).

3. *1990 Statute.* FDA reproposed its Aug. 1987 regulations in 55 Fed. Reg. 5176 (Feb. 13, 1990), but the new provisions of the 1990 Nutrition Labeling and Education Act, *supra* p. 209, required that they be reconsidered.

4. *State Law.* When Kellogg marketed its breakfast cereal HeartWise containing psyllium prior to enactment of the NLEA, the Texas Department of Health

detained packages on the ground that the product made drug claims and was therefore an illegal new drug. *Kellogg Co. v. Mattox*, 763 F. Supp. 1369 (N.D. Tex. 1991).

COMMENT: FTC REGULATION OF FOOD ADVERTISING

Section 5 of the Federal Trade Commission Act provides that "unfair or deceptive acts or practices in or affecting commerce, are declared unlawful." 15 U.S.C. 45 (2000), 38 Stat. 717 (1914). The Wheeler–Lea Amendments of 1938 added sections 14 and 15, which expressly prohibit any food advertisement, other than labeling, which is "misleading in a material respect." 52 Stat. 111 (1938). From its inception, the FTC regarded false or misleading labeling and advertising of food products as unfair acts or practices which violate section 5, and the courts have upheld that position. *E.g., Fresh Grown Preserve Corp. v. FTC*, 125 F.2d 917 (2d Cir. 1942), *FTC v. Good–Grape Co.*, 45 F.2d 70 (6th Cir. 1930); *Royal Baking Powder Co. v. FTC*, 281 F. 744 (2d Cir. 1922). For an overview of the FTC regulation of food advertising, see Peter Barton Hutt, *Government Regulation of Health Claims in Food Labeling and Advertising*, 41 FOOD DRUG COSM. L.J. 3, 9–20 (1986).

The FTC has issued three important policy statements describing the circumstances under which an advertising claim will be found to violate the FTC Act. In a letter to Congress in December 1980, reprinted in 104 F.T.C. 1070 (1984), the Commission stated that, to constitute an illegal "unfair act or practice," an advertisement must be evaluated to determine whether it results in substantial consumer injury, violates public policy, or constitutes unethical or unscrupulous conduct. In October 1983, in another letter to Congress, reprinted in 103 F.T.C. 174 (1984), the Commission stated that, in evaluating whether an advertisement violates the FTC Act, it will be examined "from the perspective of a consumer acting reasonably in the circumstances." And in a 1984 policy statement, reprinted in 104 F.T.C. 839 (1984), the Commission reaffirmed the requirement that advertisers must "have a reasonable basis for advertising claims before they are disseminated" and stated that "what constitutes a reasonable basis depends, as it does in an unfairness analysis, on a number of factors relevant to the benefits and costs of substantiating a particular claim." *See also* "FTC's Authority over Deceptive Advertising," Hearing before the Subcommittee for Consumers of the Senate Committee on Commerce, Science, and Transportation, 97th Cong., 2d Sess. (1982); "Deception: FTC Oversight," Hearing before the Subcommittee on Oversight and Investigations of the House Committee on Energy and Commerce, 98th Cong., 2d Sess. (1984); Roger E. Schechter, *The Death of the Gullible Consumer: Towards a More Sensible Definition of Deception at the FTC*, 1989 U. ILL. L. REV. 751.

Based upon these policies, the FTC encouraged what it regarded as nondeceptive disease prevention claims when they first appeared in food advertising in the mid–1980s. The preamble to FDA's reproposed regulations on disease prevention claims for food, 55 Fed. Reg. 5176, 5186 (Feb. 13, 1990), attempted to reconcile the obvious disparity between the flexible FTC "reasonable basis" standard for advertising claims and FDA's more stringent standard of scientific proof for labeling claims in the following terms.

> FDA is not convinced that [FTC's "reasonable basis"] standard is adequate for determining the appropriateness of claims on the food label. As several comments pointed out, it is important that consumers maintain confidence in the food label. Consumers view food labeling as more reliable and trustworthy than food advertising. The existence of this dichotomy in consumer perception of the information from these two sources is supported by the results of several surveys and confirmed by a number of experts in the area of advertising and communication.

> Food labeling has a high degree of acceptance among the general public. For example, when asked in a 1984 Roper Survey what sources of information about the nutritional content of food they thought most useful, labels on food packages were the most widely used source, mentioned by 57 percent of the public. Advertisements were considered the most useful source by only 4 percent. These results are essentially unchanged from a 1976 survey. Similarly, a 1980 FDA survey indicated that the perceived honesty/integrity/truthfulness of the food label is very high. Only 1 percent of respondents reported ever having bought a food product that was falsely labeled. In a 1981 survey about what FDA activities were most worthwhile, the two highest rated activities (tied for first) were "making sure food is safe to eat" and "making sure food labeling is honest."

Following enactment of the Nutrition Labeling and Education Act of 1990, the FTC published its *Enforcement Policy Statement on Food Advertising* in 59 Fed. Reg. 28388 (June 1, 1994) to emphasize that it would follow FDA's lead on nutrient descriptors and disease prevention claims for food. Some influence still runs in the opposite direction, however. FDA has adopted the FTC's "reasonable person" standard and has also raised the question whether the FTC "competent and reliable scientific evidence" standard should be used in evaluating disease claims. 67 Fed. Reg. 78002, 78003–04 (Dec. 20, 2002), 69 Fed. Reg. 64962 (Nov. 9, 2004).

In a letter from Mary K. Engle, Associate Director, FTC Advertising Practices, to Gary Ruskin (Feb. 10, 2005), the FTC stated that it did not intend to require disclosure that promotion of consumer products by placement in television programs is paid advertising.

2. STRUCTURE/FUNCTION CLAIMS

Peter Barton Hutt, *U.S. Government Regulation of Food With Claims for Special Physiological Value*

In Mary K. Schmidl and Theodore P. Labuza, eds., ESSENTIALS OF FUNCTIONAL FOODS, Ch. 16 (2000).

> ... The term *drug* is defined in basically two ways: an article intended to prevent or treat disease and an article (other than food) intended to

affect the structure or any function of the body. Quite clearly any explicit disease claim automatically classifies a food as a drug. Because of the statutory exclusion of food from the structure-function portion of the drug definition, however, structure-function claims may lawfully be made for a food without classifying the food as a drug.

For many years, FDA took the position that any structure-function claim was an implied drug claim that would render a food illegal. Although this position was declared "untenable" by a court in the starch blocker cases, the food industry is very conservative and thus generally has not pursued structure-function claims for conventional food products.

In the final regulations promulgated by FDA to implement the Nutrition Labeling and Education Act in January 1993, FDA made an initial step to bring the claims permitted for conventional food into conformity with the structure-function claims explicitly permitted for dietary supplements under the Dietary Supplement Health and Education Act. The agency stated that a structure-function claim would be permitted for a conventional food if there was no express or implied reference to any dysfunction of or damage to the body or any biological parameter that is a recognized risk factor for disease. Because this discussion in the preamble had no counterpart in the regulation itself and was written so obscurely, it had very little impact at the time.

In the preamble to the FDA regulations promulgated to implement the labeling requirements of the Dietary Supplement Health and Education Act of 1994, FDA explicitly abandoned the position that it had taken earlier in the starch blocker litigation. FDA stated that it was committed to as much parity between dietary supplements and conventional food as was possible within the statute. The agency concluded that a proper structure-function claim could be made for a conventional food, such as cranberry juice cocktail, without resulting in the product's being classified as a drug, whether the cranberry juice cocktail was marketed as a conventional food or as a dietary supplement. FDA pointed out that, because Congress changed the law explicitly to permit dietary supplements to be marketed in food form, it is up to the manufacturer of a product, through labeling statements, to determine whether the article is represented as a dietary supplement or as a conventional food. Regardless of which form is taken, the same structure-function claim can be made.

FDA did propose to limit structure-function claims for conventional food to those that directly relate to the nutritive value of the food. There is no statutory or other basis for such a limitation, however, and it is doubtful that this proposal is enforceable.

FDA published proposed regulations in April 1998 and promulgated final rules in January 2000 to distinguish between a permitted structure-function claim for conventional food and dietary supplements and an illegal disease claim. . . .

Finally, it should be noted that a conventional food—whether or not it is the subject of a structure-function claim—is fully subject to the food additive requirements of the FD&C Act. If the identical claim is made for the identical product labeled as a dietary supplement, on the other hand, any dietary ingredients in the dietary supplement will be exempt from the food additive requirement and will instead be subject to the more flexible safety provisions of the Dietary Supplement Health and Education Act of 1994. For some dietary ingredients, this distinction may be of substantial importance. On the other hand, although a dietary supplement must bear the statutory disclaimer discussed below* and must be the subject of a notification to FDA about any structure-function claim, these two requirements do not apply when structure-function claims are made for conventional food. For some products, this may also be a significant consideration . . .

NOTES

1. *Court Decision.* The District Court decision rejecting the FDA contention that structure/function claims are implied drug claims is *American Health Products Co., Inc. v. Hayes*, 574 F. Supp. 1498, 1507 (S.D.N.Y. 1983), *supra* p. 34 Note 1.

2. *Statements of Nutritional Support.* DSHEA added Section 403(r)(6) to the FD&C Act to authorize what the statute refers to as "statements of nutritional support" for dietary supplements. Four types of these statements are authorized: (1) a claimed benefit related to a classical nutrient deficiency disease, (2) a description of the role of a nutrient or dietary ingredient intended to affect the structure or function in humans (a "structure/function" claim), (3) a characterization of the documented mechanism by which a nutrient or dietary ingredient acts to maintain the structure or function in humans, and (4) a description of general well-being from consumption of a nutrient or dietary ingredient. In 69 Fed. Reg. 64962 (Nov. 9, 2004) FDA issued a Draft Guidance on Substantiation for Dietary Supplement Claims Made Under Section 403(r)(6) of the Federal Food, Drug, and Cosmetic Act.

———

In 1998, FDA promulgated proposed regulations to define valid structure/function claims for dietary supplements and to differentiate them from drug claims.

Regulations on Statements Made for Dietary Supplements Concerning the Effect of the Product on the Structure or Function of the Body

63 Fed. Reg. 23624 (April 29, 1998).

The Dietary Supplement Health and Education Act of 1994 (the DSHEA) authorizes manufacturers of dietary supplements to make certain types of statements about the uses of their products. Among the types of permitted statements are certain claims that, prior to enactment of the DSHEA, could have rendered the product a "drug" under the Federal Food, Drug, and Cosmetic Act (the act). Specifically, section 403(r)(6) of the act, added by the DSHEA, allows dietary supplement labeling to bear a

---

* "This statement has not been evaluated by the Food and Drug Administration. This product is not intended to diagnose, treat, cure, or prevent any disease."

statement that "describes the role of a nutrient or dietary ingredient intended to affect the structure or function in humans" or that "characterizes the documented mechanism by which a nutrient or dietary ingredient acts to maintain such structure or function." . . .

Certain other types of statements about dietary supplements continue, under the DSHEA, to cause the product to be regulated as a drug. Statements permitted under section 403(r)(6) of the act "may not claim to diagnose, mitigate, treat, cure, or prevent a specific disease or class of diseases," except that such statements may claim a benefit related to a classical nutrient deficiency disease, provided that they also disclose the prevalence of the disease in the United States. Such statements are generally referred to as "disease claims." FDA notes that certain statements that pertain to a disease or health-related condition are permitted on food products, including dietary supplements. These statements are known as health claims and describe the relationship between a nutrient and a disease or health-related condition. Unlike structure/function claims, health claims must be authorized by FDA before they may be used on the label or in the labeling of a food or dietary supplement. Thus, certain claims about disease may be made for foods and dietary supplements without causing these products to be regulated as drugs, provided the claim has been authorized for use by FDA in accordance with the applicable regulations. . . .

A dietary supplement manufacturer who wishes to make a permitted structure/function statement under section 403(r)(6) of the act must have substantiation that the statement is truthful and not misleading, and must include in the statement the following disclaimer: "This statement has not been evaluated by the Food and Drug Administration. This product is not intended to diagnose, treat, cure, or prevent any disease." The DSHEA requires the manufacturer of a dietary supplement bearing a statement under section 403(r)(6) of the act to notify FDA, no later than 30 days after the first marketing of the dietary supplement with the statement, that such a statement is being made for the product. . . .

Diseases, by definition, adversely affect some structure or function of the body, and it is possible to describe most products intended to treat or prevent disease in terms of their effects on the structure or function of the body. The DSHEA, thus, does not authorize the use of all claims that describe the effect of a dietary supplement on the structure or function of the body. Instead, section 403(r)(6) of the act authorizes only those structure/function claims that describe an effect of a product on the structure or function of the body but that are not also disease claims. Because the distinction between allowable structure/function claims and disease claims is not always obvious, the dietary supplement industry has requested clarification from FDA on structure/function claims that can be made for dietary supplements under section 403(r)(6) of the act. To develop clarifying criteria for such claims, FDA has reviewed the notification letters that have been submitted to FDA under section 403(r)(6) of the act. In addition, FDA has reviewed the report of the Commission [on Dietary Supplement Labels], which was established by the DSHEA to provide guidance and recommendations for the regulation of label claims and statements for dietary supplements.

The Commission's final report contains the following guidance (the guidance) on the scope of permissible structure/function claims:

GUIDANCE

While the Commission recognizes that the context of a claim has to be considered on a case-by-case basis, the Commission proposes the following general guidelines:

1. Statements of nutritional support should provide useful information to consumers about the intended use of a product.

2. Statements of nutritional support should be supported by scientifically valid evidence substantiating that the statements are truthful and not misleading.

3. Statements indicating the role of a nutrient or dietary ingredient in affecting the structure or function of humans may be made when the statements do not suggest disease prevention or treatment.

4. Statements that mention a body system, organ, or function affected by the supplement using terms such as "stimulate," "maintain," "support," "regulate," or "promote" can be appropriate when the statements do not suggest disease prevention or treatment or use for a serious health condition that is beyond the ability of the consumer to evaluate.

5. Statements should not be made that products "restore" normal or "correct" abnormal function when the abnormality implies the presence of disease. An example might be a claim to "restore" normal blood pressure when the abnormality implies hypertension.

6. Health claims are specifically defined under NLEA as statements that characterize the relationship between a nutrient or a food component and a specific disease or health-related condition. Statements of nutritional support should be distinct from NLEA health claims in that they do not state or imply a link between a supplement and prevention of a specific disease or health-related condition.

7. Statements of nutritional support are not to be drug claims. They should not refer to specific diseases, disorders, or classes of diseases and should not use drug-related terms such as "diagnose," "treat," "prevent," "cure," or "mitigate."

The guidance thus focuses on the distinction between allowable structure/function claims and claims that a product can diagnose, treat, prevent, cure, or mitigate disease (disease claims), and makes clear that structure/function claims made for dietary supplements should not imply treatment or prevention of disease. The guidance also provides examples of types of structure/function claims that do and do not imply disease claims....

... FDA believes that the Commission's guidelines provide a useful framework for clarifying the sometimes difficult distinction between structure/function claims and disease claims. Based upon the Commission's advice and the agency's experience in reviewing notification letters submitted under section 403(r)(6) of the act, FDA has developed proposed regulations to define the types of claims that are "disease claims" and thus not acceptable as structure/function claims....

In 2000, FDA promulgated a final rule on structure/function statements for dietary supplements. 65 Fed. Reg. 1000 (Jan. 6, 2000), codified at 21 C.F.R. 101.93(f). In the preamble, the agency observed: "FDA received over 235,000 submissions in response to the proposed rule. Many of these were form letters, but over 22,000 were individual letters from the dietary supplement industry, trade associations, health professional groups, and consumers. Almost all the comments from the dietary supplement industry and from individuals, which made up the vast majority of the comments, objected to all or part of the proposed rule, arguing that it inappropriately restricted the structure/function claims that could be made for dietary supplements."

The preamble filled fifty pages in the Federal Register, while the regulation itself occupied only one page. The final rule made several significant changes to the proposed version, but it continued to follow the same general approach laid out by the Commission on Dietary Supplement labeling. A trade publication, THE TAN SHEET, Vol. 8, No. 3, pp. 12–13 (Jan. 17, 2000), extracted from the preamble all of the examples of permitted structure/function claims and prohibited disease claims for dietary supplements. The resulting list is reproduced *infra* p. 282.

NOTES

1. *The "Natural State" Exception.* FDA concluded that it is not appropriate to treat common nonserious conditions associated with natural states as diseases. These conditions include adolescence, the menstrual cycle, pregnancy, menopause, and aging. The agency therefore permitted, as valid structure/function claims, such conditions as "(1) Morning sickness associated with pregnancy; (2) leg edema associated with pregnancy; (3) mild mood changes, cramps, and edema associated with the menstrual cycle; (4) hot flashes; (5) wrinkles; (6) other signs of aging on the skin, *e.g.*, liver spots, spider veins; (7) presbyopia (inability to change focus from near to far and vice versa) associated with aging; (8) mild memory problems associated with aging; (9) hair loss associated with aging; and (10) noncystic acne." The following are examples of conditions that remain disease claims: "(1) Toxemia of pregnancy; (2) hyperemesis gravidarum; (3) acute psychosis of pregnancy; (4) osteoporosis; (5) Alzheimer's disease, and other senile dementias; (6) glaucoma; (7) arteriosclerotic diseases of coronary, cerebral or peripheral blood vessels; (8) cystic acne; and (9) severe depression associated with the menstrual cycle." 65 Fed. Reg. at 1020.

2. *Pregnancy and the "Natural State" Exception.* Immediately upon issuing its dietary supplement structure/function rule, FDA received comments expressing concern about the agency's statement that common and mild conditions associated with the "natural state" of pregnancy, such as morning sickness, would not be treated as diseases. These comments pointed out the significant risks that dietary supplements might pose to unborn children. FDA quickly responded to these concerns by advising dietary supplement manufacturers "not to make any claims related to pregnancy on their products based on the agency's recently issued structure/function rule." *FDA Statement Concerning Structure/Function Rule and Pregnancy Claims* (Feb. 9, 2000).

FDA EXAMPLES OF ACCEPTABLE AND UNACCEPTABLE
DIETARY SUPPLEMENT CLAIMS

Structure/Function Claim Examples

"Helps promote digestion"
"For relief of occasional constipation"
Laxative
"Improves absentmindedness"
Stress and frustration
"Helps support cartilage and joint function"
"Maintains healthy lung function"
"Helps to maintain cholesterol levels that are already
     within the normal range"
Morning sickness associated with pregnancy
Leg edema associated with pregnancy
Mild mood changes, cramps and edema associated with
     the menstrual cycle
Hot flashes
Wrinkles
Other signs of aging on the skin, e.g., liver spots, spider
     veins
Presbyopia (inability to change focus from near to far and
     vice versa) associated with aging
Mild memory problems associated with aging
Hair loss associated with aging
Noncystic acne
"Supports a normal, healthy attitude during PMS"
"Supportive for menopausal women"
"A good diet promotes good health and prevents the onset
     of disease"
"Better dietary and exercise patterns can contribute to
     disease prevention and better health"
"Appetite suppressant"
"Tonic"
"Antispasmodic"
"Supports the immune system"
"Helps maintain intestinal flora"
Pain associated with nondisease states, e.g., muscle pain
     following exercise
"Boosts stamina, helps increase muscle size and helps
     enhance muscle tone"
"Smoking alternative"; "Temporarily reduces your desire
     to smoke"; "Mimics the oral sensations of cigarette
     smoke" if context does not imply treatment of
     nicotine addiction

"Relief of sour stomach"
"Upset stomach"
"Occasional heartburn"
"Occasional acid indigestion"
"Alleviates the symptoms referred to as gas"
"Alleviates bloating"
"Alleviates pressure"
"Alleviates fullness"
"Alleviates stuffed feeling"
"For the prevention and treatment of the nausea, vomiting or
     dizziness associated with motion"
"For the relief of occasional sleeplessness"
"Helps restore mental alertness or wakefulness when
     experiencing fatigue or drowsiness"
"Occasional simple nervous tension"
"Nervousness due to common every day overwork and fatigue"
"A relaxed feeling"

"Calming down and relaxing"
"Gently soothe away the tension"
"Calmative"
"Resolving that irritability that ruins your day"
"Helps you relax"
"Restlessness"
"Nervous irritability"
"When you're under occasional stress, helps you work relaxed"

"Arouses or increases sexual desire and improves sexual
     performance"
"Digestive aid"
"Stool softener"
"Weight control"
"Menstrual"
"Treatment and/or prevention of nocturnal leg muscle cramps,
     i.e., a condition of localized pain in the lower extremities
     usually occurring in middle life and beyond with no
     regular pattern concerning time or severity"
"Helps maintain regularity"
"Calcium helps build strong bones"

Disease Claims Examples

"Promotes low blood pressure"
"Relieves crushing chest pain" (angina or heart attack)
"Improves joint mobility and reduces joint inflammation
     and pain" (rheumatoid arthritis)
"Heals stomach or duodenal lesions and bleeding" (ulcers)
"Anticonvulsant" (epilepsy)
"Relief of bronchospasm" (asthma)
"Prevents wasting in persons with weakened immune
     systems" (AIDS)
"Prevents irregular heartbeat" (arrhythmias)

"Prevents shortness of breath, an enlarged heart, inability
     to exercise, generalized weakness and edema"
     (congestive heart failure)
"Maintaining a tumor-free state"
"Maintain normal bone density in post-menopausal
     women"
"Maintains healthy lungs in smokers"
"Lowers cholesterol"
"Promotes cholesterol clearance"
Toxemia of pregnancy
Hyperemesis gravidarum
Acute psychosis of pregnancy
Osteoporosis
Alzheimer's disease and other senile dementia
Glaucoma
Arteriosclerotic diseases of coronal, cerebral or peripheral
     blood vessels
Cystic acne
Severe depression associated with the menstrual cycle
"Helps to maintain normal urine flow in men over 50
     years old"
"Promotes good health and prevents the onset of disease"
"Anti-inflammatory"
"To maintain a healthy blood sugar level"

"Controls blood sugar in persons with insufficient insulin"
     (diabetes)
"Prevents the spread of neoplastic cells" (prevention of cancer
     metastases)
"Antibiotic" (infections)
"Herbal Prozac" (depression)
Alcohol intoxication
"According to the National Cancer Institute, ingredient X
     protects smokers' lungs"
"Inhibits platelet aggregation"
"Joint pain"
"Supports the body's antiviral capabilities"
"Helps individuals using antibiotics to maintain normal
     intestinal flora"
"Deters bacteria from adhering to the wall of the bladder and
     urinary tract"

"Dietary support during the cold and flu season"
"Promotes general well-being during the cold and flu season"
"To be used as a dietary adjunct in conjunction with your
     smoking cessation plan"
"Relief of heartburn"; Recurrent" or "persistent" heartburn
"Relief of acid indigestion"
"Helps to reduce difficulty falling asleep"
"Nervous tension headache"
"Helps restore sexual vigor, potency and performance"
"Improves performance, staying power and sexual potency"
"Builds virility and sexual potency"
"To relieve the symptoms of benign prostatic hypertrophy, e.g.,
     urinary urgency and frequency, excessive urinating at night
     and delayed urination"
"Relieve excessive secretions of the nose and eyes" (hay fever)
"Nasal decongestant" (colds, flu and hay fever)
"Expectorant" (colds, flu and bronchitis)
"Bronchodilator" (asthma)

3. *Use of Heart Symbol.* In the preamble, FDA stated that the heart symbol could be used in labeling of a dietary supplement in conjunction with a structure/function claim relating to maintenance of healthy circulation or some other function that does not imply treatment or prevention of disease. 65 Fed. Reg. at 1021–22. FDA reiterated this position in a letter from Robert J. Moore, Chief of the Dietary Supplements Branch of the Division of Compliance and Enforcement in the Office of Nutritional Products, Labeling and Dietary Supplements of the FDA Center for Food Safety and Applied Nutrition, to Alan G. Minsk (Apr. 23, 2002).

4. *Statutory Disclaimer and Notification.* Section 403(r)(6)(C) of the FD&C Act requires that the label of any dietary supplement bearing a structure/function claim must bear the following disclaimer: "This statement has not been evaluated by the Food and Drug Administration. This product is not intended to diagnose, treat, cure, or prevent any disease." Within 30 days after the first marketing of a dietary supplement with a structure/function claim, the manufacturer must notify FDA that the claim is being made. 21 C.F.R. 101.93. If FDA objects to the claim, the agency will respond with a so-called "courtesy letter" stating its objections. When structure/function claims are made in conventional food labeling, however, they are subject to none of these requirements.

5. *Animal Dietary Supplements.* For a discussion of dietary supplements for animals, see Jeannie Perron & Eugene I. Lambert, *DSHEA and Structure/Function Claims for Animal Feed*, 55 Food & Drug L.J. 151 (2000). *See also* Todd Harrison, *The Regulatory Situation for Pet Nutraceuticals*, 2 Nutraceuticals World, No. 4, at 20 (July/Aug. 1999).

COMMENT: STRUCTURE/FUNCTION CLAIMS FOR DIETARY SUPPLEMENTS VS. CONVENTIONAL FOOD

The preamble to the final rule declared: "This rule applies to claims for dietary supplements only.... FDA advises, however, that for consistency, the agency is likely to interpret the dividing line between structure/function claims and disease claims in a similar manner for conventional foods as for dietary supplements."

FDA has stated that structure/function claims may be made for dietary ingredients that have no nutritive value, but that such claims may be made for conventional food only if based on the nutritive value of the food. FDA has also stated that a conventional food may bear a structure/function claim in accordance with the "other than food" exclusion from the structure/function prong of the drug definition in section 201(g)(1)(C) of the FD&C Act but that dietary supplements may bear such a claim only under section 403(r)(6) and not under section 201(g)(1)(C). *See* 65 Fed. Reg. 1000, 1033–34 (Jan. 6, 2000); *see also* 62 Fed. Reg. 49859, 49860–61 (Sept. 23, 1977). The practical impact of this interpretation—which is strongly contested by the regulated industry—is that it would require all dietary supplements bearing a structure/function claim to (1) also bear the statutory disclaimer that "This statement has not been evaluated by the Food and Drug Administration. This product is not intended to diagnose, treat, cure, or prevent any disease" and (2) submit to FDA a notice of the claim within thirty days after first marketing.

Conventional food for which structure/function claims are made is often called "functional" food. This is a marketing term, not a separate regulatory category of food. *See* Julie Melissa Baher, *What Can Your Food Do For You? (And Should FDA Let It?): An Overview of the Regulatory Regime (or Lack Thereof) Surrounding Functional Foods* (2006), in Chapter V(D)(5) of the Electronic Book. FDA for the first time acknowledged the existence of functional foods, discussed their regulatory status under the FD&C Act, and posed questions about potential future regulatory initiatives to be discussed in a public hearing announced in 71 Fed. Reg. 62400 (October 25, 2006).

3.   DISEASE PREVENTION CLAIMS

a.   GENERAL PRINCIPLES

Since 1938, the definition of a "drug" in section 201(g)(1)(B) has included any article intended for use in the prevention or treatment of disease. Accordingly, no disease claim could be made for a food without also subjecting the food to regulation as a drug and, more important, as a new drug that requires premarket approval prior to marketing. Faced with increasing evidence of the relation of diet to disease, as well as claims about this relationship in advertising and even labeling, FDA changed its position in 1985 and publicly stated that valid disease claims would for the first time be permitted. The agency then published proposed regulations and an interim enforcement policy. 52 Fed. Reg. 28843 (Aug. 4, 1987), 54 Fed. Reg. 32610 (Aug. 8, 1989), 55 Fed. Reg. 5176 (Feb. 13, 1990). In *United States v. Undetermined Quantities of an Article of Drug Labeled as "Exachol,"* 716 F. Supp. 787 (S.D.N.Y. 1989), the District Court held that a dietary supplement, Exachol, using a disease claim consistent with the new enforcement policy could not be singled out for a seizure action because FDA must treat all products consistently. From June 1988 to June 2000, FDA took the position that claims for beneficial cardiovascular effects of omega–3 fatty acids in food were unapproved drug claims. Letter from Ronald G. Chesemore, Associate Commissioner, FDA (June 22, 1990).

These events were overtaken by enactment of the provisions authorizing food disease claims in the Nutrition Labeling and Education Act of 1990 and the Food and Drug Administration Modernization Act of 1997. In new section 403(r)(1)(B) of the FD&C Act, Congress explicitly permitted claims that characterize the relationship of a nutrient to "a disease or health related condition." Two kinds of disease prevention claims for food may be made that do not result in the food being classified as a drug: (1) those approved by FDA under section 403(r)(3)(B)of the FD&C Act on the basis of "significant scientific agreement" and (2) those approved in "authoritative statements" by other federal health agencies or the National Academy of Sciences, as provided in section 403(r)(3)(C).

Following enactment of the NLEA, the regulations promulgated by FDA narrowly construed the statutory standard of significant scientific agreement. In particular, FDA required mature science—a virtual scientific consensus—for approval of a disease claim and rejected all claims, however truthful, based on emerging science that has not yet reached maturity. The agency's disapproval of four claims was appealed to the courts. Although the case involved claims for dietary supplements, the decision of the Court of Appeals is equally applicable to conventional food.

Pearson v. Shalala

164 F.3d 650 (D.C. Cir. 1999).

■ SILBERMAN, CIRCUIT JUDGE.

Marketers of dietary supplements must, before including on their labels a claim characterizing the relationship of the supplement to a disease or health-related condition, submit the claim to the Food and Drug Administration for preapproval. The FDA authorizes a claim only if it finds "significant scientific agreement" among experts that the claim is supported by the available evidence. Appellants failed to persuade the FDA to authorize four such claims and sought relief in the district court, where their various constitutional and statutory challenges were rejected. We reverse.

. . . Each of appellants' four claims links the consumption of a particular supplement to the reduction in risk of a particular disease:

(1) "Consumption of antioxidant vitamins may reduce the risk of certain kinds of cancers."

(2) "Consumption of fiber may reduce the risk of colorectal cancer."

(3) "Consumption of omega–3 fatty acids may reduce the risk of coronary heart disease."

(4) ".8 mg of folic acid in a dietary supplement is more effective in reducing the risk of neural tube defects than a lower amount in foods in common form."

. . . .

[T]he FDA rejected the four claims supported by appellants. . . . The problem with these claims, according to the FDA, was not a dearth of supporting evidence; rather, the agency concluded that the evidence was inconclusive for one reason or another and thus failed to give rise to "significant scientific agreement." . . .

Appellants sought relief in the district court, raising APA and other statutory claims as well as a constitutional challenge, but were rebuffed. *Pearson v. Shalala*, 14 F. Supp. 2d 10 (D.D.C. 1998). . . .

It is undisputed that FDA's restrictions on appellants' health claims are evaluated under the commercial speech doctrine. It seems also undisputed that the FDA has unequivocally rejected the notion of requiring disclaimers to cure "misleading" health claims for dietary supplements. . . . The government makes two alternative arguments in response to appellants' claim that it is unconstitutional for the government to refuse to entertain a disclaimer requirement for the proposed health claims: first, that health claims lacking "significant scientific agreement" are *inherently* misleading and thus entirely outside the protection of the First Amendment; and second, that even if the claims are only *potentially* misleading, under *Central Hudson Gas & Elec. Corp. v. Public Serv. Comm'n of New York*, 447 U.S. 557, 566 (1980), the government is not obliged to consider requiring disclaimers in lieu of an outright ban on all claims that lack significant scientific agreement.

If such health claims could be thought inherently misleading, that would be the end of the inquiry.... As best we understand the government, its first argument runs along the following lines: that health claims lacking "significant scientific agreement" are inherently misleading because they have such an awesome impact on consumers as to make it virtually impossible for them to exercise any judgment at the *point of sale*. It would be as if the consumers were asked to buy something while hypnotized, and therefore they are bound to be misled. We think this contention is almost frivolous.... We reject it. But the government's alternative argument is more substantial. It is asserted that health claims on dietary supplements should be thought at least potentially misleading because the consumer would have difficulty in independently verifying these claims. We are told, in addition, that consumers might actually assume that the government has approved such claims.

Under *Central Hudson*, we are obliged to evaluate a government scheme to regulate potentially misleading commercial speech by applying a three-part test. First, we ask whether the asserted government interest is substantial. The FDA advanced two general concerns: protection of public health and prevention of consumer fraud.... [A] substantial governmental interest is undeniable ...

The more significant questions under *Central Hudson* are the next two factors: "whether the regulation *directly* advances the governmental interest asserted," and whether the fit between the government's ends and the means chosen to accomplish those ends "is not necessarily perfect, but reasonable." We think that the government's regulatory approach encounters difficulty with both factors.

It is important to recognize that the government does not assert that appellants' dietary supplements in any fashion *threaten* consumer's health and safety. The government simply asserts its "common sense judgment" that the health of consumers is advanced *directly* by barring any health claims not approved by the FDA. Because it is not claimed that the product is harmful, the government's underlying—if unarticulated—premise must be that consumers have a limited amount of either attention or dollars that could be devoted to pursuing health through nutrition, and therefore products that are not indisputably health enhancing should be discouraged as threatening to crowd out more worthy expenditures. We are rather dubious that this simplistic view of human nature or market behavior is sound, but, in any event, it surely cannot be said that this notion—which the government does not even dare openly to set forth—is a *direct* pursuit of consumer health; it would seem a rather indirect route, to say the least.

On the other hand, the government would appear to advance directly its interest in protecting against consumer *fraud* through its regulatory scheme. . . .

The difficulty with the government's consumer fraud justification comes at the final *Central Hudson* factor: Is there a "reasonable" fit between the government's goals and the means chosen to advance those goals? The government insists that it is never obliged to utilize the disclaimer approach, because the commercial speech doctrine does not embody a preference for disclosure over outright suppression. Our understanding of the doctrine is otherwise. . . .

Our rejection of the government's position that there is no general First Amendment preference for disclosure over suppression, of course, does not determine that any supposed weaknesses in the claims at issue can be remedied by disclaimers and thus does not answer whether the subregulations are valid. . . .

We do not presume to draft precise disclaimers for each of appellants' four claims; we leave that task to the agency in the first instance. Nor do we rule out the possibility that here evidence in support of a claim is outweighed by evidence against the claim, the FDA could deem it incurable by a disclaimer and ban it outright.[10] . . .

———

Following this landmark decision, FDA construed the mandate of the Court of Appeals narrowly and continued to disapprove proposed disease claims. In particular, FDA stated that it would apply a "weight of the evidence" test in determining whether to permit a qualified health claim. 65 Fed. Reg. 59855 (Oct. 6, 2000), 67 Fed. Reg. 78002 (Dec. 20, 2002). This strategy provoked further litigation.

Whitaker v. Thompson

248 F. Supp. 2d 1 (D.D.C. 2002).

■ KESSLER, DISTRICT JUDGE. . . .

Plaintiffs challenge the FDA decision prohibiting dietary supplements' labels from including the health claim that "Consumption of antioxidant vitamins may reduce the risk of certain kinds of cancers"

The Court of Appeals in *Pearson I* strongly suggested, without explicitly holding, that Plaintiffs' Antioxidant Vitamin Claim was only "potentially misleading," not "inherently misleading," and therefore the FDA's refusal to authorize the Antioxidant Vitamin Claim (or to propose a disclaimer to accompany the Claim) violated the First Amendment. Specifically, while *Pearson I* recognized the FDA's concern that the antioxidant health claim lacked "significant scientific agreement because existing research had ex-

---

10. Similarly, we see no problem with the FDA imposing an outright ban on a claim where evidence in support of the claim is *qualitatively* weaker than evidence against the claim—for example, where the claim rests on only one or two old studies.

amined only the relationship between consumption of *foods* containing these components and the risk of these diseases," the Court stated that the FDA's concern "could be accommodated ... by adding a prominent disclaimer to the label." ...

On November 13, 2000, the *Pearson* Plaintiffs filed a lawsuit in this Court challenging the FDA's decision to prohibit inclusion of the folic acid/neural tube defect health claim at issue in *Pearson I* on dietary supplement labels. The folic acid/neural tube effects health claim was denied because the FDA thought the claim was inherently misleading even with clarifying disclaimers. See *Pearson v. Shalala*, 130 F. Supp. 2d 105, 111–12 (D.D.C. 2001) ("*Pearson II*"). The Court found that the FDA had failed to comply with *Pearson I* and granted the *Pearson* Plaintiffs' request for a preliminary injunction, remanding the case to the FDA with instructions to draft one or more accurate disclaimers.

The Court found that "the FDA simply failed to comply with the constitutional guidelines" of *Pearson I* and stated that "the agency appears to have at best, misunderstood, and at worst, deliberately ignored, highly relevant portions of the Court of Appeals Opinion." The Court concluded that the "FDA acted unconstitutionally, and particularly in violation of [*Pearson I*], in suppressing Plaintiffs' Claim rather than proposing a clarifying disclaimer to accompany the Claim."

The FDA then moved for reconsideration of the *Pearson II* decision, claiming that the decision improperly considered relevant scientific evidence and created a legal standard inconsistent with *Pearson I*. In denying the motion, this Court noted that:

> Defendants again seem to ignore the thrust of *Pearson I*. While that decision might leave certain specific issues to be fleshed out in the course of future litigation, the philosophy underlying *Pearson I* is perfectly clear: that First Amendment analysis applies in this case, and that if a health claim is not inherently misleading, the balance tilts in favor of disclaimers rather than suppression.

Pearson v. Thompson, 141 F. Supp. 2d 105, 112 (D.D.C. 2001) (*Pearson III*). The Court clarified the import of the previous *Pearson* decisions on the FDA's decision to suppress health claims by stating that both *Pearson I* and *Pearson II* "established a very heavy burden which [Defendants] must satisfy if they wish to totally suppress a particular health claim." Accordingly, the Court indicated that the FDA "*must* 'demonstrate with empirical evidence that disclaimers similar to [those] suggested ... would bewilder consumers and fail to correct for deceptiveness.'" Accordingly, on June 4, 2001, the case was dismissed after an agreement was reached that allowed the labels of dietary supplements containing folic acid to display the folic acid/neural tube defect health claim with a disclaimer proposed by the FDA and chosen by the *Pearson* Plaintiffs....

... [T]he Court concludes that a preliminary injunction is warranted in this case. Upon reviewing the FDA's Antioxidant Vitamin Decision conclusion that the Claim is "misleading and incurable by a disclaimer," the Court concludes that the FDA has failed to comply with the Court of Appeals decision in *Pearson I* and that Plaintiffs have demonstrated a substantial likelihood of success on the merits of their First Amendment claim.

The Court finds, as a matter of law, that Plaintiffs' Antioxidant Vitamin Claim is not "inherently misleading," and that the FDA therefore erred in not considering disclaimers to accompany the Claim. The FDA has failed to carry its burden of showing that suppression of Plaintiffs' Antioxidant Vitamin Claim is the least restrictive means of protecting consumers against the potential of being mislead [sic] by the Claim. As explained below, it is clear that the FDA has once again failed to comply with the constitutional guidelines outlined in *Pearson I*....

The Court of Appeals established clear guidelines for the FDA in determining whether a particular health claim may be deemed "inherently misleading" and thus subject to total suppression. The Court implied, though it did not declare explicitly, that when "credible evidence" supports a claim, that claim may not be absolutely prohibited. While the Court did not "rule out the possibility that where evidence in support of a claim is outweighed by evidence against the claim, the FDA could deem it incurable by a disclaimer and ban it outright," it is clear that the Court was alluding to a very narrow set of circumstances in which suppression would be permissible under the First Amendment.

Specifically, *Pearson I* identified two situations in which a complete ban would be reasonable. First, when the "FDA has determined that no evidence supports [a health] claim," it may ban the claim completely. Second, when the FDA determines that "evidence in support of the claim is qualitatively weaker than evidence against the claim—for example, where the claim rests on only one or two old studies," it may impose an outright ban. Even in these two situations, a complete ban would only be appropriate

> when the government could demonstrate with empirical evidence that disclaimers similar to the ones [the Court] suggested above ["The evidence in support of this claim is inconclusive" or "The FDA does not approve this claim"] would bewilder consumers and fail to correct for deceptiveness....

Thus, two conclusions emerge from a close reading of *Pearson I*. First, the Court of Appeals did not rule out the possibility that disclaimers would not be able to correct the inherent misleadingness of some health claims. Second, the Court stated that any complete ban of a claim would be approved only under narrow circumstances, *i.e.*, when there was almost no qualitative evidence in support of the claims and where the government provided empirical evidence proving that the public would still be deceived even if the claim was qualified by a disclaimer.

As the FDA has satisfied the second and the third steps of the *Central Hudson* test in the present case, the key analysis comes under *Central Hudson*'s final step—whether there is a reasonable fit between the government's goals and the means it has chosen to achieve them. In determining whether there is a reasonable fit between the FDA's goals of consumer protection and its decision to ban Plaintiffs' Antioxidant Vitamin Claim, the Supreme Court has clearly stated that "if the Government could achieve its interests in a matter that does not restrict speech, or that restricts less speech, the Government *must* do so." In its review of the relevant Supreme Court decisions, our Court of Appeals also concluded— even before issuance of *Western States* [535 U.S. 357 (2002)]—that disclaimers were "constitutionally preferable to outright suppression." In other words, more disclosure rather than less is the preferred approach, so long as commercial speech is not inherently misleading.

Given that the First Amendment "means that regulating speech must be a last—not first—resort," the burden in this case is on the FDA to prove that suppression of the Antioxidant Vitamin Claim "was a *necessary* as opposed to *merely convenient* means of achieving its interests." The Court of Appeals' earlier review of the FDA's denial of the Plaintiffs' Antioxidant Vitamin Claim found that the FDA's justifications for suppression were merely "conclusory assertions [that fell] far short" of satisfying its burden and concluded that the FDA had not chosen a less restrictive means of protecting its interests, *i.e.*, a disclaimer.

Once again in its 2001 decision, the FDA has failed to recognize that its decision to suppress the Plaintiffs' Antioxidant Vitamin Claim does not comport with the First Amendment's clear preference for disclosure over suppression of commercial speech. . . .

NOTES

1. *Commentary.* For a full discussion of the details and impact of this unprecedented litigation, see Elizabeth Martell Walsh et al., *The Importance of the Court Decision in Pearson v. Shalala to the Marketing of Conventional Food and Dietary Supplements in the United States*, in Clare M. Hasler, REGULATION OF FUNCTIONAL FOODS AND NUTRACEUTICALS, Ch. 8 (2005). *See also* Clement Dimitri Pappas, *Maintaining a Level Playing Field: The Need for a Uniform Standard to Evaluate Health Claims for Foods and Dietary Supplements*, 57 FOOD & DRUG L.J. 25 (2002). For criticism of the *Pearson* decision, see David C. Vladeck, *Devaluing Truth: Unverified Health Claims in the Aftermath of* Pearson v. Shalala, 54 FOOD & DRUG L.J. 535 (1999).

2. *Implementation of Pearson v. Shalala.* Following the decision in *Pearson v. Shalala*, FDA published a strategy for implementing the Court of Appeals decision. 64 Fed. Reg. 67289 (Dec. 1, 1999). As directed by the *Pearson* court, the agency also issued a Guidance on Significant Scientific Agreement in the Review of Health Claims for Conventional Foods and Dietary Supplements. 64 Fed. Reg. 71794 (Dec. 22, 1999).

3. *Ripeness for Judicial Review.* The HHS Agency for Healthcare Research and Quality (AHRQ) published a report on the effectiveness of a dietary ingredient in the treatment of disease. A dietary supplement manufacturer brought suit for a declaratory judgment that the use of the report would not constitute an "intended use" that would convert the dietary ingredient into a drug. In *Pearson v. Leavitt*, the Court of Appeals affirmed *per curiam* the District Court's dismissal of the action as not ripe for judicial review because FDA had not taken or threatened enforcement. Food Drug Cosm. L. Rep. (CCH) ¶ 38,894 (4th Cir. 2006).

Following the *Whitaker* decision, FDA recognized that it had no choice but to change its strategy. The agency concluded that it would have two separate and different standards for disease claims for food: (1) significant scientific agreement for "unqualified" disease claims and (2) credible scientific evidence for "qualified" disease claims. 68 Fed. Reg. 66040, 66041 (Nov. 25, 2003).

b. UNQUALIFIED DISEASE CLAIMS

The general requirements for unqualified disease claims—for which FDA determines that the scientific evidence has reached the statutory level of significant scientific agreement—were promulgated by FDA after the enactment of the NLEA. 56 Fed. Reg. 60537 (Nov. 27, 1991), 58 Fed. Reg. 2478 (Jan. 6, 1993), codified at 21 C.F.R. 101.14. The *Pearson/Whitaker* litigation did not require any change in these regulations. FDA has promulgated regulations approving 12 unqualified disease claims, including, for example, calcium and osteoporosis, sodium and hypertension, dietary saturated fat and cholesterol and risk of coronary heart disease, and fiber-containing grain products, fruits, and vegetables and cancer. 21 C.F.R. Part 101, Subpart E.

Food Labeling; General Requirements For Health Claims For Food

58 Fed. Reg. 2478 (January 6, 1993).

. . . .

The proposed definition establishes that a claim must have at least two basic elements for it to be regulated as a "health claim." First, the claim must be about a "substance" as that term is defined in proposed § 101.14(a)(2). Secondly, the claim must characterize the relationship of the substance to a "disease or health-related condition." . . .

FDA does not agree that section 403(r)(1)(B) of the act addresses health claims for only those nutrients required to be on the label of a food and does not include claims about other types of nutrients. The language of section 403(r)(1)(B) of the act is clear in that it pertains to a claim that "... characterizes the relationship of any nutrient which is *of the type* required by paragraph (q)(1) or (q)(2) to be in the label or labeling of a food" (emphasis added). Thus, claims relating to a broad range of substances are potentially subject to regulation under section 403(r)(1)(B) of the act. . . .

. . . The agency has reviewed the legislative history of the 1990 amendments and concluded that this history does indeed contain evidence to support the conclusion that Congress intended that [whole] foods could be the subject of claims that are regulated under section 403(r) of the act. However, this legislative history also makes clear that, to be subject to section 403(r) of the act, a claim about a food must be, at least by implication, a claim about a substance in the food. . . .

Thus when a consumer could reasonably interpret a claim about the relationship of a food to a disease or health-related condition to be an implied claim about a substance in that food, that claim would satisfy the first element of a health claim.

However, a claim about the benefits of a broad class of foods that does not make an express or implied connection to any of the substances that are found in foods that comprise that class would not constitute an implied claim. Such claims about classes of foods (*e.g.*, fruits and vegetables) are not health claims because they are not about a substance.

... One comment asserted that the statutory phrase "a disease or health-related condition" does not set up two categories and maintained that the phrase "health-related" as used in the law appears to be nothing more than an expansion of the word "disease." ...

However, the inclusion of the phrase "health-related condition" in section 403(r)(1)(B) of the act in addition to the term "disease" leaves no question that Congress intended that claims about conditions other than diseases be regulated under this provision....

... Accordingly, the agency concludes that the inclusion of "a health-related condition" in the coverage of section 403(r)(1)(B) of the act means that claims about risk factors related to disease, as well as claims about a disease, can be health claims.

... In the legislative history, Congress focused only on those health claims that related to chronic diseases affected by diet, such as cancer, heart disease, and osteoporosis. There is no indication that it intended to cover classical deficiency diseases (diseases resulting directly for a deficiency of a vitamin, essential mineral, or other essential nutrient).

Some comments stated that the eligibility restrictions on the term "substance" in proposed § 101.14(b)(3)(i) are too restrictive and asked that they be removed.... A few comments contended that, if FDA retains the food eligibility restrictions in the final rule, the agency should permit a broader interpretation of what constitutes food. Another comment stated that although the phrase "taste, aroma, or nutritive value" is borrowed from the Seventh Circuit's opinion in *Nutrilab, Inc. v. Schweiker*, 713 F.2d 335, 338 (7th Cir. 1983), the court noted in that decision that these food characteristics were only the primary reasons why people consume food. The court, according to the comment, did not intend to give an all-inclusive list....

FDA disagrees with the comments' interpretation of the *Nutrilab* decision and believes that the agency's reliance on the case is justified. The *Nutrilab* court adopted a "common sense" definition under section 201(f)(1) of the act: "When the statute defines 'food' as 'articles used for food,' it means that the statutory definition of 'food' includes articles used by people in the ordinary way most people use food—primarily for taste, aroma, or nutritive value." *Nutrilab*, 713 F.2d at 338.... By describing taste, aroma, and nutritive value as the "primary" reasons for consuming food, the *Nutrilab* court acknowledged that a food consumed for one of these reasons might sometimes also be consumed for an additional purpose. 713 F.2d at 338 (giving prune juice and coffee as examples of foods that "may be consumed on occasion for reasons other than taste, aroma, or nutritive value"). Under *Nutrilab*, a substance whose uses do not include taste, aroma, or nutritive value is not a food....

NOTES

1. *Nutritive Value for Disease Claims.* In the preamble to the proposed regulations for disease claims, 56 Fed. Reg. 60537, 60542–43 (Nov. 27, 1991), and in the preamble to the final regulations excerpted above, FDA took the position that a disease claim could be made only for conventional food substances and dietary supplements that have "nutritive value." FDA regulations provide that, to be eligible for a health claim, a substance must "contribute taste, aroma, or nutritive value," or a listed "technical effect," and the rule explicitly states that this requirement applies "regardless of whether the food is a conventional food or a dietary supplement." 21 C.F.R. 101.14(b)(3)(i). Because dietary supplements ordinarily do not contain ingredients meant to contribute taste, aroma, or the technical characteristics of conventional foods, a dietary supplement manufacturer arguably could only make a health claim in connection with a substance that provides "nutritive value." The agency stated that herbs and a number of other traditional dietary ingredients other than vitamins and minerals have no nutritive value and therefore would not be eligible for disease claims. FDA has approved only one disease claim for a dietary supplement, the folate/neural tube defects claim, under 21 C.F.R. 101.79. However, FDA has announced it will permit the use of a number of qualified disease claims for dietary supplement ingredients, including selenium and cancer; antioxidant vitamins and cancer; omega–3 fatty acids and coronary heart disease; folic acid, vitamin B_6, and vitamin B_{12} and vascular disease; phosphatidylserine and dementia, and phosphatidylserine and cognitive dysfunction. At the same time, the agency has agreed to the use of structure/function claims for ingredients that have no nutritive value. *E.g.*, Jeannie Perron & Eugene I. Lambert, *DSHEA and Structure/Function Claims for Animal Feed*, 55 FOOD & DRUG L.J. 151, 154–157 (2000).

2. *Meaning of Nutritive Value.* FDA defines "nutritive value" succinctly as "a value in sustaining human existence by such processes as promoting growth, replacing loss of essential nutrients, or providing energy." 21 C.F.R. 101.14(a)(3). In practice, the line between a product's nutritive value and nonnutritive value is not clear. For example, in approving a health claim for plant sterol esters and plant stanol esters, FDA characterized the ability of these substances to *block* the absorption of dietary cholesterol as a nutritive value. The agency observed simply that the cholesterol-lowering effect of these esters is achieved through "an effect on the digestive process" and that the phrase "nutritive value" should be interpreted flexibly. 65 Fed. Reg. 54685, 54688 (Sept. 8, 2000).

3. *Records Inspection.* In 61 Fed. Reg. 3885 (Feb. 2, 1996), FDA proposed to require records inspection for all nutrient descriptor and disease claims. After the industry submitted substantial comment documenting forty years of FDA statements that the agency has no records inspection authority for the food industry, FDA has taken no further action on this proposal. When FDA proposed a disease claim for soy protein and coronary heart disease, it included a requirement for records inspection. 64 Fed. Reg. 45932 (Aug. 23, 1999), After substantial adverse comments demonstrating that FDA has no records inspection authority for food, the agency promulgated a final disease claim without a records inspection requirement. 21 C.F.R. 101.82.

4. *Disease Treatment Claims.* Section 403(r)(1)(B) authorizes claims relating to "a disease or a health-related condition." On its face, this language is not limited to disease prevention claims and could permit disease treatment claims if they are

adequately supported. The courts have held, however, that it is within FDA's discretion to interpret the disease claims provision in section 403(r)(1)(B) to relate only to disease prevention and not to disease treatment, and that this does not violate the free speech provisions of the First Amendment. *E.g., Whitaker v. Thompson*, 239 F. Supp. 2d 43 (D.D.C. 2003), *aff'd* 353 F.3d 947 (D.C. Cir. 2004).

5. *Constitutionality.* The National Health Alliance brought a facial First Amendment challenge to the DSHEA provisions regarding disease claims. The District Court upheld premarket approval against the argument that it was an unconstitutional prior restraint, but ordered FDA to impose a reasonable limit on the time within which any disease claim must be approved or disapproved. *Nutritional Health Alliance v. Shalala*, 953 F. Supp. 526 (S.D.N.Y. 1997). The Court of Appeals affirmed the District Court. It concluded that it could only determine compliance with *Central Hudson* in the context of a specific claim, but it upheld the prior restraint of up to 540 days permitted by the disease claim scheme as acceptable under commercial free speech doctrine. 144 F.3d 220 (2d Cir. 1998). A similar facial constitutional attack on the disease claims provision was dismissed because it was erroneously brought directly in the Court of Appeals. *Mineral Resources Int'l v. United States Dep't of Health and Human Services*, 53 F.3d 305 (10th Cir. 1995). Other facial challenges to the regulations were dismissed for lack of standing. *See National Council for Improved Health v. Shalala*, 122 F.3d 878 (10th Cir. 1997); *Wellife Products v. Shalala*, 52 F.3d 357 (D.C. Cir. 1995).

6. *The Qualified Nature of Unqualified Claims.* It is a misnomer to call the 12 "significant scientific agreement" claims "unqualified," because each contains qualified terms such as "___ *may* reduce the *risk* of ___" disease—a phrase that actually contains two qualifications. Perhaps for this reason the public has difficulty distinguishing between unqualified and qualified disease claims. This issue has been reopened for further consideration. 69 Fed. Reg. 24541, 24544 (May 4, 2004).

7. *Sparse Use of Claims.* Because FDA requires lengthy, detailed, and complex information to be part of an unqualified disease claim, the food industry has not often used unqualified disease claims for foods that are eligible to use them. FDA has requested public comment on the use of "abbreviated" claims. 69 Fed. Reg. 24541, 24546–47 (May 4, 2004).

8. *The Jelly Bean Rule.* Under 21 C.F.R. 101.14(e)(6), no food may make a disease claim unless it contains ten percent or more of the reference daily intake or the daily reference value for vitamin A, vitamin C, iron, calcium, protein, or fiber per reference amount customarily consumed *prior* to any nutrient addition. FDA intends this provision to preclude disease claims for foods of little nutritional value, hence the moniker "jelly bean rule." In practice, however, the provision also precludes disease claims for foods such as fruits and vegetables that many people regard as nutritious. In 60 Fed. Reg. 66206 (Dec. 21, 1995), FDA discussed this issue in detail and proposed to create an exemption for fruit and vegetables rather than to delete the rule and allow claims with full disclosure that the nutrients are added through fortification. The industry has strongly objected to the jelly bean rule on both policy and legal grounds. The rule was included in the final regulation without an opportunity for public comment in violation of the Administrative Procedure Act, and it violates commercial free speech doctrine. FDA subsequently reopened the rule for reconsideration. 69 Fed. Reg. 24541, 24543 (May 4, 2004).

9. *Disease Claim Determined by Authoritative Body.* The "authoritative body" provision for disease claims under section 403(r)(3)(C) of the FD&C Act is comparable to the same provision for nutrient descriptors. *See* Note 5, *supra* p. 217. FDA rejected the first nine authoritative body disease claims submitted to the agency, 63 Fed. Reg. 34083 (June 22, 1998), but has since agreed to a few other disease claims under this provision. Because section 403(r)(3)(C) of the FD&C Act, which governs "authoritative body" disease claims, does not by its terms embrace the "jelly bean" rule, and because FDA has not promulgated regulations imposing this restrictive

rule, it is not applicable to disease claims authorized under this provision. FDA letters agreeing to authoritative body disease claims are available only on the FDA website and are not published in the Federal Register.

10. *Folic Acid.* The "authoritative body" provision was added to the FD&C Act by the FDA Modernization Act of 1997 because FDA failed to promulgate a regulation authorizing a disease claim for folic acid and prevention of neural tube defects for four years after CDC had announced a causal relationship. H.R. REP. NO. 105–306, 105th Cong., 1st Sess. 16 (1997); *see* Kevin J. Wright, *Folic Acid and the American Food Supply: A Historical Account of the FDA's Creation of the Current Folic Acid Regulation* (2003), in Chapter V(D)(4) of the Electronic Book.

11. *Disqualifying Macronutrient Levels.* Under 21 C.F.R. 101.14(a)(4), a food is prohibited from any disease claim if it contains any of the following disqualifying nutrient levels per reference amount customarily consumed or per label serving size: 13 grams of fat, 4 grams of saturated fat, 60 milligrams of cholesterol, or 480 milligrams of sodium. Industry has strongly argued that this ban on disease claims violates free commercial speech doctrine and should be replaced with a disclosure requirement. FDA has reopened the record to reconsider this matter. 69 Fed. Reg. 24541, 24543–44 (May 4, 2004).

12. *Abbreviated Disease Claims.* Under 21 C.F.R. 101.14(d)(2)(iv), all information required to be in a disease claim must appear together in one place without other intervening material. This substantially reduces the likelihood that disease claims will be used in food labeling. In light of industry concerns, FDA reopened the record to reconsider this matter. 60 Fed. Reg. 66206 (Dec. 21, 1995), 69 Fed. Reg. 24541 (May 4, 2004). The industry has also complained that the FDA-prescribed disease claims are lengthy and detailed, and are not written in a way designed to attract consumer attention. It has been suggested that the FDA-prescribed disease claims should be guidelines, not requirements, and that industry should be permitted to use creativity to make those claims in the ways best suited to reach consumers. Thus far, however, FDA has not given serious attention to this approach.

13. *Potential Improvement.* In 69 Fed. Reg. 24541 (May 4, 2004), FDA published an advance notice of proposed rulemaking to request comment on how the existing regulations could be improved.

c. QUALIFIED DISEASE CLAIMS

Six days before the *Whitaker* decision, FDA announced that the agency would (1) "apply *Pearson* to health claims in the labeling of conventional foods as well as dietary supplements" and (2) use the standard of "weight of the scientific evidence" in evaluating qualified disease claims. 67 Fed. Reg. 78002 (Dec. 20, 2002). Following the *Whitaker* decision, FDA published notices substituting "credible evidence" for "weight of the evidence" as the proper standard for qualified disease claims. 68 Fed. Reg. 41387 (July 11, 2003), 68 Fed. Reg. 66041 (Nov. 25, 2003). The July and November 2003 notices also established two other important interim policies: (1) an evidence-based ranking system to evaluate the scientific evidence relevant to a disease claim and (2) four levels of disease claims based upon the rank of the evidence, the bottom three of which are qualified claims, with corresponding qualifying language.

A. High: significant scientific agreement

B. Moderate: evidence is not conclusive

C. Low: evidence is limited and not conclusive

D. Extremely low: little scientific evidence supporting this claim.

After conducting consumer research, FDA held a public meeting to discuss its finding that consumers could not easily distinguish among these four levels of claims. 70 Fed. Reg. 60749 (Oct. 19, 2005).

COMMENT: FDA USE OF "ENFORCEMENT DISCRETION"

In its notice published in 65 Fed. Reg. 59855 (Oct. 6, 2000) announcing its implementation of the *Pearson* decision, FDA stated that it would "exercise its enforcement discretion" to permit the use of qualified disease claims that the Court of Appeals held could not constitutionally be banned. In all subsequent notices and correspondence regarding qualified disease claims, FDA has continued to refer to "enforcement discretion" rather than forthrightly to state that these claims are constitutionally protected and that the agency has no discretion whatever in permitting their use.

NOTES

1. *Procedure.* In the 2002 and 2003 guidances, FDA established an interim regulatory guidance for a premarket notification procedure for the review of qualified disease claims, rather than the premarket approval procedure required under the NLEA for unqualified disease claims. Along with the 2003 notice, FDA published an advance notice of proposed rulemaking requesting comment on three procedural options for reviewing qualified disease claims: (1) premarket notification, (2) premarket approval, or (3) postmarket policing. 68 Fed. Reg. 66040 (Nov. 25, 2003). In *Center for Science in the Public Interest v. Food and Drug Administration*, 2004 WL 2218658 (D.D.C.2004), the District Court dismissed a challenge to the FDA guidances both as not ripe for judicial review and for the plaintiffs' lack of standing to bring the action.

2. *Publication.* Qualified disease claims approved by FDA are published on the agency's website, not in the Federal Register. Some are very modest indeed. Consider, for example, the following two approved level "D" claims:

> "One small study suggests that chromium picolinate may reduce the risk of insulin resistance, and therefore, possibly may reduce the risk of Type II diabetes FDA concludes, however, that the existence of such a relationship between chromium picolinate and either insulin resistance or type 2 diabetes is highly uncertain."

> "Two studies do not show that drinking green tea reduces the risk of breast cancer in women, but one weaker, more limited study suggests that drinking green tea may reduce this risk. Based on these studies, FDA concludes that it is highly unlikely that green tea reduces the risk of breast cancer."

4. GENERAL HEALTH CLAIMS AND DIETARY GUIDANCE

In the preamble to the final regulations on food disease claims under the NLEA, FDA stated that a disease claim contains two basic elements: (1) a substance and (2) a disease-related condition. FDA stated that it would use the term "dietary guidance" to refer to general health claims that do not contain both of these basic elements. 58 Fed. Reg. 2478, 2487 (Jan. 6, 1993). Unlike disease claims, general health claims/dietary guidance are not subject to the requirements of section 403(r)(1)(B) of the FD&C Act. Because that preamble discussion provoked little food industry response, a decade later FDA explained the importance of general health claims/dietary guidance in the following notice.

Food Labeling: Health Claims; Dietary Guidance

68 Fed. Reg. 66040 (November 25, 2003).

. . . FDA recognizes the importance of dietary guidance in assisting and encouraging the U.S. population to make better food choices and establish healthier eating patterns. Although these types of statements are not health claims, consistent and scientifically sound dietary guidance statements can be useful to consumers when they are truthful and nonmisleading. As previously mentioned, FDA has no regulatory authority to review or authorize dietary guidance statements before use. When used in labeling for foods, however, such statements must be truthful and not misleading under sections 201(n) and 403(a)(1) of the act. The agency generally has viewed most dietary guidance for the general U.S. population as originating from Federal agencies with public health missions related to diet and disease. For example, major Federal documents such as the Dietary Guidelines for Americans issued by USDA and U.S. Department of Health and Human Services exemplify government consensus about dietary recommendations. Given the important role that information on food labels can play in affecting consumers' health and dietary decisions, FDA sees a need to foster enhanced federal cooperative efforts to identify and agree upon dietary guidance that is appropriate for food labels and how such guidance may be used. . . .

FDA is seeking comment on dietary guidance statements on food labels generally and on approaches appropriate for FDA to consider under its statutory authorities. As part of this consideration, FDA is requesting comments on whether providing a list of dietary guidance statements that FDA recommends for inclusion on food labels would be desirable or useful to manufacturers. In addition, FDA is requesting comments on these topics: (1) Whether and how the agency should partner with other Federal agencies to identify and agree upon recommended dietary guidance statements for food labeling, (2) the appropriate criteria for evaluating the scientific validity of dietary guidance statements that appear on products in the marketplace, and (3) whether and how the agency should address dietary guidance statements from non-federal sources (*e.g.*, States, trade associations, professional associations, etc.). . . .

H.   FOOD SANITATION

1.   HISTORY

Peter Barton Hutt, *The Importance of Analytical Chemistry to Food and Drug Regulation*

68 JOURNAL OF THE ASSOCIATION OF OFFICIAL ANALYTICAL CHEMISTS 147 (1985).

Ancient Greece and Rome. Adulteration of the food and drug supply was rampant in the ancient world. Numerous Greek and Roman writers documented this adulteration over several centuries. . . .

But knowledge of extensive adulteration of food and drugs, and laws to prohibit it, are useless unless they are enforceable.... The ancient treatises that have survived through the centuries do reveal substantial discussion of analytical methodology. Cato (234–149 B.C.) suggested a method "to determine whether wine has been watered." After his description of widespread adulteration, Pliny contended that "these adulterations can be detected ... by smell, color, weight, taste, and the action of fire." Together, Pliny and Dioscorides described several dozen methods of detecting adulteration, all of which depended solely or partly on the qualitative judgment of the individual person conducting the analysis. Galen suggested methods for determining whether such common articles as pepper were adulterated.

It is all too easy, in this day of scientific sophistication, to dismiss these ancient beginnings of analytical chemistry as sheer speculation. No less an authority than C.A. Browne, who served as president of AOAC in 1925, stated in an article published in 1909 that those in the ancient world who relied on "sense perceptions" to determine adulteration "were unquestionably better judges of the purity of many articles of food than we are today." Browne also concluded that the flame test, ring test, color reactions, and other physical detection methods identified by Pliny and Dioscorides had clear scientific underpinnings and reflected "a large amount of reliable chemical knowledge." ...

The Dark Ages and Middle Ages. After the fall of Rome, nontheological scholarship was discontinued, and the scientific progress begun in Greece and Rome was lost for centuries. The adulteration of food and drugs continued, however, and thus required the use of analytical methods and regulatory controls to contain it. Throughout the Dark Ages and Middle Ages, there was a thriving spice trade, originating among the Mediterranean countries and ultimately reaching England. Then even more than now, spices were extraordinarily valuable and presented an irresistible opportunity for fraudulent profit. Government inspectors—called "garblers"—were therefore employed to remove both natural and artificial adulterants from spices. Although the origin of garbeling is now lost in history, records from the very early 1300s demonstrate that the practice was already well established in England at that time....

As the centuries progressed, adulteration became more sophisticated and thus even more difficult to detect. Because of the lack of detection methods, only gross contamination could be prevented, such as the inclusion of stones, charcoal, dust, and straw in particular products, or the putrefaction of fish and meat. This lack of effective detection methodology, and the resulting poor enforcement of the laws prohibiting food and drug adulteration, was a source of continuing problems and complaints.... In 1592, the Grocers of London submitted a petition to the Lord Mayor of London complaining that the garbelers were doing an inadequate job of enforcement, and suggesting specific standards and procedures that should be followed to improve their regulatory efforts.

The Emergence of Chemistry from Alchemy. In its purely technological (as contrasted with philosophical and theological) aspects, alchemy was the origin of the field of chemistry. But it took the work of Paracellsus in the 16th century and Robert Boyle in the 17th century to break away from the mysticism of alchemy and establish the foundations of modern experimental chemistry.

One year before he died, Boyle wrote the first modern tract on the use of analytical chemistry to detect the adulteration of food and drugs. This work, published in 1690, used the principle of specific gravity to determine "How by the Weight that divers Bodies, us'd in Physick, have in Water; one may discover Whether they be Genuine or Adulterate." In effect, Boyle did no more than apply the principle of specific gravity used by Archimedes to determine the adulteration of gold, for the purpose of determining the adulteration of food and drugs. In so doing, however, he established a scientific foundation for food and drug regulation. A test for adulteration relying on the specific gravity of a substance no longer depended on individual opinion, as did most of the earlier tests identified by Pliny and Dioscorides. On the basis of Boyle's work, other chemists soon made substantial progress in chemical analysis.

The Accum Treatise. Frederick Accum, a German-trained scientist working in England, published a landmark treatise on chemical methods of analyzing adulteration of food and drugs in 1820. Accum not only documented extensive adulteration of the food and drug supply, but offered detailed chemical methods for their detection.... Shortly after, Arthur Hassall began his extensive investigations of food and drug adulteration in England. By introducing use of the microscope (which had been invented two centuries earlier) into food and drug analysis, Hassall led regulation into a new era. Forms of adulteration that could not be detected in any other way were easily found....

Wiley and the 1906 Act. The work undertaken by Hassall in England was mirrored in the United States by Harvey W. Wiley and the Division (later Bureau) of Chemistry in the United States Department of Agriculture.... The 1906 Act was the result largely of the development of extensive documentation of the adulteration of the American food and drug supply. This evidence, which ultimately overwhelmed the congressional reluctance to enact the legislation, resulted from the painstaking and persistent work of the Division of Chemistry and the AOAC.

The Past 35 Years. It is undoubtedly true that there has been more progress in the field of analytical chemistry in the past 35 years than in the prior 20 centuries. Our more detailed understanding of the chemical composition of the food and drug supply has compelled major changes in the regulation of food and drugs.

NOTE

See also James F. Bush, *"By Hercules! The More Common the Wine, the More Wholesome!" Science and the Adulteration of Food and Other Natural Products in Ancient Rome,* 57 FOOD & DRUG L.J. 573 (2002).

Ruth Lamb, *American Chamber of Horrors*
(1936).

Common foods are sometimes produced under sanitary conditions that beggar description. Even when processing removes any immediate health menace, there remains a background of filth to make the product repulsive to self-respecting consumers....

... Butter that looked perfectly clean and wholesome to the naked eye disclosed a history of filth leading all the way back to the farm. Hay; fragments of chicken feathers; maggots; clumps of mold—blue, green, white and black; grasshoppers; straw chaff; beetles; cow, dog, cat and rodent hairs; moths; grass and other vegetable matter; cockroaches; dust; ants; fly legs; broken fly wings; metallic filings; remains of rats, mice and other animals were revealed to the astonished eye—all impregnated with yellow dye from the butter.... In a single pound of packing-stock butter consigned to a candy factory, so many maggots were found that if they had been placed end to end their length would have approximated eleven feet, nine inches.... Examination of the cream at stations everywhere—North, East, South and West—yielded some strange and wonderful prizes. Flies and their maggots were the most common find; but mice, rats, cats and chickens in various stages of decomposition were by no means rare....

NOTE

For a history of the scientific and regulatory difficulties in FDA enforcement of the decomposition and filth prohibitions in the 1906 Act, see Suzanne White Junod, *Catching Up With Tomato Catsup Under the Microscope: Burton J. Howard and the Howard Mold Count*, FDLI Update, Aug. 2000, p. 20; James Harvey Young, *The Campaign for Clean Salmon*, 50 J. AFDO, No. 2, at 9 (June 1996).

Federal Food Inspections are Lagging

THE NEW YORK TIMES, December 20, 1971, at 1.

... Dozens of incidents such as the following cases are turned up each month by F.D.A. inspectors:

Some 3,982 cases of Beech–Nut baby food manufactured in Rochester were found to contain cockroach fragments. Federal agents supervised the destruction of all the product. About $2,400 worth of Italian macaroni was confiscated when inspectors found it contaminated with "insects, insect fragments, human hair, paint and metal fragments and other foreign materials." In Seattle inspectors seized an unspecified quantity of frozen shrimp because it had been prepared and packed under unsanitary conditions. Laboratory tests showed it to contain live staphylococci bacteria....

Dr. Virgil Wodicka, director of F.D.A.'s Bureau of Foods, concedes that although there were 355 food recalls and 267 seizures through the courts last year, his inspections turned up only a fraction of the existing violations.... Another indication of the magnitude of the food hazard problem is the count of reported food poisoning cases, ranging from the rare fatal botulism to the vastly more common cases of mild nausea and vomiting caused by Clostridium perfringens, a bacterial cousin of the microbe that causes botulism, Clostridium botulinum. Although the number of reports received by the Federal Center for Disease Control hovers around 25,000 from year to year, public health experts say that because most cases are never reported, the true magnitude of food poisoning is far greater. Estimates range from two million to 10 million cases annually....

Such facts, viewed against the background of recent food scares, suggest that food is less safe today than it was years ago. There is, in fact, no clear evidence that this is the case. . . . There are even reasons to believe that in some areas food is safer today. This is because more food is manufactured with the aid of automated quality-control equipment than ever before and because, under a new Federal law, many of the inadequate meat inspection programs run by state governments have either been upgraded to meet Federal standards or have been taken over by Federal inspectors. . . .

FDA OVERSIGHT—FOOD INSPECTION

Hearings Before the Subcommittee on Public Health and Environment of the House Committee on Interstate and Foreign Commerce, 92d Congress, 1st Session (1971)

. . . .

FDA Commissioner Charles Edwards. . . . Every time an emergency situation or a natural disaster occurs, it is necessary for us to suspend food inspections, suspend planned food analyses and our normal program operations. For example, in the Bon Vivant case, the 125 man-years consumed by this emergency effort to date could have been used to inspect 2,300 food plants. This means that in this fiscal year, FDA will probably not inspect 2,300 plants which might otherwise have been investigated and their products sampled and analyzed. . . .

. . . [O]ne of our problems in the food field is not unlike the problem in the drug field. We have no registration system, so when a new firm is established and a new product marketed, we have no idea it is happening unless we just happen to run on to it. . . .

Mr. Roy. How many food plants are presently subject to your inspection?

Dr. Edwards. We figure there are approximately 60,000 food establishments which come under our jurisdiction. Now, of that 60,000 about 30,000 of them are manufacturers, per se. Others might be packagers or processors. But there are 60,000 total in terms of our responsibility.

Mr. Roy. And you presently have 250 inspectors in the field? . . .

Mr. Rogers. Doctor, what is your need for manpower to do an effective job in inspecting the 60,000 food plants coming within your jurisdiction; 1,500 inspectors, is that a sufficient figure?

Dr. Edwards. I think in that order of magnitude; yes. . . .

Mr. Rogers. That would amount to how much money?

Dr. Edwards. $75 to $85 million.

Mr. Rogers. About the amount of your total budget now?

Dr. Edwards. It is getting fairly close; yes. . . .

NOTES

1. *FDA Inspection Force.* In FY 1971–1972, FDA employed 588 inspectors, 242 of whom handled food inspections. In FY 1979–1980, the agency had 992 inspectors

of whom 413 were assigned for food activities. As a result of congressional concern about the possibility of bioterrorism through poisoning of the food supply following the attacks of September 11, 2001, FDA received supplemental funding in FY 2002 which allowed the agency to hire 673 new employees for counterterrorism work, more than 60 percent of whom were assigned to food. *See* Note 2, *infra* p. 465. Since then, the number of FDA field personnel, including food inspectors, has been cut back, but FDA has sought to maintain its food bioterrorism work at the FY 2002 level authorized by Congress. *See* "Agriculture, Rural Development, Food and Drug Administration, and Related Agencies Appropriations for 2006," Hearings before a Subcommittee of the House Committee on Appropriations, 109th Cong., 1st Sess. 291–293 (2005).

2. *Constitutionality.* The constitutionality of statutory terms as "filthy," "putrid," "decomposed," and "unfit for food" was upheld against a claim of unconstitutional vagueness in the context of a criminal prosecution under the Federal Meat Inspection Act. *United States v. Agnew*, 931 F.2d 1397 (10th Cir. 1991).

3. *Commentary.* For additional discussion of food sanitation, see GAO, DIMENSIONS OF INSANITARY CONDITIONS IN THE FOOD MANUFACTURING INDUSTRY, Rep. No. B–164031(ii) (Apr. 18, 1972); GAO, PROCESSED FRUITS AND VEGETABLES: POTENTIALLY ADULTERATED PRODUCTS NEED TO BE BETTER CONTROLLED AND SANITATION IN SOME PLANTS NEEDS IMPROVEMENT, Rep. No. B–164031(ii) (Feb. 21, 1973); GAO, LEGISLATIVE CHANGES AND ADMINISTRATIVE IMPROVEMENTS SHOULD BE CONSIDERED FOR FDA TO BETTER PROTECT THE PUBLIC FROM ADULTERATED FOOD PRODUCTS, Rep. No. HRD–84–61 (Sept. 26, 1984); GAO, EVALUATION OF SELECTED ASPECTS OF FDA'S FOOD MANUFACTURING SANITATION INSPECTION EFFORTS, Rep. No. HRD–84–65 (Aug. 30, 1984); GAO, FOOD INSPECTIONS: FDA SHOULD RELY MORE ON STATE AGENCIES, Rep. No. HRD–86–2 (Feb. 19, 1986); GAO, DOMESTIC FOOD SAFETY: FDA COULD IMPROVE INSPECTION PROGRAM TO MAKE BETTER USE OF RESOURCES, Rep. No. HRD–89–125 (Sept. 1989); GAO, FOOD SAFETY AND QUALITY: RISK-BASED INSPECTION SYSTEM NEEDED TO ENSURE SAFE FOOD SUPPLY, GAO/RCED–92–152 (June 26, 1992); GAO, FUNDAMENTAL CHANGES NEEDED TO IMPROVE FOOD SAFETY, GAO/RCED–97–249R (Sept. 9, 1997); GAO, OPPORTUNITIES TO REDIRECT FEDERAL RESOURCES AND FUNDS CAN ENHANCE EFFECTIVENESS, GAO/RCED–98–224 (Aug. 6, 1998).

The problem of food sanitation has two distinct aspects. First, there is the aesthetic problem of "filth" in food. Although filth was once regarded as a potential indicator of contamination by pathogenic microorganisms, and thus evidence of a potential health hazard, modern food technology allows products to be processed in a way that eliminates any risk of disease. Nonetheless, even sterilized filth, however harmless, is prohibited on aesthetic grounds alone. Second, all food contains microorganisms. And insanitation can facilitate the growth of pathogenic microorganisms that present a substantial risk to human health.

2. AESTHETIC ADULTERATION

a. FILTH

United States v. 484 Bags, More or Less
423 F.2d 839 (5th Cir. 1970).

■ GODBOLD, CIRCUIT JUDGE.

This case concerns whether molded green coffee is adulterated, within the meaning of ... 21 U.S.C. § 342(a)(3)....

The coffee was imported from Brazil, admitted to the United States, and stored in a warehouse in New Orleans. Three or four days after arrival in Sept., 1965 it was damaged by water during Hurricane Betsy. In an effort to impede the growth of mold on the beans the consignee had them run through a dryer and resacked.... After an evidentiary hearing the District Court found that the beans were fit for food, under the standards of the New York Coffee Exchange, and were neither contaminated nor injurious to health....

The District Court used an erroneous standard in concluding that the coffee was in compliance with the Act and need not be destroyed....

21 U.S.C. § 342(a)(3) provides that a food is deemed adulterated "if it consists in whole or in part of any filthy, putrid or decomposed substance, or if it is otherwise unfit for food." The District Court read the first clause of the quoted provision as being elucidated by the second so that the amount of decomposition made unlawful thereby is that "which would, with reasonable certainty, render the article unfit for food." This court, along with others, has long held that the two clauses are independent and complementary, so that a food substance may be condemned as decomposed, filthy, or putrid even though it is not unfit for food, or condemned as unfit for food even though not decomposed, filthy or putrid."...

We turn to consideration of the standards to be used in determining if coffee beans are adulterated. The appellee contends that the statute lays down a rule of reason, allowing seizure and condemnation of only foods which deviate from the norm of purity to the extent of going beyond fair and safe standards. We recognize that "It [the first phrase of Section 342(a)(3)] sets a standard that if strictly enforced, would ban all processed food from interstate commerce. A scientist with a microscope could find filthy, putrid, and decomposed substances in almost any canned food we eat." But the majority, in fact almost unanimous, rule is that the Act confers the power to exclude from commerce all food products which contain in any degree filthy, putrid or decomposed substances....

Unjustifiably harsh consequences of a completely literal enforcement are tempered by discretion given the Secretary.... He is allowed to adopt administrative working tolerances for violations of which he will prosecute.[1] The courts may accept the administrative tolerance as a proper judicial measure of compliance with the Act.

Part of the government's evidence at the evidentiary hearing, after the claimant has sought to bring the coffee into compliance with the Act, was that it permitted a tolerance of ten per cent moldy beans in coffee, and that the percentage in tested samples of this coffee averaged 15.1. It is undisputed that the claimant had no actual notice of the administrative tolerance

---

1. In some instances the courts have softened the impact of literal enforcement by imposing a *de minimis* qualification on the statute. *United States v. 133 Cases of Tomato Paste*, 22 F. Supp. 515 (E.D. Pa. 1938). It has been recognized that the allowed administrative tolerances may be themselves an acceptable administrative determination of what is *de minimis*.

and that it had not been published in the Federal Register. The claimant insists that the government may not employ in support of condemnation an unpublished standard of allowable tolerances, known only to itself and sprung upon the unsuspecting merchant at a condemnation hearing and after efforts to rehabilitate the food substance. His complaint is not without equity, if for no other reason than that the provisions of § 334(d) governing release of goods to the owner to be brought into compliance with the Act require that rehabilitation be under the supervision of the government and with the expense of supervision paid by the owner.

In view of the disposition which we make of the case, and of amendments to the Administrative Procedure Act the effect of which have not been considered or briefed by the parties, we do not reach the issue of publication.[3]

We remand the case to the District Court for it to determine under a correct reading of the statute whether the coffee is adulterated. It may accept as a judicial standard the allowable tolerances now permitted by the Secretary, whether published or not. A court may apply a stricter standard than the Secretary and hold a food substance adulterated though within the Secretary's tolerances. Considering the positive command of the statute, the power of the court to allow a greater departure from purity than the administrative tolerances is less certain.*

For all future purposes of this case the claimant is entitled to be told what the allowable tolerances are....

COMMENT: DE MINIMIS FILTH

Some courts have been skeptical about giving Section 402(a)(3) as broad an interpretation as its language would permit. In *United States v. 1,500 Cases ... Tomato Paste*, 236 F.2d 208 (7th Cir. 1956), for example, the court questioned the expansive majority view of the provision, although it ultimately embraced it.

We find it impossible to agree with the accepted interpretation of Section 342(a)(3), without ignoring completely the word "otherwise" therein.... It has ... been suggested that Congress wanted to protect "the aesthetic tastes and sensibilities of the consuming public," and therefore intended that food containing "any filthy, putrid, or decomposed substance" be deemed adulterated whether it was "unfit for food" or not. Congress may also have wanted to set a standard of purity well above what was required for the health of the consuming public, knowing that not every food product can be individually inspected. If the standard is set at the level of what is "fit for food" or not injurious to health, the occasional substandard item that slips by both industry and Government scrutiny will be hazardous to the health of the consumer.

---

3. In his dissent in *United States v. 449 Cases, Etc.*, 212 F. 2d 567, 575 (2d Cir. 1954), Judge Frank urged that unpublished tolerances violated the Administrative Procedure Act, 5 U.S.C. § 551 et seq.

* [On remand, the District Court adopted FDA's tolerance and determined that the coffee beans were within that tolerance. 1969–1974 FDLI Jud. Rec. 76 (E.D. La. 1971).]

A minimum standard of purity above what is actually the level of danger will, however, allow fewer products to drop below that level. A high standard will also have the same effect by encouraging more careful industry inspection. Therefore, we prefer to follow the general rule in interpreting Section 342(a)(3), although admitting that we are unable to answer ... why Congress put the word "otherwise" in the section.

The interpretation we have chosen has one serious disadvantage which most courts have recognized. It sets a standard that if strictly enforced, would ban all processed food from interstate commerce. A scientist with a microscope could find filthy, putrid, and decomposed substances in almost any canned food we eat. (The substances which it is claimed render the respondent "adulterated" were visible only through a microscope.) The conclusion is inescapable that if we are to follow the majority of the decisions which have interpreted 21 U.S.C. § 342(a)(3), without imposing some limitation, the Pure Food and Drug Administration would be at liberty to seize this or any other food it chose to seize.... The Food and Drug Administration should set definite standards in each industry which if reasonable and in line with expressed Congressional intent, would have the force of law.

See also United States v. 133 Cases of Tomato Paste, 22 F. Supp. 515 (E.D. Pa. 1938):

... [T]he claimant argues that [section 402(a)(3)] ... is directed only to filth which is perceptible by the consumer.... To so interpret this section of the statute would largely deprive the public of the protection it seeks to give. The consumer ordinarily requires no government aid to protect him from the use of food products the filthy adulteration of which he can see, taste, or smell. What he really needs is government protection from food products the filthy contamination of which is concealed within the product.

In 1972, faced with a request under the Freedom of Information Act, FDA made public all of its "filth guidelines," which it renamed "unavoidable natural defect guidelines." The Director of the FDA Bureau of Foods was quoted as stating, somewhat defensively, that if food were required to be totally pure, "there would be no food sold in the United States." WASH. POST, Mar. 29, 1972, at B2.

Natural or Unavoidable Defects in Food for Human Use That Present No Health Hazard: Public Availability of Information

37 Fed. Reg. 6497 (March 30, 1972).

... Objective findings of [the presence of natural or unavoidable defects above the stated defect levels] without evidence of the history of the production of the food render the product adulterated, even though no health hazard is presented. Thus, appropriate regulatory action is taken whenever the stated defect levels are exceeded. Whether the level of defect in the food was acquired during the growth, processing, storage, or shipment is immaterial. When evidence of insanitary conditions of production or storage is known, action may be taken against products with lower defect levels. . . .

Few foods contain no natural or unavoidable defects. Even with modern technology, all defects in goods cannot be eliminated. Foreign material cannot be wholly processed out of foods, and many contaminants introduced into foods through the environment can be reduced only by reducing their occurrence in the environment. . . . The defect levels set by the Commissioner of Food and Drugs represent a level below which the defect is both unavoidable under current technology and presents no health hazard. The Commissioner has concluded that the public is entitled to this information. . . .

Natural or Unavoidable Defects in Food for Human use that Present no Health Hazard

21 C.F.R. § 100.110.

(a) Some foods, even when produced under current good manufacturing practice, contain natural or unavoidable defects at low levels that are not hazardous to health. The Food and Drug Administration establishes maximum levels for these defects in foods produced under current good manufacturing practice and uses these levels in deciding whether to recommend regulatory actions. . . .

(c) Compliance with defect action levels does not excuse violation of the requirement in section 402(a)(4) of the act that food not be prepared, packed, or held under unsanitary conditions or the requirements in this part that food manufacturers distributors, and holders shall observe current good manufacturing practice. Evidence indicating that such a violation exists causes the food to be adulterated . . . even though the amounts of natural or unavoidable defects are lower than the currently established defect action levels. . . .

NOTES

1. *Illustrative Action Levels.* The following current defect action levels are illustrative of those disclosed by FDA in 1972:

Product	Defect Action Level
Bay Leaves	Average of 5% or more pieces by weight are moldy; or average of 5% or more pieces by weight are insect infested; or average of 1 milligram or more mammalian excreta per pound after processing.
Cloves	Average of 5% or more stems by weight.

Product	Defect Action Level
Curry Powder	Average of 100 or more insect fragments per 25 grams or average of 4 or more rodent hairs per 25 grams.
Hops	Average of more than 2500 aphids per 10 grams.
Chocolate and Chocolate Liquor	Average is 60 or more insect fragments per 100 grams when 6 100–gram subsamples are examined; or any 1 sample contains 90 or more insect fragments.
	Average of 1 or more rodent hairs per 100 grams in 6 100–gram subsamples examined; or any 1 subsample contains 3 or more rodent hairs.
Popcorn	1 or more rodent execreta pellets are found in 1 or more subsample and 1 or more rodent hairs are found in 2 or more other subsamples; or 2 or more rodent hairs per pound and rodent hair is found in 50% or more of the subsamples; or 20 or more gnawed grains per pound and rodent hair is found in 50% or more of the subsamples.
Puree, Apricot, Peach and Pear	Average mold count is 12% or more.

2.   *Current FDA Action Levels.* FDA makes available on its website its current Food Defect Action Levels. In the past, FDA has periodically announced in the Federal Register new or revised requirements for specific foods. *E.g.*, 66 Fed. Reg. 55000 (Oct. 31, 2001), 65 Fed. Reg. 37791 (June 16, 2000) (patulin in apple juice); 60 Fed. Reg. 39754 (Aug. 3, 1995) (histamine in tuna and mahi-mahi); 53 Fed. Reg. 1520 (Jan. 20, 1988) (insect fragments in wheat flour other than durum wheat flour and in macaroni and noodle products); 51 Fed. Reg. 31840 (Sept. 5, 1986) (mold in catsup and rot fragment count in tomato products); 51 Fed. Reg. 12931 (Apr. 16, 1986) (mold, insect filth, and rodent filth in ground paprika); 49 Fed. Reg. 3140 (Jan. 25, 1984) (thrips in sauerkraut); 46 Fed. Reg. 39221 (July 31, 1981) (decomposition in imported canned and cooked or frozen shrimp); 42 Fed. Reg. 35899 (July 12, 1977) (guideline lowered from 1 rodent excreta pellet per pint of wheat to 9 mg. of rodent excreta pellets per kg. or approximately 0.4 mouse excreta pellets per pint).

3.   *Judicial Review of Action Levels.* After initially upholding the FDA defect action level for garlic in *Caribbean Produce Exchange, Inc. v. Department of Health and Human Services*, Food Drug Cosm. L. Rep. (CCH) ¶ 38,100 (D.P.R. 1988), the court reversed its position on rehearing, Food Drug Cosm. L. Rep. (CCH) ¶ 38,110, determining that the test the agency used to establish violation of the defect action level was arbitrary and capricious and was illegally adopted as a substantive regulation without compliance with the Administrative Procedure Act. The case was later remanded, 893 F.2d 3 (1st Cir. 1989), and was dismissed by the District Court as moot because the garlic had been distributed. Food Drug Cosm. L. Rep. (CCH) ¶ 38,268; FDA CONSUMER, Dec. 1993, at 48.

4.   *Procedure for Adoption.* In 47 Fed. Reg. 41637 (Sept. 21, 1982), FDA announced that it would allow a one-year period for comment on any new or revised defect action levels, during which the announced levels would be effective on an interim basis. The agency later revised this procedure, shortening to 60 days the time for comment but suspending enforcement of new or revised levels during this

period. 51 Fed. Reg. 12931 (Apr. 16, 1986). FDA has made no statement about the impact on this procedure of the *Caribbean Produce* decision, *supra* Note 3.

United States v. Capital City Foods, Inc.

345 F. Supp. 277 (D.N.D. 1972).

■ VAN SICKLE, DISTRICT JUDGE.

This is a criminal prosecution by information, based on a claimed violation of [t]he Federal Food, Drug and Cosmetic Act. Specifically, the defendants are charged with having introduced, or delivered for introduction, into interstate commerce, food that was adulterated. The food is claimed to be adulterated because it consisted in part of a filthy substance, *i.e.*, insect fragments. . . .

I apply § 342(a)(3) disjunctively. . . . That is, I do not require that the food is, by virtue of filth, unfit for human consumption. But, the presentation of this case has squarely raised these problems:

1.   Since the Food and Drug Administration has not promulgated standards of allowable foreign matter in butter, is that not in itself a standard of zero allowance of foreign matter?

2.   If the standard is zero allowance of foreign matter, is such a standard reasonable?

3.   In any event, has the government proved sufficient foreign matter to raise its proof above the objection of the maxim de minimis lex? . . .

The foreign matter found was mainly miniscule fragments of insect parts. They consisted of 12 particles of fly hair (seta), 11 unidentified insect fragments, 2 moth scales, 2 feather barbules, and 1 particle of rabbit hair. The evidence showed that some of these particles were visible to the naked eye, and some, the fly hair, would require a 30x microscope to see. They were identifiable with the aid of a 470x microscope. The only evidence as to size showed that there was one hair, 1 1/2 millimeters long, and one unidentified insect fragment 0.02 millimeters by 0.2 millimeters.

In all, 4125 grams (9.1 lbs.) of butter were checked and 28 miniscule particles were found. This is an overall ratio of 3 miniscule particles of insect fragments per pound of butter.

Thus, there having been no standard established, and no showing that this number of miniscule fragments is excludable in the manufacturing process, I find that this contamination is a trifle, not a matter of concern to the law.

The defendants are found not guilty. Judgment will be entered accordingly.

———

Two University of Chicago economists proposed a very different approach to controlling filth in food.

Melvin J. Hinich & Richard Staelin, *Regulation of the U.S. Food Industry*

In Study on Federal Regulation, Volume VI.
Senate Document No. 96–14, 96th Congress, 1st Session (1978).

... How much effort should be spent guaranteeing that our food is processed using ingredients and under conditions which are "sanitary" (even though bacteria associated with unsanitary conditions are rendered harmless when the food is later processed correctly), versus guaranteeing that the food is free from substances which cannot be rendered harmless by the proper processing by the manufacturer or consumer? Instead of taking legal action related to aesthetic adulteration, what would happen if all producers were required to affix a label which indicated the level of aesthetically unpleasant contamination? This label probably would be in terms of grades although it could also be more explicit by detailing the exact levels of contamination. If a firm felt that a lower grade label would be detrimental to the marketability of its produce, it would take the necessary steps to insure that its ingredients and manufacturing process met the higher standards. On the other hand, the firm might believe that consumers did not want to pay for extra protection since the food is safe (this occurs during the normal processing). In this case the firm may want to reduce costs (and price) and not meet the higher FDA sanitation grading standards. Consequently, consumers could use the presence or absence of such a label as an indication of the level of sanitation in the plant....

... [C]onsumers are not now getting "pure" food since such food would be prohibitively expensive. The question then is should the FDA ban food when it exceeds the admittedly arbitrary defect action levels or should they allow "informed" consumers to make the choice? (Remember exceeding the allowable levels does not usually imply any safety hazard.) This is particularly important if the FDA tightens the sanitation standards since they would in effect be banning foods which before the new standards were acceptable to both the FDA and the consumer. Moreover, these limits can have deleterious side effects. For instance Professor Donald Kennedy of Stanford University [later FDA Commissioner] after a four year study on insecticide adulteration sponsored by the National Research Council pointed out that the FDA's DAL [defect action level] requirements for insect infestation in fruits and vegetables have caused farmers to use increased amounts of insecticide....

In summary then there would seem, on theoretical grounds, to be some benefit to the labeling approach versus banning since the labeling would allow the consumer to make the ultimate choice with respect to aesthetic adulteration. However, the approach has some drawbacks. First as mentioned above, the lower grades may not be in high demand, thus consumers would in reality still be offered just one grade. Also institutions, etc. may buy the lower-graded product and serve unknowing customers.... Finally, unless the FDA was given the power to require the producer to affix such a label without going through a legal procedure, the label probably would not be any more cost effective than present regulatory procedures which now require the FDA to go to the judiciary to confiscate contaminated foods. However, it represents an interesting combination of standards and consumer information....

NOTES

1. *Update.* FDA has never proposed or even discussed the Hinich and Staelin labeling approach.

2. *Other Labeling Approaches. Cf.* Peter Barton Hutt, *The Basis and Purpose of Government Regulation of Adulteration and Misbranding of Food*, 33 FOOD DRUG COSM. L.J. 505, 520–22 (1978).

COMMENT: PREDACEOUS INSECTS

In July 1988, the Director of Compliance of FDA's Center for Food Safety and Applied Nutrition provided the following response to an inquiry from a Texas grain storage facility:

> This responds to your letter of March 28, 1988, concerning predaceous insects added to stored grain. . . .
>
> . . . The [statutory] word "filth" includes insects and insect related contaminants such as insect excreta and insect fragments. The presence of insects in the food constitute adulteration whether or not the insects attack the food product itself. We recognize that certain low levels of natural and unavoidable defects such as field insects may be present in certain foods even if handled in a sanitary manner. The deliberate addition of insects to food is, however, neither natural nor unavoidable. We have not, therefore, endorsed the practice of intentionally adding "beneficial" insects to foods to control insect pests. Indeed we have considered this simply as either substituting one adulterant for another, or as changing the nature of the adulteration. . . .
>
> Please note that because the intended use of these insects is to kill other insects, such use may be considered a pesticide by EPA. . . .
>
> We emphasize that whether these insects are considered to be pesticides or food additives, the laws enforced by both FDA and EPA require the submission of adequate scientific data to support premarket approval for "substances" added to food. If EPA determines that these insects are not pesticides and you submit a food additive petition containing safety and efficacy data, FDA would be willing to consider approval of the use of predaceous insects.

Following a highly critical story on March 25, 1990 on CBS's "60 Minutes," FDA reversed this decision. With the concurrence of FDA and USDA, EPA exempted parasitic and predaceous insects used to control insect pests from the requirement of a tolerance. *See* 56 Fed. Reg. 234 (Jan. 3, 1991), 57 Fed. Reg. 14644 (Apr. 22, 1992), codified at 40 C.F.R. 180.1101.

b.   DECOMPOSITION

United States v. An Article of Food . . . 915 Cartons of Frog Legs

Food Drug Cosmetic Law Reports (CCH) ¶ 38,102 (S.D.N.Y. 1981).

■ CANNELLA, J.M., DISTRICT JUDGE. . . .

Charles Cardile, an FDA chemist, testified that on December 13, 1977, he and Albert Weber, another trained FDA organoleptic examiner, conducted a joint organoleptic analysis of the eighteen subsamples to determine whether the shrimp were decomposed.[5] Their analysis consisted of thawing the eighteen subsamples, selecting 100 shrimp from each subsample, and then breaking the flesh of each shrimp and smelling it. On the basis of their training and pursuant to FDA Guidelines, the examiners then classified each shrimp as either class one, good commercial shrimp, class two, decomposed shrimp, or class three, shrimp in advanced stages of decomposition. Under the FDA Guidelines establishing tolerances for decomposition, a subsample is classified as decomposed if (1) five percent or more of the shrimp tested is class three, (2) twenty percent or more of the shrimp tested is class two, or (3) the percentage of class two shrimp plus four times the percentage of class three shrimp equals or exceeds twenty percent. The FDA will take legal action against the entire shipment when four or more of the eighteen subsamples are found to be decomposed. Based upon their examination of the eighteen subsamples at issue, Cardile and Weber found seven of the eighteen subsamples to be decomposed. . . .

Since the results of the FDA's joint organoleptic analysis revealed that seven of the subsamples tested contained more than the 20% decomposition tolerated by the FDA, with at least two subsamples scoring as high as 100% and 170%, the Court concludes that more than a *de minimis* amount of decomposition was present in the frozen shrimp and that it is "adulterated" within the meaning of 21 U.S.C. § 342(a)(3). . . .

NOTES

1. *Decomposition After Shipment.* In *United States v. Allbrook Freezing & Cold Storage, Inc.,* 194 F.2d 937 (5th Cir. 1952), the court upheld a seizure of decomposed and filthy berries after shipment from Louisiana to Mississippi, rejecting the contention that the reprocessed berries in Mississippi were a different food that had not themselves been shipped in interstate commerce.

2. *Proof of Decomposition.* In *Bruce's Juices, Inc. v. United States,* 194 F.2d 935 (5th Cir. 1952), the Court of Appeals held that, when FDA proves that a food is decomposed, it need not also prove that the food is unfit for human consumption. The Court also held that, in a decomposition case, the claimant had no right to have the jury taste and smell the product because decomposition "was not a matter cognizable by the senses." *See also* K. L. Bett & C. P. Dionigi, *Detecting Seafood Off-Flavors: Limitations of Sensory Evaluation,* 51 FOOD TECH., No. 8, at 70 (Aug. 1997).

3. *Summary Judgment.* In *United States v. 302 Cases . . . Frozen Peeled Shrimp,* 25 F. Supp. 2d 1352 (M.D. Fla. 1998), the District Court granted summary judgment to FDA in a case involving shrimp adulterated through decomposition and filth.

5. It has been said that decomposition, like drunkenness, "is easy to detect, but hard to define." *United States v. 1,200 Cans, Etc., Pasteurized Whole Eggs,* 339 F. Supp. 131, 137 (N.D. Ga. 1972). Decomposition is "a bacterial separation or breakdown in the elements of the food so as to produce an undesirable disintegration or rot." It is well recognized that organoleptic analysis of food, whereby the examiner relies upon his trained sense of smell to detect different types of offensive food, if honestly administered, is a valid scientific test for decomposition.

4. *Electronic Noses*. Food technologists have sought to replace organoleptic evaluation of decomposition with modern technology. *E.g.*, Philip N. Bartlett et al., *Electronic Noses and Their Application in the Food Industry*, 41 FOOD TECH., No. 12, at 44 (Dec. 1997); Linda L. Leake, *Electronic Noses and Tongues*, 60 FOOD TECH., No. 6, at 96 (June 2006). At this writing, however, FDA regards such devices as research tools that are not yet ready to aid regulatory decision making.

c. INSANITARY CONDITIONS

United States v. 1,200 Cans ... Pasteurized Whole Eggs, etc.

339 F. Supp. 131 (N.D. Ga. 1972).

■ SMITH, CHIEF JUDGE.

These five actions were brought in different parts of the United States ... to condemn and destroy as adulterated various lots of pasteurized frozen whole eggs and sugar yolks processed and introduced into interstate commerce by the Golden Egg Products, Inc. ... [T]he government contends that the lots were "adulterated" in one or more of the definitions prescribed by Congress in [21 U.S.C. § 342(a)(1), (3), and (4)]....

Golden Egg is a so-called frozen egg breaking plant, the purpose of which is to remove eggs from their shells, process the egg magma, and package and freeze it in a variety of combinations for sale to manufacturers. Its principal use is in the baking, dairy products and vegetable oil industries....

I. *Poisonous substances under 21 U.S.C. § 342(a)(1)....*

Salmonella ... is a well-recognized pathogen. There are some 1400 types, all felt by medical scientists to be deleterious. As such, salmonella constitutes a serious threat to public health, particularly to the old, the young, and the sickly.... The presence of salmonella in frozen eggs is a deleterious and poisonous additive which is dangerous to health within the meaning of 21 U.S.C. § 342(a)(1). Such fact is stipulated here. Accordingly, Lot 1941 is subject to condemnation under this section.

II. *Decomposed Substances under 21 U.S.C. § 342(a)(3)....*

... [A] food substance may be condemned under the present statute as decomposed, filthy, or putrid even though it is not unfit for food....

Indicative of this attribute is the almost universal acceptance of organoleptic tests for determining decomposition. All of the experts in this case agree that, honestly administered, they are valid.... Organoleptic smell tests have worked extremely well on unpasteurized egg products for years. The product is either "passable" or "rejected." However, the pasteurization process, which basically arrests decomposition, has posed a new problem.

The pasteurization process, universal since 1966, plus refinements in the freezing process have masked decomposition odors and made the test much more difficult.... Thus, it is extremely difficult to effect a satisfactory organoleptic test on lots of pasteurized frozen eggs. Conversely, however, the presence of a test failure under these conditions would be strong evidence of decomposition.

In this case, only two lots (Can Codes 1935 and 1937) were subjected to and failed such tests. In most lots, two subsamples for laboratory use were taken from ten random cans for a total of 20 subsamples in each lot. Lot 1935 had two such series taken.... In them, a competent organoleptic examiner found two clear rejects in each series. Out of ten subsamples in Lot 1937, another competent examiner found two passable, five rejects, and three possibles, or borderlines.

Recognizing the validity of the tests and the accuracy of the results, the court is concerned only with the quantum of the proof.... What, if any, percent of the total lot must be shown to be decomposed to condemn the entire lot? ... Recognizing that the trend is to order condemnation if the lot is decomposed "to any degree", the court is still not satisfied that the organoleptic evidence is sufficient to conclude that the entire lots in question are decomposed....

Because of these difficulties and the fact that not all decomposition is discoverable under organoleptic tests, interested parties have for years sought a more scientific method for establishing and measuring decomposition.... [T]he government here relies on evidence of Direct Microscopic Count (DMC) alone.

There can be little dispute that the presence of large numbers of bacteria in a product indicates a greater possibility of activity than a small number. Accordingly, the DMC tests proceed on the basis of ascertaining the actual count in any given product by random sampling. Under acceptable AOAC [Association of Official Analytical Chemists] methods, a precise amount of the product is spread on a slide over a given area, stained, and placed under a high-powered microscope.... Years of testing has indicated that DMC counts of 5,000,000 or more coupled with the presence of certain acid measurements are proof of decomposition in unpasteurized eggs.

Here, however, the government seeks to establish the reliability of a DMC count alone. The evidence presented at trial convinces the court that this standard is not acceptable. Firstly, the DMC count if scientifically accurate only measures the presence of both live and dead bacteria and not their activity (as do the acid tests).... Moreover, by reason of the irregular distribution of bacteria throughout frozen eggs and the inherent difficulty in counting those actually observed through the microscope, the DMC is subject to significant variances in different tests run on the same sample.... Thus on the unconvincing original premise that a DMC result may prove actual decomposition under Section (a)(3) and on the substantial test variances on the lots in question, the court concludes that the government's case on this basis fails....

III.   *Insanitary Conditions under 21 U.S.C. § 342(a)(4).*

"A food shall be deemed to be adulterated—if it has been prepared, packed, or held under insanitary conditions whereby it may have become contaminated with filth, or whereby it may have been rendered injurious to health."

While there are many similarities between (a)(3) and (a)(4) proceedings, the legislative thrust of the latter is entirely different.... [T]he (a)(4) section allows the condemnation of foods processed under insanitary conditions, whether they have actually decomposed or become dangerous to health or not. The objective of (a)(4) is to "require the observance of a reasonably decent standard of cleanliness in handling of food products" and to insure "the observance of those precautions which consciousness of the obligation imposed upon producers of perishable food products should require in the preparation of food for consumption by human beings." It almost reaches the aim of removing from commerce those products produced under circumstances which would offend a consumer's basic sense of sanitation and which would cause him to refuse them had he been aware of the conditions under which they were prepared....

Again, it would be helpful if there were specific plant standards or tolerances to guide the court.... Some argument has been made that the [FDA's good manufacturing practice] regulations promulgated in 1969 answer this purpose. With a few exceptions, they are inadequate to do so in that they fail to specify just what is "necessary", "needed", "effective", "sufficient", or the like....

In the absence of particular standards, the question must be determined from the totality of the circumstances as revealed by the evidence. In this regard, it is not necessary that the evidence of insanitary conditions absolutely coincide with the dates of processing provided they are not too remote in time or space. The proof should, however, justify the inference that such conditions actually existed on the dates in question.

Measured by the above, the test has been met in this case. Reviewing the evidence as a whole, the court must conclude that the conditions existing at the Golden Egg plant on the critical dates were exactly those the Congress sought to prevent by the passage of (a)(4).... While some extreme dates such as the 1969 inspections some 6–12 months before processing ought to be eliminated, the evidence during 1970 compels the finding of insanitary conditions. This evidentiary history reveals a consistent unsuccessful effort by the Food and Drug Administration enforcement officials over a long period of time to eliminate an intolerable situation at this plant....

... [I]n varying degrees the following conditions existed at the times in question: improper refrigeration in the transportation and storage of breaking stock; the use of fiber filler flats in the breaking room; no segregation of breaking stock prior to presenting it to the breaker for breaking; the regular failure to wash, sanitize, and candle the breaking stock before it was sent to the breaking room; the regular breaking of unsanitized and unwashed eggs; the breaking of leaking eggs and eggs with maggots, adhering fecal, and other foreign matter on the shells; ineffective instruction with regard to personal and equipment sanitation; breakers with uncovered open sores breaking eggs; the breaking of eggs without even a sniff to detect rotten eggs; instances where breakers failed to sanitize their hands after handling insanitary objects while breaking eggs; failure to reject rotten eggs; improperly maintained breaking trays that did not permit the breaker to properly observe broken eggs before they dropped into the collecting buckets; paper and rusty parts used on the breaking tray that consistently came into contact with the liquid egg magma; dirty shells in the breaking room strainer; flies, in varying numbers, in the breaking and transfer rooms; evidence of mice in the plant; and improper cleanup and maintenance.

That such conditions still existed on the dates of production is amply borne out by the evidence obtained in the July 24, 1970, FDA inspection, the July 15, 1970, National Sanitation Institute inspection, and the testimony of plant employees presented by both sides at trial....

Moreover and perhaps most importantly, the DMC evidence in the case is convincing on the question of insanitary conditions and resulting filth. While there is considerable doubt in the court's mind about the valid use of manufacturing conditions to establish decomposition under (a)(3) by the DMC method as advocated by the government, the reverse is assuredly true. The claimant's own experts agree that a high DMC count is scientific proof of the exposure of the product to filth and of production under insanitary conditions.... All together, the evidence amply authorizes the inference of insanitary production conditions to a degree prohibited by the Act. Accordingly, the court finds that all lots are subject to condemnation under Section (a)(4)....

United States v. Certified Grocers Co–op.

546 F.2d 1308 (7th Cir. 1976).

■ Tone, Circuit Judge.

In this food-adulteration prosecution ... the government appeals under 18 U.S.C. § 3731 from a judgment of acquittal entered after a bench trial. The defendants, relying upon that section's provision that "no appeal shall lie where the double jeopardy clause of the United States Constitution prohibits further prosecution," have moved to dismiss the appeal for lack of jurisdiction. The question of jurisdiction, under the standard set forth in *United States v. Jenkins*, 420 U.S. 358 (1975), is intertwined with the merits. On the authority of that case we dismiss the appeal.

The defendants, Certified Grocers Co-op and two of its principal officers, were charged in a two-count information with violating § 301(k) ... by permitting flour held in their warehouse to become adulterated and permitting it to become exposed to adulteration.... The court found the following facts: ...

A Food and Drug Administration inspection on September 19 and 29, 1972, while these 252 bags were being held for sale in the warehouse, disclosed that at least eight of them contained holes gnawed by rodents. These holes were approximately evenly divided between the General Mills flour described in Count I and the Pillsbury flour described in Count II. Only two of the individual two-pound bags were actually sampled, one from each lot. The General Mills bag contained two rodent excreta pellets and one rodent hair; the Pillsbury bag contained 10 rodent excreta pellets. Near the bales and elsewhere in the warehouse were several hundred rodent excreta pellets and several rodent bait boxes, one of which showed "recent rodent activity." Two dead rodents were "lying about outside the packaged food." There were numerous rodent burrows in the ground near the outside of the warehouse walls.

Notwithstanding the foregoing findings, the court acquitted the defendants. With respect to actual contamination (§ 342(a)(3)), the judge concluded that the government had not proved when the rodent activity in the warehouse occurred or whether the two packages which actually contained excreta were breached and contaminated before or after they arrived at the warehouse. . . .

With respect to the possibility of contamination (§ 342(a)(4)), the judge found that the presence, while the flour was being held in the warehouse, of "the gnawed holes and the rodent pellets and hairs and the two dead rodents lying about the packaged food . . . was no doubt an insanitary condition," but that "there was no reason to suppose that any of these things could or would enter the packages." He "attach[ed] somewhat less importance" to the lack of evidence of when the rodent activity occurred than he had with respect to the (a)(3) issue, and said "it may be inferred that some significant portion of that activity" occurred while the flour was present. . . .

Recognizing that the standard required for conviction under (a)(4) . . . is whether the insanitary conditions made it "reasonably possible" that the flour would become contaminated, the judge stated that "one might conclude that insanitary conditions . . . made it reasonably possible that a mouse would enter [two packages of flour] . . . and deposit therein . . . rodent excreta pellets and one rodent hair. . . ." Because of the "elusive" nature of the conviction standards, he then stated that "the ultimate question appears to be how the word 'contaminated' in § 342(a)(4) is to be construed, in conjunction with 'reasonably possible.' " He construed "contaminated," as he had the language of (a)(3), to permit the presence of contaminants within a "range of tolerance contemplated by the statute." He concluded that the filth described in the findings, which he calculated were the product of "about seven full mouse-days, so to speak," and was contained in a 100,000–square–foot warehouse, was within that range of tolerance.

Despite our misgivings about the District Court's interpretation of the statute[5] and the acquittal itself, we conclude that we are required to dismiss the appeal for want of jurisdiction. . . . The double-jeopardy clause precludes review. . . . However clear it may appear to us that the inference

---

5. . . . The Act does not provide for the setting of tolerances under (a)(4) as it does with respect to poisonous or deleterious substances under (a)(1) and (2), and §§ 346 and 346(a). The Secretary is vested, however, with the discretion not to prosecute, or even not to institute libel or injunctive proceedings against, "minor violations" of the statute. 21 U.S.C. § 336. Although we would prefer that this broad discretion be regulated by administratively promulgated standards governing industry practices, "there would seem no authority for us to waive statutory violation perhaps beyond the principal of *de minimus.* . . ." *United States v. 449 Cases, Containing Tomato Paste.* Thus, subsections (a)(3) and (4) do not appear to incorporate a "tolerance," permitting some minimal level of filth contamination in food. . . .

of a reasonable possibility of contamination should have been drawn, that inference could only be drawn by the trier of fact....

NOTES

1. *Government's Burden of Proof.* In *Berger v. United States*, 200 F.2d 818 (8th Cir. 1952), the court held that under section 402(a)(4), FDA must establish a "reasonable possibility," not just a "mere possibility," that the insanitary condition will result in contamination. For an illustration of the difficulty of demonstrating that particular sanitation practices violate sections 402(a)(3) and (a)(4), in the absence of regulations prescribing specific good manufacturing practices, see *United States v. General Foods Corp.*, 446 F. Supp. 740 (N.D.N.Y.), *aff'd* 591 F.2d 1332 (2d Cir. 1978). There the District Court refused to find that geotrichum mold found on equipment used to process canned green beans demonstrated that the beans had been processed under such conditions as to present a reasonable possibility that they could have become contaminated with filth. The District Court relied on testimony that mold is common in such facilities. It also rejected FDA's charge under section 402(a)(3):

> ... There is little or no evidence whatsoever to show that the levels of Geotrichum discovered in defendants' finished product were avoidable through the use of current good manufacturing practices, as exist within the industry. Finally, it is uncontroverted that Geotrichum, at the levels with which we are dealing, is not harmful when consumed by humans. This Court therefore finds that, while the Geotrichum found in samples of defendant's frozen french-style green beans constitutes filth, the amount is *de minimis*, and does not therefore constitute an (a)(3) violation.

In *United States v. 155/137 Pound Burlap Bags*, 4 FDLI Food and Drug Rep. 784 (E.D. Va. 1993), the District Court denied a government motion for summary judgment in a section 402(a)(4) case. The District Court held that FDA must only prove a reasonable possibility of contamination rather than actual contamination, but concluded that there were genuine issues of fact as to (i) whether the threshold level of possible contamination of the cocoa beans had been achieved, in light of the fact that the beans are necessarily cleaned and processed before human consumption and (ii) whether there was a reasonable possibility that each separate cell in the warehouses was contaminated.

2. *Compliance Policy.* Following adverse rulings in the *General Foods* case, *supra* Note 1, and in a similar case, FDA sent a directive to its field force in January 1979 limiting future legal action under section 402(a)(4):

> Inspections that do not involve pathogens can be developed as 402(a)(4) cases based on observed sanitary conditions concerning visible filth....
>
> In all 402(a)(4) situations other than those involving pathogens, inspections will be conducted using inspectional observations of organoleptically detectable (by sight and/or smell) filth and collection of physical filth exhibits. For the present, we are not prepared to approve cases based on conditions demonstrable only by bacteriological analysis....

In 54 Fed. Reg. 32395 (Aug. 7, 1989), FDA issued Compliance Policy Guide No. 7153.04 on Reconditioning Food Adulterated Under Section 402(a)(4).

3. *Microbiological Quality Standards.* In 37 Fed. Reg. 20038 (Sept. 23, 1972), FDA proposed to establish "quality" standards for two foods by prescribing limits for nonpathogenic microorganisms under section 401 of the Act, "Definitions and Standards for Food." It published final regulations in 38 Fed. Reg. 20726 (Aug. 2, 1973), which it then stayed in response to objections and requests for hearing, 41

Fed. Reg. 33249 (Aug. 9, 1976). *See* John W. Farquhar, *The Role of Microbiology in the Integrity of Foods*, 31 FOOD DRUG COSM. L.J. 17 (1976). FDA withdrew both proposals in 43 Fed. Reg. 9272 (Mar. 7, 1978), but it did not abandon this approach. In 45 Fed. Reg. 37422 (June 3, 1980), FDA announced it would issue microbiological standards of quality as recommendations rather than as regulations. It announced microbiological defect action levels for raw breaded shrimp in 48 Fed. Reg. 43223 (Sept. 22, 1983), and withdrew levels for langostinos in 54 Fed. Reg. 51079 (Dec. 12, 1989).

4. *FDA/USDA Cooperation.* In AN EVALUATION OF THE ROLE OF MICROBIOLOGICAL CRITERIA FOR FOODS (1985), the National Academy of Sciences recommended establishment of a committee to review microbiological quality standards for food. In 52 Fed. Reg. 43216 (Nov. 10, 1987), USDA, in cooperation with FDA, announced the establishment of this committee, now named the National Advisory Committee on Microbiological Criteria for Foods, which has been meeting ever since and has played an important role in advising FDA on microbiological matters.

5. *Reconditioning.* FDA announced a guideline for reconditioning food adulterated under section 402(a)(4) in 54 Fed. Reg. 32395 (Aug. 7, 1989). Damaged food is often sold to the food salvage industry, which either reconditions it for human use or sells it for other purposes. *See* GAO, NEED FOR REGULATING THE FOOD SALVAGE INDUSTRY TO PREVENT SALE OF UNWHOLESOME AND MISBRANDED FOODS TO THE PUBLIC, No. MWD–75–64 (May 20, 1975); GAO, FOOD SALVAGE INDUSTRY SHOULD BE PREVENTED FROM SELLING UNFIT AND MISBRANDED FOOD TO THE PUBLIC, No. HRD–79–32 (Feb. 14, 1979). In cooperation with the Association of Food and Drug officials, FDA developed a model food salvage code. 44 Fed. Reg. 74921 (Dec. 18, 1979), 49 Fed. Reg. 31952 (Aug. 9, 1984). For a discussion of FDA authority to require reconditioning as part of the salvage of adulterated food, see *United States v. 1,638 Cases of Adulterated Alcoholic Beverages*, 624 F.2d 900 (9th Cir. 1980).

6. *Permanent Injunction.* For an example of a consent decree of permanent injunction against a bakery operating under insanitary conditions, see *United States v. Manhattan Bakery*, Food Drug Cosm. L. Rep. (CCH) ¶ 38,163 (N.D. Ga. 1982).

7. *Case Law.* For other decisions interpreting Sections 402(a)(3) and (4), *see, e.g., United States v. Gel Spice Co., Inc.*, 773 F.2d 427 (2d Cir. 1985), *aff'g* 601 F. Supp. 1205 (E.D.N.Y. 1984); *Salamonie Packing Co. v. United States*, 165 F.2d 205 (8th Cir. 1948); *United States v. 1851 Cartons . . . H. & G. Famous Booth Sea Foods Whiting Frosted Fish*, 146 F.2d 760 (10th Cir. 1945); *A.O. Andersen & Co. v. United States*, 284 Fed. 542 (9th Cir. 1922); *Dade v. United States*, 40 App. D.C. 94 (D.C. Cir. 1913); *United States v. Manhattan Bakery*, Food Drug Cosm. L. Rep. (CCH) ¶ 38,163 (N.D. Ga. 1982); *United States v. 1800 Cases . . . "Field's 'World's Best' Pecan Pie . . .",* Food Drug Cosm. L. Rep. (CCH) ¶ 38,098 (N.D. Tex. 1981); *United States v. Corbi*, Food Drug Cosm. L. Rep. (CCH) ¶ 38,040 (D. Md. 1979); *United States v. 900 Cases Peaches*, 390 F. Supp. 1006 (E.D.N.Y. 1975), *aff'd without opinion sub nom. United States v. Noroian*, 556 F.2d 562 (2d Cir. 1977); *United States v. An Article of Food . . . 51 Cases*, 1969–1974 FDLI Jud. Rec. 145 (E.D. La. 1973); *United States v. 233 Tins . . . "Grove Brand * * * Whole Blakemore Strawberries,"* 175 F. Supp. 694 (W.D. Ark. 1959); *United States v. Roma Macaroni Factory*, 75 F. Supp. 663 (N.D. Cal. 1947); *United States v. 184 Barrels Dried Whole Eggs*, 53 F. Supp. 652 (E.D. Wis. 1943); *United States v. 1,375 Cases of Tomato Paste*, 1938–1964 FDLI Jud. Rec. 13 (D. Conn. 1942).

8. *Commentary.* Representative articles on food sanitation include L. M. Beacham, *Organoleptic Examination of Processed Foods*, 5 FOOD DRUG COSM. L.J. 400 (1950); E. M. Foster, *An Evaluation of the Salmonella Problem*, 25 FOOD DRUG COSM. L.J. 60 (1970); L. B. Jensen, *Bacterial Food Poisoning*, 11 FOOD DRUG COSM. L.J. 631 (1956); George P. Larrick, *The Challenge: Improving Controls in Frozen*

Foods, 19 FOOD DRUG COSM. L.J. 290 (1964); George P. Larrick, *Enforcement of the Sanitation Provisions of the Federal Food, Drug, and Cosmetic Act*, 3 FOOD DRUG COSM. L.Q. 237 (1948); George P. Larrick, *Comments on the Food and Drug Administration's Sanitation Program*, 3 FOOD DRUG COSM. L.Q. 510 (1948); Kenneth L. Milstead, *FDA Enforcement Problems in the Fishery Industry*, 16 FOOD DRUG COSM. L.J. 274 (1961).

9. *Transport Sanitation.* For discussions of the problems of sanitation in railroad cars used to transport food, see the articles in 29 FOOD DRUG COSM. L.J. 492 *et seq.* (1974). The Sanitary Food Transport Act of 1990, 104 Stat. 1213, authorized the Department of Transportation to issue regulations to prevent the contamination of food and other FDA-regulated products by nonfood substances during shipments. DOT published an advance notice of proposed rulemaking in 56 Fed. Reg. 6934 (Feb. 20, 1991) and a proposed regulation in 58 Fed. Reg. 29698 (May 21, 1993) that would have imposed stringent rules on the use of designated railway cars exclusively for food products. In 61 Fed. Reg. 59372 (Nov. 22, 1996), FDA and USDA published an advance notice of proposed rulemaking seeking comment on approaches to foster food safety improvements in the transportation and storage of potentially hazardous food. DOT then published a supplemental proposal simply to reference in its regulations the requirements of USDA and FDA without imposing its own independent requirements. 69 Fed. Reg. 76423 (Dec. 21, 2004). DOT concluded that "the expertise for ensuring the safety of our nation's food supply, including transportation, lies with USDA and FDA." USDA and FDA have taken no further action on this matter. The Sanitary Food Transportation Act of 2005, 119 Stat. 1144, 1911, added section 416 to the FD&C Act to require FDA to promulgate regulations for the safe and sanitary transportation of food. The new law gives FDA inspection authority for food transportation records required to be maintained under section 416. DOT withdrew its proposed regulations following the enactment of the Sanitary Food Transportation Act. 70 Fed. Reg. 76228 (Dec. 23, 2005). FDA has not yet proposed regulations to implement the new statute.

d.   OTHERWISE UNFIT FOR FOOD

United States v. 298 Cases ... Ski Slide Brand Asparagus

88 F. Supp. 450 (D. Ore. 1949).

■ McCULLOCH, DISTRICT JUDGE.

Defendant is an asparagus packer. One of his products is the center cut of the asparagus. This retails for 20¢ per can (1 lb. 3 oz.) containing 95 to 100 cuts, as compared with 40 to 45 cents per can for the choicer tips. The Government contends that defendant's center cuts are fibrous and woody beyond the permissible limits set up by the Federal Food, Drug and Cosmetic Administration. Three witnesses for the Government said that they had eaten a can (or attempted to) of defendant's cuts. The composite of their testimony was that 25% or more of the cuts were inedible, and the Government's witnesses condemned them as a food product.

On the other hand, the Director of Mary Cullen's Cottage found only 5 or 6 pieces out of 100 that she had to lay aside. Confronted with this conflict in testimony, I obtained counsels' consent to eat a can. This I have done, although I confess had I understood all the difficulties of the undertaking, I might not have been so bold.

To eat a can of asparagus, hand-running, as the saying is, is quite a chore. I took three days to eat the can. That, I can now state, is as much as an old protein user should attempt on his first venture into herbalism. I suspect the Government witnesses tried to eat their cans all at one time, and that may explain the severity of their judgment about defendant's asparagus. I can see where after 50 or 60 cuts, eaten without spelling oneself, one might become very particular.

My test more than confirmed Miss Laughton's good opinion of the cuts. She found 5 or 6 per cent inedible, whereas I ate all of my can, and felt that I was helped by it. There was one runty, tough piece and two or three slivers, but I treated them as de minimis. I agree with the Director of Mary Cullen's Cottage that this is an excellent product, particularly considering its low price. Not everybody in this country can "keep up with the Joneses" and eat only asparagus tips. Indeed it seems strange to me that the Government should be interested in keeping from the market a moderately priced, wholly nutritious food product. I should think in this period of declining income the Government's interest would be the other way. If Mr. Prendergast [the lawyer for the defendant] will prepare appropriate findings, I will give his client's center cuts a clean bill of health. They deserve it.

NOTES

1. *Judicial Standards.* In *United States v. 24 Cases, More or Less*, 87 F. Supp. 826 (D. Me. 1949), the District Court held that for food to be unfit, it "must be proved to be so tough and rubbery that the average, normal person, under ordinary conditions, would not chew and swallow it." In *United States v. 71/55 Gallon Drums ... Stuffed Green Olives in Brine*, 790 F. Supp. 1379 (N.D. Ill. 1992), FDA seized olives on the ground that they were "unfit for food." FDA demonstrated that the products contained yeast, but the claimant argued that this is normal and harmless. Claimant asserted that all olives are in this condition when stored in bulk but are cleaned prior to consumer sale. The District Court rejected this argument, holding that a food which is adulterated may be condemned even though it is intended to have the adulteration eliminated by a future process. But the District Court held that an "unfit for food" decision rests upon consumer perception of the article, and it denied motions for summary judgment on the ground that whether the olives were unfit for food was a triable issue of fact.

> In cases such as these, where the condemnation of an article of food is sought even though the article has not been alleged to be injurious to the public, the decision hinges on consumer perception. While the product's appearance is a factor in consumer perception, the decisive factor rests on the taste and expectations of the consumer.

The court ordered a bench trial at which time a taste test would be conducted. The parties then entered into a consent decree that "condemned the article and authorized its release to the claimant for bringing into compliance with the law." 28 FDA CONSUMER, No. 3, at 33 (Apr. 1994).

2. *Candy Choking Hazard.* Beginning with "FDA Warns Consumers About Imported Jelly Cup Type Candy that Poses a Potential Choking Hazard," Talk Paper No. T01–38 (Aug. 17, 2001), FDA issued more than a dozen press releases and talk papers on the choking hazard caused by "konjac" jelly cups imported from Asia, which do not readily dissolve when placed in the mouth. The product caused

the death of several children. When one company refused to recall its konjac candy products, FDA brought a seizure action alleging that the products were "unfit for food because they pose a serious choking hazard." *See* "FDA Seizes New Choice Food Gel Candies," Press Release P02–16 (May 22, 2002). The company entered into a consent decree of condemnation and destruction.

3. *Peanut Butter.* Based on a 1983 unpublished report by the American Academy of Pediatrics on "Foods and Choking in Children," funded by FDA, Citizen Petition No. 90P–0395 was submitted to the agency requesting a warning label on peanut butter about the danger of choking by small children. The petition cited *Fraust v. Swift & Co.*, 610 F. Supp. 711 (W.D. Pa. 1985), a case denying summary judgment to a peanut butter manufacturer in a failure to warn tort action brought by a young choking victim. FDA denied the citizen petition, contending that peanut butter does not pose "a significant risk of choking in children." Letter from Ronald G. Chesemore, Associate Commissioner for Regulatory Affairs, to Anthony R. Martin (Apr. 27, 1998).

4. *Fish Protein.* FDA has frequently been confronted with proposals to market foods from sources that may affront the sensibilities of many consumers. In the 1950s, scientists began exploring more effective means to exploit marine sources of protein for use in human food. In 1961, FDA published a proposal to establish a standard of identity for "fish protein concentrate, whole fish flour," a product made by processing intact fish. 26 Fed. Reg. 8641 (Sept. 15, 1961). Comments on the proposal objected that the product would include the viscera, intestines, and other portions of the fish that are not normally used for food. The agency's final standard permitted the product to be made only from edible species of cleaned fish, after discarding "the heads, tails, fins, viscera, and intestinal contents." 27 Fed. Reg. 740 (Jan. 25, 1962). Objections to the standard resulted in a stay pending a public hearing. Before a hearing could be held, the entire matter was referred to a committee of the National Academy of Sciences, which eventually endorsed the concept of making protein concentrate, or flour, from whole fish for human consumption. Its report implied that requiring the cleaning of the fish prior to processing would be so expensive as to jeopardize the economic viability of this technology for producing a very cheap source of protein. Accordingly, in 1967 FDA published a regulation under the Food Additives Amendment authorizing the production and sale of whole fish protein concentrate:

> The Commissioner of Food and Drugs, taking cognizance of the findings relative to the suitability of fish protein concentrate ... deems it desirable to make this economical source of protein available for consumers. Individual consumers are entitled to the opportunity of choice in the matter of whether they desire to include this item in their diets; therefore, the product, to be readily distinguishable, should be more properly identified as "whole fish protein concentrate," and for domestic distribution it should be packaged for household use in consumer sized units not exceeding 1 pound net weight.

The regulation permitted processing "without removal of heads, fins, tails, viscera, or intestinal contents." 32 Fed. Reg. 1173 (Feb. 2, 1967), codified at 21 C.F.R. 172.385.

5. *Worms.* On April 26, 1977, FDA's Bureau of Foods replied to an inquiry that probed the limits of the "otherwise unfit for food" language of section 402(a)(3):

Pat L. Smith
Smitty's Worm Hatchery
1005 S. College Avenue
College Place, WA 99324

. . . .

Worms are not commonly recognized as a source of food in the United States. We believe the vast majority of consumers would view them as aesthetically objectionable in food or as food, just as insects are viewed as aesthetically objectionable by most people. There are certain specialty items, such as fried agave worms, baby beees [sic], and chocolate covered fried ants that have been sold in this country for many years, but such products are not widely accepted or consumed and are viewed primarily as novelty items. We have not objected to the sale of such items when properly labaled [sic] and otherwise in compliance with the law, because the purchaser is aware of the nature of the items purchased and because they have been consumed with apparent safety. . . .

From an aesthetic viewpoint, we would probably view the sale of worms or products derived from them in the same manner we view these specialty [sic] items mentioned above. However, before worms or products derived from them could be marketed as food in this country, we would have to insist that they be considered under the food additive provisions of the FD&C Act to assure that consumption of these products would be safe. . . .

When FDA issued a Warning Letter to the manufacturer of "Sugar–Free Hotlix Tequila Flavored Candy with Genuine Worm," the agency objected to the failure to include "insect larva" in the statement of ingredients, but not to the inclusion of the worm itself. Letter from Elaine C. Messa, Director of the FDA Los Angeles District Office, to Larry Peterman, Warning Letter WL–56–3 (Apr. 28, 1993). *See also* Michael E. Ruane, *Insects in Suckers, Bugs in a Bag: Company Has Six Legs Up on the Candy Competition*, WASH. POST, Nov. 5, 1999, at B1.

6. *DES Residues.* Faced with the difficulty of proving that a trace amount of DES in beef was an added poisonous or deleterious substance that may render the food injurious to health, the government tried the additional argument that the DES residue rendered the product "unfit for food." In *United States v. 2,116 Boxes of Boned Beef*, 516 F. Supp. 321 (D. Kan. 1981), the District Court ruled that "[t]he allegation of unfitness must be independent of the allegation of injuriousness" and that "unfit for food" includes such conditions as discoloration or a bad smell but does not include intentional additions of substances to food. The government did not appeal. *See also Millet, Pit and Seed Co., Inc. v. United States*, 436 F. Supp. 84 (E.D. Tenn. 1977) (holding that apricot kernels naturally containing amygdalin are not "unfit for food" because FDA failed to prove that they were "inedible for the average person under ordinary conditions").

7. *Cattle Materials.* Because of concern about transmission of "mad cow disease" (bovine spongiform encephalopathy), FDA banned specified cattle materials as unfit for use in human food and promulgated recordkeeping requirements to enforce the ban. 69 Fed. Reg. 42256 & 42275 (July 14, 2004), 70 Fed. Reg. 53063 (Sept. 7, 2005), 71 Fed. Reg. 59653 (Oct. 11, 2006), codified at 21 C.F.R. 189.5. To buttress its legal authority, FDA also relied on sections 402(a)(2)(C), 402(a)(4), 402(a)(5), and 409.

8. *Commentary. See generally* Paul M. Steffy, *"Otherwise Unfit for Food"—A New Concept in Food Adulteration*, 4 FOOD DRUG COSM. L.Q. 552 (1949).

3. THE ISSUE OF "BLENDING"

Section 110.110(d) of the FDA regulations provides:

The mixing of a food containing defects above the current defect action level with another lot of food is not permitted and renders the final food adulterated ... regardless of the defect level of the final food.

FDA's longstanding opposition to "blending" of above-tolerance and below-tolerance lots of contaminated food has continually been subject to reexamination.

Sugarman v. Forbragd

267 F. Supp. 817 (N.D. Cal. 1967).

■ ZIRPOLI, DISTRICT JUDGE.

... These coffee beans were being transported from Colombia to Japan when a fire aboard the ship MS Gunhild Torm required the Captain to change his course and enter a distress port at Long Beach, California.... The unloading of the coffee began on March 28 and was completed by April 3. The bags of coffee were torn, ripped, and split at the seams due to the swelling of the cargo and the coffee beans were therefore unloaded in bulk, commingled with other cargo; at that time the coffee beans were blackened, heated, and in a steaming condition....

On April 11, 1966, Petitioner Sugarman, together with three other joint venturers, purchased "the damaged coffee beans for salvage" for the sum of $600. The coffee beans were then transported to Turlock, California, where they were "cleaned" and sacked and thereafter offered for import.... On March 30, 1967, Respondent Forbragd [an FDA officer] wrote to the attorney for the Petitioner, incorporating verbatim the following letter which Mr. Forbragd had received from the Food and Drug Administration in Washington, D.C.:

> "We agree that the claimant's proposal to salvage this article under detention by grinding and blending it with other ground coffee is completely unacceptable, since this would amount to nothing more than diluting a legal article of food with an article which is unfit for food to make a low grade unfinished product.
>
> Although you have approved the claimant's application to attempt to salvage a portion of this article either by extracting the caffeine or by processing into soluble coffee, we doubt that a satisfactory soluble coffee can be produced.... If this coffee is to be utilized in making soluble coffee the firm should not blend this with other coffee beans to prepare the soluble coffee...."

[The court's discussion of the procedures available to importers of food and of the availability of judicial review appears *infra* p. 1371.]

Petitioner's real objective appears to be an effort to parlay an "as is" $600 investment "for salvage" plus additionally incurred expenditures for transportation, reconditioning and storage, into a gross return of some $40,000 at the expense of the ultimate consumer, by mixing these damaged beans with normal beans in the production of blended coffee....

Petitioner's proposal to blend the charred coffee beans with normal coffee beans is in reality a proposal to adulterate the good coffee beans, by substituting in part a cheapened and worthless commodity for genuine coffee beans. It is as though the proposal were to make a blend of *used coffee grounds* with freshly ground coffee. No doubt a skillful "blending" of the charred coffee beans with genuine coffee beans, or of used coffee grounds with freshly ground coffee, would enable a coffee producer to palm off the finished product on an unsuspecting public as coffee. . . .

Under these circumstances, the agency action in question cannot be said to be "arbitrary or capricious." If Petitioner's request to make a coffee blend had been granted, the Food and Drug Administration would have been grossly derelict in the performance of its duties. . . .

NOTE

As Peter Barton Hutt observed in *The Basis and Purpose of Government Regulation of Adulteration and Misbranding of Food*, 33 FOOD DRUG COSM. L.J. 505 (1978):

> . . . This policy was pursued by the Agency because of the fear that condoning the practice of "blending" would discourage sound sanitation practices and would result in great quantities of good food being blended with poor food, thus resulting in a general esthetic debasement of the food supply. . . .

> . . . Competing concerns about the availability and cost of food to feed the world must, however, also be considered. Perhaps it would be possible to permit blending at least for animal feed, or under other limited circumstances, in order to determine the impact that any change in this policy would in fact have. Blind adherence to this longstanding policy is, in any event, no longer justifiable.

See also Colleen A. Brennan, *Use of Blending as a Method to Bring Filth Content Within Defect Action Levels: An Idea Whose Time Has Come?*, in Ch. V(H)(2) of the Electronic Book.

COMMENT: BLENDING FOR MYCOTOXIN CONTAMINATION

In 1978, FDA confronted a situation in the southeastern United States that caused it to relax its opposition to "blending" despite its genuine concerns about food safety. Heavy rains during the 1977 harvesting season led to above-tolerance levels of aflatoxin contamination on as much as 40 percent of the region's corn crop. (Aflatoxins, a class of mycotoxins, are toxic and carcinogenic metabolites produced by fungi on crops.) On January 30, 1978, FDA Commissioner Donald Kennedy responded to one commodity dealer's request for permission to blend several contaminated lots with below-tolerance corn for use as animal feed:

> . . . Tolerances and action levels for poisonous or deleterious substances such as aflatoxin apply only to unavoidable levels of contamination. Intentional blending of a violative article with an uncontaminated article is wholly avoidable and not authorized by such tolerances or action levels. Accordingly, the law does not permit you to blend adulterated corn with unadulterated corn as proposed in your letter. . . .

> We recognize that farmers and elevator operators in the southeastern United States face an unusual and economically-devastating problem with respect to aflatoxin contamination in the

1977 corn harvest. It appears that over half of the 1977 corn crop in the southeastern United States (Alabama, Florida, Georgia, Mississippi, North Carolina, South Carolina, and Virginia) may exceed the 20 ppb action level.... Since it may be difficult for farmers in this area to find adequate supplies of corn for use in feeding animals if the law is enforced fully, the Commissioner has determined that he will not recommend regulatory action for violation of the FD&C Act with respect to blending of such corn for use as animal feed if *all* of the following conditions are met:

(1) A technically feasible plan for blending must be provided, the plan to be approved by the FDA district office in Atlanta, Georgia, before blending operations commence.... The blending must be accomplished under Federal or State supervision, and ... [i]t must be demonstrated to the satisfaction of the supervising Federal or State authority that the aflatoxin level of the blended lot is below 20 ppb.

(2) The aflatoxin-contaminated corn must not have been shipped in interstate commerce prior to FDA approval of the blending plan....

(3) The blended lot must be offered for use only for animal feed for mature poultry, swine and beef animals other than milk-producing animals.... Because aflatoxin is such a potent carcinogen, FDA will not under any circumstances authorize the blending for human consumption of corn exceeding the aflatoxin action level.

(4) This approval for limited blending applies only to corn harvested in the southeastern United States (Alabama, Florida, Georgia, Mississippi, North Carolina, South Carolina, and Virginia) during the 1977 harvest....

This decision, subsequently published in 43 Fed. Reg. 14122 (Apr. 4, 1978) in accordance with 21 C.F.R. 109.4(c)(2), was issued without prior notice or opportunity for comment. FDA followed the same procedure when it approved blending for a second time under similar circumstances in 46 Fed. Reg. 7447 (Jan. 23, 1981).

The latter action triggered a lawsuit by the Community Nutrition Institute (CNI), which argued that FDA's action levels for aflatoxin were unlawful because they had not been established through formal rulemaking under section 406 and Section 701(e), or even through notice-and-comment rulemaking. CNI also claimed that blending was a violation of the FD&C Act. The Court of Appeals' holding that FDA had no authority to substitute action levels for formal tolerances under section 406, *Community Nutrition Institute v. Young*, 757 F.2d 354 (D.C. Cir. 1985), was reversed by the Supreme Court, 476 U.S. 974 (1986), *infra* p. 381. On remand, the Court of Appeals, 818 F.2d 943, 949–50 (D.C. Cir. 1987), held:

... The *intentional* blending of contaminated corn obviously cannot in reason be considered unavoidable. Surely there can be little doubt that blended corn therefore stands branded as "adulterated" for purposes of the FDC Act.... But as FDA goes on to point out, a conclusion that a particular food product is "adulterated," in the abstract, means little other than that FDA could choose to initiate enforcement proceedings . . .

Upon analysis, therefore, the gravaman of CNI's complaint is that FDA failed to initiate enforcement proceedings. But as the Supreme Court held in *Heckler v. Chaney* [*infra* p. 1211], FDA enjoys complete discretion not to employ the enforcement provisions of the FDC Act, and those decisions are not subject to judicial review.

When the southeast was again faced with widespread aflatoxin contamination of the corn crop, FDA announced that it was retaining its 20 ppb action level for human food but raising its action levels for animal feed. *See* "Aflatoxin Contamination," FDA Talk Paper No. T88–73 (Oct. 4, 1988); "Drought Increases Aflatoxin Problem for Farmers, Processors," FDA Talk Paper No. T89–13 (Feb. 27, 1989). Explaining that action levels constitute only guidance and not binding requirements, FDA again announced that blending would be permitted. 54 Fed. Reg. 22622 (May 25, 1989).

NOTES

1. *Rationale for FDA Policy*. In Compliance Policy Guide No. 7120.14 (Oct. 1, 1980), FDA took the position that the deliberate mixing of adulterated food with good food renders the finished product adulterated regardless of the final concentration of contaminants in the finished food. When FDA promulgated its final food GMP regulations, it specifically declined to revise 21 C.F.R. § 110.110(d), which prohibits the blending of food to comply with an action level for defects presenting no health hazard. 51 Fed. Reg. 22458, 22474 (June 19, 1986). Now that the agency has approved the blending of food contaminated with a potent carcinogen, even if limited to food used as animal feed, should it continue to prohibit all blending of aesthetically contaminated human food when there is no risk to human health?

2. *Congressional Testimony*. FDA defended its policy of permitting the blending of mycotoxin-contaminated food for animal feed use in "Review of the U.S. Department of Agriculture's Crop Disaster Assistance and 1993 Crop Quality Issues," Hearing before the Subcommittee on General Farm Commodities of the Committee on Agriculture, House of Representatives, 103d Cong., 1st Sess. (1993).

3. *Scientific Report*. For a Scientific Status Summary by the Institute of Food Technologists on mycotoxins, see *Understanding Mycotoxins*, 60 FOOD TECH., No. 6, at 51 (June 2006).

4. PATHOGENIC MICROORGANISMS

All food contains microorganisms. Most are harmless. Nonpathogenic microorganisms are an essential part of the bacterial fermentation process needed to produce such common food products as cheese, yogurt, and pickles. As described in Note 3 at p. 317 *supra*, FDA has considered establishing standards for harmless microorganisms to protect food quality.

The scientific study of food poisoning through pathogenic contamination of food began with the publication of G.M. DACK, FOOD POISONING (1943). With rare exceptions, FDA has always taken regulatory action against any food containing any detectable level of a pathogenic microorganism. For example, Compliance Policy Guide No. 7106.08 (Oct. 10, 1980, as amended) authorizes seizure of any dairy product containing any detectable amount of salmonella, campylobacter jejuni, campylobacter coli, yersinia enterocolitica, or listera monocytogenes, or greater than a specified level of enteropathic escherichia coli. The following table of typical illnesses caused by common food pathogens, from David W. K. Acheson & Anthony E. Fiore, *Preventing Foodborne Disease—What Clinicians Can Do*, 350 NEW ENG. J. MED. 437, 439 (2004), illustrates the impact of pathogens in food.

Table. Selected Clinical and Epidemiologic Characteristics of Typical Illnesses Caused by Common Foodborne Pathogens.*

Pathogen	Typical Incubation Period†	Duration	Typical Clinical Presentation‡	Associated Foods§
Bacterial				
Salmonella species	1–3 Days	4–7 Days	Gastroenteritis	Undercooked eggs or poultry, produce
Campylobacter jejuni	2–5 Days	2–10 Days	Gastroenteritis	Undercooked poultry, unpasteurized dairy products
Escherichia coli O157:H7	1–8 Days	5–10 Days	Gastroenteritis	Undercooked beef, produce, unpasteurized dairy products
E. coli, enterotoxigenic	1–3 Days	3–7 Days	Gastroenteritis	Many foods
Shigella species	1–2 Days	4–7 Days	Gastroenteritis	Produce, egg salad
Listeria monocytogenes	2–6 Wk	Variable	Gastroenteritis, meningitis, abortion¶	Deli meat, hot dogs, unpasteurized dairy products
Bacillus cereus	1–6 Hr	<24 Hr	Vomiting, gastroenteritis	Fried rice, meats
Clostridium botulinum	12–72 Hr	Days–months	Blurred vision, paralysis	Home-canned foods, fermented fish
Staphylococcus aureus	1–6 Hr	1–2 Days	Gastroenteritis, particularly nausea	Meats, potato and egg salads, cream pastries
Yersinia enterocolitica	1–2 Days	1–3 Wk	Gastroenteritis, appendicitis-like syndrome	Undercooked pork, unpasteurized dairy products
Viral				
Norovirus	1–2 Days	12–60 Hr	Gastroenteritis	Undercooked shellfish
Hepatitis A virus	15–50 Days	Weeks–months	Hepatitis	Produce, undercooked shellfish
Parasitic				
Cryptosporidium parvum	2–10 Days	Weeks	Gastroenteritis	Produce, water
Cyclospora cayetanensis	1–11 Days	Weeks	Gastroenteritis	Produce, water
Toxoplasma gondii	5–23 Days	Months	Influenza-like illness, lymphadenopathy	Food contaminated by cat feces, undercooked meat
Giardia lamblia	1–4 Wk	Weeks	Gastroenteritis	Water
Taenia solium	Variable	Variable	Asymptomatic, cysticercosis	Raw pork

* Adapted from "Diagnosis and Management of Foodborne Illnesses: A Primer for Physicians" (available at http://www.ama-assn.org/ama/pub/category/3629.html).
† Incubation periods may vary; the average periods are given, but wider ranges have been reported.
‡ Gastroenteritis typically includes nausea, vomiting, diarrhea (which may be bloody), fever, and abdominal pain.
§ These foods are among those most commonly implicated in epidemiologic investigations. For some pathogens, person-to-person transmission or transmission through foods prepared by an infected person is more common.
¶ L. monocytogenes may also cause gastroenteritis with a short (two-to-three-day) incubation period.

In the past quarter century, three events have led FDA and the public to focus on foodborne illness caused by pathogens: (1) the unexpected discovery in 1982 that, using more sensitive detection methodology, listeria contamination can be found in many common food products, (2) the January 1993 contamination of undercooked hamburgers by a new strain of E.coli, 0157:47, at a Jack in the Box restaurant in Washington State, which caused the death of four children and the hospitalization of many others, and (3) the October 1996 contamination with E.coli 0157:47 of Odwalla fresh unpasteurized apple cider marketed on the west coast, which lead to the death of one child and the hospitalization of many others. For comprehensive reviews of foodborne illness, see Chryssa V. Deliganis, *Death by*

Apple Juice: The Problem of Foodborne Illness, the Regulatory Response, and Further Suggestions for Reform, 53 FOOD & DRUG L.J. 681 (1998); Richard A. Merrill & Jeffrey K. Francer, *Reforming Food Safety Regulation*, 31 SETON HALL L. REV. 64 (2000).

Sanford A. Miller, *The Saga of Chicken Little and Rambo**

51 JOURNAL OF THE ASSOCIATION OF FOOD AND DRUG OFFICIALS 196 (1987).

... [T]he most perplexing and hazardous problems of food safety remain today as they always have been, problems of assuring microbiological safety.

For example, there was [sic] in 1980 alone, more than one million cases of acute diarrhea in children under five in the developing world. These children died at a rate of ten diarrheal deaths every minute of every day of every year. The majority of these illnesses are caused by food, directly by microbial contamination and indirectly by reducing nutritional status in marginally nourished children. When, to this total, is added the nondiarrhetic foodborne diseases, such as botulinum, typhoid and parasitism, as well as the chronic effects of chemical contamination of foods, the number of people affected and the impact of food contamination on function, well being and economic status is appalling.

Even in the industrialized countries, foodborne diseases are a significant cause of morbidity. Relatively high standards of environmental sanitation, personal hygiene and refrigerator storage of food in most homes has virtually eliminated several serious foodborne diseases, such as typhoid fever. Nonetheless, major outbreaks of such diseases do occur occasionally. Indeed, the incidence of such diseases appears to be on the increase in these countries, in part due to transformation of organisms thought to be benign to those having characteristics which current practices may not entirely protect against. Outbreaks of relatively less serious illness, such as salmonellosis, are not uncommon, usually as the result of an error at one or more stages in the chain of food processing, preparation, distribution and storage in commercial enterprises, public institutions and private homes.

... [O]f much greater concern is the apparent, sudden appearance of a new generation of pathogenic organisms in the food supply. For example, a decade ago, organisms such as *Campylobacter jejuni, Aeromonas hydrophilia, Listeria monocytogenes, Yersinia* sp., *Shiigilla* sp., enteropathogenic and hemorrhagic serotypes of E. *coli*, rotoviruses and several protozoans were thought to be rare causes of disease in developed countries. Today, they are among the most common pathogens associated with foods. There are many reasons for this. Among these may be better methods of detection and identification, changing environmental conditions, normal transformation processes, improper use of antibiotics, etc. What is certain, however, is that the pathogenic environment in food is changing. While it appears that

* [Dr. Miller was the Director of the FDA Center for Food Safety and Applied Nutrition.]

current good manufacturing practices involving appropriate and rigorously applied sanitation as well as the proper use of pasteurization and other thermal processing techniques will control these organisms, it is also true that there is not much "forgiveness" in the system....

These concerns are not only of academic interest. For example, scientists at the Center for Food Safety and Applied Nutrition of the USFDA estimated that as many as 81 million or more cases of diarrhea disease of foodborne origin occurs [sic] in the United States each year. They also estimated that the average cost for such food-associated illnesses falls close to 164 billion dollars per year. If one adds indirect costs to the economy resulting from such illnesses, they may equal or even double these direct patient-related costs....

It is the acute effects of such illnesses that are generally considered to be the most significant outcomes of their presence. Recent research, however, has emphasized the fact that virtually all of these organisms can also produce or contribute to chronic disorders of many kinds. Thus, certain salmonella, in addition to producing acute enteric disease, may also be associated with the development of rheumatoid problems of various kinds. Certain other organisms may also be associated with the development of neoplasia in the gastrointestinal tract....

There is a parenthetical issue that needs to be addressed. Have we devoted too large a share of our treasure to the problems of chemical contamination of the food supply thus effectively ignoring the considerable problem of microbiological hazard? Public *perception* implies that we have not overreacted. Indeed there are many who say we haven't committed enough to deal with chemical hazards. Recent studies of nearly 1600 food chemicals by the CFSAN of FDA provides [sic] an interesting, even "eye opening" perspective on the problem. Among other factors, CFSAN scientists calculated what we call the "Assurance of Safety ratio, 'R' ". This ratio relates exposure to potency as determined by appropriate animal tests. Three observations emerge.

First, the R value (or margin of safety) most likely to be found in this group of food chemicals was 10^5 or a 100,000 fold margin of safety. Second, more than 99% of the values fall above a margin of safety of 1000. Third, for most compounds, only the simplest studies may be required to establish safety since, on the basis of the structure, exposure and potency data obtained in short-term tests, they fall into concern categories that predict high margins of safety. Since the 1600 compounds studied represent that part of the food chemical inventory having the highest probability of significant toxicity, it is likely that the remaining compounds are of even less concern. Based on these and other analysis the time has come, I believe, for a renewed emphasis of microbial issues and some reduction in concern with food chemicals.

NOTES

1.   *Commentary. See also* Douglas L. Archer, *The New Foodbourne Pathogens,* 52 J. AFDO, No. 4, at 5 (Oct. 1988); Paul D. Frenzen, *Deaths Due to Unknown Foodborne Agents,* 10 EMERGING INFECTIOUS DISEASES 1536 (Sept. 2004).

2. *Listeria.* With the discovery through new detection methodology of widespread listeria contamination of food products in 1982, FDA imposed and enforced a strict zero tolerance level. USDA adopted the same zero tolerance level. 52 Fed. Reg. 7464 (Mar. 11, 1987), 54 Fed. Reg. 22345 (May 23, 1989). In 53 Fed. Reg. 44148 (Nov. 1, 1988), FDA took the unusual step of publishing a revised methodology for detecting and confirming the presence of listeria in food, and in 55 Fed. Reg. 2556 (Jan. 25, 1990) CDC invited proposals to develop tests for the rapid and specific detection of listeria in food. USDA also proposed to require special testing for this pathogen. *See* 64 Fed. Reg. 28351 (May 26, 1999).

3. *Risk Assessments for Pathogens.* As is inevitable, increasingly sensitive analytical methodology can detect pathogens at increasingly lower levels. Although FDA has not altered its zero tolerance policy, the agency has prepared risk assessments on pathogens. *E.g.*, 66 Fed. Reg. 5515 (Jan. 19, 2001), 68 Fed. Reg. 61006 (Oct. 24, 2003) (listeria); 70 Fed. Reg. 41772 (July 20, 2005) (vibrio parahaemolyticus in raw oysters). For discussion of the FDA listeria risk assessment, see Clark D. Carrington et al., *Putting a Risk Assessment Model to Work: Listeria Monocytogenes "What If" Scenarios*, 68 J. AFDO, No. 1, at 5 (Mar. 2004). *See generally* Council for Agricultural Science and Technology, *Using Risk Analysis to Inform Microbial Food Safety Decisions*, CAST Issue Paper No. 31 (June 2006).

4. *Salmonella.* Salmonella contamination of food in general, and of poultry and eggs in particular, has been a major problem. *See, e.g.*, GAO, SALMONELLA IN RAW MEAT AND POULTRY: AN ASSESSMENT OF THE PROBLEM, No. B–164031(2) (July 22, 1974); *Update: Salmonella enteritidis Infections and Grade A Shell Eggs—United States, 1989*, 38 MORBIDITY & MORTALITY WEEKLY REP. 877 (Jan. 5, 1990).

5. *Label Warnings for Eggs.* In 2000, as part of a joint egg safety initiative with USDA to reduce the risk of salmonella in shell eggs and egg products, FDA promulgated regulations in 21 C.F.R. Part 115 requiring refrigeration of shell eggs held for retailed distribution. As part of the same initiative, FDA promulgated 21 C.F.R. 101.17(h) under the authority of section 361 of the Public Health Service Act, requiring that all shell eggs, whether in intrastate or interstate commerce, bear the following statement:

> SAFE HANDLING INSTRUCTIONS: To prevent illness from bacteria: keep eggs refrigerated, cook eggs until yolks are firm, and cook foods containing eggs thoroughly.

63 Fed. Reg. 27502 (May 19, 1998), 63 Fed. Reg. 45663 (Aug. 27, 1998), 64 Fed. Reg. 36492 (July 6, 1999), 65 Fed. Reg. 76092 (Dec. 5, 2000). Shell eggs that have been specifically processed to destroy all viable salmonella prior to marketing are exempt from this requirement. Even though other food products may become contaminated with pathogenic microorganisms as a result of unsafe handling, shell eggs remain the only food for which FDA has required this type of warning. FDA subsequently promulgated a food additive regulation for the safe use of irradiation for the reduction of salmonella in fresh shell eggs. 65 Fed. Reg. 45280 (July 21, 2000), codified at 21 C.F.R. 179.26(b)(9). *See generally* "Egg Safety: Are There Cracks in the Federal Food Safety System?," Hearing before the Oversight of Government Management, Restructuring and the District of Columbia Subcommittee of the Committee of Governmental Affairs, United States Senate, 106th Cong., 1st Sess. (1999).

6. *Sociogenic Illness.* Not all reported food poisoning episodes are authentic. Hysteria can also trigger false reports of public illness. *See, e.g.*, *Mass Sociogenic Illness in a Day–Care Center—Florida*, 39 MORBIDITY & MORTALITY WEEKLY REP. 301 (May 11, 1990).

7. *Basis for Legal Action.* Although the presence of pathogenic microorganisms in food can be the basis for regulatory action under sections 402(a)(3) and (4), it can also violate section 402(a)(1)'s prohibition against any "poisonous or deleterious substance." The D.C. Circuit declared in *American Public Health Ass'n v. Butz,* 511 F.2d 331 (D.C. Cir. 1974), that "the presence of salmonellae in meat does not constitute adulteration" because the American consumer understands that meat is not sterile and can cause illness if not handled properly. Eight years later the same Court of Appeals determined in *Continental Seafoods, Inc. v. Schweiker,* 674 F.2d 38 (D.C. Cir. 1982), that salmonella in shrimp constitutes an "added substance" that results in adulteration under section 402(a)(1).

8. *History of Bacteriology.* For a brief history of the foundation of modern bacteriology, see Philip P. Mortimer, *The Bacteria Craze of the 1880s,* 353 LANCET 581 (1999). The continuing search for previously undetected pathogens, using current scientific methodology, is described in David A. Relman, *The Search for Unrecognized Pathogens,* 284 SCIENCE 1308 (May 21, 1999).

COMMENT: THE COST OF FOODBORNE ILLNESS

In *Preliminary Estimates of Costs of Foodborne Disease in the United States,* 52 J. FOOD PROTECTION 595 (1989), Ewen Todd concluded:

> Although the full economic impact of foodborne diseases has yet to be measured, preliminary studies show that the cost of illness, death, and business lost is high indeed. This impact is probably greatest in developing countries, but few facts are known. For the United States, preliminary estimates are 12.6 million cases costing $8.4 billion. These may seem excessive but other authors have postulated even higher case and dollar figures. Microbiological diseases (bacterial and viral) represent 84% of the United States' costs, with salmonellosis and staphylococcal intoxication being the most economically important diseases (annually $4.0 billion and $1.5 billion, respectively.) Other costly types of illnesses are toxoplasmosis ($445 million), listeriosis ($313 million), campylobacteriosis ($156 million), trichinosis ($144 million), *Clostridium perfringens* enteritis ($123 million), and *E. coli* infections including hemorrhagic colitis ($223 million). Botulism has a high cost per case ($322,200), but its total impact is only $87 million because relatively few cases occur (270). This is because the food industry has been able to introduce effective control measures. Salmonellosis, however, is much more widespread (2.9 million cases) and affects all sectors of the food industry.

See also "Foodborne Illnesses and Deaths," Hearing Before the Senate Committee on Agriculture, Nutrition, and Forestry, 100th Cong., 1st Sess. (1987); *Foodborne Disease Outbreaks, 5–Year Summary, 1983–1987,* 39 MORBIDITY & MORTALITY WEEKLY REP., No. SS–1 (Mar. 1990).

The most recent CDC estimate is that about 76 million American suffer food poisoning each year, 300,000 of whom are hospitalized, and that about 5,000 die as a result. Paul S. Mead et al., *Food-Related Illness and Death in the United States,* 5 EMERGING INFECTIOUS DISEASES 607 (Sept.-Oct. 1999); *Diagnosis and Management of Foodborne Illnesses: A Primer for Physicians and Other Health Care Professionals,* 53 MORBIDITY & MORTALITY

WEEKLY REP., No. RR04 at 1 (Apr. 16, 2004). In April 2005, CDC reported a 30–45 percent decrease in the most common forms of foodborne illness since the late 1990s. *Preliminary FoodNet Data on the Incidence of Infections with Pathogens Transmitted Commonly Through Food—10 Sites, United States, 2004*, 54 MORBIDITY & MORTALITY WEEKLY REP. 352 (Apr. 15, 2005).

———

Even basic food products may be the source of pathogenic microorganisms. Milk was consumed raw until, following Louis Pasteur's discovery that heat treatment destroys bacteria, the dairy industry began in the 1920s to embrace this principle through pasteurization of milk. Over the ensuing decades, pasteurized milk gradually drove raw milk out of the market. When FDA revised the food standards for milk and cream in 1973, it required that all fluid milk products moving in interstate commerce be pasteurized. 37 Fed. Reg. 18392 (Sept. 9, 1972), 38 Fed. Reg. 27924 (Oct. 10, 1973). In response to an objection contending that certified raw milk was safe and should not be banned, FDA stayed the pasteurization requirement for certified raw milk, but not for all other fluid milk products, pending the required administrative hearing. 39 Fed. Reg. 42351 (Dec. 5, 1974).

In response to a petition from the Public Citizen Health Research Group requesting a ban on raw milk sales, FDA announced a hearing in 49 Fed. Reg. 31065 (Aug. 3, 1984) to determine whether to permit the continued marketing of certified raw milk. After the District Court ordered FDA to respond to the petition, *Public Citizen v. Heckler*, 602 F. Supp. 611 (D.D.C. 1985), the agency denied it, and Public Citizen returned to court.

Public Citizen v. Heckler

653 F. Supp. 1229 (D.D.C. 1986).

■ JOHNSON, DISTRICT JUDGE. . . .

From 1974 to 1982 the FDA collected and evaluated scientific and medical information to determine if the outbreak of certain diseases was associated with the consumption of certified raw milk. . . .

The process of collecting and reviewing data and information led the FDA to conclude that the consumption of certified raw milk and all forms of raw milk and raw milk products was linked to the outbreak of serious disease. In 1982, the FDA began drafting a proposed regulation banning the interstate sale of all raw milk and raw milk products.

On April 23, 1983, then-FDA Commissioner Arthur Hull Hayes sent a memorandum to the Secretary requesting her approval of the proposed rule. [H]owever, Commissioner Hayes proposed that new regulations be issued under the Public Health Service Act which "would provide a more uniform and efficient regulatory mechanism than a standard of identity proceeding, to assure public health protection."

[O]n October 11 and 12, 1984, an informal hearing was held by HHS on two issues: (1) whether the consumption of raw milk is a public health concern; and (2) if so, whether requiring pasteurization of all raw milk is the most reasonable regulatory option.... The October hearing resulted in a 330 page transcript and well over 300 comments totalling [sic] approximately 4000 pages. Those testifying against any Federal regulation of certified raw milk and certified raw milk products pointed out that many other foods (for example, raw meat) against which no Federal action was contemplated, are also sources of exposure to harmful microorganisms. It was made clear, however, that those other unregulated food products are normally cooked before consumption, and the cooking process kills the salmonella bacteria.

Comments opposing a pasteurization requirement included several witnesses' testimony that in the absence of a definitive case-control study, there was no way to determine whether the apparent association between drinking raw milk and being infected by harmful microorganisms was causal and encouraged HHS to sponsor such a study. Other proponents of raw milk testified that raw milk offers nutritional benefits that are destroyed by pasteurization and that raw milk tastes better than pasteurized milk....

On January 29, 1985, the FDA again urged the Secretary to "require the pasteurization of all milk and milk products moving in interstate commerce" because such a requirement "is supported by the administrative record compiled as a result of the [October 1984] hearing." The FDA transmitted to the Secretary a proposed rule banning interstate sales of raw milk and supported this proposed rule by stating that "there is a strong association between the consumption of certified raw milk and the outbreak of disease."

The Secretary rejected the FDA's recommendation and directed the FDA to deny Public Citizen's petition in its entirety. By letter dated March 15, 1985, the Commissioner of the FDA denied the petition, stating that the agency would not ban either interstate or intrastate sales of raw milk. The letter acknowledged that "raw milk, including certified raw milk, is a vehicle for the transmission and spread of numerous diseases" and there is no "scientifically confirmed benefit established for the consumption of raw milk, including certified raw milk." The FDA concluded that "a federal ban would not be the most effective or appropriate means of dealing with the health problems posed by unpasteurized milk and milk products...."

  . . . .

The crux of the Secretary's explanation for her decision to deny plaintiff's petition is that since a greater amount of raw milk is marketed and consumed locally, rather than shipped interstate, and most illness occurs within the producing locality, the problem is one more appropriately dealt with at the state level. The Secretary claims that interstate sales of certified raw milk are "negligible"....

Federal regulation is warranted regardless of the absolute volume of certified raw milk sold interstate....

The Secretary's reason for her decision has no rational connection to the undisputed facts in the record. As such, her decision cannot be upheld. . . .

. . . The appropriate remedy in this case is an order compelling the agency to promulgate a regulation prohibiting the interstate sale of certified raw milk and certified raw milk products, and non-certified raw milk and raw milk products. . . .

Public Citizen asks this Court to compel the agency to promulgate a rule banning both interstate and intrastate sales of raw milk. While we must agree that a rule banning the interstate sale of raw milk is appropriate, at this time there is no indication that a rule banning the intrastate sale of raw milk is necessary to effectuate the interstate ban. Accordingly, the Court declines to order the promulgation of a rule banning intrastate sales of raw milk. Assuming the interstate ban is effective without an intrastate ban, it is up to the individual states to decide on such matters of purely local concern. Should it appear that the interstate sale of raw milk continues, it is within HHS's authority at that time to institute an intrastate ban as well. . . .

NOTES

1. *Subsequent Proceedings.* FDA subsequently promulgated a final regulation requiring pasteurization of all milk shipped in interstate commerce and at the same time terminated as moot the December 1974 stay of the pasteurization requirement under the standard of identity. 52 Fed. Reg. 22340 (June 11, 1987), 52 Fed. Reg. 29509 (Aug. 10, 1987), codified at 21 C.F.R. 1240.61. The FDA regulation was not based upon Section 401 and did not establish or amend the standard of identity for milk. It was based instead on the Public Health Service Act, 42 U.S.C. 216, 243, 264, and 271. Intrastate sale of certified raw milk remains lawful in those states that permit the product.

2. *Review of Inaction.* This case is one of only two judicial decisions directing FDA to issue a regulation of specified content. Would the court have been prepared to order such relief if the administrative record had not shown that the Secretary of HHS had twice overruled an FDA recommendation to ban all interstate shipment of unpasteurized milk?

3. *Commentary.* For discussion of the continuing controversy about raw milk and raw milk cheese, see Dominique L. Castro, *Raw Milk, Cheeses: Historical Overview, Current Regulations, and the Battle to Preserve Artisinal Cheesemaking* (2005), Laura Knoll, *Origins of the Regulation of Raw Milk Cheeses in the United States* (2005), and Alex Sundstrom, *Resistance to FDA Regulation of Raw Milk* (2005), in Chapter V(I)(2) of the Electronic Book. Following an article by Barry Newman, *Will U.S. Lift Longtime Ban on Cheese Imports?*, WALL ST. J., Dec. 24, 2004, at A7, FDA provided a clear response in a statement released on March 14, 2005: "FDA further advises that there is some risk of infection from a number of pathogenic bacteria for anyone who eats raw milk soft cheese from any source."

COMMENT: FDA COOPERATIVE FOOD SANITATION PROGRAMS

Section 361(a) of the Public Health Service Act, 42 U.S.C. 264, authorizes FDA to promulgate whatever regulations are "necessary to prevent the introduction, transmission, or spread of communicable diseases. . . ." Pursuant to this authority, the Public Health Service (PHS) undertook a number of important food sanitation programs beginning in the 1920s. Administration of these programs was later transferred to FDA. 33 Fed. Reg. 9909 (July 10, 1968).

1. *The Pasteurized Milk Ordinance (PMO) and Code.* In 1923, the PHS established an Office of Milk Investigations, and in 1924, in cooperation with state public health officials, it published its first pasteurized milk ordinance. A code of interpretative regulations was added in 1927. Periodically revised, the PMO has been adopted in most states, counties, and cities. *See, e.g.,* 44 Fed. Reg. 51337 (Aug. 31, 1979) (announcing the 1978 PMO and the related documents that implement it).

To complement the PMO, a National Conference on Interstate Milk Shipments was established to rate farms and milk processing plants for compliance with the PMO. A Memorandum of Understanding between FDA and the National Conference on Interstate Milk Shipments, establishing the responsibility of both, was published in 42 Fed. Reg. 47261 (Sept. 20, 1977). *See* GAO, FOOD AND DRUG ADMINISTRATION INTERSTATE MILK SHIPPERS PROGRAM, Rep. No. HRD–86–54FS (Dec. 1985).

The PMO has proved generally successful in assuring a sanitary milk supply. Nonetheless, cities, counties, and states have continued to use restrictive sanitation requirements to protect local milk supplies from distant competition. *See, e.g., Dean Milk Co. v. Madison,* 340 U.S. 349 (1951). An attempt to solve this problem through federal legislation was unsuccessful. *See* "National Milk Sanitation Act of 1957," Hearings Before a Subcommittee of the House Committee on Interstate and Foreign Commerce, 85th Cong., 2d Sess. (1958). Following the transfer of responsibility for the PMO to FDA in 1968, FDA contemplated codifying the PMO in regulations, but abandoned this approach in response to objections by state officials who feared it would undermine federal-state cooperation. *See* Peter Barton Hutt, *FDA Court Actions and Recent Legal Developments,* 39 AFDO Q. BULL. 11, 15 (1975).

2. *The National Shellfish Sanitation Program (NSSP).* The PHS established the NSSP in 1925 as a cooperative program among the federal and state governments and the shellfish industry to assure sanitary shellfish products. For assessments of the NSSP's success, see GAO, PROTECTING THE CONSUMER FROM POTENTIALLY HARMFUL SHELLFISH (CLAIM, MUSSELS, AND OYSTERS), Rep. No. B–164031(2) (Mar. 29, 1973); GAO, NEED TO ASSESS QUALITY OF U.S.–PRODUCED SEAFOOD FOR DOMESTIC AND FOREIGN CONSUMPTION, Rep. No. CED–81–20 (Oct. 15, 1980); GAO, FOLLOWUP ON THE NATIONAL MARINE FISHERIES SERVICE'S EFFORTS TO ASSESS THE QUALITY OF U.S.–PRODUCED SEAFOOD, Rep. No. CED–81–125 (June 22, 1981); GAO, PROBLEMS IN PROTECTING CONSUMERS FROM ILLEGALLY HARVESTED SHELLFISH (CLAMS, MUSSELS, AND OYSTERS), Rep. No. HRD–84–36 (June 14, 1984); GAO, SEAFOOD SAFETY: SERIOUSNESS OF PROBLEMS AND EFFORTS TO PROTECT CONSUMERS, Rep. No. RCED–88–135 (Aug. 10, 1988); "Shellfish Contamination," Hearings before the Subcommittee on Fisheries and Wildlife Conservation and the Environment of the House Committee on Merchant Marine and Fisheries, 100th Cong., 2nd Sess. (1988); GAO, FOOD SAFETY: FDA'S IMPORTED SEAFOOD SAFETY

PROGRAM SHOWS SOME PROGRESS, BUT FURTHER IMPROVEMENTS ARE NEEDED, Rep. No. GAO–04–246 (Jan. 2004).

Following the transfer of responsibility for the NSSP to FDA in 1968, the agency sought to codify the program in regulations. A draft was made available in 38 Fed. Reg. 34353 (Dec. 13, 1973), and regulations were proposed in 40 Fed. Reg. 25916 (June 19, 1975). Although FDA initially stated that it would repropose the regulations, 40 Fed. Reg. 58883 (Dec. 19, 1975), it instead withdrew them, 50 Fed. Reg. 7797 (Feb. 26, 1985). Subsequently, FDA and the industry developed an Interstate Shellfish Sanitation Conference (ISSC) patterned after the National Conference on Interstate Milk Shipments. 49 Fed. Reg. 12751 (Mar. 30, 1984). FDA continues periodically to revise and make available the Manual of Operations for the NSSP. *E.g.*, 54 Fed. Reg. 7281 (Feb. 17, 1989).

Section 10A of the 1906 Food and Drugs Act, which was added in 48 Stat. 1204 (1934) and amended in 49 Stat. 871 (1935), was the only provision not repealed in 1938. This provision, now codified in 21 U.S.C. 372a, authorizes FDA to examine and inspect seafood products upon the payment of a fee. To implement this provision, FDA promulgated regulations codified in 21 C.F.R. Part 197 for canned oysters and processed shrimp. Although 90 percent of the canned shrimp packers operated under this program when it began in 1934, only two canneries operated under it in 1957 and the program became inactive at the end of fiscal year 1957, when no firms applied for inspection. HEW ANN. REP. 200 (1957).

The National Marine Fisheries Service (NMFS) of the National Oceanic and Atmospheric Administration (NOAA) in the Department of Commerce operates a voluntary inspection and grading program under 7 U.S.C. 1622(h), paid for by subscribing members of the fishing industry. The NMFS inspection service covered about 18 percent of seafood consumed in 1983, but only 11 percent by 1987. The NMFS regulations include standards for grades of various types of fish products. 50 C.F.R. Part 260 *et seq.*

Congress has frequently considered legislation to establish a continuous factory inspection program for fish similar to those established for meat, poultry, and eggs. Compare "Fishery Products Protection Act of 1967," Hearings before the Consumer Subcommittee of the Senate Committee on Commerce, 90th Cong., 1st Sess. (1967); "Wholesome Fish and Fishery Products Act and Assistance Needed to Implement It," Hearings before the Consumer Subcommittee of the Senate Committee on Commerce, 90th Cong., 2nd Sess. (1968); "Imported Shrimp," Hearing before the Subcommittee on Oversight and Investigations of the House Comm. on Energy and Commerce, 100th Cong., 2nd Sess. (1988); "Seafood Safety," Hearing before the Subcommittee on Oversight and Investigations of the House Committee on Energy and Commerce, 101st Cong., 1st Sess. (1989); and "Seafood Inspection System," Hearing before the Subcommittee on Fisheries and Wildlife Conservation and the Environment of the House Committee on Merchant Marine and Fisheries, 101st Cong., 1st Sess. (1989).

Congressional consideration of proposed fish inspection legislation during 1989–1990 pitted FDA, NOAA, and USDA in a struggle over regulatory turf. In an attempt to resolve the matter administratively, FDA and NOAA issued an advance notice of proposed rulemaking announcing their intent to establish a joint voluntary fish inspection program. 55 Fed. Reg. 26334 (June 27, 1990).

To allay consumer concerns about fish safety, FDA promulgated hazard analysis and critical control point (HACCP) regulations for fish and fishery products in 1995, with the support and cooperation of the seafood industry. 59 Fed. Reg. 4142 (Jan. 28, 1994), 60 Fed. Reg. 65096 (Dec. 18, 1995), codified at 21 C.F.R. Part 123. The agency also announced the availability of a Fish and Fishery Products Hazards and Controls Guide, incorporating the seafood HACCP principles. 59 Fed. Reg. 12949 (Mar. 18, 1994), 59 Fed. Reg. 16655 (Apr. 7, 1994), 60 Fed. Reg. 65096 (Dec. 18, 1995). The use of HACCP as part of good manufacturing practices (GMP) is discussed further in Part 5 of this Subchapter.

Congressional hearings on seafood legislation continued into the 1990s, but ultimately no legislation was reported out of committee in either the House or the Senate. *See* "Seafood Safety" Hearing before the Subcommittee on Fisheries and Wildlife Conservation and the Environment of the Committee on Merchant Marine and Fisheries, House of Representatives, 102d Cong., 1st Sess. (1991); "S. 2538, The Consumer Seafood Safety Act," Hearing before the National Ocean Policy Study of the Committee on Commerce, Science, and Transportation, United States Senate, 102d Cong., 2d Sess. (1992); "Seafood Safety," Hearing before the Subcommittee on Fisheries Management of the Committee of Merchant Marine and Fisheries, House of Representatives, 103d Cong., 1st Sess. (1993). Two factors undoubtedly contributed to the lack of legislation. First, FDA made seafood safety a high priority, creating a new Office of Seafood in the Center for Food Safety and Applied Nutrition. *See* "Seafood Office Established in CFSAN," FDA Talk Paper No. T91–11 (Mar. 7, 1991). Second, as noted above, FDA promulgated regulations imposing HACCP for the entire seafood industry. FDA and NMFS also engaged in mutually beneficial cooperative efforts, undoubtedly because the Director of the FDA Office of Seafood Safety was recruited from that agency. On November 22, 2004, FDA released a draft guidance that proposes to refer requests for the certification of fish products for export to the European Union to the NOAA seafood inspection program.

See generally Sharon M. Remmer, *One Hundred Years of Shellfish Regulation* (1998); Daniel Grooms, *"Not in a Month without an 'R' in Its Name": An Historical Overview of 20th Century Seafood Regulation with a Glimpse of the Challenges at the Beginning of the 21st* (2002); and Cindy H. Feng, *Beyond Nigiri and Anisakiasis, The Tale of Sushi: History and Regulation* (2006), in Chapter V(Q) of the Electronic Book.

3. *Food Code.* In 1935, in cooperation with the Conference of State and Territorial Health Officials and the National Restaurant Code Authority, the PHS prepared a Food Service Sanitation Ordinance, which was later expanded to include a Food Service Sanitation Code of regulations as well. In 1957, the PHS added a Vending of Food and Beverages Ordinance and later a complementary Code. Following transfer of these functions in 1968, FDA in cooperation with the Association of Food and Drug Officials prepared a Retail Food Service Sanitation Code in 1978, a Food and

Beverage Vending Code in 1978, and a Retail Food Store Sanitation Code in 1982.

Because section 301(k) of the FD&C Act extends FDA jurisdiction to the adulteration of food while held for sale after shipment in interstate commerce, FDA technically has jurisdiction over all restaurants, food vendors, automatic vending machines, and retail food stores in the United States. Lacking the resources to police the hundreds of thousands of establishments involved, however, the agency has concentrated its efforts on food manufacturing, processing, and wholesale warehouses, and has relied on state and local enforcement of the model ordinances and codes to protect against insanitary food conditions at the retail level. This conforms with FDA's responsibility under 42 U.S.C. 243 to provide assistance to state and local governments with respect to the prevention of communicable disease.

Criticized that it was not doing enough at the retail level, *e.g.*, GAO, FEDERAL SUPPORT FOR RESTAURANT SANITATION FOUND LARGELY INEFFECTIVE, Rep. No. MWD–76–42 (Dec. 8, 1975), FDA converted its Food Service Sanitation Ordinance and Code into proposed regulations in 39 Fed. Reg. 35438 (Oct. 1, 1974). But in response to objections that the proposal abridged the understanding between the states and the federal government regarding the regulation of the food service industry, FDA later withdrew it and announced that it would instead continue to rely on the development and periodic revision of model sanitation codes. 42 Fed. Reg. 15428 (Mar. 22, 1977).

Restaurant inspection has long been the primary responsibility of local public health officials. In some jurisdictions restaurants have been required to post the sanitation grade given by local inspectors in the front window. With the advent of the internet, the full reports of restaurant inspections can now be posted online. *See, e.g.*, Marc Santora, *Is That Restaurant Spotless? City Puts More Data Online*, N.Y. TIMES, Jan. 19, 2006, at B2.

Over time, the distinctions between food service, vending, and retail food stores have become blurred. All three functions are often performed in the same establishment. The Conference for Food Protection in 1986 therefore endorsed the development of a Food Protection Unicode, combining all of the other food protection ordinances and codes. FDA announced this project in 52 Fed. Reg. 11885 (Apr. 13, 1987) and made the draft Unicode available for public comment in 53 Fed. Reg. 16472 (May 9, 1988). The first Food Code was then issued by FDA in 59 Fed. Reg. 4085 (Jan. 28, 1994). Between 1993 and 2001 the Food Code was updated and reissued every two years. It is now updated every four years. *E.g.*, 66 Fed. Reg. 63713 (Dec. 20, 2001); "2005 Food Code Updates Food Safety Guidelines," FDA Press Release No. PO5–63 (Sept. 26, 2005). For differing views on state and local adoption of the Food Code, see Caroline Smith DeWall & Elizabeth Dahl, *Adoption of the 1995 FDA Food Code: A Survey of 45 State and Local Health Departments*, 61 J. AFDO, No. 4, at 15 (Dec. 1987); C. Thomas Leitzke, *Obtaining Uniform Adoption of the FDA Food Code by State and Local Regulatory Agencies: A Perspective from the Conference for Food Protection*, 60 J. AFDO, No. 4, at 75 (Dec. 1996); Charles A. Stoffers,

State Level Adoption of the FDA Food Code, 60 J. AFDO, No. 4, at 79 (Dec. 1996).

————

Two Institute of Medicine reports commissioned by USDA emphasized the human risk from pathogens in meat and poultry: MEAT AND POULTRY INSPECTION: THE SCIENTIFIC BASIS OF THE NATION'S PROGRAM (1985) and POULTRY INSPECTION: THE BASIS FOR A RISK-ASSESSMENT APPROACH (1987). Based on a recommendation in a third Institute of Medicine report, AN EVALUATION OF THE ROLE OF MICROBIOLOGICAL CRITERIA FOR FOODS AND FOOD INGREDIENTS (1985), USDA and FDA established a National Advisory Committee on Microbial Criteria for Foods (NACMCF) in 1988, which has provided advice on the microbial safety of food ever since. A fourth Institute of Medicine report, EMERGING INFECTIONS: MICROBIAL THREATS TO HEALTH IN THE UNITED STATES (1992), emphasized the ongoing threat of emerging infectious diseases. In response, CDC developed an Emerging Infections Program (EIP) and, as part of that program, in 1995 established a FoodNet Surveillance Program to monitor foodborne disease across the country. In Fed. Reg. 7235 (Feb. 15, 1994), FDA announced nine public meetings across the country to promote public understanding of its food safety initiative. An overview of the total Federal Food Safety Program was published in Tanya Roberts & Laurian Unnevehr, *New Approaches to Regulatory Food Safety*, 17 FOOD REVIEW, No. 2, at 2 (May–Aug. 1994).

Following national publicity about the death of children from E.coli 0157:H7 as a result of the Jack in the Box hamburger contamination in January 1993 and the Odwalla apple cider contamination in October 1996, President Clinton announced a new food safety initiative to address the problem of foodborne illness.

The White House Radio Address of the President to the Nation
Saturday, January 25, 1997.

33 WEEKLY COMPILATION OF PRESIDENTIAL DOCUMENTS 95 (February 3, 1997)

THE PRESIDENT: Good morning. Today I'm pleased to announce a major new step toward protecting the health and safety of all Americans, especially our children.

... Hard-working American parents deserve the peace of mind that comes from knowing that the meal they set before their children is safe.

That's why I was so concerned by what happened in Washington State and in two other Western States this fall. Apple juice contaminated with a deadly strain of E. coli bacteria reached supermarket shelves. More than a dozen children, some as young as 2, were hospitalized, and one child died.

I'm sure just about every parent in America remembers what E. coli can do. Four years ago this month, tragedy struck hundreds of families in the Western United States when they took their children to fast-food restaurants that served them hamburgers tainted by the E. coli bacteria. Five hundred people became ill, some of them severely, and four children lost their lives.

... That's why today I'm announcing new steps to use cutting-edge technology to keep our food safe and to protect our children from deadly bacteria. We must continue to modernize the food safety system put in place at the dawn of the 20th century so that it can meet the demands of the 21st century.

First, we will put in place a nationwide early warning system for foodborne illness. . . .

Second, we will see to it that the early warning system uses state-of-the-art technology to keep our food safe. . . .

Third, I'm directing Secretary of Agriculture Dan Glickman, Secretary of Health and Human Service Donna Shalala, and the Administrator of the Environmental Protection Agency, Carol Browner to work with communities, farmers, businesses, consumer protection groups, and all levels of government to come up with additional measures to improve food safety. I want them to pay special attention to research and public education efforts. I want them to focus on what sort of partnerships the Government can form with the private sector to meet our goals. And I want them to report back to me with their findings within 90 days. . . .

COMMENT: THE NATIONAL FOOD SAFETY INITIATIVE

President Clinton's National Food Safety Initiative produced a whirlwind of activity during his second term. FDA (together with USDA, CDC, and EPA) announced a public hearing to develop for the President a comprehensive plan to reduce foodborne illness. 62 Fed. Reg. 13589 (Mar. 21, 1997). In May 1997, the agency submitted a report to the President on "Food Safety From Farm to Table: A National Food Safety Initiative." FDA described the initiative in 277 J.A.M.A. 1664 (June 4, 1997). The President weighed in again with a new initiative to insure the safety of imported and domestic fruits and vegetables on October 2, 1997. The White House conducted a briefing for the press on the food safety initiative in February 1998, and later that month HHS and USDA submitted a report to the President in response to his October 1997 directive on insuring the safety of imported food. In May 1998, FDA released a three-year plan for research in support of the National Food Safety Initiative and the Produce and Imported Foods Safety Initiative. FDA announced the availability of a draft guidance to minimize microbial hazards for fresh fruits and vegetables in 63 Fed. Reg. 27584 (May 19, 1998). The agency announced another public hearing on the initiative in 63 Fed. Reg. 45922 (Aug. 17, 1998).

In August 1998, President Clinton signed Executive Order No. 13100, establishing the President's Council on Food Safety. Following the publication of GAO, FOOD SAFETY: WEAK AND INCONSISTENTLY APPLIED CONTROLS ALLOW UNSAFE IMPORTED FOOD TO ENTER U.S. COMMERCE, Rep. No. GAO/T–RCED–98–271 (Sept. 10, 1998), President Clinton issued a memorandum to the Secretaries of HHS and the Treasury announcing that his food safety efforts would be expanded to include six action items relating to imported food. The memorandum requested a report from the Secretaries by October 1 of that year. FDA issued a first-year report on the agency's accomplishments under the Food Safety Initiative in January 1999. In 65 Fed. Reg. 54056 (Sept. 6, 2000), FDA announced the availability of a Report of the FDA Retail Food Program Database of Foodborne Illness Risk Factors, based upon inspections conducted by FDA in 1998–1999.

As part of the early work under the Food Safety Initiative, USDA contracted with the Institute of Medicine to prepare an analysis of food safety issues. The IOM issued its report on ENSURING SAFE FOOD FROM PRODUCTION TO CONSUMPTION in 1998, and the President's Council on Food Safety sent its assessment of that report to President Clinton in March 1999. In March 1999, FDA initiated a sampling survey for 1,000 imported fresh produce samples, pursuant to the president's directive. In order better to coordinate their food safety programs, and undoubtedly in response to proposals to combine the two agencies, FDA and USDA entered into a Memorandum of Understanding to facilitate an exchange of information. *See* 64 Fed. Reg. 27274 (May 19, 1999). The next month, the President's Council on Food Safety released five draft food safety goals that were intended to create the framework for the Food Safety Strategic Plan, and it announced another public hearing to discuss development of the plan. 64 Fed. Reg. 32788 (June 17, 1999). In 64 Fed. Reg. 70168 (Dec. 15, 1999), an additional meeting of the Council was announced to obtain comment on a preliminary strategic plan.

In May 2000, President Clinton issued a directive to reduce listeria-related disease by 50 percent by the year 2005. FDA and USDA issued a joint response establishing a plan to reduce illness from listeria, then a draft risk assessment, and finally, in October 2003, a final risk assessment on the relationship between food borne listeriosis and human health. The final produce safety action plan was released by FDA in October 2004.

The progress of the Food Safety Initiative was the subject of periodic reports to the Association of Food and Drug Officials. *E.g.*, Susan Hutchcroft, *The Food Safety Initiative*, 62 J. AFDO, No. 1, at 10 (Mar. 1998); Catherine Woteki, *USDA Keynote Address: The "State of the Union" on Food Safety*, 62 J. AFDO, No. 2, at 9 (July 1998); Joseph A. Levitt, *FDA's Food Program*, 65 J. AFDO, No. 3, at 24 (Sept. 2001); Janice F. Oliver & LeeAnne Jackson, *The Application of Risk Management Principles*, 65 J. AFDO, No. 3, at 29 (Sept. 2001); Robert L. Buchanan & Sherri B. Dennis, *Microbial Risk Assessment: A Tool for Regulatory Decision Making*, 65 J. AFDO, No. 3, at 36 (Sept. 2001). On April 18, 2002, CDC released new data that showed a twenty-three percent overall drop in bacterial foodborne illnesses since 1996. 51 MORBIDITY & MORTALITY WEEKLY REP. 325 (Apr. 19, 2002). The most recent report indicates that progress has leveled off since 2000. 55 MORBIDITY & MORTALITY WEEKLY REP. 392 (Apr. 14, 2006). An outbreak of E. coli 0157:H7 in spinach in September 2006 caused a nationwide recall. *See* "FDA Announces Findings From Investigation of Foodborne E. coli 0157:H7 outbreak in Spinach," FDA News No. P06–152 (Sept. 29, 2006) and related documents on the FDA website.

NOTES

1. *Congressional Hearings*. The Jack in the Box contamination in January 1993 triggered immediate congressional hearings. "Food Safety and Government Regulation of Coliform Bacteria," Hearing Before the Subcommittee on Agricultural Research, Conservation, Forestry, and General Legislation of the Senate Committee of Agriculture, Nutrition, and Forestry, 103d Cong., 1st Sess. (1993); "U.S. Department of Agriculture Meat Inspection Program," Joint Hearing before the Subcommittee on Department Operations and Nutrition and the Subcommittee on Livestock of the House Committee of Agriculture, 103d Cong., 1st Sess. (1993). Additional hearings were also held to consider further changes in the food safety system. "Reinventing the Federal Food Safety System," Hearings before the Human Resources and Intergovernmental Relations Subcommittee and Joint Hearing before the Human Resources and Intergovernmental Relations Subcommittee and the Information, Justice, Transportation, and Agriculture Subcommittee of the House Committee on Government Operations, 103d Cong., 1st & 2d Sess., Vol. 1 & 2, (1994); "The Federal Meat Inspection Program," Hearings before the Subcommittee on Agricultural Research, Conservation, Forestry, and General Legislation of the Senate Committee on Agriculture, Nutrition, and Forestry, 103d Cong., 2d Sess (1994); "U.S. Meat and Poultry Inspection Issues," Joint Hearing before the Subcommittee on Department Operations and Nutrition and the Subcommittee on Livestock of the House Committee of Agriculture, 103d Cong., 2d Sess. (1994); "How Should Our Food Safety System Address Microbial Contamination?," Hearing before the Senate Committee on Agriculture, 106th Cong., 2d Sess. (2000). The president's initiative on food imports received particular attention in "The Safety of Food Imports," Hearings before the Permanent Subcommittee on Investigations of the Senate Committee on Governmental Affairs, 105th Cong., 2d Sess., Parts I–IV (1998).

2. *Other Reports on Food Safety*. Other nongovernmental food and agriculture scientific organizations also contributed analysis of the challenges in controlling food borne illness. *E.g.*, the Institute of Food Technologists' Expert Panel on Food Safety and Nutrition, *Foodborne Disease Significance of Escherichia coli 0157:H7 and Other Enterohemorrhagic E.coli*, 51 FOOD TECH., No. 10, at 69 (Oct. 1997); Institute of Food Technologists Expert Panel on Emerging Microbiological Food Safety Issues, *Emerging Microbiological Food Safety Issues: Implications for Control in the 21st Century* (2002); Council for Agricultural Science and Technology, *Intervention Strategies for the Microbiological Safety of Foods of Animal Origin*, Issue Paper No. 25 (Jan. 2004); Council for Agricultural Science and Technology, *Foodborne Pathogens: Risk and Consequences* (1994); Council for Agricultural Science and Technology, *Foodborne Pathogens: Review of Recommendations* (1998).

3. *Impact of Contamination*. The Jack in the Box and Odwalla contaminations had a lasting impact on food regulatory policy. USDA promulgated regulations requiring HACCP for meat and poultry. 60 Fed. Reg. 6774 (Feb. 3, 1995), 61 Fed. Reg. 38806 (July 25, 1996), codified at 9 C.F.R. Part 417. USDA subsequently implemented its HACCP requirements through the promulgation of additional standards. 64 Fed. Reg. 28351 (May 26, 1999), 66 Fed. Reg. 12589 (Feb. 27, 2001), 68 Fed. Reg. 34208 (June 6, 2003). FDA promulgated HACCP regulations for fruit and vegetable juices. 62 Fed. Reg. 45593 (Aug. 28, 1997), 63 Fed. Reg. 20450 (Apr. 24, 1998), 66 Fed. Reg. 6137 (Jan. 19, 2001), codified at 21 C.F.R. Part 120. FDA accompanied its juice HACCP requirements with regulations mandating a warning statement on fruit and vegetable juice products that have not been processed to prevent, reduce, or eliminate pathogenic microorganisms. 62 Fed. Reg. 45593 (Aug. 28, 1997), 63 Fed. Reg. 20450 (Apr. 24, 1998), 63 Fed. Reg. 37030 (July 8, 1998), codified at 21 C.F.R. 101.17(g). Both the HACCP and the warning statement

regulations were the subject of President Clinton's weekly radio address on July 4, 1998, 34 Weekly Comp. Pres. Doc. 1327 (July 13, 1998). The labeling regulation requires that any juice that has not been pasteurized to achieve a five-log reduction in microorganisms (*i.e.*, a 100,000–fold reduction) must bear the following warning statement:

> WARNING: This product has not been pasteurized and, therefore, may contain harmful bacteria that can cause serious illness in children, the elderly, and persons with weakened immune systems.

The processing requirements to avoid use of this warning are discussed in Randy W. Worobo et al., *Apple Cider: Treatment Options to Comply With New Regulations*, 62 J. AFDO, No. 4, at 19 (Dec. 1998).

4. *Continuous Factory Inspection for Meat and Poultry.* Since 1906, USDA has imposed a system of continuous premarket inspection for meat and poultry, whereas FDA has relied on periodic factory inspection and postmarket surveillance for the rest of the food supply. For more than four decades, there has been controversy about whether the federal meat and poultry statutes require continuous factory inspection and individual carcass examinations, and whether there are more effective and efficient ways to assure the safety of meat and poultry. In 1996, USDA introduced a system under which meat and poultry processors would perform the organoleptic inspections themselves, and USDA inspectors would monitor the processors to ensure that they were complying with the inspection requirements. The American Federation of Government Employees challenged the USDA's new approach, contending that the federal inspection statutes require USDA inspectors personally to inspect each and every carcass, not just to oversee others performing such a task. The District Court held that the USDA program was lawful. *American Federation of Government Employees v. Glickman*, 127 F. Supp. 2d 243 (D.D.C. 2001). On appeal, however, the Court of Appeals reversed the District Court and held that USDA was illegally "inspecting people not carcasses" and thus in violation of the statutory requirements. *American Fed'n of Gov't Employees v. Glickman*, 215 F.3d 7 (D.C. Cir. 2000). In response, USDA modified its inspection programs to assure that at least one government inspector, in addition to industry inspectors, is responsible for examining each carcass. The District Court then upheld the revised USDA inspection program, 127 F. Supp. 2d 243 (D.D.C. 2001), and the Court of Appeals affirmed, 284 F.3d 125 (D.C. Cir. 2002).

5. *CDC Monitoring.* The role of CDC in monitoring foodborne illness is a critical part of a comprehensive food safety program. "Food Safety: Oversight of the Centers for Disease Control Monitoring of Foodborne Pathogens," Hearing before the Subcommittee on Human Resources and Intergovernmental Relations on the Committee on Government Reform and Oversight, House of Representatives, 104th Cong., 2d Sess. (1996); Jason W. Glicksman, *CDC Surveillance of FDA–Regulated Products* (2003), in Chapter I(G)(2) of the Electronic Book.

6. *Advances in Pathogen Detection Methodology.* Research to develop reliable and fast methods of pathogen detection have accelerated as a result of the recent emphasis on foodborne illness. *See, e.g.*, Phillip Belgrader et al., *PCR Detection of Bacteria in Seven Minutes*, 284 Science 449 (Apr. 16, 1999); A. Garth Rand et al., *Optical Biosensors for Food Pathogen Detection*, 56 Food Tech., No. 3, at 32 (Mar. 2002); Antje Baeumner, *Nanosensors Identify Pathogens in Food*, 58 Food Tech., No. 8, at 51 (Aug. 2004).

7. *Irradiation of Meat and Poultry.* To provide an additional processing method for reducing contamination of meat and poultry with pathogenic microorganisms, FDA approved the use of irradiation in poultry in 52 Fed. Reg. 6391 (Mar. 3, 1987), 55 Fed. Reg. 18538 (May 2, 1990), 62 Fed. Reg. 64102 (Dec. 3, 1997), and in meat in 59 Fed. Reg. 43848 (Aug. 25, 1994), 62 Fed. Reg. 64107 (Dec. 3, 1997).

8. *Sprouted Seeds*. In response to substantial evidence of pathogenic contamination of raw spouts, FDA announced two guidance documents on reducing this problem in 64 Fed. Reg. 57893 (Oct. 27, 1999). FDA approved a food additive petition for the safe use of irradiation to control microbial pathogens in seeds for sprouting in 65 Fed. Reg. 64605 (Oct. 30, 2000), codified at 21 C.F.R. 179.26(b)(10).

9. *Product Liability*. The product liability implications of foodborne illness are analyzed in Jean C. Buzby et al., *Product Liability and Microbial Food Borne Illness*, USDA AGRIC. ECON. REP. No. 799 (Apr. 2001).

5. GOOD MANUFACTURING PRACTICE (GMP)

During the 1960s, FDA experimented with a number of techniques to standardize its enforcement of section 402(a)(4) and to provide food producers better guidance about the requirements of this provision. The agency developed a plant evaluation (PEV) system in which inspectors used standardized forms to evaluate particular segments of the food industry. These forms focused on the sanitation practices about which FDA was principally concerned. Later, FDA issued good manufacturing practice guidelines for specific commodities to advise both its inspectors and food manufacturers.

In 32 Fed. Reg. 17980 (Dec. 15, 1967), FDA proposed the first "umbrella" good manufacturing practice (GMP) regulations for the food industry. The agency explained that these regulations were intended to interpret the "insanitary conditions" provisions of section 402(a)(4). FDA issued a reproposal in 33 Fed. Reg. 19023 (Dec. 20, 1968) and ultimately promulgated final GMP regulations in 34 Fed. Reg. 6977 (Apr. 26, 1969), codified at 21 C.F.R. Part 110. These general regulations were not challenged in court. When FDA subsequently adopted, and then sought to enforce, GMP regulations for specific commodities, however, it was forced to defend their legality.

United States v. Nova Scotia Food Products Corp.

568 F.2d 240 (2d Cir. 1977).

■ GURFEIN, CIRCUIT JUDGE.

This appeal involving a regulation of the Food and Drug Administration is not here upon a direct review of agency action. It is an appeal from a judgment of the District Court for the Eastern District of New York . . . enjoining the appellants, after a hearing, from processing hot smoked whitefish except in accordance with time-temperature-salinity (T–T–S) regulations contained in 21 C.F.R. Part 122 (1977). . . .

Government inspection of appellants' plant established without question that the minimum T–T–S requirements were not being met. There is no substantial claim that the plant was processing whitefish under "insanitary conditions" in any other material respect. Appellants, on their part, do not defend on the ground that they were in compliance, but rather that the requirements could not be met if a marketable whitefish was to be produced. They defend upon the grounds that the regulation is invalid (1) because it is beyond the authority delegated by the statute; (2) because the

FDA improperly relied upon undisclosed evidence in promulgating the regulation and because it is not supported by the administrative record; and (3) because there was no adequate statement setting forth the basis of the regulation. We reject the contention that the regulation is beyond the authority delegated by the statute, but we find serious inadequacies in the procedure followed in the promulgation of the regulation and hold it to be invalid as applied to the appellants herein.*

The hazard which the FDA sought to minimize was the outgrowth and toxin formation of Clostridium botulinum Type E spores of the bacteria which sometimes inhabit fish. . . .

The argument that the regulation is not supported by statutory authority cannot be dismissed out of hand. The sole statutory authority relied upon is § 342(a)(4). . . . Nor is the Commissioner's expressed reliance solely on § 342(a)(4) a technicality which might be removed by a later and wiser reliance on another subsection. For in this case, as the agency recognized, there is no other section or subsection that can pass as statutory authority for the regulation. . . .

Appellants contend that the prohibition against "insanitary conditions" embraces conditions only in the plant itself, but does not include conditions which merely inhibit the growth of organisms already in the food when it enters the plant in its raw state. They distinguish between conditions which are insanitary, which they concede to be within the ambit of § 342(a)(4), and conditions of sterilization required to destroy micro-organisms, which they contend are not.

It is true that on a first reading the language of the subsection appears to cover only "insanitary conditions" "*whereby* it [the food] may have been rendered injurious to health" (emphasis added). And a plausible argument can, indeed, be made that the references are to insanitary conditions in the plant itself, such as the presence of rodents or insects. . . .

. . . [S]o far as the category of harmful micro-organisms is concerned, there is only a single provision, 21 U.S.C. § 344, which directly deals with "micro-organisms." That provision is limited to emergency permit controls dealing with any class of food which the Secretary finds, after investigation, "may, by reason of contamination with micro-organisms *during* the manufacture, processing or packing thereof in any locality, be injurious to health, and that such injurious nature cannot be adequately determined after such articles have entered interstate commerce, [in which event] he then, and in such case only, shall promulgate regulations providing for the issuance . . . of permits. . . ." (Emphasis added.) It may be argued that the failure to mention "micro-organisms" in the "adulteration" section of the Act, which includes § 342(a)(4), means that Congress intended to delegate no further authority to control micro-organisms than is expressed in the "emergency" control of Section 344.

On the other hand . . . the manner of processing can surely give rise to the survival, with attendant toxic effects on humans, of spores which would not have survived under stricter "sanitary" conditions. In that sense . . .

---

* [The portion of the court's opinion discussing the agency's procedure in promulgating the T–T–S regulation is set out *infra* p. 1550.]

the interpretation of the District Court ... is a fair reading, emphasizing that the food does not have to be actually contaminated during processing and packing but simply that "it may have been rendered injurious to health," § 342(a)(4), by inadequate sanitary conditions of prevention. . . .

We do not discount the logical arguments in support of a restrictive reading of § 342(a)(4), but we perceive a larger general purpose on the part of Congress in protecting the public health.

We come to this conclusion, aside from the general rules of construction noted above, for several reasons: First, until this enforcement proceeding was begun, no lawyer at the knowledgeable Food and Drug bar ever raised the question of lack of statutory delegation or even hinted at such a question. Second, the body of data gathered by the experts, including those of the Technical Laboratory of the Bureau of Fisheries manifested a concern about the hazards of botulism. . . .

Lastly, a holding that the regulation of smoked fish against the hazards of botulism is invalid for lack of authority would probably invalidate, to the extent that our ruling would be followed, the regulations concerning the purity of raw materials before their entry into the manufacturing process in 21 C.F.R. Part 113 (1977) (inspection of incoming raw materials for microbiological contamination before thermal processing of low-acid foods packed in hermetically sealed containers), in 21 C.F.R. Part 118 (1977) (pasteurization of milk and egg products to destroy Salmonella micro-organisms before use of the products in cacao products and confectionery), and 21 C.F.R. Part 129 (1977) (product water supply for processing and bottling of bottled drinking water must be of a safe, sanitary quality when it enters the process).

The public interest will not permit invalidation simply on the basis of a lack of delegated statutory authority in this case. A gap in public health protection should not be created in the absence of a compelling reading based upon the utter absence of any statutory authority, even read expansively. Here we find no congressional history on the specific issue involved, and hence no impediment to the broader reading based on general purpose. We believe, nevertheless, that it would be in the public interest for Congress to consider in the light of existing knowledge, a legislative scheme for administrative regulation of the processing of food where hazard from micro-organisms in food in its natural state may require affirmative procedures of sterilization. . . .

NOTE

The identical "insanitary conditions" language in section 402(a)(4) of the FD&C Act was enacted in the Federal Meat Inspection Act, 21 U.S.C. 601(m)(4). In *Supreme Beef Processors, Inc. v. USDA*, the District Court struck down a section of the USDA meat HACCP regulations that established a salmonella performance standard, and the Court of Appeals affirmed. 113 F. Supp. 2d 1048 (N.D. Tex. 2000), *aff'd* 275 F.3d 432 (5th Cir. 2001). The Court of Appeals ruled that salmonella is not a per se adulterant because it is found in all meat and meat plants and thus does not constitute evidence of insanitary conditions. It held that the statute's insanitary conditions provision may not be used to regulate the characteristics of raw materials. The Court of Appeals distinguished the *Nova Scotia Food Products* decision on the ground that the FDA regulation involved in that case required the use of processing procedures whereas the USDA regulation was directed at pre-existing characteristics of raw materials before they are processed. Supreme Beef's confrontation with USDA resulted in bankruptcy and further litigation over the harm done to the company. *Zayler v. United States*, 279 F. Supp. 2d 805 (E.D. Tex. 2003); *In re Supreme Beef Processors, Inc.*, 391 F.3d 629 (5th Cir. 2004).

———

In 1979, drawing on its experience with GMP regulations for specific food commodities, FDA proposed amendments to the 1969 umbrella GMP regulations.

Current Good Manufacturing Practice in Manufacturing, Processing, Packing, or Holding Human Food: Proposed Rulemaking

44 Fed. Reg. 33238 (June 8, 1979).

... FDA's 1977 annual report estimates the overall number of food processing, manufacturing, and warehouse facilities regulated by the agency at 77,000, and FDA conducts approximately 19,000 food establishment inspections annually.... FDA ceased relying exclusively on case-by-case litigation in the late 1960's and adopted a combined policy of promulgating regulations, relying on self-regulation by the industry, and, within the limits of available resources, enforcing regulations when the industry fails to comply with them....

The agency's experience ... has shown that problems to be addressed by [current good manufacturing practice regulations for specific segments of the food industry] are common throughout all segments of the food industry, *e.g.*, personnel, plant construction, and sanitation. Accordingly, the agency believes that the most efficient way to proceed now is to revise the umbrella CGMP regulations rather than repetitively to propose identical regulations for numerous segments of the industry....

The CGMP regulations already in effect detail the practices to be followed to ensure (1) that food is manufactured, processed, packed, and held under conditions that are sanitary, and (2) that such food is safe, clean, and wholesome. In general, this notice proposes to revise and update the requirements for plant personnel; plant design and construction; sanitary operations, facilities, and controls; equipment and utensils; regulating and recording controls; processing operations; and coding and recordkeeping....

Under section 701(a) of the act, FDA has the authority to promulgate regulations for the efficient enforcement of that act, and such regulations have been held to have the force and effect of law. The courts have also expressly held that FDA has the authority to promulgate substantive regulations defining current good manufacturing practices for the food industry. Furthermore, since the promulgation of the CGMP regulations in 1969, the Secretary of Health, Education, and Welfare has delegated authority to exercise the functions vested in the Secretary under section

361 of the Public Health Service Act (42 U.S.C. 264) to the Commissioner of Food and Drugs. Under this provision, the Commissioner is authorized to issue and enforce regulations for any measures that, in the Commissioner's judgment, are necessary to prevent the introduction, transmission, or spread of food-borne communicable diseases from one State to another. Because this authority is designed to eliminate the introduction of diseases such as typhus from one State to another, this authority must of necessity be exercised upon the disease-causing substance within the State where the food is manufactured, processed, or held. Due to the nationwide, interrelated structure of the food industry, communicable diseases may, without proper intrastate food controls, easily spread interstate.... The Commissioner therefore assumes authority to promulgate regulations under the Public Health Service Act to assure that foods are manufactured, processed, packed, or held under sanitary conditions so as to be safe, wholesome, and otherwise fit for food. Regulations promulgated under that statute also have the force and effect of law....

... [N]ew § 110.91 (21 CFR 110.91) deals expressly with product coding. In § 110.80(i) of the current umbrella GMP regulations, which this proposal would supersede, the agency suggests that meaningful coding of products should be used to enable positive lot identification.... In the past decade, voluntary product recalls by manufacturers have become one of FDA's most useful regulatory tools.... In fiscal year 1975 there were 133 recalls of food products, including misbranding violations, and 163 in fiscal year 1976. These experiences have shown that product coding is an essential element of this regulatory tool....

Section 110.100 (21 CFR 110.100) lists current recordkeeping requirements, amended to conform to those promulgated and upheld in the candy CGMP's. These recordkeeping requirements are correlated with the other CGMP requirements and require the affected parties to maintain (a) records on the results of examinations or copies of supplier guarantees or certifications verifying that the raw materials comply with the basic act and other FDA regulations under proposed § 110.80(a); (b) records of processes that are specified in proposed § 110.80(b) and are intended to destroy or prevent the growth of micro-organisms of public health significance in the foods; and (c) distribution records that identify initial distribution of finished food under proposed § 110.93 to facilitate recalls. The agency proposes that these records be kept for 2 years or for the shelf life of the product, whichever is shorter....

NOTES

1. *Final Regulations.* Regulations based upon this proposal were promulgated in 51 Fed. Reg. 22458 (June 19, 1986).

2. *Shipping Records.* When FDA promulgated GMP regulations for cacao products and confectionary, the agency included requirements that each shipping container be marked with a code identifying the plant where the candy was packed and its production or packing lot, and that the records of the initial distribution of the candy be kept for a period exceeding its shelf life but not more than two years. *See* 38 Fed. Reg. 32554 (Nov. 26, 1973), 40 Fed. Reg. 24162 (June 4, 1975). These requirements were upheld in *National Confectioners Ass'n v. Califano*, 569 F.2d 690

(D.C. Cir. 1978). FDA's proposed revision of the umbrella GMP regulations included similar requirements for all food products, but the final regulations omitted these provisions, based on the following reasoning:

> The purpose of proposing coding and recordkeeping was to facilitate a manufacturer's recall of suspect products in case such a recall was recommended by FDA. Although such information is potentially useful in determining the production time period which is effected by a recall, thereby limiting manufacturers' risk exposure, it is not needed to protect consumers from products that have been purchased but not ingested. Furthermore, all manufacturers either currently code all their products or keep shipping records in the ordinary course of business, or do both. As these sources can provide most of the information which would have been required in the proposed rule, and all of the information needed for a recall, it is not necessary to impose other economically burdensome recordkeeping requirements. This decision will save manufacturers and consumers approximately $80.5 million annually (1985 dollars) in foregone costs. . . .

> For consumer protection, the most effective safeguard is product, not lot, identification and swift dissemination of such information by mass media. . . .

> In addition, the products most likely to involve risk of recall (low acid food) are already subject to coding and recordkeeping requirements.

51 Fed. Reg. 22458 (June 19, 1986).

3. *Revocation of Product Specific GMP Regulations.* Once FDA decided to revise the umbrella regulations, it revoked its GMP regulations for smoked fish, 48 Fed. Reg. 48836 (Oct. 21, 1983), 49 Fed. Reg. 20484 (May 15, 1984); for cacao products and confectionary, 44 Fed. Reg. 52257 (Sept. 7, 1979), 51 Fed. Reg. 22481 (June 19, 1986); and for frozen raw breaded shrimp, 51 Fed. Reg. 22482 (June 19, 1986), 51 Fed. Reg. 41615 (Nov. 18, 1986).

4. *Infant Formula GMPs.* For a discussion of the GMP requirements for infant formula products, see *supra* p. 240.

5. *Dietary Supplement GMPs.* DSHEA added Section 402(g) to the FD&C Act to authorize FDA to promulgate GMP regulations for dietary supplements, modeled after the food GMP regulations. In 68 Fed. Reg. 12157 (Mar. 13, 2003), FDA proposed dietary supplement GMP regulations, which the industry criticized as being modeled on the drug GMP regulations rather than the food GMP regulations.

6. *PCB Contamination.* Although FDA initially proposed to limit the level of PCBs in sealed electrical equipment in food processing and storage facilities to prevent contamination of food, 45 Fed. Reg. 30984 (May 9, 1980), it subsequently withdrew this proposal, 50 Fed. Reg. 29233 (July 18, 1985), on the ground that controls over PCBs established by EPA adequately protect the public health.

7. *AIDS–Infected Personnel.* Section 110.10(a) of FDA's GMP regulations states that any person who has an illness or infection by which there is a "reasonable possibility of food, food-contact surfaces, or food-packaging materials becoming contaminated" must be excluded from any food operation. Soon after acquired immune deficiency syndrome (AIDS) was first identified in this country, in the late 1970s, the question was raised whether individuals infected with the human immunodeficiency virus (originally HTLV and now HIV) should be excluded from employment in food manufacturing and service establishments. The Centers for Disease Control responded by issuing *Recommendations for Preventing Transmission of Infection with Human T-lymphotropic Virus Type III/lymphadenopathy-*

associated Virus in the Workplace, 34 MORBIDITY & MORTALITY WEEKLY REP. 682, 693–94 (Nov. 15, 1985):

> *Food-service workers (FSWs).* FSWs are defined as individuals whose occupations involve the preparation or serving of food or beverages (*e.g.*, cooks, caterers, servers, waiters, bartenders, airline attendants). All epidemiologic and laboratory evidence indicates that bloodborne and sexually transmitted infections are not transmitted during the preparation or serving of food or beverages, and no instances of HBV or HTLV–III/LAV transmission have been documented in this setting.
>
> All FSWs should follow recommended standards and practices of good personal hygiene and food sanitation. All FSWs should exercise care to avoid injury to hands when preparing food. Should such an injury occur, both aesthetic and sanitary considerations would dictate that food contaminated with blood be discarded. FSWs known to be infected with HTLV–III/LAV need not be restricted from work unless they have evidence of other infection or illness for which any FSW should also be restricted.
>
> Routine serologic testing of FSWs for antibody to HTLV–III/LAV is not recommended to prevent disease transmission from FSWs to consumers.

This recommendation has not since been changed, and there has been no evidence of AIDS transmission through food. Nonetheless, the House of Representatives adopted a provision during debate on the 1990 Americans with Disabilities Act permitting the food industry to exclude HIV positive workers from food-handling jobs, 136 CONG. REC. H2484 (daily ed. May 17, 1990), and the Senate instructed its conferees to accept this amendment, 136 CONG. REC. S7449 (daily ed. June 6, 1990). The provision was deleted in conference, however.

8. *Hand Sanitizers.* The use of hand sanitizers to protect against transmission of microorganisms is common throughout the food industry. The legal status of these products, however, requires an understanding of three separate regulatory concepts. Under the Federal Insecticide, Rodenticide, and Fungicide Act (FIFRA), 7 U.S.C. 136 *et seq.*, the Environmental Protection Agency (EPA) regulates all "pesticides." Although a pesticide is defined under 7 U.S.C. 136(t) and (u) as any substance that destroys microorganisms, EPA has issued regulations in 40 C.F.R. 152.8(a) excluding microorganisms "in or on living man or animals." Thus, EPA has narrowed its jurisdiction to exclude FDA-regulated products.

Under section 201(g)(1)(B) of the FD&C Act, a product intended to prevent disease is a drug. Applying this definition, FDA has regulated antimicrobial soap and other topical antimicrobial products as drugs. In the OTC Drug Review tentative final monograph for these products, FDA set forth its position on proposed labeling claims that these products "disinfected" or "sanitized" the skin:

> The Commissioner realizes that these terms are intended to imply cleansing of human tissue. However, there is some discrepancy between the commonly understood or lay meaning of these terms and their scientific meaning. The Commissioner is concerned that, as he attempts to set general standards in this area, terms and claims not be ambiguous or have dual meanings. . . .
>
> The Commissioner concludes that to assure clarity and conciseness of the meaning of these claims, as well as to eliminate the confusion caused by the dual meaning, their use should be limited to denoting antimicrobial action only on inanimate objects. Therefore, the above claims (or similar claims) will be considered misleading when applied to the use of topical antimicrobial products on humans.

43 Fed. Reg. 1210, 1229 (Jan. 6, 1978). The food GMP regulations, however, provide that one should, as a part of "maintaining cleanliness" ... "(3) Wash[] hands thoroughly (and sanitize[e] if necessary to protect against contamination with undesirable microorganisms)...." 21 C.F.R. 110.10(b)(3).

In *Farquhar v. FDA*, 616 F. Supp. 190 (D.D.C. 1985), the District Court held that the marketing of a hand sanitizing product for food handlers did not provide a predicate to consideration of the product under the OTC Drug Review, *infra* p. 788.

9. *National Sanitation Foundation.* The NSF sponsors a voluntary program to establish consensus standards and certification of compliance for food contact equipment and articles. *See* Nina I. McClelland, *The National Sanitation Foundation: Its Mission, Programs, and Goals*, 48 J. AFDO, No. 2, at 93 (Apr. 1984).

In July 2002, FDA established an internal Food CGMP Modernization Working Group to review the existing GMP regulations and consider revision. The Working Group held public meetings, announced in 69 Fed. Reg. 29220 (May 21, 2004), and made available on the FDA website an analysis of recent food recalls and a report on current food safety problems. The Working Group then issued its report titled *Food CGMP Modernization—A Focus on Food Safety* (Nov. 2, 2005). The report recommended modernization of the current food GMP in seven areas: (1) training requirements, (2) food allergen controls, (3) Listeria controls, (4) written sanitation procedures, (5) agricultural produce, (6) records maintenance and access, and (7) temperature controls.

6. HAZARD ANALYSIS AND CRITICAL CONTROL POINTS (HACCP)

In the early 1960s, the quality control personnel in a major food manufacturer devised a new science-based system for quality control called Hazard Analysis and Critical Control Points (HACCP). Many food manufacturers voluntarily applied HACCP as part of their GMP programs. When FDA revised its GMP regulations in June 1986, the agency included the use of HACCP principles as one approach to GMP.

> (2) All food manufacturing, including packaging and storage, shall be conducted under such conditions and controls as are necessary to minimize the potential for the growth of microorganisms, or for the contamination of food. One way to comply with this requirement is careful monitoring of physical factors such as time, temperature, humidity, a_w, pH, pressure, flow rate, and manufacturing operations such as freezing, dehydration, heat processing, acidification, and refrigeration to ensure that mechanical breakdowns, time delays, temperature fluctuations, and other factors do not contribute to the decomposition or contamination of food.

21 C.F.R. 110.80(b)(2).

Around the same time, at the request of USDA, the Institute of Medicine issued two reports that recommended strengthening the regulation of meat and poultry. MEAT AND POULTRY INSPECTION: THE SCIENTIFIC BASIS OF THE NATION'S PROGRAM (1985); POULTRY INSPECTION: THE BASIS FOR A RISK-

ASSESSMENT APPROACH (1987). In response, USDA announced hearings to determine how to incorporate HACCP systems into its meat and poultry inspection operations. 55 Fed. Reg. 21765 (May 29, 1990).

As concern about pathogen contamination of the food supply increased during the early 1990s, USDA and FDA promulgated regulations requiring HACCP for the meat, poultry, fish, and juice industries, *see supra* p. 342, Note 3, and FDA published an advance notice of proposed rulemaking to consider whether and how the agency should apply HACCP to the entire food industry as the principal focus of a new comprehensive food safety assurance program.

Food and Drug Administration Development of Hazard Analysis Critical Control Points for the Food Industry

59 Fed. Reg. 39888 (August 4, 1994).

. . . .

Although the current food safety assurance program has generally functioned effectively, it currently faces new stresses and challenges. New food processing and packaging technologies, new food distribution and consumption patterns, increasing public health concerns about low levels of certain chemical contaminants, and new microbial pathogens all contribute to today's food safety challenge. . . .

One of the most important challenges to FDA's current food safety assurance program is the increasing number of new food pathogens. Although food borne illness has always been a public health problem, such illness appears to be on the rise, and new pathogens are appearing. In addition, because foods are more extensively processed and handled, there is now a greater opportunity for food to be contaminated. . . .

Pathogens are not the only potential contaminants of food, however. The extensive use of industrial chemicals, coupled with past failures to deal adequately with chemical waste, have resulted in significant chemical pollution of the environment in some regions. Many of these chemicals have found their way into the food chain. The legal use of pesticides in agriculture may also result in residues in food. Naturally occurring chemicals, such as toxic elements and mycotoxins, can also be found in food at levels of concern. . . .

The size and diversity of the food industry adds to the stress on the current food safety assurance program. FDA's current inventory lists over 30,000 food manufacturers and processors, and in excess of 20,000 food warehouses. The number of foreign manufacturers and processors shipping food products to the Untied States continues to increase. In 1992, there were well over 1 million food import entries into the United States. . . .

For all of these reasons, FDA believes that it is appropriate at this time for the agency to consider improvements to its food safety assurance program to focus the program on prevention of food safety risks and problems. . . .

Although the agency has reached no final conclusions about how its regulatory programs should be revised to make food as safe as possible, FDA has tentatively concluded that the improvements in the agency's current food safety assurance program should be based on a state-of-the-art preventive approach know as HACCP. . . .

The HACCP concept is a systematic approach to the identification, assessment of risk (likelihood of occurrence and severity), and control of the biological, chemical, and physical hazards associated with a particular food production process or practice. HACCP is a preventive strategy. It is based on development by the food producer of a plan that anticipates food safety hazards and identifies the points in the production process where a failure would likely result in a hazard being created or allowed to persist; these points are referred to as critical control points (CCP's). Under HACCP, identified CCP's are systematically monitored, and records kept of that monitoring. Corrective actions are taken when control of a CCP is lost, including proper disposition of the food produced during that period; and these actions are documented. . . .

HACCP has been endorsed by the National Advisory Committee on Microbiological Criteria for Foods (NACMCF) as an effective and rational means of ensuring food safety from harvest to table. . . .

The NACMCF has developed the following seven principles that describe the HACCP concept:

1. Hazard Analysis

The first step in the establishment of a HACCP system for a food process or practice is the identification of the hazards associated with the product. The NACMCF defines a hazard as a biological, chemical, or physical property that may cause a food to be unsafe for consumption. The hazard analysis step should include an assessment of both the likelihood that such a hazard will occur and its severity if it does occur. This analysis should also involve the establishment of preventive measures to control identified hazards.

2. Identification of CCP's

A CCP is a point, step, or procedure at which control can be applied, the result being that a potential food safety hazard can be prevented, eliminated, or reduced to acceptable levels. Points in the manufacturing process that may be CCP's include cooking, chilling, specific sanitation procedures, product formulation control, prevention of cross contamination, and certain aspects of employee and environmental hygiene.

3. Establishment of Critical Limits for Preventive Measures Associated with Each Identified CCP

This step involves establishing a criterion that must be met for each preventive measure associated with a CCP. Critical limits can be thought of as boundaries of safety for each CCP and may be set for preventive measures such as temperature, time, physical dimensions, moisture level, water activity, pH, and available chlorine.

4. Establishment of Procedures to Monitor CCP's

Monitoring is a planned sequence of observations or measurements to assess whether a CCP is under control and to produce an accurate record for use in future verification procedures. Continuous monitoring is possible with many types of physical and chemical methods. When it is not possible to monitor a critical limit on a continuous basis, monitoring intervals must be frequent enough to permit the manufacturer to determine whether the step/process/procedure designed to control the hazard is under control.

5. Establishment of Corrective Actions To Be Taken When Monitoring Shows That a Critical Limit Has Been Exceeded

While the HACCP system is intended to prevent deviations in a planned process from occurring, total prevention can rarely, if ever, be achieved. Therefore, there must be a corrective action plan in place to ensure appropriate disposition of any food produced during a deviation, to fix or correct the cause of noncompliance to ensure that the CCP is once again under control, and to maintain records of corrective actions taken.

6. Establishment of Effective Recordkeeping Systems That Document the HACCP System

This principle requires the preparation and maintenance of a written HACCP plan that lists the hazards, CCP's, and critical limits identified by the firm, as well as the monitoring, recordkeeping, and other procedures that the firm intends to use to implement the plan. This principle also requires the maintenance of records generated during the operation of the plan.

7. Establishment of Procedures to Verify That the HACCP System is Working

This process involves verifying that the critical limits are adequate to control the hazards identified, ensuring that the HACCP plan is working properly and verifying that there is documented, periodic revalidation of the plan to confirm that the plan is still performing its intended function under existing plant conditions at any point in time . . .

NOTES

1. *Pilot Program.* In the same issue of the Federal Register, FDA announced a pilot program in which volunteers from the industry would adopt the HACCP system. 59 Fed. Reg. 39771 (Aug. 4, 1994).

2. *Subsequent Proceedings.* The food industry supported voluntary adoption of HACCP but opposed its mandatory imposition. FDA had proposed HACCP regulations for the fish industry just prior to publishing this advance notice of proposed rulemaking, and it promulgated final regulations for that industry a short time later, followed by HACCP regulations for the juice industry. *See supra* p. 342, Note 3. In both of those industries, however, the specific food products had been the subject of major media focus as sources of significant contamination with pathological microorganisms, the industry had suffered economically, and the trade associations had requested FDA to undertake HACCP programs as part of a public relations program to regain public confidence. Segments of the food industry which did not have similar problems saw no compelling need for additional regulation. *See generally* Margaret Glavin, *Update on Implementation of the Final Rule on Patho-*

gen Reduction and HACCP, 52 FOOD & DRUG L.J. 323 (1997); George Hoskin & Susan J. Hutchcroft, *FDA's Seafood Safety Program*, 56 J. AFDO, No. 4, at 16 (Oct. 1992); George C. Nardi, *HACCP and the Seafood Industry*, 57 J. AFDO, No. 1, at 15 (Jan. 1993); Caroline Smith DeWaal, *Delivering on HACCP's Promise to Improve Food Safety: A Comparison of Three HACCP Regulations*, 52 FOOD & DRUG L.J. 331 (1997); Philip C. Spiller, *Status of Seafood HACCP*, 52 FOOD & DRUG L.J. 327 (1997); Seth Axelrod, *Why FDA Has Adopted HACCP Regulations to Ensure the Safety of Food*, in Chapter V(H)(1) of the Electronic Book.

3. *Enforcement of Seafood HACCP.* In *United States v. Blue Ribbon Smoked Fish, Inc.*, 179 F. Supp. 2d 30 (E.D.N.Y. 2001), the District Court granted FDA's motion for a summary judgment and entered an injunction against the company requiring it to take steps, including the implementation an adequate seafood HACCP plan, to prevent listeria contamination of smoked fish. In an extensive opinion, the District Court documented insanitary conditions and listeria contamination, and it entered a permanent injunction until FDA certifies that the plant has been brought into compliance. On appeal, the Court of Appeals affirmed the District Court decision and FDA's zero tolerance policy for listeria but vacated the part of the injunction that prohibited the company officers from any processing and marketing of smoked fish even outside of the Blue Ribbon plant. Food Drug Cosm. L. Rep. (CCH) ¶ 38,719 (2d Cir. 2003).

4. *Fresh Fruit and Vegetables.* In addition to its 80–year-old voluntary inspection and certification program for the fresh fruit and vegetable industry, the USDA Agricultural Marketing Service established a HACCP-based voluntary program for the fresh-cut industry. Kenneth C. Clayton, *USDA's Agricultural Marketing Service HACCP Certification Program*, 61 J. AFDO, No. 3, at 45 (Sept. 1997).

5. *Continuing Consideration.* FDA continues to raise the possibility of mandatory HACCP for the entire food industry, but the industry continues to oppose it.

7.   EMERGENCY PERMIT CONTROL
FOOD AND DRUG ADMINISTRATION

For Immediate Release:
Friday, October 29, 1971

PUBLIC WARNING

The Food and Drug Administration issued an urgent warning today to consumers who may have eaten or have in their homes cans of Stokely–Van Camp Finest French Style Green Beans in eight ounce cans with the code number SB 72/E213D. The suspected code of the product is being recalled by Stokely–Van Camp, Inc., Indianapolis, Indiana.

The Agency warning is based upon preliminary results of tests conducted by the National Center for Disease Control in Atlanta. The tests suggested the presence of botulinum toxin Type B in the serum of an eight-year-old Pensacola, Florida, boy. The boy and his father noticed an off-flavor after each ate two or three beans from a swollen can. Both were then purged at a local hospital. Tests on the serum from the father were negative for botulinum toxin. Neither have [sic] developed any symptoms of botulism. . . .

FOOD AND DRUG ADMINISTRATION

For Immediate Release:
Monday, November 1, 1971

Weekend testing by the Center for Disease Control, Public Health Service, Atlanta, Georgia, has failed to confirm preliminary evidence of botulinum toxin in the blood serum of a Pensacola, Florida boy or in a can of green beans from which the eight-year old and his father ate last Wednesday. FDA, therefore, is rescinding its warning to consumers against eating Stokely–Van Camp Finest French Style Sliced Green Beans, Code Number SB 72/E213D. Recall of the product no longer is considered necessary. . . .

FDA Commissioner Charles C. Edwards, M.D. said: "In dealing with life or death problems like botulism, there are times when the public interest demands action before the scientific case is complete. The decision always must be made in favor of consumer protection. Such decisions are always difficult, both for Government and the industry."

Nancy L. Ross, *Remember That Vichyssoise?*

The Washington Post, June 25, 1972, at K1.

One year ago next Friday a Bedford, N.Y. banker named Samuel Cochran, Jr. died after eating a poisonous can of Bon Vivant vichyssoise and federal officials feared a national epidemic of deadly botulism. The worst did not happen. Yet the events surrounding that tragedy were to have profound repercussions:

- Mrs. Cochran, who also sampled the soup, was partially paralyzed, and is suing Bon Vivant and Gristede's, the grocery store which sold the soup, for more than one million dollars;

- Bon Vivant Soups, Inc. declared bankruptcy, and is still trying to prove its product is safe to eat to prevent the Food and Drug Administration from ordering the destruction of its entire remaining stock of 1.4 million cans;

- Two major food producers, Campbell Soup and Stokely–Van Camp, were involved in botulism scares, the second of which was a false alarm set off by nervous federal officials; . . .

- The National Canners Association, shaken by a crisis in consumer confidence, devised stricter regulations to guard against botulism and asked the FDA to enforce them;

- The FDA, embarrassed by the revelation its inspectors had not visited the Bon Vivant plant in six years, made food inspection and safety a priority item, and plans to double the number of inspectors next year;

- Meanwhile, despite official warnings to home canners to prepare food properly, 11 other Americans died in that year from botulism.

When the normally harmless bacterium Clostridium botulinum breeds in an airless, low-acid environment, due to improper cooking of food in vacuum containers, it can be transformed into botulin toxin. A few ounces of this concentrated poison would suffice to depopulate the earth. In the past 50 years 15 people in this country have died from botulism caused by

commercially-prepared food, although hundreds more have died from improperly sterilized home-canned products....

... Bon Vivant's owners, Andrew Paretti, 47, and his wife Maria,
appeared most anxious to tell their side of the story to correct what they
feel has been biased reporting.... Venomous words like "incredible persecution, unfair treatment, vendetta panic, overreaction" punctuated a two-
hour interview. Most of this was aimed at the FDA's action in seizing Bon
Vivant's entire inventory and thereby bankrupting his 108–year-old company, which had always had a "clean" record, on the basis of one mistake. No
company in FDA history had ever had its entire stock confiscated. That
mistake, traced to human error in setting the cooking timer, resulted in
one lot of vichyssoise not being thoroughly sterilized—and eventually the
death of a man. Botulin toxin was found by FDA chemists in only five cans
of vichyssoise, yet his whole line of 90 different products was seized by the
agency which claimed it had found an unusually high percentage of
abnormal cans....

[The Parettis'] bitterness is aggravated by the government's treatment
of the Campbell Soup Company after the firm's labs discovered botulin
toxin in a batch of its chicken vegetable. Campbell's was then allowed to
effect its own recall of the soup at its own expense—an estimated $5
million. No one became ill. Bon Vivant, on the other hand, could not
finance a voluntary recall, so its products were seized by federal marshals.
The rest of Campbell's stock remained untouched because inspectors found
the plant that produced the poisonous soup to be above reproach....

David McVey, senior vice president of Stokely–Van Camp, the third
largest canner in the country, also expressed anger at the false botulism
alarm that cost his company millions of dollars in recalls. "When you
defame a product label to 200 million people watching television and
reading newspapers it takes a long time to rebuild it," he said....

––––––––

Section 404 of the FD&C Act authorizes FDA to impose special
controls over producers of food subject to microbiological contamination.
Following the Bon Vivant, Stokely, and Campbell Soup episodes, FDA
issued regulations designed to forestall similar problems in the future. In
this instance, the initiative came from the industry itself. The regulations,
issued after notice and comment but without a formal evidentiary hearing,
reflected FDA's efforts to avoid the formal rulemaking procedures of
section 701(e) of the Act.

Emergency Permit Control: Definitions and Procedures

39 Fed. Reg. 3748 (January 29, 1974).

The Commissioner of Food and Drugs published in the FEDERAL REGIS-
TER of May 14, 1973 (38 FR 12716) a final order establishing the requirements and conditions for compliance with, or exemption from, section 404
... with respect to thermally processed low-acid foods in hermetically

sealed containers. A ruling on the objections received in response to this order is published elsewhere in this issue....

The Commissioner also published in the FEDERAL REGISTER of May 14, 1973 (38 FR 12720) ... proposed definitions and procedures to govern implementation of the emergency permit control authority contained in section 404 of the act....

The Commissioner reaffirms the position that Subpart A of Part 90 is procedural in nature and designed to provide the mechanism for implementation of Part 90 [now 21 C.F.R. Part 108]. Subpart B, which at present consists only of § 90.20 [now 108.35] relating to thermally processed low-acid canned foods in hermetically sealed containers, contains the substantive requirements established under section 404 of the act for any particular food or class of foods. The Commissioner has concluded that section 702(e)(1) of the act provides an opportunity for a public hearing only on the substantive regulations applicable to a particular food or class of foods authorized by section 404(a) of the act, and that the procedural regulations generally implementing the emergency permit control system of section 404 are authorized by section 701(a) of the act, which does not provide for a public hearing....

Therefore, ... Chapter I of Title 21 of the Code of Federal Regulations is amended by adding a new subpart A to Part 90 to read as follows: ...

§ 90.2 [now 108.19] Establishment of requirements for exemption from section 404 of the act.

(a) Whenever the Commissioner finds after investigation that the distribution in interstate commerce of any class of food may, by reason of contamination with micro-organisms during the manufacture, processing, or packing thereof in any locality, be injurious to health, and that such injurious nature cannot be adequately determined after such articles have entered interstate commerce, he shall promulgate regulations in Subpart B of this part establishing requirements and conditions governing the manufacture, processing, or packing of the food necessary to protect the public health....

(b) A manufacturer, processor, or packer of a food for which a regulation has been promulgated in Subpart B of this part shall be exempt from the requirement for a permit only if he meets all of the mandatory requirements and conditions established in that regulation.

§ 90.3 [now 108.5] Determination of the need for a permit.

(a) Whenever the Commissioner determines after investigation that a manufacturer, processor, or packer of a food for which a regulation has been promulgated in Subpart B of this part does not meet the mandatory conditions and requirements established in such regulation, he shall issue to such manufacturer, processor, or packer an order determining that a permit shall be required before the food may be introduced or delivered for introduction into interstate commerce by that person.

(1) The manufacturer, processor, or packer shall have 3 working days after receipt of such order within which to file objections.... If such

objections are filed, the determination is stayed pending a hearing to be held within 5 working days after the filing of objections on the issues involved unless the Commissioner determines that the objections raise no genuine and substantial issue of fact to justify a hearing.

(2) If the Commissioner finds that there is an imminent hazard to health, the order shall contain this finding and the reasons therefore [sic], and shall state that the determination of the need for a permit is effective immediately pending an expedited hearing. . . .

(c) Within 5 working days after the hearing, and based on the evidence presented at the hearing, the Commissioner shall determine whether a permit is required and shall so inform the manufacturer, processor, or packer in writing, with the reasons for his decision. . . .

§ 90.4   [now 108.7] Issuance or denial of permit.

(a) After a determination and notification by the Commissioner ... that a manufacturer, processor, or packer requires a permit, such manufacturer, processor, or packer may not thereafter introduce or deliver for introduction into interstate commerce any such food manufactured, processed, or packed by him unless he holds a permit issued by the Commissioner or obtains advance written approval of the Food and Drug Administration. . . .

NOTES

1. *Denial of Hearing.* In the same issue of the Federal Register that these Subpart A procedural regulations appeared, FDA ruled on the objections to its "final" Subpart B substantive regulations governing thermal processing of low-acid foods in hermetically sealed containers. Under section 701(e) of the Act, regulations requiring emergency permits for the production of any class of food must be promulgated through formal rulemaking. FDA concluded, however, that none of the objections to Subpart B raised factual issues that justified a formal evidentiary hearing. 39 Fed. Reg. 3750 (Jan. 29, 1974).

2. *Acidified Food.* FDA subsequently extended this approach to include acidified food. 41 Fed. Reg. 30442, 30457 (July 23, 1976), 44 Fed. Reg. 16235 (Mar. 16, 1979), codified at 21 C.F.R. Part 114.

3. *Pet Food.* The requirements for low acid canned food apply to pet food as well. *See* 44 Fed. Reg. 48598 (Aug. 17, 1979), codified at 21 C.F.R. Part 507.

4. *Salmon Contamination.* The importance of extreme care in the production of low acid canned food was dramatically illustrated by a single incident involving the Alaska canned salmon industry. In February 1982, a Belgian citizen died of botulism poisoning after eating canned Alaska salmon. The contamination with botulinum toxin occurred as a result of a hole in the can caused by defective canning equipment. The Alaska salmon industry undertook a worldwide recall to retrieve other damaged cans, at considerable cost to both the industry and FDA. GAO, FDA's OVERSIGHT OF THE 1982 CANNED SALMON RECALLS, Rep. No. HRD–84–77 (Sept. 12, 1984).

5. *USDA Processing Requirements.* USDA has established similar requirements for canned meat and poultry products. 49 Fed. Reg. 14636 (Apr. 12, 1984); 51 Fed. Reg. 45602 (Dec. 19, 1986).

6. *Canned Meat and Poultry.* When USDA promulgated its meat and poultry HACCP regulations, the agency exempted canned meat and poultry products that are subject to the emergency permit requirements for canned food, on the premise that the emergency permit requirements provide protection against pathogenic microorganisms. A proposal by USDA in 66 Fed. Reg. 12590 (Feb. 27, 2001) to replace the canned meat and poultry requirements with a new performance standard was greeted by a storm of protest from the industry, which argued that the emergency permit regulations have been spectacularly successful for some thirty years and should not be replaced.

7. *Handling in the Home.* Virtually all botulism contamination of food occurs through improper home canning or refrigeration. *See, e.g.,* "FDA Consumer Advisory on Refrigeration of Carrot Juice: Three Cases of Botulism Possibly Caused by Improper Refrigeration," FDA News No. P06–135 (Sept. 17, 2006).

I. SAFETY OF FOOD CONSTITUENTS

One of FDA's most controversial activities is the regulation of the safety of food constituents—materials that occur naturally in agricultural commodities, that are intentionally added to food during processing, or that migrate to food as the result of industrial activity. There is no single food safety standard. The food safety provisions of the FD&C Act are an aggregation of authorities enacted over a period of 100 years, each directed at a distinct category of constituents. *See* Richard A. Merrill, *Regulating Carcinogens in Food: A Legislator's Guide to the Food Safety Provisions of the Federal Food, Drug, and Cosmetic Act*, 77 MICH. L. REV. 171 (1979); GAO, MONITORING AND ENFORCING FOOD SAFETY—AN OVERVIEW OF PAST STUDIES, No. RCED-83-153 (Sept. 9, 1983).

1. HISTORICAL AND STATUTORY BACKGROUND

The Food and Drugs Act of 1906 declared adulterated any food that contained "any added poisonous or other added deleterious ingredient which may render such article injurious to health." The early law did not deal with hazards posed by constituents that were not "added" to food, a concept that was not defined in the 1906 Act but was understood to embrace substances incorporated as ingredients or used during processing.

When Congress wrote the present FD&C Act in 1938, it expanded the 1906 Act's controls over toxicants in food. Section 402(a)(1) declares adulterated any food that "bears or contains any poisonous or deleterious substance which may render it injurious to health ...," without apparent limitation to "added" substances. Late in the legislative process, Congress qualified this standard by appending: "but in case the substance is not an added substance such food shall not be considered adulterated under this clause if the quantity of such substance in such food does not ordinarily render it injurious to health." The FD&C Act thus retained the 1906 Act's distinction between substances that are "added" and those that are not, but made the latter subject to FDA regulation for the first time.

The statutory standard applicable to nonadded substances has remained unchanged since 1938. The "ordinarily injurious" test is the legal measure of whether such a constituent adulterates food. The test is more permissive of potentially toxic constituents than other provisions of the Act. Because the Act does not define "added," moreover, FDA has exercised broad discretion in determining which food constituents qualify for evaluation under the "ordinarily injurious" test.

Congress also recognized that certain added substances required more comprehensive control than would be achieved under the "may render injurious" test of section 402(a)(1)—a standard it expected FDA to enforce in court. Section 406 was therefore included in the 1938 Act to empower FDA to establish tolerances sufficient to protect the public health for unavoidable or necessary added "poisonous or deleterious" substances, such as pesticide residues on raw agricultural commodities.

The 1938 Act thus contained three standards applicable to potentially toxic substances in food: (1) the section 402(a)(1) "ordinarily injurious" standard applied to constituents that were not added; (2) the section 402(a)(1) "may render injurious" standard applied to added constituents that were neither necessary nor unavoidable; and (3) under section 406, FDA could set tolerances "for the protection of public health" for added constituents whose use was "necessary in the production of a food" or whose occurrence was "unavoidable by good manufacturing practice."

This original triad of controls has been augmented by several subsequent amendments to the 1938 Act. Each of these amendments deals with a specific category of the broad class of added food constituents and establishes a system under which FDA is empowered—by administrative order or regulation—to limit the use, or the occurrence, of potentially toxic substances in or on food. The first of these amendments was the Miller Pesticide Amendments of 1954, which added section 408 of the Act. This provision was intended to complement the authority then residing in the Department of Agriculture to register pesticides under the Federal Insecticide, Rodenticide, and Fungicide Act (FIFRA). The Amendments provide that a raw agricultural commodity shall be deemed adulterated if it bears any residue of a pesticide that does not conform to a tolerance established under section 408, and they create an elaborate procedure for the establishment of tolerances. It should be noted that section 408 does not cover pesticides that contaminate foods for which their use is not approved. Such contamination often occurs as a result of drift during application or persistence in the environment.

In 1958 Congress carved out another category of added constituents of food for special treatment. The Food Additives Amendment, which added section 409 of the Act, establishes a licensure scheme, similar to that for pesticide residues, for substances that are intended to be used as ingredients in formulated foods. The Amendment also applies to substances such as packaging materials that, through use in contact with food, become or "may reasonably be expected to become" components of food. A food that bears or contains a food additive whose use FDA has not approved as "safe," or that contains an approved food additive in a quantity exceeding the limits specified by the agency, is adulterated under section 402(a)(2)(C).

The food additive provisions do not apply to all intentional ingredients of food or to all substances that may migrate to food. Excepted from its coverage are (1) substances whose use in food is "generally recognized as safe by qualified experts," referred to by the acronym GRAS—an exception that embraces a large number of familiar substances such as sugar and salt—and (2) substances that either FDA or USDA had approved for use in food prior to 1958, so-called "prior sanctioned" substances.

The famous Delaney Clause was added to the FD&C Act as part of the Food Additives Amendment. This clause precludes FDA from approving as "safe" any food additive found to induce cancer in man or in animals when administered by ingestion or other appropriate test. Because the Delaney Clause is drafted as a limitation on FDA's approval authority under section 409, however, it technically applies only to substances that fall within the statutory definition of a "food additive." The issues involved in the regulation of carcinogens are examined in detail in Chapter IX.

In 1960 Congress addressed the more limited problem of substances used to color foods—as well as colorings for drugs and cosmetics. The Color Additive Amendments apply to all substances used primarily for the purpose of imparting color to food. They contain no exceptions for color additives that may be generally recognized as safe or that were authorized for use prior to 1960. The 1960 Amendments require FDA approval, or "listing," for use of a color additive. A food that bears or contains a color additive whose use has not been approved by FDA, or whose use deviates from the terms of any approval, is adulterated. A second Delaney Clause prohibits the listing of any color additive that has been shown to induce cancer in man or animals.

The next relevant modification of the 1938 Act occurred as part of the Animal Drug Amendments of 1968. After the enactment of the Food Additives Amendment of 1958, drugs for food-producing animals were regulated under a combination of statutory provisions—the Food Additives Amendment coupled with the new drug approval section for all animal drugs administered through animal feed, and section 409 alone for animal drugs with other modes of administration that "could reasonably be expected" to leave residues in human food. FDA took the position (as it had with respect to packaging regulation under the Food Additives Amendment) that testing to determine if residues were present satisfied the quoted language and triggered the dual new drug-food additive approval system. In 1968 Congress simplified the procedure for evaluating animal drugs by prescribing a unified licensure system under section 512 of the Act. The Food Additives Amendment Delaney anti-cancer clause was made applicable to all animal drugs, whether or not administered through feed.

Almost forty years later, in the Dietary Supplement Health and Education Act of 1994, Congress recognized dietary supplements as a distinct subcategory of food and established separate safety criteria for "dietary ingredients." Dietary ingredients are excluded from the Food Additives Amendment. Dietary supplements and dietary ingredients continue, however, to be subject to section 402(a)(1)'s "may render injurious" and "ordinarily injurious" standards for poisonous or deleterious substances—with the condition that this adulteration be "under the conditions of use recommended or suggested in the labeling." DSHEA also prohibits the marketing of any dietary supplement or dietary ingredient that presents a "significant or unreasonable risk of illness or injury" under recommended or suggested conditions of use, and it authorizes the Secretary of HHS to impose an immediate ban of a product or ingredient that poses an imminent hazard. FDA bears the burden of proving that a dietary supplement is adulterated, and requires that a reviewing court decide the issue of adulteration on a de novo basis. Anyone who proposes to market a new (post-1994) dietary ingredient must notify FDA at least 75 days in advance unless the ingredient has been present in the food supply as an article used for food in a form in which the food has not been chemically altered. There is no GRAS exception from premarket notification for a new dietary ingredient.

Thus, Congress through its amendments has subdivided the universe of added food constituents into several categories, each of which is subject to distinct regulatory requirements. In FDA's view, however, the categories of food constituents that Congress has dealt with in special legislation since 1938 do not exhaust the universe of added substances in food. None of the post-1938 amendments covers exogenous substances, such as PCBs or mercury, whose occurrence in food is unintended and undesired. Such contaminants accordingly are regulated under the provisions of the original 1938 Act.

2. Poisonous or Deleterious Substances

As enacted in 1938, and unchanged since, section 402(a)(1) defines as adulterated any food that contains an "added" poisonous or deleterious substance which may render it injurious to health or a "nonadded" poisonous or deleterious substance which ordinarily renders it injurious to health. The statute, however, contains no definition of the term "added."

a. ADDED SUBSTANCES

United States v. Lexington Mill & Elevator Co.
232 U.S. 399 (1914).

■ Mr. Justice Day delivered the opinion of the court.

The petitioner, the United States of America, proceeding under § 10 of the Food and Drugs Act (June 30, 1906), ... sought to seize and condemn 625 sacks of flour in the possession of one Terry.... The amended libel charges that the flour had been treated by the "Alsop Process," so called, by which nitrogen peroxide gas, generated by electricity, was mixed with atmospheric air and the mixture then brought in contact with the flour, and that it was thereby adulterated under ... § 7 of the act ... in that the flour had been caused to contain added poisonous or other added deleterious ingredients, to-wit, nitrites or nitrite reacting material, nitrogen peroxide, nitrous acid, nitric acid and other poisonous and deleterious substances which might render the flour injurious to health....

A special verdict to the effect that the flour was adulterated was returned and judgment of condemnation entered....

The case requires a construction of the Food and Drugs Act. Parts of the statute pertinent to this case are:

"Sec. 7. That for the purposes of this act an article shall be deemed to be adulterated: . . .

"In the case of food: . . .

"Fifth. If it contain any added poisonous or other added deleterious ingredient which may render such article injurious to health". . . .

Without reciting the testimony in detail it is enough to say that for the Government it tended to show that the added poisonous substance introduced into the flour by Alsop Process, in the proportion of 1.8 parts per million, calculated as nitrogen, may be injurious to the health of those who use the flour in bread and other forms of food. On the other hand, the testimony for the respondent tended to show that the process does not add to the flour any poisonous or deleterious ingredients which can in any manner render it injurious to the health of a consumer. On these conflicting proofs the trial court was required to submit the case to the jury. . . .

It is evident . . . that the trial court regarded the addition to the flour of any poisonous ingredient as an offense within this statute, no matter how small the quantity, and whether the flour might or might not injure the health of the consumer. . . . The testimony shows that the effect of the Alsop Process is to bleach or whiten the flour and thus make it more marketable. If the testimony introduced on the part of the respondent was believed by the jury they must necessarily have found that the added ingredient, nitrites of a poisonous character, did not have the effect to make the consumption of the flour by any possibility injurious to the health of the consumer. . . .

. . . [I]n considering this statute, we find that the fifth subdivision of § 7 provides that food shall be deemed to be adulterated: "If it contain any added poisonous or other added deleterious ingredient *which may render such article injurious to health.*" The [jury] instruction of the trial court permitted this statute to be read without the final and qualifying words, concerning the effect of the article upon health. If Congress had so intended the provision would have stopped with the condemnation of food which contained any added poisonous or other added deleterious ingredient. In other words, the first and familiar consideration is that, if Congress had intended to enact the statute in that form, it would have done so by choice of apt words to express that intent. It did not do so, but only condemned food containing an added poisonous or other added deleterious ingredient when such addition might render the article of food injurious to the health. . . .

It is not required that the article of food containing added poisonous or other added deleterious ingredients must affect the public health, and it is not incumbent upon the Government in order to make out a case to establish that fact. The act has placed upon the Government the burden of establishing, in order to secure a verdict of condemnation under this statute, that the added poisonous or deleterious substances must be such as may render such article injurious to health. The word "may" is here used in its ordinary and usual signification, there being nothing to show the intention of Congress to affix to it any other meaning. . . . In thus describing the offense Congress doubtless took into consideration that flour may be used in many ways, in bread, cake, gravy, broth, etc. It may be consumed, when prepared as a food, by the strong and the weak, the old and the young, the well and the sick; and it is intended that if any flour, because of any added poisonous or other deleterious ingredient, may possibly injure the health of any of these, it shall come within the ban of the statute. If it cannot by any possibility, when the facts are reasonably considered, injure the health of any consumer, such flour, though having a small addition of poisonous or deleterious ingredients, may not be condemned under the act. This is the plain meaning of the words and in our view needs no additional support by reference to reports and debates, although it may be said in passing that the meaning which we have given to the statute was well expressed by Mr. Heyburn, chairman of the committee having it in charge upon the floor of the Senate:

> "As to the use of the term 'poisonous,' let me state that everything which contains poison is not poison. It depends on the quantity and the combination. A very large majority of the things consumed by the human family contain, under analysis, some kind of poison, but it depends upon the combination, the chemical relation which it bears to the body in which it exists as to whether or not it is dangerous to take into the human system." . . .

It follows that the judgment of the Circuit Court of Appeals reversing the judgment of the District Court must be affirmed, and the case remanded to the District Court for a new trial.

NOTES

1. *Codification of Lexington Mill.* When Congress enacted the 1938 Act, reproducing the language of the 1906 statute in the first clause of section 402(a)(1), it clearly intended to incorporate as well the Supreme Court's interpretation of the "may render injurious" standard in *Lexington Mill. See Flemming v. Florida Citrus Exchange*, 358 U.S. 153, 161 (1958).

2. *Other Authority.* In *United States v. Forty Barrels and Twenty Kegs*, 241 U.S. 265 (1916), the Supreme Court held that caffeine is an added substance in soft drinks and that whether it meets the "may render injurious" standard is a question of fact for the jury. *W. B. Wood Mfg. Co. v. United States*, 286 F. 84 (7th Cir. 1923), held that arsenic present as a contaminant in a color additive was an "added" substance but that FDA had failed to establish that the amount present in the food was sufficient to violate the "may render injurious" standard.

3. *DES Residues.* Even after FDA banned diethylstilbestrol (DES) in food-producing animals, *infra* p. 1131, some ranchers continued to implant cattle with the drug. The government seized the beef from treated cattle, contending that it contained an added poisonous or deleterious substance in violation of the Federal Meat Inspection Act, 21 U.S.C 601(m)(1), whose language is identical to Section 402(a)(1). In *United States v. 2,116 Boxes of Boned Beef*, 516 F. Supp. 321 (D. Kan. 1981), however, the court ruled that the government failed to carry its burden of proving that the levels of DES present in the beef could render the beef injurious to health under the *Lexington Mill* standard, or that the beef was otherwise adulterated. The government did not appeal.

4. *Benzene in Soft Drinks*. Beginning about 1990, the soft drink industry informed FDA that trace levels of benzene, a carcinogen, could form in soft drinks containing both benzoate preservatives and vitamin C. Because subsequent studies have shown that the vast majority of sampled beverages contain either no detectable benzene or levels below the 5 ppb limit for drinking water, FDA has taken no action on this matter. Letter from Robert E. Brackett, Director, FDA Center for Food Safety and Applied Nutrition, to Richard Wiles (Mar. 21, 2006).

5. *Acrylamide in Cooked Food*. In April 2002, Swedish researchers announced that they had detected acrylamide in a number of fried and baked foods, including french fries, potato chips, cookies, breakfast cereals, and bread. Acrylamide is toxic at high doses, and its safety at low doses is uncertain. FDA has concluded that there is insufficient information for the agency to issue a public warning or take other regulatory action until additional scientific information becomes available. *See* Council for Agricultural Science and Technology, *Acrylamide in Food*, CAST Issue Paper No. 32 (June 2006).

6. *Proof of Hazard*. The key issue under the "may render injurious" standard is the quantity of the added substance in the food. In *United States v. Commonwealth Brewing Corp.*, 1938–1964 F.D.L.I. Jud. Rec. 310 (D. Mass. 1945), the court observed that the quantity of a substance is likely to determine whether it may be harmful and therefore concluded that "quantity would be the test" under section 402(a)(1). Quantity would appear to be an essential element under the "ordinarily injurious" standard as well. The chief distinctions between the two standards in section 402(a)(1) appear to be the greater probability of harm that the government must show to restrict a natural constituent and the government's ability, under the "may render" standard, to take account of specially vulnerable segments of the population.

7. *Mixed, Not Added*. The court in *Cavalier Vending Corp. v. United States*, 190 F.2d 386 (4th Cir. 1951), held that the mingling of candy and trinkets in a vending machine did not fall within section 402(a)(1) because the candy did not "contain" the trinkets.

b.   NONADDED SUBSTANCES

United States v. 1232 Cases American Beauty Brand Oysters

43 F. Supp. 749 (W.D. Mo. 1942).

■ REEVES, DISTRICT JUDGE.

This is a proceeding by the process of libel to condemn an alleged adulterated food product. Such food consists of 1232 cases of oysters, each case containing 24 cans, marked "American Beauty Brand Oysters."

 As a basis for condemnation, it is alleged by the government that said article "contains shell fragments, many of them small enough to be swallowed and become lodged in the esophagus, and that said shell fragments are sharp and capable of inflicting injury in the mouth."

The provision of the law invoked by the government is section [402(a)(1)]. . . .

The claimant appeared to deny the averments of the libel and assert ownership of the product. The evidence in the case showed that in the processing of oysters for food there is a constant effort to eliminate shells and fragments thereof from the product. For this purpose many means and devices are used to reduce as nearly to a minimum as possible such shells and fragments in the product. The evidence, however, on behalf of both the government and the defense was that with present known means and devices it was impossible to free the product entirely from the presence of part shells and shell fragments.... The shells, therefore, are not artificially added for the purpose of growth or to aid in the processing operations....

The ... statute ... contemplates that there may be of necessity food products containing deleterious substances. No one who has had the experience of eating either fish or oysters is unfamiliar with the presence of bones in the fish (a deleterious substance) and fragments of shell in the oysters (also a deleterious substance). The Congress, however, withdrew such foods from the adulterated class "if the quantity of such substance in such food does not ordinarily render it injurious to health."

The evidence on both sides was that by the greatest effort, and in the use of the most modern means and devices, shell fragments could not be entirely separated from an oyster food product. The government, in its brief, quite aptly and concisely stated its point by using the following language: "It is the character, not the quantity of this substance that controls its ability to injure."

This concession on the part of the government, properly made, upon the evidence removes the case immediately from that portion of the statute which says: "... such food shall not be considered adulterated under this clause if the quantity of such substance in such food does not ordinarily render it injurious to health."

Since it is the "character, not the quantity of this substance that controls its ability to injure," as stated by the government, then in the view that it is impossible to eliminate shell fragments in toto from the product, the use of oysters as a food must be entirely prohibited or it must be found that the presence of shell fragments is not a deleterious substance within the meaning of the law and must be tolerated. [T]o reject oyster products as a food is unthinkable. It would be as reasonable to reject fish because of the presence of bones. Even if a greater percentage of shells and shell fragments were found in claimant's product than in that of other processors, yet this fact, under the theory of the government, would not add to the deleterious nature of claimant's product....

Upon the evidence in this case it must be found that the presence of shell fragments in the article sought to be condemned does not ordinarily render it injurious to health....

NOTES

1. *Other Authority.* In *Evart v. Suli*, 259 Cal. Rptr. 535 (Cal. Ct. App. 1989), the court held that a hamburger containing a piece of bone beef is not adulterated as a matter of law, because the bone is a naturally occurring substance. *See also Millet, Pit and Seed Co., Inc. v. United States*, 436 F. Supp. 84 (E.D. Tenn. 1977) (holding that the amygdalin that occurs naturally in apricot kernels is a nonadded substance and that FDA failed to carry its burden of proving that the amount present was sufficient to render the apricot kernels ordinarily injurious to health).

2. *Legislative History*. The legislative history of the 1938 Act provides little guidance on the interpretation of the second clause of section 402(a)(1). Congress evidently was aware that some foods naturally contain substances that, if consumed in excess, can be harmful, and it obviously intended to establish a demanding standard for FDA enforcement. The court's ruling in *American Beauty Brand Oysters* assumes that, notwithstanding the risk of choking or other injury from oyster shell fragments, Congress would value oysters highly enough to preclude a finding of adulteration. While the Act does not explicitly authorize any weighing of "benefits," the court's approach is consistent with the few illustrations contained in the legislative history of the second clause of section 401(a)(1). The 1906 Act declared food adulterated "[i]f it contain[s] any added poisonous or other added deleterious ingredient which may render such article injurious to health." Most of the early bills to reform the law would have changed that language to define food as adulterated "[i]f it bears or contains any poisonous or deleterious substance which may render it dangerous to health." *E.g.*, S. 2000, 73d Cong., 2nd Sess. § 3(a)(1) (introduced Jan. 4, 1934); S. 5, 74th Cong., 1st Sess. § 301(a)(1) (reported in the House May 31, 1935); S. 5, 75th Cong., 1st Sess. § 11(a)(1) (introduced Jan. 6, 1937). The language Congress ultimately adopted to deal with naturally occurring adulterants appeared in a bill reported on August 14, 1938, as a substitute for the bill (S. 5) passed by the Senate several months earlier. While the House Report, H.R. REP. NO. 213, 75th Cong., 2d Sess. (1938), does not explain why this wording was added, the legislative record of the earlier bills may suggest an answer.

The earliest proposed bills had deleted the word "added" from the language of the 1906 Act to allow the FDA to regulate any food that might present a risk to consumers, whether the deleterious constituent occurred naturally or was put in food by artifice. "Federal Foods, Drugs and Cosmetics," Hearing on S. 2800 before the Senate Committee on Commerce, 73d Cong., 2d Sess. (1934). The bills also substituted the word "dangerous" for "injurious." FDA's Walter G. Campbell pointed out that the 1906 Act left such foods as poisonous mushrooms and particularly toxic varieties of West Coast mussels, which acquire their injurious properties naturally, beyond federal control. The word "dangerous" was intended to differentiate "between those products which may be injurious to health in a mild way and those that are unquestionably dangerous to health in a very definite way." "Foods, Drugs, and Cosmetics," Hearing before a Subcommittee of the House Committee on Interstate and Foreign Commerce, 74th Cong., 1st Sess. 58 (1935).

The final wording of section 402(a)(1) returned to the word "injurious," but omitted "added" from the second clause—in order to reach naturally occurring poisons. "Injurious" had been the standard for all FDA enforcement actions under the 1906 Act, and Congress was reluctant to change language that the courts had already interpreted. But to prevent over-zealous enforcement against foods that naturally contained a deleterious substance, the House Committee added the proviso requiring the Government to prove that a substance was harmful when consumed in ordinary quantities. Statements during hearings indicate that foods such as coffee, tea, rhubarb (which naturally contains oxalic acid), and cocoa were not to be regulated. Congress wanted to reach only foods such as the poisonous mushrooms, mussels, and Burma beans that FDA witnesses had cited as examples of foods that are highly toxic in their natural state.

———

To facilitate enforcement, FDA has sought to regulate a number of naturally-occurring environmental contaminants of food as "added" rather than "nonadded" substances. Beginning in 1970, FDA established and

began to enforce an action level of 0.5 ppm mercury in fish, resulting in a
virtual ban of swordfish. Note, *Health Regulation of Naturally Hazardous
Foods: The FDA Ban on Swordfish*, 85 HARV. L. REV. 1025 (1972). This
action level was calculated to protect the 99th percentile fish consumers in
the country, who eat virtually nothing else, and it thus afforded a very wide
margin of safety for all other consumers. To clarify the distinction between
added and nonadded substances, FDA later promulgated regulations which
took the position that only a substance "that is an inherent natural
constituent of the food and is not the result of environmental, agricultural,
industrial, or other contamination" is a nonadded substance. 39 Fed. Reg.
42746 (Dec. 6, 1974), 42 Fed. Reg. 52814 (Sept. 30, 1977), codified at 21
C.F.R. 109.3(c). Under this definition, all mercury in fish is "added." At the
time it proposed these regulations, FDA also proposed to establish the 0.5
ppm action level for mercury in fish through informal rulemaking. 39 Fed.
Reg. 42738 (Dec. 6, 1974).

United States v. Anderson Seafoods, Inc.

622 F.2d 157 (5th Cir. 1980).

■ WISDOM, CIRCUIT JUDGE. . . .

In April 1977, the United States sought an injunction against
Anderson Seafoods, Inc., and its president, Charles F. Anderson, to prevent
them from selling swordfish containing more than 0.5 parts per million
(ppm) of mercury, which it considered adulterated under the meaning of
§ 342(a)(1). . . . Anderson responded in May 1977 by seeking a declaratory
judgment that fish containing 2.0 ppm of mercury or less are not adulterated. . . .

The district court denied the injunction that the government sought.
In Anderson's suit, the court also denied an injunction, but issued a
declaratory judgment that swordfish containing more than 1.0 ppm mercury is adulterated under § 342(a)(1). In doing so, the court determined that
mercury is an *"added* substance" under the Act and rejected Anderson's
contention that a level of 2.0 ppm is acceptable. . . .

In the trial of this case three theories about the meaning of the term
"added" emerged. The Food and Drug Administration sponsored the first
theory. It argues that an "added substance" is one that is not "inherent".
According to FDA regulations:

> (c) A "naturally occurring poisonous or deleterious substance" is a
> poisonous or deleterious substance that is an inherent natural
> constituent of a food and is not the result of environmental,
> agricultural, industrial, or other contamination.

> (d) An "added poisonous or deleterious substance" is a poisonous
> or deleterious substance that is not a naturally occurring poison-
> ous or deleterious substance. . . .

21 C.F.R. §§ 109.3(c)(d). Under this theory, all the mercury in swordfish is
an added substance, because it results not from the creature's bodily
processes but from mercury in the environment, whether natural or introduced by man.

② direct agency
[Anderson]

③ de minimus
by pollution
[district
court]

Anderson put forward a second theory. A substance, under this theory, is not an added substance unless it is proved to be present as a result of the direct agency of man. Further, only that amount of a substance the lineage of which can be so traced is "added". If some mercury in swordfish occurs naturally, and some is the result of man-made pollution, only that percentage of the mercury in fish proved to result directly from pollution is an added substance.

The district court adopted a third theory. Under the court's theory, if a de minimis amount of the mercury in swordfish is shown to result from industrial pollution, then all of the metal in the fish is treated as an added substance and may be regulated under the statute's "may render injurious" standard. The legislative history and case law, though sparse, persuade us that this is the proper reading of the statute.

Determining that man must appear on the stage before a substance is an added one does not determine the size of the role he must play before it is. The dichotomy in § 342(a)(1) is between two clear cases that bracket the present case. The Act considers added things such as lead in coloring agents or caffeine in Coca Cola. It considers not-added things like oxalic acid in rhubarb or caffeine in coffee. The Act did not contemplate, however, the perhaps rare problem of a toxin, part of which occurs "naturally", and part of which results from human acts. The section is designed, of course, to insure the scrutiny of toxins introduced by man....

Since the purpose of the "may render injurious" standard was to facilitate regulation of food adulterated by acts of man, we think that it should apply to all of a toxic substance present in a food when any of that substance is shown to have been introduced by man. Anderson argues that this reading of the statute would result "in the anomalous situation where a substance in a food can be 90 percent natural and 10 percent added [but] the entire substance is considered as added". There is no anomaly, however, in such a situation. The Act's "may render it injurious to health" standard is to be applied to the food, not to the added substance. The food would not be considered adulterated under our view unless the 10 percent increment creates or increases a potentiality of injury to health. If the increment does create or increase such a potentiality, then, because the increment that triggered the potentiality was introduced by man, the Food and Drug Administration ought to be able to regulate it under the standard designed to apply to adulterations of food caused by man. Anderson's argument proves too much. Anderson would argue that if a swordfish contained 0.99 ppm of natural mercury, and 0.99 ppm of mercury from human sources, the fish could be sold although it contained nearly twice as much mercury as the district court found to be a safe level....

In sum, we hold that where some portion of a toxin present in a food has been introduced by man, the entirety of the substance present in the food will be treated as an added substance and so considered under the "may render injurious to health" standard of the Act....

There was sufficient evidence to show that some mercury is attributable to the acts of man. There was evidence that mercury is dumped into rivers and washes onto the continental shelf, where some of it is methylated by bacteria and taken up by plankton. It thereby enters the food chain of

swordfish, for the plankton is consumed by small organisms and fish, such as copepods, herring, and hake, which are in turn eaten by larger organisms, and eventually by swordfish, a peak predator. This evidence was enough to trigger the Act's "may render injurious to health" standard.*
. . .

NOTES

1. *Mercury Action Level.* Following the District Court's decision and before the Court of Appeals ruled, FDA announced that it would adopt as its own action level the 1.0 ppm level determined by the District Court to be safe. 44 Fed. Reg. 3990 (Jan. 19, 1979). Based upon new methodology, FDA subsequently revised the 1.0 ppm action level to encompass only methyl mercury and not total mercury. 49 Fed. Reg. 45663 (Nov. 19, 1984). Following the District Court's decision, the agency also stated that it would adhere to its own definition of an "added" substance in 21 C.F.R. 109.3 pending the Court of Appeals' decision. Even though the Fifth Circuit rejected the definition as too broad, FDA still has not amended it. *See* Paul M. Hauge, *FDA Regulation of Mercury in Fish* (1995), in Chapter V(Q) of the Electronic Book. In March 2004, FDA and EPA issued their current joint Consumer Advisory on Methylmercury in Fish, and in June 2006 the two agencies announced that "the 2004 advisory remains current and that FDA and EPA stand behind it." The agencies deliberately issued their recommendations in the form of a consumer advisory rather than a warning because "fish and shellfish are an important part of a healthy diet and can contribute to heart health and children's proper growth and development." *See* Dariush Mozaffarian & Eric R. Rimm, *Fish Intake, Contamination, and Human Health*, 296 J.A.M.A. 1885 (2006).

2. *Other Added Substances.* The following substances have been held to be "added": aflatoxin in corn, *United States v. Boston Farm Center, Inc.*, 590 F.2d 149 (5th Cir. 1979) (by implication); salmonella in shrimp, *Continental Seafoods, Inc. v. Schweiker*, 674 F.2d 38 (D.C. Cir. 1982); and, in two other cases, mercury in swordfish, *United States v. An Article of Food Consisting of Cartons of Swordfish*, 395 F. Supp. 1184 (S.D.N.Y. 1975); *United States v. Globe Fish Co.*, Food Drug Cosm. L. Rep. (CCH) ¶ 38,129 (D. Mass. 1981), ¶ 38,263 (D. Mass. 1984).

3. *Bottled Water.* In 62 Fed. Reg. 60721 (Nov. 12, 1997), FDA published a notice requesting public comment on the feasibility of appropriate methods of informing consumers about the level of contaminants in bottled water.

3. ENVIRONMENTAL CONTAMINANTS

No provision of the FD&C Act explicitly provides a mechanism for regulating substances that become constituents of food through environmental contamination. Yet such materials—which include mercury, polychlorinated biphenyls (PCBs), polybrominated biphenyls (PBBs), and aflatoxins—may pose serious risks to human health. Controlling their occurrence in food raises difficult scientific and economic, as well as administrative, issues.

Section 402(a)(1) does not specifically provide for the promulgation of implementing regulations. It is a "policing" provision that appears to call for court enforcement. FDA might have relied on the "ordinarily injurious"

---

* [The Court of Appeals also affirmed the District Court's establishment of 1.0 ppm as the limit for mercury in swordfish. *See infra* p. 377, Note 1]

language of section 402(a)(1) as the basis for court actions to control environmental contaminants, on the premise that since such contaminants are not purposely incorporated in or intentionally used in proximity with food, they should not be considered "added." An alternative would have been to rely exclusively on the first clause of section 402(a)(1), which condemns food containing an added poisonous or deleterious substance if the food "may" be injurious to health. The agency has rejected both approaches. Its objective has been to find a statutory rationale that allows it to determine administratively what level of contamination renders food adulterated. Achievement of this objective promises uniformity in enforcement and contributes to certainty among sellers of food. Furthermore, it assigns responsibility for evaluation of the health risks posed by a contaminant to the agency's scientific experts rather than to the district courts.

As enacted in 1938, Section 406 of the FD&C Act authorized FDA to establish tolerances for added poisonous or deleterious substances that are "required" in the production of food or "cannot be avoided by good manufacturing practice." The level of a tolerance must be set "for the protection of public health." The primary purpose of this provision was to permit FDA to set tolerances for pesticide residues in food. *E.g.*, H.R. REP. No. 2139, 75th Cong., 3rd Sess. 6 (1938). To promulgate a tolerance under section 406, however, the agency was obliged to proceed under section 701(e), which requires that objectors to any regulation be given an opportunity for a formal administrative hearing.

As its first action under section 406, FDA initiated a major rulemaking in 1944 to determine appropriate tolerances for residues of fluorine that remained in food treated with pesticide compounds containing this element. Although the resulting tolerance was upheld, the court effectively nullified it by interpreting it to apply only to elemental fluorine and not to compounds containing fluorine. *Washington State Apple Advertising Comm'n v. Federal Security Adm'r*, 156 F.2d 589 (9th Cir. 1946).

After World War II, FDA, joined by the American Medical Association, voiced growing concern about the safety of pesticide residues in the food supply, and it began preparation for further hearings to establish appropriate tolerances under section 406. *See* Tom Bellis, *Rule-Making Under Section 406(a) of the Federal Food, Drug, and Cosmetic Act*, 4 FOOD DRUG COSM. L.Q. 488 (1949); Paul B. Dunbar, *The Food and Drug Administration Looks at Insecticides*, 4 FOOD DRUG COSM. L.Q. 233 (1949); W. B. White, *Protection Afforded the Consumer Against Added Chemicals in Foods*, 4 FOOD DRUG COSM. L.Q. 478 (1949); James R. Wilson, *Pesticide Residues in Food as Health Hazards*, 3 FOOD DRUG COSM. L.Q. 561 (1948). When the ensuing hearing had ended in the early 1950s, however, FDA decided that the toxicological evidence was so poor and the record so confusing that the tolerances should be withdrawn. The agency made no other efforts to set tolerances for pesticides until after the enactment of the Miller Pesticide Amendments of 1954, discussed *infra* p. 383.

Beginning in the 1960s, however, evidence of a variety of other contaminants in food began to accumulate. The contaminants that raised the greatest concern were mercury in fish (resulting from both industrial pollution and natural sources), aflatoxin in nuts, grain, and other food crops (resulting from the growth of a fungus on the crops before harvest or during storage), and polychlorinated biphenyls (PCBs) in a variety of foods (resulting from industrial disposal and accidents). Remembering its prior unsuccessful efforts to set formal tolerances under section 406, FDA chose instead to establish informal "action levels," *i.e.*, levels of contamination that would trigger court enforcement action. FDA began to rely on action levels in the mid–1960s and refined their use through regulations that will be discussed further *infra* p. 381.

Confronting growing concern over the widespread contamination of food with PCBs, however, FDA decided to establish formal tolerances for this compound under section 406. *See* 37 Fed. Reg. 5705 (Mar. 18, 1972), 38 Fed. Reg. 18096 (July 6, 1973). After objections to FDA's tolerance for PCBs in paper food packaging material were filed, the agency stayed the tolerance pending a formal hearing, but also announced that it would seize as adulterated under section 402(a)(1) any packaging material shipped in interstate commerce containing higher than the specified level. 38 Fed. Reg. 22794 (Aug. 24, 1973). This policy was subsequently upheld in *Natick Paperboard Corp. v. Weinberger*, 525 F.2d 1103 (1st Cir. 1975), which also held that FDA could establish an action level and institute seizures against paper packaging before the material was used, as long as the agency could demonstrate a likelihood that the material would in fact be used for food packaging. The agency proceeded to deny a hearing on some objections and grant a hearing on others. 40 Fed. Reg. 11563 (Mar. 12, 1975). It subsequently settled the matter without a hearing and adopted the tolerance for PCBs in paper food packaging material as amended to comply with this settlement. 48 Fed. Reg. 37020 (Aug. 16, 1983), 48 Fed. Reg. 45544 (Oct. 6, 1983).

While this administrative proceeding was ongoing, FDA amended the regulations to reduce the tolerance for PCBs in fish. 42 Fed. Reg. 17487 (Apr. 1, 1977), 44 Fed. Reg. 38330 (June 29, 1979). After receiving objections, it conducted a formal hearing. 46 Fed. Reg. 24551 (May 1, 1981). The agency later released the Administrative Law Judge's Initial Decision, Food Drug Cosm. L. Rep. (CCH) ¶ 38,159 (1982), and then issued a final regulation reducing the tolerance in 49 Fed. Reg. 21514 (May 22, 1984). The tolerances for PCBs, codified in 21 C.F.R. 109.30, remain the only formal tolerances ever adopted under section 406. *See generally* GAO, FURTHER FEDERAL ACTION NEEDED TO DETECT AND CONTROL ENVIRONMENTAL CONTAMINATION OF FOOD, No. CED–81–19 (Dec. 31, 1980).

Poisonous or Deleterious Substances in Food: Notice of Proposed Rulemaking

39 Fed. Reg. 42743 (December 6, 1974).

. . . .

"Added" is a statutory term of art encompassing all ingredients which are not inherent and intrinsic parts of a food.... Although the word chosen implies that the statute is concerned with the act of addition, the legislative history makes clear that the term seeks rather to establish a standard based upon the necessary and inherent normal condition of the food....

The legislative history ... identifies examples of foods naturally containing poisonous or deleterious substances and thus not subject to the "added" provisions of section 402(a)(1) of the act. These examples are Burma beans, which contain a glucoside that yields prussic or hydrocyanic acid; rhubarb, which contains oxalic acid; and coffee and tea. Except for substances whose deleterious nature is inherent to the natural state of the food, and thus similar in origin to these examples, all poisonous and deleterious components are "added" within the meaning of the act. Moreover, when a naturally occurring poisonous or deleterious substance is increased to abnormal levels through mishandling or other intervening act, it is "added" to the extent of such increase....

Section 406 was included in the 1938 act to permit the establishment of tolerances for added poisonous or deleterious substances which are required in the production of food or otherwise cannot be avoided by good manufacturing practice.... Although formal tolerances under section 406 have not been used by the Food and Drug Administration, except for the tolerance for PCB's published in the FEDERAL REGISTER of July 6, 1973 (38 FR 18096), informal action levels have frequently been utilized to implement this provision of the law and a number of those action levels exist today....

The definition of "food additive" established in section 201(s) of the act is not limited to intentional additives. The breadth of the language in section 201(s) of the act includes any food substance and excludes only those substances which cannot reasonably be expected to become a component of food....

When the Food Additives Amendment of 1958 was enacted, the provisions of section 406 of the act were not repealed. Although all added poisonous or deleterious ingredients are food additives, except when they appear in food accidentally and unforeseeably or are exempted under section 201(s) of the act because they are otherwise regulated under the act, the tolerance-setting provisions of section 406 of the act were left intact to deal with those unavoidably added poisonous or deleterious ingredients that could not meet the high standards for issuance of a regulation under the authority of section 409 of the act. A number of added poisonous or deleterious substances, which are also food additives within the meaning of section 201(s) of the act, are unavoidable but cannot meet the requirements for a section 409 regulation because their safety cannot be demonstrated and because they serve no functional purpose. A prominent example is lead, which was one of the contaminants most frequently mentioned in the legislative history of the 1938 act and one of the prime contaminants with which section 406 was enacted to deal. Lead cannot be the subject of a food additive regulation under section 409 of the act even at trivial levels because it serves no functional purpose.* Section 406 of the act, therefore,

---

* [FDA withdrew this statement as "incorrect" in 44 Fed. Reg. 51233 (Aug. 31, 1979), stating: "The appropriate inquiry into the functionality of such substances is whether they have a purpose in the food-contact article ... not whether they have a purpose of a function in the food."]

remains in force to control the use of such substances, since there would otherwise be no statutory means available to recognize their unavoidability and to exercise reasonable control over their presence. . . .

The Commissioner proposes to establish procedures for controlling all poisonous or deleterious substances. Basic reliance on the provisions of section 409 for regulating use of such substances remains unchanged. . . . However, when a food contaminant is unavoidable but cannot be approved under the criteria of section 409 of the act, a formal procedure is being proposed to control its use under authority of sections 306 [now section 309], 402(a), and 406 of the act.

. . . The Commissioner is not required to establish a tolerance for every added poisonous or deleterious substance, as is indicated by the language of section 406 of the act recognizing that an adulteration charge can be made under section 402(a)(1) of the act when no tolerance is in effect. Section 306 of the act has long been interpreted to permit the Food and Drug Administration to establish action levels in implementing the adulteration provisions of the act. . . .

When the factors required to be considered prior to promulgation of a section 406 tolerance are rapidly changing, it would be inappropriate to set such a formal tolerance. The procedures required by section 406 of the act, including a public hearing and requirement of substantial evidence to support the tolerance, contemplate ample evidence to consider, and a relatively stable situation where the evidence will be of more than transient significance and where the tolerance eventually promulgated will be appropriate for a relatively long period of time. . . .

When it is not appropriate to promulgate a tolerance under section 406 . . . the Commissioner will consider promulgating an action level under authority of sections 306, 402(a), and 406 of the act.

Such action levels are similar to a formal tolerance in basis and effect. In setting an action level, the Commissioner considers evidence indicating when the presence of an added poisonous or deleterious substance may render food injurious to health, which is the standard in section 402(a)(1) of the act. In addition, the Commissioner takes into account the question of its unavoidability, a policy embodied in section 406 of the act. Thus, an action level is based on the same criteria as a tolerance, except that an action level is temporary until the appearance of more stable circumstances makes a formal tolerance appropriate. . . .

The proposal also prescribes a method of issuing regulations to deal with foods containing naturally occurring poisonous or deleterious substances. Where appropriate, the Commissioner may identify foods which, because of their inherent components, are deemed to be adulterated within the meaning of section 402(a)(1) of the act. These regulations would, of course, not constitute a complete list of such foods. . . .

NOTES

1. *Final Regulations.* FDA's final regulations reflected no significant change in the agency's interpretation of the applicable statutory provisions. 42 Fed. Reg.

52813 (Sept. 30, 1977), codified at 21 C.F.R. Part 109 ("Unavoidable Contaminants in Food for Human Consumption and Food Packaging Material"). The agency elaborated its understanding of the term "added" and concluded that action levels should be established simply by notice in the Federal Register rather than by informal rulemaking.

2. *Contaminant or Food Additive.* The preamble to the final regulations set forth FDA's theory of the relationship between Section 406 tolerances (or action levels) and Section 409 food additive regulations. The agency stated that a tolerance or action level should not be established for a direct or indirect food additive that is intentionally added to serve a functional purpose unless it is unavoidable in a particular food, but that an action level or tolerance may be established for an intentionally added GRAS or prior sanctioned substance. For example, as discussed at *infra* at p. 379, action levels have been established to control lead migration from pottery and from soldered cans, where the substances containing the lead are intentionally used in the food-contact surface.

3. *Update.* PCBs remain ubiquitous in the environment. *See, e.g.*, ENVIRONMENTAL WORKING GROUP, PCBs IN FARMED SALMON (July 30, 2003). In order to harmonize advice given by different jurisdictions to consumers of sport-caught fish from the Great Lakes, eight states agreed on consensus recommendations. *See* Michael A. Kamrin & Lawrence J. Fischer, *Current Status of Sport Fish Consumption Advisories for PCBs in the Great Lakes*, 29 REGULATORY TOXICOLOGY AND PHARMACOLOGY 175 (1999).

———————

In the same December 6, 1974 Federal Register in which it proposed the procedure for establishing tolerances and action levels for unavoidable contaminants, FDA published a proposed tolerance for aflatoxin in shelled peanuts and peanut products, 39 Fed. Reg. 42748 (later withdrawn in 56 Fed. Reg. 67440, 67446 (Dec. 30, 1991)); a proposed tolerance for lead in canned evaporated milk, 39 Fed. Reg. 42740 (later withdrawn at 58 Fed. Reg. 33871 (June 21, 1993)); and a proposed action level for mercury in fish, 39 Fed. Reg. 42738 (later withdrawn in 44 Fed. Reg. 3990 (Jan. 19, 1979)). The mercury proposal, which precipitated the *Anderson Seafood* litigation, *supra* p. 369, illustrates the agency's approach.

Action Level for Mercury in Fish and Shellfish

39 Fed. Reg. 42738 (December 6, 1974).

. . . .

Most of man's exposure to mercury arises from the contamination of food and possibly drinking water.... Except in occupational exposure, the contribution of inhaled mercury is insignificant in relation to intake from food. The amount of methylmercury (the most toxic organic form of mercury) found in fruits, vegetables, grains, meat and dairy products is very small. Of all the commodities analyzed for mercury by the Food and Drug Administration (FDA) in a survey of 10 basic foods and in the food commodity classes of the FDA total diet study, fish was the only commodity shown to present a potential hazard to man. Other data show levels of mercury in shellfish (mollusks and crustaceans) similar to the levels in some vertebrate fish. The total human intake of mercury from food sources other than fish and shellfish is insignificant....

Methylmercury and other forms of mercury serve no essential function in fish and shellfish. They are not normal inherent constituents, but are found in aquatic species because of environmental, industrial, and agricultural contamination....

Methylmercury poisoning may lead to progressive blindness, deafness, incoordination, intellectual deterioration, and death.... In all mammals, concentrations of 5 to 10 micrograms per gram (mcg/g) of brain tissue may be associated with neurological symptoms....

... [A]n action level of 0.5 ppm permits a daily consumption of 60 grams of fish and shellfish contaminated to that extent, while still maintaining a tenfold margin of safety over the level of mercury intake known to be toxic. The 60 g/day figure is based on a mercury concentration of 0.5 ppm in all fish and shellfish consumed, but because actual concentrations are much less in most fish and shellfish, there is an additional safety margin. In addition, the average consumption of fish and shellfish in this country is regarded as considerably less than 60 grams per day.

A National Marine Fisheries Service (NMFS) survey determined that only 1.8 percent of the population consumes an average of more than 60 grams of fish and shellfish per day. The vast majority of the population is therefore protected by the tenfold margin of safety. Additional protection is provided by the fact that actual concentrations in most fish and shellfish are below 0.5 ppm mercury and the fact that consumption is less than an average of 60 grams per day.

It is not possible, however, to provide this same high level of protection to every person without excluding a great amount of fish and shellfish from the market. The NMFS survey indicated that 1 percent of the participants in the survey consumed an average of 77 grams daily and 0.1 percent consumed 165 grams daily. At the very high consumption of 165 grams per day, the tenfold margin of safety is reduced to less than four; although, it may be increased above that figure by the additional margin resulting from consumption of fish and shellfish with less contamination than 0.5 ppm mercury....

In balancing the unavoidability of mercury in fish and shellfish against the need for protection of the public health, the Commissioner concludes that it would be inappropriate to exclude a vast amount of fish and shellfish from the market in order to provide a large margin of safety for those who consume far more than the average person. The Commissioner notes that a person would have to consume every day the extraordinarily high amount of 600 grams of fish and/or shellfish contaminated at the full 0.5 ppm level to reach the blood levels where symptoms have been known to occur. Thus some margin of safety is still provided for even the largest consumers of these foods....

NOTES

1. *Judicial Review.* In *United States v. Anderson Seafoods, Inc.,* 447 F. Supp. 1151 (N.D. Fla. 1978), *aff'd,* 622 F.2d 157 (5th Cir. 1980), *supra* p. 369, the court

rejected both FDA's 0.5 ppm mercury action level and the industry-proposed 2.0 ppm safe level, and determined instead that mercury concentrations of 1.0 ppm or less would not be considered adulterated. While the case was pending appeal, FDA withdrew its December 1974 proposal to establish an action level for mercury and accepted the court-determined level of 1.0 ppm as its new action level. 44 Fed. Reg. 3990 (Jan. 19, 1979). The agency withdrew its proposed tolerance for aflatoxin in peanuts in 56 Fed. Reg. 67440 (Dec. 30, 1991) and for lead in evaporated milk in 58 Fed. Reg. 33871 (June 21, 1993), and it issued an action level for aflatoxin in peanuts for animal feed in 70 Fed. Reg. 17383 (Apr. 12, 1994), Compliance Policy Guide (CPG) No. 7126.33, and for peanut products in CPG 7112.02.

2. *Mercury in Drugs and Food.* Section 113 of the Food and Drug Administration Modernization Act of 1997 requires FDA to compile a list of drugs and foods that contain intentionally introduced mercury and provide a quantitative and qualitative analysis of the listed compounds. FDA announced the availability of the list and analysis in 64 Fed. Reg. 63323 (Nov. 19, 1999) and requested information to update it in 68 Fed. Reg. 5300 (Feb. 3, 2003).

3. *Mercury in Fish.* To reduce inconsistency among analytical laboratories, FDA announced guidelines for the sampling of imported swordfish for mercury residues in 52 Fed. Reg. 37659 (Oct. 8, 1987). Section 413 of the Food and Drug Administration Modernization Act of 1997 required FDA to conduct a study of mercury compounds in food and drugs. In 63 Fed. Reg. 68775 (Dec. 14, 1998) and 64 Fed. Reg. 23083 (Apr. 29, 1999), FDA requested data and information in order to prepare this report. In March 2004, FDA and EPA jointly announced a revised Consumer Advisory on methylmercury in fish. "FDA and EPA Announce the Revised Consumer Advisory on Methylmercury in Fish," FDA Press Release No. PO4–33 (Mar. 19, 1004). In announcing this Consumer Advisory, the agencies balanced the health benefits of eating fish with the health risks posed by methyl-mercury. The announcement caused substantial public controversy.

4. *Regulatory Alternatives.* Note, *Health Regulation of Naturally Hazardous Foods: The FDA Ban on Swordfish*, 85 HARV. L. REV. 1025 (1972), suggested alternative ways of protecting consumers from excessive levels of mercury:

> ... A crude approach is to advise limited consumption of the food through a frequency warning, as New York has done in recommending that sportfishermen eat their catch only once a week.... A content warning system would provide better protection. It would require that the labels state both the maximum allowable weekly levels of the contaminant and the amount contained in the food in the package. Consumers could keep track of their mercury intake just as many count calories. Though it would be impractical to test each package for its precise concentration, average levels for the food would appear to provide sufficient information to be useful, since the problem is one of average intake over time....

> ... [There is] a second alternative to a ban for regulating naturally toxic foods: food by prescription. One objectionable characteristic of a ban, its denial of the positive health values of regulated foods, would be alleviated by permitting physicians to prescribe such foods, with appropriate dosage instructions, to patients.... Because only long-term intake must be controlled, consumer rationing, the traditional means of controlling access to food in wartime, appears a more reasonable third alternative....

5. *Labeling Environmental Contaminants.* For a proposal to require the labeling of environmental contaminants, see Mara A. Guagliardo, *Reexamining Food Labels: A Proposal for Labeling Environmental Information on Food Products* (2001), in Chapter V(B)(1) of the Electronic Book.

6. *Detection of Dioxin.* As the result of improvements in detection methodology and more comprehensive sampling of the food supply, environmental contaminants are often found unexpectedly. For example, although FDA had been monitoring the dioxin content of fish, *see* "Dioxin in Fish," FDA Talk Paper No. T81–32 (Aug. 28, 1981) and "Dioxin—the Impact on Human Health," Hearings before the Subcommittee on Natural Resources, Agricultural Research and Environment of the House Committee on Science and Technology, 98th Cong., 1st Sess. 78, 81 (1983), the agency learned in 1985 that trace amounts were also detectable in paper food packaging and discovered in 1988 that dioxin could migrate from paperboard cartons into milk. *See* "Dioxin Contamination of Food and Water," Hearing before the Subcommittee on Health and the Environment of the House Committee on Energy and Commerce, 100th Cong., 2nd Sess. (1988). FDA's own tests confirmed that the dioxin contamination was "well below 1 part per trillion," and it announced that production changes undertaken by the paper industry would reduce this level so that paper would "contribute essentially no dioxin to the milk and other foods they packaged." HHS News No. P89–38 (Sept. 1, 1989):

> Most contaminant measurements are in parts per million or parts per billion. FDA tests had to be modified to detect the dioxin in the milk, which was found in amounts far below 1 part per trillion. A ppt is 1/1,000,000,-000,000, or one part in a millionth of a million, and the dioxin was less than a tenth of that.

See also "Dioxin Contamination of Milk," Hearing before the Subcommittee on Health and the Environment of the House Committee on Energy and Commerce, 101st Cong., 1st Sess. (1989); "Progress in Eliminating Dioxin from Packaging," FDA Talk Paper No. T90–21 (Apr. 30, 1990). As a result of production changes undertaken by the paper industry, FDA announced that a new survey of milk conducted during 1991–1992 found no samples with a detectable level of dioxin using analytical methods with detection limits in the range of 2–10 ppt. 59 Fed. Reg. 17384 (Apr. 12, 1994). The results of FDA's yearly monitoring for dioxin are available on the FDA website.

7. *Radionuclides.* Following the Chernobyl nuclear accident, FDA issued Compliance Policy Guide No. 7119.14 to establish Levels of Concern for radionuclides in imported food. 51 Fed. Reg. 23155 (June 25, 1986). In 63 Fed. Reg. 43402 (Aug. 13, 1998), FDA announced Recommendations to State and Local Agencies on Derived Intervention Levels for radionuclides in food. The agency later combined these two documents into a revised CPG No. 7119.14. *See* 69 Fed. Reg. 2146 (Jan. 14, 2004); 69 Fed. Reg. 45336 (July 29, 2004).

8. *FDA Monitoring.* Since the early 1960s, FDA has conducted yearly monitoring for environmental contaminants in food by chemical analysis of typical diets. *See* Anthony Celeste, *F.D.A. Total Diet Program*, 46 J. AFDO, No. 3, at 195 (July 1982).

COMMENT: LEAD CONTAMINATION

Like mercury, lead is both ubiquitous in the environment and toxic to humans. Lead occurs in food as a result of natural background, environmental pollution, and food processing and packaging (from soldered cans and foodware articles). FDA has sought to reduce lead residues in food chiefly through two approaches. The first approach focused on soldered cans. The agency attempted to reduce the migration of lead from solder and ultimately to reduce the use of soldered cans themselves. *See, e.g.,* 39 Fed. Reg. 42740 (Dec. 6, 1974), 44 Fed. Reg. 51233 (Aug. 31, 1979), 57 Fed.

29734 (July 6, 1992), 58 Fed. Reg. 17233 (Apr. 1, 1993). It banned lead soldered food cans in 58 Fed. Reg. 33860, 33871 (June 21, 1993), 60 Fed. Reg. 33106 (June 27, 1995), codified at 21 C.F.R. 189.240. *See also* 57 Fed. Reg. 55485 (Nov. 25, 1992), 61 Fed. Reg. 4816 (Feb. 8, 1996), codified at 21 C.F.R. 189.301 (banning lead foil for wine bottles). FDA's second approach focused on foodware articles. The agency prepared a Compliance Policy Guide and established action levels and regulations for migration of lead from food utensils and ceramicware. *E.g.*, 43 Fed. Reg. 58633 (Dec. 15, 1978), 44 Fed. Reg. 47162 (Aug. 10, 1979), 54 Fed. Reg. 23485 (June 1, 1989), 57 Fed. Reg. 29734 (July 6, 1992), 59 Fed. Reg. 1638 (Jan. 12, 1994) codified at 21 C.F.R. 109.16; 60 Fed. Reg. 63721 (Dec. 12, 1995). *See* "Lead in Housewares," Hearings before the Subcommittee on Oversight and Investigations of the House Committee on Energy and Commerce, 100th Cong., 2nd Sess. (1988); "FDA Issues New Guidance on Lead in Ceramicware," FDA Talk Paper No. T91–70 (Nov. 12, 1991); Edward Groth, *Lead in Canned Food*, III Agric. and Human Values 91 (1986); Kirk A. Johnson, *Perspective Paper: Lead in Canned Food*, III Agric. and Human Values 146 (1986); H. Thomas Austern & Harry C. Mussman, *Container-Contributed Lead as Part of Environmental Exposure to Lead*, III Agric. and Human Values 157 (1986). In compliance with the Lead Contamination Control Act of 1988, 102 Stat. 2884, EPA has published lists of drinking water coolers that are not lead free. *See* 54 Fed. Reg. 14320 (Apr. 10, 1989); 55 Fed. Reg. 1773 (Jan. 18, 1990).

The agency announced in 58 Fed. Reg. 38129 (July 15, 1993) that the Food Chemicals Codex had adopted a policy to reduce lead limits to the lowest extent feasible for all food substances that are the subject of FCC monographs. As part of its initiative to reduce lead in the food supply, FDA published an advance notice of proposed rulemaking to obtain information on the lead content in food additives, GRAS ingredients, and color additives. 59 Fed. Reg. 5363 (Feb. 4, 1994). Legislation to reduce lead in consumer products and the environment was considered in 1993 and was favorably reported and passed in the Senate, but was not the subject of serious consideration in the House. *See* "Lead in Ceramicware and Crystal: An Avoidable Risk," Hearing before the Ad Hoc Subcommittee on Consumer and Environmental Affairs of the Senate Committee on Governmental Affairs, 102d Cong., 2d Sess. (1992); S. Rep. No. 103–152, 103d Cong., 1st Sess. (1993); 140 Cong. Rec. 11710–11722 (May 25, 1994).

Following litigation under California Proposition 65, two competing petitions were submitted to FDA regarding the agency's limits on lead content in food and drug products. The Natural Resources Defense Council requested FDA to establish a limit of no more than 0.5 mcg of lead in the recommended daily dose of dietary calcium supplements. FDA Docket No. 97P–0034 (Jan. 27, 1997). The Council for Responsible Nutrition requested that FDA maintain the current system for establishing lead limits for food and drug ingredients and refrain from adopting a 0.5 mcg limit for calcium ingredients used in dietary supplements and calcium-containing antacids. FDA Docket No. 97P–0233 (June 10, 1997). FDA responded to both petitions on September 28, 1999, declining to adopt new lower lead limits for calcium-containing dietary supplement and drug products at that time but supporting the general concept that lead levels of calcium-containing products should be as low as practicable. FDA has taken no further action on this matter. A similar petition was submitted in May 2002 to establish a maximum level of 0.02 ppm of lead in cocoa and chocolate products, which were also the subject of litigation under California Proposition 65. FDA Docket No. 02P–0211 (May 7, 2002). In June 1995, FDA issued a letter warning about lead in candy wrappers, stating that lead levels exceeding 0.5 ppm in a candy product "would constitute a basis for regulatory action." In July 2004, the Consumer Product Safety Commission sent letters warning that lead in candy wrappers violated the Federal Hazardous Substances Act, 15 U.S.C. 1261. FDA released a draft guidance in December 2005 recommending that lead levels in candy likely to be consumed frequently by small children not exceed 0.1 ppm. FDA has determined that children's lunchboxes made from lead-contaminated polyvinyl chloride (PVC) violate the FD&C Act. Letter from Linda Tarantino, Director, FDA CFSAN Office of Food Additive Safety (July 20, 2006). For an intriguing hypothesis that lead poisoning led to the fall of Rome, see S. C. Gilifillan, *Lead Poisoning and the Fall of Rome*, 7 J. Occupational Med., No. 2, at 53 (Feb. 1965).

———

In December 1974, FDA proposed to establish Section 406 action levels through notice-and-comment rulemaking, but its final regulations provided only that action levels could be adopted or changed at any time and announced in the Federal Register, with opportunity for comment, as soon as practicable thereafter. *See* 42 Fed. Reg. 52814 (Sept. 30, 1977). In challenging FDA's decision to allow higher levels of aflatoxin in animal feed, *supra* p. 324, Public Citizen argued that the agency had authority to implement Section 406 only by formal tolerances.

Young v. Community Nutrition Institute

476 U.S. 974 (1986).

■ Justice O'Connor delivered the opinion of the Court.

We granted certiorari in this case to determine whether the Court of Appeals for the District of Columbia Circuit correctly concluded that the Food and Drug Administration's longstanding interpretation of 21 U.S.C. § 346 was in conflict with the plain language of that provision. We hold that, in light of the inherent ambiguity of the statutory provision and the reasonableness of the Food and Drug Administration's interpretation thereof, the Court of Appeals erred. We therefore reverse. . . .

Section 346 states:

"Any poisonous or deleterious substance added to any food, except where such substance is required in the production thereof or cannot be avoided by good manufacturing practice shall be deemed to be unsafe for purposes of the application of clause (2)(A) of section 342(a) of this title; but when such substance is so required or cannot be so avoided, the Secretary shall promulgate regulations limiting the quantity therein or thereon to such extent as he finds necessary for the protection of public health, and any quantity exceeding the limits so fixed shall also be deemed to be unsafe for purposes of the application of clause (2)(A) of section 342(a) of this title. While such a regulation is in effect . . . food shall not, by reason of bearing or containing any added amount of such substance, be considered to be adulterated. . . ."

. . . .

The parties do not dispute that, since the enactment of the Act in 1938, the FDA has interpreted 21 U.S.C. § 346 to give it the discretion to decide whether to promulgate a regulation, which is known in the administrative vernacular as a "tolerance level." Tolerance levels are set through a fairly elaborate process, similar to formal rulemaking, with evidentiary hearings. On some occasions, the FDA has instead set "action levels" through a less formal process. In setting an action level, the FDA essentially assures food producers that it ordinarily will not enforce the general adulteration provisions of the Act against them if the quantity of the harmful added substance in their food is less than the quantity specified by the action level. . . .

The FDA's longstanding interpretation of the statute that it administers is that the phrase "to such extent as he finds necessary for the protection of public health" in § 346 modifies the word "shall." The FDA therefore interprets the statute to state that the FDA shall promulgate regulations to the extent that it believes the regulations necessary to protect the public health. Whether regulations are necessary to protect the public health is, under this interpretation, a determination to be made by the FDA.

Respondents, in contrast, argue that the phrase "to such extent" modifies the phrase "the quantity therein or thereon" in § 346, not the word "shall." Since respondents therefore view the word "shall" as unqualified, they interpret § 346 to require the promulgation of tolerance levels for added, but unavoidable, harmful substances. The FDA under this interpretation of § 346 has discretion in setting the particular tolerance level, but not in deciding whether to set a tolerance level at all.

Our analysis must begin with *Chevron U.S.A. Inc. v. Natural Resources Defense Council, Inc.*, 467 U.S. 837 (1984). . . .

While we agree with the Court of Appeals that Congress in § 346 was speaking directly to the precise question at issue in this case, we cannot agree with the Court of Appeals that Congress unambiguously expressed its intent through its choice of statutory language. The Court of Appeals' reading of the statute may seem to some to be the more natural interpretation, but the phrasing of § 346 admits of either respondents' or petitioner's reading of the statute. As enemies of the dangling participle well know, the English language does not always force a writer to specify which of two possible objects is the one to which a modifying phrase relates. . . .

. . . We find the FDA's interpretation of § 346 to be sufficiently rational to preclude a court from substituting its judgment for that of the FDA.

To read § 346 as does the FDA is hardly to endorse an absurd result. Like any other administrative agency, the FDA has been delegated broad discretion by Congress in any number of areas. To interpret Congress' statutory language to give the FDA discretion to decide whether tolerance levels are necessary to protect the public health is therefore sensible. . . .

Finally, we note that our interpretation of § 346 does not render that provision superfluous, even in light of Congress' decision to authorize the FDA to "promulgate regulations for the efficient enforcement of [the] Act." 21 U.S.C. § 371(a). Section 346 gives the FDA the authority to choose whatever tolerance level is deemed "necessary for the protection of public health," and food containing a quantity of a required or unavoidable substance less than the tolerance level "shall not, by reason of bearing or containing any added amount of such substance, be considered to be adulterated." Section 346 thereby creates a specific exception to § 342(a)'s general definition of adulterated food as that containing a quantity of a substance that renders the food "ordinarily . . . injurious to health." Simply because the FDA is given the choice between employing the standard of § 346 and the standard of § 342(a) does not render § 346 superfluous. . . .

NOTE

The plaintiffs also contended that if FDA were allowed to enforce the Act by means of action levels, they must be established by notice-and-comment rulemaking. The Supreme Court remanded this claim to the Court of Appeals, which ruled that FDA action levels for poisonous or deleterious substances operated as legislative rules that constrained the agency rather than as general statements of policy and therefore that these levels must be promulgated through informal rulemaking. *Community Nutrition Institute v. Young*, 818 F.2d 943 (D.C. Cir. 1987). In response, FDA published a notice declaring that in the future it would regard action levels as prosecutorial guidelines and not binding rules. 53 Fed. Reg. 5043 (Feb. 19, 1988). FDA later amended its regulations to incorporate this policy. 54 Fed. Reg. 16128 (Apr. 21, 1989), 55 Fed. Reg. 20782 (May 21, 1990).

4. PESTICIDE RESIDUES

The 1910 Insecticide Act, 36 Stat. 331, regulated the labeling of insecticides. The core of the current Federal Insecticide, Fungicide, and Rodenticide Act (FIFRA), 7 U.S.C. 136 *et seq.*, was enacted in 61 Stat. 163 (1947) to replace the 1910 Act. FIFRA requires premarket approval ("registration") of all pesticides distributed or sold in the United States. Like the FD&C Act, FIFRA has been amended on several occasions, including three times in the 1970s, again in 1988, and most recently in 1996, and it has become an environmental and health protection statute.

Regulation of pesticide residues in food implicates both FIFRA and the FD&C Act. First, no pesticide may be sold for use on food crops or in food processing unless it has been registered under FIFRA. Second, any pesticide intended for use on a raw agricultural commodity must be the subject of a tolerance established under section 408 of the FD&C Act, which was added by the Miller Pesticides Amendment, 68 Stat. 511 (1954). Third, as a result of the Food Quality Protection Act of 1996, 110 Stat. 1489, 1513 a pesticide approved for use in or on a raw agricultural commodity is exempt from the requirement of a food additive regulation under section 409 of the Act when the raw commodity is used in a processed food. This amendment thus excluded pesticides from the Delaney Clause of the Food Additive Amendments. *See infra* p. 1183. Fourth, where a pesticide is lawfully applied to a "target" commodity but a residue also occurs in another "nontarget" food—*e.g.*, because the wind has transported it, or it has been absorbed from the soil in a later growing season—a section 406 action level must be established to control it.

Administration of FIFRA and the FD&C Act is bifurcated. Prior to 1970, USDA was responsible for implementing FIFRA. Reorganization Plan No. 3 of 1970, 84 Stat. 2086, established the Environmental Protection Agency and transferred primary responsibility for pesticide functions to the new agency. EPA and FDA have reached agreement on their mutual responsibilities., 36 Fed. Reg. 24234 (Dec. 22, 1971), 38 Fed. Reg. 24233 (Sept. 6, 1973), 40 Fed. Reg. 25078 (June 12, 1975). Briefly summarized, EPA registers pesticides under FIFRA, establishes pesticide tolerances under section 408, and recommends action levels for pesticide contaminants to FDA. It is FDA that establishes action levels under section 406 and enforces the limits EPA has established for pesticide residues in food.

United States v. Bodine Produce Co.

206 F. Supp. 201 (D. Ariz. 1962).

■ Boldt, District Judge....

The case arose as a misdemeanor criminal action under the Federal Food, Drug, and Cosmetic Act.... [T]he defendant was charged with having violated that Act by causing adulterated lettuce to be introduced and delivered for introduction into interstate commerce at Glendale, Arizona, consigned to Milwaukee, Wisconsin.

The lettuce was alleged to be adulterated within the meaning of 21 U.S.C. § 342(a)(2)(B) in that it was a raw agricultural commodity and it contained a pesticide chemical, namely DDT, which was unsafe within the meaning of 21 U.S.C. § 346a(a) since the quantity of such pesticide chemical on the lettuce was not within the limits of the tolerance for DDT prescribed by regulations of the Secretary of Health, Education, and Welfare. Pertinent regulations of the Secretary, issued by statutory authority, established a tolerance or permissible limit of 7 parts per million for DDT on lettuce.

Upon the evidence adduced at the trial, the jury obviously concluded that the lettuce shipped by the defendant in this instance contained DDT in excess of 7 parts per million....

 In a judicial proceeding to enforce the regulation, it is only necessary for the Government to prove a violation of the regulation, *not danger to health*. Otherwise this law could not be effectively enforced.

... In the present case, the ... Government does not have the burden of showing that the DDT in this particular shipment of lettuce could be injurious to health. DDT may not be present in lettuce unless it meets a

higher standard, namely, conformity to an administrative tolerance which
has resulted from a broad and all-inclusive evaluation of DDT and other
pesticide chemicals in foods. . . .

United States v. Roggy

76 F.3d 189 (8th Cir. 1996).

■ WOLLMAN, CIRCUIT JUDGE.

After a jury found Y. George Roggy guilty of mail fraud in violation of
18 U.S.C. § 1341, adulteration of a raw agricultural commodity in violation
of 21 U.S.C. §§ 331(k) and 333(a)(2), and using a pesticide in a manner
contrary to its label in violation of 7 U.S.C. § 136(j), the district court
sentenced him to sixty months' imprisonment, three years of supervised
release, and 200 hours of community service. Roggy appeals his conviction
and sentence. We affirm.

[handwritten margin note: Jury found guilty]

Roggy was a licensed pesticide applicator and distributor in Minnesota
and elsewhere. He owned and operated a pesticide application business
named Fumicon, Inc. and a pesticide distribution business named Aggesch,
Inc. Roggy was regarded by his peers as an expert in the field of pesticide
application.

In 1989, General Mills, Inc. hired Roggy to apply pesticide to raw oats
that were to be used in making cereal. General Mills initially purchased the
pesticide Reldan and instructed Roggy to use it on the oats. Reldan was
approved by the Environmental Protection Agency (EPA) for use on raw
oats. In 1993, General Mills asked Roggy to purchase Reldan himself and
bill General Mills for the product and his services accordingly.

Instead of purchasing Reldan, however, Roggy purchased and used
Dursban, a product that was not approved by the EPA for use on raw oats.
Roggy submitted invoices for his services to General Mills over the course
of thirteen months. The invoices stated that Reldan had been applied at an
approximate cost of $173 per gallon, when Roggy had actually used Durs-
ban, which cost approximately $83 per gallon. The difference between the
cost of Dursban and the invoice price for Reldan was approximately
$85,000.

[handwritten margin note: billed for more costly pesticide]

In 1994, the Food and Drug Administration (FDA) detected the presence of chlorpyrifos-ethyl in some of General Mills' oats while taking
random samples from various grain elevators. Chlorpyrifos-ethyl is not
approved for use on raw oats and is found in the pesticide Dursban.
Further testing by the FDA revealed that all of General Mills' grain
processing facilities in the Twin Cities and Duluth, Minnesota, and in
Superior, Wisconsin, had been contaminated. In addition, widespread Dursban contamination was found in oats and oat flour from these facilities, in
finished cereal products, and in a spraying apparatus owned by Roggy and
located at the Superior facility. Approximately 16 million bushels of oats
and 160 million boxes of cereal were tainted by the unapproved pesticide. . . .

The conviction and sentence are affirmed.

NOTES

1. *Unconstitutionally Vague Labeling.* Where the EPA-approved label for a pesticide stated "To avoid spray drift, do not apply under windy conditions," and the defendant engaged in spraying that resulted in drift, the District Court dismissed the criminal prosecution on the grounds that the label standard was unconstitutionally vague. *United States v. Wabash Valley Service Co.*, 426 F. Supp. 2d 835 (S.D. Ill. 2006).

2. *FIFRA–FD&C Act Inconsistency.* Prior to enactment of the Food Quality Protection Act of 1996, the two key statutes, FIFRA and the FD&C Act, could and did produce inconsistent results. *See* NATIONAL ACADEMY OF SCIENCES, REGULATING PESTICIDES IN FOOD: THE DELANEY PARADOX (1987). The primary purpose of the 1996 Act was to establish a single, consistent, science-based safety standard for pesticide residues permitted in food. For a comprehensive review of the 1996 Act, see *infra* p. 1183 and James R. Smart, *All the Stars in the Heavens Were in the Right Places: The Passage of the Food Quality Protection Act of 1996*, 17 STAN. ENVTL. L.J. 273 (1998).

3. *Pesticides in Imported Food.* In 65 Fed. Reg. 35069 (June 1, 2000) EPA published detailed guidance on applying current data requirements for pesticide residue tolerances in imported food. EPA later made available a NAFTA Guidance Document on the same subject. 65 Fed. Reg. 17099 (Apr. 5, 2006).

4. *Nonfood Application of FIFRA.* FIFRA regulates all pesticides and thus potentially applies to all FDA-regulated products. Congress twice addressed this FDA/EPA regulatory overlap, in 110 Stat. 1489, 1502 (1996) and 112 Stat. 3035 (1998), and the two agencies have worked together on this issue. *See* Jonathan M. Lindsay, *Working Out the Bugs in Pesticide Regulation: A Survey of the Joint Efforts of the EPA and FDA* (1999), in Chapter V(K) of the Electronic Book.

Controlling pesticide residues that occur in food as a result of environmental contamination, rather than through purposeful application, has proved difficult. Generally, FDA has relied upon enforcement of section 406 action levels. On two occasions, FDA attempted to formulate a legal position that would permit enforcement of an action level for DDT in fish without the sort of challenge that it later encountered to its action level for mercury in swordfish, *supra* p. 369. In *United States v. Goodman*, 486 F.2d 847 (7th Cir. 1973), the agency successfully argued that, in the absence of a section 408 tolerance, any residue of DDT in raw fish was illegal and that it could lawfully establish an action level of 5 ppm as an exercise of enforcement discretion under section 306 [now 309]. In the related case of *United States v. Ewig Brothers Co.*, 502 F.2d 715 (7th Cir. 1974), the agency charged that a residue of DDT in smoked fish (a processed food) in excess of the 5 ppm action level was an unapproved "food additive" that was automatically illegal because it was not the subject of an approved food additive regulation. Because the Food Quality Protection Act of 1996 excluded pesticides in both raw and processed food from the definition of a food additive, however, FDA is now left with section 406 action levels as its sole enforcement authority for environmental contamination from pesticides.

Community Nutrition Institute, supra p. 381, forced the agency to characterize action levels as enforcement guidelines rather than binding limits. Legislation to provide FDA with increased authority to prevent food contamination twice passed the Senate during the 1970s but never received formal consideration in the House. *See* Peter Barton Hutt, *Food Legislation in Perspective*, 34 FOOD DRUG COSM. L.J. 590, 597 (1979).

———

Prior to the 1980s, when EPA cancelled registrations for pesticides under FIFRA, it generally retained the section 408 tolerances and section 409 food additive regulations as long as residues could occur in food as the result of environmental contamination. With the following notice, however, EPA abandoned this practice.

Tolerances and Exemptions From Tolerances for Pesticide Chemicals in or On Raw Agricultural Commodities

47 Fed. Reg. 42956 (September 29, 1982).

AGENCY: Environmental Protection Agency . . .

This notice sets forth a policy regarding the revocation of formal tolerances for cancelled pesticides and, where necessary, the establishment of action levels for these pesticides. The Food and Drug Administration (FDA), and the Agricultural Marketing Service (AMS) and Food Safety and Inspection Service (FSIS) of the U.S. Department of Agriculture have reviewed and agreed with the policy statement. . . .

Food sometimes contains pesticide chemical residues not because of purposeful, direct application, but rather because the pesticide persists in the environment and subsequently contaminates the food. Thus, the presence of the residue in the food cannot be prevented or removed by good agricultural or manufacturing practice. Consequently, residues of pesticides may be present long after cancellation has occurred. In the absence of a tolerance, FDA, FSIS, and AMS rely on an action level recommended by the EPA in determining whether the pesticide chemical is present at levels which make it unsafe and whether regulatory action should be taken. This level is then applied by the FDA, FSIS, and AMS in their regulatory programs. . . .

When a pesticide's registration for a food or feed use is cancelled because of concern about the safety of the pesticide, the associated tolerance for use or food additive regulation is no longer justified and logically should be revoked. The tolerance revocation should discourage misuse, *i.e.*, the illegal application of a cancelled pesticide, as well as discourage persons in other countries from exporting to the United States food bearing residues of pesticides which can no longer be legally used in the United States because of safety reasons. For pesticides which degrade rapidly in the environment, particularly in the soil, revoking the tolerance should cause no problem because any pesticide residues remaining from applications prior to the cancellation action would not be expected to be present at detectable levels. However, for pesticides which persist in the environment, *i.e.*, which take long periods of time to degrade, crops may contain detectable residues of these pesticides, perhaps even at or near the tolerance levels, for many years after the application of the cancelled pesticide has ceased. Similarly, the meat of animals fed crops containing such residues may also contain such residues. If the formal tolerances for persistent pesticides were revoked and no other action were taken, land to which the cancelled pesticides have been applied could be unavailable for crop use for many years to come. Therefore, in order to avoid unfairly penalizing food producers whose commodities may still contain unavoidable residues of persistent pesticides which can no longer be legally applied, the agencies have agreed to establish action levels to replace formal tolerances that will be revoked. The action levels will be reviewed periodically and lowered as the chemicals dissipate from the environment....

NOTES

1. *EPA Actions on Other Pesticides.* For other examples of EPA actions and recommended action levels for pesticides, *see, e.g.,* 50 Fed. Reg. 10070 and 10077 (Mar. 13, 1985) and 51 Fed. Reg. 46616 and 46658 (Dec. 24, 1986) (DDT); 50 Fed. Reg. 23717 (June 5, 1985) and 51 Fed. Reg. 46665 (Dec. 24, 1986)(chlordane); 50 Fed. Reg. 10080 (Mar. 13, 1985) and 51 Fed. Reg. 46662 (Dec. 24, 1986)(aldrin and dieldrin); 54 Fed. Reg. 6129 (Feb. 8, 1989)(carbon disulfide, carbon tetrachloride, and ethylene dichloride); 54 Fed. Reg. 33690 (Aug. 16, 1989)(heptachlor); 55 Fed. Reg. 20416 (May 16, 1990)(EBDCs).

2. *FDA Action Levels.* FDA's section 406 action levels for pesticide residues in food are contained in Compliance Policy Guide No. 7141.01, which is updated regularly to reflect EPA recommendations. *See, e.g.,* 51 Fed. Reg. 11840 (Apr. 7, 1986)(reaffirming action levels for Kepone); 51 Fed. Reg. 11349 (Apr. 2, 1986)(revocation of action levels for DBCP); 52 Fed. Reg. 18025 (May 13, 1987)(new action levels for aldrin and dieldrin, chlordane, DDT, TDE, and DDE); 51 Fed. Reg. 34503 (Sept. 29, 1986) and 52 Fed. Reg. 2611 (Jan. 23, 1987)(revision of the entire guide); 54 Fed. Reg. 50025 (Dec. 4, 1989)(new action levels for heptachlor). In 55 Fed. Reg. 14359 (Apr. 17, 1990), FDA listed all existing pesticide action levels and announced that they represent only enforcement guidelines. For an example of FDA enforcement action, see *United States v. Barnett*, 587 F.2d 252 (5th Cir. 1979).

3. *Monitoring and Enforcement.* Enforcement of pesticide residue limits on imported and domestic food requires analysis of thousands of products. This resource-intensive effort is subject to ongoing reassessment by FDA and the target of critics who claim the agency is not doing enough. *See, e.g.,* "Cancer-Causing Chemicals—Part 2: Chemical Contamination of Food," Hearings before the Subcommittee on Oversight and Investigations of the House Committee on Interstate and Foreign Commerce, 95th Cong., 2nd Sess. (1978); GAO, BETTER REGULATION OF PESTICIDE EXPORTS AND PESTICIDE RESIDUES IN IMPORTED FOOD IS ESSENTIAL, No. CED–79–43 (June 22, 1979). In 1979, FDA formed an internal study group to recommend improvements in monitoring, analysis, and enforcement. 44 Fed. Reg. 57500 (Oct. 5, 1979). Criticism of the program has continued, however. *See, e.g.,* GAO, PESTICIDES: BETTER SAMPLING AND ENFORCEMENT NEEDED ON IMPORTED FOOD, No. RCED–86–219 (Sept. 26, 1986); GAO, PESTICIDES: NEED TO ENHANCE FDA'S ABILITY TO PROTECT THE PUBLIC FROM ILLEGAL RESIDUES, No. RCED–87–7 (Oct. 27, 1986); "Pesticides in Food," Hearing before the Subcommittee on Oversight and Investigations of the House Committee on Energy and Commerce, 100th Cong., 1st Sess. (1987).

Two incidents during the 1980s focused public attention on pesticide residues in food. In 1983, Florida banned the sale of food containing any residues of ethylene dibromide (EDB), even though, based on their assessments of the risk, EPA and FDA had concluded that the problem did not merit action. When other states joined Florida in restricting or banning EDB residues, *e.g., American Grain Products Processing Institute v. Department of Public Health*, 467 N.E.2d 455 (Mass. 1984), EPA banned its use. 48 Fed. Reg. 46228 (Oct. 11, 1983), 49 Fed. Reg. 4452 (Feb. 6, 1984). Concurrently, FDA established action levels for EDB in food. *See* 49 Fed. Reg. 13195 (Apr. 3, 1984), 49 Fed. Reg. 18624 (May 1, 1984), 50 Fed. Reg. 180 (Jan. 2, 1985). *See also* "Contamination from Ethylene Dibromide (EDB)," Hearing before the Subcommittee on Toxic Substances and Environmental Oversight of the Senate Committee on Environment and Public Works, 98th Cong., 2nd Sess. (1984); "Government Regulation of the Pesticide Ethylene Dibromide (EDB)," Joint Hearings before Certain Subcommittees of the House Committee on Government Operations, 98th Cong., 2nd Sess. (1984). For a critical analysis of the government's failure to reassure the public about the insignificance of the risk posed by EDB residues, see Harold I. Sharlin, *EDB: A Case Study in Communicating Risk*, 6 RISK ANALYSIS 61 (1986).

Later in the decade, the Natural Resources Defense Council (NRDC) targeted daminozide (Alar), a plant growth regulator, as a health hazard. EPA's denial of a petition to ban the pesticide in 1986 was upheld on procedural grounds in *Nader v. EPA*, 859 F.2d 747 (9th Cir. 1988). In response to claims that it was not protecting the public health, EPA reduced the tolerance for daminozide on apples. 51 Fed. Reg. 12889 (Apr. 16, 1986), 52 Fed. Reg. 1909 (Jan. 16, 1987), 54 Fed. Reg. 6392 (Feb. 10, 1989). Still not satisfied, Massachusetts banned daminozide residues in apples. *See Processed Apples Institute, Inc. v. Department of Public Health*, 522 N.E.2d 965 (Mass. 1988).

How a PR Firm Executed the Alar Scare

THE WALL STREET JOURNAL, October 3, 1989, at A22.

After this year's stir over use of the chemical Alar on apples, political publicist David Fenton celebrated the work of his firm in a lengthy memo to interested parties. He wrote of a "sea change in public opinion" that has "taken place because of a carefully planned media campaign, conceived and implemented by Fenton Communications with the Natural Resources Defense Council." Extracts are reprinted below:

"In the past two months, the American public's knowledge of the dangers of pesticides in food has been greatly increased. Overnight, suppliers of organic produce cannot keep up with demand. Traditional supermarkets are opening pesticide-free produce sections. . . .

"Our goal was to create so many repetitions of NRDC's message that average American consumers (not just the policy elite in Washington) could not avoid hearing it—from many different media outlets within a short period of time. The idea was for the 'story' to achieve a life of its own, and

make public aware

continue for weeks and months to affect policy and consumer habits. Of course, this had to be achieved with extremely limited resources....

"In October of 1988 NRDC hired Fenton Communications to undertake the media campaign for its report.... The report marked the first time anyone—inside government or out—had calculated children's actual exposure levels to carcinogenic and neurotoxic pesticides. The study showed one of the worst pesticides to be daminozide, or Alar, used primarily on apples and peanuts....

"[L]ast fall, Meryl Streep contacted NRDC, asking if she could assist with some environmental projects. Ms. Streep read the preliminary results of the study and agreed to serve as a spokesperson for it.... It was agreed that one week after the study's release, Streep and other prominent citizens would announce the formation of NRDC's new project, Mothers and Others for Pesticide Limits. This group would direct citizen action at changing the pesticide laws, and help consumers lobby for pesticide-free produce at their grocery stores. The separation of these two events was important in ensuring that the media would have two stories, not one, about this project. Thereby, more repetition of NRDC's message was guaranteed.

"As the report was being finalized, Fenton Communications began contacting various media. An agreement was made with 60 Minutes to 'break' the story of the report in late February. Interviews were also arranged several months in advance with major women's magazines like Family Circle, Women's Day and Redbook (to appear in mid-March). Appearance dates were set with the Donahue Show, ABC's Home Show, double appearances on NBC's Today show and other programs.

"On February 26th CBS' 60 Minutes broke the story to an audience of 40 million viewers.... The next morning, NRDC held a news conference attended by more than 70 journalists and 12 camera crews. Concurrently, NRDC coordinated local news conferences in 12 cities around the country also releasing the report.... On March 7 Meryl Streep held a Washington news conference to announce the formation of NRDC's Mothers and Others for Pesticide Limits....

"Coverage of Mothers and Others that week included USA Today (cover); The Today Show on NBC; The Phil Donahue Show (10 million viewers); Women's Day (6 million copies sold); Redbook (4 million); Family Circle (6 million); Organic Gardening (1.5 million); New Woman (1.7 million); People Magazine; USA TODAY Television (200 markets); Entertainment Tonight (18 million viewers); ABC's Home Show (3 million viewers); Cable News Network and numerous radio networks, newspaper chains, broadcast chains, wire services and other media around the nation. In addition, we arranged for Meryl Streep and Janet Hathaway of NRDC to grant 16 interviews by satellite with local TV major market anchors....

"In the ensuing weeks, the controversy kept building. Articles appeared in food sections of newspapers around the country. Columnists and cartoonists took up the story. MacNeil/Lehrer, the New York Times and Washington Post did follow-up stories, as did the three network evening programs and morning shows. Celebrities from the cast of L.A. Law and thirtysomething joined NRDC for a Los Angeles news conference.

"Soon school systems began banning apples (which is not what NRDC intended or recommended). Three federal agencies (EPA, USDA and FDA) issued an unusual joint statement assuring the public that apples were safe (although to children who consume a great deal, these assurances are not entirely true). . . .

"And the industry struck back. NRDC's credibility was, as expected, questioned by industry 'front groups' such as the American Council on Science and Health. A major corporate pr firm, Hill and Knowlton, was hired for $700,000 by the apple growers, which also put forward a $2 million advertising budget. Stories began appearing (including a Washington Post cover piece) saying that the levels of Alar in apples were below federal standards, and charging the media with exaggerating the story. . . .

industry retaliates

"Usually, it takes a significant natural disaster to create this much sustained news attention for an environmental problem. We believe this experience proves there are other ways to raise public awareness for the purpose of moving the Congress and policymakers."

NOTES

1. *The Alar Ban.* EPA and FDA found only low levels of daminozide in apples and attempted to reassure the public. *See* "Little Pesticide Residue Found In Foods Children Eat," FDA Talk Paper No. T89–14 (Feb. 27, 1989); "Extremely Low Levels Of Alar Found By Consumers Union," FDA Talk Paper No. T89–19 (Mar. 30, 1989). Nevertheless, reaction to the NRDC campaign caused EPA to ban daminozide. *See* 54 Fed. Reg. 6392 (Feb. 10, 1989), 54 Fed. Reg. 22558 (May 24, 1989), 54 Fed. Reg. 37278 (Sept. 7, 1989), 54 Fed. Reg. 47492 (Nov. 14, 1989), 55 Fed. Reg. 10218 (Mar. 19, 1990). The impact of the daminozide controversy on public confidence in food safety was examined in "Chemicals and Food Crops," Hearing before the Subcommittee on Toxic Substances, Environmental Oversight, Research and Development of the Senate Committee on Environment and Public Works, 101st Cong., 1st Sess. (1989) and "Produce Safety and Nutrition," Hearing before the Subcommittee on Domestic Marketing, Consumer Relations, and Nutrition of the House Committee on Agriculture, 101st Cong., 1st Sess. (1989). Damages were unsuccessfully sought in an action brought by Washington State apple growers against the news media for false statements made about the cancer risk from Alar. *Auvil v. CBS "60 Minutes,"* 67 F.3d 816 (9th Cir. 1995).

2. *Pesticide Reregistration Issues.* The statutory requirements for reregistering old pesticides imposed by the FIFRA Amendments of 1988, 102 Stat. 2654, placed formidable burdens on EPA. *See, e.g.,* the lists of pesticides required to be reregistered in 54 Fed. Reg. 7740 (Feb. 22, 1989), 54 Fed. Reg. 22706 (May 25, 1989), 54 Fed. Reg. 30846 (July 24, 1989). *See also* GAO, Pesticides: EPA's Formidable Task To Assess And Regulate Their Risks, No. RCED–86–125 (Apr. 1986).

3. *Human Testing.* It is common for direct food additives to be tested in human volunteers, and Section 409(i) of the FD&C Act contemplates such testing. When EPA issued a press release reversing a longstanding policy and banning consideration of the results of human testing in evaluating the safety of pesticides, there was a sharp division of opinion on the matter. In *CropLife America v. EPA,*

329 F.3d 876 (D.C. Cir. 2003), the Court of Appeals invalidated the new policy on the ground that it could only be adopted through notice-and-comment rulemaking.

COMMENT: EPA REGULATION OF PESTICIDES FOR FOOD USE

EPA registration of pesticides for food use resembles FDA premarket approval of food additives, color additives, and new drugs. As most recently established by the Food Quality Protection Act of 1996, however, several distinctive features merit attention.

• FIFRA applies to all pesticides distributed or sold in the United States, including those sold in intrastate commerce.

• The standard under section 408(b)(2)(A)(i) for approval of a pesticide residue in food is that the residue must be safe, which is defined as a reasonable certainty of no harm. This standard was borrowed from the Food Additives Amendment.

• EPA must specifically find under section 408(b)(2)(C) that any pesticide tolerance is safe for infants and children.

• Under section 408(b)(2)(B), EPA is authorized to retain an existing tolerance for a pesticide residue posing greater than a negligible risk if the pesticide protects consumers from a greater health risk than that posed by the pesticide or use of the pesticide is necessary to avoid a significant disruption in domestic production of an adequate, wholesome, and economical food supply.

• Risk assessments must be based on actual treatment practices and documented residue levels rather than maximum allowable levels.

• FIFRA contains complex provisions governing the disclosure of registration data submitted by the pioneer manufacturer and its use by subsequent "me too" manufacturers. 7 U.S.C. 136a(c)(1)(D). The "me too" registrant must in some instances compensate the originator for use of the data under 40 C.F.R. Part 152, Subpart E. Disputes relating to data compensation are subject to compulsory arbitration. 29 C.F.R. Part 1440.

• EPA imposes user fee charges for registration activities. 40 C.F.R. Part 152, Subpart U.

• Under 7 U.S.C. 136v, a state may forbid the sale or use of a pesticide registered by EPA but may not impose any labeling or packaging requirements in addition to or different from those established by EPA and may not allow any use on food or animal feed that is not lawful under the FD&C Act. Political subdivisions are barred from any form of pesticide regulation. See *Maryland Pest Control Ass'n v. Montgomery County, Maryland*, 646 F. Supp. 109 (D. Md. 1986), *aff'd without opinion*, 822 F.2d 55 (4th Cir. 1987).

• Under section 408(n), states and local governments are preempted from setting pesticide tolerances more stringent than those set by EPA on the basis of the 1996 safety standard, but there is no preemption of warning or labeling requirements.

• Where EPA suspends and subsequently cancels registration of a pesticide, any person who owned any quantity of the pesticide immediately before the suspension notice is entitled to be indemnified under 7 U.S.C. 136m. *See, e.g.*, 49 Fed. Reg. 49796 (Dec. 21, 1984).

• FDA may impose civil money penalties through administrative proceedings under section 303(g) as an alternative (not in addition) to its other enforcement remedies.

See "The Impact of the Food Quality Protection Act Implementation on Public Health," Hearing before the Subcommittee on Department Operations, Oversight, Nutrition, and Forestry of the House Committee on Agriculture, 106th Cong., 1st Sess. (1999); "The Status of Implementation of the Food Quality Protection Act of 1996," Hearing before the Subcommittee on Environment and Hazardous Materials of the House Committee on Energy and Commerce, 107th Cong., 2d Sess. (2002).

5. INTENTIONAL FUNCTIONAL INGREDIENTS

Before World War II, relatively few functional ingredients were used in food. Even then, however, they were viewed with suspicion and concern. *See, e.g.*, O. FOLIN, PRESERVATIVES AND OTHER CHEMICALS IN FOODS: THEIR USE AND ABUSE (1914); Wallace F. Janssen, *Inside the Poison Squad: How Food Additive Regulation Began*, 51 J. AFDO, No. 2, at 68 (Apr. 1987). The immediate post-war period saw a proliferation of functional food ingredients and a revolution in food technology. In 1950, Representative Frank B. Keefe (R–Wisc.) introduced a resolution to establish a select committee to investigate the use of chemicals in food products. 96 CONG. REC. 8933. Because he was of the minority party and in poor health, Keefe persuaded Representative James Delaney (D–N.Y.) to sponsor the resolution and serve as chairman of the committee. The Report of the Delaney Committee was released in 1952.

Investigation of the Use of Chemicals in Foods and Cosmetics

House of Representatives Report No. 2356, 82d Congress, 2d Session (1952).

At this stage of our civilization, there is a genuine need for the use of many chemicals in connection with our food supply. Many of the chemicals directly added to foods have proved to be of substantial value to the consumer, and constitute a necessary adjunct to modern civilization. Few would quarrel now with the advisability of enriching various staple foods with certain vitamins and minerals, or with the addition of other chemicals which enhance the nutritive value of the products in which they are incorporated.... The progress that has been made in food technology, however, has been attended by a certain degree of hazard, since some quantity of many of the new chemicals utilized in the production and processing of foods is inevitably ingested by the consuming public. It is essential that this risk be kept to a minimum.

... Chemical substances are being introduced into the production, processing, storage, packaging and distribution of food at an ever-increasing rate. There is hardly a food sold in the market place today which has not had some chemicals used on or in it at some state in its production, processing, packaging, transportation, or storage. . . .

The indirect addition of chemicals to our food supply also raises serious problems. For example, cattle are being treated with antibiotic drugs in the control of mastitis, anthrax, and other diseases. There is a question whether the presence of small amounts of antibiotics in milk and milk products has any effect on the consumer; that is, whether the consumer develops a sensitivity or resistance to these chemicals. . . .

The United States Food and Drug Administration, in collaboration with the United States Public Health Service, revealed that approximately 842 chemicals are used, have been used, or have been suggested for use in foods. Of this total, it was estimated that 704 are employed today, and that of these 704 only 428 are definitely known to be safe. Thus, there are approximately 276 chemicals being used in food today, the safety of which has not been established to the satisfaction of many groups concerned with the health and safety of the public.

The Surgeon General of the Public Health Service pointed out that the extent of this problem cannot be fully visualized, because of a lack of adequate information on the chronic effects of chemical substances currently in use. He testified that the toxic effects of many of these chemicals, and of the compounds which they form when introduced into food, are unknown. . . .

a.   THE FOOD ADDITIVES AMENDMENT

Stimulated by the Delaney Committee, Congress enacted the Food Additives Amendment, 72 Stat. 1784 (1958).

Food Additives Amendment of 1958

Senate Report No. 2422, 85th Congress, 2d Session (1958).

. . . [U]nder existing law the Federal Government is unable to prevent the use in foods of a poisonous or deleterious substance until it first proves that the additive is poisonous or deleterious. To establish this proof through experimentation with generations of mice or other animals may require 2 years or even more on the part of the relatively few scientists the Food and Drug Administration is able to assign to a particular problem. Yet, until that proof is forthcoming, an unscrupulous processor of foodstuffs is perfectly free to purvey to millions of our people foodstuffs containing additives which may or may not be capable of producing illness, debility, or death.

. . . This huge loophole is 1 of 2 flaws in existing law which, through this measure, we are attempting to fill. This bill, if enacted, will require the processor who wants to add a new and unproven additive to accept the responsibility now voluntarily borne by all responsible food processors of first proving it to be safe for ingestion by human beings.

The second flaw in existing law which has proved detrimental to consumers, to processors, and to our national economy and which this bill seeks to remove is a provision [section 402(a)] which has inadvertently served to unnecessarily proscribe the use of additives that could enable the housewife to safely keep food longer, the processor to make it more tasteful and appetizing, and the Nation to make use of advances in technology calculated to increase and improve our food supplies. Your committee agrees with the Food and Drug Administration that existing law should be changed to permit the use of such additives as our technological scientists may produce and which may benefit our people and our economy when the proposed usages of such additives are in amounts accepted by the Food and Drug Administration as safe. . . .

The legislation also covers substances which may reasonably be expected to become a component of any food or to affect the characteristics of any food. These substances are generally referred to as "incidental additives." . . .

On the other hand, substances which may accidentally get into a food, as for example, paints or cleaning solutions used in food processing plants, are not covered by the legislation. . . . If accidental additives do get into food, the provisions of the Food, Drug, and Cosmetic Act dealing with poisonous and deleterious substances would be applicable. . . .

The concept of safety used in this legislation involves the question of whether a substance is hazardous to the health of man or animal. Safety requires proof of a reasonable certainty that no harm will result from the proposed use of an additive. It does not—and cannot—require proof beyond any possible doubt that no harm will result under any conceivable circumstances. . . .

In determining the "safety" of an additive scientists must take into consideration the cumulative effect of such additive in the diet of man or animals over their respective life spans together with any chemically or pharmacologically related substances in such diet. Thus, the safety of a given additive involves informed judgments based on educated estimates by scientists and experts of the anticipated ingestion of an additive by man and animals under likely patterns of use. . . .

The Senate Report went on to quote the following statement from the Department of HEW on the Delaney Clause, which precluded the approval of any food additive found to induce cancer in man or in animals.

... We would like ... to call attention to the fact that the Committee on Interstate and Foreign Commerce of the House of Representatives, before bringing the bill to a vote in the House, decided to add to its previously approved bill the [Delaney Clause]. . . . We have no objections to that amendment whatsoever, but we would point out that in our opinion it is the intent and purpose of this bill, even without that amendment, to assure our people that nothing shall be added to the foods they eat which can reasonably be expected to produce any type of illness in humans or animals. . . . In short, we believe, the bill reads and means the same with or without the inclusion of the clause referred to. This is also the view of the Food and Drug Administration.*

NOTES

1. *Transitional Provisions.* The 1958 Amendment contained transitional provisions under which all food additives were required to be subject to a food additive regulation within two and one-half years. Congress later extended this transitional period in the Food Additives Transitional Provisions Amendment of 1961, 75 Stat. 42, and the Food Additives Transitional Provisions Amendment of 1964, 78 Stat. 1002, to December 31, 1965.

2. *Investigational Exemptions.* Section 409(j) requires the Secretary to issue regulations exempting food additives intended solely for investigational use by qualified experts. FDA has never issued such regulations, but has not objected to the investigational use of food additives under conditions similar to those for investigational new drugs. It is now common for new food additives intended to be directly added to food to be tested in humans prior to FDA approval of a food additive petition.

3. *Proposed Amendments.* The substantive requirements of the Food Additives Amendment have remained unchanged since 1958. A bill to amend several food safety provisions, including Section 409, was introduced with the support of the Reagan Administration, 127 Cong. Rec. 13969 (June 25, 1981), but resulted only in general oversight hearings, "Oversight of Food Safety, 1983," Hearings before the Senate Committee on Labor and Human Resources, 98th Cong., 1st Sess. (1983).

COMMENT: CONSIDERATION OF UTILITY

A major issue during congressional consideration of the 1958 Amendment was whether an additive should be approved for use if it did not convey some benefit to consumers. The Administration bill would have required a finding by FDA that a food additive has "functional value" in order to be approved, if the additive was a poisonous or deleterious substance. H.R. 6747, 85th Cong., 1st Sess. (1957). Industry opposed this approach. The House Committee adopted a compromise suggested in Bernard L. Oser, *The Functional Value of Food Additives*, 13 Food Drug Cosm. L.J. (1958), under which FDA must find that the additive accomplishes its intended physical or other technical effect. H.R. Rep. No. 2284, 85th Cong., 2d Sess. 5–6 (1958). Section 409, as enacted, requires a food additive petition to contain "all relevant data bearing on the physical or other technical effect such additive is intended to produce, and the quantity of such additive required to produce such effect." The Committee stated that this functionality requirement referred to "the objective effect" of the additive and "does not involve any judgment on the part of the Secretary of whether such effect results in any added value to the consumer of such food or enhances the marketability from a merchandising point of view." If no quantitative limitation is required to assure that the use of the additive will be safe, FDA may not consider functionality. Testifying in 1972 on a bill to require that food additives be proved effective and necessary, FDA officials favored the current requirement of functionality and objected to additional requirements that would require the agency to make economic or social

---

* [The Delaney Clause is considered separately in Chapter IX.]

decisions. "Nutrition and Human Needs—1972," Hearings before the Senate Select Committee on Nutrition and Human Needs, 92d Cong., 2d Sess., Part 4B (1972).

b. FOOD ADDITIVES

The definition of a "food additive" in section 201(s) of the FD&C Act is the key to understanding the operation of the premarketing licensure system that Congress established. The term broadly includes all substances that may reasonably be expected to become components of food, but then expressly excludes a substantial portion, probably the majority, of such substances. The substances excluded are those that (1) are generally recognized as safe ("GRAS"), (2) are subject to an approval (a "prior sanction") given before 1958 by FDA under the FD&C Act or by USDA under the Federal Meat Inspection Act or the Poultry Products Inspection Act, or (3) fall within specific exceptions for pesticides, color additives, new animal drugs, and dietary ingredients used in dietary supplements. Each of these excluded categories is explored below.

[handwritten margin note: excluded from food additive]

For a substance that is a "food additive" (as defined by the Act as contrasted with the colloquial use of the term), section 409 requires the submission of a petition demonstrating the substance's safety. Only after FDA has approved the petition and promulgated a food additive regulation may the substance be used in food.

United States v. An Article of Food ... FoodScience Labs

678 F.2d 735 (7th Cir. 1982).

■ CUMMINGS, CHIEF JUDGE.

... The defendant food comprises numerous cases containing tablets of Aangamik 15.... According to the government's complaint, the tablets are an adulterated food under 21 U.S.C. § 342(a)(2)(C) of the Federal Food, Drug and Cosmetic Act in that they contain a food additive—N,N–Dimethylglycine hydrochloride ("DMG")—which allegedly is unsafe under 21 U.S.C. § 348(a)....

Even though DMG is quite clearly a "substance" that has become a "component" of Aangamik 15, FoodScience [the claimant] would have us read into the definition of "food additive" an exception for substances that become "principal ingredients" of the food to which they are added. Although DMG is the lesser of two active components of the tablets and accounts for less than 4% of each tablet's weight, FoodScience argues that DMG is a "principal ingredient" because the tablets' consumers are particularly hopeful of "the potential usefulness of DMG as a metabolic enhancer (whether or not it is a nutrient in the strict sense)...." Since many ordinary additives come in relatively small quantities and food manufacturers often attempt to make their presence inconspicuous, an exception from the definition for "principal ingredients" might agree with the notion of "food additive" used in common parlance. But had Congress intended the

[handwritten margin note: FoodSciences reading principle ingredient exception]

Congressional Intent [handwritten margin note]

Food and Drug Administration and the courts to rely on common parlance it would not have so carefully crafted the foregoing definition of the term.

FoodScience argues it is apparent from the statutory definition that Congress intended to limit the definition of "food additive" to substances that become a component of or affect food in some subtle or incidental fashion, such as substances "intended for use in producing, manufacturing, packing, processing etc." ... FoodScience's argument is that because Congress was concerned with small amounts of unsafe substances, Congress could not similarly be concerned with unsafe substances present in relatively larger quantities. But the definition itself shows the absurdity: "[t]he term 'food additive' means any substance the intended use of which results ... in its becoming a component ... of any food...." The term "component" of course includes large quantities of unsafe substances as well as small quantities....

additive → burden on FoodScience
if not → FDA [handwritten margin notes]

The practical effect of holding that DMG is an additive is to place the burden of showing safety upon FoodScience. In order to avoid the label "food additive," FoodScience must now show that DMG is "generally recognized as safe," whereas if DMG were not an "additive," the Food and Drug Administration would have the burden under 21 U.S.C. § 342 of proving by a preponderance of the evidence that DMG is "injurious to health."....

■ CUDAHY, CIRCUIT JUDGE, concurring.

I concur fully in Chief Judge Cummings' conclusion that the government in this case properly condemned defendant's "Aangamik 15" tablets as an adulterated food because they contain an unsafe "food additive"—DMG—for which no exempting regulations have been issued. I write separately only to emphasize that, in my view, characterizing DMG as a "food additive" depends critically on its being added to or sold in combination with other active ingredients. Because FoodScience consistently represented to the public, and maintained throughout the pre-trial stages of this proceeding, that its "Aangamik 15" tablets contained *two* active and beneficial ingredients—DMG and calcium gluconate—I agree that the district court properly found DMG to be a "food additive" within the meaning of 21 U.S.C. § 321(s) (1976). I believe, however, as did the district court, that this would be a far different case if DMG were being marketed as a single food ingredient. In that case, the FDA would not be entitled to rely on the "food additive" presumption to condemn plaintiff's product but would instead be obligated to shoulder its normal burden of proving, by a preponderance of the evidence, that DMG was an "adulterated food" within the meaning of 21 U.S.C. § 342(a)(1) (1976) or that the product was "misbranded" under the standards set forth in 21 U.S.C. § 343 (1976)....

———

A decade later Judge Cudahy was presented with the opportunity to elaborate upon his concurring opinion.

United States v. Two Plastic Drums . . . Black Currant Oil

984 F.2d 814 (7th Cir. 1993).

■ CUDAHY, CIRCUIT JUDGE. The Food and Drug Administration ("FDA") brings this in rem seizure action under the Food, Drug and Cosmetic Act seeking to condemn and destroy two drums of black currant oil as adulterated under 21 U.S.C. § 342(a)(2)(C) for being a food additive not recognized as safe. The district court granted summary judgment against the FDA, and the government appeals. We affirm.

Black currant oil ("BCO") is extracted from the seeds of the black currant berry and is marketed as a dietary supplement for its unique fatty-acid structures. The FDA argues that BCO is a food additive not generally recognized as safe ("GRAS") and seeks to seize and condemn two drums of BCO pursuant to sections 334 and 342 of the Act. A food is adulterated and subject to seizure under section 334 "if it is, or it bears or contains, any food additive which [the Secretary has not recognized as safe pursuant to section 348]." The determination of whether a substance is a food additive is critical in establishing the safety of the substance because, if the substance is deemed a food additive, it is presumed to be unsafe, and the processor has the burden of showing that the substance in GRAS. On the other hand, if a substance is not a food additive, but food in the generic sense, then the substance is presumed safe and the FDA has the burden of showing that the substance is injurious to health. . . .

The FDA contends that BCO is a food additive because it is a "component" of food when it is combined with the gelatin and glycerin used to market the BCO in capsules. The gelatin and glycerin encase the BCO to prevent it from becoming rancid. The FDA concedes that if the BCO alone was marketed in bottles for teaspoon consumption, it would not be a food additive, and the FDA would bear the burden of proving that BCO is injurious to health. But the combination of BCO with glycerin and gelatin, the FDA maintains, creates a food consisting of three components, and thus, three food additives. . . .

Although we are mindful of the deference due the FDA in construing the statute it administers, deference here is unwarranted since its interpretation is contrary to the language and intent of the Act. As an initial matter, we question whether BCO can even be considered a "component" under the Act. The term "component," commonly understood and defined as . . . "a constituent part" or "ingredient," loses its meaning when applied to foods used in conjunction with inactive ingredients, as this case amply evidences. There, the dietary supplement (the food) is nothing but BCO combined with glycerin and gelatin—two inactive substances used for marketing the BCO in capsule form. The gelatin and glycerin do not interact with or change the character of the BCO, but merely act as a container comparable to a bottle containing liquids marketed for teaspoon consumption. The BCO in question is the dietary supplement and the dietary supplement is the BCO. Therefore, to hold that BCO is a component of the dietary supplement would be to find that BCO is a component of itself. Such an interpretation would defy logic and common sense.

But even assuming that a single active "ingredient" of food can be considered a component of the food, the statutory language does not indicate that every component of food is necessarily a food additive. The Act defines "food additive" as a substance "becoming a component *or otherwise affecting the characteristics of any food*." The FDA interpretation of this provision implies that the language "or otherwise" is used disjunctively in such a way that a substance is a food additive if it (1) is a component of any food, or (2) affects the characteristics of a food. We think that this interpretation, however, distorts the plain meaning of the provision. The phrase "or otherwise," as employed here, is not used to express two alternative definitions of a food additive. Rather, it is used in a way to clarify or elaborate, such that "otherwise" is correctly read as "similarly." ... Therefore, simply becoming a "component" of food does not, in and of itself, satisfy the definition of a food additive. To be a food additive, a substance must not only be added to food, but it must also have the purpose or effect of altering a food's characteristics.

When two or more active ingredients comprise a food, each component is arguably different from the food in such a way that the addition of each has affected the characteristics of the other components and of the food. . . . But when there is only one active component, as is the case here, that single component does not affect the characteristics of the food in question—rather, it constitutes the food. Thus, even if we were to find that BCO was a component of the BCO dietary supplement capsules, the language of the Act indicates that it is not a food additive because, as the single active ingredient, it does not affect the characteristics of any food. . . .

NOTES

1. *Second Case.* Shortly thereafter the First Circuit reached the same decision in another black current oil case. *United States v. 29 Cartons of . . . An Article of Food*, 987 F.2d 33 (1st Cir. 1993).

2. *Dietary Supplements.* In *United States v. 42/30 Tablet Bottles . . . "Nature's Plus Coenzyme Q10 Complex"*, 779 F. Supp. 253 (E.D.N.Y. 1991), the District Court held both substances in a combination of Coenzyme Q10 and Germanium are unapproved food additives. The parties stipulated that the GRAS status of the ingredients would not be litigated in this action. In *Dietary Supplement Coalition, Inc. v. Sullivan*, 978 F.2d 560 (9th Cir. 1992), the Court of Appeals held that a declaratory judgment action to declare that Coenzyme Q10 is a food or a GRAS food ingredient was premature even though FDA had seized products containing this ingredient on the ground that it was an illegal food additive. 978 F.2d 560 (9th Cir. 1992). These issues were made moot by enactment of the Dietary Supplement Health and Education Act of 1994, which exempted all dietary ingredients from the food additive provisions of the FD&C Act.

3. *Commentary. See* Stephen David Foley, *A Brief Survey of the Legislative History Concerning the Definition of Food Additives* (1997), in Chapter V(A) of the Electronic Book.

FDA may not approve a food additive unless it has been shown to be safe under the conditions of its intended use. Section 409(c)(3)(A), as elaborated by the legislative history of the Food Additives Amendment, *supra* p. 394, requires a demonstration that, with "reasonable certainty," the additive will not harm the health of consumers. *See generally* Daryl M. Freedman, *Reasonable Certainty of No Harm: Reviving the Safety Standard for Food Additives, Color Additives, and Animal Drugs*, 7 ECOLOGY L.Q. 245 (1978). FDA is empowered by Section 409(c)(1)(A) to prescribe conditions necessary to assure that an additive's use will be safe. Such conditions typically include limitations on the levels of use and can also include restrictions on the foods to which it is added or on the purposes for which it may be used. Occasionally, FDA may also prescribe the form in which an additive may be marketed, *e.g.*, solely as a tabletop sweetener. 42 Fed. Reg. 19996 (Apr. 15, 1977) (saccharin); 39 Fed. Reg. 27317 (July 26, 1974) (aspartame). And the act explicitly permits the agency to prescribe labeling for the additive, apparently to provide information to commercial users. In addition, FDA has occasionally prescribed special labeling requirements for the finished foods in which an additive is used. *E.g.*, 21 C.F.R. 172.110(c) (BHA); 21 C.F.R. 172.175(b) (sodium nitrite); 21 C.F.R. 172.375(b) (potassium iodide).

COMMENT: RAW AGRICULTURAL COMMODITIES

The 1958 Amendment focused on man-made chemicals added to food to perform specific technological functions. There is little evidence suggesting how Congress expected the Amendment to apply to agricultural commodities. Presumably, an apple, sold as such, is not within the reach of the Amendment because it is itself a distinct food, and does not become a "component" of any other food when it is sold in its unprocessed form. When an apple is incorporated in applesauce or in an apple pie, however, it presumably becomes subject to the same analysis under the 1958 Amendment as any other "added" food constituent.

FDA has not published a definitive regulation on this issue, and there is no pertinent case law. However, during the hearings on the 1958 Amendment, "Food Additives," Hearings before a Subcommittee of the House Committee on Interstate and Foreign Commerce, 85th Cong., 2d Sess. 461–462 (1958), FDA submitted a partial list of GRAS substances, which included such common food items as butter, coffee, lemon juice, olive oil, salt, and sugar. In "Nutrition and Human Needs—1972," Hearings before the Senate Select Committee on Nutrition and Human Needs, 92d Cong., 2d Sess., Part 4B (1972), FDA officials stated that when raw agricultural commodities are used in processed food they become subject to the food additive provisions of the law and thus must be GRAS, prior sanctioned, or the subject of a food additive regulation.

The issue has arisen most directly in FDA's attempts to regulate sassafras tea. In the 1950s, agency scientists determined that safrole, which was widely used as a flavor ingredient in root beer and other soft drinks, is an animal carcinogen. The agency therefore prohibited its addition to food. 25 Fed. Reg. 12412 (Dec. 3, 1960). Sassafras tea is made by stripping the bark from the roots of sassafras trees and steeping the bark in hot water for several minutes. One of the principal constituents of sassafras bark is safrole. Following ineluctable logic from its 1960 rule, FDA concluded that sassafras bark should no longer be permitted to be marketed for use in making sassafras tea. It thus banned the product. *See* 38 Fed. Reg. 20040 (July 26, 1973), 39 Fed. Reg. 26748 (July 23, 1974), 39 Fed. Reg. 34172 (Sept. 23, 1974), 41 Fed. Reg. 19207 (May 11, 1976), codified at 21 C.F.R. 189.180.

In *United States v. Articles of Food ... Select Natural Herb Tea, Sassafras, etc.* (C.D. Cal.), 12 FDA Consumer, No. 9, at 32 (Nov. 1978), FDA contended that the product was a food that was, or contained, an unsafe food additive within the meaning of sections 201(s) and 409(a) of the Act. But the agency's claim raised a problem. Safrole in sassafras bark is a natural constituent of a vegetable substance. Many natural foodstuffs contain substances that, if extracted and added to other food, would be both unhealthful and illegal. Spinach, for example, contains oxalic acid. If oxalic acid were extracted from spinach and added to another food, it would be a "food additive," rendering the food to which it was added adulterated. Yet oxalic acid in spinach is not regulated as a food additive. Nor had the agency previously suggested that the addition of spinach to other foods raised food additive issues with respect to the oxalic acid that is necessarily added as part of the spinach.

FDA nonetheless insisted that safrole in sassafras tea was a food additive. While not a food additive as long as it remains in the bark, the agency conceded, safrole becomes a food additive when it emerges into the water. Even if confined to safrole, this view poses problems. Safrole is a natural constituent of a number of food substances, including nutmeg. When nutmeg is added to eggnog, the safrole must emerge from the nutmeg to flavor the eggnog. If safrole were regarded as a food additive in eggnog, presumably cholesterol would be considered a food additive in every food containing milk.

To avoid this result, FDA took the position that sassafras bark is not a food in its own right, but serves essentially as a vehicle to convey safrole into water. Nutmeg, although not a food that can be eaten alone, does have food value independent of its safrole content. Likewise spinach and milk are independent foods that can be consumed as such. The components of those foods have no separate legal status in the regulatory scheme for food additives.

Although FDA vigorously pressed these distinctions in the *Select Tea* case, the court declined to rule on the agency's summary judgment motion. In 1977, the judge ordered the case tried. The claimant, over the government's objections, thereupon successfully moved to withdraw its claim. On June 12, 1978, the judge defaulted the tea. Thus, the sassafras tea regulation remains unchallenged, perhaps because FDA has not enforced it since.

NOTES

1. *Food Additive Regulations.* The FDA food additive regulations are found in 21 C.F.R. Parts 170 *et seq.*

2. *Cyclamate.* After FDA removed the noncaloric sweetener cyclamate from the GRAS list in 34 Fed. Reg. 17063 (Oct. 21, 1969) because of evidence of carcinogenicity in animals, the manufacturer continued to test it and eventually petitioned for approval of its use under section 409. *See* 34 Fed. Reg. 17063 (Oct. 21, 1969). The agency denied the petition, 41 Fed. Reg. 43754 (Oct. 4, 1976), but granted the manufacturer's demand for a hearing, 42 Fed. Reg. 12515 (Mar. 4, 1977). The Administrative Law Judge ruled that the petition was properly denied, Food Drug Cosm. L. Rep. (CCH) ¶ 38,199 (1978), but the Commissioner remanded the matter for further evidence, 44 Fed. Reg. 47620 (Aug. 14, 1979).

Frustrated by the lack of progress, the manufacturer successfully sought discovery to determine whether nonstatutory factors were being considered by the agency. *Abbott Laboratories v. Harris*, 481 F. Supp. 74 (N.D. Ill., 1979). The Administrative Law Judge reopened the administrative hearing, took additional evidence, and issued a revised initial decision again upholding the denial of the food additive petition. Food Drug Cosm. L. Rep. (CCH) ¶ 38,026 (1980). The District Court refused to enjoin the further administrative proceedings because the materials obtained through discovery did not establish that the agency's deliberations had been dominated by political rather than scientific considerations or that it had been acting in bad faith. *Abbott Laboratories v. Harris*, Food Drug Cosm. L. Rep. (CCH) ¶ 38,046 (N.D. Ill. 1980). The District Court hinted, however, that it would be prepared to compel a prompt disposition of the matter, and the Commissioner issued a final decision denying the food additive petition in 45 Fed. Reg. 61474 (Sept. 16, 1980).

Rather than appeal this ruling, the manufacturer undertook yet additional studies and analysis and submitted a new food additive petition. 47 Fed. Reg. 51227 (Nov. 12, 1982). In 1984, FDA announced that the National Academy of Sciences would hold hearings and issue a report on the matter. 49 Fed. Reg. 24953 (June 18, 1984). In "Cyclamate Update," FDA Talk Paper No. T89–35 (May 16, 1989), FDA acknowledged that both its own Cancer Assessment Committee and the NAS had concluded that cyclamate is not a carcinogen, but it also reported that the NAS was unable to determine whether it may be a tumor promoter or a co-carcinogen. FDA has taken no further action on this matter. As of January 1, 1996, under European Union Directive 94/35/EC (June 30, 1994), cyclamates became lawful throughout Europe.

3. *Saccharin.* After FDA proposed to ban saccharin, 42 Fed. Reg. 19996 (Apr. 15, 1977), Congress enacted legislation in November 1977 to suspend any further action. For a history of subsequent events, including the eventual repeal of the November 1977 legislation, *see supra* p. 141, Note 3, & *infra* p. 1160. This statutory moratorium represents the only time Congress has enacted legislation to prevent FDA from banning a food additive. For accounts of the saccharin controversy, see "Food Safety: Where Are We?", Senate Committee on Agriculture, Nutrition and Forestry Committee Print, 96th Cong., 1st Sess. (1979); Richard A. Merrill & Michael R. Taylor, *Saccharin: A Case Study of Government Regulation of Environmental Carcinogens*, III AGRIC. & HUMAN VALUES 33 (1986); William B. Schultz, *The Bitter Aftertaste of Saccharin*, III AGRIC. & HUMAN VALUES 83 (1986); Elizabeth M. Whelan & William R. Havender, *Saccharin and the Public Interest*, III AGRIC. & HUMAN VALUES 74 (1986); *see also* Sharon R. Flanagam, *Taking the Bitter with the Sweet: A History of Saccharin* (1996), in Chapter V(I)(1) of the Electronic Book.

4. *Aspartame.* The food additive petition for aspartame as a sugar substitute for table use and for use in certain dry food applications was filed in 1973. 38 Fed. Reg. 5921 (Mar. 5, 1973). FDA approved the petition and published a food additive regulation in 39 Fed. Reg. 27317 (July 26, 1974). Though FDA initially declined to stay its approval in response to demands for an evidentiary hearing, the agency

later reversed itself because of suspicions about the reliability of the studies submitted by the manufacturer. 40 Fed. Reg. 56907 (Dec. 5, 1975). After an independent audit validated the study results, FDA announced a hearing before a public board of inquiry. 44 Fed. Reg. 31716 (June 1, 1979), 45 Fed. Reg. 2908 (Jan. 15, 1980). The board's decision recommended that aspartame not be approved because of unresolved questions regarding its capacity to cause brain tumors in rodents. *See* Food Drug Cosm. L. Rep. (CCH) ¶ 38,072 (1980). The Commissioner, however, reversed the public board of inquiry and approved the additive. 46 Fed. Reg. 38284 (July 24, 1981), 46 Fed. Reg. 50947 (Oct. 16, 1981).

In the years since, FDA has approved additional uses of aspartame in food, which are codified in 21 C.F.R. 172.804. After approving the sweetener for use in soft drinks, 48 Fed. Reg. 31376 (July 8, 1983), the agency denied requests for an administrative hearing. 49 Fed. Reg. 6672 (Feb. 22, 1984). Its decision was upheld in *Community Nutrition Institute v. Young*, 773 F.2d 1356 (D.C. Cir. 1985). CNI continued to object to aspartame's approval and FDA continued to overrule those objections and to deny a public hearing. *E.g.*, 53 Fed. Reg. 6595 (Mar. 2, 1988). For discussion of the controversy, see GAO, REGULATION OF THE FOOD ADDITIVE ASPARTAME, Rep. No. MWD–76–111 (Apr. 8, 1976); FOOD AND DRUG ADMINISTRATION: SIX FORMER HHS EMPLOYEES' INVOLVEMENT IN ASPARTAME'S APPROVAL, Rep. No. HRD–86–109BR (July 22, 1986); FOOD AND DRUG ADMINISTRATION: FOOD ADDITIVE APPROVAL PROCESS FOLLOWED FOR ASPARTAME, Rep. No. HRD 87–46 (June 18, 1987); " 'Nutra-Sweet'—Health and Safety Concerns," Hearing before the Senate Committee on Labor and Human Resources, 100th Cong., 1st Sess. (1987); Vikas Arora, *FDA Policymaking in Light of Scientific Uncertainty: The Bittersweet Approval of Aspartame* (1997), Laura P. Stout, *Let Them Eat Cake?: A Historical Analysis of FDA's Decision to Approve Aspartame* (1997), Ashley G. Nill, *The History of Aspartame* (2000), in Chapter V(I)(1) of the Electronic Book. Following the publication of a medical journal article raising the question whether aspartame is associated with brain tumors, FDA issued a Talk Paper stating that the National Cancer Institute public data base "does not support an association between the use of aspartame and increased incidence of brain tumors." FDA Talk Paper No. T96–75 (Nov. 18, 1996). A complete review of the safety of aspartame was published in 35 REG. TOXICOLOGY AND PHARMACOLOGY, No. 2, Part 2 (Apr. 2002).

5. *Sucralose.* In 1998, FDA approved sucralose, a sweetening ingredient, after extensive testing. *See* 63 Fed. Reg. 16417 (Apr. 3, 1998), codified at 21 C.F.R. 172.831. On April 3, 2006, Citizens for Health submitted a citizen petition, FDA Docket No. 2006P–0158, requesting FDA to revoke this approval or to investigate its safety further.

6. *Other Controversial Additives.* See Steven J. Benerofe, *The Approval of Olestra as a Food Additive: Delays in the Process* (1996), Marc A. Cavan, *MSG: The Controversy* (1997), Monica Singh, *Fact or Fiction?: The MSG Controversy* (2005) in Chapter V(I)(1) of the Electronic Book.

7. *Fluoride.* The safety of fluoride added to water has long been controversial. EPA sets the standards for fluoride in drinking water under the Safe Drinking Water Act, 42 U.S.C. 300f et seq. *See also* 40 Fed. Reg. 59566 (Dec. 24, 1975), 50 Fed. Reg. 20164 (May 14, 1985), 50 Fed. Reg. 47142, 47156 (Nov. 14, 1985), 51 Fed. Reg. 11396 (Apr. 2, 1986). Under 21 C.F.R. 170.45, FDA prohibits all fluorine-containing compounds from food except as permitted by EPA for drinking water and by FDA for bottled water. *See generally* Mary Tieman, *Fluoride in Drinking Water: A Review of Fluoridation and Regulation Issues*, CRS Rep. No. RL 33280 (June 23, 2006).

8. *Radiation.* The definition of a food additive in section 201(s) specifically includes "any source of radiation" in food processing. After years of research, FDA

promulgated several food additive regulations approving food irradiation in 21 C.F.R. Part 179. A major point of debate was the need for special labeling to identify irradiated food. FDA determined that food containing an irradiated ingredient would not require special labeling, but that food which itself had been irradiated would require both the international "Radura" logo and, in addition, for two years, a statement that the product has been "treated with radiation" or "treated by irradiation." The obligation to include this statement was subsequently extended to April 1990. 53 Fed. Reg. 4856 (Feb. 18, 1988), 53 Fed. Reg. 12756 (Apr. 18, 1988). In 1990, FDA made the radiation statement a permanent requirement, at least until it can be shown that the logo alone is sufficient to convey to consumers that the product has been irradiated. 55 Fed. Reg. 646 (Jan. 8, 1990), 55 Fed. Reg. 14413 (Apr. 18, 1990).

Members of Congress have taken opposing positions on the practice of irradiation. Compare "The Status of the Technical Infrastructure to Support Domestic Food Irradiation," Hearing before the Subcommittee on Energy Research and Production of the House Committee on Science and Technology, 98th Cong., 2d Sess. (1984), "Federal Food Irradiation Development and Control Act of 1985," and Hearing before the Subcommittee on Department Operations, Research, and Foreign Agriculture of the House Committee on Agriculture, 99th Cong., 1st Sess. (1985), with "Food Irradiation," Hearing before the Subcommittee on Health and the Environment of the House Committee on Energy and Commerce, 100th Cong., 1st Sess. (1987). Under section 403C of the FD&C Act, as added by the Food and Drug Administration Modernization Act of 1997, Congress determined that the FDA-required radiation disclosure statement could not be required to be more prominent than the statement of ingredients. FDA amended its labeling requirement to comply with this requirement. 63 Fed. Reg. 43875 (Aug. 17, 1998). The conference report relating to this provision also directed FDA to obtain public comment on whether the radiation disclosure regulations should be revised or should expire at a specified date in the future. H.R. Rep. 105–39, 105th Cong., 1st Sess. 98–99 (1997). FDA therefore published an advance notice of proposed rulemaking. 64 Fed. Reg. 7834 (Feb. 17, 1999). In 66 Fed. Reg. 17183 (Mar. 29, 2001), FDA reopened the labeling issue by submitting to OMB under the Paperwork Reduction Act of 1995 a proposed focus group study of radiation disclosure statement options for foods treated with ionizing radiation.

The fact that radiation is specifically included within the definition of a food additive does not mean that it could not be found to be GRAS and thus excluded from the requirement for a food additive regulation. The GRAS exclusion from the requirement of a food additive regulation applies to all substances that fall within the broad food additive definition in section 201(s).

See generally Stanford M. Lin, *A Continuing Controversy: Labeling Requirements on Irradiated Foods* (1994), Steven J. Benerofe, *the Legislative History of Food Irradiation in the Food Additives Amendment of 1958* (1996), Matthew E. Freedman, *Irradiation: Too Many Risks, Too Few Benefits* (1998), Paul W. Browning, *Food Irradiation Labeling* (1991), Jonathan E. Prejean, *Food Irradiation: Why Aren't We Using It?* (2001), in Chapter V(N) of the Electronic Book.

9. *Testing Guidelines.* Although FDA established general principles governing toxicity testing for food ingredients as early as the 1940s, *see* Arnold J. Lehman et al., *Procedures for the Appraisal of the Toxicity of Chemicals in Foods*, 4 FOOD DRUG COSM. L.Q. 412 (1949), for many years it resisted issuing specific toxicology guidelines. At the completion of its review of the GRAS list, however, the agency developed a set of toxicological standards for safety evaluation of food additives and color additives, which it subsequently made publicly available in 47 Fed. Reg. 46141 (Oct. 15, 1982) as the "Red Book." FDA periodically revises the Red Book. Although

the agency formerly announced the availability of revisions in the Federal Register, *e.g.*, 58 Fed. Reg. 16536 (Mar. 29, 1993), the updated Red Book 2000 is now issued as a guidance. *E.g.*, 68 Fed. Reg. 16523, 16538 (Apr. 4, 2003); 70 Fed. Reg. 824, 896 (Jan. 5, 2005). For a bibliography of seminal works on human health risk assessment for chemicals, see Margaret H. Whittaker, *Human Health Risk Assessment: Required Reading*, 10 HUMAN AND ECOLOGICAL RISK ASSESSMENT 753 (2004).

10. *Accidental Additives. Compare Gerber Products Co. v. Fisher Tank Co.,* 833 F.2d 505 (4th Cir. 1987)(holding that a liner on the interior of a hot water storage tank used in processing baby foods was an indirect and unapproved food additive, thereby rendering all processed products adulterated), with *Burke Pest Control, Inc. v. Joseph Schlitz Brewing Co.,* 438 So. 2d 95 (Fla.App. 1983)(holding that a pesticide introduced into food during fumigation of the food plant was not a food additive but an accidental additive, whose legal status must be determined under section 402(a)(1) rather than under section 409).

11. *Specifications for Food Additives.* Many food additive regulations contain chemical specifications. FDA has supported the National Academy of Sciences' development of the FOOD CHEMICALS CODEX, a compilation of monographs establishing food grade specifications for food substances. FDA occasionally publishes notices providing an opportunity for public comment on changes to Codex monographs. *E.g.*, 50 Fed. Reg. 49131 (Nov. 29, 1985); 60 Fed. Reg. 28413 (May 31, 1995); 65 Fed. Reg. 48521 (Aug. 8, 2000). The agency also adopts specific specifications for particular substances. *E.g.*, 53 Fed. Reg. 13134 (Apr. 21, 1988), 53 Fed. Reg. 51272 (Dec. 21, 1988) (aspartame); 60 Fed. Reg. 48890 (Sept. 21, 1995) (maltodextrin derived from potato starch).

12. *Diethylene Glycol.* In July 1985, FDA and BATF discovered that some imported wine contained a highly toxic industrial chemical, diethylene glycol. This was the very chemical that, 48 years earlier, had been used as a solvent in the elixir sulfanilamide product that killed more than 100 people and galvanized Congress to enact the new drug provisions as part of the 1938 Act. *See infra* p. ___. The substance had been deliberately added to sweeten the wine and thus was an illegal food additive. The actions taken by the two agencies to protect against further importation of wine containing diethylene glycol or other contaminants were discussed in "Federal Efforts to Identify and Remove Contaminated Imported Wines," Hearing before a Subcommittee of the House Committee on Government Operations, 99th Cong., 2nd Sess. (1986).

13. *Cyclic Review.* In the late 1970s, FDA announced its intention to undertake a "cyclic review" of all food additives, to assure that past food safety decisions remained currently justifiable. "Food Additives: Competitive, Regulatory, and Safety Problems," Hearings before the Senate Select Committee on Small Business, 95th Cong., 1st Sess. (1977). Although originally intended to be a public process governed by formal procedures, *see* Alan M. Rulis & Richard J. Ronk, *Cyclic Review—Looking Backward or Looking Forward?*, 36 FOOD DRUG COSM. L.J. 156 (1981), to the extent that any review has been conducted it has been done internally on an ad hoc basis without published priorities, procedures, timetables, or criteria other than perhaps the toxicological standards made available in the Red Book.

14. *Patent Term Extension.* Under the Patent Term Restoration and Drug Price Competition Act of 1984, *infra* p. 754, food additives are eligible for patent term extension. *See, e.g.*, 54 Fed. Reg. 38289 (Sept. 15, 1989)(extension of the patent life of anionic polyurethane); 69 Fed. Reg. 40946 (July 7, 2004) (neotame).

COMMENT: INTERIM FOOD ADDITIVES

In 35 Fed. Reg. 12062 (July 28, 1970), FDA permitted the continued use of a food additive, brominated vegetable oil (BVO), in fruit-flavored beverages on what was characterized as an interim basis pending additional testing to resolve issues about its safety. This order was upheld in *Jacobson v. Edwards*, Food Drug Cosm. L. Rep. (CCH) ¶ 40,817 (D.D.C. 1971):

> The standard here is not a standard of safety in the sense of absolute, unqualified safety. It is in all of these matters conditional because, obviously, the kind of use, the nature of the use, the amount of the use cannot be dissociated from the absolute question as to whether or not a particular additive may be harmful to animals or harmful to human beings, inasmuch as almost anything is harmful to animals or human beings if used in sufficient quantity and in sufficient concentration.

> I think a fair reading of the Statute as a whole justifies the action that has been taken here in issuing an interim order, inasmuch as the findings contained in the letter of January 5, 1971 make it clear that the Commissioner has determined that the evidence available demonstrates with reasonable certainty that no harm will result from the interim use of BVO, and that the public health is being protected as long as the conditions set forth in that letter are complied with. . . .

The District Court also concluded that the case had been improperly filed in the district court. The D.C. Circuit affirmed the District Court in an unpublished order on December 15, 1972. Subsequently, FDA promulgated criteria and procedures for issuing interim food additive regulations. 37 Fed. Reg. 6207 (Mar. 25, 1972), 37 Fed. Reg. 25705 (Dec. 2, 1972), codified at 21 C.F.R. Part 180. Section 180.1 of these regulations sets forth the following criteria for an interim food additive regulation.

§ 180.1   General.

(a) Substances having a history of use in food for human consumption or in food contact surfaces may at any time have their safety or functionality brought into question by new information that in itself is not conclusive. An interim food additive regulation for the use of any such substance may be promulgated in this subpart when new information raises a substantial question about the safety or functionality of the substance but there is a reasonable certainty that the substance is not harmful and that no harm to the public health will result from the continued use of the substance for a limited period of time while the question raised is being resolved by further study.

(b) No interim food additive regulation may be promulgated if the new information is conclusive with respect to the question raised or if there is a reasonable likelihood that the substance is harmful or that continued use of the substance will result in harm to the public health.

The interim food additive order for brominated vegetable oil was extended in 39 Fed. Reg. 14611 (Apr. 25, 1974) and 39 Fed. Reg. 36113 (Oct. 8, 1974), and it remains in effect, codified at 21 C.F.R. 180.30, more than thirty years after it was promulgated.

c.   GENERALLY RECOGNIZED AS SAFE (GRAS) SUBSTANCES

The FD&C Act does not prescribe procedures for determining whether a food substance is GRAS and does not require approval or even knowledge by FDA of the GRAS status of a food substance. The statutory definition of a food additive in section 201(s) is self-executing. Just prior to enactment of the Food Additives Amendment, FDA submitted to Congress a partial list of "chemical food additives" that it would regard as GRAS, including such common food substances as brandy, butter, citric acid, cloves, coffee, cream, gelatin, lard, margarine, molasses, mustard, paprika, pepper, salt, sugar, vinegar, and wine. Shortly after the passage of the Food Additives Amendment, FDA issued, and from time to time has amended, a nonexclusive list of ingredients that the agency was prepared to acknowledge were GRAS— and therefore could lawfully be used without affirmative approval. *E.g.*, 23 Fed. Reg. 9511 (Dec. 9, 1958); 24 Fed. Reg. 9368 (Nov. 20, 1959); 25 Fed. Reg. 880 (Feb. 2, 1960); 25 Fed. Reg. 7332 (Aug. 4, 1960); and 26 Fed. Reg. 938 (Jan. 31, 1961). FDA has stated that these GRAS lists, now codified at 21 C.F.R. Parts 182 and 184, "do not include all substances that are generally recognized as safe for their intended use in food" and that "it is impracticable to list all such substances that are GRAS." 21 C.F.R. 170.30(d). Accordingly, FDA has acknowledged that a food manufacturer may determine for itself whether an ingredient that it desires to use can be considered GRAS. *See* 50 Fed. Reg. 27294 (July 2, 1985); 53 Fed. Reg. 16544 (May 10, 1988); 62 Fed. Reg. 18938, 18941–18942 (Apr. 17, 1997); *see also* Eugene P. Grisanti, *Legal Aspects of Technical Problems and Chemical Additives*, 26 FOOD DRUG COSM. L.J. 588 (1971).

In the first two decades after enactment of the Food Additive Amendments, this theoretical freedom of food processors to determine initially which food ingredients require FDA licensure had little practical significance for widely used ingredients. Very few processors would purchase ingredients for which the supplier could not provide documentation of FDA approval or acknowledgement as GRAS. Manufacturers feared that if they independently concluded that an ingredient was GRAS, they ran the risk that FDA might disagree and initiate regulatory action against their products.

United States v. An Article of Food

752 F.2d 11 (1st Cir. 1985).

■ WEIGEL, SENIOR DISTRICT JUDGE.

This is an appeal from the district court's grant of summary judgment. Appellant Coco Rico, Inc., manufactures in Puerto Rico a coconut concentrate called Coco Rico for use as an ingredient in soft drinks. The Coco Rico concentrate sold to beverage bottlers in Puerto Rico contains potassium nitrate, added for the purpose of developing and fixing a desirable color and flavor. On March 10, 1982, the United States instituted *in rem* proceedings against three lots of bottled soft drinks located on the premises of Puerto Rican bottlers. The soft drinks contained Coco Rico concentrate. The government charged that potassium nitrate constitutes an "unsafe" food additive, making the beverages "adulterated" and subject to forfeiture....

Coco Rico submitted one affidavit in opposition to the motion for summary judgment, that of food chemist Algeria B. Caragay.... Nitrates have been approved by the FDA for use in curing meat....

First, Coco Rico claims that Caragay's affidavit is sufficient to show the existence of a factual issue as to whether potassium nitrate is "generally recognized" by qualified experts as having been scientifically shown to be safe. To fall within this exception, the substance must be generally recognized as safe *under the conditions of its intended use.* The burden of proving general recognition of safe use is placed on the proponent of the food substance in question. Caragay's affidavit contained only statements to the effect that she knows of no conclusive scientific evidence that the use of potassium nitrate in beverages is *unsafe*, or that the health effects of potassium nitrate when used in beverages differ from those caused by its use in meats. Even if these allegations are true, they are insufficient to meet Coco Rico's burden of proving that the use of potassium nitrate in beverages is generally recognized by experts as *safe* based on scientific evidence.

For similar reasons, Coco Rico's second argument based on "common use" of potassium nitrate must also fail. Again, a substance may be excluded from classification as a "food additive" only if experience based on common use provides a basis for general recognition by scientists that the substance is safe *under the conditions of its intended use.* The evidence submitted by Coco Rico tends to show that nitrates are naturally present in many foodstuffs, particularly vegetables, and that they have been used for many centuries to cure meats. No evidence was submitted to show that potassium nitrate has long been added to beverages. Consequently, there is no issue of fact as to whether common experience could show that potassium nitrate is not a "food additive" when used in beverages....

NOTES

1. *Lack of GRAS Status.* In *United States v. Articles of Food ... Buffalo Jerky,* the courts concluded that patties made from buffalo (bison) meat, sodium nitrate, sodium nitrite, and other ingredients violated section 409 because nitrate and nitrite are not GRAS and no food additive regulation permitted their use for this purpose, even though they recognized that FDA had approved these substances for use in pork products. 456 F. Supp. 207 (D. Neb. 1978), *aff'd per curiam,* 594 F.2d 869 (8th Cir. 1979). *See also United States v. An Article of Food,* 678 F.2d 735 (7th Cir. 1982); *United States v. Article of Food ... Orotic Acid,* 414 F. Supp. 793 (E.D. Mo. 1976).

2. *Simplesse.* As a result of nationwide publicity about Simplesse on the TV program *Nightline*, FDA asked for a GRAS affirmation petition for an ingredient that consisted only of microparticularized egg and milk protein. Eighteen months later the agency affirmed its GRAS status. 55 Fed. Reg. 6384 (Feb. 23, 1990).

3. *Other GRAS Ingredients.* FDA has affirmed the GRAS status of oils from menhaden fish, one of the most widely consumed fish in the world. *See* 54 Fed. Reg. 38219 (Sept. 15, 1989); "Menhaden Oils Recognized as Safe," FDA Talk Paper No. T89–74 (Nov. 30, 1989). The agency has also affirmed the GRAS status of an

enzyme, chymosin, produced by recombinant DNA technology for use in making cheese. *See* 55 Fed. Reg. 10932 (Mar. 23, 1990); "Enzyme for Producing Cheese," FDA Talk Paper No. T90–15 (Mar. 26, 1990).

4. *GRAS and Prior Sanction Exceptions.* More than one critic has proposed that regulation of direct food additives should be tightened by eliminating the exclusion of GRAS and prior sanctioned substances from the food additive definition. *E.g.*, GAO, NEED FOR MORE EFFECTIVE REGULATION OF DIRECT ADDITIVES TO FOOD, Rep. No. HRD–80–90 (Aug. 14, 1980). When closely scrutinized, however, support for this proposition has faded in the face of the vast number of raw agricultural commodities and other common food substances that would have to be subjected to animal toxicity tests, the resulting thousands of petitions requiring safety evaluations, and the development of food additive regulations specifying safe conditions of use.

COMMENT: THE GRAS LIST REVIEW

FDA does not have a comprehensive inventory of GRAS ingredients, and it lacks complete information about the extent and levels of their use. Following FDA's removal of cyclamate from GRAS status in 34 Fed. Reg. 17063 (Oct. 21, 1969), President Nixon ordered a complete review of the GRAS list in his Consumer Message of October 30, 1969. "Consumer Protection," 5 WEEKLY COMP. PRES. DOC. 1516 (Nov. 3, 1969). In response, FDA contracted with the Federation of American Societies for Experimental Biology (FASEB) to conduct the initial safety reviews. The agency issued regulations establishing the procedures for this review and the criteria for determining GRAS status, as well as regulations codifying the substantive results of the review.

FDA announced a National Academy of Sciences survey of industry production and use of GRAS substances in 36 Fed. Reg. 20546 (Oct. 23, 1971). *See also* 42 Fed. Reg. 30894 (June 17, 1977) (announcement of additional NAS survey). The agency later promulgated procedures for affirmation of GRAS status and for the determination of food additive (i.e, not GRAS) status. Under these procedures, either determination can be made on the petition of an interested person or on FDA's own initiative. 37 Fed. Reg. 6207 (Mar. 25, 1972), 37 Fed. Reg. 25705 (Dec. 2, 1972), codified at 21 C.F.R. 170.35, 170.38. The procedures also allow the establishment of interim food additive regulations requiring additional study while a substance remains on the market. 21 C.F.R. 180.1. Substances affirmed by FDA as GRAS under this procedure were deleted from the old GRAS list in 21 C.F.R. Part 182 ("Substances Generally Recognized as Safe") and are identified instead in 21 C.F.R. Part 184 ("Direct Food Substances Affirmed as Generally Recognized as Safe"). A comprehensive status report on the GRAS list review was published in 38 Fed. Reg. 20054 (July 26, 1973).

As part of the GRAS List Review, FDA initially concluded that it would be appropriate to include in the resulting regulations limitations on the uses of such substances. Accordingly, the agency undertook to define 43 general food categories and 32 general physical or technical functional effects for which ingredients may be added to foods. 38 Fed. Reg. 20044 (July 26, 1973), 39 Fed. Reg. 34173 (Sept. 23, 1974), codified at 21 C.F.R. 170.3(n), (o). Initially, all of the regulations promulgated in 21 C.F.R. Part

184 affirming particular substances as GRAS were required to contain specific use level limitations based upon the various NAS food consumption surveys and other information available to the agency. Later FDA revised its regulations to require that use of all affirmed GRAS substances must comply with current good manufacturing practice and to allow flexibility in deciding when use limitations need to be included in GRAS affirmation regulations. *See* 47 Fed. Reg. 39199 (Sept. 7, 1982), 48 Fed. Reg. 48457 (Oct. 19, 1983).

Determining the criteria for GRAS status was a major issue confronting FDA. The agency initially adopted GRAS criteria in 35 Fed. Reg. 18623 (Dec. 8, 1970) and 36 Fed. Reg. 12093 (June 25, 1971). FDA proposed to revise these regulations in 39 Fed. Reg. 34194 (Sept. 23, 1974) and two years later, in the Federal Register document excerpted below, promulgated final regulations, now codified at 21 C.F.R. 170.30.

General Recognition of Safety and Prior Sanctions for Food Ingredients

41 Fed. Reg. 53600 (December 7, 1976).

. . . .

The Commissioner proposed to (1) Require that general recognition of safety through scientific procedures must ordinarily be based upon published literature; (2) Recognize that GRAS status based on scientific procedures requires the same quality and quantity of scientific evidence as would be required for approval of a food additive regulation; (3) Define "common use in food" as used in section 201(s) of the act to mean a substantial history of consumption of a substance by a significant number of consumers in the United States; (4) Recognize that GRAS status based upon common use in food does not require the same quality or quantity of scientific evidence that would be required for approval of a food additive regulation; (5) Recognize three categories of ingredients affirmed as GRAS; (6) Recognize that GRAS affirmation proceedings should consider the manufacturing process involved; and (7) Provide for procedures for considering the applicability of prior sanctions. . . .

One comment . . . argued that longtime use by consumers does not establish safety, and that FDA should not permit use of a substance in food unless it had been established as safe by appropriate scientific studies. . . . The Commissioner notes that the criteria set forth in [§ 170.30] interpret section 201(s) of the act as requiring the same quantity and quality of scientific evidence to establish that a substance is GRAS as is required to establish the safety of a newly used food additive, if the substance was first used in food after January 1, 1958. For substances in common use in food before January 1, 1958, however, the act is explicit in requiring FDA to consider experience based on such use in determining whether a substance is GRAS. Indeed, the act permits a manufacturer to determine that a substance is GRAS considering only experience based on common use in food if the substance was used in food before January 1, 1958. Thus, for those substances that were widely used before 1958, under the terms of the statute FDA must consider available data and may not prohibit use of a substance merely because tests that would be required for new food additives have not been performed....

Comments opposed the criterion ... providing that the benefit contributed by a substance shall be considered in determining whether it is "safe" for use. One comment stated that the social utility of a substance is not to be judged by FDA, but is a determination specifically reserved for the consumer to make in a free and open marketplace....

The Commissioner concludes that it is appropriate to recognize that the benefit contributed by a substance is inevitably a factor to be considered in determining whether a particular substance is "safe" (or generally recognized as "safe") for its intended use. The term "safe" is to be given its ordinary meaning, and in its common usage the term is understood to carry an assessment of benefits and risks. It is true, as the comment states, that minor food additives are not approved at levels that may present a hazard to the normal consumer. This result is required by the act because the benefit of a minor food additive is too small to justify the imposition of a known risk to normal consumers; use of such ingredient at levels that may present a hazard to the normal consumer would not be "safe." However, this result does not necessarily follow in the case of important food additives. For example, if it were found that a major food source such as meat or grain was associated with the development of chronic diseases in normal individuals, it would not necessarily follow that the food was unsafe within the meaning of the act. The ordinary understanding of the term "safe" would require some benefit-to-risk analysis in such circumstances.

Another example relates to the incidence of allergic reactions to particular food ingredients. Adverse reactions caused by allergy are clearly a consideration in determining whether a food ingredient is safe. Ordinarily, the incidence of allergic reactions from a food additive cannot be considered because data and test protocols do not exist. When data exist, however, they may be considered, and an assessment of benefits and risks becomes relevant. For example, if it were determined that both a particular emulsifier and a particular fruit resulted in the same unusually high incidence of allergic reactions, one might reasonably conclude that the emulsifier was not safe but that the fruit was safe. Such conclusions would simply represent common understanding of the concept of safety....

The Commissioner has, however, deleted from the regulations the reference to consideration of benefits on the ground that this separate consideration is legitimately included within the concept of safety as used in the act. Furthermore, explicitly retaining the criterion of benefit in the regulations might be construed as requiring routine formal analysis of a factor that the agency will only occasionally need to take into account, because the agency's general guidelines will result in disapproval of food additives that may cause toxic effects in normal individuals.*

* [FDA Commissioner Donald Kennedy repudiated the views expressed in this paragraph in his first decision on DES, 44 Fed. Reg. 54852, 58482–83 (Sept. 21, 1979), *infra* p. 1136.]

One comment opposed the provision in [§ 181.5(d)] requiring any person who intends to assert or rely on a prior sanction of which the Commissioner is not aware to submit proof of its existence when that prior sanction is inconsistent with a proposed affirmation of GRAS status or a proposed food additive regulation. . . .

The Commissioner concludes that it is necessary for proper functioning of the agency's ingredient review program to require that persons holding prior sanctions make their existence known when the agency is proposing regulations that are inconsistent with the continued use of an ingredient in accordance with a prior sanction. . . . Several factors support the Commissioner's conclusion: First, it is inequitable if one manufacturer who knows of a prior sanction is permitted to take advantage of it, while his competitors are restrained by regulations arising from the agency's review of ingredient safety. If the prior-sanctioned use is safe, all users should be permitted to rely upon it. If it is not safe, it should be brought to the agency's attention so that appropriate conclusions can be made. Second, enforcement would be highly inefficient if defenses to the agency's conclusions made during rule making are not raised until the time of enforcement. . . . Third, the issue of whether a prior-sanctioned use continues to be safe should be dealt with in an administrative proceeding, in which all relevant data and information may be economically marshaled and considered, rather than in a judicial trial, which requires the testimony of expert witnesses and in which the finder of fact is a layman. . . .

The Commissioner notes that the specification of manufacturing methods in GRAS affirmation regulations represents a basic difference between GRAS affirmation and food additive regulations, but does not represent an inconsistency. Both food additive and GRAS affirmation petitions require that methods of manufacture be carefully evaluated, as this information may be related to the final purity and safety of the product. Any change in the manufacturing process for a food additive requires a new food additive regulation if the process introduces new substances that are not GRAS into food. Thus, the policy for food additives and GRAS substances is identical. However, in the case of food additives, the manufacturing process is not generally specified in the regulation because under section 301(j) of the act confidential production information may not be disclosed. . . .

NOTES

1. *Legislative History.* In Congressional testimony two years before the Food Additives Amendment was enacted, FDA Commissioner Larrick explained that "[t]here are hundreds of substances in our dietary that have been used for 40, 50, 60, 70, or 80 years, but they have never been tested. There has been no occasion to test them because the common acceptance of them as safe has come about through long usage, but you could not prove through scientific methods whether they are safe or not. . . ." "Federal Food, Drug, and Cosmetic Act (Chemical Additives in Food)," Hearings before a Subcommittee of the House Committee on Interstate and Foreign Commerce, 84th Cong., 2d Sess. 204 (1956).

2. *Change in Status.* Under section 201(s), a food additive can acquire GRAS status and thus no longer require a food additive regulation. FDA has not yet revoked any food additive regulation on this ground, and is unlikely to do so. FDA and food manufacturers have, however, concluded that new uses of long-used food additives are GRAS. *E.g.*, 21 C.F.R. 175.105 and GRAS Notice No. GRN 000003 (sodium bisulfite); 21 C.F.R. 173.350 and GRAS Notice No. GRN 000083 (carbon monoxide); 21 C.F.R. 177.1670 and GRAS Notice No. GRN 000141 (polyvinyl alcohol). Conversely, GRAS status does not permanently exempt a substance from the definition of "food additive." FDA has revoked a GRAS determination on the basis of new data relating to safety. *E.g.*, 34 Fed. Reg. 17063 (Oct. 21, 1969) (cyclamate). Citizen Petition No. 2005P–0459/CPI (Nov. 15, 2005) requests FDA to revoke its acceptance of the GRAS notification for the use of carbon monoxide in fresh meat packaging on the ground that it helps simulate the red color of fresh meat.

3. *Procedural Rights.* An approved food additive enjoys greater procedural protection than does a GRAS ingredient. Revocation of a substance's GRAS status can be accomplished summarily by court enforcement action or by informal rule-making to add it to the list of banned food substances. 38 Fed. Reg. 20040 (July 26, 1973), 39 Fed. Reg. 34172 (Sept. 23, 1974), codified at 21 C.F.R. Part 189. In contrast, any revocation of a food additive regulation is subject to objection and a demand for a formal evidentiary hearing under section 409.

4. *Applicability of Delaney Clause.* Because GRAS ingredients do not fall within the definition of a food additive, they are not technically subject to the Delaney Clause, *infra* Chapter IX. In practice, before the mid–1970s, the Delaney principle prevented the introduction or continued use of a GRAS ingredient that was found in appropriate tests to induce cancer in experimental animals. Such a finding was regarded as undermining any basis for general expert recognition of the safety of the ingredient, thereby rendering it a food additive for which affirmative FDA approval was required. This analysis explains FDA's actions in the case of cyclamate, which prior to 1970 had been widely used based on FDA's determination that it was GRAS. A report by the principal manufacturer that cyclamate might be an animal carcinogen was viewed as destroying its GRAS status, making its continued use unlawful overnight.

Beginning in the mid–1970s, however, as evidence accumulated that virtually all food contains at least one substance that is carcinogenic in test animals, FDA began to rethink this approach. Although officials continued to state publicly that a carcinogenic food substance would not be regarded as GRAS, the agency has never challenged GRAS ingredients that have been shown to contain carcinogenic constituents. *See, e.g.*, "Agriculture, Rural Development and Related Agencies Appropriations for 1984," Hearings before a Subcommittee of the House Committee on Appropriations, 98th Cong., 1st Sess., Part 4, at 473–77 (1983) (listing FDA's responses to questions relating to natural carcinogens in the food supply).

5. *Prior Sanction Status.* The cyclamate episode illustrates an important distinction between ingredients that are excepted from the food additive definition because they are GRAS and ingredients that are permanently exempt because FDA or USDA sanctioned their use prior to 1958. An ingredient's status as GRAS is always vulnerable to the discovery of new evidence casting doubt on its safety. An ingredient that ceases to be GRAS falls automatically within the definition of a food additive, and must then be approved by FDA for its use to be lawful. A prior sanction, however, is a permanent exemption from food additive status.

6. *Indirect Uses.* FDA has clarified that any substance affirmed as GRAS for direct food use is also regarded as GRAS for indirect food use. 47 Fed. Reg. 27817 (June 25, 1982), 48 Fed. Reg. 48456 (Oct. 19, 1983).

7. *Options Open to FDA Prior to 1997.* Before 1997, FDA, operating pursuant to 21 C.F.R. 170.35, could take one of three actions upon receiving a GRAS affirmation petition: (1) determine that the substance was GRAS and indicate this GRAS affirmation in part 182,184, or 186 of the C.F.R., (2) determine that the substance was a safe food additive and promulgate a regulation under section 409, or (3) determine that the substance was a food additive for which there was inadequate evidence of safety and ban its use. *See, e.g.,* 42 Fed. Reg. 26467 (May 24, 1977) (determining that a high intensity sweetener, miracle fruit, is not GRAS and is an unapproved food additive); 50 Fed. Reg. 3890 (Jan. 29, 1985) (determining that a quaternary ammonium chloride combination is not GRAS but is a safe and approved food additive).

8. *Options Open to FDA Since 1997.* Because of the deterioration of the GRAS affirmation process, discussed *infra* p. 423, FDA issued proposed regulations in 62 Fed. Reg. 18938 (Apr. 17, 1997) to convert that process to a simple premarket notification procedure for virtually all substances for which a company seeks GRAS affirmation. The agency immediately implemented the proposal and has not promulgated final regulations. Under the post-1997 procedure, the company submits a notice stating its determination that the substance involved is GRAS for its intended use. If FDA does not disagree, the agency sends a letter to the company stating that it has "no questions" regarding the company's GRAS determination but has not made its own GRAS determination. The FDA letter is then placed on the agency's website but is not published in the Federal Register.

COMMENT: SULFITE

Sulfites are sulfur-based preservatives. Based upon a FASEB evaluation, FDA proposed in 47 Fed. Reg. 29956 (July 9, 1982) to affirm the GRAS status of sulfiting agents in food. After receiving reports of allergic reactions to sulfites, however, the agency announced the formation of an Ad Hoc Advisory Committee on Hypersensitivity to Sulfiting Agents in Food. 49 Fed. Reg. 15021 (Apr. 16, 1984). In 49 Fed. Reg. 27994 (July 9, 1984), the agency announced that it would reconsider the GRAS status of sulfites on the basis of a report to be prepared by a different body, the Ad Hoc Review Panel on the Reexamination of the GRAS Status of Sulfiting Agents. The tentative report of the Ad Hoc Review Panel was made available for comment in 49 Fed. Reg. 42984 (Oct. 25, 1984). As an interim measure, FDA notified distributors of shrimp products that shrimp may contain no more than 100 ppm of sulfite and that the presence of sulfite must be declared. 50 Fed. Reg. 2957 (Jan. 23, 1985). After receiving the final report of the Ad Hoc Review Panel, 50 Fed. Reg. 9131 (Mar. 6, 1985), FDA proposed to revoke the GRAS status of sulfite for use on fruits and vegetables intended to be served or sold raw to consumers. 50 Fed. Reg. 32830 (Aug. 14, 1985), 51 Fed. Reg. 25021 (July 9, 1986). The agency proposed also to revoke the GRAS status of sulfite for use in fresh potatoes served or sold unpackaged and unlabeled to consumers, 52 Fed. Reg. 46968 (Dec. 10, 1987), and to place specific limits on the use of sulfites in particular food categories, 53 Fed. Reg. 51065 (Dec. 19, 1988). When FDA revoked the GRAS status of sulfites for use on fresh unlabeled potatoes in 55 Fed. Reg. 9826 (Mar. 15, 1990), the industry initiated litigation that continued for three years.

While FDA was addressing the safety of sulfites, it was concurrently dealing with their labeling. Based upon the advice of the Ad Hoc Advisory Committee, the agency required that any added sulfite that is detectable at 10 ppm or more must be labeled as an ingredient. 50 Fed. Reg. 13306 (Apr. 3, 1985), 51 Fed. Reg. 25012 (July 9, 1986), codified at 21 C.F.R. 101.100(a)(4). BATF imposed a similar requirement for alcoholic beverages. 50 Fed. Reg. 26001 (June 24, 1985), 51 Fed. Reg. 34706 (Sept. 30, 1986). FDA also specifically proposed to extend the labeling requirement to any sulfite in a standardized food. 53 Fed. Reg. 51062 (Dec. 19, 1988). Remarkably, FDA accomplished all this with a single congressional hearing. *See* "Sulfites," Hearing before the Subcommittee on Oversight and Investigations of the House Committee on Energy and Commerce, 99th Cong., 1st Sess. (1985).

In the first few months of 1983, FDA took the position that, under its three model food sanitation codes, *supra* p. 334, the use of sulfite on fresh fruits, fresh vegetables, and other raw food is considered safe only if consumers are informed by signs or some other form of public notice. The National Restaurant Association notified its members, who responded by abandoning use of sulfites for salad bars and other related purposes. "Sulfiting Agents Update," FDA Talk Paper No. T83–12 (Mar. 11, 1983); "Sulfiting Agents—Update," FDA Talk Paper No. T83–15 (Apr. 5, 1983).

In *Hanover Potato Products, Inc. v. Sullivan*, plaintiffs sought an injunction to prohibit FDA from enforcing regulations promulgated in 1990 to prohibit the use of sulfites on "fresh" potatoes, *i.e.*, potatoes peeled and processed by a producer and then sold to restaurants and institutions. The District Court for the Middle District of Pennsylvania denied the plaintiffs' motion for a preliminary injunction. Food Drug Cosm. L. Rep. (CCH) ¶ 38,165 (1990). On a motion for reconsideration, the District Court ordered FDA to assemble the complete administrative record in accordance with 21 C.F.R. 10.40(g). When the District Court learned that most of the administrative record had never been made publicly available, it *sua sponte* gave FDA fifteen days to show cause why summary judgment should not be entered for plaintiffs because of the agency's failure to timely compile and file a proper administrative record in support of the regulation. After due consideration, the District Court entered summary judgment on the grounds that FDA had violated its own regulations and the Administrative Procedure Act. Food Drug Cosm. L. Rep. (CCH) ¶ 38,175 (1990). On appeal, a panel of the Third Circuit remanded the issue to the District Court, ordering it to re-try the issue based on the administrative record that was available at the deadline for filing comments. 2 Food and Drug Law Reports 78 (Mar. 1991). In a rehearing *en banc* before ten judges, however, an equally divided Court of Appeals affirmed the District Court's grant of summary judgment against the agency. Following this result, the District Court denied the award of attorney's fees to counsel for the plaintiffs, but the Court of Appeals overturned that decision under the Equal Access to Justice Act. *Hanover Potato Products, Inc. v. Shalala*, 989 F.2d 123 (3d Cir. 1993). While the case was ongoing, FDA took the position that, independent of the litigation, there was no basis for a determination that the use of sulfiting agents on fresh potatoes is GRAS. Letter from L. Robert Lake, Director, Office of Compliance in the FDA Center for Food Safety and

Applied Nutrition, to W. Gary Flamm (Aug. 13, 1991). After the *en banc* Court of Appeals upheld the District Court's judgment for the plaintiff, however, FDA withdrew the 1990 regulations revoking the GRAS listing of sulfite for use on fresh potatoes. 59 Fed. Reg. 65938 (Dec. 22, 1994).

In a 1990 state tort action against the operator of a grocery store, the plaintiff argued that he was injured by ingesting celery hearts that had been treated with sulfite. He alleged that defendant was guilty of negligence per se based upon FDA's determination that sulfite is not safe when used on raw fruits or vegetables. The trial court awarded summary judgment to the defendant. The Alabama Supreme Court overturned the trial court decision, holding that although the FD&C Act provides no private cause of action this does not preclude use of the FDA determination in a tort case. *Allen v. Delchamps, Inc.*, 624 So. 2d 1065 (Ala. 1993).

COMMENT: CAFFEINE

FDA placed caffeine on the original GRAS list, 26 Fed. Reg. 938 (Jan. 31, 1961), and it remains listed, 21 C.F.R. 182.1180. Following a report from FASEB recommending that caffeine no longer be considered GRAS in cola beverages, FDA proposed to revoke its GRAS status and to promulgate an interim food additive regulation requiring additional studies. 45 Fed. Reg. 69816 (Oct. 21, 1980). When FDA extended the time for public comment, a consumer group sued to compel the agency to ban caffeine immediately. The District Court dismissed the action, holding that the FASEB report was not binding on FDA, which in any case was not guilty of undue delay. *Federation of Homemakers, Inc. v. Harris*, Food Drug Cosm. L. Rep. (CCH) ¶ 38,100 (D.D.C. 1981).

FDA subsequently undertook an audit of the pivotal teratogenicity study on caffeine, which revealed serious flaws. 46 Fed. Reg. 32453 (June 23, 1981). In the meantime, users of caffeine, with the aid of the Freedom of Information Act, scoured FDA archives for correspondence relating to caffeine and found several FDA documents that they claimed supported a prior sanction. On May 20, 1987, FDA proposed to recognize a prior sanction for caffeine in nonalcoholic carbonated beverages, 52 Fed. Reg. 18923, but this proposal was withdrawn in 69 Fed. Reg. 68831, 68833 (Nov. 26, 2004). *See Caution Light on Caffeine*, 14 FDA CONSUMER, No. 8, at 6 (Oct. 1980); "Caffeine Content Evaluation Updated," FDA Talk Paper No. T83–42 (Oct. 19, 1983); Gwendolyn Prothro, *Caffeine Consumption and Regulation in the United States*, 27 CUMB. L. REV. 65 (1996/1997); David M. Mrazik, *Reconsidering Caffeine: An Awake and Alert New Look at America's Most Commonly Consumed Drug* (2004), in Chapter V(I)(1) of the Electronic Book.

Fmali Herb, Inc. v. Heckler

715 F.2d 1385 (9th Cir. 1983).

■ FLETCHER, CIRCUIT JUDGE....

Appellant Fmali Herb, Inc., is an importer of Chinese food products. In its business, Fmali wishes to import foods containing herbs traditional in

China that have never been widely used in the United States. One such food is a jelly or honey-like product, known as renshenfengwangjiang, which normally contains schizandra seed. The FDA has ruled that renshenfengwangjiang may be sold in the United States only if it does not contain schizandra seed, because schizandra seed has not been scientifically tested and because it was not commonly used in the United States prior to 1958. The FDA held that evidence of long and widespread use of schizandra seed in China is not admissible in aid of establishing that schizandra seed is safe for human consumption.

By promulgating the regulation defining "common use in food" to mean only common use within the United States, the FDA has imposed a restriction not required by the literal terms of the statute. The FDA's reasons for doing so were expressed at the time the regulation was issued:

> The Commissioner believes that the type of experience based on common use in food that will support a GRAS determination must involve use in the United States, and not solely in foreign countries. Reported use in foreign countries often cannot be verified, and in any event the experience based on such use cannot be monitored or evaluated. Food consumption patterns and differences between cultures make it impossible to assess whether a history of use abroad would be comparable to a history of use in the United States.

39 Fed. Reg. 34,195 (1974).

We agree for the most part with the concerns expressed by the FDA. Many residents of areas outside the United States have shorter life expectancies than do Americans. Foreign populations also suffer from higher incidences of some diseases, so that generalizations about the safety of their dietary habits may be unreliable. But it is an illogical and, we think, unwarranted constriction of the statute to rule that evidence of long use of a substance in food outside the United States can *never* provide probative evidence of safety. Counsel for the FDA admitted this point in argument before the district court, when he stated that "there are countries in the world, like West Germany or something, where one might be able to accept" prior use of an ingredient to establish safety, but added that the FDA does not believe that evidence of use in "Guam" or "Southeast Asia" could be accepted. The statute provides no basis for a purely ethnocentric distinction of this kind, divorced from demographic considerations. . . .

NOTE

Following the *Fmali Herb* case, FDA revised its GRAS regulations to recognize that a substance that was used in food prior to 1958 can be shown to be GRAS through experience based on its common use in food outside, as well as inside, the United States. 50 Fed. Reg. 27294 (July 2, 1985), 53 Fed. Reg. 16544 (May 10, 1988), codified in 21 C.F.R. 170.30(c)(2). The preambles, however, left little doubt about the agency's continued reluctance to accept foreign use as adequate evidence of GRAS status.

d. PRIOR SANCTIONED SUBSTANCES

Section 201(s)(4) constitutes a genuine "grandfather" clause for food substances that FDA or the Department of Agriculture had affirmatively approved prior to the 1958 enactment of section 409. These "prior sanctions" can be under the 1938 FD&C Act (but not the 1906 Act), the Poultry Products Inspection Act, or the Federal Meat Inspection Act. While prior to 1958, FDA lacked statutory authority to license food ingredients for general use, it routinely responded, as did USDA, to requests for opinions about the safety of individual ingredients. In addition, FDA exercised premarket control over, and thus approved, ingredients permitted to be used in foods covered by standards of identity. USDA issued formal regulations describing permitted uses of many ingredients in meat and poultry products, *see* 13 FOOD DRUG COSM. L.J. 834, 840, 860 (1958), and in some instances FDA formally acknowledged that USDA had approved certain substances for food use. An ingredient's prior sanction status does not depend upon a contemporary evaluation of its utility or its safety, but rests solely on the fact of prior approval by one of the two agencies.

Proposal Regarding Regulation of Prior–Sanctioned Food Ingredients

37 Fed. Reg. 16407 (August 12, 1972).

... [A] food ingredient subject to a prior sanction may not be regulated under the food additive provisions of the law. Such an ingredient may, however, be regulated under the general adulteration and misbranding provisions of the Act, and in particular may be banned from food if found to be a "poisonous or deleterious substance" in violation of Section 402(a)(1) of the Act.

The Food and Drug Administration, between 1938 and 1958, reaffirmed many sanctions or approvals granted under the Federal Food and Drugs Act of 1906, and also granted additional sanctions and approvals. The U.S. Department of Agriculture has similarly granted many sanctions and approvals. Not all of these sanctions and approvals can be ascertained because of the destruction of old records and the retirement of personnel involved in these matters. The Food and Drug Administration has requested information on prior sanctions (35 F.R. 5810) in an effort to make its files on these matters more complete.

Whether or not a food ingredient is used as a result of a determination that it is GRAS, or pursuant to a food additive regulation, or as a result of a prior sanction, the basis for such use should be a matter of public record. The Commissioner has therefore determined to expand Subpart E under Part 121 [now 21 C.F.R. Part 181] within which will be established regulations governing all prior-sanctioned direct and indirect food ingredients known to the Commissioner.

New scientific information requires, on occasion, that additional limitations be placed on the use of prior-sanctioned ingredients. Accordingly, the Commissioner has concluded that a procedure should also be established under which a regulation in Subpart E stating the existence of a prior sanction may be established or amended to impose limitations upon the use of the ingredient when scientific data justify such limitations. . . .

NOTES

1. *Final Regulations.* FDA's final regulations, promulgated in 38 Fed. Reg. 12737 (May 15, 1973) and amended in 39 Fed. Reg. 42746 (Dec. 6, 1974) and 42 Fed. Reg. 52814 (Sept. 30, 1977), afford the agency substantial control over prior-sanctioned food ingredients.

§ 181.1   General

(a) An ingredient whose use in food or food packaging is subject to a prior sanction or approval within the meaning of section 201(s)(4) of the act is exempt from classification as a food additive. The Commissioner will publish in this part all known prior sanctions. Any interested person may submit to the Commissioner a request for publication of a prior sanction, supported by evidence to show that it falls within section 201(s)(4) of the act.

(b) Based upon scientific data or information that shows that use of a prior-sanctioned food ingredient may be injurious to health, and thus in violation of section 402 of the act, the Commissioner will establish or amend an applicable prior sanction regulation to impose whatever limitations or conditions are necessary for the safe use of the ingredient, or to prohibit use of the ingredient.

(c) Where appropriate, an emergency action level may be issued for a prior-sanctioned substance, pending the issuance of a final regulation in accordance with paragraph (b) of this section. Such an action level shall be issued pursuant to section 402(a) of the act to identify, based upon available data, conditions of use of the substance that may be injurious to health. Such an action level shall be issued in a notice published in the FEDERAL REGISTER and shall be followed as soon as practicable by a proposed regulation in accordance with paragraph (b) of this section. Where the available data demonstrate that the substance may be injurious at any level, use of the substance may be prohibited. The identification of a prohibited substance may be made in Part 189 of this chapter when appropriate.

2. *Sanctions Under the 1906 Act.* Section 201(s)(4) only recognizes prior sanctions "granted . . . pursuant to this [the FD&C] Act," the Poultry Products Inspection Act, and the Federal Meat Inspection Act. Sanctions granted under the 1906 Act and not revoked under the 1938 Act are included, however, if FDA continued to rely upon them after the enactment of the 1938 Act.

3. *Lead in Tin Cans.* In 44 Fed. Reg. 5123 (Aug. 31, 1979), FDA issued an advance notice of proposed rulemaking requesting evidence of a prior sanction for lead in lead-soldered tin cans as food packaging. Since then, FDA has banned lead for this use under section 402(a)(1), as related in *supra* p. 379.

4. *Caffeine.* Although FDA proposed in 45 FR 69817 (Oct. 21, 1980) to find that there was no prior sanction for caffeine in soft drinks, it reversed that position and proposed to find such a prior sanction in 52 Fed. Reg. 18923 (May 20, 1987). The agency withdrew both of these this proposals, with little explanation, in 69 Fed. Reg. 68831, 68833 (Nov. 26, 2004). Caffeine continues to be treated as GRAS. *See supra* p. 417.

COMMENT: NITRITE AND NITRATE

Nitrite and nitrate (referred to here by the single term "nitrite") are two of the oldest functional food ingredients. Nitrite has been used to preserve meat since prehistoric times. Early in the 20th century, it gained popularity as an agent to impart flavor and color. Nitrite also inhibits the growth of the bacterial spores that cause botulism. In the 1960s, it was discovered that nitrite can combine with amines, substances naturally found in many food products, to produce nitrosamines, some of which cause cancer in laboratory animals. Indeed, the nitrates that occur naturally throughout the human food supply are converted to nitrite and combine with naturally occurring amines to produce nitrosamines in the human gut.

In the early 1970s, Congress conducted hearings on the safety of nitrite. *See* "Regulation of Food Additives and Medicated Animal Feed," Hearings before a Subcommittee of the House Committee on Government Operations, 92d Cong., 1st Sess. (1971); "Regulation of Food Additives— Nitrites and Nitrates," H.R. REP. No. 92–1338, 92d Cong., 2d Sess. (1972). Following these hearings, FDA proposed to prohibit nonessential uses of nitrite. 37 Fed. Reg. 23456 (Nov. 3, 1972). In this notice, however, the agency stated that "nitrite and nitrate ... have prior sanction for use as curing agents in meat and poultry products." A decade later, the FDA Commissioner responsible for this action acknowledged that nitrite had not been banned in November 1972 not only because of its usefulness in preventing botulism, but also "because of its importance in maintaining the characteristics of cured meat that are expected and demanded by consumers." "Oversight of Food Safety, 1983," Hearings before the Senate Committee on Labor and Human Resources, 98th Cong., 1st Sess. (1983). The agency subsequently banned the combination of nitrite with spice in curing premixes because it resulted in nitrosamines. 38 Fed. Reg. 19218 (July 19, 1973).

In 1972, consumer groups petitioned USDA to ban or restrict the use of nitrite in meat. After the USDA denial of the petition was upheld, *Schuck v. Butz*, 500 F.2d 810 (D.C. Cir. 1974), USDA created an Expert Panel on Nitrites and Nitrosamines whose recommendations led it to propose modifications in the use of nitrite in meat and poultry products. 40 Fed. Reg. 52614 (Nov. 11, 1975).

Following the 1976 election, USDA reevaluated the status of nitrite and subsequently advised FDA that there was no prior sanction for nitrite in poultry. FDA therefore issued a statement tentatively determining that nitrite used in poultry products is a food additive and requested information on its safe use. 42 Fed. Reg. 44376 (Sept. 2, 1977). This was followed by a request from USDA for information on the safe use of nitrite in meat products. 42 Fed. Reg. 55626 (Oct. 18, 1977). Simultaneously, users of nitrite sought a declaratory judgment requesting a determination that a prior sanction for nitrite did exist. In *Tyson Foods, Inc. v. USDA*, Food Drug Cosm. L. Rep. (CCH) ¶ 38,249 (W.D. Ark. 1979), the court held that, because FDA had stated it would take no regulatory action until it made a final decision on the prior sanction issue, the suit was premature.

USDA issued a final regulation in 43 Fed. Reg. 20992 (May 16, 1978), restricting the use of nitrite in bacon and, more important, prohibiting any *new tech*

detectable amount of nitrosamines. A year earlier, a new device for analyzing nitrosamines, called the thermal energy analyser (TEA), had improved the detection sensitivity for nitrosamines by an order of magnitude. The USDA regulation required TEA analysis sensitive to 10 ppb, and within one year it had reduced this limit to 5 ppb. Development of the TEA machine had an impact far beyond meat and poultry products, for it detected nitrosamines in other food and consumer products, and indeed in the ambient air in all urban areas. FDA took action to control inadvertent nitrosamine contamination of cosmetics, 44 Fed. Reg. 21365 (Apr. 10, 1979), malt beverages, 45 Fed. Reg. 39341 (June 10, 1980), and rubber baby bottle nipples, 48 Fed. Reg. 57014 (Dec. 27, 1984), 49 Fed. Reg. 26149 (June 26, 1984), 49 Fed. Reg. 50789 (Dec. 31, 1984). EPA took action to control nitrosamines in pesticides. 45 Fed. Reg. 42854 (June 25, 1980), 47 Fed. Reg. 33777 (Aug. 4, 1982).

Faced with the emergence of TEA technology, USDA promulgated regulations permitting meat food products traditionally preserved with nitrite to be prepared without nitrite and to be labeled with the same name with only the addition of the term "uncured." 43 Fed. Reg. 18193 (Apr. 28, 1978); 44 Fed. Reg. 48959 (Aug. 21, 1979). This regulation was upheld in *National Pork Producers Council v. Bergland*, 631 F.2d 1353 (8th Cir. 1980), *rev'g* 484 F. Supp. 540 (S.D. Iowa 1980).

Until mid–1978, the sole documented scientific concern about nitrite related to the formation of nitrosamines. In August 1978, however, FDA and USDA announced that an animal feeding study "strongly suggests nitrite produces cancer of the lymphatic system in test animals." HEW News No. P78–28 (Aug. 11, 1978). The two agencies stated that "the need to balance two kinds of health risks—one by taking nitrite out of food and the other by leaving it in—creates a difficult challenge," and they made the results of the animal bioassay publicly available for comment. The Department of Justice advised the agencies that if nitrite were determined to be a carcinogen, they had the discretion to adopt timetables and procedures to assure the orderly removal of nitrite from commerce but did not have the discretion to phase out its use over a long period of time. 43 Op. Atty. Gen. No. 19 (Mar. 30, 1979). Producers of meat and poultry products were thus faced with a potentially serious problem. *See* "Nitrite Restrictions on Poultry," Hearing before the Subcommittee on Dairy and Poultry of the House Committee on Agriculture, 95th Cong., 2d Sess. (1978); "USDA/FDA Announcement on Nitrites and Related Issues," Hearing before the House Committee on Agriculture, 96th Cong., 2d Sess. (1980).

To resolve mounting questions about the validity of the nitrite bioassay, FDA conducted a public meeting announced in 44 Fed. Reg. 19538 (Apr. 3, 1979). Meanwhile, GAO criticized the agency's delay in resolving the matter. GAO, Does Nitrite Cause Cancer? Concerns About Validity of FDA-Sponsored Study Delay Answer, Rep. No. HRD–80–46 (Jan. 31, 1980). Following USDA's promulgation of its 1978 regulations, consumer groups challenged the action as inadequate. In *Public Citizen v. Foreman*, 631 F.2d 969 (D.C. Cir. 1980), the Court of Appeals upheld the USDA regulations on the basis that nitrite had a prior sanction as a preservative in cured meat products.

Following the District Court decision in *Foreman*, 471 F. Supp. 586 (D.D.C. 1979), which held that the status of nitrite as a color additive had to first be presented to FDA before the courts could rule on it, the plaintiffs petitioned the agency to declare nitrite a color additive (and thus unlawful because it lacked either a provisional or permanent listing). FDA initially proposed to determine that although nitrite was capable of imparting color to bacon and other red meat, and thus met the threshold criterion of color additive status, it was used in bacon solely for purposes other than coloring. 44 Fed. Reg. 75659 (Dec. 21, 1979). This proposal prompted another lawsuit, which was dismissed for the failure to exhaust administrative remedies. *See Public Citizen v. Goyan*, 496 F. Supp. 364 (D.D.C. 1980). FDA subsequently concluded that while nitrite "fixes" color, it does not "impart" color either to bacon or other red meat, and thus is not a color additive. 45 Fed. Reg. 77043 (Nov. 21, 1980). This conclusion was eventually upheld. *Public Citizen v. Hayes*, Food Drug Cosm. L. Rep. (CCH) ¶ 38,161 (D.D.C. 1982). In 44 Fed. Reg. 75662 (Dec. 21, 1979), FDA had proposed to determine that no prior sanction exists for nitrite in poultry. After another change in administration, however, the agency withdrew this proposal, as well as its November 1972 proposal to ban nonessential uses of nitrite. 48 Fed. Reg. 9299 (Mar. 4, 1983). FDA's withdrawal of these proposals was based upon USDA's report that a prior sanction did in fact exist for use of nitrite in both cured meat and cured poultry products. *See* 48 Fed. Reg. 1702 (Jan. 14, 1983), codified at 21 C.F.R. 181.33, 181.34. The prior sanction now recognized for nitrite does not, however, extend to all uses. In *United States v. An Article of Food ... Coco Rico, Inc.*, 752 F.2d 11 (1st Cir. 1985), the Court of Appeals determined that potassium nitrate is not subject to a prior sanction for use in soft drinks.

In 1980, after a complete review of the animal study results that had been released in August 1978, FDA announced that "insufficient evidence exists to support a conclusion that nitrite induced cancer in rats." 45 Fed. Reg. 58970 (Sept. 5, 1980). *See* Philip J. Hilts, *The Day Bacon Was Declared Poison*, WASH. POST, Apr. 26, 1981, at 18, *reprinted in* 127 CONG. REC. 7980, (Apr. 30, 1981), 13992 (June 25, 1981). FDA's determination did not end the matter, however. USDA authorized the use of other additives to inhibit formation of nitrosamines. 50 Fed. Reg. 27573 (July 5, 1985), 51 Fed. Reg. 35630 (Oct. 7, 1986). USDA also amended its regulations to authorize alternative procedures for controlling the levels of nitrite added to bacon. 51 Fed. Reg. 21731 (June 16, 1986). Three years later, it clarified and tightened its restrictions on nitrite. *See* 54 Fed. Reg. 1371 (Jan. 13, 1989), 54 Fed. Reg. 43041 (Oct. 20, 1989).

e. THE DETERIORATION OF THE FOOD ADDITIVE APPROVAL PROCESS

Peter Barton Hutt, *Regulation of Food Additives in the United States*

In Larry Branen et al., eds., FOOD ADDITIVES, Ch. 8 (2d ed. 2001).

Four decades ago, the United States explored and ultimately adopted a new and untried approach under the Federal Food, Drug, and Cosmetic Act

Two categories (1) food (2) food additive)

(FD&C Act). Congress divided the food supply into two different regulatory categories. The first regulatory category remained subject only to the same policing controls that had been used for centuries. This category included food itself (*e.g.*, raw agricultural commodities) and functional substances added to the food supply that were either approved by the United States Department of Agriculture (USDA) or the Food and Drug Administration (FDA) during 1938–1958 or that were generally recognized as safe (GRAS) for their intended uses. The second regulatory category required the obtaining of premarket approval from FDA prior to marketing for all new food additives that did not fall within the first category and all color additives.

Now we find that half of the system has been a complete success, and the other half is a complete failure. The GRAS process has worked extraordinarily well. The food additive and color additive approval process has broken down completely and requires fundamental reform. . . .

. . . [F]or those pre-1958 substances that were not prior-sanctioned or GRAS, and thus properly fell within the definition of a food additive, Congress included a transitional period within which the manufacturers were required to submit and obtain FDA approval of a food additive petition. . . .

pre-1958

The handling of all of the pre-1958 direct human food additive petitions in seven years reflected a heroic effort by FDA. It required the development and organization of a group of dedicated scientists within FDA, close daily cooperation between FDA and the regulated industry, and a commitment by everyone involved to work through the inevitable problems that arose in a practical and realistic way. No one either in industry or in FDA had the luxury of sitting around for months or years on end, debating theoretical issues. There was a job to be done, and it was done extraordinarily efficiently and with unprecedented success. Not a single additive that was approved during that time has since been removed from the market for lack of safety. The people who participated in that effort, many of whom still are alive today, deserve far greater recognition than they have been given to date.

By the time this transitional process was completed, FDA had promulgated 185 separate direct human food additive regulations, along with an additional 93 indirect food additive regulations, five regulations governing radiation of food, the lists of GRAS substances, and additional lists of prior-sanctioned substances, and effective dates were confirmed. It was an extraordinary outpouring of regulatory science. The productivity of FDA at that time in history stands in stark contrast to the inefficiency and paralysis of today. . . .

Once FDA completed its work on pre-1958 transitional food additives, it seems the agency lost heart on food additive matters. Since that time the record of FDA approval of new food additives is appalling. It is useful to review the FDA record on approving new direct human food additives over the past thirty years, from 1970 to the present. Research indicates only eight new direct human food additives during that time:

    1. TBHQ, 1972

2. Aspartame, 1981

3. Polydextrose, 1981

4. Acesulfame K, 1988

5. Gellan gum, 1990

6. Olestra, 1996

7. Sucralose, 1998

8. Sucrose acetate isobutyrate, 1999

Eight direct human food additives in thirty years. That is embarrassing. It represents a serious problem for food technology in the United States. Just at the time when we are learning more about the relationship between diet and health, and new food ingredients could contribute greatly to healthy improvements in our daily diet, we have adopted a regulatory system that has virtually destroyed the incentive to innovate and the ability to get new food additives to the market.

Let us also examine the history of one of the new food additives that languished in the FDA pipeline almost nine years prior to FDA approval: olestra. Information published on olestra shows that it was invented in 1968, the first meetings with FDA were held in the early 1970s, and it was the subject of continuing testing and negotiations with FDA until approved in 1996....

The lesson taught by the problems encountered by these hapless compounds has been learned by the entire food industry. The food additive approval process in America is dead. It has been killed by FDA. No food company of which I am aware would even consider beginning research today on a new food additive.

The lesson learned is that there is only one type of food substance worth considering: a GRAS substance that can immediately be marketed. If a new food substance cannot be determined to be GRAS, it is simply discarded. Only if it can be regarded as GRAS will it be pursued....

When FDA established its GRAS affirmation procedures as part of the GRAS List Review in the early 1970s, the agency recognized that it did not have the statutory authority either to preclude self-determination of GRAS status or to prevent marketing while the agency reviewed a self-determination of GRAS. In establishing its GRAS affirmation procedure, the agency deliberately and explicitly adopted a policy of recognizing that industry had the legal right to market a new food substance following a self-determination of GRAS, even if the manufacturer then concluded to submit a GRAS affirmation petition to FDA. The purpose of the agency was to encourage submission of GRAS affirmation petitions to FDA in order to assist the agency in its surveillance of the food supply and to settle any safety issues that might arise with the use of new food substances. This was a purposeful tradeoff. FDA gave industry the assurance that it could market products after a self-determination of GRAS, and in return industry began to submit GRAS affirmation petitions in order to demonstrate to potential customers and to FDA that the new substance had been thoroughly evaluated and was in fact GRAS.

GRAS not a priority

While reasonable in concept, FDA implementation of this program broke down almost from the beginning. GRAS affirmation was a process created by FDA, not by statute. There was no statutory deadline for FDA action and thus no priority within FDA. In many instances, FDA seemed to be more intent upon receiving a GRAS affirmation petition than it was upon evaluating and acting upon it. As a result, FDA became simply a dumping ground for GRAS affirmation petitions. The backlog of GRAS affirmation petitions for direct food substances, in various stages of consideration, grew every year. These could undoubtedly have been handled swiftly by FASEB, but the agency was incapable of delegating this function.

Nonetheless, the program was still a resounding success from the standpoint of public policy, precisely because FDA involvement was not needed to make it work. Self-determination of GRAS permits immediate marketing, whether or not a GRAS affirmation petition is filed and whether or not FDA ever acts on it . . . .

ex high fructose corn syrup

Perhaps there is no better example of the success of the GRAS approach than the history of high fructose corn syrup. High fructose corn syrup was the subject of a thorough scientific evaluation and a self-determination of GRAS in the mid–1960s. It was immediately marketed, without asking FDA for an opinion or even informing the agency. Once one manufacturer began to market it, others followed suit. By the early 1970s, it was in widespread use throughout the food industry. It proved to have excellent functional properties and to be an extremely important addition to the food supply . . . .

One should stop to consider what would have happened if high fructose corn syrup had been handled through a food additive petition rather than a self-determination of GRAS. By any standard, this substance is what we now refer to as a macronutrient. It can be consumed at a substantial level in the daily diet, if one selects a diet of processed food sweetened only with this substance (as assumption that FDA routinely makes in evaluating food additives). High fructose corn syrup was a contemporary of olestra. These two macronutrients were subject to initial research and development at the same time, during the mid–1960s. One took the GRAS superhighway to market, and the other followed the meandering food additive path through the FDA woods. One was freely marketed more than 25 years for unlimited food use before the other was allowed to be marketed for very limited food use. In many ways, this simple comparison tells the entire story.

By 1995, it was apparent that the FDA GRAS affirmation process was no longer operable. At its June 1995 meeting, the Institute of Food Technologists sponsored a major symposium to analyze food regulatory policy. Three of the papers presented at the symposium focused on the major problems with the current regulation of food additives and GRAS substances in the United States. Congress held a hearing to investigate the matter later that month and subsequently issued a report highly critical of the FDA performance. A year later the International Society of Regulatory Toxicology and Pharmacology (ISRTP) sponsored a workshop on optimizing the review process of food additive and GRAS petitions. The following year, the Institute of Medicine Food Forum held a workshop on the subject, focusing on a major commissioned academic analysis of the entire food additive/GRAS process. Although it was difficult to interpret the FDA data presented at the House hearings and the ISRTP workshop, it was clear that the FDA backlog for direct and indirect food additive petitions and GRAS affirmation petitions was very large and increasing each year. As of June 1995, there was a backlog of 295 pending petitions. This backlog was broken down into approximately 70 direct food additive petitions, 150 indirect food additive petitions, and 75 GRAS affirmation petitions. The oldest food additive petition was filed in 1971 and the oldest GRAS affirmation petition was filed in 1972. At the ISRTP workshop a year later, the FDA data presented a slightly improved picture but FDA was quick to point out that the situation was still inadequate. . . .

Partly as a response to the findings about the deterioration of the FDA process for review of food petitions, Congress included in the Food and Drug Administration Modernization Act of 1997 a new section 909 of the FD&C Act, explicitly authorizing FDA to enter into contracts with outside experts to review and evaluate any application or submission (including a petition or notification) submitted under the FD&C Act, including those for food additives and GRAS substances. . . .

In 1997, FDA proposed to replace the entire GRAS affirmation process with a GRAS notification procedure. Under the proposed new procedure, a person would submit a GRAS notification based on the person's determination that a substance is GRAS for its intended use. The GRAS notification would include a detailed summary of the scientific data on which the GRAS determination is based, but not the raw data. Within 90 days of receipt of the notification, FDA would be required to respond in writing either that the agency has no current objection to the notification or that it does have an objection. Although FDA has not yet promulgated a final regulation for this procedure, it has declined to accept new GRAS affirmation petitions, has encouraged those who submitted old GRAS affirmation petitions to convert them to GRAS determination notifications, and has accepted new GRAS determination notifications and taken action on them. In short, FDA is already implementing this proposal. . . .

Looking back on the past four decades, it is easy to discern areas of success and areas of failure in the regulation of food substances, food additives, and color additives.

Regulation of GRAS substances under the Food Additives Amendment of 1958 has been an enormous success, largely because it has been implemented outside FDA. It is a classic free market approach. The Food and Drug Administration is not the only access to the market. There are alternative approaches, through equally competent and respected scientific organizations that are much more efficient, less costly, and thus far preferable. Individual companies are free to make their own determinations based upon their own scientific expertise; independent academic experts are available; private companies that specialize in GRAS determinations can be used; and FASEB itself has now, after completing the FDA GRAS List Review, agreed to conduct private GRAS evaluations for the food industry. These compete among each other and with FDA. Under the inexorable rules of competition, in a free enterprise environment, the most effective and efficient organization will ultimately be used.

One must question whether leaving these issues to the free market compromises public health and safety. The evidence over the past four decades provides unequivocal testimony that the public health and safety has been fully protected and not in any way compromised. Not a single food substance that has been added to the food supply under a private GRAS determination based on a thorough and well-documented scientific evaluation since 1958 has been taken off the market by FDA because of a public health or safety problem. The program, in short, has been a complete success.

The failure of the food additive approval process during the past four decades scarcely needs further elaboration. It is a closed process within FDA, not subject to public scrutiny even through an FDA advisory committee, and is solely within the control of the agency. Because there is no other lawful route to the marketplace for a food additive or color additive, manufacturers have no alternative but to do whatever FDA commands. And for the same reason, FDA can demand whatever it wishes, with or without sound scientific justification, without fear of peer review, public scrutiny, or accountability to anyone else. The resulting statistics, documented earlier, are the inevitable result.

One might consider retaining such an approach if it produced better results—that is, safer food—than other approaches might achieve. A comparison with the GRAS self-determination approach, however, demonstrates that this is not true. Far more new direct human food substances have been marketed since 1970 after an industry self-determination of GRAS than after FDA approval of a food additive or color additive petition. No product in either category has proved to present a public health hazard. The highly conservative approach of FDA thus contributes nothing more than delay, higher costs to the public for those products that eventually are approved, and a more restricted choice for consumers because the entire process has choked off innovation in this very important field. . . .

NOTES

1. *Congressional Oversight. See* "Delays in the FDA's Food Additive Petition Process and GRAS Affirmation Process," Hearings before the Subcommittee on Human Resources of the Committee of Government Reform and Oversight, House of Representatives, 104th Cong., 1st Sess. (1995); "The FDA Food Additive Review Process: Backlog and Failure to Observe Statutory Deadline," H.R. Rep. No. 104–436, 104th Cong., 1st Sess. (1995).

2. *Update.* In the 5 years since this article was written, FDA has approved only one arguably new direct human food additive or color additive, neotame. 67 Fed. Reg. 45300 (July 9, 2002). Like aspartame, neotame is a derivative of phenylalamine and thus could well have been the subject of a self-determination of GRAS status. Most direct human food additive regulations are obtained for commercial reasons—to satisfy the requests of customers for some type of FDA approval—rather than because they represent a truly unique new technology.

3. *GRAS Notification.* FDA has not yet promulgated its final GRAS notification regulations.

4. *Competitive Objections*. On occasion competitors will object to new food additive regulations in an attempt to maintain a commercial advantage. *E.g.*, 70 Fed. Reg. 15756 (Mar. 29, 2005).

6. FOOD PROCESSING AND PACKAGING SUBSTANCES

More than 10,000 substances are used in proximity with food—*e.g.*, in food packaging, in equipment used to process or store food, in compounds used to clean such equipment—in ways that permit small amounts to migrate to, and become a part of, food. The full premarket approval requirements of the Food Additives Amendment as enacted in 1958 were applicable to food additives that migrate to food from food-contact surfaces. Since 1999, however, premarket approval has been replaced by premarket notification under the amendments enacted as a part of the Food and Drug Administration Modernization Act of 1997.

A migrating food contact material is excluded from food additive classification if it is GRAS or if it is the subject of a prior sanction. Some established packaging materials fall within these exceptions. The basic statutory safety criteria for approval are the same for indirect and direct food additives. Thus, an indirect food additive must be shown, with reasonable certainty, to be safe, and no weight may be accorded the benefits of its use. Similarly, the Delaney Clause applies to indirect food additives. For comprehensive reviews of the regulation of food packaging, see Jerome H. Heckman, *Fathoming Food Packaging Regulation: A Guide to Independent Industry Action*, 42 FOOD DRUG COSM. L.J. 38 (1987); Jerome H. Heckman & Deobrah W. Ziffer, *Fathoming Food Packaging Regulation Revisited*, 56 FOOD AND DRUG L. J. 179 (2001); Jerome H. Heckman, *Food Packaging Regulations in the United States and the European Union*, 42 REG. TOXICOLOGY AND PHARMACOLOGY 96 (2005).

Many household articles come into contact with food. These include pots, pans, cooking and eating utensils, home food preparation machines such as blenders and grinders, plates and glasses, and even the surfaces on which food is often laid during the stages of its preparation, such as counter tops. Generally FDA has chosen not to regulate these articles as food additives. When in the early 1970s the agency learned that high levels of lead were leaching from ceramic pottery into food, however, it initiated a formal compliance program to enforce a limit of 7 ppm on lead migration from pottery to food.

United States v. Articles of Food Consisting . . . of Pottery

370 F. Supp. 371 (E.D. Mich. 1974).

■ FEIKENS, DISTRICT JUDGE.

The United States has filed a Complaint for Forfeiture against: (a) 668 cases, each containing one 20–piece set, of Cathy Rose pattern pottery, (b) 466 cases, each containing one 45–piece set, of Cathy Rose pattern Pottery, and (c) 187 display sets of Cathy Rose pattern pottery. . . . In its Complaint for Forfeiture the government alleges that more than 1,000 sets of pottery dinnerware, each containing plates, bowls, cups, and saucers and intended to be used in the service of foods for human consumption, contain a lead substance. The complaint alleges that some or all of this lead, which is unsafe for human consumption, may migrate from the pottery dinnerware to the food which is being served and thus cause harm.

Intervening defendant, Mount Clemens China Company, ... claims in substance that the pottery is not "food" nor can the lead be considered a "food additive" as those terms are defined in the Act.

Intervening defendant's motions must be denied.... The legislative history leading to the Food Additives Amendment of the Act shows a clear Congressional intent that substances which are subject to being ingested by human beings because of migration are "food additives" and thus "foods" within the meaning of the Act....

COMMENT: HOUSEWARES

Following this decision, FDA proposed in 39 Fed. Reg. 13285 (Apr. 12, 1974) to revoke its longstanding "housewares exemption," a policy of not applying the requirements of the Food Additives Amendment to utensils and other articles used for cooking and eating in the home:

> Since enactment of the Food Additives Amendment of 1958, letters and oral opinions have at times been issued by personnel of the Food and Drug Administration advising that ordinary houseware articles such as cutting boards, pots and pans, and eating utensils, as well as agents used to clean such housewares, are not subject to regulation under section 409....
>
> The definition of a food additive is extremely broad and easily covers all substances which may reasonably be expected to migrate to food from food-contact articles. Section 201(s) provides ... no basis for an exemption for any houseware, food service, or food dispensing article or cleaning agent, and shows clearly that Congress meant to regulate all substances not generally recognized by experts as having been shown to be safe which become or which may reasonably be expected to become, directly or indirectly, a component of any food unless specifically exempted.... Had Congress meant to exempt specific articles such as dinnerware and cooking utensils from the coverage of the act, therefore, it would have been a simple matter for it to do so....
>
> It is not possible to make an accurate determination of the cumulative effect of an additive without taking into account all means by which that additive may reasonably be expected to enter man's diet. Any reports of adverse effects resulting from migration of unsafe chemical additives from articles such as dinnerware and eating utensils would require prompt regulatory action. Therefore, to exempt dinnerware, eating utensils and other housewares, food service, and food dispensing articles which may reasonably be expected to contribute significant amounts of harmful additives at the final and, arguably, most critical stage of food processing (*i.e.*, immediately before being ingested by the consumer) at the very

time when technological advancements have vastly improved methods of detection and evaluation of their effect in man, would be in direct conflict with the express mandate of section 409(c)(5)(B) of the act. . . .

Concern about the burden of processing several hundred food additive petitions caused FDA to vacillate about this proposal and ultimately to withdraw it. 69 Fed. Reg. 68833 (Nov. 26, 2004). FDA has, however, taken regulatory actions against cookware and ceramic dinnerware containing leachable lead or cadmium. *See supra* p. 379.

didn't revoke houseware exemption

―――――

Following enactment of the Food Additives Amendment, it was a matter of dispute whether food packaging material falls within the jurisdiction of the FD&C Act before it is actually used to package food. *See, e.g.,* John G. Kuniholm, *Are Empty Containers Food?*, 15 FOOD DRUG COSM. L.J. 637 (1960). After FDA became aware of the widespread contamination of paper food packaging with PCBs, it took the position that food packaging materials constitute "food" that can be regulated even before they are put to that use. This position was upheld in the case excerpted below.

Natick Paperboard Corp. v. Weinberger

525 F.2d 1103 (1st Cir. 1975).

■ THOMSEN, SENIOR DISTRICT JUDGE. . . .

PCB's are a group of toxic chemical compounds, which find their way into industrial waste, and thence into various products, including recycled paper products. If such a product is used for packaging food, PCB's are likely to migrate into the food unless the food is protected from such migration by an impermeable barrier.

PCB's in food packaging

The affidavits before the district court justify the conclusions that PCB's are toxic, that they tend to migrate from paper packaging material to the contained food by a vapor phase phenomenon, that paper packaging material containing PCB's in excess of 10 ppm is not generally recognized as safe for packaging food for human consumption unless the food is protected from such migration by an impermeable barrier, and that if so used, without such barrier, paper food packaging containing PCB's "may reasonably be expected to result, directly or indirectly, in its becoming a component or otherwise affecting the characteristics of . . . food" within the meaning of sec. 321(s).

Since, therefore, paper food packaging material containing PCB's in excess of 10 ppm will in many instances be an "unsafe food additive" within the meaning of the Act, we proceed to the central issue of this case: whether such material is "adulterated food" under sec. 342 and thus, under sec. 334(a)(1) and (b), subject to seizure by FDA.

issue

. . . Plaintiffs argue that, although PCB's may be introduced into food by migration from the packaging, such introduction is not intentional and therefore the packaging is not "used for components" of food within sec.

321(f)(3). FDA replies that intentional introduction is not required to meet the definition, and refers to the "food additive" definition in sec. 321(s), . . . and to the legislative history. . . .

It would defeat the policy of the Act to require, as plaintiffs contend, that FDA must wait until the unsafe food additive has actually entered or come in contact with food before it can be seized; it is enough that FDA has reasonable cause to expect that the additive will be used in such a way as to enter or otherwise come in contact with food. To wait until actual contamination occurs, in the warehouse of the food processor, on the shelf of a grocery store, or in a family kitchen would effectively deny FDA the means to protect the public from adulterated food.

We do not hold, however, that FDA can properly take steps to seize any and all paperboard containing PCB's in excess of 10 ppm wherever it is located and whatever its intended use may be. The district court properly limited its judgment to paper *food packaging* material. We interpret this to mean that the FDA must be able to prove that any paperboard intended to be seized before it has actually been used as a container for food is either in the hands of the packager of food or in transit to, ordered by, or being produced with the intention that it be sold to a packager of food, or that its intended use otherwise meets the test of sec. 321(s). If the packager or other claimant can show that the food placed in or to be placed in the paper container is or will be insulated from PCB migration by a barrier impermeable to such migration, so that contamination cannot reasonably be expected to occur, the paperboard would not be a food additive and would not be subject to seizure under the Act. . . .

———

With the increasing sensitivity of analytical detection methodology, migration of substances from food-contact articles can be found or reliably predicted at levels as low as 1 part per trillion (ppt) or even lower. As detection methodology improved, FDA was forced to reevaluate both its interpretation of the "may reasonably be expected to result . . . in its becoming a component" phrase in section 201(s) and its application of the safety criteria in section 409.

The following landmark court decision on the interpretation of the statutory definition of food additive, as it applies to materials used in contact with food, involved acrylonitrile copolymers used to fabricate plastic beverage bottles. Acrylonitrile was prior sanctioned for some food packaging uses, *see* 39 Fed. Reg. 38907 (Nov. 4, 1974), 41 Fed. Reg. 23940 (June 14, 1976), and it had also come into wide use in a variety of food contact applications pursuant to food additive regulations issued by FDA. In 40 Fed. Reg. 6489 (Feb. 12, 1975), the agency approved a petition to use the material in the production of bottles for nonalcoholic beverages. The following year, because of increased concern about the potential migration of acrylonitrile into foods, FDA issued an interim food additive regulation pursuant to which it required further toxicological study as a condition of continued approval. 41 Fed. Reg. 23940 (June 14, 1976). The Natural Resources Defense Council (NRDC) filed formal objections, requesting both a stay of the food additive regulation and a formal evidentiary hearing on the safety of acrylonitrile.

In early 1977, after preliminary reports of ongoing toxicological studies suggested that acrylonitrile might be unsafe, FDA stayed the regulation approving the use of acrylonitrile in producing plastic beverage bottles pending evaluation of the tests in progress. 42 Fed. Reg. 13546 (Mar. 11, 1977). The agency claimed it was acting on the basis of the pending NRDC request for a stay. The manufacturers sought review of this order in the Court of Appeals, which concluded, in light of the passage of time between the filing of the NRDC objections and the stay order, that FDA had in fact been acting on its own initiative and was obligated to afford the manufacturing parties an evidentiary hearing. *Monsanto Co. v. Gardner*, Food Drug Cosm. L. Rep. (CCH) ¶ 38,098 (D.C. Cir. 1977).

The agency thereupon convened a formal evidentiary hearing to deal with two principal issues: (1) whether beverage containers fabricated from acrylonitrile copolymers were properly considered food additives and (2) whether such containers had been shown, with reasonable certainty, to be safe. *See* 42 Fed. Reg. 17529 (Apr. 1, 1977). The Commissioner's final decision determined that acrylonitrile was a food additive when used to make plastic beverage bottles and that it had not been shown to be safe for this use. 42 Fed. Reg. 48528 (Sept. 23, 1977); *see* GAO, FOOD ADDITIVE, ACRYLONITRILE, BANNED IN BEVERAGE CONTAINERS, No. HRD–78–9 (Nov. 2, 1977). The manufacturers appealed this decision to the Court of Appeals.

Monsanto Co. v. Kennedy

613 F.2d 947 (D.C. Cir. 1979).

■ LEVENTHAL, CIRCUIT JUDGE.

This case arises on a petition for review of a Final Decision and Order of the Commissioner of Food and Drugs in which he ruled that a substance used to fabricate unbreakable beverage containers, acrylonitrile copolymer, is a "food additive," within the meaning of section 201(s) of the Federal Food, Drug, and Cosmetic Act (the Act)....

The FDA determination that acrylonitrile copolymers used in beverage containers are "food additives" within the statute is based on the finding that such containers invariably retain a residual level of acrylonitrile monomer that has failed to polymerize completely during the manufacturing process and that will migrate from the wall of the container into the beverage under the conditions of intended use. Although the administrative proceedings focused on beverage containers with a residual acrylonitrile monomer (RAN) level equal to or greater than 3.3 parts per million (ppm), the Commissioner made findings and conclusions applicable to all beverage containers manufactured with acrylonitrile, and the Final Order prohibited manufacture of such containers irrespective of their RAN levels....

At the administrative hearing, petitioners introduced results from tests on a newly developed acrylonitrile beverage container having an RAN level of approximately 3.3 ppm. Tests on the container, employing a detection method sensitive to 10 ppb, detected no migration of acrylonitrile monomer. Nevertheless, the administrative law judge found that acrylonitrile copolymer was a "food additive," since migration had been detected from beverage containers composed of the same chemical compounds, though with higher RAN levels than those present in the "new" container....

This case brings into court the second law of thermodynamics, which C. P. Snow used as a paradigm of technical information well understood by all scientists and practically no persons of the culture of humanism and letters. That law leads to a scientifically indisputable prediction that there will be *some* migration of *any* two substances which come in contact. The Commissioner's Final Decision, which upheld the ALJ's determination, is unclear on whether and to what extent reliance was placed on this "diffusion principle" rather than on a meaningful projection from reliable data. At one point in the Final Decision the Commissioner stated: "the migration of any amount of a substance is sufficient to make it a food additive"—a passage evocative of the diffusion principle. Elsewhere, the Commissioner stated that he was able to make a finding of migration based on a projection from actual data—on the assumption that a roughly linear relationship (as a function of time and temperature) existed between the RAN levels in a container and the concentration of acrylonitrile that would migrate into a test fluid. On this premise, though migration from the 3.3 ppm RAN container was itself below the threshold of detectability (10 ppb), it could be projected from the testing data obtained from containers with higher RAN levels.

This was a troublesome aspect of the case. As it was presented to us, the Commissioner had made a projection of migration from 3.3 ppm RAN containers without the support of any actual data showing that migration had occurred from such containers. One of petitioner's experts put it that the relationship might not be linear at very low RAN levels; but this was dismissed by the Commissioner as "speculative." One could not say that the expert's contention of no migration from very low RAN containers was improbable as a concept of physical chemistry, but it was put to us that the validity of this contention could neither be demonstrated nor refuted for 3.3 ppm RAN containers because, under the conditions of intended use, migration was projected to occur in amounts below the threshold of detectability.

... [T]his court requested post-argument memoranda from the parties on whether tests had been performed, or would be feasible, to confirm by actual data the hypothesis that migration occurs from containers with an RAN level of 3.3 ppm. The responses to our inquiry have revealed the probable existence of data unavailable to counsel during the administrative proceedings that bear importantly upon the assumptions made by the Commissioner in reaching his findings and conclusions. This discovery buttressed our earlier conclusion that the Commissioner did not have sufficient support for his decision to apply the "food additive" definition in this case.

In light of the inadequacy of the agency's inquiry and in light of our view that the Commissioner has a greater measure of discretion in applying the statutory definition of "food additive" than he appears to have thought, we remand this proceeding for further consideration.

The proceedings at hand are dramatic testimony to the rapid advance of scientific knowledge in our society. At the time of the administrative proceedings, the lowest concentration of acrylonitrile in a test fluid that could be detected with an acceptable degree of confidence was 10 ppb. There are now analytical techniques available that can detect acrylonitrile concentration of 0.1 ppb, an improvement of two orders of magnitude. Thus, on the issue of migration of acrylonitrile monomer it is now possible to generate "hard" data previously unobtainable.

In his post-argument testimony, Monsanto's expert claims, on the basis of such "hard" data, that the hypothesis which the Commissioner labeled as "speculative" may accurately describe the migration characteristics of containers with very low RAN levels, to wit, that in such containers the acrylonitrile monomer is so firmly affixed within the structure of the copolymer that no migration will occur under the conditions of intended use. If these assertions can be demonstrated to the satisfaction of the Commissioner, a modification of the current regulation is a likely corollary. The actual issuance of a regulation approving the production of a beverage container with an acceptable RAN level would presumably require both a container that had been developed and the appropriate petition. However, the Commissioner would have latitude to issue a statement of policy based upon the results of the proceeding on remand that would specify what in his review was an acceptable RAN level. This would serve a technology-forcing objective.

. . . [W]e turn to certain other important questions that . . . are ripe for resolution.

. . . The statutory definition of "food additive" . . . contains a two part test. First, the *component* element of the definition states that the intended use of the substance must be reasonably expected to result in its becoming a component of any food. Second, the *safety* element of the definition states that the substance must be not *"generally recognized [as] safe* under the conditions of its intended use."

. . . Congress did not intend that the component requirement of a "food additive" would be satisfied by a mere recitation of the diffusion principle, a mere finding of any contact whatever with food. . . .

For the component element of the definition to be satisfied, Congress must have intended the Commissioner to determine with a fair degree of confidence that a substance migrates into food in more than insignificant amounts. We do not suggest that the substance must be toxicologically significant; that aspect is subsumed by the safety element of the definition. Nor is it necessary that the level of migration be significant with reference to the threshold of direct detectability, so long as its presence in food can be predicted on the basis of a meaningful projection from reliable data. Congress has granted to the Commissioner a limited but important area of discretion. Although as a matter of theory the statutory net might sweep within the term "food additive" a single molecule of any substance that finds its way into food, the Commissioner is not required to determine that the component element of the definition has been satisfied by such an exiguous showing. The Commissioner has latitude under particular circumstances to find migration "insignificant" even giving full weight to the public health and welfare concerns that must inform his discretion.

Thus, the Commissioner may determine based on the evidence before him that the level of migration into food of a particular chemical is so negligible as to present no public health or safety concerns, even to assure a wide margin of safety. This authority derives from the administrative discretion, inherent in the statutory scheme, to deal appropriately with *de minimis* situations. However, if the Commissioner declines to define a substance as a "food additive," though it comes within the strictly literal terms of the statutory definition, he must state the reasons for exercising this limited exemption authority. In context, a decision to apply the literal terms of the statute, requires nothing more than a finding that the elements of the "food additive" definition have been satisfied.[27]

In the case at hand, the Commissioner made specific rulings that the component element of the definition was satisfied with respect to acrylonitrile beverage containers having an RAN level of 3.3 ppm or more. These rulings were premised on a projection, based on an extrapolation from reliable data, of migration of acrylonitrile monomer in then-undetectable amounts. In light of the supplementary submission made in response to the post-argument inquiry of this court, we find that the determination can be made for the 3.3 ppm RAN containers with an appropriate degree of confidence, and with the support of the required quantum of evidence.

Turning to the safety element of the definition, the Commissioner determined that the scientific community had insufficient experience with acrylonitrile to form a judgment as to safety. Based on this lack of opinion, the Commissioner made a finding that acrylonitrile was not generally recognized as safe within the meaning of the statute. The Commissioner acted within his discretion in making such a finding, but we note that the underlying premise may be affected, perhaps weakened, perhaps strengthened, with time and greater experience with acrylonitrile. [29] This finding on the safety element will be open to reexamination on remand at the discretion of the Commissioner. He would have latitude to consider whether acrylonitrile is generally recognized as safe at concentrations below a certain threshold, even though he has determined for higher concentrations that in the view of the scientific community acrylonitrile is not generally recognized as safe.

Petitioners also made a claim of discriminatory treatment—that the Commissioner is applying policies in the petitioners' case that have not been applied in other similar circumstances. However, there is no claim that the Commissioner was motivated by discriminatory intention to bring the petitioners before the agency and to focus on their product. Petitioners

---

27. Absent a showing of bad faith or other extraordinary circumstances, a court will not consider meritorious the claim that the Commissioner has abused his discretion in declining to exercise his exemption authority for *de minimis* situations. This is an area of discretion by its nature committed to the informed discretion of the Commissioner.

29. Like the "component" element of the definition, the "safety" element may at times call for more rigorous examination. Thus, the Commissioner has discretion in determining when the statute applies to a given substance, but substances that do fall within its term should be so identified.

came before the agency in the ordinary course. Once the Commissioner undertook scrutiny, he shifted the lens of his microscope to a higher power—but that is no ground for objection, so long as the final action remains within the legitimate scope of discretion. . . .

NOTES

1. *Subsequent Proceedings.* Following its adoption of the "constituents policy" for carcinogenic components of food additives, *infra* p. 1154, FDA reiterated its conclusion that it is reasonable to expect some migration of acrylonitrile to food from plastic nonalcoholic beverage bottles, but at the same time it promulgated a food additive regulation establishing the conditions under which acrylonitrile can safely be used in such bottles. 49 Fed. Reg. 36635 (Sept. 19, 1984). The agency later also approved a food additive regulation for its use in plastic containers of alcoholic beverages. 52 Fed. Reg. 33802 (Sept. 8, 1987). In 55 Fed. Reg. 8476 (Mar. 8, 1990), FDA published an advance notice of proposed rulemaking to obtain public comment on potential revision of the various food additive regulations governing acrylonitrile on the basis of new toxicology data suggesting that the existing regulations do not ensure the continued safe use of acrylonitrile for all regulated and prior-sanctioned food contact applications. After receiving the requested public comment, FDA withdrew the ANPR. 69 Fed. Reg. 68831 (Nov. 26, 2004).

2. *Polyvinyl Chloride.* FDA proposed to restrict the use of polyvinyl chloride as an indirect food additive, based on a determination that this polymer contains residual vinyl chloride monomer, a carcinogen, which migrates to food from packaging materials. 40 Fed. Reg. 40529 (Sept. 3, 1975). FDA proposed to prohibit some food contact uses of polyvinyl chloride and to restrict other uses. Following the *Monsanto* decision and the agency adoption of the constituents' policy, FDA withdrew the September 1975 proposal and proposed new regulations for polyvinyl chloride in 51 Fed. Reg. 4173, 4177 (Feb. 3, 1986), which were later withdrawn in 69 Fed. Reg. 68831 (Nov. 26, 2004).

3. *Structural Similarity.* FDA once revoked its approval for an indirect food additive, based solely on its close chemical relationship to another compound that had caused neurological damage in dogs. 39 Fed. Reg. 13667 (Apr. 16, 1974); 44 Fed. Reg. 34513 (June 15, 1979); 52 Fed. Reg. 33929 (Sept. 9, 1987); 54 Fed. Reg. 7188 (Feb. 17, 1989).

4. *Heat Susceptors.* New technology may force FDA to reevaluate existing requirements for indirect food additives. Following the development of microwave ovens, makers of food packaging began to incorporate "heat susceptor" components into their products. These components resulted in a higher temperature than used in conventional ovens, thus raising the possibility that previously-approved food packaging materials might migrate into food at higher levels than the agency had anticipated or that migrating substances could degrade into unanticipated byproducts. In 54 Fed. Reg. 37340 (Sept. 8, 1989), FDA requested information on the use and safety of this form of packaging. The agency has taken no further action on this matter.

5. *Shopping Bags.* Although shopping bags come in contact with food and thus are within FDA jurisdiction, the agency does not regard food contact for such a short period of time to require regulation. *See* "Degradable Commodity Plastics Procurement and Standards Act of 1989," Hearing before the Senate Committee on Governmental Affairs, 101st Cong., 1st Sess. 21, 23 (1989).

6. *Disposal of Plastic Packaging.* In addition to safety issues, there is public concern about the solid waste problems that plastic packaging materials create. *See,*

e.g., Gordon Graff, *The Looming Crisis in Plastic Waste Disposal*, 4 ISSUES IN SCI. AND TECH., No. 2, at 105 (Winter 1988). Because FDA must consider the environmental consequences of its actions, *see infra* p. 1608, these concerns could become a matter of importance for FDA as well.

COMMENT: THRESHOLD OF REGULATION

For many years, even prior to the 1979 decision in *Monsanto v. Kennedy*, the food packaging industry concluded that migration of a component of food packaging to food at "trace" levels (which ranged at various times from 2 ppm to 2 ppb to the low ppt) should be regarded as "toxicologically insignificant" and thus not subject to the Food Additives Amendment. FDA initially declined to accept this approach, although it acknowledged that some approach to determining a "threshold of regulation" should be established. *See* Jerome H. Heckman, *Fathoming Food Packaging Regulation: A Guide to Independent Industry Action*, 42 FOOD DRUG COSM. L.J. 38 (1987); Alan M. Rulis, *De Minimis and the Threshold of Regulation*, *in* FOOD PROTECTION TECHNOLOGY 29 (C. W. Felix, ed., 1986).

In 1995, FDA decided that a substance migrating to food from a food contact article is exempt from a requirement of a food additive regulation if (1) it is not a carcinogen and (2) it results in dietary concentrations at or below 0.5 ppb. 58 Fed. Reg. 52719 (Oct. 12, 1993), 60 Fed. Reg. 36582 (July 17, 1995), codified at 21 C.F.R. 170.39. The regulations provide for the request for a written FDA exemption, but it is clear that any migration at this low level could also be the subject of a self-determination of GRAS status. *See* M.A. Cheeseman, *Thresholds as a Unifying Theme in Regulatory Toxicology*, 22 FEED ADDITIVES AND CONTAMINANTS, No. 10, at 900 (Oct. 2005).

COMMENT: PREMARKET NOTIFICATION FOR INDIRECT FOOD ADDITIVES SINCE 1999

Acknowledging the deterioration of the FDA food additive approval process, Congress included in the Food and Drug Administrative Modernization Act of 1997 an entirely new approach for handling indirect food additives. Under the 1958 Food Additives Amendment, no distinction was made between direct and indirect food additives. Under section 409(h) of the FD&C Act as added by the 1997 Act, however, a new premarket notification procedure was established for indirect food additives to replace the old premarket approval procedure. The new procedure was the result of a successful negotiation between the regulated industry and FDA.

The new law provides that a manufacturer of an indirect food additive may, at least 120 days prior to shipment, notify FDA of the identity and intended use of the substance and of the manufacturer's determination that it is safe for its intended use. All pertinent scientific information must be submitted with this notification. The notification becomes effective 120 days after its receipt by FDA. The substance may then be shipped unless FDA determines that use of the substance has not been shown to be safe. FDA may also promulgate regulations prescribing a procedure by which the agency may deem a notification to be no longer effective, based on new information. FDA maintains a list of effective food contact notifications on its website and does not publish them in the Federal Register.

Existing indirect food additive regulations continue in effect. The agency may also require that a food additive petition rather than a notification be submitted if it concludes that this is necessary to assure safety. It seems likely, however, that a food additive petition will rarely be required. The GRAS, prior sanction, and threshold of regulation provisions also remain applicable to indirect food additives.

In 2002, FDA promulgated regulations to implement the new procedure. 65 Fed. Reg. 43269 (July 13, 2000), 67 Fed. Reg. 43269 (July 13, 2000), 67 Fed. Reg. 35724 (May 21, 2002), codified at 21 C.F.R. Part 170, Subpart D. Guidance on chemistry and toxicology information to be included in a food contact notification (FCN) were announced in 64 Fed. Reg. 61648 (Nov. 12, 1999) and 67 Fed. Reg. 17703 (Apr. 11, 2002). FDA issued an advance notice of proposed rulemaking on whether the agency should establish regulations permitting a manufacturer to transfer its right to manufacture a food contact substance (FCS) under the new system to others, 67 Fed. Reg. 35764 (May 21, 2002), but later withdrew the notice as unnecessary. 69 Fed. Reg. 58371 (Sept. 30, 2004).

As initially passed by the Senate, the legislation would have included user fees to assure that FDA had sufficient resources to regulate indirect additives. The user fee provisions were deleted by the Conference Committee, which stated that the new procedure would be implemented by appropriated funds but that "implementation is to be triggered only when the FDA receives an appropriation sufficient to fund the program." H.R. Rep. No. 105–399, 105th Cong., 1st Sess. 99 (1997). The agency issued a report to Congress on the anticipated costs of the program and held a public meeting, announced in 64 Fed. Reg. 8577 (Feb 22, 1999), to consider implementation of the new procedure. The required appropriation was enacted on October 22, 1999. The new FCN procedure substantially reduced FDA resources needed to handle indirect food additive petitions.

7. Color Additive Regulation

a. THE 1906 ACT

Official concern about the safety of food colorings surfaced as early as 1900, when Congress appropriated funds for USDA "to investigate the character of proposed food preservatives and coloring matters; to determine their relation to digestion and to health, and to establish the principles which should guide their use." 31 Stat. 191, 196. USDA commissioned Dr. Bernhard Hesse, a German dye expert, to investigate the toxicity of coal tar colors used in food. Dr. Hesse determined that little was known about the safety of the some 695 coal tar colors then available. Following passage of the 1906 Act, USDA acknowledged only seven coal tar colors as safe for use in food. "Dyes, Chemicals, and Preservatives in Food," Food Inspection Decision (FID) No. 76 (June 18, 1907). The department established a program to certify that individual batches of these colors met specifications. "Certificate and Control of Dyes Permissible for Use in Coloring Foods and Foodstuffs," FID No. 77 (Sept. 16, 1907). It was another three years before producers were able to provide colors that qualified for certification. All of these requirements were imposed on the basis of the ongoing work of Dr. Hesse, who eventually published his findings in a remarkable report, COAL TAR COLORS USED IN FOOD PRODUCTS, USDA BUREAU OF CHEMISTRY BULL. No. 147 (1912).

USDA took the position that its certification program was mandatory, but the issue was never tested in court. The agency enforced the safety provisions of the 1906 Act against coal tar color additives by charging a violation of the Act itself rather claiming that a specific additive was not from a certified batch. *E.g., W.B. Wood Mfg. Co. v. United States*, 292 F. 133 (8th Cir. 1923). By 1938, FDA had recognized 15 colors as certifiable for use in food.

NOTE

In *W.B. Wood Mfg. Co. v. United States*, 286 Fed. 84 (7th Cir. 1923), the Court of Appeals concluded that the government failed to show that the amount of arsenic in a coal tar color may be injurious to health, noting that when used in food "one would be required to drink 150,000 bottles of soda before he would have consumed a quantity of arsenic sufficient to equal the 'dose'" ordinarily prescribed by physicians.

b. THE 1938 ACT

Section 406(b) of the original 1938 Act provided that "[t]he Secretary shall promulgate regulations providing for the listing of coal-tar colors which are harmless and suitable for use in foods." ... Following the Act's enactment, unfavorable publicity stemming from the association in the public mind of food colors with "thick, black, sticky" coal tars and from the Delaney Committee's 1950 investigation of the use of chemicals in foods caused FDA to tighten its enforcement of this provision. The agency promulgated regulations that required more animal studies with higher feeding levels before it would certify a color additive. More importantly, it redefined "harmless" to mean "substances incapable of producing harm in test animals in any quantity under any conditions." Under this unrealistic definition, eight color additives were delisted between 1956 and 1960, and the status of 19 others was placed in jeopardy. Pressure for a change in the law grew after the Supreme Court upheld the FDA definition of "harmless" and its ban on three important color additives in *Flemming v. Florida Citrus Exchange*, 358 U.S. 153 (1958).

NOTE

Following the *Florida Citrus Exchange* decision, Congress passed emergency legislation, 73 Stat. 3 (1959), to permit the use of FD&C Red No. 2 to color oranges until September 1961. By then, the Color Additive Amendments had been enacted.

c. THE COLOR ADDITIVE AMENDMENTS OF 1960

In response to the *Florida Citrus Exchange* decision, Congress enacted the Color Additive Amendments of 1960, 74 Stat. 397, codified primarily in section 721 (formerly 706) of the FD&C Act. While the Amendments also apply to substances used to color drugs, devices, and cosmetics, the following discussion focuses on colors that are used in food.

definition

Section 201(t)(1)(B) defines a color additive as any material that, when added to food, is capable of imparting color, "except ... any material which the Secretary, by regulation, determines is used (or intended to be used) solely for a purpose or purposes other than coloring." Soon after the enactment of the Amendments, FDA adopted a regulation limiting the circumstances in which the concluding "except" clause might apply:

> For a material otherwise meeting the definition of "color additive" to be exempt from section 706 of the act, on the basis that it is used (or intended to be used) solely for a purpose or purposes other than coloring, the material must be used in a way that any color imparted is clearly unimportant insofar as the appearance, value, marketability, or consumer acceptability is concerned. (It is not enough to warrant exemption if conditions are such that the primary purpose of the material is other than to impart color.)

26 Fed. Reg. 679 (Jan. 24, 1961), 28 Fed. Reg. 6439 (June 22, 1963), codified at 21 C.F.R. 70.3(g).

The regulatory requirements applicable to color additives resemble those applicable to food additives, with important differences. The Color Additive Amendments require premarket safety testing and FDA approval of all color additives, with no exceptions for GRAS or prior-sanctioned colors. The manufacturer or would-be user of a color additive may petition the agency for the issuance of a regulation permitting the color to be used in food. Before it may approve, or "list," a color additive, FDA must find, with reasonable certainty, that the additive poses no risk to human health, that it accomplishes the intended effect, and that its use will not result in deception of consumers. The agency is authorized to impose restrictions on the use of a color additive to assure that these criteria are satisfied. These restrictions may include limitations on levels of use, a requirement that individual batches of the color be certified by FDA to assure that the color additive used is identical to the substance tested, and specification of the products in which a color may be used.

The Color Additive Amendments contain a Delaney Clause very similar in language to the clause that appears in section 409, which is studied closely in Chapter IX *infra*. Because the Amendments do not recognize any GRAS colors or exclude substances that were sanctioned or used prior to 1960, Section 721 applies to all food coloring agents except those that are only provisionally listed while further safety testing is being conducted.

NOTES

1. *Colors Used in Food Packaging.* Color additives used in food packaging are subject to the food additive provisions of the law. *See, e.g.,* 44 Fed. Reg. 7149 (Feb. 6, 1979); 53 Fed. Reg. 11402 (Apr. 6, 1988).

2. *Colors Used in Pet Food.* Section 721(b)(6) prohibits the listing of colors if the proposed use would "promote deception of the consumer." In 44 Fed. Reg. 28418 (May 15, 1979), FDA denied a petition, previously announced in 42 Fed. Reg. 64440 (Dec. 23, 1977), to prohibit color additives in dog and cat food. The petition alleged that use of color in these products promotes consumer deception by masking the amount of meat these products contain. FDA stated that section 721(b)(6) generally applies "where the use of color cannot be readily discerned and the use of a label declaration of its presence would not prevent deception of the consumer," citing examples used in the legislative history such as the use of color in food to hide a deficiency. The agency found no evidence that use of color in pet food was deceptive. FDA's subsequent denial of a formal evidentiary hearing, 46 Fed. Reg. 7443 (Jan. 23, 1981), was not challenged.

3. *Drugs Used to Color Poultry.* The use of new animal drugs to provide acceptable pigmentation to poultry poses a similar problem. *See, e.g.*, 47 Fed. Reg. 31429 (July 20, 1982), 49 Fed. Reg. 38193 (Sept. 27, 1984).

4. *Deceptive Coloring of Human Food.* Deceptive use of color additives in human food has been a persistent concern. When FDA updated the standards of identity for bakery products, a major issue was the use of color additives, and of colored butter, margarine, and spices, to impart a yellow color to final bakery products that would suggest a higher butter or egg content. After conducting a full administrative hearing, *see* 41 Fed. Reg. 6242 (Feb. 12, 1976); Food Drug Cosm. L. Rep. (CCH) ¶ 38,239 (1979); 48 Fed. Reg. 51448 (Nov. 9, 1983); 49 Fed. Reg. 13690 (Apr. 6, 1984), FDA determined that, except for such color as is naturally present in spices, butter, or margarine, coloring may not be added as such or as part of another ingredient to standardized bakery products. 21 C.F.R. 136.110(c)(16), (17).

5. *Approval by Product Category.* A color additive must have approval for each product category in which it is to be used. For example, an additive approved for cosmetic use cannot be used in a product that is both a cosmetic and a drug until it has also been approved for drug use. *See, e.g., United States v. Eight Unlabeled Cases . . . Cosmetic*, 888 F.2d 945 (2d Cir. 1989); 52 Fed. Reg. 29664 (Aug. 11, 1987). The combination of letters "F," "D," and "C" in the name of a color additive (*e.g.*, D&C Yellow No. 10 or FD&C Red. No. 3) indicates the approved uses for that color.

6. *Power to Allocate Uses.* Section 721(b)(8) authorizes FDA to ration the use of a color additive among competing products if safety data do not establish that exposure from all products would be safe. The only time FDA has considered this provision potentially applicable, it requested submissions on all uses of FD&C Red No. 3 as a first step toward allocating the allowable safe uses if this should become necessary. 52 Fed. Reg. 44485 (Nov. 19, 1987). FDA ultimately did not use this approach, however.

7. *Commentary. See* Alan H. Kaplan, *The Color Additive Amendments of 1960 Revisited*, 22 Food Drug Cosm. L.J. 553 (1967); Winton B. Rankin, *Color Additives*, 13 Food Drug Cosm. L.J. 772 (1958); *Color Additive Amendments of 1960*, 15 Food Drug Cosm. L.J. 432 (1960). *See also* Adam Burrows, *The Palette of Our Palates: A Brief History of Food Coloring and its Regulation* (2006), in Chapter V(I)(4) of the Electronic Book. For a general discussion of the use of color in food, see National Academy of Sciences, Food Colors (1971). For an account of color additive regulation since 1900, see Sheldon Hochheiser, Synthetic Food Colors in the United States: A History Under Regulation (U. Wisc. Ph.D. Thesis 1982).

———

While Congress did not "grandfather" color additives that were already in use in 1960, it did accord them special, though ostensibly temporary, status. Section 203 of the Color Additive Amendments, 74 Stat. 397, 404 (1960), which is not part of the codified FD&C Act, authorized FDA "provisionally" to list colors then in use that were believed to be safe to allow manufacturers time to conduct the kind of toxicological testing required to support approval under the new law. Only colors that were in use in 1960 are eligible for provisional listing. Section 203 of the Amendments makes no provision for adding a post-1960 color to the provisional list to permit continued use while tests are being conducted to resolve new safety questions. FDA has maintained a list of provisionally approved color additives for 45 years, deleting those whose safety came under serious challenge, and permanently listing others as scientific data were submitted to confirm their safety.

Certified Color Manufacturers Association v. Mathews

543 F.2d 284 (D.C. Cir. 1976).

■ WILKEY, CIRCUIT JUDGE.

This appeal is a challenge to the action of the Commissioner of Food and Drugs in terminating provisional approval of the color additive FD&C Red No. 2 pursuant to the Transitional Provisions of the 1960 Color Additives Amendments....

In order to avoid a statutory presumption that all additives not permanently listed at the date of enactment were unsafe, Title II of the Amendments ("Transitional Provisions") provided for the continued use of commercially established additives—such as Red No. 2—on an interim basis. This was allowed only "to the extent consistent with the public health, pending completion of the scientific investigations needed as a basis for making determinations" on the safety of the additive for permanent approval. This provisional listing was to expire on a "closing date" which was established as either 12 January 1963 ("initial closing date"), or such later date as the Commissioner determined. The original closing date could be postponed "if in the [Commissioner's] judgment such action [was] consistent with the objective of carrying to completion in good faith, as soon as reasonably practicable" the investigation needed for making the safety determination.

Throughout this transitional period, while the permanent safety determinations were being made, the Commissioner was granted broad discretionary authority summarily to terminate a provisional listing "forthwith whenever in his judgment such action [was] necessary to protect the public health." During the period following postponement of the closing date, the Commissioner additionally was given broad authority to terminate that postponement "at any time" if he found that, *inter alia*, the basis for the postponement no longer existed because of a change in circumstances....

In the instant case, the Commissioner exercised both of these powers. He terminated the postponement of the closing date of Red No. 2, and additionally terminated its provisional listing.

Red No. 2 is a petroleum derived color additive widely used in this country artificially to create or brighten the white, brown, purple, or red colors of various foods, drugs, and cosmetics.... It has been widely used in this country under federal regulatory control for nearly seventy years. Since the initiation of more sophisticated scientific investigations following enactment of the 1960 Color Additive Amendments, it has failed to receive FDA permanent approval for safety.

Acting pursuant to his authority under the Transitional Provisions, the Commissioner has postponed the closing date a total of fifteen times, either at the request of interested parties or on his own initiative. The most recent postponement occurred 5 January 1976 and was to expire 30 September 1976. A petition for permanent listing pursuant to 21 U.S.C. § 376 has been under active consideration since late 1968, but had not been acted on prior to the action here challenged. At one point the agency was on the verge of affirmatively acting on the petition; before such action could be taken, however, information became available on several studies undertaken in the Soviet Union which raised new concerns over the safety of Red No. 2. One study concluded that amaranth, the generic name for Red No. 2, was poisonous to the reproductive organs of laboratory rats; the remaining studies concluded that amaranth was carcinogenic, that is, it caused cancer.

While FDA scientists questioned the validity of the Soviet tests, the new studies pointed out the absence of information on the effects of Red No. 2 on reproductive physiology and raised concern over its possible carcinogenicity. Accordingly, the FDA undertook its own chronic feeding study over a two-and-one-half year period in which Osborne–Mandel rats were fed Red No. 2 in their diet at concentrations of 3%, 0.3%, 0.003%, and 0%. The duration of that study and the follow-up evaluations have been the primary reason for postponing the closing date of Red No. 2's provisional listing for the last several years....

Following receipt of [a report based on the FDA study concluding that Red No. 2 may be carcinogenic,] on 19 January the Commissioner prepared, and gave notice of intent to publish, a regulation to terminate the provisional listing of Red No. 2....

Appellants ... argue that, under the transitional provision, a postponement of the closing date taken to allow for the evaluation of data for a determination of safety may not be terminated on the basis of a change in "circumstances" when in fact the evaluation has not ceased at the time of termination. While this argument is initially appealing, we believe that it is based on a much too confined interpretation of the statute and of the Commissioner's actions. It will be recalled that the statutory authority to grant a postponement is couched in broad, discretionary language and allows for the interplay of judgmental factors. While the statute speaks in terms of completing the necessary "scientific investigations," there is also a pervasive legislative gloss that the postponement must also be consistent with the protection of the public health....

The primary thrust of appellants' statutory argument is that the standard authorizing the Commissioner to act "forthwith whenever in his judgment such action is necessary to protect the public health" requires that there be an actual threat to the public, amounting for all practical purposes to an imminent health hazard. We believe this argument is without foundation. When Congress has intended so to restrict the discretion available to an agency to take regulatory action similar to that involved here, it has not hesitated to indicate that intent by the inclusion of appropriately restrictive language. Here Congress attached no such "qualifiers" and chose instead to provide for a much broader standard, designed, we think, to allow for precautionary or prophylactic responses to perceived risks....

Our review of the record, in light of the broad discretion conferred on the Commissioner, convinces us that there was no abuse of discretion in terminating the provisional listing of Red No. 2....

NOTES

1. *Subsequent Proceedings.* The FDA denial of the color additive petition for FD&C Red No. 2 was upheld by the Administrative Law Judge after an extended administrative hearing, Food Drug Cosm. L. Rep. (CCH) ¶ 38,168 (1978), and affirmed on appeal by the Commissioner, 45 Fed. Reg. 6252 (Jan. 25, 1980).

2. *Sale of Food Containing Delisted Color.* When it has revoked provisional or permanent listing of a color additive, FDA has generally permitted existing stocks of food products containing the color additive to be marketed and has allowed existing stocks of labeling listing that color additive to be used up even after the prohibited color additive has been removed from the food. *E.g.*, 43 Fed. Reg. 45611 (Oct. 3, 1978) (Orange B); 41 Fed. Reg. 41857 (Sept. 23, 1976) (carbon black); 53 Fed. Reg. 26766, 26768 (July 15, 1988) (D&C Red Nos. 8, 9, and 19, and D&C Orange No. 17). Following FDA's ban of FD&C Red No. 2, however, food containing that color additive was held to be in violation of the Act and was ordered to be destroyed rather than exported even though the color additive remained approved in the country of destination. *See United States v. An Article of Food Consisting of 12 Barrels ... Lumpfish Roe*, 477 F. Supp. 1185 (S.D.N.Y. 1979).

3. *Regulation of Cosmetics.* One explanation for FDA's long delay in resolving the status of color additives on the provisional list was its attempt to use the Color Additive Amendments to strengthen its controls over the safety of cosmetics. Industry challenges to this attempt took nine years to resolve. *See Toilet Goods Ass'n v. Finch*, 419 F.2d 21 (2d Cir. 1969), *infra* p. 1115.

4. *Use Outside Approval.* In *United States v. Eight Unlabeled Cases ... "French Bronze Tablets,"* 888 F.2d 945 (2d Cir. 1989), the Court of Appeals held that a color additive approved for use in food and drugs could not lawfully be used in cosmetics until FDA also approved cosmetic use.

———

Sixteen years after enactment of the Color Additive Amendments, FDA realized that the tests previously conducted on most of the color additives on the provisional list were out-of-date, and it concluded that new testing, using modern protocols, should be required.

Provisionally Listed Color Additives: Notice of Proposed Rulemaking

41 Fed. Reg. 41860 (September 23, 1976).

The Commissioner of Food and Drugs, on [his] own initiative, is proposing to postpone the closing date for the use of certain provisionally listed color additives beyond December 31, 1976. The postponement would be conditioned on the undertaking of appropriate scientific investigations and the submission of data to the Food and Drug Administration (FDA) on a prescribed schedule. . . .

Final determinations have been made on 12 of the 84 provisionally listed color additives on the basis of the Bureau of Foods' review of the petitions seeking "permanent" listing for them. . . . The available data on 20 of [the remaining] 72 provisionally listed color additives are adequate to support final determinations of safety and regulations "permanently" listing the color additives are being prepared. The Commissioner antici-pates that these regulations will be issued before December 31, 1976. The remaining 52 provisionally listed color additives cannot be "permanently" listed at this time because the available data are inadequate to make final determinations. The Commissioner concludes, however, that there are no significant questions of safety regarding any of these 52 color additives, and that continued provisional listing for them presents no risk to the public health. . . .

Proposed § 8.505 would require that each of the petitioners agree in writing within 30 days of the effective date of the regulation to undertake the scientific investigations necessary to permit FDA to make final determi-nations on the color additives, and that the petitioners or other interested persons undertake those scientific investigations, file progress reports with FDA, and submit the final results within fixed time periods prescribed in the regulation. Additionally, the petitioners would be required to notify FDA immediately of any findings that indicate a potential for a color additive to cause adverse effects. . . .

NOTES

1. *Delisting of Red. No. 4.* At the same time it issued this decision, FDA terminated the provisional listing of FD&C Red No. 4 for use in maraschino cherries and ingested drugs. 41 Fed. Reg. 41852 (Sept. 23, 1976). The Commissioner ultimately upheld the Administrative Law Judge's decision sustaining the agency's action. Food Drug Cosm. L. Rep. (CCH) ¶ 38,208 (1978), *aff'd* Food Drug Cosm. L. Rep. (CCH) ¶ 38,238, 48 Fed. Reg. 48533 (Oct. 19, 1983). This left manufacturers of maraschino cherries with a single color capable of producing a stable red color in the product. That color additive, FD&C Red No. 3, was also under attack. *See infra* p. 447.

2. *Red No. 40.* No color has received closer scrutiny than FD&C Red No. 40, whose safety was under intense agency review for several years. *See* 42 Fed. Reg. 8005 (Feb. 8, 1977), 42 Fed. Reg. 61630 (Dec. 6, 1977), 43 Fed. Reg. 18258 (Apr. 28, 1978), 44 Fed. Reg. 30437 (May 25, 1979).

––––––––

Following FDA's final decision to require that most provisionally listed color additives be retested using modern protocols, 42 Fed. Reg. 6992 (Feb. 4, 1977), the Health Research Group began a continuous but unsuccessful effort to force the agency to remove from the market all those colors for which it had concluded that the existing safety data were inadequate.

[handwritten: Health Grap tried to remove]

HRG initially brought suit in 1977, contending that Congress intended that provisional listing could last no longer than two and one-half years. This argument was rejected in *Health Research Group v. Califano*, Food Drug Cosm. L. Rep. (CCH) ¶ 38,125 (D.D.C. 1977). HRG also filed a petition requesting immediate revocation of regulations permanently listing six color additives. 42 Fed. Reg. 33807 (July 1, 1977). This petition was denied on the basis of a detailed analysis of the toxicological information available on each color. 43 Fed. Reg. 54990 (Nov. 24, 1978). On November 21, 1979, FDA by letter denied a subsequent petition for reconsideration. FDA agreed "that the toxicological data previously considered to support the safety of the color additives may be inadequate by modern-day criteria" but stated that this "general finding" is insufficient to require additional studies for these permanently listed colors. HRG did not challenge this decision in court, but in 1980 it again sued FDA, contending that continued provisional listing of any color additive was unlawful. In *McIlwain v. Hayes*, 690 F.2d 1041 (1982), the Court of Appeals upheld the continued provisional listing:

> We hold that the Commissioner's latest extensions for proving the safety of these color additives are within his lawful authority and secretion. Undoubtedly, in 1960 many members of Congress anticipated that color additive testing would be completed more rapidly than has been the case with respect to some additives. Just as certainly, however, Congress foresaw that unavoidable delays were possible and provided a statutory mechanism for the Commissioner to cope with such problems. Most significantly, for the issues in this case, Congress provided no limit upon the number of times postponements could be made....

Judge Mikva dissented:

> Some twenty-two years later, the majority is willing to let the FDA and industry go some more tortured miles to keep color additives that have not been proven safe on the market. The majority has ignored the fact that Congress has spoken on the subject and allows industry to capture in court a victory that it was denied in the legislative arena. The 1960 Color Additive Amendments have been made inoperative by judicial fiat.

Undiscouraged, HRG sued again, contending that the continued provisional listing for color additives found to be carcinogenic in test animals was illegal. This claim was also rejected. *Public Citizen v. Department of HHS*, 632 F. Supp. 220 (D.D.C. 1986), *aff'd sub. nom. Public Citizen v. Young*, 831 F.2d 1108 (D.C. Cir. 1987). The last remaining color additive provisional listing, for FD&C Red No. 3, was terminated in 55 Fed. Reg. 3516 (Feb. 1, 1990), but 16 years later the FD&C lakes (water-insoluble form of the dyes) remain provisionally listed.

COMMENT: FD&C RED NO. 3

The history of FD&C Red No. 3 is complex. The color was permanently listed for food and ingested drug uses in 1969. 34 Fed. Reg. 7446 (May 8, 1969), 34 Fed. Reg. 11542 (July 12, 1969). Its cosmetic and external drug uses were provisionally listed. In 1977, FDA decided to require retesting using modern protocols. When retested, FD&C Red No. 3 was found to be carcinogenic, a conclusion that ordinarily would have triggered cancellation of both the permanent and provisional listings. In 48 Fed. Reg. 45237 (Oct. 4, 1983), however, FDA announced that it was uncertain whether FD&C Red No. 3 was a primary or a secondary carcinogen and that therefore it was seeking the advice of the Board of Scientific Councilors of the National Toxicology Program (NTP). *See generally* "The Regulation by the Department of Health and Human Services of Carcinogenic Color Additives," Hearing before a Subcommittee of the House Committee on Government Operations, 98th Cong., 2d Sess. (1984). Although the NTP report was not officially released, FDA eventually reported that the Board had concluded that the evidence was insufficient to support a determination that FD&C Red No. 3 was a secondary, rather than primary, carcinogen. 52 Fed. Reg. 44485 (Nov. 19, 1987).

In the meantime, FDA had referred the issue to a panel of Public Health Service scientists. *See* 50 Fed. Reg. 26377 (June 26, 1985). The panel concluded that the carcinogenicity of FD&C Red No. 3 is "more likely to be the result of an indirect (secondary) mechanism" and there is "insufficient evidence" of human carcinogenicity "but this possibility cannot be ruled out." *See* 52 Fed. Reg. 29728 (Aug. 11, 1987). Anticipating that it might eventually be required to ration the aggregate uses, FDA requested data on specific uses of FD&C Red No. 3. 52 Fed. Reg. 44485 (Nov. 19, 1987).

Less than two years later, however, FDA announced its intention not to allow time for further testing of FD&C Red No. 3. 54 Fed. Reg. 27640 (June 30, 1989). Within days, the House Appropriations Committee included in its report on the agency's budget the following statement:

> The Committee expects the Food and Drug Administration to provide the technical expertise necessary for the development and design of protocols for a long-term study to determine if the secondary mechanism effect can be confirmed for FD&C Red No. 3. Such study shall be financed by the affected industries. The Committee further expects the Food and Drug Administration to review the results of this study, in addition to any other scientifically-based findings which may emerge, prior to making any decision relating to changes in the provisionally or permanently approved uses of this color.

H.R. REP. NO. 101–137, 101st Cong., 1st Sess. 126 (1989). The Senate Appropriations Committee gave FDA no directions on this matter, S. REP. NO. 101–84, 101st Cong., 1st Sess. (1989), but the Conference report both reproduced the statement from the House report and added:

> The managers on the part of the Senate believe that the FDA should reach its final decision on Red Dye No. 3 solely under the standards of the Food, Drug, and Cosmetic Act (21 U.S.C. 376 and the transitional provisions thereto, 74 Stat. 397–203), and section 10(e) of the Administrative Procedure Act, 5 U.S.C. 706.

H.R. REP. NO. 101–361, 101st Cong., 1st Sess. 34 (1989). During the House debate on the agency's budget, Appropriations Committee Chairman Whitten acknowledged, in a response to Representative Weiss, that the statement in the Committee report did not legally require FDA to retain the provisional listing. 135 CONG. REC. 14943 (July 18, 1989). FDA revoked the provisional listing for FD&C Red No. 3 in cosmetics and external drugs in 55 Fed. Reg. 3516 (Feb. 1, 1990), but has not taken action to revoke the permanent listings for food and ingested drugs in 21 C.F.R. 74.303 and 74.1303.

Under the ingredients labeling provision in section 403(i)(2) as enacted in 1938, all added coloring could be declared in the statement of ingredients simply as "color." However, under the Color Additive Amendments, FDA could impose conditions of use on a listed color, including "directions or other labeling or packaging requirements." FD&C Act 721(b)(3).

FD&C Yellow No. 5: Labeling in Food and Drugs for Human Use

44 Fed. Reg. 37212 (June 26, 1979).

In the FEDERAL REGISTER of May 8, 1969, the Food and Drug Administration (FDA) issued an order listing FD&C Yellow No. 5 (also commonly known as tartrazine) for use in foods under § 74.705 and for use in ingested drugs under § 74.1705. This action was supported by safety data in a color additive petition and other relevant data.... At the time of listing for food and ingested drug use, no specific restrictions were placed on the use of FD&C Yellow No. 5 other than that it be subject to batch certification by FDA.... Because of mounting evidence of allergic-type reactions to FD&C Yellow No. 5, the agency believes it is now appropriate to require that the presence of the color be specifically identified on the label of products in which it is used.

The evidence concerning the relationship between ingestion of FD&C Yellow No. 5 and allergic-type reactions was discussed in the FEDERAL REGISTER of February 4, 1977 (42 FR 6835), when FDA proposed regulations concerning the use of FD&C Yellow No. 5 in foods and ingested drugs. For food, the proposal would require a label declaration for all foods containing FD&C Yellow No. 5. For ingested drugs, however, FDA set forth two alternative proposals. Drug Proposal I was to require a warning statement on the labels of both over the counter (OTC) and prescription drugs. Drug Proposal II was to ban the use of FD&C Yellow No. 5 in certain categories of OTC and prescription drug products frequently used by persons with allergic disorders and to require a warning statement on the labels of all other OTC and prescription drugs containing FD&C Yellow No. 5....

This final rule requires the label of all foods containing FD&C Yellow No. 5 to declare the presence of the color additive as FD&C Yellow No. 5. In the case of drugs, a slightly different label declaration is required. The presence of FD&C Yellow No. 5 must be declared by both names by which it is known (FD&C Yellow No. 5 and tartrazine) for OTC and prescription drug products which are administered orally, nasally, rectally, or vaginally, but not for topical or other externally applied drug products. In addition, labeling for the prescription drug products subject to the rule will be required to contain a precautionary statement on possible allergic reactions to the use of FD&C Yellow No. 5....

Since FD&C Yellow No. 5 was listed for use in food and ingested drugs, evidence has accumulated of allergic-type responses in humans, not rats, caused by ingestion of foods or drugs containing the color. There have been increasing numbers of reports that these responses to FD&C Yellow No. 5 occur primarily in patients who also have aspirin intolerance. The phenomenon of aspirin intolerance in certain persons with underlying allergic disorders, including bronchial asthma, nasal polyposis, vasomotor rhinitis, and skin allergies to various substances, has been known for over 50 years. Both the aspirin and the FD&C Yellow No. 5 reactions are manifested by asthmatic symptoms, urticaria, angioedema, or nasal symptoms....

.... Several comments contended that color additives provide no "benefit" to the public and that their use is purely cosmetic and concluded, therefore, that their use should not be sanctioned by FDA.... Congress has made the judgment that color additives that have been shown to be safe should be permitted in food. The role of FDA under the act is not to make the value judgment about whether color additives are "beneficial," but rather to evaluate the data submitted in support of color additive petitions and to approve for use in foods, drugs, cosmetics, and devices those colors that the agency is reasonably certain are safe. Congress has made the collective judgment that color additives are "beneficial" and should be permitted to be used if shown to be safe...

The primary basis for this action is section 706(b)(3) [now 721(b)(3)] of the Federal Food, Drug, and Cosmetic Act, which provides that regulations for the listing of a color additive shall "prescribe the conditions under which such additive may be safely employed for such use or uses (including, but not limited to ... and directions or other labeling or packaging requirements for such additive)." ...

NOTES

1. *Yellow No. 6.* FDA's efforts to require label declaration of FD&C Yellow No. 6 because of similar allergic reactions were unsuccessful. *See supra* p. 133.

2. *Specific Labeling.* Section 7 of the Nutrition Labeling and Education Act of 1990, 104 Stat. 2353, 2364, amended section 403(i)(2) to provide that only "colors not required to be [batch] certified" can be listed simply as "colorings" in the ingredient statement. Moreover, FDA has interpreted the Act to authorize the agency to require specific identification by name of colors not subject to certification if they are significant allergens.

8.   DIETARY INGREDIENTS IN DIETARY SUPPLEMENTS

Peter Barton Hutt, *Regulation of Food Additives in the United States*

In A. Larry Branen et al., eds., FOOD ADDITIVES, Ch. 8 (2d ed. 2001).

.... Since the 1920s, when dietary supplements were first marketed, FDA and the dietary supplement industry have been in a continuous

regulatory war about both the promotional claims and the safety of these
products. When FDA sought to impose stricter standards for dietary
supplements in the 1960s and early 1970s. Congress enacted the Vitamin–
Mineral Amendments of 1976 to overrule the FDA restrictions. The 1976
Amendments, however, made no change in the safety standards applicable
to dietary supplements.

reg. war re: supplements

   Following enactment of the Nutrition Labeling and Education Act of
1990, FDA sought to use this statutory authority to impose new limitations
for dietary supplements. Ignoring a congressional invitation to establish
separate standards and requirements for dietary supplements, FDA instead
used the new statutory authority to deny all disease prevention claims for
dietary supplements, and threatened to impose stringent food additive
requirements on important dietary supplement ingredients. The dietary
supplement industry marshalled its formidable political power and obtained
enactment of the Dietary Supplement Health and Education Act of 1994,
over the strong objection of FDA. The 1994 Act was the most humiliating
defeat for FDA in its entire history. In addition to broadly defining dietary
supplements and explicitly authorizing strong new claims for these products, Congress exempted the dietary ingredients in dietary supplement
products from the food additive requirements of the FD&C Act and
substituted more flexible food safety provisions that place the burden on
FDA to demonstrate a lack of safety. Old pre-1994 dietary ingredients may
be used in dietary supplement products as long as FDA cannot prove that
they present a significant or unreasonable risk of illness or injury. New
post-1994 dietary ingredients that have not previously been marketed or
present in the food supply are required to be subject to a premarket
notification submitted to FDA at least 75 days before marketing. FDA may
take action against a new dietary ingredient if FDA can prove that the
petition shows that there is inadequate information to provide reasonable
assurance that the ingredient does not present a significant or unreasonable risk of illness or injury. Thus, for this one category of direct food
substances, Congress has repealed the premarket approval requirements of
the 1958 Amendment and replaced it with a premarket notification process.

pre/post 1994

———

   The 1994 Dietary Supplement Health and Education Act (DSHEA)
added section 402(f) to the FD&C Act. This new subsection provides that a
food is adulterated if:

   (1) If it is a dietary supplement or contains a dietary ingredient
   that—

      (A) presents a significant or unreasonable risk of illness or
   injury under—

         (i) conditions of use recommended or suggested in label-
      ing, or

         (ii) if no conditions of use are suggested or recommended
      in the labeling, under ordinary conditions of use;

(B) is a new dietary ingredient for which there is inadequate information to provide reasonable assurance that such ingredient does not present a significant or unreasonable risk of illness or injury;

(C) the Secretary declares to pose an imminent hazard to public health or safety, except that the authority to make such declaration shall not be delegated . . .; or

(D) is or contains a dietary ingredient that renders it adulterated under paragraph (a)(1) under the conditions of use recommended or suggested in the labeling of such dietary supplement.

In any proceeding under this subparagraph, the United States shall bear the burden of proof on each element to show that a dietary supplement is adulterated. The court shall decide any issue under this paragraph on a de novo basis.

NOTES

1. *Limitation to Dietary Ingredients.* The safety provisions of the Dietary Supplement Health and Education Act of 1994 apply only to the dietary ingredients in a dietary supplement, not to the accompanying functional ingredients such as preservatives, fillers, stabilizers, and other components.

2. *Ephedra.* In 1997, based on adverse event reports, FDA proposed to set limits on the use of ephedra in dietary supplements under section 402(f)(1)(A), as added by DSHEA, and to require label warnings under section 403(f). 62 Fed. Reg. 30678 (June 4, 1997). After adverse public comment and a critical report on the proposal, GAO, DIETARY SUPPLEMENTS: UNCERTAINTIES IN ANALYSES UNDERLYING FDA'S PROPOSED RULE ON EPHEDRINE ALKALOIDS (July 1999), FDA withdrew parts of the June 1997 proposal. 65 Fed. Reg. 17474 (Apr. 3, 2000). *See* "How Accurate is the FDA's Monitoring of Supplements Like Ephedra?" Hearing before the House Committee on Government Reform, 106th Cong., 1st Sess. (1999). In 65 Fed. Reg. 17409 (Apr. 3, 2000) and 68 Fed. Reg. 10417 (Mar. 5, 2003) FDA updated the administrative record with new information. *See* "Issues Relating to Ephedra–Containing Dietary Supplements," Hearings before the Subcommittee on Oversight and Investigations and the Subcommittee on Commerce, Trade, and Consumer Protection of the House Committee on Energy and Commerce, 108th Cong., 1st Sess. (2003). In 69 Fed. Reg. 6788 (Feb. 11, 2004), FDA banned the marketing of any dietary supplement containing any amount of ephedrine alkaloids under section 402(f). FDA determined that even the amount of ephedra that it permits in tea bags for making ephedra tea, a conventional food, must be banned from dietary supplements. The agency interpreted the "significant or unreasonable risk" standard in section 402(f)(1)(A) to authorize a benefit-risk determination. On judicial review, the District Court found no scientific basis for banning low levels of ephedra and determined that the benefit-risk approach used by FDA violated the statute. *Nutraceutical Corp. v. Crawford*, 364 F. Supp. 2d 1310 (D. Utah 2005). The Court of Appeals, however, reversed the District Court and upheld the FDA's complete ban of all ephedra. *Nutraceutical Corp. v. Von Eschenbach*, 459 F.3d 1033 (10th Cir. 2006). *See* Donna V. Porter, *Dietary Supplements: Ephedra*, CRS Rep. No. RL 30750 (Aug. 28, 2006).

3. *De Novo Judicial Review.* The final sentence of section 402(f)(1), as added by DSHEA, provides that in a court enforcement action under this provision the court shall decide the issue of adulteration of a dietary supplement "on a de novo

basis." In *NVE Inc.* v. *Department of Health and Human Services*, Food Drug Cosm. L. Rep. (CCH) ¶ 38,847 (3d Cir. 2006) the Court of Appeals held that this provision does not apply to a challenge to rulemaking brought under the Administrative Procedure Act.

4. *New Dietary Ingredients.* A "new dietary ingredient" is defined in section 413(c) as a dietary ingredient that was not marketed in the United States before October 15, 1994, ten days prior to enactment of DSHEA. Under section 413(a)(1), however, a new dietary ingredient is not required to submit a notice to FDA 75 days before marketing if it has been "present in the food supply as an article used for food in a form in which the food has not been chemically altered." In a letter from Lynn A. Larsen, Director, FDA CFSAN Office of Special Nutritionals Division of Programs and Enforcement Policy, to John C. Young (Nov. 20, 1998), FDA took the position that the mere incidental presence of components of a dietary ingredient as inherent components of a food marketed in the United States before October 15, 1994 does not satisfy this requirement. The letter stated that the company would have to show that the dietary ingredient itself has been used as a food or as an ingredient in a food without chemical alteration. The dietary supplement industry, however, interprets this provision to exempt inherent constituents in food from the need for a new dietary ingredient notification. FDA held a public meeting to consider the proper interpretation of this provision, but has not taken further action on the matter. 69 Fed. Reg. 61680 (Oct. 20, 2004) (announcing meeting).

5. *Compared to Food Safety Provisions.* Even with the changes made in the safety provisions applicable to dietary ingredients by DSHEA in 1994, the FD&C Act arguably provides somewhat greater regulatory authority over the safety of dietary supplements than over the safety of conventional food—or at least conventional food containing only GRAS substances. For example, there is no GRAS exception to the required premarket notification of new dietary ingredients, and FDA has authority to declare a dietary supplement but not a conventional food to be an imminent hazard. *See* Peter Barton Hutt, *FDA Statutory Authority to Regulate the Safety of Dietary Supplements*, 31 AM. J. OF LAW & MED. 155 (2005). It is important to remember, however, that dietary ingredients are explicitly excluded from the food additive definition, FD&C Act 201(s)(6), and thus exempted from the requirement of premarket approval. In this respect, FDA has much less authority to regulate the safety of dietary supplements than the safety of conventional foods.

9. ANIMAL DRUG RESIDUES

When a drug is used in a food producing animal (*e.g.*, a cow), some residue of that drug, or a metabolite of the drug, may appear in the food produced by the animal (i.e., the milk or meat). Regulation of animal drugs combines features of both food safety regulation and drug regulation. This subject is considered *infra* Chapter V.

10. GENETICALLY MODIFIED INGREDIENTS

Background information on the development and uses of genetic engineering of food is presented *supra* p. 143 and is not discussed further here. Regulation of the safety of genetically modified food is divided between USDA and FDA. USDA has jurisdiction over the planting of all genetically modified raw agricultural commodities. FDA has jurisdiction to determine whether those commodities, and any other genetically modified food ingredients, may be marketed in the United States.

a. USDA SAFETY REGULATION

Prior to June 2000, USDA regulated agricultural biotechnology under the statutory authority provided by a number of old laws, principally the Plant Quarantine Act of 1912, the Federal Pest Act of 1957, and the Federal Noxious Weed Act of 1974. In June 2000, Congress enacted the Plant Protection Act 114 Stat. 358,438, 7 U.S.C. 7701 *et seq.* as part of the Agriculture Risk Protection Act, to consolidate and supersede these three earlier laws and a number of other related statutory provisions. Accordingly, all USDA authority to regulate agricultural biotechnology is now concentrated in this single new statute. To make certain that there would be no loss of continuity, Congress explicitly provided that regulations issued under the prior statutory authority will remain in effect until USDA issues superseding regulations.

There is very little legislative history for this new statute. Legislation of this type was introduced in the Senate as early as 1995 and was the subject of one Senate hearing in 1999, but it was not otherwise considered. The Plant Protection Act was not included in either the House or the Senate legislation that ultimately became the Agricultural Risk Protection Act of 2000, nor was it added during the floor debate. Instead, it was added during the House–Senate conference. The only provisions in the new Plant Protection Act that specifically relate to biotechnology are the finding in section 7701(2) that biological control is often a desirable means of controlling plant pests and in the expanded definitions included in section 7702. The legislative history clearly states that USDA assisted in the drafting of the legislation, and thus it must be assumed that USDA has concluded that, with the expanded provisions, its authority to regulate agricultural biotechnology is strengthened and clarified under the new statute. Since enactment of the new Plant Protection Act, USDA has not changed either its regulations regarding agricultural biotechnology or the way that it implements those regulations.

In the mid–1980s, USDA published policy statements as part of the U.S. Office of Science and Technology Policy (OSTP) Coordinated Federal Framework for Regulation of Biotechnology. 49 Fed. Reg. 50897 (Dec. 31, 1984); 51 Fed. Reg. 23336 (June 26, 1986). Later, under its prior statutory authority, USDA established regulations that provide two approaches for the introduction (including transportation, development, and field trials) of genetically engineered agricultural plants: (1) a simple notification process for plants that are determined to meet both the six safety requirements and the six performance standards set forth in the regulations, which USDA has concluded are sufficient to assure that there will be no adverse agricultural or environmental impact, and (2) for other genetically engineered plants, a more complex permit process that requires submission of an application to USDA with substantial supporting scientific data, a detailed risk assessment by USDA, and ultimately the requirement by USDA of all conditions appropriate for approval of the permit for field testing. 51 Fed. Reg. 23352 (June 26, 1986); 52 Fed. Reg. 22892 (June 16, 1987). Recognizing the need for transparency, USDA announced that all records of notifications and permits would be publicly available on its website. 60 Fed. Reg. 27490 (May 24, 1995).

COMMENT: PHARMACEUTICAL PLANTS

Scientific advances in biotechnology permit genetic modification of agricultural plants not only to enhance their properties in order to improve their use as traditional food products, but also to produce substances intended for use as active ingredients in pharmaceutical products. In short, agricultural plants are being developed, through genetic engineering, into pharmaceutical plants. The chemical synthesis and biological processing currently performed in large pharmaceutical manufacturing establishments to produce chemical and biological active ingredients may soon also take place in bioengineered crops.

This new use of agricultural plants is neither surprising nor inherently threatening to the American food supply. The current industrial production methods for pharmaceutical active ingredients can be extremely expensive. This is particularly true for biological drugs. Use of agricultural biotechnology to reduce these production costs is therefore a logical and expected approach.

The transformation of agricultural plants through biotechnology into pharmaceutical plants that produce pharmaceutical active ingredients is in its infancy. Scientific development has progressed to the point of small scale field testing of the ability of a few specific agricultural plants to produce desired pharmaceutical active ingredients. These agriculturally-produced active ingredients have not yet been tested in humans, however, let alone been submitted to FDA for ultimate approval as marketed drugs. Because of the substantial economic value of this new approach, however, it can be anticipated that human testing and submission to FDA for marketing approval will occur fairly soon.

It is therefore important that the regulatory controls intended to prevent contamination of food plants by pharmaceutical plants be reviewed and determined to be adequate and appropriate. These regulatory controls should be designed to permit the rapid expansion of the use of agricultural plants to produce pharmaceutical active ingredients while also preventing the contamination of food plants.

Based on information provided by USDA, four food plants are being field tested with genetically engineered organisms that produce pharmaceutical active ingredients: barley, corn, rice, and sugarcane. Thus, the initial experimentation with pharmaceutical plants includes not only nonfood plants like tobacco, but also agricultural plants that have long been used as a source of human food. Without some form of containment, these experimental pharmaceutical plants could contaminate their corresponding food plants.

USDA requires that all pharmaceutical plant field testing be conducted under its more rigorous permit process rather than the simpler notification process. The USDA regulations require agricultural plants with genetically engineered organisms to be contained during interstate movement, while in the receiving facility, and during a field test. The issue that remains is whether, under the general regulations and the specific conditions established in a permit, the containment measures required by USDA are sufficient to prevent cross-contamination between a pharmaceutical plant and a food plant.

Under the permit process, each applicant must propose plant-specific containment measures. The USDA regulations establish only the general requirement that those containment measures be sufficient to prevent contamination, release, and dissemination of the particular plant involved. The USDA scientists then review the permit application and determine whether the proposed containment measures are adequate. Like each applicant's containment proposal, each USDA review and decision is based on a case-by-case risk assessment. USDA has also determined that the biological characteristics of some agricultural plants make them inappropriate for any use as pharmaceutical plants.

In May 2002, USDA issued a summary of containment measures currently used for the four pharmaceutical plants now in field testing. USDA characterizes these as "risk mitigation" measures.

Although the USDA physical containment measures imposed through the permit process are grounded on what the USDA and industry scientists presently believe to be sound scientific principles, they do not constitute a solid barrier, nor does USDA profess that they totally preclude the possibility of contamination. For example, pharmaceutical barley can be planted as close as 500 feet from food barley; pharmaceutical corn can be planted a mile away from food corn; pharmaceutical rice must have border rows of food rice to "dilute" pollen and an isolation distance of 100 feet from food rice; and pharmaceutical sugarcane flowering must be bagged during the anticipated flowering season. Thus, pharmaceutical plants and food plants are explicitly permitted in the same agricultural vicinity. Under these circumstances, the probability of some type of cross-contamination remains significant. Once pharmaceutical plant production proceeds to large scale commercialization, this probability will increase.

Other forms of more severe physical containment could reduce the possibility of cross-contamination. A requirement that field testing be conducted within a greenhouse or other structure would substantially reduce the potential for gene flow. Far greater isolation distances (*e.g.*, 100 miles) could be imposed. USDA could mandate greater use of bagging plants prior to flowering and greater use of guard and border rows. Finally, all pharmaceutical plant material, both before and after growing, could be required to be kept in separately labeled containers wherever they are stored or transported. Other possible measures beyond those presently being used include the use of male sterile lines and a requirement of different flowering times. If biological containment is not utilized, however, contamination of food plants by pharmaceutical plants will occur unless strong physical containment measures are taken.

As a result of well-publicized incidents of cross-contamination, OSTP outlined more stringent containment measures for field testing in 67 Fed. Reg. 50578 (Aug. 2, 2002). The following month, FDA and USDA issued a Draft Guidance on pharmaceutical products derived from genetically modified plants. 67 Fed. Reg. 57828 (Sept. 12, 2002). In 68 Fed. Reg. 11337 (Mar. 10, 2003) USDA tightened controls over field testing of plants genetically engineered to produce pharmaceutical active ingredients or industrial chemicals. However, in *Center for Food Safety v. Johanns*, 451 F. Supp.2d 1165 (D. Haw. 2006), the District Court held that USDA violated both the National Environmental Policy Act and the Endangered Species Act in granting four permits authorizing companies to plant corn and sugarcane that had been genetically modified to produce experimental pharmaceutical active ingredients.

b. FDA SAFETY REGULATION

The history and FDA policy regarding the labeling of genetically modified food is discussed *supra* at p. 143. The initial FDA policy statement, issued in 1986, made it clear that "FDA proposes no new procedures or requirements" for the safety evaluation of genetically modified food ingredients, and it broadly described existing GRAS and food additive provisions. 51 Fed. Reg. 23309 (June 26, 1986). In its subsequent Statement of Policy on Foods Derived from New Plant Varieties, FDA established an unequivocal presumption that a genetically modified version of a raw agricultural commodity would be GRAS, and thus would not require a food additive regulation, absent the introduction of toxic material into the food. 57 Fed. Reg. 22984 (May 29, 1992).

Food and Drug Administration Statement of Policy Foods Derived From New Plant Varieties

57 Fed. Reg. 22984 (May 29, 1992).

. . . .

The United States today has a food supply that is as safe as any in the world. Most foods derived from plants predate the establishment of national food laws, and the safety of these foods has been accepted based on extensive use and experience over many years (or even centuries). Foods derived from new plant varieties are not routinely subjected to scientific tests for safety, although there are exceptions. For example, potatoes are generally tested for the glycoalkaloid solanine. The established practices that plant breeders employ in selecting and developing new varieties of plants, such as chemical analyses, taste testing, and visual analyses, rely primarily on observations of quality, wholesomeness, and agronomic characteristics. Historically, these practices have proven to be reliable for ensuring food safety. The knowledge from this past experience coupled with safe practices in plant breeding has contributed to continuous improvements in the quality, variety, nutritional value, and safety of foods derived from plants modified by a range of traditional and increasingly sophisticated techniques. Based on this record of safe development of new varieties of plants. FDA has not found it necessary to conduct, prior to marketing, routine safety reviews of whole foods derived from plants.

Nevertheless, FDA has ample authority under the act's food safety provisions to regulate and ensure the safety of foods derived from new plant varieties, including plants developed by new techniques.... Under section 402(a)(1) of the act, a food is deemed adulterated and thus unlawful if it bears or contains an added poisonous or deleterious substance that may render the food injurious to health or a naturally occurring substance that is ordinarily injurious. . . .

FDA has relied almost exclusively on section 402(a)(1) of the act to ensure the safety of whole foods. Toxins that occur naturally in food and that render the food ordinarily injurious to health (such as poisons in certain mushrooms), and thus adulterated, rarely required FDA regulatory action because such cases are typically well known and carefully avoided by food producers.

. . . Added substances are subject to the more stringent "may render [the food] injurious" safety standard. . . . The "may render injurious" standard would apply to a naturally occurring toxin in food if the level of the toxin in a new plant variety were increased through traditional plant breeding or some other human intervention. . . .

. . . Until 1958, [402(a)(1)] was the principal tool relied upon by FDA to regulate the safety of food and food ingredients. In 1958, in response to public concern about the increased use of chemicals in foods and food processing and with the support of the food industry, Congress enacted the Food Additives Amendment (the amendment) to the act. Among other provisions, the amendment established a premarket approval requirement for "food additives." . . .

In enacting the amendment, Congress recognized that many substances intentionally added to food do not require a formal premarket review by FDA to assure their safety, either because their safety had been established by a long history of use in food or because the nature of the substances and the information generally available to scientists about the substance are such that the substance simply does not raise a safety concern worthy of premarket review by FDA. Congress thus adopted a two-step definition of "food additive." The first step broadly includes any substance the intended use of which results in its becoming a component of food. The second step, however, excludes from the definition of food additive substances that are GRAS. It is on the basis of the GRAS exception of the "food additive" definition that many ingredients derived from natural sources (such as salt, pepper, vinegar, vegetable oil, and thousands of spices and natural flavors), as well as a host of chemical additives (including some sweeteners, preservatives, and artificial flavors), are able to be lawfully marketed today without having been formally reviewed by FDA and without being the subject of a food additive regulation. The judgment of Congress was that subjecting every intentional additive to FDA premarket review was not necessary to protect public health and would impose an insurmountable burden on FDA and the food industry. . . .

FDA considers the existing statutory authority under sections 402(a)(1) and 409 of the act, and the practical regulatory regime that flows from it, to be fully adequate to ensure the safety of new food ingredients and foods derived from new varieties of plants, regardless of the process by which such foods and ingredients are produced. The existing tools provide this assurance because they impose a clear legal duty on producers to assure the safety of foods they offer to consumers; this legal duty is backed up by strong enforcement powers; and FDA has authority to require premarket review and approval in cases where such review is required to protect public health.

In the Federal Register of June 28, 1986 (51 FR 23302), FDA, in conjunction with the Office of Science and Technology Policy in the Executive Office of the President, described FDA's current food safety authorities and stated the agency's intention to regulate foods produced by new methods, such as recombinant DNA techniques, within the existing statutory and regulatory framework. This notice reaffirms that intention. The following paragraphs explain briefly how the current framework will apply specifically to foods derived from new plant varieties, including plants developed by recombinant DNA techniques. . . .

In regulating foods and their byproducts derived from new plant varieties, FDA intends to use its food additive authority to the extent necessary to protect public health. Specifically, consistent with the statutory definition of "food additive" and the overall design of FDA's current food safety regulatory program, FDA will use section 409 of the act to require food additive petitions in cases where safety questions exist sufficient to warrant formal premarket review by FDA to ensure public health protection.

With respect to transferred genetic material (nucleic acids), generally FDA does not anticipate that transferred genetic material would itself be subject to food additive regulation. Nucleic acids are present in the cells of every living organism, including every plant and animal used for food by humans or animals, and do not raise a safety concern as a component of food. In regulatory terms, such material is presumed to be GRAS. Although the guidance provided [*infra* in this notice] calls for a good understanding of the identity of the genetic material being transferred through genetic modification techniques, FDA does not expect that there will be any serious question about the GRAS status of transferred genetic material.

FDA expects that the intended expression product or products present in foods derived from new plant varieties will typically be proteins or substances produced by the action of protein enzymes, such as carbohydrates, and fats and oils. When the substance present in the food is one that is already present at generally comparable or greater levels in currently consumed foods, there is unlikely to be a safety question sufficient to call into question the presumed GRAS status of such naturally occurring substances and thus warrant formal premarket review and approval by FDA. Likewise, minor variations in molecular structure that do not affect safety would not ordinarily affect the GRAS status of the substances and, thus, would not ordinarily require regulation of the substance as a food additive.

It is possible, however, that the intended expression product in a food cold be a protein, carbohydrate, fat or oil, or other substance that differs significantly in structure, function, or composition from substances found currently in food. Such substances may not be GRAS and may require regulation as a food additive. For example, if a food derived from a new plant variety contains a novel protein sweetener as a result of the genetic modification of the plant, that sweetener would likely require submission of a food additive petition and approval by FDA prior to marketing. FDA invites comments on substances, in addition to proteins, carbohydrates, and fats and oils, that in the future may be introduced into foods by genetic modification. . . .

FDA has long regarded it to be a prudent practice for producers of foods putting new technologies to work cooperatively with the agency to ensure that the new products are safe and comply with applicable legal requirements. It has been the general practice of the food industry to seek informal consultation and cooperation, and this practice should continue with respect to foods produced using the newer techniques of genetic modification. . . .

NOTES

1. *Consultation Process.* FDA issued Consultation Procedures to implement this Statement of Policy in June 1996. FDA has stated that, although consultation is not mandatory, the agency is not aware that any genetically modified food has been marketed in the United States without prior consultation. FDA proposed to make such consultation mandatory in 66 Fed. Reg. 4706 (Jan. 18, 2001), but no further action has been taken on the proposal.

2. *Safety Evaluation.* In 71 Fed. Reg. 35688 (June 21, 2006) FDA announced a final Guidance on Recommendations for the Early Food Safety Evaluation of New Non–Pesticidal Proteins Produced by New Plant Varieties Intended for Food Use.

3. *Genetically Modified Food.* A substantial portion of the current United States food supply is genetically modified or contains a genetically modified ingredient. *See* SUJATHA SANKULA, NATIONAL CENTER FOR FOOD AND AGRICULTURAL POLICY, QUANTIFICATION OF THE IMPACTS ON U.S. AGRICULTURE OF BIOTECHNOLOGY-DERIVED CROPS PLANTED IN 2005 (Dec. 2005). For a discussion of genetically modified corn, see Drew L. Kershen, *Health and Food Safety: The Benefits of Bt–Corn,* 61 FOOD & DRUG L.J. 197 (2006). *See generally* Geoffrey S. Becker & Tadlock Cowan, *Agricultural Biotechnology: Background and Recent Issues,* CRS Rep. No. RL 32809 (Aug. 28, 2006).

4. *Use in Animal Feed.* In 2006, at least 70 percent of the corn and soybean crops fed to farm animals were obtained from genetically modified crops. The Council for Agricultural Science and Technology concluded that this does not present a human or animal safety concern. CAST, *Safety of Meat, Milk, and Eggs from Animal Fed Crops Derived from Modern Biotechnology,* Issue Paper No. 34 (July 2006).

———

The GRAS presumption for genetically modified food, as stated in the May 1992 Federal Register notice excerpted above, was challenged in court.

Alliance for Bio–Integrity v. Shalala

116 F. Supp. 2d 166 (D.D.C. 2000).

■ KOLLAR-KOTELLY, DISTRICT JUDGE. . . .

In their challenge to the FDA's Statement of Policy, Plaintiffs further claim that the Statement of Policy's presumption that rDNA-engineered foods are GRAS violates the GRAS requirements of the Federal Food, Drug, and Cosmetic Act and is therefore arbitrary and capricious....

In the Statement of Policy, FDA indicated that, under § 321(s),

> it is the intended or expected introduction of a substance into food that makes the substance potentially subject to food additive regulation. Thus, in the case of foods derived from new plant varieties, it is the transferred genetic material and the intended expression product or products that could be subject to food additive regulation, if such material or expression products are not GRAS.

Accordingly, FDA reasoned that the only substances added to rDNA engineered foods are nucleic acid proteins, generally recognized as not only safe but also necessary for survival. ("Nucleic acids are present in the cells of every living organism, including every plant and animal used for food by humans or animals, and do not raise a safety concern as a component of food"). Therefore, FDA concluded that rDNA engineered foods should be presumed to be GRAS unless evidence arises to the contrary....

This Court's evaluation of the FDA's interpretation of § 321(s) is framed by *Chevron U.S.A.* v. *Natural Resources Defense Council*....

... To resolve the issue, "the question for the reviewing court is whether the agency's construction of the statute is faithful to its plain meaning, or, if the statute has no plain meaning, whether the agency's interpretation 'is based on a permissible construction of the statute.'" ...

When Congress passed the Food Additives Amendment in 1958, it obviously could not account for the late twentieth-century technologies that would permit the genetic modification of food....

Nonetheless, the statute exempts from regulation as additives substances that are "generally recognized ... to be safe under the conditions of its intended use...." § 321(s). Plaintiffs have not disputed FDA's claim that nucleic acid proteins are generally recognized to be safe. Plaintiffs have argued, however, that significant disagreement exists among scientific experts as to whether or not nucleic acid proteins are generally recognized to be safe when they are used to alter organisms genetically. Having examined the record in this case, the Court cannot say that FDA's decision to accord genetically modified foods a presumption of GRAS status is arbitrary and capricious....

To be generally recognized as safe, a substance must meet two criteria: (1) it must have technical evidence of safety, usually in published scientific studies, and (2) this technical evidence must be generally known and accepted in the scientific community. *See* 21 C.F.R. § 170.30(a-b); 62 Fed. Reg. 18940. Although unanimity among scientists is not required, "a severe conflict among experts ... precludes a finding of general recognition." Plaintiffs have produced several documents showing significant disagreements among scientific experts. However, this Court's review is confined to the record before the agency at the time it made its decision. Therefore, the affidavits submitted by Plaintiffs that are not part of the administrative record will not be considered.

. . . Plaintiffs have failed to convince the Court that the GRAS presumption is inconsistent with the statutory requirements.

NOTES

1. *Existing Regulatory Statutes.* Once biotechnology moved beyond the research stage, its applications were potentially subject to the array of existing statutes designed to protect health and safety. *See* Peter Barton Hutt, *Existing Regulatory Authority to Control the Processes and Products of Biotechnology, in* Banbury Report No. 22 (1985). For other references to statutes available to control biotechnology, see 49 Fed. Reg. 50856, 50859–77 (Dec. 31, 1984); 50 Fed. Reg. 47174, 47177–95 (Nov. 14, 1985); Frances L. McChesney & Reid G. Adler, *Biotechnology Released from the Lab: The Environmental Regulatory Framework*, 13 ENVTL. L. REP. 10366 (1983). For a skeptical assessment of the adequacy of this battery of health and safety laws to control the hazards of biotechnology, see Gregory A. Jaffee, *Inadequacies in the Federal Regulation of Biotechnology*, 11 HARV. ENVTL. L. REV. 491 (1987).

2. *Potential Food Applications.* In February 1988, the FDA Office of Planning and Evaluation and the Center for Food Safety and Applied Nutrition reported that during the previous two years, 155 firms had applied the new scientific principles of biotechnology to the improvement of food or food sources. Experts consulted by FDA identified more than 1200 examples of future food biotechnology advances, most of which were expected to be technically feasible by 1990. FDA, FOOD BIOTECHNOLOGY: PRESENT AND FUTURE, Vol. I (PB88–177–993), Vol. II (PB88–178–009) (Feb.1988). FDA and USDA sponsored a conference on scientific issues associated with the development of transgenic plants intended for food use, 53 Fed. Reg. 28674 (July 29, 1988), and FDA contracted with the Federation of American Societies for Experimental Biology (FASEB) to establish criteria for determining the regulatory status of food and food ingredients produced by new technologies, 53 Fed. Reg. 33182 (Aug. 30, 1988). The biotechnology industry has been criticized on the ground that genetically engineered crops have primarily benefited farmers by controlling weeds and pests but have not produced healthier foods for consumers. *See, e.g.*, Andrew Pollack, *Biotech's Sparse Harvest*, N.Y. TIMES, Feb. 14, 2006, at C1.

3. *Specific Food Applications.* In 51 Fed. Reg. 10571 (Mar. 27, 1986), FDA published a notice of the filing of a GRAS affirmation petition for alpha-analuse enzyme made from recombinant DNA techniques, for use as an ingredient of human food. The first substance made from recombinant DNA processes that FDA approved was chymosin, an enzyme for use in making cheese and other food products, which the agency affirmed as GRAS in 1990. *See* 53 Fed. Reg. 3792 (Feb. 9, 1988), 55 Fed. Reg. 10932 (Mar. 23, 1990), codified at 21 C.F.R. 184.1685. For notices of filings of other GRAS affirmation petitions for substances made from recombinant DNA techniques, *see* 53 Fed. Reg. 5319 (Feb. 23, 1988); 53 Fed. Reg. 16191 (May 5, 1988); 54 Fed. Reg. 20203 (May 10, 1989).

4. *Commentary. See generally* Warren Ausubel, *Federal Regulation of Genetically Engineered Food Additives and Pesticides*, 4 HIGH TECH. L.J. 114 (1989); David T. Bonk, *FDA Regulation of Food and Food Additive Biotechnology*, 43 FOOD DRUG COSM. L.J. 67 (1988); A.S. Clausi, *Interfaces of the Food Industry with Biotechnology*, 40 FOOD DRUG COSM. L.J. 259 (1985); Jeffrey N. Gibbs & Jonathan S. Kahan, *Federal Regulation of Food and Food Additive Biotechnology*, 38 ADMIN. L. REV. 1 (1986); Daniel D. Jones, *Commercialization of Gene Transfer in Food Organisms: A Science–Based Regulatory Model*, 40 FOOD DRUG COSM. L.J. 477 (1985); Daniel D. Jones, *Genetic Engineering in Domestic Food Animals: Legal and Regulatory Considerations*, 38 FOOD DRUG COSM. L.J. 273 (1983); Stephen Paul Mahinka &

Kathleen M. Sanzo, *Biotechnology Litigation and Federal Regulation: Status and Implications*, 42 FOOD DRUG COSM. L.J. 500 (1987); Stephen H. McNamara, *FDA Regulation of Food Substances Produced by New Techniques of Biotechnology*, 42 FOOD DRUG COSM. L.J. 50 (1987); Note, *Regulation of Genetically Engineered Foods Under the Federal Food, Drug, and Cosmetic Act*, 33 AM. U. L. REV. 899 (1984).

5. *Animal Biologicals.* USDA's licensure under the Virus–Serum–Toxin Act of an animal vaccine produced through recombinant DNA technology was the subject of a congressional hearing into whether the department and the company had acted properly. "USDA Licensing of a Genetically Altered Veterinary Vaccine," Joint Hearing Before the Subcommittee on Investigations and Oversight of the House Committee on Science and Technology and the Subcommittee on Department Operations, Research, and Foreign Agriculture of the House Committee on Ariculture, 99th Cong. 2nd Sess. (1986). USDA has undertaken public reviews of genetically engineered animal vaccines. 54 Fed. Reg. 161 (Jan. 4, 1989); 54 Fed. Reg. 9241 (Mar. 6, 1989).

6. *NEPA.* The Foundation on Economic Trends, an organization opposed to any uses of biotechnology that may present the potential for public hazard, has been partially successful in suits to force both research and regulatory agencies to adhere to the procedural requirements of the National Environmental Policy Act (NEPA), but unsuccessful in preventing the underlying experimentation or product approval. *See, e.g., Foundation on Economic Trends v. Lyng*, 817 F.2d 882 (D.C. Cir. 1987); *Foundation on Economic Trends v. Thomas*, 661 F. Supp. 713 (D.D.C. 1986); *Foundation on Economic Trends v. Johnson*, 661 F. Supp. 107 (D.D.C. 1986); *Foundation on Economic Trends v. Heckler*, 756 F.2d 143 (D.C. Cir. 1985). *See also* R. Burns Israelson, *Portrait of a Professional Plaintiff: Jeremy Rifkin's Crusade Against Biotechnology* (1997) and Paul S. Naik, *Jeremy Rifkin: An Examination of the Efforts of an Anit–Biotechnolgy Activist* (1999), in Chapter XII(A) of the Electronic Book.

7. *Congressional Hearings.* Committees of both the Senate and the House have conducted hearings on numerous facets of biotechnology. A sampling of relevant hearings includes "Biotechnology: Vaccine Development," Subcommittee on Oversight and Investigations of the House Committee on Energy and Commerce, 99th Cong. 1st Sess. (1985); "Biotechnology and Agriculture," "The Use of Human Biological Materials in the Development of Biomedical Products," and "Planned Releases of Genetically–Altered Organisms: The Status of Government Research and Regulation," Subcommittee on Investigations and Oversight, House Committee on Science and Technology, 99th Cong., 1st Sess. (1985); " 'Ice–Minus': A Case Study of EPA's Review of Genetically Engineered Microbial Pesticides," and "The Biotechnology Science Coordination Act of 1986," Subcommittee on Oversight and Investigations, House Committee on Science and Technology, 99th Cong. 2d Sess. (1986); "Coordinated Framework for Regulation of Biotechnology," Subcommittee on Investigations and Oversight, on Natural Resources, Agriculture Research and Environment, and on Science Research and Technology, House Committee on Science and Technology, 99th Cong., 2d Sess. (1986); "USDA Licensing of a Genetically Altered Veterinary Vaccine," Joint Hearing before the Subcommittee on Investigations and Oversight, House Committee on Science and Technology, and the Subcommittee on Department Operations, Research, and Foreign Agriculture, House Committee on Agriculture, 99th Cong., 2d Sess. (1986); "The Commercial Development of Medical Biotechnology," Technology Policy Task Force, House Committee on Science, Space, and technology, 100th Cong., 1st Sess. (1987); "The Use and Regulation of Biotechnology in Agriculture," Joint Hearing before the Senate Committee on Agriculture, Nutrition, and Forestry and the Subcommittee on Technology and the Law of the Senate Committee on the Judiciary, 100th Cong., 1st Sess. (1987); "Federal Oversight of Biotechnology," Subcommittee on Hazard-

ous Wastes and Toxic Substances of the Senate Committee on Environment and Public Works, 100th Cong., 1st Sess. (1987); "Field Testing Genetically–Engineered Organisms," Subcommittee on Natural Resources, Agricultural Research and Environment of the House Committee on Science, Space, and Technology, 100th Cong., 2d Sess. (1988); "Biotechnology and Technology Transfer" and "Commercialization of Biotechnology," Subcommittee on Technology and Competitiveness, and "Biotechnology in a Global Economy," Subcommittee on Environment, House Committee on Science, Space, and Technology, 102d Cong., 1st Sess. (1991). For a general summary of issues from the congressional perspective, see "Issues in the Federal Regulation of Biotechnology: From Research to Release," Report Prepared by the Subcommittee on Investigations and Oversight of the House Committee on Science and Technology, 99th Cong., 2d Sess. (1986).

11. RANKING FOOD RISKS

The assessment by FDA officials of the relative hazards posed by the food supply has not changed significantly in the past three decades. Compare the ranking offered in 1972 by Dr. Virgil Wodicka, Director of the agency's Bureau of Foods, with the estimates in 1989 by Dr. Frank Young, Commissioner of Food and Drugs.

Wodicka		Young	
1.	Food-borne disease	1.	Food-borne disease
[2.	Malnutrition]		
3.	Environmental contaminants	2.	Environmental contaminants
4.	Naturally occurring toxins	3.	Naturally occurring toxins
5.	Pesticide residues	4.	Additives
6.	Deliberate additives	5.	Pesticide residues

See Virgil O. Wodicka, *FDA's Objectives in Food Today*, 27 FOOD DRUG COSM. L.J. 59 (1972); Frank E. Young, *Weighing Food Safety Risks*, 23 FDA CONSUMER, No. 7, at 8 (Sept. 1989).

J. THE THREAT OF BIOTERRORISM

Following the attacks of September 11, 2001, Congress became concerned about the security and safety of the American food supply in an era of terrorism. Not only is food susceptible to intentional contamination with pathogenic microorganisms, but it is also susceptible to deliberate sabotage with other highly toxic chemicals.

As part of the Public Health Security and Bioterrorism Preparedness and Response Act of 2002, Congress included several provisions to protect the food supply. 116 Stat. 594, 662–675. Very briefly, the new legislation contained the following authority and requirements for FDA.

1. The President's Council on Food Safety, established by Executive Order No. 13100, was resurrected and directed to develop a crisis communication and education strategy with respect to bioterrorist threats to the food supply.

2. Section 801 of the FD&C Act was amended to place a high priority on increasing the number of FDA inspections and to improve FDA's information management systems related to imported food.

3. Section 304 of the Act was amended to give FDA administrative detention authority for any food that "presents a threat of serious adverse health consequences or death."

4. The existing permissive debarment provisions in section 306 of the Act were expanded to include debarment for repeated or serious food import violations.

5. A new section 415 requires the registration of all food establishments, both domestic and foreign.

6. A new section 414 authorizes FDA to require maintenance and retention of records relating to the manufacture and distribution of food and to allow FDA to inspect records relating to any food that presents a threat of serious adverse health consequences or death.

7. To help FDA manage inspection of imported food, section 801 of the Act was amended to require that FDA be given prior notice of imported food shipments.

8. The import provisions in section 801 of the Act were amended to provide that any food that has been refused admission must be labeled "United States: Refused Entry," and section 402 was amended to prohibit the import of food that has previously been refused admission unless it can be established that the food now complies with the applicable requirements of the Act.

9. FDA is required to provide notices to states regarding any food that presents a threat of serious adverse health consequences or death and is authorized to make grants to states to conduct inspections and other food safety surveillance work.

NOTES

1. *Congressional Hearings.* Congress held hearings on food security immediately after September 11. *See* "Food Safety and Security: Can Our Fractured Food Safety System Rise to the Challenge?," Hearing before the Oversight of Government Management, Restructuring, and the District of Columbia Subcommittee of the Senate Committee on Governmental Affairs, 107th Cong., 1st Sess. (2001). *See also* "Bioterrorism, 2001," Hearings before a Subcommittee of the Senate Committee on Appropriations, 107th Cong., 1st Sess. (2001); "Science of Bioterrorism," Hearing before the House Committee on Science, 107th Cong., 1st Sess. (2001); "Agroterrorism: The Threat to America's Breadbasket," Hearing before the Senate Committee on Governmental Affairs, 108th Cong., 1st Sess. (2003).

2. *Increased Appropriations.* Congress enacted counterterrorism supplemental funding of $151.1 million for FDA in FY 2002, which allowed the agency to hire 673 new employees to improve its capacity to respond to terrorist threats and attacks regarding all FDA-regulated products. More than 60 percent of this supplemental funding was allocated to food. *See* FDA, *FY 2003 Budget Summary* 10–12 (Feb. 2002); "Agriculture, Rural Development, Food and Drug Administration, and Related Agencies Appropriations for 2006," Hearings before a Subcommittee of the House Committee on Appropriations, Part 9, 109th Cong., 1st Sess. 31, 291–293 (2005).

3. *Administrative Detention*. FDA has promulgated regulations governing its new administrative detention authority for food. 68 Fed. Reg. 25242 (May 9, 2003), 69 Fed. Reg. 31659 (June 4, 2004), codified at 21 C.F.R. 1.377 et seq.

4. *Establishment Registration*. FDA has also promulgated food establishment registration regulations. 68 Fed. Reg. 5378 (Feb. 3, 2003), 68 Fed. Reg. 58893 (Oct. 10, 2003) codified at 21 C.F.R. 1.225 et seq. At the request of the food packaging industry, FDA exempted food packaging establishments from the registration requirement.

5. *Food Records*. Regulations regarding the maintenance and inspection of food records, codified at 21 C.F.R. 1.326 et seq., were promulgated in 68 Fed Reg. 25188 (May 9, 2003) and 69 Fed. Reg. 71561 (Dec. 9, 2004).

6. *Prior Notice of Import*. FDA has issued regulations requiring prior notice of imported food shipments. 68 Fed Reg. 5428 (Feb. 3, 2003), 68 Fed. Reg. 58974 (Oct. 10, 2003), codified at 21 C.F.R. 1.276 et seq. Food for which notice prior to importation is not provided within the time specified (2 hours by land, 4 hours by train or air, 8 hours by sea) will not be admitted.

7. *Guidance*. FDA has issued guidance to assist industry compliance with these new requirements.

———

FDA has strongly encouraged the food industry to adopt standard operating procedures to prevent any attempt at bioterrorism. It appears unlikely that widespread intentional contamination of the food supply could be achieved, but small isolated incidents of food tampering would be very difficult to prevent and would result in substantial public alarm.

NOTES

1. *Food Tampering*. Ever since the well-publicized Tylenol poisoning incident, *infra* p. 812, there have been numerous examples of food product tampering. FDA has adopted the policy of not publicizing these incidents for fear that publicity would only encourage copycats. One exception involved the tampering in June 1993 of Diet Pepsi with a syringe containing a needle, an incident in which the perpetrator engaged in substantial publicity. *See United States v. Levine*, 41 F.3d 607 (10th Cir. 1994); *Knight v. FDA*, 938 F. Supp. 710 (D. Kan. 1996). The difficulties in handling product tampering are discussed in Thomas N. Gates & William P. Ward, *Product Tampering—The Dilemma*, 51 J. AFDO, No. 3, at 129 (July 1987).

2. *Tamper-Resistant Packaging*. Although FDA once administered the Poison Prevention Packaging Act, that responsibility was transferred to the Consumer Product Safety Commission by the Consumer Product Safety Act in 1972. Mandatory tamper resistant packaging can be ordered only by the CPSC, not by FDA. *See Nutritional Health Alliance v. FDA*, 318 F.3d 92 (2d Cir. 2003). Many food companies have voluntarily adopted tamper resistant packaging to assure the integrity of their products.

CHAPTER IV

HUMAN DRUGS

A. HISTORICAL BACKGROUND

The Federal Food and Drugs Act of 1906 was the first law providing for national regulation of all human drugs, but Congress had been concerned about the safety and performance of medications for nearly a century. In 1813, it enacted legislation to assure the dissemination of genuine smallpox vaccine. 2 Stat. 806. *See* Rohit K. Singla, *Missed Opportunities: The Vaccine Act of 1813* (1998), in Chapter I(A) of the Electronic Book. In 1902, it enacted legislation to regulate all biological drugs. *See infra* Chapter VI.

Prior federal measures to regulate medical products were not limited to biologicals. In 1848, Congress passed the following law to prevent the importation of "adulterated and spurious drugs and medicines."

> *Be it enacted by the Senate and House of Representatives of the United States of America in Congress assembled,* That from and after the passage of this act, all drugs, medicines, medicinal preparations, including medicinal essential oils, and chemical preparations used wholly or in part as medicine, imported into the United States from abroad, shall, before passing the custom-house, be examined and appraised, as well in reference to their quality, purity, and fitness for medical purposes, as to their value and identity specified in the invoice.

9 Stat. 237 (1848). Although passed overwhelmingly by both the House and Senate, the 1848 Act did not have universal support. During the House debate, Representative Dickinson expressed doubts which forecast arguments that did not receive serious attention until the 1960s:

> Mr. Dickinson said this bill belonged to that class of legislation which attempts to put the bell on the cat. He had no faith in it. The materials would be brought here, and the spurious drugs would be manufactured. If we could stop the compounding of these drugs, interdict patients from taking, and physicians from prescribing, we might do some good. He would not oppose the bill, but he had no faith in this legislation.

Congressional Globe 858 (June 20, 1848). The 1848 law was not supplanted by the 1906 Food and Drugs Act, 36 Op. Att'y Gen. 311 (July 17, 1907), but it ultimately was repealed as part of the enactment of the Tariff Act of 1922, 42 Stat. 858, 989. *See* Angela Walch, *A Spurious Solution to a Genuine Problem: An In–Depth Look at the Import Drugs Act of 1848* (2002), in Chapter I(A) of the Electronic Book; Wesley J. Heath, *America's*

First Drug Regulation Regime: The Rise and Fall of the Import Drug Act of 1848, 59 FOOD DRUG COSM. L.J. 169 (2004).

Peter Barton Hutt, *The Regulation of Drug Products by the United States Food and Drug Administration*

In THE TEXTBOOK OF PHARMACEUTICAL MEDICINE (John P. Griffin & John O'Grady, eds., 5th ed. 2006).

The first legislation to establish comprehensive nationwide regulation of all food and drugs was introduced in Congress in 1879. Largely because regulation of food and drugs was at that time thought to be a matter for state and local control, Congress debated this legislation for 27 years, ultimately enacting the Federal Food and Drugs Act in 1906. This law broadly prohibited any adulteration or misbranding of drugs marketed in interstate commerce. Although it was quite short, and very broad and general in nature, it was extremely progressive for its time and included sufficient authority to permit FDA to take strong enforcement action against the unsafe, ineffective and mislabeled products that flooded the United States market in the late 1800s. Unlike the Biologics Act of 1902, however, it contained no provisions requiring premarket testing or approval for new drug products. An attempt by FDA to obtain this type of authority in 1912 was unsuccessful. Thus, Congress initially provided premarket approval authority for biological drugs but not for other drugs.

premarket testing for biologics only

James C. Munch, *A Half–Century of Drug Control*

11 FOOD DRUG COSMETIC LAW JOURNAL 305 (1956).

... It should be appreciated that much of the educational and preventive work in drug control is reflected in the decrease in the number of legal actions undertaken, following cooperative efforts of industry with the Administration.

Statistical information in [FDA annual] reports from 1907 through 1939 reveals development of control under the 1906 Act. For the ten years 1930 through 1939, there were 12,016 drug imports detained, of a total of 49,402 offered, or 24 per cent. This may be compared with the data for the four years 1909–1912 ... during which there were 1,350 rejections of a total of 1,931 drug imports offered, or approximately 70 per cent. In the early years, enforcement was largely by [criminal] prosecution under section 2: it was necessary to establish rules and regulations for enforcement, and to obtain judicial interpretations of many sections of the Act. Reports show that during the five years 1908–1912, there were 841 prosecutions dealing with drugs, drug products, preparations and medicines, or approximately 25 per cent of the total 3,350 prosecutions. Similar figures for seizure actions under section 10 were not included in these reports. However, greater use was made of the seizure provisions as enforcement continued. During the last ten-year interval of the 1906 Act, from 1930 through 1939, there were 3,201 prosecutions representing drug control, or 36 per cent of the total 8,804 prosecutions, similarly, there were 3,620 seizures, or 23 per cent of the total 15,666 seizures made. In establishing the project system in 1933, one quarter of the time of the field staff was allocated to drug control projects; percentages for the next seven years ranged from 25 per cent to 33 per cent, averaging 29 per cent.

NOTES

1. *Sources on History. See also* James F. Hoge, *The Drug Law in Historical Perspective*, 1 Food Drug. Cosm. L.Q. 48 (1946); Morris L. Yakowitz, *The Evolution of the Drug Laws of the United States 1906–1964*, 19 Food Drug. Cosm. L.J. 296 (1964); Peter Barton Hutt, *Drug Regulation in the United States*, 2 Int'l J. of Tech. Assessment in Health Care 619 (1986). For accounts of problems with drugs that led to the 1938 Act, *see* Morris Fishbein, Fads And Quackery In Healing (1932); Arthur Kallet & Frederick J. Schlink, 100,000,000 Guinea Pigs: Dangers In Every-day Foods, Drugs, And Cosmetics (1933); Arthur J. Cramp, Nostrums And Quackery And Pseudo-Medicine (1936); Ruth Lamb, American Chamber Of Horrors: The Truth About Food And Drugs (1936); James Harvey Young, The Toadstool Millionaires (1961) and The Medical Messiahs (1967).

2. *Supreme Court Support.* Ever since the enactment of the 1906 Act, the United States Supreme Court's decisions have generally supported FDA's drug regulatory policies. *See* Daniel Park Chung, *Ideals and Issues from a Critical View of the Supreme Court's Jurisprudence in FDA Regulation of Human Drugs* (2003), in Chapter I(C) of the Electronic Book.

B.   Definition of "Drug"

The definition of a drug, and in particular the FD&C Act's distinction between a drug and the other products regulated by FDA, is discussed in Chapter II *supra*.

C.   General Requirements for Drugs

1.   Regulation of Therapeutic Claims

Section 502(a) of the FD&C Act provides that a drug "shall be deemed to be misbranded ... if its labeling is false or misleading in any particular." Until 1962, this language, which represented an expansion of the FDA authority that existed under the 1906 Act, formed the primary basis for FDA regulation of therapeutic claims for drugs.

Early efforts to regulate drug claims were hampered by narrow interpretations of the state of medical science and therefore also of the government's authority to regulate claims of therapeutic effectiveness. In the famous case *American School of Magnetic Healing v. McAnnulty*, 187 U.S. 94 (1902), the plaintiff was engaged in the business of healing human diseases through appeals to the mind. A large part of the plaintiff's business consisted of providing "treatment" by letter to people throughout the United States. The Postmaster General directed the local postmaster to return all letters addressed to the school to the original senders with the word "fraudulent" stamped on the outside, and to refuse payment of any postal order drawn to the order of the school. The authority relied on to justify the order was a federal statute, 26 Stat. 465, 466 (1890), granting the Postmaster General discretion to instruct local postmasters to take such preventive steps against any person found to be engaged in a "... scheme or device for obtaining money through the mail by means of false or fraudulent pretenses, representations or promises...."

The plaintiff school sought to enjoin the local postmaster from continuing to comply with the Postmaster General's order. The lower court sustained the local postmaster's demurrer and dismissed the complaint for insufficiency in law and equity. The Supreme Court reversed, however, in an opinion that questioned the government's authority to regulate the truth of therapeutic claims.

> ... Just exactly to what extent the mental condition affects the body, no one can accurately and definitely say.... The claim of the ability to cure may be vastly greater than most men would be ready to admit, and yet those who might deny the existence or virtue of the remedy would only differ in opinion from those who assert it. There is no exact standard of absolute truth by which to prove the assertion false and a fraud. We mean by that to say that the claim of complainants cannot be the subject of proof as of an ordinary fact; it cannot be proved as a fact to be a fraud or false pretense or promise, nor can it properly be said that those who assume to heal bodily ills or infirmities by a resort to this method of cure are guilty of obtaining money under false pretenses, such as are intended in the statutes, which evidently do not assume to deal with mere matters of opinion upon subjects which are not capable of proof as to their falsity....
>
> As the effectiveness of almost any particular method of treatment of disease is, to a more or less extent, a fruitful source of difference of opinion, even though the great majority may be of one way of thinking, the efficacy of any special method is certainly not a matter for the decision of the Postmaster General within these statutes relative to fraud. Unless the question may be reduced to one of fact as distinguished from mere opinion, we think these statutes cannot be invoked for the purpose of stopping the delivery of mail matter....

The Federal Food and Drugs Act of 1906, 34 Stat. 768, prohibited any drug claim that was "... false or misleading in any particular...." The Supreme Court was soon called upon to interpret this provision.

United States v. Johnson

221 U.S. 488 (1911).

■ MR. JUSTICE HOLMES delivered the opinion of the court.

This is an indictment for delivering for shipment from Missouri to Washington, D.C., packages and bottles of medicine bearing labels that stated or implied that the contents were effective in curing cancer, the defendant well knowing that such representations were false....

The question is whether the articles were misbranded within the meaning of § 2 of the Food and Drugs Act of June 30, 1906, making the delivery of misbranded drugs for shipment to any other State or Territory or the District of Columbia a punishable offense.... By § 8, the term misbranded "shall apply to all drugs, or articles of food, ... the package or label of which shall bear any statement, design, or device regarding such article, or the ingredients or substances contained therein, which shall be false or misleading in any particular...."

... [W]e are of opinion that the phrase is aimed not at all possible false statements, but only at such as determine the identity of the article, possibly including its strength, quality and purity, dealt with in § 7.... It should be noticed ... that by § 4 the determination whether an article is misbranded is left to the Bureau of Chemistry of the Department of Agriculture, which is most natural if the question concerns ingredients and kind, but hardly so as to medical effects.

In view of what we have said by way of simple interpretation we think it unnecessary to go into considerations of wider scope. We shall say nothing as to the limits of constitutional power, and but a word as to what Congress was likely to attempt. It was much more likely to regulate commerce in food and drugs with reference to plain matter of fact, so that food and drugs should be what they professed to be, when the kind was stated, than to distort the uses of its constitutional power to establishing criteria in regions where opinions are far apart. *See School of Magnetic Healing v. McAnnulty....*

———

Congress responded to the decision in *Johnson* by enacting the Sherley Amendment to the 1906 Act, 37 Stat. 416 (1912). This amendment added a new provision to section 8 of the Act making "false and fraudulent" claims regarding "curative or therapeutic effect" a misbranding violation. This provision was also promptly reviewed by the Supreme Court.

Seven Cases of Eckman's Alterative v. United States

239 U.S. 510 (1916).

■ MR. JUSTICE HUGHES delivered the opinion of the court.

Libels were filed by the United States, in December 1912, to condemn certain articles of drugs (known as "Eckman's Alterative") as misbranded in violation of § 8 of the Food & Drugs Act.... Section 8 of the Food & Drugs Act, as amended by the act of August 23, 1912, c. 352, 37 Stat. 416, provides, with respect to the misbranding of drugs, as follows:

> ... an article shall ... be deemed to be misbranded. In case of drugs:....

> "Third. If its package or label shall bear or contain any statement, design, or device regarding the curative or therapeutic effect of such article or any of the ingredients or substances contained therein, which is false and fraudulent."

The [Sherley] amendment of 1912 consisted in the addition of paragraph "Third," which is the provision here involved....

... The libel charges that the statement "effective as a preventative for pneumonia" is "false, fraudulent and misleading in this, to-wit, that it conveys the impression to purchasers that said article of drugs can be used as an effective preventative for pneumonia, whereas, in truth and in fact said article of drugs could not be so used"; and that the statement, "we know it has cured" and that it "will cure tuberculosis" is "false, fraudulent and misleading in this, to-wit, that it conveys the impression to purchasers that said article of drugs will cure tuberculosis, or consumption, whereas, in truth and in fact said article of drugs would not cure tuberculosis, or consumption, there being no medicinal substance nor mixture of substances known at present which can be relied upon for the effective treatment or cure of tuberculosis, or consumption." ...

... [T]he statute is attacked upon the ground that it enters the domain of speculation (*American School of Magnetic Healing v. McAnnulty*, 187 U.S. 94 (1902)) and by virtue of consequent uncertainty operates as a deprivation of liberty and property without due process of law in violation of the Fifth Amendment of the Constitution, and does not permit of the laying of a definite charge as required by the Sixth Amendment. We think that this objection proceeds upon a misconstruction of the provision. Congress deliberately excluded the field where there are honest differences of opinion between schools and practitioners. It was, plainly, to leave no doubt upon this point that the words "false *and fraudulent*" were used. This phrase must be taken with its accepted legal meaning, and thus it must be found that the statement contained in the package was put there to accompany the goods with actual intent to deceive—an intent which may be derived from the facts and circumstances, but which must be established.... It is said that the owner has the right to give his views regarding the effect of his drugs. But state of mind is itself a fact, and may be a material fact, and false and fraudulent representations may be made about it.... Congress recognized that there was a wide field in which assertions as to curative effect are in no sense honest expressions of opinion but constitute absolute falsehoods and in the nature of the case can be deemed to have been made only with fraudulent purpose. The amendment of 1912 applies to this field and we have no doubt of its validity....

NOTE

In spite of the difficulties posed by *American School of Magnetic Healing*, the *Johnson* case, and the Sherley Amendment, FDA enforced the drug misbranding provisions of the 1906 Act vigorously and with significant success. *E.g., United States v. Antikamnia Chemical Co.*, 231 U.S. 654 (1914); *Simpson v. United States*, 241 Fed. 841 (6th Cir. 1917); *Abbott Bros. Co. v. United States*, 242 Fed. 751 (7th Cir. 1917); *Hall v. United States*, 267 Fed. 795 (5th Cir. 1920); *United States v. Chichester Chemical Co.*, 298 Fed. 829 (D.C. Cir. 1924); *United States v. John J. Fulton Co.*, 33 F.2d 506 (9th Cir. 1929); *United States v. 17 Bottles ... "B. & M.",* 55 F.2d 264 (D. Md. 1932); *United States v. William H. Rorer, Inc.*, 27 F. Supp. 671 (E.D. Pa. 1936).

When Congress enacted the Federal Food, Drug and Cosmetic Act in 1938, to replace the 1906 Act, it omitted the Sherley Amendment language and reverted to the 1906 Act's original "false or misleading in any particular" standard. FD&C Act 502(a). Importantly, section 201(n) of the FD&C Act provides that, in determining whether labeling or advertising is misleading, "there shall be taken into account . . . not only representations made or suggested . . . but also the extent to which the labeling or advertising fails to reveal facts material in the light of such representations. . . ."

David Cavers, *The Food, Drug and Cosmetic Act of 1938: Its Legislative History and Its Substantive Provisions*

6 Law & Contemporary Problems 2 (1939).

The new Act preserves the broad definition of misbranding contained in the old Act, *viz.*, "false or misleading in any particular." . . . In the old Act, however, this definition was supplemented by a special requirement, applicable to therapeutic claims, which had been added in 1912 by the Sherley Amendment and which compelled proof that claims were both "false *and* fraudulent." This provision in effect accorded a license to the ignorant nostrum vendor who sold inefficacious drugs in good faith. Moreover, fraud is always difficult to prove, and the F & DA was driven to elaborate investigations and costly trials to secure even the seizure of drugs for which outrageous label claims were made. But since the truth or falsity of therapeutic claims must often rest on opinion evidence and since expert opinion may differ, it was felt essential to provide a criterion of opinion evidence sufficiently definite to avoid the risk that the provision would be held unconstitutional for want of certainty. In S. 1944, therefore, the general definition of misbranding was supplemented, as to drugs, by the following: "if its labeling bears any representation, directly or by ambiguity or inference, concerning the effect of such drug which is contrary to the general agreement of medical opinion." Where no such agreement existed, of course the government's burden of proof could not be sustained. With respect to most claims which called for prosecution, general agreement could normally be anticipated, but recognition of the fact that, as to new products, medical opinion might not have crystallized, resulted in the addition, in S. 2000, of an alternative criterion, "demonstrable scientific facts." This was retained in S. 5 as introduced in 1935, and passed by the Senate that year with minor changes. In S. 5, 1937 model, however, the provision was completely eliminated and did not reappear in the bill.

Concern was not felt that this omission would cause constitutional objection in cases where medical opinion agreed, or scientific fact demonstrated, that the claims at issue were false, but the risk that the defendant might produce one or two experts whose opinion ran counter to the greater weight of scientific opinion was still present. The inclusion of section 201(n) in S. 5, as reported by the House Committee in 1938, was thought to meet this difficulty. That section, as may be recalled, requires disclosure of those material facts essential to prevent representations from being misleading. Where claims for a product are not generally supported by medical opinion, the fact that some expert opinion supports them will prevent them from being held false, but unless the prevailing opinion contrary to those claims is disclosed, the labeling can properly be regarded as misleading. Through full disclosure the manufacturer can protect himself against the uncertainties of opinion evidence—and in so doing protect the public as well....

Research Laboratories, Inc. v. United States

167 F.2d 410 (9th Cir. 1948).

■ GARRECHT, CIRCUIT JUDGE....

In November, 1944, a libel was filed in the United States District Court for the Western District of Missouri, Western Division pursuant to which there were seized by the United States Marshal about 600 units of Nue–Ovo, each unit containing three bottles.... Pursuant to the same libel there were also seized at the same time stocks of circulars entitled "information on Nue–Ovo and its value in Arthritic and other Rheumatoid symptoms." ...

Summarized, the [appellant company's] attacks upon the judgment below are as follows:

1. The court below erred in submitting issues to the jury, since every statement in the labeling as to the effectiveness of the product is a statement of opinion, and at the conclusion of the case the record showed nothing more than a difference of opinion among qualified medical experts as to the effectiveness of the product....

3. The court erred in instructing the jury as to the elements to be taken into account in determining whether the labeling is misleading, under 21 U.S.C.A § 321(n), *infra*.

....

It cannot be assumed that the Supreme Court [in *McAnnulty*] intended to reach out a dead hand over the power of Congress to pass legislation in the future setting up a well-equipped Federal agency capable of arriving at a professional conclusion as to the adulteration or misbranding of drugs "when introduced into or while in interstate commerce." In the *McAnnulty* case the court not only pointed out that "as the case arises on demurrer, all material facts averred in the bill are, of course, admitted," but throughout the opinion doubt was expressed as to the qualifications of a *postmaster general* to pass on medical questions....

In contrast to the meager technical facilities for the determination of medical questions possessed by the Postmaster General—at least at the time that the *McAnnulty* case was decided—we find that the Federal Security Agency [the agency encompassing FDA] has at its disposal almost unlimited professional resources with which to carry out its investigations in the enforcement of the Federal Food, Drug, and Cosmetic Act....

Much of the appellee's evidence in the instant case consisted of "controlled clinical studies" conducted by eminently qualified physicians and surgeons....

Testimony of experts that is based upon tests or experiments made by them does not come within the ambit of the *McAnnulty* rule. . . .

It is generally agreed that testimony as to the consensus of medical opinion may [also] be considered in drug-misbranding cases. . . .

In this circuit and elsewhere, it has been held that expert testimony even in its broadest sense—i.e., where the witness has neither tested the product nor purports to report the consensus of medical opinion—is admissible on the question of therapeutic value. . . .

The evidence in this case included the three types that we have discussed hereinabove: Testimony by experts based on (a) tests made of the product itself; (b) the consensus of medical opinion as to the various ingredients used in Nue–Ovo; and (c) the expert witnesses' personal opinions regarding the effectiveness of such ingredients. Altogether, there was ample evidence to support the verdict of the jury. . . .

It is well settled that the 1938 act was intended to make the provisions against misbranding stricter and not more lenient than they had been in pre-existing laws. The new statute was not designed to provide the misbrander of drugs with additional technical loopholes for escape, but to batten down those already existing. . . .

. . . The appellant contends that "the instant libels make no general charge of misbranding under which the appellee is entitled to rely upon Section 201(n) of the Act, (21 U.S.C.A. § 321(n)) supra," but that the present charge is "merely that the product is not effective." . . .

In making this attack upon the court's instruction as to the subsection in question, the appellant seems to forget the half-truths in the labeling to which we have referred in a preceding section herein. [T]hough the appellant announced in its label that its "Analysis of Ingredients" was based chiefly on the United States Dispensatory, the Pharmacopoeia, and various textbooks, and although it did indeed quote verbatim from some of these authorities, it unfairly omitted unfavorable comments regarding some of Nue–Ovo's ingredients.

It was to cover precisely such tricky omissions and suppressions that Section 321(n) was designed.

Furthermore, in *any* case where "an article is alleged to be misbranded because the labeling is misleading" in *any* respect, it is made mandatory by § 321(n) itself that the jury "shall" take into account such omissions or suppressions. . . .

Accordingly, it was not only not erroneous for the court to instruct the jury on § 321(n), but, under the facts of this case and under the terms of the subsection itself, it was the court's duty to do so. . . .

NOTES

1. *Disclaimers. Research Laboratories* demonstrates that FDA may proceed against misleading claims of therapeutic value masquerading as assertions of opinion. Cases decided under the 1938 Act hold that deception may result from label statements that are technically accurate but misleading in overall impression. Thus,

a disclaimer may not be availing. For example, the statement "this preparation does not contain any known therapeutically useful constituent," did not prevent a finding of misbranding in *Pasadena Research Laboratories v. United States*, 169 F.2d 375 (9th Cir. 1948).

2. *Deceptive Names.* The name of a product may imply a claim of effectiveness that, if false, may render it misbranded. In one case, the use of the term "prophylactics" was sufficient to support the government's seizure upon a finding that several of the claimant's articles contained holes. *United States v. 43 1/2 Gross . . . "Xcello's Prophylactics,"* 65 F. Supp. 534 (D. Minn. 1946), *infra* p. 1273.

3. *Attributed Claims.* Even under the 1906 Act (following passage of the Sherley Amendment), a manufacturer could not escape by attributing false representations of a drug's effectiveness to third parties. In *United States v. John J. Fulton Co.*, 33 F.2d 506 (9th Cir. 1929), for example, the manufacturer claimed only that "we have received many letters from physicians reporting" success with this drug. The court characterized such labeling as even more obnoxious than false express claims of therapeutic benefit.

4. *Symptoms v. Underlying Conditions.* Another common deception has been found in labeling for products capable of treating minor ailments such as constipation, whose labeling also proclaims an ability to relieve symptoms that accompany more serious conditions for which the product is of no use whatever. *United States v. Six Dozen Bottles . . . "Dr. Peter's Kuriko,"* 158 F.2d 667 (7th Cir. 1947).

5. *Section 201(n).* In addition to providing support for FDA enforcement proceedings based on section 502(a), section 201(n) has become significant as a supplementary source of authority for regulations imposing affirmative disclosure requirements. *See National Nutritional Foods Association v. Califano, infra* p. 1579; *Cosmetic, Toiletry and Fragrance Association, Inc. v. Schmidt*, 409 F. Supp. 57 (D.D.C. 1976). For a discussion of the origin of section 201(n), see Edward Brown Williams, *Failure to Reveal Material Facts in Labeling*, 3 FOOD DRUG. COSM. L.Q. 64 (1948).

6. *Case Law.* Cases involving false or misleading drug claims under the 1938 Act are legion. Some of the more colorful include *United States v. 11 1/4 Dozen Packages . . . "Mrs. Moffat's Shoo Fly Powders for Drunkenness,"* 40 F. Supp. 208 (W.D.N.Y. 1941); *Empire Oil & Gas Corp. v. United States*, 136 F.2d 868 (9th Cir. 1943); *Pasadena Research Laboratories, Inc. v. United States*, 169 F.2d 375 (9th Cir. 1948); *Colusa Remedy Co. v. United States*, 176 F.2d 554 (8th Cir. 1949); *United States v. Hoxsey Cancer Clinic*, 198 F.2d 273 (5th Cir. 1952); *United States v. Wier*, 281 F.2d 850 (5th Cir. 1960); *United States v. 4 Cases Slim–Mint Chewing Gum*, 300 F.2d 144 (7th Cir. 1962).

7. *Internet Sites.* Any information on a company-sponsored website is regarded by FDA as labeling, advertising, or both. In order to avoid FDA scrutiny of foreign website information that may contain uses not approved in the United States, there should be a prominent disclosure that the information on the website applies only to the foreign country or countries and is not intended for United States audiences. Where there is a substantial difference between approved uses for a specific drug, there should be no direct link between the United States website and the foreign website.

8. *Commentary. See* Alan H. Kaplan, *Therapeutic Claims and the Federal Government*, 11 FOOD DRUG. COSM. L.J. 219 (1956); John G. Kuniholm, *Constitutional Limitations on the Regulation of Therapeutic Claims under 1938 Federal Food, Drug, and Cosmetic Act*, 9 FOOD DRUG. COSM. L.J. 629 (1954).

COMMENT: CURRENT FDA ENFORCEMENT STRATEGY

Court enforcement of section 502(a) no longer plays a major role in FDA's efforts to combat false or misleading therapeutic claims for drugs because the Drug Amendments of 1962 require premarket proof of the effectiveness of all "new drugs," including new drugs marketed prior to 1962. For all post-1962 prescription drugs, FDA has controlled therapeutic claims through the new drug approval process, where it may force a manufacturer to recast or omit proposed labeling claims before allowing a drug to be marketed. Claims for nonprescription drugs are subject to FDA regulation under the OTC Drug Review, *infra* p. 788. For both prescription and OTC drugs, FDA court enforcement actions since 1962 have uniformly charged a violation of the new drug provisions of the Act, rather than, or occasionally in addition to, the misbranding provisions. A claim that a drug is a new drug marketed without an FDA-approved New Drug Application (NDA) can be sustained based on affidavits that the drug is not *generally recognized* as safe and effective for the claims made. The court need not adjudicate the validity of the claims themselves. *See infra* p. 590.

FDA's use of its licensing authority to regulate label claims in advance of marketing, however, has not obviated scrutiny of the claims made for drugs once they are marketed. FDA has focused its attention on claims made in prescription drug advertising which, under section 502(n) as enacted by the Drug Amendments of 1962, falls within its jurisdiction. One of the agency's remedies has been to require the manufacturer to disseminate "corrective" advertisements through the same channels (usually another advertisement or a letter to physicians) as the original message. Very rarely has it gone to court. Whether correction is necessary and what form it should take are questions ordinarily worked out in private negotiations between FDA and the manufacturer. FDA's regulation of prescription drug advertising is considered in more detail at *infra* pp. 535 & 555. FDA lacks jurisdiction over the advertising of OTC drugs, which is the province of the FTC.

Recognizing that it cannot take action against all illegal drug claims, FDA in Compliance Policy Guide No. 7150.12 (Dec. 14, 1978) established the following priorities for initiating legal action against drug "quackery": (1) direct health hazard, (2) indirect health hazard, (3) major economic frauds, and (4) minor economic cheats.

Although section 502(j) of the Act provides that a drug is misbranded if it is dangerous to health when used in accordance with its labeling, FDA has seldom invoked this provision, because violations of other overlapping sections are easier to prove. A case that applies this section is *United States v. 62 Packages ... Marmola Prescription Tablets*, 142 F.2d 107 (7th Cir. 1944).

COMMENT: COMPETITOR SUITS TO CONTEST PRODUCT CLAIMS

Not infrequently a company finds that competitors are making claims that are false or misleading, including claims making unjustified comparison against the company's own product. There are a limited number of actions that the company can take to contest such claims.

1. *Complain to FDA.* One option is to bring the matter to the attention of FDA and request that the agency take appropriate regulatory action. Unfortunately, even in egregious cases, FDA often replies that it has very few resources and that this type of competitive problem is a low priority for the agency. If FDA does take action, it is almost always limited to a warning letter, and the competitive claim usually remains in place for a lengthy period of time.

2. *Complain to the FTC.* As with the FDA, it is not easy to persuade the FTC to challenge a competitive claim. Even if the FTC ultimately decides to act, it may take months to persuade the agency and much longer before final agency action occurs.

3. *Complain to the NAD.* The National Advertising Division of the Better Business Bureau conducts a program under which the company may initiate a proceeding in which the NAD reviews the competitive claim and offers an opinion on it. In most instances, the party making the competitive claim will comply with the NAD opinion. If it does not, the NAD will then refer the matter to the FTC or the FDA, where it receives a much higher priority than if the complaining company went to these agencies in the first place. An NAD proceeding can, however, take several months, during which the competitor may continue to make the claim. *See generally* Jeffrey S. Edelstein, *Self–Regulation of Advertising: An Alternative to Litigation and Government Action*, 43 IDEA: THE J. OF LAW AND TECH. 509 (2003).

4. *Complain to the Broadcast Media.* A complaint to the broadcast media can produce faster action if the matter is clear-cut. The FTC has been known to include advertising agencies and broadcast companies in false advertising proceedings. The media must therefore take seriously complaints about clearly misleading advertising.

5. *A Lanham Act Lawsuit.* Finally, the company may have a cause of action against a competitor under section 43(a) of the Lanham Act, 15 U.S.C. 1125(a). The Lanham Act provides a private right of action for unfair competition based on false or misleading claims in labeling or advertising. It does not provide a remedy for failure to adhere to the FD&C Act or FDA regulations per se, but it does offer a strong remedy against false or misleading competitive claims. *E.g., Zeneca Inc. v. Eli Lilly and Co.*, 1999 WL 509471 (S.D.N.Y. 1999). *But see Pfizer, Inc. v. Miles, Inc.*, 868 F. Supp. 437 (D. Conn. 1994). *See* Paul Lantieri, *Regulating Food and Drug Companies Privately: A Review of Lanham Act Cases Brought Against FDA–Regulated Products* (2001), and Jessica L. Turko, *The Lanham Act and the FD&C Act: Shaping the Law of False Advertising Into a Tool for Drug Manufacturers to Self–Regulate Their Industry and Protect Consumers* (2001), in Chapter II(T) of the Electronic Book.

2. PRESCRIPTION DRUG LABELING

a. THE DEFINITIONS OF "LABEL" AND "LABELING"

The definitions of "label" and "labeling" in the FD&C Act apply to food, drugs, devices, and cosmetics without differentiation. Thus the *Kordel* and *Urbuteit* cases, *supra* p. 99, are germane to the statutory requirements examined in this chapter. Indeed, most of the cases that have dealt with the scope of the Act's requirements for "labeling" have involved drugs.

b. ADEQUATE DIRECTIONS FOR USE

Section 502(f)(1) of the FD&C Act requires that the labeling of a drug bear "adequate directions for use."

Alberty Food Products Co. v. United States

185 F.2d 321 (9th Cir. 1950).

■ Bone, Circuit Judge.

Appellee filed a libel under which it seized appellant's drug here involved (33 bottles of Ri–Co Tablets) charging therein that the drug was "misbranded" in violation of 21 U.S.C. § 352(f)(1) of the Federal Food, Drug, and Cosmetic Act.... The specific ground of complaint was that the "labeling" of the drug failed to bear adequate directions for use since it did not state the purpose or condition for which the drug was intended. The only directions for use on the label attached to the bottle read as follows: "Three tablets with a cupful of hot water. Take four times daily. Before meals and on going to bed."

At the hearing below two newspaper advertisements from daily publications in large cities were introduced. These ads show that appellant's drug was there represented and recommended by appellant [f]or use in the treatment, mitigation, and cure of arthritis and rheumatism....

Appellant appeared as claimant of the drug and filed exceptions to the libel. In essence the exceptions were that the Act does not require the labeling of a drug to state the disease condition for which it is to be used. In this connection it contended that the misbranding here charged was merely a failure to include upon the label of the container information to consumers which was not required by the Act to be included thereon either as directions for its use or otherwise....

[A]ppellant relied exclusively upon ... "outside sources," namely, the newspaper advertisements, to provide all of the information which could possibly enlighten prospective purchasers of its drug concerning "the conditions" for which the drug was to be used by them.

As we understand the doctrine announced in [*Kordel* and *Urbeteit*, *supra* p. 99] it is that where literature [containing statements relative to the use and efficacy of drugs] is shipped in interstate commerce and distributed to consumers as part of an integrated distribution program, the literature which thus accompanies the drug and is distributed with it, constitutes an essential supplement to the label attached to the package containing the drug although this literature may have been shipped separately and at a different time than the drug.

... Appellant did not resort to the distribution of any sort of "literature" to ultimate purchasers as a "supplement" to its package label. Neither did it distribute such "literature" to purchasers, actual or prospective, to promote sales and to describe and advertise the therapeutic qualities of its drug. Appellant used only the newspaper advertisements and we think that it cannot be said that these advertisements "accompanied" appellant's drug into interstate commerce, and were "distributed" by vendors, or otherwise, to ultimate purchasers of the drug as part of an "integrated distribution program." . . .

What we have already said leads us to disagree with appellant's contention that by employing these "remote" newspaper advertisements it fully supplied a legally adequate "labeling" which described the *use* of the drug in the treatment or alleviation of arthritic or rheumatic conditions. It seems to us that supporting appellant's views would be a long and drastic step toward nullifying what we regard as salutary protective features of the act which Congress designed to control and regulate the sale of drugs to a helpless public—helpless because it is uninformed. . . . The logic of the *Kordel* and *Urbuteit* cases would seem to repel the conclusion that the therapeutic claims made only in random newspaper advertisements, *must* be considered and deemed to be a part of, and to be "accompanying" and "supplementing," the brief dosage statement appearing on the bottles containing appellant's drug. . . .

. . . We proceed upon the assumption that the "adequate directions for use" mandate of Sec. 352(f)(1) requires that *all* who might want to use a drug to relieve the pains of arthritis and rheumatism are at least entitled to a chance to somewhere find and examine a "label" which is complete enough to give them information which would lead them to purchase a drug for that purpose, or, in other words, provide sufficient information at the time of purchase upon which intelligent determination might be made as to whether the drug is one which is prescribed, recommended, or suggested for their particular form of arthritic or rheumatic ailment. We are persuaded that the law requires this much.

Can't hold: info on label insufficient

NOTES

1. *Relevance of Advertising Claims.* In a later proceeding, *Alberty Food Products v. United States*, 194 F.2d 463 (9th Cir. 1952), the company unsuccessfully argued that, if directions for use contained in advertising are insufficient to satisfy section 502(f)(1), advertising claims similarly cannot be considered in determining the intended uses of a drug for which the labeling must bear adequate directions. The Court of Appeals responded:

> . . . It is asserted by appellants that a consideration by the trial court of . . . advertisements is an invasion of a field exclusively under the jurisdiction of the Federal Trade Commission, which has control of false advertising. This contention fails to grasp the scope and purpose of the inquiry with which the Court was concerned. It is not the truth or falsity of the literature and advertising which is challenged; it is merely consideration, as evidence, of claims promulgated by the manufacturer in measuring whether the information communicated by means of the label adequately describes the diseases or conditions for which the drug was intended as well as relevant facts containing dosage.
>
> In order for the labeling of a drug to bear "adequate directions for use" within the meaning of 21 U.S.C. § 352(f)(1) it must, among other things, state the purposes and conditions for which the drug was intended

and sufficient information to enable a layman to intelligently and safely attempt self medication.

While appellants agree with this construction they argue that such fact must be determined from the labeling alone. This contention is without merit. It is not sufficient that the labeling contain a minimum of information and the use of the drug be induced by elaborate collateral representations. To permit the operation of such an escape valve would render the aims and purposes of labeling requirements nugatory....

2. *FDA's "Squeeze Play."* If Alberty had sought to comply with section 502(f)(1) by including indications for arthritis and rheumatism in its labeling for Ri–Co Tablets, FDA would then have claimed that the product was misbranded under section 502(a). The FDA approach reflected in this case has come to be referred to as the "squeeze play." For additional examples of the "squeeze play," *see V.E. Irons, Inc. v. United States*, 244 F.2d 34 (1st Cir. 1957); *United States v. Hohensee*, 243 F.2d 367 (3d Cir. 1957); *United States v. 38 Dozen Bottles ... Tryptacin*, 114 F. Supp. 461 (D. Minn. 1953). *See also* Arthur A. Dickerman, *"Adequate Directions for Use,"* 7 FOOD DRUG. COSM. L.J. 738 (1952); Carson Gray Frailey, *Observations on Section* 502(f)(1), 3 FOOD DRUG. COSM. L.Q. 255 (1948); Charles L. Nelson, *Control of Advertising by Section* 502(f)(1), 7 FOOD DRUG. COSM. L.J. 579 (1952).

3. *Relation to New Drug Provisions.* Just like section 502(a), reliance on section 502(f)(1) in FDA court enforcement proceedings has been largely superseded by allegations based on the new drug provisions of the Act. *United States v. Articles of Drug*, 625 F.2d 665 (5th Cir. 1980), is thus unusual for a post-1962 case, because there FDA successfully charged a violation of section 502(f)(1), as interpreted in 21 C.F.R. 201.5, rather than of section 505, the provision forbidding the introduction of an unapproved new drug into interstate commerce. As the agency explained, because it had seized the products before they were shipped in interstate commerce, it could not bring a new drug charge. Under these circumstances, state authorities may also take action. *E.g., Demarco v. Commonwealth of Pennsylvania*, 397 A.2d 61 (Pa. Commw. Ct. 1979). The limitation of section 505 to the introduction of an article into interstate commerce similarly compels FDA to resort to the misbranding and adulteration provisions of section 501 and section 502 when bringing an action against a person selling or distributing a drug solely within a state. *See, e.g., U.S. v. Courtney*, 362 F.3d 497 (8th Cir. 2004) (criminal charges of adulteration and misbranding brought against a pharmacist who diluted chemotherapy drugs).

United States v. Article of Drug ... Designated B–Complex Cholinos Capsules

362 F.2d 923 (3d Cir. 1966).

■ KIRKPATRICK, DISTRICT JUDGE.

... The misbranding charged by the Government was that the labeling of the products was not in compliance with section 352(f)(1) of the Act in that it failed to bear "adequate directions for use." The appellant, Foods Plus, Inc., the manufacturer and owner of the seized articles, filed a claim for them in the District Court.... The trial judge found as a fact that the articles seized (which comprised various quantities of some 43 different formulas of vitamin, mineral and other dietary preparations) were drugs—a finding not now disputed.

The labeling in this case consisted of a catalog of the vitamin and mineral products offered for sale by the claimant, it having been stipulated that its catalogs were labels within the meaning of the Act.

Whether labeling contains "adequate directions for use" of an article necessarily depends upon what it is intended to be used for. In this case, although the catalogs were in a general way suggestive of therapeutic values for the products, they contained nothing whatever to indicate for what diseases or conditions the various preparations were supposed to be beneficial and, in consequence, nothing to show how they were to be used or administered. . . . The Government undertook to show that the claimant intended its vitamin products to be used as medicaments for the prevention, mitigation or cure of various diseases in man, and the Court made a finding to that effect. Whether the evidence was sufficient to support the finding is the point upon which this case turns.

The evidence consisted mainly of transcripts of a series of radio broadcasts by one Carlton Fredericks whom the claimant described in its catalog as an "internationally prominent nutritionist." The broadcasts were commentaries covering the general subject of public health, principally in the field of nutrition, with heavy emphasis being placed upon the therapeutic value of vitamins and of food products fortified by vitamins, the central idea being that many of the ills of man, from simple malaise to serious disease, can be beneficially treated by the use of vitamins and minerals as dietary supplements.

Neither Foods Plus, Inc., nor the trade name of any of its products was mentioned in any of the Fredericks broadcasts. However, advertisements of Foods Plus vitamins were presented in commercials, some of which immediately succeeded the Fredericks programs. Whenever a listener responded to Fredericks' broadcast invitations to write to him for nutritional information, advice or literature, the claimant, which had Fredericks under contract to turn over to it all such letters, would send the listener its catalog.

Fredericks' picture, together with a statement of his academic degree and his fame as a nutritionist, appeared on the first page of the catalog as well as the fact that he was the claimant's "Chief Consultant" and that he had "scientifically formulated the exclusive formulas in this catalog" and that he personally endorsed the product. In addition to the above, it was in evidence that he was employed by the claimant by written agreement as its consultant to (among other things) "aid in the sale and promotion of the products of Foods Plus." . . .

Upon evidence of the foregoing facts, the Court found that there existed a close relationship between Fredericks and the claimant, that the claimant adopted as its own representation Fredericks' broadcast claims that vitamins were efficacious for the prevention and treatment of human disease, and that the claimant intended its products to be used for the purposes recommended by Fredericks. The facts were practically undisputed and we find no reason to disturb the inference drawn from them by the trial judge or the conclusion that the articles seized in this section were misbranded as alleged in the libel. . . .

The appellant sees in the decision of the lower court an expansion of the power and jurisdiction of the Food and Drug Administration into areas of free speech and expresses the fear that such ruling would make independent commentaries broadcast over the radio subject to regulatory control by government agencies. It would seem that this argument is based upon a misconception of what is here decided. There is nothing new or alarming in a ruling that statements made by a lecturer employed by a party and adopted by that party as its own representations may be taken in a civil action as evidence of that party's intention as to matters in which the intention is a material issue. Nor does the fact the representations were made in a radio broadcast affect the situation. . . .

appellant; free speech

NOTES

1. *FDA Authority Over OTC Drug Advertising.* Pursued to its extreme, this decision would allow FDA to regulate all therapeutic claims made in advertising for nonprescription drugs. Its practical effect is limited, however, because FDA and the FTC have agreed that the FTC has primary jurisdiction over advertising, *supra* pp. 98 & 275, and FDA therefore no longer brings cases of this kind.

2. *Interpretive Regulations.* FDA's current regulation interpreting section 502(f)(1), 21 C.F.R. 201.5, provides:

> "Adequate directions for use" means directions under which the layman can use a drug safely and for the purposes for which it is intended . . . Directions for use may be inadequate because, among other reasons, of omission, in whole or in part, or incorrect specification of:
>
> (a) Statements of all conditions, purposes, or uses for which such drug is intended, including conditions, purposes, or uses for which it is prescribed, recommended, or suggested in its oral, written, printed, or graphic advertising, and conditions, purposes, or uses for which the drug is commonly used; except that such statements shall not refer to conditions, uses, or purposes for which the drug can be safely used only under the supervision of a practitioner licensed by law and for which it is advertised solely to such practitioner. . . .

3. *Use of Foreign Languages.* All mandatory drug labeling must appear in English. 21 C.F.R. 201.15(c)(1). Foreign languages are optional, but some have argued that they should be mandatory. *See* Kimberly A. Yahr, *Foreign–Language Labeling of Food and Drugs in the Wake of Ramirez v. Plough Inc.: Is an Official Language the Solution for America?* (1994), Keila M. Legree, *Ser O No Seas: A Non–Prescription Drug Manufacturers Duty to Warn in a Foreign Language* (1996), and Ryan Arai, *English is Not Enough: The Language of Food and Drug Labels* (2002), in Chapter VI(D)(3) of the Electronic Book.

c.   PHYSICIAN LABELING

As a direct consequence of the statutory requirement of adequate directions for use, FDA requires a prescription drug manufacturer to prepare an information sheet for the physician containing, in one place, a summary of all information known about the drug. From 1938 to 1962 this physician labeling was relatively short and simple. Since 1962, the physician labeling has become much longer and more complex. Once FDA and the courts made it clear that all marketed prescription drugs required some form of NDA, FDA gained complete control over the labeling. Section

505(b)(1)(F) requires every NDA to contain the proposed labeling for the new drug, and section 505(d)(7) authorizes FDA to disapprove an NDA if the labeling is false or misleading in any particular. Moreover, the FDA-approved physician labeling constitutes the bounds of permissible advertising for the drug.

Because of the central importance of the physician labeling, FDA, the medical profession, and the pharmaceutical industry have focused substantial attention on the appropriate form and content of this information. The agency conducted a major revision of its requirements in 39 Fed. Reg. 8964 (Mar. 7, 1974), 40 Fed. Reg. 15392 (Apr. 7, 1975), 44 Fed. Reg. 37434 (June 26, 1979). It recently revised these requirements again. 65 Fed. Reg. 81082 (Dec. 22, 2000), 71 Fed. Reg. 3922 (Jan. 24, 2006), codified at 21 C.F.R. 201.56–7. In 71 Fed. Reg. 3999 (Jan. 24, 2006), FDA announced the availability of two guidances: CLINICAL STUDIES SECTION OF LABELING FOR HUMAN PRESCRIPTION DRUG AND BIOLOGICAL PRODUCTS—CONTENT AND FORMAT and ADVERSE REACTIONS SECTION OF LABELING FOR HUMAN PRESCRIPTION DRUG AND BIOLOGICAL PRODUCTS—CONTENT AND FORMAT. In 71 Fed. Reg. 3998 (Jan. 24, 2006), the agency announced the availability of two draft guidances: LABELING FOR HUMAN PRESCRIPTION DRUG AND BIOLOGICAL PRODUCTS—IMPLEMENTING THE NEW CONTENT AND FORMAT REQUIREMENTS and WARNINGS AND PRECAUTIONS, CONTRAINDICATIONS, AND BOXED WARNINGS SECTIONS OF LABELING FOR HUMAN PRESCRIPTION DRUG AND BIOLOGICAL PRODUCTS—CONTENT AND FORMAT. The January 2006 regulations are to be phased in for all prescription drugs through June 2013.

Among the more important features of the January 2006 revisions in the physician labeling regulations are the requirement of a "highlights" section at the beginning of the insert, which is limited to one-half page; a requirement of a table of contents for the full prescribing information that must list all of the headings and subheadings; a requirement that FDA-approved patient labeling must either be reprinted at the end of the insert or accompany the insert; detailed requirements for format and font size; and a statement by the agency in the preamble to the final rule that FDA labeling requirements are intended to preempt conflicting state law requirements, whether these state requirements arise by statute, administrative rule, or product liability actions. The agency's preemption statement is discussed *infra* p. 1495.

NOTES

1. *FDA Approval of Drug Labeling. See* Richard A. Merrill, *Compensation for Prescription Drug Injuries*, 59 VA. L. REV. 1 (1973):

> The FDA not only decides whether a drug may be marketed, it also determines how it may be promoted and sold. The agency approves, and for practical purposes prescribes, the labeling that the drug must bear. The label typically includes information concerning dosages, directions for administration, conditions for which the drug is effective, contraindications (disease conditions in which the drug may be harmful), and warnings about known or suspected side effects and adverse reactions. In this critical part of the approval process the FDA attempts to refine and articulate its initial weighing of hazards and benefits. It believes, and indeed tort law assumes,

that the information conveyed by the labeling will effectively control the use of a drug and thereby limit risks and enhance benefits ...

2. *Physician's Desk Reference.* In *United States v. Abbott Laboratories*, 1965–1968 FDLI Jud. Rec. 315 (N.D. Ill. 1968), a prosecution for misbranding, FDA charged that the information about a drug that the defendants supplied to the *Physician's Desk Reference* was not "substantially the same" as the FDA-approved package insert, as required by agency regulations. The District Court held that the *PDR* is labeling and upheld the FDA regulations against a variety of attacks, but it concluded that FDA had failed to prove beyond a reasonable doubt that the *PDR* monograph differed significantly from the approved labeling in this case. The regulations were subsequently changed to require that all such labeling contain "the same" information as the approved physician labeling. 33 Fed. Reg. 10283 (July 18, 1968), 33 Fed. Reg. 15023 (Oct. 8, 1968), codified at 21 C.F.R. 201.100(d)(2).

3. *Bar Code on Drug Labels.* In 68 Fed. Reg. 12500 (Mar. 14, 2003), 69 Fed. Reg. 9120 (Feb. 26, 2004), 21 C.F.R. 201.25, FDA required the labels of drugs used in hospitals to bear a bar code that contains at least the product's National Drug Code (NDC) number in order to reduce medication errors. FDA issued GUIDANCE FOR INDUSTRY: BAR CODE LABEL REQUIREMENTS—QUESTIONS AND ANSWERS in 71 Fed. Reg. 24856 (Apr. 27, 2006), 71 Fed. Reg. 58739 (Oct. 5, 2006).

4. *Trademark for Misbranded Drug.* In a trademark suit, plaintiff alleged that its brand name Supra was infringed by defendant's brand name Suprax. The District Court granted defendant's motion for summary judgment on the ground that plaintiff's drug was misbranded in violation of the FD&C Act. *Erva Pharmaceuticals, Inc. v. American Cyanamid Co.*, 755 F. Supp. 36 (D.P.R. 1991).

d. LIMITATION TO PRESCRIPTION SALE

Until the end of the 19th century, professional pharmacists dominated the compounding of drugs and had equal status with physicians in prescribing their use. In the late 1800s, however, two groups arose to challenge this authority. Commercial firms were organized to manufacture and sell drug products, usually without prescription. Organized medicine also began to assert itself, contending that only licensed physicians were qualified to prescribe drugs, as part of the practice of medicine.

Federal laws enacted by Congress to regulate drugs during the 19th century and the first half of the 20th century were designed to assure the integrity of drug products and did not address the prescription/nonprescription issue. The legislative histories of the Vaccine Act of 1813 and the Import Drugs Act of 1848 reveal a congressional concern only with the quality of the drugs made available to the Americans public. Under the Biologics Act of 1902 and the Federal Food and Drugs Act of 1906, the status of a drug as prescription or nonprescription was left entirely to the manufacturer. Even in the FD&C Act of 1938, Congress made no attempt to resolve this matter. Only in the Harrison Narcotic Act of 1914 and subsequent statutes controlling narcotics did Congress specifically designate drugs as available only on the prescription of a licensed physician.

FDA invented the concept of mandatory prescription status in regulations promulgated in 1938. Congress subsequently confirmed FDA's policy in the Durham–Humphrey Amendments of 1951. Like the requirement of physician labeling, the requirement of a physician prescription was the direct consequence of the statutory requirement of adequate directions for use.

Peter Temin, *The Origin of Compulsory Drug Prescriptions*

22 JOURNAL OF LAW & ECONOMICS 91 (1979).

. . . The FDA promulgated regulations to enforce the [FD&C Act] before the end of 1938. And among these regulations were those making clear the scope of the exemption from labeling requirements set forth in section 502(f) of the act. . . . The FDA said a shipment or delivery of a drug or device was exempt from these requirements:

> If the label of such drug or device bears the statement *"Caution: To be used only by or on the prescription of a* _____*"* (the blank to be filled in by the word *'Physician,' 'Dentist,'* or *'Veterinarian,'* or any combination of such words), and all representations or suggestions contained in the labeling thereof with respect to the conditions for which such drug or device is to be used appear only in such medical terms as are not likely to be understood by the ordinary individual, and if such shipment or delivery is made for use exclusively by, or on the prescription of, physicians, dentists, or veterinarians licensed by law to administer or apply such drug or device; but such exemption shall expire when such shipment or delivery, or any part thereof, is offered or sold or otherwise disposed of for any use other than by or on the prescription of such a physician, dentist, or veterinarian. [3 Fed. Reg. 3168 (Dec. 28, 1938)]. . . .

The act said elsewhere (section 503) that drugs sold by prescription were exempt from the labeling requirements, but it did not say which drugs were to be sold by prescription or that there were any drugs that could not be sold without a prescription. This regulation is different. It says that drugs with certain kinds of labels—*"Warning . . ."*—can only be sold by prescription. It allows the drug companies to create a class of drugs that cannot legally be sold without a prescription by putting the appropriate label on them.

This is a stunning change in the ways drugs were to be sold. Before this regulation took effect, consumers could get any nonnarcotic drug they desired without going to see a doctor. . . . After this regulation became effective, the consumer could no longer buy some drugs without seeing a doctor first and getting his approval. Which drugs were now beyond the consumer's reach? The drug companies would decide, although the FDA could sue them for mislabeling if it disagreed with their choices. The consumers became passive recipients of this decision. . . .

The FDA's assumptions were new to the drug market. Had they arisen from a change in the technology of producing drugs, from the availability of many new and complex drugs? The answer is no. The drug revolution came after 1938. . . . The FDA's *Annual Report* for 1939 identifies the regulation as the result of "an administrative conclusion of some moment." The conclusion resulted from a conflict the FDA saw within the new law. On the one hand, the law said that all drugs must be labeled adequately, adding that any drug that was dangerous to health when used as the label suggested was automatically misbranded. On the other hand, the report asserted, "Many drugs of great value to the physician are dangerous in the hands of those unskilled in the uses of drugs. The statute obviously was not intended to deprive the medical profession of potent but valuable medicaments."

The conflict was created by the assumption underlying the first of the two sentences quoted. The FDA assumed that adequate directions for self-medication could not be written for some drugs. The reasons for this assumption are not given. . . .

The 1938 regulation does not seem to have aroused much discussion at the time, and its effect on the function of prescriptions was never tested in the courts. . . . [T]he distinction between prescription and "over-the-counter" drugs was simply accepted. . . .

United States v. El–O–Pathic Pharmacy

192 F.2d 62 (9th Cir. 1951).

■ McAllister, Circuit Judge.

This is an appeal from an order of the district court denying permanent injunctions in consolidated cases in which the government sought to restrain appellees from introducing certain allegedly misbranded drugs, known as hormones, into interstate commerce. . . .

. . . It appears that the hormones in question are manufactured by pharmaceutical corporations in the eastern part of the United States and shipped to appellees in California with labeling that states, in part, "Caution: To be dispensed only by or on the prescription of a physician." Thereafter, the appellees relabel the drugs to eliminate this prescription statement; and the new labeling, it was claimed, caused the drugs to become misbranded within the meaning of the statute. . . .

The district court held that the warnings on the cartons containing the drugs were sufficient in that they stated that the hormones were for use by adult males deficient in male hormone when small dosages are prescribed or recommended by a physician for palliative relief of such symptoms; that the maintenance dosage could be extended from three to six months under supervision of a physician; [and] that before taking the hormone, a physician should be consulted, since the hormone would not aid or relieve symptoms not associated with male hormone deficiency; and that children and young adults must not use the hormone except under constant, direct supervision of a physician. . . .

It is the claim of the government that it has sustained the burden of proving that the hormones in this case are inherently dangerous; that they are not safe and efficacious for use except under the supervision of a physician; that they are not suitable for self-medication, since a layman could not know when they should be used and when they should not be used; that adequate directions for unsupervised lay use cannot be written;

and that such drugs, if sold legally in interstate commerce, must be dispensed only upon prescription of a physician, in accordance with the regulations of the Federal Security Administrator. The government further contends that the proofs disclose that the drugs in question failed to bear adequate directions for use, in that they are offered to the public as efficacious remedies for many conditions which are not mentioned in the labeling or directions for use. . . .

. . . [I]t is to be remarked that appellees' labels themselves set forth that it is impossible for a layman to determine whether he has a male hormone deficiency; that before taking testosterone, a physician should be consulted; that children or young adults must not use the drug except under constant direct supervision of a physician; that it should not be taken by anyone with cancer of the prostate, or defects of spermatogenesis; and that it is for use by adult males deficient in male hormone, when small dosages are prescribed or recommended by a physician. These labels themselves . . . clearly demonstrate that adequate directions for unsupervised use can not be written; and the testimony of the government's medical witnesses, which we accept, only strikingly emphasizes this important and crucial fact. Obviously, in such cases, the direction on the label that "a physician should be consulted," and the directions that the drug be used when dosages are prescribed or recommended by a physician, are not enough to constitute "adequate directions for use" within the meaning of the statute. . . .

NOTE

"Consult a Physician." In this case, the Court of Appeals held that the label direction that "a physician should be consulted" does not constitute adequate directions for use. By contrast, the OTC vitamin-mineral drug panel recommended in 1979 that all OTC vitamin-mineral drug products be labeled "For use in the prevention (or treatment) of vitamin (or mineral) deficiency when the need for such therapy has been determined by a physician." 44 Fed. Reg. 16126 (Mar. 16, 1979). The same requirement for physician diagnosis of disease prior to use of an OTC drug has been included in the labeling for cholecystokinetic OTC drugs, 45 Fed. Reg. 9286 (Feb. 12, 1980), 47 Fed. Reg. 37068 (Aug. 24, 1982), 48 Fed. Reg. 27004 (June 10, 1983), codified at 21 C.F.R. 357.250(d)(1); anti-asthmatic bronchodilator OTC drugs, 42 Fed. Reg. 38212 (Sept. 9, 1976), 47 Fed. Reg. 47520 (Oct. 26, 1982), codified at 21 C.F.R. 341.76(c)(1); and other OTC drugs pursuant to the OTC Drug Review.

COMMENT: THE DURHAM–HUMPHREY AMENDMENTS

In 1951 Congress enacted the Durham–Humphrey Amendments, 65 Stat. 648, revising section 503(b) of the FD&C Act to codify the FDA regulations distinguishing between prescription and nonprescription drugs. The primary purpose of the 1951 Amendments was to prevent the same drug from being marketed simultaneously as a prescription drug and as a nonprescription drug. The amended section 503(b) provided:

(1) A drug intended for use by man which—

(A) is a habit-forming drug to which section 502(d) applies; or

(B) because of its toxicity or other potentiality for harmful effect, or the method of its use, or the collateral measures necessary to its use, is not safe for use except under the supervision of a practitioner licensed by law to administer such drug; or

(C) is limited by an approved application under section 505 to use under the professional supervision of a practitioner licensed by law to administer such drug,

shall be dispensed only [upon prescription].... The act of dispensing a drug contrary to the provisions of this paragraph shall be deemed to be an act which results in the drug being misbranded while held for sale.

The subparagraph concerning habit-forming drugs was deleted in 1997, but section 503(b)(1) otherwise remains unchanged since 1951.

NOTES

1. *Senate Report.* The Senate Report on the Durham–Humphrey Amendments, S. Rep. No. 946, 82d Cong., 1st Sess. 4 (1951), provides this explanation:

The word "safe," as used in the definition, is intended to have its ordinary meaning. For example, nontoxic drugs like quinidine sulfate, intended for heart disease, or penicillin, for infections, are not safe for self-medication because their unsupervised use may indirectly cause injury or death. The language of the definition clearly shows that toxicity is only one factor to be considered by the courts in determining whether a particular drug is safe for use without medical supervision. The definition requires the court to consider also other potentialities for harmful effect, the method by which the drug is used, and the collateral measures that may be necessary in order to use the drug safely....

In order to give this general definition a more precise meaning so that it may be applied with greater uniformity by the drug trade, the Administrator can exercise the authority he has under section 701(a) of the Federal Food, Drug, and Cosmetic Act to issue interpretative regulations. It is to be understood that the inclusion of the statutory definition does not, of course, in any way derogate from the Administrator's authority to interpret and enforce the definition through the issuance of any regulations necessary or appropriate to protect the public from indiscriminate dispensing of drugs over the counter when they may be unsafe for use without the supervision of a practitioner licensed by law to administer such drugs.

... S. 1186 would have authorized the Federal Security Administrator to list by name or class the drugs which he considered within the statutory definition. The grant of such administrative authority was objected to as an unnecessary regulation of the drug industry, and the committee concluded that administrative listing is not necessary at this time. It was felt that the statutory definition, together with the authority to make interpretative regulations, could bring an end to the existing confusion in drug labeling and that uniformity can be achieved through cooperative efforts of the drug industry and the Food and Drug Administration working under the statutory plan.

2. *Different Dosages.* FDA's initial administrative exception to Durham–Humphrey was to acknowledge that the same drug could be sold both prescription and nonprescription at different dosages. *e.g.*, under the OTC Drug Review a panel

recommended that the antihistamine doxylamine—formerly limited to prescription status—be switched to nonprescription use at a dosage level of 7.5 to 12.5 mg, but retained as a prescription drug at higher levels. 41 Fed. Reg. 38312, 38385 (Sept. 9, 1996). FDA initially concluded to limit doxylamine to nonprescription use at 7.5 mg, 41 Fed. Reg. at 38313, but later increased the dosage to 12.5 mg, 52 Fed. Reg. 31892, 31893 (Aug. 24, 1987), 59 Fed. Reg. 4216 (Jan. 28, 1994), 21 C.F.R. 341.72(d)(8).

3. *Different Indications.* In 1989, FDA for the first time agreed that it could approve, at the same dosage level, one indication of a drug as prescription only and another indication as nonprescription, when it initially approved the switch of some—but not all—indications of clotrimazole from prescription to nonprescription status in 1989. A year later, all of the remaining indications were switched.

4. *Different Ages.* In considering the switch of the emergency contraceptive Plan B from prescription to nonprescription status, FDA announced a public meeting in 70 Fed. Reg. 52050 (Sept. 1, 2005) to consider whether the agency could designate the drug, at the same dosage level and for the same indication, as prescription for women under 17 years of age and nonprescription for 17 years and older. The agency subsequently approved the NDA with an age restriction of 18 rather than 17.

5. *The Prescription Legend.* As enacted in 1951, section 503(b)(4) required a prescription drug to bear the legend "Caution: Federal law prohibits dispensing without prescription." 65 Stat. 648, 649. The legend was changed in 1997 to "Rx only." 111 Stat. 2296, 2327.

6. *Section 503(b).* For discussion of the Durham–Humphrey Amendments, which added section 503(b) to the Act, see Charles Wesley Dunn, *The New Prescription Drug Law*, 6 FOOD DRUG. COSM. L.J. 951 (1951); Sol A. Herzog, *Durham–Humphrey—Two Years Later*, 10 FOOD DRUG. COSM. L.J. 119 (1955); Peter Barton Hutt, *A Legal Framework for Future Decisions on Transferring Drugs from Prescription to Non-prescription Status*, 37 FOOD DRUG. COSM. L.J. 427 (1982). For a detailed legislative history of the Durham–Humphrey Amendments, see Gregory W. Reilly, *The FDA and Plan B: The Legislative History of the Durham–Humphrey Amendments and the Consideration of Social Harms in the Rx/OTC Switch* (2006), in Chapter VI(D)(1) of the Electronic Book. Under section 503(b)(1)(B) of the FD&C Act, dispensing a drug in contravention of section 503(b) "shall be deemed to be an act which results in the drug being misbranded while held for sale." This provision reaches a pharmacist who dispenses a drug without the required labeling long after it has moved in interstate commerce. *See United States v. Sullivan*, 332 U.S. 689 (1948).

e. THE REQUIREMENT OF A VALID PRESCRIPTION

Section 503(b)(1) of the FD&C Act requires a written prescription by a licensed practitioner for any drug limited by FDA to prescription status, or an oral prescription that is promptly reduced to writing. If a pharmacy fails to abide by this prescription requirement, section 503(b) declares that the drug is misbranded. Section 503(b) relies upon state law to determine what professional training is required for licensure to administer prescription drugs.

There is substantial judicial precedent interpreting the prescription requirement under comparable provisions in federal drug abuse statutes and under the FD&C Act. The first statute specifically to regulate narcotic drugs was the Harrison Narcotic Act of 1914. The 1914 Act required that the doctor issue a prescription "in the course of his professional practice only." After upholding the validity of the Act in *United States v. Doremus*, 249 U.S. 86 (1918), the Supreme Court decided two cases which interpreted and defined the prescription requirement. According to these two decisions, narcotic drugs regulated by the Act could be dispensed only under a valid doctor/patient relationship and in the course of legitimate medical treatment.

In *Webb v. United States*, 249 U.S. 96 (1919), the Court declared that a narcotic drug may be prescribed and dispensed only for legitimate medical purposes pursuant to a valid doctor/patient relationship, not to fulfill a drug addiction. The Court found that the defendant doctor issued the order without "consideration of the applicant's individual case ... and in such quantities as the applicant desired for the sake of continuing his accustomed use." The Court denied the legitimacy of the prescription, finding that "to call such an order for the use of morphine a physician's prescription would be so plain a perversion of meaning that no discussion of the subject is required."

In 1920, the Court returned to the requirements of the Harrison Narcotic Act in *Jin Fuey Moy v. United States*, 254 U.S. 189 (1920) and again emphasized the need for a valid doctor/patient relationship in order to meet the "professional practice" standard. The Court upheld the conviction of a doctor who prescribed a "prohibited drug" to an individual with whom he had no physician/patient relationship. The Court found that such activity was "not according to the usual practice of medical men":

> ... the phrases "to a patient" and "in the course of his professional practice only" are intended to confine the immunity of a registered physician ... strictly within the appropriate bounds of a physician's professional practice, and not to extend it to include a sale to a dealer or a distribution intended to cater to the appetite or satisfy the craving of one addicted to the use of the drug.

The Fifth Circuit later relied on these requirements in deciding a case under the prescription drug provisions of the FD&C Act. In *Brown v. United States*, 250 F.2d 745 (5th Cir. 1958), the Court of Appeals relied on the professional practice standard to uphold the conviction of a doctor who issued amphetamines to truck drivers. The Court of Appeals highlighted several key facts, including that the doctor did not inquire into the physical health of the driver, that he issued the drugs without a physical examination, and that he issued drugs without a dosage restriction. The Court of Appeals emphasized that the absence of a professional relationship "bears on the question whether there had been a 'prescription.'" *See also De Freese v. United States*, 270 F.2d 730 (5th Cir. 1959).

In 1965, Congress enacted the Drug Abuse Control Amendments of 1965, 79 Stat. 226, which amended the FD&C Act to forbid any person acting outside "the ordinary and authorized course of his business, profession, occupation, or employment" to "sell, deliver, or otherwise dispose of any depressant or stimulant drug." In *White v. United States*, 399 F.2d 813 (8th Cir. 1968), the Eighth Circuit continued to rely on the prescription requirements articulated under the earlier statutes and case law. In *White*, a doctor issued amphetamines to federal agents without a prescription and without any inquiry into their medical condition. The doctor also issued a prescription for one individual whom he had never met and who was not present at the time of the prescription. The Court of Appeals upheld the doctor's conviction, accepting the precedent that subjected doctors to punishment when they act outside of a bona fide doctor/patient relationship.

In 1970, Congress enacted the Comprehensive Drug Abuse Prevention and Control Act of 1970, 84 Stat. 1236. Included in the 1970 Act was the Controlled Substances Act, which established requirements relating to the manufacture, prescription, and distribution of any controlled substance. Under section 829 of the Act, "except when dispensed directly by a practitioner, other than a pharmacist, to an ultimate user, no controlled substance in schedule II [or III or IV] which is a prescription drug as determined under the Federal Food, Drug, and Cosmetic Act, may be dispensed without the written prescription of a practitioner." In *United States v. Rosen*, 582 F.2d 1032 (5th Cir. 1978), the Fifth Circuit relied on prior case law to determine the liability of a doctor who prescribed amphetamine diet pills to individuals without an examination or a legitimate doctor/patient relationship. The Court of Appeals noted that the doctor conducted only a cursory examination of the individual, prescribed large quantities of the controlled substances, and often used street slang in describing the substances. Relying on these factors, the Fifth Circuit upheld the finding that the doctor acted without a legitimate medical purpose in violation of the Controlled Substances Act.

Similarly, in *United States v. Kaplan*, 895 F.2d 618 (9th Cir. 1990), the Ninth Circuit upheld the conviction of a physician, holding that a doctor may be liable for prescribing controlled substances outside the usual bounds of professional practice. The evidence showed that the doctor issued numerous prescriptions for controlled substances without conducting a physical examination. The defendant in *United States v. Nelson*, 383 F.3d 1227 (10th Cir. 2004) was convicted of selling controlled substances over the internet.

FDA relied on this legal theory to prosecute physicians who distributed anabolic steroids and androgenic hormones to athletes outside a genuine doctor-patient relationship. *See, e.g., Doe v. United States*, 801 F.2d 1164 (9th Cir. 1986); "Five Arrested for Steroid Distribution," FDA Talk Paper No. T87–47 (Oct. 21, 1987); "Steroid Makers in Florida, Coach in South Carolina Charged," FDA Talk Paper No. T89–23 (May 1, 1989); "San Jose Grand Jury Indicts Three For 'Steroids'," FDA Talk Paper No. T89–48 (July 25, 1989). The Anti–Drug Abuse Act of 1988, 102 Stat. 4181, 4230, added section 303(e) to the FD&C Act to prohibit distribution of any anabolic steroid for use in humans other than by prescription for the treatment of disease and provided for imprisonment of up to three years (up to six years for distribution to a minor). In 104 Stat. 4789, 4853 (1990) the 1988 statute was repealed and a new section 303(e) was enacted to regulate the distribution of human growth hormone.

Thus, according to the relevant case law, a valid prescription is one granted after a sufficient medical examination and consideration of the patient's individual needs. There must be a valid doctor/patient relationship as well as a good faith determination that the prescribed medication is medically necessary.

A pharmacist also bears a burden for not dispensing a drug where the pharmacist knows that there is no valid prescription. In *Webb*, the Supreme Court upheld the indictment under the Harrison Narcotic Act of the pharmacist as well as the doctor in a scheme to provide morphine to habitual users. Similarly, in *United States v. Guerrero*, 650 F.2d 728 (5th Cir. 1981), the Fifth Circuit found under the Controlled Substances Act that, although "the responsibility for the proper prescribing and dispensing of controlled substances is upon the prescribing practitioner, ... a corresponding responsibility rests with the pharmacist who fills the prescription." The Court of Appeals found that such responsibility arose only in the case where a pharmacist knew that the prescription was invalid. *See also United States v. Green*, 511 F.2d 1062 (7th Cir. 1975); *United States v. Leal*, 75 F.3d 219 (6th Cir. 1996); *United States v. Munoz*, 430 F.3d 1357 (11th Cir. 2005); *United States v. Kim*, 298 F.3d 746 (9th Cir. 2002), 2006 WL 903214, 1421115 (9th Cir. 2006).

pharmacist burden

NOTES

1. *State Authorization to Prescribe Drugs.* As noted previously, Section 503(b) relies upon state law to determine what professional training is required for licensure to administer prescription drugs. *United States v. Shock*, 379 F.2d 29 (8th Cir. 1967), held that a District Court should look to state law to determine whether a chiropractor is an authorized practitioner. *See* James L. J. Nuzzo, *Independent Prescribing Authority of Advanced Practice Nurses: A Threat to the Public Health?*, 53 FOOD & DRUG L.J. 35 (1998). Practitioners of naturopathy have been unsuccessful in their attempts to force FDA and state agencies to recognize their discipline as a healing art separate from but of equal standing with orthodox medicine. *See Idaho Association of Naturopathic Physicians, Inc. v. FDA*, 582 F.2d 849 (4th Cir. 1978), and cases cited therein.

2. *Dependent Pharmacist Prescribers.* To allow immediate access to emergency contraception or other prescription medication, some states have enacted laws authorizing a pharmacist to dispense drugs pursuant to a protocol established with a physician. *See* Heather M. Field, *Increasing Access to Emergency Contraceptive Pills Through State Law Enabled Dependent Pharmacist Prescribers*, 11 U.C.L.A. WOMEN'S L.J. 141 (2000).

3. *Power to Establish Prescription Status by Regulation.* In *National Nutritional Foods Association v. Weinberger*, 512 F.2d 688 (2d Cir. 1975), FDA's authority to issue substantive regulations restricting an entire class of drugs to prescription sale was in principle upheld.

4. *Refills for Schedule II Prescription Drugs.* The Controlled Substances Act prohibits a prescription for more than a 30 day supply, and the refilling of a prescription, for a Schedule II drug. The Drug Enforcement Administration (DEA) recently established a policy of allowing a physician to provide a patient with three 30–day prescriptions at one office visit. *See* 69 Fed. Reg. 67170 (Nov. 16, 2004), 70 Fed. Reg. 50408 (Aug. 26, 2005), 71 Fed. Reg. 52724 (Sept. 6, 2006).

f.   WARNINGS FOR PRESCRIPTION DRUGS

Section 502(f)(2) of the Act requires, in addition to adequate directions for use, "such adequate warnings against use in those pathological condi-

warnings for conditions & kids

tions or by children where its use may be dangerous to health, or against unsafe dosage or methods or duration of administration or application ... as are necessary for the protection of users...." This logical requirement presents difficult problems of implementation. In this chapter, we consider only the issues related to warnings that arise under the FD&C Act. Product liability considerations, and their impact on warnings, are considered separately in Chapter XIII, *infra.*

Section 201.57(c)(6) of the FDA regulations establishes the requirements for the warnings that must be contained in the physician package insert for a prescription drug.

(6) *Warnings and precautions.* (i) *General.* This section must describe clinically significant adverse reactions (including any that are potentially fatal, are serious even if infrequent, or can be prevented or mitigated through appropriate use of the drug), other potential safety hazards (including those that are expected for the pharmacological class or those resulting from drug/drug interactions), limitations in use imposed by them (*e.g.,* avoiding certain concomitant therapy), and steps that should be taken if they occur (*e.g.,* dosage modification). The frequency of all clinically significant adverse reactions and the approximate mortality and morbidity rates for patients experiencing the reaction, if known and necessary for the safe and effective use of the drug, must be expressed.... [T]he labeling must be revised to include a warning about a clinically significant hazard as soon as there is reasonable evidence of a causal association with a drug; a causal relationship need not have been definitely established. A specific warning relating to a use not provided for under the "Indications and Usage" section may be required by FDA in accordance with sections 201(n) and 502(a) of the act if the drug is commonly prescribed for a disease or condition and such usage is associated with a clinically significant risk or hazard.

In addition to information specifically designated as "warnings," the physician package insert is also required to contain warning-related sections devoted to contraindications; adverse reactions; drug interactions; effect on pregnancy, labor, delivery, and lactation; pediatric and geriatric use; and nonclinical toxicology including carcinogenesis, mutagenesis, and impairment of fertility. It has been recognized for many years that these requirements result in a lengthy, complex, and highly conservative summary of the drug's safety.

Peter Barton Hutt, *Regulation of the Practice of Medicine Under the Pure Food and Drug Laws*

33 JOURNAL OF THE ASSOCIATION OF FOOD AND DRUG OFFICIALS OF THE UNITED STATES 3 (1969).

... The prescribing brochure has been described, quite accurately, as a "conservative consensus" between the pharmaceutical manufacturer and FDA. Organized medicine and the individual medical practitioner are not parties to that decision.

FDA is obviously under substantial pressure from Congress, which is only too happy to second-guess the difficult judgments that must be made on the safety and effectiveness of new drugs....

Broad approval of an NDA for a harmful new drug could also result in Governmental liability under the Federal Tort Claims Act for the damage the product subsequently causes to a consumer who uses it. It is therefore not surprising that FDA takes a quite conservative approach to the prescribing brochure.

Pharmaceutical manufacturers are also under new pressures to be more conservative in their prescribing brochures. Recent court decisions indicate that Governmental requirements are only a minimum standard and that compliance with them does not guarantee immunity from product liability suits. Some manufacturers are therefore voluntarily including broader contraindications, precautions, and warnings in their prescribing brochures than they formerly did.

If both FDA and the pharmaceutical industry continue the trend toward protecting their own interests, there is a grave danger that the medical profession could become exposed and vulnerable to malpractice litigation. It is not unlike the committee member who is absent from the meeting and finds himself elected chairman.

———

These warnings, moreover, are seen regularly by the American public. With the advent of patient labeling, direct-to-consumer advertising (which must contain at least a "brief summary" of the physician labeling), popular sales of the *Physician's Desk Reference* (which contains all physician labeling inserts), and instant access to all this information through the internet, the public is as familiar with warnings for prescription drugs as it is for nonprescription drugs.

Lars Noah, *The Imperative to Warn: Disentangling the "Right to Know" from the "Need to Know" about Consumer Product Hazards*

11 YALE JOURNAL ON REGULATION 293 (1994).

. . . .

The use of warning statements in the labeling of consumer products appears, at first blush, to be a relatively simple and straightforward response to product hazards. Indeed, this evident simplicity has made labeling requirements a preferred option for Congress, federal agencies, state lawmakers, and the courts. When viewed in isolation, many of the warning requirements imposed by each class of decisionmakers seem more or less defensible. Considered in their entirety, however, many of these risk communication efforts appear to be seriously misguided.

It is imperative, therefore, that the primary responsibility for labeling decisions be vested in a single group of decisionmakers. Federal administrative agencies are best suited for this task, and their decisions on the

[handwritten note in left margin: Fed agency should dec'd w/ warning labels]

necessity of warnings on labels should preempt state requirements arising under statutory or common law. Congress could express such a judgment through new legislation directed to consumer product labeling generally, or each agency could take the initiative and declare that its warning requirements preempt sate law. States would retain the power to impose warning requirements for products not subject to federal regulation, and courts could entertain products liability claims in cases where manufacturers fail to comply with federal and state requirements.

For their part, federal regulators will have to reexamine their own labeling requirements, placing a greater emphasis on selectivity and consistency. To date, agency efforts have been uneven. Better coordination might be achieved through the creation of an interagency task force or working group directed to address these problems. Among the most coherent and comprehensive product warning strategies are FDA's regulation of prescription drug labeling, EPA's control over pesticide labeling, and, to lesser extent, CPSC requirements for hazardous substances. Package inserts and pesticide labels convey concrete and balanced information about substantiated risks in a format that organizes this information by level of severity. Ironically, courts have accorded little or no respect to agency judgments about appropriate labeling for these categories of products. As noted above, an essential element of any coherent risk communication system would be the preemption of state requirements.

The real question, however, is whether decisions about the risk labeling of other consumer products can be informed by the approaches used with prescription drugs and pesticides. The same agency that has done such a thoughtful job with package inserts has done a relatively poor job in designing risk labeling for cosmetic products. Although difficulties would arise if consumer labeling were modeled on an approach designed for physicians, agencies and courts could develop improved strategies for communicating risk information to product users. Warning statements should be reserved for those risks that can best be minimized by conveying information through labeling, namely by providing instructions for safe use (to avoid acute hazards) or by serving as a means for disclosing important risk information to a clearly identified segment of potential users. Otherwise, the crazy quilt of warning statements on product labels will continue to grow, at least until courts either penalize manufacturers for diluting serious warnings with trivia or refrain from second guessing federal regulators who have undertaken the difficult task of designing meaningful product labels.

———

It is therefore not surprising that the leading court challenge to an FDA-required warning was brought by a group of physicians, not by the affected drug manufacturers.

Bradley v. Weinberger

483 F.2d 410 (1st Cir. 1973).

■ COFFIN, CHIEF JUDGE.

Plaintiffs, 178 physicians who treat diabetes and one diabetes patient who use oral hypoglycemic agents to control the disease by lowering the blood sugar level, brought suit to enjoin the defendants Secretary of Health, Education and Welfare and the Commissioner of the Food and Drug Administration (FDA) from enforcing and the defendant drug companies from complying with the FDA's proposal for altering the labeling of those drugs....

This controversy revolves around a long-term, federally funded study undertaken by the University Group Diabetes Program (hereafter the UGDP study) to determine the effects of oral hypoglycemic agents on vascular complications in patients with adult-onset diabetes.... [T]he study concluded that the combination of diet and either tolbutamide or phenformin was no more effective than diet alone in prolonging life but that those oral agents might be more hazardous than diet or diet plus insulin insofar as cardiovascular mortality was concerned....

After the study received much publicity and criticism ... the FDA concluded that protection of the public required a strong warning to physicians recommending use of an oral agent only if other treatments were inadvisable and noting the UGDP's findings regarding the apparently increased danger of cardiovascular mortality....

On October 7, 1971, the Committee on the Care of the Diabetic, consisting of eminent doctors and experts in the field including some of the plaintiff doctors, submitted through its counsel a petition to the FDA. It asked the FDA to rescind its labeling recommendation, insure that all future FDA comments on the UGDP study include references to its alleged deficiencies and controversial nature, provide petitioners with the complete raw data of the study, and, "in accord with its policy of fair balance," disseminate with equal emphasis and frequency studies and individual expert opinions differing with the study....

In the May, 1972, *Drug Bulletin*, the FDA published the "Final Labeling Approved for Oral Hypoglycemic Drugs," which proposed changes in the "indications" section of the label and the addition of a "special warning" section....

This suit was filed on August 11, 1972 and a temporary restraining order issued that day. After a hearing and submission of affidavits of experts by both sides, the emergency district judge denied the preliminary injunction....

On October 17, 1972, the litigation entered an entirely new phase. On that date, plaintiffs filed a motion for leave to amend their complaint, supported by 13 affidavits by diabetes experts attesting to the controversy over the UGDP study, and new motions for a temporary restraining order and a preliminary injunction. The motions presented for the first time the argument that the FDA's proposed label was itself misleading and thus rendered the drug misbranded in violation of the statute, because it failed to reveal the existence of a "material weight of contrary opinion" among "experts qualified by scientific training and experience" as allegedly required by the agency's own regulation, 21 C.F.R. § 1.3. After oral argument ... the district court in a Memorandum and Order granted on November 3,

1972, the motions to amend the complaint and for a preliminary injunction. . . .

... Courts are not best equipped, as both sides here readily agree, to judge the merits of the scientific studies and the objections to them. Specialized agencies like the FDA are created to serve that function. In this case, the regulation which, in their motion to amend, plaintiffs contend specifically governs the content of a balanced label, 21 C.F.R. § 1.3, was never presented to the Commissioner [in connection with the October 1971 petition] nor referred to in the administrative record. It is the significance of this omission that governs our disposition. . . .

Most significantly, this is an unprecedented argument. As plaintiffs' counsel readily admitted in oral argument before the district court, there appears to be no prior case in which an FDA drug labeling decision was challenged not by the producer but by concerned medical practitioners, and no case in which the misbranding statutes and regulations were sought to be applied not to the manufacturer's label but to the FDA's proposal for alteration of the label in light of new information. . . .

... The ... statute (21 U.S.C. § 321(n)) provides: "If an article is alleged to be misbranded because the labeling is misleading, then in determining whether the labeling is misleading there shall be taken into account (among other things) not only representations made or suggested ... but also the extent to which the labeling fails to reveal facts material in light of such representations or material with respect to consequences which may result from the use of the article to which the labeling relates." Implementing [this] definition is regulation 1.3:

> "The existence of a difference of opinion, among experts qualified by scientific training and experience, as to the truth of a representation made or suggested in the labeling is a fact (among other facts) the failure to reveal which may render the labeling misleading, if there is a material weight of opinion contrary to such representation."

> . . . .

The Commissioner never considered the meaning of this regulation, its relationship to the substantial evidence test, the intersection of the safety, effectiveness, and misbranding requirements, or the applicability of the misbranding requirements, both statutory and regulatory, to an FDA proposal for re-labeling, for the simple reason that the issue was not presented to him. . . .

Because the plaintiffs failed to exhaust their administrative remedies regarding the issues they now present and, consequently, the district court reviewed the agency decision on something other than the administrative record, we must vacate the injunction. . . .

NOTES

1. *History of Dispute.* This opinion describes the inception of one of the most contentious episodes in FDA's administration of federal drug law. *See* Gina Kolata,

Controversy over Study of Diabetes Drugs Continues for Nearly a Decade, 203 SCIENCE 986 (1979).

2. *Physician Opposition.* It is notable that it was a group of physicians, rather than the manufacturers of tolbutamide and phenformin, who initially resisted FDA's efforts to require label warnings about the increased risk of cardiovascular mortality ostensibly revealed by the UGDP study. The opposition of the Committee for the Care of the Diabetic reflected profound disagreement with the findings of the study and suspicion about the way in which it had been conducted. Clinicians specializing in the treatment of diabetes, and known for their espousal of the oral hypoglycemic drugs, believed that the UGDP findings were unreliable, hence their initial demand that FDA provide access to the individual patient records from the study. Committed as they were to continued use of the drugs, the *Bradley* plaintiffs were obviously also concerned about the liability implications of an FDA-prescribed warning cautioning against their routine use and alluding to a heightened risk of cardiovascular disease—a condition that besets many diabetics anyway. Traditionally courts have accorded significant weight to FDA-approved labeling as evidence of the standard of physician care, *see infra* Chapter XIII.

3. *UGDP Study Records.* From the time of the earliest reports of the UGDP study, the Committee on the Care of the Diabetic had contended that the findings were unreliable and sought access to all of the study records in order to verify their charges. Ultimately this demand was submitted to NIH and FDA in the form of a Freedom of Information Act request, which the agencies denied on the ground that they did not have custody of the records—which were kept by the study coordinator, Dr. Christian Klimpt, a biostatistician at the University of Maryland Medical School. This denial was upheld in *Forsham v. Califano,* 587 F.2d 1128 (D.C. Cir. 1978). The Court of Appeals expressly left open the question whether FDA could validly prescribe final labeling for the oral hypoglycemic drugs based upon the UGDP findings without affording critics access to the study records. The Court of Appeals' ruling was affirmed by the Supreme Court in *Forsham v. Harris,* 445 U.S. 169 (1980).

———

The *Bradley* ruling, and the failure to reach agreement with the plaintiffs on labeling for the drugs, caused FDA to alter its legal approach. As a first step, the agency proposed to revise 21 C.F.R. 1.3, its regulation interpreting section 201(n) of the Act.

Labeling: Failure to Reveal Material Facts

39 Fed. Reg. 33229 (September 16, 1974).

... Although there was extensive congressional discussion and debate [during Congressional consideration of the FD&C Act] on the requirements for adequate directions and warnings, there was no suggestion whatever that differing medical opinions about them might be required to be reflected in the labeling. Indeed, from the beginning the legislation required warnings where the drug "may" be dangerous to health. It was nowhere suggested that there be proof of a health hazard before a warning could be required or that, absent such proof, any warning describe varying opinions as to the degree of hazard involved. ...

... Drug warnings, by their very nature, warn only about possible danger. Although they are often the subject of intense debate, the Food and Drug Administration has never permitted drug labeling to reflect such debate. That debate and disagreement is properly the subject of scientific discussion in professional journals and symposia, but not in drug labeling....

... 21 CFR 1.3 is inconsistent with relevant statutory requirements and contemporary medical and scientific principles. The Commissioner has concluded that the use of medical opinion in product labeling must be limited and particularized accordingly.

Congress has determined that the effectiveness of new drugs and new animal drugs must be established by substantial evidence. Thus, a difference of medical opinion with respect to a labeling claim of effectiveness for these products is legally insufficient and is not a material fact, within the meaning of section 201(n) of the act, unless such opinion is itself supported by evidence which meets the statutory standard....

... § 1.3 is [also] inconsistent with the statutory standard established in section 502(f) of the act. An adequate warning of possible danger must appear in all such labeling. Without such a warning, a product is misbranded. The statute presupposes a difference of medical opinion since the danger need not be established and absolute, but rather merely potential. Thus, there is no basis to permit warnings to be discounted by an opinion that the warning is really not necessary at all. Providing for medical controversy with respect to a warning undermines the public health impetus of section 502(f) of the act. Where potential danger is the statutory standard, a warning must be unencumbered and unambiguous.

The degree of scientific uncertainty about a possible hazard, or its frequency of occurrence, or other similar related information may, of course, accompany or be part of a warning. It is common for a warning to state the product "may" cause a hazard, where the relationship is not yet conclusively proven, or to point out that the relationship between adverse animal findings and human consequences has not yet been determined. However, presentation of such factual information, which is helpful to the physician in evaluating the significance of a warning, does not permit additional statements of conflicting medical opinion relating to the warning.

... The Commissioner concludes that, where warnings are required, disclamatory opinions necessarily detract from the warning in such a manner as to be confusing and misleading. In this way, differences of medical opinions regarding warnings for foods and cosmetics would render the products to be misbranded within the meaning of section 402(a) and 602(a) of the act....

Therefore ... the Commissioner proposes that [the C.F.R.] be amended by revising § 1.3 to read as follows: ...

(c) Paragraph (a) of this section does not:

(1) Permit or require a statement of differences of opinion with respect to warnings (including contraindications, precautions, adverse reactions, and other information relating to possible prod-

uct hazards) required in labeling for food, drugs, devices, or cosmetics under the act.

(2) Permit or require a statement of differences of opinion with respect to the effectiveness of a drug unless each of the opinions expressed is supported by substantial evidence of effectiveness as defined in sections 505(d) and 512(d) of the act.

NOTES

1. *Final Regulation.* The final version of this regulation, 21 C.F.R. 1.21, was promulgated in 40 Fed. Reg. 28582 (July 7, 1975).

2. *Relabeling of Oral Hypoglycemic Drugs.* At the same time FDA published its final regulation interpreting section 201(n), it published comprehensive proposed labeling requirements for oral hypoglycemic drugs, 40 Fed. Reg. 28587 (July 7, 1975), and announced a legislative-style public hearing on the issues. Persistent accusations of poor design in the UGDP study and mistakes in recording the experience of patients finally led FDA and the sponsor of the study, NIH, to undertake an audit of the accuracy of the transcription of the so-called "raw data" of the study—the actual patient records—into the published reports. The agencies completed this audit in 1978, concluding:

> ... [W]hile there are certain errors and discrepancies between the data file of the UGDP study and the published reports, none of these appears of sufficient frequency or magnitude to invalidate the finding that cardiovascular mortality was higher in the groups of patients treated with tolbutamide plus diet and phenformin plus diet compared to the groups treated with placebo or insulin.

In 43 Fed. Reg. 52732 (Nov. 14, 1978), FDA announced the availability of the audit team's report and reopened the comment period on the proposed labeling.

More than five years later, FDA published its final regulation establishing a warning for this class of drugs and announced the availability of a class labeling guideline. *See* 49 Fed. Reg. 14303, 14441 (Apr. 11, 1984), codified at 21 C.F.R. 310.517. The prescribed warning, citing the UGDP study, states that oral hypoglycemic drugs have been "reported to be associated with increased cardiovascular mortality as compared to treatment with diet alone or diet plus insulin," and that:

> Despite controversy regarding the interpretation of these results, the findings of the UGDP study provide an adequate basis for this warning. The patient should be informed of the potential risks and advantages of [name of drug] and of alternative modes of therapy.

Finally, the regulation states that the warning is applicable to all marketed oral hypoglycemic drugs even though only one, tolbutamide, was included in the UGDP study. Because FDA approval of NDAs for glyburide, a new oral hypoglycemic drug of the sulfonylurea class, was held up for a full decade as a result of this controversy, glyburide was granted statutory patent term extension for eight years beyond the May 1, 1984 date of approval. 98 Stat. 3434 (1984).

3. *Subsequent Studies.* The adverse results found in the UGDP trial have not been confirmed in subsequent studies. *E.g.,* UK Prospective Diabetes Study Group, *Intensive Blood–Glucose Control with Sulfonylureas or Insulin Compared with Conventional Treatment and Risk of Complications in Patients with Type 2 Diabetes*, 352 LANCET 837 (Sept. 12, 1998); Francis M. Collins, *Current Treatment Approaches to Type 2 Diabetes Mellitus: Successes and Shortcomings*, 8 AM. J. OF MANAGED CARE S460 (Oct. 2002).

4. *Banning of Phenformin.* In the interim, separate regulatory action was taken to remove from the market phenformin, the other drug involved in the UGDP study. HEW Secretary Califano suspended marketing of phenformin as an "imminent hazard" on other grounds even before holding an administrative hearing. *See infra* p. 740.

5. *Other Drug Warnings.* Other examples of warnings for prescription drugs imposed by FDA regulations appear in 21 C.F.R. Part 201, Subpart G. The agency formerly prescribed warnings in the Federal Register notices implementing the NAS drug effectiveness study, *infra* p. 580, but now prescribes warnings almost exclusively in the NDA process.

6. *Mailed Drug Warnings.* FDA has not required the use of detail men to disseminate important drug information. Because of the agency's concern about the effectiveness of such information when mailed to physicians, however, it has specified a uniform size and format for the envelope and the format, size, font, and wording of various statements of information required to appear on the envelope, *e.g.*, "Important Drug Warning." 32 Fed. Reg. 7127 (May 11, 1967), 33 Fed. Reg. 12138 (Aug. 28, 1968), codified at 21 C.F.R. 200.5.

7. *General Requirements for Physician Labeling.* FDA has established regulations specifying the format and content of the physician labeling for all human prescription drugs. 39 Fed. Reg. 8946 (Mar. 7, 1974), 40 Fed. Reg. 15392 (Apr. 7, 1975), 44 Fed. Reg. 37434 (June 26, 1979), 65 Fed. Reg. 81082 (Dec. 22, 2000), 71 Fed. Reg. 3922 (Jan. 24, 2006), codified at 21 C.F.R. 201.56–57. *See* J. Richard Crout, *In Praise of the Lowly Package Insert*, 29 FOOD DRUG. COSM. L.J. 139 (1974); Henry E. Simmons, *FDA Looks at the Package Insert*, 27 FOOD DRUG. COSM. L.J. 117 (1972). When FDA revised the physician labeling in January 2006 to make it more readable, the agency did not amend the definition of a warning or change its conservative approach to drug labeling.

Among the more important of these recent revisions to the physician labeling requirements are: a mandatory "highlights" section at the beginning at the insert, limited to one-half page; a mandatory table of contents for the full prescribing information, which must list all of the headings and subheadings required in the insert; a requirement that FDA-approved patient labeling be reprinted at the end of the insert or accompany the insert; detailed requirements for the format and font size of the labeling; and an obligatory statement that FDA labeling requirements are intended to preempt conflicting state law requirements, whether arising by statute, administrative rule, or product liability actions.

8. *Class Labeling.* FDA has long had the goal of achieving uniform, indeed near-identical, labeling ("class labeling") for all identical, similar, or related drugs. This policy was originally implemented by imposing consistent labeling requirements through the DESI program, *infra* p. 580. In the early 1980s, FDA began issuing class labeling guidelines. *See, e.g.*, 45 Fed. Reg. 76356 (Nov. 18, 1980) (single-entity barbiturates); 46 Fed. Reg. 49205 (Oct. 6, 1981) (topical corticosteroids); 47 Fed. Reg. 29878 (July 9, 1982) (thyroid hormones); 48 Fed. Reg. 50167 (Oct. 31, 1983) (sodium heparin). The agency abandoned this practice and currently pursues the goal of labeling uniformity through the NDA and abbreviated NDA process. FDA has also sought to prescribe similar labeling for competing products used for the same therapeutic purposes, but with less success. In light of recent scientific evidence that even closely related drugs demonstrate differences in both safety and effectiveness, *e.g.*, the Cox–2 inhibitor class of drugs, FDA is reconsidering its class labeling approach.

9. *Accutane Labeling.* Because of the substantial toxicity, and consequent narrow benefit/risk ratio, of many modern prescription drugs, their labeled contraindications and warnings can be quite frightening. Accutane (isotretinoin) is

uniquely effective in treating severe cystic acne, but is teratogenic (produces deformed babies). As part of a comprehensive program to assure its safe use, the physician labeling bears the following information:

**CAUSES BIRTH
DEFECTS**

**DO NOT GET
PREGNANT**

CONTRAINDICATIONS AND WARNINGS

Accutane must not be used by female patients who are or may become pregnant. There is an extremely high risk that severe birth defects will result if pregnancy occurs while taking Accutane in any amount, even for short periods of time. Potentially any fetus exposed during pregnancy can be affected. There are no accurate means of determining whether an exposed fetus has been affected.

Birth defects which have been documented following Accutane exposure include abnormalities of the face, eyes, ears, skull, central nervous system, cardiovascular system, and thymus and parathyroid glands. Cases of IQ scores less than 85 with or without other abnormalities have been reported. There is an increased risk of spontaneous abortion, and premature births have been reported.

Documented external abnormalities include: skull abnormality; ear abnormalities (including anotia, micropinna, small or absent external auditory canals); eye abnormalities (including microphthalmia); facial dysmorphia; cleft palate. Documented internal abnormalities include: CNS abnormalities (including cerebral abnormalities, cerebellar malformation, hydrocephalus, microcephaly, cranial nerve deficit); cardiovascular abnormalities; thymus gland abnormality; parathyroid hormone deficiency. In some cases death has occurred with certain of the abnormalities previously noted.

If pregnancy does occur during treatment of a female patient who is taking Accutane, Accutane must be discontinued immediately and she should be referred to an Obstetrician-Gynecologist experienced in reproductive toxicity for further evaluation and counseling.

Special Prescribing Requirements

Because of Accutane's teratogenicity and to minimize fetal exposure, Accutane is approved for marketing only under a special restricted distribution program approved by the Food and Drug Administration. This program is called iPLEDGE™. Accutane must only be prescribed by prescribers who are registered and activated with the iPLEDGE program. Accutane must only be dispensed by a pharmacy registered and activated with iPLEDGE, and must only be dispensed to patients who are registered and meet all the requirements of iPLEDGE (see **PRECAUTIONS**).

FDA has imposed a risk management plan for Accutane under 21 C.F.R. 314.520, described on the FDA website. *See* "Accutane—Is This Acne Drug Treatment Linked To Depression And Suicide?", Hearing before the House Committee on Government Reform, 106th Cong., 2d Sess. (2000). *See also* Cassandra L. Curry, *Preserving Access for Pregnable Women to Medically Valuable Teratogenic Drugs* (1996), Elizabeth L. Mitchell, *Miracle Drugs and Teratogens: An Exercise in Risk*

Management (1997), Julia Green, *Babies, Blemishes and FDA: A History of Accutane Regulation in the United States* (2002), and Steve C. Lee, *The Controversy
Surrounding Accutane: Regulation, Litigation, and Dangerous Side Effects* (2003),
in Chapter VI(C)(2) of the Electronic Book; Gina M. Petrocelli, *Accutane: Post–
Approval Drug Regulation in a Risk Management Framework* (2002), in Chapter
VI(C)(5) of the Electronic Book. Compare Howard B. Yeon, *Thalidomide Revisited*
(1998), and Kristina E. Lutz, *From Tragedy to Triumph: The Approval of Thalidomide* (1999), in Chapter VI(C)(2) of the Electronic Book; Sol Barer, *Celegene: The
Pharmaceutical Phoenix*, 24 CHEMICAL HERITAGE, No. 4, at 6 (Winter 2006/2007).

10. *Antibiotic Resistance Warning.* In 2003, FDA promulgated a regulation
requiring new warning information in the labeling of all systemic antibacterial drug
products. 65 Fed. Reg. 56511 (Sept. 19, 2000), 68 Fed. Reg. 6062 (Feb. 6, 2003),
codified at 21 C.F.R. 201.24. Directly under the product name, the labeling must
state:

> To reduce the development of drug-resistant bacteria and maintain the
> effectiveness of [insert name of antibacterial drug product] and other
> antibacterial drugs, [insert name of antibacterial drug product] should be
> used only to treat or prevent infections that are proven or strongly
> suspected to be caused by bacteria.

In the "precautions" section of the physician labeling, under "information for
patients," the labeling is required to state that patients should be counseled that
antibacterial drugs should only be used to treat bacterial infections, not viral
infections such as the common cold, and that the drug should be taken exactly as
directed because skipping doses decreases the effectiveness of the immediate treatment and increases the likelihood that bacteria will develop resistance.

11. *Effectiveness of Warnings.* There is substantial controversy about the
effectiveness of the warnings required by FDA to be included in drug product
labeling. Studies have shown that changing the labeling on a drug does not
necessarily change prescribing practices. For example, Walter Smalley et al., *Contraindicated Use of Cisapride: Impact of Food and Drug Administration Regulatory
Action*, 284 J.A.M.A. 3036 (2000), concluding that a warning about life-threatening
cardiac arrhythmias caused by cisapride through a boxed warning and a "Dear
Healthcare Professional" letter from the drug manufacturer "had no material effect
on contraindicated cisapride use." On the other hand, others argue that the lack of
an impact of a drug warning on prescribing practices may indicate that the use of
the drug remains important to patients in spite of the potential adverse events.

12. *Black Box Warning.* According to 21 C.F.R. 201.57(e), "Special problems,
particularly those that may lead to death or serious injury, may be required by
[FDA] to be placed in a prominently displayed box." In a study reported in Karen E.
Lasser, *Timing of New Black Box Warnings and Withdrawals for Prescription
Medications*, 287 J.A.M.A. 2215 (2002), it was found that of a total of 548 new
chemical entities approved in 1975–1999, 8.2 percent acquired one or more black
box warnings and 2.9 percent were withdrawn from the market. Over 25 years, the
probability of acquiring a new black box warning was 20 percent. In a study of
324,548 outpatients who received at least one prescription during calendar year
2002, researchers found that 33,778 patients were prescribed a medication that had
a black box warning. The report concluded that 2,354 of the prescriptions were
written in violation of the black box warning and that about 90 percent of the
violations involved patients who had a disease for which use of the drug was not
recommended. The report noted that in some cases physicians may have purposely
chosen to override the warning.

In commenting on the Lasser study, two respected FDA officials put the matter
quite succinctly:

Premarketing trials in a few thousand (usually relatively uncomplicated) patients do not detect all of a drug's adverse effects, especially relatively rare ones. Frequent post marketing labeling changes are therefore inevitable and should be anticipated. Sometimes the new information is so important it fundamentally changes the place of the drug in therapy (*e.g.*, leads to second-line status) and sometimes the post marketing discoveries cause the drug to be withdrawn.

Robert J. Temple & Martin H. Immel, *Safety of Newly Approved Drugs: Implications for Prescribing*, 287 J.A.M.A. 2273 (May 1, 2002). After a thorough criticism of the Lasser analysis, the FDA officials concluded that "the rate of serious injury has been relatively low" and that "there is no duration of use that allows a physician complete assurance that additional toxicity will not emerge." Although FDA continues to recognize the importance of labeling changes and other communications with the medical profession about new safety information, the agency recognizes that physicians often base their decisions on their own experience and therefore discount agency warnings. Accordingly, FDA has sought alternative means of risk management for drug safety problems.

13. *"Dear Doctor" Letters*. Two plaintiffs in a tort action against a pharmaceutical manufacturer moved for an injunction to require the company to send an emergency notice to physicians and patients about safety problems with the drug. In *Bernhardt v. Pfizer, Inc.*, Food Drug Cosm. L. Rep. (CCH ¶ 38,639), 2000 WL 1738645 (S.D.N.Y. 2000), the District Court denied the motion on the ground that the matter was within the primary jurisdiction of FDA and referred the matter to the agency.

14. *Nonprescription vs. Prescription Drug Warnings*. There is a substantial difference between the standards for a labeling warning for a prescription and a nonprescription drug. The standard for a prescription drug warning in 21 C.F.R. 201.57(c)(6) states, "[T]he labeling must be revised to include a warning about a clinically significant hazard as soon as there is reasonable evidence of a causal association with a drug; a causal relationship need not have been definitely established."

FDA often requires warnings in prescription drug labeling where there is in fact no evidence of causality or where there is a single known case of an adverse event. In contrast, label warnings for nonprescription drugs must be shown to deal with proven risks. FDA has stated that nonprescription label warnings must be "scientifically documented, clinically significant, and important for the safe and effective use of the products by the average consumer." 47 Fed. Reg. 54750, 54754 (Dec. 3, 1982); 53 Fed. Reg. 46204, 46213 (Nov. 16, 1988). Accordingly, when a drug is switched from prescription to nonprescription status it is entirely possible that the labeled warnings will change.

15. *Child Resistant Packaging*. The Poison Prevention Packaging Act of 1970, 84 Stat. 1670, 15 U.S.C. 1471, was enacted to prevent poisoning of children through accidental ingestion of toxic household substances, including drugs. Experience, particularly with aspirin, had demonstrated that label warnings were inadequate to prevent such poisonings. Congress therefore authorized the requirement of special "child-restraint" packaging designed to prevent young children from inadvertently obtaining access to dangerous household substances. The Consumer Product Safety Commission (CPSC), which administers the Poison Prevention Packaging Act, has promulgated regulations requiring essentially all prescription drugs, as well as aspirin and a relatively small number of other nonprescription drugs, to comply with the Act. 21 C.F.R. 1700.14(a)(10), 1700.15.

Peter Carlson, *Hey, Don't Say They Didn't Warn You* ...

THE WASHINGTON POST, September 1, 2006, at C1.

WARNING: Do not read this newspaper while driving a motor vehicle, operating machinery or piloting an aircraft. Do not read newspaper over an open flame. Do not hold newspaper close to face while smoking a cigar the size of a billy club. Do not use newspaper as a flotation device. Newspaper may be harmful if taken internally. Reading newspaper articles may cause irritation, nausea, drowsiness, uncontrollable laughter, weeping, cynicism, confusion, depression or existential despair. Keep out of reach of children.

Okay, you've been warned. Now we can proceed to the article at hand, which is about warning labels.

They're everywhere. Warning labels appear on toothpaste tubes, music CDs, restaurant menus, dog leashes, rented movies, bottles of water, bottles of champagne, bottles of bubble bath and biology textbooks.

Warning labels inform Americans that cigarettes are unhealthy, that coffee is hot, that sleeping pills can cause drowsiness, that Tide laundry detergent is not a good food source, that baking dishes get hot in the oven, that bottles of seltzer "may spray or fizz while opening" and that it is not a good idea to eat the toner used in laser printers. . . .

We are living in the Golden Age of the Warning Label.

It began in 1992, when Stella Liebeck, then 81, bought a cup of coffee at a McDonald's drive-thru window in Albuquerque. As she wedged the cup between her legs and removed its cap, her grandson drove off. The coffee spilled, causing third-degree burns to her legs. She sued McDonald's, and a jury awarded her almost $3 million. (After appeals, the company settled with Liebeck for an undisclosed sum.)

That verdict, which got more publicity than a Super Bowl and Tipper Gore combined, persuaded McDonald's and other coffee vendors to put labels on coffee cups warning that hot coffee is hot.

After that, the floodgates burst. Terrified of lawsuits, American businessmen began plastering their products with labels that belabored the obvious. . . .

But not all the new labels warned of dangers that were absurdly obvious. Some warned of dangers that were absurdly bizarre.

Listerine mouthwash, for a while, carried this warning: "Do not swallow. In case of accidental overdose, seek professional assistance or contact a poison control center immediately."

Crest toothpaste warned: "If more than used for brushing is accidentally swallowed, get medical help or contact a Poison Control Center right away."

And jars of Metamucil bear this warning: "Taking this product without adequate fluid may cause it to swell and block your throat or esophagus and may cause choking."

(Have you ever attended the funeral of somebody who OD'd on Listerine or choked on Metamucil? Me, neither. Obviously, these warnings are working.) . . .

American magazines have swelled with prescription drug ads that include FDA-mandated warnings about possible side effects. These ads are delightfully two-faced. On the front, in big bold letters, are lyrical paeans to the drug's miraculous healing powers. On the back, in type the size of nits, are endless lists of "adverse events," the industry's euphemism for side effects.

Some of these side effects are obvious: Lunesta, a sleeping pill, can cause "drowsiness."

Some are ironic: Advair, an asthma medicine, can cause "severe asthma episodes."

Some are scary: Celebrex, an arthritis medicine, can cause heart attacks, strokes, kidney failure and asthma attacks, among other maladies.

And some are just plain weird: Toprol–XL, a hypertension medicine, can cause "mental confusion" and "depression progressing to catatonia." Lunesta can cause "strange behavior" and "unusual and/or disturbing thoughts." And Caduet, a drug for high blood pressure, can inspire "abnormal dreams."

Inevitably, the plague of warnings led to a plethora of parodies. . . .

Go ahead, laugh. Maybe it will make you feel better. But the grim truth is this: The human body is a frail vessel, and the world is full of stuff that can cut, bruise, break, smash, crash, shatter, batter, mangle, maim, mutilate, poison, sicken and kill it. Sooner or later, one of them will get you.

Consider yourself warned.

g. NAME OF MANUFACTURER

Section 502(b) of the FD&C Act requires that the label of a drug bear the name and place of business of the manufacturer, packer, or distributor. With the advent of specialized manufacturing techniques in the pharmaceutical industry, this seemingly simple requirement became a matter of some complexity. FDA adopted an informal policy that any of the firms which perform an important manufacturing operation could be identified as *the* manufacturer. In addition, the agency established a "man-in-the-plant" policy, under which a drug company could lease the facilities of, or contract with, another firm to manufacture a drug and still identify itself as the manufacturer if it placed its own employees in the manufacturing facility to supervise production. Both policies came in for criticism. *See* "Competitive Problems in the Drug Industry," Hearings before the Subcommittee on Monopoly and Anticompetitive Activities of the Senate Select Committee on Small Business, 95th Cong., 1st Sess., Pt. 33 (1977); "Man-in-the-Plant— FDA's Failure to Regulate Deceptive Drug Labeling," Hearings before the Subcommittee on Oversight and Investigations of the House Committee on Interstate and Foreign Commerce, 95th Cong., 2nd Sess. (1978); "Man-in-the-Plant—FDA's Failure to Regulate Deceptive Drug Labeling," Report together with Separate Views by the Subcommittee on Oversight and Investigations of the House Committee on Interstate and Foreign Commerce, 95th Cong., 2nd Sess., Comm. Print 95–73 (1978); " 'Man-in-the-Plant' Revisited—A Deceptive Drug Labeling Practice Continues," Hearings before the Subcommittee on Oversight and Investigations of the House Committee on Interstate and Foreign Commerce, 96th Cong., 2nd Sess. (1980).

Faced with this chorus of criticism, FDA in 1978 proposed a new regulation to clarify who may be considered the "manufacturer" of a drug. 43 Fed. Reg. 45614 (Oct. 3, 1978). After consulting the Department of Justice, FDA reopened the public record for comment on the possible anticompetitive effects of the proposed regulation. 44 Fed. Reg. 37234 (June 26, 1979). The agency promulgated a final regulation in 45 Fed. Reg. 25760 (Apr. 15, 1980), but then stayed it in part in 46 Fed. Reg. 2977 (Jan. 13, 1981). In 1983, FDA promulgated a final amended regulation, which is still in effect. 47 Fed. Reg. 24735 (June 8, 1982), 48 Fed. Reg. 37620 (Aug. 19, 1983), codified at 21 C.F.R. 201.1. This complex rule abolishes the "man-in-the-plant" policy and allows a firm to be designated as the manufacturer of a drug only if it performs *all* manufacturing operations (with certain limited exceptions, such as encapsulating or sterilizing, that are commonly contracted out). A firm that performs more than half of the important manufacturing operations may be designated as the manufacturer if the label also states that "certain manufacturing operations have been performed by other firms." Alternatively, all firms that contribute to production may be listed as "joint manufacturers," or a single firm may simply be listed as the distributor.

h.   PATIENT LABELING FOR PRESCRIPTION DRUGS

Both FDA's historical practice and court decisions have reinforced the proposition that information about prescription drugs—both indications for use and warnings about possible side effects and adverse reactions—is to be directed to physicians and other medical professionals empowered by state law to authorize their dispensing. In the last four decades, however, FDA, with the support of many consumer organizations, has moved in the direction of requiring that more information be provided directly to the patients who use prescription drugs. In 1970, the agency devised the "patient package insert" (PPI), a concept that soon generated a body of secondary literature. *See generally* Joseph Barrows, *Prescription Drug Labeling for Patients*, 30 FOOD DRUG. COSM. L.J. 98 (1975); Marsha Wertzberger Gardner, *Increasing Patient Awareness in Drug Therapy: Ramifications of a Patient Package Insert Requirement*, 66 GEO. L.J. 837 (1978); Richard A. Guarino, *Patient Package Inserts*, 34 FOOD DRUG. COSM. L.J. 116 (1979); Frank Hermann et al., *Package Inserts for Prescribed Medicines: What Minimum Information Do Patients Need?*, 2 BRIT. MED. J. 1132 (1978); Louis A. Morris & Jerome A. Halperin, *Effects of Written Drug Information on Patient Knowledge and Compliance: A Literature Review*, 69 AM. J. PUB. HEALTH 47 (1979); Louis A. Morris et al., *A Survey of Patient Sources of Prescription Drug Information*, 74 AM. J. PUB. HEALTH 1161 (Oct. 1984);

Howard M. Rowe, *Patient Package Inserts: The Proper Prescription?*, 50 FOOD & DRUG L.J. 95 (1995).

Statement of Policy Concerning Oral Contraceptive Labeling Directed to Users

35 Fed. Reg. 9001 (June 11, 1970).

On April 10, 1970, there was published in the FEDERAL REGISTER, 35 F.R. 5962, a notice of proposed rule-making to establish new labeling requirements for oral contraceptives which would assure that the user is provided information necessary for her safe use of these drugs....

Organized medicine ... generally opposed the statement of policy, on the grounds that (1) it would interfere with the physician-patient relationship by introducing a barrier, and by exerting an undue influence on the physician's prescribing decision and the patient's acceptance of the drugs; (2) that it would confuse and alarm the patient to the extent that persons who should take the drugs for health reasons would not do so; (3) that the package insert cannot provide all of the needed information and is not an appropriate means of informing patients; (4) that the physician is the proper person to provide [this] kind of information to his own patient on an individualized, need-to-know, basis; and (5) that the regulations should not control what information the prescriber gives to the patient by a labeling statement that certain points had been discussed with the patient when the drug was prescribed....

A number of physicians took the opposite view, that information about the hazards of the use of oral contraceptive drugs would serve the cause of patient protection, would enable the patient to make a conscientious choice of this method of contraception, and would not be unduly alarming....

Consumer spokesmen also were divided. Most support much more extensive patient information to assure informed consent to the use of the drugs, but a few spoke of the need to encourage the use of oral contraceptives in family planning among persons for whom unwanted pregnancy would pose a special hazard....

[T]he following new section is added ...

§ 130.45   Oral contraceptive preparations; labeling directed to the patient.

(a) The Food and Drug Administration is charged with assuring both physicians and patients that drugs are safe and effective for their intended uses.... [T]he Administration has reviewed the oral contraceptive products, taking into account the following factors: The products contain potent steroid hormones which affect many organ systems; they are used for long periods of time by large numbers of women who, for the most part, are healthy and take them as a matter of choice for prophylaxis against pregnancy, in full knowledge of other means of contraception; and there is no present assurance that persons for whom the drugs are prescribed or dispensed are uniformly being provided the necessary information for safe and effective use of the drugs.

(b) In view of the foregoing, it is deemed in the public interest to present to users of the oral contraceptives a brief notice of the nature of the drugs, the fact that continued medical supervision is needed for safe and effective use, that the drugs may cause side effects and are contraindicated in some cases, that the most important complication is abnormal blood clotting which can have a fatal outcome, that the physician recognizes an obligation to discuss the potential hazards of using the drugs with the patient, that he has available for the patient written material discussing the effectiveness and the hazards of the drugs, and that users of the oral contraceptives should notify their physicians if they notice any unusual physical disturbance or discomfort.

(c) The Commissioner agrees that the physician is the proper person for providing use information to his patients, and these regulations will provide him a balanced discussion of the effectiveness and the risks attendant upon the use of oral contraceptives for his use in discussing the drugs with his patients.

(d)(1) ... [T]he Commissioner concludes that it is necessary in the best interests of users that the following printed information for patients be included in or with the package dispensed to the patient: ...

Do Not Take This Drug Without Your Doctor's Continued Supervision

The oral contraceptives are powerful and effective drugs which can cause side effects in some users and should not be used at all by some women. The most serious known side effect is abnormal blood clotting which can be fatal.

Safe use of this drug requires a careful discussion with your doctor. To assist him in providing you with the necessary information,   (firm name)   has prepared a booklet (or other form) written in a style understandable to you as the drug user. This provides information on the effectiveness and known hazards of the drug including warnings, side effects and who should not use it. Your doctor will give you this booklet (or other form) if you ask for it and he can answer any questions you may have about the use of this drug.

Notify your doctor if you notice any unusual disturbance or discomfort.

NOTES

1. *Content of Patient Labeling.* This patient package insert (PPI) for oral contraceptives represented a dramatic contraction of the agency's proposed 600–word version, which itself fell far short of the scope and detail of the labeling then directed at physicians. For the current, more comprehensive requirements for patient labeling of oral contraceptives, see 38 Fed. Reg. 26809 (Sept. 26, 1973), 40 Fed. Reg. 5351 (Feb. 5, 1975), 41 Fed. Reg. 53630 (Dec. 7, 1976), 42 Fed. Reg. 27303 (May 27, 1977), 43 Fed. Reg. 4214 (Jan. 31, 1978), 52 Fed. Reg. 13107, 13132 (Apr. 21, 1987), 54 Fed. Reg. 22585, 22624 (May 25, 1989) (oral contraceptives), codified at 21 C.F.R. 310.501.

2. *Oral Contraceptive Labeling.* In *Turner v. Edwards,* 1969–1974 FDLI Jud. Rec. 471, 493 (D.D.C. 1970 & 1971), the plaintiffs sought an injunction against

FDA's original oral contraceptive PPI regulation on the ground that the short warning was inadequate. The plaintiffs asked the court to require that the longer pamphlet be placed in all oral contraceptive packages. The court granted FDA's motion for summary judgment. In *Kushner v. Mathews*, 1975–1977 FDLI Jud. Rec. 537 (S.D.N.Y. 1977), the court declined to order the agency to complete a pending rulemaking to revise the patient labeling for oral contraceptives, despite a claim that the agency had failed to meet commitments for prompter action made before Congress.

3. *Carcinogenicity Warning*. In 1989, FDA revised the PPI for oral contraceptives to delete a specific warning that estrogen has

> ... been shown to cause cancer in animals, which showing justifies the inference that estrogens may cause cancer in humans.

52 Fed. Reg. 13107 (Apr. 21, 1987), 54 Fed. Reg. 22585 (May 25, 1989), codified at 21 C.F.R. 310.501 (1989). A women's health organization petitioned FDA to reinstate a cancer warning (FDA Docket No. 92P–0088/CPI), but FDA denied the petition. In *Henley v. FDA*, 873 F. Supp. 776 (E.D.N.Y. 1995), *aff'd* 77 F.3d 616 (2d Cir. 1996), the courts upheld the FDA decision that "the inclusion of an animal carcinogen warning is not warranted in light of current scientific studies on humans."

4. *Patient Labeling for Other Drugs*. In 1975, FDA was petitioned by a public interest group to prescribe patient labeling for several broad classes of prescription drugs. The agency published the petition in 40 Fed. Reg. 52075 (Nov. 7, 1975) and invited comments on a long list of issues, which suggested a number of then-perceived obstacles to implementation of patient labeling for all prescription drugs.

Although no pharmaceutical manufacturer challenged FDA's patient labeling for oral contraceptives, suit was filed when the agency promulgated a regulation to require patient labeling for prescription drug products containing estrogens. 41 Fed. Reg. 43108 (Sept. 29, 1976), 42 Fed. Reg. 37636 (July 22, 1977), codified at 21 C.F.R. 310.515.

Pharmaceutical Manufacturers Association v. FDA*

484 F. Supp. 1179 (D. Del. 1980), *aff'd per curiam* 634 F.2d 106 (3d Cir. 1980).

■ STAPLETON, DISTRICT JUDGE: . . . .

The regulation . . . outlined several categories of information which must be included in a patient package insert, and required that such an insert be provided to a patient every time the drug was dispensed or administered (*i.e.*, injected). . . . The agency's action came as a result of several studies published in 1975 which indicated an association between the use of conjugated estrogens and an increased risk of endometrial cancer in women. . . .

Plaintiffs and plaintiff-intervenors raise a number of challenges to the regulation. First, they contend that the FDA lacks statutory authority to

---

* [An earlier opinion denying a preliminary injunction appears at 1975–1977 FDLI Jud. Rec. 378 (D. Del. 1977).]

require patient packaging inserts for prescription drugs. They next assert that such a requirement is an unconstitutional interference with the practice of medicine. Finally, they challenge the adequacy of the FDA's findings and conclusions embodied in the preamble to the regulation and argue that, based on the administrative record, the regulation is "arbitrary, capricious, an abuse of discretion, or otherwise not in accordance with law." Because I find that the FDA does have statutory authority to require patient labeling, that such a requirement does not interfere with any constitutionally protected rights of physicians, that the agency's reasoning is sufficiently articulated and that the record adequately supports its judgment, I will grant the defendants' motion for summary judgment and deny that of the plaintiffs....

... [Sections 502(a), 502(f), and 201(n) of the FD&C Act], combined with section 701(a), provide direct support for the challenged regulation. Among other things, they reflect a clear Congressional objective that the users of drugs, whether prescription or non-prescription, shall receive facts "material ... with respect to consequences which may result from the use of the ... [drug] under the conditions of use prescribed in the labeling thereof or under such conditions of use as are customary or usual." The Commissioner, in furtherance of this objective, has seen fit in the challenged regulation to require that information concerning consequences which may result from the use of estrogen drugs be provided to the users thereof on their labeling. I think it clear that section 701(a) authorizes him to do so....

While it is true that one of the important applications of section 201(n) relates to the problem of misleading affirmative claims, nothing in the [1938 House] Report suggests that the section is limited in its application to such claims. Indeed, the text of section 201(n) itself demonstrates that its scope is not so limited. Plaintiffs focus on that portion of the section which defines as misleading any failure to "reveal facts material in light of ... [the] representations" made on the labeling. But section 201(n) goes on to require the disclosure of "facts ... material with respect to consequences which may result from the use" of the drug. This language would be rendered meaningless if this Court were to adopt the construction favored by the plaintiffs.

Finally, plaintiffs argue that any authority which the FDA may have had under the 1938 Act with respect to patient labeling of prescription drugs was withdrawn by Congress in 1951. One of the amendments adopted in that year exempted prescription drugs from the "warnings against misuse" requirement and the "adequate directions for use" requirement of Section 502(f) in those situations where the label contains certain specified information.... According to plaintiffs, the adoption of this exemption as Section 503(b)(2) of the Act was intended by Congress to deprive the Secretary of authority to require that patient labeling for prescription drugs contain information regarding possible undesirable effects of the prescribed use. I do not agree....

It is ... true that the 1951 exemption of prescription drugs from the requirements of section 502(f) was enacted with the idea that prescribing physicians would be the primary source of adequate directions for use and adequate warning against misuse or overuse. It does not necessarily follow, however, that Congress meant to strip the Commissioner of the regulatory authority he had possessed for thirteen years over prescription drug labeling. Plaintiffs' argument glosses over the fact that while prescription drugs were exempted from the requirements of section 502(f) in 1951, they were not exempted from the requirement of section 502(a) that their labels not be misleading. . . .

Court disagrees G still cen't be misleading

The government also argues that the challenged regulation furthers the Congressional objectives reflected in Section 505(d) [which] requires the Secretary to disapprove a new drug application if he or she finds that: ". . . (6) based on a fair evaluation of all material facts, (the proposed) labeling is false or misleading in any particular. . . ." The government argues that the regulation came as a result of new studies which showed that estrogen may be "unsafe for use" under the conditions prescribed in the labeling, and that the Commissioner determined in light of these studies that labeling which did not disclose the risks involved would be misleading.

gov't furthers Congress in 505

While I agree that [section 505(d)], and particularly the addition in 1962 of the sixth ground for disapproval, reflects Congress' continuing concern that drug labeling should be both truthful and complete, I cannot agree that it provides independent support for the challenged regulation. Section 505(d) cannot fairly be read to encompass authority for requiring the delivery of written material to the patient at the time of dispensing. As the FDA itself has explained, the provisions of section 505, as contrasted with the mislabeling provisions of the Act, "apply only at the moment of shipment in interstate commerce and not to action taken subsequent to shipment in interstate commerce."

Court ↄ §505 doesn't help gov't argument)

. . . Plaintiffs argue that the mandatory nature of the regulation interferes with the doctor-patient relationship, and thus with the practice of medicine, by requiring the physician to communicate information emanating from Washington without regard to his or her professional judgment concerning the accuracy of the advice or the desirability of the patient being exposed to it.

π doctor patient relationship

To the extent that the plaintiffs' claim of unconstitutional interference with the right to practice medicine is founded on a notion of federalism which reserves all rights over such regulation to the states, it is without merit. It is undisputed that the practice of medicine is subject to the exercise of state police power where such regulation furthers a legitimate state interest. . . .

Turning to plaintiff's view of a physician's right to exercise professional judgment, it is important to focus on what the challenged regulation does not do. The regulation at issue here does not forbid a physician from prescribing conjugated estrogen drugs, or limit the physician's exercise of professional judgment in that regard. Nor does it limit the information the physician may impart to his or her patients concerning estrogens. If the physician disagrees with a perceived "slant" of the labeling provided by the manufacturer, or with the facts stated therein, he or she is free to discuss the matter fully with the patient, noting his own disagreement and views.

The sample labeling encourages the patient to have this kind of open discussion with her doctor.

When these limitations on the effect of the challenged regulation are considered, it becomes apparent that the plaintiffs urge recognition not of a right to exercise judgment in prescribing treatment, but rather of a right to control patient access to information.... There simply is no constitutional basis for recognition of a right on the part of physicians to control patient access to information concerning the possible side effects of prescription drugs. The cases cited by plaintiffs do contain language referring to a doctor's right to practice medicine, but the rights there recognized were only those necessary to facilitate the exercise of a right which patients were found to possess. The physician rights discussed are thus derivative of patient rights and do not exist independent of those rights....

The patient rights recognized in the line of cases relied upon by plaintiffs flow from a constitutionally protected right of privacy. As the Supreme Court noted in *Whalen v. Roe* [429 U.S. 589 (1977)], this right encompasses the individual's "interest in independence in making certain kinds of important decisions".... To the extent these cases have any bearing on the present issue, then, their rationale would appear to support the challenged regulation.... The asserted right to limit patient access to such information can hardly be said to facilitate the patient's "interest in independence" in decision making....

NOTES

1. *Evaluation of PPIs.* For a critical review of the PPI for estrogens, based upon a survey of women who had received it, *see* Gail P. Udkow et al., *The Safety and Efficacy of the Estrogen Patient Package Insert*, 242 J.A.M.A. 536 (Aug. 10, 1979). The response of women to the estrogen PPI is described in Elizabeth Siegel Watkins, *"Dr., Are You Trying to Kill Me?": Ambivalence About the Patient Package Insert for Estrogen*, 76 BULL. HIST. MED. 84 (2002). *See also* INSTITUTE OF MEDICINE, EVALUATING PATIENT PACKAGE INSERTS (1979).

2. *Estrogen PPI.* The PPI for estrogens has since been revised. 52 Fed. Reg. 37802 (Oct. 9, 1987), 55 Fed. Reg. 18722, 18761 (May 4, 1990). In 45 Fed. Reg. 37455 (June 3, 1980), FDA exempted from its patient labeling requirement for progestational drugs any product labeled solely for treatment of cancer. *See also Schlieter v. Carlos*, Civ. No. 87–0955 SC (D.N.M. 1989) (medical institutions as well as physicians have a duty to distribute estrogen PPIs to patients).

———

FDA then proposed to expand PPIs to prescription drugs.

Prescription Drug Products: Patient Labeling Requirements

44 Fed. Reg. 40016 (July 6, 1979).

The Food and Drug Administration (FDA) is proposing regulations that would require manufacturers to distribute labeling to patients for most prescription drug products for human use, including biological products licensed under the Public Health Service Act of 1944 [42 U.S.C. 262]. The regulations would require dispensers of prescription drug products to provide the labeling to patients when the products are dispensed. This action is being taken because FDA believes that prescription drug labeling that is directed to patients will promote the safe and effective use of prescription drug products and that patients have a right to know about the benefits, risks, and directions for use of the products. . . .

The agency believes . . . that providing patients with written information about the proper use of a prescription drug product including information on the benefits and risks the drug product presents to the patient will result in reduced potential liability. This result is likely not only because patients will receive necessary warnings about the product, but also because the availability of written labeling should improve patient compliance with physician directions and improve patient monitoring of adverse reactions, two factors that may actually decrease drug induced injuries. Patient labeling may also reduce the overall number of malpractice actions, because patients will be more aware that certain risks inevitably accompany drug therapy and that not all adverse effects are caused by deficiencies in the drug product or mistakes by the prescriber.

The proposed regulations set forth general patient labeling requirements that would apply to most prescription drug products. The regulations would require the manufacturer of the product to prepare and distribute patient labeling that physically accompanies the product. The labeling would be written in nontechnical language, would not be promotional in tone or content, and would be based primarily on the physician labeling for the drug product. The patient labeling would contain both a summary of information about the product and more detailed information that identifies the product and the person responsible for the labeling, the proper uses of the product, circumstances under which it should not be used, serious adverse reactions, precautions the patient should take when using the product, information about side effects, and other general information about the proper uses of prescription drug products. The agency would be permitted to exempt the labeling for a particular drug product from any of the specific requirements. The regulations would also establish minimum printing specifications for patient labeling.

Patient labeling for a prescription drug product would be required to be based primarily on the physician labeling required for the product under § 201.100(d). . . . As a legal matter, statements in patient labeling cannot conflict with statements in physician labeling without misbranding the drug product. At the same time, the proposed requirements recognize that there may be substantial differences between the physician and patient labeling for a particular product. For example, the patient labeling may not discuss each of the subjects discussed in the product's physician labeling; and may not contain as thorough a discussion of a subject as the physician labeling. On the other hand, some information that does not appear in physician labeling may be required to appear in patient labeling, such as the consequences of the patient's failure to follow the prescribed regimen. . . .

The patient labeling would also be required to contain a statement that the physician labeling for the drug product (. . . that is, the drug product's "package insert") is available from the patient's pharmacist or physician. Many persons, including some pharmacists and physicians, erroneously believe that State or Federal law prohibits providing a drug product's official package insert to patients. No such prohibition exists. . . . Although the package insert for a drug product may be too technical for most patients to easily understand, patients should not be denied access to this information. . . .

———

On August 30, 1979, the Joint Commission of Pharmacy Practitioners, which represents over 90 percent of the licensed pharmacists in the United States, wrote President Carter to request that he prevent FDA from issuing a final regulation on patient package inserts. The JCPP contended that the cost of the FDA proposal would be large and the benefits uncertain, and that a patient education program conducted by the pharmacy profession "can do a better job at lower cost than any Federal patient education program." *See* Linda E. Demkovich, *FDA in Hot Water Again Over Cost of Proposed Drug Labeling Rule*, 11 Nat'l J. 1568 (Sept. 22, 1979). The next year, FDA nonetheless published final regulations establishing requirements for the preparation and distribution of PPIs for 10 high priority classes of human prescription drugs as a three-year pilot program. 45 Fed. Reg. 60754 (Sept. 12, 1980). The agency promptly began publishing guideline PPIs for the 10 classes of drug products. 45 Fed. Reg. 60785 (Sept. 12, 1980), 45 Fed. Reg. 78514, 78516 (Nov. 25, 1980), 45 Fed. Reg. 80740 (Dec. 5, 1980), 46 Fed. Reg. 28, 160 (Jan. 2, 1981). A RAND study sponsored by the agency concluded, however, that patients could be provided with information about prescription drugs more effectively and efficiently by the private sector than by a mandatory PPI program. Within a few months after President Reagan took office, FDA, in 46 Fed. Reg. 23739, 23815 (Apr. 28, 1981), temporarily stayed the effective dates of the PPI requirements for the five specific drugs for which final guidelines had been published, pending "additional review of these requirements" under President Reagan's Executive Order No. 12291, 46 Fed. Reg. 13193 (Feb. 19, 1981). A consortium of consumer organizations brought suit to set aside that stay. In *Public Citizen v. Department of HHS*, 671 F.2d 518 (D.C. Cir. 1981), the court allowed FDA 30 days to decide its course of action on the matter. The agency then published a notice explaining its stay, outlining the benefits and costs of the program, and stating that the matter was still under regulatory review. 47 Fed. Reg. 1773 (Jan. 13, 1982). A month later, FDA proposed to revoke the PPI regulation. 47 Fed. Reg. 7200 (Feb. 17, 1982). Following an opportunity for public comment, it issued a final decision.

Prescription Drug Products: Revocation of Patient Package Insert Requirements

47 Fed. Reg. 39147 (September 7, 1982).

. . . .

In the proposal to revoke the final rule, the agency explained that the Commissioner of Food and Drugs had carefully reviewed the entire adistrative record of the patient package insert program, the results of a 3–year study conducted under contract for the agency by the RAND Corp. on the effects of prototype PPI's, and information presented at public meetings FDA held on September 30 and October 1, 1981, to solicit views on PPI's.

Based on this review, the proposal noted, the agency believed it could no longer justify the PPI pilot program. First, the agency had been persuaded that the program would not likely have achieved a principal objective, that of enabling FDA to determine whether a mandatory, pharmacy-oriented, drug leaflet program was the most practical way of increasing patient knowledge about prescription drugs. Secondly, the agency pointed out that, since the promulgation of the pilot program, the private sector had provided new initiatives in patient information and was currently developing others. The various private sector initiatives, if effectively implemented, were considered likely to provide consumers with the same type of information about prescription drugs as would have been provided by the agency's pilot program. Moreover, as these initiatives would not be limited to 10 drugs or drug classes, or to pharmacy-distributed leaflets, it was believed possible that they would be capable of providing more information than the agency's pilot program. Also, the agency stressed that cooperation with the private sector would encourage experimentation with diverse systems for delivering patient information, thereby promoting innovation in delivery systems. . . .

The agency received 602 comments on the proposal. . . . On the basis of the information in the proposal, a review of the comments, and other information received by the agency through its Committee on Patient Education (COPE), the agency believes that encouraging diverse private sector efforts for providing consumers with adequate prescription drug information is now preferable to implementing a single, mandated Federal program. . . .

The agency agrees with the comments that written information, which the patient can retain and refer to later, is very useful to most patients. It stresses, however, that most current and planned private sector programs will provide this type of written information, to be available either at the pharmacy in the form of pamphlets, tear-off sheets, etc., or directly from the prescribing physician. With respect to special problems of the elderly, private sector efforts appear capable of offering information systems at least as effective as that which the mandatory program might have provided. A mail-order pharmacy service operated by a national organization of retired persons has developed leaflets that are similar to the originally mandated PPI's and that will be mailed with the drugs to patients. Unlike the mandated program, however, this program is able not only to emphasize drugs used mostly by the elderly, but to tailor the information provided in the leaflets to the particular needs of the elderly. . . .

A consortium of major health professional, trade, and consumer groups are forming a National Council on Patient Information and Education. The Council will encourage health professionals to provide more information to patients about prescription drugs, and will sponsor a national advertising campaign that will encourage patients to seek more information about drug use. . . .

Revocation of the program will have a reasonable effect. Patients will have access to a variety of programs of drug education and information. Pharmacists will not bear an undue share of the managerial and cost burdens associated with patient information services. At least one alternative program under development—the AMA's—will provide patient information at the time a drug is prescribed. This means of patient education, which is recognized as superior to providing patient labeling at the time of dispensing, would likely not be used if PPI's were Federally mandated.

Revocation of the PPI program is consistent with the law. The argument that absence of PPI's misbrands prescription drugs is based on a misunderstanding of the manner in which FDA utilizes its broad statutory authority in support of specific regulations. A regulation, such as the PPI program, is issued under FDA's authority to promulgate regulations for the efficient enforcement of the Federal Food, Drug, and Cosmetic Act. Such a regulation must also be justified by other, more specific, authority in the act, in this case the prohibition against misbranding. After a regulation is promulgated, failure to adhere to the regulation causes a violation of the specific statutory authority on which the regulation is based. In the absence of the regulation, however, violation of that specific authority does not necessarily occur by conduct that the regulation would have covered. To suggest that it does is tantamount to saying that all regulations issued under section 701(a) of the act are merely interpretive, for substantive regulations would be redundant of the legal requirements inherent in other provisions of the act. This view is plainly wrong. FDA has issued numerous substantive regulations under section 701(a) of the act. Most of these regulations created new legal requirements of general applicability and did not simply explain existing requirements. . . .

NOTES

1. *Lack of Judicial Challenge.* FDA's decision to revoke its PPI initiative was not contested in the courts. At the same time, FDA revoked the five final guideline PPIs and withdrew the five draft guideline PPIs that had previously been published. 47 Fed. Reg. 39249 (Sept. 7, 1982).

2. *Voluntary PPIs.* Since 1982, pharmaceutical manufacturers have voluntarily distributed PPIs for a number of drugs that present unique safety questions.

3. *PPI Content and Civil Liability.* Throughout the debate, it was assumed that a PPI would not contain all of the information required to be included in the physician package insert. However, some thought the failure to provide a consumer with *all* information could expose a manufacturer to liability for at least compensatory damages, and perhaps also for punitive damages, to any consumer who suffered an injury warned about in the physician package insert but not in the PPI.

4. *FDA Promotion of Voluntary Patient Information Efforts.* FDA's Committee on Patient Education (COPE) has been disbanded, but the agency's Office of Consumer Affairs continues to foster patient education activities by providing Patient Information Sheets on its website. The National Council on Patient Information and Education (NCPIE) remains active in supporting programs to increase

consumer understanding about prescription drugs. During 1982–1994, the AMA issued Patient Medication Instructions (PMIs) covering more than 80 prescription drugs, but this program was terminated because of diminished demand. Beginning in 1980, USP annually published two volumes of monographs for marketed drugs, one for health care professionals and the other for patients, under the name "USP DI," *i.e.*, Dispensing Information. Since 1998, they have been published by Thomson Micromedex. Since 1980, USP has also published a yearly compilation of ADVICE FOR THE PATIENT: DRUG INFORMATION IN LAY LANGUAGE. The PHYSICIAN'S DESK REFERENCE, which contains the full physician's package insert and is republished yearly, is sold in substantial numbers in bookstores throughout the country. Patient labeling is now commonly provided by groups other than the manufacturers of the drugs, such as pharmacies, private vendors, and healthcare associations. In 71 Fed. Reg. 40724 (July 18, 2006), FDA announced the availability of a guidance titled USEFUL WRITTEN CONSUMER MEDICATION INFORMATION. This guidance is intended to assist entities such as pharmacies, private vendors, and health care associations who develop patient labeling, because neither FDA nor the manufacturer of the drug reviews or approves this information.

COMMENT: PATIENT MEDICATION GUIDES

In 1998, FDA promulgated regulations governing a new program for patient package inserts, renamed "medication guides," or "MedGuides" for short. 60 Fed. Reg. 44182 (Aug. 24, 1995), 63 Fed. Reg. 66378 (Dec. 1, 1998), codified at 21 C.F.R. Part 208. FDA stated its continuing concern that "[i]nadequate access to appropriate patient information is a major cause of inappropriate use of prescription medications, resulting in serious personal injury." FDA defined a medication guide in 21 C.F.R. 208.3(h) as "FDA-approved patient labeling" and established in 21 C.F.R. 208.20 general requirements for the content and format of a medication guide. In effect, medication guides are patient package inserts with a different name.

In its 1995 proposal, FDA stated that, by the year 2000, 75 percent of consumers should be receiving "adequate and useful information about their medication" when they first pick up their new prescriptions, and that this should be increased to 95 percent by 2006. FDA decided it would permit the private sector to attempt to reach these goals on its own. If the goals were not met, FDA said that it would consider a mandatory program of medication guides.

When it published the final regulations in 1998, FDA estimated that approximately 70 percent of pharmacies supplied patient information with prescriptions. In the final regulations, FDA mandated that those pharmacies that were not providing medication guides voluntarily would be required to do so, but only under one or more of the following circumstances:

(1) The drug product is one for which patient labeling could help prevent serious adverse effects.

(2) The drug product is one that has serious risk(s) (relative to benefits) of which patients should be made aware because information concerning the risk(s) could affect patients' decision to use, or to continue to use the product.

(3) The drug product is important to health and patient adherence to directions for use is crucial to the drug's effectiveness.

21 C.F.R. 208.1(c). In accordance with these provisions, FDA has required medication guides for a number of prescription drugs. In the preamble to its final regulations, FDA estimated that it would require a medication guide only on limited occasions, approximately five to ten drugs per year. A review of the FDA website listing drugs for which FDA has required medication guides indicates that FDA is presently at the lower end of this estimate.

i. DISTINGUISHING BETWEEN PRESCRIPTION AND NONPRESCRIPTION DRUGS

Applying the criteria in section 503(b)(1) of the FD&C Act to determine whether a specific drug for a particular indication is a prescription or a nonprescription product is not always a simple matter.

United States v. Article of Drug ... "Decholin"

264 F. Supp. 473 (E.D. Mich. 1967).

■ FREEMAN, DISTRICT JUDGE. . . .

The Government commenced the case by filing a libel of information for condemnation of seventy-three packages bearing approximately ten thousand tablets, each of which contained 250 milligrams (3 3/4 grains) of dehydrocholic acid and was marketed under the trade name "Decholin." Ames Company, Inc., the manufacturer of Decholin, intervened in this in rem proceeding as claimant of the seized articles. . . .

The only substantive provision of concern is Federal Food, Drug and Cosmetic Act, § 503, as amended, reading in pertinent part:

(b)(1) A drug intended for use by man which—

. . . .

(B) because of its toxicity or other potentiality for harmful effect, or the method of its use, or the collateral measures necessary to its use, is not safe for use except under the supervision of a practitioner licensed by law to administer such drug . . .

(C) . . . shall be dispensed only [upon prescription]. . . .

The reverse side of the containers gives this . . . information: "INDICATIONS: Indigestion . . . after-meal discomfort and fullness (particularly after fatty meals) . . . excessive belching constipation. . . . CAUTION: Consult your physician should symptoms persist or severe abdominal pain, nausea and vomiting appear." . . .

There is only one fundamental issue presented by these [cross] motions [for summary judgment]: is Decholin unsafe as a drug intended for human use without a prescription? Nevertheless, recognizing that in section 503(b)(1)(B) Congress listed a number of ostensibly different reasons why a drug may be unsafe for self-medication and attempting to deal with the parties' arguments in an organized fashion, the motions will be viewed as raising two issues. First, is the pharmacological effect of Decholin such that, unless it is taken pursuant to and in accordance with a physician's directions, reactions sufficient to cause the product to be unsafe may result from its ingestion? This will be called the "toxicity question." Second, does the fact that Decholin may be taken by a person who, although experiencing the indications set out on the label, has an ailment which Decholin cannot cure, coupled with the fact such an individual may postpone a visit to his physician in reliance upon the over-the-counter availability of Decholin, cause the drug to be unsafe? Because the gist of the Government's argument on this issue is that an immediate professional diagnosis to detect the underlying cause of the symptoms in a particular case is a step which must precede or accompany use in order for the drug to be considered safe, this point will be called the collateral measures question....

At the basis of both questions lies the fact that the indications mentioned on the Decholin container can stem from any one of what, for present purposes, will be considered as three types of causes: biliary tract obstruction, organic disease and various minor factors. These last include a host of elements ranging from pregnancy through dietary indiscretions, such as skipping meals, and on to old age. Claimant willingly agrees with the Government that Decholin would not be prescribed by a physician to cure either a tract obstruction or an organic disease.

Toxicity Question

If the record showed clearly why a practitioner would not order Decholin for a person suffering from an obstruction or an organic disease, the toxicity question could be in better posture for summary disposition. However, the affidavits of the experts suggest different reasons which may be grounded upon conflicting views on a factual issue, the pharmacological effect of the drug. The statements of claimant's authorities suggest that they would not prescribe Decholin in the presence of one of these major ailments primarily, if not exclusively, just because the drug would do no good for the patient. However, these experts are quick to point out that they have never heard of an instance in which a person with either an obstruction or an organic disease sustained any ill effect from self-medication with Decholin; and at least several of them doubt that harm would ever come to an individual who takes the drug under these circumstances....

... [T]he affidavit of Dr. Manuel Sklar ... is most helpful in showing why the Government considers the drug properly dispensed only on prescription... [I]n his opinion, the product solely by virtue of its composition can be injurious to an individual with an ailment giving rise to Decholin's indications but beyond Decholin's power to cure...).

Even the Government's most helpful spokesman, Dr. Sklar, did not mention that he knew or had heard of a case in which Decholin or any article of similar composition had done harm in any perceptible degree to a layman who had taken the preparation, without consulting a physician upon experiencing the indications listed on the Decholin label. This is not surprising since the Government admitted in answer to interrogatories that it knew of no actual cases of harm attributable to the product.[3] On the other hand, statements made by three of the claimant's experts leave the strong impression that the principal reason why they would consider Decholin safe for self-medication is the fact that their experiences have taught them that a person suffering from an organic disease or a biliary tract obstruction will feel so ill that, as a matter of course, he will seek professional help. Therefore, claimant's experts do not seem to be so much of the opinion that home treatment with Decholin *cannot* cause harm as they do of the view that it *will not*; whereas the Government's affiants stress that Decholin could cause harm to the uninformed lay user, while the Government itself all but concedes that if future unadvised laymen act as their predecessors have, the drug will not be responsible for any serious consequences. . . .

Even if it were apparent from the record that both sides conceded the theoretical possibility of harm from self-medication with Decholin but admitted that, as a practical matter, the likelihood of ill effects is virtually nonexistent, the Court would not feel confident in granting either motion until it has been made aware of the nature of the factors which claimant would say separate the practical order from the theoretical. . . .

The legislative history of the 1951 amendment, which gave birth to section 503(b)(1)(B), shows that Congress did not desire to proscribe self-medication with a product just because under some set of circumstances—and especially hypothetical conditions—the drug may be harmful if taken without professional supervision. . . .

Collateral Measures Question. . . .

The Government in this case has raised the point that a layman cannot determine whether he is suffering from a disorder such as a tract obstruction or a disease like jaundice, although he can compare his symptoms with the indications mentioned on the Decholin label. However, . . . the pertinent question is not whether an individual is able to detect the cause of his ailment, but rather whether the symptoms described on the package as reasons for him to visit a physician are sufficient to alert him to the possibility that his illness may require professional attention. . . .

As the foregoing discussion indicates, there are not only differences of opinion in the record concerning pertinent factual issues, but also an absence from the record at this time of evidence relating to many of the factors which must be considered before the outcome of this case can be decided. For these reasons, both motions for summary judgment are denied.

NOTE

Following the denial of the cross-motions for summary judgment, the case was dismissed with prejudice to FDA and the seized drug was ordered released to Ames.

---

3. The record shows that the use of Decholin-type medicines has been extensive. Since 1926, claimant and its predecessor corporations alone have sold over six-tenths of a billion dehydrocholic acid tables under one or another tradename.

2 FDA Papers, No. 9, at 34 (Nov. 1968). *See also United States v. General Nutrition, Inc.*, 638 F. Supp. 556 (W.D.N.Y. 1986).

j. SWITCH FROM PRESCRIPTION TO NONPRESCRIPTION STATUS

Section 503(b)(1)(C) provides that FDA may require a new drug to be sold only on prescription as part of its decision to approve a new drug application. Virtually all new chemical entity new drugs come on the market initially as prescription drugs, and become eligible for consideration for switch after at least five years of marketing. This assures FDA that there are unlikely to be major undiscovered adverse events. Switches of Rx drugs to OTC status will therefore provide virtually all new nonprescription drugs in the future. *See* Peter Barton Hutt, *Drugs for Self–Medication in the Future: Their Source and the Social, Political, and Regulatory Climate*, 19 DRUG INFO. J. 195 (1985); Stephen Paul Mahinka & M. Elizabeth Bierman, *Direct-to-OTC Marketing of Drugs: Possible Approaches*, 50 FOOD & DRUG L.J. 49 (1995).

A drug may be switched from Rx to OTC status in four ways. First, the holder of an NDA (including a section 505(b)(2) NDA or an abbreviated NDA) may submit a supplemental application requesting FDA to approve the switch. Second, after a prescription drug goes off patent any person may submit a section 505(b)(2) NDA to switch the drug from Rx to OTC. Third, the manufacturer or any other person may petition FDA for an Rx/OTC switch under 21 C.F.R. 310.200. Drugs that FDA has switched to OTC status in response to a petition under this provision are listed in 21 C.F.R. 310.201. Fourth, a switch in status may occur through the mechanisms of the OTC Drug Review established in 21 C.F.R. Part 330 (subject to the specific conditions established in 330.13) or by amendment of an established OTC drug monograph. After an OTC drug monograph is established, all Rx/OTC switches of drugs within the class that are not accomplished through a supplemental NDA or supplemental ANDA are likely to be effected by amendment of the monograph. The petition procedure and list in sections 310.200 and 310.201 will thus fall into disuse.

Peter Barton Hutt, *A Legal Framework for Future Decisions on Transferring Drugs from Prescription to Nonprescription Status*

37 FOOD DRUG COSMETIC LAW JOURNAL 427 (1982).

... FDA has never enunciated either in published regulations or in other written documents the kind of operational rules that would provide clear policy and result in consistent decisions on the prescription/nonprescription status of drugs in this country. The statutory definition of a prescription drug enacted in the 1951 Amendments [FD&C Act 503(b)] has three components: (A) habit-forming drugs listed in section 502(d) of the Act and their derivatives, (B) drugs not safe for use except under a practitioner's supervision, and (C) drugs limited to prescription sale under an NDA.... The first component applies only to the 17 specific habit-forming chemicals listed in section 502(d) or their derivatives.* The third component simply covers those new drugs that, because they meet the statutory factors set out in the second component, are limited to prescription status where FDA approves an NDA for the drug. Thus, all future consideration of prescription/nonprescription status is properly limited to the factors set out in the second component of the statutory definition.

In turn, that second component contains three factors to be considered in determining the prescription/nonprescription status of a drug: (1) toxicity, (2) potentiality for harmful effect, and (3) the method of use or collateral measures necessary to use....

1. Toxicity. The first factor, toxicity, is perhaps the most easily understood and applied. Drugs that have a low margin of safety, and which must therefore be titrated carefully to achieve an adequate level of effectiveness without endangering patient safety, are appropriately placed in prescription status. With increasing scientific sophistication in the field of pharmacology, and the recognition that life-threatening drugs may be needed to treat life-threatening disease, there will undoubtedly always be at least some drugs too toxic for OTC marketing.

At the same time, it must be recognized that the mere possibility that a drug could be misused, with toxic results, is not sufficient by itself to retain that drug in prescription status. As the court recognized in the *Decholin* case, virtually any drug can be misused with some toxic results....

As with all of the factors described in this paper, it is not feasible now, and undoubtedly will not be feasible in the future, to derive operational definitions or empirical formulas for determining appropriate margins of safety. Toxicity, like each of the other factors described below, is simply one factor to be considered as part of an integrated decision....

2. Other potentiality for harmful effect. The statute does not limit FDA to questions simply relating to toxicity in considering the prescription/nonprescription status of a drug. Rather, FDA is permitted a broad inquiry into other potentiality for harmful effects as well....

It is undoubtedly not feasible to anticipate all of the various possible considerations that fall within this factor of potential for other harmful effects. It is important, however, to note that some considerations that represent valid public health concerns do not properly fall within this factor. Two that immediately come to mind are the potential for tampering with OTC drug products and the possibility that some OTC drug ingredients might be substituted for serious drugs of abuse in counterfeit drug sales on the street....

3. Method of use and collateral measures necessary to use. Congress intended this factor to have the broadest possible scope. It encompasses all aspects of the circumstances under which a drug is used, including broad questions of social policy. There is perhaps no issue involving drug use that cannot properly be brought into consideration under this factor.

* [The subparagraph concerning habit-forming drugs was deleted from section   503(b) in 1997.]

a. Self-diagnosis. Many people erroneously believe that a drug must be placed on prescription status for any condition for which self-diagnosis is not feasible. In fact, self-diagnosis is not a statutory prerequisite for OTC status and the law has not been applied by FDA in that way. FDA did successfully urge that interpretation upon the court in the *El–O–Pathic* case in 1951, but has not pursued it since that time.

Numerous OTC drugs are presently available for conditions that are not susceptible to self-diagnosis to lay people. The classic example is insulin. No lay person would be trusted to diagnose diabetes. Nor is that an isolated example. Many minor conditions for which OTC drugs are available could be the result of a wide variety of diseases. Differential diagnosis by specialized expert professionals would be required to pinpoint the cause with precision. Upset stomach, after all, could be caused by food poisoning, gastric cancer, too much alcoholic beverage or rich food, excess stomach acid, or an ulcer. Yet no one questions the OTC status of appropriate home remedies for this condition. And analgesics are available for headaches even though no lay person is capable of diagnosing the difference between a headache caused by simple stress and a headache caused by a concussion or a brain tumor. . . .

b. Self-treatment and self-care. Another consideration frequently mentioned as a major element in any prescription/nonprescription determination is the need for a doctor to supervise the administration of the drug and to monitor the patient's progress. In earlier days, this might well have been true. Today, it remains one consideration, but not nearly as important as it once was. . . .

With rare exception, self-administration of any drug by a lay person is entirely feasible. It is useful to remember that a major OTC drug, insulin, is administered by injection. . . .

The vast majority of our population is now fully capable of listening to, understanding, and complying with instructions for self-treatment and self-care. Most people—and particularly those suffering from chronic illness, who must take drugs for long periods of time and perhaps the rest of their lives—are quite capable of appreciating the interaction of daily self-treatment and periodic visits to a physician who can then monitor overall progress. . . .

c. Adequate labeling. This consideration is receiving more attention than ever before, and undoubtedly will become, with toxicity and abuse potential, the most important consideration in determining prescription/nonprescription status in the future. The quintessential requirement for any OTC drug must be adequate directions for use.

We are just now beginning to face up to the true meaning of that requirement for many products that have long been considered appropriate only for prescription status. It is likely that, with time, OTC drug labeling will become far more lengthy and detailed than it is at the present. . . .

d. Social policy. Neither the FD&C Act nor its legislative history includes, in specific terms, any reference to broad social policy. It is readily apparent, however, that many determinations of prescription/nonprescription status depend in large measure upon unarticulated principles of social policy.

Societal concerns must always be considered in any decision on prescription/nonprescription status. The panel that considered the prescription/nonprescription status of oral contraceptives, as part of the OTC Drug Review, undoubtedly spent more time discussing broad questions of social policy than narrow questions of toxicity. The status of drugs used to treat venereal disease would undoubtedly raise similar considerations.

The importance of having particular drugs available readily and cheaply for public use is also a major consideration.... The cost of adequate professional care for the poor and the elderly will undoubtedly be a major factor in future decisions about the possibility of transferring drugs used in chronic disease from prescription to OTC status. These are valid considerations, to be encouraged rather than discouraged, as society attempts to come to grips with the need to provide the best possible medical care for its divergent population at the least possible cost.

The concerns of the medical and pharmacy professions must also be considered. Physicians are torn between their concern about permitting important prescription drugs to leave their control, and their realization that many unproductive and unrewarding routine office visits could be avoided if, after a disease was once diagnosed, appropriate medication were readily available on an OTC basis....

Pharmacists, like physicians, are concerned about their eroding position as recognized experts in drug therapy. Ultimately, however, that position must be stabilized and rebuilt not on the basis of a legalized monopoly, but on the basis of demonstrated ability and hard-won public confidence. An increase in the number of drugs transferred from prescription to nonprescription status provides no greater justification for a so-called "third class of drugs," which would be available on an OTC basis only in pharmacies, than did the argument, rejected by FDA and the Department of Justice in 1974, that all OTC drugs with safety warnings should be sold only through pharmacies.

Finally, industry concerns must also be appreciated. The relative profitability of a drug when sold on prescription and nonprescription status will have a significant impact on the approach of the drug industry to any particular decision in this area. The relationship of the drug industry to physicians and pharmacists, and their concern about the potential impact of any prescription nonprescription decision upon that relationship, is too important to be ignored. Nor is the potential change in product liability when a drug is transferred from prescription to prescription status a matter of insignificance....

NOTES

1. *OTC Drug Review Switches.* After its establishment in 1972, the OTC Drug Review process became the principal means for switching drugs from Rx to OTC status. Both the Consumer Healthcare Products Association (formerly the Nonprescription Drug Manufacturers Association) and FDA have periodically released lists of drugs switched from Rx to OTC by decisions taken in the course of the OTC Drug

Review. Through this process, more than 50 active drug ingredients have become available without prescription. *See, e.g.*, 55 Fed. Reg. 6932 (Feb. 27, 1990) (relating the history of FDA's consideration of the switch of hydrocortisone from Rx to OTC status). Since the time FDA finished publishing all the tentative final OTC monographs in the Federal Register, however, virtually all Rx–OTC switches have occurred through the NDA process.

2. *Immediate Switch Under the OTC Drug Review.* FDA's OTC Drug Review regulations provide that, where an active ingredient was limited to prescription status prior to May 11, 1972 (the date the regulations were promulgated), and an OTC Drug Review panel recommends its switch to OTC status, it may be so marketed following publication of the panel report if FDA does not specifically disagree with the panel recommendation, but that such marketing is subject to the risk that FDA may subsequently disagree and insist that the ingredient remain limited to prescription status. 21 C.F.R. 330.13. Promethazine hydrochloride illustrates this process. The FDA OTC Cough and Cold Drug Panel recommended it be switched to OTC status, 41 Fed. Reg. 38312 (Sept. 9, 1976), but FDA objected to that recommendation, and it thus did not become effective. By the time FDA published the tentative final monograph, it had changed its mind and permitted the OTC marketing of promethazine. 53 Fed. Reg. 30522 (Aug. 12, 1988). However, adverse comments on the tentative final monograph persuaded the agency to reverse field again, and it ruled that OTC marketing should not be permitted until it had studied the matter further. 54 Fed. Reg. 36762 (Sept. 5, 1989), 57 Fed. Reg. 58356 (Dec. 9, 1992). No further action has been taken by FDA on this matter.

3. *Benylin Case.* The process of switching an Rx drug to OTC status can be treacherous and contentious. Parke, Davis & Co. initially received FDA approval of an NDA for diphenhydramine hydrochloride (DPH) in 1948 as a prescription expectorant drug under the brand name "Benylin." The OTC Drug Review panel recommended its switch to OTC status in September 1974. Two months later, the company submitted a supplemental NDA seeking approval for the switch. Before FDA acted on the supplemental NDA, however, the company began marketing Benylin as an OTC drug. A year later, in the preamble to the proposed monograph on OTC cough and cold drugs, FDA stated that the Rx–OTC status of DPH as an antitussive (cough drug) would be decided through the supplemental NDA. 41 Fed. Reg. 38312, 38313 (Sept. 9, 1976). A month later, the agency disapproved the supplemental NDA, announced its disagreement with the OTC Drug Review panel, and offered the manufacturer a hearing on the denial of approval of its supplemental NDA. 41 Fed. Reg. 52536, 52537 (Nov. 30, 1976). In an action for declaratory judgment brought by the company, the Court of Appeals held that the FDA enforcement actions against Benylin could not be enjoined. *Parke, Davis & Co. v. Califano*, 564 F.2d 1200 (6th Cir. 1977). When the company did not appear to defend seizures of the product, the actions went by default. *United States v. An Undetermined Quantity of an Article of Drug Labeled as Benylin Cough Syrup*, 583 F.2d 942 (7th Cir. 1978). Following a full evidentiary hearing on FDA's denial of the Parke, Davis supplemental NDA, the Administrative Law Judge determined that Benylin is effective for its recommended use and safe for OTC distribution. However, FDA Commissioner Kennedy reversed the Administrative Law Judge and determined that Benylin had not been shown to be effective for use in the treatment of cough. 44 Fed. Reg. 51512 (Aug. 31, 1979). Commissioner Kennedy did not resolve the issue of OTC status, but he did state that, if Benylin were found to be effective, the risks "might not be so severe as to require a prescription." 44 Fed. Reg. at 51523. FDA then proposed to withdraw approval of the existing NDA for DPH. 44 Fed. Reg. 57497 (Oct. 5, 1979). After the company submitted evidence of effectiveness of the drug, however, FDA approved the supplemental NDA for the product as an OTC drug in August 1981 and withdrew the notice of opportunity for

hearing. 47 Fed. Reg. 18669 (Apr. 30, 1982). DPH therefore never appeared in the monograph for OTC antitussive drugs, 48 Fed. Reg. 48576 (Oct. 19, 1983), 53 Fed. Reg. 30042 (Aug. 12, 1987), 21 C.F.R. Part 341, and can now be marketed only pursuant to an abbreviated NDA.

4. *Ibuprofen.* FDA's much-publicized decision in May 1984 to switch ibuprofen from Rx to OTC status, by approving NDAs for Nuprin and Advil, was immediately subjected to two different types of legal challenge. A competitor unsuccessfully challenged FDA's decision to effect this switch by approval of NDAs rather by amendment of the OTC drug monograph. *Chattem, Inc. v. Heckler*, Food Drug Cosm. L. Rep. (CCH) ¶¶ 38,293, 38,294, 38,339 (D.D.C. 1984, 1985), *aff'd per curiam* 1985–1986 FDLI Jud. Rec. 326 (D.C. Cir. 1986). Consequently, ibuprofen can now be marketed only under FDA approval of an abbreviated NDA. In *McNeilab, Inc. v. Heckler*, Food Drug Cosm. L. Rep. ¶¶ 38,290 & 38,317 (D.D.C. 1984, 1985), the District Court held that another competitor could challenge the legal basis of FDA's switch of ibuprofen from Rx to OTC but upheld the agency on the merits. As part of its approval of the NDAs, FDA obtained assurances from the two applicants that their advertising would not undercut the approved OTC labeling. McNeilab contended that, since FDA has jurisdiction only over labeling and may only approve a drug for OTC status if it can be safely marketed as *labeled*, the switch from Rx to OTC status was unlawful. The District Court held, however, that it was proper for FDA to discuss advertising with the two applicants and that the record demonstrated that it had found ibuprofen to be safe as *labeled*.

5. *Metaproterenol.* FDA has had to be sensitive to the views of physicians and pharmacists when it considers an Rx to OTC switch. Without consulting either the medical profession or the manufacturer, in the tentative final monograph for OTC bronchodilator drugs, the agency announced that metaproterenol sulfate in a metered-dose inhaler for use as a bronchodilator could immediately be switched from Rx to OTC status. 47 Fed. Reg. 47520 (Oct. 26, 1982). Following objections from the medical community and an adverse vote by an advisory committee, the agency rescinded the switch. 48 Fed. Reg. 24925 (June 3, 1983). *See* Leslie Hendeles & Miles Weinberger, *Nonprescription Sale of Inhaled Metaproterenol—Deja Vu*, 310 NEW ENG. J. MED. 207 (Jan. 19, 1984); "FDA's Prescription to Over-the-Counter Drug Switch," Hearing before the Subcommittee on Oversight and Investigations of the House Committee on Energy and Commerce, 98th Cong., 1st Sess. (1983).

6. *Forced Switch.* In June 1998, Wellpoint Health Networks, a medical insurance company, filed a citizen petition with FDA (Docket No. 1998P–0610/CPI) requesting that the agency switch the three largest selling allergy drugs (Claritin, Allegra, and Zyrtec) from Rx to OTC. Wellpoint had a major economic interest in obtaining a switch because, if the three drugs were switched, they would no longer be reimbursable. All three drugs still enjoyed patent protection, and the manufacturers opposed the petition. When the companies rebuffed the agency's pressure to cooperate with a switch, FDA threatened to grant the Wellpoint petition and do a "forced switch" by rulemaking under 21 C.F.R. 310.200. The three companies responded that any action to force a switch would require a notice of opportunity for a formal evidentiary hearing under section 505(e). To add to the pressure, other companies submitted section 505(b)(2) NDAs to switch Claritin to OTC status upon expiration of the patent. The matter was resolved when Schering–Plough switched Claritin in November 2002, just prior to the expiration of the patent, and the pending section 505(b)(2) NDAs were promptly approved when the patent expired. It appears that the FDA threat of a forced switch was only the agency's way of increasing the pressure for a voluntary switch, and that the agency had no intention of actually devoting the resources necessary to implement such a contentious approach. FDA's authority to force a switch through rulemaking therefore remains unresolved. *See* Holly M. Spencer, Comment: *The RX-to-OTC Switch of Claritin,*

Allegra, and Zyrtec: An Unprecedented FDA Response to Petitioners and the Protection of the Public Health, 51 Am. U. L. Rev. 999 (2002)

7. *Emergency Contraceptive.* No Rx/OTC switch in history has attracted more industry, public, and political attention than the switch of the emergency contraceptive, "Plan B," from prescription to nonprescription status. The proposed switch raised high emotions on both sides and delayed Senate consideration of the nominations of both Lester Crawford and Andrew von Eschenbach as FDA Commissioners. An NDA to switch the emergency contraceptive from prescription to nonprescription status was initially submitted to FDA in April 2003. In December 2003 a joint meeting of two FDA advisory committees recommended approval of the application by a vote of 23 to 4. The FDA review staff recommended approval, but the Acting Director of CDER signed a not-approvable letter in May 2004 because of concerns about unsupervised use by women under 16 years of age. FDA then requested public comment on the circumstances under which the drug could be marketed as an OTC drug for women 17 years and older and as a prescription drug for women under 17 years of age. 70 Fed. Reg. 52050 (Sept. 1, 2005). An investigation by the Government Accountability Office (GAO) described the process followed by FDA as "unusual." GAO, Food and Drug Administration Decision to Deny Initial Application for Over-the-Counter Marketing of the Emergency Contraceptive Drug Plan B Was Unusual, GAO–06–109 (Nov. 2005). It provoked a District Court into ordering unprecedented document discovery from FDA and depositions of top FDA officials in a case brought by consumers to contest the lengthy delay in the handling of the NDA. *Tummino v. Von Eschenbach*, 427 F. Supp. 2d 212 (E.D.N.Y. 2006). The matter was ultimately resolved by FDA approving the Rx/OTC switch of the emergency contraceptive for women 18 years of age and older but requiring that the OTC version of the drug be available only behind the counter and not on an open shelf. "FDA Approves Over-the-Counter Access for Plan B for Women 18 and Older," FDA News No. P06–118 (Aug. 24, 2006). *See* Marian Lee, *When Plan A Fails, We Need Plan B* (2004), in Chapter VI(H) of the Electronic Book; Gregory W. Reilly, *The FDA and Plan B: The Legislative History of the Durham–Humphrey Amendments and the Consideration of Social Harms in the Rx–OTC Switch* (2006), in Chapter VI(D)(2) of the Electronic Book. *See also* Ada A. Dekhtyar, *A Difficult Proposition: Oral Contraceptives' Switch from Prescription to Over-the-Counter Status* (1997), and Susan R. Lewis, *Oral Contraceptives: The Road to Over-the-Counter Availability* (1999), in Chapter VI(D)(1) of the Electronic Book.

8. *Considerations for Switch.* FDA CDER Director Carl C. Peck and FDA CDER Office of Nonprescription Drugs Director Michael Weintraub offered the following considerations for an Rx/OTC switch:

Peck Switch Considerations
- Is there special toxicity in its class?
- Is there a large margin of safety?
- Does dosing frequency affect safe use?
- Is the safety profile defined at high doses?
- Has the safety profile been characterized by extensive Rx marketing?
- What is the worldwide marketing experience?
- Is it OTC in foreign markets? What is the experience in these markets?
- What do use data show?
- Has a rigorous risk analysis been performed?
- Does literature support expected

Weintraub Switch Considerations
- Is absorption rapid and complete?
- Is there a low-level of first-pass hepatic extraction and metabolism?
- Are elimination patterns straightforward?
- Are there small variations in ADME?
- Does the active have a primary pharmacological effect leading to a defined clinical response?
- Have safety data been collected on the OTC dose?
- Is there potential masking of a serious disease state that would dangerously delay physician involvement?
- Is there potential for misuse in terms of duration and dose?

Peck Switch Considerations
usage and labeling?

- Is there a full understanding of pharmacodynamics?
- Is the minimally effective OTC dose known?
- Have potential drug interactions been characterized?

Weintraub Switch Considerations

- Are early stages of adverse reactions recognizable by the patient?

Mark B. Gelbert, *Making the Rx-to-OTC Switch: What You Need to Know*, 1 REG. AFFAIRS FOCUS, No. 10, at 18 (October 1996).

FDA CDER Office of Drug Evaluation V Director Robert DeLap offered the following 12 considerations for a switch:

"Fundamentals"

- Can the condition be adequately self-diagnosed?
- Can the condition be successfully self-treated?
- Is the self-treatment product safe and effective for consumer use, under conditions of actual use?

"Points to Consider"

- Is there a need for physician evaluation of the condition?
- What is the nature and severity of adverse effects of consumer misdiagnosis, and delay in correct diagnosis?
- Regarding effective product use, what is the nature of consumer understanding of product use?
- What is the consumer understanding of the expected benefit?
- Does the consumer have the ability to assess treatment effect?

"Safe Product Use"

- What is the consumer understanding of product directions for safe use?
- What is the consumer understanding of what to do if the product isn't working?
- What is the consumer ability to identify adverse effects, and the consumer ability to determine when adverse events may require professional care?
- What is the consumer expectation of safety?

DeLap's "12 Principles of OTCness," NDMA EXECUTIVE NEWSLETTER 3 (Nov. 20, 1998). *See also* Eric P. Brass, *Changing the Status of Drugs from Prescription to Over-the-Counter Availability*, 345 NEW ENG. J. MED 810 (Sept. 13, 2001).

9. *Reimbursement.* As discussed in Note 6, prescription drugs are reimbursed but OTC drugs are not. Section 503(b) does not include reimbursement or any other economic factor as a criterion for consideration of a potential switch. Yet reimbursement is often raised by interested parties. FDA and its advisory committees, although not addressing this issue directly, could easily be influenced by it in evaluating a potential switch.

10. *Unsuccessful Attempts to Switch.* FDA and its advisory committees have thus far declined to approve switch petitions filed by the pioneer manufacturers of two types of very successful Rx drugs. Burroughs Welcome (now part of Glaxo-SmithKline) proposed to switch its very successful drug, Zovirex, for herpes, but was turned down after two advisory committees failed to support the switch. Merck proposed to switch its anticholesterol statin drug, Mevacor, and Bristol Myers also proposed to switch its statin, Pravachol, but both were unsuccessful after two

advisory committee meetings. *See* Brian L. Strom, *Statins and Over-the-Counter Availability*, 352 NEW ENG. J. MED. 1403 (Apr. 7, 2005); Niteesh K. Choudry & Jerry Avorn, *Over-the-Counter Statins*, 142 ANNALS OF INTERNAL MED. 910 (June 7, 2005). The patents for all of these drugs are now expired.

11. *Required Testing for Switch.* Before it will consider switching a prescription drug to OTC status, FDA almost always requires (1) a label comprehension study to demonstrate that consumers can understand the indications, warnings, and directions for use and (2) a home use study to demonstrate that consumers will follow the label information. A home use study has been determined by FDA to qualify the applicant for 3 years of market exclusivity. See letter from Janet Woodcock, Director, FDA CDER, to Gary L. Yingling (Oct. 31, 1996).

12. *Aspirin for Stroke and Heart Disease.* Faced with clear evidence of the safety and effectiveness of aspirin for various cardiovascular and related conditions, FDA resorted to the use of professional labeling rather than patient labeling. *See* 53 Fed. Reg. 46204 (Nov. 16, 1988), 63 Fed. Reg. 56802 (Oct. 23, 1998), codified at 21 C.F.R. 343.80.

13. *Exocrine Pancreatic Insufficiency Drugs.* FDA rejected a switch of these drugs, not on the ground that a physician's diagnosis is necessary, but because of the need for a physician to monitor the condition, cystic fibrosis, for which they are used. 44 Fed. Reg. 75666 (Dec. 21, 1979), 50 Fed. Reg. 46594 (Nov. 8, 1985), 56 Fed. Reg. 32282 (July 15, 1991).

14. *State Reverse Switch.* In *Northwest Connection, Inc. v. Board of Pharmacy*, 814 P.2d 191 (Or. Ct. App. 1991), the court upheld a decision of the State Board of Pharmacy to switch ephedrine from nonprescription to prescription status. As added by the FDA Modernization Act of 1997, section 751(c)(1)(B) of the FD&C Act specifically excludes such state switches from the requirement of national uniformity for nonprescription drugs.

15. *Commentary.* For a broad-ranging discussion of the issues surrounding the switch of drugs from Rx to OTC status *see* Gerald M. Rachanow, *The Switch of Drugs from Prescription to Over-the-Counter Status*, 39 FOOD DRUG COSM. L.J. 201 (1984); *The Impact of the Rx-to-OTC Switch Process—Present and Future*, 19 DRUG INFO. J., No. 2 (1985); *Symposium, Rx-to-OTC Switch*, 24 DRUG INFO. J. 1 (1990); Linda M. Katz, *Prescription to Over-the-Counter Switches*, 48 FOOD & DRUG L.J. 567 (1993); Lars Noah, *Treat Yourself: Is Self–Medication the Prescription for What Ails American Health Care?*, 19 HARV. J.L. & TECH. 359 (2006).

3.   DRUG ESTABLISHMENT REGISTRATION AND DRUG LISTING

The Drug Amendments of 1962 added section 510 of the FD&C Act, which requires the registration of all drug establishments. 76 Stat. 780, 793. The Drug Listing Act of 1972, 86 Stat. 559, added section 510(j) of the FD&C Act to require the submission to FDA of lists of the drug products made in those establishments. *See* Robert L. Banse, *Drug Listing Act of 1972*, 28 FOOD DRUG COSM. L.J. 255 (1973). It took almost a decade before the information submitted under the Drug Listing Act became computer-accessible.

The drug establishment registration and drug product listing regulations are codified in 21 C.F.R. Part 207. A report by the HHS Office of Inspector General, *The Food and Drug Administration's National Drug Code Directory*, No. OEI–06–05–00060 (Aug. 2006), found that FDA's list of marketed drug products is seriously deficient:

Problems w/ list of marketed drugs

The Directory is incomplete, with an estimated 9,187 prescription drug products missing, primarily due to insufficient reporting by drug firms. . . .

An estimated 5,150 marketed drug product listings are pending, primarily because drug firms failed to submit complete listing information and because of submission errors. . . .

The Directory is not accurate, with an estimated 34,257 drug products no longer on the market or listed in error, primarily because drug firms failed to report drugs taken off the market. . . .

FDA's drug product listing process and lack of oversight contribute to deficiencies in the Directory. . . .

In response, FDA published a proposed complete revision of its regulations, under which drug establishment registration and drug product listing would be required to be done electronically through the internet. 71 Fed. Reg. 51276 (Aug. 29, 2006). A public meeting on this proposal was announced in 71 Fed. Reg. 63726 (Oct. 31, 2006).

For an unusual case sustaining a criminal conviction for failure to register a drug establishment, see *United States v. Antosh*, 172 F.3d 877 (9th Cir. 1999).

4.   PRESCRIPTION DRUG PROMOTION

a.   GENERIC NAME DISCLOSURE

From December 1959 until his death in August 1963, Senator Estes Kefauver presided over extensive hearings investigating pricing, promotion, and patent practices of the pharmaceutical industry. The legislation he introduced to promote competition within the industry was languishing in Congress before it was revived by the thalidomide tragedy in mid–1962. The grim reports of deformed infants born to many European women who had taken thalidomide during pregnancy revitalized Kefauver's bill, converted it into legislation to increase FDA's authority over the safety and effectiveness of drugs, and assured its enactment as the Drug Amendments of 1962, 76 Stat. 780. *See* RICHARD. HARRIS, THE REAL VOICE (1964); THE INSIGHT TEAM, SUFFER THE CHILDREN: THE STORY OF THALIDOMIDE (1979).

One of the few of Kefauver's original proposals that survived the legislative process was the requirement in section 502(e) of the FD&C Act that manufacturers disclose the generic name of the active ingredient in their products in labeling and in advertising. Kefauver explained the reason for this provision as follows:

Administered Prices—Drugs

Senate Report No. 448, 87th Congress, 1st Session (1961).

In addition to patent controls and the vast amounts spent on advertising and promotion, the control of the market by the large drug companies stems from a third source of power; this is their remarkable success in persuading physicians to prescribe by trade names rather than generic names. Where this is done the small manufacturer is automatically excluded from the market, regardless of whether the drugs are patented or nonpatented, and the opportunity for price competition disappears. This state of affairs is furthered by anything which causes the physician to be apprehensive of, or have difficulty in, prescribing by generic names. . . .

The new so-called synthetic penicillin illustrates the problem. The chemical name for this product is alpha-phenoxyethyl penicillin potassium. This set of syllables is also used as a generic name. In addition, there are two other generic names—potassium penicillin 152 and phenethicillin potassium. Since the product is protected by patent, there are only six sellers, each of whom markets under his own trade name. Thus the prescribing physician is bombarded with promotional material for Syncillin, Darcil, Alpen, Chemipen, Dramcillin–S, and Maxipen. All of these are, of course, the same chemical compound. . . .

In this example the busy practitioner is confronted with three generic names, six brand names used as the name of the drug itself, and at least five different colors. Thus, there are 14 different identification symbols for the identical drug. In terms of nomenclature, each product stands isolated: indeed, there is an attempt to conceal the identical nature of the drug. . . .

———

Pharmaceutical manufacturers opposed adoption of section 502(e). When the FDA adopted regulations to implement the provision in 1963, the major drug companies promptly took the agency to court. *See* Harry A. Sweeney, Jr., *The "Generic Every Time" Case: Prescription Drug Industry In Extremis*, 21 FOOD DRUG COSM. L.J. 226 (1966). The regulations would have required manufacturer labeling and advertising to disclose the generic name—termed the "established name" in section 502(e)—of the drug every time the trade name was used. The manufacturers sought a declaratory judgment that the regulations were invalid and an injunction against their enforcement in advance of any attempt by FDA to initiate compliance proceedings against any firm or drug. The District Court held the regulations invalid. *Abbott Laboratories v. Celebrezze*, 228 F. Supp. 855 (D. Del. 1964). Neither the Court of Appeals for the Third Circuit, which reversed the District Court, 352 F.2d 286 (1965), nor the Supreme Court reached the merits of the case. The Supreme Court's decision in *Abbott Laboratories v. Gardner*, 387 U.S. 136 (1967), p. 1535 *infra*, remains the seminal judicial discussion of "ripeness" of agency action for judicial review. The Court held that the regulations were reviewable in a preenforcement suit and remanded the case for consideration of the legality of FDA's "every time" requirement.

Following the Supreme Court's remand, the parties reached a settlement a few days before the case was scheduled for reargument before the Third Circuit. The resulting regulation, 21 C.F.R. 201.10(g), requires that the generic name appear, in type that is at least half the size as the brand name, whenever the brand name is "featured," and at least once when the brand name is used "in the running text."

NOTES

1. *Official Names.* The Drug Amendments of 1962 also added section 508 to the FD&C Act, which authorizes FDA, when necessary, to designate a drug's official name. FDA established a procedure for designating official names in 21 C.F.R. Part 299 and initially promulgated a number of official names. The agency later revoked these names, however, and adopted the policy of relying upon the drug names established by United States Adopted Names (USAN). 47 Fed. Reg. 31008 (July 16, 1982), 49 Fed. Reg. 37574 (Sept. 25, 1984), 53 Fed. Reg. 5368 (Feb. 24, 1988). USAN is published by a consortium of private organizations, in consultation with FDA and international organizations.

2. *FDA Change in Official Name.* In *Novartis v. Leavitt*, 435 F.3d 344 (D.C. Cir. 2006), the Court of Appeals held that FDA may lawfully change an official name without notice-and-comment rulemaking.

3. *Brand Name.* The manufacturer of a drug may choose any brand name that is not false or misleading. FDA has successfully challenged brand names as misleading. *E.g., United States v. 70 1/2 Dozen Bottles . . . "666"*, 1938–1964 FDLI Jud. Rec. 89 (M.D. Ga. 1944). If disclaimers are adequate to prevent a brand name from being misleading, however, the manufacturer has the right to use the disclaimer. *E.g.*, 39 Fed. Reg. 11298 (Mar. 27, 1974). *See* Angela A. Sun, *A Drug by Any Other Name: The Power of Naming and the Medical and Regulatory Impact of Misnaming Prescription Drugs* (2001), in Chapter (VI)(B)(1) of the Electronic Book. Multiple brand names for the same active ingredient may also be used in nonmisleading ways. *See* Antonella Lozito, *U.S. Regulatory Environment: Multiple Trade Names for Same Active Moiety*, 10 REG. AFFAIRS FOCUS, No. 11, at 17 (Nov. 2005).

COMMENT: USP, NF, AND HP OFFICIAL COMPENDIA

The FD&C Act establishes a special, but very limited, status for three official compendia: the United States Pharmacopeia (which incorporates the National Formulary) and the Homeopathic Pharmacopeia. Section 501(b) of the FD&C Act provides that a drug that purports to be or is represented as a drug the name of which is recognized in one of the official compendia is adulterated if its strength differs from, or its quality or its purity falls below, the standards set in the compendium. The provision specifically authorizes USP or HP to establish tests or methods of assays to determine the strength, quality, or purity of a drug. The compendia have no authority, however, to issue regulations or any other form of binding guidance regarding the labeling, methods of manufacture, or other aspects of a drug. Any compendial requirements must be in a drug standard and must be limited to determinations of strength, quality, or purity.

Under sections 501(b) and 502(e)(3)(B), a drug that does not meet a compendial standard with respect to strength, quality, or purity has two options. First, if it chooses to use the official compendial name, the label must state that the drug differs from the standard of strength, quality, or purity set forth in the compendium. Second, it may choose to use a different established name, in which case the label need not state that the drug differs from the compendium standard.

USP publishes "General Notices and Requirements" governing a number of aspects of drug manufacture and labeling that extend beyond its legal authority. These constitute recommendations that are not enforceable. USP also includes dietary supplements in its compendium. None of the provisions applicable to drugs, outlined above, apply to dietary supplements, and none of the provisions in the USP monograph relating to dietary supplements is enforceable.

b. PRESCRIPTION DRUG ADVERTISING AND PROMOTION TO PROFESSIONALS

i. *Print Advertising to Professionals*

The Drug Amendments of 1962 gave FDA authority to regulate advertising for prescription drugs in section 502(n) of the FD&C Act. Regulations to implement this grant of authority, however, must be promulgated in accordance with the formal rulemaking procedures of section 701(e). As a consequence, FDA has issued general regulations for prescription drug advertising on only two occasions, and then only after it agreed to revisions that persuaded the Pharmaceutical Manufacturers Association (now the Pharmaceutical Research and Manufacturers of America) to withdraw its demand for a formal hearing. *See* Irving H. Jurow, *Prescription–Drug Advertising—Blight or Light?*, 23 FOOD DRUG COSM. L.J. 242 (1968); Richard B. Ruge, *Regulation of Prescription Drug Advertising: Medical Progress and Private Enterprise*, 32 LAW & CONTEMP. PROBS. 650 (1967).

The original prescription drug advertising regulations were promulgated shortly after enactment of the 1962 Drug Amendments. 28 Fed. Reg. 1448 (Feb. 14, 1963), 28 Fed. Reg. 6375 (June 20, 1963), 28 Fed. Reg. 9837 (Sept. 10, 1963), 28 Fed. Reg. 10993 (Oct. 15, 1963), 29 Fed. Reg. 257 (Jan. 10, 1964). Later in the decade, as a result of FDA Commissioner James L. Goddard's strong personal concerns about pharmaceutical advertising, FDA revised those regulations to prohibit specific practices to which the agency had strong objections. 32 Fed. Reg. 7533 (May 23, 1967), 33 Fed. Reg. 9393 (June 27, 1968), 34 Fed. Reg. 7802 (May 16, 1969). *See* FDA, *Compendium of Medical Advertising*, FDA Pub. No. 40 (June 1967), James L. Goddard, *The Administrator's View*, 22 FOOD DRUG COSM. L.J. 449, 452 (1967). The revised regulations are excerpted below.

Prescription–Drug Advertisements

21 C.F.R. 202.1.

(e)(6) *Advertisements that are false, lacking in fair balance, or otherwise misleading.* An advertisement for a prescription drug is false, lacking in fair balance, or otherwise misleading, or otherwise violative of section 502(n) of the act if it:

(i) Contains a representation or suggestion, not approved or permitted for use in the labeling, that a drug is better, more effective, useful in a broader range of conditions or patients (as used in this section *patients* means humans and in the case of veterinary drugs, other animals), safer, has fewer, or less incidence of, or less serious side effects or contraindications than has been demonstrated by substantial evidence or substantial clinical experience ... whether or not such representations are made by comparison with other drugs or treatments, and whether or not such a representation or suggestion is made directly or through use of published or unpublished literature, quotations, or other references.

(ii) Contains a drug comparison that represents or suggests that a drug is safer or more effective than another drug in some particular when it has not been demonstrated to be safer or more effective in such particular by substantial evidence or substantial clinical experience.

(iii) Contains favorable information or opinions about a drug previously regarded as valid but which have been rendered invalid by contrary and more credible recent information, or contains literature references or quotations that are significantly more favorable to the drug than has been demonstrated by substantial evidence or substantial clinical experience.

(iv) Contains a representation or suggestion that a drug is safer than it has been demonstrated to be by substantial evidence or substantial clinical experience, by selective presentation of information from published articles or other references that report no side effects or minimal side effects with the drug or otherwise selects information from any source in a way that makes a drug appear to be safer than has been demonstrated.

(v) Presents information from a study in a way that implies that the study represents larger or more general experience with the drug than it actually does.

(vi) Contains references to literature or studies that misrepresent the effectiveness of a drug by failure to disclose that claimed results may be due to concomitant therapy, or by failure to disclose the credible information available concerning the extent to which claimed results may be due to placebo effect (information concerning placebo effect is not required unless the advertisement promotes the drug for use by man).

(vii) Contains favorable data or conclusions from nonclinical studies of a drug, such as in laboratory animals or in vitro, in a way that suggests they have clinical significance when in fact no such clinical significance has been demonstrated.

(viii) Uses a statement by a recognized authority that is apparently favorable about a drug but fails to refer to concurrent or more recent unfavorable data or statements from the same authority on the same subject or subjects.

(ix) Uses a quote or paraphrase out of context to convey a false or misleading idea.

(x) Uses literature, quotations, or references that purport to support an advertising claim but in fact do not support the claim or have relevance to the claim.

(xi) Uses literature, quotations, or references for the purpose of recommending or suggesting conditions of drug use that are not approved or permitted in the drug packaging labeling.

(xii) Offers a combination of drugs for the treatment of patients suffering from a condition amenable to treatment by any of the components rather than limiting the indications for use to patients for whom concomitant therapy as provided by the fixed combination drug is indicated, unless such condition is included in the uses permitted under paragraph (e)(4) of this section.

(xiii) Uses a study on normal individuals without disclosing that the subjects were normal, unless the drug is intended for use on normal individuals.

(xiv) Uses "statistics" on numbers of patients, or counts of favorable results or side effects, derived from pooling data from various insignificant or dissimilar studies in a way that suggests either that such "statistics" are valid if they are not or that they are derived from large or significant studies supporting favorable conclusions when such is not the case.

(xv) Uses erroneously a statistical finding of "no significant difference" to claim clinical equivalence or to deny or conceal the potential existence of a real clinical difference.

(xvi) Uses statements or representations that a drug differs from or does not contain a named drug or category of drugs, or that it has a greater potency per unit of weight, in a way that suggests falsely or misleadingly or without substantial evidence or substantial clinical experience that the advertised drug is safer or more effective than such other drug or drugs.

(xvii) Uses data favorable to a drug derived from patients treated with dosages different from those recommended in approved or permitted labeling if the drug advertised is subject to section 505, 507, or 512 of the act, or, in the case of other drugs, if the dosages employed were different from those recommended in the labeling and generally recognized as safe and effective. This provision is not intended to prevent citation of reports of studies that include some patients treated with dosages different from those authorized, if the results in such patients are not used.

(xviii) Uses headline, subheadline, or pictorial or other graphic matter in a way that is misleading.

(xix) Represents or suggests that drug dosages properly recommended for use in the treatment of certain classes of patients or disease conditions are safe and effective for the treatment of other classes of patients or disease conditions when such is not the case.

(xx) Presents required information relating to side effects or contraindications by means of a general term for a group in place of disclosing each specific side effect and contraindication (for example employs the term *blood dyscrasias* instead of "leukopenia," "agranulocytosis," "neutropenia," etc.) unless the use of such general term conforms to the provisions of paragraph (e)(3)(iii) of this section.

Provided, however, That any provision of this paragraph shall be waived with respect to a specified advertisement as set forth in a written communication from the Food and Drug Administration....

(7) *Advertisements that may be false, lacking in fair balance, or otherwise misleading.* An advertising may be false, lacking in fair balance, or otherwise misleading or otherwise violative of section 502(n) of the act if it:

(i) Contains favorable information or conclusions from a study that is inadequate in design, scope, or conduct to furnish significant support for such information or conclusions.

(ii) Uses the concept of "statistical significance" to support a claim that has not been demonstrated to have clinical significance or validity, or fails to reveal the range of variations around the quoted average results.

(iii) Uses statistical analyses and techniques on a retrospective basis to discover and cite findings not soundly supported by the study, or to suggest scientific validity and rigor for data from studies the design or protocol of which are not amenable to formal statistical evaluations.

(iv) Uses tables or graphs to distort or misrepresent the relationships, trends, differences, or changes among the variables or products studied; for example, by failing to label abscissa and ordinate so that the graph creates a misleading impression.

(v) Uses reports or statements represented to be statistical analyses, interpretations, or evaluations that are inconsistent with or violate the established principles of statistical theory, methodology, applied practice, and inference, or that are derived from clinical studies the design, data, or conduct of which substantially invalidate the application of statistical analyses, interpretations, or evaluations.

(vi) Contains claims concerning the mechanism or site of drug action that are not generally regarded as established by scientific evidence by experts qualified by scientific training and experience without disclosing that the claims are not established and the limitations of the supporting evidence.

(vii) Fails to provide sufficient emphasis for the information relating to side effects and contraindications, when such information is contained in a distinct part of an advertisement, because of repetition or other emphasis in that part of the advertisement of claims for effectiveness or safety of the drug.

(viii) Fails to present information relating to side effects and contraindications with a prominence and readability reasonable comparable with the presentation of information relating to effectiveness of the drug, taking into account all implementing factors such as typography, layout, contrast, headlines, paragraphing, white space, and any other techniques apt to achieve emphasis.

(ix) Fails to provide adequate emphasis (for example, by the use of color scheme, borders, headlines, or copy that extends across the gutter) for the fact that two facing pages are part of the same advertisement when one page contains information relating to side effects and contraindications.

(x) In an advertisement promoting use of the drug in a selected class of patients (for example, geriatric patients or depressed patients), fails to present with adequate emphasis the significant side effects and contraindications or the significant dosage considerations, when dosage recommendations are included in an advertisement, especially applicable to that selected class of patients.

(xi) Fails to present on a page facing another page (or on another full page) of an advertisement on more than one page, information relating to side effects and contraindications when such information is in a distinct part of the advertisement.

(xii) Fails to include on each page or spread to an advertisement the information relating to side effects and contraindications or a prominent reference to its presence and location when it is presented as a distinct part of an advertisement.

(xiii) Contains information from published or unpublished reports or opinions falsely or misleadingly represented or suggested to be authentic or authoritative.

NOTES

1. *Brief Summary and Fair Balance.* The FDA prescription drug advertising regulations contain two significant requirements for all prescription drug advertising. 21 C.F.R. 202.1(e)(1) requires that each prescription drug advertisement contain a brief summary relating to side effects, contraindications, and effectiveness. In effect, this requires the familiar second page of every print advertisement for a prescription drug, summarizing the physician labeling information. 21 C.F.R. 202.1(e)(5)(ii) requires that the text of the advertisement present a "fair balance" between information relating to side effects and contraindications and information relating to effectiveness. It is this requirement that is most often cited in warning letters sent by FDA to prescription drug advertisers.

2. *Comparative Claims.* In 40 Fed. Reg. 15392 (Apr. 7, 1975), 44 Fed. Reg. 37434 (June 26, 1979), FDA revised its prescription drug advertising and labeling regulations to specify the conditions under which comparative effectiveness claims may be made. The filing of formal objections stayed the advertising regulations, 44 Fed. Reg. 74817 (Dec. 18, 1979), and they have not been the subject of further FDA action. The labeling amendments, promulgated under Section 701(a), became effective six months after publication. *See* Lloyd G. Millstein, *FDA Policy on Comparative Prescription Drug Advertising*, 17 DRUG INFO. J. 63 (1983). Pharmaceutical companies seldom test their own drugs against competitive products in direct head-to-head comparative clinical trials. To obtain this type of information, Congress included section 1013 in the Medicare Prescription Drug, Improvement, and Modernization Act of 2003, 117 Stat. 2066, 2438, 42 U.S.C. 2996-7, to require the HHS Agency for Healthcare Research and Quality (AHRQ) to conduct and support research on the comparative clinical effectiveness of prescription drugs.

3. *Reminder Advertisements.* Section 202.1(e)(2)(i) of the regulations recognizes a category of "reminder advertisements," which "call attention to the name of the drug product but do not include indications or dosage recommendations...." Such advertisements need not include a summary of information about side effects and contraindications unless the agency has specifically required that a drug's labeling and promotional literature contain a boxed warning relating to a serious hazard associated with its use.

4. *Corrective Advertisements.* In 1972, FDA took issue with a medical journal advertisement for a tranquilizer, which began with the banner headline "For The Anxiety that Comes from Not Fitting In," followed by this text:

> The newcomer in town who *can't* make friends. The organization man who *can't* adjust to altered status within his company. The woman who *can't* get along with her new daughter-in-law. The executive who *can't* accept retirement.

> These common adjustment problems of our society are frequently intolerable for the disordered personality, who often responds with excessive anxiety.

Serentil is suggested for *this* type of patient. Not simply because its tranquilizing action can ease anxiety and tension, but because it benefits personality disorders in general. And because it has not been found habituating.

The opposite page depicted a completed jigsaw puzzle with a single piece missing through which stared an anxious face—presumably that of the reader's patient.

FDA found this advertisement deceptive and persuaded the manufacturer to run a corrective version, which appeared under the caption "Published to Correct a Previous Advertisement which the Food and Drug Administration Considered Misleading."

The Food and Drug Administration has requested that we bring to your attention a recent journal advertisement for Serentil (mesoridazine) which featured the headline "For the anxiety that comes from not fitting in."

The FDA considers the advertisement misleading in several respects. For example:

The FDA states that the principal theme of the ad suggests unapproved uses of Serentil for relatively minor or everyday anxiety situations encountered often in the normal course of living. THE FACT IS THAT SERENTIL, A PHENOTHIAZINE DRUG, IS LIMITED IN ITS USE TO CERTAIN DISEASE STATES (SEE OPPOSITE PAGE FOR INDICATIONS) IN WHICH THE RISK OF PHENOTHIAZINE THERAPY IS JUSTIFIED IN THE OPINION OF THE PHYSICIAN.

We have taken steps to withdraw the advertisement in question.

5. *Overpromotion.* In *Love v. Wolf*, 38 Cal. Rptr. 183 (Cal. Ct. App. 1964), the court held that the manufacturer of Chloromycetin, then the only marketed version of the potent antibiotic chloramphenicol, could be held liable for the plaintiff's bone marrow depression if the jury were persuaded that the company's heavy promotion of the drug effectively submerged its own warnings about the hazard:

... It appears in evidence that the company knew that many physicians in the United States had been prescribing chloromycetin for conditions less than serious. It does not appear that the detail men were told to attempt to do anything to curtail this. It *was* told them by the company president that "the fact that a drug was administered prior to development of a aplasia is by no means proof that the drug is the offender. At this time, there are absolutely no cases known to us in which such proof is extant." He said that there was "no valid scientific proof" that aplasia resulted from chloromycetin. The detail men were told that this was the position of the company and they were told so to inform the doctors they visited. They were also told (and presumably were told to relay): "Chloromycetin has been officially cleared by the FDA and the National Research Council with no restrictions on the number or the range of diseases for which Chloromycetin may be administered." These statements may have expressed literal truth. They did not, however, express "the whole truth, and nothing but the truth" as a fair warning which, according to plaintiff's experts, Parke–Davis should have been giving the medical profession....

Following a retrial, Parke Davis was found liable for Mrs. Love's injuries and appealed without success. "[T]here was evidence that the overpromotion of chloromycetin by Parke–Davis caused doctors, including Dr. Wolf, to disregard the warnings, even the 1961 warning, and hence Parke–Davis' liability is based more on this overpromotion than on the failure to include in the 1952 warning the matter included in the later warning." 58 Cal. Rptr. 42 (Cal. Ct. App. 1967). *See also*

Stevens v. Parke, Davis & Co., 507 P.2d 653 (Cal. 1973); Cohen, *Stevens v. Parke, Davis & Co.*, 10 U.S.F. L. Rev. 683 (1976).

6. *FDA Review of Guidelines.* Following the Drug Amendments of 1962, FDA issued a large number of formal and informal guidances regarding drug advertising and promotion. In 62 Fed. Reg. 14912 (Mar. 28, 1997), FDA published a list of 65 of these guidance documents that the agency intended to rescind or revise, and asked for public comment. No further action has been taken by FDA on this matter.

7. *Healthcare Economic Information.* In 1995, FDA announced two public hearings to consider the regulation of health care economic information. 60 Fed. Reg. 13778 (Mar. 14, 1995), 60 Fed. Reg. 41,891 (Aug. 14, 1995). *See* Steven K. Stranne, *Cost–Effectiveness Determinations and the FDA* (1994), Zion Shohet, *Identifying Cost–Effective Regulations to Cost–Effectiveness Studies: An Economic Analysis of a Proposed Set of Regulations* (1995), in Chapter VI(B)(6) of the Electronic Book; Peter Neumann, *The FDA and Regulation of Cost Effectiveness Claims*, 15 Health Affairs 54 (Fall 1996). Congress then enacted section 502(a) of the FD&C Act as part of the Food and Drug Administration Modernization Act of 1997, which declared that health care economic information provided to a formulary committee or other similar entity is not to be considered as false or misleading if it directly relates to an indication approved under an NDA and is based on "competent and reliable scientific evidence." *See* Ryan T. Scarborough, *Will Healthcare Economic Information Lead to Therapeutic Class Warfare or Welfare?*, 111 Harv. L. Rev. 2384 (1998). This provision has had only a modest impact on the number of pharmacoeconomic studies undertaken by the pharmaceutical industry.

8. *Constitutionality of Prescription Drug Advertising Regulations.* Section 505(d) of the FD&C Act provides that FDA must withhold approval of an NDA unless the sponsor provides "substantial evidence that the drug will have the effect it purports or is represented to have under the conditions of use, prescribed, or recommended or suggested in the proposed labeling." Section 505(d)(5) defines "substantial evidence" to mean "evidence consisting of adequate and well-controlled investigations." Under the FDA regulations set forth above, drug product claims supported by some lesser quantum of evidence categorically violate the law, whether or not they are in fact misleading, whether or not the statements are qualified with appropriate disclaimers, and whether or not the nature of the supporting evidence and the existence of countervailing evidence are made clear. Under the landmark decision in *Pearson v. Shalala*, 164 F.3d 650 (D.C. Cir. 1999), there is a reasonable argument that qualified prescription drug claims should be permitted on the same basis that qualified food disease claims are permitted, *supra* p. 285.

9. *Consent Decree.* Under a consent decree entered in *United States v. Kabi Pharmacia, Inc.*, Food Drug Cosm. L. Rep. (CCH) ¶ 38343 (D.N.J. 1993), Kabi agreed (1) not to use any advertising or promotional materials for a specified drug for one year without the prior approval of FDA, (2) not to represent the use of the drug for off-label purposes, (3) not to represent that it is superior to a competitive drug, and (4) to undertake a remedial advertising campaign.

———

FDA's current drug advertising regulations are codified at 21 C.F.R. Part 202. Their primary objective, as the portions quoted above suggest, is to curb overstatement in product claims and encourage balanced disclosure of side effects, contraindications, and warnings—the central thrust of section 502(n). The primary problems posed by advertising for prescription drugs, however, do not appear easily redressable by the authority to issue regulations or, indeed, to invoke the formal enforcement sanctions provided by the FD&C Act.

ii. Other Forms of Prescription Drug Promotion to Professionals

In addition to the traditional print advertising in medical journals, pharmaceutical companies have expanded their product marketing to a wide variety of other promotional practices.

Competitive Problems in the Drug Industry: Summary and Analysis

Subcommittee on Monopoly of the Senate Select Committee on Small Business
92d Congress, 2d Session (1972).

... In order to obtain sales, drug companies must first make prescribers aware of the existence of the drug.... More important, the successful drug firm must succeed in persuading physicians to choose its products from the multitude of other drugs or drug products which are available to them. To achieve these objectives, drug companies have developed a variety of promotional practices designed to differentiate the products of one company from those of their competitors.

Broadly speaking, promotionally-achieved product differentiation efforts undertaken by pharmaceutical houses encompass many different kinds of activities. For example, the drug industry makes extensive use of trade-names, not only to distinguish one drug from another, but also to differentiate different versions of the same drug from one another. Another feature of the present drug promotion system involves the use of a large number of company salesmen who deal directly and on a personal basis with prescribers and with others in the health community involved in the selection or purchase of prescribed drugs. Companies engage in extensive drug advertising campaigns in professional journals and magazines subscribed to by physicians and other prescribers. Direct mail programs and the distribution of sample products are other ways in which drug companies seek to make practitioners aware of their particular products....

Promotionally-achieved product differentiation efforts are especially effective where consumers, or in this case, physicians, face the difficult task of sorting out competing claims about a variety of products or drugs which often purport to be or do substantially the same thing....

... [M]anufacturers seeking to increase the overall sales of specific drugs find it in their interest to promote substances as widely as possible and for as many conditions for which the drug can be shown to be indicated. To achieve this objective, critics note that manufacturers tend to emphasize the benefits and good points of particular drugs while, at the same time, minimizing the less desirable and often serious side-effects or adverse reactions that may result from using such drugs....

If manufacturers are successful in promoting the sale of certain drugs by emphasizing their widest possible uses, they are unlikely suddenly to consider engaging in equally intensive campaigns to point out to prescribers those shortcomings in drugs that would cause physicians to reduce or stop their use of these products. Nor is it realistic to expect manufacturers to emphasize that the competition's newer drugs are either more effective, or less hazardous, than their own products in various prescribing situations. . . .

NOTES

1. *Oral Promotion.* As one author observed in 1967: "The amended statute does not specifically give the FDA authority over oral promotional statements made by detail men. These salesmen are also an important source of information about new drugs, making an estimated 18 to 20 million calls a year on doctors and druggists. . . . The FDA does, however, have jurisdiction over literature left by detailers with doctors. . . ." Richard B. Ruge, *Regulation of Prescription Drug Advertising: Medical Progress and Private Enterprise*, 32 Law & Contemp. Probs. 650 (1967).

2. *Gifts and Other Promotional Practices.* Following Congressional hearings on unprofessional drug promotion practices, "Examination of the Pharmaceutical Industry, 1973–74," Hearings before the Subcommittee on Health of the Senate Committee on Labor and Public Welfare, 93rd Cong., 1st & 2nd Sess., Pt. 3 (1974), the Pharmaceutical Manufacturers Association endorsed federal legislation to eliminate such practices as giving gifts to physicians to encourage them to prescribe specific drugs. "PMA's Positive Program," 36 FDC Reports ("The Pink Sheet"), no. 14, at A1 (Apr. 8, 1974). Criticism of pharmaceutical promotional practices has not abated, however. *See, e.g., Undesirable Marketing Practices in the Pharmaceutical Industry*, 313 New Eng. J. Med. 54 (July 4, 1985); *One Drug Company's Sales Technique*, 313 New Eng. J. Med. 270 (July 25, 1985).

3. *Medicare–Medicaid Prohibitions.* The Medicare–Medicaid Anti–Fraud and Abuse Amendments, 91 Stat. 1175 (1977), made it a felony to solicit or receive any remuneration for purchasing any product for which government reimbursement may be made under Medicare or Medicaid. This statute was initially implemented by the Health Care Financing Administration (HCFA, now renamed CMS), but was transferred to the HHS Office of Inspector General (OIG) in 48 Fed. Reg. 21662 (May 13, 1983). All related OIG regulations were then codified in 42 C.F.R. Part 1001. 51 Fed. Reg. 34764 (Sept. 30, 1986). Because of the broad reach of the criminal provisions of the 1977 statute as interpreted by the courts, *e.g., United States v. Greber*, 760 F.2d 68 (3d Cir. 1985), Congress added a civil sanction in the Medicare and Medicaid Patient and Program Protection Act of 1987, 101 Stat. 680, and ordered OIG to establish safe harbors for practices determined not to constitute illegal kickbacks. The 1977 provision was repealed and a comparable provision reenacted in 42 U.S.C. 1320a–7b(b), which makes it a felony either to pay or to receive any remuneration of any kind to induce the order or purchase of a drug for which reimbursement is made under Medicare or Medicaid. Because it is not feasible to determine in advance whether a particular drug will be subject to Medicare or Medicaid reimbursement, all current pharmaceutical industry promotional practices are potentially subject to these provisions. Regulations to implement the statute were promulgated in 54 Fed. Reg. 3088 (Jan. 23, 1989), 56 Fed. Reg. 35952 (July 29, 1991), 55 Fed. Reg. 12205 (Apr. 2, 1990), 57 Fed. Reg. 3298 (Jan. 29, 1992), 42 C.F.R. Part 1001.

COMMENT: CONTINUING PRESCRIPTION DRUG PROMOTION CONTROVERSIES

The pharmaceutical industry is highly competitive. It is a unique market, which relies on a limited group of "learned intermediaries"—

healthcare professionals who are authorized under state law to prescribe prescription drugs. Pharmaceutical companies employ diverse tactics to convince physicians to prescribe their products. Many people believe that any lawful method of marketing should be open to the industry, while many others believe that the unique importance of prescription drugs requires strong limitations on their promotion. The following illustrate some of the more prominent issues that arise in this continuing debate.

1. *Continuing Medical Education (CME)*. Although the constitutional and regulatory aspects of CME have been clarified, there remains controversy about whether any pharmaceutical industry grant to even an independent CME organization can be regarded as anything other than product promotion in general and off-label promotion in particular. It has been pointed out that drug companies would not support CME if they were not expecting an increase in their sales.

2. *Inducements for Physicians*. Many believe that the provision of meals by detail men, support for travel to conferences, and consultant arrangements improperly influence physician prescribing. It is argued that prescribing decisions then become based at least in part on financial considerations rather than strictly on scientific evidence.

3. *Marketing to Medical Students and Residents*. One study reports that at least 80 percent of medical students routinely received small to modest gifts, as well as lunches, from drug companies. More than 50 percent received free dinners, and a significant minority received funding to attend conferences or participate in writing papers. It is maintained that these activities influence the choices of these young physicians.

4. *Incomplete Information*. There is a perception that drug companies provide physicians with incomplete information, or manipulate that information, in order to influence physician prescribing choices. It is argued that greater restrictions should be placed on these interactions.

5. *Designer Diseases*. Some critics suggest that drug companies manipulate or invent disease states in order to increase prescribing. It is contended that the medical profession should maintain tighter control over the designation of new diseases.

6. *Newly Marketed Drugs*. It is argued that drug companies focus marketing efforts on newer and more expensive drugs, causing doctors to abandon older and less expensive generic drugs even where there is little evidence that the new drug provides a meaningful advantage. Tighter controls over advertising have been suggested.

7. *Inducements to Non–Physicians*. The drug industry also enlists the help of pharmacists and other healthcare professionals to encourage physicians and patients to switch from a competitor product to the company's product. Restrictions on detailing to non-physician healthcare personnel have been urged.

8. *Uncontrolled Studies As Marketing Tools*. FDA has alleged in warning letters that companies contract with physicians to conduct uncontrolled studies as a form of inducement to increase their prescribing of the products involved. It has been suggested that these are illegal marketing tactics that should be prohibited.

In response to these continuing controversies, three organizations have prepared guidance to address them.

The OIG Guidelines. In May 2003, the HHS Office of Inspector General issued a *Compliance Program Guidance for Pharmaceutical Manufacturers.* 66 Fed. Reg. 31246 (June 11, 2001), 67 Fed. Reg. 62057 (Oct. 3, 2002), 68 Fed. Reg. 23731 (May 5, 2003). Although the OIG Guidelines apply to all forms of pharmaceutical industry activity, they have particular application to pharmaceutical promotion practices. The Guidelines establish seven basic compliance program elements: (1) written standards of conduct, policies, procedures, and protocols, (2) designation of a compliance officer and corporate compliance committee, (3) regular education and training programs (4) an effective line of communication between the compliance officer and all employees, (5) audits and other risk evaluation techniques to monitor compliance, (6) policies and procedures addressing individuals excluded from participation in federal healthcare programs and the enforcement of appropriate disciplinary action, and (7) investigation of identified instances of noncompliance or misconduct. The OIG Guidelines then address kickbacks and other illegal remuneration to induce or reward the referral or generation of federal health care business, using numerous specific examples. *See* Susan Chimonas & David J. Rothman, *New Federal Guidelines for Physician–Pharmaceutical Industry Relations: The Politics of Policy Formation*, 24 HEALTH AFFAIRS 949 (2005).

The PhRMA Code. Effective July 1, 2002, the Pharmaceutical Research and Manufacturers of America (PhRMA) adopted a voluntary *Code on Interactions with Healthcare Professionals.* The document addresses nine basic aspects of the relationship between the pharmaceutical industry and healthcare professionals, and it answers questions with respect to a wide variety of appropriate and inappropriate educational and promotional activities. PhRMA, *Code On Interactions With Healthcare Professionals* (July 2002, revised January 2004). The PhRMA Code was endorsed by the OIG Guidelines as a "good starting point for compliance purposes."

The AMA Policy. The American Medical Association (AMA) has also issued guidelines regarding the funding of medical education activities. The purpose is to make certain that these activities are legitimate scientific meetings, not a mechanism for improper payments to physicians. AMA, *Code of Ethics Opinion E–8.061: Gifts to Physicians from Industry*, revised periodically. *See* The Council on Ethical and Judicial Affairs of the American Medical Association, *Guidelines on Gifts to Physicians from Industry: An Update*, 56 FOOD & DRUG L.J. 27 (2001).

c. PROMOTION OF UNAPPROVED USES

The dissemination by manufacturers of information about unapproved drugs, or unapproved uses of approved drugs, has presented vexing problems for FDA. Section 202.1(e)(4) of the FDA advertising regulations, *supra*, provides that advertising cannot recommend or suggest any use that is not in the labeling in an approved NDA. Section 312.7(a) of the Investigational New Drug Application (IND) regulations, on the other hand, though prohibiting any representation "in a promotional context" that an investigational drug is safe and effective, goes on to state:

This provision is not intended to restrict the full exchange of scientific information concerning the drug, including dissemination of scientific findings and scientific or lay media.

Reconciling these provisions, in an era of near-instantaneous dissemination of new scientific information, has not proved easy.

Speech by Kenneth R. Feather*

Annual Meeting of the PMA Marketing Section (Mar. 14, 1989).

Promotional activities for prescription drugs have expanded far beyond the materials traditionally thought of as advertising; *i.e.* advertisements in journals, mailers, and detail ads. We now see newspaper articles, interviews on TV talk shows, multi-city seminars (traveling road shows), supplements to medical journals, and press conferences being used to promote drugs. This poses new problems for the FDA in its enforcement of the Act and regulations to ensure truthful and complete promotional discussions of prescription drugs. . . .

We feel the definitions for labeling and advertisements, as found in the Act and in the regulations, can cover virtually all activities disseminating information about a drug which are done by *or on behalf of* the manufacturer. I realize there can be honest debate about that concept, especially since the regulations also tell us (FDA) that we are not to inhibit the "free exchange of scientific information." Let me address this issue.

First, that quoted statement comes from the section of the regulations dealing with IND drugs, not approved, marketed drugs. It is clear that during this investigational phase, information should flow freely between researchers in order to conduct and evaluate more fully, studies and data from this research. To the extent that the promotional regulations restrict information, this provision is clearly meant to remove that restriction in this important special case. We think this means a firm can communicate fully with their researchers; that investigators can publish the results of their research in medical and other scientific journals; and that investigators can present their research in seminars and symposia (more on this later). Does an article in the *Wall Street Journal* fall into this category?

We do not think that section in the regulations means a firm can disseminate any information it wishes simply because they disguise it as a seminar or call it "education." What "scientific" purpose does it serve to hold a press conference for the lay press (or even trade press) to announce the preliminary results of a study? . . . .

Many times it appears these activities are designed, not for scientific dialogue, but to try to get a drug used for a wide variety of uses which the company knows they will not get approval for. As an example, for several years information about studies and "logical projections" of the actions of prostaglandins in treating and preventing ulcers have appeared in exhibits, sole sponsored publications, medical press articles, and other materials. This systematically disseminated scientific information discussed these

* [Acting Director, FDA Division of Drug Advertising and Labeling.]

actions in treating and preventing ulcers caused by almost any factor, usually extolling its effectiveness and safety in these areas. It was known these products would not be approved for all of these uses.

This was justified on the basis that the physician must be kept informed so he/she can properly use the drug when approved. But if most of these uses are not going to be adequately studied and proven, how can this information help a physician use the drug "properly?" ... Doesn't this look more like a way to make sure the drug is used for all of these problems, without the company having to do the studies to properly prove them?....

We are often asked if a directly firm sponsored seminar is proper. We have always recommended that seminars and symposia be held under the auspices of a university, a medical school or a professional association, with that body through an editorial board having the responsibility for selecting speakers and perhaps, topics to be discussed. They should also be responsible for editing and disseminating written materials based on this seminar. The sponsoring firm should have little or no influence in this process....

Of even more concern is [sic] similar activities for new uses of currently marketed drugs. Obviously since there is a drug on the market, it can be used for this new purpose. The law prohibits a manufacturer from promoting unapproved uses for an NDA'd drug, so firms turn to these methods of getting this information out....

There's a recent example of discussing a new use for a marketed drug dealing with a press conference.... This involved one short term (6 weeks) small (16 patients) study for a product approved for treating severe acne. The study dealt with using the product to remove or reduce wrinkling and the appearance of aging in the skin. The study was published in a prestigious national medical journal, so the medical/scientific community was made aware of the results of this study. We understand the investigator wanted to have a press conference. He is free to do so. I think it is fair to say that had he called a press conference, very few people would have shown up. The firm paid for a press conference, and this study got national, lay press coverage. By the subject of the study I think you can visualize the headlines resulting from this press conference.... [D]id this serve to promote the product for an unapproved use? The answer to that question is, yes. In fact they can't keep the product on the pharmacy shelves, the demand for it is so high.

The essence of the regulations applying to promotional activities is that the information be accurate, truthful and balanced.... We think these general criteria can be applied to all of these things....

Even though we think most of these activities fall within the jurisdiction of the FDA, it is unlikely we will take action or impose the full range of the regulations if the information is complete and balanced....

NOTES

1. *FDA Policy Statements.* Rather than amend the prescription drug advertising regulations, FDA has issued a number of "policy statements" on various types

of advertising and promotional practices that do not fall within the existing regulations.

2. *Journal Articles.* In Compliance Policy Guide 7132b.17 (Aug. 15, 1989), FDA determined that an article about a prescription drug in an independent publication is not to be regarded as advertising (or labeling) for the drug—whether or not the drug is also separately advertised in the same publication—if the manufacturer makes no contribution to the article and does not use the article for promotional purposes.

3. *Congressional Hearings. See* "Promotion of Drugs and Medical Devices for Unapproved Uses," Hearing before the Human Resources and Intergovernmental Relations Subcommittee of the House Committee on Government Operations, 102d Cong., 1st Sess. (1991); "Questionable Sales Practices in the Drug Industry," Hearing before the Subcommittee on Regulation, Business Opportunities and Technology of the House Committee on Small Business, 103d Cong. 2d Sess. (1994).

4. *Commentary. See Symposium on Promotional and Marketing Activities: Preapproval, Time of Approval, Postapproval*, 23 DRUG INFO. J., No. 4 (1989); Robert H. Pritchard, *Off–Label Uses of Approved Drugs: A New Compromise is Needed* (1995), in Chapter VI(K) of the Electronic Book.

COMMENT: UNAPPROVED INFORMATION PROVIDED IN RESPONSE TO AN UNSOLICITED PHYSICIAN REQUEST

Since the early 1980s, FDA has taken the position that the agency will not regulate as labeling any information provided by a pharmaceutical company to a physician in response to an unsolicited request. *E.g.*, 59 Fed. Reg. 59820, 59823 (Nov. 18, 1994). As part of the FDA Modernization Act of 1997, Congress added section 557(a) to the FD&C Act to affirm this policy by exempting dissemination of "information in response to an unsolicited request from a healthcare provider" from the new requirements applicable to distribution of off-label reprints. The FDA regulations implementing the 1997 statute reflected this policy. 63 Fed. Reg. 31143 (June 8, 1998), 63 Fed. Reg. 64555 (Nov. 20, 1998), codified at 21 C.F.R., 99.1(b). Although FDA stated in 62 Fed. Reg. 14912, 14916 (Mar. 28, 1997) that it would issue a guidance on this matter, it did not do so. Some companies have implemented this policy with their regular sales force, while others employ "medical sales liaisons" to respond to unsolicited requests or use their medical departments for this purpose. Although section 557(a) of the FD&C Act—along with sections 551–556—sunsetted on September 30, 2006, FDA has taken no action to change its longstanding policy on this matter.

―――――

Underlying FDA's ambivalence about restricting the promotional dissemination of scientific information was awareness of the First Amendment issues that would arise if it were to attempt to ban discussion of unapproved uses of investigational or approved new drugs. When FDA sought by guidance to restrict industry-supported continuing medical education (CME) programs, 62 Fed. Reg. 64074 (Dec. 3, 1997) and industry distribution of textbooks and medical journal articles, 61 Fed. Reg. 52800 (Oct. 8,

1996), however, the conflict between free speech and FDA regulation could not be ignored.

Section 505(d) of the FD&C Act provides that a drug sponsor must demonstrate that the drug is safe and effective for its intended use under the conditions described in the labeling submitted with the NDA. Upon approval of the NDA, the FDA-approved labeling serves as the basis for all lawful "on-label" statements by the company and its employees about the drug. Thus, a pharmaceutical company is limited to the four corners of the approved physician package insert for all of its drug advertising and other promotional activities. Since 1962, FDA has taken the position that the company owning an NDA violates section 502 of the FD&C Act if it promotes the drug for unapproved uses, often called "off-label" uses.

FDA has a regulatory mechanism for monitoring a company's use of promotional labeling and advertising for a new drug. Under 21 C.F.R. 314.81(b)(3)(i), at the time of initial dissemination of promotional labeling or initial publication of an advertisement, manufacturers must submit a specimen of the material to FDA with a transmittal form, Form FDA 2253. Information on unapproved uses of an approved new drug is therefore seldom included in promotional labeling or advertising.

Until recently, the FD&C Act provided a highly restrictive mechanism by which information about unapproved uses of a drug could lawfully be provided to physicians. The FDA Modernization Act of 1997 added sections 551–557 to the FD&C Act. These sections explicitly authorized the provision of off-label information to healthcare practitioners, pharmacy benefit managers, health insurance issuers, group health plans, and federal or state government agencies, but only if the following six conditions were met: (1) the drug was approved, (2) the information was not false or misleading, did not otherwise render the drug misbranded, was in the form of an unabridged reprint from a peer-review journal or reference publication, and would not pose a significant risk to public health, (3) the information was not derived from another manufacturer's research (absent permission), (4) the manufacturer submitted the information to FDA 60 days before its distribution, (5) the manufacturer had submitted a supplemental NDA to FDA for approval of the use described (or certified that a supplemental NDA would be submitted within six months), and (6) the reprint included a prominent statement that the use had not been approved, a copy of the approved labeling, certain disclosures, a bibliography, and a statement if applicable that other products had been approved for the use discussed in the reprint. In 1998, FDA promulgated regulations implementing these provisions. 63 Fed. Reg. 31143 (June 8, 1998), 63 Fed. Reg. 64556 (Nov. 20, 1998), codified at 21 C.F.R. Part 99. For obvious reasons, industry rarely used them. In accordance with section 401(e) of the FDA Modernization Act of 1997, these provisions sunsetted on September 30, 2006, and thus are no longer available.

Today, there are thus only two ways that information about unapproved uses of a drug can lawfully be provided to physicians.

First, this information can be provided in response to an unsolicited request from a health care professional, as described above.

Second, this information can also be provided to a healthcare professional as commercial free speech protected by the First Amendment. One of the main reasons why industry did not use the provisions in 21 C.F.R. Part 99 is that, in litigation instituted in 1998, the Washington Legal Foundation successfully challenged the FDA policy on prohibiting the dissemination of off-label information. *Washington Legal Foundation v. Friedman*, 13 F. Supp. 2d 51 (D.D.C. 1998), *injunction amended*, 36 F. Supp. 2d 418 (D.D.C. 1999). FDA then raised the potential impact of the newly-enacted provisions in the FDA Modernization Act of 1997. The result was the following decision and injunction.

Washington Legal Foundation v. Henney

56 F. Supp. 2d 81 (D.D.C. 1999).

■ LAMBERTH, DISTRICT JUDGE....

The facts of this case are set forth in detail in the Court's July 30, 1998 memorandum opinion. *See WLF v. Friedman*, 13 F. Supp. 2d 51 (D.D.C. 1998). In that decision, the Court granted summary judgment against the defendants, holding that the FDA was violating the First Amendment rights of plaintiff's members by unduly limiting the manner in which drug manufacturers may disseminate information relating to unapproved—or "off-label"—uses of FDA-approved drugs.

At the time of this Court's July 30, 1998 decision, the FDA's unconstitutional policies were embodied in three Guidance Documents regulating the dissemination of journal articles and reference texts and manufacturer support of continuing medical education (CME) activities. However, as the Court anticipated in its July 30, 1998 decision, the Guidance Documents were superseded on November 21, 1998 by the Food and Drug Administration Modernization Act (and implementing regulations issued by the FDA). The provisions of the FDAMA perpetuate in part and modify in part the policies contained in the Guidance Documents....

Upon review, the Court is persuaded that the decisions of July 30, 1998 and February 16, 1999 did and do correctly state the law applicable to this case, and the Court incorporates its prior review of the caselaw without repeating it here. The question before the Court, therefore, is whether the FDA's policies as currently embodied in the FDAMA are unconstitutional under the legal standard stated by the Court in those decisions....

As in its previous decision of July 30, 1998, the Court will analyze the constitutionality of the FDA's policies (as now contained in the FDAMA) under the four-prong inquiry articulated by the Supreme Court in *Central Hudson Gas & Electric Corp. v. Public Service Commission of New York*, 447 U.S. 557 (1980). Under *Central Hudson*, the court looks first to determine whether the speech at issue is false or inherently misleading. If the speech is truthful and nonmisleading, the government must demonstrate a substantial interest that is directly advanced by the regulation without burdening substantially more speech than necessary....

First, the Court reiterates its prior holding that the speech at issue here is neither false nor inherently misleading. It is a difficult contention indeed that the medical and scientific articles and reference texts at issue in this case are "inherently misleading." To the contrary, the defendants themselves admit to the importance of ensuring the availability of such information to physicians and health care providers making prescription and treatment decisions. Rather, the defendants argue that the manufacturers' dissemination of such information is likely to be misleading because manufacturers have an incentive to disseminate information that presents their drugs only in a positive light, omitting negative information and failing to provide the "balance" that the FDA would prefer.

This argument must fail, for at least two reasons previously stated by the Court. First, "potentially misleading" speech is not proscribable under the First Amendment. The FDA may not restrict speech based on its perception that the speech could, may, or might mislead. Rather, for the protections of the First Amendment to fall away, the government must demonstrate that the restricted speech, by nature, is more likely to mislead than to inform, a demonstration which the defendants have not made here. Second, defendants' true perception of the speech at issue here is revealed by their attitude toward the same speech disseminated under other circumstances. For example, defendants have no concern over the exchange of article reprints and reference texts among physicians; more telling, defendants do not even object to a manufacturer providing such information to a health care provider upon such person's request. Only when the manufacturer initiates the exchange does the FDA choose to label the speech false or inherently misleading. . . .

In its July 30, 1998 decision, this Court identified two governmental interests at issue in this case: 1) ensuring that physicians receive accurate and unbiased information upon which to make prescription decisions, and 2) encouraging drug manufacturers to seek FDA-approval of off-label uses. The Court found the first of these interests unavailing and the second substantial, a determination that the Court reaffirms today. . . .

. . . The government, however benign its motivations, simply cannot justify a restriction of truthful nonmisleading speech on the paternalistic assumption that such restriction is necessary to protect the listener from ignorantly or inadvertently misusing the information. . . .

The majority of [the FDAMA] provisions (for example, that requiring attachment of a bibliography of related information) directly advance the FDA's stated goal of ensuring that physicians receive accurate and balanced information. As explained above, however, that is not a substantial interest that might justify the FDA's restrictions on speech.

In contrast, only one requirement of the FDAMA can be said to directly advance the substantial governmental interest in encouraging supplemental drug applications. The FDAMA states that a manufacturer may disseminate information on off-label uses only if it has met one of the following three requirements: 1) it has submitted a supplemental application for approval of the off-label use, 2) it has certified to the FDA that such supplemental application will be forthcoming as provided in the statute, or 3) the Secretary has determined that the manufacturer is exempt from this requirement because the supplemental application would be economically prohibitive or would require unethical studies. It is abundantly clear that this requirement directly advances the interest in encouraging supplemental applications. Indeed, any manufacturer that wishes to disseminate article reprints or reference texts (on its own initiative) has no choice but to submit a supplemental application.

The problem with FDAMA is not its effectiveness in encouraging supplemental drug applications, but rather the means by which it encourages such applications. The supplemental application requirement of the act amounts to a kind of constitutional blackmail—comply with the statute or sacrifice your First Amendment rights. It should go without saying that the tactic cannot survive judicial scrutiny.

In conclusion, the Court finds that the FDAMA unconstitutionally restricts protected commercial speech.... The Court will ... amend the [July 30, 1998] order sua sponte to explicitly declare unconstitutional and unenforceable the FDAMA and its implementing regulations ...

FINAL AMENDED ORDER GRANTING SUMMARY JUDGMENT AND PERMANENT INJUNCTION

THE COURT FINDS AND DECLARES that the policies, rules and regulations of the United States Food and Drug Administration ("FDA") set forth in the Guidance to Industry on Dissemination of Reprints of Certain Published, Original Data, 61 Fed. Reg. 52800 (Oct. 8, 1996) (the "Textbook Guidance"), and Final Guidance on Industry Supported Scientific and Educational Activities, 62 Fed. Reg. 64074 (Dec. 3, 1997) (the "Final CME Guidance"), are contrary to rights secured by the United States Constitution and therefore must be set aside pursuant to 5 U.S.C. § 706(2)(B) except insofar as they are consistent with the injunctive provisions below.

THE COURT FURTHER FINDS AND DECLARES that the policies, rules and regulations of the United States Food and Drug Administration ("FDA") set forth in the Food and Drug Administration Modernization Act, 21 U.S.C. §§ 360aaa through 360aaa–6, and in the FDA's Final Rule on the Dissemination of Information on Unapproved/New Uses for Marketed Drugs, Biologics, and Devices, 21 C.F.R. Part 99, are contrary to rights secured by the United States Constitution and therefore must be set aside pursuant to 5 U.S.C. § 706(2)(B) except insofar as they are consistent with the injunctive provisions below.

THE COURT HEREBY ENJOINS Defendants, their successors, and all persons acting in concert with them or otherwise purporting to act on behalf of the United States (collectively "Defendants") from application or enforcement of any regulation, guidance, policy, order or other official action, as follows:

1. Defendant SHALL NOT in any way prohibit, restrict, sanction or otherwise seek to limit any pharmaceutical or medical device manufacturer or any other person:

a) from disseminating or redistributing to physicians, or other medical professionals any article concerning prescription drugs or medical devices previous [sic] published in a bona fide "peer-reviewed professional journal, regardless of whether such article includes a significant or exclusive focus on unapproved uses for drugs or medical devices that are approved by FDA for other uses and regardless of whether such article reports the original study on which FDA approval of the drug or device in question was based;

b) from disseminating or redistributing to physicians or other medical professionals any reference textbook (including any medical textbook or compendium) or any portion thereof published by a bona fide independent publisher and otherwise generally available for sale in bookstores or other distribution channels where similar books are normally available, regardless of whether such reference textbook or portion thereof includes a significant or exclusive focus on unapproved uses for drugs or medical devices that are approved by FDA for other uses.

c) from suggesting content or speakers to an independent program provider in connection with a continuing medical education seminar program or other symposium regardless of whether unapproved uses for drugs or medical devices that are approved by FDA for other uses are to be discussed.

2. For purposes of this injunction, a "bona fide peer-reviewed journal" is a journal that uses experts to objectively review and select, reject, or provide comments about proposed articles. Such experts should have demonstrated expertise in the subject of the article under review, and be independent from the journal.

3. For purposes of this injunction a "bona fide independent publisher" is a publisher that has no common ownership or other corporate affiliation with a pharmaceutical or medical device manufacturer and whose principal business if [sic] the publication and distribution of books through normal distribution channels.

4. For purposes of this injunction an "independent program provider" is an entity that has no common ownership or other corporate affiliation with a pharmaceutical or medical device manufacturer, that engages in the business of creating and producing continuing medical education seminars, programs or other symposia and that is accredited by a national accrediting organization pertinent to the topic of the seminars, programs or symposia.

5. Nothing herein shall be construed to limit Defendants' application or enforcement of any rules, regulations, guidances, statutes or other provisions of law that sanction the dissemination or redistribution of any material that is false or misleading. In addition, Defendants may require any pharmaceutical or medical device manufacturer that sponsors or provides financial support for the dissemination or redistribution of articles or reference textbooks or for seminars that include references to unapproved uses for drugs or medical devices that are approved by FDA for other uses to disclose (i) its interest in such drugs or devices, and (ii) the fact that the use discussed has not been approved by FDA.

6. Defendants shall cause the injunction to be published in the Federal Register within 15 days of the date here.

———

During oral argument before the Court of Appeals, FDA reversed its position and contended that both the 1997 statutory provisions and the

FDA CME guidance are only "safe harbors" and do not independently authorize FDA to prohibit or to sanction speech. Accordingly, the court dismissed FDA's appeal and vacated the District Court decisions and injunctions. Nonetheless, the court stressed, "In disposing of the case in this manner, we certainly do not criticize the reasoning or conclusions of the district court." *Washington Legal Foundation v. Henney*, 202 F.3d 331 (D.C. Cir. 2000).

Shortly after the Court of Appeals decision, FDA published a notice about the outcome of the litigation. In this notice, the agency declared that it still may, when appropriate, "proceed, in the context of case-by-case enforcement, to determine from a manufacturer's written materials and activities how it intends that its products be used." 65 Fed. Reg. 14286 (Mar. 16, 2000). A drug manufacturer's intent to promote an unapproved use may be the basis for a misbranding case. The Washington Legal Foundation promptly asked the District Court to reopen the matter and to confirm its continuing injunction. Because the injunction had been dissolved by the Court of Appeals, however, the District Court dismissed the case. At the same time, it lamented that "[a]fter six years' worth of briefs, motions, opinions, Congressional acts, and more opinions, the issue remains 100% unresolved, and the country's drug manufacturers are still without clear guidance as to their permissible conduct." The District Court characterized the FDA Federal Register notice as a "farce" and predicted that the Court would be called upon to review the matter again before the controversy is concluded. *Washington Legal Foundation v. Henney*, 128 F. Supp. 2d 11 (D.D.C. 2000). Following this decision, however, FDA determined as a matter of policy that it would not bring legal action against any off-label promotion that complied with the now-dissolved injunction of the District Court. "Because FDA must choose carefully where to deploy its limited resources, FDA is unlikely to initiate an enforcement action where the only evidence of an unapproved intended use is the distribution of enduring materials or sponsorship of CME." Letter from Margaret M. Dotzel, FDA Associate Commissioner for Policy, to Daniel J. Popeo & Richard A. Samp (Jan. 28, 2002). *See* Peggy Chen, *Education or Promotion?: Industry–Sponsored Continuing Medical Education (CME) as a Center for the Core/Commercial Speech Debate*, 58 FOOD & DRUG L.J. 473 (2003).

The Washington Legal Foundation did not rest following dismissal of the litigation. In June 2005, it initiated a project to review and contest letters sent to drug companies by the FDA Division of Drug Marketing, Advertising and Communications (DDMAC) objecting to promotional activities. As a result of its first full year of monitoring warning and untitled letters issued by DDMAC, WLF submitted a citizen petition requesting FDA to review its policies and practices regarding prescription drug advertising in order to ensure compliance with the First Amendment. FDA Docket No. 2006P–0319 (Aug. 7, 2006).

COMMENT: ENFORCEMENT OF THE PROHIBITION AGAINST PROMOTION OF UNAPPROVED USES

The prohibition against promotion by the manufacturer of an off-label use of an approved new drug can be enforced in several different ways:

1. *The FD&C Act.* FDA can enforce this policy by warning letters, formal court proceedings, and action to withdraw the NDA, on the ground that such promotion causes the manufacturer to violate section 505 of the FD&C Act.

2. *The Fraud and Abuse Statute.* The HHS Office of Inspector General, the Department of Justice, and private whistleblowers can enforce this policy under the Medicare Fraud and Abuse provisions, 42 U.S.C. 1320a–7b(b)(2), and *qui tam* cases under the False Claims Act, 31 U.S.C. 3729, which prohibits the submission of false claims to the government. The theory supporting such enforcement is that off-label representations by the manufacturer fraudulently induce patients, pharmacists, and physicians to submit requests for reimbursement for unlabeled uses that are not reimbursable under Medicare or Medicaid. *See, e.g., United States ex rel. Franklin v. Parke–Davis,* 147 F. Supp. 2d 39 (D. Mass. 2001), 210 F.R.D. 257 (D. Mass. 2002). *See also* Michael A. Steinman et al., *Narrative Review: The Promotion of Gabapentin: An Analysis of Internal Industry Documents,* 145 ANNALS OF INTERNAL MED. 284 (Aug. 15, 2006); Maya Alperowicz, *A Case at a Crossroad: United States ex rel. Franklin v. Parke–Davis and the Intersection of Regulating Promotion of Off–Label Uses and Medicaid Fraud and Abuse* (2004), and Robert Kaufman, *The Neurontin Controversy: The Saga of Off–Label Drug Promotion Continues* (2004), in Chapter VI(B)(5) of the Electronic Book; John Rouse, *Whistleblower Protections for FDA and Private–Sector Employees* (2005), in Chapter I(M) of the Electronic Book; Mark S. Davis, *The Effects of False Claims Act Whistleblowers on the Pharmaceutical Industry* (2006), in Chapter I(G)(11) of the Electronic Book; Michael K. Loucks, *Pros and Cons of Off–Label Promotion Investigations and Prosecutions,* 61 FOOD AND DRUG L.J. 577 (2006); Linda Pissott Reig et al., *Between a Rock and a Hard Place,* 11 REG. AFFAIRS FOCUS, No. 11, at 8 (Nov. 2006).

3. *Medicaid Rebate Statute.* The same government officials can similarly bring action for fraudulent inducement of reimbursement claims under the Medicaid program.

4. *State Unfair Competition and Consumer Deception Laws.* State Attorneys General can bring cases on the ground that dissemination of off-label information represents an unfair business practice under state laws.

5. *Lanham Act.* Competitors can bring lawsuits charging that the company is making unwarranted claims that result in competitive harm under 15 U.S.C. 1125(a).

The FD&C Act does not prohibit any person other than the person(s) marketing a drug from promoting an unapproved use. Indeed, federal agencies—in particular, the National Institutes of Health—routinely recommend off-label uses of new drugs.

d. PRESCRIPTION DRUG ADVERTISING TO CONSUMERS

With growing government interest in promoting prescription drug price competition, FDA concluded in the early 1970s that the advertising regulations required revision to allow communication of price comparisons to consumers. In 1975, FDA promulgated a rule authorizing advertising of consumer prices for prescription drugs so long as no representations are made concerning the safety, effectiveness, or indications of the advertised products. 38 Fed. Reg. 32140 (Nov. 21, 1973), 39 Fed. Reg. 21165 (June 19, 1974), 40 Fed. Reg. 58794 (Dec. 18, 1975), codified at 21 C.F.R. 200.200.

Nearly a decade later, in a speech to the Pharmaceutical Advertising Council, FDA Commissioner Arthur Hayes appeared to encourage direct advertising of prescription drugs to consumers. This type of advertising has come to be known as "direct to consumer" or DTC advertising. Because both section 502(n)(3) of the FD&C Act and the implementing regulations, 21 C.F.R. 202.1(e), require advertisements to include a "brief summary relating to side effects, contraindications, and effectiveness," broadcast advertisements confronted difficulties that advertisements in print media did not. The first television advertisement for a prescription drug provoked an immediate regulatory letter. "Rx Advertising to Consumers," FDA Talk Paper No. T83–23 (May 23, 1983). The company revised its television advertisement to carry only price information, but it went forward with newspaper advertising that carried the full "brief summary" in compliance with FDA regulations. On September 2, 1983, Commissioner Hayes issued a "Statement of Policy" in which he requested a suspension of all advertising of prescription drugs to consumers "in order to permit time for a reasoned assessment of this complex issue."

There followed an intense public debate and exploration of the issues. *See, e.g.*, Professional Postgraduate Services, PRESCRIPTION DRUG ADVERTISING TO THE CONSUMER: WHAT ARE THE ISSUES? (1984); "Prescription Drug Advertising to Consumers," Staff Report prepared for the use of the Subcommittee on Oversight and Investigations of the House Committee on Energy and Commerce, 98th Cong., 2nd Sess., Comm. Pt. 98–DD (1984); Alison Masson & Paul H. Rubin, *Matching Prescription Drugs and Consumers: The Benefits of Direct Advertising*, 313 NEW ENG. J. MED. 513 (Aug. 22, 1985); Louis A. Morris, PRESCRIPTION DRUG ADVERTISING TO CONSUMERS: BRIEF SUMMARY FORMATS FOR TELEVISION AND MAGAZINE ADVERTISEMENTS (FDA, 1984), *summarized in* Louis A. Morris & Lloyd G. Millstein, *Drug Advertising to Consumers: Effects of Formats for Magazine and Television Advertisements*, 39 FOOD DRUG COSM. L.J. 497 (1984). Two years later FDA issued the following notice.

Direct–to–Consumer Advertising of Prescription Drugs; Withdrawal of Moratorium

50 Fed. Reg. 36677 (September 9, 1985).

The Food and Drug Administration (FDA) is withdrawing the voluntary moratorium on direct-to-consumer advertising of prescription drugs first requested in 1983. FDA has concluded that, for the time being, current regulations governing prescription drug advertising provide sufficient safeguards to protect consumers....

The moratorium was intended to allow time for a dialogue among consumers, health professionals, and industry on the issue of direct-to-consumer advertising of prescription drugs. It was also intended to allow time for the conduct and interpretation of research by interested parties on aspects of consumer-oriented drug advertising. These two principal purposes for which FDA sought the voluntary moratorium have now been realized....

———

Following FDA withdrawal of the moratorium, prescription drug advertising to consumers progressed largely through print media, because the requirement of a brief summary relating to side effects, contraindications, and effectiveness required reprinting the physician package insert or a major portion of it. The broadcast media could not meet this requirement except by scrolling the complete package insert in commercials run during programs after midnight. In 1995, FDA, faced with threats of legal challenge to its policy regarding DTC advertising, published a background document and asked for comments. 60 Fed. Reg. 42581 (Aug. 16, 1995). The agency conducted a public hearing in October 1995 and published a follow-up document in 61 Fed. Reg. 24314 (May 14, 1996). The agency then published the following notice in August 1997.

Draft Guidance for Industry: Consumer–Directed Broadcast Advertisements

62 Fed. Reg. 43171 (August 12, 1997).

Section 502(n) of the Federal Food, Drug, and Cosmetic Act requires that advertisements for prescription drugs for humans and animals and human biological products include information in brief summary relating to side effects, contraindications, and effectiveness. This is known as the "brief summary" requirement. The prescription drug advertising regulations in § 202.1(e)(1) and (e)(3)(iii) further require that the brief summary disclose all the risk-related information in a product's approved package labeling (package insert or product package insert).

The regulations for advertising prescription drugs through broadcast media, such as radio, television, or telephone communications systems, however, modify the disclosure requirements somewhat. All prescription drug broadcast advertisements must include information about the major risks of the advertised drug (the "major statement") in either the audio or audio and visual parts of the presentation. Instead of presenting a "brief summary" in connection with the broadcast advertisement, a sponsor may make adequate provision for the dissemination of the approved package labeling in connection with the broadcast presentation (§ 202.1(e)(1)). This alternative requirement is referred to as the "adequate provision" requirement.

The "adequate provision" requirement recognizes the inability of broadcast advertisements of reasonable length to present and communicate effectively the extensive information that would be included in a brief summary; it instead specifies that presentation of the advertised product's most important risk information as part of the "major statement," together with "adequate provision" for the dissemination of the approved labeling, can fulfill the risk information disclosure mandated by the act....

Previously, FDA had not described how prescription drug and biological product sponsors could fulfill the "adequate provision" requirement for consumer-directed broadcast advertising....

... In light of the agency's increased experience and recent public input, FDA has reconsidered the issue of adequate provision as it relates to consumer-directed broadcast advertising. Therefore, FDA is publishing a draft guidance entitled, "Consumer–Directed Broadcast Advertisements." ... This draft guidance is intended to provide consumers with adequate communication of required risk information, while facilitating the process used by sponsors to advertise their products to consumers.

The draft guidance on DTC broadcast advertisements stated that the "adequate provision" requirements could be satisfied "by providing an effective mechanism by which the majority of a potentially diverse audience can receive the advertised product's approved labeling." An acceptable mechanism was described as providing the following four components: (1) a toll-free telephone number for consumers to call for the physician package insert, (2) a statement in the broadcast advertisement that additional product information is provided with print advertisements appearing concurrently in print media, (3) a statement that pharmacists and physicians may provide additional information, and (4) an internet website address that provides access to the physician package insert. FDA, DRAFT GUIDANCE FOR INDUSTRY: CONSUMER–DIRECTED BROADCAST ADVERTISEMENTS (July 1997). As a result, the now-familiar prescription drug DTC advertising began to appear regularly on television and the radio.

NOTES

1. *Growth of DTC Advertising.* DTC prescription drug advertising has undergone phenomenal growth. From a base of about $12 million in 1997, it has grown to approximately $4.1 billion in 2005. Rich Thomaselli, *Ten Years Later: Direct to Consumer Drug Advertising*, 77 ADVERTISING AGE 51 (Oct. 1, 2006).

2. *FDA Review.* Although FDA did not require premarket review of DTC advertising, the agency clearly encouraged this approach in order to minimize the need for regulatory action. Companies that did not submit DTC advertising for FDA review were frequently the subject of warning letters.

3. *Relationship to Drug Prices.* The relationship of DTC advertising to the increased price of prescription drugs has provoked heated debate. Some argue that drug prices have been substantially increased because of this advertising. Others argue that prices either have not been affected or have been kept down as a result of the increase in sales attributed to DTC advertising.

4. *The Doctor–Patient Relationship.* There is an equally heated debate about the impact of DTC advertising on the doctor-patient relationship. Some argue that patients pressure their doctors into prescribing drugs the patients heard about on TV, even if they do not need these drugs. Others argue that advertising informs patients about new drugs that may help them and drives them into the doctor's

office to have useful and meaningful discussions about the utility of additional medication.

5. *Lack of Fair Balance.* One of the strongest attacks on DTC advertising, both by FDA and by critics, has been its emphasis on effectiveness and its inadequate mention of risk information. As a result, the industry trade association, PhRMA, has issued voluntary *Principles on Direct-to-Consumer Advertising*, and the pharmaceutical industry has improved its balance in DTC advertising between risk information and effectiveness claims.

6. *Continuing Controversy.* DTC advertising for prescription drugs continues to be controversial. The NEW ENGLAND JOURNAL OF MEDICINE staged a debate on the matter between consumer activist Sydney M. Wolfe and PhRMA President Alan F. Holmer. 346 NEW ENG. J. MED. 523–28 (Feb. 14, 2002). Congress has held several hearings on the matter. *E.g.*, "Direct to Consumer Advertising (DTC)," Hearing before the Subcommittee on Consumer Affairs, Foreign Commerce and Tourism of the Senate Committee on Commerce, Science, and Transportation, 107th Cong. 1st Sess. (2001); "Direct-to-Consumer Advertising of Prescription Drugs: What Are the Consequences?," Hearing before the Senate Special Committee on Aging, 108th Cong., 1st Sess. (2003); "The Impact of Direct-to-Consumer Drug Advertising on Seniors' Health and Health Care Costs," Hearing before the Senate Special Committee on Aging, 109th Cong., 1st Sess. (2005).

7. *Legality of DTC Advertising.* Third-party payers are understandably concerned that DTC advertising informs patients about the availability of potentially helpful prescription drugs and thus increases reimbursement payments. In *Pennsylvania Employee Benefit Trust Fund v. Zeneca, Inc.*, 2005 WL 2993937 (D. Del. 2005), the plaintiffs brought suit against the manufacturer of Prilosec and Nexium on the ground that, after the Prilosec patent had expired and was subject to generic competition which substantially reduced the price, the company used misleading DTC advertising to persuade consumers that the more expensive new Nexium was an improved drug. The District Court determined that the Nexium DTC advertising was consistent with the FDA-approved labeling, and that the action was preempted by FDA jurisdiction over the labeling of Nexium.

8. *Moratorium on DTC Advertising for Selected Drugs?* For some drugs, critics have argued that all DTC advertising is inappropriate. Such drugs would include (1) newly-marketed drugs for the first year after launch, (2) drugs with black box warnings, (3) narrow therapeutic index drugs, (4) drugs subject to risk management programs, and (5) other drugs with significant toxicity. Some pharmaceutical companies have decided not to advertise such products on a voluntary basis. There is a serious question, however, whether such restrictions would survive First Amendment scrutiny if the government made them mandatory.

9. *DTC Advertising for Controlled Substances.* The FDA regulations and guidance documents regarding DTC advertising do not distinguish between prescription drugs that are scheduled under the Controlled Substances Act and prescription drugs that are not so scheduled. The Drug Enforcement Administration (DEA) has sent letters objecting to DTC advertising for various controlled substances. Some companies have agreed to discontinue their DTC advertising for controlled substances, but others have continued to advertise. The DEA relies on the Convention on Psychotropic Substances of 1971, which states in article 10 that "[e]ach Party shall, with due regard to its constitutional provisions, prohibit the advertisement of such substances to the general public." A government ban on DTC advertising for all prescription drug controlled substances would be unlikely to withstand judicial scrutiny under the First Amendment, however.

In August 1999, FDA issued the final GUIDANCE FOR INDUSTRY: CONSUMER-DIRECTED BROADCAST ADVERTISEMENTS. Five years later, the agency issued three draft guidances addressing the information that should be provided to consumers in DTC advertising. 69 Fed. Reg. 6308 (Feb. 10, 2004). In 70 Fed. Reg. 54054 (Sept. 13, 2005), FDA announced a public hearing on DTC advertising in order to obtain comment on how the current requirements for DTC advertising could be improved.

5. COUNTERFEIT, IMITATION, STREET ALTERNATIVE, AND DIVERTED PRESCRIPTION DRUGS

a. COUNTERFEIT DRUGS

FDA has been concerned about the illicit distribution of legitimate drugs and the distribution of counterfeit drugs ever since the mid–1960s, when it was responsible for enforcement of the Drug Abuse Control Amendments of 1965, 79 Stat. 226 (superseded by the Controlled Substances Act, 84 Stat. 1236, 1242, 1281–82 (1970), enforced by DEA). The 1965 Amendments added to the FD&C Act section 201(g)(2), defining the term "counterfeit drug," and section 301(i)(2), prohibiting counterfeiting and the distribution of counterfeit drugs. FDA vigorously enforced these provisions. *See, e.g., United States v. Jamieson–McKames Pharmaceuticals, Inc.*, 651 F.2d 532 (8th Cir. 1981); *United States v. Articles of Drug in Bulk*, Food Drug Cosm. L. Rep. (CCH) ¶ 38,155 (M.D. Fla. 1982); *United States v. All Equipment Including ... An Encapsulating Machine*, 475 F. Supp. 39 (E.D. Mo. 1979); "Counterfeit Drug Cases," FDA Talk Paper, T87–42 (Sept. 30, 1987) (describing cases involving counterfeit contraceptives, analgesic, and antibiotic drug products). *See also* "International Operation Nabs Iranian Dealer and Counterfeit Drugs," FDA Talk Paper T88–55 (Aug. 12, 1988) (recounting undercover operations to stop international trade in counterfeit drugs). *See generally* J. B. Hallagan et al., *Anabolic–Androgenic Steroid Use by Athletes*, 321 NEW ENG. J. MED. 1042 (Oct. 12, 1989).

Congress addressed the growing issue of counterfeit drugs by enactment of the Prescription Drug Marketing Act (PDMA) of 1987, 102 Stat. 95, as modified by the Prescription Drug Amendments of 1992, 106 Stat. 941.

Prescription Drug Marketing Act Pedigree Requirements; Effective Date and Compliance Policy Guide; Request for Comment

71 Fed. Reg. 34249 (June 14, 2006).

The Prescription Drug Marketing Act of 1987 (the PDMA), as modified by the Prescription Drug Amendments of 1992, establish, among other things, requirements related to the wholesale distribution of prescription drugs. A primary purpose of the PDMA was to increase safeguards to prevent the introduction and retail sale of substandard, ineffective, and counterfeit drugs in the U.S. drug supply chain.

Section 503(e)(1)(A) of the act establishes the so-called "pedigree" requirement for prescription drugs. A drug pedigree is a statement of origin that identifies each prior sale, purchase, or trade of a drug, including the dates of those transactions and the names and addresses of all parties to them. Under the pedigree requirement, each person who is engaged in the wholesale distribution of a prescription drug in interstate commerce, who is not the manufacturer or an authorized distributor of record for that drug, must provide to the person who receives the drug a pedigree for that drug. The PDMA states that an authorized distributor of record is a wholesaler that has an "ongoing relationship" with a manufacturer to distribute that manufacturer's drug. However, the PDMA does not define "ongoing relationship."

In 1999, FDA published final regulations implementing the PDMA. The regulations were to take effect in December 2000.... Based on concerns raised by various stakeholders, the agency delayed the effective date ... several times.

Most recently, in February 2004, FDA delayed the effective date ... until December 1, 2006, in part because we were informed by stakeholders in the U.S. drug supply chain that the industry would voluntarily implement electronic track and trace technology by 2007. If widely adopted, this technology could create a de facto electronic pedigree documenting the sale of a drug product from its place of manufacture through the U.S. drug supply chain to the final dispenser. If properly implemented, an electronic record could thus meet the pedigree requirements in section 503(e)(1)(A) of the act. Based on a recent fact-finding effort by FDA to assess the use of e-pedigree across the supply chain, however, it appears that industry will not fully implement track and trace technology by 2007.

Today, the agency is announcing that it does not intend to delay the effective date ... beyond December 1, 2006....

We are issuing a draft CPG [Compliance Policy Guide] that describes how we plan to prioritize our enforcement actions during the next year with respect to these new requirements. To this end, FDA is announcing the availability of a new CPG section 160.900, entitled "Prescription Drug Marketing Act Pedigree Requirements Under 21 CFR Part 203." This CPG, which the agency is publishing in draft for comment, lists factors that FDA field personnel are expected to consider in prioritizing FDA's pedigree-related enforcement efforts during the next year. Consistent with our risk-based approach to the regulation of pharmaceuticals, these factors focus our resources on drug products that are most vulnerable to counterfeiting and diversion or that are otherwise involved in illegal activity.

FDA has not provided in the CPG a list of drug products that have been counterfeited in the past. We solicit comment on the merit of providing such a list....

NOTES

1. *An Increasing Problem.* As drug prices have increased, the problem of counterfeit drugs has grown exponentially. And as technology has become more sophisticated, it has become increasingly difficult even for the manufacturer of the

genuine drug to differentiate the genuine from the counterfeit. Some companies have begun to embed special markers in drugs or their labeling or to take other measures to allow an instant determination of whether a drug is genuine or counterfeit.

2. *The FDA Counterfeit Drug Task Force.* FDA established a Counterfeit Drug Task Force in 2003. The Task Force issued its first report in February 2004 and its second report in May 2005. Following a public meeting in February 2006 to gather additional information, the Task Force issued its most recent report in June 2006. All of these documents are available on the FDA website.

3. *RFID.* The use of radio frequency identification (RFID) has often been suggested as the solution to establishing a pedigree for each prescription drug. *See* Afia K. Asamoah, *Not As Easy As It May Appear: Using RFID to Fulfill PDMA's Elusive Pedigree Requirement*, 61 FOOD & DRUG L.J. 385 (2006); Jennifer A. Lee, *Counterfeit Drugs: A Growing Public Health Risk in Need of a Multi–Factored Solution* (2005), and Daniell Newman, *The Next Big Thing: Identification Technology in Industries Regulated by the Food and Drug Administration* (2005), in Chapter VI(P) of the Electronic Book.

4. *Congressional Hearings.* See "Counterfeit Bulk Drugs," Hearings before the Subcommittee on Oversight and Investigations of the House Committee on Commerce, 106th Cong. 2d Sess. (2000); "Canadian Prescription Drug Importation: Is There a Safety Issue?," Hearing before the Subcommittee on Human Rights and Wellness of the House Committee on Government Reform, 108th Cong., 1st Sess. (2003); "Sick Crime: Counterfeit Drugs in the United States," Hearing before the Subcommittee on Criminal Justice, Drug Policy, and Human Resources of the House Committee on Government Reform, 109th Cong., 1st Sess. (2005).

5. *The Federal Criminal Code.* A statutory provision outside the FD&C Act, 18 U.S.C. 2320, broadly prohibits any traffic in counterfeit goods. This provision has been applied to counterfeit prescription drugs. *See, e.g., United States v. Milstein*, 401 F.3d 53, 59 (2d Cir. 2005).

6. *Liability for Counterfeit Drugs.* As the problem of counterfeit drugs has escalated, patients harmed by these drugs have sought remedies in the courts. In *Fagan v. AmerisourceBergen Corp.*, 356 F. Supp. 2d 198 (E.D.N.Y. 2004), a patient who was prescribed Epogen following a liver transplant, and who received a counterfeit drug, brought suit against the manufacturer of Epogen, the wholesale drug distributor, and the pharmacy, to recover damages for personal injuries, under common law theories of tort and contracts.

7. *Sentence.* In *United States v. Cambra, Jr.*, 933 F.2d 752 (9th Cir. 1991), the Court of Appeals upheld a sentence based on the crime of fraud and deceit, a more serious offense than the violation of the counterfeit drug provisions of the FD&C Act.

8. *State Law.* In *Ferndale Laboratories, Inc. v. Cavendish*, 79 F.3d 488 (6th Cir. 1996), the Court of Appeals upheld an Ohio registration requirement imposed on out-of-state drug wholesalers on the ground that it was not an impermissible burden on interstate commerce.

b.   IMITATION DRUGS

Section 502(i)(2), as enacted in 1938, prohibits the sale of any imitation drug. FDA has enforced this provision against a variety of drugs made in imitation of, and sold on the street in substitution for, illegal controlled substances. *See, e.g., United States v. Articles of Drug*, 633 F. Supp. 316 (D. Neb. 1986); "National Illegal Drug Scheme Halted," FDA Talk Paper No.

T86–25 (Apr. 3, 1986), describing the seizure of 24 million tablets and capsules of imitation amphetamines which contained primarily caffeine. The District Court imposed an injunction prohibiting the defendant from marketing imitation drugs. The Court of Appeals rejected the defendant's claim that the statute was void for vagueness because it did not define the term "imitation." The court held that a product is an imitation if it is identical in shape, size and color, or similar or virtually identical in gross appearance, or similar in effect to a controlled substance, but not if it is only "similar in concept." The Court of Appeals remanded the case, however, instructing the District Court to more clearly define the prohibited acts. *United States v. Articles of Drug*, 825 F.2d 1238 (8th Cir. 1987). For the decision on remand, see *United States v. Articles of Drug*, Food Drug Cosm. L. Rep. (CCH) ¶ 38,089 (D. Neb. 1988). On a second appeal, *United States v. Midwest Pharmaceuticals, Inc.*, 890 F.2d 1004 (8th Cir. 1989), the Court of Appeals upheld the scope of the revised injunction. In *New Mexico v. Castleman*, 863 P.2d 1088 (N.M. App. 1993), the New Mexico Court of Appeals upheld the state imitation drug statute against a charge that it was unconstitutionally vague.

c. STREET DRUG ALTERNATIVES

FDA has also been confronted with the problem of street drug alternatives that do not fit the narrow definition of an imitation drug. In 65 Fed. Reg. 17512 (Apr. 3, 2000), the agency announced the availability of a guidance stating its position on these products. FDA explained that street drug alternatives are herbal products that claim to mimic the euphoric effects of illegal street drugs. The agency took the position that these products constitute unapproved new drugs and misbranded drugs, and that they do not fall within the definition of a dietary supplement because they are intended to modify the psychological states of the user rather than to supplement the diet. The FDA's position was upheld in *United States v. Undetermined Quantities of Articles of Drug, Street Drug Alternatives*, 145 F. Supp. 2d 692 (D. Md. 2001).

d. DIVERTED DRUGS

In two early cases, courts held that diverted prescription drugs labeled as "physician's sample—not to be sold" did not become misbranded in the possession of wholesalers who obtained them with the intention of selling them to retail druggists to fill prescriptions. *United States v. Various Articles of Drugs Consisting of Unknown Quantities of Prescription Drugs*, 332 F.2d 286 (3d Cir. 1964); *United States v. Various Articles of Drugs Consisting of Unknown Quantities of Prescription Drugs*, 207 F. Supp. 480 (S.D.N.Y. 1962). *See also Miami–Luken, Inc. v. Ohio State Board of Pharmacy*, Food Drug Cosm. L. Rep. (CCH) ¶ 38,106 (Ohio Ct. App. 1987). Similarly, a company that repackaged tablets from the manufacturer's original package and resold them was not required to obtain separate FDA approval when the manufacturer already had an approved NDA. *United States v. Kaybel, Inc.*, 430 F.2d 1346 (3d Cir. 1970). These decisions made it very difficult for FDA to prevent the adulteration and misbranding of diverted samples.

Congressional investigations brought to light a related problem involving pharmaceutical products exported from the United States and later reimported. *See* "Dangerous Medicine: The Risk to American Consumers from Prescription Drug Diversion and Counterfeiting," Report by the Subcommittee on Oversight and Investigations of the House Committee on Energy and Commerce, 99th Cong., 2nd Sess., Comm. Print 99–Z (1966). In September 1985, FDA adopted a policy of automatic detention of imports of U.S.-produced drugs in order to confirm that they had not become adulterated or misbranded while abroad. 52 Fed. Reg. 706 (Jan. 8, 1987). Because this policy was adopted without the opportunity for public comment, it was declared invalid in *Bellarno International Ltd. v. FDA*, 678 F. Supp. 410 (E.D.N.Y. 1988).

The Prescription Drug Marketing Act of 1987, 102 Stat. 95, added section 801(d)(1) to the FD&C Act, making the importation of American drugs by anyone other than the manufacturer illegal. The PDMA also added section 503(c), prohibiting the sale of drug samples and the resale of drug products initially sold to health care institutions; 503(d), allowing the distribution of drug samples by pharmaceutical manufacturers, but only in response to a written request and if a receipt is obtained; and 503(e), requiring state licensure of wholesale distributors of prescription drugs. FDA's steps to implement these provisions can be traced in 53 Fed. Reg. 29776 (Aug. 8, 1988), 53 Fed. Reg. 35325 (Sept. 13, 1988), 53 Fed. Reg. 44954 (Nov. 7, 1988), 55 Fed. Reg. 7778 (Mar. 5, 1990).

NOTES

1. *Drug Samples.* For cases involving illegal distribution of drug samples, *see United States v. Dino*, 919 F.2d 72 (8th Cir. 1990); *Parke–Davis & Co. v. Ricci*, 587 So. 2d 589 (Fla. Dist. Ct. App. 1991).

2. *Kaybel.* The *Kaybel* decision applies only to solid oral dosage forms of a drug, and does not apply when a liquid drug is diluted or pooled. *United States v. Baxter Healthcare Corp.*, 712 F. Supp. 1352 (N.D. Ill. 1989), *aff'd* 901 F.2d 1401 (7th Cir. 1990); FDA Compliance Policy Guide No. 7132c.06 (January 18, 1991).

3. *State Registration.* Ohio's law requiring registration of all prescription drug wholesalers was upheld against the charge that it represented an unconstitutional burden on out-of-state distributors. *Ferndale Laboratories, Inc. v. Cavendish*, 79 F.3d 488 (6th Cir. 1996).

6.   INTERNET PHARMACY

The extraordinary growth of the internet in the past decade has produced a nightmare for the regulation of drug products and an enormous growth in the distribution of counterfeit and imitation drugs. So-called "rogue" internet sites bombard the country with advertising for inexpensive versions of costly new drugs. Most of the drugs are counterfeit drugs that are made abroad and have no approved NDA. Many have no active ingredient. For most, there is no pretense of a doctor's prescription. When a prescription is written, it is done over the telephone without a valid doctor-patient relationship. Because these rogue internet sites are difficult to trace and can easily move their location, enforcement is a complex matter.

Jody Feder, *Legal Issues Related to Prescription Drug Sales on the Internet*

Congressional Research Service (CRS) Report No. RS–21711 (June 7, 2006).

With the advent of the Internet, many individuals have turned to online pharmacies to purchase prescription drugs, and an increasing number of physicians have incorporated the Internet and email into their medical practice. Use of this technology has many advantages for both the doctor and the patient, including cost savings, convenience, accessibility, and improved privacy and communication. Although many online pharmacies are legitimate businesses that offer safe and convenient services similar to those provided by traditional neighborhood pharmacies and large chain drugstores, other online pharmacies—often referred to as "rogue sites"—engage in practices that are illegal, such as selling unapproved or counterfeit drugs or dispensing drugs without a prescription. Some rogue sites operate in a legal gray area in which the online pharmacy, as mandated by federal law, requires a prescription before dispensing prescription drugs, but allows patients to secure a prescription by completing an online questionnaire that is reviewed by a doctor who never examines or speaks to the patient. . . .

Current regulation of online pharmacies and doctors consists of a patchwork of federal and state laws in an array of areas. At the federal level, the Food and Drug Administration regulates prescription drugs under the Federal Food, Drug, and Cosmetic Act (FFDCA), which governs, among other things, the safety and efficacy of prescription medications, including the approval, manufacturing, and distribution of such drugs. It is the FFDCA that requires that prescription drugs may be dispensed only with a valid prescription. The Drug Enforcement Agency (DEA) enforces the Controlled Substances Act, which is a federal statute that establishes criminal and civil sanctions for the unlawful possession, manufacturing or distribution of certain addictive or dangerous substances, including certain prescription drugs that share these properties such as narcotics and opiates. At the state level, state boards of pharmacy regulate pharmacy practice, and state medical boards oversee the practice of medicine. Thus, some of the laws that govern online pharmacies and doctors vary from state to state. . . .

The current legal framework for regulating online pharmacies and doctors is a patchwork of federal and state laws regarding controlled substances, prescription drugs, pharmacies, and the practice of medicine. Although many doctors and pharmacies who use the Internet prescribe and dispense drugs in a safe and legal fashion, others have exploited gaps in the current system to prescribe and dispense potentially dangerous quantities of highly addictive prescription drugs. To combat such abuses, legislators and interest groups have proposed an array of solutions, including establishing a federal definition of what constitutes a valid prescription, requiring doctors to conduct in-person examinations, mandating that online pharmacies disclose identifying information about themselves and their employees, establishing state prescription drug monitoring programs to track data regarding the prescription and use of controlled substances, giving state prosecutors the authority to seek nationwide injunctions against rogue sites, educating consumers about the potential dangers of buying drugs online, establishing certification programs to identify legitimate online pharmacies, and regulating search engines and shipping companies that enable rogue sites to do business.

NOTES

1. *Initial FDA Reaction to the Internet.* When the internet first became a prominent method of communication a decade ago, FDA announced a public hearing to consider its impact on promotion of FDA-regulated medical products. 61 Fed. Reg. 48707 (Sept. 16, 1996). At that time, the agency's sole focus was on the promotion of legitimate drugs. The problem of rogue internet sites had not yet arisen.

2. *Conviction of Physician.* In *United States v. Nelson*, 383 F.3d 1227 (10th Cir. 2004), a physician who operated an internet pharmacy was convicted for a conspiracy to distribute controlled prescription drugs outside the usual course of professional practice. Although all patients requesting prescription drugs were required to fill out a medical history questionnaire, the defendant signed thousands of prescriptions without ever examining a patient.

3. *Congressional Hearings.* Congress has examined the problem of internet sales of prescription drugs on several occasions, but thus far has enacted no legislation to address the matter. *See, e.g.,* "Point, Click, Self–Medicate: A Review of Consumer Safeguards on Internet Pharmacy Sites," Hearing before the House Committee on Government Reform, 108th Cong., 1st Sess. (2003); "A Prescription for Safety: The Need for H.R. 3880, the Internet Pharmacy Consumer Protection Act," Hearing before the House Committee on Government Reform, 108th Cong., 2nd Sess. (2004); "Buyer Beware: The Danger of Purchasing Pharmaceuticals Over the Internet," Hearings before the Senate Permanent Subcommittee on Investigations of the Committee on Governmental Affairs, 108th Cong., 2nd Sess. (2004); "Internet Pharmacy and Drug Importation: Exploring Risks and Benefits," Hearing before the Senate Special Committee on Aging, 109th Cong., 1st Sess. (2005); "Safety of Imported Pharmaceuticals: Strengthening Efforts to Combat the Sales of Controlled Substances Over the Internet," Hearing before the House Subcommittee on Oversight and Investigations of the Committee on Energy and Commerce, 109th Cong., 1st Sess. (2005).

7. GOOD MANUFACTURING PRACTICE (GMP)

In contrast to the food sanitation provisions of the FD&C Act, which do not expressly mandate good manufacturing practice, section 501(a)(2)(B) of the Act, added by the Drug Amendments of 1962, explicitly declares a drug to be adulterated if it is not manufactured "in conformity with current good manufacturing practice." FDA initially implemented this authority in 1963. 28 Fed. Reg. 1459 (Feb. 14, 1963), 28 Fed. Reg. 6385 (June 20, 1963).

United States v. An Article of Drug ... White Quadrisect

484 F.2d 748 (7th Cir. 1973).

■ PER CURIAM.

... The lower court condemned the shipment because the defendant's production procedure violated the "current good manufacturing practice"

(GMP) provision of the Act, 21 U.S.C. § 351(a)(2)(B). Appellant contends that that provision is unconstitutional under the Due Process Clause of the Fifth Amendment because of its alleged vagueness.

[handwritten: appellant (Δ) argues]

The GMP provision stems from congressional concern over the danger that dangerously impure drugs might escape detection under a system predicated only on seizure of drugs shown to be in fact adulterated. In order to insure public safety, Congress determined in 1962 that it was necessary to regulate the means of production themselves.... By way of implementation, the FDA has promulgated detailed regulations to spell out the precise requirements of the section.

[handwritten: why rule]

The district court found violations of GMP standards by defendant which include the failure to keep basic production records, inadequate testing of active ingredients before use, and insufficient tests of the finished product prior to shipment. These findings are not contested on appeal and we therefore consider them established....

[handwritten: lower court found]

... We conclude that the term "current good manufacturing practice" adequately defines a standard which the Administrator was authorized to particularize in interpretative regulations. Defendant does not deny that the regulations, which he has plainly violated, were adequate to notify him that his conduct was prohibited.

Defendant's argument is based on attacks on the statutory terms "current" and "good." ... We have no trouble with the use of the words in § 351(a)(2)(B). The term "current" fixes the point in time when the acceptability of the relevant production practices must be determined. Thus, the statute does not permit prosecution for failure to follow safety practices which were not recognized prior to the production of the subject drugs.[4] The term "good" likewise acquires adequate meaning when read in context even though, as defendant observes, a good dictionary lists a good many definitions of the word. Alternative definitions do not create impermissible ambiguity if the relevant definition is capable of interpretation by reference to objective criteria.... The word "good," as used in the GMP provision, is not unduly subjective.

[handwritten: Δ]
[handwritten: court says look @ context]

The Constitution requires only a reasonable degree of certainty in statutory language.... Appellant also ignores the detailed regulations promulgated by the FDA which considerably illuminate the statutory language.[5]

---

4. Appellant also argues that even if the section has a definite meaning, it creates a standard subject to such rapid change that a drug manufacturer is unable to ascertain at any point in time what is expected of him. This argument overlooks the interpretative regulations. In our opinion it is appropriate for the statute to authorize changes in regulations to reflect the Administrator's evaluation of "current" practice. We think the GMP standard is sufficiently fixed.

5. "[T]he Secretary's interpretative regulations as to good manufacturing practice for purposes of judging the adequacy of the methods, facilities, and controls would be prima facie evidence of what constitutes current good manufacturing practice in any proceeding involving [§ 351(a)(2)] of the Food, Drug, and Cosmetic Act as amended by the bill." 1962 U.S. Cong. & Admin. News, p. 2890.

In view of the customary presumption of constitutionality and the established high regard for the purposes of the Act, we readily sustain the GMP provision. The language utilized by Congress in this statute is neither less certain nor more difficult to interpret than language elsewhere in the same Act which has been upheld....

Moreover, an argument identical to defendant's was made and rejected in *United States v. Bel–Mar Laboratories, Inc.*, 284 F. Supp. 875 (E.D.N.Y. 1968). Judge Mishler's treatment of the constitutional question in that case is thorough and persuasive; we adopt his views.... We hold that defendant violated reasonably stable, definite, and ascertainable standards of current good manufacturing practice designed to insure the production of unadulterated drugs....

Once the constitutionality of the original GMP regulations was upheld, FDA moved to expand them.

Human and Veterinary Drugs: Current Good Manufacturing Practice in Manufacture, Processing, Packing, or Holding

43 Fed. Reg. 45014 (September 29, 1978).

In the FEDERAL REGISTER of February 13, 1976 (41 FR 6878), the Commissioner of Food and Drugs proposed to revise the CGMP regulations, Parts 210 and 211, issued under section 501(a)(2)(B) of the Federal Food, Drug, and Cosmetic Act, to update them in light of current technology and to adopt more specific requirements to assure the quality of finished drug products....

A number of comments addressed the so-called "how to" versus the "what" argument; that is, the proposed CGMP regulations describe "how" a particular requirement should be achieved rather than specifying "what" it is that is to be achieved. Many comments recommended that the regulations establish only objectives or specifications and allow each manufacturer to determine the best method of attaining the objective or meeting the specification....

The Commissioner believes that, with relatively few exceptions, the CGMP regulations do describe "what" is to be accomplished and provide great latitude in "how" the requirement is achieved. For example, written records and procedures are required, but FDA will recognize as satisfactory any reasonable format that achieves the desired results. Because of the need for uniformity in certain areas of the CGMP regulations that have presented problems in the past, however, there are some instances where it is desirable to specify the manner in which requirements are to be accomplished....

The requirement for written procedures is intended to provide additional assurance of effective communication of appropriate information from firm management to line personnel and of regular performance of a firm's established programs and procedures. It is not enough that employees "know their jobs." Key personnel may be absent without warning; personnel substitutions involving less experienced employees may be necessary; and new or revised instructions to employees must be adequately conveyed to those who need to know. These situations are not usual, but may occur frequently. The most appropriate method for reliably relating policies and procedures to those who must know them is to have them set down in writing, readily available, and presented in a manner easily understood. The Commissioner does not believe this is a burdensome requirement....

Several comments argued that § 210.1 [stating that failure to comply with any of the CGMP requirements shall render a drug adulterated under FD&C Act 501(a)(2)(B)] should be deleted because it is based on the erroneous proposition that CGMP regulations can be substantive. The comments urged that regulations issued under section 501(a)(2)(B) of the act are only interpretive.

Because of the fervor reflected by these objections and because the Commissioner foresees identical objections being made to proposals to issue binding CGMP regulations for specific classes of drug products in the future, the Commissioner has decided that a lengthy exposition of the basis for his concluding that FDA has legal authority to promulgate such regulations is warranted....

Based on ... complete review of the legislative history of section 501(a)(2)(B) of the act, the Commissioner concludes that there is no support for the proposition that Congress intended that CGMP regulations should be merely interpretive. At the least, Congress wanted CGMP regulations to have the same force and effect as other regulations issued under section 701(a) of the act. To the extent that a stronger Congressional mandate can be gleaned from the various reports, amendments, and debates, it appears that binding standards were to be issued by FDA and issued through the less cumbersome-notice-and-comment rulemaking procedures of section 701(a) of the act rather than the more complex section 701(e) mechanism. Therefore, the Commissioner rejects the argument that § 210.1 exceeds the authority conferred by Congress under sections 501(a)(2)(B) and 701(a) of the act....

... [I]f each CGMP requirement has to receive a de novo hearing in each and every enforcement proceeding, the burden of litigation that would result would not be in the public interest, nor would it be equitable to competing manufacturers who were not involved in such litigation....

... The Commissioner notes that [*National Confectioners Association*, 569 F.2d 690 (D.C. Cir.1978), and *Nova Scotia, supra* p. 344] dealt specifically with the validity of CGMP regulations issued under the statutory standards relating to adulterated foods, which do not explicitly refer to "current good manufacturing practice." It would indeed be anomalous that those regulations could be issued as legally binding if regulations amplifying section 501(a)(2)(B) could not be....

With regard to the alleged lack of flexibility in the enforcement of "binding" CGMP regulations, the Commissioner believes that the comments have confused the question of whether a violation exists with the question of whether FDA will take action upon the violation.... It should be noted, however, that even in the absence of any CGMP regulations, whether binding or not, the doing of or failure to do any particular act which is inconsistent with current good manufacturing practice results in the product being legally adulterated, even if no legal action is brought....

NOTES

1. *Drug GMP Cases.* FDA has in most instances found the courts to be receptive to its GMP cases, even when criminal charges are included. *United States v. Bel–Mar Laboratories, Inc.*, 284 F. Supp. 875 (E.D.N.Y. 1968); *United States v. Lanpar Co.*, 293 F. Supp. 147 (N.D. Tex. 1968); *United States v. Kendall Co.*, 324 F. Supp. 628 (D. Mass. 1971); *United States v. Lit Drug Co.*, 333 F. Supp. 990 (D.N.J. 1971); *United States v. Dianovin Pharmaceuticals, Inc.*, 342 F. Supp. 724 (D.P.R. 1972), *aff'd*, 475 F.2d 100 (1st Cir. 1973); *United States v. Medwick Laboratories, Inc.*, 416 F. Supp. 832 (N.D. Ill. 1976); *United States v. Articles of Drug ... Labeled ... Colchicine*, 442 F. Supp. 1236 (S.D.N.Y. 1978); *United States v. Morton–Norwich Products, Inc.*, 461 F. Supp. 760 (N.D.N.Y. 1978); *United States v. K–N Enterprises, Inc.*, 461 F. Supp. 988 (N.D. Ill. 1978); *United States v. Jamieson–McKames Pharmaceuticals, Inc.*, 651 F.2d 532 (8th Cir. 1981); *United States v. Sopcak*, Food Drug Cosm. L. Rep. (CCH) ¶ 38,162 (E.D. Mich. 1990); *United States v. Bhutani*, 175 F.3d 572 (7th Cir. 1999). GMP problems can also lead to recalls and other forms of voluntary compliance. *E.g.*, "Lilly Recalls Drugs Following FDA Inspections," FDA Talk Paper No. T89–55 (Sept. 15, 1989), "Lilly Reaches Compliance Agreement with FDA," FDA Talk Paper No. T89–72 (Nov. 3, 1989).

2. *History of Drug GMP Regulations.* The evolution of FDA's regulations may be traced from 28 Fed. Reg. 1459 (Feb. 14, 1963), through 28 Fed. Reg. 6385 (June 20, 1963), 30 Fed. Reg. 932 (Jan. 29, 1965), 34 Fed. Reg. 13553 (Aug. 22, 1969), 36 Fed. Reg. 601 (Jan. 15, 1971), 41 Fed. Reg. 6878 (Feb. 13, 1976), 43 Fed. Reg. 45014 (Sept. 29, 1978), and 54 Fed. Reg. 26394 (June 23, 1989). FDA proposed GMP regulations for large volume parenteral drugs in 41 Fed. Reg. 22202 (June 1, 1976), and at the same time questioned whether similar requirements should apply to small volume parenterals, 41 Fed. Reg. at 22219, but took no further action on this matter. The GMP regulations were held to have the force of law in *National Association of Pharmaceutical Manufacturers v. FDA*, 637 F.2d 877 (2d Cir. 1981). For the origin of the concept of drug GMP, *see* John P. Swann, *The 1941 Sulfathiazole Disaster and the Birth of Good Manufacturing Practices*, 40 PHARMACY IN HIST., No. 1, at 17 (1999).

3. *Interpretive Guidelines.* FDA has also issued a number of guidelines interpreting the GMP regulations, including guidelines concerning the preparation of compressed medical gases, general principles of process validation, expiration dating and stability testing, computerized drug processing, sterile drug products by aseptic processing, content uniformity testing of tablets and capsules, and parametric release of terminally heat sterilized drug products.

4. *Denial of NDA Approval.* In a relatively unusual action, FDA refused to approve three NDAs for failure to comply with GMPs in 53 Fed. Reg. 18905 (May 25, 1988). The agency has also successfully withdrawn approval of NDAs for failure to comply with GMPs. *See* 52 Fed. Reg. 7318 (Mar. 10, 1987), 52 Fed. Reg. 29274 (Aug. 6, 1987), *aff'd*, *Copanos and Sons, Inc. v. Food and Drug Administration*, 854 F.2d 510 (D.C. Cir. 1988).

5. *Commentary.* See Richard E. Williams, *Counsel's Role in Current Good Manufacturing Practice*, 23 FOOD DRUG COSM. L.J. 71 (1968); Seymour B. Jeffries, *Current Good Manufacturing Practice Compliance—A Review of the Problems and an Approach to Their Management*, 23 FOOD DRUG COSM. L.J. 580 (1968); Roscoe P. Kandle, *Application of Current Good Manufacturing Practices*, 24 FOOD DRUG COSM. L.J. 9 (1969); Irwin S. Shupe, *GMPs—An Industry Point of View*, 24 FOOD DRUG COSM. L.J. 14 (1969); Robert W. Elkas, *Revised Good Manufacturing Practice Regulations*, 25 FOOD DRUG COSM. L.J. 78 (1970); Robert W. Jennings, *Revised Good Manufacturing Practice Regulations*, 25 FOOD DRUG COSM. L.J. 107 (1970); Patrick V. Gibbons, *Legal Implications of Good Manufacturing Practice Regulations*, 31 FOOD DRUG COSM. L.J. 473 (1976); J. J. Wittick, *Proposed Revisions of the Current GMP Regulation*, 32 FOOD DRUG COSM. L.J. 109 (1977); Beth F. Goldstein, *Current Good Manufacturing Practices* (1995), and Peter J. Schildkraut, *The Regulation of Drug Manufacturing Changes: Past, Present, and Foreign* (1997), in Chapter VI(C)(6) of the Electronic Book.

6. *Compendial Standards.* At one time, standards set by the three drug compendia recognized by section 501(b) of the FD&C Act were important regulatory tools. *See* George Urdang, *The Development of Pharmacopoeias*, 8 FOOD DRUG COSM. L.J. 69 (1953); Martin I. Blake, *The Role of the Compendia in Establishing Drug Standards*, 31 FOOD DRUG COSM. L.J. 276 (1976). Although the constitutionality of section 501(b) has been questioned, *see* Thomas W. Christopher, *Validity of Delegation of Power to a Private Agency—The Pharmacopoeia Provisions*, 6 FOOD DRUG COSM. L.J. 641 (1951), the compendial standards were the basis for hundreds of FDA regulatory actions under both the 1906 Act and the 1938 Act. *See, e.g., United States v. King & Howe, Inc.*, 78 F.2d 693 (2d Cir. 1935); *Woodard Laboratories, Inc. v. United States*, 198 F.2d 995 (9th Cir. 1952); *United States v. Lanpar Co.*, 293 F. Supp. 147 (N.D. Tex. 1968). As FDA has relied increasingly upon specifications established through the new drug approval process and bioavailability/bioequivalence requirements, compendial standards have declined in regulatory importance. Monitoring of drug quality through product analysis, however, remains an important function of the agency. *See* Daniel Banes, *The National Center for Drug Analysis*, 25 FOOD DRUG COSM. L.J. 135 (1970).

In spite of the substantial success of FDA GMP enforcement, courts remain reluctant to cripple a drug manufacturer by completely closing down its manufacturing establishment, as the following strongly contested case illustrates.

United States v. Barr Laboratories, Inc.

812 F. Supp. 458 (D.N.J. 1993).

■ WOLIN, DISTRICT JUDGE.

Currently before the Court is plaintiff's application for a preliminary injunction directing defendants to suspend, recall or revamp numerous products in their current product line. Plaintiff filed this action in the United States District Court in the Southern District of New York on June 12, 1992, alleging that defendants violated the Federal Food, Drug, and Cosmetic Act. In accordance with the first-filed rule, the case was transferred to the District of New Jersey on June 26, 1992, where it was consolidated with an action defendants brought against plaintiff on April 24, 1992, seeking relief from allegedly *ad hoc* drug regulations.... Beginning on August 17, 1992, and continuing intermittently to October 12, 1992, through the testimony of inspectors, experts and employees, the parties presented exhaustive but conflicting views of defendants' business practices....

Each day with confidence and hope millions of people in the United States and other countries reach for pills, powders, capsules and syrups to relieve or prevent an infinite number of physical and mental ailments. The weighty task of ensuring the integrity of these products, frequently unquestioned by most consumers, falls to the Food and Drug Administration, which monitors the practices of the drug industry through a system of approvals and investigations. Built into this maze of often ambiguous rules, however, is the recognition that drug manufacturers are businesses, which must follow efficient as well as effective procedures.

The current conflict surrounding these rules is best characterized as a confrontation between a humorless warden and his uncooperative prisoner. Exchanging heavy blows, the parties generated a record of more than twenty-three hundred pages of testimony, almost four hundred exhibits and numerous lengthy declarations....

The divergent views presented to the Court reflect not only a difference of perspective, but also the changes made at Barr Laboratories since the first threat of this litigation. As a result, the record is a composite of two trials: the case that was and the case that is. As such, the bases upon which some of the government's criticisms rest have disappeared during the course of this litigation. Wary of this timing element, the Court has reviewed the lengthy record and the parties' proposed findings with the dual desire to protect an unsuspecting public and to avoid unnecessarily burdensome rules and now makes the following findings of fact and conclusions of law....

... Congress codified the public interest in safe and effective drugs with the Act and expressly granted the Court injunctive powers to protect this interest....

Courts entering injunctions under the Act have required the government to show: (1) violations of the Act on the part of the defendant; and (2) a cognizable danger of recurrent violations....

Even if the Court were to find that Barr violated the Act in the past and that future violations are likely, an injunction automatically will not issue. Because the language of section 332(a) is not mandatory, the Court retains discretion to grant or deny equitable relief....

The Court concludes that the government has demonstrated that it is likely to succeed on the merits. With regard to past violations, there can be no dispute that Barr has violated the Act by failing to follow manufacturing practices that comply with CGMP as required under section 351(a)(2)(B) and, therefore, has introduced adulterated drugs into commerce in violation of section 331(a). Until recently, for example, Barr did not conduct failure investigations, released batches on the basis of selective data, and refused to validate its cleaning processes, thereby ignoring specific provisions of the

CFR. Barr's own attempts to remake itself through a vigorous overhaul prevents any other conclusion.

Turning to future violations, the government has demonstrated that a threat of recurrence exists, as a consideration of the appropriate factors illustrates. First, defendants' violations properly are characterized as "recurrent" and not "isolated." Problems at Barr persisted despite repeated criticism from the FDA over at least a four-year period.

Barr's reluctance to ameliorate its methods in the face of these warnings is troublesome. This behavior requires the Court to attach a greater degree of scienter to Barr's actions. Further, Barr's refusal to comply with the recommendations of the government casts doubt on Barr's recognition of the wrongful nature of its conduct as well as the genuineness of its efforts to conform to the law.

While defendant has made many improvements, these efforts are long overdue. Because the threat of this litigation served as the catalyst for Barr's renovation, the Court cannot with confidence conclude that Barr's current efforts are the product of a new philosophy rather than a reflection of a desire to deflect this suit.

Due to established past violations and the risk of future violations, the Court now must consider whether an injunction is required under the particular facts of this case.

The Court concludes that injunctive relief is necessary to safeguard the public interest. Many of the practices the Court condemns today are used in the day-to-day operations of Barr and memorialized in standard operating procedures. Examples include Barr's blend sampling strategy, retesting procedure, outlier technique and reliance on averaging. Only through an injunction can the Court be confident that these forbidden methods, defended with vigor by Barr's employees, will be abandoned and the products made under their auspices shielded from the public....

The government cites Barr for general CGMP-compliance problems. Although the Court recognizes that Barr has had much difficulty satisfying the often reasonable demands of the FDA, injunctive relief must be used sparingly, to prevent future harm, and not to punish past violations.

In light of Barr's recent makeover, both personal and physical, the Court is unwilling to order a temporary shut-down. While Barr's transformation from an ugly duckling to a swan is neither natural nor complete, the Court cannot ignore Barr's remedial efforts, as reflected in the satisfaction of many of the concerns of its experts.

Of more concern, however, are the specific products. To the extent that Barr relied upon investigations which do not satisfy section 211.192, as construed by the Court, to release batches or to complete retrospective and prospective validation studies, these actions and studies are invalid. Reliance on faulty methods cannot be cured by subsequent compliance....

Based on these findings, the Court will order Barr to validate its products. This order will reach only those products of particular concern to the government....

The Court may recall any drug product found to be manufactured in violation of the Act that has been released to the public for distribution. Although not authorized expressly in the Act, this remedy is consistent with the broad equitable relief powers district courts enjoy.

Citing a variety of failures, the government asks the Court to recall fifteen batches of ten different drug products. In a batch-by-batch defense, Barr attempts to refute these charges. [The District Court then determined which batches must and need not be recalled.]

NOTES

1. *Neither Party Satisfied.* Both FDA and Barr—as well as most of the pharmaceutical industry—regarded this decision as a setback. FDA failed to get the type of injunction it sought, and Barr did not prevail on a number of the detailed GMP issues. The District Court set a standard of judicial inquiry that made both parties uncomfortable.

2. *Successful Litigation for FDA.* For an equally intense GMP case, *see United States v. Richlyn Laboratories, Inc.*, 817 F. Supp. 26, 822 F. Supp. 268, 827 F. Supp. 1145 (E.D. Pa. 1992–1993), where the District Court entered a temporary restraining order, a preliminary injunction, and then a permanent injunction in favor of FDA during five months of litigation.

3. *Failure to Meet GMP.* A seizure of bulk antibiotics was upheld in *United States v. Various Articles of Drug, Bulk Antibiotics*, Food Drug Cosm. L. Rep. (CCH ¶ 38,471) (D. Md. 1996) because of the failure of the manufacturer to comply with GMP. The District Court held that the drugs could not legally be exported because they did not comply with all of the requirements of section 801(3)(1) of the FD&C Act.

4. *Whistleblower Case.* In *Rheinecker v. Forest Laboratories, Inc.*, 813 F. Supp. 1307 (S.D. Ohio 1993), an allegation that a drug manufacturer violated drug GMP requirements was sufficient for a state whistleblower complaint to survive a summary judgment motion.

————

After *Barr*, FDA had the opportunity to revise its GMP regulations to incorporate both the guidance documents that it had periodically issued (in particular, the guidance on process validation) and the lessons learned from *Barr* itself. It chose not to do so. The agency did, however, begin striving to avoid additional protracted and expensive GMP litigation of the kind illustrated by *Barr*. For the next decade, it sought to negotiate relatively flexible consent decrees for GMP violations rather than force the companies into litigation. *See, e.g.*, the consent decree for the American National Red Cross, Food Drug Cosm. L. Rep. ¶ 38,313 (D.D.C. 1993), and the unpublished decrees for Warner–Lambert (Aug. 1993), Eli Lilly (July 1995), Abbott Laboratories (Nov. 1999), Wyeth–Ayerst (Oct. 2000), Schering–Plough (May 2002), and GlaxoSmithKline (Apr. 2005). Nonetheless, both FDA and the pharmaceutical industry realized that, because the GMP regulations had not significantly been altered since 1979, it was time for a thorough review to determine policy for the future. In August 2002, FDA released the following concept paper covering a new agency initiative to enhance pharmaceutical GMP.

Pharmaceutical cGMP for the 21st Century: A Risk–Based Approach

August 21, 2002.

FDA oversees the quality of drug products using a two-pronged approach involving review of information submitted in applications as well as inspection of manufacturing facilities for conformance to requirements for current Good Manufacturing Practice (cGMP). These two programs have served the country well by helping to ensure the quality of drug products available in the US. Now, as we approach the 25th anniversary of the last major revision to the drug cGMP regulations, it is time to step back and evaluate the currency of these programs so that:

- the most up-to-date concept of risk management and quality systems approaches are incorporated while continuing to ensure product quality;
- the latest scientific advances in pharmaceutical manufacturing and technology are encouraged;
- the submission review program and the inspection program operate in a coordinated and synergistic manner;
- regulation and manufacturing standards are applied consistently;
- management of the program encourages innovation in the pharmaceutical manufacturing sector; and
- FDA resources are used most effectively and efficiently to address the most significant health risks.

To these ends, FDA is undertaking an initiative, "Pharmaceutical cGMPs for the 21st Century: A Risk–Based Approach."

. . . The following principles will guide implementation of the reappraisal:

Risk-based orientation In order to provide the most effective public health protection, FDA must match its level of effort against the magnitude of risk. Resource limitations prevent uniformly intensive coverage of all pharmaceutical products and production. Although the agency has been implementing risk-based programs, a more systematic and rigorous risk-based approach will be developed.

Science-based policies and standards Significant advances in the pharmaceutical sciences and in manufacturing technologies have occurred over the last two decades. While this knowledge has been incorporated in an ongoing manner into FDA's approach to product quality regulation, the fundamental nature of the changes dictates a thorough evaluation of the science base to ensure that product quality regulation not only incorporates up-to-date science, but also encourages further advances in technology. Recent science can also contribute significantly to assessment of risk.

Integrated quality systems orientation Principles from various innovative approaches to manufacturing quality that have been developed in the past decade will be evaluated for applicability, and cGMP requirements and related pre-approval requirements will be evaluated according to applicable principles. In addition, interaction of the pre-market CMC [chemistry, manufacturing, and controls] review process and the application of cGMP requirements will be evaluated as an integrated system.

International cooperation The globalization of pharmaceutical manufacturing requires a global approach to regulation. FDA will collaborate with other regulatory authorities, via ICH and other venues.

Strong Public Health Protection The initiative will strengthen the public health protection achieved by FDA's regulation of drug product manufacturing and will not interfere with strong enforcement of the existing regulatory requirements, even as we are examining and revising our approach to these programs. . . .

––––––––

On February 24, 2003, FDA released a "Summary Progress Report" that listed completed milestones, ranging from centralizing FDA review of all drug GMP warning letters in headquarters and implementation of a technical dispute resolution process for GMP disputes, to prioritizing inspections on a risk-based approach and including GMP specialists on inspection teams. By this time, FDA had made the decision that it would implement its "Pharmaceutical cGMPs for the 21st Century" initiative through guidance and related documents rather than through amendment of the GMP regulations themselves. A second progress report was released in September 2003, and the final report on the initiative was issued a year later, in September 2004. In 71 Fed. Reg. 31194 (June 1, 2006), FDA withdrew five GMP guidances and revised two others to make them consistent with the GMP initiative. The agency issued its final GMP Guidance, QUALITY SYSTEMS APPROACHES TO PHARMACEUTICAL CURRENT GOOD MANUFACTURING PRACTICE (CGMP) REGULATIONS, in September 2006. FDA's progress reports continued to emphasize a "risk-based" and "science-based" approach to GMP, but none articulated what those phrases mean in practice. The now–25–year–old GMP regulations remain unchanged. The pharmaceutical industry has seen no difference in the way that FDA inspects pharmaceutical manufacturing facilities or enforces GMP requirements. And the agency has continued to negotiate consent decrees in the same way that it did before the initiative was announced.

D.   FDA LICENSURE OF NEW DRUGS

1.   BACKGROUND

Since 1938, the law has required some premarket review by FDA for all new drugs. Under the present Act, this licensure process necessitates FDA approval of each individual product that falls within the "new drug" definition. The approval process leads to more extensive agency involvement in the decisionmaking of private manufacturers than any other provision of the Act. FDA's performance of this function has been the target of persistent criticism, both from those who have regarded the agency as insufficiently rigorous, and more recently, from advocates of reduced regulation who contend that the agency—or the statutory pre-market approval requirement itself—has added excessively to the cost of drug development and delayed the introduction of important new therapies.

As enacted in 1938, the FD&C Act provided for premarket notification—as contrasted with premarket approval—for all new drugs. Under the 1938 Act, a drug sponsor submitted its premarket notification for a new drug—called a new drug application (NDA)—and if FDA did not affirmatively disapprove it, the NDA became effective 60 days later and the drug could immediately be marketed. This changed when, in the Drug Amendments of 1962, Congress replaced premarket notification with premarket approval. Since 1962, no new drug can be marketed until FDA specifically approves it as safe, effective, and properly labeled.

On average, it now takes 10 to 15 years to develop a new chemical entity (NCE) new drug, from initial chemical synthesis to FDA approval of an NDA. Of every 5,000 chemicals that enter preclinical testing, only five proceed to clinical testing and only one ultimately gains FDA approval. Averaging the total costs of all this research as well as the opportunity costs, an approved NDA today costs well over $1 billion. In short, the FDA licensure process is lengthy and expensive.

Following the Republican takeover of the House and Senate in November 1994, Congress enacted the FDA Modernization Act of 1997 (FDAMA) with the avowed intent of reforming and speeding up the IND/NDA process. The success of that effort remains in debate. Two hearings have been held on the impact of FDAMA. *See* "FDA Modernization Act: Implementation of the Law," Hearing of the Senate Committee on Health, Education, Labor, and Pensions, 106th Cong., 1st Sess. (1999); "Evaluating the Effectiveness of the Food and Drug Administration Modernization Act," Hearing before the Subcommittee on Health of the House Committee on Energy and Commerce, 107th Cong., 1st Sess. (2001).

David F. Cavers, *The Food, Drug, and Cosmetic Act of 1938: Its Legislative History and its Substantive Provisions*

6 LAW AND CONTEMPORARY PROBLEMS 2 (1939).

[In 1937] ... a tragedy occurred which was directly responsible for adding a new and important proviso to the drug control legislation. At least 73, perhaps over 90, persons in various parts of the country, although chiefly in the South, died as a result of taking a drug known as "Elixir Sulfanilamide," manufactured and sold by the S. E. Massengill Company of Bristol, Tennessee. This product had been prepared in order to render the valuable new drug, sulfanilamide, available in liquid form. Diethylene glycol was used as a solvent. Investigation later showed that the pharmacist on the manufacturer's staff checked the product merely for appearance, flavor, and fragrance. Tests on animals or even an investigation of the published literature would have revealed the lethal character of the solvent.... Yet the only legal basis for the F & DA's intervention was the fact that the preparation was not an "elixir" since that term may properly be applied only to an alcoholic solution. The product was therefore misbranded. The label, incidentally, did not mention the presence of the fatal ingredient, diethylene glycol.

Even if any of the bills ... had been enacted previously it is quite possible that this disaster would have occurred.... Accordingly, Senator Copeland introduced a bill ... which forbade the introduction into interstate commerce of "any drug ... not generally recognized as safe for use" under the conditions prescribed in the labeling thereof "unless the packer of such drug holds a notice of finding by the Secretary that such drug is not unsafe for use."....

———

Another drug tragedy occurred in 1962, when it was discovered that thalidomide, a drug approved for marketing in various European countries, was a teratogen, *i.e.*, it resulted in babies with various types of deformities. Although the pending NDA in the United States was not allowed to become effective, Congress promptly amended the FD&C Act to strengthen the licensure system for new drugs. Under the Drug Amendments of 1962, premarket approval replaced premarket notification.

Note, *Drug Efficacy and the 1962 Drug Amendments*
60 Georgetown Law Journal 185 (1971).

... The crux of the [1938 Act's] premarketing review scheme was the designation of certain drugs as "new drugs." A new drug was defined as one not generally recognized by experts "as safe for use under the conditions prescribed, recommended, or suggested in the labeling thereof" or one which had become generally recognized as safe but "which [had] not ... been used to a material extent or for a material time." In order for a new drug to be marketed, it had to be the subject of an "effective" (not disapproved) new drug application (NDA) under section 505(a)....

Within the next decade, two important additions were made to the 1938 Act that bore on the matter of drug efficacy. Section 506, dealing with drugs containing insulin, and section 507, concerning certain antibiotic drugs, bypassed the new drug procedures of section 505 in favor of a batch certification system. Under that system, batches of drugs would be certified for marketing upon determination by the Secretary that the batch had such "characteristics of strength, quality and purity as ... to adequately insure safety and efficacy of use."....

The efficacy provisions of the 1962 Amendments were inserted in the framework of the "new drug" procedure. First, the definition of new drug was extended to comprise drugs not generally recognized as safe and effective. Second ... [t]he data reporting requirements of the new drug procedure were amended to require submission of data showing efficacy.

Furthermore, in place of automatic approval of NDAs not disapproved, a positive act of approval is required to make an NDA approved.

The most important changes in section 505, however, occurred in subsections (d) and (e). Under subsection (d), the Secretary ... is now required to refuse approval of any NDA if, after notice and opportunity for hearing, he determines that on the basis of information before him with respect to the drug in question "there is a lack of substantial evidence that the drug will have the effect it purports or is represented to have under the conditions of use prescribed, recommended or suggested in the proposed labeling thereof...." Furthermore, section 505(e) was modified to require the Secretary to withdraw approval of any drug after notice and opportunity for hearing if he finds that "on the basis of new information before him" substantial evidence of efficacy is lacking. Significantly, this subsection also added a proviso permitting the Secretary, in the event of an imminent hazard to health, to withdraw approval of an NDA even before holding a hearing....

2.   FDA IMPLEMENTATION OF THE NEW DRUG PREMARKET APPROVAL REQUIREMENT

The complex history of FDA's implementation of the new drug provisions of the Drug Amendments of 1962 defies unitary treatment. A chronological account would frustrate legal analysis, while a wholly conceptual structure would obscure recurrent themes. Accordingly, we have combined these approaches. We first summarize in this part the history of FDA's efforts, and we then examine in subsequent parts, through the key materials that document this history, the basic elements of the process for regulating new drugs.

Marketing of Drugs Under the 1938 FD&C Act

Section 505 of the 1938 Act gave FDA the authority to refuse to let a new drug application (NDA) become effective, although it did not mandate affirmative FDA approval prior to marketing. By 1941, 4,128 NDAs had been submitted to FDA. Because it was unable to cope with this volume, the agency began in 1942 to examine each application to determine whether the product covered was indeed a "new drug," *i.e.*, whether it was generally recognized as safe (GRAS) and thus excluded from the section 201(p) definition of new drug. FDA declined to accept NDAs for drugs that the agency concluded were generally recognized as safe (GRAS) and thus not new drugs. Manufacturers in turn responded by seeking FDA's opinion in advance, or by making their own GRAS determinations. These practices ultimately led to a reduction in the number of full NDAs submitted, though the agency's workload still remained substantial. By June 30, 1962, NDAs for 9,457 individual products had become effective for nonprescription and prescription human and animal drugs.

In addition to new drug products with effective NDAs, many thousands of similar formulations entered the market as "old drugs" during this period. Manufacturers of these products either concluded independently that they were GRAS because an NDA was in effect for a version manufactured by another company or obtained an opinion from FDA that their drugs were GRAS and thus not "new." Though the agency kept no record of these "old drug" opinions, it issued several thousand between 1942 and 1962. An original NDA'd drug product came to be referred to as the "pioneer," and all subsequent versions were described as generic or "me-too" drugs. By 1962, for every pioneer drug with an effective NDA, many additional me-too copies were on the market without an effective NDA.

The Drug Amendments of 1962 and the NAS Review

Although thalidomide was never allowed to be marketed in the United States, Congress enacted the Drug Amendments of 1962, 76 Stat. 780, hurriedly in the crisis atmosphere of the thalidomide tragedy. In addition to requiring that FDA affirmatively determine that new agents be demonstrated to be effective by "substantial evidence," as well as shown to be safe, the 1962 Amendments required FDA to review all NDAs that had become effective during the previous 24 years to determine whether the products met the new effectiveness standard. No one in the agency or outside fully appreciated the consequences of this requirement when President Kennedy signed the Amendments into law on October 10, 1962.

Because the 1962 Amendments expanded the coverage of section 505, FDA immediately began to receive an increased volume of NDAs and investigational new drug (IND) submissions, which soon overwhelmed its review capacity. The agency at first did nothing to implement Congress's mandate to review NDAs that had previously become effective. In 1964, however, FDA issued regulations requiring reports on those pre-1962 drugs. 29 Fed. Reg. 2790 (Feb. 28, 1964), 29 Fed. Reg. 7019 (May 28, 1964). The major pharmaceutical manufacturers promptly contested the regulations insofar as they might apply to drugs that the firms regarded as grandfathered under the 1962 Amendments. FDA stayed the reporting requirements pending the outcome of the manufacturers' court challenge. 29 Fed. Reg. 12872 (Sept. 12, 1964). Although the companies provided some of the requested information in 1965, they argued that any review of pre-1962 NDAs should be performed by an independent scientific authority, not by the agency. In June 1966, FDA contracted with the National Academy of Sciences—National Research Council (NAS/NRC) to conduct such a review. Holders of NDAs were requested to submit information supporting the claims for their products. 31 Fed. Reg. 9425 (July 9, 1966), 31 Fed. Reg. 13014 (Oct. 6, 1966). The manufacturers thereafter withdrew their lawsuit.

Of the 9457 pre-1962 effective NDAs, about 400 were for human nonprescription drugs and the rest were evenly divided between human prescription drugs and animal drugs. The NAS review was performed by thirty panels of experts in specific drug categories. The NAS established guidelines delineating the functions of the panels and identifying the following sources of evidence for evaluation of effectiveness: (1) information available in the scientific literature; (2) information available from FDA, from the manufacturer, or other sources; and (3) the experience and informed judgment of the members of the panels. The NAS also established six ratings to serve as the basis for evaluating each claim made for a drug:

(1) *Effective.*

(2) *Probably effective.* Additional evidence required to be determined. Remedy could be additional research or modification of claims or both.

(3) *Possibly effective.* Little evidence of effectiveness, but possibility of additional evidence should not be ruled out.

(4) *Ineffective.* No acceptable evidence to support claim of effectiveness.

(5) *Effective, but ...* Effective for claimed indication but not approved form of treatment because better, safer or more conveniently administered drugs available.

(6) *Ineffective as a fixed combination.* Combination drugs for which there is no substantial reason to believe that each ingredient adds to the effectiveness of the combination.

The NAS transmitted its first evaluation to FDA in October 1967, and continued to submit monthly reports until midsummer 1968. *See* NAS, DRUG EFFICACY STUDY: FINAL REPORT TO THE COMMISSIONER OF FOOD AND DRUGS (1969). The panels reviewed approximately 4,000 different human drug formulations. The panels found roughly seven percent of the drugs ineffective for all claims, many effective for all claims, and the majority somewhere in between. The breakdown of ratings, by claim, was as follows:

Rating	No. of Claims	% of Claims
Ineffective	2,442	14.7
Possibly effective	5,778	34.9
Probably effective	1,204	7.3
Effective	3,159	19.1
Effective, but	3,990	24.0
Total	16,573	100%

As the body with ultimate responsibility for determining drug effectiveness, FDA undertook to review the NAS findings. It refused, however, to release the panel reports before completing its own evaluations.

The Commencement of NDA–Withdrawal Proceedings

The agency's first implementation notice, covering all bioflavonoid drugs, was published in 1968. FDA announced that, based on NAS's report finding no effectiveness for these drugs, the agency intended to publish a notice of opportunity for a hearing on a proposal to withdraw approval of all bioflavonoid NDAs. 33 Fed. Reg. 818 (Jan. 23, 1968). (FDA's subsequent withdrawal of approval for these drugs without a hearing was later overturned in *USV Pharmaceutical Corp. v. Secretary of HEW*, 466 F.2d 455 (D.C. Cir. 1972).) FDA next turned its attention to fixed dosage combination antibiotic products. In 33 Fed. Reg. 12904 (Dec. 24, 1968), the agency proposed to initiate proceedings to withdraw approval of Panalba, the first of many of these drugs that NAS had rated "ineffective as a fixed combination." FDA invited submission of pertinent data. In 34 Fed. Reg. 7687 (May 15, 1969), FDA withdrew approval of the drug and offered an opportunity for an administrative hearing. The manufacturer promptly obtained a judicial order enjoining FDA from withdrawing approval of the drug until after it had ruled on the firm's request for a formal evidentiary hearing. *Upjohn Co. v. Finch*, 303 F. Supp. 241 (W.D. Mich. 1969). One month later, another manufacturer obtained a similar injunction. *American Home Products Corp. v. Finch*, 303 F. Supp. 448 (D. Del. 1969).

Thus, by mid–1969, FDA confronted the prospect of having to conduct a long series of formal administrative hearings before it could implement the 1962 effectiveness standard. The agency therefore decided to adopt a new policy. In 34 Fed. Reg. 14598 (Sept. 19, 1969), FDA entered an order concluding that Upjohn had failed to show reasonable grounds for an evidentiary hearing and withdrawing approval of Panalba. Simultaneously, the agency published regulations embodying two features that became central in its subsequent efforts to implement the 1962 Amendments. First, the regulations defined the essential elements of an "adequate and well-controlled clinical investigation" necessary to constitute substantial evidence of effectiveness under sections 505(d) and (e). Second, they required the submission of at least two such studies to avoid summary judgment, *i.e.*, withdrawal of approval without a hearing. 34 Fed. Reg. 14596 (Sept. 19, 1969). In the initial court test of its new approach, FDA's order withdrawing approval of Panalba was sustained. *Upjohn Co. v. Finch*, 422 F.2d 944 (6th Cir. 1970).

Meanwhile, the major pharmaceutical manufacturers challenged FDA's regulations defining adequate and well-controlled clinical studies. *Pharmaceutical Manufacturers Association v. Finch*, 307 F. Supp. 858 (D. Del. 1970), held that FDA had violated section 553 of the Administrative Procedure Act by failing to provide an opportunity to comment on the regulations. The agency thereupon reproposed the regulations, 35 Fed. Reg. 3073 (Feb. 17, 1970), and after receiving comments, promulgated them in final form, 35 Fed. Reg. 7250 (May 8, 1970), 21 C.F.R. 314.126. In *Pharmaceutical Manufacturers Association v. Richardson*, 318 F. Supp. 301 (D. Del. 1970), the regulations were upheld on their merits.

Armed with this decision, which PMA did not appeal, FDA began publishing hundreds of so-called DESI (Drug Effectiveness Study Implementation) notices. The agency also required DESI evaluations to be included in drug labeling and advertising. 35 Fed. Reg. 15761 (Oct. 7, 1970), 36 Fed. Reg. 11022 (June 8, 1971), 36 Fed. Reg. 19978 (Oct. 14, 1971), 37 Fed. Reg. 3176 (Feb. 12, 1972). Orders withdrawing approval of combination antibiotic drugs were upheld in *Pfizer, Inc. v. Richardson*, 434 F.2d 536 (2d Cir. 1970) and *Ciba–Geigy Corp. v. Richardson*, 446 F.2d 466 (2d Cir. 1971). *See also Diamond Laboratories, Inc. v. Richardson*, 452 F.2d 803 (8th Cir. 1972). In two other cases, *American Cyanamid Co. v. Richardson*, 456 F.2d 509 (1st Cir. 1971), and *Bristol Laboratories v. Richardson*, 456 F.2d 563 (1st Cir. 1971), the companies withdrew their appeals after failing to obtain a judicial stay of the agency's withdrawal order. In 1971, FDA promulgated regulations codifying its combination drug policy. 36 Fed. Reg. 3126 (Feb. 8, 1971), 36 Fed. Reg. 20037 (Oct. 15, 1971), codified at 21 C.F.R. 300.50.

The Problem of "Me-Too" Drugs

In 1968, FDA for the first time addressed the issue of "me-too" drugs. At a government-industry conference, the agency announced that it would apply the applicable NAS findings not only to the pioneer NDA drug, but also to all subsequently marketed me-too products. FDA realized that the "old drug" opinions it had issued for me-too versions of NDA drugs before 1962 presented a major obstacle to its efforts to exert control over these copies. The agency therefore issued a statement of policy withdrawing all those opinions. 33 Fed. Reg. 7758 (May 28, 1968), codified at 21 C.F.R. 310.100. At the same time, it proposed to establish a new procedure for determining old drug status, under which many me-too products would presumably be held not to require NDAs. 33 Fed. Reg. 7762 (May 28, 1968).

In 1969, FDA sharpened its policy respecting pre-1962 me-too products. To assure that these drugs would be brought under regulatory control, it created the "abbreviated" NDA, requiring information only on biological availability and manufacturing controls. 34 Fed. Reg. 2673 (Feb. 27, 1969), 35 Fed. Reg. 6574 (Apr. 24, 1970). The agency then issued a general notice establishing uniform conditions for the marketing of all new drugs covered by a DESI notice and requiring the submission of an NDA or abbreviated NDA for any product whose rating justified continued marketing. 35 Fed. Reg. 11273 (July 14, 1970). In 1972, the agency adopted a regulation explicitly stating that every DESI notice and notice of opportunity for hearing applies both to the pioneer drug and to all identical, related, and similar me-too drug products. 37 Fed. Reg. 2969 (Feb. 10, 1972), 37 Fed. Reg. 23185 (Oct. 31, 1972), codified at 21 C.F.R. 310.6. The agency took the position that the failure of the manufacturer of a me-too drug product to respond to a DESI notice or a notice of opportunity for hearing covering the pioneer drug barred any subsequent dispute respecting the status of that drug. *See* L. M. Baukin, *Related Drugs Under DESI*, 27 FOOD DRUG COSM. L.J. 124 (1972). Because it was having difficulty learning what me-too drugs were marketed, FDA persuaded Congress to enact the Drug Listing Act of 1972, 86 Stat. 559. This legislation, which amended section 510 of the FD&C Act, requires all manufacturers to submit lists of their drugs and thus provides the agency a complete inventory of all marketed products. *See supra* p. 531.

Manufacturers Challenge DESI in Court

By the end of 1971, FDA had disposed of dozens of requests for hearings on the revocation of NDAs. In no instance had it found a manufacturer's supporting data sufficient to justify a hearing. One explanation for this striking consistency is that the agency's substantial evidence regulations embodied requirements for clinical investigations that few pre-1962 studies could meet. The drugs it initially selected for withdrawal—those evaluated by the NAS as "ineffective"—also presented the easiest targets. But it was becoming obvious that any manufacturer would have to make an overwhelming showing to persuade FDA to expend the resources even one hearing would demand.

In 1972, three rulings by the U.S. Court of Appeals for the Fourth Circuit threatened to undermine FDA's basic approach. In *Hynson, Westcott & Dunning, Inc. v. Richardson*, 461 F.2d 215 (4th Cir. 1972), the court held that the petitioner was statutorily entitled to a hearing on the effectiveness of its drug, Lutrexin, before its NDA could be withdrawn. In *Bentex Pharmaceuticals, Inc. v. Richardson*, 463 F.2d 363 (4th Cir. 1972), the same court ruled that FDA lacked jurisdiction to determine whether a product is a new drug, and that therefore the issue could be raised *de novo* by a declaratory judgment suit. And in *USV Pharmaceutical Corp. v. Richardson*, 461 F.2d 223 (4th Cir. 1972), the court held that the status of a me-too drug was not dependent on the status of the pioneer, even when the latter's NDA was withdrawn. FDA sought and obtained certiorari in all three Fourth Circuit cases, and it also supported the successful petition for certiorari in *Ciba–Geigy Corp. v. Richardson*, 446 F.2d 466 (2d Cir. 1971), which had upheld FDA's summary order withdrawing approval of an NDA drug. In June 1973, in opinions reproduced below, *infra* pp. 601, 605, 745, the Supreme Court sustained FDA on all of the legal issues involved. *See* Peter Barton Hutt, *Views on Supreme Court/FDA Decisions*, 28 FOOD DRUG COSM. L.J. 662 (1973). FDA later revised its summary judgment procedures to reflect the Supreme Court opinions. 38 Fed. Reg. 35024 (Dec. 21, 1973), 39 Fed. Reg. 9750 (Mar. 13, 1974).

The Supreme Court decisions did not end litigation or resolve all of FDA's problems in implementing the 1962 Amendments. The Supreme Court concluded that Hynson itself had presented sufficient evidence to justify a hearing. Several subsequent agency denials of hearings were upheld, but others were reversed with instructions to hold a hearing. Compare *Agri–Tech, Inc. v. Richardson*, 482 F.2d 1148 (8th Cir. 1973); *North American Pharmacal, Inc. v. Department of HEW*, 491 F.2d 546 (8th Cir. 1973); *Cooper Laboratories, Inc. v. Commissioner*, 501 F.2d 772 (D.C. Cir. 1974); *Masti–Kure Products Co. v. Califano*, 587 F.2d 1099 (D.C. Cir. 1978), with *E.R. Squibb & Sons, Inc. v. Weinberger*, 483 F.2d 1382 (3d Cir. 1973); *Hess & Clark v. FDA*, 495 F.2d 975 (D.C. Cir. 1974); *Chemetron Corp. v. Department of HEW*, 495 F.2d 995 (D.C. Cir. 1974); *Sterling Drug, Inc. v. Weinberger*, 503 F.2d 675 (2d Cir. 1974), *connected case at* 509 F.2d 1236 (2d Cir. 1975); *Edison Pharmaceutical Co. v. FDA*, 513 F.2d 1063 (D.C. Cir. 1975), *rehearing en banc denied*, 517 F.2d 164 (1975); *Smith-Kline Corp. v. FDA*, 587 F.2d 1107 (D.C. Cir. 1978); *American Cyanamid Co. v. FDA*, 606 F.2d 1307 (D.C. Cir. 1979); *Brandenfels v. Heckler*, 716 F.2d 553 (9th Cir. 1983).

Attempts to Speed Implementation

Even before the Supreme Court vindicated FDA's basic approach, some consumer groups had become impatient with FDA's slow progress in implementing the 1962 Amendments and sued to force prompter action. In *American Public Health Association v. Veneman*, 349 F. Supp. 1311 (D.D.C. 1972), *infra* p. 603, the District Court held FDA's performance unlawful in several respects and issued a detailed order requiring it to complete the DESI process within four years. This ruling imposed a new and, as it developed, unfulfillable demand on the agency, a demand ironically inflated by FDA's own decision to extend the NAS findings to all pre-1962 me-too drugs.

FDA had difficulty developing a consistent approach to this facet of the problem. In May 1968, as noted *supra* p. 583, it proposed a procedure for determining old drug status for some pre-1962 products me-too drugs, but never made this proposal final. The agency later determined that me-too drugs which had been found to be effective under the DESI program could be the subject of an "abbreviated" NDA, which need contain only labeling and manufacturing information, but not data relating to safety and effectiveness. 34 Fed. Reg. 2673 (Feb. 27, 1969), 35 Fed. Reg. 6574 (Apr. 24, 1970). This approach rested on the theory that the active ingredients in such products had become generally recognized as safe and effective and thus that FDA only had to require assurance that individual versions were properly labeled and manufactured. When concern about the bioavailability and bioequivalence of these me-too drugs emerged, FDA issued separate regulations to address these issues. *See infra* p. 755. As the DESI program progressed, new abbreviated NDAs began to swamp the agency. By June 1975, it had received over 6000 abbreviated NDAs, of which roughly 1100 had been acted on. To meet this backlog, FDA informally adopted a policy of permitting the marketing of every me-too drug upon submission of an abbreviated NDA, even before the application was approved. This decision was destined to bring the agency into court once more.

In 40 Fed. Reg. 26142 (June 20, 1975), FDA proposed comprehensive regulations governing the status of me-too drugs. The agency had long planned to develop "old drug monographs" for pre-1962 prescription drugs. *See* Mary A. McEniry, *Drug Monographs*, 29 FOOD DRUG COSM. L.J. 166 (1974). In the June 1975 proposal, the agency stated that it would soon propose a new procedure for establishing old drug monographs for drugs that had been found safe and effective through the DESI program. In summary, the agency stated that a me-too version of a drug determined to be effective under the DESI program would require neither an NDA nor an abbreviated NDA if it presented no bioavailability, bioequivalence, or special manufacturing problem. And the agency announced that, on an interim basis, it would follow these criteria in its enforcement of the FD&C Act. *See* Robert L. Spencer, *New Concepts in Abbreviated NDAs*, 30 FOOD DRUG COSM. L.J. 426 (1975).

FDA's new approach was promptly challenged in *Hoffmann–LaRoche, Inc. v. Weinberger*, 425 F. Supp. 890 (D.D.C. 1975), *infra* p. 595. The court ruled that FDA could not sanction the marketing of me-too drugs without an individualized determination of old drug status. The agency therefore withdrew its interim enforcement policy. 40 Fed. Reg. 43531 (Sept. 22, 1975), 41 Fed. Reg. 9001 (Mar. 2, 1976). It never acted on the June 1975 proposal. In 1976, FDA announced the availability of a guideline explaining the agency's policy for implementing the *Hoffman–LaRoche* decision. This document, codified as Compliance Policy Guide 7132c.02, set forth the agency's process for bringing regulatory action against me-too drugs being marketed without an approved NDA or abbreviated NDA. 41 Fed. Reg. 41770 (Sept. 23, 1976).

This enforcement policy was in turn challenged by the manufacturers of generic me-too drugs. In two cases, *United States v. Articles of Drug . . . Lannett Co.*, 585 F.2d 575 (3d Cir. 1978), and *Premo Pharmaceutical Laboratories, Inc. v. United States*, 629 F.2d 795 (2d Cir. 1980), the Courts of Appeals split on the question whether a generic version of an approved pioneer drug was no longer a new drug and could therefore be marketed without an NDA or abbreviated NDA. In *United States v. Generix Drug Corp.*, 460 U.S. 453 (1983), *infra* p. 597, the Supreme Court resolved this conflict, holding that the Act's definition of "drug" includes inactive as well as active ingredients and therefore that a generic version of a pioneer drug requires its own NDA or abbreviated NDA if it differs in any significant respect from the pioneer. The Supreme Court did not, however, reach the issue of what sorts of differences would be significant.

As the end of the 1970s approached, therefore, FDA had adopted the following enforcement policy with respect to generic drugs. First, the agency was prepared to approve an abbreviated NDA for any generic version of a pre-1962 pioneer drug that had been found effective under the DESI program. Second, it would initiate regulatory action against any generic drug on the market without an approved NDA or abbreviated NDA. Third, it would not approve an abbreviated NDA, but rather would insist on a full NDA, for a generic version of any post-1962 new drug.

Paper NDAs and Abbreviated NDAs for Post-1962 Generics

This last facet of the enforcement policy resulted from the requirements of data confidentiality. From 1938, FDA had consistently taken the position that each NDA was an individual license, and that the accompanying safety and effectiveness information constituted confidential commercial information that was not disclosable to the public or available for use by another applicant under section 301(j) of the FD&C Act, the Freedom of Information Act, or the Federal Trade Secrets Act, 18 U.S.C. 1905. The proposed Drug Regulation Reform Act, considered by Congress during 1977–1980, would have authorized abbreviated NDAs for post-1962 new drugs, but this measure was not enacted. The agency thus found itself caught between two important and longstanding policies. It had been successful in requiring an NDA or abbreviated NDA for every prescription drug on the market. But it could not approve abbreviated NDAs for post-1962 new drugs without violating the confidentiality provisions of the law.

In an attempt to break the impasse, the agency announced in July 1978 that it would approve "paper" NDAs for generic copies of pioneer new drugs, whether pre-1962 or post-1962, based upon *published* scientific data concerning the pioneer products' safety and effectiveness. In 45 Fed. Reg. 82052 (Dec. 12, 1980), FDA denied a petition to withdraw this new policy, which was later upheld in the face of claims that it had not been adopted through APA informal rulemaking. *Burroughs Wellcome Co. v. Schweiker*, 649 F.2d 221 (4th Cir. 1981). In *Upjohn Manufacturing Co. v. Schweiker*, 681 F.2d 480 (6th Cir. 1982), the Court of Appeals sustained the policy's application to a specific drug product. Despite these victories, FDA recognized that its paper NDA policy could not apply to more than a small fraction of the ever-increasing number of post-1962 new drugs. For most post-1962 new drugs, the published literature contained inadequate data on animal toxicity and human clinical trials to justify approval of a paper NDA. *See, e.g.*, 49 Fed. Reg. 15824 (Apr. 19, 1984).

After the collapse of efforts in Congress to amend the new drug provisions of the FD&C Act in the late 1970s, FDA in 1983 began to work on a proposed regulation to establish the basis for some form of abbreviated NDA procedure for post-1962 new drugs. When this proposal did not surface quickly, the National Association of Pharmaceutical Manufacturers, an association of generic drug manufacturers, brought suit seeking a declaratory judgment that the agency could lawfully approve abbreviated NDAs for post-1962 new drugs without any change in the FD&C Act.

Meanwhile, makers of innovative new drugs had become increasingly concerned about the gradual shrinkage of the remaining effective patent life for pioneer products after they completed the rigorous development and testing program and emerged from the NDA approval process. *See* Peter Barton Hutt, *The Importance of Patent Term Restoration to Pharmaceutical Innovation*, 1 HEALTH AFFAIRS, No. 2, at 6 (Spring 1982). In 1984, Representative Henry Waxman introduced a proposal that combined patent term restoration, favored by pioneer manufacturers, with authority for FDA to approve abbreviated NDAs (ANDAs) for post-1962 new drugs, favored by the generic industry. This legislation was ultimately enacted as the Drug Price Competition and Patent Term Restoration Act of 1984, 98 Stat. 1585. *See infra* p. 754. This statute, commonly referred to as "Hatch–Waxman," finally broke the two-decade old impasse over the marketing of generic versions of post-1962 drugs.

Non–DESI, Pre-1962 Drugs

A final category of prescription drugs—pre-1962 prescription products not subject to the DESI program—further complicated the landscape that FDA confronted after enactment of the Drug Amendments of 1962. Some of these drugs were first marketed before 1938 and had never been the subject of an NDA because they were eligible for a "grandfather" clause in the 1938 Act. Others, which had entered the market without an NDA after 1938, based on a GRAS determination by their manufacturers, were now deemed by their manufacturers not to require DESI review because they qualified for a grandfather clause in the 1962 Amendments. Still others drugs were covered by pre-1962 NDAs but not reviewed by the NAS panels because their manufacturers did not respond to the agency's request for information. Finally, some post-1962 drugs avoided both the DESI and NDA processes on the basis of their manufacturers' own determinations that they were generally recognized as safe (GRAS) and effective (GRAE) and thus did not require NDAs.

In CPG 7132c.02 (1976), FDA stated that it would systematically handle each one of these non-DESI, unapproved new drugs on a priority basis. The agency stated that, if one of these drugs were approved through some form of NDA, it would remove all the remaining drugs in that class from the market, thus providing an incentive for the manufacturers of these products to submit NDAs for them as well. In fact, however, no such NDAs were submitted until the early 2000s. *See infra* p. 613. In 40 Fed. Reg. 53609 (Nov. 19, 1979), FDA listed some of the NDAs whose holders had chosen not to submit effectiveness data, or had neglected to do so, in response to the agency's 1966 request for data. The agency reinvited these NDA holders to submit data and stated that the effectiveness of these drugs would be reviewed internally by the agency.

In early 1984, prescription drugs that were on the market despite never having been the subject of any form of NDA became a high priority for FDA. An intravenous vitamin E product marketed without an NDA produced serious adverse reactions that required a nationwide recall. *See* "E–Ferol Update," FDA Talk Paper No. T84–30 (Apr. 27, 1984); "FDA's Regulation of the Marketing of Unapproved New Drugs: The Case of E–Ferol Vitamin E Aqueous Solution," Hearing before a Subcommittee of the

House Committee on Government Operations, 98th Cong., 2d Sess. (1984); "Deficiencies in FDA's Regulation of the Marketing of Unapproved New Drugs: The Case of E–Ferol," H.R. Rep. No. 98–1168, 98th Cong., 2d Sess. (1984). Based on information obtained under the Drug Listing Act, FDA estimated that there were approximately 5000 prescription drugs marketed without an approved NDA of any kind. Some 1800 of these products were identical or similar to drugs reviewed by NAS under the DESI program, whereas 2400 had avoided DESI review altogether. The remainder fell into a variety of additional categories. Lacking the resources to require an NDA for all of these drugs, FDA promulgated a regulation requiring the maintenance of records and submission of reports of adverse drug reactions for all prescription drugs marketed without approved NDAs. 50 Fed. Reg. 11478 (Mar. 21, 1985), 51 Fed. Reg. 24476 (July 3, 1986), codified at 21 C.F.R. 310.305.

FDA recently published a GUIDANCE FOR FDA STAFF AND INDUSTRY: MARKETED UNAPPROVED DRUGS–COMPLIANCE POLICY GUIDE (2006). The agency released this document as part of a new initiative against the "several thousand drug products," both prescription and OTC, that are "marketed illegally without required FDA approval." 71 Fed. Reg. 33466, 33467 (June 9, 2006) (announcing availability of the guidance).

The Elusive Goal of DESI Completion

Throughout these events FDA continued, albeit in desultory fashion, to press ahead to complete implementation of the DESI Review. Having missed the original four-year deadline imposed by the court in *American Public Health Association v. Veneman*, 349 F. Supp. 1311 (D.D.C. 1972), *infra* p. 603, the agency entered into an agreement with the plaintiffs establishing a new timetable. *American Public Health Association v. Harris*, Food Drug Cosm. L. Rep. (CCH) ¶ 38,068 (D.D.C. 1980). The semiannual reports that FDA submitted to the court through 1989 confirmed that the agency continued to be in violation of the new agreement, as well as the 1972 order. The 1989 reports stated that five drugs remained for further action, two were the subject of administrative hearings, and one was in litigation. On that basis, the case was formally closed. Seventeen years later, some of these remaining drugs have not yet had administrative hearings and some of the administrative hearings remain unresolved. Nearly 40 years after the DESI Review began, it is still not completed.

In response to court orders in specific cases, and on its own initiative in others, FDA has held a number of hearings on the withdrawal of approval of pre-1962 pioneer NDAs. *See, e.g.,* 44 Fed. Reg. 11835 (Mar. 2, 1979) (Alevaire); 44 Fed. Reg. 75718 (Dec. 21, 1971) (oral proteolytic enzymes); 47 Fed. Reg. 23564 (May 28, 1982) (combination antibiotic and antifungal drugs); 49 Fed. Reg. 33173 (Aug. 21, 1984) (Vioform HC); 49 Fed. Reg. 36439 (Sept. 17, 1984) (Mycolog); 49 Fed. Reg. 36439 (Sept. 17, 1984) (Marax); 49 Fed. Reg. 38363 (Sept. 28, 1984) (Vasodilan); 49 Fed. Reg. 40212 (Oct. 15, 1984) (Parafon Forte); 49 Fed. Reg. 40972 (Oct. 18, 1984) (Cyclospasmol); 49 Fed. Reg. 50788 (Dec. 31, 1984) (Mepergan Fortis); 51 Fed. Reg. 20551 (June 5, 1986) (Deprol). The process of withdrawing approval of a pre-1962 NDA can be protracted, to put it mildly. For example, in 1989, an Administrative Law Judge upheld the

FDA's withdrawal of approvals of NDAs and abbreviated NDAs for pentaer-ythritol tetranitrate, a process commenced in 1972. FDC L. Rep. ¶ 38,120 (May 10, 1989). The appeal to the Commissioner has not yet been acted upon, however, and the drug thus remains on the market. In no instance has a manufacturer challenging the withdrawal of an NDA prevailed before an Administrative Law Judge or the Commissioner. In the few cases appealed to the courts, the Commissioner's rulings have been sustained. *Warner–Lambert Co. v. Heckler*, 787 F.2d 147 (3d Cir. 1986) (oral proteolytic enzymes); *E.R. Squibb and Sons, Inc. v. Bowen*, 870 F.2d 678 (D.C. Cir. 1989) (mysteclin).

With all other avenues foreclosed, manufacturers have been left with only one plausible defense to an enforcement action challenging a prescription drug product on the ground that it is an illegal new drug marketed without an approved NDA—the claim that the product is generally recognized as safe (GRAS) and effective (GRAE) and therefore does not require an approved NDA. In *Weinberger v. Bentex Pharmaceuticals, Inc.*, 412 U.S. 645, 652–653 (1973), *infra* p. 605, the Supreme Court stated that, in some cases, general recognition that a drug is effective might be made without the kind of scientific support necessary to obtain approval of an NDA. No court has ever applied this "*Bentex* exception," however. *See United States v. 50 Boxes More or Less*, 909 F.2d 24, 27–28 (1st Cir. 1990) (remarking on non-use of the exception); *see also United States v. 225 Cartons ... Fiorinal*, 871 F.2d 409, 418–419 (3d Cir. 1989).

Despite the courts' consistent rejection of claims that drugs subject to enforcement actions are GRAE, drug manufacturers continue to advance this defense. *See, e.g., United States v. An Article ... "Furestrol Vaginal Suppositories"*, 415 F.2d 390 (5th Cir. 1969); *Tyler Pharmacal Distributors, Inc. v. U.S. Department of HEW*, 408 F.2d 95 (7th Cir. 1969); *Durovic v. Richardson*, 479 F.2d 242 (7th Cir. 1973); *United States v. 1,048,000 Capsules ... Afrodex*, 494 F.2d 1158 (5th Cir. 1974); *United States v. Mosinee Research Corp.*, 583 F.2d 930 (7th Cir. 1978); *United States v. X-Otag Plus Tablets*, 602 F.2d 1387 (10th Cir. 1979); *United States v. Articles of Drug ... 5,906 Boxes*, 745 F.2d 105 (1st Cir. 1984); *United States v. Articles of Drug ... Promise Toothpaste for Sensitive Teeth*, 826 F.2d 564 (7th Cir. 1987); *United States v. Atropine Sulfate 1.0 mg. (Article of Drug) Dey–Dose*, 843 F.2d 860 (5th Cir. 1988); *United States v. Undetermined Quantities of a Drug ... Anucort HC Suppositories*, 857 F.2d 1466 (3d Cir. 1988), *aff'g* 709 F. Supp. 511 (D.N.J. 1987); *United States v. 225 Cartons ... Fiorinal With Codeine No. 1*, 871 F.2d 409 (3d Cir. 1989), *aff'g* 687 F. Supp. 946 (D.N.J. 1988); *United States v. 50 Boxes More or Less*, 909 F.2d 24 (1st Cir. 1990), *aff'g* 721 F. Supp. 1462 (D. Mass. 1989); *Merritt Corp. v. Folsom*, 165 F. Supp. 418 (D.D.C. 1958); *United States v. Articles of Drug Labeled "Quick–O–Ver"*, 274 F. Supp. 443 (D. Md. 1967); *United States v. An Article of Drug ... "Wynn 30 Sustained–Medication Tablets Quinaglute,"* 268 F. Supp. 245 (E.D. Mo. 1967); *United States v. An Article of Drug ... Excedrin P.M.*, Food Drug Cosm. L. Rep. (CCH) ¶ 40,486 (E.D.N.Y. 1971); *United States v. An Article of Drug ... "Mykocert"*, 345 F. Supp. 571 (N.D. Ill. 1972); *United States v. Articles of Drug ... Colchicine*, 442 F. Supp. 1236 (S.D.N.Y. 1978), *aff'd without opinion sub nom. United States v. Consolidated Midland Corp.*, 603 F.2d 215 (2d Cir. 1979); *United*

States v. K–N Enterprises Inc., *461 F. Supp. 988 (N.D. Ill. 1978);* United States v. Sene X Eleemosynary Corp., Inc., *479 F. Supp. 970 (S.D. Fla. 1979),* aff'd, *Food Drug Cosm. L. Rep. (CCH) ¶ 38,207 (11th Cir. 1983); United States v. Articles of Drug ... Hormonin,* 498 F. Supp. 424 (D.N.J. 1980); *United States v. 1,834/100 Capsule Bottles ... New Formula Hauck G–2 Capsules,* Food Drug Cosm. L. Rep. (CCH) ¶ 38,058 (N.D. Ga. 1987); United States v. 118/100 Tablet Bottles, *662 F. Supp. 511 (W.D. La. 1987); Lederle Laboratories v. Department of HHS,* Food Drug Cosm. L. Rep. (CCH) ¶ 38,088 (D.D.C. 1988); *United States v. Seven Cardboard Cases....* "100 Capsules NDC, ESGIC, with Codeine Capsules," 716 F. Supp. 1221 (E.D. Mo. 1989); *United States v. 675 Cases ... "Damason–P,"* Food Drug Cosm. L. Rep. (CCH) ¶ 38,156 (C.D. Cal. 1989); *United States v. Vital Health Products, Ltd.,* 786 F. Supp. 761 (E.D. Wisc. 1992); *United States v. Nine Cases ... Endodontic Formula,* Food Drug Cosm. L. Rep. (CCH) ¶ 38,460 (D. Conn. 1996).

Of course, the new drug requirements enacted in the Drug Amendments of 1962 also apply to post-1962 drugs. Indeed, all new prescription entities introduced since 1962 have been required to go through the new drug approval process. In this respect, the coverage of the law has ceased to be an important issue. Nor, typically, has FDA, with respect to post-1962 drugs, confronted claims to procedural rights like those advanced against its implementation of the effectiveness standard with respect to pre-1962 drugs. The controversial issues have involved the agency's internal processes for evaluating and acting on NDAs and the impact of those requirements on the availability of drugs and the health of patients.

3.   COVERAGE OF THE NEW DRUG PROVISIONS

The expansive authority conferred by the Drug Amendments of 1962 is confined to "new drugs." Section 201 of the Act defines a "new drug" as "[a]ny drug ... the composition of which is such that such drug is not generally recognized, among experts qualified by scientific training and experience to evaluate the safety and effectiveness of drugs, as safe and effective for use under the condition prescribed, recommended, or suggested in the labeling thereof...." Since both the scope of FDA's power and the costs, in terms of testing expense and marketing delay, of a manufacturer's compliance are dependent on a product's status as a new drug, the statutory definition has been the focus of continuous debate and litigation.

a.   THE GENERAL STANDARD

The following case is typical of those in which the manufacturer marketed a drug on its own determination that it was generally recognized as safe (GRAS) and effective (GRAE), but FDA disputed that determination and took court enforcement action on the ground that an NDA was required.

United States v. Article of Drug ... "Mykocert"
345 F. Supp. 571 (N.D. Ill. 1972).

■ MAROVITZ, DISTRICT JUDGE....

The Complaint alleges that the seized article of drug was misbranded while held for sale after shipment in interstate commerce within the meaning of the Act, 21 U.S.C. as follows:....

§ 352(f)(1) in that it is a drug and its labeling fails to bear adequate directions for use and it is not exempt from such requirement, under the regulations, 21 CFR 1.106(g), since the article is a new drug subject to the provisions of 21 U.S.C. § 355, and no approval of an application filed pursuant to 21 U.S.C. § 355(b) is effective with respect to such drug, and no notice of claimed investigational exemption under 21 U.S.C. § 355(i) and regulations [sic] 21 CFR 130.3 is on file for such drug. . . .

The seeming complexity of this action diminishes, once the critical issue around which the entire case revolves is isolated. The drug here in question consists of a tampon impregnated with 14 mgs. of the chemical ingredient 9–aminoacridine hydrochloride and a "binder" of 14 mgs. of polyvinylpyrrolidone which Beutlich markets as a prescription drug for the alleviation of various vaginal infections. . . .

. . . . [The defense] chosen by claimant is that Mykocert is not a "new" drug as defined in 21 U.S.C. § 321 and 21 CFR § 130.1 and that even though § 352(f)(1) is inapplicable because of the drug's prescriptive nature the non-newness of the drug exempts it from any . . . requirements . . . such as application or filing with the Federal Drug Administration. Thus the entire crux of the case is dependent on the one critical decisive issue as whether Mykocert is or is not a new drug.

A drug not new

The regulations in 21 CFR § 130.1(h) [now § 310.3(h)] . . . indicate the various conceivable manifestations of "newness":

(h) The newness of a drug may arise by reason (among other reasons) of:

"Newness"

(1) The newness for drug use of any substance which composes such drug, in whole or in part, whether it be an active substance or a menstruum, excipient, carrier, coating, or other component.

(2) The newness for drug use of a combination of two or more substances, none of which is a new drug.

(3) The newness for drug use of the proportion of a substance in a combination, even though such combination containing such substance in other proportion is not a new drug.

(4) The newness of use of such drug in diagnosing, curing, mitigating, treating, or preventing a disease, or to affect a structure or function of the body, even though such drug is not a new drug when used in another disease or to affect another structure or function of the body.

(5) The newness of a dosage, or method or duration of administration or application, or other conditions of use prescribed, recommended, or suggested in the labeling of such drug, even though such drug when used in other dosage, or other method or duration of administration or application, or different condition, is not a new drug. . . .

One indication that a drug is not generally recognized among qualified experts as safe and effective for its intended use, that some Courts have accepted, is the absence of any published medical or scientific literature relating to the usage of the drug since the lack of documented sources of information perforce curtails the widespread knowledge of the drug's effectiveness or safety. This test by itself has been recognized as determinative of "newness" by several cases especially in this district.

Other courts have searched for proof of general recognition in different, other directions and have required a higher degree of proof to establish non-recognition. The most common procedure is the disposition of the cause in drug cases of this nature on cross-motions for summary judgment which are accompanied by various affidavits attesting to the non-recognition or general recognition of the drug as the case may be. These affidavits must be directed not at the "safe and effective" portion of 21 U.S.C. § 321(p) but at the "generally recognized" portion and actual safety and effectiveness is not at issue under this test. Thus actual safety proven by a small sampling short of general recognition is not sufficient to cure violations of the regulations applying to new drugs.

Some difficulty has been encountered by the courts in determining precisely what degree of recognition both in quantity and quality constitutes "general recognition" under the statute and that task is rendered all the more difficult when it must be accomplished within the strict confines of the summary judgment rule on the basis of conflicting affidavits which all claim expertise in the field. Some cases have taken the position that the mere existence of conflict between qualified experts in supporting affidavits establishes a lack of general recognition as a matter of law (see *Merritt Corp. v. Folsom*, 165 F. Supp. 418 (D.D.C. 1958)) while other courts in dicta attempted to soften the mere conflict rule where a genuine difference of opinion exists since general recognition ought not mean unanimous recognition. *United States v. 7 Cartons ... Ferro–Lac*, 293 F. Supp. 660 (S.D. Ill. 1968); *AMP v. Gardner*, 389 F.2d 825 (2d Cir. 1968).

In addition to the various rules that have evolved in regard to the weight given affidavits in such an action certain guidelines developed pertaining to the qualifications of the affiants and the content of the affidavits. Some courts have pointed out that the personal opinions of experts are not adequate to establish general recognition and that the affidavits should instead attest to the existence of the opinion or recognition in the general community. Furthermore the affiant expert must be one qualified by scientific training and experience to evaluate the safety and effectiveness of drugs and cannot simply be a medical practitioner whose only knowledge is based on prescribing the drug for his own patients.

... It must be noted that many of the problems encountered in determining general recognition are a result of the limitations of the summary judgment procedure. While we do not in any way dispute the validity of the absence-of-a-body-of-literature test, or express an opinion as to soundness of the mere conflict of affidavits test, or in any way cast doubt on the continuing viability of summary judgment disposition of drug cases where appropriate, it must be admitted that there is greater leeway available to the Court where it can decide subjective facts in addition to applying objective tests. The opportunity to decide facts as well as law allows for a broader range of information and evidence to be taken into consideration. . . .

Claimant's contention that Mykocert is not a new drug can only succeed if it is recognized by experts in the field as safe and effective. There are two possible alternatives that would substantiate claimant's assertions. Either a Mykocert type drug in its exact form, dosage, and application must be recognized by experts (even though that drug may be marketed under a different name) or each of the component parts of Mykocert must be recognized with the critical caveat that the combination of these parts does not in any way create a new drug under 21 CFR § 130(h). . . .

can also be components

Literature on Mykocert in its exact form is virtually non-existent, no less a body of literature, and there is no expert opinion available as to the general recognition of a 14 mgs. dosage of 9–aminoacridine applied in a tampon form and claimant therefore cannot succeed with the contention that a Mykocert type drug itself is recognized. Without going into great detail the few affidavits that address themselves to Mykocert itself rather than to its component parts are inadequate, since they focus on safety and effectiveness rather than general recognition and furthermore are by practitioners prescribing the drug for patients rather than experts in the field.

literature

→ *problem w/ affidavits*

In addition it is difficult for this court to acknowledge the general recognition of Mykocert when the chairmen of the Obstetrics and Gynecology Departments at Chicago Medical School; State University of New York, Downstate Medical Center; Northwestern University Medical School; and Loyola University Medical Center all swear that Mykocert is not generally recognized. While we do not express an opinion as to whether a "mere" conflict in expert opinion constitutes lack of general recognition, it cannot be denied that the affidavits of five of the leading doctors in the field which deny general recognition creates more than a "mere" conflict. It is inconceivable that a drug such as this could be considered generally recognized in the face of such learned non-recognition.

testimony against GRAS

Yet even if these experts claim that Mykocert is not generally recognized in its present state, claimants might still attempt to salvage Mykocert by using the other avenue available—that absence of recognition for Mykocert as such is irrelevant given the fact that its component parts are generally recognized. Claimant does in fact place great faith in this contention by directing a vast amount of literature to the effectiveness and recognition of tampons and aminoacridines generally for use on infections. In order for this argument to succeed Mykocert in its present state must be similar enough in form, dosage, purpose, and application to the general usage of aminoacridines so as to be within the genre "aminoacridine" and the general recognition attributed to that genre. If Mykocert deviates in any substantial degree from previous forms of aminoacridine usage then it cannot rely on the general recognition of its component parts. The regulations in fact indicate that combinations of "old" drugs may be a "new" drug as is stated in 21 CFR 130.1(h)(1) through (5).

what about components?

Simply stated *under the drug laws the whole of a drug may be greater or "newer" than all of its parts.* How critical this factor becomes to our case is evidenced in the fact that the vast majority of claimants' affidavits and documents are directed at the recognition of the component parts of Mykocert rather than to the exact form and dosage of Mykocert. . . . [I]f we determine that Mykocert is more than just the component parts of tampons and aminoacridines, claimant is practically foreclosed from succeeding based on its almost total reliance on affidavits directed at the component parts rather than the whole.

In adding up the tampon and aminoacridine usage we do not come up with a total of Mykocert. In view of the fact that the 14 mgs. dosage of Mykocert is a much larger dosage than used in other aminoacridine medications for vaginal infections; given the tampon form of application which is unlike gell tablet and cream form of application of vaginal infection medication; that the element of polyvinylpyrrolidone is added as a chemical binder, we hold that Mykocert is a new drug as defined in 21 CFR § 130.1(h)(5). . . .

We believe that the new dosage and form of application creates greater risks and questions of safety and effectiveness than previously recognized forms of medication for vaginal infections and given the delicate area of its application—warrants a finding of "newness." . . .

NOTES

1. *Summary Judgment. See Lemmon Pharmacal Co. v. Richardson*, 319 F. Supp. 375 (E.D. Pa. 1970), where the District Court observed:

> The cited cases, in my opinion, require a discriminating analysis of the affidavits submitted by the parties to determine whether there really is a triable issue as to general recognition. Not every conflict in medical opinion is necessarily adequate to negative general recognition. . . .
>
> Plaintiff's affiants, Drs. Gordon and Danowski, both acknowledge that the medical educational community in this country does not teach the use of thyroid except for thyroid deficiency. This fact, coupled with the specific dangers pointed out by the government's affiants as being inherent in Obestat because of its thyroid content, and the non-responsiveness of the plaintiff's affidavits to these specific dangers, justifies the conclusion that no genuine issue of fact exists for trial. . . .

The *Lemmon* case involved an FDA regulation, 21 C.F.R. 250.11, that declared thyroid-containing drugs intended for the treatment of human obesity new drugs. The court implied that this determination lay properly within FDA's primary jurisdiction. The issue of who may determine whether a drug is a new drug for which marketing approval is required is considered at *infra* p. 605.

2. *Evidence of General Recognition.* In 1973, the Supreme Court approved FDA's position that "general recognition" of safety and effectiveness must be based upon the same quantity and quality of scientific evidence that would be needed to obtain an NDA. *Weinberger v. Hynson, Westcott & Dunning, Inc.*, 412 U.S. 609, 631–632 (1973); *Weinberger v. Bentex Pharmaceuticals, Inc.*, 412 U.S. 645, 653 (1973).

When FDA sought to permit the interim marketing of pre-1962 generic drugs while an abbreviated NDA was pending review by FDA, however, the agency found itself in conflict with its own interpretation of the statute.

Hoffmann–LaRroche, Inc. v. Weinberger

425 F. Supp. 890 (D.D.C. 1975).

■ JUNE L. GREEN, DISTRICT JUDGE....

Plaintiff, Hoffmann–LaRoche, Inc., has brought suit for declaratory and injunctive relief.... Specifically, Hoffmann–LaRoche challenges the FDA's policy of permitting the introduction of a new drug in interstate commerce without first approving a new drug application for such drug as required by 21 U.S.C. §§ 331, 355 (1970)....

... Hoffmann–LaRoche is the holder of three approved new drug applications for compounds which contain chlordiazepoxide or chlordiazepoxide hydrochloride (both hereafter referred to as "chlordiazepoxide"). Plaintiff markets these drugs under the trademark "Librium." Since 1959, when Hoffmann–LaRoche first filed a new drug application for chlordiazepoxide, Hoffmann–LaRoche has marketed the drug only after it has obtained approval by the FDA of its new drug applications.

On January 20, 1975, plaintiff filed suit in the United States District Court for the District of New Jersey against Zenith Laboratories, Inc. and its subsidiary, Paramount Supply Corp., alleging infringement of plaintiff's patent on chlordiazepoxide. During the course of pretrial discovery in that case, plaintiff learned from officials of the defendant companies that they had begun to ship chlordiazepoxide capsules in interstate commerce. In March 1973, Zenith filed an abbreviated new drug application with the FDA on chlordiazepoxide. On February 27, 1975, plaintiff filed this action in district court. The FDA approved the new drug application submitted by Zenith Laboratories on March 7, 1975....

The crux of this controversy is the use by the FDA of the new drug application procedure as a sort of administrative holding action to regulate the sale and manufacture of "me-too" drugs. Me-too drugs are drugs which are chemically equivalent to a pioneer drug for which a full new drug application is in effect. It is estimated that five to thirteen me-too drugs exist for every new drug that has a FDA approved new drug application. It is the present policy of the FDA, termed an interim policy, to require the filing of an abbreviated new drug application by the manufacturers of each me-too drug where the pioneer drug has a full new drug application approved pursuant to 21 U.S.C. § 355 (1970). The FDA's position is that marketing of these drugs may be permitted without the approval of each individual new drug application.

The FDA advances two principal arguments to justify its policy. First, it claims that its compliance resources are limited and must be concentrated primarily in those areas where a potential health problem exists. Thus, the FDA has directed its compliance activities toward those drug products which have been found ineffective rather than toward those which have been found effective. Second, for those drugs that the NAS/NRC have found effective and are widely recognized as safe and effective and no bioavailability or special manufacturing problem is known or suspected, the need to police their distribution is minimal. Additionally, the FDA claims that it would have a difficult time in court contending that a specific version is a new drug within the meaning of 21 U.S.C. § 321(p) (1970).

On the contrary, Hoffmann–LaRoche argues that the FDA's action is another example of its failure to follow the 1962 New Drug Amendments. Like the situation condemned in *American Public Health Assoc. v. Veneman*, 349 F. Supp. 1311 (D.D.C. 1972), the FDA is again acting contrary to the clear statutory directives of section 355. Plaintiff contends that the plain meaning of section 355 dictates that once the FDA requires a new drug application to be filed, then the approval process must be completed before such drug can be marketed. . . .

Reaching the merits of plaintiff's statutory argument, the Court holds that the FDA's policy of permitting new drugs to be marketed without an approved new drug application contravenes the clear statutory requirement of preclearance mandated by 21 U.S.C. § 355 (1970). The FDA's choice of policy is not within the intendment of the 1962 New Drug Amendments and the legislative scheme they embody.

. . . The Court recognizes that the FDA is to be given the administrative flexibility to make regulations and to determine the new drug status of individual drugs or classes of drugs. Certainly it has the power to promulgate regulations that adopt a monograph procedure for human prescription drugs similar to that adopted for over-the-counter drugs whereby a drug or drugs may be declared to be no longer new drugs. *See* 21 C.F.R. § 330.10 (1974). The FDA can regulate the bioequivalence and special manufacturing problems through its general rule-making power. However, the argument that the FDA lacks the administrative resources to insure compliance with section 355 cannot be permitted to postpone to some indefinite future date the implementation of the required preclearance approval of new drug applications. . . .

Summary judgment will therefore be entered for the plaintiff. Defendants will be permanently enjoined from implementing its policy which permits the introduction into interstate commerce without an approved new drug application of prescription drugs which the FDA has previously declared to be new drugs within the meaning of 21 U.S.C. § 321(p).

NOTES

1. *Abbreviated NDAs.* The FDA policy rejected by Judge Green represented an effort by FDA to assure that the abbreviated NDA requirement did not specially burden new manufacturers of me-too drugs, who otherwise would have to delay marketing while the bureaucratic machinery ground its way through the flood of applications, while similar "yet to be approved" products remained on the market simply because they were there when the process began. FDA did not appeal Judge Green's ruling. Compare *Public Citizen v. Schmidt*, FDLI 1975–1977 Jud. Rec. 359 (D.D.C. 1976), which held that the new drug status of chloroform "was not an 'open and shut' case" and thus that FDA had authority to phase out its use through a rulemaking proceeding. No court ruled on the legality of FDA's abbreviated NDA policy—a policy that permitted the agency to approve the marketing of a me-too

version of a pre-1962 new drug without the submission of full reports of safety and effectiveness and without formal release of the safety and effectiveness data supporting the pioneer product—before the Drug Price Competition and Patent Term Restoration Act of 1984 codified this policy.

2. *"Paper NDAs" for Post-1962 Drugs.* Prior to the enactment of the Drug Price Competition and Patent Term Restoration Act of 1984, FDA refused to accept abbreviated NDAs for post-1962 drugs. The agency was, however, concerned that an approach that required redundant preclinical and clinical testing of generic equivalent products would not increase protection of consumers and would burden scarce testing facilities. In 1978, it announced the following "paper NDA" policy for approval of duplicates of post-1962 new drugs:

> A drug marketed for the first time after 1962 under an approved New Drug Application may be marketed by a second firm only after the second firm has received the approval of a full New Drug Application for that purpose. Current Agency policy does not permit ANDAs for this purpose. Present interpretation of the law is that no data in the NDA can be utilized to support another NDA without express permission of the original NDA holder. Thus, in the case of duplicate NDAs for already approved post–62 drugs, the Agency will accept published reports as the main supporting documentation for safety and effectiveness. The Agency will not interpret the "full reports of investigations" phrase in the law as requiring either case reports or an exhaustive review of all published reports on the drug. Depending upon the quality of the published data, selected preclinical and perhaps additional clinical studies may be required of the new sponsor prior to NDA approval.

Memorandum from FDA Bureau of Drugs Associate Director of New Drug Evaluation (July 31, 1978). This policy was upheld in *Burroughs Wellcome Co. v. Schweiker*, 649 F.2d 221 (4th Cir. 1981), and *Upjohn Manufacturing Co. v. Schweiker*, 681 F.2d 480 (6th Cir. 1982), and later revoked (as superseded) by the preamble to FDA's proposed regulations to implement the 1984 Act. 54 Fed. Reg. 28872, 28890 (July 10, 1989).

3. *Bioequivalence of Me-Too Drugs.* The driving force behind FDA's ultimately successful assertion that all prescription drugs must have an approved NDA or abbreviated NDA was the agency's need to be able to represent that all generic versions of a drug have been shown to be bioequivalent and thus clinically interchangeable. *See infra* p. 755; F. Kaid Benfield, *Life After Lannett: Open Season For "Me-too" Drugs?*, 34 FOOD DRUG COSM. L.J. 212 (1979); Eugene I. Lambert, *Law, Power and Money: A Generic Trinity*, 35 FOOD DRUG COSM. L.J. 306 (1980).

Following substantial litigation in which generic drug manufacturers sought to market their products without any form of NDA approval, the Supreme Court settled the matter.

United States v. Generix Drug Corp.

460 U.S. 453 (1983).

■ JUSTICE STEVENS delivered the opinion of the Court.

The question presented is whether the statutory prohibition against the marketing of a "new drug" without the prior approval of the Food and

Must A be approved before market?

define drug

Drug Administration (FDA) requires respondent Generix Drug Corp. to have approved new drug applications (NDA's) before it may market its generic drug products. In statutory terms, we are required to determine whether the term "drug" as used in the relevant sections of the Federal Food, Drug, and Cosmetic Act (Act), as amended, 21 U.S.C. § 301 *et seq.* (1976 ed. and Supp. V), refers only to the active ingredient in a drug product or to the entire product. We hold that Congress intended the word to have the broader meaning. . . .

In examining [FD&C Act 201(g)(1), the statutory definition of the term "drug"], the Court of Appeals was persuaded that only active ingredients come within the terms of subsection (A). Unfortunately, the [Court of Appeals] did not analyze the entire definition. If it had done so, it would have noted both that the terms of subsections (A), (B), and (C) are plainly broad enough to include more than just active ingredients, and that they *must* do so unless subsection (D) is to be superfluous. Because the definition is disjunctive, generic drug products are quite plainly drugs within the meaning of the Act.

In this case we are not required to determine what types of differences between drugs would be significant or insignificant under the statute. Respondent Generix argued only that its products are not new drugs under the theory that "drug" means "active ingredient"; it does not argue that its complete products—active ingredients and excipients together—are the same as previously approved products. The latter argument would, of course, have been unavailing on the facts before us; for the respondent has not questioned the District Court's finding of a reasonable possibility that its products are not bioequivalent to any previously approved products. We thus do not reach the issue of whether two demonstrably bioequivalent products, containing the same active ingredients but different excipients, might under some circumstances be the same "drug."

In summary, a generic drug product is a "drug" within the meaning of § 201(g)(1) of the Act. Such a product is therefore a "new drug," subject to the requirements of § 505, until the product (and not merely its active ingredient) no longer falls within the terms of § 201(p). . . .

NOTES

1. *Post-1962 Drugs.* This decision prompted FDA officials to begin development of a policy for approval of abbreviated NDAs for post-1962 generic drugs and eventually provoked a suit by generic drug manufacturers to force the agency to issue such a policy. One year after *Generix*, the legislation ultimately enacted as the Drug Price Competition and Patent Term Act of 1984 was introduced.

2. *Exceptions to Generix.* In *United States v. Atropine Sulfate 1.0 mg. (Article of Drug)*, 843 F.2d 860 (5th Cir. 1988), the Court of Appeals rejected the claimant's argument that its generic product was "uniquely equivalent" to the pioneer new drug and thus fell within the exception left open by the Supreme Court in the *Generix* decision.

b.   THE "GRANDFATHER" CLAUSES

When Congress, in 1938, first required that new drugs be proved safe for the conditions of their intended use, it specified in section 201(p)(1) that this requirement would not apply to any drug marketed under the Federal Food and Drugs Act of 1906 (*i.e.*, prior to 1938) so long as its labeling continued to contain "the same representations concerning the conditions of its use." This "grandfather" clause for pre-1938 drugs was not changed in 1962.

The 1962 Amendments contained their own so-called transitional provisions designed to provide either permanent or temporary exemption from the new effectiveness requirement for certain classes of drugs first marketed after 1938. These transitional provisions appeared in section 107(c) of the Drug Amendments of 1962, 76 Stat. 780, 788–89, but are not codified in the FD&C Act.

United States v. Allan Drug Corp.

357 F.2d 713 (10th Cir. 1966).

■ MURRAH, CHIEF JUDGE.

In this consolidated libel action the Colorado District Court condemned as misbranded a drug labeled "Halsion, A Plan of Medication and Care for Acne and Pimples" and returned the seized articles to the intervening claimant to be brought into compliance with the drug law under the supervision of a representative of the Secretary of Health, Education and Welfare.[3] This appeal is from an order of the court approving the relabeling and authorizing the marketing of the product as relabeled over the protest of the Federal Food, Drug and Cosmetic Administration. . . .

On trial of the case the Court found "That the labeling material in its net effect represented to prospective purchasers . . . that the 'Halsion Plan' in and of itself is an adequate and effective treatment for acne and pimples and would give lasting relief from these conditions . . . [and] that 'These representations were misleading. . . .' " Amenable to the requirements of § 334(d), the order return[ed] the seized articles for relabeling. . . .

In a letter responding to the [claimant's] proposed relabeling the Secretary took the position that the labeling did not comply with the Court's guidelines. . . . Finally, the Secretary took the position that the requirements of § 334(d) made it necessary to consider the marketing status of the Halsion tablets under the Drug Amendments of 1962. In that regard the Secretary contended that having shown to the satisfaction of the Court that the drug was not generally recognized by experts as effective for its intended uses, it cannot now be legally marketed unless its effectiveness has been established pursuant to a "New Drug application" in accordance with the statutory procedure. . . .

For reasons we shall attempt to demonstrate we are of the considered opinion that when, based on the facts, the trial court held the Halsion labeling false and misleading, hence misbranded, it became a "new drug"

---

3. § 334(d) reads in pertinent part as follows: ". . . the court may by order direct that such article be delivered to the owner thereof to be destroyed or brought into compliance with the provisions of this chapt[er] under the supervision of an officer or emp[loy]ee duly designated by the Secretary. . ."

within the meaning of § 321(p)(1), as amended, and was subject to the administrative procedures prescribed in § 355 as amended. . . .

. . . The exception or the Grandfather Clause [from the 1938 Act] was perpetuated verbatim [by the 1962 Amendments] so that a drug not generally recognized as safe or effective on the date of the Amendment would not be deemed to be a new drug on that date if its labeling contained the same representations concerning the conditions of its use. Additionally, and under another and different section of the amending Act [section 107(c)(4) of the Drug Amendments of 1962] pertaining to the effective dates of the Amendments, the Grandfather Clause was restated, "In the case of any drug which, on the day immediately preceding the enactment date (A) was commercially used or sold in the United States . . . the amendments to section 201(p) . . . shall not apply to such drug when intended solely for the use under conditions prescribed, recommended, or suggested in labeling with respect to such drug on that day." While the exempting language of the basic Act and the Amendment is verbally different, they are undoubtedly intended to mean the same thing. . . .

The trial court construed the critical words "solely for use under conditions prescribed, recommended, or suggested in labeling" to mean that the Amendments should apply to a new or different area of use under conditions prescribed in the labeling. He did not think Congress intended the Amendments to apply to a mere change in the labeling after the effective date of the Act, thus imposing upon a drug manufacturer the onerous burden of the new drug procedures when, as in this case, the effect of the change in the labeling was merely to reduce the use of the drug under conditions prescribed or recommended in the labeling. . . .

Since we are dealing with a Grandfather Clause exception, we must construe it strictly against one who invokes it. . . .

Judged in this context, we construe the critical language of the Grandfather Clauses to exempt drugs not generally recognized as effective if on the effective date of the Act the labeling contained the same representations concerning its use, and thus confine the exemption to drugs intended solely for use under conditions prescribed on the effective date of the Act. Given this interpretation, the condemned article loses the immunity of the Grandfather Clause and becomes a new drug subject to § 355. This is not to say that every change in labeling must necessarily result in the manufacturer filing a new drug application to reintroduce the article into interstate commerce. It may well be that a condemned drug may be brought into compliance with the provisions of the Drug Act under the supervision of the Secretary by relabeling the article for another use for which it is generally recognized as effective. . . . But, we need not speculate on the effective uses for which this article may be properly relabeled. It is ~ough to say that where, as here, an article has been condemned as ~abeled in fact and misbranded in law, it can be brought into compliance ~introduced for the same or similar use only as a new drug under the ~es prescribed in § 355. . . .

~senting opinion is omitted.]

NOTES

1. *Representative Court Decision.* In *United States v. An Article of Drug ... "Bentex Ulcerine,"* (S.D. Tex. 1970, 1971), *aff'd*, 469 F.2d 875 (5th Cir. 1972), the District Court rejected the claimant's contention that its drug was protected by the transitional provisions of the Drug Amendments of 1962:

> The claimant's evidence shows De–Nol was distributed to only a very limited extent before October 9, 1962. Between 1958 and June 30, 1963, a total of only four thousand bottles were imported....

> Claimant's evidence on this issue is not impressive. At best, it tends to show that the drug was used, prescribed and enthusiastically endorsed by a few physicians in Memphis, Tennessee (including the importer); and sold to no more than perhaps 150 to 200 doctors in some two or three neighboring states.

> Bearing in mind that the test is whether the drug was *generally recognized* as safe on the date in question (not whether in fact it *was* safe), I am simply unable to find its use or reputation was sufficiently widespread at that time as to qualify.

2. *Other Decisions.* See also *United States v. 1,048,000 Capsules ... "Afrodex,"* 494 F.2d 1158 (5th Cir. 1974), *aff'g* 347 F. Supp. 768 (S.D. Tex. 1972); *United States v. Articles of Drug ... 5,906 Boxes,* 745 F.2d 105 (1st Cir. 1984); *United States v. Undetermined Quantities of an Article of Drug ... Anucort HC Suppositories,* 709 F. Supp. 511 (D.N.J. 1987), *aff'd without opinion*, 857 F.2d 1466 (3d Cir. 1988); *United States v. 50 Boxes More or Less,* 909 F.2d 24 (1st Cir. 1990), *aff'g* 721 F. Supp. 1462 (D. Mass. 1989); *United States v. Articles of Drug ... "Colchicine,"* 442 F. Supp. 1236 (S.D.N.Y. 1978); *United States v. 675 Cases ... "Damason–P,"* Food Drug Cosm. L. Rep. (CCH) ¶ 38,156 (C.D. Cal. 1989); *United States v. Vital Health Products, Ltd.,* 786 F. Supp. 761 (E.D. Wisc. 1992). No drug has yet been judicially determined to fall within the 1938 or 1962 grandfather clause.

One of the important issues raised in the four Supreme Court cases in 1973 was whether the pioneer drug's approved NDA "covered" generic "me-too" copies. A holding that they were "covered" would deny them the protection of the grandfather clause and subject them to the requirement of proof of effectiveness under the Drug Amendments of 1962.

USV Pharmaceutical Corp. v. Weinberger

412 U.S. 655 (1973).

■ MR. JUSTICE DOUGLAS delivered the opinion of the Court.

Petitioner sells a line of drugs containing, as a principal active ingredient, citrus bioflavonoid, which is an extract from fruit skins. The drugs are sold in capsules, syrup, and tablets. In the 1950's ... [NDA's] were filed and became effective for seven of them; two, however, were sold without any NDA. In 1961 the ... [FDA] advised petitioner that two of the products, when distributed under the existing labels, were not new drugs. After the 1962 amendments ..., these products, together with a large number of other bioflavonoid products, were examined by FDA for drug effectiveness....

Based upon the NAS–NRC reports and its own evaluation, FDA gave notice of opportunity for hearing on its proposal to withdraw approvals of NDA's for all drugs containing these compounds, alone or in combination with other drugs. Petitioner thereupon brought suit in the District Court.... The administrative proceedings went forward, FDA refusing a stay pending the judicial proceedings. Petitioner submitted no evidence of "adequate and well-controlled investigations" ... to support its claims of effectiveness. The Commissioner made findings and withdrew petitioner's NDA's....

The District Court found that two of the products had never been covered by effective NDA's and that, while seven had been covered, their applications had later been withdrawn by petitioner.... It therefore concluded that, as of the day the 1962 amendments became effective, petitioner's products were not new drugs, were not covered by effective applications within the meaning of § 107 (c)(4), and hence were exempt from the effectiveness criterion....

The Court of Appeals ... reversed....

Section 107(c)(4) exempted drugs from the new effectiveness requirements so long as their composition and labeling remained unchanged. This exemption, however, applies only to a product that, on the day before the 1962 amendments became effective, (A) was used or sold commercially in the United States, (B) was generally recognized by the experts as safe; and (C) was not "covered" by an "effective" application.

.... [W]e agree with the Government that "any drug" when used in § 107(c)(4) is used in the generic sense, which means that the "me-too's," whether products of the same or of different manufacturers "covered" by an "effective" NDA, are not exempt from the efficacy requirements of § 201(p). If that were not true, then ... the "me-too's" of one manufacturer covered by an NDA of another manufacturer would be exempt from regulation, while the "me-too's" of the manufacturer holding the NDA could be regulated. That seems to be a reading of § 107(c)(4) that is discriminatory....

The second question presented by this case is whether an applicant could have withdrawn or "deactivated" an NDA prior to the 1962 amendments so that its drug was no longer "covered by an effective application" and thus is now exempt from efficacy regulation by reason of § 107(c)(4)....

Congress rejected an approach that would have exempted from the efficacy requirements of the 1962 amendments all drugs then marketed which had become generally recognized as safe. It now would be irrational for us to construe § 107(c)(4) of the amendments to exempt a drug merely because the manufacturer had taken some formal steps totally unrelated to the drug's effectiveness to indicate that the drug was no longer a "new drug" under the pre-1962 standards. The result would be that some drugs for which an NDA had been filed would be subject to the efficacy requirements and some would not, even though one could not differentiate between the drugs on the grounds of effectiveness.... It would be totally inconsistent with the statutory scheme and the policy underlying the 1962 amendments, as well as patently unjust, to conclude that some manufacturers could continue to market their bioflavonoid products, but others could not. We cannot attribute such an intention to Congress and, accordingly, cannot agree with petitioner that its NDA's had been withdrawn prior to 1962 so that its bioflavonoid products were no longer "covered by an effective application."

NOTE

USV prevailed in its appeal from FDA's denial of a hearing on the withdrawal of approval of the bioflavonoid NDAs. *USV Pharmaceutical Corp. v. Secretary of HEW*, 466 F.2d 455 (D.C. Cir. 1972). FDA thereafter published a notice of opportunity for hearing under its revised summary judgment procedures, 36 Fed. Reg. 24935 (July 8, 1974), and this time the company did not contest the withdrawal of the NDAs. 42 Fed. Reg. 10066 (Feb. 18, 1977).

———

A decade after enactment of the Drug Amendments of 1962, and five years after the NAS had begun to submit its evaluations of pre-1962 new drugs, consumer organizations challenged FDA's procedure and timetable for implementing the Amendments.

American Public Health Association v. Veneman

349 F. Supp. 1311 (D.D.C. 1972).

■ BRYANT, DISTRICT JUDGE....

In January, 1968, the FDA began implementation of the NAS–NRC reports. The procedure adopted has been to evaluate each report and to release it to the public only after the FDA evaluation is completed. When the FDA completes its evaluation of an NAS–NRC report, an announcement is made in the Federal Register that the FDA has concluded that the drugs involved are "effective," "probably effective," "possibly effective," or "lack substantial evidence of effectiveness." ...

In response to the court's inquiry the defendants advised the court on February 2, 1972, that 814 reports still had not been evaluated by the FDA. Of these outstanding reports, 327 had been returned to NAS–NRC for further evaluation in early 1971 and were reported on by NAS–NRC in October, 1971; they are presently being reevaluated by the FDA....

... [FDA's] enforcement stance must be well balanced, but nevertheless effective. A timid approach can vitiate whatever protection the Congress has created for the consumer. On the other hand, an overly zealous approach can ruin a drug manufacturer by destroying public confidence in its products. Thus, it is understandable that the agency might have legitimate concern for drug manufacturers who must comply with new statutory requirements, and surely the question of time necessary to adduce new evidence of efficacy is an important consideration in creating an administrative scheme for implementation of the statute.

However, the FDA must remember that ... [a]t the very outset the Congress also was sensitive to this problem, and allowed a two-year grace period before the 1962 amendments were to become effective. When, as is the case here, the Congress has shown an awareness of a problem and has acted accordingly, it seems inappropriate for an agency to adopt procedures which extend the grace period far beyond that envisioned by the statute, and which effectively stay implementation of the Congressional mandate that drugs in the marketplace be both safe and effective.

Based upon the entire record in this case, the court concludes that there is no compelling reason why the remaining NAS–NRC reports should not be immediately released, that it would be an abuse of agency discretion to refuse to make such reports public, and that the court should set a deadline for the FDA to complete its evaluation of all drugs with regard to efficacy....

Counsel are directed to present an appropriate order.

NOTES

1. *Veneman Court Order.* FDA did not appeal this ruling because its top officials believed that judicial oversight could galvanize the agency staff into action. The District Court subsequently entered an order, drafted by government counsel, which established a schedule for completion of the DESI Review. The order required agency action, in descending order of priority, on drugs rated by the NAS panels and FDA as "ineffective," "possible effective," and "probably effective." The entire task was to be finished by 1976. OTC drugs and medically important prescription drugs were exempted. FDA was required to file semi-annual progress reports with the court. *See* 37 Fed. Reg. 26623 (Dec. 14, 1972).

2. *Paragraph XIV Drugs.* The order entered by the District Court is in many significant respects inconsistent with the *Veneman* opinion, revealing that many practical problems in implementing the 1962 Amendments were not appreciated when the opinion was written. Paragraph XIV of the order—under which the marketing of drugs with important medical uses was allowed to continue until studies meeting contemporary standards could be conducted to verify their effectiveness—is an example. FDA's implementation of this provision can be traced through a series of notices, *e.g.*, 37 Fed. Reg. 26623 (Dec. 14, 1972), 38 Fed. Reg. 18477 (July 11, 1973), 41 Fed. Reg. 32937 (Aug. 6, 1976), 42 Fed. Reg. 43127 (Aug. 26, 1977), 42 Fed. Reg. 44286 (Sept. 2, 1977), 42 Fed. Reg. 56156 (Oct. 21, 1977), 43 Fed. Reg. 7044 (Feb. 17, 1978), 43 Fed Reg. 26489 (June 20, 1978), 44 Fed. Reg. 40933 (July 13, 1979), and 45 Fed. Reg. 4471 (Jan. 22, 1980).

3. *Failure to Meet Schedule.* FDA failed to meet the mandated four-year schedule. By the end of 1976, it had largely completed work on the higher-rated drugs, by inducing manufacturers to revise label claims or, in some instances, by upgrading its own evaluation. It had revoked NDAs for drugs whose manufacturers had not submitted any additional evidence of effectiveness. But it had fallen behind in two areas: (1) It had not ruled on several requests for formal hearings nor held any hearings, because these tasks were the most resource-intensive, and relatively few employees had the knowledge necessary to attend to them; (2) As the District Court's order permitted, it had created a substantial backlog of so-called Paragraph XIV drugs. In many instances, clinical investigations had not commenced because FDA had been unable to devise appropriate testing protocols.

4. *Revised Order*. In March 1979, the *Veneman* plaintiffs moved to reopen the proceedings to seek further relief. In an agreement reached by the parties, *American Public Health Association v. Harris*, Food Drug Cosm. L. Rep. (CCH) ¶ 38,068 (D.D.C. 1980), FDA agreed to "make a good faith effort to assure a more expeditious resolution of matters covered by the [1972] Court Order" and to "attempt to achieve" specific new goals "to the maximum extent feasible." FDA continued to submit semiannual reports to the District Court on its progress.

5. *Final Resolution*. FDA filed its 32d and 33d reports in June 1989. These reports stated that FDA had removed 6813 drug products from the market pursuant to the District Court order. They also acknowledged that five drugs remained for further action, two were the subject of administrative hearings, and one was in litigation. On that basis, the case was formally closed. The status of some of these eight drugs remains unresolved even today.

6. *Federal Reimbursement for Less–Than–Effective Drugs*. In 45 Fed. Reg. 37858 (June 5, 1980), the Health Care Financing Administration (HCFA) proposed to prohibit the use of federal funds to pay for any drug that FDA had, in a final administrative ruling, found to be less than effective. Before HCFA had an opportunity to promulgate a final regulation, Congress included in the Omnibus Budget Reconciliation Act of 1981, 95 Stat. 357, 787, an amendment to the Social Security Act prohibiting the expenditure of federal funds under Medicare and Medicaid for drugs for which FDA has published a notice of opportunity for hearing to withdraw approval of the NDA. That provision, codified at 42 U.S.C. 1395y(c), was implemented by HCFA in 46 Fed. Reg. 48550 (Oct. 1, 1981), 46 Fed. Reg. 51646 (Oct. 21, 1981), 46 Fed. Reg. 53664, 54304 (Oct. 30, 1981), codified at 42 C.F.R. 410.29.

c. JURISDICTION TO DETERMINE NEW DRUG STATUS

Prior to the Drug Amendments of 1962 and the four Supreme Court cases of 1973, the courts had never been presented with the question whether FDA has "primary jurisdiction" over the matters delegated to the agency under the FD&C Act and thus is entitled to judicial deference on jurisdictional issues. Although the following decision arose in the context of determining the new drug status of a particular drug product, the principle it enunciated has been of crucial importance in establishing FDA as a strong and authoritative administrative agency.

Weinberger v. Bentex Pharmaceuticals, Inc.

412 U.S. 645 (1973).

■ MR. JUSTICE DOUGLAS delivered the opinion of the Court.

In this case Bentex and some 20 other firms . . . filed this suit for a declaratory judgment that their drugs containing pentylenetetrazol are generally recognized as safe and effective, and thus not "new drugs" within the meaning of § 201(p)(1). . . . They also sought exemption from the new effectiveness requirements by reason of § 107(c)(4) [the "Grandfather clause"] of the 1962 amendments. . . .

. . . [T]hree separate National Academy of Sciences–National Research Council (NAS–NRC) panels reviewed the evidence concerning these drugs, and each concluded that the drug was "ineffective" for the indicated use. The Commissioner concluded there was a lack of substantial evidence that these drugs were effective for their intended uses and gave notice of his

FDA withdraws approval for NDAs

intention to initiate proceedings to withdraw approval of the new drug applications (NDA's). FDA had taken the position that withdrawal of approval of an NDA would operate to remove marketing approval for all drugs of similar composition, known as "me-too" drugs, whether or not they were expressly covered by an effective NDA.... The Commissioner [then] issued orders withdrawing approval of the three NDAs; no appeal was taken. This suit in the District Court followed. It appears that all of the parties to this suit market "me-too" drugs, none of which was expressly covered by an effective NDA....

Court of Appeals

The Court of Appeals ... held that FDA has no jurisdiction, either primary or concurrent, to decide in an administrative proceeding what is a "new drug" for which an NDA is required. In its view the 1962 Act established two forums for the regulation of drugs: an administrative one for premarketing clearances for "new drugs" or withdrawal of previously approved NDA's, with the right of appeal; and, second, a judicial one for enforcement of the requirement that "new drugs" be cleared as safe and effective before marketing by providing the Government with judicial remedies of seizure, injunction, and criminal prosecution available solely in the District Court.

We reverse the Court of Appeals....

... The line sought to be drawn by the Court of Appeals is FDA action on NDA's pursuant to § 505(d) and § 505(e), on the one hand, and the question of "new drug" determination on the other. We can discern no such jurisdictional line under the Act. The FDA ... may deny an NDA where there is a lack of "substantial evidence" of the drug's effectiveness, based ... on clinical investigation by experts. But the "new drug" definition under § 201(p) encompasses a drug "not generally recognized, among experts qualified by scientific training and experience to evaluate the safety and effectiveness of drugs, as safe and effective for use." Whether a particular drug is a "new drug," depends in part on the expert knowledge and experience of scientists based on controlled clinical experimentation and backed by substantial support in scientific literature. One function is not peculiar to judicial expertise, the other to administrative expertise. The two types of cases overlap and strongly suggest that Congress desired that the administrative agency make both kinds of determination. Even where no such administrative determination has been made and the issue arises in a district court in enforcement proceedings, it would be commonplace for the court to await an appropriate administrative declaration before it acted. It may, of course, be true that in some cases general recognition that a drug is efficacious might be made without the kind of scientific support necessary to obtain approval of an NDA. But ... the reach of scientific inquiry under both § 505(d) and § 201(p) is precisely the same.

We think that it is implicit in the regulatory scheme, not spelled out *in haec verba*, that FDA has jurisdiction to decide with administrative finality, subject to the types of judicial review provided, the "new drug" status of individual drugs or classes of drugs. The deluge of litigation that would follow if "me-too" drugs and OTC drugs had to receive *de novo* hearings in the courts would inure to the interests of manufacturers and merchants in drugs, but not to the interests of the public that Congress was anxious to

*problems w/
case-by-case*

protect by the 1962 amendments, as well as OTC drugs and drugs covered by the 1972 [Drug Listing] Act. We are told that FDA is incapable of handling a caseload of more than perhaps 10 or 15 *de novo* judicial proceedings a year. Clearly, if FDA were required to litigate, on a case-by-case basis, the "new drug" status of each drug now marketed, the regulatory scheme of the Act would be severely undermined, if not totally destroyed. Moreover, a case-by-case approach is inherently unfair because it requires compliance by one manufacturer while his competitors marketing similar drugs remain free to violate the Act. . . .

. . . The determination whether a drug is generally recognized as safe and effective within the meaning of § 201(p)(1) necessarily implicates complex chemical and pharmacological consideration. Threshold questions within the peculiar expertise of an administrative agency are appropriately routed to the agency, while the court stays its hand. . . .

NOTES

1. *Concurrent Decision.* In *CIBA Corp. v. Weinberger*, 412 U.S. 640, 644 (1973), the Supreme Court reiterated its position on this issue:

> . . . [T]he Act does not create a dual system of control—one administrative, and the other judicial. Cases may arise where there has been no formal administrative determination of the "new drug" issue, it being first tendered to a district court. Even then, however, the district court might well stay its hand, awaiting an appropriate administrative determination of the threshold question. Where there is, however, an administrative determination, whether it be explicit or implicit[,] in the withdrawal of an NDA, the tactic of "reserving" the threshold question (the jurisdictional issue) for later judicial determination is not tolerable. . . . [P]etitioner, having an opportunity to litigate the "new drug" issue before FDA and to raise the issue on appeal to a court of appeals, may not relitigate the issue in another proceeding.

2. *Primary Jurisdiction.* The Supreme Court's holding in *Bentex* and *CIBA* that FDA has "primary jurisdiction" to determine new drug status was a major victory for the agency. Ironically, the opinions have provided the pretext for challenges to FDA's use of its traditional court enforcement weapons to enforce the new drug requirements. *See infra* p. 1567.

3. *Subsequent Proceedings.* Following the *Bentex* decision, FDA determined that the "me-too" pentylenetetrazol drugs in question were "new drugs" and published a notice of opportunity for hearing on this issue in 41 Fed. Reg. 4625 (Jan. 30, 1976). In 47 Fed. Reg. 19208 (May 4, 1982), the agency denied a hearing and finally declared the pentylenetetrazol drugs to be unapproved new drugs. The denial of a hearing was overturned in *Boots Pharmaceuticals, Inc. v. Schweiker*, Food Drug Cosm. L. Rep. (CCH) ¶ 38,200 (W.D. La. 1982), but this ruling was summarily reversed without opposition on appeal and no hearing was ever held.

d. THE PRACTICE OF PHARMACY

Long before there were independent drug manufacturers, apothecaries, now known as pharmacists, compounded drugs both for their own patients and in response to prescriptions of physicians. Companies engaged in the manufacture and distribution of drugs did not emerge in the United States until the latter half of the 19th century. Today, the vast majority of prescription drugs are produced in finished form by drug manufacturers and only dispensed by pharmacists, but the compounding of prescription drugs still occupies a distinctive place under the FD&C Act.

Nothing in the FD&C Act of 1938 excluded pharmacy compounding from the requirements of the statute. *See United States v. Herold*, 136 F. Supp. 15 (E.D.N.Y. 1955) (upholding FDA's authority to inspect pharmacies under the FD&C Act). Pharmacies have since been exempted from the drug establishment registration section and from one sentence of the establishment inspection provisions, FD&C Act 510(g)(1), 704(a)(2), but they remain subject to all the other pertinent provisions of the Act. The two exemptions mentioned in the prior sentence apply only to pharmacies that do not manufacture, prepare, propagate, compound, or process drugs for sale other than in the regular course of their business of dispensing or selling drugs at retail.

Concerned that some rogue pharmacies were undertaking commercial-scale compounding, FDA initially brought enforcement action and then issued Compliance Policy Guide No. 7132.16 (Mar. 16, 1992), which stated that lawful compounding consisted only of filling an individual prescription as received. According to the CPG, if a compounding pharmacy prepared a bulk quantity of a compounded drug in anticipation of prescriptions from physicians, the drug became an illegal new drug. This CPG was upheld in *Professionals and Patients for Customized Care v. Shalala*, 847 F. Supp. 1359 (S.D. Tex. 1994), *aff'd* 56 F.3d 592 (5th Cir. 1995), against an allegation that it was an illegal substantive regulation that failed to comply with the Administrative Procedure Act. For a discussion of the pharmacy manufacturing practices that led FDA to issue the original version of this CPG in March 1992, *see* Jon R. May, *The Role of FDA in the Practice of Pharmacy*: Parts I & II, 57 J. AFDO, No. 1, p. 54 (Jan. 1993) & No. 2, p. 27 (Apr. 1993).

When Congress was considering enactment of the FDA Modernization Act of 1997, the pharmacy profession sought to obtain explicit statutory recognition of compounding. Congress added section 503A to the FD&C Act, establishing regulatory standards for lawful pharmacy compounding. One of those standards provided that "a drug may be lawfully compounded only if the pharmacy does not advertise or promote the compounding of any particular drug or class or type of drug, but the pharmacy may advertise and promote the fact that it is a compounding pharmacy." This provision was subsequently struck down as an unconstitutional infringement on commercial free speech under the First Amendment to the United States Constitution. *Thompson v. Western States Medical Center*, 535 U.S. 357 (2002). Because the Court of Appeals had determined that the advertising prohibition could not be severed from the remainder of the entire provision, *Western States Medical Center v. Shalala*, 238 F.3d 1090 (9th Cir. 2001), the net effect was to invalidate all of section 503A.

Prior to the *Western States* litigation, FDA had implemented section 503A only to the extent of establishing a list of drug products that could not be compounded because they were withdrawn from the market for reasons of safety or effectiveness. 63 Fed. Reg. 54082 (Oct. 8, 1998), 64 Fed. Reg. 10944 (Mar. 8, 1999), codified at 21 C.F.R. Part 216. In *Medical Center*

Pharmacy v. Gonzales, 451 F. Supp. 2d 854 (W.D. Tex. 2006), the District Court disagreed with the Ninth Circuit's decision on severability in *Western States* and held that the unconstitutional advertising prohibition could be severed from the remainder of section 503A. The *Medical Center Pharmacy* court thus reinstated the remaining provisions of that section, at least in the Fifth Circuit. The District Court upheld FDA's policy on pharmacy compounding in all other respects, in particular the agency's view that legitimate compounding involves only reasonable quantities made upon receipt of a valid prescription for an individual patient from a licensed practitioner. The severability issue is presently on appeal.

The 1997 enactment of section 503A led FDA to rescind the March 1992 Compliance Policy Guide. 64 Fed. Reg. 1207 (Jan. 8, 1999). Shortly after the Supreme Court decision in the *Western States* case, FDA issued a new CPG to replace it.

Compliance Policy Guides Section 460.200: Pharmacy Compounding

May 2002.

This document provides guidance to drug compounders and the staff of the Food and Drug Administration (FDA) on how the Agency intends to address pharmacy compounding of human drugs in the immediate future as a result of the decision of the Supreme Court in Thompson v. Western States Medical Center, No. 01–344, April 29, 2002. FDA is considering the implications of that decision and determining how it intends to regulate pharmacy compounding in the long term. However, FDA recognizes the need for immediate guidance on what types of compounding might be subject to enforcement action under current law. This guidance describes FDA's current thinking on this issue.

On March 16, 1992, FDA issued a compliance policy guide (CPG), section 7132.16 (later renumbered as 460.200) to delineate FDA's enforcement policy on pharmacy compounding. That CPG remained in effect until 1997 when Congress enacted the Food and Drug Administration Modernization Act of 1997.

On November 21, 1997, the President signed the Food and Drug Administration Modernization Act of 1997 (Pub. L. 105–115) (the Modernization Act). Section 127 of the Modernization Act added section 503A to the Federal Food, Drug, and Cosmetic Act (the Act), to clarify the status of pharmacy compounding under Federal law. Under section 503A, drug products that were compounded by a pharmacist or physician on a customized basis for an individual patient were entitled to exemptions from three key provisions of the Act: (1) the adulteration provision of section 501(a)(2)(B) (concerning the good manufacturing practice requirements); (2) the misbranding provision of section 502(f)(1) (concerning the labeling of drugs with adequate directions for use); and (3) the new drug provision of section 505 (concerning the approval of drugs under new drug or abbreviated new drug applications). To qualify for these statutory exemptions, a compounded drug product was required to satisfy several requirements, some of which were to be the subject of FDA rulemaking or other actions.

Section 503A of the Act took effect on November 21, 1998, one year after the date of the enactment of the Modernization Act....

The Supreme Court [in *Western States*] affirmed the 9th Circuit Court of Appeals decision that found section 503A of the Act invalid in its entirety because it contained unconstitutional restrictions on commercial speech (*i.e.*, prohibitions on soliciting prescriptions for and advertising specific compounded drugs). The Court did not rule on, and therefore left in place, the 9th Circuit's holding that the unconstitutional restrictions on commercial speech could not be severed from the rest of section 503A. Accordingly, all of section 503A is now invalid.

FDA has therefore determined that it needs to issue guidance to the compounding industry on what factors the Agency will consider in exercising its enforcement discretion regarding pharmacy compounding.

FDA recognizes that pharmacists traditionally have extemporaneously compounded and manipulated reasonable quantities of human drugs upon receipt of a valid prescription for an individually identified patient from a licensed practitioner. This traditional activity is not the subject of this guidance.

FDA believes that an increasing number of establishments with retail pharmacy licenses are engaged in manufacturing and distributing unapproved new drugs for human use in a manner that is clearly outside the bounds of traditional pharmacy practice and that violates the Act. Such establishments and their activities are the focus of this guidance.... [T]he practices of many of these entities seem far more consistent with those of drug manufacturers and wholesalers than with those of retail pharmacies. For example, some firms receive and use large quantities of bulk drug substances to manufacture large quantities of unapproved drug products in advance of receiving a valid prescription for them. Moreover, some firms sell to physicians and patients with whom they have only a remote professional relationship. Pharmacies engaged in activities analogous to manufacturing and distributing drugs for human use may be held to the same provisions of the Act as manufacturers....

[W]hen the scope and nature of a pharmacy's activities raise the kinds of concerns normally associated with a drug manufacturer and result in significant violations of the new drug, adulteration, or misbranding provisions of the Act, FDA has determined that it should seriously consider enforcement action. In determining whether to initiate such an action, the Agency will consider whether the pharmacy engages in any of the following acts:

1. Compounding of drugs in anticipation of receiving prescriptions, except in very limited quantities in relation to the amounts of drugs compounded after receiving valid prescriptions.

2. Compounding drugs that were withdrawn or removed from the market for safety reasons....

3. Compounding finished drugs from bulk active ingredients that are not components of FDA approved drugs without an FDA sanctioned investigational new drug application (IND)....

4. Receiving, storing, or using drug substances without first obtaining written assurance from the supplier that each lot of the drug substance has been made in an FDA-registered facility.

5. Receiving, storing, or using drug components not guaranteed or otherwise determined to meet official compendia requirements.

6. Using commercial scale manufacturing or testing equipment for compounding drug products.

7. Compounding drugs for third parties who resell to individual patients or offering compounded drug products at wholesale to other state licensed persons or commercial entities for resale.

8. Compounding drug products that are commercially available in the marketplace or that are essentially copies of commercially available FDA-approved drug products.

9. Failing to operate in conformance with applicable state law regulating the practice of pharmacy....

NOTES

1. *Judicial Support.* In *Cedars North Towers Pharmacy, Inc. v. United States,* 1978–1980 FDLI Jud. Rec. 668 (S.D. Fla. 1978), a pharmacy which prepared, packaged, and shipped to physicians throughout the country various drugs formulated by a physician, sought a declaratory judgment that these activities fell within the practice of pharmacy. The court held that the pharmacy was a drug manufacturer and that the drugs were new drugs under the FD&C Act. *See also United States v. Sene X Eleemosynary Corp., Inc.,* 479 F. Supp. 970 (S.D. Fla. 1979), *aff'd per curiam,* 1983–1984 FDLI Jud. Rec. 123 (11th Cir. 1983) (rejecting a defense to an injunction action based upon the practice of pharmacy); *In the Matter of Establishment Inspection of: Wedgewood Village Pharmacy, Inc.,* 270 F. Supp. 2d 525 (D.N.J. 2003), *aff'd sub nom. Wedgewood Village Pharmacy, Inc. v. United States,* 421 F.3d 263 (3d Cir. 2005) (holding that FDA has a statutory right to inspect a pharmacy where there is probable cause to conclude that the pharmacy's compounding constitutes commercial manufacturing). In *United States v. Algon Chemical Inc.,* 879 F.2d 1154, 1159 (3d Cir. 1989), the Court of Appeals held that physicians may compound drugs only from "legally acquired materials" and not from "unapproved drug substances."

2. *Parenteral Nutrition.* Perhaps the most important application of the pharmacy exemption covers parenteral nutrition. FDA has long taken the position that any parenteral nutrition product is inherently a drug. *E.g.,* FDA Trade Correspondence 2–A (Nov. 5, 1945); E. M. Nelson, *Amino Acid Preparations,* 1 FOOD DRUG COSM. L.Q. 178 (1946). In 1978, FDA issued a rule that requires an NDA for any parenteral drug product in a plastic container. 39 Fed. Reg. 39473 (Nov. 7, 1974), 43 Fed. Reg. 58557 (Dec. 15, 1978), codified at 21 C.F.R. 310.509. As part of the DESI Program, FDA reviewed the pre-1962 NDAs for parenteral nutrition products. Based upon guidelines prepared by the American Medical Association, *see* American Medical Association Department of Foods and Nutrition, *Multivitamin Preparations for Parenteral Use,* 3 J. OF PARENTERAL & ENTERAL NUTRITION 258 (Aug. 1979), FDA ultimately established criteria for approval of NDAs for safe and effective parenteral

nutrition solutions. *See* 37 Fed. Reg. 15027 (July 27, 1972), 37 Fed. Reg. 26623 (Dec. 14, 1972), 44 Fed. Reg. 40933 (July 13, 1979), 47 Fed. Reg. 44022 (Oct. 5, 1982), 48 Fed. Reg. 2835 (Jan. 21, 1983), 49 Fed. Reg. 36446 (Sept. 17, 1984), 50 Fed. Reg. 8193 (Feb. 28, 1985). These standardized NDAd nutritional solutions are shipped to a local pharmacy—usually owned by the pharmaceutical company that makes the solutions—where they are modified by adding nutrition components to meet the needs of an individual patient based upon the prescription of a physician.

3. *Regional Compounding of Parenteral Nutrition Solutions.* As part of the practice of pharmacy, a parenteral nutrition solution may be modified by adding one or more prescription drugs pursuant to the order of a physician for a particular patient. Beginning in the mid–1980s, one company undertook to perform this function in regional compounding centers rather than at local pharmacies, reasoning that this would reduce the possibility of compounding error and product contamination. However, in an enforcement action by the United States, the court held that this was outside the practice of pharmacy and that, because the new drugs being added to the parenteral nutrition solutions were being used outside the approved NDAs, the practice violated the FD&C. *United States v. Baxter Healthcare Corp.*, 712 F. Supp. 1352 (N.D. Ill. 1989), *aff'd*, 901 F.2d 1401 (7th Cir. 1990).

4. *Large Volume Parenterals.* Beginning in mid–1986, FDA conducted a nationwide inspection of pharmacies manufacturing large volume parenteral solutions to determine if they were exceeding the practice of pharmacy. *See* Memorandum from Center for Drugs and Biologics Consumer Safety Officer R. L. Sorensen to Regional Food and Drug Directors on Inspections of Pharmacies Manufacturing Large–Volume Parenterals, and Other Products (July 8, 1986).

5. *Mail Order Pharmacy.* The FD&C Act does not distinguish among the various types of pharmacy practice, and thus embraces mail order pharmacy, an activity that community and hospital pharmacy organizations have gone to great efforts to discourage. *See, e.g., Federal Prescription Service, Inc. v. American Pharmaceutical Association*, 663 F.2d 253 (D.C. Cir. 1981).

6. *Scope of Practice of Pharmacy.* In Regulatory Letter No. CHI–379–85 (June 27, 1985), FDA took the position that "compounding and dispensing prescription drug products specifically compounded on the basis of a valid prescription issued by a duly licensed practitioner for a specific patient" was within the practice of pharmacy, but that performing this function for other pharmacies falls outside the practice of pharmacy.

7. *Citizen Petition.* The Consumer Health Alliance for Safe Medication submitted a citizen petition requesting that FDA require all pharmacy-compounded aqueous-based drugs for inhalation be labeled as (1) not approved by FDA, (2) compounded in a pharmacy, (3) not in compliance with FDA standards for sterility, and (4) not demonstrated to be safe or effective. FDA Docket No. 2005P–0116 (Mar. 24, 2005). FDA has taken no action on the petition.

8. *Commentary. See* Roger A. Fairfax, *"Phederalism": The Regulation of Pharmacy Compounding and Two Years in the Regulatory Turf War Between Pharmacy and the Food and Drug Administration* (1998), and Rebecca J. Riley, *The Regulation of Pharmaceutical Compounding and the Determination of Need: Balancing Access and Autonomy with Patient Safety* (2004), in Chapter VI(C)(7) of the Electronic Book.

On July 13, 2006, Senator Charles Grassley wrote a letter to CMS Director Mark B. McClellan and FDA Acting Commissioner Andrew C. von

Eschenbach expressing concern that commercial compounding of unapproved prescription inhalation drugs violated both the Medicare/Medicaid laws and the FD&C Act. In response, CMS announced that it was drastically reducing reimbursement for compounded inhalation drugs, while FDA issued warning letters and published the following press release.

FDA Warns Three Pharmacies to Stop Mass–Producing Unapproved Inhalation Drugs

FDA News No. P06–113 (Aug. 10, 2006).

The Food and Drug Administration (FDA) has warned three firms, RoTech Healthcare, Inc., CCS Medical, and Reliant Pharmacy Services, to stop manufacturing and distributing thousands of doses of compounded, unapproved inhalation drugs nation-wide. Responsible officials at firms that do not properly address violations identified in FDA warning letters risk further enforcement, including injunctions that prevent further violations and seizure of their products that violate the law.

The three firms warned by FDA say that they produce inhalation drugs as part of the practice of pharmacy compounding. Traditional pharmacy compounding typically involves pharmacies preparing drugs that are not commercially available, such as a unique medicine for a patient who is allergic to an ingredient in a FDA-approved drug. This kind of compounding follows a physician's decision that his or her patient has a special medical need that cannot be met by FDA-approved drugs. FDA normally permits traditional pharmacy compounding and the agency's action is not targeting this practice. . . .

FDA believes that, in compounding mass amounts of inhalation drugs, a number of pharmacies go well beyond traditional compounding. FDA is aware of certain pharmacies compounding millions of doses of inhalation drugs per year. These compounded drugs often simply copy FDA-approved, commercially available drugs, and any differences from FDA-approved drugs do not appear to be related to patients' medical needs. . . .

e.   NON–DESI UNAPPROVED NEW DRUGS

Under the Drug Amendments of 1962, FDA was required to review the roughly 9500 NDAs that had become effective during 1938–1962, to determine whether the drugs were effective as well as safe. Approximately 400 of those NDAs covered nonprescription drugs, which are discussed *infra* at p. 788. Of the remaining NDAs, approximately 4000 covered human prescription drugs, each of which was the subject of the NAS DESI Review. Even though FDA successfully took the position that all related, similar, and identical me-too drugs were also automatically covered by the DESI Review of the pioneer NDA, there were six categories of drug products remaining on the market without an NDA that never went through the DESI Review: (1) drugs grandfathered under the 1938 grandfather clause, (2) drugs grandfathered under the 1962 grandfather clause, (3) drugs marketed prior to 1962 on the basis of an FDA determination that they were "old drugs," (4) drugs marketed prior to 1962 on the manufacturer's determination that they were "old drugs," (5) drugs marketed subsequent to 1962 on the manufacturer's determination that they were "old drugs," and (6) drugs marketed subsequent to 1962 on the manufacturer's determination that they were the same or closely related to drugs in any of the prior categories. All of these drugs, collectively, are known as non-DESI unapproved new drugs. FDA has always known of their existence, but the agency was so overwhelmed with the DESI Review and other priorities that it had never had an opportunity or the resources necessary to address them on a systematic basis.

As early as October 1976, FDA established Compliance Policy Guide No. 7132c.08 to implement the *Hoffman–LaRoche* decision, *supra* p. 595. The CPG was expanded and reissued as No. 7132c.02 in April 1981, revised in September 1984, May 1987, and March 1995, and later codified as section 440.100 of the FDA Compliance Policy Guides. Ever since its publication of the April 1981 version of the CPG, FDA has made clear its enforcement position that (1) all of these non-DESI unapproved new drugs are in fact new drugs for which FDA can require an NDA or force the products off the market at any time, (2) an unapproved non-DESI drug product first marketed prior to the Drug Amendments of 1962 may be copied by any competitor, and will be subject to the same requirements imposed on the original drug product, (3) each of these products may remain on the market until FDA makes a final determination relating to the class of drugs under which the product falls, and (4) if any manufacturer obtains some form of an NDA for one of these products, FDA will promptly remove all other products in that category from the market. At the time of the 1984 E–Ferol incident and the subsequent Congressional investigation, FDA estimated that there were approximately 5,000 of these non-DESI unapproved new drugs being marketed, that roughly half would ultimately be brought within the DESI Review, but that approximately 2400 would never be subject to the DESI Review. In July 1984, FDA submitted to Congress a computer-generated list from the Drug Listing System of products that it thought fell into this category at that time, and in September 1987 it prepared a second list. Both lists were substantially incomplete. FDA's position that all non-DESI unapproved new drugs are illegal was upheld in *United States v. Hiland*, 909 F.2d 1114 (8th Cir. 1990), sustaining the criminal convictions of those responsible for marketing E–Ferol.

A few of the non-DESI unapproved new drugs were sufficiently important to prompt FDA to institute regulatory action to require NDAs. Three prominent examples are Digoxin, 39 Fed. Reg. 2491 (Jan. 22, 1974), 62 Fed. Reg. 43535 (Aug. 14, 1997); levothyroxine, 62 Fed. Reg. 43535 (Aug. 14, 1997); and exocrine pancreatic insufficiency products, 69 Fed. Reg. 23410 (Apr. 28, 2004). When FDA determined in its final OTC monograph for non-prescription wart remover drug products that no existing products were effective, the agency pulled all the prescription non-DESI unapproved new drugs from the market as well. 55 Fed. Reg. 33246 (Aug. 14, 1990). FDA has proposed to take the same regulatory action for all nonprescription and prescription skin bleaching drug products. 71 Fed. Reg. 51146 (Aug. 29, 2006). And the agency has opportunistically removed individual non-DESI unapproved new drugs from the market when taking enforcement action against them for other reasons, even while leaving equally illegal competitive products alone. *United States v. Sage Pharmaceuticals, Inc.*, 210 F.3d 475 (5th Cir. 2000). But no program has been established by FDA to review all of the non-DESI unapproved new drugs on a comprehensive or systematic basis.

In July 2002, FDA approved a section 505(b)(2) NDA for an extended release guaifenesin drug product, which was a non-DESI unapproved new drug. The company promptly requested FDA to take all of the other unapproved competitive products off the market, pursuant to the agency policy established in CPG 7132c.08. In October, FDA issued approximately 66 warning letters to implement its policy, prompting a citizen petition requesting that the agency reopen the DESI program to review all non-DESI unapproved new drugs on a systematic basis. FDA Docket No. 02P–0483 (Nov. 12, 2002). In February 2003, FDA issued a second letter to the 66 recipients of the October 2002 warning letters, providing a final date of November 30, 2003, by which all of the products had to be completely removed from the market.

FDA published a draft guidance and CPG to replace the September 1984 version in 68 Fed. Reg. 60702 (Oct. 23, 2003), and it announced the final version in 71 Fed. Reg. 33466 (June 9, 2006). The agency accompanied the June 2006 announcement with a determination that non-DESI unapproved carbinoxamine drug products had to be removed from the market within one month if they were intended for young children and within three months otherwise. 71 Fed. Reg. 33462 (June 9, 2006).

The companies who received the 66 FDA warning letters in October 2002 lobbied Congress to pass legislation barring FDA from taking enforcement action against them. They were not successful in this effort, but they did succeed in having a paragraph inserted in the House and Senate Reports accompanying the FDA appropriations legislation for fiscal year 2004. That paragraph requested a report from FDA regarding the feasibility and cost of the type of systematic review of non-DESI unapproved drugs that the citizen petition requested. H.R. Rep. 108–193, 108th Cong., 1st Sess. 86 (2003); S. Rep. No. 108–107, 108th Cong., 1st Sess. 157 (2003). FDA responded with a report dated July 2004 concluding that the approach advocated by the citizen petition would be "scientifically infeasible ... and the costs would be prohibitive." The Senate Appropriations Committee Reports for 2005 and 2006 therefore simply directed FDA to devise an alternative approach. S. Rep. No. 109–92, 109th Cong., 1st Sess. 155 (2005); S. Rep. No. 109–266, 109th Cong., 2d Sess. 146 (2006).

The purpose of the FDA policy at issue in the guaifenesin dispute is to provide an inducement for manufacturers of non-DESI unapproved new drugs to submit NDAs for these products, thus resulting in removal of competitive unapproved products from the market and a significant period of market exclusivity before these competitors can obtain their own approvals and come back on the market. This strategy, however, works only if FDA in fact takes immediate regulatory action to remove competitive products from the market once an NDA has been approved. Thus far, this has not occurred, and the niche drug industry that manufactures these products therefore remains skeptical about the FDA policy.

In 2006, after an article stated that almost two percent of prescriptions, or as many as 73 million, were for non-DESI unapproved new drugs, and two members of Congress sent letters to FDA demanding detailed information on this category of products, FDA announced a public workshop on the matter. *See* Justin Blum, *Drugs Slip Through FDA Cracks, Sell Unapproved by the Millions*, BLOOMBERG NEWS (Oct. 11, 2006); letters from Senator Charles E. Grassley & Representative Edward J. Markey to Andrew C. von Eschenbach, FDA Acting Commissioner (Oct. 11, 2006); 71 Fed. Reg. 64284 (Nov. 1, 2006) (announcing January 2007 workshop).

NOTES

1. *Exocrine Pancreatic Insufficiency Drugs.* In 1995, when FDA issued its final determination that all nonprescription exocrine pancreatic insufficiency drugs have not been determined to be safe and effective, 50 Fed. Reg. 46594 (Nov. 8, 1985), 56 Fed. Reg. 32282 (July 15, 1991), 60 Fed. Reg. 20162 (Apr. 24, 1995), it stated that similar non-DESI unapproved new drug products marketed by prescription should also have an approved NDA and promised to address the subject further in a future Federal Register notice. It was ten years before FDA returned to this matter and required NDAs for the prescription products. 69 Fed. Reg. 23410 (Apr. 28, 2004). Manufacturers were given four years to obtain an approved NDA.

2. *Hormone Drugs.* In 68 Fed. Reg. 17953 (Apr. 14, 2003), FDA published a notice of opportunity for hearing on the removal of estrogen-androgen combination drugs and other non-DESI unapproved hormone drugs remaining on the market without an NDA. No further action has been taken on this matter.

3. *Increase in Non–DESI Unapproved New Drugs.* Because FDA did nothing to implement its 1984 CPG, the number of non-DESI unapproved new drugs has grown from the estimated 2400 at that time to about 12,000–16,000 at the present. It is these drugs that have fueled the growth of the niche drug industry in the United States.

4. *Lanham Act Cases.* It has become common for generic drug companies to market "generic" versions of "branded" non-DESI unapproved new drugs, because there is no need to obtain FDA approval of an abbreviated NDA, and the cost of knocking off the "branded" non-DESI unapproved new drug is thus trivial. Not surprisingly, the "generic" version is promoted as equivalent to the "branded" drug and soon cannibalizes its market. In order to preserve its market, the "branded" version of the drug is forced to initiate protracted litigation, with highly unpredictable results. *E.g., Florida Breckenridge, Inc. v. Solvay Pharmaceuticals, Inc.,* 174 F.3d 1227 (11th Cir. 1999); *Ethex Corp. v. First Horizon Pharmaceutical Corp.,* 228 F. Supp. 2d 1048 (E.D. Mo. 2002); *Healthpoint, Ltd. v. Stratus Pharmaceuticals, Inc.,* 273 F. Supp. 2d 769 (W.D. Tex. 2001); *Healthpoint, Ltd. v. Ethex Corp.,* 273 F. Supp. 2d 817 (W.D. Tex. 2001); *Healthpoint, Ltd. v. Ethex Corp.,* 2001 WL 34897840 & 34907460 (W.D. Tex. 2001); *Sirius Laboratories, Inc. v. Rising Pharmaceuticals, Inc.,* 2004 WL 51240 (N.D. Ill. 2004); *Solvay Pharmaceuticals, Inc. v. Global Pharmaceuticals,* 298 F. Supp. 2d 880 (D. Minn. 2004); *Solvay Pharmaceuticals, Inc. v. Ethex Corp.,* 2004 WL 742033 (D. Minn. 2004); *Healthpoint, Ltd. v. Ethex Corp.,* 2004 WL 2359420 & 2359509 (W.D. Tex. 2004); *Healthpoint, Ltd. v. River's Edge Pharmaceuticals, LLC,* 2005 WL 356839 (W.D. Tex. 2005); *Schwarz Pharma, Inc. v. Breckenridge Pharmaceutical, Inc.,* 388 F. Supp. 2d 967 (E.D. Wis. 2005); *Pediamed Pharmaceuticals, Inc. v. Breckinridge Pharmaceutical, Inc.,* 419 F. Supp. 2d 715 (D. Md. 2006); *Solvay Pharmaceuticals, Inc. v. Global Pharmaceuticals,* 419 F. Supp. 2d

1133 (D. Minn. 2006); *Solvay Pharmaceuticals, Inc. v. Ethex Corp.*, 2006 WL 738095 & 2255375 (D. Minn. 2006).

5. *Judicial Criticism.* In one case involving two non-DESI unapproved new drugs, the Court of Appeals criticized both parties for failing to inform the District Court that neither drug was the subject of an approved NDA. *Florida Breckenridge, Inc. v. Solvay Pharmaceuticals, Inc.*, 174 F.3d 1227 (11th Cir. 1999).

6. *FD&C Act Preemption.* In *Autin v. Solvay Pharmaceuticals, Inc.*, 2006 WL 889423 (W.D. Tenn. 2006), the District Court dismissed a consumer suit alleging that the company's non-DESI unapproved new drug, Estratest, was being illegally marketed, on the ground that the FD&C Act preempted the suit.

7. *Levothyroxine.* In 62 Fed. Reg. 43535 (Aug. 14, 1997), FDA announced that NDAs would be required for all currently marketed orally administered levothyroxine sodium drug products. The original deadline of August 14, 2000 was extended by a year in 65 Fed. Reg. 24488 (Apr. 26, 2000). Following approval of an NDA for one of these products, Unithroid, FDA posted on its website information from the NDA that constituted trade secrets. Thereafter, FDA again postponed the NDA deadline for an additional two years. 66 Fed. Reg. 36794 (July 13, 2001). The manufacturer of Unithroid, Jerome Stevens Pharmaceuticals, brought suit against FDA challenging the further delay and seeking damages for disclosure of trade secrets. In *Jerome Stevens Pharmaceuticals, Inc. v. FDA*, 402 F.3d 1249 (D.C. Cir. 2005), the Court of Appeals affirmed the District Court's dismissal of the count relating to FDA's continuing extension of time for competitors to submit NDAs, but it reversed the dismissal of the counts relating to unlawful disclosure of the company's trade secrets. Knoll, the original manufacturer of the leading levothyroxine drug, Synthroid, and Abbott Laboratories, the company that purchased Knoll, missed the original deadline for submitting an NDA. On July 12, 2001 FDA ordered Abbott to cut its distribution of Synthroid pills to wholesalers as a novel penalty for missing the deadline. *See* Gardiner Harris, *Abbott Pushes Its Synthroid, But Should It?*, WALL ST. J., July 17, 2002, at B1.

8. *Digoxin.* When Bertek Pharmaceutical obtained an approved NDA for digoxin and FDA failed to remove competitive unapproved digoxin products from the market, the company sued the agency, requesting a declaratory judgment and injunctive relief. The parties agreed to a consent decree in the form of a declaratory judgment that FDA would take action against the unapproved products "within a reasonable time." *Bertek Pharmaceuticals Inc. v. Henney*, Civ. No. 1:00CV02393 (D.D.C. October 4, 2000).

9. *Criteria For NDAs.* In letters from FDA CDER Director Steven Galson to Peter Barton Hutt dated May 25, 2005 and December 23, 2005, FDA promised not to target a firm or a marketed non-DESI unapproved drug for enforcement action simply because the firm meets with FDA to discuss an NDA for the product. The agency expressed a flexible procedure to discuss NDAs for these products.

f. HOMEOPATHIC DRUGS

The concept of homeopathy was invented by Samuel Hahnemann in the late 1700s. Homeopathy is based on the principle that "like cures like" and thus that a drug that produces symptoms in a healthy subject is capable of curing the illness underlying the same symptoms in a sick patient. This concept came to be known as the "law of similars." Homeopathic drugs are subject to "provings," in which healthy volunteers take doses of the agent and record their symptoms to help establish the drug's full remedy picture.

Homeopathic drugs were not mentioned in the Federal Food and Drugs Act of 1906. Because Senator Royal S. Copeland, M.D., the Senate sponsor during 1933–1938 of the legislation that ultimately became the FD&C Act, was a homeopathic physician, the Homeopathic Pharmacopeia was included in section 501(b) of the 1938 Act as one of the three official drug compendia recognized by statute. *See generally* Natalie Robins, Copeland's Cure: Homeopathy and The War Between Conventional And Alternative Medicine (2005). Although this single reference to the Homeopathic Pharmacopeia does not technically require FDA to exempt homeopathic drugs from any of the drug provisions of the FD&C Act, FDA has as a practical matter always interpreted it that way.

By 1972, when FDA initiated its OTC Drug Review, homeopathic drugs had almost disappeared from the United States market. FDA could locate only five homeopathic pharmacies in the entire country, and no other drug stores sold homeopathic drugs. FDA therefore exempted homeopathic drugs from the Review. Three factors have contributed to the remarkable growth in homeopathic drugs since that decision was made. First, all forms of complementary and alternative medicine have had a resurgence in public interest, as individuals seek more natural and holistic approaches to personal health. For example, the March 2002 publication of a final report by the White House Commission on Complimentary and Alternative Medicine Policy led to the establishment of an Office of Complementary and Alternative Medicine in the National Institutes of Health. Second, FDA has, as a matter of policy, not required NDAs for homeopathic drugs and has declined to take action against homeopathic drugs directly competing with drug products that are subject to an approved NDA. *See, e.g.*, Citizen Petition, FDA Docket No. 98P–0084/CP1 (Feb. 10, 1998) (complaining to FDA about a homeopathic drug for smoking cessation, marketed in competition with drugs for that indication approved through the NDA process). Third, because homeopathic drugs were also exempted from the FDA OTC Drug Review, their manufacturers need not be concerned about compliance with an OTC drug monograph.

In 1988, as commercial and public interest in homeopathic drugs rose, FDA published Compliance Policy Guide No. 7132.15, stating its regulatory position on these products. The CPG imposed the same labeling and manufacturing requirements on OTC and prescription homeopathic drugs as those that apply to allopathic drugs, but it did not mention compliance with OTC drug monographs or with the IND/NDA approval system. The FDA policy has not changed since this CPG was issued.

NOTES

1. *FDA Jurisdiction.* FDA's authority to regulate homeopathic drugs was confirmed in *United States v. Writers & Research, Inc.*, 113 F.3d 8 (2d Cir. 1997).

2. *Congressional Hearings.* Following the revelation that a large portion of Americans use various forms of complementary and alternative medicine, Congress held hearings to explore this area of health care. *See* "Patient Access to Alternative Treatments: Beyond the FDA," Hearings before the House Committee on Government Reform and Oversight, 105th Cong., 2d Sess. (1998); "Complementary and

Alternative Medicine in Government–Funded Health Programs," Hearing before the House Committee on Government Reform, 106th Cong., 1st Sess. (1999).

3. *Commentary.* For discussions of FDA regulation of homeopathic drugs, *see* Ayla A. Lari, *FDA Regulation Of Homeopathy: Past, Present, and Future* (1996) and Rebecca J. Gelfond, *Regulating Homeopathic Drugs: Pragmatic Solutions for the Food and Drug Administration* (1999), in Chapter VI(J)(1) of the Electronic Book; Susan White Junod, *Homeopathy, Royal Copeland, and Federal Drug Regulation*, 42 PHARMACY IN HIST. 13 (2000).

g.   TRADITIONAL CHINESE MEDICINE

Like homeopathy, traditional Chinese medicine (TCM) is a form of complementary and alternative medicine. TCM drugs have long been sold in the United States, almost exclusively in Chinese pharmacies. They are labeled in Chinese and bear little or none of the labeling information the FD&C Act requires for drugs. No TCM drug has ever been approved by FDA through an NDA, and none has been considered under the OTC Drug Review. FDA has traditionally ignored TCM products except when some type of safety problem has emerged. Because virtually all of these products come from China, the agency has simply informed the Chinese government whenever there has been a problem, and the shipment of the products has immediately stopped. Because there has been no interest in expanding TCM products beyond the traditional Chinese market, FDA has not found it necessary to issue a compliance policy guide or any other form of policy statement about these products.

NOTES

1. *Commentary.* See Enoh T. DeGraff, *FDA Regulation of Imported Non–Compliant Chinese Herbal Remedies* (1997), and Anna L. Kim, *Searching For A Cure: The FDA's Regulatory Approach to Traditional Chinese Herbal Medicine* (1997), in Chapter VI(J)(2) of the Electronic Book; Weishi Li, *Botanical Drugs: A Future for Herbal Medicines*, 19 J. CONTEMP. HEALTH L. & POL'Y 117 (2002); Shein–Chung Chow et al., *On Traditional Chinese Medicine Clinical Trials*, 40 DRUG INFO. J. 395 (2006).

2. *FDA Guidance for Botanical NDAs.* For several years, FDA promised to provide guidance on a flexible approach toward NDAs for botanical products. When this guidance was issued in 65 Fed. Reg. 49247 (Aug. 11, 2000), 69 Fed. Reg. 32359 (June 9, 2004), it was widely regarded as providing only slight relief from the normal NDA requirements. From 1982 to June 2006, FDA received 286 INDs for botanical drugs. After at least three companies tried and failed to develop botanical drugs through the IND/NDA process, the first botanical drug NDA—for Polyphenon E, an extract of green tea leaves for topical use to treat external and perianal genital warts—was approved on October 31, 2006. *See FDA Botanical Review Team Clears Green Tea–Based Drug As First Approval*, 14 TAN SHEET, No. 45, at 10 (Nov. 6, 2006).

3. *Dietary Supplements.* Some botanical ingredients used in TCM products have been marketed to the general public as dietary supplement products.

h.   SPECIFICALLY EXCLUDED PRODUCTS

As originally enacted, the FD&C Act contemplated substantial overlap among the various categories of products defined in the Act. In the intervening years, however, Congress has amended the Act to reduce this overlap.

Food: Under the Nutrition Labeling and Education Act of 1990, Congress added section 403(r)(i)(B) to the FD&C Act to authorize FDA to promulgate regulations permitting the use of disease claims in food labeling. *See supra* p. 284. In order to prevent these disease claims from converting the food into a drug, Congress also amended the drug definition in section 201(g)(i) to exclude these claims.

Dietary Supplements: In order to emphasize that dietary supplements are to be regulated as food and not as drugs, the Dietary Supplement Health and Education Act of 1994 included in the definition of a dietary supplement under section 201(ff) of the FD&C Act that these products are to be regulated as food unless they meet the definition of a drug, *i.e.,* unless they bear claims to prevent or treat disease.

Cosmetics: When the Drug Amendments of 1962 were enacted, Congress added section 509 to the FD&C Act to confirm that cosmetics are not drugs unless they meet the definition of a drug, *i.e.,* unless they bear claims to prevent or treat disease or to affect the structure or function of the human body.

Medical Devices: As part of the Medical Device Amendments of 1976, Congress revised the definition of a "device" in section 201(h) of the FD&C Act in order to differentiate between a drug and a device.

E.   NONCLINICAL FORMULATION AND TESTING

Before clinical (human) testing may begin on an investigational new drug, substantial nonclinical testing must be completed. FDA does not directly regulate nonclinical testing, but it indirectly affects all preclinical work because drug sponsors must ultimately conduct whatever nonclinical testing FDA determines to be necessary to justify allowing the drug to proceed to human testing. This initial phase of testing requires at least two years and can last much longer.

1.   SYNTHESIS AND PURIFICATION

The first step in the lengthy and costly process of the development of a new drug is the synthesis and purification of an active pharmaceutical ingredient (API).

Preclinical Research: Synthesis and Purification

In THE CDER HANDBOOK, *The New Drug Development and Review Process.*
FDA Website.

The research process is complicated, time-consuming, and costly and the end result is never guaranteed. Literally hundreds and sometimes thousands of chemical compounds must be made and tested in an effort to find one that can achieve a desirable result....

There is no standard route through which drugs are developed. A pharmaceutical company may decide to develop a new drug aimed at a specific disease or medical condition. Sometimes, scientists choose to pursue an interesting or promising line of research. In other cases, new findings from university, government, or other laboratories may point the way for drug companies to follow with their own research.

New drug research starts with an understanding of how the body functions, both normally and abnormally, at its most basic levels. The questions raised by this research help determine a concept of how a drug might be used to prevent, cure, or treat a disease or medical condition. This provides the researcher with a target. Sometimes, scientists find the right compound quickly, but usually hundreds or thousands must be screened. In a series of test tube experiments called assays, compounds are added one at a time to enzymes, cell cultures, or cellular substances grown in a laboratory. The goal is to find which additions show some effect. This process may require testing hundreds of compounds since some may not work, but will indicate ways of changing the compound's chemical structure to improve its performance.

Computers can be used to simulate a chemical compound and design chemical structures that might work against it. Enzymes attach to the correct site on a cell's membrane, which causes the disease. A computer can show scientists what the receptor site looks like and how one might tailor a compound to block an enzyme from attaching there. But even though computers give chemists clues as to which compounds to make, a substance must still be tested within a living being.

Another approach involves testing compounds made naturally by microscopic organisms. Candidates include fungi, viruses and molds, such as those that led to penicillin and other antibiotics. Scientists grow the microorganisms in what is known as a "fermentation broth," with one type of organism per broth. Sometimes, 100,000 or more broths are tested to see whether any compound made by a microorganism has a desirable effect.

It is important to purify and characterize the API even at this early stage, in order to make certain that nonclinical and clinical studies on the compound are conducted using the same active moiety.

2.   Nonclinical Testing

Prior to introducing an investigational drug into humans, nonclinical testing is conducted for three reasons. First, computer and animal modeling are pursued to obtain preliminary confirmation that the API has the potential for effectiveness. Second, chemical analysis and manufacturing controls are further refined to assure that the drug can be reliably reproduced. Third, toxicity testing in laboratory systems and in animals is essential to obtain sufficient safety data to justify human testing.

Preclinical Research

In The CDER Handbook, *The New Drug Development and Review Process.* FDA Website.

Under FDA requirements, a sponsor must first submit data showing that the drug is reasonably safe for use in initial, small-scale clinical studies. Depending on whether the compound has been studied or market-ed previously, the sponsor may have several options for fulfilling this requirement: (1) compiling existing nonclinical data from past *in vitro* laboratory or animal studies on the compound; (2) compiling data from previous clinical testing or marketing of the drug in the United States or another country whose population is relevant to the U.S. population; or (3) undertaking new preclinical studies designed to provide the evidence neces-sary to support the safety of administering the compound to humans.

During preclinical drug development, a sponsor evaluates the drug's toxic and pharmacologic effects through *in vitro* and *in vivo* laboratory animal testing. Genotoxicity screening is performed, as well as investiga-tions on drug absorption and metabolism, the toxicity of the drug's meta-bolites, and the speed with which the drug and its metabolites are excreted from the body. At the preclinical stage, the FDA will generally ask, at a minimum, that sponsors: (1) develop a pharmacological profile of the drug; (2) determine the acute toxicity of the drug in at least two species of animals, and (3) conduct short-term toxicity studies ranging from 2 weeks to 3 months, depending on the proposed duration of use of the substance in the proposed clinical studies.

NOTES

1. *FDA Guidance.* FDA has issued a GUIDANCE FOR INDUSTRY: NONCLINICAL SAFETY STUDIES FOR THE CONDUCT OF HUMAN CLINICAL TRIALS FOR PHARMACEUTICALS (1997). *See also* Geoff Goodfellow, *Nonclinical Safety Assessment of New Drugs and Therapeutic Proteins*, 10 REG. AFFAIRS FOCUS, No. 12, at 7 (Dec. 8, 2005).

2. *Animal Welfare.* All animal testing must be conducted in accordance with the requirements established in the Animal Welfare Act, 80 Stat. 350 (1966), 84 Stat. 1560 (1970), 7 U.S.C. Chapter 54, as implemented by USDA regulations in 9 C.F.R. Subchapter A. *See* Adam I. Mandelbaum, *The Origin and Development of the Animal Welfare Act* (1999), in Chapter I(J) of the Electronic Book.

3. *Animal Rights Activists.* Activists for animal rights, such as People for the Ethical Treatment of Animals and the Animal Liberation Front, believe that animals have the same rights as humans and should not be the subject of experimentation. *See, e.g.*, PETA, WASTED MONEY, WASTED LIVES: A LAY PERSON'S GUIDE TO THE PROBLEMS WITH RODENT CANCER STUDIES AND THE NATIONAL TOXICOLOGY PROGRAM (2006). Some activists have threatened scientists and their families, have raided laboratories to free test animals, and have engaged in other terrorist activities in order to dramatize their position. To protect companies and individuals against terrorism by animal rights activists, Congress enacted the Animal Enter-prise Protection Act of 1992, 106 Stat. 928, and the Animal Enterprise Terrorism Act, 120 Stat. 2652 (2006).

4. *Alternatives to Animal Testing.* In spite of substantial international effort to develop validated alternatives to animal toxicity testing, progress over the past two decades has been modest. *See* Richard A. Becker, et al., *Report of an ISRPT Workshop: Progress and Barriers to Incorporating Alternative Toxicological Methods in the U.S.*, 46 REG. TOXICOLOGY & PHARMACOLOGY 18 (Oct. 2006); Marisa B. Nye, *Progress Toward Replacing Animals in Toxicity Testing for Cosmetics* (2006), in Chapter I(J) of the Electronic Book.

5. *Federal Efforts to Establish Alternatives to Animal Testing.* In 2000, Con-gress enacted the ICCVAM Authorization Act, 114 Stat. 2721, formally recognizing

the previously-established Interagency Coordinating Committee on the Validation of Alternative Methods. The purpose of the ICCVAM is to identify and validate alternative testing methods. *See* 71 Fed. Reg. 66172 (Nov. 13, 2006) (requesting public comment on a five-year plan for ICCVAM).

3.   Good Laboratory Practices

In 1976, FDA discovered substantial fraud in a prominent animal testing laboratory. *See United States v. Keplinger*, 776 F.2d 678 (7th Cir. 1985). The agency subsequently established comprehensive good laboratory practice (GLP) regulations governing all forms of preclinical testing. 41 Fed. Reg. 51206 (Nov. 19, 1976), 43 Fed. Reg. 59986 (Dec. 22, 1978), 49 Fed. Reg. 43530 (Oct. 29, 1984), 52 Fed. Reg. 33768 (Sept. 4, 1987), codified at 21 C.F.R. Part 85. Any report of preclinical testing submitted with an IND or NDA must either comply with GLP or explain why compliance could not be achieved. The failure to comply may result in the report being rejected by FDA.

4.   Request for Designation

In many instances, the classification of a product as a "drug" under the FD&C Act and its regulation by the Center for Drug Evaluation and Research (CDER) are clear. However, because of the often uncertain jurisdictional lines that divide drugs, biological products, and medical devices—particularly when two of these categories are combined into a single product—FDA has in the past few years sought to clarify in what FDA center particular types of products are regulated and to establish a mechanism for determining the proper locus of regulation when it is unclear or disputed.

Beginning in the 1980s, the centers responsible for drugs, biological products, and medical devices entered into Intercenter Agreements with respect to their individual jurisdiction. These agreements, which have been revised over the years, are available on the FDA website. The FDA ombudsman was initially charged with responsibility for implementing the Intercenter Agreements.

As combination products became more numerous, however, Congress determined that the matter should be handled on a more comprehensive basis. The Safe Medical Devices Act of 1990 therefore added section 503(g) to the FD&C Act to require that FDA establish a mechanism for assigning combination products to particular FDA centers according to the products' "primary mode of action." In 1991, FDA issued regulations implementing this new statutory mandate. 56 Fed. Reg. 58754 (Nov. 11, 1991), codified at 21 C.F.R. Part 3. Under these regulations, the sponsor of any combination product may submit a request for designation (RFD) to clarify where the product is to be regulated within FDA. A letter of designation will then be issued within 60 days after the request is accepted for filing.

In many instances, companies find that it is more efficient to work informally with a particular center to determine where a product should be regulated rather than to submit a formal request for designation. Nonetheless, the existence of 21 C.F.R. Part 3 has helped greatly in clarifying the jurisdiction of the individual centers in situations in which disputes have slowed product development in the past. For a comprehensive review of the history and current status of this subject, *see* Danielle C. Schillinger, *The Office of Combination Products: Its Roots, Its Creation, and Its Role* (2005), in Chapter IX(A)(7) of the Electronic Book.

F. CLINICAL TESTING: INVESTIGATIONAL NEW DRUG APPLICATION

1. PURPOSE AND FORM OF THE IND

In order to market a new drug, a manufacturer must first obtain FDA approval of a new drug application (NDA). Before submitting an application, the manufacturer must conduct, or arrange to be conducted, clinical studies designed to demonstrate that the drug is safe and effective under the criteria established in section 505(d) of the FD&C Act. Usually this will require shipment of the drug in interstate commerce, *e.g.*, to researchers at medical schools across the country. But section 505(a) prohibits the shipment of any new drug for which FDA has not approved an NDA. To enable sponsors of new drugs to carry out the clinical testing necessary to support FDA approval of an NDA, Congress in section 505(i) permitted FDA to exempt a drug from this prohibition for the limited purpose of conducting clinical investigations.

Before the submission of an NDA, all new chemical entities used in prescription drugs introduced in this country are required to go through the investigational new drug (IND) process outlined in the following materials. The clinical investigation of a new chemical entity (NCE) new drug requires five to ten years. It is often estimated that, for every 5,000 chemicals screened, five will proceed to clinical testing and one will survive to approval of an NDA. And for every 100 drugs for which an IND is submitted to FDA, 70 will successfully complete Phase I clinical testing and proceed to Phase II, 33 will proceed to Phase III, and 20 will be approved for marketing.

NOTES

1. *Development of IND Regulations.* Prior to 1962, the IND regulations were brief and basic. No IND application was required to be submitted to FDA. Following enactment of the Drug Amendments of 1962, FDA promulgated extensive regulations governing the submission and review of an IND and the obligations of sponsors and investigators. 27 Fed. Reg. 7990 (Aug. 10, 1962), 28 Fed. Reg. 179 (Jan. 8, 1963). Twenty years later, as part of the IND–NDA review undertaken when the attempt to revise all of section 505 under the Drug Regulation Reform legislation of 1977–1980 failed, FDA promulgated the current IND regulations. 44 Fed. Reg. 58919 (Oct. 12, 1979), 48 Fed. Reg. 26720 (June 9, 1983), 52 Fed. Reg. 8798 (Mar. 19, 1987), codified at 21 C.F.R. Part 312.

2. *Responsibility to Test.* The FD&C Act places responsibility for testing new drugs on the manufacturer who desires FDA approval for marketing. Manufacturers in turn fund independent medical experts, most of whom are affiliated with teaching hospitals, to conduct these tests. Suspicion of manufacturer bias has

prompted some critics of FDA and of the industry to advocate that responsibility for testing be removed from private hands and taken over by the government or some other independent testing institution.

3. *Exemptions.* Under 21 C.F.R. 312.2(b), FDA exempts from the requirement of an IND a clinical investigation of a drug product that is already lawfully marketed in the U.S. if it meets five conditions. In 21 C.F.R. 312.2(d), FDA exempts from the requirements of an IND the use of an approved new drug for an unlabeled indication in the practice of medicine. FDA has adopted a guidance for industry on IND Exemptions for Studies of Lawfully Marketed Cancer Drug or Biological Products. 67 Fed. Reg. 17078 (Apr. 9, 2002) (availability of draft guidance), 68 Fed. Reg. 53984 (Sept. 15, 2003) (availability of guidance).

4. *Form of IND.* The IND form is set forth in 21 C.F.R. 312.23.

5. *Date of Effectiveness.* An IND goes into effect under 21 C.F.R. 312.40(b)(1) 30 days after FDA receives it, unless FDA notifies the sponsor that the IND is subject to a clinical hold. In many instances, FDA officials will raise informal questions about an IND within the 30-day post-submission period but will not institute a formal clinical hold. Companies often delay starting a clinical trial until these informal discussions are completed.

6. *Oversight of Clinical Investigators.* Because FDA has often encountered fraudulent reporting of clinical studies of investigational new drugs, the IND regulations provide for disqualification of clinical investigators. 21 C.F.R. 312.70. FDA has recommended criminal prosecution of several clinical investigators for violation of the False Reports to the Government Act, 18 U.S.C. 1001. *See, e.g., United States v. Smith,* 740 F.2d 734 (9th Cir. 1984); "New Jersey Doctor Pleads Guilty to Drug Testing Fraud," FDA Talk Paper No. P88–78 (Oct. 25, 1988). *United States v. Garfinkel,* 29 F.3d 1253 (8th Cir. 1994), upheld the conviction of a physician who engaged in fraud while conducting a clinical trial under 18 U.S.C. 1001, which prohibits false statements to the government, and 18 U.S.C. 1341 & 1346, the mail fraud statute. The agency has also initiated prosecutions for fraudulent animal testing of new drugs. *See, e.g., United States v. Keplinger,* 776 F.2d 678 (7th Cir. 1985). In 47 Fed. Reg. 52228 (Nov. 19, 1982), FDA published guidelines for reinstating previously disqualified clinical investigators.

7. *Financial Disclosure.* To minimize bias in clinical studies, FDA regulations require the disclosure of the financial arrangements between sponsors and clinical investigators and of any financial interests the clinical investigators have in the product under study or in the sponsor of the study. 59 Fed. Reg. 48708 (Sept. 23, 1994), 63 Fed. Reg. 5233 (Feb. 2, 1998), codified at 21 C.F.R. Part 54. *See* Kevin W. Williams, *Managing Physician Financial Conflicts of Interest in Clinical Trials Conducted in the Private Practice Setting,* 59 Food & Drug L.J. 45 (2004).

8. *FDA Power to Mandate Testing.* FDA has no authority to require any person to investigate a new drug, however promising the drug may be, nor can any citizen compel FDA or the federal government to undertake studies of a drug or to permit a drug to be made available for treatment. *E.g., Marinoff v. Department of HEW,* 456 F. Supp. 1120 (S.D.N.Y. 1978); *Kulsar v. Ambach,* 598 F. Supp. 1124 (W.D.N.Y. 1984); *DeVito v. HEM, Inc.,* 705 F. Supp. 1076 (M.D. Pa. 1988); *National Gay Rights Advocates v. United States Department of HHS,* Food Drug Cosm. L. Rep. (CCH) ¶ 38,080 (D.D.C. 1988). Patients are required to follow the same drug approval process as pharmaceutical companies. *Duncan v. United States,* 590 F. Supp. 39 (W.D. Okla. 1984). For an understanding of the frustration felt by physicians and patients when a manufacturer declines to develop what they believe is a promising drug, see Amy Dockser Marcus, *Different Rx: A Doctor's Push for Drug Pits Him Against Its Maker,* Wall St. J., Nov. 13, 2006, at. A1.

9. *CDER Guidance.* CDER issues a very large number of guidances about specific and general subjects involving the investigation and development of new drugs. In addition to following the FDA Good Guidance Practice (GGP) Policy, 62 Fed. Reg. 8961 (Feb. 27, 1997), 65 Fed. Reg. 56468 (Sept. 19, 2000), 21 C.F.R. 10.115, CDER has its own process for developing guidance. CDER Manual of Policies and Procedures (MAPP) No. 4000.2. CDER MAPP No. 6030.1 (May 1, 1998) governs *IND Process and Review Procedures.*

10. *Consent of Test Subjects.* Section 505(i) requires that FDA's regulations condition the IND exemption upon assurance by the sponsor of an investigation that all investigators

> will inform any human beings to whom such drugs, or any controls used in connection therewith, are being administered, or their representatives, that such drugs are being used for investigational purposes and will obtain the consent of such human beings or their representatives, except where they deem it not feasible or, in their professional judgment, contrary to the best interests of such human beings.

Based upon this language, and the remainder of section 505(i), FDA has established an elaborate system of controls over the conduct of clinical drug investigations. The present regulations, which require written consent of test subjects in virtually all cases and the approval of a local institutional review board (IRB) for any study conducted in an institutional setting, appear at 21 C.F.R. Part 312. In 1987, after a decade of consideration, FDA promulgated a comprehensive revision of these regulations. 48 Fed. Reg. 26720 (June 9, 1983), 52 Fed. Reg. 8798 (Mar. 19, 1987). In general, the new IND regulations codified existing practice and reorganized the old regulations to make them more easily understandable, but did little to reduce regulatory requirements or to speed up the investigation and approval of new drugs. *See generally* "Problems in Securing Informed Consent of Subjects in Experimental Trials of Unapproved Drugs and Devices," Hearing before the Subcommittee on Regulation, Business Opportunities, and Technology of the House Committee on Small Business, 103d Cong., 2d Sess. (1994); "Oversight of NIH and FDA: Bioethics and the Adequacy of Informed Consent," Hearing before the Subcommittee on Human Resources of the House Committee on Government Reform and Oversight, 105th Cong., 1st Sess. (1997); "Harnessing Science: Advancing Care by Accelerating the Rate of Cancer Clinical Trial Participation," Hearing before the House Committee on Government Reform, 108th Cong., 2d Sess. (2004).

11. *Discovery of IND Information.* In *United States v. Wood*, 57 F.3d 733 (9th Cir. 1995), the conviction of the defendants for a conspiracy to dispense an unapproved drug, GHB (the so-called "date rape drug"), was remanded because the contents of INDs that might have exonerated the defendants were not made available to them under a protective order. On remand, the District Court determined that the failure of the government to disclose the IND information was not prejudicial to Wood, a ruling summarily reversed by the Court of Appeals. 112 F.3d 518 (9th Cir. 1997).

2. MEETINGS WITH FDA

Perhaps the most important determinant of the success of the IND/NDA development process is the frequency and candor of meetings with FDA. Both experience and actual studies have determined that open communication with the agency is essential for an efficient and effective IND/NDA process.

Since enactment of the Drug Amendments of 1962, FDA policy regarding meetings with the pharmaceutical industry has varied from commissioner to commissioner. At some times, FDA has sought to distance itself from the regulated industry and thus to keep meetings both infrequent and formal. At other times, FDA has understood that meetings are essential to the regulatory process and has been more open and forthcoming in granting them.

In March 1996, CDER adopted MAPP No. 4512.4, governing formal meetings between CDER and the regulated industry. As part of the FDA Modernization Act of 1997, section 505(b)(4)(B) was added to the FD&C Act, directing FDA to meet with the pharmaceutical industry for the purpose of reaching agreement on the design and size of clinical trials intended to form the primary basis for NDA approval. This provision, which resulted in the FDA Special Protocol Assessment (SPA) program, is discussed further at page 637, *infra*. The pharmaceutical industry also reached agreement with FDA in conjunction with the 1997 reauthorization of the Prescription Drug User Fee Act (PDUFA) on specific performance goals for the management of meetings. As a result, in February 2000 FDA issued the following guidance.

Guidance for Industry: Formal Meetings With Sponsors and Applicants for PDUFA Products

(2000).

. . . .

There are three categories of meetings between sponsors or applicants for PDUFA products and CDER or CBER staff: Type A; Type B; and Type C. Each type of meeting will be subject to different procedures, as described below.

A.   *Type A Meeting*

A Type A meeting is one that is immediately necessary for an otherwise stalled drug development program to proceed (*i.e.*, a *critical path* meeting).

Type A meetings generally will be reserved for dispute resolution meetings, meetings to discuss clinical holds, and special protocol assessment meetings that are requested by sponsors after FDA's evaluation of protocols in assessment letters . . . .

B.   *Type B Meeting*

Type B meetings are (1) pre-IND meetings (21 CFR 312.82), (2) certain end of Phase I meetings (21 CFR 312.82), (3) end of Phase 2/pre-Phase 3 meetings (21 CFR 312.47), and (4) pre-NDA/BLA meetings (21 CFR 312.47) . . . .

C.   *Type C Meeting*

A Type C meeting is any meeting other than a Type A or Type B meeting between FDA and a sponsor or applicant regarding the development and review of a product in a human drug application as described in section 735(1) of the Act [added by PDUFA]. Meetings that do not pertain to the review of human drug applications for PDUFA products (*e.g.*, most meetings about advertising and promotional labeling for approved drug products except meetings about launch activities and materials, postmarketing safety evaluation meetings) are not Type C meetings and are not addressed in this guidance document. . . .

NOTES

1. *Schedule for Meetings*. Under the guidance, a Type A meeting will occur within 30 days, Type B within 60 days, and Type C within 75 days.

2. *Additional Guidance*. The guidance, in addition to establishing the three types of meetings, gives detailed advice regarding procedures for requesting meetings, the information to be included in a request, the timing of the submission of information for the meeting, procedures for the conduct of meetings, documentation by minutes, and dispute resolution.

3. *Criticism of the FDA Meeting Policy*. Critics have argued that the 30, 60, and 75–day wait for a meeting with FDA is unconscionably long. No private business would ever conduct discussion on that type of lengthy schedule. The impact on the cost of new drugs is substantial. If one of the roughly 2000 small biotechnology companies in the United States must wait two months to discuss a protocol with FDA, and the company's burn rate (*i.e.*, the amount of money needed simply to keep the doors open) is $1 million per month, the cost of just a simple meeting with FDA is $2 million. And if, as often happens, a second meeting is needed, the cost becomes extremely high. Indeed, the cost of meetings with FDA to discuss a protocol for a clinical trial can exceed the cost of the clinical trial itself. Because it is essential to meet with FDA to discuss clinical protocols, however, pharmaceutical companies have no option other than to follow the February 2000 guidance.

3. PHASES OF CLINICAL TESTING

At one time, clinical testing proceeded through three very distinct and separate phases: Phases I, II, and III. In recent years, however, the distinctions between these phases have broken down. Some trials have characteristics of two phases at the same time. Nonetheless, it is useful to describe the basic concepts of these three phases—as well as the new Phase zero—to understand the types of clinical trials that must be undertaken in order to obtain sufficient safety and effectiveness information for NDA approval.

a. PHASE ZERO

FDA created a new category of clinical trial, termed "exploratory IND studies," in the following draft guidance, announced in 70 Fed. Reg. 19764 (Apr. 14, 2005).

Draft Guidance for Industry, Investigators, and Reviewers: Exploratory IND Studies
(2005).

. . . .

For purposes of this guidance the phrase *exploratory IND study* is intended to describe a clinical trial that occurs very early in phase I, involves very limited human exposure, and has no therapeutic intent (*e.g.*, screening studies, microdose studies). Such exploratory IND studies are conducted prior to the traditional dose escalation, safety, and tolerance studies that ordinarily initiate a clinical drug development program. The duration of dosing in an exploratory IND study is expected to be limited (*e.g.*, 7 days). This guidance applies to early phase I clinical studies involving investigational new drug and biological products that assess feasibility for further development for a drug or biological product.

Typically, during pharmaceutical development, large numbers of molecules are generated in very small quantities with goal of identifying the most promising candidates for further development. These molecules are generally related in some way, either as a single active ingredient with multiple salts or esters, or closely related active moieties. Promising candidates are often selected using in vitro testing models that examine binding to receptors, effects on enzyme activities, toxic effects, or other in vitro pharmacological parameters. Candidates that are not rejected during these early tests are prepared in greater quantities for in vivo animal testing for efficacy and safety. Commonly, a single candidate is selected for an IND application and introduction into human subjects, often healthy volunteers.

Before the human studies can begin, an IND must be submitted to the Agency containing, among other things, information on any risks anticipated based on the results of pharmacological and toxicological data collected during studies of the drug in animals (21 CFR 312.23(a)(8)). These basic safety tests are most often performed in rats and dogs. The studies are designed to permit the selection of a safe starting dose for humans, to gain an understanding of which organs may be the targets of toxicity, to estimate the margin of safety between a clinical and a toxic dose, and to predict pharmacokinetic and pharmacodynamic parameters. These early tests are usually resource intensive, requiring significant investment in product synthesis, animal use, laboratory analyses, and time. Many resources are invested in, and thus wasted on, drug candidates that subsequently are found to have unacceptable profiles when evaluated in humans. Fewer than 10 percent of INDs for new molecular entities (NME) progress beyond the investigational stage. In addition, animal testing does not always predict performance in humans, and potentially effective candidates may not be developed because of resource constraints.

Existing regulations allow a great deal of flexibility in terms of the amount of data that need to be submitted with any IND application, depending on the goals of an investigation, the specific human testing being proposed, and the expected risks. The Agency believes that sponsors have not taken full advantage of that flexibility. As a result, limited, early phase I studies, such as those described in this guidance, are often supported by a more extensive preclinical database than is required by regulations. This guidance is intended to clarify what preclinical and clinical approaches (including chemistry, manufacturing, and controls) should be considered when planning exploratory IND studies in humans, including studies of closely related drugs or therapeutic biological products, under an investigational new drug (IND) application (21 CFR 312).

Exploratory IND studies ... can help sponsors

- Gain an understanding of the relationship between a specific mechanism of action and the treatment of a disease
- Provide important information on pharmacokinetics, including, for example, biodistribution of a candidate drug
- Select the most promising lead product from a group of candidates designed to interact with a particular therapeutic target in humans
- Explore a product's biodistribution characteristics using various imaging technologies.

Whatever the goal of the study, exploratory IND studies can help identify, early in the process, promising candidates for continued development, and eliminate those lacking promise. As a result, exploratory IND studies may help reduce the number of human subjects and resources, including the amount of candidate product, needed to select promising drugs....

b. PHASE I

Phase I Clinical Studies

In THE CDER HANDBOOK, *The New Drug Development and Review Process.*
FDA Website.

Phase 1 includes the initial* introduction of an investigational new drug into humans. These studies are closely monitored and may be conducted in patients, but are usually conducted in healthy volunteer subjects. These studies are designed to determine the metabolic and pharmacologic actions of the drug in humans, the side effects associated with increasing doses, and, if possible, to gain early evidence on effectiveness. During Phase 1, sufficient information about the drug's pharmacokinetics and pharmacological effects should be obtained to permit the design of well-controlled, scientifically valid, Phase 2 studies.

Phase 1 studies also evaluate drug metabolism, structure-activity relationships, and the mechanism of action in humans. These studies also determine which investigational drugs are used as research tools to explore biological phenomena or disease processes. The total number of subjects included in Phase 1 studies varies with the drug, but is generally in the range of twenty to eighty.

NOTES

1. *Phase I Safety.* Phase I is regarded as the safest phase of human testing, because it customarily begins with low doses and is conducted under close medical supervision. However, two recent Phase I incidents, involving one death and six very serious adverse events, have served to remind clinical pharmacologists that

---

* [This description was prepared before the development by FDA of Phase zero.]

human experimentation with highly active modern drugs can produce unexpected toxic reactions. S.E. Raper et al., *Fatal Systemic Inflammatory Response Syndrome in an Ornithine Transcarbanylase Deficient Patient Following Adenoviral Gene Transfer*, 80 MOLECULAR GENETICS METABOLISM 148 (2003) (the death of Jesse Gelsinger at the University of Pennsylvania); Ganesh Suntharalingam et al., *Cytokine Storm in a Phase I Trial of the Anti–CD28 Monoclonal Antibody TGN1412*, 355 NEW ENG. J. MED. 1018 (Sept. 7, 2006) (serious adverse reactions in six healthy volunteers in England).

2.   *Reasons for Clinical Hold.* In Phase I studies, CDER can impose a clinical hold (*i.e.*, prohibit the study from proceeding or stop a trial that has started) for reasons of safety, or because of a sponsor's failure accurately to disclose the risk of the study to investigators. Although CDER often provides advice on nonsafety aspects of protocols, investigators may choose to ignore any advice regarding the design of Phase I studies in areas other than patient safety.

3.   *Deregulation of Phase I.* It has been proposed that regulation of Phase I clinical testing be subject only to IRB supervision, and that an IND be required only for Phases II and III. *See* Kingsley L. Taft, *Deregulation of Investigational New Drug Applications* (1996), in Chapter VI(C)(1) of the Electronic Book.

c.   PHASE II

Phase II Clinical Studies

In THE CDER HANDBOOK, *The New Drug Development and Review Process.*
FDA Website.

Phase 2 includes the early controlled clinical studies conducted to obtain some preliminary data on the effectiveness of the drug for a particular indication or indications in patients with the disease or condition. This phase of testing also helps determine the common short-term side effects and risks associated with the drug. Phase 2 studies are typically well-controlled, closely monitored, and conducted in a relatively small number of patients, usually involving several hundred people.

d.   PHASE III

Phase III Clinical Studies

In THE CDER HANDBOOK, *The New Drug Development and Review Process.*
FDA Website.

Phase 3 studies are expanded controlled and uncontrolled trials. They are performed after preliminary evidence suggesting effectiveness of the drug has been obtained in Phase 2, and are intended to gather the additional information about effectiveness and safety that is needed to evaluate the overall benefit-risk relationship of the drug. Phase 3 studies also provide an adequate basis for extrapolating the results to the general population and transmitting that information in the physician labeling. Phase 3 studies usually include several hundred to several thousand people.

In both Phase 2 and 3, CDER can impose a clinical hold if a study is unsafe (as in Phase 1), or if the protocol is clearly deficient in design in meeting its stated objectives. Great care is taken to ensure that this determination is not made in isolation, but reflects current scientific knowledge, agency experience with the design of clinical trials, and experience with the class of drugs under investigation.

NOTES

1. *Government–Sponsored INDs.* The federal government has a long history of supporting academic and industry scientists in the development of new drugs and of licensing new drugs to industry for commercialization. *See, e.g.*, John P. Swann, *Biomedical Research and Government Support: The Case of Drug Development*, 31 PHARMACY IN HISTORY, No. 3, at 103 (1989). The National Cancer Institute (NCI) has participated in the development of a number of important anticancer drugs. The National Technical Information Service (NTIS) of the Department of Commerce and the National Institutes of Health regularly publish notices in the Federal Register of the availability of federal government patents on pharmaceutical products available for licensing and of exclusive licenses subsequently granted to pharmaceutical companies to develop the drugs involved. The exclusive license for a particularly important anticancer drug was renewed over the objections of competitors who argued that any license should be nonexclusive. 48 Fed. Reg. 5313 (Feb. 4, 1983), 48 Fed. Reg. 53177 (Nov. 25, 1983). NIH has made a number of potential AIDS drugs available for licensing. *E.g.*, 53 Fed. Reg. 40134 (Oct. 13, 1988), 54 Fed. Reg. 39815 (Sept. 28, 1989).

2. *Regulations Governing Drug Tests.* FDA proposed new regulations governing the responsibilities of sponsors and monitors of clinical investigations in 42 Fed. Reg. 49612 (Sept. 17, 1977) and new regulations governing the obligations of clinical investigators in 43 Fed. Reg. 35210 (Aug. 8, 1978), but they have never been promulgated in final form. A guideline for monitoring clinical investigators was made available in 53 Fed. Reg. 4723 (Feb. 17, 1988). Regulations governing institutional review boards were promulgated in 43 Fed. Reg. 35186 (Aug. 8, 1978), 44 Fed. Reg. 47713 (Aug. 14, 1979), 46 Fed. Reg. 8942 (Jan. 27, 1981), revising 21 C.F.R. Part 56. FDA has also published good laboratory practice (GLP) regulations governing preclinical testing of food additives, human drugs, and animal drugs. 41 Fed. Reg. 51206 (Nov. 19, 1976), 43 Fed. Reg. 59986 (Dec. 22, 1978), 49 Fed. Reg. 43530 (Oct. 29, 1984), 52 Fed. Reg. 33768 (Sept. 4, 1987), codified at 21 C.F.R. Part 58. In 1980, FDA issued regulations that sharply limit the use of prisoner volunteers in clinical testing of new drugs. 43 Fed. Reg. 19417 (May 5, 1978), 45 Fed. Reg. 36386 (May 30, 1980). *See generally* Richard F. Kingham, *History of FDA Regulation of Clinical Research*, 22 DRUG INFO. J. 151 (1988).

3. *Poison Prevention Packaging.* The Consumer Product Safety Commission (CPSC) administers the Poison Prevention Packaging Act (PPPA) and its regulations. These regulations require poison prevention packaging for all prescription drugs for human use intended for oral administration. 16 C.F.R. 1700.14(a)(10). The CPSC interprets this provision to apply to all investigational drugs whose clinical trials involve household use. *See* letter from Geri Niebauer, CPSC Compliance Officer, to Daphne Allen (June 22, 2000).

4. *No Constitutional Right to Investigational Drugs.* In *Dahl v. HEM Pharmaceuticals Corp.*, 7 F.3d 1399 (9th Cir. 1993), the plaintiffs contracted to enroll in a double-blind study of an investigational drug in return for a promise that, if the study found the drug to be effective, those on the drug would receive a free supply of the drug for a year after the test ended and those on placebo would be switched to the drug. At the conclusion of the study, FDA denied a treatment IND but allowed an open label study. The District Court ordered the defendant to honor the contract, and the Court of Appeals affirmed the decision. Absent an explicit

contractual provision stating that the trial will be continued or that the investigational drug will continue to be provided to the test subjects, however, no such obligation exists. *See, e.g., Abney v. Amgen, Inc.*, 443 F.3d 540 (6th Cir. 2006); *Suthers v. Amgen, Inc.*, 372 F. Supp. 2d 416 (S.D.N.Y. 2005), 441 F. Supp. 2d 478 (S.D.N.Y. 2006).

5. *Suits Against the Government.* An individual who was terminated from a federally funded clinical trial has no cause of action against the government or government employees. *Kraemer–Katz v. Public Health Service*, 872 F. Supp. 1235 (S.D.N.Y. 1994). The District Court went on to discuss the existence of compassionate use of investigational drugs for treatment purposes, however, and stated that a "federal agency's denial of permission to obtain such [investigational] medications would support standing to seek review of the decision."

6. *No "Practice of Medicine" Exemption.* In *Cowan v. United States*, 5 F. Supp. 2d 1235 (N.D. Okla. 1998), the District Court held that the "practice of medicine exception" from the IND/NDA requirements of the FD&C Act only applies to a drug substance that is subject to an approved NDA for a different use and that "[n]othing in the FDCA or the case law suggests that the exception was intended to be expanded to permit doctors to test unapproved drugs," citing *United States v. Algon Chemical, Inc.*, 879 F.2d 1154 (3d Cir. 1989).

7. *Ambiguity of FDA Role.* There has long been controversy over whether the FDA's responsibility is solely to protect the safety of human subjects or also to assure that the clinical protocol is adequately designed to yield data that can support ultimate approval of an NDA. The revised IND regulations, 21 C.F.R. 312.22(a), state:

> FDA's primary objectives in reviewing an IND are, in all phases of the investigation, to assure the safety and rights of subjects, and in Phase 2 and 3, to help assure that the quality of the scientific evaluation of drugs is adequate to permit an evaluation of the drug's effectiveness and safety.

This declaration notwithstanding, FDA reviewers often comment on the scientific adequacy of protocols for Phase I studies.

8. *Protocol Guidelines and Guidance.* Since enactment of the 1962 Drug Amendments, FDA has repeatedly stated that one of the major reasons for the length of time required for development and approval of new drugs has been the failure of sponsors and clinical investigators to utilize adequate protocols for clinical trials. The agency in the early 1970s began to develop model protocols for clinical trials for different therapeutic classes of drugs. To forestall concern that these model protocols would stifle innovation in clinical investigation, FDA initially issued the protocols as "guidelines." They are now issued as "guidance."

9. *Enriched Trials.* An "all-comers" clinical trial enrolls anyone in the trial who meets relatively general inclusion criteria, without regard to whether they are more or less likely to benefit from the investigational drug. In an enriched trial, however, the inclusion criteria are narrowed in an attempt to enroll only those patients who are most likely to benefit from the drug, with the intent of demonstrating a stronger proof of effectiveness with fewer people in the trial. Some enriched trials have an initial run-in period after which only the responders are randomized into the trial.

10. *Adaptive Trials.* In a traditional clinical trial, patients are randomized to one or more dose levels of the investigational drug or to a placebo (the "arms" of the trial), and no one knows which patients are on which regimen. In an adaptive trial, an independent Data Monitoring Committee (DMC) reviews the patient responses to their regimens and can alter the number of patients in each arm to reflect the interim results. If one arm shows poor results and another shows

excellent results, patients in the former arm can be added to the latter to obtain a faster and more reliable determination of effectiveness. There is controversy about how strongly FDA can rely on this trial design. *See* Bridget M. Kuehn, *Industry, FDA Warm to "Adaptive" Trials*, 296 J.A.M.A. 1955 (Oct. 25, 2006); PhRMA Working Group on Adaptive Designs, *White Paper* and related articles, 40 Drug Info. J. 421–84 (2006).

11. *Noninferiority Trials.* Rather than testing an investigational drug against a placebo, a noninferiority trial tests it against an approved effective agent. This is often required where use of a placebo would be unethical. If the investigational drug is shown to be superior, there is no issue. If it is only shown not to be inferior, however, there is scientific debate whether this is adequate for approval, because the investigational drug might be slightly less effective but still within the statistical definition of equivalence.

12. *Patient Reported Outcomes.* FDA issued Guidance for Industry: Patient-Reported Outcome Measures in 71 Fed. Reg. 5862 (Feb. 3, 2006) for studies intended to support the clinical effectiveness of a drug.

4.   Institutional Review Board Approval

There is a lengthy history of the development of protection of human subjects by FDA. When Congress enacted the Drug Amendments of 1962, it required in section 505(i)(4) that any IND be conditioned upon informed consent by human subjects. FDA initially implemented this obligation by publishing a statement of policy concerning consent for use of investigational new drugs on humans. 31 Fed. Reg. 11415 (Aug. 30, 1966). FDA promulgated more comprehensive Institutional Review Board (IRB) requirements by amending the IND regulations in 34 Fed. Reg. 13552 (Aug. 22, 1969), 36 Fed. Reg. 5037 (Mar. 17, 1971). The agency later promulgated a separate set of institutional review regulations to cover all clinical investigations subject to FDA jurisdiction. 43 Fed. Reg. 35186 (Aug. 8, 1978), 46 Fed. Reg. 8942, 8958 (Jan. 27, 1981), codified at 21 C.F.R. Parts 50, 56. *See* Christi J. Williams, *A History of Institutional Review at the U.S. Food and Drug Administration: 1960–2001* (2001), in Chapter VI(C)(1) of the Electronic Book.

21 C.F.R. Part 56 establishes the functions and operations of an IRB, required records and reports, and FDA administrative action for noncompliance with the regulations. Over the quarter century since these regulations were promulgated, the duties and responsibilities of IRBs have substantially increased. Whereas once an IRB simply reviewed a protocol to assure that the clinical testing met ethical standards, today an IRB is expected to give a much harder look at protocols, assure that the written informed consent form is sufficiently simple and clear to be understood by the test subjects, monitor the progress of the testing, and maintain substantial records of these activities. An IRB must meet in person, not by telephone, and must devote substantial time to its responsibilities.

NOTES

1. *Commentary. See* HHS Office of Inspector General, Institutional Review Boards: A Time for Reform, No. OEI–01–97–00193 (1998); Julie K. Taitsman, *Regulation of Informed Consent in Human Subject Research: Past, Present, and*

Future *(1998), and Michelle R. Wandler,* The History of the Informed Consent Requirement in United States Federal Policy *(2001), in Chapter VI(C)(1) of the Electronic Book; Markus Schott,* Medical Research on Humans: Regulation in Switzerland, the European Union, and the United States of America, *60 FOOD & DRUG L.J. 45 (2005); Lars Noah,* Informed Consent and the Illusive Dicotomy Between Standard and Experimental Therapy, *28 AM. J.L. & MED. 361 (2002); Lars Noah,* Deputizing Institutional Review Boards to Police Biomedical Research, *25 J. LEGAL MED. 267 (2004).*

2. *IND Deregulation.* Some have argued that Phase I studies should only require approval by a local IRB. This is the approach used for investigational studies of non-significant risk medical devices. *See infra* p. 1004; 21 C.F.R. 812.2. Although it entertained this possibility in its preamble to a proposed revision of the IND regulations, 48 Fed. Reg. 26720, 26722 (June 9, 1983), FDA expressed the preliminary view that the other changes might make it unnecessary. In the preamble to the final regulations, 52 Fed. Reg. 8798, 8805–8806 (Mar. 19, 1987), the agency concluded that the issue required additional study. *See* Kingsley L. Taft, *Deregulation of Investigational New Drug Applications* (1996) in Chapter VI(C)(1) of the Electronic Book.

3. *Investigational Research on Prisoners.* In 45 Fed. Reg. 36386 (May 30, 1980) FDA promulgated regulations severely limiting the use of prisoners in drug clinical trials. FDA stayed the effective date of these regulations in 46 Fed. Reg. 35085 (July 7, 1981) and later reproposed them with fewer restrictions in 46 Fed. Reg. 61666 (Dec. 18, 1981), but then revoked the regulations completely in 61 Fed. Reg. 2192, 2194 (Jan. 25, 1996), 62 Fed. Reg. 39439, 39440 (July 23, 1997). The Department of HHS has promulgated regulations governing the use of prisoners as research subjects where the research is conducted or supported by the Department. 45 C.F.R. Part 46, Subpart C. *See generally* Institute of Medicine, *Ethical Considerations for Research Involving Prisoners* (2006).

4. *Recruiting Clinical Trial Subjects.* FDA has no regulations or guidance regarding the recruitment of individuals to participate in a clinical trial. Accordingly, the methods used to recruit trial subjects, the compensation to be paid them, and related matters are within the discretion of the IRB.

5. *IRB Ethical Standards.* Each IRB may impose its own ethical standards. It is not unusual for one IRB to approve a clinical trial that another IRB has disapproved. This is consistent with the concept that IRBs reflect local community ethical standards. *Biomedical Research,* 25 J. LEGAL MED. 267 (2004). FDA proposed in 67 Fed. Reg. 10115 (Mar. 6, 2002) to require that an IRB be informed of any prior IRB reviews, but then withdrew the proposal in 71 Fed. Reg. 2493 (Jan. 17, 2006).

6. *False Claims Act.* In *United States ex rel. Gross v. AIDS Research Alliance– Chicago,* 415 F.3d 601 (7th Cir. 2005), a clinical trial subject alleged fraudulent negligence by the IRB supervising the study. The Court of Appeals affirmed the District Court in dismissing the complaint for failure to plead negligence with specificity. *See also United States ex rel. Chandler v. Hektoen Institute for Medical Research,* 35 F. Supp. 2d 1078 (N.D. Ill. 1999), 118 F. Supp. 2d 902 (N.D. Ill. 2000); Joseph Corkery, *Primum Non Nocere: The Continuing Evolution of Safety Monitoring in Human Subjects Research* (2006), in Chapter VI(C)(1) of the Electronic Book.

7. *Inadequate Informed Consent.* In *Iron Cloud v. Sullivan,* Food Drug Cosm. L. Rep. (CCH) ¶ 38,287. (D.S. Dak. 1993), the District Court held that a person alleging that inadequate information was provided to participants in a clinical trial of a hepatitis A vaccine on Native American children had to request FDA action through a citizen petition before resorting to the courts. The Court of Appeals

declared the matter moot because the clinical trial was terminated before it heard the case. 984 F.2d 241 (8th Cir. 1993).

8. *Placebo–Controlled Trials.* There is a long-running debate about the ethics of using a placebo rather than an active drug as the control in a clinical trial. FDA adheres to the position that placebo-controlled trials are the gold standard. When the declaration of Helsinki was amended in October 2000 to require the use of an active control unless none exists, FDA issued a guidance stating that it would not adopt the October 2000 amendment.

9. *Investigational Drugs in the Military.* In advance of the 1991 Operation Desert Shield/Desert Storm military operations in Kuwait, FDA published, in response to a request from the Department of Defense, an interim final regulation authorizing the FDA Commissioner to determine that obtaining informed consent from individual military personnel is not feasible in specific situations involving combat or the immediate threat of combat. 55 Fed. Reg. 52814 (Dec. 21, 1990), codified at 21 C.F.R. 50.23(d). The regulation was upheld in *Doe v. Sullivan*, 756 F. Supp. 12 (D.D.C. 1991), *aff'd*, 938 F.2d 1370 (D.C. Cir. 1991). *See also* "Chemical and Biological Weapons Threat: The Urgent Need for Remedies," Hearings before the Senate Committee on Foreign Relations, 101st Cong., 1st Sess. (1989); Brenda Jarrell, *FDA Regulation and the Military: Is There a Compromise in the Battle Over Investigational Drugs* (1997), and Christopher J. Lovrien, *Investigational Drug Use Among the Troops: The Waiver of Informed Consent in Cases of Military Combat Exigencies* (1997), in Chapter VI(C)(1) of the Electronic Book.

10. *FDA Clinical Research.* In 2006, the Inspector General of HHS subjected the clinical research conducted by FDA to a critical review. OFFICE OF INSPECTOR GENERAL, REVIEW OF CORRECTIVE ACTIONS CONCERNING THE HUMAN SUBJECT RESEARCH PROGRAM, No. A–06–06–00042 (2006).

5.   THE CLINICAL HOLD

Although FDA has used clinical holds since 1962 to prevent trials from beginning or to stop trials that are already underway, the statutory authority for a clinical hold in section 505(i)(3) was not added to the FD&C Act until the FDA Modernization Act did so in 1997.

Clinical Hold Decision

In THE CDER HANDBOOK, *The New Drug Development and Review Process.*
FDA Website.

A clinical hold is the mechanism that CDER uses when it does not believe, or cannot confirm, that the study can be conducted without unreasonable risk to the subjects/patients. If this occurs, the Center will contact the sponsor within the 30–day initial review period to stop the clinical trial. CDER may either delay the start of an early-phase trial on the basis of information submitted in the IND, or stop an ongoing study based on a review of newly submitted clinical protocols, safety reports, protocol amendments, or other information. When a clinical hold is issued, a sponsor must address the issue that is the basis of the hold before the order is removed.

CDER's authority concerning clinical holds is outlined in Federal regulations. The regulations specify the clinical hold criteria that CDER applies to various phases of clinical testing. In addition, all clinical holds are reviewed by upper management of CDER to assure consistency and scientific quality in the Center's clinical hold decisions.

NOTES

1. *FDA Regulations.* The FDA regulations governing clinical holds and requests for modification are codified at 21 C.F.R. 312.42. CDER MAPP Nos. 6030.1 & 6031.1 govern FDA policy relating to the issuance, monitoring and resolution of clinical holds. Following enactment of section 505(i)(3) in 1997, FDA promulgated a direct final regulation in 63 Fed. Reg. 68676 (Dec. 14, 1998) amending 21 C.F.R. 312.42 to require that the agency respond to a request to lift a clinical hold within 30 days of receiving a complete response to the FDA clinical hold letter.

2. *FDA Guidance.* In 63 Fed. Reg. 26809 (May 14, 1998), FDA announced the availability of GUIDANCE FOR INDUSTRY: SUBMITTING AND REVIEWING COMPLETE RESPONSES TO CLINICAL HOLDS, which was updated in October 2000.

3. *Frequency of Clinical Holds.* Between 1980 and 1988, FDA placed between 5 and 15 percent of new commercial INDs on clinical hold. Letter from Robert Temple, Director, FDA CDER Office of Drug Evaluation, to Dr. E. Stonehill, National Cancer Institute (Sept. 28, 1989). In 55 Fed. Reg. 20802 (May 21, 1990), FDA proposed to expand its authority to impose clinical holds and to terminate an IND, for the stated purpose of exerting control over protocols for expanded use of investigational drugs in general and AIDS drugs in particular.

6. SPECIAL PROTOCOL ASSESSMENT

For the first 35 years of operating under the Drug Amendments of 1962, the pharmaceutical industry was constantly frustrated by what came to be known as the "moving target syndrome," *i.e.*, repeated changes in agency advice about the studies needed to obtain FDA approval of an NDA. A number of factors contributed to this problem, including (1) recurring changes in personnel, (2) poor records of prior FDA advice, (3) the lack of significant written FDA guidance, (4) the lack of consistent supervision by higher FDA officials over the decisions of lower officials, (5) the ability of lower-level FDA personnel to take any position on a matter without supervisory control, (6) the pharmaceutical industry's fear of retaliation if a lower decision was appealed to a higher level, and (7) the lack of any realistic deadlines for FDA decisions on INDs and NDAs.

This situation changed partly with enactment of the Prescription Drug User Fee Act of 1992, which brought significant deadlines to the process, and partly with the enactment of the FDA Modernization Act of 1997, which added section 505(b)(4)(B) and (C) to the FD&C Act, establishing what is now referred to as the "Special Protocol Assessment" (SPA) program. Section 505(b)(4)(B) states that FDA "shall" meet with a sponsor or applicant "if the sponsor or applicant makes a reasonable written request for the purpose of reaching agreement on the design and size of clinical trials intended to form the primary basis of an effectiveness claim." Section 505(b)(4)(C) states: "Any agreement regarding the parameters of the design and size of clinical trials of a new drug under this paragraph that is reached between [FDA] and a sponsor or applicant shall be reduced to writing and ... shall not be changed after the testing begins" except in specified limited circumstances. FDA implemented these statutory provisions through the following guidance, issued in 65 Fed. Reg. 6377 (Feb. 9, 2000), 67 Fed. Reg. 35122 (May 17, 2002).

Guidance for Industry: Special Protocol Assessment
(2002)

. . . .

The PDUFA goals for special protocol assessment and agreement [performance goals agreed to by FDA in conjunction with PDUFA reauthorization in 1997] provide that, upon request, FDA will evaluate within 45 days certain protocols and issues relating to the protocols to assess whether they are adequate to meet scientific and regulatory requirements identified by the sponsor. Three types of protocols related to PDUFA products are eligible for this special protocol assessment under the PDUFA goals: (1) animal carcinogenicity protocols, (2) final product stability protocols, and (3) clinical protocols for phase 3 trials whose data will form the primary basis for an efficacy claim if the trials had been the subject of discussion at an end-of-phase 2/pre-phase 3 meeting with the review division, or in some cases, if the division agrees to such a review because the division is aware of the developmental context in which the protocol is being reviewed and the questions are being answered. The clinical protocols for phase 3 trials can relate to efficacy claims that will be part of an original new drug application (NDA) or biologics license application (BLA) or that will be part of an efficacy supplement to an approved NDA or BLA. . . .

Section 119(a) of the Modernization Act amends section 505(b) of the Act (21 U.S.C. 355(b)). New section 505(b)(4)(B) of the Act directs FDA to meet with sponsors, provided certain conditions are met, for the purpose of reaching agreement on the design and size of clinical trials intended to form the primary basis of an efficacy claim in a marketing application submitted under section 505(b) of the Act or section 351 of the Public Health Service Act (42 U.S.C. 262). Such marketing applications include NDAs, BLAs, and efficacy supplements to approved NDAs and BLAs.

Under new sections 505(b)(4)(B) and (C) of the Act, if a sponsor makes a reasonable written request to meet with the Agency for the purpose of reaching agreement on the design and size of a clinical trial, the Agency will meet with the sponsor. If an agreement is reached, the Agency will reduce the agreement to writing and make it part of the administrative record. An agreement may not be changed by the sponsor or FDA after the trial begins, except (1) with the written agreement of the sponsor and FDA, or (2) if the director of the FDA reviewing division determines that "a substantial scientific issue essential to determining the safety or effectiveness of the drug" was identified after the testing began (section 505(b)(4)(C) of the Act). If a sponsor and the Agency meet regarding the design and size of a clinical trial under section 505(b)(4)(B) of the Act and the parties cannot agree that the trial design is adequate to meet the goals of the sponsor, the Agency will clearly state the reasons for the disagreement in a letter to the sponsor. However, the absence of an articulated disagreement on a particular issue should not be assumed to represent an agreement reached on that issue. . . .

CDER and CBER generally recommend that a sponsor submit a protocol intended for special protocol assessment to the Agency at least 90 days prior to the anticipated start of the study. The protocol should be complete, and enough time should be allowed to discuss and resolve any issues before the study begins. SPECIAL PROTOCOL ASSESSMENT WILL NOT BE PROVIDED AFTER A STUDY HAS BEGUN. Protocols for studies that have already begun can be evaluated by CDER and CBER, but they do not qualify for the 45–day time frame described in the PDUFA goals. . . .

As stated in the PDUFA goals for special protocol assessment and agreement,

> having agreed to the design, execution, and analyses proposed in protocols reviewed under this process [i.e., carcinogenicity protocols, stability protocols, and phase 3 protocols for clinical trials that will form the primary basis of an efficacy claim], the Agency will not later alter its perspective on the issues of design, execution, or analyses unless public health concerns unrecognized at the time of protocol assessment under this process are evident.

Thus, documented special protocol assessments should be considered binding on the review division and should not be changed at any time, except as follows:

- Failure of a sponsor to follow a protocol that was agreed upon with the Agency will be interpreted as the sponsor's understanding that the protocol assessment is no longer binding on the review division.

- If the relevant data, assumptions, or information provided by the sponsor in a request for special protocol assessment change are found to be false statements or misstatements or are found to omit relevant facts, the review division will not be bound by any assessment that relied on such data, assumptions, or information.

- A documented special protocol assessment can be modified if (1) FDA and the sponsor agree in writing to modify the protocol (section 505(b)(4)(C) of the Act) and (2) such modification is intended to improve the study. A special protocol assessment modified in this manner will be considered binding on the review division, except under the circumstances described below.

- A clinical protocol assessment will no longer be considered binding if the director of the review division determines that a substantial scientific issue essential to determining the safety or efficacy of the drug has been identified after the testing has begun (section 505(b)(4)(C) of the Act). If the director of the review division makes such a determination, (1) the determination should be documented in writing for the administrative record and should be provided to the sponsor, and (2) the sponsor should be given an opportunity for a meeting at which the review division director will discuss the scientific issue involved (section 505(b)(4)(D) of the Act).

7. CLINICAL ENDPOINTS, SURROGATE ENDPOINTS, AND BIOMARKERS

In designing a clinical trial, it is important to determine the endpoints that will be evaluated in the course of the study. There are two types of endpoints relevant to determining the effectiveness of a new drug: (1) clinical endpoints, such as mortality and serious morbidity, and (2) surrogate endpoints, which are physiological assessments that are recognized as validated indicators of clinical benefit. Clinical endpoints are the gold standard for demonstrating the effectiveness of a drug, but for many diseases it is not feasible to test for changes in clinical endpoints, and surrogate endpoints must therefore suffice. In both situations, biomarkers—objectively measured indicators of normal biological or pathogenic processes or pharmacologic responses to a therapeutic intervention—are used in studies to evaluate activity and develop dose-response relationships. Thus, a surrogate endpoint is a biomarker that has been sufficiently validated to substitute for a clinical endpoint.

James Bilstad, M.D.,* *Surrogate Endpoints*

Talk at the Institute of Medicine AIDS Roundtable (March 12, 1990).

Faced with the tragic consequences of HIV infection and AIDS, we all want to determine as efficiently as possible which investigational agents effectively treat the disease and which do not. A discussion of the role of surrogate endpoints is a very important step in examining the drug evaluation process for potential therapeutic agents for HIV infection. . . .

To be considered for a surrogate endpoint, the parameter being measured or evaluated must be therapeutically rational and biologically plausible. It must be consistent with what is known about the pathophysiology and pathogenesis of the disease. . . .

Although the vast majority of drugs that are approved by the FDA for marketing are approved on the basis of efficacy demonstrated by significant clinical benefits, there are a number of drug classes in which we have accepted surrogate markers as a basis for approval. Anti-hypertensive drugs have long been approved on the basis of demonstrated effect in lowering blood pressure. It had been known for decades that untreated hypertension was associated with increased cardiovascular mortality and morbidity, primarily from accelerated atherosclerosis but also from end organ damage related to the hypertension itself. Although demonstrating a decrease in cardiovascular mortality and morbidity were the obvious endpoints of interest in evaluating the effects of anti-hypertensive therapy, these studies were very difficult to carry out. They required large numbers of patients to be followed over prolonged periods. . . .

Another area in which we have accepted endpoints other than the clinical endpoint of most interest is for drugs to treat osteoporosis. The clinical endpoint of primary interest is the reduction of the incidence of fractures. . . .

Again, we have the problem that the vent rate is relatively low, and a large number of patients need to be followed over a prolonged period. . . .

* [Dr. Bilstead was Director of the FDA CDER Office of Drug Evaluation when he gave this talk.]

Based on a number of studies evaluating the techniques for assessing bone structure, we did accept measurements of bone density using photon absorption in the case of estrogens and total body calcium by neutron activation analysis in the case of calcitonin. These studies involved multiple measurements over relatively long periods, at least two years. In these cases, we considered the data convincing that the drugs were having an effect directly on maintaining the bone structure.

A third area in which we have used surrogate endpoints, the vaccines [sic]. I will use influenza vaccine as an example. The initial clinical trials with the crude vaccine were started in the 1940's. A number of antibodies to the virus were evaluated for correlation with disease prevention. After considerable testing, the one that seemed to correlate the best with prevention was the antibody to the hemagglutinin glycoprotein on the viral envelope which is responsible for the attachment of the virus to receptor cells. . . .

A fourth drug class in which we have accepted surrogate endpoints, the lipid altering drugs [sic]. The FDA has long approved drugs that lower serum cholesterol based only on demonstrated efficacy at lowering cholesterol levels. Epidemiologic studies have established the association between elevated cholesterol level and increased cardiovascular mortality and morbidity. Obviously, the endpoints of interest in evaluating the effects of lowering serum cholesterol by drug therapy relate to demonstrating a decrease in cardiovascular mortality and morbidity. However, these studies are very difficult to do because of the relatively low number of events in the study population and therefore the large number of patients that must be followed for prolonged periods. . . .

A fifth class in which the agency has accepted surrogate markers of effectiveness is for the anti-arrhythmic drugs. The most important clinical benefit expected from these drugs is again to decrease the frequency of sudden death. Approval for anti-arrhythmics has not been based on demonstration of decreased cardiac mortality but rather approval has relied heavily on 24–hour holter monitoring for the frequency and duration of arrhythmias. These studies may involve either symptomatic or asymptomatic individuals but at least some information has also been required for recent approvals on symptom reduction. For example, decreased frequency of palpitations or syncopal episodes. . . .

A sixth area in which we have accepted a surrogate endpoint is with the alpha one proteinase inhibitor. Alpha one antitrypsin deficiency is a hereditary disease that in the more serious aphenotryptic variants can lead to severe emphysema starting in the third and fourth decades of life. There are only about 400 patients affected with the severe variant in the United States. The alpha one antitrypsin, the proteinase inhibitor blocks the action of an elastase released by nutraphils in the lower respiratory track. In absence of the inhibitor, elastase leads to breakdown of the structural integrity of the alveolae.

The FDA recently approved an alpha one proteinase inhibitor derived from pooled plasma to be given intravenously weekly to patients with the deficiency and early evidence of emphysema. The approval was based not on a demonstration of maintenance of pulmonary function and prevention of emphysema but on demonstrated levels of the proteinase inhibitor in blood and on evaluation of bronchial alveolar washings for proteinase inhibitor activity as reflected by elastase activity. Secondly, on decrease nutraphil counts and thirdly a decrease in other inflammatory mediators. . . .

Tissue plasminogen activator or TPA is an example of a therapeutic agent in which we did not accept a surrogate endpoint as a basis for approval. The initial application included only data demonstrating an effect on thrombolysis by coronary arteriography. In the agency's judgment, there was insufficient evidence to correlate these findings with clinical benefit. The product license application was later approved on the basis of a decreased incidence of overt congestive heart failure and an increase in the ventricular ejection fraction.

In addition to establishing that there is a correlation between a surrogate endpoint and a significant clinical endpoint, the surrogate endpoint must be carefully validated. This usually means that the drug must be studied for its effect on the clinical endpoint and on the surrogate marker in well-designed prospective studies. This process is helped if other drugs in the same class demonstrate similar effects.

NOTES

1. *Cancer Drug Endpoints.* For discussion of FDA's views on appropriate endpoints for approval of new cancer drug NDAs over the last thirteen years, *see* John R. Johnson et al., *Endpoints and United States Food and Drug Administration Approval of Oncology Drugs*, 21 J. CLINICAL ONCOLOGY 1404 (2003).

2. *Commentary. See also* Robert J. Temple, *A Regulatory Authority's Opinion about Surrogate Endpoints*, in CLINICAL MEASUREMENT IN DRUG EVALUATION (Walter S. Nimmo & Geoffrey Tucker eds., 1995); Robert J. Temple, *Are Surrogate Markers Adequate to Assess Cardiovascular Disease Drugs?*, 282 J.A.M.A. 790 (1999); Raymond Huml et al., S*urrogate Markers versus Biological Markers: Different Roles in Drug Approval*, 9 REG. AFFAIRS FOCUS, No. 6, at. 47 (June 2004).

8.   CLINICAL TESTING ON SUBPOPULATIONS

Clinical testing of new drugs has traditionally been conducted on white, middle-aged males on the premise that they are less vulnerable to potential harm, are relatively reliable test subjects, and are more likely to be available for follow up. Consequently, few drugs have been tested in children, women, the elderly, and racial subgroups. Both FDA and Congress have taken steps to change this paradigm.

a.   CHILDREN

By not testing on children, the pharmaceutical industry made them therapeutic orphans. Any use of a drug in children was inherently experimental. The pharmaceutical industry, however, was reluctant to test investigational drugs in children before it had full safety information in adults, because of fear that it could seriously harm this vulnerable population. Sponsors therefore chose simply to label their products with statements that the safety and effectiveness of the drug in children had not yet been established.

FDA's first step in addressing this problem was to promulgate a regulation in 1994 clarifying that to qualify for a pediatric label, a manufacturer did not necessarily have to complete pediatric clinical tests. 57 Fed. Reg. 47423 (Oct. 16, 1992), 59 Fed. Reg. 64240 (Dec. 13, 1994), codified at 21 C.F.R. 201.57. FDA stated that adult studies in combination with pharmacokinetics, safety, and pharmacodynamics data could satisfy pediatric labeling requirements. This regulation was unsuccessful, however, for two reasons. First, it did not resolve the ethical concerns about testing in children. Second, it did not address the fact that the patents for many drugs were near or beyond expiration and thus sponsors had no economic incentive to undertake even limited efforts to qualify for pediatric labeling.

In 1998, FDA promulgated a new regulation requiring pediatric testing of new and marketed drugs. 62 Fed. Reg. 43900 (Aug. 15, 1997), 63 Fed. Reg. 66632 (Dec. 2, 1998). At the same time that FDA was pursuing an administrative approach to the matter, Congress included in the FDA Modernization Act of 1997 a new section 505A of the FD&C Act to provide six months of market exclusivity, beginning at the end of the patent term, for any drug for which pediatric testing was conducted at the request of FDA. This was a substantial incentive for many drugs, and it resulted in a major increase in pediatric studies. In its January 2000 report to Congress on pediatric exclusivity, FDA stated, "The pediatric exclusivity provision has done more to generate clinical studies and useful prescribing information for the pediatric population than any other regulatory or legislative process to date." Because section 505A was subject to a five-year sunset provision, in January 2002 Congress extended it for another five years under the Best Pharmaceuticals for Children Act, 115 Stat. 1408. As of April 2006, FDA had received 467 proposed pediatric study requests from manufacturers, issued 320 written requests, granted six-month exclusivity to 118 drugs, and added new pediatric information to 109 labels. CDER, REPORT TO THE NATION 2005, 23 (2006).

In its December 1998 regulations, FDA had broadly asserted the legal authority to require pharmaceutical manufacturers to conduct any form of testing that the agency concluded to be justified. This conflicted with prior FDA statements, including a speech by Commissioner David Kessler. A physicians group dedicated to deregulating medicine filed suit challenging the FDA regulations. In *Association of American Physicians & Surgeons, Inc. v. FDA*, 226 F. Supp. 2d 204 (D.D.C. 2002), the District Court declared the December 1998 pediatric regulations unlawful and enjoined enforcement. FDA decided not to appeal the matter and instead to seek a legislative solution. Congress responded by enacting the Pediatric Research Equity Act of 2003, 117 Stat. 1936, which added section 505B to the FD&C Act. This section requires all new NDAs to contain a pediatric assessment unless FDA grants a waiver or deferral and also authorizes FDA to require holders of already-approved NDAs to conduct pediatric studies for marketed drugs. FDA issued draft guidance on these provisions in 2005. 70 Fed. Reg. 53233 (Sept. 7, 2005).

As part of the 2002 Best Pharmaceuticals for Children Act, Congress also included a mechanism for pediatric testing of drugs whose patents have expired. NIH is required to publish an annual list of these drugs, and FDA then issues requests for testing proposals to be supported by government funds.

NOTES

1. *FDA Regulations.* In 2001, FDA published regulations to provide additional safeguards for children in clinical investigations. 66 Fed. Reg. 20598 (Apr. 24, 2001), codified at 21 C.F.R. Part 50, Subpart D. FDA issued draft guidance for implementation of this process in May 2006.

2. *Scope of Market Exclusivity.* FDA interpreted the market exclusivity provisions for pediatric testing in section 503B of the FD&C Act to extend to a manufacturer's entire line of drug products having the same active moiety. This interpretation was upheld in *National Pharmaceutical Alliance v. Henney*, 47 F. Supp. 2d 37 (D.D.C. 1999).

3. *Availability of Information.* All of the information regarding requests for pediatric testing under the Best Pharmaceuticals for Children Act of 2002 and the Pediatric Research Equity Act of 2003 is readily available on the FDA website. As required by the Best Pharmaceuticals for Children Act, FDA periodically publishes notices announcing the availability of summaries of medical and clinical pharmacology reviews of pediatric studies conducted pursuant to that statute. *E.g.*, 71 Fed. Reg. 61484 (Oct. 18, 2006). But publication of pediatric studies in the medical literature remains limited. Daniel K. Benjamin et al., *Peer–Reviewed Publication of Clinical Trials Completed for Pediatric Exclusivity*, 296 J.A.M.A. 1266 (2006).

4. *Sunset.* Section 505A of the FD&C Act, enacted as part of the FDA Modernization Act of 1997, sunsets on October 1, 2007. This provision, and only this provision, authorizes six months of market exclusivity for drugs whose sponsors undertake pediatric testing. Section 505B, which was added by the Pediatric Research Equity Act of 2003, is subject to sunset on the same date. This provision, and only this provision, authorizes FDA to require pediatric testing for new drugs.

5. *Commentary. See* Lauren Hammer Breslow, *The Best Pharmaceuticals for Children's Act of 2002: The Rise of the Voluntary Incentive Structure and Congressional Refusal to Require Pediatric Testing*, 40 HARV. J. ON LEGISL. 133 (2003); I. Glenn Cohen, *Therapeutic Orphans, Pediatric Victims? The Best Pharmaceuticals for Children Act and Existing Pediatric Human Subject Protection*, 58 FOOD & DRUG L.J. 661 (2003).

b.   WOMEN

During the past decade, FDA has made progress on the inclusion of women in clinical trials. In 1977, FDA adopted a policy restricting the participation of women with childbearing potential in early clinical trials. In 1993, FDA withdrew the 1977 policy and published a GUIDELINE FOR THE STUDY AND EVALUATION OF GENDER DIFFERENCES IN THE CLINICAL EVALUATION OF DRUGS. 58 Fed. Reg. 39406 (July 22, 1993). The 1993 FDA policy affirmatively encouraged inclusion of women in clinical trials and stated that researchers were expected to analyze potential gender-related differences in the patients included in clinical studies.

Four years later, FDA published a proposal that would have authorized the agency to place a clinical hold on any clinical trial relating to a life-threatening illness if men or women with reproductive potential who have the disease are excluded from any phase of the trial because of a risk of reproductive toxicity. 62 Fed. Reg. 49946 (Sept. 24, 1997). While this proposal was pending, Congress added section 505(b)(1) to the FD&C Act as part of the FDA Modernization Act of 1997. This provision directed FDA, in consultation with NIH and the pharmaceutical industry, to "review and development guidance, as appropriate, on the inclusion of women and minorities in clinical trials." In 1998, FDA amended its IND and NDA regulations to require that reports of studies for both safety and effectiveness present data by gender, age, and racial subgroups. 60 Fed. Reg. 46794 (Sept. 8, 1995), 63 Fed. Reg. 6854 (Feb. 11, 1998). This is required even if the study is not sufficiently powered to permit statistical analysis. *See* Patricia F. Kaufman, *A Critique of the Food and Drug Administration's 1993 Guideline Concerning the Inclusion of Fertile Women in Early Clinical Testing of New Drug Therapies* (1994), Jonathan A. Roskes, *The Inclusion of Women in Clinical Studies: Yesterday and Today* (1994), and Stacey E. Parker, *From Protectionism to Access: Women's Participation in Clinical Trials—Conflict, Controversy and Change* (2002), in Chapter VI(C)(1) of the Electronic Book.

c.   THE ELDERLY

FDA has also recognized that separate information on geriatric use of a new drug may be important to the elderly. In 1997, FDA established a "geriatric use" subsection in the physician labeling. 55 Fed. Reg. 46134 (Nov. 1, 1990), 62 Fed. Reg. 45313 (Aug. 27, 1997), codified at 21 C.F.R. 201.57(c)(9)(v). Although specific testing on the elderly is not required, age is one of the categories that must be broken out separately in all clinical trial reports submitted to FDA under the agency's February 1998 revision of the IND and NDA regulations. As FDA stated in 58 Fed. Reg. at 39410, "Patients in clinical trials should, in general, reflect the population that will receive the drug when it is marketed."

d.   ETHNIC AND RACIAL GROUPS

Although there is no statutory or regulatory requirement that special testing be conducted in ethnic or racial subpopulations, FDA expects that members of these groups will be included in clinical trials and requires that they be separated out for purposes of analysis in study reports submitted to the agency.

In June 2005, FDA approved a new drug, BiDil, for severe heart failure. The FDA-approved labeling provides that the drug is intended "for the treatment of heart failure as an adjunct to standard therapy in self-identified black patients." This is the only drug approved by FDA for a discrete racial group. For thoughtful analyses of the issues raised by this approval, see Alpana Gupta, *The Emerging Field of Race–Based Genetic Research: Can We Trust It?* (2006), and Stephanie A. Yonker, *FDA Drug Approval: A Black and White Issue?* (2006), in Chapter VI(C)(3) of the Electronic Book. In 68 Fed. Reg. 4788 (Jan. 30, 2003), FDA announced a draft guidance on "collection of race and ethnicity data in clinical trials." For scientific criticism of FDA's suggestion that ethnicity and race data will "enhance the early identification of differences in physiological response among racial and ethnic subgroups," *see* Susanne B. Haga & J. Craig Venter, *FDA Races in Wrong Direction*, 301 SCIENCE 466 (July 25, 2003).

9.   GMP FOR INVESTIGATIONAL DRUGS

Collection of the chemical, manufacturing, and controls (CMC) information ultimately needed to assure compliance with good manufacturing practice (GMP) of the finished pharmaceutical product begins even before an IND is submitted. This process continues during the investigational studies. In effect, GMP is on a continuum of improved compliance, beginning with preclinical work and extending through to final validation studies during NDA review or even after NDA approval.

FDA issued a GUIDELINE ON PREPARATION OF INVESTIGATIONAL NEW DRUG PRODUCTS in 1991, which required drugs under an IND to meet the commercial GMP standards established in 21 C.F.R. Part 211. This guideline made no distinction in the GMP requirements for the three different phases of clinical investigation. As a practical matter, however, FDA never enforced full Part 211 GMP compliance on Phase I clinical trials, nor would such compliance have been achievable.

In 71 Fed. Reg. 2458 (Jan. 17, 2006), FDA issued a direct final regulation (*i.e.*, a rule issued without complying with APA notice-and-comment requirements) to exempt investigational drugs for Phase I clinical trials from the commercial GMP requirements. At the same time, the agency announced the availability of a draft guidance titled INDs—APPROACHES TO COMPLYING WITH CGMP DURING PHASE I. 71 Fed. Reg. 2552 (Jan. 17, 2006). According to this draft guidance, the pharmaceutical industry should implement:

> manufacturing controls that are appropriate for the stage of development. The use of this approach recognizes that some controls and the extent of controls needed to achieve appropriate product quality differ not only between investigational and commercial manufacture, but also among the various phases of clinical studies.

Because FDA received significant adverse comments to the January 2006 direct final rule, the agency withdrew it with the intent of developing a final rule using APA procedures. 71 Fed. Reg. 25747 (May 2, 2006). *See* Larry Rosania, *Streamlining cGMP Standards for Phase I Clinical Trial—An Example of Unintended Consequences*, 11 REG. AFFAIRS FOCUS, No. 9, at 42 (Sept. 2006).

NOTE

In the FDA Modernization Act of 1997, Congress added section 505(c)(4) to the FD&C Act to provide that a drug manufactured in a pilot or other small facility may be used for clinical investigation to demonstrate safety and effectiveness and to obtain NDA approval prior to manufacture of the drug in a larger facility. This reflected the concern of Congress that small companies cannot afford to build large manufacturing facilities in full compliance with drug GMP requirements prior to NDA approval.

10.   DATA MONITORING COMMITTEE

An IRB reviews a clinical protocol before it is initiated and exercises general supervision over the trial as it is conducted. The primary function of an IRB, which is comprised of lay people as well as scientists, is to assure compliance with local community ethical standards.

Beginning in the 1960s, consideration was also given to the need for independent review of the data emerging from large clinical studies to determine whether the study should be stopped, either because of safety problems or because the drug was so effective that it would be unethical not to give it to the control group as well. The sponsors themselves could not perform this role, because it would unblind their trials. IRBs did not have the pharmacological and statistical competence to conduct adequate safety reviews. Thus, drug sponsors began to use what came to be called Data and Safety Monitoring Boards (DSMBs) to perform this function. FDA now calls this type of group a Data Monitoring Committee (DMC).

Guidance for Clinical Trial Sponsors: Establishment and Operation of Clinical Trial Data Monitoring Committees

(2006)

. . . .

A clinical trial DMC is a group of individuals with pertinent expertise that reviews on a regular basis accumulating data from one or more ongoing clinical trials. The DMC advises the sponsor regarding the continuing safety of trial subjects and those yet to be recruited to the trial, as well as the continuing validity and scientific merit of the trial. When a single DMC is responsible for monitoring multiple trials, the considerations for establishment and operation of the DMC are generally similar to those for a DMC monitoring a single trial, but the logistics may be more complex. For example, multiple conflict of interest determinations may be needed for each DMC member.

Many different models have been proposed and used for the operation of DMCs. Although different models may be appropriate and acceptable in different situations, experience has shown that some approaches have particular advantages or disadvantages. In this document, we highlight these advantages and disadvantages, with particular attention to the setting in which investigational products are being evaluated for possible marketing approval in well-controlled clinical trials. The intent of this guidance document is to ensure wide awareness of acceptable practices and of potential concerns regarding operation of DMCs that may arise in specific situations. . . .

Few trials sponsored by the pharmaceutical/medical device industry incorporated DMC oversight until relatively recently. The increasing use of DMCs in industry-sponsored trials is the result of several factors, including:

- The growing number of industry-sponsored trials with mortality or major morbidity endpoints;
- The increasing collaboration between industry and government in sponsoring major clinical trials, resulting in industry trials performed under the policies of government funding agencies, which often require DMCs;
- Heightened awareness within the scientific community of problems in clinical trial conduct and analysis that might lead to inaccurate and/or biased results, especially when early termination for efficacy is a possibility, and need for approaches to protect against such problems;
- Concerns of IRBs regarding ongoing trial monitoring and patient safety in multicenter trials. . . .

NOTES

1. *Mandatory DMC.* Although some clinical trials sponsored by NIH are required to incorporate a DMC, FDA has no requirement for the use of a DMC other than under 21 C.F.R. 50.24(a)(7)(iv), for research studies in an emergency setting in which informed consent is not required.

2. *Commentary.* See Susan S. Ellenberg et al., DATA MONITORING COMMITTEES IN CLINICAL TRIALS: A PRACTICAL PERSPECTIVE (2002), Joseph Corkery, *Primum Non Nocere: The Continuing Evolution of Safety Monitoring in Human Subjects Research* (2005), in Chapter VI(C)(1) of the Electronic Book.

3. *Patient Advocates.* Because of the increasing focus on protection of human subjects in clinical trials, some sponsors have also begun to use an ombudsperson or patient advocate whose duty it is to ensure the well-being of the research subjects, from the time that the protocol is first reviewed by the IRB, through the actual conduct of the study, and including the post-trial period as well.

11.   EXPEDITED DEVELOPMENT OF LIFESAVING DRUGS

a.   SUBPART E

Faced with the AIDS epidemic in the mid–1980s, FDA promulgated an interim regulation to establish an official policy on expedited development of new drugs for life-threatening and severely debilitating diseases. 53 Fed. Reg. 41516 (Oct. 21, 1988), codified at 21 C.F.R. Part 312, Subpart E.

Investigational New Drug, Antibiotic, and Biological Drug Product Regulations: Procedures For Drugs Intended to Treat Life–Threatening and Severely Debilitating Illnesses

53 Fed. Reg. 41516 (October 21, 1988).

. . . The purpose of these new procedures (§ 312.80) is to expedite the development, evaluation, and marketing of new therapies intended to treat persons with life-threatening or severely-debilitating illnesses, especially where no satisfactory alternative therapies exist. . . .

The scope of the new procedures (§ 312.81) will apply to new drugs, antibiotics, and biological products that are being studied for their safety and effectiveness in treating life-threatening or severely-debilitating illnesses. Within the context of these procedures, the term "life-threatening" is defined to include diseases where the likelihood of death is high unless the course of the disease is interrupted (*e.g.*, AIDS and cancer), as well as diseases or conditions with potentially fatal outcomes where the end point of clinical trial analysis is survival (*e.g.*, increased survival in persons who have had a stroke or heart attack). The term "severely-debilitating" refers to diseases or conditions that cause major irreversible morbidity (*e.g.*, blindness or neurological degeneration).

A key component of the procedures is early consultation between FDA and drug sponsors (§ 312.82) to seek agreement on the design of necessary preclinical and clinical studies needed to gain marketing approval. Such consultation is intended to improve the efficiency of the process by preventing false starts and wasted effort that could otherwise result from studies that are flawed in design. Most important, at the end of early (phase 1) clinical testing, FDA and the sponsor will seek to reach agreement on the proper design of phase 2 controlled clinical trials, with the goal that such research will be adequate to provide sufficient data on the product's safety and effectiveness to support a decision on its approvability for marketing. . . .

If the preliminary analysis of test results appears promising, FDA may ask the sponsor (§ 312.83) to submit a treatment protocol to be reviewed under the treatment IND regulations. Such a treatment protocol, if submitted and granted, would serve as a bridge between the completion of early stages of clinical trials and final marketing approval.

Once phase 2 testing and analysis is completed by the sponsor and a marketing application is submitted, FDA will evaluate the data utilizing a medical risk-benefit analysis (§ 312.84). As part of this evaluation, FDA will consider whether the benefits of the drug outweigh the known and potential risks of the drug and the need to answer remaining questions about risks and benefits of the drug, taking into consideration the severity of the disease and the absence of satisfactory alternative therapy. In making decisions on whether to grant marketing approval for products that have been the subject of an end-of-phase 1 meeting under this rule, FDA will usually seek the advice of outside expert scientific consultants or advisory committees. . . .

Finally, when approval or licensing of a product is being granted, FDA may seek agreement from the sponsor (§ 312.85) to conduct certain post-marketing (phase 4) studies to delineate additional information about the drug's risks, benefits, and optimal use. These studies could include, but would not be limited to, studying different doses or schedules of administration than were used in phase 2 studies, use of the drugs in other patient populations or other stages of the disease, and use of the drug over a longer period of time. . . .

b.   FAST TRACK

As part of the FDA Modernization Act of 1997, Congress added section 506 to the FD&C Act to codify the agency's expedited development initiative. Congress gave the term "Fast Track" to this program, although the program remained unchanged from the original October 1988 FDA Subpart E regulations. FDA published a guidance in September 1998 to implement the new Fast Track program and a revision in July 2004. One advantage of Fast Track status is that FDA will accept a continuous marketing application under which reviewable units of an NDA may be submitted before the full NDA is prepared. FDA issued a guidance in October 2003 for a pilot program to test this concept. A second, and perhaps the single most important, advantage is frequent scientific feedback and interactions based on a prospectively defined agreement between FDA and the applicant. This guarantees the types of interactive meetings that result in the most efficient and effective development of a new drug. *See supra* p. 626. FDA also developed a guidance on this interactive approach in October 2003.

12. Clinical Testing Conducted Overseas

An investigational new drug may be used in clinical trials abroad under either of the following two circumstances. First, if the drug is manufactured abroad by or for a United States company, it is not subject to the FD&C Act and must meet only the requirements of the foreign country. Second, if the drug is manufactured in the United States, it may be exported under section 802(c) of the FD&C Act, as added by the FDA Drug Export Reform and Enhancement Act of 1996, to any of the countries listed in section 802(b)(1)(A) without the need to comply with any of the United States investigational drug provisions.

When the Drug Amendments of 1962 were first implemented, it was unusual for a sponsor to conduct clinical studies abroad. FDA officials were at first reluctant to accept the results of foreign clinical trials, but they gradually came to consider them in a way similar to United States trials. In 1975, FDA made it clear that there would be no discrimination against foreign clinical trials submitted to support NDAs as long as the trials were conducted under the ethical standards of the Declaration of Helsinki. 38 Fed. Reg. 24220 (Sept. 6, 1973), 40 Fed. Reg. 16053 (Apr. 9, 1975), codified at 21 C.F.R. 312.120.

In the 1980s, the pharmaceutical industry began to move many of its early stage clinical trials abroad because the regulatory requirements were substantially less than those in the United States. FDA responded by attempting to streamline the information required for a United States IND. In the past decade, however, an increasing number of clinical trials have been conducted abroad for both regulatory and cost reasons. Not only are the regulatory requirements less burdensome in some foreign countries, but the cost is only a fraction of what a clinical trial costs in the United States. Clinical testing abroad has therefore spread from Western Europe to Eastern Europe and now to India and China. Fewer trials are conducted in the United States. Recognizing this trend, many have raised concerns about the protection of human subjects overseas and the quality of the trials themselves. *E.g.*, Office of DHHS Inspector General, The Globalization of Clinical Trials: A Growing Challenge in Protecting Human Subjects, No. OEI–01–00–00190 (2001).

13.   USE OF INVESTIGATIONAL DRUGS FOR THERAPY

Section 505(i) of the FD&C Act was included in the statute in 1938, and expanded in 1962, solely to authorize clinical trials designed to obtain data relating to safety and effectiveness sufficient to justify FDA approval of an NDA. It was never intended to authorize the use of investigational drugs for the treatment of ill patients outside a clinical trial. From the very beginning, however, it has been widely used to provide therapy for sick patients in situations in which there is little or no pretense of gathering data for an NDA.

Since 1938, FDA has consistently taken the position that an unapproved new drug may not lawfully be "commercialized" prior to approval. Before the Drug Amendments of 1962, the agency's regulations specified that investigational drugs were to be made available "solely for investigational use by or under the direction of, an expert qualified by scientific training and experience to investigate the safety of such drug." 21 C.F.R. 130.2(a)(2)(1962). The use of investigational drugs for therapy, rather than for investigational purposes, was not specifically addressed in FDA publications or contemporary articles describing the new drug process. The original IND regulations provided that the sponsor must not "commercially distribute nor test-market" the drug prior to approval and that an IND could be terminated if FDA found that the drug "is being or is to be sold or otherwise distributed for commercial purposes not justified by the requirements of the investigation." 27 Fed. Reg. 7990 (Aug. 10, 1962), 28 Fed. Reg. 179 (Jan. 8, 1963), codified at 21 C.F.R. 130.3(a)(11), 130.3(d)(8). The IND form itself, beginning in 1963, required that the sponsor provide

> If the drug is to be sold, a full explanation why sale is required and should not be regarded as the commercialization of a new drug for which an application is not approved.

FDA thus embraced two related enforcement principles. First, investigational drugs were to be used solely for investigational purposes and not for treatment. Second, investigational drugs were to be made available without charge, except under unusual circumstances that were fully justified in the IND.

As new drugs began to be developed to treat serious diseases for which no alternative therapy was available, FDA discarded the rule that an investigational drug could not be used for treatment purposes. Although the agency did not amend the IND regulations to reflect this change in policy, it allowed the use of investigational drugs in patient treatment while clinical trials were ongoing, on various terms.

One goal of FDA's revision of the IND regulations in the 1980s was to rationalize these exceptions to the general ban on commercialization of an investigational drug. *See* 48 Fed. Reg. 26720 (June 9, 1983), 52 Fed. Reg. 8798 (Mar. 19, 1987). The agency's 1983 proposal contained new sections on "treatment use" and "emergency use" that did no more than codify existing agency practice. By the time the final regulation was promulgated in March 1987, however, the AIDS epidemic had forced FDA to reevaluate these provisions. The emergency use provision was retained as it appeared in the March final rule, 21 C.F.R. 313.36, but the treatment use provision was reproposed in more detailed form and promulgated just two months later as a final regulation. 52 Fed. Reg. 19466 (May 22, 1987).

The use of investigational drugs for active therapy, rather than for clinical trials, is common. There is no single term used to describe this phenomenon, but "expanded access" is a fair description. One reason for the confusion and resulting proliferation of terminology to describe the various types of expanded access programs is that the majority of these programs are not referred to in the IND regulations, and some of those that are referred to are not defined. Accordingly, the terminology, definitions, and descriptions set forth below are an attempt to bring some order into an otherwise very confusing field. The only thing that can be said with certainty is that the purpose of each of the programs described *below* is to provide active therapy to sick patients, not to obtain data to justify approval of an NDA.

As part of the FDA Modernization Act of 1997, Congress added section 561 to the FD&C Act to authorize expanded access to unapproved new drugs. This provision covers only three of the various types of expanded access programs that actually exist under the current IND regulations. Reflecting the confused state of the FDA regulations, guidance, and policy in this area, the National Coalition for Cancer Survivorship and the American Society of Clinical Oncology recently submitted a Citizen Petition to request FDA to issue guidance outlining procedures and standards for initiating an expanded access program for unapproved drugs. FDA Docket No. 2006P–0135/CP1 (Mar. 27, 2006).

In light of increasing public concern about the unavailability of investigational drugs to treat desperately sick patients, FDA is reconsidering its rules in this area. *See* Anna Wilde Mathews, *FDA May Broaden Access to Experimental Drugs*, Wall St. J., Nov. 9, 2006, at A3. On December 14, 2006, FDA published two proposed regulations relating to investigational drugs. The first would create a new 21 C.F.R. Part 312, Subpart I to clarify the existing regulations and identify other types of expanded access for treatment use that are not described in the present regulations. 71 Fed. Reg. 75147 (Dec. 14, 2006). The second would add a new 21 C.F.R. 312.8 to clarify and expand the circumstances in which charging for an investigational drug in a clinical trial is appropriate and generally to permit sponsors to charge for investigational drugs in expanded access programs for treatment use. 71 Fed. Reg. 75168.

a. INDIVIDUAL PATIENT IND

FDA has long granted "single patient exceptions" to allow the use of investigational drugs outside the protocols of the approved IND. In 1978, a program for compassionate use of marijuana was established as a single patient IND to settle a civil lawsuit against the government. The program grew to 13 participants in 1992, when DHHS decided to add no new participants and to phase out the program as people died or voluntarily left. In *Kuromiya v. United States*, 37 F. Supp. 2d 717, 78 F. Supp. 2d 367 (E.D. Pa. 1999), the DHHS action was upheld. In *Smith v. Shalala*, 954 F. Supp. 1 (D.D.C. 1996), the court held that where a terminally ill cancer patient had failed to try available FDA-approved drugs for his condition, the agency could, under 21 C.F.R. 312.42(b)(1)(i), properly disallow a single patient exception for an investigational drug. *Smith v. Shalala*, 954 F. Supp. 1 (D.D.C. 1996).

Under section 561(b) of the FD&C Act, added in 1997 by the FDA Modernization Act, any person may ask a sponsor for access to an investigational drug for the treatment of a serious disease or condition if there is no satisfactory alternative therapy available, there is sufficient evidence of safety and effectiveness to support the use of the investigational drug, FDA determines that provision of the investigational drug will not interfere with clinical investigations to support NDA approval, and the sponsor or clinical investigator submits to FDA a clinical protocol consistent with the IND regulations. This provision of the statute is consistent with FDA practice since 1962, and it thus did not expand access to investigational drugs beyond what already existed.

b. EMERGENCY USE IND

Under section 561(a) of the FD&C Act, also added by the FDA Modernization Act, FDA may authorize the shipment of investigational drugs (or devices) for the treatment of a serious disease or condition in emergency situations. Like section 561(b), this provision codifies prior FDA practice extending back to 1962. FDA promulgated regulations formally establishing the emergency use IND in 1987. 52 Fed. Reg. 8798, 8820–8821 (Mar. 19, 1987), codified at 21 C.F.R. 312.36. An emergency use IND is exempt from prior IRB approval and, in some instances, from informed consent. 21 C.F.R. 56.104(c), 50.23(a). IRB approval must be obtained, however, and an IND must be submitted promptly.

Following the terrorism attacks of September 11, 2001, Congress enacted the Project BioShield Act of 2004, 108 Stat. 276, which added section 564 to the FD&C Act to allow FDA to authorize the use of an unapproved new drug during a declared domestic, military, or national security emergency. FDA has twice issued an authorization of emergency use of anthrax vaccine by military personnel at the request of the Department of Defense. *See* 70 Fed. Reg. 5450 (Feb. 2, 2005), 70 Fed. Reg. 44657 (Aug. 3, 2005).

c. TREATMENT IND

Section 561(c), another component of the FDA Modernization Act of 1997, authorizes FDA to permit the use of an investigational drug under a treatment protocol (referred to in the provision as an "expanded access protocol") for the treatment of a serious or immediately life-threatening disease or condition. This provision simply codifies the prior FDA regulations governing the treatment IND. The 1983 proposed revisions of the IND regulations had a section on treatment use, and FDA reproposed this section in broader form in 52 Fed. Reg. 8850 (March 19, 1987). The agency promulgated the final treatment use regulation in 52 Fed. Reg. 19466 (May 22, 1987), just as the AIDS crisis reached a peak in the United States. A prominent feature of the final regulation is the authority for sponsors to charge for investigational drugs under a treatment IND if the drug is not being commercially promoted or advertised and the sponsor of the drug is actively pursuing marketing approval with due diligence.

In all cases, the final rule provides that the sponsor may not commercialize an investigational drug by charging a price larger than necessary to recover the costs of manufacture, research, development, and handling of the investigational drug. The same standard is currently applied to charging for investigational medical devices.

The treatment IND was initially used by several drug sponsors. However, when CMS and third party payors refused to reimburse for any drugs used under a treatment IND on the ground that it represented experimental use, this approach fell into disuse.

NOTES

1. *Publication of Treatment INDs.* For several years, FDA periodically published a list of all drugs subject to treatment INDs. *See, e.g.,* "Treatment IND Update," FDA Talk Paper T90–14 (Mar. 20, 1990). *See generally* Myron L. Marlin, *Treatment INDs A Faster Route to Drug Approval?*, 39 AM. U. L. REV. 171 (1989); David M. Cocchetto, *Issues Regarding Compassionate Treatment With Investigational New Drugs*, 23 DRUG INFO. J. 87 (1989).

2. *The AIDS Amendments.* The AIDS Amendments of 1988 essentially ratified the treatment IND policy adopted by FDA. The Amendments, 102 Stat. 3048, 3066–67, codified at 42 U.S.C. 300cc–12, require FDA to encourage submission of an IND for clinical trials, and submission of a treatment IND for individuals not in clinical trials, for any investigational drug when there is "preliminary evidence that the drug has effectiveness in humans" in the prevention or treatment of AIDS. FDA is specifically authorized to provide technical assistance, directly or through grants or contracts, to facilitate submission of INDs for these purposes.

3. *Continuing Demands.* These statutory and regulatory initiatives did not satisfy all the agency's critics. *See* "FDA Responds to Act Up Demands," FDA Talk Paper No. T88–74 (Oct. 5, 1988). Some contended that the agency applied the treatment IND regulations more restrictively than their wording promised. These critics claimed that rather than allowing a treatment IND for any drug that "may" be effective for some AIDS victims, FDA approved a treatment IND for a drug only after the sponsor had already submitted substantial evidence of safety and effectiveness, as a "bridge" to NDA approval. Many argued that treatment INDs should be granted much earlier, even if this allowed the use of some drugs that were later found to be unsafe or ineffective. According to a news article:

> Even as the FDA was easing its rules, AIDS sufferers were still suffering for a cure on the black market for unapproved drugs. It was revealed last week that an underground network of doctors in four cities has been conducting a clandestine trial of a drug known as Compound Q. In test tubes, it can destroy cells infected with the AIDS virus, but it has not yet been proved to be safe and effective in humans. In the unofficial trial, 42 patients have received Compound Q, which is derived from a Chinese cucumber-like plant. . . .

> The secret study, organized by a San Francisco-based group of AIDS activists called Project Inform, came to light after one of the patients died. He went into a coma, later awoke but then choked while vomiting—ten days after his first Compound–Q treatment. The FDA has launched an investigation of the study.

The Compound–Q affair has heightened concern about the widespread use of unproven drugs. "There is always a tension between treatment of a patient and the need for solid drug testing," says Dr. Frank Young, the FDA commissioner. But AIDS has increased that tension. . . .

Although FDA officials dispute the notion, some experts are concerned that the use of unproven medications may be getting out of control. So many AIDS patients are taking a pharmacological stew of approved and experimental drugs and potions that it is difficult to gauge the effectiveness of any single drug. Underground studies of experimental drugs, like the Compound–Q effort, confuse an already complex situation and frustrate scientists. "They're violating all the standards of safe testing of new compounds," says Dr. Paul Volberding, an AIDS specialist at the University of California at San Francisco. The haphazard use of experimental drugs may help some AIDS patients in the short run, but it will slow down the quest to discover the best ways to treat the many people who will contract the disease in the future.

Drugs from the Underground, Time Mag., July 10, 1989, at 49.

d.   PARALLEL TRACK IND

As a result of continuing pressure from the AIDS community, and at the personal recommendation of NIH–NIAID Director Anthony Fauci, the Public Health Service and FDA in 1990 announced a "parallel track mechanism" permitting the use of investigational drugs by people with AIDS and HIV-related diseases who are both unable to benefit from existing standard therapies and unable to participate in ongoing clinical trials. 55 Fed. Reg. 20856 (May 21, 1990), 57 Fed. Reg. 13250 (Apr. 15, 1992). This policy can be found only in the Federal Register; it is not codified in the C.F.R. An investigational new drug may not be released under a parallel track protocol before patient enrollment in an FDA-approved Phase II clinical trial for that drug is initiated. A parallel track protocol must comply with the requirements generally applicable to other protocols for investigational new drugs.

e.   GROUP C CANCER TREATMENT IND

The National Cancer Institute (NCI) plays a major role in the discovery and development of anticancer drugs. *See, e.g.*, GAO, Improvements Needed in Clinical Testing of Anticancer Drugs, No. HRD–83–52 (Sept. 26, 1983); "Oversight of Drug Development Program of the National Cancer Institute," Hearing before the Subcommittee on Investigations and General Oversight of the Senate Committee on Labor and Human Resources, 97th Cong., 2d Sess. (1982). Since 1976, NCI has furnished qualified physicians the most promising investigational drugs, called "Group C" drugs, to treat their patients outside any clinical trial. These drugs appear in a Master File submitted to FDA. NCI includes on this list only those drugs that it concludes are likely to obtain NDA approval. *See* NCI, *Understanding the Approval Process for New Cancer Treatments* (Jan. 6, 2004); FDA, *Report to Congress on Patient Access to New Therapeutic Agents for Pediatric Cancer* (Dec. 2003). This is an informal program, not codified in regulations. The program was incorporated in a Memorandum of Understanding between the two agencies published in 44 Fed. Reg. 25510 (May 1, 1979). Beginning in October 1980, Group C drugs were made eligible for Medicare reimbursement, despite their investigational status.

In 1988, FDA determined that NCI would continue to use the designation "Group C" for these drugs, that FDA would use the designation "treatment IND/Group C," and that FDA "will treat NCI applications for Group C status as treatment IND requests, no matter what name they come under, and utilize the standards that we would ordinarily use for such a request." Under the program, NCI may submit an application to FDA for authorization to distribute the investigational new drug for a specific indication. If approved, NCI ships the drug to appropriately trained physicians who have provided adequate assurance that their patients qualify under the protocol. Patients are not charged for the investigational new drugs they receive pursuant to a Group C IND. To facilitate the exchange of clinical research information between NCI and FDA, the two agencies entered into a Memorandum of Understanding establishing a secure electronic database for clinical investigator information. 71 Fed. Reg. 54286 (Sept. 14, 2006).

f. OPEN LABEL IND

Open label INDs trace their origin back to 1962, but have never been codified in FDA regulations. There are two types of open label INDs. First, when a placebo-controlled clinical trial is completed and there is no formal followup as part of the protocol, it is common to continue the treatment arm, and switch the placebo arm to treatment, under an open label protocol. Second, an open label protocol is used under a wide variety of other circumstances for the treatment of ill patients. In both instances, safety data are collected and reported to FDA under the IND and as part of the NDA.

g. COMPASSIONATE USE IND

Like the term "expanded access," "compassionate use" is a broad and undefined term. It applies to situations in which the use of an investigational new drug for patient therapy does not fall within any other specific expanded access IND program. Since 1962, FDA has taken a very liberal and flexible approach to compassionate use INDs where there is a clear medical need. The term "compassionate IND" is regarded by some as synonymous with an "open protocol." H.R. Rep. No. 97–840, 97th Cong. 2nd Sess., 11 (1982). Section 2312 of the Public Health Service Act, 42 U.S.C. § 300cc–12, provides that FDA shall encourage "an application to use the drug in the treatment of individuals" as part of the IND where "there is preliminary evidence that a new drug has effectiveness in humans with respect to the prevention or treatment of acquired immune deficiency syndrome."

h. ORPHAN DRUG IND

Prior to the enactment of the Orphan Drug Act of 1983, orphan drugs (*i.e.*, drugs for rare diseases or conditions) seldom proceeded from an IND to an approved NDA. In some instances, there were too few patients to satisfy FDA testing requirements for an NDA, and in other instances, the market for the drug was too small to justify the investment needed to obtain an approved NDA. As a result, orphan drugs were relegated to a continuing IND status that FDA and the sponsor tacitly agreed would probably be permanent. Section 528 of the FD&C Act requires FDA to encourage the sponsor of an orphan drug to design "open protocols" for "persons with the disease or condition who need the drug to treat the disease or condition and who cannot be satisfactorily treated by available alternative drugs." Although the Orphan Drug Act has reduced the number of permanent orphan drug INDs, they have not been eliminated completely.

i. TROPICAL DRUG IND

Although FDA has long permitted drugs for tropical diseases to be the subject of clinical trials in the United States, the agency, until fairly recently, rarely approved NDAs for exclusively tropical new drugs, on the ground that there was no need for such drugs in this country. Thus, like the orphan drug INDs, a tropical drug IND was tacitly assumed to be permanent. With increased international travel and immigration, the rationale for not approving NDAs for tropical drugs has now largely disappeared.

j. SPECIAL EXCEPTION IND

When an individual is ineligible to enroll in a clinical trial of an investigational drug, the sponsor may request that FDA permit a special exception from the IND protocol to permit the excluded individual to receive treatment. Although this special exception IND is not reflected in any FDA regulation or guidance, the agency does permit such exceptions. Because the patient falls outside the inclusion criteria for the study, the data regarding the patient are excluded from the reported study results.

k. CONSTITUTIONAL RIGHT TO EXPANDED ACCESS?

Individuals afflicted with serious or life-threatening diseases have, since 1962, been frustrated by their inability to obtain investigational new drugs that offer the promise, or at least the hope, of useful therapy. Small companies with limited funds and a supply of an experimental drug sufficient only to conduct FDA-required animal and clinical studies usually cannot afford to provide the drug free to terminally ill patients. And the demand for such drugs is often great. For example, between the time that FDA initially determined the NDA for the cancer drug Erbitux to be approvable and the time that the agency finally approved the drug for marketing, the manufacturer received 8500 requests for compassionate use. Justin Gillis, *Patients Press Pleas for Cancer Drugs: Experimental Medicine in Short Supply*, WASH. POST, Apr. 7, 2002, at A1. Congress sought to address this problem in the FDA Modernization Act of 1997 by providing in new section 561(b) that any person acting through a licensed physician may obtain an investigational drug from the sponsor if all the requirements of an individual patient IND are met. This provision did nothing more than codify longstanding FDA policy. It stopped short of overruling FDA's ban on the sale of investigational drugs, codified at 21 C.F.R. 312.7.

21 C.F.R. 312.7(d) prohibits charging for an investigational drug without the prior written approval of FDA. In requesting approval, the sponsor must provide a full written explanation of why charging is necessary in order for it to undertake or continue the clinical trial. The needs of desperately ill patients are not considered. For that reason, the Abigail Alliance brought suit against FDA to contest the constitutionality of this prohibition.

Abigail Alliance for Better Access to Developmental Drugs v. von Eschenbach

445 F.3d 470 (D.C. Cir. 2006), *reh'g denied* 469 F.3d 129 (D.C. Cir. 2006), *reh'g en banc granted, judgment vacated*, U.S. App. LEXIS 28974 (D.C. Cir. Nov. 21, 2006).

■ ROGERS, CIRCUIT JUDGE.

The Abigail Alliance for Better Access to Developmental Drugs ("the Alliance") seeks to enjoin the Food and Drug Administration ("FDA") from continuing to enforce a policy barring the sale of new drugs that the FDA has determined, after Phase I trials on human beings, are sufficiently safe for expanded human testing (hereafter "post-Phase I investigational new drugs"). More specifically, the Alliance seeks access to potentially life-saving post-Phase I investigational new drugs on behalf of mentally competent, terminally ill adult patients who have no alternative government-approved treatment options (hereafter "terminally ill patients"). The Alliance contends that the FDA's policy violates the substantive due process rights to privacy, liberty, and life of its terminally ill members. The complaint presents the question of whether the Due Process Clause protects the right of terminally ill patients to decide, without FDA interference, whether to assume the risks of using potentially life-saving investigational new drugs that the FDA has yet to approve for commercial marketing but that the FDA has determined, after Phase I clinical human trials, are safe enough for further testing on a substantial number of human beings.

Upon applying the Supreme Court's test for addressing substantive due process claims set forth in *Washington v. Glucksberg*, 521 U.S. 702, 710 (1997), we hold that the district court erred in dismissing the Alliance's complaint pursuant to Federal Rule of Civil Procedure 12(b)(6) for failure to state a claim. First, the right at issue, carefully described, is the right of a mentally competent, terminally ill adult patient to access potentially life-saving post-Phase I investigational new drugs, upon a doctor's advice, even where that medication carries risks for the patient. Second, we find, upon examining "our Nation's history, legal traditions, and practices," *Glucksberg*, 521 U.S. at 710, that the government has not blocked access to new drugs throughout the greater part of our Nation's history. Only in recent years has the government injected itself into consideration of the effectiveness of new drugs. Third, Supreme Court precedent on liberty indicates that the right claimed by the Alliance can be inferred from the Court's conclusion in *Cruzan v. Director, Missouri Department of Health*, 497 U. S. 261, 278 (1990), that an individual has a due process right to refuse life-sustaining medical treatment. Here, the claim implicates a similar right—

the right to access potentially life-sustaining medication where there are no alternative government-approved treatment options. In both instances, the key is the patient's right to make the decision about her life free from government interference.

Because the question remains whether the FDA's challenged policy has violated that right, we reverse the dismissal of the Alliance's complaint and remand the case to the district court to determine whether the FDA's policy "is narrowly tailored to serve a compelling [governmental] interest," *Glucksberg*, 521 U.S. at 721 (quoting *Reno v. Flores*, 506 U.S. 292, 302 (1993))....

. . . .

[Dissenting opinion omitted.]

NOTES

1. *En Banc Reconsideration.* A petition for rehearing was denied, 2006 WL 3359334, but the Court of Appeals has ordered an en banc reargument.

2. *Unproven Drugs for the Terminally Ill.* The arguments for and against a "right to treatment" have special force when applied to unproven remedies sought by terminally ill patients. *See* "Adequacy of Access to Investigative Drugs for Seriously Ill Patients," Hearing before the Subcommittee on Oversight and Investigations of the House Committee on Commerce, 105th Cong., 1st Sess. (1997); Jerome Groopman, *The Right to a Trial: Should Dying Patients Have Access to Experimental Drugs?*, THE NEW YORKER, Dec. 18, 2006, at 40; Norman F. Carlin, *Informing Public Choice: Risk Perception Heuristics, Agency Paternalism, and Individual Autonomy in Food and Drug Safety Regulation* (1994), Andrew F. Schmolka, *In Search of the Optimal Balance: FDA's Safety Mandate and the Autonomy Rights of Individuals* (1994), and Madeline Blot, *The Right to Stay Alive?* (1994), in Chapter I(D) of the Electronic Book; Mary M. Flannery, *Research on the Terminally Ill: A Balancing Act between Facilitating Access to Innovative Therapies and Protecting Vulnerable Subjects in Search of One Last Hope for Survival* (2003), in Chapter VI(C)(1) of the Electronic Book.

COMMENT: USE OF LAETRILE FOR CANCER

For more than a decade, from 1975 through 1987, cancer patients, often aided by producers, sought the same right to use unproven remedies that spokespersons for AIDS patients have now won. Their central target was Laetrile (amygdalin), a poorly-characterized natural constituent of apricot kernels. FDA first seized quantities of Laetrile in 1960 at the Hoxsey Cancer Center in Dallas, Texas. Laetrile was one of a number of unproven drugs made and administered by Dr. Ernst T. Krebs of San Francisco, with whom FDA had engaged in litigation as early as the 1920s.

Unproven cancer remedies have been the focus of major FDA enforcement actions since the mid–1900s. Following enactment of the Drug Amendments of 1962, the new statutory requirements provided FDA with important new enforcement tools. For example, the agency successfully ended the marketing of Krebiozen on the ground that it was an illegal new drug. *Tutoki v. Celebrezze*, 375 F.2d 105 (7th Cir. 1967); *Rutherford v.*

American Medical Ass'n, 379 F.2d 641 (7th Cir. 1967); *Durovic v. Richardson*, 479 F.2d 242 (7th Cir. 1973).

In 1975, two cancer victims sued to enjoin FDA from interfering with their personal use of Laetrile. The District Court determined that the plaintiffs were incapable of complying with the new drug approval requirements of FDA and thus were entitled to an injunction against the agency to preserve their free choice of treatment. *Rutherford v. United States*, 399 F. Supp. 1208 (W.D. Okla. 1975). On appeal, the Tenth Circuit (2–1) upheld the injunction pending a formal determination by FDA of Laetrile's regulatory status. 542 F.2d 1137 (10th Cir. 1976).

The District Court thereafter remanded the matter to FDA for preparation of an appropriate administrative record and meanwhile reaffirmed its injunction. 424 F. Supp. 105 (W.D. Okla. 1977). The District Court later also certified the case as a class action, a ruling FDA did not appeal. 429 F. Supp. 506 (W.D. Okla. 1977). Following a public hearing, commenced at 42 Fed. Reg. 10066 (Feb. 18, 1977), the FDA Commissioner determined that Laetrile was not GRAS and GRAE and was not exempt from the new drug provisions of the FD&C Act under either grandfather clause. 42 Fed. Reg. 39768 (Aug. 5, 1977). *See* "Banning of the Drug Laetrile from Interstate Commerce by FDA," Hearing before the Subcommittee on Health and Scientific Research of the Senate Committee on Human Resources, 95th Cong., 1st Sess. (1977).

When the dispute returned to court, the district judge held that Laetrile was grandfathered under the FD&C Act and concluded that in any case the plaintiffs had a constitutional right of privacy to use the drug in the treatment of their disease. 438 F. Supp. 1287 (W.D. Okla. 1977). On appeal, the Tenth Circuit held that, wholly apart from any constitutional issues, the new drug requirements of the FD&C Act have no application to terminally ill cancer patients:

> ... [W]hat can "generally recognized" as "safe" and "effective" mean as to such persons who are so fatally stricken with a disease for which there is no known cure? What meaning can "effective" have in the absence of anything which may be used as a standard? Under this record Laetrile is as effective as anything else. What can "effective" mean if the person, by all prevailing standards, and under the position the Commission takes, is going to die of cancer regardless of what may be done. Thus there has been no standard here advanced by the Commission against which to measure the safeness or effectiveness of the drug as to the plaintiffs. Clearly the terms have no meaning under these circumstances, and certainly not the abstract meaning sought to be applied by the Commission....

> It would not seem difficult to define the group to which this determination of a legal issue applies. A licensed medical practitioner can express an opinion as to whether, under the present state of the art, a particular person is terminally ill with cancer, and to so certify....

We do not reach the constitutional aspects which were applied by the district court. We conclude, however, that the permanent injunction granted by the district court should be continued but be limited only to permit procurement of intravenous injections administered by a licensed medical practitioner to persons who are certified by a licensed medical practitioner to be terminally ill of cancer in some form.

582 F.2d 1234, 1237 (10th Cir. 1978). *Cf. United States v. Mosinee Research Corp.*, 583 F.2d 930 (7th Cir. 1978).

A unanimous Supreme Court reversed this decision, holding that the FD&C Act "makes no special provision for drugs used to treat terminally ill patients." *United States v. Rutherford*, 442 U.S. 544 (1979). The Supreme Court accepted FDA's arguments that it was important to protect individuals suffering from a potentially fatal disease from rejecting conventional therapy in favor of a drug with no demonstrable curative properties, and to protect the public generally from "the vast range of self-styled panaceas that inventive minds can devise." The Court remanded the case to the Court of Appeals.

When the case returned to the Tenth Circuit, it rejected the District Court's constitutional ruling:

It is apparent in the context with which we are here concerned that the decision by the patient whether to have treatment or not is a protected right, but his selection of a particular treatment, or at least a medication, is within the area of governmental interests in protecting public health. The premarketing requirement of the Federal Food, Drug and Cosmetic Act, 21 U.S.C. § 355, is an exercise of Congressional authority to limit the patient's choice of medication.

Rutherford v. United States, 616 F.2d 455 (10th Cir. 1980). *See also Carnohan v. United States*, 616 F.2d 1120 (9th Cir. 1980); *Judkins v. United States*, Food Drug Cosm. L. Rep. (CCH) ¶ 38,179 (D. Or. 1978).

But the battle over Laetrile was not over. The District Court dismissed the complaint and dissolved its injunctions in March 1984, 1983–1984 FDLI Jud. Rec. 173 (W.D. Okla. 1984), but two months later it granted a motion to reopen the case. In March 1985, the District Court entered an order determining that the consent order between the parties and the government must be enforced and that, because Laetrile is GRAS and GRAE for the reduction of cancer pain, the injunction against FDA interference in the use of Laetrile by cancer patients would be reinstated. Food Drug Cosm. L. Rep. (CCH) ¶ 38,312 (W.D. Okla. 1985). This time, the Tenth Circuit quickly reversed the District Court, determined that the consent order had been dissolved, and ordered the District Court to dismiss the action and dissolve all injunctions. 806 F.2d 1455 (10th Cir. 1986). On remand, the District Court complied, finally bringing a decade of litigation to a close. Food Drug Cosm. L. Rep. ¶ 38,030 (W.D. Okla. 1987). *See* "Postscript on Laetrile," FDA Talk Paper No. T87–27 (June 18, 1987).

Throughout this judicial sparring, supporters of Laetrile also sought its legalization through state legislation. More than one-third of the states ultimately legalized use of the drug within their borders. *See also Wickwire v. N.Y. State Dep't of Health*, Food Drug Cosm. L. Rep. (CCH) ¶ 38,166 (N.Y. 1978) (allowing a patient to be treated with Laetrile over the objections of the Department of Health). Laetrile also remains available from foreign sources.

NOTES

1. *Other Cancer Product Controversies.* For reviews of other cancer products that have been the subject of FDA regulatory action, see Wallace F. Janssen, *Cancer Quackery: Past and Present*, 11 FDA CONSUMER, No. 6, at 27 (July–Aug. 1977); Richard E. McFadyen & James Harvey Young, *The Koch Cancer Treatment*, 53 J. OF THE HIST. OF MED. 254 (1998); Eric S. Junhkie, *Quacks and Crusaders: The Fabulous Careers of John Brinkley, Norman Baker, and Harry Hoxsey* (2002), in Chapter VI(C)(12) of the Electronic Book. For another nonchemotherapy approach to treating cancer see Michael Specter, *The Outlaw Doctor*, THE NEW YORKER, Feb. 5, 2001, at 48. *See also United States v. Sopeak*, Food Drug Cosm. L. Rep. (CCH) ¶ 38,162 (E.D. Mich. 1990).

2. *Stanislaw V. Burzynski, M.D., Ph.D.* Dr. Burzynski began using antineoplastons in the treatment of cancer patients in 1977, without an IND or approved NDA. In 1983, FDA obtained an injunction prohibiting him from shipping antineoplastons in interstate, but not intrastate, commerce. *United States v. Burzynski Cancer Research Institute*, No. H–83–2069 (S.D. Tex. 1983). After extensive further litigation, *e.g., United States v. Burzynski Cancer Research Institute*, 819 F.2d 1301 (5th Cir. 1987), *Burzynski v. Aetna Life Insurance Co.*, 967 F.2d 1063 (5th Cir. 1992), *modified*, 989 F.2d 733 (5th Cir. 1993), *Trustees of the Northwest Laundry v. Burzynski*, 27 F.3d 153 (5th Cir. 1994), the Texas State Board of Examiners suspended his license to practice medicine but stayed that action and placed him on probation for ten years conditioned on compliance with federal and Texas law regarding the manufacture and distribution of drugs. This action was upheld in *Texas State Board of Medical Examiners v. Burzynski*, 917 S.W.2d 365 (Tex. Ct. App. 1996). In 1997, FDA prosecuted Burzynski for violating the FD&C Act, but the jury acquitted him. *See* Matthew L. Stennes, *The Criminalization of Innovation: FDA Misdirection in the Najarian and Burzynski Cases* (1997) in Chapter VI(K) of the Electronic Book. For a detailed report on the cost to FDA of investigating and prosecuting Buryznski, see *Agency Spent Over $2 Million Pursuing Cancer Researcher Burzynski*, 3 FDA WEEK, No. 31, at 4–9 (Aug. 1, 1997).

3. *John S. Najarian, M.D.* Dr. Najarian, a research scientist at the University of Minnesota, developed a biological drug, antilymphocyte globulin (ALG), for use in preventing the rejection of transplanted organs. He conducted clinical investigation of the drug and distributed it to other physicians for their use without an IND or NDA. Motions to dismiss a criminal indictment were denied, *United States v. Najarian*, 915 F. Supp. 1460 (D. Minn. 1996), Food Drug Cosm. L. Rep. (CCH) ¶ 38,461 (D. Minn. 1996), but the District Court directed a verdict of acquittal for Najarian at the end of the government's case.

14.   EMERGENCY RESEARCH

In 1996, FDA established regulations governing the narrow circumstances under which emergency clinical research may be conducted without informed consent, *e.g.*, because of a life-threatening condition for which there is no available alternative and the person is unconscious. 60 Fed. Reg. 49086 (Sept. 21, 1995), 61 Fed. Reg. 51498 (Oct. 2, 1996), codified at 21

C.F.R. 50.24. A decade later, on the basis of approximately 60 INDs for emergency research, FDA issued a draft guidance and conducted a public hearing on this subject, announced in 71 Fed. Reg. 51143, 51198 (Aug. 29, 2006). *See* Robert V. Ciccone, *Medical Research and the Protection of Individuals Incapable of Providing Consent* (1999), in Chapter XI(C)(1) of the Electronic Book.

15.   Investigator Fraud

Ever since Congress enacted the Drug Amendments of 1962, requiring proof of the effectiveness of a drug before FDA will approve an NDA, the pharmaceutical industry has been plagued by sporadic instances of investigator fraud during clinical trials, especially Phase III trials. On occasion, the sponsoring company has uncovered this fraud. FDA investigators have also occasionally been the first to find such problems. Regardless of how the fraud is discovered, it can have a devastating effect on drug development and thus on the economic viability of both the drug and the company involved. FDA has issued Guidance for Industry and Clinical Investigators: The Use of Clinical Holds Following Clinical Investigator Misconduct (2004).

Virtually every type of fraud imaginable has been uncovered by companies and the FDA. Some investigators have fabricated the names and data for some or all of the trial subjects. Others have used the names of deceased patients. Still others have used the names of actual patients but have "penciled" (*i.e.*, made up) the data, either without administering the test drug at all or by substituting fraudulent data for the actual data.

On occasion, it has been difficult to determine whether questionable data are in fact valid or fraudulent. Attempts to validate data after the trial is complete can be extremely time-consuming and costly, and thus can have a major impact on a trial even if the data are in fact validated. Whenever data are found by FDA to be suspect, it is unlikely that the agency will rely upon those data as pivotal evidence for an NDA in the absence of unequivocal validation.

The clinical monitoring that has commonly been used for the past 40 years to assure the integrity of clinical trials offers only modest safeguards against fraudulent investigator activity. For the most part, sponsoring companies rely upon clinical research associates (CRAs) to talk to investigators periodically and to review the clinical report forms (CRFs) for individual patients. A clever and determined investigator, however, can easily hide fraudulent material from random and relatively superficial oversight of this type. Indeed, even a relatively rigorous inquiry by a CRA can easily miss systematic and continuing fraud in clinical research.

Because FDA has often encountered fraudulent reporting of clinical studies of investigational new drugs, the IND regulations provide for disqualification of clinical investigators. 21 C.F.R. 312.70. FDA has recommended criminal prosecution of several clinical investigators for violation of the False Reports to the Government Act, 18 U.S.C. § 1001. *See, e.g.*, *United States v. Smith*, 740 F.2d 734 (9th Cir. 1984); "New Jersey Doctor Pleads Guilty to Drug Testing Fraud," FDA Talk Paper No. P88-78 (Oct.

25, 1988). The agency has also initiated prosecutions for fraudulent animal testing of new drugs. *See, e.g., United States v. Keplinger*, 776 F.2d 678 (7th Cir. 1985). In 1982, FDA published guidelines for reinstating previously disqualified clinical investigators. 47 Fed. Reg. 52228 (Nov. 19, 1982).

16. IMPORTATION OF INVESTIGATIONAL NEW DRUGS FOR PERSONAL USE

FDA first adopted a personal import policy for drugs in 1954. Since 1977, the FDA Regulatory Procedures Manual provisions for mail importation (Ch. 9–71–00) and personal baggage (Ch. 9–72–00) have stated that FDA will not detain unapproved new drugs imported for personal use. At the same time, however, the Manual has continued to prohibit the importation of any "new drugs that are not covered by an approved NDA" and of any product subject to an Import Alert because of concerns about safety or fraud. Faced with a large number of unapproved AIDS drugs being imported for personal use, in July 1988 the agency issued the following guidance:

> Because of the desire to acquire articles for treatment of serious and life-threatening conditions like AIDS and cancer, individuals have been purchasing unapproved products from foreign sources.... Such products are often shipped to the purchaser by mail.
>
> Even though such products are subject to refusal, we may use our discretion to examine the background, risk, and purpose of these products before making a final decision....
>
> 2. A product entered for personal use, which meets the criteria in item 4 below, may proceed without sampling or detention.
>
> 3. Products that are not identified, or are not accompanied by documentation of intended use, should be detained. Other reasons for detention may include: size of the shipment (amount inconsistent with personal use), fraudulent promotion or misrepresentation, or an unreasonable health risk due to either toxicity or possible contamination....
>
> 4. Following detention, shipments may be released to an individual if the following criteria can be satisfied and there is no safety risk or evidence of fraud:
>
> • the product was purchased for personal use
>
> • the product is not for commercial distribution and the amount of product is not excessive (*i.e.*, 3 months supply of a drug)
>
> • the intended use of the product is appropriately identified
>
> • the patient seeking to import the product affirms in writing that it is for the patient's own use and provides

> the name and address of the doctor licensed in the U.S. responsible for his or her treatment with the product

5. If the district should encounter a situation suggesting promotional and/or commercial activity that falls within our health fraud guideline, the district should recommend that an Import Alert be issued for the automatic detention of the product and identification of the promoter involved.

FDA Office of Regional Operations, Pilot Guidance for Release of Mail Importations (1988).

NOTES

1. *Policy Interpretation.* In a letter from FDA Associate Commissioner for Legislative Affairs H. C. Cannon to Representative John Dingell (Aug. 19, 1988), FDA stated that the new importation policy applied whether the drugs were approved or unapproved in the country of origin; included any drug for the treatment of serious and life-threatening conditions; applied to both individuals and organizations; applied whether or not an IND has been submitted to FDA; and permitted FDA to deny entry wherever there was an unreasonable risk to patients. In accordance with this policy, AIDS patients organized buying groups to purchase unapproved drugs from abroad.

2. *Drugs on Import Alert.* The FDA importation policy does not apply to drugs that have been made the subject of an Import Alert. FDA has issued some 40 Import Alerts for medical products that are unsafe or clearly fraudulent. *See* "Policy on Importing Unapproved AIDS Drugs for Personal Use," FDA Talk Paper No. T88–51 (July 27, 1988).

3. *Importation of Unapproved RU486.* On July 20, 1988, FDA revised Chapter 9–71 of its Regulatory Procedures Manual (RPM) to authorize a pilot program for importation of unapproved AIDS and cancer drugs for personal use. FDA issued Import Alert 66–813 on September 26, 1988, clarifying that the personal import policy did not apply to RU486 (the "abortion pill"). On February 1, 1989, FDA expanded the July 1988 program to drugs for all life-threatening or serious conditions (not just AIDS and cancer) and to drugs for other medical conditions when the drug is not known to represent a significant health risk. In *Benten v. Kessler*, 799 F. Supp. 281 (E.D.N.Y. 1992), plaintiffs contested the seizure by FDA of RU486 imported for personal use. After severely criticizing FDA for its failure to establish its policies by notice-and-comment rulemaking, the District Court ordered FDA to return the RU486 to the plaintiffs.

4. *FDA Denial of Personal Use Import.* The District Court in *Garlic v. FDA*, 783 F. Supp. 4 (D.D.C. 1992), held that a person denied permission to import an investigational drug for personal use must first exhaust administrative remedies by submitting a citizen petition to FDA requesting the agency to reverse its refusal to permit importation before bringing an injunction and declaratory judgment action in court. The District Court also held that a person with Alzheimer's disease has no constitutional right to obtain unapproved medications. *See also Sifre v. Robles*, 917 F. Supp. 133 (D.P.R. 1996).

5. *Illegal Commercial Importation.* In *United States v. Haas*, 171 F.3d 259 (5th Cir. 1999), the Court of Appeals affirmed the conviction of a defendant for illegally importing unapproved versions of approved prescription drugs. The court held that the importation was for commercial purposes that did not fall within the FDA personal use exception. In *In re: Canadian Import Antitrust Litigation*, 470

F.3d 785 (8th Cir. 2006), the Court of Appeals affirmed the District Court's dismissal of an antitrust case brought against nine large pharmaceutical companies alleging a conspiracy to suppress the importation of Canadian prescription drugs for personal use.

6. *Commentary. See* Susan Thaul & Donna U. Vogt, *Importing Prescription Drugs: Objectives, Options, and Outlook*, CRS REP. No. RL 32511 (Dec. 8, 2005); Suzan Thaul, *Drug Safety and Effectiveness: Issues and Action Options after FDA Approval*, CRS REP. No. RL 32797 (Mar. 21, 2006); Jody Feder, *Prescription Drug Importation and Internet Sales: A Legal Overview*, CRS REP. No. RL 32191 (May 25, 2006).

————

FDA has declined to initiate regulatory action against various activities by organized nonprofit AIDS groups that would almost surely trigger enforcement immediately if engaged in by commercial enterprises. For example, on July 23, 1988, in a speech to the Second International Lesbian and Gay Health Conference & AIDS Forum in Boston, FDA Commissioner Frank Young declared:

> The absence of an effective AIDS therapy has led to promotion of a number of unproven remedies or unproven drugs. Most of these products will be cast aside as ineffective after they have been popular for awhile. . . .
>
> Traditionally, FDA has not interfered with individuals that use unproven substances in self-treatment. Nor have we interfered when doctors prescribed drugs for other than their approved use. On the other hand, we have acted against promoters or seized products when there was a fraudulent promotion, or when the product represented an unreasonable risk. FDA's new policy regarding self-help, nonprofit clinics is similar to our policy regarding the use of unproven substances in self-treatment—that is, not to interfere as long as patients are not being harmed, clinics do not promote unproven products outside the clinic, and the clinic does not serve as a subterfuge for a commercial enterprise.

Gina Kolata, *An Angry Response to Actions on AIDS Spurs F.D.A. Shift*

THE NEW YORK TIMES, June 26, 1988, at A1.

Ripples of fear and resentment spread among AIDS patients and their advocates last week as the Food and Drug Administration threatened to restrict access to a substance thousands of patients are taking in the hope it might help fight their disease. On Monday, without publicity, the agency acted to stop two companies from selling AL–721, a substance made from eggs and soybeans that is being marketed as a food but is widely used as a possible treatment against the AIDS virus on the basis of slim anecdotal evidence. Then, on Thursday, as spreading word of the actions led to protests, the agency partly reversed itself. It allowed the companies to continue selling AL–721 but warned them not to suggest in their marketing that it was a drug. . . .

As last week's action and retreat against the two companies suggested, F.D.A. officials feel AL–721 puts them in a quandary. The agency is struggling to balance its mandate to protect the public from useless and perhaps harmful drugs against the understandable demand by the AIDS community for freer access to possible treatments for those facing death from acquired immune deficiency syndrome. . . .

In the last two years the use of AL–721 by AIDS virus carriers and AIDS patients has soared, promoted and organized by an impressive network. As many as 19 buyers clubs have sprung up around the country, purchasing AL–721 in bulk and even testing shipments to be sure they are pure. While it may not be dangerous, the substance is not cost-free. Patients pay about $135 to $250 a month for it, and taking it disrupts their lives. AL–721 requires refrigeration and, according to some, should not be taken within two hours of a meal.

It was developed about three years ago by Dr. Meir Shinitzky and his colleagues at the Weizmann Institute of Science in Rehovot, Israel. Dr. Shinitzky explained in a telephone interview that the substance was composed of three lipids, fats found in egg yolks, soybeans and some other foods. The theory is that the compound reduces the level of cholesterol in the membranes of blood cells and the AIDS virus. This makes the membranes more fluid, which Dr. Shinitzky and others postulate hampers the ability of the AIDS virus to attach to and invade body cells. . . .

When Dr. Shinitzky began making claims for AL–721 about two years ago, AIDS patients flew to Israel for the substance. Then, some began making a version of it for themselves, extracting it from egg yolks with acetone heated to near boiling. Later, they discovered a supplier in Japan and imported the substance. And finally, in the last year, as many as a half dozen companies in this country began openly marketing AL–721 as a food, which allowed them to skirt F.D.A. regulations for licensing drugs.

Yet calling AL–721 a food is the thinnest of guises, AIDS patients and their advocates say. Everyone is winking and nodding as buyers clubs purchase huge amounts of the substance and sell it to people infected with the AIDS virus. In New York City, the People With AIDS Health Club sells a ton of AL–721 a month—enough to treat nearly 1,000 people, according to Mr. Callen.

On Monday, New Jersey officials, acting at the request of the F.D.A., entered a warehouse in South Plainfield, N.J. and put an embargo on 41 cases of AL–721, made by the Ethigen Corporation of Los Angeles. Also on Monday, the agency sent a letter to Nutricology, Inc. of San Leandro, Calif., telling the company to stop selling its version of the substance, which it calls Pe 9+. In both instances, the agency felt that the companies were selling AL–721 as an AIDS drug, not food.

As word of the action spread through the AIDS community, people felt panicked and outraged. Almost immediately, lawyers for gay support groups called the agency, and some AIDS patients began stockpiling AL–721. By Thursday, the agency called off the embargo and informed Nutricology that if it would comply with agency regulations and stop implying that the substance is useful against AIDS, it could resume selling the product.

NOTES

1. *Compound Q.* In June 1989, FDA announced it was investigating the distribution of "Compound Q," another putative treatment for AIDS:

> Trichosanthin is a plant protein, which researchers think may be an effective agent against the AIDS virus. An FDA-sanctioned clinical study of GLQ–223, a refined form of trichosanthin, was started at San Francisco General Hospital in May 1989. This initial human study is designed to test the safety of this drug's use in treating AIDS patients, and particularly to determine at what dose levels the drug can be tolerated.

> According to media reports, Project Inform, a San Francisco-based AIDS activist group initiated distribution of a trichosanthin-based preparation imported from China, supposedly to test its efficacy in AIDS patients.... There have been several media reports that the death of one patient and the serious adverse reactions of other patients participating in this informal study have been either directly or indirectly linked to this trichosanthin-based product....

> The agency feels that the concerns raised by this operation point out the need to conduct clinical studies in a scientific manner, that includes careful study design, institutional monitoring mechanisms and consistent reporting channels. Such studies assure the acquisition of good clinical data in the shortest possible time, and ensure the safety of patients.

"FDA Statement on Unauthorized AIDS Drug Study," FDA Talk Paper No. T89–40 (June 28, 1987).

2. *Commercial Cancer Clinics.* Compare FDA's actions with respect to AIDS treatments to its efforts to shut down for-profit cancer clinics using unproven cancer drugs. *United States v. Hoxsey Cancer Clinic*, 198 F.2d 273 (5th Cir. 1952); *United States v. Burzynski Cancer Research Institute*, 819 F.2d 1301 (5th Cir. 1987).

3. *Commentary. See* Katherine S. Bolland, *AIDS Buyers Clubs* (1994), Julie A. Grow, *Expanding Access to New AIDS Drugs: Wise Policy or Wrong Direction?* (1996), and Julie L. Strom, *The Cure at a Crossroads: The Intersection of Ethics and Ambition in AIDS Research* (2003), in Chapter VI(C)(1) of the Electronic Book.

COMMENT: THE FUTURE OF THE FDA PERSONAL IMPORT POLICY

With the increased availability of FDA-approved cancer and AIDS drugs in the United States and the substantial problem of foreign counterfeit drugs, FDA has concluded that the personal import policy should be either drastically reduced or eliminated. *See* "Errata: Comparative Pricing of Prescription Drugs Sold in the United States and Canada and the Effects on U.S. Customers," Hearing before the Subcommittee on Consumer Affairs, Foreign Commerce and Tourism of the Senate Committee on Commerce, Science, and Transportation, 107th Cong., 1st Sess. 10 (2001). Although FDA began discussing this with the Secretary of HHS several years ago, for obvious political reasons no action has been taken to change the July 1988 policy.

During the same time that FDA has sought to narrow or eliminate its personal import policy, Congress, in light of the price differential between domestic and foreign drugs, has enacted two statutes designed to increase imports of less expensive drugs from abroad. *See infra* p. 779. Those two statutes failed because the Secretaries of HHS in two administrations refused to certify that importation of drugs not approved by FDA would pose no additional risk to public health and would result in a significant reduction in cost to consumers. As political pressure increased prior to the November 2006 elections, it became clear that a compromise was essential in order to forestall more damaging legislation. Congress therefore enacted section 535 of the FY 2007 appropriations statute for the Department of Homeland Security, 120 Stat. 1355 (2006), to provide, for one year, that an individual entering the country from Canada may bring up to a 90–day supply of any drug except a controlled substance or a biological product. *See generally* Peter S. Reichertz & Melinda S. Friend, *Hiding Behind Agency Discretion: The Food and Drug Administration's Personal Use Drug Importation Policy*, 9 CORNELL J.L. & PUB. POL'Y 493 (2000).

17. CLINICAL TRIALS DATABANK

During the 1980s, FDA began publishing a list of all AIDS drugs in clinical trial under an IND. In the AIDS Amendments of 1988, enacted as part of the Health Omnibus Programs Extension of 1988, 102 Stat. 3048, 3062, 3072, 42 U.S.C. 300cc–17(d) & (e), Congress directed FDA to establish, as part of a databank on AIDS drugs, a registry of clinical trials of AIDS drugs conducted under an IND. The Department of HHS announced the availability of the databank and IND registry, located in NIH, in "AIDS Clinical Trials Lists Completed," HHS News No. P89–33 (July 18, 1989).

The FDA Modernization Act of 1997 added section 402(j) to the Public Health Service Act, 42 U.S.C. 282(j), to require the Director of NIH to establish a databank of information on clinical trials for drugs for serious or life-threatening diseases and conditions. The databank was required to include a registry of clinical trials and information pertaining to experimental treatments under a treatment IND or as a Group C cancer drug. NIH, through the National Library of Medicine, established the databank at clinicaltrials.gov. It is currently the most comprehensive source of clinical trials in the country. In March 2002, FDA issued a GUIDANCE FOR INDUSTRY: INFORMATION PROGRAM ON CLINICAL TRIALS FOR SERIOUS OR LIFE–THREATENING DISEASES AND CONDITIONS to address statutory and procedural issues relating to the databank, but implementation of the statutory requirement for the pharmaceutical industry to participate in the databank has been hindered by the absence of enforcement remedies for noncompliance. *See* FDAMA SECTION 113: STATUS REPORT ON IMPLEMENTATION (2005), FDA Website (reporting that only 35 percent of the trials that should have been listed in the database had been).

The clinical trials databank mandated by section 402(j) of the PHS Act is limited to drugs for serious or life-threatening diseases. Almost immediately, patients and physicians began to call for a more expanded clinical trials databank, to cover all diseases and to provide more information on the clinical trial protocols involved, as well as to cover the results of trials as soon as they became available. A consortium of respected medical journals announced that they would not publish the results of clinical trials that were not fully registered in the databank. Catherine D. DeAngelis et al., *Clinical Trial Registration: A Statement from the International Committee of Medical Journal Editors*, 292 J.A.M.A. 1363 (Sept. 15, 2004). The Pharmaceutical Research and Manufacturers of America published *Principles for the Conduct of Clinical Trials and the Communication of Clinical Trial Results* in 2002, launched a *Clinical Study Results Database* in 2004, and adopted a Policy Paper on *Principles Regarding the Disclosure of Clinical Trial Information* in 2005. Individual companies have also established their own databanks. Nonetheless, all clinical trial databanks remain voluntary and they vary widely in the type and detail of the information they contain.

In one well-publicized case, New York sued GlaxoSmithKline (GSK) alleging that the company had committed fraud in violation of state statutes by (1) withholding data from clinical trials showing that Paxil was no more effective than a placebo in adolescents and children and was more likely to cause suicidal thoughts, (2) selectively publishing only data from trials with favorable results, and (3) making promotional claims inconsistent with the study results that were suppressed. GSK settled the matter by paying a small fine of $2.5 million and agreeing to establish an online registry with summaries of results for all clinical trials conducted after December 27, 2000.

18.   GENETICS, GENOMICS, AND PERSONALIZED MEDICINE

Drugs behave differently in different people. A drug may be effective in some and ineffective in others. It may be safe in some but toxic in others. These variations among individuals are potentially explainable by the genetic differences among individuals in a large population. The emergence of the science of genetics and genomics therefore has important implications for clinical trials for drugs, as the following article by two respected FDA drug officials relates.

Larry J. Lesko & Janet Woodcock, *Pharmacogenomic–Guided Drug Development: Regulatory Perspective*

2 THE PHARMACOGENOMICS JOURNAL 20 (2002).

Pharmacogenetics (PGt) and now the more global term, pharmacogenomics (PGx), have come to the forefront after an evolutionary period of more than 30 years. Several transforming events in the past 5 years, not the least of which was the completion of the human genome sequence in 2001, have created an expectation that genetic and genomic information will produce sweeping changes in the practice of medicine and the prescribing of drugs. The almost daily press reports of new gene discoveries lend credence to the argument that personal genetic/genomic profiles will have a tremendous impact on health by the year 2010.

Genomic information has the potential to revolutionize pharmacologic therapies at many levels. The process of drug discovery may be transformed by this knowledge. Extensive genetic data will promote understanding of the molecular genetic contribution to many diseases. Genes and gene products suspected of being involved in disease pathogenesis will become new targets for intervention, and will stimulate new drug discovery programs. Conversely, gene expression profiling is being used currently to gain new insights into the molecular mechanism of drug actions, and the drug-disease interaction. Taken together, these techniques are expected to yield major advances in identifying drug candidates.

Genomic information will be increasingly used in the preclinical phases of drug development. There is great interest in using gene expression profiling to develop markers for both desired pharmacologic actions and toxic effects. Batteries of markers will then be used to characterize drug candidates and to aid in selection of those with optimal properties for further development, thus improving the effectiveness of drug development.

At the clinical level, the hope is for true individualization of therapy, which would maximize benefit and minimize toxicity. Currently, clinicians have few tools for predicting who will respond to a drug, or who will suffer ill effects. Although such differential responses have long been characterized as "idiosyncratic", clearly there are underlying reasons for them, and many have a genetic component. It is believed then most chronic diseases represent a heterogeneous group of disorders at the molecular level. This heterogeneity is one of the reasons that not all people with a disease respond to a given drug. One contribution of genomic science could be to provide a much more precise diagnosis, based either on underlying genotype, or on gene expression profiles. Similarly, some differences in drug efficacy response, and some toxicities, are based on variability in exposure or in pharmacodynamic response, caused by genetic differences. The ability to predict and account for such differences could markedly improve the therapeutic index of many drug interventions. Finally, it is hoped that genetically-based mechanisms of toxicity can be elucidated, and adverse effects avoided, by application of pharmacogenomic information.

We are not aware of any consensus on the definition of PGt and PGx, and in fact there are many different definitions in the scientific literature. Occasionally, these terms are used interchangeably. For the purposes of this article, we will consider PGx to be the global science of using genetic information from an individual or population for the purpose of: (1) explaining interindividual differences in pharmacokinetics (PK) and pharmacodynamics (PD); (2) identifying responders and non-responders to a drug; and (3) predicting the efficacy and/or toxicity of a drug. Also, we will consider PGt to be a scientific subset of PGx in which there are genetic variations (*e.g.*, polymorphism in cytochrome P–450 metabolizing enzymes) to drug doses and dosing regimens that result in different systemic drug exposure patterns (PK) in individuals or populations.

Over the past 5 years, many have expressed the concern that human clinical efficacy and safety trials in a traditional drug development program are challenging, time-consuming and increasingly more expensive to conduct. The relatively high rate of failure of drug candidates entering the clinical phases of drug development add significantly to these estimated costs. More recently, new drug candidates have been filtered from the discovery and development pipeline because their hepatic metabolism requires CYP–450 enzymes subject to genetic polymorphism. Several experts in the science of drug development perceive the increasing costs, and recent decreasing return on investment, as a significant threat to the viability of the pharmaceutical industry in the next 10 years.

Conventional wisdom suggests that PGx-guided clinical trials would shift the drug development paradigm toward a more efficient and informative process, resulting in a lower attrition rate of new drug candidates, and an overall lower development cost to the sponsor, albeit in the long-run. Furthermore, many believe that drug therapy based on the genetic profile of individuals could provide public health benefits such as better management of post-approval risks, and a decreased incidence of drug-induced morbidity and mortality. PGx could also reduce the incidence of drug product market withdrawals due to serious or fatal adverse events by allowing pre-selection, in advance of prescribing the drug, those patients who will be predisposed to toxicity.

It is hoped that more extensive use of PGx/PGt information will be utilized in future clinical trials. However, there are many unanswered questions about the FDA's regulation of clinical development programs using various elements of PGx/PGt. The following issues and questions, which need further discussion, are among the major concerns of the industry with regard to drug development:

● What are the regulatory implications of genetic profile screening of patients during investigational drug therapy?

● Is it acceptable to the FDA to stratify patients entering into a clinical trial *a priori* based on a PGx/PGt test?

● What are the statistical ramifications when using PGx/PGt to define patient subsets?

● If a PGx/PGt test is used to enrich a patient cohort receiving a certain dose and dosing interval during a clinical trial, will the label for that drug require a PGx/PGt diagnostic test?

● Would the Agency require the drug sponsor to submit an application for approval for the PGx/PGt diagnostic test at the time of approving the drug?

● What are the performance and statistical requirements for the PGx/PGt diagnostic that would be used for this purpose?

● What use would the Agency allow for a *post hoc* subset analysis based on a PGx/PGt diagnostic test in a clinical trial that failed to demonstrate efficacy or had an unacceptably high rate of adverse events?

● What information would be expected in those patient subgroups excluded from the pivotal clinical trials based on a PGx/PGt test?

● What PGx/PGt testing might be required for drugs currently approved and in the marketplace as new "genetic/genomic" information is discovered?

● When is it appropriate to prescreen in, or out, subjects for bioavailability, bioequivalence, drug interaction and other clinical pharmacology studies?

Ideally, a regulatory agency should be able to meet its public health mandate without stifling new technology that might lead to better drugs including the "customized medicines" of the PGx/PGt era. It should be noted that the FDA went on record of supporting the basic idea of "customized medicines" for a patient subset, back in 1998, as evidenced by its approval of trastuzumab (Hercept). The approved indication of trastuzumab, a recombinant DNA-derived humanized monoclonal antibody, was for the treatment of only those patients with metastatic breast cancer whose tumors overexpress the protein, HER2, in large amounts. This patient subset represents up to 30% of all women with breast cancer. The FDA has also approved one prognostic PGt assay and two PGx immunohistochemical assays to measure HER2/neu protein overexpression to be used in patient selection before prescribing trastuzumab treatment. It is likely that FDA would not have approved Hercept without the accompanying diagnostic test. Also, the recent approval of Gleevec (imatinib mesylate) in May 2001 for late phase chronic myelogenous leukemia (CML) is another example that the CDER is well aware of, and open to, individualization of drug therapy using PGx or other research strategies. The discovery and development of imatinib, while not strictly PGx-driven, is a good example of the type of molecular targeting to abnormal proteins, in this case in CML cells, that is possible with the help of PGx information. In addition, the Center for Biological Evaluation and Research (CBER) has extensive experience with gene therapy development for over 10 years and has reviewed applications for genetically engineered protein drugs for such indications as sepsis and hemophilia.

At present, patient genomic/genetic data from prospective clinical and clinical pharmacology studies are necessary to: (1) evaluate the role that PGx can play in drug development; (2) identify issues that will trigger more urgent and extensive discussion between the Agency and industry; (3) focus the regulatory review on the important science/clinical questions and determine what evidence is necessary to support label claims. We continue to be concerned that despite the widespread availability of simple PGx/PGt tests to determine a patient's phenotype and/or genotype with regard to polymorphism in drug metabolizing enzymes, there has been little use of this information to tailor drug doses and dosing regimens to individual patient subgroups in clinical practice before using the drug. Together, all of the stakeholders in PGx/PGt need to work on ways to assure that this does not happen with the second and third generation of PGx/PGt diagnostic tests. We conclude that the bridge between the current and emerging PGx/PGt research in drug development and regulatory review practices, and related policy, needs to be built systematically and on a sound scientific foundation. The gap between research and the use of PGx/PGt in clinical practice remains very wide, but we are encouraged with the progress that is being made to close this gap.

NOTES

1. *FDA Guidance.* FDA announced its GUIDANCE FOR INDUSTRY: PHARMACOGENOMIC DATA SUBMISSIONS in 70 Fed. Reg. 14698 (Mar. 23, 2005) and issued a Draft

Concept Paper, *Recommendations for the Generation and Submission of Genomic Data*, in November 2006.

2. *Warfarin Study.* A study by three FDA officials concluded that integrating genetic testing into therapy with the anticoagulant warfarin would reduce health care spending by about $1.1 billion annually. *See* Andrew McWilliam et al., *Health Care Savings from Personalizing Medicine Using Genetic Testing: The Case of Warfarin*, AEI–Brookings Joint Center for Regulatory Studies Working Paper No. 06–23 (Nov. 2006).

3. *Commentary. See* Lars Noah, *The Coming Pharmacogenomics Revolution: Tailoring Drugs to Fit Patients' Genetic Profiles*, 43 JURIMETRICS 1 (Fall 2002); Valerie Gutmann, *A New Era in Drug Development: Legal and Ethical Implications of Pharmacogenomics* (2005), in Chapter XII(C) of the Electronic Book.

19.   THE FDA CRITICAL PATH INITIATIVE

Concerned by the slowdown in the industry's submission of INDs and NDAs, in March 2004, FDA issued a report titled CHALLENGE AND OPPORTUNITY ON THE CRITICAL PATH TO NEW MEDICAL PRODUCTS "to address the growing crisis in moving basic discoveries to the market where they can be made available to patients." The report "highlights examples of Agency efforts that have improved the critical path and discusses opportunities for future efforts." *See also* 29 Fed. Reg. 21839 (Apr. 22, 2004); Janet Woodcock, *FDA's Approach to the Pipeline Problem*, 9 REG. AFFAIRS FOCUS, No. 9, at 6 (Sept. 2004). When, as part of its critical path initiative, FDA announced a public workshop "to explore approaches and potential obstacles to developing drugs," 70 Fed. Reg. 44660 (Aug. 3, 2005), it stated that the 2004 Critical Path report was "aimed at identifying potential problems and solutions to ensure that breakthroughs in medical science can be efficiently translated to safe, effective, and available medical products." After the workshop, FDA published a CRITICAL PATH OPPORTUNITIES REPORT AND LIST (Mar. 2006), identifying "targeted research that we believe, if pursued, will increase efficiency, predictability, and productivity in the development of new medical products." As one example of such a research project, FDA has established with Duke University the Cardiac Safety Research Consortium, to identify indicators of cardiac risk, predict adverse cardiovascular events, and improve biomarkers as diagnostic and assessment tools that will facilitate the development of safer and more effective cardiovascular drugs and diagnostic products. 71 Fed. Reg. 60732 (Oct. 16, 2006).

G.   THE NEW DRUG APPLICATION

Richard A. Merrill, *The Architecture of Government Regulation of Medical Products*

82 VIRGINIA LAW REVIEW 1753 (1996).

. . . .

The 1962 Amendments transformed the new drug review process that Congress had first authorized in 1938. Three changes were critically important. First, the 1962 Amendments converted what had been a premarket *notification* system, under which the maker of a new drug could commence marketing after the statutorily prescribed 180 days unless FDA challenged its safety, into a premarket *approval* system, in which the maker was obliged to wait for agency officials to affirm the drug's safety *and* effectiveness. The law thus gave FDA an effective veto over the marketing of any drug about which it had reservations. Not only was it harder for a manufacturer to satisfy FDA because effectiveness as well as safety had to be shown, the agency now had to be *convinced* before a drug could be marketed. Drug makers thus were held hostage to reviewers' indecision, to their preoccupation with other work, or to Congress's failure to provide FDA the resources necessary to handle its workload.

Second, the Amendments obviously raised the standard that a new drug had to satisfy by explicitly directing FDA to confirm its effectiveness as well as its safety. FDA now had express authority to examine the evidence supporting all therapeutic claims made for a drug. Congress accordingly broadened the statutory definition of "new drug" to include any drug that was not generally recognized by experts as safe *and* effective.

The effectiveness requirement dramatically expanded the scope of the new drug approval process. Once FDA was convinced that a new therapeutic agent was safe for a particular indication, the manufacturer could reasonably conclude—and FDA might even agree—that it was "generally recognized as safe" for other uses. But for any active ingredient, novel or familiar, many therapeutic uses are possible, each of which, under the law's broadened definition of a "new drug," potentially required FDA review.

The 1962 Amendments enlarged the fixed time limit for FDA to rule on an application to 180 days, after which the applicant could, in theory, demand a final decision. And, if that decision was adverse, the applicant could take the matter to court. These procedural safeguards proved to be empty promises; FDA made it a practice to restart the clock each time an applicant submitted new information, even if the agency had requested the information. Reviewers resisted any pressure to rush to rule on completed applications. Almost without exception, applicants for approval have been unwilling to press for a timely decision when the answer might be "no," and they have displayed no inclination whatever to challenge in court an agency refusal to approve drugs.

The third important change made by the 1962 Amendments was to enlarge FDA's authority over the design and conduct of clinical trials of new drugs, the experiments undertaken to generate the data that the agency requires to decide whether a drug is safe and, centrally, effective. Section 505(d) of the Act specifies that the effectiveness of a drug must be shown by "substantial evidence," which the statute defines as "evidence consisting of adequate and well-controlled investigations, including clinical investigations, by experts qualified . . . to evaluate the effectiveness of the drug involved. . . ." The 1962 Amendments also gave FDA explicit authority to establish standards under which experimental drugs may be shipped to investigators who agree to conduct clinical trials.

These two grants of authority have made FDA the ultimate arbiter of how clinical trials should be designed. In interpreting the "substantial evidence" requirement and in reviewing applications for "investigational exemptions" from the premarket approval requirement, the agency has inevitably played a dominant role in deciding how to determine whether new drugs work as claimed. At the end of the day, drug makers must persuade FDA reviewers that they have submitted sufficient evidence to prove that a drug works. As a result, the agency has become the most influential source of guidance on the design of clinical drug studies in the country, and perhaps in the world.

Under the 1906 law, FDA had relatively little influence over the therapeutic claims made for drugs. Its authority was exerted, if at all, after a drug was on the market and evidence had accumulated that it might not work. The 1938 Act gave the agency a gatekeeper role, which permitted officials to examine and sometimes question a drug's clinical utility. The 1962 Amendments completed the law's reversal of the burden of proof. Since the passage of the Amendments, FDA has been responsible for judging, on the basis of evidence that it prescribed and makers supplied, whether new drugs worked. This shift in responsibility transformed the way in which drugs are developed, tested and marketed.

With the shift came a more subtle change in FDA's own view of its consumer protection role. Citizens may complain when local police fail to curtail unlawful or violent activity, but few believe that even the best-functioning police force can solve, much less prevent, all crimes. FDA is believed to have a different role, a responsibility to prevent harm before it occurs. The law makes it unlawful, without proof of intent or demonstration of actual injury or deception, to market drugs that the agency has not approved. In some sense, the agency becomes a warrantor of manufacturer compliance with the rules that govern drug development and marketing. This responsibility is implicitly acknowledged in the agency's own publications, is frequently referred to in press accounts of its performance, and historically has permeated the dialogue between the agency and congressional oversight committees. FDA is repeatedly reminded, and often reminds us, that it shares responsibility for any drug that causes harm. Many observers claim that this perception of FDA's role has made agency officials responsible for allowing drugs to reach the market exceptionally, and inappropriately, cautious....

1.   PURPOSE AND FORM OF THE NDA

Peter Barton Hutt, *The Regulation of Drug Products by the United States Food and Drug Administration*

In THE TEXTBOOK OF PHARMACEUTICAL MEDICINE (John P. Griffin & John O'Grady, eds., 5th ed. 2006).

After the sponsor has completed all non-clinical and clinical testing necessary to demonstrate the safety and effectiveness of the drug, the test results must be compiled in an NDA for submission to FDA. As with the IND, the content and format of the NDA are set forth in the FDA regulations and must be followed in detail. The NDA must begin with a summary, to be followed by technical sections relating to (1) chemistry, manufacturing and controls, (2) non-clinical pharmacology and toxicology,

(3) human pharmacokinetics and bioavailability, (4) microbiology, (5) clinical data and (6) statistics. Proposed labeling must also be included. The typical NDA comprises tens of thousands or even hundreds of thousands of pages.

The statute requires that a new drug should be shown to be both safe and effective. Because no drug has ever been shown to be completely safe or effective, in all cases this has been interpreted to mean that the benefits of the drug outweigh its risks under the labeled conditions of use for a significant identified patient population. The statute is very broadly worded with respect to the required proof for safety and effectiveness, and FDA has exercised substantial discretion in applying these requirements. New drugs have been approved on the basis of only one study, on the basis of Phase II studies that have never progressed to Phase III, on the basis of foreign studies alone and with results that could not be regarded as definitive from a scientific standpoint.

In most instances, FDA requires more than one adequate and well-controlled clinical trial. In the FDA Modernization Act of 1997 however, Congress clarified the law by providing that FDA may base the approval of an NDA on data from one adequate and well-controlled clinical investigation and confirmatory evidence.

The FDA has in practice implemented this provision only when the single adequate and well-controlled clinical investigation has statistical significance that is an order of magnitude greater than is normally required, that is, 0.005 or greater than 0.05.

Under the FD&C Act, FDA has always been required to evaluate the NDA and approve or disapprove it within 180 days. Until 1992, this almost never occurred. The average time for approval of an NDA was between 2 and 3 years. This time remained largely unchanged for the years between 1962 and 1994, in spite of repeated promises and attempts by FDA to speed up the process. FDA was able to avoid the 180–day statutory time deadline in several ways. First, the agency started the clock when it accepted the NDA for filing, not when it was submitted. Second, FDA stopped the clock, and restarted it, whenever new submissions were made. Third, FDA requested an extension of time from the applicant, who had no choice but to agree. Fourth, FDA simply ignored the 180–day deadline, and there was nothing that the applicant could do about it anyway.

NOTES

1. *NDA Regulations.* Following its success in the four Supreme Court cases in 1973, FDA planned to undertake a total revision of its IND and NDA regulations. This work was interrupted, first by investigations growing out of allegations of improper FDA handling of new drug decisions during the fall of 1974, "Examination of the Pharmaceutical Industry, 1973–74," Joint Hearings before the Subcommittee on Health of the Senate Committee on Labor and Public Welfare and the Subcommittee on Administrative Practice and Procedure of the Senate Committee on the Judiciary, 93rd Cong., 2nd Sess., Part 7 (1974), and later by Congressional consideration of the Drug Regulation Reform legislation in 1977–1980. FDA promulgated new NDA regulations in 44 Fed. Reg. 58919 (Oct. 12, 1979), 47 Fed. Reg. 46622 (Oct. 19, 1982), 50 Fed. Reg. 7452 (Feb. 22, 1985), completely revising 21 C.F.R.

Part 314. Thereafter, FDA made available several guidelines on compliance with the new provisions. *E.g.*, 50 Fed. Reg. 26411 (June 26, 1985), 53 Fed. Reg. 39524 (Oct. 7, 1988).

2. *NDA Filing.* An NDA is not "filed" when it is submitted to FDA. It becomes "filed" only after it has been reviewed and the agency concludes that it is complete enough to be acted on. This procedure, which dates back to 1938, was upheld in *Newport Pharmaceuticals International, Inc. v. Schweiker*, Food Drug. Cosm. L. Rep. (CCH) ¶ 38,148 (D.D.C. 1981).

3. *Data Supporting Approval.* In an unusual situation, one party to a joint venture to develop recombinant erythropoietin (EPO) for two separate indications sued the other to require that the data supporting both indications be submitted to FDA. *Ortho Pharmaceutical Corp. v. Amgen, Inc.*, 709 F. Supp. 504 (D. Del. 1989). The court granted the requested injunction, which was honored by the defendant, but the agency approved the drug for only one of the two requested indications.

4. *Studies of NDA Process.* The new drug approval process has been the subject of dozens of studies and reports. *See* Peter Barton Hutt, *Investigations and Reports Respecting FDA Regulation of New Drugs*, 33 CLINICAL PHARMACOLOGY AND THERAPEUTICS 537 (Part I), 674 (Part II) (1983). The early implementation of section 505 is discussed in Carl M. Anderson, *The "New Drug" Section*, 1 FOOD DRUG COSM. L.Q. 71 (1946); Erwin E. Nelson, *New Drug Requirements of the Federal Food, Drug and Cosmetic Act*, 4 FOOD DRUG COSM. L.Q. 227 (1949), *Development of New Drugs*, 5 FOOD DRUG COSM. L.J. 238 (1950), *Twelve Years of the New Drug Section*, 6 FOOD DRUG COSM. L.J. 344 (1951); Robert T. Stormont, *Application of the Federal Act to New Drugs*, 2 FOOD DRUG COSM. L.Q. 490 (1947); Walton Van Winkle, *The Safety of New Drugs*, 2 STAN. MED. BULL. 103 (Aug. 1944); *Laboratory and Clinical Appraisal of New Drugs*, 126 J.A.M.A. 958 (Dec. 9, 1946). *See also* the FDA testimony in "Drug Safety (Part 1)," Hearings before a Subcommittee of the House Committee on Government Operations, 88th Cong., 2d Sess. (1964); "The Food and Drug Administration's Process for Approving New Drugs," Report of the Subcommittee on Science, Research and Technology of the House Committee on Science and Technology, 96th Cong., 2d Sess. (1980).

5. *Reform of the NDA Approval System.* Since the investigations and reports described in Hutt, *supra* Note 4, there have been an equally large number of studies and reports on reforming the NDA approval system. *See, e.g.*, FINAL REPORT OF THE NATIONAL COMMITTEE TO REVIEW CURRENT PROCEDURES FOR APPROVAL OF NEW DRUGS FOR CANCER AND AIDS (Aug. 15, 1990), prepared pursuant to a request by President George H. W. Bush to the President's Cancer Panel of the National Cancer Institute; REINVENTING REGULATION OF DRUGS AND MEDICAL DEVICES (Apr. 1995), prepared as part of the National Performance Review ordered by Presidents Clinton and Vice President Gore; Note, *FDA Reform and the European Medicines Evaluation Agency*, 108 HARV. L. REV. 2009 (1995); Blanchard Randall, *Drug Regulation: Historical Overview and Current Reform Proposals*, CRS REP. No. 95–962 SPR (Sept. 11, 1995).

2. USER FEES

The General Accounting Office had long favored the imposition of user fees to finance the increasingly expensive IND/NDA process outside the annual FDA appropriations. The Office of Management and Budget raised the question in 1982, the President's Private Sector Survey on Cost Control issued a task force report recommending FDA user fees in 1983, and the Reagan administration proposed FDA user fees as part of the fiscal year budgets of both 1985 and 1986. In 1985, pursuant to administration policy to raise additional funds without new taxes, FDA—in a reversal of its longstanding opposition to user fees— proposed to establish user fees in the amount of $126,200 for a full NDA, $16,400 for a supplemental NDA, and $9900 for an abbreviated NDA. 50 Fed. Reg. 31726 (Aug. 6, 1985). From the mid–1980s to 1992, the administration routinely requested user fees as part of the FDA appropriations process, but the pharmaceutical industry opposed them and Congress consistently rejected them. The industry's resistance to these early user fee proposals was based largely on the fact that revenue from the fees would have substituted for, rather than supplemented, revenues appropriated from general funds.

By 1992, it was apparent that Congress would not provide sufficient funding to allow timely review of INDs and NDAs and adequate opportunity for industry-FDA interaction on these applications. Average NDA review and approval times reached a high of three years. Thus, industry put aside its antipathy toward user fees and agreed to cooperate on a workable legislative approach.

There was agreement between FDA and industry that the fees must supplement, rather than replace, existing FDA baseline appropriations. There was also agreement that, in return for industry paying user fees to support the IND/NDA process, FDA would commit to improved performance goals in the operation of this process. Industry wanted those goals to be included in the legislation, but FDA insisted that they be set forth in a separate letter from the Commissioner or the HHS Secretary to the appropriate House and Senate Committees. The first Prescription Drug User Fee Act (PDUFA) was passed in 1992, 106 Stat. 4491. *See* Bruce N. Kuhlik, *Industry Funding of Improvements in the FDA's New Drug Approval Process: The Prescription Drug User Fee Act of 1992*, 47 FOOD & DRUG L.J. 483 (1992). PDUFA was initially authorized for five years, and it was reauthorized for another five years under the Food and Drug Administration Modernization Act of 1997, 111 Stat. 2296, and another five years under the Prescription Drug User Fee Amendments of 2002, 116 Stat. 594, 687. *See* James L. Zelenay, Jr., *The Prescription Drug User Fee Act: Is a Faster Food and Drug Administration Always a Better Food and Drug Administration?*, 60 FOOD & DRUG L.J. 261 (2005); Alusheyi J. Wheeler, *The Prescription Drug User Fee Act: A Solution to the Drug Lag?* (2003), in Chapter III(G) of the Electronic Book.

The legislation provides for three types of user fees: (1) drug applications, (2) drug products, and (3) drug establishments. These fees have allowed FDA to more than double the number of personnel reviewing NDAs. The average time for NDA approval under user fees was initially halved. In 1999 and 2000, however, this trend was reversed and the time for approval began to increase. As a response to this increase in approval time, FDA began its current practice of issuing "approvable" letters within the user-fee time guidelines and then taking substantial additional time to negotiate remaining issues, often including labeling, before a final approval letter is sent.

The initial performance goals focused on the time required for FDA review of an NDA. Industry realized, however, that the amount of time required for nonclinical and clinical testing was increasing at a greater rate than the NDA review time was being reduced. Consequently, subsequent performance goals have focused on pre-NDA requirements as well. FDA issued the following White Paper in November 2005, summarizing the agency performance goals under the three successive PDUFA statutes.

Prescription Drug User Fee Act (PDUFA): Adding Resources and Improving Performance in FDA Review of New Drug Applications

November 10, 2005.

The Prescription Drug User Fee Act (PDUFA) program is the cornerstone of modern FDA drug review. User fees currently fund about half of new drug review costs. By providing needed funds, PDUFA ended slow and unpredictable review and approval of new drug applications, while keeping FDA's high standards.

PDUFA funds allowed FDA to accomplish a number of important goals. FDA hired more review and support staff to speed review. The number of full-time equivalent (FTE) staff devoted to the new drug review process has nearly doubled, growing from 1,277 FTE in 1992 to 2,503 FTE in 2004. FDA upgraded its data systems and gave industry guidance to help minimize unnecessary trials and generally improve drug development. FDA gave industry guidance on how to improve the quality of applications, with the goal to reduce misunderstandings and the need for sponsors to rework and resubmit applications. Finally, FDA improved procedures and standards to make review more rigorous, consistent, and predictable.

Taken together, all of these steps ensure that the time and effort patients put in to clinical trials provide useful data. They also lowered drug development costs and shortened review times. For example, the median approval time for priority new drug applications and biologics license applications decreased from 13.2 months on 1993 to 6.4 months in 2003. Ultimately these developments enabled FDA to ensure that needy American patients get fast access to novel drugs—faster, in fact, than citizens of other countries. Since the start of PDUFA, FDA has approved over 1,000 new drugs and about 100 new biologics. Under the currently authorized program (PDUFA 3) 50 percent of new drugs are launched first in the United States, compared to only 8 percent in the years pre-PDUFA....

Table 4.1 Expansion of FDA Performance Commitments Since Enactment of PDUFA		
PDUFA 1 **Industry paid a fee** • Per submitted NDA/BLA, per establishment, and per product	**PDUFA 2** **Industry paid a fee** • Per submitted NDA/BLA per establishment, and per product	**PDUFA 3** **Industry paid a fee** • Per submitted NDA/BLA, per establishment, and per product
Goals by FY97 • **Backlog:** Eliminate • **Priority reviews:** 90% in 6 months	**Goals by FY02** • **Priority Reviews:** 90% in 6 months • **Standard reviews:** 90% in 10 months	**Goals by FY07** • **Priority reviews:** 90% in 6 months • **Standard reviews:** 90% in 10 months

• **Standard Reviews:** 90% in 12 months	• **Formal Meetings:** schedule 90% within 14 days, convene 90% within 30/60/75 days • **Clinical hold response:** 90% in 30 days • **Special protocol evaluation:** 90% in 45 days • **Electronic Submissions:** Able to receive by end of FY02	• **Formal Meetings:** schedule 90% within 14 days; convene 90% within 30/60/75 days. • **Clinical hold response:** 90% in 30 days • **Special protocol evaluation:** 90% in 45 days • **Electronic Submissions:** Able to receive by end of FY02 • **Continuous Marketing Application** • **Pre- and Peri-NDA/BLA Risk Management** Plan Activities • **Independent Consultants** for Clinical Trials • **Good Review Management Principles (GRMPs)** for First Cycle Review Performance • **Improved Performance Management** • **Electronic Applications & Submissions**

The user fees established under the PDUFA program have increased substantially.

	1993	1997	2002	2007
Product	$12,000	$13,200	$21,630	$49,750
Establishment	$60,000	$115,700	$140,109	$313,100
NDA	$100,000	$205,000	$313,320	$896,200

Under all PDUFA statutes, congressional appropriations have been required to be maintained at the 1992 level, indexed for inflation. In reality, however, PDUFA fees have gradually become the predominant source of the FDA budget for the review of human new drugs.

	User Fees %	Appropriations %
1992	0	100
1993	7	93
1994	23	77
1995	35	65
1996	36	64
1997	36	64
1998	40	60
1999	43	57
2000	47	53
2001	50	50
2002	47	53
2003	49	51
2004	53	47
2005	56	44

Steve Usdin, *Cinderella's Glass Slipper*, BIOCENTURY, Sept. 18, 2006, at A1, A2. The IOM Report, A DRUG SAFETY SYSTEM PROMOTING AND PROTECTING THE HEALTH OF THE PUBLIC (2006), recommended that the IND/NDA regulatory system be funded by congressional appropriations rather than by user fees.

Steve Usdin, *Diminishing Returns*

BIOCENTURY, February 13, 2006, at A1.

PDUFA must again be reauthorized in 2007, which will require the development of new performance goals. It will also provide the opportunity for other statutory reforms of the IND/NDA process to be added to the legislation.

Data from the Prescription Drug User Fee Act are clear in one respect: most of the progress in reducing review and approval times was made in the first two years—between 1993 and 1995. Since then, despite ever-larger infusions of cash and increasing requirements that are intended to make FDA more responsive and collaborative, the agency and industry have been treading water.

Drugs aren't getting developed or approved any faster than when user fees were much lower and FDA's workload, as measured by new drug and biologics applications, was larger. In part, this is because user fees have replaced taxpayer funding, even though PDUFA income was designed to supplement government investments in the agency.

During the first five-year PDUFA round, the $292.3 million paid by drug sponsors covered about 30% of the costs for reviewing human drug applications. For the first two years of PDUFA III, user fees covered 49% and 53% of the costs in fiscal years 2003 and 2004, respectively.

Thus, all signs lead to the conclusion that the easy gains have been made.

As industry and FDA now prepare for PDUFA IV, some efficiency still could be squeezed out of the system. There is scope for cutting approval times for standard applications, particularly by reducing the number of review cycles. Review practices could be made more consistent across divisions. And it is important to remain vigilant to detect backsliding.

But to get more drugs approved faster, the focus of regulatory innovation must widen to include the entire time from preclinical to marketing. A sea change, something on the order of the 60% reduction accomplished through PDUFA in review and approval times for priority new molecular entities, can come only by attenuating the period from preparing an IND to submitting an NDA or BLA.

Although proposals to add user fees to improve sponsor-agency dialog during the development process will be discussed as part of PDUFA IV, most of the big ideas for cutting drug development times require forging consensus among FDA, industry and academic researchers, rather than the enactment of legislation.

3.   MEETINGS WITH FDA

Just as it is important to have substantive meetings between sponsors and FDA throughout the IND process, *supra* p. 626, it is equally important to continue having these meetings while the NDA is in preparation and under review. These meetings are used to help prepare an NDA that will meet the expectations of the agency, to respond to questions that arise during FDA's review of the NDA, and to maintain continuing dialogue about all aspects of the review process. *See* Joseph A. DiMasi & Michael Manocchia, *Initiatives to Speed New Drug Development and Regulatory Review: The Impact of FDA–Sponsor Conferences*, 31 DRUG INFO. J. 771 (1997).

One indicator of a successful NDA review process is whether the NDA review is completed, and final action by FDA is taken, within the performance goal established by PDUFA, *e.g.*, within 10 months for a standard NDA. At the end of the time established by PDUFA for review of the NDA, the agency is obligated to send the applicant a letter either approving the NDA or stating what needs to be done in order to obtain approval. The first ten-month period is called the first "cycle." Subsequent review periods are called the second cycle, the third cycle, and so on.

As one of the performance goals under PDUFA III, FDA agreed to retain an independent expert consultant to evaluate the factors that contribute to first cycle approval. In 71 Fed. Reg. 6284 (Feb. 7, 2006), FDA announced the availability of the resulting final report, excerpted below:

Booz Allen Hamilton, Inc., *Independent Evaluation of FDA's First Cycle Review Performance—Retrospective Analysis*

January 2006.

. . . .

FDA reviewer team members agree that early on-going dialog with sponsors is the most important factor in identifying issues and potentially providing an opportunity for timely resolution, ideally before first action is taken. All divisions interviewed routinely strive to start discussions with sponsors before the submission. These efforts meet with mixed success: End-of-Phase 2 meetings appear to significantly contribute to first-cycle approval while Pre-NDA/BLA meetings had a lesser impact. In some instances, substantial deficiencies were not documented/identified until the review phase, potentially preventing first-cycle approval despite the possible availability of pertinent information at the time of Pre-BLA/NDA meetings. This finding may be attributed to the general focus of these meetings on application formatting rather than review of development results. When issues are identified, there is often insufficient time to adequately address these as submission timelines are generally not delayed. This may be due to sponsors' unwillingness to adopt FDA suggestions or lack of clarity in FDA communications on the severity of the issues raised. There are also examples where sponsors are able to resolve issues via a different path than originally recommended by the FDA. These findings point to broad issues around coverage of problem areas prior to submission, ineffective communication between the FDA and sponsors, and unclear prioritization of issues and/or problem resolution requirements.

An approach to address this challenge is the development of an open and accountable communication system centered around issue resolution. This system may include a pre-submission check-list and follow-up responsibilities that will guide FDA–Sponsor discussions and ensure that these communications are better leveraged to achieve agreement on issue resolution. This system—termed in this report as check-and-follow up communication—will increase consistency and reduce the risk of overlooking key issues at pre-submission stages....

FDA has stated that meetings require FDA personnel to spend extensive time in preparation and attendance—time that is not adequately reflected in PDUFA funding. It is the uniform experience of the pharmaceutical industry, however, that between ten and twenty FDA personnel typically attend these meetings, but only two or three people actually participate in the discussion. If FDA were to limit meetings to the agency employees who will actually participate, and were to communicate the results through accurate and detailed minutes, the agency could hold far more meetings with the same amount of resources.

4. REFUSAL TO FILE

From the inception of the NDA review process under the 1938 Act, it was FDA practice to declare as "incomplete" any application it regarded as inadequate and not to take any form of action on it until the applicant submitted a new application that the agency deemed to be complete. When FDA promulgated the current NDA regulations as part of the IND/NDA rewrite in 1985, it included in 21 C.F.R. 314.101 a detailed regulation governing its refusal to file an application because it is not "sufficiently complete to permit a substantive review." 47 Fed. Reg. 46622 (Oct. 19, 1982), 50 Fed. Reg. 7452 (Feb. 22, 1985). FDA issued a guidance on its refuse-to-file policy in July 1993. Around the same time, the agency established a Refuse-to-File (RTF) Review Committee. The Review Committee held two pilot meetings and then two regular meetings, 58 Fed. Reg. 28983 (May 18, 1993), 58 Fed. Reg. 52497 (Oct. 8, 1993), but there have been no further announced meetings. In general, if a sponsor has held adequate pre-NDA meetings with FDA, it should have little concern the agency will refuse to file the NDA.

5.   THE SAFETY STANDARD

Section 505(d) of the FD&C Act directs FDA to withhold approval of an NDA unless the sponsor's evidence shows the drug to be safe "by all methods reasonably applicable to show whether or not such drug is safe for use under the conditions of use prescribed, recommended, or suggested" in the proposed labeling. The Act does not say how safety is to be determined, and FDA has never attempted to spell out in regulations the criteria that it employs.

The term "safety" appears in many provisions of the FD&C Act. With respect to food, for example, FDA has always applied it as an absolute standard, ignoring any potential benefit that the food may have. *See supra* p. 360. With respect to drugs, on the other hand, FDA has relatively consistently taken into account a product's potential benefit. As the following testimony by former FDA Commissioner George Larrick illustrates, even before enactment of the Drug Amendments of 1962, when FDA could disapprove an NDA on safety grounds alone, the agency implicitly considered the effectiveness of the product in making its safety decisions.

Testimony of FDA Commissioner George Larrick

"Drug Safety," Hearings Before a Subcommittee of the House Committee on Government Operations, 88th Congress 2d Session (1964).

The 1938 new drug section of the law did not require a manufacturer to prove that his new drug would yield the benefits claimed on its label. It spoke only of safety. Thus, many of the Government's decisions allowing drugs to be marketed had to be made without access to the full facts a physician would want in deciding whether to use the product. . . .

Of course the question of benefit was an integral part of the safety question in dealing with a product to be used in a life-threatening disease such as pneumonia or in dealing with a drug presenting grave risks. We required information about effectiveness for such drugs in order to reach a decision about safety. But many fairly innocuous new drugs offered for ailments that were not life-threatening were presented to us for evaluation without evidence that they would do what the label claimed. We had no power in such case to require submission of efficacy data. . . .

In evaluating risk we need, to the extent it is available, and in many of these areas the extent of the available science is quite deficient, information on such things as:

1.   The interaction of the drug with body processes, including: hormonal, enzymic, metabolic, and reproductive processes.

2.   The manner in which the drug is absorbed, distributed in body tissues, and inactivated or excreted. . . .

3.   Whether active compounds arise from the metabolism of the drug by the body.

4.   The influence of other chemicals, such as other drugs or even articles of food or drink upon the activity of the drug in question.

5.   How the activity of the drug in animals compares with its activity in man. . . .

No plan of clinical investigation, even the most expensive, can be expected to give all of the information that will be revealed by general marketing and use of a new drug. . . . General use involves more patients than can possibly be employed in clinical trial. Whereas the clinical trial may expose hundreds or at most thousands of people to a new product, general use may involve several million. Physicians who investigate a drug before it is marketed, even in the widespread tests just before marketing, are generally selected because of their specialized superior training and skill and because of their interest in clinical testing. After release the drug will be used by some physicians with less training, less skill, and less opportunity to make sure they are adhering to all of the suggestions in the labeling of the drug.

In fact, the early period following general marketing of a new drug must be regarded as a final step in the testing of the product. There is no way to duplicate fully in clinical trials the great variety of use conditions under which a new drug will be employed when it is finally approved. . . .

———

Four decades later the safety decision has not fundamentally changed.

Bernadine Healy, M.D., *What is a "Safe" Drug?*

U.S. NEWS & WORLD REPORT, December 13, 2004, at 37.

One of the most vivid lessons I learned in medical school came from an otherwise dry course in pharmacology. Our professor sobered a class of eager 20–somethings just aching to have prescription pads in their hands with his opening pronouncement: "Drugs are dangerous." If there's any lesson for the public in the current firestorm surrounding the recalled anti-inflammatory drug Vioxx, it should be that. Whether it's the century-old aspirin or the recently disgraced Vioxx—designed as a safer form of aspirin—all drugs come with unwanted and often unexpected side effects.

Unfortunately, the public theater of Vioxx's demise omits such messy details. Within moments of the recall, media stories rushed to sing good riddance to a "bad drug," tort lawyers set out in hot pursuit of the injured "class," and critics assailed the drug maker for greed and deception and the FDA for lack of vigilance. Wall Street analysts wrapped the entire COX–2 drug class in black crepe. Would that it were this simple.

I predict that the COX–2 inhibitors will survive. They are too important a tool to be dumped from the medicine chest. In addition to their pain-relieving capabilities, they show great promise in preventing and treating a wide array of deadly tumors, including those of the colon, lung, pancreas, stomach, brain, and breast. There's reason for this: To take hold and spread, some cancer cells have learned how to hijack the body's inflammatory pathways by producing overactive COX–2 genes. The COX–2 inhibitors offer a unique and targeted weapon against this banditry. Celebrex has already been approved for the prevention of colon cancer. Remember thalidomide? Once a notorious drug because it caused birth defects, it is now a lifesaver for those with certain cancers, like multiple myeloma.

Vioxx is no demon drug. And the FDA does not turn a blind eye to danger. Were safety the only measure, the agency's job would be easy—and our medicine chests would be empty. As we watch the Vioxx fallout, we should be wary of a scalping party that could leave us so safe we are not safe at all.

NOTES

1. *Commentary. See also* John P. Swann, *Sure Cure: Public Policy on Drug Efficacy Before 1962, in* THE INSIDE STORY OF MEDICINES: A SYMPOSIUM 223 (Gregory J. Higby & Elaine C. Stroud, eds., 1997).

2. *Procedures for Disapproval.* A notable example of FDA disapproval of an NDA for a prescription drug on the ground of lack of safety is medroxyprogesterone acetate (Depo–Provera). In 1974, in anticipation of approval of the NDA for Depo–Provera for use as an injectable contraceptive, FDA established patient package inserts for the drug. 39 Fed. Reg. 11680 (Mar. 29, 1974), 39 Fed. Reg. 32907 (Sept. 12, 1974), codified as 21 C.F.R. 310.501a. Soon thereafter, however, the FDA commissioner delayed approval of the drug based on concerns it presented a risk of cancer. 39 Fed. Reg. 38226 (Oct. 30, 1974) (delaying approval), 40 Fed. Reg. 12830 (Mar. 21, 1975) (announcing open meeting). In 43 Fed. Reg. 28555 (June 30, 1978), FDA published a notice of opportunity for hearing on its intent to disapprove the NDA, based on its carcinogenicity. The applicant elected a hearing before a public board of inquiry, 44 Fed. Reg. 44274 (July 27, 1979), which recommended against approval of the NDA. Food Drug Cosm. L. Rep. (CCH) ¶ 39,291 (Oct. 17, 1984); 49 Fed. Reg. 43507 (Oct. 29, 1984) (announcement of availability of decision). The company then withdrew its NDA. 51 Fed. Reg. 37651 (Oct. 23, 1986). FDA revoked the PPI for Depo–Provera in 52 Fed. Reg. 13109 (Apr. 21, 1987), 54 Fed. Reg. 22585 (May 25, 1989). In 1992, however, the carcinogenicity issue was resolved and FDA approved the NDA.

3. *Withdrawal of NDA Approval for Safety Reasons.* The separate issue of FDA withdrawal of an NDA approval for safety reasons after the drug has been marketed is discussed *infra* p. 745.

4. *Competitive Safety Studies.* On occasion, companies will conduct safety studies on each other's drugs and submit the results to FDA, in an attempt to slow down the NDA approval for competitive products. Companies have made presentations to advisory committees arguing that a competitor's drug was unsafe and

should be disapproved or at least bear a strong warning label, perhaps with a black box. Some of these efforts have been successful. Others have been viewed as competitive tactics that should be given little or no weight.

5. *Private Right of Action With Regard to Safety.* In *Hawkins v. Upjohn Company*, 890 F. Supp. 609 (E.D. Tex. 1994), plaintiffs alleged a fraudulent conspiracy by the defendants to withhold safety information from FDA for the purpose of inducing the agency to approve the marketing of two drugs. The District Court held that, although plaintiffs could not assert a private right of action for enforcement of the FD&C Act, they could properly allege a conspiracy both to commit fraud and to market a known unreasonably dangerous product.

6. The Effectiveness Standard

Section 505(d) also specifies that the FDA shall withhold approval of a new drug unless the sponsor provides "substantial evidence that the drug will have the effect it purports or is represented to have under the conditions of use prescribed, recommended, or suggested in the proposed labeling." The section defines "substantial evidence" of effectiveness as

> evidence consisting of adequate and well-controlled investigations, including clinical investigations, by experts qualified by scientific training and experience to evaluate the effectiveness of the drug involved, on the basis of which it could fairly and responsibly be concluded by such experts that the drug will have the effect it purports or is represented to have under the conditions of use prescribed, recommended, or suggested in the labeling or proposed labeling thereof.

In 1970, FDA promulgated a regulation defining adequate and well-controlled clinical studies. 34 Fed. Reg. 14596 (Sept. 19, 1969), 35 Fed. Reg. 3073 (Feb. 17, 1970), 35 Fed. Reg. 7250 (May 8, 1970). It did so not in order to provide guidance to the pharmaceutical industry in designing protocols for future NDAs, but rather to enable the agency to withdraw pre-1962 new drugs from the market under the DESI Review without the need for an administrative hearing. *See supra* p. 581. Nonetheless, these regulations have remained unchanged for more than 35 years and continue to guide both FDA and the pharmaceutical industry in their daily decisions.

Adequate and Well–Controlled Studies

21 C.F.R. 314.126.

(a) The purpose of conducting clinical investigations of a drug is to distinguish the effect of a drug from other influences, such as spontaneous change in the course of the disease, placebo effect, or biased observation.... Reports of adequate and well-controlled investigations provide the primary basis for determining whether there is "substantial evidence" to support the claims of effectiveness for new drugs and antibiotics. Therefore, the study report should provide sufficient details of study design, conduct, and analysis to allow critical evaluation and a determination of whether the characteristics of an adequate and well-controlled study are present.

(b) An adequate and well-controlled study has the following characteristics:

(1) There is a clear statement of the objectives of the investigation and a summary of the proposed or actual methods of analysis in the protocol for the study and in the report of its results. . . .

(2) The study uses a design that permits a valid comparison with a control to provide a quantitative assessment of drug effect. The protocol for the study and report of results should describe the study design precisely; for example, duration of treatment periods, whether treatments are parallel, sequential, or crossover, and whether the sample size is predetermined or based upon some interim analysis. Generally, the following types of control are recognized:

(i) *Placebo concurrent control.* The test drug is compared with an inactive preparation designed to resemble the test drug as far as possible. A placebo-controlled study . . . usually includes randomization and blinding of patients or investigators, or both.

(ii) *Dose-comparison concurrent control.* At least two doses of the drug are compared. . . . Dose-comparison trials usually include randomization and blinding of patients or investigators, or both.

(iii) *No treatment concurrent control.* Where objective measurements of effectiveness are available and placebo effect is negligible, the test drug is compared with no treatment. No treatment concurrent control trials usually include randomization.

(iv) *Active treatment concurrent control.* The test drug is compared with known effective therapy; for example, where the condition treated is such that administration of placebo or no treatment would be contrary to the interest of the patient. . . . Active treatment trials usually include randomization and blinding of patients or investigators, or both.

(v) *Historical control.* The results of treatment with the test drug are compared with experience historically derived from the adequately documented natural history of the disease or condition, or from the results of active treatment, in comparable patients or populations. Because historical control populations usually cannot be as well assessed with respect to pertinent variables as can concurrent control populations, historical control designs are usually reserved for special circumstances. Examples include studies of diseases with high and predictable mortality (for example, certain malignancies) and studies in which the effect of the drug is self-evident (general anesthetics, drug metabolism).

(3) The method of selection of subjects provides adequate assurance that they have the disease or condition being studied, or evidence of susceptibility and exposure to the condition against which prophylaxis is directed.

(4) The method of assigning patients to treatment and control groups minimizes bias and is intended to assure comparability of the groups with respect to pertinent variables such as age, sex, severity of disease, duration of disease, and use of drugs or therapy other than the test drug. . . .

(5) Adequate measures are taken to minimize bias on the part of the subjects, observers, and analysts of the data. . . .

(6) The methods of assessment of subjects' response are well-defined and reliable. . . .

(7) There is an analysis of the results of the study adequate to assess the effects of the drug. . . .

NOTES

1. *Meaning of Substantial Evidence.* The Senate Report on the 1962 Drug Amendments provides this description of the proof of effectiveness requirement:

> When a drug has been adequately tested by qualified experts and has been found to have the effect claimed for it, this claim should be permitted even though there may be preponderant evidence to the contrary based upon equally reliable studies. There may also be a situation in which a new drug has been studied in a limited number of hospitals and clinics and its effectiveness established only to the satisfaction of a few investigators qualified to use it. There may be many physicians who deny the effectiveness simply on the basis of a disbelief growing out of their past experience with other drugs or with the diseases involved. Again the studies may show that the drug will help a substantial percentage of the patients in a given disease condition but will not be effective in other cases. What the committee intends is to permit the claim for this new drug to be made to the medical profession with a proper explanation of the basis on which it rests.
>
> In such a delicate area of medicine, the committee wants to make sure that safe new drugs become available for use by the medical profession so long as they are supported as to effectiveness by a responsible body of opinion.

S. Rep. No. 1744, 87th Cong., 2nd Sess., Part. 1 at 16 (1962).

2. *One or More Studies.* Prior to 1997, section 505(d) referred only to "investigations," including clinical "investigations." This wording raised the question whether there must be at least two clinical investigations to support approval of an NDA. The regulations FDA promulgated immediately following the 1962 Drug Amendments stated that "ordinarily" more than one clinical study would be required. 28 Fed. Reg. 1449 (Feb. 14, 1963), 28 Fed. Reg. 6377 (June 20, 1963). In implementing the DESI program, however, FDA summarily withdrew approval of an NDA only where there was *no* adequate and well-controlled clinical study. In 39 Fed. Reg. 9750, 9755 (Mar. 13, 1974), FDA declined to adopt a requirement that two, rather than just one, adequate and well-controlled clinical studies be identified in order to demonstrate a drug's effectiveness. When it revised the NDA regulations in 1985, FDA retained the provision that summary revocation of an NDA will not occur where at least one adequate and well-controlled clinical investigation has been identified. 21 C.F.R. 314.200(g)(1). In the years prior to 1997, FDA officials testified more than once that the agency has authority to approve an NDA on the basis of a single adequate and well-controlled clinical study. "Use of Advisory Committees by the Food and Drug Administration," Hearings before a Subcommittee of the House Committee on Government Operations, 93rd Cong., 2nd Sess. 122 (1974); "The Regulation of New Drugs by the Food and Drug Administration: The New Drug Review Process," Hearings before a Subcommittee of the House Committee on Government Operations, 97th Cong., 2nd Sess. 37 (1982). Nonetheless, for most NDAs, FDA required at least two adequate and well-controlled clinical studies.

In the FDA Modernization Act of 1997, Congress added to section 505(d) a new sentence stating that:

> If the Secretary determines, based on relevant science that data from one adequate and well-controlled clinical investigation and confirmatory evidence (obtained prior to or after such investigation) are sufficient to establish effectiveness, the Secretary may consider such data and evidence to constitute substantial evidence for purposes of the preceding sentence.

This provision has been applied by FDA only in situations where a single study demonstrates statistical significance at the .005–.001 level. FDA has issued no guidance on this matter. A significant number of NDA and supplemental NDA submissions have been based on a single controlled trial since 1997. *See, e.g.,* Tuft's Center for the Study of Drug Development, 3 Impact Report, No. 5 (Sept./Oct. 2001).

3. *Clinical Testing Guidelines.* To advise manufacturers and investigators on testing protocols that will satisfy the agency's requirements for adequate and well-controlled clinical studies, FDA began issuing clinical testing guidelines for several types of drugs in the 1970s. *E.g.,* 44 Fed. Reg. 20796 (Apr. 6, 1979). All of these have now been converted to guidance, and numerous other guidances have been issued by FDA on appropriate clinical testing.

4. *Relative Efficacy.* The history of the 1962 Amendments reveals a Congressional decision that FDA not refuse to approve a drug on the ground of "relative efficacy," *i.e.,* that a more effective drug is available. *E.R. Squibb and Sons, Inc. v. Bowen,* 870 F.2d 678 (D.C. Cir. 1989); Thomas E. Knauer, *The Regulation of Drugs on the Basis of Relative Effectiveness,* 42 Food Drug Cosm. L.J. 323 (1987). While FDA has formally observed this mandate, it has taken other actions that have a similar impact. First, it has disapproved drugs on the ground of relative safety. *See, e.g.,* John C. Ballin, *Who Makes the Therapeutic Decisions?* 242 J.A.M.A. 2875 (1979). Second, it has stated that the labeling of a less effective drug may be required to specify the drug of choice. Third, it has taken the position that, to be found "effective," a drug must be shown to have a clinically significant effect. *See* 44 Fed. Reg. 51512 (Aug. 31, 1979).

5. *Combination Drugs.* In 1971, FDA promulgated a policy for evaluating the effectiveness of combination prescription drugs. 36 Fed. Reg. 3126 (Feb. 18, 1971), 36 Fed. Reg. 20037 (Oct. 15, 1971), codified at 21 C.F.R. 300.50. *See* E. Carrington Boggan, *The FDA's Combination Drug Policy,* 30 Food Drug Cosm. L.J. 276 (1975).

6. *Assessing Effectiveness.* For examples of the complex judgments involved in the evaluation of drug effectiveness, *see* William B. Hood, *More on Sulfinpyrazone After Myocardial Infarction,* 306 New Eng. J. Med. 988 (1982), and the FDA reconsideration of the safety and effectiveness of Ilosone (erythromycin estolate) in 44 Fed. Reg. 69670 (Dec. 4, 1979), 47 Fed. Reg. 22547 (May 25, 1982).

7. *Statistical Analysis.* To minimize bias and maximize statistical power, FDA relies on the so-called "intent-to-treat" analysis of large clinical trials. Under this approach, all patients who are included in the control or treatment group, without exception, must be included in the ultimate analysis of the results, regardless of whether additional information reveals that they failed to follow the protocol instructions or otherwise do not represent appropriate subjects. For example, patients who are instructed to take the drug according to a specified regimen, but who fail to take it, are included in the analysis even though they obviously could not have exhibited any benefits from the drug. Accordingly, the results of an "intent-to-treat" analysis provide an average of those subjects who comply with the protocol and those who do not. Depending upon the extent of noncompliance with the protocol, the results may accurately reflect the effectiveness of the drug or may be

seriously misleading. More accurate analysis can be obtained by stratifying the clinical data according to the level of patient compliance with the prescribed drug regimen. The physician package insert for Questran (cholestyramine), for example, provides information on the reduction in cholesterol in relation to the amount of the drug taken in a clinical trial, *i.e.*, the patient compliance with the drug regimen established in the protocol:

Packet Count	Total Cholesterol Lowering	Reduction in Coronary Heart Disease Risk
0–2	4.4%	10.9%
2–5	11.5%	26.1%
5–6	19.0%	39.3%

8. *Clinical and Surrogate Endpoints.* In determining effectiveness, the ultimate endpoint of interest is the survival of the patient. Clinical trials studying only patient survival may, however, require large numbers of subjects and take many years to complete. For that reason, researchers seek "surrogate" endpoints that will demonstrate, at a much earlier stage, whether the drug is effective. These surrogate endpoints are typically physiological parameters that correlate with the progress of the disease. *See, e.g.*, Robert E. Wittes, *Antineoplastic Agents and FDA Regulations: Square Pegs for Round Holes?*, 71 CANCER TREATMENT REP. 795 (Sept. 1987). For some diseases, the correlation between particular physiological parameters and the disease is sufficiently well-established that the parameters are accepted as surrogate endpoints. For example, reduction in serum cholesterol is now accepted as a surrogate endpoint to demonstrate the effectiveness of a drug in reducing the risk of coronary heart disease. For cancer and AIDS, however, there is substantial debate about what surrogate endpoints have been sufficiently validated to permit approval of drugs for these indications without more direct evidence of their effect on morbidity and mortality. For a more detailed discussion of this topic, see *supra* p. 639.

9. *Exemptions.* The FDA regulations permit the agency to exempt a drug, in writing, from the requirement for controlled studies. FDA granted one of these rare exemptions for the approval of AZT for use in children with AIDS. *See* Ellen Cooper, Remarks at Institute of Medicine Workshop on Drug Development for Pediatric HIV Infection and AIDS (June 29, 1990).

10. *Effectiveness of Oncology Drugs.* There is no more controversial field in the FDA review of NDAs than oncology. Many believe that the agency has been too strict and that promising drugs have inappropriately been held back from approval, thus unnecessarily killing thousands of cancer victims every year. Yet there has been a significant decline in cancer in the United States, undoubtedly in part due to improved cancer detection and treatment. *E.g.*, Brad Rodu and Philip Cole, *The 50–Year Decline of Cancer in America*, 19 J. CLINICAL ONCOLOGY 239 (Jan. 2001). FDA has repeatedly defended its record of cancer drug approvals. Steven Hirschfeld & Richard Pazdur, *Oncology Drug Development: United States Food and Drug Administration Perspective*, 42 CRITICAL REVS. IN ONCOLOGY, HEMATOLOGY 137 (2002); Ramzi Dagher et al., *Accelerated Approval of Oncology Products: A Decade of Experience*, 96 J. NAT'L CANCER INSTITUTE 1500 (Oct. 20, 2004). For a different view of FDA policy on cancer drugs, see a remarkable series of editorials by Antonio J. Grillo–Lopez, published under the title *The ODAC Chronicles*, beginning in 4 EXPERT REV. OF ANTICANCER THERAPEUTICS (2004), which provide rare insight into the work of the FDA Oncology Drugs Advisory Committee. *See also* "An Inquiry into the ImClone Cancer–Drug Story," Hearings before the Subcommittee on Oversight and Investigations of the House Committee on Energy and Commerce, 107th Cong., 2d Sess.

(2002); Benjamin M. Hron, *Placebo or Panacea: The FDA's Rejection of ImClone's Erbitux Licensing Application* (2003), and Andrew J. Sung, *Expediting Oncology Drug Approvals: The Public Backlash Against the FDA and Opportunities to Reform* (2005), in Chapter VI(C)(3) of the Electronic Book.

11.   *Longer Term Studies.* The length of a clinical trial to study the effectiveness of a new drug is almost always determined by FDA. There is no objective way to set the required length of a trial. It is a matter of subjective judgment. For example, drugs to treat major depressive disorder are typically studied in a placebo-controlled trial for six to twelve weeks. Longer-term effectiveness studies are then routinely conducted following NDA approval, to confirm safety but not to study effectiveness. When FDA proposed to require longer-term effectiveness trials prior to NDA approval, the pharmaceutical industry strongly objected, and an advisory committee of experts voted 12–0 against the proposal because it would result in patients being denied important new medication. *See* Jennifer Corbett Dooren, *FDA May Scrap Plan to Require Longer Psychiatric Drug Studies*, WALL ST. J., Oct. 26, 2005, at D5.

7.   INTERNAL AGENCY REVIEW PROCESS

No two NDAs are alike, and thus no two review processes are similar. Each is an ad hoc negotiation that varies widely among different FDA review divisions, within a single review division, and among individual reviewers. Each is fact dependent, *i.e.*, it depends on the specific data and information contained in the particular NDA for the product. All clinical trials are different, all manufacturing information is highly specific to the individual company and the specific drug, and the labeling claims sought in the NDA are unique because they depend solely on the data in the application. It is therefore treacherous to generalize from one NDA to the other. The most that can be done is to describe, in broad terms, the overall process.

Before the NDA is submitted, there should have been a series of meetings of the type described *supra* p. 683. When the NDA is submitted, the first issue is whether it will survive a refuse-to-file screening by the agency. Assuming the drug is subject to standard rather than priority review, there is almost always a period of complete silence from the agency. At some point, the agency will communicate with the sponsor asking various questions, relying on every known form of communication—letter, telephone, e-mail, and fax. These inquiries will intensify as the PDUFA date approaches. There may also be personal meetings between the applicant and FDA. The hope is that, when the first cycle is complete, the drug will be approved. If it is not, some other type of letter will be received, with any of several different titles—an approvable letter, a not-approvable or nonapproval letter, an action letter, a complete response letter, or even a letter that has no title of any kind. There is little, if any, practical difference attached to these different titles. In 69 Fed. Reg. 43351 (July 20, 2004), FDA proposed to standardize these types of letters, but no further action has been taken on this matter.

Whatever title the letter bears, two points are clear. First, the letter is no more than a tentative position of the agency and an invitation to begin a serious negotiation. Even a not-approvable or nonapproval letter can be turned into an ultimate NDA approval. Second, the burden is on the company to respond to all issues raised in the letter if it hopes to persuade FDA that the NDA should be approved.

The most difficult letter the applicant may receive is one stating that one or more additional lengthy and expensive clinical trials must be conducted in order to demonstrate effectiveness. Particularly for a small biotechnology company, this can be devastating news, requiring substantial additional financing in the face of a falling stock price caused by the SEC-required disclosure of the FDA request. Even if there is no request for an additional trial, this does not mean that the remaining issues are easily resolved. It may still take months to gather all of the information requested by FDA. Fortunately, the FDA letters are detailed and candid, spelling out every issue needed to resolve FDA's remaining questions and thus obtain NDA approval. But from beginning to end, this dialogue is a riveting, exhausting, and all-consuming process that is frightening even for those who have gone through it on more than one occasion, because ultimately it means the success or failure of the entire enterprise.

NOTES

1. *Good Review Management Principles and Practices.* The FDA Modernization Act of 1997 added section 505(d)(4)(A) to the FD&C Act. This provision requires FDA to issue guidance for the individuals who review NDAs, which shall relate to promptness in conducting the review, technical excellence, lack of bias and conflict of interest, and knowledge of regulatory and scientific standards. In response to this statutory requirement, FDA issued GUIDANCE FOR REVIEW STAFF AND INDUSTRY: GOOD REVIEW MANAGEMENT PRINCIPLES AND PRACTICES FOR PDUFA PRODUCTS (2005). 68 Fed. Reg. 44345 (July 28, 2003), 70 Fed. Reg. 16507 (Mar. 31, 2005). The Guidance breaks down the typical NDA first cycle review to five phases: (1) filing determination and review planning, (2) review, (3) advisory committee meeting, (4) action, and (5) post-action. The Guidance offers an excellent list of references to the FDA regulations, guidance, and other policies that apply throughout the NDA review process.

2. *Antagonistic Medical Review Officer.* As occasionally occurs in all organizations, an FDA medical review officer can be biased and antagonistic. Higher FDA officials have gone so far as to remove an abusive member of a medical review team.

3. *FDA Regulatory Briefing.* When an NDA raises an issue that CDER regards as novel, important, or particularly difficult, or simply the subject of substantial public controversy, top CDER officials will participate in a "regulatory briefing" to analyze the matter and reach a conclusion. Regulatory briefings are relatively uncommon but can be an important mechanism for resolving difficult matters. *See, e.g., Lyrica Reviewer Concerns on Vision, Skin Lead to Consults with Top FDA Staff,* 68 THE PINK SHEET, No. 34, at 10 (Aug. 21, 2006).

4. *Company Resubmissions.* FDA has issued GUIDANCE FOR INDUSTRY: CLASSIFYING RESUBMISSIONS IN RESPONSE TO ACTION LETTERS (1998) that sets forth the PDUFA performance goals regarding FDA review of these second cycle and subsequent submissions relating to an NDA.

8.   BALANCING BENEFIT AND RISK

Under the 1938 Act, an applicant had to submit sufficient data to demonstrate the safety of the new drug. That requirement was not amended when Congress enacted the Drug Amendments of 1962. Under the 1962 Amendments, a separate and independent provision was added to require the applicant also to submit substantial evidence of effectiveness. The new provision made no reference to the preexisting safety requirement.

Confronted with these two independent and separate requirements in 1962, FDA could have interpreted section 505 in two different ways. First, the agency could have interpreted the statute the way it was written. The agency could have concluded that Congress intended FDA separately to evaluate the safety information and the evidence of potential benefit presented in the NDA, to require that information regarding both be set forth in the physician labeling in a truthful and nonmisleading way, and then to allow the physician and the patient jointly to make a benefit-risk judgment whether the doctor should prescribe the drug for the patient, in light of the individualized disease situation confronting the patient. In other words, the physician and patient would make the benefit-risk determination, not FDA. Second, FDA could have decided to take the benefit-risk determination away from the physician and patient, and to make that decision itself. Under this approach, it would deny drugs to patients that they might rationally want to have available for their own individualized disease situation, even if the drug might be regarded as unsafe or ineffective for other patient populations or for the country as a whole.

Without public participation of any type, FDA Commissioner George Larrick announced how the agency would implement its new authority under the Drug Amendments of 1962 at a Congressional hearing held in March 1964.

Testimony of FDA Commissioner George Larrick

"Drug Safety," Hearings Before a Subcommittee of the House Committee on Government Operations, 88th Congress 2d Session 150, 153, 154 (1964).

The decisionmaking process can conveniently be regarded as a three-step operation....

Step 1. Determine the benefit to be derived from the drug;

Step 2. Determine the risk; and

Step 3. Weigh the benefit against the risk and decide whether it is in the public interest to approve the drug for marketing or to withdraw approval if the product is already on the market....

The decision to approve a drug for marketing, or to withdraw an earlier approval requires a weighing of the benefit to be expected from use of the product against the risk inherent in its use.... The Government must make a judgment as to the hazards likely to be encountered when the drug is employed: by physicians of varying skills and abilities, in patients with a multitude of disease processes, many occurring concurrently, and in patients incorrectly diagnosed or inadequately tested with accepted laboratory procedures....

We seek to make decisions about drugs solely on the basis of scientific consideration. But over a period of time, the direction of Government's decisions will inevitably be influenced by public reaction.... The judgments of society are not necessarily consistent with scientific facts. Neither are they always logical. They can be and sometimes are arbitrary. Even so, neither the executive nor the legislative branches of government can long ignore them. If it should become the overwhelming public view that society should drastically limit the risk no matter how much good a drug can do, then we would be forced to remove from the market many drugs whose good far outweighs their harm. Carried too far, such developments would seriously impede the progress of medicine....

NOTES

1.   *Risk v. Benefit.* David L. Cavers, *The Legal Control of Clinical Investigation of Drugs: Some Political, Economic, and Social Questions*, 98 DAEDALUS 427 (1969), characterized the agency's analytical process as follows:

> ... [T]his evaluation does not call for a simple "yes" or "no" judgment. One dosage level may be safe, another questionable, but the safer dosage level may be of doubtful efficacy. A satisfactory answer may lie in between. Negotiation follows. The reports of clinical trials may include some evidence of hazard, but was the reported condition the consequence of the drug's administration or of other factors? There may have been side effects disclosed in the trials, but ought these merely to be listed as such or was their association with a given condition such as to require its listing in the labeling as a contraindication? The FDA must evaluate the sponsor's statistical work; it may have to decide whether a sponsor was justified in downgrading a side effect as "rare" or "infrequent."

2.   *The FDA Judgment Factor.* The benefit-risk decision embodied in the choice whether to approve an NDA is purely impressionistic and judgmental. It cannot be justified by modeling or other objective criteria. It is, pure and simple, an "I know it when I see it" type of decision. For that reason alone, patient advocacy groups and individual patients often question the authority of FDA to make a decision that may determine whether they will live or die.

3.   *Physician/Patient Benefit–Risk Decision.* It is only after FDA has substantially reduced the available drugs for a particular indication that physicians and their patients are permitted to make their own benefit-risk decision regarding the remaining available medication. *See* STEVEN MARKS, AMERICAN COUNCIL ON SCIENCE AND HEALTH, WEIGHING BENEFITS AND RISK IN PHARMACEUTICAL USE: A CONSUMER'S GUIDE (2005).

———

Regulation of antidepressant drugs presents a particularly useful illustration of the difficulty in making benefit-risk judgments for drugs used in serious diseases. FDA must balance the risk that an antidepressant drug may increase suicide against the risk that the failure to use the drug may also increase the risk of suicide. There are no hard data documenting the degree of either of these risks, but the latter appears to be larger than the former. *See, e.g.,* "FDA's Role in Protecting the Public Health: Examining FDA's Review of Safety and Efficacy Concerns in Anti–Depressant Use by Children." Hearing before the Committee on Oversight and Investigations of the House Committee on Energy and Commerce, 108th Cong. 2d Sess. (2004).

Thomas M. Burton, *Risk vs. Benefit: FDA Weighs Antipsychotic*

THE WALL STREET JOURNAL, October 14, 1996, at B1.

"I think that this is a dangerous drug," declared senior Food and Drug Administration official Raymond Lipicky at an FDA advisory committee hearing in July.

As head of the FDA's division of cardio-renal drug products, Dr. Lipicky used this unusually harsh language to describe sertindole, a new antipsychotic drug from Abbott Laboratories. The drug, trade-named Serlect, may cause sudden cardiac death, he contended. Yet earlier this month, North Chicago, Ill.-based Abbott received an FDA letter suggesting that the agency will soon approve marketing of the drug.

This case illustrates the FDA's dilemma in balancing potentially lethal side effects against possibly powerful therapeutic benefits—particularly when no existing drug cures an illness. The FDA evaluates "safety and efficacy" in a delicate risk-benefit analysis and sometimes makes decisions before the full scope of potential risk can be known. "Safety in our terms," says Robert Temple, an FDA director of drug evaluation, means that a drug's "benefits outweigh its risks when used as labeled."

Sertindole is among the first of a new class of antipsychotic medications that offer hope for millions of people. About 1% of the world's population, including some 2.5 million adult Americans, suffer from schizophrenia. They are tormented by hallucinations, such as voices torturing them or visions of dead relatives. They're plagued by delusions of persecution and of being followed by strangers. Such terrors are alleviated to varying degrees by older generic medications like haloperidol, and by newer drugs like Sandoz AG's Clozaril and Johnson & Johnson's Risperdal.

But an estimated 40% to 60% of patients develop drug-induced side effects such as debilitating tremors or muscle rigidity. Perhaps half of those with side effects drop off medication as a result, psychiatrists estimate. Clozaril, generically called dozapine, tends to be effective in patients who aren't helped by other drugs, but it can lead to a sometimes-fatal condition called agranulocytosis, a blood disorder characterized by fever and weakness.

As a result, psychiatrists and pharmaceutical companies are searching for new therapies. "We need all the help we can get," says Harvard University psychiatry professor William M. Glazer. And University of Maryland psychiatry professor Carol A. Tamminga says sertindole holds promise because of its "potent antipsychotic effects."

But during Abbott's clinical trials on 2,194 patients using sertindole for an average of about six months, 27 patients died. Of these, Dr. Lipicky identified at least six as possible sudden cardiac deaths ...

Ultimately, the FDA's advisory committee voted, 4 to 2, that sertindole was safe enough to allow it on the U.S. market; the FDA usually follows the directives of its advisory committees....

Among the options now available for the FDA regarding sertindole is to put restrictions in the labeling of the drug, warning of a possibly fatal side effect—though researchers don't yet know whether they pose more risks for some types of patients than others....

NOTES

1. *Commentary. See* "FDA's Role in Protecting the Public Health: Examining FDA's Review of Safety and Efficacy Concerns in Anti–Depressant Use by Children," Hearing before the Subcommittee on Oversight and Investigations of the House Committee on Energy and Commerce, 108th Cong., 2d Sess. (2004); Katherine Wray, *Combating Depression: A History and Analysis of FDA Regulation of Selective Serotonin Reuptake Inhibitors* (2004), in Chapter VI(C)(3) of the Electronic Book.

2. *Ritalin.* The use of Ritalin for attention deficit disorder has also been controversial. *See* Marina Bonanni, *The Invasion of Ritalin: A Call for Federal Regulation* (2004), and Kenneth Shaitelman, *Overload: Regulating the Sources of Information about Attention–Deficit/Hyperactivity Disorder* (2005), in Chapter VI(C)(3) of the Electronic Book.

9.   ENVIRONMENTAL CONSIDERATIONS

Under the National Environmental Policy Act of 1969, *infra* p. 1608, all federal agencies must consider the environmental impact of any major action that may significantly affect the quality of the environment. FDA has promulgated regulations in 21 C.F.R. Part 25 to implement this statutory requirement. 21 C.F.R. 25.20(1) requires the preparation of an environmental assessment for every NDA unless it is subject to a categorical exclusion under 21 C.F.R. 25.31. Section 411 of the FDA Modernization Act of 1997 added section 746 to the FD&C Act to confirm that an environmental impact statement prepared in accordance with 21 C.F.R. Part 25 meets the requirements for a detailed environmental statement under section 102(2)(C) of the National Environmental Policy Act. FDA formerly periodically published notices of the availability of these environmental assessments in the Federal Register, *e.g.*, 57 Fed. Reg. 18887 (May 1, 1992), but in 1999, FDA announced that it would no longer publish these notices because all environmental assessments are now available through the CDER Electronic Reading Room. 64 Fed. Reg. 25046 (May 10, 1999).

NOTE

In accordance with the Montreal Protocol on Substances that Deplete the Ozone Layer of September 16, 1987, FDA has promulgated regulations for an orderly phaseout of the use of chlorofluorocarbons in inhaled drugs administered by metered dose inhalers. 62 Fed. Reg. 10242 (Mar. 6, 1997), 64 Fed. Reg. 47719 (Sept. 1, 1999), 67 Fed. Reg. 48370 (July 24, 2002), 71 Fed. Reg. 70870 & 70912 (Dec. 7, 2006), codified at 21 C.F.R. 2.125. *See* "Regulatory Efforts to Phaseout Chlorofluorocarbon–Based Metered Dose Inhalers," Hearing before the Subcommittee on

Health and Environment of the House Committee on Commerce, 105th Cong., 2d Sess. (1998).

10. DRUGS TO COMBAT TERRORISM

Following the events of September 11, 2001, Congress enacted the Public Health Security and Bioterrorism Preparedness and Response Act of 2002, 116 Stat. 594. Section 122 authorizes the Secretary of HHS to designate an antiterrorism drug, including one whose approval may be sought solely on the basis of animal studies, as a Fast Track product under section 506 that will be given priority review. Section 123 ordered FDA to complete its rulemaking regarding drugs approved solely on the basis of animal trials, *see* below.

Section 511 of an earlier law, the Antiterrorism and Effective Death Penalty Act of 1996, 110 Stat. 1214, 1284, directed the Secretary of HHS to maintain a list of biological agents and toxins that have "the potential to pose a severe threat to public health and safety." *See* "Interstate Transportation of Human Pathogens," Hearing before the Senate Committee on the Judiciary, 104th Cong., 2d Sess. (1996). This list and related regulations were published in 61 Fed. Reg. 55190 (Oct. 24, 1996) and codified at 42 C.F.R. Part 72. Section 201 of the Bioterrorism Preparedness and Response Act of 2002 codified the 1996 Act as part of the Public Health Service Act and strengthened control over the biological agents included on that list. At the same time, section 201 required that the HHS regulations include measures to ensure the "appropriate availability of biological agents and toxins for research." Drug products subject to an NDA are exempt from transfer and possession restrictions promulgated under the statute. Drug products subject to an IND may be exempted on an individual basis.

Section 321 of the 2002 Act also amends section 510 of the FD&C Act to require that foreign drug establishments update their registrations annually and include information about each importer or carrier transporting drugs into the United States. Any drug imported into the United States may be refused admission if it does not identify the establishment registration, and section 301 of the FD&C Act was amended to make importation without establishment registration a prohibited Act. The import-for-export provisions in section 801(d)(3) of the FD&C Act were also tightened to assure appropriate identification of the imported article.

Both the Bioterrorism Act of 2002 and the Project BioShield Act of 2004, 118 Stat. 835, were intended to stimulate research and development of drugs to combat terrorism. For critiques of these statutes, see Sara Kasper, *The National Strategic Stockpile: Will it Really Protect the Nation Against Bioterrorism?* (2006), and Janet Temko, *The Project Bioshield Act of 2004: An Innovative Failure* (2006), in Chapter II(Y) of the Electronic Book; Frank Gottron, *Project BioShield*, CRS REP. No. RS 21507 (Sept. 27, 2006). *See also* "Germs, Toxins and Terror: The New Threat to America," Hearing before the Subcommittee on Technology, Terrorism, and Government Information of the Senate Committee on the Judiciary, 107th Cong., 1st Sess. (2001).

11.   THE "ANIMAL RULE"

FDA has always recognized that there are some drugs for which human clinical trials, and particularly controlled clinical trials, cannot be conducted ethically. The paradigm example is a snake bite remedy. Such drugs have been approved by FDA on the basis of animal studies.

In 1999, FDA proposed what has come to be known as the "animal rule," under which the effectiveness of a new drug to reduce or negate the toxicity of chemical, biological, radiological, or nuclear substances is permitted to be tested only in animals because it would be unethical to expose individuals to these lethal or permanently disabling toxic substances in clinical trials. 64 Fed. Reg. 53960 (Oct. 5, 1999). Following the September 11, 2001 attacks, FDA promulgated a final regulation. 67 Fed. Reg. 37988 (May 31, 2002), codified at 21 C.F.R. Part 314, Subpart I. The animal rule removes a major obstacle to the development of new drugs to counter bioterrorism. *See* Carrie Campbell, *No Humans Have Been Injured in the Testing of this Drug: The New Animal Efficacy Rule* (2004), in Chapter VI(C)(2) of the Electronic Book.

Nonetheless, the pharmaceutical industry has expressed concern about its potential liability arising from the development or use of drugs for which only animal models are available to support effectiveness. In the Public Readiness and Emergency Preparedness Act, 119 Stat. 2680, 2818 (2005), Congress conferred immunity from tort liability for the clinical investigation or marketing of any antiterrorism drug used under a declaration of emergency by the Secretary of HHS pursuant to section 564 of the FD&C Act. This immunity is lost only if the company has engaged in willful misconduct and enforcement action has been brought by FDA and resolved in favor of the agency.

12.   REQUEST FOR DESIGNATION

In most instances, the proper FDA center for regulating a product is determined at the investigational stage, as described *supra* p. 623, because one center asserts jurisdiction or the sponsor files a request for designation pursuant to 21 C.F.R. Part 3. It is entirely possible, however, that this intercenter jurisdictional issue will only arise when a product application is submitted. In that event, the matter can still be resolved either by informal agreement or through a request for designation.

FDA strives to ensure that similar products are treated in the same way, in order to avoid competitive inequity, but it is not always successful. This problem is illustrated by *Bracco Diagnostics, Inc. v. Shalala*, 963 F. Supp. 20 (D.D.C. 1997), where three manufacturers of injectable contrast imaging agents for use with diagnostic ultrasound equipment in the diagnosis of cardiac dysfunction brought suit against FDA on the ground that they were required to obtain NDAs while a competitor with virtually identical technology was regulated as a medical device. The District Court found that CDER and CDRH (the device center) were applying very different standards to assess safety and effectiveness of essentially identical products. It granted the plaintiffs' motion for injunctive relief, concluding that FDA has discretion under section 503(g) of the FD&C Act to determine whether to regulate these products as drugs or devices, but that "what the FDA is not free to do ... is to treat them dissimilarly and to permit two sets of similar products to run down two separate tracks, one more treacherous than the other, for no apparent reason." Because the "disparate treatment of functionally indistinguishable products is the essence of the meaning of arbitrary and capricious," the District Court enjoined FDA from continuing any approval or review procedure with respect to the medical device product until the agency determined how all of the products should be regulated. The court also enjoined the agency from taking any further review action with respect to the three drug products until the jurisdictional issue was resolved. FDA subsequently declared that it would regulate all ultrasound contrast agents as drugs. The District Court then determined that all of the pending lawsuits were moot and should be dismissed. Food Drug Cosm. L. Rep. (CCH) ¶ 38,537 (D.D.C. 1997).

13.   ORPHAN DRUGS

The requirements for approval of a new drug present special obstacles for the development of drugs intended to treat rare diseases whose potential sales are not large enough to justify funding the necessary nonclinical and clinical tests. For several years, FDA kept many such drugs indefinitely in "orphan IND" status, contrary to the intent of section 505(i), while allowing them to be used for patient treatment. One goal of FDA's revision of the IND regulations in the late 1970s was to establish a formal regulatory status for these orphan INDs.

A 1979 report of an HHS interagency task force, SIGNIFICANT DRUGS OF LIMITED COMMERCIAL VALUE, outlined new mechanisms for spurring the development of orphan drugs. Soon after, Congress enacted the Orphan Drug Act, 96 Stat. 2049 (1983), to provide two types of incentives for the development of orphan drugs. First, the Act amended the Internal Revenue Code to provide tax credits for expenditures for clinical testing. 26 U.S.C. 44H. Second, it added four new sections, 525–528, to the FD&C Act. These provisions require FDA to provide sponsors written recommendations for the animal and clinical investigations needed for approval of an NDA, authorize FDA to designate those drugs that qualify as orphan drugs, provide seven years of postapproval market exclusivity for any unpatentable orphan drug (during which even a full NDA for an identical drug cannot be approved by FDA), and direct the agency to encourage open label INDs for orphan drugs under which patients suffering from the disease can obtain the drug for treatment. The pharmaceutical industry's response to the 1983 Act surpassed expectations, in part because several orphan drugs had already been identified and were thus available for immediate development.

To provide additional incentives for manufacturers to expand research into new clinical areas, Congress made two other important changes to the FD&C Act in the mid–1980s. In the Health Promotion and Disease Prevention Amendments of 1984, 98 Stat. 2815, 2817, section 526(a)(2) was revised to define a "rare disease or condition" as one that affects fewer than 200,000 persons in the United States. This change greatly expanded the number of diseases that could be regarded as "rare" and thus the number of drugs that could qualify as orphan drugs. The Orphan Drug Amendments of 1985, 99 Stat. 387, expanded the provision for market exclusivity to include patented as well as unpatentable drugs. As a result, pharmaceutical companies began to compete to become the first to obtain FDA approval of NDAs for lucrative orphan drugs.

Genentech, Inc. v. Bowen

676 F. Supp. 301 (D.D.C. 1987).

■ STANLEY S. HARRIS, DISTRICT JUDGE.

This matter is before the Court on the separate, but similar, motions of plaintiff Genentech, Inc. (Genentech) [and] intervenor-defendant Ares–Serono, Inc. (Serono) . . . for partial summary judgment. In its complaint, Genentech, the manufacturer and marketer of a synthetic human growth hormone produced through recombinant DNA technology, alleges that the recent decision of the Food and Drug Administration (FDA) . . . to approve a recombinant DNA human growth hormone product manufactured by intervenor-defendant Eli Lilly and Company (Lilly) violated the Administrative Procedure Act, the Orphan Drug Act, and the Fifth Amendment to the United States Constitution. The pending motions challenge the validity of the FDA's designation, prior to marketing approval, of Lilly's drug as an orphan drug. . . . [T]he motions for partial summary judgment are denied. . . .

Human growth hormone (hGH) is a protein naturally produced and secreted by the human pituitary gland. In some children, between 6,000 and 15,000 in the United States, the pituitary gland does not produce enough hGH, resulting in stunted growth. Since 1958, the condition had been treated by supplementing a patient's natural hGH with hGH derived from the pituitary glands of human cadavers. However, in 1985, use of pituitary-derived hGH was effectively eliminated by the discovery that three hGH patients who had been treated with hGH provided by NHPP had developed Creutzfeldt–Jakob Disease, an extremely rare but fatal condition, apparently due to exposure to a pathogen transmitted by the pituitary-derived hGH. Although no cases of Creutzfeldt–Jakob Disease have ever been linked to hGH distributed by Serono or KabiVitrum, neither has distributed pituitary-derived hGH in the United States since 1985.[13]

On October 17, 1985, the FDA granted Genentech, a pharmaceutical developer that specializes in the use of biotechnology (popularly known as "gene splicing"), marketing approval for a human growth product known commercially as Protropin. Genentech's product differs from pituitary-derived hGH in two important respects. First, it is synthesized through a

---

13. Although Serono's and KabiVitrum's NDAs were not cancelled by the FDA pursuant to 21 U.S.C. § 355(e), it is not clear to the Court whether those companies' withdrawals were purely voluntary, or whether there was a degree of informal compulsion exerted by the FDA. It is undisputed, however, that the withdrawals were occasioned by the linking of Creutzfeldt–Jakob Disease to pituitary-derived hGH, and that they effectively eliminated the supply of supplemental hGH in this country.

recombinant DNA process utilizing *E. coli* bacteria, rather than produced in a human gland. Second, Genentech's "r-hGH" product includes an amino acid group not commonly found in pituitary-derived hGH. In terms of chemical structure, Genentech's r-hGH has the same sequence of 191 amino acids found in hGH, with an additional methionine amino acid group attached to one end of the molecule. Because Genentech's drug apparently does not present the risk of Creutzfeldt–Jakob Disease associated with pituitary-derived hGH, its approval in 1985 filled an important health need. On December 12, 1985, the FDA designated Protropin as an orphan drug, thus granting Genentech marketing exclusivity, pursuant to 21 U.S.C. § 360cc, until December 12, 1992. . . .

On June 12, 1986, the FDA designated an r-hGH drug developed by intervenor-defendant Lilly as an orphan drug for the treatment of human growth hormone deficiency. Unlike Genentech's r-hGH product, the chemical structure of Lilly's product is identical to that of natural, pituitary-derived hGH; that is, Lilly's drug does not contain the additional methionyl group found in Protropin. On October 15, 1986, Lilly submitted to the FDA a New Drug Application (NDA) for its r-hGH product, seeking permission to market the drug commercially.

On November 3, 1986, Genentech submitted a "citizen petition" to the FDA. In it, Genentech took the position that Lilly's drug was, for the purposes of the Orphan Drug Act, the same as Protropin and therefore ineligible for marketing approval until 1992. . . . Genentech . . . requested an administrative stay of approval of any new r-hGH products. . . .

When Genentech learned that the FDA was preparing to approve the NDA for Lilly's methionyl-free r-hGH product, known commercially as Humatrope, Genentech sought an emergency stay from the FDA. When that request was denied, Genentech filed suit in this Court on March 6, 1987, seeking temporary, preliminary, and permanent injunctive relief, in addition to a declaratory judgment that the FDA's application of the Orphan Drug Act violated Genentech's statutory and constitutional rights.

. . . On March 8, the FDA approved Lilly's NDA for Humatrope, thereby authorizing Lilly to market the drug commercially and triggering the orphan drug exclusivity provision of 21 U.S.C. § 360cc. . . .

Movants contend that Humatrope's orphan drug designation violated both the Orphan Drug Act and the FDA's binding regulations implementing the Act. Their argument is based on the contention that Humatrope and pituitary-derived hGH are the same drug. In light of the peculiar facts of this case, the Court cannot accept movants' contention, and therefore must uphold the Humatrope designation. . . .

Two related aspects of this particular case convince the Court that if Congress had been presented with the facts of this case, it would have considered Humatrope and pituitary-derived hGH different drugs for the purposes of § 360bb(a). First, Humatrope, by virtue of its synthetic origin, does not present the danger of contamination with the Creutzfeldt–Jakob prion that is associated with hGH obtained from human cadavers. . . . [A]ny pituitary-derived hGH product presents a risk (albeit unquantifiable) of lethal side effects not associated with r-hGH products such as Protropin and Humatrope.

Second, the industry's response to the linking of Creutzfeldt–Jakob Disease to pituitary-derived hGH—withdrawal from the United States market—meant that regardless of the status of the Serono and Kabi NDAs, methionyl-free hGH would not be available to hGH-deficient children in this country. The legislative history is replete with references to the fundamental need to provide treatment for presently untreated patients; the fact that NDAs for pituitary-derived hGh were technically still valid would not have convinced Congress that growth hormone deficiency was not a condition in need of new treatments. One need only imagine a world without methionyl r-hGH (plaintiff's Protropin) to appreciate the unacceptable ramifications of movants' argument when applied to this case. Without Protropin, children in need of supplemental hGH would go without treatment, while movants offered assurances that no additional orphan drug designations were necessary because valid, but unused, NDAs remained in effect. In enacting the Orphan Drug Act, Congress clearly focused on the availability of treatments, not the existence of prior NDAs. . . .

In finding that Humatrope and pituitary-derived hGH are different drugs for the purposes of orphan drug designation under 21 U.S.C. § 360bb, and that therefore the Humatrope designation is valid, the Court's holding is narrow and confined to the particular facts of this case. The Court expresses no opinion on the still-pending issue of whether Protropin's orphan drug exclusivity barred approval of Humatrope, and, in particular, sets down no universal rule for determining whether two drugs are "different": for the purposes of the Orphan Drug Act. . . .

NOTES

1. *Consistent Decisions.* In two other cases, the courts reached the same conclusion as the District Court in *Genentech.* In *Berlex Laboratories, Inc. v. Food and Drug Administration*, 942 F. Supp. 19 (D.D.C. 1996), Berlex was given market exclusivity of its drug under the Orphan Drug Act, but FDA approved an NDA for a competitor's product on the ground that it was "clinically superior" because the pioneer drug had a higher rate of injection site necrosis. In *Sigma–Tau Pharmaceuticals, Inc. v. Schwetz*, 288 F.3d 141 (4th Cir. 2002), FDA approved a generic version of the pioneer drug in spite of the seven-year period of orphan exclusivity for the pioneer, because the FDA approval was only for an indication that was no longer protected by market exclusivity. The Court of Appeals held that the seven-year period of orphan drug exclusivity applies on an indication basis, not for the entire drug and all of its uses. As the Court of Appeals stated, the market exclusivity granted under the orphan drug is "disease-specific, not drug-specific."

2. *Implementing Regulations.* In 1984, FDA published notices of the availability of interim guidelines to implement the Orphan Drug Act. 48 Fed. Reg. 40784 (Sept. 9, 1983), 50 Fed. Reg. 19583 (May 9, 1985). In 1986, the agency published a notice of its intent to initiate rulemaking to implement the Act. 51 Fed. Reg. 4505 (Feb. 5, 1986). These regulations were completed in 1992. 56 Fed. Reg. 3338 (Jan. 29, 1991), 57 Fed. Reg. 62076 (Dec. 29, 1992), codified at 21 C.F.R. Part 316.

3. *Timing of Claim of Orphan Status.* FDA initially concluded that a drug was eligible for orphan drug designation if a petition was received before the agency *approved* an NDA for use of the drug to treat the rare disease. The Orphan Drug Amendments of 1988, 102 Stat. 90, amended section 526 to require that a petition for orphan drug designation be made before the *submission* of an NDA for the orphan drug use.

4. *List of Orphan Drugs.* FDA periodically published a cumulative list of orphan drug designations. *E.g.,* 54 Fed. Reg. 16294 (Apr. 21, 1989), 55 Fed. Reg. 11438 (Mar. 28, 1990). That list is now available on the FDA website.

5. *Orphan Products Board.* As originally enacted, the Orphan Drug Act created an Orphan Products Board, composed entirely of officials of the Department of HHS, to promote the development of drugs and devices for rare diseases and conditions. 96 Stat. 2049, 2052 (1983). The Orphan Drug Amendments of 1985 substituted a new National Commission on Orphan Diseases, with nongovernmental membership, to assess governmental and nongovernmental activities with respect to rare diseases. 99 Stat. 387, 388. FDA has generally heeded the recommendations of the National Commission. *See, e.g.,* "Orphan Product Development Policies," FDA Talk Paper No. T89–30 (May 8, 1989).

6. *Seven Year Exclusivity.* As illustrated in the *Genentech* case, the assurance of seven years of market exclusivity is of major commercial importance. An amendment to allow exceptions to this provision passed by Congress was vetoed by President George H. W. Bush on the ground that it would undermine the commercial incentive to develop orphan drugs. 26 WEEKLY COMP. OF PRES. DOC. 1796 (Nov. 8, 1990).

7. *Proposed Legislation.* Because some orphan drugs have been very profitable, legislation has been proposed to revise various provisions of the law. *See, e.g.,* "Anticompetitive Abuse of the Orphan Drug Act: Invitation to High Prices," Hearing before the Subcommittee on Antitrust, Monopolies and Business Rights of the Senate Committee on the Judiciary, 102d Cong., 2d Sess. (1992); "Orphan Drug Amendments of 1991," Hearing before the Senate Committee on Labor and Human Resources, 102d Cong., 2d Sess. (1992); "Orphan Drug Reauthorization," Hearing before the Subcommittee on Health and the Environment of the House Committee on Energy and Commerce, 103d Cong., 2d Sess. (1994). *See also* John S. Gardner, *Profit Windfall or Patient Windfall? The Orphan Drug Act and Proposals for Its Reform* (1994), and Anton Leis Garcia, *Is the Copy Better Than the Original? The Regulation of Orphan Drugs: A US–EU Comparative Prospective* (2004), in Chapter VI(G) of the Electronic Book.

8. *Commentary. See* Martha J. Carter & Alan R. Bennett, *Developments in Orphan Drugs*, 44 FOOD DRUG COSM. L.J. 627 (1989); Donna Brown Grossman, *The Orphan Drug Act: Adoption or Foster Care?*, 39 FOOD DRUG COSM. L.J. 128 (1984); Rosanne Apfeldorf Hurwitz, *Legal and Ethical Issues in the Clinical Testing of Drugs for Rare Diseases*, 40 FOOD DRUG COSM. L.J. 396 (1985); Patricia J. Kenney, *The Orphan Drug Act—Is it a Barrier to Innovation? Does it Create Unintended Windfalls?*, 43 FOOD DRUG COSM. L.J. 667 (1988); Robert A. Bohrer & John T. Prince, *A Tale of Two Proteins: The FDA's Uncertain Interpretation of the Orphan Drug Act*, 12 HARV. J.L. & TECH. 365 (1999).

Marlene E. Haffner, *Adopting Orphan Drugs—Two Dozen Years of Treating Rare Diseases*

354 NEW ENGLAND JOURNAL OF MEDICINE 445 (2006).

In the 24 years since this law was passed, 282 [orphan] drugs and biologic products, providing treatment for more than 14 million patients in the United States, have come to market under its aegis. In the 8 to 10 years before 1982, by contrast, only 10 treatments for rare diseases had been approved by the FDA and brought to market....

Orphan drugs must go through the same development process as any other drug and must be shown to meet the same standards for effectiveness and safety as a drug for a common condition. Indeed, because of the small number of patients available to be enrolled in clinical trials of orphan drugs, these products must be even more effective than the average drug if a statistically significant benefit is to be established. . . .

The research and development encouraged by the Orphan Drug Act have brought needed therapies to millions of patients in the United States, but these products are not free from controversy. One criticism concerns the high cost of some orphan drugs—although other drugs developed by means of biotechnology are equally expensive. . . .

14.   BIOTECHNOLOGY DRUGS

Beginning with Watson and Crick's discovery of the double helix structure of DNA, *supra* p. 143, recombinant DNA technology and other forms of biotechnology have played significant roles in pharmaceutical research and development. Every large pharmaceutical company has entered the field, but the unexpected development has been the explosive growth of startup companies financed by venture capital. Today there are approximately 2000 small companies of this kind, most of which are private and are building toward the day when they can launch an initial public offering (IPO) that will give them access to the public financial markets.

At least at the beginning of the biotechnology revolution, these small companies were formed on the hypothesis that they could avoid the huge investment made by large pharmaceutical companies to obtain approval of an NDA, by staying lean and picking only those drug targets that their scientific founders and consultants concluded would have a high likelihood of success. They also harbored the belief that FDA would assist them, both with timely advice and more rapid review and approval. They have been disappointed in both respects. FDA treats small companies no differently from large companies. Taking into account all the failed biotechnology products and companies, the cost of the average biotechnology NDA is not significantly different from the cost of the average NDA obtained by a large pharmaceutical company. Thus, the biotechnology industry has had to cope with the same rules governing preclinical and clinical research and employ the same strategies in negotiating NDAs with FDA as the large pharmaceutical companies.

Nonetheless, the importance of the emerging biotechnology industry should not be ignored. Small companies are invariably formed on the basis of cutting-edge scientific developments in academia. If a substantial percentage of the drugs now under development in these small companies survive to become the subject of approved NDAs, it will be the most dramatic leap forward in human medicine that the world has ever seen.

Davis P. Hamilton, *Dose of Reality—Biotech's Dismal Bottom Line: More Than $40 Billion Losses*

THE WALL STREET JOURNAL, May 20, 2004, at A1.

Since the first biotechnology company went public a quarter-century-ago, stock-market investors have put somewhere close to $100 billion into the industry.

The results so far: More than a hundred new drugs and vaccines, several hundred million people helped by biotech medicines,—and cumulative net losses of more than $40 billion for the industry's public companies.

Biotechnology, which harnesses the science of genetics to develop medicines may yet turn into an engine of economic growth and cure deadly diseases. But it's hard to argue that it's a good investment. Not only has the biotech industry yielded negative financial returns for decades, it generally digs its hole deeper every year.

Home runs in biotechnology are scarce, but they can be lucrative. A $1,000 investment in Amgen Inc. at its initial offering in 1983 would now be worth almost $150,000. . . .

"Biotechnology is the people's lottery," says Thomas Eadington, a medical-technology entrepreneur turned investor in Newport Beach, Calif. "It's like the ultimate roulette game. If you hit it, the returns are astronomical."

A few biotechnology companies have achieved undeniable success. Amgen, the most successful biotech to date, earned $2.3 billion in net profit last year. Its nearest rival, Genentech Inc., earned $563 million. Overall, however, publicly traded biotech companies in the U.S. posted a net loss of $3.2 billion in 2003, thanks to vast research and development spending.

The biotech industry traces its origins to the mid–1970s, when Genentech created a scientific sensation by splicing genes into bacteria to produce human proteins. Since then, the term biotech has generally referred to such genetic engineering. Scientists insert a stretch of synthetic or human-derived DNA into living cells, which then interpret that genetic code and produce large amounts of a protein useful in treating diseases.

Every success, however, is accompanied by far more failures. Since it is almost impossible to tell which of the thousands of promising ideas will turn into a hit, the losers of the biotech lottery effectively fund the windfalls of the handful of lucky winners. . . .

Biotechnology research spending now consumes roughly $18 billion a year, more than the federal National Institutes of Health spends on heart disease, cancer and infectious disease, and close to two-thirds of the pharmaceutical industry's research spending. Taxpayers fund the NIH, while buyers of profitable prescription drugs pay for the billions that companies such as Merck & Co. and Pfizer Inc. plow into research.

The primary driver of biotechnology research, by contrast, is the apparently boundless optimism of investors. Biotech's mostly small, research-driven start-ups can spend years on basic science studies before they even start testing a drug, yet investors nurture hopes of huge-rewards far in the future.

The biotechnology industry also draws financial support from venture capitalists and drug-industry partners seeking access to promising experimental drugs. . . .

Almost one-sixth of the more than 350 U.S. biotechs that have gone public over the past two decades either were bought out for pennies on the dollar, dissolved themselves or had filed for bankruptcy protection by the end of 2003. Names that once raised hopes of medical miracles are now forgotten: Escagenetics, Advanced Tissue Sciences, ImmuLogic, Gliatech.

These are the headstones in a graveyard of investors' dreams. Early in the industry's history, biotech pioneers argued that genetic engineering could cut short the years-long testing process that traditional pharmaceuticals must go through. Since biotech drugs are often versions of the body's own proteins, the thinking was that they'd sail through safety tests. That didn't turn out to be the case, and these days genetically engineered medications generally take 10 to 15 years to win approval, much the same as other drugs.

A decade later, drugs made from bioengineered antibodies were touted as potential magic bullets against cancer and other diseases. Such antibodies have only come into general medical use within the past five years or so.

By the turn of the millennium, the deciphering of the complete human genetic code or genome appeared to herald a new age of treatments personalized for individual genetic differences. This sparked an astonishing 170% rise in biotech stock prices in just four months—followed by a steep crash over the next year. Four years later, such treatments are still mostly hypothetical.

Biotechnology companies are essentially research and fund-raising machines devoted to selling their scientific and medical "story" to investors and spending the resulting cash on laboratory studies and clinical testing. Some companies survive as long as two decades on investors' largesse without developing a revenue-producing drug. Like the dot-coms that populated the landscape during the late 1990s, the vast majority of biotechs have neither profits nor meaningful revenue—and no guarantee they'll ever have either.

To biotech enthusiasts, that merely underscores the need for investors to have patience. "Amgen and Genentech are just the ones to finish the race. They hold the promise of what so many of these companies could become," says Laurence Bleicher, an analyst for portfolio managers at Marsico Capital Management LLC.

NOTE

See also Gary P. Pisano, *Can Science Be a Business?: Lessons from Biotech*, 84 HARV. BUS. REV., No. 10, at 114 (Oct. 2006).

15. PRIORITY REVIEW

FDA has always regularly accorded expedited consideration to applications for important new medicines. *See Providing a Breakthrough for Drugs With Promise*, 13 FDA CONSUMER, No. 6, at 25 (July–Aug. 1979). In 1974, FDA formalized this logical, if not expressly authorized, practice by establishing a complex matrix to classify NDAs according to chemical type and therapeutic potential to determine their priority for review. *See* FDA Bureau of Drugs, *Staff Manual Guide* BD4820.3 (1974). In 1996, FDA replaced the 1974 priority system with the following, much simpler approach.

CDER Manual of Policies and Procedures 6020.3, Priority Review Policy

April 22, 1996.

BACKGROUND

The NDA classification system provides a way of describing drug applications upon initial receipt and throughout the review process and prioritizing their review.

DEFINITIONS

Review Priority Classification. A determination that is made based on an estimate of its therapeutic preventive or diagnostic value. The designations "Priority" (P) and "Standard" (S) are mutually exclusive. Both original NDAs and effectiveness supplements receive a review priority classification but manufacturing supplements do not.

- *P—Priority review*

The drug product, if approved, would be a significant improvement compared to marketed products [approved (if such is required), including non-"drug" products/therapies] in the treatment, diagnosis, or prevention of a disease. Improvement can be demonstrated by, for example: (1) evidence of increased effectiveness in treatment, prevention, or diagnosis of disease; (2) elimination or substantial reduction of a treatment-limiting drug reaction; (3) documented enhancement of patient compliance; or (4) evidence of safety and effectiveness of a new subpopulation.

- *S—Standard review*

All non-priority applications will be considered standard applications.

POLICY . . .

- Because the review priority classification determines the review time frame the application receives, the review priority classification should be determined and assigned at the 45–day meeting if the application is to be filed.

- The final review classification of a new drug may change from "P" to "S" during the course of the review of a marketing application (NDA), either because of the approval of other agents or because of availability of new data; however, the review priority classification assigned at the time of filing will not change during the first review cycle and the user fee time frame of the original review cycle will be that based on the original priority.

- The review priority classification determines the overall approach to setting review priorities and user fee review time frames but is not intended to preclude work on other projects. It does not imply that staff working on a priority application cannot work on other projects, such as 30–day safety reviews of a newly submitted investigational new drug application (IND), preparation for end-of-phase 2 conferences, etc. . . .

NOTES

1. *Authority to Prioritize*. A priority review policy necessarily means that NDAs for drugs assigned a low classification will be reviewed more slowly than those with a higher classification, even though they may be economically important to the applicant. Section 505 makes no reference to prioritizing NDAs for review. It does specify that FDA is to reach a final decision on any NDA within 180 days, a schedule the agency very rarely meets even for drugs of great therapeutic promise.

2. *Challenge to FDA Priorities*. FDA did not establish this priority classification system by public rulemaking, and the agency has not provided a procedure by which an applicant may dispute its initial classification of a drug. Nor has any applicant formally contested FDA's classification of its NDA or the agency's review in accordance with its priority classification.

16.   ACCELERATED APPROVAL—SUBPART H

In 1992, FDA promulgated regulations establishing two forms of accelerated approval of an NDA: (1) approval based on evidence of the drug's effect on a surrogate endpoint that reasonably suggests clinical benefit or on evidence of the drug's effect on a clinical endpoint other than survival or irreversible morbidity, and (2) approval of an effective drug that can be used safely only if distribution or use is modified or restricted. 57 Fed. Reg. 13234 (Apr. 15, 1992), 57 Fed. Reg. 58942 (Dec. 11, 1992), codified at 21 C.F.R. Part 314, Subpart H. In both situations, the approval is determined by FDA to meet the requirements for safety and effectiveness and thus is a full NDA approval under section 505 of the FD&C Act.

a.   APPROVAL BASED ON A SURROGATE ENDPOINT

As the discussion *supra* p. 639 showed, FDA has for many years approved NDAs on the basis of *validated* surrogate endpoints. Accelerated approval, however, is based upon an *unvalidated* surrogate endpoint that nonetheless is reasonable likely, based on epidemiologic, therapeutic, pathophysiologic, or other evidence, to predict clinical benefit or on the basis of an effect on a clinical endpoint other than survival or irreversible morbidity. NDA approval will therefore be subject to the requirement of a further clinical trial to verify clinical benefit, when there is uncertainty as to the relation of the surrogate endpoint to clinical benefit or of the observed clinical benefit to ultimate outcome. As the following article authored by five FDA officials with responsibility for the regulation of oncology drug products reflects, this accelerated approval mechanism has been very successful. If there is any criticism, it is that it has not been used as often as it could be. *E.g., FDA's Handling of UFT Raises Questions about Agency's Isolation, Grasp of Science*, 26 THE CANCER LETTER, No. 29 (July 21, 2000); Jacob W. Stahl, *A History of Accelerated Approval: Overcoming the FDA's Bureaucratic Barriers in Order to Expedite Desperately Needed Drugs to Critically Ill Patients* (2005), in Chapter IX(C)(2) of the Electronic Book.

Ramzi Dagher et al., *Accelerated Approval of Oncology Products: A Decade of Experience*

96 Journal of the National Cancer Institute 1500 (2004).

In 1992, Accelerated Approval Subpart H was added to the new drug application regulations. This addition allows accelerated approval of drugs for serious or life-threatening diseases if the drug appears to provide a benefit over available therapy [and] the benefit is determined by the drug's effect on a surrogate endpoint that is reasonably likely to predict clinical benefit or on evidence of an effect on a clinical benefit other than survival. . . .

In general, the FDA has considered an effect on survival or relief of patient symptoms as evidence of clinical benefit in oncology. Objective tumor response rates and time-to-progression have often been viewed as surrogate endpoints that are reasonably likely to predict clinical benefit. Objective response rates and/or time-to-progression have been accepted as evidence of clinical benefit in some circumstances—for example, when relatively nontoxic products are evaluated, such as hormonal therapies for breast cancer and some biologic products. Durable complete responses have been accepted as evidence of clinical benefit in hematologic malignancies when response has been associated with an established clinical benefit parameter, such as improved survival, reduced rate of infection, or reduced need for transfusion (3–5). These endpoints have also been accepted for other malignancies, such as testicular cancer, because the response was of sufficient magnitude and duration that it appeared to be associated with improved survival. . . .

From January 1992 through January 2004, 18 different anticancer drugs or biologic products for 22 indications were approved under Subpart H regulations. Since the first accelerated approval for an oncology drug was granted in 1995, six accelerated approval oncology drugs have subsequently been converted to regular approval. Of the remaining 16 applications, 11 accelerated approvals were granted on the basis of studies without an active comparator group (*i.e.*, single-arm studies or studies comparing two dose levels) and five accelerated approvals were granted on the basis of randomized studies with an active or placebo control group. . . .

In conclusion, the accelerated approval program in oncology has been successful in making 18 different products available to patients for 22 different cancer treatment indications. The use of single-arm studies for accelerated approval allows for the rapid evaluation of novel agents, usually in patients with refractory disease. Randomized studies allow for the evaluation of populations with less refractory disease, add-on designs, confirmation of clinical benefit in the same population as that used for accelerated approval, a larger and more precise safety database, and the examination of time-to-event endpoints.

Both single-arm studies and randomized studies may provide evidence to support accelerated approval. It is useful to discuss development plans including the design, conduct, and analysis of confirmatory studies with the FDA early in the development process. These studies are viewed as part of a comprehensive drug development plan that includes studies that might lead to accelerated approval and the confirmatory studies.

NOTE

The FDA website lists all Subpart H NDA accelerated approvals based on a surrogate endpoint.

b.   APPROVAL CONDITIONED ON RESTRICTED DISTRIBUTION

The second provision in Subpart H authorizes FDA to approve an effective drug that can be used safely only if distribution or use is modified or restricted. Because of the holding in *American Pharmaceutical Association v. Weinberger*, 377 F. Supp. 824 (D.D.C. 1974), *infra* p. 829, *aff'd per curiam*, 530 F.2d 1054 (D.C. Cir. 1976), that FDA has no authority under the FD&C Act to restrict distribution as a condition of NDA approval, this provision can be invoked by FDA only at the request or with the agreement of the NDA applicant. FDA has approved fewer than ten drugs with restricted distribution programs under subpart H. Examples include thalidomide, RU–486, GHB (the "date rape" drug), and a highly addictive pain medication. Each of the restricted distribution programs is uniquely tailored to the specific drug, and is described in detail on the FDA website.

NOTES

1.   *Impact of Restricted Distribution.* The risk management requirements of a restricted distribution program can substantially hinder those who wish to use it. *See, e.g.*, Sandra G. Booman, *Too Hard To Take: A Strict New Program May Prevent Birth Defects But Many Complain It Also Drives People Away From a Potentially Life-Transforming Treatment*, Wash. Post, Sept. 5, 2006, at F1; Jennifer Corbett Cooren, *Restrictions Curb Use of Powerful Acne Drug*, Wall St. J., Sept. 12, 2006, p. D1.

2.   *FDA Approval of Promotional Materials.* 21 C.F.R. 314.550 requires that all promotional materials intended to be used within 120 days after approval of an NDA under Subpart H be approved by FDA prior to NDA approval, and that all subsequent promotional materials be submitted to FDA at least 30 days prior to use. *See* Guidance for Industry: Accelerated Approval Products—Submission of Promotional Materials (1999).

3.   *Commentary. See* Monica R. Gerber, *Restrictions on Distribution on Use of Prescription Drugs: Current Practices and Future Products* (2003), in Chapter VI(L) of the Electronic Book.

17.   Fast Track

The FDA Fast Track program has two dimensions. The first facilitates expedited development during the IND phase of a new drug, as discussed *supra* p. 648. The second provides the opportunity to submit what is often called a "rolling NDA." The Fast Track program is open to any drug that is intended to address an "unmet medical need." In its Guidance for Industry: Fast Track Drug Development Programs—Designation, Development, and Application Review, FDA has clarified that a drug addresses an unmet medical need if the only available treatments are unapproved uses of approved drugs or are approved under the accelerated approval program in Subpart H. In order to evaluate the "rolling NDA," FDA undertook a pilot program pursuant to an October 2003 GUIDANCE FOR INDUSTRY: CONTINUOUS MARKETING APPLICATIONS: PILOT 1—REVIEWABLE UNITS FOR FAST TRACK PRODUCTS UNDER PDUFA. This pilot program is available through September 30, 2007, in order to determine the added cost and utility of this approach and its impact on the efficiency of the development process.

A Fast Track designation applies only to a specific drug for a specific indication. The indication must be for a serious or life-threatening condition and must be intended to meet an unmet medical need not adequately addressed by existing therapy. Although a Fast Track designation is independent from priority review, the definitions are sufficiently similar that a Fast Track NDA will almost always be able to obtain priority review. Separate requests must be submitted for each of these programs.

18.   RISK MANAGEMENT

FDA has engaged in risk management for new drugs since it began reviewing NDAs. The earliest and still most prevalent form of risk management is the agency's insistence on accurate and non-misleading physician labeling, particularly with regard to the pharmacology, toxicology, and adverse event information. For especially troublesome adverse reactions, the agency insists on using the contraindication designation. And for the most serious contraindications, FDA mandates a black box warning.

FDA's most recent risk management program, however, is of a different nature. In 1999, Public Citizen Health Research Group charged that time pressures caused by the PDUFA performance goals and the FDA initiatives to speed up the review and approval of new drugs was resulting in an increased number of unsafe drugs being introduced onto the market, and thus an increased number of unsafe drugs required to be taken off the market. In response, FDA Commissioner Jane Henney established a Task Force on Risk Management to evaluate this allegation. The resulting report, MANAGING THE RISKS FROM MEDICAL PRODUCT USE: CREATING A RISK MANAGEMENT FRAMEWORK (1999), rejected the allegations:

> The results of our comparison of the data showed that there has been no increase in the rate of *drug withdrawals* in the United States since PDUFA was enacted. As the graph at the end of this section shows, the nation has experienced a 1–to 3.5–percent rate of post marketing withdrawals for new products during the last several decades. In most cases, withdrawals occurred during the first or second year following approval. But there have been cases where drugs were withdrawn three, four and up to five years after approvals.
>
> The rate of serious adverse events has also decreased.
>
> The task force has found that available evidence does not support the charge that *unanticipated serious adverse events* are occurring at a higher rate since the implementation of PDUFA. We found that under PDUFA, there has been a lower rate of serious adverse events identified during the post approval phase (30.3% of

products) than during the 1976–1985 baseline years (51.5% of products).

See also Michael A. Friedman et al., *The Safety of Newly Approved Medicines: Do Recent Market Removals Mean There Is A Problem?*, 281 J.A.M.A. 281 (May 12, 1999).

But the Task Force report did not stop there. It went on to review the FDA mechanisms for risk management in the approval of NDAs and concluded that the agency could do a more effective job of risk management. The report identified numerous ways that FDA could improve these programs. FDA held a public hearing on the report, announced in 67 Fed. Reg. 18230 (Apr. 15, 2002).

The Task Force report had an immediate impact on FDA requirements for clinical trials. The pharmaceutical industry soon found that FDA was requesting more nonclinical studies and more clinical trials, of longer duration, with more subjects, containing more arms for additional dosage levels, with more diverse subjects, and longer follow up. The result was a significant reduction in NDAs submitted to the agency and an approximate doubling of the average cost of an NDA. In June 2001, stock analysts at SalomonSmithBarney, citing ten negative developments at FDA, headed its analysis: "FDA Goes Hostile."

In 2004, to implement its risk management program, FDA announced three draft guidances for industry relating to risk management practices during the development of new drugs: PREMARKETING RISK ASSESSMENT, DEVELOPMENT AND USE OF RISK MINIMIZATION ACTION PLANS, and GOOD PHARMACOVIGILANCE PRACTICES AND PHARMACOEPIDEMIOLOGIC ASSESSMENT. 69 Fed. Reg. 25130 (May 5, 2004). The following year, FDA announced the final versions of these guidances. 70 Fed. Reg. 15866 (Mar. 29, 2005), and CDER made available MAPP No. 6700.1 on RISK MANAGEMENT PLAN ACTIVITIES IN OND AND ODS (Sept. 8, 2005). Because this array of risk management policies is still relatively recent, it is unclear how much of an impact they will have on drug development in the United States.

19.   POISON PREVENTION PACKAGING

The Consumer Product Safety Commission (CPSC) implements the Poison Prevention Packaging Act of 1970, 84 Stat. 1670, under which child-resistant packaging is required. In 16 C.F.R. 1700.14(a)(10), the CPSC requires child resistant packaging for all human prescription drugs, with rare exceptions. In *Nutritional Health Alliance v. FDA*, 318 F.3d 92 (2d Cir. 2003), the Court of Appeals held that CPSC has exclusive jurisdiction over poison prevention packaging and therefore that FDA has no jurisdiction to require unit dose packaging for drugs and dietary supplements.

20.   RADIOPHARMACEUTICAL DRUGS

Radiopharmaceutical drugs receive distinctive regulatory treatment. Few of these drugs have been the subject of NDAs, and it is not feasible to regulate all radioactive-tagged drugs through the new drug process. FDA has established an old drug monograph approach, 21 C.F.R. 310.503 & Part

361, in cooperation with the Nuclear Regulatory Commission. *See* 37 Fed. Reg. 21026 (Nov. 3, 1971), 39 Fed. Reg. 26143 (July 17, 1974), 39 Fed. Reg. 27538 (July 29, 1974), 40 Fed. Reg. 31298 (July 25, 1975), 41 Fed. Reg. 7747 (Feb. 20, 1976), 41 Fed. Reg. 35171 (Aug. 20, 1976), 41 Fed. Reg. 42947 (Sept. 29, 1976), 42 Fed. Reg. 23161 (May 6, 1977), 43 Fed. Reg. 11208 (Mar. 17, 1978), 44 Fed. Reg. 8242 (Feb. 9, 1979), 45 Fed. Reg. 24920 (Apr. 11, 1980), 46 Fed. Reg. 46403 (Sept. 18, 1981), 49 Fed. Reg. 24949 (June 18, 1984). The NRC regulations governing licensing of individuals and institutions for medical use of radioactive material were overhauled in 50 Fed. Reg. 30616 (July 26, 1985), 51 Fed. Reg. 36932 (Oct. 16, 1986), and more recently in 62 Fed. Reg. 42219 (Aug. 6, 1997), 63 Fed. Reg. 43516 & 43580 (Aug. 13, 1998), 67 Fed. Reg. 20250 (Apr. 24, 2002), 68 Fed. Reg. 19321 (Apr. 21, 2003), 10 C.F.R. Part 35. The NRC has established training and experience criteria for physicians who request authorization to engage in nuclear medicine. 47 Fed. Reg. 3228 (Jan. 22, 1982), 47 Fed. Reg. 54376 (Dec. 2, 1982).

When FDA sought to increase its regulation of one form of radiopharmaceutical product, positron emission tomography (PET), in response to the forthcoming INSTITUTE OF MEDICINE, RADIATION IN MEDICINE: A NEED FOR REGULATORY REFORM (1996), it met with strong opposition from the nuclear medicine industry.

Syncor International Corporation v. Shalala

127 F.3d 90 (D.C. Cir. 1997).

■ SILBERMAN, CIRCUIT JUDGE: . . .

Positron emission tomography (PET) is a diagnostic imaging method that uses a subset of radioactive pharmaceuticals, called PET drugs, to determine biochemistry, physiology, anatomy, and pathology within various body organs and tissues by measuring the concentration of radioactivity in a targeted area of the body. The active component of PET drugs is a positron-emitting isotope. This component has a short half-life, so the drug remains effective for only brief periods of time. As a consequence, PET drugs are not manufactured by pharmaceutical companies; instead, they are prepared by physicians and pharmacists operating accelerators in facilities known as nuclear pharmacies, which most often are part of major teaching hospitals or their adjacent universities, and always are located very near to the place where the PET drug will be administered to patients. These nuclear pharmacists compound the isotope with a chemical solution called a substrate. The substrate is used to carry the isotope to the targeted organ or tissue, and the precise solution used depends on the targeted area. For example, a nuclear pharmacist might combine an isotope with a glucose substrate if the brain was being targeted, since the brain is an area of high glucose uptake. In part for this reason, PET drugs are compounded pursuant to a prescription.

On February 25, 1995, FDA announced that PET radiopharmaceuticals "should be regulated" under the drug provisions of the Federal Food, Drug, and Cosmetic Act. In this publication, labeled a "Notice," and referred to alternatively in its text as "guidance" and a "policy statement," FDA indicated that it would require PET "radiopharmaceutical manufacturers" to comply with the adulteration provision of § 501(a)(2)(B) of the Act (drugs are considered adulterated unless manufactured in conformance with current good manufacturing practices); the misbranding provision of § 502 of the Act (drugs are considered misbranded if the product labeling is false or misleading, if the drug is dangerous to health when used as suggested in the labeling, or if the labeling fails to include certain required information); the new drug provision of § 505 of the Act (new drugs must be the subject of approved new drug applications or abbreviated new drug applications before marketing); and the registration and listing provisions of § 510 of the Act (drug establishment must register with FDA, and file a list of all drugs that it makes or processes). *See* Regulation of Positron Emission Tomography Radiopharmaceutical Drug Products; Guidance; Public Workshop, 60 Fed. Reg. 10594, 10595 (1995).

FDA indicated that its 1995 publication was to supersede its prior 1984 publication—which had been directed at all nuclear pharmacies, not just those compounding PET radiopharmaceuticals—entitled "Nuclear Pharmacy Guideline; Criteria for Determining When to Register as a Drug Establishment." The 1984 Guideline had unequivocally stated that nuclear pharmacists who operated an accelerator to produce radioactive drugs to be dispensed under a prescription—which precisely describes the process by which nuclear pharmacies compound PET radiopharmaceuticals—were not required to register under § 510 of the Act. The Guideline also indicated that if a nuclear pharmacist was not required to register, that other of the Act's requirements, including the new drug provision and compliance with current good manufacturing practices, would not apply.

Syncor filed suit in the district court challenging FDA's 1995 publication. Syncor brought three claims, alleging that: (1) FDA lacked jurisdiction over PET drugs under the new drug provision of § 505 of the Act, which requires premarket approval for drugs introduced or delivered for introduction into interstate commerce, because PET drugs do not move in interstate commerce; (2) FDA violated the Tenth Amendment to the United States Constitution by regulating pharmacies in the absence of clear congressional authorization to do so, since pharmacy is an area traditionally reserved for state regulation; and (3) FDA violated the Administrative Procedure Act's requirement that an agency engaged in rulemaking give notice of its proposed rulemaking to the public and "give interested persons an opportunity to participate in the rule making through submission of written data, views, or arguments." The district judge granted summary judgment in FDA's favor on all three claims. We consider the APA claim first since if notice and comment are required we think it prudent to defer deciding the other two issues which presumably would be explored in a future rulemaking. . . .

The APA exempts from notice and comment interpretative rules or general statements of policy. 5 U.S.C. § 553(b)(3)(A). . . .

We have long recognized that it is quite difficult to distinguish between substantive and interpretative rules. . . . An agency policy statement does not seek to impose or elaborate or interpret a legal norm. It merely represents an agency position with respect to how it will treat—typically enforce—the governing legal norm. By issuing a policy statement, an agency simply lets the public know its current enforcement or adjudicatory approach. The agency retains the discretion and the authority to change its position—even abruptly—in any specific case because a change in its policy does not effect the legal norm. We thus have said that policy statements are binding on neither the public nor the agency. The primary distinction between a substantive rule—really any rule—and a general statement of policy, then, turns on whether an agency intends to bind itself to a particular legal position.

An interpretative rule, on the other hand, typically reflects an agency's construction of a statute that has been entrusted to the agency to administer. The legal norm is one that Congress has devised; the agency does not purport to modify that norm, in other words, to engage in lawmaking. . . .

A substantive rule has characteristics of both the policy statement and the interpretative rule; it is certainly in part an exercise of policy, and it is a rule. But the crucial distinction between it and the other two techniques is that a substantive rule modifies or adds to a legal norm based on the agency's own authority. That authority flows from a congressional delegation to promulgate substantive rules, to engage in supplementary lawmaking. And, it is because the agency is engaged in lawmaking that the APA requires it to comply with notice and comment.

It is apparent to us, in light of the foregoing discussion, that FDA's 1995 publication is not an interpretative rule. It does not purport to construe any language in a relevant statute or regulation; it does not interpret anything. Instead, FDA's rule uses wording consistent only with the invocation of its general rulemaking authority to extend its regulatory reach. . . .

The reasons FDA has advanced for its rule—advancement in PET technology, the expansion of procedures in which PET is used, and the unique nature of PET radiopharmaceuticals—are exactly the sorts of changes in fact and circumstance which notice and comment rulemaking is meant to inform. . . .

Accordingly, we reverse and remand to the district court with instructions to enter summary judgment in Syncor's favor, and to vacate FDA's rule as not in accordance with law. The district court should also dismiss Syncor's substantive claims without prejudice.

NOTES

1. *Congressional Direction.* Section 121 of the FDA Modernization Act of 1997, 111 Stat. 2296, 2320, added section 201(ii) to the FD&C Act to define the term "compounded positron emission tomography drug" and added section 501(a)(1)(C) to authorize FDA to promulgate GMP requirements for these drugs. Congress explicitly revoked 60 Fed. Reg. 10594 (Feb. 27, 1995) (guidance on regulation of PET products), 60 Fed. Reg. 10593 (Feb. 27, 1995) (draft guideline on PET product compliance with CGMP), and 62 Fed. Reg. 19493 (Apr. 22, 1997) (final rule allowing requests for exceptions to CGMP requirements). Congress also directed the agency to adopt appropriate procedures for the approval of PET drugs under section 505 of the FD&C Act, taking into account the "special characteristics of

positron emission tomography drugs and the special techniques and processes required to produce these drugs.''

2. *Revoked Notices.* In accordance with the 1997 Act, FDA revoked the notices and regulations of 1995 and 1997. 62 Fed. Reg. 66636 & 66522 (Dec. 19, 1997). The agency released a preliminary draft of new PET GMP requirements in 64 Fed. Reg. 51274 (Sept. 22, 1999), 67 Fed. Reg. 15344 (Apr. 1, 2002) and announced a draft guidance on PET DRUG PRODUCTS—CURRENT GOOD MANUFACTURING PRACTICE in 67 Fed. Reg. 15404 (Apr. 1, 2002). In 2005, FDA published comprehensive proposed new PET GMP regulations. 70 Fed. Reg. 55038 (Sept. 20, 2005).

21.   INSULIN AND ANTIBIOTIC DRUGS

The 1938 Act contained no provisions relating specifically to insulin or antibiotic drugs. Congress added section 506 to provide for the certification of insulin, 55 Stat. 851 (1941), and section 507 to provide for certification of the first antibiotic drug, penicillin, in 59 Stat. 463 (1945). Section 507 was later amended to include streptomycin in 61 Stat. 11 (1947), aureomycin, chloramphenicol, and bacitracin in 63 Stat. 409 (1949), and to substitute chlortetracycline for aureomycin in 67 Stat. 389 (1953). The Drug Amendments of 1962, 76 Stat. 780, 785 amended section 507 to include all antibiotic drugs.

Because antibiotics are produced from microorganisms, individual batch certification was thought necessary to assure the identity, and thus the safety and effectiveness, of these drugs. Antibiotic drugs were also subject to the same IND and NDA requirements under 21 C.F.R. Parts 312 and 314 as other new drugs. Because of the high level of manufacturer compliance with antibiotic standards, in 1982, FDA exempted all classes of antibiotic drugs from batch certification. 47 Fed. Reg. 19954 (May 7, 1982), 47 Fed. Reg. 39155 (Sept. 7, 1982). *See* GAO, FDA SHOULD REDUCE EXPENSIVE ANTIBIOTIC TESTING AND CHARGE FEES WHICH MORE CLOSELY REFLECT COST OF CERTIFICATION, No. HRD–82–11 (Oct. 28, 1981). Thereafter, antibiotic new drugs were regulated on the same terms as nonantibiotic new drugs.

Recognizing that there was no longer a reason to distinguish insulin or antibiotics from other new drugs, Congress repealed sections 506 and 507 in the FDA Modernization Act of 1997, 111 Stat. 2296, 2325. As a result, these drugs are now regulated as new drugs, except that Congress specifically provided that they could continue to be exported solely under the requirements of Section 801(e)(1). FDA is presently determining what standards should be applied for abbreviated NDAs for insulin, a naturally derived protein.

NOTES

1. *Regional Compounding.* In *United States v. Baxter Healthcare Corp.*, 901 F.2d 1401 (7th Cir. 1990), the courts reviewed the practice of antibiotic manufacturers of obtaining an approved NDA for antibiotics in powder and liquid form and then reconstituting, repackaging, and freezing those drugs in final dosage form at regional compounding facilities for distribution to hospitals. Both courts upheld the FDA position that an NDA was needed for the final products produced at the regional compounding facilities. Under these decisions, all preparation of final dosage form antibiotics must be undertaken by the hospitals.

2. *Antibiotic Resistance.* As a result of antibiotic overuse and improper use, bacteria can develop resistance to existing antibiotic drugs, making infections difficult if not impossible to treat. Legislative and other solutions have been proposed to stimulate research and development on new antibiotic drugs that would address this problem. *See* Infectious Diseases Society of America, *Bad Bugs, No Drugs: As Antibiotic Discovery Stagnates a Public Health Crisis Brews* (2004); George H. Talbot et al., *Bad Bugs Need Drugs: An Update on the Development Pipeline from the Antimicrobial Availability Task Force of the Infectious Diseases Society of America*, 42 CLINICAL INFECTIOUS DISEASES 657 (2006). FDA has been accused of discouraging the development of new antibiotics. Paul H. Rubin, *The FDA's Antibiotic Resistance*, in 27 REGULATION, No. 4, at 34 (Winter 2004–2005); Joseph Gottfried, *History Repeating: Avoiding a Return to the Pre-Antibiotic Age* (2005), in Chapter VI(C)(3) of the Electronic Book.

22. PRESCRIPTION DRUG CONTROLLED SUBSTANCES

Before 1970, federal control of narcotic drugs, marijuana, and other drugs used for recreational and nonmedical purposes was shared among several agencies and rested on a haphazard cluster of laws enacted since the Harrison Narcotic Act of 1914, 38 Stat. 785. FDA was responsible for enforcement of the Drug Abuse Control Amendments of 1965, 79 Stat. 226, to prevent abuse of depressant and stimulant drugs, such as the amphetamines and barbiturates, which also have legitimate medical use. In 1970, Congress repealed the earlier statutes and enacted a new comprehensive law, the Controlled Substances Act, 84 Stat. 1236, 1242, 21 U.S.C. 801 *et seq.* Responsibility for enforcement of the Controlled Substances Act rests with the Drug Enforcement Administration (DEA) of the Department of Justice, which has the statutory obligation to consult with FDA on the scheduling of controlled substances. FDA's recommendations are binding on scientific and medical matters, and DEA may not schedule a drug if FDA recommends against it. 21 U.S.C. 201(b). FDA is required to request public comment on drug scheduling. *E.g.*, 70 Fed. Reg. 73775 (Dec. 13, 2005).

The Controlled Substances Act establishes five schedules of controlled substances, which can be summarized as follows: Schedule I includes drugs with a high potential for abuse that have no currently accepted medical use (*e.g.*, heroin). Schedule II includes drugs with a high potential for abuse with a currently accepted medical use. Schedule III includes drugs with a moderate potential for abuse and accepted medical use. Schedule IV includes substances with a low potential for abuse and accepted medical use. Schedule V includes substances with the lowest potential for abuse and currently accepted medical use.

The Act prohibits domestic distribution of all Schedule I drugs. The controls used to regulate distribution of drugs on Schedules II–V are calibrated to the degree of danger. Because the controls over scheduled drugs increase with the schedule to which they are assigned, scheduling decisions are of major importance to the pharmaceutical industry. *See, e.g., Grinspoon v. DEA*, 828 F.2d 881 (1st Cir. 1987); *Reckitt & Colman, Ltd. v. DEA*, 788 F.2d 22 (D.C. Cir. 1986); *Hoffmann-LaRoche, Inc. v. Kleindienst*, 478 F.2d 1 (3d Cir. 1973); *United States v. Hovey*, 674 F. Supp. 161 (D. Del. 1987). DEA may also establish production quotas for Schedule I and Schedule II drugs. *Western Fher Laboratories v. Levi*, 529 F.2d 325 (1st Cir.

1976). Although the requirements established under the Controlled Substances Act may impose extra burdens upon manufacturers, physicians, and pharmacists, they do not prevent FDA from approving an NDA for any controlled substance that has a legitimate medical use. *See generally* Anthony Vieux, *Regulatory Requirements under the Controlled Substances Act*, CRS REP. No. RX22487 (Aug. 2, 2006).

NOTES

1. *Medical Marijuana.* The efforts of the National Organization for the Reform of Marijuana Laws (NORML) are reflected in more than three decades of continuing administrative and judicial consideration of the appropriate scheduling of marijuana and tetrahydrocannabinol (THC), the principal active ingredient in marijuana, which is not yet completed. DEA denied the first NORML petition to move marijuana from Schedule I to Schedule II in 37 Fed. Reg. 10897 (Sept. 1, 1972), but the matter was remanded for an administrative hearing in *NORML v. Ingersoll*, 497 F.2d 654 (D.C. Cir. 1974). After a hearing, DEA again denied the NORML petition, 40 Fed. Reg. 44164 (Sept. 25, 1975), but the court remanded the matter once more with instructions to refer the petition to the Secretary of HHS for medical and scientific evaluation. *NORML v. DEA*, 559 F.2d 735 (D.C. Cir. 1977). After receiving FDA's evaluation and recommendations through HHS, DEA again denied the NORML petition in 44 Fed. Reg. 36123 (June 20, 1979). And again the court disagreed, remanding with directions that FDA take into account new evidence concerning medical use of THC. *NORML v. DEA*, No. 79–1660 (D.C. Cir., October 16, 1980). In 47 Fed. Reg. 10080 (Mar. 9, 1982), FDA recommended to the Department of HHS that THC remain in Schedule I until an NDA for THC was approved for medical purposes. In May 1985, FDA approved an NDA for a drug containing synthetic THC. In 51 Fed. Reg. 17476 (May 13, 1986), DEA classified this formulation in Schedule II. DEA then announced hearings on the NORML petition to reschedule marijuana. 51 Fed. Reg. 22946 (June 24, 1986). An administrative law judge recommended that marijuana be rescheduled from Schedule I to Schedule II, but the DEA Administrator rejected this recommendation and denied the NORML petition in 54 Fed. Reg. 53767 (Dec. 29, 1989). Previous constitutional challenges to the classification of marijuana in Schedule I failed. *NORML v. Bell*, 488 F. Supp. 123 (D.D.C. 1980); *Hartz v. Bensinger*, 461 F. Supp. 431 (E.D. Pa. 1978). *See also Productos Medix, S.A. v. U.S. Treasury Dept.*, Food Drug Cosm. L. Rep. (CCH) ¶ 38,131 (S.D. Tex. 1989), *aff'd*, 915 F.2d 1567 (5th Cir. 1990). *See* INSTITUTE OF MEDICINE, MARIJUANA AND MEDICINE: ASSESSING THE SCIENCE BASE (1999); "Marijuana and Medicine: The Need for a Science–Based Approach," Hearing before the Subcommittee on Criminal Justice, Drug Policy and Human Resources of the House Committee on Government Reform, 108th Cong., 2d Sess. (2004); Linda L. LeCraw, *Alternate Routes of Reformist Activism: Medial Marijuana As a Case Study of Initiatives Within and Beyond Statutorily Prescribed Channels* (1996), E. Laurita Finch, *The History of Medical Marijuana in the United States and Its Implications for the Current Legal Impediments to the Medical Use of Marijuana in the United States* (1997), Dean W. Leckie, *State Medical Marijuana Initiatives: A Justification and Analysis* (1998), and Jesse J. Ransom, *"Anslingerian" Politics: The History of Anti–Marijuana Sentiment in Federal Law and How Harry Anslinger's Anti–Marijuana Politics Continue to Prevent the FDA and Other Medical Experts from Studying Marijuana's Medical Utility* (1998), in Chapter VI(I) of the Electronic Book. State attempts to legalize medical marijuana were thwarted by the decision in *Gonzales v. Raich*, 545 U.S. 1 (2005), which upheld Congress's power, through the Controlled Substances Act, to prohibit intrastate, noncommercial cultivation and possession of cannabis for personal medical purposes as recom-

mended by a patient's physician pursuant to California law. In an attempt to discourage use of smoked marijuana as a medicine, FDA released a statement on April 20, 2006 stating that "FDA has not approved smoked marijuana for any condition or disease indication" and that "FDA, as the federal agency responsible for reviewing the safety and efficacy of drugs, DEA as the federal agency charged with enforcing the CSA, and the Office of National Drug Control Policy, as the federal coordinator of drug control policy do not support the use of smoked marijuana for medical purposes."

2. *Peyote for Religious Use.* The use of an otherwise banned Schedule I controlled substance as part of a religious ceremony has also provoked litigation. The plaintiff in *Peyote Way Church of God, Inc. v. Smith*, 556 F. Supp. 632 (N.D. Tex. 1983), 742 F.2d 193 (5th Cir. 1984), 698 F. Supp. 1342 (N.D. Tex. 1988), 922 F.2d 1210 (5th Cir. 1991), has thus far been unsuccessful in gaining permission to use peyote in its ceremonies despite its claims of discrimination because members of the Native American Church may use the drug pursuant to federal and state statutory exceptions. *See also Oregon Dept. of Human Resources v. Smith*, 494 U.S. 872 (1990) (state is not barred by the First Amendment from prohibiting sacramental use of peyote); *Olsen v. DEA*, 878 F.2d 1458 (D.C. Cir. 1989) (rejecting a religious use exemption for marijuana). In *Gonzales v. O Centro Esprita Beneficente Uniao Do Vegetal*, 544 U.S. 973 (2005), however, the Supreme Court interpreted the Religious Freedom Restoration Act of 1993, 107 Stat. 1488, which prohibits the federal government from substantially burdening a person's exercise of religion unless it represents the least restrictive means of advancing a compelling interest, to require DEA to allow a bona fide religious sect to receive communion by drinking a sacramental tea, hoasca, brewed from plants that naturally contain DMT, a Schedule I hallucinogen under the Controlled Substances Act.

3. *Hemp.* Sterilized hemp seed and oil, and cake derived from hemp seed, are used in manufacturing food and cosmetic products. These products contain trace amounts of THC, the active ingredient in marijuana. In 66 Fed. Reg. 51530 (Oct. 9, 2001) DEA issued an interpretative rule stating that any product that contains any amount of THC is a banned controlled substance, and in 68 Fed. Reg. 14114 (Mar. 21, 2003) DEA revised its regulations to ban natural as well as synthetic THC. In *Hemp Industries Association v. DEA*, 333 F.3d 1082 (9th Cir. 2003) & 357 F.3d 1012 (9th Cir. 2004), the Court of Appeals held that DEA may not regulate naturally-occurring THC not contained within or derived from marijuana; *i.e.*, nonpsychoactive hemp products.

4. *Control of Methamphetamine.* The United States has been subject to an epidemic of illegal methamphetamine use. Because methamphetamine can be derived from common cold remedies containing pseudoephedrine, Congress enacted a law limiting the amount of pseudoephedrine that can lawfully be purchased at retail. *E.g., United States v. Kim*, 298 F.3d 746 (9th Cir. 2002) & 449 F.3d 933 (9th Cir. 2006); *PDK Laboratories, Inc. v. DEA*, 438 F.3d 1184 (D.C. Cir. 2006); *United States v. Youngblood*, 949 F.2d 1065 (10th Cir. 1991). When those restrictions proved inadequate and the epidemic continued to grow, Congress enacted the Combat Methamphetamine Epidemic Act of 2005, 120 Stat. 192, 256, imposing still tighter restrictions on the retail sale of lawful nonprescription drugs containing ephedrine, pseudoephedrine, or phenylpropanolamine.

5. *Pain Medication.* Many important prescription drugs for serious pain are scheduled under the Controlled Substances Act. This has provoked repeated confrontations between DEA, which wants to reduce the use of these drugs, and the medical profession, which wants to assure that patients receive adequate medication for chronic pain. In August 2004, DEA initially published on its website a statement on "Prescription Pain Medications: Frequently Asked Questions and Answers for Healthcare Professionals and Law Enforcement Personnel," and then took the

unusual step of publicly disavowing and refuting it in 69 Fed. Reg. 67170 (Nov. 16, 2004). In 2005, DEA published what it characterized as a clarification of the legal requirements governing the prescribing of schedule II controlled substances, which include most of the pain medications at issue. 70 Fed. Reg. 2883 (Jan. 18, 2005), 70 Fed. Reg. 50408 (Aug. 26, 2005). *See* "Oxycontin: Balancing the Risks and Benefits," Hearing of the Senate Committee on Health, Education, Labor, and Pensions, 107th Cong., 2d Sess. (2002); "Legal Drugs, Illegal Purposes: The Escalating Abuse of Prescription Medications," Hearing before the Senate Committee on Government Affairs, 108th Cong., 1st Sess. (2003); Lars Noah, *Challenges in the Federal Regulation of Pain Management Technologies*, 31 J. LAW, MED. & ETHICS 55 (2003); Ronald T. Libby, *Treating Doctors as Drug Dealers: The DEA's War on Prescription Pain Killers*, CATO Institute Policy Analysis No. 545 (June 16, 2005); "Oxycontin and Beyond: Examining the Role of FDA and DEA in Regulating Prescription Pain Killers," Hearing before the House Subcommittee on Regulatory Affairs of the Government Reform Committee, 109th Cong., 1st Sess. (2005).

6. *DTC Advertising*. DEA has objected to several DTC advertisements for products scheduled under the Controlled Substances Act, but has taken no formal legal action. FDA had previously cleared each of the advertisements in question, and it has not supported the DEA position.

7. *GHB*. While GHB was being developed as a treatment for narcolepsy under an IND, Congress scheduled it as a controlled substance in Schedule I because of its notoriety as a "date rape" drug but determined that it would be rescheduled to Schedule III upon approval of an NDA. 114 Stat. 7 (2000). *See* "Date Rape Drugs," Hearing before the Subcommittee on Oversight and Investigations of the House Committee on Commerce, 106th Cong., 1st Sess (1999). GHB was subsequently approved by FDA. The sponsor agreed to a risk management plan to prevent diversion of the drug. *See* Ariel Neuman, *GHB's Path to Legitimacy: An Administrative and Legislative History of Xyrem* (2004), in Chapter VI(C)(3) of the Electronic Book.

23. PREAPPROVAL PROMOTION

As NDA approval approaches, a company may wish to begin advising the medical profession that the drug may soon be available. 21 C.F.R. 312.7(a), however, prohibits a sponsor from representing "in a promotional context" that an investigational new drug is safe or effective and from otherwise promoting the drug. Prior to NDA approval, FDA takes the position that there may be a "full exchange of scientific information" relating to an investigational drug but that promotion of the drug constitutes illegal commercialization. Nonetheless, press releases that merely announce events in the regulatory approval process are unlikely to raise FDA concern. Similarly, press releases that merely report factual data relating to scientific studies, and that avoid any statement that the drug is safe or effective, have raised no FDA objections.

In a Guidance on PRE-APPROVAL PROMOTION, originally issued in 1982 and later revised and reissued in April 1986, FDA stated that preapproval promotion is not allowed except in one of the following two ways: (1) institutional promotions stating that a specifically named drug company is conducting research in a therapeutic area to develop new and important drugs, without mentioning any drug name and (2) "coming soon" promotions announcing the name of a new product that will be available soon, but without any direct or implied representations concerning the safety, effectiveness, or intended use of the product. FDA stated that a sponsor could not use both types of advertisements simultaneously or switch types during the promotional campaign prior to product approval. This guidance was issued before recent judicial decisions applying the First Amendment to FDA advertising policy, however, and it is uncertain that it would withstand constitutional scrutiny. Accurate, truthful, and nonmisleading preapproval promotion of a drug not yet approved for any use might well be constitutionally protected, because the drug is not yet marketed and thus the government would have difficulty articulating a valid governmental interest in suppressing free speech.

24.   PREAPPROVAL INSPECTION

Beginning in 1980, FDA conducted a preapproval inspection (PAI) of the drug manufacturer before approving any NDA, to assure compliance with GMP and with the CMC (chemistry, manufacturing, and controls) sections of the NDA, under Compliance Program Guidance Manual No. 7346.832 (Oct. 1, 1980). Following the generic drug scandal of the 1980s, the PAI program was intensified. This new policy of mandatory preapproval inspection (PAI) was not codified in the FD&C Act or FDA regulations at that time or subsequently. It was first formally announced in preambles to regulations requiring every NDA applicant to submit a review copy of the CMC section of the NDA for use by FDA field investigators during the PAI to audit application commitments and statements against actual manufacturing practices used by the applicant. 56 Fed. Reg. 3180 (Jan. 28, 1991), 58 Fed. Reg. 47340 (Sept. 8, 1993).

The PAI program inevitably led to delays in approval of NDAs. FDA attempted to address these in its Compliance Program Guidance Manual for Pre-Approval Inspections, CPG No. 7346.832 (Aug. 1984). Congress directly addressed this issue in the FDA Modernization Act of 1997, adding a provision, now FD&C Act 505(b)(5)(F), stating:

> No action by the reviewing division may be delayed because of the unavailability of information from or action by field personnel unless the reviewing division determines that a delay is necessary to assure the marketing of a safe and effective drug.

As a result of improved electronic communications within FDA, up to 90 percent of NDA approvals no longer require a PAI because the agency can determine from the GMP compliance history that an inspection is not warranted.

25.   ADVISORY COMMITTEE REVIEW

FDA has several permanent prescription drug advisory committees. The agency has discretion whether to require advisory committee review of any NDA.

Peter Barton Hutt, *The Regulation of Drug Products by the United States Food and Drug Administration*

In THE TEXTBOOK OF PHARMACEUTICAL MEDICINE (John P. Griffin & John O'Grady, eds., 5th ed. 2006).

There is no statutory requirement that FDA review the approval of an NDA with an advisory committee before final action is taken. Since the

1970s, however, this has been the customary practice, particularly with important new drugs. This prompted Congress to enact a specific provision dealing with the establishment of drug advisory committees under the FDA Modernization Act of 1997.

The review of an NDA by an advisory committee is an extremely important step in the approval process. It represents the best opportunity that the applicant has to address the agency and the public about the evidence of safety and effectiveness and the importance of the drug to public health. In the vast majority of cases, FDA accepts the recommendation of the advisory committee for approval, further testing or outright disapproval. Where the advisory committee recommends approval and FDA disagrees, however, the agency will almost always take a long time to implement the advisory committee recommendations, or may even add additional testing requirements before approval is eventually obtained. The importance of advisory committee review is widely recognized in the pharmaceutical industry, and it is common for a company to engage in extensive preparation for the company presentation and to seek supportive statements from independent outside experts and patients as well.

NOTES

1. *FDA Statutory Authority and Guidance.* The FDA Modernization Act of 1997 added section 505(n) to the FD&C Act explicitly to authorize scientific advisory committees to provide expert advice on IND and NDA issues. FDA has issued a Guidance for Industry on ADVISORY COMMITTEES: IMPLEMENTING SECTION 120 OF THE FOOD & DRUG ADMINISTRATION MODERNIZATION ACT OF 1997 (1998). The general FDA advisory committee regulations are codified in 21 C.F.R. Part 14, *see infra* p. 1573.

2. *Disclosure of Materials Sent to Advisory Committee.* In *Public Citizen Health Research Group. v. FDA*, Food Drug Cosm. L. Rep. (CCH) ¶ 15,427 & ¶ 38,614 (D.D.C. 1999), FDA entered into a stipulation that it would make publicly available all the materials provided to advisory committee members prior to or at the committee meetings, subject to applicable exemptions under the Freedom of Information Act (FOIA). In accordance with these stipulations, FDA issued a draft guidance, DISCLOSING INFORMATION PROVIDED TO ADVISORY COMMITTEES IN CONNECTION WITH OPEN ADVISORY COMMITTEE MEETINGS ... CONVENED BY THE CENTER FOR DRUG EVALUATION AND RESEARCH, BEGINNING ON JANUARY 1, 2000 (1999).

3. *Financial Conflict of Interest.* There has been substantial controversy about possible conflicts of interest among advisory committee members. Experts in a particular medical discipline are often consultants to, or investigators for, the pharmaceutical industry. As a consequence, they would be precluded from serving on advisory committees if FDA did not grant a waiver that allowed them to participate. The appropriations legislation for fiscal years 2006 and 2007 contain provisions requiring all FDA waivers of conflict of interest to be made public. Public Citizen Health Research Group published an article analyzing the voting patterns of drug advisory committee members and concluded that a "weak relationship between certain types of conflict and voting behaviors was detected, but excluding advisory committee members and voting consultants with conflicts would not have altered the overall vote outcome at any meeting study." Peter Lurie et al., *Financial Conflict of Interest Disclosure and Voting Patterns at Food and Drug Administration Drug Advisory Committee Meetings*, 295 J.A.M.A. 1921 (2006). Analyzing the data in that report, FDA released a "comment" concluding that "[a]dvisory committee

members and voting consultants with financial ties to pharmaceutical companies tend to vote against the financial interest of those companies. This result suggests that fears that disclosed conflicts of interest are leading to tainted, unreliable recommendations are unfounded."

4. *Strengthening the Advisory Committee Process.* In July 2006, FDA announced several steps to help make its advisory committee processes more effective: (1) the issuance of a guidance identifying more clearly the conditions under which conflict of interest waivers are granted, (2) the issuance of a guidance specifying when waivers of conflict of interest will be disclosed to the public and what information will be made available, (3) the issuance of a guidance specifying when briefing materials used at advisory committees will be made publicly available, (4) greater public dissemination of advisory committee schedules through increased mailing to public groups and electronic notifications, and (5) implementation of a more streamlined approach to the appointment of members of the advisory committees.

26.   LABELING REVIEW

Every NDA must include proposed labeling for physicians. FDA invariably leaves negotiation about the exact wording of this labeling until the last few days before NDA approval. As added by the Drug Amendments of 1962, section 505(d)(7) of the FD&C Act provides that FDA shall disapprove an NDA if "based on a fair evaluation of all material facts, such labeling is false or misleading in any particular period."

House of Representatives

107 CONGRESSIONAL RECORD 21065 (September 27, 1962).
87th Congress, 1st Session.

Mr. JARMAN. Mr. Chairman, I rise to propound an inquiry in respect to one provision of section 102 which will sharply modify long-established relationships between industry and the Food and Drug Administration. . . .

The distinguished chairman of our committee will recall that, when we substituted the Senate-approved language for the original provisions of section 102, included in that language was an entirely new provision which gives the Secretary of Health, Education, and Welfare a new basis for disapproving a new-drug application, even when the drug is unquestionably safe and unquestionably effective. Under section 102, the Secretary may now disapprove a new-drug application on the ground that a proposed labeling is "false or misleading." A parallel provision, authorizes the Secretary to withdraw already-approved applications on the same ground.

Today, where the safety of a drug is clearly established, compliance with the broadly phrased statutory rules on labeling remains the manufacture's responsibility. A charge that any label wording is "false or misleading" must be judicially determined on objective facts produced in open court. Under this bill, however, a manufacturer can be stopped from marketing a new drug, not because the drug is unsafe or ineffective, but because the proposed label of an acknowledgedly safe and effective drug is considered "false or misleading."

Now, in committee we recognized that the granting to FDA of a new authority of this kind could open the door to possible administrative abuse. To meet this contingency, we adopted an amendment requiring that a finding that a proposed label is "false or misleading" have an objective base—that is, the finding by the Secretary must be based on a fair evaluation of all material facts.

The question I now raise with the distinguished chairman of our committee is our intent in adopting this amendment. I construe it to mean this—that we have precluded a refusal of a new drug application or a revocation of an effective application on false or misleading grounds if the departmental objection is merely a subjective interpretation of a proposed label or any particular word appearing therein. We have required that there must be, to warrant a disapproval or a revocation, objective facts of record which make the proposed labeling demonstrably false or demonstrably misleading.

May I inquire of the distinguished chairman of our committee if this construction of this particular amendment fairly and accurately explains what our committee has sought to do? . . .

Mr. HARRIS. Mr. Chairman, if I understand correctly the question of the gentleman I would answer in the affirmative. However, I think if you read the language it is self-explanatory. The language provides a new basis for refusing to approve a new drug application. The gentleman quoted the language correctly "based on a fair evaluation of all material facts." I think that would be the prevailing language in the interpretation. It is true that to warrant a disapproval or a revocation of the application objective facts of record which makes the proposed labeling is false or misleading would be necessary—demonstrably false or misleading. That is true. That must be a part of the consideration which would be given to this particular problem.

Mr. JARMAN. The concern that I have had, Mr. Chairman, is the danger that the departmental objection might be merely a subjective interpretation. My own understanding of the words that we put into the bill with this amendment is that we intended that it be based on objective facts of record that are clear and more definite than simply a matter of individual interpretation.

Mr. HARRIS. We must presume and certainly the Congress expects any Secretary of Health, Education and Welfare Administering this program to be fair in his decision and the administration of the law. The gentleman raises the question of subjective decisions and objective decisions. We expect the Secretary to have wide latitude in his decisions. Certainly we do not expect by this language for any Secretary in the administration of the law to be arbitrary in his decisions but to be objective, after consideration of all the material facts then to make the best decision objectively that he can make on it. . . .

NOTES

1. *First Amendment.* Although Representative Jarman did not justify his position in First Amendment terms, his emphasis on "objective facts" as opposed to a "subjective interpretation" foretells current First Amendment jurisprudence.

2. *Trademarks*. For many years, FDA officials objected to trademarks that they believed could be misleading. Reacting to recent First Amendment decisions and the requirement of objective facts, this FDA practice has substantially diminished. Based on a full factual record, on the other hand, the Court of Appeals in *Kos Pharmaceuticals, Inc. v. Andrx Corp.*, 369 F.3d 700 (3d Cir. 2004) determined that the Andrx trademark Altocor was confusingly similar to the Kos trademark Advicor and thus should be enjoined.

3. *Black Box Warnings*. The most serious type of warning that FDA may prescribe in labeling is a black box warning. In 21 C.F.R. 201.57(c)(1), FDA has stated that a black box warning must be the first item in a physician package insert. The black box is only used for contraindications or serious warnings, particularly those that may lead to death or serious injury. Ordinarily such a warning must be based on clinical data, but serious animal toxicity may also suffice. Other than the general statements in this rule, FDA has issued no guidance on the criteria applied by FDA in imposing a black box warning. In Judith E. Beach et al., *Black Box Warnings in Prescription Drug Labeling: Results of a Survey of 206 Drugs*, 53 FOOD & DRUG L.J. 403 (1998), the authors reviewed all 206 black box warnings for drugs that were listed in the 1995 Physician's Desk Reference. As a result of FDA's heightened interest in risk management, there has been a substantial increase in black box warnings.

27. POSTAPPROVAL TESTING COMMITMENTS

The FD&C Act does not explicitly authorize FDA to require additional postapproval nonclinical or clinical studies as a condition for NDA approval, or even as a condition for FDA not taking the drug off the market after approval. Nonetheless, FDA has in fact been taking these actions since the late 1960s. On the rare occasions when the agency has specified the statutory basis for these actions, it has cited section 505(e) (the provision for withdrawal of approval of an NDA) and 505(k) (the provision authorizing FDA to require NDA applicants to establish and maintain records). FDA imposed postapproval testing requirements by regulation on only two occasions. *See infra* p. 728, Note 2. In all other instances, it has been a matter of informal negotiation between the applicant and the agency.

Postapproval testing commitments—commonly referred to as "Phase IV" studies—are generally established in the following way. At the very end of the NDA review process, often within the last few days or even hours, one or more of the FDA review team will inform the applicant that the application is ready for approval, but that FDA would like assurance that additional specified Phase IV testing will be undertaken after approval to assure safety and effectiveness. The unmistakable implication is that the NDA will be approved immediately if the commitments are made, but that otherwise, the NDA review will continue and there is no certainty when or whether the NDA will be approved. Under these circumstances, applicants understandably commit to any postapproval testing suggested by FDA, in order to assure the fastest possible NDA approval. There is little or no discussion about the matter between the applicant and the FDA personnel, and virtually no supervision or attempt at consistent policy at even relatively low FDA management levels.

Not surprisingly, the result has been chaotic. Applicants frequently agree to undertake tests for which there is no reasonable possibility of patient accrual once the drug is marketed. Many of the Phase IV tests have little or no scientific rationale or become moot once the drug is marketed without significant adverse events. There is no mechanism for systematic review of these commitments either before or after the NDA is approved, no appeal mechanism that would not hold up NDA approval, and no mechanism for reconsideration of these commitments after the drug has been marketed. For a discussion of the problems that this has caused, *see infra* p. 738 and Charles Steenburg, *The FDA's Use of Postmarketing (Phase IV) Study Requirements: Exception to the Rule?*, 61 FOOD & DRUG L.J. 295 (2006).

NOTES

1. *Commentary. See also* Nancy Mattison & Barbara W. Richard, *Postapproval Research Requested by FDA at the Time of NCE Approval, 1970–1984*, 21 DRUG INFORMATION J. 309 (1987): Barbara W. Richard et al., *Postapproval Research as a Condition of Approval: An Update, 1985–1986*, 3 J. CLINICAL RES. & DRUG DEV. 247 (1989).

2. *FDA Regulations.* FDA issued general regulations governing postmarketing research in 35 Fed. Reg. 14784 (Sept. 23, 1970), 37 Fed. Reg. 201 (Jan. 7, 1972), codified at 21 C.F.R. 310.303. The regulation prescribing postapproval studies of levodopa was issued at the same time but later repealed in 40 Fed. Reg. 54252 (Nov. 21, 1975), 41 Fed. Reg. 9546 (March 5, 1976). FDA also established postapproval research requirements for methadone, which remain in 21 C.F.R. 310.304(b). Since 1976 the agency has not used the procedure established in § 310.303.

3. *Postmarketing Toxicological Testing.* Whether to demand additional animal testing for a marketed drug is often a difficult scientific question. In 41 Fed. Reg. 14888 (April 8, 1976), 42 Fed. Reg. 37538 (July 22, 1977), FDA required additional animal studies on the potential of inhalation anesthetic drugs to cause cancer and reproductive toxicity. In response to a petition from the affected drug manufacturers, FDA stayed, 44 Fed. Reg. 11753 (March 2, 1979), and later revoked, the regulation. 46 Fed. Reg. 43465 (Aug. 28, 1981), 47 Fed. Reg. 49014 (Oct. 29, 1982).

28. FDA/EMEA COOPERATION

As part of the integration of countries into the European Union (EU), the EU, in January 1995, established the European Medicines Evaluation Agency (EMEA), located in London, to centralize European evaluation of novel drugs. In September 2003, FDA and the EMEA issued a public statement relating to confidentiality arrangements to allow closer collaborative discussion. In 70 Fed. Reg. 69977 (Nov. 18, 2004) this was extended to the European Commission as well. In March 2006, the three organizations announced that the initial program had been successful and would be extended.

Beginning in January 2005, FDA and the EMEA established a parallel scientific advice program under which a drug sponsor seeking marketing approval from both agencies can obtain a telephone conference with both to discuss a harmonized approach. In the first two years of the program there has been about one call every three months. *See* Kate Rawson, *Parallel*

Advice: A False Step in the March to Globalized New Drug Reviews?, 1 RPM REPORT, No. 11, at 28 (Nov. 2006).

In June 1997, the United States and the European Community entered into an Agreement on Mutual Recognition. Under that agreement, FDA promulgated regulations to govern mutual recognition of GMP inspections where FDA determines that the specific EU country involved has an inspection system equivalent to the FDA inspection system. 63 Fed. Reg. 17744 (Apr. 10, 1998), 63 Fed. Reg. 60122 (Nov. 6, 1998), codified at 21 C.F.R. Part 26.

At the same time, the International Conference on Harmonization (ICH)—a cooperative joint effort by the United States, Europe, and Japan—has been working on detailed guidance on all aspects of the drug development process and has been proceeding toward a common technical document (CTD) that can be submitted to regulatory agencies throughout the world in order to secure marketing approval. For the past 20 years, these remarkably successful cooperative efforts have proceeded both on a formal level and through informal communications among medical review officials in countries everywhere.

These efforts are consistent with section 803(c) of the FD&C Act, added by the FDA Modernization Act of 1997, which encourages international harmonization efforts in general and mutual recognition agreements in particular. Harmonization is a realistic goal at this time, although mutual recognition by one country of another country's regulatory determination on a new drug is unlikely to be realized in the near future, if ever.

NOTE

See also Theodore W. Ruger, Note, *FDA Reform and the European Medicines Evaluation Agency*, 108 HARV. L. REV. 2009 (1995); Richard A. Merrill, *The Importance and Challenges of "Mutual Recognition,"* 29 SETON HALL L. REV. 736 (1998); Linda Horton, *Mutual Recognition Agreements and Harmonization*, 29 SETON HALL L. REV. 692 (1998); Ellen Hochberg, *The Need for Comprehensiveness and Increased Enforceability in the Standardization of International Pharmaceutical Regulations* (2002), and Nibal Fayad, *Harmonizing Pharmaceutical Regulation Among the United States, the European Union, and Japan: The ICH Initiative* (2003), in Chapter II(C)(6) of the Electronic Book.

29.   FDA/SEC COOPERATION

The rise of venture capital-financed biotechnology companies resulted in a substantial increase in initial public offerings (IPOs) to gain sufficient funding to support the heavy research and development costs leading to submission and approval of an NDA. The documents submitted to the Securities and Exchange Commission (SEC) supporting these IPOs and subsequent financings typically made representations about the status of INDs and NDAs pending at FDA and about discussions with agency officials. While prior to 2004, FDA and the SEC cooperated informally in reviewing these documents, during that year the two agencies announced a more formal collaborative program.

FDA and SEC Work to Enhance Public's Protection From False and Misleading Statements

FDA NEWS No. P04–15 (February 5, 2004).

The Food and Drug Administration (FDA) is announcing new measures designed to improve the manner by which FDA assists the Securities and Exchange Commission (SEC), whose primary mission is to protect the investing public and maintain the integrity of the securities market. In addition to implementing administrative improvements to make FDA technical and scientific support of the SEC and its staff more efficient, FDA is for the first time establishing a centralized procedure for FDA personnel to use in referring to the SEC statements by FDA-regulated firms that may be false or misleading.

"The SEC and its staff have primary responsibility for enforcing the rules requiring truth in the securities market, which is essential for its proper functioning," said Commissioner of Food and Drugs Mark B. McClellan, M.D., Ph.D. "Unfortunately, companies sometimes violate the public trust by issuing false or misleading statements about FDA-related issues, such as the progress of FDA's premarket review. When we identify suspected misstatements, we have a new process to bring them to the attention of the SEC staff as quickly and efficiently as possible."

Under the new referral procedure, any FDA employee who believes a publicly held, FDA-regulated firm has made a false or misleading statement to the investment public concerning a matter within FDA's authority can initiate a process for referring the matter to the SEC Division of Enforcement. FDA's mission is to promote and protect the public health, and FDA employees will not be expected routinely to police statements by publicly held, FDA-regulated companies. However, FDA can be in a position to identify statements that may be of interest to the SEC and its staff, and FDA employees will now have a centralized procedure to make SEC referrals if, in the normal course of their activities, they come to believe that a company may have made a false or misleading statement to the investing public.

NOTES

1. *FDA Referrals.* Since the establishment of the new cooperative procedure, FDA has in fact referred matters to the SEC for investigation and the SEC has requested FDA to review company securities documents for accuracy.

2. *Securities Litigation.* In *In re Carter–Wallace, Inc. Securities Litigation*, 150 F.3d 153 (2d Cir. 1998), the Court of Appeals held that false drug advertisements in medical journals may be considered in a securities fraud case if financial analysts considered them in evaluating the stock of the company.

3. *Commentary.* For a review of SEC disclosure requirements, *see* Mikko Heinonen, *Disclosure of the Dealings between Drug Developing Companies and the FDA Under the Federal Securities Laws* (2002), in Chapter I(G)(9) of the Electronic Book.

30.   Final Approval or Denial

Section 505 does not require FDA to explain its approval of an NDA. In its public information regulations, however, FDA announced that, beginning in July 1975, it would release a summary of the basis of approval (SBA) for every NDA, instead of disclosing internal agency memoranda prepared in the course of reaching its decision. 39 Fed. Reg. 44602, 44635–36 (Dec. 24, 1974). Under FOIA, FDA is also required to release non-confidential records reflecting the administrative review of the NDA. Since 1996, FDA has posted the SBA and supporting materials on its website.

An FDA decision to *approve* a drug has seldom been contested in court. When FDA approved an NDA for an OTC version of ibuprofen, two competitors of the applicant challenged this action. *See supra* p. 528, Note 4. Neither was successful. Patients injured by an approved drug have similarly failed in attempts to obtain damages from FDA for wrongfully approving the drug. *See infra* p. 734, Note 9.

Perhaps surprisingly, court challenges to decisions refusing approval have been equally rare. Manufacturers who anticipate denial focus all their efforts on attempting to persuade the agency to change its mind, realizing that recourse to judicial review of an adverse determination is almost certain to be futile.

Ubiotica Corp. v. FDA

427 F.2d 376 (6th Cir. 1970).

■ Combs, Circuit Judge. . . .

Petitioner originally filed its new drug application and claim for investigational exemption in June, 1963. The new drug is proposed for treatment of mongolism. . . .

In November, 1963, the Commissioner notified petitioner that, since certain conditions had not been met, the investigational exemption allowing clinical testing of the drug was terminated. Petitioner unsuccessfully sought to enjoin and vacate this order in *Turkel v. Food and Drug Administration*, 334 F.2d 844 (6th Cir. 1964). We held there that 21 U.S.C. § 355(h) does not permit review of the withdrawal of an investigational exemption except on appeal from a subsequent order of the Secretary refusing to approve a new drug application. However, prior to our decision in *Turkel*, petitioner withdrew the new drug application which it had submitted in June, 1963.

Then, in June, 1966, petitioner submitted a second new drug application which was designated as supplemental to the previously withdrawn new drug application. After extended correspondence, petitioner was notified that the Commissioner proposed to issue an order refusing approval of the new drug application. A hearing was held, and subsequently the order was issued which is the subject of this appeal. The record before us consists of numerous exhibits and in excess of 6,000 pages of transcript. On this appeal we are asked to review the Commissioner's action in refusing to approve the new drug application and also in terminating petitioner's investigational exemption. . . .

In enacting section 355, Congress clearly placed on the applicant the burden of establishing that the drug proposed to be distributed in interstate commerce is both safe and effective for the intended use. Here, the hearing examiner properly phrased the issues in terms of the statutory grounds for rejection set forth in section 355(d), and the Government came forward with proof as to why petitioner had not satisfied the burden of proof required of a new drug applicant under section 355. The Commissioner adopted the findings of the hearing examiner and concluded that the new drug application should not be approved in that it was deficient in each of the five respects enumerated above under section 355(d). The question here is whether those findings are supported by substantial evidence. We conclude that they are and that the Commissioner properly refused to approve the new drug application. . . .

NOTES

1. *Exhaustion of FDA Procedures.* The ruling earlier in the same case, *sub. nom. Turkel v. FDA,* that the sponsor of a clinical investigation whose IND is terminated may only obtain judicial review of that action by filing an NDA and then seeking review of FDA's subsequent denial of approval, seems questionable. Other "exhaustion" cases suggest that it would not be followed today. *See, e.g., Rosado v. Wyman,* 397 U.S. 397 (1970); *Leedom v. Kyne,* 358 U.S. 184 (1958). *See also AMP Inc. v. Gardner,* 275 F. Supp. 410 (S.D.N.Y. 1967), *aff'd,* 389 F.2d 825 (2d Cir. 1968).

2. *Judicial Review of FDA Denial of NDA.* The Court of Appeals' perfunctory scrutiny of FDA's denial of Ubiotica's NDA is paralleled in one of the two other court challenges to FDA's refusal to approve a drug. In *Unimed, Inc. v. Richardson,* 458 F.2d 787 (D.C. Cir. 1972), the Court of Appeals' full opinion, after describing the applicant's argument, consisted of the following paragraph:

> We have examined the record of the administrative hearing on this point with care, particularly with a view to grasping as best we can the nature of the divergences between the differing expert witnesses. Although the matter seems to us one not entirely free from doubt, we remind ourselves that our role in the Congressional scheme is not to give an independent judgment of our own, but rather to determine whether the expert agency entrusted with regulatory responsibility has taken an irrational or arbitrary view of the evidence assembled before it. We are unable to say that it has; and, accordingly, the petition for review is denied.

3. *The Cothyrobal Litigation.* The third court challenge to FDA's refusal to approve a drug has a unique history. A physician, Dr. Murray Israel, developed an injectable drug, Cothyrobal, for hypercholesterolemia and hypothyroidism. Frustrated by the agency's skeptical and desultory handing of his NDA, he unsuccessfully sued the agency and a competitor, alleging a conspiracy to keep the drug off the market. *Israel v. Baxter Laboratories, Inc.,* 466 F.2d 272 (D.C. Cir. 1972). Following FDA's eventual denial of approval and its refusal to grant an administrative hearing, the court set aside the agency's decision and ordered it to hold an evidentiary hearing on the issue. *Edison Pharmaceutical Co., Inc. v. FDA,* 513 F.2d 1063 (D.C. Cir. 1975). The agency's ultimate denial of the NDA, following the hearing, was upheld. *Edison Pharmaceutical Co., Inc. v. FDA,* 600 F.2d 831 (D.C. Cir. 1979).

In sum, judicial review of the new drug approval process has been not only casual, but infrequent. No sponsor has successfully sought reversal of an FDA refusal to approve its drug. The lesson has not been lost on applicants, who understand that the only way to secure approval of an NDA is to satisfy the agency.

4. *Proper Court for Judicial Review.* Challenges to FDA's final decisions under sections 505(d) and (e) must be filed in the court of appeals for the appropriate circuit. A district court thus lacks jurisdiction to order FDA to approve an NDA, but may entertain a case seeking to force FDA to rule on an NDA within a specified period of time. *IMS Limited v. Schweiker*, Food Drug Cosm. L. Rep. (CCH) ¶ 38, 104 (C.D. Cal. 1981).

5. *Grounds for Disapproval.* A 1980 FDA analysis of NDA rulings during the 1970s produced the surprising findings that 61 percent of the deficiencies cited in nonapproval letters during 1977 and 1978 related to the chemistry, manufacturing, and controls (CMC) portions of the NDA, and that nearly 90 percent of such letters identified such deficiencies. Only 22 percent of the deficiencies related to the applicant's evidence of safety and effectiveness. Jonathan D. Cook et al., *Approvals and Non–Approvals of New Drug Applications During the 1970s*, FDA OPE STUDY No. 57 (Dec. 1980). A 1988 FDA report examined the fate of 174 new chemical entity (NCE) drugs for which INDs were filed during 1976–1978. Nine percent had been discontinued before the commencement of Phase I studies, 20 percent had been discontinued during Phase I studies, 39 percent during Phase II studies, and 5 percent during Phase III studies. Twenty-seven percent had become the subject of a submitted NDA, and nearly all of these—85 percent—ultimately gained approval. Steven A. Tucker et al., *The Outcome of Research on New Molecular Entities Commencing Clinical Research in the Years 1976–1978*, FDA OPE STUDY No. 77 (May 1988).

6. *NDAs Invited by FDA.* On rare occasions, FDA has formally announced that it would approve NDAs for particular drugs if and when they were submitted. In 38 Fed. Reg. 26809 (Sept. 26, 1973), 40 Fed. Reg. 5351 (Feb. 5, 1975), FDA stated that NDAs would be approved for diethylstilbestrol (DES) as a postcoital contraceptive. FDA had hoped that this announcement would induce DES manufacturers to submit abbreviated NDAs to add postcoital contraception as an approved indication, but the plausible fear of liability deterred all potential applicants. In 1989, FDA deleted this provision because there were still no marketed drugs approved for this use. 52 Fed. Reg. 13107 (Apr. 21, 1987), 54 Fed. Reg. 2285 (May 25, 1989). DES products approved for other uses thus continue to be prescribed for this still unapproved use as well. In 1997, FDA announced that combined oral contraceptives containing ethinyl estradiol and norgestrel or levonorgestrel are safe and effective for use as postcoital emergency contraceptives and requested submission of NDAs for this use. 62 Fed. Reg. 8610 (Feb. 25, 1997).

In 1980, FDA announced that it had approved two NDAs for potassium iodide as a thyroid-blocking agent for use in radiation emergencies. 45 Fed. Reg. 11912 (Feb. 22, 1980). These NDAs were received after the agency had invited manufacturers to seek approval as part of an emergency preparedness program for possible accidents at nuclear facilities. 43 Fed. Reg. 58798 (Dec. 15, 1978). The agency later announced the availability of draft recommendations for administering potassium iodide to the general public in a radiation emergency. 46 Fed. Reg. 30199 (June 5, 1981), 47 Fed. Reg. 28158 (June 29, 1982).

7. *FDA Control Over Packaging.* FDA control over the safety and effectiveness of a new drug extends to the packaging as well. See 49 Fed. Reg. 4040 (Feb. 1, 1984), announcing the availability of a draft guideline on the documentation needed in an NDA to support the safety of drug packaging.

8. *Publicity about NDA Approvals.* Section 301(l) of the 1938 Act prohibited any representation that FDA has approved an NDA for a drug. Despite repeated arguments that this provision was an anachronism, attempts to repeal it prior to 1997 failed. *E.g.,* H.R. Rep. No. 98–431, 98th Cong., 1st Sess. (1983), H.R. Rep. No. 99–143, 99th Cong., 1st Sess. (1985). Section 421 of the FDA Modernization Act of 1997 finally repealed this provision. 111 Stat. 2296, 2380.

9. *Federal Tort Claims Act.* In *Forsyth v. Eli Lilly & Co.,* 904 F. Supp. 1153 (D. Haw. 1995), the District Court dismissed an action for damages against FDA for negligently approving the NDA for a new antidepressant drug that allegedly caused a man to kill his wife and then commit suicide, on the ground that the approval of an NDA falls within the discretionary function exception to the Federal Tort Claims Act. The District Court in *Nichols v. FDA,* Food Drug Cosm. L. Rep. (CCH) ¶ 38,325 (S.D. Ohio 1993), held that, before suing FDA for damages because his health deteriorated after taking an FDA-approved drug, the plaintiff must first file a claim with FDA and receive a denial. Plaintiff's request for an injunction to remove the drug and related drugs from the market was dismissed for failure to exhaust administrative remedies.

10. *Suits to Force FDA Approval.* FDA cannot be sued by a private party to force the agency to approve an NDA. *Garlic v. FDA,* 783 F. Supp. 4 (D.D.C. 1992), *appeal dismissed* 986 F.2d 546 (D.C. Cir. 1993).

11. *FDA Alert List.* Any drug establishment found by FDA inspection not to be in compliance with GMP regulations is placed by the agency on an "alert list." It is standard FDA procedure not to approve any NDA or abbreviated NDA of any firm which is on the alert list. FDA's immediate withdrawal of approval of an abbreviated NDA on the same day an inspection resulted in placing the company on the alert list was upheld in *American Therapeutics, Inc. v. Sullivan,* Food Drug Cosm. L. Rep. (CCH) ¶ 38,159 (D.D.C. 1990).

12. *Judicial Enforcement of 180–Day Deadline.* Section 505(c)(1) of the FD&C Act unequivocally states that FDA shall either approve the application or give notice of opportunity for an administrative hearing whether the application is approvable with 180 days. This provision is mandatory, not discretionary. Its enforceability has been considered in two cases. In *In re Barr Laboratories, Inc.,* 930 F.2d 72 (D.C. Cir. 1991), the Court of Appeals concluded that, although section 505(c)(1) is mandatory, the Court would not issue an injunction against FDA where the delay was roughly 489 days and FDA demonstrated that it did not have sufficient resources to act faster. In *Sandoz, Inc. v. Leavitt,* 427 F. Supp. 2d 29 (D.D.C. 2006), the District Court concluded that a delay of roughly 1000 days did justify a court order requiring FDA to take action on the pending NDA in light of the fact that FDA now has sufficient funds under PDUFA. FDA promptly approved the NDA, but has appealed the District Court's ruling.

13. *Rationing a Newly Approved Drug.* On occasion, the demand for an important new drug outpaces the manufacturing capacity. In these situations, it is common to conduct a lottery to determine which patients will receive the drug. *E.g.,* Michael Manocchi & Louis Lasagna, *Issues in Pharmaceutical Lotteries: The Case of Interferon Beta–1b,* 62 CLINICAL PHARMACOLOGY & THERAPEUTICS 241 (Sept. 1997).

H. POSTAPPROVAL OBLIGATIONS

Following NDA approval, the manufacturer of a new drug becomes subject to a new set of regulatory requirements and prohibitions.

1.   Postapproval Submissions to FDA

a.   SUPPLEMENTAL NDAs

Under 21 C.F.R. 314.70, any significant change from the detailed terms and conditions specified in the approved NDA must be the subject of a supplemental NDA and may not be put into effect until approved by FDA. The only changes in an approved NDA that may be made without approval of a supplemental NDA are set forth in the FDA regulations, and those exceptions must be reflected in the annual report for the NDA submitted to FDA, discussed *infra* p. 737. If FDA finds that changes have been made from an approved NDA beyond those permitted without a supplemental NDA, very stringent regulatory action can be taken, including recall of the product and the suspension of manufacture until the unapproved changes are eliminated or approved.

FDA rigorously enforces the requirement for a supplemental NDA. *See, e.g., United States v. Sardesai*, Food Drug Cosm. L. Rep. (CCH) ¶ 38,536 (4th Cir. 1997) (criminal prosecution for failure to submit and obtain approval of a supplemental NDA prior to making manufacturing changes); *United States v. Marcus*, 82 F.3d 606 (4th Cir. 1996) (criminal prosecution for failure to submit and obtain approval of a supplemental NDA prior to making a change in the inactive ingredients of the drug); *United States v. 1500 90–Tablet Bottles ... Genendo Pharmaceutical N.V.*, 384 F. Supp. 2d 1205 (N.D. Ill. 2005) (seizure for repackaging without an approved supplemental NDA). Two types of supplemental NDAs are particularly important: (1) labeling changes and (2) manufacturing changes.

i.   *Labeling Changes*

FDA maintains control and surveillance over product labeling and advertising in three ways. First, any change in the actual labeling of the product—*e.g.*, a new indication for the drug, a change in the dosing schedule, or any other significant change in the physician labeling—must be the subject of a supplemental NDA. Second, under 21 C.F.R. 314.81(b)(3)(i), the NDA holder is required to submit specimens of all promotional labeling and advertising at the time of initial dissemination, accompanied by form FDA 2253. Third, under 21 C.F.R. 314.81(b)(2), the NDA holder must submit an annual report containing currently used professional labeling, patient brochures, package inserts, and package labels. Thus, FDA maintains a file of the complete history and current status of all prescription drug labeling used under the NDA.

ii.   *Manufacturing Changes*

The pharmaceutical industry has long felt that FDA has been too stringent in requiring supplemental NDAs for manufacturing changes. Prior to 1997, the industry found it easier to continue obsolete manufacturing methods in establishments producing drugs for the United States market rather than to seek FDA approval of a supplemental NDA. In contrast, manufacturers were free to make substantial manufacturing changes, reflecting the latest technology, in establishments producing the same drugs for foreign markets. In the FDA Modernization Act of 1997, Congress added section 506A to the FD&C Act to make changes in manufacturing more flexible. Under section 506A, a major manufacturing change may be made only pursuant to a supplemental NDA, but all other manufacturing changes may be made based on the manufacturer's validation, so long as the change is reported to FDA either at the time it is made or as part of the NDA annual report. The implementation of this new provision, as reflected in 21 C.F.R. 314.70 and FDA guidance, has substantially streamlined the regulatory process for manufacturing changes.

b.   ADVERSE EVENT REPORTING

Under 21 C.F.R. 314.80, an NDA holder must report to FDA any adverse event "associated with" the use of a drug in humans, whether or not drug related, in one of the following ways. First, an adverse event that is both serious and unexpected, whether foreign or domestic, must be reported as soon as possible but in no event later than 15 calendar days after initial receipt of the information. The company is required to promptly investigate all 15–day alert reports and submit additional new information to FDA. Second, all other adverse drug experiences must be reported to FDA at quarterly intervals for the first three years under the NDA and at annual intervals thereafter. Both of these types of reports must be submitted using form FDA 3500A. These reports should not include information that would identify individual patients.

NOTES

1.   *Economic Impact.* In compliance with the requirements for OMB review and clearance under the Paperwork Reduction Act of 1995, 44 U.S.C. 3507, FDA must prepare a yearly analysis of the economic burden of its recordkeeping and reporting requirements. For an analysis of the adverse drug experience reporting requirements *see* 70 Fed. Reg. 22882 (May 3, 2005), 71 Fed. Reg. 6281 (Feb. 7, 2006).

2.   *The MedWatch Program.* The FD&C Act requires drug manufacturers to submit adverse reports to FDA, but FDA has no authority to require physicians or medical institutions to require such reports. For many years FDA has maintained and widely publicized a MedWatch program for voluntary reporting of adverse drug events by health care professionals and institutions. *See generally,* Philip Routledge, *150 Years of Pharmacovigilance,* 351 LANCET 1200 (Apr. 18, 1998).

3.   *Contract Requirement.* In 68 Fed. Reg. 12406 (Mar. 14, 2003), FDA proposed to amend its postmarket adverse event reporting regulations to add a requirement that "a contract between the applicant and a contractor must specify the post marketing safety reporting responsibilities of the contractor." If this proposal becomes final, the pharmaceutical industry must amend its contracts to require contractors to report all adverse events to the company.

4.   *Preemption of Confidentiality.* In a product liability case a Texas trial judge ordered Eli Lilly to disclose the names and addresses of all persons who submitted adverse reaction reports relating to the drug. In *Eli Lilly and Co. v. Marshall,* Food Drug Cosm. L. Rep. ¶ 38,304 (Sup. Ct. Tex. 1993), the Texas Supreme Court, taking into account an FDA statement of interest supporting the Eli Lilly position, reversed the trial court. Because this issue arose repeatedly in product liability litigation throughout the country, FDA determined in 58 Fed. Reg. 31596 (June 3, 1993), 60 Fed. Reg. 16962 (Apr. 3, 1995), 21 C.F.R. 20.63(f)(2) to preempt all state

and local requirements that permit or require disclosure of the identities of a voluntary reporter or other person named in an adverse event report.

5. *Different Types of Adverse Reactions.* Timothy Brewer & Graham A. Colditz, *Post Marketing Surveillance and Adverse Drug Reactions: Current Perspectives and Future Needs*, 281 J.A.M.A. 824 (Mar. 3, 1999), argue that adverse drug reactions should be divided into two categories: (1) events that otherwise occur rarely in the population and (2) events that represent an increased frequency over a relatively common rate in the general population. Adverse event reports are extremely helpful in revealing the former, but controlled studies are needed to find the latter type of adverse events. The increased risk of heart disease attributed to some Cox–2 inhibitors could not be found with the former type of reporting but came to light when controlled studies were conducted.

6. *Improved Safety Surveillance.* The concentrated focus on postmarket drug safety surveillance as a result of the Cox–2 inhibitor drug issues during 2004–2005 spawned a series of reports on methods to improve the effectiveness of FDA's safety decisionmaking following NDA approval. *E.g.,* GAO, *Improvement Needed in FDA's Postmarket Decision-making and Oversight Process*, GAO–06–402 (Mar. 2006); Susan Thaul, *Drug Safety and Effectiveness: Issues and Action Options After FDA Approval*, CRS Rep. No. RL 32797 (Mar. 21, 2006); Institute of Medicine, *The Future of Drug Safety: Promoting and Protecting the Health of the Public* (Sept. 2006). *See also* Barbara A. Noah, *Adverse Drug Reactions: Harnessing Experiential Data to Promote Patient Welfare*, 49 Cath. U. L. Rev. 449 (2000); Barbara A. Noah & David B. Brushwood, *Adverse Drug Reactions in Elderly Patients: Alternative Approaches to Postmarket Surveillance*, 33 J. Health L. 383 (2000).

c.   OTHER POSTMARKET REPORTS

Two other types of postmarketing reports are also required under the FDA regulations.

i.   *Field Alert Reports*

Under 21 C.F.R. 314.81, the NDA holder must submit to FDA a field alert report within three working days of receipt of information concerning (1) the drug being mistaken for another article or (2) bacteriological or other change or deterioration in a distributed drug product or any failure to meet specifications.

ii.   *Annual Report*

The NDA holder must submit an annual report that summarizes all significant new information from the previous year that might affect the safety, effectiveness, or labeling of the drug, as well as the distribution data, labeling and advertising, changes in CMC, nonclinical studies, clinical data, and the status of any postmarketing study commitments. 21 C.F.R. 314.81(b)(2).

d.   VOLUNTARY WITHDRAWAL OF LIFE–SUPPORTING DRUG

Because of concern about sudden interruptions in the availability of important drugs, the FDA Modernization Act of 1997 added section 506C to the FD&C Act to require that a sole manufacturer of a drug that is life-supporting, live-sustaining, or used in the prevention of a debilitating disease or condition must notify FDA at least six months prior to the date of discontinuance unless there are good reasons for a shorter notification.

e. PHASE IV TESTING COMMITMENTS

As noted *supra* p. 727, in accordance with section 506B of the FD&C Act, the annual report for an NDA drug must identify each Phase IV commitment and describe the progress being made until the commitment is completed or terminated. The reasons for any delay in fulfilling a study commitment must be specified. FDA has internal procedures to facilitate the tracking and review of Phase IV commitments in the CDER MAPP No. 6010.2 (Oct. 1, 1996).

As previously noted, Congress and FDA have expressed concern about the failure of NDA holders to keep Phase IV commitments. In Office of Inspector General, *FDA's Monitoring of Postmarketing Study Commitments*, OIG REP. No. OEI–01–04–00390 (June 2006), the OIG reported that 48 percent of NDAs approved during 1990–2004 involved at least one Phase IV commitment and 74 percent of these commitments were for clinical studies. The OIG concluded that the FDA tracking of these commitments was lax and is not a high priority. Although FDA has both informal and formal authority to enforce these commitments, up to and including withdrawal of approval of the NDA, this authority has not been exercised.

In 71 Fed. Reg. 10978 (Mar. 3, 2006), FDA issued its annual report on the status of postmarketing study commitments. FDA reported that, as of September 2005, there were 154 NDAs with 1,231 open Phase IV commitments and presented a breakdown of these figures into the current status of those commitments. Less than a month later FDA announced a study of the entire Phase IV program. *See* "FDA Awards Contract to Assess Postmarketing Study Commitment Decision-making Process: Analysis Will Lead to More Standardized Approach," FDA News No. PO6–52 (Apr. 5, 2006). A study by the Tufts Center for the Study of Drug Development reported that FDA requested Phase IV studies in 73% of new drug approvals during 1998–2003. *See* "Post marketing Studies Becoming Essential to New Drug Development in the U.S., According to the Tufts Center for the Study of New Drug Development," Tufts CSDD News Release (July 6, 2004).

2. DRUG SAFETY OVERSIGHT BOARD

Following the controversy about the Cox–2 inhibitor drugs, FDA announced on February 15, 2005 that the agency was creating an independent Drug Safety Oversight Board (DSOB) to oversee the management of important drug safety issues within CDER. "FDA Improvements in Drug Safety Monitoring," FDA Fact Sheet (Feb. 15, 2005). CDER issued MAPP No. 4151–3 (May 4, 2005) to describe the organizational structure, roles, and responsibility of the DSOB. The membership was announced the same month, "FDA Announces Membership of Drug Safety Oversight Board," FDA Talk Paper No. T05–22 (May 18, 2005), and the DSOB began to meet almost immediately. The DSOB is comprised only of government employees and thus is not subject to the Federal Advisory Committee Act requirements for open public meetings. Its meetings are closed except when it invites representatives of a pharmaceutical company to discuss a specific safety issue relating to one of its products. In its first year, the DSOB held nine meetings. A public summary of each meeting is available on the FDA website.

In the same announcement, FDA stated that it would initiate a Drug Watch program under which it would post on the FDA website new drug safety information as it became available. When substantial objections were raised to this approach on the ground that unverified and unanalyzed information would do more harm to physicians and patients than good, FDA agreed to place this initiative on hold until it could be studied further. In 70 Fed. Reg. 24606 (May 10, 2005), FDA announced the availability of a draft Guidance: FDA's "Drug Watch" for Emerging Drug Safety Information, but this guidance remains on hold pending FDA reconsideration of the program.

3.   The Applications Integrity (Fraud) Policy

Peter Barton Hutt, *The Regulation of Drug Products by the United States Food and Drug Administration*

In The Textbook of Pharmaceutical Medicine (John P. Griffin & John O'Grady, eds., 5th ed. 2006).

As a result of the generic drug scandal ... where generic drug manufacturers submitted fraudulent data and bribed FDA officials, the FDA adopted a "fraud policy" in September 1991, which was later called the Applications Integrity Policy, to cover situations where FDA concluded that an applicant who had engaged in a wrongful act would need to take corrective action to establish the reliability of data submitted to FDA in support of pending applications and to support the integrity of products already on the market. Under this policy, FDA issues a formal letter invoking the policy and requiring the applicant to cooperate fully with the FDA investigation. The applicant is required to identify all individuals associated with the wrongful act and to ensure that they are removed from any substantive authority on matters under FDA jurisdiction. A credible internal review must be conducted to identify all instances of wrongful acts, to supplement FDA's own investigation. The internal review should involve an outside consultant or team qualified by training and experience to conduct such a review. Finally, the applicant must commit in writing to developing and implementing a correction action operating plan. Although this fraud policy was developed in response to the generic drug scandal, it also applies to pioneer drug companies and to data in full NDAs.

NOTES

1. *Origin of Fraud Policy.* The FDA fraud policy was established in the aftermath of the generic drug scandal, as an additional enforcement mechanism. *See* 55 Fed. Reg. 52323 (Dec. 21, 1990), 56 Fed. Reg. 46191 (Sept. 10, 1991), Compliance Policy Guide No. 120.100.

2. *Publicity.* When FDA makes a formal determination to place a company under the fraud policy, the company is included in the fraud policy list on the agency's website.

3. *Due Process.* Although companies are given the opportunity to meet with FDA and make submissions demonstrating that they should not be placed under the fraud policy, FDA has not provided any specific administrative or judicial remedy to contest a fraud policy determination. Presumably such a determination could be contested in a district court under the Administrative Procedure Act, but no company has chosen to pursue that remedy.

4.   SUMMARY BAN OF AN "IMMINENT HAZARD"

As part of the Drug Amendments of 1962, Congress provided to the Secretary of HHS nondelegable authority to suspend the NDA approval for any drug determined to be an "imminent hazard" to health.

Forsham v. Califano

442 F. Supp. 203 (D.D.C. 1977).

■ CORCORAN, DISTRICT JUDGE.

Plaintiffs are seven physicians who specialize in the treatment of diabetes and six diabetic patients taking phenformin hydrochloride (phenformin) prescribed by their physicians as part of their diabetic therapy. Phenformin is an orally administered drug designed to control blood sugar levels in patients with adult-onset diabetes who are not dependent on insulin and who cannot or will not reduce their daily caloric intake....

The defendant is the Secretary of Health, Education and Welfare (the Secretary) who, pursuant to section 505(e) of the Federal Food, Drug and Cosmetic Act, has suspended new drug applications for phenformin on grounds that the drug poses an "imminent hazard." ...

Plaintiffs seek to enjoin the Secretary from implementing his suspension order. They also seek a declaratory judgment that the suspension order is outside the scope of the Secretary's authority, is arbitrary and capricious, and violates their Fifth Amendment due process rights, the Administrative Procedure Act and the Food and Drug Administration's regulations....

In considering the likelihood of success on the merits, it should be noted at the outset that the review by this Court of the Secretary's decision to suspend phenformin pursuant to his authority under 21 U.S.C. § 355(e) is limited to a determination of whether that decision was arbitrary and capricious, an abuse of discretion, or otherwise not in accordance with the law.... In other words, [the plaintiffs] must demonstrate the substantial likelihood that the decision was "a clear error of judgment" by the Secretary and that he failed to articulate any rational connection between the facts submitted to him and the choice he made....

While acknowledging the existence of "conflicting testimony" on the incidence of lactic acidosis among phenformin patients and the view expressed by the manufacturers that labeling changes made in January, 1977 would reduce the incidence of phenformin-related lactic acidosis, the Secretary nonetheless deemed that the following factors necessitated his decision to suspend:

1. The discontinued marketing of phenformin in Norway and Canada based on the experience in those countries with phenformin related lactic acidosis cases.

2. Adverse reports of phenformin-related lactic acidosis in Finland, Sweden, New Zealand, and Australia.

3. The discontinued use of phenformin by several diabetes clinics in major U.S. hospitals.

4. The unanimous October, 1976 recommendation by the FDA Endocrinology and Metabolism Advisory Committee that phenformin be removed from the market.

5. The May 6, 1977 decision by the FDA's Bureau of Drugs to seek withdrawal of approval of NDA's for phenformin.

6. Calculations submitted by the FDA's Bureau of Drugs based on information it had received from phenformin manufacturers, research conducted in other countries, studies conducted in a group of university based medical centers and reports from individual hospitals. Those calculations indicated that:

   a. Between 0.25 and four cases of lactic acidosis arose per 1,000 phenformin users per year with an approximate mortality rate of fifty per cent.

   b. That the estimated incidence of death due to lactic acidosis in phenformin users is between 0.125 and 2 deaths annually per 1,000 patients—a rate 5 to 80 times higher than that of other widely used drugs known to cause fatalities even when properly used.

   c. That between four and 60 patients would die each month from phenformin-induced lactic acidosis.

   d. That final administrative action on withdrawal of the NDA's for phenformin could take from six to twelve months during which time anywhere from 10 to 700 people could die from phenformin associated lactic acidosis.

. . . . [P]laintiffs allege that the standards used by the Secretary in determining that phenformin posed an imminent hazard under the statute do not comport either with the standards dictated by Congress[4] or with those set forth in the FDA's own regulation.[5]

---

4. Plaintiffs cite the Senate Judiciary Report accompanying the 1962 Amendments . . . which added the imminent hazard provision to the effect that the Secretary's power should be exercised "only in the exceptional case of an emergency which does not permit the Secretary to correct it by other means." S. Rep. No. 1744, Pt. 2, 87th Cong., 2d Sess. p. 7 (1962).

Reference is also made to the consideration of the amendments by the Senate where it was noted that the imminent hazard authority "should only be exercised under the most extreme conditions and with the utmost care." 108 Cong. Rec. 16304 (Aug. 23, 1962).

5. The FDA regulation defines imminent hazard as one, "(1) that should be corrected immediately to prevent injury and (2) that should not be permitted to continue while a hearing or other formal proceeding is being held. The 'imminent hazard' may be declared at any point in the chain of events which may ultimately result in harm to the public health. The occurrence of the final anticipated injury is not essential to establish

As recited in the Order, the criteria used by the Secretary to determine the imminence of the hazard included:

1.   The severity of the harm that could be caused by the drug during the completion of customary administrative proceedings to withdraw the drug from the general market.

2.   The likelihood that the drug will cause such harm to users while the administrative process is being completed.

3.   The risk to patients currently taking the drug that might be occasioned by the immediate removal of the drug from the market taking into account the availability of other therapies and the steps necessary for patients to adjust to these other therapies.

4.   The likelihood that after the customary administrative process is completed, the drug will be withdrawn from the general marketing [sic].

5.   The availability of other approaches to protect the public health.

Upon reviewing these criteria, the Court is not persuaded either that they improperly reflect the intent of Congress or are at substantial variance with the FDA regulation. And, even if there may exist some discrepancy between the Secretary's criteria and those set forth in 21 CFR § 2.5, we would note that the regulation was designed to guide the FDA Commissioner in making his *recommendations* to the Secretary with respect to the existence of an imminent hazard, and would not necessarily bind the Secretary in making his nondelegable decision to suspend. Further we are not inclined to adopt plaintiff's "crisis" interpretation of imminent hazard. Rather we are more persuaded by defendant's suggested analogy to cases interpreting the imminent hazard provisions of the Federal Insecticide, Fungicide and Rodenticide Act which caution "against any approach to the term imminent hazard ... that restricts it to a concept of crisis" and adopt the view that "It is enough that there is substantial likelihood that serious harm will be experienced during ... any realistic projection of the administrative process." *See Environmental Defense Fund v. Environmental Protection Agency*, 510 F.2d 1291 (1975) (E.D.F. II); *Environmental Defense Fund v. Environmental Protection Agency*, 465 F.2d 528 (1972) (E.D.F. I).

We decide accordingly that the Secretary's criteria for evaluating the existence of an imminent hazard were not improper. There remains to be determined whether a rational connection exists between the facts on which he relied and his decision to suspend. Keeping in mind that "invocation of this emergency power is a matter which is peculiarly one of judgment," this Court cannot say that the facts on which the Secretary relied, particularly the calculations provided by the Bureau of Drugs, do not adequately support his decision to suspend. . . .

that an 'imminent hazard' of such occurrence exists." 21 C.F.R. § 2.5(a).

The regulation also noted that in determining the existence of an imminent hazard, the number, nature, severity and duration of the injury will be considered.

Assuming, as we must at this juncture, the validity of the Bureau of Drug's projection of between four and 60 phenformin related deaths each month, we cannot find that the Secretary's conclusion that labeling changes "cannot be expected to achieve a needed reduction in the usage of phenformin within any reasonable time frame ... with so many lives at stake," was either arbitrary or unreasonable. Nor was it made so by his decision to act first on phenformin rather than some other drug which may pose a hazard of similar magnitude....

... [P]laintiffs also object to what it [sic] alleges is the unprecedented and unlawful attempt by the Secretary to create within the suspension order a voluntary system of limited distribution to those small number of patients for whom it may be determined that phenformin's benefits outweigh its risks. Plaintiffs voice similar objections to the Secretary's 90 day delay in implementing his order. In view of the fact that the Secretary's power to suspend under section 355(e) has never been exercised, it is obvious that any method of implementation used would be unprecedented.... It appears to us that the Secretary's dual concerns of an orderly withdrawal of the use of the drug from the majority of patients now using it, and of accommodating the small number of patients for whom the benefits outweighed the risks were eminently reasonable and that the power to deal with them in the manner in which he did could fairly be implied from his power to suspend.

... [T]he Court concludes that it must deny plaintiffs' Motion for a Preliminary Injunction....

NOTES

1. *Limited Distribution.* As the District Court noted, Secretary Califano's suspension of the NDAs for phenformin was the first time this nondelegable suspension authority had ever been exercised. The action came in response to a petition and threatened lawsuit by the Public Citizen Health Research Group, and it followed FDA's publication of a notice proposing to withdraw approval of the NDAs. 42 Fed. Reg. 23170 (May 6, 1977). Secretary Califano instructed FDA to attempt to negotiate an arrangement with the two manufacturers under which phenformin could continue to be supplied to the relatively small number of patients for whom it was believed the therapy of choice. These negotiations failed, but the firms continued to distribute small quantities of phenformin under a compassionate use IND.

2. *Standing to Challenge NDA Withdrawal.* After the District Court declined to overturn Secretary Califano's suspension order, a full evidentiary hearing was held on the proposed withdrawal of the NDAs, following which the Commissioner ordered the NDAs withdrawn. 43 Fed. Reg. 54995 (Nov. 24, 1978). Forsham subsequently sought review of this order as well as review of the District Court's original ruling. The Court of Appeals dismissed the appeal regarding the suspension order as moot and ruled that Forsham and his co-plaintiffs, prescribing physicians and patients, lacked standing to seek review of the Commissioner's withdrawal order under section 505(h) of the FD&C Act because "only an 'applicant' may petition a Court of Appeals to review the ... withdrawal of [the Commissioner's] approval of a new drug application." *Forsham v. Califano,* Food Drug Cosm. L. Rep. (CCH) ¶ 38,241 (D.C. Cir. 1979).

3. *Petition to Suspend Propoxyphene.* Secretary Califano's willingness to exercise the previously dormant "imminent hazard" authority prompted a similar petition a year later from the Public Citizen Health Research Group, which this time sought suspension of the drug propoxyphene because of fatalities attributed to overdose. The Secretary denied the petition pending consideration of rescheduling of the drug under the Controlled Substances Act and strengthened label warnings, including patient labeling, against the risks of misuse. *In re Petition to Suspend New Drug Applications for Propoxyphene: Order of the Secretary Denying Petition* (Feb. 15, 1979). After a public hearing on the safety and effectiveness of the drug, 44 Fed. Reg. 11837 (Mar. 2, 1979), the company voluntarily agreed to revise the drug's labeling and distribute a PPI. And to show its persistence, more than 25 years later, on February 28, 2006, the Public Citizen Health Research Group submitted a citizen petition to FDA again requesting that the agency immediately begin the phased removal from the market of propoxyphene. FDA Docket No. 2006P–0090/CP1. *See generally* Iris Lan, *Placing Sidney Wolfe's Public Citizen Health Research Group in the Context of the American Consumer Movement* (2002), in Chapter I(M) of the Electronic Book.

4. *Butazolidin, Tandearil, and Feldene.* In response to a petition to ban the nonsteroidal anti-inflammatory drugs Butazolidin (phenyllbutazone) and Tandearil (oxyphenbutazone), FDA conducted a hearing to develop recommendations for the HHS Secretary. 49 Fed. Reg. 1939 (Jan. 16, 1984). On FDA's recommendation, the Secretary denied the petition. FDA Docket No. 84N–0014 (Aug. 7, 1984). In response to a petition to ban Feldene (prioxicam), FDA again conducted a public hearing to develop recommendations for the Secretary. 51 Fed. Reg. 3658 (Jan. 29, 1986). In this case, too, the Secretary adopted FDA's recommendation and denied the petition. FDA Dkt No. 86P–0023 (July 7, 1986). Three months later, a second petition, to require stronger warnings for Feldene, was filed, but it was never acted upon. FDA Dkt No. 86P–0450. Since 1986, there have been no other petitions to the Secretary to invoke the imminent hazard provision, but there have been many petitions to FDA, particularly from the Public Citizen Health Research Group, requesting that FDA take allegedly unsafe drugs off the market. *E.g.*, in May 1988 FDA, rather than HHS, was petitioned to declare Accutane (isotretinoin) an imminent hazard. The agency denied the petition. FDA Dkt No. 88P–0191/CP (May 2, 1989).

5. *Impact of Tort Liability.* In recent years, it has no longer been necessary for FDA to take legal action to remove an unsafe drug from the market. As soon as serious toxicity is encountered—often discovered by the company rather than by FDA—the manufacturer will voluntarily remove the product from the market as quickly as possible to avoid, or at least reduce, product liability exposure. Often these drugs are very effective, and in some people they are uniquely effective. FDA has frequently requested that companies continue to serve unmet medical needs with these drugs on a compassionate IND basis, but companies are reluctant to do so.

6. *Patients' Need for Unsafe Drugs.* Drugs removed from the market for safety reasons frequently have a very low rate of toxicity (*e.g.*, one in one million) of an extremely serious adverse event (*e.g.*, death). If a drug is removed on this basis, an individual patient will lose the opportunity to use the drug, even though using it would be entirely rational on a personal benefit-risk basis. Patients do everything they can to keep obtaining some drugs that have been removed from the market, often turning to rogue internet sources. *See, e.g., Ill Patients Fight to Keep Receiving Banned Drug*, N.Y. TIMES, Dec. 12, 2000, at F9 (Propulsid); Denise Grady, *F.D.A. Pulls a Drug, and Patients Despair*, N.Y. TIMES, Jan. 30, 2001, at F1 (Lotronex); Bill Saporito, *My Most Difficult Choice*, TIME, May 23, 2005, at 64 (Vioxx).

7. *Imminent Hazard Criteria.* FDA's definition of "imminent hazard" is codified at 21 C.F.R. 2.5. 35 Fed. Reg. 18679 (Dec. 9, 1970), 36 Fed. Reg. 12516 (July 1, 1971). In 44 Fed. Reg. 48979 (Aug. 12, 1979) the Secretary of HHS proposed new criteria and procedures for implementing the imminent hazard provisions of the Act, but no further action has been taken on this proposal.

5.   WITHDRAWAL OF NDA APPROVAL

FDA withdrawal of approval of an NDA is a rare event. Almost all withdrawals have occurred under the DESI program.

Weinberger v. Hynson, Westcott & Dunning, Inc.

412 U.S. 609 (1973).

■ MR. JUSTICE DOUGLAS delivered the opinion of the Court.

... Hynson, Westcott & Dunning, Inc., had filed an application under the 1938 Act for a drug called Lutrexin, recommended by Hynson for use in the treatment of premature labor, threatened and habitual abortion, and dysmenorrhea. FDA informed Hynson that Hynson's studies submitted with the application were not sufficiently well controlled to justify the claims of effectiveness and urged Hynson not to represent the drug as useful for threatened and habitual abortion. But FDA allowed the application to become effective, since the 1938 Act permitted evaluation of a new drug solely on the grounds of its *safety*.... When the 1962 amendments became effective and NAS–NRC undertook to appraise the efficacy of drugs theretofore approved as safe, Hynson submitted a list of literature references, a copy of an unpublished study, and a representative sample testimonial letter on behalf of Lutrexin. The panel of NAS–NRC working in the relevant field reported to FDA that Hynson's claims for effectiveness of the drug were either inappropriate or unwarranted in the absence of submission of further appropriate documentation. At the invitation of the Commissioner of Food and Drugs, Hynson submitted additional data. But the Commissioner concluded that this additional information was inadequate and published notice of his intention to withdraw approval of the NDA's covering the drug, offering Hynson the opportunity for a prewithdrawal hearing [in accordance with section 505(e) of the Act]. Before the hearing could take place, Hynson brought suit in the District Court for a declaratory judgment that the drugs in question were exempt from the *efficacy* review provisions of the 1962 amendments or, alternatively, that there was no lack of substantial evidence of the drug's *efficacy*. The Government's motion to dismiss was granted, the District Court ruling that FDA had primary jurisdiction and that Hynson had failed to exhaust its administrative remedies.

While the District Court litigation was pending, FDA promulgated new regulations establishing minimal standards for "adequate and well-controlled investigations" and limiting the right to a hearing to those applicants who could proffer at least some evidence meeting those standards. Although Hynson maintained that it was not subject to the new regulations because its initial request for a hearing predated their issuance, it renewed its request and submitted the material which it claimed constituted "substantial evidence" of Lutrexin's effectiveness. The Commissioner denied the request for a hearing and withdrew the NDA for Lutrexin. He ruled that Lutrexin is not exempt from the 1962 amendments and that Hynson had not submitted adequate evidence that Lutrexin is not a new drug or is effective. The Court of Appeals reversed, holding that while the drug in question was not exempt, Hynson was entitled to a hearing on the substantial-evidence question.

Section 505(e) directs FDA to withdraw approval of an NDA if the manufacturer fails to carry the burden of showing there is "substantial evidence" respecting the *efficacy* of the drug.... The Act and the Regulations, in their reduction of that standard to detailed guidelines, make FDA's so-called administrative summary judgment procedure appropriate.

The general contours of "substantial evidence" are defined by § 505(d) of the Act to include "evidence consisting of adequate and well-controlled investigations, including clinical investigations, by experts qualified by scientific training and experience to evaluate the effectiveness of the drug involved, on the basis of which it could fairly and responsibly be concluded by such experts that the drug will have the effect it purports or is represented to have under the conditions of use prescribed, recommended, or suggested in the labeling or proposed labeling thereof." Acting pursuant to his "authority to promulgate regulations for the efficient enforcement" of the Act, § 701(a), the Commissioner has detailed the "principles ... recognized by the scientific community as the essentials of adequate and well-controlled clinical investigations. They provide the basis for the determination whether there is 'substantial evidence' to support the claims of effectiveness for 'new drugs'...." 21 CFR § 130.12(a)(5)(ii) [now § 314.111(a)(5)(ii)].... [T]he regulation provides that "[u]ncontrolled studies or partially controlled studies are not acceptable as the sole basis for the approval of claims of effectiveness. Such studies, carefully conducted and documented, may provide corroborative support.... Isolated case reports, random experience, and reports lacking the details which permit scientific evaluation will not be considered."

... [I]t is not disputed here that [these regulations] express well-established principles of scientific investigation. Moreover, their strict and demanding standards, barring anecdotal evidence indicating that doctors "believe" in the efficacy of a drug, are amply justified by the legislative history....

To be sure, the Act requires FDA to give "due notice and opportunity for hearing to the applicant" before it can withdraw its approval of an NDA. FDA, however, by regulation, requires any applicant who desires a hearing to submit reasons "why the application ... should not be withdrawn, together with a well-organized and full-factual analysis of the clinical and other investigational data he is prepared to prove in support of his opposition to the notice of opportunity for a hearing.... When it clearly appears from the data in the application and from the reasons and factual analysis in the request for the hearing that there is no genuine and substantial issue of fact ..., *e.g.*, no adequate and well-controlled clinical investigations to support the claims of effectiveness," the Commissioner may deny a hearing and enter an order withdrawing the application based solely on these data. What the agency has said, then, is that it will not provide a formal hearing where it is apparent at the threshold that the applicant has not tendered *any* evidence which *on its face* meets the statutory standards as particularized by the regulations.

The propriety of such a procedure was decided in *United States v. Storer Broadcasting Co.*, 351 U.S. 192, and *FPC v. Texaco, Inc.*, 377 U.S. 33. We said in *Texaco*:

> "[T]he statutory requirement for a hearing under § 7 [of the Natural Gas Act] does not preclude the Commission from particularizing statutory standards through the rulemaking process and barring at the threshold those who neither measure up to them nor show reasons why in the public interest the rule should be waived."

There can be no question that to prevail at a hearing an applicant must furnish evidence stemming from "adequate and well-controlled investigations." We cannot impute to Congress the design of requiring, nor does due process demand, a hearing when it appears conclusively from the applicant's "pleadings" that the application cannot succeed[17] . . .

Our conclusion that the summary judgment procedure of FDA is valid does not end the matter, for Hynson argues that its submission to FDA satisfied its threshold burden. In reviewing an order of the Commissioner denying a hearing, a court of appeals must determine whether the Commissioner's findings accurately reflect the study in question and if they do, whether the deficiencies he finds conclusively render the study inadequate or uncontrolled in light of the pertinent regulations. There is a contrariety of opinion within the Court concerning the adequacy of Hynson's submission. Since a majority are of the view that the submission was sufficient to warrant a hearing, we affirm the Court of Appeals on that phase of the case. . . .

. . . The Court of Appeals suggested that only a district court has authority to determine whether Lutrexin is a "new drug." The Government contends that the Commissioner has authority to determine new drug status in proceedings to withdraw approval of the product's NDA under § 505 (e).

[FDA's] determination that a product is a "new drug" or a "me-too" drug is, of course, reviewable. But its jurisdiction to determine whether it

---

17. This applies, of course, only to those regulations that are precise. For example, the plan or protocol for a study must include "[a] summary of the methods of analysis and an evaluation of data derived from the study, including any appropriate statistical methods." 21 CFR § 130.12(a) [314.111(a)(5)(ii)(a)(5)]. A mere reading of the study submitted will indicate whether the study is totally deficient in this regard. Some of the regulations, however, are not precise, as they call for the exercise of discretion or subjective judgment in determining whether a study is adequate and well-controlled. For example, § 130.12(a) [314.111(a)(5)(ii)(a)(2)(i)] requires that the plan or protocol for the study include a method of selection of the subjects that provide [sic] "*adequate* assurance that they are suitable for the purposes of the study." (Emphasis added.) The qualitative standards "adequate" and "suitable" do not lend themselves to clear-cut definition, and it may not be possible to tell from the face of a study whether the standards have been met. Thus, it might not be proper to deny a hearing on the ground that the study did not comply with this regulation.

has jurisdiction is as essential to its effective operation as is a court's like power.... The heart of the new procedures designed by Congress is the grant of primary jurisdiction to FDA, the expert agency it created....

The thrust of § 201(p) [the definition of "new drug"] is both qualitative and quantitative. The Act, however, nowhere defines what constitutes "general recognition" among experts. Hynson contends that the "lack of substantial evidence" is applicable only to proof of the *actual* effectiveness of drugs that fall within the definition of a new drug and not to the initial determination under § 201(p) whether a drug is "generally recognized" as effective. It would rely solely on the testimony of physicians and the extant literature, evidence that has been characterized as "anecdotal." We agree with FDA, however, that the statutory scheme and overriding purpose of the 1962 amendments compel the conclusion that the hurdle of "general recognition" of effectiveness requires at least "substantial evidence" of effectiveness for approval of an NDA....

It is well established that our task in interpreting separate provisions of a single Act is to give the Act "the most harmonious, comprehensive meaning possible" in light of the legislative policy and purpose. We accordingly have concluded that a drug can be "generally recognized" by experts as effective for [its] intended use within the meaning of the Act only when that expert consensus is founded upon "substantial evidence" as defined in § 505(d). We have held ... however, that the Commissioner was not justified in withdrawing Hynson's NDA without a prior hearing on whether Hynson had submitted "substantial evidence" of Lutrexin's effectiveness. Consequently, any ruling as to Lutrexin's "new drug" status is premature and must await the outcome of this hearing....

NOTES

1. *Subsequent Proceedings.* Following this decision, FDA published a notice of hearing in 39 Fed. Reg. 15341 (May 2, 1974) and subsequently held a formal evidentiary hearing. The Commissioner's ultimate decision withdrawing approval of the NDAs for Lutrexin, 41 Fed. Reg. 14406 (Apr. 5, 1976), was not challenged.

2. *New Drug Status.* The *Hynson* decision effectively renders every new chemical entity drug introduced since 1962 a "new drug," for it holds that no drug can be generally recognized as effective in the absence of the "adequate and well-controlled" clinical studies that are required for approval of an NDA.

3. *Withdrawal by Statute.* Congress has only once ordered FDA to withdraw approval of an NDA. It took this action to ban methaqualone (Quaalude) after the sponsor had already discontinued marketing. *See* "Drug Abuse: Quaaludes," Hearing on H.R. 1097 before the Subcommittee on Health and the Environment of the House Committee on Energy and Commerce, 98th Cong., 1st Sess. (1983); 98 Stat. 280 (1984); 49 Fed. Reg. 36441 (Sept. 17, 1984).

4. *NDA Withdrawal for Untrue Statements of Material Fact.* In 60 Fed. Reg. 32982 (June 26, 1995), FDA withdrew three NDAs from one company because the company had submitted false and misleading information in the applications.

5. *Withdrawal of Obsolete NDAs.* In 1998, FDA withdrew approval of Seldane on the ground that it was no longer shown to be safe because a safer version, Allegra, containing the primary active derivative of Seldane produced in the body when Seldane is taken, was shown to be a safer drug. 62 Fed Reg. 1889 (Jan. 14,

1997), 63 Fed. Reg. 53444 (Oct. 5, 1998). *See* "FDA Proposes to Withdraw Seldane Approval," FDA Talk Paper No. T97–3 (Jan. 13, 1997). FDA has stated that Rezulin is another example of an obsolete drug because newer drugs have a better safety profile. "Rezulin is Outmoded Drug, Not an Example of System Failure—FDA's Lumpkin," 12 HEALTH NEWS DAILY, No. 96, at 1 (May 19, 2000).

6.   *Rescission of NDA Approval Because of a Mistake.* In a very unusual case, *American Therapeutics, Inc. v. Sullivan,* Food Drug Cosm. L. Rep. (CCH) ¶ 38,159, 755 F. Supp. 1 (D.D.C. 1990), FDA approved an NDA on June 23 and then rescinded the approval on August 3 on the ground that approval had issued through "an inadvertent mistake." The District Court held that even though FDA lacked statutory authority to correct a mistake of this kind, it would defer to the agency and thus dismiss the complaint.

As the *Hynson* case illustrates, lack of substantial evidence of effectiveness was the chief reason for withdrawal of approval of many pre-1962 new drugs. For a number of effective drugs approved since 1962, however, the problem has been infrequent but serious adverse reactions revealed only with use of the drug in a large patient population.

Parnate, an antidepressant, was the first drug to be withdrawn from the market because of a safety issue following enactment of the Drug Amendments of 1962.

Statement of Joseph F. Sadusk, Jr., M.D.*

"Drug Safety," Hearings Before the Intergovernmental Relations Subcommittee of the House Committee on Government Operations, 89th Congress, 1st Session (1965).

Soon after the introduction of Parnate to the market [in 1961] a few cases of hypertensive reaction with headache were reported.... In the summer of 1961 the labeling was revised to call attention to this reaction. Approximately 1 year later another supplemental [new drug] application was processed to provide for further changes in the labeling which in part cautioned against the use of Parnate with other drugs....

It became apparent late in 1962 and early in 1963 that the number of severe reactions associated with the use of Parnate was increasing.... In a meeting of September 17, 1963, of FDA with representatives of the firm, the latter presented new information on adverse reactions and proposed to send a warning letter to physicians.... By February 1964, approximately 400 cases of hypertensive reaction, including 50 cerebrovascular accidents with 16 deaths, had been reported....

... [A] meeting with representatives of the firm was held in the office of Commissioner Larrick on February 18, 1964. Following a general discussion of the situation the visitors were informed of our intention to issue a notice of hearing on a proposal to withdraw approval of the drug.... The proposal that a panel of experts be appointed to consider the matter was again made by the company. Mr. Larrick explained that FDA had already

* [Dr. Sadusk was the FDA Medical Director.]

canvassed outside experts and for this reason would not be willing to substitute an advisory committee for the hearing procedure or to delay this procedure for the formation of an advisory committee.

Six days following the meeting, Mr. Munns, president of Smith, Kline & French, informed Mr. Rankin by phone that the firm had decided to withdraw Parnate from the market, but not to voluntarily withdraw the NDA.... The action of FDA which resulted in withdrawal of Parnate from the market was followed by many letters from physicians, who had used the drug, protesting the action. Several were from psychiatrists of recognized eminence. The consensus of this correspondence was to the effect that Parnate was an effective antidepressant for certain patients, it was irreplaceable by other available drugs, and its adverse effects were outweighed by its value in converting invalidism to a useful life and in the prevention of suicides....

Our FDA studies up through the May–June 1964 period indicated that 38 strokes had been reported in the United States, among which 21 deaths resulted in patients who were on Parnate. A careful review of these cases by the Bureau of Medicine staff responsible for the analysis of these cases indicated that in only 6 of these 38 strokes would there appear to be a highly probable causal relationship between stroke and the use of Parnate, although the attending physicians involved in care of the patients considered 19 of the cases to be causal....

Our records reveal that up to August 1964 a total of 216 strokes were reported from both domestic and foreign sources in patients who were receiving Parnate before the labeling change. Of these 216 patients, 146 were from the United States. Most of these reports came in during the summer of 1964....

In final summary of the question of efficacy, it was our opinion that Parnate is an effective drug within the meaning of the 1962 Drug Amendments to the Federal Food, Drug, and Cosmetic Act. Consequently, I stated to the Commissioner that it was my carefully considered opinion that Parnate should be returned to the market under the condition of acceptance by Smith Kline & French of a drastic revision of their previous labeling....

... [T]he revised labeling called for a number of factors of safety....

1. Parnate is to be used only in cases of severe depression.

2. Parnate is to be used only in patients who are either hospitalized or in patients who are under close observation and in whom electroconvulsive therapy is not indicated or other medication had been found to be ineffective.

3. Parnate is not to be used in patients over 60 years of age or in patients in whom there is evidence of history of hypertension or other cardiovascular disease.

4. The maximum dosage of Parnate was to be significantly reduced, employing a recommended top level of 30 milligrams per day as compared to a top level of 60 milligrams per day which was endorsed in the previous level of September 1963.

5. Parnate is not to be used in combination with many other potent drugs.

... Particular warning was also given to the need for the patient to abstain from cheese while on Parnate....

Subsequent to the time that Parnate reappeared on the market, namely, August 1, 1964, a careful analysis has been continued of severe adverse reactions reported to us from use of this drug. This analysis indicates that from August 1, 1964, through May 31, 1965 (a period of 9 months) there have been reported to FDA 18 strokes and 25 hypertensive reactions without serious sequela.... In the 18, there were 7 fatalities—4 from the United States, 3 from foreign sources. The four fatalities in this country involved use of the drug prior to August 1, 1964. There have been no reported deaths which have come to our attention involving the use of Parnate in the United States since Parnate was returned to the market with revised labeling....

NOTES

1. *Failure to Report Adverse Reactions.* During the Bureau of Medicine's reevaluation of Parnate in the summer of 1964, an agency toxicologist discovered "discrepancies" in the firm's original reporting of cerebrovascular lesions in animals to which the drug had been administered in preclinical tests. While acknowledging that the firm may have been attempting to avert concern about Parnate's safety, Dr. Sadusk adhered to his conclusion that the drug should be permitted back on the market. In a similar case, FDA sought to initiate proceedings to withdraw approval of the underlying NDA on the ground that the application had contained an "untrue statement of a material fact." 41 Fed. Reg. 45605 (Oct. 15, 1976) (Naprosyn Tablets).

2. *Return to Market.* Parnate was the first drug to be taken off the market and later returned. Four decades later, Lotronex and Tysabri similarly were withdrawn from marketing and then returned.

3. *Congressional Reactions.* The discovery of serious adverse reactions after a drug is marketed, and thus in wide use, is not an uncommon event, and its occurrence almost invariably prompts outraged reactions from members of Congress, who view FDA as responsible. *See, e.g.,* "Corporate Criminal Liability," Hearings before the Subcommittee on Crime of the House Committee on the Judiciary, 96th Cong., 1st and 2nd Sess. (1980) (Selacryn); "The Regulation of New Drugs by the Food and Drug Administration: The New Drug Review Process," Hearings before a Subcommittee of the House Committee on Government Operations, 97th Cong., 2d Sess. (1982); "Deficiencies in FDA's Regulation of the New Drug 'Oraflex'," H.R. Rep. No. 98–511, 98th Cong., 2d Sess. (1983); "The Regulation of New Drugs by the Food and Drug Administration: The New Drug Review Process," Hearings before a Subcommittee of the House Committee on Government Operations, 97th Cong., 2d Sess. (1982) (Feldene); "FDA's Regulation of Zomax," H.R. Rep. No. 98–584, 98th Cong., 1st Sess. (1983); "Oversight of the New Drug Review Process and FDA's Regulation of Merital," Hearing before a Subcommittee of the House Committee on Government Operations, 99th Cong., 2d Sess. (1986), "FDA's Regulation of the New Drug Merital," H.R. Rep. No. 100–206, 100th Cong., 1st Sess. (1987); "FDA's Regulation of the New Drug Suprol," Hearings before a Subcommittee of the House Committee on Government Operations, 100th Cong., 1st Sess. (1987); "FDA's Regulation of the New Drug Versed," Hearings before a Subcommittee of the House Committee on Government Operations, 100th Cong., 2d

Sess. (1988), "FDA's Deficient Regulation of the New Drug Versed," H.R. Rep. No. 100–1086, 100th Cong., 2d Sess. (1988). In many cases where marketing of the drug was suspended, the company acted voluntarily. In some instances, the agency has specifically requested the manufacturer to make the drug available for compassionate use when no effective alternative existed.

4. *Postmarketing Adverse Reactions.* Because an investigational new drug is tested in only a relatively few patients before an NDA is approved, low frequency adverse reactions will almost certainly be discovered when use becomes widespread. In FDA DRUG REVIEW: POSTAPPROVAL RISKS 1976–85, PEMD–90–15 (1990), the General Accounting Office found that of 198 drugs approved by FDA during this period, about half had serious postapproval risks as evidenced by labeling changes or market withdrawal. All but six of the drugs studied were still being marketed in 1989, based upon the agency's determination that the benefits outweighed the risks.

5. *Evaluating Adverse Reactions.* For a case study of the problems involved in assessing and responding to reports of postmarketing adverse reactions, *see* Seymour Shubin, *Triazure and Public Drug Policies*, 22 PERSP. IN BIOLOGY AND MED. 185 (Winter 1979); "FDA's Regulation of the Drug 'Triazure'," Hearing Before a Subcommittee of the House Committee on Government Operations, 94th Cong., 2d Sess. (1976).

6. *Sales Abroad.* Voluntary removal of a drug from the United States market does not necessarily result in removal from markets in other countries. Different countries can make different benefit-risk judgments. *See, e.g.*, Joanne McManus & Trish Saywell, *Not in Our Backyard: Medicines Deemed Unsafe for Americans by Federal Regulators are Still Being Sold and Prescribed Throughout Asia*, FAR EASTERN ECON. REV. (Aug. 3, 2000).

———

The Parnate scenario has been reenacted numerous times since 1964, most recently with the Cox–2 inhibitor drugs.

Statement of Sandra L. Kweder, M.D.*

"FDA, Merck, and Vioxx: Putting Patient Safety First?" Hearing before the Senate Committee on Finance, 108th Cong., 2d Sess. (2004).

FDA approved Vioxx in May, 1999 for the reduction of signs and symptoms of osteoarthritis, as well as for acute pain in adults for the treatment of primary dysmenorrhea. Vioxx received a 6–month priority review because the drug potentially provided a significant therapeutic advantage over existing approved drugs due to fewer gastrointestinal side effects, including bleeding. A product undergoing a priority review is held to the same rigorous standards for safety, efficacy, and quality that FDA expects from all drugs submitted for approval.

As with many other new molecular entities, this product was taken before the Arthritis Advisory Committee, April 20, 1999, prior to its approval. It was the second of a new class (Cox–2 selective) of non-steroidal anti-inflammatory drugs (NSAIDs) approved by FDA. The original safety database for this product included approximately 5,000 patients on Vioxx and did not show an increased risk of heart attack or stroke.

    * [Dr. Kweder is Deputy Director of the CDER Office of New Drugs.]

In the clinical trials conducted before approval, the risk of gastrointestinal (GI) side effects was determined through the use of endoscopy. At the time that FDA approved Vioxx, the available evidence from these endoscopy studies showed a significantly lower risk of gastrointestinal ulcers, a significant source of serious side effects such as bleeding and death, in comparison to ibuprofen.

After Vioxx was approved in 1999, Merck continued studies of Vioxx designed to look at clinically meaningful GI effects, such as stomach ulcers and bleeding (Vioxx Gastrointestinal Outcomes Research, or VIGOR study)....

VIGOR did not have a placebo group because to do so would have meant patients with rheumatoid arthritis would have been randomized to receive no pain relief. Use of a placebo would have been intolerable, because untreated patients would have suffered and left the study. The study also excluded subjects taking low dose aspirin for cardiovascular (CV) prevention because use of aspirin might have contributed to increased rates of GI bleeding in the study and confound the results. However, the exclusion of patients on low dose aspirin may have influenced CV events in the study, since low dose aspirin has been shown to reduce CV risk

In April, 2002, FDA approved extensive labeling changes to reflect the findings from the VIGOR study. These labeling changes included detailed information about the increase in risk of cardiovascular events relative to naproxen, including heart attack....

In the years following the 1999 FDA approval of Vioxx, Merck began conducting a serious of clinical trials exploring other potential indications of this product. All trials for chronic use were designed to monitor carefully for CV safety, and included data safety monitoring committees as well as blinded experts to assess all CV events in the trials....

Merck contacted FDA on September 27, 2004, to request a meeting to discuss with the Agency the Data Safety Monitoring Board's decision to halt Merck's long-term study of Vioxx in patients at increased risk of colon polyps. Merck and FDA officials met the next day, September 28, and during that meeting the company informed FDA of its decision to remove Vioxx from the market voluntarily. The data presented demonstrated an increase in cardiovascular risk and stroke starting at the 18–month timepoint compared to placebo. This was the first demonstration of a difference in comparison to a placebo group, and supported the previous signal seen in the VIGOR trial and some of the epidemiologic studies....

NOTES

1. *Cox–2 Inhibitor Decisions.* At a subsequent FDA Advisory Committee hearing, the committee voted 31 to 1 to retain Celebrex on the market, 17 to 13 to retain Bextra on the market, and 17 to 15 to bring Vioxx back to the market. Because of the widespread publicity surrounding the withdrawal of Vioxx and the results of this Advisory Committee meeting, FDA took the unprecedented step of releasing a memorandum prepared jointly by FDA CDER Office of New Drugs Director John K. Jenkins and FDA CDER Office of Pharmacoepidemiology and Statistical Science Director Paul J. Seligman (Apr. 6, 2005) recommending that

FDA: (1) allow Celebrex to remain on the market, (2) request Pfizer voluntarily to withdraw Bextra from the market or face a formal withdrawal procedure, and (3) carefully review any proposal from Merck for resumption of the marketing of Vioxx. *See generally* "FDA, Merck, and Vioxx: Putting Patient Safety First?," Hearing before the Senate Committee on Finance, 108th Cong., 2d Sess. (2004); "Ensuring Drug Safety: Where Do We Go From Here?," Hearing of the Senate Committee on Health, Education, Labor, and Pensions, 109th Cong., 1st Sess. (2005); "Risk and Responsibility: The Roles of FDA and Pharmaceutical Companies in Ensuring the Safety of Approved Drugs, Like Vioxx," Hearing before the House Committee on Government Reform, 109th Cong., 1st Sess. (2005); Lan Tran, *Untangling the Vioxx–Celebrex Controversy: A Story About Responsibility* (2005), Daniel Zahler, *Preventing the Next Public Health Crisis: New Drug Approval After Vioxx* (2005), and McCauley Mancinelli, *Placing Blame for the Vioxx Debacle* (2006), in Chapter VI(C)(3) of the Electronic Book.

    2. *Trasylol.* Two years after the Cox–2 inhibitor controversy became public, postmarket studies raised safety questions about the antifibrinolytic drug Trasylol. *See* Jerry Avorn, *Dangerous Deception—Hiding the Evidence of Adverse Drug Effects*, Williams R. Hiatt, *Observational Studies on Drug Safety—Aprotinin and the Absence of Transparency*, Jeffrey M. Drazen, *Research Replication*, 355 NEW ENG. J. MED. 2169, 2171, & 2252 (Nov. 23, 2006).

    3. *Approval Speed v. Safety Withdrawal.* A study has shown no link between NDA approval speed and subsequent withdrawal for safety reasons:

Decade	% Withdrawn For Safety Reasons
1980s	3.2%
1990s	3.5%
2000s	1.6%

Tufts Center for Study of Drug Development, *Drug Safety Withdrawals in the U.S. Not Linked to Speed of FDA Approval*, 7 IMPACT, No. 5 (Sept./Oct. 2005). The study found that the rate of drug safety withdrawals has not increased since the user fee era began in 1993 and that faster approval times do not correlate with increased drug safety withdrawals.

I. THE GENERIC NEW DRUG PROCESS

1. FDA REGULATION AND PROMOTION OF GENERIC DRUGS

    The primary goal of the investigations begun by Senator Estes Kefauver in 1959 was to reduce drug prices by increasing competition in the pharmaceutical industry. Although the only element of Kefauver's proposed legislation that became part of the Drug Amendments of 1962 was the requirement that drug labeling and advertising disclose the generic name, the federal government's growing financial responsibility for drug purchases has led FDA to assume a role in promoting the use of generic drugs that extends beyond its narrow statutory mandate.

    The Social Security Amendments of 1965, 79 Stat. 286, established federal programs to provide medical benefits to the elderly and disabled (Medicare) and, in cooperation with the states, to the needy (Medicaid). Medicare covers the costs of medical care provided in two contexts. Part A primarily covers inpatient hospitalization services, including drugs. Part B is a voluntary program of supplemental medical insurance which includes drugs provided incidental to a physician's care that cannot be self-administered. Although each state has its own Medicaid rules, most cover outpatient prescription drugs for needy patients. The costs to both federal and state governments for reimbursing prescription drug purchases have continued to increase, and accordingly the incentive to encourage price competition and contain costs has been substantial. *See, e.g.,* John G. Giumarra, *Drug Amendments of 1962—Generic–Name Prescribing: Drug Price Panacea?,* 16 STAN. L. REV. 649 (1964); Note, *Consumer Protection and Prescription Drugs: The Generic Drug Substitution Laws,* 67 KY. L.J. 384 (1978–1979).

Soon after the NAS began to deliver its DESI reports to FDA in 1967, FDA devised the abbreviated NDA to secure control over, and at the same time allow marketing of, generic copies of pre-1962 prescription drugs. 34 Fed. Reg. 2673 (Feb. 27, 1969). One requirement for approval of an abbreviated NDA was proof of "biological availability." Faced with competitors that had FDA approval, manufacturers of pioneer drugs questioned the quality, and thus the clinical effectiveness, of generic products. In DRUG BIOEQUIVALENCE (1974), the Office of Technology Assessment concluded that "current standards and regulatory practices do not insure bioequivalence for drug products" and that "present compendial standards and guidelines for Current Good Manufacturing Practice do not insure quality in uniform bioavailability for drug products."

Just as these questions were being raised, FDA encountered the first major bioavailability/bioequivalence problem with an important prescription drug, digoxin, versions of which were being marketed without approved NDAs. FDA promptly adopted stringent conditions for testing and labeling of digoxin drugs. 39 Fed. Reg. 2471 (Jan. 22, 1974), codified at 21 C.F.R. 310.500. Following a public hearing, 39 Fed. Reg. 9129, 9184 (Mar. 8, 1974), it revised the labeling, 41 Fed. Reg. 43135 (Sept. 30, 1976), and reimposed the requirement of an abbreviated NDA for all generic versions.

In the 1970s, FDA promulgated general regulations governing drug bioavailability and bioequivalence. 38 Fed. Reg. 885 (Jan. 5, 1973), 40 Fed. Reg. 26164 (June 20, 1975), 42 Fed. Reg. 1624 (Jan. 7, 1977), 42 Fed. Reg. 42311 (Aug. 23, 1977), codified at 21 C.F.R. Part 320. *See* Bernard Cabana, *Bioavailability/Bioequivalence,* 32 FOOD DRUG COSM. L.J. 512 (1977); James T. Doluisio, *A Definition of Bioequivalence/Bioavailability and a Historical Perspective,* 32 FOOD DRUG COSM. L.J. 506 (1977); Robert Spencer, *Bioequivalence/Bioavailability—The FDA's Plans,* 31 FOOD DRUG COSM. L.J. 32 (1976). 21 C.F.R. 320.1 defines the critical terms as follows:

> (a) "Bioavailability" means the rate and extent to which the active drug ingredient or therapeutic moiety is absorbed from a drug product and becomes available at the site of drug action.

> (b) "Drug product" means a finished dosage form, *e.g.,* tablet, capsule, or solution, that contains the active drug ingredient, generally, but not necessarily, in association with inactive ingredients.

(c) "Pharmaceutical equivalents" means drug products that contain identical amounts of the identical active drug ingredient, *i.e.*, the same salt or ester of the same therapeutic moiety, in identical dosage forms, but not necessarily containing the same inactive ingredients, and that meet the identical compendial or other applicable standard of identity, strength, quality, and purity, including potency and, where applicable, content uniformity, disintegration times and/or dissolution rates.

(d) "Pharmaceutical alternatives" means drug products that contain the identical therapeutic moiety, or its precursor, but not necessarily in the same amount or dosage form or as the same salt or ester. . . .

(e) "Bioequivalent drug products" means pharmaceutical equivalents or pharmaceutical alternatives whose rate and extent of absorption do not show a significant difference when administered at the same molar dose of the therapeutic moiety under similar experimental conditions, either single dose or multiple dose. Some pharmaceutical equivalents or pharmaceutical alternatives may be equivalent in the extent of their absorption but not in their rate of absorption and yet may be considered bioequivalent because such differences in the rate of absorption are intentional and are reflected in the labeling, are not essential to the attainment of effective body drug concentrations on chronic use, or are considered medically insignificant for the particular drug product studied.

FDA also set forth a procedure for establishing bioequivalence requirements for specific drugs and proposed regulations for eleven drug clusters, the first for anticonvulsants, 42 Fed. Reg. 39675 (Aug. 5, 1977), and the last for quinidine, 45 Fed. Reg. 72200 (Oct. 31, 1980). The agency later determined simply to set bioequivalence requirements through the abbreviated NDA process rather than by regulations. 54 Fed. Reg. 28823, 28872, 28911 (July 10, 1989).

With greater assurance of the quality and clinical effectiveness of generic drugs, the Department of HEW established procedures for fixing the maximum allowable cost (MAC) that the federal government would reimburse for any multi-source drug dispensed to patients under Medicare and other programs. 39 Fed. Reg. 40302 (Nov. 15, 1974), 40 Fed. Reg. 32284 (July 31, 1975). Under these procedures, a new body, the Pharmaceutical Reimbursement Board, would establish a "MAC" for a drug based on the "lowest unit price at which the drug is widely and consistently available from any formulator or labeler." The MAC did not apply where "the prescriber has certified in his own handwriting [that a particular brand] is medically necessary for that patient." For a single-source drug, reimbursement was based on the actual cost of the product. The MAC regulations withstood legal challenge. *American Medical Association v. Mathews*, 429 F. Supp. 1179 (N.D. Ill. 1977); *Hoffmann–LaRoche, Inc. v. Califano*, 453 F. Supp. 900 (D.D.C. 1978). Nonetheless, following a public meeting on the MAC regulations, 48 Fed. Reg. 35506 (Aug. 4, 1983), HHS later revoked them, on the grounds that they had had little impact on drug costs and that alternative approaches to encouraging generic prescribing under Medicaid would be more cost-effective. 51 Fed. Reg. 29560 (Aug. 19, 1986), 51 Fed. Reg. 33086 (Sept. 18, 1986), 52 Fed. Reg. 28648 (July 31, 1987)

During the 1970s, many states also sought to promote the use of generic drugs under Medicaid. To assist the states in developing formularies listing drugs appropriate for reimbursement, FDA initially disseminated lists of all drugs it had approved for marketing. 41 Fed. Reg. 5539 (Feb. 5, 1976), 43 Fed. Reg. 28557 (June 30, 1978). Soon afterwards, it prepared a list of "therapeutically equivalent drugs," including prices, and proposed that it be distributed to all physicians and pharmacists to aid them in making comparisons among products containing the same generic active ingredients. 44 Fed. Reg. 2932 (Jan. 12, 1979). Following an unsuccessful attempt to halt the rulemaking, *Pharmaceutical Manufacturers Association v. Kennedy*, 471 F. Supp. 1224 (D. Md. 1979), FDA issued a final regulation in 45 Fed. Reg. 72582 (Oct. 31, 1980), codified at 21 C.F.R. 20.117(a)(3), making available a list of all approved drugs together with "an evaluation of the therapeutic equivalence of the drug products covered by such applications." The Drug Price Competition and Patent Term Restoration Act of 1984—often referred to as the Hatch–Waxman Act—added section 505(j)(6) to the FD&C Act to require FDA to publish such a list as a way of identifying drugs eligible for abbreviated NDAs. In accordance with that provision, the agency published a yearly list of approved drugs, with monthly revisions, commonly referred to as the "Orange Book," which has now been replaced with an electronic version on the FDA website.

The Orange Book contains two types of therapeutic equivalence evaluations. A drug given an "A" rating is considered by FDA to be "therapeutically equivalent to other pharmaceutically equivalent products." Drugs that "FDA does not at this time consider to be therapeutically equivalent to other pharmaceutically equivalent products, *i.e.*, drug products for which actual or potential bioequivalence problems have not been resolved by adequate evidence of bioequivalence," are rated "B." FDA arrives at these ratings without consultation with manufacturers and without notice-and-comment rulemaking. When FDA considered changing the classification of a generic antihypertensive drug from "A" to "B" because of uncertainty about therapeutic equivalence, however, it first provided an opportunity for the manufacturer to respond. *See* "FDA to Propose Withdrawal of Bolar's Generic Antihypertensive," FDA Talk Paper No. T89–53 (Aug. 28, 1989); "FDA Officially Changes Rating of Bolar's Antihypertensive," FDA Talk Paper No. T89–57 (Sept. 28, 1989).

As the rate of applications for approval of generic versions of post-1962 new drugs rose following the Drug Price Competition and Patent Term Restoration Act, manufacturers of pioneer drugs amplified their criticisms of generic products. In 1986, FDA established a Bioequivalence Task Force and scheduled a public hearing on the subject. 51 Fed. Reg. 23476 (June 27, 1986), 51 Fed. Reg. 46721 (Dec. 24, 1986), 53 Fed. Reg. 6036 (Feb. 29, 1988). One conclusion of the Task Force was that FDA should improve its procedures to detect and evaluate reports of drug product therapeutic failure that could be indicative of product inequivalence. In response FDA established a Therapeutic Inequivalence Act Coordinating Committee. 53 Fed. Reg. 35562 (Sept. 14, 1988). For a history of some of the controversies over generic drugs, see Frank J. Ascione et al., *Historical Overview of Generic Medication Policy*, 41 J. AM. PHARMACEUTICAL ASS'N 567 (July/August 2001).

In 1988, the House Subcommittee on Oversight and investigations launched an investigation into allegations by some manufacturers of generic drugs that their applications were not being processed fairly or expeditiously by FDA. "Misconduct Allegations in Generic Drug Reviews," FDA Talk Paper No. T88–48 (July 6, 1988); "FDA's Generic Drug Approval Process (Parts 1–3)," Hearings before the Subcommittee on Oversight and Investigations of the House Committee on Energy and Commerce, 101st Cong., 1st Sess. (1989). The Subcommittee found that some employees of the FDA Division of Generic Drugs of the Office of Drug Standards had accepted illegal gratuities from manufacturers, that some manufacturers conducted (and submitted) bioavailability and bioequivalence studies using the pioneer drug rather than their own generic products, and that significant discrepancies occurred in the testing and manufacture of some generic drugs. The agency employees and responsible officials of the implicated manufacturers were prosecuted and the suspect products were recalled. *See, e.g.,* "Vitarine Suspends Distribution of Drugs After Inquiry," FDA Talk Paper No. T89–36 (June 1, 1989); "Generics Firm Recalls Diuretic," FDA Talk Paper No. T89–47 (July 24, 1989). FDA withdrew, or proposed to withdraw, the approval of the abbreviated NDAs for the suspect products, and it undertook investigations of manufacturing facilities and testing of products to verify the quality and clinical effectiveness of the generic drug supply. *See* "FDA Testing Generics of Top Thirty Drugs," FDA Talk Paper No. T89–51 (Aug. 16, 1989): "FDA Inspections of Makers of Generic Drugs," FDA Talk Paper No. T89–52 (Aug. 23, 1989); 54 Fed. Reg. 35535 (Aug. 28, 1989); 54 Fed. Reg. 40740 (Oct. 3, 1989); 54 Fed. Reg. 42367 (Oct. 16, 1989); 54 Fed. Reg. 48026 (Nov. 20, 1989); 55 Fed. Reg. 5074 (Feb. 13, 1990); 55 Fed. Reg. 8995 (Mar. 9, 1990); 55 Fed. Reg. 9360 (Mar. 13, 1990); 55 Fed. Reg. 21103 (May 22, 1990); 55 Fed. Reg. 25712 (June 22, 1990); 55 Fed. Reg. 24934 (June 19, 1990); 55 Fed. Reg. 25712 (June 22, 1990); 55 Fed. Reg. 46245 (Nov. 2, 1990); 55 Fed. Reg. 47542 (Nov. 14, 1990); 55 Fed. Reg. 47919 (Nov. 16, 1990); 56 Fed. Reg. 2528 (Jan. 23, 1991). FDA made management changes and upgraded the Division of Generic Drugs. "Temporary Changes Made in Generic Drugs Management," FDA Talk Paper No. T89–34 (May 15, 1989); 54 Fed. Reg. 32014 (Aug. 3, 1989).

On August 18, 1989, the Secretary of HHS and the FDA Commissioner issued statements announcing intensified analyses of generic drugs and their manufacturers, strengthened generic drug review procedures, and the creation of an independent ombudsman to assure fairness in decisionmaking on product approval. As part of its program to reassure the public about the safety and effectiveness of generic drugs, FDA issued AN INTERIM REPORT ON GENERIC DRUGS (Nov. 17, 1989), established an advisory committee on generic drugs, 55 Fed. Reg. 5838 (Feb. 20, 1990), requested public comment on the generic drug program, 55 Fed. Reg. 6049 (Feb. 21, 1990), held a public meeting on new policies and procedures for generic drugs, 55 Fed. Reg. 38583 (Sept. 19, 1990), and established a public file with all pertinent records on the agency's generic drug policies, 55 Fed. Reg. 42654 (Oct. 22, 1990). An interim regulation on retention of bioavailability and bioequivalence testing samples was promulgated in 55 Fed. Reg. 47034 (Nov. 8, 1990).

For a personal recollection of the generic drug scandal by an FDA employee reassigned as temporary Director of the Generics Review Division to solve the problems created by the scandal, see Richard A. Terselic, *The Generic Drugs Scandal Revisited*, 11 DICKINSON'S FDA REVIEW, No. 7, at 2 (July 2004). *See generally* Frank J. Ascione, *Historical Overview of Generic Medication Policy*, 41 J. AM. PHARMACEUTICAL ASS'N 567 (July/August 2001).

Legislation was introduced in May 1990 to provide increased penalties, including debarment, against individuals and corporations who defrauded FDA in generic drug applications. This legislation was enacted two years later as the Generic Drug Enforcement Act of 1992, 106 Stat. 149. A study commissioned by the generic drug industry made recommendations for improving FDA regulation of the industry. BLUE RIBBON COMMITTEE ON GENERIC MEDICINES, GENERIC MEDICINES: RESTORING PUBLIC CONFIDENCE (Nov. 15, 1990). By early 1991, five FDA employees had been convicted of bribery or perjury, eight generic drug companies had been found to have submitted applications to FDA containing fraudulent data, and investigations by both FDA and congressional oversight committees were continuing. *See* "FDA's Generic Drug Enforcement and Approval Process," Hearing before the Subcommittee on Oversight and Investigations of the House Committee on Energy and Commerce, 102d Cong., 1st Sess. (1991); *United States v. Marcus*, 849 F. Supp. 417 (D. Md. 1994); *United States v. Chatterji*, 46 F.3d 1336 (4th Cir. 1995); *United States v. Shulman*, Food Drug Cosm. L. Rep. (CCH) ¶ 38,504 (4th Cir. 1997). Companies which did not engage in the fraudulent activities sued for damages for the harm done by their competitors in submitting fraudulent applications and bribing FDA officials to approve them. *E.g., Mylan Laboratories, Inc. v. Azko*, 770 F. Supp. 1053 (D. Md. 1991), *aff'd* 2 F.3d 56 (4th Cir. 1993); *Mylan Laboratories, Inc. v. Matkari*, 7 F.3d 1130 (4th Cir. 1993); *Barr Laboratories, Inc. v. Quantum Pharmics, Inc.*, 827 F. Supp. 111 (E.D.N.Y. 1993); *Eli Lilly and Co. v. Roussel Corp.*, 23 F. Supp. 2d 460 (D.N.J. 1998).

There are two statutory mechanisms for FDA approval of generic copies of pioneer new drugs: (1) the abbreviated NDA under section 505(j) of the FD&C Act and (2) the section 505(b)(2) NDA. Congress enacted both of these provisions, together with patent term restoration, in the Drug Price Competition and Patent Restoration Act of 1984, 98 Stat. 1585.

2.   ABBREVIATED NDA's

All of the requirements for an abbreviated NDA that FDA had developed in the late 1960s as part of the implementation of the Drug Amendments of 1962, and all of the proposed changes that FDA considered to adapt those requirements to post-1962 new drugs, were eliminated when Congress enacted the Drug Price Competition and Patent Term Restoration Act of 1984. The 1984 Act established detailed requirements that supersede everything that went before.

Under the 1984 Act, FDA may approve an abbreviated NDA for a generic version of a pioneer new drug after (1) all relevant product and use patents have expired for the pioneer drug and (2) all relevant periods of market exclusivity for the pioneer drug have also expired. The statute contains detailed and complex rules for determining precisely how this system works. No attempt will be made here to discuss the specific provisions, but they are extremely important in determining the commercial value of a pioneer new drug, because they govern when the drug will become subject to generic competition. In the FDA Modernization Act of 1997, as extended by the Best Pharmaceutical for Children Act of 2002, Congress expanded the length of protection granted pioneer drugs by providing an extra six months of market exclusivity at the end of the extended patent term (or market exclusivity term, if the patent has already expired) when the sponsor conducts pediatric testing requested and approved by FDA.

There are basically two types of situations in which an abbreviated NDA may be submitted. The first situation is where the generic version is the same as the pioneer version in all material respects. In these instances, the sponsor of the generic product simply submits the abbreviated NDA, and FDA may approve it without further consideration about the basic safety and effectiveness of the drug. The second situation is where the generic version is different from the pioneer drug in any significant respect (e.g., a different active ingredient, route of administration, dosage form, or strength). In these circumstances, the generic applicant must first submit to FDA a "suitability petition" demonstrating that the difference between the drugs is not sufficient to preclude an abbreviated NDA, and that additional studies to show safety and effectiveness are not needed. If FDA grants the suitability petition, an abbreviated NDA may be submitted. If the agency denies the suitability petition, the applicant must submit either a section 505(b)(2) NDA or a full NDA. In all other respects, the regulations and requirements for an abbreviated NDA are the same as those for a full NDA.

Peter Barton Hutt, *Landmark Pharmaceutical Law Enacted*

1 HEALTH SCAN, No. 3, p. 11 (1984).

. . . [T]he Drug Price Competition and Patent Term Restoration Act of 1984 . . . caps fifteen years of controversy about the procedures to be used by the Food and Drug Administration (FDA) in approving the marketing of generic drugs, and about the incentives for developing important new pioneer drugs, given the erosion of patent protection resulting from lengthy regulatory processes. . . . The legislation applies to all drugs marketed in the United States and to all patents granted in the United States, regardless of whether the drug is imported, or the new drug application (NDA) or patent is owned abroad. . . .

The new statute keeps abbreviated NDAs and paper NDAs [i.e., section 505(b)(2) NDAs] separate, but applies the ... same rules to both.... Accordingly, the rest of this article refers only to abbreviated NDAs, but must be understood to encompass paper NDAs as well.

The statute amends the FD&C Act to establish a new procedure for abbreviated NDAs. Unlike a pioneer NDA, which must contain full animal and human data to establish the safety and effectiveness of the drug, an abbreviated NDA need only contain sufficient information to demonstrate that the generic version of the drug is bioavailable and is bioequivalent to the pioneer drug. In return, however, the statute provides three new statutory protections for manufacturers of pioneer new drugs; protection against release of safety and effectiveness information, protection against an abbreviated NDA becoming effective before all relevant product and use patents for the pioneer drug have expired, and protection against an abbreviated NDA becoming effective during specified periods of market exclusivity that are independent of the patent status of the pioneer drug.

Part of the disagreement about abbreviated NDAs for post-1962 drugs during the past several years has been a dispute about the status of the safety and effectiveness information submitted in the pioneer NDA. The FDA has consistently stated ... that this information constitutes trade secrets which cannot be released to the public or used to approve a generic drug. The new statute provides that such information will retain its trade secret status and cannot be released to the public at least up to the point where an abbreviated NDA for a generic version could be made effective by FDA. Thereafter, the status of such information continues to enjoy protection against disclosure as trade secrets or other confidential commercial information. Under all circumstances, however, such information—even if not disclosable to the public—can be used by FDA to approve an abbreviated NDA for a generic drug.

Although FDA can approve an abbreviated NDA for a patented pioneer drug, that approval cannot be made effective (and thus the generic version cannot be marketed) until all relevant product and use patents have expired. Thus, a patented product or use (but not a patented process) will be protected by FDA until the relevant patents expire, because FDA is precluded from making an abbreviated NDA for a generic drug effective during the life of those patents. This is an entirely new concept under the FD&C Act. Previously, FDA approved all forms of NDAs without any consideration of patent status.

The new statute does permit a generic company to challenge a product or use patent which the pioneer NDA holder identifies as precluding the marketing of generic versions. The generic company which wishes to initiate such a challenge must submit an abbreviated NDA to FDA certifying that any relevant patent is invalid or will not be infringed, must notify the patent owner of that certification, and must specify the legal and factual basis for it. If the patent owner takes no action within 45 days, FDA may proceed to handle the abbreviated NDA like any other abbreviated NDA and the patent owner remains free to initiate or not initiate any form of patent litigation once the drug is approved by FDA and marketed. If the patent owner chooses to challenge the certification of patent invalidity or noninfringement and keep the generic version off the market, however, it must bring suit within 45 days of receiving the generic company's notification. If that is done, FDA is precluded from making the abbreviated NDA effective for a period of 30 months while the matter is being litigated or until the trial court decides the matter. If at the end of that 30 months the litigation is not concluded, an approved abbreviated NDA will become effective, and the generic drug can be marketed subject to the outcome of the pending litigation, unless the court itself enjoins marketing.

In addition to protection of trade secret data and product and use patents, the statute sets specified time periods during which abbreviated NDAs for generic drugs cannot become effective and thus generic versions cannot be marketed....

- All pioneer drugs approved by FDA during 1962–1981 are subject to abbreviated NDAs immediately.

- Abbreviated NDAs for new chemical entity (NCE) drugs approved during 1982–1984 cannot become effective for ten years after the date of approval of the pioneer NDA.

- Abbreviated NDAs for non-NCE drugs approved during 1982–1984 cannot be made effective for two years following the date of enactment of the legislation.

- Abbreviated NDAs for post-enactment NCE drugs cannot be submitted to (or accepted by) FDA for five years following the date of approval of the pioneer NDA, except that an abbreviated NDA challenging a patent for a pioneer drug can be submitted after four years.

- Abbreviated NDAs for post-enactment, non-NCE drugs cannot become effective for three years following the date of approval of the pioneer NDA if the FDA approval of the pioneer NDA is based upon new clinical investigations.

- Abbreviated NDAs covering changes in pioneer NDAs (*e.g.*, new uses, new dosages, or new processes) approved by FDA after the date of enactment cannot become effective for three years after such FDA approval if the supplemental NDA submitted by the pioneer NDA holder to obtain approval of those changes is based upon reports of new clinical investigations.

All of these provisions also apply, as already noted, to paper NDAs. These time periods apply regardless of the status of any patents for the pioneer drug. If, at the end of the applicable period of market exclusivity, any product or use patent for the pioneer drug remains unexpired, however, no approval of an abbreviated NDA could be made effective by the FDA for that drug until the last such patent expires.

The biotechnology industry requested Congress to include in this legislation a specific provision prohibiting an abbreviated NDA for any pioneer NDA utilizing recombinant DNA technology for a period of ten years following approval of the pioneer NDA. This [proposal] was not accepted. Drugs made from recombinant DNA technology are therefore subject to the other provisions of the new law. If such a drug is an NCE drug, no abbreviated NDA may be submitted for five years after approval of the pioneer NDA (or four years, if a patent is being challenged). If it is a non-NCE drug, an abbreviated NDA cannot be made effective until three years after approval of the pioneer NDA....

Under the new statute (which amends the patent law) the patent for any drug approved by FDA after the date of enactment is potentially eligible for patent term extension....

Any product, use, or process patent is potentially subject to extension. The patent may be a broad genus patent, or a narrow species patent. The decision as to which patent to extend is up to the patent owner. No patent may be extended more than once, and only one patent may be extended for any regulatory review. Moreover, the marketing or use of the product permitted by the regulatory review must represent the first permission for that marketing or use, and cannot previously have been permitted by an earlier regulatory review. The only exception to this rule is for a new process using recombinant DNA technology, where the production of the product permitted by an earlier regulatory review does not preclude the extension of a process patent for making the product through recombinant DNA technology as a result of a second regulatory review.

Patent term extension may be obtained for the length of the regulatory review period as defined in the statute, subject to three important limitations. The regulatory review period for a drug is defined as half the IND (human clinical study) time, plus the whole time during which FDA is reviewing the NDA. Thus, if the IND time is eight years and the NDA time is two years, the regulatory review period would be 6 years (half the 8–year IND time *plus* the full two-year NDA time).

The three important limitations to the length of patent term extension are as follows. First, under no circumstances may it exceed five years.... Second, the total effective patent life (defined as the time from the date of the pioneer NDA approval to the conclusion of patent protection, including the extended patent term) may not exceed a total of fourteen years. Third, the regulatory review period is to be reduced by any amount of time during which the NDA applicant has not exerted "due diligence" in attempting to obtain FDA approval of the NDA. The statute defines "due diligence" in terms of usual industry practice and requires FDA to initiate a due diligence investigation only upon petition of an interested person showing good cause.

In order to obtain patent term restoration, the patent holder must submit an application to the Patent Office within sixty days of approval of the NDA. The Patent Office is directed to take action upon the application solely on the basis of information contained in the application, in order to reduce the burden placed on it by the legislation.

NOTES

1. *Implementing Regulations.* For a more detailed discussion of the 1984 statute, *see* Ellen J. Flannery & Peter Barton Hutt, *Balancing Competition and Patent Protection in the Drug Industry: The Drug Price Competition and Patent Term Restoration Act of 1984*, 40 FOOD DRUG COSM. L.J. 269 (1985); Elizabeth

Stotland Weiswasser & Scott D. Danzis, *The Hatch–Waxman Act: History, Structure, and Legacy*, 71 ANTITRUST L.J. 585 (2003). FDA promulgated detailed regulations to implement the generic drug provisions of the statute in 54 Fed. Reg. 28872 (July 10, 1989), 57 Fed. Reg. 17950 (Apr. 28, 1992), codified at 21 C.F.R. Part 314, Subpart C.

2. *Eligibility for Abbreviated NDA.* When a pioneer drug is withdrawn from marketing by its manufacturer for reason of safety, it is automatically withdrawn from the FDA-approved drug list and can no longer be the subject of an abbreviated NDA. *See, e.g.,* 51 Fed. Reg. 21981 (June 17, 1986) (nomifensine maleate).

3. *Effect of Generic Drugs on Price.* FDA conducted a study, Generic Competition and Drug Prices (Apr. 4, 2006), in which the agency determined that the first generic competitor results in only about a 5 percent reduction in price, whereas the second brings the price down to about 50 percent of the pioneer drug price. By the sixth competitor, the price is only about 25 percent of the pioneer price. With a large number of competitors it can reach 10 percent or lower.

4. *Patent Term Restoration.* The Patent and Trademark Office has promulgated regulations implementing the patent provisions of the 1984 statute. 51 Fed. Reg. 27205 (July 30, 1986), 52 Fed. Reg. 9386 (Mar. 24, 1987), 59 Fed. Reg. 56015 (Nov. 10, 1994), 60 Fed. Reg. 25615 (May 12, 1995), codified at 37 C.F.R. 1.710 et seq. FDA promulgated regulations implementing the patent provisions of the 1984 statute for which it is responsible in 51 Fed. Reg. 25338 (July 11, 1986), 53 Fed. Reg. 7298 (Mar. 7, 1988), codified at 21 C.F.R. Part 60. FDA and the Patent and Trademark Office entered into a Memorandum of Understanding to coordinate implementation of these regulations. 52 Fed. Reg. 17830 (May 12, 1987). FDA regularly publishes in the Federal Register notices of the determinations of regulatory review periods for purposes of patent term extension.

5. *Statutory Extensions.* In addition to the general statutory patent term restoration provided by the 1984 statute, specific patent term extensions have been granted by congressional enactment for Forane in 97 Stat. 831, 832–33 (1983), Impro in 98 Stat. 3430 (1984), glyburide in 98 Stat. 3434 (1984), and Lopid in 102 Stat. 1107, 1569–70 (1988).

6. *Time and Cost for Development.* Development of the average NCE NDA drug takes some 15 years from preclinical research through NDA approval and costs in excess of $1.5 billion. The average generic drug takes 3–5 years from formulation through FDA approval of an abbreviated NDA and costs up to $500,000. Thus, a generic drug can be sold at a fraction of the cost of the pioneer drug. All of the research and development must be undertaken by the pioneer company. The generic company relies on that information and need only prove that its version of the drug is bioequivalent.

7. *Economic Impact.* In the first twenty years after enactment of the 1984 statute, FDA has approved over 8000 abbreviated NDAs. As more major pioneer drugs lose patent protection and are displaced by generic versions, and fewer pioneer drugs are being approved by FDA to take their place, *infra* p. 777, some have questioned whether the pioneer drug industry can sustain its current level of research and development. Even after patent term restoration under the 1984 Act, the current average effective patent life of an NCE NDA drug is only 11–12 years. This relatively brief period of market protection may not be long enough for a drug's sponsor to recoup the full research and development investment made in the drug other than by charging extremely high prices. *See infra* p. 776. At some point, Congress must reconsider the compromise made in the 1984 Act and find a new mechanism for assuring adequate market protection for NCE NDA drugs that will provide sufficient incentive for investment in research and development. *See* "Im-

proving Access to Generic Drugs," Hearing before the Senate Special Committee on Aging, 109th Cong. 2d Sess. (2006).

8. *Due Diligence*. Under 35 U.S.C. 156(d)(2)(B) any interested person may request a hearing to determine whether the NDA applicant has failed to act with "due diligence" in pursuing FDA approval. It appears that this provision has never formally been invoked.

9. *Correction of Regulatory Review Period*. In 2002, FDA initially determined the regulatory review period for Mifeprex and then, in response to a request for revision, recalculated the applicable regulatory review period. 67 Fed. Reg. 3724 (Jan. 25, 2002), 67 Fed. Reg. 65358 (Oct. 24, 2002). *See also* 65 Fed. Reg. 31010 (May 15, 2000).

10. *The 30–Month Stay*. Faced with criticism from the FTC and the generic drug industry, FDA amended its regulations to clarify the types of patents that must and may not be listed in the Orange Book and revised the declaration that NDA applicants must provide regarding their patents to help ensure that only appropriate patents are listed. 67 Fed. Reg. 65448 (Oct. 24, 2002), 68 Fed. Reg. 36676 (June 18, 2003). The new regulations stated that there would be only one opportunity for a 30–month stay in the approval date of an ANDA or section 505(b)(2) NDA as the result of patent litigation. This change was a response to pioneer companies' practice of obtaining multiple patents covering different features or variants of the same drug, listing them in the Orange Book at different times, and thus enjoying numerous sequential 30–month stays. These regulations were subsequently superceded by Congress in 117 Stat. 2066, 2448 (2003), discussed *infra* at p. 768.

11. *In Vivo Bioequivalence Test*. The conventional test to determine the bioequivalence of a generic drug involves giving oral doses to 24–36 healthy human volunteers. The 90 percent confidence intervals for the peak serum concentration (Cmax) and area under the plasma concentration-time curve (AUC) of a generic formulation must fall within 80 percent to 125 percent of those of the reference listed drug (RLD) specified in the Orange Book. In a letter from FDA Associate Commissioner for Regulatory Affairs Dennis Baker to Sharon W. Brown & Mary Mathisen, FDA Docket No. 98P–0434/CPI & PSAI (Mar. 17, 2000), the agency defended the use of these criteria to determine bioequivalence. An FDA-approved ANDA drug with an "A" rating is bioequivalent to the pioneer drug. A "B" rated ANDA drug has not been shown to be bioequivalent to the reference pioneer by an in vivo test and therefore is not considered by FDA to be therapeutically equivalent to the pioneer RLD. All "A" rated drugs are considered by FDA to be therapeutically equivalent to the RLD.

12. *Orange Book Listing*. With judicial approval, FDA has taken the position that its task of listing submitted patents in the Orange Book is ministerial and that it is not obligated to determine the relevance or accuracy of the patent information submitted to it.

13. *Change in Bioavailability Standards*. FDA has on occasion sought to relax the bioequivalence requirements for generic drugs. For example, FDA has previously required in vivo testing to demonstrate the bioequivalence of antibiotic drugs, which treat serious life-threatening infections. In a letter from FDA CDER Office of Generic Drugs Director Gary J. Buehler to Timothy J. Smith (Mar. 7, 2006) FDA announced that it would waive in vivo bioequivalence testing if the generic drug is rapidly dissolving under the conditions specified in an FDA guidance. The manufacturer of the pioneer RLD contested this decision by submitting a citizen petition. FDA Docket No. 2006P–0124 (May 31, 2006).

14. *First Generic Drug Market Exclusivity.* Section 505(j)(5)(B)(iv) provides that the first generic applicant to file a "Paragraph IV certification"—a certification in the ANDA that the pioneer's listed patent is invalid or will not be infringed—receives 180 days of market exclusivity for its generic drug, during which no other abbreviated NDA for the same generic drug product may be approved. This period of market exclusivity is extremely valuable. As the FDA statistics mentioned *supra* in Note 3 demonstrate, generic manufacturers typically undercut the price of the pioneer drug by only about 5 percent during their exclusive marketing period, but then are forced to reduce the price by 50 percent or more as other generic manufacturers receive approvals of their abbreviated NDAs. For a thorough analysis of this statutory provision and its numerous judicial interpretations, *see* Erika King Lietzan, *A Brief History of 180-Day Exclusivity Under the Hatch–Waxman Amendments*, 59 FOOD & DRUG L.J. 287 (2004); Erika King Lietzan & David E. Korn, *Issues in the Interpretation of 180-Day Exclusivity*, 62 FOOD & DRUG L.J. 49 (2007).

15. *Citizen Petitions.* It is common for the manufacturer of a pioneer drug to submit a citizen petition asking FDA to adopt rigorous testing requirements for a generic applicant to demonstrate bioequivalence to the pioneer drug. In 64 Fed. Reg. 66822 (Nov. 30, 1999), FDA proposed significantly to restrict the use of citizen petitions. Because citizen petitions are the very heart of the FDA administrative procedure regulations, however, the agency took no further action on this proposal. Nonetheless, the agency continues to consider ways in which citizen petitions for bioequivalence requirements could be limited. When FDA decides to deny a citizen petition, it usually does so on the same day that it approves the abbreviated NDA for the generic drug. The pioneer manufacturer inevitably immediately brings suit and requests a temporary restraining order. *E.g., Somerset Pharmaceuticals, Inc. v. Shalala*, 973 F. Supp. 443 (D. Del. 1997).

16. *Extensive Litigation.* Because of the large economic impact of the 1984 statute, all aspects of this legislation have provoked extensive litigation. We focus here on a few leading cases, and make no attempt to cite or summarize all of the voluminous court decisions that have resulted.

17. *Eligibility for Extension.* In the first cases it decided under the 1984 Act, the United States Court of Appeals for the Federal Circuit held that 35 U.S.C. 156(a)(5)(A) precludes patent term restoration for a second approved use after the new drug was initially approved for another use, and that the provisions in 35 U.S.C. 271(e)(1) allow a manufacturer to test a patent holder's device (or drug) to obtain information to support FDA approval of a substitute product, prior to expiration of the patent. *Fisons plc v. Quigg*, 876 F.2d 99 (Fed. Cir. 1989); *Eli Lilly and Co. v. Medtronic, Inc.*, 872 F.2d 402 (Fed. Cir. 1989), *aff'd* 496 U.S. 661 (1990).

18. *Copyright.* In *SmithKline Beecham Consumer Healthcare v. Watson Pharmaceuticals, Inc.*, 211 F.3d 21 (2d Cir. 2000), the pioneer drug company sought to prevent a generic competitor from using copyrighted materials developed for its nonprescription drug product that was subject to an NDA. The Court of Appeals held that the Drug Price Competition and Patent Term Restoration Act of 1984 requires generic drug manufacturers to use the same labeling as the pioneer drug even if that use may infringe a copyright held by the pioneer drug company. The Court of Appeals further held that the pioneer company may not obtain damages. *But see* John C. O'Quinn, *Protecting Private Intellectual Property from Government Intrusion: Revisiting SmithKline and the Case for Just Compensation*, 29 PEPP. L. REV. 435 (2002).

19. *Authorized Generic Drugs.* When a pioneer NDA drug approaches the end of its patent coverage, a common response by the pioneer manufacturer is to license a generic drug company immediately to begin marketing a generic version in order to preserve as much of the market as possible. If another generic company has

challenged the pioneer company's patent for the drug and as a result obtained the statutory right to a 180–day period of market exclusivity before any other generic product may be approved by FDA, the licensing of the authorized generic drug substantially reduces the value of this period of market exclusivity. Nonetheless, the courts have upheld the legality of immediate marketing of an authorized generic. *E.g., Teva Pharmaceuticals Industries Ltd. v. Crawford*, 410 F.3d 51 (D.C. Cir. 2005). *See* John R. Thomas, *Authorized Generic Pharmaceuticals: Effects on Innovation*, CRS REP. No. RL33605 (Aug. 8, 2006). Under the Deficit Reduction Act of 2005, 120 Stat. 4 (2006), the average manufacturer price (AMP) and the best price for the pioneer manufacturer's drug under the Medicaid Rebate Law must take into account the price of the authorized generic drug. *See* Jeffrey N. Wasserstein & Kurt R. Karst, *New Law Reigns In "Authorized Generics" Despite Generic Industry Court Losses, But Leaves Several Ambiguities*, 11 REG. AFFAIRS FOCUS, No. 6, at 8 (June 12, 2006).

20. *Complex Mixtures.* For generic versions of several complex mixtures, FDA has required the submission of a section 505(b)(2) NDA or a full NDA rather than an abbreviated NDA, because the generic version could not be shown to be the same as the pioneer drug. Examples include digoxin, Premarin, and levothryoxine. In *Serono Laboratories, Inc. v. Shalala*, 158 F.3d 1313 (D.C. Cir. 1998), however, the Court of Appeals upheld the legality of an abbreviated NDA for a complex mixture extracted from the urine of post-menopausal women where the generic version had demonstrable differences from the pioneer drug.

21. *The Research Use Exemption.* The Supreme Court has broadly interpreted the research use exemption from the patent law in 35 U.S.C. 271(e)(1), which allows a manufacturer to test a competitor's patented drug prior to expiration of the patent to obtain information to support FDA approval of a generic product. In *Eli Lilly and Co. v. Medtronic, Inc.*, 496 U.S. 661 (1990), the Supreme Court held that this exemption applies to medical devices as well as to drugs. In *Merck KGaA v. Integra Lifesciences I, Ltd.*, 545 U.S. 193 (2005), the Supreme Court held that drug discovery using a patented research tool is similarly eligible for this exemption. The lower courts have also provided broad interpretations of this exemption.

22. *New Indications For Use.* It is common for a pioneer drug manufacturer to seek FDA approval of new indications through submission of supplemental NDAs following FDA approval of the original NDA. In *Bristol–Myers Squibb Co. v. Shalala*, 91 F.3d 1493 (D.C. Cir. 1996), the Court of Appeals held that FDA may approve an abbreviated NDA for the original indication, for which the patent and market exclusivity have expired, even if later indications retain patent protection or market exclusivity. The approved abbreviated NDA must be limited to indications for which there is no patent or market exclusivity protection. As a practical matter, however, this means that a physician may prescribe the generic drug for all of the indications, including those protected by a patent or market exclusivity, and thus the additional indications obtained by the pioneer company's supplemental NDAs are of little value. It is for this reason that pioneer manufacturers do not submit supplemental NDAs for new indications unless there is a substantial amount of patent protection time remaining on the original NDA.

23. *Statutory Patent Term.* At the time that the Drug Price Competition and Patent Term Restoration Act was enacted, the statutory patent term was 17 years from the date of issue. In 1994, to comply with an international treaty, Congress enacted the Uruguay Round Agreements Act, 108 Stat. 4809 (1994), 35 U.S.C. 156, to extend the patent term in the United States to 20 years from the filing of the patent. In 60 Fed. Reg. 37652 (July 21, 1995), FDA announced that pre-1995 patent holders could not take advantage of the additional three years of patent extension. *Merck & Co., Inc. v. Kessler*, 80 F.3d 1543 (Fed. Cir. 1996), overruled FDA on this

matter. FDA then revised its policy to conform with the court's decision. 62 Fed. Reg. 12216 (Mar. 14, 1997). *See also DuPont Merck Pharmaceutical Co. v. Bristol–Myers Squibb Co.*, 62 F.3d 1397 (Fed. Cir. 1995).

In 2003, FDA amended its regulations on Orange Book listings and the availability of 30–month stays on the approval of ANDAs containing Paragraph IV certifications. 67 Fed. Reg. 65448 (Oct. 24, 2002), 68 Fed. Reg. 36676 (June 18, 2003). The amended regulations accomplished the following FDA objectives. First, they permitted only one 30–month stay per NDA or section 505(b)(2) NDA. Second, they prevented the submission of information on patents claiming packaging, intermediates, or metabolites. Third, they permitted the submission of patents claiming alternate polymorphic forms of the active ingredient found in the NDA and required information demonstrating that a drug product containing the polymorph will perform the same as the drug product described in the NDA. Fourth, they amended the patent information required to be submitted to FDA and provided declaration forms for submitting that information to ensure that only those patents claiming the approved drug product and its approved uses are listed in the Orange Book. Fifth, except in the case of method-of-use-patents, the regulations did not require a claim-by-claim declaration. All of these changes were designed to reduce what FDA regarded as abuse of the 1984 Act by the pioneer pharmaceutical industry.

Congress then amended the Drug Price Competition and Patent Term Restoration Act of 1984 as part of the Medicare Prescription Drug, Improvement, and Modernization Act of 2003, 117 Stat. 2066, 2448. First, Congress codified the FDA regulation providing that only one 30–month stay is permitted for each abbreviated NDA. Second, an abbreviated NDA applicant who makes a Paragraph IV certification must give notice to the pioneer manufacturer and the patent owner within 20 days after FDA files the abbreviated NDA. (It is this notice that starts the 45–day period during which the pioneer manufacturer must bring suit in order to obtain a 30–month stay.) Third, if the pioneer manufacturer does not exercise its right to bring a patent infringement suit within the 45–day period, the statute permits an abbreviated NDA applicant to bring a declaratory judgment action to determine the validity of the patent. (Many concluded that this provision is unconstitutional because, if the pioneer manufacturer does not bring suit for infringement, there is no case or controversy to be adjudicated.) Fourth, if the pioneer manufacturer sues the generic drug manufacturer, the latter may bring a counterclaim seeking an order requiring the pioneer manufacturer to delete from the Orange Book any patent that does not claim the approved drug or method of using the drug. Fifth, the 180–day market exclusivity that is of such economic importance to a generic manufacturer begins on the date of first commercial marketing of either the abbreviated NDA product or the NDA product (in the event that the generic manufacturer enters into an agreement with the pioneer manufacturer to market the NDA product instead of the generic version). Sixth, if the generic manufacturer fails to market its drug in a timely manner, the 180–day market exclusivity period is subject to forfeiture, as it is under other specified conditions. Seventh, when two abbreviated NDAs are submitted on the same day, each will share the 180–day market exclusivity, which will begin whenever either first begins marketing. Finally, to permit monitoring under the antitrust laws, agreements between pioneer and generic manufacturers that could violate the antitrust laws are required to be filed with the FTC and the Department of Justice within ten days of their execution.

In 69 Fed. Reg. 64314 (Nov. 4, 2004), FDA announced the availability of a Draft Guidance titled LISTED DRUGS, 30–MONTH STAYS, AND APPROVAL OF ANDAS AND 505(B)(2) APPLICATIONS UNDER HATCH-WAXMAN, AS AMENDED BY THE MEDICARE PRESCRIPTION DRUG, IMPROVEMENT, AND MODERNIZATION ACT OF 2003— QUESTIONS AND ANSWERS. The purpose of the Draft Guidance was to implement the earlier FDA regulations and the more recent statutory amendments. For a discussion of the problems intended to be addressed by the new FDA regulations and the congressional solutions, see "Examining Issues Related to Competition in the Pharmaceutical Marketplace: A Review of the FTC Report, Generic Drug Entry Prior to Patent Expiration," Hearing before the Subcommittee on Health of the House Committee on Energy and Commerce, 107th Cong., 2d Sess. (2002); "Closing the Gaps in Hatch–Waxman: Assuring Greater Access to Affordable Pharmaceuticals," Hearing before the Senate Committee on Health, Education, Labor, and Pensions, 107th cong., 2d Sess. (2002); Aidan Hollis, *Closing the FDA's Orange Book*, 24 REGULATION, No. 4, at 14 (Winter 2001); Hassen A. Sayeed, *A Summary of Recent Changes to the Drug Price Competition and Patent Term Restoration Act of 1984* (2004), in Chapter VI(C)(4) of the Electronic Book; Wendy H. Schacht & John R. Thomas, *The Hatch–Waxman Act: Legislative Changes in the 108th Congress Affecting Pharmaceutical Patents*, CRS REP. No. RL 32377 (Apr. 30, 2004).

NOTES

1. *Alternative Methods of Demonstrating Bioequivalence.* Section 505(j)(8)(B) provides that a drug shall be considered to be bioequivalent to an RLD if the rate and extent of absorption of the drug do not show a significant difference from rate and extent of absorption of the listed drug or if the extent of absorption does not show a significant difference and the difference in the rate of absorption is intentional, reflected in the proposed labeling, and medically insignificant. In *Schering Corp. v. FDA*, 782 F. Supp. 645 (D.D.C. 1992), 995 F.2d 1103 (D.C. Dir. 1993), 51 F.3d 390 (3d Cir. 1995), the Third Circuit agreed with FDA that, for a non-systemically effective drug (NSED) that derives its effectiveness from application directly at the site of drug action rather than through systemic absorption into the bloodstream, the agency may substitute for the statutory reference to rate and extent of drug absorption the rate and extent to which a drug becomes available at the site of drug action. In *Pfizer, Inc. v. Shalala*, 1 F. Supp. 2d 38 (D.D.C. 1998), the District Court held that FDA was justified in finding that a generic version of a sustained-release drug provided the "same" dosage as the RLD despite a different release mechanism. *See also Bristol–Myers Squibb Co. v. Shalala*, 923 F. Supp. 212 (D.D.C. 1996); *Zeneca Inc. v. Shalala*, 1999 WL 728104 (D. Md. 1999).

2. *The Active Ingredient.* In *Glaxo Operations UK Limited v. Quigg*, 894 F.2d 392 (Fed. Cir. 1990), the Court of Appeals concluded that, in determining whether an active ingredient is the same as a previously-approved active ingredient or is a

new active ingredient, the statute refers to the substance as it is formulated in the drug product and not as it is subsequently metabolized in the gut.

3. *Market Exclusivity for a New Indication.* Section 505(j)(5)(F)(iv) provides that a supplemental NDA containing reports of new clinical investigations (other than bioavailability studies) "essential" to the approval of the supplement and conducted by the sponsor is entitled to three years of market exclusivity from the date of approval of the supplemental NDA. In *Upjohn Co. v. Kessler*, 938 F. Supp. 439 (W.D. Mich. 1996), the District Court held that the administrative record supported the conclusion that the study conducted by the company was not "essential" to approval.

4. *Recalculation of Patent Extension.* In *Astra v. Lehman*, 71 F.3d 1578 (Fed. Cir. 1995), the Court of Appeals held that the PTO could not be required to recalculate the applicable patent extension under the 1984 Act because the statute assigns exclusive authority to HHS to determine the regulatory review period, and the manufacturer did not contest that determination.

5. *Case or Controversy.* In *Teva Pharmaceuticals USA, Inc. v. Pfizer, Inc.*, 395 F.3d 1324 (Fed. Cir. 2005), the Court of Appeals held that there was no constitutionally-required case or controversy where the pioneer manufacturer did not sue the generic applicant within the 45–day period.

6. *FDA Waiver.* As part of its regulations, FDA included 21 C.F.R. 320.22(b), which authorizes FDA to waive the submission of evidence demonstrating in vivo bioequivalence. The courts have upheld the authority of FDA to grant such a waiver. *E.g.*, *Fisons Corp. v. Shalala*, 860 F. Supp. 859 (D.D.C. 1994). *See also Somerset Pharmaceuticals, Inc. v. Shalala*, 973 F. Supp. 443 (D. Del. 1997).

7. *Patent Notice in Labeling.* In order to prevent innocent infringement of patents, Congress enacted 35 U.S.C. 287 to provide for notice that an article is patented by placing on the article the word "patent" or the abbreviation "pat." together with the number of the patent. Absent such notice, no damages may be recovered by the patentee in any action for infringement unless the infringer was notified of the infringement.

3.   SECTION 505(b)(2) NDAs

When Congress enacted the Drug Price Competition and Patent Term Restoration Act of 1984, it included a provision modeled after, and arguably meant to codify, the concept of a paper NDA, but which FDA has interpreted expansively. The former paper NDA is therefore now called a section 505(b)(2) NDA, after the statutory provision that created it. It provides for applications in those situations where a pioneer drug has lost patent protection and market exclusivity but the modified drug differs in some way from the pioneer drug. A section 505(b)(2) NDA relies on the pioneer NDA for all required information except the data needed to support the difference. Thus, a section 505(b)(2) NDA need not include any data supporting the basic safety and effectiveness of the drug, except insofar as the difference between the pioneer drug product and the applicant's modification of that drug product bears upon safety or effectiveness.

As discussed p. 760 *supra*, FDA may approve an abbreviated NDA for a generic drug that differs in minor ways from the RLD in response to the filing of a "suitability petition". If the differences are substantial, however, FDA will deny the suitability petition and require a more complete application. In these circumstances, the section 505(b)(2) paper NDA will suffice, and a full NDA will not be required. Thus, the section 505(b)(2) NDA is mid-way between a full NDA and an abbreviated NDA. The same requirements apply to a section 505(b)(2) paper NDA under the 1984 Act as apply to a full NDA. FDA interprets section 505(b)(2) to authorize the agency to rely on confidential commercial information in a pioneer NDA in order to approve a generic competitor's version of the drug. The pioneer pharmaceutical industry takes the position that this would be unlawful under the FD&C Act. This disagreement must ultimately be resolved in the courts.

NOTES

1. *Frequency of Use.* For the decade following its enactment, section 505(b)(2) was rarely used. Since the 1990s, however, generic drug companies have sought to use it in innovative ways. First, competitors to a pioneer prescription drug have sought to switch the drug to OTC status using the section 505(b)(2) NDA. Second, competitors have also sought to add a new indication, change the dosage or delivery form, or make other changes to a pioneer drug through a section 505(b)(2) NDA.

2. *Substitution.* As noted *supra* Note 11 p. 765, a generic drug that is the "same" as and "bioequivalent" to a pioneer drug is rated "A" and thus can be substituted by doctors and pharmacists for the pioneer drug. In contrast, a drug approved under section 505(b)(2) cannot be rated "A" because it is not therapeutically equivalent to the pioneer drug and thus cannot be substituted in the same way as an abbreviated NDA drug.

3. *Application to Biological Products.* As discussed in greater detail p. 891 *infra*, Congress explicitly determined to exclude biological products from sections 505(b)(2) and (j) when it enacted the Drug Price Competition and Patent Term Restoration Act of 1984. FDA has stated that the Act must be amended before generic biological products can lawfully be approved through either of these two provisions. *See, e.g.,* "The Law of Biologic Medicine," Hearing before the Senate Committee on the Judiciary, 108th Cong., 2d Sess. 133–34 (2004). This was confirmed with the passage of the FDA Modernization Act of 1997, in which Congress added section 351(j) to the Public Health Service Act stating that a biological product is not subject to the NDA provisions of FD&C Act 505 and, in an uncodified provision, mandated that FDA minimize differences in the review and approval of products required to have an approved biologics license under section 351 of the Public Health Service Act and products required to have an approved NDA under section 505(b)(1) of the FD&C Act, but not sections 505(b)(2) or (j). FDA Modernization Act 123(f), 111 Stat. 2296, 2324,

4. *Biological Products Subject to an NDA.* A small number of biological products are marketed pursuant to an NDA rather than a biological products license (BLA). These include human growth hormone (HGH), for which an NDA was obtained as one of the earliest approvals for a drug made through recombinant DNA, and insulin, which became subject to an NDA when Congress repealed former section 506 of the FD&C Act as part of the FDA Modernization Act of 1997. Because these products are subject to NDAs, FDA must handle applications for generic versions of them and a few others. On May 30, 2006, FDA approved a section 505(b)(2) NDA for a generic version of recombinant HGH. In doing so, FDA emphasized that this was not a precedent for generic biological products licensed under section 351 of the Public Health Service Act.

J. IMPACT OF THE 1962 DRUG AMENDMENTS

1. THE "DRUG LAG"

Within a few years after enactment of the Drug Amendments of 1962 physicians began to complain that, because of the new drug approval process, drugs were being introduced into foreign markets substantially earlier than into the United States. This became known as the "drug lag."

Statement of Sam Peltzman*

"Competitive Problems in the Drug Industry," Hearings before the Subcommittee on Monopoly of the Senate Small Business Committee, 93d Cong., 1st Sess. (1973).

[T]he benefits provided by the [1962] amendments seem clearly outweighed by the costs they have engendered.... As I hope to make clear, consumers could not have avoided losses under the most efficient and well-intentioned administration of the law....

It is beyond dispute that new drug innovation in the United States has declined since 1962. The 15 years prior to 1962 saw an average of 42 new chemical entities marketed per year compared to 16 in the subsequent decade. What is in dispute is the connection of this decline to the 1962 amendments. Innovation was declining from 1959 to 1962, and it is sometimes thought that the post-1962 experience might simply be a continuation of a previous trend. However, my research has led me to reject this explanation. I found that prior to 1962 there was a regular, highly predictable relationship between the rate of drug innovation in any year and previous growth in the market for drugs.... Subnormal growth in prescription sales led—with a lag of about two years, that being the average development time for new drugs—to subnormal innovation. That relationship held closely in the 1959–62 period and accounts fully for the decline in innovation: growth of the drug market peaked in the mid 1950's and declined to about 1960. However, unlike the pre-1962 period, the resumption of drug market growth in the early 1960s did not subsequently lead to increased innovation....

... [I]t appears that the Amendments are preventing development of something like 25 new chemical entities for the U.S. drug market annually. I will argue subsequently that only a small fraction of the sales of those drugs would likely prove ineffective.... [This] means that the amendments' proof of efficiency and clinical testing requirements impose costs on the drug development process which discourage new drug development. I have estimated that the R. & D. costs for developing a new chemical entity have been about doubled by the added testing and information requirements of the Amendments.... It is simply unreasonable to expect a cost increase of this magnitude not to discourage development of new drugs,

* [Sam Peltzman is a Professor of Economics at the University of Chicago Graduate School of Business.]

effective as well as ineffective.... Even if an effective new drug could be developed, neither the FDA nor the consumer will hear of it if its prospective returns cannot defray added development costs....

... If the pre-1962 rate of innovation had been maintained, annual sales of new drugs in their initial full year of marketing would, given the larger size of today's drug market, approximate $125 million.... The comparable post-1962 figure is about $50 million.... [I]f one assumes that about 10 percent of the pre-1962 drug sales were for ineffective drugs ... and that none of the post-1962 drugs are ineffective ... then the decline in sales of effective new drugs due to the Amendments is over $60 million per year. My net benefit estimate of 50 percent of sales then applies a benefit loss exceeding $30 million on new drugs in their initial year of marketing. This loss will recur each year that new drugs remain on the market and sales remain $60 million lower.... [A]ssuming that these new drugs have level sales and a market life of 15 years ..., the total benefits sacrificed due to reduced innovation in a single year would exceed $450 million into a present value of about $250 million.... In addition ... because the amendments have been such an effective barrier to new competition for existing drugs, price rivalry in the drug market has been weakened. My estimate of the consumer cost of the resulting high prices for old and new drugs is about $50 million per year.

The benefits attributable to the Amendments must, of course, be set against this ... cost. I used two approaches to estimate the waste on ineffective new drugs prior to 1962. One was the test of the marketplace.... If a new drug is ineffective, one would expect some reduction in prescribing for it as physicians accumulate evidence ... of its ineffectiveness.... If the Amendments screened ineffective drugs out, one would then find sales of pre-1962 new drugs taken together growing more slowly over time than their post-1962 counterparts.... I will not burden the committee with this calculation, because the plain fact is that the difference in market acceptance between pre-and post-1962 drugs is trivial....

... I turned to drug evaluations by experts—specifically the AMA Council on Drugs. A highly skeptical layman's reading of their *Drug Evaluations* turned up 16 of 80 new chemical entities introduced 1960–62 which could be labeled either ineffective, or no more effective than a cheaper alternative. The total consumer waste on these drugs—expenditures on the eight ineffective drugs, and the price premium for the eight equally effective but more expensive drugs—scaled to the 1970 drug market was under $20 million annually.... [U]nlike most new drugs, sales of the ineffective drugs decline markedly over time.... Taking both this decline and the difference between present and future losses into account, I arrive at a present value of well under $100 million for the total waste imposed on consumers....

The extravagant potential costs of the risk-tradeoff in the Amendments can be illustrated by first examining its potential benefits in forestalling something like the thalidomide tragedy.... [T]he thalidomide tragedy was, in fact, forestalled in the United States without the Amendments. But if we ... consider what might have been, and ... assume that the thalidomide tragedy here might have been as widespread as it was in West Germany ...

we could have expected the birth of about 20,000 phocomelic infants on a 1970 population base. . . . If we further make the extreme assumption that none of these infants would be at all productive in adulthood, I estimate the present value of the economic cost of this hypothetical event at between $150 and $500 million. . . . Now, if we are going to assume that the Amendments completely eliminate the potential for such tragedies, we must gauge the frequency with which such a tragedy could otherwise be expected to occur in order to evaluate the prospective benefits. . . . Since a tragedy as profound as thalidomide has in fact never occurred in the United States, this must be largely conjectural. . . . [W]e could attribute to the Amendments a potential for preventing something like 10,000 deaths or serious disabilities and an economic loss of something like $300 million perhaps once per decade. . . .

NOTES

1. *FDA Risk Aversion.* Peltzman's study prompted Professor Milton Friedman to write in the January 8, 1973 issue of *Newsweek:*

> Put yourself in the position of an FDA official charged with approving or disapproving a new drug. You can make two very different kinds of serious mistakes:
>
> 1. Approve a drug that turns out to have unanticipated side effects resulting in death or serious impairment of a sizable number of persons.
>
> 2. Refuse approval of a drug that is capable of saving many lives or relieving great distress and has no untoward side effects. . . .
>
> With visions of the thalidomide episode dancing in your head and the knowledge of the fame and acclaim that came to the woman who held up approval of thalidomide in the U.S., is there any doubt which mistake you will be more anxious to avoid? With the best will in the world, you will be led to reject or postpone approval of many a good drug in order to avoid even a remote possibility of approving a drug that will have newsworthy side effects. . . .

2. *Drug Lag Literature.* The literature dealing with the "drug lag" is extensive, and the conclusions reached about the impact of FDA's implementation of the 1962 Amendments conflicting. For statements of both sides of the issue, compare Donald Kennedy, *A Calm Look at "Drug Lag,"* 239 J.A.M.A. 423 (1978), with William M. Wardell, *A Close Inspection of the "Calm Look,"* 239 J.A.M.A. 2004 (1978). In addition to Peltzman's work, see William M. Wardell and Louis C. Lasagna, REGULATION AND DRUG DEVELOPMENT (AEI, 1975). In June 1979, representatives of the General Accounting Office provided a prepublication look at a study it had undertaken, which concluded that Americans wait significantly longer than citizens of other developed countries for important new drugs to obtain approval. *See* "Review of the United States General Accounting Office of the Food and Drug Administration's Drug Approval Process," Subcommittee on Science, Research and Technology of the House Committee on Science and Technology, 96th Cong., 1st Sess. (1979). The final GAO report expressed the same view. FDA DRUG APPROVAL—A LENGTHY PROCESS THAT DELAYS THE AVAILABILITY OF IMPORTANT NEW DRUGS (1980). *See also* Hans Berlin & Bengt Jonsson, *International Dissemination of New Drugs: A Comparative Study of Six Countries,* 7 MANAGERIAL & DECISION ECON. 235 (1986); Arthur E. Hass, et al., *A Historical Look at Drug Introductions on a Five–Country*

Market: A Comparison of the United States and Four European Countries (1960–1981), FDA OPE Study No. 60 (Mar. 1982); Louis C. Lasagna, *The Development and Regulation of New Medications*, 200 Science 871 (1978); Nancy Mattison et al., *New Drug Development in the United States, 1963 through 1984*, 43 Clinical Pharmacology & Therapeutics 290 (Mar. 1988); Loren Miller et al., *Delays in the Drug Approval Process: Recent Trends*, 2 J. Clinical Res. & Drug Dev. 31 (1988); National Academy of Sciences, The Competitive Status of the U.S. Pharmaceutical Industry (1983); J.E.S. Parker, *Regulating Pharmaceutical Innovation: An Economist's View*, 32 Food Drug Cosm. L.J. 160 (1977); David Seidman, *The Politics of Policy Analysis: Protection or Overprotection in Drug Regulation?*, 1 Regulation, No. 1, at 22 (July/August 1977); Leonard G. Shifrin and Jack R. Tayan, *The Drug Lag: An Interpretive Review of the Literature*, 7 Int. J. of Health Serv. 359 (1977); Joseph M. Jadlow, *Competition and "Quality" in the Drug Industry: The 1962 Kefauver-Harris Drug Amendments as Barriers to Entry*, 5 Antitrust L. & Econ. Rev. 103 (Winter 1971–72); William M. Wardell, *More Regulation or Better Therapies?*, Regulation (Sept./October 1979), at 25; David L. Weimer, *Safe—And Available—Drugs, in* Instead of Regulation (R. W. Poole, Jr., ed., 1982); S.N. Wiggins, *The Cost of Developing a New Drug* (PMA 1987). Some critics have even urged that the Act should be amended to repeal the requirement that new drugs be proved effective. *See* Richard Dorsey, *The Case of Deregulating Drug Efficacy*, 242 J.A.M.A. 1755 (1979).

3. *The Continuing Drug Lag Debate.* It is impossible to capture the enormous literature on the drug lag, but the following five studies will illustrate what has occurred in the past 15 years. First, FDA released a report on Timely Access To New Drugs In The 1990s: An International Comparison (Dec. 1995) which showed that of 214 NCEs approved in the United States, England, or both, 29 were approved in England but not the United States and 18 were approved in the United States but not England; of the 214 new drugs approved in the United States, Germany, or both, 34 have been approved in Germany but not the United States and 32 have been approved in the United States but not in Germany; and of the 214 new drugs that have been approved in the United States, Japan, or both, 82 have been approved in Japan but not in the United States and 62 have been approved in the United States but not in Japan. Of the 185 drugs that have been approved in at least one of the four countries from 1990 through 1994, Japan had first approval for 43 percent, the United States for 24 percent, England for 22 percent, and Germany for 11 percent. FDA argued that its report showed that the agency does not delay consumer access to important new drugs compared to other countries. Second, in Julie C. Defalco, Treatment Delayed, Treatment Denied: Therapeutical Lag and FDA's Performance, Competitive Enterprise Institute Healthcare Reform Project (Feb. 1997), the Competitive Enterprise Institute listed numerous new drugs approved elsewhere but not available in the United States, or approved much later in the United States than abroad, in order to dispute FDA's 1995 study. Third, in Tufts Center for the Study of Drug Development, *European and U.S. Approval Times for New Drugs are Virtually Identical*, 1 Impact Report 1 (Nov. 1999), it was concluded that the mean total approval time for 30 new drugs approved both by the EMEA (370 days) and the FDA (366 days) was virtually identical. Fourth, Kenneth I. Kaitin & Jeffrey S. Brown, *A Drug Lag Update*, 29 Drug Information J. 361 (1995) found that the United States continues to lag behind other countries in the introduction of new pharmaceutical products. Fifth, a study by Henry G. Grabowski & Y. Richard Wang, *The Quantity and Quality of Worldwide New Drug Introductions, 1982–2003*, 25 Health Affairs 452 (2006), concluded that the United States has become the leading market for first launch of high-quality NCEs.

4. *Congressional Budget Office.* For a thorough study of all aspects of the economics of drug development *see* CBO, RESEARCH AND DEVELOPMENT IN THE PHARMACEUTICAL INDUSTRY (2006).

5. *Impediments to Drug Research.* For a discussion of the political, social and regulatory (including liability) climate that inhibits contraceptive research in the United States, *see* Carl Djerassi, *The Bitter Pill*, 245 SCIENCE 356 (July 28, 1989).

2.   IND/NDA STATISTICS

To understand the impact of the Drug Amendments of 1962 and the regulatory requirements that law has spawned, it is necessary briefly to review the statistics relating to the average cost of an approved NDA, the annual number of approved NDAs, and the time devoted to IND testing and NDA review. Together, these statistics illustrate the enormous investment in time and money that is required to obtain FDA approval of an NDA for a new chemical entity (NCE) new drug.

a.   COST OF AN APPROVED NCE DRUG

There is as much debate about the cost of an approved NDA as there is about other aspects of the impact of the Drug Amendments of 1962. The most rigorous studies conducted on this issue make two key assumptions. First, they include all the research and development costs from failed or abandoned research along with the costs of successful research. Second, they include the opportunity costs, *i.e.*, the interest expense of the money invested in this research that could have been deployed elsewhere. Under these assumptions, researchers have arrived at the following figures:

Year of Survey	Author	Average Cost of NCE NDA
1976	Hansen	$137 million
1987	DiMasi	$319 million
1990	U.S. OTA	$445 million
1996	Lehman Brothers	$608 million
2000	DiMasi	$802 million
2000–2002	Bain & Co.	$1.7 billion

DiMasi also conducted a study, based on a 2005 survey, which determined that the average cost to develop a new biotechnology drug is $1.2 billion. Joseph A. DiMasi & Henry G. Grabowski, *The Cost of Biopharmaceutical R & D: Is Biotech Different?* (in press). Regardless of how each of these was calculated, it is apparent that the cost of an approved NCE NDA has risen far faster than inflation in the past three decades.

b.   NUMBER OF APPROVED NCE NDAs

The number of approved NCE NDAs from 1990 to 2005, according to the published FDA statistics, is disappointing when viewed in the light of the amount invested in research and development by the pharmaceutical industry and NIH, as shown on their respective websites.

Year	Approved NCE NDAs	Total PhRMA Members R&D Foreign & Domestic ($ Millions)	Total NIH Budget ($ Millions)
1990	23	8.4	7.6
1991	30	9.7	8.3
1992	26	11.5	8.9
1993	25	12.7	10.3
1994	21	13.4	11.0
1995	29	15.2	11.3
1996	53	17.0	12.0
1997	39	19.0	12.7
1998	30	21.0	13.6
1999	35	22.7	15.6
2000	27	26.0	17.8
2001	24	29.8	20.4
2002	17	31.0	23.3
2003	21	34.4	27.0
2004	36	37.0	27.9
2005	20	39.4	28.5
2006	18	N.A.	N.A.

These statistics confirm that the productivity of pharmaceutical research has declined substantially.

c. TIME DEVOTED TO IND TESTING AND NDA REVIEW

The median number of months taken by FDA to review and approve an NCE NDA over the past twenty years shows that user fees—first imposed in 1993—have had a substantial impact.

Year	Months
1986	32.9
1987	29.9
1988	27.2
1989	29.3
1990	24.3
1991	22.1
1992	22.6
1993	23.0
1994	17.5
1995	15.9
1996	14.3
1997	13.4
1998	12.0
1999	11.6
2000	15.6
2001	14.3
2002	16.3
2003	9.9
2004	11.5

Thus, under PDUFA, FDA has cut the NCE NDA review time by slightly less than 50 percent. The NCE NDA review time is, however, the smaller portion of the entire development time for a drug. Total development time must also take into consideration the time for nonclinical and clinical testing. Two studies by the Tufts Center for the Study of Drug Development considered the average clinical time alone—without considering the time for nonclinical testing required by FDA before an IND can be submitted. The first, Janice M. Reichert, *Trends in Development and Approval Times for New Therapeutics in the United States*, 2 NATURE REVIEWS 695 (2003), found the following average months of IND testing time from 1970 through 2001.

Year	Months of IND Time
1970–1971	39.9
1972–1973	41.9
1974–1975	50.5
1976–1977	65.3
1978–1979	55.4
1980–1981	42.7
1982–1983	61.6
1984–1985	71.7
1984–1987	64.4
1988–1989	86.3
1990–1991	76.2
1992–1993	82.4
1994–1995	92.5
1996–1997	79.4
1998–1999	70.9
2000–2001	63.6

In a subsequent study, the Tufts Center found that the average months of IND testing time had risen to 84.0 months in 2002–2004, thus cancelling out the gain made in the NDA review time under PDUFA. Tufts Center for the Study of Drug Development, *Longer Clinical Times are Extending Time to Market for New Drugs in U.S.*, 7 IMPACT REP., No. 6 (Nov./December 2005). Another study shows that the total drug development time—including nonclinical research and development as well as the IND/NDA time—was 8.1 years in 1960, 11.6 years in the 1970s, and 14.2 years in the 1980s and 1990s. Joseph A. DiMasi, *New Drug Development in the United States 1963 to 1999*, 69 CLINICAL PHARMACOLOGY & THERAPEUTICS 286 (2001)

3.   COST OF DRUGS FOR PATIENTS

Patients living in the United States pay a higher price for prescription new drugs than patients living anywhere else in the world. This is because the United States is the only country where the government does not set the price of drugs. We allow the free market to set the price, which means that the full cost of the research and development for a new drug is borne by United States citizens. We subsidize the research and development for these lifesaving products for the rest of the world.

With an annual budget of more than $28 billion, the National Institutes of Health (NIH) provides funds, often supplemented by university funds, for substantial university research that results in exclusive licenses to private companies who turn that research into profitable drugs. Some view this as an appropriate use of public tax dollars and academic funds, but others complain that the government and universities should control the price of the drugs resulting from their funding and should receive a larger royalty. *See* "Transfer of Technology from Federal Laboratories," Hearing before the Subcommittee on Technology and Competitiveness of the House Committee on Science, Space, and Technology, 102d Cong., 1st Sess. (1991); "The Federal Government's Investment in New Drug Research and Development: Are We Getting Our Money's Worth?," Hearing before the Senate Special Committee on Aging, 103d Cong., 1st Sess. (1993); "Pricing of Drugs Codeveloped by Federal Laboratories and Private Companies," Hearing before the Subcommittee on Regulation, Business Opportunities, and Technology of the House Committee on Small Business, 103d Cong., 1st Sess. (1993); Kenneth Sutherlin Dueker, *Biobusiness on Campus: Commercialization of University–Developed Biomedical Technologies*, 52 FOOD & DRUG L.J. 453 (1997); Christine G. Solt, *Conflicts of Interest in Industry–Sponsored Pharmaceutical Research at Academia Institutions: The Need for a Regulatory Approach to Conflict Management* (1995), Andrew Z. Michaelson, *The Law of the Lab: Using Zerit to Inform Technology Transfer* (2002), and Peter J. Klein, *An Empirical Analysis of Technology Transfer from U.S. Academic Medical Centers* (2005), in Chapter VI(C)(10) of the Electronic Book. To assure that government-sponsored research is translated into useful products for the country, Congress has passed a number of statutes, including the Stevenson–Wydler Technology Innovation Act of 1980, 94 Stat. 2311, the Bayh–Dole Act, 94 Stat. 3015 (1980), the Federal Technology Transfer Act of 1986, 100 Stat. 1785, and the National Technology Transfer Competitiveness Act of 1989, 103 Stat. 1352, 1674.

Surprisingly, once a drug loses its patent protection and market exclusivity in the United States, generic competition drives the price down to a point below the generic drug prices in virtually all other countries. Thus, we have a system that features very high prices for patented new drugs and very low prices for generic old drugs.

The high price of drugs in the United States has frustrated and angered citizens. Because of the large differential between the price of a drug in the United States and in all other countries, many consumers have sought to find sources of cheaper drugs from abroad. Americans' desire for more affordable foreign drugs has led to legislation to permit the lawful import of unapproved versions of NDA'd drugs, to the creation of organized programs to obtain these drugs, and to resort to internet pharmacies.

a.   STATUTORY LEGALIZATION OF IMPORTATION OF UNAPPROVED DRUGS

Congress has on three occasions enacted legislation to address this matter: (1) the Medicine Equity and Drug Safety Act of 2000, 114 Stat. 1549A–35, adding section 804 to the FD&C Act, (2) the Medicare Prescription Drug, Improvement and Modernization Act of 2003, 117 Stat. 2066, 2464, which replaced section 804 with a virtually identical substitute provision, and (3) section 535 of the FY 2007 appropriations statute for the Department of Homeland Security, 120 Stat. 1355 (2006), which for one year permits individuals personally to bring up to a 90–day supply of any drug from Canada, except for a biological product or a controlled substance. In both of the first two statutes, Congress required that, before the provision could take effect, the Secretary of HHS had to certify to Congress that its implementation would impose no risk to the public health and safety and that it would result in a significant reduction of the cost of prescription drugs to the American consumer. The Secretaries of HHS in both the Clinton and Bush Administrations determined that these certifications could not be made, and thus these laws have never been implemented. Nonetheless, Congress has continued to consider legislation of this type, particularly in election years. Interest has been particularly high among members of Congress from border states, whose constituents can see lower drug prices just a few miles away. The third provision simply codified the FDA personal import policy first adopted by the agency in 1954. For a more detailed discussion of these legislative measures, see Chapter XI.

NOTE

For a full discussion of drug importation as a solution to the high price of prescription drugs in the United States, *see* John E. Calfee, *The Grim Economics of Pharmaceutical Importation* (AEI, November 2003); Yee–Ho Irene Chan, *Reimportation of U.S. Pharmaceuticals: Political, Economic and Legal Perspectives* (2002), Rene J. Theriault, *Drug Reimportation: Prescription, Placebo or Poison?* (2002), Jennifer Pomerantz, *Reimportation: The Solution to the High Cost of Prescription Drugs?* (2004), Bryan Lee, *Reimportation: A First Step or Fake Step toward Transparency in the Prescription Drug Market?* (2005), Janna Kimberly Fishman, *Blame Canada? State Prescription Drug Importation Programs, the Federal Response, and Why Lawmakers Are Up in Arms* (2006), and Lauren Kim, *Reimportation of Prescription Drugs—Legislative, Executive, Judicial and Local Responses* (2006), in Chapter II(C)(2) of the Electronic Book.

b.   ORGANIZED IMPORT PROGRAMS AND INTERNET PHARMACY SALES

A wide variety of illegal programs have been established to import cheaper drugs into the United States. Some have been set up by counties and states, and others have relied on internet pharmacies in Canada and elsewhere. FDA considers all of these illegal. In the cases brought by state and local governments to obtain declaratory judgments, and in the cases brought by FDA to shut down rogue pharmacies, the agency has been uniformly successful. *See, e.g., In Re: Canadian Import Antitrust Litigation*, 385 F. Supp. 2d 930 (D. Minn. 2005), *aff'd* 2006 WL 3436309 (8th Cir. 2006); *United States v. Rx Depot, Inc.*, 290 F. Supp. 2d 1238, 297 F. Supp. 2d 1306 (D. Okla. 2003). The REPORT OF THE HHS TASK FORCE ON DRUG IMPORTATION, ordered by statute, strongly supported the FDA position on drug importation. *See* "Drug Importation: The Realities of Safety and Security," Hearing before the Senate Committee on Health, Education, Labor, and Pensions, 109th Cong., 1st Sess. (2005). *See generally* Jana

Kimberly Fishman, *Blame Canada?: State Prescription Drug Importation Programs, the Federal Response, and Why Lawmakers are Up in Arms* (2006), in Chapter II(C)(2) of the Electronic Book.

Malcolm Gladwell, *High Prices*

THE NEW YORKER, October 25, 2004, at 86.

. . . .

The problem with the way we think about prescription drugs begins with a basic misunderstanding about drug prices. The editorial board of the *Times* has pronounced them much too high; Marcia Angell calls them "intolerable." The perception that the drug industry is profiteering at the expense of the American consumer has given pharmaceutical firms a reputation on a par with that of cigarette manufacturers.

In fact, the complaint is only half true. The "intolerable" prices that Angel writes about are confined to the brand-name sector of the American drug marketplace. As the economists Patricia Danzon and Michael Furukawa recently pointed out in the journal *Health Affairs*, drugs still under patent protection are anywhere from twenty-five to forty per cent more expensive in the United States than in places like England, France, and Canada. Generic drugs are another story. Because there are so many companies in the United States that step in to make drugs once their patents expire, and because the price competition among those firms is so fierce, generic drugs here are among the cheapest in the world. And, according to Danzon and Furukawa's analysis, when prescription drugs are converted to over-the-counter status no other country even comes close to having prices as low as the United States.

It is not accurate to say, then, that the United States has higher prescription-drug prices than other counties. It is accurate to say only that the United States has a different pricing system from that of other countries. Americans pay more for drugs when they first come out and less as the drugs get older, while the rest of the world pays less in the beginning and more later. Whose pricing system is cheaper? It depends. If you are taking Mevacor for your cholesterol, the 20–mg. pill is two-twenty-five in America and less than two dollars if you buy it in Canada. But generic Mevacor (lovastatin) is about a dollar a pill in Canada and as low as sixty-five cents a pill in the United States. Of course, not every drug comes in a generic version. But so many important drugs have gone off-patent recently that the rate of increase in drug spending in the United States has fallen sharply for the past four years. And so many other drugs are going to go off-patent in the next few years—including the top-selling drug in this country, the anti-cholesterol medication Lipitor—that many Americans who now pay more for their drugs than their counterparts in other Western countries could soon be paying less.

The second misconception about prices has to do with their importance in driving up over-all drug costs. In one three-year period in the mid-nineteen-nineties, for example, the amount of money spent in the United States on asthma medication increased by almost a hundred per cent. But none of that was due to an increase in the price of asthma drugs. It was largely the result of an increase in the *prevalence* of usage—that is, in the number of people who were given a diagnosis of the disease and who then bought drugs to treat it. Part of that hundred-per-cent increase was also the result of a change in what's known as the *intensity* of drug use: in the mid-nineties, doctors were becoming far more aggressive in their attempts to prevent asthma attacks, and in those three years people with asthma went from filling about nine prescriptions a year to filling fourteen prescriptions a year. Last year, asthma costs jumped again, by twenty-six per cent, and price inflation played a role. But, once again, the big factor was prevalence. And this time around there was also a change in what's called the therapeutic mix; in an attempt to fight the disease more effectively, physicians are switching many of their patients to newer, better, and more expensive drugs, like Merck's Singulair.

Asthma is not an isolated case. In 2003, the amount that Americans spent on cholesterol-lowering drugs rose 23.8 per cent, and similar increases are forecast for the next few years. Why the increase? Well, the baby boomers are aging, and so are at greater risk for heart attacks. The incidence of obesity is increasing. In 2002, the National Institutes of Health lowered the thresholds for when people with high cholesterol ought to start taking drugs like Lipitor and Mevacor. In combination, those factors are having an enormous impact on both the prevalence and the intensity of cholesterol treatment. All told, prescription-drug spending in the United States rose 9.1 per cent last year. Only three of those percentage points were due to price increases, however, which means that inflation was about the same in the drug sector as it was in the over-all economy. Angell's book and almost every other account of the prescription-drug crisis take it for granted that cost increases are evidence of how we've been cheated by the industry. In fact, drug expenditures are rising rapidly in the United States not so much because we're being charged more for prescription drugs but because more people are taking more medications in more expensive combinations. It's not price that matters; it's volume.

This is a critical fact, and it ought to fundamentally change the way we think about the problem of drug costs. Last year, hospital expenditures rose by the same amount as drug expenditures—nine percent. Yet almost all of that (eight percentage points) was due to inflation. That's something to be upset about: when it comes to hospital services, we're spending more and getting less. When it comes to drugs, though, we're spending more and we're getting more, and that makes the question of how we ought to respond to rising drug costs a little more ambiguous. . . .

The fact that volume matters more than price also means that the emphasis of the prescription-drug debate is all wrong. We've been focussed on the drug manufacturers. But decisions about prevalence, therapeutic mix, and intensity aren't made by the producers of drugs. They're made by the consumers of drugs. . . .

NOTES

1. *Antitrust Issues.* For an unsuccessful attempt to attack the legality, under the antitrust laws, of a 478 percent increase in the price of an AIDS drug, see *Schor v. Abbott Laboratories Inc.*, 457 F.3d 608 (7th Cir. 2006).

2. *The Medicare Prescription Drug Benefit.* Under the Medicare Prescription Drug, Improvement, and Modernization Act of 2003, 117 Stat. 2066, 2071, Congress created an outpatient prescription drug benefit under Part D of the Social Security Act. Previously, only an inpatient prescription drug benefit was available under Part B. Under Part D, Medicare reimburses 75 percent of the cost of prescription drugs for $250 to $2,250 per year, nothing for $2,250 to $3,600, and 95 percent over $3,600. Private plans may negotiate prices with pharmaceutical manufacturers for drugs listed on their formularies, but the federal government may not do so. Part B remains unchanged. *See* Thomas M. Conroy Jr., *What's New in Medicare and Medicaid Reimbursement for Pharmaceuticals?*, 11 REG. AFFAIRS FOCUS, No. 6, at 20 (June 2006); William Gonzalez, *An Analysis of the Medicare Prescription Drug Improvement and Modernization Act of 2003: A Win–Win for the Elderly and the Prescription Drug Industry?* (2004), in Chapter VI(M)(2) of the Electronic Book;.

3. *Congressional Hearings.* Virtually all of the numerous hearings held by Congress during the past decade to consider legislation to permit the importation of unapproved foreign drugs have been in response to concern about the cost of prescription drugs. *See also* "Earning a Failing Grade: A Report Card on 1992 Drug Manufacturer Price Inflation," Staff Report to the Senate Special Committee on Aging, S. Print No. 103–14, 103d Cong., 1st Sess. (1993); "Prescription Drug Prices: Out–Pricing Older Americans," Hearing before the Senate Special Committee on Aging, 103d Cong., 1st Sess. (1993); "Drug Pricing: Poor Prescription for Consumers and Taxpayers?," Hearing before the Senate Committee on Governmental Affairs, 103d Cong., 2d Sess. (1994); "Prescription Drug Costs: What Drives Increases?," Hearing of the Senate Committee on Health, Education, Labor, and Pensions, 106th Cong., 2d Sess. (2000).

4. *Commentary.* For discussion of prescription drug pricing issues, see George H. Sung, *Should Prescription Drug Prices in the United States be Regulated? A Public Policy Debate* (1996), Bradley J. Fiorenzo, *Prescription Drug Pricing: How Much is Too Much?* (2000), Tarak Shah, *Equitable Division of International Joint Costs in Pharmaceutical Research and Development* (2004), and Patricia Young, *Perfect Price Discrimination for the Global Drug Market: Applying Economic Principles to Drive Innovation and Ensure Global Access* (2005), in Chapter VI(M)(1) of the Electronic Book. For discussion of the unique issues raised by the need to provide expensive patented AIDS drugs to Africa, see Theresa June Chung, *Shocking the Conscience of the World: International Norms and the Access to AIDS Treatment in South Africa* (2002), Andrew J. Chen, *U.S. Global AIDS Policy: Solutions in the National Interest* (2003), and John Doulamis, *Getting Back on the Path to Life: Negotiating the International Patent Regime to Provide Access to HIV Medicine to Africa* (2004), in Chapter II(C)(4) of the Electronic Book.

4. PATIENT "FREEDOM OF CHOICE"

Government control of market access for prescription drugs is designed to accomplish two objectives: (1) to prevent distribution of drugs that may affirmatively harm some consumers, and (2) to protect consumers against drugs that fail to perform as claimed. But these objectives are not achieved without costs to consumers.

Tutoki v. Celebrezze

375 F.2d 105 (7th Cir. 1967).

■ KILEY, CIRCUIT JUDGE. . . .

The original plaintiff, now deceased, was Geraldine Roy, a cancer patient residing in Arizona. . . .

The gist of the various claims is that defendants, under color of the Federal Food, Drug and Cosmetic Act of 1938, prevented the interstate shipment of Krebiozen and are continuing to do so by their unconstitutional and unlawful acts, to the detriment of plaintiffs, who are cancer patients.... The plaintiffs allege that defendants, acting under color of law but beyond their authority, coerced Dr. Stevan Durovic, sponsor of the drug Krebiozen, into withdrawing his application for an exemption to ship Krebiozen interstate; that defendants have imposed discriminatory, harsh and severe standards in testing Krebiozen so that it cannot obtain approval and were predetermined to refuse Krebiozen an exemption; that as a result plaintiffs, advised by their physicians to receive treatment with Krebiozen, have been forced to leave their homes in other states of their residence and come to Illinois to receive the necessary treatment, which has benefited them; that as a result defendants by this conduct have subjected plaintiffs to irreparable injury through "cruel and unusual punishment," violated their constitutional rights and caused physiological, psychological and proprietary damage; and that plaintiffs have no adequate remedy at law.

In the first five counts plaintiffs seek a declaratory judgment with respect to their rights and defendants' liabilities, and a declaratory judgment that section 505 of the Act is unconstitutional as applied to them and to Krebiozen. They also seek an injunction to restrain defendants from enforcing the section 505(a) prohibition against interstate shipment of Krebiozen....

The present posture of Krebiozen vis-a-vis the Food and Drug Administration (FDA) is that it is not approved under or exempted from section 505. The FDA has promulgated no order with respect to the drug, and no application of plaintiffs is pending before the agency.

An essential element of proof by plaintiffs would be a showing that if the FDA has passed upon Krebiozen according to statutory and constitutional standards, it would have been approved or exempted. The relief sought by plaintiffs therefore presupposes a determination by the district court that Krebiozen should be approved for interstate shipment or exempted from the prohibition pursuant to the standards Congress enacted in the Food, Drug and Cosmetic Act. This determination is a matter within the primary jurisdiction of the FDA....

... We hold that the district court did not err in dismissing the complaint....

NOTES

1. *Related Cases.* See also *Rutherford v. American Medical Association*, 379 F.2d 641 (7th Cir. 1967); *Durovic v. Richardson*, 479 F.2d 242 (7th Cir. 1973) (rejecting suits to restrain FDA from removing Krebiozen from commerce).

2. *Due Process of Law.* See the *Abigail Alliance* decision, *supra* p. 658, for a judicial decision applying the Due Process Clause to entitle terminally ill patients to purchase investigational drugs if the manufacturer is willing to sell them.

Peter Barton Hutt, *Laetrile Decision Ignores Constitutional Question*

LEGAL TIMES OF WASHINGTON, July 2, 1979.

Because of the obvious distasteful implications of an unproven cancer cure, it is all too easy to overlook the serious moral and ethical issues, and their constitutional implications, raised in the Laetrile litigation.... [C]ommercialization of an unproven anticancer drug, raising false hopes in the terminally ill is unconscionable.

Preemptory denial of a cancer victim's last wishes, on the other hand, raises equally serious questions....

It would be possible for the courts to fashion, from long-established constitutional doctrines, a requirement that FDA adopt the least stringent requirements for control of Laetrile necessary to achieve the intended beneficial purposes of the 1938 Act and the 1962 Amendments, *i.e.*, to prevent any commercialization of Laetrile or exploitation of cancer patients....

... [T]he rigid approach taken by FDA with Laetrile thus far has had other serious ramifications. A number of States have enacted laws designed to legalize Laetrile within their borders. Because Laetrile can readily be prepared from apricot seeds at any location, the interstate commerce requirements of the FD&C Act can easily be avoided....

NOTES

1. *Right of Privacy.* See People v. Privitera, 591 P.2d 919 (Cal. 1979), holding (5–2) that the constitutional right to privacy does not protect a cancer patient's desire to obtain and use Laetrile. While many cases were brought to enjoin FDA action against Laetrile, the agency itself mounted a vigorous enforcement effort against persons responsible for commercializing the drug. *See, e.g., United States v. Mosinee Research Corp.,* 583 F.2d 930 (7th Cir. 1978); *United States v. Spectro Foods Corp.,* 544 F.2d 1175 (3d Cir. 1976); *United States v. General Research Laboratories,* 397 F. Supp. 197 (C.D. Cal. 1975). In *Importation of Amygdalin,* FDA CONSUMER (Dec. 1979–January 1980), at 40 (S.D. Cal. 1977), the District Court ordered FDA to permit the importation of Laetrile solely for use by an individual *"who, by conclusive proof, is shown to be terminally ill with cancer and unresponsive to any recognized treatment presently available in the United States."* (Emphasis in original.)

2. *Commentary.* See Randi E. Block, *Laetrile: Individual Choice for Cancer Patients,* 7 N.Y.U. REV. L. & SOC. CHANGE 313 (1978); Barbara J. Clinite, *Freedom of Choice in Medical Treatment: Reconsidering the Efficacy Requirement of the FDCA,* 9 LOYOLA U. CHI. L.J. 205 (1977); Cecilia H. Eddy, *The Laetrile Controversy: Background and Issues,* 20 ARIZ. L. REV. 825 (1978); Note, *Restrictions on Unorthodox Health Treatment in California: A Legal and Economic Analysis,* 24 UCLA L. REV. 647 (1977); Note, *Laetrile: Statutory and Constitutional Limitations on the Regulation of Ineffective Drugs,* 127 U. PA. L. REV. 233 (1978). See also Thomas H. Jukes, *Laetrile on Trial,* 242 J.A.M.A. 719 (1979); Janardan D. Khandekar & Harlan Edelman, *Studies of Amygdalin (Laetrile) Toxicity in Rodents,* 242 J.A.M.A. 169 (1979); William Regelson, *The "Grand Conspiracy" Against the Cancer Cure,* 243 J.A.M.A. 337 (1980); Susan J. Tius, *Constitutional and Legislative Challenges to the Federal Pre-market Proof of Drug Effectiveness Requirement,* 13 NEW ENG. L.

REV. 279 (1977); Gregory P. Drescher, *What's in an Apricot?: The Seeds of Life and Death* (1995), Erik S. Groothuis, *Laetrile: The Power of Hope* (1996), and Lindsay Blohn, *Dr. Koch: A Cancer Quack?* (2006), in Chapter VI(C)(12) of the Electronic Book.

Richard J. Crout,* *The Nature of Regulatory Choices*

33 FOOD DRUG COSMETIC LAW JOURNAL 413 (1978).

. . . .

There was a time, not very long ago, when I thought the quality of public discussion on our drug regulatory system in the United States was extraordinarily low. In those days it was typical for most critics of the FDA to cast all criticism into one of two models, depending upon their point of view. The first of these might be called the "political" model and is highly popular among physicians, clinical investigators, and the drug industry. According to this construct, the regulation of drugs is conducted by slow, unimaginative bureaucrats who are intent on disapproving drugs so as to avoid criticism by Congressional committees for approving anything with risks. By combining such qualities as lack of perspective, overconcern with safety, and inefficiency, they manage to bog down all of drug regulation into a mire of technicalities. Admirers of this model tend to see regulatory decisions as contests between science and politics, and they plead for an FDA which is "more scientific" and "more reasonable."

The other model might be called the "sellout" model and is particularly popular among consumer activists, certain congressional committees, and the press. According to this formulation, the Agency is also slow and bureaucratic—a point on which all critics seem to agree—but largely because it lacks commitment in enforcing the law. Because of personal allegiance to the medical profession and the drug industry, the regulator is seen as quick to approve new drugs without adequate evidence for safety or effectiveness but as slow and inept in withdrawing drugs from the market. The new effect is an industry-dominated Agency which fails to enforce the law. . . .

Each of these models has the virtue of being readily understandable and is inherently plausible. It appeals to the biases of nearly everyone to view regulatory controversies as basically one-on-one contests between the virtuous and the untrustworthy. . . .

If drug development is to move faster in this country, the public must come to accept the idea that less control over research is, in the long run, safer than the alternative, because freedom is essential to discovery and insight. This is a sophisticated concept, not easily explained to the public, and certainly not about to be readily accepted by those already suspicious of science and technology, and of physicians. The challenge to those concerned about the innovative process is to defend that point of view in public on its merits, not to promote some simplistic, extraneous "solution" such as repeal of the effectiveness requirement. . . .

* [Dr. Crout was Director of the FDA Bureau of Drugs, now CDER.]

In contrast to those concerned about the effect of regulation on innovation, the laetrile supporters really do want, I suspect, simple repeal of the effectiveness requirement.... It may not be wise ... to continue the pretense that substances such as laetrile must either be accepted as therapeutic drugs or be suppressed. The drug regulatory law deals with science, and to risk its essential features in the political arena over relatively innocuous products is to court a serious long-term setback to the rational control of powerful chemicals in our society. We may well be better off to tolerate a few follies in the marketplace. But again the choice is between competing good values—do we want scientific rationality or personal freedom? And if we want the latter, are we willing to pay the price of a few frauds here and there?

Scott Gottlieb, M.D., *The Price of Too Much Caution*

THE NEW YORK SUN, December 22, 2004, at 8.

... Over the last 50 years, we have added successive layers of testing and monitoring before new drugs are approved for sale to patients, to the point where the average development time for a new drug can span 10 years and cost almost $1 billion.

The result is that today we have the safest system in the world, but few glaring gaps to easily improve on. When it comes to making new drugs safer, most of the obvious solutions are already accounted for and we have reached the flat part of a curve that measures incremental safety against the additional cost. We can make our drug development system a little safer, but only at a very big cost.

This trade-off is at issue, after the pain medications Vioxx and Celebrex, known as Cox–2 inhibitors, were traced to small but higher risks of heart attacks among patients who use them....

Consumers are angry that these problems were not unearthed earlier. But the higher risk of heart attacks caused by Vioxx, for example, was on the order of about six or seven heart attacks for every 1,000 patients who took the drug. In an older-patient population that already suffered more heart attacks, such a risk could have been easily missed, even with a clinical trial that included 10,000 patients or more. With this additional testing, the benefits of an off chance of discovering a rare side effect before a new drug is approved is eventually outweighed by the cost of keeping promising drugs from patients.

Even delaying seemingly ordinary drugs can have dramatic consequence on the public health. The first non-sedating anti-allergy medicine, Claritin, took almost seven years to get approved, while sleepy drivers with sniffles continued to cause car accidents. Each of the popular anti-cholesterol drugs known as statins that today prevent 15% to 30% of heart attacks took several years to get approved. How many people died waiting? The math is straightforward.

Or consider this math: It's estimated more than 20,000 people died between 1985 and 1987 waiting for streptokinase, the first drug that could be intravenously administered to reopen the blocked coronary arteries of heart attack victims. Between 1988 and 1992, about 3,500 kidney cancer patients died waiting for Interleukin–2, which was available in several European countries. In 1988 alone, it is estimated between 7,500 and 15,000 people died from gastric ulcers caused by aspirin and other non-steroidal anti-inflammatory drugs, waiting for the FDA to approve miso-prostol, which was already available in 43 countries. . . .

K.   REGULATION OF NONPRESCRIPTION DRUGS

From the enactment of the 1938 Act, FDA has drawn clear distinctions between prescription and nonprescription drugs—or over-the-counter (OTC) drugs, as they are commonly called. This part explores the special problems FDA has encountered in applying the new drug requirements, and specifically the 1962 effectiveness standard, to OTC drugs.

1.   THE OTC DRUG REVIEW

Prior to 1972, no country had ever attempted to conduct a systematic review of nonprescription drugs or to establish a comprehensive regulatory program for these products. When FDA found that it was required by the Drug Amendments of 1962 to review the effectiveness of OTC drugs for which an NDA had become effective during 1938–1962, the agency realized that a new approach would have to be established.

a.   RATIONALE AND PROCEDURES OF THE REVIEW

Congress's mandate in the Drug Amendments of 1962 to review all previous effective NDAs extended to OTC as well as prescription drugs. Most OTC drugs could not be considered "covered" by effective NDAs, however, and FDA concluded that case-by-case challenges to individual products on the ground that they were unapproved "new drugs" would exhaust its resources and fail to assure their safety and effectiveness. In 1972, FDA proposed a new approach which featured expert advisory committees and relied on the agency's claim to primary jurisdiction to determine new drug status.

Over–the–Counter Drugs: Proposal Establishing Rule Making Procedures for Classification

37 Fed. Reg. 85 (January 5, 1972).

. . . . The NAS–NRC reviewed 420 OTC drugs which were broadly representative of the whole range of the OTC market. The NAS–NRC panels' conclusions, which were based upon supporting data submitted by manufacturers, were that approximately 25 percent of the drugs reviewed had an indication that was classifiable as effective.

Estimates of the number of OTC drug products on the market vary from 100,000 to one-half million. Extremely few of these drugs have been approved through the new-drug procedures set forth in section 505 of the act. Some OTC drugs may be excluded from the definition of a new drug by reasons of the so-called 1938 grandfather clause in section 201(p)(1) of the act, and others may be excluded from application of the Drug Amendments of 1962 by reason of the so-called 1962 grandfather clause in section 107(c) of those amendments. Any OTC drug excluded from new-drug status by reason of the 1938 or 1962 grandfather clause is, however, subject to other requirements for drugs in Chapter V of the act, and in particular may not be misbranded under section 502.

The Food and Drug Administration intends to require that all unapproved new drugs and misbranded drugs either be reformulated and/or relabeled to meet all requirements of the act or be removed from the market. In carrying out its responsibilities in this area, the Food and Drug Administration may either initiate a separate court action with respect to each violative OTC drug or deal with all OTC drugs through rulemaking by therapeutic classes on an industry wide basis. It has been determined that the latter approach should be pursued. In making this decision, the following factors were considered:

1.   The limited resources of the Food and Drug Administration would be overwhelmed by attempting to review separately the labeling and the data on the safety and effectiveness for each OTC drug now on the market. . . .

2.   Litigation to remove violative OTC preparations from the market would necessarily be on a drug-by-drug basis. . . . Such litigation is time-consuming and expensive and is sometimes ineffective because manufacturers may change the formulation of the drug in question and/or its labeling claims and reintroduce the product into the market, thus requiring still further litigation.

3.   Litigation to delineate the precise scope of the 1938 and 1962 grandfather clauses in order to determine exactly which of the thousands of OTC drugs on the market may validly claim exemption from new-drug status under those clauses and then to determine on a drug-by-drug basis which of those grandfathered claims and formulations are safe and effective under the prescribed, recommended, or suggested conditions of use, and thus not misbranded, would more than exhaust all present resources of the agency. . . .

4.   Of paramount concern is the inadequate consumer protection produced by a product-by-product review and case-by-case litigation against each drug. . . .

5.   It is impossible to proceed simultaneously by litigation against all manufacturers of similar preparations or their drugs. . . .

6.   Practically all of the thousands of OTC drugs now marketed are compounded from only an estimated 200 active ingredients which are used either alone or in varying combinations. Many thousands of these drugs are readily comparable in that the labeling is similar and the active ingredients are the same, or are essentially the same, but are present in slightly different dosages. Although each is a separate product, the same scientific and medical evidence is relevant in reviewing all OTC drugs within a given therapeutic class. . . .

Accordingly, the Commissioner proposes to establish procedures for rule making which will result in classifying some OTC drugs as generally recognized among qualified experts as safe and effective and not misbranded under prescribed, recommended, or suggested conditions of use. Any OTC drug not meeting the requirements established for such drugs pursuant to this procedure will have to be the subject of an approved new-drug application prior to marketing. (Since a grandfathered drug that is found to be misbranded would be required to change its formulation and/or labeling and thus lose its grandfathered status, any such product must either meet the applicable monograph or be the subject of an approved new-drug application in order to be legally marketed.) A deviation from a monograph will be approved for an individual manufacturer through approval of a new-drug application justifying such a deviation. Shipment of a non-conforming OTC drug (one neither classified as generally recognized as safe and effective and not misbranded, nor subject to an approved NDA) in interstate commerce will be prohibited. . . .

————

The agency made modifications in only a few provisions in the proposed regulations and quickly promulgated the final regulations, 21 C.F.R. Part 330. Section 330.10, laying out the procedures for classification of OTC drugs, appears *infra*, after the following excerpt from the preamble to the final rule.

Procedures for Classification of Over–the–Counter Drugs

37 Fed. Reg. 9464 (May 11, 1972).

. . . .

Some comments have contended that the Food and Drug Administration does not have the authority to regulate drugs by therapeutic class, because the authority to do so has not been given by Congress . . . These comments also argue that the category reviews are not legally proper, since it is a subversion of the NDA procedures (21 U.S.C. 355), which call for a drug-by-drug review. The regulations however do not state that the OTC drugs reviewed are new drugs which have been approved, but instead provide for monographs which will include those drugs that do not require an NDA. Nothing in the act prohibits the use of the therapeutic category approach to defining those OTC drugs that are generally recognized as safe and effective and not misbranded. . . .

A number of comments would delete the words "generally recognized" before the words "safe" and "effective". Under the law, however, a drug that is safe and effective but not generally recognized as such would require an NDA unless it is grandfathered. If it is grandfathered it may not be misbranded or adulterated. Thus, only those drugs that are generally recognized as safe and effective and that are not misbranded or adulterated may be lawfully marketed without an NDA. . . .

Many comments stated that the proposed regulations would extend the new drug requirements of the 1962 Amendments to include those OTC drugs that were grandfathered under the 1962 and 1938 acts. This is not the situation. The Commissioner seeks to determine which nongrandfathered OTC drugs are generally recognized as safe and effective and which grandfathered OTC drugs are not misbranded. The grandfather clauses exempt those drugs to which they are applicable from the new drug provisions of the act but not from the misbranding provisions....

There was also comment that the required proof of effectiveness is far too rigorous and in effect adopts for OTC drugs a standard that should apply only to prescription drugs. It was urged that OTC drugs do not require the same sophistication in research and analysis as prescription drugs to prove their effectiveness.... There can be no question, however, that the best possible data would consist of adequate and well controlled clinical studies of the drug ..., and in any event the regulation allows for a waiver where there is a showing that such studies are unnecessary or inappropriate....

Comments argued that section 503(b) of the act determines prescription status and that this is not a question that should be asked of a panel. This issue is fundamentally no different, however, from the other issues being considered by the panels. Each panel is being asked for its reviews on the safety and effectiveness of OTC drugs, and it may well be that they will decide that a drug is generally recognized as safe and effective but that because of adverse reaction or side effects it is not safe and effective for OTC use....

... Although the data submitted by interested parties are to relate only to OTC drugs, the panel is charged with making recommendations with respect to all drugs that should be on OTC status. Any interested person may, of course, submit data and views suggesting that a prescription drug be moved to OTC status....

Another comment objects to the statement ... that the proposed monograph would specify a reasonable period of time within which drugs falling within subdivision (iii) could be marketed while the data necessary to evaluate the drug is being obtained for evaluation by the Food and Drug Administration.... There can be no justification to allow the continued marketing of a drug when the Commissioner finds it to be ineffective. On the other hand there is justification as provided in subdivision (iii) for allowing an interested party time to prove a drug safe and effective, if the evidence is insufficient for the Commissioner to make a proper determination.... It is intended that reasonable time will be provided as long as testing is in progress that is adequate to resolve the medical issues raised by the panel and the Commissioner....

Almost every comment contended that the Food and Drug Administration lacks legal authority under the act to promulgate OTC drug monographs that constitute binding substantive rules and that the agency's authority is limited to issuing interpretive guidelines. Section 701(a) of the act expressly grants "the authority to promulgate regulations for the efficient enforcement of this Act." Numerous Supreme Court cases, interpreting comparable legislative authorization in other regulatory statutes, have upheld the right to proceed by substantive rule making rather than on a case-by-case basis, to particularize general statutory standards....

Some comments stated that, even if there were authority to issue substantive regulations, the proposed OTC drug procedures fail to meet Constitutional requirements, because they do not provide for an evidentiary hearing or cross-examination and there is no written record available for review. The regulations promulgated in this order governing the OTC review meet all of the requirements of the Administrative Procedure Act and of due process of law.... In the OTC drug review procedures, far greater procedural rights are granted than are required under the Administrative Procedure Act. Instead of a simple notice of proposed rule making giving the substance of the proposed rule, all interested persons have an opportunity, prior to any court review, to submit the data on which the proposed rule will be based and to request an oral hearing before the panel, to provide written comments and objections to the Commissioner, and to request an oral hearing before the Commissioner. In addition, interested organizations have an opportunity to recommend lists of experts to serve on the panels themselves....

The comments argued that, even if the Food and Drug Administration had the authority to determine by rule making which drugs are generally recognized as safe and effective, there is no authority to set a standard to determine which drugs are misbranded, because the statute specifically provides for court adjudication of this issue. The legal authority to utilize a rule making rather than a case-by-case adjudication approach with respect to misbranding stands on no different footing than the legal authority to exercise rule making with respect to new drug status. Both instances involve explication, particularization, and definition of general statutory requirements as they apply to large numbers of products now on the market....

Similarly, most comments argued that, even if the agency has the authority to establish binding substantive rules, the 1938 and 1962 grandfather clauses preclude review of OTC drugs protected by them. The grandfather clauses apply only to the new drug provisions of the act, however, and not to the adulteration or misbranding provisions. The review contained in these regulations is designed to particularize not just the new drug provisions of the act, but also the misbranding provisions....

Over–the–Counter Human Drugs Which are Generally Recognized as Safe and Effective and not Misbranded

21 C.F.R. Part 330.

§ 330.10 Procedures for classifying OTC drugs as generally recognized as safe and effective and not misbranded, and for establishing monographs

. . . .

(a) *Procedure for establishing OTC drug monographs.* (1) *Advisory review panels.* The Commissioner shall appoint advisory review panels of qualified experts to evaluate the safety and effectiveness of OTC drugs, to review OTC drug labeling, and to advise him on the promulgation of monographs establishing conditions under which OTC drugs are generally recognized as safe and effective and not misbranded.... The members of a panel ... may include persons from lists submitted by organizations representing professional, consumer, and industry interests....

(3) *Deliberations of an advisory review panel.* An advisory review panel will ... review the data submitted to it and ... prepare a report containing its conclusions and recommendations to the Commissioner with respect to the safety and effectiveness of the drugs in a designated category of the OTC drugs. A panel may consult any individual or group. Any interested person may request an opportunity to present oral views to the panel; such request may be granted or denied by the panel.... Any interested person may present written data and views which shall be considered by the panel....

(4) *Standards for safety, effectiveness, and labeling.* The advisory review panel ... shall apply the following standards ...:

(i) Safety means a low incidence of adverse reactions or significant side effects under adequate directions for use and warnings against unsafe use as well as low potential for harm which may result from abuse under conditions of widespread availability. Proof of safety shall consist of adequate tests by methods reasonably applicable to show the drug is safe under the prescribed, recommended, or suggested conditions of use. This proof shall include results of significant human experience during marketing. General recognition of safety shall ordinarily be based upon published studies which may be corroborated by unpublished studies and other data.

(ii) Effectiveness means a reasonable expectation that, in a significant proportion of the target population, the pharmacological effect of the drug, when used under adequate directions for use and warnings against unsafe use, will provide clinically significant relief of the type claimed. Proof of effectiveness shall consist of controlled clinical investigations as defined in § 314.111(a)(5)(ii) of this chapter, unless this requirement is waived on the basis of a showing that it is not reasonably applicable to the drug or essential to the validity of the investigation and that an alternative method of investigation is adequate to substantiate effectiveness. Investigations may be corroborated by partially controlled or uncontrolled studies, documented clinical studies by qualified experts, and reports of significant human experience marketing.... General recognition of effectiveness shall ordinarily be based upon published studies which may be corroborated by unpublished studies and other data.

(iii) The benefit-to-risk ratio of a drug shall be considered in determining safety and effectiveness.

(iv) An OTC drug may combine two or more safe and effective active ingredients and may be generally recognized as safe and effective when each active ingredient makes a contribution to the claimed effect(s); when combining of the active ingredients does not decrease the safety or effectiveness of any of the individual active ingredients; and when the combination, when used under adequate directions for use and warnings against unsafe use, provides rational concurrent therapy for a significant proportion of the target population....

(5) *Advisory review panel report to the Commissioner....* Included within this report shall be:

(i) A recommended monograph or monographs covering the category of OTC drugs and establishing conditions under which the drugs involved are generally recognized as safe and effective and not misbranded (Category I)....

(ii) A statement of active ingredients, labeling claims or other statements, or other conditions reviewed and excluded from the monograph on the basis of the panel's determination that they would result in the drug's not being generally recognized as safe and effective or would result in misbranding (Category II).

(iii) A statement of active ingredients, labeling claims or other statements, or other conditions reviewed and excluded from the monograph on the basis of the panel's determination that the available data are insufficient to classify such condition under either paragraph (a)(5)(i) or (ii) of this section and for which further testing is therefore required (Category III)....

(6) *Proposed monograph.* After reviewing the conclusions and recommendations of the advisory review panel, the Commissioner shall publish in the FEDERAL REGISTER a proposed order containing:

(i) A monograph or monographs establishing conditions under which a category of OTC drugs or a specific or specific OTC drugs are generally recognized as safe and effective and not misbranded (Category I).

(ii) A statement of the conditions excluded from the monograph on the basis of the Commissioner's determination that they would result in the drug's not being generally recognized as safe and effective or would result in misbranding (Category II).

(iii) A statement of the conditions excluded from the monograph on the basis of the Commissioner's determination that the available data are insufficient ... (Category III).

(iv) The full report(s) of the panel to the Commissioner.... Any interested person may, within 90 days after publication of the proposed order ... file ... written comments....

(7) *Tentative final monograph.*

(i) After reviewing all comments, reply comments, and any new data and information or, alternatively, after reviewing a panel's recommendations, the Commissioner shall publish in the FEDERAL REGISTER a tentative order containing a monograph establishing conditions under which a category of OTC drugs or specific OTC drugs are generally recognized as safe and effective and not misbranded. Within 30 days, any interested party may file ... written objections specifying with particularity the omissions or additions requested.... A request for an oral hearing may accompany such objections....

(8) *Oral hearing before the Commissioner.* After reviewing objections filed in response to the tentative final monograph, the Commissioner, if he finds reasonable grounds in support thereof, shall ... schedule an oral hearing. . . .

(9) *Final monograph.* After reviewing the objections ... and considering the arguments made at any oral hearing, the Commissioner shall publish in the FEDERAL REGISTER a final order containing a monograph establishing conditions under which a category of OTC drugs or a specific or specific OTC drugs are generally recognized as safe and effective and not misbranded. . . .

(11) *Court appeal.* The monograph contained in the final order constitutes final agency action from which appeal lies to the courts. . . .

(b) *Regulatory action.* Any product which fails to conform to an applicable monograph after its effective date is liable to regulatory action.

. . . .

NOTES

1. *Legality of OTC Drug Review.* Surprisingly, the legality of the OTC Drug Review, while questioned, has never been squarely challenged in the courts. Several court opinions have referred approvingly to the Review. *E.g. Weinberger v. Bentex Pharmaceuticals, Inc.*, 412 U.S. 645 (1973); *Warner–Lambert Co. v. FTC*, 361 F. Supp. 948 (D.D.C. 1973); *United States v. Articles of Food and Drug ... Coli–Trol 80 Medicated*, 372 F. Supp. 915 (N.D. Ga. 1974); *Farquhar v. FDA*, 616 F. Supp. 190 (D.D.C. 1985). Two features of the Review procedures were later challenged. FDA's initial use of closed panel meetings, with confidential transcripts, was upheld by one court and declared unlawful by another before the issue was mooted by the enactment of the Federal Advisory Committee Act, *infra* p. 1573. The agency's approval for continued marketing of Category III drugs was enjoined in *Cutler v. Kennedy, infra* p. 799.

2. *FDA Request for Data.* Because FDA has no statutory power to require a manufacturer to submit any information to, or otherwise participate in, the OTC Drug Review, the agency feared that companies might submit only favorable information. FDA's initial requests for data on specific drug categories therefore included this language in the mandatory format for data submissions:

> ... If the submission is by a manufacturer, a statement signed by the person responsible for such submission, that to the best of his knowledge it includes unfavorable information, as well as any favorable information, known to him pertinent to an evaluation of the safety, effectiveness, and labeling of such a product. Thus, if any type of scientific data is submitted, a balanced submission of favorable and unfavorable data must be submitted. . . .

E.g., 37 Fed. Reg. 26842 (Dec. 16, 1972) (antimicrobial drugs).

3. *General Requirements for OTC Drugs.* The general conditions for all OTC drugs in 21 C.F.R. 330.1 were promulgated in 38 Fed. Reg. 8714 (Apr. 5, 1973), 38 Fed. Reg. 31258 (Nov. 12, 1973), 39 Fed. Reg. 19880 (June 4, 1974), 40 Fed. Reg. 11717 (Mar. 13, 1975).

4. *Combination OTC Drugs.* The conditions under which combination OTC drugs are permitted have long been in dispute. 21 C.F.R. 330.10(a)(4)(iv) paraphrases the prescription combination drug regulation, 21 C.F.R. 300.50. Because of the

significant differences between OTC and Rx drugs, however, many more combinations have been permitted for OTC drugs. To promote uniformity among the several review panels, FDA issued a guideline for OTC combination drug products. 43 Fed. Reg. 55466 (Nov. 28, 1978).

5. *New Combination Products.* Because most new OTC drug products utilize combinations of active ingredients, FDA has paid particular attention to the marketing of new combinations not explicitly recognized in an OTC drug monograph. In Compliance Policy Guide 7132b.16 (Oct. 1, 1980), the agency took the position that no new OTC combination drug not on the market before May 11, 1972 may be marketed before it has been classified in Category I in a proposed monograph and the Commissioner has not dissented, unless the agency has announced in the Federal Register that the combination is permitted. In the face of this guidance, a company unsuccessfully attempted to market a toothpaste containing both an anticaries active ingredient and a tooth desensitizer, a combination not sanctioned by the report of the OTC Dental Drug Panel. *United States v. Articles of Drug ... Promise Toothpaste for Sensitive Teeth*, 826 F.2d 564 (7th Cir. 1987). *See also Farquhar v. FDA*, 616 F. Supp. 190 (D.D.C. 1985).

6. *Encouraged Reformulation.* FDA encouraged manufacturers to reformulate and relabel their products to conform to proposed monographs even before the monographs are promulgated in final form. The agency adopted a regulation, 21 C.F.R. 330.12(d), stating that it would not take action against such products, pending promulgation of a final monograph, if such changes resulted in loss of grandfather protection. FDA also persuaded the court in *American Public Health Association v. Veneman*, 349 F. Supp. 1311 (D.D.C. 1972), *supra* p. 603, to exempt all OTC drugs from its implementation order. *See* 37 Fed. Reg. 26623, 26624 (Dec. 14, 1972) (¶ XV of reprint of District Court implementation order). *See also* 37 Fed. Reg. 7807 (Apr. 20, 1972), 39 Fed. Reg. 1580 (Jan. 11, 1974).

7. *Homeopathic Drugs.* FDA decided to defer consideration of homeopathic drugs, for which there is scant evidence of effectiveness, because they represented such a small volume. *See* 37 Fed. Reg. 9464, 9466 (May 11, 1972). In the interim, *Meserey v. United States*, 447 F. Supp. 548 (D. Nev. 1977), confirmed that homeopathic drugs are subject to all the drug provisions of the FD&C Act. Compliance Policy Guide 7132.15 (May 31, 1988) sets forth FDA's policy on the conditions under which homeopathic drugs may be marketed. *See supra* p. 617.

8. *Outstanding NDAs.* In order to mesh the NDA procedures with the OTC Drug Review procedures, FDA withdrew all NDAs for OTC antacid drugs upon promulgation of the first final monograph for antacids. 39 Fed. Reg. 19882 (June 4, 1974), 39 Fed. Reg. 39591 (Nov. 8, 1974).

9. *FDA Enforcement Policy.* A well-understood premise of the OTC Drug Review was that FDA would not devote its resources to enforcement actions against individual OTC products even though they might technically be unapproved new drugs. In short, the agency would tolerate continued marketing of most OTC drug products pending completion of the Review. But FDA added two caveats. It would take action against an individual OTC product if it believed the product posed a significant health hazard or was likely to defraud consumers. *See* Compliance Policy Guide No. 7132b.15 (Oct. 1, 1980). In addition, the agency made clear that it would not hesitate to act outside the scope and schedule of the review to deal with ingredients that were found by the panels, or otherwise demonstrated, to be health hazards. Thus FDA has dealt specially with hexachlorophene, an antimicrobial ingredient used in cleansing products, 37 Fed. Reg. 219 (Jan. 7, 1972), 37 Fed. Reg. 20160 (Sept. 27, 1972), codified at 21 C.F.R. 250.250; TBS, an antibacterial ingredient, 39 Fed. Reg. 33102 (Sept. 13, 1974), 40 Fed. Reg. 50527 (Oct. 30, 1975), codified at 21 C.F.R. 310.508; zirconium, an antiperspirant ingredient, 40 Fed. Reg.

24328 (June 5, 1975), 42 Fed. Reg. 41374 (Aug. 16, 1977), codified at 21 C.F.R. 310.510; chloroform, 41 Fed. Reg. 15026 (Apr. 19, 1976), 41 Fed. Reg. 26842 (June 29, 1976), codified at 21 C.F.R. 310.513; and methapyrilene, an ingredient of sleep-aid products found by the national Cancer Institute to be carcinogenic in animals. The agency has also transferred to category II, and thus banned, a number of active ingredients for which the OTC drug industry expressed no further interest. *E.g.*, 55 Fed Reg. 46914 (Nov. 7, 1990); 58 Fed. Reg. 27636 (May 10, 1990); 67 Fed. Reg. 31123 & 31125 (May 9, 2002); codified at 21 C.F.R. 310.545.

10. *Daytime Sedatives.* In 44 Fed. Reg. 36378 (June 22, 1979), FDA issued a final order dealing with OTC daytime sedative products. The document set forth FDA's conclusion that "any ingredient when labeled for use as an over-the-counter daytime sedative is not generally recognized as safe and effective for this intended use." The agency's conclusion, which precludes the marketing of any OTC product for use as a daytime sedative, was based on findings that the ingredients used in such products were either ineffective at the dosages used (and potentially toxic at higher dosages) or only capable of rendering the user sleepy. The agency's ruling relied on concerns about potential societal abuse as a basis for its conclusion that no daytime OTC sedative can be generally recognized as safe and effective.

11. *Premature Marketing.* Once the nonprescription drug industry began to appreciate the commercial opportunities created by the OTC Drug Review, companies closely followed each panel and anticipated the results of the Review by marketing new products that previously were not permitted (*e.g.*, drugs previously limited to prescription status or marketed for a different indication or containing less of the active ingredient) even before the panel submitted its report. After FDA forced the nationwide recall of a new product marketed in anticipation of a panel conclusion with which it disagreed, *supra* p. 527, Note 3, the agency promulgated a rule governing the conditions under which manufacturers may safely follow the recommendations of an OTC drug panel before a final monograph has been promulgated. 40 Fed. Reg. 56675 (Dec. 4, 1975), 41 Fed. Reg. 32480 (Aug. 4, 1976), codified at 21 C.F.R. 330.13. The FDA policy was amended in 47 Fed. Reg. 17738 (Apr. 23, 1982) to provide that, when the Commissioner agrees that a new product meets all the requirements for Category I and provides notice of that determination in the Federal Register, marketing may begin before promulgation of a final monograph.

12. *The Flexibility of the OTC Drug Review.* Although criticized as rigid, in truth the OTC Drug Review exhibited notable flexibility. For example, 21 C.F.R. 330.10(a)(5) authorized a panel to recommend in a monograph any conditions of any kind relating to an OTC drug. The recommended labeling indications and other conditions need not have been marketed prior to 1972. No FDA policy has ever adopted a May 1972 cut-off for monograph approval of OTC drug conditions. Indeed, panels routinely considered and recommended approval of conditions not marketed prior to May 1972. The agency's flexibility with respect to new conditions of use is limited only by the material extent or material time provision of the new drug definition, which FDA has liberally construed. Many final monographs recognize conditions that did not exist in 1972.

13. *Switch from NDA to Monograph Status.* Although a large number of important drugs have been switched from prescription to non-prescription status through the NDA process, very few have then been switched from NDA to monograph status. An exception is clotrimazole, whose manufacturers submitted a citizen petition requesting monograph status. Clotrimazole was switched to the antifungal monograph for all uses except vaginal yeast infection. 66 Fed. Reg. 29059 (May 29, 2001), 67 Fed. Reg. 5942 (Feb. 8, 2002).

14. *Professional Labeling.* Some OTC drugs have prescription as well as nonprescription indications. In such instances, the applicable monographs specifically provide for "professional labeling" containing these prescription indications. *See, e.g.,* 21 C.F.R. 331.80, relating to peptic ulcer claims for antacid products, and 21 C.F.R. 332.31, permitting postoperative gas pain claims for antiflatulent products.

15. *Reopening the OTC Drug Review.* In general, FDA has resisted reopening the OTC Drug Review to include additional ingredients. In 1989, however, the agency requested the submission of data for ingredients contained in eyewash drug products used for emergency first aid treatment of chemical burns of the eye, because these important products were missed by earlier panel reports. 54 Fed. Reg. 50240 (Dec. 5, 1989). The next year, FDA also reopened the Review to consider products for which dental plaque and gingivitis claims are made. 55 Fed. Reg. 38560 (Sept. 19, 1990). In 68 Fed. Reg. 75585 (Dec. 31, 2003), FDA published a request for data and information on products it characterized as OTC drugs eligible for the original OTC Drug Review but that had not been reviewed by FDA to date. Included in the list were a number of products that industry has long marketed as cosmetics. Many companies did not respond to the notice, and others who did respond objected to the list. FDA has taken no further action on this matter.

16. *Mailing OTC Drugs.* The Drug and Household Substance Mailing Act of 1990, 104 Stat. 1184, prohibits the mailing of a "household substance" (which includes OTC drugs) which does not comply with any special child-resistant packaging requirements established for the product under the Poison Prevention Packaging Act of 1970.

17. *First Amendment Considerations.* In two final monographs, serious First Amendment issues were raised. When the final monograph for OTC sunscreen drug products was promulgated in 64 Fed. Reg. 27666 (May 21, 1999) the affected companies threatened to bring a lawsuit to contest the constitutionality of restrictions on truthful and nonmisleading labeling claims. Because the monograph was stayed for other reasons, the issue has not yet been resolved. Similarly, when the OTC antiperspirant drug product final monograph was promulgated in 68 Fed. Reg. 34273 (June 9, 2003) an affected manufacturer objected on the ground that it permitted only 48–hour duration claims even if longer durations were fully supported by scientific data. In the face of a constitutional objection, FDA stayed the effectiveness of that portion of the final monograph. No further action has been taken on the matter.

18. *Nanotechnology.* In a citizen petition filed with FDA by environmental organizations, FDA was requested to determine that nanomaterial versions of traditional OTC sunscreen drug active ingredients manufactured with the use of nanotechnology constitute new drugs that require a separate NDA. FDA Docket No. 2006P0210 (May 17, 2006). Other interested persons have submitted substantial responses disputing this petition. FDA held a public meeting announced in 71 Fed. Reg. 19524 (Apr. 14, 2006), 71 Fed. Reg. 56158 (Sept. 26, 2006), on the impact of nanotechnology on the agency's regulatory programs. *See also* NATIONAL ACADEMY OF SCIENCES, A MATTER OF SIZE: TRIENNIAL REVIEW OF THE NATIONAL NANOTECHNOLOGY INITIATIVE (2006).

19. *OTC Drug Active Ingredients and Categories of Products Not Generally Recognized as Safe and Effective.* When FDA determines that an OTC drug active ingredient or product category is not generally recognized as safe and effective, in addition to stating that determination in the preamble to the final monograph, the agency publishes a separate regulation summarizing that conclusion. 21 C.F.R. 310.519–310.548.

20. *Commentary.* For analyses of the OTC drug review, *see* Charles Ames & Steven McCracken, *Framing Regulatory Standards to Avoid Formal Adjudication:*

The FDA as a Case Study, *64 CAL. L. REV. 14 (1976); Dan R. Harlow,* The FDA's OTC Drug Review: The Development and Analysis of Some Aspects of the Procedure, *32 FOOD DRUG COSM. L.J. 248 (1977); David Selmer, Note:* FDA's Over-the-Counter Drug Review: Expeditious Enforcement By Rulemaking, *11 MICH. J. OF L. REFORM 142 (1977); Kenneth C. Baumgartner,* A Historical Examination of the FDA's Review of the Safety and Effectiveness of Over-the-Counter Drugs, *43 FOOD DRUG COSM. L.J. 463 (1988). For histories of particular OTC drug monographs, see Perham Gorji,* OTC Sunscreen Drug Products: Toward Greater Protection *(1997), and Michael B. Sandier,* The Regulation of Toothpaste *(1997), in Chapter VI(D)(2) of the Electronic Book.*

b. LEGALITY OF CATEGORY III

Another controversial feature of the OTC Drug Review was the provision allowing continued marketing of products containing ingredients classified by final FDA monographs in Category III while additional testing was being conducted. Authorizing continued marketing during testing of drugs for which available data were insufficient to permit a determination of general recognition of safety and effectiveness was thought necessary to persuade many drug manufacturers to accede to the basic concept of the Review. FDA also hoped to avoid litigation over the status of individual OTC drug products under the 1938 and 1962 grandfather clauses. In its brief in *USV Pharmaceutical Corp. v. Weinberger, supra* p. 601, FDA acknowledged that a significant number of OTC drug ingredients enjoyed grandfather status as long as no change in formulation or labeling occurred. By establishing a transitional category, FDA hoped to induce the manufacturers of these products to conduct further testing which would then permit a definitive determination of their safety and effectiveness.

Thus, Category III was designed as a bridge between the status quo and GRAS/GRAE status for ingredients for which the requisite evidence could be obtained. As the schedule for completion of the OTC Drug Review lengthened, however, pressure on FDA to depart from its systematic approach or curtail the marketing of Category III ingredients mounted.

Cutler v. Kennedy

475 F. Supp. 838 (D.D.C. 1979).

■ SIRICA, DISTRICT JUDGE. . . .

Plaintiffs Mimi Cutler, Pamela S. Ellsworth, and Stephen D. Annand are each consumers of various OTC drugs. . . . Plaintiffs' basic rationale can be quite simply stated. Under the OTC regulations, drugs are not placed in Category III unless there is insufficient evidence to determine that they are generally recognized as safe and effective. Given the *Hynson* case and the strict requirements for "general recognition," they say this means that Category III drugs lack substantial evidence of effectiveness, are necessarily new drugs, and, under the Act, cannot be marketed without an NDA. . . .

Plaintiffs also apparently contend, although their papers are considerably less clear on this point, that once having concluded, in effect, that Category III drugs are not supported by substantial evidence of safety or efficacy, the Commissioner has a statutory *duty* to take action to remove such drugs from the market. . . .

Defendants' basic position is equally straightforward. Only Category II, not Category III, contains drugs which the agency has finally determined to be not generally recognized as safe and effective. . . .

Under the Act, with very limited exceptions not here relevant, drugs can be lawfully marketed in only two ways. They are either new drugs which must be licensed, or they are generally recognized by experts as safe and effective, and are therefore not subject to active regulation. The goal of the Act is to insure that *every* marketed drug is both safe and effective. There are no other possibilities, no interim provisions under which safe, but only potentially effective drugs can be marketed pending testing. Even assuming that defendants are correct that Category III drugs are not *necessarily* unlawful new drugs, there is no question that they are *potentially* unlawful new drugs. To say that the Commissioner has the authority under the Act to affirmatively sanction the marketing of such drugs, effectively exempting them from the enforcement provisions of the Act for periods ranging from two to at least five years, is nothing less than a frontal assault on the premarket licensing scheme of the Food, Drug, and Cosmetic Act. . . .

The question of appropriate relief raises an additional, and difficult, issue. As noted above, part of plaintiffs' requested relief is an order directing the Commissioner "to take all appropriate steps" to remove any Category III drug from the market which is not covered by an NDA. The assumption underlying this request is apparently that the Commissioner, in addition to exceeding his statutory authority by authorizing the marketing of Category III drugs, has violated a statutory duty or abused his discretion by not moving to do just the opposite—removing them from the market.

The Court is sympathetic to plaintiffs' frustrations with the history of enforcement of the Drug Amendments of 1962. . . . On balance, however, even assuming that placement of a drug in Category III, absent grandfather status or coverage by an NDA, is tantamount to a finding of illegality under the Act, the Court cannot agree with plaintiffs that the Commissioner must move to take such drugs off the market. . . .

It should be emphasized, however, that the FDA may not lawfully maintain Category III in any form in which drugs with Category III conditions (as Category III conditions are presently defined) are exempted from enforcement action. Informally, of course, the FDA will be free to exercise its discretion to seek enforcement actions or not to seek enforcement actions. It may thus be argued that the Court's ruling simply permits the agency to accomplish informally and indirectly what it cannot accomplish in a formal order. But that is the system Congress created. . . .

NOTES

1. *Testing Category III Ingredients.* Prior to the *Cutler* decision, FDA was forced to decide the conditions under which Category III active ingredients could be tested. The agency concluded that the manufacturer must make a fundamental

choice at the beginning of testing: either (1) discontinue marketing the ingredient, test it under an IND, and file an NDA to obtain approval of its use; or (2) continue marketing the ingredient while testing is in progress, in which case no NDA may be obtained and any approval will be in the form of an amendment to the monograph. 40 Fed. Reg. 49097 (Oct. 21, 1975), 42 Fed. Reg. 19137 (Apr. 12, 1977).

2. *Subsequent Proceedings.* Neither FDA nor the industry intervenor defendants appealed the *Cutler* decision. FDA revised its regulations to comply with the decision. 44 Fed. Reg. 61608 (Oct. 26, 1979), 45 Fed. Reg. 31422 (May 13, 1980), 46 Fed. Reg. 47739 (Sept. 29, 1981). The revised regulations deleted the authorization to market Category III ingredients after publication of a final monograph and required testing of ingredients to be completed prior to such publication in order to be eligible for Category I. At the same time, FDA published a policy statement announcing that it would welcome meetings with industry representatives to study protocols and test results for Category III ingredients, and promising to comment on the adequacy of study results to upgrade an ingredient to Category I while it was being considered as part of the monograph process. 46 Fed. Reg. 47740 (Sept. 29, 1981). In substance, therefore, the *Cutler* decision resulted in Category III ingredients being tested and FDA decisions on those ingredients reached before, rather than after, publication of the final monograph.

c. COMPLETION OF THE OTC DRUG REVIEW

The OTC Drug Review has been one of the most challenging rulemaking efforts undertaken by any government agency. As the Review has progressed, and manufacturers of OTC drugs have responded by reformulating and relabeling their products, often even before final monographs have been promulgated, the program's priority on FDA's agenda has fallen. *See* GAO, FDA's APPROACH TO REVIEWING OVER THE COUNTER DRUGS IS REASONABLE, BUT PROGRESS IS SLOW, No. HRD–82–41 (Apr. 26, 1982).

Cutler v. Hayes

818 F.2d 879 (D.C. Cir. 1987).

■ ROBINSON, CIRCUIT JUDGE:

This case presents a challenge by consumers of over-the-counter drugs to the program undertaken by the Food and Drug Administration comprehensively to review these drugs for their safety and effectiveness. The consumers allege (1) that the regulations implementing this program violate the Food, Drug, and Cosmetic Act of 1938, as amended by the Drug Amendments of 1962, pursuant to which they were promulgated; (2) that FDA's policy of nonenforcement of the efficacy requirement for marketing over-the-counter drugs in interstate commerce violates the agency's statutory duty; and (3) that FDA's lack of progress in completing the review program and the unlikelihood that the review will be completed in the near future infringes the provisions of the Administrative Procedure Act disapproving unreasonable agency delay. The District Court granted appellees' motion for summary judgment on all counts. While we affirm the District Court's judgment on appellants' first two claims, we vacate the judgment on the charge of unreasonable delay and remand the case to the District Court for reconsideration in accordance with this opinion....

As we understand their argument, appellants assert that FDA has abdicated its statutory duty by (1) postponing enforcement of the Act's efficacy requirement and substantially limiting enforcement of the safety mandate until the completion of the OTC drug review program, and (2) then delaying completion of the program unreasonably....

... The FDC Act imposes no clear duty upon FDA to bring enforcement proceedings to effectuate either the safety or the efficacy requirements of the Act. Without a doubt, FDA has a responsibility under the Act to identify drugs generally recognized as safe and effective and require premarketing clearance for all others. But Congress has not given FDA an inflexible mandate to bring enforcement actions against all violators of the Act....

Nor does FDA's policy of postponing enforcement of the efficacy requirement until after publication of final monographs afford a basis for intervention under *Heckler v. Chaney*. Particularly as an agency with limited resources, FDA reasonably may assign enforcement of a statutory requirement designed to prevent unnecessary consumer expense to a lower priority than that accorded one concerned with identifying and eliminating threats to human life....

As we have already stated, the 1962 amendments to the FDC Act obligate FDA to review all nonexempt OTC drugs for their therapeutic efficacy as well as their safety. Concededly, FDA has broad discretion in deciding how to achieve this objective. The District Court erred, however, in equating the agency's freedom to exercise its discretion with voluntariness. Although FDA's discretion extends to review of OTC drugs by ingredient rather than by product—a choice implicitly approved by the Supreme Court in *Bentex* Pharmaceuticals—the agency lacks authority to simply do nothing to effectuate the purpose of the Act.

Once FDA elected to respond to its legislative directive by establishing the OTC drug review program, the APA imposed an obligation to proceed with reasonable dispatch....

The agency must justify its delay to the court's satisfaction. If the court determines that the agency delays in bad faith, it should conclude that the delay is unreasonable. If the court finds an absence of bad faith, it should then consider the agency's explanation, such as administrative necessity, insufficient resources, or the complexity of the task confronting the agency....

In 1962, Congress ordained that only those drugs generally recognized as safe and effective could be marketed without premarketing clearance. Because, a quarter-century later, this mandate has not yet been fully satisfied, close scrutiny must be paid to appellants' claim that FDA has unreasonably delayed its completion of the OTC drug review program....

NOTES

1. *Proceedings on Remand.* On remand, at the request of the District Court, FDA submitted A HISTORICAL EXAMINATION OF FDA's REVIEW OF THE SAFETY AND EFFECTIVENESS OF OVER-THE-COUNTER DRUGS (Sept. 22, 1987). In a memorandum

submitted to the District Court on September 25, 1989, to support a motion for summary judgment, plaintiffs complained that FDA was late in publishing many OTC Drug Review documents and thus that the current agency schedule, which projected completion in 1993, could not be met. The District Court granted FDA's motion for summary judgment in September 1995 and dismissed the case with prejudice.

2. *Progress of OTC Review.* FDA passed one landmark in the OTC Drug Review on October 7, 1983, when it published the last of the 58 reports prepared by the 17 advisory panels. The 17 panels held 508 meetings over 1047 days and reviewed some 20,000 volumes of data on more than 700 active ingredients used in over 300,000 nonprescription drug products. HHS News No. P83–22 (Oct. 7, 1983). The agency passed a second landmark when it published the last of the tentative final monographs a decade later. Nonetheless, it still has final monographs to promulgate. Because most OTC drugs are reformulated and relabeled to comply with the panel reports soon after, and sometimes even before, their publication, the major impact of the OTC Drug Review has already been reflected in the market-place.

3. *The Work of the Panels.* The OTC Drug Review panels reviewed some 722 active ingredients for approximately 1,454 specific uses. They rated roughly 30 percent as Category I for the intended use, 34 percent as Category II, and 36 percent as Category III. The agency later upgraded many Category III active ingredients to Category I based upon new information. William Gilbertson, THE PRESCRIPTION TO OTC SWITCH: FDA VIEW 5 (Apr. 1986).

4. *Monitoring Progress.* The progress of the OTC Drug Review can be monitored through FDA's Semiannual Regulatory Agenda. *E.g.,* 52 Fed. Reg. 14314 (Apr. 27, 1987), 55 Fed. Reg. 44470 (Oct. 29, 1990), 68 Fed. Reg. 30228 (May 27, 2003), 71 Fed. Reg. 22554 (Apr. 24, 2006).

5. *Exclusion of Unimportant Ingredients.* To speed up completion of the OTC Drug Review, FDA has deleted from further consideration several Category II and III active ingredients on which the agency has received no public comment. *See supra* p. 796, Note 9.

6. *Public Hearing.* In 65 Fed. Reg. 24074 (Apr. 27, 2000), FDA announced a public hearing on the agency's approach to regulating OTC drugs. A wide variety of views were presented, but most emphasized the need to complete the OTC Drug Review and to emphasize the switch of prescription drugs to OTC status.

2.   INACTIVE INGREDIENTS

FDA deferred review of inactive ingredients used in OTC drug products until evaluation of all active ingredients was completed. As one of the general conditions for recognition of an OTC drug as safe, effective, and not misbranded under 21 C.F.R. 330.1(e), all inactive ingredients must be suitable, safe in the amounts administered, and not interfere with the effectiveness or with suitable tests or assays to determine if the product meets its professed standards. In 42 Fed. Reg. 19156 (Apr. 12, 1977), the agency proposed general conditions for use and labeling of inactive ingredients pending such review. No further action was taken on this proposal. In 1984, the nonprescription drug industry established its own voluntary program for the labeling of inactive ingredients on OTC drug labels. *See* PROPRIETARY ASSOCIATION, GUIDELINES FOR DISCLOSURE OF INACTIVE INGREDIENTS IN OTC MEDICINES (1984). As part of the FDA Modernization Act of 1997, Congress amended section 502(e)(1)(A)(iii) of the FD&C Act to require all inactive ingredients to be listed on an OTC drug label in alphabetical order. *See* 21 C.F.R. 201.66(c)(8).

There are three types of inactive ingredients: (1) those that are inert and serve no functional purpose in the product, (2) those that facilitate the activity of the active ingredients but that exert no activity of their own, and (3) those that serve as a pharmacological adjuvant and therefore are regulated as an active ingredient. Although the line between each of these categories is not always clear, the preambles to several proposed, tentative final, and final monographs discuss these three categories and draw distinctions among them.

3.   OTC DRUG "TIME AND EXTENT" APPLICATIONS

In 2002, FDA promulgated regulations establishing a new mechanism for adding foreign ingredients to OTC drug monographs. 61 Fed. Reg. 51625 (Oct. 3, 1996), 64 Fed. Reg. 71062 (Dec. 10, 1999), 67 Fed. Reg. 3060 (Jan. 23, 2002), codified at 21 C.F.R. 330.14. The agency did so in response to the 1983 *FMALI Herb* decision, *supra* p. 417, which held that marketing experience abroad must be considered in determining whether a food ingredient is a "food additive," and in recognition of the fact that there are safe and effective OTC drug ingredients that have been marketed abroad for decades. Under section 201(p)(2) of the FD&C Act, a drug is a "new drug" even if it is generally recognized as safe and effective based on scientific investigations if it has not been used "to a material extent or for a material time." Thus, the application under the new procedure is called a "time and extent application" (TEA). The information that must be included with a TEA is voluminous, and the procedure established by FDA for consideration of a TEA is complex. Nonetheless, at least ten companies have submitted these applications and some have met with success. *E.g.*, 69 Fed. Reg. 7652 (Feb. 18, 2004); 69 Fed. Reg. 28932 (May 19, 2004); 69 Fed. Reg. 63482 (Nov. 2, 2004); 70 Fed. Reg. 72447 (Dec. 5, 2005); 70 Fed. Reg. 72449 (Dec. 5, 2005).

4.   OTC DRUG LABELING

Two aspects of OTC drug labeling must be considered: (1) the restrictions established under the OTC Drug Review and (2) the "Drug Facts" format for general labeling established in 1999.

a.   OTC DRUG REVIEW RESTRICTIONS

At the outset of the OTC Drug Review, FDA intended that the only label claims that could lawfully be made for an OTC drug were those specified in a final monograph for the class of drugs or approved by the agency in a new drug application. The agency took the position on several occasions that a manufacturer must use the precise terminology set forth in the monograph in describing the indications for use of a product or in providing warnings about misuse. 38 Fed. Reg. 31260, ¶¶ 17, 49 (Nov. 12, 1973); 39 Fed. Reg. 19868, ¶ 50 (June 4, 1974); 40 Fed. Reg. 11718 (Mar.

13, 1975). This so-called "exclusivity" policy did not prevent the use of accurate and non-misleading descriptive phrases or adjectives, *e.g.*, "sparkling" antacid. 40 Fed. Reg. 11718 (Mar. 13, 1975).

Manufacturers of OTC drugs opposed FDA's exclusivity policy for a decade, arguing that greater flexibility should be permitted for both legal and policy reasons. After a public hearing announced in 47 Fed. Reg. 29002 (July 2, 1982), the FDA published the following proposal.

Labeling of Drug Products for Over–the–Counter Human Use

50 Fed. Reg. 15810 (April 22, 1985).

. . . .

The policy of limiting monograph labeling terminology to specific words and phrases considered and approved by FDA has been the subject of comment throughout the OTC drug review process. With the publication of the tentative final monograph for OTC antacid drug products in the Federal Register of November 12, 1973 (38 FR 31280), FDA responded to comments proposing that terms other than those specified in the monograph should be allowed in the product labeling. The agency concluded that the terms recommended by the panel fully met the intent of the regulation. The agency also stated that allowing each manufacturer to select words other than those set forth in the monograph would result in continued consumer confusion and deception (38 FR 31264). . . .

The objections to the exclusivity policy were resubmitted with respect to nighttime sleep-aid and stimulant drug products after publication of the tentative final monographs for these products, and an oral hearing was requested. . . .

The notice of hearing defined the scope of the hearing broadly as encompassing all aspects, both practical and legal, of the exclusivity policy and its possible alternatives. . . .

The agency has decided . . . that the present exclusivity policy, while legally supportable, should not be continued for policy reasons. FDA specifically rejects the assertions in the submitted comments that the present policy is legally deficient on constitutional grounds, is in violation of the Administrative Procedure Act (APA), or contrary to the Federal Food, Drug, and Cosmetic Act. . . .

As discussed in detail below, the new labeling requirements would allow for a[n] alternative labeling of OTC drug products. The label and labeling would be required to contain, in a prominent and conspicuous location, either (1) within a boxed area that is designated "APPROVED USES" the specific wording set out in the indications for use section of an applicable OTC drug monograph, or (2) within a nonboxed area alternative wording relating to indications for use that is not false or misleading. As a third alternative, monograph language would be used in the boxed area and the label and labeling could contain elsewhere alternative wording describing indications for use, so long as the alternative wording was not false or misleading.

The agency believes that labeling established in an OTC drug monograph would continue to serve a vital purpose. It would represent the agency's determination, following extensive notice and comment rulemaking, of the specific indications for which an OTC drug product would be generally recognized as safe and effective, and not misbranded. Because the monographs would provide a definitive explanation of those uses a particular drug is good for, FDA would be able to determine whether nonmonograph language is an accurate description of a drug's properties. . . .

The agency emphasizes, as described below in the discussion of the proposed regulation, that it will use the monograph language as a regulatory benchmark. FDA will carefully examine any alternative language to ensure that it does not go beyond the approved indications, thereby causing the drug to become a "new drug" or misbranded, or both, under the act. Language that is so nondescriptive as to be meaningless, or that indicates uses for a new indication, would cause the product to be misbranded, a new drug, or both. . . .

NOTE

The final regulation was promulgated in 51 Fed. Reg. 16258 (May 1, 1986), codified at 21 C.F.R. 330.1(c)(2). The regulation specifies that flexibility is allowed only for labeled "indications" and not for any other required features of OTC drug labeling.

b.   OTC "DRUG FACTS" FORMAT

Drawing on its food labeling initiative, in February 1997 FDA proposed to standardize OTC drug labeling.

Over-The-Counter Human Drugs; Proposed Labeling Requirements

62 Fed. Reg. 9024 (February 27, 1997).

Under the Federal Food, Drug, and Cosmetic Act, OTC Drug products must be safe and effective in order to be marketed. The agency is conducting a comprehensive review of these drug products, which are available to consumers without a prescription. As a result of this review, the agency has required specific language to be included in the labeling of many OTC drug products, describing the uses, directions, warnings, drug interaction precautions, active ingredients, and other information, so that consumers can use these products safely and effectively.

As a result of escalating health care costs and the increasing availability of OTC drug products, some of which were once available only by prescription, more consumers are engaging in self-medication. Thus, it is increasingly important that consumers read and understand the information on drug product labeling.

On January 6, 1993, the agency issued final regulations to help consumers read and understand the information on food product labeling. . . .

FDA believes it is equally important for consumers to be able to make reasoned decisions about the drugs they take. On August 24, 1995 (60 FR 44182), FDA proposed a comprehensive program to increase the distribution and quality of easy to read and easy to understand written information about prescription drugs to patients. Recently enacted legislation provides that various private entities will work to transform these goals into a satisfactory program. FDA is now proposing to improve the way that information on the labeling of OTC drug products is communicated.

The design, format, and placement of required labeling information varies considerably among OTC drug products. As a result, consumers often have difficulty finding, reading, and understanding this labeling information. Modifying and simplifying the manner in which the information is presented can improve the legibility and understandability of OTC drug product labeling. FDA is, therefore, proposing to establish a standardized format for the labeling of all marketed OTC drug products. This action is intended to enable consumers to better read and understand OTC drug product labeling and to apply this information to the safe and effective use of OTC drug products.

The agency is proposing five types of labeling changes for OTC drug products. First, the proposal would require that OTC drug product labeling include standardized headings and subheadings presented in a standardized order, as well as standardized graphical features such as the Helvetica type style, minimum standards for type size, leading (*i.e.*, space between two lines of text), kerning (spacing between letters), upper and lower case letters, and graphical highlights.

Second, the proposal would permit manufacturers, packers, or distributors to delete specific terms, referred to for purposes of this rulemaking as "connecting terms," that are currently required in OTC drug product labeling. . . . Typically, such terms are found within quotation marks in OTC drug monographs and in specific regulations. Deletion of these terms would only be permitted where deletion would not change the meaning of the information. . . .

Third, the proposal would expand the list of "interchangeable terms" found in the current regulations, to facilitate the use of more concise, easier to understand statements on the labeling of OTC drug products. . . .

Fourth, the proposal would amend specific warning language required under current monographs and regulations (the pregnancy-nursing warning, the "keep out of reach of children" warning, and the overdose/accidental ingestion warning) make the warnings easier to understand and more concise.

Finally, in order to ensure OTC drug product labeling is easier to read and understand, and to ensure the safe and effective use of OTC drug products, FDA is proposing to preempt State and local rules that establish different or additional format or content requirements than those in this proposed rule. . . .

The final regulations, promulgated in 64 Fed. Reg. 13254 (Mar. 17, 1999), 21 C.F.R. 201.66, closely followed the proposal, except that FDA deleted the preemption provision because Congress had in the interim enacted section 751 of the FD&C Act under the Food and Drug Administration Act of 1997. *See infra* p. 1454. One of the sample OTC drug labels used by FDA to illustrate the new format follows.

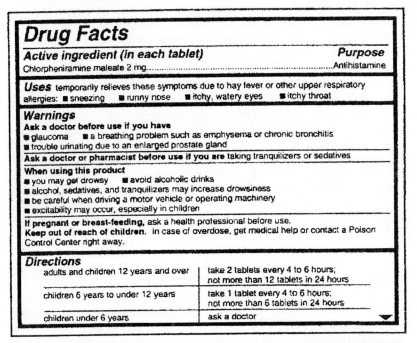

c. LABEL WARNINGS

As discussed *supra* p. 505, Note 14 there are significant differences between prescription and nonprescription drug warnings. Prescription drug warnings include a number of potential adverse events for which causality and materiality have not been established. Physicians can then evaluate this information and use it to select appropriate medication for their patients. OTC drug warnings, in contrast, are directed at the consumer, not the physician. Accordingly, as FDA has stated, OTC drug warnings are limited to those that are "scientifically documented, clinically significant and important for the safe and effective use of the products by consumers." 47 Fed. Reg. 54750, 54754 (Dec. 3, 1982); 53 Fed. Reg. 46204, 46213 (Nov. 16, 1988). *See* R. William Soller, *When To Warn*, 2 REG. AFFAIRS FOCUS, No. 10 at 18 (Oct. 1997).

NOTES

1. *Pre–OTC Drug Review Warnings.* Prior to the OTC Drug Review, recommended and required warnings for OTC drugs were published in 21 C.F.R. Parts 201 and 369. The Review, however, has provided a vehicle for examining the need for, and content of, required warnings for all OTC drugs.

2. *Aspirin Warnings.* In *Public Citizen Health Research Group v. Commissioner*, 740 F.2d 21 (D.C. Cir. 1984), the Court of Appeals declined to order FDA to require a warning on aspirin-containing products about the risk of Reye Syndrome. FDA ultimately did prescribe such a warning. 47 Fed. Reg. 57886 (Dec. 28, 1982), 50 Fed. Reg. 51400 (Dec. 17, 1985), 51 Fed. Reg. 8180 (Mar. 7, 1986), 53 Fed. Reg. 1796 (Jan. 22, 1988), 53 Fed. Reg. 21633 (June 9, 1988), codified at 21 C.F.R. 201.314(h).

3. *Aspirin Flavoring and Packaging.* In 1967, FDA issued a statement of policy recommending that the flavoring of five-grain aspirin tablets or other adult aspirin tablets be discontinued. 32 Fed. Reg. 3340 (Mar. 2, 1967), codified at 21 C.F.R. 201.314. Following enactment of the Poison Prevention Packaging Act of 1970, FDA (which was responsible for implementing the PPPA before the Consumer Product Safety Commission was established) issued a regulation requiring that aspirin products be marketed in child-resistant packaging. 37 Fed. Reg. 3127 (Feb. 6, 1972), codified at 16 C.F.R. 1700.14(a)(1), 1700.15. These actions substantially reduced the frequency of cases of accidental childhood ingestion of aspirin.

4. *Other OTC Drug Warnings.* Additional pregnancy warnings were promulgated for aspirin in 55 Fed. Reg. 27776 (July 5, 1990), and warnings were proposed for all OTC drugs containing water-soluble gums as active ingredients in 55 Fed. Reg. 45782 (Oct. 30, 1990).

5. *Proposition 65 Warnings.* Under California Proposition 65, nicotine products are required to bear a warning about reproductive toxicity. Under the NDA for nicotine smoking cessation products, however, FDA concluded that such a warning was inappropriate and could not be used. In *Dowhal v. SmithKline Beecham Consumer Healthcare*, 88 P.3d 1 (Cal. 2004), the California Supreme Court held that, under these circumstances, the FDA determination preempted the California law.

6. *Adverse Event Reporting.* In late 2006, Congress enacted the Dietary Supplement and Nonprescription Drug Consumer Protection Act, 120 Stat. 3469, which added sections 760 and 761 to the FD&C Act to require serious adverse event reporting to FDA for both dietary supplements and nonprescription drugs. The law provides that such a report does not constitute an admission that the product caused the adverse event, and it preempts any non-identical state law.

5. FTC REGULATION OF OTC DRUG ADVERTISING

Congress declined in 1938 to give FDA jurisdiction to regulate drug advertising and instead confirmed the advertising authority of the Federal Trade Commission. *See* Charles O. Jackson, FOOD AND DRUG LEGISLATION IN THE NEW DEAL (1970); David Cavers, *The Food, Drug, and Cosmetic Act of 1938: Its Legislative History and Its Substantive Provisions*, 6 LAW & CONTEMP. PROBS. 2 (1939); Note, *The FTC's Injunctive Authority Against False Advertising of Food and Drugs*, 75 MICH. L. REV. 745 (1977). Congress created exceptions to this general allocation of jurisdiction by granting FDA authority to regulate advertising for prescription drugs under FD&C Act 502(n) in the Drug Amendments of 1962, *supra* p. 535, and advertising for vitamins and minerals under FD&C Act 403(a)(2) and 707 in the Vitamin–

Mineral Amendments of 1976, *supra* p. 256. With respect to OTC drugs, however, FTC retains the jurisdiction that Congress conferred in 1938.

The two agencies are supposed to cooperate in exercising their abutting responsibilities. *See* FDA–FTC Memorandum of Understanding, 36 Fed. Reg. 18539 (Sept. 16, 1971). FDA's commencement of the OTC Drug Review promised new opportunities for collaboration. In determining what label claims for OTC drugs were supported by legally adequate evidence of effectiveness and would not render drugs misbranded, FDA would inevitably examine evidence that might be pertinent to a determination of whether advertising claims for a drug were deceptive. Both agencies hoped that the FTC would be able to make use of FDA's monographs in a fashion that would limit claims in advertising to those approved for labeling.

Based on FDA's adoption of the "exclusivity" policy, *supra* p. 804, the FTC proposed a trade regulation rule (TRR) under sections 5 and 12 of the Federal Trade Commission Act, 15 U.S.C. 45, 52, that would translate FDA's OTC drug monographs into commensurate restrictions on advertising. 40 Fed. Reg. 52631 (Nov. 11, 1975). Under the terms of the rule as proposed, it would be a violation of the FTC Act to disseminate an advertisement for an OTC drug in any drug category

> for which an applicable final monograph has been established by the Food and Drug Administration ... which advertisement makes any claim, directly or by implication, which the Commissioner of Food and Drugs has determined, in a final order accompanying such monograph, may not appear in the labeling of such drug.

As the FTC rulemaking progressed, it became evident that counsel supporting the proposed rule were seeking the broadest possible construction of FDA's monographs. They argued that in the course of approving label claims in a final monograph, FDA necessarily concluded that other terminology would not convey the same message to consumers, and accordingly that drugs bearing other terminology would not be generally recognized as safe and effective and not misbranded. From this premise it was a small step to the conclusion that advertising using nonconforming terminology to describe a drug's performance would be deceptive.

The presiding officer's report largely rejected the staff position. 44 Fed. Reg. 1123 (Jan. 4, 1979). Although the staff persevered, 44 Fed. Reg. 31241 (May 31, 1979), the full Commission terminated the proceeding in 46 Fed. Reg. 24584 (May 1, 1981) with the following explanation:

> The Commission has concluded that in advertising a drug for a permissible (*i.e.*, FDA-approved) purpose, advertisers should not always be limited (as they would have been under the original proposed rule) to the labeling language approved by FDA.

The Commission declared that it would continue to review advertising for OTC drugs, in the light of FDA monographs, to determine whether further action was necessary.

NOTES

1. *Commentary.* For further discussion of the FTC "claims" TRR, see Robert Altman, *Labeling and Advertising Trends*, 34 FOOD DRUG COSM. L.J. 569 (1979);

Frank DiPrima, *Some Partisan Musings on the OTC Review and the Advertising TRRs*, 32 FOOD DRUG COSM. L.J. 405 (1977); Richard Herzog, *The FTC's Proposed Rule on OTC Drug Advertising*, 31 FOOD DRUG COSM. L.J. 147 (1976).

2. *FDA Label Warnings.* The FTC proposed a second TRR to require that some of the label warnings required by the final FDA monograph for antacid drugs also appear in advertising. 41 Fed. Reg. 14534 (Apr. 6, 1976), 43 Fed. Reg. 38851 (Aug. 31, 1978). *See* Frank DiPrima, *Advertising of OTC Drugs: Proposed TRR on Warnings*, 32 FOOD DRUG COSM. L.J. 96 (1977); Herbert Dym, *Affirmative Disclosure of Warning Information in OTC Drug Advertising*, 34 FOOD DRUG COSM. L.J. 564 (1979); Richard Herzog, *The Antacid Warning—Rulemaking at the FTC*, 32 FOOD DRUG COSM. L.J. 76 (1977). Following a public hearing, publication of the staff report, 48 Fed. Reg. 36273 (Aug. 10, 1983), and an oral hearing before the Commissioners, the FTC terminated this proceeding. 49 Fed. Reg. 46156 (Nov. 23, 1984). The Commission concluded that the record did not support the staff's contention that antacid advertisements would be deceptive or unfair if they failed to contain warnings similar to those required by FDA in labeling.

3. *Defensive Use of OTC Panel Report.* For an unsuccessful attempt by a respondent before the FTC to use the tentative conclusions of an OTC Drug Review panel defensively, see *Warner–Lambert Co. v. FTC*, 562 F.2d 749 (D.C. Cir. 1977).

4. *Claim Substantiation.* In *Pfizer, Inc.*, 81 F.T.C. 23 (1972), the FTC enunciated the policy that it is unfair and deceptive for a manufacturer to make any affirmative drug product claim without having a "reasonable basis" for it. Relying on the prevailing view of experts in the field, the Commission has required at least two clinical studies to substantiate OTC drug advertising claims. *See Thompson Medical Co., Inc.*, 104 F.T.C. 648 (1984), *aff'd*, 791 F.2d 189 (D.C. Cir. 1986); *Bristol–Myers Co.*, 102 F.T.C. 21 (1983), *aff'd*, 738 F.2d 554 (2d Cir. 1984); *American Home Products Corp.*, 98 F.T.C. 136 (1981), *aff'd*, 695 F.2d 681 (3d Cir. 1982).

5. *Corrective Advertising.* In *Warner–Lambert Co. v. FTC*, 562 F.2d 749 (D.C. Cir. 1977), the FTC for the first time required corrective advertising for an OTC drug. It was not until *Novartis Corp. v. FTC*, 223 F.3d 783 (D.C. Cir. 2000), that the FTC used this remedy for a second time.

6.   THE NDA DEVIATION

A final OTC drug monograph represents only the state of the evidence provided to FDA at the time the monograph is promulgated. FDA recognized that improvements in OTC drugs would occur continuously. The agency therefore included in 21 C.F.R. 330.11 a procedure for an "NDA deviation" from an applicable monograph. This provision specifically authorizes the use of an NDA to request approval of an OTC drug deviating in any respect from a final monograph. The NDA need address only the requirement of the monograph for which the deviation is requested, and it may omit all information except that pertinent to the deviation. The concept is analogous to a section 505(b)(2) NDA for a prescription drug. FDA granted one NDA deviation to permit an aerosol pediculicide (lice treatment), where the final monograph permitted only a non-aerosol dosage formulation. In response to a citizen petition requesting that the cough and cold monograph be amended to include a chewing gum dosage form for a topical antitussive drug, FDA responded that the appropriate mechanism would be to submit an NDA deviation under 21 C.F.R. 330.11. Letter from

FDA Associate Commissioner for Regulatory Affairs Dennis E. Baker to David L. Rosen (Nov. 9, 2001), FDA Docket No. OIP–0253/CPI.

7. THIRD CLASS OF DRUGS?

Nonprescription drugs may be sold at any kind of retail store in the United States, ranging from a pharmacy to a grocery store to a gasoline station. There are no criteria for or limitations on their method of distribution and sale. Pharmacy groups have contended that FDA should establish a "third class" of drugs that would be available only through a pharmacy, and they have pointed to prescription drugs that are in the process of being switched to nonprescription status as one example of the need for such a new class. FDA has declined to establish such a third class, on both policy and legal grounds. First, FDA has stated that any drug switched by the agency from prescription to nonprescription status is sufficiently safe for sale in any retail establishment and that a requirement limiting sale to a pharmacy would provide an unjustified monopoly to pharmacists. Second, FDA has stated that the FD&C Act provides no authority for FDA to restrict distribution of a nonprescription drug to pharmacies. *See, e.g.,* 39 Fed. Reg. 19880, 19881 (June 4, 1974). *See also* Gregory M. Fisher, *Third Class of Drugs—A Current View*, 46 FOOD DRUG COSM. L.J. 583 (1991); GAO, NONPRESCRIPTION DRUGS: VALUE OF A PHARMACIST-CONTROLLED CLASS HAS YET TO BE DEMONSTRATED, No. PEMD–95–12 (Aug. 1995). *But see* Leland L. Price, *Sweetening the Bitter Pill: Rx to OTC Switches via a Third Class of Drugs* (1995), in Chapter VI(D)(1) of the Electronic Book. In *Carey v. Population Services International*, 431 U.S. 678 (1977), the Supreme Court invalidated a New York statute making it a crime for anyone other than a pharmacist to distribute contraceptives.

8. OTC DRUG PRODUCT TAMPERING

In response to purposeful cyanide contamination of Tylenol resulting in the death of several persons in Chicago, FDA promptly promulgated final regulations to require tamper-resistant packaging for non-prescription drugs and cosmetics.

Tamper–Resistant Packaging Requirements for Certain Over–the–Counter Human Drug and Cosmetic Products

47 Fed. Reg. 50442 (November 5, 1982).

FDA is issuing final regulations to require tamper-resistant packaging for certain over-the-counter (OTC) drug and cosmetic products. OTC drug products subject to these regulations include all OTC drug products except dermatologics (*i.e.*, products applied to the skin), dentifrices, and insulin. The OTC drug products that are covered by these regulations include oral (except dentifrices), nasal, otic, ophthalmic, rectal, and vaginal drug products. Cosmetic products covered by these regulations are liquids that are used orally, such as mouthwashes, gargles, breath fresheners, etc., and vaginal cosmetic products. The agency is requiring that the packaging of these products be capable of providing consumers with visible evidence of package tampering. . . .

On September 30, 1982, FDA was advised that several persons living in the Chicago metropolitan area had died from cyanide poisoning after taking Extra–Strength Tylenol capsules. Capsules taken from bottles of Extra–Strength Tylenol in the possession of the victims were chemically analyzed by local authorities, and some of the capsules in these bottles were found to contain lethal amounts of potassium cyanide. By October 1, several more Chicago area residents had died from cyanide poisoning after ingesting Tylenol Extra–Strength capsules, bringing the total of deaths to seven.

On September 30, government authorities and the manufacturer of Tylenol, McNeil Consumer Products, Fort Washington, PA, began an investigation to determine the manner in which the capsules had become contaminated with cyanide. The capsules involved in the seven deaths were manufactured in two plants, one in Pennsylvania and one in Texas. FDA investigators immediately inspected both plants. Based on the plant inspections, FDA concluded that the contamination had not occurred at either plant, but rather was the result of tampering after the capsules had been shipped to distribution points and, most likely, after they had reached the retail shelves. . . .

Since the Tylenol poisonings, several cases of serious injuries have been reported resulting from the use of products that have been tampered with. These incidents, although not the initial impetus for these regulations, further demonstrate the need for their prompt implementation.

The poisoning fatalities make plain the gravity of the risk to which the nation's population is exposed from malicious tampering with drug products sold over-the-counter to the consumer. The Tylenol incident occurred in the Chicago area, but it was followed by others elsewhere in the country. Nor is the potential for such tampering confined to one manufacturer's products. Incidents of OTC drug product tampering have occurred in recent weeks. The combined incidents demonstrate that the need for adequate product security is national in scope and requires an industrywide response. . . .

The agency defines a tamper-resistant package as one having an indicator or barrier to entry which, if breached or missing, can reasonably be expected to provide visible evidence to consumers that tampering has occurred. Tamper-resistant packaging may involve immediate-container/closure systems or secondary-container/carton systems or any combination thereof intended to provide a visual indication of package integrity when handled in a reasonable manner during manufacture, distribution, and retail display. The visual indication is required to be accompanied by appropriate illustrations or precautionary statements to describe the safeguarding mechanism to the consumer. To reduce the possibility that the security mechanism can be restored after tampering, the agency is also requiring that either the tamper-resistant feature be designed from materials that are generally not readily available (*e.g.*, an aerosol system) or that barriers made from readily obtainable material (*e.g.*, plain tape, paper seals, clear plastic) carry a distinctive design or logo.

The agency stresses that tamper-*proof* packaging is not possible. Although the requirements in this final rule will reduce the potential for tampering, they cannot eliminate it. Neither the agency nor manufacturers can guarantee protection against malicious tampering but can only make tampering more difficult by making product packaging more *resistant* to tampering. For this reason, the agency will consider any labeling statement suggesting that the package is tamper-proof, as contrasted with tamper-resistant, to be false and misleading. Consumers must act to protect themselves from injury by inspecting the condition of the packages they buy, the tablets and capsules they take, and the liquids they drink....

Under the Federal Food, Drug, and Cosmetic Act, FDA is authorized to impose requirements necessary to assure that drugs meet the requirements of the act for identity, strength, quality, and purity. Such requirements may be imposed as current good manufacturing practice (CGMP) (21 U.S.C. 351(a)(2)(B))....

... The requirements set forth in FDA's CGMP regulations for pharmaceutical products represent those measures needed to ensure that drugs purchased by the people of this country meet all statutory requirements at the time of purchase. Such measures must now include provision for container and package design that provides protection against intentional product adulteration by means of tampering.

FDA's authority to issue Federal standards for tamper-resistant drug packaging is also derived from other provisions of the act relating to drug adulteration. Under section 501(b) of the act, drugs are required to meet applicable compendial standards for strength, quality, and purity. Under section 501(c) of the act, drugs not subject to compendial standards are required to possess the strength, quality, and purity they are represented to have. Because contamination of drugs by tampering causes these requirements to be violated, FDA is authorized to impose packaging requirements reasonably designed to prevent such contamination....

NOTES

1. *Preemption.* In order to make certain that state and local governments would not enact different or additional anti-tampering requirements, FDA included a specific administrative determination of federal preemption. 47 Fed. Reg. at 50447–48.

2. *Anti–Tampering Act.* In response to the Chicago Tylenol poisonings, Congress enacted the Federal Anti–Tampering Act, 97 Stat. 831 (1983), codified at 18 U.S.C. § 1365, which makes it a crime to tamper with a consumer product with reckless disregard for the risk of persons or with intent to cause injury to a business. The statute also prohibits communication of false information that a consumer product has been tainted and threats to tamper with a consumer product. For examples of prosecution under this statute, *see United States v. Garnett*, 122 F.3d 1016 (11th Cir. 1997); *United States v. Moyer*, 985 F. Supp. 924 (D. Minn. 1997); *United States v. Acosta*, Food Drug Cosm. L. Rep. (CCH) ¶ 38,294 (S.D.N.Y. 1992).

3. *Incidents of Tampering.* Despite the efforts of the agency and of Congress, tampering with FDA-regulated products continues to occur. In 1986, the agency

acknowledged that reports of tampering had "decreased significantly" following the actions taken in 1982, but it then recounted more recent incidents:

> In February 1986, FDA again received a report of a death linked to the tampering of Tylenol capsules with cyanide. In the following months, FDA has been embroiled in a widespread series of investigations of tampering incidents that include dozens of products such as Gerber baby food, Girl Scout cookies, Ac'cent flavor enhancer, and other OTC drugs including Contac, Teldrin, Dietac, Excedrin and Anacin–3. . . .

> . . . FDA will continue to support the criminal investigation of tamperings and falsely reported tamperings. In addition, FDA, with assistance from the Proprietary Association and other industry and consumer groups, will continue to focus efforts on public education since investigation of tampering incidents shows that current packaging is indeed very tamper-evident and has usually offered a signal to users that the product has been tampered with. The report also says that FDA will work with the pharmaceutical industry to encourage and emphasize the rapid adoption of improved tamper-resistant packaging including the utilization of more than one tamper-resistant feature per package, phasing out weaker tamper-resistant packaging technologies such as glued cartons, and bringing uniformity to tamper-resistant packaging within the product lines of companies. . . .

"Agency Report on Tampering Available," FDA Talk Paper No. 786–49 (July 9, 1986). The agency devoted $2.85 million to OTC drug tampering problems during fiscal year 1986. "Cost of Tampering and Other Emergencies," FDA Talk Paper No. T87–10 (Feb. 18, 1987).

4. *CPSC Regulations.* In 2001, the CPSC promulgated a requirement of child resistant packaging on all drugs approved by FDA for OTC sale that contain active ingredients formerly available only by prescription. 65 Fed. Reg. 52678 (Aug. 30, 2000), 66 Fed. Reg. 40111 (Aug. 2, 2001), codified at 16 C.F.R. 1700.14(a)(30). Under section 4(a) of the Poison Prevention Packaging Act, 15 U.S.C. 1473(a), manufacturers have the right to package a nonprescription drug in one size of non-child-resistant packaging as long as the company also supplies the drug in child-resistant packaging of a popular size, and the noncomplying package bears a conspicuous statement that "this package for households without young children." This exception does not apply to prescription drugs, but samples distributed to physicians are not required to be in child-resistant packaging. 49 Fed. Reg. 8008 (Mar. 5, 1984).

5. *Commentary. See* Steven D. Weatherhead, *Rethinking Product Tampering* (1996), and Michelle L. Woollen, *"Do Not Use If Seal Is Broken:" Product Tampering and the Case Against Private Tort Liability* (1996), in Chapter II(Z) of the Electronic Book.

L. REGULATING PHYSICIAN PRESCRIBING

1. PHYSICIAN PRESCRIBING HABITS

As defined by the FD&C Act, a prescription drug is a drug for which adequate directions for use cannot be written, because laypersons lack the scientific understanding needed to diagnose their disease or to use the drug in treating it. As we have suggested, *supra* p. 523, this rationale for restricting drugs to sale only by prescription is beginning to erode. With the spread of patient labeling and other educational materials, combined with direct-to-consumer advertising and the internet, patients have become more knowledgeable about prescription drugs and often participate with their physicians in treatment decisions.

From the time of its creation of a mandatory category of prescription drugs in 1939, FDA has sought to protect consumers of these drugs in two distinct ways. First, it has attempted to assure through the new drug approval process and other regulatory controls that prescription drugs are safe and effective. Second, the agency has sought to provide physicians, through labeling addressed specifically to them, increasingly detailed information about drug use in patients. The FDA-approved physician labeling has now become a summary of all that is known about the safety and effectiveness of a drug. It represents a distillation of the results of testing arrived at through negotiations between agency officials and the drug's sponsor. Both FDA and pharmaceutical manufacturers assume that this labeling will influence the physician's decisions about use of the drug. The wisdom of FDA's reliance upon the physician labeling thus depends on the validity of that assumption.

There seems little doubt that the FDA-approved physician labeling significantly influences how prescription drugs are used. But it is also clear that every prescription drug is sometimes, and perhaps frequently, administered for conditions that fall outside the FDA-approved labeling. There are several reasons for this. The physician labeling describes only those conditions that have been systematically studied, and not all possible conditions of use. Physicians who routinely confront the duty to care for seriously ill patients are impelled to try new methods of treatment. Medical need invariably outpaces controlled clinical evaluation. New uses of established drugs often gain acceptance before controlled studies are launched, supplemental NDAs submitted, and FDA approval obtained. Once a drug goes off patent, there is no economic incentive for either the pioneer or a generic company to invest in clinical trials for off-label uses. On the other extreme, use of a drug for an unapproved indication can also represent poor judgment, inattention to warnings, or inadequate medical training.

Thus, FDA is often faced with the following dilemma. Some unapproved uses represent sound medical care, sometimes even the only promising treatment. Other unapproved uses seem reckless. Initially, the agency took the position that only the information contained in the FDA-approved physician labeling represents reliable information about a new drug and cautioned physicians not to stray beyond it. When pressed, however, FDA backed away from the proposition that prescribing a new drug for an indication not approved in the FDA-approved physician labeling constitutes a violation of the FD&C Act. Instead, the agency took the more limited position that the manufacturer may not promote an approved drug for unapproved uses.

2.   FDA INFLUENCE OVER PHYSICIAN PRESCRIBING

FDA initially sought to discourage any unapproved use of an approved new drug.

New Drugs Used for Nonapproved Purposes
(Methotrexate for Psoriasis)

Hearings Before a Subcomm. of the House Comm. on Government Operations, 92d Congress, 1st Sess. (1971).

Mr. Rosenthal. . . . If you find . . . that physicians who are not part of the IND studies are dispensing a drug improperly, is it also your attitude that nothing can be done?

Mr. Goodrich [FDA Chief Counsel]. We could have done more than we did. The problem here was the physicians were using the drug on the basis of literature reports. The company was saying that it was not promoting the drug. We examined the evidence; we thought they did.

. . . We found out that when a physician out in the prescribing territory asked the detail man about Methotrexate for psoriasis then that would be reported back to Lederle and Lederle would send the physician a letter and reprints. They would send a disclaimer that they were not promoting the drug for that purpose, but that they would supply the information that it had been used; it had been used successfully by simply reporting out of the literature, and they would give him some information about the dose.

Mr. Rosenthal. That was not legal, what they were doing?

Mr. Goodrich. No, it was not. . . .

And Dr. Ley's approach, Mr. Rosenthal, was that it should be dealt with as an educational program with the profession. He encouraged the American Medical Association Journal to run an editorial on this. . . .

Mr. Grant [FDA Deputy Commissioner]. . . . Methotrexate is not the only drug that is being used for conditions for which it is not approved or labeled. Drugs approved for marketing for one purpose sometimes are found in ingenuity or by accident or have other uses. . . .

Our problem in dealing with the use of drugs for conditions in which they are not approved involves both the manufacturer and the prescribing physician. We have direct control over the manufacturer. We can take legal and administrative actions to assure that any drug is labeled for all of the conditions for which it is intended to be used, whether that intent is openly expressed in the promotional literature and promotional practices, or whether it is demonstrated by the manufacturer supplying a drug for purposes not covered in the approved labeling.

As to the physician, no less a group than the Council on Drugs of the American Medical Association has taken the position that it is within the physician's sole discretion to choose and to prescribe a drug for his own patient. . . .

What physicians need to know is that when they prescribe outside the limits of safety and effectiveness that have been established through the adequate and well-controlled clinical investigations required by the new drug procedures, they are using the drug investigationally on their patients. If any untoward reaction or adverse effect occurs, the physician may well be called upon to defend the reasonableness of his therapy. . . .

Following this hearing, FDA's position changed in two respects. First, FDA agreed that a company could properly respond with information about an off-label use of a drug to an unsolicited question by a physician. *See supra* p. 548. Second, the agency published the following proposed regulation to state its policy on physician prescribing for off-label uses.

Legal Status of Approved Labeling for Prescription Drugs; Prescribing for Uses Unapproved by the Food and Drug Administration: Notice of Proposed Rule Making

37 Fed. Reg. 16503 (August 15, 1972).

The widespread use of certain prescription drugs for conditions not named in the official labeling has led to questions concerning the legal responsibilities of the prescribing physicians and the position of the Food and Drug Administration with respect to such use. . . .

Section 505 of the Federal Food, Drug, and Cosmetic Act prohibits the introduction or delivery for introduction into interstate commerce of any new drug without the filing of an investigational new drug plan or approval of a new drug application. Unlike the adulteration and misbranding provisions of the Act, the new drug provisions apply only at the moment of shipment in interstate commerce and not to action taken subsequent to shipment in interstate commerce. In *United States v. Phelps Dodge Mercantile Co.*, 157 F.2d 453 (9th Cir. 1946) [*infra* p. 1226], the court held that violations while products are held for sale after interstate shipment did not come within the jurisdiction of the Act. As a result of that decision, Congress enacted the Miller amendment of 1948, amending section 301(k) of the Act to extend the reach of the adulteration and misbranding provisions of the Act to violations after interstate shipment. The 1948 amendment did not, however, also extend the reach of the new drug provisions of the Act, which are separate from the adulteration and misbranding provisions, to action taken after interstate shipment.

The major objective of the drug provisions of the Federal Food, Drug, and Cosmetic Act is to assure that drugs will be safe and effective for use under the conditions of use prescribed, recommended, or suggested in the labeling thereof. . . . When a new drug is approved for marketing, the conditions of use that have been approved are required to be set forth in detail in the official labeling. This labeling must accompany the drug in interstate shipment and must contain adequate information for safe and effective use of the drug. . . . It presents a full disclosure summarization of drug use information, which the supplier of the drug is required to develop from accumulated clinical experience, and systematic drug trials consisting of preclinical investigations and adequate well-controlled clinical investigations that demonstrate the drug's safety and the effectiveness it purports or is represented to possess.

If an approved new drug is shipped in interstate commerce with the approved package insert, and neither the shipper nor the recipient intends that it be used for an unapproved purpose, the requirements of section 505 of the Act are satisfied. Once the new drug is in a local pharmacy after interstate shipment, the physician may, as part of the practice of medicine, lawfully prescribe a different dosage for his patient, or may otherwise vary the conditions of use from those approved in the package insert, without informing or obtaining the approval of the Food and Drug Administration.

This interpretation of the Act is consistent with congressional intent as indicated in the legislative history of the 1938 Act and the drug amendments of 1962. Throughout the debate leading to enactment, there were repeated statements that Congress did not intend the Food and Drug Administration to interfere with medical practice and references to the understanding that the bill did not purport to regulate the practice of medicine as between the physician and the patient. . . .

[A]lthough it is clear that Congress did not intend the Food and Drug Administration to regulate or interfere with the practice of medicine, it is equally clear that it did intend that the Food and Drug Administration determine those drugs for which there exists substantial evidence of safety and effectiveness and thus will be available for prescribing by the medical profession, and additionally, what information about the drugs constitutes truthful, accurate, and full disclosure to permit safe and effective prescription by the physician. As the law now stands, therefore, the Food and Drug Administration is charged with the responsibility of judging the safety and effectiveness of drugs and the truthfulness of their labeling. The physician is then responsible for making the final judgment as to which, if any, of the available drugs his patient will receive in the light of the information contained in their labeling and other adequate scientific data available to him.

Although the Act does not require a physician to file an investigational new drug plan before prescribing an approved drug for unapproved uses, or to submit to the Food and Drug Administration data concerning the therapeutic results and the adverse reactions obtained, it is sometimes in the best interests of the physician and the public that this be done. The physician should recognize that such use is investigational, and he should take account of the scientific principles, including the moral and ethical considerations, applicable to the safe use of investigational drugs in human patients. . . .

Where the unapproved use of an approved new drug becomes widespread or endangers the public health, the Food and Drug Administration is obligated to investigate it thoroughly and to take whatever action is warranted to protect the public. Several alternative courses of action are available to the Food and Drug Administration under these circumstances, depending upon the specific facts of each case. These actions include: Requiring a change in the labeling to warn against or to approve the unapproved use, seeking substantial evidence to substantiate the use, restricting the channel of distribution, and even withdrawing approval of the drug and removing it from the market in extreme cases. When necessary, the Food and Drug Administration will not hesitate to take whatever action of this nature may be required to bring possible harmful use of an approved drug under control.

Section 1.106 of the regulations [now 21 C.F.R. § 201.5] requires the labeling to contain appropriate information with respect to all intended uses of the drugs. Thus, where a manufacturer or his representative, or any person in the chain of distribution, does anything that directly or indirectly suggests to the physician or to the patient that an approved drug may properly be used for unapproved uses for which it is neither labeled nor advertised, that action constitutes a direct violation of the Act and is punishable accordingly. . . .

NOTES

1. *Subsequent Proceedings.* FDA first announced this policy in response to a question posed during a congressional hearing. "Regulation of Diethylstibestrol (DES)," Hearings before a Subcommittee of the House Committee on Government Operations, 92d Cong., 1st Sess., Part 1, at 102–103 (1971). The agency has taken no further action on the proposed regulation, but it has not been revoked and the agency continues to refer to this proposal as expressing its established policy. *See, e.g.,* "Use of Approved Drugs For Unlabeled Indications," 12 FDA DRUG BULL. 4 (Apr. 1982). *See also* 40 Fed. Reg. 15392, 15393–94 (Apr. 7, 1975). When FDA undertook its comprehensive revision of the IND regulations in the 1980s, it incorporated this policy. 48 Fed. Reg. 26720 (June 9, 1983), 52 Fed. Reg. 8798 (Mar. 19, 1987), codified at 21 C.F.R. 312.2(d) ("This part does not apply to the use in the practice of medicine for an unlabeled indication of a new drug. . . ."). The Supreme Court recognized the legitimacy and medical importance of off-label uses in *Buckman Co. v. Plaintiffs' Legal Comm.*, 531 U.S. 341, 350 (2001).

2. *Extent of Unapproved Use.* In its report on OFF-LABEL DRUGS: REIMBURSEMENT POLICIES CONSTRAIN PHYSICIANS IN THEIR CHOICE OF CANCER THERAPIES (1991), the GAO found that 44 of the 46 FDA-approved cancer drugs were prescribed for off-label uses and that almost all types of cancer were treated by unapproved uses of approved drugs. *See also* "Supplemental Indications for Approved Prescription Drugs," Hearing before the Subcommittee on Human Resources and Intergovernmental Relations of the House Committee on Government Reform and Oversight, 104th Cong., 2d Sess. (1996). Questions have been raised whether the agency should exercise regulatory control over unapproved uses. *See* "Is the FDA Protecting Consumers from Dangerous Off-Label Uses of Medical Drugs and Devices?," Fortieth Report by the House Committee on Government Operations, H. Rep. 102–1064, 102d Cong., 2d Sess. (1992).

3. *Use of Anticancer Drugs in Combination.* Few cancer drugs have been approved by FDA with labeling that explicitly recommends use in combination with any other cancer drug. The National Cancer Institute (NCI) not only recommends and makes available a number of Group C investigational cancer drugs for routine cancer therapy, *see supra* p. 655, but also recommends that virtually all cancer drugs be used in various combination in order to achieve the most effective therapy. In distributing or referring to standard NCI materials, pharmaceutical manufacturers are thus clearly recommending their drugs for unapproved uses. For years FDA has taken no action to prevent this activity, although in early 1991 the agency issued a letter objecting to the practice. Letter from K. R. Feather, Acting Director, FDA CDER Division of Drug Advertising and Labeling, to R. L. Gelb (Jan. 25,

1991). In light of current First Amendment jurisprudence, it is unlikely that FDA would take the same position today.

4. *Prohibition of Unapproved Use.* The only drug for which Congress has expressly prohibited all off-label use is human growth hormone (HGH). Section 303(e)(1) of the FD&C Act makes it a criminal offense for a physician to distribute HGH for any use other than the FDA-approved labeled use.

5. *Unapproved New Drugs.* Although unapproved uses of an FDA-approved new drug are lawful, any use of an unapproved new drug is unlawful. *See, e.g., United States v. Hiland,* 909 F.2d 1114 (8th Cir. 1990).

6. *State Law.* A related issue is whether the unapproved use of an approved new drug complies with state law. Relying upon FDA's position, states that have considered the matter have determined that the physician is not bound by the approved physician package insert. *E.g.,* Opinion of California Attorney General E. J. Younger, CV 76/212 and 77/236 (May 2, 1978); Opinion of California Legislative Counsel B. M. Gregory No. 8182 (May 26, 1981).

7. *Depo–Provera.* The Department of HHS has itself officially used approved drugs for unapproved purposes. The Indian Health Service prescribed Depo–Provera for contraceptive use even after FDA specifically disapproved this indication, as described *supra* p. 687, Note 2. *See* "Use of the Drug, Depo Provera, by the Indian Health Service," Oversight Hearing before the Subcommittee on General Oversight and Investigations of the House Committee on Interior and Insular Affairs, 100th Cong., 1st Sess. (1987). The military also uses approved drugs for unapproved purposes. *See, e.g.,* Matthew A. Hoffman, *The Military's Need for "Speed:" A Case Study on the FDA's Regulation of Off–Label Prescriptions* (2003), in Chapter VI(B)(5) of the Electronic Book.

8. *Generic Drugs.* Relying upon the FDA policy, the Chairman of the Subcommittee on Health and the Environment of the House Committee on Energy and Commerce took the position that a generic drug may lawfully be prescribed for a use for which only the pioneer drug has been approved, without added risk of liability on the part of the pharmacist or the physician. *See* letter from Representative Henry A. Waxman to F. S. Mayer (Nov. 25, 1985).

9. *Reimbursement for Unapproved Uses.* Even though FDA has stated that a physician may lawfully prescribe a new drug for an unapproved use, reimbursement for such uses under Medicare, Medicaid, and private insurance programs is not available unless a special rule states otherwise. *See* GAO, OFF-LABEL DRUGS: REIMBURSEMENT POLICIES CONSTRAIN PHYSICIANS IN THEIR CHOICE OF CANCER THERAPIES, Rep. No. PEMD–91–14 (1991); *see also* Gina M. Mazzariello Plaue, *Third Party Reimbursement for Participation in Cancer Clinical Trials: A Proposal for Legislation* (1999), in Chapter VI(C)(1) of the Electronic Book. This has caused the federal government to bring cases against drug manufacturers who promote unapproved uses.

10. *Physician Distribution.* Although a physician does not violate section 505 of the FD&C Act by *prescribing* an approved new drug for an unapproved use, a physician who distributes either unapproved drugs or approved drugs for unapproved uses is fully subject to the requirements of section 505. *See, e.g., United States v. Sartori,* Food Drug Cosm. L. Rep. (CCH) ¶ 38,196 (D. Md. 1982). Where the requisite interstate commerce is lacking, misbranding or adulteration charges may properly be brought against the illegal drug.

11. *Diversion of Drugs Exempted for Studies in Animals.* FDA's August 1972 policy apparently does not provide a basis for the diversion of experimental drugs from animal testing to human use. In 1983, FDA discovered that interferon, a biological drug which was being shipped for investigational use only in laboratory

animals or in vitro studies, was being diverted to human use. The agency published a notice warning that such diversion constituted a violation of section 351 of the Public Health Service Act. 48 Fed. Reg. 52644 (Nov. 21, 1983).

12. *FTC Enforcement.* When physicians began to advertise unapproved uses of approved new drugs, the FTC sought to prevent it. In 1975, the FTC sought to enjoin a weight reduction clinic from advertising human chorionic gonadotropin or any other unapproved drug for use in its treatment program. Citing FDA's August 1972 policy, however, the District Court ruled that advertising a treatment program that utilizes an unapproved new drug does not violate the FD&C Act. *F.T.C. v. Simeon Management Corp.*, 391 F. Supp. 697 (N.D. Cal. 1975), *aff'd*, 532 F.2d 708 (9th Cir. 1976).

13. *DEA Concern.* Just as DEA has attempted to discourage DTC advertising of scheduled prescription drugs, *supra* p. 559, Note 9, it has also threatened to penalize physicians who prescribe these drugs off-label. 51 Fed. Reg. 17476 (May 13, 1986).

14. *Commentary.* For a detailed analysis of the pertinent legislative history and the controversy that led to the August 1972 proposal, *see* Peter Barton Hutt, *Regulation of the Practice of Medicine under the Pure Food and Drug Laws*, 33 Q. BULL. ASS'N OF FOOD & DRUG OFFICIALS, No. 1, at 3 (1969); *see also* Mary A. McEniry & Sidney H. Willig, *The Federal Food, Drug, and Cosmetic Act and the Medical Practitioner*, 29 FOOD DRUG COSM. L.J. 548 (1974); David A. Kessler, *Regulating the Prescribing of Human Drugs for Nonapproved Uses under the Food, Drug, and Cosmetic Act*, 15 HARV. J. ON LEGIS. 693 (1978); William L. Christopher, *Off–Label Drug Prescription: Filling the Regulatory Vacuum*, 48 FOOD & DRUG L.J. 247 (1993); Steven R. Salbu, *Off–Label Use, Prescription, and Marketing of FDA–Approved Drugs: An Assessment of Legislative and Regulatory Policy*, 51 FLA. L. REV. 181 (1999).

On occasion, FDA has sought to prevent physicians from systematic off-label prescribing.

United States v. An Article of Drug . . . Diso–Tate

1975–1977 FDLI Judicial Record 239 (E.D. La. 1976).

■ GORDON, J., DISTRICT JUDGE.

This suit was originally instituted as a forfeiture action for the seizure and condemnation of the drug Disodium Edetate (EDTA), which is held for sale at Meadowbrook Hospital, on the ground that the drug was misbranded after shipment in interstate commerce. . . . However, as the prayer for injunctive relief indicates, the Government is now not only attempting to enjoin the misbranding of EDTA, but also its administration. The issuance of the injunction will avoid the necessity of the Government making multiple, and perhaps daily, seizures of EDTA in order to prevent the misbranding of EDTA.

The evidence is undisputed that the defendants have used EDTA in the treatment of arteriosclerosis and other circulatory diseases (chelation therapy). . . . [N]ot only does the labeling [of EDTA] fail to bear adequate direction for its use in the treatment of circulatory diseases, but also it is specifically contraindicated for that type of treatment. . . .

Testimony at the injunction hearing established that Dr. Evers has held a press conference and distributed promotional literature advocating EDTA therapy for cardiovascular therapy, and that promotional literature of a same sort was distributed at a convention of the National Health Federation. It was shown that Dr. Evers continued to distribute chelation therapy advertising to prospective patients and both he and Meadowbrook Hospital enjoy a national reputation as employing EDTA in the treatment of arteriosclerosis.

Accordingly, it is this Court's conclusion that the intended use of EDTA at Meadowbrook Hospital is in the treatment of arteriosclerosis and that the failure of the drug's label to comply with 21 C.F.R. § 200.100 causes it to be misbranded within the meaning of 21 U.S.C.A. § 352(f)(1)....

As a general proposition, the Food and Drug Administration is charged with the responsibility of removing misbranded drugs from the market. Normally, this is done by seizure of the article in question. However, in the case at bar, the Government wishes to go one step further by enjoining the actual administration of EDTA by Dr. Evers and his employees at Meadowbrook Hospital. Initially, the Court expressed concern over the possibility that such an injunction would constitute an unwarranted interference with the practice of medicine. However, a closer analysis of the jurisprudence and the particular facts of this case reveal that the injunctive relief as requested by the Government is not only lawful but also compelled....

In the case at bar, the Court feels that the requested injunction is justified as the only possible means of removing the misbranded drugs from interstate commerce....

The Court is of the further opinion that such an injunction will not interfere with or regulate the practice of medicine in any degree greater than it is already regulated under the Food, Drug and Cosmetic Act. As noted above, the Food and Drug Administration is charged with the responsibility of removing misbranded drugs from the flow of interstate commerce. The injunction as prayed for by the Government is the only practical and equitable means of carrying out that responsibility in the case at bar.[3] ...

——————

Two years later, a different district court reached a different result.

United States v. Evers

453 F. Supp. 1141 (M.D. Ala. 1978).

■ VARNER, DISTRICT JUDGE.

... The Plaintiff, the United States of America, spear-headed by the Federal Drug Administration, filed this proceeding against Dr. H. Ray

3. This is not to say that a licensed physician cannot utilize a drug for experimental or investigational uses, which would otherwise cause the drug to be misbranded. To use a drug in such a way, the physician is obligated to follow the procedure set forth at 21 U.S.C.A. § 355(i) and the complementing regulations found at 21 C.F.R. § 312.1. Suffice it to say that such procedures were not followed in this case.

Evers, a licensed physician in the State of Alabama, alleging (1) that Defendant has been engaged in promoting and administering calcium disodium versenate in treatment for arteriosclerosis; (2) that the labeling of the drug, commonly called the package insert, which is prescribed and approved by the Federal Drug Administration, indicates that the drug is recommended for treatment of heavy metal poisons but not for other things here relevant; (3) that patients being treated by the Defendant are subjected to an unwarranted risk of grave physical injury or death as a result of said treatment; and (4) that the promotion and administering of said drug, after having utilized interstate commerce in obtaining the same, amounts to a mislabeling of the drug under the provisions of Title 21, U.S.C. §§ 331(k) and 352(f)(1)....

The defense is that Defendant is not using the drug for other than treatment of metal poisoning, its recommended use, and that, in any event, the Defendant is a licensed physician in the State of Alabama and that licensed physicians have a right and a duty to use drugs in prescribing for their patients' usage in accordance with their best judgment as physicians and that the Federal Food and Drug Act does not prohibit a licensed physician's using a drug for a disease or weakness in a patient in any manner which is not contraindicated on the package insert....

The legal issues presented by this cause, in the opinion of this court, place squarely before this court the question of whether a licensed physician may be enjoined from prescribing for his patient a drug of which the package insert is silent as to whether the drug is indicated or contraindicated for the patient's illness....

In response to Dr. Evers' contention that the Federal Drug Administration has no power to direct how he shall treat his own patients, the government relies upon *United States v. Hoxsey Cancer Clinic*, 198 F.2d 273 (5th Cir. 1952), in which a layman, Hoxsey, was advertising and shipping drugs in interstate commerce as a cancer cure and the court found that the literature distributed constituted mislabeling of the drugs within the meaning of the act because it contained misleading statements and therefore the drugs were misbranded and Hoxsey was enjoined from the continuation of such interstate commerce. The *Hoxsey* case is comparable to the instant case in that the Hoxsey Clinic was staffed by licensed physicians but Hoxsey was shipping the drugs in interstate commerce to other than his patients after having advertised them for unapproved usage while Dr. Evers, after having received a drug in interstate commerce, holds them for prescribed use on his patients....

The government also relies on the case of *United States of America v. An Article of Drug ... Diso–Tate, Etc., H. Ray Evers, and Meadowbrook Hospital*, No. 75–1790 (E.D. La., Sept. 28, 1976) [*supra* p. 822].... In that case, Dr. Evers again was advertising in interstate commerce and receiving shipments of drugs to effect the chelation of patients as a treatment for arteriosclerosis. Two obvious differences appeared in that case as compared with the instant case. The drug used for chelation in Louisiana was contraindicated for arteriosclerosis on the label and Dr. Evers himself was not a licensed physician and was operating as a layman in Louisiana. That case, therefore, has limited authority in the instant case. It is notable, however, that that court expressed its concern about any unwarranted interference with the practice of medicine even though Dr. Evers was not licensed to practice in Louisiana at that time. . . .

Perhaps the government's position is best exemplified by the explanation of the purposes of the Federal Food and Drug Administration's interest in practices such as those enjoyed by Dr. Evers in the Federal Register for August 15, 1972 (Vol. 37, No. 150, p. 16503). That position is that once a drug is in a local pharmacy, after interstate shipment, a physician may, as part of the practice of medicine, lawfully prescribe a different dosage for his patients or may vary the conditions of use from those approved in the package insert, without informing or obtaining the approval of the Food and Drug Administration. Congress did not intend the Food and Drug Administration to interfere with medical practice as between the physician and the patient. Congress recognized a patient's right to seek civil damages in the courts if there should be evidence of malpractice, and declined to provide any legislative restrictions upon the medical profession. It appears to this Court that such a restriction would exceed the powers of Congress. There is no federal prohibition of transportation of an approved drug in interstate shipment with the approved package insert when neither the shipper nor the recipient intends that it be used for an unapproved purpose. If the illegal purpose is devised after termination of interstate shipment, the matter passed from federal jurisdiction, but jurisdiction may well apply if the shipper or the recipient intends an illegal use at the time of the deposit of the shipment in interstate commerce. Then the act and the illegal contention may coincide so as to furnish federal jurisdiction over interstate commerce. . . .

It is well-recognized that a package insert may not contain the most up-to-date information about a drug and the physician must be free to use the drug for an indication not in the package insert when such usage is part of the practice of medicine and for the benefit of the patient. Hopefully the physician would welcome a well-documented package insert because he finds it useful because the information in it is supported by substantial documented evidence. However, the physician can ascertain from medical literature and from medical meetings new and interesting proposed uses for drugs marketed under package inserts not including the proposed usages. The package insert's most important educational value derives from the fact that it is a well-reviewed, authoritative document. New uses for drugs are often discovered, reported in medical journals and at medical meetings, and subsequently may be widely used by the medical profession. But the Federal Drug Administration does not permit the package insert to be amended to include such uses unless the manufacturer submits convincing evidence supporting the change. The manufacturer may not have sufficient commercial interests or financial wherewithal to warrant following the necessary procedures to obtain FDA approval for the additional use of the drug. When physicians go beyond the directions given in the package insert it does not mean they are acting illegally or unethically and Congress did not intend to empower the FDA to interfere with medical practice by limiting the ability of physicians to prescribe according to their best judgment....

This court is, therefore, of the opinion ... that Dr. Evers is not misbranding the drug in question and that the relief prayed by the plaintiff should be denied. Judgment will enter in accordance with this memorandum opinion.

NOTE

The District Court later dismissed a suit by Evers against the FDA District Director, finding the latter was immune from liability for his actions in initiating the investigations that resulted in both of the above-described enforcement actions. *Evers v. White*, FDLI 1978–1980 Jud. Rec. 764 (M.D. Ala. 1979).

On appeal, the Court of Appeals affirmed the District Court, but on other grounds.

United States v. Evers

643 F.2d 1043 (1981).

■ RANDALL, CIRCUIT JUDGE:

In this action the government charges a licensed Alabama physician with a violation of section 301(k) of the Federal Food, Drug, and Cosmetic Act. That section prohibits, *inter alia*, the misbranding of a drug which is held for sale after shipment in interstate commerce. The government charges that the drug at issue, which is a prescription drug, was misbranded under section 502(f)(1) of the Act, which deems a drug to be misbranded unless its labeling contains "adequate directions for use." In particular, the government alleges that the physician promoted and administered a drug for a use that is not approved by the Food and Drug Administration (the FDA), without providing adequate directions for such use to his patients. The district court found that the physician had indeed failed to provide adequate directions for the intended use of the drug, but held that the physician's actions were within "the practice of medicine" and therefore beyond the constitutional reach of federal power and beyond the intended reach of the Act....

We do not reach the issue on which the district court's opinion rests, for we find that the government has not established a violation of section 301(k) of the Act. Since prescription drugs are required by regulations promulgated pursuant to section 502(f)(1) of the Act to bear adequate information for use by physicians but not for use by patients, and since the physician charged in this case was administering the drug to his own patients but not distributing it to other physicians, we hold that Dr. Evers has not violated section 301(k) of the Act by his failure to provide such "adequate directions for use" as are required by section 502(f)(1) of the Act....

The government contends that Dr. Evers violated section 301(k) of the Act, which prohibits any act with respect to a drug which "is done while such [drug] is held for sale (whether or not the first sale) after shipment in interstate commerce and [which] results in such article being ... misbranded." The government must therefore establish two separate elements: (1) that the act in question occurred while the drug was held for sale after shipment in interstate commerce; and (2) that the act resulted in the article being misbranded. The focus of the government's case, as well as of Dr. Evers' defense and of the district court's opinion, is the second of these elements. In order to establish this element, that is, to demonstrate that Dr. Evers has "misbranded" Calcium EDTA, the government relies solely on section 502(f)(1) of the Act. That section deems a drug to be misbranded "unless its labeling bears ... adequate directions for use." In brief, the government contends that Dr. Evers failed to provide "adequate directions for use" when he promoted and prescribed Calcium EDTA for the treatment of circulatory disorders, a use for which the drug has not been approved by the FDA.

In response to this charge, Dr. Evers (as well as certain of his patients, as intervenors) argues that as a licensed physician he has a right to prescribe any lawful drug for any purpose, whether or not that purpose has been approved by the FDA. The district court agreed with Dr. Evers and held that no misbranding could result from a doctor's prescription of a lawful drug to his own patients....

However, the analysis urged by Dr. Evers and adopted by the district court misapprehends the thrust of the government's case against Dr. Evers, for the FDA has at no point contended, and the government does not argue on appeal, that the misbranding provisions of the Act prohibit a doctor from prescribing a lawful drug for a purpose for which the drug has not been approved by the FDA. To the contrary, the FDA has explicitly informed Dr. Evers that he could legally prescribe chelating drugs for the treatment of circulatory disorders....

The object of the government's case against Dr. Evers is not, therefore, his *prescription* of Calcium EDTA for use in the treatment of circulatory disorders. Instead, the government seeks to challenge Dr. Evers' *promotion* and *advertising* of chelating drugs for that use. According to the government, Dr. Evers "misbranded" Calcium EDTA when he publicly advocated his use of chelating drugs for an unapproved purpose without providing "adequate directions" for such a use....

The government argues that Dr. Evers' prescription and promotion of Calcium EDTA for the treatment of circulatory disorders meets both of the above requirements of section 301(k) of the Act. In the first place, the government contends that Dr. Evers "held (Calcium EDTA) for sale" when he maintained a supply of the drug for use on his own patients at the Ra–Mar Clinic. To support this position, the government relies on cases ... which did indeed hold that a doctor who had held drugs for use in his practice had held those drugs for sale within the meaning of the Act. In the second place, the government contends that Dr. Evers misbranded Calcium EDTA within the meaning of section 502(f)(1) of the Act by failing to provide "adequate directions for use".... It is undisputed that Dr. Evers did in fact fail to provide adequate directions for either lay or professional use; Dr. Evers does not contend that his booklets contained "adequate directions for lay use" within the meaning of the regulations, and he does not appear to have made any attempt to meet the terms of either the regulatory or the statutory exception for prescription drugs.

When each of the two elements of the offense with which Dr. Evers is charged is examined individually, Dr. Evers does indeed seem to have violated the statute. A different picture emerges, however, when the two elements are considered together. Since Calcium EDTA is a prescription drug, the FDA can establish an act of misbranding under section 502(f)(1) of the Act only by proving that Dr. Evers did not provide adequate information *for use by physicians*, as is required by the exceptions to that section. The information provided by Dr. Evers to his patients is irrelevant to the question at hand, for according to FDA regulations there is *no* information which could have been provided about this prescription drug which would have constituted "adequate directions for [lay] use." However, the government argues that Dr. Evers "held [Calcium EDTA] for sale" within the meaning of section 301(k) because he maintained a supply of the drug for use *on his own patients;* the government does not contend that Dr. Evers was distributing Calcium EDTA to other licensed physicians. The government therefore must find itself in an awkward position: while the misbranding violation it urges is based on Dr. Evers' failure to provide adequate information to licensed physicians, it seeks to include his actions within the reach of section 301(k) of the Act by virtue of his distribution to patients.

The requirement which the FDA seeks to impose is nonsensical. Since Calcium EDTA is a prescription drug, the misbranding provision under which Dr. Evers was charged requires him to provide adequate information for use by prescribing physicians. However, Dr. Evers was the only physician who used the Calcium EDTA in question. The government's application of the statute may therefore be reduced to the following proposition: Dr. Evers did not provide adequate information to himself. It is doubtful at best that this interpretation was intended by the drafters of the statute.

In more specific terms, the government's interpretation of the Act breaks down over its use of the phrase "held for sale after shipment in interstate commerce." Although Dr. Evers was holding Calcium EDTA for sale in the sense that he was distributing it *to his own patients*, he was not holding it for sale *to physicians*. Section 301(k) of the Act cannot reasonably be read to require a physician who is holding a drug for sale only to patients to provide adequate information to physicians to whom he is not distributing the drug. We think it clear that a single doctor may be holding drugs for sale to one group of purchasers but not to another. If the doctor is not holding the drug for sale to the party to whom he owes a statutory obligation of full disclosure (in this case other prescribing physicians), then it makes no sense to impose the requirements of the statute. No legitimate purpose is served when a statutory provision requiring disclosure to one particular group of purchasers is invoked on the basis of sales made to a different group. Since Dr. Evers was holding Calcium EDTA, a prescription drug, for sale only to his patients, and since section 502(f)(1) of the Act does not require any disclosure to patients regarding prescription drugs, we conclude that Dr. Evers did not violate section 301(k) of the Act.[16]

NOTE

For a discussion of physician civil liability for deviating from the package insert, *see* Chapter XIII, *infra*.

3. CONTROLS OVER PRESCRIPTION DRUG DISTRIBUTION

The addictive drug methadone was originally approved by FDA as an analgesic. When it was discovered that methadone was effective in blocking the euphoria caused by heroin and therefore could be used in the treatment of heroin addiction, physicians throughout the country began to prescribe it for this off-label use without adequate consideration of the drug's own addictive properties. To bring the drug's use back under control, FDA promulgated regulations restricting distribution to hospital pharmacies. 37 Fed. Reg. 6940 (Apr. 6, 1972), 37 Fed. Reg. 26790 (Dec. 15, 1972).

American Pharmaceutical Association v. Weinberger

377 F. Supp. 824 (D.D.C. 1974).

■ PRATT, DISTRICT JUDGE . . . .

. . . Plaintiffs challenge the validity of certain provisions of the Food and Drug Administration's methadone regulations. . . . Specifically, plaintiffs object to those parts of the regulations which purport to restrict the distribution of methadone to direct shipments from the manufacturer to (a) approved maintenance treatment programs, (b) approved hospital pharmacies, and (c) in cases where hospital pharmacies are unavailable in a particular area, to selected community pharmacies. Plaintiffs include the American Pharmaceutical Association (APhA), a professional association of

---

16. One might argue that although Dr. Evers did not distribute Calcium EDTA to other physicians, he nevertheless "labeled" the drug to the medical community at large through his public promotional and advertising efforts, and that he therefore caused the drug to be "misbranded" because the drug's label did not meet the full disclosure requirements of the regulatory exception to section 502(f)(1) with respect to the new use advocated for the drug by Dr. Evers. This seems to be the theory on which the District Court for the Eastern District of Louisiana found a misbranding violation in the government's earlier suit against Dr. Evers. *See United States v. An Article of Drug . . . Diso–Tate.* This approach relies on the promotion *per se* of the drug, and seems to ignore altogether the fact that misbranding under section 301(k) of the Act can occur only with respect to particular drugs "held for sale after shipment in interstate commerce." At base, this theory equates *promotion* with sale, and therefore brings into question the legality of a physician's advocacy of any medical program involving drugs not approved for the advocated use by the FDA, even when the physician does not himself sell or even dispense the drug. But the Act was intended to regulate the distribution of drugs in interstate commerce, not to restrain physicians from public advocacy of medical opinions not shared by the FDA. We believe, therefore, that a doctor who merely advocates to other doctors a lawful prescription drug for a use not approved by the FDA, and does not distribute that drug to other doctors, is not holding that drug for sale within the meaning of the statute and therefore is not in violation of section 301(k) of the Act.

pharmacists with a membership in excess of 50,000, three individual professional pharmacists and an individual physician. . . .

The drug methadone, a synthetic substitute for morphine, is a "new" drug within the meaning of section 201(p) of the Federal Food, Drug and Cosmetic Act and, as a new drug, requires FDA's approval of a NDA, filed with the Commissioner of Food and Drugs pursuant to section 505(b) of the Act. The drug was first approved by FDA in the 1950's as safe for use as an analgesic and antitussive agent as well as for short-term detoxification of persons addicted to heroin. Subsequently, investigation of methadone for use in long-term maintenance of narcotic addicts (methadone maintenance) was approved by FDA pursuant to its authority under 21 U.S.C. § 355(i), the investigational new-drug (IND) exemption. . . . [In 1972] FDA determined that "retention of the drug [methadone] solely on an investigational status appears to be no longer warranted" and published a notice of proposed rulemaking which resulted, with certain modifications, in the regulations now in question.

The final regulation gave notice that pursuant to FDA's authority under 21 U.S.C. § 355(e), the Commissioner was withdrawing approval of all outstanding NDA's because of "a lack of substantial evidence that methadone is safe and effective for detoxification, and analgesia, or antitussive use *under the conditions of use that presently exist.*" Having withdrawn all approved NDA's, the Commission's new regulatory scheme is presently the exclusive means of distribution for the drug methadone. The Commissioner has thereby created an admittedly unique classification for methadone since on the one hand he has determined that methadone should not be limited solely to investigational status while at the same time concluding that the drug is inappropriate for regular NDA approval. As statutory support for this novel solution to the methadone dilemma, defendants rely on an expansive interpretation of the Commissioner's NDA authority under § 355 of the Act. . . .

The defendants point out . . . that § 355(d) gives the Secretary the authority to refuse to approve an NDA where the reports of the investigations submitted do not include adequate tests showing whether the new drug is "safe for use under the conditions prescribed, recommended, or suggested in the proposed labeling thereof." Defendants argue that the term "safe" should be interpreted with reference not only to the inherent qualities of the drug under consideration but also in the sense of the drug's being secure from possible misuse. Such a broad interpretation would, according to defendants' theory, serve as the statutory foundation for FDA's exercise of authority in restricting methadone's channels of distribution because FDA's principal rationale for restricting distribution was "to help reduce the likelihood of diversion."

. . . As noted above, the term "safe" is used in conjunction with the phrase "for use under the conditions prescribed, recommended, or suggested in the proposed labeling thereof." When taken in this context, a determination of whether a drug is "safe" is premised on the drug's use in the "prescribed, recommended, or suggested" manner. Thus the context of the statute indicates that the term "safe" was intended to include only the inherent safety of the drug when used in the manner intended. Moreover,

... [§ 355(d)(3)] extends the Secretary's authority to pass on the adequacy of methods, facilities and *controls* only with respect to *manufacturing, processing* and *packaging*. Under the doctrine of "expressio unius est exclusio alterius" any stage of the drug's genesis not specifically mentioned in provision (3) was presumably intended to be excluded from the Secretary's authority. Thus ... the Court concludes that the term "safe" was intended to refer to a determination of the inherent safety or lack thereof of the drug under consideration when used for its intended purpose.[9] ...

In addition to being a "new" drug and thus within the jurisdiction of the FDA, methadone is a controlled substance within Schedule II of the Controlled Substances Act, 21 U.S.C. § 812. Under this Act the Attorney General is made responsible for the registration of any person who manufactures, distributes or dispenses any controlled substance....

The Court concludes that Congress intended to create two complementary institutional checks on the production and marketing of new drugs. At the production or pre-marketing stage, the FDA is given the primary responsibility in determining which new drugs should be permitted to enter the flow of commerce.... When an IND exemption is approved, the Commissioner may, of course, severely restrict the distribution of the exempted drug to bona fide researchers and clinicians. But once a drug is cleared for marketing by way of an NDA-approval, for whatever uses the Commissioner deems appropriate, the question of permissible distribution of the drug, when that drug is a controlled substance, is one clearly within the jurisdiction of the Justice Department.... To allow the challenged portions of the methadone regulations to stand, therefore, would be to abrogate the collective judgment of Congress with regard to the appropriate means of controlling unlawful drug diversion....

NOTES

1. *Subsequent Proceedings.* On appeal, the District Court decision was affirmed *per curiam*, 530 F.2d 1054 (D.C. Cir. 1976). Although he concurred in the judgment, Judge McGowan was not content simply to affirm the lower court's opinion:

> ... The FDA contends that where there exists a documented pattern of drug misuse contrary to the intended uses specified in the labelling, the drug is unsafe for approval unless controls over distribution are imposed. As a corollary, it asserts that for a drug such as methadone, for which there is substantial evidence of misuse, the FDA must have the power to restrict distribution to avoid the dilemma of either disapproving a drug with important therapeutic benefits or of placing on the market a drug likely to be misused. The FDA claims that ... the regulations at issue differ only in degree from a prescription-only restriction....

9. Even if the Court were to agree with defendant's interpretation of the term "safe," this alone would not provide a statutory basis for the regulations challenged herein. At most such an interpretation would authorize FDA to deny or withdraw any methadone NDA based on a finding that the drug could not be "safely" distributed. As outlined in the Court's opinion, FDA's discretion under the Act's NDA provisions is limited to either approving or denying NDA's and nowhere is FDA empowered to approve an NDA upon the condition that the drug be distributed only through specified channels.

Although these arguments have some weight, I do not find them ultimately convincing. The word "safe" in section 355(d) is, to my mind, best interpreted as requiring the labelling to include the evidence from drug testing, and the inferences therefrom, indicating the therapeutic benefits, possible dangers, and uncertainties involved in use of a drug, as an aid to a conscientious physician in determining appropriate medical treatment. That view seems to me to accord with both the most reasonable interpretation of the statutory language and the common understanding of the FDA's mission. Thus, methadone is safe for its intended use notwithstanding the possibility that it will be employed in unintended fashions. . . .

There would be almost no limit to the FDA's authority were its view adopted. If, for example, it had concluded before 1970 that without restrictions on methadone of the sort now contained in the Controlled Substances Act the possibility of drug misuse remained high, there would be no barrier under its argument to its having established a regulatory scheme of the complexity of that ultimately adopted in that Act. . . .

2. *Methadone Regulations.* FDA subsequently revised its methadone regulations by deleting the restrictions on distribution to pharmacies. 41 Fed. Reg. 28261 (July 9, 1976). The regulations were recodified in 42 Fed. Reg. 46698 (Sept. 16, 1977) and significant amendments were adopted in 41 Fed. Reg. 17926 (Apr. 29, 1976), 42 Fed. Reg. 56897 (Oct. 28, 1977), and 45 Fed. Reg. 62694 (Sept. 19, 1980). Additional changes were adopted in 48 Fed. Reg. 41049 (Sept. 13, 1983), 52 Fed. Reg. 37046 (Oct. 2, 1987), and 54 Fed. Reg. 8954 (Mar. 2, 1989). Largely in response to the spread of AIDS among heroin users, FDA proposed further revisions in 54 Fed. Reg. 8973 (Mar. 2, 1989) and 54 Fed. Reg. 50226 (Dec. 4, 1989). In 2001, HHS repealed the narcotic treatment regulations enforced by FDA and created a new regulatory system based on an accreditation model, under the oversight of the Substance Abuse and Mental Health Services Administration (SAMHSA). 64 Fed. Reg. 39810 (July 22, 1999); 66 Fed. Reg. 4076 (Jan. 17, 2001).

3. *Distribution Restrictions.* For a discussion of several proposed control mechanisms to restrict drug distribution and prescribing, *see* Peter Barton Hutt, *The Legal Requirement That Drugs Be Proved Safe and Effective Before Their Use,* *in* CONTROVERSIES IN THERAPEUTICS 495 (Louis C. Lasagna, ed., 1980). The Drug Regulation Reform Act of 1979, which passed the Senate but was never adopted by the House, would have explicitly authorized FDA to restrict distribution of drugs. S. Rep. No. 96–321, 96th Cong., 1st Sess. (1979).

4. *Voluntary Restrictions.* Although *American Pharmaceutical Association* held that FDA may not restrict distribution as a condition of approving an NDA, the courts did not state that a pharmaceutical manufacturer could not *voluntarily* limit distribution or that FDA could not approve labeling that incorporated such voluntary controls. In fact, FDA now frequently approves physician labeling that contains various limitations on the type of pharmacy at which the drug will be available, the conditions under which pharmacies will be permitted to stock the drug, or the qualifications of the physicians who will be permitted to prescribe the drug. Consider, for example, the restrictions voluntarily imposed by Sandoz for clozapine (Clozaril) for use in schizophrenia, under which the drug was not available through pharmacies and had to be administered by trained home health care workers. *Clozapine for Schizophrenia*, 32 THE MEDICAL LETTER 3 (Jan. 12, 1990). As a result of pressure from pharmacists and state health care agencies, and following the filing of an antitrust suit by several state attorneys general, Sandoz abandoned this plan in early 1991.

5. *Accutane Restrictions*. In addition to providing stringent warnings for Accutane (isotretinoin) to reduce potential side effects, *see supra* p. 503, the manufacturer engaged in an extensive physician education campaign and, in accordance with FDA directives, specified that physicians should obtain informed consent from patients. *See* R. S. Stern, *When A Uniquely Effective Drug is Teratogenic: The Case of Isotretinoin*, 320 NEW ENG. J. MED. 1007 (Apr. 13, 1989); 321 N. ENG. J. MED. 756 (Sept. 14, 1989). FDA's Dermatologic Drugs Advisory Committee has reviewed the agency's handling of Accutane on numerous occasions, most recently to endorse a highly restrictive risk management plan.

6. *Subpart H Regulations*. As described p. 712 *supra*, because of concern about the methadone decision, FDA's distribution controls under 21 C.F.R. Part 314, Subpart H ("Accelerated Approval of New Drugs for Serious or Life Threatening Illnesses") apply only if the applicant voluntarily agrees. If the applicant were to refuse to agree, of course, FDA might not approve the NDA.

7. *Controlled Substances and Medical Devices*. Distribution of prescription drug controlled substances is subject to restriction under the Controlled Substances Act, *supra* p. 719. The Medical Device Amendments of 1976 explicitly authorize FDA by regulation to restrict distribution of a device pursuant to section 520(e) of the FD&C Act.

———

As drug safety issues mount, FDA intrudes still further into the practice of medicine.

Scott Gottlieb, M.D.,* *Speech Before the American Medical Association*

June 12, 2006.

Clearly there is a renewed focus on issues of drug safety. One of the questions that the public has is whether or not the FDA is doing enough to find out about new safety issues that marketed drugs might have, and whether we are communicating these things quickly enough. Those are fair concerns, and we have been doing a lot at FDA to address them. People are rightly concerned when it takes many years to find out that a marketed drug had a rare but serious side effect....

But there is a second question that I am equally concerned with, and it has to do with how we confront situations where we already know that a drug has a certain side effect at the time of approval, or shortly after. Especially in cases where we know there are some common sense precautions physicians and patients can take to mitigate, or even nearly eliminate the chances of someone suffering these side effects. Yet patients continue to succumb to it anyway, whether it is a cardiac rhythm problem or a liver toxicity problem that is potentiated by a drug-drug interaction or by some pre-diagnosed comorbidity, or something more closely linked to the manner in which a drug is administered.

This challenge cuts directly to issues related to the practice of medicine, and sometimes tugs at where the boundary is between our role at

* [Dr. Gottlieb was FDA Deputy Commissioner for Medical and Scientific Affairs.]

FDA and the role of practicing doctors. I am worried that this boundary has become increasingly blurry to an outside view, and we at FDA are being increasingly asked by some groups and by political bodies to occasionally step across it, when drug safety issues arise and where our role in influencing how a drug is prescribed can be reasonably assumed to cut down on that risk. I am talking in particular about the increasing number of risk management plans that are becoming part of new drug approvals. These plans attempt to mitigate a certain risk by directly influencing or controlling how a drug is used. Now I think if you look at the places where we have implemented these plans, I think you would agree we have been balanced and careful to respect practice issues. These plans also allow us to often put drugs on the market or keep drugs on the market that otherwise we would not feel comfortable with. But I worry about the future.

My concern is that even though we do not have the legal authority to impose these plans on drug sponsors, they are nonetheless becoming an increasingly prominent condition of certain approvals as we negotiate final labeling over newly approved drugs. It is fair to say, I believe, that these plans are sometimes a less-than-optimal response to more systemic systems problems in the delivery of medical care. But that does not change the final calculus, that there are some real needs that these plans address but also some real challenges we face if these plans continue to become a common feature of drug approvals. In particular, there is a cumulative burden they impose that could encroach on medical practice decisions that doctors make and on patient discretion. This could be especially true when it comes to patients who already have a hard time getting access to specialty care or to the most innovative safe and effective medicines. Patients for example who may receive care in urban settings where busy clinics may not have the time and resources to comply with these plans, or patients who do not have access to specialists who are favored prescribers under some of these plans, or access to pharmacies able to subsidize all of the requirements. We are especially sensitive to these kinds of concerns when working on the design of these plans.

The good news is I think there are some steps we can take working together to make sure that the laudable medical safety goals that these risk management plans aim to achieve can be accomplished without FDA being directly involved every time. But addressing these healthcare systems problems is going to require a lot more involvement and collaboration of organized medical bodies as well as individual physicians in our work than we have enjoyed in the past. . . .

. . . A lot of these drug safety questions are difficult for us to address directly at FDA, because they deal with personal prescribing decisions. The more we promulgate plans that attempt to guide or even control these decisions, the more we encroach on professional autonomy, and the responsibilities doctors have as a profession to address these kinds of practice issues through their own vehicles so that they can continue to personalize care to their patients' individual preferences.

NOTE

See also Lars Noah, *Ambivalent Commitments to Federalism in Controlling the Practice of Medicine*, 53 U. KAN. L. REV. 149 (2004).

CHAPTER V

FOOD AND DRUGS FOR ANIMALS

A. GENERAL STATUTORY REQUIREMENTS

The 1938 FD&C Act, like the 1906 statute, drew no distinction between food and drugs for humans and food and drugs for animals. Thus, most of the requirements imposed by Chapters IV and V of the original Act are potentially applicable to products marketed for use in livestock or for feeding or treating companion animals. Moreover, the elusive statutory boundary between human food and drugs also separates animal food from animal drugs.

United States v. Articles of Drug for Veterinary Use

50 F.3d 497 (8th Cir. 1995).

■ HANSEN, CIRCUIT JUDGE.

The United States appeals the judgment entered on a jury verdict rendered in favor of the defendant, Immuno–Dynamics, Inc. (Immuno–Dynamics), in the United States' attempt to condemn six products manufactured by Immuno–Dynamics as unsafe and adulterated new animal drugs under the Federal Food, Drug, and Cosmetic Act (FDCA). The United States contends that the district court erred by not granting its motion for judgment as a matter of law or alternatively, that the jury verdict is not supported by the evidence. We affirm.

This action began when the United States filed a complaint for forfeiture of six products manufactured by Immuno–Dynamics at its Perry, Iowa, plant, contending that the products were "adulterated" "new animal drugs." The United States seized the six products, as well as some written literature found at the plant. The seized products had not been approved by the United States Food and Drug Administration (FDA). Immuno–Dynamics protested the need for such approval, contending that these products are mere nutritional supplements or food and not drugs subject to FDCA regulation.

The six products seized (Bio–Stim Calf Boluses, Bio–Stim Cattle Boluses, Feed Supplement, ID–Vita Pak, VP–127, and VeGa–1) are made from dried colostrum with an added preservative. Colostrum, the first milk produced by a mammal after giving birth, is generally recognized for its high content of protein and antibodies that supply essential immunities to the newborn. To manufacture the seized products, Immuno–Dynamics collects colostrum from dairy cows, sanitizes it, adds a preservative to prevent spoilage, formulates the colostrum into a cheese, extracts the whey (the watery part of milk that is separated from the curd in making cheese), and defats it through a drying process. Immuno–Dynamics then markets the colostral whey in both a powdered and a liquid form. Of the six products seized, some are powder and some are liquid; all must be mixed with either feed or water and orally ingested by young calves or cattle.

. . . Immuno–Dynamics argued that the seized products were not intended for drug uses and therefore were not adulterated new animal drugs under the FDCA. . . .

The dispute in this case centers around claims made in written literature seized at the plant but not affixed to the products seized. The United States seized written literature consisting of a brochure, two University and Field Trial Results booklets, a pamphlet, and an advertisement. This literature described colostrum-based products in general and made various claims about the seized products, including that they increase the chance of survival in young animals, improve circulatory flow, increase circulatory cell volume, regulate the body defense system, improve the quality of blood flow, lessen the severity of scours and pneumonia, and act as a digestive stimulant to improve appetite after stress. There is little doubt that these claims, if used in promotional material, can be said to indicate an intent to "affect the structure or any function of the body of" animals within the FDCA's broad definition of "drug." 21 U.S.C.A. § 321(g)(1)(C). . . .

. . . [T]he record in this case establishes a material factual dispute about whether the written materials found at the plant were promotional in nature, whether they were ever distributed in relation to the six products seized, and if distributed only in the past whether any customers were still relying on the past representations as relating to the six products seized. Thus, whether the written materials evidenced the vendor's intent that the products be used for drug purposes was properly a question of fact in this case and was properly submitted to the jury.

Even if the product labeling or written literature evidenced some intended drug purpose, a product is not a new animal drug within the meaning of the FDCA if its composition is such that it is generally recognized among experts as safe and effective for use as suggested in the product's label or if, as a result of investigations to determine its safety and effectiveness, it has become recognized as safe and effective for the recommended use. . . .

There was evidence at trial that the seized products consisted solely of dried colostrum and a preservative, and experts testified that colostrum is generally recognized as safe and beneficial to animals. Immuno–Dynamics presented evidence that it has conducted approximately 75–100 controlled field investigations of its products and that numerous published articles exist in scientific literature indicating that colostrum products are safe and effective for use in the animal industry. One government expert testified that there is no general recognition by qualified experts that the actual products seized were effective for their intended use because there is a lack of published studies on these products. We conclude that this evidence created a genuine dispute of fact concerning whether the products were generally recognized as safe and effective for their intended use, and thus, the issue was properly submitted to the jury.

NOTE

See also United States v. Undetermined Quantities ... of Veterinary Drug, 22 F.3d 235 (10th Cir. 1994) (holding that a product, "Pets Smellfree," that promised to control pets' body odor was "intended to affect the structure or function" of the animals); United States v. Pro–Ag, Inc., 968 F.2d 681 (8th Cir. 1992) (holding that the defendants' promotional literature demonstrated that its products were intended to improve feed efficiency and increase milk production, making them drugs).

COMMENT: OTHER APPLICATIONS OF THE GENERAL FOOD AND DRUG PROVISIONS TO ANIMAL FOOD AND DRUGS

Adulteration. Numerous seizure actions under the 1906 Act charged economic adulteration of animal feed, but in recent years FDA has focused its attention on the safety of animal feed, particularly as the composition of feed administered to livestock may affect the safety of human food. For example, FDA declared animal feed adulterated if it is contaminated with salmonella microorganisms. This statement of policy, however, did nothing to diminish the incentives to make use of recycled animal waste in animal feed. After debating the health implications of this practice internally, FDA published a notice containing background information in 42 Fed. Reg. 64662 (Dec. 27, 1977), and requested comments on whether and how the practice should be restricted. But in 45 Fed. Reg. 86272 (Dec. 30, 1980), the agency announced that it was leaving the regulation of the use of recycled animal waste to the states.

In 42 Fed. Reg. 49468 (Sept. 27, 1977), FDA proposed to establish a new section of the regulations that would list all substances prohibited from use in animal feed or pet food. The agency proposed to list trichloroethylene, a carcinogen in test animals, as the first prohibited substance. FDA ultimately withdrew its proposal to prohibit trichloroethylene, 56 Fed. Reg. 67440 (Dec. 30, 1991). However, as of October 1, 2006, FDA regulations prohibit the use of three other substances in animal feed or food: gentian violet in all animal feed, propylene glycol in cat food, and animal proteins in ruminant feed. 21 C.F.R. Part 589, Subpart B.

Misbranding. For examples of FDA's successful enforcement of the Act's misbranding provisions against animal feed; see, e.g., United States v. Dr. David Roberts Veterinary Co., 104 F.2d 785 (7th Cir. 1939); United States v. 14 105 Pound Bags ... Mineral Compound, 118 F. Supp. 837 (D. Idaho 1953); United States v. 18 Cases ... "Barton's Cannibalism Remedy," 1938–1964 FDLI Jud. Rec. 1335 (D. Neb. 1956). See also United States v. An Article of Drug ... "Misty Dog Food....," 1969–1974 FDLI Jud. Rec. 108 (D.D.C. 1972); United States v. An Article of Food ..., "Medi–Matic Free Choice Poultry Formula (Medicated)" 1965–1968 FDLI Jud. Rec.1 (W.D. Ark. 1968). As in other areas, FDA has come to rely on rulemaking to correct label deceptions. For example, in 39 Fed. Reg. 25229 (July 9, 1974), the agency promulgated a regulation, 21 C.F.R. 500.52, governing the use of terms such as "tonic," "toner," or "conditioner" in labeling of preparations intended for use in or on animals.

New Drug Approval Pre-1968. Prior to the enactment of the 1968 Animal Drug Amendments, new drugs for animal use were subject to the same premarket approval requirements as new drugs for human use. And as with human drugs, FDA often found itself enmeshed in protracted litigation over the "new" status of veterinary drugs. *See, e..g., United States v. 7 Cartons ... "Ferro–Lac Swine Formula Concentrate (Medicated),"* 293 F. Supp. 660 (S.D. Ill. 1968), *aff'd on other grounds,* 424 F.2d 1364 (7th Cir. 1970). Animal drugs that FDA had approved between 1938 and 1962 were subject to the National Academy of Sciences review and the FDA drug efficacy study implementation (DESI) program. Similarly, before 1968, new animal drugs, like other substances added to food, were subject to the same requirements as food additives for human food use. Thus, unless GRAS or prior sanctioned, a drug added to animal feed the feed of animals grown for human food required an approved food additive regulation under section 409 of the Act. *See, e.g., United States v. Seven Cartons ... "Ferro–Lac Swine Formula Concentrate,"* 424 F.2d 1364 (7th Cir. 1970).

Pet Food. An unwritten understanding between FDA and state regulatory officials has for many years governed the regulation of pet food. Content standards and labeling requirements for pet food are established by the Association of American Feed Control Officials, and are enforced by both FDA and state agencies. Pet food labels must comply with the same labeling requirements under the FD&C Act as human food. Accordingly, when exemptions from these requirements are needed, FDA must be directly involved. *See* 48 Fed. Reg. 2136 (Jan. 18, 1983), 51 Fed. Reg. 11456 (Apr. 3, 1986) (FDA denying an industry request for the use of class or collective names for pet food ingredients, rather than the individual common or usual name for each ingredient); 41 Fed. Reg. 15731 (Apr. 14, 1976) (FDA denying an industry request to declare water at the end of the list of ingredients rather than in order of predominance). *See generally* Justine S. Patrice, *Deconstructing the Regulatory Façade: Why Confused Consumers Feed their Pets Ring Dings and Krispy Kremes* (2006), in Chapter VII of the Electronic Book.

B.   THE 1968 ANIMAL DRUG AMENDMENTS

To eliminate the overlapping regulatory requirements imposed by section 409, section 505, and the antibiotic drug provisions of section 507, Congress in 1968 enacted the Animal Drug Amendments, 82 Stat. 342 (1968), which added section 512 to the Act. In broad terms the criteria and procedures for approval of new animal drugs remained similar to those for new human drugs, but the 1968 Amendments introduced some important formal distinctions reflecting differences in the way animal drugs are manufactured, distributed, and administered. The following excerpt from the legislative history describes Congress' basic objectives.

Animal Drug Amendments

H.R. Rep. No. 875, 90th Cong., 1st Sess. (1967).

The bill would consolidate into one place in the law all of the principal provisions of the Federal Food, Drug, and Cosmetic Act which relate to premarketing clearance of new drugs for administration to animals, either directly or in their feed and water....

In many cases, the requirements for clearance of new drugs for administration to animals are more complicated than the clearance procedures for new human drugs. These complexities have in some instances led to long delays in the clearance of new animal drugs, and the purpose of the bill is to provide a single procedure for clearance of these drugs....

In the past 15 years the animal feed industry in the United States has been virtually revolutionized through the use of drugs and other additives in the feed of animals. Drugs are used to promote growth and combat disease, and as a result of the increasing use, animals today add more meat per pound to feed in a much shorter time than has ever been true in the past. This means that the price of meat and poultry is much less than it otherwise would be. For example, in 1950 broiler production was about 630 million birds whereas in 1965 it was well over 2 billion. The average retail price of broilers has dropped from 57 cents a pound in 1950 to approximately 39 cents today. This results from two factors. First, a few years ago, broiler producers had 15 to 20 percent of their chicks die before they reached maturity whereas today it is not unusual for broiler producers to raise 99 to 100 percent of the chicks started.

In addition, broilers are ready for market weeks earlier today than a few years ago, and they consume less feed per pound of added body weight than was true a few years ago. Similar developments have taken place in the beef producing industry and in the production of swine, lambs, and other animals.

... Yet the farmer even today suffers enormous losses in disease, parasites, and insects, losses estimated by the Department of Agriculture at $2.8 billion per year. These losses not only reduce farm income, but, by reducing the supply of food, affect the availability of meat, poultry, eggs, and milk and increase the cost of the basic foods to the consumer. Each delay in the clearance of safe and effective products for animal health perpetuates these losses. Every duplication of unnecessary controls adds to the ultimate cost of providing food for the consumer. Every lack of administrative coordination adds needlessly to the time required to provide the farmer with the resources he needs to feed an ever-growing population....

Subsection (a) of the proposed new section 512 provides in general that a new animal drug shall be considered as adulterated unless there is in effect an approval of an application with respect to the drug. In general, this subsection follows corresponding provisions in sections 409(a), 505, and 507 of the act.

Subsection (b) corresponds to section 505(b) of the act, and details the requirements for an application with respect to a new animal drug....

Subsection (i) requires publication of a notice in the Federal Register of information with respect to approved applications for use of new animal drugs in manufacture of animal feed. The application must refer to the regulation published pursuant to subsection (i) on which the application relies, together with other information. . . .

In general, the procedure prescribed in this subsection for approval of an application is similar to that set out for approval of the basic application, and the same is true with respect to withdrawal of approval, except that an order granting approval for use of an animal drug in feed manufacture shall be disapproved automatically when the basic animal drug application is disapproved. Since disapproval of the basic application may occur only after notice and opportunity for a hearing, the feed manufacturer may intervene in that proceeding. . . .

NOTES

1. *New Drug Status.* The 1968 Amendments did not end litigation over the new drug status of particular products. *E.g., United States v. An Article of Drug Consisting of 4,680 Pails*, 725 F.2d 976 (5th Cir. 1984); *United States v. Undetermined Quantities of Various Articles of Drug . . . Equidantin Nitrofurantoin Suspension*, 675 F.2d 994 (8th Cir. 1982); *United States v. Western Serum Co.*, 666 F.2d 335 (9th Cir. 1982); *United States v. An Article of Drug . . . "Cap–Chur–Sol,"* 661 F.2d 742 (9th Cir. 1981).

FDA has frequently issued notices determining the status of specific products or ingredients, ordinarily after affording an opportunity for public comment. For example, 21 C.F.R. 510.455 prescribes the new animal drug requirements for medicated feed blocks and other "free-choice" feeds. *See* 38 Fed. Reg. 30746 (Nov. 7, 1973); 41 Fed. Reg. 32213 (Aug. 2, 1976); 42 Fed. Reg. 23149 (May 6, 1977); 44 Fed. Reg. 10790 (Feb. 23, 1979); 49 Fed. Reg. 45593 (Nov. 19, 1984); 51 Fed. Reg. 19826 & 19898 (June 3, 1996). *See also* 41 Fed. Reg. 52482 (November 30, 1976), 42 Fed. Reg. 44225 (September 2, 1977), 21 C.F.R. 510,413, which required that any animal drug containing chloroform must be the subject of an approved new animal drug application.

2. *Investigational Animal Drugs.* Under 21 C.F.R. 511.1, an investigational new animal drug application (INAD) is required only for field trials and not for laboratory animal research, which can include research on the target species.

3. *Proving Effectiveness.* Until 1996, FDA's implementation of the effectiveness requirement of section 512 has closely paralleled its implementation of section 505's effectiveness standard for new human drugs. *See, e.g., Masti–Kure Products Co. v. Califano*, 587 F.2d 1099 (D.C. Cir. 1978); *Agri–Tech, Inc. v. Richardson*, 482 F.2d 1148 (8th Cir. 1973); *Diamond Laboratories, Inc. v. Richardson*, 452 F.2d 803 (8th Cir. 1972); *Masti–Kure Products Co. v. Weinberger*, 1969–1974 FDLI Juc. Rec. 655 (D.D.C. 1974); *United States v. Articles of Food and Drug Coli–Trol 80 Medicated*, 372 F. Supp. 915 (N.D. Ga. 1974); *United States v. An Article of Drug . . . "Entrol–C Medicated,"* 362 F. Supp. 424 (S.D. Cal. 1973). The agency's interpretation of the "substantial evidence" of effectiveness standard in section 512(d)(3) paralleled its interpretation of this standard for new human drugs. *See* 21 C.F.R. 514.111(a)(5); 35 Fed. Reg. 7569 (May 15, 1970); 36 Fed. Reg. 18375 (Sept. 14, 1971), 21 C.F.R. 514.111(a)(5).

4. *Combination Drugs.* The requirement that each active ingredient be shown to contribute to the effect of drug, 21 C.F.R. 514.1(b)(8)(v), 35 Fed. Reg. 7569 (May

15, 1970), 36 Fed. Reg. 18375 (Sept. 14, 1971), 21 C.F.R. 514.1(b)(8)(v), was explained in guidelines FDA announced in 43 Fed. Reg. 46375 (Oct. 8, 1978), 48 Fed. Reg. 19472 (Apr. 29, 1983), 48 Fed. Reg. 51537 (Nov. 9, 1983). *See* Edward Allera, *FDA's Combination Animal Drug Policy–Is It Feasible? Or Should Elsie be the Only One Getting Milked?* 33 FOOD DRUG COSM. L.J. 267 (1978). Congress modified this standard for animal drugs in 1996. *See* p. 872 *infra.*

5. *Agency Approval.* As CDER did has done for human drugs, FDA's Center for Veterinary Medicine (CVM) has issued guidance establishing a "fast track" classification for expediting review of important new animal drugs, 45 Fed. Reg. 56919 (Aug. 26, 1980).

6. *Publication of Approval.* Section 512 requires approvals of new animal drugs, unlike approvals of new human drugs, to be published in the Federal Register. Such notices appear regularly and are codified in 21 C.F.R. Subchapter E. CVM has established guidelines for the preparation of a "Freedom of Information summary" of safety and effectiveness data that is to be made publicly available after an NADA is approved. 41 Fed. Reg. 21498 (May 26, 1976), 48 Fed. Reg. 37711 (Aug. 19, 1983), 50 Fed. Reg. 33641 (Aug. 20, 1985). Though drafted by the applicant this summary must be approved by the agency.

7. *Drugs for Minor Uses.* Critics of the approval process have argued that many animal drugs have "minor uses" for which development of full-blown NADAs cannot be justified economically. FDA has made available special guidelines to facilitate review of such drugs, 21 C.F.R. 514.1(d), 44 Fed. Reg. 42716 (July 20, 1979), 48 Fed. Reg. 1922 (Jan. 14, 1983). The agency makes funds available for research on minor uses. *See, e.g.,* 49 Fed. Reg. 18359 (Apr. 30, 1984); 50 Fed. Reg. 9718 (Mar. 11, 1985). It also establishes a public master file of safety and effectiveness data for use by any applicant for approval of a minor use NADA. *See, e.g.,* 51 Fed. Reg. 12930 (Apr. 16, 1986); 52 Fed. Reg. 4968 (Feb. 18, 1987); 54 Fed. Reg. 6758 (Feb. 14, 1989); 55 Fed. Reg. 9771 (Mar. 15, 1990).

8. *Good Manufacturing Practice.* Animal feed and drugs are also subject to FDA's general GMP regulations for food and for drugs. The agency has brought court enforcement action against animal products that violated these requirements and has withdrawn approval of NADAs for non-compliance. *See United States v. Articles of Drug ... Manufactured or Labeled by Goshen Laboratories, Inc.*, Food Drug Cosm. L. Rep. (CCH) ¶ 38,174 (S.D.N.Y. 1982); *United States v. Bronson Farms, Inc.*, Food Drug Cosm. L. Rep. (CCH) ¶ 38,354 (M.D. Fla. 1986). *See also* 52 Fed. Reg. 7311 (Mar. 10, 1987), 52 Fed. Reg. 29274 (Aug. 6, 1987).

9. *Animal Feed Additives.* The 1968 Amendments did not eliminate the need for petitions requesting approval, under section 409, of non-drug additives to animal feed. *See, e.g.,* the food additive regulation for selenium, 21 C.F.R. 573.920, 38 Fed. Reg. 10458 (Apr. 27, 1973), 39 Fed. Reg. 1355 (Jan. 8, 1974), 46 Fed. Reg. 43415 (Aug. 28, 1981), 46 Fed. Reg. 49115 (Oct. 6, 1981), 52 Fed. Reg.10887 (Apr. 6, 1987), 21 C.F.R. 573.920; the proposed food additive regulation for copper, 38 Fed. Reg. 25694 (Sept. 14, 1973); and the notices discussing the legal status of vitamin K, 41 Fed. Reg. 35009 (Aug. 18, 1976), 48 Fed Reg. 16748 (Apr. 19, 1983). *See also Heterochemical Corp. v. FDA*, 644 F. Supp. 271 (E.D.N.Y. 1986).

10. *Antibiotic Certification.* Section 507 of the FD&C Act, which was added to the statute in 1945 to require FDA to certify individual batches of penicillin and later other antibiotics, did not distinguish between human and animal drugs. The 1968 Amendments incorporated the provisions of section 507 into new section 512. FDA later determined that batch-by-batch certification was no longer required to assure the safety of animal antibiotics, and revoked requirements for certification. 47 Fed. Reg. 39155 (Sept. 7, 1982). In the Generic Animal Drug and Patent Term

Restoration Act of 1988, 102 Stat. 3971, Congress repealed all antibiotic certification requirements for animal drugs.

11. *Animal Drugs and FIFRA.* There is substantial overlap between the new animal drug provisions of the FD&C Act and the pesticide registration provisions of the Federal Insecticide, Fungicide, and Rodenticide Act (FIFRA) administered by EPA. *See United States v. Articles of Drug in Possession of Nip–Co Mfg., Inc.*, Food Drug Cosm. L. Rep. (CCH) ¶ 38,233 (S.D.N.Y. 1979). The two agencies have entered into a Memorandum of Understanding to reduce duplication. 36 Fed. Reg. 24234 (Dec. 22, 1971); 38 Fed. Reg. 24233 (Sept. 6, 1973). In 41 Fed. Reg. 26734 (June 29, 1976), FDA assumed exclusive jurisdiction of new animal drugs that are also pesticides. Nonetheless, EPA adopted a statement of policy, 44 Fed. Reg. 15768 (Mar. 15, 1979), 44 Fed. Reg. 62940 (Nov. 1, 1979), respecting the application of FIFRA to veterinarians who use or dispense pesticides in the course of their practice. A new MOU published in 48 Fed. Reg. 22799 (May 20, 1983) gave FDA exclusive jurisdiction over new animal drugs that are also pesticides, but it was stayed in 48 Fed. Reg. 37077 (Aug. 16, 1983) and remains unexecuted.

12. *Commentary.* For contrasting evaluations of FDA's implementation of the 1968 Amendments, *see* John T. Craig, *The Animal Drug Amendments of 1968—In Retrospect*, 34 FOOD DRUG COSM. L.J. 228 (1979); Lester Crawford, *Animal Drug Amendments—Ten Years After*, 34 FOOD DRUG COSM. L.J. 196 (1979); Donald Van Houweling, *Looking Back at the Animal Drug Amendments of the Act*, 34 FOOD DRUG COSM. L.J. 199 (1979). 43 FOOD DRUG COSM. L.J., No. 6 (1988) contains a 20–year retrospective of the 1968 Amendments. *See also* "Human Food Safety and the Regulation of Animal Drugs," H.R. Rep. No. 99–461, 99th Cong., 1st Sess. (1985).

COMMENT: ANIMAL BIOLOGICAL DRUGS

In 1913 Congress enacted a separate animal Virus, Serum, and Toxin Act to regulate animal biological drugs, 37 Stat. 832, 21 U.S.C. 151–158. This statute is administered by USDA, not FDA. To avoid regulatory duplication, 21 C.F.R. 511.1(b)(5) and 510.4 exempt animal biologics from section 512 of the FD&C Act if they comply with the provisions of the 1913 statute. Because the 1913 statute applied only to the interstate shipment of finished products, FDA asserted jurisdiction over animal biological drugs that were not shipped in interstate commerce but contained components that were so shipped. *Animal Health Institute v. USDA*, 487 F. Supp. 376 (D. Colo. 1980); *Grand Laboratories, Inc. v. Harris*, 660 F.2d 1288 (8th Cir. 1981) (en banc), *aff'g* 644 F.2d 729 (8th Cir. 1981). FDA and USDA subsequently entered into a Memorandum of Understanding defining their respective jurisdictions. 47 Fed. Reg. 26458 (June 18, 1982). The Food Security Act of 1985, 99 Stat. 1354, 1654 (1985), made both intrastate and exported animal biologics subject to the 1913 statute and strengthened USDA's enforcement authority, thus ousting FDA from jurisdiction over animal biological products, which are USDA's exclusive responsibility.

C. REGULATION OF CARCINOGENIC DRUGS ADMINISTERED TO ANIMALS RAISED FOR HUMAN FOOD

For several decades, FDA has devoted substantial attention to regulating carcinogenic animal drugs that are used in food-producing animals and thus may leave carcinogenic residues in human food derived from the animals. This effort has been an important component in the evolution of FDA's comprehensive approach to regulating carcinogens, which is the subject of Chapter IX.

D.   HUMAN HEALTH HAZARDS OF LIVESTOCK PRODUCTION PRACTICES

1.   ANTIBIOTICS USED IN LIVESTOCK PRODUCTION

For more than three decades, FDA officials have wrestled with claims that the subtherapeutic use of antibiotics in the feed of food-producing animals, such as cattle, swine, and poultry—a practice widespread in the United States and several other countries—poses a risk to human health by inducing resistance to disease-producing organisms the drugs might otherwise combat. The story begins in the early 1970s and continues to this day. The attempt to assess the risk posed by this practice has taken the agency to the frontiers of science, while action to restrict the use of these drugs probes the limits of the concept of "safety" in section 512 of the FD&C Act.

Harold C. Hopkins, *Keeping the Kick in Antibiotics*

FDA Papers (June 1972).

The dual use of antibiotics—at concentrated or therapeutic dosages in humans and animals to treat diseases, and at low levels in feeds to promote faster growth in food-producing animals—has been widely discussed in recent years. The problem is that some bacteria exposed to low levels of antibiotics for prolonged periods in animals develop a resistance to some of these drugs.... If the resistant bacteria find their way into the human system, they may successfully fight off antibiotic treatment, making it less effective for treatment of humans.... Humans may become exposed to these large numbers of antibiotic-resistant bacteria from animals which are a major source of our food. After this resistance develops, antibiotic treatment may be less effective in humans....

———

The concern described by Mr. Hopkins was first identified by public health authorities in the United Kingdom in the late 1960s and elaborated in a famous document titled the Swann Report. In 1972, FDA took what turned out to be the first of several halting steps to characterize and manage the risk. *See* Antibiotic and Sulfonamide Drugs in Animal Feed: Proposed Statement of Policy, 37 Fed. Reg. 2444 (Feb. 1, 1972) (declaring that the agency would revoke "currently permitted uses of subtherapeutic and/or growth promotant uses of antibacterial agents in feeds ... when such drugs are also used in human clinical medicine unless data are submitted which establish their safety and effectiveness").

The following year the agency sounded a more cautious note, acknowledging that the withdrawal of all antibacterial approvals could have significant economic impact, but at the same time directing sponsors of such drugs to undertake field studies to determine the reality and magnitude of the risk. Continued attention to the issue, coupled with accumulation of research findings, seemed to enlarge rather than narrow uncertainty. Years passed without any decisive regulatory action.

Antibiotic and Sulfonamide Drugs in the Feed of Animals

38 Fed. Reg. 9811 (April 20, 1973).

The commercial animal and poultry production practices used in this country today, including the use of medication in feed administered to the entire herd or flock, have made it possible to effectively concentrate large numbers of animals into small areas without serious losses in production efficiency. From such concentration and intensified production, benefits accrue in terms of efficient land usage, labor savings, and more efficient conversion of animal feed to animal protein, thereby making a major contribution to the abundance of food from animals.... Immediate and total withdrawal of these drugs from animal feeds could seriously disrupt the quality and quantity of an important portion of our total human diet....

It would be chaotic, and is clearly not feasible, to withdraw approval of all food or drug substances merely because new questions have arisen, new testing is considered scientifically appropriate, or new studies raise issues that require further exploration. That is the situation involved here....

1.   The antibacterial drugs commonly used in animal feed and which are recognized to cause transferable drug resistance and are commonly used to treat human and animal diseases include the tetracyclines, streptomycin, dihydrostreptomycin, the sulfonamides, and penicillin. The use of these drugs in feeds may also affect the reservoir of salmonella organisms in food animals. An assessment of the effect of subtherapeutic levels of these drugs in feed on the salmonella reservoir can be completed in a relatively short time. Therefore, continued marketing of products containing any of these named drugs will be dependent on completion of salmonella reservoir studies by no later than 1 year following the effective date of this order. A determination that the drug promotes a significant increase in the salmonella reservoir will be considered sufficient grounds for proceeding to withdrawal [sic] approval of that drug.

2.   The approval for the use of antibiotic and sulfonamide drugs in animal feeds at subtherapeutic levels will be withdrawn, unless by no later than 2 years following the date of this order there has been submitted conclusive evidence demonstrating that no human or animal health hazard exists which can be attributed to such use....

FDA withdrew product approvals held by firms that had not complied with the information requirements of this regulation. 41 Fed. Reg. 8282 (Feb. 25, 1976). The next year, Donald Kennedy, Stanford Professor of Human Biology, became FDA Commissioner. Within a month FDA announced that the Bureau of Veterinary Medicine would soon propose:

1.   To terminate all subtherapeutic use of penicillin in all feed;

2.   To restrict the use of the tetracyclines to situations where there are no viable alternatives;

3.   To impose restrictions on the distribution and use of the remaining uses of penicillin and tetracycline; and

4.   To expedite implementation of the drug efficacy study implementation (DESI) notices proposing to withdraw approval of all penicillin and tetracycline combination products that lack evidence of effectiveness. . . .

42 Fed. Reg. 27264 (May 27, 1977).

FDA published detailed notices of opportunity for hearing on subtherapeutic uses of penicillin and tetracycline in animal feed in 42 Fed. Reg. 29999 (June 10, 1977), 42 Fed. Reg. 43772 (Aug. 30, 1977), and 42 Fed. Reg. 56264 (Oct. 21, 1977), and announced its intention to conduct hearings in 43 Fed. Reg. 53827 (Nov. 17, 1978).

In the meantime the General Accounting Office issued a report criticizing FDA's failure to disapprove the subtherapeutic use of several antibiotics. NEED TO ESTABLISH SAFETY AND EFFECTIVENESS OF ANTIBIOTICS USED IN ANIMAL FEEDS, HRD–77–81 (1977). However, the House Appropriations Committee, sensitive to the needs of agriculture, instructed the agency to delay any regulatory action pending a study by the National Academy of Sciences. The NAS concluded that it was not possible to conduct a single comprehensive epidemiological study to resolve the issues, but suggested studies that could advance understanding of the potential risk. NAS, THE EFFECTS ON HUMAN HEALTH OF SUBTHERAPEUTIC USE OF ANTIMICROBIALS IN ANIMAL FEED (1980).

In November 1984, the Natural Resources Defense Council petitioned the Secretary of HHS to suspend the NADAs for all the drugs approved for subtherapeutic use on the ground that their continued use constituted an imminent hazard to public health. After a public hearing, 49 Fed. Reg. 49645 (Dec. 31, 1984), the petition was denied. Surprisingly, no court challenge to the Secretary's denial was filed. Opening another legal front, the Animal Legal Defense Fund of Boston sued a Wisconsin veal producer, alleging that the defendant raised calves in confined pens, fed them iron-deprived diets, and gave them subtherapeutic doses of drugs that may be dangerous to humans, and that failing to tell consumers about these practices was unfair and deceptive under Massachusetts law. The court entered summary judgment for the defendant, finding that there is no private right of action under the Massachusetts animal cruelty statutes and that FDA regulation of animal drugs preempted Massachusetts law on this subject. *Animal Legal Defense Fund Boston, Inc. v. Provimi Veal Corp.*, 626 F. Supp. 278 (D. Mass. 1986), *aff'd without opinion* 802 F.2d 440 (1st Cir. 1986).

Meanwhile the Centers for Disease Control (CDC) continued investigations of reports suggesting a link between antibiotic resistant salmonella and the use of subtherapeutic antibiotics in animal feed. S. D. Holmberg et al., *Drug–Resistant Salmonella From Animals Feed Antimicrobials*, 311 NEW ENG. J. MED. 617 (Sept. 6, 1984); S. E. Levy, *Playing Antibiotic Pool: Time to Tally the Score*, 311 NEW ENG. J. MED. 663 (Sept. 6, 1984); J. S. Spika et al., *Chloramphenicol–Resistant Salmonella Newport Traced Through Hamburger to Dairy Farms: A Major Persisting Source of Human Salmonellosis in California*, 316 NEW ENG. J. MED. 565 (Mar. 5, 1987).

In February 1989, the Institute of Medicine, a unit of the NAS, issued yet another report, HUMAN HEALTH RISKS WITH THE SUBTHERAPEUTIC USE OF PENICILLIN OR TETRACYCLINES IN ANIMAL FEED. The IOM committee concluded that it was "unable to find data directly implicating the subtherapeutic use of feed antimicrobials in human illness and that much of the available evidence was primarily circumstantial, often ambiguous, and sometimes conflicting," but it put forward a novel risk assessment model that estimated the possible number of excess deaths per year under a variety of assumptions. Debate over the risks posed by subtherapeutic users of antibiotics in livestock continued into the current century, as recounted in FDA's decision to ban enrofloxacin, set forth below.

NOTES

1. *Sulfonamide Drugs.* Sulfonamide drugs are a class of synthetic antibacterials. Thirty-five years ago, FDA required residue depletion data to permit the establishment of an adequate withdrawal period to assure that edible products from animals treated with sulfonamide-containing drugs were safe for consumption. 35 Fed. Reg. 16538 (Oct. 23, 1970). Interim marketing was permitted while approved NADAs were being obtained for all sulfonamide drugs. 38 Fed. Reg. 19404 (July 20, 1973); 39 Fed. Reg. 26633 (July 22, 1974); 42 Fed. Reg. 62211 (Dec. 9, 1977); 43 Fed. Reg. 19385 (May 5, 1978). FDA ended interim marketing and announced the requirement of an approved NADA for these drugs in 49 Fed. Reg. 27543 (July 5, 1984). *See also* 55 Fed. Reg. 32390 (Aug. 9, 1990) (removal of regulation allowing interim marketing of sulfonamide drugs). After sulfamethazine was found to be carcinogenic in both mice, 53 Fed. Reg. 9492 (Mar. 23, 1988), and rats, 53 Fed. Reg. 17850 (May 18, 1988), FDA announced a public hearing in 53 Fed. Reg. 17852 (May 18, 1988) to determine a proper course of action on that drug. Following the hearing, FDA acted to prevent further use of any sulfonamide-containing drugs in food-producing animals. It refused to approve all the pending NADAs for sulfonamide drugs, not on the specific ground of carcinogenicity, but on the more general ground that the data were inadequate to support the safety of the drug either in animals or in people who consumed edible products from treated animals. 53 Fed. Reg. 46050 (Nov. 15, 1988); 53 Fed. Reg. 51950 (Dec. 23, 1988); 54 Fed. Reg. 10725 (Mar. 15, 1989); 54 Fed. Reg. 22015 (May 22, 1989), 54 Fed. Reg. 38442 (Sept. 18, 1989).

2. *Residue Monitoring.* USDA shares responsibility with FDA for monitoring the residues of animal drugs in livestock. *See* 49 Fed. Reg. 23602 (June 7, 1984); 50 Fed. Reg. 32162 (Aug. 9, 1985); 52 Fed. Reg. 2101 (Jan. 20, 1987); 53 Fed. Reg. 52177 (Dec. 27, 1988); 55 Fed. Reg. 7472 (Mar. 2, 1990) (adding 9 C.F.R. 310.21, relating to USDA post-mortem inspection of carcasses suspected of containing sulfamethazine and antibiotic residues); 45 Fed. Reg. 63930 (Sept. 16, 1980), 50 Fed. Reg. 20796 (May 20, 1985), & 53 Fed. Reg. 52177 (Dec. 27, 1988) (recording

FDA's and USDA's concern about the continuing occurrence of above-tolerance sulfamethazine residues in swine). *See also United States v. Nelson Farms, Inc.,* Food Drug Cosm. L. Rep. (CCH) ¶ 38,019 (D. Vt. 1987). Animal drug residues are a subject of constant FDA interest. In 52 Fed. Reg. 165 (Jan. 2, 1987), FDA announced the availability of funds to support studies on the development and improvement of analytical methodologies for residues of high priority animal drugs in tissues. *See* Gary E. Stefan, *FDA's Role in Combatting Animal Drug Residues,* 52 J. AFDO, No. 3, at 45 (July 1988). FDA, USDA, and EPA have a Memorandum of Understanding covering monitoring for, and control of, drug and pesticide residues in food. 50 Fed. Reg. 2304 (Jan. 16, 1985).

———

In 1996, FDA approved an NADA submitted by Bayer for enrofloxacin to reduce Campylobacter infections in chickens and turkey. Almost immediately, the agency became concerned about the development of Campylobacter resistance in humans and four years later it proposed to withdraw approval. Bayer demanded the evidentiary hearing to which the Act entitled it, leading to the ruling of an Administrative Law Judge described in the following decision of the Acting Commissioner, Dr. Lester Crawford.

Withdrawal of Approval of the New Animal Drug Application for Enrofloxacin in Poultry: Final Decision of the Commissioner

FDA Docket No. 2000N–1571.

Enrofloxacin is an antimicrobial drug belonging to a class of drugs known as fluoroquinolones. On October 31, 2000, the Center for Veterinary Medicine (CVM) of the U.S. Food and Drug Administration (FDA) published a Notice of Opportunity for Hearing (NOOH) proposing to withdraw the approval of the new animal drug application (NADA) 140.828 for the use of enrofloxacin in chickens and turkeys. 65 Fed. Reg. 64,954 (2000). On November 29, 2000, Bayer Corporation (Bayer), the sponsor of enrofloxacin (sold under the trade name Baytril® 3.23% Concentrate Antimicrobial Solution), requested a hearing on the proposed withdrawal.... On March 21, 2002, the Animal Health Institute (AHI) submitted a Notice of Participation pursuant to 21 CFR § 12.45, identifying itself in part as "the national trade association representing research based manufacturers of animal health products."

. . . .

On March 16, 2004, the ALJ [Administrative Law Judge] issued an Initial Decision pursuant to 21 CFR § 12.120. The ALJ found, among other things, that more than a million people annually suffer from infections caused by Campylobacter, a genus of bacteria; that poultry is a source of *Campylobacter* infections; that the use of enrofloxacin in poultry results in the emergence and dissemination of fluoroquinolone-resistant *Campylobacter*; that fluoroquinolone-resistant *Campylobacter* in poultry can be transferred to humans and "can contribute to" fluoroquinolone-resistant *Campylobacter* infections in humans; and that fluoroquinolone-resistant *Campylobacter* infections in humans "have the potential to adversely affect human health." ... Based on these and other findings, the ALJ determined that "Bayer has not shown Baytril use in poultry to be safe" as set out in § 512(e)(1)(B) of the Federal Food, Drug, and Cosmetic Act (FDCA), 21 U.S.C. § 360b(e)(1)(B).

. . . .

After reviewing the evidentiary record of the hearing, I find that the record supports the ALJ's determination. . . . However, my reasoning varies in several regards from that of the ALJ. I therefore am withdrawing the approval of the NADA for use of enrofloxacin in poultry for the reasons set forth more fully in this Final Decision. . . .

CVM proposed to withdraw approval of enrofloxacin pursuant to § 512(e)(1)(B) of the FDCA, which provides:

The Secretary shall, after due notice and opportunity for hearing to the applicant, issue an order withdrawing approval of an application filed pursuant to subsection (b) with respect to any new animal drug if the Secretary finds . . .

(B) that new evidence not contained in such application or not available to the Secretary until after such application was approved, or tests by new methods, or tests by methods not deemed reasonably applicable when such application was approved, evaluated together with the evidence available to the Secretary when the application was approved, shows that such drug is not shown to be safe for use under the conditions of use upon the basis of which the application was approved. . . .

I agree with the Initial Decision's general description of the allocation of the burdens between CVM and Bayer. CVM, as the proponent of withdrawal of approval of the use of enrofloxacin in poultry, has the burden of making the first showing; in other words, CVM has the initial burden of production. Once this threshold burden has been satisfied, the burden passes to Bayer, as the sponsor of enrofloxacin, to demonstrate its safety. *Rhone–Poulenc, Inc. v. FDA*, 636 F.2d 750, 752 (D.C. Cir. 1980) (*per curiam*); *Hess & Clark*, 495 F.2d at 992; 21 CFR § 12.87(d).

. . . .

By arguing that the standard of proof that applies to both participants' burdens is preponderance of the evidence, Bayer also seems to be implying that CVM has the burden of persuasion. If that is what Bayer means, I disagree. Bayer, as the sponsor of enrofloxacin, has the ultimate burden of persuasion regarding the safety of the drug. . . .

As Bayer acknowledges, the evidentiary standards set out in *Daubert v. Merrell Dow Pharmaceuticals, Inc.*, 509 U.S. 579 (1993), and its progeny are not binding in administrative adjudications.

As will be clear in reviewing the discussion of the evidence below, however, the principles of *Daubert* are useful to this proceeding. Furthermore, I find that consideration of those principles leads me to conclude that the epidemiologic and other research CVM presented is reliable. . . .

Bayer also asserts that the FDA and Office of Management and Budget (OMB) guidelines issued pursuant to the Information Quality Act (IQA), Pub. L. No. 106–554, § 515 (2000), provide "useful guideposts" for evaluating the testimony and evidence relied on by CVM. Bayer further argues that a risk assessment relied on by CVM, described in more detail below, must satisfy FDA's guidelines to be considered reliable evidence in this proceeding.

I disagree with both arguments. The stated intent of the IQA is to ensure and maximize the quality of data "disseminated" by Federal agencies and to allow "affected persons" to request correction of such information—not to impose new evidentiary standards in administrative proceedings. Indeed, OMB's guidelines specify that such requests for correction should serve to address the genuine and valid needs of outside parties without disrupting agency processes, and information used in and findings made in adjudications are expressly exempted by the FDA Guidelines. Furthermore, on its face, the FDA guidance makes clear that it, like all FDA guidance documents, does not "create or confer any rights for or on any person or bind FDA or the public." *See also* 21 CFR § 10.115(d).

... If I were to agree with Bayer's interpretation of the role of the FDA's IQA guidelines in this proceeding, I would in effect be ruling that in any formal administrative proceeding the IQA guidelines should replace longstanding and well-established statutory provisions and judicial doctrine about the admissibility and reliability of expert testimony and scientific evidence. Bayer's IQA argument would also require me to evaluate the evidence on which CVM relies differently from that on which Bayer relies.... I do not believe that Congress would have chosen such an indirect means of changing the formal adjudication provisions of the APA and drug approval and withdrawal provisions of the FDCA. The factors I look to in evaluating the reliability of the scientific evidence do not change depending on which participant is relying on it....

III.   DISCUSSION

. . . .

A.   Human Campylobacter Infections in the United States

The U.S. Centers for Disease Control and Prevention (CDC) estimated in 1999 that food borne infections cause 76 million illnesses, 325,000 hospitalizations, and 5,000 deaths each year. Food borne illnesses may be caused by viruses, bacteria, parasites, toxins, metals, and prions. CDC estimated that bacterial agents are associated with approximately 30.2% of food borne illnesses and a majority of resulting hospitalizations (59.9%) and deaths (71.7%). *Campylobacter* is a genus of bacteria with many different species, a number of which are known to cause illness in humans, although two, *Campylobacter jejuni* (abbreviated as *C. jejuni*) and *Campylobacter coli* (*C. coli*), are identified as the cause of almost all cultured human infections. *Campylobacter* is recognized as a leading cause of gastroenteritis in many developed and developing countries. In the United States, the most important, in terms of human infection, is *C. jejuni*. ...

Based on data from 1996–1997 (adjusted for underreporting), in 1999 CDC [U.S. Centers for Disease Control and Prevention] estimated that 2.4 million illnesses in the United States each year are caused by *Campylobacter*, of which approximately 80% were food borne infections. In that analysis, CDC estimated that about 14.2% of food borne illness in the United States annually is caused by *Campylobacter* infection, making it the leading bacterial source of food borne illness in this country.

... [A]lthough the incidence of these infections has declined in recent years, I find that the record demonstrates that *Campylobacter* infections remain a major cause of food borne illness in the United States.

Campylobacter infections in humans are characterized by fever, headache, abdominal pain, and diarrhea (bloody or watery), usually 24–72 hours after ingestion of the contaminated food. Less frequently, patients may suffer from muscle aches and vomiting.

Campylobacter infection in humans can be self-limiting, *i.e.*, it may resolve without antibiotics or other pharmaceutical treatment. However, in some patients the illness may be prolonged or more severe. In addition, *Campylobacter* infections can occasionally result in significant and sometimes long term adverse health outcomes. First, extraintestinal infections, such as meningitis, peritonitis, and bloodstream infection, are possible, although rare.

More commonly, *Campylobacter* infection can cause reactive arthritis and Guillain–Barré syndrome (GBS)....

Finally, there is a very low possibility of death associated with *Campylobacter* infections. Mortality in the United States associated with *Campylobacter* is low, with estimates ranging from 8 per 10,000 to 24 per 10,-000....

I find that the record demonstrates that fluoroquinolones, such as ciprofloxacin, are widely used to treat gastroenteritis, because they are generally well-tolerated, can be prescribed on an outpatient basis, and are effective against a broad range of bacteria....

B. Enrofloxacin use and Campylobacter in poultry

On October 4, 1996, FDA approved NADA 140–828 under § 512 of the FDCA, authorizing the use of enrofloxacin (Baytril® 3.23% Concentrate Antimicrobial Solution) to control mortality in chickens associated with *Escherichia coli* (*E. coli*) and mortality in turkeys associated with *E. coli* and *Pasteurella multocida* (fowl cholera). FDA approved the use of enrofloxacin only by prescription and under veterinary supervision, and only for therapeutic treatment (*i.e.*, not for growth promotion). FDA prohibited the extra-label use of enrofloxacin for all food-producing animals, including poultry....

... I find that commercially produced chickens and turkeys in the United States are frequently colonized with *Campylobacter*, and that the colonization of *Campylobacter* persists until slaughter. I further find that the selection for fluoroquinolone-resistant *Campylobacter* occurs rapidly in poultry following initiation of fluoroquinolone treatment, and that fluoroquinolone-resistant *Campylobacter* persist until slaughter.

In contrast, I find the absence of fluoroquinolone treatment of poultry to be associated with a very low level of fluoroquinolone resistance in such untreated poultry, despite the fact that the actual mutation occurs spontaneously. This is important evidence linking the use of enrofloxacin in poultry to the emergence of resistant *Campylobacter* infections in poultry and exposure of humans to resistant *Campylobacter*.

C. Poultry consumption as a risk factor for human Campylobacter infection

In addition to the data on persistent colonization of live poultry with susceptible *Campylobacter* and resistant *Campylobacter*, the presence of susceptible and resistant *Campylobacter* in and on broilers and turkeys presented for slaughter, and the frequency of contamination of poultry carcasses with susceptible and resistant *Campylobacter*, there is substantial other evidence supporting my determination that, in the United States, poultry consumption is a primary risk factor for human infections with *Campylobacter*, including fluoroquinolone-resistant *Campylobacter*. . . .

. . . .

In sum, the record shows that illness can occur at very low levels of exposure to *Campylobacter*. I find that there is no scientific justification for disregarding the retail meat studies because they do not provide a measure of bacterial load. The retail meat studies show that the contamination of poultry meat persists to and after the point of purchase, providing further evidence in the link between fluoroquinolone use in poultry and fluoroquinolone-resistant *Campylobacter* infections in humans. We know from these studies that, in different areas of the country and over a range of recent years, all researchers investigating retail meat contamination have found that a large proportion of retail poultry products is contaminated with *Campylobacter*. Moreover, recent studies consistently have shown that a large proportion of the products is contaminated with *Campylobacter* that are resistant to fluoroquinolones. This is important evidence linking human infections to poultry consumption. . . .

Several case-control studies from the United States and elsewhere have shown that the risk of *Campylobacter* infection is significantly elevated with respect to: consumption of poultry generally; poultry consumption in restaurants; consumption of undercooked or raw poultry; handling of raw chicken; and failure to clean food preparation or cutting board surfaces. The association between poultry and *Campylobacter* infections in humans is generally consistent across studies, despite broad differences in size, methodology, and sample population. . . .

The epidemiologic studies I have described thus far identified risk factors for acquiring *Campylobacter* infections, without consideration of the susceptibility or resistance of the bacteria to fluoroquinolones. However, the record demonstrates, and I find, that there are no significant biologic reasons that transmission of fluoroquinolone-resistant *Campylobacter* infections from animals to humans is different from transmission of fluoroquinolone-susceptible infections. As a result, it can be expected that when resistance to fluoroquinolones emerges in *Campylobacter* in animals, resistant *Campylobacter* will be transmitted to humans, and investigations have shown temporally that this in fact occurs.

. . . .

I also find that data from several countries, including the United States, indicate that a rise in human *Campylobacter* infections that are resistant to fluoroquinolones has consistently followed the introduction of enrofloxacin in poultry production in that country.... [A]n indication that an exposure precedes the outcome of interest is consistent with a causal association....

CVM introduced into evidence a quantitative assessment of the human health impact of fluoroquinolone-resistant *Campylobacter* infections attributed to the consumption of contaminated chicken. The question the risk assessment addresses was whether the use of fluoroquinolones in poultry introduced a significant human health burden associated with a specific prevalence of fluoroquinolone resistance in poultry carcasses, and, if so, whether any action by CVM would significantly reduce that burden. Using the risk assessment model, CVM estimated that in 1998 about 8,678 people and in 1999 about 9,261 people were expected to be infected with fluoroquinolone-resistant *Campylobacter* from consuming chicken, receive fluoroquinolone treatment, and experience a longer duration of illness because of the decreased effectiveness of the antibiotic.

. . . .

The risk assessment was not published in a peer reviewed journal. It was, however, subject to extensive public review and layers of expert review within and outside of FDA. The process began with draft guidance to industry in November 1998 on antimicrobial use in food-producing animals. In December 1998, CVM issued a discussion document called ''A Proposed Framework for Evaluating and Assuring the Human Safety of the Microbial Effects of Antimicrobial New Animal Drugs Intended for Use in Food Producing Animals.'' FDA also developed the quantitative risk assessment model used in the CVM risk assessment, which was released publicly in December 1999. At that time the draft risk assessment document, as well as two spreadsheet models—one for use with Microsoft Excel and a second version, in an Microsoft Excel spreadsheet, for use with the software package @Risk (Palisades Corp, NY)—were posted on the FDA–CVM website. CVM held a public conference exclusively to discuss and present the risk assessment that included panel discussions involving food safety and risk assessment experts. Comments collected at the conference and submitted in writing were organized, assembled, and summarized by CVM, and were addressed in the final version of the model and the report. Thus, the conference offered an opportunity for peer review of the document by providing critical evaluations of the science, data and information, and methodologies used to develop the risk assessment.

. . . .

Although I have found that the [Information Quality Act] does not afford Bayer any legal basis to challenge the reliability of any of CVM's evidence in the context of this administrative proceeding, under the unique circumstances of this proceeding, I now have pending before me AHI's IQA request for correction and request for reconsideration, accessible at the website noted in the preceding paragraph, and the formal adjudication. I am therefore taking the unusual step of also resolving, in this Final Decision, AHI's request for correction of the CVM risk assessment....

Based on several factual findings set forth in this Final Decision, I find that, even assuming that the risk assessment is properly considered "influential" under FDA's Guidelines, and is otherwise subject to the IQA, the process by which the risk assessment was produced (which predated the enactment of the IQA and the issuance of OMB, HHS, and FDA guidelines), was nonetheless consistent with the FDA Guidelines, even those for influential information, and that no correction of the risk assessment is warranted.

First, CVM used the "best available science and supporting studies conducted in accordance with sound and objective scientific practices" and relied on "data collected by accepted methods." *See* FDA Guidelines. The data were robust, peer reviewed, and/or compiled by federal agencies, but not for regulatory action or the withdrawal hearing.

Second, the risk assessment underwent a stringent expert and public review process. Third, the risk assessment process, including the methodology used, the data relied on, assumptions made, and uncertainties, was transparent, reproducible, and replicable. In the assessment CVM highlighted critical assumptions and limitations, and posted the draft and final assessment model on its website. Anyone familiar with the commonly used Microsoft Excel software program is able to use the model, incorporating different assumptions and data. The stated purpose of the assessment was to estimate the nominal mean number of patients with fluoroquinolone-resistant *Campylobacter* infections who sought treatment, were treated with fluoroquinolones, and were affected by the resistance of their infection to fluoroquinolones, for the years 1998 and 1999, and gave appropriate confidence intervals for this estimate. In the risk assessment, CVM clearly identified the potentially affected population; analyzed uncertainties, both in the assessment and in underlying data; and identified and relied on relevant peer-reviewed studies.

. . . .

IV. DISCUSSION OF LEGAL ISSUES

A. New evidence

... § 512(e)(1)(B) of the FDCA requires withdrawal of a new animal drug application if the Commissioner finds that "new evidence not contained in [a new animal drug] application or not available to the [Commissioner] until after such application was approved, or tests by new methods, or tests by methods not deemed reasonably applicable when such application was approved, evaluated together with the evidence available to the [Commissioner] when the application was approved" shows that the new animal drug is no longer shown to be safe. . . .

In its exceptions, Bayer contests whether there is "new evidence" on enrofloxacin use in poultry. Bayer argues that evidence about a drug that is generated after approval of the drug cannot be "new evidence" under § 512(e)(1)(B) of the FDCA unless it "points to a different conclusion that was not contained in the original application. . . ." In effect, Bayer argues that if FDA is aware that a human health risk could occur or exists when it approves a new animal drug, then post-approval evidence relating to that risk cannot be "new evidence."

... While it is clear that the content of the evidence is critical to my determination of whether CVM has met its burden to produce evidence raising serious questions about enrofloxacin's safety, I do not find support for such a content-driven definition of "new" in the statute or its legislative history. To the contrary, § 512(e)(1)(B) requires that I must make my determination about whether an animal drug "is not shown to be safe" based on "new evidence ... evaluated together with the evidence available to [me] when the application was approved." 21 U.S.C. § 360b(e)(1)(B). In other words, I must find both that there is "new" evidence, and that that the collective weight of the evidence in front of me, old and new, shows that the drug in question is no longer shown to be safe.

. . . .

B.   The meaning of "safe"

A central issue in the proceeding is whether, under § 512(e)(1)(B) of the FDCA, enrofloxacin "is not shown to be safe for use under the conditions of use upon the basis of which the application was approved...." The ALJ determined that "safe" in the context of assessing the human food safety of a new animal drug means that there is a "reasonable certainty of no harm." The ALJ also held that "the safety concern in this matter is limited to human food safety and human health impact, and the proper risk-benefit analysis considers only whether the benefits to human health from the use of enrofloxacin in poultry are proven to outweigh the risk to human health from such use." The ALJ noted that there are effective alternatives to enrofloxacin and that FDA is not required to put humans at risk to benefit animals. The ALJ thus declined to weigh animal health and welfare benefits against risks to humans. Finally, citing two Supreme Court rulings, *American Textile Manufacturers Institute, Inc. v. Donovan*, 452 U.S. 490 (1981), and *Whitman v. American Trucking Ass'ns*, 531 U.S. 457 (2001), for the proposition that costs cannot be considered as part of a safety or health assessment without explicit authorization, the ALJ rejected consideration of economic costs of the decision to withdraw approval of the use of enrofloxacin in poultry.

... I agree with the ALJ that when assessing whether food from animals treated with a new animal drug is safe for human consumption, it is correct to frame the meaning of "safe" as presenting a "reasonable certainty of no harm." I conclude, as FDA has before, that an assessment of the human health impacts of the use of a particular drug in food-producing animals under the "reasonable certainty of no harm" standard involves a straightforward evaluation of the human safety of the animal drug; it does not encompass any weighing of costs and benefits, including any weighing of human safety concerns (in other words, health risks) against human health benefits. I find that the FDCA as a whole, as well as its legislative history, makes clear that Congress did not intend to allow FDA to weigh costs or benefits associated with the use of a new animal drug in deciding whether its use has been shown to be safe for humans when used in food-producing animals.

When FDA reviews an application for approval of a use of a new animal drug in a food-producing animal, the agency must find: 1) that the drug is safe and effective in the target animal, and 2) that food from the animal is safe for human consumption....

The target animal safety standard of § 512 originated from the new drug safety standard used in § 505 which, until 1968, applied to both human and animal drugs. Thus, FDA, when implementing the 1968 Animal Drug Amendments, continued to use, and still uses, this same standard when it is reviewing whether a new animal drug is safe for use in or on the target animal. Thus, FDA may, in evaluating a NADA, look at both the risks and benefits a new animal drug will have with respect to the target animal. Section 505 however, provides no direct insight into the process by which FDA evaluates the human food safety of animal drugs....

... Section 409(a), 21 U.S.C. 348(a), requires that uses of "food additives" be approved by FDA as safe prior to their use in food.... This broad definition of food additive included drugs used in animal feed and food-producing animals. Therefore, these animal drugs were subject to § 409's safety standard.

Congress defined "safe" for purposes of § 409. Section 201(t) (now § 201(u)) provided: "The term 'safe' as used in paragraph (s) of this section [the definition of food additive] and in section 409, has reference to the health of man or animal." ...

By framing the safety standard as "reasonable certainty of no harm," [the] legislative history [of § 409] makes it clear that weighing costs and benefits, including any weighing of health risks and benefits, was not envisioned by Congress as part of the assessment of the safety of food additives.

Furthermore, Congress explicitly rejected consideration of benefits as part of the food additive approval process.

. . . .

Because the human food safety standard of § 512 originated from the "reasonable certainty of no harm" standard used in § 409, FDA, when implementing the 1968 Animal Drug Amendments, continued to use, and still uses, this same standard when it is reviewing whether food from an animal treated with a new animal drug is safe for human consumption. Thus, in making a determination ... whether food from animals treated with a new animal drug is safe for human consumption, FDA looks only at whether there are human health risks from the use of the drug and does not consider whether there are any benefits to humans from the use of the drug.

. . . .

Bayer relies on two D.C. Circuit cases, *Hess & Clark, Inc. v. FDA*, 495 F.2d 975 (D.C. Cir. 1974), and *Rhone–Poulenc, Inc. v. FDA*, 636 F.2d 750 (D.C. Cir. 1980), in support of its argument that, in assessing human food safety, I must weigh all of these alleged benefits of enrofloxacin's use in poultry against the human health risks such use poses. The ALJ found that these D.C. Circuit cases implicitly have been overruled by two Supreme Court rulings, *Donovan*, 452 U.S. 490 (1981), and *American Trucking*, 531 U.S. 457 (2001)....

... Based on my review, I conclude that the Supreme Court has effectively overruled those parts of *Hess & Clark* and *Rhone–Poulenc* that address consideration of costs and benefits as part of a withdrawal of approval of a new animal drug based on human food safety risks.

Hess & Clark involved a challenge to FDA's decision to withdraw, without a hearing, the approval of the new animal drug diethylstilbestrol (DES) for use in cattle and sheep. After ruling that FDA had not given the sponsors adequate notice of the grounds for withdrawal, the D.C. Circuit stated:

> Outside of the *per se* rule of the Delaney Clause, the typical issue for the FDA is not the absolute safety of a drug. Most drugs are unsafe in some degree. Rather, the issue for the FDA is whether to allow sale of the drug, usually under specific restrictions. Resolution of this issue inevitably means calculating whether the benefits which the drug produces outweigh the costs of its restricted use. In the present case, DES is asserted to be of substantial benefit in enhancing meat production. . . .

In *Rhone–Poulenc*, the D.C. Circuit upheld FDA's withdrawal of DES after additional notice and a hearing, but rebuffed FDA's efforts to revisit the meaning of "safe"; the court noted that it was "bound by the holding of the *Hess & Clark* court until we are instructed otherwise by the Supreme Court or an *en banc* decision of this court."

A year after *Rhone–Poulenc* was decided, the Supreme Court decided *Donovan*. At issue was whether the Occupational Safety and Health Administration (OSHA) was required to compare costs and benefits when setting a standard for harmful agents under § 6(b)(5) of the Occupational Safety and Health Act (OSH Act), 29 U.S.C. § 655(b)(5). This provision states that OSHA is to set a standard "which most adequately assures that, to the extent feasible . . . no employee will suffer material impairment of health or functional capacity even if such employee has regular exposure to the hazard dealt with by the standard for the period of his working life." The Supreme Court concluded that this provision did not permit comparison of costs and benefits. First, based on the plain meaning of "feasible," the Court reasoned that Congress had directed an analysis of ability to achieve the level of protection, not a balancing of benefits and costs. By contrast, the Court said, "[w]hen Congress has intended that an agency engage in cost-benefit analysis, it has clearly indicated such intent on the face of the statute." After citing numerous examples, some as far back as 1936, the Court concluded that these examples "demonstrate that Congress uses specific language when intending that an agency engage in cost benefit analysis." The Court also determined that other provisions of the OSH Act did not suggest a different result, finding that to interpret the other parts of the statute as calling for a cost-benefit analysis essentially would render § 6(b)(5) largely meaningless. In the *Nitrofurans* Final Decision, FDA Commissioner David Kessler concluded that *Donovan* is "ample authority for the proposition that clauses like the [FDCA's] general safety clause do not permit, much less invite, cost/benefit analysis." I agree.

. . . .

C.   Bayer's evidence on costs and benefits

Because I conclude that CVM has met its initial burden of coming forward with evidence to show that there are serious questions about enrofloxacin's safety, the burden then shifts to Bayer to show that the use of enrofloxacin in chickens and turkeys is safe and that FDA should continue to approve such use. I conclude, as described more fully below, that Bayer has not met its burden.

Bayer sought to introduce the testimony of G. Thomas Martin, Jr. as an expert in the economics of poultry processing. In his testimony Mr. Martin presented a projection of the potential economic impacts of the withdrawal of enrofloxacin from the U.S. market. The ALJ excluded Mr. Martin's testimony, holding broadly that "[e]conomic and environmental evidence is not relevant to the issues in this proceeding," and specifically striking the testimony of Mr. Martin and a number of other witnesses. The ALJ noted that Mr. Martin's testimony was stricken "because it was found to be altogether unreliable, and not just on the issue of economic effects of Baytril's withdrawal."

Although, as discussed at length above, I find the issue of economic benefit has no relevance to this proceeding, I have nonetheless reviewed Mr. Martin's proffered written direct testimony, and I agree with the ALJ that, even if it were relevant, this testimony is not sufficiently reliable to be given any weight.

. . . .

NOTE

Commentary. *See* Elizabeth A. Barclay, *Subtherapeutic Use of Antibiotics in Animal Feed: In Light of an Unresolved Clash of Expert Paradigms Should We Punt to the Consumer in Decade Four?* (1998), in Chapter VII of the Electronic Book; Neal J. Suit, *Antibiotic Resistance: Proposals to Deal with the New Wrinkles on an Old Problem* (2000), in Chapter VII of the Electronic Book.

2.   Mad Cow Disease

In the late 1980s Britain was swept by fear that a newly-identified disease in cattle, bovine spongiform encephalopathy (BSE), which erodes an animal's nervous system, could be transmitted to humans who drank milk or ate meat from afflicted cows. It was soon learned that cattle could contract BSE from feed that included bone meal from diseased ruminants, usually sheep. In 1989 a working party established by Britain's Ministries of Health and Agriculture concluded that "the risk of transmission of BSE to humans appears remote," but it acknowledged that the possibility "cannot be ruled out." Report of the Working Party on Bovine Spongiform Encephalopathy 14 (Feb. 1989).

Events soon shattered this sanguine assessment. By the mid–1990s, the British government had ordered (and paid for) the destruction of more than 100,000 head of potentially diseased cattle and stringently limited the permissible source of feed for livestock. By the end of the decade BSE had been reported among cattle in most European countries as well as Japan and Canada. Japan, a major customer for imported beef, announced that it would not accept imports from any country that had not established a fail-safe for preventing the disease—including the United States.

It was not the risk to livestock that prompted government action; it was the fear, and soon the realization, that consumption of meat from BSE-infected animals could produce an analogous form of the disease—dubbed "mad cow disease" and officially labeled variant Creutzfeld–Jacob Disease (vCJD)—in humans. By the end of the decade British health authorities had identified more than 100 cases of vCJD, most of them attributed to consumption of meat from diseased cattle. Isolated cases had also been discovered in other countries. In the United States, FDA and USDA had adopted a series of measures—summarized in the following Federal Register excerpt—designed to prevent the occurrence of BSE in domestic cattle and sheep. In addition, FDA had imposed restrictions on blood donations by persons who have resided in Britain for six months or more since 1989, during which time they might have consumed meat from diseased animals.

As of February 2007 there have been no reports of cases of vCJD linked to consumption of meat from BSE-infected cows in the United States, but two cases of BSE in older cows have been confirmed. One of the cows came from Canada. Both apparently were born before segregated ruminant feed requirements were imposed by FDA in 1997. 62 Fed. Reg. 30936, 21 C.F.R. 589 (2000). The press coverage accorded these discoveries contributed to the additional measures that FDA and USDA announced in 2005. For a critical account of the measures taken by U.S. authorities to avert problems on a scale comparable to Britain's, *see* Caroline Smith DeWaal & Leora Vegosen, *Bovine Spongiform Encephalopathy: The Importance of Precautionary Measures to Protect the Food Supply*, 58 FOOD & DRUG L.J. 537 (2003).

Substances Prohibited From Use in Animal Food or Feed

70 Fed. Reg. 58570 (October 6, 2005).

SUMMARY: The Food and Drug Administration (FDA) is proposing to amend the agency's regulations to prohibit the use of certain cattle origin materials in the food or feed of all animals. These materials include the following: The brains and spinal cords from cattle 30 months of age and older, the brains and spinal cords from cattle of any age not inspected and passed for human consumption, the entire carcass of cattle not inspected and passed for human consumption if the brains and spinal cords have not been removed, tallow that is derived from the materials prohibited by this proposed rule that contains more than 0.15 percent insoluble impurities, and mechanically separated beef that is derived from the materials prohibited by this proposed rule. These measures will further strengthen existing safeguards designed to help prevent the spread of bovine spongiform encephalopathy (BSE) in U.S. cattle....

I. Background

    A.   *Bovine Spongiform Encephalopathy*

BSE belongs to the family of diseases known as transmissible spongiform encephalopathies (TSEs). In addition to BSE, TSEs also include scrapie in sheep and goats, chronic wasting disease (CWD) in deer and elk, and Creutzfeldt–Jakob disease (CJD) in humans. The agent that causes BSE and other TSEs has yet to be fully characterized. The most widely accepted theory in the scientific community is that the agent is an abnormal form of a normal cellular prion protein.... There is currently no available test to detect the disease in a live animal.

Since November 1986, there have been more than 180,000 confirmed cases of BSE in cattle worldwide. Over 95 percent of all BSE cases have occurred in the United Kingdom, where the epidemic peaked in 1992/1993, with approximately 1,000 new cases reported per week. In addition to the United Kingdom, the disease has been confirmed in native-born cattle in 22 European countries and in some non-European countries, including Japan, Israel, Canada, and the United States.

. . . .

In 1996, a newly recognized form of the human disease CJD, referred to as variant CJD (vCJD), was reported in the United Kingdom. Scientific and epidemiological studies have linked vCJD to exposure to the BSE agent, most likely through human consumption of beef products contaminated with the agent. To date, approximately 150 probable and confirmed cases of vCJD have been reported in the United Kingdom, where there had likely been a high level of contamination of beef products. It is believed that in the United States, where measures to prevent the introduction and spread of BSE have been in place for some time, there is far less potential for human exposure to the BSE agent. The Centers for Disease Control and Prevention (CDC) ... has not detected vCJD in any resident of the United States that had not lived in or traveled to the United Kingdom for extended periods of time....

B.   Current Animal Feed Safeguards in the United States

In the Federal Register of June 5, 1997 (62 FR 30936), FDA published a final rule to provide that animal protein derived from mammalian tissues is prohibited for use in ruminant feed....

The 1997 ruminant feed final rule (§ 589.2000) prohibits the use of mammalian-derived proteins in ruminant feed, with the exception of certain proteins believed at that time not to pose a risk of BSE transmission. These exceptions to the definition of "protein derived from mammalian tissues" included: Blood and blood products; gelatin; inspected meat products which have been cooked and offered for human food and further heat processed for feed (such as plate waste and used cellulosic food casings), referred to herein as "plate waste"[;] milk products (milk and milk protein); and any product whose only mammalian protein consists entirely of porcine or equine protein....

C.   Risk of BSE in North America

In April 1998, the United States Department of Agriculture (USDA) contracted with the Harvard Center for Risk Analysis (HCRA) at Harvard University and the Center for Computational Epidemiology at Tuskegee University to conduct a comprehensive investigation of the BSE risk in the United States....

The Harvard–Tuskegee Study concluded that the most effective measures for reducing potential introduction and spread of BSE are as follows: (1) The ban placed by USDA's Animal and Plant Health Inspection Service on the importation of live ruminants and ruminant meat-and-bone meal from the United Kingdom since 1989 and all of Europe since 1997 and (2) the feed ban instituted in 1997 by FDA to prevent recycling of potentially infectious cattle tissue. The Harvard–Tuskegee Study further indicated that, if introduction of BSE had occurred via importation of live animals from the United Kingdom before 1989, mitigation measures already in place would have minimized exposure and begun to eliminate the disease from the cattle population even assuming less than complete compliance with the feed ban. . . .

On December 23, 2003, USDA announced that a dairy cow in Washington State had tested positive for BSE. The results were confirmed on December 25, 2003, by the Veterinary Laboratories Agency in Weybridge, England. Immediately after the diagnosis was confirmed, USDA, FDA, and other Federal and State agencies initiated an epidemiological investigation, and began working together to trace any potentially infected cattle, trace potentially contaminated rendered product, increase BSE surveillance, and take additional measures to address risks to human and animal health. The epidemiological investigation and DNA test results confirmed that the infected cow was born and most likely became infected in Alberta, Canada, before Canada's 1997 implementation of a ban on feeding mammalian protein to ruminants. . . .

In December 2004, Canada announced that a third North American cow tested positive for BSE. An ongoing epidemiologic investigation found that this animal, an 8–year-old, non-ambulatory dairy cow, originated in Alberta, Canada and was born before the Canadian feed ban went into effect in August 1997. Shortly thereafter, in January 2005, another cow in Alberta was found to be positive for BSE. This case involved a beef cow born in March 1998, 6 months after the Canadian feed ban went into effect. . . .

In June 2005, USDA announced that a 12–year-old beef cow, born and raised in Texas, was confirmed BSE positive. The BSE-positive cow most likely became infected before FDA's implementation of the 1997 ruminant feed final rule. . . .

D. Additional Measures Considered to Strengthen Animal Feed Safeguards

. . . .

In response to the BSE case identified in Washington State, USDA published an interim final rule in the Federal Register of January 12, 2004 (69 FR 1861), excluding high-risk tissues from human food. The interim final rule prohibited the use of SRMs and certain other cattle material in USDA-regulated human food. USDA defined SRMs as brain, skull, eyes, trigeminal ganglia, spinal cord, vertebral column (excluding the vertebra of the tail, the transverse processes of the thoracic and lumbar vertebrae, and the wings of the sacrum), and dorsal root ganglia (DRG) of cattle 30 months of age and older, and the tonsils and distal ileum of the small intestine of cattle of all ages. . . .

On January 26, 2004, FDA announced its intention to implement additional measures to strengthen existing BSE safeguards for FDA-regulated products.... The interim final rule would have implemented four specific measures related to animal feeds. These measures included the elimination of the exemptions for blood and blood products and "plate waste" from the 1997 ruminant feed rule, a prohibition on the use of poultry litter in ruminant feed, and a requirement for dedicated equipment and facilities to prevent cross-contamination.

. . . .

Consistent with measures implemented by USDA to exclude high-risk cattle tissues from human food (69 FR 1861), FDA published an interim final rule on July 14, 2004 (69 FR 42255), prohibiting a similar list of risk materials from FDA-regulated human food, including dietary supplements, and cosmetics.

. . . .

II.   Proposed Measures to Strengthen Animal Feed Safeguards

... Even though strong control measures have been put in place and compliance with the current BSE feed regulation is high by renderers, protein blenders and feed mills, the Agency is concerned, as discussed further below, about such issues as the presence of high risk material in the non-ruminant feed supply and cross-contamination of ruminant feed during the rendering or feed manufacturing process. For example, without fully dedicated equipment, it may not be possible to verify that there is zero carryover of feed or feed ingredients in equipment, even where a firm's cleanout procedures have been judged to be adequate. In addition, resource constraints limit FDA's ability to assure full compliance by all segments of the industry that are subject to the current BSE feed regulation. For example, resources are not available to the FDA and its state counterparts to fully verify compliance on over 1 million farms where cattle are being fed.

. . . .

B.   *Additional Measures to Further Strengthen Feed Protection*

The United States and Canadian feed regulations implemented in 1997 were necessary because of uncertainty about whether BSE infectivity had already been introduced into North America before new import restrictions on live cattle and meat and bone meal from Europe were put in place. It is now clear from the five North American BSE cases that the BSE agent was introduced into the North American animal feed supply at some point in time.... [T]he recent cases are an indication that additional animal feed protections are needed to remove residual infectivity that may be present in the animal feed supply. FDA also believes that of all the options considered since publication of the 2002 ANPRM, excluding the highest risk tissues from all animal feed is the best approach to address the risks of BSE in the United States. In the 2004 ANPRM, FDA announced its tentative conclusion that it should propose a prohibition on the use of SRMs in all animal feed.

. . . .

In reaching a decision about what specific additional measures should be proposed at this time, FDA considered the magnitude of the BSE risk in the United States. While the recent North American cases clearly show the BSE agent was introduced, the USDA enhanced BSE surveillance program indicates that the prevalence of the disease in the United States is very low. As of July 2005, USDA has tested over 418,000 high-risk cattle under its enhanced BSE surveillance program, and has found one positive animal in addition to the cow identified in Washington State in December 2003. Therefore, FDA believes that the additional measures being proposed are appropriate at this time. The agency proposes to prohibit from use in all animal feed the brains and spinal cords from cattle 30 months of age and older, the brains and spinal cords from all cattle not inspected and passed for human consumption, and the entire carcass of cattle not inspected and passed for human consumption from which brains and spinal cords were not removed. The agency also proposes to prohibit from use in all animal feed mechanically separated beef and tallow that are derived from materials prohibited by the rule. However, the rule proposes to exempt tallow from this requirement if it contains no more than 0.15 percent insoluble impurities. . . .

D. Cattle Materials Proposed to be Prohibited From Use in All Animal Food and Feed

. . . .

In reaching the decision to propose to exclude only the brain and spinal cord from animal feed, FDA considered information regarding the tissue distribution of BSE infectivity. Under field conditions, BSE infectivity has been found in the brain, spinal cord, and retina of the eye in animals with clinical disease. The Scientific Steering Committee (SSC) of the European Union has also reported on the proportion of total infectivity in various tissues. According to the report, in an animal with clinical BSE, approximately 64 percent of the infectivity is in the brain, 26 percent is in the spinal cord, 4 percent is in the dorsal root ganglia, 2.5 percent is in the trigeminal ganglia, and 3 percent is in the distal ileum. The eyes are estimated to contain less than 1 percent of the infectivity. Although available data are limited on the distribution of tissue infectivity, data from both naturally infected and experimentally infected cattle support the finding that the brain and spinal cord are the tissues with the highest level of infectivity.

Because available data indicate that the brain and spinal cord contain about 90 percent of BSE infectivity, FDA believes that the most appropriate course of action is to concentrate efforts on excluding these highest risk tissues from animal feed. . . . The measures proposed by this rule will effectively reinforce existing ruminant feed protection measures by removing the tissues with the highest infectivity from all animal feed. As a result, these measures greatly minimize BSE risks if cross-contamination of ruminant feed with non-ruminant feed, or diversion of non-ruminant feeds to ruminants, were to occur.

. . . .

European surveillance data indicate that cattle found dead or culled onsite, where the carcass was submitted to rendering (fallen stock), and cattle with health-related problems unfit for routine slaughter (emergency slaughter) have a greater incidence of BSE than healthy slaughter cattle. Surveillance data in the European Union in 2002 showed that there were 27.95 positive animals per 10,000 emergency slaughter bovine animals tested and 6.15 positive animals per 10,000 fallen stock bovine animals tested compared to 0.31 positive animals per 10,000 healthy slaughter animals tested. In Switzerland, the odds of finding a BSE case in fallen stock and emergency slaughter cattle were found to be 49 and 58 times higher, respectively, compared to the odds of finding a BSE case through passive surveillance. These findings suggest that cattle not inspected and passed for human consumption are more likely to test positive for BSE than healthy cattle that have been inspected and passed for human consumption.

Because cattle not inspected and passed for human consumption are included in the population of cattle at highest risk for BSE, and processes are currently not established in the rendering industry for verifying the age of such cattle through inspection, the agency is proposing to define brains and spinal cords from all cattle not inspected and passed for human consumption, regardless of age, to be cattle materials prohibited in animal feed.

. . . .

III. . . .

D. Legal Authority

FDA is issuing this proposed regulation on animal feed under the food adulteration provisions in sections 402(a)(2)(C), (a)(3), (a)(4), (a)(5), 409, and 701(a) of the Federal Food, Drug, and Cosmetic Act. The term "food" is defined to include articles used for food "for man or other animals." See section 201 of the act. We note that the material that would be prohibited under this proposed rule from use in animal feed continues to meet the definition of food. Therefore, this material would be adulterated or mis-branded under the act based on violations of the proposed rule, as well as any animal feed or feed ingredients that were manufactured from, processed with, or otherwise contained, the prohibited material.

. . . [S]ection 402(a)(3) . . . does not require that a food be filthy, putrid, or decomposed for it to be "otherwise unfit for food." . . . Because of the possibility of intentional or unintentional use of the materials that would [be] prohibited under this proposed rule in ruminant feed and the risk of BSE to ruminants and humans from these materials, we have tentatively concluded that these materials would be "otherwise unfit for food" under section 402(a)(3) of the act.

Under section 402(a)(5) of the act, food is deemed adulterated "if it is, in whole or in part, the product . . . of an animal which has died otherwise than by slaughter." Some cattle are not inspected and passed because they are diseased or have died before slaughter. Material from these cattle that are diseased or that die otherwise than by slaughter that is used as animal feed would render that feed adulterated under section 402(a)(5) of the Act.

FDA has traditionally exercised enforcement discretion with regard to the use of such animals in animal feed. FDA intends to continue exercising such discretion for the use in animal feed of the remaining material from cattle that are diseased or that die other than by slaughter when the brain and spinal cord are removed.

We are also relying on the adulteration provision in section 402(a)(2)(C)(i) of the act. Section 402(a)(2)(C)(i) deems a food adulterated if it is or bears or contains a food additive that is unsafe under section 409 of the act....

For the reasons discussed in other sections of this document, the agency is tentatively concluding that cattle materials prohibited in animal feed under this proposed rule are not GRAS by qualified experts for use in animal food and, therefore, would be food additives.... Under section 409(a), a food additive is unsafe unless a food additive regulation or an exemption is in effect with respect to its use or its intended use....

NOTE

1. *Final Regulations.* As of February 2007, FDA had not yet promulgated final regulations.

2. *Commentary. See* Kannon K. Shanmugam, *America and the BSE Scare: Near Misses, Future Lessons* (1997), Brent G. Schlotthauer, *Bovine Spongiform Encephalopathy: The Past, Present, and Future of Mad Cow Disease in the United States* (1998), Alison E. Cantor, *Adequacy of FDA's Response to Mad Cow Disease* (1999), in Chapter VII of the Electronic Book.

E. REGULATION OF THE USE OF PRESCRIPTION ANIMAL DRUGS

Before 1988, the animal drug provisions did not contain a counterpart of section 503(b), which specifies that some human drugs are available only with a doctor's prescription. However, FDA created a class of prescription animal drugs by regulation. After an initial setback, the agency's regulation was upheld as a valid interpretation of section 502(f)(1)'s requirement for "adequate directions for use." *United States v. Colahan*, 635 F.2d 564 (6th Cir. 1980), *rev'g* Food Drug Cosm. L. Rep. (CCH) ¶ 38,004 (N.D. Ohio 1979).

The distinction between Rx and OTC status for animal drugs is more complex than for human drugs. The FD&C Act's new drug provisions are violated only when an unapproved new human drug is shipped in commerce. A physician who prescribes an approved drug for a use that FDA has not sanctioned in the package insert, therefore, does not violate the Act. In the case of new animal drugs, however, the statutory scheme differs. A new animal drug that is "unsafe" under section 512 is deemed adulterated, 21 U.S.C. 351(a)(5), 360(a)(1), and its use adulterates the food derived from the treated animal (or even the animal itself). 21 U.S.C. 342(a)(2)(C)(ii). The FDA can take action against such "adulteration" at any point in the chain of distribution of the drug or the animal.

Prior to the Animal Drug Amendments of 1968, veterinarians routinely used drugs that had been developed and approved for human use, and used animal drugs in ways not provided for in the drugs' labeling. Over the years, the FDA did not take exception to these practices. The 1968 Amendments, however, borrowing from the Food Additives Amendment, required that a new animal drug not only be approved but that "[its] use conform" to its FDA approval, thus creating a legal dichotomy between veterinary and human medicine practice. 21 U.S.C. 360(a)(1), triggering extra-label drug use adulteration under 21 U.S.C. 342(a)(2)(C)(ii), and placing the veterinarian at risk for "causing" the violation. 21 U.S.C. 331(k). Nonetheless FDA continued to condone the use of human drugs in veterinary medicine as long as veterinarians took responsibility for the decisions to use these agents. *See* FDA, Compliance Policy Guide No. 7125.35 (Mar. 19, 1991). *See also* FDA, Compliance Policy Guide No. 7125.05 (July 1, 1982). In recent years, the agency has taken the position that the statutory admonition applies directly to veterinarians treating food-producing animals, unless the veterinarian meets a series of tests designed to give an assurance that an "extra-label use" will not result in unsafe residues in meat, milk, or eggs. FDA, Compliance Policy Guide No. 7125.06 (Mar. 9, 1984). The FDA's position became increasingly strict in part due to congressional criticism in light of the statutory prohibition on extra-label use. *E.g., "Regulation of Animal Drugs by the Food and Drug Administration," Hearings Before a Subcomm. of the House Comm. on Government Operations*, 99th Cong., 1st Sess. 221–75 (1985). The requirements set forth in the Compliance Policy Guides include establishing what the American Veterinary Medical Association refers to as a valid veterinarian-client-patient relationship (requiring actual and continued oversight of the animal), determining that the unapproved usage is medically necessary, and ensuring that a prolonged withdrawal time is observed to protect against residues.

Takhar v. Kessler

76 F.3d 995 (9th Cir. 1996).

■ Fletcher, Circuit Judge:

Santokh Takhar, a California-licensed veterinarian with a large-animal practice, challenges two Food and Drug Administration (FDA) Compliance Policy Guides (CPG) as exceeding the agency's statutory mandate by regulating veterinarians' extra-label drug use. He claims they contravene Congressional intent to exempt the practice of veterinary medicine from the Food, Drug and Cosmetic Act (FDCA).

"Extra-label" drug use consists of using a drug in a manner not indicated on the FDA-approved manufacturer's label; this can include the use of a drug for a condition, in a dosage, or in an animal species for which the drug has not received FDA approval. The plaintiff asserts that extra-label drug use is common in veterinary medicine because no FDA-approved drugs exist for many diseases in many species; about 30,000 drugs have been approved for human use, while only about 2,000 drugs have been approved for animal use.

By at least 1977, the FDA took the position that while extra-label drug use by veterinarians was technically illegal under the FDCA, its Bureau of Veterinary Medicine did not object to such use in non-food-producing animals as long as the veterinarian legally obtained the drug and had no approved alternative drug available, and as long as the use posed no obvious hazard to the animal's health. The FDA stated that extra-label drug use by veterinarians in food-producing animals was not sanctioned and was the responsibility of the veterinarian, and advised that it would take regulatory action where such use resulted in illegal drug residues in edible animal tissue.

In 1984, the FDA revised its compliance policy and issued CPG 7125.06 regarding extra-label use of animal drugs in food-producing animals. CPG 7125.06 announced that a finding of illegal drug residues in food would no longer be a prerequisite to regulatory action against extra-label drug use by veterinarians. "Nevertheless," the agency stated, "extra-label drug use in treating food-producing animals may be considered by a veterinarian when the health of animals is immediately threatened and suffering or death would result from failure to treat the affected animals." The agency then provided criteria and precautions for such extra-label drug use and announced that as long as those criteria were met and those precautions followed, the FDA "would not ordinarily" consider regulatory action against veterinarians' extra-label drug use. The current version of those criteria and precautions provides that regulatory action will not ordinarily be considered where:

1) a medical diagnosis is made by an attending veterinarian within a valid veterinarian-client-patient relationship;

2) no approved drug or dosage is available to treat the condition effectively in the animals affected;

3) the animals treated are carefully identified;

4) an extended withdrawal period is assigned and observed before the marketing of food produced by the animal and no illegal residues occur in the food; and

5) the extra-label drug is adequately labeled by the prescribing veterinarian.

In addition, the FDA indicated that certain drugs could not be used in food-producing animals even when the outlined criteria and precautions were met and followed. The 1984 CPG specified that such drugs included chloramphenicol and DES, and the 1992 version of CPG 7125.06 lists use of seven additional types of drugs in food-producing animals as among the highest-priority extra-label drug uses for regulatory attention. . . .

In 1991, the FDA issued CPG 7125.35 regarding the use of human drugs in animal medicine. The agency noted that most such use occurs in non-food pets and that "many of the maladies of pets cannot be treated in accordance with current standards of veterinary practice without the use of human drugs since veterinary versions of many human drugs do not exist." Concern was expressed about increasing promotion and distribution of human drugs for use in, and actual use of such drugs in, food-producing animals. The criteria and precautions in CPG 7125.06 for extra-label animal-drug use in food-producing animals were incorporated by reference to guide enforcement of extra-label human-drug use in such animals, and the FDA announced its intent to take aggressive regulatory action to discourage such use, while stating that extra-label human-drug use in non-food-producing animals would not ordinarily prompt regulatory action. The current version of CPG 7125.35 specifies that food-animal veterinarians should consider extra-label human-drug use only when:

1) a medical diagnosis is made by an attending veterinarian within a valid veterinarian-client-patient relationship;

2) no approved drug or dosage is available to treat the condition effectively in the animals affected; and

3) adequate steps are taken to prevent illegal residues from occurring in food.

Even when these criteria and precautions are met and followed, the agency stated that it would consider regulatory action if an illegal residue occurred in food because of the extra-label drug use.

On October 22, 1994, after briefing in this case but before oral argument, the Animal Medicinal Drug Use Clarification Act of 1994 became law. Pub. L. No. 103–396, 1994 U.S.C.C.A.N. (108 Stat.) 4153. The Act amended the FDCA to allow extra-label use of approved drugs in the practice of veterinary medicine in accordance with regulations to be promulgated by the Secretary of Health and Human Services. . . .

On July 16, 1993, Takhar filed a Complaint for Declaratory Judgment and Injunctive Relief against FDA officials, including David Kessler, M.D. and Gerald Guest, D.V.M. Takhar asked the court (1) to declare that licensed veterinarians are exempt from certain registration, labeling, and prescription requirements under 21 U.S.C. §§ 360(g)(2) and 353(f) when using prescription drugs solely in the course of their professional practices; (2) to declare that the FDA lacked the authority to prosecute veterinarians for violating provisions of the CPGs regarding specific drugs because the agency failed to follow notice-and-comment procedures in promulgating the CPGs; and (3) to enjoin the FDA from enforcing CPG 7125.35 in violation of the alleged practice-of-medicine exemption. . . . After a hearing in January 1994, the district court dismissed the First Amended Complaint for lack of ripeness and standing.

. . . .

Takhar alleges that if he were prosecuted again for extra-label drug use, he would be subject to felony penalties and to a fine up to five hundred times greater than that he faced in his previous prosecution. While this fact would increase the severity of injury to Takhar if he were facing a threat of prosecution, the possible consequences of a criminal violation by Takhar do not confer standing on him to challenge the CPGs in the absence of a showing that he faces any concrete threat of enforcement. Takhar also alleges that he suffered three years of legal vulnerability while awaiting clarification from the FDA regarding its policy regarding gentamicin, which he began to use in cattle, even though such use is extra-label, when the FDA began to investigate Takhar's and Jacobs' practice for use of chloramphenicol. While it is regrettable that the FDA did not respond to Takhar's inquiries more promptly, he has now received the "clarification" that CPG 7125.06 accurately states the agency's policy on extra-label use of gentamicin, and therefore does not suffer any continuing uncertainty. The uncertainty that Takhar experienced while waiting for clarification from the FDA is not an injury in fact sufficient to confer standing on Takhar to challenge the CPGs.

NOTES

1. *FDA Enforcement.* In *Cowdin v. Young*, 681 F. Supp. 366 (W.D. La. 1987), the court granted FDA's motion to dismiss a court action challenging the compliance policy guide on the grounds that the issues were not ripe and that veterinarians did not have standing to challenge the guide. In *United States v. Blease*, Food Drug Cosm. L. Rep. (CCH) ¶ 38,095 (D.N.J. 1988), FDA obtained an injunction, and in *United States v. Jacobs*, Food Drug Cosm. L. Rep. CCH ¶ 38,113 (E.D. Cal. 1989), the agency successfully opposed a motion to dismiss a criminal indictment, in cases involving extra-label use of new animal drugs.

2. *Withdrawal of Chloramphenicol.* Because of evidence of widespread extra-label use in food-producing animals, FDA withdrew approval of the NADAs for chloramphenicol oral solution. The drug had been approved only for use in dogs because of its known human toxicity. 50 Fed. Reg. 27059 (July 1, 1985); 51 Fed. Reg. 1367, 1441 (Jan. 13, 1986).

3. *Shipment of Bulk Drugs.* FDA has long taken the position that unapproved bulk drugs for veterinary use may not be sold to veterinarians and may only be sold to holders of approved NADAs. After an internal task force report, made available in 48 Fed. Reg. 34512 (July 29, 1983), FDA proposed to adopt new procedures under which NADAs could be approved for bulk new animal drug substances that are to be compounded into finished dosage form by or on the prescription of licensed veterinarians for use in their professional practices. 50 Fed. Reg. 27016 (July 1, 1985). FDA withdrew this proposal in 54 Fed. Reg. 12454 (Mar. 27, 1989) on the grounds, among others, that veterinarians may lack the necessary qualifications for compounding complex drug formulas and are not subject to GMP requirements. Two district courts initially held that a bulk animal drug supplied to veterinarians for use within the scope of the practice of their profession is not subject to the requirements for new animal drugs, but FDA prevailed in both cases on appeal. *United States v. 9/1 Kg. Containers, More or Less, of an Article of Drug for Veterinary Use*, 854 F.2d 173 (7th Cir. 1988), *rev'g* 674 F. Supp. 1344 (C.D. Ill. 1987); *United States v. Algon Chemical, Inc.*, 879 F.2d 1154 (3d Cir. 1989), *rev'g* 689 F. Supp. 394 (D.N.J. 1988). Accordingly, veterinarians have access only to approved prescription animal drugs and must ordinarily use those drugs within the confines of the FDA-approved label.

4. *Rx to OTC Switch.* In 41 Fed. Reg. 51078 (Nov. 19, 1976), FDA issued a notice of opportunity for hearing on a proposal to deny a supplemental NADA to switch a new animal drug from Rx to OTC status. Although the agency concluded that a hearing was not warranted, 42 Fed. Reg. 46595 (Sept. 16, 1977), this decision was overturned. *American Cyanamid Co. v. FDA*, 606 F.2d 1307 (D.C. Cir. 1979). Following the court-ordered hearing, the Administrative Law Judge and subsequently the Commissioner upheld the agency's initial decision. 49 Fed. Reg. 26311 (June 27, 1984), *aff'd, American Cyanamid Co. v. Young*, 770 F.2d 1213 (D.C. Cir. 1985). *See also* 46 Fed. Reg. 46396 (Sept. 18, 1981) (FDA denial of another petition to switch an animal drug from Rx to OTC status). In October 1988, the agency's Veterinary Medicine Advisory Committee recommended to FDA criteria for deter-

mining Rx and OTC status, and FDA has established an internal committee to reevaluate the matter.

———

The ostensible illegality of extra-label drug use, even in companion and exotic animals for which there were limited approvals, and the risk of per se malpractice exposure from "violating" the FD&C Act sparked concern among veterinarians. This led to the passage of the Animal Medicinal Use Clarification Act of 1994 (AMDUCA); Pub. L. No. 103–396, 108 Stat. 4153, (principally codified as 21 U.S.C. 360(a)(4)–(5)) which largely established the lawfulness of the practices the FDA permitted under existing policies but also provided the FDA with new authority, when justified by safety concerns, to inspect veterinarian records of extra-label drug use. Thus, AMDUCA leaves veterinarians regulated differently under the FD&C Act than physicians.

The availability of veterinary drugs remains in a state of tension. While the passage of AMDUCA largely eliminated the constraints imposed on veterinarians by the Animal Drug Amendments, they still must vie for clientele with knowledgeable laymen who have considerable experience in animal husbandry, and for whom adequate directions for use can be written for a wide variety of drugs. It can be expected that, as food animal production becomes more professional and integrated, there will be increasing tension over the right of animal-care professionals who are not veterinarians to make therapeutic drug choices.

COMMENT: CONGRESS AUTHORIZES ABBREVIATED GENERIC NEW ANIMAL DRUGS

During the 1980s, FDA approved abbreviated NADAs for generic versions of pre-1962 animal drugs that had been rated effective in the DESI review, e.g., 46 Fed. Reg. 36254 (July 14, 1981), but it did not adopt a formal policy allowing abbreviated or paper NADAs for post-1962 generic animal drugs. Congress, however, was eventually persuaded to fill this gap, as explained in the following excerpt by a leading expert on animal drug regulation:

> The Generic Animal Drug and Patent Term Restoration (GADPTR) Act [of 1988] differs in a number of respects from the 1984 human drug legislation. The principal differences recognized the human food safety concerns inherent in using drugs in food producing animals, as well as the greater expenditure of time normally required to obtain the initial approval of such drugs. This led to changes in both the FDA approval process for abbreviated applications as well as the availability of additional options for patent term restoration. In the case of the approval process, for example, the FDA was authorized to go beyond requiring bioavailability and bioequivalence data to demonstrate that a generic applicant's product was equivalent to the pioneer drug it was emulating. FDCA section 512(c)(2)(H) authorizes the FDA to require (as scientific principles dictate) bioequivalence studies in

each species for which the drug is approved, tissue residue studies in each such species, "or such other data or studies as [the FDA] considers appropriate based on scientific principles." Under the patent term restoration provisions, a company could choose between an initial companion animal approval and a subsequent food animal approval in seeking a patent term extension.

There also was a total exclusion from both the generic approval process and the patent extension process of animal drugs produced by biotechnology. This exclusion was to permit the biotechnology industry to demonstrate that patents in their area did not provide the same protection, and thus different incentives, as patents on chemically defined drugs. . . .

The GADPTR Act also contained a special provision dealing with the release of data on the safety and efficacy of drugs that are eligible for abbreviated applications; both the initial requester and any person to whom the data are transferred must submit verified statements to the FDA that the data will not be used to market the drug outside the United States. . . .

Additionally, controls on the use of animal drugs were altered by the new Act. Until its passage, there had been no parallel to section 503(b) to set standards for "prescription" animal drugs. Rather, the FDA successfully relied on its regulations exempting those drugs for which directions for safe effective lay use could not be written from the statutory requirement for "adequate directions for use;" FDCA § 502(f)(1); *see United States v. Colahan*, 635 F.2d 564 (6th Cir. 1980), *cert. denied*, 454 U.S. 831 (1981); the effect was to limit such drugs "to use by or on the order of a licensed veterinarian." 21 C.F.R. § 201.105(b)(1). The GADPTR Act codified FDA practice in a new statutory provision that draws, as is the case with human drugs, an obvious line between those drugs limited to use by or on the order of a veterinarian, and those available without such an order.

Eugene I. Lambert, *Food and Drugs for Animals Other than Man, in* 1 FUNDAMENTALS OF LAW AND REGULATION: AN IN-DEPTH LOOK AT FOODS, VETERINARY MEDICINES, AND COSMETICS 295–96 (1997).

F. COMPLETION OF THE REGULATORY FRAMEWORK

Eugene I. Lambert, *The Reformation of Animal Drug Law: The Impact of 1996*

52 FOOD & DRUG LAW JOURNAL 277 (1997).

Before 1968, there was no separate "animal drug" law. There was only "new drug" law, "antibiotic" law, and "food additive" law, because drugs used in animals were subject to one or more of these regulatory provisions. . . . This system involved three separate statutory provisions; three separate administrative procedures; three separate parts of the agency.

Especially for drugs intended to be used in food-producing animals, it was an administrative maelstrom.

As a result of efforts that began in 1962, the Animal Drug Amendments were passed in 1968, coalescing the three regulatory systems into a single provision governing approvals for drugs used in animals.

The basic licensing system came from the new drug provisions, with an overlay of antibiotic batch certification for certain antibiotics, and an interweaving of food additive concepts, including the Delaney anticancer clause and its diethylstilbestrol (DES) proviso. In addition to the Delaney Clause, food additive concepts included the requirements that animal drugs be used only in accordance with their approval, that optimal doses be determined, and that approvals be published as regulations. . . .

Enactments in 1988 and 1994 started the process of looking at animal drug law as separate from other drug regulation. These initial steps recognized some unique aspects of animal drug regulation that were distinct from human drug regulation.

[The Generic Animal Drug and Patent Term Restoration Act of 1988, Pub. L. 100–670, 102 Stat. 3971] recognized the distinction between drugs used in food producing animals and other animal drugs, by providing, both in the drug approval process and in the patent extension process, that an applicant first obtaining an approval for nonfood-animal use, could waive the "new chemical entity" period of exclusivity and the right to obtain an extended patent, and exercise those rights upon the later approval of the same drug in food-producing animals. Second, it repealed the then-obsolete antibiotic certification provisions; all animal drugs that are or contain antibiotics are controlled simply as new animal drugs. Third, it granted the Food and Drug Administration (FDA) additional authority to require human safety information concerning the inactive ingredient composition of generic animal drugs. Fourth, it created new safeguards against the use of data submitted in support of new animal drug approvals being used by a competitor to obtain foreign approval for the use of the drug. . . . Finally, it created a separate provision defining veterinary drugs limited to use by or on the order of a licensed veterinarian. . . .

[The Animal Medicinal Drug Use Clarification Act of 1994, Pub. L. 103–396, 108 Stat. 4153] was the product of veterinarian frustration and concern with the difference between their prescribing rights and those accorded other physicians with respect to licensed drugs. . . . FDA tried to ameliorate the strictness of the statute by announcing, as a matter of enforcement discretion, that it would not object to the use of any approved human or animal drug in nonfood animals, *e.g.*, pets, and would permit extralabel use in food-producing animals where there was a valid veterinarian-client-patient relationship, extended withdrawal times were used, and approved drug conditions of use were found to ineffective. . . .

Veterinarians remained concerned that prescribing rights essentially were at the sufferance of the agency, and that their prescribing actions still were in facial violation of the Act. . . . Their goal in supporting passage of AMDUCA was to codify, and thus legitimize, the extralabel use practices sanctioned by the various Compliance Policy Guides.

AMDUCA and its implementing regulations maintain the effective distinction between the prescribing authority of veterinarians and physicians by recognizing the public health significance of off-label use of drugs in food-producing animals, and thus the limitations on the discretion of veterinarians in those circumstances. While extralabel use of approved animal and human drugs in nonfood-animals is permitted with minimal restrictions, extralabel use in food-producing animals is subject both to current limitations and prospective ones.

Current limitations include the requirements that where data do not exist to provide for an extended safe withdrawal time, the animal be withheld from the food supply; that an animal drug be used in an extralabel fashion before a human drug may be so used; that there be "an appropriate medical rationale" for the extralabel use; and that an enumerated list of drugs not be used at all in an extralabel fashion in food-producing animals. Prospectively, FDA may condition extralabel use on the maintenance of certain records by veterinarians and the availability of those records to FDA, or on the adoptions of specific residue requirements based on existing or required new analytical methods (or prohibit extralabel use if such methods are not developed), or the agency may add drugs to the list of ones prohibited from extralabel use.

While the goal of veterinarians was symmetry between their practice and physicians', the enacted legislation reflected real differences between the regulation of animal drugs where there can be an impact on human health over which consumers would have no control, and the regulation of human drugs in the context of a physician-patient relationship. With the passage of AMDUCA came the recognition that there was a longer term goal of making more drugs available for animal treatment, rather than just using available drugs in an extralabel fashion. . . .

Another major step forward was the 1996 passage of the [Animal Drug Availability Act, Pub. L. 104–250, 110 Stat. 3151]. . . . [T]he ADAA altered the efficacy criteria, including the definition of "substantial evidence" of effectiveness, altered the approval criteria for combination drugs, created a process for achieving greater certainty in drug research and development, created a new class of feed drugs limited to use under the "directive" of a veterinarian, permitted the establishment of residue tolerances for animal drugs not approved in the United States, and changed the regulation of medicated feed from product licenses to establishment licenses. . . .

In borrowing the definition of "substantial evidence" from the new drug provision of the Act, and the "optimal dose" provision from the food additive provision of the Act, animal drug producers were faced (as was FDA) with restrictions and requirements that went beyond what was necessary, especially in the case of food producing animals, to establish that the drug worked. The substantial evidence definition always required a minimum of two studies, one of which had to be a field trial; for some kinds of drugs, a single well-designed study in the target species, but not under field conditions, could establish efficacy. The optimal dose provision—that no approval could exceed what was reasonably necessary to achieve the drug's intended effect—led to laborious dose titrations that were as exact as they were misleading. . . .

What both industry and the agency sought was more flexibility in designing the right studies to evaluate efficacy, without a "punchlist" that had to be completed. This was achieved in the amendments made by the ADAA. First, the definition of "substantial evidence" was rewritten to reflect the range of studies, from *in vitro* laboratory studies through laboratory animal studies (including in the target species), to other target species studies, including a field trial when needed. Second, the optimal dose provision was rewritten to focus on a safety cap, *i.e.*, the effective dose must not leave a residue in excess of the established tolerance. . . .

While "fixed combination drugs" are well recognized in both human and animal medicine, animal drugs also are combined in feed, and so fed in combination, even if the drugs have different sponsors and uses. Chickens may receive an anticoccidial drug together with a growth promotant; swine may be treated for scours while fed for efficiency and growth promotion. In most cases, the individual drugs had been approved previously, and users— that is, animal producers—wanted to be able to use various combinations, often for disparate purposes. The FDA approval process provided no flexibility or alternative; producers were faced with redoing both safety and efficacy studies.

The ADAA created an entirely new approach to combination drug approvals, whether in dosage form or as feed-use recommendations. By starting with the requirement that each component will previously have been approved, the new provision of the Act specifies just what new or additional data are needed to ensure safety and effectiveness. Thus, on the safety side, the ADAA focuses on interference with methods of analysis, or altering residue patterns, or any safety issue raised by submitted studies or newly-identified in the scientific literature. On the efficacy side, the new provision distinguishes between dosage form products and drugs intended to be used in animal feed or drinking water.

There is one major difference between dosage form and feed drugs: the new rules do not apply when a systemic combination dosage form—*e.g.*, injectable, implant, or bolus—contains an "antibacterial" drug. If that limitation does not apply, and each of the drugs has at least one use different than the other drugs in the combination, the issue is solely whether the [dosage form] combination "provides appropriate concurrent use for the intended target population." If all of the uses are the same, the issue is whether there is "substantial evidence," as newly defined, that each drug "makes a contribution to the labeled effectiveness." If, based on "scientific information," FDA determines that the drugs are physically incompatible in the combination, or if their dosing schedules are "disparate," *e.g.*, one of the drugs is to be administered before feeding and the other after, the combination can be disapproved.

The two basic criteria are the same in the case of combinations of drugs to be used in feed: if the uses are different, the issue is "appropriate concurrent use," and where the uses are the same, the issue is "substantial evidence" of "contribution to effectiveness." Similarly, if "scientific information" shows a combination in drinking water to be "physically incompatible," the combination may be disapproved. . . .

Over the years, drug sponsors have been concerned by the concept of a "moving target" for approval. Studies would be planned and executed. Then, between the time of planning and results, new FDA reviewers would make "suggestions" for additional data. Sometimes testing concepts would change, with questions raised concerning the adequacy of the design. One of the provisions of the ADAA was intended to provide greater certainty to the research process; a new provision was added to the Act to provide for *binding* presubmission conferences.

The language of the new provision makes clear, as does the congressional report, that what is provided is a *process* for reaching agreement, rather than an *event* called a "presubmission conference." The new provision grants an applicant "one or more conferences . . . to reach an agreement acceptable to [CVM] establishing a submission or an investigational requirement. . . ." This is "a forum for the applicant and FDA to discuss what studies the applicant needs to conduct to support FDA's finding that the new animal drug is safe and effective. . . . The binding nature of the . . . agreement gives the sponsor assurance that development time and resources will be used efficiently and predictably." . . .

Since enactment of the current [FD&C Act], FDA has provided an exemption from the requirement of adequate directions for use for veterinary drugs requiring the intervention of a veterinarian for their safe use. All feed-administered drugs, however, remained available without veterinarian control, despite one attempt by FDA to adopt such controls administratively. In light of growing FDA pressure for veterinarian control over the use of some new antibiotics, but recognizing the impracticality of treating feed mixing the same as pharmacist compounding, industry groups proposed first the administrative, and then the legislative, creation of a new set of controls for feed-administered drugs. In the ADAA, this took the form of "veterinary feed directives" (VFDs).

While drugs subject to VFD controls require the intervention of a veterinarian before they can be used, they are not limited to special channels of distribution, as are veterinarian-order drugs. The label, labeling, and advertising for a VFD-limited drug will have to contain a uniform notification that the drug is limited to use pursuant to a VFD. The VFD provision requires that a veterinarian issue a VFD before a drug limited to VFD-use can be fed to an animal; the seller of the feed retains a copy, and the purchaser-user of the feed retains a copy, as does the veterinarian, and these records are subject to FDA inspection. Although this sounds very much like a "prescription" drug, the Act specifies that neither these drugs nor feeds containing them "shall be deemed to be a prescription article under any Federal or State law."

. . . .

Before there was an animal drug law, FDA took the position that mixing an active ingredient into feed form was manufacturing a final dosage form drug, requiring a new drug approval if the active ingredient was a new drug. Although the Animal Drug Amendments of 1968 changed that system, it left feed mills with the requirement for medicated feed applications for each new animal drug mixed into feed. Both FDA and industry chafed under the administrative burden of those applications, and

FDA by successive administrative actions reduced the number of drugs and persons subject to the application requirement. The ADAA further reduces both the industry and FDA burden by eliminating individual drug applications for feed mills.

In its place, the ADAA calls for the licensing of feed mills based on their compliance with current good manufacturing practices. In addition, the FDCA now specifically authorizes FDA to exempt mills from licensing. Each licensed mill will be able to mix any drug, limited by its approval to mixing in a licensed facility, *i.e.*, the "Category II" drugs under the Second Generation of Medicated Feed Controls. Every current holder of any approved medicated feed application is deemed to have a license for the manufacturing site of the feed, and is required in the eighteen months after enactment to submit a feed mill license application that "shall be deemed to be approved upon receipt by" FDA.

. . . .

CHAPTER VI

BIOLOGICS: VACCINES, BLOOD, TISSUE TRANSPLANTS, AND CELLULAR THERAPIES

A. HISTORICAL BACKGROUND

Smallpox was once the most feared disease, with the highest mortality rate, in human history. Its devastating effects are widely chronicled. Near the end of the Middle Ages halting efforts began to prevent the disease. Based on the observation that victims who survived never got smallpox again, the practice known as "variolation"—inoculation with smallpox puss or scabs—arose in the Far East. By the 16th century the practice had spread to Europe. During a severe smallpox epidemic in Boston in 1721, Cotton Mather persuaded Dr. Zabdiel Boylston to use variolation for the first time in North America. Initially resisted by the medical profession, variolation eventually became common practice in this country too.

In the late eighteenth century, English physician Edward Jenner, observing that milkmaids rarely got smallpox, inoculated several Gloucestershire children with cowpox taken from an infected milkmaid and then challenged them by inoculation with live smallpox. All displayed resistance to smallpox. Following publication of Jenner's results in 1798, Dr. Benjamin Waterhouse conducted confirmatory tests in Boston by inoculation with the cowpox vaccine and subsequent challenge with injection of live smallpox. Thereafter, the use of Jenner's vaccine spread rapidly. *See generally* FRANK FENNER ET AL., SMALLPOX AND ITS ERADICATION (1988).

Inevitably, spurious smallpox vaccine appeared in the market. Frequently, neither physicians nor the general public could distinguish the genuine product. A crusading Baltimore physician, James Smith, persuaded the Maryland legislature to establish a public lottery to raise funds so that he could distribute "genuine vaccine matter" free to everyone. L. Md., Ch. 123 (1809). Dr. Smith later persuaded Congress to enact similar legislation. 2 Stat. 806 (1813). The federal law gave the President authority to appoint a Vaccine Agent "to preserve the genuine vaccine matter, and to furnish the same to any citizen of the United States, whenever it may be applied for, through the medium of the post office. . . ." Smith was appointed the first (and only) Vaccine Agent of the United States. Following an outbreak of smallpox in North Carolina that was attributed to vaccine Smith had furnished, H.R. Rep. No. 48, 17th Cong., 1st Sess. (1822), H.R. Rep. No. 93, 17th Cong., 1st Sess. (1822), Congress repealed the 1813 Act on the premise that it was "better to commit the subject altogether to the local authorities...." 3 Stat. 677 (1822).

By the late 19th century diphtheria had become the third most common cause of death in the United States. The causative agent was identified and, through injection into animals who built up an immunity, an "antitoxin" was produced. In 1902, an outbreak of tetanus in St. Louis was traced to contaminated diptheria antitoxin. This followed an outbreak of tetanus in Camden, New Jersey, the previous year that was traced to contaminated smallpox vaccine. *See generally* JONATHAN LIEBENAU, MEDICAL SCIENCE AND MEDICAL INDUSTRY: THE FORMATION OF THE AMERICAN PHARMACEUTICAL INDUSTRY (1987). Spurred by these episodes, Congress enacted the law that today still underpins federal regulation of biological products for human use, commonly called the Biologics Act. 32 Stat. 728 (1902). The Biologics Act was reenacted in 1944 as part of the recodification of the Public Health Service Act, 58 Stat. 682, 702 (1944) and further revised by the FDA Modernization Act of 1997, 111 Stat. 1991, Pub. L. 105–115. It is now codified at 42 U.S.C. 262.

The past 20 years have been a period of dramatic advances in understanding of human biology, which have in turn made possible major improvements in human health and welfare. A cursory listing provides a glimpse of the technological advances that FDA has confronted: human cloning, prenatal genetic diagnosis, germ line engineering, embryonic stem cell research, xenotransplantation, and various aids to human reproduction. FDA has not attempted to regulate all of these technologies. Some have not reached the stage at which the agency could plausibly assert jurisdiction. Others have reached the clinical trial stage but not yielded commercial products whose safety and effectiveness the agency might assess. But many of these new technologies are recognized subjects of governmental regulation.

B. FDA ACQUIRES RESPONSIBILITY FOR BIOLOGICS

When the omnibus Public Health Service Act was recodified in 1944, a major issue was the status of biological products under the FD&C Act. During hearings on the recodification bill, Alanson W. Willcox, Acting General Counsel of the Federal Security Agency, predecessor of the Department of Health, Education, and Welfare, initially recommended the addition of the following language:

> *The persons and the products to which this section is applicable shall be subject also to the provisions of the Federal Food, Drug, and Cosmetic Act.*

Later Wilcox went on to explain:

> That, I am convinced, is the present law, though there has been some difference of opinion on the subject. The wording has caused some alarm in the industry for fear it would mean duplication of administrative control, which is the last thing we want or anybody

else wants. I am going to suggest that subsection be revised to read this way:

Nothing contained in this Act shall be construed as in any way affecting, modifying, repealing, or superseding the provisions of the Federal Food, Drug, and Cosmetic Act.

We are making that suggestion only because we are confident that it does now apply. The controls which the Public Health Service exercises are, I think, very effective but there is also a possibility in anything of that sort that some product which is dangerous to life may inadvertently get out into the market. The Federal Food and Drug [Act], unlike this act, contains seizure of power [sic]. We are very firmly of the opinion that the authority in law to pick up off the market any dangerous product that might have gotten out despite the most rigid controls should be continued and, as I say, it is only because of our confidence that this revised wording would continue that, that we are willing to suggest the revised wording. . . .

Hearings before a Subcomm. Of the Senate Comm. On Education and Labor, 78th Cong., 2d Sess. 48 (1944).

The biological products licensing section of the Public Health Service Act has been amended several times since 1944, most significantly in 1997. The relevant provisions of the current version follow, as does the section of the Public Health Service Act which empowers FDA to promulgate regulations to prevent the spread of communicable diseases:

Licensing of Biological Products

42 U.S.C. § 262.   Regulation of biological products

(a) Biologics license.

(1) No person shall introduce or deliver for introduction into interstate commerce any biological product unless—

(A) a biologics license is in effect for the biological product; . . .

(C) The Secretary shall approve a biologics license application—

(i) on the basis of a demonstration that—

(I) the biological product that is the subject of the application is safe, pure, and potent; and

(II) the facility in which the biological product is manufactured, processed, packed, or held meets standards designed to assure that the biological product continues to be safe, pure, and potent; and

(ii) if the applicant (or other appropriate person) consents to the inspection of the facility that is the subject of the application, in accordance with subsection (c).

(3) The Secretary shall prescribe requirements under which a biological product undergoing investigation shall be exempt from the requirements of paragraph (1).

. . . .

(g) Construction with other laws. Nothing contained in this Act shall be construed as in any way affecting, modifying, repealing, or superseding the provisions of the Federal Food, Drug, and Cosmetic Act. . . .

(i) "Biological product" defined. In this section, the term "biological product" means a virus, therapeutic serum, toxin, antitoxin, vaccine, blood, blood component or derivative, allergenic product, or analogous product, or arsphenamine or derivative or arsphenamine (or any other trivalent organic arsenic compound), applicable to the prevent, treatment, or cure of a disease or condition of human beings.

(j) Application of other law. The Federal Food, Drug, and Cosmetic Act applies to a biological product subject to regulation under this section, except that a product for which a license has been approved under subsection (a) shall not be required to have an approved application under section 505 of such Act.

Quarantine and Inspection

42 U.S.C. § 264.   Regulations to control communicable diseases

(a) Promulgation and enforcement by Surgeon General. The Surgeon General, with the approval of the Administrator [Secretary], is authorized to make and enforce such regulations as in his judgment are necessary to prevent the introduction, transmission, or spread of communicable diseases from foreign countries into the States or possessions, or from one State or possession into any other State or possession. For purposes of carrying out and enforcing such regulations, the Surgeon General may provide for such inspection, fumigation, disinfection, sanitation, pest extermination, destruction of animals or articles found to be so infected or contaminated as to be sources of dangerous infection to human beings, and other measures, as in his judgment may be necessary.

———

During its first half century, the biologics control program was the responsibility of the director of the Hygienic Laboratory, the predecessor of the National Institutes of Health (NIH). In 1948 the program was made a part of the National Microbiological Institute, a unit of NIH. In 1955, after several cases of polio resulted from vaccine containing undetected live virus, the need for closer oversight became clear and a new organization, the Division of Biologics Standards (DBS), was established within NIH.

In early 1972, Dr. Anthony Morris, a DBS scientist, charged publicly that the DBS's combination of research and regulatory functions created an inherent conflict of interests. According to Nicholas Wade, *Division of Biologics Standards: Scientific Management Questioned*, 175 SCIENCE 966 (1972):

The common theme of the ... charges is that in numerous instances, amounting to a "pattern of administrative insensitivity," the DBS management has suppressed or ignored scientific findings that would adversely affect the vaccine market. The motive for this alleged behavior is ascribed ... to a "passionate commitment to vaccine therapy" on the part of the DBS leadership....

In a later article, *Division of Biologics Standards: The Boat That Never Rocked*, 175 SCIENCE 1225 (1972), Wade described the DBS decision-making environment:

... Federal responsibility for vaccines does not rest solely on the DBS, but is diffused over a handful of committees with interlocking memberships. Thus, if the mass annual inoculations against influenza were indeed the "forcing on the public [of] a bogus situation....," it is not too clear whether responsibility would lie with the DBS for certifying an inefficacious vaccine or with a second body, the Center for Disease Control's Advisory Committee on Immunization Practices (ACIP), whose function is to decide who should be vaccinated against what....

... [F]ederal responsibility for vaccine development should be clarified, in a way that ensures the DBS does not develop vaccines in-house. There should be some court of appeal against the director's decisions. Since the DBS acts, in effect, for the academic community on behalf of the public, there should be a stronger connection with the academic world than occasional ad hoc conferences and a rubber-stamp board of scientific counselors....

A contemporaneous General Accounting Office investigation resulted in charges of improper certification of influenza vaccine:

... The GAO investigators discovered that on the evidence of the DBS's own records, 130 of the 221 lots of influenza vaccine released by the DBS in 1966 failed to meet the standards of potency required by the agency's own regulations. One hundred and fifteen of these lots were subpotent according to the test results submitted to the DBS by the manufacturers themselves. Another 15 lots were potent according to the manufacturers' tests and failed the tests conducted by DBS scientists, yet were released for public use by the DBS management....

The precise effect of the DBS policy of releasing subpotent vaccines is hard to estimate but probably some 67 million doses of influenza vaccine were used in the United States during the 3 years covered by the GAO report. If half of these vaccines failed the DBS's own standards, and the cost to each recipient was $1 a head (a conservative estimate), then the DBS has allowed citizens to spend more than $30 million on subpotent vaccines....

Nicholas Wade, *DBS: Agency Contravenes Its Own Regulations*, 176 SCIENCE 34 (1972).

As a result of these criticisms the DBS was transferred from NIH to FDA in 1972 and renamed the Bureau of Biologics. 37 Fed. Reg. 12865

(June 23, 1972). *See* "Consumer Safety Act of 1972," Hearings Before the Subcomm. on Executive Reorganization of the Senate Comm. on Government Affairs, 92d Cong. 2d Sess. (1972); Hearings Before the OK Subcomm. on Health of the Senate Comm. on Labor and Human Resources, 92d Cong., 2d Sess. (1972). *See* Margaret Pittman, *The Regulation of Biologic Products, 1902–1972*, NATIONAL INSTITUTE OF ALLERGY AND INFECTIOUS DISEASE, INTRAMURAL CONTRIBUTIONS, 1887–1987 (Oct. 1987).

The Bureau of Biologics remained a separate administrative unit within FDA from the time of its transfer from NIH in 1972 until it was merged with the Bureau of Drugs in 1982, 47 Fed. Reg. 26913 (June 22, 1982). The combined unit was named the National Center for Drugs and Biologics, later shortened to the Center for Drugs and Biologics. In 1988, the two parts were again separated and the biologics unit given its present title, the Center for Biologics Evaluation and Research. 52 Fed. Reg. 38275 (Oct. 15, 1987); 53 Fed. Reg. 8978 (Mar. 18, 1988).

NOTES

1. *Commercial Sale.* Unlike the FD&C Act, the Biologics Act applies only to commercial production or sale of biologics. For that reason, investigational biologics are subject to the IND requirements of section 505(i) of the FD&C Act prior to their licensure for marketing. *See* 21 C.F.R. 312.2(a).

2. *Veterinary Biologics.* Congress enacted a separate Animal Virus, Serum, and Toxin Act to regulate veterinary biological products in 1914, 37 Stat. 828, 832B33, codified in 21 U.S.C. 151 *et seq.* The law is administered by the U.S. Department of Agriculture.

3. *Commentary. See* Parke M. Banta, *Federal Regulation of Biologicals Applicable to the Diseases of Man*, 13 FOOD DRUG COSM. L.J. 215 (1958); Leroy E. Burney, *Human Biological Drugs and Basic Drug Research*, 14 FOOD DRUG COSM. L.J. 621 (1959); William David Hardin, *Poliomyelitis Vaccine—History, Regulations and Recommendations*, 40 FOOD DRUG COSM. L.J. 145 (1985); Hope Hopps, *The Bureau of Biologics: What It Is and What It Does*, 33 FOOD DRUG COSM. L.J. 198 (1978); Harry Meyer, *Biologicals and FDA*, FDA CONSUMER, Apr. 1973, at 12; Eugene M. Timm, *75 Years Compliance with Biological Product Regulations*, 33 FOOD DRUG COSM. L.J. 225 (1978).

C.   FDA REGULATION OF THERAPEUTIC BIOLOGICS

The 1972 GAO report concluded that DBS had failed to apply the FD&C Act's requirements for proof of effectiveness. According to Nicholas Wade:

> ... The GAO report states that ... 75 of the 263 products licensed by the DBS are generally not recognized as effective by most of the medical profession. The GAO report reveals that [DBS] ... was advised by HEW counsel in February 1969 that the DBS possessed authority under ... [the Drug Amendments of 1962] to enforce vaccine efficacy. Murray [Director of DBS] refused to use the [FD&C] act ... on the grounds that to do so would strengthen the

argument of those who wished to merge the DBS with the FDA into a single control agency. . . .

Wade, *DBS: Agency Contravenes Its Own Regulations*, 176 SCIENCE at 34.

1. THE BIOLOGICS REVIEW

In anticipation of the GAO findings, HEW Secretary Richard Schweiker redelegated authority to administer the drug provisions of the FD&C Act for all biological products concurrently to FDA and DBS. 37 Fed. Reg. 4004 (Feb. 25, 1972). NIH then announced its intention to review the effectiveness of all licensed biologicals and called for manufacturers to submit "substantial evidence of effectiveness" meeting the requirements of FDA's Bureau of Drugs. 37 Fed. Reg. 5404 (Mar. 15, 1972). When responsibility for administering the Biologics Act was delegated to FDA alone, the agency revoked NIH's notice and proposed new procedures for the review of the safety, effectiveness, and labeling of all licensed biologicals.

Biological Products: Procedures for Review of Safety, Effectiveness, and Labeling

37 Fed. Reg. 16679 (August 18, 1972).

This proposal will establish a procedure under which the safety, effectiveness, and labeling of all biological products presently licensed under section 351 of the Public Health Service Act will be reviewed. Advisory review panels comprised of independent experts will provide their conclusions and recommendations to the Commissioner of Food and Drugs, who then will review and implement them. . . .

The review procedure proposed in this notice relies for legal authority on both the Federal Food, Drug, and Cosmetic Act and section 351 of the Public Health Service Act. . . .

The Commissioner of Food and Drugs is aware of the unique problems involved in applying the requirement of "substantial evidence of effectiveness" to biological products, under the Federal Food, Drug, and Cosmetic Act. Where adequate and well-controlled studies are not feasible, and acceptable alternative scientific methods of demonstrating effectiveness are available, the latter will be sufficient. The advisory review panels convened under the procedure proposed in this notice will initially develop the standard and methodology for effectiveness for a particular class of biological products, . . . subject to review by the Commissioner of Food and Drugs. . . . Each review panel will determine those biological products that are and are not safe, effective, and not misbranded, as well as those for which further study is required. The applicable product licenses will then be confirmed, revoked, or permitted to remain in effect on an interim basis pending further study. . . .

———

FDA issued requests for data relating to the eight classes of biologics under review in 37 Fed. Reg. 16690 (Aug. 18, 1972) (bacterial vaccines and bacterial antigens with no U.S. standard of potency); 38 Fed. Reg. 5358 (Feb. 28, 1973) (bacterial vaccines and toxoids with standards of potency); 38 Fed. Reg. 5359 (Feb. 28, 1973) (viral and rickettsial vaccines); 39 Fed. Reg. 1082 (Jan. 4, 1974) (allergenic biological products); 39 Fed. Reg. 7445 (Feb. 26, 1974) (skin test antigens); 39 Fed. Reg. 21176 (June 19, 1974) (distributing remaining biological products among the existing panels); and 39 Fed. Reg. 43413 (Dec. 13, 1974) (blood, blood components, and derivatives).

The process that FDA thus set in motion took much longer than the agency originally forecast.

Biological Products: Bacterial Vaccines and Toxoids; Implementation of Efficacy Review

70 Fed. Reg. 75018 (December 19, 2005).

The purpose of this document is to: (1) categorize those bacterial vaccines and toxoids licensed before July 1972 according to the evidence of their safety and effectiveness, thereby determining whether they may remain licensed and on the market; (2) issue a final response to recommendations made in the Panel's report.[1] These recommendations concern conditions relating to active components, labeling, tests required before release of product lots, product standards, or other conditions considered by the Panel to be necessary or appropriate for assuring the safety and effectiveness of the reviewed products; and (3) revise the standard for potency of Tetanus Immune Globulin in § 610.21.

II. Background

In the Federal Register of February 13, 1973 (38 FR 4319), FDA issued procedures for the review by independent advisory review panels of the safety, effectiveness, and labeling of biological products licensed before July 1, 1972. This process was eventually codified in § 601.25 (21 CFR 601.25) (38 FR 32048 at 32052, November 20, 1973). Under the panel assignments published in the Federal Register of June 19, 1974 (39 FR 21176), FDA assigned the biological product review to one of the following groups: (1) bacterial vaccines and bacterial antigens with "no U.S. standard of potency," (2) bacterial vaccines and toxoids with standards of potency, (3) viral vaccines and rickettsial vaccines, (4) allergenic extracts, (5) skin test antigens, and (6) blood and blood derivatives.

Under § 601.25, FDA assigned responsibility for the initial review of each of the biological product categories to a separate independent advisory panel consisting of qualified experts to ensure objectivity of the review and public confidence in the use of these products. Each panel was charged with preparing an advisory report to the Commissioner of Food and Drugs which was to: (1) Evaluate the safety and effectiveness of the biological products for which a license had been issued, (2) review their labeling, and (3) identify the biological products that are safe, effective, and no misbranded.

---

1. The Panel was convened on July 12, 1973, in an organizational meeting, followed by multiple working meetings until February 2, 1979. The Final Report of the Panel was completed in August 1979.

Each advisory panel report was also to include recommendations classifying the products reviewed into one of three categories.

- Category I, designating those biological products determined by the panel to be safe, effective, and not misbranded.

- Category II, designating those biological products determined by the panel to be unsafe, ineffective, or misbranded.

- Category III, designating those biological products determined by the panel not to fall within either Category I or Category II on the basis of the panel's conclusion that the available data were insufficient to classify such biological products, and for which further testing was therefore required. Category III products were assigned to one of two subcategories. Category IIIA products were those that would be permitted to remain on the market pending the completion of further studies. Category IIIB products were those for which the panel recommended license revocation on the basis of the panel's assessment of potential risks and benefits.

. . . .

III. Categorization of Products—Final Order

Category I. Licensed biological products determined to be safe and effective and not misbranded. Table 1 of this document is a list of those products proposed in December 2004 by FDA for Category I.

. . . .

Category II. Licensed biological products determined to be unsafe or ineffective or to be misbranded and which should not continue in interstate commerce. FDA did not propose that any products be placed in Category II and in this final rule and final order does not categorize any products in Category II.

Category IIIB. Biological products for which available data are insufficient to classify their safety and effectiveness and should not continue in interstate commerce. Table 2 of this document is a list of those products proposed by FDA for Category IIIB. . . .

IV. FDA's Responses to Additional Panel Recommendations

. . . .

The Panel recommended that actions be taken to improve the reporting and documentation of adverse reactions to biological products. The Panel particularly noted the need to improve the surveillance systems to identify adverse reactions to pertussis vaccine.

Since publications of the Panel's report, the Vaccine Adverse Event Reporting System (VAERS) was created as an outgrowth of NCVIA and is administered by FDA and the Centers for Disease Control and Prevention (CDC). VAERS accepts from health care providers, manufacturers, and the public, reports of adverse events that may be associated with the U.S.-licensed vaccines. Health care providers must report certain adverse events included in a Reportable Events Table and any event listed in the vaccine's package insert as a contraindication to subsequent doses of the vaccine. Health care providers also may report other clinically significant adverse events. FDA and CDC receive about 1,000 reports each month under the

VAERS program. A guidance document is available which explains how to complete the VAERS form (Ref. 2).

. . . .

NOTE

One of the products reviewed by the Panel on Review of Bacterial Vaccines and Toxoids was Anthrax Vaccine Adsorbed, which had been produced by the Michigan Department of Public Health and distributed pursuant to a license issued by the Division of Biologics Standards in 1970. See 50 Fed. Reg. 51002, 51059 (Dec. 13, 1985). After lengthy evaluation the panel recommended and FDA proposed in 1985 to assign AVA to Category I (safe and effective). Some nineteen more years would pass before the agency acted on this proposal and confirmed that the vaccine was effective as well as safe. Three circumstances slowed and complicated FDA's decision making. First, in the late 1990s the product's sponsor, the Michigan Department of Public Health, sold its facility and business to a private firm, BioPort, which took over all dealings with FDA. Thos dealings became contentious when FDA inspectors reported that BioPort's facilities and operation failed to satisfy the agency's good manufacturing practice requirements. Finally, while FDA and BioPort were in discussions over GMP requirements the company, and indirectly FDA, came under pressure to confirm AVA's safety and effectiveness so that it could lawfully be administered to U.S. military personnel who faced deployment in the first Gulf War. For a reasonably dispassionate review of these events, *see* INSTITUTE OF MEDICINE, THE ANTHRAX VACCINE IS IT SAFE? DOES IT WORK? (2004). The controversy surrounding the Defense Department's determination to administer the vaccine despite FDA's reluctance to confirm its safety and effectiveness until relevant studies were concluded and GMP requirements were met is chronicled in *Doe v. Rumsfeld*, 297 F. Supp. 2d 119 (D.D.C. 2003), 341 F. Supp. 2d 1 (D.D.C. 2004).

2.   FDA APPROVAL OF NEW BIOLOGICS

Section 123(f) of the FDA Modernization Act of 1997, which is not codified, requires the agency processes for reviewing BLAs and NDAs to be parallel. This provision culminated 25 years of biologics law assimilation into FDA. The section reads:

> The Secretary of Health and Human Services shall take measures to minimize differences in the review and approval of products required to have approved biologics license applications under section 351 of the Public Health Service Act (42 U.S.C. 262) and products required to have approved new drug applications under section 505(b)(1) of the Federal Food, Drug and Cosmetic Act (21 U.S.C. 355(b)(1)[subsec. (b)(1) of this section]).

An application for approval of a biologics license (BLA) resembles a new drug application described in detail in Chapter IV and the agency's criteria are similar even if couched in the language—"safe, pure, and potent"—of the Biologics Act. The user fee legislation that has fueled FDA's approval process for drugs applies to biologics as well. Clinical trials of investigational biologics must satisfy the agency's IND standards. And biologics are eligible for orphan drug status if they satisfy that law's requirements.

For many years, FDA's requirements for obtaining marketing approval of a biologic differed from the requirements for drugs in one important respect; the agency required approval of both a biologics product license application (PLA) and an establishment license application (ELA). This approach reflected the agency's long-standing concern about whether a biologic applicant's production processes would assure identity and consistency from batch to batch. In the 1990s this dual requirement came to be regarded as unnecessarily burdensome. The Clinton administration, as part of its "Reinventing Government" initiative to simplify government operations, chaired by Vice President Gore, proposed to conflate the two licenses into one. This reform was endorsed and expanded by Congress in the FDA Modernization Act and soon implemented by the agency.

Reinventing Regulation of Drugs Made From Biotechnology

FDA Press Release, November 9, 1995.

The Food and Drug Administration today is proposing several measures that will reduce costs for manufacturers of biotechnology derived pharmaceuticals, increase the agency's efficiency and continue to protect the public health. The six proposals—which constitute FDA's most significant overhaul of biotech regulations to date—complement and build on the drug and medical device reforms announced last spring as part of the Clinton Administration's National Performance Review.

. . . .

The proposals include the following changes:

● Elimination of establishment license application (ELA) for well-characterized therapeutic biotech drugs. . . .

● Elimination of FDA's lot-by-lot release for well-characterized therapeutic biologic drugs that are licensed for marketing. . . .

● Consolidation of 21 different approval application forms into a single, user-friendly format. . . .

● Elimination of the need for approval of promotional labeling before launching a new product. . . .

● FDA commitment to review and respond within 30 days to information submitted in response to a clinical hold on a study of an investigational drug or biologic. . . .

● Revision of the manufacturers' requirements to appoint a "responsible head" for compliance and official contacts with FDA. . . .

Elimination of Establishment License Application for Specified Biotechnology and Specified Synthetic Biological Products

61 Fed. Reg. 24227 (May 14, 1996).

I. Background

In the Federal Register of January 29, 1996, FDA proposed to amend the biologics regulations to eliminate the ELA requirement for well-characterized biotechnology products licensed under the PHS Act. In that document, FDA proposed to use the general phrase "well-characterized biotechnology product," to describe products that would be eligible for a single license application so that the regulatory language would accommodate categories of products that might later be considered to be well-characterized as scientific knowledge progresses. . . .

The agency noted that technical advances over the last 15 years have greatly increased the ability of manufacturers to control and analyze the manufacture of many biotechnology-derived biological products. After over a decade of experience with these products, the agency has found that it can review the safety, purity, potency, and effectiveness of most well-characterized biotechnology products without requiring submission of a separate ELA. Accordingly, FDA proposed procedures under which CBER would approve most well-characterized biotechnology products by requiring a single biologics license application. FDA noted that the proposed procedures would significantly reduce burdens without reducing the safety or effectiveness of these products. . . .

After considering the public comments received on the interim definition, the discussion at the workshop, and the many requests the agency has received for further clarification of the term "well-characterized," FDA has determined that it may not be possible to achieve a sufficiently clear and specific understanding of this term to adequately apprise potential applicants of the applicability of the new procedures. Accordingly, in this final rule, FDA is specifying, in lieu of the term "well characterized biotechnology product," the categories of products to which this final rule will be applicable. . . .

II. Proposed Rule

In the January 29, 1996, proposed rule, FDA proposed to amend § 601.2(a) and to add a new paragraph (c) to create a licensing scheme for well-characterized biotechnology products that differs from the current licensing scheme for biological products in four fundamental ways. First, an applicant seeking marketing approval for a product that falls within the scope of the rule would submit a single biologics license application to CBER and would be issued a single license. Second, for these products, many of the establishment and product standards set forth in parts 600 through 680 (21 CFR parts 600 through 680) would not be applied. The current good manufacturing practice (CGMP) regulations found at parts 210 and 211 (21 CFR parts 210 and 211), in addition to the information included in a chemistry, manufacturing, and controls (CMC) section of the biologics license application, would constitute the bulk of the applicable establishment standards for these products. Third, in lieu of reviewing an ELA, FDA proposed to evaluate whether establishment standards had been met by reviewing information submitted in the biologics license application and by inspecting the facilities in which the product is manufactured for compliance with applicable requirements, including CGMP's. Fourth, FDA proposed to amend § 600.3(t) to broaden the term "manufacturer" as it is used in parts 600 through 680 to include an applicant for a license for a well-characterized biotechnology product who may or may not own the facilities engaged in significant manufacturing steps. This amendment would allow a single license applicant to take responsibility for compliance with the requirements in parts 600 through 680 applicable to manufacturers and would eliminate the requirement that each contract facility engaged in significant manufacturing obtain its own license. Instead, each well-characterized biotechnology product could be covered by a single biologics license application, which lists all manufacturing locations, regardless of how many separate companies are involved in its manufacture.

. . . FDA is expanding the scope of this final rule to include additional products, based on the technology of the manufacturing process and the proposed use of the products. At this time, FDA has determined that it has sufficient experience in reviewing investigational and product applications to eliminate the ELA requirements for the following categories of products: therapeutic DNA plasmid products; therapeutic synthetic peptide products of 40 or fewer amino acids; monoclonal antibody products for in vivo use; and therapeutic recombinant DNA-derived products. Methodologies are now available to characterize these products in a much more rigorous fashion, allowing the products to be more clearly evaluated by end product testing. . . .

FDA disagrees that vaccines and in vitro diagnostic (IVD) products should be included within the scope of this rule at this time because these products raise additional concerns in assessing safety, purity, and potency. For vaccines, safety is a critical concern due to the intended use in a healthy population. For IVD products, FDA believes that the product and establishment standards necessary to ensure continued safety, purity, and potency may differ from those applicable to products included in this rule.

FDA agrees that blood and blood components, including plasma, plasma derivatives, and stem cells, are products which should not fall within the scope of this rule. FDA believes that license applications for these and other naturally derived products should continue to include establishment information at this time. FDA believes that a license application that includes detailed information on the facilities and controls may be necessary to assess the continued safety, purity, and potency of these products. Because these products involve complex issues, such as a risk of contamination with infectious agents, their review requires special expertise and adequate time in order to assess the adequacy of controls in place at the facility. In addition, end product testing of naturally derived products may not be sufficient to detect contamination with infectious agents. . . .

Biological Products Regulated Under Section 351 of the Public Health Service Act; Implementation of Biologics License; Elimination of Establishment License and Product License

64 Fed. Reg. 56441 (October 20, 1999).

. . . .

On November 21, 1997, the President signed into law FDAMA (Pub. L. 105–115). Section 123 of FDAMA, in pertinent part, amended section 351 of the PHS Act to specify that a biologics license shall be in effect for a biological product prior to such product's introduction into interstate commerce. FDAMA thereby statutorily codified FDA's administrative BLA/biologics license "Reinventing Government" initiative. Section 123(a)(1) of FDAMA further states that the Secretary of Health and Human Services (the Secretary)(delegated to the Commissioner of Food and Drugs at 21 CFR 5.10(a)(5)) shall approve a "biologics license application" on the basis of a demonstration that the biological product that is the subject of the application is safe, pure, and potent; and the facility in which the biological product is manufactured, processed, packed, or held meets standards designed to ensure that the biological product continues to be safe, pure, and potent.

With the consolidation of the ELA's and PLA's into a single BLA, the amount of information formerly included in the ELA will be reduced, but not eliminated. Much of the information previously reviewed in an ELA at FDA will be reviewed by FDA investigators at the manufacturing site during a preapproval inspection. Some information formerly included in the ELA will now be submitted as "chemistry, manufacturing, and controls" (CMC) information or under the "establishment description" section of Form FDA 356h. The type and amount of information related to the establishment will vary according to the specific biological product for which licensure is being requested.

Under the proposed rule, a manufacturer applying for approval to market a biological product under section 351 of the PHS Act would submit to FDA the appropriate establishment and product information on the recently approved Form FDA 356h. Manufacturers would no longer be required to submit product or establishment information on one of the many different PLA and ELA forms formerly in use. Upon approval of the BLA, FDA would issue an approval letter that in general terms states that FDA grants the licensed manufacturer a biologics license to manufacture the particular biological product. FDA would not issue license certificates separate from the approval letter as is current agency practice. The approval letter would serve as the functional equivalent of a biologics license within the meaning of section 351 of the PHS Act.

Under proposed § 601.2(a), manufacturers would list in the BLA the addresses of all locations of manufacture of a biological product. FDA believes this will simplify and clarify the licensing processes by having necessary establishment information in the BLA and also by allowing FDA to approve all locations involved in the manufacture of the product without having to issue an establishment license for each location.

Under proposed § 601.9(c), for manufacturers of some biological products that would be able to list multiple products in a single BLA, (such as blood and blood components and nonstandardized allergenic products) and for which FDA will issue a single biologics license to the manufacturer for more than one product, FDA would be able to license compliant locations and products and exclude noncompliant locations.

. . . .

1.   A comment was supportive of the concept of a BLA and use of the Form FDA 356h but strongly urged FDA to ensure that the intended paperwork reduction and efficiency goals are achieved. The comment stated that the simplification of the BLA will be affected by how supplemental applications are handled and expressed concern that this be adequately addressed. . . .

FDA agrees that it is important to implement the rule in a manner that will reduce unnecessary burdens; accordingly the agency is implementing several mechanisms for ensuring that this is the case. Manufacturers of some biological products will be able to list multiple products in a BLA and FDA will issue a single biologics license to the manufacturer for more than one product. FDA intends to use this approach generally with products that both have been on the market for a long period of time and that FDA has considerable knowledge and expertise regulating. Currently, only products such as blood and blood components and nonstandardized allergenic products will be handled in a single BLA. Therefore, a manufacturer of blood and blood components will only need to submit one BLA to request approval to market one or more blood or blood components, (*e.g.*, Whole Blood, Platelets, Plasma, Red Blood Cells, and Cryoprecipitated AHF). . . .

With regard to manufacturing changes, the BLA system will simplify submission of supplements to blood and blood component applications. Currently, manufacturers desiring to make a single manufacturing change that would affect multiple products are required to submit a supplement to each individual product and establishment application. Under the final rule, a manufacturer would only need to submit one supplement to the BLA. For example, under the current PLA/ELA system if a manufacturer desired to make a single change to the irradiation procedure for its Whole Blood, Red Blood Cells, Platelets, and Plasma products manufactured at 3 locations, the manufacturer would be required to submit 12 supplements to 4 PLA's, *i.e.*, a separate supplement for each blood component manufactured at each location. Under the final rule, the manufacturer would only be required to submit one supplement to the BLA describing the change for all of the products and locations involved. . . .

––––––––

After President George W. Bush took office, his appointees to DHHS and FDA implemented another reform designed to exploit what they saw as CDER's superior performance in meeting the product approval targets adopted pursuant to the Prescription Drug User Fee Act. On June 30, 2003, FDA transferred some of the therapeutic biological products that had been reviewed and regulated by CBER to the Center for Drug Evaluation and Research (CDER). CDER now has regulatory responsibility, including premarket review and continuing oversight, over the transferred products, which include:

Monoclonal antibodies for in vivo use.

Proteins intended for therapeutic use, including cytokines (*e.g.* interferons), enzymes (*e.g.* thrombolytics), and other novel proteins, except for those that are specifically assigned to CBER (*e.g.*, vaccines and blood products). This category includes therapeutic proteins derived from plants, animals, or microorganisms, and recombinant versions of these products.

Immunomodulators (non-vaccine and non-allergenic products intended to treat disease by inhibiting or modifying a pre-existing immune response).

Growth factors, cytokines, and monoclonal antibodies intended to mobilize, stimulate, decrease or otherwise alter the production of hematopoietic cells in vivo.

CBER remains responsible for the following products:

Cellular products, including products composed of human, bacterial or animal cells (such as pancreatic islet cells for transplantation), or from physical parts of those cells (such as whole cells, cell fragments, or other components intended for use as preventative or therapeutic vaccines).

Gene therapy products. . . .

Vaccines (products intended to induce or increase an antigen specific immune response for prophylactic or therapeutic immunization, regardless of the composition or method of manufacture).

Allergenic extracts used for the diagnosis and treatment of allergic diseases and allergen patch tests.

Antitoxins, antivenins, and venoms.

Blood, blood components, plasma derived products (for example, albumin, immunoglobulins, clotting factors, fibrin sealants, proteinase inhibitors), including recombinant and transgenic versions of plasma derivatives, (for example clotting factors), blood substitutes, plasma volume expanders, human or animal polyclonal antibody preparations including radiolabeled or conjugated forms, and certain fibrinolytics such as plasma-derived plasmin, and red cell reagents.

"Transfer of Therapeutic Products to the Center for Drug Evaluation and Research," FDA–CBER website (updated Nov. 17, 2005).

3. FDA REVIEW OF BLAS

The process followed by FDA's Center for Biologics Evaluation and Research in reviewing BLAs for compliance with the requirements of 21 U.S.C. 262 does not differ in any fundamental way from that followed by CDER in evaluating NDAs. See the account of CDER's procedures in Chapter IV.

4. GENERIC BIOLOGICS

As many therapies produced through genetic engineering approach the end of their patent protection, interest has focused on the question whether Hatch–Waxman applies to biologics, *i.e.*, whether ANDAs can be approved for copies of biologic drugs. As this edition went to press the answer to this question had not been resolved. Some FDA officials had signaled their hope that an affirmative response might be found, but the former Commissioner (then only Acting Commissioner) Lester Crawford stated the following in testimony before Congress, providing this summary of the law:

> The FD&C Act provides the ANDA and 503(b)(2) abbreviated approval pathways for drugs approved under section 505 of the Act. However, the PHS Act has no similar provision. That is, unlike section 505 of the FD&C Act, there is no provision under the PHS Act for an abbreviated application that would permit approval of a "generic" or "follow-on" biologic based on the Agency's earlier approval of another manufacturer's application.

"The Law of Biologic Medicine," Hearing before the Senate Comm. on the Judiciary, 108th Cong., 2d Sess. 11 (2004). Crawford went on to suggest that for a few biological products for which FDA had approved marketing under section 505, such as "simple peptide or protein products," the agency might have the authority to accept abbreviated applications for generic versions.

Shawn Glidden, *The Generic Industry Going Biologic*

20 BIOTECHNOLOGY LAW REPORT 172 (2001).

. . . Traditional pharmaceutical drugs are small molecules, generally produced through chemical synthesis. These compounds are relatively simple to characterize with current technologies. Pharmaceutically, these drugs have been characterized as identical or different on the basis of their active moiety.

Biotechnology brings with it the ability to go right to the source of many human ailments by replacing or augmenting defective genes, proteins, glycoproteins, or antibodies in the patient with biologic drugs that mimic those deficient or defective macromolecules. However, one problem that has surfaced with this transformation is the ability to ascertain precisely and effectively the composition of the biologic drug.

Biologic drugs are macromolecules consisting of proteins (including antibodies) and glycoproteins. Proteins are strings of amino acid molecules covalently bonded. The function of the protein is determined by its structure, which is described in terms of four levels of organization. The primary structure is the amino acid sequence. The secondary structure is the spatial arrangement of the amino acid chain. The tertiary level of organization is the folding of the amino acid chain into a three-dimensional structure. The manner in which the amino acid chain folds is dependent on the linear order of the amino acids aligned in the chain. Different amino acids have different chemical structures and bonding forces and therefore attract and repel each other differently. Finally, the quaternary structure is the interaction of one fully folded amino acid chain with others. Thus, the structure and function of proteins is determined by the amino acid sequence because variations in the sequence create different binding affinities and therefore different folding characteristics resulting in different biologic activity.

There are 20 different amino acids in the human body. However, not all amino acid substitutions will produce a different finished product: some are interchangeable, so that the substitution does not affect the protein's function. On the other hand, certain amino acids are critical to the specific protein organization and function. In the body, a change of a critical amino acid as the result of mutation can lead to disease, as is the case with sickle-cell anemia.

. . . .

The enormous amount of variation in these biologic macromolecules is far from characterized, and the impact of various modifications on the molecule's pharmacologic activity is not fully understood. . . . The problem, when making these molecules in the laboratory as drug candidates, is that, depending on the temperature of the reactions and the cell lines, media, and organisms employed, the proteins will fold differently, glycosylation patterns will differ, and antibody variable regions will differ. In effect, the biologic activity of an end product is largely dependent on the process used to create that product.

. . . .

In 1997, the Food and Drug Administration Modernization Act . . . eliminated § 507 of the FD&C Act and moved the approval of antibiotic drugs to § 505. Under § 505, antibiotics became subject to ANDA procedures for generics. Some observers thought that the FDAMA also allowed biologics to come under § 505 and therefore allow the filing of an ANDA for generic biologics. However, Senators Jeffords (R–Vt.) and Kennedy (D–Mass.), two proponents of the FDAMA, contacted the Commissioner for the FDA to state that the legislative intent of the FDAMA was not to shift biologics in their relation to the Hatch–Waxman Act ANDA procedures. . . .

So biologics are not subject to Hatch–Waxman Act process for two reasons. First, biologics are not approved under § 505 of the FD&C Act, which approves drugs through the NDA: they are approved under § 351 of the Public Health Service Act through a BLA and therefore not appropriate for the filing of an ANDA. Second, the FDA does not have any procedures in place for the approval of generic biologics. . . .

But this does not answer the question: why is there no process and abbreviated form in place for biologics?

The approval of a generic form of a traditional drug is dependent on the showing that the drug is the equivalent of or contains the same active moiety as an approved drug such that the generic can be predicted to function safely and effectively. However, the current capability of science and technology in relation to biologics is not sufficient to determine the bioequivalence and pharmacologic equivalence of biologic macromolecules without extensive clinical testing. This is so because biologic macromolecules are not easily classifiable. . . . Therefore, the FDA cannot approve "generic" biologics on the basis of the innovator drug's clinical trial data, which could have been based on a molecule that is chemically and pharmacologically different from that produced by the generic manufacturer.

For biologic macromolecule drugs, the FDA presumes the drugs are the same if they have the "same principal molecular structure." The "principal molecular structure" expression used in this definition is quite broad and arbitrary. With respect to proteins, the FDA's [Orphan Drug Act] regulations make a presumption of sameness between any two proteins that have primarily the same amino acid sequence. To rebut this presumption, one must show a clinical difference between or superiority of the new biologic drug and the one that was the first to market. This demonstration generally requires clinical trials.

. . . .

With respect to modern day biotechnology and biologic drug patents, the effect of present law has come to be a monopoly for longer than the statutory period. Because a biologic drug's pharmacologic activity is largely defined by its process of manufacture, a generic manufacturer would need either to complete its own clinical trials with its version of the biologic or to indistinguishably copy the innovator's manufacturing process. However, current patent law does not require a biologic drug innovator to disclose its manufacturing process with particularity. Furthermore, it is so costly and time consuming to develop and approve a biologic through the FDA's full clinical trial process that the rewards of developing a generic biologic do not outweigh the burdens.

NOTE

For further exploration of this puzzle, *see* Edward Korwek, *Towards Understanding the "Generic" Debate About Biologics*, J. BIOLAW & BUS. 27, No. 4 (2004); David Dudzinski, *Reflections on Historical, Scientific, and Legal Issues Relevant to Designing Approval Pathways for Generic Versions of Recombivant Protein–Based Therapeutics and Monoclone Antibodies*, 60 FOOD & DRUG L.J. 143 (2005).

D.   REGULATING AND PROMOTING VACCINES

The most prominent activity of the Division of Biologics Standards, which became FDA's Bureau of Biologics in 1972, dealt with vaccines. The DBS's responsibility for vaccine safety was just one element of a larger public health effort to promote the development and use of agents to prevent infectious disease. This has been a goal of the federal public health apparatus for more than a century and, as later excerpts illustrate, it has achieved some dramatic successes. Consider, for example, FDA's recent approval of a new vaccine to prevent cervical cancer. *FDA Licenses New Vaccine for Prevention of Cervical Cancer and Other Diseases in Females Caused by Human Papillovirus*, FDA News, No. P06–77 (June 8, 2006).

Edward Mortimer, *Immunization Against Infectious Disease*

200 SCIENCE 902 (1978).

. . . In the United States since the turn of the century life expectancy has increased remarkably. Expected duration of life for individuals born in

1900 was 47.3 years; in 1970 it was 70.9 years. The age-adjusted death rate in 1900 was 17.2 deaths per thousand population, whereas in 1970 it was 9.5 per thousand, a reduction in mortality of 45 percent. . . .

. . . [T]he decrease in mortality has been most pronounced in younger age groups. . . . The mortality rate in children 1 to 4 years of age declined 96 percent between 1900 and 1970, whereas that in the population aged between 65 and 74 years declined by only a little more than a third. . . . [M]uch of this change in mortality in younger age groups is due to a decrease in deaths from certain infectious diseases, including the common contagious diseases of childhood, tuberculosis, meningitis, pneumonia, and epidemic diseases such as typhoid fever, plague, and smallpox . . . [I]n children older than 1 year of age, approximately two-thirds of the decreased mortality can be attributed to a decline in deaths from the above-specified infectious diseases.

. . . Clearly, there are multiple reasons for the decline in mortality due to infectious diseases in the United States in this century, and in many instances it is impossible to determine the relative importance of different factors. . . . To a considerable extent in some diseases, the decline in mortality can be attributed to man's intervention in terms of sanitary control of water supplies and refuse and proper food handling. An example of such a disease is typhoid fever. . . .

Control of nonhuman vectors has been responsible for much of the decline in mortality from some diseases, such as rabies, typhus fever, and malaria in the United States. Antimicrobial drugs effective against certain bacterial diseases have certainly contributed to the decline in mortality from infection since their development and widespread use during, and subsequent to, World War II. . . .

In view of the above, what has been the contribution of immunization to the decreased mortality from infectious disease in the United States? In the case of a number of diseases, immunization—though available and of some effect—has been of negligible importance. These diseases include typhoid fever, cholera, epidemic typhus fever, and plague. . . . The disappearance of mortality from one disease (smallpox) and the rarity of deaths from two others (tetanus and poliomyelitis) can be attributed almost entirely to active immunization. . . .

The lack of visibility of vaccine-preventable diseases in the United States has . . . resulted in a certain amount of complacency in both health professionals and the public. In 1975 only 116 deaths were reported from diseases against which children are routinely immunized. This has resulted in less than the optimum number of children being immunized. For example, in 1975 only 64.8 percent of 1 to 4 year old children had received three or more doses of poliomyelitis vaccine, compared to 73.9 percent in 1965. The low was 1973 with 60.4 percent. Only 75.2 percent of 1 to 4–year–olds had received three or more doses of diphtheria and tetanus toxoids and pertussis vaccine, and 65.5 percent measles vaccine. This latter deficit resulted in localized outbreaks of measles with more than 41,000 cases in 1976; how small the proportions of the population immune to poliomyelitis and diphtheria must be before substantial outbreaks occur is unknown. . . .

1.   Government Support for Immunization

The federal vaccine program involves more than FDA review and approval of the agents used in immunization programs. Through many organizations, the federal and state governments help develop vaccines; encourage and in some cases require their use (*see Jacobson v. Commonwealth of Massachusetts*, 197 U.S. 11 (1905)); subsidize their distribution; and assume responsibility for anticipating disease threats for which prophylactic agents should be used or, if need be, devised. Currently, officials confront two major challenges. Scientists at the Centers for Disease Control anticipate the possibility of a major flu pandemic in the near future, possibly the result of the spread of an avian flu virus, first to humans in Asia and then, inexorably, around the world. The last major flu pandemic, at the end of World War I, claimed more than 10 million lives in the U.S. alone. The other threat is a possible sequel to 9/11, the purposeful exposure of the U.S. population to an infectious agent for which no reliable prevention is now available. Anthrax and smallpox are two of several agents that lawmakers have directed public health authorities to address.

In short, vaccines represent a technology that government not only regulates but promotes. The responsible agencies often face conflicts in the performance of their regulatory functions because some of the most effective vaccines are capable, in rare cases, of causing the very disease they are supposed to prevent. One result has been legal claims brought by individuals who suffered adverse reactions from vaccines. These claims in turn have generated programs designed to compensate the "victims" of government-sponsored or encouraged immunization programs and, in various ways, to cushion the impact of potential liability on the dwindling number of private firms still engaged in manufacturing vaccines.

Rank A. Sloan, et al., *The Fragility of the U.S. Vaccine Supply*

351 New England Journal of Medicine 23 (2004).

The number of companies that produce vaccines for the United States has declined markedly since the 1960s. Today only five companies produce all routine vaccines for this market, and for each of eight of these vaccines—including the measles, mumps, and rubella (MMR); diphtheria, pertussis, and tetanus (DPT); and polio vaccines—there is only one supplier. Should one of these suppliers cease production, it could take years to have a replacement vaccine licensed and publicly available.

The dearth of suppliers has decreased the availability of vaccines. In 2001–2002, the United States had shortages of 8 of the 11 recommended childhood vaccines: DPT, MMR, varicella, and pneumococcal conjugate vaccines. In 2004, the country again had a shortage of pneumococcal conjugate vaccine, prompting the Centers for Disease Control and Prevention (CDC) to recommend suspension of the third and fourth doses.

Several explanations for the small number of vaccine suppliers seem plausible. Developing a new vaccine is costly and risky. It can cost $700 million to bring a new vaccine from concept to market. Phase 3 trials for pneumococcal vaccines and *Haemophilus influenzae* type b vaccine required tens of thousands of subjects. Some observers have suggested that the licensure requirements of the Food and Drug Administration (FDA) are excessively stringent and unnecessarily limit the entry of new suppliers into the market. Unlike pharmaceutical manufacturers, vaccine producers must obtain a license in advance to produce a vaccine at a particular site, and the FDA encourages creation of commercial production capacity before the license is granted, a stipulation that puts the company at substantial financial risk.

Vaccine suppliers also face increasingly stringent regulation of production. Suppliers undergo frequent FDA inspections of their production facilities, individual product batches require separate approval for release, and slight modifications to production processes or even the packaging of products may trigger expensive product reviews. The FDA requires frequent upgrades of vaccine production to reflect state-of-the-art manufacturing processes. In the mid–1990s, the FDA implemented Team Biologics, a new inspection process that imposed new record-keeping and administrative requirements. This regulatory approach is likely to increase the costs of producing vaccines, add to the uncertainty of rewards for investment in research and development and in production capacity, and discourage the entry of new suppliers.

. . . .

Despite intensive regulation of quality, vaccine companies are vulnerable to product-liability lawsuits. A surge of lawsuits in the 1980s resulted in a serious concern about the supply of DPT and other vaccines. . . .

Pharmaceutical companies cannot justify investment in vaccines if their risk-adjusted returns on investment are low, and vaccine profitability appears to be relatively low. The prices of childhood vaccines have remained flat for two decades, the result of federal price caps and the federal government's exercise of its considerable purchasing power. The cost of immunizing children has risen dramatically in recent years because of a few new high-priced vaccines, such as the varicella and pneumococcal conjugate vaccines, rather than because of a general increase in the prices of vaccines.

. . . .

In response to recurrent shortages of vaccines for children and adults since 2001, a number of proposals for reform have been advanced. These include expanding stockpiles of vaccines; establishing better communication among the CDC, manufacturers, the FDA, and states regarding potential disruptions in supplies; streamlining the FDA's regulatory process, including its review of new vaccine applications; strengthening the Vaccine Injury Compensation Program; requiring that manufacturers notify the U.S. government of an intention to withdraw a product; harmonizing international standards for vaccine licensure; removing price caps for vaccines; making vaccines from Vaccines for Children available at all public clinics, rather than just at federally qualified health centers; and creating incentives for vaccine production and development.

Far-reaching structural changes have also been proposed, such as extending the mandate for Vaccines for Children to underinsured children and adults, providing for universal coverage through a federal purchase program, providing for direct control of vaccine production by the government through an approach similar to that used by the military, and mandating universal insurance coverage of immunization. Most proposals would increase government intervention in the vaccine market with the goal of stabilizing supplies through direct control. But they also run the risk of discouraging the development of vaccines and entry into this market by companies that are wary of federal regulation. The other approach is a federal mandate that insurers must cover immunizations, which would increase coverage of underinsured children. But if insurers increase premiums to cover the higher expected expenditure, families may lose or drop insurance coverage altogether. . . .

Institute of Medicine, Financing Vaccines in the 21st Century: Assuring Access and Availability (2003)

. . . .

The federal government currently purchases between 52 and 55 percent of the childhood vaccines distributed in the United States, primarily for children who are uninsured or Medicaid-eligible. Nearly 20 doses of vaccines against 11 diseases are required for childhood immunization, at a cost of about $400 at the discounted prices available to the public sector (up to $600 at private-sector prices). This investment strains the ability of both the public and private sectors to immunize a daily birth cohort of more than 11,000 babies. Additional funds are required for the administration of the vaccines, as well as the vaccine shipping and storage costs.

In the 10–year period between 1988 and 1997, public-sector expenditures for vaccine purchases doubled from $100 to $200 per child through age 6. The cumulative public-sector cost doubled again in less than 5 years between 1997 and 2001, from $200 to almost $400 per child. The addition to the recommended childhood schedule of the expensive new pneumococcal conjugate vaccine for infants resulted in a doubling of the budget between 2000 and 2002 (from $500 million to over $1 billion in 2000) for the Vaccines for Children (VFC) entitlement—the major government vaccine purchase program for disadvantaged children. Continued cost increases can be expected as a result of the array of new vaccines now in development.

. . . .

The uneven nature of health plan vaccine benefits and the limited data on insurance practices with respect to immunization create significant uncertainties in designing national finance strategies for vaccine purchases. The population of underinsured—those who have health care insurance that covers major medical expenses but does not include benefits for vaccines—is a source of increasing concern and uncertainty. Furthermore, some health plans that do include vaccine benefits require out-of-pocket expenses in the form of high deductibles of copayments.

. . . .

Recent vaccine shortages that were unprecedented in their scope and severity, as well as diminishing numbers of vaccine suppliers for the U.S. market, are early warning signs of other problems that require systemic remedies to assure a healthy and reliable vaccine supply system. While temporary production problems appear to have eased, the potential for disruption remains. The problem of vaccine shortages has raised concerns about the relationships among the size of the government vaccine market, low vaccine prices, and the scale of investment in the production of current vaccines and the development of new vaccine products. The ability of the government to negotiate low prices for recommended vaccines is important to public health agencies and others that are trying to stretch tight budgets to cover both traditional vaccines and a growing array of new and higher-priced vaccine products. On the other hand, adequate financial incentives are necessary to sustain private investment in the vaccine production and licensing processes if the vaccine industry is to remain competitive and have the capacity to innovate within a global vaccine market.

. . . .

Ultimately, the [Institute of Medicine] committee determined that the best strategy would be to formulate a comprehensive plan that can address multiple goals. This plan would encompass a mandated insurance benefit strategy that includes a subsidy for insurers; a decentralized, private market for vaccines; and a voucher program for the uninsured....

The proposed plan, referred to as the *vaccine payment system*, consists of five core components that should be considered an integrated strategy for achieving the key objectives of access to and availability of vaccines:

- Federal legislation would be required to establish a vaccination coverage mandate for all public and private health plans....

- The federal government would create a new federal subsidy to reimburse public and private health plans and providers for mandated vaccine costs and associated vaccine administration fees.

- The federal government would also create a voucher system for vaccines and vaccine administration fees for designated uninsured populations.

- The insurance mandate, subsidy, and voucher would apply principally to vaccines that have substantial spillover effects as a result of their ability to prevent highly contagious diseases. Vaccines without substantial spillover effects, such as therapeutic vaccines, would be considered for inclusion only in cases of exceptional societal benefit.

- The amount of the subsidy and voucher would be determined both for vaccines currently on the immunization schedule and for vaccines that are not yet available. The subsidy for new vaccines would be based on an estimate of their societal benefit. The subsidy for vaccines already in use would be based on a formula that would take into account both current market prices and the vaccines' calculated societal benefit. The mandate would not apply to vaccines priced above the subsidy amount.

The prospect of a guaranteed public subsidy for selected vaccines would provide economic incentives that would encourage manufacturers to invest in the clinical trial, licensing, and production processes necessary to move a vaccine product from the early stage of discovery to its use in routine medical care. Reducing the financial uncertainties associated with these processes would stimulate the market and encourage the development of new and effective vaccine products. . . .

2. Manufacturer Liability for Vaccine Injuries

Reyes v. Wyeth Laboratories
498 F.2d 1264 (5th Cir. 1974).

■ Wisdom, Circuit Judge:

. . . .

I.

Twenty or thirty years ago poliomyelitis was a dread disease that especially attacked the very young. In 1952 alone, there were 57,879 reported cases of polio in the United States; 21,269 of these resulted in crippling paralysis to the victims. By 1970, when Anita Reyes contracted polio, the number of those stricken by polio had diminished dramatically; she was one of just 33 individuals to be afflicted during that year. Credit for this precipitous decline must go primarily to the medical researchers who discovered the viral nature of the disease, and were able to isolate and reproduce the virus in an inactivated or an attenuated form. But credit for this remarkable achievement must also be given to such laboratories as Wyeth, which processed the polio vaccine, and to massive federal-state public health programs for the administration of the vaccine.

On May 8, 1970, Anita Reyes was fed two drops of Sabin oral polio vaccine by eye-dropper at the Hidalgo County Department of Health clinic in Mission, Texas. The vaccine was administered to Anita by a registered nurse; there were no doctors present. Mrs. Reyes testified that she was not warned of any possible danger involved in Anita's taking the vaccine. Mrs. Reyes has a seventh grade education, but her primary language is Spanish. She signed a form releasing the State of Texas from "all liability in connection with immunization". The form contained no warning of any sort, and it is apparent from her testimony that she either did not read the form or lacked the linguistic ability to understand its significance. About fourteen days after the vaccine was administered, Anita Reyes became ill. On May 23, 1970, she was admitted to the McAllen (Texas) General Hospital, where her disease was diagnosed as Type I paralytic poliomyelitis. As a result of the polio, at the time of trial Anita was completely paralyzed from the waist down, her left arm had become atrophied, and she was unable to control her bladder or bowel movements.

The vaccine given Anita Reyes in the Mission clinic on May 8, 1970 was part of a "lot", No. 15509, prepared by Wyeth. Lot No. 15509 was trivalent oral polio vaccine that Wyeth had titered (mixed) from Types I, II, and III monovalent vaccine provided by Pfizer, Ltd. In response to an order placed by the Texas State Department of Health on December 23, 1969, Wyeth shipped 3500 vials of Lot No. 15509 vaccine to the State Health Department which in turn transferred 400 vials to the Hidalgo County Health Department. The jury found that vaccine from one of these vials was given to Anita Reyes. Included with every vial, each of which contained ten doses of vaccine, was a "package circular" provided by Wyeth which was intended to warn doctors, hospitals, or other purchasers of potential dangers in ingesting the vaccine. Mrs. Lenore Wiley, the public health nurse who administered the vaccine to Anita Reyes, testified that she had read the directions on this package insert, but that it was not the practice of the nurses at the Mission Health Clinic to pass on the warnings to the vaccines or to their guardians. She testified that she gave Mrs. Reyes no warning before she administered the vaccine to Anita.

On October 7, 1970, Epifanio Reyes, individually and as next friend of his minor daughter, brought this action on theories of strict products liability, breach of warranty, and negligence. In his complaint he alleged that his daughter had contracted polio from the live virus in Wyeth's vaccine, and that Wyeth's failure to warn him or his wife that this might occur rendered it liable for Anita's injuries....

II.

... Our inquiry is bounded by the jury's finding that Wyeth's vaccine was the producing cause of Anita Reyes's polio, and by those principles of products liability law we conclude would be applied by the courts of Texas.

... Texas courts recognize both tort and warranty theories of products liability. This case was tried, briefed, and argued on appeal entirely on the tort theory of strict liability. Thus the differences between the two approaches, and whatever contractual trappings of warranty have not been destroyed with the crumbling of the citadel of privity, need not detain us. Rather, we turn to the theory of strict products liability as embodied in Section 402A of the *Restatement (Second) of Torts* (1965), and approved by the Supreme Court of Texas in *McKisson v. Sales Affiliates*, Tex.Sup.Ct. 1967, 416 S.W.2d 787.

Basically, Section 402A subjects to liability the seller or manufacturer of a product sold "in a defective condition unreasonably dangerous" to an ultimate user or consumer whose person or property is physically harmed by the product....

We begin the inquiry by asking whether the vaccine was unreasonably dangerous, that is, in a defective condition when Anita Reyes received it. It is clear, of course that the vaccine was not itself defective. Wyeth Vaccine Lot No. 15509 was exactly what its makers and the Texas public health authorities intended it to be: trivalent live-virus Sabin oral polio vaccine. The live virus which the jury concluded caused Anita's poliomyelitis was not inadvertently included in the mixture. Indeed, it is the presence of the living but attenuated Type I, II, and III viruses which makes the Sabin vaccine so effective

Although the living virus in the vaccine does not make the vaccine defective, it does make it what the Restatement calls an "unavoidably unsafe product", one which cannot be made "safe" no matter how carefully it is manufactured. Such products are not necessarily *"unreasonably* dangerous", for as this Court has long recognized in wrestling with product liability questions, many goods possess both utility and danger. Rather, in evaluating the possible liability of a manufacturer for injuries caused by his inevitably hazardous products, a two-step analysis is required to determine first, whether the product is so unsafe that marketing it at all is "unreasonably dangerous per se", and, if not, whether the product has been introduced into the stream of commerce without sufficient safeguards and is thereby "unreasonably dangerous as marketed". . . .

Since Sabin oral polio vaccine is not "unreasonably dangerous per se", we move to the second step of our analysis to determine whether it is "unreasonably dangerous as marketed", for to conclude that the maker of an unavoidably unsafe product did not act unreasonably in placing it on the market is not to relieve him of the responsibility to market it in such a way as to prevent unreasonable danger. In the case of a product such as Sabin oral polio vaccine, this translates into a duty to provide proper warnings in selling the product. As comment k to Section 402A instructs, an unavoidably unsafe product is neither defective nor *unreasonably* dangerous if such a product is "properly prepared, and is accompanied by proper directions and warning". Consequently, the Restatement requires a seller who has reason to believe that danger may result from a particular use of his product to provide adequate warning of the danger in order that the product's potential for harm may be reduced. Failure to give such a warning when it is required will itself present a "defect" in the product and will, without more, cause the product to be "unreasonably dangerous as marketed".

Issue is joined then, on the question whether Wyeth was under a duty to warn the parents of Anita Reyes that there was a possibility, however remote, that she might contract polio from the drug designed to immunize her. If such a duty existed, the vaccine was "defective" and unreasonably dangerous as marketed, for such cautions as Wyeth advanced did not, and were not intended to, reach the Reyes family. *See Davis v. Wyeth Laboratories, Inc.*, 399 F.2d 121, 129 (9th Cir. 1968).

Wyeth does not deny that its vaccine is "unavoidably unsafe", or contend that it was unaware of the danger. Rather, the appellant contends that if it had a duty to warn at all, that duty was discharged by the warning contained on the package insert which accompanied the vials of vaccine sold to the Texas State Department of Health. This is so, Wyeth asserts, because the Sabin trivalent oral polio vaccine in issue here is a "prescription drug", and those who prepare such drugs are not required to warn the ultimate consumer. If the warning to the dispensing physician or authorities (here the Texas and Hidalgo County Public Health Departments) was adequate, Wyeth is not liable for any harm caused by the vaccine. Resolution of these contentions is crucial; Wyeth concedes in its brief that "since it is undisputed that Wyeth did not warn Reyes, but only the Texas State Department of Health, a finding that the vaccine was not a prescription drug establishes as a matter of law the defectiveness of the vaccine for purposes of a prima facie case in strict products liability."

We cannot quarrel with the general proposition that where *prescription* drugs are concerned, the manufacturer's duty to warn is limited to an obligation to advise the prescribing physician of any potential dangers that may result from the drug's use. This special standard for prescription drugs is an understandable exception to the Restatement's general rule that one who markets goods must warn foreseeable ultimate users of dangers inherent in his products. Prescription drugs are likely to be complex medicines, esoteric in formula and varied in effect. As a medical expert, the prescribing physician can take into account the propensities of the drug, as well as the susceptibilities of his patient. His is the task of weighing the benefits of any medication against its potential dangers. The choice he makes is an informed one, an individualized medical judgment bottomed on a knowledge of both patient and palliative. Pharmaceutical companies then, who must warn ultimate purchasers of dangers inherent in patent drugs sold over the counter, in selling prescription drugs are required to warn only the prescribing physician, who acts as a "learned intermediary" between manufacturer and consumer.

Although there is no question that Sabin oral vaccine is licensed for sale only as a prescription drug, the district court, in its charge to the jury, noted that the vaccine was not administered as a prescription drug at the Mission Clinic. The court charged: "if you [the jury] find that a warning should have been given, the warning had to be given to Anita and her parents, not to Mrs. Wiley, that Public Health nurse, somebody else ... The ultimate consumer is the one that had to be warned." The district court apparently based this instruction on the leading federal case in the area, *Davis v. Wyeth Laboratories*. In *Davis*, the plaintiff had allegedly contracted polio from Wyeth oral vaccine distributed at a public clinic. The Ninth Circuit held that where no individualized medical judgment intervenes between the manufacturer of a prescription drug and the ultimate consumer, "it is the responsibility of the manufacturer to see that warnings reach the consumer, either by giving warning itself or by obligating the purchaser to give warning. Where there is no physician to make an "individualized balancing ... of the risks", the Court reasoned, the very justification for the prescription drug exception evaporates. Thus, as in the case of patent drugs sold over the counter without prescription, the manufacturer of a prescription drug who knows or has reason to know that it will not be dispensed as such a drug must provide the consumer with adequate information so that he can balance the risks and benefits of a given medication himself. Moreover, just as the manufacturer cannot make this choice for its ultimate consumers, it cannot allow its immediate purchaser to choose for them. In sum, then, the manufacturer is required to warn the ultimate consumer, or to see that he is warned.

Wyeth does not resist the Ninth Circuit's holding in *Davis*, but asserts that the instant case can be distinguished on four grounds. First, the appellant argues, Davis received his vaccine during a mass immunization program, whereas Anita Reyes ingested her vaccine at her parents' request. Second, Wyeth stresses the fact that Davis received his vaccine from a pharmacist, but Reyes's was administered by a public health nurse. Third, Wyeth's active participation in the mass immunization program involved in the *Davis* case is contrasted to its relatively passive role here. Finally,

Wyeth urges that unlike the situation in *Davis*, here it had no knowledge that the vaccine would not be administered as a prescription drug.

None of these asserted grounds for distinguishing *Davis* justifies a different result here. The first two arguments are admittedly distinctions between *Davis* and the instant controversy, but they have no bearing on the *rationale* of the *Davis* opinion. Whether vaccine was received during a mass immunization or an on-going program, whether it was administered by nurse or pharmacist, it was, in both these cases, dispensed without the sort of individualized medical balancing of the risks to the vaccinee that is contemplated by the prescription drug exception. The third and fourth asserted bases for distinguishing *Davis* from this case are essentially the same: Wyeth took no active part in the vaccination process here, and did not know that its vaccine would be dispensed without procedures appropriate for distribution of prescription drugs.

Were we to conclude that Wyeth neither knew nor had reason to know that its vaccine would be dispensed without prescription drug safeguards, we might be required to hold that the *rationale* in *Davis* is inapplicable here. But Wyeth had ample reason to foresee the way in which its vaccine would be distributed. . . .

Viewed in this light, the present controversy, however it differs from *Davis* factually, invites application of the *Davis* principles, and the conclusion that Wyeth was under a duty to warn Anita Reyes's parents of the danger inherent in its vaccine. Wyeth knew or had reason to know that the vaccine would not be administered as a prescription drug, and therefore was required to warn foreseeable users, or see that the Texas Department of Health warned them. Wyeth's failure to warn was a breach of its duty and made the vaccine "defective"—hence "unreasonably dangerous"—as marketed.

[Prior cases] . . . suggest a test for cases such as the one now before the Court: Where a consumer, whose injury the manufacturer should have reasonably foreseen, is injured by a product sold without a required warning, a rebuttable presumption will arise that the consumer would have read any warning provided by the manufacturer, and acted so as to minimize the risks. In the absence of evidence rebutting the presumption, a jury finding that the defendant's product was the producing cause of the plaintiff's injury would be sufficient to hold him liable.

. . . The legal presumption . . . thus operates here to provide the final element necessary to hold Wyeth Laboratories liable for Anita Reyes' poliomyelitis. Aware of its unavoidable dangers and cognizant that it foreseeably would not be dispensed as a prescription drug, Wyeth nonetheless failed to warn Mrs. Reyes that its vaccine could cause polio in some few of the millions receiving the medication. Administered without a warning, the vaccine was "defective", hence unreasonably dangerous. According to the test we have distilled above, we must assume in the absence of evidence to the contrary that Anita's parents would have acted on the warning, had it been given. Perhaps this would have prevented her polio. It unquestionably would have avoided Wyeth's liability.

V.

In closing, we feel that we should comment on the important policy considerations raised in the briefs of the amici curiae, the American Academy of Pediatrics [AAP] and the Conference of State and Territorial Epidemiologists [CSTE]. Both insist that the holding we reached is "dangerous" to the nation's preventive medicine programs and contravenes a strong public policy favoring large-scale participation in immunization efforts to combat infectious disease. The crucial points of the argument are two: first, that any effort to warn vaccines will be futile and frightening, leading only to confusion, and second, that a warning is unnecessary once epidemiologists have reached a deliberate medical judgment that universal vaccination is necessary. These public health policy questions cut across the law. We realize their importance.

Citing a recent Texas statute which requires that all Texas schoolchildren receive polio vaccine, the AAP insists that this renders any warnings futile. This argument assumes, of course, that the only options available are to ingest the oral vaccine at the clinic or to eschew immunity. Obviously, however, one can choose to be inoculated with killed-virus Salk vaccine, either to provide complete immunity or as a precautionary prelude to ingesting oral vaccine. The AAP also insists that the warnings would be so complex or misleading as to confuse and frighten potential vaccines. This is possible. Yet we believe that a warning advising a patron of a public health clinic of the relative risk of contracting polio from a "wild" source against the slight chance of contracting it from the vaccine would not be terrifying or confusing. . . .

This position raises a policy consideration scarcely less urgent than the need for mass immunization from disease; the right of the individual to choose and control what risk he will take, in the absence of an individualized medical judgment by a physician familiar with his needs and susceptibilities. Recognition of this right counters the argument advanced in the CSTE's brief that once an epidemiological balancing of the risks of immunization has been made, no warning is required. Clearly, the rationale excusing warnings to ultimate consumers of prescription drugs whose physicians have balanced the risk for them, cannot be extended to a medical determination that statistical probabilities justify universal immunization. . . .

Here, the qualitative risk was great, the quantitative risk minute. The end sought to be achieved—immunization—is important both to the individual and society. Striking the balance in this case is difficult, but by adding two elements to the *Davis* calculus we conclude that a sufficient "true choice judgment" was involved here to lend strong policy support to our holding. First, the risk here was foreseeable statistically, although unknowable individually. Thus, unlike the abreaction cases, here there was a basis for rational choice. Second, a choice here, if given, had an opportunity to be efficacious, since reasonable alternatives to taking the oral vaccine were available. . . .

. . . Statistically predictable as are these rare cases of vaccine-induced polio, a strong argument can be advanced that the loss ought not lie where it falls (on the victim), but should be borne by the manufacturer as a foreseeable cost of doing business, and passed on to the public in the form of price increases to his customers.

Contrary to the assertions of the AAP and the CSTE, we feel strongly that our holding is in accord with public policy considerations. We recognize both the essential role the city health clinic and the rural county clinic play in the nation's public health scheme, and the dangers that their depersonalized medical treatment pose. We do not then, lay down an absolute duty to warn all who receive medication at public clinics. Instead, we hold that in the case of a prescription drug which is unavoidably unsafe, and as to which there is a certain, though small, risk throughout the population, there must be *either* a warning—meaningful and complete so as to be understood by the recipient—*or* an individualized medical judgment that this treatment or medication is necessary and desirable for this patient. Anita's parents received neither. Wyeth is therefore liable for the consequence of its failure to market its unavoidably unsafe product in such a way as to warn Anita's parents of its unreasonably dangerous condition.

NOTES

1. *Congressional Alteration of* Reyes *Decision*. In the National Childhood Vaccine Injury Compensation Act of 1986, discussed *infra* p. 912, Congress overrode *Reyes* by declaring that childhood vaccine manufacturers need provide warnings of unavoidable side effects only to the administering physician or nurse.

2. *Givens v. Lederle*, 556 F.2d 1341 (5th Cir. 1977), affirmed a jury verdict against the defendant manufacturer of Sabin oral live virus polio vaccine and in favor of an unvaccinated plaintiff, who contracted paralytic poliomyelitis after her infant daughter had been given the vaccine by a private pediatrician. The court found that the manufacturer's package insert failed to reach the consumer and warn of the risks of taking a live vaccine. Though in this case a private physician administered the dose, the court held that the warning language did not sufficiently alert even the physician of the risks.

3. GOVERNMENT LIABILITY FOR VACCINE INJURIES

As the *Reyes* case illustrates, public campaigns to achieve wide immunization can produce cases of diseases that are attributable to the vaccine itself. In addition to seeking recovery from vaccine manufacturers, victims of these "accidents" have occasionally sought recovery from the government agencies responsible for a vaccine's release and use. In the following opinion, the Supreme Court addresses this issue and at the same time provides a close look at the workings of FDA's vaccine approval process.

Berkovitz v. United States

486 U.S. 531 (1988).

■ MARSHALL, J., delivered the opinion for a unanimous Court.

The question in this case is whether the discretionary function exception of the Federal Tort Claims Act (FTCA or Act), 28 U.S.C. § 2680(a), bars a suit based on the Government's licensing of an oral polio vaccine and on its subsequent approval of the release of a specific lot of that vaccine to the public.

On May 10, 1979, Kevan Berkovitz, then a 2–month–old infant, ingested a dose of Orimune, an oral polio vaccine manufactured by Lederle Laboratories. Within one month, he contracted a severe case of polio. The disease left Berkovitz almost completely paralyzed and unable to breathe without the assistance of a respirator. The Communicable Disease Center, an agency of the Federal Government, determined that Berkovitz had contracted polio from the vaccine.

Berkovitz, joined by his parents as guardians, subsequently filed suit against the United States in Federal District Court.[1] The complaint alleged that the United States was liable for his injuries under the FTCA, because the Division of Biologic Standards (DBS), then a part of the National Institutes of Health, had acted wrongfully in licensing Lederle Laboratories to produce Orimune and because the Bureau of Biologics of the Food and Drug Administration (FDA) had acted wrongfully in approving release to the public of the particular lot of vaccine containing Berkovitz's dose. According to petitioners, these actions violated federal law and policy regarding the inspection and approval of polio vaccines.

The Government moved to dismiss the suit for lack of subject-matter jurisdiction on the ground that the agency actions fell within the discretionary function exception of the FTCA....

FTCA, 28 U.S.C. § 1346(b), generally authorizes suits against the United States for damages

> "for injury or loss of property, or personal injury or death caused by the negligent or wrongful act or omission of any employee of the Government while acting within the scope of his office or employment, under circumstances where the United States, if a private person, would be liable to the claimant in accordance with the law of the place where the act or omission occurred."

The Act includes a number of exceptions to this broad waiver of sovereign immunity. The exception relevant to this case provides that no liability shall lie for

> "any claim ... based upon the exercise or performance or the failure to exercise or perform a discretionary function or duty on the part of a federal agency or an employee of the Government, whether or not the discretion involved be abused." 28 U.S.C. § 2680(a).

... [T]he discretionary function exception will not apply when a federal statute, regulation, or policy specifically prescribes a course of action for an employee to follow. In this event, the employee has no rightful option but to adhere to the directive. And if the employee's conduct cannot appropriately be the product of judgment or choice, then there is no discretion in the conduct for the discretionary function exception to protect.

---

1. Petitioners also sued Lederle Laboratories in a separate civil action. That suit was settled before the instant case was filed.

Moreover, assuming the challenged conduct involves an element of judgment, a court must determine whether that judgment is of the kind that the discretionary function exception was designed to shield. The basis for the discretionary function exception was Congress' desire to "prevent judicial 'second-guessing' of legislative and administrative decisions grounded in social, economic, and political policy through the medium of an action in tort." The exception, properly construed, therefore protects only governmental actions and decisions based on considerations of public policy. In sum, the discretionary function exception insulates the Government from liability if the action challenged in the case involves the permissible exercise of policy judgment.

. . . .

Petitioners' suit raises two broad claims. First, petitioners assert that the DBS violated a federal statute and accompanying regulations in issuing a license to Lederle Laboratories to produce Orimune. Second, petitioners argue that the Bureau of Biologics of the FDA violated federal regulations and policy in approving the release of the particular lot of Orimune that contained Kevan Berkovitz's dose. We examine each of these broad claims by reviewing the applicable regulatory scheme and petitioners' specific allegations of agency wrongdoing. Because the decision we review adjudicated a motion to dismiss, we accept all of the factual allegations in petitioners' complaint as true and ask whether, in these circumstances, dismissal of the complaint was appropriate.

Under federal law, a manufacturer must receive a product license prior to marketing a brand of live oral polio vaccine. In order to become eligible for such a license, a manufacturer must first make a sample of the vaccine product. This process begins with the selection of an original virus strain. The manufacturer grows a seed virus from this strain; the seed virus is then used to produce monopools, portions of which are combined to form the consumer-level product. Federal regulations set forth safety criteria for the original strain. Under the regulations, the manufacturer must conduct a variety of tests to measure the safety of the product at each stage of the manufacturing process. Upon completion of the manufacturing process and the required testing, the manufacturer is required to submit an application for a product license to the DBS. In addition to this application, the manufacturer must submit data from the tests performed and a sample of the finished product.

In deciding whether to issue a license, the DBS is required to comply with certain statutory and regulatory provisions. The Public Health Service Act provides:

"Licenses for the maintenance of establishments for the propagation or manufacture and preparation of products [including polio vaccines] may be issued only upon a showing that the establishment and the products for which a license is desired meet standards, designed to insure the continued safety, purity, and potency of such products, prescribed in regulations, and licenses for new products may be issued only upon a showing that they meet such standards. All such licenses shall be issued, suspended, and re-

voked as prescribed by regulations...." § 351(d), 42 U.S.C.
§ 262(d).

A regulation similarly provides that "[a] product license shall be issued
only upon examination of the product and upon a determination that the
product complies with the standards prescribed in the regulations...." In
addition, a regulation states that "an application for license shall not be
considered as filed" until the DBS receives the information and data
regarding the product that the manufacturer is required to submit. These
statutory and regulatory provisions require the DBS, prior to issuing a
product license, to receive all data the manufacturer is required to submit,
to examine the product, and to make a determination that the product
complies with safety standards.

Petitioners' first allegation with regard to the licensing of Orimune is
that the DBS issued a product license without first receiving data that the
manufacturer must submit showing how the product, at the various stages
of the manufacturing process, matched up against regulatory safety standards. The discretionary function exception does not bar a cause of action
based on this allegation. The statute and regulations described above
require, as a precondition to licensing, that the DBS receive certain test
data from the manufacturer relating to the product's compliance with
regulatory standards. The DBS has no discretion to issue a license without
first receiving the required test data; to do so would violate a specific
statutory and regulatory directive. Accordingly, to the extent that petitioners' licensing claim is based on a decision of the DBS to issue a license
without having received the required test data, the discretionary function
exception imposes no bar.

Petitioners' other allegation regarding the licensing of Orimune is
difficult to describe with precision. Petitioners contend that the DBS
licensed Orimune even though the vaccine did not comply with certain
regulatory safety standards. This charge may be understood in any of three
ways. First, petitioners may mean that the DBS licensed Orimune without
first making a determination as to whether the vaccine complied with
regulatory standards. Second, petitioners may intend to argue that the DBS
specifically found that Orimune failed to comply with certain regulatory
standards and nonetheless issued a license for the vaccine's manufacture.
Third, petitioners may concede that the DBS made a determination of
compliance, but allege that this determination was incorrect. Neither
petitioners' complaint nor their briefs and argument before this Court
make entirely clear their theory of the case.

If petitioners aver that the DBS licensed Orimune either without
determining whether the vaccine complied with regulatory standards or
after determining that the vaccine failed to comply, the discretionary
function exception does not bar the claim. Under the scheme governing the
DBS's regulation of polio vaccines, the DBS may not issue a license except
upon an examination of the product and a determination that the product
complies with all regulatory standards. The agency has no discretion to
deviate from this mandated procedure. Petitioners' claim, if interpreted as
alleging that the DBS licensed Orimune in the absence of a determination
that the vaccine complied with regulatory standards, therefore does not

challenge a discretionary function. Rather, the claim charges a failure on the part of the agency to perform its clear duty under federal law. When a suit charges an agency with failing to act in accord with a specific mandatory directive, the discretionary function exception does not apply.

If petitioners' claim is that the DBS made a determination that Orimune complied with regulatory standards, but that the determination was incorrect, the question of the applicability of the discretionary function exception requires a somewhat different analysis. In that event, the question turns on whether the manner and method of determining compliance with the safety standards at issue involve agency judgment of the kind protected by the discretionary function exception. Petitioners contend that the determination involves the application of objective scientific standards, whereas the Government asserts that the determination incorporates considerable "policy judgment." In making these assertions, the parties have framed the issue appropriately; application of the discretionary function exception to the claim that the determination of compliance was incorrect hinges on whether the agency officials making that determination permissibly exercise policy choice.... We therefore leave it to the District Court to decide, if petitioners choose to press this claim, whether agency officials appropriately exercise policy judgment in determining that a vaccine product complies with the relevant safety standards.

The regulatory scheme governing release of vaccine lots is distinct from that governing the issuance of licenses. The former set of regulations places an obligation on manufacturers to examine all vaccine lots prior to distribution to ensure that they comply with regulatory standards. These regulations, however, do not impose a corresponding duty on the Bureau of Biologics. Although the regulations empower the Bureau to examine any vaccine lot and prevent the distribution of a noncomplying lot, they do not require the Bureau to take such action in all cases. The regulations generally allow the Bureau to determine the appropriate manner in which to regulate the release of vaccine lots, rather than mandating certain kinds of agency action.

Given this regulatory context, the discretionary function exception bars any claims that challenge the Bureau's formulation of policy as to the appropriate way in which to regulate the release of vaccine lots. In addition, if the policies and programs formulated by the Bureau allow room for implementing officials to make independent policy judgments, the discretionary function exception protects the acts taken by those officials in the exercise of this discretion. The discretionary function exception, however, does not apply if the acts complained of do not involve the permissible exercise of policy discretion. Thus, if the Bureau's policy leaves no room for an official to exercise policy judgment in performing a given act, or if the act simply does not involve the exercise of such judgment, the discretionary function exception does not bar a claim that the act was negligent or wrongful....

Viewed in light of these principles, petitioners' claim regarding the release of the vaccine lot from which Kevan Berkovitz received his dose survives the Government's motion to dismiss. Petitioners allege that, under the authority granted by the regulations, the Bureau of Biologics has adopted a policy of testing all vaccine lots for compliance with safety standards and preventing the distribution to the public of any lots that fail to comply. Petitioners further allege that notwithstanding this policy, which allegedly leaves no room for implementing officials to exercise independent policy judgment, employees of the Bureau knowingly approved the release of a lot that did not comply with safety standards.... If those allegations are correct—that is, if the Bureau's policy did not allow the official who took the challenged action to release a noncomplying lot on the basis of policy considerations—the discretionary function exception does not bar the claim....

NOTES

1. *Proceedings on Remand.* The court of appeals denied the government's motion to dismiss and remanded the case for a trial on the merits. 858 F.2d 122 (3d Cir. 1988). Thereafter the case was consolidated with several other suits seeking damages for injuries resulting from the administration of Orimune. *In re Sabin Polio Vaccine Products Liability Litigation*, 743 F. Supp. 410 (D.Md.1990). There is no record of further legal proceedings but newspapers reported later that one Kevan Berkowitz was paid $4.45 in April of that year to settle the case. Donna Shaw, *All Polio in U.S. Now Caused by Vaccine*, SEATTLE TIMES, June 10, 1993, at A1.

2. *Related Theory of Government Liability.* In *Griffin v. United States*, 500 F.2d 1059 (3d Cir. 1974), the court sustained recovery against the government for the severe injuries suffered following administration of a dose of Sabin polio vaccine that the Division of Biological Standards had licensed. The DBS had promulgated a regulation establishing specifications that its employees were to apply in determining nonvirulence of batches of the vaccine—specifications that many outside experts had criticized as unnecessarily stringent. The DBS had released the batch of vaccine administered to Mrs. Griffin even though it did not meet these specifications. The court disagreed with the government's contention that the decision whether to release the vaccine was discretionary and that the DBS regulation required a judgmental determination:

> We acknowledge that under DBS' construction of the regulation, the implementation called for a judgmental determination as to the degree to which each of the enumerated criteria indicated neurovirulence.... The judgment, however, was that of a professional measuring neurovirulence. It was not that of a policy-maker promulgating regulations by balancing competing policy considerations in determining the public interest.... At issue was a scientific, but not policy-making, determination as to whether each of the criteria listed ... was met and the extent to which each such factor accurately indicated neurovirulence. DBS' responsibility was limited to merely executing the policy judgments of the Surgeon General....
>
> ... The Government's release of Lot 56 was predicated upon its reliance on a factor called "biological variation." Reliance on this factor, however, was not authorized by the regulations. We therefore conclude ... that DBS' activity was not immunized from judicial review.

3. *FDA Oversight of Vaccines.* The Supreme Court's description of the steps in DBS's approval of polio vaccine provides a window on a distinctive facet of the regulatory process for vaccines. Because most vaccines are the byproduct of natural biological processes, successive batches may differ in their composition and thus in their effects. This means that a batch produced today by the same process used to produce the doses used in clinical trials may diverge, slightly or even significantly,

from the tested formula. To deal with this problem, DBS (and later FDA) called for individual testing of each successive batch—both by the manufacturer and then by the agency itself. In short, FDA often plays two roles to assure the safety of vaccines: it evaluates and approves the results of tests on the "model" of the product and then, repeatedly over time, examines successive reproductions to assure that—as closely as can be—they mimic the "model."

4. COMPENSATING VACCINE INJURIES

On three occasions Congress has passed legislation creating a program for compensating recipients of vaccines who suffer adverse reactions. And, as Professor Greenberger suggests, Congress faces pressure to repeat the gesture.

Michael Greenberger, *The 800 Pound Gorilla Sleeps: The Federal Government's Lackadaisical Liability and Compensation Policies in the Context of Pre–Event Vaccine Immunization Programs*
8 Journal of Health Care Law & Policy 7 (2005).

The United States government has implemented three primary vaccine liability and compensation schemes over recent years. . . .

A.   The National Swine Flu Immunization Program of 1976.

The National Swine Flu Immunization Program of 1976 [hereinafter the Swine Flu Act] was the federal government's first foray into a vaccine liability and compensation program. Fear of a flu pandemic began in January of 1976 when four cases of swine flu were discovered at Fort Dix, New Jersey. This raised grave concerns in the public health community, because it feared a repeat of the swine flu pandemic that had killed millions in 1918–19. While neither a swine flu epidemic nor a pandemic materialized in the early months of 1976 (the flu season generally runs from September though March), Congress quickly authorized the procurement of nearly 200 million doses of the swine flu vaccine in April of 1976.

Concerns over vaccine manufacturer liability did not arise until insurers declared that they would end coverage for vaccine manufacturers as of June 30, 1976. This refusal stemmed in large part from the case of *Reyes v. Wyeth Laboratories*, 498 F.2d 1264 (5th Cir. 1974), which held polio vaccine manufacturers strictly liable for failing to provide product warnings directly to vaccines which would allow vaccines to assess the risks of the vaccine. . . .

. . . As a result, swine flu manufacturers stopped producing the vaccine that would potentially save the lives of thousands, if not millions, of Americans if the swine flu returned for the fall flu season. However, Congress eventually passed the Swine Flu Act on August 12, 1976. . . .

The Swine Flu Act protected manufacturers and distributors of the swine flu vaccine, as well as those who administered the vaccine. Plaintiffs asserted claims directly against the United States through the Federal Tort Claims Act, rather than against the alleged "wrongdoer," and the United

States would assume the liability of manufacturers, distributors, and vaccinators, "based on any theory of liability ... including negligence, strict liability in tort, and breach of warranty." In addition, the courts consistently interpreted the "any theory of liability" language as establishing a no-fault compensation system that made the government liable to all plaintiffs who could demonstrate that their injuries were caused by the swine flu vaccine. However, the United States would seek indemnification from negligent organizations or individuals covered by the Swine Flu Act's liability protections.

. . . Because the Swine Flu Act used the Federal Tort Claims Act as a vehicle for liability and compensation, claimants first had to file an administrative claim with the agency, before proceeding to federal district court. The Swine Flu Act did not place limits on the amount of an award that could be obtained.

The swine flu vaccination program was successful in terms of getting a large number of people vaccinated in a short period. During the two-month run of the program, over 40 million Americans—nearly a third of the adult population of the United States—received the swine flu vaccination. However, a vast field of vaccine injury litigation subsequently began in which attorneys and medical experts readily attributed injuries to the vaccine. By 1985, the government had paid out $90 million to those that developed Guillain–Barre syndrome, an often reversible but sometimes fatal form of paralysis, which had been attributed to the swine flu vaccine. . . .

B. National Childhood Vaccine Injury Compensation Act of 1986

Prior to 1986, the number of manufacturers making childhood vaccines had "declined significantly." In addition, the early 1980's exhibited an increase in vaccine tort litigation, which in part grew out of the fact that injuries previously unrecognized as arising from childhood vaccines were starting to be connected with those vaccines. . . . At the time, vaccine manufacturers faced grave difficulty in obtaining liability insurance, which caused one vaccine manufacturer to stop producing vaccines temporarily in 1984. Others were threatening to follow suit. Because "the withdrawal of even a single manufacturer would present the very real possibility of vaccine shortages," Congress once again involved the federal government in vaccine liability and compensation through the National Childhood Vaccine Injury Compensation Act of 1986 [hereinafter NCVICA]. However, NCVICA's liability and compensation provisions were crafted differently from the Swine Flu Act, largely due to the government's increasing reluctance to accept financial responsibility.

Specifically, NCVICA established a two-stage, no fault compensation system for specific childhood vaccines (exclusive of the smallpox vaccine). The first stage was a mandatory "no-fault" system, administered by a special master of the federal district court, which compensated specific injuries resulting from childhood vaccination. This administrative hearing provided compensation regardless of the party alleged to have caused the injury, and the respondent was always the United States.

However, unlike the Swine Flu Act of 1976 which did not limit awards, NCVICA capped certain types of awards. Under NCVICA's no-fault system, the plaintiff could recover actual unreimbursable and reasonable projected unreimbursable expenses, such as medical expenses, lost wages, reasonable attorneys' fees, and secondary transmission costs; but, "actual and project-ed" pain and suffering were limited to $250,000. Awards for a vaccinee's death were capped at $250,000. Both of the aforementioned caps were adjusted for inflation in accordance with the Consumer Price Index. Lost wages were explicitly limited to "compensation for actual and anticipated loss of earnings determined in accordance with generally recognized actuar-ial principles and projections" for those injured by a vaccine after turning 18 years old. Those injured before turning 18 could recover lost wages in anticipation of turning 18 in amounts based on "the average gross weekly earnings of workers in the private, non-farm sector, less appropriate taxes and the average cost of a health insurance policy." Although this was a limitation, injured parties could generally recover lost wages, without the benefit of knowing what their actual wages would have been.

If unsatisfied with an administrative award (or not even a recipient of an award under NCVICA's first stage), the plaintiff could enter NCVICA's second stage and commence traditional tort litigation against the vaccine manufacturer.... If a plaintiff chose litigation, Congress made certain alterations to traditional tort law to protect vaccine manufacturers, as the government would not pay awards that arose from litigation. First, the manufacturer was not liable for injuries or death that resulted from "unavoidable" side effects that were inherent in properly prepared, labeled, and administered vaccines. Next, Congress legislatively altered the *Reyes v. Wyeth Laboratories* rule by declaring that childhood vaccine manufacturers were not liable for failing to provide such warnings. Rather, simply provid-ing those warnings to the administering physician or nurse was ade-quate.... Finally, a manufacturer was immune from punitive damages in a civil trial if it complied with the Federal Food, Drug, and Cosmetic Act and the Public Health Service Act when manufacturing the vaccine, unless the manufacturer engaged in fraudulent, wrongful, or criminal action when submitting information for the vaccine's approval....

A final retreat from the generosity of the Swine Flu Act was that NCVICA made its compensation secondary to state and private sources of compensation as well as federal sources. NCVICA clearly stated that the federal government had liability in this area secondary to state compensa-tion programs; private or public health benefit; private insurance; or federal or state "health benefits program." ...

C. Phase I Smallpox Vaccination Program

Believing that regimes hostile to the United States may possess *Variola major*, the etiological agent of smallpox, President Bush announced the Phase I smallpox vaccination program in December of 2002—a program which aspired to vaccinate 500,000 first responders against smallpox. While the smallpox vaccine had been used routinely in America until 1972, few people in today's medical field have any experience administering the smallpox vaccine. In addition, the smallpox vaccine has been referred to as the "least safe human vaccine" available today.

... Congress and the President knew they had to protect a variety of entities and persons from liability and compensate those injured or killed by the vaccine. Otherwise, the Phase I smallpox vaccination program would likely fail. However, for reasons discussed below, Congress cobbled together Phase I's liability and compensation program over the course of several months during the implementation of Phase I. Even when Congress completed the package, it was insufficient to attract vaccines and/or providers to the Phase I program.

Initially, the Phase I smallpox vaccination program relied upon Section 304 of the Homeland Security Act of 2002 (passed in November 2002) as its vehicle for providing liability protection and compensation to injured vaccinees. However, the liability protection afforded was ambiguous and the compensation available to those injured was inadequate.

With regards to liability, Section 304 provided protection to manufacturers, distributors, persons authorized to administer the vaccine, or an "official, agent, or employee of a person described" in the first three categories. While this clearly gave liability protection to some, others questioned their coverage under section 304. For example, it was unclear if persons involved in activities ancillary to administering the vaccine, such as infection control or contraindication screening, were covered under section 304's liability provisions. As a result, the entire purpose of Section 304—ensuring that those involved with making, distributing, and administering the smallpox vaccine to first responders were protected from liability was unclear to key players, and it clearly hindered the preemptive vaccination effort.

. . . .

With regards to compensation, Section 304 failed to provide an adequate scheme for those injured by the vaccine. In fact, unlike the Swine Flu Act or NCVICA, Congress did not create an administrative no fault system to remedy injuries and deaths occasioned by the smallpox vaccine. Assuming that a party had coverage under section 304, the United States would insert itself in place of the defendant in lawsuits against covered parties, and would assume liability for negligent conduct only that caused injury or death to a smallpox vaccine recipient. Therefore, a person injured by a properly manufactured and distributed vaccine, which was properly prepared and administered, would not receive compensation under Section 304, even though the vaccine has inherent side effects of varying severity, including death. As a result, parties injured by a smallpox vaccination under Phase I had little likelihood of recovering under Section 304. . . .

It was not until April 2003—three months after Phase I began—that Congress passed a law, the Smallpox Emergency Personnel Protection Act of 2003 [hereinafter SEPPA], to improve upon the compensation provisions of Section 304. Specifically, SEPPA aimed to "provide benefits and other compensation for certain individuals with injuries resulting from administration of smallpox countermeasures." Like the Swine Flu Act and NCVICA, SEPPA created a no fault compensation program for vaccinees injured or killed by the smallpox vaccine. SEPPA supplied medical benefits, death benefits, and lost income benefits for covered injuries, resulting from countermeasures administered to those volunteering before a confirmed active case of smallpox is discovered anywhere in the world.

However, there are limits to SEPPA's compensation. For example, like NCVICA, SEPPA's benefits are also secondary to all other sources of compensation and, the sections of SEPPA limiting lost employment and death benefits are worded identically, differing only in reference to the benefit they limited. In addition, SEPPA imposed caps on those awards, caps which are more stringent than previous federal vaccine compensation and liability laws. In particular, SEPPA limited compensation for lost employment income to 2/3 of the vaccinee's income, providing an additional 8.3% of their income if the person had one or more dependants, while NCVICA allowed lost income awards equivalent to "actual and anticipated loss of earnings." SEPPA further limited lost income awards to a maximum of $50,000 per year and a lifetime total of $262,000 if injuries were not permanently disabling. Finally, lost income benefits ceased to be payable if the injured person died and the survivors collected SEPPA's death benefits. These death benefits were limited to a lump sum of $262,100 or a maximum annual payment of $50,000 until the deceased's youngest dependant reached 18 years of age.

. . . .

Ultimately, the liability protection offered to vaccine providers and the compensation available to first responders were the major inhibitors to the program's success. Even SEPPA's no fault compensation package and added liability protections were not enough to invigorate the federal Phase I vaccination program. As of July 31, 2004 (the most recent data available online as of this writing), only 39,584 first responders have been vaccinated—far short of the government's goal of 500,000. . . .

D.   The Support Anti-terrorism by Fostering Effective Technologies Act

Cognizant of SEPPA's shortcomings, some experts are belatedly suggesting that the solution to the dilemma of vaccine liability protection and compensation lies in the Support Anti-terrorism by Fostering Effective Technologies Act [hereinafter SAFETY Act]. The SAFETY Act was passed by Congress in November of 2002 (as part of the Homeland Security Act of 2002) as a response to the growing concern of liability protection for technologies developed to combat terrorism. Through passage of the Act, Congress aimed to ensure that the threat of liability would not discourage potential development of technologies that could significantly reduce the risks or mitigate the effects of large-scale acts of terrorism.

However, the SAFETY Act is not an attractive option for a biodefense vaccine liability and compensation scheme due to the following three reasons. First, as its legislative history illustrates, the Act was not drafted with biodefense vaccines in mind. Rather, the purpose of the Act was to encourage the development of anti-terrorism hardware such as computer systems, explosion detection services, and audio/video identifiers. Accordingly, the drafters gave little if any thought to the issue of injury compensation because, unlike biodefense vaccines, those technologies lacked intimate contact with people. Second, even if the SAFETY Act were applicable to biodefense vaccines, the Act's procedural and insurance requirements are overly burdensome. In fact, the entire basis of liability protection in the vaccine context hinges upon the provider's ability to obtain private insurance, which is virtually impossible. Thus, it would be extremely difficult to obtain protection for pre-event biodefense vaccination programs under the Act. Third, even if the procedural and insurance requirements are satisfied, the level of liability protection available under the Act is far too broad and provided at the expense of those injured by the vaccine....

While several factors have contributed to the federal Phase I [smallpox] vaccination program's collapse, the ... most significant reason is the ineffective liability and compensation scheme created by Congress....

Beginning with the Swine Flu Act of 1976 and continuing with NCVICA in 1986, it is clear that vaccine manufacturers (and others in the chain of distribution) demand liability protection from the federal government in the absence of insurance coverage. Congress largely gave manufacturers and distributors the needed liability protection. However, as the failure of Section 304 demonstrated, it is crucial to define the scope of coverage unambiguously....

Unambiguous liability protection certainly will be more important in future pre-event biodefense vaccination programs because the vaccine's risks may be relatively unknown. In contrast, the efficacy, side-effects, and contraindications of the smallpox vaccine were well documented (with the exception of the cases of myocarditis and periocarditis allegedly linked to the smallpox vaccine), and parties could estimate fairly well the number of injuries. However, we will not know exactly how well a vaccine performs until a vaccinated human is exposed to a certain agent. It is unethical for researchers to intentionally expose humans to diseases such as smallpox that do not exist in nature. Accordingly, the effectiveness of a vaccine can only truly be determined for diseases that are naturally occurring, such as Ebola, by vaccinating persons likely to come in contact with the disease. But, as a result, claims will inevitably arise that allege the vaccine did not provide a suitable level of protection. Furthermore, side-effects that did not present themselves during testing may become apparent during a vaccination program, such as the emergence of Guillian–Barre syndrome frequently associated with the swine flu vaccine....

In terms of a liability regime's procedure in a pre-event context, the government should insert itself as the defendant in any claim, so that manufacturers, distributors, and administrators need not be directly involved in litigating claims. Liability, as well as compensation, should be handled exclusively in an administrative hearing process, much like that of the NCVICA. This would reduce the risk of litigation to vaccine administrators and provide vaccines with a greater guarantee of compensation in the event that they are injured by the vaccination. Both of these suggestions would sharply curtail the transactional costs associated with litigating claims. Finally, unlike what transpired in the Phase I smallpox program, a full liability and compensation scheme should be in place *before* any "preemptive" vaccination program begins.

... The Phase I smallpox vaccination program taught us an important lesson that without adequate compensation, it will be difficult to attract volunteer vaccinees. Indeed, days before President Bush formally announced the Phase I vaccination program, Service Employees International Union (SEIU), America's largest health care worker union, demanded that a "simple and fair compensation system—like [NCVICA]—should be made available to assist anyone who is injured from receiving the vaccine or coming into contact with someone who received it." The compensation package offered by Section 304 failed to successfully encourage first responders to volunteer for vaccination. Furthermore, even SEPPA's improved compensation scheme did little to increase participation in the program. In particular, the limits and caps SEPPA placed on awards were more stringent than the previous federal vaccination programs, and thus less attractive to first responders.

Compensation should also restore an injured vaccinee to their [sic] position before being harmed. As mentioned above, SEPPA generally offered benefits that were less generous than either NCVICA or the Swine Flu Immunization Program. . . .

E.   BLOOD AND BLOOD PRODUCTS

1.   REGULATORY JURISDICTION

Before 1970 the Biologics Act did not expressly cover blood products. Two earlier cases had produced conflicting answers to the question of whether blood products are "biological products." In *United States v. Steinschreiber*, 219 F. Supp. 373 (S.D.N.Y.1963), *aff'd per curiam*, 326 F.2d 759 (2d Cir.1964), the court held that human blood plasma is analogous to a therapeutic serum and is thus properly regulated under the Biologics Act. The court also concluded that processing and drying liquid blood constituted sufficient steps in the "manufacture" or "preparation" of the final product to subject those activities to the Act. *See also* 218 F. Supp. 426 (S.D.N.Y.1962) (same case). But *Blank v. United States*, 400 F.2d 302 (5th Cir.1968), held that citrated whole blood (human) and packed red blood cells (human) were not analogous to a therapeutic serum. The court concluded that only immunological agents were covered by the Biologics Act. However, it sustained the defendant's conviction under the FD&C Act for interstate shipment of a misbranded drug. Following the Fifth Circuit's ruling, Congress amended the Biologics Act specifically to include blood and blood components or derivatives. 84 Stat. 1297, 1308 (1970).

2.   THE REGULATORY MECHANISM

Blood and processed blood derivatives, such as plasma and clotting factors, are licensed biological products under the PHS Act. Prior to 1997 the statute prescribed two levels of licensure for blood products, as for other biologics. A processor—such as a blood bank—required an establishment license from FDA confirming that its facilities and procedures could produce products that, in the statute's words, were "safe, pure, and potent." However, it also needed a license for each product that it manufactured or distributed, specifying requirements designed to assure satisfaction of that statutory standard. (Now, pursuant to the FDA Modernization Act's directive to combine product and establishment licenses, a distributor of a blood product need only a product license, but this requires proof that its facilities are equipped to produce a compliant product.) While some biologics product licenses were proprietary, like an NDA, others could be—

and for blood products typically are—generic. Numerous establishments can hold essentially identical licenses for the same generic product, such as "source plasma, human."

The reason why licenses for similar blood products are essentially identical should be obvious. Distributors all draw upon the same source of supply—donated or in some circumstances purchased whole human blood or blood fractions. In this respect blood is more like a commodity than a proprietary product. To be sure, all units of whole blood are not identical, as is demonstrated by the division of blood into different types—A, AB, B, and O, each in two forms, – and +. But within these categories units of whole blood are essentially interchangeable.

The primary goals of blood regulation are easy to state but hard to achieve. For most blood products, clinical utility is established by long clinical experience; safety is the central concern. And the task for regulators is to assure that source material does not transmit disease infecting the donor and to enforce measures that prevent it from being contaminated in the distribution process. Thus, much of the regulatory effort is focused on the screening and testing of donors and tracking the distribution of individual units.

A relatively small share of blood is used in the form in which it was collected, *i.e.*, as single units transfused into individual patients. Here the risk of disease transmission is confined; only the recipient of a contaminated unit of blood is potentially vulnerable. But most blood is fractionated, pooled, and processed to yield a variety of useful products. Thus factor H, a product used to stimulate clotting in hemophiliacs, is produced in batches that combine several thousand individual donations. If only one donor to the pool has a transmissible disease, the population at risk is multiplied several fold.

A unique concern for blood regulators is potential scarcity of source material. The United States is nearly self-sufficient when it comes to blood; less than 3 percent of total annual usage comes from foreign sources. This margin between need and supply, however, is not evenly spread across the country or during the calendar year. During bad weather, for example, donations typically decline while demand for blood rises. Thus, regulators are sometimes faced with circumstances in which measures to prevent life-threatening disease may threaten the supply of life-sustaining material.

United States General Accounting Office, Blood Supply: FDA Oversight and Remaining Issues of Safety

February 1997.

... The Commissioner of the Food and Drug Administration, the agency that has main responsibility for regulating the safety of blood products, described "five layers of safety" that were present throughout the blood industry to help ensure safe blood:

1. screening donors,

2. maintaining donor deferral registries to eliminate unsuitable donors from the rolls,

3. testing blood,

4. quarantining blood until tests and control procedures establish its safety, and

5. monitoring and investigating adverse incidents to ensure that deficiencies are corrected.

. . . .

About 8 million volunteers donate approximately 14 million units of whole blood each year. This whole blood is rarely transfused into patients. Instead, blood services in the blood industry separate each unit of whole blood into an average of 1.8 specialized components that, in blood-banking terminology, are "products" consisting of various types of blood cells, plasma, and special preparations of plasma. Health care facilities transfuse the resulting 23 million components—4 to 5 units at a time, on average—into as many as 4 million patients to treat specific conditions such as anemia and hemophilia. Donors give an additional 12 million units of plasma each year, for a total of approximately 26 million annual blood donations.

. . . .

In addition to separating blood into component products, plasma facilities manufacture "derivative products" by fractioning plasma chemically into concentrated proteins. These include albumin, used to treat shock; immune globulin, used to prevent certain infectious diseases and to treat deficiencies of protein; clotting factor concentrates, used to control bleeding in patients with clotting factor deficiencies; and specific immune globulins, prepared from plasmas collected from donors with antibodies to specific diseases and then used to prevent those diseases in others. Derivatives are commonly made by commercial manufacturers. Depending on the product, they may pool plasma from as many as 60,000 donors for fractionation in order to produce sufficient amounts of the final concentrated material cost-effectively. These therapies processed from plasma also undergo viral and bacterial removal and inactivation procedures that are effective in destroying most of these agents.

The blood services industry has a volunteer and a commercial sector. Voluntary donors are unpaid and usually donate whole blood. Commercial facilities collect plasma from paid donors for manufacturing various derivatives. Table 1.1 outlines the different types of blood collection services and the amount of blood they collect annually.

Type of facility	Volunteer sector		Commercial sector[a]
	Licensed	Unlicensed	Plasma center
Number of facilities	308	2,274	463
Number of units collected	12.6	1.4	12

[a]All plasma centers are licensed

The three types of facilities in the volunteer section are (1) regional and community blood centers, which usually collect and distribute blood and blood components to hospitals within circumscribed geographical areas; (2) hospital blood facilities, which collect and transfuse whole blood and blood components; and (3) hospitals, which primarily store and transfuse blood but do not collect it.

. . . .

The volunteer sector is represented by three organizations: the American Association of Blood Banks (AABB), the American Red Cross (ARC), and America's Blood Centers (ABC), formerly known as the Council of Community Blood Centers (CCBC). ABC member centers collect approximately 45 percent of all blood, ARC collects another 45 percent, and independent facilities collect the remaining 10 percent. The members of the AABB include both ARC and the majority of ABC member centers.

AABB is the professional society of blood facilities and transfusion services and it also includes individual members such as physicians, scientists, nurses, and administrators, among others. ABC is a council of community based blood-collection facilities. ARC is a single corporation consisting of all ARC blood centers. Until 1994, ARC served as an organizational framework for its centers, each operating somewhat independently and self-sufficiently. In an organizational change that began in 1994 and was completed in 1995, ARC centralized and standardized its operations, reducing the number of regions and limiting testing to a few centralized laboratories.

The commercial sector, which is generally called the "source plasma sector" and receives plasma from paid donors, has three main components: (1) collectors, or plasmapheresis centers; (2) fractionators; and (3) brokers. (Brokers do not collect source plasma.) The plasmapheresis centers collect plasma that they either sell to U.S. fractionators (who manufacture derivatives such as albumin from it) or export to fractionators in Europe, Japan, and South America. . . .

Plasma brokers purchase and market recovered plasma from whole-blood facilities (that is, the volunteer section) and sell this directly to fractionators. Plasma is "recovered" after components have been removed from whole blood or after whole blood has become outdated.

. . . .

The five layers of safety are designed to overlap so that they will prevent the distribution of contaminated blood and blood products. . . .

The first layer is designed to prevent the donation of blood by persons who have known risk factors or other conditions such as low blood pressure. High-risk donors, those whose blood may pose a health hazard, are encouraged to exclude themselves. Everyone who seeks to donate blood must answer a series of behavioral and medical questions. If the answers indicate high risk, the prospective donor is deferred. These requirements are completed before the donor is allowed to give blood. If the questions are answered truthfully, they isolate about 90 percent of all persons whose risk of having HIV is too recent for their bodies to have produced sufficient antibodies or antigen to be detected by viral screening tests.

The safeguard of this layer is the constant updating of lists, known as "donor deferral registries," of unsuitable donors and the checking of names of donors with the names in the donor deferral registry to prevent blood being used from donors previously determined to be unsuitable. Individuals who were entered into a deferral registry are those who were found not to meet donor suitability requirements during screening or who have had a positive test for any of the diseases checked at a previous donation. Services that collect blood must check the donor deferral registry for each donor, and if they find a donor listed, they do not distribute that person's blood. The deferral registry includes the names of donors who have donated in the past 8 weeks and are, thus, ineligible to donate until this 8–week period has expired. The deferral registry may be checked either before or after blood is donated.

After a donor's blood has been drawn in a donation, it is tested for an ABO group and Rh type. Additionally, viral testing, the third safety layer, and perhaps the most widely recognized layer, may be the most critical link in protecting the public from the risk of receiving contaminated blood transfusions. Screening tests are performed for hepatitis B surface antigen (HBsAg), hepatitis B core (HBc), hepatitis C (HCV), human immunodeficiency virus (antibody for HIV–1 and HIV–2 and antigen for HIV–1), human T-lymphotropic virus type I (HTLV–I), and syphilis.[3]

Blood facilities also notify the consignee (the facility that receives the product) if the product is from a donor who may have been in the "window period" at the time of his or her last donation—that is, repeat donors who subsequently test positive for HIV.[4] Even though the previous donations may have met all test requirements at the time of donation, recipients of blood from such donors may need to be tested to determine whether a disease has been transmitted to them. Additionally, consignees may be notified if they have received blood from donors who subsequent to their donation disclose historical information that would have compromised their eligibility as donors.

Two tests—one for alanine aminotransferase (ALT) and one for hepatitis B core—(HBc)—were introduced as "markers" for the major viruses noted above. That is, donors with elevated ALT counts or those found to be positive for Hbc have, at times, been found positive for viruses such as HCV and HIV. These two tests were introduced when more specific tests for hepatitis C and HIV had not yet been developed. A positive result on the syphilis test is considered by some to be a surrogate marker for high-risk behavior, since it may be a sign of behavior that increases the risk of infection from HIV. However, more specific tests for hepatitis C have since been developed, and a 1995 National Institutes of Health (NIH) consensus

3. HIV antibody tests detect antibodies that the human body produces as an immune response to HIV, whereas HIV antigen tests detect the actual presence of HIV. HTLV is a retrovirus that can lead to neurologic disease or adult T-cell leukemia and lymphoma. The test for human lymphotropic virus type II (HTLV–II) uses the HTLV–I test, although the HTLV–I test is not specific for HTLV–II, it is the closest test now available for this virus

4. The window period is the time from infectivity to the point at which currently licensed test kits can ascertain antibodies or antigens to certain viruses tested for by blood facilities.

development conference recommended discontinuing the use of ALT as a surrogate. AABB also recommended that the ALT test be dropped for donated blood, and FDA has stated that it will not object if it is dropped.

. . . .

The fourth safety layer that FDA enforces is the quarantine of all donated blood until tests and other controls have established its safety. This means that blood units cannot be used, except in emergencies, until all the requirements of the three preceding layers have been satisfied. At the fourth layer, blood facilities maintain separate storage for untested units of blood and for units that are suitable and units that are unsuitable for use. "Autologous" units are also stored separately from "allogeneic" units. . . . Autologous donation is often made when a person plans for elective surgery.

Blood facilities are obligated to monitor and investigate errors and accidents in their procedures, to audit their systems, and to correct deficiencies. Licensed blood facilities—those that may engage in the sale, barter, or exchange of blood products across state lines—must file "error and accident reports" (EARS) with FDA in order to notify it of problems. Unlicensed blood facilities—those that do not ship blood products across state lines—are not required to report EARS to FDA but may do so voluntarily. However, unlicensed blood facilities must follow the same safety procedures as licensed facilities.

All members of the blood industry are also obligated to determine the causes of errors and accidents and to institute changes to make sure such problems do not recur. Finally, this layer includes FDA inspections of blood facilities to monitor compliance with federal requirements.

Michael Rodell, *Overview of the Regulatory Process in the Manufacture of Plasma and Plasma Derivatives*

34 FOOD DRUG COSMETIC LAW JOURNAL 208 (1979).

Each facility involved in the manufacture of biological products is inspected annually by members of the [Center for Biologics Evaluation and Research] . . . or, in the case of licensed blood banks and plasmapheresis centers, by FDA field personnel. . . .

Unless specifically exempted, samples of each lot of biological product must be submitted to the [Center], along with a signed copy of test results, prior to the distribution of the lot. . . . Upon receipt of written notification of release, the manufacturer may then distribute the lot. . . .

Another powerful control tool is the [Center's] authority to promulgate regulations and standards. Whereas regulations can cover a wide range of activities, from how a sterility or general safety test is performed to good manufacturing practices, standards are generally confined to an individual product or group of products and delineate acceptable criteria for such products. Standards may include potency and purity requirements for a product, and how to determine such parameters; they may include source material requirements; they may include required processing steps. . . .

NOTES

Following its assumption of responsibility for the Biologics Act in 1972, FDA took steps to apply several provisions of the FD&C Act to blood products:

1. *Establishment Registration and Inspection.* FDA required registration of blood establishments. The frequency of the inspection of blood establishments was changed from at least once every year to at least once every two years.

2. *Good Manufacturing Practice.* FDA promulgated regulations governing current good manufacturing practices (GMP) in the collection, processing, and storage of human blood and blood components, 40 Fed. Reg. 53532 (Nov. 18, 1975). By combining the jurisdictional and regulatory provisions of the Biologics Act and the FD&C Act, FDA brought all blood and blood products produced and used in the United States under uniform Federal requirements.

3. *Container Regulation.* Responsibility for regulation of containers for collection or processing of blood and blood components, with or without ingredients such as anticoagulant solutions, was established in 40 Fed. Reg. 33971 (Aug. 13, 1975). FDA's current regulations governing the composition and configuration of containers for blood appear at 21 C.F.R. Part 606.

4. *Adverse Reaction Reports.* Regulations requiring the submission of error and accident reports by licensed and unlicensed blood establishments appear at 21 C.F.R.606.171.

5. *Investigational Blood Products.* FDA clarified the relationship between the Biologics Act and section 505(i) of the FD&C Act insofar as they relate to investigational products in 45 Fed. Reg. 73922 (Nov. 7, 1980).

6. *FDA/HCFA Collaboration.* FDA and HCFA executed a Memorandum of Understanding, published in 45 Fed. Reg. 19316 (Mar. 25, 1980), to coordinate their inspection of blood banks and transfusion services. FDA exempted from its establishment registration requirements all transfusion services and clinical laboratories that are regulated by HCFA (now CMS) under Medicare, 45 Fed. Reg. 64601 (Sept. 30, 1980), 45 Fed. Reg. 85727 (Dec. 30, 1980). HCFA in turn adopted FDA's blood regulations, 46 Fed. Reg. 41059 (Aug. 14, 1981), to assure uniform regulation of these facilities.

3.   PROTECTING THE SAFETY OF THE BLOOD SUPPLY

Blood Donor Classification Statement, Paid or Volunteer Donor

Food and Drug Administration Compliance Policy Guide Sec. 230.150
(updated Dec. 12, 2005).

The purpose of this compliance guidance document is to update the Compliance Policy Guide of the same title issued May 7, 2002. It is based on guidance provided to industry representing the Agency's current thinking on blood donor classification statements. It does not create or confer any rights for or on any person and does not operate to bind FDA or the public. An alternative approach may be used if such approach satisfies the requirements of the applicable statutes and regulations....

BACKGROUND:

In a Federal Register notice dated January 13, 1978 (43 FR 2142), the Agency issued a final rule which required that blood and blood components intended for transfusion include a donor classification statement on the labels to indicate whether the products were collected from paid or volunteer donors. This labeling requirement appears at 21 CFR 606.121(c)(5). The regulation defines a "paid donor" as a person who receives monetary payment for a blood donation (21 CFR 606.121(c)(5)(i)). A volunteer donor is a person who does not receive monetary payment for a blood donation.

The regulation also defines certain benefits that do not constitute monetary payment. Those benefits include time off from work, membership in blood assurance programs, and cancellation of non-replacement fees, as long as the benefits are not readily convertible to cash (21 CFR 606.121(c)(5)(iii)).

The requirement that the label of blood and blood components indicate whether the product came from a volunteer or a paid donor applies only to blood and blood components intended for transfusion, such as Whole Blood, Red Blood Cells, Fresh Frozen Plasma, Platelets, and Cryoprecipitated AHF. The donor classification labeling requirement does not apply to products that will be used for further manufacturing, such as Source Plasma.

As used in this document, the term incentive means anything a donor receives for donating blood other than those items a donor would ordinarily receive during the blood donation process. For example, refreshments provided by the blood collection facility would not be considered to be a donor incentive.

POLICY:

As stated in the regulation cited above, if a donor receives monetary payment for a blood donation, all products collected during the donation at which the donor received the monetary incentive must be labeled with the "paid donor" classification statement. Monetary payment includes cash, in any amount, or items that are readily convertible to cash. The regulation does not make any distinction regarding where the payment comes from, such as the blood center or the sponsoring organization.

All monetary payments to the donor would require the blood and blood components to be labeled with a "paid donor" classification statement, regardless of the dollar value of the incentive. The nature of the population (the type of people) attracted by the incentive should not be considered in determining whether an incentive is a monetary payment. FDA considers all monetary payments to blood donors to require a "paid donor" label statement on the blood, whether or not the incentive is offered only to donors who are successful in donating or if all donors who present to donate receive the incentive.

If a monetary payment in any amount is made to a group to which the donor belongs, this would generally be considered a monetary payment to the donor. An exception to this is reimbursement to the sponsoring organization for costs directly associated with the blood drive, such as advertisement or refreshments for the donors. FDA would not consider reimbursement for costs directly associated with the blood drive to be a payment to the donor, even if the donor belongs to the sponsoring organization.

The regulation specifies benefits that would not require the "paid donor" classification statement, as long as the benefits are not readily convertible to cash. These benefits are 1) time off from work, 2) membership in blood assurance programs, and 3) cancellation of non-replacement fees. Products collected from blood donors who have received such benefits may be labeled with the "volunteer donor" classification statement.

Other incentives that would not require the "paid donor" classification are described in the preamble to the final regulation mentioned above. These include 1) lotteries or raffles, regardless of the value of the prize to be given away and 2) non-monetary rewards associated with product promotion.

. . . .

NOTE

See generally Alvin W. Drake et al., THE AMERICAN BLOOD SUPPLY (1982); R. Eckert & Edward L. Wallace, SECURING A SAFER BLOOD SUPPLY: TWO VIEWS (1985); GAO, PROBLEMS IN CARRYING OUT THE NATIONAL BLOOD POLICY, HRDB77B150 (1979); OTA, BLOOD POLICY & TECHNOLOGY, OTABHB260 (Jan. 1985). Even before the emergence of AIDS, regulation of the safety of the blood supply was a difficult challenge. *See* Dennis Donohue, *Blood and Blood Products: A Five Year Challenge?*, 36 FOOD DRUG COSM. L.J. 27 (1981), Linda M. Dorney, *Culpable Conduct With Impunity: The Blood Industry And The FDA's Responsibility For The Spread Of Aids Through Blood Products*, 3 J. PHARMACY & LAW 129, 139 (1994); Erica L. Niezgoda & Maureen M. Richardson, *Federal Food And Drug Act Violations*, 35 AM. CRIM. L. REV. 767 (1998).

———

Most readers will be familiar with some steps in the process by which blood or blood products make their way from source through processing to the ultimate recipient, but they could be surprised by the scope and details of the regulatory regime for which FDA is responsible. The agency's regulations address the earliest stages of donor recruitment and screening; the steps collecting agencies must take in the handling of whole blood and other source material; the maintenance of records and reporting of "errors and accidents;" the obligation to comply with good manufacturing practice; and the reporting of adverse events—to name only the prominent steps in the process of collection, delivery, and use.

The agency's expectations for blood collecting, processing, and distribution facilities are set forth in detailed regulations, 21 CFR Part 600 *et seq.* While it would be wrong to say that violations of FDA's elaborate requirements are common, the reality is that most of the major organizations involved in collecting, processing and distributing blood have from time to time had conflicts with FDA. According to press accounts, organizations responsible for fully 60 percent of the nation's blood supply currently are operating under judicially monitored consent decrees. The organization responsible for nearly half of all blood collected and used in the United States, the American Red Cross, has been a particular target of FDA scrutiny and enforcement. For accounts of the Red Cross's troubled relationship with FDA, *see Food and Drug Administration Recent Developments*, HOSPITAL BUSINESS WEEK, Nov. 15, 2006, p. 1298; Mark McCarty, *Red Cross Boosting IT Systems, Recruiting to Reduce FDA Snags*, MEDICAL DEVICE WEEK, Nov. 30, 2006.

As the following case illustrates, FDA has two responsibilities in the efforts to assure the safety of blood and blood products. First, as discussed above, it regulates the entities that collect, process, and distribute blood, and in that capacity ultimately determines—under the Biologics Act—what screening and testing procedures must be followed. Second, because most test methods are themselves diagnostic products subject to regulation under the Medical Device Amendments, FDA is responsible for confirming their reliability and sensitivity.

R.F. and R.F. v. Abbott Laboratories

745 A.2d 1174 (N.J. Sup. Ct. 2000).

■ GARIBALDI, J.

In September 1986, plaintiff, R.F., received a transfusion of blood incident to surgery, that was infected with the human immunodeficiency virus ("HIV"), causing her to subsequently test positive for the presence of that virus. The blood which was transfused into R.F. had been previously screened for HIV infection at the Bergen Community Blood Center ("BCBC") with the first commercially-available HIV blood screening test, manufactured by defendant, Abbott Laboratories ("Abbott")....

R.F. and her husband (collectively, "plaintiffs"), claim that the HIV blood test used by the BCBC was defective under N.J.S.A. 2A:58C–2, because its package insert failed to provide adequate instructions or warnings regarding the sensitivity limitations allegedly inherent in Abbott's test. Specifically, plaintiffs contend that in light of its knowledge that the test was not 100% sensitive, Abbott should have instructed blood banks to retest samples that were negative yet "borderline," meaning samples that had yielded results close to the test's "cutoff value." The cutoff value was a value defined by the federal Food and Drug Administration ("FDA") in the test's instructional pamphlet, to be used by blood bank technicians to measure whether the HIV antibody was present in a donated blood sample.

... The primary issue presented in this appeal is whether federal regulation of Abbott's HIV blood screening test preempts plaintiffs' cause of action for defective design and failure to warn....

As the agency responsible for the safety of the blood supply, the FDA took action quickly to contain the AIDS epidemic by seeking help from both public and private sources. Initially, the FDA turned to the National Cancer Institute ("NCI"), where in May 1984, Dr. Robert Gallo had published the first description of a screening test that could detect the HIV infection in blood samples. Dr. Gallo's prototype screening test was an "ELISA" or "EIA" test, a generic term that describes "Enzyme Linked Immunoabsorbant Assays." ELISA tests, which had been used for the detection of other blood-borne viruses such as hepatitis, function by detecting the body's immune response (or antibodies) to a virus or its antigen components, rather than the virus itself. . . . The prototype was approximately 85% effective in detecting infected samples. The government applied for, and ultimately received, a patent for Dr. Gallo's HIV ELISA test.

On May 3, 1984, soon after Dr. Gallo's publication, the United States government published a solicitation in the Federal Register ("Notice") seeking private manufacturers who could further develop, manufacture, and mass-distribute Dr. Gallo's prototype HIV screening test to the nation's blood banks. . . .

On May 9, 1984, Abbott filed a response to the Notice demonstrating its capacity to develop and manufacture Dr. Gallo's prototype. . . .

Four other manufacturers also were selected to develop Dr. Gallo's prototype. . . .

Although the FDA considered the blood screening test as a "device" under the Medical Device Amendments of 1976, the development, manufacturing, and field performance of the HIV test, was overseen by the FDA's Office of Biologics Research and Review ("OBRR"). That is consistent with the FDA's 1982 designation of the Bureau of Biologics as "the lead Bureau for regulating certain medical devices used in the processing or administration of biological products," such as the test kit. Therefore, although the test kit was largely regulated by the OBRR as a biologic (because the virus was the main component of the test) the OBRR required that the test be listed as a medical device, and its package insert drafted pursuant to Labeling for In Vitro Diagnostic Products, 21 C.F.R. § 809.10(b) (1985), a medical device regulation.

. . . During December 1984, Abbott conducted clinical trials of its proposed assay that included approximately 10,000 random donors, including a sample group of AIDS and ARC patients (ARC patients are infected with the virus yet do not exhibit the symptoms of full-blown AIDS). The results of the trials using AIDS and ARC patients showed that the test was 98.3% effective in detecting the antibody in AIDS patients, and 65% effective in detecting the antibody in ARC patients. In addition, the FDA collected 30,000 samples from across the United States, distributing 6,000 samples to each of the five manufacturers developing Dr. Gallo's prototype. . . .

On December 19, 1984, Abbott sent all of its clinical data to Dr. Esber, Director of the OBRR Center for Drugs & Biologics, with the product license application for the proposed test. . . .

As part of the product license application, Abbott submitted a draft of the test's package insert. In the December 19, 1984 draft, Abbott suggested that the package insert state: *"Specimens with absorbance values within a plus or minus 10% range of the Cutoff Value should be retested to confirm the initial results."* (emphasis added). However, in their January 29, 1985 response, . . . the FDA "mandated that [this provision] be deleted." Dr. Heller testified that the FDA decided not to instruct blood banks to retest "borderline" negative samples because: (1) there was no scientific basis for the belief that samples close to the borderline were more likely to be false-negative than negative samples with results well-below the cutoff; and (2) such a provision would effectively redefine the cutoff to the lower value for which there would be associated a new set of "borderline samples."

Dr. Heller testified that in defining the test's cutoff value, the FDA "specifically indicated [to Abbott] that they had reentered all of the raw data and redid the statistical analysis to determine that the cutoff was in the appropriate place." During this process, the FDA and Abbott balanced the goal of maximized sensitivity with the problem of having an abundance of false-positive results. The appearance of false-positive results was a major concern throughout the development of the First and Second Generation Tests, since false-positive results not only caused a blood bank to destroy that particular sample, but also disqualified the donor from future blood donations, thereby further limiting the qualified source of donated blood.

The FDA's active role in setting the test's cutoff was confirmed by [the agency's] Dr. Meyer who testified that, although Abbott contributed to the discussion, the FDA ultimately determined the appropriate cutoff value. . . .

. . . [T]he FDA essentially authored three critical sections of the test's package insert entitled: "INTERPRETATION OF RESULTS," "LIMITATIONS OF PROCEDURE," and "SENSITIVITY AND SPECIFICITY." Those sections appeared in identical form in each of the five manufacturers' package inserts; none of them mentioned "borderlines," and none of them instructed users to retest initially negative samples. . . .

Both the LIMITATIONS OF PROCEDURE and the SENSITIVITY AND SPECIFICITY sections indicated that the Test was not 100% sensitive in detecting the HIV antibody in truly infected blood samples. Specifically, the LIMITATIONS OF PROCEDURE section states in part: "*A negative test result does not exclude the possibility of exposure to or infection with HTLV III*" (emphasis supplied). Similarly, the SENSITIVITY AND SPECIFICITY section sets forth a textual explanation of Abbott's clinical trials which revealed:

1. Sensitivity based on an assumed 100% prevalence of HTLV III antibody in AIDS patients is estimated to be 98.3%.

2. Specificity based on an assumed zero prevalence of HTLV III antibody in random donors is estimated to be 99.8%.

. . . .

On March 1, 1985, after the package insert was completed, the OBRR issued a license that "authorized Abbott to manufacture and sell in interstate and foreign commerce HTLV III in an in vitro ELISA test," hereinafter referred to as the "Test" or the "First Generation Test." . . .

In addition, the FDA's letter accompanying the license specifically indicated that if Abbott sought to amend the labeling or package insert of the Test, "it would be necessary . . . to submit an amendment to either [the] product or establishment license application for review and approval prior to implementation." Moreover, the Test's labeling was subject to a similar promulgated FDA regulation for biologics. . . .

As indicated by its drafting of the package insert warnings, the FDA was aware of the limitations of Abbott's First Generation Test (and ELISA tests in general) at the time of its development. Specifically, the FDA understood that since all ELISA tests detected the presence of antibodies to virus, and not the presence of viruses themselves, the tests were by design subject to a "window period" during which an infected individual does not have detectable levels of antibodies, causing the test to produce false-negative results. That "window period" is the length of time required for the body to produce enough antibodies to be detected. In 1985–86, the scientific community could not predict precisely how long the window period was for HIV. The FDA understood that it was possible that there were individuals infected with the HIV virus who had not yet produced HIV antibodies and, therefore, could donate infected blood (fully-capable of spreading the disease) that could not be screened by any of the manufacturers' ELISA tests.

Accordingly, prior to the introduction of the Test onto the market, the FDA conducted a mass-mailing campaign to blood banks and physicians regarding the use and limitations of the first HIV blood screening tests.... The FDA's memorandum, summarizing an attached copy of the CDC's January 11, 1985 newsletter, explicitly described the limitations of the tests as follows:

> ... [A] negative antibody test result does not necessarily mean that one is free from virus. Antibody may not have developed, or be undetectable, if infection was recent. There is at least one report that 4 of 96 individuals carried the virus for 6 months without developing detectable antibodies.

Soon thereafter, the FDA sent out a similar "Dear Doctor" letter to all licensed physicians in the United States, including R.F.'s physician, expressly warning of the above limitations.[9]

. . . .

In this case, both (1) the FDA's exercise of control and initiative over the Test's development, packaging, and field performance monitoring, and (2) the unique circumstances under which the Test arose (a national health crisis surrounding the emergence of the AIDS epidemic and the loss of a safe national blood supply), give rise to implied preemption of the plaintiffs' state law claims under each of the three categories of implied preemption.

... It is undisputed that: (1) the FDA took an active role in, and then later scrutinized, the development and clinical trials of Abbott's proposed HIV blood test; (2) the FDA dictated the Test's warning labels, and explicitly rejected the additional warnings and instructions regarding borderline negative samples that the plaintiffs claim were required by state

---

9. However, in spite of its limitations, the ELISA blood screening tests were effective. A paper published in the journal *Transfusion* in 1993 shows that in 1984, prior to the use of the ELISA tests, there were 714 new cases of AIDS caused by transfusion. However, after the first full year of the use of the ELISA test (1986), the number of AIDS cases associated with transfusion dropped to below 20 per year. *See* R.M. Selik, et al., *Trends in Transfusion–Associated Acquired Immunodeficiency Syndrome in the United States, 1982–1991*, Transfusion, Vol. 33, No. 11 (1993).

law; (3) the FDA continued to closely monitor the Test's field performance both through information received from Abbott, and information received directly from the nation's blood banks and scientific publications; (4) based on that information, the FDA believed throughout the relevant time period (1985–86) that the Test's field performance was consistent with the FDA's expectations and also with the warnings, limitations, and clinical results published in the Test's package insert; and (5) Abbott's product license, and 21 C.F.R. § 601.12, specifically prohibited it from unilaterally altering the Test's package insert or disseminating additional warnings through "Dear Doctor" letters or otherwise.

. . . .

First, the extensive control and continuous scrutiny of the Test by the FDA was so pervasive as to make reasonable the inference "that [the FDA] left no room for the states to supplement it." Secondly, requiring blood banks to retest the "borderline" samples, and to warn that borderline results were inherently dangerous, would have been in direct conflict with the specific mandates of the FDA. The FDA dealt directly with the issue of how to define the cutoff, and concluded that false-negative results were not clustered around the cutoff, but were randomly spread over the entire scale of negative results. Additionally, the FDA did not only scrutinize the language required in the package insert warning, but also in large part, dictated the wording of the insert. Moreover, the FDA's regulations and its specific mandates restricted Abbott's ability to amend the package insert.

The plaintiffs' state law cause of action based on a claim of inadequate warnings, where those warnings are dictated by the FDA, is "inconsistent" with federal regulation, and is therefore preempted. . . .

■ STEIN, J., dissenting.

. . . .

The Court's opinion, which meticulously recites the facts concerning the FDA's supervisory role in reviewing the Abbott blood test prior to licensing in March 1985, attempts to diminish the significance of the trial testimony elicited by plaintiffs to demonstrate that after licensure, and specifically between September 1985 and July 1986,—the crucial period before plaintiff's transfusion—Abbott acquired information suggesting that its test frequently failed to detect blood that was confirmed to be HIV positive, and that in two scientific studies its test was shown to be substantially less capable of detecting HIV positive blood than were the blood tests of its primary competitors.

. . . Although the Court's opinion attempts to justify federal preemption not on the basis of Congressional action but rather on the basis of a national health emergency concerning a safe blood supply, experience informs us that Congress knows how to mandate federal preemption in the context of a national health emergency. . . .

Second, the Court either overlooks or disregards that the plaintiffs' focus is not on the FDA's regulation prior to licensure, but on Abbott's after-acquired knowledge in the summer of 1986 that its test's tendency to record false negatives around the cutoff required prompt remediation. The record demonstrates that during this post-licensure period Abbott was concerned about its test, not only because of safety concerns, but because the blood tests of competitors appeared, according to some research reports, to be more sensitive in detecting HIV contaminated blood. Abbott knew enough about its test's deficiencies to propose to the FDA in July 1986 a modified test that "would be better able to detect positive samples that were 'borderline or negative' by the First Generation Test." . . .

———

The New Jersey Supreme Court's opinion reveals the technical complexity of testing for the presence of pathogens in blood (and indirectly for the presence of disease in donors). It took several years and much effort for testing to move beyond the search for antibodies to the detection of the HIV virus itself. And complicating this essentially scientific inquiry is the realization that improvement in the test methodology may shrink the available supply of blood. This gloomy possibility is at the heart of Justice Stewart Pollock's opinion in the next case. His opinion reveals how many institutions and personalities have roles in the deliberations by which the several "architects" of U.S. blood policy arrive at decisions.

Snyder v. American Association of Blood Banks

676 A.2d 1036 (N.J. Sup. Ct. 1996).

■ The opinion of the Court was delivered by Pollock, J.

Plaintiff William Snyder contracted Acquired Immune Deficiency Syndrome (AIDS) from a transfusion of blood that the Bergen Community Blood Center (BCBC), a non-profit blood bank, had provided to St. Joseph's Hospital. The BCBC is a member of defendant, the American Association of Blood Banks (AABB), an association of blood banks and blood-banking professionals. . . .

I

. . . .

At the time, no direct test existed to determine whether blood was infected with Human Immunodeficiency Virus (HIV), the cause of AIDS. Other means of making that determination, however, were available. Starting in 1985, the enzyme-linked immunoabsorbent-assay-screening test (the ELISA test) enabled blood banks to screen for HIV.

Under a nation-wide "look-back" program instituted that year, blood banks could determine whether a prospective donor who tested positive for HIV had donated blood before the development of the ELISA test. As part of the "look-back" program sponsored by the AABB, BCBC ascertained in 1986 that the donor of unit 29F0784 was HIV positive. That same year BCBC so informed St. Joseph's Hospital. St. Joseph's, in turn, informed Snyder's doctor, who notified him in 1987. . . .

Ultimately, all defendants other than the AABB either settled or obtained dismissals. At the trial, the critical issue was whether the AABB had breached a duty of care to Snyder. Hence, the trial focused on the

AABB's role in the blood-banking industry and the reasonableness of its response to increasing evidence that blood or blood products could transmit AIDS.

. . . .

II

Crucial to the assessment of the AABB's alleged duty of care is its role in the blood-banking industry in 1983–84. . . .

The AABB describes itself as a "professional, non-profit, scientific and administrative association for individuals and institutions engaged in the many facets of blood and tissue banking, and transfusion and transplantation medicine." . . . In the early 1980s, the AABB centers collected about half of the nation's blood supply and transfused eighty percent of the blood to patients. Its institutional members were mainly hospitals and non-profit blood centers.

According to the AABB's executive director, Joel Solomon, the general purpose of the AABB is "to develop and recommend standards on the practice of blood banking, to help promote the public health, . . . and to conduct numerous programs for communication and education among organization members and the public at-large." The AABB discharges its educational mission by conducting workshops and seminars, and by publishing books, newsletters, pamphlets, and a peer-review journal, *Transfusion* . . . .

Significantly, the AABB annually inspects and accredits member institutions. It conditions accreditation on compliance with standards published in its *Standards for Blood Banks and Transfusion Services* and procedures outlined in its *Technical Manual*. According to the annual report, AABB standards often become FDA standards. . . .

Both the state and federal government, as well as the blood-banking industry, generally accept AABB standards as authoritative. Consequently, blood banks throughout the nation rely on those standards. . . .

In the early 1980s, the AABB led the blood industry. Dr. George F. Grady, an expert in blood-banking procedures and transfusion-related viruses, testified that the AABB had established itself as the leader in setting blood-banking standards. The AABB, moreover, was an active member of the FDA's influential Blood Products Advisory Council and advised the FDA on issues concerning the blood industry. In a recent study of the FDA's response to the threat of AIDS, the Committee to Study HIV Transmission Through Blood and Blood Products (the Committee) of the Institute of Medicine found that "in the early 1980s, the FDA appeared too reliant upon analyses provided by industry-based members of the Blood Products Advisory Council."

. . . .

At the state level, the DOH [New Jersey Department of Health], when renewing blood-bank licenses, accepted reports of AABB inspections in lieu of its own inspections. DOH also accepted AABB's standards for obtaining medical histories and conducting physical examinations of donors.

The picture that emerges is of a private, tax-exempt organization with substantial power over the operation of blood banks, including BCBC. That the blood banks would accept direction from the AABB is understandable: it was their organization. . . .

The first report of severe immune deficiency among homosexuals surfaced in 1981. In 1985, the DHHS [United States Department of Health and Human Services] approved the ELISA test. Snyder received his transfusion in 1984. Our initial inquiry is whether the BCBC should have known in 1984 that blood and blood products could carry the HIV virus. . . .

Plaintiffs presented several expert witnesses who explained the evolution of the discovery that blood and blood products could carry the AIDS virus. Dr. Donald Francis, a virologist and epidemiologist, served as director of the AIDS Task Force laboratory in the early 1980s and as assistant director of the CDC's [Centers for Disease Control] hepatitis-B effort in the 1970s. He testified that in 1982 the CDC detected a pattern in the transmission of AIDS and in the identification of the persons at risk. The pattern revealed that early homosexual AIDS patients were infecting others through sexual contact. Also apparent was an incubation period varying from several months to several years. The CDC postulated in June 1982 that the cause of the disease was an infectious agent, such as a virus.

. . . .

Dr. Ernest Simon, an expert in blood-banking and transfusion medicine, as well as the deputy director of the FDA's blood division from 1976 to 1980, also testified. He stated that during the early 1980s, "seven to ten percent of individuals who were transfused . . . would [subsequently] show evidence of liver dysfunction probably related to transmissibility of viral hepatitis." Members of the AIDS Task Force, noting the epidemiological similarity between AIDS and hepatitis B, feared that blood and blood products could carry AIDS.

. . . .

In its July 16, 1982, report in the MMWR [*Morbidity and Mortality Weekly Report*], the CDC concluded that "although the cause of [AIDS] is unknown, the occurrence among the three hemophiliac cases suggests the possible transmission of an agent through blood products." . . . Dr. Francis explained that the realization that the infectious agent was a virus that could be transmitted by blood "was a red flag and concerned us greatly about the potential for blood-borne transmission of other therapeutic blood products."

On July 27, 1982, the PHS [Public Health Service] held a national meeting of blood and blood-product collectors to discuss the threat of AIDS. At that meeting, members of the CDC Task Force reported their findings to blood-industry organizations, including the AABB.

. . . .

In November 1982, the CDC became concerned about the special risk that AIDS posed to doctors, nurses, and other hospital personnel who were exposed regularly to blood. Consequently, the CDC alerted them that "hepatitis-B virus infections occur very frequently among AIDS cases." The

CDC warned that "at present, it appears prudent for hospital personnel to use the same precautions when caring for" AIDS patients as when caring for patients with hepatitis B.

. . . .

Alarmed at the prospect of AIDS in the blood supply, the CDC called an emergency workshop in Atlanta for January 4, 1983. The purpose of the meeting was to ascertain how to prevent the transmission of AIDS through blood and blood products. Representatives of government, the AABB, the American Red Cross, the Council for Community Blood Banks, the National Hemophilia Foundation, the National Gay Task Force, and other organizations attended the meeting. The AIDS Task Force was convinced that AIDS was blood-transmissible, and that its epidemiology mirrored that of hepatitis B, "involving the same high-risk groups and in the same proportions."

. . . .

At the January 4, 1983, meeting, the AABB and other blood-banking representatives strenuously disagreed with the CDC. Dr. Joseph Bove, chairman of the AABB Committee on Transfusion Transmitted Disease, stated that he was unconvinced that blood could transmit AIDS. He argued that surrogate testing was unnecessary and that direct questioning was improper.

Dr. Francis rejoined that the AABB's response was "remarkably obstructive." He recognized the response as "basically an attempt to deny that there was a threat." The AABB nonetheless persisted in arguing that surrogate testing and direct questioning would be too costly and would lead to the rejection of too much blood. . . .

Throughout 1983, the evidence continued to mount. On March 4, 1983, the PHS reported in MMWR that "the occurrence of AIDS among IV drug users" supports a finding that "blood products or blood appear responsible for AIDS among hemophilia patients." The PHS recognized the need for, but did not recommend, surrogate testing.

A month later, the AABB issued a set of standard operating procedures that required only the distribution of AIDS educational material to donors and continued medical history screening. The AABB refused to require surrogate testing or direct questioning of donors.

That refusal ... belied internal concerns within the AABB. In December 1982, Dr. Bove wrote an internal memo indicating a growing concern that AIDS could cause "major problems in the blood collecting sector." He continued that his "current best guess is that we are dealing with an infectious agent able to be spread by blood and blood products and that individuals who receive large quantities of factor concentrate are at an increased risk."

. . . .

The plasma industry, which relies on paid donors, took a much more cautious view. Whenever a plasma donor later developed AIDS, the industry would withdraw all coagulation products made from that donor's blood.

Consistent with that approach, the FDA, in a March 24, 1983, memorandum to licensed manufacturers of plasma derivatives, prohibited use of plasma "collected from donors suspected of being at increased risk of transmitting AIDS" from being used to produce "derivatives already known to have a risk of transmitting infectious diseases," such as the clotting factors used in treating hemophilia. Thus, the memorandum evidences the decision of the federal government to exclude high-risk donors, specifically sexually-active homosexuals. Existing regulations already excluded IV drug users. In sum, the FDA's recommendation reflected its growing concern about AIDS contamination of blood and blood products.

Beginning in 1983, some blood banks began to institute surrogate testing. . . .

In July 1984, the [FDA] Blood Products Advisory Committee's Hepatitis B Core Antibody Testing Study Group (study group) reported its findings on the core test. The study group consisted of eleven members representing the FDA, plasma fractionators, and major blood-industry associations, including the AABB. The majority of the study group, including the AABB, rejected the core test. It contended that the core test would lead to the rejection of too many healthy donors, was not sufficiently specific, and cost too much. Further, the majority contended that self-screening was working. A minority recommended adoption of the core test. It asserted that self-screening was not working and urged that the core test would exclude sixty to eighty percent of high-risk donors. As a matter of policy, the minority concluded that concerns about blood safety outweighed concerns about a diminishing blood supply or excessive costs.

On April 24, 1984, Secretary Margaret Heckler of the DHHS announced that researchers had isolated the AIDS virus and had developed a blood test for AIDS. She believed that the test, now known as the ELISA test, would be available within six months. In fact, the DHHS approved the ELISA test on March 4, 1985, seven months after Snyder received his transfusion.

III

. . . .

By words and conduct, the AABB invited blood banks, hospitals, and patients to rely on the AABB's recommended procedures. The AABB set the standards for voluntary blood banks. At all relevant times, it exerted considerable influence over the practices and procedures over its member banks, including BCBC. On behalf of itself and its member banks, the AABB lobbies legislatures, participates in administrative proceedings, and works with governmental health agencies in setting blood-banking policy. In many respects, the AABB wrote the rules and set the standards for voluntary blood banks.

. . . The severity of the risk of transfusion-related AIDS is a function of the mortality rate and the infection rate. In 1984, the overall mortality rate of AIDS was forty percent, but for those who had AIDS for more than three years, the rate approached nearly 100%. The infection rate was increasing exponentially. . . . Thus, the risk that blood transfusions could transmit AIDS was severe.

The risk also was foreseeable. Epidemiologists at the CDC believed as early as 1982 that the AIDS virus could be transmitted by blood and blood products. In January 1984, Dr. Curran's article in the *New England Journal of Medicine* confirmed that belief. Thus, before Snyder received his transfusion, the AABB should have foreseen that a blood transfusion could transmit AIDS.

We are unpersuaded by the AABB's argument that because the evidence was inconclusive, it owed no duty to Snyder. The foreseeability, not the conclusiveness, of harm suffices to give rise to a duty of care. By 1983, ample evidence supported the conclusion that blood transmitted the AIDS virus. In early 1984, the AABB knew that AIDS was a rapidly spreading, fatal disease and that apparently healthy donors could infect others. The AABB also knew that blood and blood products probably could transmit AIDS and that each infected blood donor could infect many donees. Thus, the AABB knew, or should have known, in 1984 that the risk of AIDS infection from blood transfusions was devastating. We agree with the lower courts that the record establishes that the AABB owed Snyder a duty of care.

The AABB claims that considerations of public policy and fairness negate the imposition of a duty of care extending to Snyder. Specifically, the AABB contends that it should not be found liable for taking the "wrong side" of a debate involving medical uncertainties and public policy....

The AABB also alleges that the imposition of a duty contravenes the public policy of fostering open debate on health issues. It warns that imposition of such a duty would chill debate on public-health issues and impair scientific discourse. According to the AABB, the imposition of a duty of care would engender fear of liability that would result in the adoption of ill-conceived standards. Finally, the AABB contends that it did not accept the core test because of concerns about the effect that such a test would produce on the availability and cost of blood.

These concerns, however, should not have diverted the AABB from its paramount responsibility to protect the safety of the blood supply. Recognition of that responsibility should have led the AABB to consider more carefully the risks to recipients from the transfusion of infected blood. When balanced against the devastating risks from a disease such as AIDS, the imposition of a duty of care on the AABB does not, in our opinion, offend the public policy favoring open debate on controversial scientific issues.

Relevant also to the determination of the AABB's duty of care is its role in the governmental regulation of the blood-banking industry. In 1984, the AABB was more than a trade association. It was the governing body of a significantly self-regulated industry....

V

. . . .

The record reveals that the AABB led the charge against direct questioning of donors and surrogate testing. Viewed most favorably to the AABB, the evidence suggests that it was concerned that such questioning and testing would be of limited effectiveness and could diminish the supply of blood and blood products. A less favorable view suggests that the AABB resisted surrogate testing because it did not want to suffer the added inconvenience and costs of such testing. . . .

On the record, the jury could have concluded that the AABB in 1984 unreasonably resisted recognizing that blood transmits HIV. That resistance led the AABB to sacrifice an uncontaminated supply of blood for one that was contaminated, but more readily available. The jury could have found that if the AABB had not been so intransigent, its members, particularly the BCBC, would have instituted surrogate testing. Further, the jury could have found that if the BCBC had instituted surrogate testing, it would have rejected Unit 29F0784. Rejecting that unit could have prevented the transfusion of contaminated blood to William Snyder. It could have saved his health and his life. Against this background, we believe that the imposition of liability on the AABB is both fair and reasonable. . . .

[The dissenting opinion of Justice Garibaldi is omitted.]

NOTES

1. *Deciding Whether to Screen for AIDS.* The decision-making process that Justice Pollack describes was the focus of a critical report by the Institute of Medicine, which recommended major reforms. *See* INSTITUTE OF MEDICINE, HIV AND THE BLOOD SUPPLY: AN ANALYSIS OF CRISIS DECISION MAKING (1995).

2. *Umbilical Cord Blood.* Blood circulating in the placenta prior to birth and thus present in—and recoverable from—the umbilical cord following birth is a rich source of stem cells, which might later be used in the treatment of diseases displayed by the newborn or discovered as late as adulthood. In the early 1990s entrepreneurs offered recovery and long-term storage services to expectant parents as a form of insurance. Calls for regulation of this activity led FDA to assert jurisdiction, but instead of applying the requirements of the Biologics Act, the agency declared cord blood a type of human tissue transplant subject to its general plan for tissue and cellular therapies, described at p. 941 *infra*.

3. *Home Tests for HIV.* In 53 Fed. Reg. 46118 (Nov. 16, 1988), FDA made available a draft "points to consider" regarding labeling and premarket submission of in vitro diagnostic devices for use in the home, and shortly thereafter, in 54 Fed. Reg. 7279 (Feb. 17, 1989), announced an open public meeting to discuss whether FDA should approve blood collection kits and home test kits designed to detect the HIV antibody. The announcement reiterated the agency's position that none of these HIV antibody testing kits is "substantially equivalent" to any pre-1976 medical device and its policy that premarket approval would currently be granted only for professional use, subject to conditions previously announced. The public meeting was to consider whether this policy should be changed, and it provoked substantial controversy. A year later, based upon the development of new technology, FDA announced that it would begin to review applications for approval of home test kits for AIDS. *See* Gardiner Harris, *F.D.A. to Weigh At–Home Testing for AIDS Virus*, N.Y. TIMES, Oct. 13, 2005, at A1.

F. HUMAN TISSUE TRANSPLANTS

1. REGULATORY AUTHORITY

Since the 1960s, transplantation of organs (*e.g.*, heart, liver, and kidneys) and other human tissues (*e.g.*, skin, bone, semen) has become common. *See, e.g.,* the widely reported surgical repair of the knee of Cincinnati Bengals' quarterback Carson Palmer with the Achilles tendon of a deceased victim of an automobile accident. N.Y. Times, Aug. 9, 2006, at D2. However, regulatory oversight of cadaver tissues has lagged behind their medical use. In 1983 FDA was asked by Congress to address its authority under existing law to oversee whole organ transplantation. In the following statement unnamed FDA officials tried to explain why the agency had not asserted jurisdiction over these products.

Statement by the Food and Drug Administration Concerning its Legal Authority to Regulate Human Organ Transplants and to Prohibit Their Sale

Submitted to the Subcommittee on Investigations and Oversight, House Committee on Science and Technology, 98th Congress,1st Session (1983).

... The Food and Drug Administration has never had occasion formally to address the issue of its authority to regulate the sale of human organs. This statement constitutes the FDA's first examination of that issue.

The Federal Food, Drug, and Cosmetic Act defines the term "drug" in part as "articles intended for use in the diagnosis, cure mitigation, treatment, or prevention of disease in man ...", and "articles (other than food) intended to affect the structure or any function of the body of man...."

A human organ intended for use in transplantation arguably could be regulated as a drug because it falls within the literal language of these provisions. Although Congress could not have had human organ transplants in mind when it defined the term "drug" in 1938, the case law suggests that the definition is not limited to the types of substances used as drugs prior to 1938....

Although the case law has interpreted the term "drug" very broadly, no court has held that a human organ intended for use in transplantation is a drug. Such an interpretation, while arguably supportable, would extend the legal definition well beyond the traditional medical concept of the term "drug." The unprecedented nature of this interpretation necessarily means that considerable uncertainty would be associated with a conclusion by FDA that the definition of the term "drug" includes human organ transplants. Adding to this uncertainty is FDA's current administrative interpretation of the term "drug," which cannot be read to include human organs. That interpretation states: "[a] drug ... is a chemical or a combination of chemicals in liquid, paste, powder, or other drug dosage form that is ingested, or instilled into body orifices, or rubbed or poured onto the body in order to achieve its intended medical purpose." 47 FR 46139. Although this administrative interpretation would not be conclusive, it would be given deference by a reviewing court.

Section 201(h) of the FDC Act, as amended by the Medical Device Amendments of 1976, defines the term "device" as "an instrument, apparatus, implement, machine, contrivance, implant, in vitro reagent, or other similar or related article ... which is ... intended for use in the diagnosis of disease or other conditions, or in the cure, mitigation, treatment, or prevention of disease" or which is "intended to affect the structure or any function of the body," *and* "which does not achieve any of its principal intended purposes through chemical action within or on the body" or by "being metabolized." 21 U.S.C. 321(h). A human organ transplant could be regarded as within the literal language of the statute, for a transplanted organ is a type of "implant."

On the other hand, the definition's list of things that are "devices"— "instrument, apparatus, implement, machine, contrivance, implant, in vitro reagent"—implies that Congress understood the term "device" to refer to the product of human artifice. Except for implants and in vitro reagents, the items in the list are man-made products that generally are constructed of materials such as metal or plastic. Although some devices regulated by FDA consist in part of organic material, the material is usually either a part of a man-made device, or it is treated to make it useful for its intended purpose rather than simply being substituted for its equivalent material in the human body. In vitro reagents often use organic material, but as part of a system designed to diagnose diseases or conditions. There are many man-made devices that are "implants." Cardiac pacemakers, artificial joints, and intraocular plastic lenses fall into this category. The legislative intent underlying the definition of "device" is, therefore, probably limited to artificial implants. This view is consistent with the principle of statutory construction that a word is known by the company it keeps (*noscitur a sociis*).

. . . .

The Public Health Service Act, 42 U.S.C. 262, *et seq.*, authorizes the licensure of a class of products that has come to be known as "biological products." Although the term is undefined, the Act includes the following as subject to licensure: ". . . any virus, therapeutic serum, toxin, antitoxin, vaccine, blood, blood component or derivative, allergenic product, or analogous product . . . applicable to the prevention, treatment, or cure of diseases or injuries of man. . . ."

Whether a human organ transplant is a biological product depends on whether solid organs, such as the heart, liver, or kidneys, are "analogous" to blood or blood derivatives. If the term "analogous" is interpreted in its broadest sense, FDA arguably could regulate human organ transplants as biological products. Blood is essentially a liquid organ. Blood performs vital functions comparable to the functions performed by solid organs. Blood is composed of tissue cells, which are similar but not identical to the tissue cells of solid organs.

The legislative history of the PHS Act suggests, however, that a narrower interpretation of the term "analogous" would be more in keeping with the legislative design for the regulation of "biological products." The predecessor of the PHS Act, the Viruses, Serums, and Toxins Act of 1902 ("VSTA"), defined a biological product as "any virus, therapeutic serum, toxin, antitoxin, or analogous product." In 1970, Congress amended the VSTA by adding to the definition the terms "blood" and "blood component or derivative." The legislative history of the 1970 amendment states that Congress added these terms because ". . . the products and processes involved in blood transfusions were not known in 1902 when the "Virus–

Toxin law," which preceded section 351 [42 U.S.C. § 262(as)], was enacted
... [and] Congress [therefore] could not have intended that they be
included." 116 Cong. Rec. 31017 (1970) (remarks of Sen. Dominick). Under
this rationale, the definition of "analogous products" would be limited to
those human organs for which transplantation had become known at the
time of the enactment of the 1970 amendments to the VSTA. By 1970,
kidney and bone marrow transplants had become fairly common and liver
and heart transplants had been performed, but were still in the experimental stages.

NOTE

It is by no means clear that, by adding the words "blood, blood component or
derivative," Congress intended to include as "analogous" products the entire range
of human organs then known to be capable of transplantation. Kidney and bone
marrow transplants were known to be part of the developing field of organ
transplants, yet those organs were not mentioned by name in the 1970 amendment.
Although as a matter of human physiology blood is correctly regarded as a "liquid
organ," it seems improbable that those who drafted the amendment viewed blood as
simply one of the several organs or organ systems that make up the human body.
The more plausible assumption is that Congress believed that blood should be
subject to regulation, and included it in the list of biological substances for which a
license was required as a means of authorizing necessary governmental controls.
Under this view, the term "analogous product" would include analogous blood
products, not solid organs that are "analogous" because blood is also, in a broader
sense, a human "organ," albeit a liquid organ.

The following year Congress enacted the National Organ Transplant, Pub. L.
98–507, which established the framework for whole organ recovery and allocation
that operates today. The system, described in IOM, Organ Donation: Opportunities
for Action (2006), does not deal with tissue recovery, processing, or use, and it
accords no role to FDA.

2.   FDA's Regulation of Cells and Tissues

In addition to the few thousand recipients of organ transplants each
year, more than one million Americans receive allogeneic (from another)
tissue transplants. Bone is the most common transplanted tissue. Thoroughly cleansed, demineralized, and then pulverized, cadaver bone is widely
used in reconstructive dental surgery. Intact bone segments are used by
orthopedic surgeons in spinal restoration and joint repair. Soft tissues—
such as tendons—are the material of choice in some procedures to repair
joint damage.

Like organs, almost all of the tissues in question come from deceased
donors. Some donors may have willed their bodies to medical research or
for use in treatment. More commonly, it is the families of persons who die
abruptly from traumatic injury who consent to recovery of usable body
parts. To be transplantable, organs must be recovered within a few hours of
death. Other tissues do not deteriorate as quickly, but most must be
recovered within 24 hours. Most tissue banks are affiliated with organ
procurement organizations (OPO's), and it is routine for teams representing both to collaborate in the recovery operation.

Until the 1980s, the surgical use of cadaver tissue was regarded as a facet of the "practice of medicine" that FDA did not regulate. Many of the earliest tissue "banks" were established by surgical teams and maintained as part of hospital operations. In time, however, these surgeon-managed operations took on independent status; supplying tissues for surgery was out-sourced. Contemporaneously, innovations in tissue preservation and manipulation expanded the procedures in which human-source materials could be used. Demand expanded and tissue banks responded. What had been an in-hospital service for surgeons became an independent industry—a source of materials that offered unique functionality or served as alternatives to man-made replacement parts.

In some respects the regulatory regime that FDA has constructed for tissue resembles the agency's program for blood. Prevention of disease transmission has been a primary goal of the agency's requirements. But blood is collected from living donors who can be tested again after donation. Testing of cadaveric donors of tissue is more complicated, and investigation of their experience and habits prior to death must generally rely on surrogates—the same next of kin whose consent must be obtained.

John J. Zodrow, *The Commodification of Human Body Parts: Regulating the Tissue Bank Industry*

32 SOUTHWESTERN UNIVERSITY LAW REVIEW 407 (2003).

... Researchers and practitioners are developing more uses for an assortment of human tissues, including dura matter, veins, nerves, corneas, fascia lata (muscle sheath), pituitary tissue, bone, cartilage, tendons, temporal bone cores from the middle ear, skin, marrow, semen, and blood.

. . . .

A survey of members of the leading trade group for tissue banks illustrates important details of the tissue procurement and transplantation process. Results show that donors typically come from organ procurement organizations, coroners' offices, hospital morgues, and (familial) donations. The average age of the donor was thirty-five. However, every bank is different. For instance, a Virginia tissue bank—one of the largest banks in the country—is a free-standing, non-profit bank that supplies everything from nerves to veins to mandibles. The United States Navy's tissue bank, which is the oldest tissue bank in existence today, recovers and stores only skin, dura, fascia, bone, and tendons. The Miami tissue bank, at the University of Miami, primarily supplies bone, skin, and cartilage, for use by physicians throughout the country. The Virginia tissue bank uses technicians to harvest tissue, and processes tissue for other banks. The Miami tissue bank utilizes surgeons to perform recovery.

Usually, the procurement process begins when a bank is informed that donor tissue is available. About one-half of donors are rejected for a variety of reasons, including the patient's age or medical history. When the donor is suitable, a team of technicians travels to the hospital the same day. Although tissue recovery is not as urgent as organ recovery, it must be carried out without delay.

. . . Upon arrival at the hospital, the technicians review the patient's record, thus beginning the screening process. Cultures are taken and analyzed during the recovery procedure. Recovery may take from two to four hours, "depending on how much tissue is being donated." Preparing the skin to ensure sterility can take quite a while because when bones are removed, large areas are exposed. The actual harvesting lasts about thirty minutes.... The tissues are cultured again before they are released for transplantation. After final culturing, the tissues are "processed and either freeze-dried or fresh frozen for storage." . . .

Richard A. Merrill, *Human Tissues and Reproductive Cloning: New Technologies Challenge FDA*

3 HOUSTON JOURNAL OF HEALTH LAW & POLICY 1 (2002).

. . . .

The question whether FDA could regulate human tissue apparently first arose in 1973.... This was an era when FDA rarely shrank from new challenges, and the response of the Chief Counsel to whom the question was first put, Peter Barton Hutt, was predictable: Human tissues as well as whole organs, could be considered "analogous" to materials such as blood, over which FDA had authority under section 351 of the Public Health Service Act. Hutt went further:

> In any event, whether human semen, human tissues and organs are or are not biological products, they clearly are drugs when used for therapeutic purposes or to affect any bodily function and accordingly are subject to the requirements of the FD&C Act. The decision as to which Bureau within FDA handles these products is entirely an administrative matter that raises no legal issue.

Several years were to pass before FDA took any formal position regarding its authority to regulate tissue.... According to FDA's one-time Associate Commissioner for Health Affairs, Stuart Nightingale, representatives of the three bureaus (now "Centers") responsible for regulating medical products in 1976 "met to discuss possible regulation of tissue banks." They apparently were not able to identify clear criteria that could justify and at the same time limit FDA's assertion of jurisdiction: "[N]o one system seemed applicable to all of the potential products that fall under the rubric of transplantable tissues. It was [therefore] decided that FDA jurisdiction over tissues would be asserted only in response to an immediate need."

. . . .

In 1979, two incidents occurred which led the agency to again review the possible need to regulate the banking of allogeneic materials. In one incident, gonorrhea had been transmitted by contaminated fresh semen used in artificial insemination, and in the other incident a thirty-seven year old woman contracted rabies and died a month after she had received a corneal transplant.

Once again the question of legal authority was referred to FDA's Chief Counsel, then Richard Cooper, who declared that "any residual doubt about (FDA's) authority can be put aside," implying that whether and how to regulate were questions of science and policy. Once more, the decision was made not to assert jurisdiction. . . .

. . . Nightingale records that during the 1980s some officials were of the view that the Agency was obliged to regulate tissue. They may have recognized that tissue transplants were being used for purposes identical to those for which man-made—and comprehensively regulated—product were being used. . . .

Others recognized, however, that regulating by analogy would have far-reaching implications. The statutory definition of "device" is very broad. It would not be easy to confine regulation to tissue implants that resembled artificial products designed for similar use. . . .

Furthermore, the requirements FDA would be obliged to impose if tissues were drugs or medical devices did not seem well-matched for the operations of tissue recovery and processing or well-suited to address the concerns that might justify regulation in the first place. If human tissues were "drugs," virtually every one would be a "new drug" for which FDA approval was required. Few tissue banks had the resources to fund the sort of clinical studies that FDA would require. . . .

Classifying tissues as "devices" would also present problems for FDA. Not all medical devices require premarket approval by FDA; only those classified in Class III, and then only after the Agency calls for applications. The device law would thus appear to afford a "window" during which suppliers could conduct the studies needed to gain Agency approval. But this avenue was available only for devices that were in commercial distribution prior to 1976 or were "substantially equivalent" to a device then in distribution. For any tissue first provided to surgeons after 1976, it would have been difficult for FDA to fashion even a temporary exemption from the Act's premarket approval requirement.

. . . .

In 1985 the family of a 22–year old Virginia man, who had died from gunshot wounds, agreed to donate his organs and tissues for transplantation. Tests of the donor for HIV were negative. His tissues were processed and distributed by LifeNet Transplant Services of Virginia Beach. Over the next few years several dozen individuals received grafts from the Virginia donor. Some time thereafter seven of them tested positive for the HIV antibody. Their infections were attributed to the common donor, who at the time he died had been infected but apparently fell within the "window" between exposure to the AIDS virus and the development of detectable antibodies.

. . . [I]n December 1993, FDA published general regulations governing human tissue intended for transplantation. "To help prevent the transmission of AIDS and hepatitis through human tissue used in transplantation," the Agency mandated screening of tissue donors, testing of individual tissues for infectious disease, and maintenance of records to enable FDA inspectors to confirm compliance with the requirements for screening and testing. Thus, in a single stroke, FDA asserted control over as many as 200 institutions whose activities had previously largely escaped federal regulation. . . .

. . . FDA defined the category [of "human tissue"] as including "musculoskeletal and integumentary materials that may be recovered from living or cadaveric donors," which "largely consist of bone, ligaments, tendons, fascia, cartilage, corneas, and skin" used in disease treatment or reconstructive surgery. The new regulations did not apply to "tissues already regulated . . . as drugs, biological products, or medical devices," or to vascularized organs and bone marrow (overseen by other parts of the Public Health Service) and human milk. Significantly, FDA also specifically excluded "semen [and] other reproductive tissue," without identifying any other federal agency with oversight authority.

From the outset a critical issue for tissue banks was whether processing that altered the appearance or form, or facilitated the use, of a tissue would cause it to fall outside the coverage of the new regulations—and under the more stringent requirements for drugs or medical devices. FDA's treatment of this issue was not altogether reassuring. The Agency stated that its regulations applied to tissue processed or stored "by methods not intended to change tissue structure or functional characteristics." . . .

Perhaps the most significant feature of FDA's "interim" regulations was its decision not to rely on the FDCA for legal authority. Instead, the Agency invoked Section 361 of the Public Health Service Act, an old provision of awesome breadth. In its current form, Section 361 reads:

> The Surgeon General [i.e., FDA] . . . is authorized to make and enforce such regulations as in his judgment are necessary to prevent the introduction, transmission, or spread of communicable diseases from foreign countries into the States or possessions, or from one State or possession into any other State or possession. For purposes of carrying out and enforcing such regulations, the Surgeon General may provide for such inspection fumigation, disinfection, sanitation, pest extermination, destruction of animals or articles found to be so infected or contaminated as to be sources of dangerous infection to human beings, and other measures, as in his judgment may be necessary.

> . . . .

The interim regulations that FDA promulgated in December 1993 proved to be just the first installment in the Agency's development of an elaborate program for regulating human tissue and "tissue-based products." . . .

. . . [In 1997 FDA] released for discussion an unusual document, titled "A Proposed Approach to the Regulation of Cellular and Tissue–Based Products." . . .

FDA's plan set forth the Agency's thinking about a critical issue: When should a tissue-based product require premarketing proof of safety and effectiveness? In other words, when should a product be regulated as a new drug or Class III medical device? . . .

. . . Essentially, FDA embraced the principle of familiarity. If a donated tissue was expected to perform in the recipient the same function it performed in the donor, its effectiveness could be assumed and its safety could be assured if appropriate screening and testing were conducted. In an effort to capture this concept, the Agency said it would ask whether a tissue had been more than "minimally manipulated" and whether it was intended for other than a "homologous use." Significant changes in the form of a tissue or implantation in a different part of the body to perform a novel function would, the Agency suggested, undermine the presumption of clinical utility and safety. . . .

Current Good Tissue Practice for Human Cell, Tissue, and Cellular and Tissue-Based Product Establishments; Inspection and Enforcement

69 Fed. Reg. 68612 (November 24, 2004).

In February 1997, FDA proposed a new, comprehensive approach to the regulation of human cellular and tissue-based products (now called human cells, tissues, and cellular and tissue-based products or HCT/Ps). . . .

Since that time, the agency has published two final rules and one interim final rule to implement aspects of the proposed approach. On January 19, 2001, we issued regulations to create a new, unified system for registering HCT/P establishments and for listing their HCT/Ps (registration final rule, 66 FR 5447). . . . On January 27, 2004 (69 FR 3823), we issued an interim final rule to except human dura mater and human heart valve allografts from the scope of that definition until all of the tissue rules became final. On May 25, 2004, we issued regulations requiring most cell and tissue donors to be tested and screened for relevant communicable diseases (donor-eligibility final rule, 69 FR 29786). . . .

FDA is issuing these new regulations under the authority of section 361 of the PHS Act. . . .

Section 361 of the PHS Act authorizes FDA to issue regulations necessary to prevent the introduction, transmission, or spread of communicable diseases. Certain diseases, such as those caused by the human immunodeficiency virus (HIV) and the hepatitis B and C viruses (HBV and HCV respectively), may be transmitted through the implantation, transplantation, infusion, or transfer of HCT/Ps derived from infected donors. . . . However, donor screening and testing, although crucial, are not sufficient to prevent the transmission of disease by HCT/Ps. Rather, each step in the manufacturing process needs to be appropriately controlled. Errors in labeling, mix-ups of testing records, failure to adequately clean work areas, and faulty packaging are examples of improper practices that could produce a product capable of transmitting disease to its recipient. Similarly, . . . improper handling of an HCT/P can lead to bacterial or other pathogenic contamination of the HCT/P, or to cross-contamination between HCT/Ps, which in turn can endanger recipients. The agency has determined that the procedural provisions of this rule are necessary to ensure that the important protections created by these regulations are actually effected and are not simply empty promises. Only manufacturing conducted in accordance with established procedures can assure that HCT/Ps meet the standards in these rules. . . .

The record requirements of this rule are similarly necessary. A single donor may be the source of a large number of HCT/Ps. It may be discovered, long after the donation and transplantations have been completed, that, due to an error in processing, the donor tissue was infected and capable of spreading communicable disease. Although it might be too late to prevent infections in the recipients, it would not be too late for the recipient to obtain treatment and take steps to avoid infecting others, such as close family members. Unless adequate records were maintained, and maintained for the period of time throughout which infections may be identified, it would be impossible to identify the recipients potentially infected by the donor's HCT/Ps. This would be a critical breakdown in the prevention of disease transmission. Moreover, a single processing error, such as an improper practice that permitted bacterial contamination of all tissue processed at a location during a limited period of time, may also have wide ranging effects. Without reporting and study of adverse events involving the transmission of communicable disease, or involving the release of HCT/Ps presenting an increased risk of such transmission, common causes of seemingly isolated incidents would never come to light. Affected HCT/Ps would continue to place patients at risk of communicable disease. Accordingly, FDA has also determined that HCT/P tracking, maintenance and retention of records, and reporting of adverse reactions and HCT/P deviations are necessary to prevent the transmission of communicable disease through HCT/Ps.

The CGTP [Current Good Tissue Practices] regulations govern the methods used in, and the facilities and controls used for, the manufacture of HCT/Ps. CGTP requirements are a fundamental component of FDA's risk-based approach to regulating HCT/Ps. HCT/Ps regulated solely under section 361 of the PHS Act and the regulations in part 1271 are not regulated under the [FD&C] act or section 351 of the PHS Act (42 U.S.C. 262). By requiring that HCT/Ps meeting the criteria listed in Sec. 1271.10 (361 HCT/Ps) be manufactured in compliance with CGTP, in combination with the other requirements in part 1271, the agency can ensure that 361 HCT/Ps are subject to sufficient regulatory controls to protect the public health.

HCT/Ps regulated as drugs, devices, and/or biological products, and not as 361 HCT/Ps, must be manufactured in accordance with CGTP, in addition to existing requirements. The CGTP regulations supplement the current good manufacturing practice (CGMP) and quality system (QS) regulations applicable to drugs, devices, and biological products in parts 210, 211, and 820 (21 CFR parts 210, 211, and 820). . . . Thus, . . . those HCT/Ps regulated as drugs, devices, and/or biological products are subject to CGMP regulations as well as to CGTP regulations. . . .

The proposed CGTP requirements were intended, in part, to prevent the introduction, transmission, or spread of communicable disease by helping to ensure that the function and integrity of HCT/Ps are not impaired through improper manufacturing. Many of the provisions of the proposed rule contained requirements intended to help ensure HCT/P function and integrity. . . .

. . . Approximately nine comments objected to the proposed rule's provisions on function and integrity. Some of these comments criticized our justification for these provisions as weak or theoretical; these comments questioned whether the impairment of an HCT/P's function and integrity actually increases the risk of disease transmission. Other comments argued that section 361 of the PHS Act cannot be interpreted to cover an HCT/P's function and integrity. . . .

. . . To increase clarity, and because of the confusion expressed by comments about the term "function and integrity," we have removed from the regulations all references to function or integrity. For the same reason, we have also removed references to the related terms, "deterioration" and "adverse effect."

. . . .

§ 1271.150   Current good tissue practice requirements. . . .

(b) *Core CGTP requirements.* The following are core CGTP requirements:

(1) Requirements relating to facilities in § 1271.190(a) and (b);

(2) Requirements relating to environmental control in § 1271.195(a);

(3) Requirements relating to equipment in § 1271.200(a);

(4) Requirements relating to supplies and reagents in § 1271.210(a) and (b);

(5) Requirements relating to recovery in § 1271.215;

(6) Requirements relating to processing and process controls in § 1271.220;

(7) Requirements relating to labeling controls in § 1271.250(a) and (b);

(8) Requirements relating to storage in § 1271.260 (a) through (d);

(9) Requirements relating to receipt, predistribution shipment, and distribution of an HCT/P in § 1271.265(a) through (d); and

(10) Requirements relating to donor eligibility determinations, donor screening, and donor testing in §§ 1271.50, 1271.75, 1271.80, and 1271.85.

. . . .

(a) Upon an agency finding that there are reasonable grounds to believe that an HCT/P is a violative HCT/P because it was manufactured in violation of the regulations in this part and, therefore, the conditions of manufacture of the HCT/P do not provide adequate protections against risks of communicable disease transmission; or the HCT/P is infected or contaminated so as to be a source of dangerous infection to humans; or an establishment is in violation of the regulations in this part and, therefore, does not provide adequate protections against the risks of communicable disease transmission, the Food and Drug Administration (FDA) may take one or more of the following actions:

(1) Serve upon the person who distributed the HCT/P a written order that the HCT/P be recalled and/or destroyed, as appropriate, and upon persons in possession of the HCT/P that the HCT/P must be retained until it is recalled by the distributor, destroyed, or disposed of as agreed by FDA, or the safety of the HCT/P is confirmed;

(2) Take possession of and/or destroy the violative HCT/P; or

(3) Serve upon the establishment an order to cease manufacturing until compliance with the regulations of this part has been achieved. When FDA determines there are reasonable grounds to believe there is a danger to health, such order will be effective immediately. In other situations, such order will be effective after one of the following events, whichever is later:

. . . .

§ 1271.440 Orders of retention, recall, destruction, and cessation of manufacturing. . . .

(e) The recipient of an order issued under this section may request a hearing in accordance with part 16 of this chapter. To request a hearing, the recipient of the written order or prior possessor of such HCT/P must make the request within 5 working days of receipt of a written order for retention, recall, destruction, and/or cessation (or within 5 working days of the agency's possession of an HCT/P under paragraph (a)(2) of this section), in accordance with part 16 of this chapter. An order of destruction will be held in abeyance pending resolution of the hearing request. Upon request under part 16 of this chapter, FDA will provide an opportunity for an expedited hearing for an order of cessation that is not stayed by the Commissioner of Food and Drugs.

NOTE

FDA's tissue regulations, like its 1993 "interim rule," rely on Section 361 of the PHS Act for legal authority. That provision allows FDA to use virtually any means to accomplish the congressional objective—prevention of disease transmission. But that goal arguably limits the measures that FDA might adopt. Unless a requirement can be justified as contributing to the prevention of communicable disease, Section 361 presumably does not provide the necessary legal support.

COMMENT: FASHIONING REGULATORY REQUIREMENTS

FDA's tissue regulations, 21 C.F.R. Part 1271, of which the foregoing "good tissue practice" regulations are a major component, apply to tissues that are only "minimally manipulated" and are intended for a "homologous use." These are FDA's main criteria for deciding whether an implant derived from cadaver tissue should be subject only to the tissue requirements promulgated under section 361, or instead should be required to demonstrate its safety and—critically—its clinical effectiveness, either as a biological drug or a Class III medical device. The common theme here is

novelty—or its absence. FDA defines "homologous use" as "the replacement or supplementation of a recipient's cells or tissues with a HCT/P that
performs the same basic function or functions in the recipient as in the
donor." 21 C.F.R. 1271.3(c). The agency defines "minimal manipulation" of
structural tissue as "processing that does not alter the original relevant
characteristics of the tissue relating to the tissue's utility for reconstruction, repair, or replacement." 21 C.F.R. 1271.3(f)(1). It defines "minimal
manipulation" with respect to cells and nonstructural tissues as "processing that does not alter the relevant biological characteristics of cells or
tissues." 21 C.F.R. 1271.3(f)(2). In September 2006, FDA issued guidance
describing its approach to the issue of "minimal manipulation." Its brief
discussion includes the following paragraphs:

> For purposes of determining whether a structural tissue product is
> minimally manipulated, a tissue characteristic is "original" if it is
> present in the tissue in the donor. A tissue characteristic is
> "relevant" if it could have a meaningful bearing on how the tissue
> performs when utilized for reconstruction, repair, or replacement.
> A characteristic of structural tissue would be relevant when it
> could potentially increase or decrease the utility of the original
> tissue for reconstruction, repair or replacement.

> Accordingly, FDA's determination of whether structural tissue is
> eligible for regulation solely under section 361 of the PHS Act has
> encompassed a consideration of all the potential effects, both
> positive and negative, of the alteration of a particular characteris-
> tic on the utility of the tissue for reconstruction, repair or replace-
> ment, *i.e.*, changing the characteristic could improve or diminish
> the tissue's utility. Once FDA has determined, based on the data
> and information before it, that processing has altered an original
> characteristic of a structural tissue, and that the characteristic is
> relevant in that it has a potential effect on the utility of the tissue
> for reconstruction, repair, or replacement, the agency has consid-
> ered the tissue to be more than minimally manipulated and not
> eligible for regulation solely under section 361 of the PHS Act. In
> such a case the structural tissue will be regulated as a drug, device
> and/or biological product under the Federal Food, Drug and Cos-
> metic Act and/or section 351 of the PHS Act.

OFFICE OF COMBINATION PRODUCTS AND CENTER FOR BIOLOGICS EVALUATION AND
RESEARCH, GUIDANCE FOR INDUSTRY AND FDA STAFF: MINIMAL MANIPULATION OF
STRUCTURAL TISSUE JURISDICTIONAL UPDATE (2006).

FDA has established an institutional mechanism for determining
whether a tissue product implicates either of the so-called "kick-up factors." In guidance the agency describes the composition and processes of
this mechanism, known as the Tissue Reference Group.

> ... The TRG is composed of three representatives from the Center
> for Biologics Evaluation and Research (CBER) and three from the
> Center for Devices and Radiological Health (CDRH), including the
> product jurisdiction officer at each Center. An executive secretary
> carries out the functions described below. A liaison from the
> Ombudsman's Office and the Office of the Chief Counsel attends

meetings. Other FDA staff are asked to attend meetings as needed, to discuss issues related to HCT/Ps in their area of expertise.

CBER and CDRH intend to provide a single reference point for product-specific questions received by the Centers or the Ombudsman's Office from the manufacturers and sponsors or their designated representatives regarding existing or investigational products containing or consisting of HCT/Ps.... Questions the TRG considers include whether HCT/Ps meet the criteria for regulation solely under section 361 of the PHS Act, are a device or biologic, or what the primary mode of action of a combination product is. The TRG does not publicly release correspondence received or TRG responses because of limits on disclosure of confidential information as contained in the Freedom of Information Act and the Privacy Act.

. . . .

• The executive secretary of the TRG may be contacted directly by sponsors or manufacturers, concerning regulation of HCT/Ps.... The executive secretary, when appropriate, may inform the sponsor or manufacturer whether there is insufficient information to respond to the inquiry. The executive secretary may advise the sponsor or manufacturer what, if any, information would be helpful for the TRG to respond to the specific inquiry. Such information may relate to the factors specified in 21 CFR Part 1271.10 that determine whether an HCT/P will be regulated solely under section 361 of the Public Health Service (PHS) Act.

• Inquiries concerning regulation of products already designated as biologics or devices through regulation, policy statements, or other agency communications, are not within the scope of the TRG issues and will be directed to the appropriate reviewing Division with product responsibility. Inquiries that involve trade complaints will be forwarded to the respective CBER/CDRH Office of Compliance.

• Inquiries, with accompanying information about the product, are placed on the agenda for the next scheduled TRG meeting and should be reviewed in order of receipt. The TRG attempts to respond within 60 calendar days of receiving an inquiry in writing.... A sponsor or manufacturer may request to meet with the TRG to present information. When the TRG reaches a recommendation, the TRG executive secretary prepares a draft response letter, which reflects the recommendation and the reasons supporting the recommendation....

• If the TRG cannot reach a recommendation in applying the factors in 21 CFR Part 1271.10, the matter is placed on the agenda of the TAP Core Team for discussion at its next scheduled meeting. If the TAP Core Team cannot reach a recommendation, the matter is referred to the Center Directors, with a summary of the TRG and TAP Core Team deliberations, for resolution.

• If the sponsor or manufacturer does not agree with the TRG or Center Directors recommendation, the sponsor or manufacturer may submit a Request for Designation (RFD) to the Ombudsman's Office, as provided under 21 CFR Part 3.

COMMENT: CORD BLOOD

FDA has chosen to treat umbilical cord blood as transplantable human tissue subject to its general requirements for tissue, rather than as donated whole blood subject to the Biologics Act. *See* David A. Suski, *Frozen Blood, Neonates, and FDA: The Regulation of Placental Umbilical Cord Blood*, 84 VA. L. REV. 715 (1998). FDA's implicit reliance on section 361—the legal predicate for its tissue regulations—suggests that it is chiefly concerned about disease transmission rather than clinical performance. Most uses of cord blood were thought to contemplate autologous administration, *i.e.*, return of blood to its original donor. *See* Eligibility Determination for Donors of Human Cells, Tissues, and Cellular and Tissue–Based Products, 69 Fed. Reg. 29786 (May 25, 2004). However, FDA held upon the possibility of more rigorous regulation if recovered blood underwent significant manipulation to enhance its therapeutic properties.

G.   OTHER CELLULAR TECHNOLOGIES

This concluding section of the chapter surveys a series of emerging medical technologies over which FDA exercises some level of regulatory authority. The technologies have two things in common. Each of them utilizes materials recovered from living organisms, human or animal. And, though the case for FDA jurisdiction in each instance seems plausible, the agency was at first slow to respond to claims that it could or should exert control.

1.   GENE THERAPY

The remarkable advances in mapping the human genome and understanding the role of specific genes in the genesis of disease have spurred development of therapeutic applications of genetic material. These efforts have raised questions on several fronts. What agency or agencies should be responsible for overseeing attempts at gene therapy? What controls should public entities impose to protect patients and at the same time facilitate promising research? And, more recently, are the early applications of gene therapy yielding evidence to support the optimistic predictions of the technology's pioneers?

Joseph M. Rainsbury, *Biotechnology on the RAC: FDA/NIH Regulation of Human Gene Therapy*

55 FOOD & DRUG LAW JOURNAL 575 (2000).

Gene therapy, a procedure in which healthy genes are spliced into the cells of sick patients, represents the cutting edge of medical research. If successful, it will constitute a revolution in medicine. It already has pushed the limits of regulatory science. . . .

On April 11, 1983, the RAC [Recombinant DNA Advisory Committee at NIH] established a Working Group on a Response to the Splicing Life Report. . . .

. . . FDA began to take notice of the emerging technology of gene therapy. In 1984, the agency announced that it intended to regulate rDNA-derived products. In 1986, it specifically asserted jurisdiction over human gene therapy products, while acknowledging that it might share regulatory duties with NIH. . . .

The opening salvo in the regulatory battles to get particular gene therapy treatments approved occurred on April 24, 1987, when Dr. W. French Anderson submitted what he styled a Preclinical Data Document to the RAC that detailed his proposal to treat Severe Combined Immunodeficiency (SCID) with ex vivo modification of extracted blood cells. Anderson sought to use a retroviral vector to splice a functioning copy of the defective gene into the blood cells of a SCID victim, thus enabling the patient herself to manufacture the protein. In this initial quasi-protocol, Anderson targeted blood cells in the bone marrow, hoping to transduce blood stem cells with copies of the healthy gene. Unfortunately, the results from Anderson's animal studies were less than promising. Among other things, half of the (otherwise healthy) monkeys subjected to the treatment died. Professional reaction to the Phonebook (the name given to Anderson's 500–page document) was withering, and at its December 7, 1988 meeting the RAC made it clear that it was nowhere near approving Anderson's protocol. . . .

Not long after gene therapy trials began, it became clear that the technique could be employed to fight diseases other than rare, single-gene, hereditary defects like SCID. In particular, cancer and AIDS began to emerge as potential targets. Consequently, the number of gene therapy protocols approved by the RAC rose exponentially. With these diseases came large and, particularly with AIDS, well-organized, vocal, and powerful activist groups. Because the RAC and its Human Gene Therapy Subcommittee met only three or four times a year, the work soon began to exceed their processing capacity. More importantly, many of the new protocols raised no new ethical or safety issues. The work was becoming mundane, stuff for full-time regulators at FDA, not for the all-star staff assembled at the RAC.

. . . .

As the RAC's role in overseeing human gene therapy clinical trials gradually waned, FDA's responsibility correspondingly waxed. . . . FDA had asserted jurisdiction over human gene therapy products as early as 1986. The agency, however, was vague about both the legal authority underlying this jurisdiction and the content of the technical standards the agency intended to deploy. As human gene therapy trials commenced, FDA began to clarify both.

Unlike NIH, FDA was not a source of funding for human gene therapy clinical trials. Thus, it could not ensure compliance with its gene therapy policies simply by withholding funding from violator researchers/institutions. Instead, it had to rely on its statutory authority to prevent the shipment of misbranded drugs, devices, or biologics. Human gene therapy products defy easy classification under the existing regulatory schemata of drugs, devices, or biologics. Nevertheless, FDA determined early that it would regulate this class of therapeutic agents as biologics. By doing so, FDA maximized its control over such products. . . . Moreover, under the Public Health Service Act (PHS Act), FDA did not need to demonstrate an interstate nexus to exert its regulatory power.

> . . . .

The gene therapy field lost its innocence on September 17, 1999. On that date, eighteen year-old Jesse Gelsinger died from complications arising out of a Phase I safety trial of a gene therapy treatment for ornithine transcarbamylase (OTC) deficiency. Unlike previous gene therapy fatalities, researchers ascribed Gelsinger's death to his treatment, not to the underlying disease being treated. Worse, Gelsinger was a (reasonably) healthy volunteer. The incident therefore cast a harsh spotlight on the legal safeguards in place to protect patients at the frontier of medicine.

Jesse Gelsinger was the eighteenth of nineteen patients scheduled to be treated in the University of Pennsylvania (UPenn) OTC deficiency study. Although earlier volunteers had suffered temporary liver toxicities, three of these serious enough to trigger the protocol's "stopping rule," Gelsinger's reaction appeared to be idiosyncratic. The actual cause of death was acute respiratory distress syndrome brought on by a severe immunological response to the adenovirus vector. The precise physiological basis for his reaction remains unclear. After Gelsinger's death, FDA put the UPenn study on a clinical hold pending further investigation. Scrutiny of the OTC deficiency study revealed that UPenn researchers had deviated from both the protocol approved by the RAC and the IND approved by FDA. Although there is little evidence that these deviations contributed to Gelsinger's death, their revelation in the wake of the disaster provided a lightning rod for those critical of the UPenn team in particular and of the conduct of gene therapy researchers in general.

Public attention also focused on the institutions responsible for regulating gene therapy. An issue that dominated headlines was widespread industry non-compliance with NIH disclosure requirements. Although NIH had stripped the RAC of approval authority for gene therapy protocols, it retained a provision in the Guidelines that required investigators to submit adverse event reports to ORDA [NIH's Office of Recombinant DNA Activities]. This rule was honored mostly in the breach. This is not to say the researchers were keeping adverse events hidden from regulators. FDA has nearly identical requirements for adverse-event reporting, and had reported no serious compliance problems among gene therapy researchers. A major explanation for this difference appears to have been industry concerns about proprietary information. Unlike the RAC, FDA treats sponsor-provided clinical data as confidential information that cannot be disclosed publicly without prior sponsor approval. Compounding this problem was confusion in the gene therapy community about what information needed to be sent to the RAC. Whatever the motives, the failure of so many researchers to comply with NIH requirements gave the appearance of a major regulatory breakdown. . . .

———

In addition to causing regulators to reassess their requirements, the death of Jesse Gelsinger and the manifestation of cancer among gene therapy patients in France prompted some critics to question the early predictions of the promise of gene therapy.

Fifteen years ago, scientists heralded gene therapy as a medical revolution that would quickly bring cures for crippling and deadly diseases. After more than 900 clinical trials, however, gene scientists can claim few real successes, and even the technology's longtime supporters say gene therapy has developed far more slowly than they had expected. Treatment comes with a cost. Experts say the story of the treatment of 10 sick children at a Paris hospital, which made news in March, illustrates the technology's promise as well as its challenges. The boys were born with a rare and lethal genetic disorder that left them without working immune systems.

... Instead of treating the symptoms, French doctors hoped to correct the source of the illness by providing the boys with working copies of a gene that helps the immune system develop. Almost all the children got better. Today, most of them are healthy. . . . The French trial began in 1999, and in 2002, two of the children developed leukemia. Doctors discovered that the new genes either settled next to or inside a gene that spurs growth. . . . Recently, French doctors announced that one of the children died and a third has developed a condition that appears similar to leukemia. "This is the first example of a really effective, robust treatment of anything by gene therapy," Friedmann says. "But that treatment carries an enormous cost." Science seeks the answer. Yet scientists say they have not given up. Children treated in similar experiments in England appear healthy. . . . Many new medical treatments—from heart transplants to cancer drugs—took decades to perfect, doctors say. Chemotherapy and radiation treatments that cure cancer often lead to heart damage or even second tumors. Scientists still are struggling to deliver genes in "the right way, at the right time in a regulated way." . . . Other gene therapy experiments have failed because the body rejects the genes themselves as foreign. . . . Some investors are not willing to wait for scientists to solve these problems. Other investors lost faith in gene therapy in 1999 when teenager Jesse Gelsinger died after he was injected with a modified virus carrying a gene in an experiment at the University of Philadelphia. The number of gene trials in the USA, which peaked at 91 that year, fell sharply. . . . Scientific companies are shifting efforts away from rare disorders and toward more common maladies such as cancer, blindness and Parkinson's disease because of the larger potential markets, says

Mark Kay, a researcher at Stanford University and president-elect of the gene therapy society. . . .

Liz Scabo, *Gene therapy's slow path: What started as a revolution has run into roadblocks*, USA TODAY, Apr. 5, 2005 at 7D. *See* FDA, GUIDANCE FOR HUMAN SOMATIC CELL THERAPY AND GENE THERAPY (Mar. 1998); FDA, GUIDANCE FOR INDUSTRY, GENE THERAPY CLINICAL TRIALS–OBSERVING PARTICIPANTS FOR DELAYED ADVERSE EVENTS (Aug. 2005).

2.   ASSISTED REPRODUCTION

Lars Noah, *Assisted Reproductive Technologies and the Pitfalls of Unregulated Biomedical Innovation*

55 FLORIDA LAW REVIEW 603 (2003).

. . . .

ART [Assisted Reproductive Technology] now encompasses several distinct methods, though they often are used in combination. Artificial insemination (AI), also referred to as intrauterine insemination (IUI), has the longest history and requires the least technological sophistication: the procedure introduces sperm (spermatozoa)—from either the husband or a donor—into the woman's uterus. Gamete intrafallopian transfer (GIFT), which delivers the sperm and harvested eggs (ova or oocytes) directly into the woman's fallopian tube, represents a more complicated method of insemination requiring the use of a laparoscope through an abdominal incision. . . .

In vitro fertilization (IVF), first accomplished a quarter of a century ago, represents the paradigmatic form of ART. Basically, the procedure involves harvesting oocytes from the patient, mixing them with sperm in a petri dish containing a culture medium in order to achieve extracorporeal fertilization, and then transferring one or more embryos back into the patient. Several permutations are, however, possible: the sperm and/or eggs may come from donors, the embryos may be transferred into a woman shortly after fertilization or cryopreserved (frozen) for possible future use, they may be transferred back into the woman who supplied the eggs or into an unrelated surrogate, and they may be transferred into the woman's uterus or, typically at an earlier stage of embryonic development, into her fallopian tubes.

. . . .

In recent years, ARTs have become an increasingly popular medical intervention. . . . Almost 400 fertility clinics currently operate in the United States. Some of these are free-standing entrepreneurial facilities, while other clinics are housed within larger health care institutions. Much like other fee-for-service operations such as elective cosmetic surgery, hospitals may establish fertility clinics as lucrative profit centers. . . .

Unlike other medical technologies, ARTs arrive on the scene with little or no rigorous testing of their safety and effectiveness. . . . The government plays essentially no role in reviewing new medical procedures—as opposed to new products—in advance of their use in patients, leaving the task of scrutinizing the safety and effectiveness of innovative techniques for biomedical researchers and professional self-regulation, perhaps with tort litigation serving as a backstop.

As a result, patient demand coupled with the lack of any evidence suggesting intrinsic hazards associated with these procedures led to the increasing use of ARTs to treat infertility. As experience accumulates, researchers can try to assess these technologies after they have come into widespread clinical use.

As a number of researchers have documented, fertility drugs and IVF increase the incidence of multiple births. Such pregnancies pose a variety of significant health risks to both mothers and children. For instance, prematurity and low birth weight can result in long-term developmental harms in offspring. Before recent advances in neonatology, "preemies" often failed to survive. Nowadays, after lengthy and costly stays in neonatal intensive care units (NICUs), many premature infants leave the hospital only to face significant physical and cognitive disabilities....

Multifetal pregnancies pose numerous maternal risks as well, including gestational diabetes and preeclampsia. In addition, ART procedures raise a variety of other safety concerns for the mother, ranging from acute and chronic side effects associated with the use of fertility drugs, including a suspected increased risk of ovarian cancer, to complications involved in the harvesting procedure, and higher rates of ectopic pregnancies. In short, although uncertainties remain about the frequency of these adverse effects, ARTs are hardly innocuous medical interventions, and little doubt remains about their contribution to (or the negative consequences of) multifetal pregnancies.

Apart from the consequences of prematurity and low birth weight after multifetal pregnancy, initial studies reached equivocal conclusions about the suspected link between particular ARTs and birth defects....

Until recently, the FDA had not asserted regulatory jurisdiction over IVF or other fertility procedures. Indeed, scholars who wrote about the regulation of ARTs had paid no attention to the agency, and, when Congress passed the Fertility Clinic Success Rate and Certification Act of 1992, it suggested no role for the FDA....

Nonetheless, in 1998, the FDA announced, and subsequently reiterated, that its proposed rule governing cellular and tissue-based products would apply to ARTs as well:

> Most aspects of cellular and tissue product manufacturing in the reproductive tissue industry would become newly regulated under the proposed CGTP [current good tissue practices] rule. The affected establishments within this industry include sperm banks and ART facilities. Reports of the sensitivity of product quality to variations in tissue collection, technician skill, processing methods, environmental conditions, and other factors, indicate that the risk of communicable disease transmission would be reduced by improving the proposed overall product quality, and economic benefits would be seen through improved patient outcomes from facility

compliance with the proposed CGTP requirements. . . . Despite the increasing effectiveness of infertility treatment through ART, problems can occur in tissue processing. Adverse outcomes owing to problems with product quality can result from contamination that produces infection (*e.g.*, HIV transmission) in the infertility patient. Problems with ART facility processing of sperm or oocytes can also lead to reduced rates of fertilization. . . . [66 Fed. Reg. 1508, 1542–43 (2001).]

. . . .

More controversially . . . the FDA also asserted jurisdiction over other aspects of ARTs, claiming that it had the authority to subject human reproductive tissues to premarket review—and to demand proof of their safety and effectiveness—in the event that they had undergone more than minimal manipulation. After the publication of its proposed CGTP rule, the agency sent warning letters to several fertility clinics ordering them to cease using techniques that entail any kind of alteration of human genetic material, including cloning, genetic engineering, and ooplasmic transfer (a.k.a. IVONT). . . .

3.   Searching for Stem Cells

Committee on the Biological and Biomedical Applications of Stem Cell Research, Stem Cells and the Future of Regenerative Medicine

National Academy Press, 2001.

. . . .

The conditions listed below occur in many forms and thus not every person with these diseases could potentially benefit from cell-based therapies. Nonetheless, the widespread incidence of these conditions suggests that stem cell research could help millions of Americans.

Condition	Number of patients
Cardiovascular disease	58 million
Autoimmune diseases	30 million
Diabetes	16 million
Osteoporosis	10 million
Cancers	8.2 million
Alzheimer's disease	5.5 million
Parkinson's disease	5.5 million
Burns (severe)	0.3 million
Spinal-cord injuries	0.25 million
Birth defects	0.15 million/year

The Committee placed off limits the issue of reproductive cloning, which is sometimes linked to stem cell research because in both cases, the somatic cell nuclear transfer (SCNT) technique can be used to create embryos. The interest in this technique for stem cell research is related to the possibility of producing stem cells for regenerative therapy that are genetically matched to the person needing a tissue transplant. The immune system is poised to reject tissue transplants from genetically non-identical people, and immunological rejection poses serious clinical risks that can be life-threatening. Overcoming the threat of immunological rejection is thus one of the major scientific challenges to stem cell transplantation—and, indeed, for transplantations of any sort. The SCNT technique offers the possibility of deriving stem cells for transplantation from the recipient's own cells. Such cells would produce only the patient's own proteins and would not cause an immunological reaction when transplanted into their patient.

. . . .

Embryonic stem cells (ESCs) are derived from an early-stage embryo. Fertilization of an ovum by a sperm results in a zygote, the earliest embryonic stage. The zygote begins to divide about 30 hours after fertilization and by the third-to-fourth day, the embryo is a compact ball of 12 or more cells known as the morula. Five-to-six days after fertilization, and after several more cycles of cell division, the morula cells begin to specialize, formed a hollow sphere of cells, called a blastocyst, which is about 150 microns in diameter (one-seventh of a millimeter). The outer layer of the blastocyst is called the trophoblast and the cluster of cells inside the sphere is called the inner cell mass. At this stage, there are about 70 trophoblast cells and about 30 cells in the inner cell mass. The cells of the inner cell mass are multipotent stem cells that give rise to all cell types of the major tissue layers (ectoderm, mesoderm, and endoderm) of the embryo. In the last 3 years, it has become possible to remove these stem cells from the blastocyst and maintain them in an undifferentiated state in cell culture lines in the laboratory. To be useful for producing medical therapies, cultured ESCs will need to be differentiated into appropriate tissues for transplantation into patients. Researchers are just beginning to learn how to achieve this differentiation.

Fetal stem cells are primitive cell types in the fetus that eventually develop into the various organs of the body, but research with fetal tissue so far has been limited to only a few cell types: neural stem cells, including neural crest cells; hematopoietic stem cells, and pancreatic islet progenitors. Neural stem cells, which are numerous in the fetal brain, can be isolated and grown in an undifferentiated form in culture, and they have been shown to differentiate into the three main types of brain cells. These cells have been used in rodent models of Parkinson's disease. Neural crest cells arise from the neural tube and migrate from it throughout the developing fetus. They are able to develop into multiple cell types, including the nerves that innervate the heart and the gut, non-neural cells of hormone-secreting glands, pigment cells of the skin, cartilage and bone in the face and skull, and connective tissue in many parts of the body. Neural crest cells from mice have been cultured in the laboratory.

The fetal liver and blood are rich sources of hematopoietic stem cells, which are responsible for generating multiple cell types in blood, but their properties have not been extensively investigated. Although not part of the fetus, the umbilical cord and placenta are also rich sources of hematopoietic stem cells. Tissue extracted from the fetal pancreas has been shown to stimulate insulin production when transplanted into diabetic mice, but it is not clear whether this is due to a true stem cell, a more mature progenitor cell, or to the presence of fully mature insulin-producing pancreatic islet cells themselves. Finally, multipotent cells called primordial germ cells have been isolated from the gonadal ridge, a structure that arises at an early stage of the fetus that will eventually develop into eggs or sperm in the adult. Germ cells can be cultured in vivo and have been shown to give rise to multiple cell types of the three embryonic tissue layers.

Adult stem cells are undifferentiated cells that occur in a differentiated tissue, such as bone marrow or the brain, in the adult body. They can renew themselves in the body, making identical copies of themselves for the lifetime of the organism, or become specialized to yield the cell types of the tissue of origin. Sources of adult stem cells include bone marrow, blood, the eye, brain, skeletal muscle, dental pulp, liver, skin, the lining of the gastrointestinal tract, and pancreas. Studies suggest that at least some adult stem cells are multipotent. For example, it has been reported that stem cells from the bone marrow, a mesodermal tissue, can give rise to the three major types of brain cells, which are ectodermal derivatives, and that stem cells from the brain can differentiate into blood cells and muscle tissue, but these findings require verification. It is not clear whether investigators are seeing adult stem cells that truly have plasticity or whether some tissues contain several types of stem cells that each give rise to only a few derivative types. Adult stem cells are rare, difficult to identify and purify, and, when grown in culture, are difficult to maintain in the undifferentiated state. It is because of those limitations that even stem cells from bone marrow, the type most studied, are not available in sufficient numbers to support many potential applications of regenerative medicine. Finding ways to culture adult stems cells outside the body is a high priority of stem cell research. . . .

4. REPRODUCTIVE CLONING

Richard A. Merrill, *Human Tissues and Reproductive Cloning: New Technologies Challenge FDA*
3 HOUSTON JOURNAL OF HEALTH & POLICY 1 (2003).

. . . The first signal that FDA would seek to regulate cloning was sent during a radio interview of Acting FDA Commissioner Dr. Michael Friedman. . . . He went on to say that FDA viewed human cloning as analogous to gene therapy, over which the Agency had years before asserted regulatory control.

. . . .

[Later, in congressional testimony, the head of CBER] described the Agency's concerns and outlined the regulatory requirements that, she asserted, existing law imposed. . . .

FDA has the authority to regulate medical products, including biological products, drugs, and devices. The use of cloning technology to clone a human being would be subject to both the biologics provisions of the Public Health Service (PHS) Act and the drug and device provisions of the Federal Food, Drug, and Cosmetic

(FD&C) Act.... Before such research could begin, the researcher must submit an IND request to FDA, which FDA would review to determine if such research could proceed. FDA believes that there are major unresolved safety questions on the use of cloning technology to clone a human being and therefore would not permit any such investigation to proceed at this time.

Advocates for FDA regulation [had earlier] suggested that the Agency could rely on [section 361 of the PHSA] to regulate human cloning because of the risk of transmission of HIV and other infectious diseases from the donor(s) of cellular material to a clone or its "mother." While not facially implausible, this theory would have confronted two difficulties that may explain FDA's failure to adopt it. First, while the measures authorized by Section 361 are broadly described, the end at which such measures must be aimed is not; the only goal that Congress has authorized the Agency to pursue is the prevention of communicable disease-a narrower target than the manifold concerns about cloning. Moreover, and more importantly, FDA could have invoked Section 361 only if it had been prepared to initiate rulemaking in accordance with the APA....

A second option pressed on FDA ... was to rely on the "FDA plan for cellular and tissue-based products." ... [E]ven if FDA had been prepared to argue that the cellular material used to produce a human clone fell within its definition of "human tissue," this conclusion would not have enabled the Agency to require advance approval of any clinical experiments....

FDA's "plan for cellular and tissue-based products" does contemplate that some tissues will require clinical studies to demonstrate safety and effectiveness—a requirement that would be triggered by a determination that a tissue is a biological drug or Class III device. FDA's plan can therefore be read as predicting how the Agency might view human cloning but, standing alone, it cannot provide authority for the restrictions the Agency later sought to impose.

———

In 1998, an unidentified FDA employee prepared the following analysis of the agency's legal authority to regulate—and prohibit—human cloning.

FDA's Jurisdiction Over Human Cloning Activities
April 16, 1998.

... The conclusion that FDA has jurisdiction over somatic cell clones under the PHS Act and the FD&C Act is consistent with the statutory purpose of public health protection. Courts have recognized that remedial statutes, such as the FD&C Act and the PHS Act, are to be liberally construed consistent with their public health purpose. See United States v. An Article of Drug ... Bacto–Unidisk, 394 U.S. 784 (1968).

FDA regulates biological products under section 351 of the PHS Act. 42 U.S.C. § 262. That section applies to "any virus, therapeutic serum, toxin, antitoxin, vaccine, blood, blood component or derivative, allergenic product, or analogous product, or arsphenamine or its derivatives (or any other trivalent organic arsenic compound), applicable to the prevention, treatment or cure of diseases or injuries of man ..." Section 123(d) of the Food and Drug Administration Modernization Act of 1997 (FDA Modernization Act) amends the PHS Act by including within the definition of biological products "conditions" as well as diseases. 42 U.S.C. § 262(I) (effective February 19, 1998).

... A somatic cell clone used to create a cloned human being for an infertile individual is a product applicable to the treatment of infertility. Likewise, a somatic cell clone used to create a cloned human being to avoid transmission of a genetic disease from a prospective parent is a product applicable to the prevention of that genetic disease in the cloned human being. In addition, significant safety questions have been raised regarding whether the cloning process will produce a healthy human being who will develop normally. For example, the cloned human being might have defects from the donor or during development, such as genetic, biochemical, or cellular defects.

A somatic cell clone is not one of the specifically listed products in section 351 of the PHS Act. It is, however, an "analogous product" under the PHS Act and thus falls within the scope of this section.

... A somatic cell clone has similarities in composition and function with blood and blood components. A somatic cell clone is analogous to white blood cells, a component of blood, in that both cells are similarly composed because they are somatic cells that contain a nucleus. A somatic cell clone is also like blood and blood components in that they contain cellular elements derived from a living human being and are applicable to diseases or conditions of human beings.

. . . .

Under the FD&C Act, the term "drug" is defined as "articles (other than food) intended to affect the structure or any function of the body." . . . As described above, a somatic cell clone is a product intended to affect the structure or function (including the diseases or conditions) of the cloned human being. The continued growth and development of the cloned human being are the result of the maturation of the somatic cell clone. In addition, a somatic cell clone could be viewed as a product intended to affect the structure or function of the woman into whose uterus the somatic cell is to be implanted.

A product also is a "drug" if it is "intended for use in the diagnosis, cure, mitigation, treatment, or prevention of disease in man or other animals." A somatic cell clone used to create a cloned human being in order to avoid transmission of a genetic disease from a prospective parent with the disease would be an article intended to prevent the transmission of disease to the cloned human being and thus would fall within this definition. A somatic cell clone used with the intent to create a cloned human being for an infertile couple also could fall within this drug definition in that the product would be used to treat infertility.

. . . .

In the regulatory approach [the agency had proposed for tissue in 1997], FDA addressed reproductive tissues and noted that such tissues have a long history of use in the medical community. FDA also recognized that such tissues raised a number of less substantial issues than those raised by other tissues that have a systemic effect on the body. As a result, FDA stated that such tissues would be subject to less regulation than other tissues that have a systematic effect on the body. Unlike the reproductive tissues discussed in the regulatory approach, tissues and cells for cloning of human beings raise additional significant health concerns not raised by processes in place for the reproductive tissues used in the past. Consistent with the tiered approach for cellular and tissue-based products, a somatic cell clone would be subject to FDA premarket review and approval because it is more than minimally manipulated.

Under the authorities of both Acts, FDA promulgated regulations to allow clinical research on investigational drugs and biological products. Clinical research on these products can proceed only when an investigational new drug application (IND) is in effect. Before such research may begin, the sponsor of the research is required to submit to FDA an IND describing the proposed research plan. The sponsor also is required to obtain authorization to proceed from an institutional review board (an independent group of experts and consumers which reviews the proposed study from a scientific and ethical perspective). Thus, before an egg is removed from a woman or the cell containing the nucleus to be inserted into the egg is removed from the prospective genetic parent for the purpose of creating a cloned human being, an IND should be in place and informed consent obtained.

NOTE

For further discussion of FDA's authority to regulate—and if appropriate to prohibit—human cloning, *see* Christine Willgoos, *FDA Regulation: An Answer to the Questions of Human Cloning and Germline Gene Therapy*, 27 AM. J. OF LAW & MED. 101 (2001); Hank Greely, *Cloning and Government Regulation*, 53 HASTINGS L.J. 1085 (2002); Elizabeth Price, *Does the FDA Have Authority to Regulate Human Cloning?*, 11 HARV. J.L. & TECH. 619 (1998); Gregory Rokosz, *Human Cloning: Is the Reach of FDA Authority Too Far a Stretch?*, 30 SETON HALL L. REV. 464 (2002). As of October 1, 2006, there is no firm evidence that any U.S. researcher has risked FDA enforcement action by attempting to clone a human being.

5.   XENOTRANSPLANTATION

When in 1990 FDA asserted jurisdiction over human heart valves as medical devices, it had already ordered the manufacturers of artificial heart valves and providers of porcine (pig) valves to submit premarket approval applications for these "devices." 52 Fed. Reg. 18162 (May 13, 1987). FDA's later approval of PMAs for porcine valves is clear evidence that the agency has jurisdiction over at least some implants derived from animals—known as xenotransplants. Although the technology is still in the investigational stage, there continues to be interest in the possibility that animals may be, or may be made to become, sources of tissues or possibly even organs for humans. The scarcity of cadaver organs for transplantation helps fuel this interest. The development of drugs to suppress the body's rejection of foreign materials, which has been key to the success of human organ transplants, has also stimulated xenotransplantation research. More than two dozen clinical trials using animal source materials have been undertaken in the United States, pursuant to INDs approved by FDA. None has yet led to an application for marketing approval.

Because this research involves human subjects, there has been little question that it is subject to FDA oversight. Whether categorized as drugs, biologics, or medical devices, materials derived from animals implanted in human subjects fall under FDA's authority to regulate the clinical investigation of medical products.

Jodi K. Frederickson, *He's All Heart* ... *and a Little Pig Too: A Look at the FDA Draft Xenotransplant Guideline*

52 FOOD AND DRUG LAW JOURNAL 429 (1997).

Xenotransplantation is the transplanting of organs or tissues across species, and is by no means a new concept. Xenotransplantation was first attempted in 1905. Advances in scientific technology and increasing efficacy of antirejection therapy in allogeneic transplants allowed xenotransplants to come closer to being a reality in the 1960s. Early efforts involved attempts to transplant baboon organs into human recipients. The baboons were chosen because the similarity between human and baboon physiology gave rise to the hope that the two species could accept one another's organs with minimal rejection. These early attempts were largely unsuccessful, but laid the groundwork and identified the issues researchers needed to confront in future attempts.

. . . .

In 1995, the University of Pittsburgh Medical Center performed the first baboon-to-human liver transplants on two patients dying of Hepatitis B. The first recipient lived for seventy-one days before dying of a brain hemorrhage stemming from a fungal infection, and the second recipient died of sepsis, a common cause of death in transplant patients, twenty-six days after the transplant. According to surgeons, neither death was attributable to the source of the livers, but rather was due to complications associated with transplants in general. The surgeons used a combination of four drugs intended to prevent hyper-acute rejection, at levels that may have contributed to the patients' deaths. In 1984, Baby Fae received a baboon heart to replace her congenitally defective heart, in hopes that her immune system would be too immature to mount an immune response. She died a mere twenty days later of graft rejection and infection.

Human organ transplants have become almost commonplace due to the arsenal of drugs designed to combat rejection of transplanted tissues. The increasing efficacy of these agents has made the transplantation of organs that are not closely matched a realistic option, and it permits science to move one step closer to utilizing organs that are not only non-HLA [human leukocyte antigen] matched, but also are harvested from entirely different species.

. . . .

The potential of xenotransplants is phenomenal, but does not come without associated, and potentially catastrophic, risks. The issue of paramount concern is the potential for viruses to use transplanted organs as vehicles into the human body, where they may develop into new diseases with epidemic potential. The gravity of these concerns escalates when viewed in light of the recent outbreaks of HIV, Ebola virus, and hantavirus that have killed thousands, and the looming possibility of unknown viruses waiting for an opportunity to strike. Also, given the etiology of viral infections, a xenotransplant recipient unknowingly may be a carrier and/or a vector for a strange new virus due to the long incubation period of some viruses (as was the case with HIV and other retroviruses). Of greater concern is that, during this latency period, a carrier may act as a "Typhoid Mary," passing the virus along to unwitting victims. HIV carriers, for example, may harbor the virus for years before exhibiting any of the symptoms of AIDS, and subsequently may pass the virus on to unsuspecting recipients. Such concerns with xenotransplants, therefore, are not unwarranted.

The similarities of certain species, such as primates, increase the likelihood that a virus may cross over into humans. Infections are a major concern following any transplant, without regard to organ source, and are much more likely to take hold in transplant recipients due to the concomitant immunosuppressive therapy to combat rejection....

The draft guideline addresses xenotransplantation protocol issues by delineating the qualifications of the transplantation team, the parameters for clinical review of the protocol, health surveillance plans, and requirements for informed consent. The draft guideline also provides requirements for animal sources by procurement parameters, biomedical research animal facilities, preclinical screening for known infectious agents, herd/colony health maintenance and surveillance, individual source animal screening and qualification, procurement and screening of xenografts, and archives or source medical records and specimens. Clinical issues are addressed by setting parameters for the xenotransplant recipient, contacts of the recipient (i.e., family and intimate contacts), control of infection within the hospital, and maintenance of health care records. The public health is preserved by the establishment of a national registry, and the archiving of serum and tissue samples.

. . . .

The development of a draft guideline was deemed an acceptable compromise between competing interests—those representing the risks and the promise of xenotransplantation. FDA regulations direct that use of a guideline is nonbinding on the industry, but will be considered the appropriate minimum standard of care. The decision to use a guideline rather than a regulation is indicative of FDA's policy to allow for greater flexibility as the industry develops, while providing insight into FDA views. A guideline, such as the xenotransplant draft guideline, is readily adaptable and may be updated as technology progresses, whereas a regulation must comply with notice-and-comment procedures for its initial promulgation as well as all substantive changes.... Although draft guidelines do not carry the force and effect of law, they provide strong evidence of the standard FDA will apply in compliance considerations. . . .

The draft guideline suggests that patients be informed of specific risks associated with xenotransplants. The recipient should be informed that there is the potential for infection from zoonotic agents, including those infections known to be associated with the donor species and those yet to be identified. Furthermore, the patient must be made aware of the uncertainty as to the risks, including the likelihood of a latency period with any infectious agents, and that any resulting clinical diseases may be unknown. The draft guideline also suggests that the recipient should be adequately informed that there exists a risk of transmission of xenogeneic infectious agents to his or her close contacts, including family members and particularly sexual contacts. Recipients must be informed and understand that they may be isolated while hospitalized and that there are special precautions to be adhered to after discharge from the hospital.

The patient will be required to consent to life-long surveillance, including physical examinations and tissue sampling, and the recipient and his/her close contacts will be required to report to a physician immediately the event of any unexplained physical illnesses. The recipient must keep the transplant investigator abreast of address and telephone number changes to facilitate life-long surveillance. The team also should discuss the eventual need to perform a complete autopsy on the recipient; this discussion should include family members so as to ensure that the recipient's wishes ultimately are carried out. The recipient must understand that his or her medical records will be accessible by public health authorities, but that confidentiality of those records will be maintained. Finally, the recipient should never donate blood, tissues, or fluids. . . .

NOTES

1. *FDA Guidance for Xenotransplant Studies.* FDA has published its advice on the design and conduct of clinical studies employing animal tissues in a series of guidances. *See, e.g,* Source Animal, Product, Preclinical and Clinical Issues Concerning the Use of Xenotransplantation Products in Humans, Final Guidance (Apr. 2003); Public Health Issues Posed by the Use of Nonhuman Primate Xenografts in Humans, Draft Guidance (Apr. 1999).

As of October 1, 2006, FDA acknowledged having received approximately two dozen INDs for clinical applications of xenotransplantation, of which perhaps fifteen were still active. *Cf. Campaign for Responsible Transplantation v. U.S. Food and Drug Administration*, 219 F. Supp. 2d 106 (D.D.C. 2002).

2. *Risks and Potential Benefits.* For a comprehensive yet balanced summary of risks and benefits, *see* Jack M. Kress, *Xenotransplantation: Ethics and Economics*, 53 Food & Drug L.J. 353 (1998). With respect specifically to the public health risks, *see* Parik Florencio & Erik Ramantham, *Legal Enforcement of Xenotransplantation Public Health Standards*, 32 J.L. Med. & Ethics 117 (2004); F.H. Bach, et al., *Uncertainty in Xenotransplantation: Individual Benefit Versus Collective Risk*, 4 Nature Med.141 (1998)(emphasizing that not only the recipient of animal tissue but also her family, friends, and neighbors could be exposed to pathogens harbored by the source animals); *Xenotransplantation,*18 Nature Biotechnology IT53 (2000) (listing companies reported to be sponsoring xenograft studies).

CHAPTER VII

MEDICAL DEVICES

FDA's regulation of medical devices has gone through two distinct phases. The first phase began with enactment of the 1938 Act and extended to the mid–1970s. The second and still evolving phase opened with enactment of the Medical Device Amendments of 1976. This chapter reviews FDA's enforcement of the medical device provisions of the 1938 Act, explores the reasons why the 1976 Amendments were enacted, and examines the first three decades of FDA's implementation of the new regulatory regime.

A. HISTORICAL BACKGROUND

Medical devices were made subject to the 1938 Act largely because of congressional concern about the growing number of fraudulent—and in many instances implausible—instruments being marketed during the 1930s. This problem, however, was not new.

Wallace F. Janssen, *The Gadgeteers*
Chapter 16 of Barrett & Knight, THE HEALTH ROBBERS (1980).*

When Benjamin Franklin published his discoveries on electricity he also helped open the door for two of the most famous frauds in medical history.... In 1784, while representing the United States in France, Franklin was appointed to a royal commission to investigate the hypnotist Antoine Mesmer, whose treatments had become the rage of Paris. Mesmer, clad in a lilac suit, carrying a metal wand and playing a harmonica, healed by what he called "animal magnetism." Patients sat around a huge vat or "battery," holding iron rods which were immersed in a solution. The treatments went on for hours, accompanied by shouts, hysterical laughter and convulsions. The Franklin commission, after conducting some experiments, reported no electricity in Mesmer's tub. Nor could they detect the current known as "animal magnetism." A royal decree banned further treatments, but Mesmer was allowed to take his winnings to England....

Ten years later, Elisha Perkins, a mule trader turned physician, secured a patent for "Perkins Tractors." ... The tractors, two pointed rods about three inches long, one gold-colored, the other silver, were simply drawn downward across the afflicted part of the anatomy, in a sort of scratching motion. This, it was theorized, would draw off the "noxious

* Copyright 1980, George F. Stickley Co.,
Philadelphia, Pa. 19106.

fluid" (electricity) which was alleged to cause disease. "Tractoration," of course, was universal therapy—good for everything. For a time, the Perkins treatment enjoyed amazing popularity. Ministers, college professors and Congressmen gave enthusiastic endorsement. The Chief Justice of the Supreme Court bought a pair and President Washington himself is supposed to have been a customer. The medical profession was initially impressed; but in 1796 the Connecticut Medical Society condemned the treatment as "gleaned from the miserable remains of animal magnetism." In the following year the Society expelled Dr. Perkins from membership. In 1799, Dr. Perkins voluntarily served in a yellow fever epidemic in New York, caught the disease, and died. Tractoration withered away.

But electrical health gadgetry marched on—through the 19th century and into the 20th.... In the 1920's, Albert Abrams, M.D., invented the system of diagnosis and healing he called "Radionics." Soon more than 3,000 local practitioners, mainly chiropractors, were sending dried blood specimens from patients to be inserted in Abrams' "Radioscope." The diagnosis would come back on a postcard, with recommended dial settings for treatment with other Abrams machines....

Albert Abrams had many imitators, among them Ruth Drown, a Los Angeles chiropractor. One of her many nonsensical inventions was the Drown Radio-therapeutic Instrument. With this little black box and *two* blood spots, Mrs. Drown claimed to be able to "tune in" specific organs of the body and treat a patient by remote control anywhere in the world! ...

Wilhelm Reich, M.D., one-time pupil of psychiatrist Sigmund Freud, claimed to have discovered "orgone energy," the most powerful force in the universe, and wrote extensively of its manifestations.... Soon after coming to the United States in 1934, Reich designed and built "orgone accumulators." Most of them were boxes of wood, metal and insulation board about the size of a telephone booth. Disease, he claimed, could be cured simply by sitting inside the box and absorbing the orgone. Hundreds of the boxes were sold or leased to practitioners and laymen for treatment of all kinds of diseases including cancer. Rentals were around $250 per month....

NOTES

1. *History of Device Regulation.* For a history of device regulation, *see* Peter Barton Hutt, *A History of Government Regulation of Adulteration and Misbranding of Medical Devices*, 44 FOOD DRUG COSM. L.J. 99 (1989).

2. *Legislative History.* The key legislative history of the device provisions of the 1938 Act is summarized in *United States v. An Article of Drug ... Bacto–Unidisk*, 394 U.S. 784 (1969).

B.   REGULATION OF DEVICES UNDER THE 1938 FD&C ACT

The 1938 Act gave FDA jurisdiction over medical devices, but did not give the agency authority to review them for safety or effectiveness prior to marketing, nor to establish and enforce performance standards. FDA's power over devices prior to 1976 was thus limited primarily to pursuit of judicial remedies by actions brought in federal district court charging violations of the 1938 Act's basic misbranding and adulteration provisions. Probably the most important provision was section 502, which declares a drug or device to be misbranded "[i]f its labeling is false or misleading in any particular." The 1976 Medical Device Amendments gave FDA important new authorities, including premarket review, but the Act's basic adulteration and misbranding provisions remain important regulatory tools.

Medical Device Legislation—1975

House Committee on Interstate and Foreign Commerce.
94th Congress, 1st Session (1975).

The medical devices in use during the late 1930's and through the late 1940's were of relatively simple and basic design. Seizure and injunction actions by FDA were generally limited to actions against a persistent series of "quack" devices. Legitimate devices were generally only reviewed for the accuracy of labeling. Between 1939 and 1941, the FDA initiated roughly 100 seizure actions against devices. At that time, several dangerous devices, such as lead nipple shields which caused nursing infants to incur lead poisoning, contraceptives which often caused genital infection and injury, and vaporizers which caused sinus and eustachian tube infections were removed from the market. . . .

The post-war years brought forth a wide variety of "quack" devices utilizing colored lights, dangerous gases such as ozone and chlorine, radio waves, heat, and vibration with claims of treatment and cure for virtually every disease known to man. One such device was a simple galvanometer which was encased in an impressive box and purportedly could diagnose any illness known to man. But when tested by the FDA on a corpse, the device registered a reading. It cost only a few dollars to produce, yet sold for hundreds of dollars.

The post-war revolution in biomedical technology also resulted in the introduction of a wide variety of sophisticated but legitimate devices. New developments in the electronic, plastics, metallurgy, and ceramics industries, coupled with progress in design engineering, led to invention of the heart pacemaker, the kidney dialysis machine, defibrillators, cardiac and renal catheters, surgical implants, artificial vessels and heart valves, intensive care monitoring units, and a wide spectrum of diagnostic and therapeutic devices. The increased sophistication of medical products, coupled with a stronger authority to regulate drugs, caused FDA to classify some of the new products as drugs. During the 1950s and 1960s, FDA encountered increasing difficulty in proving why certain dangerous or ineffective medical devices should be removed from the market. Device manufacturers were increasingly inclined to challenge FDA actions in the courts as the Diapulse Litigation illustrates.

COMMENT: DIAPULSE LITIGATION

In November 1965, FDA instituted its first seizure of a Diapulse, beginning litigation that lasted more than 20 years and exposed central deficiencies of the 1938 Act. The Diapulse was designed to produce a high frequency electrical pulse, similar to a conventional diathermy unit, but with lower output. FDA took the position that it was a misbranded device because it did not produce sufficient heat to provide the claimed therapeutic benefit. Although the government prevailed at trial, *United States v. An Article of Device . . . Diapulse Manufacturing Corp. of America*, 269 F. Supp. 162 (D. Conn. 1967), and on appeal, 389 F.2d 612 (2d Cir. 1968), the violations continued. FDA therefore secured a permanent injunction against further sales. *United States v. Diapulse Corp. of America*, 457 F.2d 25 (2d Cir. 1972). *See* Comment, *U.S. v. The Diapulse Corporation of America*, 8 NEW ENG. L. REV. 111 (1972).

In October 1973, FDA advised Congress: "The *Diapulse* cases require us to expend an inordinate amount of the resources allocated to device regulation, and thereby restrict investigative effort with respect to other dangerous or useless devices." "Medical Devices," Hearings before the Subcomm. on Public Health and Environment of the House Comm. on Interstate and Foreign Commerce, 93d Cong., 1st Sess. 155 (1973). Indeed, the litigation did not end with the Second Circuit's 1972 decision; FDA enforcement activities continued into 1976. A criminal contempt action failed, but the court strengthened the injunction. *United States v. Diapulse Corp. of Am.*, 365 F. Supp. 935 (E.D.N.Y. 1973), 514 F.2d 1097 (2d Cir. 1975). FDA then lost a seizure action in a District Court, but won on appeal. *United States v. Articles of Device . . . "Diapulse,"* 527 F.2d 1008 (6th Cir. 1976), *reh'g denied*, 532 F.2d 1056 (6th Cir. 1976). When FDA again initiated seizures, the claimant, a physician, acknowledged misbranding violations, but the District Court declined to condemn the devices and instead allowed them to be relabeled over the agency's objections. The Court of Appeals ruled that the trial court had incorrectly conducted a de novo trial on the validity of the relabeling rather than first requiring the claimant to submit a compliance proposal to FDA. *United States v. An Article of Device . . . Diapulse*, 650 F.2d 908 (7th Cir. 1981). On remand, the District Court affirmed FDA's refusal to accept the relabeling. *See United States v. An Article of Device . . . Diapulse*, 768 F.2d 826 (7th Cir. 1985).

In the interim, based on FDA's approval (pursuant to the 1976 Medical Device Amendments) of a higher-powered diathermy device marketed by a competing company, the Diapulse Corporation persuaded the District Court to permit it to market a modified Diapulse device similar to the newly approved device. That ruling against FDA was upheld on appeal. *United States v. Diapulse Corp. of America*, 748 F.2d 56 (2d Cir. 1984). Rather than market a Diapulse identical to the approved competitor device, however, the Diapulse Corporation continued research on its own lower-powered version. It ultimately obtained FDA's agreement to a narrower claim, "for adjunctive use in the palliative treatment of post-operative edema and pain in superficial tissues." 13 Medical Devices, Diagnostics & Instrumentation Rep. (the "Gray Sheet"), No. 16, at I & W–12 (Apr. 20, 1987).

———

In 1950, L. Ron Hubbard, a science-fiction writer, published a bestselling book titled *Dianetics: The Modern Science of Mental Health*. Dianetics was a purely secular approach to self-improvement. Hubbard soon began to add religious elements to his theory, however, and in 1953, he founded the Church of Scientology. Over ensuing decades, the Church of Scientology grew into a global organization.

The Hubbard Electrometer, or E-meter, is used in the Church of Scientology's "auditing" process, by which adherents strive to purge from their minds negative memories known as "engrams." The Church of Scientology's assertion that the E-meter plays an essential part in the practice of religion complicated FDA's attempts to enforce the FD&C Act against what the agency saw as a worthless device.

Founding Church of Scientology v. United States

409 F.2d 1146 (D.C. Cir.), *cert. denied*, 396 U.S. 963 (1969).

■ J. SKELLY WRIGHT, CIRCUIT JUDGE.

This is an appeal from a judgment and decree of condemnation and destruction against several electrical instruments and a large quantity of literature owned by claimants-appellants, The Founding Church of Scientology of Washington, D.C. and various individual adherents of that organization. The instruments and literature were seized by the Food and Drug Administration as "devices" with accompanying "false and misleading labeling" subject to condemnation under the Food, Drug and Cosmetic Act. The Government further charged that the instruments were "devices" lacking "adequate directions for use," in further violation of the Act. After a jury trial, a general verdict "for the Government" was returned, and a judgment and decree of condemnation was entered.

Appellants contend that ... the proceedings interfered with the free exercise of their religion, and that the evidence was insufficient to sustain the verdict. Because we find that much of the literature relied on by the Government to establish misbranding was not "labeling" within the meaning of the statute as interpreted in the light of the First Amendment, we reverse....

... The Government has charged that the instruments seized, Hubbard Electrometers or "E-meters," are "devices" as defined in the Act, that the literature seized constitutes "labeling" of the device, in that it is "written, printed, or graphic matter ... accompanying" the device; and that this "labeling" is false or misleading....

Appellants in this case, claimants to the seized materials, are individual and corporate adherents to the movement known as Scientology. The movement apparently rests almost entirely upon the writings of one man, L. Ron Hubbard, an American who maintained the headquarters of the movement in England at the time this action was brought. In the early 1950's, Hubbard wrote tracts elucidating what he called "Dianetics." Dianetics is a theory of the mind which sets out many of the therapeutic techniques now used by Scientologists, including techniques attacked by the Government in this case as false healing....

Dianetics is not presented as a simple description of the mind, but as a practical science which can cure many of the ills of man. It terms the ordinary person, encumbered by the "engrams" of his reactive mind, as a "preclear," by analogy to a computer from which previously programmed instructions have not been erased. The goal of Dianetics is to make persons "clear," thus freeing the rational and infallible analytical mind....

From the evidence developed at trial, it appears that a major activity of the Founding Church and its affiliated organizations in the District of Columbia is providing "auditing," at substantial fees (at the time of trial $500 for a 25–hour course), to persons interested in Scientology.... There is no membership in the Church as such; persons are accepted for auditing on the basis of their interest in Scientology (and presumably their ability to pay for its benefits).

The Hubbard Electrometer, or E-meter, plays an essential, or at least important, part in the process of auditing. The E-meter is a skin galvanometer, similar to those used in giving lie detector tests. The subject or "preclear" holds in his hands two tin soup cans, which are linked to the electrical apparatus. A needle on the apparatus registers changes in the electrical resistance of the subject's skin. The auditor asks questions of the subject, and the movement of the needle is apparently used as a check of the emotional reaction to the questions. According to complex rules and procedures set out in Scientology publications, the auditor can interpret the movements of the needle after certain prescribed questions are asked, and use them in diagnosing the mental and spiritual condition of the subject. The E-meters are sold for about $125, and are advertised in Scientology publications available at the Distribution Center adjoining the Church....

In its legal arguments the Government has contended from the outset that whether or not Scientology is a religion, and whether or not auditing or processing is a practice of that religion, are entirely irrelevant to the case. Religious beliefs, it is argued, are entirely protected by the First Amendment, but action in the name of religion is susceptible to legal regulation under the same standards and to the same degree as it would be if entirely secular in purpose.

Appellants have argued from the first that the entire case must fall as an unconstitutional religious persecution. In their view, auditing or processing is a central practice of their religion, akin to confession in the Catholic Church, and hence entirely exempt from regulation or prohibition. They have made no attempt to contradict the expert testimony introduced by the Government. They have conceded that the E-meter is of no use in the diagnosis or treatment of disease as such, and have argued that it was never put forward as having such use. Auditing or processing, in their view, treats the spirit of man, not his body, though through the healing of the spirit the body can be affected....

The principles enunciated in [prior decisions of the Supreme Court] ... at least raise a constitutional doubt concerning the condemnation of instruments and literature apparently central to the practice of religion. That doubt becomes more serious when we turn to the decision of the Supreme Court in *United States v. Ballard*, 322 U.S. 78 (1944)....

... Here the E-meter has been condemned, not because it is itself harmful, but because the representations made concerning it are "false or misleading." And the largest part of those representations is contained in the literature of Scientology describing the process of auditing which appellants have claimed, without contest from the Government, is part of the doctrine of their religion and central to its exercise. Thus if their claims to religious status are accepted, a finding that the seized literature misrepresents the benefits from auditing is a finding that their religious doctrines are false. To construe the Food, Drug and Cosmetic Act to permit such a finding would ... present the gravest constitutional difficulties. . . .

By far the greatest bulk of the material alleged to be "false labeling" of the E-meter consists of the general literature of Scientology, which presents in an integrated manner the theory sketched earlier concerning the human mind, the sources of various sorts of unhappiness, personality disorder and psychosomatic complaints, and the way in which the process of auditing can alleviate these ills. . . .

Were the literature here introduced clearly secular, we might well conclude that under existing law it constituted "labeling" for purposes of the Act. . . . However, such broad readings are not favored when they impinge upon constitutionally sensitive areas, especially in the absence of a showing of legislative intent to regulate these areas. . . .

Finally, we come to the vexing question: is Scientology a religion? On the record as a whole, we find that appellants have made out a *prima facie* case that the Founding Church of Scientology is a religion. . . .

(1) We do not hold that the Founding Church is for all legal purposes a religion. Any *prima facie* case made out for religious status is subject to contradiction by a showing that the beliefs asserted to be religious are not held in good faith by those asserting them, and that forms of religious organization were erected for the sole purpose of cloaking a secular enterprise with the legal protections of religion.

(2) We do not hold that, even if Scientology is a religion, all literature published by it is religious doctrine immune from the Act.

(3) We do not hold that public health laws in general, or the Food, Drug and Cosmetic Act in particular, have no application to the activities of religion. For instance, it may well be that adulterated foods, drugs or devices used in religious practices can be condemned under the Act. It may be that a drug or device used in religion is subject to condemnation as "misbranded" if its labeling is found to lack, for instance, adequate directions for use, as was charged in this case. Our holding prevents only a finding of false labeling on the basis of doctrinal religious literature.

(4) Finally, we made no holding concerning the power of Congress to deal generally with the making of false claims by religions deemed injurious to the public health or welfare. . . .

■ McGOWAN, CIRCUIT JUDGE (dissenting):

     . . . .

This proceeding did not involve an inquisition into the validity of any personal religious beliefs, or the infliction of a punishment upon any person for holding or disseminating such beliefs. It was a proceeding against property under a Congressional statute aimed at protecting the unsophisticated against not only wasting their money but, more importantly, endangering their lives by relying upon misbranded machines. There is, as the majority points out, a well-recognized distinction between the good faith holding of a religious belief, however bizarre, and unlimited freedom to implement that belief by conduct. I do not believe that the Government was required, at least in a statutory *in rem* proceeding of the kind here involved, to show that, over and above the misbranding of the device, the religious pretensions of its sponsors were fraudulent.

NOTES

1. *Subsequent Proceedings.* Upon retrial following remand, the District Court held that the Founding Church of Scientology had met its burden of establishing its status as a bona fide religion. It also found the E-meter to be misbranded. The court's decree returned the devices and literature to the church for use only in bona fide religious counseling. *United States v. An Article of Device ... "Hubbard Electrometer,"* 333 F. Supp. 357 (D.D.C. 1971). Its order, designed to assure observance of this limitation, would have required the following statement to be affixed to every E-meter:

> The E-meter is a device which has been condemned by Order of a Federal Court for misrepresentation and misbranding, in violation of the Federal Food, Drug, and Cosmetic Act. Use of the E-meter is permitted only as part of bona-fide religious activity. The E-meter is not medically or scientifically useful for the diagnosis, treatment, or prevention of any disease. It is not medically or scientifically capable of improving the health or bodily functions of anyone. Any person using, selling or distributing the E-meter is forbidden by law to represent, state or imply that the E-meter is useful in the diagnosis, treatment, or prevention of any disease.

The court order would also have required a similar version of the statement to be signed by every recipient of auditing services and to appear in the Church's E-meter literature. 969–1974 FDLI Jud. Rec. 90 (D.D.C. 1971).

Upon appeal once more, the Court of Appeals, per curiam, concluded that the lower court's order "would involve the Government and the courts in an excessive entanglement with religion ... in circumstances in which the legitimate governmental interest in law enforcement can be protected by a narrower remedy." It therefore modified the order to read as follows:

> 1. E-meters shall be used or sold or distributed only for use in bona fide religious counseling.

> 2. Each E-meter shall bear the following warning, printed in 11–point leaded type, permanently affixed to the front of the E-meter so that it is clearly visible when the E-meter is used, sold, or distributed:

>> The E-meter is not medically or scientifically useful for the diagnosis, treatment, or prevention of any disease. It is not medically or scientifically capable of improving the health or bodily functions of anyone.

> 3. Any and all items of written, printed, or graphic matter which directly or indirectly refers [sic] to the E-meter or to Dianetics and/or Scientology and/or auditing or processing shall ... bear the following prominent printed warning ... :

WARNING

The device known as a Hubbard Electrometer, or E-meter, used in auditing, a process of Scientology and Dianetics, is not medically or scientifically useful for the diagnosis, treatment, or prevention of any disease. It is not medically or scientifically capable of improving the health or bodily functions of anyone.

1969–1974 FDLI Jud. Rec. 131 (D.C. Cir. 1973).

2. *Other E–Meter Cases.* Courts in *Church of Scientology of California v. Richardson*, 437 F.2d 214 (9th Cir. 1971), and *Church of Scientology of Minnesota v. Department of HEW*, 459 F.2d 1044 (8th Cir. 1972), *aff'g* 341 F. Supp. 563 (D. Minn. 1971), upheld FDA's summary detention of imported E-meters based on charges, *inter alia*, that their labeling failed to bear "adequate directions for use." Both decisions relied on the broad authority over imports granted to FDA by section 801(a) of the FDCA.

3. *Enforcement Against Quack Devices.* Although most FDA seizures under the device provisions of the 1938 Act have resulted in default or consent decrees, actions against so-called "quack" devices often precipitated protracted litigation. *See, e.g., United States v. Urbuteit*, 335 U.S. 355 (1948); *United States v. Articles of Device . . . "Kuf Diatherapuncteur"*, 481 F.2d 434 (10th Cir. 1973); *United States v. Ellis Research Laboratories, Inc.*, 300 F.2d 550 (7th Cir. 1962); *Drown v. United States*, 198 F.2d 999 (9th Cir. 1952), *discussed in* Tobias G. Klinger, *Conflict with Quackery*, 8 Food Drug Cosm. L.J. 777 (1953); *United States v. Ghadiali*, 165 F.2d 957 (3d Cir. 1948); *United States v. One Device . . . Colonic Irrigator*, 160 F.2d 194 (10th Cir. 1947); *United States v. Relaxacizor, Inc.*, 340 F. Supp. 943 (C.D. Cal. 1970); *United States v. 46 Devices Labeled "Dynatone,"* 315 F. Supp. 588 (D. Minn. 1970); *United States v. An Article of Device . . . "Cameron Spitler Amblyo–Syntonizer . . . ,"* 261 F. Supp. 243 (D. Neb. 1966); *United States v. "2000 Plastic Tubular Cases . . . Each Containing 2 Toothbrushes,"* 231 F. Supp. 236 (M.D. Pa. 1964); *United States v. 24 Devices . . . "Sunflo Flowing Air Purifier,"* 202 F. Supp. 147 (D.N.J. 1962); *United States v. Article of Device . . . "110 V Vapozone . . . ,"* 194 F. Supp. 332 (N.D. Cal. 1961); *United States v. 22 Devices . . . Halox Therapeutic Generator*, 98 F. Supp. 914 (S.D. Cal. 1951); *United States v. 6 Devices, "Electreat Mechanical Heart,"* 38 F. Supp. 236 (W.D. Mo. 1941). *See also* FDA, Recent Enforcment Actions Involving Therapeutic Devices, January 1–December 31, 1963 (1964).

4. *Organizational Responsibility.* The same FDA unit was responsible for regulating drugs and medical devices until the device program was transferred from the Bureau of Drugs to the Office of the Associate Commissioner for Medical Affairs in 1971. David M. Link & Larry R. Pilot, *FDA's Medical Device Program*, FDA Papers, May 1972, at 24 (1972). In 1974, in anticipation of the enactment of the Medical Device Amendments, the device program was transferred to a new Bureau of Medical Devices and Diagnostic Products. 39 Fed. Reg. 5812 (Feb. 15, 1974). In 1982, this bureau was combined with the Bureau of Radiological Health to form the National Center for Devices and Radiological Health (CDRH), 47 Fed. Reg. 44614 (October 8, 1982).

COMMENT: THE DRUG–DEVICE DISTINCTION

According to Professor David F. Cavers, *The Food, Drug, and Cosmetic Act of 1938: Its Legislative History and Its Substantive Provisions*, 6 Law & Contemp. Probs. 2 (1939):

The definition of "drug" in the old [1906] Act was defective in two respects. It did not cover (1) products designed to affect the structure or functioning of the body where disease was not involved or (2) mechanical devices used either for such purposes or in the diagnosis or treatment of disease. Consequently the [FDA] was powerless to combat a host of both types of products which appeared on the market under misleading claims and which in some instances were positively dangerous to the user. Accordingly the term "drug" was redefined in S.1944 so as to include these products. The simple tactic, far from uncommon in statutory definition, of giving a special meaning to an ordinary term, evoked unexpected opposition, and ultimately separate definitions were provided for "drug" and "device" [in the 1938 Act]. . . .

Under the 1938 Act, the definition of "device" in section 201(h) was: "instruments, apparatus [sic], and contrivances, including their components, parts, and accessories, intended (1) for use in the diagnosis, cure, mitigation, treatment, or prevention of disease in man or other animals; or (2) to affect the structure or function of the body of man or other animals." The distinction between a drug and a device was fuzzy, because the definition of "device" did not yet include the proviso, added by the Medical Device Amendments of 1976 (MDA), that a device "does not achieve any of its principal intended purposes through chemical action within or on the body of man or other animals and which is not dependent upon being metabolized for the achievement of any of its principal intended purposes."

Before the enactment of the 1976 Amendments, devices, unlike new drugs, were never required to obtain premarket approval from FDA. The agency thus classified a handful of device-like products as drugs rather than devices in order to exercise this higher level of regulatory control over them. In *AMP, Inc. v. Gardner*, 389 F.2d 825 (2d Cir. 1968), *cert. denied*, 393 U.S. 825 (1968), the Second Circuit upheld FDA's contention that the two products described below were drugs:

Both of the products are intended to be used in a new method of tying off, or ligating, severed blood vessels during surgery. The conventional ligating method is to hand-tie ligatures around severed vessels by means of a surgeon's knot (which is a reef knot). AMP's products both consist of a disposable applicator, a nylon ligature loop, and a nylon locking disk. . . . The ligature is applied by inserting the hemostat or tube into the body and placing the loop around the severed vessel, then tightening the loop and locking it in place with the disk. The excess nylon thread is cut off, and the disk and the rest of the thread remain in the patient's body.

In *United States v. An Article of Drug . . . Bacto–Unidisk*, 394 U.S. 784 (1969), *supra* p. 29, the Supreme Court upheld FDA's categorization of an antibiotic sensitivity disc as a drug rather than as a device. With the Court's endorsement of the agency's authority to categorize products so as to protect the public health, FDA's counsel announced that with regard to medical products falling "in the middle ground or the grey area, where they are not clearly one or the other, [the agency has] complete discretion at this

time to decide whether it will handle those products as drugs or devices. . . ." Remarks by Peter Barton Hutt at the FDA Medical Device
Conference of April 11, 1972, 34 FDC Reports (the "Pink Sheet"), No. 16,
at 18–20 (April 17, 1972).

The following are examples of device-like products that FDA classified
as drugs: surgical sutures, contacts lenses, injectable silicone, pregnancy
test kits, and bone cement. The 1976 amendments labeled these products
as "transitional devices." For a complete list, *see* 56 Fed. Reg. 57960,
57961–62 (Nov. 14, 1991). Because the amendments permit FDA to require
premarket approval for many devices, the decision of whether to classify a
product as a drug or device, while still significant, is less critical than it
used to be.

NOTES

1. *In Vitro Diagnostics.* Following the *Bacto–Unidisk* decision, FDA could have
required the submission of NDAs for all in vitro diagnostic products. Instead,
mindful of both the resources it would need and the impact on the industry and the
public health, FDA explicitly declined to determine whether these products would
be regulated as drugs or devices. Rather, the agency prescribed detailed labeling
requirements to assure that users would have accurate and reliable information. 37
Fed. Reg. 819 (Jan. 19, 1972), 37 Fed. Reg. 16613, (Aug. 17, 1972), 38 Fed. Reg.
7096 (Mar. 15, 1973), 21 C.F.R. Part 807 (1989). *See* Adrien L. Ringuette, *Regulatory Aspects of Reagents*, 27 FOOD DRUG COSM. L.J. 557 (1972); *The Future of
Diagnostic Kits and Reagents*, 29 FOOD DRUG COSM. L.J. 246 (1974). Because of the
importance of reliable diagnoses of gonorrhea and cancer, however, FDA announced
that any diagnostic test for these diseases would require an approved NDA 38 Fed.
Reg. 10488 (Apr. 27, 1973), 39 Fed. Reg. 3705 (Jan. 29, 1974).

2. *Commentary.* For discussion of the *AMP* and *Bacto–Unidisk* decisions, see
Vincent A. Kleinfeld, *Surgical Implants: Drugs or Devices, and New Device Legisla-
tion*, 23 FOOD DRUG COSM. L.J. 510 (1968); Ronald L. Styn, *A Dichotomy in Consumer
Protection—The Drug–Device Definition Dilemma*, 44 IND. L.J. 503 (1969); Steven
Weitzman, *Drug, Device, Cosmetic?* (pts. I–II), 24 FOOD DRUG COSM. L.J. 226, 320
(1969).

C. THE 1976 MEDICAL DEVICE AMENDMENTS

1. BACKGROUND

Congress first seriously considered device legislation in 1962. Following
the thalidomide tragedy, Congress focused on enacting the Drug Amend-
ments of 1962 and deferred device legislation. After years of internal
discussion, the Department of HEW established a Study Group on Medical
Devices to consider what form such legislation should take. The Study
Group on Medical Devices (the "Cooper Committee") issued its report in
September 1970. *See* Theodore H. Cooper, *Device Legislation*, 26 FOOD DRUG
COSM. L.J. 165 (1971); Peter Barton Hutt, *A HISTORY OF GOVERNMENT
REGULATION OF ADULTERATION AND MISBRANDING OF MEDICAL DEVICES*, 44 Food
Drug Cosm. L.J. 99 (1989).

Theodore H. Cooper,* *Device Legislation*

26 FOOD DRUG COSMETIC LAW JOURNAL 165 (1971).

By 1937, there were 463 manufacturers of surgical, medical and dental instruments and supplies, and the value of their shipments was a little over one million dollars. The industry grew rather slowly over the next decade. By 1947, the number of manufacturers picked up in the Census count had about doubled—to 980 establishments—while the value of shipments had more than tripled—to $372 million.

In the late 1950's and early 1960's, medical devices rapidly became both more numerous and more complex. Starting with the introduction of monitoring equipment into coronary care units, and automation into laboratories, electronics came to medicine. New implanted devices such as pacemakers, modern anesthetic equipment, and a myriad of diagnostic and therapeutic instruments began to appear. By 1963, there were over 1,300 manufacturers, and the value of shipments had grown to over $1 billion.... By 1967, comparable Census data showed almost 1,500 manufacturers with shipments valued at over $1.5 billion. Census estimates that the 1970 value of shipments was more than $2 billion, and that by 1975, the $2.8 billion, or almost the $3 billion mark will be reached. Census staff emphasize that all of these may be underestimates because of the characteristics of their accounting system.

Today, Census estimates that more than half of the total value of medical device shipments is accounted for in surgical appliances and supplies, including familiar consumable items such as sutures and dressings. Surgical and medical instruments—including X-ray machines and EKG machines—account for slightly less than one-third of the Census totals, with dental supplies and equipment coming in third....

Medical Device Amendments of 1976

House Report No. 853, 94th Congress, 2d Session (1976).

FDA began focusing more attention on hazards from legitimate medical devices around 1960.... New developments in the electronic, plastic, metallurgy, and ceramics industries, coupled with progress in design engineering, led to invention of the heart pacemaker, the kidney dialysis machine, defibrillators, cardiac and renal catheters, surgical implants, artificial vessels and heart valves, intensive care monitoring units, and a wide spectrum of other diagnostic and therapeutic devices. Although many lives have been saved or improved by the new discoveries, the potential for harm to consumers has been heightened by the critical medical conditions in which sophisticated modern devices are used and by the complicated technology involved in their manufacture and use. In the search to expand medical knowledge, new experimental approaches have sometimes been tried without adequate premarket clinical testing, quality control in materials selected, or patient consent.

* [Dr. Theodore Cooper, Director of the National Heart and Lung Institute, chaired the Department of HEW Study Group on Medical Devices in 1969–70. He served as Assistant Secretary for Health from 1974 to 1976.]

An example ... is the Dalkon Shield. In November 1970, the Dalkon Shield was introduced to the medical profession as a safe effective contraceptive device.... In less than two years the Shield had been adopted by 1,497 family planning clinics in the United States and was also being used in world population control programs. The manufacturer reported that more than one million Shields had been sold. In May of 1972, the Family Planning Digest, an official HEW publication, reported that, based on an eighteen month study of 937 patients in family planning programs in California, the pregnancy rate with the Shield was 5.1%, the removal rate for medical reasons was 26.4%, the infection rate was 5%, and the continuation rate after eighteen months was under 60%. By mid–1975 the Shield had been linked to sixteen deaths and twenty-five miscarriages. Presently, more than 500 lawsuits seeking compensatory and punitive damages totalling more than $400 million are pending against the manufacturer of the Shield, which is no longer being marketed....

Experience with two other types of devices further demonstrates the need for increased statutory authority. Significant defects in cardiac pacemakers have necessitated 34 voluntary recalls of pacemakers, involving 23,000 units, since 1972. A recent investigation in four states of eleven patients who experienced unusual eye infections following implantation of intraocular lenses revealed serious impairment of vision in all patients and the necessity to remove the eyes of five patients....

Study Group on Medical Devices, Medical Devices: A Legislative Plan

Department of Health, Education and Welfare (1970).

The variety of medical devices already in use are produced from an equally wide variety of materials. Moreover, the bases of scientific data range from almost pure empiricism to reasonably well systematized information. As a result, there are many scientific and technical issues involved in the evaluation of medical devices that require judgment by expert professionals all along the developmental continuum from research through development to testing, evaluation, and preparation for sale. Accordingly, unilateral decisions by government agencies without expert advice would be as unwise as unilateral decisions by developers or producers....

The study group agrees that definition and classification are important, and that there are inherent differences between drugs and devices— differences in the state of the art, and the size and scope of manufacture. Therefore, the study group believes that a new regulatory plan is needed, one which is specifically adapted to the needs of devices.... By drawing upon the advice of appropriate scientific organizations, the Department can determine an appropriate basis for decisions about which devices are so well recognized as safe and effective as to require neither standards nor pre-clearance. It can also identify devices or characteristics of devices for which *standards* should and can be developed and applied. With continuing assistance of the scientific and medical community, a system for *review of objective data prior to clinical application* can be devised for new and unproven critical devices that are at the leading edge of technological innovation and biomedical explorations to assure the safety and reliability of devices offered to the profession.

NOTES

1. *Anticipatory Implementation.* FDA began to implement the recommendations of the Cooper Committee even before the 1976 Amendments were enacted. *See* David M. Link, *Cooper Committee Report and Its Effect on Current FDA Medical Device Activities*, 27 FOOD DRUG COSM. L.J. 624 (1972).

2. *Legislative History.* The House Report's explanation of the 1976 Amendments consumes 87 pages, H.R. Rep. No. 853, 94th Cong., 2d Sess. (1976). The legislation itself runs 45 pages, 90 Stat. 539 (1976), more than doubling the length of the original FD&C Act.

3. *FDA Implementation Plan.* Seven days after President Ford signed the 1976 Amendments, FDA published a notice in 41 Fed. Reg. 22620 (June 4, 1976) outlining its plan for implementing the new law.

2. OVERVIEW OF THE 1976 AND LATER AMENDMENTS

The Medical Device Amendments added more than a dozen provisions to the 1938 Act. Together, they create a complex and novel system for regulating the development, introduction, and marketing of medical devices. Subsequent statutes have made numerous adjustments to the 1976 structure without modifying the basic regulatory approach that it established. *See* Safe Medical Devices Act of 1990, Pub. L. No. 101–629; Medical Device Amendments of 1992, Pub. L. No. 102–300; Food and Drug Administration Modernization Act of 1997, Pub. L. No. 105–115; Medical Device User Fee and Modernization Act of 2002, Pub. L. No. 107–250. The new regime can best be understood by focusing on six key features.

First, the 1976 Amendments revised the definition of a "device" to achieve two purposes. The new definition was intended to convert some medical products then being regulated as drugs to devices. The definition was also broadened to include products intended to diagnose physiological conditions that are not ordinarily regarded as diseases, such as pregnancy.

Second, the FDA was required to classify all medical devices in accordance with the relative degree of assurance of their safety and effectiveness. Class I includes those devices for which neither special controls nor premarket approval is warranted because the general regulatory controls available under the FD&C Act are sufficient to assure safety and effectiveness. Class II includes those devices for which general controls are not sufficient but for which enough information exists to develop special controls. Class III includes those devices for which general controls are not sufficient to assure safety and effectiveness and there is not sufficient information to establish a performance standard. Class III also includes all devices introduced after the enactment of the 1976 Amendments (postamendment devices) that are not substantially equivalent to a device marketed prior to enactment (preamendment devices).

Third, the 1976 Amendments provide for comprehensive control over the market introduction of all medical devices, a system which operates independently of the classification scheme. After 1976, a device may lawfully be marketed in only one of three ways: (1) a device may be the subject of a premarket notification (PMN) to FDA under section 510(k) which demonstrates that it is "substantially equivalent" to a preamendment device or may be exempt from this requirement; (2) it may be the subject of a premarket approval (PMA) application under Section 515; or (3) upon petition to FDA under section 513(f)(2)(A), it may be reclassified from Class III to Class II or I.

Fourth, two classes of preamendment medical devices are subject to special requirements. A Class II medical device must comply with any special controls established by FDA for that device under section 514. A Class III device must be the subject of an application, eventually approved by FDA, demonstrating its safety and effectiveness and submitted once the agency promulgates a regulation requiring the submission of applications for that type of device.

Fifth, all medical devices, regardless of class and regardless of the manner of market introduction, are subject to the general regulatory controls established under the 1938 Act and amplified by the 1976 and subsequent amendments. These "general controls" include the basic adulteration and misbranding provisions as well as applicable good manufacturing practice (GMP) regulations, banned device regulations, and notification and repair, replacement, or refund requirements.

Sixth, Congress has enacted special rules for specific types of devices. Examples include requirements for custom devices and provisions for extending the patent term for certain Class III devices.

NOTE

See Linda Horton, *Medical Devices: Strengthening Consumer Protection*, FDA CONSUMER, October 1976, at 4; John C. Villforth, *The Medical Device Amendments: 10 Years After*, 20 FDA CONSUMER, May 1986, at 28; William F. Weigel & Charles J. Raubicheck, *How to Comply With the New Medical Device Law*, 31 FOOD DRUG COSM. L.J. 312 (1976).

3. THE DEFINITION OF "DEVICE" SINCE 1976

a. THE LINE BETWEEN DRUG AND DEVICE

As discussed in the chapter on product definitions, *supra* p. 39, the definition of "device" at FD&C Act 201(h) closely mirrors the definition of "drug" at 201(g)(1). This has been the case ever since the device definition was added to the Act in 1938. Indeed, subsequent amendments to the definition have been designed largely to address the distinction between these two categories of products.

The definition of "device" at section 201(h) of the 1938 FD&C Act embraced "instruments, apparatus, and contrivances ... intended (1) for use in the diagnosis, cure, mitigation, treatment, or prevention of disease in man or other animals; or (2) to affect the structure or any function of the body of man or other animals." The 1976 Medical Device Amendments amended the device definition to provide that a device could not achieve "any of its principal purposes" through chemical action or metabolization.

It also expanded the list of device types to: "instrument, apparatus, implement, machine, contrivance, implant, in vitro reagent, or similar or related article." The Safe Medical Devices Act of 1990 further amended the definition to state that an article is a device only if it does not achieve "its primary intended purposes" (rather than "any of its principal purposes") through chemical action within or on the body or by being metabolized. Moreover, the 1990 Act removed an explicit exclusion of devices from the definition of "drug."

The current definition of "device" does not always make clear whether an article will be regulated as a drug or as a device. However, FDA must regulate similar products consistently. *Bracco Diagnostics, Inc. v. Shalala*, 963 F. Supp. 20, 28 (D.D.C. 1997). In *Bracco*, FDA had regulated some injectable contrast imaging agents as drugs and others as devices. Manufacturers challenged the agency's actions, complaining that it was applying different standards to assess the safety and effectiveness of these similar products. The District Court agreed, stating:

> The MBI products and plaintiffs' products all likely meet both the definition of a drug and the definition of a device under the Federal Food, Drug and Cosmetic Act, and the FDA therefore has discretion in determining how to treat them.... What the FDA is not free to do, however, is to treat them dissimilarly and to permit two sets of similar products to run down two separate tracks, one more treacherous than the other, for no apparent reason. Plaintiffs merely maintain that the same tests and studies should be required of each product before it is approved and that the result is impossible so long as the FDA treats one as a device subject to the regimen established by the CDRH and the other three as drugs subject to the more rigorous regimen established by the CDER. The Court agrees.

COMMENT: DRUG–DEVICE COMBINATIONS

Medical products that combine a drug and a device (or combine either of these types of product with a biologic) present special challenges. One important type of combination product is a device (such as a stent or catheter) coated with a drug (such as an antibiotic). Another prominent type is a prefilled drug delivery device, such as a syringe, metered dose inhaler, or transdermal patch.

Section 503(g), added by the Safe Medical Devices Act of 1990, directs FDA to assign "primary jurisdiction" to regulate combination products to the agency's drug, device, or biologics center based on the product's "primary mode of action." The Medical Device User Fee and Modernization Act of 2002 (MDUFMA) modified section 503(g) to require the establishment of an Office of Combination Products within the Office of the Commissioner. FDA created the office that year. The purpose of the Office of Combination Products is to ensure the prompt assignment of combination products to agency components, the timely and effective premarket review of such products, and consistent and appropriate postmarket regulation of combination products. The center to which a specific combination product is assigned (CDER, CBER, or CDRH) retains primary regulatory responsibility for the product. *See* FDA News, *FDA Establishes Office of*

Combination Products, Dec. 31, 2002; Danielle Schillinger, *The Office of Combination Products: Its Roots, Its Creation, and Its Role*, in Chapter IX(A)(7) of the Electronic Book.

In 2004, FDA proposed to amend its combination product regulations to define "mode of action" and "primary mode of action." The proposed rule also sets forth principles the agency would use to assign combination products to a Center when the agency cannot determine with reasonable certainty which mode of action provides the most important therapeutic action of the combination product. 69 Fed. Reg. 25527 (May 7, 2004).

b. DIAGNOSTIC DEVICES

Prior to 1976 FDA had declared certain diagnostic products to be drugs, as in *Bacto–Unidisk*. *See* 38 Fed. Reg. 10488 (Apr. 27, 1973) (test for cancer regulated as drug); 39 Fed. Reg. 3705 (Jan. 29, 1974) (test for gonorrhea regulated as drug). In 1975, however, the agency confronted the limits of this approach when a federal district court ruled that a pregnancy test was not a drug. *U.S. v. An Article of Drug ... Ova II*, 414 F. Supp. 660 (D.N.J. 1975), *aff'd* 535 F.2d 1248 (3d Cir. 1976). The case was a seizure action against a pregnancy test kit sold for home use. The government claimed that this *in vitro* diagnostic product, consisting of vials of sodium hydroxide and hydrochloric acid, was a new drug under the Act. The trial court disagreed, concluding that it fell outside all three dimensions of the Act's definition of "drug," even though both its ingredients appear in the U.S. Pharmacopeia and the National Formulary. The court stated, "The OVA II kit is not ... related to the diagnosis of disease," since "the existence or non-existence of pregnancy ... is not of itself a disease." The court also held that because the product was to be used *in vitro* it was not intended "to affect the structure or any function of the body."

The *OVA II* decision threatened to undermine FDA's efforts to assert control over the reliability, and thus the safety, of a host of *in vitro* diagnostics. In 1976, Congress broadened the definition of "device" to include articles "intended for use in the diagnosis of disease *or other conditions*." FD&C Act 201(h)(2) (emphasis added). Second, the amendments added "in vitro reagent" to the list of articles categorized as devices. Finally, the Amendments imposed a premarket approval regime on many types of medical devices. Today FDA regulates most diagnostic products (and all articles that diagnose "conditions" rather than "diseases") as medical devices.

Pregnancy Test Kits: Transfer of Responsibility From the Bureau of Biologics to the Bureau of Medical Devices
44 Fed. Reg. 10133 (February 16, 1979).

The Medical Device Amendments of 1976 ... expanded the definition of "device" in section 201(h) of the act to include in vitro reagents and similar articles intended for use in the diagnosis of disease or other conditions....

. . . Although FDA believes that the *OVA II* decision is not a sound precedent for future cases because it adopts an unduly restrictive interpretation of the definition of "drug," the precise issue in that case, FDA's authority to regulate pregnancy test kits has been addressed by the Medical Device Amendments of 1976, which expanded the definition of "device" in section 201(h) of the Act to include in vitro products for the diagnosis of any "condition" as well as for the diagnosis of disease. . . .

Because FDA has clear and adequate authority to regulate in vitro products for the determination of pregnancy as devices, FDA has concluded that Anti–HCG serum products for assisting in the determination of pregnancy will be regulated only under the device provisions of the Federal Food, Drug, and Cosmetic Act. Accordingly, by this notice, Anti–HCG serum intended for assisting in the determination of pregnancy is no longer subject to the licensing requirements of section 351 of the Public Health Service Act. All existing licenses for Anti–HCG serum intended for use in assisting in the determination of pregnancy are hereby revoked.

NOTE

Diagnostic Biologic. In 55 Fed. Reg. 5892 (Feb. 20, 1990), FDA announced that in vitro diagnostic test kits that are used to detect total antibody to hepatitis B core antigen in blood will be regulated as biologics rather than as medical devices, because the major use has changed from clinical diagnostic use to screening blood intended for transfusion.

4.   CLASSIFICATION

a.   PROCEDURE

Following enactment of the 1976 Amendments, FDA promulgated new classification procedures to meet the requirements of new section 513 of the FD&C Act. 42 Fed. Reg. 46028 (Sept. 13, 1977), 43 Fed. Reg. 32988 (July 28, 1978), 21 C.F.R. Part 860.

Medical Devices: Classification Procedures

42 Fed. Reg. 46028 (September 13, 1977).

Anticipating eventual enactment of medical device legislation, FDA initiated in 1973 a preliminary classification of medical devices. A list of approximately 8,000 devices had been compiled in 1971, and 13 classification panels, plus a Diagnostic Products Advisory Committee, had been established by 1975. The panels made recommendations for classifying medical devices into different classes of regulatory control using criteria contained in legislative proposals before Congress during this period. . . .

The panels were organized according to the various fields of clinical medicine and fundamental sciences in which devices intended for human use are used. The panels were composed of experts of diverse backgrounds, skilled in the use of, or experienced in the development, manufacture, or use of, medical devices.

Under section 513(b) of the act, the Commissioner may either establish classification panels or use panels established before the date of enactment of the amendments. The Commissioner finds that the objectives of the 13 classification panels established before enactment satisfy the requirements of the amendments. He has, however, rechartered each panel and directed it to reconsider its previous recommendations in light of the statutory classification criteria and other requirements of the legislation....

Section 513 of the act establishes three classes of regulatory control for medical devices and requires FDA to classify all devices intended for human use into one of those classes. They are: Class I, General Controls; Class II, Performance Standards; and Class III, Premarket Approval.

Section 513(a)(1)(A) of the act defines Class I devices as those devices (1) for which there is sufficient information to determine that the provisions of the act with respect to adulteration; misbranding; registration; banning; defect notification; repair, replacement, or refund; records and reports; and good manufacturing practices (referred to as "general controls" hereafter) will provide reasonable assurance of the safety and effectiveness of the device or (2) for which there is insufficient information to determine that general controls are sufficient to provide reasonable assurance of the safety and effectiveness of the device or to establish a performance standard to provide such assurance but which are not purported or represented to be for a use in supporting or sustaining human life or for a use which is of substantial importance in preventing impairment of human health and do not present a potential unreasonable risk of illness or injury. Class I devices are to be regulated under the general controls provisions of the act.

Section 513(a)(1)(B) of the act defines Class II devices as those devices for which general controls alone are insufficient to provide reasonable assurance of safety and effectiveness and for which there is sufficient information to establish a performance standard to provide such assurance. Class II devices will be subject to performance standards to be established under section 514 of the act....

Section 513(a)(1)(C) of the act defines Class III devices as those devices for which there is insufficient information to determine that general controls will assure their safety and effectiveness and for which there is insufficient information to establish a performance standard to provide such assurance, and which are purported or represented to be for a use in supporting or sustaining human life or for a use which is of substantial importance in preventing impairment of human health, or which present a potential unreasonable risk of illness or injury. Class III devices are subject, under section 515 of the act, to premarket approval....

The classification procedures contained in section 513(b)–(d) of the act ... apply to the initial classification of "old" devices, i.e., those which either were in commercial distribution before the date of enactment of the amendments or are substantially equivalent to devices in commercial distribution before that date. Section 513(f) of the act contains special provisions for the classification of "new" devices, i.e., those which were not in commercial distribution before the date of enactment and are not substantially equivalent to any which were in distribution. Such a device is automatically classified in Class III unless it is substantially equivalent to another new device that has been reclassified to Class I or II . . . .

Section 513(d) of the act requires the Commissioner to publish in the FEDERAL REGISTER panel recommendations and proposed classification regulations. After providing an opportunity for comment, the Commissioner must by final regulation classify the device. . . .

COMMENT: THE CLASSIFICATION PROCESS

FDA began the process of classifying devices even before enactment of the 1976 Amendments but then had to start over again following the procedures prescribed by the new statute. Classification of the diverse universe of devices took longer than either FDA or Congress had anticipated. By 1984, FDA had completed classification of products in 11 out of 19 categories (comprising about 1700 types) of devices and had issued proposed classifications for the other eight. Of these 1700 types, roughly 30 percent were placed in Class I, 60 percent in Class II, and 10 percent in Class III. Office of Technology Assessment, FEDERAL POLICIES AND THE MEDICAL DEVICES INDUSTRY, OTA–H–230, at 105–106 (Oct. 1984) (hereinafter OTA DEVICES REPORT). FDA completed the classification process with a final rule classifying general and plastic surgery devices, 53 Fed. Reg. 23856 (June 24, 1988). There have been no formal legal challenges to the results of this classification process, perhaps because, in the vast majority of cases, a device's classification does not control when and on what terms it can be marketed.

FDA's classification process proved responsive to a wide variety of societal interests. For example, in response to comments questioning the agency's proposal to place in Class II the electroconvulsive therapy device used in psychiatric patients and voicing doubts about this method of treatment, the agency ultimately classified the device in Class III. 44 Fed. Reg. 51726 (Sept. 4, 1979).

FDA has issued rules identifying and classifying almost 1,800 types of medical devices. Excerpted below are just three of these classification regulations, all from the category of dental devices. They offer examples of a Class I, Class II, and Class III device and hint at the range of technological sophistication illustrated by the universe of devices regulated by FDA.

21 C.F.R. Part 872—Dental Devices

Sec. 872.6390 Dental floss.

(a) Identification. Dental floss is a string-like device made of cotton or other fibers intended to remove plaque and food particles from between the teeth to reduce tooth decay. The fibers of the device may be coated with wax for easier use.

(b) Classification. Class I (general controls). The device is exempt from the premarket notification procedures in subpart E of part 807 of this chapter subject to Sec. 872.9.

Sec. 872.3570   OTC denture repair kit.

(a) Identification. An OTC denture repair kit is a device consisting of a material, such as a resin monomer system of powder and liquid glues, that is intended to be applied permanently to a denture to mend cracks or breaks. The device may be available for purchase over-the counter.

(b) Classification. Class II. The special controls for this device are FDA's:

(1) "Use of International Standard ISO 10993 'Biological Evaluation of Medical Devices—Part I: Evaluation and Testing," and

(2) "OTC Denture Reliners, Repair Kits, and Partially Fabricated Denture Kits."

Sec. 872.3940   Total temporomandibular joint prosthesis.

(a) Identification. A total temporomandibular joint prosthesis is a device that is intended to be implanted in the human jaw to replace the mandibular condyle and augment the glenoid fossa to functionally reconstruct the temporomandibular joint.

(b) Classification. Class III.

(c) Date PMA or notice of completion of a PDP is required. A PMA or a notice of completion of a PDP is required to be filed with the Food and Drug Administration on or before March 30, 1999, for any total temporomandibular joint prosthesis that was in commercial distribution before May 28, 1976, or that has, on or before March 30, 1999, been found to be substantially equivalent to a total temporomandibular joint prosthesis that was in commercial distribution before May 28, 1976. Any other total temporomandibular joint prosthesis shall have an approved PMA or a declared completed PDP in effect before being placed in commercial distribution.

NOTE

PDPs. The "total temporomandibular joint prosthesis" rule refers to "notice of completion of a PDP" as a path to market entry. PDP stands for "Product Development Protocol," a rarely-used form of PMA approval mentioned in every Class III device regulation. The concept will be discussed below, *infra* p. 1019.

b.   EQUITABLE TREATMENT OF OLD AND NEW DEVICES

When FDA officials were engaged in drafting the legislation that became the 1976 Device Amendments, they faced a familiar issue in the design of new health and safety legislation—whether to discriminate between old and new devices. (For a general discussion of the law's propensity to apply more stringent standards to new technologies, *see* Peter Huber, *The Old–New Division in Risk Regulation*, 69 VA. L. REV. 1025 (1983)). Congress was not prepared to require that every preamendment Class III device be pulled from the market immediately upon classification, to be reintroduced only when the manufacturer established safety and effectiveness through a PMA. Such an approach would create an enormous backlog of unapproved PMAs and would keep many well-established and important devices off the market for years.

But if Congress postponed the imposition of the new statutory requirements only for preamendment Class III devices, and not for similar products introduced after 1976, the result would be an untenable discrimination between old and new devices. A preamendment Class III device would remain *on* the market while the manufacturer gathered and FDA evaluated evidence of safety and effectiveness. And a counterpart postamendment device would remain *off* the market while the same evidence was being obtained and evaluated. Furthermore, once the postamendment device was approved by FDA, it would enter the market to compete with preamendment counterparts whose safety and effectiveness FDA had not yet approved.

To avoid this result, FDA advocated, and Congress endorsed, the following policy. Sections 513(f)(1)(A) and 515(b)(1) provide that a preamendment Class III device, and any postamendment Class III device that is substantially equivalent to a preamendment Class III device, need not secure FDA approval of safety and effectiveness until FDA promulgates a regulation triggering the approval requirement for the specific type of device. Thus, a postamendment Class III device that is substantially equivalent to a preamendment Class III not yet subject to a call for PMAs can go on the market immediately, with only the submission of a section 510(k) notification. Once on the market, the post-1976 device will be subject only to the same general controls as its preamendment counterpart (and other medical devices). When FDA orders the submission of PMA applications for devices of that type, the requirement applies equally to both preamendment and postamendment products.

An understanding of this process clarifies subsection (c) of the "total temporomandibular joint prosthesis" rule reprinted above. 21 C.F.R. 872.3940(c), *supra* p. 987. The PMA requirement for this type of device became effective on March 30, 1999. Prior to that date, total temporomandibular joint prostheses that were already in commercial distribution when the MDA became effective on May 28, 1976 could remain on the market, subject only to general controls. Moreover, between May 28, 1976 and March 30, 1999, new devices of this type could enter the market based on the filing of a section 510(k) notification showing substantial equivalence to a preamendments total temporomandibular joint prosthesis. Since March 30, 1999, however, it has been illegal to sell any total temporomandibular joint prosthesis without an approved PMA.

Congress did not anticipate the huge number of postamendments Class III devices that would successfully take advantage of the section 510(k)/substantial equivalence route to market entry, nor did it expect FDA to take as long as it did to commence, let alone complete, the PMA proceedings. FDA did not even issue a final regulation setting forth PMA procedures until 1986. 45 Fed. Reg. 81769 (July 22, 1986). To the dismay of some commentators, many Class III devices, both old and new, thus remained on the market for years without establishing safety and effectiveness through a PMA. *See Robert B. Leflar, Public Accountability and Medical Device Regulation*, 2 HARV. J.L. & TECH. 1 (1989); Robert Adler, *The 1976 Medical*

Device Amendments: A Step in the Right Direction Needs Another Step in the Right Direction, 43 FOOD DRUG COSM. L.J. 511 (1988). In the Safe Medical Devices Act of 1990, Congress directed that, by December 1, 1995, every preamendment Class III device either be downclassified to Class I or Class II or retained in Class III and, within a year, scheduled for imposition of the PMA requirement under section 515(i). The agency failed to meet these deadlines. In fact the process is still not finished.

Today, the awkward transition into the modern regulatory regime for preamendment Class III devices and their post-amendment substantial equivalents is finally almost complete. There are roughly two-dozen types of preamendments Class III devices for which FDA has not issued a call for PMAs.

c. RECLASSIFICATION OF PREAMENDMENTS DEVICES

Section 513(e) authorizes FDA, upon the petition of any interested person or upon its own initiative, to change the classification of a preamendments device. The agency has only ever reclassified about ten types of preamendments devices under this provision. This is not to say that FDA has not reclassified numerous preamendments Class III devices to Class II or Class I. Most of these reclassifications, however, have happened pursuant to section 515(i), a decision-forcing provision added to the FD&C Act by the Safe Medical Devices Act of 1990 (SMDA).

In 1990, fourteen years into the new device regime, Congress was unhappy with the relatively large number of preamendment devices FDA had placed in Class III, the dearth of successful section 513(e) reclassification petitions, and FDA's slowness in demanding the submission of PMAs for Class III devices. SMDA thus required the agency to reconsider the classification of all Class III devices. More specifically, new section 515(i) required FDA to order the submission of safety and effectiveness data for every preamendments Class III device not yet subject to a PMA call and, by December 1995, either to downclassify it or to keep it in Class III and schedule it for imposition of the PMA requirement.

In 1994, FDA announced the availability of a document setting forth its strategy for implementing section 515(i) with respect to the 116 preamendments Class III devices not yet subject to the PMA requirement. 59 Fed. Reg. 23731 (May 6, 1994). Under this plan, the agency divided these devices into three groups (not to be confused with the three classes): Group 1 devices, which FDA believed raised significant questions of safety and/or effectiveness, but were no longer used or were in very limited use; Group 2 devices, which FDA believed had a high potential for being reclassified into Class II; and Group 3 devices, which FDA believed were not likely candidates for reclassification. The agency dealt fairly promptly with the Group 1 products; in 1996, it published a final rule requiring the filing of a PMA for most of them. 61 Fed. Reg. 50704 (Sept. 27, 1996).

FDA has not been nearly so efficient with respect to the 73 Group 2 and Group 3 Class III devices. By 1997, it had issued orders under section 515(i) requiring manufacturers of all the devices in both groups to submit a summary of, and citation to, all safety and effectiveness information known or otherwise available to them respecting such devices. 60 Fed. Reg. 41986 (Aug. 14, 1995), 62 Fed. Reg. 32352 (June 13, 1997). Not until 1999 did the agency start publishing significant numbers of final rules either downclassifying the Group 2 and Group 3 devices or retaining them in Class III and imposing the PMA requirement. This process continues today, though it is finally largely complete. To date, FDA has retained about fifteen of the devices in Class III and established the effective date for the PMA requirement. The agency has also issued final orders downclassifying some 45 other Group 2 and Group 3 devices. Interestingly, FDA has taken no further SMDA compliance action with regard to about 15 of the devices identified in the 1994 strategy memorandum, including some that the agency identified as "high priority" Group 3. *See, e.g.,* 21 C.F.R. 882.5940 (electroconvulsive therapy device; Group 2), 870.3600 (external pacemaker pulse generator, Group 3); 888.3320 (hip joint metal/metal constrained, with a cemented acetabular component, High Priority Group 3). There are also about a dozen preamendments Class III devices not identified in the 1994 strategy memorandum that have not been subjected to PMA calls.

d.   REGULATION OF "TRANSITIONAL" DEVICES

As discussed above, *supra* p. 976, FDA had regulated approximately twenty types of devices as new drugs prior to enactment of the 1976 Amendments. In the legislation, Congress, at the agency's urging, automatically assigned these devices, generally referred to as "transitional" devices, to Class III under section 520(l)(1). The agency, which identified the transitional devices in 42 Fed. Reg. 63472 (Dec. 16, 1977), took the position that these products and their postamendment counterparts would remain in Class III unless and until reclassified. Moreover, in a major exception to the nondiscrimination policy between old and new Class III devices discussed above, FDA determined that no postamendment version of any Class III transitional device could come on the market without FDA approval of a PMA application, even if it were substantially equivalent to a preamendment product not yet required to submit a PMA.

The resulting treatment of transitional devices was unsatisfactory in several respects. First of all, many of these products did not seem to raise safety and effectiveness concerns sufficient to warrant their placement into Class III. Second, the discriminatory treatment of postamendment transitional devices created a disincentive for new manufacturers and technological improvements. Finally, the requirement that manufacturers of new transitional devices gain PMA approval before entering the market overburdened FDA. Some sixty percent of PMAs filed with the agency were for transitional devices, and about fifty percent of these were for contact lens products. Robert Adler, *The 1976 Medical Device Amendments*, 43 FOOD DRUG COSM. L.J. at 526; 56 Fed. Reg. 57960, 57960 (Nov. 14, 1991). These proportions were strikingly high, not only because transitional devices represented only a small slice of the device market (and transitional contact lens products an even smaller slice), but also because many transitional devices presented fewer risks than most non-transitional Class III products for which FDA had not yet demanded PMAs.

Section 520(l)(2) offered a potential escape from this quandary, namely, the reclassification of low-risk transitional devices from Class III to Class II or Class I. But by 1991, FDA had downclassified only seven types of transitional devices, and it had considered and explicitly declined to downclassify about eight others. 56 Fed. Reg. at 57960. In the Safe Medical Devices Act of 1990 (SMDA), Congress attempted to resolve the transitional device problem by requiring FDA to reconsider the classification of each Class III transitional device and, by December 1, 1993, to issue a regulation either downclassifying it or keeping it in Class III. FD&C Act 520(l)(5). Moreover, section 4(b)(3) of the SMDA specified that two types of transitional device—soft and rigid daily wear contact lenses—had to be downclassified to Class II unless FDA affirmatively ruled otherwise by November 28, 1993.

Although FDA nearly satisfied the deadline for contact lenses, it did not come close to meeting the deadline for the other transitional devices. As of October 1, 2006, the agency had issued post-SMDA rules classifying or reclassifying only about ten types of transitional devices. In each instance, FDA either placed a transitional device it had never considered into Class II or downclassified a transitional device it had earlier placed into Class III. However, there remain numerous transitional devices that FDA expressly classified into Class III prior to 1990 that the agency has not reconsidered, and even some transitional devices that remain automatically in Class III because FDA has never classified them at all.

D.   REGULATION OF MARKET ENTRY

1.   INTRODUCTION

Under the regulatory structure established by the 1976 Amendments, there were only four ways a new medical device could lawfully be introduced: (1) as a device for which FDA had cleared a section 510(k) premarket notification (PMN) demonstrating, under section 513(f)(1), that the device was substantially equivalent to a preamendment Class I or Class II device; (2) as a device for which FDA had cleared a 510(k) notification, under section 515(b)(1), that the device was substantially equivalent to a preamendment Class III device on which the agency had not yet imposed the PMA requirement; (3) as a Class III device for which FDA had approved a premarket approval (PMA) application under section 515; (4) as a device that FDA had reclassified from Class III (the Class by default of all new devices without a substantially equivalent predicate) into Class I or Class II pursuant to a section 513(f) reclassification petition.

After the implementation of the new regime, the 510(k) notification demonstrating substantial equivalence became the dominant route of market entry to a degree never contemplated by Congress. Between 1976 and 1990, more than 98 percent of new medical devices entered the market by demonstrating substantial equivalence to a preamendment device.

In the Food and Drug Administration Modernization Act of 1997 (FDAMA), Congress established two additional paths for introducing a device into the market. First, new section 513(f)(2) established, as a supplement to the reclassification petition process, a procedure for requesting that FDA *initially* classify a device with no substantially equivalent predicate into Class I or Class II instead of Class III (the default classification in this situation). Second, and more important, Congress automatically exempted most Class I devices from the 510(k) premarket notification requirement and authorized FDA also to exempt Class II devices where appropriate. Consequently, today FDA does not oversee the market entry of many low-risk devices at all.

For those devices for which premarket filings are still required, section 510(k) remains the dominant mode of market entry. In 2005, FDA cleared 3,148 premarket notifications while approving only 32 PMAs. In other words, 98.99% of new devices cleared for marketing by FDA that year were cleared under section 510(k) rather than by a PMA. The number of devices initially marketed pursuant to reclassification petitions or initial classification requests is negligible. In 2005, FDA granted only eight section 513(f)(2) requests, and it granted no section 513(f)(3) reclassification petitions.

Each of these premarket pathways is examined below. For now, it is important only to grasp the basic features of the different pathways and to recognize that section 510(k) offers a route to market that is usually faster and smoother than any other.

Jonathan S. Kahan, *Premarket Approval Versus Premarket Notification: Different Routes to the Same Market*

39 FOOD DRUG COSMETIC LAW JOURNAL 510 (1984).

. . . .

Gaining premarket approval is not an easy process. . . . The sponsor is obliged to include in the PMA sufficient data to prove the effectiveness and safety of the device. . . . [I]n practice, this almost always means conducting clinical trials. . . .

. . . Unless the device is a nonsignificant risk device, a company must first obtain FDA approval to conduct a clinical investigation of the device. . . .

Once the investigational data are gathered, they must be analyzed by the sponsor, and then reported to FDA in some statistically meaningful way. . . .

Actual submission of the PMA does not, however, end the process. FDA will review the submission for completeness. If the agency believes that additional information is needed, it will be requested. FDA does, in fact, routinely ask sponsors to supplement PMAs. . . .

Once FDA decides that the PMA is complete, the agency will refer the approval question to one of several expert outside panels. . . .

After the panel issues its report on the device, FDA also conducts its own in-depth review. In addition to a careful examination of the safety and effectiveness data, this review will include close scrutiny of the labeling claims. . . . If FDA ultimately decides to grant the application, that decision is published in the *Federal Register*, and a summary of the evidence must be prepared.

. . . Some companies have elected to seek reclassification of a device. Essentially, this mechanism allows a device that would otherwise be placed into Class III to be regulated as a Class II or Class I device. This obviates the need for a PMA. . . . However, the common perception is that the data required by FDA for approval of a petition to reclassify may in many cases be tantamount to the data required for a PMA. This may be one reason that this procedure has been invoked infrequently. . . .

The simplest, least costly, and fastest way to place a new device into commercial distribution is to file a "510(k) notification." For these reasons, the 510(k) submission has become the option of choice for bringing a new device to market. . . .

A.   Less Information is Required in a 510(k) Submission

In implementing the Medical Device Amendments, FDA has adopted regulations that delineate, to some extent, the data requirements for a 510(k) notification. Compared to the PMA, comparatively little is directly required by FDA regulation.

One of the few substantive requirements in the regulation is that the applicant provide information supporting the claim of substantial equivalence to a pre-amendment device. . . .

On its face, this FDA 510(k) regulation is far easier to satisfy than its PMA counterpart, section 515 of the Amendments. For one thing, safety and effectiveness data are not explicitly required. Thus, unlike the PMA sponsor, under a literal reading of the 510(k) provisions . . . [a] showing of substantial equivalence should suffice. Thus, with the few exceptions . . . where FDA has converted the 510(k) into a mini-PMA, an applicant submitting a 510(k) notification should be relieved of the enormous expense and delay associated with generating clinical data. . . .

B.   510(k)s Have a Better Chance of Gaining FDA Acceptance

. . . Over the years, FDA has consistently had a very high rate of finding post-amendment devices to be substantially equivalent to pre-amendment devices. Of the approximately 20,650 510(k)s FDA had reviewed by the end of 1983, only 2 percent were found not to be substantially equivalent.

Comparable statistics for PMA approval rates are not readily available. However, PMAs plainly fare less well. . . .

C.   Speed of Disposition of the Application

Additionally, not only is a 510(k) more likely to result in a favorable disposition than a PMA, but it is likely to do so more quickly. By statute, FDA has 90 days in which to respond to a 510(k) notification. FDA generally meets that deadline. . . .

. . . In 1981, Acting Commissioner Novitch wrote that the average PMA review time was 7.9 months, slightly longer than the 180 days allowed by statute. Currently, FDA estimates that the median [PMA] approval time since 1976 has been approximately 8½ months. This figure, though, tends to understate the length of the total review process.... FDA does not consider the statutory clock to start ticking until a complete PMA has been filed. Many PMAs are returned to the sponsor for additional data....

NOTES

1. *Recent Data.* In the five years from 2000 to 2004, FDA received 20,652 premarket notifications claiming substantial equivalence and rejected only 369 of these (approximately 1.8%). In the same period, FDA made 338 approval decisions on original PMAs, of which 41 (approximately 12.1%) were "not approvable." (Some sponsors receiving "not approvable" letters may have corrected the identified deficiencies and ultimately received PMA approval.) In the years between 2000 and 2004, the average amount of time that elapsed between submission of a section 510(k) premarket notification and a substantial equivalence decision by FDA ranged from 96 days (2001 and 2003) to 102 days (2000). By contrast, the average total time from submission to decision for PMAs ranged from 359 days (2003) to 436 days (2004). Compiled from FDA–CDRH, Office of Device Evaluation Annual Reports (FY 2000–2004).

2. *Patent Term Restoration.* The Drug Price Competition and Patent Term Restoration Act of 1984, *supra* p. 760, provided stronger protection for drug patents and easier entry of generic drugs into the market once the pioneer's patent and any period of market exclusivity has expired. The 1984 Act also offered patent term restoration of up to five years for medical devices subject to a regulatory review period that would otherwise reduce their effective patent life. Some premarket approval devices have, in fact, been awarded extensions of their patent term under this statute. *E.g.*, 63 Fed. Reg. 24557 (May 4, 1998); 58 Fed. Reg. 42560 (Aug. 10, 1993). *Eli Lilly & Co. v. Medtronic, Inc.*, 496 U.S. 661 (1990), held that 35 U.S.C. 271(e)(1), which states that research conducted with a patented drug to develop information for submission to FDA does not constitute infringement, applies to medical devices as well as to drugs.

2. SUBSTANTIAL EQUIVALENCE

The 1976 Amendments did not include a definition of "substantially equivalent." The legislative history, however, indicates that substantial equivalence was meant to be assessed not merely in terms of physical characteristics and intended use, but also in terms of safety and effectiveness:

> The term "substantially equivalent" is not intended to be so narrow as to refer only to devices that are identical to marketed devices nor so broad as to refer to devices which are intended to be used for the same purposes as marketed products. The Committee believes that the term should be construed narrowly where necessary to assure the safety and effectiveness of a device but not so narrowly where differences between a new device and a marketed device do not relate to safety and effectiveness. Thus, differences between "new" and marketed devices in materials, design, or energy source, for example, would have a bearing on the adequacy of information as to a new device's safety and effectiveness, and such devices should be automatically classified into Class III. On the other hand, copies of devices marketed prior to enactment, or

devices whose variations are immaterial to safety and effectiveness would not necessarily fall under the automatic classification scheme.

H.R. Rep. No. 853, 94th Cong., 2d Sess. 36–37 (1976). Thus, the concept of substantial equivalence was left for FDA to interpret, but it was clearly intended to embrace some inquiry into the safety and effectiveness of a new device.

Congress also concluded that the manufacturer of a new device should not have the authority to resolve the issue of substantial equivalence unilaterally, without FDA oversight. Section 510(k), as originally written, thus required every person who planned to market a new device to submit to FDA a notification of such intent at least 90 days in advance. This PMN, still required for many devices, is required to set forth the legal basis on which the device is being introduced. The House Report, at p. 37, provided the following explanation:

> The proposed Bill contains provisions designed to insure that manufacturers do not intentionally or unintentionally circumvent the automatic classification of "new" devices. These provisions, included in amendments to Section 510 of Act, would require all persons to advise the Secretary ninety days before they intend to begin marketing a device as to whether the device has been classified under Section 513. This provision will enable the Secretary to assure that "new" devices are not marketed until they comply with premarket approval requirements or are reclassified into Class I or II.

Accordingly, the regulatory structure created by the 1976 Amendments was organized around three principles. First, a postamendment device that is substantially equivalent to a preamendment device (a predicate device) should meet the same standards of safety and effectiveness as the predicate device, on the same schedule. Second, a postamendment device that has no preamendment counterpart, and thus cannot establish substantial equivalence to a predicate device, should presumptively be required to obtain approval of a PMA before it is allowed on the market. Third, a mechanism such as section 510(k)'s PMN requirement should be established to allow FDA to review a manufacturer's decision to introduce a device and thereby prevent the introduction of novel devices that have not undergone official assessment.

This is the scheme that FDA attempted to implement prior to 1990. Soon after enactment of the 1976 Amendments FDA issued regulations governing the premarket notification process. 41 Fed. Reg. 37458 (Sept. 3, 1976), 42 Fed. Reg. 42520 (Aug. 23, 1977). However, these regulations did not include any definition of "substantial equivalence." In 1986, FDA issued a guidance that, for the first time, spelled out in detail the agency's approach to assessing substantial equivalence. FDA, GUIDANCE ON THE CENTER OF DEVICES AND RADIOLOGICAL HEALTH'S PREMARKET NOTIFICATION REVIEW PROGRAM (June 30, 1986). According to this memorandum, one device could be substantially equivalent to another only if it had the same intended use. If a new device had the same intended use as a predicate device, and also the same technological characteristics, it was substantially equivalent.

Moreover, a new device could be substantially equivalent to a predicate device even if it had different technological characteristics—but only if the section 510(k) notification demonstrated that these new technological characteristics did not diminish safety or effectiveness. *Id.*

In the Safe Medical Devices Act of 1990, Congress amended section 513(i) of the FD&C Act, essentially to codify the substantial equivalence policy stated in the 1986 document. Soon thereafter, FDA issued a rule incorporating these SMDA requirements into the existing medical device regulations. 57 Fed. Reg. 58400 (Dec. 10, 1992). The resulting regulatory definition of substantial equivalence reads:

(b) FDA will determine that a device is substantially equivalent to a predicate device using the following criteria:

(1) The device has the same intended use as the predicate device; and

(2) The device:

(i) Has the same technological characteristics as the predicate device; or

(ii)(A) Has different technological characteristics, such as a significant change in the materials, design, energy source, or other features of the device from those of the predicate device;

(B) The data submitted establishes that the device is substantially equivalent to the predicate device and contains information, including clinical data if deemed necessary by the Commissioner, that demonstrates that the device is as safe and as effective as a legally marketed device; and

(C) Does not raise different questions of safety and effectiveness than the predicate device.

21 C.F.R. 807.100. *See generally* Benjamin A. Goldberger, *The Evolution of Substantial Equivalence in FDA's Premarket Review of Medical Devices*, 56 FOOD & DRUG L. J. 317 (2001).

In FDAMA (1997), Congress revolutionized the 510(k) process by automatically exempting many devices from the premarket notification requirement. According to new section 510(l): "A report under subsection (k) is not required for a device that ... is within a type that has been classified into Class I," unless the device "is intended for a use which is of substantial importance in preventing impairment of human health, or ... presents a potential unreasonable risk of illness or injury." FDAMA also authorizes FDA to identify types of Class II devices for which a PMN 510(k) is not necessary under section 510(l) & (m). Today, under this regime as implemented by FDA, most Class I devices and some Class II devices are exempt from the premarket notification requirement. Congress has thus retreated significantly from its initial intention, in 1976, to have FDA assess the legality of the market introduction of all devices without PMAs. Under the current system, manufacturers of less risky devices routinely determine substantial equivalence for themselves.

NOTES

1. *Safety and Effectiveness Data.* The 1990 Act specifically authorized FDA to require clinical data in a section 510(k) notification. Many PMN's include such data. Indeed, FDA would be unlikely to clear a PMN for a product incorporating new technologies that could affect safety or effectiveness if the notification did not contain clinical investigation data. Nevertheless, FDA assiduously avoids mentioning safety or effectiveness in letters clearing PMNs, and the agency clings to its position that a 510(k) clearance reflects a determination of equivalence, not safety and effectiveness. This distinction was critical in the Supreme Court's conclusion that a PMN clearance does not preempt a state tort action based on a device's allegedly defective design. *Medtronic v. Lohr*, 518 U.S. 470, 492–94 (1996), excerpted *infra* at 1442.

2. *PMN Summary Versus PMN Statement.* A section 510(k) notification must include either a "510(k) Summary" or a "510(k) Statement." The former is a summary of the information upon which the person filing the notification bases a claim of substantial equivalence. A 510(k) statement is a certification that the 510(k) owner will provide safety and effectiveness information supporting the FDA finding of substantial equivalence to any person within 30 days of a written request. 21 C.F.R. 807.92 & 807.93.

3. *User Fees.* Under the authority granted it by the Medical Device User Fee and Modernization Act of 2002 (MDUFMA), P.L. 107–250, FDA assesses fees for the review of 510(k)s, as well as PMAs.

4. *Abbreviated PMN.* In 1998, FDA developed a "New 510(k) Paradigm" to streamline the premarket notification process. FDA–CDRH, THE NEW 510(K) PARADIGM: ALTERNATE APPROACHES TO DEMONSTRATING SUBSTANTIAL EQUIVALENCE IN PREMARKET NOTIFICATIONS (1998). Under this paradigm, FDA invites any device manufacturer submitting a PMN to include a "summary report" outlining its product's compliance with an FDA guidance document or special control, or a declaration of conformity to a national or international standard (consensus standard) that FDA has recognized pursuant to section 514(c). Such a notification is known as an "Abbreviated 510(k)." While FDA does not put Abbreviated 510(k)s on a special processing track, it states that their review will generally be more efficient than the review of traditional section 510(k) submissions. *Id.* at 9.

5. *Special 510(k)s.* FDA's 1998 "New 510(k) Paradigm" also established the use of "Special 510(k)s" for certain device modifications. FDA regulations have long required the submission of 510(k)s for devices that are already in commercial distribution but are about to be "significantly changed or modified in design, components, method of manufacture, or intended use." 21 C.F.R. 807.81(a)(3). In 1997, FDA also began to require manufacturers of Class I, Class II, and some Class III devices to follow design control procedures when introducing devices or when modifying them. 21 C.F.R. 820.30. In establishing the "Special 510(k)" process, FDA recognized that many of the questions traditionally addressed in a traditional 510(k) notification for a device modification would now be addressed in the verification and validation studies performed by the manufacturer pursuant to design control procedure requirements. A Special 510(k) contains a declaration of conformity with design control requirements. FDA promises to process Special 510(k)s within 30 days of receipt. The agency will not, however, accept Special 510(k)s for modifications that affect the intended use of the device or alter its fundamental scientific technology.

6. *Third Party Review.* In 1997, FDAMA added section 523 to the Act, requiring FDA to accredit external organizations to review section 510(k) notifications and make recommendations to FDA regarding the agency's response to these

submissions. (FDA began experimenting with this approach prior to 1997 under a pilot program.) These accredited third parties, which may be used only at the request of the person submitting the PMN, are not authorized to review Class III devices or various types of Class II devices. According to FDA, in 2002, PMNs reviewed by Accredited Persons received FDA marketing clearance, on average, 29 percent faster than comparable PMNs reviewed entirely by FDA. Another advantage to using third-party review is that submissions reviewed by Accredited Persons are not subject to a FDA user fee for PMNs, which was $3502 in fiscal year 2005.

COMMENT: "PIGGYBACKING"

To enter the market without a PMA, must a postamendment device be substantially equivalent to a preamendment device, or is it sufficient to be substantially equivalent to an earlier postamendment device that itself was found to be equivalent to a device on the market prior to 1976? The latter approach, especially if carried through several generations, may lead to the marketing of new devices that bear little resemblance to any preamendment products. Nevertheless, FDA permitted PMNs to take this approach prior to 1990 even without explicit statutory authorization, leading to a phenomenon known colloquially as "piggybacking" or "equivalence creep." Various commentators criticized this approach to determining substantial equivalence. *See, e.g.*, Robert B. Leflar, *Public Accountability and Medical Device Regulation*, 2 HARV. J. L. & TECH. 1 (1989). Others praised it. *See, e.g.*, John J. Smith, *Physician Modification of Legally Marketed Devices: Regulatory Implications Under the Federal Food, Drug, and Cosmetic Act*, 55 FOOD & DRUG L.J. 245, 247 (2000) (noting that piggybacking "permits evolutionary change effectively avoiding the more demanding premarket approval process for incrementally-improved devices").

Prior to 1990, FDA denied that it permitted piggybacking, but it nevertheless allowed it as a practical matter. Consider, for example, the following passage from the 1986 guidance on premarket notification:

> . . . The Center does not routinely require that . . . all 510(k)s initially provide information on a predicate device. Instead, the Center requires submitters to provide information that compares the new device to a marketed device of a similar type, regardless of whether this marketed device was marketed before or after enactment of the Amendments, or before or after a type of post-Amendments device was reclassified.

> This means that the manufacturer can submit a 510(k) comparing a new device to a device that has been found to be SE. It does not mean, however, that the Center finds new devices SE to devices that have been found SE. It only reflects the agency's position that the similarity of a new device to a marketed device is evidence that can be considered in determining that the new device is, as is the marketed device to which it is compared, SE to a predicate device. . . .

GUIDANCE ON THE CENTER OF DEVICES AND RADIOLOGICAL HEALTH'S PREMARKET NOTIFICATION REVIEW PROGRAM. Despite the agency's insistence that a new device could not, as a formal matter, be found SE to a postamendment device, the 1986 Guidance permitted 510(k)s to be drafted largely in reference to postamendment devices that themselves had been found to be substantially equivalent to preamendment products.

The 1990 Act specifically authorized piggybacking. The current statutory definition of "substantial equivalence," added in 1990, states that a device with technological characteristics different from a predicate device is nonetheless substantially equivalent if the PMN "contains information ... that demonstrates that the device is as safe and effective as a *legally marketed device* and does not raise different questions of safety and effectiveness than the predicate device" (emphasis added). Section 513(i)(1)(A)(ii). If this amendment left any ambiguity regarding the permissibility of piggybacking, FDA eliminated it in its 1994 regulations implementing the 1990 Act. Under these regulations, which are still in effect: "A legally marketed device to which a new device may be compared for a determination regarding substantial equivalence is a device that was legally marketed prior to May 28, 1976, or a device which has been reclassified from Class III to Class II or I (the predicate), or a device which has been found to be substantially equivalent through the 510(k) premarket notification process." 21 C.F.R. 807.92(a)(3) (1994) (promulgated at 59 Fed. Reg. 64287 (Dec. 14, 1994)).

———

The question of whether a new device is "substantially equivalent" to a particular predicate device is distinct from the question of whether it falls within a generic type of device that FDA has defined in a classification regulation. Sometimes both questions arise with respect to a single product. Consider the saga of the female condom.

Obstetrical and Gynecological Devices; Proposed Classification of Female Condoms

64 Fed. Reg. 31164 (June 10, 1999).

The Food and Drug Administration (FDA) is proposing to classify the preamendments female condom intended for contraceptive and prophylactic purposes. Under this proposal, the preamendments female condom would be classified into Class III (premarket approval)....

In the FEDERAL REGISTER of April 3, 1979 (44 FR 19894), FDA published a proposed rule classifying all known obstetrical and gynecological preamendments devices, including condoms.... Subsequently, in the FEDERAL REGISTER of February 26, 1980 (45 FR 12710), FDA published a final rule classifying certain obstetrical and gynecological preamendments devices, including classifying the condom into Class II (21 CFR 884.5300). The condom encompasses preamendments barrier-type sheaths that cover the entire shaft of the penis for purposes of contraception (preventing pregnancy), prophylaxis (preventing transmission of sexually transmitted diseases (STD's)), or semen collection (diagnostic testing)....

Following classification of the condom into Class II, FDA received two 510(k) notifications for "female condoms" intended to be inserted into the vagina and held in place to line the vaginal walls for purposes of contraception and prophylaxis. These 510(k) notifications claimed substantial equivalency to the condom identified in § 884.5300. Initially, in late 1987, in response to a 510(k) notification submitted by the Energy Basin Clinic to market a "barrier female condom," FDA concurred that this condom, later called the Bikini Condom, was substantially equivalent to the Class II condom. Subsequently, in 1989, the agency received a 510(k) notification from the Wisconsin Pharmacal Co. for the WPC–333 female use condom-like device (WPC–333 device), later called the Femshield/Reality (Intra-) Vaginal Pouch and Reality Female Condom....

The Wisconsin Pharmacal Co. claimed in its 510(k) notification that its WPC–333 device was substantially equivalent to the condom identified in § 884.5300 as well as to another preamendments device known as the Gee Bee Ring. Documentation in the 510(k) notification indicated that the Gee Bee Ring was a double-ringed pouch-type preamendments device intended for insertion into the vagina to line the walls of the vagina for contraceptive (pregnancy prevention) and prophylactic (prevention of STD's transmission) purposes.

. . . .

During an open meeting held on March 7, 1989, the Panel reviewed all available information concerning the classification of a barrier-type pouch device that is inserted into the vagina prior to coitus and lines the vaginal wall and external cervix. Such available information indicated that the preamendments device, known as the Gee Bee Ring, was distributed, beginning in the 1930's and for some years thereafter, as a female condom, *i.e.*, as a "modified condom placed in the hands of the female ... for proper insertion and use." The Panel determined that this particular device represented a generic type of preamendments device that the Panel identified as the vaginal pouch, rather than the condom, noting that the classification regulation for the condom device (§ 884.5300) identifies the condom as "a sheath *which completely covers the penis* with a *closely fitting membrane*" (emphasis added). The regulation also states that the condom is used "for contraceptive and for prophylactic purposes (preventing transmission of sexually transmitted disease)" and "to collect semen to aid in the diagnosis of infertility." Because an intravaginal pouch loosely lines the interior of the vagina, rather than closely fitting the penis, and because there is no data to establish the safe and effective use of the intravaginal pouch, the Panel recommended that FDA not include the intravaginal pouch in the condom classification (§ 884.5300), but classify this generic type of device as a device that is distinct from condoms.

Subsequently, in April 1989, in response to the Wisconsin Pharmacal Co. 510(k), FDA advised the firm that its WPC–333 device is not substantially equivalent to either the condom identified in § 884.5300 or the Gee Bee Ring, due to design differences. As a result, in accordance with section 513(f) of the act, the device was automatically classified into Class III. In April 1989, FDA also advised the Energy Basin Clinic that the agency's response to the firm's 510(k) was incorrect, in that the firm's "barrier female condom" is not substantially equivalent to the condom as defined in § 884.5300. . . .

. . . .

On May 29, 1993, FDA approved the PMA for the Wisconsin Pharmacal Co. "Reality" Female Condom.

. . . .

On its own initiative, FDA is proposing to change the name of the generic type of device identified by the Panel from "intravaginal pouch" to "female condom." FDA agrees with the Panel's finding that the female condom represents a type of preamendments device that has different technological characteristics than the preamendments condom identified in § 884.5300 and concurs with the Panel's recommendation that the female condom not be considered a type of device that falls within the classification category of condom (§ 884.5300).

FDA believes that the proposed name, "female condom," better connotes the intended female use and purposes of the device than does the term, "intravaginal pouch," . . . Adequate labeling for female condoms, including adequate directions for use, and actual usage by female users will make clear to sexual partners the differences between female condoms and male condoms.

. . . .

FDA notes that differences in technological characteristics and design among devices within the same generic type of device may raise new questions of safety and effectiveness that prevent the devices from being substantially equivalent to one another. Such was the case for the 510(k) notifications for certain postamendments female condoms claiming substantial equivalence to the preamendments female condom, the Gee Bee Ring. In the preamble of the final rule setting forth classification procedures (43 FR 32988 at 32989, July 28, 1978), FDA noted that "The term 'generic type of device' describes FDA's grouping, for reasons of administrative convenience, of devices that are to be regulated in the same way because they present *similar safety and effectiveness concerns*. A generic type of device will include devices that may or *may not be* 'within a type' and 'substantially equivalent' to each other." (Emphasis added.)

FDA believes the female condom should be classified into Class III because general controls and special controls would not provide reasonable assurance of the safety and effectiveness of the device and the device is purported or represented to be for a use in supporting or sustaining human life or for a use which is of substantial importance in preventing impairment of human health, or presents a potential unreasonable risk of illness or injury. . . .

FDA agrees with the Panel's conclusions and recommendations regarding the unproven contraceptive effectiveness of the preamendments female condom and its indeterminate efficacy in protecting against the transmission of STD's. The agency has neither received nor found in the literature valid scientific evidence from laboratory tests, preclinical studies, or clinical investigations that does the following: (1) Demonstrates the biocompatibility of materials used in the preamendments female condom; (2) measures performance characteristics, such as displacement, dislodgement, bursting, and tearing; (3) assesses the contraceptive safety and effectiveness of the preamendments device in preventing pregnancy, in terms of reported failure or pregnancy rates based upon usage; or (4) demonstrates the prophylactic efficacy of the preamendments device in protecting against the transmission of STD's, including HIV. The agency believes that the present voluntary industry standard and the agency's methodology for testing conventional condoms for pinhole leaks are not suitable for testing the female condom for leaks without significant modification and validation. . . .

. . . [I]t is proposed that 21 CFR part 884 be amended as follows. . . . Section 884.5330 is added to subpart F to read as follows:

§ 884.5330—Female condom.

(a) *Identification.* A female condom is a sheath-like device that lines the vaginal wall and is inserted into the vagina prior to the initiation of coitus. It is indicated for contraceptive and prophylactic (preventing the transmission of sexually transmitted diseases) purposes.

(b) *Classification.* Class III (premarket approval).

(c) *Date premarket approval application (PMA) or notice of completion of a product development protocol (PDP) is required.* No effective date has been established of the requirement for premarket approval for the devices described in paragraph (b) of this section. . . .

NOTES

1. *Final Rule.* In 2000, FDA issued a final rule that formally added the proposed "female condom" classification, 21 C.F.R. 884.5330, to the medical device regulations. 65 Fed. Reg. 31454 (May 18, 2000). To date, FDA has not yet called for PMAs for these Class III devices, but to no effect, because no female condom manufacturers have attempted temporarily to avoid filing a PMA by claiming substantial equivalence to the preamendment Gee Bee Ring.

2. *Approval of the Female Condom.* The Reality Female Condom, for which FDA approved a PMA in 1993, remains on the market, manufactured by the Female Health Company under the brand name FC Female Condom. Most sales are to international health organizations for distribution in the developing world, especially Africa.

3. *Male Condoms.* As FDA mentions, male condoms (known simply as "condoms") are Class II. 21 C.F.R. 884.5300. The rise of AIDS in the 1980s led FDA to tighten its regulation of this device. Late in the decade, the agency announced a strengthened inspection program, a more stringent defect standard, and a new labeling guideline for condoms. 52 Fed. Reg. 12605 (Apr. 17, 1987), 53 Fed. Reg. 573 (Jan. 8, 1988). In 2005, FDA proposed to amend the classification regulation for condoms by a guidance document entitled Class II Special Controls Guidance Document: Labeling for Male Condoms Made of Natural Rubber Latex. 70 Fed. Reg. 69102 (Nov. 14, 2005).

COMMENT: REPROCESSED SINGLE–USE DEVICES

Traditionally, most medical devices used in hospital settings were considered to be reusable. Users would routinely clean, disinfect, and sterilize glass, rubber, and metal devices and use them again and again. In the 1970s, however, manufacturers increasingly began to sell devices labeled as "single-use devices" (SUDs). The market for these products developed in response to the emergence of new plastics and a demand for disposable equipment. Hospitals, however, to save costs and prevent the accumulation of medical waste, often chose to reprocess SUDs and reuse them. Hospitals and health care facilities reprocessed many SUDs themselves. In addition, by the late 1970s, a new industry of third-party reprocessors developed.

The rise of reprocessing raised a complicated question for FDA. Should it regulate reprocessors according to the regime it imposed on original device manufacturers? More particularly, should the agency require reprocessors to submit PMNs for reprocessed versions of original devices that themselves were subject to the premarket notification requirement? FDAMA, which exempted Class I devices from PMN obligations, made the latter question irrelevant for commonly reprocessed Class I SUDs, such as surgical saw blades, drill bits, and staplers. But it remained an important unresolved question for frequently reprocessed Class II SUDs, such as catheters and tracheal tubes.

Through the 1990s, FDA left hospital reprocessing operations virtually unregulated, despite declaring in a Compliance Policy Guide that "there is a lack of data to support the general reuse of disposable medical devices," and that "any [health care] institution or practitioner who resterilizes and/or reuses a disposable medical device must bear full responsibility for its safety and effectiveness." FDA, REUSE OF MEDICAL DISPOSABLE DEVICES, Compliance Policy Guide 300.500 (1977). As for third party reprocessors, the agency considered them to be subject to the full panoply of requirements applicable to original device manufacturers, including premarket notification. Nevertheless, although FDA issued warning letters to third-party reprocessors for some types of violations, it exercised its enforcement discretion with regard to section 510(k) notification and never took action against a third-party reprocessor for failing to comply with this requirement. FDA–CDRH, FDA PROPOSED STRATEGY ON REUSE OF SINGLE–USE DEVICES 2–5 (1999), availability announced at 64 Fed. Reg. 59782 (Nov. 3, 1999); Kurt R. Karst, *Going 90 in a 55 M.P.H. Speed Zone: Reprocessing of Used Single–Use Medical Devices and the Food and Drug Administration's Non–Enforcement of the Food, Drug, and Cosmetic Act*, 56 FOOD & DRUG L.J. 57 (2001).

The age of unregulated device reprocessing ended at the turn of the millennium. In 2000, FDA announced its intention to phase in enforcement of the premarket submission requirements on third-party and hospital reprocessors. 65 Fed. Reg. 49583 (Aug. 14, 2000). Reprocessors of Class III devices would have to file premarket applications, and reprocessors of nonexempt Class II and Class I devices would have to file PMNs. Then, in 2002, MDUFMA added section 510(o) to the FD&C Act. This provision, which assumes that reprocessed single use devices are fully subject to the premarket submission requirements, instructs FDA to identify SUDs for which PMNs must include validation data concerning cleaning, sterilization, and functional performance. The validation data are intended to ensure that the reprocessed devices are substantially equivalent to their predicate devices. The provision further provides that the PMN requirement, including validation data, will apply to formerly exempt critical and semi-critical devices identified by the agency. FDA has since promulgated lists of SUD types requiring validation data and of critical and semicritical SUDs whose PMN exemption has been terminated.

3. INVESTIGATIONAL DEVICES

All PMAs for Class III devices require clinical data demonstrating safety and effectiveness. *See* section 515(c)(1)(A). Moreover, as noted above, some PMNs require such data. In most instances, a manufacturer seeking to introduce a device to the market by either route must itself generate the necessary clinical data. The following question thus arises: how can a manufacturer legally ship for investigative purposes a postamendment device that has been neither cleared nor approved by FDA?

Like new drugs, the FD&C Act and FDA regulations allow the investigational use of a new postamendment device in order to obtain the safety and effectiveness data required to support a PMA application or section 510(k) notification. A sponsor seeking to perform clinical studies on an unapproved device must qualify for an investigational device exemption (IDE). The IDE system resembles the IND system for clinical testing of new drugs (discussed *supra* p. 624), with one major difference. FDA may require agency approval of an IDE application, in addition to approval by a local institutional review board (IRB), only if the agency "finds that the process of review by such committee is inadequate." Section 520(g)(3)(A). FDA has implemented this provision by dividing investigational devices into two categories: those that represent a "significant risk" and those that do not. The IDE application requirements for a device in the "significant risk" category are similar to the IND process for new drugs. For a device in the second category, however, an investigation will be "considered to have" an approved IDE based solely on IRB approval and the satisfaction of several other requirements, and the sponsor need not submit an application to FDA. 21 C.F.R. 812.2(b). A sponsor has the authority initially to determine whether its device is a "significant risk" device, but either the IRB or FDA may disagree and redesignate it. 21 C.F.R. 812.2(b)(1), 812.20(a), 812.66. *See* Marc H. Bozeman, *The Clinical Investigation of Medical Devices—A Preliminary Guide for Manufacturers*, 34 FOOD DRUG COSM. L.J. 289 (1979); FDA, SIGNIFICANT RISK AND NONSIGNIFICANT RISK MEDICAL DEVICE STUDIES (1995).

An IDE, whether actually approved or "considered approved," exempts an investigator from a wide range of statutory and regulatory requirements, including, for example, those concerning misbranding, registration and listing, performance standards, adverse event reporting, and good manufacturing practices. Section 520(g)(2)(A), 21 C.F.R. 812.1. Most notably, a sponsor with an approved IDE does not have to comply with premarket approval or premarket notification requirements. An IDE thus permits a device manufacturer legally to ship an investigative device that has received neither PMN clearance nor PMA approval.

COMMENT: FEASIBLITY STUDIES

Often only a limited "feasibility" study is conducted on a significant risk investigational device to determine whether a full investigation is warranted. As FDA has explained:

> In a developmental process, a device is designed to meet a clinical need and testing begins in the laboratory using animal and/or bench methodology. Once the design and operating parameters have been subject to adequate preclinical tests, the developer may wish to conduct an initial limited study in humans to confirm the design and operating specifications before beginning an extensive clinical trial. The initial study may indicate that minor or major changes in the device or its manufacture are necessary before proceeding. It may also indicate that the device does not meet expectations and it will be terminated. The performance of the device in the limited study serves to establish the parameters for the larger clinical study, such as sample size and indices of measurement.

> Inherent in the utility of the limited study is the importance of maintaining sufficient flexibility for the researcher to make adjustments in the device, its manufacture or the investigational plan in the early stages of clinical testing without the need for repeated prior FDA approval.

GUIDANCE MEMORANDUM: REVIEW OF IDEs FOR FEASIBILITY STUDIES (1989).

Because FDA's IDE regulations impose substantial obligations even for such a limited test, in 1986 the American Society of Artificial Internal Organs petitioned the agency to reduce the requirements for such a "feasibility" investigation. FDA published the petition for comment, 51 Fed. Reg. 11266 (Apr. 1, 1986), and subsequently announced a comprehensive review of the IDE regulations, 51 Fed. Reg. 26830 (July 25, 1986). FDA ultimately responded to the ASAIO petition by issuing guidance on May 17, 1989, adopting a flexible approach to the review of IDE applications for feasibility studies.

COMMENT: "RESEARCH USE ONLY" EXEMPTION

An exemption from the IDE requirements in 21 C.F.R. 812.2(c)(2) allows the sale of a diagnostic device labeled "For Research Use Only" or "For Investigational Use Only" if the testing is noninvasive, does not require an invasive sampling procedure that presents a significant risk, does not introduce energy into a subject, and is not used without confirmation by another established diagnostic product or procedure. In a consent decree entered in *United States v. Centocor, Inc.*, Civ. No. 85–5613 (E.D. Pa. 1986), 22 FDA CONSUMER, No. 7, at 44 (Sept. 1989), the defendant agreed not only to label a diagnostic device "For Research Use Only," but also to obtain from each researcher a written agreement that the device would not be used for investigation involving clinical use, including diagnosis or monitoring, and that results of tests would not be used in conjunction with any patient records or treatment. The consent decree prohibited shipment to any researcher before this agreement was executed. FDA has since used this consent decree as a model for regulating diagnostic products sold for research use only. *See* DRAFT COMPLIANCE POLICY GUIDE, COMMERCIALIZATION OF IN VITRO DIAGNOSTIC DEVICES LABELED FOR RESEARCH USE ONLY OR INVESTIGATION- AL USE ONLY 14 (1998).

NOTES

1. *Other IDE Exemptions.* In addition to exempting some diagnostic devices from the IDE requirement, 21 C.F.R. 812(c) also exempts, with some qualifications, preamendment nontransitional devices being investigated in accordance with their 1976 labeling; devices determined to be substantially equivalent to such preamend- ment devices; devices undergoing nonrisky consumer preference testing; veterinary devices; devices shipped solely for research on laboratory animals; and custom devices. In accordance with section 520(g)(6) (added by FDAMA), the regulations do not require FDA approval of "developmental changes" in a device subject to an IDE, if these changes "do not constitute a significant change in design or in basic principles of operation" and are "made in response to information gathered during the course of an investigation." 21 C.F.R. 812.35(a)(3)(i).

2. *Early Collaboration on IDEs.* In 1995, FDA established a "Pre–IDE" program to increase the approval rate and reduce the time to approval. This informal program encourages IDE sponsors to meet with agency staff before submitting IDE applications for review, to submit portions of the IDE to FDA preliminarily for guidance before making the formal submission, and to communi- cate frequently with the agency during the review process. *See* GOALS AND INITIATIVES FOR THE IDE PROGRAM (1995) (IDE Memorandum D95–1). The informal Pre–IDE program is still in effect, but it now coexists with a formal system of "early collaboration meetings" established in 1997 by FDAMA. These meetings are also intended to take place prior to submission of the IDE. FDA must grant requests for formal early collaboration meetings, reduce the resulting determinations or agree- ments to writing, and generally treat these written conclusions as binding. Meetings under FD&C Act 513(a)(3)(D) (termed "Determination Meetings" by FDA), be- tween the agency and individuals intending to submit PMAs address what type of scientific evidence will be necessary to establish the effectiveness of the device in question. Meetings under FD&C Act 520(g)(7) ("Agreement Meetings") are between FDA and individuals intending to file PMAs or PMNs for Class III or implantable devices. Agreement Meetings are meant to reach agreement regarding the key parameters of the investigational plan. *See* EARLY COLLABORATION MEETINGS UNDER FDAMA; FINAL GUIDANCE (2001).

———

The IDE system appears to have worked satisfactorily for routine long term investigations of new devices, but it seems less well-suited to studies of devices that are deployed infrequently and usually in an emergency. For example, FDA had approved an IDE for the Jarvik–7 artificial heart, setting stringent protocol conditions, months before Dr. William DeVries implanted it in Dr. Barney Clark on December 1–2, 1982. After four permanent implants of the Jarvik–7 heart, however, an FDA advisory committee reviewed the program and recommended that "FDA should assume a more direct oversight role as the clinical trial proceeds, and should approve subsequent implants on a case-by-case basis." "FDA Sets New Requirements For Permanent Artificial Heart Program," FDA Talk Paper No. T86–3 (January 7, 1986).

In the interim, however, the exigencies of patient care overcame FDA's IDE requirements for another type of artificial heart.

Cristine Russell, *Temporary Heart Implanted: Tucson Operation Lacked FDA Approval*

WASHINGTON POST, Thursday, March 7, 1985, at A1.

Doctors at a University of Arizona teaching hospital yesterday implanted a new type of temporary artificial heart in a dying 32–year–old man while they tried to locate a human heart for transplant.... Dr. Allan Beigel, a university vice president and spokesman for the University Medical Center hospital, said last night that the mechanical device, designed by a Chinese dentist, "had not been tested in humans" and does not have government approval, but was implanted anyway because "the alternative was that the patient would die." The recipient, identified only as a Caucasian divorced father of two, had rejected a human heart transplant earlier in the day and had been placed on a heart-lung machine. Beigel said time was of the utmost concern because the patient was reaching the point where continued use of the machine risked causing irreparable damage.

The patient was reported in critical but stable condition after the three-hour implant procedure, which has not been approved by the federal Food and Drug Administration. Asked at a news briefing last night whether FDA approval was needed for the operation, Dr. Jack Copeland, head of the hospital's heart-transplant team, said: "Ideally, they should have, but you can't think of everything." Later, he added, "We did not set out to do a human experiment. We set out to do a heart transplant. We were faced with a patient who had no alternative except death."

The mechanical heart used, called the Phoenix heart, was developed at St. Luke's Hospital in Phoenix, where it has been under study for about two years, Beigel said. It was one of three devices—including the Jarvik–7 artificial heart, which has been implanted into three permanent artificial-heart recipients—rushed to Tucson when the patient's condition began deteriorating.

An FDA spokesman said last night that the agency had informed the university yesterday that federal permission was needed for human experimentation with unproven medical devices, but that the university failed to obtain the approval. University spokesman Mike Letson said "there was not time" to obtain permission, adding, "The legal ramifications will have to come along later."

FDA spokesman David Duarte said the agency "is waiting to hear the facts from the university." He said the FDA response could range from a reprimand to taking the matter to court.

After FDA completed an investigation of the episode, on May 10, 1985, John Villforth, Director of the Center for Devices and Radiological Health, wrote to the administrator of the University of Arizona's hospital:

> FDA understands the situation that occurred at the University of Arizona Hospital and the reasons why Dr. Copeland took the actions he did to save the patient's life; however, we also believe that all of the patients who might benefit from such a device are best served when the device is used in a planned clinical investigation, where the device's safety and effectiveness can be studied....

> Although the Medical Device Amendments to the Food, Drug, and Cosmetic Act do not provide for the emergency use of unapproved devices, FDA has discretion to withhold consideration of regulatory action in appropriate circumstances. Because we believe that the situation at the University of Arizona Hospital constitutes such a circumstance, no further action by FDA is indicated and we consider the matter closed.

> We would be pleased to assist you in obtaining FDA approval for investigations of artificial hearts, should you wish to conduct such studies. We are now encouraging sponsors of investigations to include in their investigations therapeutic use of life-saving devices in situations where no alternative exists.... This will allow physicians to have access to life-saving devices, while at the same time, ensuring that physicians participate in an approved investigation....

To govern future emergencies of this sort, FDA then published a guidance permitting emergency use of unapproved devices without an IDE when the patient is in a life-threatening condition and no alternative treatment is available. Guidance for the Emergency Use of Unapproved Medical Devices, announced in 50 Fed. Reg. 42866 (Oct. 25, 1985).

A manufacturer may prospectively obtain an IDE for emergency use of an unapproved device. Indeed, in 1996 FDA finalized a rule, discussed *supra* p. 653, permitting IRBs to approve emergency protocols for investigational devices or drugs with an exception to the informed consent requirement when obtaining such consent is not feasible. 21 C.F.R. 50.24. Nevertheless, situations may still arise in which a device with no approved IDE represents a patient's final chance. A revised version of FDA's Guidance for Emergency Use of Unapproved Devices thus remains in effect:

Guidance for Institutional Review Boards and Clinical Investigators: Emergency Use of Unapproved Medical Devices (1998)

... The Food and Drug Administration (FDA) recognizes that emergencies arise where an unapproved device may offer the only possible life-saving alternative, but an IDE for the device does not exist, or the proposed use is not approved under an existing IDE, or the physician or institution is not approved under the IDE. Using its enforcement discretion, FDA has not objected if a physician chooses to use an unapproved device in such an emergency, provided that the physician later justifies to FDA that an emergency actually existed.

Each of the following conditions must exist to justify emergency use:

1. the patient is in a life-threatening condition that needs immediate treatment;

2. no generally acceptable alternative for treating the patient is available; and

3. because of the immediate need to use the device, there is no time to use existing procedures to get FDA approval for the use.

... The physician may not conclude that an "emergency" exists in advance of the time when treatment may be needed based solely on the expectation that IDE approval procedures may require more time than is available. Physicians should be aware that FDA expects them to exercise reasonable foresight with respect to potential emergencies and to make appropriate arrangements under the IDE procedures far enough in advance to avoid creating a situation in which such arrangements are impracticable.

In the event that a device is to be used in circumstances meeting the criteria listed above, the device developer should notify the Center for Devices and Radiological Health (CDRH), Program Operation Staff by telephone ... immediately after shipment is made. [An unapproved device may not be shipped in anticipation of an emergency. EDS.] Nights and weekends, contact the FDA Office of Emergency Operations....

FDA would expect the physician to follow as many subject protection procedures as possible. These include:

1. obtaining an independent assessment by an uninvolved physician;

2. obtaining informed consent from the patient or a legal representative;

3. notifying institutional officials as specified by institutional policies;

4. notifying the Institutional Review Board (IRB); and

5. obtaining authorization from the IDE holder, if an approved IDE for the device exists.

. . . .

Subsequent emergency use of the device may not occur unless the physician or another person obtains approval of an IDE for the device and its use. If an IDE application for subsequent use has been filed with FDA and FDA disapproves the IDE application, the device may not be used even if the circumstances constituting an emergency exist. Developers of devices that could be used in emergencies should anticipate the likelihood of emergency use and should obtain an approved IDE for such uses.

Even for an emergency use, the investigator is required to obtain informed consent of the subject or the subject's legally authorized representative unless both the investigator and a physician who is not otherwise participating in the clinical investigation certify in writing all of the following [21 C.F.R. 50.23(a)]:

1. The subject is confronted by a life-threatening situation necessitating the use of the test article.

2. Informed consent cannot be obtained because of an inability to communicate with, or obtain legally effective consent from, the subject.

3. Time is not sufficient to obtain consent from the subject's legal representative.

4. No alternative method of approved or generally recognized therapy is available that provides an equal or greater likelihood of saving the subject's life.

    . . . .

The conduct of planned research in life-threatening emergent situations where obtaining prospective informed consent has been waived, is provided by 21 CFR 50.24. The research plan must be approved in advance by FDA and the IRB, and publicly disclosed to the community in which the research will be conducted. Such studies are usually not eligible for the emergency approvals described above. . . .

4.   PREMARKET APPROVAL APPLICATIONS

After the sponsor of a novel Class III device has obtained the requisite safety and effectiveness data, it must submit a PMA application to FDA for review and approval. FDA has promulgated regulations governing the PMA process in 45 Fed. Reg. 81769 (Dec. 12, 1980), 51 Fed. Reg. 26342 (July 22, 1986), 21 C.F.R. Part 814.

a.   COMPARISON OF PMAs AND NDAs

The PMA process is similar to the new drug application (NDA) process discussed in Chapter IV. After the agency determines that the PMA is complete and accepts it for filing, it proceeds to perform a comprehensive review of the information contained within. As discussed below, FDA must refer the PMA to an advisory committee if the applicant requests, and it may do so on its own initiative. As is the case with new drugs, the primary questions for the advisory committee, and ultimately for FDA itself, are safety and effectiveness under the conditions of use in the proposed labeling.

Despite these similarities, the statutory standards for determining the safety and effectiveness of devices differ from the comparable standards for drugs in several respects. First, section 513(a)(1)(C) of the FD&C Act provides that premarket approval of devices is intended to provide "reasonable assurance" of safety and effectiveness. The drug provisions do not contain similar qualifying language.

Second, section 513(a)(2) explicitly mandates that when assessing the safety and effectiveness of a device, FDA consider: (1) the persons for whose use the device is intended, (2) the "conditions of use" prescribed in the labeling, and (3) the "probable benefit to health from the use of the device [weighed] against any probable risk of injury or illness." Such enumerated factors do not appear in the new drug provisions of the Act, although FDA routinely takes them into account when reviewing NDAs.

Third, the Act sets a standard for establishing the effectiveness of devices that seems more flexible than the "substantial evidence" standard applicable to drugs. Section 513(a)(1)(C) states that effectiveness may be established "on the basis of well-controlled investigations, including clinical investigations *where appropriate....*" Section 513(a)(3)(A) (emphasis added). Paragraph (B) then provides an alternative method for proving a device's effectiveness.

> If the Secretary determines that there exists valid scientific evidence (other than evidence derived from [well-controlled investigations])—
>
> (i) which is sufficient to determine the effectiveness of a device, and
>
> (ii) from which it can fairly and responsibly be concluded by qualified experts that the device will have the effect it purports or is represented to have under the conditions of use prescribed, recommended, or suggested in the labeling of the device,
>
> then ... the Secretary may authorize the effectiveness of the device to be determined on the basis of such evidence.

There are a number of reasons why Congress, when drafting the 1976 Amendments, may have been inclined to subject medical device manufacturers seeking premarket approval to a more flexible standard of proof of safety and effectiveness than new drug sponsors. Because devices are not metabolized, their interaction with the body tends to be less complex than is the case with drugs. Moreover, as noted by one witness at hearings preceding the enactment of the 1976 Amendments: "In the determination of efficacy, drug studies permit measurements of dosages, biological levels, and responses in relation to these, whereas in devices these relationships are not present and effectiveness must often be evaluated by professional judgment rather than measurable responses." "Medical Device Amendments of 1975," Hearings before the Subcomm. on Health and the Environment of the House Comm. on Interstate and Foreign Commerce, 94th Cong., 1st Sess. 298–99 (1975) (statement by Vallee I. Willman, M.D). Finally, double-blind placebo-controlled clinical investigations are sometimes simply not feasible or appropriate for medical devices. Surgically implanting a nonfunctioning dummy device in a patient obviously raises different issues than does administering a sugar pill.

The House Report accompanying the bill that was eventually enacted stated the following when discussing the section 513(a)(3)(B) alternative to well-controlled investigations:

> Devices vary widely in type and in mode of operation, as well as in the scope of testing and experience they have received. Thus, the Committee has authorized the Secretary to accept meaningful data developed under procedures less rigorous than well-controlled investigations in instances in which well-documented case histories assure protection of the public health or in instances in which

well-controlled investigations would present undue risks to subjects or patients.

H.R. Rep. No. 853, 94th Cong., 2d Sess. 17 (1976).

During the first 15 years of the new device regime, FDA frequently
approved devices based on evidence that would have been deemed insufficient for approval of a new drug. *See* Richard A. Merrill, *The Architecture of
Government Regulation of Medical Products*, 82 Va. L. Rev. 1753, 1823
(1996). In the mid–1990s, however, the agency began to assert that it
expected studies for Class III devices to be as rigorous, and often as
elaborate, as those required for new drugs. *Id.* This apparent shift in policy
followed the 1993 publication of an FDA committee report critical of the
device review process. Final Report of the FDA Committee for Clinical
Review (1993), *reprinted in* "Less Than the Sum of Its Parts: Reforms
Needed in the Organization, Management, and Resources of the Food and
Drug Administration's Center for Devices and Radiological Health," Subcomm. on Oversight and Investigations, House Comm. on Energy and
Commerce, 103d Cong., 1st Sess., 98–163 (Comm. Print 1993). The committee was chaired by Dr. Robert Temple, the Director of CDER's Office of
Drug Evaluation, and was composed almost entirely of CDER scientists.
FDA Commissioner David Kessler established the Temple Committee in
the midst of widespread criticism of the agency's regulation of silicone
breast implants and commentary alleging a lack of rigor in CDRH's
assessment of devices.

Based on its examination of a small sample of pending and approved
applications for medical devices, the Temple Committee identified "certain
patterns of deficiencies in the design, conduct, and analysis of clinical
studies . . . in enough of the applications to suggest that these deficiencies
represent a common problem." Although the committee did not directly
criticize CDRH's performance, the very fact that the center had approved
such flawed applications raised questions about the center's thoroughness
and competence. The committee's formal recommendations included more
systematic integration of biostatisticians into the review process, development of "guidance" on clinical study design for manufacturers and agency
reviewers, and "adherence to the principles of sound study design throughout the review of device applications and in final decisionmaking." Importantly, the committee stated that "[t]he fundamental principles underlying
evaluation of any therapeutic intervention, whether it is a drug [or a]
device . . . are the same." Commissioner Kessler endorsed the report and
promised that its recommendations would be implemented. David A. Kessler, *FDA's Revitalization of Medical Device Review and Regulation*, 28
Biomed. Instrumentation & Tech. 220, 223 (1994).

Although the conclusion is difficult to document, it seems fair to say
that FDA sets the bar higher for PMA sponsors today than it did in the
years following the enactment of the Medical Device Amendments. Nevertheless, the device approval process remains less rigorous than the drug
approval process. After all, the differences in the statutory standards
remain. The authors of a recent article observed:

> The device statute merely requires "reasonable assurance" of
> safety and efficacy, while the drug statute requires "substantial

evidence of efficacy." Yet we are inclined to think that the differences in testing requirements for drugs and devices are justified by the difference in difficulty of finding adverse effects due to the toxic quality of drugs as opposed to the physical effects of medical devices. Perhaps one might describe device regulation as a watered-down version of drug regulation, even if there is genuine disagreement about the amount of water that passes under the device-regulatory bridge.

Michael D. Green & William B. Schultz, *Symposium: Regulatory Compliance as a Defense to Products Liability: Tort Law Deference to FDA Regulation of Medical Devices*, 88 GEO. L.J. 2119, 2137 (2000). *See also* Peter Barton Hutt, Richard A. Merrill & Alan M. Kirschenbaum, *The Standard of Evidence Required for Premarket Approval Under the Medical Device Amendments of 1976*, 77 FOOD & DRUG L.J. 605 (1992).

b. ADVISORY COMMITTEE REVIEW

Whereas FDA's use of advisory committees in the review of NDAs, BLAs, and food additive petitions is entirely discretionary, the agency ordinarily must refer a PMA to an advisory committee if the applicant asks that it do so. Under section 515(c)(3), added by the 1990 Act, FDA may refer a PMA application to an expert panel on its own initiative, and it must do so on the request of the applicant unless the agency finds that the information in the application substantially duplicates information which has previously been reviewed by a panel. FDA describes its application of this provision of the Act as follows:

> In general, all PMAs for the first-of-a-kind device are taken before the appropriate advisory panel for review and recommendation. However, as soon as FDA believes that (1) the pertinent issues in determining the safety and effectiveness for the type of medical device are understood and (2) FDA has developed the ability to address those issues, future PMAs for devices of that type are not be taken before an advisory panel unless a particular application presents an issue that can best be addressed through panel review.

FDA Website, Device Advice: Review Process (June 11, 2003).

The panel to which FDA must refer a PMA is the appropriate classification panel organized by clinical category pursuant to section 513(b). The workload of these panels originally was dominated by the task of classifying the universe of preamendment devices into Class I, Class II, or Class III, but they now dedicate much of their time to making reports and recommendations respecting approval of PMAs. Section 513(b)(2) imposes certain requirements on these panels:

> The Secretary shall appoint to each panel ... persons who are qualified by training and experience to evaluate the safety and effectiveness of the devices to be referred to the panel and who, to the extent feasible, possess skill in the use of, or experience in the development, manufacture, or utilization of, such devices. The Secretary shall make appointments to each panel so that each panel shall consist of members with adequately diversified exper-

tise in such fields as clinical and administrative medicine, engineering, biological and physical sciences, and other related professions. In addition, each panel shall include as nonvoting members a representative of consumer interests and a representative of interests of the device manufacturing industry. Scientific, trade, and consumer organizations shall be afforded an opportunity to nominate individuals for appointment to the panels. No individual who is in the regular full-time employ of the United States and engaged in the administration of this Act may be a member of any panel....

c.   FDA ACTION ON PMAs

By statute, FDA has only 180 days after receipt of a PMA to issue an order approving or denying approval. In fact, the time from initial submission of a PMA to ultimate approval or denial can be quite a bit longer. First, FDA measures the 180-day period from the date it files the PMA, having made a threshold determination that the application is sufficiently complete to permit a substantive review. 21 C.F.R. 814.40–42. Second, the submission of any "major" PMA amendment restarts the 180-day clock, and FDA may request such an amendment. 21 C.F.R. 814.37(a)–(c). Finally, FDA does not commit itself to issuing an actual approval or denial order within the mandatory period. It deems itself compliant with the 180-day requirement if it issues an "approvable letter" or a "not approvable letter" within that time. 21 C.F.R. 814.40. An approvable letter is sent if the PMA "substantially meets the requirements [of the PMA regulations] and the agency believes it can approve the application if specific additional information is submitted or specific conditions are agreed to by the applicant." 21 C.F.R. 814.44(e). A not approvable letter, which is sent if "the agency believes that the application may not be approved," "describes the deficiencies" and, "where practical ... identif[ies] measures required to place the PMA in approvable form." 21 C.F.R. 814.45(f). An applicant may respond to either type of letter by amending its PMA, withdrawing its PMA, or considering the letter to be a denial of approval and requesting administrative review of that denial. 21 C.F.R. 814.44(e)(2) & (f).

COMMENT: USER FEES, PERFORMANCE GOALS, AND PMA REVIEW TIMES

FDA's implementation of the premarket approval provisions of the 1976 Amendments proved largely uncontroversial for the first decade of the new device regime. The time required for FDA review of a PMA application was approximately half that for review of an NDA. No doubt the agency's prompt processing of PMAs was in part attributable to the relatively small number of Class III postamendment devices required to go through the premarket approval process. By the late 1980s, however, these time frames had begun to lengthen significantly. The device industry and its supporters in Congress began to call for measures to quicken the PMA review process. An obvious model for achieving this goal appeared with the enactment of Prescription Drug User Fee Act of 1992, in which Congress authorized user fees to fund the drug review process and tied these fees to the achievement of performance goals. It took almost a decade, however, for Congress to institute a parallel system for devices.

The Medical Device User Fee and Modernization Act of 2002, 116 Stat. 1588, FD&C Act (sections 737–38), amended the FD&C Act to provide FDA with the authority to assess fees for the premarket review of PMAs and PMNs, as well as various other types of premarket submissions, for the five year period between 2002 and 2007. According to section 101(3) of MDUFMA, "the fees authorized by this title will be dedicated to meeting the goals identified in the letters from the Secretary of Health and Human Services to the [appropriate House and Senate Committees], as set forth in the Congressional Record." DHHS Secretary Thompson's identical letters to Congress, generally referred to together as the "FDA commitment letter," set forth annual performance goals for the number of days within which FDA should respond to and decide the various categories of premarket submissions. The letter is available on FDA's website.

Secretary Thompson's 2002 commitment letter included special performance goals for expedited PMA submissions. FDA has had some form of expedited review for medical devices since 1994. The practice was mandated by Congress in 1997, when FDAMA revised the FD&C Act to state:

> In order to provide for more effective treatment or diagnosis of life-threatening or irreversibly debilitating human diseases or conditions, the Secretary shall provide review priority for devices—
>
> (A) representing breakthrough technologies,
>
> (B) for which no approved alternatives exist,
>
> (C) which offer significant advantages over existing approved alternatives, or
>
> (D) the availability of which is in the best interest of the patients.

Section 515(d)(5). Although this provision applies only to PMAs, the agency performs expedited review of all types of premarket submissions for devices that satisfy the statutory criteria. FDA–CDRH, EXPEDITED REVIEW OF PREMARKET SUBMISSION FOR DEVICES: GUIDANCE FOR INDUSTRY AND FDA STAFF (2003). The submitter may request expedited review, but it is FDA that determines whether the device qualifies for such treatment. A PMA, PMN, or other submission granted expedited review status is moved to the front of the review queue and may receive additional review resources.

MDUFMA also codified FDA's policy of accepting "Modular PMAs." In 1998, FDA began to allow applicants to submit discrete completed sections, or "modules," of a PMA before completing the entire PMA. This approach permitted applicants to submit, and the agency to review, preclinical data and manufacturing information while clinical data were still being collected and analyzed. The 2002 amendments sanctioned this policy by adding section 515(c)(4), which provides: "Prior to submission of [a PMA], the Secretary shall accept and review any portion of the application that the applicant and the Secretary agree is complete, ready, and appropriate for review." *See* PREMARKET APPROVAL APPLICATION MODULAR REVIEW (2003).

NOTES

1. *Use of Data from a Prior PMA Application.* Under the 1976 Amendments, the data contained in a PMA application were considered confidential and thus could not be used by FDA or relied on by another applicant to support approval of a PMA application for an identical or similar device. The 1990 Act added new section 520(h)(4), which, as amended by FDAMA, authorizes FDA, six years after approving a PMA, to refer to clinical and preclinical data in the application, but not descriptions of methods of manufacture or product composition, to approve a subsequent PMA application.

2. *Implanted Devices.* Not surprisingly, FDA gives close scrutiny to any device intended to be implanted in the body. In 53 Fed. Reg. 5469 (Feb. 24, 1988), FDA announced the availability of a guideline prepared jointly by regulatory officials in the United Kingdom, Canada, and the United States, on testing of medical devices to establish human biocompatibility.

3. *Extended Review Period for Public Health—Breast Implants.* Section 515(d)(1)(B)(i) provides that FDA may extend the period for taking action on a PMA beyond the statutory 180–days if it "finds that the continued availability of the device is necessary for the public health."

Silicone gel-filled breast implants are preamendment devices. In 1988, the agency classified them into Class III, and in 1991, it required their manufacturers to file PMAs. Four manufacturers submitted applications. In October 1992, FDA, concerned about reports of a possible association between the implants and autoimmune disorders, denied the PMAs for cosmetic augmentation of healthy breasts. With respect to the use of silicone gel-filled breast implants for reconstructive purposes, however, FDA invoked section 515(d)(1)(B)(i) and extended the review period indefinitely. During the extended review period, FDA permitted the use of silicone gel-filled implants in any woman seeking breast reconstruction, so long as she enrolled in an open scientific protocol. Manufacturers distributed the devices for purely cosmetic purposes only under an approved IDE. *See* 57 Fed. Reg. 45812 (Oct. 5, 1992); FDA Commissioner David A. Kessler, Statement Regarding FDA's Decision on the Distribution and Use of Silicone Gel–Filled Implants (Apr. 16, 1992). In 2002–03, FDA received two new PMAs for silicone gel-filled implants. FDA sent both manufacturers "approvable" letters in 2005 and approved both on November 17, 2006.

4. *Administrative Review of a PMA Decision.* If FDA denies or withdraws approval of a PMA, the applicant may petition for review of the decision. Section 515(d)(4), (e)(2). Moreover, any interested person, including any member of the public, may petition the agency for reconsideration of a PMA approval. A petitioner may seek one of two types of administrative review. First, under section 515(g)(1) the petitioner may request a formal evidentiary public hearing. *See, e.g.,* 47 Fed. Reg. 7877 (Feb. 23, 1982) (announcing a public hearing on a petition to withdraw premarket approval of three gonorrhea antibody test kits). Alternatively, under section 515(g)(2) the petitioner may request review by an independent advisory committee of experts. *See, e.g.,* 51 Fed. Reg. 19610 (May 30, 1986) (granting advisory committee review of FDA denial of PMA for antibiotic bone cement). The reviewing committee provided in the second option must be distinct from the section 513(b) panels that advise FDA on classification and initial PMA decisions. Section 515(g)(2)(B). *See* 52 Fed. Reg. 3865 (Feb. 6, 1987) (establishing special committee for reconsideration of antibiotic bone cement PMA). FDA may deny a request for either type of review if it concludes that a hearing is not warranted.

5. *Temporary Suspension of Approval.* The 1990 Act added new section 515(e)(3), which authorizes FDA to suspend approval of a PMA application if, after

providing an opportunity for an informal hearing, it determines there is reasonable probability that use of the device would cause serious adverse health consequences or death. The agency must then proceed "expeditiously" to provide an opportunity for a hearing on whether to withdraw approval of the PMA permanently. *See* 21 C.F.R. 814.47.

COMMENT: POSTAPPROVAL REQUIREMENTS

As discussed earlier, *supra* p. 727, 829, FDA does not have formal statutory power to condition approval of a new drug on the manufacturer's adherence to distribution restrictions (other than prescription status) or other postapproval requirements. For devices, FDA's authority to impose such conditions is clear. The Act explicitly provides that an order approving a PMA "may require as a condition to such approval that the sale and distribution of the device be restricted ... to the extent [they] may be restricted under a regulation under section 520(e)." Section 515(d)(1)(B)(ii). Section 520(e), examined *infra* p. 1045, empowers FDA to issue regulations that restrict a device to sale, distribution, or use only upon prescription or "upon such other conditions as the Secretary may prescribe in such regulation."

FDA believes that its authority to impose postapproval requirements under the 1976 Amendments is not limited to restrictions on the sale, distribution, or use of a device. In its PMA regulations, the agency asserts the power to impose a wide variety of postapproval requirements, either in the PMA order itself or by regulation. 21 C.F.R. 814.82. The most common type of postapproval requirement imposed by FDA is mandatory postmarketing evaluation, reporting, or both regarding the safety and effectiveness of a device. According to its regulations, FDA may also require the prominent display of warnings or other information in the labeling of any device and in the advertising of a restricted device; the use of identification codes; the maintenance of records, including patient records; batch testing; and "[s]uch other requirements as FDA determines are necessary to provide reasonable assurance, or continued reasonable assurance, of the safety and effectiveness of the device." *Id*.

When FDA proposed its initial PMA rules, some comments challenged the agency's right to impose postapproval requirements other than restrictions on sale or distribution. FDA dismissed these arguments, responding that "FDA interprets section 515 of the act ['Premarket Approval'] as authorizing imposition of postapproval requirements and has imposed such requirements in PMA approval orders since the enactment of the amendments." 51 Fed. Reg. 26342, 26359 (July 22, 1986). FDA also relied on section 519, which authorizes FDA to issue regulations requiring manufacturers to maintain records and make reports necessary to assure the safety and effectiveness of devices.

Subsequent amendments to the FD&C Act have provided FDA with explicit authority to impose other types of postapproval requirements. For example, FDAMA amended section 522 to authorize FDA to order a manufacturer to conduct postmarketing surveillance of a Class III or Class II device if the device's failure is "reasonably likely to have serious adverse health consequences" and the device is either (1) intended to be implanted for more than one year or (2) is a life sustaining or life supporting device used outside a device user facility. *See* 21 C.F.R. 822 (implementing FD&C Act 522); FDA–CDRH, GUIDANCE FOR INDUSTRY AND FDA STAFF: POSTMARKETING SURVEILLANCE UNDER SECTION 522 (2006).

COMMENT: REGULATION OF IN VITRO DIAGNOSTIC DEVICES

FDA defines "in vitro diagnostic products" (IVDs) as "those reagents, instruments, and systems intended for use in the diagnosis of disease or other conditions, including a determination of the state of health, in order to cure, mitigate, treat, or prevent disease or its sequelae. Such products are intended for use in the collection, preparation, and examination of specimens taken from the human body." 21 C.F.R. 809.3(a). The regulation of IVDs presents distinctive issues, and a separate office within CDRH, known as the Office of In Vitro Diagnostic Device Evaluation and Safety (OIVD), is dedicated to these products. The Center for Biologics Evaluation and Research (CBER), rather than CDRH, regulates IVD devices involved in the collection, processing, testing, manufacture, and administration of blood, blood components, and cellular products. CBER also regulates all HIV test kits used either to screen blood and cellular products or to diagnose and treat people with HIV and AIDS.

FDA has issued regulations focused solely on IVD devices. For example, FDA rules establish an exemption from the IDE requirements for diagnostic devices labeled "For Research Use Only" or "For Investigational Use Only," *supra* p. 1005. FDA has also, by rule, created a special labeling regime for IVD products. 21 C.F.R. 809.10. Moreover, the agency has issued two restricted device regulations regulating the sale, distribution, and use of particular types of IVD devices. 21 C.F.R. 809.30 & 40.

FDA acknowledges that a PMA for an IVD presents unique issues:

> PMA approval is based on scientific evidence providing a reasonable assurance that the device is safe and effective for its intended use or uses. For IVDs, there is a unique link between safety and effectiveness since the safety of the device is not generally related to contact between the device and patient. For IVD products, the safety of the device relates to the impact of the device's performance, and in particular on the impact of false negative and false positive results, on patient health.

Although the agency has not formally established any special PMA, BLA, or PMN requirements for IVDs, it has published numerous guidance and draft guidance advising manufacturers on the investigation of IVD products and the preparation of successful premarket submissions for them. *See, e.g.,* FDA–CDRH, IN VITRO DIAGNOSTIC DEVICES: GUIDANCE FOR THE PREPARATION OF 510(K) SUBMISSIONS (1997). FDA–CDRH, DRAFT GUIDANCE FOR INDUSTRY AND FDA: PREMARKET APPROVAL APPLICATIONS FOR IN VITRO DIAGNOSTIC DEVICES PERTAINING TO HEPATITIS C VIRUSES (2003); FDA–CBER, GUIDANCE FOR INDUSTRY: CONTENT AND FORMAT OF CHEMISTRY, MANUFACTURING AND CONTROLS INFORMATION AND ESTABLISHMENT DESCRIPTION INFORMATION FOR A BIOLOGICAL IN VITRO DIAGNOSTIC PRODUCT (1999).

In 1988, Congress enacted the Clinical Laboratory Improvement Amendments (CLIA), 102 Stat. 2903, which established quality standards for laboratory testing and an accreditation program for clinical laboratories. Although the Centers for Medicare & Medicaid Services (CMS) (formerly the Health Care Financing Administration (HCFA)) has primary responsibility for overseeing the CLIA program, FDA's Office of In Vitro Diagnostic Device Evaluation and Safety also has an important role in implementing the law.

Under CLIA, it is illegal for a laboratory that has not been federally certified to "solicit or accept materials derived from the human body for ... examination." Laboratories are subject to different levels of regulation depending on the nature of the tests they perform. CLIA and its implementing regulations, 43 C.F.R. Part 493, establish three categories of testing based on the complexity of the testing methodology: (1) waived tests, (2) tests of moderate complexity, and (3) tests of high complexity. Laboratories performing only waived tests are subject to minimal regulation, whereas laboratories performing moderate or high complexity tests are subject to specific laboratory standards governing personnel, proficiency testing, patient test management, quality assurance, quality control, and inspections. Although FDA was initially given the task of categorizing commercially marketed in vitro diagnostic products for CLIA purposes, it delegated it to the Centers for Disease Control (CDC) in 1994. In 2000, FDA reassumed this responsibility. 64 Fed. Reg. 73561 (Dec. 30, 1999). OIVD, the in vitro product office within CDRH, determines the appropriate complexity categories for clinical laboratory devices as it evaluates premarket submissions.

5.   PRODUCT DEVELOPMENT PROTOCOLS

At the urging of makers of cardiac pacemakers, in 1976 FDA acquiesced in the inclusion of section 515(f), which provides an alternative track for the consideration and approval of a Class III device, termed a "product development protocol" (PDP). Under this rarely-used approach, one regulatory mechanism embraces both the investigation of the device and its marketing approval. FDA and the applicant agree in advance upon a testing program which, if completed with successful results, will result in approval. The requirements for proof of safety and effectiveness are as stringent for the PDP procedure as for PMAs; FDA may not declare a protocol complete (the equivalent of PMA approval) if it finds that "there is a lack of a showing of reasonable assurance of the safety and effectiveness of the device under the conditions of use prescribed, recommended, or suggested in the proposed labeling." Section 515(f)(6)(B)(iii). Section 513(C)(2), elaborating on the calculation of safety and effectiveness under section 515 (for example, by requiring a risk/benefit analysis), applies equally to PDPs and PMAs. The PDP is in many respects the model for the SPA used for new drugs, p. 637 *supra*, but is used far less frequently.

Medical Devices; Product Development Protocol Availability of Guidelines
45 Fed. Reg. 62555 (September 19, 1980).

The purpose of a PDP is to encourage the development of innovative devices, to reduce development time and costs by combining the conventional two-step investigatory and premarket development procedure into one regulatory mechanism, to aid small manufacturers, and to provide sponsors greater certainty that a testing approach will be acceptable to FDA. The guideline is intended to assist persons submitting PDP's to the agency to meet these objectives.

PDP's are optional; FDA cannot require a sponsor to submit a PDP rather than a premarket approval application (PMA) when seeking approval for a device. However, a sponsor may gain major advantages in using a PDP. For example, a sponsor can obtain FDA assistance in designing the testing procedures and protocols. Also, the sponsor receives a commitment from FDA that if the testing is done under these approved procedures and protocols and the test results are satisfactory, the device will be approved by FDA for marketing. Small manufacturers are likely to benefit from FDA assistance particularly for products that are used in limited circumstances....

There are five steps in the PDP process. Step I is a presubmission conference with FDA. The presubmission conference is designed to ensure that a PDP is appropriate for a particular device rather than an IDE and PMA (or reclassification of the device). Step II is FDA's determination that a PDP is appropriate. In this step, FDA formally determines whether a PDP that has been submitted by a sponsor is appropriate for the device. Step III is filing and approving a PDP. FDA will file a PDP if the PDP is suitable for submission to an advisory panel for review. To be suitable, the PDP must be designed to develop, or in fact contain, sufficient data to permit an evaluation of the device's safety and effectiveness. Upon filing of a suitable PDP, FDA will refer the PDP to an advisory panel for a recommendation. Subsequently, FDA will evaluate the PDP and the panel's recommendation and either approve or disapprove the PDP. Step IV is the submission of pre-clinical test results. After a PDP is approved, the sponsor may submit pre-clinical test data for FDA evaluation prior to beginning clinical trials. Although a PDP may be approved before pre-clinical testing, FDA will authorize the initiation of clinical trials only after reviewing the pre-clinical test results. After pre-clinical test results are evaluated, FDA will inform sponsors whether they may begin clinical tests with human subjects. This part of Step IV is similar to what happens when a sponsor seeks approval of an IDE. PDP sponsors must comply with the IDE requirements set forth in Part 812 including recordkeeping, institutional review board (IRB) review, and informed consent. Step V is the submission of clinical test results. This step is similar to what happens when a sponsor applies for approval of a PMA. FDA will review pre-clinical and clinical data together with manufacturing data and determine whether the device is suitable for marketing. After evaluating the data, FDA will declare the PDP "completed" or "not completed."

A significant difference between the PDP and IDE/PMA procedure is in the time schedules. A PDP must be approved or disapproved within 120 days of the date it is filed by FDA. An IDE, however, is deemed approved 30 days after receipt by FDA. There is no statutory time limit for FDA review of PDP preclinical data submitted to obtain FDA authorization to begin clinical trials....

NOTES

1.   *Advisory Panels.* It is no longer the case that FDA must refer every PDP to an advisory panel prior to approval. In 1997, FDAMA brought the PDP process into line with the PMA process by stating that the FDA need not refer a protocol to an advisory committee if "the proposed protocol and accompanying data which would be reviewed by such panel substantially duplicate a product development protocol and accompanying data which have previously been reviewed by such panel." Section 515(f)(2).

2.   *Frequency of Use of PDPs.* Despite early expectations, only a few Class III devices have completed—or even started down—the PDP path to market. In 1991, the author of an article on the PDP process reported that, since 1976, FDA had declared only two devices appropriate for PDP treatment, and neither manufacturer had completed the PDP procedure. Bradley Merrill Thompson, *Resurrecting the Product Development Protocol for Medical Devices*, 46 FOOD DRUG COSM. L.J. 187, 196 (1991). More recently, the popularity of the PDP process appears to have increased, though only slightly. From 1995 to 2005, 13 PDPs WERE RECEIVED AND APPROVED BY FDA, BUT ONLY TWO WERE ULTIMATELY DECLARED "COMPLETED." *SEE* ODE FISCAL YEAR REPORTS, 1995 THROUGH 2004; 71 FED. REG. 37082 (NOTING ONE PDP RECEIVED IN 2005).

6.   HUMANITARIAN DEVICE EXEMPTIONS

In the 1990 Act, Congress added section 520(m), to encourage the development of devices intended to benefit patients in the treatment and diagnosis of diseases that affect fewer than 4,000 individuals in the United States. FDA regulations implementing this section dub these Class III products "humanitarian use devices" (HUDs). 21 C.F.R. Part 814, Subpart H. Under these regulations, a device manufacturer may apply for a "humanitarian device exemption" (HDE) that allows a HUD to be marketed "notwithstanding the absence of reasonable assurance of effectiveness that would otherwise be required under sections 514 and 515 of the act." 21 C.F.R. 814.100(a)(2).

To acquire a HDE, a sponsor must first request a formal designation of HUD status from FDA's Office of Orphan Products Development. To receive such designation, the sponsor must provide sufficient evidence to establish that the disease or condition intended to be treated or diagnosed by the device affects fewer than 4,000 people in the United States per year. If the agency designates the product a HUD, the sponsor then files a HDE application to CDRH. The application generally must contain all the information required to be in a PMA, except that it need only include "reasonably obtainable" clinical data. 21 C.F.R. 814.104(b)(4). The HDE applicant must aver that no "comparable" device is available to treat or diagnose the condition. Like a PMA applicant, a person submitting an HDE application must provide "reasonable assurance that the device is safe under the conditions of use prescribed, recommended, or suggested in the labeling." But instead of also providing reasonable assurance of effectiveness, a HDE application need only satisfy FDA that "there is a reasonable basis from which to conclude that the probable benefit to health outweighs the risk of injury or illness, taking into account the probable risks and benefits of currently available devices and alternative forms of treatment." *See* GUIDANCE FOR INDUSTRY AND FDA STAFF, HUMANITARIAN DEVICE EXEMPTIONS

(HDE) Regulation: Questions and Answers (JULY 12, 2001); MAX SHERMAN ET AL., *HUMANITARIAN USE DEVICES*, 57 Food Drug L.J. 95 (2002).

A HDE constitutes full marketing approval. Unlike a device with an approved IDE, an approved HUD is not an investigational device and does not require informed consent. Section 520(m)(4) requires, however, that except in emergency situations, a device granted a HDE may be used only in facilities in which an IRB has approved its use.

A recent example of the HDE regime is FDA's approval of Fetoscopy Instrument Sets, a device used to treat fetuses with twin-to-twin transfusion syndrome (TTTS), a rare disorder involving uneven blood flow between identical twins in the womb. *See FDA Approves Humanitarian Device Exemption for Treatment of Fetuses with Twin-to-Twin Transfusion Syndrome*, FDA News No. P06–51 (April 3, 2006).

NOTE

Orphan Devices. As discussed previously, *supra* p. 701, the Orphan Drug Act of 1983 provided for financial assistance, in the form of grants and contracts, to defray the cost of developing "orphan drugs" for rare diseases (diseases suffered by fewer than 200,000 Americans). The Orphan Drug Amendments of 1988, 102 Stat. 90, extended this provision to medical devices. Consequently, under 21 U.S.C. 360ee, FDA "may make grants to and enter into contracts with public and private entities and individuals to assist in ... (2) defraying the costs of developing medical devices for rare diseases or conditions...."

COMMENT: CUSTOM DEVICES

Section 520(b) of the FD&C Act provides that the requirements of sections 514 (performance standards) and 515 (premarket approval) do not apply to any device which, to comply with the order of an individual physician or dentist, necessarily deviates from an otherwise applicable performance standard or approved PMA application. This "custom device" exemption applies only if the device is not generally available for purchase in finished form and is either made according to specifications for an individual patient or is intended to meet the special needs of the ordering physician or dentist. FDA regulations exempt custom devices from the IDE requirement "unless the device is being used to determine safety or effectiveness for commercial distribution." 21 C.F.R. 812.2(c)(7).

In *Contact Lens Manufacturers Ass'n v. FDA*, 766 F.2d 592 (D.C. Cir. 1985), the manufacturers contended that soft lenses are custom devices and thus exempt from the classification scheme. The court upheld FDA's rejection of this claim on the ground that, though individually ground to doctors' specifications for specific patients, as a class soft lenses are generally available to or used by other physicians and most prescriptions are likely to be replicated. *Cf. Sharp v. Artifex*, 110 F. Supp. 2d 388, 395 (W.D. Pa. 1999) ("We hold that given the narrow reading of the statute in *Contact Lens Manufacturers Association*, there is a material issue of fact as to whether the Defendant's [pedical screw fixation] device falls within the custom device exemption."). In a 1983 advisory opinion, FDA took the position that a custom device may not be a "standardized modification" of a marketed device, may not be "commercially distributed," and must be "made in a specific form for a patient named in the order of a physician or intended to meet the special needs of such physician in the course of his or her professional practice." FDA Associate Commissioner for Regulatory Affairs J.P. Hile to B. Gersh, FDA Docket No. 82A–0264 (March 7, 1983).

7.   Classification and Reclassification of Novel Devices

Under section 513(f)(3)(A), the manufacturer of a postamendment device that is not substantially equivalent to a preamendment device, and thus is presumptively a Class III product required to obtain premarket approval under 513(f)(1), may instead petition FDA to reclassify the device into Class II or I. If reclassified, the device may be marketed immediately. A successful reclassification petition results in a new classification regulation for that device, published in the Federal Register and later inserted into the Code of Federal Regulations.

In 1997, FDAMA created another procedural option for the manufacturer of a postamendment device with no substantially equivalent predicate. Under section 513(f)(2), if FDA responds to a PMN for a new device with a "not substantially equivalent" (NSE) determination, presumptively classifying it into Class III, the manufacturer may, within 30 days, request FDA instead to classify the device into Class I or Class II. Within 60 days of receiving such a request, the agency must classify the device by written order. If the agency classifies the device into Class I or Class II, the manufacturer is free to start marketing the device immediately. Moreover, the device becomes a predicate for other PMN submissions. Like a successful section 513(f)(3) reclassification petition, this procedure results in the addition of a new classification regulation for the device in the Code of Federal Regulations. However, the section 513(f)(2) process, as a formal matter, is not one of "reclassification," because the Act states that a classification under this provision "shall be the initial classification of the device." *See* FDA–CDRH, New Section 513(f)(2): Evaluation of Automatic Class III Designation, Guidance for Industry and CDRH Staff (1998).

Even with the advent of the section 513(f)(2) procedure, a manufacturer may still choose instead to file a reclassification petition under section 513(f)(3). The reclassification petition process does not require prior submission of a PMN, nor is it limited to requests submitted within 30 days following receipt of an NSE determination.

For the manufacturer of a new device with no substantially equivalent predicate, the key question, of course, is whether section 513(f)(3) reclassification or section 513(f)(2) classification can be accomplished more speedily or with less safety and effectiveness data than approval of a PMA application. The section 513(f)(2) process, with its 60–day time limit, may lead to quicker classifications into Class I or Class II than the older reclassification petition procedure, which presumes that FDA will routinely refer petitions to an expert panel and gives FDA up to 210 days to reach a final decision. Section 513(f)(3)(B)(i), (C)(i). (In its guidance document on 513(f)(2), FDA retains the option of requesting input from an advisory panel but recognizes that the agency must nonetheless complete its review within 60 days.) Despite its time advantages, however, the new 513(f)(2) process does not reduce the manufacturer's burden of providing data. A manufacturer making a section 513(f)(2) request must present FDA with the same types of information submitted in a traditional reclassification petition.

Reclassification of a new postamendment device by petition has rarely provided a shortcut to the market. FDA granted three such petitions in 2003, but that was the only year in the past 20 in which the agency granted more than one. Many years, FDA has granted no section 513(f)(3) reclassification petitions. The section 513(f)(2) approach introduced in 1997 has proven to be a somewhat more successful strategy. Multiple devices have reached the market this way almost every year since the birth of the procedure, and the pace is quickening; the agency granted 6 section 513(f)(2) requests in both 2004 and 2005, and at least 7 in 2006. Nevertheless, entry into the market through either initial classification into Class I or Class II or reclassification into Class I or Class II remains a minor feature in the overall scheme of device regulation.

If the MDA were read literally, section 513(f)(2) and section 513(f)(3) might have become popular methods for bringing harmless but unproven postamendment devices onto the market. The statutory definition of Class I embraces low-risk devices for nonserious conditions, regardless of the amount of safety and effectiveness data that exist. FD&C Act 513(a)(1)(A)(ii). One clever manufacturer believed that the reclassification petition offered a potential loophole by which he could introduce a new device onto the market as a Class I product.

Lake v. FDA

Med. Devices Rep. (CCH) ¶ 15,117, 1989 WL 715454 (E.D. Pa. 1989).

■ AHN, DISTRICT JUDGE.

Mr. Lake was the inventor of the Inductive Nasal Device ("IND"), which he maintained could cure the common cold and allergies. Despite these extraordinary claims and the appropriately august name attached to the invention, the IND is, essentially, a nose clip. Mr. Lake repeatedly attempted to obtain Food and Drug Administration approval to market the IND. The FDA, however, was unconvinced of the efficacy of the invention and refused to approve its sale as a cure for colds and allergies. Plaintiff now challenges the FDA decision.... [F]or the reasons that follow, defendants' motion for summary judgment will be granted.

The FDA was first called on to review the IND in 1979. The invention was automatically considered a Class III device pursuant to 21 U.S.C. § 360c(f)(1).... In order to sell the IND, Mr. Lake either had to procure approval of the PMA or get the IND reclassified out of Class III.

In 1983, Mr. Lake filed a PMA, but the FDA denied his application. The FDA cited numerous deficiencies, including a lack of scientific evidence demonstrating the safety and effectiveness of the device. Mr. Lake amended the PMA, but the FDA still found the petition lacking because no clinical trials had been held.

Realizing that the first route to market, the PMA process, had been foreclosed, Mr. Lake tried the second route; he filed a reclassification petition. He asserted the IND was properly a Class I device. Under 21 U.S.C. § 360c(f)(2) [now 360c(f)(3)], the Secretary is empowered to review reclassification petitions for "deficiencies," and if none are found, then the Secretary must refer the petition to a panel of experts for consideration. The FDA rejected Mr. Lake's original petition because it failed to conform with several agency form and content requirements set out at 21 C.F.R. § 860.123, including a failure to provide valid scientific evidence of the safety and effectiveness of the device. . . . Mr. Lake's attorney then wrote to the FDA, which responded:

> Not only is the petition devoid of "valid scientific evidence", but even if a reclassification was possible, the agency would regulate the device as misbranded. The agency's view is that no device will prevent or cure the common cold and that such a claim would be false or misleading.

The FDA took the position that a lack of scientific evidence is an infirmity which obviates the need to send the application to a reclassification panel. . . .

[The plaintiff argues] that the FDA violated the Medical Device Amendments of 1976, 21 U.S.C. §§ 360c–360k, by making it too difficult to procure reclassification into Class I.

Class I devices are defined as:

(i) A device for which [general controls] are sufficient to provide reasonable assurance of the safety and effectiveness of the device.

(ii) A device for which insufficient information exists to determine that the controls referred to in clause (i) are sufficient to provide reasonable assurance of the safety and effectiveness of the device or to establish a performance standard to provide such assurance, but because it—

> (I) is not purported or represented to be for use in supporting or sustaining human life or for a use which is of substantial importance in preventing impairment of human health, and

> (II) does not present a potential unreasonable risk of illness or injury, is to be regulated by the controls referred to in clause (i).

21 U.S.C. § 360c(a)(1)(A). Plaintiff takes the position that the IND falls within § 360c(a)(1)(A)(ii) because it presents no unreasonable risk of illness or injury. Defendant maintains that when there is no valid scientific evidence of benefit, the risk is per se unreasonable.

Plaintiff raises an interesting question of statutory interpretation. § 360(a)(1)(A)(ii) provides for the marketing of devices which are unproven to be "safe and effective" and which do not provide an "unreasonable risk of illness or injury." Thus, it is possible that a small Class of devices unproven as safe, but without demonstrable risks could be reclassified into Class I. As one court has recognized: "Congress contemplated that a device not both safe and effective might be able to enter the stream of commerce, although such a device has to meet conditions so narrow that no actual device may fall into the category." *General Medical Co. v. United States Food and Drug Admin.*, 770 F.2d 214, 222 (1985). The court in *General Medical* ... concluded that Congress intended to provide that certain devices which were unproven as to safety and effectiveness, did not purport to be of importance in improving human life, and presented no potential unreasonable risk of injury could avoid the PMA process. In applying this rule to the facts of the case, the *General Medical* court held that because there was some minimal evidence of minor harm and no benefits, the harm outweighed the benefits, and the risk of injury was therefore unreasonable.

The case at bar, however, goes one step beyond *General Medical*. There is nothing in the record demonstrating even minor harm from the IND. The FDA stands solely only on its interpretation of the statute that a lack of evidence presents an unreasonable risk.

The FDA's interpretation is valid. It could not have been the intent of Congress to allow the marketing of unproven medical devices about which no scientific evidence is available. To hold otherwise would allow people to market all manner of fraudulent devices. We are long past the day when snake oil can be sold with impunity. Plaintiff's reading of the statute would shift the burden of proof to the FDA and that is not how our public health laws are designed to work. When there is no valid scientific evidence of efficacy, and the risks are unknown, the risk is unreasonable.

The FDA interpretation does not, as plaintiff argues, read § 306c(a)(1)(A)(ii) out of existence. There are devices which may still fall into the category. The relevant subsection refers to devices about which there is insufficient evidence that the various controls of the Food and Cosmetic Act guarantee safety and effectiveness. There may well be devices about which some valid evidence of efficacy and safety exists, but the evidence is inconclusive. The controls may, therefore, not "guarantee" safety and effectiveness. However, there may be no evidence of any risks associated with use. In such a situation, the FDA may find that the minimal benefits, when combined with the lack of known risk, qualify the device for Class I status.

... Congress did not want the PMA process to be the only way a device could get to market because the required clinical studies are expensive and time-consuming. If a device has some demonstrated benefits and no risks, there is no reason to force it to jump through restrictive regulatory hoops. However, Congress did not intend that devices with no proven benefit could be marketed. Indeed, the legislative history defined "potential unreasonable risk of illness or injury" as a risk which is "simply foreseeable" and "[t]he fact that a device is being marketed without sufficient testing is an adequate basis for the Secretary's conclusion that the device presents a potential unreasonable risk to health." H.R. Rep. 853, at 36. In this case the Secretary made a determination that the lack of sufficient testing presented a potential health risk. The Secretary followed the Congressional mandate, and there is no reason to argue with his decision.

... It is not difficult to conclude from this that the FDA has the power to require [valid scientific] evidence in reclassification petitions. The FDA is empowered to check a reclassification petition for "deficiencies" before sending the petition on to a panel of experts. 21 U.S.C. § 360c(f)(2). . . . While the evaluation of the evidence is properly done by the panel, when no evidence is cited in the petition, there is nothing for the panel to review. The FDA is within its rights in demanding some scientific evidence before incurring the time and expense to process the application.

... The FDA requires that evidence in reclassification petitions be:

> [E]vidence from well-controlled investigations, partially controlled studies, studies and objective trials without matched controls, well-documented case histories conducted by qualified experts, and reports of significant human experience with a marketed device, from which it can fairly and responsible be concluded by qualified experts that there is reasonable assurance of the safety and effectiveness of a device under its conditions of use. The evidence required may vary according to the characteristics of the device, its conditions of use, the existence and adequacy of warnings and restrictions and the extent of experience with its use. Isolated case reports, random experience, reports lacking sufficient details to permit scientific evaluation, and unsubstantiated opinions are not regarded as valid scientific evidence to show safety and effectiveness.

21 C.F.R. § 860.7(c)(2). This regulation simply requires that there be some evidence from which the panel can make a logical decision. If there is no evidence, then sending the petition to the panel would be a waste of time. The taxpayers' money can be better spent elsewhere than by hiring scientific experts to review claims with no supporting evidence. . . .

In this case it is not hard to see why additional proof of safety is required. The closing of an infected or irritated nose may well have negative, not positive effects on the course of illness. In addition, anyone who fails to see an allergist because he believes the IND will help, may harm himself. Anyone who avoids bed rest believing the IND will cure him, may suffer all manner of subsequent illnesses caused by inattention to a cold. Attorneys are trained to pose hypotheticals like these, but only medical experts can answer them. I am a jurist, not a physician. It is uniquely within the ken of the FDA to make determinations of the safety and effectiveness of medical devices. For this reason, I will defer to the FDA's decision on the IND. Defendants' motion for summary judgment will be granted. . . .

NOTES

1. *Effect of Change in Law?* The court in *Lake* remarks on the absurdity of referring a petition containing no evidence to an expert panel. At the time, the FD&C Act required FDA to refer all nondeficient reclassification petitions to an advisory committee. The 1990 Act, however, made referral to a panel discretionary rather than mandatory. *See* FD&C Act 513(f)(3)(B)(i) ("Upon determining that a petition does not contain any deficiency ... the Secretary *may* for good cause shown refer the petition to an appropriate [classification panel]." (emphasis added)). Does this development undermine the *Lake* court's reasoning?

2. *Distinction from Reclassification of Preamendment Devices.* The section 513(f) procedures discussed in this subsection concern the classification and reclassification of postenactment devices with no substantially equivalent predicate. They are alternative methods for a manufacturer to get a completely new postenactment device onto the market. Section 513(f) reclassification should not be confused with section 513(e) and 515(i) reclassification of already-classified preamendment devices, discussed p. 989, *supra.*

E. SPECIAL CONTROLS FOR CLASS II DEVICES

Section 513(a)(1)(B) defines a Class II device as one:

> which cannot be classified as a Class I device because the general controls by themselves are insufficient to provide reasonable assurance of the safety and effectiveness of the device, and for which there is sufficient information to establish special controls to provide such assurance, including the promulgation of performance standards, postmarket surveillance, patient registries, development and dissemination of guidelines (including guidelines for the submission of clinical data in premarket notification submissions in accordance with section 510(k)), recommendations, and other appropriate actions as the Secretary deems necessary to provide such assurance.

As originally enacted in 1976, this provision referred only to performance standards, and not to any of the other measures now included. In the 1990 Act, Congress, recognizing that not all Class II devices justify performance standards and aware that FDA had begun the process of establishing standards for only a bare handful, revised section 513(a)(1)(B) to authorize these other types of special controls. Today, as discussed below, other sorts of special controls, particularly guidance documents, are far more important than performance standards in the regulation of Class II devices.

1. PERFORMANCE STANDARDS

FDA's reliance on performance standards actually predates the enactment of the 1976 Medical Device Amendments. Prior to 1976, FDA promulgated a standard for impact-resistant lenses in eyeglasses and sunglasses, 35 Fed. Reg. 15402 (Oct. 2, 1970), 36 Fed. Reg. 8939 (May 15, 1971), 36 Fed. Reg. 18871 (Sept. 23, 1971), 37 Fed. Reg. 2503 (Feb. 2, 1972), 21 C.F.R. 801.410. In 1972, as part of its decision to regulate in vitro diagnostic products without ruling whether they were drugs or devices, *supra* p. 977, Note 1, FDA established a procedure for establishing "product Class standards," as well as detailed labeling requirements, for IVD products. 33 Fed. Reg. 7096 (Mar. 15, 1973). In 1976, the agency made available a draft standard for IVD products intended for the detection or measurement of glucose or total sugars. 41 Fed. Reg. 22394 (June 3, 1976).

FDA also published notices requesting information to establish standards for other in vitro diagnostic products.*

The 1976 Amendments established a procedure for the formal promulgation of performance standards under new section 514, modeled on the provisions governing standards under the Consumer Product Safety Act, 15 U.S.C. 2056, 2058. As enacted, section 514 provided that FDA "may" establish performance standards. FDA officials involved in drafting the original legislation carefully chose this language to negate any implication that the agency was obligated to establish a performance standard for every Class II device or to adopt standards in accordance with any fixed schedule. It was their expectation that the provision for performance standards, like the requirement for approval of preamendment Class III devices, would be implemented in accordance with priorities to be determined in the future and in light of the resources then available to the agency. Even if FDA had been inclined to quickly issue a large number of performance standards, it could not practically have done so; the procedure originally established by section 514 for the promulgation of performance standards was extraordinarily complex and drawn-out. As one author observed: "By constructing this regulatory labyrinth and filling it with procedural snares, Congress ensured that only the bravest or most foolhardy of regulators would ever venture therein." Robert B. LeFlar, *Public Accountability and Medical Device Regulation*, 2 HARV. J. L. & TECH 1, 27 (1989).

Indeed, by the time Congress enacted the 1990 Act, FDA had not finalized a single performance standard. The 1990 Act amended section 514 to permit the agency to promulgate performance standards through ordinary notice-and-comment rulemaking, with a few special requirements. *See* FD&C Act 514(b)(1)(B) (mandating specific content in a notice of proposed rulemaking for the establishment of a performance standard); 514(b)(5)(A)(ii) (FDA must, upon request of interested person demonstrating "good cause," refer proposed performance standard to advisory committee). The agency did not respond to this invitation with great enthusiasm, however. To date, FDA has published only one final performance standard. This standard, published in 1997, applies to electrode lead wires and patient cables, which are components of devices such as breathing frequency monitors and electrocardiographs. 21 C.F.R. Part 898. The rule, intended to prevent patient contact with power sources, requires that "[a]ny connector in a cable or electrode lead wire having a conductive connection to a patient shall be constructed in such a manner as to comply with subclause 56.3(c) of [International Electrotechnical Commission (IEC) standard 601–1, Medical Electrical Equipment, general requirements for safety]." 21 C.F.R. 898.12.

NOTE

FDA has proposed, but then withdrawn, performance standards for a few devices, including vascular graft prostheses and continuous ventilators, 59 Fed. Reg.

---

* Following enactment of the 1976 Amendments, the agency revoked the separate procedure for establishing standards for in vitro diagnostic products, 45 Fed. Reg. 7474 (Feb. 1, 1980), and withdrew the proposed glucose standard, 51 Fed. Reg. 13023 (Apr. 17, 1986).

3042 (Jan. 20, 1994) (withdrawal of proposed rule), and infant apnea monitors, 65 Fed. Reg. 57303 (Sept. 22, 2000) (withdrawal of proposed rule). When withdrawing the proposed infant apnea monitor standard, the agency simultaneously announced the availability of a different special control for these devices under a guidance document. 65 Fed. Reg. 57301 (Sept. 22, 2000).

COMMENT: VOLUNTARY MEDICAL DEVICE STANDARDS

Shortly after passage of the 1976 Amendments, FDA described its activities to encourage and support the development of performance standards for devices by private organizations and associations.

> The Food and Drug Administration intends to continue to promote such voluntary efforts because they contribute to assuring the safety and effectiveness of marketed devices. Voluntary or privately recognized performance standards will not be a substitute for the formal promulgation of standards under section 514 of the act for any device that is classified in the performance standard category. However, voluntary or privately recognized standards can serve as informal standards prior to classification as well as during the development of formal standards for devices that are not candidates for immediate attention, and they may be the basis for subsequent formal FDA standards.

41 Fed. Reg. 34099, 34100 (Aug. 12, 1976).

Four years later, when FDA issued final regulations establishing its procedures for developing performance standards, it simultaneously acknowledged that it lacked the resources to establish performance standards for all Class II devices. 45 Fed. Reg. 7474 (Feb. 1, 1980), 45 Fed. Reg. 7490 (Feb. 1, 1980). The agency proposed a policy of endorsing particular voluntary standards, encouraging manufacturers of devices conforming to these standards to label them as such, and deferring development of mandatory standards if there were adequate voluntary compliance. 45 Fed. Reg. 7490 (Feb. 1, 1980). The following year, however, FDA abandoned its proposal to endorse voluntary standards, because manufacturers might mistake such standards as mandatory. The agency also discarded its suggestion that it might defer the establishment of a formal performance standard for a Class II device based solely on adequate compliance with an agency-endorsed voluntary standard. 50 Fed. Reg. 43060 (Oct. 23, 1985). "FDA now believes that it should focus its limited resources on setting priorities for, and initiating proceedings to establish, performance standards, rather than on endorsement and promotion of voluntary standards."

In FDAMA, Congress, for the first time, required FDA to recognize voluntary device standards, but as an aid to premarket submissions, not as a substitute for mandatory performance standards. According to new section 514(c), FDA "shall, by publication in the Federal Register, recognize all or part of an appropriate standard established by a nationally or internationally recognized standard development organization for which a person may submit a declaration of conformity in order to meet a premarket submission requirement or other requirement under this Act to which such standard is applicable." FDA refers to section 514(c) standards as "consensus standards" and maintains a list of those it has recognized on the CDRH website. Under section 514(c), a manufacturer filing a PMN, PMA, or other premarket submission may include a "declaration of conformity" to a recognized standard. Conformity to a recognized standard usually conclusively establishes substantial equivalence of safety and effectiveness for those aspects of a device addressed by the standard. *See* FDA–CDRH, Recognition and Use of Consensus Standards; Final Guidance for Industry and FDA (2001); FDA–CDRH, Frequently Asked Questions on the Recognition of Consensus Standards; Guidance for Industry and FDA Staff (2002).

An important recent development is FDA's frequent designation of voluntary standards as special controls for Class II devices. In the past decade, the agency has written or amended more than 25 classification regulations for Class II devices that list one or more standards established by private standard-setting organizations as special controls. At first blush, this approach seems effectively identical to the incorporation of a voluntary standard into a mandatory performance standard, as in the electrode lead wire rule discussed above. There is an important difference, however. Whereas failure to comply with a formal performance standard automatically adulterates a device under section 501(e)(1), the same is not true for violations of other types of special controls, which are discussed in more detail below.

2. Other Special Controls

While FDA has largely abandoned formal performance standards, it has liberally embraced other types of special controls for Class II devices. Although the agency acquired the statutory authority to impose special controls other than performance standards in 1990, as late as 1997, it had implemented such special controls "only sparingly." Howard M. Holstein & Edward C. Wilson, *Developments in Medical Device Regulation*, in 2 Fundamentals of Law and Regulation: An In-Depth Look at Therapeutic Products 257, 269 (David G. Adams et al. eds., 1997). Today, by contrast, approximately three-fourths of the classification regulations for Class II devices incorporate one or more special controls.

Special controls other than performance standards include: "postmarket surveillance, patient registries, development and dissemination of guidelines (including guidelines for the submission of clinical data in premarket notification submissions in accordance with section 510(k)), recommendations, and other appropriate actions." Section 513(a)(1)(B). FDA uses guidance documents far more than any other type of special control; it has issued guidances as special controls for the majority of Class II devices. The second most common type of special control is a voluntary standard set by a private standard-setting organization. FDA has also, more rarely, used other types of special controls, either alone or in combination with guidances, standards, or both. Following are examples of regulations for Class II devices that illustrate the range of mandated special controls:

§ 864.9245 Automated blood cell separator....

(b) *Classification of device operating by filtration separation principle.* Class II (special controls). The special controls for the device are that the manufacturer must file an annual report with FDA for 3 consecutive years. Each annual report must include the following:

(1) A summary of adverse donor reactions reported by the users to the manufacturer that do not meet the threshold for medical device reporting under part 803 of this chapter;

(2) Any change to the device, including but not limited to:

(i) New indications for use of the device;

(ii) Labeling changes, including operation manual changes;

(iii) Computer software changes, hardware changes, and disposable item changes, *e.g.*, collection bags, tubing, filters;

(3) Equipment failures, including software, hardware, and disposable item failures, *e.g.*, collection bags, tubing, filters....

§ 866.3332   Reagents for detection of specific novel influenza A viruses....

(b) Classification. Class II (special controls). The special controls are:

(1) FDA's guidance document entitled "Class II Special Controls Guidance Document: Reagents for Detection of Specific Novel Influenza A Viruses." See § 866.1(e) for information on obtaining this document.

(2) The distribution of these devices is limited to laboratories with experienced personnel who have training in standardized molecular testing procedures and expertise in viral diagnosis, and appropriate biosafety equipment and containment....

§ 870.5550   External transcutaneous cardiac pacemaker (noninvasive)....

(b) Classification. Class II. The special controls for this device are:

(1) "American National Standards Institute/American Association for Medical Instrumentation's DF–21 'Cardiac Defibrillator Devices'" 2d ed., 1996, and

(2) "The maximum pulse amplitude should not exceed 200 milliamperes. The maximum pulse duration should not exceed 50 milliseconds."...

§ 872.1745   Laser fluorescence caries detection device....

(b) Classification. Class II, subject to the following special controls:

(1) Sale, distribution, and use of this device are restricted to prescription use in accordance with § 801.109 of this chapter;

(2) Premarket notifications must include clinical studies, or other relevant information, that demonstrates that the device aids in the detection of tooth decay by measuring increased laser induced fluorescence; and

(3) The labeling must include detailed use instructions with precautions that urge users to:

(i) Read and understand all directions before using the device,

(ii) Store probe tips under proper conditions,

(iii) Properly sterilize the emitter-detector handpick before each use, and

(iv) Properly maintain and handle the instrument in the specified manner and condition. . . .

§ 880.5130 Infant radiant warmer. . . .

(b) Classification. Class II (Special Controls):

(1) The Association for the Advancement of Medical Instrumentation (AAMI) Voluntary Standard for the Infant Radiant Warmer;

(2) A prescription statement in accordance with § 801.109 of this chapter (restricted to use by or upon the order of qualified practitioners as determined by the States); and

(3) Labeling for use only in health care facilities and only by persons with specific training and experience in the use of the device.

§ 880.5580 Acupuncture needle. . . .

(b) Classification. Class II (special controls). Acupuncture needles must comply with the following special controls:

(1) Labeling for single use only and conformance to the requirements for prescription devices set out in 21 CFR 801.109,

(2) Device material biocompatibility, and

(3) Device sterility. . . .

§ 886.4392 Nd:YAG laser for posterior capsulotomy and peripheral iridotomy. . . .

(b) Classification. Class II (special controls). Design Parameters: Device must emit a laser beam with the following parameters: wavelength = 1064 nanometers; spot size = 50 to 100 micros; pulse width = 3 to 30 nanoseconds; output energy per pulse = 0.5 to 15 millijoules (mJ); repetition rate = 1 to 10 pulses; and total energy = 20 to 120 mJ.

F.   General Controls Applicable to All Devices

All marketed devices, regardless of their date of introduction or classification, are subject to the following general regulatory controls, unless specifically exempted from them.

1.   ADULTERATION AND MISBRANDING

The device regime established in 1976 is enforced through sections 501 and 502, the FD&C Act's adulteration and misbranding provisions for drugs and devices. For example, a device is adulterated if it is a Class II device that fails to comply with a performance standard or a Class III device that fails to conform to the premarket approval requirement. Section 501(e), (f). Similarly, a device is misbranded if its manufacturer fails to comply with the section 510(k) premarket notification requirement. Section 502(o). Failure to comply with other statutory requirements, to be discussed below, also constitutes adulteration or misbranding. *See, e.g.* section 501(g) (a banned device is adulterated); section 501(h) (violation of good manufacturing practice requirements is adulteration); section 502(q) (violation of restricted device regulations is misbranding); section 502(t) (violation of notification, repair, replacement, refund, reimbursement, recall, and adverse event reporting requirements is misbranding).

Misbranding and adulteration also retain the meanings they had under the 1938 Act. For instance, section 501(a) declares that a device (or drug) is adulterated: "[I]f it consists in whole or in part of any filthy, putrid, or decomposed substance; or if it has been prepared, packed, or held under insanitary conditions whereby it may have been contaminated with filth, or whereby it may have been rendered injurious to health." Section 502(a) provides that a device (or drug) is misbranded "[i]f its labeling is false or misleading in any particular," and section 502(f) states that it is misbranded "[u]nless its labeling bears adequate directions for use." These provisions apply to all medical devices, but they can be difficult to enforce. It is much easier for FDA to establish a violation of the PMA requirement, for example, than a violation of one of the broadly-phrased adulteration and misbranding prohibitions. The traditional adulteration and misbranding provisions are thus relatively unimportant regulatory tools for Class III devices, which are subject to the PMA mandate. For preamendment Class I and Class II devices, however, and their postamendment substantial equivalents, the agency sometimes has no choice but to rely on conventional, and often difficult to prove, charges of adulteration or misbranding.

United States v. An Article . . . Acu–dot

483 F. Supp. 1311 (N. D. Ohio 1980).

■ LAMBROS, DISTRICT JUDGE.

This action is the result of a libel of information brought by the United States of America for the condemnation of numerous cases of an over-the-counter medical device called an Acu-dot, as provided for in 21 U.S.C. § 334. . . .

. . . [T]he sole issue presented to this Court at trial was this: are the Acu-dot devices "misbranded" within the meaning of 21 U.S.C. § 352?

In simple terms, the Acu-dot is a small, pin-head sized magnet attached to the underside of a circular, adhesive patch. It is sold to the public in sheets of ten, packaged in a flat, cardboard box. Inside the box, in addition to the sheet of ten Acu-dots, can be found a four-page pamphlet, purporting to be instructions for the use of the device. The obverse of the cardboard box reads in this way:

ACU–DOT
Magnetic Analgesic Patch
For temporary relief of occasional minor aches and pains
of muscles and joints.
Contains 10 Patches

The reverse is labelled [sic] in this way:

ACU–DOT
Magnetic Analgesic Patch
Mfg. for Acu–Dot Corp. Box F 598,
Akron, Ohio 44308

Directions for use:

Apply fingertip pressure to sensitive area to determine point or points of sharpest pain or discomfort. Thoroughly clean and dry area and apply an adhesive-backed ACU–DOT to each such point.

Complete adhesion of the ACU–DOT is recommended. Leave ACU–DOT in place for a two-to five-day period, then procedure may be repeated as needed for continued symptomatic relief.

If itching, rash or other skin irritation occurs, discontinue use. If pain or soreness persists for ten days or longer, discontinue use and consult a physician. Keep this and all medicines out of the reach of children.

FOR EXTERNAL USE ONLY

MADE IN U.S.A.

Manufactured under U.S.A. Patent No. 4162672

The pamphlet insert merely enlarges on the information presented by the outer packaging, adding, however, that the device is "Not a pill. Not a drug. Easy to use."

Libellant claims that the Acu-dots are "misbranded", as that term is used in 21 U.S.C. § 352, in that the labeling is "false or misleading" (subsection (a)) and "fails to bear adequate directions for use" (subsection (f)(1)). The res is therefore subject to seizure under 21 U.S.C. § 334....

... Claimant-intervenor denied that the res was "misbranded"....

Trial of the action was held to the bench, trial by jury having been waived by claimant-intervenor so that an expedited hearing could be had.

I.

The majority of the evidence presented both by the government and by claimant-intervenor went to the first of the two "misbranding" issues—is the labeling "false or misleading in any particular"? 21 U.S.C. § 352(a). Libellant, in presenting its case, specifically attacked the descriptions of the devices as "magnetic analgesic patch(es)" and "for temporary relief of occasional minor aches and pains of muscles and joints".

Libellant offered the testimony of three experts—one biophysicist and two medical doctors. These experts were adduced to show that none of the theories offered by claimant-intervenor were valid explanations for the mechanism by which the devices were to achieve their results. Further, each expert testified to his belief that the devices could not achieve the effect alleged by the labeling, other than through a placebo effect.

On behalf of the effectiveness of the res, claimant-intervenor presented several theories for the mechanism of the device. At various times, it was suggested that the magnetic action of the device "drew" blood to the affected area, which action had the therapeutic effect; that the blood, being composed in part of iron-based chemicals, produced an electromotive force within the body when passing through the field of the magnet, much in the way electric generators produce electricity by moving an electric wire through a magnetic field; that the pressure of the device against the skin creates therapeutic effects in a way analogous to acupuncture techniques; that the ionization of molecules in the skin area under the magnet caused the therapeutic effect claimed; and, finally, that the claimed beneficial effect of the device was achieved largely as a result of the psychosomatic placebo response.[3] These various theories were suggested by the teachings of the patent said to include the res, by the theories presented in an article written by Kyoichi Nakagawa, M.D., one of a number of Japanese researchers attempting to analyze the mechanism of an identical device now in wide currency in Japan, and, most importantly, by the empirical results of an experiment conducted by Rocco Antenucci, M.D., an Akron area family physician who testified at the hearing.

The most impressive evidence on behalf of the res was the result of the Antenucci study. That study purported to be a double-blind comparison of the Acu-dots with non-magnetized facsimiles. Of the 70 patients receiving the facsimiles, 10 indicated some degree of pain relief. Of the 152 patients receiving the Acu-dots, 138 reported some degree of pain relief. These figures are impressive and argue strongly for the therapeutic claims.

However, each of the government witnesses was able to suggest major flaws in the conception and execution of the test protocol. Considerable doubt was also cast on the Nakagawa study and the Court was finally left with this problem: libellant could demonstrate that the therapeutic claims of the device could not be explained by any reasonable theory that did not

---

3. This last theory—the "placebo effect"—cannot be dismissed lightly. Expert witnesses testified that current medical theory explains the placebo relief of pain as being mediated by the release of "endorphins" within the body. A lay explanation of this process is that because the patient believes the placebo will have an analgesic effect, administration of the placebo will cause the patient's body to release small amounts of a morphine-like chemical that is usually dormant within the cells of the body. The morphine-like chemical—the "endorphin"—then produces the analgesic effect. This explanation suggests to the Court that a placebo cannot be dismissed as "ineffective" simply because it works its effect in a way more oblique than standard therapeutic treatments. As is seen *infra* in this opinion, the real difficulty of this case is that a "placebo" can work only by means of the artifice of its presentation to the patient—the patient must be misled as to its inherent effectiveness. This artifice is the heart of the negative aspects of a placebo, for the composition of the placebo is largely irrelevant to its effectiveness, and a sugar pill of minimal cost to the patient should theoretically be as effective as a $500 device. The person marketing the $500 device is misleading the buyer because the seller claims that the $500 device relieves pain, when it is really the patient's belief in the device that relieves pain. The potential for abuse is obvious.

rely on a "placebo" explanation, but had no empirical evidence of the lack of efficacy; claimant-intervenor had very weak theoretical support for the mechanism of the device, and vested its claims in unexplained empirical evidence. . . .

After careful consideration of all of the evidence, this Court finds that any therapeutic value of the res is the result of its placebo effect, and that this placebo effect is very strong in the case of ailments for which the device is claimed effective. Thus, the device often can achieve its claims of providing "temporary relief of occasional minor aches and pains of muscles and joints"; but this effect is the result of nothing more than sophisticated marketing chicanery.

This Court hastens to affirm here its belief in the right of the American public to seek any treatment it wishes, especially when that treatment is a harmless, if ineffective, drug or device. The Court further wishes to make plain that it in no way desires to allow a governmental agency to emasculate the constitutional right to seek desired medical treatment enunciated in *Roe v. Wade*, 410 U.S. 113 (1973). There is a difference, however, between the right to use a harmless, ineffective drug or device and a claimed right to promote and profit from the drug or device. . . . Judge Bohanon, speaking for the district court for the Western District of Oklahoma, explained this distinction in *Rutherford v. United States*, 438 F. Supp. 1287 (1977), at 1300–1301:

> When certain "fundamental rights" are invoked, such as the right of privacy involved herein, regulation may be justified only by a "compelling state interest," and legislative enactments "must be narrowly drawn to express only the legitimate state interests at stake," *Roe v. Wade, supra,* 410 U.S. at 155. By denying the right to use a nontoxic substance in connection with one's own personal health-care, FDA has offended the constitutional right of privacy.

> This court's decision in this case in no way portends the return of the traveling snake oil salesman. As emphasized earlier, the right to use a harmless, unproven remedy is quite distinct from any alleged right to promote such. FDA is fully empowered under other statutory provisions to combat false or fraudulent advertising of ineffectual or unproven drugs.

This Court resists the impulse to allow claimant to market a product that works only by means of a placebo effect on the basis that it nevertheless often achieves a relief of pain as claimed. The strong placebo effect may save the res from claims of "false labeling" under 21 U.S.C. § 352(a), but it does not protect the device from the charge that the labeling is "misleading" under 21 U.S.C. § 352(a), and that is all that is required to warrant condemnation of the res. The device's label is "misleading" because the device is not inherently effective, its results being attributable to the psychosomatic effect produced by the advertising and marketing of the device. A kiss from mother on the affected area would serve just as well to relieve pain, if mother's kisses were marketed as effectively as the Acu-dot device.

This Court finds that the device is "misbranded" under 21 U.S.C. § 352, and properly subject to seizure and condemnation under 21 U.S.C. § 334, even though the claims are not technically false, because the claims are inherently misleading. . . .

NOTES

1. *Other Cases.* For other post-1976 cases in which FDA has relied, at least in part, on traditional charges of adulteration or misbranding, see *United States v. Shabbir*, 64 F. Supp. 2d 479 (D. Md. 1999); *United States v. Two Units . . . of an Article or Device . . . Power Unit and a Chair*, 49 F.3d 479 (9th Cir. 1995); *United States v. An Article of Device . . . "Toftness Radiation Detector,"* 731 F.2d 1253 (7th Cir. 1984); *United States v. 789 Cases . . . Latex Surgeons' Gloves*, 799 F. Supp. 1275 (D.P.R. 1992); *United States v. An Article of Device "Theramatic"*, 715 F.2d 1339 (9th Cir. 1983); *United States v. Torigian Laboratories, Inc.*, 577 F. Supp. 1514 (E.D.N.Y. 1984); *United States v. An Article or Device Consisting of . . . Biotone Model 4 . . . Muscle Stimulator*, 557 F. Supp. 141 (N.D. Ga. 1982); *United States v. Articles of Device . . . Acuflex; Pro–Med*, 426 F. Supp. 366 (W.D. Pa. 1977).

2. *Burden of Proof.* Although the government ordinarily has the burden of proving any claim of adulteration or misbranding, the Seventh Circuit has held that the defendant bears the burden of establishing that its device falls within one of the regulatory exceptions to section 502(f)(1)'s "adequate directions for use" requirement, such as the exception for prescription devices. *United States v. Article of Device . . . "Toftness Radiation Detector"*, 731 F.2d 1253, 1258–62 (7th Cir. 1984). *Accord United States v. 45/194 Kg. Drums of Pure Vegetable Oil*, 961 F.2d 808, 812 (9th Cir. 1992).

3. *PMA Requirement.* The premarket notification requirement is another general control for medical devices, although, since 1997, most Class I devices and some Class II devices have been exempt from it. In the years following the 1976 Amendments, the premarket notification requirement proved to be a potent regulatory instrument, as FDA took action against a number of products that were misbranded under section 502(o) simply for failure to follow section 510(k). *E.g., United States v. 22 Rectangular or Cylindrical Devices . . . "The STER–O–LIZER"*, 714 F. Supp. 1159 (D. Utah 1989); *United States v. Clark Research and Development, Inc.*, Med. Dev. Rep. (CCH) ¶ 15,119, 1989 WL 140224 (E.D. La. 1989); *United States v. An Article of Device . . . Stryker Shoulder 130–10 Dacron Ligament Prosthesis*, 607 F. Supp. 990 (W.D. Mich. 1985); *United States v. Undetermined Quantities of an Article of Device . . . "Gendertest,"* 1985–1986 FDLI Jud. Rec. 30 (C.D. Cal. 1985); *United States v. An Article of Device . . . Ovutron*, 1981–1982 FDLI Jud. Rec. 92 (D. Ariz. 1982). Today, however, FDA rarely has occasion to allege section 502(o) misbranding for failure to satisfy section 510(k).

———

Using the authority under section 701(a) "to promulgate regulations for the efficient enforcement of this Act," FDA has issued rules setting forth specific labeling that must be used to avoid misbranding of particular types of devices. *See, e.g.,* 21 C.F.R. 801.405 (labeling for denture repair and refitting products); 801.420 (hearing aid labeling); 801.435 (latex condoms). FDA used this approach in prescribing labeling for menstrual tampons. Following discovery of the association between tampons, which are Class II devices, and toxic shock syndrome (TSS), FDA mandated a strong warning statement on the package label and the provision of detailed consumer information in a package insert. 45 Fed. Reg. 69840 (Oct. 21, 1980), 47 Fed. Reg. 26982 (June 22, 1982), 21 C.F.R. 801.430(a)–(d). The following year, FDA asked the American Society for Testing and Materials (ASTM) to devise a performance standard for tampons regarding absorbency testing and labeling, but the ASTM task force was unable to reach agreement. The principal tampon manufacturers then each consented to take voluntary action, but while they agreed on an absorbency testing method, they adopted differing approaches to providing label information about absorbency. FDA thus proposed to establish a uniform test for absorbency and a uniform letter designation, from A (the lowest degree of absorbency) to F (the highest degree of absorbency), for purposes of product labeling. 53 Fed. Reg. 37250 (Sept. 23, 1988). Comments from the public, however, caused the agency to revise this approach.

Medical Devices; Labeling for Menstrual Tampons; Ranges of Absorbency; Reproposed Rule

54 Fed. Reg. 25076 (June 12, 1989).

... The Food and Drug Administration (FDA) is reproposing amendments to its tampon labeling regulation. The reproposed rule would require that manufacturers of menstrual tampons determine tampon absorbency using a test method specified in the reproposal, and, based on the results of that testing, express absorbency on tampon labeling by using one of six specified absorbency terms, each of which corresponds to a range of absorbency set forth in the reproposal. The reproposed rule would enable consumers to compare the absorbency of one brand and style of tampons with the absorbency of other brands and styles before purchasing them....

Several manufacturers commented on FDA's statement in the preamble to the proposed rule that tampons are misbranded under section 502(f)(1) of the Federal Food, Drug, and Cosmetic Act because current tampon labeling does not contain any information with which a woman can determine the relative absorbency of different brands of tampons....

As the agency tentatively concluded, omission of uniform absorbency information does render tampons misbranded within the meaning of sections 201(n) and 502(a) and (f)(1) of the act. But, rather than act against individual tampons to remedy the deficiency, FDA has proposed, consistent with its authority, to address the misbranding by requiring a uniform labeling system through rulemaking.... And, as provided in § 801.430(h) of the reproposal, any tampon that is not labeled as required by any final rule and that is initially introduced or initially delivered for introduction into commerce after the effective date of the final rule would be misbranded under sections 201(n) and 502(a) and (f)(1) of the act.... FDA advises, however, that those and the other device misbranding provisions of the act are self-executing and apply to all labeling of all tampons, and that compliance with the labeling requirements of any final rule would not preclude FDA from taking action against any tampon the labeling of which misbranded the product in any respect, or which otherwise caused the product to be in violation of the act. . . .

FDA received many comments on the use of letters to designate ranges of absorbency. One manufacturer, one consumer group, and several individual consumers, opposing the use of letters, contended that their use would create confusion because consumers are accustomed to numbers, not letters, representing quantity or size, because the use of letters would require that consumers learn two systems (the letters and the numerical ranges to which they refer), and because consumers would not know whether "A" were high or low. A comment from an individual consumer argued that "A" commonly indicates "most desirable" and, thus, would be misinterpreted by consumers. By contrast, comments from two manufacturers, two consumer groups, and most individual consumers supported the use of letter designations. These comments supported the use of a labeling scheme that does not use numbers. . . .

Although the agency agrees that the use of sun protection factors on labeling for sunscreens is effective and appropriate, FDA believes that this is so because the public understands that the higher the number, the greater the blockage of ultraviolet radiation and the greater the health benefit. In the case of tampons and TSS, the reverse would be true: the higher the number the higher the risk of TSS and the lower the public health benefit. FDA, therefore, believes that the analogy to sunscreen labeling is unpersuasive. Also, the agency continues to believe that the use of single numbers to represent grams of fluid absorbed by tampons is not feasible at this time.

FDA agrees, however, with the comments that the use of letters representing numerical ranges might be confusing and that consumers might not be able to readily ascertain which letters represented high or low absorbency. . . . The agency has tentatively concluded, therefore, that letter designations would not provide to consumers the clear, nonmisleading absorbency information that was intended in the proposed rule, and, accordingly, has removed letter designations from the reproposal.

FDA, however, also agrees that a numerical system, by itself, would pose the problems discussed in other comments. The agency has tentatively concluded that a system in which [sic] a new set of standardized, clear, nonmisleading terms of absorbency, corresponding to standardized nonoverlapping ranges of absorbency, would best facilitate interbrand comparison of tampon absorbencies and selection of the least absorbent tampon needed. Accordingly, FDA now proposes to further revise § 801.430(e)(1) to require the use of the following absorbency terms in lieu of letters: low absorbency, medium absorbency, medium-high absorbency, high absorbency, very high absorbency, and highest absorbency, each corresponding to one of the six nonoverlapping ranges provided for in the initial proposal. The applicable term, which must be on the principal display panel(s), would readily convey absorbency information to consumers. In addition, reproposed § 801.430(e)(2) would permit a manufacturer to include on tampon labeling the numerical range of absorbency corresponding to the applicable term of absorbency whenever the manufacturer used a term. . . .

NOTE

Following the decision in *Public Citizen Health Research Group v. Commissioner*, 724 F. Supp. 1013 (D.D.C. 1989), criticizing FDA's seven-year delay in promulgating these regulations and ordering final regulations to be promulgated within two months, FDA published final regulations in 54 Fed. Reg. 43766 (Oct. 26, 1989). The final regulations, 21 C.F.R. 801.430, once again changed the required absorbency terms, finally settling upon the terms actually used by the industry: junior absorbency, regular absorbency, super absorbency, and super plus absorbency. In 2000, FDA required the term "ultra absorbency" for the new category of more absorbent tampons that had been introduced to the market since 1989. 65 Fed. Reg. 62282 (Oct. 18, 2000). Finally, in 2004, the agency amended the rule to change the "junior" designation to "light," to combat perceptions that the previous term meant "the tampon is only for younger or teenage women when, in fact, it may be appropriate for women of any age with light menstrual flow." 69 Fed. Reg. 52170, 52171 (Aug. 25, 2004).

2. ESTABLISHMENT REGISTRATION AND PRODUCT LISTING

Section 510 of the Act requires that "every person who owns or operates any establishment in any State engaged in the manufacture, preparation, propagation, compounding, or processing of . . . a device or devices" must register the establishment with FDA at the commencement of device production and on December 31 of each year. FD&C Act 510(b), (c). Registration of foreign establishments, which was originally voluntary, has been mandatory since 1997 under section 510(i). Every person who registers one or more device establishments must also, at the time of registration and semiannually thereafter, file with the agency a list of devices produced in these establishments. FD&C Act 510(j). The regulations regarding registration and listing are codified at 21 C.F.R. 807.20–65.

As of 2006, more than 33,000 device establishments, domestic and foreign, were registered with FDA. There are approximately 100,000 listed devices in commercial distribution.

3. ADVERSE EVENT REPORTING

Section 519 authorizes FDA to promulgate regulations requiring device manufacturers, importers, and user facilities to maintain records and submit reports necessary to assure the safety and effectiveness of devices. Under section 502(t)(2), failing to furnish information required by section 519 automatically makes a device misbranded.

FDA's regulations, borrowing language directly from the Act, require manufacturers and importers to make a medical device report (MDR) whenever they receive information from any source that "reasonably suggests" that one of their devices "[m]ay have caused or contributed to a death or serious injury" or "has malfunctioned and such device or similar device marketed by the manufacturer would be likely to cause or contribute to a death or serious injury, if the malfunction were to recur." 21 C.F.R. 803.40(a) & (b) (importers); 803.50(a) (manufacturers). Manufacturers and importers must submit an MDR within 30 days of acquiring such information, except that manufacturers must do so within five days if the reportable event "necessitates remedial action to prevent an unreasonable risk of substantial harm to the public health." 21 C.F.R. 803.40, 50 & 53.

The 1976 Amendments authorized FDA also to require medical device distributors to file adverse event reports. For many years, the agency chose not to impose such a requirement, but the 1990 Act added a new provision to section 519 mandating that distributors report adverse events to FDA and submit copies of these reports to manufacturers. The agency never issued a final rule regarding distributor reporting, but its tentative final rule became final by operation of law in 1993. *See* 56 Fed. Reg. 60024; (Nov. 26, 1991), 58 Fed. Reg. 46514 (Sept. 1, 1993). Distributors thus bore this obligation from 1993 until 1997, when FDAMA eliminated distributors from the list of entities required to report adverse device events.

The 1990 Act also mandated for the first time that device user facilities make adverse event reports. This requirement survives today. By regulation, user facilities include hospitals, ambulatory surgical facilities, nursing homes, outpatient diagnostic facilities, and outpatient treatment facilities, but not physicians' offices. 21 C.F.R. 803.3(f). User facilities must make a report to both FDA and the device manufacturer within ten days of receiving information that "reasonably suggests" that a device "has or may have caused or contributed to the death of a patient of the facility." FD&C Act 519(b)(1)(A); 21 C.F.R. 803.30(a)(1). Within the same time frame, user facilities must make reports of serious injury, rather than death, to the manufacturer of the device, if known, and otherwise to FDA. FD&C Act 519(b)(1)(B); 21 C.F.R. 803.30(a)(2). Moreover, user facilities must make annual reports to the agency summarizing all the reportable events that occurred in the facility during the year. FD&C Act 519(C); 21 C.F.R. 803.33.

FDAMA directed FDA, at some indefinite time in the future, to convert the current user facility MDR system from a universal one to one involving only a subset of user facilities. FD&C Act 519(b)(5). In response to this requirement, since February 2002 CDRH has been collecting data about medical device problems from a sample of cooperating facilities. The goal of this initiative, called the Medical Product Surveillance Network (MedSun), is to determine the impact of various incentives and types of feedback on the quantity and quality of reports. The agency has not yet implemented a nonuniversal MDR system, however, and, for the time being, all user facilities not specifically exempted from the MDR requirements must continue to comply with them.

The General Accounting Office has long been critical of FDA's device reporting regulations and its implementation of them. *See* GAO, MEDICAL DEVICES: EARLY WARNING OF PROBLEMS IS HAMPERED BY SEVERE UNDERREPORTING, PEMD–87–1 (Dec. 1986); MEDICAL DEVICES: FDA'S FORECAST OF PROBLEM REPORTS AND FTE'S UNDER H.R. 4640, PEMD–88–30 (July 1988); MEDICAL DEVICES: FDA'S IMPLEMENTATION OF THE MEDICAL DEVICE REPORTING REGULATION, PEMD–89–10 (Feb. 1989); MEDICAL DEVICE REPORTING: IMPROVEMENTS NEEDED IN FDA'S SYSTEM FOR MONITORING PROBLEMS WITH APPROVED DEVICES, GAO/ HEHS–97–21 (Jan. 1997). Commentators and FDA itself remain concerned today. Two authors recently noted: "In 2004 alone, nearly 152,000 MDR submissions were posted. While this number may seem high, underreporting of adverse events concerns FDA. The agency estimates that as few as one in every 100 medical device adverse events actually is reported to FDA, although there is no hard data to support this estimate." Edward M. Basile & Beverly H. Lorell, *The Food and Drug Administration's Regulation of Risk Disclosure for Implantable Cardioverter Defibrillators: Has Technology Outpaced the Agency's Regulatory Framework?*, 61 Food & Drug L.J. 251, 257–58 (2006).

Apart from their adverse event reporting obligations, device manufacturers, importers, and user facilities must all maintain MDR event files. 21 C.F.R. 803.18.

4.   Good Manufacturing Practice

Section 520(f) of the Act authorizes FDA to "prescribe regulations requiring that the methods used in, and the facilities and controls used for, the manufacture, pre-production design validation . . ., packing, storage, and installation of a device conform to current good manufacturing practice, as prescribed in such regulations, to assure that the device will be safe and effective and otherwise in compliance with this Act." FDA first established regulations governing current good manufacturing practices (CGMPs) for devices in 1978. 42 Fed. Reg. 11997 (Mar. 1, 1977), 43 Fed. Reg. 31508 (July 21, 1978), codified in 21 C.F.R. Part 820. These regulations governed, among other things, production and process controls; packaging and labeling controls; distribution; and recordkeeping. Notably lacking, however, were any preproduction design controls. The original CGMP regulations distinguished between "critical" and "noncritical" devices, and the most rigorous requirements applied only to the former.

In the 1990s, FDA substantially revised 21 C.F.R. Part 820 and renamed it the "Quality System" regulation. The excerpt below, from the proposed rule, highlights the most important changes.

Medical Devices; Current Good Manufacturing Practice (CGMP) Regulations; Proposed Revisions; Request for Comments

58 Fed. Reg. 61952 (November 23, 1993).

. . . Except for editorial changes to update organizational references in the regulations and revisions to the list of critical devices that was included in the preamble to the final regulations, the device CGMP requirements have not been revised since 1978. This proposed rule is the result of an effort begun in 1990 to revise these regulations.

On November 28, 1990, the Safe Medical Devices Act of 1990 became law. The SMDA amended section 520(f)(1)(A) of the act to provide clear authority to add preproduction design validation controls to the device CGMP regulations and also added a new section 803 to the act which encourages FDA to work with foreign countries toward mutual recognition of CGMP requirements. . . .

Thus, FDA's decision to revise the CGMP regulations is based on changes in the law by the SMDA, the agency's discussions with others including its Device Good Manufacturing Practice Advisory Committee, responses to ... Federal Register notices on this matter, FDA's analysis of recall data, its experience with the regulatory application of the current device CGMP regulations, and its assessment of international quality standards....

Design Controls

Over the last 9 years, FDA has identified lack of design controls as one of the major causes of device recalls. The intrinsic quality of devices, including their safety and effectiveness, is established during the design phase. Thus, FDA believes that unless appropriate design controls are observed during preproduction stages of development, a finished device may be neither safe nor effective for its intended use.... Based on its experience with administering the CGMP regulations, which currently do not include preproduction design validation controls, the agency is concerned that the current regulations provide less than an appropriate level of assurance that devices will be safe and effective....

... Therefore, FDA has concluded that it is essential that those firms and individuals who design Class II, Class III, and certain Class I medical devices ... do so under formal controls that will ensure that, for each intended use of a device, specifications are established and validated to be adequate and that the final design actually meets these validated specifications.

Purchasing Controls

The quality of purchased product and services is crucial to maintaining the intrinsic safety and effectiveness of a device. Many device failures due to problems with components that result in recall are due to unacceptable components provided by suppliers. Therefore, FDA believes that the purchasing of components, finished devices, packaging, labeling, and manufacturing materials must be conducted with the same level of planning, control, and verification as internal activities.

The appropriate level of control should be achieved, FDA believes, through a proper mix of supplier and in-house controls. Purchasing contracts, orders, or other purchasing documents must clearly and unambiguously specify the necessary requirements for the product or service ordered. This means, of course, that a manufacturer must establish and validate component requirements prior to purchasing the component....

Changes in Critical Device Requirements

....

FDA is proposing to retain the distinction between critical and noncritical devices for one regulatory purpose. Traceability will continue to be required only for critical devices....

Harmonization

FDA is proposing to reorganize the structure of the device CGMP regulations and modify some of their language in order to harmonize them with international quality standards. Thus, FDA is proposing to relocate and combine certain requirements to better harmonize the requirements with specifications for quality systems in the ISO [International Standards Organization] 9001 quality standard and to use as much common language as possible to enhance conformance with ISO 9001 terminology.

. . . .

FDA believes that revising the device CGMP regulations so they are comparable to the ISO 9001 specifications for quality systems will, once harmonization is achieved, reduce a source of competitive disadvantage to U.S. manufacturers attempting to market devices in the EC. Harmonization of FDA's device CGMP regulations with the medical device good manufacturing practice rules of the EC, and with comparable device good manufacturing practice rules being developed by Canada and Japan, will minimize the number of quality systems with which the U.S. industry must comply to compete in the international market. . . .

NOTES

1. *Final Rule.* In the final rule, FDA changed the title of the regulations from "Current Good Manufacturing Processes" to "Quality System" regulations. The agency embraced this terminology because it is used by international standard setting organizations and because it reflects the expansion of the CGMP rule to cover a comprehensive quality system, including preproduction design and purchasing and postproduction servicing. 61 Fed. Reg. 52604, 52605 (Oct. 7, 1996).

In the final rule, FDA also eliminated the term "critical device" from the rule, noting this deletion would bring the regulation in closer harmony with ISO 9001 and the quality system standards of other countries. Despite the abandonment of the "critical device" terminology, however, FDA clung to the critical/noncritical distinction in one respect:

> . . . FDA has retained the concept of distinguishing between devices for the traceability requirements in § 820.65. As addressed in the discussion under that section, FDA believes that it is imperative that manufacturers be able to trace, by control number, any device, or where appropriate component of a device, that is intended for surgical implant into the body or to support or sustain life whose failure to perform when properly used in accordance with instructions for use provided in the labeling can be reasonably expected to result in a significant injury to the user.

2. *Exemptions from Quality System Requirements.* FDA's final Quality System regulation exempts all Class I devices from the design control requirements, except for those "automated with computer software" and a few others specifically listed in the rule. 21 C.F.R. 820.30(a). The classification regulations for many types of Class I devices exempt them from all the Quality System ("CGMP") requirements, other than the general recordkeeping requirements and those concerning complaint files. *E.g.* 21 C.F.R. 880.6085 (hot/cold water bottle). Pursuant to section 520(f)(2) of the Act, a device manufacturer may petition FDA for an exemption or variance from any quality system requirement.

5.   RESTRICTED DEVICES

Section 520(e) of the Act ("Restricted Devices") provides that FDA may:

By regulation require that a device be restricted to sale, distribution, or use—

(A) only upon the written or oral authorization of a practitioner licensed by law to administer or use such device, or

(B) upon such other conditions as the Secretary may prescribe in such regulation, if, because of its potentiality for harmful effect or the collateral measures necessary to its use, the Secretary determines that there cannot otherwise be reasonable assurance of its safety and effectiveness. No condition prescribed under subparagraph (B) may restrict the use of a device to persons with specific training or experience in its use or to persons for use in certain facilities unless the Secretary determines that such a restriction is required for the safe and effective use of the device.

A restricted device is thus analogous to a prescription drug, but the statutory language was crafted to allow FDA to control distribution of a device in ways that it cannot control distribution of a drug. *See American Pharmaceutical Ass'n v. Weinberger, supra* p. 829.

FDA has issued restricted device rules pursuant to this provision in only a few instances. For example, hearing aids are "restricted devices" whose sale, distribution, and use are subject to FDA requirements governing the clinical context in which they are used and the professional and patient labeling that must be provided with them. 21 C.F.R. 801.420–21. *See also* 21 C.F.R. 809.30 (restrictions on the sale, distribution, and use of analyte specific reagents). The fact that a "restricted device" is not necessarily synonymous with a "prescription device" is illustrated by FDA's restricted device rule for over-the-counter test sample collection systems for drugs of abuse testing. 21 C.F.R. 809.40. The restrictions imposed by this rule include a requirement that sample testing be performed by a laboratory that satisfies several conditions, that the collection system bear certain specified labeling, and that there be "an adequate system to communicate the proper interpretation of test results from the laboratory to the purchaser."

The paucity of restricted device rules issued pursuant to section 520(e) does not reflect the frequency with which FDA actually restricts the sale, distribution, and use of devices. Although a section 520(e) rule is the only way FDA can impose such restrictions on a Class I device, the agency has other options in regulating Class II and Class III products. The Act provides that a performance standard for a Class II device may include "a provision requiring that the sale and distribution of the device be restricted but only to the extent [they] may be restricted under a regulation under section 520(e)." Section 514(a)(2)(B)(v). Moreover, permissible special controls for Class II devices include "other appropriate actions as the Secretary deems necessary to provide" reasonable assurance of safety and effectiveness. Section 513(a)(1)(B). Accordingly, the classification regulations for some Class II devices identify, as the applicable special controls, prescription status or other restrictions on sale, distribution, or use. *E.g.* 21 C.F.R. 862.1118 (prescription requirement for biotinidase test system); 866.3332 (distribution of reagents for detection of specific novel influenza A viruses restricted to laboratories satisfying certain conditions). Finally, and most importantly, the Act states that an order approving a PMA for a Class III device may "require as a condition to such approval that the sale and distribution of the device be restricted" to extent they may be restricted under a section 520(e) regulation. Thus, many Class III devices are prescription devices, or their distribution is otherwise restricted, as a condition of their PMA approval.

————

In the early 1970s, FDA became concerned about widespread abuses in the marketing of hearing aids. Hearing aid sales were regulated only by the states, and the state regulatory schemes were inconsistent. Some states required that a customer, before purchasing a hearing aid, receive an examination by a physician specializing in hearing disorders or by an audiologist. Other states applied such requirements only to certain age segments of the population. Still other states required no examination at all.

In 1974, the Department of HEW established a Task Force to study problems relating to the marketing of hearing aids throughout the United States. As a result of the Task Force findings, FDA undertook to develop national rules. In April 1976, just prior to the enactment of the Medical Device Amendments, the agency published proposed rules requiring an examination by a licensed physician prior to the issuance of a hearing aid. This requirement was subject to waiver in certain instances. 41 Fed. Reg. 16756 (Apr. 21, 1976). The agency maintained that it had the legal authority to impose such a requirement under the misbranding provisions of the Act combined with its section 701(a) power to promulgate regulations for the "efficient enforcement" of the Act. FDA also noted, however, that after the forthcoming enactment of the 1976 Amendments, it would consider hearing aids to be restricted devices and base its power to place conditions on their sale and distribution on the restricted device provision.

In 1977, FDA published the final hearing aid rules. 42 Fed. Reg. 9286 (Feb. 15, 1977), 21 C.F.R. Section 801.420–21. The final regulations retained the proposed rule's requirement, subject to waiver, concerning an examination by a physician. The American Speech and Hearing Association (ASHA), a national association of audiologists and speech pathologists, challenged the final rules. ASHA contended that the requirement that the pre-sale evaluations be conducted by physicians, rather than by any practitioners licensed to administer hearing aid devices, including audiologists, violated the 1976 Amendments and was arbitrary and capricious.

American Speech and Hearing Ass'n v. Califano

Civ. No. 77–1327 (D.D.C. 1977).

■ Gesell, District Judge.

. . . .

At the very heart of the substantive dispute is the fact that FDA's requirement of examination by a physician as opposed to an audiologist has threatened an important facet of the audiologist's role in the hearing aid delivery system.... A clinical audiologist is a graduate-school-trained "individual qualified to provide professional assistance concerning communication problems associated with hearing impairment." Such assistance includes prevention, identification, evaluation, and rehabilitation of people with auditory disorders....

... Plaintiffs argue that the regulation in question is invalid under subsection (A) [of section 520(e)(1)] which, in plaintiffs' opinion, requires any regulation mandating pre-sale authorization by a licensed practitioner to apply equally to all licensed practitioners. In most states audiologists, physicians, and hearing aid dealers are all licensed practitioners within the meaning of the statute....

Plaintiffs' argument has several flaws. First, it is incorrect to characterize it as one of exclusion: neither audiologists nor dealers are barred from doing anything, nor are they deprived of their status as practitioners. Second, at least in the context of hearing aid sales, plaintiffs' construction of the term "practitioner" leaves subsection (A) devoid of meaning. Hearing aids are always sold by "licensed practitioners" who, by the very act of selling have "authorized" the sale. The type of restriction comprehended by plaintiffs' interpretation of subsection (A) imposes no restriction at all.... [T]he Court ... find[s] that subsection (A) permits the FDA to distinguish among different types of practitioners and thus to authorize the type of regulation at issue.

This result accords with plain sense. The purpose of the Amendments was to empower the Secretary or his designate to root out the abuses extant under state regulation of medical devices. The regulation at issue is so obviously directed toward that goal that the Court would have to ignore the most fundamental tenets of statutory interpretation to void it....

Plaintiffs argue that ... the regulation ... is nonetheless arbitrary and capricious and thus voidable under section 10 of the APA, 5 U.S.C. § 706(2)(A). Under the Amendments the regulation is valid only if "there cannot otherwise be reasonable assurance of [the] safety and effectiveness" of hearing aid devices. Yet if this is so is it not irrational to make the examination requirement waivable in a large number of cases? And is it not irrational to allow the required examination to be performed by any physician, a Class that include podiatrists, gynecologists, and others with little familiarity with hearing disorders, yet at the same time exclude audiologists, whose expertise is in this area?

These are thoughtful questions. The record shows, however, that they were carefully considered by the FDA prior to enactment. The regulation is accompanied by detailed and conscientious findings of fact that justify the rule adopted. The seeming contradictions are actually the result of compromises between the competing demands of economy and safety. After extended and careful study, the FDA found a medical evaluation to be essential for proper diagnosis and treatment. It also found that audiologists were unable to "differentiate, diagnose, evaluate, and treat the medical cause or causes of a hearing impairment." Examinations were authorized by all physicians because of the scarcity of otologists, otolaryngologists, and other physicians specializing in hearing disorders. A required audiological examination in addition to that of a physician was rejected as too expensive and of dubious incremental benefit. The waiver provision was included to accommodate certain religious and personal beliefs as well as those with the most limited access to physicians. Those eligible to waive the examination may do so only upon signing a form strongly advising against waiver. The Court is far from convinced of the wisdom of the compromise adopted, but is mindful of the limited scope of its review and the deference due to the "informed experience and judgment of the agency to whom Congress delegated appropriate authority." Because the regulatory choice made in this case cannot be termed unconsidered, it is upheld. . . .

COMMENT: OVER–THE–COUNTER IN VITRO DIAGNOSTIC DEVICES

For years, the market for home-use tests was dominated by pregnancy tests and ovulation monitors. Today, dozens of tests are available over-the-counter for use in the diagnosis and screening of a growing number of conditions and symptoms, from cholesterol to the presence of drugs of abuse, and from glucose levels in diabetics to HIV. Most of these tests provide results for the consumer at home, but a few require the consumer to deposit a specimen in a collection device and send it to a laboratory, which then contacts the consumer with the results. On its website, FDA–CDRH's Office of In Vitro Diagnostic Device Evaluation and Safety (OIVD) lists no fewer than 60 types of tests it has approved or cleared for over-the-counter sale. Carol Lewis, *Home Diagnostic Tests: The Ultimate House Call?*, FDA CONSUMER, Nov.-Dec. 2001.

When to permit the sale of in vitro diagnostic devices for home use has long been a difficult issue for FDA. In 1985, in recognition of "the growing interest in home-use in vitro devices," FDA held a public meeting of the chairpersons and the consumer and industry representatives of four of its advisory committees to help develop "uniform evaluation criteria for home-use in vitro devices to help insure that these devices are regulated in a consistent fashion and that consumers are provided with reliable, adequately labeled products." 50 Fed. Reg. 32641 (Aug. 13, 1985). In 1988, the agency released a draft "points to consider" in formulating labeling and premarket submissions for home use in vitro diagnostic devices.

Since that time, FDA has issued restricted device regulations with regard to two types of in vitro diagnostic products. The first covers analyte specific reagents (ASRs). As described by FDA, ASRs are:

> reagents composed of chemicals or antibodies that may be thought of as the "active ingredients" of tests that are used to identify one specific disease or condition. ASR's are purchased by manufacturers who use them as components of tests that have been cleared or approved by FDA and also by clinical laboratories that use the ASR's to develop in-house tests used exclusively by that laboratory. These in-house developed tests (sometimes referred to as "home brew" tests) include those that measure a wide variety of antibodies used in the diagnosis of infectious diseases, cancer, genetic, and various other conditions.

62 Fed. Reg. 62243 (Nov. 21, 1997), 21 C.F.R. 864.4020. In 1997, FDA published a final rule classifying ASRs as Class I, II, or III, depending on their intended use. At the same time, the agency designated all ASRs as restricted devices under section 520(e) and promulgated a restricted device rule for them. Under this rule, ASRs intended for clinical use can be sold only to in vitro diagnostic manufacturers and to certain categories of laboratories qualified to perform high-complexity testing. 21 C.F.R. 809.30. Moreover, the restricted device regulation restricts ordering the use of in-house developed tests using ASRs to physicians or other health care practitioners authorized by applicable state law to access such tests. FDA explained this latter requirement as follows:

> FDA disagrees with comments that have suggested that results from in-house assays developed using ASR's are no different from other IVD test results and that OTC access to the use of ASR's in these settings does not raise issues of their safety and effectiveness. Traditionally, IVD test results are evaluated in the context of a patient's history, physical examination and other sources of diagnostic information. In many cases, those tests are approved or cleared by FDA and their performance criteria have been established. . . . By contrast, results of IVD tests using ASR's may be particularly difficult for lay persons to interpret correctly without the guidance of a physician because the performance characteristics of the individual tests often have not been cleared or approved by FDA.

62 Fed. Reg. at 62255.

The other category of IVD products subject to a restricted device rule is "OTC test sample collection systems for drugs of abuse testing." 21 C.F.R. 809.40. As revealed by the title of this regulation, however, FDA has not made these prescription devices. Rather, the restricted device regulation requires that sample testing be performed only in qualified laboratories using FDA-approved or FDA-cleared screening tests and that the systems "provide an adequate system to communicate the proper interpretation of test results from the laboratory to the lay purchaser." Note that this rule applies only to sample collection devices; FDA allows complete drug of abuse test systems to be sold to consumers over-the-counter without any restrictions on sale, distribution, or use.

For several years, perhaps the most contentious question in this area was whether test kits for HIV (the virus that causes AIDS) should be approved for home use. Although regulated as medical devices, HIV tests are under the authority of FDA's biologics center (CBER). In 1996, FDA approved a PMA for the first home collection HIV testing system. Letter from Jay S. Epstein, FDA–CBER, to Michael Wandell, Home Access Health Corporation (July 22, 1996). The approved device consists of materials for specimen collection, instructions, an educational booklet, and a mailing envelope to send the specimen to a laboratory for analysis. The distributor of the kit, which anonymizes the results and provides them over the telephone, also provides counseling and referral services. As a condition of PMA approval, the company agreed to conduct postmarketing surveillance studies and lot acceptance testing.

COMMENT: CIGARETTES AS RESTRICTED DEVICES

As discussed in Chapter II, in 1996 FDA published "Regulations Restricting the Sale and Distribution of Cigarettes and Smokeless Tobacco to Protect Children and Adolescents." 61 Fed. Reg. 44396 (Aug. 28, 1996). In this rule, the agency categorized cigarettes as combination drug-devices and determined to regulate them pursuant to its device authorities. Because the agency did not immediately classify these products under section 513, however, the only controls it could apply to them initially were the general controls applicable to all devices. FDA purported to apply the Act's full panoply of general controls, although, in the rule, it exempted cigarettes from the adequate directions for use requirement of section 502(f)(1); required adverse event reports from manufacturers "only for serious adverse events that are not well-known or well-documented by the scientific community;" and wholly exempted distributors from the registration and listing, GMP, and adverse event reporting requirements. Most of the rule consisted of restrictions on sale designed to prevent youth from gaining access to tobacco products and restrictions on advertising and promotion designed to limit the targeting of children and adolescents. To support these controls, FDA relied on section 520(e).

The tobacco industry challenged the legality of FDA's rule in federal district court. What follows are excerpts from the District Court's ruling on the industry's summary judgment motion. Earlier in his opinion, Judge Osteen held that that FDA could exercise jurisdiction over tobacco products and could regulate them as medical devices rather than as drugs. In the excerpted passages, he goes on to assess whether the Act permits the particular restrictions contained in the FDA regulation. On appeal, majorities on both the Fourth Circuit and the Supreme Court held that FDA lacked jurisdiction over tobacco products, and consequently neither addressed the legality of the agency's specific restrictions.

Coyne Beahm, Inc. v. United States Food & Drug Administration

966 F. Supp. 1374 (M.D.N.C. 1997).

■ Osteen, District Judge.

. . . .

The court has found that FDA properly regulated tobacco products pursuant to its device authorities. The question remains whether FDA has properly applied its device authorities to tobacco products. The Regulations' requirements fall into essentially three categories: restrictions on advertising and promotion,[20] restrictions on access,[21] and labeling requirements.[22]

---

20. The promotional and advertising restrictions limit certain advertising to a black-and-white text-only format, restrict the trade or brand name of certain tobacco products, prohibit the sale or distribution of brand-identified promotional nontobacco items such as hats and tee shirts, and prohib-it use of a brand name of a tobacco product to sponsor entries, teams, sporting and other events.

21. The access restrictions prohibit the sale of tobacco products to individuals under the age of 18, require retailers to verify a

22. See p. 1052 for footnote 22.

FDA promulgated the first two categories of restrictions pursuant to 21 U.S.C. § 360j(e), and the last pursuant to 21 U.S.C. § 352.

a. Section 360j(e) Does Not Authorize Restrictions on the Promotion and Advertisement of Tobacco Products.

... FDA determined that tobacco products are restricted devices within the meaning of § 360j(e) because, due to the "unique circumstances surrounding the use of tobacco products, the only way to provide a reasonable assurance of the safety of these products is to prevent children and adolescents from using and becoming addicted to them" and that, "without the restrictions contained in the Regulations, there cannot be a reasonable assurance of the safety and effectiveness of these products." FDA asserts that since tobacco products are restricted devices, it may restrict their "sale, distribution, or use," pursuant to § 360j(e). FDA further asserts that it may restrict the advertising and promotion of tobacco products, explaining that advertising and promotion constitutes an "offer of sale" and, moreover, that an "offer of sale" is part of the "sale" of a product.

Plaintiffs contend, and the court agrees, that FDA may not restrict advertising and promotion pursuant to § 360j(e). First, both as ordinarily defined and as used in the phrase "may ... be restricted to sale, distribution, or use," the word "sale" does not encompass the advertising or promotion of a product. Second, as Plaintiffs note, although Congress expressly used the words "offer for sale" and "advertising" or "advertisements" elsewhere in the FDCA, it chose not to use such language in § 360j(e).

Even if "sale," as used within § 360j(e), could be construed to encompass the advertising and promotion of a product, the court finds that the section's grant of authority to FDA to impose "other conditions" on the sale, distribution, or use of restricted devices does not authorize FDA to restrict advertising and promotion. The phrase "other conditions" must be construed within the context of § 360j(e) and other relevant sections of the FDCA. Section 360j(e) authorizes FDA to restrict the sale, distribution, or use of certain devices to prescription sale or other conditions necessary to provide a reasonable assurance of safety and effectiveness. The restriction on the advertising and promotion of a product does not fit within this framework. Furthermore, § 360j(e) must be construed in relation to 21 U.S.C. § 353(b), which Plaintiffs assert is the counterpart to § 360j(e) and which authorizes FDA to constrain certain drugs to prescription status. Section 353(b), like § 360j(e), authorizes FDA to restrict drugs to prescription sale. It is true, as FDA notes, that FDA's authority is broader under § 360j(e) than under § 353(b) because FDA may impose pursuant to the former "other conditions" on the sale, distribution, or use of a restricted

purchaser's age by photographic identification, prohibit the sale of tobacco products through vending machines and self-service displays except in facilities where individuals under the age of 18 are not permitted, prohibit distribution of free samples, and prohib-

it the sale of cigarette packages containing fewer than 20 cigarettes.

22. FDA requires tobacco product packages, cartons, and boxes to bear the established name of the product and a statement of intended use.

device. Nonetheless, the meaning of "other conditions" cannot be considered without context, and the court finds that "other conditions" cannot be so broadly construed as to encompass conditions on advertising and promotion.

In addition, the court finds that Congress' delegation to FDA of limited authority to restrict the advertising of devices elsewhere in the FDCA suggests that § 360j(e) should not be construed so as to allow FDA to restrict advertising and promotion. The court notes that just as Congress gave FDA authority to limit drugs to prescription status in § 353(b), but gave FDA authority to regulate prescription drug advertisements in § 352(n), Congress gave FDA authority to limit certain devices to prescription status in § 360j(e), but gave FDA authority to regulate the advertising of such devices in §§ 352(q) and 352(r).[29] Indeed, the fact that Congress has specifically granted to FDA the authority to regulate advertising of restricted devices in a separate section supports the court's finding that Congress did not intend to grant FDA such authority under § 360j(e)....

b.   Section 360j(e) Authorizes the Food and Drug Administration to Impose Restrictions on Access to Tobacco Products.

The court finds that § 360j(e) can be construed to authorize the access restrictions imposed by FDA. First, the access restrictions imposed by FDA, unlike its advertising and promotion restrictions, directly restrict the sale or distribution of tobacco products within the meaning of § 360j(e). Second, the court finds that such conditions on the sale or distribution of tobacco products fit within what Congress intended for FDA to impose pursuant to its authority to impose "other conditions." Thus, FDA's access restrictions will stand.

c.   Section 352 Authorizes the Food and Drug Administration to Impose Labeling Restrictions on Tobacco Products.

FDA, pursuant to § 352(r), requires tobacco products to have a statement of intended use and the established name printed on the packages. The court finds that § 352(r) clearly authorizes FDA to require restricted devices to bear the product's established name and a statement of intended use.

. . . .

———

Even if Judge Osteen was correct in holding that section 520(e) does not authorize advertising limitations of the type FDA attempted to impose on cigarettes, the agency indisputably has some power over advertising for

29. Section 352(r) requires that advertisements for any restricted device include certain information: the established name of the device; a brief statement of the intended uses of the device and relevant warnings; and, if determined necessary after a hearing, a description of the device's components. Section 352(r) further provides that "no advertisement of a restricted device ... shall, with respect to the matters specified in this paragraph or covered by regulations issued hereunder, be subject to" the Federal Trade Commission Act. Plaintiffs contend, and the court agrees, that § 352(r) reveals Congress' intention that the Federal Trade Commission have primary jurisdiction over advertising.

restricted devices. Section 502(r) requires that advertisements for restricted devices contain "a true statement of the device's established name" and "a brief statement of the intended uses of the device and relevant warnings, precautions, side effects, and contraindications." FDA has published a draft guidance on how to satisfy the latter requirement in broadcast advertisements. DRAFT GUIDANCE FOR INDUSTRY AND FDA: CONSUMER-DIRECTED BROADCAST ADVERTISING OF RESTRICTED DEVICES (Feb. 10, 2004). Moreover, section 502(q) provides that a restricted device is misbranded if "its advertising is false or misleading in any particular." Restricted devices are thus the only FDA-regulated products other than prescription drugs (and vitamins and minerals) for which the agency has authority to regulate advertising that is not also section 201(m) "labeling."

6.   BANNED DEVICES

Section 516 authorizes FDA, by regulation, to ban a device that "presents substantial deception or an unreasonable and substantial risk of illness or injury." It was included in the 1976 Amendments primarily to enable FDA to deal with the "quack" devices that occupied so much of the agency's attention in the past. The agency has adopted procedural regulations to implement this provision. 42 Fed. Reg. 42000 (Aug. 19, 1977), 44 Fed. Reg. 29214 (May 18, 1979), 21 C.F.R. Part 895. In 48 Fed. Reg. 25126 (June 3, 1983) and 49 Fed. Reg. 1177 (Jan. 10, 1984), FDA promulgated its first, and so far only, regulation under this provision, banning prosthetic hair fibers intended for implantation into the human scalp to simulate natural hair or conceal baldness. 21 C.F.R. 895.101.

7.   ADMINISTRATIVE DETENTION

Section 304(g), governing seizures, gives FDA authority, by administrative order, to detain potentially adulterated and misbranded devices discovered during a section 704 inspection for up to 30 days. FDA has established procedural regulations for such detentions. 42 Fed. Reg. 54574 (Oct. 7, 1977); 44 Fed. Reg. 13234 (Mar. 9, 1979), 21 C.F.R. 800.55. Administrative detentions are intended to prevent the distribution of devices that an inspector has reason to believe are adulterated or misbranded until the agency has had the opportunity to consider whether to institute a seizure action. This provision, too, has rarely been used.

8.   NOTIFICATION AND REPAIR, REPLACEMENT, OR REFUND

Sections 518(a)–(d) ("Notification and Other Remedies") authorize FDA to order a manufacturer, importer, or distributor to notify the public of an unreasonable risk of substantial harm from a marketed device. After offering the opportunity for an informal hearing, the agency may order a manufacturer, importer, or distributor of a device presenting an unreasonable risk to repair or replace the device or refund the purchase price. Under section 502(t)(1), a device is misbranded in the event of a failure or refusal to comply with any requirement in a section 518 order.

Section 518 was patterned on similar grants of authority to the National Highway and Traffic Safety Administration, to the Consumer

Product Safety Commission, and to FDA itself under the Radiation Control for Health and Safety Act. FDA considers the section self-executing and therefore has not promulgated implementing regulations. In 49 Fed. Reg. 11716 (Mar. 27, 1984), however, FDA did make available for public comment a draft guideline on Medical Device Notification and Voluntary Safety Alert, which sets forth the procedure that it follows in implementing section 518.

FDA has invoked its authority under these provisions on several occasions. In 1978, when a manufacturer of a dangerous defective defibrillator refused to pay for repairs in units of the device that had already been distributed to hospitals, FDA ordered the manufacturer to submit an adequate plan for repairing the defects in the distributed devices. Although the firm initially demanded a hearing on the agency's action, it subsequently submitted a plan which, after several changes, FDA accepted.

In 1980, a Minnesota public health study and a CDC study both found that users of Rely tampons, manufactured by Procter & Gamble, were at a higher risk for toxic shock syndrome than users of other tampons. After FDA threatened to issue a section 518 notification and refund order against the company, the agency and Procter & Gamble entered the following consent agreement:

In re Procter & Gamble Co.: Consent Agreement

U.S. Food and Drug Administration, September 26, 1980.

. . . .

2. Rely brand tampon ("Rely") is a device . . . .

3. Toxic Shock Syndrome ("TSS") is a recently recognized disease. The exact cause of and cure for TSS are not known, although *Staphylococcus aureus* may play an important role in the etiology of the disease. TSS is a rare disease which progresses rapidly and, in some instances, has resulted in death. The Food and Drug Administration ("FDA") believes that TSS is a significant public health problem. The Center for Disease Control ("CDC") and FDA believe there is an association between use of Rely and occurrence of TSS, a proposition which P&G vigorously disputes.

4. On September 23, 1980, FDA advised P&G that FDA was contemplating the possibility of invoking the provisions of 21 U.S.C. § 360h [FD&C Act 518] to compel the firm to engage in a notification and retrieval/refund program.

5. In settlement of actions contemplated by FDA under 21 U.S.C. § 360h, P&G and FDA enter into this Agreement, which constitutes a "requirement" for purposes of 21 U.S.C. § 352(t)(1) [FD&C Act 502(t)(1)].

6. P&G expressly denies that Rely is in any way defective or that the sale or distribution of Rely violated the Act or any other law. This agreement does not constitute an admission by P&G of any such violation.

7. By its acceptance of this Agreement, FDA does not waive any of its rights to initiate administrative or judicial enforcement under the Act or other applicable law against Rely, P&G, or any P&G officer, agent, attor-

ney, or employee should FDA, in its discretion, determine that such action is appropriate.

Therefore, IT IS AGREED that P&G shall:

8. Discontinue all sale and commercial distribution of Rely.

9. Make every reasonable effort to withdraw from all media any advertisement for Rely placed prior to September 22, 1980.

10. Conduct the consumer notification program set forth and explained as follows. . . .

11. Conduct a retrieval/refund program as follows. . . .

12. P&G shall make available to FDA for review and copying all documents related to the notification and retrieval/refund programs. . . .

13. P&G shall retain the records relating to the notification and retrieval/refund programs according to the following schedule, except that P & G is not required to retain copies of records already submitted to FDA. . . .

IT IS UNDERSTOOD that P&G has already commenced or completed certain of these undertakings prior to entering into this Agreement.

IT IS FURTHER AGREED that P&G shall advise FDA when all its undertakings and any other steps reasonably necessary to accomplish the purpose of these notification and retrieval/refund programs have been carried out. FDA will review P&G's actions and if it agrees that P&G's undertakings and the purpose of these programs have been carried out, shall notify P&G that these programs have been concluded. Thereafter, P&G shall continue to retrieve Rely and refund in accordance with the provisions of the retrieval/refund program to any consumers, distributors, or retailers who P&G learns has Rely.

IT IS FURTHER AGREED that P&G shall not reintroduce for commercial distribution nor export nor offer for export the products covered by this Agreement or identical products under any name without the prior written permission of the Director of FDA's Bureau of Medical Devices.

NOTES

1. *Private Lawsuits.* After 1980, more than 1,000 injury and death claims were brought against P&G by users of Rely tampons and their relatives. *See Northbrook Excess & Surplus Ins. Co. v. Procter & Gamble*, 924 F.2d 633, 635 (7th Cir. 1991) (resolving insurance dispute between P&G and its insurer in light of the Rely litigation). The leading reported case is *Kehm v. Procter & Gamble*, 724 F.2d 613 (8th Cir. 1983) (affirming judgment awarding compensatory damages to husband and children of Rely user who died of TSS).

2. *Medtronic Pacemakers.* On February 19, 1979, Medtronic submitted a section 510(k) notification to FDA for the Model 6972 bipolar pacemaker lead. On April 19, 1979, FDA concurred that the device was substantially equivalent to a preamendment device. Experience with the device, however, disclosed a high failure rate, which led to a full FDA investigation and a congressional hearing. "Failed Pacemaker Leads," Hearing before the Subcomm. on Oversight and Investigations of the House Comm. on Energy and Commerce, 98th Cong., 2nd Sess. (1984). After

extensive deliberation, FDA decided not to pursue possible action under section 518(b) for repair, replacement, or refund.

This decision is based on the absence here of any ongoing public health problem or concern which could be addressed by such an action. The pacemaker leads of concern are no longer being manufactured or sold, unimplanted leads have been recalled, and the firm has a program for reimbursement or elimination of out-of-pocket costs to patients who require surgery or increased monitoring because they rely on Model 6972 leads.

Memorandum from FDA Commissioner Frank E. Young to CDRH Director John C. Villforth (Aug. 19, 1985).

3. *Dalkon Shield.* In *National Women's Health Network, Inc. v. A.H. Robins Co., Inc.*, 545 F. Supp. 1177 (D. Mass. 1982) the District Court dismissed a class action for injunctive relief to require the manufacturer of the Dalkon Shield intrauterine contraceptive device (IUD) to conduct a nationwide notification and refund program. The Court held that the FD&C Act creates no private right of action and that any state cause of action would be preempted by the 1976 Amendments.

4. *Alternative Approaches.* On its webpage, CDRH has the following to say about section 518:

The procedures for repair, replacement, or refund are complex and could result in multiple orders, regulatory hearings, and much delay if FDA and the manufacturer, or other responsible person, are unable to agree on a plan for addressing a risk. The Agency must consider available alternatives. Both notification orders and repair, replacement, or refund orders are discretionary. Before ordering notification, FDA must determine that no more practical means are available under the FD&C Act to eliminate the risk. Although there is no requirement that such a determination be made before FDA orders repair, replacement, or refund, FDA must determine that notification alone is insufficient before ordering repair, replacement or refund.

FDA's alternatives to Section 518 are the following approaches:

• Legal actions (seizures, injunctions, prosecutions);

• Regulations (*e.g.*, banning or imposing restrictions on sale, distribution or use); and

• Recalls (under FDA's recall regulations).

5. *1990 Act Response to Under-Use of Section 518.* In 1990, Congress, concerned about FDA's reluctance to use its authority under section 518, added a number of postmarket powers to FDA's arsenal, including postmarket surveillance, mandatory recall, device tracking, and the requirement that manufacturers notify FDA of corrective actions. These new postmarket authorities are discussed below.

9.   POSTMARKET SURVEILLANCE

Under section 522, FDA may order the manufacturer of any Class II or Class III device to conduct postmarket surveillance if the failure of the device would be "reasonably likely to have serious adverse health consequences," if it is intended to be implanted in the body for more than one year, or if is intended to be used outside a user facility to support or sustain life. (FD&C Act 522(a); 21 C.F.R. 822.1). As defined by FDA regulations, "postmarket surveillance" is "the active, systematic, scientifically valid collection, analysis, and interpretation of data or other information about a marketed device." 21 C.F.R. 822.3(h).

Congress first gave FDA the authority to order postmarket surveillance in the 1990 Act. Section 522 was meant to compensate for underreporting of adverse events under the MDR system and for the agency's reluctance to use its postmarket authorities under section 518. *See* 65 Fed. Reg. 52376, 52377–78 (Aug. 29, 2000). Before FDA issued a final rule implementing the new section 522, Congress, in FDAMA, revised the section, giving the agency more discretion in imposing postmarket surveillance and setting a presumptive limit of three years on studies.

FDA has issued rules implementing section 522 as amended by FDA-MA MA, 65 Fed. Reg. 52376 (Aug. 29, 2000), 67 Fed. Reg. 38878 (June 6, 2002), 21 C.F.R. Part 822. After receiving a postmarket surveillance order, a manufacturer must submit a surveillance plan for FDA approval within 30 days. Failure to submit such a plan, to resubmit if FDA rejects the plan, or to conduct surveillance in accordance with the plan constitutes a misbranding violation and is prohibited under section section 301(q)(1)(C) and 502(t)(3). *See generally* FDA–CDRH, GUIDANCE FOR INDUSTRY AND FDA STAFF: POSTMARKET SURVEILLANCE UNDER SECTION 522 (2006).

10.   DEVICE TRACKING

Section 519(e) authorizes FDA to issue an order requiring the manufacturer of a Class II or Class III device to adopt a method of tracking it from manufacturer to patient if the failure of the device would be "reasonably likely to have serious adverse health consequences," if it is intended to be implanted in the body for more than one year, or if it is intended to be used outside a user facility to support or sustain life. Section 519(e)(1). Note that the subset of devices potentially subject to device tracking is precisely the same as that for which FDA may order postmarket surveillance under section 522. Failure to comply with a tracking requirement constitutes a misbranding violation and is prohibited under sections 301(e), 301(q)(1)(C), and 502(t)(2).

FDA has issued device tracking regulations implementing section 519(e). 67 Fed. Reg. 5943 (Feb. 8, 2002), 21 C.F.R. Part 821. As stated by the agency in these regulations: "Effective tracking of devices from the manufacturing facility, through the distributor network (including distributors, retailers, rental firms and other commercial enterprises, device user facilities, and licensed practitioners) and, ultimately, to the patient is necessary for the effectiveness of remedies prescribed by the act, such as patient notification (section 518(a) of the act) or device recall (section 518(e) of the act)." 21 C.F.R. 821.1(b). The list of device types that the agency has ordered to be tracked is published in FDA–CDRH, GUIDANCE FOR INDUSTRY AND FDA STAFF: MEDICAL DEVICE TRACKING 8–9 (2003).

The device tracking provision was first added to the FD&C Act by the 1990 Act. Originally, however, section 519(e) tracking was mandatory for the manufacturers of all devices fitting the statutory criteria. In 1997 FDAMA amended section 519(e) to give FDA discretion as to whether or not to require tracking for such devices. Accordingly, starting in 1998, the agency rescinded the tracking orders for fourteen types of devices. 67 Fed. Reg. 5943, 5944 (Feb. 8, 2002). The additional criteria FDA uses to determine whether to compel tracking for a device meeting the statutory criteria are "(1) The likelihood of sudden, catastrophic failure; (2) the likelihood of significant adverse clinical outcomes; and (3) the need for prompt professional intervention."

11.   MANDATORY RECALLS

Another aspect of Congress's effort to bolster FDA's postmarketing authority was the 1990 Act's addition of new subsection 518(e), giving the agency power to order device recalls. Under this provision, if FDA finds there is "a reasonable probability that [a device] would cause serious adverse health consequences or death," it must order the manufacturer, importer, distributor, or retailers to cease distribution of the device and to notify health professionals and device user facilities that they should stop using it. After providing the person subject to such an order an opportunity for an informal hearing, FDA may amend the order to require a recall. The agency may not order the recall of a device from individuals, but it must provide that notice be given to those subject to the risks associated with the device. FDA has published regulations governing the mandatory recall process. 59 Fed. Reg. 30656 (June 14, 1994), 61 Fed. Reg. 59004 (Nov. 20, 1996), 21 C.F.R. Part 810.

When one of its devices presents a serous risk, a manufacturer will usually agree to conduct a voluntary recall, thus obviating the need for FDA to issue a section 518(e) order. Nonetheless, FDA has found it necessary to order device recalls on a few occasions. *E.g.*, FDA Enforcement Report (Apr. 1, 1992), at 4–5 (mandatory recall of wheelchair lift for whirlpool bathing system); FDA Enforcement Report (Oct. 7, 1992), at 7 (mandatory recall of infant ventilating system).

12.   REPORTS OF REMOVALS AND CORRECTIONS

Under section 519(f), added by the 1990 Act, FDA must promulgate regulations requiring the manufacturer, importer, or distributor of a device to report to the agency any correction or removal of a device undertaken to reduce a risk to health or to remedy a violation of the FD&C Act which may present a risk to health. FDA has published a rule implementing this subsection. 59 Fed. Reg. 13828 (Mar. 23, 1994), 62 Fed. Reg. 27183 (May 19, 1997), 21 C.F.R. Part 806. As the agency explained when it promulgated the rule: "Section 519(f) of the act was enacted because Congress was concerned that device manufacturers, distributors, and importers were carrying out product corrections or removals without notifying FDA, or not notifying the agency in a timely fashion Congress explained that industry's failure to report corrections and removals, particularly those undertaken to reduce risks associated with the use of a device, 'denies the agency the opportunity to fulfill its public health responsibilities by evaluating device-related problems and the adequacy of corrective actions.' . . ."

Section 519(f) supplements rather than duplicates the previously-discussed MDR system implemented pursuant to section 519(a). According to FDA:

> Generally, there is expected to be little overlap between these reporting requirements. This is because MDR's are based on adverse events that have occurred (*i.e.*, deaths, serious injuries, and malfunctions) regardless of whether a remedial action (*i.e.*, correction or removal) has been undertaken by the manufacturer or distributor. Moreover, the MDR report, which is tied to the adverse event itself and its possible association with the device, will only rarely address any remedial action taken by the manufacturer because, in most cases, no such remedial action has yet occurred.

62 Fed. Reg. at 27183. The one area of potential overlap between the section 519(a) and 519(f) concerns the former's requirement that a manufacturer file an MDR within five days of becoming aware that a reportable event "necessitates remedial action to prevent an unreasonable risk of substantial harm to the public health." 21 C.F.R. 803.53. To avoid duplication, FDA has provided that a 519(f) report is not required for an event that has already been reported under 519(a). 21 C.F.R. 806.10(f).

13.   CIVIL PENALTIES

Finally, the 1990 Act added a new provision to the FD&C Act's section on penalties, stating that any person who violates the device provisions of the FD&C Act may be liable for a civil penalty in an amount not to exceed $15,000 for each violation and $1 million for all such violations adjudicated in a single proceeding. Section 303(f). FDA may assess civil penalties only after affording the person to be assessed an opportunity for a formal adjudicatory hearing. For more on civil penalties as an enforcement tool, *see infra* p. 1333.

NOTES

1. *Export of Devices.* The export provisions of the 1976 Amendments are examined in Chapter XI, *infra*.

2. *Preemption of State Regulation.* The statutory preemption provision in section 521 and its interpretation by FDA are discussed in Chapter XII, *infra*.

G.   RADIATION CONTROL

FDA's responsibility for assuring the safety and effectiveness of medical equipment is not confined to the device provisions of the FD&C Act. Under the Radiation Control for Health and Safety Act of 1968, 82 Stat. 1173, originally codified as 42 U.S.C. 263b *et seq.*, recodified and integrated into the FD&C Act by the 1990 Act as FD&C Act sections 531 *et seq.*, the agency is also responsible for regulating products that emit radiation, many of which fit the definition of a medical device. This responsibility was transferred to FDA in 1971, 36 Fed. Reg. 12803 (July 7, 1971), and combined with the medical devices program in 1982, 47 Fed. Reg. 44614 (Oct. 8, 1992).

The radiological health provisions of the FD&C Act give FDA primary authority for protecting the public from "electronic product radiation." The Act defines this term as "(A) any ionizing or non-ionizing electromagnetic or particulate radiation, or (B) any sonic, infrasonic, or ultrasonic wave, which is emitted from an electronic product as a the result of the operation of an electronic circuit in such product." Section 531(1). In its regulations, FDA provides a lengthy list of examples of electronic products subject to the Radiation Control for Health and Safety Act. 21 C.F.R. 1000.15. Many of the listed products are medical devices, but the majority are not. Medical products subject to the provisions include, among others, x-ray machines, tanning and therapeutic lamps, diathermy units, cauterizers, electromedical equipment, and medical lasers. Some of the (usually) nonmedical products on FDA's list are television receivers, accelerators, black light sources, welding equipment, infrared alarm systems, microwave ovens, radar devices, remote control devices, vibrators, sound amplification equipment, and "art-form" lasers. (With regard to the last of these, *see* FDA– CDRH, RESPONSIBILITIES OF LASER LIGHT SHOW PROJECTOR MANUFACTURERS, DEALERS, AND DISTRIBUTORS; FINAL GUIDANCE FOR INDUSTRY AND FDA (2001)). This list, published in 1973, does not include some important new categories of radiation-emitting electronic products over which FDA currently asserts authority—laser pointers and cell phones, for example.

Because FDA's activities under the Radiation Act concern the design, manufacture, and use of medical instrumentation, it is logical to provide an introduction to the program here, but there is an additional justification for treating radiation-emitting products in this chapter. FDA's ability to minimize the risks of medical devices without nullifying their benefits depends in many instances on its power to control the ways in which they are put to use by medical professionals. This theme of utilization review and control pervades the field of medical radiation.

1.   PERFORMANCE STANDARDS

FDA's most important power under the radiation provisions of the FD&C Act is the authority to issue performance standards, by regulation, "to control the emission of electronic product radiation ... if [it] determines that such standards are necessary for the public health and safety." Section 534(a)(1). The statute provides that radiation safety standards "may include provisions for the testing of such products and the measurement of their electronic product radiation emissions, may require the attachment of warning signs and labels, and may require the provision of instructions for the installation, operation, and use of such products." Unstated, but assumed, is FDA's power through such standards to control the physical characteristics of electronic products. The Act requires FDA, before issuing a radiation safety standard, to consult with an advisory committee known as the "Technical Electronic Product Radiation Safety Standards Subcommittee." Every manufacturer of an electronic product subject to a standard must, upon delivery to the dealer or distributor, certify that the product conforms to the applicable standard. 21 C.F.R. 1010.2.

Whereas FDA has published only one medical device performance standard under Section 514, it has finalized 13 radiation safety standards under section 534.

Electronic Products; Performance Standard for Diagnostic X–Ray Systems and Their Major Components; Final Rule

70 Fed. Reg. 33998 (June 10, 2005).

The Food and Drug Administration is issuing a final rule to amend the Federal performance standard for diagnostic x-ray systems and their major components (the performance standard). The agency is taking this action to update the performance standard to account for changes in technology and use of radiographic and fluoroscopic x-ray systems. . . .

The purpose of the performance standard for diagnostic x-ray systems is to improve the public health by reducing exposure to and the detriment associated with unnecessary ionizing radiation while assuring the clinical utility of the images produced.

In order for mandatory performance standards to continue to provide the intended public health protection, the standards must be modified when appropriate to reflect the changes in technology and product usage. When the performance standard was originally developed, the only means of producing a fluoroscopic image was either a screen of fluorescent material or an x-ray image intensifier tube. Therefore, the standard was written with these two types of image receptors in mind. A number of technological developments have been implemented for radiographic and fluoroscopic x-ray systems, such as solid-state x-ray imaging (SSXI) and new modes of image recording (e.g., digital recording to computer memory or other media). These developments have made the application of the current standard to systems incorporating these new technologies cumbersome and awkward. FDA is therefore amending the performance standard for diagnostic x-ray systems and their major components in 21 CFR 1020.30, 1020.31, and 1020.32 to address the recent changes in technology.

These amendments will require that newly-manufactured x-ray systems include additional features that physicians may use to minimize x-ray exposures to patients. Advances in technology have made several of these new features feasible at minimal additional cost.

. . . .

Three comments expressed concern regarding the requirement in proposed Sec. 1020.30(h)(5) that manufacturers describe specific clinical procedures or uses for which a specific mode of operation is designed or intended. The concern expressed was that the clinical use of the fluoroscopic system should not be limited by any statements required of the manufacturer regarding the purposes of any mode of operation.

FDA agrees that clinical use of the system should not be limited to the examples provided by the manufacturer. The manner of use and the decision to use a particular mode of operation are medical decisions. In addition, the requirements of the performance standard apply only to manufacturers and do not impose requirements on the users of such systems. The requirement at Sec. 1020.30(h)(5)(ii) has been modified to reflect that a manufacturer's descriptions of particular clinical procedures exemplifying the use of specific modes of operation do not limit when or how any mode may be used in actual clinical practice. . . .

. . . Executive Order 12866 directs agencies to assess all costs and benefits of available regulatory alternatives and, when regulation is necessary, to select regulatory approaches that maximize net benefits (including potential economic, environmental, public health and safety, and other advantages; distributive impacts; and equity). The agency believes that this final rule is consistent with the regulatory philosophy and principles identified in the Executive order. . . .

It is FDA's opinion that the amendments will offer public health benefits that warrant their costs. . . .

The principal costs associated with the amendments will be the increased costs to produce equipment that will have the features required by the amendments. FDA has made an estimate of potential cost. . . .

The benefits that are expected to result from these amendments are reductions in acute skin injuries and radiation-induced cancers. These benefits will result from two types of changes to the performance standard that should reduce patient dose and associated radiation detriment without compromising image quality.

The first type of change involves several new equipment features that will directly affect the intensity or size of the x-ray field. These are the requirements addressing x-ray beam quality, x-ray field limitation, limits on maximum radiation exposure rate, and the minimum source-skin distance for mini C-arm fluoroscopic systems. Almost all of the changes that directly affect x-ray field size or intensity will bring the performance standard requirements into agreement with existing international voluntary standards. To the extent that these requirements are included in voluntary standards that have a growing influence in the international marketplace, the radiological community has already recognized their benefit and appropriateness. Moreover, harmonization within a single international framework will eliminate the need for manufacturers to produce more than one line of products for a single global marketplace.

The second type of change that will be required by these amendments involves the information to be provided by the manufacturer or directly by the system itself that may be utilized by the operator to more efficiently use the x-ray system and thereby reduce patient dose. These new features are widely supported and anticipated by many knowledgeable users of fluoroscopic systems. Similar requirements were recently included in a new international voluntary standard. . . .

X-ray imaging is used in medicine to obtain diagnostic information on patient anatomy and disease processes or to visualize the delivery of therapeutic interventions. X-ray imaging almost always involves a tradeoff between the quality of the images needed to do the imaging task and the magnitude of the radiation exposure required to produce the image. Difficult imaging tasks may require increased radiation exposure to produce the images unless some significant technological change provides the needed image quality. Therefore, it is important that users of x-ray systems have information regarding the radiation exposures required for the images that are being produced in order to make the appropriate risk-benefit decisions.

Equipment meeting the new standards in the amendments will provide image quality and diagnostic information identical to equipment meeting current standards. Therefore, the clinical usefulness of the images provided will not change.... These amendments will result in x-ray systems having features that automatically provide for more efficient use of radiation or features that provide the physicians using the equipment with immediate information related to patient dose, thus enabling more informed and efficient use of radiation....

Projected benefits are quantified in table 3 of this document in terms of: (1) Collective dose savings, (2) numbers of lives spared premature death associated with radiation-induced cancer, (3) collective years of life spared premature death, (4) numbers of reports of fluoroscopic skin burns precluded, and (5) pecuniary estimates associated with the preceding four items....

Costs to manufacturers of fluoroscopic and radiographic systems will increase due to these proposals. FDA will also experience costs for increased compliance activities. Some costs represent one-time expenditures to develop new designs or manufacturing processes to incorporate the regulatory changes. Other costs are the ongoing costs of providing improved equipment performance and features with each installed unit....

. . . .

The cost-effectiveness of the final regulation using a 7–percent discount rate has a modal value of $184,400 within an estimated range of between $50,900 and $667,600 per cancer avoided....

NOTES

1. *CT Scanners.* As a result of the development and widespread use of computed tomography (CT) diagnostic x-ray systems, FDA revised the x-ray standard to include a section on this equipment. 45 Fed. Reg. 72204 (Oct. 31, 1980), 49 Fed. Reg. 34698 (Aug. 31, 1984), codified at 21 C.F.R. 1020.33.

2. *Mammography.* In the Mammography Quality Standards Act of 1992 (MQSA), 106 Stat. 3547, section 263b of the Public Health Service Act, 42 U.S.C. 2636, Congress gave FDA responsibility for certifying mammography (radiology of the breast) facilities. Under the statute, it is unlawful to operate any mammography facility in the United States, with the exception of a Department of Veterans Affairs facility, without FDA certification. To obtain FDA certification, a mammography facility must meet quality standards set forth in agency regulations and be accredited by an approved accreditation body. FDA's MQSA quality standards include requirements regarding the qualifications of facility personnel. 21 C.F.R. 900.12(a). They also include regulations concerning mammography equipment. *Id.* 900.12(b).

A mammography facility cannot be certified unless its equipment satisfies a wide variety of specific requirements, including, for example, image receptor sizes, light fields, and magnification. *Id.* Because the MQSA applies to almost all mammography facilities, these equipment quality standards are, as a practical matter, just as obligatory as device performance standards promulgated under FD&C Act 514 and radiation safety standards promulgated under FD&C Act 534. Radiographic equipment used in mammography is also directly subject to the radiation standards established by FDA for x-rays and radiographic equipment. 21 C.F.R. 1020.30, 1020.31. *See also* 21 C.F.R. 900.12(b)(2) (mandating that a mammography facility's equipment must satisfy these radiation safety standards).

3. *Baggage Screening Machines.* FDA regulations contain a separate performance standard for "cabinet x-ray systems," which include systems "designed primarily for the inspection of carry-on baggage at airline, railroad, and bus terminals, and in similar facilities." 21 C.F.R. 1020.40(a)(3).

––––––––

FDA has established a radiation safety standard for sunlamps and ultraviolet lamps intended for use in sunlamps. 42 Fed. Reg. 65189 (Dec. 30, 1977), 44 Fed. Reg. 65352 (Nov. 9, 1979), 21 C.F.R. 1040.20. The standard regulates "irradiation ratio limits," timer systems, shut-off switches, protective eyewear, lamp compatibility, and labeling. Ultraviolet lamps for tanning are also regulated as Class I medical devices. 21 C.F.R. 878.4635. This classification reflects the fact that FDA relies more on its radiation safety authorities than on its device authorities to regulate these products.

In the early 1980s, the rapid growth of commercial suntanning facilities led the agency to propose revisions to the radiation safety standard, to reflect the changes in product technology and design. 48 Fed. Reg. 22886 (May 20, 1983). The following excerpts from the preamble to the final rule focus on the labeling aspects of the proposed revised standard:

Sunlamp Products; Performance Standard

50 Fed. Reg. 36548 (September 6, 1985).

. . . .

FDA believes that irradiation of the skin with ultraviolet radiation to induce skin tanning is hazardous. The performance standard for sunlamp products was established to protect the consumer from acute burns (as evidenced by erythema) and from exposure to hazardous radiation that is unnecessary for skin tanning (in this case, UV radiation of wavelengths in air of less than 260 nanometers (nm)) and to warn the consumer of the known adverse effects to the body after exposure to ultraviolet radiation. FDA believes that the user of a sunlamp product can take appropriate action when informed of the possible adverse effects to the body from exposure to ultraviolet radiation, if the product is equipped with necessary safety performance features. . . .

A comment suggested that the warning statement required by § 1040.20(d)(1)(i) should utilize the signal word "CAUTION" rather than

"DANGER." The comment contended that the word "DANGER" implies an immediate and serious threat to life, a hazard not associated with UVA sunlamp products, *i.e.*, sunlamp products that operate in the wavelength region of 320 to 400 nm. The comment stated that there is a need for an appropriate warning label cautioning the user that certain safeguards need to be observed to avoid injury and that prolonged use has long-term risk.

The agency believes that the word "DANGER" as used on the warning statement is appropriate. Exposure to ultraviolet radiation can be an immediate threat to life for people using photosensitizing medications or cosmetics and for people with a medical condition that causes them to be sensitive to ultraviolet radiation, for example, photoallergies.

One comment urged that UVA lamps should be exempt from the provisions of § 1040.20(d) that require the warning: "As with natural sunlight, overexposure can cause eye and skin injury and allergic reactions. Repeated exposure may cause premature aging of the skin and skin cancer." The comment argued that radiation at wavelengths in air longer than 320 nm cannot induce skin cancer and that only radiation at wavelengths in air shorter than 320 nm is responsible for premature skin aging. The comment argued further that UVA radiation that does not contain measurable UVB radiation (280 to 320 nm) has positive effects, for example, a UVA tan can protect a person against the harmful UVB radiation of the sun. . . .

FDA disagrees that it has been proven that UVA does not cause skin cancer or premature skin aging, or that UVA radiation can protect humans against UVB radiation. Relatively few studies have been carried out on the long-term biological effects of UVA radiation in humans or in animals. Further studies are needed to establish clearly the long-term biological effects of UVA radiation. There are, however, reports that, under long-term continuous exposure, UVA radiation can induce skin cancer in test animals. Also, there is evidence that the incidence of skin tumors induced in animals by irradiation with a combination of UVB and UVA radiation can be increased by subsequent irradiation with UVA alone.

There is evidence that UVA radiation can enhance the photoreactivation of pyrimidine dimers in the DNA of human leukocytes. However, this effect has not been shown to provide humans protection against UVB radiation. The Task Force on Photobiology of the American Academy of Dermatology has expressed concerns about potential risks of tanning with UVA radiation.

Based on available evidence, FDA concludes that to exempt UVA lamps from the warning statement required by the standard would not promote the public health and safety.

One comment disagreed with the language of the warning statement set forth in § 1040.20(d)(1) of the proposed amendments and argued that the statement, "If you do not tan in the sun, you are unlikely to tan from the use of this product," would be inappropriate because it may confuse the sunlamp user. The comment argued that the action of direct exposure to the sun cannot be compared to that of exposure to either UVA or UVB suntanning equipment; that the current warnings already clearly and accurately provide the same information in more detail; and that the quoted statement would be redundant to the statement "Consult a physician before using lamp if taking any medication or if you believe yourself sensitive to sunlight."

The agency disagrees with the comment. The scientific literature clearly demonstrates that some people do not tan or that they tan only with great difficulty using either the sun or sunlamps. People who, when exposed to the sun, do not tan or tan only with great difficulty should be informed about the futility of exposures to potentially hazardous ultraviolet radiation....

Therefore, ... Part 1040 is amended ... [b]y revising § 1040.20, to read as follows:

§ 1040.20 Sunlamp products and ultraviolet lamps intended for use in sunlamp products.

(d) *Label requirements*....

(1) *Labels for sunlamp products*. Each sunlamp product shall have a label(s) which contains:

(i) A warning statement with the words "DANGER—Ultraviolet radiation. Follow instructions. Avoid overexposure. As with natural sunlight, overexposure can cause eye and skin injury and allergic reactions. Repeated exposure may cause premature aging of the skin and skin cancer. WEAR PROTECTIVE EYEWEAR; FAILURE TO MAY RESULT IN SEVERE BURNS OR LONG–TERM INJURY TO THE EYES. Medications or cosmetics may increase your sensitivity to the ultraviolet radiation. Consult physician before using sunlamp if you are using medications or have a history of skin problems or believe yourself especially sensitive to sunlight. If you do not tan in the sun, you are unlikely to tan from the use of this product."

NOTES

1. *Further Revisions?* In 1999, FDA published an advance notice of proposed rulemaking in which it stated its intent to propose amendments to the performance standard for sunlamp products. 64 Fed. Reg. 6288 (Feb. 9, 1999). The notice explained:

> The agency is taking this action to address concerns about the adequacy of the warnings on sunlamp products, current recommended exposure schedule to minimize risk to customers who choose to produce and maintain a tan, current labeling for replacement lamps, and current health warnings which do not reflect recent advances in photobiological research. FDA is soliciting comments and information from interested persons concerning the subject matter of the proposed amendments.

FDA has not followed up the advance notice with a proposed rule amending the standard.

2. *Violations of Sunlamp Standards.* In lengthy litigation, FDA successfully obtained an injunction and civil penalties for violations of the sunlamp standard in 47 separate suntanning booths. *Throneberry v. FDA*, 1983–1984 FDLI Jud. Rec. 242 (E.D. Tenn. 1983), 1983–1984 FDLI Jud. Rec. 382 (E.D. Tenn. 1984).

3. *Other Standards.* In addition to the x-ray and sunlamp standards, FDA has published radiation safety standards for a variety of other medical devices and common household articles, including, for example, television receivers, 21 C.F.R. 1020.10; microwave ovens, 21 C.F.R. 1030.10; medical and nonmedical laser products, 21 C.F.R. 1040.10–11; and ultrasonic therapy products, 21 C.F.R. 1050.10.

4. *Relationship to Device Statute.* The precise relationship between the standard-setting and premarket approval authority of the Medical Device Amendments and the Radiation Act's standard-setting authority is uncertain. It does seem clear that FDA is obligated to regulate radiation-emitting medical devices under the 1976 Amendments and has discretion to regulate them under the Radiation Act as well. Because all new radiation-emitting medical devices are subject to the premarket approval requirement of section 515, the agency may have few if any occasions to establish additional radiation safety standards for medical devices under the Radiation Act.

5. *Variances.* Under 21 C.F.R. 1010.4, FDA may, upon application of a manufacturer, grant a variance from all or part of any electronic product performance standard. After 20 years of publishing these variances in the Federal Register, many of them for laser light shows, FDA observed that it had never received comment on any of them and announced it was discontinuing publication. 53 Fed. Reg. 52683 (Dec. 29, 1988).

2. ENFORCEMENT OF RADIATION STANDARDS

The Radiation Act, now incorporated into the FD&C Act, provides FDA with various tools in addition to performance standards to ensure the radiation safety of electronic products. For example, section 537 states that FDA may inspect any "factory, warehouse, or establishment in which electronic products are manufactured or held" if the agency "finds for good cause that the methods, tests, or programs related to electronic product radiation safety in [the facility] may not be adequate or reliable." Section 537(a). The broad sweep of this provision is epitomized by FDA's declaration, on its website, that it may "inspect displays of laser light shows to ensure the public is protected. Producers of laser light shows are required to tell the FDA where they are planning a show so that the agency can inspect it if possible and take action if required." Frequently Asked Questions About Lasers, on FDA website. Electronic product manufacturers, and some dealers and distributors, are also subject to an array of records and reporting requirements, varying by product type. Section 537(b); 21 C.F.R. 1002.1 (chart).

Section 535(f) requires manufacturers of electronic products to notify purchasers when they discover safety defects related to the emission of radiation and to repair the defect, replace the product, or refund the cost. Section 535 (a) & (f). *See* 21 C.F.R. 1003.21 (notification to affected persons); 21 C.F.R. Part 1004 (repurchase, repairs, and replacement). When Congress gave these same additional authorities to FDA with respect to medical devices in the 1990 Act, the Radiation Act served as a model. *See supra* p. 1060.

For many years, the Radiation Act was the only statute administered by FDA that authorized civil penalties. As discussed in the chapter on enforcement, *infra* p. 1333, Congress has, since the 1980s, given FDA the power to impose civil penalties for an assortment of other types of violations, including, under the 1990 Act, violations of the FD&C Act's device requirements. There is an important distinction, however, between the civil penalties authorized by the Radiation Act and those authorized elsewhere. Under the Radiation Act, the United States must file an action in federal district court to obtain an order imposing civil money penalties, whereas under all the later civil penalty provisions, FDA can impose the monetary penalties itself, through administrative order, after notice and an administrative hearing.

FDA's civil penalties policy under the Radiation Act is set forth in Compliance Policy Guide No. 7133.23 (Mar. 1, 1983) (rev. Apr. 2005). CDRH has collected civil penalties for violations of the electronic product radiation control provisions in a few instances. *E.g., United States v. Hodges X–Ray Inc.*, 759 F.2d 557 (6th Cir. 1985) (holding that a company's president, as well as the company, may be held liable for civil penalties for violations of the x-ray standard); *Throneberry v. FDA*, 1983–84 FDLI Jud. Rec. 242, 382 (E.D. Tenn. 1983). Although the agency has not recently pursued civil penalties under the Radiation Act, it has sought and collected civil fines from mammography facilities under the Mammography Quality Standards Act. *See* HHS News, Mammography Facility Fined, Shut Down (Aug. 12, 1998); *In re Korangy Radiology Assocs.*, FDA Docket No. 2003H–0432 (Dec. 17, 2004).

3.   COLLECTION AND DISSEMINATION OF INFORMATION

Section 532(a) requires FDA to establish and carry out an "electronic product radiation control program designed to protect the public health and safety from electronic product radiation." As part of this program, the agency must not only develop and administer performance standards for electronic products, but also, for example, conduct, coordinate, and support testing and research and collect information from other agencies, industry, and professional organizations.

One important authority FDA has in this area is to "(A) collect and make available, through publications and other appropriate means, the results of, and other information concerning, research and studies relating to the nature and extent of the hazards and control of electronic product radiation; and (B) make such recommendations relating to such hazards and control as he considers appropriate." Pursuant to this provision, through the 1980s, FDA issued numerous recommendations relating to safe exposure to radiation. These recommendations were initially codified in the Code of Federal Regulations; 21 C.F.R. 1000.50 (1976) (recommendations for the use of gonad shields during x-ray); 21 C.F.R. 1000.55 (1979) (recommendations for quality assurance programs in diagnostic radiology facilities); 21 C.F.R. 1000.60 (1980) (recommendation against third-party requirements of dental x-rays with no clinical benefit to patient). In 1983, however, the agency ceased publishing its radiation exposure recommendations in the C.F.R. and instead started merely to announce their availability. Under this new system, FDA announced the availability of two additional recommendations: 50 Fed. Reg. 20011 (May 13, 1985) (quality assurance in nuclear medicine); 51 Fed. Reg. 6039 (Feb. 19, 1986) (minimizing diagnostic nuclear medicine exposure to the embryo, fetus, and breastfeeding infant.). *See also* 57 Fed. Reg. 41144 (Sept. 9, 1992) ("Suggested State Regulations for Control of Radiation").

CDRH apparently has not issued a radiation exposure recommendation or guidance document since 1992. Moreover, FDA has neither affirmed nor withdrawn the two radiation exposure recommendations it announced, but did not publish, in the Federal Register in the mid–1980s. Today, most of the guidance documents issued by the agency in the radiological health area concern manufacturer reporting requirements or procedures for the FDA field force. Occasionally, CDRH provides radiation exposure risk information and prevention advice on the FDA website. *See, e.g.,* HHS News, "FDA Issues Warning on Misuse of Laser Pointers" (Dec. 18, 1997); Whole Body Scanning Using Computed Tomography (last updated Apr. 17, 2002); Use of Wireless Communication Devices and the Risk of Brain Cancer (last updated Apr. 27, 2006).

FDA's primary initiative in the collection of radiological health data is a 25–year old survey program called the Nationwide Evaluation of X-ray Trends (NEXT). Under this program, CDRH collaborates with the Conference of Radiation Control Program Directors, an organization made up primarily of radiation professionals in state and local government. Each year, the NEXT program selects a particular radiological examination for study. State radiation control personnel then collect radiation exposure data from a nationally representative sample of U.S. clinical facilities, and CDRH compiles, analyzes, and publishes the survey results.

Because FDA has never had significant amounts of money to fund radiological health research and only occasionally publishes radiation exposure recommendations, the NEXT program and the issuance and administration of performance standards are today the most important components of the "electronic product radiation control program" mandated by section 532(a).

COMMENT: OTHER RADIATION CONTROL PROGRAMS

Several federal agencies in addition to FDA regulate exposure to radiation. While far from exhaustive, this comment describes some of these other authorities and their relationship to FDA's authority under the Radiation Act.

FCC. The Federal Communications Commission (FCC) authorizes and licenses products, transmitters, and facilities that generate radiofrequency (RF) and microwave radiation. The FCC does not itself develop radiation exposure guidelines, but instead adopts standards promulgated by other agencies and by private organizations. FCC and FDA both regulate wireless telephones. FCC ensures that all wireless phones sold in the United States follow safety guidelines that limit RF energy, while FDA monitors the health effects of wireless telephones. Each agency has the authority to take action if a wireless phone produces hazardous levels of RF energy.

NRC. The Nuclear Regulatory Commission (NRC), in addition to regulating the medical use of radioactive byproduct material, 10 C.F.R. Part 35, *see supra* p. 714, also regulates the manufacture and transfer of certain other types of products containing byproduct material. 10 C.F.R. Part 32.

FAA. Laser light radiation projected into navigable airspace, in connection with a laser light show or scientific operations, can damage the eyesight of aircraft pilots and passengers. The Federal Aviation Administration (FAA) and FDA have entered into a memorandum of understanding to coordinate their regulatory programs to prevent this danger. FAA–FDA Memorandum of Understanding (1998).

EPA. The Environmental Protection Agency (EPA), on its website, describes itself as "the primary federal agency for protecting people and the environment from harmful and avoidable exposure to radiation." EPA has authority to advise the president and other agencies on the health hazards of radiation under 42 U.S.C. 2021(h). It produces guidances and technical reports for use by both federal and state agencies responsible for radiation safety. EPA's other radiation protection activities include, among others: running radioactive waste management programs; disseminating information and issuing regulations concerning naturally occurring radioactive sources in the ground, air, and water; overseeing the cleanup of radioactive sites; and participating in nuclear emergency response plans.

Interagency Working Groups. Over the years, various interagency working groups have been established to address issues of radiation safety in a coordinated manner. For example, FDA, FCC, EPA, the National Institute for Occupational Safety and Health, the Occupational Safety and Health Administration, and the National Telecommunications and Information Administration currently participate in a working group regarding radiofrequency radiation safety.

CHAPTER VIII

COSMETICS

A. HISTORICAL AND STATUTORY BACKGROUND

Peter Barton Hutt, *A History of Government Regulation of Adulteration and Misbranding of Cosmetics*

In COSMETIC REGULATION IN A COMPETITIVE ENVIRONMENT (Norman F. Estrin & James M. Akerson eds., 2000).

The use of cosmetics began long before recorded history. The earliest cosmetics found by archaeologists are dated from about 10,000 B.C. Aboriginal societies have painted their bodies for centuries for a variety of reasons—as camouflage, a mark of status or achievement, for sexual attraction, to obtain spiritual protection, for community celebrations, and other purposes.

Historical evidence demonstrates widespread use of virtually all of the types of cosmetic products available today beginning about 5,000 B.C. in Egypt and later in ancient Greece and Rome. The best documentation of this comes from Pliny the Elder (23–79 A.D.), who recorded the use in Roman society of every form of cosmetic known to us today: hair dye, eyelash dye, eyebrow dye, freckle removers, rouge, deodorants and antiperspirants, depilatories, wrinkle removers, hair preservatives and restorers, bust firmers, sunburn products, complexion aids, moisturizers, mouthwashes and breath fresheners, toothpaste, face powder, and of course, perfume, to name only some. Pliny also described their sources, which were primarily readily available plant and animal materials.

From these ancient times to the present, cosmetics have continued to be widely used. Following Guttenberg's invention of the printing press in the fifteenth century, books began to appear on how to make and use cosmetics. At the same time, however, a Puritan movement was developing whose philosophy opposed the use of cosmetics. Books were published beginning in the late 1500s strongly criticizing those who sought to enhance their natural beauty. As the Puritan movement waned a century later, however, beauty specialists advertised their products and skills and cosmetic products appeared as commercial products in retail stores. Widely read books were also published advising women how to make their own cosmetics.

From 1700 on, cosmetic products of all types have been marketed and used throughout the world. The specific types of cosmetic products in greatest use at any time are influenced by current beauty and fashion trends and popular philosophy as well as personal taste. Some books stress the importance of personal appearance and others criticize any societal emphasis on beauty. Critics have attacked the cosmetic industry generally or offer selective reviews of particular products. Yet over the past century, hundreds of beauty books have been best-sellers, beauty magazines have been widely read, the founders of cosmetic companies and the models who appear in their advertising have become well-recognized celebrities, and a number of the largest and most successful consumer marketing companies have helped increase the annual retail sales of cosmetics in the United States from about $350,000 in 1850 to $7 million in 1900, $150 million in 1940, $1 billion in 1960 and close to $35 billion today.

———

FDA first acquired authority to regulate cosmetics in the 1938 Act. The safety of cosmetics, however, had been a concern in Congress as early as 1881. *See* H.R. Rep. No. 199, 46th Cong., 3d Sess. 2 (1881). Following the example of a Massachusetts statute (L. Mass. 1886, c. 171), Congress in 1898 amended the District of Columbia food and drug law to define the term "drug" to include cosmetics. 30 Stat. 246. The original 1897 bill to create a federal law similarly "included cosmetics in the definition of drugs, but this portion was dropped in 1900 as partial payment for support from the National Pure Food and Drug Congress." Oscar E. Anderson, *Pioneer Statute: The Pure Food and Drugs Act of 1906*, 13 J. PUB. L. 189, 195 (1964).

Senate Report No. 361

74th Congress, 1st Session (1935).

While the definition of the term cosmetic does not include devices, it is drawn in broad terms to include all substances and preparations, other than ordinary toilet or household soap, intended for cleansing, or altering the appearance of, or promoting the attractiveness of the person. Cosmetics may be used externally, orificially, or even internally as in the case of arsenic for clearing the complexion. The definition therefore must be sufficiently broad to cover potential abuses no matter how the substance or preparation is used. While soaps sold only for ordinary toilet or household use are specifically exempted from the definition of cosmetic and will not be subject to the definition of drug, soaps for which claims concerning disease are made or which are sold as pharmacopoeial articles will come within the definition of drug and will thus be subject to regulation. Likewise soaps intended for other than ordinary toilet or household use and represented, for instance, as beautifying agents, will come within the definition of cosmetic. . . .

Section [601(a)] deals with adulterated cosmetics. . . . There are on the market a number of preparations, notably hair dyes, eyelash and eyebrow dyes, complexion bleaches and depilatories, which have caused serious impairment to the health of users and, in a number of instances, have resulted in such injuries as blindness and paralysis. These injuries have been caused by such toxic substances as certain coal-tar dyes and metals like lead, arsenic, mercury, and thallium, upon which the beautifying "action" of the preparations depends. Paragraph (a) is intended to protect the user against such hazards to health.

It will be noted that in drafting this paragraph the same general form has been used, to avoid complications arising from allergic reaction to wholesome products, as was employed in dealing with food under section [401](a)(2).... [O]nly those products are considered as adulterated which contain poisonous and deleterious substances, and then only when those substances are present in such quantity which may render the product injurious. This would not prevent the marketing of a face powder or cream or any other cosmetic which did not contain poisonous or deleterious ingredients, even though such cosmetics might contain ingredients to which a certain class of unfortunate people are allergic....

Paragraph (a) of ... section [602] is identical with the general misbranding provision on food.... Paragraphs (b) and (c) ... are merely an extension to cosmetics of provisions in the food and drug chapters....

NOTES

1. *History.* For a broad history of cosmetic regulation, see Peter Barton Hutt *A History of Government Regulation of Adulteration and Misbranding of Cosmetics, in* Cosmetic Regulation in a Competitive Environment (Norman F. Estrin & James M. Akerson eds., 2000).

2. *Commentary.* For treatment of cosmetic regulation in historical context, see Hugo Mock, *Cosmetic Law: History and Observation*, 1 Food Drug Cosm. L.Q. 61 (1946). Accounts of the dangers of cosmetics which led to their inclusion in the 1938 Act may be found in Arthur Kallet & F. J. Schlink, 100,000,000 Guinea Pigs, Ch. V. (1933); Ruth deForest Lamb, American Chamber Of Horrors, Ch. 2 (1936). A defense of the industry was published by Everett G. McDonough, Truth About Cosmetics (1937).

3. *State Regulation.* The constitutionality of an early state law requiring the registration of cosmetic preparations was upheld in *Bourjois, Inc. v. Chapman*, 301 U.S. 183 (1937).

George P. Larrick,* *Some Current Problems in the Regulation of Cosmetics Under the Federal Food, Drug, and Cosmetic Act*

3 Food Drug Cosmetic Law Quarterly 570 (1948).

We do recognize that a great deal of progress has been made, but the principal object of this short talk is to emphasize the need for universal acceptance in the industry of the fact that a real scientific appraisal of the safety and suitability of materials used should be made before an ingredient is included in the composition of products designed to enhance the attractiveness of users. The same scientific approach should, of course, be followed in deciding what claims can legitimately be made....

---

* [Mr. Larrick was an FDA Associate Commissioner in 1948 and served as Commissioner from 1954 to 1965.]

There is still, in our opinion, too much secrecy concerning the precise composition of some ingredients of beautifying agents. We encounter instances wherein manufacturers or distributors of finished products do not know the composition of the preparations which they sell. . . .

This situation encourages changes in composition of the basic ingredients without the knowledge of the cosmetic firm. Scarcities or price variations are sometimes an invitation to change these compositions without notice. Occasionally, these circumstances have led to the introduction of dangerous ingredients. . . .

————

The Select Committee To Investigate the Use of Chemicals in Food Products, chaired by Representative James Delaney of New York, was established on June 20, 1950, pursuant to House Resolution 323, 81st Cong., 1st Sess. *See supra* p. 393. On October 15, 1951, the House extended the scope of the committee's authority to include "an investigation and study of the nature, extent, and effect of the use of chemicals, compounds, and synthetics in the production, processing, preparation, and packaging of cosmetics to determine the effect of the use of such chemicals, compounds, and synthetics upon the health and welfare of the Nation. . . ." A year later, the Delaney Committee issued its final report.

Investigation of the Use of Chemicals in Foods and Cosmetics

House Report No. 2182, 82d Congress, 2d Session (1952).

. . . The partial regulation of cosmetics . . . has appreciably decreased the incidence of serious harm, but insufficiently tested cosmetics still constitute a source of considerable annoyance, discomfort, and disability.

Under existing law, a dangerous cosmetic can be removed from the market by the institution of seizure proceedings. Unfortunately, the protection offered the public by this procedure is somewhat illusory. Before the government can avail itself of this remedy, data must first be assembled which will sustain the Government's burden of establishing to the satisfaction of a court and jury, by a preponderance of the evidence, that the cosmetic may cause injury to users. . . . It is clear that substances and combinations of substances have been used in cosmetics which, because of their injurious effects, would have been excluded if a law had existed requiring that adequate information concerning their safety be obtained before the cosmetics were sold to consumers. . . .

There is probably no cosmetic ingredient which can be used with impunity by every human being. In the case of virtually every cosmetic preparation, some particular person or limited number of persons may experience an unfavorable reaction, although all others may suffer no ill effects. Allowance must necessarily be made, therefore, for some incidence of untoward effects. . . .

1.   Pretesting

Most of the representatives of the cosmetic industry took the position that existing legislation was adequate to protect the public fully.... The incongruity of the position of some industry representatives is exemplified by their testimony that the companies they represent conduct rigorous and exhaustive tests, and maintain strict controls over their products, as a necessary precaution to protect both themselves and the health of their customers. Nevertheless, they were opposed to a requirement that all cosmetic manufacturers observe essentially the same safety standards....

... Your committee recommends ... that the Federal Food, Drug, and Cosmetic Act be amended to require that cosmetics be subjected to essentially the same safety requirements as now apply to new drugs. Under such an amendment, data would not be required to be submitted to the Food and Drug Administration with respect to cosmetics which are generally recognized by qualified experts as safe under the conditions of use for which they are sold....

2.   Soaps

... Soaps which have been on the market for years, and are generally recognized by competent authorities as being safe, would be unaffected by pretesting legislation. As indicated, however, inadequately tested hair shampoos have caused injury to the eye. There is an even greater possibility of injury from soaps containing new ingredients, for soaps are used to wash the face and, therefore, more readily make contact with the eye than do shampoos.... Your committee is of the opinion that the Federal Food, Drug, and Cosmetic Act is in need of amendment to bring soaps within the definition of cosmetics.

3.   Labeling of Ingredients

... Physicians who specialize in the fields of allergy and dermatology testified that the labeling of cosmetic ingredients would be most helpful in their diagnosis and treatment of patients who may be suffering from the effects of some cosmetic ingredient.... Industry representatives testified, generally, in opposition to the labeling of ingredients, on the ground that cosmetics are composed of a large number of ingredients and that a long list affixed to the product would destroy the attractiveness of the package. The committee recognizes the importance of packaging attractiveness in the sale of cosmetics, and that in some instances it would be most difficult to set forth on the label of a cosmetic preparation a list of its numerous ingredients. It is the committee's view, however, that a list of ingredients need not in all cases by physically affixed to the cosmetic. Where the number of ingredients is quite large, the list can be contained, in most instances, in the cosmetic package in the form of an accompanying circular....

4.   Coal–Tar Hair Dyes

Coal-tar hair dyes have long been a source of difficulty for cosmetic users. Paraphenylenediamine, a coal-tar color base for a large number of hair dyes, has a high sensitizing potential. There was considerable testimony that there have been reactions to this substance varying from slight dermatitis around the forehead, eyes, scalp, face, and neck, to generalized dermatitis requiring hospitalization....

Coal-tar hair dyes are permitted special privileges under [section 601(a)].... These provisions of the law have proven inadequate to provide the protection intended....

———

The cosmetic industry made the following response.

S.L. Mayham,* *Chemicals in Cosmetics*
7 FOOD DRUG COSMETIC LAW JOURNAL 184 (1952).

... The provisions of the present law, as they affect cosmetics, are entirely adequate to control any situation which is controllable with any type of law whatever....

... I have surveyed the 189 (and there are only 189) adjudicated cases on cosmetics since the enactment of the law in 1938. During those 13 years there have been 95 adjudicated cases brought under the adulteration provisions of the Act. One of these was won by the defendant, leaving 94 such cases. Of these 94 cases, only 59 were brought because of the presence of harmful or deleterious ingredients used in the manufacture of the cosmetics. The other 35 were because of the presence of filth, products being held under insanitary conditions, and for other reasons technically and legalistically classified as adulterations. Of these 59 which were brought because of the presence of a harmful ingredient, 22 came in the very early stages.... [L]et us be generous and say there were 34 cases where the presence of a chemical in a cosmetic was brought to court and proved to have done a harm.

This was over the period of 13 years since the law went into effect. During that time, the Toilet Goods Association has estimated that ... 26,301,000,000 packages of cosmetics [have been] sold and consumed in the United States. I contend that to find only 34 cases where harm has arisen from the presence of a poisonous ingredient in over 26 billion packages of cosmetics sold is not only *de minimis* but is really "much ado about nothing." ...

The first [proposal] is to write into the cosmetic section of the present law something akin to the new-drug application provision of the present law.... From my observation of the industry, I would say that more than two thirds of the present cosmetic manufacturers do not have sufficient resources to file one single new-cosmetic application should there be such a provision in the law....

The second proposal ... is to list all ingredients of every cosmetic on the label.... Let us look at this proposal for a moment and consider how it would work. First, I have examined a great many cosmetic formulas. Few of

* [Mr. Mayham was Executive Vice-President of The Toilet Goods Association, now renamed The Cosmetic, Toiletry, and Fragrance Association.]

them contain less than 15 ingredients and many of them contain 50 or more. Just where on the label or in the labeling would this list appear in distinguishable form? If you consider the perfume ingredients used in some of these products, you might well have to list 150 items on the label. The names of most of these would be completely unfamiliar to anyone who might want to read them. . . .

. . . [L]et us go back now for a moment to the lady who is allergic. She goes to a dermatologist who discovers that she is allergic possibly to lanolin, so she wants to avoid lanolin in cosmetics. If her dermatologist really knows his business he is aware of the fact that there are already a number of cosmetic manufacturers making hypo-allergenic cosmetics which exclude every possible known allergen and that these companies are willing to make up on special order at very, very reasonable prices cosmetics excluding the ingredients to which the individual may be allergic. So, the industry itself has made provision to take care of these cases of allergy and it would seem folly to insist on listing all the ingredients of a cosmetic, when absolutely nothing in the way of public protection would be accomplished by doing it. . . .

. . . I would call attention to the record of the hearings of the Delaney Committee to date. Practically every industry witness who has appeared has shown how carefully he insists upon control of the product from the time of purchase of the raw material until the ultimate consumer actually uses it. He tests the raw materials, he tests the products in process, he tests the finished product and he does so without any great love for the public, but because he knows that if a manufacturer puts out something that is harmful and poisonous he will not stay in business. . . .

A quarter of a century later, the issues dividing proponents and opponents of new cosmetic legislation had not changed.

U.S. General Accounting Office, Lack of Authority Hampers Attempts to Increase Cosmetic Safety

GAO Report No. HRD–78–139 (August 8, 1978).

About 125 ingredients available for use in cosmetics are suspected of causing cancer, according to studies. In addition, about 25 are suspected of causing birth defects and 20 may cause adverse effects on the nervous system, including headaches, drowsiness, and convulsions. . . . Although many of the reported adverse effects have not been verified, 12 of the ingredients are known to cause cancer in humans or contain impurities known to cause cancer in humans. Another 18 ingredients have been found to cause cancer in animals. . . .

Although there is increasing evidence that some cosmetic products and ingredients may carry a significant risk of injury to consumers, the Food and Drug Administration does not have an effective program for regulating cosmetics.... The act ... does NOT authorize the Food and Drug Administration to require manufacturers to

- register their plants or products,
- file data on the ingredients in their products,
- file reports of cosmetic-related injuries, or
- test their products for safety....

... [I]n 1972 and 1973 the agency asked cosmetic manufacturers, packers, and distributors to register their plants and file information on the ingredients used in their products and the injuries reported from their use. As of December 1977, about 40 percent of the manufacturers and packers had registered their plants; less than 20 percent of the manufacturers, packers, and distributors had filed ingredient listings, and less than 4 percent had filed injury reports. A Food and Drug Administration regulation requires that labeling of cosmetics that have not been adequately tested for safety include a warning to that effect. This regulation cannot be effectively enforced because the agency is not authorized to require manufacturers to test their products for safety or to make their test available to the agency. In addition, many manufacturers have refused Food and Drug Administration inspectors access to manufacturing records, such as qualitative and quantitative formulas, sales or shipping records, and consumer complaint files. The agency lacks authority to require that such records be made available....

The Food and Drug Administration has not inspected most manufacturers' plants or sampled most of their products for compliance with the Federal Food, Drug, and Cosmetic Act. Only about half the cosmetic establishments were inspected between fiscal years 1969 and 1975. Since 1975 the agency identified about 1,000 additional manufacturers, which it had never inspected because they had been unknown to the agency. The Food and Drug Administration also has not established criteria to determine whether adequate methods, facilities, and controls are used in all phases of manufacturing and distribution of cosmetics. According to an agency official, about 75 percent of a sample of over 300 firms inspected since 1976 had deficiencies in their manufacturing practices. Between 1974 and 1976 Food and Drug Administration inspectors and laboratories identified over 400 violations of the cosmetic provisions of the act which they believed warranted some form of regulatory action. Yet only 141 regulatory actions were taken; 54 involved 1 violative product. No prosecutions were started.

Establishing regulations to prohibit or limit the use of an individual ingredient or requiring the use of a specific warning on the label is an effective way to increase consumer safety with regard to a specific product or class of products. However, as of January 1, 1978, the Food and Drug Administration had established regulations governing the use of only 11 ingredients used in cosmetics and had required precautionary labeling only on feminine deodorant sprays, aerosols containing chlorofluorocarbon propellants, and aerosol cosmetics in self-pressurized containers....

Although the Food and Drug Administration cannot require cosmetic manufacturers to test the safety of their products, it can establish regulations identifying appropriate tests which should be used by manufacturers in evaluating safety. The agency said that development of appropriate tests is both difficult and resource demanding.

Some coal tar hair dyes may pose a significant risk of cancer to consumers because they contain colors known to cause or suspected of causing cancer in humans or animals. However, exemptions granted to coal tar hair dyes under the Federal Food, Drug, and Cosmetic Act prevent the Food and Drug Administration from regulating hair dyes effectively.... The Congress should repeal these exemptions....

———

The cosmetic industry again responded.

Statement of the Cosmetic, Toiletry and Fragrance Association, Inc.

"Cancer-Causing Chemicals—Part 1 (Safety of Cosmetics and Hair Dyes)," Hearings Before the Subcommittee on Oversight and Investigations of the House Committee on Interstate and Foreign Commerce, 95th Congress, 2d Session (January 26, 1978).

Cosmetic products have an enviable safety record. In September 1973, the panel on chemicals and health of the President's Science Advisory Committee issued a report published by the National Science Foundation which concluded with respect to cosmetics:

From what may be judged from human experience, the incidence of injury is small.

In the total pattern of environmental risks, those from cosmetics are both infrequent and slight.

While there are no formal pretesting or preclearance requirements for cosmetics, the total effect of individual and informal review—usually private rather than governmental—together with the innocuousness of most materials used, has made the injury rate fairly low by comparison with other widely prevalent sources of hazard.

It seems likely, though solid information is lacking, that the actual injury rate from cosmetics has declined, while the complaint rate has increased as a result of greater consumer awareness of the Food and Drug Administration as a regulatory agency, and of the existence of legal and insurance remedies.

Company records show that reactions to cosmetics are rarely serious and are almost invariably transient and reversible. We are unaware that any case of cancer has ever been shown to have been caused by any cosmetic....

The FDA regulation requiring ingredient labeling for cosmetics is effective. The regulation requires that all retail cosmetic packaging list the ingredients in descending order of predominance with the exception of flavor and fragrance. It is more informative than food ingredient labeling because it requires specific designation of color ingredients, and is far more informative than drug ingredient labeling which requires declaration only of active ingredients.

Any cosmetic which has not been adequately substantiated for safety prior to marketing is required by an FDA regulation to bear the warning statement that "the safety of this product has not been determined." . . . CTFA strongly supports the concept of safety substantiation, firmly believing that it is the obligation of every manufacturer and distributor not to market any cosmetic which has not been substantiated for safety. CTFA has not challenged the legal authority of FDA to promulgate its regulation requiring safety substantiation, and has over the years established many programs designed to help industry meet its obligation to the public even before it became a legal requirement. . . .

CTFA inaugurated its scientific program 30 years ago with the establishment of analytical standards for ingredients commonly used in cosmetics. In the past 10 years it has formed scientific committees of qualified experts to analyze and resolve scientific questions dealing with microbiology, pharmacology, and toxicology, quality assurance, color safety, hair coloring, ingredient nomenclature, and a wide variety of other subjects. CTFA regularly develops and disseminates standards for raw material specifications, testing methods, and ingredient descriptions, as well as technical guidelines to help insure the quality and safety of finished products.

CTFA initiated and submitted three major petitions to FDA, on the basis of which FDA has promulgated regulations governing voluntary registration of cosmetic product manufacturing plants, filing of cosmetic product formulas, and filing of cosmetic product experience reports. The following statistics reflect voluntary industry participation in these three programs as of September 30, 1977. About 900 cosmetic plants have been registered with FDA, representing about 85 percent of the volume of cosmetics sold in the United States. Some 23,500 cosmetic formulas have been submitted to FDA, representing about 80 percent of the volume of cosmetics sold in the United States. About 125 companies were participating in the product experience reporting program, representing about 50 percent of the volume of cosmetics sold in the United States. . . .

CTFA has recently undertaken a major program to review the safety of cosmetic ingredients. All available published and unpublished data on individual ingredients will be compiled and submitted for review by an independent expert panel of eminent scientists. The expert panel members have been required to meet the same strict conflict-of-interest standards as are applied to members of Federal Government advisory committees. The review process is modeled directly after current FDA safety review programs, and includes a consumer liaison selected by consumer organizations, an industry liaison, and an FDA contact person. . . .

NOTES

1. *Reprise.* The same debate was replayed a decade later. *See* "Potential Health Hazards of Cosmetic Products," Hearings Before the Subcomm. on Regulation and Business Opportunities of the House Comm. on Small Business, 100th Cong., 2d Sess. (1988).

2. *Legislative Proposals.* Since 1938, many bills have been introduced in Congress to amend and strengthen the cosmetic provisions of the FD&C Act. *See, e.g.*, Vincent A. Kleinfeld, *What Kind of Cosmetic Legislation?*, 19 FOOD DRUG COSM. L.J. 87 (1964); Vincent A. Kleinfeld, *The Role of Government in the Field of Cosmetics*, 20 FOOD DRUG COSM. L.J. 480 (1965); Selma M. Levine, *Cosmetics: Is New Legislation Needed?*, 29 FOOD DRUG COSM. L.J. 564 (1974); Vincent A. Kleinfeld, *Cosmetic Legislation: Benefit–Risk*, 29 FOOD DRUG COSM. L.J. 308 (1974); Joseph A. Page & Kathleen A. Blackburn, *Behind the Looking Glass: Administrative, Legislative and Private Approaches to Cosmetic Safety Substantiation*, 24 UCLA L. REV. 795 (1977). However, these proposals received serious consideration only in the Senate in 1974 and 1975. *See* "Cosmetic Safety Act of 1974," Hearings Before the Subcomm. on Health of the Senate Comm. on Labor and Public Welfare, 93d Cong., 2d Sess. (1974); "Cosmetic Safety Amendments, 1975," Hearing Before the Subcomm. on Health of the Senate Comm. on Labor and Public Welfare, 94th Cong., 1st Sess. (1975). Cosmetic legislation was reported out of committee, S. Rep. No. 94–1047, 94th Cong., 2d Sess. (1976), and passed the Senate, 122 CONG. REC. 24629 (July 30, 1976), but was never taken up by the House. *See also* "Cancer-Causing Chemicals—Part 1: Safety of Cosmetics and Hair Dyes," Hearings before the Subcomm. on Oversight and Investigations of the House Comm. on Interstate and Foreign Commerce, 95th Cong., 2d Sess. (1978).

3. *Enforcement History.* For a summary of the 205 notices of judgment in legal actions by FDA against cosmetics between 1938 and 1959, see James C. Munch & James C. Munch, Jr., *Notices of Judgment—Cosmetics*, 14 FOOD DRUG COSM. L.J. 399 (1959).

4. *Commentary.* For general discussion of the adequacy of FDA regulation of cosmetic safety, see Margaret Gilhooley, *Federal Regulation of Cosmetics: An Overview*, 33 FOOD DRUG COSM. L.J. 231 (1978); Thomas O. Henteleff, *A Cosmetic Legal Update*, 33 FOOD DRUG COSM. L.J. 252 (1978); Stephen H. McNamara, *FDA Regulation of Cosmetics in 1979: Industry Concerns*, 34 FOOD DRUG COSM. L.J. 236 (1979); Jacqueline A. Greff, *Regulation of Cosmetics That Are Also Drugs*, 51 FOOD & DRUG L.J. 243 (1996); Laura A. Heymann, *The Cosmetic/Drug Dilemma: FDA Regulation of Alpha–Hydroxy Acids*, 52 FOOD & DRUG L.J. 357 (1997); Bryan A. Liang & Kurt M. Hartman, *It's Only Skin Deep: FDA Regulation of Skin Care Cosmetics Claims*, 8 CORNELL J.L. & PUB. POL'Y 249 (1999); Nakia Elliott, *Cosmetic Regulation: The Case for Reform* (2006) and Sarah Schaffer, *Reading Our Lips: The History of Lipstick Regulation in Western Seats of Power* (2006), in Chapter X of the Electronic Book.

B.   DEFINITION OF "COSMETIC"

The definition of a "cosmetic," and its relation to the definition of a "drug," are discussed in Chapter II, *supra*.

C.   ADULTERATED COSMETICS

United States v. An Article of Cosmetic . . . "Beacon Castile Shampoo"

1969–1974 FDLI Jud. Rec. 160 (N.D. Ohio 1974).

As the case was finally submitted to me for determination, the claim of the Government narrowed to a contention that the article of commerce is adulterated in that it contains deleterious substances, namely, potassium oleate and Neutronyx 600, which may render it injurious to users under such conditions of use as are customary or usual. Thus the claim is based on the wording of Section 361(a), which declares that "a cosmetic shall be deemed to be adulterated (A) if it bears or contains ... any deleterious substance which may render it injurious to users under the conditions of use prescribed in the labeling thereof, or under such conditions of use as are customary or usual."

Government's counsel has correctly noted that the meaning of the words "may render the deleterious substance injurious" actually bears the same meaning as given or interpreted by the United States Supreme Court in the case of *United States vs. Lexington Mill and Elevator Company* [*supra* p. 363].... Further, I think it is correct and appropriate to observe and to determine here that the word "injurious" is understood to mean capable of causing physical harm when the cosmetic is rubbed or poured on or otherwise applied on the human body as intended. However, it is concluded that the physical harm which may result from the deleterious substance may be temporary as well as permanent.

However, if temporary, it should be objectively and medically demonstrable that it is damaging either externally or internally to a part of the body, including but not limited to the skin, tissues, or vessels of the body. It should be added that, as I construe the term, pain alone without objective injury would not be enough to establish the injurious character of the deleterious substance.

... Under the evidence in this case it develops that the potential harm of the subject Beacon Castile Shampoo relates to its full strength concentrate getting into the eyes of a human being. Hence it is essential to determine whether, within the second condition of 361(a), the Beacon Castile Shampoo is injurious to a user who is using the shampoo in a customary or usual manner. I, therefore, conclude that it is part of the government's burden of proof in this case to show that getting the full concentrate of shampoo into one's eyes would occur under a condition of use that is customary or usual.

There is no evidence in this record that shows exactly what condition of use is customary or usual in applying shampoo to the hair. But certainly the evidence in this record does not disclose any basis for inferring that one is likely to apply shampoo to the hair without water and, if so, that the full strength of the shampoo would trickle down undiluted into the eyes.... Similarly, I think there is no evidence here that it is a customary and usual use to apply the shampoo so closely to the eyes that it would enter the eye in a full concentrated condition.

But the Government's burden goes further. Assuming that full strength shampoo got into a user's eyes while washing his hair, it is my conclusion that it is the Government's further burden to show that the user would not then flush or wash out the eye in the customary and usual use of the shampoo.

The burden which I feel is imposed on the Government in this respect immediately takes us ... to the results of the Harris study.... [T]he

Harris report shows, with reference to each of the instillations, whether it be quarter strength, half strength, or full strength, that there was ocular burning and irritation. Surely, in the customary and usual use of shampoo, if by accident some shampoo got into one's eye and caused ocular burning and irritation, the autonomic response of a human being would be to wash out his eye. Hence the Harris report, the keystone of the Government's case, fails to show that it was conducted under circumstances that represented the customary and usual use of the Beacon Castile Shampoo.

The significance of the omission of washing as a step in the protocol of the Harris human studies becomes quite apparent when the Marzulli studies are considered together with Dr. Marzulli's oral testimony of last Saturday. Dr. Marzulli's tests of March 25th, 1970, showed corneal epithelial damage to the eye of one of two rabbits where eyes were washed 30 seconds after the instillation of full strength Beacon, and significant iritis of the eyes of two rabbits washed after 30 seconds. It was quite clear in Dr. Marzulli's testimony of last Saturday that these findings were regarded by him as essential to his conclusions, for he testified in substance as follows— and these are my notes, but in substance this is the way I took down his testimony:

> We were concerned that shampoo that causes damage despite washing should not be marketed. If an eye is unwashed and produces injury to the cornea, that shampoo should not be marketed. If, in addition, flushing the eye 30 seconds after does not prevent injury, that shampoo should not be marketed.

The absence of the washing step from the protocol of the Harris studies thus has this added result: It negatives the extrapolation of this key portion of the Marzulli rabbit studies, and thus the relevancy of the principal point in Dr. Marzulli's testimony is impaired.... Thus it is not the ocular burning that represents an injury.

There is also evidence in the human studies of mild-to-moderate injection of the conjunctiva; yet this is not deemed sufficient to constitute an injury within the contemplation of 361(a). Surely there are many soaps that might cause temporary redness to the conjunctiva, and yet I don't believe they would be subject to condemnation. Surely it is clear in the Harris studies that there is no injury to the iris of any of the 22 human subjects. And thus up to this point the human studies do not disclose any injury that I think would fall within the contemplation of 361(a).

There is, however, destruction of the corneal epithelium of Joan Hughes. This, it turned out, was a temporary destruction; and in accordance with the medical testimony that I received, the epithelium of Joan Hughes was reported by Dr. Harris as being restored in 72 hours. The evidence in the case seems to indicate that, when epithelium is destroyed, one third of it will be restored within the first 24 hours, the second third within the second 24 hours, and the third third within the third 24 hours.

This destruction of corneal epithelium is deemed to be and determined to be a sufficient injury to meet the meaning of the word "injurious" in 361(a), especially because there is certainly a basis for believing that there is a susceptibility to infection, though the evidence indicates that it is a very small possibility. And yet the possibility remains, and presumably within that very broad language of 361(a), the definition of "injurious," if there is a possibility of injury, this would constitute an injury within that term.

Then there were also two other persons of the 22 who had slight corneal staining, which is indicative of some slight corneal epithelial injury. But the significant point is that the injury of Joan Hughes occurred only when full strength shampoo was applied to her eye. And likewise, the slight corneal staining occurred only when the full strength Beacon shampoo was applied to the eyes of those two other subjects. . . . Thus the only evidence in this record that would sustain the Government's burden is the human studies as to the temporary injury that occurred to the cornea of Joan Hughes when full strength Beacon Castile Shampoo was applied to one of her eyes. Yet it is this full concentration that has previously not been proved by the Government, as I evaluate the evidence, as being shown to be a condition customary or usual in the use of a shampoo. . . .

On the entire record, as I previously have shown, the Government has not proved that the use of the full concentrate in a manner that would get into the human eye while shampooing the hair represents a customary and usual use of the shampoo. In fact, that in the usual and customary use of this shampoo the full shampoo has not gotten into the eyes of the user is certainly a fair inference to draw from the facts set forth in the stipulation.

Those facts show that the Claimant, Consolidated Royal Chemical Company, has manufactured and sold over two million gallons of shampoo of this formulation from August 11th, 1958, to the date of seizure in January, 1971. Approximately eight to ten million bottles of this product have been sold, usually in 16, 32 and 64 ounce containers. During this period neither Claimant nor its insurers received any claim of injury to the eyes of a user.

And, therefore, on the entire record, I conclude and determine that the Government has failed to establish its requisite burden of proof. . . .

NOTES

1. *Baby Shampoo.* On April 4, 1979, FDA's Associate Commissioner for Compliance sent the following letter to R. C. Stites, President, Johnson & Johnson Baby Product Company:

> On June 17, 1978, you submitted a petition requesting that the Commissioner of Food and Drugs propose regulations . . . defining the term "baby shampoo" for the purpose of cosmetic labeling and requiring that shampoos so designated comply with prescribed animal testing requirements to demonstrate ocular safety. . . . For the reasons stated below, the agency is denying your petition. . . .

> . . . Your petition contains no data to support the allegation that baby shampoos contain a deleterious substance that may render them injurious to babies' eyes under customary conditions of use. It simply notes society's emphasis upon the safety of products designed for use on babies and young children and asserts that baby shampoos should be subject to more stringent safety requirements. It is argued that baby shampoos may accidentally

spill into babies' eyes. While this may be true, you have not submitted data to support your conclusion. . . .

. . . You presented a 1976 consumer perception survey to support the allegation that a "baby shampoo" that is a potential eye irritant is misbranded because, to consumers, a "baby shampoo" is expected to be "more gentle and mild and less irritating to eyes and scalp than a product labeled 'shampoo.'" This comparative definition of the term "baby shampoo" is not adequately supported by the results of the survey. Furthermore, in our view, the survey results are undermined by the possibility of bias because an inherently comparison-oriented situation was used in conducting the survey. . . .

Finally, we agree that a rabbit eye irritation test similar to the one you propose would be capable of distinguishing between moderately or strongly irritating shampoos and those which possess little or no potential for ocular irritancy. However, it is generally recognized that the rabbit eye irritation test is not capable of making fine distinctions between degrees of irritancy. Our understanding of the standard your petition sets forth includes the requirement that "baby shampoos" are, among other characteristics, free of stinging and burning qualities. . . . These characteristics cannot be measured by the rabbit eye irritation test. . . .

21 CFR 10.30(e)(1) provides that the Commissioner shall review and rule upon a petition, taking into consideration, *inter alia*, the agency resources available to handle the category of subject matter involved and the priority assigned to the petition in relation both to the category of subject matter involved and the overall work of the agency. . . . This means that a petition such as yours must establish, by adequate supporting documentation, that a health problem exists which, in comparison with health problems that are currently being addressed by the agency, warrants the reallocation of FDA resources. Your petition fails to do this. . . .

Johnson & Johnson submitted a new citizen petition (FDA Docket No. 80P–0139/CP) on April 8, 1980, with additional information supporting its request that all baby shampoos be required to pass a standard rabbit eye safety test, but FDA again denied the petition on October 5, 1981, concluding that there was no basis for requiring baby shampoos to be safer than other shampoos, that no evidence demonstrated that baby eyes are different from adult eyes, and that available data did not demonstrate a significant difference between babies and other age groups in injury frequency from shampoos.

2. *Cosmetics for Children.* The U.S. Public Interest Research Group submitted a citizen petition to FDA requesting a ban on the use of xylene, toluene, and dibutyl phthalate in nail polish marketed for children under the age of 14. FDA Docket No. 2005P–0487/CPI (Dec. 6, 2005). FDA has taken no action on this matter.

3. *GMPs for Cosmetics.* On the need for cosmetic GMP regulations, see Edward Milardo, *Quality Assurance Guidelines—The Industry's Viewpoint*, 31 FOOD DRUG COSM. L.J. 105 (1976); Michael A. Pietrangelo, *Cosmetic Quality Assurance—Alias Cosmetic Good Manufacturing Practices*, 31 FOOD DRUG COSM. L.J. 167 (1976); John A. Wenninger, *Quality Assurance Procedures for the Cosmetic Industry—The FDA's Viewpoint*, 31 FOOD DRUG COSM. L.J. 101 (1976). CTFA submitted a citizen petition (FDA Docket No. 77P–0315) on July 28, 1977, requesting the promulgation of cosmetic GMP regulations. No action has been taken by FDA on this petition. FDA stated in October 1977 that it intended to propose GMP regulations with respect to preservative systems in mascara and other eye area cosmetic products, 42 Fed. Reg. 54837 (Oct. 11, 1977), but no action has been taken on this matter. Current FDA views with respect to cosmetic GMP are reflected in the yearly

revisions to the cosmetic provisions of the FDA Inspection Operations Manual and Compliance Program Guidance Manual and in cosmetic GMP guidance on the agency's website.

4. *GMPs for Cosmetic–Drugs.* In response to a CTFA comment urging that products that fall within both the cosmetic and the drug provisions of the Act be subject to different GMP requirements than other drug products, FDA defended the need for uniform drug GMP requirements:

> ... A number of comments, including a petition to the Commissioner, were received regarding the applicability of the proposed general CGMP regulations to a class of products identified as cosmetic-drug products and described as those which: (1) Meet the definitions of both "drug" and "cosmetic" under section 201 of the act; (2) represent a minimum health or safety risk; and (3) are marketed over-the-counter for regular and frequent consumer use without dosage limitations. Examples of these products are described as medicated skin creams, antibacterial soap, antiperspirants, and topical sunburn prevention products. Specifically, the comments requested separate CGMP regulations for this alleged class of drugs....
>
> The Commissioner has concluded that these regulations ... must apply to all products meeting the definition of drug products, whether the drug products are highly potent prescription drugs or are OTC drugs of the type described as "cosmetic-type." Past experience of the agency has demonstrated that the public has been put in a hazardous situation because of manufacturing errors in OTC products.... That many of the general CGMP regulations are applicable to and reasonable for the cosmetic-type drug products is evidenced by the fact that a majority of the specific suggestions submitted by the petitioner and others as applicable for cosmetic-type drug products duplicated in substance, a number of comments submitted by other OTC manufacturers and manufacturers of prescription drug products....

43 Fed. Reg. 45014, 45027–28 (Sept. 29, 1978).

5. *Commentary.* For an early FDA review of potential toxicity problems raised by cosmetics, see Arnold J. Lehman, *Toxicological Aspects of Certain Types of Cosmetics*, 15 FOOD DRUG COSM. L.J. 399 (1960).

In the course of the OTC Drug Review, *supra* p. 788, FDA determined that some ingredients used in both cosmetic and OTC drug products were unsafe, and it took action to ban these ingredients in both types of products.

Aerosol Drug and Cosmetic Products Containing Zirconium

42 Fed. Reg. 41374 (August 16, 1977).

... In the Federal Register of June 5, 1975 (40 FR 24328), the Commissioner proposed that any aerosol drug or cosmetic product containing zirconium is a new drug or an adulterated cosmetic....

The June 5, 1975 proposal was in response to a report submitted to the Commissioner by the over-the-counter (OTC) Panel on Review of Antiperspirant Drug Products. This panel concluded in their report that zirconium compounds have caused skin granulomas and toxic effects in the lungs and other organs of experimental animals and expressed concern about the potential toxicity of such compounds when used in humans over an extended period of time. Although extensive animal toxicity data were received, these data failed to provide a basis for establishment of a safe level for long-term use. The panel also concluded that the benefit likely to be derived from the use of zirconium-containing aerosol antiperspirants is unsupportable in view of the risks involved. . . .

Because it appears that conclusive testing to establish the safety of zirconium-containing aerosol antiperspirants would take years to accomplish, and because during that time millions of consumers would be unnecessarily subjected to risk, the Commissioner has decided to stop movement of these agents in interstate commerce until safety testing adequate for approval of a new drug application has been done, as recommended in the proposed rule making.

The available toxicological data indicate that zirconium compounds may be responsible for human skin granulomas as well as toxic effects in the lungs and other internal organs of test animals. Accordingly, these ingredients in aerosol formulations are not generally recognized as safe, and the Commissioner considers any drug product containing zirconium in aerosol form to be a new drug. Furthermore, the Commissioner believes that the available information is sufficient to show that aerosol cosmetic products containing zirconium may be injurious to users. The regulation as proposed stated that regulatory action was being taken with respect to cosmetic products "[b]ased upon the lack of toxicological data adequate to establish a safe level for use. . . ." The final regulation relating to cosmetic products has been revised to delete this phrase, to identify the risks from zirconium use that are of concern, and to refer to the statutory test for determining when a product is adulterated. . . .

§ 700.16   Use of aerosol cosmetic products containing zirconium

(a) Zirconium-containing complexes have been used as an ingredient in cosmetics and/or cosmetics that are also drugs, as, for example, aerosol antiperspirants. Evidence indicates that certain zirconium compounds have caused human skin granulomas and toxic effects in the lungs and other organs of experimental animals. When used in aerosol form, some zirconium will reach the deep portions of the lungs of users. The lung is an organ, like skin, subject to the development of granulomas. Unlike the skin, the lung will not reveal the presence of granulomatous changes until they have become advanced and, in some cases, permanent. It is the view of the Commissioner that zirconium is a deleterious substance that may render any cosmetic aerosol product that contains it injurious to users. . . .

NOTES

1. *Other Ingredients Banned from Cosmetics.* Other substances banned by FDA under the cosmetic adulteration provisions of the FD&C Act are listed at 21 C.F.R. 700.11–700.11–23. Examples include: hexachlorophene, 37 Fed. Reg. 219 (Jan. 7, 1972), 37 Fed. Reg. 20160 (Sept. 27, 1972); vinyl chloride, 39 Fed. Reg.

14215 (Apr. 22, 1974), 39 Fed. Reg. 30830 (Aug. 26, 1974); halogenated salicylanilides, 39 Fed. Reg. 33102 (Sept. 13, 1974), 40 Fed. Reg. 50527 (Oct. 30, 1975); chloroform, 41 Fed. Reg. 15026 (Apr. 9, 1976), 41 Fed. Reg. 26842 (June 29, 1976); chlorofluorocarbon propellants, 41 Fed. Reg. 52070 (Nov. 26, 1976), 42 Fed. Reg. 24536 (May 13, 1977), 43 Fed. Reg. 11301 (Mar. 17, 1978); and methylene chloride, 54 Fed. Reg. 27328 (June 29, 1989). FDA also proposed to ban 2–mercaptoimidazoline, 39 Fed. Reg. 15306 (May 2, 1974), and trichloroethylene 42 Fed. Reg. 49467 (Sept. 27, 1977). Both of these proposed regulations were withdrawn by FDA in 56 Fed. Reg. 67440 (Dec. 30, 1991).

2. *Cattle Materials.* Because of the concern about transmission of "mad cow disease" (bovine spongiform encephalopathy), FDA banned specified cattle materials from use in cosmetics and promulgated recordkeeping requirements to enforce the ban. 69 Fed. Reg. 42256 & 42275 (July 14, 2004), 70 Fed. Reg. 53063 (Sept. 7, 2005), 71 Fed. Reg. 59653 (Oct. 11, 2006), codified at 21 C.F.R. 700.27.

3. *OTC Drug Review.* The impact of the OTC Drug Review on the status of substances also used in cosmetic products is discussed in Robert P. Giovacchini, *The Significance of the Over-the-Counter Drug Review with Respect to the Safety Considerations of Cosmetic Ingredients*, 30 FOOD DRUG COSM. L.J. 223 (1975); Gary L. Yingling, *The Effect of the FDA's OTC Drug Review Program on the Cosmetic Industry*, 33 FOOD DRUG COSM. L.J. 78 (1978).

4. *Tattoos.* FDA has issued a formal advisory opinion stating that dyes and pigments for temporary or permanent tattooing are both color additives and cosmetics, and are not drugs. *See* letter from John Taylor, Associate Commissioner for Regulatory Affairs, FDA, to Robert E. Carpenter, Docket No. 81A–0315/AP (July 21, 1986). The agency has taken no action to enforce that position. *See* Carrie Griffin, *Henna Tattooing: Cultural Tradition Meets Regulation* (2002), in Chapter X of the Electronic Book. FDA has placed information on tattoos and permanent markup on its website and has on occasion issued consumer alerts about these products. *E.g.*, "FDA Alerts Consumers About Adverse Events Associated With 'Permanent Makeup'," FDA Talk Paper No. T04–20 (July 2, 2004). Regulation of tattooing varies widely among the states. Robert Louis Stauter, *Tattooing: The Protection of the Public Health*, 6 HEALTH MATRIX, No. 2 (1988).

5. *Cosmetics Sold at Flea Markets and Electronic Auctions.* In a letter from Linda M. Katz, Director, FDA CFSAN Office of Cosmetics and Colors, to Peter Barton Hutt (Nov. 25, 2003), the agency confirmed that cosmetic products resold at flea markets and electronic auctions are held to full compliance with all requirements under the FD&C Act.

6. *EC Regulation.* The European Community adopted Council Directive 76/768/EEC relating to cosmetic products, which requires that cosmetic products "must not be liable to cause damage to human health when they are applied under normal conditions of use." OFFICIAL JOURNAL OF THE EUROPEAN COMMUNITIES No. L 262, at 169 (July 27, 1976). In contrast to the United States, where the only cosmetic ingredients requiring approval before they may be used are color additives, the EC directive adopts a listing approach for all cosmetic ingredients. Thus, the EC has issued several annexes listing provisional, permanent, and restricted (including banned) substances, and substances left to regulation by individual countries.

7. *Environmentally Protected Ingredients.* On occasion, ingredients are prohibited from cosmetics for reasons other than safety. The use of spermaceti (a substance taken from the oil in the head of a sperm whale or dolphin) is prohibited under the Mammal Protection Act of 1972 and the Endangered Species Act of 1973.

At the same time that FDA expressed concern about the safety of nitrosamines in the food supply, *supra* p. 421, the agency sought to control their occurrence in cosmetics.

Nitrosamine–Contaminated Cosmetics; Call for Industry Action; Request for Data

44 Fed. Reg. 21365 (April 10, 1979).

The agency is concerned about contamination of cosmetic products with nintrosamines, particularly N-nitrosodiethanolamine (NDELA)....

Some nitrosamines are potent animal carcinogens. The carcinogenicity of NDELA at high dose levels has been established in two animal species....

A limited number of cosmetic products have been analyzed for NDELA in both private and FDA laboratories. A number of these products were found to be contaminated with NDELA. The contamination is believed to be caused by the chemical reaction between the amines used to formulate the products and a nitrosating agent.... Analytical methods for identifying nitrosamines such as NDELA at concentrations of parts per million (ppm) and parts per billion (ppb) are quite new.... Analyses were made of 29 cosmetics thought likely to contain such contamination. It was found that 27 of the 29 contained up to 48 ppm of NDELA....

Recent studies have also been conducted in FDA laboratories to determine whether NDELA penetrates the skin. The agency now has evidence that NDELA penetrates excised human skin from an aqueous vehicle. One study that has been completed demonstrated that NDELA penetrates the skin of live monkeys....

The Commissioner of Food and Drugs has therefore determined that cosmetics containing nitrosamines may be considered adulterated under section 601 of the Federal Food, Drug, and Cosmetic Act. Cosmetic manufacturers are put on notice that cosmetic products may be analyzed by FDA for nitrosamine contamination and that individual products could be subject to enforcement action. However, the Commissioner is still considering whether a compliance program is needed to reduce or eliminate nitrosamine contamination in cosmetics, and, if so, what the nature of the program should be. Three factors will influence the Commissioner's decision on how to proceed in this matter:

1. The results of FDA's continuing efforts to understand better the nature of the problem and the means of reducing or preventing it....

2. The extent to which the public health risk is alleviated by industry reformulation of products.

3. The results of FDA's continuing efforts to determine the extent of the formation of, and human exposure to, nitrosamines in cosmetics....

NOTES

1. *Nitrosamines.* FDA has continued to express concern about nitrosamines in cosmetics (as well as in food and drugs), but it has not adopted a specific tolerance

level or taken formal regulatory action against products containing nitrosamines. The Cancer Prevention Coalition petitioned FDA in 1996 to require a cancer warning on the label of any cosmetic containing diethanolamine (DEA), a commonly used ingredient, because it could react with nitrosating agents to form nitrosomines (FDA Docket No. 96P–0404). FDA has taken no action on this petition.

2. *Alpha Hydroxy Acid Labeling.* Because of concern that cosmetic products containing alpha hydroxy acids may increase skin sensitivity to the sun, FDA issued a guidance on a labeling statement for these products alerting consumers to take appropriate action. 67 Fed. Reg. 71577 (Dec. 2, 2002), 70 Fed. Reg. 1721 (Jan. 10, 2005).

3. *Enforcement History.* The following summary illustrates the variety of circumstances in which FDA has brought court enforcement action or requested recalls to protect consumers against unsafe cosmetics:

> Early in 1978, FDA received about 50 complaints of hair breakage and scalp irritation associated with a hair straightener. An investigation disclosed that a compounding error had resulted in one batch of the product containing 60% more than the intended level of free caustic (sodium hydroxide). During the course of the FDA investigation the firm recalled the product.

> In 1974 consumer complaints of fingernail injuries associated with the use of certain nail extenders led FDA to investigate the problem. It was determined that the methyl methacrylate monomer used in these products was causing the injuries. The FDA obtained a court order to seize the offending product. Similar products were voluntarily recalled by the distributors and some have since been reformulated....

> During 1976 and 1977, a number of consumer complaints that a nail hardener had caused serious allergic and irritant effects were received. An investigation and subsequent laboratory analyses demonstrated that the product contained formaldehyde at a potentially harmful concentration. The product was seized in August 1977.

> Fifteen consumer complaints of axillary irritation from a new deodorant were received during 1976. During the course of the investigation of the problem, FDA was notified by the firm that distribution of the product had been terminated. The adverse experiences reported to FDA were not serious enough to warrant regulatory action.

> During 1976–1978 an unusually large number of consumer complaints concerning one brand of suntan product were received. The ensuing investigation disclosed that the firm also had received many complaints. Many of the adverse experiences appeared to be a form of photocontact dermatitis. Research sponsored by the firm and investigations by FDA identified 6–methylcoumarin (6–MC), a fragrance ingredient in the suntan products, as a potent photocontact allergen.

> When FDA learned that 6–MC was commonly used in suntan or sunscreen products, telegrams were sent to all known domestic firms which either market suntan/sunscreen products or distribute fragrance compounds to the cosmetics industry, requesting that they immediately terminate the use of 6–MC in all topical products and recall existing stocks of suntans or sunscreen products containing 6–MC....

Martin Greif et al., *Cosmetics Regulation*, 7 FDA BY-LINES 331, 333–334 (Sept. 1979).

4. *Child Resistant Packaging.* Because of a report of accidental poisoning from ingestion of a solvent product intended for use in the removal of sculptured nails, E. Martin Caravati & Toby L. Litovitz, *Pediatric Cyanide Intoxication and Death from an Acetonitrile–Containing Cosmetic*, 260 J.A.M.A. 3470 (1988), CTFA submitted a petition and the Consumer Product Safety Commission promulgated a regulation requiring child-resistant packaging under the Poison Prevention Packaging Act to protect against accidental ingestion of acetonitrile contained in glue removers. 55 Fed. Reg. 1456 (Jan. 16, 1990), 55 Fed. Reg. 51897 (Dec. 18, 1990), codified at 16 C.F.R. 1700.14(a)(18). The Drug and Household Substance Mailing Act of 1990, 104 Stat. 1184, prohibits the mailing of any cosmetic that fails to comply with an applicable requirement for child-resistant packaging.

5. *Opposition to Animal Testing.* Paradoxically, at the same time that the public and FDA are demanding greater assurance of safety of all FDA-regulated products, animal rights activists are demanding an end to the type of animal testing used to evaluate product toxicity. The cosmetic industry has been a principal target of the animal rights proponents. For a discussion of the issues involved, see NATIONAL ACADEMY OF SCIENCES, USE OF LABORATORY ANIMALS IN BIOMEDICAL AND BEHAVIORAL RESEARCH (1988); OFFICE OF TECHNOLOGY ASSESSMENT, ALTERNATIVES TO ANIMAL USE IN RESEARCH, TESTING, AND EDUCATION, OTA–BA–273 (1986); articles in Chapter I(J) of the Electronic Book. Faced with these attacks, some cosmetic industry officials have promised to end animal testing, and some firms have promoted their products as not tested on animals (*e.g.*, "beauty without cruelty"). In a decision handed down in December 1988 by a Higher Regional Court in Frankfurt, Germany, however, the representation of "beauty without cruelty" was held to be misleading, and thus illegal, unless the manufacturer can demonstrate that neither the finished product nor any of the ingredients has *ever* been tested in animals by itself or by anyone else. Such a showing would be impossible for any ingredient in any consumer product.

6. *Mailing Fragrances.* The Drug and Household Substance Mailing Act of 1990, 104 Stat. 1184, prohibits the mailing of any fragrance advertising sample unless it is sealed or otherwise prepared to prevent individuals from being unknowingly or involuntarily exposed to the sample.

7. *California Statute.* The California Safe Cosmetics Act of 2005, California Health and Safety Code Division 104, Part 5, Chapter 7, Article 3.5, Section 111791, requires companies with aggregate worldwide cosmetic sales of more than $1 million to submit to the state a list of any cosmetics sold in California that contain an ingredient listed by the state as causing cancer or reproductive harm. The state is authorized to investigate the safety of any product containing a listed ingredient and to require manufacturers to submit pertinent requested information. The results of an investigation may be referred to the California Division of Occupational Safety and Health, which is required to establish occupational health standards if an ingredient poses an occupational safety hazard.

D. MISBRANDED COSMETICS

1. LABEL WARNINGS

FDA has no specific statutory authority to require label warnings for cosmetics. Under Sections 201(n) and 602(a) of the FD&C Act, however, the agency has determined that the failure of a label to bear an appropriate warning constitutes misbranding.

Preservation of Cosmetics Coming in Contact With the Eye: Intent to Propose Regulations and Request for Information

42 Fed. Reg. 54837 (October 11, 1977).

... FDA has received several reports of corneal ulceration associated with the use of cosmetic mascaras containing pathogenic microorganisms.... Mascaras can become contaminated with various microorganisms when the consumer uses the product and re-inserts the applicator wand into the container after application of the mascara to the eye lashes. The re-insertion of the applicator wand into the mascara is part of the intended or customary conditions of use of the products. Without an adequate preservative system, microorganisms introduced into the mascara with the applicator wand can survive and multiply inside the container. When the mascara is used again, if the microorganisms on the applicator wand come into contact with a scratched or damaged cornea, the eye may become infected....

The reported incidents all involve mascaras in which the microorganism *Pseudomonas aeruginosa* has been found. *Pseudomonas aeruginosa* is an ubiquitous bacterium that may be present on the skin as a transient microorganism. It may readily grow in a cosmetic unless the cosmetic contains a preservative adequate to prevent contamination. *Pseudomonas aeruginosa* infections, if not recognized and treated immediately, can cause corneal ulceration that leads to partial or total blindness in the injured eye....

The Commissioner believes that the preservative systems used in mascara and other eye-contact products should be adequate not only to prevent the further growth of microorganisms introduced during use but also to reduce significantly the number of microorganisms introduced during use. The Commissioner expects to promulgate all-inclusive regulations delineating good manufacturing practice for cosmetics at some point, and he intends to propose regulations regarding microbial preservation of cosmetics coming in contact with the eye as a first step....

The Commissioner also advises that he considers inadequately preserved cosmetics to be in violation of the Act. Under section 601 of the act, a cosmetic is considered adulterated if it is prepared under conditions whereby it may have been rendered injurious to health, as well as if it bears any poisonous or deleterious substance that may render it injurious to users under the conditions of use. Furthermore, under sections 201(n), 601, and 602 of the act and 21 CFR 740.10, the label must bear any warning statements that are necessary or appropriate to prevent a health hazard that may be associated with the product. Manufacturers and distributors should be advised that FDA ... does not intend to await the completion of the rule making proceeding announced in this notice of intent before taking needed regulatory action....

NOTES

1. *Update.* FDA has taken no further action on this matter.

2. *Commentary. See* Anthony D. Hitchins, *Cosmetic Preservatives and Safety*, 57 J. Ass. of Food and Drug Officials, No. 3, at 42 (July 1993).

In addition to requiring specific cosmetic product warnings, FDA has promulgated 21 C.F.R. 740.10, a generic requirement that a warning appear on the label of all cosmetics whose safety has not been adequately substantiated.

Food, Drug, and Cosmetic Products: Warning Statements

40 Fed. Reg. 8912 (March 3, 1975).

The Commissioner of Food and Drugs is establishing required warnings for certain food, drug, and cosmetic products. Products packaged in self-pressurized containers are required to bear warnings to ensure their safe use and storage. Aerosol products containing halocarbon or hydrocarbon propellants are required to bear warnings against the dangers of deliberate concentration and inhalation. Cosmetic products whose safety has not been adequately substantiated are required to warn of that fact on the label. . . .

The Commissioner concludes that section 201(n) of the act applies in those situations where abuse has become sufficiently frequent to constitute a hazard of widespread public concern. Section 201(n) of the act is applicable to require affirmative disclosures in the light of representations and also to reveal consequences of customary or usual conditions of use. The very act of representing a product for food, drug, or cosmetic use constitutes an inherent implied representation of its safety. Warnings to ensure safe use are therefore within the scope of section 201(n) of the act. Moreover, the customary or usual conditions of use of such products often involve little or no protection against their misuse, where no warning exists. Accordingly, section 201(n) of the act is applicable to assure that consumers will understand, and guard against, the potential consequences of inadvertent misuse under conditions of such customary or usual conditions of use. In addition, the Commissioner advises that "conditions of use" is not a narrow term limited to the active handling, operation, and application of a product, but rather includes the entire setting and circumstances in which a product is used. The usual conditions of use of aerosol products are, that once purchased, they are freely available to all members of a household. Thus, warnings against misuse of aerosol products may alert parents of adolescent children to take precautions to ensure that such products in the household are not misused. . . .

The availability of section 201(n) of the act to require an explicit warning against misuse was upheld in *United States v. 12 Bottles of Esterex* (E.D. Mo. 1946), reported in V. Kleinfeld & C. Dunn, Federal Food, Drug and Cosmetic Act 1938–1949 at 523, 525. . . .

Several comments request clarification of the term "adequately substantiated for safety" as used in § 740.10.

The Commissioner advises that the safety of a product can be adequately substantiated through (a) reliance on already available toxicological test data on individual ingredients and on product formulations that are similar in composition to the particular cosmetic, and (b) performance of any additional toxicological and other tests that are appropriate in the light of such existing data and information. Although satisfactory toxicological data may exist for each ingredient of a cosmetic, it will still be necessary to conduct some toxicological testing with the complete formulation to assure adequately the safety of the finished cosmetic. . . .

The Commissioner recognizes that a manufacturer of a cosmetic ingredient cannot always foresee, much less control, the uses of the ingredient in cosmetic products, and therefore cannot be held responsible for the safety of the ingredient under every possible condition of use. The manufacturer is responsible, however, for the safety of the ingredient under the conditions of use recommended in its labeling as well as reasonably expected related uses, and the safety of the ingredient must be adequately substantiated for use under these conditions if the label does not bear the warning statement required by § 740.1. . . .

One comment argued that substantiation of safety amounts to premarketing review of cosmetics since the manufacturer would have to meet the "vague" standard of adequate substantiation for safety before his cosmetics could be marketed, and would bear the burden of meeting this standard in a court review.

. . . It is the manufacturer, not the Food and Drug Administration who is responsible for having his product in compliance with the act and regulations promulgated thereunder. The act necessarily contemplates that the manufacturer has assured itself of the safety of its product, but in no way does this imply Food and Drug Administration approval or review prior to marketing. . . .

Part 740—Cosmetic Product Warning Statements

§ 740.1   Establishment of warning statements

(a) The label of a cosmetic product shall bear a warning statement whenever necessary or appropriate to prevent a health hazard that may be associated with the product.

(b) The Commissioner of Food and Drugs, either on his own initiative or on behalf of any interested person who has submitted a petition, may publish a proposal to establish or amend, under Subpart B of this part, a regulation prescribing a warning for a cosmetic. . . .

§ 740.10   Labeling of cosmetic products for which adequate substantiation of safety has not been obtained

(a) Each ingredient used in a cosmetic product and each finished cosmetic product shall be adequately substantiated for safety prior to marketing. Any such ingredient or product whose safety is not adequately substantiated prior to marketing is misbranded unless it contains the following conspicuous statement on the principal display panel:

Warning—The safety of this product has not been determined.

(b) An ingredient or product having a history of use in or as a cosmetic may at any time have its safety brought into question by new information that in itself is not conclusive. The warning required by paragraph (a) of this section is not required for such an ingredient or product if:

(1) The safety of the ingredient or product had been adequately substantiated prior to development of the new information;

(2) The new information does not demonstrate a hazard to human health; and

(3) Adequate studies are being conducted to determine expeditiously the safety of the ingredient or product.

(c) Paragraph (b) of this section does not constitute an exemption to the adulteration provisions of the act or to any other requirement in the act or this chapter.

§ 740.11   Cosmetics in self-pressurized containers

(a)(1) The label of a cosmetic packaged in a self-pressurized container and intended to be expelled from the package under pressure shall bear the following warning:

Warning—Avoid spraying in eyes. Contents under pressure. Do not puncture or incinerate. Do not store in temperature above 120 F. Keep out of reach of children.

. . . .

NOTES

1. *Judicial Affirmance.* FDA's aerosol warning was upheld in *Cosmetic, Toiletry and Fragrance Ass'n, Inc. v. Schmidt*, 409 F. Supp. 57 (D.D.C. 1976).

2. *Feminine Deodorant Sprays.* At the same time, FDA prescribed a warning statement for feminine deodorant sprays. 38 Fed. Reg. 16236 (June 21, 1973), 40 Fed. Reg. 8926 (Mar. 3, 1975), codified at 21 C.F.R. 740.12. FDA concluded that "the reported adverse reactions do not demonstrate a health hazard which is serious enough to justify removal of these products from the market" but agreed with comments that "these sprays offer no medical usefulness or hygienic benefits" and therefore stated that the use of the term "hygienic" would render the products misbranded under Section 602(a).

3. *Talcum Powders.* A citizen petition (No. 83P–0404) submitted on December 2, 1983, requesting FDA to require a label warning for cosmetic talcum powders because of their potential asbestos content, was denied by FDA on July 21, 1986.

4. *Bubble Bath.* The need for a label warning for bubble bath products provoked dispute between FDA and the cosmetic industry for a full decade. FDA proposed a label warning about irritation of the skin and urinary tract from bubble bath products in 42 Fed. Reg. 5368 (Jan. 28, 1977). Manufacturers responded that the incidence of problems was trivial. Nonetheless, FDA promulgated a final regulation requiring a warning, stating that the number of reported reactions was "sufficiently large enough to indicate a public hazard." 45 Fed. Reg. 55172 (Aug. 19,

1980), codified at 21 C.F.R. 740.17. In response to an industry petition, FDA stayed the regulation and requested further comment in 48 Fed. Reg. 7169 and 7203 (Feb. 18, 1983). After further comment, FDA reinstated the warning but excluded products labeled exclusively for adults. 51 Fed. Reg. 20471 (June 5, 1986). Industry again petitioned FDA for reconsideration, but the petition was denied and the regulation became effective.

5. *Disclosure to Dermatologists.* It is common practice for cosmetic companies to provide the components of their products to dermatologists to use in skin patch tests on patients to determine sensitivity to particular substances. *See* Cyril H. March, *Editorial: Cosmetic Formula Information*, 216 J.A.M.A. 1337 (May 24, 1971); CTFA, COSMETIC INDUSTRY ON CALL (annual publication providing dermatologists with contact information for company personnel who can provide these components). FDA encourages this practice. 21 C.F.R. 720.4(b)(4). In 51 Fed. Reg. 33664 (Sept. 22, 1986), FDA took the position that all skin patch test kits "intended for commercial marketing" are drugs or biologics that require FDA approval. The "commercial marketing" proviso allows cosmetic companies to continue their present practice.

6. *Failure to Warn as Misbranding.* See also 16 C.F.R. 1500.81(a), originally promulgated by FDA under the Federal Hazardous Substances Act before it was transferred to the Consumer Product Safety Commission, which provides that where a cosmetic "offers a substantial risk of injury or illness from any handling or use that is customary or usual it may be regarded as misbranded under the Federal Food, Drug, and Cosmetic Act because its label fails to reveal material facts with respect to consequences that may result from use of the article (21 U.S.C. 321(n)) when its label fails to bear information to alert the householder to this hazard."

2.   MISLEADING LABELING

FDA failed in its attempt to establish by rule when use of the claim "hypoallergenic" in cosmetic labeling is misleading.

Almay, Inc. v. Califano

569 F.2d 674 (D.C. Cir. 1977).

■ MARKEY, CHIEF JUDGE, United States Court of Customs and Patent Appeals: . . . .

On February 25, 1974, appellee Food and Drug Administration (FDA) in accordance with 21 U.S.C. §§ 321(m), 362(a), and 371(a), initiated informal rulemaking proceedings by publishing a proposed regulation governing hypoallergenic cosmetics, under which:

> A cosmetic may be designated in its labeling by words that state or imply that the product of any ingredient thereof is "hypoallergenic" if it has been shown by scientific studies that the relative frequency of adverse reactions in human subjects from the test product is significantly less than the relative frequency of such reactions from each reference product(s). [39 F.R. 7291.]

The lynch-pin of the regulation was its requirement for employment of "comparison testing," *i.e.*, for testing the labeled product against "reference product(s)" defined in the regulation as "similar-use competitive products in the same cosmetic product category" and representing a market share of 10%. Adoption of the comparison testing method rested entirely on the Commissioner's adoption of a comparative definition: "the term 'hypoallergenic' means to the consumer that the product causes fewer adverse reactions than other, similar-type use products" and the feeling that, while use of "hypoallergenic" has expanded over the years, the difference between "hypoallergenic" cosmetics and those not so labeled has become less distinct.

Included in the preamble were comments of the Cosmetic, Toiletry and Fragrance Association (CFTA), the Bureau of Consumer Protection of the Federal Trade Commission (FTC), and appellant Almay Corporation (Almay). CFTA alleged that "there is no demonstrated need nor is it practicable for the minimizing of allergic reactions to be an overriding consideration in all aspects of production and marketing of every cosmetic product".... Almay objected to the comparison testing method because the composition of the selected reference products could not be predicted.... [T]he FTC filed the results of a consumer survey on hypoallergenic cosmetics, and ... comments thereon by the Director of FTC's Bureau of Consumer Protection....

Comments were also submitted by a number of dermatologists, consumer groups, and individual consumers. Eight dermatologists favored testing in which a product would have to demonstrate an extremely low potential for allergic reaction to qualify as hypoallergenic. Seven dermatologists opposed the comparison test method, and one was non-committal. Four consumer groups took issue with the comparative definition as likely to cause confusion among users of hypoallergenic cosmetics. One consumer group was in general agreement with the FDA proposal....

FDA justified its decision to define "hypoallergenic" as meaning less allergenic than some competing products on what it considered confusion in the use of the term.... The district court found the Commissioner's definition supported by two factors in the administrative record: (1) a significantly greater number of consumers believed that "hypoallergenic" meant "safer than competitors" rather than "very safe," and (2) a comparative definition would be more helpful to consumers because adverse reactions to cosmetic products are relatively rare today overall....

Involved here is an informal rulemaking proceeding, in which no hearing is required. The scope of review is therefore governed by the "arbitrary or capricious" standards set out in the Administrative Procedure Act, 5 U.S.C. § 706(2)(A)....

The fact that an "arbitrary and capricious" standard applies to informal rulemaking, rather than a "substantial evidence" requirement, cannot mean that *nothing* of an evidentiary nature is needed in the administrative record to support an agency decision. On the contrary, there being no evidentiary hearing, informal rulemaking proceedings are much more susceptible to abuse, and it becomes all the more important that a rational basis for the agency's decision be found in the facts of record....

FDA relies first on the preamble to its own proposed regulation in support of the Commissioner's conclusion. Respecting the definition of "hypoallergenic," the preamble is conclusory. The only authorities cited are a dictionary which defines "hypo" to mean "under," "beneath," "down," "less than normal," of "the lowest position in a series of compounds;" and the statement of an AMA Committee on Cutaneous Health and Cosmetics that "the term 'hypoallergenic' as applied to cosmetics has outlived its usefulness, is misleading, and should be dropped from the labeling of cosmetic products."

... The dictionary definition clearly does not support the Commissioner's decision to define "hypoallergenic" as causing "fewer reactions than *some* [10% of the market] products."

... In light of the AMA report's conclusion that "hypoallergenic" should be dropped entirely, and of its further statement that "little distinction can be made between established cosmetic products as to their sensitization potential," it was inappropriate to cite the AMA report in support of any use whatever of "hypoallergenic," no matter how defined.

FDA relied also on [an FTC survey on hypoallergenic cosmetics].... In drawing inference from the FTC survey, the Commissioner failed to consider a relevant factor—the comments of the FTC's Director of the Bureau of Consumer Protection.... The Director ... stated on the record that the survey: (1) was limited in population sample and number of questions; (2) was silent in important respects; (3) lacked a breakdown between users and non-users; (4) lacked a tabulation; (5) established that consumers lacked medical knowledge sufficient to distinguish skin reactions; (6) produced results which should be used with caution; and (7) probably produced fewer "correct" definitions because it was not limited to consumers interested in the subject, *i.e.*, hypoallergenic cosmetic users. Finally, the survey defined the "correct" definition as "less likely to cause irritation than regular cosmetics," yet the Commissioner chose a different definition: "less likely to cause adverse reactions than some [10% of market] similar-use competitive products in the same category."

We are fully aware of the caveat that we must not substitute our judgment for that of the regulator, nor shall we. We are equally aware, however, of the need for rationality, in the interest not only of justice, our major concern, but in the interest of the continued viability and public acceptance of the federal regulatory scheme itself....

An aura of unreality surrounds the creation of a definition in the present case. In the apparent belief that most products are today non-allergenic, it may have been thought that producers could not find 10% of marketed products producing more reactions and that use of "hypoallergenic" would thereupon cease. If so, the cumbersome method here chosen to achieve that result is an irrational substitute for a direct prohibition of all use of "hypoallergenic." ...

NOTE

FDA revoked this regulation in 43 Fed. Reg. 10559 (Mar. 14, 1978), and it has not since initiated regulatory action against cosmetic products labeled as hypoallergenic.

———

The scope of legitimate cosmetic claims has been a source of controversy for the past forty years.

Peter Barton Hutt, *The Legal Distinction in the United States Between a Cosmetic and a Drug*

In Cosmeceuticals (Peter Elsner & Howard I. Maibach eds., 2000).

The Wrinkle Remover Cases of the 1960s

In the early 1960s, the cosmetic industry developed a line of products, broadly characterized as "wrinkle remover" products, containing ingredients intended to smooth, firm, and tighten the skin temporarily and thus to make wrinkles less obvious. In 1964, the FDA seized several of these products, alleging that they were drugs under the FD&C Act. The resulting litigation produced three decisions by U.S. District Courts and two decisions by U.S. Courts of Appeals involving three products: Line Away, Sudden Change, and Magic Secret. . . .

The OTC Drug Review

The OTC Drug Review inherently raised issues relating to the distinction between a cosmetic and a drug. All of the traditional cosmetic drug products—sunscreens, antiperspirants, antidandruff shampoos, anticaries toothpaste, skin protectants, hormone creams, acne products, and so forth—were reviewed under the OTC Drug Review. The FDA made clear that only the drug and not the cosmetic aspects of cosmetic drugs were subject to review and evaluation, and ultimately a final monograph, under this program. Thus, in many of the advisory committee meetings and subsequent reports, as well as in the preambles of the tentative final and final monographs, there has been substantial discussion about the dividing line between a drug claim and a cosmetic claim for a cosmetic drug. In several instances, the FDA has explicitly stated that a final monograph covered only products making drug claims and did not cover cosmetic claims for the product or products making only cosmetic claims. . . .

The Warning Letters of the Late 1980s

For a period of 15 years following the conclusion of the wrinkle remover cases, the FDA pursued cosmetic/drug issues largely through the OTC Drug Review and seldom, if ever, through Regulatory Letters or direct court action. Based upon new product technology and the conclusion that the consuming public was becoming increasingly sophisticated about skin-care products and their claims, the cosmetic industry gradually became more aggressive with cell rejuvenation and other antiaging promotional claims. As a result of research and development in the intervening years, new and more effective products were now on the market.

Two defining events served to initiate a new round of FDA enforcement activities against skin-care claims in the late 1980s. First, in 1986 the well-known South African heart surgeon, Christiaan Barnard, made a tour of the United States on behalf of a cosmetic company to promote its skin care product, Glycel. Barnard made extravagant claims for Glycel on the television program, Nightline, with FDA Commissioner Frank Young participating on the same program. Second, an attorney for a major cosmetic company wrote Dr. Young to protest the claims being made for Glycel. As a result, the FDA began to issue Regulatory Letters not only to manufacturer of Glycel but also to other leading members of the industry. More than 20 Regulatory Letters were sent in the first wave, and when the FDA concluded that the response was unsatisfactory the agency sent another 20....

The Alpha–Hydroxy Acid (AHA) Products of the 1990s

In the early 1990s, the cosmetic industry developed and marketed a line of products containing alpha-hydroxy acids such as glycolic, lactic, and citric acid that occurred in natural food products, to cleanse dead cells from the surface of the skin and assist moisturization. The AHAs have been used in consumer products at relatively modest levels, usually at 10% or lower, in contrast with very high levels used in professional skin peeling products. It is universally accepted that the AHA products are the most effective skin-care beauty products that the industry has ever developed. As a result, they have become extremely popular with consumers and gained substantial media and regulatory attention.

The FDA has raised two questions about the AHA products. First, the agency has questioned the claims being made. The FDA has sought to adhere to the guidelines established in the November 1987 letter on the antiaging and cell rejuvenation products. Second, the FDA has also questioned the safety of these products, not on the ground that there are known toxicological concerns but rather on the ground that their safety is unproven. In contrast with the cell rejuvenation claims of the 1980s, however, the FDA has not launched another wave of Warning Letters. A company that had obtained FDA approval of NDAs for antiaging drugs, frustrated by this lack of FDA action, brought a private false advertising case under section 43(a) of the Lanham Act against a competitor making aggressive claims for a cosmetic product, but lost in both the District Court and the Court of Appeals....

NOTES

1. *Regulation of Claims.* For discussion of FDA regulation of cosmetic claims, see Stephen H. McNamara, *Performance Claims for Skin Care Cosmetics or How Far May You Go in Claiming to Provide Youthfulness?*, 41 FOOD DRUG COSM. L.J. 151 (1986); Laura A. Heymann, *The Cosmetic/Drug Dilemma: FDA Regulation of Alpha–Hydroxy Acids*, 52 FOOD & DRUG L.J. 357 (1997); Bryan A. Liang & Kurt M. Hartman, *It's Only Skin Deep: FDA Regulation of Skin Care Cosmetics Claims*, 8 CORNELL J.L. & PUB. POL'Y 249 (1999). For a list of cosmetic claims that FDA regarded as false or misleading in 1939, see FDA Trade Correspondence 10 (Aug. 2, 1939), 1938–1949 FDLI Jud. Rec. at 566.

2. *"See Through" Labels.* FDA once proposed to ban, as misbranded, all "see-through" cosmetic labels (*i.e.*, labels that can be read only through the container and its contents), 39 Fed. Reg. 25328 (July 10, 1974), but later relented, 44 Fed. Reg. 47547 (Aug. 14, 1979).

3. *FDA Budget for Cosmetics.* The ability of the FDA to monitor and bring regulatory action with respect to claims for cosmetic products depends on the

resources available to the agency for this purpose. Because of budgetary factors, the FDA announced in 1998 that it was reducing the staff of the Office of Cosmetics and Colors by 50 percent and cutting back or eliminating many cosmetic regulatory programs. This reduction was so substantial that it propelled the cosmetic industry to request and obtain restoration by Congress of adequate funds to assure that the FDA has a credible cosmetic regulatory program.

4. *NAD Review of Cosmetic Claims*. The National Advertising Division (NAD) of the Better Business Bureau, *see supra* p. 478, frequently reviews the substantiation for cosmetic product claims. *See, e.g., Coty, Inc.* 34 NAD/CARU Case Reports 368 (July 2004).

5. *Organic Cosmetics*. USDA has determined that cosmetic products that meet the requirements established under the Organic Foods Production Act of 1990, *see supra* p. 117, are eligible for certification in accordance with that statute. *See* Memorandum on Certification of Agricultural Products that Meet NOP Standards from Barbara C. Robinson, Deputy Administrator, USDA Agricultural Marketing Service Transportation and Marketing Programs (Aug. 23, 2005).

E.   Cosmetic Ingredient Labeling

The FD&C Act contains no provision authorizing FDA to require ingredient labeling on cosmetics. FDA initially established a recommended format for voluntary cosmetic ingredient labeling. 37 Fed. Reg. 16208 (Aug. 11, 1972). The next year, the agency promulgated the following regulation imposing mandatory cosmetic ingredient labeling under Section 5(c) of the Fair Packaging and Labeling Act (FPLA) of 1966, 15 U.S.C. 1451 *et seq.*

Cosmetic Ingredient Labeling

38 Fed. Reg. 28912 (October 17, 1973).

In the FEDERAL REGISTER of February 7, 1973 (38 FR 3523), the Commissioner of Food and Drugs published two proposals concerning the labeling of cosmetic ingredients....

Several comments questioned the legal basis for the proposals, contending that [Section 5(c) of] the Fair Packaging and Labeling Act grants authority to establish ingredient labeling only on a commodity-by-commodity basis, and only as necessary to prevent consumer deception or to facilitate value comparisons.

... For the purposes of ingredient labeling, the Commissioner concludes that all cosmetics are appropriately considered a single "commodity." ...

The Commissioner also concludes that cosmetic ingredient labeling is necessary to prevent the deception of consumers and to facilitate value comparisons. Ingredient labeling can be meaningful in preventing consumer deception by precluding product claims that are unreasonable in relation to the ingredients present and by providing consumers with additional information that can contribute to a knowledgeable judgment regarding the reasonableness of the price of the product. Furthermore, while ingredient identity may not be the sole determinant of a product's value to a consumer, it is one important criterion of a product's value in comparison with others. The presence of a substance to which a consumer is allergic or sensitive, for example, may render the product worthless to that consumer. . . .

The Commissioner recognizes that section 5(c)(3) of the act does not grant authority for promulgating ingredient labeling regulations that require the divulgence of trade secrets. However, because quantitative formulas are not revealed, he does not agree that the mere listing of ingredients in descending order of their predominance is tantamount to the divulgence of a trade secret. Furthermore, the final regulation does not require declaration by name of flavors or fragrances, the two types of cosmetic ingredients which would be the most likely of any to create trade secret issues. Nevertheless, in consideration of the possibility that there may be some legitimate trade secret issues regarding the mere identity of other ingredients, the final regulation provides for an administrative review of any such claims of trade secret status and for exemption from label declaration by name for any legitimate trade secret identity. . . .

The Commissioner recognizes that many consumers may initially be unfamiliar with certain cosmetic ingredients, but concludes that increasing familiarity will be acquired. Certain ingredients have become known to consumers who, for example, are aware of their sensitivity to specific substances and who will quickly learn to utilize the ingredient statement. Ingredient labeling will have to be accompanied by the acquisition of additional information by consumers if they are to be fully informed. Ingredient labeling will, however, directly provide some of the necessary information and should help to motivate consumers to acquire the necessary additional information. . . .

Therefore, pursuant to provisions of the Fair Packaging and Labeling Act and the Federal Food, Drug, and Cosmetic Act (sec. 701(e)), Part 1 is amended by adding the following new section: [The regulation that follows is the current, slightly revised version of the rule promulgated by FDA in the above Federal Register notice.]

Designation of Ingredients

21 C.F.R. § 701.3

(a) The label on each package of a cosmetic shall bear a declaration of the name of each ingredient in descending order of predominance, except that fragrance or flavor may be listed as fragrance or flavor. An ingredient which is both fragrance and flavor shall be designated by each of the functions it performs unless such ingredient is identified by name. . . . Where one or more ingredients is accepted by the Food and Drug Administration as exempt from public disclosure pursuant to the procedure established in § 720.8(a) of this chapter, in lieu of label declaration of identity the phrase "and other ingredients" may be used at the end of the ingredient declaration.

(b) The declaration of ingredients shall appear with such prominence and conspicuousness as to render it likely to be read and understood by ordinary individuals under normal conditions of purchase. The declaration shall appear on any appropriate information panel in letters not less than 1/16 of an inch in height and without obscuring design, vignettes, or crowding. In the absence of sufficient space for such declaration on the package, or where the manufacturer or distributor wishes to use a decorative container, the declaration may appear on a firmly affixed tag, tape, or card. In those cases where there is insufficient space for such declaration on the package, and it is not practical to firmly affix a tag, tape, or card, the Commissioner may establish by regulation an acceptable alternate, *e.g.*, a smaller type size. A petition requesting such a regulation as an amendment to this paragraph shall be submitted pursuant to part 10 of this chapter.

(c) A cosmetic ingredient shall be identified in the declaration of ingredients by:

(1) The name specified in § 701.30 as established by the Commissioner for that ingredient for the purpose of cosmetic ingredient labeling pursuant to paragraph (e) of this section;

(2) In the absence of the name specified in § 701.30, the name adopted for that ingredient in the following editions and supplements of the following compendia, listed in order as the source to be utilized:....

(3) In the absence of such a listing, the name generally recognized by consumers.

(4) In the absence of any of the above, the chemical or other technical name or description.

(d) Where a cosmetic product is also an over-the-counter drug product, the declaration shall declare the active drug ingredients as set forth in § 201.66(c)(2) and (d) of this chapter, and the declaration shall declare the cosmetic ingredients as set forth in § 201.66(c)(8) and (d) of this chapter.

. . . .

NOTES

1. *Final Regulations.* FDA received objections to the cosmetic ingredient labeling rule as originally promulgated. It accommodated these objections and issued a revised final order. 39 Fed. Reg. 27181 (July 25, 1974), 40 Fed. Reg. 8918, codified at 21 C.F.R. 701.3.40. The procedure followed by the agency in promulgating these regulations, without conducting an evidentiary hearing, *see* 40 Fed. Reg. 8924 (Mar. 3, 1975), 40 Fed. Reg. 23458 (May 30, 1975), was upheld by a divided court. *Independent Cosmetic Mfrs. & Distribs., Inc. v. Califano*, 574 F.2d 553 (D.C. Cir. 1978).

2. *Determination of Trade Secret Status.* The process used by FDA to determine whether a cosmetic ingredient represents a trade secret and is therefore exempt from required label declaration was challenged in *Zotos Int'l, Inc. v. Kennedy*, 460 F. Supp. 268 (D.D.C. 1978). The district court ruled that the procedure, which did not afford an opportunity for a hearing or other form of "focused dialogue" with the agency, violated the due process clause of the Constitution. In *Carson Prods. Co. v. Califano*, 594 F.2d 453 (5th Cir. 1979), the court agreed with the *Zotos* decision but held that the revised procedures afforded Carson satisfied due process and that the facts justified FDA's conclusion that the ingredient involved was not a trade secret. The court in *Del Labs., Inc. v. United States*, 86

F.R.D. 676 (D.D.C. 1980), overturned, on procedural grounds, FDA's preliminary refusal to recognize the trade secret status of an ingredient of the plaintiff's products. To remedy the deficiencies discovered by the courts, FDA established a new procedure for considering requests for confidentiality of cosmetic ingredient identity. 47 Fed. Reg. 38353 (Aug. 31, 1982), 51 Fed. Reg. 11441 (Apr. 3, 1986). Even following these new regulations, FDA had difficulty justifying its decisions. In the continuing *Zotos* litigation, FDA again rejected trade secret status after reconsideration under the new regulations, and the District Court affirmed the FDA decision. However, the Court of Appeals reversed and remanded the matter for yet additional proceedings because the agency had given inconsistent reasons for its decision. *Zotos Int'l, Inc. v. Young*, 830 F.2d 350 (D.C. Cir. 1987).

3. *Ingredient Names.* In 42 Fed. Reg. 56757 (Oct. 28, 1977) and 45 Fed. Reg. 3574 (Jan. 18, 1980), FDA recognized the second edition of the CTFA Cosmetic Ingredient Dictionary as the primary source for cosmetic ingredient terminology but refused to adopt the CTFA names for 34 listed substances and required the description of the chemical composition of 16 listed substances. Because of the Office of the Federal Register rule that federal regulations may not incorporate documents by prospective reference, the cosmetic ingredient labeling regulations must be revised whenever a new edition of or supplement to the CTFA Cosmetic Ingredient Dictionary is published. Since 1980, FDA has failed to respond to CTFA petitions recognizing these new editions and supplements but has not taken regulatory action against use of the terminology contained in the most current edition.

4. *Color Additive Names.* In 50 Fed. Reg. 23815 (June 6, 1985), FDA permitted color additives to be designated in product labeling without their prefix, *i.e.*, "Yellow 5" rather than "FD&C Yellow No. 5," and proposed to change its regulations to reflect this policy.

5. *Commentary.* For differing views about the cosmetic ingredient labeling regulations, see Eugene I. Lambert, *Working Out Cosmetic Ingredient Labeling*, 30 FOOD DRUG COSM. L.J. 228 (1975); Murray Berdick, *Cosmetic Ingredient Labeling— The Nomenclature Problem*, 31 FOOD DRUG COSM. L.J. 125 (1976); Walter E. Byerley, *Cosmetic Ingredient Labeling—An FDA Chimera*, 31 FOOD DRUG COSM. L.J. 109 (1976); Heinz J. Eiermann, *Cosmetic Ingredient Labeling Requirements*, 31 FOOD DRUG COSM. L.J. 115 (1976); Margaret Gilhooley, *Status Report on Cosmetic Ingredient Labeling*, 31 FOOD DRUG COSM. L.J. 121 (1976).

6. *Scope of Ingredient Labeling.* The FPLA applies only to retail packaging and contains no criminal enforcement sanctions. Ingredient labeling for cosmetics is thus required to appear only on the outside labeling and only on retail packages (not on packages sold to beauty salons or institutions for use on the premises), and the requirement is enforceable only by civil action. Following congressional hearings that criticized the lack of ingredient labeling for professional cosmetic products, *supra* p. 1081 Note 1, on December 16, 1988, five cosmetic industry trade associations announced a voluntary program to provide ingredient information for all professional products manufactured on or after December 31, 1989. Under this voluntary program, the ingredient information for professional cosmetic products may be provided on the product label or in accompanying labeling, and may be provided in descending order of predominance or in alphabetical order.

F. VOLUNTARY "REGULATION" OF COSMETICS

The FD&C Act does not authorize FDA to require registration of cosmetic manufacturing establishments, submission of lists of cosmetic products and their ingredients, or filing of adverse event reports. In the early 1970s, in response to petitions from the cosmetic industry, FDA promulgated regulations governing the voluntary registration of cosmetic establishments (21 C.F.R. Part 710), voluntary filing of cosmetic product ingredient statements (21 C.F.R. Part 720), and voluntary filing of product experience reports (21 C.F.R. Part 730). The product experience report regulations were revoked in 1997.

Voluntary Registration of Cosmetic Product Establishments; Voluntary Filing of Cosmetic Product Ingredient and Cosmetic Raw Material Composition Statements

37 Fed. Reg. 7151 (April 11, 1972).

... [A] member of Congress urged that the registration and filing of ingredient statements by producers of cosmetics be mandatory [and] that foreign producers of cosmetics be subjected to the regulations.... Two other comments challenged the legality of establishing voluntary regulations under section 701(a) of the Federal Food, Drug, and Cosmetic Act and urged that the regulations issued be mandatory....

The Commissioner has considered these comments and concludes that under section 701(a) of the act he is authorized to accept the voluntary registration of cosmetic product establishments and the voluntary filing of cosmetic product ingredient statements and cosmetic raw material composition statements as set forth in the regulations established below. He also agrees that foreign producers should be included in this voluntary registration. He concludes however that promulgation of a mandatory regulation could result in lengthy litigation that would seriously delay FDA from obtaining the type of information expected as a result of this promulgation....

A dermatologist commented that the proposed regulations ... did not go far enough, particularly in the provision for providing coded samples to physicians treating persons suffering from allergic reaction. He urged establishment of a "Register" that would list all ingredients of all cosmetic products used in the United States and would be made available to every practicing dermatologist. The Commissioner concludes that a "Register" of cosmetic ingredients goes beyond the scope of the proposal and cannot be implemented by these regulations. The Commissioner considers that promulgation of labeling requirements for cosmetic ingredients will substantially satisfy the need of dermatologists for this type of data....

Voluntary Filing of Cosmetic Product Experiences

38 Fed. Reg. 28914 (October 17, 1973).

In the FEDERAL REGISTER of November 1, 1972 (37 FR 23344) a notice of proposed rulemaking to establish a procedure for the voluntary filing of cosmetic product experience was published by the Commissioner of Food and Drugs. The notice included the text of regulations suggested in a petition filed by the Cosmetic, Toiletry, and Fragrance Association, Inc. (CTFA) ... as well as regulations proposed by the Commissioner....

A number of comments agreed with the FDA proposal that all complaints alleging bodily injury received by a manufacturer, packer, or distributor should be submitted to the Food and Drug Administration. The petitioner opposed the request for the submission of all complaints and suggested that provision be made for a manufacturer, packer, or distributor to use a screening procedure for determining reportable experiences and in the absence of such a procedure to submit all alleged injury complaints received.

The Commissioner of Food and Drugs concludes that the submission of complaints that have been screened by a procedure appropriately designed to eliminate any unfounded or spurious complaints would be more meaningful and, therefore, adopts the suggestion of the petitioner. However, in order to protect against the use of screening procedures which might eliminate valid experience reports, the regulation provides that any procedure used to screen such reports should be filed with the agency and that it will be subject to public inspection....

Several comments argued for a broad definition of "reportable experience." It was asserted that any bodily injury resulting from the accidental or deliberate misuse of a cosmetic product is a valid reportable experience. The petitioner, on the other hand, opposed the inclusion of any experience not in association with the intended use of a cosmetic product.

The Commissioner is of the opinion that any information he can obtain in regard to injuries involving cosmetic products, including adverse reactions resulting from the accidental or deliberate misuse of cosmetic products, may be of use in protecting the public health, and therefore he has concluded that all such experiences should be considered reportable.

... [T]he rules governing confidentiality granted to voluntarily submitted data on cosmetic product experiences should be the same as the rules governing confidentiality for other data submitted to the agency on a voluntary basis [set forth in 21 C.F.R. 20.111]....

A public interest group requested that FDA obtain testing data on products for which complaints have been received. The regulation provides that the Commissioner may request additional information in response to reports received....

Both the Industry member and the petitioner opposed the provision in the FDA proposal for submitting a negative report for each cosmetic product by brand name for which no reportable experience had been received during a reporting period.

The Commissioner is of the opinion that statistical data obtained from the submission of reportable experiences will be meaningful only if the agency obtains sufficient information to relate the number of the reportable experiences in a product category to the total number of cosmetic product units sold in that particular product category. Such information by product categories can be obtained, however, without the need for filing a separate negative report for each product by brand name. The regulation now provides for the submission of a "Summary Report of Cosmetic

Product Experience by Product Categories." The person submitting this report need not list products by brand name, but only the total number of product units in each product category estimated to have been distributed to consumers during the reporting period, together with the number and rate of reportable experiences in each category. . . .

NOTES

1. *Confidentiality of Reports.* FDA subsequently issued final regulations under the Freedom of Information Act granting confidentiality to product experience reports. 39 Fed. Reg. 44602 (Dec. 24, 1974).

2. *Simplification of Reporting Requirements.* In an effort to improve compliance with the voluntary reporting regulations, FDA reduced the reporting burdens. 45 Fed. Reg. 73960 (Nov. 7, 1980), 46 Fed. Reg. 38073 (July 24, 1981), 50 Fed. Reg. 47760 (Nov. 20, 1985), 51 Fed. Reg. 25687 (July 16, 1986). On May 15, 1989, CTFA submitted a citizen petition to FDA (No. 89P–0180) requesting that the voluntary filing of cosmetic formulas be simplified by eliminating the requirement for semi-quantitative information, thus permitting manufacturers to submit a simple list of ingredients. FDA proposed amendments to the regulations in accordance with this petition and stated that they could be implemented immediately. 55 Fed. Reg. 42993 (Oct. 29, 1990). FDA has announced that establishment registration and product and ingredient listing may be accomplished electronically.

3. *Industry Compliance.* The industry record of compliance with the voluntary reporting regulations was a subject of debate during the 1988 House hearings on cosmetic product safety, *supra* p. 1081 Note 1. *See also* GAO, Cosmetics Regulation Information on Voluntary Actions Agreed to by FDA and the Industry, HRD–90–58 (1990).

4. *Revocation of Adverse Experience Reporting.* As part of President Clinton's "Reinventing Government" initiative, FDA revoked the voluntary adverse experience reporting regulation in 1997. 61 Fed. Reg. 29708 (June 12, 1996), 62 Fed. Reg. 43071 (Aug. 12, 1997). FDA stated that, after 23 years of adverse event reporting, even with limited industry participation, the agency now had sufficient data to calculate the baseline adverse reactions that occur for each cosmetic category and thus that the program no longer provided useful new information. FDA promised to provide "an in depth report that will be useful to both the cosmetic industry and the public in understanding adverse reaction trends for different product categories and the baseline rates for adverse reactions," but no such report has been published.

5. *Commentary.* For a description of cosmetic experience reporting from FDA's perspective, see John A. Wenninger, *Voluntary Cosmetic Product Experience Reporting—The FDA Viewpoint*, 30 Food Drug Cosm. L.J. 204 (1975). For discussion of cosmetic industry concerns about product experience reporting, see Eugene I. Lambert, *Carrot and Stick: Product Experience Reporting and Cosmetic Ingredient Labeling*, 29 Food Drug Cosm. L.J. 78 (1974); George L. Wolcott, *Cosmetics Workshop—Product Experience Reporting*, 29 Food Drug Cosm. L.J. 284 (1974); Michael Pietrangelo, *Product Experience Reporting—An Industry View*, 30 Food Drug Cosm. L.J. 219 (1975).

———

After FDA promulgated Section 740.10 of its regulations, *supra* p. 1094, requiring safety substantiation (or a warning statement) for cosmetic ingredients, CTFA initiated meetings to request FDA to undertake a review of the safety of cosmetic ingredients similar to the agency's reviews of GRAS food ingredients, *supra* p. 410, and OTC drugs, *supra* p. 788. When FDA declined to do this, CTFA, in 1976, undertook its own comprehensive review of the safety of ingredients used in cosmetic products.

Robert L. Elder, *The Cosmetic Ingredient Review—A Safety Evaluation Program*

11 JOURNAL OF THE AMERICAN ACADEMY OF DERMATOLOGY 1168 (1984).

The Cosmetic Ingredient Review (CIR) was established in 1976 by the Cosmetic, Toiletry and Fragrance Association to review and document information on the safety of ingredients as used in cosmetic products. . . .

CTFA recognized that acceptance of the program and its results would depend on three major factors: (1) the safety review process had to be conducted with no cosmetic industry bias; (2) the Panel of Experts who would review the safety test data on each ingredient had to be given complete independence; and (3) the review process, the reports, and all of the data used in the safety evaluation had to be available for public and scientific scrutiny.

These three major requirements were codified into formal, written procedures that established CIR as an independent, nonprofit organization. CIR staff and all consultants were to be separate from CTFA and the cosmetic industry and must pass the same conflict of interest requirements stipulated for special federal government employees. All reports were to be discussed and voted on in a public meeting before being released for a 90–day public comment period without prior industry review. And finally, all data, published or unpublished, used by the CIR Expert Panel would be available for public review.

Policy guidance for the CIR program is provided by a five-person Steering Committee chaired by the president of CTFA [and including two scientists] . . . appointed by the American Academy of Dermatology . . . [and] the Society of Toxicology. Two scientists from industry—the current chairman of CTFA's Scientific Advisory Committee and CTFA's senior vice-president for Science—also serve on the Committee. The Steering Committee has no input into the scientific evaluations of the CIR Expert Panel. One of the Steering Committee's major responsibilities is the selection of the seven-member CIR Expert Panel. This is done following a public announcement requesting nominees. . . .

Three nonvoting members assist the Expert Panel and attend the public meetings. These include a consumer representative (appointed by the Consumer Federation of America), an industry liaison, and a Food and Drug Administration (FDA) "contact person." . . .

The priority order of ingredient review is established by using a weighted formula that includes factors for: ingredient concentration in cosmetic products, number of products containing the ingredient, frequency of consumer use, area of use, use by sensitive population subgroups, biologic activity, estimate of penetration, and frequency of consumer complaints about products containing the ingredient.... Ingredients specifically regulated by the FDA, such as color additives, are exempt from CIR review. Any ingredient that is being evaluated by the FDA under the Over–The–Counter Drug Review (OTC) or for use as a Direct Food Additive is deferred until that review is completed. Fragrance materials are being evaluated separately in a program sponsored by the Research Institute for Fragrance Materials (RIFM) and are not included in the CIR review program. The CIR ingredient review list is developed as described and then issued for public comment before it is forwarded with all the comments to the Expert Panel for their review and approval. The Expert Panel may at any time add, delete, or change the order of ingredient review without requesting concurrence by the Steering Committee....

... [T]he review of each ingredient goes through several stages. The staff of CIR prepares a Scientific Literature Review summarizing the published information and publicly requests any relevant published or unpublished data that the review does not already include.

Individually, ingredient suppliers and cosmetic manufacturers have tested ingredients, as well as formulations, for many years. Although much of these data have been published, a significant portion are in industry files and not available for public or scientific review. The collection of these data and the test protocols used to produce the data are critical to the success of the program. At the end of a 90–day public comment period, all submitted data are incorporated into a document for consideration by a subgroup (Team) of the Expert Panel. From 25% to 75% of the data included in the CIR reports has not been published previously. Teams meet in a series of closed working sessions to evaluate the report and determine whether there are sufficient data upon which to base a conclusion. A document reflecting those considerations is then prepared for review by the full Expert Panel. After discussion of this document in public meetings of the full Panel, a Tentative Report is issued with one of three conclusions: (1) that the ingredient is safe as currently used, (2) that the ingredient is unsafe, or (3) that there is insufficient information for the Panel to make a determination of safety. It is significant that CIR procedures require documented evidence giving reasonable assurance of safety before reaching the final determination. Lack of adverse information about an ingredient is not sufficient to justify a determination of safety.

The Tentative Report is then made available for a 90–day public comment period.... A Final Report, incorporating any substantive changes resulting from public comment, is then released by the Expert Panel....

Statement of Robert L. Elder, SC.D.*

"Potential Hazards of Cosmetic Products," Hearing before the Subcommittee on Regulation and Business Opportunities House Committee on Small Business (September 15, 1988).

The CTFA Ingredient Dictionary currently lists 5000 nonfragrance ingredients. These are ingredients that are offered for use by the cosmetic industry. Many are not used in a cosmetic at any given time. It is estimated

---

* [Dr. Elder was the Director of CIR.]

that about 2300 of these nonfragrance ingredients are in actual use at any one time. Data from the FDA cosmetic voluntary reporting program indicate that approximately 700 of these 2300 ingredients have been reported to be used in 20 or more cosmetic formulations. The 700 ingredients whose reported frequency of use is greater than 20 are the ingredients that have thus far been prioritized for CIR review. Although we have prioritized only those cosmetic ingredients used in 20 or more formulations, in going through this process we have actually considered a much larger number of ingredients. We considered all ingredients in 10 or more formulations when we established the 1984 priority list, to make sure that important chemicals were not missed. And in 1987 FDA provided to the Expert Panel a list of all chemicals used in *any* cosmetic formulation, again to be sure that any important chemical was included. Thus, we have cast a wide net. One-third of these 700 ingredients are already regulated by FDA for use in food or drug products or as color additives. . . .

Wilma F. Bergfeld* et al., *Safety of Ingredients Used in Cosmetics*

52 JOURNAL OF THE AMERICAN ACADEMY OF DERMATOLOGY 125 (2005).

. . . From 1976 to September 2004, the CIR Expert Panel completed safety assessments of 1194 ingredients. These ingredients are estimated to be used in more than 100,000 cosmetic products. . . .

For 683 ingredients (approximately 58%), the conclusion was safe as used. In this context, "as used" refers to the practices of use and concentrations described in each safety assessment . . .

For 114 ingredients (approximately 33%) the conclusion was that they could be used safely in cosmetic products with qualifications. Ingredients found safe with qualifications fall into one or more of the following groups: concentration limits, inhalation or other product-use restrictions, and nitrosamine formation. Ingredients may be listed more than once if there are multiple qualifications on their safe use. . . .

For 114 ingredients (approximately 9%), the available data were insufficient to support safety. If the panel reaches an insufficient data conclusion, it does not state whether the ingredient is safe or unsafe. The panel is, however, describing a situation in which the available data do not support safety. . . .

Only 9 ingredients were found to be unsafe for use in cosmetic products (<1%). These are ingredients with specific adverse effects that make them unsuitable for use in cosmetics, in the view of the panel.

————

As of December 31, 2005, the CIR has reviewed 1,284 cosmetic ingredients and has made the following determinations.

* [Dr. Bergfeld is the Chair of the CIR Expert Panel.]

Safe	766
Safe with qualifications	408
Insufficient data for a safety determination	120
Unsafe	9

Cosmetic Ingredient Review, 2005 ANNUAL REPORT 10 (2006).

––––––––

In 1991, the Consumer Federation of America petitioned FDA to ban urocanic acid, one of the ingredients found by CIR to lack sufficient data for a safety determination.

Letter From Ronald G. Chesemore, Associate Commissioner for Regulatory Affairs, FDA, to Consumer Federation of America

FDA Docket No. 91P–0114/CP (October 25, 1996).

This replies to your citizen petition (91P–0114CP), of March 20, 1991, and filed March 21, 1991, requesting that the Food and Drug Administration (FDA) find that the cosmetic ingredient urocanic acid is a deleterious substance which may render any cosmetic product containing it injurious to users and that FDA declare any cosmetic products containing urocanic acid to be adulterated under the Federal Food, Drug and Cosmetic Act (FD&C Act). . . .

We conclude that the scientific evidence does not establish that the low level of immunosuppression by urocanic acid in humans presents a safety concern to humans. Thus, we cannot conclude that urocanic acid is a deleterious substance which, when used as a component of a cosmetic product, may render the product injurious to the user under the conditions of use prescribed in the labeling or under such conditions of use as are customary or usual. As a result, we are not prepared to say that cosmetic products containing urocanic acid are adulterated under the FD&C Act. Therefore, FDA is denying your petition.

We also conclude, however, that, while the scientific evidence reviewed for your petition does not demonstrate that use of urocanic acid is unsafe, it does raise questions whether the evidence exists to conclude that the use of this ingredient in cosmetic products is safe. These questions are significant under 21 CFR 740.10—a regulation that FDA adopted under the misbranding provisions of the FD&C Act. . . .

The safety of urocanic acid as a cosmetic ingredient has been previously reviewed by the Cosmetic Ingredient Review (CIR) Expert Panel. The CIR Expert Panel is a group of scientists that reviews the safety of cosmetic ingredients under the aegis of the Cosmetic, Toiletries and Fragrance Association (CTFA), a trade association of the cosmetics industry. As such, the CIR Expert Panel is the focus for the evaluation of the safety of ingredients by the cosmetic industry. In 1995, the CIR Expert Panel published a report of its review of the safety of urocanic acid (J Am Coll Toxicol, 14 386–423 (1995).) In its report, the CIR Expert Panel concluded that the safety of urocanic acid as a cosmetic ingredient has not been documented and substantiated. . . .

Based on the Expert Panel's report, it would seem that manufacturers that use urocanic acid would have to provide notice on the labels of those products that contain this ingredient that its safety has not been established. We recognize that additional, unpublished, studies to substantiate the safety of urocanic acid may have been performed by individual companies. If cosmetic manufacturers have not done so, then the safety of urocanic acid in cosmetic products has not been substantiated, and there may be questions about the labeling of products that contain this ingredient. . . .

NOTE

FDA subsequently sent letters to manufacturers of cosmetic products containing urocanic acid, informing them of their obligation to include the warning statement under Section 740.10, and the industry discontinued use of the ingredient.

In 2004, the Environmental Working Group (EWG) surveyed the labeling for cosmetic products and concluded that many products contain ingredients determined by CIR to be unsafe or to have insufficient data to determine safety, or to have qualifications not followed by the manufacturer. EWG issued a report, available on its website, and, on June 14, 2004, petitioned FDA to take appropriate regulatory action (Docket No. 2004P–0266/CP).

Letter From Robert E. Brackett, Director, FDA Center for Food Safety and Applied Nutrition, to CTFA

February 3, 2005.

. . . In December 2004, the Center for Food Safety and Applied Nutrition released its 2005 Program Priorities. These priorities include two items specifically aimed at ensuring that cosmetic products being marketed in the United States remain safe.

The first of these priorities addresses a citizen petition received from the Environmental Working Group (EWG) alleging that cosmetic products are currently being marketed in the United States with ingredients that have been determined by the Cosmetic Ingredient Review Expert Panel (CIR) to be unsafe, or to have insufficient data for a determination of safety, or to fall outside the qualifications for safe use. . . . We are preparing a response to the EWG citizen petition. Additionally, you should know that FDA intends to consider taking compliance action, where appropriate, regarding cosmetic products that contain ingredients that we determine have not been shown to be safe, based on findings of the CIR Expert Panel and other sources of information available to the Agency, but that are not currently labeled with the warning statement ("Warning—The safety of this product has not been determined.") required under 21 CFR 740.10. In the past we have taken appropriate action based in part on the CIR Expert Panel determination for safety.

FDA regards the CIR Expert Panel determination an important element in ensuring the safety of the cosmetic supply in the United States. Indeed, we have provided a Liaison Representative to the Expert Panel since approximately 1980 and plan to continue to provide a representative.

The second 2005 Program Priority related specifically to cosmetics is the development of draft guidance to implement 21 CFR 740.10. The guidance is intended to provide information to manufacturers on determining the adequacy of safety substantiation of ingredients in cosmetic products and on determining when the 21 CFR 740.10 warning statement would be necessary . . . .

NOTES

1. *Update.* FDA denied the EWG petition, stating that requests for enforcement action are not appropriate for a citizen petition, that EWG did not provide sufficient information for FDA to evaluate the safety of the ingredients which EWG identified, and that FDA takes enforcement action based on "the agency's priorities and available resources." Letter from Margaret O'K. Glavin, Associate Commissioner for Regulatory Affairs, FDA, to Jane Houlihan & Arianne Callender (Sept. 29, 2005).

2. *Section 740.10 Guidance.* The guidance to implement Section 740.10, promised in Dr. Brackett's letter to CTFA, has not been forthcoming and has been removed from the CFSAN annual priority list.

3. *Challenge to FDA's Role.* Before the CIR commenced, Consumers Union brought suit against FDA, contending that discussions between CTFA and FDA about plans for the program were advisory committee meetings that must comply with all of the requirements of the Federal Advisory Committee Act. *See infra* p. 1573. In *Consumers Union of United States, Inc. v. Department of HEW*, 409 F. Supp. 473 (D.D.C. 1976), *aff'd without opinion*, 551 F.2d 466 (D.C. Cir. 1977), the court concluded that CTFA was not "advising" FDA but that "CTFA in its own discretion was ultimately to decide whether or not to initiate a testing program." The District Court observed that FDA "appears to lack statutory authority to require initiation of an ingredient testing program."

4. *Fragrance Ingredients.* Fragrance ingredients used in cosmetics are exempt from the CIR program because they are subject to a separate safety review conducted by the Research Institute for Fragrance Materials. *See* Richard A. Ford, *Criteria for Development of a Database for Safety Evaluation of Fragrance Ingredients*, 31 REG. TOXICOLOGY & PHARMACOLOGY 166 (2000).

5. *Commentary.* The objectives of the cosmetic industry's self-regulation program are discussed in Murray Berdick, *The Cosmetic Industry's Approach to Voluntary Regulation—Scientific Aspects*, 27 FOOD DRUG COSM. L.J. 208 (1972); J. Richard Edmondson, *Cosmetic Industry Self–Regulation*, 27 FOOD DRUG COSM. L.J. 45 (1972). For contrasting assessments of the effectiveness of the cosmetic industry self-regulation program, compare Murray Berdick, *Cosmetic Industry Initiatives*, 33

FOOD DRUG COSM. L.J. 239 (1978), with Joseph A. Page & Kathleen A. Blackburn, *Behind the Looking Glass: Administrative, Legislative and Private Approaches to Cosmetic Safety Substantiation*, 24 UCLA L. REV. 795 (1977). *See also* Casey Daum, *Self–Regulation in the Cosmetic Industry: A Necessary Reality or a Cosmetic Illusion?* (2006), in Chapter X of the Electronic Book.

G. COAL TAR HAIR DYES

Section 601(a) of the FD&C Act exempts from the prohibition against any poisonous or deleterious substance in cosmetics a coal-tar hair dye if it is labeled with a statutorily prescribed caution statement advising that the consumer should first conduct a test for skin irritation. The special treatment accorded coal tar hair dyes by section 601(a) has been a continuing source of frustration for FDA, which periodically has sought to circumvent the provision.

Toilet Goods Association v. Finch

419 F.2d 21 (2d Cir. 1969).

Nine years ago Congress amended the Food, Drug, and Cosmetic Act by enacting the Color Additive Amendments of 1960. Nearly three years later, after appropriate rule-making proceedings, the Food and Drug Administration (FDA) published its Regulations thereunder, 28 F.R. 6439. This litigation about the validity of their provisions concerning diluents, finished cosmetics and hair-dyes has continued ever since. . . .

The two provisions of § 361 relevant to the FDA's hair-dye regulation are subdivisions (a) and (e). They say that a cosmetic shall be deemed adulterated

(a) If it bears or contains any poisonous or deleterious substance which may render it injurious to users under the conditions of use prescribed in the labeling thereof, or under such conditions of use as are customary or usual: *Provided*, That this provision shall not apply to coal-tar hair dye, the label of which bears the following legend conspicuously displayed thereon: "Caution—This product contains ingredients which may cause skin irritation on certain individuals and a preliminary test according to accompanying directions should first be made. This product must not be used for dyeing the eyelashes or eyebrows; to do so may cause blindness," and the labeling of which bears adequate directions for such preliminary testing. . . .

(e) If it is not a hair dye and it is, or it bears or contains, a color additive which is unsafe within the meaning of section 376(a) of this title.

. . . .

The Regulation held invalid by the district court, 21 C.F.R. § 8.1(u), provides:

(u) The "hair-dye" exemption in section 601(a) of the act applies to those articles intended for use in altering the color of the hair and which are, or which bear or contain, color additives with the sensitization potential of causing skin irritation in certain individuals and possible blindness when used for dyeing the eyelashes or eyebrows. The exemption is permitted with the condition that the label of any such article bear conspicuously the statutory caution and adequate directions for preliminary patch-testing. If the poisonous or deleterious substance in the "hair dye" is one to which the caution is inapplicable and for which patch-testing provides no safeguard, the exemption does not apply; nor does the exemption extend to poisonous or deleterious diluents that may be introduced as wetting agents, hair conditioners, emulsifiers, or other components in a color shampoo, rinse, tint, or similar dual-purpose cosmetics that alter the color of the hair....

Taking first things first, we agree with the invalidation of so much of the Regulation as sought to deprive coal-tar hair dyes of the exemption conferred by § 361(a) in cases where, in the view of FDA, the coal-tar color ingredient carries a danger for which patch-testing provides no safeguard. The Government's argument should indeed be appealing to a legislator— what good is the warning to make a patch test if the test will not disclose the danger? But a court must take the statute as it is, and Congress wrote with great specificity....

It is equally plain that the exemption of § 361(a) does not apply to coloring agents in hair dyes not derived from coal-tar ... We likewise see no basis for invalidating the portion of the Regulation which says that the exemption does not apply to poisonous or deleterious diluents. It is inconceivable that Congress meant to deprive the FDA of its ordinary powers with respect to other ingredients simply because they are combined with a coal-tar dye.

We think the court also erred in excluding from § 361(e) color additives in hair dyes other than those made from coal tar. The 1938 Act applied only to coal-tar colors, and the exemption of hair dyes in subdivision (e) was logical since coal-tar colors were dealt with by subdivision (a) in a supposedly adequate fashion. The modification of subdivision (e) in 1960 was part of a program to regulate all colors, and not merely coal-tar colors. But, if the statute be read with entire literalness, the unaltered introductory provision in subsection (e) now would have the effect of excluding any sanction for the use in a hair dye of an unlisted or uncertified coloring ingredient although not within the proviso to § 361(a). In the absence of any legislative history indicating an intention to broaden the exemption in § 361(e), the most sensible construction is that, despite the retention of the introductory words "if it is not a hair dye," Congress did not mean to exempt non-coal-tar color additives used in hair dyes from the requirement of listing and certification....

NOTES

1. *Origin of Exemption.* The coal tar hair dye exemption in Section 601(a) was the product of intensive lobbying during consideration of the 1938 Act by thousands

of beauty shop operators and employees who were concerned that the pending legislation would require FDA to ban coal tar hair dye products and thus seriously injure their business. The allegation that some ingredients in coal tar hair dyes are carcinogenic prompted Congressional hearings in 1978 and 1979. "Cancer-Causing Chemicals—Part 1 (Safety of Cosmetics and Hair Dyes)," Hearings Before the Subcommittee on Oversight and Investigations of the House Committee on Inter-state and Foreign Commerce, 95th Cong., 2nd Sess. (1978); "Safety of Hair Dyes and Cosmetic Products," Hearing before the Subcommittee on Oversight and Investigations of the House Committee on Interstate and Foreign Commerce, 96th Cong., 1st Sess. (1979). *See also* Anatasia Menechios, *Sixty Years Later: The Survival of the 1938 Coal Tar Hair Dye Exemption* (2000), in Chapter X of the Electronic Book. FDA regulation of carcinogenic coal tar hair dye substances is treated in depth *infra* in Chapter IX.

2. *Scope of Exemption.* The coal tar hair dye exemption extends only to products intended to dye the hair and explicitly excludes products for the eyebrow and eyelash. FD&C Act 601(a). *See Byrd v. United States*, 154 F.2d 62 (5th Cir. 1946).

3. *Deletion of Caution Statement.* FDA Trade Correspondence 103 (Feb. 29, 1940), 1938–49 FDLI Jud. Rec. at 610, states that hair dyes containing harmless coal tar colors need not bear the caution statements specified in Section 601(a) of the FD&C Act. Failure to use the statutory caution statement subjects a coal tar hair dye to Section 601(a), but as long as the product does not contain any poisonous or deleterious substance it is not unlawful. Under Section 601(e), a coal tar hair dye is exempt from the color additive requirements of Section 706 whether or not it bears the statutory caution statement.

4. *Roux Litigation.* FDA has been continually frustrated in efforts to establish that ingredients used in Roux Lash & Brow Tint Kits are hazardous color additives. Not long after enactment of the FD&C Act, FDA seized this product, contending that it contained three poisonous or deleterious substances. The first jury to hear the case was unable to agree on a verdict. A second jury returned a verdict for Roux. *See* James C. Munch & James C. Munch, Jr., *Notices of Judgment—Cosmetics*, 20 FOOD DRUG COSM. L.J. 399, 400–01 (1959). In 1968, FDA instituted another seizure of the product, charging that the three ingredients were unapproved color additives. The district court dismissed the case on the ground that it was controlled by the decision in *TGA v. Gardner*, 278 F. Supp. 786 (S.D.N.Y. 1968). This ruling was reversed on appeal and the case was remanded for trial. *United States v. Roux Labs., Inc.*, 437 F.2d 209 (9th Cir. 1971). The district court ultimately dismissed the action on the ground that a 1963 Federal Register notice exempted the substances from color additive requirements. *Roux Lash & Brow Tints*, FDA CONSUMER, Nov. 1974, at 42. In 1974, FDA brought yet another seizure, again alleging the use of unapproved color additives. The trial judge this time ruled that the 1963 Federal Register notice did not exempt the substances. Following trial of the factual question whether the ingredients were color additives or diluents, the jury returned a verdict for the claimant. *Roux Lash & Brow Tint Kits*, FDA CONSUMER, Dec. 1977–Jan. 1978, at 37.

CHAPTER IX

REGULATION OF CARCINOGENS

Perhaps the most famous provision of the FD&C Act is the Delaney Clause, a provision of the 1958 Food Additives Amendment that prohibits FDA approval of any food additive that has been shown to "induce cancer in man or other animal. . . ." Its presence in the law is largely attributable to the persistence of New York Representative James Delaney, who from 1950 to 1953 presided over a House select committee established to investigate the use of man-made chemicals in producing and marketing food. *See supra* p. 393. Representative Delaney became convinced that chemical additives—or some of them—posed serious risks to humans. And he was particularly concerned that chemicals shown to cause cancer in experimental animals could be responsible for the reported increase in U.S. cancer incidence.

In the early 1950s, when Delaney's committee concluded its work, only a small number of chemicals were believed to be carcinogenic, and few of these could be found in food. Hence, Delaney's endorsement of a clause that flatly prohibited the approval of any "food additive" that induces cancer in animals was seen as noncontroversial. A generation later, however, a different picture emerged. As the result of more comprehensive and thorough testing, more chemicals used or found in food exhibited carcinogenic potential. And dramatic advances in the sensitivity of chemical analysis were revealing the presence in food of small, often very small, quantities of hitherto unsuspected residues of chemicals used in its production, processing, and packaging. What earlier appeared to be a small problem was now seen as a serious threat to public health on the one hand and industrial agriculture on the other. In this more complicated world, the tribute colleagues paid to Representative Delaney presented a mounting regulatory challenge.

In this chapter we explore FDA's response to this challenge. We highlight FDA's embrace and exploitation of an analytical methodology for estimating the potential frequency with which a chemical capable of causing cancer might produce cancers in a population exposed to the chemical. This methodology—quantitative risk assessment—later played a central role in decision making by other agencies that share responsibility for regulating toxic substances, including EPA, the Occupational Safety and Health Administration, and the Consumer Product Safety Commission. Thus this chapter provides an introduction to cancer risk assessment as well as an account of one agency's struggle to make sense of a challenging statutory mandate.

A. HISTORICAL BACKGROUND

While cancer has gripped public attention and preoccupied regulators only since World War II, its existence as a discrete disease and the lack of effective treatments were recognized in ancient times. In the 4th century B.C., Hippocrates wrote: "It is better not to apply any treatment in cases of occult cancer; for, if treated, the patients die quickly; but if not treated, they hold out for a long time." II APHORISMS 256 (F. Adams trans., 1886). Four centuries later the Roman physician Celsus offered this pessimistic assessment of the disease's progression.

> ... [G]enerally the first stage is what the Greeks call cacothese; then from that follows a carcinoma without ulceration; then ulcer- ation, and from that a kind of wart. It is only the cacoethes which can be removed; the other stages are irritated by treatment; and the more so the more vigorous it is. Some have used caustic medicaments, some the cautery, some excision with a scalpel; but no medicament has ever given relief; the parts cauterized are excited immediately to an increase until they cause death. After excision, even when a scar has formed, none the less the disease has returned and caused death; while at the same time the majority of patients; though no violent measure are applied in the attempt to remove the tumor, but only mild applications in order to soothe it, attain to a ripe old age in spite of it. No one, however, except by time and experiment, can have the skill to distinguish a cacoethees which admits of being treated from a carcinoma which does not.

II DE MEDICINA, Book V, Chapter 28, pp. 129, 131 (W.G. Spencer translation, 1938). *See also* Frank Riddle, *Ancient and Medieval Chemotherapy for Cancer*, 76 ISIS 319 (1985).

Although more is discovered each year about the causes of cancer in humans, complete understanding of the disease remains elusive. Percivall Pott, an English physician, published the first epidemiological report identi- fying one cause of cancer in 1775. Pott described what he termed "chim- ney-sweepers' cancer," a disease "which always makes its first attack on, and its first appearance in the inferior part of the scrotum...." He advocated immediate surgery upon discovery of the lesion "for when the disease has got head, it is rapid in its progress, painful in all its attacks, and most certainly destructive in its event." CHIRURIGICAL OBSERVATIONS 64– 68. Apart from Pott's prescient finding, however, knowledge about the causes and mechanisms of cancer remained primitive throughout the 19th century. Only after researchers began using large colonies of inbred strains of rodents in toxicity studies in the early 20th century did scientific investigation of the processes of carcinogenesis itself begin in earnest. Such studies also provided a method—still the chief method—for evaluating the potential carcinogenicity of man-made substances.

Many ancient Greek and Roman writers recognized that consumption of different amounts of the same substance had quite different effects. But it was Paracelsus, an enigmatic alchemist writing in the first half of the 16th century, who articulated the relationship between dose and response: "Poison is in everything, and nothing is without poison. The dosage makes it either a poison or a remedy." H.M. PACHTER, MAGIC INTO SCIENCE: THE STORY OF PARACELSUS 86 (1951). Paracelsus' profound insight did not immediately advance societal decision making. He correctly pointed out that there is a line dividing safe from unsafe doses, but he offered no criteria for determining how to draw that line. It took several centuries before dose-response relationships assumed their present importance in regulatory risk assessment.

B.   EARLY FDA POLICY

The advent of systematic toxicity testing in laboratory animals made possible, for the first time, the formulation of an *operational* definition of safety. During the 1940s FDA scientists adopted the rough rule of thumb that a safe human dose of a substance was 1/100th of the highest dose that produced no toxic effects in test animals (the "no effect level," now known as the "no observed adverse effect level" (NOAEL)).

Arnold Lehman, et al., *Procedures for the Appraisal of the Toxicity of Chemicals in Foods*

4 FOOD DRUG COSMETIC LAW JOURNAL 412 (1949).

While it is not especially difficult to evaluate a set of pharmacological data which lead to the conclusion that the substance being investigated is a poison, it is extremely difficult to conclude that any chemical is safe for human consumption. It would be difficult, if not impossible, to set up a number of criteria which, if met, would automatically make the compound safe for use. Each chemical must be evaluated as a separate entity by individuals with adequate scientific background and experience. . . .

The first consideration is the transference of animal data to what might be expected for man. Experience has shown that if *all* of the experimental data are correlated, a good estimate of the probable effect on man can be made. In some cases, it is possible to compare the effects of the chemical with a drug or compound which has a known history on both man and animals. In other cases, the comparative biochemistry of man and the various species of animals used will serve as a guide for evaluating the data obtained. Finally, there are compounds which produce effects in animals that are so alarming that one has no hesitation in excluding such compounds from further consideration. For example, if a chemical has been shown to possess carcinogenic properties, there would be no question in applying animal data to man. . . .

The second factor that must be kept in mind is the apparent heterogeneity of man as compared with the relative homogeneity of experimental animals. Normally, laboratory animals exist under controlled conditions, are fed adequate diets, and are in good health. If a chemical is added to human food, however, it is eaten by all people, the young and old, those suffering from various pathological conditions, and those existing in border-line states of nutrition. Obviously, all of these conditions are not and cannot readily be duplicated in animal experiments. About the only compensation that can be made is the provision of an adequate margin of safety in establishing safe levels for the particular chemical in a food.

The third consideration which is all too often overlooked is the other sources of exposure to a given chemical. These other sources may include industrial exposure to the chemical, the natural occurrence of the chemical in drinking water or edible plants and animals, and existing or proposed uses of this chemical in other food products. Here also should be mentioned the possibilities that a chemical may act synergistically with other constituents of the diet, may alter intestinal absorption, may interfere with utilization of accessory food factors, and may increase the ease with which allergic conditions can be produced.

Since man is the ultimate consumer of the chemical to be added to foods, clinical trials are certainly to be desired. . . . Human volunteers even in moderate numbers are difficult to obtain; hence, considerable reliance must be placed on the results of animal experimentation, and this accounts for the emphasis placed on the objective of a 100–fold margin of safety.

Need clinical trials

———

As Dr. Lehman relates, a finding that a substance caused cancer in experimental animals was regarded as so "alarming" as to exclude it from consideration for human exposure. Accordingly, FDA used (and continues to use) the 100:1 safety factor to set permissible exposure levels only for substances that cause adverse effects other than cancer. For chemicals that caused cancer, no safety factor was ever used. The agency's goal was to prevent any use of carcinogens in human food or drugs.

Accordingly, under the statutory provision requiring certification of coal tar colors used in food, drugs, and cosmetics, FDA promptly deleted from the permitted list of colors "the only two coal-tar colors known to be capable of producing carcinogenic manifestations." Herbert O. Calvery, *Coal-Tar Colors: Their Use in Foods, Drugs, and Cosmetics*, 114 AM. J. PHARM. 324, 334 (1942). When the agency discovered that one of these colors, Butter Yellow (dimethyl-amino-azobenzene), was still being used after being delisted, it launched a comprehensive enforcement campaign, including seizures, injunctions, and criminal prosecutions. 1945 FDA ANNU-AL REPORT at 52. In 1950, FDA banned two nonnutritive sweeteners on the basis of animal experiments that showed them to be carcinogenic. 15 Fed. Reg. 321 (Jan. 19, 1950). Four years later, it banned natural tonka beans and their constituent, coumarin, because coumarin was found to be carcinogenic. 19 Fed. Reg. 1239 (Mar. 5, 1954).

Thus, it can be said that, even before the enactment of the 1958 Food Additives Amendment, with its Delaney Clause, FDA embraced a policy of prohibiting the addition of any carcinogen to food and drugs.

C. EVOLUTION OF LEGISLATIVE POLICY

1. THE INCIDENCE AND CAUSES OF CANCER

Cancer primarily afflicts older people, and thus its prevalence varies with the age of the population. In the nation's early years, average life expectancy was much shorter than it is today. Shortly before the Civil War, for example, average life expectancies at birth in Boston and New York were 21.43 and 19.6 years. LEMUEL SHATTUCK, REPORT OF THE SANITARY COMMISSION OF MASSACHUSETTS 104 (1850). By 1900, as a result of the public health measures undertaken during the previous half century, life expectancy of Americans at birth had risen to 47.3 years. Average life expectancy has continued to rise reaching 71.5 years for men and 78.3 years for women by the end of the last century.

This dramatic rise in longevity has been achieved chiefly through successful assaults on infectious diseases. The three leading causes of death in 1900 were pneumonia/influenza, tuberculosis, and diarrhea. Today, these diseases occur less frequently and rarely cause death. Now the two leading causes of death are heart disease and cancer. The sharp rise in the number of cancer fatalities is largely the result of successful attacks on infectious diseases, not of an increase in cancer incidence. Current statistics indicate that the overall prevalence of cancer in this country remains steady. Some types of cancer have become more common while others have declined in frequency, but overall, age-adjusted incidence does not appear to have changed significantly.

Based upon evidence of variations in cancer frequency among different populations, epidemiologists have contended that up to 90 percent of all cancers are "environmental" in origin. But this label can be misleading; "environmental causes" of cancer include not only air and water pollutants, but also lifestyle factors such as smoking, dietary patterns, consumption of alcoholic beverages, and sexual habits. At a 1979 conference of the American Health Foundation, a group of cancer experts produced the following consensus ranking of cancer risk factors:

Factors in Cancer, as Summarized by the Conference on the Primary Promotion of Cancer, New York, 1979

	Men	Women
	Percent of Cancers Involving the Listed Factors	
Smoking	25–35	5–10
Alcohol	7	2
Occupation	6	2
Nutrition	30	30–50
Food contaminants	0	0
Drugs	1	1
Air pollution	0	0
Ionizing radiation	3	3

	Men	Women
	Percent of Cancers Involving the Listed Factors	
Ultraviolet radiation	(skin 50)[1]	(skin 50)[1]
Heredity	10–25	10–25
Viruses	1	1
Immunodeficiency	1	1

[1] Excluded from total cancers.

M. Shimkin, Industrial and Life-Style Carcinogens 10 (1980).

In a comprehensive study commissioned by the Office of Technology Assessment, two prominent British epidemiologists reached similar conclusions:

Proportions of Cancer Deaths Attributed to Various Different Factors

Factor or class of factors	Percent of all Cancer deaths	
	Best estimate	Range of acceptable estimates
Tobacco	30	25–40
Alcohol	3	2–4
Diet	35	10–70
Food additives	1	–5[1]–2
Reproductive and sexual behavior	7	1–13
Occupation	4	2–8
Pollution	2	1–5
Industrial products	1	1–2
Medicines and medical	1	0.5–3
Geophysical factors[2]	3	2–4
Infection	10?	1–?
Unknown	?	?

[1] Allowing for a possibly protective effect of antioxidants and other preservatives.
[2] Only about 1%, not 3%, could reasonably be described as "avoidable".

Sir Richard Doll & Richard Peto, *The Causes of Cancer: Quantitative Estimates of Avoidable Risks of Cancer in The United States Today*, 66 J. Nat'l Cancer Inst. 1191, 1256 (1981).

While these tables represent estimates rather than measured frequencies, they have elicited agreement from other experts, and thus provide a concensus picture of the major causes of cancer among Americans.

2.   The Original Delaney Clause

As the number of Americans dying from cancer rose in the 1930s and 1940s, reflecting the increased longevity of the population, public anxiety about the disease grew. Inevitably, this concern stimulated congressional consideration of measures to reduce potential cancer risks. One expression of this effort was the enactment of the Delaney Clause in 1958.

A version of the Clause appears in three places in the Act: the Food Additives Amendment of 1958 (section 409(c)(3)(A)), the Color Additive Amendments of 1960 (section 721(b)(5)(B)), and the Animal Drug Amendments of 1968 (section 512(d)(1)(I)). While the three versions differ slightly in their language, their basic thrust is similar—to prohibit the addition to human food of any defined substance that has been found to induce cancer in man or laboratory animals. The language of section 409(c)(3)(A) is exemplary:

> [N]o such regulation [authorizing use of a food additive] shall issue if a fair evaluation of the data before the Secretary—
>
> (A) fails to establish that the proposed use of the food additive, under the conditions of use to be specified in the regulation, will be safe: *Provided*, That no additive shall be deemed to be safe if it is found to induce cancer when ingested by man or animal, or if it is found, after tests which are appropriate for the evaluation of the safety of food additives, to induce cancer in man or animal. . . .

While the Delaney Clause attracted attention during congressional deliberations on the Food Additives Amendment and Color Additive Amendments, it was not the central focus of debate either time. The accompanying legislative history, therefore, can be frustrating for one who wishes to divine Congress' contemporaneous understanding of the provisions that have excited so much interest since. Even now there is no agreement on how the key passages should be interpreted. This lack of agreement has played an important role in FDA's efforts to fashion a policy to regulate carcinogens. (For the views of the authors on the Delaney Clause, *see*, *e.g.*, Peter Barton Hutt, *The Basis and Purpose of Government Regulation of Adulteration and Misbranding of Food*, 33 FOOD DRUG COSM. L.J. 505 (1978); Hutt, *Public Policy Issues in Regulating Carcinogens in Food*, 33 FOOD DRUG COSM. L.J. 541 (1978); Hutt, *Unresolved Issues in the Conflict Between Individual Freedom and Government Control of Food Safety*, 33 FOOD DRUG COSM. L.J. 558 (1978); Hutt, *FDA Can Handle Food Safety Issues Most Effectively*, LEGAL TIMES OF WASH., Apr. 27, 1981, at 28; Richard A. Merrill, *FDA's Implementation of the Delaney Clause: Repudiation of Congressional Choice or Reasoned Adaptation to Scientific Progress?*, 5 YALE J. ON REG. 1 (1987); Merrill, *FDA's "Erasure" of the Delaney Clause: A Case Study in Statutory Interpretation*, 50 AFDO Q. BULL. 199 (1986); Merrill, *Regulating Carcinogens in Food: A Legislator's Guide to the Food Safety Provisions of the Federal Food, Drug and Cosmetic Act*, 77 MICH. L. REV. 171 (1978). Compare Margaret Gilhooley, *Plain Meaning, Absurd Results and the Legislative Purpose: The Interpretation of the Delaney Clause*, 40 ADMIN. L. REV. 267 (1988), with Richard M. Cooper, *Stretching Delaney Til It Breaks*, REGULATION, Nov./Dec. 1985, at 11.)

In 1950, the House of Representatives established a Select Committee to Investigate the Use of Chemicals in Food Products, chaired by Representative James Delaney. The reports of that committee did not make specific recommendations about carcinogens. No special consideration was given to carcinogens during the enactment of the Miller Pesticide Amendments of 1954, which added section 408 to the FD&C Act. Nor did the initial versions of the legislation that ultimately became the Food Additives Amendment of 1958 contain anticancer language. In 1957, however, as Congress began to focus on requirements for food additives, Delaney introduced a revised bill (H.R. 7798, 85th Cong., 1st Sess.), which contained the following clause: "The Secretary shall not approve for use in food any chemical additive found to induce cancer in man, or, after tests, found to induce cancer in animals."

[handwritten margin note: propose clause]

FDA's parent, the Department of Health, Education, and Welfare, initially objected to this provision on the following grounds:

[handwritten margin note: initial disagreement]

> We, of course, agree that no chemical should be permitted to be used in food if, as so used, it may cause cancer. We assume that this, and no more, is the aim of the sponsor. No specific reference to carcinogens is necessary for that purpose, however, since the general requirements of this bill give assurance that no chemical additive can be cleared if there is reasonable doubt about its safety in that respect.

> On the other hand, the above-quoted provisions are so broadly phrased that they could be read to bar an additive from the food supply even if it can induce cancer only when used on test animals in a way having no bearing on the question of carcinogenicity for its intended use. This, we think, would not be in the public interest. Scientists, I am advised, can produce cancer in test animals by injecting sugar in a certain manner, and they can produce cancers by injections into test animals of cottonseed oil, olive oil, or tannic acid (a component of many foods). Probably they can do the same thing with other naturally occurring foods chemicals. We think that it would be unnecessary and undesirable to rule out of the food supply sugar, vegetable oils, or common table beverages simply because, by an extraordinary method of application never encountered at the dining table, it is possible to induce cancer by injecting the substances into the muscles of test animals.

"Food Additives," Hearings before a Subcomm. of the House Comm. on Interstate and Foreign Commerce, 85th Cong. 38–39 (1958).

In July 1958, the House Commerce Committee reported out a bill requiring premarketing clearance of food additives but containing no anticancer clause. Accordingly, Representative Delaney urged the addition of the following anticancer proviso:

> *Provided*, That no additive shall be deemed to be safe if it is found to induce cancer when ingested by man or animal, or if it is found, after tests which are appropriate for the evaluation of the safety of food additives, to induce cancer in man or animal.

[handwritten margin note: New clause]

Thus, on its face the Clause Delaney championed applies only to "food additives" and does not apply to food itself or to food substances excluded from the statutory definition of a "food additive" because they are generally recognized as safe (GRAS) or were sanctioned by FDA or USDA between 1938 and 1959.

Agreed

Rather than risk possible defeat of the legislation, HEW agreed to this amendment, which became part of the statute. Assistant HEW Secretary Elliot Richardson, in a letter to the committee chairman, at once embraced Delaney's goal and stated that the anticancer language would not change the bill's meaning:

> ... This Department is in complete accord with the intent of these suggestions—that no substance should be sanctioned for uses in food that might produce cancer in man. H.R. 13254, as approved by your committee, will accomplish this intent, since it specifically instructs the Secretary not to issue a regulation permitting use of an additive in food if a fair evaluation of the data before the Secretary fails to establish that the proposed use of the additive will be safe. The scientific tests that are adequate to establish the safety of an additive will give information about the tendency of an additive to produce cancer when it is present in food. Any indication that the additive may thus be carcinogenic would, under the terms of the bill, restrain the Secretary from approving the proposed use of the additive unless and until further testing shows to the point of reasonable certainty that the additive would not produce cancer and thus would be safe under the proposed conditions of use. This would afford good, strong public health protection.
>
>   . . . .
>
> At the same time, if it would serve to allay any lingering apprehension on the part of those who desire an explicit statutory mandate on this point, the Department would interpose no objection to appropriate mention of cancer in food additives legislation. If the specific disease were referred to in the law, it would however, be important for everyone to have a clear understanding that this would in no way restrict the Department's freedom in guarding against other harmful effects from food additives.

Richardson welcomed the amendment's reference to "appropriate tests."

> [T]he language suggested by some to bar carcinogenic additives would, if read literally, forbid the approval for use in food of any substance that causes any type of cancer in any test animal by any route of administration. This could lead to undesirable results which obviously were not intended by those who suggested the language. Concentrated sugar solution, lard, certain edible vegetable oils, and even cold water have been reported to cause a type of cancer at the site of injection when injected repeatedly by hypodermic needle into the same spot in a test animal. But scientists have not suggested that these same substances cause cancer when swallowed by mouth.
>
> The enactment of a law which would seem to bar such common materials from the diet on the basis of the evidence described above, would place the agency that administered it in an untenable position. The agency would either have to try to enforce the law literally so as to keep these items out of the diet—

evidently an impossible task—*or it would have to read between the lines of the law an intent which would make the law workable,* without a clear guide from Congress as to what was meant. 104 Cong. Rec. 17415 (Aug. 13, 1958) (emphasis supplied). The bill was passed by the House with the revised amendment.

In the Senate, the House-passed bill was favorably reported without hearings. Commenting on the anticancer clause the Senate Report declared:

> We applaud Congressman Delaney for having taken this, as he has every other opportunity, to focus our attention on the cancer-producing potentialities of various substances, but we want the record to show that in our opinion the bill is aimed at preventing the addition to the food our people eat of any substances the ingestion of which reasonable people would expect to produce not just cancer but any disease or disability. In short, we believe the bill reads and means the same with or without the inclusion of the clause referred to. This is also the view of the Food and Drug Administration.

S. Rep. No. 2422, 85th Cong., 2d Sess. 10–11 (1958). The bill passed the Senate and, after minor amendments were agreed to by the House, was signed into law as the Food Additives Amendment of 1958.

3.   The Color Additives Delaney Clause

The 1960 Color Additive Amendments contain a Delaney Clause similar in language and identical in principle to the clause that appears in section 409. This clause precludes approval for food use of any color additive shown to induce cancer when ingested by experimental animals. Because the Amendments do not recognize a category of "generally recognized as safe" colors or exclude substances that were sanctioned or used prior to 1960, the Delaney Clause in section 706 applies to all food coloring agents except those that are only provisionally listed while further safety testing is being conducted.

The original House bill contained an anticancer clause; the bill initially introduced in the Senate was silent on the point. Both bills contained language comparable to the food additive law, requiring proof of the safety of a color before FDA could permanently list it. Then, just before Thanksgiving in 1959, HEW Secretary Arthur Flemming issued a statement advising the public about the possible contamination of substantial quantities of cranberries with a pesticide, aminotriazol, which FDA had recently determined was a carcinogen. Although the Act's pesticide residue provisions contain no anticancer clause, the agency determined that use of this pesticide could not be approved as safe, and that the public should be warned of the potential hazard. During the same period, FDA determined that the previously-approved use of the drug diethylstilbestrol (DES) in poultry resulted in detectable residues in liver and skin fat. *See* p. 1131 *infra*. Although the 1958 Delaney Clause did not apply, because DES for poultry was subject to a prior sanction and therefore not a "food additive," FDA proposed to withdraw the new drug application for this use on the ground that the finding of residues confirmed that it was unsafe.

On the heels of these two events, Secretary Flemming appeared before the House Commerce Committee in January 1960 to testify in support of the proposed color additive legislation. Anticipating that a major issue would be the desirability of including an anticancer clause, he had requested the National Cancer Institute to summarize the prevailing scientific knowledge about the etiology of cancer. The NCI report concluded:

> No one at this time can tell how much or how little of a carcinogen would be required to produce cancer in any human being, or how long it would take the cancer to develop.

"Color Additives," Hearings Before the House Comm. on Interstate and Foreign Commerce, 86th Cong., 2d Sess. 45, 52 (1960). After offering the NCI report for the record, Secretary Flemming testified:

> This is why we have no hesitancy in advocating the inclusion of the anticancer clause.

> Unless and until there is a sound scientific basis for the establishment of tolerances for carcinogens, I believe the Government has a duty to make clear—in law as well as in administrative policy—that it will do everything possible to put persons in a position where they will not unnecessarily be adding residues of carcinogens to their diet.

Flemming contended that the anticancer clause allowed greater room for scientific judgment than its critics claimed:

> It has been suggested that once a chemical is shown to induce a tumor in a single rat, this forecloses further research and forever forbids the use of the chemical in food. This is not true. The conclusion that an additive "is found to induce cancer when ingested by man or animal" is a scientific one. The conclusion is reached by competent scientists using widely accepted scientific testing methods and critical judgment. An isolated and inexplicable tumor would not be a basis for concluding that the test substance produces cancer. . . .

> This, I believe, is as far as our discretion should go in the light of present scientific knowledge. We have no basis for asking Congress to give us discretion to establish a safe tolerance for a substance which definitely has been shown to produce cancer when added to the diet of test animals. We simply have no basis on which such discretion could be exercised because no one can tell us with any assurance at all how to establish a safe dose of any cancer-producing substance.

In a subsequent colloquy with Committee Chairman Oren Harris, Flemming returned to the distinction between the exercise of scientific judgment in identifying carcinogenic activity and the discretion to set tolerance levels for carcinogens:

> When the time comes that our research reaches the place where that threshold can be identified, where a tolerance can be established that we know will not induce cancer in man, then we

will come back and ask the Congress to give us authority to identify the threshold or to establish the tolerance.

Even with Flemming's assurances, however, some feared that the Delaney Clause was too rigid. In early 1960, the President's Special Assistant for Science and Technology convened a panel of prominent scientists to consider the regulation of carcinogens in food. The panel's report was released by the White House on May 14, 1960, just before the 1960 Amendments were to be voted on by the House and Senate. *See* PRESIDENT'S SCIENTIFIC ADVISORY COMMITTEE, REPORT OF THE PANEL ON FOOD ADDITIVES (May 1960), reprinted in 106 Cong. Rec. 15380 (July 1, 1960).

The report recounted the difficulties encountered in interpreting and administering the 1958 Delaney Clause. For example, the report pointed out that trace amounts of carcinogens occur in common food products:

> In foodstuffs, as they occur in nature, one finds traces of chemicals which in larger amounts are generally accepted as carcinogenic, such as certain inorganic arsenic compounds, radium and selenium. It can be shown by methods of analysis now available that ordinary table salt derived from rock salt contains trace amounts of radium and that foodstuffs containing iron salts are contaminated by minute quantities of arsenic. Although it cannot be stated absolutely that these traces of carcinogenic materials have never induced cancer in any human, the available evidence has not directed suspicion to these trace amounts as significant to the over-all cancer morbidity.

The panel report concluded with this advice:

> In applying the provisions of Section 409(c)(3) of the Food Additives Amendment ... the enforcing agency must employ the "rule of reason" based on scientific judgment in order to carry out the intent of the Congress to protect the public from the possibility of increasing cancer risks through the diet.
>
> The definition of a carcinogen implicit in the language of Section 409(c) requires discretion in its interpretation because so many variables enter into a judgment as to whether a particular substance is or is not carcinogenic.
>
> It is to be emphasized that the present difficulty in establishing whether there are permissible levels for certain possibly carcinogenic food additives is accentuated by the limited relevant scientific information available. From the experience obtained in animal experiments and study of humans who have been exposed to carcinogens in the course of their work such as cited above, the panel believes that the probability of cancer induction from a particular carcinogen in minute doses may be eventually assessed by weighing scientific evidence as it becomes available.
>
> The special emphasis placed by the Congress on the protection of the public from the dangers resulting from the addition of possible carcinogens to food calls for prudent administration of section 409(c).... Since an area of administrative discretion based on the rule of reason is unavoidable if the clause is to be workable,

it is essential that this discretion be based on the most informed
and expert scientific advice available. Until the causes of carcinogenesis are better understood, each situation must be judged in the
light of all applicable evidence. In this way the protection of public
health can best be assured.

    ... If existing legislation does not permit the Secretary of
Health, Education, and Welfare to exercise discretion consistent
with the recommendations of this report, it is recommended that
appropriate modifications in the law be sought.

Id. at 8–9. This report was widely disseminated during the congressional
debate on the 1960 Delaney Clause.

    The House Commerce Committee, reporting the bill ultimately enact-
ed, H. R. Rep. No. 1761, 86th Cong., 2d Sess. 13–14 (1960), discussed
several proposed amendments to the Color Additives anticancer clause and
explained why no changes were made:

    One industry witness objected to any anticancer clause. An-
other witness argued that it is possible to establish safe tolerance
levels for substances that produce cancer when fed to test animals.
Some would have the ban on cancer producers apply only to colors
that induce cancer when ingested in an amount and under conditions reasonably related to their intended use. And another witness proposed that the cancer clause be taken out of its present
position in the bill and added with material language changes to
section 706(b)(5)(A) so that it would become simply one of the
factors for the Secretary to consider in evaluating the safety of a
color additive.

    It is evident that such proposed changes are intended to give
the Secretary the right to establish tolerances for presumed safe
levels of colors that produce cancer when tested under appropriate
laboratory conditions. Thus, any of the proposals, if adopted,
would weaken the present anticancer clause in the reported bill.
For this reason all of the proposed changes were rejected by the
committee....

    Some of the panel members have suggested that despite these
difficulties, in extraordinary cases, the Secretary of Health, Education, and Welfare should have the authority to decide that a
minute amount of a cancer-producing chemical may be added to
man's food after a group of scientists consider all the facts and
conclude that the quantity to be tolerated is probably without
hazard....

    In view of the uncertainty surrounding the determination of
safe tolerances for carcinogens, the committee decided that the
Delaney anticancer provision in the reported bill should be retained without change.

    A qualification that any test demonstrating carcinogenicity be appro-
priate was incorporated in the enacted version of the anticancer clause. The
clause contains two parts: A color additive that will or may result in
ingestion is deemed unsafe if it is found to cause cancer when ingested or if

it is found to cause cancer after tests "which are appropriate for the evaluation of the safety of additives for use in food." A color additive that will not be ingested, on the other hand, falls within the proscription of the anticancer clause only if it is found to cause cancer "after tests which are appropriate for the evaluation of the safety of additives for such [non-ingestion] use, or after other relevant exposure of man or animal to such additive."

Prior to the 1970s FDA invoked either Delaney Clause only twice, both times to ban unimportant indirect food additives, 32 Fed. Reg. 5675 (Apr. 7, 1967) (1,2–dihydro–2, 2, 4–trimethylquinoline, polymerized), and 34 Fed. Reg. 19073 (Dec. 2, 1968) (4,4–methylenebis(2–choroanaline)). In that era few substances were systematically tested for carcinogenicity, the customary test protocols were less rigorous than those now in use, and available analytical methods were not sufficiently sensitive to detect trace amounts of known or suspected carcinogens in consumer products. The 1970s, however, brought changes on several fronts: More chemicals were subjected to toxicological evaluation in accordance with better designed and more carefully executed study protocols; a significant percentage of these exhibited the capacity to produce tumors in one or more test species; and analytical chemists improved by several orders of magnitude their methods for detecting and measuring trace chemicals in environmental media—including food. The collective result of these developments was to expand the universe of chemicals to which one of the versions of the Delaney Clause might apply.

D. REGULATION OF DIETHYLSTILBESTROL

In the 1940s and 1950s, FDA approved a number of new drug applications for the use of diethylstilbestrol (DES) as a growth promotant in poultry, cattle, and sheep. As discussed in Chapter V, new drugs for animal use were, prior to the passage of the Animal Drug Amendments of 1968, subject to the same section 505 licensure requirements as new drugs for human use. After the enactment of the Food Additive Amendments of 1958, animal drugs intended for food-producing animals were also subject to the food additive regime of section 409. Therefore, when FDA became highly concerned about the carcinogenicity of DES residues in meat in the late 1950s, section 409's Delaney Clause was an obvious tool to address the problem. This tool was unavailable with respect to the NDAs that had been approved before section 409 went into effect, however, because FDA concluded that these uses of DES were "prior sanctioned" uses exempt from the food additive definition and thus from the Delaney Clause as well. *See* FD&C Act 201(s)(4). In attempting to withdraw approval of these older NDAs, FDA thus had to rely on the general drug safety standard of section 505, a tactic challenged by an animal drug manufacturer in the case below.

Bell v. Goddard

366 F.2d 177 (7th Cir. 1966).

■ SWYGERT, CIRCUIT JUDGE....

In July 1957 the petitioner filed a new drug application for "Stilbo-serts" covering the manufacture and sale of a pellet of his own formula containing diethylstilbestrol and intended for use in producing caponette poultry. The application became conditionally effective on January 11, 1958 and fully effective on March 24, 1959.

On December 10, 1959 the Secretary of Health, Education, and Welfare announced that a recently completed re-examination of the use of stilbestrol in the poultry industry had led him to the conclusion that it was desirable to eliminate a potential cancer hazard to the consuming public occasioned by the ingestion of stilbestrol-treated poultry. Shortly thereafter, this administrative proceeding was initiated by the Commissioner of Food and Drugs pursuant to 21 U.S.C. § 355(e) [FD&C Act 505(e)] to determine whether new drug applications covering drugs containing DES for use in poultry production should be suspended....

The drug involved, Stilboserts, consists of pellets containing either 12 or 15 milligrams of diethylstilbestrol. The pellets, to be implanted in live poultry, are designed to provide for the gradual release of DES over a period of weeks. The labeling submitted with the new drug application recommends the implantation of one tablet in chickens of any age four to six weeks before marketing, and two tablets in turkeys six weeks before marketing. Implantation is "under the loose skin just below the head." Stilboserts were recommended for poultry fattening and to produce tenderized, flavorized, upgraded poultry, and to improve feed efficiency.

DES is a synthetic estrogenic drug which was first used in medical practice in 1939; the use of natural estrogens in medicine dates to about 1920. The first new drug application for the use of DES in medicine was approved in 1941; a new drug application for use of DES in poultry production was first approved in 1947. The fact that oral administration of DES had been shown to produce cancer in test animals was known at that time, and DES was suspected of being carcinogenic to humans. It was believed, however, that no significant residue of the drug remained in the edible tissue of treated poultry.

Beginning in 1955, a team of scientists of the Food and Drug Administration headed by Dr. Ernest Umberger developed a bio-assay method of detecting and measuring the estrogenic residue remaining in edible tissues of poultry treated with drugs containing DES.... Dr. Umberger was able to calculate that the petitioner's product, Stilboserts, in 15 and 12 milligram doses, under the conditions of use in the petitioner's new drug application, results in [up to 50 ppb] residues of added DES four weeks after chickens are treated....

Based upon these facts, the Commissioner determined that the addition of diethylstilbestrol to poultry, resulting in residues in the edible portions, was unsafe to the consuming public....

[Petitioner] argues that since the quantity of stilbestrol residue in caponette tissues was deemed insignificant at [the time of approval of his application], the suspension of his application can only be attributed to the change in policy embarked upon by the Secretary of Health, Education, and Welfare which was allegedly prompted by the latter's desire to achieve improper retrospective application of the so-called "Delaney clause" of the Food Additives Amendment Act of 1958....

The petitioner contends that the residues of DES found in the livers of caponettes which have been treated with Stilboserts are so minuscule as not to pose a health hazard, in other words, that Stilboserts were not shown to be "unsafe" within the meaning of section 355(e). He points to the evidence in the record that the caponette trade represented one per cent of the poultry market, an average of one caponette per year for every third family in the United States. Assuming residues of the order of forty-five parts per billion, as found by the examiner, this means, according to the petitioner, a total of six micrograms per caponette, a per capita exposure on the average of less than one microgram per year. The petitioner indicates that it is a common practice to apply a safety margin of 100 to 1. This would raise the exposure of DES in the diet per person to a maximum of 100 micrograms, which the petitioner says is an inconsequential, nonharmful residue of the drug in the diet. He further maintains that estrogen occurs in many natural foods and that, according to the evidence, the amount of estrogen exposure in the diet from a variety of common foodstuffs is greater than any exposure from caponette residues. The petitioner also points out that estrogen is produced naturally in the human body which has a regulatory mechanism that varies the amount produced, that this internal regulation in turn is affected by estrogen introduced by external sources, and that excess estrogen is detoxified and conjugated in the liver as a natural process, whatever its sources, natural or external....

The answer to the petitioner's contentions in great part is that DES is a carcinogen.... It is true that the petitioner's expert witnesses disagreed, and testified that the small amount of DES found in caponette livers is safe and would not impose a risk. But this conflict in testimony does not mean that the Commissioner's ultimate finding that the petitioner's drug was not safe is without substantial evidentiary support.

Although the actual number or percentage of chickens treated with DES is unknown, it is a known fact that the consumption of caponettes is not evenly spread over the population.

Therefore, attempting to assess the safety factor by averaging per capita consumption in order to show the lack of exposure and hazard, as the petitioner suggests, is not justified. Secondly, even though estrogen occurs naturally in certain foodstuffs, such as beef liver, eggs, and lettuce, there is as yet no knowledge of the amounts which are contained in such foods. The existence of natural estrogen in foodstuffs does not warrant the intake of DES by a deliberate means of exposure through the implantation of such drug in a chicken so as to make it tastier and to save feed costs. If estrogens are contained naturally in certain items of diet, there is no justification for adding more by an artificial method....

Following enactment of the 1958 Food Additives Amendment, FDA took the position the Delaney Clause precluded it from approving any new DES uses or products. But, as noted above, the agency also concluded that the Delaney Clause did not apply to existing DES approvals because they covered "prior sanctioned" uses exempt from the Act's definition of food additive. Indeed, even after the agency withdrew approval of the DES pellets for poultry, various approvals of DES implants and feed premixes for cattle and sheep remained in effect. Faced with this discrepancy, Congress in 1962 enacted the so-called "DES proviso" to allow FDA to resume approving DES for use in livestock as long as no residue could be found in human food produced from the animals. *See* 108 Cong. Rec. 21077–81 (Sept. 27, 1962). The proviso appears in section 409(c)(3)(A) of the Act and reads as follows:

> [E]xcept that [the Delaney] proviso shall not apply with respect to the use of a substance as an ingredient of feed for animals which are raised for food production, if the Secretary finds (i) that, under the conditions of use and feeding specified in proposed labeling and reasonably certain to be followed in practice, such additive will not adversely affect the animals for which such feed is intended, and (ii) that no residue of the additive will be found (by methods of examination prescribed or approved by the Secretary by regulations, which regulations shall not be subject to subsections (f) and (g)) in any edible portion of such animal after slaughter or in any food yielded by or derived from the living animal.

Congress, in 1962, also added essentially identical language to the color additive Delaney Clause. *See* FD&C Act 721(b)(5)(B).

The Animal Drug Amendments of 1968 contain their own Delaney Clause, with the same DES proviso. FD&C Act 512(d)(1)(I). In the early 1970s, after the enactment of the Amendments, USDA monitoring of livers of slaughtered steers detected small residues of DES used in their feed. FDA therefore ordered that the withdrawal period for DES (*i.e.*, the time between the last use of DES in the feed of an animal and the date of slaughter) be extended from 48 hours to seven days. 36 Fed. Reg. 23292 (Dec. 8, 1971). USDA simultaneously required written certification that this new withdrawal period was in fact followed. On March 11, 1972, FDA announced the opportunity for a hearing on a proposal to withdraw approval for use of DES in liquid animal feed premixes, 37 Fed. Reg. 526 (Jan. 13, 1972). Because of continuing reports of residues, the agency announced the opportunity for a hearing to determine whether *any* approvals for DES uses in animal feed or as implants could be continued, 37 Fed. Reg. 12251 (June 21, 1972).

Meanwhile, USDA undertook new analytic studies using a more sensitive radioactive tracer method to determine whether DES residues occurred only when the prescribed withdrawal period was not adhered to. When the new studies revealed residues even under the approved conditions of use, FDA withdrew all approvals of DES for use in animal feed while denying requests for a hearing. 37 Fed. Reg. 15747 (Aug. 4, 1972). Formal revocation of the applicable regulations was accomplished in 37 Fed. Reg. 26307 (Dec. 9, 1972). The agency later obtained similar results from a study using radioactive tagged DES implants and therefore summarily withdrew approval of all NADAs for this use as well. 38 Fed. Reg. 10485 (Apr. 27, 1973).

A week later it also revoked the regulation prescribing the official method for detection of DES residues. 38 Fed. Reg. 10926 (May 3, 1973).

Various manufacturers of DES sought direct review of the agency's orders in the District of Columbia Circuit. In *Hess & Clark, Division of Rhodia, Inc. v. FDA*, 495 F.2d 975 (D.C. Cir. 1974), the court, in an opinion by Judge Harold Leventhal, overturned FDA's withdrawal of approval of DES implants on the ground that the agency had not afforded the petitioners the evidentiary hearing that the Act guaranteed if material factual issues were in dispute. Because FDA had not shared the results of the USDA studies that triggered its action and had not established that residues could be detected using the approved assay, summary judgment was not justified.

> ... If the FDA, using an approved test method, detected residues of DES in edible portions of slaughtered animals, then it could show a violation of the Delaney Clause.
>
> In the instant case, however, despite references to the Delaney Clause, and despite continual reference in the briefs and at oral argument to the fact that DES is a carcinogen, the FDA has plainly not used the Delaney Clause theory. One possible reason for this election is that the detected residues may not be DES residues and hence the Delaney Clause may be inoperative. In any event, the USDA did not detect the residues while using an "approved" test method as required by the Delaney Clause. In its regulations, the FDA has approved only the "mouse-uterine" test. Using this test, no residues have been found in the tissues of slaughtered animals. Rather, the only method by which residues have been detected is the radioisotope tracer test, but that method has not been approved. For that reason, the Delaney Clause is plainly inapplicable, without regard to the composition of the residues.
>
> The Commissioner relies on the alternative theory of the "general safety" clause of section 360b(e)(1)(B) [512(e)(1)], contending that the new evidence from the USDA tests "shows that [DES] is not shown to be safe." ...
>
> Because he is not using the Delaney Clause, it is not enough for the Commissioner merely to show that animal carcasses contain residues and that DES is a carcinogen. Instead, the FDA must show that two different issues are resolved in its favor before it can shift to petitioners the burden of showing safety: (1) whether the detected residues are related to the use of DES implants; (2) if so, whether the residues, because of their composition, and in the amounts present in the tissue, present some potential hazard to the public health.
>
> . . . .
>
> Outside of the *per se* rule of the Delaney Clause, the typical issue for the FDA is not the absolute safety of a drug. Most drugs are unsafe in some degree. Rather, the issue for the FDA is whether to allow sale of the drug, usually under specific restric-

tions. Resolution of this issue inevitably means calculating whether the benefits which the drug produces outweigh the costs of its restricted use. In the present case, DES is asserted to be of substantial benefit in enhancing meat production, and this is not gainsaid by FDA. The FDA must consider, after hearing, whether DES pellets would be safe in terms of the amounts of residue consumed. Or the FDA might restrict such consumption by a ban on sale of liver, the only food material in which any residues have even been detected. . . .

In *Chemetron Corp. v. United States Department of HEW*, 495 F.2d 995 (D.C. Cir. 1974), decided the same day, the court reversed FDA's withdrawal of the NADAs for DES premixes because the residues detected by USDA in animals fed DES had not been identified by the mouse uterine assay method.

In 39 Fed. Reg. 11323 (Mar. 27, 1974), FDA reinstated the NADAs for DES and encouraged further precautions to reduce the possibility of residues. Simultaneously the agency took the first step toward final revocation of the NADAs by proposing to revoke the currently approved mouse uterine test method of detecting DES residues. 39 Fed. Reg. 11299 (Mar. 27, 1974). For the next 22 months the matter was held in abeyance while the agency sought to develop a general policy respecting the required sensitivity of methods of detecting residues of carcinogenic animal drugs. When that project progressed slowly, FDA published a notice of opportunity for a hearing on a proposal to withdraw approval of all NADAs for DES, 41 Fed. Reg. 1804 (Jan. 12, 1976), and later ordered a hearing with respect to those NADAs on which a hearing was requested, 41 Fed. Reg. 52105 (Nov. 26, 1976).

After a lengthy hearing, FDA's lone Administrative Law Judge issued an Initial Decision concluding that the Delaney Clause did not require withdrawal of the NADAs but that DES had not been shown to be safe. Food Drug Cosm. L. Rep. (CCH) ¶ 38,198 (Sept. 21, 1978). This ruling was appealed to Commissioner Donald Kennedy who rendered the following decision.

Diethylstilbestrol: Withdrawal of Approval of New Animal Drug Application

44 Fed. Reg. 54852 (September 21, 1979).

. . . [This] Decision discusses what might at first appear to be very small amounts of DES in edible tissues of meat from treated animals. Yet, as a respected cancer expert has testified, we have no data upon which to base the conclusion that any amount of a carcinogen above the single-molecule level would not produce a response. The risk of cancer would, of course, be expected to be lower the smaller the number of molecules of a carcinogen that are ingested. . . .

. . . [A]lthough there is evidence, discussed below, that DES used as medication in pregnant women causes cancer in some of their female offspring, it is unlikely that any individual will ever be identified as having been afflicted with cancer because he or she consumed meat containing residues of DES in the range of parts per billion.... [B]ecause our population is inevitably exposed to a variety of carcinogens, it is generally impossible (in the absence of evidence of, for example, occupational exposure to carcinogenic chemicals) to attribute any specific cancer to any specific cause. Yet this record warrants a finding that a significant (though unquantifiable) number of the cancers that do occur in this country today are associated with the use of DES in food-producing animals....

The Administrative Law Judge found that neither the approved analytical method for DES nor any other analytical method is adequate for use with DES. He was not, however, authorized to revoke the regulations setting out the approved analytical method for DES and did not purport to do so....

... I am now revoking the analytical method for DES. My decision to do so is supported by the evidence in the record that no analytical method is acceptable for DES. Because there is now no approved method of analysis for DES, I conclude that the Delaney Clause applies to the drug. I therefore withdraw approval of the DES NADA's on that ground....

... I find that evidence in the record concerning the incidence of clear cell adenocarcinoma in daughters of mothers treated with DES (the Herbst data) supports the conclusion (which may also be drawn from animal carcinogenicity data) that DES presents a human cancer risk. The evidence from the treatment of women with DES provides no basis for concluding that there is a no-effect level for DES with respect to cancer. These findings warrant the conclusions that DES has not been shown to be safe and that it is unsafe....

... Congress ... did not authorize or require consideration of the socio-economic benefits of an animal drug in determining its safety. Indeed, the language adopted by Congress, having its roots in the human drug and food additive provisions of the law, clearly reflects an intention that FDA definitely not consider socio-economic benefits in making decisions on the safety of animal drugs. I thus conclude that Congress has made the determination that an animal drug that poses a risk to humans can never be considered "safe" because it provides an economic or other social benefit to society....

... There are persuasive policy arguments against having an administrative agency such as the FDA make the kind of risk-benefit analysis sought by the manufacturing parties here. It may be that preliminary issues in this analysis are of the type that the FDA is qualified by experience and expertise to resolve. The agency is equipped, for instance, to evaluate calculations of the risk from a drug such as DES if the necessary data are available (they are not here). Once the risk and the benefits of an animal drug are determined, however, the ultimate issues require pure value judgments....

Perhaps society is willing to expose all of its meat-consuming members to a relatively small risk of cancer and other adverse effects in order to provide a small economic benefit to those consumers and a larger economic benefit to DES producers and, potentially, users. The FDA is not, however, qualified in any particular way to make that value judgment for society. The value judgment could not be supported by a record; a record could support only factual findings not value judgments. Nor could the value judgment be effectively reviewed by a court, which in general is limited to consideration of facts, law, and procedures. In a democratic system, the appropriate place for value judgments to be made is the legislature. Here, as discussed above, it is apparent that Congress has shouldered the responsibility for resolving this issue. It has decided that no economic benefit justifies use of an animal drug that presents an identifiable risk to the health of consumers.

. . . .

NOTES

1. *Judicial Affirmation.* In *Rhone–Poulenc, Inc. v. Food and Drug Administration*, 636 F.2d 750 (D.C. Cir. 1980), the Commissioner's withdrawal of the NADAs for DES was upheld. But the Court of Appeals declined to rule on the Commissioner's reliance on the Delaney Clause and went out of its way to reject his treatment of the court's earlier discussion of the role of benefits in evaluating the safety of animal drug residues.

2. *Subsequent Proceedings.* While the *Rhone–Poulenc* case was pending, FDA formally withdrew approval of the NADAs for DES in 44 Fed. Reg. 39387, 39388 & 39618 (July 6, 1979). While partial stays of the effective date of these regulations were granted, 44 Fed. Reg. 42679, 42781 (July 20, 1979), 44 Fed. Reg. 45618, 45764 (Aug. 3, 1979), the ban of DES became effective on November 1, 1979, and USDA therefore also revoked its DES certification requirements, 44 Fed. Reg. 59498 (Oct. 16, 1979).

3. *Continued Illegal Use.* The ban of DES was disregarded by many cattle growers. FDA determined that, even though continued use was illegal, "the public interest is not well served by the discard of a large number of food-producing animals that can be reconditioned" and it therefore established criteria in 45 Fed. Reg. 27014 (Apr. 22, 1980) for allowing food from illegally treated cattle to be marketed. See also 45 Fed. Reg. 51921 (Aug. 5, 1980). FDA prosecuted some producers that had illegally implanted DES, with mixed results. *See* "DES Update," FDA Talk Paper T81–11 (Apr. 20, 1981); "DES Prosecutions," FDA Talk Paper T84–94 (Dec. 24, 1984); *United States v. Cermiga*, 20 FDA CONSUMER, No. 7, at 40 (Sept. 1986). When the government attempted to condemn carcasses of cattle that had been illegally implanted, however, the District Court ruled that it failed to prove that the beef contained an added poisonous or deleterious substance that could render the food injurious to health. *United States v. 2,116 Boxes of Boned Beef*, 516 F. Supp. 321 (D. Kan. 1981). The government did not appeal this ruling.

4. *DES for Human Use.* At the same time FDA was pursuing withdrawal of approval of DES for animal use, the agency promulgated a regulation stating its willingness to approve NDAs for use of DES as a postcoital human contraceptive under carefully controlled conditions. 40 Fed. Reg. 5351 (Feb. 5, 1975). No manufacturers of human dosage forms of DES have ever sought approval in accordance with the terms of this regulation.

5. *Nitrofurans.* FDA has also taken action to revoke the NADAs for animal drugs containing nitrofurans on the ground that they are carcinogenic. FDA initially proposed to withdraw approval of the NADAs under the general safety requirements of the FD&C Act in 36 Fed. Reg. 5926 (Mar. 31, 1971), 36 Fed. Reg. 14343 (Aug. 4, 1971), then invoked the Delaney Clause as well, 41 Fed. Reg. 19907

(May 13, 1976), announced a hearing on both of these issues, 49 Fed. Reg. 34965, 34967, 34971 (Sept. 4, 1984), and began the hearing in 1985. The Administrative Law Judge handed down his Initial Decision in favor of the agency on November 12, 1986 and the manufacturer appealed to the Commissioner. The ALJ's decision was affirmed with modifications and two NADs ordered withdrawn. 56 Fed. Reg. 41902 (Aug. 23, 1991).

6. *Commentary.* For a debate on the DES controversy, *see Public Policy Panel: FDA—Diethylstilbestrol,* in Howard H. Hiatt, J.D. Watson & J.A. Winsten, Origins of Human Cancer, Vol. C, at 1651–82 (1977).

E.   FDA Embraces Quantitative Risk Assessment

Prior to 1972, the possibility that the magnitude of the risk presented by a carcinogen could be reliably estimated had been discussed in the scientific literature but had not received serious attention from regulators. In response to the problems posed by DES, however, FDA adopted quantitative risk assessment as a tool for regulating carcinogenic animal drugs. And by 1980 the agency was also relying on quantitative risk estimation in evaluating carcinogenic constituents in food, drugs, medical devices, and cosmetics.

Simply summarized, quantitative risk assessment is the mathematical extrapolation from high-dose laboratory animal data to derive estimates of the cancer risk associated with much lower human exposures from the consumer products. It is the key step in a four-step process: identifying a hazard, generally on the basis of animal studies; extrapolating from the high animal doses to estimate human response at lower doses; measuring or estimating human exposure to the substance; and characterizing the risk faced by exposed humans. This process is explained in a seminal report by the National Academy of Sciences, NAS, Risk Assessment in the Federal Government: Managing the Process (1983).

Because of uncertainties in the risk assessment process, assumptions must be made to fill gaps in the data or in the underlying scientific knowledge. Regulators generally rely on conservative assumptions at each stage of the process. For example, they assume that laboratory animals are appropriate models for human risk; choose data from the most sensitive sex of the most sensitive animal species; count benign tumors as malignant tumors; assume the relationship between dose and response to be linear; select upper bound estimates of human exposure and absorption; and assume away the uncertainties at each stage of the process at the next stage. Thus, risk assessment typically produces "worst-case" estimates that may be orders of magnitude higher than the actual risk. As the following examples illustrate, FDA has found in quantitative risk assessment an intellectual framework for estimating the magnitude of the cancer risk associated with known or predicted human exposures to chemicals thought capable of causing cancer in humans. In several instances, the agency has applied the framework in determining whether a risk merits regulatory concern, *i.e.,* whether it poses a genuine threat to human health. In addition, several of the examples present FDA with an additional question, *i.e.*, whether the applicable statutory language permits the agency to apply the framework at all.

1.   APPLIED TO ANIMAL DRUGS

Section 512(d)(1)(I) of the FD&C Act—known as the "DES proviso"—allows FDA to approve a carcinogenic animal drug for use in food-producing animals if it concludes that, when the drug is used in accordance with its label directions, "no residue" will be found in human food derived from the animals using the detection method prescribed by the agency. Obviously, the sensitivity of the detection method that FDA prescribes will influence the likelihood of finding residues.

Until the 1970s FDA had no uniform criteria for determining the level of sensitivity it should require for methods to monitor drug residues. Sometimes it simply approved the best method available for the drug in question. More often it insisted that a drug's sponsor submit a method capable of detecting a specified level of residues, typically 2 ppb. In 1973 FDA decided to rely on quantitative risk assessment to determine the sensitivity of the detection method required to allow approval of any carcinogenic animal drug. In short, the agency decided to correlate the required level of sensitivity to the risk posed by the residues of a drug that might escape detection.

The key to FDA's "sensitivity of method" (SOM) approach is the conduct of a quantitative risk assessment for the specific drug under review. In proposed regulations, 38 Fed. Reg. 19226 (July 19, 1973), the agency prescribed a modified version of the Mantel–Bryan method as the appropriate mathematical extrapolation model. It specified that residues presenting no more than one in 100 million lifetime individual risk of cancer could be considered "acceptable." Using the agency's proposed formula, one could calculate the residue level that, were it to occur undetected in the food derived from the animal, could be regarded as essentially "safe." The drug's sponsor would then be required to submit a detection method capable of measuring any residues that exceeded this level.

FDA issued final regulations, 42 Fed. Reg. 10412 (Feb. 22, 1977), which adopted a 1975 refinement of the Mantel–Bryan mathematical extrapolation model and revised the acceptable risk level to one in one million. In *Animal Health Institute v. FDA*, Food Drug Cosm. L. Rep. (CCH) ¶ 38,154 (D.D.C. 1978), the court held that these changes were substantial enough to require a remand to the agency for further findings to rectify omissions in the record. FDA subsequently revoked the 1977 regulations, 43 Fed. Reg. 22675 (May 26, 1978), and published the following revised proposal.

Chemical Compounds in Food–Producing Animals: Criteria and Procedures for Evaluating Assays for Carcinogenic Residues

44 Fed. Reg. 17070 (March 20, 1979).

. . . .

Two interpretations of the [DES] proviso are, in theory, possible. The first interpretation, which in the Commissioner's judgment is the less probable, is that Congress intended to allow FDA to approve the use of a carcinogenic compound in food-producing animals only if the agency could be absolutely positive that no traces whatever—no matter how small—would remain in edible tissues.

1st interp: no trace

This interpretation presents several difficulties, all stemming from the fact that any introduction of a compound, whether or not carcinogenic, is likely to leave in edible tissues minute residues, which are below the level of detection of any known or likely to be developed method of analysis, *i.e.*, assay.... Although different assays may have different lowest limits of measurement, all assays are subject to the same type of limitation. Thus, when a tissue is examined with an assay having a lowest limit of measurement of 1 ppb and no interpretable response is observed, the analyst can conclude only that the compound under analysis is not present at a level of 1 ppb or above. It can never be concluded that the compound is "not present" in the absolute sense. It is thus impossible to determine the conditions under which edible tissues derived from food-producing animals that have received a carcinogen will contain no residue if the phrase "no residue" is to be interpreted literally....

... [T]he "absolutely no molecules" interpretation seems, at the very least, an improbable interpretation of an amendment enacted by Congress precisely because it wanted to relieve animal drugs from the rigid strictures of the anticancer clauses. Moreover, any interpretation of a statutory provision that would render it totally inoperative should be rejected unless considerations of overwhelming persuasiveness require that interpretation....

2nd interp:

A second, and in the Commissioner's view more plausible, interpretation of the DES proviso accepts the words of the amendment and focuses on the ... language, "no residue of such drug will be found ... by methods of examination prescribed or approved by the Secretary by regulations...." Under this interpretation, a sponsored compound that is carcinogenic may be approved for use in animals if examination of edible tissues by an assay approved by FDA reveals no residues....

The Commissioner believes that the criteria to be applied in evaluating assays for carcinogenic residues in the edible tissue of food-producing animals must further the congressional intent to minimize public exposure to carcinogens, without nullifying the decision reflected in the DES proviso, as the first interpretation of the proviso would do. As explained more fully below, the criteria set forth in these regulations for evaluating assays for carcinogenic residues are minimum requirements. They are designed to identify assays that are (1) reliable and practical for use by a regulatory agency and (2) capable of measuring residues at levels that have been determined, on the basis of animal toxicity tests, to present no significant increase in human risk of cancer. An assay that does not meet both criteria cannot be approved....

... By enacting and twice re-enacting the Delaney clause, Congress made clear its willingness to ban entirely from the human food supply food additives, color additives, and animal drugs that present a carcinogenic risk to man. It enacted the DES proviso with the intent and expectation that the provision that "no residue . . . will be found" would sufficiently protect the human food supply from any significant cancer risk from food additives, color additives, and animal drugs. Thus, in enacting the DES proviso, Congress did not change in any way the policy of the Delaney clause to protect the human food supply from carcinogenic additives and animal drugs; it merely eliminated an application of the clause that it considered unnecessary to the complete achievement of that policy.

From this statutory structure and language, it is evident that any consideration of feasibility and costs is subsidiary to the overriding congressional purpose to permit no additional human cancer risk from food additives, color additives, or animal drugs. The Commissioner's discretion to establish "methods of examination" for detecting residues is to be exercised so as to carry out that congressional purpose. The factor that determines the acceptable level of measurement of an assay method is protection of the human food supply from carcinogenic risks. If, on the basis of toxicological considerations, the Commissioner determines that a certain level of assay measurement is necessary to prevent a significant human cancer risk from use of a carcinogenic substance in food animals, then a method having that level of measurement is necessary to carry out the congressional purpose. If no such method is feasible, or if it is too costly to develop or apply one, then the choice is between refusing to permit the use of the substance altogether and permitting its use despite the fact there is no method of examination that can prevent the use of the substance from presenting a significant human cancer risk. Under the general safety clause and the Delaney clause, that choice can be resolved in only one way: by refusing to permit the use of the substance. . . .

It is true that these proposed regulations will permit the approval, for use in animal feed or for use as animal drugs, of carcinogenic compounds that are likely to leave residues below the lowest level of reliable measurement of any assay meeting all the criteria of the regulation. Indeed, as a result of Congress' enacting the DES proviso, the agency will not have any certainty that these residues, in amounts below the level of detectability, are not always present. This result makes sense in practical terms, however, for a regulatory agency cannot effectively control residues—of any compound—that are so small that they escape measurement by every available assay. . . .

The Commissioner has considered three basic alternative approaches to an operational definition of the phrase ["no residue"]. Under one approach, the term "no residue" might be operationally defined as satisfied when the levels of residues fall below those that can be measured by available analytical methodology. A second approach would be to establish some low finite level (e.g., 1 part per billion) as a "practical zero" and to require assays that can reliably measure this zero, and to insist on the development of new assays if available assays are not adequate. Finally, "no residue" might be operationally defined on the basis of quantitative carcinogenicity testing of residues and the extrapolation of test data using one of a number of available procedures to arrive at levels that are safe in the total diet of test animals and that would, if they occurred, be considered safe in the total diet of man. Under this approach, the Commissioner would require assays that can reliably measure that safe level in edible tissues. For the reasons discussed below in this preamble, the Commissioner has concluded that alternative 3 should be adopted....

By adopting this approach to implementing the no-residue standard, the Commissioner has assumed that: (I) The dose-response relationship between chemical compounds and carcinogenesis can be quantified, and (ii) a dietary level of a carcinogen can be identified at which no significant human risk of carcinogenesis would derive from consuming food containing residues below this level.

... [T]he Commissioner extensively reviewed the known procedures that may be used to derive an operational definition of the no-residue standards of the act from animal carcinogenesis data. This review persuaded the Commissioner that the same scientific and technical limitations are common to all. Specifically, because the mechanism of chemical carcinogenesis is not sufficiently understood, none of the procedures has a fully adequate biological rationale. All require extrapolation of risk-dose relations from responses in the observable range to that segment of the dose-response curve where the responses are not observable. Matters are further complicated by the fact that the risk-dose relations assumed by the various procedures are practically indistinguishable in the observable range of risk ... but diverge substantially in their projections of risks in the unobservable range....

... Of the three general procedures recommended by the comments or available in the literature (the curvilinear models, linear extrapolation and the Mantel and Bryan procedure), the Commissioner has now decided that for purposes of this regulation, linear extrapolation best meets the above criteria:

(1) Of the available procedures, the linear procedure is least likely to underestimate risk. That is, at the level of acceptable risk (1 in 1 million over a lifetime), the maximum permissible dose of residues calculated by use of the linear extrapolation is usually lower than that obtained by the use of the other procedures.

(2) Linear extrapolation does not require the use of complicated mathematical procedures and can be carried out without the aid of complex computer programs....

(3) No arbitrary selection of slope is required to carry out linear extrapolation....

The 1973 proposal suggested that an acceptable level of risk for test animals, and thus for man, could be 1 in 100 million over a lifetime. Many comments argued that this level of risk was unnecessarily conservative in light of the many other cumulative, conservative restrictions already in the proposed regulations. In the February notice the Commissioner concluded that the 1 in 100 million level of risk was unduly limiting without substantial compensation in terms of public health. Consequently, the notice established the maximum risk to be used in the Mantel–Bryan calculation as 1 in 1 million....

In the Commissioner's opinion, the acceptable risk level should (1) not significantly increase the human cancer risk and (2) subject to that constraint, be as high as possible in order to permit the use of carcinogenic animal drugs and food additives as decreed by Congress.... In addition to protecting the public health and satisfying the congressional directive, the Commissioner believes the selected level of risk should be consistent with acceptable levels of risk for other materials that are considered safe, and should prevent any false sense of security in the calculations. After reviewing data on acceptable levels of risk and knowing the limitations on the procedures, the Commissioner has concluded that a level of risk of 1 in 1 million over a lifetime satisfies all of these criteria....

NOTES

1. *Translating Risk Estimates.* The product of any quantitative risk assessment for a carcinogen is the correlation of a level of risk with a given dose. This risk level is usually stated in terms of the lifetime risk of cancer faced by an exposed individual and in terms of the increased number of cancers that would occur annually in the exposed population. An individual risk of one in 100,000 means that an exposed individual faces that additional risk of developing cancer from this exposure alone during his lifetime. Roughly 4,000,000 persons are born each year in the United States. An individual lifetime risk of one in 100,000 associated with exposure to a substance would mean that 40 of these might develop cancer at some point in their lifetimes if they do not die of other causes—including cancers with other causes—first. Assuming an average lifetime of 70 years, this cohort would experience an average maximum risk of 4/7 of one cancer case each year.

2. *"Acceptable" Risk.* The level of risk that a regulatory agency ought to consider "acceptable" or "insignificant" is, as could be expected, controversial. The level of risk considered "acceptable," moreover, must be keyed to a specified mathematical extrapolation model. The more conservative the model, the higher the risk it will project for a given level of exposure. For example, it has been estimated that the risk projected by the Mantel–Bryan procedure may differ from the risk estimated by the linear model by an order of magnitude (*i.e.*, a factor of 10). It should be noted, however, that any of the mathematical extrapolation models provides the so-called "upper bound" risk, and does not purport to predict the number of cancers that will occur. Each of these mathematical models incorporates so many conservative assumptions that it is unlikely that the actual number of cancers would approach the upper-bound "worst case." For that reason, the result of a risk assessment is often depicted as a range of potential risk from zero to the number given by the quantitative risk assessment.

3. *Risk Comparisons.* Analysts have compared the risks of different occupations and other activities, and the risks of various natural and synthetic substances. So long as the distinction is made between actuarial risks, *i.e.*, measured frequencies, and calculated or estimated risks, these comparisons can be enlightening. *See, e.g.*, E.A.C. CROUCH & RICHARD WILSON, RISK/BENEFIT ANALYSIS 173 (1982); BARUCH FISCHOFF, et al., ACCEPTABLE RISK (1981); C. R. Richmond, et al., eds., HEALTH RISK ANALYSIS (1980); JOHN URQUHART & KLAUS HEILMANN, RISK WATCH: THE ODDS OF LIFE (1984); W.F. Allman, *Staying Alive in the 20th Century*, 6 SCIENCE 85 at 31 (Oct. 1985); B.L. Cohen & J.S. Lee, *A Catalog of Risks*, 36 HEALTH PHYSICS 707 (1979); C.R. Cothern & W.L. Marcus, *Estimating Risk for Carcinogenic Environmental Contaminants and its Impact on Regulatory Decision Making*, 4 REGUL. TOXICOL. & PHARMACOL. 265 (1984); E.A.C. Crouch & Richard Wilson, *Inter–Risk Comparisons*, in ASSESSMENT AND MANAGEMENT OF CHEMICAL RISKS 97 (Joseph Rodricks & Robert

Tardiff, eds., 1984); J.P. Leigh, *Estimates of the Probability of Job–Related Death in 347 Occupations*, 29 J. OCCUP. MED. 510 (June 1987); James C. Miller, *Comparative Data on Life–Threatening Risks*, 5 TOXIC SUBSTANCES J. 3 (Summer 1983); John Morrall, *A Review of the Record*, REGULATION 25 (Nov./Dec. 1986); Frederica Perera & Paola Boffetta, *Perspectives on Comparing Risks of Environmental Carcinogens*, 80 J.N.C.I. 1282 (Oct. 19, 1988); E. Pochin, *Estimates of Industrial and Other Risks*, 12 J. ROYAL COLL. PHYSN'S 210 (1978); Bert Spilker & Pedro Cuatrecasas, *Assessing Risks*, 2 DN & P, No. 2, at 69 (Mar. 1969).

4. *Estradiol.* After initially deciding to withdraw approval of estradiol, a carcinogenic animal drug, 44 Fed. Reg. 1462, 1463 (Jan. 5, 1979), FDA reversed itself and approved the drug for steers and heifers, concluding that any residues of the drug in human food represent an insignificant risk of cancer and thus are safe. 46 Fed. Reg. 24694 (May 1, 1981), 47 Fed. Reg. 51108 (Nov. 12, 1982), 48 Fed. Reg. 48659 (Oct. 20, 1983), 49 Fed. Reg. 13872 (Apr. 9, 1984), 49 Fed. Reg. 29777 (July 24, 1984). The agency approved the drug even though the sponsor failed to meet the explicit statutory requirement that there be a "regulatory method" to detect the residue in food. It concluded that the drug "is likely to leave a safe level of residue of carcinogenic endogenous hormones in the edible tissue" and thus it is "unreasonable to disapprove that product because a post slaughter method (*i.e.*, 'regulatory method') capable of monitoring such small amounts of residues has not been developed." 46 Fed. Reg. at 24696. Because no comparable data were submitted to justify use of the drug in chickens, however, FDA withdrew approval for that use. 53 Fed. Reg. 4214 (Feb. 12, 1988), 53 Fed. Reg. 15885 (May 4, 1988).

5. *Commentary.* For a scientific discussion of the SOM approach, see M.K. Perez, *Human Safety Data Collection and Evaluation for the Approval of New Animal Drugs*, 3 J. TOXICOL. & ENVT'L HEALTH 837 (1977). *See also* George Gass, *A Discussion of Assay Sensitivity Methodology and Carcinogenic Potential*, 30 FOOD DRUG COSM. L.J. 111 (1975); David S. Salsburg, *Mantel–Bryan—Its Faults and Alternatives Available After Thirteen More Years of Experimentation*, 30 FOOD DRUG COSM. L.J. 116 (1975); Robert G. Zimbelman, *Biological Perspectives on Approaches to Sensitivity of Analytical Methods for Tissue Residues*, 30 FOOD DRUG COSM. L.J. 124 (1975). For illustrations of the application of the SOM approach to individual animal drugs, see the notices of opportunity for hearing on proposals to withdraw approval of various NADAs in 41 Fed. Reg. 19907 (May 13, 1976), 41 Fed. Reg. 34891, 34899, 34908 (Aug. 17, 1976), and 44 Fed. Reg. 1463 (Jan. 5, 1979).

———

Several years later, after reviewing comments, FDA published the following revised proposal.

Sponsored Compounds in Food–Producing Animals; Criteria and Procedures for Evaluating the Safety of Carcinogenic Residues

50 Fed. Reg. 45530 (October 31, 1985).

. . . The selection of an insignificant level of risk is a choice which, although susceptible to being posed as a question of fact, cannot be answered solely by science or currently available information. It is, instead, a policy question that must be answered by weighing a number of subjective considerations.

received comments

No comments on the 1979 proposal were received that disagreed with FDA's decision that the 1 in 1 million level presents an insignificant risk to the public. No comments at all, however, were received from the general public. All comments were from regulated industry. These comments contended that the 1 in 1 million level represented an insignificant risk but that higher levels might also represent insignificant risks. The comments, however, as discussed below, failed to demonstrate that any higher level satisfied FDA's responsibility under the statute to protect the public health. FDA has carefully studied the submitted comments, the suggested alternatives, and other available information on risk assessment and has concluded that the 1 in 1 million level represents an insignificant level of risk.

FDA emphasizes that the 1 in 1 million level of risk ... does not mean that 1 in every 1 million people will contract cancer as a result of this regulation. Rather, as far as can be determined, in all probability no one will contact [sic] cancer as a result of this regulation. The 1 in 1 million level represents a (1) 1 in 1 million increase in risk over the normal risk of cancer and (2) a lifetime—not annual—risk. Furthermore, because of a number of assumptions used in the risk assessment procedure and the extrapolation model used, FDA expects that the actual risk to an individual will be between 1 in 1 million and some much lower, but indeterminable, level.

Some comments on the 1979 proposal suggested ... that a level of risk should be chosen for each compound on an individual basis. FDA disagrees. Under the suggested procedure sponsors would receive no guidance about the likelihood of approval of a compound during the expensive stage of drug development or about the factors consider in determining whether the compound should be approved. This unstructured ad hoc approach would be contrary to the interests of the public health and would result in inequitable treatment of sponsors.

Comments argued that FDA could determine a level of insignificant risk by comparing risks presented from carcinogens in food with risks individuals voluntarily assume from using their occupation, from common forms of transportation, from leisure activities, and the like....

The comments overlook the fact that when FDA approves the use of a carcinogenic compound, FDA affirmatively allows a risk to be imposed on the public. The public is not "accepting" that risk because (1) The public has no information on the risk presented by carcinogenic compounds in its food, and (2) the public has no way of avoiding that risk assuming it wishes to continue to eat meat, milk, or eggs. Furthermore, these comments do not address the growing evidence that group attitudes and group choices do not follow the same patterns as individual choices. Reliance on group preference, therefore, might cause the imposition of a risk that is unacceptable to many individuals.

... Although FDA has considered the comments and information provided, FDA concludes that the sole use of social preferences and the magnitude of involuntary risks to select an insignificant level of risk provides an incomplete basis for determining the level of risk to which the public should be exposed by substances permitted in the food supply. FDA also concludes that an increase in the level of risk to 1 in 15,000 might significantly increase the risk of cancer to people, and, until better information is provided, such a level must be viewed as unacceptable in light of current knowledge and legal standards.

... The question that logically follows is whether a level of 1 in 100,000 presents a significant risk to people. If FDA were to propose 1 in 100,000 as the insignificant level of risk, the permitted concentration of residue would increase by a factor of 10....

The 1 in 100,000 level does not carry with it the degree of concern presented by the 1 in 15,000 level. Similarly, it is not as insignificant as the 1 in 1 million level. The approval of a carcinogenic sponsored compound, at any level of risk, does not include consideration of the potential interaction or synergy between an approved compound and any other substance or substances to which people are exposed. Certainly, the more approved carcinogenic compounds that are marketed the greater is the likelihood of cancer induction in people.

In the presence of these uncertainties, FDA cannot, with assurance, state that the 1 in 100,000 level would pose an insignificant level of risk of cancer to people. FDA can state, and comments agree, that the 1 in 1 million level presents an insignificant level of risk of cancer to people. Furthermore, FDA has developed confidence in the merit of the 1 in 1 million level because in recent years the agency has considered that level as its benchmark in evaluating the safety of carcinogenic compounds administered to food-producing animals....

... Pervasive uncertainty is the primary analytical difficulty in making a risk assessment that involves trying to define the human health effects of exposure to harmful residues. Although the risk assessment procedures proposed for these regulations draw extensively on science, which has developed a basis for linking exposure to residues to potential chronic health effects, there is uncertainty in types, probability, and magnitude of the health effects that will be associated with a given compound and its residues. These problems have no immediate solutions because of the many gaps in FDA's ability to ascertain the nature or extent of the effects associated with specific exposures. Where science fails to provide solutions, FDA applies conservative assumptions to ensure that its decisions will not adversely affect the public health.

....

The risk assessment procedure used by FDA requires that the upper 95 percent confidence limit on the tumor incidence data be used to estimate the carcinogenic potency of a substance. Assuming a typical bioassay conducted on a sponsored compound (*e.g.*, 50 animals per sex per dose) and a 20 percent incidence of tumors, this requirement causes an overestimate of the most probable potency by a factor of two. In addition, data from the most sensitive species and the most sensitive sex are used, resulting in an overestimate of the most probable potency by a factor of one to four.

The risk assessment procedure used by FDA assumes that each residue is as potent as the most potent compound detected in the bioassay. This is unlikely to be true, but in the absence of a bioassay on each residue and of knowledge of the quantity of each residue in the tissue, the effect on risk to the consuming public cannot be quantified. . . .

The risk assessment procedure used by FDA assumes that a lower frequency of dosing has no effect on carcinogenic potency. This is unlikely to be true. Because the animals used in the bioassay receive a constant and daily dose, but people will most likely be exposed to sporadic doses, the carcinogenic potency to people is most likely overestimated. However, FDA has no data that will allow a reliable prediction of the magnitude of this overestimate. . . .

The risk assessment procedure used by FDA includes a calculation of the upper limit of carcinogenic potency at low dose, a dose representative of what people are exposed to. . . .

The risk assessment procedure used by FDA assumes a one to one correspondence between the carcinogenic potency of the compound in the test animals and in people. The available, but extremely limited, data submitted in a comment suggest that carcinogenic potency of a specific chemical in rodents and people may vary by an order of magnitude, but is as likely to be high as low.

The risk assessment procedure used by FDA assumes that the concentration of residue in the edible product is at the permitted concentration, that consumption of that edible product by all people is equal to the consumption by the 90th percentile eater, and that all marketed animals are treated with the carcinogen (market penetration of 100 percent). These assumptions may overestimate risk. The extent of the overestimation cannot be quantified. . . .

NOTES

1. *Conservatism in Assessing Risks.* FDA has emphasized that the mathematical extrapolation procedures used in its quantitative risk assessments are "extremely conservative statistical analyses," 51 Fed. Reg. 28331, 28344, 28346, 28360 (Aug. 7, 1986), that overstate real risk. *See, e.g.,* 47 Fed. Reg. 14464, 14466 (Apr. 2, 1982); 49 Fed. Reg. 36635, 36638 (Sept. 19, 1984).

2. *A Risk of One in One Million.* FDA adopted the one in one million level of risk without guidance from Congress or any clear empirical justification. It emphasized that a one in one million level of risk is an "extremely small, perhaps nonexistent, theoretical risk" that "represents a calculated statistical upper bound estimate of a conservative model" and "does not represent a documented experience or a real expectation." Letter from FDA Acting Commissioner Mark Novitch to Representative Theodore Weiss (Dec. 28, 1983) at 9, 10. According to the agency, a one in one million level of risk over a lifetime "imposes no additional risk of cancer to the public," 44 Fed. Reg. 17070, 17093 (Mar. 20, 1979), and "is consistent with the likelihood that no cancers will result," 46 Fed. Reg. 15500, 15501 (Mar. 6, 1981), 47 Fed. Reg. 49628, 49631 (Nov. 2, 1982).

> This computed level of risk is . . . not an actuarial risk. An actuarial risk is the risk determined by the actual incidence of an event. In contrast, the computed risk is a projection based on certain assumptions that enable the agency to estimate a risk that is too small to actually be measured. The agency uses conservative assumptions to ensure that the computation does not understate the risk.

50 Fed. Reg. 51551, 51557 (Dec. 18, 1985).

The agency has variously characterized a one in one million risk as "represent[ing] no significant carcinogenic burden in the total diet of man," 42 Fed. Reg. 10412, 10422 (Feb. 22, 1977); "for all practical purposes, zero," 50 Fed. Reg. 51551, 51557 (Dec. 18, 1985); "the functional equivalent of no risk at all," 51 Fed. Reg. 28331, 28344 (Aug. 7, 1986); "so low as to be effectively no risk," *id.;* assuring that "in all probability no one will contract cancer," 50 Fed. Reg. 45530, 45541 (Oct. 31, 1985); and "so low that there is a reasonable certainty of no harm." 51 Fed. Reg. 4173, 4174 (Feb. 3, 1986).

3. *Refusal to Reduce Risk Level.* FDA has declined to reduce its numerical measure of "insignificant" risk, once declaring: "Any gain from removing [a risk of this magnitude] from the market would be trivial or of no value." Letter from FDA Commissioner Young to S.M. Wolfe, FDA Dkt No. 84P–0429 (June 21, 1985). *See also* 50 Fed. Reg. 51551, 51557 (Dec. 18, 1985).

4. *Department of Justice Views.* In 1995, the views of the Department of Justice Office of Legal Counsel regarding FDA's and EPA's interpretation of the DES proviso were sought. In responding, Deputy Assistant Attorney General Christopher Schroeder addressed three questions:

• Could the agencies demand, as a condition of approval of a carcinogenic animal drug, that there be an analytical method capable of detecting any residues that could present a significant human cancer risk? In providing an affirmative answer, Schroeder made clear that the agencies need not require a method capable of detecting any residues at all. In this respect, he concluded, the DES proviso for animal drugs implicitly qualified the mandate of the Delaney Clause itself, as interpreted in *Public Citizen v. Young, infra.*

• Having once approved an analytical method as adequate to detect (and thus prevent human consumption of) any residue that could present a significant risk, could the agencies decline to mandate the adoption of a more sensitive method if one were developed? Schroeder advised that the law did not require the agencies to continue to press for the adoption of the most sensitive method of detection.

• Were the agencies entitled to treat actually detected residues as consistent with the proviso's "no residue" standard if they did not exceed the insignificant risk level? On this point, Schroeder's response rejected the two agencies' established understanding. He drew a distinction between the first two questions posed by FDA and EPA, which related to their discretion to approve methods of detection—a role the law assigned to the agencies but did not guide—and this final question, which focused on their discretion to interpret the "no residue" language of the FDCA itself. Schroeder concluded that in the Delaney Clause itself Congress had spoken to, and resolved, the precise issue—the discovery of *some* residue could not be compatible with the explicit directive that *no residue* may be found.

2. APPLIED TO CONTAMINANTS OF FOOD

Aflatoxins in Shelled Peanuts and Peanut Products Used as Human Foods: Proposed Tolerance

39 Fed. Reg. 42748 (December 6, 1974).

. . . .

Aflatoxins may contaminate foods whenever the producing molds grow on foods under favorable conditions of temperature and humidity.... Corn, barley, copra, cassava, tree nuts, cottonseed, peanuts, rice, wheat, and grain sorghum are subject to natural aflatoxin contamination. In the United States, aflatoxins have been detected only in corn, figs, grain sorghum, cottonseed, certain tree nuts, and peanuts.

Aflatoxins are present in peanuts and peanut products because of these contaminating molds. They are, therefore, added substances within the meaning of [section 402(a)(1) of the] Act....

... First, animals fed aflatoxins are subject to acute toxic effects. Second, and of primary concern, data ... indicate that these substances, particularly aflatoxin B_1, in some species of test animals are among the most potent liver carcinogens known....

Epidemiological studies bearing on the possible effects of aflatoxin in man have been performed on specific population groups in Southeast Asia and Africa, where there is a known high incidence of primary liver cancer.... The result of these studies is an indication of a general correlation between the incidence of primary liver cancer in humans and the exposure to aflatoxins.

... [W]hile it is not certain that aflatoxins are a cause of primary liver cancer in the United States, the Commissioner concludes that the observations of severe carcinogenic effects in experimental animals and positive correlations between dietary aflatoxins and primary human liver cancer seen in other parts of the world are sufficient justification to regard aflatoxins as poisonous or deleterious substances and to take actions to hold the human exposure to aflatoxins in the United States to the lowest level possible.... In 1965, the FDA established an informal action level of 30 ppb total aflatoxins. In 1969, it was reduced to the current level of 20 ppb total aflatoxins....

Fungicides, crop rotational practices, and other good agronomic practices can ameliorate the problem to an extent. It is impossible at this time totally to eliminate all of the breakdowns that can occur in the total process of growing, harvesting, and storing peanuts.... Processors of shelled nuts can eliminate some contaminated material by using a number of standard manual, mechanical, and electronic sorting procedures....

Survey data ... indicate that since 1971 an average of 93 percent of sampled peanut products contained aflatoxins below the 20 ppb level. The Commissioner concludes that current agricultural and manufacturing technology is capable of meeting a level below that which it is now being asked to meet. Although the immediate result of lowering the level may be the loss of a small percentage of the peanut supply, improved producer practices should compensate for any short-run loss.

Obviously, for complete protection, aflatoxins should be eliminated from food, but this is not presently feasible. Therefore, it is necessary for the Commissioner to weigh the consequences of possible levels above zero.

Setting a level at 5 or 10 ppb was considered by the Commissioner. Eleven of the 12 major U.S. manufacturers of peanut butter could meet a 10 ppb level in 90 percent of their products. The Canadian government survey of 1972 indicated that 95 percent of the samples of peanut butter could meet this standard. However, there is year-to-year variability in aflatoxin contamination of the peanut crop. The FDA survey of 1973 evidenced the fact that only 89 percent of the peanut butter samples and 82 percent of the establishments surveyed met a 10 ppb level. Of the 12 largest establishments surveyed, only seven met a 5 ppb limit in 90 percent of their samples. There are also data showing that in some years only about 60 percent of the peanut butter produced met a 5 ppb level. One bad crop year could effectively eliminate a large percentage of peanut products from the market. Thus, a move to 5 or 10 ppb could result in significant losses to producers, manufacturers, and consumers alike.

These increased losses of food would result in much higher prices or in unavailability of what is generally considered a highly nutritious and useful food.

Another important consideration concerns setting a tolerance at a level at which manufacturers have the capability to monitor their products during processing and to ensure that the finished product complies with the tolerance.... Setting a tolerance level of 5 or 10 ppb for aflatoxins in peanut products would have the effect of requiring manufacturers to employ an analytical limit of less than 1 to 5 ppb for quality control purposes. Because present sampling and analytical methodologies have considerable error at the 1–5 ppb range, analytical results obtained for such quality control samples would not accurately represent the production lot from which the sample was drawn. Therefore, the capability of manufacturers to control their production at these levels is extremely questionable, and to guard against the release of products containing levels of aflatoxins in excess of 5 or 10 ppb is not possible....

In addition, because there is no direct evidence that aflatoxins cause cancer in man or of what may be the level of no effect, the Commissioner cannot conclude that there is any tangible gain from lowering the permissible level to either 10 or 5 ppb....

The Commissioner concludes that existing agricultural and industrial technology can combine to yield finished peanut products at or below a 15 ppb level without causing significantly increased losses of food. This level will also allow manufacturers to maintain capability for monitoring their products during processing with nearly as much reliability as could be attained with a 20 ppb level ...

... Limiting an unavoidable substance through use of an action level, rather than a tolerance, is appropriate when changes are foreseeable in the near future that might affect the appropriateness of the limitation established. This, however, is not the case with aflatoxins.... There are no new procedures pending, either agronomic or technical, that will alter the present unavoidability of aflatoxins. Furthermore, it is unlikely that any new pertinent information will become available in the near future. Therefore, it is the Commissioner's preliminary conclusion that the most reasonable approach to regulating aflatoxin, in shelled peanuts and peanut products, would be a formal tolerance established under section 406.

NOTES

1. *Withdrawal of Proposed Tolerance.* FDA never finalized the proposed tolerance for aflatoxins in peanuts and peanut products, and it formally withdrew

the proposal in 1991. 56 Fed. Reg. 67440 (Dec. 30, 1991). The 20 ppb informal action level, first instituted in 1969, remains in effect. *See* CPG 570.375.

2. *Risk Assessment for Aflatoxins.* FDA later released its formal assessment of the cancer risk posed by aflatoxin in peanuts. 43 Fed. Reg. 8808 (Mar. 3, 1978). The agency's estimate of the human risk of liver cancer based on animal test data using the Mantel–Bryan mathematical model (rather than the linear model) substantially exceeded the reported incidence of liver cancer in the United States from all causes. FDA speculated that "possible explanations for these differences are: (1) the level of human exposure to aflatoxin has been overestimated; (2) the Mantel–Bryan extrapolation procedure is overly conservative in this case; and/or (3) rats may not be an appropriate model for predicting aflatoxin-induced primary liver cancer in humans." FDA, ASSESSMENT OF ESTIMATED RISK RESULTING FROM AFLATOXINS IN CONSUMER PEANUT PRODUCTS AND OTHER FOOD COMMODITIES (1978). FDA's action levels for aflatoxins in several foods are listed in a 2000 Industry Activities Staff Booklet titled Action Levels for Porsoroust or Deleterious Substance in Human Food and Animal Feed, available on FDA's website.

3. *Contamination Variability.* FDA's concern about the variability of aflatoxin contamination proved correct. Severe contamination problems in 1977–78 led FDA to issue an action level for aflatoxin in milk, 42 Fed. Reg. 61630 (Dec. 6, 1977), and to permit "blending" of aflatoxin-contaminated corn, 43 Fed. Reg. 14122 (Apr. 4, 1978). In *United States v. Boston Farm Center, Inc.*, 590 F.2d 149 (5th Cir. 1979), the court overturned a lower court ruling allowing up to 100 ppb aflatoxin in corn and upheld FDA's 20 ppb action level.

In 1980, the corn crop in southeastern United States contained a higher than usual level of aflatoxin due to an unusual combination of early drought and late rains. At the request of the States of South Carolina, North Carolina, and Virginia, FDA agreed to an exemption raising the action level for aflatoxin in corn for use solely as feed for mature nonlactating livestock and poultry from 20 ppb to 100 ppb, 46 Fed. Reg. 7447 (Jan. 23, 1981). The Community Nutrition Institute challenged this decision, both on procedural grounds and on the substantive grounds that the higher level of aflatoxin was unsafe and that the FDA policy of permitting farmers to blend corn containing high levels of aflatoxin with corn containing lower levels was illegal. In *Community Nutrition Institute v. Novitch*, 583 F. Supp. 294 (D.D.C. 1984), the 100 ppb level was upheld as "safe for consumption" and the FDA authorization for blending was held to be lawful. Following the Supreme Court's decision upholding FDA's reliance on action levels rather than tolerances, *Young v. Community Nutrition Institute*, 476 U.S. 974 (1986), *supra* p. 381, the Court of Appeals held that the intentional blending of contaminated corn constitutes adulteration but, citing *Heckler v. Chaney, infra* p. 1211, upheld FDA's discretion not to initiate enforcement proceedings. *Community Nutrition Institute v. Young*, 818 F.2d 943 (D.C. Cir. 1987). In 54 Fed. Reg. 22622 (May 25, 1989), FDA issued revised action levels for aflatoxin and its enforcement policy with respect to the blending of contaminated and noncontaminated corn from the 1988 harvest.

4. *Limits on Other Food Contaminants.* FDA has established tolerances or action levels for several other carcinogenic contaminants. The only formal section 406 tolerances ever established permit PCBs in food and food packaging. 37 Fed. Reg. 5705 (Mar. 18, 1972), 38 Fed. Reg. 18096 (July 6, 1973), 41 Fed. Reg. 8409 (Feb. 26, 1976), 42 Fed. Reg. 17487 (Apr. 1, 1977), 44 Fed. Reg. 38330 (June 29, 1979), 47 Fed. Reg. 10079 (Mar. 9, 1982), 48 Fed. Reg. 37020 (Aug. 16, 1983), 48 Fed. Reg. 45544 (Oct. 6, 1983), 49 Fed. Reg. 21514 (May 22, 1984), codified at 21 C.F.R. 109.30. The agency has set action levels for carcinogenic nitrosamines in malt beverages, 45 Fed. Reg. 39341 (June 10, 1980), barley malt contaminated with nitrosamines, 46 Fed. Reg. 39218 (July 31, 1981); and rubber baby bottle nipples

contaminated with nitrosamines, 48 Fed. Reg. 57014 (Dec. 27, 1983), 49 Fed. Reg. 26149 (June 26, 1984), 49 Fed. Reg. 50789 (Dec. 31, 1984); FDA Compliance Policy Guide No. 7117.11 (June 28, 1988). Action levels have also been established for residues of a variety of carcinogenic pesticides in foods, *e.g.*, 52 Fed. Reg. 18025 (May 13, 1987). For 2,3,7,8–TCDD (dioxin), which FDA has characterized as "the most carcinogenic substance known to science," the agency has stated that fish containing more than 50 ppt should not be consumed at all, fish containing 25–50 ppt should not be consumed more than twice each month, and that below 25 ppt there is "no public health problem." "Dioxin—The Impact on Human Health," Hearings before the Subcomm. on Natural Resources, Agriculture Research and Environment of the House Comm. on Science and Technology, 98th Cong., 1st Sess. 78, 79, 81 (1983). FDA's refusal to issue a tolerance or action level for dioxin in fish and other food was upheld in *National Wildlife Federation v. Secretary of Health and Human Services*, 808 F.2d 12 (6th Cir. 1986).

5. *Acrylonitrile.* In 1977 FDA banned acrylonitrile for use in formulating plastic beverage containers because of the possibility that some small amount could migrate from the container wall to the food it contained. In *Monsanto Co. v. Kennedy*, 613 F.2d 947 (D.C. Cir. 1979), p. 433 *supra*, the court overturned this ban because FDA had not considered the possibility that the risk faced by beverage consumers might be *de minimis*. The court stated that:

> [T]here is latitude inherent in the statutory scheme to avoid literal application of the statutory definition of "food additive" in those *de minimis* situations that, in the informed judgment of the Commissioner, clearly present no public health or safety concerns.

Upon reconsideration, FDA estimated that the human cancer risk was 1 in 3 million and therefore approved the use of acrylonitrile in plastic bottles for food use, 49 Fed. Reg. 36635 (Sept. 19, 1984), and for alcoholic beverage use, 52 Fed. Reg. 33802 (Sept. 8, 1987). In 55 Fed. Reg. 8476 (Mar. 8, 1990), however, the agency requested information on existing uses of acrylonitrile in order to determine whether additional restrictions should be imposed.

6. *Polyvinyl Chloride.* After concluding that vinyl chloride monomer (VCM) was carcinogenic, FDA banned the use of vinyl chloride in aerosol cosmetic products starting in 1975, 39 Fed. Reg. 30830 (Aug. 26, 1974), and proposed to ban or severely restrict the use of polyvinyl chloride (PVC) in food packaging, 40 Fed. Reg. 40529 (Sept. 3, 1975). Following the decision in *Monsanto*, however, the agency reassessed its position, withdrew the 1975 proposal, 51 Fed. Reg. 4173 (Feb. 3, 1986), and published a new proposal to set limits on the use of PVC in food packaging that would assure a cancer risk from VCM of less than 1 in 10 million, 51 Fed. Reg. 4177 (Feb. 3, 1986). FDA announced its intent to prepare an Environmental Impact Statement on that proposal in 53 Fed. Reg. 47264 (Nov. 22, 1988).

7. *Hair Dyes.* In 43 Fed. Reg. 1101 (Jan. 6, 1978), 44 Fed. Reg. 59509 (Oct. 16, 1979), FDA required a cancer warning on labels of, and on posters at beauty shops that used, any hair dye containing the coal tar ingredient 4–MMPD (also known as 2,4–DAA). In the preamble of the final rule, the agency reconciled its imposition of this warning with its failure to require warnings on other products containing animal carcinogens.

> It was asserted in the comments that it is inconsistent to require a warning on hair dyes containing 4–MMPD yet require no warning on other products within FDA's jurisdiction that also contain carcinogens.... [M]any of the other specific substances cited by the comments are not analogous to 4–MMPD in hair dyes in terms of the appropriateness of a warning. Some of the substances cited in the comments are inherent rather than added substances in food, and the statutory standard for prohibiting

these substances may warrant a different policy with respect to warnings (21 U.S.C. § 342(a)(1)). In the case of charcoal broiled steaks, ... the warning would have to be directed at a manner of cooking meat, a product with respect to which FDA's authority is limited under section 902(b) of the FD&C Act....

In regulating aflatoxins, FDA has been primarily concerned with the aflatoxin level above which foods with aflatoxin should be prohibited. FDA has not considered requiring a label warning. Aflatoxins are unintentional contaminants, and they do not appear in every unit of peanuts, corn, and milk, or the foods containing these ingredients. Thus, any warning on these products would have to be considered in light of the fact that no detectable levels of aflatoxin may be present in some foods affected by the warning.... Moreover, given the prevalence of foods containing milk, corn and peanuts in some form, it may be impractical and confusing to require a warning on all the foods that may be affected. Indeed, a requirement for warnings on all foods that may contain an inherent carcinogenic ingredient or a carcinogenic contaminant (in contrast to a deliberately added carcinogenic substance) would apply to many, perhaps most, foods in a supermarket. Such warnings would be so numerous they would confuse the public, would not promote informed consumer decision making, and would not advance the public health. Warnings concerning deliberately added, unbannable carcinogens do not present this difficulty....

Id. at 59512–13.

Later the agency withdrew this proposal, 43 Fed. Reg. 1101 (Jan. 6, 1978). It was clear from FDA's own statements, and from estimates prepared by its staff that became part of the rulemaking record, that the risk posed by 4–MMPD was very low, at least for persons to whose hair the dyes are applied. For evaluations of the carcinogenic risk posed by hair dyes, *see* F. Cordle & G.E. Thompson, *An Epidemiologic Assessment of Hair Dye Use*, 1 REGUL. TOXICOL. & PHARM. 388 (1981); Richard Wilson, *Risks Posed By Various Components of Hair Dyes*, 278 ARCH. DERMATOL. RES. 165 (1985). Compare "Cancer-Causing Chemicals—Part I: Safety of Cosmetics and Hair Dyes," Hearings before the Subcomm. on Oversight and Investigations of the House Comm. on Interstate and Foreign Commerce, 95th Cong., 2nd Sess. (1978); "Safety of Hair Dyes and Cosmetic Products," Hearing before the Subcomm. on Oversight and Investigations of the House Comm. on Interstate and Foreign Commerce, 96th Cong., 1st Sess. (1979).

The cosmetic industry challenged FDA's warning as arbitrary and capricious. *Carson Products Co. v. Department of Health and Human Services*, Food Drug Cosm. L. Rep. (CCH) ¶ 38,071 (S.D. Ga. 1980). Following a consent order ending the litigation, FDA stayed its regulation. 47 Fed. Reg. 7829 (Feb. 23, 1982).

3. APPLIED TO "CONSTITUENTS" OF ADDITIVES

Questions about the Delaney Clause's coverage lurk around many corners. For example, how (if at all) does it apply to a naturally-occurring carcinogenic constituent of a raw agricultural commodity? FDA offered the following analysis:

> ... [T]he detection of a trace amount of a known carcinogenic substance naturally present in a food, or unavoidably added to a food in the course of its manufacture or processing, does not invoke the anticancer clauses. It has been pointed out, for example, that there are small amounts of estrogenic substances, which

are regarded as carcinogenic, naturally present in many foods. The anticancer clauses would be applicable, however, only if the food itself (containing the naturally-occurring substance) were, upon feeding to test animals or some other appropriate test, found to induce cancer. If this were to happen, the food itself would then be prohibited for use as a "food additive"—*i.e.*, for any use other than as an unprocessed raw agricultural commodity. . . .

"Agriculture–Environmental and Consumer Protection Appropriations for 1975," Hearings before a Subcomm. of the House Comm. on Appropriations, 93d Cong., 2d Sess. (1974).

By contrast, the agency for many years proceeded more cautiously in dealing with carcinogenic impurities of synthetic food and color additives.

Policy for Regulating Carcinogenic Chemicals in Food and Color Additives: Advance Notice of Proposed Rulemaking

47 Fed. Reg. 14464 (April 2, 1982).

During the two decades that FDA has administered the food and color additive provisions, the agency has, with a few exceptions, interpreted the Food and Color Additive Amendments to ban the use of any additive that was found to contain or was suspected of containing minor amounts of carcinogenic chemicals, even if the additive as a whole had not been found to cause cancer.

For example, FDA terminated the provisional listings of carbon black (41 FR 41857; September 23, 1976) and graphite (42 FR 60734; November 29, 1977) because the agency suspected that these colors could contain polynuclear aromatic hydrocarbons (PNA's), some of which are carcinogenic. The agency removed Ext. D&C Yellow No. 1 from the provisional list (42 FR 62478; December 13, 1977) because of the possibility that it might contain as impurities 4–aminobiphenyl and benzidine, both of which have been shown to be carcinogenic in humans. FDA terminated the provisional listing of D&C Red Nos. 10, 11, 12, and 13 because the agency suspected that they might contain low levels of [beta]-naphthylamine, a known human carcinogen (42 FR 62475; December 13, 1977).

The agency has also proposed to restrict the uses of polyvinyl chloride (PVC) materials in contact with food (40 FR 40529; September 3, 1075) because of a finding that vinyl chloride monomer, a known human carcinogen, could migrate in small amounts into food from PVC bottles.

Over the past 20 years, there have been rapid developments in analytical capabilities that make it possible to decrease by orders of magnitude the levels at which the components of a substance such as a food additive or color additive are detectable and identifiable. . . . Coupled with this development has been a large increase in the number of substances that have been studied for carcinogenicity in animal bioassays. For example, Tomatis has reported that 828 chemical substances were under test for cancer throughout the world in 1975. Many of these bioassays have resulted in positive findings for carcinogenesis. . . .

... It is the agency's frank expectation that a growing number of additives will be found to contain a carcinogenic chemical in future years. If FDA continues to implement the regulatory approach that it has followed in recent years, it will be forced to refuse to approve or to terminate the approval of the use of each of these additives, even though they themselves may be safe.

However, the agency believes that there are alternatives to its current policy that will adequately protect the public health. Not all of the additives that have been or will be found to contain carcinogenic chemicals will themselves be shown to induce cancer in appropriate tests (*e.g.* D&C Green No. 6). The agency believes that a distinction can be drawn between additives that contain a carcinogenic chemical but that have not themselves been shown to be carcinogenic. Two recent developments support the agency's belief that such a distinction is appropriate.

One development was the 1979 decision by the United States Court of Appeals for the District of Columbia in *Monsanto Co. v. Kennedy*, 613 F.2d 947 (D.C. Cir. 1979). In discussing whether a substance that migrates into food is a food additive, that court expressed the view that there is "administrative discretion, inherent in the statutory scheme, to deal appropriately with *de minimis* situations." If FDA has discretion to disregard low-level migration into food of substances in indirect additives because the migration of the particular additive presents no public health concern, then the agency may also disregard, after appropriate tests, a carcinogenic chemical in a noncarcinogenic food additive or color additive, if FDA determines that there is a reasonable certainty of no harm from the chemical.

Second, the agency is now confident that it possesses the capacity, through the use of extrapolation procedures, to assess adequately the upper level of risk presented by the use of a non-carcinogenic additive that contains a carcinogenic chemical.... Many theoretical models have been developed to extrapolate from animal experimental data to the relatively low levels of possible human exposure, but they can vary widely in the risk values that they predict. Thus, knowledge of the true risk at relatively low exposures is elusive.

In the decision on D&C Green No. 6 published elsewhere in this issue of the FEDERAL REGISTER, FDA is approving a color additive that has not been shown to be a carcinogen in appropriate tests, even though it contains a carcinogenic impurity. In this advance notice of proposed rulemaking, FDA is announcing its intent to formally adopt the principles on which that decision is based as the general policy of the agency....

The policy consist of three elements:

1.   Clarifying exactly what an "additive" is;

2.   Interpreting the Delaney Clause to apply only when the additive itself has been shown to cause cancer; and

3.   Using risk assessment as one of the tools for determining whether the additive is safe under the general safety clause....

Conceivably, each chemical in the complex mixture that constitutes a food additive could itself be considered to be a food additive. Each of these chemicals in some sense becomes a component of the food of which the additive is a part. For example, in the case of an indirect food additive used in food packaging or the like, any chemical impurity that migrates from the indirect additive into food could be considered to be an additive. In the *Monsanto* case, the agency argued that the food additive definition applied to the residual acrylonitrile monomer used to fabricate the final bottle, as well as to the bottle itself, because the monomer was intended for use and was used to manufacture the copolymer bottle. However, the *Monsanto* court held that the statute does not compel the Commissioner of Food and Drugs to declare that each chemical in an additive is itself an additive....

The constituents approach ... distinguishes between the additive as a whole and its constituents for the purpose of determining when the Delaney Clause is triggered. Using this approach, the food additive would be the substance that is actually intended for use in food or for food contact. All nonfunctional chemicals present in that substance would be called the "constituents" of the additive. Similarly, the term "color additive" would mean only those substances intended for use as a dye, pigment, or other substance that is capable of imparting color.... The constituents would include residual reactants, intermediates, and manufacturing aids, as well as products of side reactions and chemical degradation. A constituent, although part of the additive as a whole, would not itself be considered to be an additive for regulatory purposes....

The Delaney Clause requires the disapproval of any food additive that has been shown to be a carcinogen in appropriate testing.... However, it does not state that an additive shall not be deemed safe if the additive "or any of the chemicals present in the additive" is found to induce cancer.... A natural reading of the language that does appear in the statute establishes that the Delaney Clause does not apply to a carcinogenic chemical in a food additive absent a finding, after appropriate tests, that the additive as a whole induces cancer. Similar reasoning would apply to the Delaney Clause in the color additive provisions of the act.

... The risk assessment procedure discussed in this advance notice would not modify currently applied requirements under the general safety clause other than to provide a procedure for determining whether a noncarcinogenic additive that contains minor amounts of a proven carcinogenic chemical is safe. The risk assessment procedure would provide a method for estimating the levels of such chemicals that meet the general safety clause standard of safety. The upper limit of acceptable exposure would be determined by carcinogenic potency and risk extrapolation by the best current scientific methods available. FDA believes that any risk assessment procedure should yield such low acceptable levels that nothing but minor levels of carcinogenic chemicals would be able to pass the screen....

FDA believes that this general policy is a sensible, scientific means of limiting the circumstances in which it will be necessary for the government to act to ban the use of a food additive or color additive, without compromising the public health protection afforded by the act. This policy, if finally adopted, is intended to be implemented solely in those instances (*e.g.*, in the case of D&C Green No. 6) where data demonstrate that there is a reasonable certainty that no harm will result from the use of an additive that contains a carcinogenic chemical....

———

The Natural Resources Defense Council objected to FDA's approval of D&C Red No. 6, but, when the agency denied a hearing, 48 Fed. Reg. 34463 (July 29, 1983), did not seek court review. However, FDA's reliance on the "constituents policy" to approve a second color additive, D&C Green No. 5, 47 Fed. Reg. 14138 (Apr. 2, 1982), 47 Fed. Reg. 24278 (June 4, 1982), triggered a court challenge that produced the following ruling.

Scott v. Food and Drug Administration

728 F.2d 322 (6th Cir. 1984).

■ PER CURIAM ...

D&C Green No. 5 contains another color additive, D&C Green No. 6, manufactured through the use of p-toluidine, which has been proven to be a carcinogenic when tested separately, and which is present in minute quantities as a chemical impurity in D&C Green No. 5. After extensive tests, the FDA determined that D&C Green No. 5, as a whole, did not cause cancer in test animals. It also determined that p-toluidine was not itself a color additive. It concluded, therefore, that the Delaney Clause ... did not bar the permanent listing of D&C Green No. 5....

The FDA first ... determined that the maximum life-time average individual exposure to p-toluidine from use of D&C Green No. 5 would be 50 nanograms per day. The FDA then extrapolated from the level of risk found in animal bioassays to the conditions of probable exposure for humans using two different risk assessment procedures. Under the first procedure, the upper limit individual's life time risk of contracting cancer from exposure to 50 nanograms per day of p-toluidine through the use of D&C Green No. 5 was 1 in 30 million; the second procedure resulted in a calculation of a 1 in 300 million risk. The agency concluded "that there is a reasonable certainty of no harm from the exposure of p-toluidine that results from the use of D&C Green No. 5."

... Petitioner does not contest the validity of the tests employed by the FDA in determining that D&C Green No. 5 was safe for its intended uses but rather asserts that the Delaney Clause, as a matter of law, prohibits approval of a color additive when it contains a carcinogenic impurity in any amount and that the FDA has no discretion to find D&C Green No. 5 "safe" under the General Safety Clause because "[it is not] possible to establish a safe level of exposure to a carcinogen." ...

We affirm the judgment of the Food and Drug Administration.... The FDA's finding that the Delaney Clause is inapplicable to the instant case because D&C Green No. 5 does not cause cancer in humans is in accordance with the law. In its final order, the FDA stated its rationale for its conclusion, and it was fully mindful of the Delaney Clause in making its decision:

> [T]he Agency does not believe that it is disregarding the Delaney Clause. In drafting the Delaney Clause, Congress implicitly recognized that known carcinogens might be present in color additives as intermediaries or impurities but at levels too low to trigger a response in conventional test systems. Congress apparently concluded that the presence of these intermediaries or impurities at these low levels was acceptable. This legislative judgment accounts for the absence of any requirement in the Delaney Clause that the impurities and intermediaries in a color additive, rather than the additive as a whole, be tested or otherwise evaluated for safety. Thus, Congress drew a rough, quantitative distinction between a color additive that is deemed unsafe under the Delaney Clause because it causes cancer, and an additive that is not subject to the Delaney Clause because it does not cause cancer even though one of its constituents does. FDA's decision on D&C Green No. 5 is consistent with this distinction.

This interpretation of the Delaney Clause case is a reasonable one, and it is consistent with its legislative history. Congress distinguished between "pure dye" and its "impurities" in its list of factors for the FDA to consider under the General Safety Clause, but omitted "impurities" as a factor under the Delaney Clause. Although the Agency's regulatory interpretation of the Delaney Clause contains the words, "color additive *including its components*," it is clear that this regulation was aimed only at those additives containing impurities that produced cancer when tested together. . . .

Since in the instant case it was determined by the FDA that D&C Green No. 5, after testing as a whole, did not cause cancer in test animals, under the plain language of the Delaney Clause and the FDA's interpretation of that Clause, the FDA was not prohibited from permanently listing D&C Green No. 5.

. . . We agree with the FDA's conclusion that since it "has discretion to find that low-level migration into food of substances in indirect additives is so insignificant as to present no public health or safety concern . . . it can make a similar finding about a carcinogenic constituent or impurity that is present in a color additive." Accordingly, we hold that the FDA did not abuse its discretion under the General Safety Clause in determining that the presence of p-toluidine in D&C Green No. 5 created no unreasonable risk of harm to individuals exposed to the color additive.

NOTES

1. *Approval of Other Carcinogenic "Constituents."* Although FDA said that it intended to publish the constituents policy as a final regulation, it has not done so. Since the decision in *Scott* the agency has approved more than 30 color additives and indirect food additives containing trace amounts of carcinogenic constituents. *E.g.,* 48 Fed. Reg. 37615 (Aug. 19, 1983), 49 Fed. Reg. 13018 (Apr. 2, 1984), 50 Fed. Reg. 49684 (Dec. 4, 1985) (dibutyltin diacetate); 50 Fed. Reg. 4643 (Feb. 1, 1985)

(dimethylnitrosamine); 50 Fed. Reg. 20406 (May 16, 1985) (C.I. Vat Yellow 4); 50 Fed. Reg. 35774 (Sept. 4, 1985) (4–aminoazobenzene, 4–aminobiphenyl, aniline, azobenzene, benzidine, and 1,3–dephenyltriazene); 51 Fed. Reg. 28930 (Aug. 13, 1986) (1,4–dioxane and ethylene oxide); 52 Fed. Reg. 19722 (May 27, 1987) (methylene chloride); 52 Fed. Reg. 29178 (Aug. 6, 1987) (hydrazine); 52 Fed. Reg. 39508 (Oct. 22, 1987) (ethylenimine and 1,2–dichloroethane); 53 Fed. Reg. 31832 (Aug. 22, 1988) (1,2–dichloroethane, epichlorohydrin, 2,4–toluenediisocyanate, and 2,4–toluenediamine);

2. *Indirect Additives.* FDA in 43 Fed. Reg. 56247 (Dec. 1, 1978) proposed to ban the use of 2–nitropropane as an indirect additive for use in food packaging because of its carcinogenicity. No further action has been taken on that proposal, but the agency has approved another indirect food additive, 2–amino–2–methyl–1–proponol which contains 2–nitropropane as a constituent, 52 Fed. Reg. 29665 (Aug. 11, 1987).

4. APPLIED TO ADDITIVES "STRAIGHT UP"

FDA's 1969 ban of the nonnutritive sweetener, cyclamate, on the ground that it had been shown in animal tests to be carcinogenic, 34 Fed. Reg. 17063 (Oct. 21, 1969), disrupted the diet food industry. The agency's effort to soften the blow by reclassifying cyclamate-containing dietary foods as drugs, and therefore not subject to the Delaney Clause, provoked ridicule and was soon abandoned. 34 Fed. Reg. 19547 (Dec. 11, 1969), 34 Fed. Reg. 20426 (Dec. 31, 1969), 35 Fed. Reg. 2774 (Feb. 10, 1970), 35 Fed. Reg. 5008 (Mar. 24, 1970), 35 Fed. Reg. 11177 (July 11, 1970), 35 Fed. Reg. 13644 (Aug. 27, 1970). Periodic attempts to persuade the agency to reapprove cyclamate have failed. 41 Fed. Reg. 43754 (Oct. 4, 1976), 42 Fed. Reg. 12515 (Mar. 4, 1977), 44 Fed. Reg. 47620 (Aug. 14, 1979), 45 Fed. Reg. 61474 (Sept. 16, 1980), 49 Fed. Reg. 24953 (June 18, 1984). In 1985 FDA's Cancer Assessment Committee concluded that cyclamate is not a carcinogen, but a report by the National Academy of Sciences stating that cyclamate may be a tumor promoter or co-carcinogen led to yet another reassessment. *See* "Cyclamate Update," FDA Talk Paper T89–35 (May 16, 1989).

Following cyclamate's removal from the market, saccharin remained the only nonnutritive sweetener approved in the U.S. Two years later FDA had before it the results of two animal studies which suggested that saccharin was a carcinogen. With candor that could not be expected of any regulator while still in office, Dr. Charles Edwards, the FDA Commissioner who declined to ban saccharin, later forthrightly explained his decision:

> Technically, I could have banned saccharin immediately under the Delaney Clause, in early 1972, on the basis of those animal studies. I did not take that step because, once again, it was clear to me that the law should not be interpreted to yield absurd results. Saccharin was, at that time, the only remaining nonnutritive sweetener on the market. American consumers demand the availability of diet food products. It is irrelevant whether these diet products produce quantifiable health benefits or whether consumers simply like them. The point is that saccharin, like nitrite and many other important food substances, has come to be accepted

and expected by the American public, and any law which does not recognize this simply will not work.

"Oversight of Food Safety, 1983," Hearings Before the Senate Comm. on Labor and Human Resources, 98th Cong., 1st Sess. 20–21 (1983).

By 1977, long after Dr. Edwards had retired, FDA once again faced a threat to saccharin's continued approval in the form of a third study, sponsored by the Canadian government, which appeared to confirm the earlier findings that saccharin induced cancer in experimental animals. This time FDA officials concluded that they had no choice but to ban the sweetener. The agency defended its action in terms that emphasized the estimated magnitude of the risk consumers faced:

> The results of the Canadian study have been evaluated by expert pathologists, including scientists from FDA and other institutions in the United States, from Great Britain, and from other European countries, as well as from Canada. The findings indicate unequivocally that saccharin causes bladder tumors in the test animals. . . .
>
> . . . Public reaction to recent publicity about the Canadian study suggests considerable misunderstanding about the nature of toxicity testing in animals and the interpretation of results. For example, it has been widely publicized that the dose of saccharin found to be carcinogenic in rats is about 1,000 times that ingested by a human in a single diet beverage (when both doses are adjusted for the difference in body weight between rats and humans). Since this amount of saccharin would clearly never be ingested chronically by any person, some have suggested that these results have no pertinence whatsoever to human risk. In the judgment of FDA, this conclusion is not valid. . . .
>
> Current scientific methods are not capable of determining the exact risk to humans of a chemical found to be carcinogenic in animals. However, techniques are available for estimating the upper limits of the risk. The Food and Drug Administration estimates that the lifetime ingestion of the amount of saccharin in one diet beverage per day results in a risk to the individual of somewhere between zero and 4 in 10,000 of developing a cancer of the bladder. If this risk is transposed to the population at large and if everyone in the United States drank one such beverage a day, this would result in somewhere between zero and 1,200 additional cases of bladder cancer each year. . . .
>
> The estimated increase in risk from this moderate use of saccharin cannot be detected in human epidemiological studies. Such studies usually can only detect increased risks of 200 to 300 percent (*i.e.*, 2 to 3 times the baseline rate) or greater. Even the best feasible epidemiologic study is not likely to detect an increased risk of only 2 to 4 percent over background incidence. . . . The Food and Drug Administration thus considers the animal data and the human epidemiological data on saccharin to be compatible. . . .

... [T]he human risk of cancer indicated by these findings is significant and cannot be ignored. The Commissioner believes that conscientious protection of the public health is not consistent with continued general use in foods of a compound shown to present the kind of risk of cancer that has been demonstrated for saccharin—regardless of the asserted benefits of its use for some individuals in the population.

Section 409(c) of the act requires that any food additive must be found to be safe for human consumption before it can be approved or, in case of an additive already approved, continue to be used in foods. Based on the accumulated evidence of hazard associated with ingestion of saccharin, culminated by the Canadian study, the Commissioner concludes that the finding required by the statute can no longer be made. . . .

Therefore, under both the general safety requirement of the Food Additives Amendment of 1958 and the Delaney anticancer clause, the Commissioner concludes that saccharin may no longer be approved as a food additive. . . .

Saccharin and Its Salts: Proposed Rule Making, 42 Fed. Reg. 19996 (Apr. 15, 1977).

Within days of FDA's proposal, it became apparent that Congress would not permit a ban to become effective. Congress soon passed, and the President signed, the Saccharin Study and Labeling Act, 91 Stat. 1451, which forbade FDA, for a period of 18 months, to take any action to prohibit or restrict the sale of saccharin sweetened foods. The Act also instructed the Department of HEW to conduct or arrange for studies of the health benefits and risks of saccharin and of the current national food safety policy. The legislation added to the FD&C Act sections 403(o) and (p), which required that warnings about the risk of cancer be placed on all food containing saccharin and in all retail stores selling food containing saccharin. 42 Fed. Reg. 59119 (Nov. 15, 1977), 42 Fed. Reg. 62209 (Dec. 9, 1977) (guidelines for labeling warning); 42 Fed. Reg. 62160 (Dec. 9, 1977), 43 Fed. Reg. 8793 (Mar. 3, 1978) (retail store warning).

NOTES

1. *NAS Studies.* The congressionally mandated studies were completed early in 1979. *See* NAS, COMM. FOR A STUDY ON SACCHARIN AND FOOD SAFETY POL'Y, SACCHARIN: TECHNICAL ASSESSMENT OF RISKS AND BENEFITS (Part One, 1978); FOOD SAFETY POLICY: SCIENTIFIC AND SOCIETAL CONSIDERATIONS (Part Two, 1979). *See also,* OTA, ASSESSMENT OF TECHNOLOGIES FOR DETERMINING CANCER RISKS FROM THE ENVIRONMENT, OTA–H–138 (June 1981); Richard A. Merrill & Michael Taylor, *Saccharin: A Case Study of Government Regulation of Environmental Carcinogens,* 5 VA. J. NAT. RES. L. 1 (1985).

2. *Other Studies of Saccharin.* An epidemiologic study of 9,000 people sponsored by the National Cancer Institute found no overall added risk from the use of nonnutritive sweeteners, but did reveal the possibility of a slightly increased risk to some subgroups. FDA took the position that this study and two others were consistent with its 1977 judgment, based on the animal studies, that saccharin is a weak carcinogen. "Saccharin Studies," FDA Talk Paper T80–12 (Mar. 7, 1980). A

congressional report observed that most epidemiological studies are only capable of detecting increased risks on the order of 200 percent and concluded that the available studies of the effects of saccharin would probably fail to detect as many as 20,000 additional cases of cancer per year. H.R. Rep. No. 348, 96th Cong., 1st Sess. 27–28 (1979).

3. *End of Ban.* The statutory moratorium on any ban of saccharin was reenacted seven times, six times for two years each, and a seventh (in 1996) for five years. During this period, concern that saccharin might cause cancer in humans declined as questions about the relevance of the original animals studies were raised and research into the experience of long-time saccharin users failed to uncover a heightened cancer risk. In supporting the 1996 extension of the moratorium, Senator Orrin Hatch declared . . .

> Frankly, Congress long ago recognized, based on the established science on the issue, that the benefits of saccharin exceed the risk. . . . Because . . . no evidence has come to light that the risk of saccharin is greater than previously thought, I see no more reason to ban this product today than existed in 1977. In fact, I understand that more recent studies indicate saccharin does not pose the cancer risk in animals that it was thought to pose 20 years ago.

142 Cong. Rec. S8608 (July 24, 1996).

Within a few years, further doubts were raised about saccharin's carcinogenicity. In 1998, the National Toxicology Program, whose duties include the biennial publication of a "report on carcinogens," invited public comments on whether saccharin should continue to be listed as a suspect carcinogen. 63 Fed. Reg. 13418 (Mar. 19, 1998). In May 2000 the NTP released its ninth list of potential human carcinogens, from which saccharin had been deleted. While the agency acknowledged that "there is evidence for the carcinogenicity in rats, . . . [the] factors thought to contribute to tumor induction . . . in rats would not be expected to occur in humans." Appendix b, *Ninth Report on Carcinogens*, available on NTP website. A few months later, Congress enacted the Saccharin Warning Elimination Via Environmental Testing Employing Science and Technology Act, dubbed the S.W.E.E.T.E.S.T. Act, which repealed the warning requirements for saccharin and saccharin-sweetened foods, effectively affirming—at least as a legal matter—the safety of saccharin as a food additive. Consolidated Appropriations Act Pub. L. 106–554, 114 Stat. 2763, 2763A–73 (2000).

Lead Acetate; Listing as a Color Additive in Cosmetics that Color the Hair on the Scalp
45 Fed. Reg. 72112 (October 31, 1980).

. . . .

Lead acetate is a metallic salt color additive which had been used in cosmetic hair dyes before the enactment of the [Color Additive] Amendments. . . .

By 1978 . . . it had been established conclusively through animal feeding testing in the 1950's and 1960's that lead acetate was an animal carcinogen in two species, the mouse and the rat. Yet, because the limited human epidemiological data were considered equivocal, a definitive conclusion whether lead was a human carcinogen could not be reached.

... In addition to passing muster under the general safety clause, a color additive must also pass the test laid down by the color additive anticancer (Delaney) clause in section 706(b)(5)(B) [now 721(b)(5)(B)] of the Amendments.... The applicable provision is the second section of the color additive Delaney Clause (section 706(b)(5)(B)(ii) of the Amendments), which states that a color additive:

> ... shall be deemed unsafe, and shall not be listed, for any use which will not result in ingestion of any part of such additive, if, after tests which are appropriate for the evaluation of the safety of additives for such use or after other relevant exposure of man or animal to such additive, it is found by the Secretary to induce cancer in man or animal.

... [T]he "non-ingestion clause," does not make an animal ingestion study demonstrating carcinogenicity an absolute bar to the approval of a petition for a non-ingested color additive. Instead, it requires the agency to make one of two additional findings:

1.   That the tests relied upon to conclude that the substance is an animal or human carcinogen are "appropriate for the evaluation of the safety of additives" for the particular use under review; or,

2.   That other exposure of man or animal "relevant" to the substance shows it to be a carcinogen.

... As discussed below, after a thorough evaluation of all available scientific evidence relevant to the issue, the agency cannot find that the animal feeding studies are either "appropriate" or "relevant" for making the safety determination for lead acetate hair dyes under section 706(b)(5)(B)(ii) of the Amendments. This conclusion is based upon the unusual combination of scientific facts peculiar to lead acetate in hair dyes, a combination which will rarely, if ever, be presented again in this context....

1.   The Combe, Inc. radioactive tracer skin absorption study, in attempting to identify whether systemic absorption of lead occurred following the application of the hair dye, demonstrated that on an average only 0.5 ug of lead per application penetrates the skin. Conventional analytical methods could not detect so small an amount of lead. Indeed, the agency believed prior to the performance of the study that absorption would not be considered significant, in an analytical sense, unless found to be greater than 1 ug. On the basis of that study, it is estimated that frequent users of lead acetate hair dyes who might apply the hair dye as often as twice per week, could have an average daily absorption of lead from that source of 0.3 ug (3/10 of one millionth of a gram).... [T]his compares to an average human absorption of lead from air, food, and water of approximately 35 ug/per day. Thus, the average user of lead acetate hair dye might increase his or her body lead burden by less than 1 percent. Such an increase of absorbed lead from hair dyes over the normal human "background" levels of lead does not augment the existing risk of acute or chronic lead toxicity, including cancer, in any clearly discernible, much less significant, manner.

2.   The scientific data submitted to FDA concerning the issue of whether lead is a human carcinogen are not sufficient for substantiating a

direct correlation between lead exposure and human carcinogenicity. However, even if a direct correlation could be made, the human cancer risk
from the use of lead acetate hair dye would be a clearly insignificant
one. . . . Using "worst case" risk estimates extrapolated from the animal
toxicity data (*i.e.*, assuming carcinogenicity), the agency calculated that the
upper limit of lifetime cancer risk from the use of lead acetate in hair dyes
was approximately two in ten million lifetimes. Dr. Wilson's risk assessment calculated that the upper limit lifetime cancer risk from lead acetate
in hair dyes was about one in eighteen and one half million lifetimes. The
disparity in the upper limit lifetime risk derived by these assessments can
be attributed to slight differences in the assumptions underlying each
assessment. These very conservative risk assessments support a conclusion
that any risk likely to result from use of lead acetate hair dye cannot be
considered significant in terms of public health protection.

. . . .

The reasoning that leads FDA to conclude that lead acetate is safe and
that the Delaney Clause cannot be invoked also justifies the conclusion that
lead acetate hair dyes satisfy the general safety provisions under section
706(b)(5)(A)(i) through (iv) of the Amendments.

———

Six months later, FDA rejected, as inadequate to require an evidentiary
hearing, the objections filed by several consumer groups, 46 Fed. Reg.
15500 (Mar. 6, 1981).

The objection stated "if the risk is 1 in a million and if more
than 1 million persons use hair dyes with lead acetate, then at
least 1 person will die as a direct consequence of the FDA's
decision." . . .

Upper limit estimates of risk using "worst case" assumptions
cannot be used to predict with mathematical precision what will
actually occur. . . . The agency's conclusion that less than 1 out of
5 million persons would be at risk from the use of this color
additive in hair dyes based upon the "worst case estimates" is
consistent with the likelihood that no cancers will result from the
topical use of this color additive. . . .

FDA's decision was not challenged in court. Noting that "there is a healthy
new skepticism about how far regulators should go without first proving
the extent of risk or the value of a ban," the *New York Times* editorialized
that "The F.D.A.'s restraint in this case is welcome." *A Carcinogen Passes*,
N.Y. Times, Nov. 9, 1980, at 18E.

Listing of D&C Orange No. 17 for Use in Externally Applied Drugs and Cosmetics
51 Fed. Reg. 28331 (August 7, 1986).

. . . .

Because FDA considers D&C Orange No. 17 to be a carcinogen when
ingested by laboratory animals, . . . the Delaney Clause (section

706(b)(5)(B)(i) of the act [now 721(b)(5)(B)(i)]) is applicable. A strictly literal application of the Delaney Clause would prohibit FDA from finding that D&C Orange No. 17 is safe and, therefore, prohibit FDA from permanently listing the color for externally applied uses in drugs and cosmetics. However ... the calculated risk for these uses of D&C Orange No. 17 is extremely low. In fact, the level is three to four orders of magnitude lower than that level of risk which the agency accepts in other areas concerning carcinogens.... With such a negligible risk, there is no gain to the public and the statutory purpose is not implemented or served by an agency action delisting the substance.

... Therefore, FDA has decided to exercise its inherent authority under the *de minimis* doctrine and concludes that the Delaney Clause does not require a ban in the case of the externally applied uses of D&C Orange No. 17. Because there are no other safety problems with this use of D&C Orange No. 17, FDA finds that the externally applied uses are safe.

. . . .

Two conditions must apply to justify an agency's exercise of its authority to interpret a legal requirement as not requiring action in *de minimis* situations. First, it must be consistent with the legislative design for the agency to find that a situation is trivial and, therefore, one that need not be regulated. *Alabama Power Co. v. Costle*, 636 F.2d 323, 360 (D.C. Cir. 1979). Second, it must be clear that the situation is in fact trivial, and that no real benefit will flow from regulating the particular situation. Both conditions apply here.

1.   The establishment of a *de minimis* exception to the Delaney Clause is consistent with the legislative design.

In *Alabama Power Co. v. Costle*, the court stated that the implication of *de minimis* authority is consistent with most statutes. The court stated that unless Congress has been extraordinarily rigid, there is likely a basis for an implication of such authority....

... [T]he Senate agreed to adopt the color additive Delaney Clause only with the understanding that the clause would be administered with "a rule of reason," premised on the expectation that scientists would be able to determine the "probability of cancer induction." Thus, far from having been "extraordinarily rigid," Congress clearly contemplated that those administering the Delaney Clause would have discretion to implement that provision in a reasonable way.

This interpretation of the Delaney Clause finds support in recent case law. In *Monsanto v. Kennedy*, the [D.C. Circuit] held that not all chemicals that become components of food need be considered food additives....

The court also held in *Monsanto* that the "*de minimis*" concept, applied to the threshold "food additive" definition, could be utilized to allow the marketing of a substance that presents no real public health risk. Thus, the court's decision in *Monsanto* has the practical effect of shielding substances that present effectively no carcinogenic risk from the Delaney Clause. Although the court did not explicitly interpret the Delaney Clause as inapplicable to such substances, the court presumably knew that if a carcinogenic chemical was disregarded as *de minimis* in relation to the food additive definition, the chemical would not be subject to the Delaney Clause, which applies only when that definition is met. Necessarily, therefore, the court regarded this consequence as legally warranted.

Moreover, in *Scott v. FDA*, the Sixth Circuit upheld the so-called constituents policy....

In addition to the foregoing precedents, the state of scientific knowledge about cancer when the Delaney Clause was passed also supports the implication of *de minimis* authority under the Delaney Clause and the fact that the provision could not possibly have been meant to be "extraordinarily rigid." In 1958, there were only four substances that were known to induce cancer in humans: soot, radiation, tobacco smoke, and *beta*-naphthylamine. Only 20 years later, scientists had identified 37 human carcinogens and over 500 animal carcinogens.

. . . .

Under these circumstances, it would not be consistent with the legislative design for FDA, today, to attempt to prohibit all added carcinogens from the food supply provided the risks presented by permitted levels are trivial....

2.   The risk from the use of D&C Orange No. 17 in externally applied drugs and cosmetics is, in fact, so trivial as to be effectively no risk.

According to the [agency] panel's revised risk estimates, the highest lifetime level of risk presented by the external uses of D&C Orange No. 17 is 1 in 19 billion, *i.e.*, 5.1×10^{-11}.... The risk from the use of D&C Orange No. 17 in externally applied drugs and cosmetics will not exceed 1 in 19 billion and is likely to be somewhere between that level and zero. The 1 in 19 billion level represents a 1 in 19 billion increase in risk over the normal risk of cancer in a lifetime—not annual—risk. FDA emphasizes that the 1 in 19 billion level of risk does not mean that 1 in every 19 billion people will contract cancer as a result. Rather, in all likelihood, no one will contract cancer as a result of this exposure. In light of the level of risk presented by the external uses of D&C Orange No. 17, FDA finds that the uses are safe, that they impose no additional risk of cancer to the public, and that any risk they may present is of no public health consequence.

The Environmental Protection Agency (EPA) in recent years has ... relied upon the 1 in 1 million lifetime level as a reasonable criterion for separating high risk problems from low risk problems presented by the wide ranging environmental contaminants EPA must regulate.... For example, under the Safe Drinking Water Act (42 U.S.C. 300f et seq.), EPA sets drinking water standards that contain maximum contaminant levels for toxicants, including carcinogens. Maximum contaminant levels for carcinogens that have been promulgated or proposed to date by EPA generally fall into lifetime risk ranges of 1 in 10,000 to 1 in 1 million. Similarly, EPA recently proposed to establish the 1 in 1 million level as the "point of departure" in determining the level of control for all known and possible carcinogenic constituents compounds resulting from hazardous waste contamination (51 FR 1602, 1635; January 14, 1986)....

Although comparisons between the safety decisions made by OSHA and EPA with those made by FDA must be tempered by the fact that the decisions are made under different statutory frameworks, the decisions support the consensus proposition that a lifetime level of 1 in 1 million presents an extremely small risk.

———

When the listing of Orange No. 17 was challenged in court, the Department of Justice expressed reluctance to defend FDA's decision on the grounds the agency had originally advanced. FDA was instructed to issue the following clarification.

Correction of Listing of D&C Orange No. 17 for Use in Externally Applied Drugs and Cosmetics
52 Fed. Reg. 5081 (February 19, 1987).

. . . .

[In the preamble to the permanent listing of D&C Orange No. 17, a]fter summarizing the animal toxicity studies for this color additive as part of its explanation of this conclusion, FDA observed that the "data and information regarding the safety of D&C Orange No. 17 support FDA's conclusion that the substance induces cancer when tested in laboratory animals." This clarification of the Final Rule is being published to make clear that FDA was not, by this observation, concluding that this additive induces cancer in animals within the meaning of the Delaney Clause. As explained in the permanent listing document, in calculating the risk to man presented by the expected use of D&C Orange No. 17, FDA concluded that absorption of the color additive through the human skin was essentially the same as oral exposure in the rat. By virtue of this essentially one-to-one correspondence in absorption between rodent and man, a conclusion for purposes of the Delaney Clause that a substance at a given level poses a *de minimis* risk to humans implicitly includes the conclusion that a *de minimis* level of risk at a comparable level of exposure is presented to animals. Accordingly, D&C Orange No. 17 cannot be said to induce cancer in animals, as well as in man, within the meaning of the Delaney Clause. When a substance causes only a *de minimis* level of risk in animals, it cannot be said to induce cancer in animals within the meaning of the Delaney Clause....

... The words "induce cancer in man or animal" as used in the Delaney Clause are terms of art intended to convey a regulatory judgment that is something more than a scientific observation that an additive is carcinogenic in laboratory animals. To limit this judgment to such a simple observation would be to arbitrarily exclude from FDA's consideration developing sophisticated testing and analytical methodologies, leaving FDA with only the most primitive techniques for its use in this important endeavor to protect public health. Certainly the language of the Delaney Clause itself cannot be read to mandate such a counterproductive limit on FDA's discharge of its responsibilities. Moreover, nothing in the legislative history indicates that Congress intended to impose such a scientifically anachronistic meaning on the words of the statute, stopping the technological clock and relegating FDA's expert regulatory judgment to outdated analytical tools. . . .

Public Citizen v. Young

831 F.2d 1108 (D.C. Cir. 1987).

■ WILLIAMS, CIRCUIT JUDGE:

. . . Assuming that the quantitative risk assessments are accurate, as we do for these purposes, it seems altogether correct to characterize these risks as trivial. For example, CTFA notes that a consumer would run a one-in-a-million lifetime risk of cancer if he or she ate *one* peanut with the FDA-permitted level of aflatoxins once every *250* days (liver cancer). Another activity posing a one-in-a-million lifetime risk is spending 1,000 minutes (less than 17 hours) every year in the city of Denver—with its high elevation and cosmic radiation levels—rather than in the District of Columbia. Most of us would not regard these as high-risk activities. Those who indulge in them can hardly be thought of as living dangerously. Indeed, they are risks taken without a second thought by persons whose economic position allows them a broad range of choice.

According to the risk assessments here, the riskier dye [D&C Orange No. 19] poses one ninth as much risk as the peanut or Colorado hypothetical; the less risky one [D&C Orange No. 17] poses only one 19,000th as much.

. . . .

The Delaney Clause of the Color Additive Amendments provides as follows:

> a color additive . . . (ii) shall be deemed unsafe, and shall not be listed, for any use which will not result in ingestion of any part of such additive, if, after tests which are appropriate for the evaluation of the safety of additives for such use, or after other relevant exposure of man or animal to such additive, it is found by the Secretary to induce cancer in man or animal. . . . 21 U.S.C. § 376(b)(5)(B) [now 21 U.S.C. § 379e(b)(5)(B)].

The natural—almost inescapable—reading of this language is that if the Secretary finds the additive to "induce" cancer in animals, he must deny listing. Here, of course, the agency made precisely the finding that Orange No. 17 and Red. No. 19 [another color additive approved by FDA on a similar rationale] "induce[ ] cancer when tested in laboratory animals." . . .

Courts (and agencies) are not, of course, helpless slaves to literalism. One escape hatch, invoked by the government and CTFA here, is the *de minimis* doctrine, shorthand for *de minimis non curat lex* ("the law does not concern itself with trifles"). The doctrine—articulated in recent times in a series of decisions by Judge Leventhal—serves a number of purposes. One is to spare agency resources for more important matters. But that is a goal of dubious relevance here. The finding of trivial risk necessarily followed not only the elaborate animal testing, but also the quantitative risk assessment process itself; indeed, application of the doctrine required additional expenditure of agency resources.

More relevant is the concept that "notwithstanding the 'plain meaning' of a statute, a court must look beyond the words to the purpose of the act where its literal terms lead to 'absurd or futile results.' " Imposition of pointless burdens on regulated entities is obviously to be avoided if possible, especially as burdens on them almost invariably entail losses for their customers: here, obviously, loss of access to the colors made possible by a broad range of dyes.

. . . Assuming as always the validity of the risk assessments, we believe that the risks posed by the two dyes would have to be characterized as "acceptable." Accordingly, if the statute were to permit a *de minimis* exception, this would appear to be a case for its application.

. . . .

Judge Leventhal articulated the standard for application of *de minimis* as virtually a presumption in its favor: "Unless Congress has been extraordinarily rigid, there is likely a basis for an implication of *de minimis* authority to provide [an] exemption when the burdens of regulation yield a gain of trivial or no value." But the doctrine obviously is not available to thwart a statutory command; it must be interpreted with a view to "implementing the legislative design." Nor is an agency to apply it on a finding merely that regulatory costs exceed regulatory benefits.

Here, we cannot find that exemption of exceedingly small (but measurable) risks tends to implement the legislative design of the color additive Delaney Clause. The language itself is rigid; the context—an alternative design admitting administrative discretion for all risks other than carcinogens—tends to confirm that rigidity. . . .

[Judge Williams then examined the legislative history of the 1960 Color Additive Amendments, searching for indications that Congress might not have intended the Delaney Clause to be applied literally in all cases.]

Like all legislative history, this is hardly conclusive. But short of an explicit declaration in the statute barring use of *de minimis* exception, this is perhaps as strong as it is likely to get. Facing the explicit claim that the Clause was "extraordinarily rigid," a claim well supported by the Clause's language in contrast with the bill's grant of discretion elsewhere, Congress persevered.

Moreover, our reading of the legislative history suggests some possible explanations for Congress's apparent rigidity. One is that Congress, and the nation in general (at least as perceived by Congress), appear to have been truly alarmed about the risks of cancer. . . .

A second possible explanation for Congress's failure to authorize greater administrative discretion is that it perceived color additives as lacking any great value. . . . [T]here is evidence that Congress thought the public could get along without carcinogenic colors, especially in view of the existence of safer substitutes. Thus the legislators may have estimated the costs of an overly protective rule as trivial.

So far as we can determine, no one drew the legislators' attention to the way in which the Delaney Clause, interacting with the flexible standard for determining safety of non-carcinogens, might cause manufacturers to substitute more dangerous toxic chemicals for less dangerous carcinogens. But the obviously more stringent standard for carcinogens may rest on a view that cancer deaths are in some way more to be feared than others.

problem

Finally, ... the House committee (or its amanuenses) considered the possibility that its no-threshold assumption might prove false and contemplated a solution: renewed consideration by Congress....

Apart from their contentions on legislative history, the FDA and CTFA assert two grounds for a *de minimis* exception: an analysis of two cases applying *de minimis* concepts in the food and drug regulation context, and contentions that, because of scientific advances since enactment, the disallowance of *de minimis* authority would have preposterous results in related areas of food and drug law....

2 grounds for de minimis?

... The opinion [in *Monsanto v. Kennedy*] makes no suggestion that anyone supposed acrylonitrile to be carcinogenic, or that the Delaney Clause governing food additives was in any way implicated. Thus the case cannot support a view that the food additive Delaney Clause (or, obviously, the color additive one) admits of a *de minimis* exception.

Monsanto → didn't discuss carcinogens

Scott v. Food and Drug Administration involved the color additive Delaney Clause, but is nonetheless distinguishable.... Application of a *de minimis* exception for *constituents* of a color additive ... seems to us materially different from use of such a doctrine for the color additive itself. As the *Scott* court noted, the FDA's action was completely consistent with the plain language of the statute, as there was no finding that the *dye* caused cancer in animals. Here, as we have observed, application of a *de minimis* exception requires putting a gloss on the statute qualifying its literal terms....

Scott → distinguishable

The CTFA also argues that in a number of respects scientific advance has rendered obsolete any inference of congressional insistence on rigidity.... If the color additive Delaney Clause has no *de minimis* exception, it follows (they suggest) that the food additive one must be equally rigid. The upshot would be to deny the American people access to a healthy food supply.

As a historical matter, the argument is overdrawn: the House committee was clearly on notice that certain common foods and nutrients were suspected carcinogens. Beyond that, it is not clear that an interpretation of the food additive Delaney Clause identical with our interpretation of the color additive clause would entail the feared consequences. The food additive *definition* contains an exception for substances "generally recognized" as safe (known as the "GRAS" exception), an exception that has no parallel in the color additive definition. That definition may permit a *de minimis* exception at a stage that logically precedes the FDA's ever reaching the food additive Delaney Clause. Indeed, *Monsanto* so holds—though, as we have noted, in a case not trenching upon the food additive Delaney Clause....

GRAS

The relationship of the GRAS exception and the food additive Delaney Clause clearly poses a problem: if the food additive definition allows the FDA to classify as GRAS substances carrying trivial risks ... but the food additive Delaney Clause is absolute, then Congress has adopted inconsistent provisions.... On the other hand, if (1) the GRAS exception does not encompass substances with trivial carcinogenic effect (especially if its special provision for substances used before 1958 does not do so for long-established substances), and (2) the food additive Delaney Clause is as rigid as we find the color additive clause to be, conceivably the consequences identified by the CTFA, or some of them, may follow. All these are difficult questions, but they are neither before us nor is their answer foreordained by our decision here.

food v. color

Moreover, we deal here only with the color additive Delaney Clause, not the one for food additives. Although the clauses have almost identical wording, the context is clearly different. Without having canvassed the legislative history of the food additive Delaney Clause, we may safely say that its proponents could not have regarded as trivial the social cost of banning those parts of the American diet that CTFA argues are at risk....

[The FDA clarification notices on the listing of Orange No.17, *supra* p. 1168, and Red No. 19] effectively apply quantitative risk assessment at the stage of determining whether a substance "induce[s] cancer in man or animal." They assert that even where a substance does cause cancer in animals in the conventional sense of the term, the FDA may find that it does not "induce cancer in man or animal" within the meaning of 21 U.S.C. § 376(b)(5)(B).

The notices acknowledged that the words "to induce cancer" had not been "rigorously and unambiguously" so limited in the previous notices. This is a considerable understatement. The original determinations were quite unambiguous in concluding that the colors induced cancer in animals in valid tests....

The plain language of the Delaney Clause covers all animals exposed to color additives, including laboratory animals exposed to high doses. It would be surprising if it did not. High-dose exposures are standard testing procedure, today just as in 1960; such high doses are justified to offset practical limitations on such tests: compared to expected exposure of millions of humans over long periods, the time periods are short and the animals few. Many references in the legislative history reflect awareness of reliance on animal testing, and at least the more sophisticated participants must have been aware that this meant high-dose testing. A few so specified.

All this indicates to us that Congress did not intend the FDA to be able to take a finding that a substance causes only trivial risk in humans and work back from that to a finding that the substance does not "induce cancer in ... animals." This is simply the basic question—is the operation of the clause automatic once the FDA makes a finding of carcinogenicity in animals?—in a new guise. The only new argument offered in the notices is that, without the new interpretation, only "primitive techniques" could be used. In fact, of course, the agency is clearly free to incorporate the latest breakthroughs in animal testing; indeed, here it touted the most recent animal tests as "state of the art." The limitation on techniques is only that the agency may not, once a color additive is found to induce cancer in test animals in the conventional sense of the term, undercut the statutory consequence. As we find the FDA's construction "contrary to clear congressional intent," *Chevron USA v. NRDC*, 467 U.S. 837, 843 n. 9 (1984), we need not defer to it.

. . . .

NOTES

1. *Subsequent Proceedings.* Following the Supreme Court's denial of certiorari, FDA delisted the color additives involved in the litigation and two other color additives that had been approved on the same basis in the interim, 53 Fed. Reg. 26766, 26768, 26881, 26884, 26885 (July 15, 1988).

2. *FDA Discretion.* A former FDA Chief Counsel later suggested that the agency erred when it attempted to reinterpret the legal meaning of the Delaney Clause rather than taking its language at face value and reaching the same result by exercising the scientific judgment inherent in "induces cancer" to treat

> tumor development in experimental animals dosed at the level of maximum tolerated dose as insufficient to prove that the additive induces cancer when ingested. The observation of tumors, even malignant ones, at this extreme boundary of the experiment should have been regarded only as part of the total scientific evidence about carcinogenicity of the color additive, and a rule of reason judgment should have been reached that the colors do not fall within the ban of the Delaney Clause. I do not believe that FDA has ever had a policy of basing a judgment on the issue of cancer causation upon the results of a study in only one strain, gender, and species, at one dose in one experiment. Indeed, that is what Secretary Flemming warned against.

Letter from W. W. Goodrich to D. W. Sigelman, Counsel to the Human Resources and Intergovernmental Relations Subcomm., House Comm. on Government Operations (Sept. 11, 1987).

4. *Dimethyl Dicarbonate.* In 53 Fed. Reg. 41325 (Oct. 21, 1988), FDA approved the use of dimethyl dicarbonate for direct use as a yeast inhibitor in wines. FDA noted that the additive could react with naturally occurring ammonia in wine to form trace amounts of methyl carbamate, a carcinogen in rats, but concluded that the risk was less than one in 42 million and thus that the additive was safe. The agency declined to apply the Delaney Clause, commenting, "An additive that has not been shown to cause cancer but that contains a carcinogenic constituent, or whose use will lead to the formation of trace amounts of a carcinogenic substance in or on food, may be properly evaluated under the general safety clause of the statute." *Id.* at 41325.

5. *Methylene Chloride.* At the same time that FDA proposed to ban the use of methylene chloride in cosmetics, it announced that it was not proposing to revoke the existing food additive regulation, 21 C.F.R. 173.255, authorizing the use of methylene chloride for decaffeination of coffee because the residue of the additive in coffee represents less than a one in one million risk, 50 Fed. Reg. 51551 (Dec. 18, 1985). In *Public Citizen v. Bowen*, 833 F.2d 364 (D.C. Cir. 1987), the court determined that this decision was not ripe for judicial review.

6. *Coverage of the Delaney Clause.* Section 409 empowers FDA to promulgate a food additive regulation under two circumstances. First, the agency is required by

section 409(c) to act on any petition submitted by an interested person under section 409(b). Second, under section 409(d) FDA may promulgate a food additive regulation on its own initiative. The Delaney Clause appears in section 409(c) and not in section 409(d). Does this mean that FDA is not bound by the Delaney Clause when it acts on its own initiative?

7. *Color Additive Advisory Committee.* Section 721(b)(5)(C) provides a unique opportunity for the petitioner or any person adversely affected to trigger advisory committee review of any question involving application of the Delaney Clause to a color additive. FDA has issued regulations governing this procedure, 21 C.F.R. 14.140 *et seq.*, but it has not been used in more than 45 years. *See* Robert Becker, *The Scientific Advisory Committee and the Administration of Color Additives*, 15 FOOD DRUG COSM. L.J. 801 (1960).

5.   APPLIED TO NATURAL FOODS

Many natural foods have been found to be carcinogenic in laboratory animals. *See, e.g.,* B. Toth & J. Erickson, *Cancer Induction in Mice by Feeding of the Uncooked Cultivated Mushroom of Commerce, Agaricus bisporue*, 46 CANCER RES. 4007 (Aug. 1986). In addition, many chemicals found to be carcinogenic in laboratory animals are constituents in important foods. For example, the NTP announced in 48 Fed. Reg. 4557 (Feb. 1, 1983) that allyl isothiocyanate, which was shown to be carcinogenic, is:

> the major component in volatile oil of mustard, a flavoring agent prepared from seed of black mustard. Allyl isothiocyanate may be present in syrups, meats, condiments, baked goods, candy, ice cream and ices, and nonalcoholic beverages. Allyl isothiocyanate is found in cabbage, broccoli, kale, cauliflower and horseradish.

In 55 Fed. Reg. 26016 (June 26, 1990), NTP announced clear evidence of the carcinogenicity of d-Limonene, "a naturally occurring monoterpene found in many volatile oils, especially citrus oils which are used as a flavor and fragrance additive for food...." *See also* Bruce Ames et al., *Ranking Possible Carcinogenic Hazards*, 236 SCIENCE 271 (Apr. 17, 1987); Bruce Ames, *Dietary Carcinogens and Anticarcinogens*, 221 SCIENCE 256 (Sept. 23, 1983).

FDA scientists have pointed out that traditional methods of cooking and preserving food often contaminate food with carcinogens. For example, charbroiling and smoking contaminate food with polynuclear aromatic hydrocarbons, and pickling produces nitrosamines.

> This is just the tip of the iceberg. The spectrum of natural carcinogenic contaminants at low levels in food is far larger than these two examples can suggest. These "added" carcinogens are officially ignored because the exposures are ubiquitous and they would be extraordinarily difficult if not impossible to control and regulate.

Robert Scheuplein et al., *New Approaches to the Regulation of Carcinogens in Foods: The Food and Drug Administration, in* HANDBOOK OF CARCINOGEN TESTING 556, 563 (Harry A. & Elizabeth Weisburger, eds., 1985). *See also* M. J. Prival, *Carcinogens and Mutagens Present as Natural Components of Food or Induced by Cooking*, 6 NUTR. CANCER 236 (1985). Dr. Scheuplein, at one time Director of the Office of Toxicological Sciences in CFSAN, has concluded that, although "we should continue to minimize exposure to carcinogens from any major source," the data suggest that almost 98% of the cancer risk from food is natural in origin.

> [E]ven a modestly effective attempt to lessen the dietary risk of natural carcinogens would probably be enormously more useful to human health than regulatory efforts devoted to eliminating traces of pesticide residues or contaminants. The risk from natural carcinogens appears to be so much greater that just reducing it a few percent ... promises a greater decrease in absolute cancer risk than the total elimination of the lesser risks.

Perspectives on Toxicological Risk: An Example: Food–Borne Carcinogenic Risk 25 (1989) (unpublished manuscript).

As early as 1954 FDA banned the use of natural tonka beans as food because of the carcinogenicity of a constituent, coumarin, 19 Fed. Reg. 1239 (Mar. 5, 1954). FDA published an order banning the use of safrole and oil of sassafras in 25 Fed. Reg. 12412 (Dec. 2, 1960) based on animal studies demonstrating carcinogenicity. This ban was extended to include natural sassafras bark marketed for use in making sassafras tea in the home in 38 Fed. Reg. 20040 (July 26, 1973), 39 Fed. Reg. 26748 (July 23, 1974), 39 Fed. Reg. 34172 (Sept. 23, 1974), 41 Fed. Reg. 19207 (May 11, 1976), 21 C.F.R. 189.180. Although a 1973 seizure of sassafras bark was initially contested, the claimant subsequently withdrew the claim and thus the validity of FDA's position was not litigated. *United States v. Articles of Food ... Select Natural Herb Tea, Sassafras, etc.*, Civ. No. 73–1370–RF (C.D. Cal., June 15, 1973). Since then, the agency has not sought to ban natural food products containing carcinogenic constituents. Although FDA has quietly ignored carcinogenicity studies of long-established food products, it has consistently taken the position that a substance found to be carcinogenic in animals *cannot* be regarded as GRAS, although a substance containing a carcinogenic constituent *can* be regarded as GRAS. *See, e.g.*, "Agriculture, Rural Development and Related Agencies Appropriations for 1984," Hearings Before a Subcomm. of the House Comm. on Appropriations, 98th Cong., 1st Sess., Part 4, at 475 (1983).

F. DECIDING WHETHER AN ADDITIVE "INDUCES CANCER"

The supporters of the Delaney Clause assumed that any chemical capable of causing cancer at high doses could cause cancer at low doses, albeit less frequently. In other words, carcinogens exhibited no threshold; any exposure carried some risk of cancer. As knowledge of cancer induction progressed, the scientific community came to believe that this generalization did not fit all carcinogens. Some were probably threshold-limited, though it was far from certain whether these could be reliably identified.

Selenium in Animal Feed; Proposed Food Additive Regulation

38 Fed. Reg. 10458 (April 27, 1973).

The Commissioner of Food and Drugs ... proposes that the food additive regulations should be amended as set forth below to provide for the safe use of selenium as a nutrient in the feed of chickens, turkeys, and swine. . . .

Selenium is an element essential for normal growth and metabolism in animals. The minimum dietary requirements for selenium in poultry and swine range from 0.1 to 0.2 p/m of available selenium in the form of sodium selenite or sodium selenate. A dietary intake of less than these quantities of available selenium may result in a variety of debilitating conditions. . . .

It has been estimated that 70 percent of domestic basic feedstuffs (corn and soybeans) contain less selenium than that required to meet the animals' nutritional needs. . . .

The applicability of the anticancer clause (sec. 409(c)(3)(A)) of the act to the addition of selenium to animal feed has been thoroughly considered. . . . Available data have been evaluated by the Food and Drug Administration and the National Cancer Institute. Based on these evaluations, it has been concluded that the judicious administration of selenium derivatives to domestic animals would not constitute a carcinogenic risk. In three of the six studies available on the subject, test animals were found to have developed neoplastic lesions. These lesions were concluded to be a consequence of the liver cirrhosis produced by frank selenium toxicity. Further evaluation of the results of these three studies was complicated by the unusually high levels of selenium that had been administered, faulty experimental design, and, or infectious conditions present in the animal colonies used. Results of the remaining three studies, all of which were well controlled investigations, were negative for carcinogenic activity.

Selenium at high dietary levels (above 2 p/m for experimental animals) is a proven hepatotoxic agent. Early studies at dietary levels of 5, 7, and 10 p/m showed liver damage and regeneration in rats and an increased incidence of hepatoma in treated animals as compared with controls. Hepatoma did not occur in the absence of severe hepatotoxic phenomena. In more recent studies, hepatotoxicity was observed in rats fed selenium at 2 p/m. At 16 p/m, more severe liver damage was observed but was not associated with hepatoma. No hepatotoxic effects were noted at 0.5 p/m or below.

In this respect, selenium is no different from a number of foods and drugs available in the marketplace today. Beverage alcohol, for example, is associated with a higher incidence of liver cirrhosis, which, in turn, is associated with a higher incidence of liver cancer.

The Commissioner is of the opinion that these foods and drugs are not, by reason of their capacity to induce liver damage when abused by being consumed at high levels, properly classified as carcinogenic because of their potential association with a higher rate of liver cancer. The various anticancer clauses contained in the act were predicated on the theory that, since we do not know the mechanisms of carcinogenesis, even one molecule of a carcinogen should not be allowed into the food supply. The anticancer clauses do not apply in the case of an agent that (1) occurs naturally in practically all foods, (2) is used in a manner such that the natural level in food is not increased, (3) has a definite hepatotoxic effect/no-effect level, and (4) has a possible carcinogenic effect which is associated only with the hepatotoxic effect.

Accordingly, the Commissioner has concluded that: (1) The available information does not support classification of selenium or its compounds as having carcinogenic activity, (2) the use of selenium as set forth below constitutes no carcinogenic risk, and (3) the limitations set forth below, while satisfying the animals' dietary need for selenium, will assure safety to animals treated with sodium selenite or sodium selenate and to consumers of edible products of such treated animals.

NOTES

1. *No Court Challenge.* FDA's selenium ruling was never challenged in court.

2. *FD&C Red No. 3.* In 52 Fed. Reg. 29728 (Aug. 11, 1987), FDA released a report by a panel of government scientists the agency had convened to evaluate FD&C Red No. 3. This color has been shown to cause cancer in experimental animals, but the proponents of listing sought to persuade FDA that its mechanism of carcinogenic action posed no cancer risk for humans who might ingest it. Three years earlier the Director of CFSAN summarized the questions the agency would have to resolve before it could approve Red No. 3:

> Even if sufficient evidence of a secondary mechanism is developed, the agency would still need to consider other scientific questions in deciding on the safety of this color additive. Among the relevant questions are: (a) whether valid scientific data demonstrate that the cancer caused by the color additive has a clearly established threshold below which cancer will not be induced; (b) whether there is an adequate margin of safety between that threshold and expected consumption levels; and (c) whether FD&C Red No. 3 has otherwise been shown to be safe for its uses.

"The Regulation by the Department of Health and Human Services of Carcinogenic Color Additives," Hearing Before a Subcomm. Of the House Comm. On Government Operations, 98th Cong.; 2d Sess. 84–85 (1984) (Letter from Sanford A. Miller, Ph.D., to National Food Processors Association) (Apr. 16, 1984). In 55 Fed. Reg. 3516 (Feb. 1, 1990), FDA terminated the provisional listing of FD&C Red No. 3 for cosmetics and external drugs, and of Red No. 3 lakes (insoluble variants) for all purposes, stating that industry had failed to prove the hypothesis that the color is a secondary carcinogen.

3. *Dioxin.* There has been continuing controversy whether 2,3,7,8–TCDD (dioxin) is a secondary carcinogen. FDA and EPA have determined that it has not yet been satisfactorily shown to be a secondary carcinogen and have continued to regulate it as a no-threshold carcinogen, relying on quantitative risk assessment. Members of the EU have accepted the evidence of a secondary mechanism and thus have set dioxin exposure limits based on safety factors. In consequence, there is a 1000–fold difference between U.S. limits on exposure to dioxin and those observed in Europe. *See* Michael Gough, *Science Policy Choices and the Estimation of Cancer Risk Associated with Exposure to TCDD*, 8 Risk Analysis 337 (1988). In the interim, the paper industry reduced dioxin contamination to an insignificant level. "Progress in Eliminating Dioxin from Packaging," FDA Talk Paper T90–21 (Apr. 30, 1990).

4. *Other Putative Secondary Carcinogens.* FDA found that the scientific evidence is insufficient to characterize either chloroform or methylene chloride as a secondary, rather than primary, carcinogen. 41 Fed. Reg. 26842, 26843 (June 29, 1976), 54 Fed. Reg. 27328, 27333 (June 29, 1989). But the agency has agreed with

EPA that melamine is a secondary carcinogen. 49 Fed. Reg. 18120 (Apr. 27, 1984), 53 Fed. Reg. 23128 (June 20, 1988), 54 Fed. Reg. 12912 (Mar. 29, 1989).

COMMENT: AGENCY DISCRETION TO REJECT LINEARITY

EPA is responsible for administering the Safe Drinking Water Act. The Act requires the agency to establish two sets of limitations on concentrations of toxic materials in public drinking water systems—one pair for each contaminant. First, the agency is to establish a "maximum contaminant level goal" (or MCLG) at a level sufficient to protect consumers from any adverse health effect. Then, because achievement of that goal might not be practical, EPA is to prescribe an enforceable "maximum contaminant level" (MCL). For contaminants the agency considered carcinogenic it had routinely set MCLGs at zero.

In the late 1990s EPA undertook to reassess several contaminants of drinking water, including chloroform, a byproduct of chlorination, for which it had established an MCLG of zero based on the premise that any level of exposure posed a finite risk of cancer. In the meantime, however, further toxicological studies had suggested that chloroform's mode of action might not be linear. A group of independent experts surveyed the data and came to the conclusion that, while carcinogenic at higher concentrations, chloroform exhibited a threshold below which it presented no risk of cancer. EPA said it agreed with this assessment. "Employing the threshold approach that it found was entailed by chloroform's mode of action, EPA then calculated an MCLG of 600 parts per billion based solely on carcinogenicity." 206 F.3d at *1288*. However, when it resumed rulemaking in 1998, the agency retained its old MCLG of zero. The Chlorine Chemistry Council promptly challenged EPA's rule in court.

The D.C. Circuit upheld the challenge. *Chlorine Chemistry Council v. Environmental Protection Agency*, 206 F.3d 1286 (D.C. Cir. 2000). It held that EPA's adherence to the no-threshold premise for carcinogenicity, in the face of its own agreement with the expert panel's assessment, violated the Drinking Water Act's directive to set MCLs and MCLGs at levels supported by "the best available evidence." By the agency's own admission, the "best available evidence" showed that chloroform's cancer-producing effects were threshold-limited. Its reluctance to take the precedent-setting step of recognizing that one carcinogen did not fit the linear model provided no justification for EPA's failure to adhere to the conclusion dictated by the science.

In 2006, the Office of Management and Budget announced that it expected all agencies responsible for regulating chronic health hazards to use quantitative risk assessment in analyzing the potential adverse health effects of products and processes. OMB made clear that it expected agencies to adhere to the "best available evidence" standard in characterizing putative health hazards, thus making the distinctive language of the Safe Drinking Water Act a universal standard for regulatory decision making. *See* Office of Management and Budget, Office of Information and Regulatory Affairs, Proposed Risk Assessment Bulletin, Jan. 9, 2006. *See also* Occupational Safety and Health Act § 6(b)(5), 29 U.S.C. 655 (b)(5).

COMMENT: FDA SCIENTIFIC ASSESSMENT

FDA has never embraced the proposition that a mere temporal association between administration of a chemical to test animals and an elevation in tumor incidence inexorably requires a finding that the chemical "induces cancer." The agency has generally subjected study results to critical scientific assessment. It considers information on other biological parameters, such as dose response, tumor progression, and tumor latency, as well as the results of other bioassays. *See, e.g.,* 51 Fed. Reg. 41765 (Nov. 19, 1986) (Yellow No. 6); 48 Fed. Reg. 5252 (Feb. 4, 1983) (Blue No. 2); 47 Fed. Reg. 24278, 24281–82 (June 4, 1982) (Green No. 5).

The agency considers whether the effects observed in an animal study are biologically significant:

> Determining that the incidence of neoplasms increases as a result of exposure to the test compound requires a full biological, pathological, and statistical evaluation. Statistics assist in evaluating the biological conclusion, but a biological conclusion is not determined by the statistical result.

52 Fed. Reg. at 49577 (quoting with approval from a report of the Interdisciplinary Panel on Carcinogenicity entitled Criteria for Evidence of Chemical Carcinogenicity, 225 Science 682, 683 (1984)). *See also* 50 Fed. Reg. at 10415 (STP guidelines emphasizing the need for biological as well as statistical significance); 45 Fed. Reg. 61474, 61478 (Sept. 16, 1980).

In approving the color additive FD&C Blue No. 2, FDA declared that it had "consistently asserted that statistical factors must be analyzed in conjunction with biological factors" in determining what conclusions can be drawn from a study. 48 Fed. Reg. at 5257. FDA based its decision that the food additive acesulfame potassium is not a carcinogen on "the weight of all of the evidence; no single point provided complete proof in determining the question of carcinogenicity." 57 Fed. Reg. 6667, 6675 (Feb. 27, 1992). In denying a subsequent petition for a hearing, FDA defended, *inter alia,* its conclusion that the incidence of mammary gland tumors in female rats was not treatment-related by pointing out that these tumors are common in old age rats of the strain used in the bioassays, that the incidence of these tumors was in the range for historical controls, and that there was no evidence of progressive tumor stages. 57 Fed. Reg. at 6674–75.

In the 1993 edition of CFSAN's *Red Book,* FDA emphasizes the importance of scientific judgment in weighing all the evidence when deciding whether a chemical is carcinogenic.

> FDA's guidelines for toxicity tests for direct food additives and color additives used in food continue to emphasize that there is no substitute for sound scientific judgment. These guidelines are recommendations—not hard and fast rules. If an investigator believes that he/she can provide the Agency with useful toxicological information by modifying a recommended study protocol, and is able to support the modification with sound scientific arguments, then the investigator should propose the modified protocol to toxicologists at CFSAN.

FDA, CFSAN, RED BOOK II (DRAFT): TOXICOLOGICAL PRINCIPLES FOR THE SAFETY ASSESSMENT OF DIRECT FOOD ADDITIVES AND COLOR ADDITIVES USED IN FOOD, Ch. 1, p. 6 (1993).

In describing FDA's approach to evaluating toxicological evidence, the *Red Book* implies that a statistically significant increase in tumors by itself without the support of corroborative evidence, would not support a finding of carcinogenicity.

> There are no universally agreed upon ways of evaluating carcinogenicity data. It is necessary that there be interaction between pathologist, toxicologist and statistician. The role of pathologist is to decide whether an observed lesion is . . . cancerous or noncancerous. The role of the toxicologist is to determine whether the lesion is related to the treatment. The statistician's role is to analyze the mathematical probability of occurrence of the tumors by chance or as a result of treatment. . . .

> Because the power of carcinogenesis bioassays that use groups of a few dozen animals is relatively weak for determining carcinogenic activity, it is not surprising that evidence of carcinogenicity is something difficult to establish [from] a single bioassay. This is so for several reasons, including problems of historical diagnosis, sensitivity of the bioassay, and variability of the background tumor incidence. For these reasons, other correlative information may be necessary to add to the weight of evidence of carcinogenicity of a chemical. In general, the extent of the evidence for carcinogenicity can be determined by considering the following evidence: the number of species or strains with an increased tumor incidence; the number of positive studies (with different routes of administration and/or doses), if tested in more than one bioassay; the degrees of tumor response (incidence, site, type, multiplicity, etc.); evidence of structure-activity relationship; prevalence of dose-response relationship; the results of short-term tests for genetic toxicity; the presence of preneoplastic lesions; and a reduced latency for tumor development or increase in the severity (malignancy) of the neoplasia.

FDA has frequently noted the difficulties involved in determining whether the tumors have been caused by exposure to the test chemical or by some other factor. In its evaluation of acesulfame potassium, FDA explained that "the presence of extensive, severe chronic respiratory disease in the lungs of rats of all groups confounded diagnosis and interpretation of lung lesions in these animals." 53 Fed. Reg. 28379, 28380 (July 28, 1988)(adding that there were "inconsistencies in the diagnostic criteria applied to the observation reported in the study"). The agency continued, "Although the data appeared to show treatment-related differences in a few of the observations, these were subsequently found to be due to the different way categories of lesions were summarized."

FDA has declined to classify a chemical as a carcinogen if its observed effects in treated animals fall within the expected range from historical controls. The preamble to the agency's listing of the color additive D&C

Green No. 5 explains its reasons for ignoring statistically significant findings:

> [T]he tumor incidence in the D&C Green No. 5 high-dose group is within the expected range for controls. On the basis of this analysis, FDA has concluded that the tumor incidence found in the high-dose group is attributable to random variation.... FDA believes that, in this instance, the p-value calculated using the concurrent controls for the trend in the incidence of hepatocellular tumors in the mouse bioassay of D&G Green No. 5 is not a crucial factor in determining whether this bioassay has shown the color additive to be a carcinogen.

47 Fed. Reg. 49628, 49630 (Nov. 2, 1982).

FDA routinely takes into account whether a compound is genotoxic or exhibits structural alerts. The majority of chemicals that are recognized carcinogens are capable of directly altering the DNA, and FDA has held that negative findings in genotoxicity tests are relevant when determining whether a chemical "induces cancer" in animals. *See, e.g.*, 51 Fed. Reg. 41765, 41773 (Nov. 19, 1986)("the predominantly negative results [in short-term tests] with FD&C Yellow No. 6 support the conclusion that the color additive is not a carcinogen."); 48 Fed. Reg. 5252, 5258 (Blue No. 2)(Feb. 4, 1983); 47 Fed. Reg. 24278, 24282 (June 4, 1982)(Green No. 5).

FDA accords evidence of decreased lifespan substantial weight, as illustrated by its decision on Green No. 5:

> A shortening of this period is considered to be one of the primary indicators of an induced carcinogenic event, and studies with many bona fide carcinogens have indicated a more dramatic relationship between latency period and treatment than between tumor incidence and treatment. 47 Fed. Reg. 24278, 24283 (because the size and type of liver neoplasms was similar in the treatment and control groups, FDA concluded that "the small increased incidence of liver tumors in the high dose group was a spurious and nonreproducible occurrence"); *see also* 50 Fed. Reg. at 10416 (STP guidelines); 43 Fed. Reg. 18258 (April 28, 1978) (rejecting statistically significant reduced time-to-tumor findings for lymphomas in mice tested with Red. No 40).

As a general rule, FDA demands corroborative evidence before it finds that a chemical "induces cancer." *See, e.g.*, 51 Fed. Reg. 41765, 41773 (Nov. 19, 1986)("None of the other chronic studies in rats, mice, and dogs displayed a suggestion of treatment-related carcinogenic effects of FD&C Yellow No. 6 of the kidney."). As a former FDA Chief Counsel later explained, the agency has never had a policy of basing a judgment on the issue of cancer causation upon the results of a study in only one strain, gender, and species, at one dose in one experiment. Letter from William B. Goodrich, former FDA Chief Counsel, to D.W. Sigelman, Counsel to the Human Resource & Intergovernmental Relations Subcomm., House Comm. On Government Operations (Sept. 11, 1987).

FDA's willingness to consider evidence relating to mechanism extends beyond selenium. In a report to Congress, the agency wrote:

The issue has arisen whether the substance tested, or some other intervening factor, has caused the cancer. If a food additive causes a pathologic change at a particular level (*e.g.*, liver damage), and it is that pathologic change (rather than the additive directly) which in turn leads to cancer, the anti-cancer clause does not preclude approval of that additive for use at levels which provide an adequate margin of safety below the point at which it causes the pathologic change involved.

FDA Study of the Delaney Clause and Other Anti–Cancer Clauses in "Agriculture—Environmental and Consumer Protection Appropriations for 1975," Hearings Before a Subcomm. of the Comm. On Appropriations, House of Representatives, 93rd Cong., 2nd Sess. Part 8 at 219 (1974).

FDA has relied on mechanistic evidence in assessing the carcinogenicity of other chemicals. A notable example is the antioxidant BHA, which in 1982 was found to be associated with a statistically-significant increase in tumors in the forestomach of the rat. To evaluate this finding, FDA convened a working group of international scientists to evaluate the test results. The scientists commented on the evidence illuminating BHA's mechanism of action.

The available evidence indicates that BHA is not a carcinogen in the classical sense, *i.e.*, it is not a primary or direct-acting carcinogen, but instead exerts and expresses its activity through some as yet unknown mechanism.

REPORT OF THE PARTICIPANTS OF THE FOUR NATIONS (CANADA, JAPAN, UNITED KINGDOM AND UNITED STATES) ON THE EVALUATION OF THE SAFETY OF BHA 2 (1982). The group's report noted the steep dose-response curve in the BHA study, BHA's lack of genotoxicity, and the evidence suggesting a possible link between a marked increase in cell proliferation at high doses of BHA and consequent hyperplasia. Based on this analysis, FDA took no action to restrict the use of BHA.

FDA also considers the "appropriateness" or "relevance" of particular test species both in recommending test protocols and in assessing whether elevated tumor occurrence warrants a finding that an additive "induces cancer." For example, it is established agency policy that positive results for certain synthetic steroids do not trigger the Delaney Clause if "tumors are observed only in endocrine-sensitive tissue and no adverse data are obtained from ... genetic toxicity tests." *See* 52 Fed. Reg. 49572, 49578 (Dec. 31, 1987). Similarly, FDA has questioned the relevance of tumors observed in the forestomach of the male rat because humans do not have a corresponding organ. Based partly on this distinction, FDA in 1982 declined to find that BHA "induces cancer" in the face of a statistically significant increase in this tumor type in the rat.

In 1981, FDA received evidence that D&C Green No. 5 caused a statistically significant increase in the incidence of liver carcinomas in male mice. However, the agency concluded that, notwithstanding the statistical significance of the increase in tumor incidence, other factors led to the conclusion that Green No. 5 did not induce cancer.

[C]ollectively there exists a significant body of "biological" evidence that strongly supports the conclusion that D&C Green No. 5 is not a carcinogen. FDA finds that this evidence, when considered in conjunction with the results of the analysis of variance conducted by the agency, refutes any inference from the low *p*-values found in the statistical analysis of the data on D&C Green No. 5 that this color additive is a carcinogen.

47 Fed. Reg. 24278 (June 4, 1982).

FD&C Yellow No. 6 provides another illustration of FDA's reliance upon biological factors in evaluating what otherwise would appear to be statistically significant bioassay findings. Female rats fed doses of Yellow No. 6 exhibited a statistically significant increase in renal tubular adenomas. FDA concluded, however, that the effect could not be directly attributed to Yellow No. 6 for three reasons: (1) the animals exhibited an underlying kidney disease that could have been exacerbated by consumption of large doses of the color additive; (2) male rats, though known to be more susceptible than females to the effect of renal carcinogens, did not exhibit any form of treatment-related changes in their kidneys; and (3) the test animals may have suffered from chronic progressive nephrosis, a disease which is generally associated with the presence of tubular cell proliferative lesions. 51 Fed. Reg. 41765 (Nov. 19, 1986).

G.   RESOLVING THE "DELANEY PARADOX"

As part of the Food Additives Amendment, Congress added to the Act language codifying FDA's practice in regulating pesticides on processed foods. Section 402(a)(2)(C) said that a residue on processed food would not render the food adulterated if the level did not exceed the tolerance that had been established under section 408 for the raw form. The statute did not say specifically what was to happen if, in processing, the concentration of pesticide did exceed the level allowed on the raw food, but there is little doubt that Congress expected the agency to regulate this elevated residue under section 409. However, section 409 contains the Delaney Clause. This meant that if the pesticide, whose level was elevated by processing, was shown to induce cancer in animals, EPA could not approve its presence— and thus any food in which residues concentrated would be adulterated.

The next case, *Les v. Reilly* exposes the implications of this statutory arrangement. The practical consequences were amplified because EPA took the position that, if a food additive tolerance could not—because of Delaney—be approved for any processed form of a food, it would be obliged to revoke its 408 tolerance for the raw commodity. The agency reasoned that it could not permit marketing of a raw commodity some of which could be converted into unlawful processed food.

Les v. Reilly
968 F.2d 985 (9th Cir. 1992).

■ SCHROEDER, CIRCUIT JUDGE.

Petitioners seek review of a final order of the Environmental Protection Agency permitting the use of four pesticides as food additives although they have been found to induce cancer. Petitioners challenge the final order on the ground that it violates the provisions of the Delaney clause, 21 U.S.C. § 348(c)(3), which prohibits the use of any food additive that is found to induce cancer.

... A food "additive" is defined broadly as "any substance the intended use of which results or may reasonably be expected to result ... in its becoming a component ... of any food." A food additive is considered unsafe unless there is a specific exemption for the substance or a regulation prescribing the conditions under which it may be used safely.

Before 1988, the four pesticide chemicals with which we are here concerned—benomyl, mancozeb, phosmet and trifluralin—were all the subject of regulations issued by the EPA permitting their use. In October 1988, however, the EPA published a list of substances, including the pesticides at issue here, that had been found to induce cancer.

The FFDCA ... contains special provisions which regulate the occurrence of pesticide residues on raw agricultural commodities. Section 402 of the FFDCA provides that a raw food containing a pesticide residue is deemed adulterated unless the residue is authorized under section 408 of the FFDCA, which allows tolerance regulations setting maximum permissible levels and also provides for exemption from tolerances under certain circumstances. When a tolerance or an exemption has been established for use of a pesticide on a raw agricultural commodity, then the FFDCA allows for the "flow-through" of such pesticide residue to processed foods, even when the pesticide may be a carcinogen. This flow-through is allowed, however, only to the extent that the concentration of the pesticide in the processed food does not exceed the concentration allowed in the raw food. The flow-through provisions are contained in section 402 which provides:

> That where a pesticide chemical has been used in or on a raw agricultural commodity in conformity with an exemption granted or a tolerance prescribed under section 346a of this title [section 408] and such raw agricultural commodity has been subjected to processing such as canning, cooking, freezing, dehydrating, or milling, the residue of such pesticide chemical remaining in or on such processed food shall, notwithstanding the provisions of sections 346 and 348 of this title [sections 406 and 409], not be deemed unsafe if such residue in or on the raw agricultural commodity has been removed to the extent possible in good manufacturing practice and the concentration of such residue in the processed food when ready to eat is not greater than the tolerance prescribed for the raw agricultural commodity.

It is undisputed that the EPA regulations at issue in this case allow for the concentration of cancer-causing pesticides during processing to levels in excess of those permitted in the raw foods.

The proceedings in this case had their genesis in October 1988 when the EPA published a list of substances, including these pesticides, that were found to induce cancer. Simultaneously, the EPA announced a new interpretation of the Delaney clause: the EPA proposed to permit concentrations *new interp. of* of cancer-causing pesticide residues ⌐greater⌐than that tolerated for raw *Delaney* foods so long as the particular substances posed only a "de minimis" risk of *clause* actually causing cancer. Finding that benomyl, mancozeb, phosmet and trifluralin (among others) posed only such a de minimis risk, the Agency announced that it would not immediately revoke its previous regulations authorizing use of these substances as food additives.

... The Agency acknowledges that its interpretation of the law is a new and changed one. From the initial enactment of the Delaney clause in 1958 to the time of the rulings here in issue, the statute had been strictly and literally enforced. The EPA also acknowledges that the language of the statute itself appears, at first glance, to be clear on its face.

The language is clear and mandatory. The Delaney clause provides that no additive shall be deemed safe if it induces cancer. The EPA states in its final order that appropriate tests have established that the pesticides at issue here induce cancer in humans or animals. The statute provides that once the finding of carcinogenicity is made, the EPA has no discretion....

This issue was litigated before the D.C. Circuit in connection with the virtually identical "color additive" prohibition of 21 U.S.C. § 376(b)(5)(B).... *Public Citizen v. Young,* 831 F.2d 1108. The court concluded that the EPA's de minimis interpretation of the Delaney clause in 21 U.S.C. § 376 was "contrary to law." The *Public Citizen* decision reserved comment on whether the result would be the same under the food additive provisions as it was under the food color provisions, but its reasoning with respect to the language of the statute is equally applicable to both.

The Agency asks us to look behind the language of the Delaney clause to the overall statutory scheme governing pesticides, which permits the use of carcinogenic pesticides on raw food without regard to the Delaney clause. Yet section 402 of the FFDCA, 21 U.S.C. § 342(a)(2)(C), expressly harmonizes that scheme with the Delaney clause by providing that residues on processed foods may not exceed the tolerance level established for the raw food. The statute unambiguously provides that pesticides which concentrate in processed food are to be treated as food additives, and these are governed by the Delaney food additive provision contained in section 409. If pesticides which concentrate in processed foods induce cancer in humans or animals, they render the food adulterated and must be prohibited.

  . . . .

The EPA contends that the legislative history shows that Congress never intended to regulate pesticides, as opposed to other additives, with extraordinary rigidity under the food additives provision. The Agency is indeed correct that the legislative history of the food additive provision does not focus on pesticides, and that pesticides are regulated more comprehensively under the Federal Insecticide, Fungicide, and Rodenticide Act (FIFRA), 7 U.S.C. §§ 136–136y.... Congress intended to regulate pesticides as food additives under section 409 of the FFDCA, at least to the extent that pesticide residues concentrate in processed foods and exceed the tolerances for raw foods.

Finally, the EPA argues that a de minimis exception to the Delaney clause is necessary in order to bring about a more sensible application of the regulatory scheme. It relies particularly on a recent study suggesting that the criterion of concentration level in processed foods may bear little or no relation to actual risk of cancer, and that some pesticides might be barred by rigid enforcement of the Delaney clause while others, with greater cancer-causing risk, may be permitted through the flow-through provisions because they do not concentrate in processed foods. *See* National Academy of Sciences, *Regulating Pesticides in Food: The Delaney Paradox* (1987). The EPA in effect asks us to approve what it deems to be a more enlightened system than that which Congress established.

The EPA is not alone in criticizing the scheme established by the Delaney clause. *See, e.g.,* Richard A. Merrill, *FDA's Implementation of the Delaney Clause: Repudiation of Congressional Choice or Reasoned Adaptation to Scientific Progress*, 5 YALE J. ON REG. 1, 87 (1988) (concluding that the Delaney clause is both unambiguous and unwise: "at once an explicit and imprudent expression of legislative will"). Revising the existing statutory scheme, however, is neither our function nor the function of the EPA. . . . If there is to be a change, it is for Congress to direct.

. . . .

————

The Ninth Circuit's rejection of EPA's effort to resolve this paradox prompted Congress to amend both the FD&C Act and the Federal Insecticide, Fungicide, and Rodenticide Act (FIFRA). The following excerpts explain the source of EPA's dilemma and the compromise that Congress adopted.

James Smart, *All the Stars in the Heavens Were in the Right Places: The Passage of the Food Quality Protection Act of 1996*

17 STANFORD ENVIRONMENTAL LAW JOURNAL 273 (1998).

. . . .

Section 408 required EPA to reduce pesticide tolerances for raw agricultural commodities "to the extent necessary to protect the public health," but the provision also instructed the Administrator to "give appropriate consideration . . . to the necessity for the production of an adequate, wholesome and economical food supply." In implementing this standard, EPA first calculated the theoretical maximum residue contribution (TMRC) for use of a pesticide on a given commodity. . . . If the pesticide was one for which a threshold or "no observable effect level" (NOEL) could be identified for any ill effect, EPA considered the dietary residue contribution of the pesticide on the crop for which a new tolerance was sought in conjunction with all other dietary residue contributions for the pesticide on other crops. Regulators then compared this aggregate total maximum residue contribution to EPA's reference dose—the acceptable exposure level.

EPA arrived at the reference dose by applying an uncertainty factor to the level at which no observable effect could be found, the NOEL. The uncertainty factor consisted of one factor of ten to account for the uncertainty in "extrapolating data from animals to humans." Another factor of ten was meant to cover "variation within the human population." A third factor of ten applied whenever testing revealed fetal developmental effects.

If the reference dose was greater than the aggregate TMRC, the pesticide use would be approved. If the commodity-specific TMRC pushed the aggregate TMRC above the reference dose, EPA usually denied a new tolerance. Nevertheless, in some instances, EPA would allow consideration of the benefits of a pesticide to tip the scales the other way.

If the pesticide were only oncogenic, EPA simply considered the magnitude of the risk posed by the use's TMRC. If the risk were below a lifetime mortality risk of one in a million, and the crop had no processed form that concentrated the pesticide to trigger the Delaney Clause, the agency would approve the use. If the risk were greater than one in ten thousand, the agency typically disallowed the use. When the risk fell between these two numbers, consideration of the benefits of the pesticide was crucial to the outcome.

Thus, the FDCA created a discrepancy between the absolute prohibition on Delaney pesticides and the risk-benefit regime for pesticide residues that do not fall under Delaney. Delaney pesticides were those cancer-inducing pesticides that concentrated during food processing. Pesticides that either did not induce cancer or did not concentrate avoided Delaney. . . .

Allison D. Carpenter, *Impact of the Food Quality Protection Act of 1996*

3 Environmental Lawyer 479 (1997).

. . . .

The Act resolves the Delaney Paradox by establishing a single standard for pesticide residues in all types of food. The Act does not repeal or amend the Delaney Clause, but redefines "food additive" and "pesticide chemical residue" to ensure that pesticide residue in all foods, including processed foods, are covered by . . . section 408 of the FFDCA. The Act then amends section 408 to provide a general safety standard to govern pesticide tolerances, defined as "reasonable certainty that no harm will result from aggregate exposure to the pesticide chemical residue."

When a pesticide residue does not meet the general safety standard, EPA still may establish a tolerance for it if it qualifies as an "eligible pesticide chemical residue." To determine that a residue qualifies as an "eligible pesticide chemical residue," EPA must (1) appropriately assess the "non-threshold" health risks associated with the pesticide through a quantitative risk assessment, and (2) determine that the "threshold" health risks for the expected level of exposure are safe.

Once a pesticide residue qualifies as an "eligible pesticide chemical residue," EPA then may establish a tolerance for it if the Agency determines that use of the pesticide is necessary to avoid a significant disruption in production of an adequate, safe and wholesome food supply, or that the health benefits from using the pesticide outweigh the risks involved.

The Act, however, establishes three limitations on EPA's authority to issue tolerances in such circumstances. First, the yearly non-threshold risk may not exceed ten times the general safety standard, and the lifetime non-threshold risk may not be greater than twice the general safety standard. Second, EPA must review tolerances established under a risk-benefit analysis after five years and, if necessary, revoke or modify the tolerances if the foregoing requirements have not been met. Third, tolerances established under the risk-benefit analysis must be consistent with the special provisions for infants and children set out in the Act.

The Act responds to the findings of a study performed by the National Academy of Sciences Board on Agriculture, *Pesticides in the Diets of Infants and Children* ("the NAS Report"). The Act requires EPA to assess risk based on children's dietary patterns, including their higher consumption of fruits and vegetables, when setting a pesticide tolerance. In addition, the Act requires EPA to consider the special susceptibility of infants and children to pesticides, and to publish a special determination regarding the safety of each pesticide for infants and children. The Act also requires EPA to use an additional tenfold margin of safety when assessing threshold risks for infants and children. . . .

COMMENT: THE MANDATE TO PROTECT CHILDREN

As the previous excerpts reveal, the Food Quality Protection Act was a classic legislative compromise. A coalition of chemical companies and agricultural interests sought, above all, to escape the "Delaney paradox" and were rewarded by amendments to Sections 402 and 408 of the Act that excluded pesticide residues from the category of food additives to which Delaney might apply. The several groups that sought stricter limits on pesticide residues in food wished to curtail if not eliminate EPA's authority to take account of the benefits of pesticide use in setting tolerances, a victory more symbolic than substantive. But they were even more eager to have the law ensure that tolerances would be low enough to protect infants and children. The amended statute accomplished this in two steps. First, it required EPA to find that any tolerance would reflect analysis of the size, maturity, and dietary exposure of these populations. And then, by way of emphasis, it instructed the agency, in setting a tolerance, to apply an additional "safety" or "uncertainty" factor of 10 unless available data supported a different safety factor.

The latter provision was soon recognized as a potential threat to pesticide use (and thus sale) and, indirectly, to agricultural practice. Rigorous application of an "extra" 10 in computing an "acceptable daily intake" (ADI, or reference dose) for a pesticide could require that allowable residues be reduced by an order of magnitude, *i.e.*, a factor of 10. This would not only cut into chemical sales to farmers but could render pesticide use futile to cope with the pest. Environmental groups grasped the practical implications of this analysis and began to lobby EPA vigorously to accept and follow a protective—and arguably literal—interpretation of the crucial statutory language.

No definitive interpretation of the "10–X" provision has thus far been endorsed by any court. *See New York v. U.S. E.P.A.*, 350 F. Supp. 2d 429 (S.D.N.Y. 2004) (challenge to EPA position for lack of subject matter jurisdiction), *aff'd NRDC v. Johnson*, 461 F.3d 164 (2d Cir. 2006) (challenge may be brought in Court of Appeals, but only after exhaustion of administrative review). *See also* Alexandra Klass, *Pesticides, Children's Health Policy, and Common Law Tort Claims*, 7 MINN. J.L. SCI. & TECH. 89 (2005). EPA has approved tolerances for several crop-pesticide combinations based on analyses that reflect special attention to infants and children, and none has so far been overturned. It is too early to venture any definitive assessment of the impact of Congress' preoccupation with the risks faced by the youngest consumers of pesticide-treated food.

H.   OTHER EFFORTS TO IDENTIFY OR REGULATE CARCINOGENS

1.   IARC AND NTP

The International Agency for Research on Cancer (IARC), a component of the World Health Organization, helps coordinate research into the causes of cancer and monitors trends in cancer incidence worldwide. IARC has produced a series of "monographs" describing the evidence for the carcinogenicity of individual chemicals. It recognizes four categories or tiers of animal evidence of carcinogenicity: (1) sufficient evidence, (2) limited evidence, (3) inadequate evidence, and (4) evidence suggesting lack of carcinogenicity. IARC MONOGRAPHS ON THE EVALUATION OF CARCINOGENIC RISKS TO HUMANS, IARC INTERNAT. TECH. REP. No. 87/001, at 30–31 (1987).

IARC classifies substances according to carcinogenic potential under four headings: Group 1 (substances carcinogenic to humans), Group 2A (substances probably carcinogenic to humans), Group 2B (substances possibly carcinogenic to humans), and Group 3 (substances not classifiable). Like the National Toxicology Program, discussed below, IARC draws no distinctions based on mechanism of action. In 1986 EPA adopted a similar classification system, which includes an additional category: Group A (human carcinogens), Group B (probable human carcinogens), Group C (possible human carcinogens), Group D (not classifiable as to human carcinogenicity), and Group E (evidence of noncarcinogenicity for humans). 51 Fed. Reg. 33992 (Sept. 24, 1986). Only for substances in Group A and Group B will EPA prepare a quantitative risk assessment.

In the United States, the National Toxicology Program (NTP), part of the National Institute of Environmental Health Sciences, has adopted a five-tier system for describing the "strength of evidence" of the experimental findings from its animal carcinogenicity studies. 51 Fed. Reg. 2579 (Jan.

17, 1986), 51 Fed. Reg. 11843 (Apr. 7, 1986). The five categories are: (1) clear evidence, (2) some evidence, (3) no evidence, (4) equivocal evidence, and (5) inadequate study. The first two categories (clear evidence and some evidence) represent positive results. Based upon the "weight" of the animal evidence, as well as any relevant human or in vitro data, NTP then classifies the substances as "known" or as "reasonably anticipated" to be human carcinogens. NTP's refusal to consider a chemical's mechanism of action in compiling the required annual report under 42 U.S.C. 241(b)(4) was upheld in *Synthetic Organic Chemical Mfrs. Ass'n v. Secretary, Dept. of HHS*, 720 F. Supp. 1244 (W.D. La. 1989).

In 1978 Congress enacted legislation that requires the Secretary of Health and Human Services to compile and annually, later biannually, publish a list of known and suspected carcinogens. Pub. L. 95–622, 92 Stat. 3412. The responsibility to discharge this duty had been assigned to NTP, now a function of the National Institute of Environmental Health Sciences. NTP's decisions whether to list a chemical and what to say about the evidence relating to chemicals that are listed are often a matter of intense interest to firms that make, sell, or use a chemical. Some NTP choices have provoked legal challenges by affected industry groups. Government claims that such decisions are not actions subject to judicial review under the Administrative Procedure Act have not been successful, but the two courts that have entertained challenges have upheld NTP's procedures and its findings on the merits. *The Fertilizer Institute v. U.S. Department of Health and Human Services*, 355 F. Supp. 2d 123 (D.D.C. 2004) (challenging listing of sulfuric acid mist); *Tozzi v. U.S. Department of Health and Human Services*, 271 F.3d 301 (D.C. Cir. 2001) (challenging NTP's listing of dioxin as a "known human carcinogen").

2.   AGENCY CANCER GUIDELINES

FDA is not the only federal agency with responsibility to protect consumers and others from chemicals that may cause cancer. As the previous section illustrates, EPA has been active in this field—and probably more active than even FDA—since its creation in 1970. Over time EPA has been given authority to discover and control toxic chemicals in a wide range of exposure settings, under a long list of health-protective statutes: the Clean Air Act; the Federal Water Pollution Control Act; the Safe Drinking Water Act; the Toxic Substances Control Act; the Hazardous Waste Act (part of the Resource Conversation and Recovery Act); and, most prominently, the Federal Insecticide, Fungicide, and Rodenticide Act (along with the companion provisions of the FD&C Act that apply to pesticides on food).

With so vast a range of authorities, EPA almost from its beginning found it useful to formulate and adhere to an agency-wide set of criteria for identifying substances that might cause cancer and a set of standards for assessing the risks posed by those that displayed this potential. In 1974, the agency announced its first "interim guidance and procedures" governing its assessment of the health risks of carcinogens and the economic impact of possible regulatory responses. 41 Fed. Reg. 21402 (May 25, 1974). This comparatively brief document provided the intellectual framework within which EPA formulated risk assessments for the next decade. By the late 1980s, however, experience had added so many refinements and qualifications that the agency was impelled to develop an updated and far more sophisticated set of "cancer guidelines." This project has undergone several iterations, resulting in the release of successive drafts coupled with invitations for public comment. The most recent, and possibly "final" (for the moment) version was released—again for comment—in 70 Fed. Reg. 10616 (Mar. 4, 2005). *See also* Questions and Answers: EPA's Guidelines for Carcinogen Risk Assessment and Supplemental Guidance from Assessing Susceptibility from Early–Life Exposure to Carcinogens, March 29, 2005.

The Occupational Safety and Health Administration (OSHA) has likewise been active in assessing and regulating carcinogenic chemicals to which workers are exposed on the job. The agency is empowered to establish and enforce workplace exposure limits for chemicals that threaten worker health under statutory language that directs it to assure, "to the extent feasible," that workers exposed to toxic chemicals experience no adverse effects on health.

Like EPA, OSHA's appreciation of its potential caseload led it to attempt to formulate criteria for carcinogen risk assessment that it could apply in case after case. In 1978 the agency launched the most ambitious effort to codify these criteria—and the remedial response that should automatically follow—through rulemaking. OSHA's criteria were to be binding rules, not simply hortatory guidelines. 45 Fed. Reg. 5002 (Jan. 22, 1980), 29 C.F.R. Part 1990. In essence, the agency accepted the no-threshold premise for all cancer-causing chemicals and said it would require that workplace exposure to any chemical found to be carcinogenic be reduced to as near zero as the affected industry could achieve by engineering methods and afford, short of bankruptcy, to pay for. In the most famous case in this field, *Industrial Union Department, AFL–CIO v. American Petroleum Institute*, 448 U.S. 607 (1980), the Supreme Court essentially rejected OSHA's decision to dispense with any attempt to quantify the risk of a carcinogen. The agency did not abandon its effort to codify its cancer criteria, but instead amended its published generic cancer policy to require risk assessment. 46 Fed. Reg. 5878 (Jan. 21, 1981) (amending 29 C.F.R. 1990 to require OSHA to demonstrate that existing levels of worker exposure to a chemical pose a significant risk before it can regulate). Although OSHA later announced that it was reconsidering further changes, 47 Fed. Reg. 187 (Jan. 5, 1982), 48 Fed. Reg. 241 (Jan. 4, 1983), the agency has taken no further steps to revise its 1980 regulation. OSHA's workplace standards for particular carcinogens reflect explicit reliance on quantitative risk assessment. *E.g., International Union, United Automobile, Aerospace and Agricultural Implement Workers of America v. Pendergrass*, 878 F.2d 389 (D.C. Cir. 1989)(formaldehyde); *Building and Construction Trades Department, AFL–CIO v. Brock*, 838 F.2d 1258 (D.C. Cir. 1988) (asbestos); *Public Citizen Health Research Group v. Tyson*, 796 F.2d 1479 (D.C. Cir.1986) (ethylene oxide); *ASARCO, Inc. v. Occupational Safety and Health Administration*, 746 F.2d 483 (9th Cir. 1984)(airborne arsenic); *Asbestos Information Association/North America v. Occupational Safety and Health Administration*, 727 F.2d 415 (5th Cir. 1984) (ambient asbestos fibers). For a thoughtful discussion of regulatory risk assessment by EPA and OSHA, see Matthew D. Adler, *Against "Individual Risk": A Sympathetic Critique of Risk Assessment*, 153 U. PA. L. REV. 1121 (2005).

Of the principal federal safety agencies, the Consumer Product Safety Commission (CPSC) has had the least experience identifying or regulating carcinogens. On the one occasion it explicitly relied on quantitative risk assessment to justify action, a ban of urea-formaldehyde foam insulation, a court set aside the Commission's action. *Gulf South Insulation v. U.S. Consumer Product Safety Commission*, 701 F.2d 1137 (5th Cir. 1983). *See generally* Richard A. Merrill, *CPSC Regulation of Cancer Risks in Consumer Products*: 1972–1981, 67 VA. L. REV. 1261 (1981). *See* 57 Fed. Reg. 46626 (1992) (the Commission's art materials rule).

3.   GOVERNMENT-WIDE POLICIES

In 1977, FDA, EPA, CPSC, and OSHA established the Interagency Regulatory Liaison Group (IRLG) whose goal was to develop common approaches to the regulation of toxic chemicals. One of the IRLG's first projects was the establishment of a Work Group on Risk Assessment. The efforts of the Work Group were complicated by interagency policy differences. Although FDA and EPA strongly supported quantitative risk assessment for carcinogens and had been using this technique for some years, OSHA had recently proposed an approach to classifying carcinogens that explicitly refrained from giving weight to carcinogenic potency or risk assessment, 42 Fed. Reg. 54148 (Oct. 4, 1977). The final IRLG report, 44 Fed. Reg. 39858 (July 6, 1979), was therefore muted. While acknowledging its limitations, the report nevertheless endorsed the use of quantitative risk assessment.

On February 1, 1979, the Office of Science and Technology Policy (OSTP) of the Executive Office of the President issued a staff paper, IDENTIFICATION, CHARACTERIZATION, AND CONTROL OF POTENTIAL HUMAN CARCINOGENS: A FRAMEWORK FOR FEDERAL DECISION-MAKING, which explicitly endorsed use of quantitative risk assessment. The since-defunct Regulatory Council, representing the four IRLB agencies and others, likewise issued a statement on regulation of chemical carcinogens in 44 Fed. Reg. 60038 (Oct. 17, 1979). It declared that, except where a statute "explicitly indicates which substances are to be controlled and how, every regulatory proposal will be accompanied by some form of risk assessment." The statement went on to say, however, that all carcinogens "will be considered capable of causing or contributing to the development of cancer even at the lowest doses of exposure."

Several years later, OSTP convened an Interagency Staff Group on Chemical Carcinogenesis, and prepared a comprehensive review of a science and associated principles governing the assessment of chemical carcinogens, 49 Fed. Reg. 21594 (May 22, 1984), 50 Fed. Reg. 10372 (Mar. 14, 1985). Most recently OMB, in consultation with OSTP, released a risk assessment bulletin to guide rulemaking agencies, 71 Fed. Reg. 2600 (Jan. 17, 2006). OMB said it relied specifically on OSTP's 1985 report. Office of Management and Budget, Proposed Risk Assessment Bulletin, Jan. 9, 2006.

I. PERSISTENT ISSUES

Peter Barton Hutt, *Food and Drug Law*: *A Strong and Continuing Tradition*

37 FOOD DRUG COSMETIC LAW JOURNAL 123 (1982).

... In 1960, at the time Congress enacted the Food Additives Amendment, the Color Additive Amendments, and the Drug Amendments, [U.S. life expectancy] stood at 69.7 years. In 1978 ... it reached 73.3 years....

Food and drug regulation was designed, from its inception, to deal with the acute causes of death.... The 1906 Act was directed against poisons in food and food-borne disease. Regulatory strategy dictated elimination of dangerous ingredients and contaminating microorganisms. It was a sound strategy then, it remained a sound strategy when the law was modernized in 1938, and it continues to be a sound strategy today.

... [T]raditional regulatory strategy involves elimination of dangerous substances from the food and drug supply. This clearly works for such substances as salmonella, botulism, and other pathogenic microorganisms. It works equally well for frank poisons that can produce demonstrable injury, such as diethylene glycol and thalidomide. The question being raised today, however, is whether that regulatory strategy applies equally well to protect the public health against the causes of chronic disease....

The burden of demonstrating safety has changed for some categories of substances but not for others. For food and color additives, and new human and animal drugs, the burden of demonstrating safety has been shifted to the regulated industry. For many other ingredients used in food and drugs, however, the burden of demonstrating a lack of safety remains on the government, where it has been for centuries. This change in strategy, however, does not seem at all related to any attempt to prevent chronic disease. There is no evidence whatever that the principal causes of heart disease and cancer fall into those categories that now require premarket approval rather than into those categories that are exempt from premarket approval. One can persuasively argue, indeed, that the reverse is likely to be true. Heart disease and cancer have existed for centuries. To the extent that these diseases are attributable to any particular substances, therefore, those substances are more likely to be in the categories of old substances that are exempt from premarket approval than in the categories of new substances that now require premarket approval....

The credibility of regulatory agencies has been severely damaged by the mounting evidence that some of the most popular items in our food supply are carcinogenic by some form of scientific test. The public is not prepared to give up charcoal-broiled steak and hamburgers, pepper, nutmeg, mustard, and coffee, much less the essential nutrients that have been implicated by this scientific evidence. The failure of traditional regulatory techniques to deal with these problems was definitely demonstrated when regulatory action was threatened against artificially sweetened food containing saccharin and cured meat containing nitrites. The government quickly learned that the public simply did not intend the food and drug laws to be applied literally when it meant the elimination of important items from the food supply.

Evidence mounts that to reduce either heart disease or cancer there must be major lifestyle changes. Where this is true, it radically alters the prospects for regulatory intervention. Regulation can require some modifications in individual items in the food supply, but it cannot reform the entire American diet. If it is the way we eat and live that is associated with cancer, rather than specific substances in our environment, the traditional approaches of a regulatory agency are obviously inappropriate. . . .

Perhaps most devastating, the eradication of cancer and heart disease would have a much smaller impact on longevity than is commonly assumed. If all cancer, from all sources, were eliminated from the United States, average life expectancy at birth would still be increased by only 2.5 years. If a 30% reduction in cancer were achieved—an obviously more realistic but still extremely difficult goal—average life expectancy at birth would be increased by 0.71 year. A 30% reduction in major cardiovascular disease would produce an increase in average life expectancy at birth of 1.98 years. Application of the same 30% reduction to the working ages, 15 to 70 years, would result in a gain for them of 0.43 year from major cardiovascular disease and 0.26 year from cancer. . . .

The question, then, is whether the heroic personal, societal, and regulatory measures that would be required to make a substantial reduction in cancer—assuming that they would be effective, an assumption that is entirely conjectural—would be worth an additional 0.26 to 0.71 year added to the end of our lives. The smallest part of the sacrifice necessary to make that effort would entail the economic cost of regulation. Much more important would be the foregone pleasures of life-style, dietary habits, and individual food items that we have all learned to enjoy.

NOTES

1. *Life Style Changes.* J.F. Fries et al., *Health Promotion and the Compression of Morbidity*, 1 LANCET 481 (1989), point out that the substantial increase in life expectancy, and our lack of ability to achieve overall life extension, require "a change of focus from quantity to quality of life—'Add Life to Your Years, Not Years to Your Life.' "

> As life-style practices continue to improve and as mortality rates at advanced years decline more slowly, there may be disillusionment about the link between risk factors and health. It is critically important to recognize that the dividends of prevention are mainly in reduction of the population illness burden and enhancement of the quality of life, and that these are very large dividends indeed. . . . The primary purpose of population interventions, risk assessment, and risk reduction in developed societies is to compress morbidity and to improve the quality and vigor of life.

2. *More and More Carcinogens.* Of 86 chronic bioassays conducted by NTP and reported between July 1981 and July 1984, half showed the chemical was carcinogenic. J.K. Haseman et al., *Results From 86 Two–Year Carcinogenicity Studies Conducted By the National Toxicology Program*, 14 J. TOX. & ENVIRON. HEALTH 621, 634 (1984). FDA has stated that the sensitivity of analytical detection

methodology increased in the period from 1958 to 1979 "between two and five orders of magnitude," *i.e.*, between 100 and 100,000 times. 44 Fed. Reg. 17070, 17075 (Mar. 20, 1979). The increase in the number of chemicals found to be carcinogenic, their easy detection, and the expenditures required to control human exposure have led some cancer experts to suggest that the strategy of regulatory control has been overemphasized. *See, e.g.*, John Higginson, *Changing Concepts in Cancer Prevention: Limitations and Implications for Future Research in Environmental Carcinogenesis*, 48 Cancer Res. 1381 (Mar. 15, 1988).

3. *Costs of Regulation.* In 1987 the Office of Management and Budget (OMB) questioned the cumulative impact of conservative assumptions used in quantitative risk assessment.

> Often each conservative assumption is made by a different scientist or analyst responsible for a portion of the risk assessment. Each may think that erring on the side of caution or conservatism is reasonable. However, the effect of these individual conservative assumptions is compounded in the final estimate of risk presented to the decisionmaker. For example, if at each of two different steps in an analysis, estimates are chosen that have a 5 percent chance of being less than the true risk, then the final risk estimate will have only a 0.25 percent chance of being less than the true risk $(0.05 + 0.05 = 0.0025)$. That is, the risk estimate will have a 99.75 percent chance of being greater than the true risk. If there were 5 steps in the analysis instead of 2 and a conservative estimate at the 5 percent level were chosen for each step then the final risk estimate would have a 0.00003 percent (0.05^5) chance of being less than the true risk, or 3 chances in 10 million. In other words, the estimate has a 99.99997 percent chance of overstating the true risk.

> In practice, there may be as many as 20 distinct stages in a risk assessment where conservative assumptions are made. A typical risk assessment would probably contain about 10. The final risk estimate derived from these compounded conservative assumptions may be more than a million times greater than the best estimate and may, thus, have a probability of being accurate that is virtually zero. . . .

OMB, Regulatory Program of the United States government, Apr. 1, 1986–Mar. 31, 1987, xx & xxv (1987).

4. *Proposition 65.* On November 4, 1986, the voters of California by a large majority enacted Proposition 65 as an initiative measure under Article II, Section 8 of the California Constitution. Codified in the California Health and Safety Code 25249.5–25249.13, Proposition 65 requires the governor to publish, and periodically revise, a list of chemicals "known to the state to cause cancer. . . ." Any listed chemical is presumed to be a health hazard, and any individual exposed to a listed chemical must be given a "clear and reasonable warning" about the exposure by the person responsible for the exposure unless that person can prove that the exposure represents "no significant risk," assuming lifetime exposure at the level in question. Within three years more than 370 natural and synthetic chemicals had been listed as carcinogens, including some essential nutrients and many natural constituents of food. The impact of this experiment in risk communication is discussed in Peter Barton Hutt, *Application of Proposition 65 to Food, Drugs, Medical Devices, and Cosmetics, in* Clean Water and toxic Waste: At What Cost for What Gain? 23 (National Legal Center for the Public Interest, 1989); Matt Kuryla, *California Proposition 65 and the Chemical Hazard Warning: Risk Management Under the New Code of Popular Outrage*, 8 Va. J. Nat. Res. L. 103 (1988).

CHAPTER X

FDA ENFORCEMENT

A. INTRODUCTION

1. SECTION 301: PROHIBITED ACTS

Section 301, which enumerates the acts prohibited by the FD&C Act, is the heart of the enforcement provisions of the Act. These prohibitions are in turn enforceable in courts by the judicial remedies provided elsewhere in the Act and by other less formal mechanisms. Broadly speaking, section 301 prohibits the violation of any of the Act's substantive proscriptions or requirements. One or more provisions of section 301 is thus involved in *every* enforcement suit initiated by FDA, and extensive treatment of each of these provisions would be redundant.

One feature of section 301 deserves separate consideration. The section's opening phrase provides that the "causing" of any prohibited act, as well as the act itself, is prohibited. Neither the legislative history of the Act nor any judicial opinion discusses the scope of this provision. It had no counterpart in the 1906 Act, and Congress gave no reason for its inclusion in the 1938 Act. The provision is most often cited in holding corporate officers criminally liable for violations of the Act, although such liability had also been sustained under the 1906 Act. See generally *George E. Harding*, The "Causing" Provision and Jurisdictional Limits, *6 FOOD DRUG COSM. L.J. 594 (1951). In* United States v. Industrial Laboratories Co., *456 F.2d 908 (10th Cir. 1972), it was assumed without discussion that a consulting laboratory that failed to perform proper tests on a drug "caused" the adulteration of the product. Presumably any person involved in a violation is brought within the Act under this provision.* See, e.g., United States v. International Exterminator Corp., *294 F.2d 270 (5th Cir. 1961), involving the liability of a pest control service for causing the introduction of contaminated food into interstate commerce.*

NOTES

1. *Enforcement History.* For analyses of FDA enforcement actions under the 1906 Act, *see* James C. Munch & James C. Munch, Jr., *Notices of Judgment—The First Thousand,* 10 FOOD DRUG COSM. L.J. 219 (1955); *Notices of Judgment—Nos. 1001 to 5000,* 11 FOOD DRUG COSM. L.J. 17 (1956); *Notices of Judgment—Nos. 5001 to 15,000,* 11 FOOD DRUG COSM. L.J. 196 (1956); *Notices of Judgment—Nos. 15,001 to 31,157,* 13 FOOD DRUG COSM. L.J. 178 (1958). For a similar series under the 1938 Act, *see* James C. Munch & James C. Munch, Jr., *Notices of Judgment—Cosmetics: C.N.J.'s Nos. 1 to 205,* 14 FOOD DRUG COSM. L J. 399 (1959); *Notices of Judgment— Foods: F.N.J.'s Nos. 1 to 23,400,* 14 FOOD DRUG COSM. L.J. 402 (1959). Many of the early drug and device notices of judgment under the 1938 Act are summarized in

James C. Munch, *A Half–Century of Drug Control*, 11 FOOD DRUG COSM. L.J. 305 (1956). Colorful examples of early enforcement activities can be found in Suzanne White, *Enforcing the 1938 Food, Drug, and Cosmetic Act: The Class of '39*, 52 J. ASS'N FOOD & DRUG OFFICIALS, No. 4, at 10 (October 1988); James Harvey Young, *From Oysters to After–Dinner Mints: The Role of the Early Food and Drug Inspector*, 42 J. HIST. MED. AND ALLIED SCI. 30 (1987).

2. *Judicial Interpretation.* Numerous Supreme Court opinions have stated that the 1906 and 1938 Acts should be construed broadly in order to achieve their intended purpose. *See, e.g., United States v. Lexington Mill & Elevator Co.*, 232 U.S. 399 (1914); *United States v. Dotterweich*, 320 U.S. 277 (1943); *United States v. Sullivan*, 332 U.S. 689 (1948); *United States v. An Article of Drug ... Bacto-Unidisk*, 394 U.S. 784 (1969); *United States v. Park*, 421 U.S. 658 (1975).

3. *Commentary. See generally* Frederic P. Lee, *The Enforcement Provisions of the Food, Drug, and Cosmetic Act*, 6 LAW & CONTEMP. PROBS. 70 (1939); *Developments in the Law—The Federal Food, Drug, and Cosmetic Act*, 67 HARV. L. REV. 632 (1954).

2. FDA REGULATORY PHILOSOPHY AND COMPLIANCE POLICY

The differences between a broad and a narrow interpretation of the FD&C Act are highlighted in the following debate between Mr. Hutt, at the time FDA Chief Counsel, and H. Thomas ("Tommy") Austern, the leading food and drug practitioner of his era (and Mr. Hutt's mentor).

Peter Barton Hutt, *Philosophy of Regulation Under the Federal Food, Drug and Cosmetic Act*

28 FOOD DRUG COSMETIC LAW JOURNAL 177 (1973).

... Congress chose for the most part to express its mandate in broad and general terms, rather than in narrow and specific terms.... Congress obviously knew in 1938 that it could not foresee future developments, and that it must proceed primarily by establishing general principles, permitting implementation within broad parameters, if regulation in this important area was to be effective.

In this respect, the Act must be regarded as a constitution. It establishes a set of fundamental objectives—safe, effective, wholesome, and truthfully-labeled products—without attempting to specify every detail of regulation. The mission of the Food and Drug Administration is to implement these objectives through the most effective and efficient controls that can be devised.

This does not mean that the Act provides unfettered discretion for the Agency to do whatever it wishes in pursuing these objectives. We may not and do not ignore the statute. In some areas, Congress did lay down very specific rules which, until changed, must control....

But the fact that Congress simply has not considered or spoken on a particular issue certainly is no bar to the Food and Drug Administration exerting initiative and leadership in the public interest. Except where expressly prohibited, I believe the Food and Drug Administration is obligated to develop whatever innovative and creative regulatory programs are reasonable and are most appropriate to achieve the fundamental objectives laid down by Congress. And in spite of the diversity of the Agency's new programs, I am not at all certain that the Food and Drug Administration has yet begun to explore the full reaches of existing statutory authority. . . .

H. Thomas Austern, *Philosophy of Regulation: A Reply to Mr. Hutt*

28 FOOD DRUG COSMETIC LAW JOURNAL 189 (1973).

. . . Despite some semantic obeisance to "unfettered discretion," [Mr. Hutt's] premise is that *except* where specifically prohibited by Congress, the FDA is free, and indeed is *obligated*, to develop whatever innovative and creative regulatory programs *it* believes are most appropriate to implement the fundamental objectives it finds in the Act.

Mr. Hutt grants that FDA cannot override Congress by administrative fiat, but he insists that simply because Congress has *not spoken* on a particular issue there is no bar to FDA exercising new authority. . . .

Some might urge that that view is contrary to experience, that on the many amendments since 1938 Congress had never objected to being bothered, or had thought that under what Mr. Hutt calls "the FDA constitution," FDA should have made new law itself rather than through careful Congressional deliberation that would strike a *legislative* balance.

It is no distortion, I hope, of his basic approach to read it as meaning: Everything *we* want to do that is not specifically prohibited can be made mandatory if we think it is in the public interest. Well, as Mr. Justice Cardozo once observed: "That is delegation running riot." . . .

We do not often indulge in government by decree or in regulation by fiat. I agree that regulation becomes futile, if not impossible, absent *enforcement*. But as a lawyer I look at Section 301 to see what Congress has specifically made a prohibited act, backed by the sanctions of seizure, injunction, and criminal penalties. . . .

NOTES

Commentary. See generally Lars Noah, *Interpreting Agency Enabling Acts: Misplaced Metaphors in Administrative Law*, 41 WM. & MARY L. REV. 1463 (2000).

———

FDA has on occasion attempted to establish its enforcement policies and priorities in formal agency documents.

FDA COMPLIANCE PHILOSOPHY

May 6, 1971.

TO: Associate and Assistant Commissioners
        Bureau and Office Directors
        Directors of Offices of Compliance

Regional Food and Drug Directors
Deputy Regional Food and Drug Directors
FROM: Charles C. Edwards, M.D., Commissioner of Food and Drugs

... [A]ll FDA managers and employees in the various headquarters and field offices should be guided by the following statement of general principles in carrying out our mandated responsibilities in consumer protection:

a. The Food and Drug Administration is a scientifically oriented law enforcement agency. Our mission is to provide consumer protection through judicious enforcement of the various laws which have been entrusted to our administration.

b. We encourage industry self regulation and will participate in cooperative programs designed to inform industry how to meet the requirements of the law and to promote voluntary compliance through preventive measures designed to keep unsafe, unfit or ineffective products from reaching the consumer, or to remove expeditiously such products from the market when found.

c. We also will fully utilize formal enforcement procedures, including the punitive provisions of the various laws under which we operate, when dealing with those sections of the regulated industry which may have chosen not to comply, or which may have been unable to comply with the requirements of the law. . . .

e. All violations of the law which come to our attention through our own activities or through other sources will be evaluated as to how best the consumer can be served, in consideration of the seriousness of the observed problem and our available resources and other priorities.

f. We will use all available compliance measures to achieve optimum consumer protection. This may include the release of information to the general public and/or professional groups; administrative action; the institution of recall; or seizure, injunction, or prosecution action.

Compliance Policy Guide 7150.10

52 Fed. Reg. 27731 (July 23, 1987).

SUBJECT: Health Fraud—Factors in Considering Regulatory Action

BACKGROUND

Health Fraud products are articles of unproven effectiveness that are promoted to improve health, well being, or appearance. They can be drugs, devices, foods or cosmetics for animal or human use. . . .

DEFINITIONS

A health fraud product presents a direct health hazard if it is likely to cause injury, death or other serious adverse effect when used as directed or in a customary manner.

A health fraud product presents an indirect health hazard if, as a result of reliance on the product, the consumer is likely to delay or discontinue appropriate medical treatment. The health hazard is indirect when it does no direct harm to the person as a result of its use, but rather denies, delays, or interferes with effective treatment. Consumers who purchase these products are misled by exaggerated or false claims that are made for the products.

POLICY

Products that pose a direct health hazard to the user shall receive the agency's highest priority attention, regardless of whether they are health fraud products.... Health fraud products for which there is not a documented direct health hazard (*i.e.*, indirect health hazard products) will still be considered for regulatory action but on a lower priority.

In evaluating regulatory actions against indirect health hazard products, the following factors should be considered by districts and the centers:

1.   Whether the therapeutic claims, or conditions to be treated are significant as interpreted by the appropriate center;

2.   Whether there are scientific data or specific information to support the safety or effectiveness of the product for its intended or customary use;

3.   The degree of vulnerability of the prospective user group, *e.g.*, the elderly, persons with illnesses for which there is no recognized effective treatment;

4.   The availability of other administrative or regulatory alternatives to bring the product or firm into compliance, *e.g.*, education, referral or cooperation with local, state or other federal agencies;

5.   The amount of agency resources required and whether they are sufficient to pursue the action to its conclusion.

6.   The source of the product, size of the industry distributing the same or similar products, and the impact of the action on that source and industry;

7.   The cost of the product, the economic impact of this cost on the target user group, as well as the profit (per sale) realized from the sale of the product;

8.   The amount (dollar and volume) of product sold, and the geographical scope of its distribution;

In most cases, the seriousness of the therapeutic claims and the nature of the indirect hazard will be obvious. We recognize that when a product with unproven therapeutic claims is first introduced, it is difficult to predict its economic impact because, whether or not a regulatory action is taken, the product may not be accepted in the marketplace. Generally, new health fraud products with undetermined economic impact and limited health significance should result in a Notice of Adverse Findings Letter to the promoter. Regulatory action should be considered for products of limited health significance when it appears there is a growing national or substantial regional market for them. The office of compliance in each center will designate a contact and a back-up person for primary consultation on health fraud action....

3. Industry-Wide Enforcement

It is well established that a regulatory agency has discretion to initiate enforcement action against fewer than all of the firms engaged in similar unlawful conduct, and to appraise and discount the impact on competition of case-by-case enforcement. *See Moog Industries, Inc. v. FTC*, 355 U.S. 411 (1958); *see also FTC v. Universal–Rundle Corp.*, 387 U.S. 244 (1967). Yet there are strong arguments favoring more comprehensive regulation.

Peter Barton Hutt, *Philosophy Of Regulation Under the Federal Food, Drug and Cosmetic Act*

28 Food Drug Cosmetic Law Journal 177 (1973).

... Standing alone, institution of legal enforcement action, resulting in costly and time-consuming litigation on a case-by-case basis, is an inadequate method of regulation. It fails to inform the regulated industry of its obligations, it involves years of delay, and the end results are often uncertain. Worst of all, it inevitably results in invidious selective enforcement, whereby one or two individuals or companies must be singled out as the test cases while the rest of the industry is left alone. By contrast, the promulgation of regulations informs an entire industry of all applicable requirements and has proved to be far more likely to induce widespread compliance. . . .

This past year has seen more new regulatory programs undertaken by detailed substantive and procedural regulations published in the *Federal Register* than at any other time in the history of the Food and Drug Administration. Indeed, those in industry who formerly complained that they could not determine what the Food and Drug Administration expected of them are now complaining that [FDA is] spelling out those requirements all too clearly. . . .

Over–the–Counter Drugs: Proposal Establishing Rule Making Procedures for Classification

37 Fed. Reg. 85 (January 5, 1972).

The Food and Drug Administration intends to require that all unapproved new drugs and misbranded drugs either be reformulated and/or relabeled to meet all requirements of the act or be removed from the market. In carrying out its responsibilities in this area, the Food and Drug Administration may either initiate a separate court action with respect to each violative OTC drug or deal with all OTC drugs through rulemaking by therapeutic classes on an industrywide basis. It has been determined that the latter approach should be pursued. . . .

Litigation to remove violative OTC preparations from the market would necessarily be on a drug-by-drug basis. . . . Such litigation is time-consuming and expensive and is sometimes ineffective because manufacturers may change the formulation of the drug in question and/or its labeling claims and reintroduce the product into the market, thus requiring still further litigation. . . .

Of paramount concern is the inadequate consumer protection produced by a product-by-product review and case-by-case litigation against each drug. It is not unreasonable to expect that a very large number of violative drugs would remain on the market for long periods of time because of the limited resources of the agency to evaluate and proceed against such drugs and the delays inherent in complicated litigation through trial and appellate courts.

It is impossible to proceed simultaneously by litigation against all manufacturers of similar preparations or their drugs. The situation will arise, as it has before, that preparations similar to those proceeded against will remain on the market long after their less fortunate counterparts have been removed. This situation must be avoided for two reasons. First, and most important, the public is not sufficiently protected when violative drugs remain on the market. Second, equitable enforcement of the law requires that the agency proceed against all manufacturers of similar preparations, since those not proceeded against would have an unfair competitive advantage.

Practically all of the thousands of OTC drugs now marketed are compounded from only an estimated 200 active ingredients which are used either alone or in varying combinations. . . . [T]he same scientific and medical evidence is relevant in reviewing all OTC drugs within a given therapeutic class. . . .

NOTES

1. *Supreme Court Support.* In *Weinberger v. Bentex Pharmaceuticals, Inc.*, 412 U.S. 645 (1973), the Supreme Court endorsed FDA's approach to implementation of the 1962 effectiveness standard:

> . . . The deluge of litigation that would follow if "me-too" drugs and OTC drugs had to receive *de novo* hearings in the courts would inure to the interests of manufacturers and merchants in drugs, but not to the interests of the public that Congress was anxious to protect by the 1962 amendments, as well as OTC drugs and drugs covered by the 1972 [Drug Listing] Act. We are told that FDA is incapable of handling a caseload of more than perhaps 10 or 15 *de novo* judicial proceedings in a year. Clearly, if FDA were required to litigate, on a case-by-case basis, the "new drug" status of each drug now marketed, the regulatory scheme of the Act would be severely undermined, if not totally destroyed. Moreover, a case-by-case approach is inherently unfair because it requires compliance by one manufacturer while his competitors marketing similar drugs remain free to violate the Act. . . .

2. *Limits on Even-Handed Enforcement.* In *United States v. Articles . . . Coli-Trol 80 Medicated*, 372 F. Supp. 915 (N.D. Ga. 1974), the claimant contested FDA's seizure of its OTC veterinary products as arbitrary and discriminatory:

> . . . . This argument is based on the fact that the Commissioner . . . has proposed a policy of taking no enforcement action against OTC drugs for human use where lack of efficacy is the issue, pending a category-by-

category review of those drugs ... while he has not done the same for OTC drugs for veterinary use....

The FDA ... explained why OTC drugs for veterinary use were not being treated in a similar manner, to wit:

"... It is undoubtedly true that OTC veterinary drugs should be reviewed in the same way as OTC human drugs. Because of limited resources, however, it is impractical at this time to review OTC veterinary drugs, the higher priority must be given to a review of OTC human drugs." ...

As a general rule laws are to some extent inherently unequal. Almost every statute or governmental regulation involves some disparity in treatment; few statutes affect everyone in the country in the same manner.... The only constitutional requirement is that any disparity in treatment caused by such classification be *reasonable*....

... The FDA's distinguishing OTC drugs for human use from OTC drugs for veterinary use appears to the court to be entirely reasonable, rational, and in keeping with the public interest whose health and welfare the agency is charged to protect....

3. *Notice.* In 1973, FDA stated its intention to withdraw NDA's covering combination amphetamine products and sent statutorily required notices of this decision and of the opportunity for a hearing to the holders of NDA's for these products. The ultimate withdrawal order, which applied to all manufacturers that had not requested a hearing, included not only NDA holders, but also manufacturers of "me-too" drugs that did not hold NDAs—even though the latter had not received individualized notice. A "me-too" combination amphetamine manufacturer who did not receive notice and did not request a hearing brought a suit challenging the application of the withdrawal order to its product, claiming that the absence of personal notice violated its due process rights. The Eighth Circuit rejected this argument, concluding that the publication of the intention to withdraw approval in the Federal Register gave "me-too" manufacturers adequate notice. *North American Pharmacal v. HEW*, 491 F.2d 546 (8th Cir. 1973).

4. ADMINISTRATIVE CONSISTENCY AND SELECTIVE ENFORCEMENT

United States v. Undetermined Quantities of an Article of Drug Labeled as Exachol

716 F. Supp. 787 (S.D.N.Y. 1989).

■ SWEET, DISTRICT JUDGE:

Plaintiff the United States Federal Food and Drug Administration ("the FDA") moves for summary judgment pursuant to Rule 56, Fed. R.Civ.P. against defendant U.S. Health Club, Inc. ("Health Club") seeking to condemn the seized Exachol as a misbranded and unapproved new drug. Because Exachol is entitled to be considered under the Health Claims for Food Policy, the motion for summary judgment is denied....

Health Club manufactures and sells a product ... distributed under the name "Exachol." Exachol is comprised of lecithin, phosphatidyl ethanolamine, phosphatidyl choline, lethicon, phosphatidyl inositol, extract of chondrus crispus, carrageenan extract, silicon, niacin, and "compounded plant extract," all apparently natural products found in food.... According to Health Club, the ingredients used in Exachol are commonly available as food supplements for which scientific data as to their effectiveness is publicly available.

In 1985, 1986 and 1987, the FDA received complaints and inquiries from physicians, consumers, and state health departments about literature being distributed by Health Club stating that Exachol is useful for the prevention and treatment of coronary disease. According to the FDA, an inspection conducted on December 8, 1986, revealed that the labelling and promotion of Exachol asserts that Exachol is effective in the prevention and treatment of coronary thrombosis, arteriosclerosis, atherosclerosis and angina....

Health Club solicits orders through a mail order brochure which states in part:

> The Exachol Program is a preventive plan designed to help you keep your cholesterol under control by a combined approach including moderate exercise, proper eating and Exachol capsules.
> It is not intended as a substitute for any medical treatment your medical condition may require.

On April 9, 1987, FDA sent Health Club a regulatory letter which stated that Exachol was a drug within Section 201(g) of the Federal Food, Drug and Cosmetic Act....

... The FDA has also sent regulatory letters to sixty-four fish oil supplement manufacturers which were promoted for use "in the treatment and prevention of heart disease, and the lowering of cholesterol and triglyceride levels."

On August 4, 1987, the FDA published the Health Claims for Food Policy in the form of a Notice of Proposed Rulemaking concerning the content of health-related claims or information placed on food labelling and the criteria applied to evaluate the propriety of such labelling. Pending the rulemaking proceeding, the FDA decided to apply the proposed criteria to any questioned labelling:

> (1) Information on the labelling must be truthful and not misleading to the consumer.

> (2) The claims should be supported by valid, reliable, scientific evidence that is publicly available (prior to any health related claim being made).

> (3) The claims must be consistent with generally recognized medical and nutritional principles.

> (4) Food labels containing a health-related claim must also contain the nutrition labelling information required by 21 CFR § 101.9.

The FDA also indicated that it would apply the same criteria to dietary supplements, noting that it may be more difficult for dietary supplements to meet the criteria.

The FDA's policy and application of the Health Claims for Food Policy to at least two products is relevant here. In 1984, the Kellogg Company

("Kellogg") began to promote its All–Bran cereal ("All–Bran") with labelling that recommended in connection with the prevention of cancer that
consumers "eat high fiber foods, eat foods low in fat, eat fresh fruits and
vegetables, eat a well-balanced diet and avoid being overweight." The FDA
drafted a regulatory letter to Kellogg's suggesting that the labelling could
be misleading and that the label promotes All–Bran as a product effective
and adequate in the prevention of cancer. The letter charged Kellogg's with
violations of both the food and drug provisions of the Act. However, the
letter was never sent, and there was no action taken against Kellogg's
regarding the All–Bran product.

On February 12, 1988, Congressman Theodore Weiss made a request
for an assessment of whether the Kellogg labelling met the standards of the
FDA's health claims proposal. The FDA responded that it would wait until
it had developed a single standard for considering health related information or food labels before determining whether Kellogg's claims were
misleading. The FDA contended that All–Bran is both a food and a drug
and that, as is its right, it will decline to treat All–Bran as a drug and will
not prosecute Kellogg on the basis of scientific evidence which indicates
that the labelling is not misleading.

With respect to the fish oil products the FDA advised the manufacturers to identify those claims each would remove from the labels and to
propose the appropriate claims they would include. On June 1, 1988 the
FDA advised the Council for Responsible Nutrition ("CRN"), an agency
which had responded on behalf of the manufacturers, that the FDA was
reviewing the scientific basis for the fish oil labelling claims and would not
initiate any proceeding until it had completed such review. This letter
further stated that the labelling would be judged by the criteria contained
in FDA's health messages proposal and that the FDA would give the
industry a fair opportunity to complete its submission of scientific evidence
substantiating the health benefits of fish oils and ninety days after the
completion of the guidelines to bring their labelling into compliance. FDA
reserved its right to bring enforcement action against those companies
making therapeutic claims for fish oils that would not be permitted under
the health messages proposal no matter how well substantiated. . . .

Health Club does not maintain that Exachol is a food within the
definition of 21 U.S.C. § 321(f). Exachol is, however, a special dietary
food. . . .

. . . The product does address a special dietary need that a person with
a high cholesterol content has. It is therefore a food for special dietary use
within the definition of 21 U.S.C. § 350(c)(3)(A).

Under the health claims policy, a company is permitted to label its food
or food supplement with appropriate health related messages without the
product being rendered "misbranded" or a "drug" under the Act. . . .

According to the FDA, this policy is inapplicable to Exachol because
Exachol is a drug. The correct inquiry, however, is whether the labelling
accompanying Exachol is consistent with the criteria discussed by FDA for
the type of health claim which does not trigger the drug provisions of the
Act.

Health Club claims that other companies such as the Kellogg Company, Mazola and Fleischmann are distributing products bearing labels with claims linking diet, nutrition, exercise and their products with health and avoidance of disease conditions. Specifically the FDA's application of the health claims rule to Kellogg's All Bran and various fish oil products before determining whether they will be regulated as drugs indicates that Health Club has been treated in a manner inconsistent with the FDA's established policy.

Health Club has shown that Exachol was similarly situated to the other two products. All–Bran is a food within the definition of 21 U.S.C. § 321(f) since it is used by man for food. Exachol too is a food, for a special dietary use. Like All–Bran, Exachol can be regulated as a drug as well. The FDA has declined to regulate All–Bran as a drug until it has developed and applied one standard for considering health related information on food labels. As a result, the Health Claims for Food Policy, which applies to foods, should be applied to both products since the effect of the current labelling of each is virtually indistinguishable.

The FDA claims that Health Club has not submitted evidence similar to Kellogg's scientific evidence upon which the FDA based its decision indicating that its labels were not misleading. However, this did not constitute grounds for the prosecution of the fish oil manufacturers. The FDA has withheld review of the scientific evidence submitted by the fish oil manufacturers and classification of the fish oil products until after the health claims policy is applied. Further the FDA has given the fish oil manufacturers additional time to compile their evidence despite the fact that at the time the regulatory letters were written to the fish oil manufacturers, the FDA was "unaware of any history of fish oil use as a food supplement" or that there was any evidence to indicate that the product was approved as safe. The FDA was also aware of scientific studies indicating possible adverse effects of prolonged consumption of the fish oil products.

The FDA has not indicated any knowledge of scientific evidence that suggests Exachol will have adverse effects upon its consumers. The FDA has apparently already reviewed Exachol's scientific evidence without awaiting the formalization of the health claims policy. There is no evidence offered here that the fish oil companies are compiling scientific data that will substantiate their claims of the health benefits of fish oils any more than the evidence which Health Club may present to substantiate its claims. Further the FDA has given no indication that the scientific evidence which Kellogg submitted, characterized in a letter responding to Congressman Weiss's request for an assessment of the Kellogg labelling, as "some epidemiological data [which] support the statements being made [and] other data, including animal and clinical studies [which] are less conclusive," will significantly differ from that which Health Club has provided or may provide. Because the FDA makes no clear distinction between the scientific evidence presented for each product it has not sufficiently disputed health Club's claim that Exachol is similarly situated to All–Bran and the fish oil products.

Finally the FDA has not set forth its criteria for distinguishing which products are similar to Exachol and which are not. The Health Club has made a sufficient showing of its similarity to products to be considered under the Health Claims for Food Policy against which judicial action was not taken.

Courts reviewing administrative action require consistency from the government—whether the context be the denial of a regulatory exemption; the denial of a license; or the issuance of a cease and desist order. In every context, the overriding principle of fairness is always the same: the government must govern with an even hand.

In *United States v. Diapulse Corp. of America*, 748 F.2d 56 (2d Cir. 1984), the same standard of evenhandedness was required. There, the Diapulse Corporation of America sought to modify an injunction issued several years earlier in an enforcement action by the FDA, which prohibited Diapulse from marketing one of its products. Diapulse had moved to modify the injunction because the FDA has subsequently approved the same product for sale by a different company. Despite FDA objection, the district court agreed to a modification of the injunction. This decision was affirmed by the Second Circuit.

In explaining its affirmance, the Second Circuit declared that the government must act "evenhandedly" and that it could "not 'grant to one person the right to do that which it denies to another similarly situated.' " In the future, the Court instructed, the government could not continue "to treat like cases differently," and "must apply to [Diapulse] the same scientific and legal standards it applies to [Diapulse's] competitors."

Because the FDA has not treated Exachol under its Health Claims for Food Policy, it has applied an uneven regulatory policy, requiring denial of the requested summary judgment....

NOTES

1. *Selective Prosecution. Cf. U.S. v. Nutri–Cology, Inc.*, 1993 WL 13585505 (N.D. Cal. 1993), in which defendants, a dietary supplement manufacturer, advanced an affirmative defense of "selective prosecution" in an action in which FDA sought to enjoin it from distributing several products the agency deemed to be unapproved new drugs.

> Defendants primarily rely upon *United States v. Undetermined Quantities of an Article of Drug Labeled as "Exachol"*, 716 F. Supp. 787 (S.D.N.Y. 1989), which they claim supports the view that an uneven regulatory approach by the FDA precludes summary judgment. In *Exachol*, the court found that the FDA had applied its own Health Claims for Food Policy unevenly and thus concluded that summary judgment was inappropriate for the government because the decision to prosecute in that case was contrary to the FDA's published enforcement policy. *Id.* at 795–96. Since this decision, however, the FDA has withdrawn its Health Claims for Food Policy. As a result, it appears that defendants' reliance on a so-called uneven regulatory approach defense lacks relevant case support. Defendants are thus left with their more traditional selective prosecution defense.

A defense of selective prosecution requires two factors: First, defendants must show that others similarly situated have not been prosecuted. Second, defendants must show that the decision to prosecute was motivated by a discriminatory purpose, such as race, religion, or other arbitrary classification. *See Wayte v. United States*, 470 U.S. 598 (1985) (citing *Bordenkircher v. Hayes*, 434 U.S. 357 (1978)).

Although the evidence may support a conclusion that the FDA is more aggressively prosecuting Nutri–Cology than other similarly-situated companies, there is a total lack of credible evidence that the government's prosecution is motivated by a discriminatory purpose. Moreover, the FDA has broad prosecutorial discretion. *See Heckler v. Chaney*, 470 U.S. 821 (1985).

As a result, the Court finds that defendants' affirmative defense of selective prosecution is without basis.

2. *Consistency Over Time.* The United States Supreme Court has recognized that "an agency must be given ample latitude to adapt their rules and policies to the demands of changing circumstances." *Motor Vehicle Mfrs. Assn. v. State Farm Mut. Auto. Ins. Co.*, 463 U.S. 29, 42 (1983). The agency changing course must only supply a "reasoned analysis." *Id.* In an influential partial concurrence-partial dissent in *Motor Vehicles*, Justice Rehnquist opined, "A change in [Presidential] administration brought about by the people casting their votes is a perfectly reasonable basis for an executive agency's reappraisal of the costs and benefits of its programs and regulations." *Id.* at 59 (Rehnquist, J., concurring in part and dissenting in part).

In *FDA v. Brown & Williamson Tobacco Corp.*, 529 U.S. 120 (2000) (*supra* p. 82), the Supreme Court overturned FDA's rule asserting jurisdiction over tobacco products as medical devices. The FDA's action represented a striking departure from the agency's earlier conclusions that it could not regulate conventional tobacco products as drugs or devices. The *Brown & Williamson* dissenters embraced Rehnquist's statement in *Motor Vehicles* and suggested that FDA should be permitted to change its policy based on a "different regulatory attitude." *Brown & Williamson*, 529 U.S. at 189 (Breyer, J. dissenting). The majority, in response, confirmed that agencies have ample latitude under *Motor Vehicles* to change positions, but it insisted that "our conclusion [in this case] does not rely on the fact that the FDA's assertion of jurisdiction represents a sharp break with its prior interpretation of the FDCA." *Id.* at 156.

Bracco Diagnostics, Inc. v. Food and Drug Administration

963 F. Supp. 20 (D.D.C. 1997).

I. BACKGROUND

The plaintiffs in these three consolidated cases are manufacturers of injectable contrast imaging agents for use with diagnostic ultrasound equipment in the diagnosis of cardiac dysfunction. Bracco's product is named BR–1; the DuPont Merck and ImaRx product is named DMP 115; and the SONUS product is named EchoGen. Each product contains fluorinated gas (perfluoropropane) encapsulated in a microsphere membrane or microbubble. Each is administered by intravenous injection into a patient's body in order to better reflect the sound waves used in ultrasound diagnostics, which in turn helps to improve the quality of the ultrasound images. After injection, the microbubbles eventually dissolve and the patient exhales the gas. Plaintiffs' products are at various stages of review by the FDA, but none presently is approved for marketing.

Molecular Biosystems, Inc. has developed a virtually identical injectable microbubble ultrasound contrast imaging agent named FSO69 (the successor to its already-approved product Albunex), which is also the subject of a pending application for approval by the FDA. MBI maintains that FSO69 is significantly different from plaintiffs' products. It points out that EchoGen and DMP 115 require some type of agitation to create the microbubbles and that while some of the microbubbles in EchoGen are formed outside the patient's body prior to injection by the action of pulling back the syringe, more microbubbles are subsequently created inside the body as the heat from the patient's body vaporizes the suspension liquid to create gas bubbles. In contrast, the microbubbles in FSO69 are all formed during the manufacturing process, outside the human body; FSO69 is not dependent upon being metabolized for the achievement of its primary intended purposes.

Plaintiffs argue that the only difference between their products and FSO69 is that the microbubbles in FSO69 are suspended in human albumin while the microbubbles in plaintiffs' products are suspended in a synthetic medium, a matter they say is of no significance. The declarations they have filed and an exhibit they submitted at oral argument, which is appended to this Opinion, demonstrate to the Court's satisfaction that the characteristics of all three of the plaintiffs' products and those of FSO69 are identical in all material respects. Indeed, on this point, the FDA has offered no counter-declarations or argument in response. . . .

Despite the similarity of the products, the FDA has chosen to regulate plaintiffs' products as new drugs and MBI's product as a device. Under the Federal Food, Drug and Cosmetic Act ("FFDCA"), there are separate provisions governing the regulation of drugs and devices, and the review provisions applicable to each differ in several respects. *Compare* 21 U.S.C. § 355 (regulating review and approval of new drugs) *with* 21 U.S.C. §§ 351(f), 360c, 360d, 360e (regulating classification, review and approval of devices). In addition, the FDA has established two distinct operating units or "Centers" to exercise the FDA's regulatory responsibilities: the Center for Drug Evaluation and Review ("CDER") is responsible for drugs; the Center for Devices and Radiological Health ("CDRH") is responsible for medical devices. Each has authority to approve products within its jurisdiction, but each Center is subject to direction by the Office of the Commissioner of the FDA.

The FDA has decided to treat MBI's product as a device and is treating plaintiffs' products as drugs; thus, both the CDER and the CDRH are regulating ultrasound contrast agents. The two Centers, however, apparently are applying very different standards to assess the safety and effectiveness of essentially identical products. Plaintiffs maintain, without contradiction, that they have been required to produce much more exhaustive scientific data demonstrating the safety and effectiveness of their ultrasound agents while MBI, in response to requests from the CDRH, has been required to submit much less rigorous information and testing results.

Plaintiffs argue that these disparate standards impose considerably greater financial and other burdens on those companies whose agents are being treated as drugs and regulated by the CDER than on MBI's product, treated as a device and regulated by the CDRH.

In January of 1982, the FDA issued a proposed rule relating to the classification of all radiological devices pursuant to the 1976 Medical Device Amendments to the FFDCA. In its preamble, which constitutes an advisory opinion binding on the agency unless repudiated by the agency, the FDA stated: "The agency has determined that all radiologic contrast media, including barium enema kits, are to be regulated by FDA as drugs under section 201(g) of the act and not as devices." Plaintiffs argue that the FDA's review of MBI's precursor to FSO69, Albunex, and of FSO69 itself as devices rather than as drugs is directly contrary to this advisory opinion and, thus, unless fully and rationally explained, is arbitrary and capricious agency action in violation of the Administrative Procedure Act.

Beginning in the summer of 1996, Bracco, DuPont Merck and SONUS began discussions with the FDA in an effort to persuade the FDA to regulate ultrasound agents under uniform standards, be they as devices or as drugs. When the informal discussions were unsuccessful, each of the plaintiffs filed a Citizen Petition pursuant to FDA regulations. Bracco was the first to file its petition on December 27, 1996. Because the FDA has 180 days to respond to citizen petitions, *see* 21 C.F.R. § 10.30(e)(2), neither Bracco nor the other plaintiffs, who filed their petitions later, have yet received responses.

In their petitions, plaintiffs requested the FDA to act promptly to eliminate the disparity in the regulation of ultrasound contrast agents and what they viewed as the "unjustified preferential treatment" given to MBI to the disadvantage of those whose products were being treated as drugs. They pointed out that the CDRH applies significantly different standards than the CDER to assess the safety and effectiveness of the agents even though the products are essentially identical. Plaintiffs requested that the FDA determine that all ultrasound contrast agents be regulated under uniform standards and procedures either as new drugs or as medical devices. DuPont Merck asked for expedited consideration of its request, presumably because it knew that MBI's product was on track for approval by mid-April 1997.

II.   DISCUSSION

. . . .

Our court of appeals has repeatedly held that "an agency must treat similar cases in a similar manner unless it can provide a legitimate reason for failing to do so." "Government is at its most arbitrary when it treats similarly situated people differently." *Etelson v. Office of Personnel Management*, 684 F.2d 918, 926 (D.C. Cir. 1982). As Judge Greene noted in a related context, "If an agency treats similarly situated parties differently, its action is arbitrary and capricious in violation of the APA." Allergan, Inc. v. Shalala, 6 Food and Drug Rep. 389, 391, No. 94–1223 (D.D.C. Nov. 10, 1994) (Greene, J.).

In this case, the Bracco, DuPont Merck, SONUS and MBI products are identical in all material respects, and the FDA has not provided a legitimate reason for failing to regulate these similar products in the same way.

Under the Administrative Procedure Act, the FDA either must provide a rational basis for treating MBI's imaging agent as a device while simultaneously regulating essentially identical agents as drugs, or it must treat all four of these similar products in the same way. A failure to do one of these two things is arbitrary and capricious agency action and therefore is a violation of the APA, 5 U.S.C. § 706(2)(A).

The MBI products and plaintiffs' products all likely meet both the definition of a drug and the definition of a device under the Federal Food, Drug and Cosmetic Act, and the FDA therefore has discretion in determining how to treat them. *See* 21 U.S.C. § 353(g) ("The Secretary shall designate a component of the Food and Drug Administration to regulate products that constitute a combination of a drug, device, or biological product.") What the FDA is not free to do, however, is to treat them dissimilarly and to permit two sets of similar products to run down two separate tracks, one more treacherous than the other, for no apparent reason. Plaintiffs merely maintain that the same tests and studies should be required of each product before it is approved and that that result is impossible so long as the FDA treats one as a device subject to the regimen established by the CDRH and the other three as drugs subject to the more rigorous regimen established by the CDER. The Court agrees. The disparate treatment of functionally indistinguishable products is the essence of the meaning of arbitrary and capricious. . . . Plaintiffs therefore are likely to succeed on this argument as a matter of law.

Defendants and defendant-intervenor make strong arguments that the public interest favors permitting an agency to proceed with its administrative process without interference and that there are public health reasons why FSO69 should be allowed to be marketed promptly after it has been thoroughly tested, passed all the tests and has been approved by the FDA. As plaintiffs point out, however, there is also a strong public interest in requiring an agency to act lawfully, consistent with its obligations under the APA, and to treat all similarly situated and regulated parties equally.

The FDA's "core function" is "the promotion and protection of the public health." If there is no rational basis for treating plaintiffs' and MBI's products differently, however, then an injectable ultrasound contrast agent may be released onto the market and used on cardiology patients after having passed less rigorous testing requirements than are required of every other ultrasound contrast agent currently under FDA review. Requiring the FDA to test similar products with the same scrutiny is consistent with the FDA's mission and is in the public interest. Requiring them to act lawfully is also very much in the public interest. Therefore, on balance, the Court concludes that the public interest is better served by issuing an injunction that will assure that the FDA meets its statutory obligations.

. . . .

5. ENFORCEMENT DISCRETION

Heckler v. Chaney

470 U.S. 821 (1985).

■ JUSTICE REHNQUIST delivered the opinion of the Court.

This case presents the question of the extent to which a decision of an administrative agency to exercise its "discretion" not to undertake certain enforcement actions is subject to judicial review under the Administrative Procedure Act, 5 U.S.C. § 501 *et seq.* (APA). Respondents are several prison inmates convicted of capital offenses and sentenced to death by lethal injection of drugs. They petitioned the Food and Drug Administration (FDA), alleging that under the circumstances the use of these drugs for capital punishment violated the Federal Food, Drug, and Cosmetic Act (FDCA) and requesting that the FDA take various enforcement actions to prevent these violations. The FDA refused their request. We review here a decision of the Court of Appeals for the District of Columbia Circuit, which held the FDA's refusal to take enforcement actions both reviewable and an abuse of discretion, and remanded the case with directions that the agency be required "to fulfill its statutory function." 718 F.2d 1174, 1191 (1983). . . .

The Court of Appeals' decision addressed three questions: (1) whether the FDA had jurisdiction to undertake the enforcement actions requested, (2) whether if it did have jurisdiction its refusal to take those actions was subject to judicial review, and (3) whether if reviewable its refusal was arbitrary, capricious, or an abuse of discretion. In reaching our conclusion that the Court of Appeals was wrong, however, we need not and do not address the thorny question of the FDA's jurisdiction. For us, this case turns on the important question of the extent to which determinations by the FDA *not to exercise* its enforcement authority over the use of drugs in interstate commerce may be judicially reviewed. That decision in turn involves the construction of two separate but necessarily interrelated statutes, the APA and the FDCA.

The APA's comprehensive provisions for judicial review of "agency actions" are contained in 5 U.S.C. §§ 701–706. Any person "adversely affected or aggrieved" by agency action, *see* § 702, including a "failure to act," is entitled to "judicial review thereof," as long as the action is a "final agency action for which there is no other adequate remedy in a court," *see* § 704. The standards to be applied on review are governed by the provisions of § 706. But before any review at all may be had, a party must first clear the hurdle of § 701(a). That section provides that the chapter on judicial review "applies, according to the provisions thereof, except to the extent that—(1) statutes preclude judicial review; or (2) agency action is committed to agency discretion by law." Petitioner urges that the decision of the FDA to refuse enforcement is an action "committed to agency discretion by law" under § 701(a)(2). . . .

This Court first discussed § (a)(2) in *Citizens to Preserve Overton Park v. Volpe*, 401 U.S. 402 (1971). . . .

[*Overton Park*] answers several of the questions raised by the language of § 701(a), although it raises others. First, it clearly separates the exception provided by § (a)(1) from the § (a)(2) exception. The former applies when Congress has expressed an intent to preclude judicial review. The latter applies in different circumstances; even where Congress has not affirmatively precluded review, review is not to be had if the statute is drawn so that a court would have no meaningful standard against which to judge the agency's exercise of discretion. In such a case, the statute ("law") can be taken to have "committed" the decisionmaking to the agency's judgment absolutely. This construction avoids conflict with the "abuse of discretion" standard of review in § 706—if no judicially manageable standards are available for judging how and when an agency should exercise its discretion, then it is impossible to evaluate agency action for "abuse of discretion." In addition, this construction satisfies the principle of statutory construction mentioned earlier, by identifying a separate class of cases to which § 701(a)(2) applies....

Overton Park did not involve an agency's refusal to take requested enforcement action. It involved an affirmative act of approval under a statute that set clear guidelines for determining when such approval should be given. Refusals to take enforcement steps generally involve precisely the opposite situation, and in that situation we think the presumption is that judicial review is not available. This Court has recognized on several occasions over many years that an agency's decision not to prosecute or enforce, whether through civil or criminal process, is a decision generally committed to an agency's absolute discretion. This recognition of the existence of discretion is attributable in no small part to the general unsuitability for judicial review of agency decisions to refuse enforcement.

The reasons for this general unsuitability are many. First, an agency decision not to enforce often involves a complicated balancing of a number of factors which are peculiarly within its expertise. Thus, the agency must not only assess whether a violation has occurred, but whether agency resources are best spent on this violation or another, whether the agency is likely to succeed if it acts, whether the particular enforcement action requested best fits the agency's overall policies, and, indeed, whether the agency has enough resources to undertake the action at all. An agency generally cannot act against each technical violation of the statute it is charged with enforcing. The agency is far better equipped than the courts to deal with the many variables involved in the proper ordering of its priorities. Similar concerns animate the principles of administrative law that courts generally will defer to an agency's construction of the statute it is charged with implementing, and to the procedures it adopts for implementing that statute.

In addition to these administrative concerns, we note that when an agency refuses to act it generally does not exercise its *coercive* power over an individual's liberty or property rights, and thus does not infringe upon areas that courts often are called upon to protect....

We of course only list the above concerns to facilitate understanding of our conclusion that an agency's decision not to take enforcement action should be presumed immune from judicial review under § 701(a)(2). For good reasons, such a decision has traditionally been "committed to agency discretion," and we believe that the Congress enacting the APA did not intend to alter that tradition. In so stating, we emphasize that the decision is only presumptively unreviewable; the presumption may be rebutted where the substantive statute has provided guidelines for the agency to follow in establishing its enforcement powers.[4] Thus, in establishing this presumption in the APA, Congress did not set agencies free to disregard legislative direction in the statutory scheme that the agency administers. Congress may limit an agency's exercise of enforcement power if it wishes, either by setting substantive priorities, or by otherwise circumscribing an agency's power to discriminate among issues or cases it will pursue....

To enforce the various substantive prohibitions contained in the FDCA, the Act provides for injunctions, 21 U.S.C. § 332, criminal sanctions, §§ 333 and 335, and seizure of any offending food, drug, or cosmetic article, § 334. The Act's general provision for enforcement, § 372, provides only that "[t]he Secretary is *authorized* to conduct examinations and investigations ..." (emphasis added).... § 332 gives no indication of when an injunction should be sought, and § 334, providing for seizures, is framed in the permissive—the offending food, drug, or cosmetic "shall be liable to be proceeded against." The section on criminal sanctions states baldly that any person who violates the Act's substantive prohibitions "shall be imprisoned ... or fined." Respondents argue that this statement mandates criminal prosecution of every violator of the Act but they adduce no indication in case law or legislative history that such was Congress' intention in using this language, which is commonly found in the criminal provisions of Title 18 of the United States Code. We are unwilling to attribute such a sweeping meaning to this language, particularly since the Act charges the Secretary only with recommending prosecution; any criminal prosecutions must be instituted by the Attorney General. The Act's enforcement provisions thus commit complete discretion to the Secretary to decide how and when they should be exercised.

Respondents nevertheless present three separate authorities that they claim provide the courts with sufficient indicia of an intent to circumscribe enforcement discretion. Two of these may be dealt with summarily. First, we reject respondents' argument that the Act's substantive prohibitions of "misbranding" and the introduction of "new drugs" absent agency approval supply us with "law to apply." These provisions are simply irrelevant to the agency's discretion to refuse to initiate proceedings.

We also find singularly unhelpful the agency "policy statement" on which the Court of Appeals placed great reliance [37 Fed. Reg. 16503 (August 15, 1972), p. 818 *supra.*]. We would have difficulty with this statement's vague language even if it were a properly adopted agency rule.... But in any event the policy statement was attached to a rule that was never adopted. Whatever force such a statement might have, and leaving to one side the problem of whether an agency's rules might under certain circumstances provide courts with adequate guidelines for informed judicial review of decisions not to enforce, we do not think the language of the agency's "policy statement" can plausibly be read to override the

4. We do not have in this case a refusal by the agency to institute proceedings based solely on the belief that it lacks jurisdiction. Nor do we have a situation where it could justifiably be found that the agency has "con-sciously and expressly adopted a general policy" that is so extreme as to amount to an abdication of its statutory responsibilities....

agency's express assertion of unreviewable discretion contained in the above rule.

Respondents' third argument, based upon [§ 309] of the FDCA, merits only slightly more consideration. That section provides:

> "Nothing in this chapter shall be construed as requiring the Secretary to report for prosecution, or for the institution of libel or injunction proceedings, minor violations of this chapter whenever he believes that the public interest will be adequately served by a suitable written notice or ruling."

Respondents seek to draw from this section the negative implication that the Secretary is *required* to report for prosecution all "major" violations of the Act, however, those might be defined, and that it therefore supplies the needed indication of an intent to limit agency enforcement discretion. We think that this section simply does not give rise to the negative implication which respondents seek to draw from it. The section is not addressed to agency proceedings designed to discover the existence of violations, but applies only to a situation where a violation has already been established to the satisfaction of the agency. We do not believe the section speaks to the criteria which shall be used by the agency for investigating *possible* violations of the Act.

We therefore conclude that the presumption that agency decisions not to institute proceedings are unreviewable under 5 U.S.C. § 701(a)(2) is not overcome by the enforcement provisions of the FDCA. The FDA's decision not to take the enforcement actions requested by respondents is therefore not subject to judicial review under the APA.... In so holding, we essentially leave to Congress, and not to the courts, the decision as to whether an agency's refusal to institute proceedings should be judicially reviewable. No colorable claim is made in this case that the agency's refusal to institute proceedings violated any constitutional rights of respondents, and we do not address the issue that would be raised in such a case. The fact that the drugs involved in this case are ultimately to be used in imposing the death penalty must not lead this Court or other courts to import profound differences of opinion over the meaning of the Eighth Amendment to the United States Constitution into the domain of administrative law.

The judgment of the Court of Appeals is *Reversed.*

[The concurring opinions of Justice Brennan and Justice Marshall are omitted.]

COMMENT: ENFORCEMENT DISCRETION AFTER CHANEY

In one of the first cases after *Heckler* in which FDA asserted non-reviewable discretion not to take an enforcement action, the district court rejected the agency's argument. In *Heterochemical Corp. v. FDA*, 644 F. Supp. 271 (E.D.N.Y. 1986), the plaintiff petitioned FDA to take regulatory action against three competitors who sold vitamin K for use in animal feed without FDA approval. After publishing the petition in 41 Fed. Reg. 35009 (August 18, 1976), the agency denied it seven years later in 48 Fed. Reg.

16748 (April 19, 1983), and the plaintiff sought judicial review. FDA took the position that *Chaney* was dispositive. The court refused to dismiss the action, however, holding that the Supreme Court had excluded from FDA's unreviewable discretion those situations where the agency had already conducted an investigation and determined that there was a violation of the FD&C Act, particularly where FDA regulations themselves established a required course of agency action. The court later determined that the agency's own regulations required it to take action with regard to the vitamin K substances, and it thus granted the plaintiff's motion for summary judgment and required the agency to proceed with its established procedures. *Heterochemical Corp. v. FDA*, 741 F. Supp. 382 (E.D.N.Y. 1990).

Heterochemical is the only instance since *Chaney* in which FDA's exercise of enforcement discretion has been judicially thwarted. In light of budget and personnel constraints, FDA always has to prioritize some enforcement goals over others, and the agency does not disguise its choices. For example, CFSAN publishes annually a "Program Priorities," report, which categorizes some activities as higher priorities than others and fails to mention other activities altogether. *E.g.*, 70 Fed. Reg. 29328 (May 20, 2005) (request for comments on 2006 priority setting). FDA's failure to take particular enforcement actions is rarely challenged in court, and the few suits that are brought are almost always unsuccessful. For example, in *Community Nutrition Institute v. Young*, 818 F.2d 943, 949–50 (D.C. Cir. 1987), the D.C. Circuit, citing *Heckler*, refused to review the agency's decision not to commence enforcement proceedings against corn into which aflatoxin-contaminated corn had been intentionally blended. In *International Center for Technology Assessment v. Thompson*, 421 F. Supp. 2d 1, 7 (D. D. C. 2006) the court rejected the plaintiff's claim that FDA was required to impose the Act's new animal drug application (NADA) provisions on the Glofish, an ornamental, glowing zebra fish for home aquariums. Citing *Heckler*, the court observed: "[T]he FDA was not acting on the basis of a mistaken belief as to its regulatory jurisdiction.... [T]he FDA is simply exercising its discretion not to take enforcement actions against these particular fish.".

FDA has designed at least one major initiative entirely and explicitly around the principle of enforcement discretion. As discussed in Chapter III, *supra* p. 295, after *Pearson v. Shalala* declared that the First Amendment limited FDA's authority to reject health claim petitions, 164 F.3d 650 (D.C. Cir. 1999), the agency established a framework to permit qualified health claims under its "enforcement discretion." The agency issued a guidance which, citing *Heckler*, laid out the circumstances "under which FDA will consider exercising its enforcement discretion to permit health claims that do not meet the 'significant scientific agreement' standard of evidence by which the health claims regulations require FDA to evaluate the scientific validity of claims." GUIDANCE FOR INDUSTRY, QUALIFIED HEALTH CLAIMS IN THE LABELING OF CONVENTIONAL FOODS AND DIETARY SUPPLEMENTS (Dec. 18, 2002). The agency calls the letters it sends to petitioners stating its intention not to object to the use of a qualified claim "letters of enforcement discretion." Two public advocacy organizations brought an action challenging FDA's qualified health claims approach, but the court dismissed the case for lack of standing and ripeness, in light of the fact that the agency had not yet issued any enforcement discretion letters at the time the plaintiffs filed their complaint. *Center for Science in the Public Interest v. FDA*, 2004 WL 2011467 (D.D.C. 2004). Although FDA has since issued a number of such letters, the plaintiffs have not refiled their action.

6. ROLE OF THE JUSTICE DEPARTMENT

Like almost all other Federal agencies, FDA must rely on the Department of Justice and local U.S. Attorneys to initiate suits to enforce the FDCA. The office within the Department of Justice that handles FDA referrals is the Civil Division's Office of Consumer Litigation. In 1972, Congress considered, but failed to enact, a bill that would have authorized FDA's counsel to represent the agency in court.

Food and Drug Administration Act

Hearings on H.R. 15315 Before the Subcommittee on Public Health and Environment of the House Committee on Interstate and Foreign Commerce.
92d Cong., 2d Sess. (1972).

Mr. Hastings [Republican Congressman from New York].... There have been many charges by many people—responsibly or not, I won't comment on—that the prosecutions of FDA violations have in fact not been as diligent or successful as they possibly could be....

. . . .

Mr. Hutt [FDA Chief Counsel] ... [A]s far as we can determine, in roughly 30 to 35 percent of the criminal cases brought, the Department of Justice has either declined to file the case or has dismissed the case over the Food and Drug Administration's objection, or has dismissed one or more individuals over the Food and Drug Administration's objection....

Mr. Kurzman [DHEW Assistant Secretary for Legislation] ... There have historically been [exceptions] where Congress has given or sought to give one or more agencies the power to go to court independently of the Department of Justice.... I believe all administrations have resisted this kind of splitting up of the litigating power....

As an ex-assistant U.S. attorney myself, I am very much aware of how our current arrangement of U.S. attorney offices is designed to bring to the Federal Government the same kind of effectiveness that private attorneys often seek.... It is wise to have, from the point of view of not only efficiency but success, attorneys on the scene who are residents of the district involved and know well the way the particular judges of that court operate and the way juries react to particular types of cases, who can assess the workload of that particular court and can make the most effective judgment as to whether they are likely to win the case asking for the particular remedy involved....

I recall making judgments of that sort, myself. It is the ultimate test of the use of court sanctions for the enforcement of the Congress' will, and I think that judgment has been wisely delegated to attorneys on the spot. So the administration, like previous administrations, prefers to keep that unitary judgment in the Department of Justice and with the U.S. attorneys' offices around the country. As I pointed out, there are 62 independent agencies, all reporting to the President, and if subagencies were to be given this power as well as all those departments, you can just imagine the duplication of effort and the tremendous fragmentation and weakening of the Government's posture before these courts and these juries if there were helter-skelter enforcement sought by attorneys out of the Washington offices of each independent agency or indeed certainly if each agency felt called upon to set up its own satellite U.S. attorney offices in the most heavily trafficked districts. . . .

Mr. Rogers [Democratic Congressman from Florida]. I am concerned, too, because I have a letter from the former counsel of HEW for Food and Drug and we wanted his experience in this area. . . .

Dear Mr. Chairman: . . . I am writing about the proposal now before your Subcommittee, H.R. 15315, which includes a provision authorizing the Agency's counsel to represent it in Court. This is an issue on which I have strong feelings arising out of my own experience as FDA's Chief Counsel. I am convinced that FDA requires a very knowledgeable and fully effective advocate in the courtroom to uphold and to enforce the laws committed to its administration. . . .

The outside interests with whom FDA litigates are able to select their own expert counsel—both trial and appellate counsel—from the best of the Nation's practitioners. Fairness to the public interest calls for an equal expertise of representation in any area involving a complex statutory scheme such as the Federal Food, Drug, and Cosmetic Act. This expertise comes from close association with, and participation in, FDA's programs as they develop. . . .

. . . This arrangement has the disadvantage of requiring trial and appellate counsel to be brought into cases after they have fully developed in the administrative agency, and does not permit Agency counsel closest to the case to represent its interest in Court except through Department of Justice counsel. Even where the Department of Justice takes the lead in the Court case, it is necessary to supply Agency counsel because of his better knowledge of the facts and the law. Duplication of legal services is both costly and unnecessary.

Moreover, the Congress holds FDA and its Commissioner responsible for the efficient administration of these laws. . . . Yet the Department of Justice has taken a role in deciding when to prosecute enforcement actions and how to settle them once they have been initiated. . . .

I think the FDA should have the right to speak through its own chosen counsel when it considers this necessary (as where the Department of Justice fails or refuses to act), and it should have the right to press any case that the Commissioner considers vital to the achievement of his program purposes.

Respectfully, William M. Goodrich. . . .

Mr. Kurzman. . . . Let me comment briefly, though, on two points. . . . I know that in the southern district of New York, which probably accounts for an enormous proportion of regulatory cases filed by all agencies because it is the headquarters of so much of American industry, the U.S. attorney office there at the time I was there in the late 1950's and early 1960's was specialized in this regard. It did have assistant U.S. attorneys who handled nothing but FDA cases and who had developed over the years enormous expertise comparable, I am sure, to what the agency itself develops. . . .

NOTE

See Charles R. McConachie, *The Role of the Department of Justice in Enforcing the Federal Food, Drug and Cosmetic Act*, 31 FOOD DRUG COSM. L.J. 333 (1976).

COMMENT: ROLE OF THE HHS INSPECTOR GENERAL

In 90 Stat. 2429 (1976), Congress created the Office of Inspector General in the Department of HEW, for the purpose of "preventing and detecting fraud and abuse" in departmental programs and operations. Two years later, in the Inspector General Act of 1978, 92 Stat. 1101, Congress created an Office of Inspector General in other departments and agencies as well. As part of the Inspector General Act Amendments of 1988, 102 Stat. 2515, the 1976 statute was repealed, and the HHS Office of Inspector General was made subject to the 1978 statute.

AGAO report, FOOD AND DRUG ADMINISTRATION: HHS INSPECTOR GENERAL SHOULD BE INVOLVED IN CRIMINAL INVESTIGATIONS, HRD–88–8 (November 19, 1987), acknowledged that the HHS Inspector General was not intended to replace the FDA regulatory function, but still recommended that the Inspector General be involved in FDA criminal investigations. Following that report, the Office of Legal Counsel in the Department of Justice issued an opinion that under the 1978 statute inspectors general do not have authority to investigate violations of regulatory statutes but rather are limited to investigating the employees and operations of a department and its contractors, grantees, and other recipients of federal funds in order to "root out waste and fraud." Memorandum from Assistant Attorney General D.W. Kmiec to Department of Labor Acting Solicitor J.G. Thorn (Mar. 9, 1989), reprinted in 3 CORP. CRIME REP., No. 32, at 18 (Aug. 14, 1989).

Nonetheless, on the heels of the generic drug scandal, the HHS Inspector General was delegated "the responsibility for conducting investigations of criminal violations of the Federal Food, Drug and Cosmetic Act for which the penalty is a felony," excluding any program inspection or "examination authority" and any other matters that "should remain a function of the Food and Drug Administration." Memorandum from HHS Secretary L.W. Sullivan to HHS Inspector General R.P. Kusserow (July 24, 1989). This action was reported to have precipitated the resignation of the FDA Chief Counsel. Hemelstein, *Top FDA Lawyer Resigns Over Policy Dispute*, LEGAL TIMES OF WASH., Aug. 7, 1989, at 6. Although the Inspector General and FDA attempted to limit the delegation to situations where there was "fraud by or upon employees of the FDA," Memorandum from HHS Inspector General R.P. Kusserow to HHS General Counsel M.J. Astrue and Commissioner of Food and Drugs F.E. Young (Oct. 2, 1989), and to situations "when FDA requests their assistance," (Aug. 18, 1989), the delegation continued to attract substantial criticism. Secretary Sullivan rescinded the delegation on December 28, 1989, on the stated basis that the generic drug "emergency" was over and its need had "passed." *See* "Naked Reverse: Secretary Sullivan's Recission of his Delegation of Investigative Authority to the Inspector General," Staff Report Prepared for the Use of the Subcomm. on Oversight and Investigations of the House Comm. on Energy and Commerce, 101st Cong., 2d Sess., Comm. Print 101–S (1990). In the early 1990s, FDA established a criminal investigations office in ORA to satisfy critics.

B. ENFORCEMENT JURISDICTION

1. INTRODUCTION

The United States Constitution grants Congress power "[t]o regulate commerce with foreign nations, and among the several States, and with the Indian tribes." U.S. CONST., Art. I, § 3. Since the early 1940s, the Supreme Court has construed the commerce clause extremely broadly. For example, the Court famously upheld Congress' authority to impose a marketing penalty on home-grown, home-consumed wheat, *Wickard v. Filburn*, 317 U.S. 111 (1942), and to prohibit racial discrimination in a restaurant frequented only by local customers, *Katzenbach v. McClung*, 379 U.S. 294 (1964).

Around the turn of the present century, the Court, in two decisions, ruled for the first time in decades that Congress had exceeded its commerce power. *United States v. Lopez*, 514 U.S. 549 (1995); *United States v. Morrison*, 529 U.S. 598 (2000). These decisions led some analysts to predict a new era of more limited federal authority over intrastate activities. But in 2005, the Court ringingly affirmed *Wickard* when it upheld the enforcement of the federal Controlled Substances Act against parties using home-grown or locally-grown marijuana for medical purposes, as permitted by California law. *Gonzales v. Raich*, 545 U.S. 1 (2005). As a constitutional matter, Congress thus appears to retain virtually unlimited power to regulate even the wholly intrastate production and sale of food, drugs, devices, and cosmetics.

Importantly, however, FDA's jurisdiction over such activities is restricted *as a statutory matter*. The scope of the FD&C Act is largely limited to products that have moved, are moving, or will be moving in interstate commerce. This is hardly surprising, for when the Act was enacted in 1938, the Supreme Court had only just begun to breathe life into the commerce power. *See NLRB v. Jones & Laughlin Steel Corp.*, 301 U.S. 1 (1937). At the time, controlling Supreme Court precedents still maintained formalistic distinctions between "commerce" and "production" and between "direct" and "indirect" effects on commerce. *See Carter v. Carter Coal Co.*, 298 U.S. 238 (1936). Moreover, the year before the enactment of the FD&C Act, the

Supreme Court had held that a product was no longer in interstate commerce after "it had come to a permanent rest within [a] State." *Schechter Poultry v. United States*, 295 U.S. 495, 543 (1935). Therefore, even if Congress had desired to regulate purely local commerce in food, drugs, and cosmetics, it would have been constrained by this older commerce clause jurisprudence.

In the years since *Wickard*, Congress has expanded FDA's power over intrastate activities. For example, as discussed below, the FD&C Act was amended in 1947 to make clear that its prohibitions apply to a product that was previously shipped in interstate commerce, even if the article has changed hands numerous times within a state after its arrival there. FD&C Act 301(k), 304(a). In 1976, Congress revised the Act to permit FDA to seize misbranded or adulterated devices without proving interstate commerce at all. FD&C Act 304(a)(2). Moreover, in 1972 FDA assumed responsibility for implementing the biological product provisions of the Public Health Service Act, and that statute's prohibition against the false labeling of biological products is not restricted to articles moving in interstate commerce. PHS Act 351(b). FDA also now has authority to prevent the spread of communicable diseases under section 361 of the PHSA, a provision with no interstate commerce limitations whatsoever.

Even in instances when the FD&C Act still requires there be a nexus to interstate commerce for FDA to have jurisdiction, the agency no longer has the initial burden to demonstrate this nexus in court. In 1997, Congress amended section 709 of the FD&C Act to state: "In any action to enforce the requirements of this Act respecting a device, food, drug, or cosmetic the connection with interstate commerce required for jurisdiction in such action shall be presumed to exist." (Prior to 1997, this section applied only to devices.) This is, however, a rebuttable presumption and not a delegation to FDA of full authority over intrastate commerce.

Thus, FDA still does not have the full degree of power Congress could constitutionally give it under the commerce clause as interpreted today. All of the "prohibited acts" listed in section 301 of the FD&C Act are (either explicitly or by reference to other provisions) limited to articles that were, are, or will be in interstate commerce. Furthermore, the agency's basic authority to seize adulterated or misbranded articles under section 304 remains (with a few exceptions, including devices) limited to articles "introduced into or while in interstate commerce or while held for sale (whether or not the first sale) after shipment in interstate commerce." FD&C Act 304(a). In short, FDA cannot exercise many of the enforcement powers discussed in this chapter unless it can demonstrate interstate commerce, as required by specific statutory provisions.

2. "Introduction Into Interstate Commerce"

United States v. 7 Barrels ... Spray Dried Whole Egg
141 F.2d 767 (7th Cir. 1944).

■ Sparks, Circuit Judge.

The Government appeals from a judgment dismissing its libel for want of jurisdiction. The libel, alleging adulteration, had been filed against one lot of seven barrels of dried eggs which it sought to condemn under the provisions of § 304(a) of the Federal Food, Drug, and Cosmetic Act. The claimant ... interposed [the defense] that the libel failed to state facts indicating that the article seized was introduced into or was in interstate commerce, at the time of the seizure....

The statute relied upon to confer jurisdiction provides: "Any article of food ... that is adulterated or misbranded when introduced into or while in interstate commerce ... shall be liable to be proceeded against while in interstate commerce, or at any time thereafter, on libel of information and condemned in any district court of the United States within the jurisdiction of which the article is found...." [FD&C Act 304(a).]

The subject of the libel was part of 150 barrels of spray-dried whole eggs tendered by appellee to the Federal Surplus Commodities Corporation in part performance of a contract between the parties....

... [T]he 7 libeled barrels ... were rejected by the FSCC.... The libeled product has never been removed from appellee's plant.

Appellant contends that the contract was a transaction in interstate commerce; that the barrels were marked and set aside as the property to be used in fulfillment of the contract, thus being brought within the exclusive dominion of the out-of-state purchaser, and thereby introduced into commerce within the meaning of the statute. It further contends that the subsequent rejection of the eggs did not remove them from the jurisdiction of the Act or divest them of their interstate character.

We are not in accord with these contentions. It is clear that the contract is quite conditional in its character. It consists of an accepted offer to deliver at appellee's plant, on or before a certain date, a prescribed amount of eggs of a described character. The eggs here libeled were part of a lot intended for delivery, if accepted, within the time, and at the place named in the contract, in part performance thereof. True, they were marked and set aside in seller's plant. However, they were not thus segregated as the property to be used in fulfillment of the contract, but for inspection and testing to determine whether they complied with the required specifications. This was necessary before there could be an acceptance of the delivery, and before acceptance there could be no dominion of the FSCC over the property.

The contract provided that the product should be considered ready for delivery on the date the inspection certificate was issued, and not sooner.... It seems to us that the only reasons for the required preliminary marking and segregation of the barrels before the inspection and test was [sic] that actual delivery might be expedited after the acceptance, and the probability of substitution for any part of the tendered produce, without the knowledge of the FSCC, would be greatly minimized.

It is quite apparent that the object of the statute is to prevent adulterated articles of food from entering interstate commerce. That object seems to have been fully accomplished long before this libel suit was filed. After the inspection certificate was issued neither party insisted upon a delivery of the seven barrels, and that was as early as a delivery could be made under Article 7 of the contract. Appellee thereupon substituted seven other barrels in their stead and the FSCC accepted them, whereupon the State of Indiana placed an embargo upon the rejected barrels, the effect of which was to prevent their removal from the plant. Hence they could never become a part of interstate commerce.

We recognize the legal principle that goods may become a part of interstate commerce before transportation begins, and may remain such after transportation ends. The cases bearing on the former enunciate the rule that where goods are purchased in one State for transportation to another, the commerce includes the purchase quite as much as it does the transportation. . . .

In the instant case, however, the contract did not provide, nor did the parties intend that the eggs segregated and marked prior to the test would then and there become a part of interstate commerce, or that such acts would amount to a sale or delivery of them. . . .

. . . Appellant also relies on *Carter v. Carter Coal Co.*, 298 U.S. 238, where the distinction was drawn in regard to federal jurisdiction between goods which were part of a contract of sale in interstate commerce and goods merely intended to be sold in another state. There the Court said: "One who produces or manufactures a commodity, subsequently sold and shipped by him in interstate commerce, whether such sale and shipment were originally intended or not, has engaged in two distinct and separate activities. So far as he produces or manufactures a commodity, his business is purely local. So far as he sells and ships, or contracts to sell and ship, the commodity to customers in another state, he engages in interstate commerce. In respect to the former, he is subject only to regulation by the state; in respect to the latter, to regulation only by the federal government."

We have never questioned the soundness of that principle. It constitutes the basis of our conclusion. We are convinced that if appellee had sold and shipped, or contracted to ship, the seven barrels of eggs to customers in another state it would be held to have engaged in interstate commerce. However, our conclusion is that appellee never sold nor shipped, nor did it contract to sell or ship, to customers in another state the seven barrels of eggs in question.

Affirmed.

NOTES

1. *Other Authorities. See also Hipolite Egg Co. v. United States*, 220 U.S. 45 (1911) (1906 Act's provision for seizure of an adulterated food "transported from one state . . . to another for sale" applies to food shipped for use in the manufacture of another food product); *United States v. 52 Drums of Maple Syrup*, 110 F.2d 914 (2d Cir. 1940) (adulterated food shipped in commerce is illegal even though intended for processing to bring it into compliance).

2. *Holding Prior to Shipment. See United States v. International Exterminator Corp.*, 294 F.2d 270 (5th Cir. 1961):

... [T]he defendants operate an exterminator and pest-control service for establishments such as warehouses, mills and dryers which store and sell foods such as beans, rice, flour, sugar, meal, salt, bakery supplies and also animal and poultry feed. In so doing, it is averred, the defendants are causing quantities of a poisonous liquid known as compound 1080 to be placed in the establishments in uncovered paper bait cups in close proximity to the foods. This, the complaint alleged, results in the foods being adulterated within the meaning of the Act "because of being held under insanitary conditions whereby they may have been rendered injurious to health prior to being introduced or delivered for introduction into interstate commerce." ...

There seems to us no question but that the complaint brings the case within the interstate commerce requirements of the Act.

United States v. Sanders

196 F.2d 895 (10th Cir. 1952).

■ HUXMAN, CIRCUIT JUDGE.

On October 17, 1951, an injunction was entered against appellee ... enjoining him from directly or indirectly introducing or causing to be introduced, and delivering or causing to be delivered, for introduction into interstate commerce, in violation of 21 U.S.C. § 331(a), a drug which was misbranded.... Thereafter this action was filed in the nature of an application for an order to show cause why he should not be prosecuted for criminal contempt for a violation of the injunction.... [The district court] denied the application for a show cause order on the ground that the allegations of the application were insufficient to state an offense.

It is admitted that the drug in question was misbranded. Appellee's position adopted by the court is that his activities do not constitute interstate commerce as prohibited by the injunction.... After the injunction ... [a]ppellee sold only to those who came to his place of business at Wanette, Oklahoma, and delivered the drugs to them there....

The application for the order to show cause ... alleged that since the issuance of the injunction appellee had ... on January 24, 1951 ... sold and delivered to Loyd Mangan of Garden City, Kansas, for introduction into interstate commerce two one quart jars of said misbranded drug, with the knowledge that Mangan intended to and would return to Garden City, Kansas, with said article of drug. The complaint alleged five other specific sales made to out of state customers and alleged that all of said sales were made with the knowledge that the purchaser was from out of the state and intended to and would return to his place of residence out of the state with said drugs. It alleged that while appellee ostensibly discontinued the practice of using salesmen or so called "runners" to solicit and fill orders from customers outside of the state of Oklahoma he had adopted the practice of selling and delivering his products at Wanette, Oklahoma, directly to out of state customers, soliciting them to return at later dates for more of the product....

... The Act must be given a reasonable construction to effectuate its salutary purposes. It prohibits not only the introduction into interstate commerce of adulterated articles but also the delivery thereof for introduction into commerce. One is as much a violation of the Act as the other.

There is a long line of cases beginning with *In re Dahnke–Walker Milling Co. v. Bondurant*, 257 U.S. 282 (1921), holding that where one purchases goods in one state for transportation to another the interstate commerce transaction includes the purchase as well as the transportation.... The decisions ... make it clear that whether delivery for transportation is made to a common carrier, a private carrier, or even to the purchaser for transportation by himself is immaterial.

To be guilty of violating the Act, it was not necessary that appellee be engaged in interstate commerce with respect to a misbranded drug. It was sufficient if he was engaged in delivering such a drug for introduction into interstate commerce. If appellee knowingly and regularly sold misbranded drugs and delivered them, knowing that they were purchased for transportation in interstate commerce, and solicited customers to return for future purchases and deliveries, he was guilty of a violation of the Act....

The judgment is Reversed and the cause is Remanded with directions to proceed in conformity with the views expressed herein.

NOTES

1. *Supporting Authority. See Drown v. United States*, 198 F.2d 999 (9th Cir. 1952) (sale to buyer known to be returning to Illinois constituted delivery for introduction into interstate commerce).

2. *Dispensing of Rx Drugs.* Compare Trade Correspondence No. 183 (March 15, 1940), in which FDA provided the following reply to a physician who treated patients in several states:

> With reference to medicines given to your patients at your hospital and transported by them to their homes in some other states for use by themselves, it is our opinion that such a transaction is not interstate commerce as that term is defined in Section 201(b) of the Act. We are still of the opinion, however, that the shipment of drugs by you to patients in other states, whether by mail, express, messenger, or otherwise, is interstate commerce, and that products so shipped are required by the statute to comply with its terms.

3. "HELD FOR SALE AFTER SHIPMENT IN INTERSTATE COMMERCE"

Whereas the cases excerpted above address when interstate commerce begins, the cases below consider when, if ever, it ends. As enacted in 1938, the FD&C Act's list of "Prohibited Acts" in section 301 included the commission of an act that resulted in an article being misbranded (though not adulterated) if such act was done "while such article [was] held for sale after shipment in interstate commerce." FD&C Act 301(k) (pre-1948). The plain language of the statute thus clearly reached articles that were misbranded after they came to rest in a state. Nevertheless, some questioned whether a product fell outside this provision if it were misbranded long after reaching a state or after multiple intrastate sales.

By contrast to section 301(k), section 304(a) of the FD&C Act, authorizing seizures, originally made no reference at all to articles "held for sale after shipment in interstate commerce." This provision thus did not reach articles that were adulterated or misbranded after they came to rest in a state.

The two cases below interpret the pre-1948 versions of sections (k) and 304(a). In 1948, Congress amended both provisions into their current forms, so as to make clear that FDA enforcement authority reaches articles adulterated or misbranded while "held for sale (whether or not the first sale) after shipment in interstate commerce."

United States v. Phelps Dodge Mercantile Co.

157 F.2d 453 (9th Cir. 1946).

■ MATHEWS, CIRCUIT JUDGE.

. . . [T]he United States, proceeded against 175 cartons of food (150 cartons of spaghetti and 25 cartons of macaroni) in possession of appellee, Phelps Dodge Mercantile Company, in the District of Arizona. . . .

Condemnation was sought under Sec. 304(a) of the Federal Food, Drug, and Cosmetic Act, 21 U.S.C.A. § 334(a), which provides: "Any article of food . . . that is adulterated . . . when introduced into or while in interstate commerce . . . shall be liable to be proceeded against while in interstate commerce, or at any time thereafter, on libel of information and condemned in any district court of the United States within the jurisdiction of which the article is found: . . ."

. . . [T]he libel stated . . . that on September 28, 1945—more than two years after it was shipped in interstate commerce—the food was adulterated. The libel did not state that the food was adulterated when introduced into or while in interstate commerce. Instead, the libel stated . . . that the food was adulterated while held in original packages by appellee at its warehouse in Douglas, Arizona. Thus it appeared that the adulteration of the food occurred after it ended its interstate journey and came to rest at appellee's warehouse.

Appellant contends that the fact that the food was adulterated while held in original packages was sufficient to warrant its condemnation. We do not agree. . . . 21 U.S.C. § 334(a), under which this proceeding was brought, provides for the condemnation of "Any article of food . . . that is adulterated . . . when introduced into or while in interstate commerce." It says nothing about original packages. The terms "interstate commerce" and "original packages" are not synonymous. Articles may be in interstate commerce without being in original packages. They may be in original packages without being in interstate commerce. They may be in both interstate commerce and original packages and, if in both, may cease to be in interstate commerce and yet remain in original packages. Hence the fact that the food was adulterated while held in original packages did not show that it was adulterated when introduced into or while in interstate commerce.

. . . .

United States v. Sullivan

332 U.S. 689 (1948).

■ MR. JUSTICE BLACK delivered the opinion of the Court.

Respondent, a retail druggist in Columbus, Georgia, was charged ... with a violation of § 301(k) of the Federal Food, Drug, and Cosmetic Act of 1938. That section prohibits "the doing of any ... act with respect to, a ... drug ... if such act is done while such article is held for sale after shipment in interstate commerce and results in such article being misbranded." Section 502(f) of the Act declares a drug "to be misbranded ... unless its labeling bears (1) adequate directions for use; and (2) such adequate warnings against use ... dangerous to health, or against unsafe dosage ... as are necessary for the protection of users." ...

The facts alleged are these: A laboratory had shipped in interstate commerce from Chicago, Illinois, to a consignee at Atlanta, Georgia, a number of bottles, each containing 1,000 sulfathiazole tablets. These bottles had labels affixed to them, which, as required by § 502(f)(1) and (2) of the Act, set out adequate directions for the use of the tablets and adequate warnings to protect ultimate consumers from dangers incident to this use. Respondent bought one of these properly labeled bottles of sulfathiazole tablets from the Atlanta consignee, transferred it to his Columbus, Georgia, drugstore, and there held the tablets for resale. On two separate occasions twelve tablets were removed from the properly labeled and branded bottle, placed in pill boxes, and sold to customers. These boxes were labeled "sulfathiazole." They did not contain the statutorily required adequate directions for use or warnings of danger.

Respondent's motion to dismiss the information was overruled, a jury was waived, evidence was heard, and respondent was convicted under both counts.

The Circuit Court of Appeals reversed. 161 F.2d 629. The court thought that as a result of respondent's action the sulfathiazole became "misbranded" within the meaning of the Federal Act, and that in its "broadest possible sense" the Act's language "may include what happened." However, it was also of the opinion that the Act ought not be taken so broadly "but held to apply only to the holding for the first sale by the importer after interstate shipment." ...

... [One] reason of the [court of appeals] for refraining from construing the Act as applicable to articles misbranded while held for retail sale, even though the articles had previously been shipped in interstate commerce, was its opinion that such a construction would raise grave doubts as to the Act's constitutionality. In support of this position the court cited. *National Labor Relations Board v. Jones & Laughlin Steel Corporation*, 301 U.S. 1, 30, and *Schechter Poultry Corporation v. United States*, 295 U.S. 495. ...

A restrictive interpretation should not be given a statute merely because ... giving effect to the express language employed by Congress might require a court to face a constitutional question. ...

... When we seek the meaning of § 301(k) from its language we find that the offense it creates and which is here charged requires the doing of some act with respect to a drug (1) which results in its being misbranded, (2) while the article is held for sale "after shipment in interstate commerce." Respondent has not seriously contended that the "misbranded" portion of § 301(k) is ambiguous. Section 502(f), as has been seen, provides that a drug is misbranded unless the labeling contains adequate directions and adequate warnings. The labeling here did not contain the information which § 502(f) requires....

Furthermore, it would require great ingenuity to discover ambiguity in the additional requirement of § 301(k) that the misbranding occur "while such article is held for sale after shipment in interstate commerce." The words accurately describe respondent's conduct here. He held the drugs for sale after they had been shipped in interstate commerce from Chicago to Atlanta. It is true that respondent bought them over six months after the interstate shipment had been completed by their delivery to another consignee. But the language used by Congress broadly and unqualifiedly prohibits misbranding articles held for sale after shipment in interstate commerce, without regard to how long after the shipment the misbranding occurred, how many intrastate sales had intervened, or who had received the articles at the end of the interstate shipment. Accordingly, we find that the conduct of the respondent falls within the literal meaning of § 301(k).

... Given the meaning that we have found the literal language of § 301(k) to have, it is thoroughly consistent with the general aims and purposes of the Act.... Its purpose was to safeguard the consumer by applying the Act to articles from the moment of their introduction into interstate commerce all the way to the moment of their delivery to the ultimate consumer. Section 301(a) forbids the "introduction or delivery for introduction into interstate commerce" of misbranded or adulterated drugs; § 301(b) forbids the misbranding or adulteration of drugs while "in interstate commerce"; and § 301(c) prohibits the "receipt in interstate commerce" of any misbranded or adulterated drug, and "the delivery or proffered delivery thereof for pay or otherwise." But these three paragraphs alone would not supply protection all the way to the consumer. The words of paragraph (k) "while such article is held for sale after shipment in interstate commerce" apparently were designed to fill this gap and to extend the Act's coverage to every article that had gone through interstate commerce until it finally reached the ultimate consumer....

Reversed.

■ Mr. Justice Frankfurter, dissenting.

... [A]n article is "misbranded" only if there is "adulteration, mutilation, destruction, obliteration, or removal of the whole or any part of the labeling of, or the doing of any act with respect to, a food, drug, device, or cosmetic." Here there was no "alteration, mutilation, destruction, obliteration, or removal" of any part of the label. The decisive question is whether taking a unit from a container and putting it in a bag, whether it be food, drug or cosmetic, is doing "any other act" in the context in which that phrase is used in the setting of the Federal Food, Drug, and Cosmetic Act and particularly of § 301(k).

As bearing upon the appropriate answer to this question, it cannot be that a transfer from a jar, the bulk container, to a small paper bag, without transferring the label of the jar to the paper bag, is "any other act" when applied to a drug, but not "any other act" when applied to candies or cosmetics.... [I]t cannot be put off to some other day to determine whether "any other act" in § 301(k) applies to the ordinary retail sale of candies or cosmetics in every drug store or grocery throughout the land....

It is this inescapable conjunction of food, drugs and cosmetics in the prohibition of § 301(k) that calls for a consideration of the phrase "or the doing of any other act," in the context of the rest of the sentence and with due regard for the important fact that the States are also deeply concerned with the protection of the health and welfare of their citizens or transactions peculiarly within local enforcing powers. So considered, "the doing of any other act" should be read with the meaning which radiates to that loose phrase from the particularities that precede it, namely "alteration, mutilation, destruction, obliteration, or removal" of any part of the label.... There is nothing in the legislative history of the Act ... to give the slightest basis for inferring that Congress contemplated what the Court now finds in the statute. The statute in its entirety was of course intended to protect the ultimate consumer. This is no more true in regard to the requirements pertaining to drugs than of those pertaining to food....

... I would affirm the judgment below....

COMMENT: THE LEGISLATIVE OVERRULING OF PHELPS DODGE

In 1948, in reaction to the *Phelps Dodge* decision, Congress revised both sections 301(k) and 304(a) of the FD&C Act in 62 Stat. 582 (1948). Each provision now extends to products misbranded or adulterated when "held for sale (whether or not the first sale) after shipment in interstate commerce."

The 1948 amendment of section 301(k) requires some explanation. After all, *Phelps Dodge* addressed only 304(a). In *Sullivan*, the Supreme Court decided that the preamended language of section 301(k), unlike that of 304(a), did in fact reach acts performed with respect to articles after they came to rest within a state. But at the time Congress drafted the amendments to the FD&C Act, the Supreme Court had not yet overturned the contrary conclusion of the court of appeals in *Sullivan*. Moreover, section 301(k) as enacted in 1938 covered acts resulting in an article being misbranded but did not include acts that resulted in a product being adulterated. Only Congress could fill this gap.

The House Report, H.R. Rep. No. 807, 80th Cong., 1st Sess. (1947), explained the 1948 amendments to sections 301(k) and 304(a) in the wake of *Phelps Dodge*:

> ... The 1906 act authorized seizure of foods and drugs that became adulterated or misbranded after interstate movement had ceased if they remained unloaded, unsold, or in original unbroken packages. Thousands of shipments of foods and drugs that became

filthy, debased, or deteriorated after interstate transportation were seized and condemned under this provision and thereby were prevented from reaching the consuming public. The authority to make seizures in such circumstances was never challenged by court contest. . . .

From time to time seizures have been made of foods contaminated with toxins produced by bacteria. Frequently it is impossible to tell whether the toxin developed before or after the end of the interstate journey. The toxins of different organisms cause illnesses of varying degrees of seriousness. That caused by the toxin of the botulinus organism is of high mortality. Such dangerous products do not appear frequently, but when they are found it is vital that there be adequate legal authority to apprehend them. The great bulk of the commodities involved in this problem are those which become contaminated by rodents, insects, and other vermin.

The insertion of the parenthetical wording "(whether or not the first sale)" in section 301(k) is not designed to change the original intended meaning of the section but would simply make it entirely clear that "held for sale" includes the first sale and any subsequent sale. As a result of a decision on May 12, 1947, by the Circuit Court of Appeals for the Fifth Circuit, in the case of *Jordan J. Sullivan v. United States*, doubts have arisen as to the ultimate judicial interpretation of the present language. . . .

The committee's recommendation that section 301(k) be amended so as to cover adulteration as well as misbranding will make this subsection coextensive with section 304(a). . . .

NOTES

1. *Proof of Shipment. Archambault v. United States*, 224 F.2d 925 (10th Cir. 1955), held that interstate commerce could be proved simply by the fact that a drug produced in one state was subsequently found in another.

2. *Commentary. See generally* William W. Goodrich, *The Applicability of the Federal Food, Drug, and Cosmetic Act to Interstate Commerce*, 3 FOOD & DRUG L. R. 332 (1948); G. H. Kemker, *The Commerce Clause and the Federal Food, Drug, and Cosmetic Act*, 10 FOOD DRUG COSM. L.J. 389 (1955).

United States v. Geborde

278 F.3d 926 (9th Cir. 2002).

■ SILVERMAN, CIRCUIT JUDGE.

Defendant Lindley Geborde manufactured and gave away to several teenagers a home-made designer drug called gamma hydroxy butyrate, commonly known as GHB [or the "date-rape drug."]. Geborde's concoction killed one of the teenage boys who drank the stuff. Geborde was convicted of manslaughter in state court and sentenced to prison. The present case involves the efforts of federal authorities to prosecute Geborde on drug charges arising out of the same events. Although GHB is now a controlled substance as defined by federal law, it wasn't at the time, and therefore, wasn't covered by the usual federal statutes dealing with illegal drugs.

Unable to bring a conventional drug case, the government charged Geborde with various violations of the Food, Drug, and Cosmetic Act ("FDCA")....
The problem is that the FDCA was not designed to deal with the wholly gratuitous distribution of homemade substances. We now have to decide whether the square pegs of Geborde's conduct can be pounded into the round holes of the FDCA.

Geborde was convicted of ... seven counts of misbranding of drugs held for sale after receipt in interstate commerce, with the intent to defraud or mislead, in violation of 21 U.S.C. §§ 331(k), 333(a)(2)....

... [T]he government failed to prove an essential statutory element of the offense—that the misbranding occurred while the drug was "held for sale." The undisputed evidence established that Geborde did not sell the GHB or hold it for sale; he gave it away, free of charge, to the ultimate users with whom he socialized. Accordingly, we reverse Geborde's convictions of Counts Two through Eight and remand with directions to enter a judgment of acquittal as to those counts.

I. Facts

In the fall of 1995, Geborde was a 25–year old aspiring disc jockey and musician from Los Angeles who moved to Yucca Valley, California and soon became something of a Pied Piper among a group of young locals. According to the testimony, he was admired as a deejay and regarded as cool....

On seven different occasions between September, 1995 and January, 1996, Geborde gave his homemade GHB to his young friends.... [I]n each instance, at a party or in some other social setting, Geborde gave his teenage groupies GHB, either straight or mixed with vodka.... Count Eight is the instance in which Geborde, while partying with his young friends ... in North Landers, California, gave GHB to 15–year-old Lucas Bielat. Bielat died from ingesting a toxic level of GHB. It is undisputed, however, that Geborde never sold or offered to sell GHB....

II. Sufficiency of the evidence

    . . . .

B. Counts II through VIII—Misbranding of drugs held for sale after receipt in interstate commerce in violation of 21 U.S.C. §§ 331(k) and 333(a)(2)

In Counts Two through Eight, Geborde was charged with misbranding of a drug after receiving it in interstate commerce, in violation of 21 U.S.C. § 331(k). The indictment also contained an allegation under 21 U.S.C. § 333(a)(2) that the offense was committed with the intent to defraud or mislead, enhancing it to a felony.

21 U.S.C. § 331(k) provides as follows:

The following acts and the causing thereof are prohibited:....

(k) The alteration, mutilation, destruction, obliteration, or removal of the whole or any part of the labeling of, or the doing of any other act with respect to, a food, drug, device, or cosmetic, *if such act is done while such article is held for sale (whether or not the first sale)* after shipment in interstate commerce and results in such article being adulterated or misbranded.

(Emphasis added.)

The government does not contend that Geborde actually sold GHB or held it for sale in the usual sense. Rather, the government's position is that "held for sale" means "not for personal consumption." At the government's request, the district court instructed the jury as follows:

> "All articles, including drugs, not intended for the sole consumption by the producer are deemed to be held for sale under the Federal Food, Drug and Cosmetic Act. If a producer possesses a drug with the intent of selling or giving it away to others, even if she or he also possess it in addition for his or her own personal consumption, he or she holds the drug for sale." . . . .

The government's main case is the 1911 decision in *Hipolite Egg Co. v. United States*, 220 U.S. 45 (1911), in which the Supreme Court held that eggs intended for use by a commercial bakery rather than for sale in unbroken packages were nevertheless "held for sale." The government also relies on *United States v. Torigian Labs. Inc.*, 577 F. Supp. 1514 (E.D.N.Y.), *aff'd* 751 F.2d 373 (2d Cir.1984), a case in which the defendants' laboratory received intra-ocular lenses from their manufacturer in order to sterilize, package, and label them before returning the lenses to the manufacturer for distribution to customers. The court rejected the defendants' argument that *the lab* wasn't holding the lenses for sale, but was just sterilizing and packaging them for the manufacturer. Both *Hipolite Egg* and *Torigian Labs.* clearly involve commercial transactions, commercial actors, and commercial products. The eggs and lenses, respectively, were products held for sale, in one form or another, to consumers who would buy them. They were not homemade items distributed free of charge to friends.

The government also cites *Chaney v. Heckler*, 718 F.2d 1174 (D.C. Cir. 1983) (*rev'd on other grounds, Heckler v. Chaney*, 470 U.S. 821 (1985)). This odd case was brought by prison inmates in Texas and Oklahoma seeking to require FDA regulation of lethal drugs used in executions. The court held that the drugs were subject to regulation even though they were not "held for sale" to the condemned inmate, described by the court as the "ultimate consumer." "Inquiry into the statutory scheme and legislative history of the FDCA and subsequent amendments reveals a specific congressional intent to prevent misbranding of drugs at each stage of the distribution process from manufacturer to patient." *Chaney*, 718 F.2d at 1181. *Chaney* sheds little light on the problem before us because it, too, involved the distribution of commercial drugs by an entity (to wit, a prison) that was in the business of administering them to the "ultimate consumer."

All of the FDCA "held for sale" cases of which we are aware involve individuals or entities who are in the business of distributing or handling the drug or product in question. We know of no case, much less a criminal case, in which the "held for sale" language of the FDCA has been applied to an individual who gave away a homespun drug or product in a wholly non-commercial setting.

... It seems clear to us that the phrase "held for sale" plainly contemplates a sale. But even if "held for sale" could somehow mean something else, in a criminal case due process requires that ambiguity be resolved against the government. The government did not have to prove that Geborde sold GHB; it would have been sufficient if the government proved that Geborde simply held the drug for sale. In this case, the government proved neither, and therefore, Geborde's convictions of Counts Two through Eight must be reversed.

By way of epilogue, we note that in March, 2000, pursuant to the Hillory J. Farias and Samantha Reid Date–Rape Drug Prohibition Act of 1999, GHB is now listed as a Schedule I controlled substance. Law enforcement authorities can now prosecute GHB cases just as they do other illegal drug cases, under the Drug Abuse Prevention and Control statutes, 21 U.S.C. § 801 et seq.

NOTES

1. *Shipment of Components in Interstate Commerce.* Although the home-brewed GHB distributed by Gebarde did not itself move in interstate commerce, the ingredients he used to make the GHB (lye and common industrial solvent) apparently had so moved. As will be discussed *infra* p. 1235, an article may be deemed "held for sale after shipment in interstate commerce" based solely on the prior movement of one or more of its components across state lines.

2. *Use in Patient Treatment.* In *United States v. An Article of Device ... "Cameron Spitler Amblyo–Syntonizer,"* 261 F. Supp. 243 (D. Neb. 1966), the court granted summary judgment for the libelant:

> Although the claimant never sold the devices in the commercial sense, the device was used in the claimant's treatment of patients. In *United States v. 10 Cartons of Black Tablets*, 152 F. Supp. 360 (W.D. Pa. 1957), the articles were not sold to patients but used as part of the treatment in the cancer clinic. The court held that such use was within the scope of the "holding for sale."

Other rulings that "held for sale" includes any use other than personal consumption include *United States v. Diapulse Corp. of America*, 514 F.2d 1097 (2d Cir. 1975); *United States v. Bronson Farms, Inc.*, Food Drug Cosm. L. Rep. (CCH) ¶ 38,354 (M.D. Fla. 1986); *United State v. Articles of Drug ... "Hydralazine HCL,"* 568 F. Supp. 29 (D.N.J. 1983); *United States v. Article of Animal Drug Containing Diethylstilbestrol*, 528 F. Supp. 202 (D. Neb. 1981); *United States v. Articles of Device [Acuflex, Pro–Med]*, 426 F. Supp. 366 (W.D. Pa. 1977); *United States v. Article of Device ... Cameron Spitler*, 261 F. Supp. 243 (D. Neb. 1966); *United States v. 10 Cartons ... "Hoxsey"*, 152 F. Supp. 360 (W.D. Pa. 1957).

3. *New Drugs.* Whereas the adulteration and misbranding provisions of the FD&C Act apply to actions taken subsequent to shipment of an article in interstate commerce, the new drug provisions apply only at the moment of shipment in interstate commerce. *See* FD&C Act 301(d), 505(a). (As discussed at pp. 818–819 *supra*, FDA has predicated its conclusion that the FD&C Act does not apply to a physician who prescribes an approved drug for an unapproved use on this stricter interstate commerce requirement applicable to new drugs.) On occasion, FDA loses sight of its own construction of the Act and seizes products as illegal new drugs that have not themselves been shipped in commerce. *E.g., United States v. Articles of Drug ... Wans*, 526 F. Supp. 703 (D.P.R. 1981).

4. *Goods in Possession of Bailee.* In *U.S. v. Wiesenfeld Warehouse*, 376 U.S. 86 (1964), a warehouse was charged under amended section 301(k) for allowing food in its possession to become contaminated with filth. Among other defenses, the warehouse contended that it was a bailee of the food, not a seller, and thus that it was not holding the food "for sale" within the meaning of section 301(k). The United States Supreme Court rejected this argument:

> The language of § 301(k) does not limit its application to one holding title to the goods, and since the danger to the public from insanitary storage of food is the same regardless of the proprietary status of the person storing it, the purpose of the legislation—to safeguard the consumer from the time the food is introduced into the channels of interstate commerce to the point that it is delivered to the ultimate consumer—would be substantially thwarted by such an unwarranted reading of the statutory language.

Id. at 92.

5. *Goods in Possession of Ultimate Consumer. United States v. Olsen*, 161 F.2d 669 (9th Cir. 1947), reversed the district court's dismissal of the government's seizure under section 304 of a misbranded device in the appellee's private home. The undisputed facts indicated that the article was misbranded when introduced into interstate commerce.

> It is immaterial, if true, that appellee had purchased and paid for the article, had it in his home, was satisfied with it and desired to keep it; that the article was not inherently dangerous or harmful; that appellee did not intend to use it commercially or permits its use by persons other than himself and his mother and brothers....

Id. at 671. In compliance with the court of appeals' mandate, the same district judge that had originally dismissed the seizure reluctantly issued a seizure order. *United States v. One Article of Device Labeled Spectrochrome*, 77 F. Supp. 50 (D. Or. 1948). In doing so, the judge deplored the adoption of a country-wide "policy of entering private homes to seize articles ... [as] governmental madness."

It is important to recognize that the basis for the section 304 seizure in this case was not that the device was misbranded by the appellee "while held for sale after shipment in interstate commerce," but rather that it had already been misbranded by others "when introduced into [and] while in interstate commerce." Consequently, although the government could seize the misbranded device in the appellee's home, it could not have penalized him under section 301(k). After all, he did not misbrand the device himself nor was he holding it for sale.

COMMENT: FDA JURISDICTION OVER RESTAURANTS AND FOOD STORES

Because section 301(k) of the FD&C Act prohibits the adulteration of an article "while such article is held for sale (whether or not the first sale) after shipment in interstate commerce," FDA's legal power to enforce food sanitation requirements clearly extends to restaurants, grocers, and food vending machines. Nonetheless, in light of the overwhelming number of retail food operations in the United States, and their traditional supervision by local authorities, FDA has ceded the regulation of such establishments to state and local governments. FDA's primary contribution has been to draft model ordinances and codes for voluntary adoption by state agencies and local departments. Starting in 1934, when the agency published recommended Restaurant Sanitation Regulations, it issued and periodically revised separate model sanitation codes for restaurants, food stores, and vending establishments.

In 1974, the agency, concerned about the lack of uniformity in federal, state, and local regulation, proposed to make the restaurant code mandatory by issuing a revision of it in the form of an administrative rule. 39 Fed. Reg. 35438 (October 1, 1974). State officials opposed this action, primarily because "it abridged a long-term understanding between the States and the Federal government regarding the regulation of the food service industry. . . ." 42 Fed. Reg. 15428 (March 22, 1977). In response to these comments, FDA withdrew the proposal, declaring that "it was never [the agency's] intention to supersede State and local regulation of food service sanitation. . . ." *Id.*

Since 1993, FDA has combined the model sanitation codes for restaurants, food stores, and vending establishments into one model "Food Code," which the agency revises every two years. As of 2005, 48 states and territories have adopted the Food Code. *See* "Real Progress in Food Code Adoptions," FDA CFSAN (March 2005).

4. Components Shipped in Interstate Commerce

Even if a food, drug, or cosmetic is itself not shipped in interstate commerce, it is almost always made from ingredients that have been so shipped.

United States v. 40 Cases . . . "Pinocchio Brand 75% Corn, Peanut Oil and Soya Bean Oil Blended With 25% Pure Olive Oil"

289 F.2d 343 (2d Cir. 1961).

■ Lumbard, Chief Judge.

The single question before us on this appeal is whether § 304(a) of the Federal Food, Drug, and Cosmetic Act authorizes the United States to proceed against and seize mislabeled or adulterated cans of blended vegetable oils mixed entirely within the State of New York from various oils shipped under proper labels from other states and foreign countries. . . . The district judge held that the blended oil was a "new product" and therefore not the same as those shipped in interstate commerce. He dismissed the libel.

In its libel . . . the United States charged that . . . the cans were labeled "25 per cent pure olive oil"; that examination showed that the cans contained little or no olive oil; and that the oil was therefore "adulterated" within the meaning of § 402(b)(2) or "misbranded" within the meaning of § 403(a) of the Federal Food, Drug, and Cosmetic Act. . . .

The United States did not in the district court or here challenge the truth of the company's assertion that the blending process was done entirely within the State of New York, nor did it claim that the blended oil was carried across any state line. It is also undisputed that the various oils from which the blend was made had been shipped under proper labels from

New Jersey, Illinois and Georgia, and that olive oil had been transported to the company's plant in Ozone Park, New York, from Spain, Italy and Tunisia. The United States contends that although the component oils were correctly labeled when shipped interstate, the misbranding or adulteration which occurred during or after the blending of the oils brought them within the compass of the federal act as articles of food held for sale after interstate shipment.

... In 1948 ... Congress amended 304(a) so as also to permit seizure of food that is adulterated or misbranded "while held for sale (whether or not the first sale) after shipment in interstate commerce." Had the company in this case not mixed the oils it received from various sources but instead pasted new misleading labels on the containers in which they were shipped in interstate commerce or otherwise adulterated the oils, seizure would have been authorized. The appellee would have us hold here that the blending of the oils which had been transported in interstate commerce took the final product out from under federal regulation although each of its separate components was being held for sale after shipment in interstate commerce. We do not agree.

... Congress sought to fill the gap in the regulatory scheme pointed out in *United States v. Phelps Dodge Mercantile Co.*, by subjecting to condemnation food which had been adulterated or misbranded after coming to rest within a state but before being sold to a consumer. The interest of the federal government in ensuring that such food meets minimum standards of purity and is not misbranded arises out of its supervisory function over interstate commerce. The House and Senate reports both referred expressly to the Congressional desire to protect the integrity of interstate products so as not to depress the demand for goods that must travel across state lines. This interest surely extends to products such as olive oil, which a New York consumer would probably recognize as out-of-state or foreign in origin.

Moreover, in this case all the components of the oil blend had been transported in interstate commerce, and the completed mixture was being held for sale as "oil"—the very same type of food which had traveled across the state line. This is not a case in which oil which was transported interstate was used as one of many ingredients in a finished product which in no way resembled the food which had crossed state lines. Oil may come in many varieties, but to the unsophisticated consumer one oil blend is much like another. We would be undermining the remedial legislative purpose of consumer protection were we to deny the power to seize misbranded articles on the ground that such foods as corn oil, peanut oil, soya bean oil and olive oil when mixed constitute a "different product" from a blend of less than all or from a pure measure of any one of them.

... [W]e reverse the order of the district court dismissing the libel.

NOTE

Supporting Authority. For other cases holding that shipment of product ingredients in interstate commerce is sufficient to confer jurisdiction on FDA, see *United States v. An Article of Food ... Coco Rico*, 752 F.2d 11 (1st Cir. 1985); *United States v. Dianovin Pharmaceuticals, Inc.,* 475 F.2d 100 (1st Cir. 1973); *United States v. Cassaro, Inc.,* 443 F.2d 153 (1st Cir. 1971); *Palmer v. United States,* 340 F.2d 48 (5th Cir. 1964); *United States v. Detroit Vital Foods, Inc.,* 330 F.2d 78 (6th Cir. 1964); *United States v. Allbrook Freezing & Cold Storage,* 194 F.2d 937 (5th Cir. 1952); *United States v. Miami Serpentarium Laboratories, Inc.,* Food Drug Cosm. L. Rep. (CCH) ¶ 38,164 (S.D. Fla. 1982); *United States v. 14 Cases ... Naremco Medi-Matic Free Choice Poultry Formula,* 374 F. Supp. 922 (W.D. Mo. 1974); *United States v. 39 Cases ... "Korleen Tablets,"* 192 F. Supp. 51 (E.D. Mich. 1961).

COMMENT: COMPONENTS AND THE "LOSS OF IDENTITY" APPROACH

In *United States v. An Article or Device ... "Gonsertron Corp.,"* 180 F. Supp. 52 (E.D. Mich. 1959), the government attempted to seize a device constructed in Michigan out of mechanical parts shipped from other states. None of the parts was made to the specifications of the claimant. The court dismissed the government's libel because the device itself was never in interstate commerce. *Id.* at 53. Two years later, however, the same judge reached an opposite conclusion regarding the seizure of drugs compounded in Michigan from ingredients that had moved in interstate commerce. *United States v. 39 Cases ... "Korleen Tablets,"* 192 F. Supp. 51 (E.D. Mich. 1961). The judge distinguished *Goserton* as follows:

> In [*Gonsertron*], the Court[ ] held that ... [a] device is not subject to the jurisdiction of the Act where the only components shipped in interstate commerce were either a minor ingredient of the final product or several commonly used components which lost their identity within the newly manufactured device. In contrast, in the case at bar, the "drugs" comprising the Korleen Tablets are the very heart of the manufactured and tableted "drug" and were proclaimed as such to the public.

More recently, the Court of Appeals for the Ninth Circuit (which does not include Michigan) rejected this "loss of identity" theory. In concluding that FD&C Act 301(k) applied to a synthetic heroin manufactured entirely in California from components shipped from other states, the Ninth Circuit concluded that *Gonserton* was incorrectly decided and "does not represent the current state of the law." *Baker v. U.S.,* 932 F.2d 813, 815 (9th Cir. 1991). The *Baker* court concluded, "Thus, whether the ingredient is a main one or minor one, or whether it is identifiable or unidentifiable after combination is inconsequential" (citing *U.S. v. Generix Drug Corp.,* 460 U.S. 453 (1983), for the principle that the term "drug" in the FD&C Act refers to both inactive and active ingredients).

5. MEDICAL DEVICES

The Medical Device Amendments of 1976 amended section 304(a) of the FD&C Act to authorize seizure (but not criminal penalties or injunctive action) against misbranded or adulterated devices without proof of interstate commerce.

United States v. Undetermined Quantities of an Article of Device ... "Depilatron Epilator"

473 F. Supp. 913 (S.D.N.Y. 1979).

■ SAND, DISTRICT JUDGE.

This action is an *in rem* proceeding ... for forfeiture and condemnation of a depilatory device. Claimant has moved to dismiss the complaint on the grounds that 21 U.S.C. § 334(a)(2) "is unconstitutional on its face as a violation of the commerce clause of the United States Constitution." ...

Section 334(a) provides for the seizure of, *inter alia*, adulterated or misbranded devices. Prior to 1976, it was a requirement of such seizures that the device in question have been introduced into interstate commerce. Subsection 334(a) was amended in 1976, however, so as to include adulterated or misbranded devices in the class of articles which are "liable to be proceeded against at any time on libel of information" without regard to interstate commerce.

Claimant concedes that "Congress may regulate not only interstate commerce, but also those wholly intrastate activities which it concludes have an affect [sic] upon interstate commerce." Claimant's contention is, rather, that where Congress seeks to regulate intrastate activities, "a proper nexus to interstate commerce must be made by Congress in order to justify [the] departure from the Commerce Clause," and that Congress has failed to make the required findings.

The legislative history of the 1976 amendment contains no express consideration of the impact of the intrastate sale and distribution of medical devices on interstate commerce. It was, however, the clear intent of Congress

> to authorize the seizure of devices which are distributed wholly in intrastate commerce. This provision will be applicable to all devices and will assist enforcement by doing away with the cumbersome and time consuming task of establishing interstate shipment. This provision will be particularly useful against quack devices.

S.Rep.No. 94–33, 94th Cong.1st Sess. 14 (1976)....

The Government argues that § 334(a)(2) is a valid exercise of Congress' power under the Commerce Clause, and that its legislative history "plainly implies [that] effective protection of the public health and safety would be sacrificed were Congress to have required that the source and destination of all allegedly adulterated or misbranded devices be determined in seizure cases." Moreover, the Government argues that

> [w]ith respect to the absence of express legislative history regarding the impact of the intrastate sale and distribution of medical devices on interstate commerce, it is enough that this Court perceive a basis upon which Congress could have predicated a judgment that such a nexus exists....

We agree that the absence of formal findings as to the nexus between intrastate sale and distribution of medical devices and interstate commerce is not fatal, as long as Congress had a rational basis for finding such a nexus. Congress alluded to the proliferation of medical devices and to the danger posed by unsafe and ineffective devices to the public health and safety. In light of the extensive hearings held by Congress with respect to the 1976 legislation, we find that Congress did have a sufficient basis for concluding that the regulation of the intrastate sale and distribution of medical devices was necessary for the proper regulation of interstate commerce. . . .

NOTE

In addition to permitting FDA to seize misbranded or adulterated devices without proving interstate commerce, the Device Amendments added a new section 709 to the Act, which provided: "In *any* action to enforce the requirements of this Act respecting a device the connection with interstate commerce required for jurisdiction in such action shall be presumed to exist." (Emphasis added.) This provision was intended to establish a rebuttable presumption in order to relieve FDA of the burden of demonstrating a connection with interstate commerce in criminal and injunction proceedings. *See* H.R. Rep. No. 94–853, 94th Cong., 2nd Sess. 15 (1976). In 1997, as noted previously, this provision was amended to embrace foods, drugs, and cosmetics, as well.

6. BIOLOGICS

The licensing requirement for biological products, like the new drug approval process, applies only to articles "introduce[ed] or deliver[ed] for introduction into interstate commerce." *Compare* section 351(a) of the Public Health Service Act, 42 U.S.C. 262(a), *with* FD&C Act 505(a). Unlike the FD&C Act's prohibitions against drug misbranding, however, the PHS Act's prohibition against "falsely labeling or marking" a biological product is not limited to articles in interstate commerce. *Compare* PHS Act 351(b), 42 U.S.C. 262(b), *with* FD&C Act 301(a)–(c), (k). Moreover, FDA's power under section 361 of the PHSA to issue regulations to prevent the introduction, transmission, or spread of communicable diseases has no interstate commerce restrictions. 42 U.S.C. 264.

United States v. Calise

217 F. Supp. 705 (S.D.N.Y. 1962).

■ CASHIN, DISTRICT JUDGE.

The voluminous eighty count indictment in the above entitled action charges defendants, John P. Calise and Westchester Blood Service, Inc., with several types of violations of the Public Health Service Act and the Federal Food, Drug and Cosmetic Act, and a conspiracy to violate those statutes. . . .

The defendants . . . assert that counts . . . alleging violations of the mislabeling provisions of 42 U.S.C. § 262(b), are not within the jurisdiction of this court because the acts complained of occurred entirely within the boundaries of the State of New York. The subsection reads as follows:

"(b) No person shall falsely label or mark any package or container of any virus, serum, toxin, antitoxin, or other product aforesaid;

nor alter any label or mark on any package or container of any virus, serum, toxin, antitoxin, or other product aforesaid so as to falsify such label or mark."

The language in subsection (b) does not indicate that Congress intended the effect of the statute to be confined merely to products moving in interstate commerce. The restrictive interpretation of subdivision (b) which the defendants urge is not persuasive, in view of the fact that Congress could very easily have expressed such an intention in the Public Health Service Act, as it was cautious to do in 21 U.S.C. § 331(k) where such an intention actually existed. Furthermore, the manner in which Congress separated the mislabeling ban of Section 262(b) from the labeling requirements of Section [262(a)(1)(B)] would seem to be indicative of an intention that Section 262(b) was to reach further in its scope from Section 262(a). To restrict Section 262(b) exclusively to products moving in interstate commerce would also be inconsistent with the general purpose of the Public Health Service Act as a whole, because such an interpretation would encourage unscrupulous distributors to sell falsely labeled products on the local market which have been marked so as to apparently meet federal standards, but which do not meet those standards. This would grant such distributors a definite advantage in competing with those who sell interstate products which fulfill the licensing and labeling requirements of 42 U.S.C. § 262(a).

. . . .

NOTES

1. *Joint Reliance on FD&C Act and Biologics Act.* In the preambles to its proposed and final GMP regulations for the collection, processing, and storage of human blood and blood components, 39 Fed. Reg. 18614 (May 28, 1974), 40 Fed. Reg. 53532 (Nov. 18, 1975), FDA invoked both the drug provisions of the FD&C Act and sections 351(b) and 361 of the Biologics Act, thus exerting regulatory control over both interstate and intrastate blood banks. More recently, FDA has followed a similar approach in designing its system for the regulation of human cellular and tissue-based products, invoking both the drug and device provisions of the FD&C Act and section 361 of the PHS Act. *E.g.*, 63 Fed. Reg. 26744, 47–48 (May 14, 1998) (proposed establishment registration rule and summary of overall approach); 69 Fed. Reg. 68612, 68613–14 (Nov. 24 2004) (current good tissue practice final rule).

2. *Turtle Ban. State of Louisiana v. Mathews*, 427 F. Supp. 174 (E.D. La. 1977), upheld FDA's ban on intrastate as well as interstate commerce in small turtles to prevent the spread of communicable disease under section 361 of the Public Health Service Act.

COMMENT: FDA JURISDICTION OVER HUMAN CLONING

As discussed previously, *supra* p. 960, FDA has asserted jurisdiction over "clinical research using cloning technology to create a human being." *See* "Dear Colleague" Letter from Stuart L. Nightingale, Associate Commissioner, FDA (Oct. 26, 1998). Without citing specific provisions, the agency claimed power under both the PHS Act and the FD&C Act to require an approved investigational new drug application (IND) for such research. *Id*. FDA has not, however, publicly addressed how these statutes authorize it to regulate human cloning that is conducted entirely intrastate.

A scientist cloning a human being would fuse an enucleated egg with the nucleus of a regular adult cell, for example a skin cell, taken from the person to be cloned. The scientist would then implant the resulting embryo in a woman. If the enucleated egg and nucleic DNA were both obtained from local people (or one local woman), and the resulting embryo were carried by a local woman (perhaps the same woman), the physician or researcher would not be introducing an unapproved drug into interstate commerce in violation of section 301(d) of the FD&C Act or an unlicensed biological product into interstate commerce in violation of section 351(a) of the PHSA.

Section 361 of the PHSA does not have any interstate commerce limitations, and, indeed, FDA based its general regulations on human cellular and tissue-based products in part on this provision. But this section is relevant only to measures designed to prevent the spread of communicable diseases and thus does not seem to empower the agency to impose an IND requirement for human cloning. FDA could clearly demand investigational device exemptions (IDEs) for the devices used in cloning experiments, assuming they moved in interstate commerce. But this tactic would only work with respect to instruments that were represented for use in cloning, or were in fact used almost exclusively for that purpose. Perhaps for this reason, the "Dear Colleague" letter on human cloning does not even mention FDA's medical device authorities.

In short, the interstate commerce limitations in the FD&C Act and PHSA raise important unanswered questions about the agency's asserted authority to prevent human cloning experiments. Scholars considering FDA's jurisdiction over cloning have focused primarily on other issues, such as whether FDA can validly categorize an embryo as a biological product, drug, or medical device. *See* Richard A. Merrill, *Human Tissues and Reproductive Cloning: New Technologies Challenge FDA*, 3 HOUS. J. HEALTH L. & POL'Y 1 (2002); Gregory J. Rokosz, *Human Cloning: Is the Reach of FDA Authority Too Far a Stretch?*, 30 SETON HALL L. REV. 464 (2000); Gail H. Javitt & Kathy Hudson, *Regulating (For the Benefit of) Future Persons; A Different Perspective on the FDA's Jurisdiction to Regulate Human Reproductive Cloning*, 2003 UTAH L. REV. 1201 (2003). Elizabeth Price, *Does the FDA Have Authority to Regulate Human Cloning?*, 11 HARV. J.L. & TECH. 619 (1998).

COMMENT: OLEOMARGARINE

The Oleomargarine Act of 1950, 64 Stat. 20 (1950), ended discriminatory federal taxation against oleomargarine, thus allowing free competition between it and butter. At the same time, Congress, to ensure there would be no consumer confusion between the products, added section 407 to the FD&C Act, regulating all "colored" (yellow) margarine sold at retail establishments or used in public eating places. The legislation mandates prominent label disclosure on all packages of colored margarine. FD&C Act

407(b). Moreover, the law requires restaurants serving colored margarine to disclose this fact on a prominent placard or menu statement, and it directs that they serve it only in triangular portions with labeling identifying the food as margarine. FD&C Act 407(c).

Because of the FD&C Act's interstate commerce language, Congress was concerned that margarine produced and sold intrastate would evade these requirements designed to prevent consumer confusion. The legislation thus also added Section 407(a), which explicitly provides, "Colored oleomargarine or colored margarine which is sold in the same State or Territory in which it is produced shall be subject in the same manner and to the same extent to the provisions of this Act as if it had been introduced in interstate commerce." The Senate Report on the law remarked as follows on the loosening of the interstate commerce nexus for federal oleomargarine regulation:

> At the present time oleomargarine which has moved in interstate commerce is required to meet the exacting requirements of the Federal Food, Drug, and Cosmetic Act with respect to labeling. There is little danger that the consumer of interstate oleomargarine will be confused as to the product he obtains. There remain however two principal levels at which confusion of identity may occur: One is at the restaurant level where the applicability of the Federal Food, Drug, and Cosmetic Act is uncertain, and the other exists with respect to oleomargarine produced and sold in the same State. The House bill (H.R. 2023) brings the regulation of colored oleomargarine squarely within the Federal Food, Drug, and Cosmetic Act, irrespective of the source of the oleomargarine, and specifically regulates the restaurant transaction of serving colored oleomargarine. Thus, intrastate colored oleomargarine would be held to the same standards respecting purity and labeling as colored oleomargarine which is shipped in interstate channels....

S. Rep. No. 81–309 (1949). *SEE UNITED STATES V. RUTSTEIN*, 163 F. SUPP. 71 (S.D.N.Y. 1958) (§ 407(B) APPLIES ONLY TO RETAIL PACKAGES). *SEE ALSO* THOMAS CHRISTOPHER, *THE OLEOMARGARINE AMENDMENT*, 5 Food Drug Cosm. L.J. 279 (1950). FOR A VIVID ACCOUNT OF THE BUTTER-MARGARINE WARS, *SEE* GEOFFREY P. MILLER, *PUBLIC CHOICE AT THE DAWN OF THE SPECIAL INTEREST STATE: THE STORY OF BUTTER AND MARGARINE*, 77 Cal. L. Rev. 83 (1989).

C.   FACTORY INSPECTION

1.   INTRODUCTION

The 1906 Act contained no provision authorizing FDA to inspect the establishments in which food and drugs were manufactured, processed, or stored. Section 704 of the 1938 Act therefore represented a major increase in the agency's enforcement authority. Section 704 provides, in part:

> (a)(1) For purposes of enforcement of this chapter, officers or employees duly designated by the Secretary, upon presenting appropriate credentials and a written notice to the owner, operator,

or agent in charge, are authorized (A) to enter, at reasonable times, any factory, warehouse, or establishment in which food, drugs, devices, or cosmetics are manufactured, processed, packed, or held, for introduction into interstate commerce or after such introduction, or to enter any vehicle being used to transport or hold such food, drugs, devices, or cosmetics in interstate commerce; and (B) to inspect, at reasonable times and within reasonable limits and in a reasonable manner, such factory, warehouse, establishment, or vehicle and all pertinent equipment, finished and unfinished materials, containers, and labeling therein.

Section 301(f) of the FD&C Act makes the "refusal to permit entry or inspection as authorized by section 704" a prohibited act. In the FD&C Act as enacted in 1938, section 704 conditioned entry and inspection on "making request and obtaining permission of the owner, operator, or custodian." The plain language of the statute thus seemed to make the refusal to allow inspection a section 301 violation only if the owner had previously granted permission. FDA nonetheless interpreted the statute as prohibiting the refusal to permit an inspection at any reasonable time, regardless of whether permission had previously been given. In 1952, the United States Supreme Court rejected this interpretation, concluding that the statute was unconstitutionally vague when construed in this way. *U.S. v. Cardiff*, 344 U.S. 174 (1952). Congress subsequently amended section 704 to remove the reference to the "permission" of the owner. Consequently, today, it is illegal for the owner of an establishment to refuse entry to an inspector who arrives at a "reasonable time" and presents appropriate credentials and notice.

NOTE

"For Purposes of Enforcement." In *R.T. French Co. v. Commissioner of Food and Drugs*, Food Drug Cosm. L. Rep. (CCH) ¶ 38,258 (D. Idaho 1984), the court held that an investigatory inspection to gather information from which FDA intended to promulgate microbiological standards for the potato industry was lawful under section 704.

FDA INVESTIGATIONS MANUAL 2007

Chapter 5: Establishment Inspection.

5.1—INSPECTION INFORMATION

5.1.1—AUTHORITY TO ENTER AND INSPECT

. . . .

It is your obligation to fulfill these requirements because failure to do so may prevent use of evidence and information obtained during the inspection.

. . . .

5.1.1.1—FDA Investigator's Responsibility

Your authority to enter and inspect establishments is predicated upon specific obligations to the firm as described below. It is your responsibility to conduct all inspections at reasonable times and within reasonable limits and in a reasonable manner. Proceed with diplomacy, tact and persuasiveness.

5.1.1.2—Credentials

Display your credentials to the top management official be it the owner, operator, or agent in charge.

. . . .

5.1.1.3—Written Notice

After showing the firm's representative your credentials, issue the original, properly executed, and signed FDA 482, Notice of Inspection, to the top management official. Keep the carbon copy for submission with your report.

5.1.1.4—Written Observations

Upon completing the inspection and before leaving the premises, provide the highest management official available your inspectional findings on an FDA 483—Inspectional Observations. See Section 704(b) of the FD&C Act.

5.1.1.5—Receipts

Furnish the top management official the original of the FDA–484—Receipt for Samples describing any samples obtained during the inspection.

. . . .

NOTES

1. *Duration of Inspection.* In *United States v. Durbin*, 373 F. Supp. 1136 (E.D. Okl. 1974), the court observed: "[D]efendant's interpretation of 21 U.S.C. § 374(a) as requiring a separate notice for each day of a multiple day inspection is incorrect. . . . [T]he Notice was dated May 31, 1973 and was effective until the inspection was completed and the required Report submitted."

2. *Time of Day.* In re *Establishment Inspection of New England Medical Center Hospital*, 1969–1974 FDLI Jud. Rec. 622 (D. Mass. 1974), authorized FDA investigators and a local medical examiner to enter the hospital any time except between 6:00 A.M. and 1:00 P.M. in order to determine what caused a radiation therapy stretcher assembly to rise and crush a patient against the ceiling. The judge concluded that the investigation could proceed more rapidly if access to the device were not limited and could continue in a closed room without disturbing other patients.

3. *Inspection Costs.* In *United States v. Tri–Bio Laboratories, Inc.*, 700 F. Supp. 223 (M.D. Pa. 1988), the court held that it has inherent equitable power to order defendants to bear the cost of FDA inspection to enforce an injunction, but declined to exercise that authority under the circumstances of this case which showed no reasonable likelihood of future violations.

4. *Third–Party Inspections.* The Medical Device User Fee and Modernization Act of 2002 added a new subsection "g" to section 704 (Factory Inspection) of the FD&C Act. This subsection requires FDA to accredit third parties to perform inspections of eligible manufacturers of Class II or III devices. Manufacturers who

meet certain conditions have the option of requesting inspection by one of these accredited third parties. This program is entirely voluntary.

2. Constitutional Limitations

United States v. Jamieson–McKames Pharmaceuticals, Inc.

651 F.2d 532 (8th Cir. 1981).

■ Arnold, Circuit Judge. . . .

Jamieson–McKames Pharmaceuticals, Inc. (Jamieson–McKames) is a Missouri corporation with its principal place of business in St. Louis, Missouri. The company manufactured, purchased, packaged, labeled, distributed, and sold drugs from before June 1972 until November 1975. . . .

On October 29, 30, and 31, and November 3, 1975, federal and state agents entered and searched the premises of Jamieson–McKames Pharmaceuticals, Inc., and Pharmacare, Inc. . . . Samples of drugs were taken, documents were taken, quantities of drugs were embargoed, the premises and contents photographed, and machinery seized. . . . Thereafter, on May 12, 1977, defendants were charged in an 11–count indictment with counterfeiting, adulterating, and misbranding drugs and conspiracy to counterfeit, adulterate, and misbrand drugs. The indictment also charged that the defendants committed all of these acts with the intent to defraud and mislead, rendering such felonies punishable under 21 U.S.C. § 333(b).

The appellants contend that their Fourth Amendment rights were violated by the failure of the court to suppress evidence seized by government agents from the defendants' business premises. . . .

The seizures at the Wentzville pharmacy were conducted on the authority of a notice to inspect authorized by 21 U.S.C. § 374(a). The employee in charge was given a copy of the notice to inspect, but no warrant to inspect was obtained.

The Supreme Court has held that warrantless searches are generally unreasonable, and that commercial premises as well as homes are within the Fourth Amendment's protection. *Marshall v. Barlow's, Inc.*, 436 U.S. 307 (1978). An exception from the search-warrant requirement has, however, been delineated for industries "long subject to close supervision and inspection," *Colonnade Catering Corp. v. United States*, 397 U.S. 72 (1970), and "pervasively regulated business[es]," *United States v. Biswell*, 406 U.S. 311 (1972). *Colonnade* involved the liquor industry, and *Biswell* the interstate sale of firearms. The threshold question therefore is whether the drug-manufacturing industry should be included within this class of closely regulated businesses.

The appellants argue that the drug-manufacturing industry is no more closely regulated than any number of industries involved in interstate commerce, and that therefore the rule of *Marshall v. Barlow's, Inc., supra,* requiring a warrant in the absence of consent before an administrative search can take place, should apply. In *Barlow's*, the Supreme Court held that warrantless searches authorized by § 8(a) of the Occupational Safety and Health Act violated the Fourth Amendment. There, however, the government sought to inspect work areas not open to the public on the premises of an electrical and plumbing contractor. In *Barlow's* the argument that all businesses involved in interstate commerce had "long been subject to close supervision" of working conditions was urged by the Secretary of Labor but explicitly rejected by the Court. In rejecting this argument and others the Court specifically preserved the *Colonnade–Biswell* exception to the warrant requirement. The Court indicated that there were other industries, covered by regulatory schemes applicable only to them, where regulation might be so pervasive that a *Colonnade–Biswell* exception to the warrant requirement could apply. Such warrantless searches are upheld because "when an entrepreneur embarks on such a business, he has chosen to subject himself to a full arsenal of governmental regulation," and "in effect consents to the restrictions placed on him." Further, in the face of a long history of government scrutiny, such a proprietor has no "reasonable expectation of privacy."

We think the drug-manufacturing industry is properly within the *Colonnade–Biswell* exception to the warrant requirement. The drug-manufacturing industry has a long history of supervision and inspection. The present Food, Drug, and Cosmetic Act has its origins in the Food and Drug Act of 1906. . . .

The *Biswell* Court acknowledged that the history of regulation of interstate firearms traffic was "not as deeply rooted" as the history of liquor regulation, but included firearms within the warrant exception because their regulation was of "central importance to federal efforts to prevent violent crime and to assist the states in regulating the firearms traffic within their borders." This passage teaches that the nature of the federal or public interest sought to be furthered by the regulatory scheme is important to our analysis. It is difficult to overstate the urgent nature of the public-health interests served by effective regulation of our nation's drug-manufacturing industry. Furthermore, virtually every phase of the drug industry is heavily regulated, from packaging, labeling, and certification of expiration dates, to prior FDA approval before new drugs can be marketed. The regulatory burdens on the drug-manufacturing industry are weighty, and that weight indicates that the drug manufacturer accepts the burdens as well as the benefits of the business and "consents to the regulations placed on him." *Marshall v. Barlow's, Inc.*, 436 U.S,. at 313.

The final lesson of *Barlow's* is that the reasonableness of warrantless searches is dependent on the "specific enforcement needs and privacy guarantees of each statute." In *Barlow's* the Court was unconvinced that requiring OSHA officials to obtain administrative warrants when consent to inspect was withheld would cripple the effectiveness of the enforcement scheme. . . .

Regulation of the drug industry differs from the OSHA situation in another significant way. The class sought to be protected by OSHA regulation of safety of work areas is made up of employees, who are in the work place itself and free to report violations at any time. The protected class in the area of drug manufacturing is the consuming public, which has no way of learning of violations short of illness resulting from the consumption of defective drug products. In this sense the enforcement needs of drug-industry regulation are considerably more critical than those before the Court in *Barlow's*.

As for privacy guarantees, the Supreme Court points out that a warrant provides assurances that the proposed "inspection is reasonable under the Constitution, is authorized by statute, and is pursuant to an administrative plan containing specific neutral criteria." *Id.* at 323 (foot-note omitted). The notice of inspection used in this case satisfies at least some of these criteria. It informs the "owner or agent in charge" (§ 374(a)) of the "scope and objects of the search." *Id.* at 323. Although the notice of inspection makes no express reference to reasonableness under the Constitution, it clearly states that notice is given pursuant to 21 U.S.C. § 374, which is enacted by the Congress. The name of the firm and address is also prominently listed. Further, the notice of inspection reproduces large portions of § 374(a), stating the areas and objects to be searched; that the inspection is to take place at reasonable times; that certain records are to be made available to the inspector; that each inspection must be made with reasonable promptness; that each inspection must be accompanied by a separate notice; and that the purpose of any inspection of a prescription-drug operation is discovery of information "bearing on whether prescription drugs (are being) adulterated or misbranded within the meaning of" the Act or on other violations of the Act. 21 U.S.C. § 374(a). Equally important, the Notice of Inspection informs the owner of what cannot be examined by the inspector. Inspections relating to prescription drugs do not extend to financial data, pricing data, and certain data regarding sales, personnel, and research.

In sum, the authorizing statute now before the Court was not painted with so broad a brush as the one rejected in *Barlow's*, the enforcement needs are more critical in the drug-manufacturing field, and the interests of the general public are more urgent. We hold that inspections authorized by § 374 are "reasonable" and therefore not inconsistent with the Fourth Amendment. Thus, this case falls within the "carefully defined classes of cases" which are an exception to the search-warrant requirement. We share, to a degree, the fears expressed by appellants that many businesses are thoroughly regulated by the United States, and that an undue extension of our rationale might obliterate much of the Fourth Amendment's protection. On balance, however, we are persuaded that the capacity for good or ill of the manufacture of drugs for human consumption is so great that Congress had power to enact § 374(a).

Having concluded that drug manufacturing is a "pervasively regulated" industry does not end our inquiry, but establishes only that Congress has broad authority to place restrictions on that industry that might otherwise violate the Fourth amendment. A question remains as to whether the conduct of the government in this case conforms with the statutory scheme provided by the Congress....

The Federal Food, Drug, and Cosmetic Act contains provisions, similar to those addressed in *Colonnade*, which punish refusals to permit inspections by imprisonment up to one year, or a fine of not more than $1,000, or both. It follows, therefore, as in *Colonnade*, that an inspection pursuant to a § 374 notice to inspect is authorized only when there is a valid consent. If consent is withheld, a separate violation of the Act occurs, and the FDA inspectors are required to obtain a warrant before the inspection can proceed. . . .

This brings us to the problem presented by the search at the Wentzville site. Here, as in *Colonnade*, the critical issue is whether there was consent to the inspection. Unfortunately this issue was not expressly resolved in the court below. . . . Therefore, as to . . . the counts as to which evidence was taken from the Wentzville site, the judgments of conviction will be vacated, and the cause remanded for the making of further findings on the issue of consent. . . .

We add a word of clarification as to the meaning of the term "consent" as we intend it in this context. We do not mean, by imposing a requirement of "consent," to require a factual determination as to whether appellants, with respect to the Wentzville site, knowingly and understandingly relinquished a known right. The question is whether appellants refused to permit entry or inspection, thereby violating 21 U.S.C. § 331(f). If they did so refuse, then FDA was obliged to obtain an administrative warrant in order to effect the inspection, and could also seek a separate criminal prosecution for the refusal itself. If appellants did not refuse to permit entry or inspection, then they "consented" to the search and seizure, as we use that term here. This formulation, while it may not answer every question that may arise with respect to searches and seizures pursuant to § 374 notices of inspection, seems to us to be the most logical way to harmonize *Biswell* and *Colonnade*. . . .

The inspection and seizures conducted at the Morganford Road site were supported not only by a statutory notice, but also by a Warrant for Inspection issued by a United States Magistrate . . . and a Warrant for Arrest of Property issued by the clerk of the district court. . . .

Appellants . . . argue that the inspections were part of an ongoing criminal investigation, and that therefore a warrant issued on less than criminal probable cause was not sufficient to authorize a search. It is our view that a warrant based on an administrative showing of probable cause is valid in this pervasively regulated industry. To hold otherwise would be inconsistent with our conclusion, already expressed, that warrantless entry under a notice of inspection does not violate the Fourth Amendment in the drug-manufacturing field. Probable-cause standards are relaxed because the business person engaged in this industry has a lesser expectation of privacy. . . .

Appellants next argue that certain statements made by the defendants to FDA agents during the searches were inadmissible at trial because *Miranda* warnings were not given. The district court held that *Miranda* was not applicable because "the evidence failed to establish that defendants . . . were in a custodial situation, subject to arrest."

Evidence presented at trial showed that FDA agents are without authority to make arrests, that the defendants' movements were not restricted during the time of the search, and that there were no threats or coercion. Evidence also indicated that appellants' employees were free to go about their business, and that consultation with attorneys was not limited. There is ample evidence to support the district court's finding, and the statements were therefore properly admitted at trial. . . .

NOTES

1. *Supporting Authority.* The Sixth and Ninth Circuits have also found the pharmaceutical industry to be so "pervasively regulated" that a warrantless search is permissible under the Fourth Amendment. *See United States v. Acklen,* 690 F.2d 70, 75 (6th Cir. 1982); *United States v. Argent Chemical Laboratories, Inc.,* 93 F.3d 572 (9th Cir. 1996). Several lower courts have applied the "pervasively regulated" reasoning to the food industry. *See, e.g., U.S. v. Del Campo Baking Mfg. Co.,* 345 F. Supp. 1371 (D. Del. 1972); United States v. New England Grocers Supply Co., 488 F. Supp. 230, 238 (D. Mass. 1980).

2. *Clinical Investigators.* In *New York v. Burger,* 482 U.S. 691 (1987), the Supreme Court upheld the warrantless inspection of an automobile junkyard under a statute regulating such businesses on the grounds that (1) the government had a substantial interest in regulating junkyards, (2) warrantless inspections were necessary to further the regulatory scheme, and (3) in certainty and regularity of its application, the statutory inspection program provided a constitutionally adequate substitute for a warrant. Applying these criteria, the court in *United States v. Fogari,* 1987–1988 FDLI Jud. Rec. 144 (D.N.J. 1988), upheld a warrantless inspection of a physician conducting clinical investigations whose results were to be submitted to FDA.

3. *Criminal Investigation.* An argument that FDA improperly used its section 704 inspection authority to gather evidence for a criminal prosecution was rejected in *United States v. Gel Spice Co., Inc.,* 773 F.2d 427 (2d Cir. 1985), for lack of evidence of bad faith. The court held that the mere fact that FDA was pursuing criminal enforcement of the FD&C Act at the same time that it conducted a section 704 inspection did not evidence bad faith because the agency has concurrent civil and criminal enforcement responsibilities.

4. *Inspection Warrants. See In re Mallard Beauty Products, Inc.,* Food Drug Cosm. L. Rep. (CCH) ¶ 38,232 (S.D. Ala. 1979), and *United States v. Roux Laboratories, Inc.,* 456 F. Supp. 973 (M.D. Fla. 1978), holding companies in civil contempt for failure to comply with an administrative warrant for inspection obtained by FDA. *But see United States v. Undetermined Quantities of Various Articles of Drugs . . . Morton Pharmaceuticals,* 1978–1980 FDLI Jud. Rec. 23 (W.D. Tenn. 1978), holding an FDA seizure invalid because it was accomplished without a court-awarded warrant.

5. *Specificity and Scope of Inspection Warrants. See In re Administrative Warrant . . . Regarding Portex, Inc.,* 585 F.2d 1152 (1st Cir. 1978); *In the Matter of Establishment Inspection of Medtronic, Inc.,* 500 F. Supp. 536 (D. Minn. 1980).

6. *Search warrants.* FDA officials are authorized to request the issuance of a search warrant under Rule 41 of the Federal Rules of Criminal Procedure pursuant to 28 C.F.R. 60.3(a)(3), promulgated in 44 Fed. Reg. 21785 (April 12, 1979).

7. *Commentary. See generally* Edward J. Allera, *Warrantless Inspections of the Food Industry,* 34 FOOD DRUG COSM. L.J. 260 (1979); Peter O. Safir, *Establishment Inspections: The Risk of Refusal,* 33 FOOD DRUG COSM. L.J. 680 (1978). A number of articles have been written on the history and interpretation of section 704 and on the practical aspects of an FDA factory inspection. In addition to those already cited, *see* Edward M. Basile, *The Law of Inspections,* 34 FOOD DRUG COSM. L.J. 20

(1979); Anthony C. Celeste, *The Inevitable FDA Inspection*, 34 Food Drug Cosm. L.J. 32 (1979); Franklin D. Clark, *Inspecting Food Processing Plants*, 18 Food Drug Cosm. L.J. 365 (1963); Linda R. Horton, *Warrantless Inspections Under the Federal Food, Drug, and Cosmetic Act*, 42 Geo. Wash. L. Rev. 1089 (1974); Peter Barton Hutt, *Factory Inspection Authority—The Statutory Viewpoint*, 22 Food Drug Cosm. L.J. 667 (1967); William L. Jackson, *FDA Inspectional Records and Freedom of Information*, 33 Food Drug Cosm. L.J. 692 (1978); Alfred S. Neely IV, *FDA Inspectional Authority—Is There an Outer Limit?*, 33 Food Drug Cosm. L.J. 710 (1978); Richard A. Shupack, *The Inspectional Process—A Statutory Overview*, 33 Food Drug Cosm. L.J. 697 (1978); W. R. M. Wharton, *Original Federal Food and Drugs Act of June 30, 1906—Its Inspection Evolution*, 1 Food Drug Cosm. L.Q. 348 (1946); Papers Presented at the 21st Annual Educational Conference of the Food and Drug Law Institute, Inc., 33 Food Drug Cosm. L.J. 100–60 (1975).

United States v. Thriftimart, Inc.

429 F.2d 1006 (9th Cir. 1970).

■ Merrill, Circuit Judge:

Appellants have been convicted of violations of the Federal Food, Drug & Cosmetic Act, 21 U.S.C. § 331(k) and § 333(a). Upon inspection, food in four company warehouses had been found to be infested with insects.... The inspectors testified that on arrival at the warehouses they approached the managers, filled out and presented their notices of inspection, requested permission to inspect and in each case were told, "Go ahead" or words of similar import....

... The precise issue raised is whether the informal and casual consent to search given by the warehouse managers made it unnecessary to secure a search warrant.... Since the managers were not warned that they had a right to refuse entry and since there was no proof that they knew they had such a right, appellants argue that the consent was not effective to remove the need for a search warrant....

... The issue in this case is whether the body of law that has grown up around the definition of consent to a search in the criminal area should mechanically be applied to the inspection of a warehouse. In a criminal search the inherent coercion of the badge and the presence of armed police make it likely that the consent to criminal search is not voluntary. Further, there is likelihood that confrontation comes as a surprise for which the citizen is unprepared and the subject of a criminal search will probably be uninformed as to his rights and the consequences of denial of entry. Finally, the consent given to a fruitful search in a criminal case is inherently suspect....

These circumstances are not present in the administrative inspection. The citizen is not likely to be uninformed or surprised. Food inspections occur with regularity. As here, the judgment as to consent to access is often a matter of company policy rather than of local managerial decision. FDA inspectors are unarmed and make their inspections during business hours. Also, the consent to an inspection is not only not suspect but is to be expected. The inspection itself is inevitable. Nothing is to be gained by

demanding a warrant except that the inspectors have been put to trouble—
an unlikely aim for the businessman anxious for administrative good will.

... Here, the managers were asked for permission to inspect; the
request implied an option to refuse and presented an opportunity to object
to the inspection in an atmosphere uncharged with coercive elements. The
fact that the inspectors did not warn the managers of their right to insist
upon a warrant and the possibility that the managers were not aware of
the precise nature of their rights under the Fourth Amendment did not
render their consent unknowing or involuntary. They, as representatives of
Thriftimart, Inc., were presented with a clear opportunity to object to the
inspection and were asked if they had any objection. Their manifestation of
assent, no matter how casual, can reasonably be accepted as waiver of
warrant.

. . . .

NOTES

1. *Supporting Authority. See also United States v. Alfred M. Lewis, Inc.*, 431
F.2d 303 (9th Cir. 1970); *United States v. Hammond Milling Co.*, 413 F.2d 608 (5th
Cir. 1969); *United States v. Stanack Sales Co.*, 387 F.2d 849 (3d Cir. 1968); *United
States v. Crescent–Kelvan Co.*, 164 F.2d 582 (3d Cir. 1948).

2. *Lack of Consent. United States v. J. B. Kramer Grocery Co., Inc.*, 418 F.2d
987 (8th Cir. 1969), held that the trial court properly suppressed evidence obtained
by an FDA inspector during a warrantless inspection of defendant's warehouse
where the evidence indicated that the inspector had so harassed and intimidated the
defendant that his consent to the inspection could not be considered voluntary. *See
also United States v. I.D. Russell Laboratories*, 439 F. Supp. 711 (W.D. Mo. 1977),
which relied upon *Kramer* to uphold the defendants' right to refuse to permit a
warrantless FDA inspection.

3. *Authority to Consent.* In *United States v. Maryland Baking Co.*, 81 F. Supp.
560 (N.D. Ga. 1948) the court held that under section 704 consent must be given by
the "owner, operator, or custodian" and not by a subordinate employee.

4. *Records Access.* In *United States v. Stanack Sales Co.*, 387 F.2d 849 (3d Cir.
1968), defendants permitted FDA inspectors to enter and inspect their premises but
refused access to their business records. The court held that, by granting access to
the premises, defendants did not waive their constitutional right to require a search
warrant or subpoena before opening their records.

3. SCOPE OF INSPECTIONS

a. RECORDS

As enacted, section 704 did not generally empower FDA to inspect
establishment records. Over time, however, Congress has repeatedly
amended the FD&C Act to grant the agency the authority to inspect an
increasingly broad array of records. The Drug Amendments of 1962 and the
Device Amendments of 1976 amended section 704(a) to authorize FDA to
inspect "records, files, papers, processes, controls, and facilities," except for
"financial data, sales data other than shipment data, pricing data, personnel data ... and research data" for prescription drugs, human OTC drugs,
and restricted devices. The 1976 device amendments also added Section

704(e), a provision giving FDA access to any records that device manufacturers, user facilities, and investigators are required to maintain under the FD&C Act. The 1980 Infant Formula Act required manufacturers to retain records and gave FDA authority to inspect these records. FD&C Act 412(b)(4); 704(a)(3). Most recently, the Bioterrorism Act of 2002 gave the agency access to records relating to an article of food when the agency has a reasonable belief that the article is adulterated and presents a threat of serious adverse health consequences or death to humans or animals. FD&C Act 414; 704(a)(1).

For some product categories, however, FDA does not have—and acknowledges that it does not have—explicit authority under the FD&C Act to inspect the records of manufacturing, processing, or storage establishments. Notable examples include food establishments in circumstances not covered by the Bioterrorism Act and cosmetics establishments. However, the absence of explicit statutory authority has not prevented FDA inspectors from requesting access to pertinent records, and often getting it. Moreover, FDA has repeatedly asserted the power to inspect food establishment records under FD&C Act provisions other than section 704.

The case below concerns an additional section of the Act that gives FDA authority to inspect records: section 703, titled "Records of Interstate Shipment." Under this section, the agency may inspect the records of shippers and receivers of FDA-regulated articles, so far as those records show "the movement in interstate commerce" of such articles, "the holding thereof after such movement," or the "quantity, shipper, and consignee thereof."

United States v. 75 Cases ... Peanut Butter, Labeled ... "Top Notch Brand"

146 F.2d 124 (4th Cir. 1944).

■ DOBIE, CIRCUIT JUDGE.

The Old Dominion Peanut Corporation (hereinafter referred to as claimant) is a corporation with its place of business in Norfolk, Virginia, engaged in manufacturing peanut butter and peanut candies. On or about October 15, 1943, one Rankin, an inspector for the Food and Drug Administration, went to claimant's plant for the purpose of making an inspection of the factory, under authority of Section 374 of the Act. He saw Stubbs, claimant's president, and revealed the purpose of his visit. Stubbs made no objection. An inspection of the factory was made and Rankin found rodent pellets and refuse in and around the food products. Chapman, claimant's plant superintendent, secured containers for Rankin and samples of the food products were taken.

After the completion of the factory inspection, Rankin asked to see the company invoices for the purpose of ascertaining where shipments of these food products were being made. Mizzell, the claimant's sales manager, produced the invoices for Rankin's inspection. No objection whatever was made by either Stubbs or Mizzell....

The District Court found, and we agree with this finding, that permission to inspect the factory was fully and freely given. Further findings were made to the effect that permission was given to Rankin to inspect the claimant's invoices; but the District Court held that this permission was secured by a method that "smacks of surprise, if not of actual misrepresentation." This finding was predicated on the Court's interpretation of the requirements of Section 373 of the Act [21 U.S.C. § 373; FDCA § 703], and was, we think, clearly erroneous.

Section 373 of the Act provides as follows: "For the purpose of enforcing the provisions of this chapter, carriers engaged in interstate commerce, and persons receiving food, drugs, devices, or cosmetics in interstate commerce or holding such articles so received, shall, upon the request of an officer or employee duly designated by the Administrator, permit such officer or employee, at reasonable times, to have access to and to copy all records showing the movement in interstate commerce of any food, drug, device, or cosmetic, or the holding thereof during or after such movement, and the quantity, shipper, and consignee thereof; and it shall be unlawful for any such carrier or person to fail to permit such access to and copying of any such record so requested when such request is accompanied by a statement in writing specifying the nature or kind of food, drug, device, or cosmetic to which such request relates."

The Court below has taken the position, that since Section 373 "meticulously" sets out the method by which information as to interstate shipments is to be obtained, should the Government choose to avail itself of any other method, it must make a full and complete disclosure to the claimant and make sure that claimant's consent is not due in any respect to a failure to understand the fullest use to which the records might be put by the Government.

While we agree that in no case should the Government be permitted to use fraudulent methods in obtaining evidence, we think that the District Court has here placed an unduly narrow construction on this statute. No such interpretation is warranted, either by the words of the Act, by its purpose, or by its legislative history.

Section 373 was enacted to provide a compulsory method by which information of interstate shipments, necessary to the enforcement of the Act, might be obtained from carriers. The need for such a method is obvious since interstate transportation is, in large part, done by common carriers. The lack of such a provision had proved a definite handicap to the enforcement of the Act. But this section does not require that investigation must be limited to the records of the classes of persons therein enumerated. Nothing in the legislative history of the Act indicates any such intent on the part of Congress.

Claimant contends here, as it did below, that since the Act provides that the records of carriers and receivers may be examined, this excludes the examination of the claimant's records. We agree with the District Court that the prescribing of certain compulsory methods of investigation does not exclude permissive investigation. The affidavit filed by Stubbs clearly shows the unfortunate result which would follow from a contrary view. The affiant there states that one of the interstate shipments involved was moved by the purchaser in his own truck. Such an instance reveals the difficulties confronted by those administering the Act, should permissive examination of the shipper's records be denied. In such cases there would be no common carrier's records to be examined. Such a view would clearly not be in conformity with the purposes of the Act.

Reversed and remanded.

NOTES

1. *Voluntary Disclosure.* Section 703 provides that "evidence obtained under this section . . . shall not be used in a criminal prosecution of the person from whom obtained. . . ." In *United States v. Arnold's Pharmacy, Inc.*, 116 F. Supp. 310 (D.N.J. 1953), the defendants were convicted of dispensing prescription drugs without a physician's authorization. The government's evidence included the pharmacy's shipping and prescription records, which the defendant had voluntarily shown to FDA inspectors. At trial, the defendants sought to suppress this evidence on the ground that it had been "obtained under" section 703 of the Act and therefore could not be used to support their prosecution. The court rejected this claim:

> . . . [T]he purpose of the provision here in question was to close an earlier loophole in the enforcement provisions of the act, which handicapped its enforcement, this handicap being caused by the refusal of certain carriers, if not others, to permit the copying of essential records. In other words, where, as was generally the case, these records were willingly made available to the Government, so that the Act could readily be enforced, the previous law was effective. But, in cases where this access and copying was refused, the section in question would apply to overcome such refusal, and eliminate such "handicap to its (the Act's) enforcement."
>
> . . .
>
> Since the evidence here was voluntarily turned over to the Government by its owners, the conditions for the applicability of the statutory provision in question did not exist, and the statute does not apply. And since the evidence was not obtained unconstitutionally, defendant's motion for the suppression, impounding and return of the evidence, is denied.

For other cases holding that section 703 applies only where the person refused to provide the requested records voluntarily and FDA requests them in writing, *see United States v. Herold*, 136 F. Supp. 15 (E.D.N.Y. 1955); *United States v. Lyon Drug Co.*, 122 F. Supp. 597 (E.D. Wis. 1954). As a result of these decisions, FDA rarely makes a written request for records under section 703.

2. *Pharmacy Exemption.* Section 704(a)(2)(A) explicitly exempts from FDA records inspection "pharmacies which maintain establishments in conformance with any applicable local laws regulating the practice of pharmacy . . . and which do not . . . manufacture, prepare, propagate, compound, or process drugs or devices for sale other than in the regular course of their business of dispensing or selling drugs or devices at retail." In *Wedgewood Village Pharmacy v. United States*, 421 F.3d 263 (3d Cir. 2005), FDA obtained a warrant to inspect a pharmacy's "production and distribution records to determine the extent to which [its] activities are consistent with those of a drug manufacturer rather than a retail pharmacy, and to evaluate the extent of violations of the [FD&C Act]." The Third Circuit rejected the pharmacy's assertion that it was eligible for the 704(a)(2)(A) exemption and that the inspection was therefore illegal. FDA's Compliance Policy Guide 460.200 sets forth a nine-factor approach for distinguishing manufacturing activities subject to FD&C Act enforcement from compounding activities outside the scope of the FDCA.

Wedgewood held that CPG 460.200's factors are reasonable and that, given the averments of the warrant application, "it was therefore reasonable for the FDA to conclude that Wedgewood may be engaged in activity inconsistent with its status as a retail pharmacy."

3. *Medical Practitioner's Exemption.* Section 704(a)(2)(B) exempts from records inspection any practitioner who is licensed by law to prescribe or administer drugs and who manufactures those drugs solely for use in his professional practice. In *United States v. Jacobs*, Food Drugs Cosm. L. Rep. (CCH) ¶ 38,123 (E.D. Cal. 1989), the court ruled against suppression despite the failure of an FDA inspector either to request the defendant physician's permission to inspect records or to inform the defendant that his inspection authority did not extend to the records of a licensed physician. Because the defendant had not objected to the inspection, the court concluded that he consented.

4. *Contract Laboratories.* Where a contract research organization assumed responsibilities for clinical trials regulated by FDA, the court held in *Leo Winter Associates, Inc. v. Department HHS*, 497 F. Supp. 429 (D.D.C. 1980), that the organization was subject to FDA inspection of its records under section 704.

COMMENT: FDA ASSERTIONS OF RECORD INSPECTION AUTHORITY

FDA has a long history of creatively establishing record inspection powers outside the explicit grant in section 704. For example, in the early 1970s, the agency was concerned about the contamination of low-acid canned foods and acidified foods with *Clostridium botulinum* toxin. It wanted processors of these products to submit detailed information about their manufacturing processes and to provide FDA inspectors with access to processing records and other documents. Since section 704 did not authorize inspection of records in food establishments, FDA turned instead to section 404 ("Emergency Permit Control"), which authorizes the agency to require permits for foods that might be dangerous because of contamination with microorganisms. Instead of directly mandating recordkeeping and access, FDA by regulation required producers of acidified foods and low-acid canned foods to disclose processing records as a condition for avoiding the imposition of emergency permit controls. 21 C.F.R. 108.25(c)(3)(ii) & (g); 108.35(c)(3)(ii) and (h).

In 1974, before section 704 was amended by the Medical Device Amendments to allow inspection of records in certain device establishments, FDA sought and was granted a permanent injunction by a federal court authorizing the agency to inspect the records of the manufacturer of the Diapulse, a misbranded device. The manufacturer appealed the injunction, contending that the 1962 amendment to section 704 specifically allowing inspection of the records of prescription drug manufacturers implied that such authority did not exist with respect to other products. The Second Circuit rejected this argument and upheld the injunction. *United States v. Diapulse Corp.*, 514 F.2d 1097 (2d Cir. 1975). *See* Eugene M. Elson, *Inspection of Records*, 5 Food Drug Cosm. L.J. 755 (1950); George McKray, *Record Inspection 1906–1963*, 18 Food Drug Cosm. L.J. 301 & 380 (1963). *See also* James Harvey Young, *From Oysters to After–Dinner Mints: The Role of the Early Food and Drug Inspector*, 42 J. Hist. Med. & Allied Sci. 30 (1987).

In the 1990s, as discussed *supra* p. 351, FDA decided to establish a Hazard Analysis and Critical Control Point (HACCP) approach to regulating seafood safety. The very concept of HACCP is premised on the assumption that an establishment will maintain accurate records of its production operations. As discussed above, the low-acid canned food and acidified food regulations gave FDA access to processing records by conditioning exceptions to the section 404 emergency permit system on the provision of such access. When FDA proposed its seafood HACCP regulations in 1994, some comments suggested that the agency should once again base its claim to records access on section 404. 60 Fed. Reg. 65096, 65101–02 (Dec. 18, 1995). The agency, however, rejected this approach, observing that the permit system applied only in emergency situations and only to hazards from micro-organisms. Instead, FDA found broader authority to demand access to seafood establishment records under section 402, the adulterated food provisions, and section 701(a), the provision giving the agency "authority to promulgate regulations for the efficient enforcement of this Act." *Id*. at 65101. The agency rejected the contention that the explicit grant of records access for drugs and devices in section 704 precluded the agency from extending its access to other types of records.

> FDA has concluded ... that these regulations are consistent with section 704 of the act and with the act as a whole. Because the preventive controls required by HACCP are essential to the production of safe food as a matter of design, the statutory scheme is benefited by agency access to records that demonstrate that these controls are being systematically applied. The case law supports FDA's authority to require such recordkeeping and to have access to such records.

Not surprisingly, nobody has challenged the records access provision of the seafood HACCP regulations (21 C.F.R. 123.10(c)) in court. Nor has anybody challenged an essentially identical provision in FDA's 2001 HACCP regulations for juices. 21 C.F.R. 120.12(d)(1). In both situations, the industries were under severe public criticism and could not risk the consequences of opposing FDA. In 2003, the agency proposed current good manufacturing practice (CGMP) regulations for dietary supplements, including record access requirements. Once again, FDA appears to be basing its record access authority on a broad reading of sections 402 and 701. 68 Fed. Reg. 12157, 12168 (March 13, 2003). Because dietary supplement manufacturers have hardly been shy about launching legal challenges against FDA regulations, a court may soon have the chance to opine on the legality of FDA's approach.

b. SAMPLES AND PHOTOGRAPHS

Triangle Candy Co. v. United States

144 F.2d 195 (9th Cir. 1944).

■ DENMAN, CIRCUIT JUDGE.

This is an appeal by defendants and appellants, Triangle Candy Company, a corporation, and Bernard G. Kennepohl, from judgments rendered against them after appellants were found guilty on six counts of violation of the Federal Food, Drug, and Cosmetic Act. . . .

There were seven counts in the information. The adulteration charge was twofold in character in all but the first count. Alleged in each count was adulteration under 21 U.S.C. § 342(a)(4), providing that a food shall be deemed adulterated "if it has been prepared, packed, or held under insanitary conditions whereby it may have become contaminated with filth, or whereby it may have been rendered injurious to health." In all counts save the first it was additionally alleged that there was adulteration of the candy involved under 21 U.S.C. § 342(a)(3), providing that a food shall be deemed to be adulterated "if it consists in whole or in part of any filthy, putrid, or decomposed substance, or if it is otherwise unfit for food." . . .

It is the contention of the appellants that Congress made the supplying to them of part of the samples whose analysis provided the basis for the charges a condition precedent to the maintenance of a prosecution under the Act. . . .

The sample provision requirement of the Act [, section 702(b), provides that, when FDA inspectors collect a sample for analysis, a portion shall be provided to the owner upon request, subject to reasonable exceptions established by regulation.]

. . . [FDA regulations, 21 C.F.R. 2.10(b), provide:] "When an officer or employee collects an official sample . . . he shall collect at least twice the quantity estimated by him to be sufficient for analysis, unless [one of the subsequent listed exceptions applies]," none of them pertinent to the facts of this case. . . .

The only testimony regarding the amount of the samples left after analysis was not from any collector but from the government's chief chemist of the Los Angeles station to whom the collector sent the collected samples. He nowhere testified that double the amount deemed needed for analysis was received. . . . All he testified to is that "the reason why samples were not furnished which the candy company requested was because all the samples at the Los Angeles station were used in the course of the analyses by the chemists involved; that there was no candy left over after the analyses [which] could be sent to them."

It is thus apparent that the government, failing to supply the demanded samples, has not brought itself within the exceptions of the regulations created under the statute. The problem thus becomes one of the effect of such failure to obey the mandate that the Administrator "shall . . . provide" the samples. . . .

We hold that the provision is not merely directory—for the guidance of the Administrator—but mandatorily gives the right to samples to the accused manufacturers, unless the Administrator brings himself within the excepting regulations. . . .

. . . If those accused under the Act are not given a portion of the sample, their power to make a complete defense is substantially curtailed. Intent is no part of the crime with which they are charged. If they have introduced the food into interstate commerce, and if it is adulterated, they are guilty, regardless of their intent or lack of knowledge as to adulteration.

It may frequently happen that the single factual issue is that of adultera-tion. Without access to a portion of the sample, they are confronted by a government analysis of that sample which they cannot refute but at best, and with difficulty, impeach by challenging the government's method of sampling and testing.

Section 372(b), then, must have been intended to provide defendants with an opportunity for independent analysis; and it is clear that the results of such analysis may be among the most important pieces of evidence defendants can offer in their own behalf. Deprival of the chance to make this test . . . prejudices defendants' substantial rights. This consider-ation, added to the statute's mandatory wording, and the analogy of cases under other acts, lead us to the conclusion that provision of a portion of the sample, save in properly excepted cases, is a condition precedent to prosecu-tion.

Since, despite seasonable written request, no samples of the food involved . . . were furnished defendants, nor any reason offered for this failure, the convictions on these counts must be reversed. . . .

NOTES

1. *Sample Size.* In *United States v. Roux Laboratories, Inc.*, 456 F. Supp. 973 (M.D. Fla. 1978), the court rejected the contention that FDA inspectors' demand for an eight-ounce total sample of expensive cosmetic ingredients was unreasonable. The court also rejected Roux's claim that the agency should be required to disclose in advance what tests it intended to conduct.

2. *FDA Analysis.* The defendant in *United States v. Durbin*, 373 F. Supp. 1136 (E.D. Okl. 1974), owner of a wholesale grocery business, asked for both a reserve sample and the FDA analysis of its samples. The court responded:

> . . . [T]he Plaintiff acknowledges that Defendant is entitled to a part of the samples but resists Defendant's request for a copy of an analysis of the samples. Though it may be arguable whether Defendant is entitled to a copy of said analysis pursuant to 21 U.S.C. § 374(d) because he is not a manufacturer, processor, or packer, it appears to the Court that such analysis would be a scientific test under Rule 16(a)(2), Federal Rules of Criminal Procedure, and is therefore discoverable under said Rule.

3. *Agency Practice. See also United States v. Gnome Bakers, Inc.*, 135 F. Supp. 273 (S.D.N.Y. 1955), which held that the requirement that FDA furnish a receipt for any sample does not apply where the agency buys the product at retail. FDA has issued regulations respecting samples in 21 C.F.R. 2.10.

Frederick H. Branding & James M. Ellis, *Underdeveloped: FDA's Authority to Take Photographs During an FDA Establishment Inspection Under Section 704*

58 FOOD & DRUG LAW JOURNAL 9 (2003).

As a guide to FDA investigators, FDA maintains an *Investigations Operations Manual* (IOM). The IOM describes to its field personnel the procedures to follow in conducting establishment inspections.

. . . IOM Subchapter 523, entitled *Photographs—Photocopies*, discusses the taking of photographs and the making of photocopies during inspections:

> Since photographs are one of the most effective and useful forms of evidence, *every one should be taken with a purpose*. Photographs should be related to insanitary conditions contributing or likely to contribute filth to the finished product, or to practices likely to render it injurious or otherwise violative.

The IOM cites seven examples of conditions or practices that may be "effectively documented by photographs.". . . .

Subchapter 523 further discusses *In-Plant Photographs* and directs investigators to assume that they have authority to take photographs. Inspectors are instructed as follows:

> Do not request permission from management to take photographs during an inspection. Take your camera into the firm and use it as necessary just as you use other inspectional equipment.

> If management objects to the taking of photographs, explain that photos are an integral part of an inspection and present an accurate picture of plant conditions. Advise management that the U.S. courts have held photographs may lawfully be taken as part of an inspection.

Section 704 of the FDCA states that the inspection must be conducted during "reasonable times," "within reasonable limits," and in a "reasonable manner." . . . The scope of an establishment inspection (*i.e.*, "reasonable time," "reasonable limits," and "reasonable manner") is rarely litigated. When an inspection is challenged, courts usually favor the agency.

When an investigator complies with the statutory requirements of section 704, FDA's right to inspect is extremely broad. Refusal to permit FDA investigators access to inspect a facility, assuming the investigator presents proper identification and a valid inspection notice, is a violation of section 301(f) of the FDCA. The refusal may be partial or total. . . .

Whether a refusal to allow photographs is an actual refusal of the inspection under section 704 is not settled. FDA considers a "refusal" to mean refusing to permit an inspection or prohibiting an investigator from obtaining information to which the agency is entitled by law. An investigator may characterize a firm's nonconsent to the taking of photographs as a refusal of the inspection or of information. In the absence of explicit legal authority in the statute, however, such nonconsent should not, as a matter of legal interpretation, be referred to as a refusal of the inspection. Nevertheless, if the refusal is of such a character that the investigator determines that he or she cannot conduct a satisfactory inspection or obtain information to which FDA is entitled under the Act, the investigator is instructed to contact his or her supervisor to determine whether an administrative inspection warrant should be requested.

When an investigator encounters either a partial or total refusal, FDA may seek an administrative inspection warrant from a federal magistrate judge. If FDA feels compelled to obtain such an order from the court, it is probable that the inspection warrant will contain language specifically authorizing the taking of photographs. . . .

FDA cites two cases in the IOM to support its authority to take photographs: *Dow Chemical v. United States*, 476 U.S. 227 (1986), and *United States v. Acri Wholesale Grocery Company*, 409 F. Supp. 529 (S.D. Iowa 1976). If management continues to refuse the taking of photographs, investigators are instructed to provide management with references to the *Dow Chemical* and *Acri Wholesale Grocery Co.* cases as support for FDA's authority to take photographs during inspections. Neither *Dow Chemical* nor *Acri Wholesale Grocery Co.* specifically addresses FDA's authority to take photographs during inspections and, more importantly, neither case addresses whether a company may refuse the taking of photographs during an inspection.

In *Dow*, the taking of aerial photographs by the Environmental Protection Agency (EPA), pursuant to the Clean Air Act, was upheld as a valid exercise of EPA's inspectional powers and not a violation of Dow Chemical's Fourth Amendment privacy rights. In support of its interpretation that photographs may lawfully be taken as part of an inspection, the IOM quotes, in part, the Supreme Court: "When Congress invests an agency with enforcement and investigatory authority, it is not necessary to identify explicitly each and every technique that may be used in the course of executing the statutory mission." The *Dow* case did not deal with FDA's authority under the FDCA, nor did the *Dow* case deal with the taking of photographs *inside* a plant during an establishment inspection. . . .

In *Acri*, the court admitted into evidence photographs taken by FDA investigators while inside a food warehouse. FDA's authority to take the photographs, however, was not at issue. In *Acri*, no objection was made to the taking of the photographs at the time of the inspection, so the court determined the company had consented to the taking of photographs. Thus, *Acri* does not support FDA's claimed right to take photographs during an establishment inspection, absent consent from the establishment.

In addition to *Dow* and *Acri*, two other cases address FDA's inspectional authority where photographs were taken during the inspections. . . .

Although neither [*United States v. Jamieson–McKames Pharmaceuticals, Inc.*, 651 F.2d 532 (8th Cir. 1981) (*supra* p. 1245)] nor [*United States v. Gel Spice Co., Inc.*, 601 F. Supp. 1214 (E.D.N.Y. 1985)], addressed the specific issue of whether section 704 authorized the taking of photographs, both decisions appear to support FDA's broad inspectional authority, based on a flexible standard of reasonableness, once consent to the inspection is given.

It also appears from the case law that once consent is given to inspect the facility, it may be too late to refuse the taking of the photographs. Under such circumstances, the issue then becomes whether the inspection (and the taking of the photographs) was reasonable. Such determinations, perhaps made at a later time by a court, are heavily influenced by the particular facts and circumstances associated with the inspection, including a firm's regulatory history.

NOTES

1. *Photographs. See* Nicholas Freitag, *Federal Food and Drug Act Violations*, 41 AM. CRIM. L. REV. 647 663–64 (2004).

2. *Tape Recording.* In *American Dietaids Co. v. Celebrezze*, 317 F.2d 658 (2d Cir. 1963), the court declined to rule on the legality of FDA inspectors' surreptitious use of tape recorders, concluding that there was no showing that the agency intended soon to reinspect the plaintiff's premises using recorders. The use of tape recorders and other electronic surveillance equipment by FDA inspectors was the subject of three days of congressional hearings, during which a number of FDA cases involving such equipment were discussed in detail. "Invasions of Privacy (Government Agencies)," Hearings on S. Res. 39 Before the Subcomm. on Administrative Practice and Procedure of the Senate Comm. on the Judiciary, Part 2, 89th Cong., 1st Sess. (1965). The agency has since adopted a policy against any use of tape recorders during an inspection.

COMMENT: THE USDA INSPECTION REGIME

The FDA method of intermittent random factory inspections, coupled with occasional "for cause" inspections, differs markedly from the continuous factory inspection by resident inspectors conducted by USDA's Food Safety and Inspection Service (FSIS). In accordance with the Federal Meat Inspection Act and the Poultry Products Inspection Act, FSIS inspectors not only conduct sanitary inspections of slaughtering and packing establishments, but also perform mandatory carcass-by-carcass inspections, apply inspection marks to carcasses and parts that pass inspection, and require the destruction of those found to be adulterated. The labor-intensiveness of this inspection regime explains why the number of inspectors at FSIS (approximately 7,400 in 2003) dwarfs the number available to FDA's Center for Food Safety and Applied Nutrition (fewer than 1,200 in 2004).

Critics have long questioned the merits of this approach. Continuous inspection of the type conducted by FSIS is extremely costly. Moreover, USDA's continuous inspection programs, with their resident inspectors, have sometimes been vulnerable to compromise by inspected firms. The *Report of the USDA Food Safety and Quality Service Task Force on Program Quality* (October 1979) concluded that continuous factory inspection "because of its structure and functions is inherently vulnerable to corruption" and recommended a new "integrity program" to combat this problem.

By the 1970s, the traditional "poke-and-sniff" approach used by FSIS inspectors began to seem inadequate in light of growing concern about the dangers of microbial pathogens undetectable by organoleptic (sight, touch, and smell) methods. USDA thus began to experiment with different forms of continuous inspection for meat and poultry, including total quality control (TQC) and partial quality control (PQC) systems that gave meat and poultry establishments more responsibility to control their own production under FSIS oversight. *See* 45 Fed. Reg. 54310 (August 15, 1980), 50 Fed. Reg. 33348 (August 19, 1985), 51 Fed. Reg. 32301 (September 11, 1986). These precursors to HACCP led finally, in 1996, to the issuance of an FSIS rule imposing HACCP requirements on meat and poultry establishments, with the stated goal of reducing pathogenic microorganisms in meat and poultry products. 60 Fed. Reg. 6774 (February 3, 1995), 61 Fed. Reg. 38806 (July 25, 1996), 9 C.F.R 417. The rule required first large plants, then small plants, then very small plants to adopt HACCP, and by 2000 the approach was mandatory for the entire industry.

Congress might have used the adoption of HACCP as an occasion to end FSIS "continuous inspection" and severely reduce the number of meat and poultry inspectors. Indeed, during the implementation of the FSIS rule, the inspectors' union warned of this result. *See* George Anthan, *Inspectors Decry New Meat System*, DES MOINES REG., Jan. 21, 1999, at B9. But to this point, carcass-by-carcass inspection remains required by law, the massive force reductions predicted by the union have not come to pass, and the primary change confronted by the inspectors has been the incorporation of HACCP-related document inspection into their traditional duties. *See American Fed. Gov't Emps. v. Glickman*, 215 F.3d 7 (D.C. Cir. 2000) (federal employees must inspect every carcass, despite implementation of HACCP); Richard A. Merrill & Jeffrey K. Francer, *Organizing Federal Food Safety Regulation*, 31 SETON HALL L. REV. 61, 100–04 (2000).

D.   SEIZURE

Section 304 of the FD&C Act, titled "Seizure," sets forth a two-step process. First, it authorizes the United States to proceed against adulterated or misbranded articles (or unapproved drugs) "on libel of information" and seize the articles. Second, the section empowers the federal district courts, after trial, to decree the "condemnation" of such articles and order them destroyed, sold, or returned to the owner for destruction, reconditioning, or, in some instances, export.

1.   THE SEIZURE PROCESS

United States of America v. Argent Chemical Laboratories, Inc.

93 F.3d 572 (9th Cir. 1996).

■ CANBY, CIRCUIT JUDGE:

Under procedures authorized by Congress, the Food and Drug Administration ("FDA") seized allegedly adulterated products from the premises of a regulated veterinary drug manufacturer, without obtaining a warrant from a judicial officer issued upon a finding of probable cause. The question before us is whether that seizure violated the Fourth Amendment. We conclude that it did not, and we reverse the judgment of the district court.

I.   The Factual Background

Argent Chemical Laboratories manufactures and repackages veterinary drugs. FDA agents inspected Argent several times between the summer of 1993 and May 1994 to ensure compliance with the Food, Drug, and

Cosmetic Act ("Act"). The FDA cited Argent for certain deficiencies. Several months after the last inspection, the FDA agents secured from the Deputy Clerk of the District Court, without the intervention of a judicial officer or a showing of probable cause, an *in rem* arrest warrant for various veterinary drugs alleged to violate the Act. FDA agents and United States Marshals then seized over $100,000 worth of veterinary drugs from Argent's premises. This condemnation action followed. Argent appeared as claimant and contested the constitutionality of the seizure. The district court held that the seizure violated the Fourth Amendment; it accordingly granted Argent's motion to quash the *in rem* arrest warrant and ordered the government to return the property. The government appealed, and the district court stayed its order pending the appeal.

II. The Statutory Scheme of Seizure

The warrant in this case was issued in accordance with the Act. Under the Act, an article "proceeded against shall be liable to seizure by process pursuant to the libel, and the procedures in cases under this section shall conform, as nearly as may be, to the procedure in admiralty...." 21 U.S.C. § 334(b). Under the Supplemental Rules for Certain Admiralty and Maritime Claims ("Supplemental Rules"), an *in rem* action begins with a complaint that must "be verified on oath or solemn affirmation" and that must "describe with reasonable particularity the property that is the subject of the action." Supplemental Rule C(2). Upon filing of the complaint, the clerk issues a warrant:

> Except in actions by the United States for forfeitures for federal statutory violations, the verified complaint and any supporting papers shall be reviewed by the court and, if the conditions for an action in rem appear to exist, an order so stating and authorizing a warrant for the arrest of the vessel or other property that is the subject of the action shall issue and be delivered to the clerk who shall prepare the warrant.
>
> . . . .
>
> *In actions by the United States for forfeitures for federal statutory violations, the clerk, upon filing of the complaint, shall forthwith issue a summons and warrant for the arrest of the vessel or other property....*

Supplemental Rule C(3) (emphasis added). Thus, because this was an action by the United States for a forfeiture for federal statutory violations, FDA agents were able to obtain a warrant without review by a judicial officer or a finding of probable cause.

III. The Fourth Amendment and the Colonnade–Biswell Exception

Argent argues that, although the drugs were seized pursuant to a warrant issued in accordance with the Act, the seizure violated the Fourth Amendment's prohibition of unreasonable searches and seizures and its requirement that warrants issue upon probable cause. We conclude, however, that Argent's argument is defeated by the nature of its business and the regulation to which it is subject.

The Fourth Amendment applies to commercial premises as well as to private homes, but under the so-called *Colonnade-Biswell* exception, warrantless searches and seizures on commercial property used in "closely regulated" industries are constitutionally permissible. *Colonnade Catering Corp. v. United States*, 397 U.S. 72 (1970); *United States v. Biswell*, 406 U.S. 311 (1972). Persons engaging in pervasively regulated industries have a diminished expectation of privacy. With regard to such industries, "Congress has broad authority to fashion standards of reasonableness for searches and seizures." *Colonnade*, 397 U.S. at 77 . . . .

Argent asserts that it is not subject to the *Colonnade-Biswell* exception for two reasons: first, its veterinary drug business is not the kind of industry that is subject to the *Colonnade-Biswell* exception; and second, the *Colonnade-Biswell* exception does not extend to a separate and particularized seizure of misbranded or adulterated goods. We reject both contentions.

IV.   *Manufacture of Veterinary Drugs as a Closely Regulated Industry*

In *New York v. Burger*, 482 U.S. 691 (1987), the Supreme Court set forth the standards for determining when the *Colonnade-Biswell* exception applies. A warrantless inspection will be deemed reasonable only if the business is closely regulated and if three criteria are met:

> First, there must be a "substantial" government interest that informs the regulatory scheme pursuant to which the inspection is made. . . .

> Second, the warrantless inspections must be "necessary to further [the] regulatory scheme." . . .

> Finally, "the statute's inspection program, in terms of the certainty and regularity of its application, [must] provide a constitutionally adequate substitute for a warrant."

We conclude that all of these standards are met in this case.

As a threshold matter, the veterinary drug industry is "closely regulated." . . .

FDA regulation of Argent's industry also meets the three enumerated criteria of *Burger*. First, there is "a 'substantial' government interest that informs the regulatory scheme pursuant to which the inspection is made." . . . Congress has seen fit, either for human safety or for economic reasons, to regulate animal drugs to ensure their safety and effectiveness. Whether the interest is human health, economic health, or both, we conclude that it is substantial.

Second, "the warrantless inspections [are] 'necessary to further [the] regulatory scheme.'" *Burger*, 482 U.S. at 702. Unannounced inspections have a deterrent effect; forcing inspectors to obtain a warrant before inspection might frustrate the purpose of the Act by alerting owners to inspections. Moreover, this court has recognized the "need for swift governmental action to remove misbranded products from the stream of commerce." . . .

Finally, the regulatory scheme, " 'in terms of the certainty and regularity of its application, [provides] a constitutionally adequate substitute for a warrant,' " thereby satisfying the third *Burger* requirement. "The regulatory statute must perform the two basic functions of a warrant: it must advise the owner of the commercial premises that the search is being made pursuant to the law and has a properly defined scope, and it must limit the discretion of the inspecting officers." *Id.* Taken as a whole, the Act, the accompanying regulations, and the Supplemental Rules for Certain Admiralty and Maritime Claims provide a constitutionally adequate substitute for a warrant. Inspections are conducted with notice furnished at the time, and their scope is limited by statute. 21 U.S.C. § 374(a)(1). Seizures are limited to drugs that are adulterated or misbranded, 21 U.S.C. § 334(a)(1), the articles to be seized must be described "with reasonable particularity," Supplemental Rules C(2), and the government's complaint must be "verified on oath or solemn affirmation." Moreover, in most cases, the seizure is subject to the approval of one of the Food and Drug Administration's district offices, the appropriate office (or "center") in the Food and Drug Administration headquarters, the Food and Drug Administration's Office of Enforcement, the Office of the Chief Counsel, and the Department of Justice. *See* FDA REGULATORY PROCEDURES MANUAL, ch. 6, at 173–85 (Aug. 1995).

We conclude, therefore, that Argent's operation, as regulated by the FDA, falls within the *Colonnade-Biswell* exception to the Fourth Amendment's warrant requirement.

V. *The Particularized Seizure and the Warrant Requirement of the Theramatic Case*

Argent next contends that, even if it is a "closely regulated" industry for purposes of the *Colonnade-Biswell* exception, that exception does not apply to the seizure in this case. To the extent that Argent's argument suggests that the *Colonnade-Biswell* exception applies only to inspections and not to seizures, the argument is untenable. It is true that *Burger* discussed its criteria for "closely regulated" industries in terms of "inspections," but it also approved the use of evidence seized in the course of the inspection. Moreover, both *Colonnade* and *Biswell* involved seizures of contraband discovered during the unwarranted inspections.... Thus, *Colonnade-Biswell* extends to seizure without warrant of what may be inspected without warrant, when Congress so authorizes.

The argument that Argent most vigorously asserts, and the one that was accepted by the district court, is based on our decision in *United States v. Device Labeled "Theramatic"*, 641 F.2d 1289 (9th Cir. 1981) (*"Theramatic I"*). In *Theramatic I*, we held that the Fourth Amendment was violated by the FDA's seizure from a physician's office of an allegedly misbranded medical device pursuant to a warrant issued under the Supplemental Rules. We emphasized that the physician was entitled to the protection of the Fourth Amendment in his office just as he was in his home. We recognized that some administrative searches could be conducted on the strength of a warrant issued on less than probable cause, but the government in *Theramatic I* was not conducting random inspections to enforce administrative standards; it was "searching a particular physician's office to seize a particular, identified device." Finally, we said that the *Colonnade-Biswell* exception to the warrant requirement did not apply because "the search at issue here was not part of any statutory program to inspect physicians' offices."

We do not draw from *Theramatic I* the same lessons that Argent and the district court did. The problem with the seizure in *Theramatic I* was that it was effectuated by an impermissible invasion of the physician's right of privacy. That is why we were careful in *Theramatic I* to point out that the case involved not only a seizure, "but a paradigmatic search—a physical intrusion by the U.S. Marshal into [the physician's] office." *Id.* at 1291. We also stated:

> It is one thing to seize without a warrant property resting in an open area or seizable by levy without an intrusion into privacy, and it is quite another thing to effect a warrantless seizure of property, even that owned by a corporation, situated on private premises *to which access is not otherwise available for the seizing officer*.

The *Colonnade–Biswell* exception did not apply because it is based largely on the diminished expectation of privacy in a closely-regulated industry, and the physician in *Theramatic I* was not closely regulated by the FDA.

The district court, however, accepted Argent's interpretation of *Theramatic I*, concluding that "although a well-defined scheme for inspecting pervasively regulated businesses may survive Fourth Amendment scrutiny, the protection against unreasonable searches and seizures may nevertheless prevent government agents from returning to conduct a particularized search and seizure without first obtaining an ordinary warrant." The District Court held that *Theramatic I* forbade agents from searching "a particular business to seize particular, identified chemicals and drugs." . . .

. . . [I]t is the invasion of privacy, not the particularity of the seizure, that is the relevant difference between Argent's case and *Theramatic I* for purposes of the *Colonnade-Biswell* exception. Argent, being closely regulated by the FDA, has a diminished expectation of privacy that was not violated by the seizure. We attach no significance to the fact that the FDA "returned" to execute its *in rem* warrant some time after its last inspection. If a random, unannounced inspection does not violate Argent's Fourth Amendment right of privacy, we see no reason why the unannounced execution of a warrant under the Supplemental Rules would do so. The seizure is from the premises of a closely regulated manufacturer and is conducted within the regulatory scheme in the manner Congress has authorized. There is no need to brigade the seizure with an inspection in order to legitimize it; Argent's expectation of privacy has not been violated.

. . . .

REVERSED.

NOTES

1. *Seizures from Non–Closely–Regulated Industries.* In the *Theramatic* decision, distinguished by the court in *Argent Chemical*, the Ninth Circuit struck down

a section 304 seizure of a diathermy machine and accompanying leaflets from a neurosurgeon's office because the seizure did not satisfy Fourth Amendment requirements. 641 F.2d 1289 (9th Cir. 1981). As the *Theramatic* court itself acknowledged, however, this decision was in tension with decisions by two other Circuits: *Founding Church of Scientology v. United States*, 409 F.2d 1146 (D.C. Cir. 1969) (seizure of devices from church facilities); *United States v. Articles of Hazardous Substance*, 588 F.2d 39 (4th Cir. 1978) (seizure of pajamas from retail store).

2. *Specificity of Warrant.* For contrasting views about the specificity needed in the warrant of seizure, compare *United States v. An Article of Food ... "Sof–T–Salt Meat Curing General Purpose Salt,"* Food Drug Cosm. L. Rep. (CCH) ¶ 38,325 (N.D. Ala. 1985), with *United States v. Articles of Drug ... Ru–Vert*, Food Drug Cosm. L. Rep. (CCH) ¶ 38,201 (W.D. La. 1982).

3. *Counterfeiting Equipment.* Under section 304(a)(2), any equipment used in counterfeiting a drug may also be confiscated. *United States v. All Equipment Including, but not Limited to, an Encapsulating Machine*, 475 F. Supp. 39 (E.D. Mo. 1979).

4. *Seizure of Labeling.* The power of seizure extends to product labeling as well as to the article itself. *E.g., United States v. 8 Cartons, Containing "Plantation 'The Original' ... Molasses,"* 103 F. Supp. 626 (W.D.N.Y. 1951). But *United States v. Vitasafe Corp.*, 345 F.2d 864 (3d Cir. 1965), held that promotional material labeling for an illegal product could not be condemned unless it had "accompanied" the product in interstate commerce.

5. *Removal of Labeling. Lee v. United States*, 187 F.2d 1005 (10th Cir. 1951), held that if a device was misbranded when introduced into interstate commerce, while in interstate commerce, or when held for sale after shipment in interstate commerce, the removal of the illegal labeling before seizure does not render the device immune from seizure and condemnation.

2.   INJUNCTIONS RESTRAINING SEIZURES OR ORDERING RELEASE OF SEIZED GOODS PRIOR TO TRIAL

Ewing v. Mytinger & Casselberry, Inc.

339 U.S. 594 (1950).

■ MR. JUSTICE DOUGLAS delivered the opinion of the Court.

This is an appeal from a three-judge District Court specially constituted on appellee's application for an injunction to restrain enforcement of a portion of an Act of Congress for repugnance to the Due Process Clause of the Fifth Amendment.

Section 304(a) of the Federal Food, Drug, and Cosmetic Act ... permits multiple seizures of misbranded articles "when the Administrator has probable cause to believe from facts found, without hearing, by him or any officer or employee of the Agency that the misbranded article is dangerous to health, or that the labeling of the misbranded article is fraudulent, or would be in a material respect misleading to the injury or damage of the purchaser or consumer."

Appellee is the exclusive national distributor of Nutrilite Food Supplement, an encapsulated concentrate of alfalfa, water cress, parsley, and synthetic vitamins combined in a package with mineral tablets. There is no claim that the ingredients of the preparation are harmful or dangerous to health. The sole claim is that the labeling [a booklet touting the curative powers of Nutrilite] was, to use the statutory words, "misleading to the injury or damage of the purchaser or consumer" and that therefore the preparation was "misbranded" when introduced into interstate commerce.

This was indeed the administrative finding behind eleven seizures resulting in that number of libel suits, between September and December, 1948.... Shortly thereafter the present suit was instituted to have the multiple seizure provision of § 304(a) declared unconstitutional and to dismiss all libel cases except the first one instituted. The District Court held that appellants had acted arbitrarily and capriciously in violation of the Fifth Amendment in instituting multiple libel suits without first affording the appellee a hearing on the probable cause issue; that the multiple seizure provision of § 304(a) was unconstitutional under the Due Process Clause of the Fifth Amendment; and that appellants should be permanently enjoined from instituting any action raising a claim that the booklet accompanying the preparation was a misbranding since it was not fraudulent, false, or misleading.

First. The administrative finding of probable cause required by § 304(a) is merely the statutory prerequisite to the bringing of the lawsuit. When the libels are filed the owner has an opportunity to appear as a claimant and to have a full hearing before the court. This hearing, we conclude, satisfies the requirements of due process....

It is said that these multiple seizure decisions of the Administrator can cause irreparable damage to a business. And so they can. The impact of the initiation of judicial proceedings is often serious.... Yet it has never been held that the hand of government must be stayed until the courts have an opportunity to determine whether the government is justified in instituting suit in the courts. Discretion of any official may be abused. Yet it is not a requirement of due process that there be judicial inquiry before discretion can be exercised. It is sufficient, where only property rights are concerned, that there is at some stage an opportunity for a hearing and a judicial determination....

Second. The District Court had no jurisdiction to review the administrative determination of probable cause.

[FDA's] determination of probable cause in and of itself had no binding legal consequence.... It took the exercise of discretion on the part of the Attorney General ... to bring it into play against appellee's business. Judicial review of such a preliminary step in a judicial proceeding is so unique that we are not willing easily to infer that it exists....

The purpose of the multiple seizure provision is plain. It is to arrest the distribution of an article that is dangerous, or whose labeling is fraudulent or misleading, pending a determination of the issue of adulteration or misbranding. The public therefore has a stake in the jurisdictional issue before us. If the District Court can step in, stay the institution of seizures, and bring the administrative regulation to a halt until it hears the case, the public will be denied the speedy protection which Congress provided by multiple seizures. It is not enough to say that the vitamin preparation in the present case is not dangerous to health. This preparation may be relatively innocuous. But the statutory scheme treats every "misbranded article" the same in this respect—whether it is "dangerous to health," or its labeling is "fraudulent," or materially "misleading to the injury or damage of the purchaser or consumer." . . . Congress weighed the potential injury to the public from misbranded articles against the injury to the purveyor of the article from a temporary interference with its distribution and decided in favor of the speedy, preventive device of multiple seizures. We would impair or destroy the effectiveness of that device if we sanctioned the interferences which a grant of jurisdiction to the District Court would entail. . . .

Reversed.

■ Mr. Justice Jackson, dissenting.

      . . . .

The trial court of three judges wrote no opinion but made forty-three detailed findings of fact. . . . The substance of these is to find that the Government instituted a multiplicity of court actions, with seizures in widely separated parts of the country, with a purpose to harass appellee and its dealers and intending that these actions and the attendant publicity would injure appellee's business *before any of the issues in such cases could be tried.* This, the court held, was justified by no emergency, the product being, at worst, harmless and having been marketed for years with knowledge of the Department.

Assuming as I do that the Act on its face is not constitutionally defective, the question remains whether it has been so misused by refusal of administrative hearing, together with such irreparable injury in anticipation of judicial hearing, as to deny appellee due process of law or to amount to an abuse of process of the courts.

      . . . . The holding of the court below and the contention of the appellee here that the Government is not entitled to so apply the statute as to bring multiple actions designed to destroy a business before it can be heard in its own defense is not frivolous, to say the least.

I am constrained to withhold assent to a decision that passes in silence what I think presents a serious issue.

NOTES

1. *Multiple Seizures. See Merritt Corp. v. Folsom*, 165 F. Supp. 418 (D.D.C. 1958). In *Dainty–Maid, Inc. v. United States*, 216 F.2d 668 (6th Cir. 1954), claimant sought dismissal of multiple seizures for misbranding, on the ground that the labeling involved was not identical to the labeling held illegal in an earlier default judgment. The court refused, holding that whether the new labeling involved the same misbranding as the earlier judgment was a factual question for the district court.

2. *Commentary. See* Lester L. Lev, *The Multiple Seizure Bludgeon*, 5 Food Drug Cosm. L.J. 535 (1950); James B. Swire, *FDA's Multiple Seizure Powers: A Time for Equity*, 34 Food Drug Cosm. L.J. 244 (1979).

Parke, Davis & Co. v. Califano

564 F.2d 1200 (6th Cir. 1977).

■ LIVELY, CIRCUIT JUDGE.

The question in this case is whether the district court properly enjoined enforcement actions by the Food and Drug Administration (FDA) which were instituted as libels for the seizure of drugs in warehouses of the plaintiff, Parke, Davis & Company (Parke Davis). The appellants contend that the judgment of the district court constitutes an unwarranted interference with a discretionary determination of the FDA commissioner, whereas the appellee argues that the district court properly exercised its authority under the Administrative Procedure Act (APA) to enjoin capricious and arbitrary action by the commissioner. . . .

The dispute in the case concerns the right of Parke Davis to market as an antitussive (cough inhibitor) a nonprescription, over-the-counter drug product containing diphenhydramine hydrochloride (DPH). [The court related that in 1948, FDA approved Parke Davis' NDA for this product for prescription use. Parke Davis subsequently pursued two approaches to "switch" the product from Rx to OTC status; through the OTC drug review and by submitting a supplemental NDA. The firm began marketing an OTC version of the product in 1975, after the OTC Cough–Cold Panel agreed to recommend that the product be available OTC and FDA's Associate Chief Counsel wrote Parke Davis indicating that the agency was extremely unlikely to initiate enforcement action. In November 1976, however, FDA disapproved Parke Davis's supplemental NDA, stated that it would not accept the review panel's recommendation, and declared that DPH-containing products marketed over-the-counter would be subject to regulatory action. EDS.] . . .

The present action was filed in the United States District Court for the Eastern District of Michigan on November 29, 1976. . . . [On November 30 and December 1, the United States filed three additional seizure actions in other districts. The probable cause determination required for multiple seizures by section 304(a) did not apply to the Michigan seizure, however, because it was the first one filed. EDS.] The district court in the present action issued a temporary restraining order on December 1, 1976 and, after hearings on December 3rd and 8th, issued a preliminary injunction on that latter date. Shortly thereafter the district court filed a memorandum opinion setting forth its reasons for granting the injunction.

. . . Emphasizing Parke Davis' reliance on assurances in the [letter from the Chief Counsel's office] that enforcement action was unlikely . . . the district court found that Parke Davis would suffer irreparable injury unless FDA were restrained, and that the action of FDA in threatening enforcement was arbitrary and capricious. . . .

When this action was filed in the district court Parke Davis had taken the necessary steps to obtain a final decision on its right to market Benylin over the counter by protesting the ruling that its supplemental NDA was not approvable. A hearing will be held before a final decision is rendered on that application, and the decision will be subject to judicial review by the appropriate court of appeals pursuant to 21 U.S.C. § 371(f)(1).

We conclude that the district court had no jurisdiction to review the decision of the FDA to initiate enforcement actions. That decision is indistinguishable from the finding of probable cause which the Supreme Court has held may not be challenged in a separate action. *Ewing v. Mytinger & Casselberry*, 339 U.S. 594 (1950).

Parke Davis argues in this court that the district court did more than review the decision of the commissioner to initiate enforcement proceedings. It contends that the district court acted properly under the Administrative Procedure Act to prevent irreparable injury from an arbitrary and capricious action of the commissioner in seizing drug products which were being distributed over the counter as a matter of right following publication of the preliminary monograph without dissent. Parke Davis relies primarily on *Upjohn Co. v. Finch*, 303 F. Supp. 241 (W.D. Mich. 1969). In *Upjohn* the FDA revoked a certificate for marketing an antibiotic which had been approved for 12 years. No enforcement action was pending and no hearing was provided prior to revocation. *Upjohn* is distinguishable in at least two respects. First, the drug in question had been approved for sale—this was not in dispute. In the present case Benylin has never received final approval as an over-the-counter drug. The "switch-over" proceedings are still in progress, and a hearing is scheduled. The OTC Review was concluded with a decision adverse to Parke Davis. Secondly, in this case enforcement proceedings were pending in other jurisdictions when the district court issued its injunctive orders. Every issue raised in this case, including the question of whether the OTC Review regulations deprived Parke Davis of due process rights by failing to provide for a hearing and failing to contain guidelines for the commissioner in determining whether to accept or dissent from a panel monograph, could have been raised in the enforcement proceedings.

Thus Parke Davis had an adequate remedy, and the district court erred in holding that it did not. Parke Davis had the same remedy which was available to the distributor in *Ewing*—the statutory right to contest the seizure of its property in the libels, four of which had been filed before the injunction was entered in the present action.... Though the district court had jurisdiction under the Administrative Procedure Act to consider the complaint of Parke Davis, insofar as it questioned the regulations and procedures of the FDA as contrasted with the mere decision to initiate enforcement proceedings, it was an abuse of discretion to enjoin the FDA in the circumstances of this case where pending enforcement actions provided an opportunity for a full hearing before a court....

NOTE

Ripeness for Judicial Review Before Condemnation. In *Natick Paperboard Corp. v. Weinberger*, 498 F.2d 125 (1st Cir. 1974), the court was called upon to reconcile the holding in *Ewing* that a seizure may not be enjoined with the holding in *Abbott Laboratories*, p. 1535 *infra*, permitting preenforcement review of an agency rule:

> We think the best accommodation of these conflicting policies is to construe § 334 as not precluding district court jurisdiction to decide the definitional question within the context of an action solely for declaratory relief. At the same time, we want to make clear that the existence of this

limited jurisdiction does not permit the district court to halt in any way the seizure of appellants' food-packaging materials while the definitional issue is being resolved....

See also United States v. Alcon Laboratories, 636 F.2d 876 (1st Cir. 1981); *Gemini Pharmaceutical v. HHS*, Food Drug Cosm. L. Rep. (CCH) ¶ 38,248 (E.D.N.Y. 1983).

United States v. 893 One–Gallon Cans ... Labeled Brown's Inhalant

45 F. Supp. 467 (D. Del. 1942).

■ LEAHY, DISTRICT JUDGE.

A libel was filed which sought seizure and condemnation of certain cans containing poultry medicine.... The claimants, who were in possession of the articles, filed an answer denying the property was misbranded. The manufacturer, Edgar W. Brown, an individual engaged in business under the name of "Brown's Poultry Products Co.," in Lancaster, Pennsylvania, was permitted to intervene on May 21, 1942, to defend the labeling on his own behalf. In the order permitting the intervention, there was a provision directing that the property be discharged from seizure and delivered to the claimant upon the claimant's filing bond; and that the claimant should not sell said property unless and until the labels were removed.... On May 26, 1942, the Government moved to amend the precipitous order of May 21, 1942, by striking out those portions which permitted a return of the seized property.

In opposing the Government's motion, both the manufacturer and claimant assert that as this is a cause in Admiralty, they should be allowed to have possession of the property before final hearing and decree by filing an appropriate bond in view of the fact that the statute provides that the procedure under Section 334(b) [FD&C Act 304(b)] "shall conform, as nearly as may be, to the procedure in admiralty; ..." The Government contends that there can be no release of seized property under the statute until "after entry of the [final] decree" of condemnation....

... The argument of the claimants that the application of the Admiralty Rules ... should control the procedure as to the release of seized products finds no support when we examine the Admiralty Rules. Rule 11 deals with release of perishable goods. Obviously this rule can hardly apply to nonperishable goods seized under Section 334(d) [FD&C Act 304(d)] ... Hence, it appears that there is no apposite Admiralty Rule or traditional practice upon the basis of which goods may be released prior to decree of condemnation....

Not only is the legislative history of Section 304 helpful in determining its meaning, but a mere examination of the statute makes it clear that (1) an article may be proceeded against by libel when it is adulterated or misbranded; (2) once such an article is seized the issue of adulteration or misbranding must be determined by the Court; (3) if the article is neither adulterated nor misbranded, it is released to the claimant; but (4) if it is adulterated or misbranded it may be disposed of only as provided by Section 304(d). Destruction or release may only be had after decree.

I reject the contention of the claimants that the articles may be released prior to judicial determination of whether they were misbranded. Accordingly, the motion of the Government to amend the Order of May 21, 1942, is granted. . . .

NOTES

1. *Supporting Authority. See United States v. Article of Device ... "110 V Vapozone ...",* 194 F. Supp. 332 (N.D. Cal. 1961) (seized product should not be returned to the claimant *pendente lite*); *United States v. Alcon Laboratories,* 636 F.2d 876, 882–85 (1st Cir. 1981) (court may not dissolve administrative seizure without first addressing the merits of the seizure proceedings initiated by FDA); *United States v. 18 Cases ... Lipodrene,* Food Drug Cosm. L. Rep. (CCH) ¶ 38,867 (N.D. Ga. 2006) (court lacks jurisdiction to issue a preliminary injunction requiring FDA to return seized dietary supplements before the court makes a determination on the merits of the case). *But see United States v. Undetermined Quantities of Drugs,* 675 F. Supp. 1113 (N.D. Ill. 1987) (ordering postseizure, precondemnation release of drugs under the court's equitable powers in light of the facts that the articles were perishable and not harmful).

2. *Perishable Commodities.* Seizure of perishable commodities may result in the articles' destruction, or a reduction in their value, even if the claimant ultimately prevails. If the seizure was reasonable, however, the claimant is not entitled to reimbursement for any loss in the commodity's value during storage. For example, in *United States v. 2,116 Boxes of Boned Beef,* 516 F. Supp. 321 (D. Kan. 1981), *aff'd,* 726 F.2d 1481 (10th Cir. 1984), the claimant prevailed in the court proceedings following a seizure of beef containing DES. Nevertheless, the claimant's attempt to recover the lost value of the food under the Tucker Act, 28 U.S.C. § 1491(a)(1), which creates a cause of action for uncompensated takings, was rejected because the Tenth Circuit had determined that the seizure was reasonable. *Jarboe–Lackey Feedlots, Inc. v. United States,* 7 Cl. Ct. 329 (1985).

3. PROOF REQUIRED FOR CONDEMNATION

In a civil seizure action the government must prove its case by a preponderance of the evidence. *See, e.g., United States v. 60 28–Capsule Bottles ... "Unitrol,"* 325 F.2d 513 (3d Cir. 1963); *United States v. 4 Cases * * * Slim–Mint Chewing Gum,* 300 F.2d 144 (7th Cir. 1962); *United States v. 449 Cases, Containing Tomato Paste,* 212 F.2d 567 (2d Cir. 1954). It is not required, however, to offer such proof with respect to every article in a seized shipment.

United States v. 43 ½ Gross Rubber Prophylactics Labeled in Part "Xcello's Prophylactics"

65 F. Supp. 534 (D. Minn. 1946).

■ NORDBYE, DISTRICT JUDGE.

. . . .

The government inspection has established that the devices tested were defective in the number indicated, and there can be no serious doubt that the strength and quality of these particular defective articles fell below that which they purported or were represented to possess....

The problem presented, however, pertains to the right of the Government to condemn the entire shipment.... The average defects ... of all the tests [made on samples randomly drawn from the shipment] is approximately 7.37 per cent. But of the entire shipment seized a fraction of one per cent is definitely shown to be defective, and claimant contends that the Government has failed to sustain the burden of proof which rests on it in these proceedings in its attempt to condemn the entire shipment. It should be pointed out that apparently the only practical tests which the government representatives are able to make with the facilities available to them results in the article's being rendered useless after the test has been made. Concededly, the burden of proof rests upon the Government. But it does not follow that each individual article in the shipment must be tested. Inspection and condemnation on the basis of samples tested is clearly contemplated by the Act. In fact, the Act speaks of samples and their availability for testing. 21 U.S.C.C. § 334(c) ... No serious question is raised in this proceeding as to the samples taken being representative. But claimant contends that the Court cannot order the condemnation of good articles, and concededly some of the remaining articles are in all probability free from defects. However, in urging this contention, claimant fails to distinguish between condemnation and the confiscation or sale of goods. Condemnation only sustains the Government's position that the goods as they were composed in interstate shipment violate the provision and purpose of the Federal Food, Drug, and Cosmetic Act. After the decree, the claimant can separate the good from the defective if it posts a bond, and thereby will be able to retain the balance of the goods. 21 U.S.C.A. § 334(d).... But it is urged that the number of defectives are so low in proportion to the total number of articles involved in this proceeding that a grave injustice would result to the claimant if the entire shipment is condemned. Again, it may be reiterated that condemnation is not confiscation.... Moreover, the Court is not required or permitted to establish any formula as to what tolerance of defects should be allowed, if any, in every type of libel proceeding before it determines that the Government has sustained the burden of proof as to any particular shipment. Suffice it to say that, on the state of the facts herein, and assuming that the same ratio of defectives would be found in the entire shipment, it would follow that over 1,500 defective articles would be found in this shipment. Such a number, if sold on the market, would constitute a potential menace to public health, and, in view of the claimed purpose and object of the devices, that is, the prevention of disease, are sufficient to sustain the libel proceedings herein.

. . . .

COMMENT: JURISDICTION AND VENUE IN CONDEMNATION PROCEEDINGS

According to section 304(a), condemnation proceedings must be brought within the federal district in which the articles in question were seized. In such actions, the court obtains *in rem* jurisdiction (over the articles seized) rather than *in personam* jurisdiction (over the owner of the articles). Consequently, the court does not have jurisdiction to hear an enforcement claim directly against the owner. However, the owner may intervene in the case and claim the goods. By doing so, the claimant submits to the personal jurisdiction of the court, and FDA may move to amend the complaint to add a request for an injunction. Moreover, the court retains *in personam* jurisdiction over a claimant even if the government later releases the seized articles. *United States v. An Article of Drug Consisting of 4,680 Pails*, 725 F.2d 976, 982–84 (5th Cir. 1984).

The seizure of articles not only establishes jurisdiction over condemnation proceedings but also usually determines the venue of the action. Because section 304(a) requires condemnation proceedings to be brought within the district where the article is found, a claimant may not ordinarily use the federal change of venue statute, 28 U.S.C. § 1404, to transfer such an action for the convenience of the parties and witnesses. *Clinton Foods, Inc. v. United States*, 188 F.2d 289, 292 (4th Cir. 1951). Nonetheless, when multiple seizures are filed in different jurisdictions, the claimant may, pursuant to section 304(b), request that the actions be consolidated in "a district of reasonable proximity to the claimant's principal place of business." The court is required to grant such a request for consolidation "unless good cause to the contrary is shown." FD&C Act 304(b). *See, e.g., United States v. 91 Packages ... Nutrilite Food Supplement*, 93 F. Supp. 763 (D.N.J. 1950). Seizure actions for misbranding are sometimes limited to a single proceeding, FD&C Act 304(a), and in such instances, the claimant may similarly request transfer of that one proceeding to a district in reasonable proximity to its principal place of business. Interestingly, the phrase "a district of reasonable proximity to the claimant's principal place of business" excludes the district within which the principal place of business is actually located. *See, e.g., United States v. 600 Units ... "Nue-Ovo"*, 60 F. Supp. 144, 145 (W.D. Mo. 1945). *See generally* Vincent A. Kleinfeld & Arthur A. Dickerman, *Removal and Consolidation in Condemnation Proceedings*, 2 Food & Drug L. J. 197 (1947).

4. Final Condemnation Decrees and Salvaging

Section 304(d) of the FD&C Act, governing final decrees in seizure and condemnation actions, provides, in part, as follows:

> Any [article] condemned under this section shall, after entry of the decree, be disposed of by destruction or sale as the court may ... direct and the proceeds thereof, if sold, less the legal costs and charges, shall be paid into the Treasury of the United States.... After entry of the decree and upon the payment of the costs of such proceedings and the execution of a good and sufficient bond ... the court may by order direct that such article be delivered to the owner thereof to be destroyed or brought into compliance with the provisions of this Act, under the supervision of an officer or employee duly designated by the Secretary....

United States v. 1,638 Cases of Adulterated Alcoholic Beverages
624 F.2d 900 (9th Cir. 1980).

■ Thornberry, Circuit Judge.

K&L Distributors, Inc. brings this appeal from a judgment for the destruction of 1,638 cases of alcoholic beverages entered by the United

States District Court for the District of Alaska under the authority of the Federal Food, Drug and Cosmetic Act (Act).... K&L asserts that the district court erred in ruling that appellant's method of reconditioning the articles must be rejected in favor of the method approved by the Food and Drug Administration (FDA)....

On November 11, 1974, a flood swept through the City of Nome, Alaska.... The flood waters caused extensive damage to the commercial district of Nome. Included in the commercial district is the Bering Sea Saloon, the location of the articles that are the subject of this controversy. The flood waters apparently burst through the back door of the saloon, resulting in merchandise being thrown to the ground and being exposed to various amounts of sea water.

The flood also destroyed the city's sewage disposal plant.... It is possible that the raw sewage was washed into the commercial district of Nome and into the Bering Sea Saloon....

This action was initiated by the United States on March 27, 1975, by filing a Complaint for Forfeiture seeking the seizure and condemnation of liquor and other articles, claiming that the items had been held under insanitary conditions which may have caused them to become contaminated with filth or may have rendered them injurious to health. The articles were seized by the United States Marshal pursuant to an arrest warrant on April 1, 1975.

... On June 9, 1976, K&L entered into [a] consent decree with respect to the cases of alcohol. First, K&L admitted that the articles under seizure were adulterated in violation of 21 U.S.C. § 342(a)(4). They were therefore condemned pursuant to 21 U.S.C. § 334(a). Second, the consent decree provided that the goods were to be released from custody for the purpose of reconditioning the articles pursuant to 21 U.S.C. § 334(d) under the supervision of the FDA. Because the alcohol may have been contaminated by raw sewage, the FDA would only approve a reconditioning plan that included redistillation of the alcohol. Appellant claimed that this plan would be economically disastrous and brought an action seeking approval and implementation of its reconditioning plan. The district court approved the FDA's plan.... The district court then ordered the condemned articles destroyed [because K&L would not recondition them in accordance with FDA's plan] but stayed the order during the pendency of this appeal.

K&L initially contends that the owner of seized goods should have the right to choose the method of reconditioning that is to be used to bring adulterated articles in compliance with the Act.

In assessing this claim, we must first examine the statutory framework surrounding this type of situation.... After it is determined that an article is "adulterated," ... [t]he article is then disposed of by destruction or sale unless, upon payment of the costs of the proceeding and execution of a sufficient bond, the court orders the articles to be delivered to the owner to be destroyed or brought into compliance with the provisions of the Act under the supervision of an officer designated by the Secretary of Health, Education and Welfare. 21 U.S.C. § 334(d)(1).

K&L admitted in the consent decree that the articles were adulterated. The consent decree provided that they were to be returned to K&L to be reconditioned under the supervision of the FDA. The only remaining question then is whether "under the supervision of" the FDA requires appellant to adopt the FDA's recommended method of reconditioning the articles. K&L suggested a plan of reconditioning that included a soap and water washing of the bottles followed by a hypochlorite dip.... K&L's proposal was found unacceptable because it would not solve the problem of the filth under the caps. If a cap was removed for additional cleaning, there would be further contamination. Therefore, the FDA provided that the only acceptable method for remedying the insanitary condition would be through a complete reprocessing of the product by redistillation.

It is the duty of the FDA to protect the health and welfare of the general public. Therefore, the courts that have dealt with the issue presented in this case have held that it is proper to rely on the scientific expertise of the FDA in determining the acceptability of a reconditioning proposal and to require FDA approval of a reconditioning plan. *United States v. Allan Drug Co.*, 357 F.2d 713 (10th Cir.), *cert. denied*, 385 U.S. 899 (1966); *United States v. 1,322 Cans, More or Less, of Black Raspberry Puree*, 68 F. Supp. 881 (N.D. Ohio 1946). In *Allan*, the Tenth Circuit addressed the meaning of the language of § 334(d)(1) as it applies to misbranded drugs. The court stated that once a district court delivers a misbranded (or adulterated) article to the owner to bring it into compliance with the law under the supervision of an officer designated by the Secretary of HEW,

> the supervisory powers committed to the Secretary undoubtedly carry broad authority to determine whether and in what manner the labeling may be brought within compliance with the act. The judicial function is concerned with the end product of the labeling process. While the final decision lies with the courts, great weight must be given to the administrative decision.

357 F.2d at 719. The district court in *1,322 Cans* reached a similar conclusion with respect to articles of adulterated food when it stated that

> The Food and Drug Administration has determined that distillation is the only process which would recondition this puree for human consumption and which it would approve. I see no abuse of discretion in making this determination. To interfere would be substituting the judgment of the court for that of the Food and Drug Administration upon a matter which it is better able to decide upon an issue which I think is not properly joined in this case.

68 F. Supp. at 881.

The district court properly deferred to the expertise of the FDA. While this court is not bound by *Allan* or *1,322 Cans*, we choose to follow the reasoning of those cases. A district court may rely on and give great weight to the FDA's finding that a reconditioning plan is not scientifically acceptable. The FDA did not abuse its discretion, even in light of the economic hardship imposed on appellants by its reconditioning plan. The district court, in its discretion, properly adopted the determination of the FDA.

AFFIRMED.

NOTES

1. *No Precondemnation Salvage Orders.* A district court may not order a seized article returned to the claimant for reconditioning prior to issuing a decree of condemnation. *See In re United States*, 140 F.2d 19 (5th Cir. 1943).

2. *Forfeiture of Bond.* Violation of a court decree permitting salvaging after condemnation will result in forfeiture of the bond posted by the claimant. *See Stinson Canning Co. v. United States*, 170 F.2d 764 (4th Cir. 1948); *Fresh Grown Preserve Corp. v. United States*, 143 F.2d 191 (6th Cir. 1944). *See generally* Thomas Haskins Jacobs, *An Analysis of the Application of the Salvaging Provision of the Food, Drug, and Cosmetic Act of 1938*, 26 FOOD DRUG COSM. L.J. 240 (1971); Vincent A. Kleinfeld, *The Salvaging of Products Condemned Under the Federal Food, Drug, and Cosmetic Act*, 2 FOOD DRUG COSM. L.Q. 335 (1947).

3. *No Compensation to Claimant for Seized Goods.* In *United States v. An Article of Food ... 55 Gallons ... Honey*, Adm. 78–6–D (D.N.H., May 15, 1979), the District Court, instead of ordering that the condemned honey be destroyed by conventional means, awarded custody of the honey to the New Hampshire Department of Fish and Game to "constructively destroy the substance in the drums by using it as bear bait." Nevertheless, It ruled that the claimant had no right to compensation for the use of the condemned goods.

4. *Costs of Litigation.* Section 304(e) provides: "When a decree of condemnation is entered against the article, court costs and fees, and storage and other proper expenses, shall be awarded against the person, if any, intervening as claimant of the article." If the claimant withdraws its claim for seized articles prior to judgment, the claimant is nonetheless properly charged for court costs and storage. *United States v. 374 100 Pound Burlap Bags ... Cocoa Beans*, Food Drug Cosm. L. Rep. (CCH) ¶ 38,119 (E.D. Pa. 1989); *United States v. An Article of Food ... "COJM Grade A,"* Food Drug Cosm. L. Rep. (CCH) ¶ 38,179 (N.D. Ill. 1982). *See United States v. An Article of Food ... Raisins*, Food Drug Cosm.L. Rep. (CCH) ¶ 38,002 (E.D. Tenn. 1979). The costs imposed on a claimant under section 304(e) may not include the costs the government incurred in proving its case. *United States v. Article of Drug*, 428 F. Supp. 278, 281–82 (E.D. Tenn. 1976),

5. *Re-export.* Section 304(d)(1) provides that an article that violates the FD&C Act at the time it is imported into the United States may be delivered to the importer for exportation in lieu of destruction, but only if the importer had no cause to believe the article was illegal before it was released from customs custody. *United States v. Articles of Drug ... 203 Paper Bags*, 634 F. Supp. 435 (N.D. Ill. 1985). As *United States v. An Article of Food ... "Basmati Rice,"* Food Drug Cosm. L. Rep. ¶ 38,009 (N.D. Cal. 1986), illustrates, a claimant has a heavy burden to prove it lacked cause to believe that the product was illegal when imported.

6. *Commentary. See generally* Vincent A. Kleinfeld, *The Seizure Section of the Federal Food, Drug, and Cosmetic Act*, 2 FOOD DRUG COSM. L.J. 21 (1947); Michael R. Taylor, *Seizures and Injunctions: Their Role in FDA's Enforcement Program*, 33 FOOD DRUG COSM. L.J. 596 (1978).

5. CHALLENGING CONDEMNATION DECISIONS

United States v. An Article of Drug Consisting of 4,680 Pails

725 F.2d 976 (5th Cir. 1984).

■ RANDALL, CIRCUIT JUDGE:

Claimant-appellant, Pfizer, Inc., appeals the district court's grant of summary judgment in this seizure action instituted by the United States under section 304 of the Federal Food, Drug, and Cosmetic Act, 21 U.S.C. § 301 *et seq.* (1982). The district court held that Neo–Terramycin Soluble Powder Concentrate was adulterated within the meaning of 21 U.S.C. § 351(a)(5) (1982). We affirm. . . .

II.

On May 15, 1979, the United States filed a complaint for forfeiture, under section 304 of the Act, praying for seizure and condemnation of a specified quantity of the animal drug Neo–Terramycin Soluble Powder Concentrate ("Neo–Terra Powder") that was shipped in interstate commerce by Pfizer, Inc. ("Pfizer"). The complaint alleged that the drug was a "new animal drug" within the meaning of section 321(w), for which an approved NADA was not in effect. After seizure pursuant to a warrant for arrest *in rem*, Pfizer intervened as claimant and filed an answer, alleging that Neo–Terra Powder is "generally recognized" as safe and effective, and is not, therefore, a "new animal drug" within the meaning of the Act. . . .

A jury trial was held from October 14, 1980 to October 23, 1980, at the conclusion of which the jury found that Neo–Terra Powder is "generally recognized" as safe and effective. On November 4, 1980, the district court issued a final judgment based upon the jury's verdict and ordered that the United States Marshal return the seized Neo–Terra Powder to Pfizer.

The next day, November 5, 1980, the United States Marshal released the drug, in violation of the automatic ten-day stay provision of Fed. R.Civ.P. 62(a). The marshal's return shows that the marshal's office called Pfizer on November 5 to notify Pfizer that the drug had been released, and then mailed Pfizer a copy of the written order. The United States was not notified of the release, although it learned informally of the release sometime during the ten-day automatic stay period. The United States did not request or obtain an order staying execution of the judgment releasing the Neo–Terra Powder to Pfizer, nor did it request or obtain an order requiring its return once improperly released.

On November 7, 1980, the United States filed a timely motion for a new trial, pursuant to Fed.R.Civ.P. 59(a). This motion was granted on May 8, 1981.

. . . On November 9, 1981, Pfizer moved to dismiss the complaint alleging that the court lacked *in rem* jurisdiction following the release and removal of the seized drug from the district. The district court denied [the] motion[ ].

The United States, on December 17, 1981, moved for summary judgment, which the district court granted on May 6, 1982. Pfizer filed a timely notice of appeal.

III.

The first issue we must address is whether the release by the United States Marshal of the 4,680 pails of Neo–Terra Powder destroyed the jurisdiction of the district court; Pfizer contends that it did. Pfizer's argument rests on the admiralty rule that *in rem* actions generally require, as a prerequisite to a court's jurisdiction, the presence of the vessel or other *res* within the territorial confines of the court. This rule is predicated upon admiralty's fiction of convenience that a ship is a person against whom suits can be filed and judgments entered, allowing actions to be brought against the vessel when her owner cannot be reached. However, in recent years this court has shied away from a strict construction of this *in rem* rule and has allowed, in certain circumstances, an *in rem* action to continue despite the absence of the *res*. Specifically, we have dispensed with strict application of this *in rem* rule when a legal fiction which exists solely to effectuate the adjudication of disputes is invoked for the opposite purpose, and we have found a substitute basis of *in personam* jurisdiction. *See, e.g., Treasure Salvors, Inc. v. Unidentified Wrecked and Abandoned Sailing Vessel*, 569 F.2d 330 (5th Cir.1978). . . .

We are presented with a similar interface of *in rem* and *in personam* jurisdiction in the instant case. Pfizer entered a general appearance in the district court. It did not, as is allowed under Admiralty Rule E(8), enter a limited appearance. Moreover, even after the release of the *res*, Pfizer voluntarily appeared before the district court. Although the *res* had been released on November 5, 1980, Pfizer submitted a memorandum in opposition to the government's new trial motion on November 26, 1980 and a response to the government's reply on December 31, 1980. On neither occasion did Pfizer make mention of the release of the drug. . . . Therefore, we find, as we did in *Treasure Salvors, supra*, that the district court had *in personam* jurisdiction over the parties, thus rendering the *res'* arrest nonessential to the court's jurisdiction.

Pfizer contends, however, that the district court did not retain jurisdiction because the release of the *res* rendered the case moot. Because the relief sought by the United States' complaint was forfeiture and destruction of the *res*, Pfizer argues, once the *res* was beyond the court's control, it could no longer grant the relief requested; accordingly, the case is moot. We do not agree. While, in form, the relief requested by the United States is the forfeiture and destruction of a specifically identified lot of Neo–Terra Powder, the action, in substance, seeks much more. The substantive character of the remedy sought in this case is not forfeiture and destruction of a specific lot of Neo–Terra Powder, but a declaration that Neo–Terra Powder is or is not a new animal drug. The effect of this finding would be *res judicata* against Pfizer in a subsequent seizure, as well as being *res judicata* in a subsequent injunction action. Conversely, a judgment in this case for Pfizer would be *res judicata* against the United States. Thus, the ultimate issue for each of the parties is whether or not Pfizer must submit Neo–Terra Powder to the FDA for premarketing approval; the effect of the court's holding goes far beyond a single lot of the drug. The fiction of bringing suit against the drug itself is invoked simply to get the issues and the parties before the court; this purpose was accomplished. With both parties before the court, the action, for all practical purposes, becomes one for a declaratory judgment to determine whether Neo–Terra Powder is a new animal drug. Therefore, we refuse, in this case, to elevate form over substance. Both the controversy and the parties being before the court, the action is not moot and need not be dismissed. Accordingly, we turn to an examination of the merits of Pfizer's appeal.

. . . .

NOTES

1. *Other Cases.* Accord *United States v. An Article of Drug Consisting of 4,680 Pails,* 725 F.2d 976, 982–84 (5th Cir. 1984). *But see United States v. 3 Unlabeled 25–Pound Bags Dried Mushrooms,* 157 F.2d 722 (7th Cir. 1946) (destruction of seized adulterated mushrooms destroyed jurisdiction and rendered case moot, despite appearance of claimant).

2. *Timing of Appeal from Condemnation.* An appeal by a claimant from an adverse district court decision must await a final decree of condemnation and an order disposing of the articles. *See United States v. 38 Cases . . . "Mr. Enzyme",* 369 F.2d 399 (3d Cir. 1966).

3. *Limited Appearance.* No reported case suggests that a claimant of goods seized under the FD&C Act may enter a limited appearance.

6.   Effectiveness of Seizures

Peter Barton Hutt, *Philosophy of Regulation Under the Federal Food, Drug and Cosmetic Act*

28 Food Drug Cosmetic Law Journal 177 (1973).

. . . [A] seizure represents a substantial expenditure of governmental resources. . . . Many seizures, involving relatively minor violations, include only a small amount of the total goods involved. During the past ten years 13% of our seizure recommendations were never executed because the product had been moved or consumed during the time taken to complete these procedures. And during this same period, 99.7% of all seizures were adjudicated by default or consent, and were not litigated through to trial. . . .

There is no question that, in many instances, the traditional seizure mechanism remains very useful. Where an entire carload or grain elevator of food is found adulterated, seizure obviously does accomplish its intended purpose. In an unfortunately large number of instances, however, seizure is a wholly ineffective and inappropriate remedy that needs to be supplemented by more efficient approaches. One particularly disturbing aspect is that, as any food and drug lawyer knows, the impact of a single seizure of a small amount of a product can be effectively blunted simply by filing a claim and engaging in the usual pre-trial discovery. The inventory of the offending product can then be relabeled, or exhausted without change, and at that point a consent decree can be accepted or the claim withdrawn and the case forfeited. In the meantime, the public is subjected to the illegal product, and the entire purpose of the seizure is substantially delayed and subverted.

There is no easy solution to these problems. Whether or not statutory changes occur, it is clear that the Food and Drug Administration will continue its use of recall and detention, in lieu of seizure, where this is the most appropriate means of enforcement available. Another approach that I favor is the increased use of a regulatory letter to a company under section

306 of the Act where relatively minor violations are involved (*e.g.*, FPLA violations, some misbranding charges, and perhaps instances of esthetic adulteration), requiring compliance with the law within a specified period of time. Failure to comply would then be subject to injunction and/or criminal action, and in some instances also seizure. . . .

NOTE

In the early 1970s, based on the above analysis, FDA began frequently to use regulatory letters in lieu of seizures, particularly in cases involving no danger to health. The agency proposed regulations to codify this approach in 43 Fed. Reg. 27498 (June 23, 1978), but later withdrew that proposal in 45 Fed. Reg. 60449 (September 12, 1980) and issued guidelines in Chapters 8–10 of the REGULATORY PROCEDURES MANUAL instead. The designation "regulatory letter" was later changed to "warning letter." *See* p. 1339 *infra*.

7.   ADMINISTRATIVE DETENTION

To prevent illegal articles from being moved or consumed while it is taking the steps necessary to accomplish a seizure, FDA often requests state officials to use their statutory powers to embargo or detain the articles by administrative order. The agency shares with USDA the authority to detain by administrative order meat, poultry, and egg products under 21 U.S.C. 679(b), 467f(b), and 1052(d), respectively. For USDA regulations implementing this authority, see 9 C.F.R. Part 329. The Bioterrorism Act Preparedness of Response Act of 2002 (Public Law 107–188) amended the FD&C Act to provide that an officer or qualified employee of FDA may order the detention of any article of food found during an inspection, examination, or investigation under the Act if he or she "has credible evidence or information indicating that such article presents a threat of serious adverse health consequences or death to humans or animals." FD&C Act 304(h)(1)(A). The agency has published a final rule implementing this provision. 69 Fed. Reg. 31660 (June 4, 2004), codified in 21 C.F.R. Part 1, Subpart K. Under the Medical Device Amendments, FDA has administrative detention authority for medical devices. FD&C Act 304(g). *See* 21 C.F.R. 800.55; *Life Design Systems, Inc. v. Sullivan*, Civ. No. CA3–90–701–D (N.D. Tex. 1990).

FDA has often asked Congress to enact administrative detention authority for all of the products it regulates. The Senate included such authority for drugs when it passed S. 1075, the Drug Regulation Reform Act of 1979, S. Rep. No. 96–321, 96th Cong., 1st Sess. (1979), but the House did not act on the bill.

E.   INJUNCTIONS

1.   INTRODUCTION

The 1906 Act did not authorize FDA to seek injunctive relief against violators. The legislative history of the 1938 Act reveals various reasons for including injunction authority. During Senate hearings on an early version of the legislation, FDA Chief Campbell testified:

> The next section ... provides for the suppression of repetitious offenses. In the present circumstances there is no way by which that can be done effectively. If an article is misbranded or adulterated the manufacturer can continue for a protracted period its production and shipment in interstate commerce because of the delay incident to the conclusion of a [criminal] prosecution. Even though a conviction were obtained, it would be impossible to bring the matter at issue to a definite determination without the lapse of an inordinate period. This section by expediting action and suppressing continued offenses is for the more adequate protection of the public....

"Food, Drugs, and Cosmetics," Hearings before a Subcomm. of the Senate Comm. on Commerce, 73d Cong., 2d Sess. 78 (1933).

The House Report on the final version of the FD&C Act discussed another benefit of adding the option of enforcement by injunction.

> Section 302 provides a new enforcement procedure for food and drug legislation by authorizing the courts to enjoin violations. This procedure will be particularly advantageous in border-line cases that cannot be settled without litigation. In many such cases it is unfair to the manufacturer to subject him to criminal trial and likewise unfair to the public to have the issue determined under the restrictions necessarily prevailing in criminal procedure. This remedy should reduce litigation. In some cases it should avoid the hardship and expense to litigants in seizure cases.... A seizure case finally decided in favor of a defendant leaves him without recourse for his losses, including court costs, storage, and other charges.

House Rep. No. 2139, 75th Cong., 3d Sess. (1938).

FDA was slow to start taking advantage of this new enforcement tool, and it has not frequently sought injunctions. *See infra* p. 1351. Nevertheless, the agency does occasionally file civil actions seeking injunctions, sometimes as the sole remedy, other times in combination with seizure. An injunction has several distinct advantages as an enforcement mechanism. The government has a lower burden of proof in an injunction suit than in a criminal prosecution. An injunction can prohibit further violations, whereas a condemnation decree after a seizure cannot, because it is issued against the seized product itself, not against any person. Moreover, FDA can seek a preliminary injunction, or even a temporary restraining order (TRO), to put a halt to violative conduct immediately, before the court decides whether to award a permanent injunction. Most injunction actions are resolved by consent decree.

The issuance of temporary restraining orders and injunctions by federal courts is regulated by Rule 65 of the Federal Rules of Civil Procedure.

NOTES

1. *Jury Trial.* A defendant is not entitled to a jury trial in an injunction suit under the Act. *See United States v. Ellis Research Laboratories, Inc.,* 300 F.2d 550

(7th Cir. 1962). Under section 302(b), however, a charge of violation of an injunction may be triable to a jury, if the violation also constitutes a violation of the FD&C Act.

2. *Animal Biologics.* The Animal Virus, Serum, and Toxin Act (VS&T Act), 21 U.S.C. § 151 *et seq.*, enacted in 1913, contains criminal penalties but no authority for injunctions. *Impro Products, Inc. v. Block*, 722 F.2d 845 (D.C. Cir. 1983), declined to find an "implied" civil remedy under the VS&T Act.

3. *Commentary. See generally* Edward M. Barrett, *Injunction Power Under the Food, Drug, and Cosmetic Act*, 5 FOOD DRUG COSM. L.J. 788 (1950); John B. Buckley, Jr., *Injunction Proceedings*, 6 FOOD DRUG COSM. L.J. 515 (1951); George M. Burditt, *The Trial of an Injunction Suit*, 25 FOOD DRUG COSM. L.J. 238 (1970); Richard Morey, *Handling FDA Injunction Actions*, 31 FOOD DRUG COSM. L.J. 366 (1976).

2.   PRELIMINARY INJUNCTIONS

United States v. Odessa Union Warehouse Co–Op

833 F.2d 172 (9th Cir. 1987).

■ CANBY, CIRCUIT JUDGE: . . . .

In April 1986, the government conducted extensive inspections of thirteen grain elevators operated by Odessa in eastern and central Washington. The inspections revealed violations of the food contamination and adulteration standards of the FDCA. The condition of Odessa's wheat at the time of the FDA inspection is uncontested. The wheat in the Odessa-operated elevators was moldy and contaminated with live and dead insect, insect larvae and rodent excreta. Various structural defects allowed for entry of rodents and birds at six of the storage stations.

Prior FDA inspections of Odessa facilities had also revealed unsanitary conditions. In May 1985, inspections showed live insect infestation at each of seven facilities. Two stations contained rodent excreta on the grain-conveying equipment. In 1983 and 1984, the Washington State Department of Agriculture, under contract with the FDA, inspected Odessa's storage facilities and discovered significant sanitary problems. As a result of these inspections, the FDA had imposed embargoes on thousands of bushels of wheat under Odessa's control.

As a result of the April 1986 inspections, the government sought a preliminary injunction to enjoin the sale and movement of wheat held in Odessa's elevators until Odessa complied with FDCA standards. In response to the filing of the injunction action by the government, and prior to the September 1986 district court hearing, Odessa took action to improve the sanitation at its facilities. Odessa's general manager testified that Odessa cleaned and fumigated the wheat, removed rodent and bird excreta from the wheat's surface, destroyed rodent tunnels, and sealed the elevators to prevent future infestation. In addition, Odessa hired a sanitation expert to recommend additional sanitation policy and procedures.

The district court, applying a standard we will set forth below, denied the government's motion for a preliminary injunction. . . .

1.   *Standard for Issuing a Preliminary Injunction*

The factors we traditionally consider in determining whether to grant a preliminary injunction in this circuit are (1) the likelihood of plaintiff's success on the merits; (2) the possibility of plaintiff's suffering irreparable injury if relief is not granted; (3) the extent to which the balance of hardships favors the respective parties; and (4) in certain cases, whether the public interest will be advanced by the provision of preliminary relief. To obtain a preliminary injunction, the moving party must show either (1) a combination of probable success on the merits and the possibility of irreparable injury or (2) that serious questions are raised and the balance of hardships tips in its favor. These two formulations represent two points on a sliding scale in which the required degree of irreparable harm increases as the probability of success decreases.

2.   *Statutory Injunctions*

The motion for preliminary injunction in this action was brought by the government pursuant to the FDCA. That fact unquestionably affects the balance of factors that determines whether an injunction should be granted. The function of a court in deciding whether to issue an injunction authorized by a statute of the United States to enforce and implement Congressional policy is a different one from that of the court when weighing claims of two private litigants. This is not to say that the violation of a federal statute automatically requires a district court to issue an injunction.... However, the fact that a federal statute is being enforced by the agency charged with that duty may alter the burden of proof of a particular element necessary to obtain injunctive relief. Once Congress, exercising its delegated powers, has decided the order of priorities in a given area, it is for the courts to enforce them when asked.

3.   *The District Court's Standard*

The district court in this case applied neither the conventional balancing test ... nor the glosses on that test that arise from the fact that a federal agency is seeking to enforce an act of Congress. Instead, the district court announced the following standard:

> "The teachings of the appellate courts list several of these conditions, but Federal judges being an independent group, this Court has developed his own list of conditions and feels that a preliminary injunction should issue only when the circumstances truly permit no other course, when the crisis is current or at least appears to be recurrent, that the response of the respondent is recalcitrant and clearly so, and that the total impact of the Order must be assessed."

Applying this standard, the district court denied the preliminary injunction on the grounds that Odessa was making improvements in its unsanitary conditions and that the granting of injunctive relief might put Odessa out of business and adversely affect the local agricultural economy.

The standard announced and applied by the district court is far too restrictive, compared with the standards for statutory injunctions set forth above....

4. *Irreparable Injury*

To obtain a preliminary injunction, the movant must ordinarily show that there exists a significant threat of irreparable injury. The district court may have imposed a variant of this requirement in insisting upon the existence of a "crisis." Whether or not the variant is a sufficient substitute is beside the point because the requirement itself is inapplicable to this case. Where an injunction is authorized by statute, and the statutory conditions are satisfied as in the facts presented here, the agency to whom the enforcement of the right has been entrusted is not required to show irreparable injury. No specific or immediate showing of the precise way in which violation of the law will result in public harm is required. The district court accordingly should have presumed that the government would suffer irreparable injury from a denial of its motion.

5. *Success on the Merits*

A second element of the test for issuance of a preliminary injunction is the moving party's probable success on the merits. However, the required degree of probable success on the merits decreases as the likelihood of irreparable harm increases. Because irreparable injury must be presumed in a statutory enforcement action, the district court needed only to find some chance of probable success on the merits. The record indicates that there is a substantial likelihood of success on the merits in this action given the uncontested evidence that Odessa remained in violation of the FDCA up until the September 1986 hearing, despite its efforts to improve sanitary conditions. Had the district court applied the correct standard, the government's likelihood of success on the merits and the presumptive finding of irreparable injury would have met the first test for issuance of a preliminary injunction. . . .

. . . Because the district court erroneously applied its own set of conditions in denying the government's motion, and because the record indicates that the government may qualify for a preliminary injunction under this circuit's standards, the district court's order must be reversed and remanded for reevaluation under the correct standards.

United States v. Nutri–cology, Inc.

982 F.2d 394 (9th Cir. 1992).

■ PREGERSON, CIRCUIT JUDGE:

. . . .

I. BACKGROUND

Nutri-cology distributes and promotes a number of products labelled as nutritional or dietary supplements. These products are allegedly promoted as useful to prevent and treat numerous diseases and conditions.

The Food and Drug Administration (the "FDA") began monitoring Nutri-cology's activities in 1982. The FDA notified defendants in writing—three times in 1982, twice in 1985, and twice in 1988—that the FDA considered Nutri-cology's products to be unapproved "drugs" and "new drugs" under the FDCA. . . .

Since 1982, Nutri-cology has maintained that its products are not "drugs" or "new drugs," under the FDCA, but are herbs, oils, vitamins, and other "foods." The FDA sent its last communication to Nutri-cology on June 16, 1988. The government filed this action three years later on May 2, 1991.

On May 8, 1991, the district court granted the government's ex parte request for a temporary restraining order enjoining Nutri-cology from further marketing nine of its products, which constituted 80% of Nutri-cology's business.

On May 23, 1991, the district court denied the government's motion for a preliminary injunction. The district court applied the following preliminary injunction standard: " 'the moving party must show either (1) a combination of probable success on the merits and the possibility of irreparable harm, or (2) that serious questions are raised and the balance of hardships tips sharply in the moving party's favor.' "

The district court made the following findings: (1) the government made a threshold evidentiary showing that Nutri-cology intended its products to be perceived as beneficial in preventing or treating diseases; (2) the government created some showing that Nutri-cology's products were "drugs" falling under the auspices of 21 U.S.C. § 321(g)(1)(B); and (3) the government made a colorable showing that Nutri-cology was violating 21 U.S.C. § 331(d) by marketing unapproved "new drugs." The court further concluded that a rebuttable presumption of irreparable harm arose from the colorable showing of an FDCA violation.

The district court then concluded that the presumption of irreparable harm was rebutted by Nutri-cology's extensive showing, through the petition signed by sixty physicians and nutritionists, in support of the merit and reliability of its products. Nutri-cology's showing was particularly persuasive because the government failed to demonstrate any harm to consumers. The district court found that two other factors weighed against granting the preliminary injunction: the FDA's nine-year delay in bringing the action, and the likelihood that an injunction would destroy Nutri-cology's business.

On July 19, 1991, the district court denied the government's motion for reconsideration. On September 10, 1991, the government filed its notice of appeal. . . .

IV. STANDARD FOR ISSUING PRELIMINARY INJUNCTIONS

The principal issue in this appeal is whether the district court applied the correct legal standard in denying the government's motion for preliminary injunction. Generally, to obtain a preliminary injunction, "the moving party must show either (1) a combination of probable success on the merits and the possibility of irreparable injury or (2) that serious questions are raised and the balance of hardships tips in its favor." *United States v. Odessa Union Warehouse Co-op*, 833 F.2d 172, 174 (9th Cir. 1987). "These two formulations represent two points on a sliding scale in which the required degree of irreparable harm increases as the probability of success decreases." *Id.*

A.   Probability of Success on the Merits

. . . .

In its preliminary determination regarding the merits of the government's claims, the district court . . . found that the government had made merely a colorable showing that Nutri-cology was violating the FDCA by marketing its products. We cannot say that the district court erred.

B.   Irreparable Injury

The government relies on our opinion in *Odessa Union* when it contends that, because this is a statutory enforcement action, it was not required to make a showing of irreparable harm. We disagree.

In *Odessa Union*, the parties conceded that the FDCA was violated. We therefore found that the conventional requirement of showing the possibility of irreparable injury was inapplicable. Specifically, we held that "[w]here an injunction is authorized by statute, *and the statutory conditions are satisfied as in the facts presented here*, the agency to whom the enforcement of the right has been entrusted is not required to show irreparable injury." (emphasis added). . . . In *Navel Orange Admin. Comm. v. Exeter Orange Co.*, 722 F.2d 449, 453 (9th Cir.1983), we did not require a showing of irreparable harm where . . . the evidence supported the conclusion that the government was likely to prevail on the merits.

In this case, the FDCA violation is substantially disputed, and has been disputed since 1982. The district court found that the government submitted "sufficient evidence to survive a motion for a directed verdict," but did not submit sufficient evidence to show that it was "likely to succeed on the merits of the case." Thus, the government's showing did not reach the level of the showing in *Odessa Union, i.e.*, of an undisputed statutory violation. Moreover, it did not even match the government's showing in *Navel Orange, i.e.*, that it was likely to prevail on the merits. Consequently, the government is not entitled to a presumption, rebuttable or otherwise, of irreparable injury.

In statutory enforcement cases where the government has met the "probability of success" prong of the preliminary injunction test, we presume it has met the "possibility of irreparable injury" prong because the passage of the statute is itself an implied finding by Congress that violations will harm the public. Therefore, further inquiry into irreparable injury is unnecessary. However, in statutory enforcement cases where the government can make only a "colorable evidentiary showing" of a violation, the court must consider the possibility of irreparable injury.

Here, the government did not show that it would probably prevail on the merits. Therefore, it was not entitled to a presumption of irreparable injury.

Relying on language in *Odessa Union*, the district court gave the government the benefit of a rebuttable presumption of irreparable injury. This was error. However, the district court would have reached the same result had it not initially presumed irreparable injury. Because the government failed to demonstrate any harm to consumers and because Nutricology submitted extensive evidence to the contrary, the district court did not abuse its discretion in finding that the government did not make the requisite showing of irreparable harm. The district court, moreover, did not abuse its discretion in denying the government's motions for preliminary injunction and for reconsideration.

Affirmed.

3. Permanent Injunctions

United States v. Laerdal Manufacturing Corp.

73 F.3d 852 (9th Cir. 1995).

■ D.W. Nelson, Circuit Judge:

Appellant Laerdal Manufacturing Corp. appeals the order of the district court that Laerdal be "perpetually restrained and enjoined from directly or indirectly . . . (f)ailing or refusing to furnish information required by or under 21 U.S.C. § 360i, in accordance with" Medical Device Recording ("MDR") regulations, 21 C.F.R. § 803. Laerdal is a manufacturer of automated external defibrillators ("AEDs"), which are applied to cardiac arrest victims in order to convert ventricular fibrillation back into regular heartbeats. In its findings of fact, the court determined that Laerdal had violated 21 C.F.R. § 803(a)(1)(i), which requires a manufacturer to file a report with the Food and Drug Administration ("FDA") "whenever information is received that reasonably suggests that a patient care device . . . may have caused or contributed to a death or serious injury."

Laerdal argues that the court improperly imposed this injunction, because there was no cognizable danger that Laerdal would violate the MDR regulation in the future. Laerdal claims that (a) the violation found by the court was an isolated incident, (b) the violation was unintentional, and (c) Laerdal has taken the necessary steps to prevent future violations. In addition, Laerdal contends that the balance of the parties' interests dictates that no injunction is warranted. We . . . affirm.

We review the scope of injunctive relief for an abuse of discretion or application of erroneous legal principles.

THE PERMANENT INJUNCTION AND THE "COGNIZABLE DANGER OF RECURRENT VIOLATION"

A district court cannot issue an injunction unless "there exists some cognizable danger of recurrent violation." *United States v. W. T. Grant Co.*, 345 U.S. 629, 633 (1953). The determination that such danger exists must "be based on appropriate findings supported by the record." *Federal Election Comm'n v. Furgatch*, 869 F.2d 1256, 1263 (9th Cir. 1989); Fed. R. Civ. P. 65(d). Factors that a district court may consider in making this finding include the degree of scienter involved; the isolated or recurrent nature of the infraction; the defendant's recognition of the wrongful nature of his conduct; the extent to which the defendant's professional and personal characteristics might enable or tempt him to commit future violations; and the sincerity of any assurances against future violations.

. . . . We find . . . that the district court did make findings that indicated a cognizable danger of recurrent violations.

We review the scope of injunctive relief for an abuse of discretion or application of erroneous legal principles.

THE NUMBER OF VIOLATIONS

Laerdal asserts that the court found only one isolated violation of the MDR regulation. This assertion does not accurately represent the whole of the court's findings. The district court specifically found that "at least one violation of the MDR regulations has occurred." The court developed at length the facts surrounding the incident in Grand Rapids that first brought Laerdal's reporting practices to the FDA's attention, but the court also found testimony in the record that Laerdal had received complaints of other instances in which a Laerdal AED failed to work properly.

On the basis of these findings the court concluded that while Laerdal's official reporting policy incorporated the language of FDA regulations, in actual practice Laerdal had an ongoing history of not implementing these procedures. . . .

Even if the district court had found evidence of only one violation, Laerdal is in error in asserting that one violation provides insufficient grounds for granting an injunction. The Supreme Court has determined that if a court has found a cognizable danger of recurrent future violations, an injunction "can be utilized even without a showing of past wrongs." *W. T. Grant Co.*, 345 U.S. at 633. . . .

INTENTION AND THE LIKELIHOOD OF RECURRENCE

Laerdal further argues that it did not intend to violate the MDR regulations, and thus, no degree of scienter was involved. In this context, Laerdal also argues that the district court made a clearly erroneous factual finding in its determination that Laerdal had received information reasonably suggesting that in the Grand Rapids incident a Laerdal AED may have caused or contributed to a death. As Laerdal concedes, 21 C.F.R. § 803 is a strict liability provision. For purposes of determining whether Laerdal violated the MDR regulations, the district court was not required to develop the issue of Laerdal's intent; however, Laerdal contends that its intent is pertinent to the likelihood of its committing future violations.

Laerdal has repeatedly argued that its actions in violating the MDR regulations were justifiable. Though Laerdal decided to file a report concerning the Grand Rapids incident two weeks before trial, the court noted that Laerdal continued to argue at trial that the circumstances of the incident did not make filing a report necessary. . . .

Though Laerdal does not appeal the court's finding that it violated the MDR regulations, Laerdal nonetheless continues to argue that its actions were justifiable. Laerdal cites as support for its failure to file a report "the ambiguous language of the regulation" and numerous unique aspects of the Grand Rapids incident that warranted its decision not to file a report. . . .

Laerdal's intransigent insistence on its own blamelessness also manifests itself in hostility toward the MDR system. At trial and on appeal, Laerdal has attempted to demonstrate the "foibles of the MDR system." It claims that "MDR reports languish for several months in a bureaucratic limbo" and that the consequences of its Grand Rapids violation were "merely trifling." . . .

Laerdal's repeated self-justification is sufficient to show a likelihood of future violation. Even if Laerdal had not intended to violate the regulation, its continued insistence on justifying its actions in committing the violation "is an important factor in deciding whether future violations are sufficiently likely to warrant an injunction." . . . That Laerdal's self-justification extends to indicting the MDR system itself reflects "the sort of extraordinary intransigence and hostility" toward the FDA and the MDR regulations that support the inference of a likelihood to commit future violations.

. . . .

BALANCING THE INTERESTS OF THE PARTIES

Laerdal asserts that the district court failed to balance the interests of the parties. Furthermore, Laerdal contends that its own interests—the reputational damage caused by the injunction and the losses due to sanctions imposed when Laerdal next violates the regulation—outweigh the public interest served by the regulation. The record shows otherwise. In the first paragraph of the "Conclusion" of the findings, the court implicitly balances the public health against the burden placed upon Laerdal, namely, that it comply with government regulations. The court's ruling in favor of the public interest is consistent with the legal standards governing the exercise of equitable discretion.

Laerdal argues that the public interest was not harmed, because FDA allegedly suffers from a backlog in filing its reports and the Grand Rapids report would have languished for several months before being filed. However, the public interest addressed by the MDR regulations centers not on the efficiency of the FDA, but on the attention manufacturers pay to evidence that their products could be causing or contributing to needless deaths. That Laerdal regards its own reputational and financial interests to be more important only reinforces the need for the injunction.

NOTE

Injunction Denied. Compare *United States v. Sars of Louisiana,* 324 F. Supp. 307, 310 (E.D. La. 1971), in which the court denied an injunction. Though the defendants did not dispute that when inspected in 1968 and 1970 their animal food product contained Salmonella microorganisms, by the time the case came to trial they had complied with all the recommendations of FDA inspectors.

> Thus, the critical determination in this case is whether or not it is reasonable to expect that the defendants will commit violative acts in the future. It is the conclusion of this Court, from the evidence at trial, that there is simply no showing that such violations are likely to reoccur. . . .

United States v. Articles of Drugs, et al., Midwest Pharmaceuticals, Inc.

825 F.2d 1238 (8th Cir. 1987).

■ McMILLIAN, CIRCUIT JUDGE.

Midwest Pharmaceuticals, Inc., Steven F. Sommers and Robert S. Leibert (collectively referred to as Midwest) appeal from a final judgment entered in the District Court for the District of Nebraska condemning as "misbranded" certain drug products seized from Midwest in April 1984. The district court held that the Midwest drugs were imitations of other drugs in violation of 21 U.S.C. §§ 331(b), 352(i)(2) and enjoined Midwest under 21 U.S.C. § 332(a) from selling or marketing any drug product similar in appearance and in effect to drugs seized in April 1984 by the Food and Drug Administration (FDA or the government).

For reversal, Midwest argues that . . . the injunction is overly broad and lacks specificity. . . .

Midwest is both a wholesale and retail distributor of generic, over-the-counter drug products containing caffeine, ephedrine . . ., and phenylpropanolamine. Midwest also sells powdery and sticky substances, which Midwest markets as "incense."

Midwest . . . usually sells its products in bulk containers of 1,000 dosage units (caplets or tablets). The drugs are shipped by mail in response to mail or telephone orders and payment is usually C.O.D. According to the government, Midwest sold over 245 million dosage units during 1984. . . . Midwest advertises its drug products in print media that the government characterizes as "subculture," "porno," "drug," and "biker" magazines. . . . Midwest in advertisements describes its drug products as "legal body stimulants" and "sleep aids." The advertisements contain pictures or photographs of the drugs, but contain no information about the ingredients or indications or contraindications, and describe the drug products by names such as "357 Magnum," "20/20," "30/30," "White Mole," "Mini–White" and "Incense." Some of these names are "street names" for various illegal drugs. . . .

On April 5, 1984, the FDA seized approximately 15 tons of drug products from Midwest. . . .

On the day of the seizure, the FDA filed a complaint alleging that Midwest drug products were "misbranded" because they were "imitations" of other drugs in violation of 21 U.S.C. § 352(i)(2) and were thus subject to *in rem* seizure under 21 U.S.C. § 334. The FDA also sought an order enjoining Midwest and its president, Sommers, under 21 U.S.C. § 332(a), from selling or marketing the same or similar products in the future. . . .

The case was tried in February 1986. . . . The government introduced evidence that Midwest's drug products were purchased in bulk, then repackaged without any information about the ingredients, and sold as "real drugs" to "youthful and unsophisticated" junior high and high school students at "real drug" prices. Midwest "dealers" thus realized a tremendous profit, approximately 20 times the actual cost of the drugs. . . .

The government also presented evidence that Midwest markets only drug products that are similar in appearance and effect to controlled substances and that the many different shapes, sizes and colors of Midwest drugs are non-functional. . . .

The district court held that the Midwest drugs, which had been seized in April 1984, were imitations of other drugs and enjoined Midwest from selling or marketing any drug similar in appearance and in effect to those seized. This appeal followed. . . .

Midwest . . . contends that the permanent injunction issued by the district court is both defective and grossly overbroad. Midwest argues that the injunction violates Fed. R. Civ. P. 65(d) because it fails to enumerate the drug products Midwest is enjoined from marketing. In addition, Midwest argues that the injunction is overbroad because it prohibits the sale of Midwest products for legal uses.

We consider first Midwest's contention that the injunction violates Fed. R. Civ. P. 65(d) which provides: "Every order granting an injunction and every restraining order shall set forth the reasons for its issuance; shall be specific in terms; shall describe in reasonable detail, and not by reference to the complaint or other document, the act or acts sought to be restrained." We agree that the injunction violates Rule 65(d). The district court order enjoins Midwest from

> selling or marketing in any way products described in CV. 84–0–206 and further are enjoined from employing marketing techniques to sell drug products identical or similar to those described in CV. 84–0–206. . . .

The injunction fails to identify the specific drug products that Midwest is prohibited from selling or marketing and fails to specify the marketing techniques that Midwest may not employ. On remand the district court should revise the injunction so that the specific acts which are prohibited are clearly defined within the order as required by Fed. R. Civ. P. 65(d).

Midwest also argues that the injunction is overbroad because it is not tailored to remedy the alleged specific harm, that is, the passing off of Midwest drug products as controlled substances. Midwest argues that there is no legal basis to enjoin the otherwise lawful sale of drug products that are capable of a lawful use to customers who act lawfully in reselling or consuming these products.

The government responds that the injunction is not overbroad because the injunction, as drafted, is necessary in order to prevent Midwest from continuing its illegal conduct. According to the government, a narrower injunction would not be effective because, even without future advertising, Midwest could continue to sell these drug products as a result of residual orders and repeat business. Thus, Midwest would reap future profits from its past illegal conduct.

Under § 332, the district court is authorized to restrain acts that are in violation of 21 U.S.C. § 331. Good faith is not a defense to the issuance of an injunction. Nor may a defendant successfully defend against the issuance of an injunction by asserting that the injunction would drive it out of business. A district court may issue an injunction if it concludes that the injunction is necessary to prevent future violations. . . .

The government presented evidence that Midwest had a pattern of noncompliance with federal drug laws. For example, the government showed that Midwest continued to sell imitation drug products, without change, after the FDA advised Midwest in regulatory letters that Midwest drug products were being passed off and after several seizures of Midwest products by the FDA. The district court could reasonably conclude that Midwest would continue the illegal acts unless restrained. We hold that the district court did not abuse its discretion in issuing an injunction barring Midwest from marketing and selling drugs in violation of 21 U.S.C. §§ 331, 352(i)(2).

NOTES

1. *Consent Decree.* A consent decree is a settlement ratified by the court, and thus enforceable by it. FDA frequently enters "consent decrees of permanent injunction." *See, e.g., United States v. Schering–Plough*, Consent Decree of Permanent Injunction 8, 23, 36 (D.N.J. filed May 20, 2002).

2. *Suits for Contempt.* Violation of an injunction may lead to a suit for contempt under section 302(b) of the Act. *See, e.g., United States v. Vale*, 140 Fed. Appx. 302 (2d Cir. 2005) (upholding criminal contempt conviction); *United States v. Syntrax Innovations, Inc.*, 149 F. Supp. 2d 880 (E.D. Mo. 2001) (denying motion for civil contempt); *United States v. Themy–Kotronakis*, 140 F.3d 858 (10th Cir. 1998) (upholding criminal contempt conviction); *United States v. 22 Rectangular or Cylindrical Finished Devices*, 941 F. Supp. 1086 (D. Utah 1996) (finding of criminal contempt); *Upjohn Co. v. Medtron Labs., Inc.*, 894 F. Supp. 126 (S.D.N.Y. 1995) (granting motion for civil contempt); *United States v. Spectro Foods Corp.*, 544 F.2d 1175 (3d Cir. 1976) (reversal of civil contempt order).

As discussed below, *infra* p. 1310, the government does not have to prove criminal intent to establish criminal liability under the FD&C Act. Whether FDA must prove intent to sustain a charge of criminal contempt of an injunction issued under the FD&C Act has not been resolved. *Cf. United States v. Schlicksup Drug Co., Inc.*, 206 F. Supp. 801 (S.D. Ill. 1962) (no proof of intent or willfulness required); *United States v. Lit Drug Co.*, 333 F. Supp. 990, 996–97 (D.N.J. 1971) (no proof of specific intent required); *with United States v. I. D. Russell Laboratories*, 439 F. Supp. 711 (W.D. Mo. 1977) (proof of willfulness required); *United States v. Themy–Kotronakis*, 140 F.3d at 864 (same).

For discussions of some of the more technical aspects of FD&C Act 302(b), the provision providing a right to a jury for some contempt proceedings, *see United States v. 22 Rectangular or Cylindrical Finished Devices*, 941 F. Supp. 1086, 1093 (D. Utah 1996); *United States v. Dean Rubber Mfg. Co.*, 72 F. Supp. 819 (W.D. Mo. 1947); *United States v. Diapulse Corp.*, 365 F. Supp. 935 (E.D.N.Y. 1973).

4. RESTITUTION AND DISGORGEMENT

William W. Vodra & Arthur N. Levine, *Anchors Away: The Food and Drug Administration's Use of Disgorgement Abandons Legal Moorings*

59 FOOD & DRUG LAW JOURNAL 1 (2004).

During the past several years, the Food and Drug Administration (FDA) has renewed a decades-old pursuit of restitution and disgorgement to enforce alleged violations of the Federal Food, Drug, and Cosmetic Act (FDCA). This effort has produced three consent decrees containing multi-million dollar payments to the U.S. Treasury that purport to represent disgorgement of ill-gotten gains.[2] To date, at least $759,000,000 has been paid under these three decrees....

FDA first attempted to marshal the equitable powers of federal courts in the enforcement of the FDCA over fifty years ago. After the Ninth Circuit rejected the use of restitution in FDA actions in 1956,[6] the agency did not attempt to seek either restitution or disgorgement for almost forty years. Then, in the 1990s, FDA sought equitable monetary remedies in three consecutive cases. The first two resulted in judicial rejections of FDA's theories. On the agency's third try, a district court denied the agency's request for disgorgement but awarded restitution as part of an injunction. The Court of Appeals for the Sixth Circuit affirmed.[9]

Why has FDA now returned to the pursuit of disgorgement? We believe that the agency is attempting to solve a dilemma in regulatory law enforcement that emerged in the 1990s. The FDCA provides three judicial mechanisms to address violations: seizure, injunction, and criminal prosecution. The first removes noncompliant products from the market; the second prohibits the further manufacture or distribution of such products; the last punishes the wrongdoer with fines and (in the case of individuals) imprisonment. In practice, FDA has rarely used criminal penalties for violations that were not willful and did not result in death or serious injury to, or blatant fraud upon, consumers. Instead, it has relied on civil actions to compel a wrongdoer to cease operations "unless and until" the alleged deficiencies are cured....

After a series of actions in the early 1990s, however, FDA found that these tools were not always appropriate or effective. Seizures and traditional prohibitory injunctions in these cases would have removed products or services that were essential, such as therapeutic drugs for which there were no adequate alternatives, blood and blood products, and food service on long-distance passenger railroads. Instead, FDA turned to "forward-looking" consent decrees of mandatory injunction that allowed necessary goods and services to continue to be provided while ordering that the defendants remediate the alleged noncompliance within time periods specified under the decree.

This response, however, produced other regulatory challenges. By its initial action that permitted the continued distribution of necessary products, FDA had effectively signaled to the defendant that, even if remediation were not accomplished under the decree, the agency would be extremely reluctant to block future sales of those products to compel compliance.

---

2. The three consent decrees are United States v. Abbott Labs., Consent Decree of Permanent Injunction (N.D. Ill. filed Nov. 2, 1999); United States v. Various Articles of Drug Identified in Attachment A & Wyeth–Ayerst Labs., Consent Decree of Condemnation and Permanent Injunction (E.D. Tenn. filed Oct. 4, 2000); and United States v. Schering–Plough Corp., Consent Decree of Permanent Injunction (D.N.J. filed May 20, 2002).

6. U.S. v. Parkinson, 240 F.2d 918 (9th Cir. 1956).

9. United States v. Universal Mgmt. Servs., Inc., 191 F.3d 750 (6th Cir. 1999), *cert. denied*, 530 U.S. 1274 (2000).

The only tools left were contempt citations (which FDA has rarely sought) or criminal prosecutions (which are enormously costly for the government). The agency was frustrated by this lack of credible judicial remedies to compel full and timely compliance under the "going-forward" decrees. At the same time, FDA was repeatedly encountering claims from companies targeted for enforcement actions that their products also were "medically necessary," such that the supply could not be safely interrupted. These companies wanted "going-forward" injunctions too. How could FDA both increase the effectiveness of such injunctions and also convince future targets that having a "medically necessary" or otherwise essential product would not be a free pass for business as usual?

FDA's creative solution to this dual challenge emerged in the Abbott consent decree and has been repeated in the Wyeth and Schering decrees. The answer was disgorgement payments of significant size. All of these decrees involved alleged violations of current good manufacturing practice (GMP) requirements in the production of medical products (*i.e.*, drugs, biologics, and medical devices). The decrees contain three separate types of payments:

(1) A "lump-sum payment" to the U.S. Treasury at the time the decree is entered. . . .

(2) "Percentage of sales" payments required if remediation is not achieved by the deadline established under the decree. The amount of these payments would be based on revenues generated by any "medically necessary" product between the expiration of the deadline and the date when, in FDA's view, compliance was finally achieved. . . .

(3) "Daily payments" required for each product or process not brought into compliance within specific deadlines determined pursuant to the decree, from the date of the deadline until compliance is actually achieved. . . .

The legal rationale for *all* of these payments was the doctrine of disgorgement, which FDA has described as a "long-recognized equitable remedy developed to prevent unjust enrichment and to deprive a defendant of ill-gotten gains." FDA's premise was that the sale of any product not made in compliance with GMP requirements generated profits to which the manufacturer was not entitled. The agency distinguished between restitution and disgorgement on the basis of where the money goes and which remedy is appropriate when the aggrieved party cannot be identified. . . .

Although often treated interchangeably, the concepts of "disgorgement" and "restitution" frequently are distinguished from each other on the basis of the primary intended purpose of each equitable remedy. The goal of restitution is to restore losses to a victim. In contrast, the objective of disgorgement is to divest from wrongdoers the gains flowing from their wrong. "The purpose of disgorgement is to deter violations by making them unprofitable. . . ."

The term "disgorgement" does not carry any specific meaning regarding the ultimate disposition of the assets divested. These monies can be— and very often are—used to offset the losses of victims. For example, when other federal agencies seek disgorgement, they have insofar as it is possible applied the funds to compensate victims for losses. The Federal Trade Commission (FTC), the Securities and Exchange Commission (SEC), and the Commodities Futures Trading Commission (CFTC) usually place recovered monies into escrow accounts for distribution to claimants who can demonstrate financial loss as a result of the wrongdoing alleged as the basis for the decrees. . . .

FDA's approach is quite different from these sister government bodies. The agency makes no attempt to compensate alleged victims. Rather, FDA relies on a restricted interpretation of "disgorgement" under which the proceeds are *intended from the outset* of the proceeding to be kept by the government. . . .

United States v. Lane Labs–USA Inc.

427 F.3d 219 (3d Cir. 2005).

■ RENDELL, CIRCUIT JUDGE.

In this case, we are called upon to decide whether a district court has the power under the Federal Food, Drug and Cosmetic Act to order a defendant found to be in violation of the Act to pay restitution to consumers. Because a district court's equitable powers in such a situation are broad, we hold that an order of restitution is properly within the jurisdiction of the court.

. . . Three products are the subject of this action: (1) BeneFin, sold in powder or tablet form as a dietary supplement and containing shark cartilage; (2) SkinAnswer, a skin cream containing glycoalkaloid; and (3) MGN–3, a dietary fiber produced by the hydrolysis of rice bran with the enzymatic extract of Shiitake mushroom, and whose main ingredient is arabinoxylan. . . .

Investigations revealed that Appellants specifically promoted the products . . . as cancer and HIV treatments. . . .

On December 10, 1999, the FDA filed a Complaint for Permanent Injunction, alleging that Labs' promotional claims brought their products under 21 U.S.C. § 321(g)(1)(B)'s definition of "drugs" and that they were "new drugs" . . . being distributed without requisite FDA approval. . . . It also alleged that the products were misbranded . . . because they lacked adequate directions for use. . . .

. . . FDA [sought] both a permanent injunction and equitable relief in the form of restitution for purchasers of the products . . . and disgorgement of profits, if such profits were not exhausted through restitution.

On July 12, 2004, the District Court granted the government's motion for summary judgment, issued a permanent injunction against the future sales of the products until a new drug application was approved for them, and ordered restitution to all purchasers of the products since September 22, 1999. . . .

. . . .

Appellants contend that the District Court did not have the authority to order restitution under the FDCA. This is a question of law, which we review de novo. Appellants urge that restitution cannot be awarded in this case because the FDCA does not expressly provide for such a remedy and restitution is inconsistent with the policy, purpose, and legislative history of the FDCA.

The District Court based its power to order restitution on 21 U.S.C. § 332(a), which states:

> The district courts of the United States and the United States courts of the Territories shall have jurisdiction, for cause shown, to restrain violations of section 331 of this title, except paragraphs (h), (i), and (j).

It is undisputed that this provision invokes the equitable jurisdiction of the District Court. Appellants claim that the specific language of § 332 that permits the District Court "to restrain violations" also limits its jurisdiction to injunctive orders that would require them to cease their offensive conduct. They argue, further, that the remedial structure of the FDCA and principles of statutory construction require us to find such a limitation to the court's power.

While arguably a close call, we conclude that applicable Supreme Court jurisprudence has mapped out the contours of a district court's equitable powers in much more expansive terms than Appellants recognize. Though the FDCA does not specifically authorize restitution, such specificity is not required where the government properly invokes a court's equitable jurisdiction under this statute. . . .

Our review of the case law begins with the Supreme Court's opinion in *Porter v. Warner Holding Company*, 328 U.S. 395 (1946). In *Porter*, the Office of Price Administration sought an injunction against the Warner Holding Company under § 205(a) of the Emergency Price Control Act of 1942 to prevent Warner from collecting rents from tenants in excess of those permitted by the applicable maximum rent regulations issued under the Act. The complaint was later amended to seek, in addition, an order of restitution to certain tenants who were entitled to a refund of any rent that exceeded the regulatory maximum. . . .

The Supreme Court held that, although the language of Section 205(a) did not explicitly grant the power to order restitution, such power was within a district court's equitable jurisdiction. The Court explained:

> Unless otherwise provided by statute, all the inherent equitable powers of the District Court are available for the proper and complete exercise of that jurisdiction. . . . Power is thereby resident in the District Court, in exercising this jurisdiction to do equity and to mould [sic] each decree to the necessities of the particular case. It may act so as . . . to accord full justice to all the real parties in interest. . . . Only in that way can equity do complete rather than truncated justice.
>
> Moreover, the comprehensiveness of this equitable jurisdiction is not to be denied or limited in the absence of a clear and valid legislative command. Unless a statute in so many words, or by a

necessary and inescapable inference, restricts the court's jurisdiction in equity, the full scope of that jurisdiction is to be recognized and applied.

Based on such clear and sweeping language, it would appear that a district court sitting in equity may order restitution unless there is an explicit statutory limitation on the district court's equitable jurisdiction and powers.... Yet, Appellants urge that the statutory language in *Porter* is distinguishable from the language of 21 U.S.C. § 332(a) in such a way as to merit a different result here. In *Porter*, § 205(a) of the Emergency Price Control Act granted jurisdiction to enter a "permanent or temporary injunction, restraining order, *or other order*" (emphasis added). Since § 332(a) makes no mention of any "other order" nor includes any language that suggests alternative equitable remedies may be available under the FDCA, Appellants claim that restitution is not authorized by the statute. This argument, however, was foreclosed by the Supreme Court in *Mitchell v. Robert de Mario Jewelry, Inc.*, 361 U.S. 288 (1960).

In *Mitchell*, the Supreme Court not only reinforced its ruling in *Porter*, but expanded its scope as well. There, ... the Secretary [of Labor] sought reimbursement for wages lost by the employee-victims of ... discrimination based on § 17 of the Fair Labor Standards Act, which grants the district courts jurisdiction "for cause shown, to restrain violations of section 15." ... The Court noted that the absence of language that could be said to support an affirmative confirmation of the power to order restitution, such as the "other order" provision in *Porter*, did not preclude the district court from ordering reimbursement.... The Court thus held that when a statutory provision gives the courts power to "enforce prohibitions" contained in a regulation or statute, Congress will be deemed to have granted as much equitable authority as is necessary to further the underlying purposes and policies of the statute.

... Thus, we must now examine the scope of the grant of equitable authority under the FDCA and the policies and purposes underlying the statute to ensure that ordering restitution furthers such purposes.

The statutory grant of equitable power of 21 U.S.C. § 332(a) at issue here is identical to the language the Supreme Court considered in *Mitchell*. Consequently, the Supreme Court's reasoning in *Mitchell* applies with equal force in the instant case. Since nothing in the FDCA creates a "necessary and inescapable inference" that the equitable power of district courts under § 332(a) is limited, we conclude that the authority given is broad enough to encompass all equitable remedies that would further the purposes of the Act.

Appellants and amicus argue that the FDA's failure to seek restitution for long periods of time, including during the first thirteen years after the FDCA's enactment, is strong evidence that such power is not granted by the statute.... However, " 'authority granted by Congress ... cannot evaporate through lack of administrative exercise.' " *BankAmerica Corp v. U.S.*, 462 U.S. 122, 131 (1983). That the FDA has rarely sought restitution under § 332(a) does not create a "necessary and inescapable inference" that Congress stripped district courts of their equitable power to award it.

Appellants argue that ordering restitution does not further the purpose of the FDCA, which they contend is limited to protecting consumers from dangerous and harmful products. They distinguish *Porter* and *Mitchell* in this regard, claiming that restitution supported the statutory purposes of the violated Acts in each of those cases in a way that it does not here. . . .

We agree that protecting consumer health and safety is a primary purpose of the FDCA. Appellants argue that since this purpose is not of a financial nature, restitution should not be ordered in equity. We are not convinced, however, that the purposes of the FDCA are as limited as Appellants suggest. The FDCA and its legislative history make it clear that Congress intended the statute to protect the financial interests of consumers as well their health.

The economic purposes of the FDCA are evidenced in part by the statute itself. . . . Indeed, the FDCA explicitly prohibits labeling and advertising that may deceive consumers as to the quality or content of products. *See* 21 U.S.C. § 331 (prohibiting the misbranding of food, drugs, devices, or cosmetics); 21 U.S.C. § 352 (defining "misbranded drugs" to include any drugs labeled or packaged in a misleading manner). Preventing such deception has as much to do with ensuring customers receive the value they expect from products as it does ensuring their safety. . . .

The legislative history likewise supports the view that one purpose of the FDCA is to protect consumers' financial interests. During its deliberations about the Act, Congress stated that prevention of deceit upon the purchasing public and protection of consumers from unscrupulous competition were among its purposes. The statute was aimed at protecting both "the consumer's health and pocketbook." H.R. Rep. No. 74–2755 at 2 (1936). . . .

Appellants and amicus argue that § 332(a) was designed only to fill a gap in the previous enactment by allowing a prompt injunctive action to prevent products from entering commerce. . . . Appellants and amicus argue that nothing in the legislative history suggests that Congress viewed § 332 as granting courts authority to order restitution, or any other backward-looking relief . . .

They also argue that construing § 332 to encompass backward-looking monetary relief such as restitution would turn Congress's intent on its head because one reason Congress added § 332 was to provide an option that was less punitive to manufacturers than the seizure provisions and criminal sanctions already in the Act. . . .

The Court of Appeals for the Sixth Circuit properly rejected this argument in *Universal Management*, reasoning that "even if Congress expressed some concern that seizure should remain the harshest relief available, there is no convincing argument that, in all cases, restitution creates a more harsh result than seizure, procedurally or substantively." *United States v. Universal Mgmt. Servs.*, 191 F.3d 750, 762 (6th Cir. 1999). The court went on to find that "even accepting the references to legislative concerns . . . these concerns are far from a clear statement of Congress's intent to exclude restitution, recalls, disgorgement, or any other traditional form of equitable relief." *Id* . . . .

Thus, both the FDCA and its legislative history support the view that protecting consumers' economic interests is an important objective of the Act. Though this economic purpose is not as central to the FDCA as protecting public health, one objective need not be the sole guide for how a court constructs a statute that has multiple purposes.

Restitution that reimburses consumers who paid for unapproved drugs, and may have been defrauded or deceived about their effectiveness, restores aggrieved parties to the same economic position they enjoyed before the Act was violated. This strengthens the financial protection offered to the public by the FDCA and enhances consumer confidence in the drug market. Whether or not Congress specifically contemplated restitution under the FDCA, the ability to order this remedy is within the broad equitable power granted to the district courts to further the economic protection purposes of the statute.

Restitution also serves a deterrent function embodied in the district court's authority to "restrain violations of section 331." 21 U.S.C. § 332(a).... Such a forward-looking deterrent effect is an important ancillary consequence of restitution. Given Appellants' repeated violations of the FDCA, committed despite numerous warnings from the FDA, it was within the District Court's equitable discretion to award restitution in order to prevent further violations.

... [T]here is case law and commentary that discusses how we should apply *Porter* and *Mitchell* to the specific context of the FDCA....

Nearly fifty years ago, in *United States v. Parkinson*, 240 F.2d 918 (9th Cir. 1956), the Court of Appeals for the Ninth Circuit rejected the government's request to collect restitution under the FDCA.... *Parkinson* does not survive *Porter* and *Mitchell*....

More recently, the Court of Appeals for the Sixth Circuit rejected the reasoning in *Parkinson* and ordered a party to pay restitution under the FDCA. *Universal Mgmt. Servs., Inc.*, 191 F.3d at 764. In that case, the defendant sold electric gas grill lighters equipped with finger grips as pain reliving devices without obtaining FDA approval. The court held that the grant of equitable power in § 332(a) was so broad that it was within the district court's authority to order restitution....

In the years since *Universal Management*, the FDA has negotiated three consent decrees with drug companies that included significant disgorgement amounts....

Amicus and other commentators have responded vigorously to these consent decrees and to the Universal Management decision. The authors of several recent articles have raised numerous arguments as to why *Porter* and *Mitchell* do not, or should not, authorize courts to order restitution or disgorgement under the FDCA. To the extent that the arguments of commentators are relevant to the instant case, their central claim is that awarding restitution under the FDCA would rewrite or improperly expand the remedies available under the statute. They argue that the ability under § 332(a) "to restrain violations" contemplates only forward-looking remedies and that this mandate excludes restitution....

... Since Congress has placed no unambiguous restriction on equity jurisdiction under § 332(a), the arguments of amicus and other commentators are little more than entreaties that we ignore or overrule *Porter* and *Mitchell*, neither of which we have the power to do.

Also, we view amicus and the commentators as making a fundamental error in analyzing whether restitution is available: they view this primarily as a question of what remedies are provided by the FDCA rather than, as we have emphasized, a question of the scope of the express legislative grant of equitable power under § 332(a). The District Court did not "discover" an implied remedy, but rather exercised the equitable power that Congress explicitly granted to it under the FDCA. . . . [T]here is a presumption that "when Congress entrusts to an equity court the enforcement of prohibitions contained in a regulatory enactment, it must be taken to have acted cognizant of the historic power of equity to provide complete relief in light of the statutory purposes." *Mitchell*, 361 U.S. at 291–92. . . .

. . . Until the Court overrules *Porter* and *Mitchell*, we are bound by the reasoning of those cases. Given the breadth and open-ended nature of § 332(a), and the direct correlation between the language of that provision and the directives in *Porter* and *Mitchell*, we hold that the District Court here did have the power to grant restitution. We will therefore AFFIRM its order.

NOTES

1. *Commentary Supporting FDA's Authority. See* Recent Case, *Statutory Interpretation—Federal Food, Drug, and Cosmetic Act—Third Circuit Holds that the FDA Can Obtain Restitution on Behalf of Consumers*, 119 HARV. L. REV. 2636 (2006).

2. *Restitution vs. Disgorgement.* In *United States v. Rx Depot, Inc.*, 438 F.3d 1052 (10th Cir. 2006), the Tenth Circuit extended the reasoning of *Lane Labs* to hold that a court may, pursuant to its equity power under the FD&C Act, impose the remedy of disgorgement. The court saw no distinction of legal significance between restitution and disgorgement.

3. *Repair, replacement, and refund.* The Medical Device Amendments, in section 518(b) of the FD&C Act, gave FDA restitution ("refund") authority respecting medical devices that present an "unreasonable risk of substantial harm to the public health." As an alternative, FDA can order repair or replacement of the device in question. FD&C Act 518(b). Section 535 of the Act requires manufacturers of electronic products to notify purchasers when they discover safety defects related to the emission of radiation and to repair the defect, replace the product, or refund the cost. FD&C Act 535(f). Regulations implementing this provision appear in 21 C.F.R. Part 1004.

4. *Restitution by Other Agencies. Heater v. FTC*, 503 F.2d 321 (9th Cir. 1974), denied the FTC authority to order restitution. *See also* John A. Sebert, Jr., *Obtaining Monetary Redress for Consumers Through Action by the Federal Trade Commission*, 57 MINN. L. REV. 225 (1972). On the reasoning in *Heater*, authority to order restitution has also been denied to the CPSC under the Flammable Fabrics Act. *Congoleum Industries, Inc. v. CPSC*, 602 F.2d 220 (9th Cir. 1979). However, the CPSC has specific statutory restitution authority under the Federal Hazardous Substances Act, 15 U.S.C. 1274, and the Consumer Product Safety Act, 15 U.S.C. 2064.

F.   RECALLS

Since before passage of the 1938 Act, FDA has used its own resources, and encouraged manufacturers, to recall illegal products from the market. The recall of the infamous Elixir Sulfanilamide accounted for 99.2 percent of the product manufactured. In 1947 the agency explained its practice:

> As soon as the [Food and Drug] Administration learns that a potentially injurious product has been distributed, its efforts to retrieve the suspect batches are abated only when every unit is accounted for. As far as possible this is accomplished through instigating adequate recalls by the shippers and checking upon their effectiveness and the safe disposition of the returned goods. When necessary, the goods are removed from consumer channels by individual visits to wholesale houses, retail drug stores, hospitals, and other consignees, with the very real assistance of State and local enforcement agencies whose efforts have been an important factor in the success of every major round-up. After the dangerous drugs have been accounted for, the firm involved is cited to a hearing with a view to criminal prosecution if the error was one which could have been avoided by good manufacturing practice or could have been corrected at an earlier stage.

FEDERAL SECURITY AGENCY, ANNUAL REPORT 525 (1947).

The question of whether a court or FDA itself can order a manufacturer to recall a product does not often arise. FDA's prevailing practice, on learning about an illegal product in commercial distribution, is informally to encourage the manufacturer to recall it from commercial channels. Almost all FDA-initiated recalls are thus denominated "voluntary." Only if the manufacturer refuses to conduct a recall, or if a volunteered recall proves to be inadequate, will FDA seek a court order or issue a mandatory administrative recall order.

Why do manufacturers almost always comply with FDA recall requests? The threat of adverse publicity is a powerful club for the agency in such situations. Moreover, regulated industries dependent on FDA approval of their products are wary about incurring the agency's wrath. But it is also important to recognize that, lying behind every FDA informal request for a recall is the implied threat that the agency might take formal legal action if the manufacturer does not cooperate. It is thus important to understand the parameters of mandatory recall authority under the FD&C Act, even though this authority is rarely invoked.

COMMENT: MANDATORY RECALLS

Originally, the FD&C Act itself said nothing about recalls. Today, because of various amendments and transfers of administrative responsibility, FDA has explicit statutory authority to mandate recalls in certain limited circumstances.

In 1971, FDA assumed responsibility for implementing the Radiation Control for Health and Safety Act of 1968, 82 Stat. 1173. The Radiation Act, which was originally codified as part of the Public Health Services Act (PHSA), was recodified by 104 Stat. 4511, 4529 (1990) as §§ 531–42 of the FD&C Act. Section 535(f) gives FDA power to mandate the repurchase, repair, or replacement of radiation-emitting electronic products. Although this provision does not explicitly mention recall, FDA has always interpreted it to authorize recall orders as well. *See, e.g.*, 21 C.F.R. 1004.4 (requiring plans for refund to include the "procedure for obtaining possession of the product for which the refund is to be made" and the "steps which the manufacturer will take to insure that the defective products will not be reintroduced into commerce").

In 1972, responsibility for administering the Biological Products portion of the Public Health Service Act (PHSA) was transferred from the National Institutes of Health to FDA. Section 351(d) of the PHSA, as then written and as amended in 1999, gives FDA the power to order recall of a biological product that presents an "imminent or substantial hazard to public health." 42 U.S.C. § 262(d).

The Infant Formula Act of 1980, 94 Stat. 1190, added current section 412(f) to the FD&C Act, directing FDA to prescribe the scope and extent of recalls of infant formulas. The 1980 statute was further strengthened by the Alcohol and Drug Abuse Amendments of 1986, 100 Stat. 3207, 3207, which added the provision now found in section 412(e)(1), requiring a manufacturer to take all actions necessary to recall an infant formula if FDA determines that it presents a risk to human health.

The Safe Medical Devices Act of 1990, 104 Stat. 4511, amended the device provisions in the FD&C Act by adding section 518(e), titled "Recall Authority." This section requires FDA to order cessation of the distribution of a device and notification of health professionals and user facilities if the agency finds that the device would cause serious health consequences or death. After an opportunity for informal hearing, the agency may amend the order to include a recall of the device.

FDA has issued relatively few mandatory recall orders under any of these provisions. *See, e.g.*, FDA ENFORCEMENT REPORT, September 25, 1991 (mandatory § 518(e) recall of enteral feeding pump); April 1, 1992 (mandatory § 518(e) recall of wheelchair lift).

With regard to food (other than infant formula), drugs, cosmetics, and devices that do not pose a serious risk to health, FDA does not itself have formal authority to demand a recall. The agency has, however, successfully sought court orders to recall illegal products, invoking section 302(a), the injunction provision. The case law is split on the question of whether district courts have the power to order recalls under this section. *Cf. United States v. C.E.B. Prods., Inc.*, 380 F. Supp. 664 (N.D. Ill. 1974) (denying authority to require recall); *United States v. Superpharm Corp.*, 530 F. Supp. 408 (E.D.N.Y. 1981) (same) *with United States v. Barr Laboratories, Inc.*, 812 F. Supp. 458, 489 (D.N.J. 1993) (affirming authority to require recall); *United States v. K–N Enterprises, Inc.*, 461 F. Supp. 988, 991 (N.D. Ill. 1978). The trend seems to be toward recognizing the courts' authority to require recalls. As the *Barr Laboratories* court observed: "Although not authorized expressly in the Act, this remedy [recall] is consistent with the broad equitable relief powers district courts enjoy."

Moreover, the reasoning of *Lane Labs*, *supra* p. 1297, in which the Third Circuit recognized the district courts' implicit power to order restitution, seems also to apply to recall. Indeed, *United States v. Universal Mgmt. Servs.*, 191 F.3d 750 (6th Cir. 1999), the other recent Court of Appeals case affirming the remedy of restitution under section 302(a), treated the questions of restitution and recall identically. Thus, interwoven with the Sixth Circuit's discussion of the remedy of restitution was the following dictum on recalls.

> Appellants also rely on a number of district court cases that determine that recalls ... are unavailable under the FDCA. Portions of the legislative history relating to the FDCA indicates [sic] that Congress was concerned about the harshness and seriousness of the remedy of seizure. Injunctive procedures, it is argued, "were viewed as a means to alleviate the hardships seizures might cause to manufacturers." *C.E.B. Prods.*, 380 F. Supp. at 668. Based on that legislative history, the court in *C.E.B. Products* reasoned that a recall provision was probably not within the court's power because it would, in the court's opinion, make an injunction as harsh as a seizure, contrary to the intent of Congress. *See C.E.B. Prods.* 380 F. Supp. at 668. . . .
>
> We reject the holdings in the ... *C.E.B. Products* line of cases. First, the existence of the remedy of seizure exists alongside an explicit authorization for injunctive relief to cure violations of the FDCA. The express provision for general equitable relief without the enumeration of any exceptions makes it difficult for this court to find any legitimate means for implicitly carving out such exceptions as we see fit. . . . [E]ven accepting the references to legislative concerns relied upon by the ... *C.E.B. Products* line, these concerns are far from a clear statement of Congress's intent to exclude ... recalls. . . .

Id. at 761–62.

NOTE

Consent decrees entered in district court by FDA and defendants sometimes require recall by the defendant. For example, the 2002 Schering–Plough consent decree, discussed above, included a number of recall provisions. *United States v. Schering–Plough*, Consent Decree of Permanent Injunction 8, 23, 36 (D.N.J. filed May 20, 2002). In November 2002, FDA entered into a consent decree with a distributor of large gel candies that presented a choking hazard for children. The consent decree provided not only that FDA would supervise the destruction of candies already seized by the United States, but also that the company would withdraw the product still on the market. *See* Press Release, FDA, *New Choice Agrees to Withdraw Remaining Gel Snacks on U.S. Market* (Nov. 6, 2002).

———

FDA's general policy and procedures for recalls, finalized in 1978, are set forth at 21 C.F.R. 7.40 et seq. *See* 43 Fed. Reg. 26202 (June 16, 1978). The following document is the 1976 preamble to the proposed regulations.

Enforcement Policy, Practices and Procedures: Recall Policy and Procedures

41 Fed. Reg. 26924 (June 30, 1976).

Most manufacturers and distributors of products subject to the jurisdiction of FDA have long recognized their responsibility to market safe and properly labeled products and to take measures to protect the public from adulterated and misbranded products that have already reached the marketplace. Indeed, it is not unusual for a firm, when it learns that a distributed product is defective, to take steps to correct the situation by removing the product from commerce or by remedying the defect. The Commissioner generally regards such responsible, voluntary action as an acceptable alternative to an agency-initiated seizure of the defective product.

Most firms honor FDA requests to recall violative foods, drugs, devices, cosmetics, or biologics. . . . Thus, the recall policy and procedures of FDA are, in part, founded upon the cooperation of firms and their willingness to remove violative products from the marketplace. . . .

The Commissioner is proposing these regulations to define more clearly FDA recall policy and procedures and to provide guidance to the regulated industry so that firms may more effectively discharge their responsibility to remove or correct violative products in commerce. The proposed regulations are authorized by section 701(a) of the Federal Food, Drug, and Cosmetic Act . . . and sections 301, 351, and 361 of the Public Health Service Act (42 U.S.C. §§ 241, 262, and 264) relating to cooperative programs for the protection of the public health, to biological products, and to interstate quarantine. The provisions of the proposed regulations that describe responsibilities of recalling firms consist of guidelines rather than enforceable requirements. In this respect, the proposed regulations do not exhaust the authority of FDA to prevent the introduction of violative products into commercial channels, facilitate recalls by manufacturers, and enable the agency to monitor recalls. If experience under the final regulations proves that mandatory requirements are necessary, the Commissioner will propose appropriate revisions.

Product recall has evolved over the years as the most expeditious and effective method of removing violative products from the marketplace, particularly those that present a danger to health. . . .

FDA–initiated recalls. There are two types of FDA-initiated recalls. First, when the agency determines that a marketed product violates the law and so informs the responsible firm, a later recall of the product by that firm is considered an "FDA-initiated recall," even though such action has not been specifically requested by the agency. Second, when use of the product presents a danger to health or significant consumer deception and immediate action is necessary, the Commissioner or his designee will formally notify the firm of this determination and of the need to begin immediately a recall of the product. Because the latter type of FDA-initiated recall is an urgent matter and must be used judiciously, the decision to request a recall shall be made only by the Commissioner or his designee.

Firm-initiated recall. A firm may, for a variety of reasons, on its own initiative remove, correct or otherwise dispose of an illegal product that it has distributed in commerce. FDA has clear authority to require notification [to the agency] that a firm has initiated a recall of new drugs, new animal drugs, biologics, foods subject to emergency permit control, electronic products subject to the Radiation Control for Health and Safety Act, and articles subject to interstate quarantine regulations.* However, the Commissioner also believes it serves the public interest for firms to notify FDA when a recall of any other FDA-regulated product is initiated....

The proposed regulations also provide that the Commissioner will continue the policy of making available to the public information on all recalls by routinely issuing the weekly "FDA Enforcement Report." ... The report is not, however, intended to serve, nor is it used by the agency, as a form of public warning or as a means of seeking publicity in the news media....

A recall involves several separate but related steps that are taken by recalling firms and by FDA. These include: evaluation of the health hazard associated with the product being recalled or being considered for recall; developing and following a recall strategy (described below in this preamble); recall communications to a firm's customers; periodic reports on the progress of the recall; and finally, termination of the recall and proper disposition or correction of the violative product. The combined purpose of these steps is to assure that a recall is conducted in a manner that achieves the orderly removal or correction of a violative product to the extent necessary to protect public health....

Recall strategy. Each recall, whether FDA-initiated or firm-initiated, requires devising a specific course of action to implement the recall....

The elements of a recall strategy include:

1.   Depth of recall. This element refers to the level of product distribution to which the recall is to extend. There are three basic options: (1) Consumer or user level (which may vary with product); (2) retail level; or (3) wholesale level....

2.   Public warnings. This element of the recall strategy refers to FDA-issued warnings to the public about a product in consumer channels that is being recalled. The purpose of a public warning is to alert consumers or users that a product presents a serious hazard to health....

3.   Effectiveness checks. The third element of recall strategy involves verification that consignees (recipients of a product being recalled) have been notified of the recall and have taken appropriate action ... [which is]

---

* [FDA now also has such authority with regard to infant formula and medical devices.]

a vital part of the overall responsibility of recalling firms. For FDA to routinely carry out industry's task of assuring recall effectiveness would represent misuse of public funds. However ... FDA will monitor the efforts of a firm to effect a recall, and where necessary, will initiate its own effectiveness checks....

Because the Commissioner considers recalls to be primarily the responsibility of manufacturers and distributors of regulated products, this notice describes ways in which they should carry out this responsibility, which can be summarized in the following steps:

1. Develop a contingency plan for a recall.

2. Develop the capability of tracing product distribution and identifying the product being recalled.

3. Promptly notify FDA when products are being removed or corrected ... and provide the agency with pertinent information on these actions.

4. Initiate a recall when it is requested by FDA.

5. Develop and follow a recall strategy for handling any recall situation.

6. Assume the responsibility and expense of conducting all aspects of a recall, including effectiveness checks.

7. Notify all consignees of initiated recalls.

8. Evaluate the circumstances causing the violation and take steps to prevent recurrence of violations and future recalls.

9. Provide periodic reports to FDA on the progress of the recall.

10. When a recall is completed, certify to FDA that the recall has been effective and that final disposition of the recalled product has been made....

NOTES

1. *Recall Procedures.* Chapter Seven of FDA's REGULATORY PROCEDURES MANUAL, titled "Recall Procedures," implements the recall regulations set forth at 21 C.F.R. 7.40 et seq. The manual provides FDA personnel with detailed policy, definitions, responsibilities, and procedures for recall actions REGULATORY PROCEDURES MANUAL (rev. ed. March 2004) (Chapter 7 rev. June 14, 2005). In addition, FDA publishes a guidance document for regulated industry on its website. *Product Recalls, Including Removals and Corrections—Industry Guidance* (Nov. 3, 2003).

2. *Infant Formula Recalls.* The recall procedures for infant formula are codified at 21 C.F.R. 107.200–280.

3. *USDA Recall Policy.* FDA and USDA have entered into a Memorandum of Understanding to coordinate their responsibilities for food recalls, published in 40 Fed. Reg. 25079 (June 12, 1975). USDA subsequently announced in 44 Fed. Reg. 56732 (Oct. 2, 1979) the availability of its own internal directive concerning recalls.

4. *Commentary.* There is an extensive literature on FDA recall authority and policy. *See, e.g.,* Michael T. Roberts, *Mandatory Recall Authority: A Sensible and Minimalist Approach to Improving Food Safety,* 59 FOOD & DRUG L.J. 563 (2004); John M. Packman, *Civil and Criminal Liability Associated with Food Recalls,* 53 FOOD & DRUG L.J. 437 (1998); Marc H. Bozeman, *Recalls—On Making the Best of a*

Bad Thing, 33 FOOD DRUG COSM. L. J. 342 (1978); Robert W. Harkins, *Product Recall*, 31 FOOD DRUG COSM. L.J. 383 (1976); Richard W. Kasperson, *Recalls Revisited*, 29 FOOD DRUG COSM. L.J. 242 (1974); Papers Presented at the 27th Annual Meeting of the Food, Drug and Cosmetic Law Section of the New York State Bar Association, reprinted in 27 FOOD DRUG COSM. L.J. 332–354 (1972); A Symposium on the Recall of Food Products presented at the 32nd Annual Meeting of the Institute of Food Technologists, reprinted in 27 FOOD DRUG COSM. L.J. 660–736 (1972).

5.   *GAO Evaluations of FDA Authority and Execution.* For specific General Accounting Office suggestions regarding FDA recall procedures, *see* GAO, LEGISLATIVE AND ADMINISTRATIVE IMPROVEMENTS SHOULD BE CONSIDERED FOR FDA TO BETTER PROTECT THE PUBLIC FROM ADULTERATED FOOD PRODUCTS, No. HRD–84–61 (Sept. 26, 1984); FDA'S OVERSIGHT OF THE 1982 CANNED SALMON RECALLS, No. HRD–84–77 (Sept. 12, 1984); MEDICAL DEVICE RECALLS: AN OVERVIEW AND ANALYSIS 1983–88, PEMD–89–15BR (Aug. 30,1989); MEDICAL DEVICE RECALLS: EXAMINATION OF SELECTED CASES, PEMD–90–6 (Oct. 1989); BLOOD SAFETY: RECALLS AND WITHDRAWALS OF PLASMA PRODUCTS, GAO/T–HEHS–98–166 (May 7, 1998); MEDICAL DEVICES: FDA CAN IMPROVE OVERSIGHT OF TRACKING AND RECALL SYSTEMS, GAO/HEHS–98–211 (Sept. 18, 1998); FOOD SAFETY: USDA AND FDA NEED TO BETTER ENSURE PROMPT AND COMPLETE RECALLS OF POTENTIALLY UNSAFE FOOD, GAO–05–51 (Oct. 7, 2004)

G.   CRIMINAL LIABILITY

1.   THE DECISION TO PROSECUTE

Sam D. Fine,* *The Philosophy of Enforcement*

31 FOOD DRUG COSM. L.J. 324 (1976).

. . . FDA, of necessity, must depend upon the entire regulated industry for a great amount of self-regulation. With its limited resources, the Agency can never hope to monitor completely the massive industries subject to its legislative mandates. . . . Can all of the FDA's enforcement be by self-regulation? I believe we can all agree that the answer is no. . . . I am persuaded that prosecution of firms can have an important and dramatic impact on their peers. . . .

In considering whether or not prosecution action should be forwarded to the next reviewing authority, and eventually to a United States Attorney, one or more of the following general conditions must exist. In most cases, more than one of the conditions does exist.

(1) The violations ordinarily are shown to be of a continuing nature; that is, previous inspections or documented incidents indicate management of the firm is aware of the problem and has failed to take steps to correct the violations. This situation requires a showing of awareness. . . .

(2) The violation is so gross that any reasonable person would conclude management must have known of the conditions. Examples include a heavily insect or rodent-infested warehouse or an obvious fraud. . . .

* [Mr. Fine was FDA Associate Commissioner for Compliance from 1969 to 1976.]

(3) The violations are such that it is obvious that normal attention by management could have prevented them; for example, those situations where violations develop because management delegates authority and does not exercise normal care....

(4) The violations are such that they are life-threatening or injuries have occurred; for example, botulism in improperly prepared products or serious drug mix-ups....

(5) The violations are deliberate attempts to circumvent the law; for instance, submission of false data, falsification of records, or deliberate short weight or subpotency....

What this means is that continuation or repetition of violations over a period of time, or a single gross or deliberate violation, generally will trigger consideration for prosecution....

NOTE

See also H. Thomas Austern, *Sanctions in Silhouette: An Inquiry Into the Enforcement of the Federal Food, Drug, and Cosmetic Act*, 51 CAL. L. REV. 38 (1963); Franklin M. Depew, *The Philosophy of Enforcement of the Federal Food, Drug and Cosmetic Act*, 18 FOOD DRUG COSM. L.J. 185 (1963); Joel Hoffman, *Enforcement Trends Under the Federal Food, Drug and Cosmetic Act—A View From Outside*, 31 FOOD DRUG COSM. L.J. 338 (1976).

2.   STANDARD OF LIABILITY

Most violations of the FD&C Act potentially carry criminal penalties. The Act's standard of criminal liability, as articulated by the United States Supreme Court in *United States v. Dotterweich*, excerpted below, does not include the *mens rea* (guilty mind) element typically required in Anglo–American criminal law. According to *Dotterweich*, the FD&C Act criminalizes the conduct of individuals without consciousness of wrongdoing if they bear a "responsible relation" to the violation. This strict liability standard has proved to be one of the most controversial features of the statute.

United States v. Dotterweich

320 U.S. 277 (1943).

■ MR. JUSTICE FRANKFURTER delivered the opinion of the Court.

This was a prosecution begun by two informations, consolidated for trial, charging Buffalo Pharmacal Company, Inc., and Dotterweich, its president and general manager, with violations of the ... Federal Food, Drug, and Cosmetic Act. The Company, a jobber in drugs, purchased them from their manufacturers and shipped them, repacked under its own label, in interstate commerce.... Three counts went to the jury—two, for shipping misbranded drugs in interstate commerce, and a third, for so shipping an adulterated drug. The jury disagreed as to the corporation and found Dotterweich guilty on all three counts. We start with the finding of the Circuit Court of Appeals that the evidence was adequate to support the verdict of adulteration and misbranding.

Two other questions which the Circuit Court of Appeals decided against Dotterweich call only for summary disposition to clear the path for the main question before us. He invoked § 305 of the Act requiring the Administrator, before reporting a violation for prosecution by a United States Attorney, to give the suspect an "opportunity to present his views." We agree with the Circuit Court of Appeals that the giving of such an opportunity, which was not accorded to Dotterweich, is not a prerequisite to prosecution.... Equally baseless is the claim of Dotterweich that, having failed to find the corporation guilty, the jury could not find him guilty. Whether the jury's verdict was the result of carelessness or compromise or a belief that the responsible individual should suffer the penalty instead of merely increasing, as it were, the cost of running the business of the corporation, is immaterial. Juries may indulge in precisely such motives or vagaries.

And so we are brought to our real problem. The Circuit Court of Appeals, one judge dissenting, reversed the conviction on the ground that only the corporation was the "person" subject to prosecution unless, perchance, Buffalo Pharmacal was a counterfeit corporation serving as a screen for Dotterweich....

The court below drew its conclusion not from the provisions defining the offenses on which this prosecution was based (§§ 301(a) and 303(a)), but from the terms of § 303(c). That section affords immunity from prosecution if certain conditions are satisfied. The condition relevant to this case is a guaranty from the seller of the innocence of his product. So far as here relevant, the provision for an immunizing guaranty is as follows:

> No person shall be subject to the penalties of subsection (a) of this section ... (2) for having violated section 301(a) or (d), if he establishes a guaranty or undertaking signed by, and containing the name and address of, the person residing in the United States from whom he received in good faith the article, to the effect, in case of an alleged violation of section 301(a), that such article is not adulterated or misbranded, within the meaning of this Act, designating this Act....

The Circuit Court of Appeals found it "difficult to believe that Congress expected anyone except the principal to get such a guaranty, or to make the guilt of an agent depend upon whether his employer had gotten one." And so it cut down the scope of the penalizing provisions of the Act to the restrictive view, as a matter of language and policy, it took of the relieving effect of a guaranty.

The guaranty clause cannot be read in isolation.... The purposes of this legislation ... touch phases of the lives and health of people which, in the circumstances of modern industrialism, are largely beyond self-protection. Regard for these purposes should infuse construction of the legislation if it is to be treated as a working instrument of government and not merely as a collection of English words. The prosecution to which Dotterweich was subjected is based on a now familiar type of legislation whereby penalties serve as effective means of regulation. Such legislation dispenses with the conventional requirement for criminal conduct—awareness of some wrongdoing. In the interest of the larger good it puts the burden of acting at hazard upon a person otherwise innocent but standing in responsible relation to a public danger. . . .

The Act is concerned not with the proprietory relation to a misbranded or an adulterated drug but with its distribution. In the case of a corporation such distribution must be accomplished, and may be furthered, by persons standing in various relations to the incorporeal proprietor. . . . To read the guaranty section, as did the court below, so as to restrict liability for penalties to the only person who normally would receive a guaranty— the proprietor—disregards the admonition that "the meaning of a sentence is to be felt rather than to be proved." It also reads an exception to an important provision safeguarding the public welfare with a liberality which more appropriately belongs to enforcement of the central purpose of the Act.

The Circuit Court of Appeals was evidently tempted to make such a devitalizing use of the guaranty provision through fear that an enforcement of § 301(a) as written might operate too harshly by sweeping within its condemnation any person however remotely entangled in the proscribed shipment. But that is not the way to read legislation. Literalism and evisceration are equally to be avoided. To speak with technical accuracy, under § 301 a corporation may commit an offense and all persons who aid and abet its commission are equally guilty. Whether an accused shares responsibility in the business process resulting in unlawful distribution depends on the evidence produced at the trial and its submission—assuming the evidence warrants it—to the jury under appropriate guidance. The offense is committed, unless the enterprise which they are serving enjoys the immunity of a guaranty, by all who do have such a responsible share in the furtherance of the transaction which the statute outlaws, namely, to put into the stream of interstate commerce adulterated or misbranded drugs. Hardship there doubtless may be under a statute which thus penalizes the transaction though consciousness of wrongdoing be totally wanting. Balancing relative hardships, Congress has preferred to place it upon those who have at least the opportunity of informing themselves of the existence of conditions imposed for the protection of consumers before sharing in illicit commerce, rather than to throw the hazard on the innocent public who are wholly helpless.

It would be too treacherous to define or even to indicate by way of illustration the class of employees which stands in such a responsible relation. To attempt a formula embracing the variety of conduct whereby persons may responsibly contribute in furthering a transaction forbidden by an Act of Congress, to wit, to send illicit goods across state lines, would be mischievous futility. In such matters the good sense of prosecutors, the wise guidance of trial judges, and the ultimate judgment of juries must be trusted. Our system of criminal justice necessarily depends on "conscience and circumspection in prosecuting officers," even when the consequences are far more drastic than they are under the provision of law before us. For present purpose it suffices to say that in what the defense characterized as "a very fair charge" the District Court properly left the question of the responsibility of Dotterweich for the shipment to the jury, and there was sufficient evidence to support its verdict.

Reversed.

■ MR. JUSTICE MURPHY, dissenting.

. . . There is no evidence in this case of any personal guilt on the part of the respondent. There is no proof or claim that he ever knew of the introduction into commerce of the adulterated drugs in question, much less that he actively participated in their introduction. Guilt is imputed to the respondent solely on the basis of his authority and responsibility as president and general manager of the corporation.

It is fundamental principle of Anglo–Saxon jurisprudence that guilt is personal and that it ought not lightly to be imputed to a citizen who, like the respondent, has no evil intention or consciousness of wrongdoing. It may be proper to charge him with responsibility to the corporation and the stockholders for negligence and mismanagement. But in the absence of clear statutory authorization it is inconsistent with established canons of criminal law to rest liability on an act in which the accused did not participate and of which he had no personal knowledge. Before we place the stigma of a criminal conviction upon any such citizen the legislative mandate must be clear and unambiguous. . . .

The dangers inherent in any attempt to create liability without express Congressional intention or authorization are illustrated by this case. Without any legislative guides, we are confronted with the problem of determining precisely which officers, employees and agents of a corporation are to be subject to his Act by our fiat. To erect standards of responsibility is a difficult legislative task and the opinion of this Court admits that it is "too treacherous" and a "mischievous futility" for us to engage in such pursuits. But the only alternative is a blind resort to "the good sense of prosecutors, the wise guidance of trial judges, and the ultimate judgment of juries." Yet that situation is precisely what our constitutional system sought to avoid. Reliance on the legislature to define crimes and criminals distinguishes our form of jurisprudence from certain less desirable ones. The legislative power to restrain the liberty and to imperil the good reputation of citizens must not rest upon the variable attitudes and opinions of those charged with the duties of interpreting and enforcing the mandates of the law. I therefore cannot approve the decision of the Court in this case.

■ MR. JUSTICE ROBERTS, MR. JUSTICE REED and MR. JUSTICE RUTLEDGE join in this dissent.

United States v. Park

421 U.S. 658 (1975).

■ MR. CHIEF JUSTICE BURGER delivered the opinion of the Court.

Acme Markets, Inc., is a national retail food chain with approximately 36,000 employees, 874 retail outlets, 12 general warehouses, and four special warehouses. Its headquarters, including the office of the president, respondent Park, who is chief executive officer of the corporation, are located in Philadelphia, Pa. In a five-count information filed in the United States District Court for the District of Maryland, the Government charged Acme and respondent with violations of the Federal Food, Drug, and Cosmetic Act. Each count of the information alleged that the defendants had received food that had been shipped in interstate commerce and that, while the food was being held for sale in Acme's Baltimore warehouse following shipment in interstate commerce, they caused it to be held in a building accessible to rodents and to be exposed to contamination by rodents. These acts were alleged to have resulted in the food's being adulterated within the meaning of 21 U.S.C. §§ 342(a)(3) and (4)....

Acme pleaded guilty to each count of the information. Respondent pleaded not guilty. The evidence at trial demonstrated that in April 1970 the Food and Drug Administration (FDA) advised respondent by letter of insanitary conditions in Acme's Philadelphia warehouse. In 1971 the FDA found that similar conditions existed in the firm's Baltimore warehouse. An FDA consumer safety officer testified concerning evidence of rodent infestation and other insanitary conditions discovered during a 12–day inspection of the Baltimore warehouse in November and December 1971. He also related that a second inspection of the warehouse had been conducted in March 1972. On that occasion the inspectors found that there had been improvement in the sanitary conditions, but that "there was still evidence of rodent activity in the building and in the warehouses and we found some rodent-contaminated lots of food items."

The Government also presented testimony by the Chief of Compliance of the FDA's Baltimore office, who informed respondent by letter of the conditions at the Baltimore warehouse after the first inspection. There was testimony by Acme's Baltimore division vice president, who had responded to the letter on behalf of Acme and respondent and who described the steps taken to remedy the insanitary conditions discovered by both inspections. The Government's final witness, Acme's vice president for legal affairs and assistant secretary, identified respondent as the president and chief executive officer of the company and read a bylaw prescribing the duties of the chief executive officer. He testified that respondent functioned by delegating "normal operating duties," including sanitation, but that he retained "certain things, which are the big, broad, principles of the operation of the company," and had "the responsibility of seeing that they all work together." ...

Respondent was the only defense witness. He testified that, although all of Acme's employees were in a sense under his general direction, the company had an "organizational structure for responsibilities for certain functions" according to which different phases of its operation were "assigned to individuals who, in turn, have staff and departments under them." He identified those individuals responsible for sanitation, and related that upon receipt of the January 1972 FDA letter, he had conferred with the vice president for legal affairs, who informed him that the Baltimore division vice president "was investigating the situation immediately and would be taking corrective action and would be preparing a summary of the corrective action to reply to the letter." Respondent stated that he did not "believe there was anything [he] could have done more constructively than what [he] found was being done."

On cross-examination, respondent conceded that providing sanitary conditions for food offered for sale to the public was something that he was "responsible for in the entire operation of the company," and he stated that it was one of many phases of the company that he assigned to "dependable subordinates." Respondent was asked about and, over the objections of his counsel, admitted receiving the April 1970 letter addressed to him from the FDA regarding insanitary conditions at Acme's Philadelphia warehouse. He acknowledged that, with the exception of the division vice president, the same individuals had responsibility for sanitation in both Baltimore and Philadelphia. Finally, in response to questions concerning the Philadelphia and Baltimore incidents, respondent admitted that the Baltimore problem indicated the system for handling sanitation "wasn't working perfectly" and that as Acme's chief executive officer he was responsible for "any result which occurs in our company."

At the close of the evidence, respondent's renewed motion for a judgment of acquittal was denied. The relevant portion of the trial judge's instructions to the jury challenged by respondent is set out in the margin.[9] Respondent's counsel objected to the instructions on the ground that they failed fairly to reflect our decision in *United States v. Dotterweich*, and to define " 'responsible relationship.' " The trial judge overruled the objection. The jury found respondent guilty on all counts of the information, and he was subsequently sentenced to pay a fine of $50 on each count.

The Court of Appeals reversed the conviction and remanded for a new trial.... The Court of Appeals concluded that the trial judge's instructions "might well have left the jury with the erroneous impression that Park could be found guilty in the absence of 'wrongful action' on his part," and that proof of this element was required by due process. It ... directed that on retrial the jury be instructed as to "wrongful action," which might be "gross negligence and inattention in discharging ... corporate duties and obligations or any of a host of other acts of commission or omission which would 'cause' the contamination of food."

9. "In order to find the Defendant guilty on any count of the Information, you must find beyond a reasonable doubt on each count....

"Thirdly, that John R. Park held a position of authority in the operation of the business of Acme Markets, Incorporated.

"... The main issue for your determination is only with the third element, whether the Defendant held a position of authority and responsibility in the business of Acme Markets....

"The statute makes individuals, as well as corporations, liable for violations. An individual is liable if it is clear, beyond a reasonable doubt, that ... the individual had a responsible relation to the situation, even though he may not have participated personally.

"The individual is or could be liable under the statute, even if he did not consciously do wrong. However, the fact that the Defendant is pres[id]ent and is a chief executive officer of the Acme Markets does not require a finding of guilt. Though, he need not have personally participated in the situation, he must have had a responsible relationship to the issue. The issue is, in this case, whether the Defendant, John R. Park, by virtue of his position in the company, had a position of authority and responsibility in the situation out of which these charges arose."

The Court of Appeals also held that the admission in evidence of the April 1970 FDA warning to respondent was error warranting reversal, based on its conclusion that, "as this case was submitted to the jury and in light of the sole issue presented," there was no need for the evidence and thus that its prejudicial effect outweighed its relevancy. . . .

We granted certiorari because of an apparent conflict among the Courts of Appeals with respect to the standard of liability of corporate officers under the Federal Food, Drug, and Cosmetic Act as construed in *United States v. Dotterweich*, and because of the importance of the question to the Government's enforcement program. We reverse. . . .

The rationale of the interpretation given the Act in *Dotterweich*, as holding criminally accountable the persons whose failure to exercise the authority and supervisory responsibility reposed in them by the business organization resulted in the violation complained of, has been confirmed in our subsequent cases. Thus, the Court has reaffirmed the proposition that "the public interest in the purity of its food is so great as to warrant the imposition of the highest standard of care on distributors." . . . Similarly, in cases decided after *Dotterweich*, the Courts of Appeals have recognized that those corporate agents vested with the responsibility, and power commensurate with that responsibility, to devise whatever measures are necessary to ensure compliance with the Act bears a "responsible relationship" to, or have a "responsible share" in, violations.

Thus *Dotterweich* and the cases which have followed reveal that in providing sanctions which reach and touch the individuals who execute the corporate mission—and this is by no means necessarily confined to a single corporate agent or employee—the Act imposes not only a positive duty to seek out and remedy violations when they occur but also, and primarily, a duty to implement measures that will insure that violations will not occur. The requirements of foresight and vigilance imposed on responsible corporate agents are beyond question demanding, and perhaps onerous, but they are no more stringent than the public has a right to expect of those who voluntarily assume positions of authority in business enterprises whose services and products affect the health and well-being of the public that supports them.[15]

The Act does not, as we observed in *Dotterweich*, make criminal liability turn on "awareness of some wrongdoing" or "conscious fraud." The duty imposed by Congress on responsible corporate agents is, we emphasize, one that requires the highest standard of foresight and vigilance, but the Act, in its criminal aspect, does not require that which is objectively impossible. The theory upon which responsible corporate agents are held criminally accountable for "causing" violations of the Act permits a claim that a defendant was "powerless" to prevent or correct the violation to "be raised defensively at a trial on the merits." *United States v. Wiesenfeld Warehouse Co.*, 376 U.S. 86, 91 (1964). If such a claim is made, the defendant has the burden of coming forward with evidence, but this

---

15. We note that in 1948 the Senate passed an amendment to § 303(a) of the Act to impose criminal liability only for violations committed "willfully or as a result of gross negligence." 94 Cong. Rec. 6760–6761 (1948). However, the amendment was subsequently stricken in conference.

does not alter the Government's ultimate burden of proving beyond a reasonable doubt the defendant's guilt, including his power, in light of the duty imposed by the Act, to prevent or correct the prohibited condition. Congress has seen fit to enforce the accountability of responsible corporate agents dealing with products which may affect the health of consumers by penal sanctions cast in rigorous terms, and the obligation of the courts is to give them effect so long as they do not violate the Constitution.

We cannot agree with the Court of Appeals that it was incumbent upon the District Court to instruct the jury that the Government had the burden of establishing "wrongful action" in the sense in which the Court of Appeals used that phrase. The concept of a "responsible relationship" to, or a "responsible share" in, a violation of the Act indeed imports some measure of blameworthiness; but it is equally clear that the Government establishes a prima facie case when it introduces evidence sufficient to warrant a finding by the trier of the facts that the defendant had, by reason of his position in the corporation, responsibility and authority either to prevent in the first instance, or promptly to correct, the violation complained of, and that he failed to do so. The failure thus to fulfill the duty imposed by the interaction of the corporate agent's authority and the statute furnishes a sufficient causal link. The considerations which prompted the imposition of this duty, and the scope of the duty, provide the measure of culpability. . . .

Our conclusion . . . suggests as well our disagreement with [the Court of Appeals] concerning the admissibility of evidence demonstrating that respondent was advised by the FDA in 1970 of insanitary conditions in Acme's Philadelphia warehouse. We are satisfied that the Act imposes the highest standard of care and permits conviction of responsible corporate officials who, in light of this standard of care, have the power to prevent or correct violations of its provisions. . . .

Respondent testified in his defense that he had employed a system in which he relied upon his subordinates, and that he was ultimately responsible for this system. He testified further that he had found these subordinates to be "dependable" and had "great confidence" in them. By this and other testimony respondent evidently sought to persuade the jury that, as the president of a large corporation, he had no choice but to delegate duties to those in whom he reposed confidence, that he had no reason to suspect his subordinates were failing to insure compliance with the Act, and that, once violations were unearthed, acting through those subordinates he did everything possible to correct them.

Although we need not decide whether this testimony would have entitled respondent to an instruction as to his lack of power, had he requested it, the testimony clearly created the "need" for rebuttal evidence. That evidence was not offered to show that respondent had a propensity to commit criminal acts or that the crime charged had been committed; its purpose was to demonstrate that respondent was on notice that he could not rely on his system of delegation to subordinates to prevent or correct insanitary conditions at Acme's warehouses, and that he must have been aware of the deficiencies of this system before the Baltimore violations were discovered. The evidence was therefore relevant since it served to rebut respondent's defense that he had justifiably relied upon subordinates to handle sanitation matters. And, particularly in light of the difficult task of juries in prosecutions under the Act, we conclude that its relevance and persuasiveness outweighed any prejudicial effect.

Reversed.

■ MR. JUSTICE STEWART, with whom MR. JUSTICE MARSHALL and MR. JUSTICE POWELL join, dissenting.

Although agreeing with much of what is said in the Court's opinion, I dissent from the opinion and judgment, because the jury instructions in this case were not consistent with the law as the Court today expounds it.

As I understand the Court's opinion, it holds that in order to sustain a conviction under § 301(k) of the Federal Food, Drug, and Cosmetic Act the prosecution must at least show that by reason of an individual's corporate position and responsibilities, he had a duty to use care to maintain the physical integrity of the corporation's food products. A jury may then draw the inference that when the food is found to be in such condition as to violate the statute's prohibitions, that condition was "caused" by a breach of the standard of care imposed upon the responsible official. This is the language of negligence, and I agree with it. . . .

The trial judge instructed the jury to find Park guilty if it found beyond a reasonable doubt that Park "had a responsible relation to the situation. . . . The issue is, in this case, whether the Defendant, John R. Park, by virtue of his position in the company, had a position of authority and responsibility in the situation out of which these charges arose." Requiring, as it did, a verdict of guilty upon a finding of "responsibility," this instruction standing alone could have been construed as a direction to convict if the jury found Park "responsible" for the condition in the sense that his position as chief executive officer gave him formal responsibility within the structure of the corporation. But the trial judge went on specifically to caution the jury not to attach such a meaning to his instruction, saying that "the fact that the Defendant is pres[id]ent and is a chief executive officer of the Acme Markets does not require a finding of guilt." "Responsibility" as used by the trial judge therefore had whatever meaning the jury in its unguided discretion chose to give it.

The instructions therefore, expressed nothing more than a tautology. They told the jury: "You must find the defendant guilty if you find that he is to be held accountable for this adulterated food." In other words: "You must find the defendant guilty if you conclude that he is guilty." . . .

. . . The instructions given by the trial court in this case . . . were a virtual nullity, a mere authorization to convict if the jury thought it appropriate. Such instructions—regardless of the blameworthiness of the defendant's conduct, regardless of the social value of the Food, Drug, and Cosmetic Act, and regardless of the importance of convicting those who violate it—have no place in our jurisprudence.

The *Dotterweich* case stands for two propositions, and I accept them both. First, "any person" within the meaning of 21 U.S.C. § 333 may include any corporate officer or employee "standing in responsible relation" to a condition or transaction forbidden by the Act. Second, a person may be convicted of a criminal offense under the Act even in the absence of "the conventional requirement for criminal conduct—awareness of some wrongdoing."

But before a person can be convicted of a criminal violation of this Act, a jury must find—and must be clearly instructed that it must find— evidence beyond a reasonable doubt that he engaged in wrongful conduct amounting at least to common-law negligence. There were no such instructions, and clearly, therefore, no such finding in this case. . . .

NOTES

1. *Prosecutorial Discretion.* The government's brief in *Park*, at pp. 30–32, offered the following account of the agency's exercise of enforcement discretion under the FD&C Act:

> In enacting the 1938 Act Congress recognized that the strict standards of liability created might operate harshly, or even unfairly. Congress therefore expressed its concern that minor violations of the Act should not be subjected to criminal prosecutions. Thus, Section 306 of the Act provides that:
>
>> Nothing in this chapter shall be construed as requiring the Secretary to report for prosecution, or for the institution of libel or injunction proceedings, minor violations of this chapter whenever he believes that the public interest will be adequately served by a suitable written notice or warning.
>
> This provision indicates that FDA was expected to exercise reasonable discretion in invoking the Act's criminal sanctions. . . .
>
> In exercising the reasonable prosecutorial discretion contemplated by Congress and this Court, FDA has applied criteria which do not result in criminal prosecutions for every violation of the statute's strict standard of criminal liability. The government is interested in the prevention and correction of conditions potentially dangerous to the public health and welfare, not in prosecution for its own sake. Accordingly, FDA's standards for reference of cases to the Department of Justice for prosecution embrace the following categories: continuing violations of law (*e.g.*, continuing insanitary conditions in a food plant); violations of an obvious and flagrant nature (*e.g.*, food warehouse overrun with rodents, birds and insects, which contains plainly contaminated products); and intentionally false or fraudulent violations.
>
> The standard for prosecution of individual corporate officials, as distinguished from the prosecution of their corporations, is based on the reasonable relationship criterion of *Dotterweich*. The government's policy is to prosecute only those individuals who are in a position and who have an opportunity to prevent or correct violations, but fail to do so. Officials who lack authority to prevent or correct violations, or who were totally unaware of any problem and could not have been expected to be aware of it in the reasonable exercise of their corporate duties, are not the subject of criminal action. Even if investigation discloses the elements of liability, and indicates that an official bears a responsible relationship to them, the agency will not ordinarily recommend prosecution unless that official, after becoming aware of possible violations, often (as with Park) as a result of notification by FDA, has failed to correct them or to change his managerial

system so as to prevent further violations. In those instances where prosecution is brought, it is brought for past, as well as the most recent, violations. . . .

See also FDA, REGULATORY PROCEDURES MANUAL ch. 8–50.

2. *Lack of Knowledge. United States v. Parfait Powder Puff Co.*, 163 F.2d 1008 (7th Cir. 1947), affirmed the defendant's conviction for introducing an adulterated cosmetic product into interstate commerce. The defendant, a cosmetics company, had entered into a contract with Helfrich Laboratories under which Helfrich would manufacture and distribute hair lacquer pads with the Parfait Powder Puff Company label. Defendant tested the first sample submitted by Helfrich and found it satisfactory. When shellac supplies became difficult to obtain, however, Helfrich made a substitution in the lacquer formula without the defendant's knowledge. Subsequently, the defendant learned of the substitution and immediately forbade its use. The defendant's argument that Helfrich was an independent contractor for whose acts it was not responsible was rejected by the court of appeals, which reasoned that the defendant incurred liability when it voluntarily selected Helfrich to manufacture and distribute a product it knew would become part of interstate commerce.

3. *Responsible Officer.* A district court's revocation of a suspended sentence for violation of the Act was sustained in *United States v. Shapiro*, 491 F.2d 335 (6th Cir. 1974). The defendant, convicted for operating the Tasty Cookie Company under unsanitary conditions, was given a probated sentence contingent upon his rectifying those conditions before continuing production. The defendant also agreed to sell the plant as soon as a buyer could be found. Following the trial court's order, the plant was temporarily closed for cleaning. Within several months the defendant entered into a formal "operations and management" agreement giving the newly found buyer complete production control until the final closing. Several days prior to that closing, FDA inspected the plant and found it infested with vermin. Acting upon the FDA's petition, the trial court revoked probation and imposed a 6–month sentence. The court was unpersuaded by the defendant's arguments that he was no longer the responsible officer because equitable title and plant control had passed to his purchaser. The court of appeals found that the trial judge had not abused his discretion in revoking probation under these circumstances because the defendant still had legal title at the time of inspection.

4. *Record of Conviction.* Where individual defendants were acquitted on all charges of intent to violate the FD&C Act, but were convicted under the *Park* doctrine that intent is not required, the court reluctantly denied the defendants' motion to expunge their criminal records in *United States v. Purity Condiments, Inc.*, Food Drug Cosm. L. Rep. (CCH) ¶ 38,276 (S.D. Fla. 1984). The court concluded that the rationale underlying the FD&C Act and the applicable precedent left no choice but to deny the motions for expungement, but characterized this lack of discretionary power as amounting to "an unreasonable and impermissible restraint on judicial authority."

COMMENT: THE DEFENSE OF IMPOSSIBILITY

In *Park*, the Court observed: "The duty imposed by Congress on responsible corporate agents is, we emphasize, one that requires the highest standard of foresight and vigilance, but the Act, in its criminal aspect, does not require that which is objectively impossible." The Supreme Court had earlier held that a defendant in a criminal action under the FD&C Act can introduce evidence at trial that he was "powerless" to prevent or correct the violation. *United States v. Weisenfeld Warehouse Co.,* 376 U.S. 86, 91 (1964). To advance the impossibility defense, the defendant must come forward with sufficient evidence of impossibility to warrant placing an additional burden on the government, namely, the burden of establishing beyond a reasonable doubt that the defendant could have prevented or corrected the prohibited condition through the exercise of extraordinary care. *See U.S. v. Gel Spice Co.,* 773 F.2d 427, 434–35 (2d Cir. 1985). *Cf. U.S. v. New England Grocers Supply Co.,* 488 F. Supp. 230, 236 (D. Mass. 1980) (suggesting that the defendant must establish that he actually exercised extraordinary care).

In practice, defendants have had trouble sustaining the impossibility defense. For example, in *United States v. Certified Grocers Co–Op,* 1968–1974 FDLI Jud. Rec. 299 (W.D. Wis. 1974), the court denied defendants' motion to dismiss the information charging violation of the Act by the holding and contamination of foods in a rodent infested warehouse. The court refused to accept the defense even though the prosecution stipulated that the defendant was doing everything possible to maintain sanitary conditions in that warehouse. The court reasoned that the defendants were helpless only for as long as they continued to use that particular warehouse.

In the wake of *Park,* courts continued to rein in the impossibility defense. The Ninth Circuit, applying the *Park* standard of "foresight and vigilance," upheld the convictions of corporate officers in two cases decided the same day in 1976. By *per curiam* opinion in *United States v. Y. Hata & Co., Ltd.,* 535 F.2d 508 (9th Cir. 1976), the court rejected the defense tendered by the company's president that he had done everything possible to correct the unsanitary warehouse conditions. Having discovered the violations months before FDA inspection, the company had attempted unsuccessfully, through various methods, to prevent access of birds to stored food. At the time of inspection, the company was awaiting shipment of materials with which it would build a huge wire cage enclosing the warehouse. The court concluded that since "a wire cage is scarcely a novel preventive device," it would not have been "objectively impossible" for the defendant to implement this effective solution earlier. Consequently, the defendant was not excused.

Rodent infestation and contamination of stored food resulted in the conviction of the corporation's secretary-treasurer in *United States v. Starr,* 535 F.2d 512 (9th Cir. 1976). The defendant advanced a two-pronged argument of objective impossibility. First, the defendant asserted that he was helpless to prevent contamination resulting from the natural flow of rodents seeking sanctuary from the plowing of a nearby field. The court rejected this argument, remarking, "One with only a minimum of foresight would recognize that rodents and insects would flee from freshly plowed fields." Second, the defendant claimed that he had instructed the janitor to correct the situation, and the janitor deliberately failed to do so. The Court of Appeals denied that this situation obligated the trial judge to give an "objective impossibility" instruction to the jury, because the defendant worked in close proximity to the scene of the violations and was therefore in a position to observe for himself whether the necessary corrections were being made. *See also United States v. Gel Spice Co., Inc.*, 773 F.2d 427 (2d Cir. 1985).

The impossibility defense does not invariably fail, however. For example, the court in *United States v. New England Grocers Supply Co.*, 488 F. Supp. 230 (D. Mass. 1980), set aside a magistrate's finding of guilt. The court held that if a defendant introduced sufficient evidence that he had exercised "extraordinary care" and still could not prevent the violation, the burden shifted to the government affirmatively to establish, beyond a reasonable doubt, that the defendant could have prevented the violation through the exercise of extraordinary care. The court remanded the case so the magistrate could apply this standard properly.

3.   THE GUARANTY CLAUSE

Under section 303(c) of the Act, a person who in good faith merely receives and later delivers an illegal article is exempt from criminal liability. And a person who introduces an illegal article into commerce is also exempt from liability if he has received the article in good faith and obtained a written guaranty that it is not in violation of the Act. In turn, the giving of a false guaranty is prohibited by section 301(h) and is thus a criminal offense.

United States v. Crown Rubber Sundries Co.

67 F. Supp. 92 (N.D. Ohio 1946).

■ FREED, DISTRICT JUDGE.

Crown Rubber Sundries Co., a partnership, and one of the partners, individually, Joseph Lader, were charged in eight counts of an information alleging violation ... in the shipment and sale of rubber prophylactics which were, in fact, ineffective for prophylactic purposes because of the presence of holes and perforations in the devices.... The defendants rely solely upon the claim that they are free from guilt because they received a guaranty given them by the L. E. Shunk Latex Products, Inc., the manufacturer, warranting that all the merchandise complied with the provisions of the Pure Food, Drug and Cosmetic Act, and authorizing them to make the same guaranty to their distributees.

The undisputed facts show that the defendants received the merchandise in bulk, that they repacked the prophylactics in individual containers bearing their own labels and shipped them to their own customers. There was some evidence tending to show that the merchandise was acquired by the purchase of a wholesale business which had in stock the prophylactics which the original owner had purchased from the Shunk company....

Assuming, for the purpose of the instant case, that the defendants did have a right to rely upon a guaranty received from someone other than the person from whom they purchased the merchandise, the question remains whether the guaranty affords a defense under the statute.

The decided cases have not dealt with the question here raised. The report of the Congressional committees ... indicates it was the intent of

Congress to relieve the manufacturer of the effect of violations of the Act that result from the processing of his products by others for whom the manufacturer should not be liable.

Neither the reported cases, nor the Committees' report deals with the question of the defense available to the shipper who holds a guaranty from the manufacturer.

It is fundamental that the purpose of the Act is to protect the consumer. Public policy casts upon those who introduce foods, drugs and cosmetics into interstate commerce the duty of rigid inspection. They are charged with absolute responsibility for proper branding of their products. Public safety demands of them not only extreme care, but definite assurance of the quality of their products.

It is the judgment of this court that no person may rely upon any guaranty unless, in introducing the product into interstate commerce, he has acted merely as a conduit through which the merchandise reaches the consumer.... The guaranty can be received in good faith, within the meaning of the statute, only if the shipper passes the product on in the same form as he received it, without repacking it or subjecting it to any new hazards of adulteration or failure which were not present when the original guaranty upon which he relies was given.

The facts in this case show the prophylactics were purchased by the defendants in bulk and that they repackaged and relabeled them. They shipped them in cartons bearing their own trade name.

When this state of facts appears, in the judgment of the court, as a matter of law, the defense of the guaranty no longer is available to the defendants....

NOTE

Guaranty with Assurances. In *United States v. Balanced Foods*, 146 F. Supp. 154 (S.D.N.Y. 1955), government agents informed a food shipper, who had received a guarantee, that the product in question was misbranded. The defendant shipper communicated this fact to the guarantor and was given assurances that the charge was a mistake. The court held that the defendant could justifiably rely on such assurances until there was an adjudication or authoritative determination that the merchandise was misbranded.

United States v. Walsh

331 U.S. 432 (1947).

■ MR. JUSTICE MURPHY delivered the opinion of the Court.

This appeal brings before us § 301(h) of the Federal Food, Drug and Cosmetic Act of 1938, which prohibits the giving of a false guaranty that any food, drug, device or cosmetic is not adulterated or misbranded within the meaning of the Act.

Appellee does business in San Diego, California, under the name of Kelp Laboratories. An information has been filed, charging appellee with having given a false guaranty in violation of § 301(h). The following facts have been alleged: In February 1943, appellee gave a continuing guaranty to Richard Harrison Products, of Hollywood, California, stating that no products thereafter shipped to the latter would be adulterated or misbranded within the meaning of the Act. On February 24, 1945, while the guaranty was in full force and effect, appellee consigned to Richard Harrison Products, at Hollywood, a shipment of vitamin products which were allegedly adulterated and misbranded—thereby making the guaranty false in respect of that shipment. . . .

Appellee moved to dismiss the information on the ground that it did not state an offense. The argument was that § 301(h) applies only to a guaranty that is false relative to an interstate shipment, whereas the alleged shipment here was to a consignee within California, the state of origin, and there was no allegation that the consignee purchased the order for someone outside California or that it intended to sell the products in its interstate rather than its intrastate business. The District Court gave an oral opinion sustaining appellee's contention and granting the motion to dismiss. The case is here on direct appeal by the United States. . . .

. . . § 301(h), with which we are concerned, does not speak specifically in interstate terms. It prohibits the "giving of a guaranty or undertaking referred to in section 303(c)(2), which guaranty or undertaking is false". . . . Nothing on the face of the section limits its application to guaranties relating to articles introduced or delivered for introduction into interstate commerce. . . .

We thus conclude that § 301(h) definitely proscribes the giving of a false guaranty to one engaged wholly or partly in an interstate business irrespective of whether that guaranty leads in any particular instance to an illegal shipment in interstate commerce. Such a construction is entirely consistent with the interstate setting of the Act. A manufacturer or processor ordinarily has no way of knowing whether a dealer, whose business includes making interstate sales, will redistribute a particular shipment in interstate or intrastate commerce. But if he guarantees that his product is not adulterated or misbranded within the meaning of the Act, he clearly intends to assure the dealer that the latter may redistribute the product in interstate commerce without incurring any of the liabilities of the Act. And the dealer is thereby more likely to engage in interstate distribution without making an independent check of the product. The possibility that a false guarantee to him may give rise to an illegal shipment by such a dealer is strong enough to make reasonable the prohibition of all false guaranties to him, even though some of them may actually result only in intrastate distribution. . . .

So construed, § 301(h) raises no constitutional difficulties. The commerce clause of the Constitution is not to be interpreted so as to deny to Congress the power to make effective its regulation of interstate commerce. . . .

[The dissenting opinion of Mr. Justice Jackson is omitted.]

NOTE

See also *Barnes v. United States*, 142 F.2d 648 (9th Cir. 1944), *United States v. Santoro & Sons, Inc.*, 1965–1968 FDLI JUD. & ADMIN. REC. 277 (E.D.N.Y. 1965); *United States v. Colosse Cheese & Butter Co.*, 133 F. Supp. 953 (N.D.N.Y. 1955).

4.   SECTION 305 HEARINGS

Enforcement Policy, Practices, and Procedures: Informal Hearing Before Report on Criminal Violation
41 Fed. Reg. 14769 (April 7, 1976).

Section 305 of the act provides that "Before any violation of this Act is reported by the Secretary to any United States attorney for institution of a criminal proceeding, the person against whom such proceeding is contemplated shall be given appropriate notice and an opportunity to present his views, either orally or in writing, with regard to such contemplated proceeding." . . .

. . . Congress recognized when it enacted the 1938 act that not all violations would warrant prosecution. Accordingly, the act included section 306, which provides that when the Secretary of Health, Education, and Welfare believes the public interest would be adequately served by a suitable written notice or warning, he need not report minor violations for the institution of prosecution, seizure, or injunction.

Many violations, including most minor violations, can be readily corrected if brought promptly to the attention of the person responsible. To deal with such violations, FDA in the past used an administrative procedure known as "citation for warning." Over the years, this practice was used for many types of violations that, in the agency's judgment, appeared to fall somewhere between those that are subject to [a § 305] informal hearing before report of a criminal violation and those that are subject to section 306 of the act.

Although the practice of citation for warning frequently achieved correction of violations, it also had an undesirable consequence. Because it was often used to deal with violations for which the agency was not prepared to recommend prosecution, citation for warning diluted the significance of section 305 hearings in situations in which prosecution was clearly appropriate. This practice has therefore been abandoned. With the addition of "recalls" and "regulatory letters" to FDA's enforcement measures, section 305 hearings are no longer used to deal with those types of violations in which some sort of warning is a proper first step. Instead, section 305 hearings are used as Congress originally intended. FDA accordingly will schedule a hearing only when criminal prosecution is seriously contemplated.

It must be recognized, however, that the failure to provide an opportunity for a section 305 hearing is not a bar to prosecution of persons who violate the act. The legislative history of the act makes clear that a section 305 hearing is not a prerequisite to prosecution, and the United States Supreme Court has upheld this position . . . *United States v. Dotterweich*,

320 U.S. 277, 278–79 (1943). [H]owever, the Commissioner will dispense with the section 305 hearing procedure only in compelling circumstances. This would occur so infrequently, if ever, that it is not prudent to attempt to illustrate the "compelling circumstances" standard by examples. . . .

Response to a Notice of Hearing, in writing or in person, is entirely voluntary. A person who receives a Notice of Hearing may elect not to respond, may respond in writing, may respond through a designated representative, or may appear personally with or without the aid of counsel. Failure by any person to respond to the Notice of Hearing will not prejudice the agency's final determination. A decision whether the matter will be referred to a United States attorney will be made solely on the evidence in the agency's possession. The Commissioner notes, however, that the opportunity for presentation of views may be important where the person who received the Notice of Hearing believes he is not responsible for the alleged violations. . . .

Sharp differences frequently appear between FDA's views as set forth in the Charge Sheet and the respondents' views expressed during the section 305 hearing. It is important that the summary of the hearing that is prepared be accurate and fairly reflect the views of the respondents. Accordingly, the proposed procedures adopt current agency practice under which the hearing officer dictates a summary of the hearing in the presence of the respondents and affords them an opportunity to make any necessary corrections or additions. Furthermore, although a section 305 hearing is not a formal hearing, either the respondent or the agency may arrange for the preparation of a verbatim transcript. The proposed regulations also permit a respondent to supplement the record of his personal appearance following the hearing. . . .

After reviewing all relevant information, FDA may conclude not to recommend prosecution of one or more persons named in a Notice of Hearing. Whenever FDA and the United States attorney both decide not to prosecute all persons names in a Notice of Hearing for the offenses charged, the Commissioner will undertake to notify such persons. No individual named in the Notice of Hearing will be notified of a decision not to seek prosecution until determination has been made that such notification will not prejudice the prosecution of any other person. . . .

NOTES

1. *FDA Regulations.* Final regulations governing section 305 hearings were promulgated in 42 Fed. Reg. 6801 (Feb. 4, 1977) and codified in 21 C.F.R. 7.84 *et seq.* Later, in 43 Fed. Reg. 20508 (May 12, 1978), FDA proposed to revise the regulations:

> Section 305 of the act, by its terms, applies only when the agency has determined that "a violation" of the act has occurred and the agency intends to refer the case to a United States attorney for a "criminal proceeding" that is, prosecution. A request for a grand jury investigation does not constitute the reporting of a violation for prosecution. Accordingly, the revised regulation, in § 7.85(a), makes clear that the agency need not hold a section 305 hearing when it is considering recommending a

grand jury investigation instead of a criminal prosecution based on the evidence then available. . . .

Since a 305 notice alerts a prospective defendant that prosecution may be imminent, it may result in the alteration or destruction of potentially incriminating evidence. . . . When FDA has reason to believe that such alteration or destruction will occur, or that a potential defendant will flee, a 305 notice need not be issued.

. . . FDA's current practice is to reference in the 305 notice other Federal statutes violated by the same conduct that violates the Federal Food, Drug, and Cosmetic Act. This practice is retained in revised § 7.84(c). However, if the agency does not contemplate proceeding with a recommendation under the Federal Food, Drug, and Cosmetic Act, no 305 hearing will be held with regard to the violation of other statutes.

The revisions resulting from this proposal were promulgated in 44 Fed. Reg. 12164 (March 5, 1979); FDA, REGULATORY PROCEDURES MANUAL ch. 8–40.

2. *Commentary*. For further treatment of hearings under section 305, *see* Raymond McMurray, *Section 305 Hearings—Defense Considerations*, 31 FOOD DRUG COSM. L.J. 386 (1976); Eugene Pfeifer, *Section 305 Hearings and Criminal Prosecutions*, 31 FOOD DRUG COSM. L.J. 376 (1976); Robert Wilmoth, *Criminal Prosecutions, Inspections and Section 305 Hearings*, 33 FOOD DRUG COSM. L.J. 360 (1978).

COMMENT: AUTHORIZED CRIMINAL PENALTIES

Under section 303(a), violations of the Act are generally misdemeanors, but they may be felonies if they constitute second offenses or are committed "with the intent to defraud or mislead." Such "intent" includes the intent to defraud or mislead not only ultimate consumers, but also state and federal government enforcement agencies. *See United States v. Bradshaw*, 840 F.2d 871 (11th Cir. 1988), *cert. denied*, 488 U.S. 924 (1988).

Section 303(a) provides criminal penalties of $1,000 or up to one year in jail for any misdemeanor violation of the Act and $10,000 or up to three years in jail for a felony violation. In the Sentencing Reform Act of 1984, 98 Stat. 1837, Congress enacted new criminal fines in 18 U.S.C. § 3571, which were made applicable to any offense under any federal statute by 18 U.S.C. § 3551. In the Criminal Fines Improvement Act of 1987, Congress amended section 3571 to raise the maximum fines. 101 Stat. 1279. The current provisions impose maximum fines for individuals of $100,000 for a misdemeanor that does not result in death and $250,000 for a misdemeanor resulting in death or for a felony. For corporations, the maximums are $200,000 for a misdemeanor that does not result in death and $500,000 for a misdemeanor resulting in death or a felony.

The Prescription Drug Marketing Act of 1987, 102 Stat. 95, 99 added section 303(b)(1), which establishes criminal penalties of not more than 10 years imprisonment or a fine of not more than $250,000 for violation of the prescription drug sample requirements in that statute. Under section 303(b)(5), moreover, a "bounty hunter" who provides information leading to the arrest and conviction of a person for a violation is entitled to one-half of the criminal fine but not more than $125,000.

NOTES

1. *Venue for Trial.* The Sixth Amendment to the Constitution provides that a criminal defendant has the right to be tried in the "district wherein the crime shall have been committed." The court in *United States v. Beach–Nut Nutrition Corp.,* 871 F.2d 1181 (2d Cir. 1989), reversed convictions for adulteration of orange juice because the adulteration did not occur in the district where the trial was held. *Cf. United States v. Taller,* 394 F.2d 435 (2d Cir. 1968).

2. *Separate Violations.* FDA may bring a separate criminal charge for each illegal action, even if all the violations arose out of a single transaction. *See United States v. H. B. Gregory Co.,* 502 F.2d 700 (7th Cir. 1974); *Akin Distributors of Florida, Inc. v. United States,* 399 F.2d 306 (5th Cir. 1968); *V.E. Irons, Inc. v. United States,* 244 F.2d 34 (1st Cir. 1957).

3. *Unsuccessful Prosecutions.* The criminal cases that FDA has lost at trial have rarely been reported. Section 705(a) requires FDA "from time to time" to publish reports summarizing all judgments, decrees, and orders rendered under the FD&C Act. The agency used to list such notices of judgment in FDA CONSUMER, but it has not done so since 2002.

4. *Interaction of Civil and Criminal Proceedings.* In *United States v. Kordel,* 397 U.S. 1 (1970), FDA instituted a seizure, served interrogatories, and then issued a notice under section 305 of the Act that the agency also contemplated criminal prosecution. The defendant objected to answering the interrogatories while the possibility of a criminal action existed, but it ultimately complied and supplied the answers, which were then used in the criminal prosecution. The Supreme Court held that this did not violate the privilege against self-incrimination or basic standards of fairness, concluding that FDA should not be required to choose between civil and criminal enforcement proceedings. *See also United States v. Gel Spice Co., Inc.,* 773 F.2d 427 (2d Cir. 1985).

5. *Commentary. See, e.g.,* Nicholas Freitag, *Federal Food and Drug Act Violations,* 41 AM. CRIM. L. REV. 647 (2004); George M. Burditt, *The Park Case in Perspective,* 31 FOOD DRUG COSM. L.J. 137 (1976); Daniel F. O'Keefe, Jr., *Criminal Liability: Park Update,* 32 FOOD DRUG COSM. L.J. 392 (1977); Daniel F. O'Keefe & C. Willard Isley, *Dotterweich Revisited—Criminal Liability Under the Federal Food, Drug, and Cosmetic Act,* 31 FOOD DRUG COSM. L.J. 69 (1976); Daniel F. O'Keefe, Jr., & Marc H. Shapiro, *Personal Criminal Liability Under the Federal Food, Drug, and Cosmetic Act: The Dotterweich Doctrine,* 30 FOOD DRUG COSM. L.J. 5 (1975); Richard A. Merrill, *The Park Case,* 30 FOOD DRUG COSM. L.J. 683 (1975); Roger M. Rodwin, *A Violation of the Federal Food, Drug, and Cosmetic Act—A Crime in Search of a Criminal,* 31 FOOD DRUG COSM. L.J. 616 (1976); S. Prakash Sethi & Robert W. Katz, *The Expanding Scope of Personal Criminal Liability of Corporate Executives—Some Implications of United States v. Park,* 32 FOOD DRUG COSM. L.J. 544 (1977).

COMMENT: OTHER STATUTES INVOKED IN CRIMINAL ENFORCEMENT OF THE FD&C ACT

Several provisions in Title 18 of the United States Code are potentially available for ancillary enforcement of the FD&C Act:

Conspiracy, 18 U.S.C. 371. United States v. Munoz, 430 F.3d 1357 (11th Cir. 2005); *United States v. Ellis,* 326 F.3d 550 (4th Cir. 2003); *United States. v. Prigmore,* 243 F.3d 1 (1st Cir. 2001); *United States v. Beech–Nut Nutrition Corp.,* 871 F.2d 1181 (2d Cir. 1989), *United States v. Automated Medical Laboratories, Inc.,* 770 F.3d 399 (4th Cir. 1985); *United*

States v. General Nutrition, Inc., 638 F. Supp. 556 (W.D.N.Y. 1986); *United States v. Haga*, 1985–1986 FDLI Jud. Rec. 146 (N.D. Tex. 1986).

False Statements, 18 U.S.C. 1001. U.S. v. C.R. Bard, Inc., 848 F. Supp. 287 (D. Mass. 1994); *United States v. Keplinger*, 776 F.2d 678 (7th Cir. 1985); *United States v. Automated Medical Laboratories, Inc.*, 770 F.2d 399 (4th Cir.1985); *United States v. Smith*, 740 F.2d 734 (9th Cir. 1984); *United States v. Velsicol Chemical Corp.*, 498 F. Supp. 1255 (D.D.C. 1980).

Mail Fraud, 18 U.S.C. 1341. U.S. v. Leahy, 438 F.3d 328 (3d Cir. 2006); *U.S. v. Livdahl*, 356 F. Supp. 2d 1289 (S.D. Fla. 2005); *U.S. v. Snyder*, 291 F.3d 1291 (11th Cir. 2002); *United States v. Beech–Nut Nutrition Corp.*, 871 F.2d 1181 (2d Cir. 1989).

Perjury, 18 U.S.C. 1623. U.S. v. Stewart, 433 F.3d 273 (2d Cir. 2006); *United States v. Lighte*, 782 F.2d 367 (2d Cir. 1986).

Federal Conspiracy Statute. FDA and the Department of Justice frequently charge a violation of the general federal conspiracy statute, 18 U.S.C. 371, as well as the FD&C Act in drug misbranding cases, because it has a long maximum sentence of 20 years and can encompass mere attempts under 18 U.S.C. 1349. Allegations of mail fraud under 18 U.S.C. 1341 and wire fraud under 18 U.S.C. 1343 are often added. The defendant's conviction for conspiracy to defraud FDA by attempting to hide the fact that he was distributing misbranded and unapproved new drugs was upheld under 18 U.S.C. 371 in *United States v. Ballistrea*, 101 F.3d 827 (2d Cir. 1996). In *United States v. Mitcheltree*, 940 F.2d 1329 (10th Cir. 1991), however, a conviction for intent to defraud and mislead under the FD&C Act and 18 U.S.C. 371 was reversed and remanded for a new trial where there was no evidence of a specific intent to defraud or mislead FDA. See also *United States v. Arlen*, 947 F.2d 139 (5th Cir. 1991); *United States v. Acosta*, 17 F.3d 538 (2d Cir. 1994); *United States v. Antosh*, 172 F.3d 877 (9th Cir. 1999).

H.   DEBARMENT

Bae v. Shalala

44 F.3d 489 (7th Cir. 1995).

■ COFFEY, CIRCUIT JUDGE.

Petitioner Kun Chae Bae, the former president of a generic drug manufacturing company, appeals the final order of the Food and Drug Administration ("FDA") under the Generic Drug Enforcement Act of 1992 ("GDEA"), 21 U.S.C. §§ 335a–335c, permanently debarring him from "providing services in any capacity to a person that has an approved or pending drug product application." The GDEA mandates permanent debarment for any individual "convicted of a felony under [f]ederal law for conduct ... relating to the development or approval, ... or ... [other] regulation of any drug product" under the Federal Food, Drug, and

Cosmetic Act.[1] The FDA debarred Bae because of his 1990 felony conviction for aiding and abetting interstate travel in aid of racketeering, which arose from allegations that, in 1987, Bae provided an FDA official with an "unlawful gratuity" in exchange for "official acts performed and to be performed" by the FDA official. This case presents the question of whether and under what circumstances a civil debarment penalty may constitute retroactive punishment prohibited by the *Ex Post Facto* Clause of the United States Constitution. We affirm.

I.   BACKGROUND

While president of My–K Laboratories, Bae submitted several abbreviated new drug applications to the FDA's Division of Generic Drugs. . . . Charles Y. Chang, the Branch Chief of the FDA's chemistry review branch in Maryland, was responsible for supervising the chemists who evaluated My–K Laboratories' abbreviated new drug applications. . . .

. . . In 1990, Bae was charged with and pleaded guilty to one felony count of aiding and abetting interstate travel in aid of racketeering. . . . The Information alleged that on or about August 21, 1987, Bae caused . . . Chang to travel from Maryland to Illinois with the intent to provide Chang with an "unlawful gratuity." The Information further alleged that during Chang's visit to Illinois, Bae gave Chang $10,000 "for and because of official acts performed and to be performed" by Chang. The statement of facts accompanying the Information asserted that Chang provided Bae "with several formulations for generic drugs which Chang had gleaned from other companies' [applications]."

By certified letter dated March 30, 1993, the FDA notified Bae that it proposed to debar him from participation in the generic drug industry pursuant to 21 U.S.C. § 335a(a)(2) based on his prior felony conviction for conduct relating to the development or approval of a generic drug product. The FDA notified Bae that he would have the opportunity for an evidentiary hearing, should he desire to contest his debarment, if he presented specific facts, in writing, demonstrating a genuine and substantial issue of fact relevant to his debarment. Bae requested a hearing, but submitted no specific facts, and instead raised the argument that the GDEA's debarment provision was punitive in nature, and that its retroactive application to him violated the constitutional prohibition against *ex post facto* laws. The FDA, after reviewing Bae's request for a hearing, denied the request, finding that Bae had failed to raise any genuine or substantial issue of fact relevant to his debarment. On December 30, 1993, the FDA issued a final order permanently debarring Bae from providing services in any capacity to a person with a pending or approved drug product application.

---

1. Section 335a(a)(2) provides that [i]f the Secretary finds that an individual has been convicted of a felony under Federal law for conduct—(A) relating to the development or approval, including the process for development or approval, of any drug product, or (B) otherwise relating to the regulation of any drug product under this chapter, the Secretary shall debar such individual from providing services in any capacity to a person that has an approved or pending drug product application.

II. DISCUSSION

. . . .

The *Ex Post Facto* Clause of the United States Constitution, Article I, § 9, clause 3, prohibits the enactment of any law "which imposes a punishment for an act which was not punishable at the time it was committed; or imposes additional punishment to that then prescribed." "[F]or a criminal or penal law to be *ex post facto* . . . it must be retrospective, that is, it must apply to events occurring before its enactment, and it must disadvantage the offender affected by it." *Weaver v. Graham*, 450 U.S. 24, 28 (1981).

A civil sanction, like the debarment provision of the GDEA, will implicate *ex post facto* concerns only if it can fairly be characterized as punishment. *United States v. Halper*, 490 U.S. 435, 447–48 (1989).

> The mark of an *ex post facto* law is the imposition of what can fairly be designated punishment for past acts. The question in each case where unpleasant consequences are brought to bear upon an individual for prior conduct, is whether the legislative aim was to punish that individual for past activity, or whether the restriction of the individual comes about as a relevant incident to a regulation of a present situation, such as the proper qualifications for a profession.

In *Halper*, the Supreme Court described the proper analysis to determine whether a given civil sanction constitutes punishment in the constitutional sense:

> . . . We have recognized in other contexts that punishment serves the twin aims of retribution and deterrence. . . . [I]t follows that a civil sanction that cannot fairly be said solely to serve a remedial purpose, but rather can only be explained as also serving either retributive or deterrent purposes, is punishment, as we have come to understand the term. . . . We therefore hold that under the Double Jeopardy Clause a defendant who already has been punished in a criminal prosecution may not be subjected to an additional civil sanction to the extent that the second sanction may not fairly be characterized as remedial, but only as a deterrent or retribution.

The aim of the GDEA was to restore consumer confidence in generic drugs by eradicating the widespread corruption in the generic drug approval process. The preamble to the GDEA focuses exclusively on its remedial purpose, *i.e.*, "to restore and to ensure the integrity of the abbreviated drug application approval process and to protect the public health." Pub.L. 102–282, § 1(c). Enactment of the GDEA was prompted by the 1988 investigation that revealed the crimes of Bae and others in connection with the FDA's generic drug approval process. . . . With these objective goals, the GDEA can fairly be said solely to serve a remedial purpose.

Bae argues that a civil sanction that serves both remedial and punitive goals must be characterized as punishment. Bae contends that debarment cannot be said to serve solely remedial purposes because debarment is triggered only by a criminal conviction, and the only basis for limiting or terminating an otherwise permanent debarment is to provide substantial assistance to the government in other criminal prosecutions. We refuse to read *Halper* so broadly. A civil sanction that can fairly be said solely to serve remedial goals will not fail under *ex post facto* scrutiny simply because it is consistent with punitive goals as well. A civil sanction will be deemed to be punishment in the constitutional sense only if the sanction "may not fairly be characterized as remedial, but *only* as a deterrent or retribution." *Halper*, 490 U.S. at 449 (emphasis added). Without question, the GDEA serves compelling governmental interests unrelated to punishment. The punitive effects of the GDEA are merely incidental to its overriding purpose to safeguard the integrity of the generic drug industry while protecting public health.

Our inquiry does not end here. We must also determine whether the legislative history of the GDEA evinces an intent to punish. Bae points out that the legislators who sponsored the GDEA repeatedly sought support for the bill in the name of deterrence.

Even though the legislative history of the GDEA is replete with references to its deterrent objective, we are unconvinced that Congress, as a whole, intended the mandatory debarment provision of the GDEA to serve solely punitive goals.... The Supreme Court has consistently required "unmistakable evidence of punitive intent" to characterize a sanction as punishment....

... [A] deterrent purpose does not automatically mark a civil sanction as a form of punishment. General deterrence is the foremost and overriding goal of all laws, both civil and criminal, and transcends the nature of any sanction. General deterrence aims to dissuade all persons from violating the laws....

Bae finally argues that his permanent debarment is overwhelmingly disproportionate to the remedial goals of the GDEA.... [W]e must determine whether Bae's permanent debarment from participation in the generic drug industry "reasonably can be viewed as a remedial measure commensurate with his wrongdoing." *Furlett*, 974 F.2d at 844.

A number of appellate courts have upheld debarments and other similar employment restrictions to serve nonpunitive, remedial goals. The employment restrictions imposed in [these cases] were of limited duration.... In contrast, petitioner Bae's debarment is permanent. However, the duration or severity of an employment restriction will not mark it as punishment where it is intended to further a legitimate governmental purpose. This court has twice upheld permanent employment bans against double jeopardy and *ex post facto* challenges....

In enacting the GDEA, Congress adopted a bright-line rule excluding from the generic drug industry all individuals with prior felony convictions relating to the approval or regulation of any generic drug product. Although Bae's permanent debarment from providing services in any capacity to a person with an approved or pending drug product application is undoubtedly harsh, it is not disproportionate to the remedial goals of the GDEA or to the magnitude of his wrongdoing. Bae's actions were both unlawful and unscrupulous. Bae lined the pockets of a high-ranking FDA official with thousands of dollars in exchange for information or preferential treatment. His contribution to the widespread corruption in the generic drug industry was by no means slight. We agree with the Tenth Circuit that

> [i]t is the clear intent of debarment to purge government programs of corrupt influences and to prevent improper dissipation of public funds. Removal of persons whose participation in these programs is detrimental to public purposes is remedial by definition. While those persons may interpret debarment as punitive, and indeed feel as though they have been punished, debarment constitutes the "rough remedial justice" permissible as a prophylactic governmental action.

. . . .

III. CONCLUSION

By enacting the mandatory debarment provision of the GDEA, Congress sought not to punish Kun Chae Bae but to safeguard the integrity of the generic drug industry. The clear and unambiguous intent of Congress in passing the GDEA was to purge the generic drug industry of corruption and to restore consumer confidence in generic drug products. The GDEA's civil debarment penalty is solely remedial, even though it "carries the sting of punishment" in the eyes of petitioner Bae. Accordingly, the FDA's final order permanently debarring Bae from providing services in any capacity to a person with an approved or pending drug product application is

AFFIRMED.

NOTES

1. *Subsequent Cases.* The reasoning of *Bae* was embraced in *DiCola v. FDA*, 77 F.3d 504 (D.C. Cir. 1996) and *Bhutani v. FDA*, 161 Fed. Appx. 589 (7th Cir. 2006).

2. *Frequency of Debarment.* Since 1993, the FDA has debarred 68 individuals and no firms. A list of debarments is available on the FDA website.

I. CIVIL PENALTIES

The 1938 FD&C Act contained no provisions authorizing civil money penalties. For many years, the only authority FDA had to seek such penalties was under the Radiation Control for Health and Safety Act of 1968, which amended the Public Health Service Act to regulate radiation-emitting electronic products. (FDA assumed responsibility for administering the Radiation Act in 1971.) Former section 360(C) of the PHS Act, now codified as section 539 of the FD&C Act, empowers FDA to seek the imposition of civil penalties for violations of the Radiation Act in federal district court. FD&C Act 539(b), (c).

Beginning in the late 1980s, Congress repeatedly amended the FD&C Act and the PHS Act to give FDA authority to impose civil money penalties for various types of violations. The National Childhood Vaccine Injury Act of 1986 added civil penalties to the PHS Act for violations of the biological product recall provision and the vaccine manufacturer recordkeeping requirements. 42 U.S.C. 262(d)(2), 300aa–28(b)(1). The Prescription Drug Marketing Act of 1987 authorizes FDA to seek civil penalties from manufacturers or distributors convicted of violations of the drug sample provisions of the FD&C Act or parallel state laws. FD&C Act 333(b)(2). *See also* FD&C Act 332(b)(3) (civil penalty for failing to report conviction under state law).

The Safe Medical Devices Act of 1990 authorizes FDA to impose civil penalties on "any person who violates a requirement of this Act which relates to devices." FD&C Act 303(f)(1)(A). *See also* FD&C Act 303(f)(1)(B) (exempting certain violations from civil money penalties). The Generic Drug Enforcement Act of 1992 added civil penalties for various categories of misconduct in connection with an Abbreviated New Drug Application. FD&C Act 307. The Food Quality Protection Act of 1996 authorizes FDA to seek civil penalties from people other than growers who introduce food containing unsafe pesticide chemicals into interstate commerce. FD&C Act 303(f)(2). Finally, the Mammography Quality Standards Acts of 1992 and 1998, amending the PHSA, include civil penalties for various violations regarding mammography facilities. 42 U.S.C. § 263b(h)(2). *See* 58 Fed. Reg. 30,680, 30,680–82 (May 26, 1993) (summarizing the civil money penalty provisions enacted to that point).

Under the Radiation Act, the United States must file an action in federal district court to obtain an order imposing civil money penalties. Under all of the later civil penalty provisions, by contrast, FDA can impose the monetary penalties itself, through administrative order, after notice and an administrative hearing. Some of the statutory provisions in question explicitly provide for administrative imposition of the civil money penalties, but even with regard to those that are "silent on whether Congress intended civil money penalties to be judicially or administrative imposed," FDA has declared that it has "the authority to choose which [approach] it believes best." 58 Fed. Reg. at 30,680. In 1995, the agency issued final regulations establishing the hearing procedures for the imposition of civil money penalty provisions. 21 C.F.R. Part 17.

FDA's most broad-ranging new power to impose civil penalties is its authority, under the Safe Medical Devices Act of 1990, to seek such sanctions for most violations of the FD&C Act relating to medical devices. The agency has extensively considered the purposes and application of this provision.

Guidance for FDA Staff: Civil Money Penalty Policy

Draft Guidance: Not for Implementation.
Center for Devices and Radiological Health, June 8, 1999.

PURPOSE:

This document is addressed to all FDA Regional and District Directors for the purpose of advising field personnel of this new guidance policy when pursuing potential Civil Money Penalty (CMP) recommendations under the Safe Medical Devices Act of 1990 (SMDA).

This guidance document ... does not create or confer any rights for or on any person and does not operate to bind FDA or the public. . . .

BACKGROUND:

... FDA has considerable latitude when applying CMP to violations involving devices. CMP cases should serve to eliminate the profit from violative activity and/or to provide non-compliant firms with the financial incentive to correct violations. . . .

GENERAL PHILOSOPHY:

The Safe Medical Devices Act of 1990 (SMDA) added civil money penalty (CMP) authority as a supplement to the existing statutory remedies of seizure, injunction, and prosecution, primarily to "take the profit out of noncompliance."

CMP is considered to be a remedial action, not punitive. This means it is designed to influence future conduct of the affected firm and/or other firms that are similarly situated, either directly, by affecting current violative conduct, or indirectly, by serving to deter future violative conduct.

When the monies spent on corrective actions will be deducted from the fine imposed, CMP action can also provide non-compliant firms with a financial incentive to come into compliance. . . . In these cases, even if the firm pays a sharply reduced fine, the remedial goal of the CMP action will have been accomplished if the firm successfully and promptly brings itself into compliance.

Pursuant to the SMDA, CMP cases that have not been settled are in the first instance resolved by administrative hearings, if the individual or company requests it by filing an answer. Hearings are held before an Administrative Law Judge in accordance with procedures contained in 21 CFR Part 17. Appeals can be heard by the Health and Human Services Departmental Appeals Board and subsequently by a United States Circuit Court of Appeals, if needed. Evidence and testimony developed for administrative hearings must be prepared as carefully and as thoroughly as if the case were being tried in federal court. Companies that wish to avoid hearings may resolve the dispute by entering into consent agreements. . . .

DECISION TREE PROCESS:

The Decision Tree is designed to assist the Office of Regulatory Affairs (ORA) ... and the Center in determining whether the evidence and information collected justifies pursuing a CMP case. . . .

The Decision Tree reflects that CMP may be considered in cases where:

- In general:
  - Other regulatory action is NOT appropriate,
  - Prior warning has been given,
  - FDA policy is clear; and

- Statutory factors in Section 303(f) support the case.

. . . .

1.   Suitability of Other Regulatory Options

First, determine whether regulatory action other than CMP is necessary to address the violations. Current violations warrant consideration of seizure or injunction. (A combination of CMP with seizure or injunction should be considered only on rare occasions and only for egregious or flagrant violations).

If other civil action is *not* deemed appropriate, consider whether prosecution is appropriate. CMP and prosecution will not be initiated for the same violative conduct. Should neither seizure, injunction, nor prosecution be appropriate, you may want to consider CMP. CMP may be used for both past violations that have since been corrected as well as for current or continuing violations.

Note that CMP action may be appropriate in situations in which all of the violations have been corrected. For example, CMP could be used for a firm that continued to violate the law for a period of time before coming into compliance. In this instance, CMP would eliminate or reduce the profit derived from the violative activity; however, in setting a penalty amount, please bear in mind that in some cases violators may deem it advantageous to distribute devices even though no short term profits are realized.

2.   Prior Warning

If other regulatory action is not appropriate, consider whether FDA has notified the firm or individual of a violation of the Act. . . . Only in rare and compelling cases should a CMP be initiated without prior warning. . . .

3.   Clarity of FDA Policy

If there has been prior warning, determine whether the Agency's expectation (policy) is clear regarding the regulatory requirements affecting the potential defendants. . . . The key is whether a neutral person would say that industry had or should have had a clear understanding of FDA's requirements.

4.   Statutory Factors

If the policy is clear, consider the statutory factors under section 303(f)(3)(B) of the Act. FDA is required to consider the following statutory factors in determining the amount of the CMP in each case: the nature, circumstances, extent, and gravity of the violations, and with respect to the violator, the ability to pay, the effect on the ability to continue to do business, any history of such prior violations, the degree of culpability, and such other matters as justice may require. . . .

Nature of the violations refers to a general evaluation of the type and seriousness of statutory or regulatory violation(s) considered in the abstract, without regard to the facts of a particular case. The general seriousness of the violation refers to the relationship of the type of violation to the different purposes of the Act.

Violations of laws and rules that relate to the Act's core purposes and the Agency's mission, *e.g.*, the premarket approval and clearance provisions and provisions that bear materially on the safety and effectiveness of the product would be very serious; violations of misbranding provisions, *e.g.*, those prohibiting false or misleading claims, may be in a mid-range of severity. Violations of provisions requiring that labels declare the identity of the manufacturer (unless the omissions were part of a plan to avoid detection) may be evaluated "low." The seriousness of GMP violations will vary. Thus, a violation of a record keeping requirement might be "low," whereas a failure to sterilize a device would probably be "high."

Circumstances of the violations refers to the context in which the violations occur and to facts extrinsic to the legal elements of the violations themselves. The circumstances of violations may include both mitigating and aggravating factors. Examples of facts to be considered in this category include the clarity and number of the prior warnings; the clarity of applicable statutes, regulations, or policies; and whether the violations were of an obvious nature.

Extent of the violations refers to the number and variety of documented violations and the length of time during which the violations continued. Although you may only use the number of *shipments* to calculate the initial penalty assessment you may consider the number of devices included within each shipment to evaluate the extent of the violations.

Gravity of the violations refers to the consequences, actual and potential, of the violations. Consider, for example, whether any patients or users were harmed or placed at risk of harm by the violation; the classification of the device (generally, violations involving class III devices will increase the gravity of the offense); whether the defendants benefited from the violation (*e.g.*, by generating sales, maintaining market position, or creating an early market niche or other advantage); and the amount of Agency or other public resources that were needed to investigate and rectify the violations.

Ability to Pay—In evaluating this factor, consider the size of the firm, including factors such as revenues (sales); assets, including accounts receivable; past and projected liabilities; and the financial position of any individual defendants. Does the firm have, at a minimum, assets that would permit it to pay the fine over time?

In assessing fines for small businesses, you must take into account the money spent to correct the violations for which the fines are being sought. (*See* Presidential Memorandum 4/21/95 (60 FR 20621) and Small Business Regulatory Enforcement Fairness Act of 1996.) . . .

Effect on Continued Business—In evaluating this factor, the most important issue is the relationship between the penalty FDA is seeking and its effect on the firm's ability to remain in business (*i.e.*, pay salaries and rent, purchase raw materials and equipment, etc.) after payment of the penalty. . . . If there is no money to pay the fine, then consider other regulatory actions. . . .

History of prior violations refers to prior conduct of the person that is similar in nature to the violations in the current case; you may consider conduct as similar even if it does not implicate the identical law or regulation. . . .

Degree of culpability refers to the level of blameworthiness. Consider, for example, whether the violations were intentional, reckless, careless, or inadvertent; whether the persons were obstructive or cooperative during the investigation and following notification; whether the violations involved were condoned by many actors or high level corporate officials; whether, upon learning of the violation, the person took timely action to correct the violation, eliminate or reduce the risk that the instant violation would cause future harm, and made restitution to any parties harmed by the violative conduct. You should also consider whether, within a reasonably prompt time after becoming aware of the offense—and before and without knowledge of the commencement of a formal investigation of that violation—the person disclosed the violation to FDA; and whether the violation occurred despite the defendant's implementation of a program designed to prevent and detect violations of law.

Other factors as justice may require is a catch-all category that permits consideration of any fact, whether aggravating or mitigating, that reasonably bears upon the evaluation of a penalty assessment. Among other factors, you may consider the factual and legal strength of the government's case, the availability and credibility of witnesses, and the amount of resources that would be required to adjudicate the case.

. . . .

NOTES

1. *Frequency of Civil Penalties Under SMDA.* Not surprisingly, FDA does not often impose civil money penalties under the SMDA. Between 1997 and 2000, for example, the agency did not collect such penalties even once. FDA, THE ENFORCEMENT STORY (2001), *available on* FDA Website. For two recent examples of civil penalties that were collected (both as a result of consent agreements), see FDA, THE ENFORCEMENT STORY (2002), "Civil Money Penalty Case for In Vitro Test Kit," *available on* FDA Website ($250,000 fine levied in 2002 against a company marketing an OTC "drugs of abuse" test kit that had been cleared only for professional use); *In re Lahaye Center for Advanced Eye Care*, Settlement Agreement (Nov. 7, 2003), *available on* FDA Website ($950,000 penalty imposed in 2003 on an eye care center using an excimer laser for vision correction outside the scope of its investigational device exemption).

2. *Frequency of Civil Penalties Under Radiation Act and MQSA.* CDRH, FDA's device center, can also seek civil penalties under the Radiation Act and the Mammography Quality Standards Act. The civil penalties policy under the Radiation Act is set forth in Compliance Policy Guide No. 7133.23 (March 1, 1983) (rev. Apr. 2005). CDRH has, on a few occasions, collected civil penalties under this Act. *See United States v. Hodges X–Ray, Inc.*, 759 F.2d 557 (6th Cir. 1985); *Throneberry v. FDA*, 1983–84 FDLI Jud. Rec. 242, 382 (E.D. Tenn. 1983). The agency has not recently pursued civil penalties under the Radiation Act. It has, however, sought and collected civil fines from mammography facilities under the Mammography Quality Standards Act. *See* HHS NEWS, Mammography Facility Fined, Shut Down (Aug. 12, 1998); *In re Korangy Radiology Assocs.*, FDA Docket No. 2003H–0432 (Dec. 17, 2004).

3. *Frequency of Other Civil Penalties.* FDA has rarely, if ever, sought civil penalties under the National Childhood Vaccine Injury Act, the Prescription Drug Marketing Act, the Generic Drug Enforcement Act, or the Food Quality Protection Act.

4. *Penalties Against Small Entities.* The Small Business Regulatory Enforcement Fairness Act of 1996, 110 Stat. 857, and a Presidential Memorandum of April 21, 1995, 60 Fed. Reg. 20,621 (Apr. 26, 1995), mandate that agencies improve the regulatory climate for small entities by establishing civil penalty reduction policies for small entities. FDA explains its decisional process for determining whether to reduce civil money penalties for small entities in its GUIDANCE FOR INDUSTRY AND FDA STAFF, REDUCTION OF CIVIL MONEY PENALTIES FOR SMALL ENTITIES (2001). *See* 66 Fed. Reg. 15,726 (Mar. 20, 2001) (notice of availability of guidance).

5. *Inflation Adjustment.* The Federal Civil Penalties Inflation Adjustment Act of 1990 Pub. L. 101–410, requires agencies to issue regulations every four years to adjust for inflation each civil money penalty provided by statutes within their jurisdiction. Therefore, the maximum amounts stated in the various civil penalty provisions of the FD&C Act and the PHSA are no longer in force. The higher, adjusted amounts currently in force are listed at 21 C.F.R. 17.2.

J. INFORMAL COMPLIANCE CORRESPONDENCE

Section 309 of the FD&C Act (formerly section 306) permits FDA to decline to institute formal enforcement proceedings for "minor violations of this Act whenever [it] believes that the public interest will be adequately served by a suitable written notice or warning." Historically, FDA relied primarily upon seizure and other formal court proceedings to enforce the FD&C Act. Beginning in the early 1970s, however, the agency developed regulatory letters and other informal compliance correspondence as alternatives to court enforcement. The agency established a two-tiered approach to such correspondence. A "Regulatory Letter" warned a violator that formal enforcement was likely in the absence of voluntary compliance. By contrast, a "Report of Investigational Finding" (also known as an "Information Letter") requested voluntary correction but made no representation that formal enforcement action was imminent. This two-tiered approach continues today, although the nomenclature has evolved: "Regulatory Letters" are now known as "Warning Letters," and "Information Letters" are now denominated "Untitled Letters."

FDA Regulatory Procedures Manual, Chapter 4 ("Advisory Actions")

March 2006.

4–1   WARNING LETTERS

4–1–1   Warning Letter Procedures

When it is consistent with the public protection responsibilities of the agency and depending on the nature of the violation, it is the Food and Drug Administration's (FDA's) practice to give individuals and firms an opportunity to take voluntary and prompt corrective action before it initiates an enforcement action. Warning Letters are issued to achieve voluntary compliance and to establish prior notice.... The use of Warning Letters and the prior notice policy are based on the expectation that most individuals and firms will voluntarily comply with the law.

The agency position is that Warning Letters are issued only for violations of regulatory significance. Significant violations are those violations that may lead to enforcement action if not promptly and adequately corrected. A Warning Letter is the agency's principal means of achieving prompt voluntary compliance with the Federal Food, Drug, and Cosmetic Act (the Act).

The Warning Letter was developed to correct violations of the statutes or regulations. Also available to the agency are enforcement strategies which are based on the particular set of circumstances at hand and may include sequential or concurrent FDA enforcement actions such as recall, seizure, injunction, administrative detention, civil money penalties and/or prosecution to achieve correction. Despite the significance of the violations, there are some circumstances that may preclude the agency from taking any further enforcement action following the issuance of a Warning Letter. For example, the violation may be serious enough to warrant a Warning Letter and subsequent seizure; however, if the seizable quantity fails to meet the agency's threshold value for seizures, the agency may choose not to pursue a seizure. In this instance, the Warning Letter would document prior warning if adequate corrections are not made and enforcement action is warranted at a later time.

Responsible officials in positions of authority in regulated firms have a legal duty to implement whatever measures are necessary to ensure that their products, practices, processes, or other activities comply with the law. Under the law such individuals are presumed to be fully aware of their responsibilities. Consequently, responsible individuals should not assume that they would receive a Warning Letter, or other prior notice, before FDA initiates enforcement action.

FDA is under no legal obligation to warn individuals or firms that they or their products are in violation of the law before taking enforcement action, except in a few specifically defined areas....

A Warning Letter is informal and advisory. It communicates the agency's position on a matter, but it does not commit FDA to taking enforcement action. For these reasons, FDA does not consider Warning Letters to be final agency action on which it can be sued.

There are instances when issuing a Warning Letter is not appropriate, and, as previously stated, a Warning Letter is not a prerequisite to taking enforcement action. Examples of situations where the agency will take enforcement action without necessarily issuing a Warning Letter include:

1. The violation reflects a history of repeated or continual conduct of a similar or substantially similar nature during which time the individual and/or firm has been notified of a similar or substantially similar violation;

2. The violation is intentional or flagrant;

3. The violation presents a reasonable possibility of injury or death;

4. The violations, under Title 18 U.S.C. 1001 [criminalizing "Fraud and False Statements"], are intentional and willful acts that once having occurred cannot be retracted. Also, such a felony violation does not require prior notice. Therefore, Title 18 U.S.C. 1001 violations are not suitable for inclusion in Warning Letters; and,

5. When adequate notice has been given by other means and the violations have not been corrected, or are continuing....

. . . .

4–1–10 Warning Letter Format

Warning Letters can vary in form, style, and content to provide the flexibility needed to accurately and effectively state the nature of the violation(s) found and the response expected. However, the elements listed below are common to Warning Letters:

1. Title: "WARNING LETTER."

. . . .

3. The Warning Letter should be addressed to the highest known official in the corporation that includes the facility that was inspected, and a copy should be sent to the highest known official at the facility that was inspected....

4. The dates of the inspection and a description of the violative condition, practice, or product in brief but sufficient detail to provide the respondent the opportunity to take corrective action. Include citation of the section of the law and, where applicable, the regulation violated....

. . . .

6. A request for correction and a written response within a specific period of time after the date of receipt of the letter, usually fifteen (15) working days. At the district's discretion, the recipient may be offered an opportunity to discuss the letter with district officials or, when appropriate, with center officials.

. . . .

10. A warning statement that failure to achieve prompt correction may result in enforcement action without further notice. Examples of such actions may be cited. Do not include a commitment to take enforcement action.

. . . .

12. Issued by the district director, division director, or higher agency official. Some program areas will require center concurrence before issuance.

. . . .

4–2 UNTITLED LETTERS

An Untitled Letter cites violations that do not meet the threshold of regulatory significance for a Warning Letter. Therefore, the format and content of an Untitled Letter should clearly distinguish it from a Warning Letter. For example:

1. The letter is not titled.

. . . .

3. The letter does not include a warning statement that failure to take prompt correction may result in enforcement action.

. . . .

5. The letter requests (rather than requires) a written response from the firm within a reasonable amount of time (*e.g.*, "Please respond within 30 days"), unless more specific instructions are provided in a relevant compliance program.

Any appropriate agency compliance official may issue an Untitled Letter.

. . . .

COMMENT: MANDATORY OCC CLEARANCE OF ENFORCEMENT CORRESPONDENCE

On November 29, 2001, the Deputy Secretary of the Department of Health and Human Services directed FDA to submit all Warning Letters and Untitled Letters to FDA's Office of Chief Counsel (OCC) prior to their issuance so that they can be reviewed for legal sufficiency and consistency with agency policy. These procedures were implemented in March 2002 and are now attached as an exhibit to Chapter 4 of the Regulatory Procedures Manual. Following the institution of the OCC review policy, the number of FDA warning letters dropped sharply.

When FDA devised Regulatory Letters in the early 1970s, the agency intended them to represent final statements of enforcement policy subject to court challenge. FDA later retreated from this position, characterizing Regulatory Letters as informal correspondence, which did not constitute final agency action, and the courts agreed. *E.g., Biotics Research Corp. v. Heckler*, 710 F.2d 1375 (9th Cir. 1983). This policy change occurred because OCC had no control over the issuance of regulatory letters and thus was not prepared routinely to defend them in court. Despite the mandatory OCC clearance policy now in effect, FDA continues to maintain, as stated in the above excerpt from Regulatory Procedures Manual: "FDA does not consider Warning Letters to be final agency action on which it can be sued."

COMMENT: SECTION 309 AND FDA ENFORCEMENT DISCRETION

The Supreme Court has cited section 309 (formerly section 306) in rejecting arguments for literal interpretation of the FD&C Act's broader provisions. *See, e.g., United States v. Dotterweich*, 320 U.S. 277 (1943); *United States v. Sullivan*, 332 U.S. 689 (1948); *United States v. Park*, 421 U.S. 658 (1975); *Heckler v. Chaney*, 470 U.S. 821 (1985). FDA itself has cited section 309 as authority for the issuance of informal tolerances for filth and other contaminants in food, and courts have accepted this argument. *See, e.g., United States v. 484 Bags, More or Less*, 423 F.2d 839, 841 (5th Cir. 1970); *Dean Rubber Mfg. Co. v. United States*, 356 F.2d 161, 164 (8th Cir. 1966).

There are, however, limits to FDA's discretion to refrain from initiating enforcement against violations of the FD&C Act. In the late 1970s, FDA proposed to continue to allow the use of nitrates in food during an indefinite phase-out period, even if they were found to be carcinogenic. The Secretary of Health, Education, and Welfare (HEW was then FDA's parent agency) sought the Attorney General's opinion regarding the legality of this approach. The Attorney General rejected the suggestion that section 306 conferred such discretion.

> The FDA has informed you that it would not regard the deliberate, continued additions of a carcinogenic substance to food—even at a controlled level—as minor violations within the meaning of [section 306]. This conclusion is compatible with the legislative history of the Delaney Clause expressing a clear congressional purpose to prevent the establishment of *any* tolerance level for a substance found to cause cancer when ingested by man or animals. Such violations would appear to be one of "substance rather than form" for which enforcement "action is necessary to effect compliance." Therefore, the proposed phasing out of nitrite use does not conform to the scope of enforcement discretion contemplated by the Congress when it enacted the Food and Drug Act....

> The proposed phasing out of nitrites through the withholding of enforcement ... would not be a mere formalization of FDA policy on the allocation of scarce enforcement resources, an identification of minor violations, or an effort to give content or limits to a vague statute. The effect of the policy—indeed its purpose— would be to authorize the continued use of nitrites in certain products under circumstances that would concededly constitute non-minor violations of the specific terms of the Food and Drug Act....

> The public health considerations underlying the desire to permit the continued addition of nitrites and nitrates to certain foods are clearly important. But the balancing of these competing health risks is a matter for the Congress in determining whether to amend the Food and Drug Act, not for the Secretary in administering the law....

43 Op. Att'y Gen. 19 (1979).

Conversely, section 309 gives FDA virtually unfettered discretion to pursue formal enforcement rather than issue a warning. Defendants' attempts to invoke the provision to challenge agency decisions to initiate enforcement proceedings have been unsuccessful. In *United States v. Hunter Pharmacy, Inc.*, 213 F. Supp. 323 (S.D.N.Y. 1963), the court responded to such an argument as follows:

... The determination of whether a violation is of such a nature as not to require criminal prosecution to vindicate the public interest is entrusted to the judgment of the Secretary. In the instant case, the reference of the matter to the United States Attorney for prosecution is indication that he deems the offenses as other than "minor," or that he believes the public interest will not be adequately safeguarded by a warning. The statute nowhere commands, with respect to this section, that he establish rules and regulations for procedures to determine whether a warning instead of a prosecution of injunction serves to vindicate the public interest. The statute itself indicates the matter rests in his discretion.

K. PUBLICITY

Unlike many regulatory laws, which leave the matter to implication, the FD&C Act in section 705 ("Publicity") expressly authorizes the issuance of information to the public. Section 705(a) obligates FDA to publish "from time to time" summaries of all formal enforcement actions resolved in court. Section 705(b) permits FDA also to disseminate information regarding regulated products "in situations involving . . . imminent danger to health, or gross deception of the consumer." *See also* PHS Act 301(b), 42 U.S.C. 242o (requiring Secretary, from time to time, to issue "information related to public health" for the public and to publish weekly reports of "health conditions . . . and other pertinent health information" for health care deliverers).

Hoxsey Cancer Clinic v. Folsom

155 F. Supp. 376 (D.D.C. 1957).

■ HOLTZOFF, DISTRICT JUDGE.

The Food and Drug Administration has issued a circular, copies of which are being posted in post offices throughout the country, warning the public that the so-called Hoxsey cancer treatment has been found worthless insofar as internal cancer is concerned. It also warns those afflicted with cancer not to be misled by the false promise that the Hoxsey cancer treatment will cure or alleviate their condition. This action is brought by Harry M. Hoxsey who claims to have treated patients afflicted with cancer, to enjoin the Secretary of the Department of Health, Education, and Welfare, and the Commissioner of the Food and Drug Administration, against the dissemination of this poster.

The defendants claim that they are acting pursuant to the authority of [Section 705(b) of the FD&C Act]. . . .

It is claimed in behalf of the plaintiff that the statute to which reference has just been made is unconstitutional as a denial of due process of law in that it does not provide for any notice or hearing, administrative or otherwise, before the Secretary disseminates information of the type described in the statute. It is elementary law, of course, that an order of an administrative agency adjudicating rights or directing someone to do or refrain from doing something must be based on a hearing after due notice. Here, however, the situation is entirely different. The defendants have made no order; they are issuing no directions. What they are doing is disseminating information and warning the public against the use of certain medicines and of a certain treatment for internal cancer. There is no basis for requiring a hearing before information can be disseminated.

But beyond that, even in the absence of this statute there would be nothing to prevent the defendants from disseminating information to the public. . . . The defendants are performing a public duty when they are urging the use of certain treatments or warning the public against the use of certain treatments. The only purpose of this statute is to place within the express scope of the duties of the Secretary something that was one of his implied functions.

If, however, the contents of the poster were erroneous then the question might arise whether they were libelous. It is a well settled rule of equity that equity does not enjoin a libel or slander, and that the only remedy for libel or slander is an action for damages if the libelous character of a statement to which objection is made can be established. . . . Naturally in a libel suit the question would arise whether there is absolute or conditional privilege, and those questions are not before the Court at this time. . . .

COMMENT: PRIVILEGE IN DEFAMATION SUITS AGAINST FDA OFFICIALS

Two years after the decision in *Hoxsey Cancer Clinic*, the United States Supreme Court addressed the question that *Hoxsey* explicitly declined to address, namely, the extent of the privilege enjoyed by government officials against common law defamation suits. In *Barr v. Mateo*, a case involving a libel suit brought against the Director of the Office of Rent Stabilization, the Court embraced a broad version of the privilege, holding that executive officers are absolutely immune from defamation claims if they issued the allegedly defamatory statements in the appropriate discretionary exercise of their official duties. 360 U.S. 564, 570–74 (1959). *Barr v. Mateo* also made clear that the privilege attaches not just to high-ranking officials, but to officers anywhere in the executive hierarchy.

The *Barr v. Mateo* doctrine poses a virtually unconquerable obstacle to individuals contemplating an action against FDA officials for the dissemination of allegedly libelous information. In *Barr*, the Court assigned importance to the fact that the "issuance of press releases was standard agency practice" for the agency in question. *Id.* at 574. For FDA, publicity is not only "standard agency practice," but a practice explicitly authorized by section 705 of the FD&C Act. Unsurprisingly, in light of this legal background, defamation claims against FDA officers are extremely rare and none has been successful. In one of the few instances, post-*Barr*, in which such a claim was advanced, the court brushed it away effortlessly, based on the plaintiffs' failure to overcome the absolute privilege. *Ajay Nutrition*

Foods, Inc. v. FDA, 378 F. Supp. 210 (D.N.J. 1974), *aff'd*, 513 F.2d 625 (3d Cir. 1975).

In 1973, based upon Ernest Gellhorn, *Adverse Publicity By Administrative Agencies*, 86 HARV. L. REV. 1380 (1973), the U.S. Administrative Conference adopted recommendations respecting the use of publicity by regulatory agencies. The primary recommendation was that agencies should adopt regulations describing the circumstances and appropriate content of agency publicity, particularly publicity related to pending administrative or judicial proceedings, and providing a procedure for retraction or correction of erroneous publicity. *See* Recommendation 73–1: Adverse Agency Publicity, 38 Fed. Reg. 16839 (June 27, 1973). FDA's proposed regulations follow:

Administrative Practices and Procedures: Publicity Policy

42 Fed. Reg. 12436 (March 4, 1977).

. . . Every citizen is affected by how FDA carries out its responsibilities to ensure the safety and nondeceptive labeling of the nation's supply of foods, drugs, devices, and cosmetics. . . . The Food and Drug Administration believes it has an affirmative obligation to see that the public knows about and understands the agency's actions and has an opportunity to participate in decisions affecting the public health and the honest marketing of products. Issuing publicity is important to FDA fulfillment of this commitment. . . .

. . . The Food and Drug Administration seeks publicity for several purposes, among which are:

1. To warn against the use of marketed products that may be hazardous.

2. To warn against gross economic deception.

3. To encourage public comment on proposed regulations or actions and other public participation in FDA activities.

4. To report to the public on adjudicated court proceedings.

5. To present to the public FDA's views on matters of public interest.

6. To report on studies or investigations that may form the basis for an FDA regulatory action.

Despite these positive objectives of publicity, there are occasions when publicity can have a negative or adverse effect. For example, an excess of negative information could make the public indifferent or insensitive to important warnings about a potentially dangerous product. Adverse publicity may prejudice a defendant's right to a fair trial in a criminal prosecution, or might improperly influence civil litigation. Under certain circumstances, the issuance of publicity could create a greater hazard than that posed by a particular violation by causing a panic-type reaction. Adverse publicity can cause economic harm to both individuals and firms. . . .

The Food and Drug Administration recognizes a clear distinction between publicity that involves the mass media and materials issued to inform and/or educate the public. Considerable information about FDA and its activities is contained in publications or audio-visual materials produced by the agency....

The Food and Drug Administration does not issue any of these publications or provide any of this information for the purpose of seeking publicity in the news media. For purposes of this regulation, these publications are not considered to be publicity. Similarly, public appearances by FDA employees at public meetings are not considered to be publicity. The Commissioner or a representative often is called to testify before congressional committees, and such appearances customarily are covered by the news media. These appearances and any subsequent release, by the committee or its staff, of materials provided to support such testimony are not publicity within the scope of these regulations....

   ....

The Administrative Conference ... recommended that disparaging terminology should be avoided in the issuance of adverse publicity. The Commissioner believes there is no way that such terminology can be entirely avoided when the purpose of the publicity is to warn of a threat to the public health or to report to the public about an action taken by FDA against a firm or product. The agency agrees that personally disparaging or gratuitously critical remarks, not required in reporting the facts of a situation, should be and will be avoided.

Issuance of information that may be adverse to an individual, firm, or product is justifiable when it is needed to fulfill the agency's primary mission. Adverse publicity also may be an unavoidable consequence of information issued for an appropriate agency purpose. In issuing press releases relating to actions of a general nature (such as rule making), specific persons, firms, or products will be named only if the Commissioner determines it is necessary to explain fully the background or consequences of the action being discussed....

The Food and Drug Administration will continue to seek publicity, when appropriate, even if there is the possibility that the information may be ignored, misinterpreted, oversimplified, overstated, or misunderstood by the media or by the public....

... The issuance of publicity that is potentially prejudicial to a defendant's right to a fair trial in a criminal prosecution may lead to a dismissal of the complaint or necessitate special measures to impanel a jury unaffected by the publicity. *United States v. Abbott Laboratories, Inc.*, 505 F.2d 565 (5th Cir. 1974).

Accordingly, FDA—on behalf of the public—has an interest in assuring that no information is issued that may endanger its ability to pursue a warranted prosecution or other appropriate enforcement action. It also has an interest in guarding against injury from unwarranted publicity about agency charges of law violations prior to the completion of administrative proceedings to resolve disputes related to the validity of the charges.

The Commissioner is not proposing to bar release of all information about court proceedings, hearings, and supporting investigations. While a total prohibition would effectively forestall any possibility of unwarranted or prejudicial publicity, it would not be in the public interest. Publicity serves various purposes ... and the need to issue publicity to promote these purposes may arise in connection with a matter that is the subject of a court proceeding, hearing, or investigation. . . .

The proposed provisions relating to publicity about litigation, administrative hearings, and related investigations would not in any way restrict the issuance of warnings to protect the public health or to avoid substantial economic harm, even if there is a possibility the publicity might prejudice a pending or future criminal trial or other proceeding. The Commissioner believes that his obligations to protect the public are paramount. If publicity were in fact prejudicial, it might be possible to cure its effects by impaneling a jury unaffected by the publicity or by other measures; but the Commissioner believes that, if need be, he must risk dismissal of a prosecution because of the impact of publicity, rather than fail to issue a warning that he believes is needed to protect the public. . . .

The Administrative Conference recommended that agencies should provide advance notice of adverse agency publicity when "practicable and consistent with the nature of the proceeding." . . . .

The proposed regulations ... define what is actually meant by "advance notice." The release of the actual text of a press release to the affected firm or individual, without making the text available upon request to all persons, would be inconsistent with the principle of equal access to public information followed by the Commissioner in administering the Freedom of Information Act. . . . To make the actual text available to the firm or individual and the mass media simultaneously would defeat the practical difficulties in making the exact text available in advance. The proposed regulations attempt to solve this dilemma by providing notice to a firm or individual that publicity on a given subject is to issue without providing the exact text. Because of the varying degrees of public hazard that may exist in different situations, specific time frames for advance notice are not proposed.

Advance notice of FDA's plans to seek publicity that may be adverse is appropriate when needed to enable affected persons to make a timely response of their own to the press. Advance notice of publicity usually will not be given to selected persons or firms regarding the agency's initiation of proposed rule making. . . . Advance notice of the initiation by FDA of enforcement action in the courts is not appropriate since it would require a prior notification about the underlying action. Disclosure of those plans in some instances might lead to the removal of products about to be seized or to the destruction or loss of evidence relating to an imminent injunction. . . .

The ... Administrative Conference calls for a retraction or correction of adverse agency publicity where it is shown to be erroneous or misleading, and when a person named in the publicity requests a retraction or correction. The Food and Drug Administration concurs in this recommendation, and ... the proposed regulations provide for such corrections or retractions....

NOTES

1. *Proposed Policy Withdrawn.* In 1991, FDA withdrew this proposed publicity policy, along with 88 other proposed rules issued prior to 1986 and never finalized. In its notice of intent to withdraw these proposals, FDA indicated that it was motivated by the age of the proposals, their low priority within the agency, and the agency's limited resources. 56 Fed. Reg. 42668 (Aug. 28, 1991). The agency received no comments with regard to the publicity policy in particular. When FDA formally withdrew the proposed rules, it remarked: "[S]ome of the withdrawn proposals still reflect current agency views and thus may still provide useful guidance. However, the withdrawn proposals no longer necessarily represent the formal position of FDA, and do not bind or otherwise obligate or commit the agency to the views expressed." 56 Fed. Reg. 67440, 67440–41 (Dec. 30, 1991). FDA had issued no other guidelines governing agency publicity.

2. *Press Release Policy.* On April 15, 1986, FDA Commissioner Young responded to an inquiry from Senator John Heinz who sought an explanation of the agency's use of press releases:

> In issuing publicity about potential risks of products we regulate, we attempt to choose a level of alert appropriate to the nature and scope of the problem. We also take into account the publicity and notifications issued by the manufacturer. Our goal is to assure that appropriate warnings are conveyed to health professionals and consumers without creating undue alarm.
>
> Often in the past we have utilized press releases and *FDA Talk Papers* to alert the public about product withdrawals. Generally, a press release is issued when we feel that the scope of the problem warrants more widespread publicity. A *Talk Paper*, on the other hand, is generally used when we believe the problem to be of a narrower scope. Although *Talk Papers* are not normally distributed to the press, they are available to the press and are often used as a source for news stories.

3. *Pollution of Jury Pool.* In *U.S. v. Abbott Laboratories*, cited above in the preamble to FDA's publicity policy, the federal district court dismissed the indictment of Abbott officials responsible for the shipment of contaminated intravenous drugs, in part because prejudicial publicity precluded a fair trial. This prejudicial publicity included an FDA press release that not only reported the indictment, but also mentioned a Center for Disease Control determination that fifty deaths were associated with use of the contaminated drugs. The Fourth Circuit reversed the dismissal of the indictment, instructing the district court to attempt to impanel an impartial jury before concluding that a fair trial was impossible. Nonetheless, the court castigated FDA for issuing "a press release containing such prejudicial material." 505 F.2d 565, 571 (4th Cir. 1974).

Lars Noah, *Administrative Arm–Twisting in the Shadow of Congressional Delegations of Authority*

1997 WISCONSIN LAW REVIEW 873, 887–91 (1997).

. . . .

The Food and Drug Administration generally lacks the statutory authority to order a recall of potentially dangerous products subject to its regulatory jurisdiction. Although Congress has granted the Agency such authority with regard to limited classes of products, and others have recommended providing it with broader recall powers, the FDA generally has resisted suggestions that the statute be amended to provide it with recall authority. Instead, the Agency prefers encouraging voluntary recalls, and it has even promulgated detailed regulations setting forth its recall procedures and policies. Even agencies with explicit recall authority often prefer negotiating settlements with regulated entities in which the companies agree to undertake voluntary recalls.

This strategy has succeeded because firms know that a failure to cooperate with an agency's request risks more serious enforcement measures authorized by statute, such as product seizures, injunctions, and even criminal penalties. Because these measures require somewhat cumbersome judicial proceedings, however, the issuance of adverse publicity may be a more effective means of inducing prompt action. Companies often prefer a voluntary recall because it allows them to exercise greater control over the nature and extent of public notification regarding any hazards associated with their particular product.

The Food, Drug, and Cosmetic (FD&C) Act expressly authorizes the issuance of adverse publicity by the FDA, though only in limited circumstances. Even when Congress has delegated such power, however, some controversy surrounds the use of adverse publicity. In particular, targets of an information campaign often have no meaningful opportunity to respond to the charges or seek judicial review. In recognition of the risk of improper use, the FDA once proposed a policy to limit the issuance of such publicity. The Agency never finalized this proposal, and it continues to rely on explicit or implicit threats of disseminating adverse publicity as a method of encouraging voluntary compliance with its various demands.

. . . .

NOTE

For discussions of FDA's public information function, *see* Donald C. McLearn, *The FDA's Office of Public Affairs: Getting the Agency's Message Out*, 48 FOOD DRUG COSM. L.J. 23 (1993); Wallace Janssen, *Public Information Under the Federal Food, Drug, and Cosmetic Act*, pts. I–IV, 12 FOOD DRUG COSM. L.J. 57, 93, 229, 566 (1957). Other articles describe the effects and debate the propriety of this function. Scott M. Fisher, *Publicity and the FDA*, 28 FOOD DRUG COSM. L.J. 436 (1973); William Goodrich, *Cranberries, Chickens and Charcoal*, 15 FOOD DRUG COSM. L.J. 87 (1960); Richard Morey, *Publicity as a Regulatory Tool*, 30 FOOD DRUG COSM. L.J. 469 (1975); Edward L. Smith, *The Cranberry Scare and Cabinet Immunity*, 16 FOOD DRUG COSM. L.J. 209 (1961).

L.   FDA ENFORCEMENT STATISTICS

Activity	1939	1951	1963	1976	1989	1994	2003
Criminal prosecution	626	347	248	43	16	8	1
Seizure	1861	1341	1049	317	144	98	25
Injunction	0	4	30	39	13	16	22
Regulatory/warning letters	N.A.	N.A.	N.A.	982	370	1594	545
Recalls	0	54	101	837	2183	3236	4627
Factory inspections	N.A.	13,357	35,539	39,870	17,740	15,179	22,543
Import inspections	16,352	39,942	30,985	71,643	102,617	93,323	139,310
Samples	39,746	40,853	103,166	57,495	71,932	22,502	15,590
Personnel	565	1000	3210	6683	7395	9370	10,327
Appropriations/budget ($millions)	2.226	5.467	29.065	201.805	487.344	934	1,381.08

FDA: A CENTURY OF CONSUMER PROTECTION 116 (2006)

Prescription for Harm: The Decline in FDA Enforcement Activity

Minority Staff of House Committee on Government Reform, 109th Cong., 2d Sess., 2006.

... The report finds that there has been a dramatic decline in FDA enforcement actions over the last five years. Enforcement statistics show that FDA sent far fewer warning letters and conducted fewer seizures in 2005 than in 2000. One reason for the decline in enforcement actions is revealed in the internal FDA files reviewed in the investigation: FDA officials in Washington repeatedly rejected the recommendations of career field officials urging enforcement actions, even in cases involving death and serious injury....

... The overall number of warning letters issued by the agency decreased from 1,154 in fiscal year 2000 to 535 in fiscal year 2005, a drop of over 50%....

The decline in the number of FDA warning letters has been consistent throughout the Bush Administration, with the number of letters declining in four of the last five years. The number of warning letters declined by 11% in 2001, 27% in 2002, and 28% in 2003. After increasing slightly in 2004, the number of warning letters again declined (by 26%) in 2005, reaching a 15–year low.

A similar trend characterizes agency seizures. The number of seizures of unsafe products conducted by FDA fell by 44%, from 36 in 2000 to 20 in 2005.

Only one enforcement measure has shown a significant increase over the last five years: the number of FDA-regulated products on the market that had to be recalled increased by 44%, from 3,716 in 2000 to 5,338 in 2005. Since one of the goals of an enforcement system is to deter violations and keep dangerous products off of the market, the increase in recalls is not a hallmark of effective enforcement.

Increased compliance by manufacturers does not appear to account for the decline in FDA enforcement activity under the Bush Administration. Whenever FDA field inspectors observe violations during an inspection, the inspectors give the firm a notice to inform them of the violations observed. These notices, referred to as "483 forms," are an indication of the number of violations observed during a given year. In 2000, FDA issued 6,334 such forms. The number of "483 forms" issued was higher for the next four years: 7,683 in 2001; 7,180 in 2002; 7,813 in 2003, and 7,137 in 2004. In 2005, FDA issued 6,268 "483 forms," almost identical to the number issued in 2000. . . .

Internal FDA documents indicate that in at least 138 cases involving drugs or biological products over the last five years, FDA failed to take enforcement actions recommended by the agency's own field inspectors. . . .

In nearly half of these cases (67 cases), FDA took no enforcement action at all against the firm identified by field inspectors. In the remaining cases, the agency took action that was weaker than recommended by the field inspectors. . . .

M.   RES JUDICATA AND RELATED DOCTRINES

1.   RES JUDICATA IN FDA ENFORCEMENT CASES

Both of the main subdoctrines of res judicata—claim preclusion and issue preclusion—can, in theory, apply with respect to judgments in FDA enforcement cases.

The application of res judicata law in the FD&C Act enforcement context is complicated by the fact that the United States files both *in rem* (seizure) and *in personam* (injunction and civil penalty) actions to enforce the Act. In an *in rem* action, the defendant is, as a formal matter, the thing being seized rather than the person who owns it. This affects the use of res judicata, because, in general, a judgment in lawsuit #1 can create claim preclusion or issue preclusion in lawsuit #2 only against an individual who was a party (or in privity to a party) in both suits. To confuse matters more, in most FD&C Act seizure actions, a claimant intervenes, subjecting himself to the court's *in personam* jurisdiction. The following questions thus arise: What is the res judicta effect of a seizure action when a claimant does not intervene? More importantly, what is the res judicata effect of such an action when a claimant participates?

Courts have not addressed these problems in detail in food and drug law cases, but they have done so with some frequency in suits in admiralty, another area in which *in rem* actions play a prominent role. The FD&C Act seizure provision explicitly provides that "the procedure in cases under this section shall conform, as nearly as may be, to the procedure in admiralty." FD&C Act 304(b). An examination of admiralty cases reveals that the *in rem* nature of a seizure action limits its claim preclusive force, but not its issue preclusive force.

Claim preclusion's prohibition against claim splitting apparently does not apply with respect to *in rem* seizure actions. Because each libel for condemnation is brought against a specifically named shipment or article, the United States' defeat in such an action does not preclude it from later proceeding against another shipment for the same adulteration or misbranding. As observed by a leading treatise: "[T]he traditional rule has been that a judgment based on property jurisdiction is binding only with respect to interests in the property brought before the court." 18 CHARLES ALAN WRIGHT & ARTHUR R. MILLER, FEDERAL PRACTICE AND PROCEDURE § 4412 (3d ed. 1998).

As noted above, claimants often intervene in condemnation proceedings, subjecting themselves to the personal jurisdiction of the court, and thus to an injunction claim against them personally. It is interesting to ask whether in such a situation the United States must seek an injunction against the intervening claimant, if at all, as part of the same lawsuit. Admiralty law seems to have embraced the principle that a plaintiff who could have joined an *in personam* claim to an *in rem* claim but elected not to do so is precluded from bringing the *in personam* claim separately in a later suit. *Id.* § 4412. Regardless of the answer to this question, however, the government apparently would not be precluded from subsequently filing a libel for condemnation against a distinct *rem*. If the later-seized article were outside the jurisdiction of the court that issued the judgment in the first suit, a separate claim against it would not be precluded by res judicata.

The FD&C Act does preclude some claim splitting. It prohibits multiple *simultaneous* condemnation proceedings in cases that do not involve dangerous or fraudulent misbranding. FD&C Act 304(a). Moreover, even where the statute permits multiple simultaneous condemnation proceedings (for adulteration or for other misbranding) it allows a claimant to demand consolidation of proceedings in one district. FD&C Act 304(b). These provisions, however, address pending cases, not cases that have already reached judgment. Indeed, the Act appears to assume that a final judgment in a condemnation proceeding will *not* have claim preclusive effect; section 304(a) expressly allows multiple simultaneous condemnation proceedings for misbranding "when such misbranding has been the basis of a prior judgment in favor of the United States, in a criminal, injunction, or libel for condemnation proceeding under this Act." FD&C Act 304(a).

All this is not to say that judgments in condemnation proceedings have no res judicata effect in later cases. To the contrary, parties have frequently asserted res judicata based on condemnation judgments, and some have prevailed in subsequent actions on this basis. But the relevant rationale is issue preclusion (collateral estoppel), not claim preclusion. A claimant who intervenes in an *in rem* proceeding, and fully litigates an issue, is generally precluded from relitigating that issue in a later case. As declared by the Restatement (Second) of Judgments: "A valid and final judgment in an action based only on jurisdiction to determine interests in a thing ... [i]s conclusive between parties, in accordance with the rules of issue preclusion,

as to any issues actually litigated by them and determined in the action."
RESTATEMENT (SECOND) OF JUDGMENTS § 30(3) (1982).

United States v. Sandoz Pharmaceuticals Corp., and 14 Boxes, More or Less, ... Fiorinal With Codeine No. 3

894 F.2d 825 (6th Cir. 1990).

■ PER CURIAM

Defendant-appellant, Sandoz Pharmaceuticals Corporation, appeals from the judgment of the [Ohio] district court in favor of plaintiff-appellee, United States of America, acting on behalf of the Food and Drug Administration, in this *in rem* seizure action filed pursuant to the Federal Food, Drug and Cosmetic Act. For the following reasons, we affirm.

Sandoz first marketed Fiorinal with Codeine (FWC)-type products in 1963, after receiving informal advice from the FDA that the products were not regarded as "new drugs." In 1968, FDA revoked all informal opinions and required manufacturers to file a "new drug application" (NDA) for any product classified as a "new drug" under 21 U.S.C. § 321(p). The NDA must be approved before a new drug may be introduced into interstate commerce. An abbreviated NDA can be used for duplicates of new drugs or closely related drugs.

In 1977, the FDA approved Fiorinal as a "new drug" effective for treating tension headaches. Thereafter, Sandoz sought approval of its FWC products through the abbreviated NDA procedure, contending that the FWC products were closely related to the previously approved drug, Fiorinal. FDA officials rejected Sandoz's arguments, finding that FWC products were "new drugs" requiring full NDA's. In November 1984, the FDA sent Sandoz a regulatory letter which stated that the FWC products were considered "new drugs," and that its continued marketing of FWC products without approval of a NDA would violate 21 U.S.C. § 355. Subsequently, Sandoz submitted a NDA for the FWC products and another request that the FDA accept an abbreviated NDA for these products. Upon preliminary review of the NDA, the FDA found that the application was not approvable, and also rejected Sandoz's request for an abbreviated procedure. Thereafter, Sandoz notified the FDA that it believed the FWC products were not new drugs and submitted several studies indicating that FWC products were both safe and effective. However, the FDA declined to reverse its position.

On June 17, 1986, the Government filed a complaint in the United States District Court for the Southern District of Ohio, and subsequently seized several boxes containing Fiorinal with Codeine No. 3 (FWC No. 3). Approximately four months later, the Government brought a separate complaint for forfeiture in the United States District Court for the Northern District of New Jersey, alleging that two other drugs distributed by Sandoz, Fiorinal with Codeine No. 1 and Fiorinal with Codeine No. 2 (FWC No. 1 and FWC No. 2) were "new drugs" that could not be marketed without FDA approval. After evaluating documentary evidence submitted by both parties (the same clinical evidence and testimony filed in the Ohio action), the New Jersey district court granted summary judgment to the Government, finding that FWC No. 1 and FWC No. 2 are "new drugs" within the meaning of 21 U.S.C. § 321(p). *United States v. 225 Cartons, More or Less, of an Article of Drug*, 687 F. Supp. 946 (D.N.J. 1988), *aff'd*, 871 F.2d 409 (3d Cir. 1989).

In the instant action, the Ohio district court ruled that Sandoz was collaterally estopped from relitigating the issue of whether FWC No. 3 is a "new drug." The court entered a permanent injunction and ordered that the seized articles be destroyed; however, these orders were stayed pending the outcome of Sandoz's appeals.

Sandoz argues that the district court erred in finding that this action is barred by the doctrine of collateral estoppel. The availability of collateral estoppel is a mixed question of law and fact which we review *de novo*. However, once it is established that the elements of collateral estoppel are present, a district court has broad discretion to determine when the doctrine should be applied offensively. *Id.*

The doctrine of collateral estoppel may be applied only if four criteria have been satisfied:

(1) the precise issue raised in the present case must have been raised and actually litigated in the prior proceeding;

(2) determination of the issue must have been necessary to the outcome of the prior proceeding;

(3) the prior proceeding must have resulted in a final judgment on the merits; and

(4) the party against whom estoppel is sought must have had full and fair opportunity to litigate the issue in the prior proceeding.

Sandoz claims that neither the first, second, nor the fourth criteria have been satisfied.

The Ohio district court properly noted that the drug at issue here (FWC No. 3) and the drugs involved in the New Jersey action (FWC No. 1 and FWC No. 2) contain four ingredients, three of which are identically formulated. The only distinction between the three drugs is the amount of the fourth ingredient, codeine. Sandoz presents two reasons why the precise issues in the Ohio case are different than those in the New Jersey action.

First, Sandoz argues that the different amounts of codeine in the FWC products require different determinations of the "new drug" status of each product. We reject this argument. Both legal actions required identical showings that each ingredient contributes to the claimed effect. In fact, in both the New Jersey and Ohio forums, Sandoz defended the efficacy of its products with the same six studies and expert declarations. The New Jersey district court found that Sandoz failed to show the contributions of the non-codeine components to the efficacy of the FWC products, the same showing required for FWC No. 3 in the Ohio proceeding. This finding renders the issue of codeine's contribution to FWC No. 3 immaterial. As a result, Sandoz has no basis for its claim that the evidence for FWC No. 3 is stronger than the evidence for FWC No. 1 and FWC No. 2.

Second, Sandoz contends that the New Jersey action involved an "unmixed" question of law, or "issues of law which arise in successive actions involving unrelated subject matter." *United States v. Stauffer Chemical Co.*, 464 U.S. 165, 170 n. 3 (1984). In such cases, the courts do not give the legal decisions collateral estoppel effect. Sandoz notes that the instant case is based on a different cause of action, predicated on a different *res*, and presents a different legal question than the New Jersey action. As such, Sandoz claims that there must be different legal evaluations of the evidence supporting the drugs' effectiveness.

We find this argument unpersuasive. The Supreme Court has severely limited the "unmixed" question of law exception. The *Stauffer* Court noted that the exception requires a determination that the " 'issue of law' arises in a successive case that is so unrelated to the prior case that relitigation of the issue is warranted." In the instant case, the factual and legal issues are almost identical. In both the New Jersey and Ohio actions, the Government seized drugs to prevent their sale and distribution pending a submission of a NDA. In addition, the judgment in both cases rested upon a determination of the validity and relevance of clinical studies, which are by *definition* fact-based evaluations, and an assessment of whether these fact-based evaluations meet the standards set forth in the FDA regulations. Thus, we find that because the New Jersey judgment was a mixed question of fact and law in an action very similar to the instant case, the application of collateral estoppel in this case was permissible.

Sandoz also argues that the second and fourth criteria for collateral estoppel were not present. Sandoz first maintains that the findings of the New Jersey district court were not necessary to the outcome of that proceeding. In particular, Sandoz claims that the only finding necessary to its judgment was that there has been no study of any new formulation of FWC No. 1 or FWC No. 2 to determine the contribution of caffeine, one of the non-codeine ingredients. This argument is unpersuasive because Sandoz submitted the six clinical studies into evidence in the New Jersey action in order to defend FWC No. 1 and FWC No. 2. Having placed the studies at issue, Sandoz cannot now argue that it was unnecessary for the New Jersey district court to rule on their relevance.

Sandoz next contends that it did not have a full and fair opportunity to litigate in New Jersey because it was denied discovery. We reject this claim. . . .

Sandoz argues that even if the elements of collateral estoppel are present, its application in the instant case would not be fair. In *Parklane Hosiery Co., Inc. v. Shore*, 439 U.S. 322, 330–31 and n. 15 (1979), the Supreme Court indicated two situations in which the application of offensive collateral estoppel can be unfair to defendants: (1) if a defendant in the first action is sued for small or nominal damages, he may have little incentive to defend vigorously; and (2) if the defendant in the first action was unable to engage in full scale discovery or call witnesses, application of offensive estoppel may be unwarranted.

Sandoz contends that it did not have an adequate incentive to defend the New Jersey action vigorously for the following three reasons: FWC No. 1 and FWC No. 2 generate lower revenues than FWC No. 3; the Ohio case was instituted before the New Jersey case; and the evidence to support FWC No. 3 was generally stronger than that supporting FWC No. 1 and FWC No. 2. Sandoz maintains that undefined time constraints and the relatively weaker case in New Jersey forced it to scale down its defense in that action.

We find these arguments unpersuasive. First, the amount of revenues at stake in the New Jersey action was not nominal, especially since sales of the drugs in question generated over three million dollars a year. Second, the record does not show that time constraints were imposed on Sandoz as a result of the New Jersey action. Finally, there is nothing in the record to indicate that the evidence presented in the New Jersey action differed from the evidence presented here. Thus, we conclude that Sandoz had ample incentive to litigate both actions vigorously as long as both actions were pending.

With respect to Sandoz's argument under the second *Parklane* situation, that full-scale discovery was not permitted, we have already concluded that the New Jersey proceeding gave Sandoz a full and fair opportunity to prove that FWC products are not "new drugs." Finally, Sandoz contends that the Government's choice of forum was unfair because it did not receive a full hearing in the New Jersey district court. However, there is no evidence that the New Jersey forum was more inconvenient than Ohio or that it deprived Sandoz of any procedural opportunities available in Ohio. *Parklane*, 439 U.S. at 332. Thus, we conclude that the application of offensive collateral estoppel against Sandoz is not unfair under the *Parklane* criteria.

. . . .

Accordingly, for above stated reasons, the judgment of the district court is AFFIRMED.

NOTES

1. *Same Issue?* In *United States v. 17 Cases . . . of Nue–Ovo*, prior decisions had held that the seized product was misbranded because of false claims of effectiveness. Despite the addition of a disclaimer to the labeling of the later-seized Nue–Ovo, the district court granted the government summary judgment based on issue preclusion. 1938–1964 FDLI Jud. Rec. 858 (N.D. Ill. 1949). *Cf. United States v. 4 Cans . . . Master Liquid*, 127 F. Supp. 243 (N.D. Iowa 1955) (relitigation of prior finding of misbranding based on false efficacy claim precluded, despite changes in the labeling and alleged changes in medical opinion). In *598 Cases . . . Tomatoes v. United States*, 211 F.2d 249 (7th Cir. 1954), the court declined to hold that an earlier injunction decree finding that the food in question was adulterated by filth was res judicata in a subsequent seizure action against the product. The court concluded there was an unresolved factual issue as to whether the food actually seized in the latter action was similarly adulterated. *United States v. 14 105 Pound Bags . . . Mineral Compound*, 118 F. Supp. 837 (D. Idaho 1953).

2. *Federal Res Judicata Law Applies.* With rare exceptions, federal courts hear FD&C Act matters. Consequently, in almost all instances, federal res judicata law (rather than the res judicata law of one of the states) determines the preclusive effects of a judgment in an FDA enforcement action. As noted in the Restatement (Second) of Judgments, "Federal law determines the effects under the rules of res

judicata of a judgment of a federal court." RESTATEMENT (SECOND) OF JUDGMENTS § 87 (1982).

3. *Issue Preclusion in Subsequent Private Lawsuits*. A judgment in favor of FDA in a civil enforcement case may be res judicata in a subsequent private civil case for damages. *See Smith v. Great Atlantic & Pacific Tea Co.*, 170 F.2d 474 (8th Cir. 1948); *Sussex Drug Products Co. v. Kanasco, Ltd.*, Food Drug Cosm. L. Rep. (CCH) ¶ 38,103 (D.N.J. 1988).

4. *Nonmutual Preclusion*. Although the United States Supreme Court has explicitly abandoned the doctrine of mutuality in res judicata, *Blonder-Tongue Labs. v. University of Illinois*, 402 U.S. 313 (1971); *Parklane Hosiery Co. v. Shore*, 439 U.S. 322 (1979), this development has few implications for FDA enforcement actions. In *United States v. Mendoza*, 464 U.S. 154 (1984), the Supreme Court forbad the use of nonmutual issue preclusion against the government. Although *Mendoza* itself concerned a private plaintiff's attempt to use nonmutual issue preclusion offensively against the government, lower courts have generally suggested that the logic behind *Mendoza* applies with equal force in cases in which private defendants attempt to use nonmutual preclusion against the government defensively. *See, e.g., Hercules Carriers, Inc. v. Claimant State of Florida*, 768 F.2d 1558, 1579 (11th Cir. 1985).

5. *Issue Preclusion Based on FDA Administrative Determinations*. In some circumstances, an administrative decision by FDA may have issue-preclusive effect in subsequent litigation. As explained by one district court:

> Evidence or arguments that contradict a factual determination made by an agency are precluded if: (1) the original action was properly before the agency; (2) the same disputed issue of fact was before the agency as is before the court; (3) the agency acted in a judicial capacity; and (4) the parties had an adequate opportunity to litigate the issues before the agency.

United States v. Caputo, 313 F. Supp. 2d 764, 768 (N.D. Ill. 2004) (citing *Meyer v. Rigdon*, 36 F.3d 1375, 1379–80 (7th Cir.1994)). In *Caputo*, the court declined to give preclusive effect to FDA's earlier determination that a modified medical device required a new 510(k) submission, because FDA did not act in a judicial capacity when making this determination. *Id.* at 768. By contrast, a determination of an issue by FDA following a full administrative hearing (for example, a hearing concerning the withdrawal of a drug approval) might preclude relitigation of the issue in a separate court proceeding. *Cf. Yacub v. Sandoz Pharmaceuticals*, 85 F. Supp. 2d 817 (S.D. Ohio 1999) (denying issue preclusion based on FDA order withdrawing NDA approval but implicitly suggesting such preclusion is possible).

United States v. Gramer

191 F.2d 741 (9th Cir. 1951).

■ STEPHENS, CIRCUIT JUDGE.

A criminal action brought by the United States ... charged Gramer, claimant herein, with the introduction into interstate commerce of misbranded drugs in violation of the Federal Food, Drug, and Cosmetic Act. After a plea of not guilty was entered a trial on the merits was had and the district judge, sitting without a jury, adjudged claimant not guilty.

In January, 1950, two libels were filed by the government in the U.S. District Court for the Western District of Washington, against separate subsequent shipments of the same preparation of drugs as was involved in the Minnesota federal district court, for seizure and condemnation pursuant to provisions of the same act. The cases were consolidated since the articles proceeded against and the charges were the same in both cases. It was undisputed that the contents of the bottles, the accompanying literature, the labeling, and all of the material issues except criminality, raised were the same as those involved in the prior 1949 criminal action. Claimant's motion for summary judgment was granted for the reason that the issues raised by the government in the cause were adjudicated in favor of Gramer in the prior criminal action. . . .

. . . [N]either the judicial doctrine of *res judicata* nor the constitutional mandate against double jeopardy operates to prevent the action here involved.

Res judicata. Where a right, question or fact has been put in issue and determined by a court of competent jurisdiction, as a ground of recovery, it cannot again be disputed in a subsequent suit between the same parties or their privies. But the Supreme Court has held that . . . the doctrine of *res judicata* [does not have] application to a situation where there has been an acquittal on a criminal charge followed by a civil action requiring a different degree of proof.

Hence, since the prior action by the government was criminal in nature, while the cause before us is civil, the doctrine of *res judicata* does not operate to make the acquittal a bar.

Double jeopardy. . . . Since it is admitted that the libels filed herein did not seek to condemn the same shipment of preparation which was involved in the prior criminal action it is immediately apparent that there is no question of double jeopardy involved. . . . In addition, the Supreme Court has held . . . that a proceeding in rem to forfeit property used in committing an offense is not punitive in character, and therefore is not barred by a prior conviction for a criminal offense involving the same transactions. This would seem especially true in a condemnation proceeding under the Federal Food, Drug, and Cosmetic Act, where the purpose is not to punish the owner of the goods but to protect the public health.

NOTES

1. *Res Judicata Effect of Acquittal on Criminal Charges. See* Arthur A. Dickerman, *Res Judicata—An Acquittal in a Criminal Case Does Not Bar Subsequent Seizure Action*, 7 FOOD DRUG COSM. L.J. 293 (1952). *Cf. Stanley v. United States*, 111 F.2d 898 (6th Cir. 1940) (holding that prior determination, in dismissal of a criminal indictment on demurrer, that label statements did not claim a curative effect within the meaning of the FD&C Act precluded relitigation of misbranding issue in a subsequent seizure action based on the same labeling); *accord United States v. 119 Packages . . . Z–G–Herbs, XXX No. 17, Double Strength*, 15 F. Supp. 327 (S.D.N.Y. 1936).

2. *Res Judicata Effect of Criminal Conviction.* Although the issue apparently has never been litigated, it is likely that a criminal conviction for violation of the FD&C Act would be res judicata in a subsequent FDA civil action. *See Developments in the Law: The Federal Food, Drug, and Cosmetic Act*, 67 HARV. L. REV. 632 (1954).

See generally *Scott E. Bohon,* Res Judicata as a Weapon of Enforcement of the Federal Food Drug, and Cosmetic Act, *9 FOOD DRUG COSM. L.J. 256 (1954).*

3. *Claim Preclusion.* Although, as discussed above, decisions in FDA enforcement actions rarely have claim preclusive effect in later enforcement suits, the doctrine of claim preclusion does sometimes arise in other types of litigation involving the FD&C Act, particularly where the government is the defendant. *See, e.g., Apotex, Inc. v. FDA,* 393 F.3d 210 (D.C. Cir. 2004) (claim preclusion bars successive challenges to FDA's interpretation and application of the Hatch–Waxman 180–day generic marketing exclusivity provision); *Keene v. United States,* Food Drug Cosm. L. Rep. (CCH) ¶ 38,233 (S.D.W. Va. 1979) (barring action seeking to prevent FDA from interfering with plaintiffs' use of Laetrile).

COMMENT: COLLATERAL EFFECT OF TRADE ASSOCIATION SUITS

On occasion FDA has prevailed in a suit for declaratory judgment brought by a trade association and later confronted attempts by individual association members to relitigate the same issue. In an attempt to forestall such claims, FDA regulation 21 C.F.R. 10.105(e) provides:

> In a court proceeding in which an organization participates, the Commissioner will take appropriate legal measures to have the case brought or considered as a class action or otherwise as binding upon all members of the organization except those specifically excluded by name. Regardless of whether the case is brought or considered as a class action or as otherwise binding upon all members of the organization except those specifically excluded by name, the Commissioner will take the position in any subsequent suit involving the same issues and a member of the organization that the issues are precluded from further litigation by the member under the doctrines of collateral estoppel or res judicata.

FDA's commitment to seek class action status for trade association suits against it is of limited significance. The Federal Rules of Civil Procedure provide no mechanism by which a defendant can force a plaintiff to bring its claim as a class action. *See* FED. R. CIV. P. 23. With regard to declaratory judgment actions in particular, dictum in one case suggests that a federal district court can deny a trade association standing to bring a declaratory judgment suit if the suit is not fashioned as a class action. *National Automatic Laundry and Cleaning Council v. Shultz,* 443 F.2d 689, 704 (D.C. Cir. 1971). Judge Leventhal reasoned that "the Government should be able to offset the diversion of enforcement resources required to defend a pre-enforcement review action by the assurance that the determination in such a litigation will have a reasonably broad *res judicata* effect." No reported decisions have embraced this dictum, however, and FDA does not seem to have pursued the tactic successfully.

FDA's broader commitment to assert res judicata against members of trade associations has a firmer legal basis. Although the state of the law is not well developed, a suit brought by an association may, in some situations, have preclusive effect in a later suit brought by one of its members. 18 CHARLES ALAN WRIGHT & ARTHUR R. MILLER, FEDERAL PRACTICE AND PROCEDURE § 4456 (3d ed. 1998). Several courts have refused to permit a second action where an unsuccessful plaintiff association was found to have the same interests as its members. *See, e.g., Expert Electric, Inc. v. Levine*, 554 F.2d 1227 (2d Cir. 1977); *Aluminum Co. of America v. Admiral Merchants Motor Freight, Inc.*, 486 F.2d 717 (7th Cir. 1973); *Acree v. Air Line Pilots Ass'n*, 390 F.2d 199 (5th Cir. 1968); *Proctor & Gamble Co. v. Byers Transportation Co.*, 355 F. Supp. 547 (W.D. Mo. 1973). *But see Spring Mills, Inc. v. Consumer Product Safety Com'n*, 434 F. Supp. 416 (D.S.C. 1977). A leading case concerned state law. *General Foods Corp. v. Massachusetts Dept. of Public Health*, 648 F.2d 784 (1st Cir. 1981), addressed the preclusive impact of an unsuccessful trade association suit challenging the validity of a state food labeling regulation. The First Circuit did not decide whether mere membership in a trade association would subject a member to res judicata in a subsequent suit, but it did find preclusion in the particular circumstances of the case.

> Here more is involved than mere membership in a trade association. General Foods, at the request of GMA, contributed $2,500 toward the expenses of the GMA litigation in the Massachusetts courts. General Foods was chargeable with knowledge that in that litigation, inasmuch as the challenged regulations did not affect the trade association itself but only its members, GMA's standing to sue depended on its claim to represent its members as the real parties in interest.... We need not decide whether a dissenting member would be bound if he gave notice or even if he did not give notice of his opposition. It is sufficient for us to say in our view Massachusetts would hold, and we do hold, that a member of a trade association who finances an action which it brings on behalf of its members impliedly authorizes the trade association to represent him in that action. It is of no significance if a member declines to intervene in the litigation in his own name.

Id. at 787–88. *Cf. Crane v. Commissioner of Dep't. of Agric.*, 602 F. Supp. 280, 285–86 (D. Me. 1985) (setting forth five-factor analysis).

2. COLLATERAL EFFECT OF SUITS BY OTHER AGENCIES

United States v. Willard Tablet Co.
141 F.2d 141 (7th Cir. 1944).

■ MAJOR, CIRCUIT JUDGE.

The United States (libelant) instituted this proceeding for condemnation of a quantity of Willard's Tablets shipped in interstate commerce on the ground that the labeling thereof was false, in violation of the Food, Drug, and Cosmetic Act, and the articles were therefore subject to seizure and confiscation.... The lower court sustained the claimant's defense of res judicata, based upon a prior proceeding before the Federal Trade Commission, and dismissed the action....

The government urges as a basis for overruling the lower court's holding that: (1) the issues herein involved were not determined by the Federal Trade Commission; (2) unaffirmed decisions of the Federal Trade

Commission do not have the finality necessary to constitute res judicata; (3) there is no mutuality of estoppel; (4) the lower court's holding would impair the enforcement of the Food, Drug, and Cosmetic Act; . . .

The facts as stipulated and adopted by the lower court effectively dispose of the government's first contention. The stipulation disclosed: (1) that the statements relied upon by the government to uphold the charge of misbranding are identical with those approved by the Federal Trade Commission; (2) that the fundamental issue of fact as to whether the Willard Tablets would give the relief claimed was considered by the Federal Trade Commission. We, therefore, have the incongruous situation of one branch of the government approving the method now pursued by the claimant and another branch seeking to condemn. That is, to say the least, placing claimant in an embarrassing situation and should be avoided if possible. . . .

As was stated by the Supreme Court in *Sunshine Coal Co. v. Adkins*, 310 U.S. 381: "A judgment is res judicata in a second action upon the same claim between the same parties or those in privity with them. There is a privity between officers of the same government so that a judgment in a suit between a party and a representative of the United States is res judicata in relitigation of the same issue between that party and another officer of the government."

The government's second contention seems to rest solely upon the provisions of the Federal Trade Commission Act that the Commission may, under certain conditions, modify its order after the expiration of time for appeal. Therefore, the contention is that such power of modification leaves an unappealed order without that finality essential to invoke the doctrine of res judicata. With this contention we do not agree.

The Act provides that an order of the Commission shall become final at the expiration of sixty days if no appeal is taken (45(g)), and further provides for heavy penalties for violation of such order (45(l)). It further provides that "the findings of the Commission as to the facts, if supported by evidence, shall be conclusive." Subd. (c). Thus, even the reviewing court in the same proceeding is bound by the findings of the Commission. To allow their finality to be attacked in a collateral proceeding would seem to run counter to the provisions and purposes of the Act. . . .

We agree with appellee's contention that mutuality of estoppel is not herein involved. We have held that the facts found by the Federal Trade Commission are conclusive and binding upon the District Court. The same result would obtain if the government were depending upon these findings to sustain its charge of misbranding. . . .

What we have heretofore said sufficiently disposes of the argument that the decisions of the Federal Trade Commission should not be allowed to impair the enforcement of the Food, Drug, and Cosmetic Act. . . .

NOTES

1. *FTC Proceedings. See George H. Lee Co. v. FTC*, 113 F.2d 583 (8th Cir. 1940), holding that a decision in a prior FDA civil action is res judicata in a subsequent FTC civil action. *See also United States v. 14 Cartons . . . Ayds Candy*, 1938–1964 FDLI Jud. Rec. 182 (E.D. Mo. 1946), holding that an earlier decision that

the advertising claims for a reducing aid did not violate the Federal Trade Commission Act, *Carlay Co. v. FTC*, 153 F.2d 493 (7th Cir. 1946), barred an FDA seizure action alleging misbranding. In *Sekov Corp. v. United States*, 139 F.2d 197 (5th Cir. 1943), the court declined to invoke res judicata on the ground that the issues in the earlier FTC proceeding were different from those in the subsequent FDA seizure. *See also United States v. Five Cases ... Capon Springs Water*, 156 F.2d 493 (2d Cir. 1946). In *United States v. An Article of Drug ... Ova II*, 414 F. Supp. 660 (D.N.J. 1975), FDA withdrew a claim that the claimant's pregnancy test kit was falsely labeled in order not to prejudice a possible future proceeding by the FTC under section 5 of the Federal Trade Commission Act.

2. *Mail Fraud Proceedings.* A decision in an action under the Mail Fraud Act, 18 U.S.C. § 1341, has been held not to be res judicata with respect to any subsequent FDA action because the Mail Fraud Act requires proof of fraudulent purpose and intent to deceive. *See United States v. 3963 Bottles ... "Enerjol Double Strength,"* 265 F.2d 332 (7th Cir. 1959); *United States v. Kaadt*, 171 F.2d 600 (7th Cir. 1948). In *United States v. 42 Jars ... "Bee Royale Capsules,"* 264 F.2d 666 (3d Cir. 1959), the court declined to apply a broader concept of "res administrata":

> ... [under this theory, a] benevolent Uncle Sam is, as the cartoons show him, to be treated as a unified individual with the addition of a degree of omniscience not accorded to him by anyone before. Furthermore, all his citizens, both natural and corporate, are included in the family of his children thus to create privity, or something akin to it, between them.
>
> ... It is hardly necessary to add that a court cannot swallow any such broad proposition as this.... [W]hile there may be cases where the administrative process works hardship, this is not one of them. As indicated above, there is not a single fibril to connect these two pieces of Government procedure except certain claims made on behalf of that product known as Bee Royale jelly....

Id. at 669. *See Kurzon v. United States Postal Service*, 539 F.2d 788 (1st Cir. 1976), holding that a decision for the government in an earlier FDA civil action did not bar a later action under the Mail Fraud Act. In *Aycock v. O'Brien*, 28 F.2d 817 (9th Cir. 1928), the court held an acquittal in an FDA criminal action not to be res judicata in a civil case brought 11 years later under the Mail Fraud Act involving the same products because the parties were different and because during the lapse of time medical knowledge may have changed.

3. *State Proceedings.* In *United States v. Depilatron Epilator*, 473 F. Supp. 913 (S.D.N.Y. 1979), FDA brought a seizure action for misleading labeling of a medical device after a state court in California had determined that the labeling was not misleading. Although FDA and the FTC had participated in the California state action, the district court held that the participation was "minimal" and thus that FDA was not collaterally estopped from bringing its own action.

4. *Commentary.* See Scott E. Bohon, *Res Judicata as a Weapon of Enforcement of the Federal Food, Drug, and Cosmetic Act*, 9 FOOD DRUG COSM. L.J. 256 (1954); Note, *Res Judicata and Two Coordinate Federal Agencies*, 95 U. PA. L. REV. 388 (1947); Annot., 152 A.L.R. 1198 (1944).

3.   SIMULTANEOUS GOVERNMENT PROCEEDINGS

Warner–Lambert Co. v. Federal Trade Commission

361 F. Supp. 948 (D.D.C. 1973).

■ JOHN H. PRATT, DISTRICT JUDGE.

. . . .

This action seeks to restrain the Federal Trade Commission from undertaking further proceedings in FTC Docket No. 8891, and to restrain the Secretary of Health, Education and Welfare and the Commissioner of Food and Drugs from further proceeding with its review of over-the-counter cold remedies, unless and until the two federal agencies take appropriate action to prevent the conduct of two simultaneous proceedings with regard to the cold and sore throat claims of Listerine Antiseptic....

Plaintiff is the respondent in an adjudicative proceeding presently pending before the FTC under FTC Docket 8891....

The complaint, in general, alleges Warner–Lambert, in its advertising, offering for sale, sale and distribution of the mouthwash preparation Listerine to retailers for resale to the public, has misrepresented by false, deceptive and misleading statements the effect of the product in the prevention, cure, treatment and mitigation of colds and sore throats....

Warner–Lambert, on August 30, 1972, filed an answer, denying the substantive averments of the FTC complaint. Hearings before the Administrative Law Judge have been scheduled to commence on September 24, 1973.

... Because of the inadequacy, great cost, and burden on the courts of proceeding against individual drugs on a case-by-case basis, the Commissioner of Food and Drugs, on December 30, 1971, proposed new regulations setting up a procedure for a thorough and complete review of all over-the-counter drugs....

... With respect to cold remedies, Listerine is one of many products to be reviewed. No monograph has yet been proposed. An invitation for all interested persons to submit data bearing on the safety and effectiveness of the ingredients of cough-cold remedies was published on August 9, 1972. As a nonprescription cough and cold remedy, Listerine will be subject to the requirements of any monograph issued by FDA pursuant to the rulemaking proceedings.

Plaintiff argues the two proceedings complained of are unlawful in that they violate a "rule" of both agencies. The "rule" which plaintiff asserts is binding upon defendants is a "Memorandum of Understanding" issued jointly by FTC and FDA and published at 36 Fed. Reg. 18539 (1971). Plaintiff's contention is erroneous. Even assuming, arguendo, the "rule" is binding on defendants, it is clear it does not apply to the proceedings in issue.

The Memorandum is an agreement between the two agencies promulgated primarily for the convenience of the agencies in carrying out their functions under two different statutes. The only parties to the agreement were the two agencies involved, and an individual private party, such as plaintiff, may not invoke the agreement in challenging these agency actions. Furthermore, in the Court's opinion, the agreement has not been breached....

As far as the proceedings themselves are concerned, it is the Court's opinion they are quite different. As has been pointed out previously, the proceeding before the Federal Trade Commission is an adversary proceeding. It is an adjudicatory proceeding. It involves only Warner–Lambert.

The proceeding before the Food and Drug Administration is a rulemaking proceeding. It involves thousands of manufacturers of over-the-counter products, including cold remedies. It is a proceeding which individual companies can participate in or decline to participate in, at their option, recognizing it may also be to their possible disadvantage.

If this Court were to require the Food and Drug Administration to exempt plaintiff from its proceeding, it seems such action would give plaintiff a discriminatory preference over the manufacturers of many products of a similar kind, namely, over-the-counter cold remedy products.

The joint proceedings which FDA and FTC agreed to limit were intended to be proceedings where the FTC would file a complaint seeking a cease-and-desist order on the basis of false and misleading claims, and where the FDA would institute a seizure proceeding seeking to condemn the product on the same grounds. It is certain that the present proceedings ... are not within the provisions of the Memorandum of Understanding. For if this were the case, then the FTC would now be foreclosed from proceeding against any of the 100,000 to 500,000 OTC drugs currently on the market, no matter how false or how misleading the claims for such a product.

The Supreme Court has long held that the same issues and parties may be proceeded against simultaneously by more than one agency.... These same principles apply to the concurrent actions of FDA and FTC which may involve the same parties or issues. The propriety of simultaneous FDA–FTC proceedings involving the same issues does not, as claimant would have this Court believe, present a novel legal issue. For in at least three cases, the courts, including this Court, have held that concurrent FDA–FTC proceedings involving the same or similar matters are proper, and that the statutory remedies of the two agencies are cumulative and not mutually exclusive....

NOTE

The FTC subsequently issued a cease and desist order against Listerine advertising which was upheld in *Warner–Lambert Co. v. FTC*, 562 F.2d 749 (D.C. Cir. 1977). In the interim between the FTC order and the court of appeals decision, FDA proposed a monograph relating to OTC cough-cold drugs in 41 Fed. Reg. 38312 (Sept. 9, 1976). In upholding the FTC order, the Court of Appeals stated: "Since the FDA did not consider the extensive record compiled in the FTC proceeding, its conclusion that there is insufficient data about the ingredients of Listerine to justify classifying it as effective or ineffective is not necessarily inconsistent with the FTC's conclusion that Listerine's advertising claims are deceptive." For other cases recognizing the propriety of concurrent FDA–FTC proceedings, *see Thompson Medical Co. v. FTC*, 791 F.2d 189, 192–93 (D.C. Cir. 1986), *cert. denied* 479 U.S. 1086 (1987); *Bristol Meyers Co. v. FTC*, 738 F.2d 554, 559 (2d Cir. 1984), *United States v. 1 Dozen Bottles ... Boncquet Tablets*, 146 F.2d 361 (4th Cir. 1944); *United States v. Research Laboratories, Inc.*, 126 F.2d 42 (9th Cir. 1942).

4.   ESTOPPEL AGAINST THE GOVERNMENT

The general doctrine of estoppel (not to be confused with the res judicata doctrine of collateral estoppel, or issue preclusion) is an equitable doctrine invoked to avoid injustice in particular cases in which one has changed his position for the worse in reasonable reliance on the misrepresentation of another. Courts are more reluctant to impose estoppel against the government than against private parties. In *Heckler v. Community Health Servs. of Crawford County*, 467 U.S. 51 (1984), the Supreme Court, while refusing to embrace a flat rule that estoppel may never run against the government, explained: "When the Government is unable to enforce the law because the conduct of its agents has given rise to an estoppel, the interest of the citizenry as a whole in obedience to the rule is undermined. It is for this reason that it is well settled that the Government may not be estopped on the same terms as any other litigant."

In the food and drug context, there are two main questions of estoppel FDA has confronted over the years. The first is whether estoppel attaches when an FDA employee has made an informal representation to a regulated entity and the entity has acted in reliance on that representation. The latter is whether the agency can bind itself with guidance documents that fall short of the Administrative Procedure Act's notice-and-comment requirements. The following case concerns the first problem.

United States v. 354 Bulk Cartons ... Trim Reducing–Aid Cigarettes

178 F. Supp. 847 (D.N.J. 1959).

■ WORTENDYKE, DISTRICT JUDGE.

. . . .

... [L]ibelant [the United States] contends that the articles seized consisted of a drug shipped in interstate commerce, misbranded in violation of 21 U.S.C. § 334(a), when introduced therein, and constituting a new drug with respect to which an effective new drug application was not on file, as required by 21 U.S.C. § 355(a)....

Respecting the requirement of 21 U.S.C. § 355(a) that no person shall introduce into interstate commerce any new drug unless an application filed pursuant to subsection (b) of that section is effective with respect to such drug, claimant's president admits in his affidavit that no such application was filed before the commencement of the sale of Trim cigarettes. He would, however, explain such failure to file such an application by the statement that it was orally excused, by telephone, by Dr. Ralph G. Smith, of the Medical Division of the Federal Drug Administration. Abbott says that before the execution of the contract between claimant and Riggio Tobacco Corporation, for the manufacture by the latter of Trim cigarettes, counsel for the manufacturer insisted that the Administration be contacted for the purpose of ascertaining whether there was anything dangerous to human beings in their proposed ingredients.... Abbott's affidavit states that Dr. Smith advised that it was unnecessary for a new drug application to be filed since the ingredients of the cigarette disclosed to him were all well-known and harmless for human use in the form prescribed.... Assuming that Dr. Smith, a Government employee, told claimant's attorney that it would be unnecessary for claimant to file a new drug application with the Administration, claimant's failure to comply with the statute in that regard cannot be excused under the theory of estoppel against the Government....

NOTE

For other cases holding that FDA is not estopped from initiating regulatory action by prior contradictory statements of agency employees, *see Bentex Pharmaceuticals, Inc. v. Richardson*, 463 F.2d 363 (4th Cir. 1972), *rev'd on other grounds*, 412 U.S. 645 (1973); *AMP, Inc. v. Gardner*, 389 F.2d 825 (2d Cir. 1968); *United States v. 154 Sacks of Oats*, 294 F. 340 (W.D. Va. 1923); *United States v. 60 28–Capsule Bottles ... "Unitrol,"* 211 F. Supp. 207 (D.N.J. 1962). In *United States v. Articles of Food ... Clover Club Potato Chips*, 67 F.R.D. 419 (D. Idaho 1975), the court stated that the validity of an alleged agreement by FDA not to seize the existing inventory of illegal food labeling in return for the company changing all future labeling "depends upon the authority of the official" at FDA who made that agreement.

———

FDA has by regulation provided for the issuance of formal advisory opinions that are binding upon the agency and thus would presumably estop contrary action. 21 C.F.R. 10.85, promulgated in 42 Fed. Reg. 4680 (Jan. 25, 1977). The preamble to the agency's 1975 proposal explained these provisions.

Administrative Practices and Procedures: Notice of Proposed Rule Making

40 Fed. Reg. 40682 (September 3, 1975).

Throughout its history, the Food and Drug Administration has issued advisory opinions in various forms. Early advisory opinions, between 1938 and 1946, were issued as trade correspondence (TC's). More recently, advisory opinions have been codified in the agency's Compliance Policy Guides manual, which is available from the Public Records and Documents Center, in other documents designated as "advisory opinions," and in preambles to FEDERAL REGISTER documents. The proposed regulations recognizing the continuing status of these prior documents as advisory opinions except to the extent that they are revoked....

Prior Food and Drug Administration policy has not distinguished between formal advisory opinions and informal oral advice and correspondence. As a result, confusion and uncertainty has been engendered both within the agency and outside as to whether opinions expressed in correspondence or orally carry the weight of the agency or only of the individual agency employee involved.

Absent specific regulations to the contrary, the statements of a government employee do not bind the government. Accordingly, because of the lack of any agency regulations on this matter, none of the correspondence or oral advice previously issued by the agency has had any binding legal effect. . . . The Commissioner would resolve the present uncertainty by the proposal of regulations that would clearly and explicitly recognize the difference between the informal opinion of an individual in the agency, which represents his best information and advice, and the formal opinion of the agency, which represents a position of the Food and Drug Administration that is binding and commits the agency to the views expressed until they are formally modified or revoked. . . .

Under [§ 10.85 as codified], a request for a formal advisory opinion would be made pursuant to a specified form. The resulting advisory opinion would have to be followed by the agency until it is amended or revoked. Amendment or revocation of an advisory opinion would be required to be made with the same degree of public dissemination as adoption of the original advisory opinion, or by publishing notice of such revocation in the FEDERAL REGISTER, which by statute constitutes adequate public notice. An advisory opinion would, however, have to be explicitly revoked. . . .

All statements or advice given by a Food and Drug Administration employee orally or in writing, but which did not constitute an advisory opinion, would represent informal communications that contain the best information and opinion available to that employee at that time, but would not have the same binding effect as an advisory opinion. Accordingly, such informal communications would in no way obligate or commit the agency to the views expressed. . . .

Ordinarily, an advisory opinion would commit the Food and Drug Administration to the position stated in the opinion, until it is amended or revoked. In unusual situations involving an immediate and significant danger to health, however, the Commissioner could take appropriate civil enforcement action contrary to an advisory opinion prior to amending or revoking it. . . .

COMMENT: GUIDANCE DOCUMENTS AND ESTOPPEL

According to 21 C.F.R. 10.85, the "advisory opinions" FDA is generally obligated to follow include not only responses to formal requests for advisory opinions, but also (1) "[a]ny portion of a Federal Register notice other than the text of a proposed or final regulation, *e.g.*, a notice to manufacturers or a preamble to a proposed or final regulation," (2) Trade Correspondence issued by FDA between 1938 and 1946, (3) Compliance policy guides issued since 1968 and codified in the Compliance Policy Guides manual, and (4) other documents specifically identified as advisory opinions. 21 C.F.R. 10.85(d)(1)–(4).

Originally, section 10.85 also listed FDA "guidelines" (now known as "guidance documents") as a type of advisory opinion. In 1997, however, FDA issued a document titled "Good Guidance Practices" (GGP), in which it stated that guidance documents themselves do not create rights or responsibilities under the law and are not legally binding on either regulated industries or the agency. 62 Fed. Reg. 8961 (Feb. 27, 1997). Later that year, in FDAMA, Congress codified certain parts of the GGP document, including the portions on legal effect. As revised by FDAMA, the FD&C Act now provides that guidance documents "shall not create or confer any rights for or on any person, although they present the views of the Secretary ..." FD&C Act 701(h)(1)(A). The FDAMA amendments also provide, however, that "[a]lthough guidance documents shall not be binding on the Secretary, the Secretary shall ensure that employees of the [FDA] do not deviate from such guidances without appropriate justification and supervisory concurrence." FD&C Act 701(h)(1)(B).

In 2000, to comply with FDAMA, FDA promulgated a final rule codifying its Good Guidance Practices. 65 Fed. Reg. 56468 (Sept. 19, 2000). In addition to echoing FDAMA's language on guidance documents' legal effect, this rule deleted 21 C.F.R. 10.85(d)(5), the paragraph that listed "guidances" as a category of usually binding "advisory opinions." In the preamble to the final rule, FDA stated:

> Two comments suggested that compliance with a guidance document should provide a company with a safe harbor from FDA enforcement action. The comments recommended that we change the regulation to require us to amend, or at least publish a proposal to amend, a guidance document before initiating an enforcement action against a company that acted in accordance with a guidance. The comments also noted that if we do not provide a safe harbor from enforcement, at a minimum, a company's action in accordance with a guidance document should be evidence of the company's intent to comply with our regulations.

> Section 701(h)(1)(B) of the act provides that guidance documents "shall not be binding on the Secretary." Creating a "safe harbor" in a guidance document that would preclude us from taking action would impermissibly bind us. In issuing enforcement-related guidance documents, we express our current thinking regarding regulatory matters and believe this provides useful information. However, you always remain independently responsible for complying with applicable statutes and regulations. Whether you have complied with the law is determined from the facts of each case.

N.   STATE ENFORCEMENT OF THE FD&C ACT

Since 1938, section 702(a) of the FD&C Act has authorized FDA to conduct examinations and investigations using state employees who have been "commissioned" as FDA officers. Under the Nutrition Labeling and Education Act of 1990, 104 Stat. 2353, states were for the first time authorized directly to enforce particular food labeling provisions of the FD&C Act in Federal courts. All of the food labeling requirements that preempt differing state requirements under section 403A of the FD&C Act are also open to state enforcement under section 310(b). To date, no state has attempted to exploit this authority.

Section 310(b) is limited to civil actions brought within the geographical area of the state. A state is precluded from bringing suit until 30 days after it provides notice to FDA of its intent to do so. If FDA commences regulatory action relating to the matter, the state must wait an additional 90 days. If at the end of those 90 days, FDA is diligently prosecuting or has settled the matter, the state is barred from bringing suit in federal court.

CHAPTER XI

REGULATION OF FOREIGN COMMERCE

A. IMPORTATION INTO THE UNITED STATES

1. FDA's GENERAL AUTHORITY OVER IMPORTATION

FDA works closely with Customs and Border Protection of the Department of Homeland Security (formerly the Customs Service of the Department of Transportation) to prevent the importation of adulterated or misbranded products, and unapproved drugs, into the United States. FDA's primary source of authority to keep such products out of the country is section 801(a) of the FD&C Act:

> The [Secretary of Homeland Security] shall deliver to the Secretary of Health and Human Services, upon his request, samples of food, drugs, devices, and cosmetics which are being imported or offered for import into the United States, giving notice thereof to the owner or consignee, who may appear before the Secretary of Health and Human Services and have the right to introduce testimony.... If it appears from the examination of such samples or otherwise that (1) such article has been manufactured, processed, or packed under insanitary conditions or, in the case of a device, [in violation of the current good manufacturing practice requirements for devices,] or (2) such article is forbidden or restricted in sale in the country in which it was produced or from which it was exported, or (3) such article is adulterated, misbranded, or in violation of section 505, then such article shall be refused admission, except as provided in subsection (b) of this section [providing for reconditioning].....

Sugarman v. Forbragd

405 F.2d 1189 (9th Cir. 1968).

■ MERRILL, CIRCUIT JUDGE:

Appellant seeks by suit for injunction to review an order of the Food and Drug Administration excluding from import as adulterated certain damaged coffee beans. In entering its order the Food and Drug Administration was acting ... pursuant to the terms of the Food, Drug and Cosmetic Act, 21 U.S.C. § 381(a) [FDCA § 801(a)]. The question presented is whether (absent arbitrary or capricious action which clearly is lacking here) such an order excluding material from import under § 381(a) is subject to judicial review. The District Court held that it was not. We agree.

Appellant contends that the Administrative Procedure Act applies to require agency notice and hearing and provide judicial review. By the terms of that Act, § 701(a)(2), it is not to apply where "agency action is committed to agency discretion by law." In our judgment that is the situation here; by 21 U.S.C. § 381(a) exclusion from import as there provided is committed to the discretion of the Secretary of Health, Education and Welfare.

We note that the prescribed procedure suggests final discretionary authority in the Secretary. His judgment must be accepted and acted upon by the Secretary of the Treasury. Further, the language of the section "if it appears" suggests discretion to be tested by a standard of arbitrariness rather than error. These suggestions in our view are compellingly borne out by the fact that the Secretary's judgment may be founded solely upon his examination of the material in question.[3] While the superficiality of tests and inspections or an arbitrary refusal to accept their results may be appropriate subjects for judicial review, a dispute as to what an examination has established or disclosed is more appropriately left to agency expertise.

The material in question was determined to be adulterated under the statutory definition for the reason that it was found to be "unfit for food." Appellant contends that to preclude arbitrary action the Secretary should promulgate regulations spelling out fitness for food. The [FDA] here determined from its examination that due to its damage the material in question was wholly lacking in recognized food values. A determination of unfitness under these facts cannot, in our judgment, be regarded as arbitrary even in absence of more explicit definition by regulation.

Judgment affirmed.

NOTES

1. *Nature of Hearing.* Although FDA is not required to give an importer a formal evidentiary hearing on the record before refusing admission to the owner's product, the agency is, in accordance with section 801(a), obligated to provide the owner notice and an opportunity to "introduce testimony." This procedure is set forth at 21 C.F.R. 1.94(a), which states: "If it appears that the article may be subject to refusal of admission, the district director [having jurisdiction over the port of entry] shall give the owner or consignee a written notice to that effect, stating the reasons therefor. The notice shall specify a place and a period of time during which the owner or consignee shall have an opportunity to introduce testimony."

2. *Requirement of Adequate Notice.* In *L&M Industries, Inc. v. Kenter*, 458 F.2d 968 (2d Cir. 1972), FDA issued a Notice of Detention and Hearing informing an importer that its detained shipment of food was misbranded. After the hearing, FDA issued a Notice of Refusal, based on its conclusion that the shipment was adulterated (rather then misbranded). The Second Circuit held: "L & M was

---

3. While provision is made to supplement the Secretary's examination with a hearing, his decision need not be determined exclusively on the record of a formal hearing. The District Court held, and we agree, that to exclude imports, no formal hearing is required either by the Food, Drug and Cosmetic Act, 21 U.S.C. § 381(a), by the Administrative Procedure Act, or by the Constitution, congressional power over foreign commerce being absolute.

effectively denied the opportunity to be heard or to introduce testimony as to this central issue for it never received a Section 381 notice that adulteration was in question. Therefore, we find that the F.D.A. exceeded its statutory authority when it determined [the shipment] to be adulterated without first providing the appellant with the opportunity to be heard on that issue."

3. *A Double Standard?* FDA's ability to interdict imports of products into the United States—in effect to prevent commercial distribution before any charge of misbranding or adulteration is adjudicated—arguably permits discrimination against foreign products.

Goodwin v. United States

371 F. Supp. 433 (S.D. Cal. 1972).

■ WALLACE, DISTRICT JUDGE. . . .

FINDINGS OF FACT

1.   Plaintiff is an American citizen who for the past two and one-half years has been engaged in the regular importation of live clams into the United States from Mexican waters in the Gulf of California.

2.   Plaintiff's live clams, once imported, have been distributed for human consumption to various markets and restaurants on the West Coast of the United States.

3.   During the two and one-half years of operation, plaintiff's live clams have been frequently tested by the Food & Drug Administration for presence of E. Coli bacteria and have been allowed to be released in the open market for sale for human consumption.

4.   Between September 22, 1971, and November 2, 1971, the United States Food & Drug Administration issued notices of detention pursuant to 21 U.S.C. § 381 against five lots of live clams offered for import by plaintiff Donald G. Goodwin.

5.   The basis for each detention was that the clams were prepared, packed or held under insanitary conditions whereby they may have been contaminated with filth and were adulterated within the meaning of 21 U.S.C. § 342(a)(4) in that they came from uncertified waters.

6.   The Food & Drug Administration, during the summer of 1971, informally established a policy, which was implemented in this area in September, 1971, which bars the importation of shellfish from any waters of a foreign country which are not from "certified" waters. . . .

7.   United States, Japan, and Canada have entered into reciprocal certification programs whereby waters within those territorial boundaries are subject to testing and certification, which comply with federal standards as set forth by the National Shellfish Sanitation Program. Waters of nations who do not participate in this program are regarded as uncertified waters.

. . . .

15.   There is no known test to determine whether shellfish, including clams, are carriers of infectious hepatitis or typhoid.

16.   There are tests which can be performed to determine whether shell-fish, including clams, are carriers of salmonellosis . . . but these tests do not provide a feasible approach to protection in that they are costly, incomplete and/or destroy the marketability of the product.

17.   Compliance with the requirements of the National Shellfish Sanitation Program is currently the most effective method of monitoring the commercial distribution of shellfish, including clams, to ensure that the public health danger associated with the consumption of contaminated shellfish is minimized.

. . . .

20.   Shellfish are known potential carriers of bacterial and viral organisms which may cause typhoid, gastroenteritis and viral hepatitis. There is a high incidence of typhoid, gastroenteritis and viral hepatitis in Mexico due to the generally unsanitary conditions prevailing there.

From the foregoing findings of fact, the Court makes the following conclusions of law.

CONCLUSIONS OF LAW

1.   The United States Food & Drug Administration has authority to bar the importation of all shellfish (including clams) which appear from examination of such shellfish, or otherwise, to have been manufactured, processed, or packed under insanitary conditions, or to be adulterated in that they may be injurious to health. 21 U.S.C. § 381(a); 21 U.S.C. § 342(a)(4).

2.   The Food & Drug Administration is not required to find that each shellfish is actually contaminated prior to barring its importation from a foreign country; rather, it is sufficient that the shellfish appear to have been grown or processed under insanitary conditions, which conclusion may be derived from an examination of the shellfish or otherwise.

. . . .

4.   This Court has jurisdiction to review the issue of whether the Food & Drug Administration acted arbitrarily or capriciously in deciding to bar the importation of all shellfish from foreign uncertified waters. *Sugarman v. Forbragd*, 405 F.2d 1189 (9th Cir. 1968).

5.   The action of the Food & Drug Administration in barring the importation of live clams from uncertified foreign waters was not an arbitrary or capricious act, in that it appears that such clams may be injurious to health and this method provides the best protection for the public. The question is whether there is statutory authority to do so.

. . . .

7.   In this case, from the combined factors of (1) the presence of E. coli bacteria in the detained loads showing that the beds from which plaintiff's clams are harvested are in proximity to possible fecal contamination, (2) the general lack of sanitary conditions and the high incidence of gastroenteritic diseases and of viral hepatitis in Mexico, and (3) the uncertainty as to a potential of danger because the waters are not certified, I cannot hold that it was an arbitrary or capricious determination that it "appears" the clams in question were grown under insanitary conditions or were "adulterated" pursuant to 21 U.S.C. § 381(a).

8.   The Food and Drug Administration is not estopped to prevent plaintiff from importing clams.

NOTES

1.   *Coordination With Customs Service.* In a Memorandum of Understanding (MOU) between the Customs Service and FDA, published in 44 Fed. Reg. 53577 (Sept. 14, 1979), FDA was given the authority under section 801 of the FD&C Act to collect samples at ports, issue notices of sampling, and issue notices of refusal of admission. The MOU stated that the FDA Commissioner would designate certain FDA officers as Customs Officers with the responsibility for performing these functions.

The Bioterrorism Act of 2002 added section 801(m) to the FD&C Act, requiring food importers to give FDA prior notice of each article of imported food. FDA's implementing regulations, which went into effect in December 2003, require this notice to be submitted electronically and to identify, among other things, the article, the manufacturer or grower of the article, and the country of origin. 21 C.F.R. 1.281, implementing section 801(m). Even before 2003, importers and brokers provided much of this information to the Customs Service, but the Bioterrorism Act mandates notice directly to FDA so it can determine whether to inspect the imported food. The introduction of this requirement impelled FDA and Customs and Border Protection to increase their level of cooperation even further. The two agencies entered an MOU allowing FDA to commission all CBP officers it deems necessary to enforce section 801(m) and the implementing regulations. Memorandum of Agreement Between CBP and FDA (Dec. 3, 2003).

2.   *Legal Challenges to FDA Importation Procedures.* Particular procedures under which FDA has regulated importation have been sharply questioned in several cases. In *Caribbean Produce Exchange, Inc. v. Secretary of HHS*, Food Drug Cosm. L. Rep. (CCH) ¶ 38,100 & ¶ 38,110 (D.P.R. 1988), *rev'd*, 893 F.2d 3 (1st Cir. 1989), the District Court enjoined the FDA detention procedure for imported garlic because its requirements had not been established through rulemaking. The Court of Appeals, however, remanded the case for an evidentiary hearing. In *Bellarno International Ltd. v. FDA*, 678 F. Supp. 410 (E.D.N.Y. 1988), the court invalidated an FDA "import alert" that provided for automatic detention of drugs that had been exported and then reimported, because of the agency's failure to engage in notice-and-comment rulemaking. In *United States v. Articles of Drugs Consisting of 203 Paper Bags*, 634 F. Supp. 435 (N.D. Ill. 1985), *vacated*, 818 F.2d 569 (7th Cir. 1987), the District Court allowed reexportation of illegal animal drugs, over FDA's protest, because the agency had failed to establish its requirements for imported drugs through rulemaking. The Court of Appeals vacated this decision as moot after the drugs had been reexported.

3.   *USDA Powers.* In *Ganadera Industrial, S.A. v. Block*, 727 F.2d 1156 (D.C. Cir. 1984), the court upheld a USDA decision to ban the importation of meat by the plaintiff Costa Rican company until the chairman of the board and controlling stockholder, who had been indicted in the United States for criminal violations of the Federal Meat Inspection Act, was removed from his management position and from control of the company through a voting trust.

2.   RECONDITIONING, DESTROYING, OR REEXPORTING GOODS REFUSED ADMISSION

Section 801(a) of the FD&C Act provides: "The Secretary of [Homeland Security] shall cause the destruction of any . . . article refused admission unless such article is exported, under regulations prescribed by the Secretary of the [Homeland Security], within ninety days of the date of notice of such refusal or within such additional time as may be permitted pursuant to such regulations." Section 801(b) creates an alternative mechanism by which FDA may defer its final determination as to the admission of an article that appears to be adulterated, misbranded, or in violation of the Act's new drug approval requirements:

> If it appears to the Secretary of Health and Human Services that [an article that appears to be adulterated, misbranded, or in violation of the Act's new drug approval requirements] can, by relabeling or other action, be brought into compliance with the Act or rendered other than a food, drug, device, or cosmetic, final determination as to admission of such article may be deferred and, upon filing of timely written application by the owner or consignee and the execution by him of a bond ... the Secretary may, in accordance with regulations, authorize the applicant to perform such relabeling or other action specified in such authorization (including destruction or export of rejected articles or portions thereof, as may be specified in the Secretary's authorization).

Carl Borchsenius Co. v. Gardner

282 F. Supp. 396 (E.D. La. 1968).

■ CASSIBRY, DISTRICT JUDGE.

The shipment of 5,000 bags of coffee, weighing 665,000 pounds with an estimated invoice value of $227,000, arrived at the Port of New Orleans from Paranagua, Brazil aboard the Mario D'Almeida on November 21, 1967. . . .

A wharf examination of the shipment by a United States Food and Drug Inspector on December 1 disclosed damp, moldy coffee in four of the six samples taken in the inspection. Approximately 1,500 bags were wet and some contained moldy coffee. The entire shipment of 5,000 bags was detained by the Food and Drug Administration. . . .

On December 1, plaintiff filed an application for authorization pursuant to 21 U.S.C. § 381(b) to attempt to bring the 5,000 bags of coffee into compliance with the Act by the procedure of "skimming the coffee to remove molded beans" and "drying the coffee out to remove wet beans." This authorization was given on December 4. . . .

Of the 5,000 bags, examination showed 2,325 to be sound, and upon request of plaintiff's representatives these bags were released under a partial release of the shipment on December 8. . . . [T]he Import Inspector's examination showed on December 21 that, of the 2,789 bags received for reconditioning, 1,730 bags were made sound and thus brought into compliance with the law, 270 bags were poor skims, 231 bags were sweepings, and 1,053 bags were too poor to skim due to mold.

On December 26, the defendant C. C. Freeman, Acting Director of the Food and Drug Administration for this District, advised the plaintiff's representative by letter that a "Release Notice" on the 1,730 bags made sound would be issued upon receipt of proof of destruction of the remaining

270 bags of poor skims, 231 bags of sweepings and 1,053 bags of moldy coffee in original bags. The plaintiff had no objection to destruction of the 270 bags of poor skims and the 231 bags of sweepings, but its representative requested on January 2, 1968 that the 1,730 bags of "made sound" coffee be released for import and that it be allowed to burnish, rebag and export the 1,053 bags which had not been reconditioned. The request to burnish, rebag and export was denied by Acting Director Freeman by letter of January 3....

The only issue before the Court is whether the defendants acted within the limits of their statutory authority in this case, and to resolve that issue the Court must determine whether the defendants have the discretion under 21 U.S.C. § 381(b) to require destruction of articles offered for import, which are rejected because they cannot be brought into compliance with the Act, without giving the applicant an opportunity to export the rejected articles....

The defendants agree that the owner or consignee could choose to export articles refused admission under the language in subsection (a) that "The Secretary of the Treasury shall *cause the destruction of any such article refused admission unless such article is exported*, ...," and they agree that had the plaintiff in this case not chosen to attempt to bring the coffee into compliance under subsection (b), it would have had the choice of exporting the entire shipment of 5,000 bags. (Italics here and elsewhere mine). They argue that such a choice is not available to an owner or consignee as to rejected articles from the attempt at compliance under the language of subsection (b) that "the Secretary of Health, Education and Welfare may, in accordance with regulations authorize the applicant to perform such relabeling or other action specified in such authorization (*including destruction nor export of rejected articles or portions thereof*, as may be specified in the Secretary's authorization)," and that the rejected articles may be ordered destroyed at their discretion.

This contention of defendants as to their discretion under 381(b) is not only at variance with the policy set by Congress as to the disposition of articles rejected for admission set out in 381(a), but is at variance with a continuing policy of Congress as to the disposition of articles refused admission for import....

There is nothing in 381(b) to indicate that the taking advantage of the opportunity to bring articles into compliance with standards for import makes those rejected from the compliance operation products involved in illegal import activity. Interpreting that statute as giving administrative discretion to destroy rejected articles would be a radical departure from the policy of Congress on this matter, and such a major change in policy could hardly be expected to appear as a parenthetical insertion in a statute. I find nothing from policy considerations to support the argument of defendants that Congress intended when a consignee elects to avail himself of the compliance provisions of 381(b) to deprive him of the choice under 381(a) to export rejected articles. From this viewpoint the contention of plaintiff that 381(a) and (b) should be read together, and that the parenthetical phrase regarding disposition of rejecting articles in (b) was not intended to depart from the disposition provision of (a) and deprive the consignee of the choice of export is logical and persuasive. . . .

The Court concludes that the defendants do not have the discretion under 381(b) to require the destruction of articles offered for import, which are rejected because they cannot be brought into compliance with the Act, without giving the applicant an opportunity to export the rejected articles upon compliance with the applicable statutes; therefore, the action in this case in refusing to grant the request for permission to export the rejected coffee, and in requiring its destruction as a condition of release of the sound coffee, was beyond their statutory authority. Judgment is rendered in accordance with these views granting to plaintiff the relief prayed for.

3.   REFUSAL OF ADMISSION COMPARED TO SEIZURE

An imported article that is adulterated, misbranded, or unapproved might be detained by the government under section 801 or seized by the government under section 304. Which remedy the government pursues has important practical implications for the importer or consignee. First of all, section 801 creates a purely administrative procedure, whereas section 304 requires the United States to seek a condemnation order from a federal district court. Second, the two procedures can potentially lead to different ultimate dispositions of the goods in question. Under either section, an importer may be given an opportunity to bring the goods into compliance with the FD&C Act. FD&C Act 304(d)(1), 801(b). Suppose, however, that the importer is not provided such an opportunity to cure, or is unable to do so? As discussed above, section 801 requires U.S. Customs and Border Protection to permit the reexportation of the goods, as an alternative to their destruction. By contrast, under section 304(d)(1), as revised in 1997, a court may permit exportation of a seized and condemned imported good only if the person seeking to export it can "establish that the article was intended for export at the time the article entered commerce." The regulation of "import for export" will be explored in more detail *infra* p. 1408. For purposes of the current discussion, the important thing to recognize is that, for goods imported for sale in the United States, reexportation is often an option under section 801 but never an option under section 304.

United States v. Food, 2,998 Cases

64 F.3d 984 (5th Cir. 1995).

■ E. GRADY JOLLY, CIRCUIT JUDGE:

This appeal presents complex, difficult, and close questions. It is, however, a case that is unlikely to arouse widespread passion. . . .

In October 1989, the Food and Drug Administration issued an "import alert"[2] for all canned mushrooms processed in China in response to a foodborne illness caused by staphylococcal enterotoxin found in canned mush-

---

2. An import alert advises FDA field offices of ongoing problems with a specific product offered for import and suggests ap-   propriate action, such as detention for inspection and sampling.

rooms produced in nine China factories. Appellee First Phoenix Group Limited, Inc., an importer of food products, purchased several orders of canned mushrooms supposedly packaged at Hwa Chen Industrial Corporation in Taiwan. In late spring 1992, First Phoenix attempted to enter two shipments of mushrooms—3,000 cases and 6,000 cases—into the United States. . . . The United States Customs Service conditionally released these mushrooms under bond pending review by the FDA. . . .

On July 10, 1992, the FDA issued a second import alert advising its field offices to detain shipments of canned mushrooms from specified Taiwanese manufactures, including Hwa Chen. The FDA issued this import alert because mushrooms labelled [sic] as packaged and produced from these specified manufacturers actually were processed and packaged in an unknown factory in China. Because of this import alert, the FDA issued Notices of Detention and Hearing for the 3,000–case shipment on July 29, and for the 6,000–case shipment on December 14. In these notices, the FDA indicated that it was acting under its power in § 381(a) of the Federal Food, Drug, and Cosmetic Act. . . . FDA . . . concluded that an unknown factory in China used Hwa Chen's can codes in a deliberate attempt to circumvent the broad import alert on canned mushrooms originating in China. The FDA then advised First Phoenix that it would likely refuse admission of the mushrooms and allow reexport only under very strict conditions. The FDA, however, issued no formal notice of refusal of admission. The FDA then conducted additional testing of a separate lot of mushrooms ostensibly packaged at Hwa Chen and shipped into the United States by First Phoenix, but not at issue in this appeal. Based on staphyloccal enterotoxin found in these mushrooms, the FDA informed First Phoenix of its decision to destroy the mushrooms, rather than allow reexport. Thus, the FDA decided to proceed under the authority provided in 21 U.S.C. § 334, instead of proceeding under 21 U.S.C. § 381.

Accordingly, on November 3, 1993, the government filed a complaint in the United States District Court for the Eastern District of Louisiana seeking seizure and condemnation of both [the 3,000–case and 6,000–case] shipments of mushrooms as adulterated and misbranded goods in interstate commerce under its authority in 21 U.S.C. § 334(a) of the FDCA. Under the district court's warrant for the arrest of both shipments, the United States Marshals Service seized and attached the shipments at the New Orleans warehouse where they were stored upon entry into New Orleans and continue to be held at the present time. On April 19, 1994, the district court granted summary judgment in favor of First Phoenix and dismissed the government's case. The district court held that the mushrooms had never entered interstate commerce as required for an action under § 334(a) because they had continually remained under Customs Service transit bonds. The district court thus determined that the Customs Service remained in control of the mushrooms since their import into the United States. Finally, the court concluded that § 381(a) was the government's exclusive authority with respect to the mushrooms and gave First Phoenix the opportunity to reexport the two shipments before being destroyed by the FDA. . . .

On appeal, the government argues that because the mushroom shipments fall within the statutory definition of "interstate commerce," it had the authority to bring a § 334 seizure and condemnation action in the district court. The government further contends that its authority to act under this statute is unaffected by the fact that the administrative remedy in § 381 is also available to it in this case. . . .

. . . We hold that the interstate commerce requirement has been satisfied in this case and that goods seized at the port of entry may be the proper subject of an action under § 334. We therefore reverse the judgment of the district court and remand for further proceedings not inconsistent with this opinion.

We first examine whether the mushrooms in this case were introduced into "interstate commerce," as required to initiate a seizure and condemnation action under § 334. . . . [T]o initiate an action for seizure and condemnation, the FDA must prove only that the goods have been introduced into interstate commerce, notwithstanding the fact that the goods may be removed at some later time from interstate commerce. The FDCA expansively defines interstate commerce as "commerce between any State or Territory and any place outside thereof." 21 U.S.C. § 321(b) Here, each shipment was shipped from a place outside the United States—Taiwan— and entered the United States at Savannah, Georgia, and Long Beach, California, respectively, where they arrived and were unloaded. There is some suggestion, however, that these mushrooms may have been effectively detained at sea by the import alert and thus were removed from the stream of commerce before they actually entered the United States. If, however, goods are destined for sale in a state other than the place from which they are shipped, then goods are in "interstate commerce" without the necessity of physically crossing a state boundary. Thus, we conclude that the mushrooms in this case undoubtedly constituted an interstate shipment from the moment they left Taiwan.

The question remaining is whether these goods, which were never released for sale in the United States from the Customs Service, were also in "commerce," as required by § 321(b). First Phoenix argues that these mushrooms could not possibly be in commerce because from the moment the goods were placed on alert, even before they arrived in the United States, and at all times thereafter, sale of these goods in the United States was prohibited by the FDA. First Phoenix additionally argues that because the mushrooms were held under Customs Service bonds[8] since arriving in the United States, they were never introduced into interstate commerce as required in § 334 for a condemnation action. First Phoenix attempts to

---

8. A Customs Service bond includes any bond required under Customs laws or regulations in order to perform a particular Customs activity. 19 C.F.R. § 113.61 (1994). Under 19 U.S.C. § 1553, "any merchandise, other than . . . merchandise the importation of which is prohibited, . . . may be entered for transportation in bond through the United States by a bonded carrier without appraisement or the payment of duties." Here, both shipments were transported under bond and to New Orleans based on § 1553. These bonds were obtained to secure duties, taxes, and other charges due on the shipments of the imported mushrooms. *See* 19 C.F.R. § 113.62 illust. a (requiring bond securing duties, taxes, and charges imposed or estimated to be due if merchandise is released from Customs custody).

place an impossibly narrow construction on a very broad statute. Regardless of the government's impediments to the sale of these goods once they reached the United States, these goods nevertheless had been shipped to the United States for the express purpose of sale when they left Taiwan. . . . In sum, we hold that these mushrooms had been introduced into interstate commerce at the time they were detained by the Customs Service, given the expansive and unrestricted definition of § 321(b).

Having determined that the mushrooms had been introduced into interstate commerce, it is plain on the face of the statute that § 334 is a judicial remedy available to the FDA in this case. We now must address, however, First Phoenix's argument that Congress intended § 334 to apply only to seizures of goods that have been released from the Customs Service. In short, First Phoenix argues that only the administrative procedures under § 381 may be invoked by the FDA when the goods are seized at the port of entry and not yet admitted into the United States. We now turn to consider this question of whether § 334 and § 381 create two mutually exclusive statutory remedies for goods under the FDCA.

As earlier discussed, § 334(a) is a judicial remedy available to the FDA allowing it to seize and condemn any goods that have been introduced into or are already in interstate commerce or after shipment is in interstate commerce, but if the FDA chooses to proceed under this statute it must prove in a court of law by a preponderance of the evidence that the goods are indeed adulterated or misbranded. Section 381, on the other hand, is purely an administrative procedure, which allows a quick and efficient means of protecting the American public from unhealthy or mislabeled imported goods. . . .

Clearly no provision of § 381 expressly restricts the authority of the FDA from proceeding judicially under § 334 when it seizes and holds goods at the port of entry in the United States.[10] If goods are, in point of time, both "in interstate commerce" [§ 334] and "being imported or offered for import into the United States," [§ 381] as the mushrooms here, the plain words of the statutes permit the government the option of proceeding under either § 334 or § 381.[11] . . .

---

10. We point out that § 381 undoubtedly only applies to goods detained at the port of entry and any seizure of imported goods after release by the Customs Service *must* submit to judicial proceedings under § 334. The question here is whether these statutes provide overlapping remedies for goods seized at the port of entry so that the government, at that point, may chose to proceed under either § 334 or § 381.

11. First Phoenix argues that the express language of § 381 mandates that adulterated goods being imported or offered for import, as here, *shall* be refused admission. Once admission is refused, First Phoenix argues, § 381 grants the importer an unqualified right to reexport the goods within ninety days of this refusal. First Phoenix contends,

and the district court agreed, that allowing the FDA the option of proceeding under § 334 or § 381 when the imported goods meet the prerequisites of both would emasculate its unqualified right granted by § 381 to reexport goods within ninety days of refusal of admission.

We acknowledge that this plain language projects a forceful argument that importers have an unequivocal right to a notice of refusal of admission. And it is true that if the FDA proceeds under § 334, as they have in this case, the importer does not receive a notice of refusal of admission and the concomitant right to reexport. Nevertheless, we are convinced that the more compelling view of the statutory scheme, for reasons we ex-

We therefore hold that the plain language of § 334 permits the FDA to initiate a seizure and condemnation action, such as the one before us, when goods are seized at the port of entry. The district court is REVERSED and the case REMANDED for further proceedings not inconsistent with this opinion.

NOTES

1. *Reexportation of Imported Goods Seized Under Section 304.* FD&C Act 304(d)(1) authorizes courts, at their discretion, to permit reexportation of seized and condemned imported articles under certain conditions, as an alternative to their destruction or reconditioning. A claimant seeking to reexport condemned imported goods must show that the adulteration, misbranding, or violation did not occur after importation; that it had no reason to believe that the articles were adulterated, misbranded, or in violation before they were released from customs custody; and that it can and will satisfy the requirements in section 801(e)(1), applicable to exported goods generally. Section 304(d)(1) explicitly forbids reexportation with regard to certain types of adulteration that render an article dangerous to health. *See, e.g., United States v. 76,552 Pounds of Frog Legs*, 423 F. Supp. 329 (S.D. Tex. 1976) (reexportation not allowed because claimant offered part of shipment for sale in domestic commerce in violation of section 801(e)(1)(D) and because the food was injurious to health).

Despite these conditions, courts could, prior to 1997, permit reexportation of a wide variety of seized imported goods that could not legally have been sold in the United States. *E.g., United States v. Articles of Drug . . . 203 Paper Bags*, 634 F. Supp. 435 (N.D. Ill. 1985) (permitting reexportation of adulterated and misbranded animal drugs). However, in the FDA Modernization Act of 1997 Congress added a further requirement that severely reduced the availability of section 304(d)(1) reexportation, namely, that the person seeking to reexport must "establish that the article was intended for export at the time the article entered commerce." Section 304 reexportation is now thus restricted to goods "imported for export." Perhaps the last ever application of the earlier, broader version of the reexportation provision was a 1998 district court order permitting the claimant to reexport three lots of adulterated frozen shrimp that were originally imported in 1997, before the new version of 304(d)(1) went into effect. The court refused to apply the amendment retroactively. *United States v. 302 Cases . . . Frozen Shrimp*, 25 F. Supp. 2d 1358 (M.D. Fla. 1998).

2. *GAO Oversight.* The General Accounting Office has been a frequent critic of FDA's enforcement against imported products. *See, e.g.,* FOOD AND DRUG ADMINISTRATION'S PROGRAM FOR REGULATING IMPORTED PRODUCTS NEEDS IMPROVING, No. HRD–77–72 (July 5, 1977); FDA IMPORT AUTOMATION: SERIOUS MANAGEMENT AND SYSTEMS DEVELOPMENT PROBLEMS PERSIST, No. AIMD–95–188 (Sept. 28, 1995); FOOD SAFETY: FEDERAL EFFORTS TO ENSURE THE SAFETY OF IMPORTED FOODS ARE INCONSISTENT AND UNRELIABLE, No. RCED–98–103 (Apr. 30, 1998); PRESCRIPTION DRUGS: ENHANCED EFFORTS AND BETTER AGENCY COORDINATION NEEDED TO ADDRESS ILLEGAL IMPORTATION No. GAO–06–175T (Dec. 13, 2005).

3. *Commentary. See generally* F. K. Killingsworth, *Import Control Under Federal Laws*, 2 FOOD DRUG COSM. L.Q. 498 (1947), 5 FOOD DRUG COSM. L.J. 205

press in this opinion, is that the FDA has an option to proceed under either statute with respect to goods detained at the port of entry, and if the government chooses to proceed under § 334, the right to a notice of refusal and opportunity to reexport provided in § 381 simply is inoperative.

(1950), and 8 Food Drug Cosm. 117 (1953); D. Joe Smith Jr., *Detention and Seizure of Imports by the Food and Drug Administration*, 33 Food Drug Cosm. L.J. 726 (1978).

4.   IMPORTATION OF PRESCRIPTION DRUGS AND DEVICES

a.   COMMERCIAL IMPORTATION

Because of the significant price differential, it became common in the early 2000s to import from Canada, for sale in the United States, cheaper unapproved versions of the FDA-approved drugs.

Warning Letter to Rx Depot
March 21, 2003.

Harry Lee Jones
Store Manager
Rx Depot, Inc. . . .

Dear Mr. Jones:

The Food and Drug Administration (FDA) has learned that you are assisting United States consumers in obtaining prescription drugs from Canada. Specifically, you are running a storefront operation that sends U.S. prescriptions, credit card information, and paperwork (including a "Patient Profile" and "Release & Limited Power of Attorney") to a Canadian pharmacy. According to information provided by you and your store, a prescription is then obtained from a medical doctor in Canada, and Canadian drugs are shipped by a pharmacy in the Canadian province of Manitoba directly to the U.S. consumer. As discussed in greater detail below, your actions violate the Federal Food, Drug and Cosmetic Act. Your actions also present a significant risk to public health, and you mislead the public about the safety of the drugs obtained through Rx Depot.

Legal Violations

Your actions violate the FD&C Act because virtually every shipment of prescription drugs from Canadian pharmacies to consumers in the U.S. violates the Act. Even if a prescription drug is approved in the U.S., if the drug is also originally manufactured in the U.S., it is a violation of the Act for anyone other than the U.S. manufacturer to import the drug into the United States (21 U.S.C. 381(d)(1)). We believe that virtually all drugs imported into the U.S. from Canada by or for individual U.S. consumers also violate U.S. law for other reasons. Generally, such drugs are unapproved (21 U.S.C. 355), labeled incorrectly (21 U.S.C. 353(b)(2)), and/or dispensed without a valid prescription (21 U.S.C. 353(b)(1)). Thus, their shipment into the U.S. from Canada violates the Act. *See, e.g.,* 21 U.S.C. 331(a), (d), (t).

The reason that Canadian or other foreign versions of U.S.-approved drugs are generally considered unapproved in the U.S. is that FDA approvals are manufacturer-specific, product-specific, and include many requirements relating to the product, such as manufacturing location, formulation, source and specifications of active ingredients, processing methods, manufacturing controls, container/closure system, and appearance. 21 C.F.R. 314.50. Frequently, drugs sold outside of the U.S. are not manufactured by a firm that has FDA approval for that drug. Moreover, even if the manufacturer has FDA approval for a drug, the version produced for foreign markets usually does not meet all of the requirements of the U.S. approval, and thus it is considered to be unapproved. 21 U.S.C. 355.

In order to ensure compliance with the Act when they are involved in shipping prescription drugs to consumers in the U.S., businesses and individuals must ensure, among other things, that they only sell FDA-approved drugs that are made outside of the U.S. and that comply with the FDA approval in all respects, including manufacturing location, formulation, source and specifications of active ingredients, processing methods, manufacturing controls, container/closure system, and appearance. 21 C.F.R. 314.50. They must also ensure that each drug meets all US. labeling requirements, including that it bears the FDA-approved labeling. 21 C.F.R. 201.100(c)(2). The drug must also be dispensed by a pharmacist pursuant to a valid prescription. 21 U.S.C. 353(b)(1).

Practically speaking, it is extremely unlikely that a pharmacy could ensure that all of the applicable legal requirements are met. Consequently, almost every time an individual or business ships a prescription drug from Canada to a U.S. consumer, the individual or business shipping the drug violates the FD&C Act. Moreover, individuals and businesses, such as Rx Depot, Inc. and its responsible personnel, that <u>cause</u> those shipments also violate the Act. 21 U.S.C. 331 ("The following acts and the causing thereof are hereby prohibited . . .").

Rx Depot's web site . . . misleadingly claims that, "United States FDA policy allows importation of approved products for personal use in quantities not to exceed three months." This is not correct. Under FDA's Personal Importation policy, as a matter of enforcement discretion in certain defined circumstances, FDA allows consumers to import otherwise illegal drugs. However, contrary to your statement, this policy is not intended to allow importation of foreign versions of drugs of which there is an FDA-approved version. This is especially true when the foreign versions of such drugs are being "commercialized" to U.S. citizens through operations such as yours.

Moreover, the policy simply describes the agency's enforcement priorities. It does not change the law, and it does not give a license to persons to import or export illegal drugs into the United States. See FDA Regulatory Procedures Manual, Chapter 9, Subchapter: Coverage of Personal Importations.

FDA's Public Health Concerns and Your Misleading Statements about Drug Safety

. . . Prescription drugs purchased from foreign countries generally are not FDA-approved, do not meet FDA standards, and are not the same as the drugs purchased in the United States. Drugs from foreign countries do not have the same assurance of safety as drugs actually regulated by the FDA. Because the medications are not subject to FDA's safety oversight, they could be outdated, contaminated, counterfeit or contain too much or too little of the active ingredient. In addition, foreign dispensers of drugs to American citizens may provide patients with incorrect medications, incorrect strengths, medicines that should not be used in people with certain conditions or with other medications, or medications without proper directions for use. These risks are exacerbated by the fact that many of the products you are soliciting United States consumers to buy are indicated for serious medical conditions. . . .

FDA is also very concerned about the importation of prescription drugs from Canada and other foreign counties because, in our experience, many drugs obtained from foreign sources that purport or appear to be the same as U.S.-approved prescription drugs are, in fact, of unknown quality. Recent examples of counterfeit products entering the U.S. marketplace also raise substantial safety questions about drugs from foreign countries. Moreover, there is a possibility that drugs which come to U.S. consumers through Canada or purport to be from Canada may not actually be Canadian drugs. In short, drugs delivered to the American public from foreign countries may be very different from products approved by FDA and may not be safe and effective. For all of these reasons, FDA believes that operations such as yours expose the public to significant potential health risks.

. . . .

Sincerely,
David J. Horowitz, Esq.
Director
Office of Compliance
Center for Drug Evaluation and
Research
Food and Drug Administration

United States of America v. Rx Depot, Inc.

290 F. Supp. 2d 1238 (N.D. Okla. 2003).

■ EAGAN, UNITED STATES DISTRICT JUDGE

. . . .

I. FINDINGS OF FACT

A. *Procedural History*

1. The plaintiff instituted this suit on September 11, 2003, by filing a complaint for injunction and a motion for a preliminary injunction. Plaintiff's complaint alleged violations by defendants of the Federal Food, Drug, and Cosmetic Act.

2. Defendants . . . moved for their own preliminary injunction against the plaintiff's attempt to enforce the FDCA. . . .

. . . .

D. *Operation of Rx Depot/Rx Canada*

11. Rx Depot assists individuals in procuring prescription medications from pharmacies in Canada. Each Rx Depot/Rx Canada location has one or two employees who accept prescriptions from U.S. customers. Customers

also are asked to fill out a medical history form and other forms provided by Rx Depot. Customers can deliver these documents to defendants' stores in person, or can mail or fax to the nearest Rx Depot/Rx Canada store.

12.   Once an Rx Depot/Rx Canada customer has submitted the required forms and prescription to defendants, the papers and the customer's credit card information or a certified check are transmitted to a cooperating pharmacy in Canada. A Canadian doctor rewrites the prescription, and the Canadian pharmacy fills the prescription, ships the prescription drugs directly to the U.S. customer, and bills the U.S. customer's credit card.

13.   Defendants receive a 10 to 12 percent commission for each sale they facilitate for the Canadian pharmacies. The defendants also receive commissions for refill orders, which generally are arranged directly between customers and the Canadian pharmacies.

14.   Defendants are essentially commissioned sales agents for Canadian pharmacies.

. . . .

E. *Prescription Drugs from Foreign Countries*

18.   Although defendants presented evidence that the amount of prescription drugs shipped from Canadian pharmacies never exceeds a ninety-day supply, that defendants do not allow Canadian pharmacies to ship temperature-sensitive drugs, and that defendants do not deal with any third parties, unapproved prescription drugs and drugs imported from foreign countries by someone other than the U.S. manufacturer do not have the same assurance of safety and efficacy as drugs regulated by the Food and Drug Administration ("FDA"). Because the drugs are not subject to FDA oversight and are not continuously under the custody of a U.S. manufacturer or authorized distributor, their quality is less predictable than drugs obtained in the United States. For instance, the drugs may be contaminated, counterfeit, or contain erratic amounts of the active ingredient or different excipients. Also, the drugs may have been held under uncertain storage conditions, and therefore be outdated or subpotent.

19.   Prescription drugs obtained through Rx Depot frequently are dispensed in greater quantities than are requested by the prescribing physician. Although defendants presented evidence that the amount of prescription drugs shipped from Canadian pharmacies never exceeds a ninety-day supply, Rx Depot advertises the availability of, and causes the importation of, preset quantities of drugs and dispenses these preset quantities regardless of the quantity of the drug the patient's U.S. physician prescribed and without directions to take the drug for only the number of days prescribed by the U.S. physician. American patients could, therefore, take a drug for many days more than their physicians intend without supervision. This practice can be dangerous in instances where drugs have potentially life-threatening side effects with continued use.

20.   Prescription drugs obtained through Rx Depot also do not contain the FDA-approved patient package inserts included with certain prescription drugs in the United States. Nor are prescription drugs obtained through Rx Depot shipped in FDA-approved unit-of-use packaging. This type of packag-

ing is used in the United States to help ensure that certain drugs received by customers arrive in designated dosages with the approved patient package insert.

21. The fact that there are currently no known cases of someone being harmed by a drug received as a result of using Rx Depot, or that plaintiff is currently unaware of anyone being harmed by prescription medications ordered through Rx Depot and imported from Canada, does not diminish the legitimate safety concerns of the FDA with unregulated commercial reimportation of U.S.-manufactured drugs by someone other than the manufacturer and importation of foreign-manufactured drugs not approved by the FDA.

. . . .

H. *Cost of Prescription Drugs* . . .

43. Because of the high cost of prescription drugs in the United States, some citizens cannot afford their medications at U.S. prices. Defendants presented three highly credible witnesses to testify to this effect at the preliminary injunction hearing. These witnesses use or used Rx Depot to purchase their medications at a significantly lower price. The high cost of prescription drugs in the United States especially impacts those on fixed incomes, such as senior citizens and the disabled. . . .

46. Not only is Congress the best forum to address the high cost of prescription drugs for U.S. citizens, but also Congress is currently considering legislation which could allow prescription drug importation from Canada.

I. *FDA Personal Use and Enforcement Discretion Policies*

47. The FDA has a personal importation policy which allows entry of foreign drugs by U.S. citizens who bring prescription drugs from foreign countries for personal use.

48. The FDA also has an "enforcement discretion policy" whereby the FDA allows small quantities of prescription drugs to be brought into the U.S. by individuals for personal use without recourse. In this regard, the FDA does not enforce the FDCA against individuals who travel to Canada or use the Internet to purchase prescription drugs from Canada for personal use. . . .

II. *CONCLUSIONS OF LAW*

. . . .

3. The defendants violate 21 U.S.C. § 331 by causing the importation of prescription drugs from Canadian pharmacies. . . .

7. Defendants violate 21 U.S.C. § 331(t) each time they cause the importation of prescription drugs in violation of 21 U.S.C. § 381(d)(1). Specifically, the defendants cause the reimportation of the U.S.-manufactured drugs, such as Sporanox, listed on their website. Reimportation of U.S.-manufactured drugs, even those approved for use in the United States, violates the FDCA, because only the manufacturer of a drug can reimport that drug into the United States. 21 U.S.C. § 381(d)(1). . . .

18. The Court recognizes that individual customers of the defendants believe that they benefit from the low prescription drug prices offered by Rx Depot/Rx Canada. This Court is not unsympathetic to the predicament faced by individuals who cannot afford their prescription drugs at U.S. prices. However, the defendants are able to offer lower prices only because they facilitate illegal activity determined by Congress to harm the public interest. Congress, not this Court, is the best forum for weighing all of the costs and benefits of the national statutory scheme regulating prescription drug importation. . . .

28. Plaintiff's motion for a preliminary injunction is granted.

29. For the same reasons described herein, defendants' motion for a preliminary injunction is denied.

NOTES

1. *Subsequent History.* The following week, the court denied Rx Depot's emergency motion to stay the order of preliminary injunction pending appeal. *United States v. Rx Depot*, 297 F. Supp. 2d 1306 (N.D. Okl. 2003). The parties then agreed to, and the district court approved, a consent decree of permanent injunction. In the consent decree, Rx Depot admitted to violating the FDCA and agreed not to resume its business operations. The consent decree left "to the discretion of [the district court] the issue of what, if any, equitable relief, including restitution and/or disgorgement, should be awarded to [the United States]." As noted *supra* p. 1302, Note 2, in *United States v. Rx Depot, Inc.*, 438 F.3d 1052 (10th Cir. 2006), the Tenth Circuit held that a court may, pursuant to its equity power under the FDCA, impose the remedy of disgorgement.

2. *Other Plans to Import Drugs from Canada.* The defendant in *Rx Depot* was not alone in trying to import prescription drugs from Canada at the time the case was decided. In 2003 and 2004, FDA exchanged a significant amount of correspondence with various types of public and private entities interested in taking advantage of lower prices for prescription drugs in our neighbor to the north. *See, e.g.,* Letter from William K. Hubbard, FDA Associate Commissioner for Policy and Planning to Robert P. Lombardi (Feb. 12, 2003) (responding to letter of inquiry from Lombardi, an attorney representing sponsor and administrators of employer-sponsored health plans considering including coverage for prescription drugs purchased outside the U.S.); Letter from Hubbard to Gregory Gonot, Deputy Attorney General, California (Aug. 25, 2003) (responding to letter of inquiry asking whether California citizens can purchase drugs from Canada and whether California public pension funds can negotiate Canadian prescription drug prices for their members); Letter from Hubbard to Ram Kamath & Scott McKibbon, Illinois Special Advocates for Prescription Drugs (Nov. 6, 2003) (unsolicited letter regarding report presented to Illinois governor regarding feasibility of Illinois employees and retirees purchasing prescription drugs from Canada); Letter from Hubbard to Charlie Ryan, Mayor, Springfield, Massachusetts (Aug. 4, 2004) (denying citizen petition in which Springfield asked FDA to exercise its enforcement discretion to allow importation of Canadian drugs). In all of this correspondence, FDA, in language similar to that used in the Rx Depot warning letter, observed (1) that 21 U.S.C. 381(d) forbids anyone other than the manufacturer to reimport drugs originally manufactured in the U.S. and (2) that virtually all foreign versions of U.S.-approved drugs are illegal under the FD&C Act because they are unapproved variants, incorrectly labeled, or dispensed without a valid prescription.

b. IMPORTATION FOR PERSONAL USE

As noted in the *Rx Depot* decision, FDA exercises its enforcement discretion with regard to personal-use quantities of imported drugs, devices, and biologics in baggage and mail. The agency instituted this policy in 1954 and updated it in 1988 with respect to mailed imports of AIDS and cancer treatments. In February 1989, FDA set forth the broader, current version of the personal importation policy in a revision to its Regulatory Procedures Manual. The subchapter on "Coverage of Personal Importations" now states, in part:

> FDA personnel may use their discretion to allow entry of shipments of violative FDA regulated products when the quantity and purpose are clearly for personal use, and the product does not present an unreasonable risk to the user. Even though all products that appear to be in violation of statutes administered by FDA are subject to refusal, FDA personnel may use their discretion to examine the background, risk, and purpose of the product before making a final decision. Although FDA may use discretion to allow admission of certain violative items, this should not be interpreted as a license to individuals to bring in such shipments.

> Commercial and promotional shipments are not subject to this guidance. Whether or not a shipment is commercial or promotional may be determined by a number of factors. . . .

> In deciding whether to exercise discretion to allow personal shipments of drugs or devices, FDA personnel may consider a more permissive policy in the following situations:

>> 1. when the intended use is appropriately identified, such use is not for treatment of a serious condition, and the product is not known to represent a significant health risk; or

>> 2. when a) the intended use is unapproved and for a serious condition for which effective treatment may not be available domestically either through commercial or clinical means; b) there is no known commercialization or promotion to persons residing in the U.S. by those involved in the distribution of the product at issue; c) the product is considered not to represent an unreasonable risk; and d) the individual seeking to import the product affirms in writing that it is for the patient's own use (generally not more than 3 month supply) and provides the name and address of the doctor licensed in the U.S. responsible for his or her treatment with the product, or provides evidence that the product is for the continuation of a treatment begun in a foreign country.

Regulatory Procedures Manual, Chapter 9, Subchapter: Coverage of Personal Importations (1989).

Soon after the February 1989 revision to the Regulatory Procedures Manual, FDA carved out a specific exception to the personal importation policy. In June 1989, under pressure from antiabortion members of Congress, the agency issued an import alert stating that the French abortifacent pill RU–486 (mifepristone) was subject to automatic detention. Three years later, a pregnant woman who sought to import a single dose of RU–486 from Great Britain for personal use had her supply seized at airport customs in accordance with the import alert. The woman obtained a preliminary injunction in federal district court requiring the government to return the drug to her. The district court accepted her argument that she was entitled to the return of her RU–486 because FDA issued the import alert without notice-and-comment procedures. *Benten v. Kessler*, 799 F. Supp. 281, 288–90 (E.D.N.Y. 1992). The judge maintained that the agency was bound to follow such procedures here even though it did not do so when it revised the Regulatory Procedures Manual to establish the broader personal importation policy.

The Second Circuit stayed the injunction, and the United States Supreme Court, *per curiam*, refused to vacate the stay. *Benten v. Kessler*, 505 U.S. 1084 (1992). Justice Stevens, dissenting, contended that the government's seizure of Benten's RU–486 constituted an undue burden on her constitutional due process right to liberty. *Id.* at 1085–86. The majority declined to express any view on the merits of Steven's assertion. In 2000, FDA approved mifepristone for termination of early pregnancy.

In the early 2000s, some of the entities seeking to participate in systematic schemes for importing drugs from Canada invoked the personal importation policy in communications with FDA. In its correspondence with these and other entities, discussed above, FDA consistently emphasized that the policy does not change the law, but only reflects the agency's enforcement priorities. Moreover, the agency emphasized that the personal importation policy does not apply to situations in which foreign drugs are commercialized and promoted to U.S. consumers, nor generally to foreign versions of U.S.-approved drugs.

In October 2006, Congress effectively legalized importation of drugs from Canada for personal use. Section 535 of the Homeland Security appropriation act for the fiscal year ending September 2007 declares: "None of the funds made available in this Act for United States Customs and Border Protection may be used to prevent an individual not in the business of importing a prescription drug ... from importing a prescription drug from Canada that complies with the [FD&C Act]: *Provided*, That this section shall apply only to individuals transporting on their person a personal use quantity of the prescription drug, not to exceed a 90–day supply." Thus Congress essentially ratified FDA's 1954 policy.

c.   IMPORTATION PURSUANT TO WAIVER

At the end of 2003, a new potential avenue for legal importation of unapproved foreign versions of prescription drugs appeared. On December 8, President Bush signed into law the Medicare Prescription Drug Improvement and Modernization Act of 2003 ("MMA"), 117 Stat. 2066 (2003). This complex legislation created Medicare Part D, providing voluntary access to prescription drug coverage for senior citizens and individuals with disabilities. MMA also included various provisions addressing the cost of drugs. Section 1121 of the legislation amended section 804 of the FD&C Act to permit individuals to import prescription drugs and devices from Canada pursuant to waivers granted by FDA by regulation or on a case-by-case basis. FD&C Act 804(j). Congress also provided, however, that section 804 will become effective only if and when the Secretary of Health and Human Services certifies to Congress that the implementation of the section will "pose no additional risk to the public's health and safety" and will "result in a significant reduction in the cost of covered products to the American consumer." FD&C Act 804(l)(1). This certification requirement was carried over from the Medicine Equity and Drug Safety Act of 2000 (MEDS Act), which first added section 804 to the FD&C Act, but limited importation to pharmacists and wholesalers. 114 Stat. 1549, 1549A–36 (codified as amended in section 21 U.S.C. § 384). Under both the 2000 and 2003 statutes successive Secretaries of Health and Human Services said they were unable to make this certification.

On December 12, 2003, just days after President Bush signed MMA, FDA received a citizen petition from the state of Vermont, asking the agency to permit the state's employee medical benefit plan to establish a program for the orderly importation, by its members, of prescription drugs from Canada. In addition to arguing that FDA should exercise its enforcement discretion, consistent with its Personal Importation Policy, Vermont urged the agency to establish regulations permitting importation from Canada under section 1121 of MMA. When FDA denied this citizen petition, Vermont challenged the denial in federal district court:

State of Vermont v. Leavitt
405 F. Supp. 2d 466 (D. Vt. 2005).

■ SESSIONS, CHIEF JUDGE

In Beebe Plains, Vermont, there is a street, appropriately named Canusa Avenue, that runs right along the United States–Canada border. Houses on the northern side of the street are in Canada while houses on the southern side are in Vermont. If a resident of the northern side of Canusa Avenue needs medication to control high cholesterol, he or she can purchase a 90–day supply of 20 milligram Lipitor for $170. On the southern side of the street, Vermont residents will have to dig much deeper if they need to purchase the same drug. The same 90–day supply of Lipitor costs about $330 in the United States.

This price differential is far from unique. On average, brand-name drug prices are approximately 70% higher in the United States. It has been estimated that United States consumers would have saved $59.7 billion if, during 2004, they had purchased all brand-name drugs at Canadian prices. To put that figure in context, it is more than the gross national products of Kuwait, Iceland and Jamaica *combined.*

Given the dramatic difference between United States and Canadian drug prices, it is unsurprising that many Americans are interested in buying prescription drugs in Canada. . . .

Vermont regulators have been concerned about high domestic drug prices and the increase in ad-hoc, personal importation of Canadian drugs by Vermont residents. In response to these concerns, plaintiff Vermont

Agency of Administration submitted a citizen petition to the Food and Drug Administration requesting that the FDA allow the Vermont State Employee Medical Benefit Plan ("VTSEMBP") to "establish a program for the orderly individual importation of prescription medications." The FDA denied this petition.

Plaintiffs ... filed this lawsuit on August 19, 2004, challenging the FDA's denial of the citizen petition. Vermont claims that the denial was arbitrary and capricious in violation of the Administrative Procedure Act. Vermont also seeks a declaratory judgment that 21 U.S.C. § 384(l)(1) violates Article I, § 1 of the United States Constitution by improperly delegating legislative power to the Executive Branch.

... For the reasons set forth below, the Court grants the Defendants' Motion to Dismiss....

A.   Importation Under the FDCA and the MMA

The MMA contains a provision that authorizes the Secretary of HHS to "promulgate regulations permitting pharmacists and wholesalers to import prescription drugs from Canada into the United States." 21 U.S.C. § 384(b). The MMA also provides that the Secretary "may grant to individuals, by regulation or on a case-by-case basis, a waiver of the prohibition of importation of a prescription drug or device or class of prescription drugs or devices, under such conditions as the Secretary determines to be appropriate." 21 U.S.C. § 384(j)(2)(A). Thus, the MMA contemplates both commercial and individual importation. These provisions of the MMA appear to become effective only if the Secretary certifies to Congress that importation will be safe and cost-effective.... 21 U.S.C. § 384(l).... Secretary Leavitt and his predecessor, former Secretary Thompson, have declined to issue a certification under this subsection.

The MMA superseded the Medicine Equity and Drug Safety Act of 2000 ("MEDS Act"). Like the MMA, the MEDS Act authorized the Secretary of HHS to pass regulations allowing commercial importation of prescription drugs. The MEDS Act also contained a certification provision conditioning importation on a certification to Congress. Former Secretaries Thompson and Shalala declined to issue a certification to Congress under the MEDS Act. Thus, when Congress enacted the MMA's certification provision, it was aware that, during the previous three years, the Secretary of HHS had declined to issue a certification under a very similar provision.

B.   Vermont's Proposed Plan Violates the FDCA

There is no question that Vermont's proposed program would violate the FDCA. For example, whenever Vermont assisted in the re-importation of a drug manufactured in the United States, it would violate 21 U.S.C. § 331(t) [prohibiting the importation of a drug in violation of FD&C Act 801(d)(1) (21 U.S.C. § 381(d)(1)), which generally bans reimportation of finished prescription drugs by parties other than the manufacturer]. This will be true regardless of whether VTSEMBP or the members themselves import the drugs. VTSEMBP will violate section 331(t) if it "causes" its members to import drugs in violation of 21 U.S.C. § 381(d)(1). Thus, as Vermont's proposed plan would be highly likely to include drugs manufactured in the United States, it would lead to violations of section 331(t).

Similarly, Vermont's plan is likely to violate 21 U.S.C. § 331(a) [prohibiting interstate commerce in adulterated and misbranded products]. Many Canadian drugs will have packaging and labeling that is not approved by the FDA. Also, many Canadian drugs may not have been manufactured according to GMP (even if these drugs are pharmacologically identical to drugs approved by the FDA). Thus, VTSEMBP would violate 21 U.S.C. § 331(a) by causing these drugs to be introduced into interstate commerce.

C.   The MMA Does Not Authorize Vermont's Plan

As Vermont's proposed plan violates the FDCA, the crucial issue is whether the MMA provides authorization for the plan. Vermont argues that its proposed program is permitted under the MMA. Vermont is incorrect. Under section 384(l), the relevant provisions of the MMA only become effective if the Secretary certifies to Congress that importation is safe and cost-effective. As the Secretary has not made this certification, the MMA offers no support for Vermont's program. . . .

NOTES

1.   *HHS Report.* In December 2004, as mandated by MMA, the Department of Health and Human Services issued a report on its study of drug importation. HHS TASK FORCE ON DRUG IMPORTATION, REPORT ON PRESCRIPTION DRUG IMPORTATION (2004). The task force's findings included, among others: (1) "It would be extraordinarily difficult and costly for 'personal' importation to be implemented in a way that ensures the safety and effectiveness of the imported drugs," (2) "Overall national savings from legalized commercial importation will likely be a small percentage of total drug spending," and (3) "Legalized importation will likely adversely affect the future development of new drugs for American consumers." *Id.* at XII–XIII (Executive Summary: "Key Findings"). In light of these conclusions, it is hardly surprising that the Secretary of HHS has not certified to Congress that the implementation of section 804 importation would "pose no additional risk to the public's health and safety" and would "result in a significant reduction in the cost of covered products to the American consumer." FD&C Act 804(l)(1). Consequently, section 804, while still part of the FD&C Act, has never gone into effect.

2.   *Partial Certification.* In *Vermont v. Leavitt, supra,* the district court explicitly declined to consider whether MMA allows a certification specific to a particular state or program. 405 F. Supp. 2d at 479. Apparently trying to exploit this potential loophole, in 2004, the governor of Oregon requested certification of the Oregon Pioneer Prescription Drug program, which would have allowed the state board of pharmacy to license and inspect Canadian pharmaceutical wholesalers, who would then have sold a limited formulary of prescription drugs to Oregon pharmacies. FDA declined to permit the program, observing, "The certification requirement in the MMA does not authorize a partial certification or a specific waiver for a discrete state pilot program." Letter from Randall W. Lutter, FDA Acting Association Commissioner for Policy and Planning, to Theodore R. Kulongoski, Governor of Oregon (Oct. 14, 2005). Using identical language, FDA subsequently rejected similar requests from the County Executive of Montgomery County, Maryland, and the Washington State Board of Pharmacy. Letter from Lutter to Douglas M. Duncan, County Executive, Montgomery County (Nov. 8, 2005); Letter to Steven M. Saxe, Director, Washington State Board of Pharmacy (Mar. 17, 2006).

B.   EXPORTATION FROM THE UNITED STATES

1.   EXPORTATION PURSUANT TO FD&C ACT § 801(e)(1)

a.   GENERAL

Section 801(e)(1) of the FD&C Act establishes an "intended for export" exception to the Statute's adulteration and misbranding provisions. Under section 801(e)(1):

> A food, drug, device, or cosmetic intended for export shall not be deemed to be adulterated or misbranded under this Act if it—
>
> (A) accords to the specifications of the foreign purchaser,
>
> (B) is not in conflict with the laws of the country to which it is intended for export,
>
> (C) is labeled on the outside of the shipping package that it is intended for export, and
>
> (D) is not sold or offered for sale in domestic commerce.

This section applies to all misbranding of every FDA-regulated product, to all adulteration of food, human drugs, and cosmetics, and to most adulteration of devices and animal drugs. However, as discussed *infra*, section 801(e)(1), by itself, does not legalize exportation of unapproved new drugs, unlicensed biologics, unapproved class III devices, or "banned" new animal drugs.

For a detailed account of the legislative history of Section 801(e)(1), see Peter Barton Hutt & Bruce N. Kuhlik, EXPORT EXPERTISE: UNDERSTANDING EXPORT LAW FOR DRUGS, DEVICES AND BIOLOGICS, Chapter 1 (Washington Business Information, Inc., 1997).

United States v. an Article . . . Enriched Rice

FDA CONSUMER, October 1976, at 36 (S.D. Tex. 1975).

. . . [C]laimant argues that it has met its burden of proving the applicability of the exemption provided by § 381(d) [now 381(e)] because the evidence it has submitted in support of the motion demonstrates that the export of the seized product would not be in violation of the laws of Chile. In view of the fact that disposition of this argument will require a consideration of facts outside of the pleadings, the Court will consider the motion to dismiss as a motion for summary judgment pursuant to Rule 56, Fed. R. Civ. P.

There appears to be little dissention between both parties that the applicable provisions of the law of Chile may be summarized as follows: (1) the importation of foodstuffs requires notification of the proper governmental authorities who may then inspect the product upon its arrival and thereafter take appropriate action in accepting, rejecting or altering the condition of the imported goods; (2) all imported foodstuffs must be accompanied by a sanitation certificate issued by a competent authority of the exporting country; (3) the manufacture, sale, [or] storage for sale of altered, contaminated, adulterated or falsified foods with risk to the health of men or animals is prohibited.

Insofar as items (1) and (2) are concerned, the Court does not find that these would prohibit the application of the export exemption to the seized goods in question here. Claimant had secured the necessary sanitation certificate prior to the seizure of the article of food in question here. Furthermore, it must be presumed that claimant will comply with the provisions requiring notice to be given to appropriate Chilean authorities in the absence of any evidence to the contrary. However, item (3) does prohibit the sale or storage for sale of altered food products. It is clearly the intention of claimant to export the seized goods for sale. . . . [T]he sale and shipment of the goods seized in this action, if altered within the meaning of Chilean law, will conflict with the laws of the receiving country.

Thus, it will be necessary for the Court to hear further evidence with respect to the Government's contention that the seized goods are in fact adulterated under the laws of the United States. It will be necessary thereafter for the claimant to demonstrate that, even if the goods are adulterated under our laws, they are not altered or adulterated within the meaning of these provisions of the Chilean law. Because the above questions present issues of fact that cannot be determined on the basis of the record now before the Court, claimant's motion for summary judgment will be denied and this matter set for hearing at a later date.

United States v. Kanasco, Ltd.

123 F.3d 209 (4th Cir. 1997).

■ MOTZ, CIRCUIT JUDGE:

The United States filed a complaint for forfeiture requesting the seizure and condemnation of approximately 104 drums of adulterated bulk antibiotics manufactured by Kanasco, Limited. . . . Following discovery, the Government moved for summary judgment maintaining that the drugs were adulterated because they were not manufactured according to "current good manufacturing practice," as defined in 21 U.S.C.A. § 351(a)(2)(B). Kanasco filed a cross-motion for summary judgment. The company did not dispute that the drugs were not manufactured according to "current good manufacturing practice;" instead, it argued that the drugs were exempt from the manufacturing requirements of § 351 because they were intended for export, and thus fell within the export exemption to the Food, Drug, and Cosmetic Act. *See* 21 U.S.C.A. § 381(e)(1).

. . . [T]he district court rejected Kanasco's argument and granted summary judgment to the Government. . . . We affirm. . . .

. . . [A] drug is not "adulterated" (and thus not subject to forfeiture) if the drug is "intended for export" and meets a four factor test. *See* 21 U.S.C.A. § 381(e)(1). A drug "intended for export shall not be deemed to be adulterated" if it:

(A) accords to the specifications of the foreign purchaser,

(B) is not in conflict with the laws of the country to which it is intended for export,

(C) is labeled on the outside of the shipping package that it is intended for export, and

(D) is not sold or offered for sale in domestic commerce.

21 U.S.C.A. § 381(e)(1).

Kanasco claims that the drugs were "intended for export" and that they satisfy the four factor test. The burden of pleading and proving the applicability of § 381(e)(1) is on Kanasco—the party that seeks the benefit of the exemption.

John Capanos, president of Kanasco, filed an affidavit stating that the seized drugs were "intended for export." Based on this affidavit, the district court held that Kanasco raised a dispute of fact as to the "threshold requirement" of § 381(e)(1) that the drugs be "intended for export." The Government does not dispute this point, and we agree that there is a factual dispute as to Kanasco's intent.

We also concur with the district court, however, that this factual dispute is not "material" because Kanasco clearly cannot satisfy the requirements of § 381(e)(1)(A) or (B). Kanasco has come forward with no evidence that the drugs seized "accord[] to the specifications of the foreign purchaser" or are "not in conflict with the laws of the country to which [they are] intended for export." 21 U.S.C.A. § 381(e)(1)(A)–(B).

Kanasco contends that § 381(e)(1) does not require that the drugs be manufactured for a specific foreign purchaser, or that the drugs comply with "the laws of" a particular country. The company asserts that Capanos' affidavit, which stated that he could find a foreign purchaser, and that the drugs met the requirements of unnamed and unspecified "foreign countries," satisfies the first two prongs of § 381(e)(1).

... Sections 381(e)(1)(A) and (B) require that in order to be deemed not adultered [sic], drugs meet "the specifications of *the* foreign purchaser," and that drugs not be "in conflict with the laws of *the* country to which" they are "intended for export." 21 U.S.C.A. § 381(e)(1)(A)–(B) (emphasis added). By using the definite article "the," Congress signaled that § 381(e)(1) requires proof that a drug accords with both the specifications of a specific foreign purchaser and the laws of a specific foreign country.

The plain language of § 381(e)(1) thus requires a particular foreign buyer and country; not a generalized assertion that the drugs can be sold to some buyer and that sale is consistent with the laws of some foreign country. Kanasco maintains that this interpretation of § 381(e)(1) subverts the objective of the export exemption because drugs that could be sold in foreign markets will instead be destroyed. This argument, however, examines the export exemption in a vacuum, ignoring the fact that it is an exception to the Food, Drug, and Cosmetic Act. "Exceptions from a general policy which a law embodies should be strictly construed."

Moreover, it is particularly appropriate to construe the export exemption narrowly, because a broad interpretation could seriously damage the "overriding purpose" of the Food, Drug, and Cosmetic Act, "to protect the public health." *United States v. Bacto–Unidisk*, 394 U.S. 784 (1969). Kanasco's expansive interpretation would undermine this purpose by crippling the effectiveness of enforcement actions against violators. Drug manufacturers could ignore the statutory quality requirements and produce adulterated drugs for sale in the United States, secure in the knowledge that if caught they could claim the export exemption and subsequently find a foreign buyer for the drugs. Manufacturers could thus produce adulterated drugs with little fear of any effective sanction.

Facing a similar argument in a case involving adulterated food, the Second Circuit reached an interpretation of the export exemption identical to ours:

> The practical aspects of the situation would seem to support this construction, for there is nowhere disclosed an intention that a violator of the Act may avoid the consequences of his wrong by then exporting the outlawed goods to some foreign country which will receive them. However laudatory may be the purpose to conserve the food supply (perhaps even of a condiment or relish such as catsup), an attempt to rewrite the Act along these lines seems likely to have the effect of nullifying its chief purposes.

United States v. Kent Food Corp., 168 F.2d 632, 634 (2d Cir. 1948).

In sum, Kanasco's interpretation of the export exemption is contrary to the plain language of § 381(e)(1), and would create an unwarranted escape hatch for violators of the Act. The district court properly rejected that interpretation.

Compliance Policy Guide No. 7127.02 (1995)

Subject: Uncertified or Delisted Colors in Foods for Export (*e.g.* FD&C Red No. 2). . . .

Policy: Colors such as FD&C Red No. 2, which have been delisted, can be used in lots of food specifically manufactured for export to a country in which its use is legal, provided all the requirements of section 801(e) of the Act are followed and provided further, that a control system is followed which insures that there is no possibility of diversion by mistake or otherwise to domestic channels, of the food containing the color. Proper control can be achieved by following the procedure set forth below:

1. Prior to start of production and for each lot produced a separate order, letter from the purchaser, and letter from an official of the country must be obtained.

The order from the purchaser must state the exact amount desired by the foreign purchaser and must state on the order or be accompanied by a letter from the purchaser stating that he desires that FD&C Red No. 2 or other specific color be used in the lot and that he is aware of its illegality in the United States. The letter from a responsible official of the country to which the lot is to be shipped shall state that the use of the color is legal in his country. Since the laws and regulations of countries are subject to change, a continuing order or letter will not be satisfactory.

2. The stock of the color to be used for export production must be kept locked up at all times, except when actually being used. Complete records must be kept accounting for all use.

3. During all stages of production, manufacture, processing and packing the lot must be kept segregated from all other production and must be clearly marked that it is "for export only."

The outside of each shipping package of the lot must be labeled [to] show it is for export.

4. All records, pertaining to such lots, including orders and letters, must be kept for at least three years and made available to any Food and Drug Administration inspector upon oral or written request.

NOTE: This policy only applies to uncertified or delisted colors that have been manufactured in this country, or entered legally into this country prior to being uncertified or delisted, and are intended to be used in foods solely for export.

NOTE

1. *Lacking Legal Authority?* FDA could point to no legal authority for the position asserted in this guide.

2. *See generally* Edward Brown Williams, *Regulation of Exports Under the Federal Food, Drug, and Cosmetic Act*, 3 FOOD DRUG COSM. L.Q. 382 (1948).

COMMENT: INTERNATIONAL TRADE AGREEMENTS

The General Agreement on Tariffs and Trade (GATT) governed international trade in agricultural, consumer, and industrial products for more than 40 years, from 1947 until 1995. The agreement successfully reduced tariff barriers to trade, but because GATT permitted each country to enact its own health and safety laws, food and drug regulatory requirements remained non-tariff barriers to trade throughout the world. Although GATT prohibited members from using health and safety measures as disguised trade barriers, the agreement offered little guidance on applying this prohibition, and there were few GATT rulings holding that particular domestic health and safety measures violated the treaty.

In 1995, GATT was succeeded by the World Trade Organization (WTO). WTO member states establish global trade rules by entering into multilateral agreements. Contrary to GATT, the WTO has a formalized dispute settlement mechanism that requires its members to resolve trade disputes arising from the WTO agreements through its dispute settlement body. Perhaps the most important WTO agreement with respect to products regulated by FDA is the Agreement on the Application of Sanitary and Phytosanitary Measures (SPS Agreement), which addresses regulations regarding food safety and diseases carried by animals and plants. Agreement on the Application of Sanitary and Phytosanitary Measures, Apr. 15, 1994, Annex 1A to Agreement Establishing the World Trade Organization. The SPS Agreement encourages member states to adopt international standards, such as the food safety standards promulgated by the Codex

Alimentarius Commission, a subsidiary of the United Nations' World Health Organization and Food and Agriculture Organization. The SPS Agreement permits individual members to set more rigorous standards, but only if there is a scientific justification for doing so, as established by approved risk assessment techniques. SPS Agreement, arts. 3.3, 5.1. In the absence of adequate scientific evidence, nations may provisionally impose precautionary measures pending the acquisition of additional information, but they must obtain this further evidence within a reasonable time. *Id.* art. 5.7. The North American Free Trade Agreement (NAFTA) contains similar, though not identical, provisions regarding SPS measures. Can.–Mex.–U.S.: North American Free Trade Agreement, Chapter 7(B) ("Sanitary and Phytosanitary Measures"), Dec. 17, 1992.

In the late 1990s, the United States brought a successful complaint in the WTO against the European Community's ban on meat and meat products derived from hormone-treated animals. The WTO ruled that the EC ban violated the SPS agreement. *See* Panel Report, *EC Measures Concerning Meat and Meat Products (Hormones), Complaint by the United States*, WT/DS26/R/USA (18 Aug. 1997); Appellate Body Report, *EC— Measures Concerning Meat and Meat Products (Hormones)*, WT/DS26/AB/R, ST/DS48/AB/R (Jan. 16, 1998) (adopted Feb. 13, 1998). When the European Union failed to act on this adverse ruling by ending the ban on hormone-treated beef, the United States retaliated by imposing tariffs against several specific European food products, such as foie gras, Roquefort cheese, and Dijon mustard. *See* James F. Smith, *From Frankenfood to Fruit Flies: Navigating the WTO/SPS*, 6 U.C. DAVIS J. INT'L L. & POL'Y 1 (2000).

In the late 1990s, the European Union instituted a moratorium on the approval of agricultural biotechnology products. In August 2003, the United States, Argentina, and Canada challenged this moratorium in the WTO, contending that the policy impermissibly blocks imports without a valid scientific basis, in violation of the SPS and other agreements. In February 2006, the WTO preliminarily concluded in favor of the United States and the other complainants. *See* Rob Portman, U.S. Trade Rep., & Mike Johanns, U.S. Agric. Sec., Joint Statement on Agricultural Biotechnology and the WTO (Feb. 7, 2006). The final WTO panel reports, confirming the preliminary verdict, were released on September 29, 2006 and are available on the organization's website. Although the EU has approved some biotechnology applications since the institution of the case in 2003, the United States maintains that a partial moratorium remains in effect.

While the WTO SPS Agreement can be an effective tool for the United States to use on behalf of American exporters, other countries could potentially use it to challenge the United States' own food safety measures, including, for example, some of the new requirements contained in the 2002 Bioterrorism Act. *See* Richard T. Ting, *Food and Drug Administration Regulation of Imported Foods and Compliance with International Trade Obligations* (2005), in Chapter II(C)(2) of the Electronic Book; Robyn E. Ridler, *Cattle, Dolphins, and the WTO: The Potential Impact of the World Trade Organization Agreements on United States Food Regulation* (1998), in Chapter II(C)(4) of the Electronic Book.

b.   EXPORT OF UNAPPROVED NEW DRUGS AND UNLICENSED BIOLOGICS

As discussed above, section 801(e)(1) can prevent a product intended for export from being deemed adulterated or misbranded. However, the act of introducing an unapproved new human drug into interstate commerce, though prohibited by the statute, is not an adulteration or misbranding violation. *See* FD&C Act 301(d), 505(a). The same is true for unlicensed biological products. *See* 42 U.S.C. 262(a)(1). Accordingly, FDA has always taken the position that section 801(e) does not legalize unapproved new drugs or unlicensed biological products intended for export, and the courts have upheld this interpretation. In 1986, as discussed *infra* p. 1403, Congress amended the Act to allow some exportation of unapproved products under new section 802. To this day, however, 801(e)(1) is not a vehicle for exportation of medical products requiring approval

United States v. An Article of Drug ... Ethionamide–INH

1965–1968 FDLI Jud. and Ad. Rec. 16 (E.D.N.Y. 1967).

■ DOOLING, DISTRICT JUDGE.

The government seized a large quantity of tablets of Ethionamide–INH in the possession of Amfre–Grant, Inc. on the ground that it was a "new drug" ... and that no approval of an application ... was effective for the drug. . . .

. . . The drug in question is a combination of equal quantities (125 mg.) of ethionamide and isoniazid or isononicotinic acid hydrazide (INH). . . . While use of ethionamide in conjunction with INH is known in the literature, it is not contended that the particular Amfre–Grant combination has been approved for use in the manner recommended in the insert included in the completed packages, or that it could qualify as not a "new drug" because it was generally recognized by qualified persons to be safe and effective for use as recommended.

Amfre–Grant has supplied the drug to Vietnam, where it has been approved for sale, in 1966 and early 1967, and the Agency for International Development has approved the drug for Vietnamese sale, and authorized the use of AID funds to pay for it. The packaging for the drug is entirely in French, and the package displays the Vietnamese registration number; the insertion sheet is in French and Vietnamese. The package indicates that the drug is to be sold on prescription only. . . .

. . . Section 381(d) [now section 381(e)] took its present form in the 1938 Act, and the legislative history is invoked to show that the primary concern of the Congress was to safeguard residents of the United States, and that the narrow focus of that concern resulted in the rejection of amendments to section 381(d) that would have required exports to be in compliance with some but not all of the standards of the Act. It is argued that the "new drug" provisions of 21 U.S.C. Sec. 355 were introduced late in the transit of the bill through the Congress, that no hearings and little debate accompanied the addition of section 355 to the Senate Bill in the

House, and that the section was added under the goad of concern over deaths caused in 1937 by using "antifreeze," diethylene glycol, as the carrier in "Elixir Sulfanilamide." . . .

The argument must yield to the language of the statute. The exemption of section 381(d) [381(e)] applies to what would otherwise be "adulterated or misbranded" within the other sections of the Act. On those words hinge the operation of the Act as it applies to foods and drugs that are not "new drugs." The "new drug" provisions, although solidly embedded in the Act, operate separately, and it is not a necessary, nor even a probable, inference that the policy considerations that led to the enactment of section 381(d) would extend to the new drug provisions. . . .

NOTES

1. *Supporting Authority.* See *United States v. Yaron Laboratories, Inc.*, 365 F. Supp. 917 (N.D. Cal. 1972).

2. *Partially Processed Biologics.* In 1996, Congress amended the Public Health Service Act to allow exportation of a limited category of unapproved biologic products, namely, "partially processed biologics." According to this amendment:

> A partially processed biological product which—
>
> (1) is not in a form applicable to the prevention, treatment, or cure of diseases or injuries of man;
>
> (2) is not intended for sale in the United States; and
>
> (3) is intended for further manufacture into final dosage form outside the United States, shall be subject to no restriction on the export of the product under this chapter or the Federal Food, Drug, and Cosmetic Act if the product is manufactured, processed, packaged, and held in conformity with current good manufacturing practice requirements or meets international manufacturing standards as certified by an international standards organization recognized by the Secretary and meets the requirements of section 801(e)(1) of the Federal Food, Drug, and Cosmetic Act.

42 U.S.C. 262(h).

2. *Drug Intermediates.* 21 C.F.R. § 310.3(g) defines "new drug substance" to exclude "intermediates used in the synthesis of such substance." Such intermediates may therefore be exported without an IND or NDA.

c.   EXPORTATION OF UNAPPROVED NEW ANIMAL DRUGS

Prior to the passage of the 1968 Animal Drug Amendments (ADA), unapproved animal drugs fell outside the scope of FD&C Act 801(d) (now 801(e)) for the same reason that human drugs did, and thus could not be legally exported. The ADA potentially changed the equation, however. Under the regulatory scheme established by the ADA, an unapproved animal drug, unlike an unapproved human drug, is adulterated by virtue of being unapproved. *See* FD&C Act 501(a)(5), 512(a)(1). Consequently, section 801(e), if not amended, would have allowed the exportation of unapproved new animal drugs that met the provision's four requirements. Indeed, the initial version of the ADA would have permitted such exportation. In the final version, however, Congress maintained the status quo regarding the illegality of the exportation of unapproved new animal drugs by amending 801(e) to exclude them explicitly.

As discussed below, the Drug Export Amendments Act of 1986 added FD&C Act 802, which created a scheme for exporting unapproved animal drugs and other types of unapproved products. In 1996, when Congress loosened export requirements for unapproved products under section 802, it also broadened the opportunity to export unapproved new animal drugs under section 801(e). Now, instead of excluding all unapproved new animal drugs from the scope of section 801(e), the Act excludes only new animal drugs that have been "banned" in the United States. FD&C Act 801(e)(3). Because there is no "banned animal drugs" section of the Act parallel to the "banned devices" provision in section 516, it is unclear precisely what the exclusion of "banned" new animal drugs means. Indisputably, however, section 801(e) now permits exportation of unapproved animal drugs for which FDA has neither rejected an NADA nor withdrawn approval of an NADA.

d. EXPORTATION OF MEDICAL DEVICES

Like unapproved new animal drugs, unapproved class III devices subject to premarket approval under section 515 are "adulterated." FD&C Act 501(f)(1). When Congress enacted the Medical Device Amendments of 1976 (MDA), however, it determined that exportation of such unapproved devices should not be permitted under section 801(e). The MDA thus amended section 801(e) to state that the provision does not generally apply to devices that violate the section 515 PMA requirement. FD&C Act 801(e)(2). This revision to 801(e) also excludes devices that fail to comply with an applicable performance standard under section 514, investigational devices subject to an IDE under section 520(g), and devices that are banned under section 516. Under section 801(e)(2), an unapproved device for which a PMA is required will be deemed adulterated, even if intended for export and in compliance with section 801(e)(1), unless "either (i) [FDA] has determined that the exportation of the device is not contrary to public health and safety and has the approval of the country to which it is intended for export or (ii) the device is eligible for export under section 802."

Despite these limitations, section 801(e) remains a viable path for exportation of many unapproved devices, even when FDA has not made a "health and safety"/foreign approval determination under section 801(e)(2). The reason why section 801(e) exportation remains an option for many manufacturers of unapproved devices is that section 801(e)(2) does not exclude devices based on their failure to comply with 510(k) marketing clearance requirements. A new device does not have to get PMA approval prior to marketing if it is "substantially equivalent" to a class I or class II device already on the market. And for class II devices (and class I devices not exempt from 510(k)), FDA makes this substantial equivalence determination based on a manufacturer's 510(k) submission. How, then, should the agency treat a class II device intended for export for which neither a PMA nor a 510(k) has been filed? FDA has declared:

Although the act prohibits exportation of ... devices requiring premarket approval unless the criteria under section 801(e)(2) of the act are met, FDA, in exercising its enforcement discretion, has not taken enforcement action against those manufacturers who have not complied with the export criteria in section 801(e)(2) of the act [i.e., FDA "health and safety"/foreign approval determination], provided that the manufacturers have reasonably concluded that, if a report under section 510(k) of the act had been submitted to FDA, FDA would have granted 510(k) marketing clearance. FDA intends to continue exercising its enforcement discretion in this manner, with respect to the requirements in section 801(e)(2) of the act. FDA emphasizes, however, that it does not intend to exercise enforcement discretion with respect to the requirements in section 801(e)(1) of the act for manufacturers who reasonably believe that their devices would receive a 510(k) marketing clearance.

FDA, DRAFT GUIDANCE FOR INDUSTRY ON EXPORTS AND IMPORTS UNDER THE FDA EXPORT REFORM AND ENHANCEMENT ACT OF 1996 (1998).

2.   EXPORTATION OF UNAPPROVED MEDICAL PRODUCTS PURSUANT TO FD&C ACT § 802

FDA, Draft Guidance for Industry: Exports and Imports Under the FDA Export Reform and Enhancement Act of 1996

February 1998.

. . . .

IV.   Statutory Background

. . . .

The [language of the] 1938 act ... led to the conclusion that section 801(d)(1) [now 801(e)(1)] of the act did not apply to new drugs. As a result, the act was interpreted as permitting the export of approved drugs, but not the export of unapproved new drugs. This interpretation was viewed as imposing hardships on the pharmaceutical industry (by impairing its ability to compete in international markets) without any accompanying public health benefits.

To remedy the situation, Congress enacted the Drug Export Amendments Act of 1986 (Pub. L. 99–960). Insofar as human drug products and biologics were concerned, the 1986 Amendments created section 802 of the act.... Under [section 802], FDA was authorized to approve an application for the export of new human and animal drugs and biologics that were not approved in the United States, so long as the drug contained the same active ingredient(s) as a product for which marketing approval in the United States was being sought or the biological product was one for which licensing was actively being pursued. Exports ... were confined to 21 specific countries listed in section 802 of the act....

The 1986 Amendments, however, presented several problems and concerns. One significant problem was that the 1986 Amendments limited exports of unapproved drugs and biologics to 21 countries. Although the 1986 Amendments provided criteria for adding more countries to the list, it did not provide any administrative mechanism for doing so. . . .

The concept in the 1986 Amendments which required FDA approval before a product could be exported generated criticism and debate as well. . . . Some firms charged that this approval process took too long; others questioned why the United States should have to approve the export of a product to a foreign country, particularly when the foreign country had its own public health authorities or had approved the product for marketing.

. . . .

The FDA Export Reform and Enhancement Act of 1996 (Pub. L. 104–134, and amended by Pub. L. 104–180) addressed industry's problems and concerns. . . . [T]he 1996 Amendments . . . [r]eplaced section 802 of the act in its entirety with a new section 802. . . .

. . . .

VII. Exports of Unapproved Drugs, Biologics, and Devices Under Section 802(b) of the Act

. . . .

Under section 802(f) of the act, the basic requirements for all drugs, biologics, and devices exported under section 802 of the act [include, among others, the following:]

- The product must be manufactured, processed, packaged, and held in "substantial conformity" with cGMP's or meet international standards as certified by an international standards organization recognized by FDA. . . .

- The product must have the strength, purity, or quality that it is represented to possess; . . .

- The product must comply with the requirements in section 801(e)(1) of the act. . . .

- The product cannot present an imminent hazard to the public health of the country to which it would be exported; and

- The product must be labeled in accordance with the requirements and conditions of use in the listed country which authorized it for marketing and the country to which it is being exported, and must be labeled in the language and units of measurement used in or designated by the country to which the drug or device is being exported. Additionally, a drug or device may not be exported if the drug or device is not promoted in accordance with these labeling requirements.

If the above requirements are not met, section 802(f) of the act states that a drug or device may not be exported. Furthermore, in determining whether a drug or device may present an imminent hazard to the public health of the foreign country or is improperly labeled or promoted, section 802(f) of the act requires FDA to consult with the "appropriate public health official in the affected country."

The principal provision authorizing the exportation of unapproved new drugs, biologics, and devices is section 802(b)(1)(A) of the act. Section 802(b)(1)(A) of the act states that a drug or device "may be exported to any country, if the drug or device complies with the laws of that country and has valid marketing authorization by the appropriate authority" in Australia, Canada, Israel, Japan, New Zealand, Switzerland, South Africa, or any member nation in the European Union or the European Economic Area.

This means that a firm whose drug or device has received marketing authorization in any of the countries listed above can export that drug or device to any country in the world as long as the drug or device meets applicable requirements of the act, without submitting an export request to FDA or receiving FDA approval to export the drug or device. Moreover, in a change from the 1986 Amendments, firms do not have to seek U.S. approval of the product as a condition of exportation. . . .

Some countries . . . have regulatory systems that permit marketing without an affirmative act or decision by the government. In such cases, FDA would consider a drug, biologic, or device to have "marketing authorization" if the listed country does not object to the product's marketing, and FDA recommends that the firm obtain a document from the relevant authority in the listed country indicating that it does not object to the product's marketing.

As for the word "drug," the drug to be exported under section 802(b)(1)(A) of the act should be the same product as the drug that received marketing authorization in the listed foreign country. Thus, the issue of whether the drug to be exported must be exactly identical to the drug authorized in the listed country may depend on the conditions surrounding market authorization in the foreign country. . . .

The list of countries in section 802(b)(1)(A) of the Act is not closed. The 1996 Amendments contain a mechanism whereby the Secretary may add other countries to the list, provided that the country meets certain criteria. . . .

The authority to add countries to the list, by law, cannot be delegated below the Office of the Secretary. Thus, FDA has no authority to add countries to the list.

If a firm intends to export an unapproved new drug (including biologics) to a foreign country, but none of the listed countries has approved the drug for marketing, it has two other options for exporting the product.

One option is in section 802(b)(2) of the act. This section permits a firm to export an unapproved drug directly to an unlisted country if:

- The drug complies with the laws of the foreign country and has valid marketing authorization by the "responsible authority" in that country, and

- The agency determines that the foreign country has statutory or regulatory requirements:

** Which require the review of drugs for safety and effectiveness by a government entity in that country and which authorizes marketing approval of drugs which trained and experienced experts have determined to be safe and effective . . . ;

** Pertaining to cGMP's;

** For reporting adverse events and for removing unsafe or ineffective drugs from the market; and

** Which require that the labeling and promotion be in accordance with the product's approval.

. . . .

The second option is in section 802(b)(3) of the act. This section permits a firm to petition the agency to approve exportation to an unlisted country if the conditions for export under section 802(b)(1) and 802(b)(2) of the act cannot be met. Under section 802(b)(3) of the act, FDA must allow exportation of the drug if:

- The person exporting the drug: (1) Certifies that the drug would not meet the conditions for approval under the Act or the conditions for approval in a listed country; and (2) provides "credible scientific evidence" that is acceptable to FDA to show that the drug would be safe and effective under the conditions of use in the country to which it is being exported . . . ; and

- The appropriate health authority in the foreign country that is to receive the drug: (1) Requests approval of the drug's exportation, (2) certifies that the health authority understands that the drug is not approved under the Act or by any listed country, and (3) concurs that the scientific evidence provided to FDA is credible scientific evidence that the drug would be reasonably safe and effective in the foreign country. . . .

VIII.   Exports of Unapproved Drugs and Devices for Investigational Use to Listed Countries Under Section 802(c) of the Act

. . . .

The 1996 Amendments . . . creat[ed] a new section 802(c) of the act. In brief, section 802(c) of the act permits a firm to export an unapproved drug for investigational use in any of the listed countries, without prior FDA approval or even an IND. The only requirements are that the drug be exported in accordance with the laws of the foreign country, and comply with the basic export requirements in section 802(f) of the act. . . .

It is important to note that FDA interprets section 802(c) of the act as applying only to investigational drugs and devices exported to the listed countries. The agency is aware that some firms have interpreted this provision as permitting transshipment to unlisted countries, but section 802(c) of the act is silent with respect to transshipment, and a more reasonable interpretation would be that transshipments are not allowed under section 802(c) of the act. . . .

Additionally, one should note that section 802(b)(1) of the act authorizes exportation to unlisted countries if the drug complies with the foreign country's laws and has valid marketing authorization in a listed country. Exports under section 802(b)(1) of the act may be made for investigational uses or for marketing purposes.

. . . .

. . . Section 802(c) of the act permits a firm to export an unapproved device for investigational use in any of the listed countries, without prior FDA approval or an IDE. However, as in the case for drugs, the device must be exported in accordance with the laws of the foreign country.

Yet, unlike the situation for drug exports, the 1996 Amendments give device manufacturers the option whether to export a device under section 801(e)(2) of the act or under section 802 of the act. The selected authority is important because each section of the act carries its own statutory requirements.

. . . .

XI.   Export Notification Under Section 802(g) of the Act

Section 802(g) of the act requires persons exporting a drug or device under section 802(b)(1) of the act to provide a "simple notification . . . identifying the drug or device when the exporter first begins to export such drug or device" to any country listed in section 802(b)(1) of the act. If the product is to be exported to an unlisted country, section 802(g) of the act requires the exporter to provide a simple notification "identifying the drug or device and the country to which such drug or device is being exported."

In all cases, section 802(g) of the act requires the exporter to maintain records of all drugs or devices exported and the countries to which they were exported.

NOTES

1. *Listed Countries.* The Secretary of Health and Human Services has not yet used his nondelegable authority to expand the list of countries in section 802(b)(1)(A).

2. *Tropical Diseases.* Section 802(e) permits the exportation, with FDA approval of an export application, of "a drug or device which is used in the diagnosis, prevention, or treatment of a tropical disease or another disease not of significant prevalence in the United States and which does not otherwise qualify for export under this section."

COMMENT: EXPORT CERTIFICATES

Firms exporting a product from the United States are often requested by foreign customers or foreign governments to supply a "certificate" containing information about the product's regulatory or marketing status. For exported drugs, biologics, animal drugs, and devices, FDA is statutorily required, if requested, to issue a certification either that the product is exportable under the requirements of FD&C Act 801(e)(1) or 802 or that it satisfies the Act's requirements for marketing in the United States. FD&C Act 801(e)(4)(A). The Act permits FDA to charge a fee for this service. *Id.*

801(e)(4)(B). A certificate that a product meets domestic requirements for marketing is called a "Certificate to Foreign Government" with respect to biologics, animal drugs, and devices and a "Certificate of a Pharmaceutical Product" with respect to human drugs. (The latter type of certificate conforms to a World Health Organization (WHO) format.) A certificate for an unapproved product that may be legally exported under 801(e) or 802 is called a "Certificate of Exportability," except with respect to human drugs, for which FDA instead issues a Certificate of a Pharmaceutical Product with a special notation that the product is unapproved. For all these sorts of certification, FDA relies on the manufacturer's self-certification that it meets the applicable legal requirements. 71 Fed. Reg. 4147 (Jan. 25, 2006); FDA, GUIDANCE FOR INDUSTRY: FDA EXPORT CERTIFICATES (2002).

FDA is not obligated to issue export certificates for foods, cosmetics, or dietary supplements, and is not empowered to charge a fee for such certificates. Nonetheless, so far as resources permit, the agency issues "Certificates for Export" for these products, attesting that they are produced and marketed in the United States in general conformity with U.S. requirements. Interestingly, other agencies with jurisdiction over food, including the Department of Agriculture, have statutory authority to collect fees associated with the issuance of export certificates. FDA, with responsibility for the majority of the food supply, does not. The burden on FDA is particularly high with regard to seafood and dairy products, for which many foreign nations require export certificates. FDA, FDA–ISSUED/SUPPORTED EXPORT CERTIFICATES FOR FOODS (2002).

C.   IMPORT FOR EXPORT

FDA Regulatory Procedures Manual, Chapter 9, Subchapter: Import for Export (2002)

... The FDA Export Reform and Enhancement Act of 1996 (Export Reform Act), Public Law 104–134[,] amended section 801(d)(3) of the Act to allow the importation of certain articles that are unapproved or otherwise do not comply with the Act, provided that those imported articles are further processed or incorporated into products that will be exported from the United States, by their initial owner or consignee in accordance with section 801(e) or section 802 of the Act or section 351(h) of the Public Health Service Act (PHSA).... [T]he Public Health Security and Bioterrorism Preparedness and Response Act of 2002 (Bioterrorism Act), Public Law 107–188 ... [further] amended section 801(d)(3) of the Act....

When a drug or device component, food additive, color additive, or dietary supplement is imported under section 801(d)(3), the importer is required to submit a statement to FDA at the time of each importation with the following information:

1. that such article (the components, parts, accessories, or articles) is intended to be further processed by the initial owner or consignee or incorporated by the initial owner or consignee into a drug, biological product, device, food, food additive, color additive, or dietary supplement that will be exported from the United States by

the initial owner or consignee in accordance with section 801(e) or section 802 of the Act or section 351(h) of the PHSA; and

2. identification of the manufacturer of such article and each processor, packer, distributor or other entity that had possession of the article in the chain of possession from the manufacturer to such importer of the article.

. . . .

The terms "further processed" and "incorporated" can cover a wide range of activities. These can include packaging or labeling of finished products and specialized processing (such as sterilization) of a product. FDA recognizes that in some instances, it may be advantageous to manufacture a product in a foreign country and then ship it to the United States for specialized packaging or labeling. Merely storing an article or product in the United States before export is not considered "further processing." . . .

Many manufacturers assemble their products in various stages. These manufacturing steps may include sending partially completed products to firms in the United States for further manufacturing or processing, but not into a finished product. Neither the statutory language of the amended section 801(d)(3) nor the legislative history of the Export Reform Act or the Bioterrorism Act require that violative components allowed to be imported must be incorporated into "finished products." Because components, or "subassemblies," are the finished product of the U.S. manufacturer (although not necessarily a consumer ready product) and would constitute a drug, biological product, device, food additive, color additive, or dietary supplement within the Act's meaning, the agency has concluded that articles imported for use in the manufacture of such products fall within the scope of the import for export provision. . . .

The new section 801(d)(3)(A)(iv) requires that the initial owner or consignee maintain records on the use or destruction of the imported articles or portions and to provide records when requested. The initial owner or consignee is also required to submit a report to FDA, upon request, that provides an accounting of the export or destruction of such imported article or portions and the manner in which such owner or consignee complied with the requirements of section 801(d)(3). . . .

CHAPTER XII

STATE REGULATORY AUTHORITY

The several states have long played important roles in regulating food, drugs, and related products. Space does not permit close examination of the law of any one state, much less a survey of them all. Instead, this chapter explores the legal doctrines surrounding the limits on state authority and the increasingly significant role of Federal preemption.

A. THE ELUSIVE GOAL OF NATIONAL UNIFORMITY

Peter Barton Hutt, *The Basis and Purpose of Government Regulation of Adulteration and Misbranding of Food*

33 FOOD DRUG COSMETIC LAW JOURNAL 505 (1978).

It was not until the establishment of the Department of Agriculture in 1862 that any segment of the agriculture industry in this country received much consideration in Congress, and . . . it was at least another 25 years before most members of Congress were willing to consider agricultural problems as national rather than local in nature. . . .

The 1906 Act and its successor, the Federal Food, Drug, and Cosmetic Act of 1938, were a reflection of the emerging nationwide food marketing system in this country. Nonetheless, in spite of a 70–year tradition of a single federal statute governing the food supply, and a marketing system that knows no political bounds, there remain today the persistent vestiges of inconsistent state and local laws and regulations reflecting the piecemeal approach to food regulation that characterized the 1800's. . . .

NOTES

1. *Drive for Uniformity.* Perhaps surprisingly, state regulatory officials have long been troubled by the diversity of state laws. The original 1884 constitution of the Association of Official Agricultural Chemists (now the Association of Official Analytical Chemists) declared it was the association's objective "to secure, as far as possible, uniformity in legislation . . . and uniformity and accuracy in the methods and results" of analysis. KENNETH HELRICH, THE GREAT COLLABORATION: THE FIRST ONE HUNDRED YEARS OF THE ASSOCIATION OF OFFICIAL ANALYTICAL CHEMISTS 9 (1984). In 1897, representatives from ten states met "for the purpose of forming a national association . . . with the end in view of producing, as nearly as conditions and laws

would permit, uniformity of action in the enforcement of such [food and drug] laws." The 1897 constitution of the resulting organization, declared that its purpose was "to promote and foster such legislation as would tend to protect public health and prevent deception ... also to promote uniformity in legislation and rulings...." William F. Reindollar, *The Association of Food and Drug Officials*, 6 FOOD DRUG COSM. L.J. 52, 53, 54 (1951).

2. *AFDO Supports Uniformity.* The consistent position of the Association of Food and Drug officials is expressed in the following statement:

Food and Drug Officials can render a national service, make regulatory work easier and more forceful, compliance simpler, and at the same time promote expansion of industry and commerce if they will:

1. Discourage the enactment of laws that make it impossible for legitimate industry of one state to engage in trade in another state under conditions which are fair and equitable.

2. Seek the repeal of discriminatory laws that now retard commerce between the states, discourage legitimate trade, prevent expansion and complicate the problem of policing industry, all to the detriment of legitimate enterprises and with no consequent benefit to the consumer.

3. Encourage the enactment of uniform laws and the adoption of uniform regulations looking toward honest protection of the consumer. If the honest consumer is adequately protected, the dishonest industry cannot prosper.

Editorial, 5 Q. BULL. AFDO No. 1, at 2 (1941). Resolutions favoring uniform federal, state, and local food and drug laws have appeared repeatedly in AFDO's Quarterly Bulletin. *See, e.g.*, 4 Q. BULL., No. 1, at 3 (1940); 31 Q. BULL., No. 1, at 73 (1967); 37 Q. BULL., No. 1, at 19 (1973).

3. *Uniform State Laws.* AFDO has sponsored the development of uniform state legislation under both the 1906 Act and the 1938 Act. Ole Salthe, *State Food, Drug and Cosmetic Legislation and its Administration*, 6 L. & CONTEMP. PROBS. 165 (1939); O.J. Wiemann, *Report on Revision of the Uniform State Food, Drug and Cosmetic Bill*, 17 FOOD DRUG COSM. L.J. 218 (1962). The current version of the Uniform State Food, Drug and Cosmetic Bill can be found in Food Drug Cosm. L. Rep. (CCH) ¶ 10,100.

4. *Conforming State Regulations.* Section 24 of the Uniform State Food, Drug, and Cosmetic Bill authorizes state authority "to make the regulations promulgated under this Act conform, insofar as practicable, with those promulgated under the Federal Act." Most state laws contain a provision that urges or requires consistency with the FD&C Act and FDA regulations. Enforcing compliance with these provisions, however, has not proved easy. In *American Grain Products Processing Institute v. Department of Public Health*, 467 N.E.2d 455 (Mass. 1984), the court decided (4–3) that, even though a state statute provided that any state standard or tolerance must conform to a federal standard or tolerance, Massachusetts could establish a tolerance for ethylene dibromide (EDB) in food in the face of a federal EPA "exemption from tolerance." In *Processed Apples Institute, Inc. v. Department of Public Health*, 522 N.E.2d 965 (Mass. 1988), the court held (5–1) that the same statute was intended to set a floor and not a ceiling and that Massachusetts could "conform" to the federal tolerance by imposing a more stringent limit on residues of the pesticide daminozide on apple products.

5. *Pre–1906 State Laws.* Surveys of state food and drug laws before enactment of the 1906 Act may be found in Willard Bigelow, *Foods and Food Control*, USDA BUR. CHEM. BULL. No. 69, Pts. I–V (1902); Alexander John Wedderburn, *Special Report on the Extent and Character of Food Adulteration*, USDA DIV. CHEM. BULL.

No. 32, at 87 (1892). *See also* Willard Bigelow, *Officials Charged with the Enforcement of Food Laws in the United States and Canada*, USDA Bur. Chem. Circ. No. 16 (1904).

6. *State Laws in 1938.* The status of state legislation at the time of enactment of the 1938 Act was reviewed in detail by Salthe, *State Food, Drug and Cosmetic Legislation, supra.* n. 3. The results of a detailed survey of state food regulations were reported in House Comm. on Government Operations, "Consumer Protection Activities of State Governments: Part 2—The Regulation of Foods and Related Products," H.R. Rep. No. 921, 88th Cong., 1st Sess. (1963).

FDA, State Programs and Services in Food and Drug Control

(1978).

No State has a single agency responsible for all program areas of food and drug control.... The extent to which the States have divided their food and drug control responsibilities varies from two to four or more agencies with the majority of States having three agencies involved....

... [T]he variability of organizational structures complicates the problems of many of the individual State agencies in accomplishing their program goals because of overlapping responsibilities and the lack of a clear delineation of responsibilities. For example, it is not uncommon to find authority granted to two agencies for some divided program segments of a single program category (*e.g.*, milk, shellfish). Frequently, two or more independent agencies of relatively equal rank are charged with enforcement of portions of the same general food and drug law. In still other States, there is no central State control over the food and drug programs. In these instances, the State agency has an unclear role as an advisor or consultant to the local government. However, the local agency may not be legally bound to follow the advice and/or direction that may be suggested by the State agency....

... Basic State food and drug laws are patterned in varying degrees after Federal food and drug laws at different stages in their evolution or after the Uniform State Food, Drug and Cosmetic Bill of the Association of Food and Drug Officials. Currently, 42 States have enacted food provisions based on the 1938 Federal FD&C Act. Approximately half of the States have updated the food provisions to include such major amendments as the Food and Color Additives Amendment and the Pesticide Amendment.... Forty one States have enacted drug provisions based upon the 1938 Federal FD&C Act. Less than a third of the States have modernized their drug legislation by the inclusion of the modern new drug amendments (Kefauver–Harris Legislation). The uniform device provisions have been enacted by 38 States and 43 have its cosmetic requirements....

Melvin Hinich & Richard Staelin, *Regulation of the U.S. Food Industry*

Appendix, VI Study on Federal Regulation, S. Doc. No. 96–14 (1st Session 1978).

Why does food regulation differ among the states? We suggest two factors: local special interest groups use their influence in state legislatures to secure a competitive advantage, and special features exist between differing locales, leading to a heterogeneity of preferences across regions. In other words the economic and social forces which affect food regulation at the national level are also present at the state and even local level. Just as U.S. producers profit from Federal regulations which raise the costs of foreign producers, local producers profit from regulations which give them a competitive edge over their competitors in other regions. The consumers pay for any profits which result from constraints on free trade, although they also get the benefits of being protected by the regulatory actions of the Government. Not all the profits, however, go to the producers; labor unions and local suppliers can also benefit at the expense of others. Since there are fewer special interest groups in a state or local region as compared to the nation as a whole, it is probably easier for these groups to organize to exert effective pressure for restrictive regulations. . . .

Arguments made for uniformity of legislation stress the desirability of modernizing food laws, regulations, and standards. Uniform legislation is said to be needed to protect consumers' health, assure high quality food, and eliminate objectionable trade barriers. . . .

Another argument for uniformity of state food laws by the food industry is that concerning productivity. Non-uniform statutes are said to necessitate additional production lines for the same product to meet different requirements, thereby reducing productivity. Some other arguments for uniformity stress that the legal interpretation of acts in state courts are [sic] unpredictable—adding more uncertainty to the business. With uniform legislation, a state can coordinate state enforcement efforts with the FDA (*e.g.*, supplementing field forces, exchange of laboratory results, and use of FDA resources where expert testimony is needed). State scientific resources can be devoted to enforcement of federally established standards, revising them as special circumstances or doubt[s] arise.

While there is general support for uniformity, this does not necessarily translate into proof that Federal pre-emption of state food and drug law is best for the consumer. States have provided much impetus for food and drug legislation and uniformity in law and regulation, have played a crucial part in enforcing Federal pre-emptive legislation, and have shown a willingness to adopt uniform regulations (*e.g.*, the Interstate Milk Shippers Program). Moreover, without any say, state legislators may be more reluctant to appropriate state funds to enforce Federal laws and regulations. Also, states have expressed a desire to retain the authority to require nutritional standards and maintain enforcement ability over and above that of the Federal government. Differing regulations also allow for different sensibilities among geographic areas in regard to ingredients in meat or other products.

As with Federal agencies, state and local units can regulate either by banning or providing information. In our opinion it seems reasonable for a local government, whose citizens have very different risk preferences from the rest of the nation, to exercise its judgment and ban a product from its region, since this does not impose costs on other consumer groups. Jurisdictional duplication and conflict about product labeling, on the other hand, cause economic losses to everyone, since there normally exist economies of scale in production and marketing which are unrealized if labeling regulations vary by region. For example, if label requirements vary by area, major food producers can not advantageously use the low mass distribution systems now available. This implies a significant economic advantage for a uniform national labeling code which would allow firms to market their products without having to worry about specific labels for individual areas. . . .

NOTE

For reports and analyses documenting the adverse economic impact of nonuniform state and Federal regulation of food and drug laws, see "An Inquiry Into Conflicting and Duplicative Regulatory Requirements Affecting Selected Industries and Sectors," 96th Cong., 2d Sess. (Joint Comm. Print 1980); R.E. Jenkins, A Comparative Study of State Food and Drug Regulatory Programs (1976) (unpublished Ph.D. dissertation, Ohio State University); REPORT ON THE WHITE HOUSE CONFERENCE ON FOOD, NUTRITION AND HEALTH, *Panel III–2: New Foods* (1969); NATIONAL COMMISSION ON FOOD MARKETING, FOOD FROM FARMER TO CONSUMER (1966); REPORT OF PUBLIC ADMINISTRATION SERVICE ON A STUDY OF STATE AND LOCAL FOOD AND DRUG PROGRAMS (1965); "Consumer Protection Activities of State Governments," H.R. Rep. No. 445, 88th Cong., 1st Sess. (1963); H.R. Rep. No. 921, 88th Cong., 1st Sess. (1963); and USDA, BARRIERS TO INTERNAL TRADE IN FARM PRODUCTS (1939).

H. Thomas Austern, *Federalism in Consumer Protection: Conflict or Coordination?*

29 BULLETIN OF THE ASSOCIATION OF FOOD & DRUG OFFICIALS OF U.S., No. 4 (1965).

. . . Two principles, I suggest, should control . . .

The first is that there is a place, indeed an important place, for State activity, and that effective consumer protection requires that there be fully deployed the corps of dedicated State and local regulatory officials who have devoted their careers to that end. . . .

The second controlling principle is that there should be no barriers to the free interstate movement of foods and drugs. As a corollary, the sophistication of modern food and drug production, and the delicacy of present-day techniques for determining pesticide residues, food additive safety, and drug efficacy, require both uniformity and the avoidance of costly duplication of research. . . .

I divide the area of needed regulatory activity into four parts. . . .

. . . [A]s to environmental sanitation. That covers not only food and drug manufacture, but also distribution and retail sale, as well as fundamental sanitation in local restaurants and food stores. Here the State and local health inspectors and health officials should play the dominant role. They can achieve the greatest degree of protection for the consuming public. . . .

Turning to the second area—the *safety* of composition of foods and drugs—the lines of responsibility begin to blend. Present-day sophistication of food manufacture and of drug technology impose too great a burden on the scientific resources of individual State agencies. . . .

When one leaves the area of environmental or compositional safety, and enters the third area of *economic* regulation, the national interest in freedom of the movement of goods usually should stay the hand of the State.... Interstate dealing, as well as the cost economies of mass production, dictate that there be a uniform package and label for all interstate distribution along with a trademark that can be nationally advertised....

Turning, finally, to the economic regulation of food composition by standardization, one finds the most discomforting area of chaos and perhaps plain rivalry.... It is not too much to hope that in this area of economic control over composition of food products, the States will yield to Federal standardization, and at the same time that the FDA will develop better and more responsive mechanisms for consultation and consideration of the views of State officials....

NOTES

1. *Prospective Adoption of Federal Regulations.* One obstacle to achievement of uniformity is the prohibition, in some states, against prospective adoption of regulations. In these states, the legislature may incorporate by reference only those FDA regulations in effect at the time it enacts legislation. *See* Thomas Christopher, *May a State Adopt Prospective Federal Regulations,* 15 FOOD DRUG COSM. L.J. 373 (1960).

2. *Federal–State Compacts.* For arguments in favor of federal-state compacts as an alternative to federal preemption, see David E. Engdahl, *Consolidation by Compact: A Remedy for Preemption of State Food and Drug Laws,* 14 J. OF PUB. L. 276 (1965).

3. *Commentary.* The literature dealing with statutory uniformity and Federal preemption is prolific. *See, e.g.,* Mark E. Barmak, *State Legislative Impact on the Drug Industry,* 33 FOOD DRUG COSM. L.J. 641 (1978); George M. Burditt, *The Importance of Uniformity Among State Food and Drug Laws,* 26 FOOD DRUG COSM. L.J. 96 (1971); *The Challenge of Uniformity,* 48 AFDO Q. BULL. 233 (1984); Thomas Christopher, *Conflicts Between State and Federal Food and Drug Laws,* 16 FOOD DRUG COSM. L.J. 164 (1961); Margery Downey, *Laboratories or Puppets? The Challenge of Federal Preemption of State Legislation,* 34 FOOD DRUG COSM. L.J. 334 (1979); David E. Engdahl, *Consolidating State and Federal Regulatory Power over Foods and Drugs,* 20 FOOD DRUG COSM. L.J. 587 (1965); William W. Goodrich, *The Applicability of the Federal Food, Drug, and Cosmetic Act to Intrastate Commerce,* 3 FOOD DRUG COSM. L.Q. 332 (1948), William W. Goodrich, *Uniformity in Federal–State Food Regulations,* 17 FOOD DRUG COSM. L.J. 305 (1962); Harvey L. Hensel, *Importance of Uniformity in the Weights and Measures Field,* 19 FOOD DRUG COSM. L.J. 274 (1964); Thomas L. Hooker, *The Impossible Dream: Maximum Uniformity with Maximum Freedom,* 48 J. AFDO, No. 2, at 74 (Apr.1984); Daniel J. Manelli, *State Legislation and the Regulation of OTC Drugs,* 33 FOOD DRUG COSM. L.J. 650 (1978); Charles P. Mitchell, *State Regulation and Federal Preemption of Food Labeling,* 45 1 FOOD DRUG COSM. L.J. 23 (1990); Jeffrey Nedelman, *Uniformity in the Regulation of Food,* 54 J. AFDO, No. 1, at 47 (Jan. 1990); Ralph P. Schipa, *The Desirability of Uniform Food Laws,* 3 FOOD DRUG COSM. L.Q. 518 (1948); Bruce A. Silverglade, *Preemption—The Consumer Viewpoint,* 45 FOOD DRUG COSM. L.J. 143 (1990); D. Joe Smith, Jr., *What Hath Rath Wrought? Federal Preemption in Food Labeling,* 33 FOOD DRUG COSM. L.J. 28 (1978); Michael R. Taylor, *Federal Preemption and Food and Drug Regulation: The Practical Modern Meaning of an Ancient Doctrine,* 38 FOOD DRUG COSM. L.J. 306 (1983).

B.   State Authority at the Dawn of Federal Regulation

A century ago the Supreme Court dealt frequently with the authority of the states to regulate products marketed interstate.

Plumley v. Massachusetts

155 U.S. 461 (1894).

■ Mr. Justice Harlan delivered the opinion of the court.

Plumley, the plaintiff in error, was convicted in the Municipal Court of Boston upon the charge of having sold in that city on the 6th day of October, 1891, in violation of the law of Massachusetts, a certain article, product and compound known as oleomargarine, made partly of fats, oils and oleaginous substances and compounds thereof, not produced from unadulterated milk or cream but manufactured in imitation of yellow butter produced from pure unadulterated milk and cream.

. . . .

The vital question in this case is . . . whether, as contended by the petitioner, the statute under examination in its application to sales of oleomargarine brought into Massachusetts from other States is in conflict with the clause of the Constitution of the United States investing Congress with power to regulate commerce among the several States. . . .

It will be observed that the statute of Massachusetts which is alleged to be repugnant to the commerce clause of the Constitution does not prohibit the manufacture or sale of all oleomargarine, but only such as is colored in imitation of yellow butter produced from pure unadulterated milk or cream of such milk. . . . It appears, in this case, that oleomargarine, in its natural condition, is of "a light-yellowish color," and that the article sold by the accused was artificially colored "in imitation of yellow butter." . . . The statute seeks to suppress false pretenses and to promote fair dealing in the sale of an article of food. It compels the sale of oleomargarine for what it really is, by preventing its sale for what it is not. Can it be that the Constitution of the United States secures to any one the privilege of manufacturing and selling an article of food in such manner as to induce the mass of people to believe that they are buying something which, in fact, is wholly different from that which is offered for sale? Does the freedom of commerce among the States demand a recognition of the right to practice a deception upon the public in the sale of any articles, even those that may have become the subject of trade in different parts of the country? . . .

If there be any subject over which it would seem the States ought to have plenary control, and the power to legislate in respect to which it ought not to be supposed was intended to be surrendered to the general government, it is the protection of the people against fraud and deception in the sale of food products. Such legislation may, indeed, indirectly or incidentally affect trade in such products transported from one State to another

State. But that circumstance does not show that laws of the character alluded to are inconsistent with the power of Congress to regulate commerce among the States. . . .

[The dissenting opinion of Chief Justice Fuller, joined by Justices Field and Brewer, is omitted.]

———

A decade earlier, in an address to the Medical Society of the State of New York, Dr. E.R. Squibb proposed enactment of a nationwide food and drug law.

> It is self-evident that a law to be most effective in preventing the adulteration of food and medicine should be general or national in order to secure universality and uniformity of action. . . .

E.R. SQUIBB, PROPOSED LEGISLATION ON THE ADULTERATION OF FOOD AND MEDICINE 3 (1879). Because of strong feelings in Congress that this was properly a matter for state and local regulation, arguments over the need for and scope of Federal legislation continued into the next century. The position of federal officials was clear. The Chief of the USDA Food Laboratory argued for national legislation because "[b]y no other means can we hope to secure laws uniform in their scope, requirements and penalties among ourselves. . . ." Willard Bigelow, *The Development of Pure Food Legislation*, 7 SCIENCE 505, 512 (1898). The Chief of the USDA Bureau of Chemistry stated that legislation was necessary "to secure uniformity in the composition of drugs. . . ." Harvey Wiley, *Drugs and Their Adulteration and The Laws Relating Thereto*, 2 WASH. MED. ANNALS 205 (1903).

> The House Report accompanying the 1906 Act stated that

> [t]he laws and regulations of the different States are diverse, confusing, and often contradictory. What one State now requires the adjoining State may forbid. Our food products are not raised principally in the States of their consumption.

> State boundary lines are unknown in our commerce, except by reason of local regulations and laws, such as State pure-food laws. It is desirable, as far as possible, that the commerce between the States be unhindered. One of the hoped-for good results of a national law on the subject of pure foods is the bringing about of a uniformity of laws and regulations on the part of the States within their own several borders.

H.R. Rep. No. 5056, 59th Cong., 1st Sess. 8–9 (1906). Nonetheless, the 1906 Act did not establish a comprehensive national regulatory scheme. It applied only to unbroken packages in interstate commerce, and only to the actual label of the product, perhaps reflecting doubt about the reach of Congress' jurisdiction.

Savage v. Jones

225 U.S. 501 (1912).

■ MR. JUSTICE HUGHES . . . delivered the opinion of the court.

The principal contention in support of this appeal is that the statute of Indiana (Acts 1907, chapter 206) . . . is an unconstitutional interference with the complainant's right to engage in interstate commerce.... The question of its constitutional validity may be considered in two aspects, (1) independently of the operation and effect of the act of Congress of June 30, 1906, known as "The Food and Drugs Act," and (2) in the light of this Federal enactment.

First. The statute relates to the sale of various sorts of food for domestic animals, embraced in the term "concentrated commercial feeding stuff" as defined in the act. It requires the filing of a statement and a sworn certificate, the affixing of a label bearing certain information, and a stamp

. . . .

The evident purpose of the statute is to prevent fraud and imposition in the sale of food for domestic animals, a matter of great importance to the people of the State.... It was not aimed at interstate commerce, but without discrimination sought to promote fair dealing in the described articles of food.... [T]he statute does not compel a disclosure of formulas or manner of combination. It does demand a statement of the ingredients, and also of the minimum percentage of crude fat and crude protein and of the maximum percentage of crude fiber, a requirement of obvious propriety in connection with substances purveyed as feeding stuffs.

... [W]hen the local police regulation has real relation to the suitable protection of the people of the State, and is reasonable in its requirements, it is not invalid because it may incidentally affect interstate commerce, provided it does not conflict with legislation enacted by Congress pursuant to its constitutional authority....

... The question remains whether the statute of Indiana is in conflict with ... the Food and Drugs Act of June 30, 1906.... It will be observed that in its enumeration of the acts, which constitute a violation of the statute, Congress has not included the failure to disclose the ingredients of the article....

Congress has thus limited the scope of its prohibitions. It has not included that at which the Indiana statute aims. Can it be said that Congress, nevertheless, has denied to the State, with respect to the feeding stuffs coming from another State and sold in the original packages, the power the State otherwise would have to prevent imposition upon the public by making a reasonable and nondiscriminatory provision for the disclosure of ingredients, and for inspection and analysis? If there be such denial it is not to be found in any express declaration to that effect....

... [T]he intent to supersede the exercise by the State of its police power as to matters not covered by the Federal legislation is not to be inferred from the mere fact that Congress has seen fit to circumscribe its regulation and to occupy a limited field. In other words, such intent is not to be implied unless the act of Congress fairly interpreted is in actual conflict with the law of the State....

... The requirements, the enforcement of which the bill seeks to enjoin, are not in any way in conflict with the provisions of the Federal act.

They may be sustained without impairing in the slightest degree its operation and effect. There is no question here of conflicting standards, or of opposition of state to Federal authority. It follows that the complainant's bill in this aspect of the case was without equity. . . .

McDermott v. Wisconsin
228 U.S. 115 (1913).

■ Mr. Justice Day delivered the opinion of the court.

The facts are that the plaintiffs in error were retail merchants in Oregon, Dane County, Wisconsin; that before the filing of the complaints against them each had bought for himself for resale as such merchant from wholesale grocers in Chicago and had received by rail from that city twelve half gallon tin cans or pails of the articles designated in the complaints, each shipment being made in wooden boxes containing the cans, and that when the goods were received at their stores the respective plaintiffs in error took the cans from the boxes, placed them on the shelves for sale at retail, and destroyed the boxes in which the goods were shipped to them, as was customary in such cases. From their nature, the articles thus canned and offered to be sold, instead of being labeled as they were, if labeled in accordance with the state law, would have been branded with the words "Glucose flavored with Refiner's Syrup," and, as the statute provides that the mixtures or syrups offered for sale shall have upon them no designation or brand which represents or contains the name of a saccharine substance other than that required by the state law, the labels upon the cans must be removed, if the state authority is recognized.

Plaintiffs in error contend that the cans were labeled in accordance with the Food and Drugs Act passed by Congress, June 30, 1906. . . . And it is insisted that the Federal Food and Drugs Act passed under the authority of the Constitution has taken possession of this field of regulation and that the state act is a wrongful interference with the exclusive power of Congress over interstate commerce, in which, it appears, the goods in question were shipped. The case presents, among other questions, the constitutional question whether the state act in permitting the sale of this article only when labeled according to the state law is open to the objection just indicated. . . .

. . . [I]t is essential to a legal exercise of possession of and traffic in such goods under the state law that labels which presumably meet with the requirements of the Federal law and for the determination of the correctness of which Congress has provided effectual means, shall be removed from the packages before the first sale by the importer. In this connection it might be noted that as a practical matter, at least, the first time the opportunity of inspection by the Federal authorities arises in cases like the present is when the goods, after having been manufactured, put up in package form and boxed in one State and having been transported in interstate commerce, arrive at their destination, are delivered to the consignee, unboxed, and placed by him upon the shelves of his store for sale. Conceding to the State the authority to make regulations consistent with the Federal law for the further protection of its citizens against impure and misbranded food and drugs, we think to permit such regulation as is embodied in this statute is to permit a State to discredit and burden legitimate Federal regulations of interstate commerce, to destroy rights arising out of the Federal statute which have accrued both to the Government and the shipper, and to impair the effect of a Federal law which has been enacted under the Constitutional power of Congress over the subject.

To require the removal or destruction before the goods are sold of the evidence which Congress has, by the Food and Drugs Act, as we shall see, provided may be examined to determine the compliance or noncompliance with the regulations of the Federal law, is beyond the power of the State. The Wisconsin act which permits the sale of articles subject to the regulations of interstate commerce only upon condition that they contain the exclusive labels required by the statute is an act in excess of its legitimate power.

It is insisted, however, that, since at the time when the state act undertook to regulate the branding of these goods, namely, when in the possession of the plaintiffs in error and held upon their shelves for sale, the cans had been removed from the boxes in which they were shipped in interstate commerce, they had therefore passed beyond the jurisdiction of Congress, and their regulation was exclusively a matter for state legislation. This assertion is based upon the original package doctrine as it is said to have been laid down in the former decisions of this court....

Congress having made adulterated and misbranded articles contraband of interstate commerce, in the manner we have already pointed out, provides in § 10 of the act that such articles may be proceeded against and seized for confiscation and condemnation while being transported from one State, Territory, district, or insular possession to another for sale, or, having been transported, remaining "unloaded, unsold, or in original unbroken packages," and the subsequent provisions of the section regulate the disposition of the articles seized.... It is enough, by the terms of the act, if the articles are *unsold*, whether in original packages or not.... The legislative means provided in the Federal law for its own enforcement may not be thwarted by state legislation having a direct effect to impair the effectual exercise of such means.

For the reasons stated, the statute of Wisconsin, in forbidding all labels other than the one it prescribed, is invalid....

NOTES

1. *State Regulation Upheld.* In *Price v. Illinois*, 238 U.S. 446 (1915), the Supreme Court upheld an Illinois statute which prohibited the marketing of a food preservative containing boric acid, a product lawful under federal law.

> ... [N]o question is presented in the present case as to the power of Congress to make provision with respect to the immediate containers (as well as the larger receptacle in which the latter are shipped) of articles prepared in one State and transported to another, so as suitably to enforce its regulations as to interstate trade. *McDermott v. Wisconsin.* It does not appear that the state law as here applied is in conflict with any Federal rule.

In *Armour & Co. v. North Dakota*, 240 U.S. 510 (1916), the Supreme Court unanimously upheld a North Dakota law requiring lard sold at retail to be packaged in specified sizes, although federal law permitted it to be sold in any size package so long as the net weight was stated on the label.

Weigle v. Curtice Bros. Co., 248 U.S. 285 (1919), required the Court once more to examine the scope of state power to regulate food that met the requirements of federal law. A Wisconsin statute prohibited the sale within the state of any food containing benzoic acid or benzoates. The plaintiff, who shipped fruit preserved with sodium benzoate in glass jars, packed in wooden crates, from New York, brought suit to enjoin enforcement of the state law. The plaintiff's argument, in substance, was that since the individual bottles sold at retail were still subject to the misbranding requirements of the Federal Food and Drugs Act of 1906, they were immune from Wisconsin law. The Court rejected this contention.

> ... For reasons stated in *McDermott v. Wisconsin*, if the State could require the label to be removed while the bottles remained in the importer's hands unsold, it could interfere with the means reasonably adopted by Congress to make its regulations obeyed. But all this has nothing to do with the question when interstate commerce is over and the articles carried in it have come under the general power of the State. The law upon that point has undergone no change.

> ... The fact that a food or drug might be condemned by Congress if it passed from State to State, does not carry an immunity of foods or drugs, making the same passage, that it does not condemn.... When objects of commerce get within the sphere of state legislation the State may exercise its independent judgment and prohibit what Congress did not see fit to forbid....

See also Hebe Co. v. Shaw, 248 U.S. 297 (1919) (sustaining an Ohio statute regulating condensed milk as construed to prohibit the sale of labeled condensed skim milk containing coconut oil).

In *Corn Products Refining Co. v. Eddy*, 249 U.S. 427 (1919), the Court held that a Kansas law requiring that a proprietary syrup mixture be labeled "compound" did not violate the equal protection clause of the Fourteenth Amendment or burden interstate commerce.

2. *Continued Advocacy of Uniformity.* Following passage of the 1906 Act, the USDA Bureau of Chemistry made repeated efforts to achieve uniform regulation of food and drugs. The Bureau's 1914 Annual Report reported cooperative efforts with state officials "for the purpose of fixing working standards for foods and drugs" that "should serve as a uniform guide in the enforcement of the food and drug laws throughout the country" and thus "should very largely overcome the lack of uniformity." 1914 USDA Ann. Rep. 1. Its 1921 Annual Report similarly recounted that "both officials and manufacturers complained greatly of the lack of uniformity in the exercise of food control by the Federal and State Governments." 1921 USDA Ann. Rep. 7.

> Lack of uniformity increases the costs of doing business, and the increased cost is usually passed on to the consumer. It arises not merely from differences in the various laws but also from differences in the interpretation of the laws by the officials and in the application by them of different standards to the same product in different jurisdictions.

C. The 1938 Act and State Authority

In 1938, there was broad support for relaxing the earlier law's limitations on federal jurisdiction. At the same time, senators debated the desirability of amending the existing statute rather than enacting an entirely new law:

> One of the innumerable objections originating with those who are opposed to any new food and drug legislation is that the bill is in the form of a revision rather than amendments to the present law. It is urged that by appropriate amendments court decisions under the old law will be preserved and that uniformity with existing State laws will be promoted....
>
> It is true that many State laws are modeled after the existing Federal law. But the problem of uniformity is not more easily solved by amendment than by revision. The contrary is true. In bringing their own laws in line with modern requirements the States would encounter the same difficulties your committee has found in efforts to amend. The States have unanimously urged the Federal Government to take leadership in modernizing existing law. Greater uniformity can be guaranteed by the logical, orderly form of this bill than by a confusion of amendments.

S. Rep. No. 74–361 (1st Sess. 2–3 1935). However, a minority took a different view of the matter:

> It is not disputed that the present law is an effectual statute in its existing scope and extent. The criticism of it, advanced in support of new legislation, is that it requires strengthening and extension or, in the President's words, "practical improvements." That is quite possible without discarding the statute in its entirety and, with one stroke, wiping out the clarity and certainty that exist under the court decisions and the uniformity in Federal and State statutes.

In *United States v. Phelps Dodge Mercantile Co.*, 157 F.2d 453 (9th Cir. 1946) (excerpted *supra* p. 1226), the Court of Appeals for the Ninth Circuit sharply restricted FDA's enforcement authority under the 1938 Act. The court affirmed a District Court order dismissing the libel brought by the United States against cartons of macaroni and spaghetti held for two years in the defendant's Arizona warehouse. Release of the food was appropriate because the plaintiff did not prove that it "was adulterated when introduced into or while in interstate commerce," even though the food was adulterated while held in the original packages. Within a year Congress amended sections 301(k) and 304(a) of the Act, 52 Stat. 582 (1948), extending federal jurisdiction to products that become adulterated or misbranded after shipment in interstate commerce. The 1948 amendments did not, however, forestall continued litigation.

Cloverleaf Butter Co. v. Patterson

315 U.S. 148 (1942).

■ MR. JUSTICE REED delivered the opinion of the Court.

The petitioner, Cloverleaf Butter Company, is engaged at Birmingham, Alabama, in the manufacture of process or renovated butter from packing stock butter. It obtains 25% of its supplies of packing stock butter from the farmers and country merchants of Alabama and 75% from those of other states, and it ships interstate 90% of its finished product. The production of renovated butter is taxed and regulated by the United States. . . .

The respondents, Alabama officials charged with the duty of enforcing the Alabama laws in regard to renovated butter, entered petitioner's factory and, in a little more than a year, seized on sixteen separate occasions a total of over twenty thousand pounds of packing stock butter, the material from which the finished product is made. Defendants also seized some butter moving to the factory in interstate commerce. . . .

The test to be applied to the action of the state in seizing material intended solely for incorporation into a product prepared for interstate commerce is the effect of that action upon the national regulatory policy declared by the federal statute. . . . The rule is clear that state action may be excluded by clear implication or inconsistency. Its application to individual cases creates difficulties. The differentiation between cases where the assumption of federal power is exclusive and where it admits state action is narrow. . . .

Coming finally to the query whether the state's claim interferes or conflicts with the purpose or provisions of the federal legislation, we determine that it does. The manufacture and distribution in interstate and foreign commerce of process and renovated butter is a substantial industry which, because of its multi-state activity, cannot be effectively regulated by isolated competing states. Its wholesome and successful functioning touches farm producers and city consumers. Science made possible the utilization of large quantities of packing stock butter which fell below the standards of public demand and Congress undertook to regulate the production in order that the resulting commodity might be free of ingredients deleterious to health. It left the states free to act on the packing stock supplies prior to the time of their delivery into the hands of the manufacturer and to regulate sales of the finished product within their borders. But, once the material was definitely marked for commerce by acquisition of the manufacturer, it passed into the domain of federal control.

Inspection of the factory and of the material was provided for explicitly. Confiscation of the finished product was authorized upon a finding of its unsuitability for food through the use of unhealthful or unwholesome materials, a finding that might be based upon visual or delicate laboratory tests, or upon observation of the use of such materials in the process of manufacture. By the statutes and regulations, the Department of Agriculture has authority to watch the consumer's interest throughout the process of manufacture and distribution. It sees to the sanitation of the factories in such minutiae as the clean hands of the employees and the elimination of objectionable odors, inspects the materials used, including air for aerating the oils, and confiscates the finished product when materials which would be unwholesome if utilized are present after manufacture. Confiscation by the state of material in production nullifies federal discretion over ingredients. . . .

■ MR. CHIEF JUSTICE STONE, dissenting. . . .

The decision of the Court appears to me to depart radically from the salutary principle that Congress, in enacting legislation within its constitutional authority, will not be deemed to have intended to strike down a state statute designed to protect the health and safety of the public unless the act, in terms or in its practical administration, conflicts with the act of Congress or plainly and palpably infringes its policy. . . .

. . . [N]ot only is there a complete want of conflict between the two statutes and their administration, but it seems plain that the Alabama statute, both by its terms and in its practical administration, aids and supplements the federal regulation and policy. Consequently there is no room for any inference that Congress, by its enactment, sought to stay the hands of the state in the exercise of a power with which the federal act does not conflict. The basic and identical concern of both governments is to protect the consuming public from contaminated butter. If the state seizes unfit packing stock, the federal authorities are relieved of the necessity of detecting it and of seizing the renovated product which it contaminates. . . .

Florida Lime & Avocado Growers, Inc. v. Paul
373 U.S. 132 (1963).

■ MR. JUSTICE BRENNAN delivered the opinion of the Court.

Section 792 of California's Agricultural Code, which gauges the maturity of avocados by oil content, prohibits the transportation or sale in California of avocados which contain "less than 8 per cent of oil, by weight . . . excluding the skin and seed." In contrast, federal marketing orders approved by the Secretary of Agriculture gauge the maturity of avocados grown in Florida by standards which attribute no significance to oil content. This case presents the question of the constitutionality of the California statute insofar as it may be applied to exclude from California markets certain Florida avocados which, although certified to be mature under the federal regulations, do not uniformly meet the California requirement of 8% of oil. . . .

. . . In adopting his calendar test of maturity for the varieties grown in South Florida the Secretary expressly rejected physical and chemical tests as insufficiently reliable guides for gauging the maturity of the Florida fruit.

. . . Whether a State may constitutionally reject commodities which a federal authority has certified to be marketable depends upon whether the state regulation "stands as an obstacle to the accomplishment and execution of the full purposes and objectives of Congress," *Hines v. Davidowitz*, 312 U.S. 52, 67 (1941). By that test, we hold that § 792 is not such an obstacle; there is neither such actual conflict between the two schemes of regulation that both cannot stand in the same area, nor evidence of a congressional design to preempt the field. . . .

A holding of federal exclusion of state law is inescapable and requires no inquiry into congressional design where compliance with both federal and state regulations is a physical impossibility for one engaged in interstate commerce.... No such impossibility of dual compliance is presented on this record, however....

The issue under the head of the Supremacy Clause is narrowed then to this: Does either the nature of the subject matter, namely the maturity of avocados, or any explicit declaration of congressional design to displace state regulation, require § 792 to yield to the federal marketing orders? The maturity of avocados seems to be an inherently unlikely candidate for exclusive federal regulation.... On the contrary, the maturity of avocados is a subject matter of the kind this Court has traditionally regarded as properly within the scope of state superintendence....

It is true that more recently we sustained a federal statute broadly regulating the production of renovated butter. But we were scrupulous in pointing out that a State might nevertheless—at least in the absence of an express contrary command of Congress—confiscate or exclude from market the processed butter which had complied with all the federal *processing* standards, "because of a higher standard demanded by a state for its consumers." A state regulation so purposed was, we affirmed, "permissible under all the authorities." *Cloverleaf Butter Co. v. Patterson*, 315 U.S. 148, 162 (1942).... Federal regulation by means of minimum standards of the picking, processing, and transportation of agricultural commodities, however comprehensive *for those purposes* that regulation may be, does not of itself import displacement of state control over the distribution and retail sale of those commodities in the interests of the *consumers* of the commodities within the State....

... While it is conceded that the California statute is not a health measure, neither logic nor precedent invites any distinction between state regulations designed to keep unhealthful or unsafe commodities off the grocer's shelves, and those designed to prevent the deception of consumers....

[Justice Brennan concluded that the record was inadequate to permit a judgment about whether the California statute unreasonably burdened interstate commerce. Justice White, in a dissenting opinion joined by Justices Black, Douglas, and Clark, concluded that California's statute was inconsistent with, and thus preempted by, federal law. EDS.]

NOTES

1. *State Regulation Displaced.* For examples of cases in which courts deemed state laws to be preempted by the FD&C Act or regulations promulgated pursuant to the Act, *see Borden Co. v. Liddy*, 239 F. Supp. 289 (S.D. Iowa 1965); *Gorolin Corp. v. City of New York*, Food Drug Cosm. L. Rep. (CCH) ¶ 7116 (S.D.N.Y. 1949). *But see People v. Breen*, 40 N.W.2d 778 (Mich. 1950) (upholding state law prohibiting sale of yellow margarine in face of FDA standard of identity permitting such coloring). *Cf. Dean Foods Co. v. Wisconsin Dept. of Agriculture*, 478 F. Supp. 224 (W.D. Wis. 1979) (state law prohibiting sale of product "purporting to be" milk but containing fat other than milkfat struck down as applied under the dormant Commerce Clause for unduly burdening interstate commerce).

2. *Statutory Preemption for Meat, Poultry, Eggs.* Congress has preempted any "additional" or "different" state requirement in the Federal Meat Inspection Act,

21 U.S.C. 678, the Poultry Products Inspection Act, 21 U.S.C. 467e, and the Egg Products Inspection Act, 21 U.S.C. 1052. Following enactment of 21 U.S.C. 678, the meat industry waged a successful 14–year war to have the courts invalidate the Michigan Comminuted Meat Law, which established ingredient requirements for various meat products that differed from the USDA requirements. Michigan then amended its statute to require grocery stores and restaurants that sell meat products whose ingredients do not meet the state standards to notify consumers by a "clearly visible" placard or by a notice printed on menus. The District Court determined that the Michigan law violated the dormant Commerce Clause. 550 F. Supp. 285 (W.D. Mich. 1982), *aff'd sub nom. American Meat Institute v. Pridgeon*, 724 F.2d 45 (6th Cir. 1984). *See also Mario's Butcher Shop and Food Center, Inc. v. Armour and Co.*, 574 F. Supp. 653 (N.D. Ill. 1983) (holding that state consumer fraud statutes were preempted). *But see Chicago–Midwest Meat Ass'n v. City of Evanston*, 589 F.2d 278 (7th Cir. 1978) (holding that a municipal ordinance authorizing the inspection of meat delivery vehicles did not violate either 21 U.S.C. 678 or the Commerce Clause).

Jones v. Rath Packing Co.

430 U.S. 519 (1977)

■ MR. JUSTICE MARSHALL delivered the opinion of the Court.

Petitioner Jones is Director of the Department of Weights and Measures in Riverside County, Cal. In that capacity he ordered removed from sale bacon packaged by respondent Rath Packing Co. and flour packaged by three millers, respondents General Mills, Inc., Pillsbury Co., and Seaboard Allied Milling Corp. (hereafter millers). Jones acted after determining by means of procedures set forth in 4 Cal. Admin. Code c. 8, Art. 5, that the packages were contained in lots whose average net weight was less than the net weight stated on the packages. The removal orders were authorized by Cal. Bus. & Prof. Code § 12211 (West Supp. 1977). . . .

In its present posture, this litigation contains no claim that the Constitution alone denies California power to enact the challenged provisions. We are required to decide only whether the federal laws which govern respondents' packing operations preclude California from enforcing § 12211, as implemented by Art. 5. . . .

Section 12211 . . . applies to both Rath's bacon and the millers' flour. The standard it establishes is straightforward: "[T]he average weight or measure of the packages or containers in a lot of any . . . commodity sampled shall not be less, at the time of sale or offer for sale, than the net weight or measure stated upon the package." . . .

Rath's bacon is produced at plants subject to federal inspection under the Federal Meat Inspection Act (FMIA or Act). . . . Among the requirements imposed on federally inspected plants, and enforced by Department of Agriculture inspectors, are standards of accuracy in labeling. On the record before us, we may assume that Rath's bacon complies with these standards. . . .

The Secretary of Agriculture has used his discretionary authority [under 21 U.S.C. 601(n)(5)(B)] to permit "reasonable variations" in the accuracy of the required statement of quantity:

"The statement [of net quantity of contents] as it is shown on a label shall not be false or misleading and shall express an accurate statement of the quantity of contents of the container exclusive of wrappers and packing substances. Reasonable variations caused by loss or gain of moisture during the course of good distribution practices or by unavoidable deviations in good manufacturing practice will be recognized. Variations from stated quantity of contents shall not be unreasonably large." 9 CFR § 317.2(h)(2) (1976).

Thus, the FMIA, as implemented by statutorily authorized regulations, requires the label of a meat product accurately to indicate the net weight of the contents unless the difference between stated and actual weights is reasonable and results from the specified causes.

Section 408 of the FMIA prohibits the imposition of "[m]arking, labeling, packaging, or ingredient requirements in addition to, or different than, those made under" the Act. This explicit pre-emption provision dictates the result in the controversy between Jones and Rath. California's use of a statistical sampling process to determine the average net weight of a lot implicitly allows for variation from stated weight caused by unavoidable deviations in the manufacturing process. But California makes no allowance for loss of weight resulting from moisture loss during the course of good distribution practice. Thus, the state law's requirement—that the label accurately state the net weight, with implicit allowance only for reasonable manufacturing variations—is "different than" the federal requirement, which permits manufacturing deviations *and* variations caused by moisture loss during good distribution practice.... We therefore conclude that with respect to Rath's packaged bacon, § 12211 and Art. 5 are pre-empted by federal law.

The federal law governing net-weight labeling of the millers' flour is contained in two statutes, the Federal Food, Drug, and Cosmetic Act (FDCA) and the Fair Packaging and Labeling Act (FPLA), 15 U.S.C. §§ 451–1461. For the reasons stated below, we conclude that the federal weight-labeling standard for flour is the same as that for meat.

... [The net weight labeling requirement in FDCA 403(e)] is identical to the parallel provision in the FMIA, except that the FDCA mandates rather than allows the promulgation of implementing regulations. The regulation issued in response to this statutory mandate is also substantially identical to its counterpart under the FMIA....

Since flour is a food under the FDCA, its manufacture is also subject to the provisions of the FPLA.... [T]he FPLA bans the distribution in commerce of any packaged commodity unless it complies with regulations

"which shall provide that—

"(2) The net quantity of contents (in terms of weight, measure, or numerical count) shall be separately and accurately stated in a uniform location upon the principal display panel of [the required] label." § 1453(a).

The FPLA also contains a saving clause which specifies that nothing in the FPLA "shall be construed to repeal, invalidate, or supersede" the FDCA. § 1460....

The *amici* States contend that since the FPLA does not allow any variations from stated weight, there is no difference between federal law governing labeling of flour and California law. The Court of Appeals, however, held that because of the saving clause, compliance with the FDCA, which does allow reasonable variations, satisfies the requirements of the FPLA.... We can only conclude that under the FPLA, as under the FDCA, a manufacturer of food is not subject to enforcement action for violation of the net-weight labeling requirements if the label accurately states the net weight, with allowance for the specified reasonable variations.

The FDCA contains no pre-emptive language. The FPLA, on the other hand, declares that

> "it is the express intent of Congress to supersede any and all laws of the States or political subdivisions thereof insofar as they may now or hereafter provide for the labeling of the net qua[nt]ity of contents of the package of any consumer commodity covered by this chapter which are less stringent than or require information different from the requirements of section 1453 of this title or regulations promulgated pursuant thereto." 15 U.S.C. § 1461....

The Court of Appeals, although recognizing that this section leaves more scope for state law than does the FMIA, concluded that § 12211, as implemented by Art. 5, is pre-empted because it is less stringent than the Federal Acts.

The basis for the Court of Appeals' holding is unclear.... [T]he Court of Appeals may have found California's approach less stringent because the State takes no enforcement action against lots whose average net weight *exceeds* the weight stated on the label, even if that excess is not a reasonable variation attributable to a federally allowed cause.

We have some doubt that by pre-empting less stringent state laws, Congress intended to compel the States to expend scarce enforcement resources to prevent the sale of packages which contain more than the stated net weight. We do not have to reach that question, however, because in this respect California law apparently differs not at all from federal law, as applied.... Since neither jurisdiction is concerned with overweighting in the administration of its weights and measures laws, we cannot say that California's statutory lack of concern for that "problem" makes its laws less stringent than the federal.

Respondents argue that California's law is pre-empted because it requires information different from that required by federal law.... Respondents attribute to the [FPLA] ban on requiring different information a broad meaning, similar in scope to the pre-emption provision of the FMIA. They contend that since California law requires the label to state the minimum net weight, it requires "information different from" the federal laws, which demand an accurate statement with allowance for the specified reasonable variations. The legislative history, however, suggests that the statute expressly pre-empts as requiring "different information" only state laws governing net quantity labeling which impose requirements inconsistent with those imposed by federal law. Since it would be possible to comply with the state law without triggering federal enforcement action we conclude that the state requirement is not inconsistent with federal law. We therefore hold that 15 U.S.C. § 1461 does not pre-empt California's § 12211 as implemented by Art. 5.

That holding does not, however, resolve this case, for we still must determine whether the state law "stands as an obstacle to the accomplishment and execution of the full purposes and objectives of Congress." As Congress clearly stated, a major purpose of the FPLA is to facilitate value comparisons among similar products. Obviously, this goal cannot be accomplished unless packages that bear the same indicated weight in fact contain the same quantity of the product for which the consumer is paying. The significance of this requirement for our purposes results from the physical attributes of flour. . . .

The moisture content of flour does not remain constant after milling is completed. If the relative humidity of the atmosphere in which it is stored is greater than 60%, flour will gain moisture, and if the humidity is less than 60%, it will lose moisture. The federal net-weight labeling standard permits variations from stated weight caused by this gain or loss of moisture.

Packages that meet the federal labeling requirements and that have the same stated quantity of contents can be expected to contain the same amount of flour solids. Manufacturers will produce flour with a moisture content fixed by the requirements of the milling process. Since manufacturers have reason not to pack significantly more than is required and federal law prohibits underpacking, they will pack the same amount of this similarly composed flour into packages of any given size. Despite any changes in weight resulting from changes in moisture content during distribution, the packages will contain the same amount of flour solids when they reach the consumer. This identity of contents facilitates consumer value comparisons.

The State's refusal to permit reasonable weight variations resulting from loss of moisture during distribution produces a different effect. In order to be certain of meeting the California standard, a miller must ensure that loss of moisture during distribution will not bring the weight of the contents below the stated weight. Local millers, which serve a limited area, could do so by adjusting their packing practices to the specific humidity conditions of their region. For example, a miller in an area where the humidity is typically higher than 60% would not need to overpack at all. By contrast, a miller with a national marketing area would not know the destination of its flour when it was packaged and would therefore have to assume that the flour would lose weight during distribution. The national manufacturer, therefore, would have to overpack.

Similarly, manufacturers who distributed only in States that followed the federal standard would not be concerned with compensating for possible moisture loss during distribution. National manufacturers who did not exclude the nonconforming States from their marketing area, on the other hand, would have to overpack. Thus, as a result of the application of the California standard, consumers throughout the country who attempted to compare the value of identically labeled packages of flour would not be comparing packages which contained identical amounts of flour solids. Value comparisons which did not account for this difference—and there would be no way for the consumer to make the necessary calculations—would be misleading.

We therefore conclude that with respect to the millers' flour, enforcement of § 12211, as implemented by Art. 5, would prevent "the accomplishment and execution of the full purposes and objectives of Congress" in passing the FPLA. Under the Constitution, that result is impermissible, and the state law must yield to the federal....

■ MR. JUSTICE REHNQUIST, with whom MR. JUSTICE STEWART joins, concurring in part and dissenting in part.

I agree that with respect to Rath's packaged bacon, § 12211 of the Cal. Bus. & Prof. Code and Art. 5 of 4 Cal. Admin. Code, c. 8, are pre-empted by the express pre-emptive provision of the Federal Meat Inspection Act.... I am unable to agree, however, with the implicit pre-emption the Court finds with respect to the flour....

... It is virtually impossible to say, as the Court does, that "neither the State nor the Federal Government is concerned with overweighting," and yet conclude that state-induced overweighting conflicts with a "value comparison" purpose, while, presumably, other overweighting does not. In viewing such a purpose to be sufficient to require pre-emption while the very purpose is ignored in practice by the administering federal agency reverses the normal presumption against finding pre-emption. The reasoning process which leads the Court to conclude that there is no express pre-emption leads me to conclude that there is no implied pre-emption....

The assumptions in the Court's opinion not only are insufficient to compel a finding of implied pre-emption, they suggest an approach to the question of pre-emption wholly at odds with that enunciated in *Florida Lime & Avocado Growers, Inc. v. Paul*, 373 U.S. 132 (1963). There, this Court ... rejected a test which looked to the similarity of purposes, and noted instead that a manufacturer could have complied with both statutes by modifying procedures somewhat, which demonstrated that there was "no inevitable collision between the two schemes of regulation, despite the dissimilarity of the standards." Nothing has been shown to demonstrate that this conclusion is not equally justified in the instant case....

NOTES

1. *Rival Interpretations of "Imitation".* Grocery Mfrs. of America, Inc. v. Gerace, 755 F.2d 993 (2d Cir. 1985), involved a collision between state and national definitions of the term "imitation."

> The text of New York's section 63, enacted in 1982, ... requires that alternative cheese products feature labels that display prominently the descriptive term "imitation." It also directs that anyone who sells prepared foods containing cheese alternatives, whether for carry out or for consumption on the premises, must display a sign that discloses in three inch letters

those foods that contain "imitation cheese." Further, it provides that restaurant menus must append the words "contains imitation cheese" to the item designation of any offering containing alternative cheese. And, finally, alternative cheese products available for use by customers on the premises—as, for example, something resembling grated parmesan—must be conspicuously labeled as "imitation cheese." Section 63 does not define imitation. The regulations promulgated pursuant to the statute define "imitation cheese" as any food simulating "cheese" as described or standardized by regulation but failing to meet that description or standard. Neither the statute nor any of its regulations is concerned with nutritional values.

The federal scheme implicated here, which establishes the requisite information content of package labels for foods shipped in interstate commerce, involves three federal statutes and two federal agencies.... [The court summarized the FDA and USDA requirements for labeling substitute and imitation foods, *supra* p. 218, which restrict the term "imitation" to foods that are nutritionally inferior to the foods for which they are substitutes.]

If we were addressing the validity of the FDA regulation in or about 1973, the year of its promulgation, we might be inclined to reject it. But the regulation has been in effect for eleven years. Congress' failure during this period to alter the relevant statutory language or to otherwise condemn the regulatory definition, while not a fail-safe guide, allows us at least to infer that it has acquiesced in the FDA's construction.... The FDA's definition of imitation is entitled to our deference.

Thus, as applied to alternative cheese, the New York labeling scheme is in direct conflict with its federal counterpart. Including the term "imitation" on the label of a nutritionally superior alternative cheese in order to comply with New York law, would render the product misbranded under federal law. Compliance with both the state and federal requirements is impossible. To the extent that it attempts to regulate the labeling of alternative cheese, the New York law is preempted.

. . . .

Even if it should be classified as an interpretive rule or a statement of general policy, rather than as a formal rule adopted via adjudication, the USDA's practice of following the FDA definition of imitation when reviewing meat and poultry product labels is valid.... Consequently, the New York requirements are "different from" the federal requirements, as administered, and they are therefore preempted.

Notwithstanding the conflict created by its use of "imitation," the New York law imposes other labeling requirements that are "in addition to[ ] or different than" the federal requirements.... New York's section 63 mandates the precise size of the letters in and relative location of the word "imitation" on package labels. These requirements do not comport exactly with the federal specifications. Therefore, the state requirements are preempted.

2. *Chlorofluorocarbon Propellants.* In *Cosmetic, Toiletry and Fragrance Ass'n v. Minnesota*, 440 F. Supp. 1216 (D. Minn. 1977), *aff'd per curiam* 575 F.2d 1256 (8th Cir. 1978), the District Court struck down as preempted a Minnesota statute

that required the following label warning on products using chlorofluorocarbon propellants:

> Warning: Contains a chlorofluorocarbon that may harm the public health and environment by reducing ozone in the upper atmosphere.

Inspired by the same scientific findings that had animated the Minnesota legislators, FDA had previously adopted a regulation under the FD&C Act that mandated the very same warning on foods, drugs, and cosmetics that incorporated chlorofluorocarbon propellants. The FDA rule required the warning to appear on any panel on which it was likely to be seen by the purchaser at the time of purchase. The state statute, by contrast, required the warning to appear on the immediate container.

The District Court began with the conclusion that FDA's decision to address the risk of ozone damage by requiring a label warning effectively precluded the state from requiring any other measure or form of words. It credited FDA's repeated statements that "uniformity in labeling is required to meet the dual national goal of the most effective warning at the least possible cost." And it was not persuaded by the state's argument that placement on a product's immediate container of the very words FDA had prescribed would be both more effective and not incompatible with federal policy. It concluded that FDA's outer package requirement reflected a judgment that consumers should be warned when they considered purchase of a product. "The responsible federal administrative agency has determined that the federal policy is purchase awareness and that a policy of use awareness would require more time and expense and cause more disruption." The state's labeling requirement, therefore, was "an obstacle to full effectuation of the federal purpose," and accordingly unconstitutional under the Supremacy Clause of the Constitution.

3. *Labeling of Dairy Products. Lever Brothers Co. v. Maurer*, 712 F. Supp. 645 (S.D. Ohio 1989), invalidated, as preempted by the FD&C Act and the Commerce Clause, a state statute precluding use of the word "butter" on the label or in the labeling of any substitute for butter. In *Committee for Accurate Labeling and Marketing v. Brownback*, 665 F. Supp. 880 (D. Kan. 1987), the District Court held that the Kansas Artificial Dairy Products Act, which required any "artificial" dairy product to be labeled as such, was preempted under the Supremacy Clause because it stood as an obstacle to the accomplishment of the FDA regulation of food labeling generally and the agency's definition of an "imitation" in particular.

4. *Pennsylvania Bakery Legend.* One of the most notorious state food labeling provisions was 43 Pennsylvania Statutes § 405, which required every "bakery product" to bear a "Registered with Pennsylvania Department of Agriculture" legend in full text or an approved abbreviated form. Enacted in 1933, this statute was never judicially challenged before it was repealed in the last years of the 20th century. What if other states had followed Pennsylvania's example?

Hillsborough County v. Automated Medical Laboratories, Inc.

471 U.S. 707 (1985).

■ JUSTICE MARSHALL delivered the opinion of the Court.

The question presented is whether the federal regulations governing the collection of blood plasma from paid donors pre-empt certain local ordinances. Appellee Automated Medical Laboratories, Inc., is a Florida corporation that operates, through subsidiaries, eight blood plasma centers in the United States.... Appellee's plasma centers collect blood plasma from donors by employing a procedure called plasmapheresis.... Appellee sells the plasma to pharmaceutical manufacturers.

Vendors of blood products, such as TPC, are subject to federal supervision. Under § 351(a) of the Public Health Service Act, such vendors must be licensed by the Secretary of Health and Human Services (HHS). Licenses are issued only on a showing that the vendor's establishment and blood products meet certain safety, purity, and potency standards established by the Secretary. HHS is authorized to inspect such establishments for compliance. Pursuant to § 351 of the Act, the Food and Drug Administration (FDA), as the designee of the Secretary, has established standards for the collection of plasma....

In 1980, Hillsborough County adopted Ordinances 80–11 and 80–12.... Ordinance 80–12 establishes a countywide identification system, which requires all potential donors to obtain from the County Health Department an identification card, valid for six months, that may be used only at the plasmapheresis center specified on the card. The ordinance incorporates by reference the FDA's blood plasma regulations, but also imposes donor testing and recordkeeping requirements beyond those contained in the federal regulations. Specifically, the ordinance requires that donors be tested for hepatitis prior to registration, that they donate at only one center, and that they be given a breath analysis for alcohol content before each plasma donation....

In arguing that the Hillsborough County ordinances and regulations are pre-empted, appellee faces an uphill battle. The first hurdle that appellee must overcome is the FDA's statement, when it promulgated the plasmapheresis regulations in 1973, that it did not intend its regulations to be exclusive. In response to comments expressing concern that the regulations governing the licensing of plasmapheresis facilities "would pre-empt State and local laws governing plasmapheresis," the FDA explained in a statement accompanying the regulations that "[t]hese regulations are not intended to usurp the powers of State or local authorities to regulate plasmapheresis procedures in their localities."

The FDA's statement is dispositive on the question of implicit intent to pre-empt unless either the agency's position is inconsistent with clearly expressed congressional intent, or subsequent developments reveal a change in that position. Given appellee's first argument for implicit pre-emption—that the comprehensiveness of the FDA's regulations evinces an intent to pre-empt—any pre-emptive effect must result from the change since 1973 in the comprehensiveness of the federal regulations. To prevail on its second argument for implicit pre-emption—the dominance of the federal interest in plasmapheresis regulation—appellee must show either that this interest became more compelling since 1973, or that, in 1973, the FDA seriously underestimated the federal interest in plasmapheresis regulation.

The second obstacle in appellee's path is the presumption that state or local regulation of matters related to health and safety is not invalidated under the Supremacy Clause. Through the challenged ordinances, Hillsborough County has attempted to protect the health of its plasma donors by preventing them from donating too frequently. It also has attempted to ensure the quality of the plasma collected so as to protect, in turn, the recipients of such plasma. "Where ... the field that Congress is said to have pre-empted has been traditionally occupied by the States 'we start with the assumption that the historic police powers of the States were not to be superseded by the Federal Act unless that was the clear and manifest purpose of Congress.'" Of course, the same principles apply where, as here, the field is said to have been pre-empted by an agency, acting pursuant to congressional delegation....

Given the clear indication of the FDA's intention *not to pre-empt* and the deference with which we must review the challenged ordinances, we conclude that these ordinances are not pre-empted by the federal scheme.

We reject the argument that an intent to pre-empt may be inferred from the comprehensiveness of the FDA's regulations at issue here.... The FDA has not indicated that the new regulations affected its disavowal in 1973 of any intent to pre-empt state and local regulation, and the fact that the federal scheme was expanded to reach other uses of plasma does not cast doubt on the continued validity of that disavowal.

We are even more reluctant to infer pre-emption from the comprehensiveness of regulations than from the comprehensiveness of statutes. As a result of their specialized functions, agencies normally deal with problems in far more detail than does Congress. To infer pre-emption whenever an agency deals with a problem comprehensively is virtually tantamount to saying that whenever a federal agency decides to step into a field, its regulations will be exclusive....

Moreover, because agencies normally address problems in a detailed manner and can speak through a variety of means, including regulations, preambles, interpretive statements, and responses to comments, we can expect that they will make their intentions clear if they intend for their regulations to be exclusive. Thus, if an agency does not speak to the question of pre-emption, we will pause before saying that the mere volume and complexity of its regulations indicate that the agency did in fact intend to pre-empt....

Appellee's second argument for pre-emption of the whole field of plasmapheresis regulation is that an intent to pre-empt can be inferred from the dominant federal interest in this field. We are unpersuaded by the argument. Undoubtedly, every subject that merits congressional legislation is, by definition, a subject of national concern. That cannot mean, however, that every federal statute ousts all related state law. Neither does the Supremacy Clause require us to rank congressional enactments in order of "importance." ...

Instead, we must look for special features warranting pre-emption. Our case law provides us with clear standards to guide our inquiry in this area. For example, in the seminal case of *Hines v. Davidowitz*, 312 U.S. 52 (1941), the Court inferred an intent to pre-empt from the dominance of the federal interest in foreign affairs because "the supremacy of the national power in the general field of foreign affairs ... is made clear by the Constitution," and the regulation of that field is "intimately blended and intertwined with responsibilities of the national government." Needless to say, those factors are absent here. Rather, as we have stated, the regulation of health and safety matters is primarily, and historically, a matter of local concern.

. . . .

Appellee's final argument is that even if the regulations are not comprehensive enough and the federal interest is not dominant enough to pre-empt the entire field of plasmapheresis regulation, the Hillsborough County ordinances must be struck down because they conflict with the federal scheme. Appellee argues principally that the challenged ordinances impose on plasma centers and donors requirements more stringent than those imposed by the federal regulations, and therefore that they present a serious obstacle to the federal goal of ensuring an "adequate supply of plasma." We find this concern too speculative to support pre-emption. . . .

Finally, the FDA possesses the authority to promulgate regulations pre-empting local legislation that imperils the supply of plasma and can do so with relative ease. Moreover, the agency can be expected to monitor, on a continuing basis, the effects on the federal program of local requirements. Thus, since the agency has not suggested that the county ordinances interfere with federal goals, we are reluctant in the absence of strong evidence to find a threat to the federal goal of ensuring sufficient plasma. . . .

NOTES

1. *State Regulation of Blood Products.* On remand, the Hillsborough ordinances were upheld. *Immuno International, A.G. v. Hillsborough County, Florida,* 775 F.2d 1430 (11th Cir. 1985). Compare *State v. Interstate Blood Bank, Inc.,* 222 N.W.2d 912 (Wis. 1974), which overturned the defendant's conviction for unlawfully operating a commercial blood bank, declaring Wisconsin's statute unconstitutional under the Commerce and Supremacy Clauses. While conceding that protecting the health of both donors and recipients was a legitimate objective of the police power, the court held that the statute unduly burdened interstate commerce because other similarly federally licensed blood banks relied on defendant to supply blood interstate and the purpose of federal regulations was also to insure the safety, purity and potency of the product. *See also Samuels v. Health & Hospital Corp. of the City of New York,* 432 F. Supp. 1283 (S.D.N.Y. 1977) (holding that classification of blood as a "drug" under the FD&C Act does not preempt a different classification for purposes of state product liability law).

2. *Agency Purpose to Preempt.* The Supreme Court, relying upon *United States v. Shimer,* 367 U.S. 374 (1961), has frequently emphasized that an agency's intent to preempt state regulation, if clear, will usually be decisive. *See, e.g., City of New York v. FCC,* 486 U.S. 57, 64 (1988); *Capital Cities Cable, Inc. v. Crisp,* 467 U.S. 691, 698–700 (1984); *Fidelity Federal Savings & Loan Association v. de la Cuesta,* 458 U.S. 141, 152–54 (1982).

3. *Scope of Agency Preemption.* Professor Susan Bartlett Foote argues that Federal agencies like FDA should preempt only product design/performance standards, minimum safety requirements, and requirements applicable to interstate packaging, and should leave the states free to impose more stringent safety requirements, labeling requirements, and other conditions of sale, and restrictions on use (including a ban). Susan Bartlett Foote, *Administrative Preemption: An Experiment in Regulatory Federalism,* 70 VA. L. REV. 1429 (1984).

D. FDA AUTHORITY TO PREEMPT STATE LAW

In *Hillsborough County*, the Supreme Court confidently declared that FDA "possess[es] the authority to promulgate regulations preempting local legislation that imperils the supply of plasma." However, no provision of the Biologics Act (or the FD&C Act for that matter) confers such authority in so many words. Arguably the agency can rely on section 701(a) of the FD&C Act, which authorizes regulations that aid "efficient enforcement," but this language falls short of an explicit conferral of power to preempt. Moreover, section 701(a) does not apply to the Biologics Act, the statute under which FDA regulates blood. Nonetheless, the modern cases appear to assume, and some expressly declare, that FDA has authority to nullify any state law or regulation that it believes might interfere with the implementation of federal requirements.

Beginning in the late 1970s, the California Department of Health proposed to require that all nonprescription drugs include a warning that the drug's safety during pregnancy or nursing is unknown, unless the manufacturer secured an exemption by submitting substantial evidence that the warning was not needed. On four occasions, FDA opposed issuance of the proposed regulation. The California Office of Administrative Law disapproved the regulation, but California Governor Brown overruled that decision in October 1981. The matter was then resolved by the enactment of an amendment to Section 10381 of the California Health and Safety Code, effective November 18, 1992, which required the label of any nonprescription drug intended for systemic absorption into the human body to include the following warning:

Caution: If pregnant or nursing a baby, consult your physician or pharmacist before using this product.

Two months earlier, in 47 Fed. Reg. 39470 (Sept. 7, 1982), FDA proposed a similar warning for all systemically absorbed nonprescription drugs. The agency invited comments on the preemptive effect the proposed warning should have on state labeling requirements. Three months later it issued a final regulation.

Pregnant or Nursing Women; Amendment of Labeling Requirements for Over-the-Counter Human Drugs

47 Fed. Reg. 54750 (December 3, 1982).

. . . .

Several comments that were submitted in response to the agency's invitation for comments on the preemptive effect the FDA warning would have on the California and other similar State OTC drug labeling requirements supported FDA's view that a Federal pregnancy-nursing warning requirement would preempt State pregnancy-nursing warnings. . . .

A comment submitted by the California Department of Health Services, however, opposed the statements in the proposal on the preemptive effects of the FDA warning on general legal and policy grounds.... The Federal Food, Drug, and Cosmetic Act does not expressly preempt State activity relating to OTC drug labeling. Therefore, in determining whether FDA's pregnancy-nursing warning preempts California's warning, the doctrine of implied preemption must be applied. As stated in the proposed rule, a single national pregnancy-nursing warning with a specified text is necessary to ensure that OTC drugs are used safely and for their intended purposes. A single national warning will help ensure that consumers receive clear, unambiguous, and consistent information on the labeling of OTC drugs concerning use by pregnant or nursing women. Differing State requirements could conflict with the Federal warning, cause confusion to consumers, and otherwise weaken the Federal warning. FDA believes that differing State OTC drug pregnancy-nursing warning requirements would prevent accomplishment of the full purpose and objectives of the agency in issuing the regulation and that, under the doctrine of implied preemption, these State requirements are preempted by the regulation as a matter of law.

As noted in the proposal, the California warning allows for the use of pregnancy-nursing warnings that are "substantially similar" to the California requirement. In view of comments made by the California Department of Health Services, the FDA warning would appear to meet the California "substantially similar" exception. Therefore, under these circumstances, the issue appears to be academic: manufacturers who use the FDA warning would also be in compliance with the California requirement.

FDA shares the concerns of the comments that States may elect to regulate aspects of OTC drug labeling other than pregnancy-nursing warnings. The agency is concerned that a proliferation of such State requirements may weaken FDA's efforts to develop comprehensive national labeling and other requirements for OTC drugs. The current regulation, however, is intended to apply only to one aspect of OTC drug labeling: pregnancy-nursing warnings....

The California warning requirement becomes effective on November 18, 1982. FDA regards the California requirement as preempted as of the date of publication of this regulation....

NOTES

1. *FDA's Legal Rationale?* Why, if California law would be satisfied by the warning that FDA has prescribed, did the agency consider it necessary to add the final sentence quoted above? And what is the effect of FDA's statement that it regards the California requirement as preempted? Does this determination have the force of law, or is it simply FDA's prediction of how a court would—or should—rule in an actual case?

2. *Tamper–Resistant Packaging.* Following the purposeful cyanide contamination of Extra–Strength Tylenol capsules in Chicago, FDA promulgated tamper-resistant packaging requirements for other OTC drugs. In the preamble to the final rule, the agency declared:

> FDA intends that the regulations issued in this document preempt State and local packaging requirements that are not identical to it in all respects,

including those relating to the use of alternative tamper-resistant packaging systems, the coverage of the regulations within the product categories addressed, the label statement alternating [sic] consumers, exemptions, and effective dates.

47 Fed. Reg. 50442, 50447–48 (Nov. 5, 1982). Does this language suggest that FDA believes it has the independent authority to preempt state law?

3. *Reye Syndrome Warning.* In 50 Fed. Reg. 51400 (Dec. 17, 1985), FDA proposed to require that the labeling of oral nonprescription aspirin products bear a warning about the risk of Reye syndrome. In response to comments, the agency announced in the preamble to the final regulation that "FDA intends that the regulations issued in this document preempt State and local packaging requirements that are not identical to it." 51 Fed. Reg. 8180, 8181 (Mar. 7, 1986).

4. *Reagan Era Federalism.* President Reagan encouraged efforts to return responsibility for many governmental activities to the States. However, C. Boyden Gray, Counsel to Vice President Bush, wrote that the President recognized

> that state and local administration of regulatory programs may conflict in some instances with other goals of regulatory relief or with other important federal interests. For example, individual states may operate specific programs more effectively than the federal government, but the combined effect of disparate state regulatory standards may intolerably burden interstate commerce, thus requiring uniform federal regulation.

Acknowledging "the need for a strong central government to promote commerce and other federal interests," Gray distinguished between those activities that are primarily local and those that involve such "burdens on interstate commerce" that national uniformity is required. C. Boyden Gray, *Regulation and Federalism*, 1 YALE J. ON REG. 93, 95–96 (1983).

The FINAL REPORT OF THE PRESIDENTIAL TASK FORCE ON REGULATORY RELIEF 51 (Aug. 11, 1983) declared:

> [R]egulating the safety of drugs and food additives is appropriate to the federal government, since the products being regulated are usually marketed on a nationwide basis, differing state standards could impose large costs on interstate commerce, and benefits of multiple approaches to screening new drugs are small.

Four years later, in 52 Fed. Reg. 41685 (Oct. 30, 1987), President Reagan issued Executive Order No. 12612 on Federalism. The order encouraged "healthy diversity" in the public policies among the several states. Federal action limiting the policy making discretion of the states is to be taken only where "the national activity is necessitated by the presence of a problem of national scope." Agencies were directed to preempt local regulation "only when the statute contains an express preemption provision or there is some other firm and palpable evidence compelling the conclusion that the Congress intended preemption of State law, or when the exercise of State authority directly conflicts with the exercise of Federal authority under the Federal statute." *See also* President George H. W. Bush's "Memorandum on Federalism" 26 Week. Comp. Pres. Doc. 264 (Feb. 16, 1990).

E. STATUTORY PREEMPTION

1. THE SILENT 1962 DRUG AMENDMENTS

During the debates on the bill that eventually became the Drug Amendments of 1962, 108 Cong. Rec. 21083 (Sept. 27, 1962), the House adopted language explicitly declaring that:

"Nothing in the Federal Food, Drug, and Cosmetic Act, as amended, shall be construed as invalidating any provision of State law which would be valid in the absence of such Act unless there is a direct and positive conflict between such Act and such provision of State law." . . .

The Conference Committee revised this provision to make it applicable only to the legislation immediately under consideration. H.R. Rep. No. 2526 87th Cong., 2d Sess. 15 (1962).

The provision that Congress ultimately enacted, 76 Stat. 793 (1962), states:

Nothing in the amendments made by this Act to the Federal Food, Drug, and Cosmetic Act shall be construed as invalidating any provision of State law which would be valid in the absence of such amendments unless there is a direct and positive conflict between such amendments and such provision of State law.

In light of this language it is hardly surprising that no case has interpreted the 1962 Amendments, or any provision thereof, as independently preempting state statutes or regulations absent a direct conflict.

2. THE AMBIGUOUS MEDICAL DEVICE AMENDMENTS

In the 1976 Medical Device Amendments, Congress attempted to define the federal and state roles in the regulation of medical instrumentation. The result is section 521 of the FD&C Act, which reads:

Sec. 521(a) Except as provided in subsection (b), no State or political subdivision of a State may establish or continue in effect with respect to a device intended for human use any requirement—

(1) which is different from, or in addition to, any requirement applicable under this Act to the device, and

(2) which relates to the safety or effectiveness of the device or to any other matter included in a requirement applicable to the device under this Act.

(b) Upon application of a State or a political subdivision thereof, the Secretary may, by regulation promulgated after notice and opportunity for an oral hearing, exempt from subsection (a), under such conditions as may be prescribed in such regulation, a requirement of such State or political subdivision applicable to a device intended for human use if

(1) the requirement is more stringent than a requirement under this Act which would be applicable to the device if an exemption were not in effect under this subsection; or

(2) the requirement

(A) is required by compelling local conditions, and

(B) compliance with the requirement would not cause the device to be in violation of any applicable requirement under this Act.

Medical Device Amendments of 1976: House Report No. 94–853

94th Congress, 2d Session (1976).

In the absence of effective Federal regulation of medical devices, some States have established their own programs. The most comprehensive State regulation of which the Committee is aware is that of California, which in 1970 adopted the Sherman Food, Drug, and Cosmetic Law. This law requires premarket approval of all new medical devices, requires compliance of device manufacturers with good manufacturing practices and authorizes inspection of establishments which manufacture devices. . . .

Because there are some situations in which regulation of devices by States and localities would constitute a useful supplement to Federal regulation, the reported bill authorizes a State or political subdivision thereof to petition the Secretary for exemptions from the bill's general prohibition of non-Federal regulation. . . .

In the Committee's view, requirements imposed under the California statute serve as an example of requirements that the Secretary should authorize to be continued (provided any application submitted by a State meets requirements pursuant to the reported bill). . . .

———

Soon after passage of the Amendments, FDA proposed, 42 Fed. Reg. 30383 (June 14, 1977), and later promulgated, regulations describing its understanding of section 521.

Exemptions From Federal Preemption of State and Local Device Requirements

43 Fed. Reg. 18661 (May 2, 1978).

. . . .

Many comments stated that there is no basis in the act or in the legislative history to justify the interpretation of section 521 of the act set forth in the first sentence of proposed § 808.1(d). That sentence stated that State and local requirements are preempted only when FDA has established specific counterpart regulations or there are other specific requirements applicable to a particular device under the act, thereby making any existing divergent State or local requirements applicable to the device different from, or in addition to, the specific FDA requirements. . . .

. . . [F]rom a plain reading of section 521 of the act it is clear that the scope of preemption is limited to instances where there are specific FDA requirements applicable to a particular device or class of devices. . . . [A] prime example is the preemption of divergent State or local requirements relating to hearing aid labeling and conditions for sale, which occurred when the new FDA hearing aid regulations took effect on August 25, 1977. Here, only requirements relating to labeling and conditions for sale were preempted, not all State or local requirements regulating other facets of hearing aid distribution....

... [I]nterpretations urged by the comments would provide less public protection from unsafe and ineffective medical devices because State and local regulation of medical devices would be reduced or eliminated before compensating FDA regulations could become effective....

The Commissioner also believes that the [agency's] interpretation ... will not cause an undue burden on interstate commerce because it merely allows State and local requirements to continue in effect until FDA establishes a national policy on the regulation of specific devices. Thus, since there is no duplication between FDA and State programs, there is no greater burden on interstate commerce than if the Amendments had not been enacted.

Several comments stated that there is no basis in the act or in the legislative history for the statement in proposed § 808.1(d)(2) that section 521(a) does not preempt State or local requirements that are equal to, or substantially identical to, requirements imposed by or under the Act.... The Commissioner believes that a common sense reading of section 521 of the act supports the "substantially identical" concept in § 808.1(d)(2). Thus, while a State or local requirement may differ in some nonessential manner from an FDA requirement, if it is substantially identical to an FDA requirement it is not "different from" the FDA requirement within the meaning of section 521, and therefore not preempted....

The Commissioner also cannot accept the argument that an identical State or local requirement is preempted because it is "in addition to" the FDA requirement. Such an interpretation of section 521 renders meaningless the "different from" language of section 521 because under this theory any State and local requirement would be preempted whether or not it was actually "different from" an FDA requirement....

The Commissioner believes that State laws relating to inspection, registration, and licensing usually are not requirements "with respect to a device" within the meaning of section 521 of the act because they generally pertain either to persons who manufacture or distribute devices or to places where devices are manufactured, and not directly to devices. In order for a State provision to be a requirement with respect to a device within the meaning of section 521 of the act—and thereby a candidate for preemption—it must relate to the device itself....

NOTES

1. *California Exemption Application.* In 1977, FDA received an application from California for an exemption from section 521's preemption of its medical device requirements. In 42 Fed. Reg. 9186 (Feb. 15, 1977), the agency published a proposed regulation to grant the application, with one exception. After reproposing the regulation, FDA, in 45 Fed. Reg. 67321 (Oct. 10, 1980), issued a final rule granting some exemptions while denying others.

2. *FDA Exemption Regulations.* FDA's regulations governing exemptions from preemption of state medical device laws, and the specific exemptions that have been granted, are codified in 21 C.F.R. Part 808.

3. *Successful State Petitions.* As of October 2006, FDA had received 47 petitions from states to exempt their device laws from preemption. It had granted 22 and denied 25. Twenty-two states have had one or more requirements restored through this process.

4. *Hearing Aid Controls.* In response to the applications of Massachusetts and Rhode Island for exemptions from preemption of state hearing aid requirements, FDA issued proposed regulations in 44 Fed. Reg. 22119 (Apr. 13, 1979) and, after a public hearing, promulgated final regulations in 45 Fed. Reg. 67325 (Oct. 10, 1980). Massachusetts challenged FDA's denial of its application for an exemption for two provisions of its statute governing the sale of hearing aids, contending that the agency's published criteria for exemptions were invalid because they permit broad consideration of "the best interest of public health, taking into account the potential burden on interstate commerce." 21 C.F.R. 808.25(g)(3). The First Circuit approved both FDA's criteria for exemptions from preemption and its action on the Massachusetts application. *Commonwealth of Massachusetts v. Hayes,* 691 F.2d 57 (1st Cir. 1982). For a discussion of the circumstances under which state hearing aid requirements are not preempted, see 55 Fed. Reg. 23984 (June 13, 1990). State hearing aid requirements were upheld in *Smith v. Pingree,* 651 F.2d 1021 (5th Cir. 1981); *New Jersey Guild of Hearing Aid Dispensers v. Long,* 384 A.2d 795 (N.J. 1978).

5. *Suntanning Equipment.* In 1988, in response to a request for an advisory opinion on whether a city may ban the use of indoor commercial tanning equipment, FDA said it had to consider both section 521 of the FD&C Act and the preemption provisions applicable to radiation-emitting electronic products under section 360F of the Public Health Service Act (now FD&C Act section 541). FDA advised that section 521 does not preempt the city ordinance because the agency had not promulgated any requirements under the FD&C Act applicable to the use of sun tanning equipment, and that section 360F does not preempt because the ordinance does not establish a standard applicable to the performance of suntanning equipment. Letter from J. M. Taylor to D. R. Kalins, FDA Dkt. No. 87A–0201 (June 20, 1988).

Medtronic, Inc. v. Lohr

518 U.S. 470 (1996).

■ JUSTICE STEVENS announced the judgment of the Court and delivered the opinion of the Court with respect to Parts I, II, III, V, and VII, and an opinion with respect to Parts IV and VI, in which JUSTICE KENNEDY, JUSTICE SOUTER, and JUSTICE GINSBURG join.

Congress enacted the Medical Device Amendments of 1976, in the words of the statute's preamble, "to provide for the safety and effectiveness of medical devices intended for human use." 90 Stat. 539. The question presented is whether that statute pre-empts a state common-law negligence action against the manufacturer of an allegedly defective medical device....

I.

Throughout our history the several States have exercised their police powers to protect the health and safety of their citizens....

Despite the prominence of the States in matters of public health and safety, in recent decades the Federal Government has played an increasingly significant role in the protection of the health of our people. . . .

In response to the mounting consumer and regulatory concern, Congress enacted the statute at issue here: the Medical Device Amendments of 1976 (MDA or Act). The Act classifies medical devices in three categories based on the risk that they pose to the public. . . . Pacemakers are Class III devices.

Before a new Class III device may be introduced to the market, the manufacturer must provide the FDA with a "reasonable assurance" that the device is both safe and effective. Despite its relatively innocuous phrasing, the process of establishing this "reasonable assurance," which is known as the "premarket approval," or "PMA" process, is a rigorous one.

Not all, nor even most, Class III devices on the market today have received premarket approval because of two important exceptions to the PMA requirement. First, Congress realized that existing medical devices could not be withdrawn from the market while the FDA completed its PMA analysis for those devices. The statute therefore includes a "grandfathering" provision which allows pre-1976 devices to remain on the market without FDA approval until such time as the FDA initiates and completes the requisite PMA. Second, to prevent manufacturers of grandfathered devices from monopolizing the market while new devices clear the PMA hurdle, and to ensure that improvements to existing devices can be rapidly introduced into the market, the Act also permits devices that are "substantially equivalent" to pre-existing devices to avoid the PMA process.

II.

As have so many other medical device manufacturers, petitioner Medtronic took advantage of § 510(k)'s expedited process in October 1982, when it notified the FDA that it intended to market its Model 4011 pacemaker lead as a device that was "substantially equivalent" to devices already on the market. (The lead is the portion of a pacemaker that transmits the heartbeat-steadying electrical signal from the "pulse generator" to the heart itself.) On November 30, 1982, the FDA found that the model was "substantially equivalent to devices introduced into interstate commerce" prior to the effective date of the Act, and advised Medtronic that it could therefore market its device subject only to the general control provisions of the Act, which could be found in the Code of Federal Regulations. . . .

Cross-petitioner Lora Lohr is dependent on pacemaker technology for the proper functioning of her heart. In 1987 she was implanted with a Medtronic pacemaker equipped with one of the company's Model 4011 pacemaker leads. On December 30, 1990, the pacemaker failed, allegedly resulting in a "complete heart block" that required emergency surgery. . . .

In 1993 Lohr and her husband filed this action in a Florida state court. Their complaint contained both a negligence count and a strict liability count. The negligence count alleged a breach of Medtronic's "duty to use reasonable care in the design, manufacture, assembly, and sale of the subject pacemaker" in several respects, including the use of defective materials in the lead and a failure to warn or properly instruct the plaintiff or her physicians of the tendency of the pacemaker to fail, despite knowledge of other earlier failures. The strict-liability count alleged that the device was in a defective condition and unreasonably dangerous to foreseeable users at the time of its sale. . . .

Medtronic removed the case to Federal District Court, where it filed a motion for summary judgment arguing that both the negligence and strict-liability claims were pre-empted by 21 U.S.C. § 360k(a). . . .

III.

. . . While the pre-emptive language of § 360k(a) [FD&C Act section 521] means that we need not go beyond that language to determine whether Congress intended the MDA to pre-empt at least some state law, we must nonetheless "identify the domain expressly pre-empted" by that language. Although our analysis of the scope of the pre-emption statute must begin with its text, our interpretation of that language does not occur in a contextual vacuum. Rather, that interpretation is informed by two presumptions about the nature of pre-emption.

First, because the States are independent sovereigns in our federal system, we have long presumed that Congress does not cavalierly pre-empt state-law causes of action. . . .

Second, our analysis of the scope of the statute's pre-emption is guided by our oft-repeated comment that the purpose of Congress is the ultimate "touch-stone" in every pre-emption case. . . .

IV.

In its petition, Medtronic argues that the Court of Appeals erred by concluding that the Lohrs' claims alleging negligent design were not pre-empted by 21 U.S.C. § 360k(a). That section provides that "no State or political subdivision of a State may establish or continue in effect with respect to a device intended for human use any requirement (1) which is different from, or in addition to, any requirement applicable under this chapter to the device, and (2) which relates to the safety or effectiveness of the device or to any other matter included in a requirement applicable to the device under this chapter." Medtronic suggests that any common-law cause of action is a "requirement" which alters incentives and imposes duties "different from, or in addition to," the generic federal standards that the FDA has promulgated in response to mandates under the MDA. In essence, the company argues that the plain language of the statute pre-empts any and all common-law claims brought by an injured plaintiff against a manufacturer of medical devices.

Medtronic's argument is not only unpersuasive, it is implausible. Under Medtronic's view of the statute, Congress effectively precluded state courts from affording state consumers any protection from injuries resulting from a defective medical device. Moreover, because there is no explicit private cause of action against manufacturers contained in the MDA, and no suggestion that the Act created an implied private right of action, Congress would have barred most, if not all, relief for persons injured by defective medical devices. Medtronic's construction of § 360k would therefore have the perverse effect of granting complete immunity from design defect liability to an entire industry that, in the judgment of Congress, needed more stringent regulation in order "to provide for the safety and effectiveness of medical devices intended for human use," 90 Stat. 539 (preamble to Act). It is, to say the least, "difficult to believe that Congress would, without comment, remove all means of judicial recourse for those injured by illegal conduct," and it would take language much plainer than the text of § 360k to convince us that Congress intended that result.

. . . .

An examination of the basic purpose of the legislation as well as its history entirely supports our rejection of Medtronic's extreme position. The MDA was enacted "to provide for the safety and effectiveness of medical devices intended for human use." Medtronic asserts that the Act was also intended, however, to "protect innovations in device technology from being 'stifled by unnecessary restrictions,' " and that this interest extended to the pre-emption of common-law claims. While the Act certainly reflects some of these concerns, the legislative history indicates that any fears regarding regulatory burdens were related more to the risk of *additional* federal and state regulation rather than the danger of pre-existing duties under common law. Indeed, nowhere in the materials relating to the Act's history have we discovered a reference to a fear that product liability actions would hamper the development of medical devices. . . .

V.

Medtronic asserts several specific reasons why, even if § 360k does not pre-empt all common-law claims, it at least pre-empts the Lohrs' claims in this suit. In contrast, the Lohrs argue that their entire complaint should survive a reasonable evaluation of the pre-emptive scope of § 360k(a). . . .

Design Claim

The Court of Appeals concluded that the Lohrs' defective design claims were not pre-empted because the requirements with which the company had to comply were not sufficiently concrete to constitute a pre-empting federal requirement. Medtronic counters by pointing to the FDA's determination that Model 4011 is "substantially equivalent" to an earlier device as well as the agency's continuing authority to exclude the device from the market if its design is changed. These factors, Medtronic argues, amount to a specific, federally enforceable design requirement that cannot be affected by state-law pressures such as those imposed on manufacturers subject to product liability suits.

The company's defense exaggerates the importance of the § 510(k) process and the FDA letter to the company regarding the pacemaker's substantial equivalence to a grand-fathered device. . . . "[S]ubstantial equivalence determinations provide little protection to the public. These determinations simply compare a post-1976 device to a pre-1976 device to ascertain whether the later device is no more dangerous and no less effective than the earlier device. If the earlier device poses a severe risk or is ineffective, then the later device may also be risky or ineffective." The design of the Model 4011, as with the design of pre-1976 and other "substantially equivalent" devices, has never been formally reviewed under the MDA for safety or efficacy.

The FDA stressed this basic conclusion in its letter to Medtronic finding the 4011 lead "substantially equivalent" to devices already on the market. That letter only required Medtronic to comply with "general standards"—the lowest level of protection "applicable to all medical devices," and including "listing of devices, good manufacturing practices, labeling, and the misbranding and adulteration provisions of the Act." It explicitly warned Medtronic that the letter did "not in any way denote official FDA approval of your device," and that "any representation that creates an impression of official approval of this device because of compliance with the premarket notification regulations is misleading and constitutes misbranding."

Thus, even though the FDA may well examine § 510(k) applications for Class III devices (as it examines the entire medical device industry) with a concern for the safety and effectiveness of the device, it did not "require" Medtronics' pacemaker to take any particular form for any particular reason; the agency simply allowed the pacemaker, as a device substantially equivalent to one that existed before 1976, to be marketed without running the gauntlet of the PMA process. In providing for this exemption to PMA review, Congress intended merely to give manufacturers the freedom to compete, to a limited degree, with and on the same terms as manufacturers of medical devices that existed prior to 1976.

Identity of Requirements Claims

... Although the precise contours of [the Lohrs'] theory of recovery have not yet been defined (the pre-emption issue was decided on the basis of the pleadings), it is clear that the Lohrs' allegations may include claims that Medtronic has, to the extent that they exist, violated FDA regulations. At least these claims, they suggest, can be maintained without being preempted by § 360k, and we agree.

Nothing in § 360k denies Florida the right to provide a traditional damages remedy for violations of common-law duties when those duties parallel federal requirements. Even if it may be necessary as a matter of Florida law to prove that those violations were the result of negligent conduct, or that they created an unreasonable hazard for users of the product, such additional elements of the state-law cause of action would make the state requirements narrower, not broader, than the federal requirement. While such a narrower requirement might be "different from" the federal rules in a literal sense, such a difference would surely provide a strange reason for finding pre-emption of a state rule insofar as it duplicates the federal rule. The presence of a damages remedy does not amount to the additional or different "requirement" that is necessary under the statute; rather, it merely provides another reason for manufacturers to comply with identical existing "requirements" under federal law.

The FDA regulations interpreting the scope of § 360k's pre-emptive effect [21 CFR 808.1] support the Lohrs' view, and our interpretation of the pre-emption statute is substantially informed by those regulations. The different views expressed by the Courts of Appeals regarding the appropriate scope of federal pre-emption under § 360k demonstrate that the language of that section is not entirely clear. In addition, Congress has given the FDA a unique role in determining the scope of § 360k's pre-emptive effect.... [P]re-emption under the MDA does not arise directly as a result of the enactment of the statute; rather, in most cases a state law will be pre-empted only to the extent that the FDA has promulgated a relevant federal "requirement." Because the FDA is the federal agency to which Congress has delegated its authority to implement the provisions of the Act, the agency is uniquely qualified to determine whether a particular form of state law "stands as an obstacle to the accomplishment and execution of the full purposes and objectives of Congress," and, therefore, whether it should be pre-empted.... The ambiguity in the statute—and the congressional grant of authority to the agency on the matter contained within it—provide a "sound basis" for giving substantial weight to the agency's view of the statute. *See Chevron U.S.A. Inc. v. Natural Resources Defense Council, Inc.*, 467 U.S. 837 (1984).

The regulations promulgated by the FDA expressly support the conclusion that § 360k "does not preempt State or local requirements that are equal to, or substantially identical to, requirements imposed by or under the act." ...

Manufacturing and Labeling Claims

... The Court of Appeals believed that these claims would interfere with the consistent application of general federal regulations governing the labeling and manufacture of all medical devices, and therefore concluded that the claims were pre-empted altogether.

The requirements identified by the Court of Appeals include labeling regulations that require manufacturers of every medical device, with a few limited exceptions, to include with the device a label containing "information for use, ... and any relevant hazards, contraindications, side effects, and precautions." Similarly, manufacturers are required to comply with "Good Manufacturing Practices," or "GMP's," which are set forth in 32 sections and less than 10 pages in the Code of Federal Regulations. In certain circumstances, the Court of Appeals recognized, the FDA will enforce these general requirements against manufacturers that violate them.

While admitting that these requirements exist, the Lohrs suggest that their general nature simply does not pre-empt claims alleging that the manufacturer failed to comply with other duties under state common law. In support of their claim, they note that § 360k(a)(1) expressly states that a federal requirement must be "applicable to the device" in question before it has any pre-emptive effect. Because the labeling and manufacturing requirements are applicable to a host of different devices, they argue that they do not satisfy this condition. They further argue that because only state requirements "with respect to a device" may be pre-empted, and then only if the requirement "relates to the safety or effectiveness of the device or to any other matter included in a requirement applicable to the device," § 360k(a) mandates pre-emption only where there is a conflict between a specific state requirement and a federal requirement "applicable to" the same device.

The Lohrs' theory is supported by the FDA regulations, which provide that state requirements are pre-empted "only" when the FDA has established "specific counterpart regulations or ... other specific requirements applicable to a particular device." 21 C.F.R. 808.1(d). They further note that the statute is not intended to pre-empt "State or local requirements of general applicability where the purpose of the requirement relates either to other products in addition to devices ... or to unfair trade practices in which the requirements are not limited to devices." ...

Although we do not believe that this statutory and regulatory language necessarily precludes "general" federal requirements from ever pre-empting state requirements, or "general" state requirements from ever being pre-empted, it is impossible to ignore its overarching concern that pre-emption occur only where a particular state requirement threatens to interfere with a specific federal interest.... The statute and regulations, therefore, require a careful comparison between the allegedly pre-empting federal requirement and the allegedly pre-empted state requirement to determine whether they fall within the intended pre-emptive scope of the statute and regulations.

Such a comparison mandates a conclusion that the Lohrs' common-law claims are not pre-empted by the federal labeling and manufacturing requirements. The generality of those requirements make this quite unlike a case in which the Federal Government has weighed the competing interests relevant to the particular requirement in question, reached an unambiguous conclusion about how those competing considerations should be resolved in a particular case or set of cases, and implemented that conclusion via a specific mandate on manufacturers or producers. Rather, the federal requirements reflect important but entirely generic concerns about device regulation generally, not the sort of concerns regarding a specific device or field of device regulation that the statute or regulations were designed to protect from potentially contradictory state requirements.

Similarly, the general state common-law requirements in this suit were not specifically developed "with respect to" medical devices. Accordingly, they are not the kinds of requirements that Congress and the FDA feared would impede the ability of federal regulators to implement and enforce specific federal requirements. The legal duty that is the predicate for the Lohrs' negligent manufacturing claim is the general duty of every manufacturer to use due care to avoid foreseeable dangers in its products. Similarly, the predicate for the failure to warn claim is the general duty to inform users and purchasers of potentially dangerous items of the risks involved in their use. These general obligations are no more a threat to federal requirements than would be a state-law duty to comply with local fire prevention regulations and zoning codes, or to use due care in the training and supervision of a work force. These state requirements therefore escape pre-emption, not because the source of the duty is a judge-made common-law rule, but rather because their generality leaves them outside the category of requirements that § 360k envisioned to be "with respect to" specific devices such as pacemakers. As a result, none of the Lohrs' claims based on allegedly defective manufacturing or labeling are pre-empted by the MDA.

VI.

In their cross-petition, the Lohrs present a final argument, suggesting that common-law duties are never "requirements" within the meaning of § 360k and that the statute therefore never pre-empts common-law actions. . . .

. . . [W]e do not respond directly to this argument for two reasons. First, since none of the Lohrs' claims is pre-empted in this suit, we need not resolve hypothetical cases that may arise in the future. Second, given the critical importance of device specificity in our (and the FDA's) construction of § 360k, it is apparent that few, if any, common-law duties have been pre-empted by this statute. It will be rare indeed for a court hearing a common-law cause of action to issue a decree that has "the effect of establishing a substantive requirement for a specific device." Until such a case arises, we see no need to determine whether the statute explicitly pre-empts such a claim. Even then, the issue may not need to be resolved if the claim would also be pre-empted under conflict pre-emption analysis, see *Freightliner Corp. v. Myrick*, 514 U.S. 280 (1995).

■ JUSTICE BREYER, concurring in part and concurring in the judgment.

This action raises two questions. First, do the Medical Device Amendments of 1976 (MDA) to the Federal Food, Drug, and Cosmetic Act ever pre-empt a state-law tort action? Second, if so, does the MDA pre-empt the particular state-law tort claims at issue here?

I.

My answer to the first question is that the MDA will sometimes pre-empt a state-law tort suit. . . . The statute's language, read literally, supports that conclusion. . . .

One can reasonably read the word "requirement" as including the legal requirements that grow out of the application, in particular circumstances, of a State's tort law.

. . . .

. . . [A] contrary holding would have anomalous consequences. Imagine that, in respect to a particular hearing aid component, a federal MDA regulation requires a 2-inch wire, but a state agency regulation requires a 1-inch wire. If the federal law, embodied in the "2-inch" MDA regulation, pre-empts the state "1-inch" agency regulation, why would it not similarly pre-empt a state-law tort action that premises liability upon the defendant manufacturer's failure to use a 1-inch wire (say, an award by a jury persuaded by expert testimony that use of a more than 1-inch wire is negligent)? The effects of the state agency regulation and the state tort suit are identical. To distinguish between them for pre-emption purposes would grant greater power (to set state standards "different from, or in addition to," federal standards) to a single state jury than to state officials acting through state administrative or legislative lawmaking processes. Where Congress likely did not focus specifically upon the matter, I would not take it to have intended this anomalous result.

. . . .

II.

The answer to the second question turns on Congress' intent. Although Congress has not stated whether the MDA does, or does not, pre-empt the tort claims here at issue, several considerations lead me to conclude that it does not.

First, the MDA's pre-emption provision is highly ambiguous. . . .

Second, this Court has previously suggested that, in the absence of a clear congressional command as to pre-emption, courts may infer that the relevant administrative agency possesses a degree of leeway to determine which rules, regulations, or other administrative actions will have pre-emptive effect. To draw a similar inference here makes sense, and not simply because of the statutory ambiguity. The Food and Drug Administration (FDA) is fully responsible for administering the MDA. That responsibility means informed agency involvement and, therefore, special understanding of the likely impact of both state and federal requirements, as well as an understanding of whether (or the extent to which) state requirements may interfere with federal objectives. The FDA can translate these understandings into particularized pre-emptive intentions accompanying its various rules and regulations. It can communicate those intentions, for example, through statements in "regulations, preambles, interpretive statements, and responses to comments," as well as through the exercise of its explicitly designated power to exempt state requirements from pre-emption.

Third, the FDA has promulgated a specific regulation designed to help. That regulation says:

> "State . . . requirements are preempted only when . . . there are . . . *specific* [federal] requirements applicable to a particular device . . . thereby making any existing *divergent* State . . . requirements applicable to the device different from, or in addition to, the *specific* [federal] requirements." 21 C.F.R. 808.1(d) (emphasis added).

The regulation does not fill all the statutory gaps, for its word "divergent" does not explain, any more than did the statute, just when different device-related federal and state requirements are closely enough related to trigger pre-emption analysis. But the regulation's word "specific" does narrow the universe of federal requirements that the agency intends to displace at least some state law.

Insofar as there are any applicable FDA requirements here, those requirements, even if numerous, are not "specific" in any relevant sense. Hence, as the FDA's above-quoted pre-emption rule tells us, the FDA does not intend these requirements to pre-empt the state requirements at issue here. At least in present circumstances, no law forces the FDA to make its requirements pre-emptive if it does not think it appropriate.

. . . .

Fourth, ordinary principles of "conflict" and "field" pre-emption point in the same direction. Those principles make clear that a federal requirement pre-empts a state requirement if (1) the state requirement actually conflicts with the federal requirement–either because compliance with both is impossible, or because the state requirement "stands as an obstacle to the accomplishment and execution of the full purposes and objectives of Congress,"—or (2) the scheme of federal regulation is "so pervasive as to make reasonable the inference that Congress left no room for the States to supplement it."

. . . .

Insofar as these basic principles inform a court's interpretation of the statute and regulation, they support the conclusion that there is no pre-emption here. I can find no actual conflict between any federal requirement and any of the liability-creating premises of the plaintiffs' state-law tort suit; nor, for the reasons discussed above, can I find any indication that either Congress or the FDA intended the relevant FDA regulations to occupy entirely any relevant field.

. . . .

■ JUSTICE O'CONNOR, with whom THE CHIEF JUSTICE, JUSTICE SCALIA, and JUSTICE THOMAS join, concurring in part and dissenting in part.

. . . If § 360k's language is given its ordinary meaning, it clearly pre-empts any state common-law action that would impose a requirement different from, or in addition to, that applicable under the FDCA—just as it would pre-empt a state statute or regulation that had that effect. JUSTICE BREYER reaches the same conclusion.

. . . .

I disagree, however, with the Court's conclusion that the Lohrs' claims survive pre-emption insofar as they would compel Medtronic to comply with requirements different from those imposed by the FDCA. Because I do not subscribe to the Court's reading into § 360k the additional requisite of "specificity," my determination of what claims are pre-empted is broader. Some, if not all, of the Lohrs' common-law claims regarding the manufacturing and labeling of Medtronic's device would compel Medtronic to comply with requirements different from, or in addition to, those required by the FDA. The FDA's Good Manufacturing Practice (GMP) regulations impose comprehensive requirements relating to every aspect of the device-manufacturing process, including a manufacturer's organization and personnel, buildings, equipment, component controls, production and process controls, packaging and labeling controls, holding, distribution, installation, device evaluation, and recordkeeping. The Lohrs' common-law claims regarding manufacture would, if successful, impose state requirements "different from, or in addition to," the GMP requirements, and are therefore pre-empted. In similar fashion, the Lohrs' failure to warn claim is pre-empted by the extensive labeling requirements imposed by the FDA. These extensive federal manufacturing and labeling requirements are certainly applicable to the device manufactured by Medtronic. Section 360k(a) requires no more specificity than that for pre-emption of state common-law claims. . . .

NOTES

1. *Deference to FDA's Interpretation of Section 521.* Both Justice Stevens and Justice Breyer accord some deference—though possibly not *Chevron* deference—to FDA's regulations interpreting of Section 521. In adopting its interpretation, FDA was aware that an expansive interpretation—one that displaced numerous state regulations—would leave consumers less well-protected than if the Device Amendments had never been passed. For it quickly became obvious that years, even decades, would pass before the agency could fully deploy and enforce all of the authorities the new law provided.

On the heels of the Supreme Court's decision in *Medtronic v. Lohr*, FDA proposed changes in its regulations designed to limit the Amendments' preemptive effect on product liability claims based on state law. 62 Fed. Reg. 65384 (Dec. 12, 1997). A central feature of FDA's proposal was the declaration that, to preempt, a federal requirement had not only to apply to a specific device or type of device, but also had to be embodied in a regulation. Because FDA approval of a PMA for a Class III device does not take the form of a regulation, this interpretation would permit states to impose additional requirements for devices whose safety and effectiveness the agency had reviewed and approved. The agency's proposed approach may have been inspired by a conviction among agency officials that persons injured by FDA-approved devices should not be barred from recovery. When comments pointed out that the agency's understanding of section 521 would allow state regulatory bodies to apply their own—and additional—premarket approval requirements, FDA had second thoughts. It withdrew its proposal to amend its regulation less than a year after its publication. 63 Fed. Reg. 39789 (July 24,1998).

2. *Did Congress Intend to Preempt State Civil Causes of Actions?* In *Medtronic v. Lohr*, the Supreme Court was faced with a claim that the Device Amendments preempted a major slice of the states' common law of torts, a body of judge-made law whose fate had never been mentioned in the legislative history and that could be said to embody the states' front line of protection of consumers of medical products. Justice Stevens makes no secret of his unwillingness, absent a very clear directive from Congress, to recognize such a claim. And there seems little doubt that the draftsmen of section 521 had statutory and administrative "requirements" in mind. Nonetheless, the subsequent case law, not to mention *Medtronic* itself, has confirmed the proposition that a tort verdict can constitute a "requirement" that section 521 may preempt. We explore this fiercely contested body of law in Chapter XIII, *infra*.

3. *State Enforcement Remedies.* FDA has issued an advisory opinion stating that section 521 of the FD&C Act does not preempt application of state law injunctive remedies to medical devices generally or to IUDs in particular. Letter from FDA Associate Commissioner for Regulatory Affairs J.P. Hile to National Women's Health Network, Dkt. No. 83A–0140/AP (Mar. 8, 1984). The advisory opinion explained that section 521 preempts only state requirements that relate specifically to medical devices, and that there is no indication that Congress intended to preempt the application of general state law remedies that apply to many products including devices. *But see National Women's Health Network, Inc. v. A.H. Robins Co., Inc.*, 545 F. Supp. 1177 (D. Mass. 1982) (holding that state action to require a national notification and recall campaign for IUDs would be preempted by the FD&C Act).

3.   PREEMPTION UNDER THE NUTRITION LABELING AND EDUCATION ACT

The 1990 Nutrition Labeling and Education Act (NLEA), 104 Stat. 2353, expressly prohibits any state or local government from directly or indirectly establishing any food labeling requirement of the type governed by sections 403(b)–(k), (q), and (r) of the FD&C Act that is not identical to FDA requirements. This preemption provision was designed to become effective in stages. (1) It was effective immediately upon enactment for food standards. (2) It became effective one year after enactment for imitation labeling, declaration of ingredients, declaration of net quantity of contents, and the name and address of the manufacturer. (3) State requirements for nutrition labeling, nutrient descriptors, and disease prevention claims became preempted when FDA regulations implementing the new authorities of sections 403(q) and (r) became effective. (4) The remainder of the Act's food labeling provisions would become preemptive after a study required to be conducted by FDA, thirty months after enactment.

In response to members of Congress who believed FDA had been slow to require nutrition information on food labels, NLEA's drafters offered the states a role in enforcing the statute's new requirements. NLEA added a new paragraph (b) to what had been section 307 and is now section 310 of the FD&C Act. That section in its entirety now reads:

SEC. 310 [337].   PROCEEDINGS IN NAME OF UNITED STATES; PROVISION AS TO SUBPOENAS.

(a) Except as provided in subsection (b), all such proceedings for the enforcement, or to restrain violations, of this Act shall be by and in the name of the United States. Subpoenas for witnesses who are required to attend a court of the United States, in any district, may run into any other district in any proceeding under this section.

(b)(1) A State may bring in its own name and within its jurisdiction proceedings for the civil enforcement, or to restrain violations, of section 401, 403(b), 403(d), 403(e), 403(f), 403(g), 403(h), 403(i), 403(k), 403(q), or 403(r) if the food that is the subject of the proceedings is located in the State.

(2) No proceeding may be commenced by a State under paragraph (1) B

(A) before 30 days after the State has give notice to the Secretary that the State intends to bring such proceeding,

(B) before 90 days after the State has given notice to the Secretary of such intent if the Secretary has, within such 30 days, commenced an informal or formal enforcement action pertaining to the food which would be the subject of such proceeding, or

(C) if the Secretary is diligently prosecuting in court pertaining to such food, has settled such proceeding, or has settled the informal or formal enforcement action pertaining to such food.

In any court proceeding described in subparagraph (C), a State may intervene as a matter of right.

Section 310(b) draws on the model of the "citizen suit" provisions found in the nation's major environmental laws, including the Clean Air

Act and Federal Water Pollution Control Act. These laws authorize suits by individuals and organizations who are affected by polluting conduct that violates statutory requirements. Section 310(b) confers on state officials, but not private citizens, the authority to sue to enforce federal labeling requirements. FDA must be given notice of any such suit, however, and has the right to take over responsibility for the case.

The addition of Section 310(b) drew relatively little attention during consideration of the NLEA. It attracted just two sentences during the debate on the Senate floor, 136 Cong. Rec. § 16607–02, § 16608, and none in the House. The House Report contains the following brief discussion:

> The bill also contains a provision that would prevent State and local governments from adopting inconsistent requirements with respect to the labeling of nutrients or with respect to the claims that may be made about the nutrients in foods. However, these governmental entities are explicitly permitted to enforce Federal requirements with respect to nutrition labeling.

H.R. Rep. No. 538 101st Cong. (1990), p. 8. No state or state official has brought suit pursuant to this authority.

NOTES

1. *Restaurant and Retail Food.* Because foods consumed in restaurants and foods prepared in retail stores (*e.g.*, bread baked on the premises in a grocery store) are exempt from the food labeling requirements of sections 403(q) and (r), state and local requirements governing such foods are not subject to preemption.

2. *State Petitions.* Under FD&C section Act 403A(b), a state or local government may petition FDA to exempt a specific requirement from preemption by the NLEA. FDA may grant the petition if the requirement would not cause any food to be in violation of the FD&C Act, would not unduly burden interstate commerce, and is designed to address a particular need for information that is not met by the FD&C Act. Since 1990, only six state petitions have been submitted to FDA and none has been granted.

4.   PREEMPTION UNDER THE FOOD AND DRUG ADMINISTRATION MODERNIZATION ACT

Amy E. Semet, *Toward National Uniformity for FDA– Regulated Products* (2000)

In Chapter IV(B) of the Electronic Book.

... [I]n 1997, Congress passed the Food and Drug Administration Modernization Act ("FDAMA") in order to mandate "national uniformity" for the regulation of over-the-counter ("OTC") drugs and cosmetics. Under FDAMA, states may not pass "any requirement" that differs from federal standards for OTC drugs. In contrast, state labeling on cosmetics is preempted, but states remain free to pass cosmetic safety standards as long as the federal government has not acted. Why is there a difference in the preemption standards for OTC drugs and cosmetics? As Senator Jeffords noted during the FDAMA debates, OTCs are not "any different" from cosmetics for "all intents and purposes," yet preemption of OTCs was not nearly as objectionable as preemption of cosmetics. . . .

———

The provisions added by FDAMA follow:

FD&C ACT § 751. NATIONAL UNIFORMITY FOR NONPRE-SCRIPTION DRUGS.

(a) IN GENERAL.—Except as provided in subsection (b), (c)(1), (d), (e), or (f), no State or political subdivision of a State may establish or continue in effect any requirement—

(1) that relates to the regulation of a drug that is not subject to the requirements of section 503(b)(1) or 503(f)(1)(A); and

(2) that is different from or in addition to, or that is otherwise not identical with, a requirement under this Act, the Poison Prevention Packaging Act of 1970 (15 U.S.C. 1471 et seq.), or the Fair Packaging and Labeling Act (15 U.S.C. 1451 et seq.).

(b) EXEMPTION.—

(1) IN GENERAL.—Upon application of a State or political subdivision thereof, the Secretary may by regulation, after notice and opportunity for written and oral presentation of views, exempt from subsection (a), under such conditions as may be prescribed in such regulation, a State or political subdivision requirement that—

(A) protects an important public interest that would otherwise be unprotected, including the health and safety of children;

(B) would not cause any drug to be in violation of any applicable requirement or prohibition under Federal law; and

(C) would not unduly burden interstate commerce.

(2) TIMELY ACTION.—The Secretary shall make a decision on the exemption of a State or political subdivision requirement under paragraph (1) not later than 120 days after receiving the application of the State or political subdivision under paragraph(1).

(c) SCOPE.—

(1) IN GENERAL.—This section shall not apply to—

(A) any State or political subdivision requirement that relates to the practice of pharmacy; or

(B) any State or political subdivision requirement that a drug be dispensed only upon the prescription of a practitioner licensed by law to administer such drug.

(2) SAFETY OR EFFECTIVENESS.—For purposes of subsection (a), a requirement that relates to the regulation of a drug shall be deemed to include any requirement relating to public information or any other form of public communication relating to a warning of any kind for a drug.

(d) EXCEPTIONS.—

(1) IN GENERAL.—In the case of a drug described in subsection (a)(1) that is not the subject of an application approved under section 505 or section 507 (as in effect on the day before the date of enactment of the Food and Drug Administration Modernization Act of 1997) or a final regulation promulgated by the Secretary establishing conditions under which the drug is generally recognized as safe and effective and not misbranded, subsection (a) shall apply only with respect to a requirement of a State or political subdivision of a State that relates to the same subject as, but is different from or in addition to, or that is otherwise not identical with—

(A) a regulation in effect with respect to the drug pursuant to a statute described in subsection (a)(2); or

(B) any other requirement in effect with respect to the drug pursuant to an amendment to such a statute made on or after the date of enactment of the Food and Drug Administration Modernization Act of 1997.

(2) STATE INITIATIVES.—This section shall not apply to a State requirement adopted by a State public initiative or referendum enacted prior to September 1, 1997.

(e) NO EFFECT ON PRODUCT LIABILITY LAW.—Nothing in this section shall be construed to modify or otherwise affect any action or the liability of any person under the product liability law of any State.

(f) STATE ENFORCEMENT AUTHORITY.—Nothing in this section shall prevent a State or political subdivision thereof from enforcing, under any relevant civil or other enforcement authority, a requirement that is identical to a requirement of this Act.

FD&C ACT § 752. PREEMPTION FOR LABELING OR PACKAGING OF COSMETICS.

(a) IN GENERAL.—Except as provided in subsection (b), (d), or (e), no State or political subdivision of a State may establish or continue in effect any requirement for labeling or packaging of a cosmetic that is different from or in addition to, or that is otherwise not identical with, a requirement specifically applicable to a particular cosmetic or class of cosmetics under this Act, the Poison Prevention Packaging Act of 1970 (15 U.S.C. 1471 et seq.), or the Fair Packaging and Labeling Act (15 U.S.C. 1451 et seq.).

(b) EXEMPTION.—Upon application of a State or political subdivision thereof, the Secretary may by regulation, after notice and opportunity for written and oral presentation of views, exempt from subsection (a), under such conditions as may be prescribed in such regulation, a State or political subdivision requirement for labeling or packaging that—

(1) protects an important public interest that would otherwise be unprotected;

(2) would not cause a cosmetic to be in violation of any applicable requirement or prohibition under Federal law; and

(3) would not unduly burden interstate commerce.

(c) SCOPE.—For purposes of subsection (a), a reference to a State requirement that relates to the packaging or labeling of a cosmetic means any specific requirement relating to the same aspect of such cosmetic as a requirement specifically applicable to that particular cosmetic or class of cosmetics under this Act for packaging or labeling, including any State requirement relating to public information or any other form of public communication.

(d) NO EFFECT ON PRODUCT LIABILITY LAW.—Nothing in this section shall be construed to modify or otherwise affect any action or the liability of any person under the product liability law of any State.

(e) STATE INITIATIVE.—This section shall not apply to a State requirement adopted by a State public initiative or referendum enacted prior to September 1, 1997.

NOTES

1. *Reason for Difference.* The OTC drug and cosmetic national uniformity provisions in the FDA Modernization Act were the result of classic political bargaining. FDA agreed to support national uniformity only if the regulated industry agreed to a provision giving the agency the authority to inspect records that FDA has sought for half a century. The OTC drug industry agreed to this deal. However, the cosmetic industry rejected the bargain and still pressed for national uniformity over FDA's opposition. The food industry likewise spurned the compromise and decided to pursue national uniformity in separate legislation.

2. *Food Uniformity Legislation.* Local interest group politics and special geographical considerations have encouraged divergent food regulations among the fifty states. In the early 1990s, over 380 state agencies had responsibilities similar to the FDA. These agencies devoted most of their resources to food regulation; indeed, a 1989 study found that food regulation constituted 74% of the $196.06 million spent for all food and drug control activities by the states.

Food processors have been urging Congress to pass legislation to prohibit states from requiring warnings for ingredients that FDA deems safe. They contend the uniformity legislation would "ensure consumers have access to the same accurate, science-based food safety information regardless of where they live," while state regulators and consumer groups contend such legislation would gut state food safety laws. Legislation providing for national uniformity for food was reported favorably in 2000, S. Rep. No. 106–504, 106th Cong., 2d Sess., but was not considered on the Senate floor. Similar legislation was endorsed in H.R. Rep. No. 108–770, 108th Cong., 2d Sess. (2004), but was not taken up by the House. Most recently, uniformity legislation was endorsed in H.R. Rep. No. 109–379, 109th Cong., 2d Sess. (2006), and passed by the House but was not considered by the Senate.

3. *The Latest if Not the Last Word on Preemption.* The Supreme Court has confronted preemption-based challenges to the application of state law in several recent cases. Most have involved private liability suits against makers or distributors of federally-regulated products, but others have pitted state regulatory policies against claims that Congress has provided for regulation that is both comprehensive and exclusive. For the Court's most recent treatments, see *Bates v. Dow Agrosciences LLC*, 544 U.S. 431 (2005); *Buckman Co. v. Plaintiff's Legal Committee*, 531 U.S. 341 (2001); *Alexis Geier v. American Honda Motor Co., Inc.*, 529 U.S. 861 (2000), and Chapter XII, *infra*.

CHAPTER XIII

CIVIL LIABILITY AND FEDERAL REGULATION

While this book chiefly focuses on statutes and regulations administered by FDA (*i.e.*, federal law), sellers of food, drugs, devices, and cosmetics are subject to other limits that are chiefly the creation of state law. These take two forms. One consists of rules adopted by state legislatures or agencies that express policies that often mimic and sometimes supplement policies expressed in federal law. We consider this form of state regulation in Chapter XII. The other form is found in the reported decisions of state courts (or federal courts applying state law) in suits brought by private plaintiffs seeking some remedy for harms claimed to be caused by such products.

Sellers of foods and medical products are of course not alone in their interest in the liability rules that apply to their products. Makers of most consumer products face the prospect of private suits by consumers. However, makers of FDA regulated products confront unusually complex demands because their products are subject to extensive federal regulation. The obligations imposed by these distinct bodies of law, in harmony, are sometimes in tension. This chapter explores both possibilities. It is concerned with the relationship between FDA's regulatory role and the legal principles that govern the liability of sellers of products the agency regulates.

A. TORT LIABILITY OF SELLERS OF FOOD OR DRUGS

In the following excerpt Professor David Owen describes the principles that American courts apply in adjudicating claims that a food or a medicine was the cause of physical harm.

David G. Owen, *Products Liability Law*

Thomson–West 2005.

To recover for injuries from ingesting food or drink, a plaintiff must establish that the food contained some dangerous element that rendered it unwholesome or "defective." The concept of defectiveness in food and drink cases is basically the same as in other contexts. Thus, a food or beverage item generally is defective, and a seller generally is subject to liability in negligence, warranty, and strict liability in tort for selling it, if the food product's condition is dangerous in a manner neither intended by the seller nor expected by the consumer. . . .

Defective[ness] is clear enough . . . if food or drink contains a foreign object, such as glass, steel, bugs, or when the food is spoiled or otherwise contaminated. Yet the parties' expectations and legal responsibility may be quite different with respect to hazards that are natural to certain types of food, such as clamshells in clam chowder, cherry pits in cherry pies, and fish bones in fish fillets. To the extent that such naturally occurring objects are dangerous, food purveyors ordinarily attempt to keep them out of the food and drink they sell. But sometimes their efforts are unsuccessful and a food consumer is injured by a naturally occurring object of this type. The question in such cases is whether the food should be considered defective or whether such naturally occurring objects should be expected, and thus the responsibility of the consumer.

. . . .

The principal effect of § 7 [of the Restatement (Third) of Torts: Products Liability], the special section on food products, is its explicit adoption of the so-called "consumer expectations" test of liability for food containing injurious matter, such as the proverbial mouse in a bottle of Coke or a nail or a fish bone in a can of fish soup. . . . [C]ourts have largely switched to the more functional, and more flexible, consumer expectations test in food cases of this type. . . .

§ 7. *Liability of Commercial Seller or Distributor for Harm Caused by Defective Food Products*

One engaged in the business of selling or otherwise distributing food products who sells or distributes a food product that is defective under § 2, § 3, or § 4 is subject to liability for harm to persons or property caused by the defect. Under § 2(a), a harm-causing ingredient of the food product constitutes a defect if a reasonable consumer would not expect the food product to contain that ingredient.

. . . .

Prescription drugs are paradoxical: as one of the greatest triumphs of the twentieth century, their powerful chemicals and biologics save many millions of humans from suffering and death; yet, these same chemicals also cause great suffering and death. All prescription drugs, that is, possess substantial costs as well as benefits. This is because most drug hazards are inherent and unavoidable. . . .

Outside of tort law, our medico-legal systems address this conundrum, the bad-comes-with-the-good aspect of prescription drugs, in two basic ways. First, prior to being allowed onto the market, prescription drugs must undergo rigorous analysis, laboratory testing, and clinical trials, the results of which are closely scrutinized by the FDA, to assure both the safety and efficacy of all new drugs. . . .

The second relevant feature of our medico-legal system is that it positions experts in diagnosis and drug therapy, doctors and nurse practitioners, between beneficial yet dangerous prescription drugs, on the one hand, and the lay public who need drug therapy, on the other. The role of such health care professionals, such "learned intermediaries," is to connect individual drugs and patients—to choose from among the panoply of available prescription drugs the one with the highest benefit-risk ratio for each particular patient's needs and wants. . . .

The question of interest here is what role, if any, does the medico-legal system just described leave for the law of torts and products liability? Because the system just described breaks down in many ways in practice, the answer to the question must be that products liability law has a powerful role to play in compensating persons harmed unnecessarily by defective drugs, and some role (if a lesser one) in deterring their sale and promoting drug safety. . . .

. . . In a nutshell, comment k [of the Restatement (Second) of Torts] provides that manufacturers are not subject to strict liability in tort for harm caused by certain "unavoidably unsafe" but useful products, notably prescription drugs, solely on the basis of their inherent hazards that cannot feasibly be designed away. . . .

In 1998, the ALI promulgated a liability standard for defective drug designs that is unusual, to say the least. Section 6(c) of the Products Liability Restatement provides:

> (c) A prescription drug or medical device is not reasonably safe due to defective design if the foreseeable risks of harm posed by the drug or medical device are sufficiently great in relation to its foreseeable therapeutic benefits that reasonable health-care providers, knowing of such foreseeable risks and therapeutic benefits, would not pre-scribe the drug or medical device for any class of patients.

. . . [T]his standard leaves a very small window for design defect claims for prescription drugs, a window so tiny that almost no drug claim could fit through it. . . .

Most prescription drug litigation properly is based on the adequacy of warnings and instructions provided to the doctor about the drug, because the best place to locate a drug manufacturer's responsibility is in the information it provides to doctors—information which must be clear, complete, and properly conveyed. In the great majority of cases, a challenge to a drug's design can easily be reformulated as a defect in a warning or instruction. If a drug's adverse effects are not reasonably foreseeable, the manufacturer should not be responsible for its untoward effects. . . . If such adverse effects in fact are reasonably discoverable by a manufacturer properly performing its research and development obligations, then it will have a duty to provide adequate warnings to doctors of those effects. . . .

If a prescription drug is dispensed under circumstances where a health professional does not render the type of individualized balancing of risks and benefits contemplated by the learned intermediary doctrine, warnings may have to be provided directly to the patient. Thus, when the rationale for the learned intermediary doctrine falls away, the general rule requiring manufacturers to warn consumers directly reappears. . . .

The principles of adequacy applicable to warnings generally . . . apply as well to prescription drugs. All material information on possible risks must be conveyed to the doctor, comprehensible to the general practitioner as well as to the specialist, or to consumers, comprehensible to them, if the circumstances warrant. For a drug warning to be "adequate," it must describe the scope of the danger; the effects of misuse, including the failure to follow instructions; and the physical aspects of the warning, and broader method of conveyance, must be likely to alert recipients to the danger. . . .

Courts have only infrequently held prescription drug manufacturers liable for design defects, and the new Products Liability Restatement mirrors this perspective by strictly limiting design liability in § 6(c) to cases where a drug is shown to have no net value for any class of patient. Section 6(d) restates the widely accepted "learned intermediary" doctrine for warnings cases, by which a manufacturer generally is obligated to provide a warning only to the prescribing physician, not directly to the patient. . . .

§ 6. Liability of Commercial Seller or Distributor for Harm Caused by Defective Prescription Drugs and Medical Devices

(a) A manufacturer of a prescription drug or medical device who sells or otherwise distributes a defective drug or medical device is subject to liability for harm to persons caused by defect. A prescription drug or medical device is one that may be legally sold or otherwise distributed only pursuant to a healthcare provider's prescription.

(b) For purposes of liability under Subsection (a), a prescription drug or medical device is defective if at the time of sale or other distribution the drug or medical device:

(1) contains a manufacturing defect as defined in § 2(a); or

(2) is not reasonably safe due to defective design as defined in Subsection (c); or

(3) is not reasonably safe due to inadequate instructions or warnings as defined in Subsection (d).

(c) A prescription drug or medical device is not reasonably safe due to defective design if the foreseeable risks of harm posed by the drug or medical device are sufficiently great in relation to its foreseeable therapeutic benefits that reasonable health-care providers, knowing of such foreseeable risks and therapeutic benefits, would not prescribe the drug or medical device for any class of patients.

(d) A prescription drug or medical device is not reasonably safe due to inadequate instructions or warnings if reasonable instructions or warnings regarding foreseeable risks of harm are not provided to:

(1) prescribing and other health-care providers who are in a position to reduce the risks of harm in accordance with the instructions or warnings; or

(2) the patient when the manufacturer knows or has reason to know that health-care providers will not be in a position to reduce the risks of harm in accordance with the instructions or warnings.

NOTES

1. *Proving Causation.* To recover damages from the manufacturer of a drug, or of food for that matter, a plaintiff must convince the jury (or judge sitting as trier of fact) that the manufacturer's defective product caused her injury. Sometimes this is self-evident, but often it is not. For example, if the "defect" consists of failure to warn of the product's side effects, the jury must be persuaded that the plaintiff might have escaped injury had an adequate warning been provided. *See* Sherrill Calabro, *Breaking the Shield of the Learned Intermediary Doctrine: Placing the Blame Where It Belongs*, 25 CARDOZO L. REV. 2241, 2291 (2004). Establishing causation can also be challenging where the plaintiff's injury is of a kind also suffered by persons who have never used the defendant's product. The plaintiff's challenge, then, is to distinguish her injury from the "background" exhibited by unexposed individuals. For many such injuries it is not possible to distinguish product-caused cases from natural or background cases by physical diagnosis. In such circumstances the plaintiff must often rely on statistical evidence, *i.e.*, evidence comparing the frequency with which such harms occur spontaneously with the frequency manifested by the population of product users. *See* Mark Geistfeld, *Scientific Uncertainty and Causation in Tort Law*, 54 VAND. L. REV. 1011 (2001).

2. *Scientific Evidence.* As the previous note suggests, the plaintiff in a product liability suit must often rely on evidence produced and explained by scientists. The principles governing the admission and interpretation of such evidence have undergone a revolution in the last generation, a revolution triggered by the Supreme Court's ruling in *Daubert v. Merrell Dow Pharmaceuticals*, 509 U.S. 579 (1993), and accelerated by two later Court rulings (*General Electric Co. v. Joiner*, 522 U.S. 136 (1997); *Kumho Tire Co. Ltd. v. Carmichael*, 526 U.S. 137 (1999)) and an avalanche of lower court decisions purporting to understand and apply the Supreme Court's rulings. This burgeoning body of law is far too vast to recount here, but its basic lessons can be summarized as follows: (1) for scientific evidence to be admitted it must be shown to reflect the principles and practices of the scientific community and its purported findings must be relevant to factual issues in the case of hand, (2) responsibility for assuring that evidence offered by a party satisfies these standards lies with the trial judge, and (3) the judge's decision to admit or exclude evidence can be overturned only if clearly erroneous. For some of the best of many good treatments of Daubert and its progeny, *see* Margaret A. Berger, *Procedural Paradigms for Applying the Daubert Test*, 78 MINN. L. REV. 1345 (1994); Troyen Brennan, *Causal Chains and Statistical Links: The Role of Scientific Uncertainty in Hazardous–Substance Litigation*, 73 CORNELL L. REV. 469 (1988); Troyen Brennan, *Helping Courts with Toxic Torts: Some Proposals Regarding Alternative Methods for Presenting and Assessing Scientific Evidence in Common Law Courts*, 51 U. PITT. L. REV. 1 (1989); Gerald W. Boston, *A Mass–Exposure Model of Toxic Causation: The Content of Scientific Proof and the Regulatory Experience*, 18 COLUM. J. ENVTL. L. 181 (1993). *See also* Margaret A. Berger, *Eliminating General Causation: Notes towards a New Theory of Justice and Toxic Torts*, 97 COLUM. L. REV. 2117 (1997).

3. *Class Action Eligibility.* Because several high-profile liability suits against makers of prescription drugs and medical devices have been duplicates, *i.e.*, one of many involving the same product, similar types of harm, and similar allegations of fault or effect, it should be no surprise that many plaintiffs' lawyers and some courts have sought to aggregate similar claims pursuant to the federal class action rules. Courts have certified classes in some of these cases, but they have more often rejected class treatment, frequently on the ground that the harms experienced—and their attribution to a single defendant's product—have been too diverse to satisfy the commonality standards of Rule 23. For contrasting views on these issues, *see* Young K. Lee, *Beyond Gatekeeping: Class Certification, Judicial Oversight, and the*

Promotion of Scientific Research in "Immature" Pharmaceutical Torts, *105 COLUM. L. REV. 1905 (2005); David Rosenberg,* Decoupling Deterrence and Compensation Functions in Mass Tort Class Actions for Future Loss, *88 VA. L. REV. 1871 (2002).*

4. *Other Commentary. See, e.g., Richard A. Merrill, Compensation for Prescription Drug Injuries,* 59 VA. L. REV. 1 (1973).

COMMENT: THE LEARNED INTERMEDIARY DOCTRINE AND EXCEPTIONS

As Professor Owen emphasizes, the duty of a manufacturer of prescription drugs to warn about its risks is a duty owed the patient, the ultimate consumer, but fulfilled by communication with the prescribing physician, the so-called "learned intermediary." Nearly every state has embraced this doctrine as a governing principle. *See Larkin v. Pfizer, Inc.,* 153 S.W.3d 758 (Ky. 2004). A drug manufacturer thus usually fulfills its legal obligation to warn by providing adequate warnings to the health-care provider. At the same time there has been a growing willingness to recognize exceptions—and hold that the consumer is entitled to be warned directly—in at least two, and perhaps three, circumstances.

First, where a drug is administered in a setting where individual physician diagnosis and attention to individual patients cannot be expected, the manufacturer is expected to assure that patients get warned directly. The leading case is *Reyes v. Wyeth Laboratories,* 498 F.2d 1264 (5th Cir. 1974), *supra* p. 900, which imposed liability on Wyeth for failing to take steps to assure that parents of youngsters who were vaccinated at a public health clinic were alerted to the slim but real possibility that the polio vaccine could actually cause the disease.

Second, the courts, as well as the American Law Institute, have also endorsed the proposition that users of birth control pills (and no doubt other drugs that serve health needs or personal goals, but do not treat or prevent disease) are entitled to be warned about their risks. Restatement (Third) of Torts § 6 Comment; *Odgers v. Ortho Pharm. Corp.,* 609 F. Supp. 867 (E.D. Mich. 1985). It is not entirely clear whether this "exception" to the learned intermediary doctrine rests on the distinctive characteristics of these products or on the fact that FDA for 30 years has required oral contraceptives to be accompanied by a detailed "patient insert." *See MacDonald v. Ortho,* 475 N.E.2d 65 (Mass. 1985), *infra* p. 1475.

Finally, there is some support for the proposition that when a manufacturer of a prescription drug chooses to promote the product in advertisements directed at consumers, it should be obligated to provide adequate warnings to its customers. *See Perez v. Wyeth Laboratories, Inc.,* 734 A.2d 1245 (N.J. 1999) (discussed *infra* p. 1486).

Those who assert the need for adequate warnings directly to consumers contend that manufacturers that communicate directly with consumers should not escape liability simply because the decision to prescribe the drug was made by the health-care provider. Proponents of the learned intermediary rule argue that, notwithstanding direct communications to the consumer, drugs cannot be dispensed unless a health-care provider makes an individualized decision that a drug is appropriate for a particular patient, and that it is for the health-care provider to decide which risks are relevant to the particular patient. The Restatement leaves to developing case law whether exceptions to the learned intermediary rule in these or other situations should be recognized.

B.   THEORIES OF PRIVATE LIABILITY

1.   NO PRIVATE CAUSE OF ACTION UNDER THE FD&C ACT

Numerous federal statutes, in addition to empowering the Department of Justice (or a specialized agency like EPA or the FTC) to enforce their substantive requirements, also authorize suits by persons harmed by violative activity. For example, the Clayton Act, 15 U.S.C. 15(a), specifically provides for private damage suits against violators of the antitrust laws. To win a suit under the Clayton Act, a private plaintiff must be able to prove that the defendant's conduct not only violated the law but also harmed his interests. As an incentive for such "private enforcement suits" the Act permits a successful plaintiff to recover three times his actual damages.

Most of the nation's environmental laws—including the Clean Air Act, the Federal Water Pollution Control Act, and the Resource Conservation and Recovery Act, to name prominent examples—provide for so-called "citizen suits."

> Every major federal environmental law passed since 1970 has contained a citizen suit provision.... Under the citizen suit provisions, individuals and organizations can pursue two new categories of lawsuits not authorized by the Administrative Procedure Act. First, they can sue anyone, either public and private, alleged to be in violation of an environmental law, serving in effect as private attorneys general. Environmental groups have used this opportunity actively both to supplement the government's limited enforcement resources and to pursue violations that the government is ignoring.... Secondly, individuals or groups can sue the EPA administrator or other relevant governmental officials who are failing to carry out non-discretionary Congressional obligations.

James Salzman & Barton H. Thompson Jr., ENVIRONMENTAL LAW AND POLICY 69–70 (2003).

As the following excerpt explains, citizen suits have become a popular method of enforcing some federal environmental laws, most notably the Federal Water Pollution Control Act.

> While action-forcing litigation against EPA played a major role in the development of environmental law during the 1970s, citizen enforcement actions against private parties who violated environmental regulations were rarely filed during this period. This changed in 1982 due to concern over a dramatic decline in governmental enforcement effort during the early years of the Reagan administration. The Natural Resources Defense Council initiated a national project to use citizen suits to fill the enforcement void.

The citizen suit project focused on enforcement of the Clean Water Act because it was easy to prove violations. Dischargers are required to file discharge monitoring reports (DMRs), which are available to the public and can serve as prima facie evidence of NPDES permit violations. Joined by local environmental groups, NRDC systematically scrutinized DMRs and sent 60–day notice letters to dischargers who reported violations of permit limits. Notice letters were then followed by citizen suits. As a result of this project, the total number of citizen suits brought under the Clean Water Act increased from 6 in 1981 to 62 in 1983, surpassing the 56 Clean Water Act cases referred by EPA to the Justice Department for prosecution that year.

Robert V. Percival et al., ENVIRONMENTAL REGULATION LAW, SCIENCE, POLICY 997 (4th ed. 2003). For a skeptical view of citizen suits see Michael S. Greve, *The Private Enforcement of Environmental Law*, 65 TUL. L. REV. 339 (1990).

For several decades the federal courts, led by the Supreme Court, endorsed a role for private suits to enforce statutes that make no specific reference to the possibility. The seminal case was *J. I. Case v. Borak*, 377 U.S. 426 (1964), in which the Court upheld the right of shareholders to seek judicial relief from actions of corporate officers who allegedly violated the Securities Exchange Act's ban on misleading prospectuses. Although the statute said nothing about the possibility of such suits, the Court, encouraged by an overworked SEC, reasoned that suits by private investors would provide a useful supplement to enforcement by the Commission. A series of cases, chiefly in the securities and civil rights arenas, took *Borak*'s lead, so that by 1970 many judges assumed that most regulatory statutes could support private enforcement suits even if they did not mention the possibility.

Against this background, the plaintiff's argument in the following case drew upon what many lawyers saw as robust line of judicial precedent. The court's response to Broward County's claim that the FD&C Act "impliedly authorized" private enforcement suits, however, relied on more recent authority and the particular language used in the Act.

State of Florida ex rel. Broward County v. Eli Lilly & Co.

329 F. Supp. 364 (S.D. Fla. 1971).

■ ATKINS, DISTRICT JUDGE.

This cause has come on to be heard on defendants' motions to dismiss the First Amended Complaint and the Second Amended Complaint. By its First Amended Complaint, the State of Florida, appearing by a Special Assistant Attorney General, brought suit on its own behalf and on behalf of class of consumers and purchasers against the defendants to recover damages allegedly sustained in connection with the purchase, administration and use of certain fixed-ratio combination drugs claimed to have been manufactured and sold by the defendants. In essence, the Florida complaint charged that the defendants fraudulently induced the plaintiff to purchase drugs by falsely representing their effectiveness and side effects and by failing to provide adequate directions for and warnings against their use. Such conduct was claimed to be actionable under provisions of the Federal Food, Drug, and Cosmetic Act, 21 U.S.C. § 301 et seq. The complaint also charged the defendants with common law fraud, negligence and breach of warranty. This Court's jurisdiction was invoked pursuant to 28 U.S.C. §§ 1331 and 1337 and 28 U.S.C. § 1332.

The defendants moved to dismiss the First Amended Complaint....

Upon consideration of the aforesaid motion to dismiss and of the memoranda in support thereof and in opposition thereto, and after oral argument, the Court granted the motion to dismiss. The Court concluded:

1. The Federal Food, Drug, and Cosmetic Act does not create a private right of action and the claims pleaded in the First Amended Complaint do not, therefore, arise under federal law. Section 310(a) of the Act, 21 U.S.C. § 337(a), provides that "all" proceedings for the enforcement or to restrain violations of the Act shall be brought by the United States. Section 302(a), 21 U.S.C. § 332(a), limits the jurisdiction of district courts under the Act to injunctive proceedings involving purely prospective relief. The legislative history of the Act indicates that an express provision for a private right of action for damages was included in an early version of the bill but was omitted from all later versions after being attacked on the ground that it would create an unnecessary federal action duplicative of state remedies. Thus, the terms and legislative history of the statute compel the conclusion that Congress did not intend to allow private rights of action for damages under the statute.

This conclusion is reinforced by the decisions of the only two other courts that have squarely faced this issue, *Clairol, Inc. v. Suburban Cosmetics, Inc.*, 278 F. Supp. 859 (N.D. Ill. 1968); *Wells v. Wells*, 240 F. Supp. 282 (W.D. Ky. 1965), and by the several other federal decisions which, in viewing the relationship between the Federal Food, Drug, and Cosmetic Act and applicable state remedies, have clearly indicated that violations of the Act do not constitute an independent basis for federal question jurisdiction, *Orthopedic Equipment Co. v. Eutsler*, 276 F.2d 455 (4th Cir. 1960); *Herman v. Smith, Kline & French Laboratories*, 286 F. Supp. 694 (E.D. Wis. 1968).

Plaintiff's reliance upon cases arising under other federal regulatory statutes is misplaced. First, the federal statutes involved in those cases had neither provisions requiring all actions to be brought by the United States nor ones restricting federal district court jurisdiction to injunctive actions. Secondly, those decisions did not deal with legislative history like that of the Food, Drug and Cosmetic Act, showing an explicit rejection by Congress of a provision for private actions. Finally, such decisions typically involve claims for which no corresponding civil remedies are available in state courts....

NOTES

1. *The Search for a Federal Right.* It is not entirely clear what the county's attorneys thought they would gain from recognition of a right to sue under the

FD&C Act itself. This was only one of their claims, and not the most prominent. The court's opinion suggests that the county saw this theory—that the FD&C Act implicitly provided for private suits—as helpful to their aim of establishing United States District Court jurisdiction. The county's other claims could not have been independently brought in federal court, and it may have doubted that a state court would be sympathetic to the underlying merits.

2. *FD&C Act Cases.* Other cases echo the ruling in *Broward County. See Fiedler v. Clark*, 714 F.2d 77 (9th Cir. 1983); *Gelley v. Astra Pharmaceutical Products, Inc.*, 466 F. Supp. 182 (D. Minn.), *aff'd*, 610 F.2d 558 (8th Cir. 1979); *Raye v. Medtronic Corp.*, 696 F. Supp. 1273 (D. Minn. 1988); *Griffin v. O'Neal, Jones & Feldman, Inc.*, 604 F. Supp. 717 (S.D. Ohio 1985); *Munson v. Eli Lilly and Co.*, 1987–1988 FDLI Jud. Rec. 760 (D. Minn. 1987); *National Women's Health Network Inc. v. A.H. Robins Co., Inc.*, 545 F. Supp. 1177 (D. Mass. 1982); *American Home Products Corp. v. Johnson and Johnson*, 436 F. Supp. 785 (S.D.N.Y. 1977); *Powell v. Kull*, 329 F. Supp. 193 (M.D. Pa. 1971). For discussion of private suits under the FD&C Act, *see* Richard Cole & Mark Shapiro, *Private Litigation Under the Federal Food, Drug, and Cosmetic Act: Should the Right to Sue be Implied?*, 30 FOOD DRUG COSM. L.J. 576 (1975); Bruce D. Sales, *Does the FDC Act Create a Private Right of Action?* 28 FOOD DRUG COSM. L.J. 501 (1973). Any remaining doubts were resolved by *Buckman v. Plaintiffs' Legal Committee*, 531 U.S. 341, 349 n. 4 (2001), p. 1508 *infra*, where the Supreme Court declared that only the federal government may enforce the FD&C Act.

3. *Implied Rights Under Other Statutes. Pacific Trading Co. v. Wilson & Co., Inc.*, 547 F.2d 367 (7th Cir. 1976), held that no private cause of action could be implied under the Packers and Stockyards Act, the United States Warehouse Act, or the Federal Meat Inspection Act. A private cause of action under the Federal Meat Inspection Act was also rejected in *Shoultz v. Monfort of Colorado, Inc.*, 754 F.2d 318 (10th Cir. 1985); *Mario's Butcher Shop and Food Center, Inc. v. Armour and Co.*, 574 F. Supp. 653 (N.D. Ill. 1983). *Cross v. Board of Supervisors of San Mateo County*, 326 F. Supp. 634 (N.D. Cal. 1968), rejected private claims based on the Federal Trade Commission Act and the Federal Hazardous Substances Act, as well as the FD&C Act. *Holloway v. Bristol–Myers Corp.*, 485 F.2d 986 (D.C. Cir. 1973), and *Carlson v. Coca–Cola Co.*, 483 F.2d 279 (9th Cir. 1973), denied a private cause of action under the Federal Trade Commission Act. *See* Note, *Judicial Refusal to Imply a Private Right of Action Under the FTCA*, 1974 DUKE L.J. 506. Nor is a private right of action provided by the Federal Insecticide, Fungicide, and Rodenticide Act, *Fiedler v. Clark*, 714 F.2d 77 (9th Cir. 1983); *In re "Agent Orange" Product Liability Litigation*, 635 F.2d 987 (2d Cir. 1980).

4. *The Supreme Court's Retreat.* In *Cort v. Ash*, 422 U.S. 66 (1975), the Court began a retreat from *Borak*. It enunciated four factors for determining whether a private cause of action will be inferred under federal regulatory statutes. Later decisions stressed that the central inquiry is whether Congress intended to permit private enforcement of a regulatory statute. The Court's prevailing deeply skeptical treatment of implied private right claims is chronicled in Jerry L. Mashaw et al., ADMINISTRATIVE LAW: THE AMERICAN PUBLIC LAW SYSTEM 1207–1223 (5th ed. 2003).

2. INFORMER SUITS TO ENFORCE THE FD&C ACT

The case law thus confirms that the FD&C Act does not independently provide a basis for private suits alleging that a defendant has violated the law's requirements. But this does not necessarily mean that a citizen who discovers conduct that he believes violates the Act is without any remedy.

In the following case the "relator" (Franklin) sought to exploit an ancient theory in a modern context.

United States ex. rel. Franklin v. Parke–Davis

147 F. Supp. 2d 39 (D. Mass. 2001).

■ SARIS, J.

In this qui tam action, Relator Dr. David Franklin brings a claim under the False Claims Act, 31 U.S.C. §§ 3729 et seq., alleging that Defendant Parke–Davis (Franklin's former employer) promoted the drug Neurontin for uses not approved by the Food and Drug Administration, resulting in federal reimbursement payments for Neurontin prescriptions that were ineligible under Medicaid. Parke–Davis moves for summary judgment. The government, which has not intervened, has filed a Statement of Interest. After hearing, Parke–Davis's motion is DENIED.

. . . .

The False Claims Act ("FCA") imposes liability on any person who, inter alia:

> (1) knowingly presents, or causes to be presented, to an officer or employee of the United States Government or a member of the Armed Forces of the United States a false or fraudulent claim for payment or approval; [or]

> (2) knowingly makes, uses, or causes to be made or used, a false record or statement to get a false or fraudulent claim paid or approved by the Government

31 U.S.C. § 3729(a).

Parke–Davis argues that it can only be held liable under the FCA if Relator proves that Parke–Davis intentionally made a material false statement that led to the filing of a false claim. Under Parke–Davis's interpretation, the FCA contains a double falsehood requirement: An FCA plaintiff must prove a false statement that led to a false claim. . . .

Parke–Davis's legal argument is inconsistent with the text of the FCA. While § 3729(a)(2) contains a double-falsehood requirement ("knowingly makes, uses, or causes to be made or used, a false record or statement to get a false or fraudulent claim paid or approved by the Government"), FCA liability under § 3729(a)(1) arises when a defendant "knowingly presents, or causes to be presented . . . a false or fraudulent claim." Thus, there is no double falsehood requirement under § 3729(a)(1). . . .

Because Relator has not limited his FCA claim to § 3729(a)(2), he need not show two falsehoods to prevail. Under § 3729(a)(1), Relator is not required to present evidence that Parke–Davis lied to physicians about Neurontin's off-label efficacy or safety to induce them to prescribe Neurontin for uses ineligible under Medicaid. Though such evidence would be probative as to whether Parke–Davis caused to be presented false Medicaid claims, truthful off-label marketing (ineligible for federal safe harbors) and financial incentives like kickbacks would suffice.

Parke–Davis contends that Relator cannot prove the sine qua non of a False Claims Act violation: the existence of a false claim. In the early phases of this litigation, "Defendant did not dispute that an off-label prescription submitted for reimbursement by Medicaid is a false claim within the meaning of the FCA." Now Parke–Davis argues that forty-two state Medicaid programs permit reimbursement for off-label, non-compendium drug prescriptions, and that therefore claims for Medicaid reimbursement for off-label Neurontin prescriptions in those states were not false claims. Parke–Davis contends that the Medicaid statute gives states the discretion to provide reimbursement for such prescriptions; in particular, Parke–Davis points to 42 U.S.C. § 1396r–8(d)(1)(B): "A state may exclude or otherwise restrict coverage of a covered outpatient drug if—(I) the prescribed use is not for a medically accepted indication...." Parke–Davis argues that the language "may exclude or otherwise restrict" indicates that states have the option not to exclude (*i.e.*, may provide) coverage for drugs for which the prescribed use is not for a medically accepted indication.

Relator contends that Parke–Davis is wrong as to the scope of Medicaid coverage in the forty-two states. Indeed, Relator argues that the Medicaid statute does not authorize states to provide such broad coverage. Relator emphasizes that the Medicaid statute allows states to "exclude or otherwise restrict coverage of a covered outpatient drug," 42 U.S.C. § 1396r–8(d)(1)(B) (emphasis added), implying that states are given discretion only within the category of "covered outpatient drugs." The Medicaid statute defines this category to exclude drugs for which the prescribed use is not a medically accepted indication....

The debate may be immaterial. If the Medicaid statute gives states the discretion to cover off-label, non-compendium prescriptions, and a state exercised its discretion to cover such prescriptions, then an off-label Neurontin prescription in that state would not be a false claim. On the other hand, if the Medicaid statute does not give states the discretion to cover off-label, non-compendium prescriptions, but a state misconstrued the statute and authorized coverage of such prescriptions, an FCA action against Parke–Davis in that state would likely fail, as it would be difficult to establish Parke–Davis's scienter.

In any event, even Parke–Davis concedes that eight states do not provide reimbursement for off-label drug prescriptions not included in a medical compendium, and in those states, a Medicaid-reimbursement request for an off-label, non-compendium prescription constitutes a false claim. Thus, at best Parke–Davis's argument goes to the amount of damages, and does not provide a basis for summary judgment of no liability under the FCA....

Parke–Davis also raises a factual argument about why Relator cannot show a false claim: Parke–Davis points out that the Medicaid reimbursement claim forms for prescription drugs do not require the claimant to list the indication for which the drug is being prescribed. Thus, Parke–Davis argues, Relator cannot show that any Medicaid claim sought reimbursement for an off-label, non-compendium use. But the Relator has provided analysis linking patients' treatment histories to Neurontin prescriptions that generated reimbursement claims; Relator contends this analysis demonstrates that many reimbursement claims must have been for off-label, non-compendium indications, given the patients' treatment histories. Parke–Davis has submitted expert testimony contesting the reliability of comparing data from pharmacy claim forms with diagnosis data from patient medical-services claim forms. Relator's expert evidence suffices to survive summary judgment.

The text of § 3729(a)(1) requires a causal connection between Parke–Davis's actions and the false claims at issue. Parke–Davis contends that the Relator must show that Parke–Davis "either exerted 'control over' or otherwise directly influenced, the submission of a false claim." Parke–Davis argues that Relator cannot meet this standard, as the causal chain includes several links: Parke–Davis markets Neurontin to doctors, who prescribe it for their patients, who take the prescriptions to their pharmacists, who file claims for Medicaid reimbursement.

But Parke–Davis misstates the legal standard for causation. The FCA does not provide a special definition for causation, and neither the Supreme Court nor any Circuit Court of Appeals has grafted such a special definition on the FCA. Absent an FCA-specific definition of causation, the Court will apply common-law tort causation concepts. . . .

Whether Parke–Davis's conduct was a substantial factor in causing the presentation of false Medicaid claims is a question of fact. Relator has produced enough evidence on this score to create at least a genuine issue of material fact. In particular, Relator has produced circumstantial evidence (*e.g.*, the rates of off-label prescriptions before and after physician conferences hosted by Parke–Davis) and direct evidence (the "Verbatim" market-research reports recording doctors' state of mind after marketing meetings).

Parke–Davis also disputes that Relator can reliably extrapolate the prescription activities of a small sample of ten doctors to the off-label prescription rates of over 3000 physicians in fifty states, and, as discussed above, Parke–Davis challenges the reliability of the underlying data used to determine whether a prescription is for off-label uses. But the Court will defer the daunting task of determining whether a reliable statistical method exists for measuring nation-wide damages. . . .

NOTES

1. *History of Qui Tam Suits.* "Qui tam" (standing for "qui tam pro domino rege quam pro se ipso"—"he who as much on behalf of the king as on behalf of himself") is a common-law action in which a private individual, the "relator," sues on behalf of himself and the government, and the two share the proceeds. *See Qui Tam Suits Under the Federal False Claims Act: Tool of the Private Litigant in Public Actions*, 67 Nw. U. L. Rev. 446, 451 (1972) (student author); Valerie Park, *The False Claims Act, Qui Tam Relators, and the Government: Which Is the Real Party to the Action?*, 43 Stan. L. Rev. 1061, 1064 (1991); Robert W. Fischer, Jr., *Qui Tam Actions: The Role of the Private Citizen in Law Enforcement*, 20 UCLA L. Rev. 778, 780 (1973).

The U.S. Congress in its first decade enacted some dozen qui tam provisions for enforcement of criminal statutes. Qui tam actions fell by the wayside as federal law enforcement capacity increased and as the action became an object of suspicion in the eyes of a public that saw private involvement in public suits as meddling and abusive. Currently, the only qui tam cause of action authorized by federal law is to enforce the False Claims Act (FCA). The FCA allows individuals with knowledge of fraud against the government to sue for treble damages and to keep fifteen to twenty-five percent of any award. The Justice Department has welcomed suits like that by Franklin as part of a stepped-up effort to punish and deter fraud in federal health care programs. *Justice Department Gears Up for Health Care Fraud Litigation*, FDA WEEK, Vol. 12, No. 9 (Mar. 3, 2006); *Medicaid Fraud Control Unit Recovers $171 Million*, US STATES NEWS (Oct. 17, 2005); Jonathan K. Henderson & Quintin Cassady, *Drug Deals in 2006: Cutting Edge Legal and Regulatory Issues in the Pharmaceutical Industry*, 15 ANNALS OF HEALTH LAW 107 (2006). The qui tam action to enforce the FCA had lain dormant for nearly fifty years when Congress revitalized the FCA in 1986.

Although qui tam suits originated in England at common law, in the United States they have always been statutory. Thus, such suits are a mechanism for enforcing specific statutes passed by the legislature. And there is a general consensus that they must be explicitly authorized, which means that Congress not only created the law that expresses the standard of legality but has also expressly authorized private suits to enforce that standard.

2. *Qui Tam Enforcement of the False Claims Act.* Franklin's lawsuit did not seek a remedy for violation of the FD&C Act. The statute he alleges Parke–Davis violated is the False Claims Act. That statute prohibits submitting, or causing to be submitted, any false or fraudulent claim for payment by the government. It also provides that persons who provide information about violations may sue on their own behalf and recover a portion of the government's loss. The supposedly false claims in question were those submitted by providers of medical care—in this case prescription drugs—for reimbursement for drugs prescribed by participating physicians. Many, or at least some, of those claims were ineligible for payment because the drugs had been prescribed for indications that FDA had not approved. Franklin alleged that Parke–Davis was responsible for many if not all of these off-label prescriptions (and resulting claims) because it encouraged physicians to prescribe for off-label use. This complex line of reasoning was plausible enough to withstand Parke–Davis's summary judgment motion. *See* Stephanie Greene, *False Claims Act Liability for Off–Label Promotion of Pharmaceutical Products*, 110 PENN ST. L. REV. 41 (2005); Mark S. Davis, *The Effects of False Claims Act Whistleblowers on the Pharmaceutical Industry* (2006), in Chapter I(G)(11) of the Electronic Book.

3. *The Plaintiff's Burden of Proof.* As the District Court acknowledges, however, Franklin faces another hurdle in establishing the dollar value of the claims he alleges were false. He must be able to identify which prescriptions were for indications that, although lacking FDA's approval, are still eligible for reimbursement under state standards. And to do this he must establish what indication particular prescriptions were for. That information does not appear on the prescription form itself. Physicians presumably know why they want a patient to use a drug and may record this information in the patient's record, but the form they sign for delivery to the pharmacist does not call for any description of the purpose for which the drug is prescribed. Franklin claimed to have solved this problem by developing an instrument or algorithm that permits estimates of the share of any drug's use that is off-label. Finally, Franklin must find a way of estimating the share of such off-label use that is attributable to Parke–Davis's unlawful promotion rather than to physicians' self-informed decisions.

4. *Settlement.* Franklin and Parke–Davis ultimately settled the dispute. A Stipulation of Dismissal states that the United States will pay Relator Franklin

$24,640,000 (in accordance with the Relator Share Agreement between the U.S. and Franklin) after defendant Parke–Davis pays the agreed upon settlement amount. A status report dated February 5, 2004, references a January 22, 2004, Investor News Release in which Pfizer announced that it is taking a charge of $427 million dollars in connection with investigations into Warner–Lambert's promotion of Neurontin to "resolve all outstanding federal and state governmental investigations related to Neurontin as well as the pending civil qui tam suit concerning this matter."

3. THE FD&C ACT AS A STATE LAW STANDARD OF CARE

Although the FD&C Act does not provide an independent basis for suits by injured consumers, proof that the defendant violated the Act may materially assist the plaintiff, as the following case illustrates.

Orthopedic Equipment Co. v. Eutsler

276 F.2d 455 (4th Cir. 1960).

■ SOBELOFF, CHIEF JUDGE.

... On March 30, 1956, the twenty-one year old plaintiff was helping his father take down a tree on a farm near Orange, Virginia. He was injured by the tree falling upon him. At the University of Virginia Hospital, it was found that he had sustained a fracture of the leg and other injuries. In the judgment of the surgeons, the treatment indicated for the fracture was an operation known as intra medullary nailing by use of a Kuntscher Cloverleaf Intramedullary Nail. This involves the insertion of a long metal rod or nail into the medullary canal (containing the [m]arrow) of the femur (or thigh bone), in order to stabilize the broken fragments. The advantage sought by this method is an early union and weight-bearing without the necessity of a plaster cast.

A team of orthopedists, experienced in this technique, operated on April 3, 1956. Having prepared the canal by use of a 9mm. medullary reamer or drill, the surgeons began to insert into the medullary canal a Kuntscher Cloverleaf intramedullary nail manufactured by the defendant. These Kuntscher nails usually have imprinted upon them two figures signifying their dimensions, e.g., 9 + 40, 10 + 42, but the imprint or label does not explain the meaning of these figures. It is agreed by the parties that the larger figure is understood to represent the length of the nail in centimeters. According to the plaintiff's expert witnesses, the interpretation placed upon the smaller figure by orthopedists is that the nail will fit into a hole having a width or diameter corresponding in millimeters to the figure on the nail. This follows from the necessity that the nail shall fit tightly into the canal previously prepared by a reamer of corresponding diameter. These witnesses also testified that after the canal is reamed, the nail is selected on the basis of the measurement on its "label," or imprint, conforming to the measurement of the reamer used. Furthermore, plaintiff's experts testified, orthopedic surgeons invariably rely upon the figures imprinted on the nail, when there are figures imprinted, without making independent measurements. Thus, according to the surgeons, they relied in this instance too on the accuracy of the marking, "OEC 9 + 40," in selecting the nail.

As the nail was driven down the canal of the upper fragment of the thigh bone, the surgeons at first met normal resistance. When it penetrated further, however, greater resistance was encountered. Nevertheless, the doctors did not regard this as unusual, since they knew that they had used a 9mm. reamer and the nail was marked to indicate 9mm.; they concluded that it must merely have met some slight obstruction which, as in past operations, would be passed or overcome without difficulty. Accordingly, as was customary in such cases, two or three slightly heavier blows were then struck.

Because the nail would progress no further even after these heavier blows, the surgeons decided to remove it. However, when persistent efforts to dislodge the nail proved unavailing, the portion of the nail protruding below the canal of the upper fragment was cut off, the wound closed, and a plaster cast applied in the hope that in a few weeks the bone would atrophy sufficiently to loosen the nail and permit its withdrawal.

About a month later, on May 4, the surgeons again tried to extract the nail, but were unsuccessful. Thereupon, one of the doctors designed a new instrument, and by its use removal of the nail was finally accomplished in a third operation on June 5. Measurements of cross-sections of the nail, as testified to by a machinist, varied from a minimum of 9.27mm. to a maximum of 10.12mm.

Due to the nail's impaction, incurable osteomyelitis or bone infection resulted. The plaintiff has permanently lost the use of his leg, and its ultimate amputation is expected.

This action was brought against defendant for alleged "negligent manufacture, labeling and launching on the market of said nail ...," plaintiff presumably at first intending to charge ordinary common law negligence only. Later, however, it was stipulated by counsel that, without formal amendment, the complaint should also be regarded as alleging a violation of the Federal Food, Drug, and Cosmetic Act....

Defendant contends, for two reasons, that the District Judge erred in basing his charge to the jury on the Federal Food, Drug, and Cosmetic Act, 21 U.S.C.A. §§ 301–392. It asserts first, that the evidence of misbranding is insufficient....

We think that the evidence was sufficient to raise a jury question of misbranding. Notwithstanding the defendant's expert testimony to the contrary, the testimony of plaintiff's experts as to the understanding of the medical profession of the number 9 on the nail certainly presented an issue for the jury as to the "true" meaning of the number.

Furthermore, the defendant points out that its catalogue was available in the hospital, but the surgeons performing the operation admittedly had not read it. However, that the defendant claims the catalogue would show, namely that the figure on the nail refers to its "width," does not seem to aid the defendant's argument. Even if, as defendant argues, the number did refer to the "width" of the nail, and assuming for the sake of the argument that "width" is different from diameter, it is undisputed that the nail was actually more than 9mm. wide. Properly, it was left to the jury to judge the weight of the testimony offered by the plaintiff and the answering explanations advanced by the defendant, and the jury was clearly warranted in concluding that the labeling was false or misleading.

. . . .

It is urged by defendant that the regulations issued pursuant to [21 U.S.C. § 352(f); FD&C Act § 502(f)] nevertheless exempt manufacturers from the obligation to give directions for the use of surgical instruments since such devices are designed for use by a skilled profession. This specific exemption of surgical instruments from section 352(f), however, does not relieve the defendant from compliance with other provisions of the Act, including the remainder of section 352, and seems to us rather to indicate a contrary intention. In short, while the Act imposed no obligation upon defendant to label its nail, once it undertook to do so the Act required it to avoid misbranding.

. . . The Federal Food, Drug, and Cosmetic Act does not expressly provide a civil remedy for injured consumers. However, the statute imposes an absolute duty on manufacturers not to misbrand their products, and the breach of this duty may give rise to civil liability.

The basic question is whether a violation of the strict duty created by the Act shall be deemed negligence per se under Virginia law, assuming as we must from the submission made to the jury and from its verdict, that the violation was the proximate cause of the plaintiff's injury. The majority of American courts which have passed on this question, in cases arising under state laws resembling the Federal Act, have held violations to be negligence per se. Apparently the Supreme Court of Appeals of Virginia has not had occasion to decide whether a violation of the Virginia Food Act, or the state statutory provisions dealing with misbranding and adulteration of drugs and cosmetics, constitutes negligence per se. The Virginia Court, however, has stated, in a case involving a motor vehicle statute, that:

> "The violation of a statute, although negligence per se, will not support a recovery for damages unless such violation proximately causes or contributes to the injury complained of." *Reid v. Boward*, 1943, 181 Va. 718, 723, 26 S.E.2d 27, 29.

Since Virginia law seems to regard violation of motor vehicle statutes as negligence per se, again assuming from the jury's verdict here that the violation was found to be a proximate cause of the injury, and in light of the decisions in other states passing on this question, we think that a violation of the Federal Food, Drug, and Cosmetic Act is negligence per se in Virginia, and that the District Judge correctly based his charge on that premise.

. . . .

NOTES

1. *State Claims Incorporate Federal Law. Eutsler* was in federal court based on diversity jurisdiction. It is thus the law of Virginia, as interpreted by the U.S. Court of Appeals, that establishes that the FD&C Act's definition of misbranding is one measure of the device manufacturer's common law duty. The Court of Appeals suggested that proof that the company misbranded its nail under the FD&C Act will

establish beyond dispute, *i.e.*, per se, that it breached its common law duty to exercise care in the manufacture and packaging of its product. In short, state law determines whether federal regulatory requirements should be consulted in determining what standard of care should apply in a tort suit, as well as what weight, *e.g.*, "some evidence of negligence" or "negligence per se," should attach to proof of its violation. State courts may, however, be influenced by the reasoning federal regulators offer for such requirements. *See, e.g., MacDonald v. Ortho Pharmaceutical Corporation*, 475 N.E.2d 65 (Mass. Sup. Ct. 1985), below.

2. *Other FD&C Act Cases. Stanton v. Astra Pharmaceutical Products, Inc.*, 718 F.2d 553 (3d Cir. 1983), sustained a jury award to an injured consumer based upon the company's failure to submit adverse reaction reports to FDA. *See also Toole v. Richardson–Merrell Inc.*, 60 Cal. Rptr. 398 (1967). For commentary, *see* William Kaplan, *Variations on a Single Theme—The Impact of the Pure-Food Statutes on Civil Liability*, 13 Food Drug Cosm. L.J. 11 (1958); William Woods, *The Effect of the Food, Drug and Cosmetic Act on Private Litigation*, 8 Food Drug Cosm. L.J. 511 (1953).

3. *The Advantages of a Regulatory Standard.* Plaintiffs' attorneys commonly search for evidence of possible statutory or regulatory violations. If there is any ground for questioning whether the defendant's product was properly designed or appropriately labeled, evidence that it did not satisfy FDA's requirements can materially strengthen the plaintiff's case and perhaps even end debate over what standard of care should apply.

4. *Jurisdictional Implications.* For many years it was assumed that if a plaintiff in a state tort action asserted that the defendant violated a federal regulatory requirement, the action was one "arising under the laws ... of the United States" and was thus eligible for federal question jurisdiction under 28 U.S.C. 1331. However, in *Merrell Dow Pharmaceutical v. Thompson*, 478 U.S. 804 (1996), the Supreme Court squarely rejected this reading of Section 1331 and ruled that the plaintiff's reliance on alleged violations of the FD&C Act did not convert what was essentially a state law dispute into a federal question case.

C.   FEDERAL LAW LIMITS ON STATE LAW CLAIMS

In most of the cases treated in Part B, it was the plaintiff—the alleged victim of a regulatory violation—who sought to invoke the federal standard. But sometimes it is the defendant who asks a court to reconcile disparities between federal regulatory duties and state common law obligations by holding that compliance with FDA's demands should fulfill its duties under state law.

1.   REGULATORY COMPLIANCE AS A DEFENSE

MacDonald v. Ortho Pharmaceutical Corporation

475 N.E.2d 65 (Mass. 1985)

■ Abrams, Justice

This products liability action raises the question of the extent of a drug manufacturer's duty to warn consumers of dangers inherent in the use of oral contraceptives. The plaintiffs brought suit against the defendant,

Ortho Pharmaceutical Corporation (Ortho), for injuries allegedly caused by Ortho's birth control pills, and obtained a jury verdict in their favor. The defendant moved for a judgment notwithstanding the verdict. The judge concluded that the defendant did not owe a duty to warn the plaintiffs, and entered judgment for Ortho. The plaintiffs appealed. We transferred the case to this court on our own motion and reinstate the jury verdict.

We summarize the facts. In September, 1973, the plaintiff Carole D. MacDonald (MacDonald), who was twenty-six years old at the time, obtained from her gynecologist a prescription for Ortho–Novum contraceptive pills, manufactured by Ortho. As required by the then effective regulations promulgated by the United States Food and Drug Administration (FDA), the pill dispenser she received was labeled with a warning that "oral contraceptives are powerful and effective drugs which can cause side effects in some users and should not be used at all by some women," and that "[t]he most serious known side effect is abnormal blood clotting which can be fatal."[3] The warning also referred MacDonald to a booklet which she obtained from her gynecologist, and which was distributed by Ortho pursuant to FDA requirements. The booklet contained detailed information about the contraceptive pill, including the increased risk to pill users that vital organs such as the brain may be damaged by abnormal blood clotting.[4] The word "stroke" did not appear on the dispenser warning or in the booklet.

---

3. FDA regulations in effect during the time period relevant to this litigation required that the following warning be included in or with the pill dispenser:

"Do Not Take This Drug Without Your Doctor's Continued Supervision.

The oral contraceptives are powerful and effective drugs which can cause side effects in some users and should not be used at all by some women. The most serious known side effect is abnormal blood clotting which can be fatal.... "

4. Applicable FDA regulations required that the booklet contain "information in lay language, concerning effectiveness, contraindications, warnings, precautions, and adverse reactions," including a warning "regarding the serious side effects with special attention to thromboembolic disorders and stating the estimated morbidity and mortality in users vs. nonusers." Ortho's booklet contained the following information:

"About blood clots

Blood clots occasionally form in the blood vessels of the legs and the pelvis of apparently healthy people and may threaten life if the clots break loose and then lodge in the lung or if they form in other vital organs, such as the brain. It has been estimated that about one woman in 2,000 on the pill each year suffers a blood clotting disorder severe enough to require hospitalization. The estimated death rate from abnormal blood clotting in healthy women under 35 not taking the pill is 1 in 500,000; whereas for the same group taking the pill it is 1 in 66,-000. For healthy women over 35 not taking the pill, the rate is 1 in 200,-000 compared to 1 in 25,000 for pill users. Blood clots are about three times more likely to develop in women over the age of 34. For these reasons it is important that women who have had blood clots in the legs, lungs or brain not use oral contraceptives. Anyone using the pill who has severe leg or chest pains, coughs up blood, has difficulty breathing, sudden severe headache or vomiting, dizziness or fainting, disturbances of vision or speech, weakness or numbness of an arm or leg, should call her doctor immediately and stop taking the pill."

MacDonald's prescription for Ortho–Novum pills was renewed at subsequent annual visits to her gynecologist. The prescription was filled annually. On July 24, 1976, after approximately three years of using the pills, MacDonald suffered an occlusion of a cerebral artery by a blood clot, an injury commonly referred to as a stroke. The injury caused the death of approximately twenty per cent of MacDonald's brain tissue, and left her permanently disabled. . . .

MacDonald testified that, during the time she used the pills, she was unaware that the risk of abnormal blood clotting encompassed the risk of stroke, and that she would not have used the pills had she been warned that stroke is an associated risk.[6] The case was submitted to a jury on the plaintiffs' theories that Ortho was negligent in failing to warn adequately of the dangers associated with the pills and that Ortho breached its warranty of merchantability. These two theories were treated, in effect, as a single claim of failure to warn. [T]he jury found . . . that Ortho was negligent and in breach of warranty because it failed to give MacDonald sufficient warning of such dangers.

After the jury verdict, the judge granted Ortho's motion for judgment notwithstanding the verdict, concluding that, because oral contraceptives are prescription drugs, a manufacturer's duty to warn the consumer is satisfied if the manufacturer gives adequate warnings to the prescribing physician, and that the manufacturer has no duty to warn the consumer directly.

The rule in jurisdictions that have addressed the question of the extent of a manufacturer's duty to warn in cases involving prescription drugs is that the prescribing physician acts as a "learned intermediary" between the manufacturer and the patient, and "the duty of the ethical drug manufacturer is to warn the doctor, rather than the patient, [although] the manufacturer is directly liable to the patient for a breach of such duty." Oral contraceptives, however, bear peculiar characteristics which warrant the imposition of a common law duty on the manufacturer to warn users directly of associated risks. Whereas a patient's involvement in decision making concerning use of a prescription drug necessary to treat a malady is typically minimal or nonexistent, the healthy, young consumer of oral contraceptives is usually actively involved in the decision to use "the pill," as opposed to other available birth control products, and the prescribing physician is relegated to a relatively passive role.

Furthermore, the physician prescribing "the pill," as a matter of course, examines the patient once before prescribing an oral contraceptive and only annually thereafter. Thus, the patient may only seldom have the opportunity to explore her questions and concerns about the medication with the prescribing physician. Even if the physician, on those occasions, were scrupulously to remind the patient of the risks attendant on continua-

6. Subsequent to the events in this case, the FDA regulation was amended by 43 Fed. Reg. 4221 (1978), which replaced the regulation requirement of a specified warning on the pill dispenser, see Note 3, *supra*, with a requirement that the dispenser contain a warning "of the serious side effects of oral contraceptives, such as thrombophlebitis, pulmonary embolism, myocardial infarction, retinal artery thrombosis, *stroke*, benign hepatic adenomas, induction of fetal abnormalities, and gallbladder disease" (emphasis added).

tion of the oral contraceptive, "the patient cannot be expected to remember all of the details for a protracted period of time."

Last, the birth control pill is specifically subject to extensive Federal regulation. The FDA has promulgated regulations designed to ensure that the choice of "the pill" as a contraceptive method is informed by comprehensible warnings of potential side effects. These regulations, and subsequent amendments, have their basis in the FDA commissioner's finding, after hearings, that "[b]ecause oral contraceptives are ordinarily taken electively by healthy women who have available to them alternative methods of treatment, and because of the relatively high incidence of serious illnesses associated with their use ... users of these drugs should, without exception, be furnished with written information telling them of the drug's benefits and risks." The FDA also found that the facts necessary to informed decisions by women as to use of oral contraceptives are "too complex to expect the patient to remember everything told her by the physician," and that, in the absence of direct written warnings, many potential users of "the pill" do not receive the needed information "in an organized, comprehensive, understandable, and handy-for-future-reference form."

The oral contraceptive thus stands apart from other prescription drugs in light of the heightened participation of patients in decisions relating to use of "the pill"; the substantial risks affiliated with the product's use; the feasibility of direct warnings by the manufacturer to the user; the limited participation of the physician (annual prescriptions); and the possibility that oral communications between physicians and consumers may be insufficient or too scanty standing alone fully to apprise consumers of the product's dangers at the time the initial selection of a contraceptive method is made as well as at subsequent points when alternative methods may be considered. We conclude that the manufacturer of oral contraceptives is not justified in relying on warnings to the medical profession to satisfy its common law duty to warn, and that the manufacturer's obligation encompasses a duty to warn the ultimate user.

... Ortho contends initially that its warnings complied with FDA labeling requirements, and that those requirements preempt or define the bounds of the common law duty to warn. We disagree. The regulatory history of the FDA requirements belies any objective to cloak them with preemptive effect. In response to concerns raised by drug manufacturers that warnings required and drafted by the FDA might be deemed inadequate by juries, the FDA commissioner specifically noted that the boundaries of civil tort liability for failure to warn are controlled by applicable State law. Although the common law duty we today recognize is to a large degree coextensive with the regulatory duties imposed by the FDA, we are persuaded that, in instances where a trier of fact could reasonably conclude that a manufacturer's compliance with FDA labeling requirements or guidelines did not adequately apprise oral contraceptive users of inherent risks, the manufacturer should not be shielded from liability by such compliance. Thus, compliance with FDA requirements, though admissible to demonstrate lack of negligence, is not conclusive on this issue, just as violation of FDA requirements is evidence, but not conclusive evidence, of negligence. We therefore concur with the plaintiffs' argument that even if the conclusion that Ortho complied with FDA requirements were inescapable, an issue we need not decide, the jury nonetheless could have found that the lack of a reference to "stroke" breached Ortho's common law duty to warn.

The common law duty to warn, like the analogous FDA "lay language" requirement, necessitates a warning "comprehensible to the average user and . . . convey[ing] a fair indication of the nature and extent of the danger to the mind of a reasonably prudent person." Whether a particular warning measures up to this standard is almost always an issue to be resolved by a jury; few questions are "more appropriately left to a common sense lay judgment than that of whether a written warning gets its message across to an average person." . . .

Ortho argues that reasonable minds could not differ as to whether MacDonald was adequately informed of the risk of the injury she sustained by Ortho's warning that the oral contraceptives could cause "abnormal blood clotting which can be fatal" and further warning of the incremental likelihood of hospitalization or death due to blood clotting in "vital organs, such as the brain." We disagree. . . . We cannot say that this jury's decision that the warning was inadequate is so unreasonable as to require the opposite conclusion as a matter of law. The jury may well have concluded, in light of their common experience and MacDonald's testimony, that the absence of a reference to "stroke" in the warning unduly minimized the warning's impact or failed to make the nature of the risk reasonably comprehensible to the average consumer. Similarly, the jury may have concluded that there are fates worse than death, such as the permanent disablement suffered by MacDonald, and that the mention of the risk of death did not, therefore, suffice to apprise an average consumer of the material risks of oral contraceptive use.

Ortho's argument that, as a matter of law, there was insufficient evidence that MacDonald's injury was proximately caused by a deficiency in the warnings is substantially similar to its argument on the issue of the adequacy of the warnings, and is likewise unavailing. . . .

■ O'CONNOR, J. (dissenting).

. . . While I would choose the "prescription drug" rule [i.e, the "learned intermediary" rule] over the rule announced today by the court, I recognize that the FDA has promulgated regulations governing the provision of printed information to users of oral contraceptives. I would not consider the imposition of tort liability for failure to comply with those regulations, designed to further consumer protection, unfair nor unduly burdensome to contraceptive pill manufacturers. However, in my view, the evidence in this case would not support a finding that Ortho failed to comply with those regulations. The FDA required Ortho to place on every oral contraceptive pill dispenser a warning stating that the "most serious known side effect [of the oral contraceptive pill] is abnormal blood clotting which can be fatal." 21 C.F.R. § 130.45(d)(1), 35 Fed. Reg. 9002–9003 (1970). Ortho complied in every way with that requirement. The FDA also required that Ortho make available to physicians for patients who requested it "information in lay language, concerning effectiveness, contraindications, warnings, precautions, and adverse reactions." 21 C.F.R. § 130.45(e), 35 Fed. Reg. 9003 (1970). Ortho provided Carole MacDonald's physician with a booklet that stated: "Blood clots occasionally form in the blood vessels of the legs and pelvis of apparently healthy people and may threaten life if the clots break loose and then lodge in the lung or if they form in other vital organs, such as the brain." MacDonald's physician gave Ortho's booklet to MacDonald. The court finds it unnecessary to decide whether Ortho complied with FDA's "lay language" requirement, but I do not believe that any rational trier of fact could have concluded that Ortho failed to comply with the regulation.

The court states only that the jury "could have found that the lack of reference to 'stroke' breached Ortho's common law duty to warn." Surely, the statement in Ortho's booklet that the contraceptive pill could cause life threatening blood clots to form in the brain, even though it did not contain the word "stroke," satisfied the court's requirement that Ortho provide "written warnings conveying reasonable notice of the nature, gravity, and likelihood of known or knowable side effects." I would affirm the judgment for Ortho.

NOTES

1. *Rejection of Learned Intermediary Defense.* The *MacDonald* court's rejection of Ortho's claim that it had no duty to warn consumers directly about the risk of stroke is consistent with the Restatement and with other judicial authority. The reasons the court offers for holding that Ortho had a duty to warn patients as well as physicians are similar to those on which FDA relied when it decided to require makers of oral contraceptives to provide "patient package inserts." Of course, as a result of FDA's decision, Ortho had no choice in the matter. Federal law required the very communication Mrs. MacDonald claimed that Massachusetts common law mandated. It is therefore not clear whether this obligation arises from federal or state law.

2. *Rejection of FDA's Mandated Labeling.* More problematic, perhaps, is the court's holding that the jury was entitled to conclude that Ortho's unquestioned compliance with FDA's prescribed form and wording was not sufficient to satisfy its common law duty to warn. The court's reasoning, redolent of the "minimum standards" theory, does not quite do justice to the company's defense. FDA had considered the very risk that Mrs. MacDonald experienced. The risk of stroke had long been apparent. Furthermore, the agency wrestled with the question of how best to warn patients about this risk. It prescribed the words Ortho used after considering other possibilities. Consumers may have understood other words, including the word "stroke," more readily, but the court offers no reason to believe that a jury would be better equipped than FDA to select the best verbal formula. And consider another issue: Would Ortho's product have been misbranded if it had used words in its patient insert that did not match those FDA had prescribed? See FDA's discussion in its 2006 prescription drug labeling rule, p. 1495 *infra*.

MacDonald is rather unusual in focusing on the adequacy of the company's efforts to warn about a risk that both it and FDA (and later the plaintiff) agreed should be the subject of a warning. More often the debate is over whether the risk experienced by the plaintiff is sufficiently well documented to require a warning at all. *MacDonald* is not atypical, however, in presenting the court (and potentially the jury) with a clear challenge to a decision previously reached by FDA.

Tobin v. Astra Pharmaceutical Products, Inc.

993 F.2d 528 (6th Cir. 1993).

■ RALPH B. GUY, JR., CIRCUIT JUDGE.

. . . .

In 1986, Kathy Tobin was 19 years old and pregnant with twins. Her expected date of delivery was in early April 1987. Other than a mitral valve prolapse, or heart murmur, a rather common finding in reproductive-age women, Tobin was a healthy young woman. In mid-October 1986, Tobin was hospitalized for dehydration. She was having difficulty keeping down food and fluids and required hydration. Her condition was diagnosed as viral in origin. She was released after a few days and her pregnancy progressed. In January 1987, Tobin was admitted to the hospital for management of preterm labor. She was given an injection of magnesium sulphate and then was placed on an oral maintenance dose of ritodrine. Dosage levels varied, being increased when contractions returned.

Tobin testified that after each dose of ritodrine her pulse would race and her heart felt as if "it was going to jump out of my skin"; her face would also flush and her hands and legs would swell. She was advised that these symptoms were normal side effects of ritodrine. On March 9, 1987, Tobin's obstetricians reduced the dosage because of her rapid heart rate. On March 16, 1987, Tobin informed her doctors that she could not breathe when lying down, and she was told to further reduce the ritodrine dosage. At 1:30 a.m. on March 17, she was admitted to the hospital with symptoms of tachypnea (rapid breathing), dyspnea (shortness of breath), and a gallop rhythm of the heart. At this time, it also was noted that Tobin had a grade I/IV systolic murmur of the heart. X-rays revealed that she had pulmonary edema (fluid in the lungs) and cardiomegaly (enlargement of the heart) caused by congestive heart failure. An electrocardiogram revealed advanced dilated cardiomyopathy. Ritodrine was discontinued, and that afternoon plaintiff delivered healthy twins having a gestational age of 37 weeks.

On March 20, Tobin was discharged from the hospital with instructions to follow up with a cardiologist. The next day she was readmitted for treatment of congestive heart failure, cardiomyopathy, and pulmonary edema. After five days in the hospital, she was again released. She was readmitted on April 10, and on April 15 a mechanical heart, or ventricular assist device, was inserted until a donated heart for a heart transplant could be found. On April 16, Tobin underwent a heart transplant.

Plaintiff filed suit against Duphar B.V., the corporation in the Netherlands that manufactures ritodrine, and against Astra Pharmaceutical, Duphar's United States distributor. After removal to federal court on diversity grounds, the district court granted Duphar's motion to dismiss for lack of personal jurisdiction. Plaintiff proceeded against Astra. After a two-week trial, the jury returned a verdict in favor of the plaintiff. The jury awarded Tobin approximately $4.5 million, finding Astra liable on the basis of defective design and failure to warn for the conditions that led to her heart transplant. . . . The district court denied Astra's motion for j.n.o.v. or in the alternative for a new trial, and Astra timely appealed.

. . . .

Having concluded that plaintiff's evidence of causation was appropriate expert testimony from which the jury could find causation, we turn to the two theories of liability offered by the plaintiff. The jury was instructed that it should find for the plaintiff if:

(a) ritodrine, as manufactured and marketed by Astra and as used by the plaintiff, was in a defective condition unreasonably dangerous to the user, and

(b) the defective and unreasonably dangerous condition of the ritodrine was a substantial factor in causing the plaintiff['s] injuries.

. . . .

Under Kentucky law, the test for whether a product is in a defective condition and unreasonably dangerous to the user is whether an ordinarily prudent manufacturer, being fully aware of the risks, would have placed the product on the market. . . .

In the context of her defective design claim, plaintiff's arguments regarding the weighing of the risks against the benefits of ritodrine were not improper, given the evidence presented in this case. . . .

In a nutshell, plaintiff claims that oral ritodrine is bereft of benefits as far as improving neonatal outcome. Weighing no benefits against the serious risks posed by the drug and suffered by the plaintiff, it is clear, plaintiff asserts, that the risks outweigh the benefits and thus no "ordinarily prudent manufacturer" would put the drug on the market. Astra maintains that oral ritodrine is effective in prolonging pregnancy, and therefore in improving neonatal outcome, and that the risks to maternal and fetal health associated with oral ritodrine are outweighed by the benefits of reducing neonatal morbidity and mortality. Astra also maintains that, because of FDA approval, ritodrine's effectiveness is not open to question.

Plaintiff's expert in this area was Dr. Mortensen. Dr. Mortensen, a pediatrician with a master's degree in pharmacology and trained in toxicology, reviewed the test results that were submitted to the FDA with the New Drug Application in 1974. Dr. Mortensen also reviewed several articles discussing betamimetic drugs in general and ritodrine in specific.

Before addressing the arguments concerning efficacy, we must first address whether plaintiff should have been allowed to litigate the efficacy issue at all. Defendant argues that "plaintiff should not have been permitted to litigate this issue, because it is a mockery of the scientific analysis employed by the FDA and the Advisory Committee which conclusively found that ritodrine was efficacious." We reject the argument that FDA approval preempts state product liability claims based on design defect.

While this circuit has not directly ruled on whether a plaintiff in a product liability action may litigate an FDA finding that a drug is efficacious, the Fifth Circuit has ruled that the Food, Drug and Cosmetic Act, 21 U.S.C. § 301 et seq., does not preempt state law claims based on defective design. *Hurley v. Lederle Lab. Div. of Am. Cyanamid Co.*, 863 F.2d 1173, 1176–77 (5th Cir. 1989). In so holding, the Fifth Circuit reversed the district court's finding of preemption, noting that "the great majority of United States district courts which have addressed this issue have ruled against preemption."

FDA approval is evidence which the jury may consider in reaching its verdict. The jury may weigh FDA approval as it sees fit, especially in a case where the plaintiff has presented evidence to support an articulable basis for disregarding an FDA finding—in this case the finding that ritodrine was effective. Tobin presented an articulable basis for disregarding the FDA's finding that ritodrine was effective in improving neonatal outcome: the individual studies relied on by the FDA were insufficient to support a finding of efficacy as found by the FDA Advisory Committee, and the pooled data requested by the Advisory Committee was statistically invalid.

To understand the arguments of the parties concerning ritodrine's effectiveness, it is necessary to review the New Drug Application that was submitted to the FDA and the results of the required clinical trials, along with subsequent articles that have been published discussing ritodrine.... The required clinical studies on ritodrine consisted of Phase I (16 studies in healthy patients to determine safety), Phase II (5 studies in preterm labor patients to determine efficacy), and Phase III (11 studies in preterm labor patients comparing ritodrine patients to non-ritodrine controls to determine safety and efficacy).

The clinical trials were designed to measure a gain in days in the length of pregnancy as a measure of efficacy under the assumption that any increase in the gestational period would reduce neonatal morbidity and mortality. The Phase III studies consisted of tests of oral ritodrine's effectiveness based on three separate testing procedures: a placebo series, in which oral ritodrine was compared to the use of a placebo; an ethanol series comparing ritodrine to the use of ethanol; and a series referred to as the "Creasy studies," in which all patients were treated with injections of intramuscular ritodrine and then half received oral maintenance doses of ritodrine while the other half received placebos. In the Creasy studies, any recurrences of premature labor were treated with injections of intramuscular ritodrine.

After the data from these studies was submitted to the FDA, the FDA Advisory Committee on Fertility and Maternal Health Drugs found that the required clinical trials failed to demonstrate efficacy. Specifically, "the tenor of the committee was that there was not substantial data to support the efficacy of ritodrine for the treatment of premature labor." The Advisory Committee found that three of the Phase III placebo-controlled studies were flawed because they included women who were not actually in preterm labor. Because the remaining individual studies did not have a sufficient number of patients to establish statistical significance regarding improvement in neonatal outcome, the Advisory Committee requested the data be pooled and resubmitted. The initial data was presented in terms of gain in days; it did not include statistics on neonatal outcome or mortality. The Advisory Committee requested that, when the data was resubmitted, it should include such information. The manufacturer was asked to pool the data from all the studies for an all-patient analysis; stratify all of the patients by gestational age; and analyze neonatal mortality, birth weight, and the incidence of respiratory distress syndrome.

Dr. Peter, who participated in the proceedings before the FDA, testified at trial that this pooled data does not represent statistically valid results. Dr. Barden, one of Astra's experts, said he was not surprised that one of the members of the Advisory Committee stated the pooled studies were not statistically valid

> because the problem with the pooled studies, as you well know, were that some of the patients had rather than placebo, the treatment with ethanol or alcohol, which is another treatment of premature labor. So that tends to mean that by pooling the data, they were mixing apples and oranges in a sense.

Comments made by various members of the Advisory Committee recognized the inappropriateness of pooling data: "So, strictly speaking, the statistical tests are not valid for the pooled studies. The statistical tests would presume that the groups randomized were similar in every respect but for the treatments received, and here we have a combination of different controls and different treatment regimens for ritodrine patients." Dr. Little of the committee commented that "obviously, it is not reasonable to pool data." Yet, on the basis of the originally submitted data, which the Advisory Committee had found did not contain substantial evidence to support a finding of efficacy, and the newly reworked data, the committee recommended approval.

The FDA made its own determination regarding efficacy. FDA regulations require that efficacy be established by "at least two 'adequate and well-controlled' studies." The FDA determined that four studies of the Phase III studies met this test, and approved ritodrine in 1980. The four studies are referred to by the names of the project leaders: Fuchs, Barden, Creasy, and Sivasambo. Plaintiff introduced evidence regarding the methodology and conclusions of each study.

In the Fuchs study, the control group of mothers were treated with intravenous ethanol and no follow-up, while ritodrine patients were given initial intravenous doses of ritodrine and follow-up oral doses. The control group was further along in gestation based on each mother's last menstrual period, and the group was found to be in more advanced labor, in that they were more dilated, than the ritodrine group. The Sivasambo study compared ritodrine to librium, which, according to recent studies actually increases uterine activity. The Creasy study, described above, did not have an adequate control group, in that all patients were given intramuscular injections of ritodrine at the onset of premature labor and again if contractions returned. In a later publication, Dr. Creasy stated that "further studies have not proved that oral maintenance will decrease the incidence of preterm birth.... They do show that such an approach will decrease the need for repetitive hospitalization, thus improving the overall quality of life for the remainder of the pregnancy." The final study relied on by the FDA, the Barden study, involved a total of only 25 patients—some given oral ritodrine and others given a placebo.

Astra's evidence focused on the effect of oral ritodrine in prolonging the term of pregnancy, and then separately showed that extending the term of pregnancy improves neonatal outcome. Plaintiff refuted this claim with evidence that, while ritodrine may produce a short-term gain in prolonging pregnancy, there is no evidence of improved neonatal outcome. Plaintiff introduced articles written after the FDA approval. One of those articles concluded that "the lack of any suggestion of an effect on [neonatal] mortality and respiratory morbidity remains noteworthy, particularly given the clear short-term effect of tocolytic treatment on duration of gestation." James F. King et al., *Beta-mimetics in preterm labour—an overview of the randomized controlled trials*, 95 British Journal of Obstetrics and Gynecology 211, 220 (1988). Other articles have come to similar conclusions....

We do not sit to review the findings of the FDA; our only role in this appeal is to decide if there was sufficient evidence on which the jury could base its verdict. Plaintiff introduced evidence, through the cross-examination of Astra officials, that a reasonably prudent manufacturer would not market ritodrine if the evidence of its efficacy was inconclusive. Plaintiff also introduced sufficient evidence regarding the various clinical studies concerning the efficacy of ritodrine. The jury found that ritodrine, as manufactured and marketed by Astra, was in a defective condition and unreasonably dangerous to plaintiff. We find that there was sufficient evidence before the jury to conclude that a prudent manufacturer knowing all the risks would not market ritodrine.

Defendant argues that if the warning accompanying ritodrine was adequate then it cannot be held strictly liable. The cases cited by defendant to support its position, that a drug manufacturer should be shielded from liability, so hold based on comment k of the Restatement (Second) of Torts § 402A. Comment k provides that the seller of "unavoidably unsafe products" "is not to be held to strict liability for unfortunate consequences attending their use...." For comment k to apply, however, the product must be "an apparently useful and desirable product." It is the useful or effective nature of ritodrine which plaintiff has called into question.... A drug that prolongs pregnancy in order to reduce infant morbidity and mortality, if effective, is a highly useful and desirable product. Plaintiff, however, has attacked the linchpin of this theory—effectiveness—with various evidence. The jury was instructed:

> A product such as ritodrine is not in a defective condition unreasonably dangerous if it cannot be made completely safe for all users, but is nevertheless a useful and desirable product which is accompanied by proper directions and warnings.

> The jury verdict rejecting this argument is supported by the evidence that was presented.

The jury verdict rejecting this argument is supported by the evidence that was presented....

NOTE

The Court of Appeals' account of FDA's decision ultimately to approve the drug that injured Ms. Tobin leaves little doubt that it was a close call. Indeed, the Court appears convinced that it was a wrong call, or at least that the jury was entitled so to determine. In short, the jury concluded that FDA had made an error in approving the drug in the first place. This result does not appear to have rested on new evidence about risk or benefit. So far as one can tell, the jury was presented with the same evidence that had been before FDA.

It is not uncommon for a federal appeals court to conclude that an agency decision is not supported by the evidence it assembled or had presented to it. Ordinarily, however, such rulings are the product of a process for judicial review that has been prescribed by Congress, either in the agency's own statute or in the Administrative Procedure Act. This process usually designates the pathway into court, specifies the court or courts entitled to entertain such suits, and accords the agency some benefit of the doubt by stipulating that its decision is to be upheld if supported by "substantial evidence" or not "arbitrary or capricious." In *Tobin*, by contrast, the court gives little or no deference to FDA's conclusion that ritodrine is effective.

COMMENT: COMPLIANCE WITH FEDERAL LAW AS A DEFENSE UNDER STATE LAW

The decisions in *MacDonald* and *Tobin* illustrate the proposition that a defendant's compliance with FDA's requirements usually will not be a defense to tort liability. An important recent decision by the New Jersey Supreme Court, however, suggests that this is not universally true. *Perez v. Wyeth Laboratories, Inc.*, 734 A.2d 1245 (N.J. 1999), was a suit against the manufacturer of Norplant, an implantable contraceptive. The plaintiff claimed that the use of Norplant entailed severe discomfort and risks to health about which Wyeth had failed to warn her.

The company sought refuge in the learned intermediary doctrine. Ms. Perez asked the court to recognize a new exception to the doctrine which would impose a duty to warn patients directly if a product was advertised directly to consumers. She pointed to Wyeth's persistent efforts to reach consumers through advertisements in print and electronic media. Her advocacy of another exception to the learned intermediary doctrine convinced a majority of the New Jersey court, whose lengthy opinion has become a leading, if so far not widely accepted, additional justification for requiring that consumers themselves be warned about the risks of prescription drugs and devices.

The court recognized, however, that its general declaration that consumers of widely advertised products were entitled to receive information about their risks left open the question of implementation. How should—indeed how could—Wyeth fulfill this obligation when Norplant was provided and implanted by the physician and the company had no direct dealings with the patient? The court's response embraced a form of regulatory compliance defense, accepting Wyeth's argument that it would fulfill its duty if, in its advertisements, it included the information about risks that FDA's guidelines for DTC (direct to consumer) advertisements recommended.

We have no doubt of the profound public interest in developing new products for reproductive services. We intend no disparagement of the product when we recite plaintiffs' claims concerning the efficacy of Norplant. The procedural posture that brings this case before us requires that we accept as true plaintiffs' version of the facts. . . .

According to plaintiffs, Wyeth began a massive advertising campaign for Norplant in 1991, which it directed at women rather than at their doctors. Wyeth advertised on television and in women's magazines such as *Glamour, Mademoiselle* and *Cosmopolitan*. According to plaintiffs, none of the advertisements warned of any inherent danger posed by Norplant; rather, all praised its simplicity and convenience. None warned of side effects including pain and permanent scarring attendant to removal of the implants. Wyeth also sent a letter to physicians advising them that it was about to launch a national advertising program in magazines that the physicians' patients may read.

. . . [H]aving spent $1.3 billion on advertising in 1998, drug manufacturers can hardly be said to "lack effective means to communicate directly with patients," when their advertising campaigns can pay off in close to billions in dividends.

In August 1997, the FDA released a Draft Guidance, which specifically addresses consumer-directed broadcast advertisements such as radio, television and telephone communications. Broadcast advertisements must contain a "major statement" of the major risks of the drug. Instead of presenting a brief summary with the broadcast, which is not as feasible as in the print media, the Guidance proposes an alternative requirement known as the "adequate provision" requirement. That provision provides that the manufacturer "may make adequate provision for the dissemination of the approved package labeling in connection with the broadcast presentation (§ 202.1(e)(1))." The Guidance explains that four components must be present to meet the "adequate provision" requirement in broadcasts—a toll-free number that provides information concerning where consumers might find information about package labeling; an alternative mechanism for obtaining package labeling information for consumers who do not have access to technology such as the Internet; a statement directing consumers to pharmacists and/or physicians; and an Internet web-page address.

FDA regulations are pertinent in determining the nature and extent of any duty of care that should be imposed on pharmaceutical manufacturers with respect to direct-to-consumer advertising. Presently, any duty to warn physicians about prescription drug dangers is presumptively met by compliance with federal labeling. That presumption is not absolute. Nevertheless, FDA regulations serve as compelling evidence that a manufacturer satisfied its duty to warn the physician about potentially harmful side effects of its product.

We believe that in the area of direct-to-consumer advertising of pharmaceuticals, the same rebuttable presumption should apply when a manufacturer complies with FDA advertising, labeling and warning requirements. That approach harmonizes the manufacturer's duty to doctors and to the public when it chooses to directly advertise its products, and simultaneously recognizes the public interest in informing patients about new pharmaceutical developments. Moreover, a rebuttable presumption that the duty to consumers is met by compliance with FDA regulations helps to ensure that manufacturers are not made guarantors against remotely possible, but not scientifically-verifiable, side-effects of prescription drugs, a result that could have a "significant anti-utilitarian effect."

Perez v. Wyeth Laboratories, Inc., 734 A.2d at 1247–59.

NOTE

In this opinion it is the New Jersey Supreme Court—and not FDA, or Congress, or any federal court—that determines that a drug manufacturer who complies with FDA's guidelines for advertisements addressed to consumers should be presumed to have fulfilled its duty to warn about the drug's risks. In other words, it is state law that dictates what weight, if any, should be accorded proof of compliance with federal regulatory compliance. This does not mean, however, that federal lawmakers do not or should not take an interest in the issue or that Congress may not resolve the issue by statute. The following cases explore the reasons why Congress might wish to appropriate the issue for itself. *See generally* Lars Noah, *Reconceptualizing Federal Preemption of Tort Claims as the Government Standards Defense*, 37 WM. & MARY L. REV. 9903 (1996). Mitchell S. Berger, *A Tale of Six Implants: The Perez v. Wyeth Laboratories Norplant Case and the Applicability of the Learned Intermediary Doctrine to Direct-to-Consumer Drug Promotion*, 55 FOOD & DRUG L.J. 525 (2000).

2.   EXPRESS FEDERAL PREEMPTION

Medtronic Corp. v. Lohr

518 U.S. 470 (1996).

[The opinions are reproduced in Chapter XII, *supra* p. 1442.]

NOTES

1. *Tort Law Duties as "Requirements."* All nine Justices in *Lohr* agreed that none of Mrs. Lohr's claims was preempted by the Medical Device Amendments. Justice Stevens voiced doubt whether Congress, in enacting FD&C Act 521 (28 U.S.C. 360k), intended to preempt any common law duties. However, he and three colleagues refrained from holding that the term "requirement" could not include tort law rulings by state courts. At the same time, the remaining five Justices left no doubt that the term could embrace a tort law ruling if it were device-specific and that such a ruling could be preempted by FDA-imposed requirements designed to assure the safety of the same type of device. In sum, a majority of Justices accepted the principle that section 521 could preempt some common law duties, but they left unanswered the questions of how narrowly focused such duties must be and what legal form they must take to be vulnerable to preemption.

2. *History of the Term "Requirement."* Congress earlier used the term "requirement" in amendments to legislation regulating the sale and advertising of cigarettes. There Congress sought to bar the enactment of local statutes and regulations that went beyond any "requirements" it was prescribing. 15 U.S.C. 1334(b). In due course, the question arose whether this language precluded product liability claims against makers of cigarettes whose products met the federal requirements for manufacture and sale. In *Cipollone v. Liggett Group, Inc.*, 505 U.S. 504 (1992), the son of a long-time smoker who had died from lung cancer sued several cigarette manufacturers, claiming that they were responsible for his mother's death. His complaint asserted several state law claims, including design defect, failure to warn, negligence, express warranty, fraudulent misrepresentation, and conspiracy to defraud consumers by denying the public scientific information showing the perils of smoking. The defendants argued that all of Cipollone's claims were preempted by the Federal Cigarette Labeling and Advertising Act of 1965, 79 Stat. 282, and the Public Health Cigarette Smoking Act of 1969, 84 Stat. 87, which spelled out warnings for cigarette labels, packaging, and advertising and prohibited any regulation of cigarette advertising by state and local governments.

The Supreme Court rejected the companies' contention that the 1965 Act preempted Cipollone's claim. That Act said that "[n]o statement relating to smoking and health shall be required in the advertising of [properly labeled] cigarettes." This language, the Court held, "only pre-empted state and federal rulemaking bodies from mandating particular cautionary statements" and did not preempt common law damage actions. But the Court reached a different conclusion with respect to the 1969 Act, whose language was "much broader" in two respects. The word "statement" was replaced by "requirement[s] or prohibitions ... imposed under state law." Furthermore, the 1969 Act encompassed obligations "with respect to the advertising or promotion" of cigarettes. The Court held that the "phrase '[n]o requirement or prohibition' ... suggests no distinction between positive enactments and common law; to the contrary, those words easily encompass obligations that take the form of common-law rules." Accordingly, the Court held that some of Cipollone's failure to warn claims—those based on representations that the companies made in conformity with the 1969 Act—were preempted.

3. *FDA's Reaction to* Lohr. Soon after the Supreme Court's opinion in *Lohr* issued, FDA published in the Federal Register a notice setting forth its interpretation of the decision and addressing the circumstances in which a state requirement, *e.g.*, a requirement embodied in a court's imposition of tort liability, might be preempted by section 521. 62 Fed. Reg. 65384 (Dec. 12, 1997). The notice acknowledged that the agency had rarely expressed its views of products liability suits, but with its attention now drawn, FDA embraced a narrow reading of section 521. The agency opined that for a state law duty to be vulnerable to preemption, it must differ from or add to a "requirement" FDA had already prescribed for the particular type of device. General duties applicable to all devices or to a class of devices would not qualify. The agency went on to declare that a "requirement" must appear in a regulation duly promulgated in the Federal Register or must be imposed by an administrative order that was the product of a formal adjudicatory proceeding involving a specific device. No other duties or conditions that FDA might impose would constitute "requirements" for purposes of section 521. *See* Margaret Jane Porter, *The Lohr Decision, FDA Perspective and Position*, 52 FOOD & DRUG L.J. 7 (1997).

This view essentially neutered section 521 as a source of limitations on state tort law. It also, inadvertently, eviscerated the preemptive scope of section 521 in the context where it was unquestionably intended to apply, *i.e.*, in evaluating "requirements" imposed by state legislatures and regulatory agencies. Thus, comments pointed out, FDA's view would permit a state to require and deny premarket approval for devices that FDA had already approved. A little over a year later FDA withdrew its 1997 notice. 63 Fed. Reg. 39789–01 (July 24, 1998).

4. *Preempted State Requirements.* Lawsuits have continued to probe the contours of section 521's language. The decided cases generally accept Justice Stevens' reasoning in *Lohr*—that until FDA imposes safety-related obligations for a type of device, no state requirement is preempted. This has meant, as the Court's ruling forecast, that FDA's confirmation that a device is "substantially equivalent" to another marketed device under Section 510(k) does not impose any "requirements" that preempt state controls. However, under the PMA process, the Act requires the maker of a Class III device to supply evidence that convinces FDA that it will be safe and effective in use. The evidence typically submitted to FDA derives from a series of studies of the specific device with fixed design and materials; modification of any feature would require additional studies. While FDA's approval letter may not say that no feature of the tested product may be changed without approval, the statute and regulations require FDA approval of a supplemental PMA before any significant change may be made. This view has been accepted by every circuit but the Eleventh. *E.g., Gomez v. St. Jude Medical Diag Division Inc.*, 442 F.3d 919 930 (5th Cir. 2006); *Riegel v. Medtronic*, 451 F.3d 104 (2d Cir. 2006). *See* Michael K. Brown & Lisa M. Baird, *Appeals Court Ruling Embraces "PMA" Device Preemption*, 14 WASHINGTON LEGAL FOUNDATION COUNSEL'S ADVISORY No. 9 (July 21, 2006).

5. *The Supreme Court's Latest Word On Preemption.* The Supreme Court grappled with another statutory preemption provision in *Bates v. Dow Agrosciences*, 544 U.S. 431 (2005), producing a decision suggesting that a majority may now take a narrow view of claims that common law duties are preempted. The statute in question, the Federal Insecticide, Fungicide, and Rodenticide Act, or FIFRA, contains a provision declaring that states "shall not impose or continue in effect any requirements for labeling or packaging in addition to or different from those required under this subchapter." 7 U.S.C. § 136v(b). The case involved claims by Texas peanut growers that their crop had been damaged by Dow's "Strongarm" weed killer, which, they alleged, had been misleadingly promoted as useful and safe "in all areas where peanuts are grown." The plaintiffs sought damages under Texas law; Dow responded that acceptance of their claims would inevitably require changes in the Strongarm label and thus would impose "requirements ... in addition to" those EPA had prescribed when it approved Strongarm.

Writing for five colleagues, Justice Stevens—the author of *Medtronic*—rejected Dow's categorical argument that FIFRA's preemption clause precluded enforcement of any common law duty that might force a pesticide producer to make changes in its label. In remanding the case for exploration of whether any of Bates' several theories would necessitate relabeling and, if so, would require changes that conflicted with EPA's label requirements, Stevens conceded that the statutory term "requirement" could include some common law duties as well as legislative and administrative mandates. Stevens emphasized that common law duties, to be subject to preemption, had to command conduct that went beyond or conflicted with the requirements EPA imposed. This condition was not met by a showing that, if liability were imposed, pesticide makers would be likely to change their labels. "This effect-based test finds no support in the text of § 136v(b), which speaks only of 'requirements'. A requirement is a rule of law that must be obeyed; an event, such as a jury verdict, that merely motivates an optional decision is not a requirement."

Later, addressing the mindset with which courts should approach claims of preemption, Justice Stevens quoted from *Medtronic*, where he had written: "[B]ecause the States are independent sovereigns in our federal system, we have long presumed that Congress does not cavalierly pre-empt state-law causes of action.... In areas of traditional state regulation, we assume that a federal statute has not supplanted state law unless Congress has made such an intention 'clear and manifest.' "

The *Bates* majority's narrow reading of the FIFRA preemption clause was, according to Stevens, the position EPA had held prior to this litigation, citing an amicus brief filed on behalf of the United States in an earlier case. Stevens thus acknowledged, but at the same time dismissed, the government's new litigating position, which may have prompted Justice Breyer's brief separate concurrence. Breyer called attention to his statement in *Medtronic* that FDA "had legal authority within ordinary administrative constraints to promulgate agency rules and to determine the preemptive effect of those rules in light of the agency's special understanding of 'whether (or the extent to which) state requirements may interfere with federal objectives.' ... The EPA enjoys similar authority here." This exchange exposes what may be a vulnerability in the government's position in *Bates*. It was the Department of Justice—and not EPA—that first acknowledged the validity of Dow's preemption argument.

For assessments of the Court's ruling in *Bates* and its general attitude toward preemption claims, see Note, *Preemption of State Common Law*, 119 HARV. L. REV. 376 (2005); Leslie A. Brueckner, *Turning Of The Tide For Preemption*, TRIAL, Nov. 2005, at 28 (2005); Andrew M. Siegel, *The Court Against the Courts: Hostility to Litigation As an Organizing Theme in the Rehnquist Court's Jurisprudence*, 84 TEX. L. REV. 1097, 1166 (2006).

3. CONFLICT PREEMPTION

For decades FDA tried to avoid any involvement in private suits involving products that it regulated. The agency on request provided courts its view on the meaning of the statutes it enforces or the regulations it has promulgated, but it otherwise refrained from injecting itself into private litigation. In the last decade, however, FDA has asked for leave to participate as an amicus in at least four cases, and in each it has urged the court to find the plaintiffs' state law damages claim preempted. *Motus v. Pfizer*, 358 F.3d 659 (9th Cir. 2004); *Dowhal v. SmithKline Beecham Consumer*, 88 P.3d 1 (Cal. 2004); *In re Paxil Litigation*, 2002 WL 31375497 (C.D. Cal. 2002); *Murphree v. Pacesetter, Inc.*, 2005 WL 4668517 (D. Minn. 2005), appeal docketed, No. W2004–01432 (Tenn. Ct. App.). The agency's argument prevailed in *Dusek v. Pfizer Inc.*, 2004 WL 3631155 (S.D. Tex. 2004) a case whose facts are very similar to *Witczak, supra. See also Horn v. Thoratec*, 376 F.3d 163 (3d Cir. 2004). As the following decision shows, however, the agency's amicus arguments were not always persuasive.

Witczak v. Pfizer, Inc.

377 F. Supp. 2d 726 (D. Minn. 2005).

■ ROSENBAUM, CHIEF JUDGE.

Defendant, a prescription drug manufacturer, seeks summary judgment claiming federal preemption bars plaintiff's state law failure-to-warn claim. Defendant's motion is denied.

On August 6, 2003, Timothy Michael Witczak committed suicide. His suicide occurred shortly after he began taking Zoloft, a drug manufactured by defendant. Plaintiff is Mr. Witczak's surviving spouse, and claims his suicide was caused by known side effects of Zoloft. She further claims defendant is liable for wrongful death damages because, among other things, it failed to warn of Zoloft's association with "suicidality."

Zoloft is one of a class of drugs known as Selective Serotonin Reuptake Inhibitors ("SSRIs"). Defendant initially submitted the product for Food and Drug Administration ("FDA") approval in 1988. In 1991, the FDA granted approval for the drug's use in treating adult depression. The FDA-approved label did not warn of an association between Zoloft and suicidality. Instead, the label's "Precautions" section noted suicide as an inherent risk of depression.

Since granting original approval, the FDA has reapproved Zoloft several times for treatment of other disorders.... During the reapprovals, the FDA never suggested that Zoloft's label was deficient for failing to warn of a link to suicidality.

Claims of an association between SSRIs and suicidality have been made since the drugs were first introduced. In the past 15 years, the FDA has considered three petitions to remove Prozac, another SSRI, from the market because of the claimed association. Each petition was denied.[2]

The FDA changed its position on March 22, 2004, when it issued a Public Health Advisory recommending that all SSRIs carry a warning calling for "close observation of adult and pediatric patients treated with these agents for worsening depression or the emergence of suicidality." Defendant complied with the FDA's recommendation. Later that year, an FDA panel issued another Public Health Advisory directing that all SSRI labels carry a "black-box warning"—the most serious kind—warning of "increased risk of suicidality . . . in children and adolescents."

Defendant moves for summary judgment, claiming plaintiff's state law failure-to-warn claim—upon which her other claims allegedly depend—is preempted by the federal Food, Drug, and Cosmetics Act ("FDCA"), and FDA regulations promulgated pursuant to it.... Defendant claims plaintiff's case is barred by conflict preemption.

. . . .

According to defendant, plaintiff's failure-to-warn claim conflicts both directly and indirectly with federal food and drug laws. Defendant first argues that the state law duty-to-warn requirement directly conflicts with both the FDA's requirement that it use "verbatim" the label specified by the agency, and with the FDA's prohibition on "false and misleading" labels. Defendant alternatively argues that the failure-to-warn claim indirectly conflicts with the FDCA's goal of providing only scientifically accurate drug-label information. Defendant's contentions are without merit.

---

2. In 2002, the FDA filed an amicus brief in a separate action. *See Motus v. Pfizer*, 358 F.3d (9th Cir. 2004). Its brief in that case said any change in the warning to reflect a causal link between Zoloft and suicidality would create a "false and misleading" label, in violation of federal law.

Defendant argues that if it had warned of an association between Zoloft and suicidality, it would have violated the FDA's order to use the FDA-approved warning-label language "verbatim."[4] But FDA regulations explicitly permitted defendant to unilaterally strengthen its warning label at any time without regulatory pre-approval. 21 C.F.R. § 314.70(c)(6)(iii)(A). This particular regulation was promulgated precisely to allow drug-makers to quickly strengthen label warnings when evidence of new side effects are discovered. Thus, as the FDA has noted, the regulation "permits the addition to the drug's labeling or advertising of information about a hazard without advance approval" by the FDA.

Defendant denies that § 314.70 defeats preemption because it gives manufacturers only temporary authority to strengthen their labels. The Court does not agree. The FDA's regulations do grant it the power to later disapprove a label strengthened pursuant to § 314.70. But the regulation "does not require that FDA take any action when a manufacturer" makes a change pursuant to § 314.70(c); if the FDA does nothing, the change remains in effect. Further, even if exercised, the power to disapprove does not retroactively make the manufacturer's strengthened label a violation of any law. Rather, if the FDA exercises its power to disapprove, the manufacturer simply stops distributing the new label.

Thus, the Court finds no absolute duty to use the FDA-approved label "verbatim." Pursuant to § 314.70(c), defendant could have strengthened its label to warn of the alleged association between Zoloft and suicidality at any time. Accordingly, it was not "impossible for [defendant] to comply with both state and federal requirements."

Defendant next asserts that a unilateral change in its warning label which suggested a link between SSRIs and suicidality would have rendered the label "false and misleading," and in direct conflict with 21 U.S.C. § 355(e), the misbranding statute. Defendant bolsters this argument by pointing to a series of FDA pronouncements. The flaw in defendant's argument is that, as set forth below, none of the FDA's statements has the force of law. So none made it "impossible" for defendant to comply with Minnesota's failure-to-warn law.

Defendant proffers the FDA's amicus brief in *Motus v. Pfizer* in support of its position. There, the FDA—which has since modified its own position—avers that it would have deemed any warning of a causal link between Zoloft and suicidality to be false and misleading. These assertions do not preempt state law.

The FDA is authorized to promulgate regulations which have the preemptive force of law, so long as the regulations are properly adopted and in accord with its statutory authority. And an agency's interpretations of its own regulations are ordinarily entitled to great deference.

The Court, however, declines to treat statements from a single FDA legal brief as declarations afforded the preemptive force of law. First, the propositions defendant cites from the *Motus* brief were not even addressed or considered by the *Motus* court itself. Second, the FDA has since dis-

---

4. The word "verbatim" appears only in the FDA "approvable letter" to Pfizer— not in any of the misbranding statutes or regulations.

tanced itself from the substance of the *Motus* brief by recommending labeling changes that, in fact, reflect concerns about the association between SSRIs and suicidality....

Furthermore, even if the Court credited the *Motus* brief as an attempt by the FDA to articulate an official agency position, it would still fail to preempt plaintiff's claim. This is because the FDA has no authority to declare, ipse dixit, that a label is false an/d misleading. Rather, the government must initiate an enforcement action to establish that the drug is in fact misbranded. For all of these reasons, the statements in the *Motus* brief are insufficient to preempt plaintiff's failure-to-warn claim.

Defendant next suggests the FDA would have regarded any unilateral label change to be "false and misleading" by pointing to the FDA's frequent reapproval of Zoloft without any changes to its warnings or its label. This suggestion fails to recognize that "FDA regulations are generally minimum standards of conduct" unless Congress has expressed clear intent to preempt state common law, which it has not done here. *Hill v. Searle Laboratories*, 884 F.2d 1064, 1068 (8th Cir. 1989); *see also Wells v. Ortho Pharm. Corp.*, 788 F.2d 741, 746 (11th Cir. 1986) ("An FDA determination that a warning is not necessary may be sufficient for federal regulatory purposes but still not be sufficient for state tort law purposes."). As a result, rather than acting as a mandate, the reapprovals merely confirmed the minimum labeling requirements. They do not prove that a label strengthened pursuant to § 314.70(c)(6)(iii)(A) would necessarily be "false and misleading."

In sum, Pfizer's claim of direct conflict rests on its own assumptions of what the FDA would have done if defendant had unilaterally strengthened its warning label. The validity and authority of state law, however, does not depend on speculative hypotheticals. The Court cannot find that defendant has established a direct conflict.

Defendant also claims that complying with Minnesota's duty-to-warn regime would have created an indirect conflict. It claims any warning of a possible link between Zoloft and suicidality would have frustrated Congress's goal of ensuring the scientific validity of drug label information. Specifically, defendant posits that failure-to-warn laws pressure drug manufacturers to paper their labels with unsubstantiated warnings in order to avoid lawsuits. Defendant claims this undercuts the FDA's mission to provide only scientifically valid warnings, and over-deters the use of efficacious drugs. The Court considers this a public policy argument gone awry.

It is obvious that state failure-to-warn laws do not pressure manufacturers to include false or invalid warnings. Instead, they give drug manufacturers every incentive to warn of real, known risks as soon as they are discovered—even before any FDA action. This does not conflict with the FDCA's purposes and objectives. To the contrary, FDA regulations allow drug manufacturers to § strengthen warning labels "in the interest of drug safety" at any time without FDA pre-approval precisely so that new warnings can be "placed into effect at the earliest possible time" and "to enable prompt adoption of such changes." 30 Fed. Reg. 993 (Jan. 30, 1965).

....

The FDA itself vindicated Congress's protective intent when it issued its March 22, 2004, Public Health Advisory, recommending that SSRI labels be modified to reflect potential suicide risks. The FDA noted in the Advisory that it had "not concluded that [SSRI side effects] are a precursor to either worsening of depression or the emergence of suicidal impulses," but it still recommended the label change to alleviate "concern." In other words: "Safety first."

State consumer-protection law compliments, rather than frustrates, the FDA's protective regime. This is especially apparent when one considers that prescription drugs were once marketed primarily to trained health care providers—sophisticated and discerning intermediaries. Today, on the other hand, pill-rolling apothecaries and the mortar and pestle have disappeared. They have been replaced by drug manufacturers who urge the use of their drugs in mass-market print and television advertisements targeted directly at the public. Defendant, for example, advertises the drug involved in this case by personifying it as a happy, bouncing-oval cartoon character.

This new drug-marketing environment calls out for enhanced consumer protection. But defendant urges the Court to find Congress intended to obviate the very state laws that provide remedies to consumers harmed by dangerous products and deceptive marketing. The Court finds this proposition untenable in the absence of a clear and compelling Congressional statement. *See Bates v. Dow Agrosciences L.L.C.*, 544 U.S. 431 (2005) ("If Congress had intended to deprive injured parties of a long available form of compensation, it surely would have expressed that intent more clearly.").

. . . .

Finally, defendant's argument that it should not be exposed to fifty-one separate tort-law regimes also rings hollow. Most mass merchants in this nation's economy sustain this burden as a cost of doing business. If Congress intends to create a class of protected businesses, it has the means and ability to do so. The Court finds no proof that it has done so here. . . .

———

In January 2006 FDA reiterated the arguments made in its amicus briefs in final regulations revising the requirements for physician labeling for all prescription drugs.

Requirements on Content and Format of Labeling for Human Prescription Drug and Biological Products

71 Fed. Reg. 3922 (January 24, 2006).

. . . .

This final rule amends part 201 (21 CFR part 201) of FDA regulations by revising the requirements for the content and format of labeling for prescription drug products. . . .

A. Content and Format of Labeling....

1. Highlights of Prescribing Information

Like the proposed rule, the final rule requires that the labeling for new and more recently approved products include introductory information entitled "Highlights of Prescribing Information."

The final rule requires the same headings for Highlights as proposed, except that, in response to comments, FDA moved "Most Common Adverse Reactions" from "Warnings and Precautions" to a new heading entitled "Adverse Reactions." Like the proposed rule, the final rule requires that Highlights, except for the boxed warning, be limited in length to one-half of the page.

FDA has revised, on its own initiative, the heading for this portion of the labeling to read "Full Prescribing Information" instead of proposed "Comprehensive Prescribing Information." FDA made this change to more accurately reflect that this portion of prescription drug labeling contains the information that FDA determined is necessary for the safe and effective use of the drug, but may not contain all known information about the drug (*e.g.*, details of all clinical trials).

. . . .

In addition, FDA has revised, on its own initiative, "Contraindications" to emphasize that the section must only describe situations in which the potential risks associated with drug use outweigh any possible benefit. FDA believes that including relative or hypothetical hazards diminishes the usefulness of the section. For clarity and emphasis, FDA is requiring that "none" be stated when no contraindications are known....

. . . .

D. Comments on Product Liability Implications of the Proposed Rule

. . . .

FDA believes that under existing preemption principles, FDA approval of labeling under the act, whether it be in the old or new format, preempts conflicting or contrary State law. Indeed, the Department of Justice (DOJ), on behalf of FDA, has filed a number of amicus briefs making this very point. In order to more fully address the comments expressing concern about the product liability implications of revising the labeling for prescription drugs, we believe it would be useful to set forth in some detail the arguments made in those amicus briefs. The discussion that follows, therefore, represents the government's long standing views on preemption, with a particular emphasis on how that doctrine applies to State laws that would require labeling that conflicts with or is contrary to FDA-approved labeling.

Under the act, FDA is the expert Federal public health agency charged by Congress with ensuring that drugs are safe and effective, and that their labeling adequately informs users of the risks and benefits of the product and is truthful and not misleading. Under the act and FDA regulations, the agency makes approval decisions based not on an abstract estimation of its safety and effectiveness, but rather on a comprehensive scientific evaluation of the product's risks and benefits under the conditions of use prescribed, recommended, or suggested in the labeling. FDA considers not only complex clinical issues related to the use of the product in study populations, but also important and practical public health issues pertaining to the use of the product in day-to-day clinical practice, such as the nature of the disease or condition for which the product will be indicated, and the need for risk management measures to help assure in clinical practice that the product maintains its favorable benefit-risk balance. The centerpiece of risk management for prescription drugs generally is the labeling which reflects thorough FDA review of the pertinent scientific evidence and communicates to health care practitioners the agency's formal, authoritative conclusions regarding the conditions under which the product can be used safely and effectively. FDA carefully controls the content of labeling for a prescription drug, because such labeling is FDA's principal tool for educating health care professionals about the risks and benefits of the approved product to help ensure safe and effective use. FDA continuously works to evaluate the latest available scientific information to monitor the safety of products and to incorporate information into the product's labeling when appropriate.

Changes to labeling typically are initiated by the sponsor, subject to FDA review, but are sometimes initiated by FDA. Under FDA regulations, to change labeling (except for editorial and other minor revisions), the sponsor must submit a supplemental application fully explaining the basis for the change. FDA permits two kinds of labeling supplements: (1) Prior approval supplements, which require FDA approval before a change is made (21 CFR 314.70(b)); and (2) "changes being effected" (CBE) supplements, which may be implemented before FDA approval, but after FDA notification (21 CFR 314.70(c)). While a sponsor is permitted to add risk information to the FPI [Full Prescribing Information] without first obtaining FDA approval via a CBE supplement, FDA reviews all such submissions and may later deny approval of the supplement, and the labeling remains subject to enforcement action if the added information makes the labeling false or misleading under section 502(a) of the act. Thus, in practice, manufacturers typically consult with FDA prior to adding risk information to labeling. . . .

Since the proposed rule was published, FDA has learned of several instances in which product liability lawsuits have directly threatened the agency's ability to regulate manufacturer dissemination of risk information for prescription drugs in accordance with the act. In one case, for example, an individual plaintiff claimed that a drug manufacturer had a duty under California State law to label its products with specific warnings that FDA had specifically considered and rejected as scientifically unsubstantiated. In some of these cases, the court determined that the State law claim could not proceed, on the ground that the claim was preempted by Federal law, or was not properly before the court by operation of the doctrine of primary jurisdiction. In some cases, however, the court has permitted the claim to proceed.

State law actions can rely on and propagate interpretations of the act and FDA regulations that conflict with the agency's own interpretations and frustrate the agency's implementation of its statutory mandate. For example, courts have rejected preemption in State law failure-to-warn cases on the ground that a manufacturer has latitude under FDA regulations to revise labeling by adding or strengthening warning statements without first obtaining permission from FDA. (*See, e.g., Eve v. Sandoz Pharm. Corp.*, 2002 U.S. Dist. LEXIS 23965 (S.D. Ind. 2002); *Ohler v. Purdue Pharma, L.P.*, 2002 U.S. Dist. LEXIS 2368 (E.D. La. 2002); *Motus v. Pfizer Inc.*, 127 F. Supp. 2d 1085 (C.D. Cal. 2000); *Bansemer v. Smith Labs., Inc.*, 1988 U.S. Dist. LEXIS 16208 (E.D. Wis. 1988); *McEwen v. Ortho Pharm Corp.*, 528 P.2d 522 (Ore. 1974).) In fact, the determination whether labeling revisions are necessary is, in the end, squarely and solely FDA's under the act. A manufacturer may, under FDA regulations, strengthen a labeling warning, but in practice manufacturers typically consult with FDA before doing so to avoid implementing labeling changes with which the agency ultimately might disagree (and that therefore might subject the manufacturer to enforcement action).

Another misunderstanding of the act encouraged by State law actions is that FDA labeling requirements represent a minimum safety standard. . . . In fact, FDA interprets the act to establish both a "floor" and a "ceiling," such that additional disclosures of risk information can expose a manufacturer to liability under the act if the additional statement is unsubstantiated or otherwise false or misleading. Given the comprehensiveness of FDA regulation of drug safety, effectiveness, and labeling under the act, additional requirements for the disclosure of risk information are not necessarily more protective of patients. Instead, they can erode and disrupt the careful and truthful representation of benefits and risks that prescribers need to make appropriate judgments about drug use. Exaggeration of risk could discourage appropriate use of a beneficial drug.

State law requirements can undermine safe and effective use in other ways. In the preamble accompanying the proposal, FDA noted that liability concerns were creating pressure on manufacturers to expand labeling warnings to include speculative risks and, thus, to limit physician appreciation of potentially far more significant contraindications and side effects. FDA has previously found that labeling that includes theoretical hazards not well-grounded in scientific evidence can cause meaningful risk information to "lose its significance." Overwarning, just like underwarning, can similarly have a negative effect on patient safety and public health. Similarly, State-law attempts to impose additional warnings can lead to labeling that does not accurately portray a product's risks, thereby potentially discouraging safe and effective use of approved products or encouraging inappropriate use and undermining the objectives of the act.

State law actions also threaten FDA's statutorily prescribed role as the expert Federal agency responsible for evaluating and regulating drugs. State actions are not characterized by centralized expert evaluation of drug regulatory issues. Instead, they encourage, and in fact require, lay judges and juries to second-guess the assessment of benefits versus risks of a specific drug to the general public—the central role of FDA—sometimes on behalf of a single individual or group of individuals. That individualized reevaluation of the benefits and risks of a product can result in relief—

including the threat of significant damage awards or penalties—that creates pressure on manufacturers to attempt to add warnings that FDA has neither approved nor found to be scientifically required. This could encourage manufacturers to propose "defensive labeling" to avoid State liability, which, if implemented, could result in scientifically unsubstantiated warnings and underutilization of beneficial treatments.

. . . .

As noted previously, DOJ has made submissions to courts in a number of cases in which private litigants asserted a State law basis for challenging the adequacy of risk information provided by manufacturers for drugs in accordance with FDA requirements under the act. . . . The practice of addressing conflicting State requirements through participation in litigation (including product liability cases) in which the Government is not a party is not new. For example, DOJ participated on FDA's behalf in favor of pre-emption in *Jones v. Rath Packing Company*, 430 U.S. 519 (1977), *Grocery Manufacturers of America, Inc. v. Gerace*, 755 F.2d 993 (2d Cir. 1985), *Eli Lilly & Co., Inc. v. Marshall*, 850 S.W.2d 155 (Tex. 1993), and *Buckman Co. v. Plaintiffs' Legal Comm.*, 531 U.S. 341, 352–53 (2001). FDA believes that State laws conflict with and stand as an obstacle to achievement of the full objectives and purposes of Federal law when they purport to compel a firm to include in labeling or advertising a statement that FDA has considered and found scientifically unsubstantiated. In such cases, including the statement in labeling or advertising would render the drug misbranded under the act (21 U.S.C. 352(a) and (f)). The agency believes that State law conflicts with and stands as an obstacle to achievement of the full objectives and purposes of Federal law if it purports to preclude a firm from including in labeling or advertising a statement that is included in prescription drug labeling. By complying with the State law in such a case and removing the statement from labeling, the firm would be omitting a statement required under 201.100(c)(1) as a condition on the exemption from the requirement of adequate directions for use, and the omission would misbrand the drug under 21 U.S.C. 352(f)(1). The drug might also be misbranded on the ground that the omission is material within the meaning of 21 U.S.C. 321(n) and makes the labeling or advertising misleading under 21 U.S.C. 352(a) or (n).

Consistent with its court submissions and existing preemption principles, FDA believes that at least the following claims would be preempted by its regulation of prescription drug labeling: (1) Claims that a drug sponsor breached an obligation to warn by failing to put in Highlights or otherwise emphasize any information the substance of which appears anywhere in the labeling; (2) claims that a drug sponsor breached an obligation to warn by failing to include in an advertisement any information the substance of which appears anywhere in the labeling, in those cases where a drug's sponsor has used Highlights consistently with FDA draft guidance regarding the "brief summary" in direct-to-consumer advertising; (3) claims that a sponsor breached an obligation to warn by failing to include contraindications or warnings that are not supported by evidence that meets the standards set forth in this rule; (4) claims that a drug sponsor breached an obligation to warn by failing to include a statement in labeling or in advertising, the substance of which had been proposed to FDA for inclusion in labeling, if that statement was not required by FDA at the time plaintiff claims the sponsor had an obligation to warn (unless FDA has made a finding that the sponsor withheld material information relating to the proposed warning before plaintiff claims the sponsor had the obligation to warn); (5) claims that a drug sponsor breached an obligation to warn by failing to include in labeling or in advertising a statement the substance of which FDA has prohibited in labeling or advertising; and (6) claims that a drug's sponsor breached an obligation to plaintiff by making statements that FDA approved for inclusion in the drug's label (unless FDA has made a finding that the sponsor withheld material information relating to the statement). Preemption would include not only claims against manufacturers as described above, but also against health care practitioners for claims related to dissemination of risk information to patients beyond what is included in the labeling. . . .

NOTES

1. *The Courts' Responses to FDA's Preamble.* In the brief time since FDA's publication of its views on preemption, only a few courts have addressed its implications. In *Abramowitz v. Cephalon, Inc.*, 2006 WL 560639 (N.J. Super. Ct. 2006), a New Jersey trial judge dismissed the plaintiff's failure to warn claim against the maker of Actiq, a drug approved for cancer pain, relying explicitly on the agency's preamble. Compare *Jackson v. Pfizer, Inc.*, 21 BNA TOXICS LAW REP. 560 (D. Neb. 2006), *with Laisure–Radke v. Par Pharmaceutical, Inc.*, 2006 WL 901657 (W.D. Wash. 2006).

2. *Reactions to FDA's Preamble.* FDA's emphatic view of the threat to national uniformity and the agency's recognized expertise have provoked an avalanche of commentary, with supporters and critics roughly equally divided. *E.g.*, Catherine M. Sharkey, *Preemption by Preamble: Federal Agencies and the Federalization of Tort Reform*, 56 DEPAUL L. REV. (forthcoming 2007); Allison M. Zieve & Brian Wolfman, *The FDA's Argument for Eradicating State Tort Law: Why It is Wrong and Warrants No Deference*, 21 BNA TOXICS LAW REP. 516 (2006); David Singh, *Preamble to New FDA Prescription Drug Regulations Strengthens Manufacturers' Preemption Argument*, 21 BNA TOXICS LAW REP. 334 (2006); *Preemption: "Silent Tort Reform" or "Federal Uniformity,"* 20 PIKE & FISHER AD. L. BULL. 1 (2006).

COMMENT: QUALIFIED SUPPORT FOR A COMPLIANCE DEFENSE

In 1990, the American Law Institute released the report of a blue ribbon panel of torts and administrative law scholars entitled REPORTER'S STUDY: ENTERPRISE LIABILITY FOR PERSONAL INJURY. So controversial were some of its recommendations that the Institute members were never asked to vote on any part of the report, but it gained a reputation for insightful scholarship. The report included an extensive treatment and endorsement of a regulatory compliance defense in carefully defined circumstances.

We believe that a regulatory compliance defense should shield the defendant from negligence liability upon satisfaction of the following requirements:

First, the risk must have been placed under regulatory control by a specialized administrative agency, a body with statutory authority to monitor and assess risk creating activities in its area of responsibility, and with a mandate to establish and revise regularly specific regulatory controls on enterprise behavior. Under a system of regulatory screening, a risk or category of risks is placed under regulatory control after accurate up-to-date data on such risks are provided to the responsible agency by the enterprise or otherwise obtained by the agency; the data and risks are evaluated by the agency in accordance with authoritative criteria; clearance is granted upon a reasoned determination that the risk is acceptable; and there is an ongoing system of agency monitoring and review in place to deal with new information or changed circumstances. Under a system of regulatory standards the criteria are essentially the same, except that the standards adopted must be intended to limit and must limit, directly or indirectly, the amount of such risks that may be generated.

Second, the enterprise in question must have complied with all relevant regulatory requirements.

Third, the defendant must have publicly disclosed to the relevant regulatory agency any material information in its possession (or of which it has reason to be aware) concerning the risks posed by the defendant's activities and/or the means of controlling them. This requirement would extend to information indicating that agency standards or tests may be inadequate or inappropriate. . . .

. . . Pharmaceuticals present a special combination of circumstances justifying such a defense. They are products with public health benefits that depend heavily on innovation; the regulatory regime carefully balances therapeutic risk and benefit in approving products on a case by case basis; there are inevitably some residual harms that cannot be prevented; there are also pervasive reporting requirements, a comprehensive and detailed regime of regulatory controls, and strong market incentives to generate safer products; and the activity in question is the manufacture and sale of a uniform, nationally marketed product. . . .

NOTE

Would the ALI Report's third condition—that the manufacturer have disclosed to FDA all it knew about the effects of a drug—assure that FDA's conditions for continued marketing reflected an expert and current assessment of the drug's risks and how to minimize them? Suppose, after receiving the manufacturer's latest report, FDA took no steps to require changes in the drug's labeling, *e.g.*, to discourage certain uses or make certain warnings? Could we be confident that the terms of FDA approval represented a sound assessment of benefits and risks?

4.   STATE RECOGNITION OF A COMPLIANCE DEFENSE

There is no statutory counterpart to FD&C Act 521 (the medical device preemption provision) for drugs. The Act's silence, however, does not limit the authority of state courts or state legislatures to recognize defenses based on compliance with federal law.

Grundberg v. The Upjohn Company

813 P.2d 89 (Utah 1991).

■ DURHAM, JUSTICE:

. . . .

We hold that a drug approved by the United States Food and Drug Administration ("FDA"), properly prepared, compounded, packaged, and distributed, cannot as a matter of law be "defective" in the absence of proof of inaccurate, incomplete, misleading, or fraudulent information furnished by the manufacturer in connection with FDA approval. . . .

. . . Mildred Lucille Coats died at age 83 from gunshot wounds inflicted by her daughter, Ilo Grundberg, on June 19, 1988. Grundberg and Janice Gray, the personal representative of Coat's estate, brought this action, alleging that Grundberg shot her mother as a result of ingesting the drug Halcion, a prescription drug manufactured by defendant Upjohn to treat insomnia.

. . . .

The parties agree that the Restatement (Second) of Torts section 402A, comment k (1965) and the principles it embodies provide an exemption from strict liability for a claimed design defect in the case of products that are "unavoidably unsafe." In moving for partial summary judgment, Upjohn argued that public policy supporting the research and development of new drugs requires a holding that *all* FDA-approved prescription medications are "unavoidably unsafe products" under comment k and, as such, manufacturers of those drugs would not be liable for a claim based on defective design. Plaintiffs argue that whether a drug is "unavoidably unsafe" must be determined on a case-by-case basis, with a determination in each case of whether the specific drug's benefit exceeded its risk at the time it was distributed. . . .

In its entirety, comment k [to Section 402A] reads:

k. *Unavoidably unsafe products.* There are some products which, in the present state of human knowledge, are quite incapable of being made safe for their intended and ordinary use. These are especially common in the field of drugs. . . . It is . . . true in particular of many new or experimental drugs as to which, because of lack of time and opportunity for sufficient medical experience, there can be no assurance of safety, or perhaps even of purity of ingredients, but such experience as there is justifies the marketing and use of the drug notwithstanding a medically recognizable risk. The seller of such products, again with the qualification that they are properly prepared and marketed, and proper warning is given, where the situation calls for it, is not to be held to strict liability for unfortunate consequences attending their use, merely because he has undertaken to supply the public with an apparently useful and desirable product, attended with a known but apparently reasonable risk.

. . . .

We agree with comment k's basic proposition—that there are some products that have dangers associated with their use even though they are used as intended. We also agree that the seller of such products, when the products are properly prepared and marketed and distributed with appropriate warnings, should not be held strictly liable for the "unfortunate consequences" attending their use. Thus, we adopt comment k's basic policy as the law to be applied in this state and must now turn to the issue of how to apply that policy.

. . . .

Because prescription drugs are chemical compounds designed to interact with the chemical and physiological processes of the human body, they will almost always pose some risk of side effects in certain individuals. Despite these risks, new drugs are continually approved by the FDA because of their social benefit in saving lives and alleviating human suffering. The health care system and general standard of living in this country, for example, would be seriously impaired without such essential drug products as antibiotics that allow quick recovery from ailments that were once debilitating or even fatal.

. . . .

Despite inherent risks, *and in contrast to any other product*, society has determined that prescription medications provide a unique benefit and so should be available to physicians with appropriate warnings and guidance as to use. The federal government has established an elaborate regulatory system, overseen by the FDA, to control the approval and distribution of these drugs. No other class of products is subject to such special restrictions or protections in our society.

. . . .

Elaborate premarket screening, however, does not ensure review of approved prescription medications where adverse reactions may appear after extensive preapproval testing. For this reason, the FDA also conducts extensive post-market surveillance. *All* reports of adverse drug reactions ("ADRs") must be reported to the FDA, regardless of whether the physician, the manufacturer, or others believe the reaction to be drug-related. The manufacturer must also periodically submit reports as to what actions it took in response to ADRs and must submit data from any post-marketing studies, reports in the scientific literature, and foreign marketing experience. The FDA has authority to enforce these reporting requirements; any failure to comply may subject a manufacturer to civil and criminal penalties. In response to its surveillance findings, the FDA may require labeling changes or if necessary withdraw NDA approval and thereby revoke the license to market the medication.

We find this extensive regulatory scheme capable of and appropriate for making the preliminary determination regarding whether a prescription drug's benefits outweigh its risks. The structured follow-up program imposed by law ensures that drugs are not placed on the market without continued monitoring for adverse consequences that would render the FDA's initial risk/benefit analysis invalid. Allowing individual courts and/or juries to continually reevaluate a drug's risks and benefits ignores the processes of this expert regulatory body and the other avenues of recovery available to plaintiffs.

We note that the Utah Legislature has recognized the value of the FDA approval process and the public interest in the availability and affordability of prescription drugs by restricting the extent of liability for injuries resulting from the use of those drugs. Utah Code Ann. § 78–18–2(1) (Supp. 1990) states that "punitive damages may not be awarded if a drug causing the claimant's harm: (a) received premarket approval or licensure by the Federal Food, Drug, and Cosmetic Act, 21 U.S.C. Section 301 et seq. . . . ." This policy, designed to avoid discouraging manufacturers from marketing FDA-approved drugs, applies even to drugs marketed with inadequate warnings.

The legislature has also acknowledged the important role of governmental standards in Utah Code Ann. section 78–15–6(3). In that section, the legislature declared that there is a rebuttable presumption that a product which fully complies with the applicable government standards at the time of marketing is not defective.[8]

Our prior case law supports this approach as well. . . .

Finally, we do not believe that a trial court in the context of a products liability action is the proper forum to determine whether, as a whole, a particular prescription drug's benefits outweighed its risks at the time of distribution. In a case-by-case analysis, one court or jury's determination that a particular drug is or is not "defectively designed" has no bearing on any future case. As a result, differences of opinion among courts in differing jurisdictions leaves unsettled a drug manufacturer's liability for any given drug. Although the FDA may have internal differences of opinion regarding whether a particular new drug application should be approved, the individuals making the ultimate judgment will have the benefit of years of experience in reviewing such products, scientific expertise in the area, and access to the volumes of data they can compel manufacturers to produce. Nor is the FDA subject to the inherent limitations of the trial process, such as the rules of evidence, restrictions on expert testimony, and scheduling demands.

Although we do not accept the notion that courts are unsuited to address design defect claims in any products liability action, we do agree that prescription drug design presents precisely this type of "polycentric" problem. A drug is designed to be effectively administered to specific

---

8. Plaintiffs argue that immunizing drug manufacturers from strict liability for design defects is contrary to this statute, because that conclusion would establish an "irrebuttable presumption" that the drug was not defective or unreasonably dangerous. We disagree. Plaintiffs may still recover under a strict liability claim by demonstrating that the product was unreasonably dangerous due to an inadequate warning, a manufacturing flaw, mismarketing, or misrepresenting information to the FDA. We cite these statutes only to demonstrate the legislature's similar deference to the expertise of certain governmental agencies, particularly that of the FDA.

individuals for one or a number of indications. To determine whether a drug's benefit outweighs its risk is inherently complex because of the manufacturer's conscious design choices regarding the numerous chemical properties of the product and their relationship to the vast physiologic idiosyncracies [sic] of each consumer for whom the drug is designed. Society has recognized this complexity and in response has reposed regulatory authority in the FDA. Relying on the FDA's screening and surveillance standards enables courts to find liability under circumstances of inadequate warning, mismanufacture, improper marketing, or misinforming the FDA—avenues for which courts are better suited. Although this approach denies plaintiffs one potential theory on which to rely in a drug products liability action, the benefits to society in promoting the development, availability, and reasonable price of drugs justifies this conclusion.

....

■ STEWART, JUSTICE (dissenting):

....

Numerous congressional investigations have demonstrated that the FDA has often approved drugs in complete ignorance of critical information relating to the hazards of such drugs which was contained either in its own files or in the published medical literature, or both....

Although the FDA has a mechanism for the withdrawal of pharmaceutical agents which are found to be dangerous, 21 U.S.C. § 355(e) (1988), the mechanism is slow and sometimes unreliable....

In relying on the efficacy of FDA approval procedures as the basis for dispensing with the judicial remedy of product liability, the majority simply ignores FDA failures to protect the public against unnecessary and unacceptable risks....

Proposals before Congress and rules promulgated by the FDA to make it easier for pharmaceutical companies to obtain FDA approval for new drugs would dilute even further the safety and efficacy standards for FDA approval of drugs. Perhaps truly unavoidably unsafe drugs intended to treat life-threatening ailments should be more easily available to the public, but a lessening of safety standards is an argument for strict liability, not against. Profit motivation is likely to lead to many more unnecessarily dangerous drugs.

Furthermore, not a shred of evidence has been presented to this Court that indicates that liability under the tort system has deterred pharmaceutical companies from introducing new drugs. Even if that were the case, the question that must be answered, given the majority's holding, is why comment k does not provide a proper accommodation of all the competing policy interests involved in the issue before the Court. Why should those who are seriously injured or suffer because of the death of another have to stand the expense of such losses to support the high profit margins in the drug industry? ...

NOTES

1. *Is Grundberg Persuasive?* Chief Justice Durham offers several justifications for the court's ruling that FDA approval is a complete defense to design defect

claims, including FDA's superior expertise in evaluating drug safety and effectiveness and the agency's capacity to learn about and take measures to minimize risks that become manifest only after a drug is marketed. Are you persuaded by her account and reasoning? Does she respond adequately to Justice Stewart's more skeptical account of FDA's capabilities and performance?

2. *Liability Disincentives.* Chief Justice Durham worries that liability will discourage drug companies from developing and marketing new drugs while Justice Stewart contends that the pre-*Grundberg* rules do not appear to have discouraged manufacturers from continuing to develop and market new drugs. Who has the better of this debate? Does either judge cite convincing evidence? Does such evidence exist? *See* W. Kip Viskusi & Michael Moore, *Product Liability, Research and Development, and Innovation,* 101 J. POL. ECON. 161 (1993). *See also* Catherine T. Struve, *The FDA and the Tort System: Postmarketing Surveillance, Compensation, and the Role of Litigation,* 5 YALE J. HEALTH POL'Y & ETHICS 587 (2005).

COMMENT: STATE STATUTORY LIMITS ON DRUG MANUFACTURERS' LIABILITY

Several states have enacted statutes that provide legal protection to manufacturers whose products comply with FDA regulations. These laws fall into two general categories: (1) those that bar awards of punitive damages, often with an exception for a manufacturer that knowingly withheld or misrepresented relevant information, *see* ARIZ. REV. STAT. ANN. § 12–701 (2006); COLO. REV. STAT. § 13–64–302.5(5) (2006); N.J. STAT. ANN. § 2A:58C–5(c) (2006); N.D. CENT. CODE § 19–02.1–26(1) (2006); OHIO REV. CODE ANN. § 2307.80(C) (2006); OR. REV. STAT. § 30.927(1) (2006); UTAH CODE ANN. § 78–18–2(1) (2006); and (2) those that create a rebuttable presumption that a compliant drug is not defective or provides adequate warnings, *see* N.J. STAT. ANN. § 2A:58C–4 (2006); TEX. CIV. PRAC. & REM. CODE § 82.007(a) (2006). The Michigan legislature has gone further. It has enacted a controversial statute that creates a complete defense to liability "if the drug was approved for safety and efficacy by the United States Food and Drug Administration, and the drug and its labeling were in compliance with the United States Food and Drug Administration's Approval at the time the drug left the control of the manufacturer or seller." MICH. COMP. LAWS § 600.2946(5) (2006). *See generally* Daniel E. Troy, STATE-LEVEL PROTECTION FOR GOOD-FAITH PHARMACEUTICAL MANUFACTURERS (2006), available at http://www.fed-soc.org/pdf/fdapaper.pdf.

Most of these statutes have been the target of legal challenge. For example, in *Taylor v. Gate Pharm.,* 639 N.W.2d 45, 53 (Mich. Ct. App. 2001), the Michigan Court of Appeals held that the statute constituted "an unconstitutional delegation of legislative authority" because "[i]t places the FDA in the position of final arbiter with respect to whether a particular drug may form the basis of a products liability action in Michigan." The Supreme Court of Michigan later reversed, finding that the statute is not a delegation if it "merely provides that specific legal consequences under Michigan law will result from an act or determination by a federal agency of a fact that has independent significance." *Taylor v. Smithkline Beecham Corp.,* 658 N.W.2d 127, 129 (Mich. 2003).

Manufacturers have successfully limited the exception, present in several of these statutes, for manufacturers that knowingly withhold information from or misrepresent information to FDA. Since the Supreme Court held in *Buckman Co. v. Plaintiffs' Legal Committee*, 531 U.S. 341, 348 (2001), p. 1508 *infra*, that the FD&C Act preempts state law fraud-on-the-FDA claims, lower courts have refused to apply this exception unless FDA has made an administrative finding of fraud. *See Garcia v. Wyeth–Ayerst Labs.*, 385 F.3d 961, 966 (6th Cir. 2004) (construing MICH. COMP. LAWS. § 600.2946(5)); *Zammit v. Shire US, Inc.*, 415 F. Supp. 2d 760, 767 n.6 (E.D. Mich. 2006) (same); *Kobar v. Novartis Corp.*, 378 F. Supp. 2d 1166, 1174–75 (D. Ariz. 2005) (construing ARIZ. REV. STAT. § 12–701).

Several states provide a general regulatory compliance defense that creates a rebuttable presumption that any product conforming to a government standard is not defective. *See* COLO. REV. STAT. § 13–21–403(1)(b) (2006); FLA. STAT. § 768.1256(1) (2006); IND. CODE ANN. § 34–30–5–1(2) (2006); KAN. STAT. ANN. § 6–3304 (2006)(a); MICH. COMP. LAWS ANN. § 600.2946(4) (2006); N.D. CENT. CODE § 28–01.3–09 (2006); TENN. CODE ANN. § 29–28–104 (2006); UTAH CODE ANN. § 78–15–6(3) (2006). Other state statutes merely restate the common-law rule that the trier of fact may consider compliance with governmental safety standards as evidence that the product is not defective. *See* ARK. CODE ANN. § 16–116–105(a) (2006); N.C. GEN. STAT. § 99B–6(b)(3) (2006); OHIO REV. CODE ANN. § 2307.75(B)(4) (2006); WASH. REV. CODE ANN. § 7.72.050(1) (2006).

Courts are currently divided over whether regulatory compliance statutes should protect manufacturers from liability for injuries caused by off-label uses. *Compare Griffus v. Novartis Pharms. Corp.*, 2006 WL 2583129 *1 (E.D. Mich. 2006) (holding that Mich. Comp. Laws § 600.2946(5) applies to off-label uses) *with Ehlis v. Shire Richwood, Inc.*, 233 F. Supp. 2d 1189, 1199 (D.N.D. 2002) (refusing to grant summary judgment to defendant under N.D. Cent. Code § 28–01.3–09 because plaintiffs' presentation of evidence that defendant knew of off-label use rebutted the statute's presumption against defects), *aff'd on other grounds*, 363 F.3d 1013 (8th Cir. 2004).

The variety of state statutes has led to forum shopping by plaintiffs. For example, Michigan plaintiffs have filed suit in other jurisdictions in an attempt to circumvent their state's complete bar to liability. *See, e.g., Stupak v. Hoffman–La Roche, Inc.*, 287 F. Supp. 2d 968 (E.D. Wis. 2003). This strategy can backfire, however, since courts in other states may decide, under their own choice-of-law principles, that Mich. Comp. Laws § 600.2946(5) is substantive, not procedural, and thus applies in their forum. *See Alli v. Eli Lilly & Co.*, 854 N.E.2d 372 (Ct. App. Ind. 2006). The diversity of state laws may also defeat class certification of nationwide punitive damages claims. *See In re Baycol Prods. Litig.*, 218 F.R.D. 197, 215–16 (D. Minn. 2003).

D. EXCLUSIVITY OF FEDERAL ENFORCEMENT

In the following case, the Supreme Court agrees that allowing private suits to enforce the FD&C Act's prohibition against misrepresentations to

FDA would interfere with the government's capacity to investigate and punish such conduct, and accordingly it holds such suits are preempted.

Buckman Co. v. Plaintiffs' Legal Committee

531 U.S. 341 (2001).

■ CHIEF JUSTICE REHNQUIST delivered the opinion of the Court.

Respondent represents plaintiffs who claim injuries resulting from the use of orthopedic bone screws in the pedicles of their spines. Petitioner is a consulting company that assisted the screws' manufacturer, AcroMed Corporation, in navigating the federal regulatory process for these devices. Plaintiffs say petitioner made fraudulent representations to the Food and Drug Administration (FDA or Administration) in the course of obtaining approval to market the screws. Plaintiffs further claim that such representations were at least a "but for" cause of injuries that plaintiffs sustained from the implantation of these devices: Had the representations not been made, the FDA would not have approved the devices, and plaintiffs would not have been injured. Plaintiffs sought damages from petitioner under state tort law. We hold that such claims are pre-empted by the Federal Food, Drug, and Cosmetic Act (FDCA), as amended by the Medical Device Amendments of 1976.

I.

. . . It is not disputed that the bone screws manufactured by AcroMed are Class III devices.

. . . The PMA process is ordinarily quite time consuming because the FDA's review requires an "average of 1,200 hours [for] each submission."

An exception to the PMA requirement exists for devices that were already on the market prior to the MDA's enactment in 1976. The MDA allows these "predicate" devices to remain available until the FDA initiates and completes the PMA process. In order to avoid the potentially monopolistic consequences of this predicate-device exception, the MDA allows other manufacturers to distribute (also pending completion of the predicate device's PMA review) devices that are shown to be "substantially equivalent" to a predicate device.

Demonstrating that a device qualifies for this exception is known as the "§ 510(k) process," which refers to the section of the original MDA containing this provision. . . .

In 1984, AcroMed sought § 510(k) approval for its bone screw device, indicating it for use in spinal surgery. The FDA denied approval on the grounds that the Class III device lacked substantial equivalence to a predicate device. In September 1985, with the assistance of petitioner, AcroMed filed another § 510(k) application. "The application provided additional information about the . . . device and again indicated its intended use in spinal surgery. The FDA again rejected the application, determining that the device was not substantially equivalent to a predicate device and that it posed potential risks not exhibited by other spinal-fixation systems." In December 1985, AcroMed and petitioner filed a third § 510(k) application.

> "AcroMed and [petitioner] split the . . . device into its component parts, renamed them 'nested bone plates' and '[cancellous] bone screws' and filed a separate § 510(k) application for each component. In both applications, a new intended use was specified: rather than seeking clearance for spinal applications, they sought clearance to market the plates and screws for use in the long bones of the arms and legs. AcroMed and Buckman claimed that the two components were substantially equivalent to predicate devices used in long bone surgery. The FDA approved the devices for this purpose in February 1986."

Pursuant to its designation by the Judicial Panel on Multidistrict Litigation as the transferee court for *In re Orthopedic Bone Screw Liability Litigation*, MDL No. 1014, the District Court for the Eastern District of Pennsylvania has been the recipient of some 2,300 civil actions related to these medical devices. Many of these actions include state-law causes of action claiming that petitioner and AcroMed made fraudulent representations to the FDA as to the intended use of the bone screws and that, as a result, the devices were improperly given market clearance and were subsequently used to the plaintiffs' detriment. The District Court dismissed these "fraud-on-the-FDA" claims, first on the ground that they were expressly pre-empted by the MDA, and then, after our decision in *Medtronic*, on the ground that these claims amounted to an improper assertion of a private right of action under the MDA.

A divided panel of the United States Court of Appeals for the Third Circuit reversed, concluding that plaintiffs' fraud claims were neither expressly nor impliedly pre-empted. . . .

II.

Policing fraud against federal agencies is hardly "a field which the States have traditionally occupied, such as to warrant a presumption against finding federal pre-emption of a state-law cause of action." To the contrary, the relationship between a federal agency and the entity it regulates is inherently federal in character because the relationship originates from, is governed by, and terminates according to federal law. Here, petitioner's dealings with the FDA were prompted by the MDA, and the very subject matter of petitioner's statements were dictated by that statute's provisions. Accordingly . . . no presumption against pre-emption obtains in this case.

Given this analytical framework, we hold that the plaintiffs' state-law fraud-on-the-FDA claims conflict with, and are therefore impliedly pre-empted by, federal law. The conflict stems from the fact that the federal statutory scheme amply empowers the FDA to punish and deter fraud against the Administration, and that this authority is used by the Administration to achieve a somewhat delicate balance of statutory objectives. The balance sought by the Administration can be skewed by allowing fraud-on-the-FDA claims under state tort law.

As described in greater detail above, the § 510(k) process sets forth a comprehensive scheme for determining whether an applicant has demonstrated that a product is substantially equivalent to a predicate device.... To achieve its limited purpose, the § 510(k) process imposes upon applicants a variety of requirements that are designed to enable the FDA to make its statutorily required judgment as to whether the device qualifies under this exception.

Accompanying these disclosure requirements are various provisions aimed at detecting, deterring, and punishing false statements made during this and related approval processes. The FDA is empowered to investigate suspected fraud, and citizens may report wrongdoing and petition the agency to take action. In addition to the general criminal proscription on making false statements to the Federal Government, the FDA may respond to fraud by seeking injunctive relief and civil penalties, seizing the device[,] and pursuing criminal prosecutions. The FDA[4] thus has at its disposal a variety of enforcement options that allow it to make a measured response to suspected fraud upon the Administration.

This flexibility is a critical component of the statutory and regulatory framework under which the FDA pursues difficult (and often competing) objectives. For example, with respect to Class III devices, the FDA simultaneously maintains the exhaustive PMA and the more limited § 510(k) processes in order to ensure both that medical devices are reasonably safe and effective and that, if the device qualifies under the § 510(k) exception, it is on the market within a relatively short period of time. Similarly, "off-label" usage of medical devices (use of a device for some other purpose than that for which it has been approved by the FDA) is an accepted and necessary corollary of the FDA's mission to regulate in this area without directly interfering with the practice of medicine. Indeed, a recent amendment to the FDCA expressly states in part that "[n]othing in this chapter shall be construed to limit or interfere with the authority of a health care practitioner to prescribe or administer any legally marketed device to a patient for any condition or disease within a legitimate health care practitioner-patient relationship." Thus, the FDA is charged with the difficult task of regulating the marketing and distribution of medical devices without intruding upon decisions statutorily committed to the discretion of health care professionals.

State-law fraud-on-the-FDA claims inevitably conflict with the FDA's responsibility to police fraud consistently with the Administration's judgment and objectives. As a practical matter, complying with the FDA's detailed regulatory regime in the shadow of 50 States' tort regimes will dramatically increase the burdens facing potential applicants—burdens not contemplated by Congress in enacting the FDCA and the MDA. Would-be applicants may be discouraged from seeking § 510(k) approval of devices with potentially beneficial off-label uses for fear that such use might expose the manufacturer or its associates (such as petitioner) to unpredictable civil

---

4. The FDCA leaves no doubt that it is the Federal Government rather than private litigants who are authorized to file suit for noncompliance with the medical device provisions: "[A]ll such proceedings for the enforcement, or to restrain violations, of this chapter shall be by and in the name of the United States." 21 U.S.C. 337(a).

liability. In effect, then, fraud-on-the-FDA claims could cause the Administration's reporting requirements to deter off-label use despite the fact that the FDCA expressly disclaims any intent to directly regulate the practice of medicine, and even though off-label use is generally accepted.

Conversely, fraud-on-the-FDA claims would also cause applicants to fear that their disclosures to the FDA, although deemed appropriate by the Administration, will later be judged insufficient in state court. Applicants would then have an incentive to submit a deluge of information that the Administration neither wants nor needs, resulting in additional burdens on the FDA's evaluation of an application. As a result, the comparatively speedy § 510(k) process could encounter delays, which would, in turn, impede competition among predicate devices and delay health care professionals' ability to prescribe appropriate off-label uses.

. . . .

Respondent also suggests that we should be reluctant to find a preemptive conflict here because Congress included an express pre-emption provision in the MDA. To the extent respondent posits that anything other than our ordinary pre-emption principles apply under these circumstances, that contention must fail in light of our conclusion last Term in *Geier v. American Honda Motor Co.*, 529 U.S. 861 (2000), that neither an express pre-emption provision nor a saving clause "bar[s] the ordinary working of conflict pre-emption principles."

. . . .

In sum, were plaintiffs to maintain their fraud-on-the-agency claims here, they would not be relying on traditional state tort law which had predated the federal enactments in questions. On the contrary, the existence of these federal enactments is a critical element in their case. For the reasons stated above, we think this sort of litigation would exert an extraneous pull on the scheme established by Congress, and it is therefore pre-empted by that scheme. The judgment of the Court of Appeals is reversed.

■ JUSTICE STEVENS, with whom JUSTICE THOMAS joins, concur in the judgment.

NOTES

1. *Bypassing Section 521*. Even though the defendant's alleged misrepresentations were part of overtures designed to convince FDA that a device was substantially equivalent to an already marketed device, the Supreme Court is careful not to rely on FD&C Act section 521, the device preemption provision, suggesting that the result would be the same if Congress had never enacted the provision.

2. *Buckman Critiqued*. Professor Thomas McGarity is troubled by the Court's ruling in *Buckman* and offers the following limiting interpretation of the case:

> One of the considerable advantages of a tort reparations regime is its capacity to get to the truth of the matter in ways that are largely unavailable to regulatory agencies. Private attorneys are adept at uncovering evidence of fraud and misrepresentation in the discovery that precedes common law trials, and they are willing to spend the resources necessary to

copy and organize documents, take deposition, and fight the company's efforts to resist discovery.... Buckman arose under peculiar institutional and procedural settings. Institutionally, the statute that required federal approval for a product for a particular use did not allow the federal agency to limit the actual use of approved products to the approved uses. This odd regulatory setting is the result of the historical political power of the medical profession. Everyone recognizes that medical devices should be regulated to protect the public against negligent and deceitful manufacturers of medical devices, but the medical profession has thus far successfully persuaded Congress that the practice of medicine is a matter that is exclusively subject to state regulations and that doctors are capable of protecting their patients from the risks posed by putting medical devices to unapproved uses. Procedurally, the plaintiffs had originally sued both Buckman and AcroMed, the manufacturer and marketer of the bone screws that injured the plaintiffs, but had subsequently dismissed AcroMed pursuant to a global settlement. In addition to fraud on the agency claims, the claims against AcroMed had included traditional common law claims for negligence and strict liability. The plaintiffs' only claims against Buckman relied upon its novel "fraud on the FDA" theory.

Given its peculiar institutional and procedural posture, courts in the future should limit *Buckman's* precedential effect to the claims against companies that assist manufacturers in obtaining federal agency approval of products, like medical devices and drugs, that may lawfully be used for unapproved uses. Under *Medtronic* and its predecessors, plaintiffs should ordinarily be able to base actions against manufacturers of risky products on traditional common law negligence and strict liability theories without fear of preemption. As cases based upon negligence and strict liability go forward, evidence of attempts by the defendant to manipulate the regulatory process through fraudulent or misleading means should be admissible even if wrongful manipulation may not support an independent claim for relief. For example, wrongful manipulation would appear relevant to the issue of cause-in-fact in cases where the plaintiff may plausibly argue that but for the wrongful manipulation of the federal agency the product would not have been marketed and the plaintiff would not have been injured. At the very least, evidence of wrongful manipulation should be admissible to rebut any direct or indirect implication by the defendant that the product was not defective because it was government-approved.

Furthermore, a strong argument exists for limiting the *Buckman* precedent to cases in which the government has decided not to initiate action against the company that allegedly defrauded a federal agency. In *Buckman*, the government either did not consider Buckman's action fraudulent or did not think that any fraud was worth punishing. In such a situation, the argument that judicial recognition of a common law action based upon wrongful manipulation of the regulatory process conflicts with the "delicate balance" of considerations that governs the decision whether or not to prosecute fraud is much stronger than in a case in which the federal government has decided to prosecute an alleged fraud under one of its enforcement authorities.

Thomas McGarity, *Beyond Buckman: Wrongful Manipulation of the Regulatory Process in the Law of Torts*, 41 WASHBURN L.J. 549, 571–93 (2002). *See also* Jean Macchiaroli Eggen, *Shedding Light on the Preemption Doctrine in Product Liability Actions: Defining the Scope of Buckman and Sprietsma*, 6 DEL. L. REV. 143 (2003).

3. *Geier v. American Honda.* Reading *Buckman,* one hears echos of the Court's approach in an earlier case involving a statute that contained an express preemption clause. In *Geier v. American Honda,* 529 U.S. 861 (2000), the Supreme Court held that a private suit to recover for injuries attributable to Honda's failure to equip the plaintiff's automobile with air bags was preempted. The statute in question, the National Highway Traffic Safety Act, 49 U.S.C. 30103(b), expressly preempts any state "safety standard" that differs from or adds to a standard adopted by the Secretary of Transportation. Acting through the National Highway Traffic Safety Administration, the Secretary had adopted a standard for passive restraints that required manufacturers to equip at least 10 percent of their new cars with air bags. Honda without question complied with this standard. Later it faced Geier's claim that it should have so-equipped the model he purchased. Conceding that a jury's imposition of tort liability for failure to equip Geier's car with air bags would not constitute the adoption of a "safety standard," Justice Breyer nonetheless found that allowing such suits would undermine the delicate political/regulatory compromise that the Secretary had struck when he demanded that only 10 percent of a manufacturer's new cars be equipped with air bags.

Desiano v. Warner–Lambert & Co.

467 F.3d 85 (2d Cir. 2006).

■ CALABRESI, CIRCUIT JUDGE:

It has long fallen within the province of states to safeguard the health and safety of their citizens. Consonant with the "historic primacy of state regulation" of these matters, the power of states to govern in this field is considerable and undisputed. Historically, common law liability has formed the bedrock of state regulation, and common law tort claims have been described as "a critical component of the States' traditional ability to protect the health and safety of their citizens." *Cipollone v. Liggett Group, Inc.,* 505 U.S. 504 (1992) (Blackmun, J., concurring in part and dissenting in part). In recent years, some states, in exercising their traditional authority with respect to the pharmaceutical industry, have narrowed common law liability in order to insulate drug companies from burdensome litigation. *See generally* David G. Owen, *Special Defenses in Modern Products Liability Law,* 70 Mo. L. REV. 1, 22–23 (2005)....

In 1995, the State of Michigan enacted legislation immunizing drugmakers from products liability claims so long as the Food and Drug Administration ("FDA") approved the pharmaceutical product at issue. Michigan's immunity scheme contains an exception that preserves liability if the pharmaceutical company withheld or misrepresented information that would have altered the FDA's decision to approve the drug....

BACKGROUND

A. Michigan's Immunity Statute

. . . .

In 1995, Michigan's legislature amended the law in order to confer immunity upon drugmakers in product liability suits where the FDA had approved the drug in question.... The relevant provision states:

> In a product liability action against a manufacturer or seller, a product that is a drug is not defective or unreasonably dangerous,

and the manufacturer or seller is not liable, if the drug was approved for safety and efficacy by the United States food and drug administration, and the drug and its labeling were in compliance with the United States food and drug administration's approval at the time the drug left the control of the manufacturer or seller.

M.C.L. § 600.2946(5). In addition to several qualifications not relevant to the case before us, the immunity provision contains an important exception:

This subsection does not apply if the defendant at any time before the event that allegedly caused the injury does any of the following:

(a) Intentionally withholds from or misrepresents to the United States food and drug administration information concerning the drug that is required to be submitted under the federal food, drug, and cosmetic act and the drug would not have been approved, or the United States food and drug administration would have withdrawn approval for the drug if the information were accurately submitted.

M.C.L. § 600.2946(5)(a). Hence, under these provisions, so long as a drug company did not withhold or misrepresent information that would have affected the FDA's approval of a putatively harmful drug, the company can successfully defend itself against products liability litigation by establishing that its product received the FDA's approval and complied with the FDA's labeling and substantive requirements.

B.   Procedural History

Appellants in this case are all Michigan residents alleging injuries caused by Rezulin, a drug marketed and sold by Appellees for the treatment of Type–2 diabetes. The FDA originally approved Rezulin in 1997. After adverse liver-related effects were documented in patients taking Rezulin, Appellees agreed to a series of label changes, which were authorized by the FDA on four occasions between November 1997 and June 1999. In March 2000, apparently at the FDA's request, Appellees withdrew Rezulin from the United States market.

. . . .

In the District Court, Appellees moved for judgment on the pleadings on the ground that liability was foreclosed under Michigan state law. To support their motion, Appellees emphasized *Buckman* and the Sixth Circuit's decision in *Garcia v. Wyeth–Ayerst Labs.*, 385 F.3d 961 (6th Cir. 2004), *which held (on the basis of* Buckman) *that the "fraud" exception in Michigan's statute was impliedly preempted by two federal laws—the Food, Drug and Cosmetic Act ("FDCA"), et seq., and the Medical Device Act ("MDA"), and therefore had to be severed from the rest of the Michigan law.*

DISCUSSION

We review *de novo* a district court's dismissal of a suit pursuant to a motion for judgment on the pleadings. . . .

This appeal raises two separate and significant questions. First, ... must we follow our sister circuit's holding in *Garcia* because the Sixth Circuit's decision involved the laws of Michigan, a state within its circuit? Second, even if we are not required to defer conclusively to *Garcia*, should we nonetheless conclude, applying the logic of *Buckman*, that Appellants' common law claims—preserved by Michigan's exception—conflict with, and are therefore preempted by, federal law?

I.

. . . .

But [precedent] instructed us to defer conclusively to another circuit's judgment only when that court of appeals' decision addressed questions of *state* law from a state within that circuit. It asserted no obligation to defer to a foreign circuit's views on *federal* law. As to issues of federal law, we are permitted—indeed, required—to reach our own conclusions....

. . . .

The problem, therefore, with the District Court's decision and with the position taken by Appellees is that both fail to appreciate that this appeal ... is not governed primarily, and certainly not exclusively, by state law. Rather, the question of whether federal law impliedly preempts part of Michigan's statutory scheme depends on significant issues of federal law including, *inter alia*, the meaning of Supreme Court precedents, *e.g.*, *Buckman*, and the scope of federal statutes, *e.g.*, FDCA....

. . . .

II.

In *Buckman*, the Supreme Court considered whether federal law—specifically, the FDCA and the MDA—preempted state "fraud-on-the-FDA" claims. The plaintiffs in *Buckman* contended that a medical device manufacturer had obtained FDA approval for its product only after making fraudulent misrepresentations to the federal agency. Claiming that the FDA would not have approved the device but for these misrepresentations, the plaintiffs sought damages under California state law. The Court began by stating what is undoubtedly true that "[p]olicing fraud against federal agencies is hardly a field which the States have traditionally occupied." As a result, the presumption against federal preemption of a state law cause of action did not apply to fraud-on-the-FDA claims.

In the absence of any presumption against preemption, the Court found that fraud-on-the-FDA claims conflicted with, and were therefore impliedly preempted by, federal law. "The conflict stems from the fact that the federal statutory scheme amply empowers the FDA to punish and deter fraud against the Administration, and that this authority is used by the Administration to achieve a somewhat delicate balance of statutory objectives." In other words, *policing fraud on the FDA* through a tort action could interfere with how the FDA might wish to police that kind of fraud itself.

The *Buckman* Court went on to express its concern that the potential conflict between federal law and the competing regulatory regimes of 50 states would unduly burden drug companies seeking to obtain FDA approval for their products. The Supreme Court worried that these companies, fearful of state liability, would file "a deluge of information" that the FDA does not require, thereby burdening the federal agency as well. But the Court ended by emphasizing that the plaintiffs' claims before it were not rooted in traditional state law, and were instead derivative of federal law:

> In sum, were plaintiffs to maintain their fraud-on-the-agency claims here, they would not be relying on traditional state tort law which had predated the federal enactments in questions. On the contrary, the existence of ... federal enactments is a critical element in their case.

For these reasons, the Court invalidated the plaintiffs' fraud-on-the-FDA claims as impliedly preempted by federal law.

Echoing the conclusion of the Sixth Circuit, Appellees argue that there is no meaningful difference between the fraud-on-the-FDA claims struck down in *Buckman* and Appellants' claims under Michigan tort law. We disagree. There are three differences between the nature of the claim which M.C.L. § 600.2946(5) exempts from abolition and the claim in *Buckman* . . . .

A.   *Presumption Against Preemption*

First, the presumption against federal preemption of state law obtains in the case before us. . . . In *Buckman*, the Court held that this presumption did not apply *because "[p]olicing fraud against federal agencies is hardly a field which the States have traditionally occupied."*

In the case before us, instead, the cause of action (which survives the changes made by M.C.L. § 2946(5)) cannot reasonably be characterized as a state's attempt to police fraud against the FDA. ... Rather, M.C.L. § 600.2946(5) did not invent new causes of action premised on fraud against the FDA. The object of the legislative scheme was rather to regulate and restrict when victims could continue to recover under preexisting state products liability law.

The Michigan legislature's desire to rein in state-based tort liability falls squarely within its prerogative to "regulat[e] matters of health and safety," which is a sphere in which the presumption against preemption applies, indeed, stands at its strongest. . . . As a result, while there may be reasons to override that presumption, the existence of the presumption in the instant case requires an altogether different analysis from that made in *Buckman*.

B.   *Traditional Common Law Liability*

Second, Appellants here are not pressing "fraud-on-the-FDA" claims, as the plaintiffs in *Buckman* were understood by the Supreme Court to be doing. They are, rather, asserting claims that sound in traditional state tort law. . . .

The *Buckman* Court suggested that the source and "vintage" of the *duty* the drug maker is accused of breaching in "fraud-on-the-FDA" claims is different from the source and "vintage" of the duty that obtains in traditional tort claims. . . .

Significantly, all of the claims advanced by Appellants in this case are premised on traditional duties between a product manufacturer and Michigan consumers. None of them derives from, or is based on, a newly-concocted duty between a manufacturer and a federal agency. As a result, were we to conclude that Appellants' claims were preempted, we would be holding that Congress, without any explicit expression of intent, should nonetheless be taken to have modified (and, in effect, gutted) traditional state law duties between pharmaceutical companies and their consumers. We see no reason, nor can we identify any precedent, to justify such a result.

The second difference between common law actions and "fraud-on-the-FDA" claims, suggested in *Buckman*, is that in FDA-fraud cases, proof of fraud against the FDA is *alone sufficient* to impose liability. In *Buckman*, there were no freestanding allegations of wrongdoing apart from the defendant's purported failure to comply with FDA disclosure requirements. And *Buckman* explicitly distinguished *Medtronic* on this ground....

As in *Medtronic*, the plaintiffs' claims in the case before us "parallel federal safety requirements" but are not premised principally (let alone exclusively) on a drug maker's failure to comply with federal disclosure requirements. On the contrary, the plaintiffs' complaints allege a wide range of putative violations of common law duties long-recognized by Michigan's tort regime. These pre-existing common law claims survive under *M.C.L. § 600.29466(5)* because there is also evidence of fraud in FDA disclosures....

Significantly, this reading of *Buckman* reflects the position the pharmaceutical industry articulated at oral argument in *Buckman*. Thus, the industry's presentation to the Supreme Court began by stressing the unusual and narrow claim before the *Buckman* Court:

> The plaintiffs in this case are people who underwent back surgery in which particular medical devices were used. They brought this suit under State law to recover for injuries allegedly caused by their—by these devices, but this is a very unusual form of State law product liability action. The plaintiffs don't claim that these devices were in any way defective. There's no claim here of manufacturing defect. There's no claim here of design defect. The plaintiffs also don't claim that the surgeons who used these devices did anything wrong. There's no claim here of medical malpractice.

> Instead, the plaintiffs' sole claim in this case is the following. They assert that the Federal Food & Drug Administration was deceived into giving regulatory clearance to these devices, that, absent this deception, these devices would never have been on the market, and that, if the devices had never have been on the market, they wouldn't have been used in their surgeries and they wouldn't have suffered any injuries.

Oral Argument Transcript, *Buckman*, 531 U.S. 341, 346–47 (No. 98–1768).

C.   *Immunity as Affirmative Defense*

Third, and once more unlike *Buckman*, the Michigan Supreme Court has indicated that proof of fraud against the FDA is not even an *element* of a products liability claim like the one here brought. The existence of properly-obtained FDA approval becomes germane *only* if a defendant company chooses to assert an affirmative defense made available by the Michigan legislature in M.C.L. § 600.2946(5). Thus, in *Taylor*'s discussion of M.C.L. § 2946(5), Michigan's highest court offered this characterization of the statute: "[A] manufacturer or seller of a drug that has been approved by the FDA has an absolute *defense* to a products liability claim if the drug and its labeling were in compliance with the FDA's approval at the time the drug left the control of the manufacturer or seller." (emphasis added). And, throughout its opinion, the *Taylor* court spoke of the *defendant's* references to the *FDA's* findings, suggesting again that it is the defendant that must invoke the FDA's decision to approve its drug if it wishes to insulate itself from liability. We take this to mean that the Michigan law in question does no more than create a defense that drug makers may invoke, if they so decide, and that it is not up to the plaintiff to prove fraud as an element of his or her claim.

Finding preemption of traditional common law claims where fraud is not even a required element—but may be submitted to neutralize a drugmaker's use of an affirmative defense available under state law—would result in preemption of a scope that would go far beyond anything that has been applied in the past. Until and unless Congress states explicitly that it intends invalidation of state common law claims merely because issues of fraud may arise in the trial of such claims, we decline to read general statutes like the FDCA and the MDA as having that effect.

* * *

The *Buckman* Court did, however, mention practical concerns with allowing "fraud-on-the-FDA" suits to go unpreempted. Specifically, it said that permitting such suits would result in a deluge of information that could swamp FDA administrators. The *Garcia* court, in applying *Buckman* to a suit like the one before us, made reference to these same concerns. But these worries, if deemed controlling, would prove too much. They would result in preemption of a scope that no one is contemplating, let alone advocating.

In terms of deluging the FDA, there is little difference between (a) causes of action, like the instant one, where proof of fraud against the FDA is not the basis of the cause of action but is necessary to negate a limitation on state liability, and (b) causes of action where proof of fraud against the FDA is permitted but not conclusive (as it was under the precursor to the Michigan law at issue here, *see supra*, and as it presumably is in most states in the country). So long as a court or jury is *allowed to consider* evidence of fraud against the FDA in an ordinary common law tort suit, and so long as juries are likely to react to such evidence, there will be substantial inducements on the pharmaceutical industry to provide the federal agency with just the kind of information that troubled the *Buckman* and *Garcia* Courts. Requiring such evidence when a plaintiff seeks to counter a statutory defense from liability would not significantly alter that incentive. Only when proof of fraud is by itself *sufficient* to impose liability—and indeed is the sole basis of liability (as it was in *Buckman*)— does the incentive to flood the FDA appreciably escalate.

In other words, the incentive to supply additional data to the FDA under the Michigan law before us is no greater than the incentive that exists whenever evidence of what a company submitted, or failed to submit, to the FDA is admissible and probative of liability. It follows that under *Garcia*'s reading of *Buckman*, unless a state barred the submission of evidence of fraud against the FDA in run of the mill tort cases, the policy concerns that *Buckman* expressed in a very narrow context would seemingly justify invalidating any product liability suit brought against a drugmaker. We do not believe *Buckman* meant to go anywhere near so far.[9]

III.

Because of its important role in state regulation of matters of health and safety, common law liability cannot be easily displaced in our federal system. *Buckman* underscored this fact, finding implied preemption of a newly-fashioned state cause of action only where (1) no presumption against federal preemption obtained, and (2) the cause of action, by assigning liability *solely* on the basis of fraud against the FDA, imposed significant and distinctive burdens on the FDA and the entities it regulates. The appeal before us presents a very different set of circumstances, one in which there is a clear presumption against preemption of long-standing common law claims. In the presence of this presumption, because Michigan law does not in fact implicate the concerns that animated the Supreme Court's decision in *Buckman*, and because Appellants' lawsuits depend primarily on traditional and preexisting tort sources, not at all on a "fraud-on-the-FDA" cause of action created by state law, and only incidentally on evidence of such fraud, we conclude that the Michigan immunity exception is not prohibited through preemption. It follows that common law liability is not foreclosed by federal law, and Appellants' claims should not have been dismissed.

E.   GOVERNMENT LIABILITY

FDA's involvement in the development, evaluation, and marketing of products covered by the FD&C Act can make the government a target for

---

9. Since we heard oral argument in this case, the FDA issued a final rule governing the content and format of drug product labeling. In the amended regulation, the FDA announced its view that FDA labeling requirements preempt state law claims that impose additional or different requirements: "[The] FDA believes that under existing preemption principles, FDA approval of labeling under the act, whether it be in the old or new format, preempts conflicting or contrary State law." In so doing, the FDA apparently confined its view that state claims undermine federal law to circumstances "when [state laws] purport to compel a firm to include in labeling or advertising a statement that [the] FDA has considered and found scientifically unsubstantiated."

Although any statement by a federal agency carries persuasive weight, the FDA's recent pronouncement does not ultimately affect our analysis in this case. First, the FDA's statement seemingly concerns only preemption of state laws that impose additional *labeling* requirements. Appellants' claims rest on far broader allegations, *e.g.*, defective design and manufacturing.

Second, even to the extent that the FDA's statement might bear peripherally on the claims asserted in this case, it is not clear what, if any, deference would be owed to the FDA's view. Assertions of implied preemption arguably originate in statutory ambiguity as to which an agency's interpretations may be accorded deference....

But, whatever deference would be owed to an agency's view in contexts where a presumption against federal preemption does apply, an agency cannot supply, on Congress's behalf, the clear legislative statement of intent required to overcome the presumption against preemption.

suits when its agents play a significant role in the approval or use of products that cause harm. *Berkovitz v. United States*, 486 U.S. 531 (1988), p. 906 *supra* explores the United State's potential liability under the Federal Torts Claims Act and in the process reveals the complexity of the questions the agency must resolve.

NOTES

1. *Subsequent History.* On remand, the Court of Appeals denied the government's motion to dismiss and remanded the case to the district court for a trial on the merits, 858 F.2d 122 (3d Cir.1988). Thereafter the case was consolidated with several other suits seeking damages for injuries resulting from the administration of Orimune. *In re Sabin Oral Polio Vaccine Products Liability Litigation*, 743 F. Supp. 410 (D. Md.1990).

2. *Another Theory of Liability.* In *Griffin v. United States*, 500 F.2d 1059 (3d Cir. 1974), the Court of Appeals sustained recovery against the government for the severe injuries suffered following administration of a dose of Sabin polio vaccine that the Division of Biological Standards (now CBER) had licensed. The DBS had promulgated a regulation establishing specifications that its employees were to apply in determining nonvirulence of batches of the vaccine, specifications that many outside experts had criticized as unnecessarily stringent. The DBS had released the batch of vaccine administered to Mrs. Griffin even though it did not meet these specifications. The court disagreed with the government's contention that the decision whether to release the vaccine was discretionary and that the DBS regulation required a judgmental determination:

> We acknowledge that under DBS' construction of the regulation, the implementation called for a judgmental determination as to the degree to which each of the enumerated criteria indicated neurovirulence.... The judgment, however, was that of a professional measuring neurovirulence. It was not that of a policy-maker promulgating regulations by balancing competing policy considerations in determining the public interest.... At issue was a scientific, but not policy-making, determination as to whether each of the criteria listed ... was met and the extent to which each such factor accurately indicated neurovirulence. DBS' responsibility was limited to merely executing the policy judgments of the Surgeon General....
>
> ... The Government's release of Lot 56 was predicated upon its reliance on a factor called "biological variation." Reliance on this factor, however, was not authorized by the regulations. We therefore conclude ... that DBS' activity was not immunized from judicial review.

3. *Government Liability for Approving DES.* In *Gray v. United States*, 445 F. Supp. 337 (S.D. Tex. 1978), where the court concluded that FDA's approval of DES was not open to reexamination in a suit based on the Federal Tort Claims Act. The District Court distinguished *Griffin* by contrasting the open-ended standard for approval of drugs generally with the detailed and explicit regulations governing the release of lots of a vaccine. *See also Gelley v. Astra Pharmaceutical Prods., Inc.*, 466 F. Supp. 182 (D. Minn.1979), *aff'd* 610 F.2d 558 (8th Cir. 1979):

> Generally, plaintiff's theory of liability against the government is that the FDA negligently failed to withdraw its prior approval of xylocaine and negligently failed to enforce the provisions of the Food, Drug and Cosmetic Act and its own regulations relating to information collection and labeling changes, thereby allowing xylocaine to remain in interstate commerce in a misbranded and/or adulterated condition....

... [A]s the Federal Tort Claims Act makes explicit, the law of the place where the act or omission occurred which gives rise to the claim is the foundation upon which federal governmental liability is predicated.... The law of the District of Columbia does not impose a tort duty on private persons to perform activities required by the FDA regulatory scheme. Regulatory activity engaged in by FDA personnel simply has no counterpart in private activity and thus cannot give rise to liability under the common law of the District of Columbia or elsewhere.... The result of the plaintiff's argument, if accepted, would be to impose liability on the federal government for the failure of its regulatory employees to protect the public in general against third party violations of federal law. This result would cast the federal government in the role of an insurer against violations of regulatory law, certainly a result not contemplated by Congress in enacting the Federal Tort Claims Act.

4. *Additional Authority.* FDA has been held to be immune from suit under the FTCA for assertedly negligent approval of a new drug, *Bailey v. Eli Lilly Co.*, 607 F. Supp. 660 (M.D. Pa. 1985), for wrongful refusal to approve a new drug, *Hogan v. FDA*, 1965–1968 FDLI Jud. Rec. 376 (S.D. Cal. 1965), and for allegedly negligent inspection, *Anglo–American and Overseas Corp. v. United States*, 242 F.2d 236 (2d Cir. 1957). *See generally* Richard A. Merrill, *Compensation for Prescription Drug Injuries*, 59 VA. L. REV. 1 (1973).

CHAPTER XIV

ADMINISTRATIVE PRACTICE AND PROCEDURE

A. FDA's RELIANCE ON REGULATIONS

1. OVERVIEW

For most regulatory agencies, the number and scope of their regulations grow over time. For much of its history FDA fit this pattern. The agency's regulations occupied nearly 250 pages in the Code of Federal Regulations in 1948, they reached 585 pages by 1956, and they ballooned to 1,718 pages in 1969 and to 1,951 pages in 1979. By the publication of our second edition in 1991, FDA regulations had expanded to nearly 3,790 pages. Since then, however, what had seemed inexorable growth in regulatory text has slowed and stabilized. As of July 1, 2006, FDA's regulations occupied 3800 CFR pages.

The growth in FDA regulations in the 1970s and the early 1980s reflects an earlier change in the agency's approach to enforcing the FD&C Act. For several decades FDA relied on court enforcement as its main method for assuring compliance. This approach was feasible, perhaps appropriate, because the issues facing the agency were typically less complex and its ambitions were more modest. In the area of food labeling, for example, FDA was responsible for enforcing a handful of explicit mandatory requirements (the name of the food, the name and address of the manufacturer, the net quantity of contents, and the statement of ingredients) along with the Act's general prohibition against false or misleading statements. Later, however, the agency was expected to establish labeling requirements that would allow consumers to evaluate the composition and nutritional quality of food. While court enforcement fulfilled FDA's former role, it could not suffice as public and congressional expectations changed.

Starting around 1970, FDA implemented the FD&C Act primarily through rulemaking. It continued to rely on court enforcement to deal with traditional problems of filth in food or fraudulent labeling, and to assure compliance with promulgated regulations. But new substantive law was rarely made through court action. The Second Circuit endorsed the agency's approach.

> [O]ver the last decade rule-making has been increasingly substituted for adjudication as a regulatory technique, with the support and encouragement of courts, at least where the regulation involves specialized scientific knowledge. Where the objective is essentially legislative, *i.e.*, to establish rules or principles by

which an entire industry may be governed, the case-by-case adversary proceeding, in which the agency confronts a single alleged offender selected for suit with respect to a specific factual situation, has frequently proved to be an unsuitable method of enforcing the law, since it often resolves narrow issues of importance only to the immediate adversaries rather than broad questions of interest to the industry or the public. The rule-making proceeding, on the other hand, provides the agency with an opportunity first to receive a wide spectrum of views proffered by all segments affected by the proposed rule (*e.g.*, manufacturers, vendors, doctors, consumers) and then in a legislative fashion to consider and choose from several alternatives or options rather than limit its decisions to narrow issues controlling a particular case. Furthermore, once binding regulations are promulgated, the industry and public are put on notice and may be guided accordingly rather than speculate as to the outcome of a seizure or enforcement suit.

National Nutritional Foods Ass'n v. Weinberger, 512 F.2d 688 (2d Cir. 1975).

FDA pioneered rulemaking as the primary instrument of regulation, issuing numerous new rules to particularize the Act's substantive requirements. An example was the regulation establishing the required type, size and location for mandatory information on food labels, 38 Fed. Reg. 2124 (Jan. 19, 1973), 38 Fed. Reg. 6950 (Mar. 14, 1973). Previously, the agency had relied on enforcement actions in court to implement section 403(f)'s requirement that this information appear "prominently" and "with such conspicuousness (as compared with other words, statements, designs, or devices in the labeling) and in such terms as to render it likely to be read and understood by the ordinary individual under customary conditions of purchase and use." By mandating a specific type size and establishing rules for placement of this information on the label, FDA eliminated uncertainty and thus obviated court action except against firms that did not follow the prescribed standards. *See generally* Stephen McNamara, *The New Age of FDA Rule–Making*, 31 FOOD DRUG COSM. L.J. 393 (1976); Richard A. Merrill, *Administrative Rule–Making*, 30 FOOD DRUG COSM. L.J. 478 (1975).

In addition to such substantive rulemaking, FDA designed—by regulation—a variety of nonstatutory procedures for resolving issues that were not foreseen when the FDCA was passed. A good example of this use of rulemaking is the OTC Drug Review, discussed *supra* in Chapter IV. In the 1970s, FDA also issued detailed regulations specifying how it will interpret and apply laws of government-wide applicability, such as the Freedom of Information Act, the National Environmental Policy Act, and the Federal Advisory Committee Act. FDA's Public Information Regulations, for example, list all of the numerous types of documents in its files and specify exactly how each type will be dealt with under the FOIA.

This capsule account largely explains the proliferation of regulations reflected in the figures set forth above. But, as noted above, the pace of rulemaking at FDA has slackened in recent decades. According to Professor Todd Rakoff, in the 1990s FDA's output of regulations declined by 50 percent. *See The Choice Between Formal and Informal Modes of Adminis-*

trative Regulation, 52 ADMIN. L. REV. 159 (2000), below. An examination of annual indices of the Federal Register from 1970 to 2005 reveals the following:

- From 1970 to 1978, FDA produced roughly 700 proposed and final rules each year.

- After 1978 its annual production of proposed and final rules never again passed 600 and exceeded 500 only once (in 1983).

- The agency's productivity progressively declined through the latter half of the 1980s and the 1990s, as FDA's annual output of proposed and final rules averaged 270 through the end of the century.

- FDA's production of proposed and final rules fell below 200 in 2001—where it has remained every year since.

In the procedural regulations it adopted in 1975, FDA identified a category of official but nonbinding documents intended to reflect the agency's position on regulatory matters but not purporting to be legal requirements. The agency initially labeled these documents "guidelines" but later named them "guidance." Most were developed to assist the pharmaceutical industry to meet the agency's expectations for adequate NDAs.

Todd D. Rakoff, *The Choice Between Formal and Informal Modes of Administrative Regulation*

52 ADMINISTRATIVE LAW REVIEW 159 (2000).

On February 8, 1997, the United States Food and Drug Administration (FDA) issued a document entitled "Good Guidance Practices" that set forth the agency's "policies and procedures for the development, issuance, and use of guidance documents."[1] The details are, of course, of special interest to lawyers who practice food and drug law. From a broader standpoint, the document is important because it frankly recognizes and treats a category of administrative action called "guidance."

"Guidance" as a named, identified legal category is something new in American administrative law. . . .

During the 1950s and 1960s, most major regulation took place through formal adjudicatory proceedings. This emphasis on developing law by deciding individual cases proved deficient in three respects. First, it was costly. Second, even though American lawyers are skilled in handling case law, the law that could be extracted from agency decisions often proved to be vague or contradictory. Third, the newer goals of regulation that developed in the 1960s, such as protection of the environment, depended on establishing generally applicable standards with precise contours. Such standards are difficult to establish in the context of a single case.

---

1. The Food and Drug Administration's Development, Issuance, and Use of Guidance Documents, 62 Fed. Reg. 8961 (1997). The approach taken by the FDA received congres- sional approval in the Food and Drug Administration Modernization Act of 1997 (codified as amended at 21 U.S.C. § 360bbb–1 (Supp. III 1997)).

The response was to shift the emphasis of the system from adjudicating cases to promulgating rules. This was done partly by Congress when it mandated rulemaking in various environmental, health, and safety statutes.

The upshot of these developments was a surge of administrative rulemaking. . . .

With so much regulating being done by rulemaking rather than by adjudication, one might think that the system as a whole had become less formal. Indeed, if one reads the plain text of the APA [Administrative Procedure Act], it does seem that the less formal rulemaking process, while certainly not left entirely to agency discretion, is not too demanding.

. . . The American legal culture, however, could not tolerate such lack of formality once rulemaking of this sort became the paradigmatic case of agency action. In light of the large substantive discretion many agencies had been given, doing so would seem to authorize highhanded agency behavior. As a result, partly through legislative and executive action, but primarily led by judges, these provisions were given increasingly burdensome interpretations.

For example, agencies were required to provide the public from the start, not only the substance of the proposed rule, but also the data on which the agency relied to justify the rule. Agencies were also required to explain why they rejected at least the most forceful comments made by regulated parties or the public; otherwise, they had not adequately explained the basis for the rule. And on review, judges increasingly ask the agency to justify the specific regulatory choice it had made, rather than merely showing that the agency had not been, in the ordinary sense of the term, arbitrary.

These developments were exacerbated by the new political culture that developed after the inauguration of Ronald Reagan as President in 1981. The organized bureaucracy of the government—the administrative agencies—were seen by many in the Reagan Administration as the representatives of entrenched interests that opposed the Chief Executive's program of deregulation. Further procedural requirements were imposed in order to give the President's close advisors more control over the agencies. That these requirements made rulemaking yet more cumbersome did not dissuade an administration interested in less, not more, regulation. . . .

In short, notice-and-comment rulemaking—already more formal than the rulemaking process in some other countries—has now become (even though still known as "informal" rulemaking) an even more formal, more burdensome, and more expensive process. . . . Promulgating a major rule often takes years and represents a substantial commitment of an agency's resources. . . .

If we compare the mid–1990s with the late 1970s or early 1980s, we find that the number of FDA regulations adopted each year in accordance with the APA's rulemaking procedures declined by about fifty percent. By contrast, since the start of this decade [the 1990s] there has been a striking increase in the number of FDA-issued documents intended to give guidance to the regulated industry but not adopted through public procedures. . . .

This decrease in the number of enacted rules, and this increase in the number of guidance documents led to cries that the required procedures were being subverted. Under pressure from industry, and to some extent from the courts as well, the FDA responded with a substantial, public proceeding—much like a rulemaking proceeding—in order to develop the very procedures by which this new process would be carried out.

The scope of the matter can be seen from the definition of the term "guidance documents" that the agency ultimately adopted. While speeches or warning letters were not included, the term does cover documents directed either to the agency's own staff or to the public that relate to: the evaluation or approval of proposed new drugs; the production and testing of regulated products; the agency's inspection and enforcement procedures; or documents that broadly describe "the agency's policy and regulatory approach to an issue." At the same time, the FDA takes pains to state that guidance documents "are not legally binding on the public or the agency. Rather, they explain how the agency believes the statutes and regulations apply to certain regulated activities." ... In short, guidance documents are meant to be statements of no legal consequence but immense practical consequence about virtually everything the agency regulates.

. . . .

The "Good Guidance Practices" statement divides guidance documents into two groups. The documents in the first, more important, group "set forth first interpretations of statutory or regulatory requirements, changes in interpretation or policy that are of more than a minor nature, unusually complex scientific issues, or highly controversial issues." The stipulated procedures for this group provide that the agency will publish a notice of the draft guidance in the Federal Register, accept written comments and perhaps hold public meetings regarding the draft, review the comments, and "make changes to a guidance document in response to comments as appropriate." It would not be far-fetched to rephrase these matters by saying that the FDA now proposes to issue its important regulations mostly in accordance with the notice-and-comment rulemaking procedure set forth in the APA, as it was understood before 1970.

The only difference is that, at least in the agency's view, the entire matter will be beyond the purview of the courts. The promulgated policies will not legally bind the agency or regulated parties, and the stipulated procedures are not intended to confer procedural rights. But is that such a difference? The FDA appears to thinks it is not, as it proposes to set forth new interpretations of statutory requirements and other regulatory changes "of more than a minor nature" in this fashion. It appears that the industry thinks it is not a great difference either, since it participated extensively in the proceeding to establish these "good guidance practices." In this highly regulated industry, in which all the players—including the agency, the drug companies, and even the representatives of consumers—are repeat players, it may well be that "the force of law," in the strict sense of enforceability in court, is of little value compared to "the force of law" in the practical sense as dictated by existing relationships....

NOTES

1. *Obstacles to Rulemaking.* The production of legislative rules is not an easy process. Agency officials must reach agreement on the policy they wish to adopt as well as the words used to express it. Federal law requires that consideration be given to implications for small business, for the environment, for the reporting and record keeping burdens on citizens, for federal-state relations, and then of course to the costs and benefits of the codified policy. For many rules, FDA can expect questions and perhaps opposition from the Office of Management and Budget (OMB) and must contemplate the possibility of court review (and possible rejection). All this takes time. FDA's location within the Department of Health and Human Services creates additional obstacles which potentially can duplicate those implicit in OMB review. The frequent turnover in agency leadership means that the average Commissioner often cannot expect to see the process through from start to finish. Finally, embodying a policy in an APA-compliant rule entails a commitment for the future, for it can only be changed or abandoned by commencing anew the process that produced the rule in the first place. Little wonder that FDA, and many other agencies, have increasingly turned to less formal ways of describing their expectations for those firms they regulate.

2. *Rulemaking vs. Guidance.* There are important differences between these two approaches. Rulemaking is a formal process that, under the Administrative Procedure Act, requires publication of a proposed regulation with an explanatory preamble, followed by an opportunity for public comment, and then promulgation of a final regulation accompanied by responses to the comments. Once promulgated, assuming Congress has so authorized, a regulation has the force of law. A "guidance," by contrast, requires no preamble and no publication, and can be modified or revoked by FDA at any time. And it does not have the force of law.

3. *FDA's Guidance Procedures.* The agency's preference for what it calls "guidance" has produced its own internal logic—the increasing formalization of the process by which guidances are developed and adopted. Partly in response to complaints that the agency's reliance on guidance, rather than APA rulemaking, left interested members of the public ignorant of its policies and with no opportunity to share their views as to what policies ought to be adopted, FDA has developed a set of so-called "good guidance practices." 62 Fed. Reg. 8961 (Feb. 27, 1997); 65 Fed. Reg. 7321 (Feb. 14, 2000); 65 Fed. Reg. 56468 (Sept. 19, 2000).

4. *OMB Standardization and Oversight of Agency Guidance.* In late 2005 the Office of Management and Budget—perhaps concerned that reliance on guidance in lieu of rulemaking was allowing agencies to evade cost-benefit scrutiny under the Presidents' several Executive Orders—released a draft bulletin describing the process that, in OMB's view, agencies should follow in issuing new guidances. "Proposed Bulletin for Good Guidance Practice," 70 Fed. Reg. 71866 (Nov. 30, 2005). OMB issued the final bulletin at 72 Fed. Reg. 3432 (Jan. 25, 2007).

5. *Commentary.* For analyses of FDA's reliance on and production of guidances, *see, e.g.,* Lars Noah, *The FDA's New Policy on Guidelines: Having Your Cake and Eating It Too,* 47 Cath. U.L. Rev. 113 (1997); Erica Seiguer & John J. Smith, *Perception and Process at the Food and Drug Administration: Obligations and Trade–Offs in Rules and Guidances,* 60 Food & Drug L.J. 17 (2005). For discussion of the "guidance phenomenon" across the government, *see, e.g.,* Andrew P. Morriss, Bruce Yandle & Andrew Dorchak, *Choosing How to Regulate,* 29 Har. Envtl. L. Rev. 179 (2005); David Zaring, *Best Practices,* 81 N.Y.U. L. Rev. 294 (2006); "Use of Alternatives to Conventional Notice and Comment Rulemaking," Symposium at the American University Center for the Study of Rulemaking, March 16, 2005.

2.   REGULARIZING AGENCY PROCEDURES

In 40 Fed. Reg. 22950 (May 27, 1975), FDA published comprehensive regulations governing a wide range of administrative procedures. Consisting of 34 pages of preamble and 62 pages of codified rules, the regulations were made effective 60 days later, without time for comment, on the premise that, as procedural regulations, they were exempt from the APA's rulemaking requirements. Suit was promptly brought seeking a declaration that the regulations were unlawful because of the agency's failure to provide an opportunity for public comment. *American College of Neuropsychopharmacology v. Weinberger*, Food Drug Cosm. L. Rep. (CCH) ¶ 38,025 (D.D.C. 1975), held that even though exclusively concerned with agency procedures, the regulations were so substantial that they could not lawfully be issued without complying with 5 U.S.C. 553, the APA section governing rulemaking. 40 Fed. Reg. 33063 (Aug. 6, 1975).

Following this ruling, FDA republished the entire document as a proposal, 40 Fed. Reg. 40682 (Sept. 3, 1975). After receiving comments, the agency proceeded to promulgate final regulations in stages: 41 Fed. Reg. 26636 (June 28, 1976), 41 Fed. Reg. 48258 (Nov. 2, 1976), 41 Fed. Reg. 51706 (Nov. 23, 1976), 41 Fed. Reg. 52148 (Nov. 26, 1976), 42 Fed. Reg. 4680 (Jan. 25, 1977). The regulations were later reorganized and recodified, with different section numbers. 42 Fed. Reg. 15553 (Mar. 22, 1977). And later still, as part of HEW's "operation common sense," FDA promulgated revisions to "incorporate editorial changes" to the procedural regulations and to make them "more concise and readable," 53 Fed. Reg. 51966 (Nov. 7, 1978), 44 Fed. Reg. 22318 (Apr. 13, 1979).

Because of their length and detail, it is not feasible to summarize even the important issues addressed by FDA's procedural regulations. The following paragraphs provide essential references.

1.   FDA's general administrative practices and procedures are set out in 21 C.F.R. Part 10, 42 Fed. Reg. 4680 (Jan. 25, 1977). *See* Stuart Pape, *Meetings and Correspondence, Including FOI Considerations*, 32 FOOD DRUG COSM. L.J. 226 (1977); Michael Peskoe, *Submissions and Petitions under the FDA's Procedural Regulations*, 32 FOOD DRUG COSM. L.J. 216 (1977); William Van Brunt, *Advisory Opinions*, 32 FOOD DRUG COSM. L.J. 304 (1977).

2.   Regulations governing formal evidentiary hearings, 41 Fed. Reg. 51706 (Nov. 23, 1976), 21 C.F.R. Part 12.

3.   Regulations governing FDA advisory committees, 41 Fed. Reg. 52148 (Nov. 26, 1976), 21 C.F.R. Part 14.

4.   Regulations governing legislative-type hearings before the Commissioner or other officials appear at 21 C.F.R. Part 15, 41 Fed. Reg. 48258 (Nov. 2, 1976). *See* Alan Bennett, *Committee or Commissioner*, 32 FOOD DRUG COSM. L.J. 323 (1977).

5.   Regulations governing informal regulatory hearings, 41 Fed. Reg. 48258 (Nov. 2, 1976), 21 C.F.R. Part 16. *See* Ronald Greene, *Informal FDA Hearings*, 32 FOOD DRUG COSM. L.J. 354 (1977).

6.   Regulations prescribing standards of conduct and defining conflicts of interest appear at 21 C.F.R. Part 19, 41 Fed. Reg. 48258 (Nov. 2, 1976).

For a sampling of views regarding FDA's efforts to codify its procedures, *see generally* Marcia Greenberger, *A Consumer Advocate's View of the FDA's Procedures and Practices*, 32 FOOD DRUG COSM. L.J. 293 (1977); Joel Hoffman, *The FDA's New Forms of Public Hearing—Choosing Among the Alternatives*, 32 FOOD DRUG COSM. L.J. 330 (1977); Louis Rothschild, *The FDA's Regulations—A Model for the Future?*, 32 FOOD DRUG COSM. L.J. 344 (1977); Merrill Thompson, *Public Hearings—A View from the Bar*, 32 FOOD DRUG COSM. L.J. 312 (1977).

B. DEALING WITH MAKERS OF REGULATED PRODUCTS

Throughout its history the relationship that does, or should, prevail between agency officials and organizations that market regulated products has been a source of controversy. Academic theorists have argued that the relationship would become too conciliatory with the passage of time. Relations between FDA and the firms it regulates have been more contentious than this "capture" theory predicts. Nevertheless, concerns that FDA may be too receptive to industry claims have persisted. Because compliance with the FD&C Act requires voluntary action by regulated firms, frequent informal communications are inevitable.

One well known episode is illustrative of this controversy. In August 1974, eleven employees of the Bureau of Drugs (now CDER), testified at a Senate hearing that FDA officials had harassed them when they made decisions adverse to drug manufacturers. "Examination of the Pharmaceutical Industry, 1973–74," Joint Hearings Before the Subcomm. on Health of the Senate Comm. on Labor and Public Welfare and the Subcomm. on Administrative Practice and Procedure of the Senate Comm. on the Judiciary, 93rd Cong., 1st & 2nd Sess., Pt. 7 (1974). Commissioner Alexander Schmidt vigorously disputed the charges. "Regulation of New Drug R&D by the Food and Drug Administration, 1974," 93rd Cong., 2nd Sess. (1974). Nonetheless, HEW Secretary David Mathews was persuaded to appoint a panel of outside experts to investigate the charges that FDA was too close to regulated firms and that the industry exerted undue influence over agency decisions.

Review Panel on New Drug Regulation, Final Report
Department of Health, Education and Welfare, 1977.

... FDA employees and industry representatives frequently discuss INDs and NDAs in telephone conversations and at meetings. Industry representatives also make numerous unscheduled visits to FDA reviewers to drop off materials, chat, and check on the status of their companies' applications....

FDA employees and industry representatives have stated that oral communications are essential because many scientific issues are not easily resolved through written correspondence. Nevertheless, such a system has led to questions about the influence exerted by the pharmaceutical industry on agency decisions, especially in light of FDA's trade secrets policy.

The ... Panel agrees that non-written communication at times can be a more efficient means of resolving complex scientific questions than written communication.... However, the Panel found no justification for much of the informal, non-written contact which takes place between FDA staff and industry representatives....

... Because the system is *ad hoc*, Bureau procedures for communicating with industry vary from division to division and sometimes from reviewer to reviewer. Although FDA staff are required to prepare memoranda of their communications with industry representatives, the Panel found that reviewers differed in the extent to which they documented such contacts and in the amount of detail they provided in memoranda.

The Panel recommends that FDA institute a more formalized system of contact, in which written correspondence is the preferred means of communication. Such a system, using a minimum of oral, informal communications, is appropriate for FDA to assure both its regulatees and the public that it is performing its function fairly and objectively. It also is necessary to produce a well-documented record of FDA decision-making. Finally, written correspondence is consistent with the Bureau of Drugs' duty to approve or disapprove new drugs solely on the basis of the scientific data presented....

———

Several years later, a similar advisory body, chartered to identify ways to expedite the development of new drugs, offered a different view.

Final Report of the National Committee to Review Procedures for Approval of New Drugs for Cancer and Aids

Department of Health and Human Services, 1990.

If the drug development and approval process is to proceed expeditiously, it is essential that there be free and open communication between FDA and drug sponsors at all times. The relationship between FDA reviewers and drug sponsors must be informal, highly interactive, and foster a spirit of mutual cooperation. An atmosphere of arms-length formality will slow down the process, raise artificial barriers to drug development and approval, and seriously harm the public health. The development and approval of AIDS and cancer drugs depends upon helpful cooperation, not adversarial isolation. Communications should most frequently be by telephone, fax, and computer, to provide current information, quick responses to important questions, and a feeling of genuine partnership. The artificial barriers that have been erected through years of criticism on the part of both the regulators and the regulated have created a serious threat to rapid development and approval of new drugs, and can no longer be tolerated....

———

A similar theme was sounded during a 2005 conference sponsored by the FDA and Association of American Medical Colleges on "Drug Development Science." The conference was inspired by a March 2005 white paper issued by the agency on the need to improve the system for developing and regulating medical products, titled "Innovation or Stagnation: Challenge and Opportunity on the Critical Path to New Medical Products." The conference dealt with a wide range of issues, among them the now-familiar debate over the appropriate relationship between regulators and the regulated. While the AAMC/FDA report called for earlier and faster collaboration, it acknowledged a continuing concern about agency capture, a concern fueled by the controversy over FDA's handling of the Cox–2 inhibitor, VIOXX.

> In exploring novel preclinical research approaches, industry would like to improve the level of dialogue with FDA on the design and implementation of innovative early study designs. Some industry researchers find that discussions with FDA during the pre-approval research process tend to be highly orchestrated. Multiple rules of engagement across different CDER and CBER offices and differing toxicology requirements in FDA review divisions make it needlessly difficult for industry to address the dynamic process of moving from pre-clinical animal testing to human experimentation. . . .

The report went on to recommend that communication between sponsors and FDA be improved.

NOTES

1. *Ex Parte Communications.* FDA's regulations, 21 C.F.R. 10.65, 10.70, and 10.80, permit essentially unlimited contact between agency employees and private individuals, including representatives of regulated firms, but at the same time require that all significant communications be summarized and disclosed. All memoranda summarizing meetings or telephone conversations are available to the public and are required to be made part of the pertinent administrative record. *Cf. Home Box Office, Inc. v. FCC*, 567 F.2d 9 (D.C. Cir. 1977). If a draft regulation is made available to any outside person, it is available to everyone. *See, e.g.*, 37 Fed. Reg. 24117 (Nov. 14, 1972); 40 Fed. Reg. 12535 (Mar. 19, 1975).

2. *Generic Drug Scandal.* For a discussion of a genuine scandal involving bribes paid by some generic drug manufacturers to induce FDA employees to act favorably on their applications, see "FDA's Generic Drug Approval Process (Parts 1 and 2)," Hearings Before the Subcomm. on Oversight and Investigations of the House Comm. on Energy and Commerce, 101st Cong., 1st Sess. (1989).

C.   FDA's Relations With Other Agencies

Since 1970, the proliferation of new regulatory statutes and agencies has enlarged the need for FDA to coordinate activities with other agencies. Numerous memoranda of understanding (MOU) and interagency agreements (IAG) have been published in the Federal Register.

Mutually Exclusive Jurisdiction. FDA-regulated products are often explicitly excluded from other regulatory statutes. For example, the Toxic Substances Control Act (TSCA), 15 U.S.C. 2602(2)(B)(vi), excludes FDA-regulated products, and EPA has interpreted this exclusion as extending to all aspects of these products, including raw materials. *See, e.g.,* 42 Fed. Reg. 13130 (Mar. 9, 1977); 42 Fed. Reg. 64572 (Dec. 23, 1977); 43 Fed. Reg. 11318 (Mar. 17, 1978). Because jurisdictional lines are not always easy to draw, however, FDA has on occasion entered into agreements with other regulatory agencies to allocate responsibilities. For example, FDA and the Consumer Product Safety Commission (CPSC) have agreed that, to the extent that food containers and utensils that do not become components of food present a hazard, they are subject to regulation by CPSC. 41 Fed. Reg. 34342 (Aug. 13, 1976).

Overlapping Jurisdiction. FDA-regulated products are not always exempt from other regulatory statutes. Congress has often addressed the jurisdictional issue ambiguously or not at all. For example, the jurisdictional divisions between USDA and FDA for meat, and between BATF (now TTB) and FDA for alcoholic beverages, have been the subject of intense controversy and not even now definitively resolved. To guide agency officials and regulated firms following the creation of EPA by Executive Order in 1970, FDA and EPA entered into a series of agreements regarding matters of mutual responsibility. 36 Fed. Reg. 24234 (Dec. 22, 1971); 38 Fed. Reg. 24233 (Sept. 6, 1973); 40 Fed. Reg. 25078 (June 12, 1975). An attempt to explain the joint regulation of pesticides that are also new animal drugs, 48 Fed. Reg. 22799 (May 20, 1983), was stayed in 48 Fed. Reg. 37077 (Aug. 16, 1983). FDA and BATF (TTB) have entered into an MOU defining their responsibilities for adulterated alcoholic beverages. 52 Fed. Reg. 45502 (Nov. 30, 1987). FDA and the Patent and Trademark Office (PTO) have entered into an MOU establishing procedures for their mutual responsibilities under the Drug Price Competition and Patent Term Restoration Act of 1984. 52 Fed. Reg. 17830 (May 12, 1987).

Concurrent Jurisdiction. As discussed *supra,* in Chapter XI, FDA and the Customs Service of the Department of Treasury (now Customs and Border Protection of the Department of Homeland Security), which jointly enforce the import provisions of the FD&C Act, have established a working relationship on sampling and refusal of imports. 44 Fed. Reg. 53577 (Sept. 14, 1979); 69 Fed. Reg. 924 (Jan. 7, 2004).

National Shellfish Sanitation Program. The Interstate Shellfish Sanitation Conference (ISSC) is a voluntary national organization of state shellfish regulatory officials, which provides guidance and counsel on matters for the sanitary control of shellfish. FDA has entered into an MOU with the ISSC, 49 Fed. Reg. 12751 (Mar. 30, 1984), which was one factor in FDA's recision of a proposed national shellfish safety program. *See* 50 Fed. Reg. 7797 (Feb. 26, 1985).

The National Shellfish Sanitation Program (NSSP) is a federal/state cooperative program recognized by the FDA and the ISSC for the sanitary control of shellfish. The purpose of the NSSP is to promote and improve the sanitation of shellfish (oysters, clams, mussels, and scallops) moving in interstate commerce through federal/state cooperation and uniformity of state shellfish programs. Participants in the NSSP include agencies from shellfish producing states, FDA, and the shellfish industry. Under international agreements with FDA, foreign governments also participate in the NSSP. Other components of the NSSP include program guidelines, state growing area classification and dealer certification programs, and FDA evaluation of state program elements.

In 1984, the FDA entered into an MOU with the ISSC to provide a formal structure for state regulatory authorities to participate in establishing updated regulatory guidelines and procedures for uniform state application of the NSSP. The ISSC has adopted formal procedures for state representatives to review shellfish sanitation issues and develop regulatory guidelines. Following FDA concurrence, these guidelines are published in revisions of the NSSP Model Ordinance.

Service To Other Agencies. FDA provides services to several other agencies as a part of its regulatory activities. For example, FDA has agreed to inspect toxicology testing laboratories for compliance with EPA's Good Laboratory Practice requirements, 43 Fed. Reg. 14124 (Apr. 4, 1978), and has assumed the responsibility to assure that drugs and biologics procured by Department of Defense are of appropriate quality, FDA Compliance Policy Guide No. 7155d.02 (Oct. 1, 1980).

D.   FDA's Authority to Adopt Binding Rules

1.   The Statutory Framework

FDA's reliance on rulemaking to implement the FD&C Act beginning in the 1970s, *see supra* p. 1522 *et seq.*, assumed that the statute conferred authority to adopt regulations that have the force of law. By the end of that decade, the agency could point to several court victories that supported this proposition. Previously, however, FDA's authority to adopt binding rules was uncertain. To appreciate this uncertainty, we must examine the text of the original 1938 Act.

The core of the Act was a series of descriptions of conditions that would render an article—a food, drug, device, or cosmetic—"adulterated" or "misbranded." For example, section 403(a) provided (and still does) that a food is misbranded "if its labeling is false or misleading in any particular." Elsewhere the statute provided remedies for this and other forms of adulteration or misbranding—specifically seizure, injunction, or criminal prosecution.

Certain of the Act's misbranding or adulteration descriptions, however, specifically provided that FDA must adopt regulations to make the law's obligations concrete. Thus, for example, section 403(j) provided that a food intended for special dietary use would be misbranded unless its label conveyed information about its dietary properties that FDA by regulation prescribed. In short, for section 403(j), and nine other misbranding or adulteration definitions, the 1938 Act conferred on FDA the authority to determine—by regulation—what the law required. Agency regulations implementing these specific definitions were understood to have the force of law. Furthermore, because such regulations would be binding, Congress prescribed special procedures for their adoption. These procedures, set forth in section 701(e) of the Act, were intended to give persons subject to binding regulations an opportunity to contest the factual assumptions and policy judgments embodied in the regulations. Briefly, section 701(e) required (and still requires) FDA to establish the factual and legal bases for specified regulations in a formal evidentiary hearing.

Thus, the 1938 FD&C Act's substantive requirements—embodied in its definitions of misbranding and adulteration—took two forms. Most imposed obligations or prohibited conduct described in the text of the statute itself. But ten misbranding or adulteration provisions did not impose primary obligations; instead they directed FDA to issue regulations to carry out the policies set forth in the statute. And in fulfilling this responsibility, FDA was required to conduct a trial-type hearing.

Most of the 1938 Act's self-sufficient misbranding and adulteration provisions were couched in general language which did not clearly describe the conduct that Congress meant to prescribe or prohibit. For example, the directive to avoid label statements that might mislead provided little concrete guidance. An obvious issue, then, was whether FDA had the authority to promulgate regulations translating this prohibition into concrete obligations. And if it could, would such regulations be binding, too?

From the time of the Act's passage, few doubted that FDA could issue regulations that interpreted statutory provisions that did not themselves call for regulations. Section 701(a) gives FDA the authority to issue regulations "for the efficient enforcement of the Act." But until 1967, this language was assumed, by both agency counsel and industry, to authorize only "interpretative" regulations, *i.e.*, regulations that could influence but could not bind. This assumption rested on those provisions of the Act like section 403(j) that specifically authorized the agency to issue regulations but required that they be the product of a formal evidentiary hearing. In short, section 701(e)'s procedural obligations were thought to be Congress's indispensable condition for its delegation of authority to adopt binding regulations.

2. JUDICIAL ACKNOWLEDGMENT OF FDA'S RULEMAKING AUTHORITY

In a series of decisions, commencing with the Supreme Court's opinion in *Abbott Laboratories v. Gardner*, 387 U.S. 136 (1967), set forth below, FDA won judicial acceptance for the proposition that section 701(a) was a general grant of authority to adopt binding regulations implementing any of the FD&C Act's substantive requirements for which the statute did not mandate formal rulemaking.

In *Abbott Laboratories*, pharmaceutical manufacturers sought a declaratory judgment that FDA regulations issued pursuant to section 701(a) exceeded the agency's authority. FDA countered that the regulations were only interpretive and could only be challenged by way of defense in a court enforcement action brought by the government. The Supreme Court held that the regulations were immediately reviewable under the Administrative

Procedure Act and in so doing implied, without analysis, that section 701(a) regulations could have the force of law.

Abbott Laboratories v. Gardner

387 U.S. 136 (1967).

■ MR. JUSTICE HARLAN delivered the opinion of the Court.

In 1962 Congress amended the Federal Food, Drug, and Cosmetic Act to require manufacturers of prescription drugs to print the "established name" of the drug "prominently and in type at least half as large as that used thereon for any proprietary name or designation for such drug," on labels and other printed material. . . . After inviting and considering comments submitted by interested parties the Commissioner promulgated the following regulation for the "efficient enforcement" of the Act, § 701(a):

> "If the label or labeling of a prescription drug bears a proprietary name or designation for the drug or any ingredient thereof, the established name, if such there be, corresponding to such proprietary name or designation, shall accompany each appearance of such proprietary name or designation."

A similar rule was made applicable to advertisements for prescription drugs.

The present action was brought by a group of 37 individual drug manufacturers and by the Pharmaceutical Manufacturers Association, of which all the petitioner companies are members, and which includes manufacturers of more than 90% of the Nation's supply of prescription drugs. They challenged the regulations on the ground that the Commissioner exceeded his authority under the statute by promulgating an order requiring labels, advertisements, and other printed matter relating to prescription drugs to designate the established name of the particular drug involved every time its trade name is used anywhere in such material.

. . . .

The first question we consider is whether Congress by the Federal Food, Drug, and Cosmetic Act intended to forbid pre-enforcement review of this sort of regulation promulgated by the Commissioner. The question is phrased in terms of "prohibition" rather than "authorization" because a survey of our cases shows that judicial review of a final agency action by an aggrieved person will not be cut off unless there is persuasive reason to believe that such was the purpose of Congress. . . .

. . . [W]e are wholly unpersuaded that the statutory scheme in the food and drug area excludes this type of action. The Government relies on no explicit statutory authority for its argument that pre-enforcement review is unavailable, but insists instead that because the statute includes a specific procedure for such review of certain enumerated kinds of regulations, not encompassing those of the kind involved here, other types were necessarily meant to be excluded from any pre-enforcement review. The issue, however, is not so readily resolved; we must go further and inquire whether in the context of the entire legislative scheme the existence of that circumscribed remedy evinces a congressional purpose to bar agency action not within its purview from judicial review....

In this case the Government has not demonstrated such a purpose; indeed, a study of the legislative history shows rather conclusively that the specific review provisions were designed to give an additional remedy and not to cut down more traditional channels of review....

We conclude that nothing in the Food, Drug, and Cosmetic Act itself precludes this action.

A further inquiry must, however, be made. The injunctive and declaratory judgment remedies are discretionary, and courts traditionally have been reluctant to apply them to administrative determinations unless these arise in the context of a controversy "ripe" for judicial resolution. Without undertaking to survey the intricacies of the ripeness doctrine it is fair to say that its basic rationale is to prevent the courts, through avoidance of premature adjudication, from entangling themselves in abstract disagreements over administrative policies, and also to protect the agencies from judicial interference until an administrative decision has been formalized and its effects felt in a concrete way by the challenging parties. The problem is best seen in a twofold aspect, requiring us to evaluate both the fitness of the issues for judicial decision and the hardship to the parties of withholding court consideration.

As to the former factor, we believe the issues presented are appropriate for judicial resolution at this time. First, all parties agree that the issue tendered is a purely legal one: whether the statute was properly construed by the Commissioner to require the established name of the drug to be used *every time* the proprietary name is employed.... It is suggested that the justification for this rule might vary with different circumstances, and that the expertise of the Commissioner is relevant to passing upon the validity of the regulation. This of course is true, but the suggestion overlooks the fact that both sides have approached this case as one purely of congressional intent, and that the Government made no effort to justify the regulation in factual terms.

Second, the regulations in issue we find to be "final agency action" within the meaning of § 10 of the Administrative Procedure Act, 5 U.S.C. 704, as construed in judicial decisions. An "agency action" includes any "rule," defined by the Act as "an agency statement of general or particular applicability and future effect designed to implement, interpret, or prescribe law or policy," §§ 2(c), 2(g). The cases dealing with judicial review of administrative actions have interpreted the "finality" element in a pragmatic way....

... The regulation challenged here, promulgated in a formal manner after announcement in the Federal Register and consideration of comments by interested parties is quite clearly definitive. There is no hint that this regulation is informal, or only the ruling of a subordinate official, or tentative. It was made effective upon publication, and the Assistant General Counsel for Food and Drugs stated in the District Court that compliance was expected.

The Government argues, however, that the present case can be distinguished on the ground that in [prior cases] ... the agency involved could implement its policy directly, while here the Attorney General must authorize criminal and seizure actions for violations of the statute. In the context of this case, we do not find this argument persuasive. These regulations are not meant to advise the Attorney General, but purport to be directly authorized by the statute. Thus, if within the Commissioner's authority, they have the status of law and violations of them carry heavy criminal and civil sanctions. Also, there is no representation that the Attorney General and the Commissioner disagree in this area; the Justice Department is defending this very suit. It would be adherence to a mere technicality to give any credence to this contention. Moreover, the agency does have direct authority to enforce this regulation in the context of passing upon applications for clearance of new drugs, § 505, or certification of certain antibiotics, § 507.

This is also a case in which the impact of the regulations upon the petitioners is sufficiently direct and immediate as to render the issue appropriate for judicial review at this stage. These regulations purport to give an authoritative interpretation of a statutory provision that has a direct effect on the day-to-day business of all prescription drug companies; its promulgation puts petitioners in a dilemma that it was the very purpose of the Declaratory Judgment Act to ameliorate.... The regulations are clear-cut, and were made effective immediately upon publication; as noted earlier the agency's counsel represented to the District Court that immediate compliance with their terms was expected. If petitioners wish to comply they must change all their labels, advertisements, and promotional materials; they must destroy stocks of printed matter; and they must invest heavily in new printing type and new supplies. The alternative to compliance—continued use of material which they believe in good faith meets the statutory requirements, but which clearly does not meet the regulation of the Commissioner—may be even more costly. That course would risk serious criminal and civil penalties for the unlawful distribution of "misbranded" drugs....

NOTES

1. *Interpretive or Legislative.* Justice Harlan's statement that FDA's regulations, if within the scope of the agency's substantive authority, "have the status of law" could be read as endorsing a position the agency in its brief did not assert—or rejecting a claim that the industry challengers did not advance. In both the District Court and Court of Appeals, the government acknowledged that the regulations—authorized if at all by section 701(a)—were not binding rules, and the industry challengers did not claim that the regulations were of a type section 701(a) did not authorize. However, FDA was not slow to recognize that the Court's ruling, though an immediate defeat for the agency, held the seeds of a larger victory. Years later, in recalling his days as the agency's lead lawyer, William W. Goodrich provided the following account of the litigation:

> In arguing the case in Wilmington before the judge, he said to me, "you adopted this as a binding rule, and you have every intention to enforce it?" I said, "Yes, that's true." And he says, "Sounds like it has the

force and effect of law." I said, "Judge, if you'll rule that, I'll take my hat, leave, thank you, and be satisfied with it." . . .

It went up to the court of appeals. The solicitor general was Archibald Cox. . . . And when we recommended the appeal, he said, "Well, I agree with you. That interpretive regulation is subject to these other things, and they have to be challenged in the enforcement." So we appealed and we won there. . . .

Then it went to the Supreme Court. . . . Again, we really had more to win by that by making those regulations a binding regulation than we had to lose. You know, it wouldn't really help us much to open the rules up for challenge at some undefined time, when we could get it all settled and have it as force and effect of law. So I consider the *Abbott* and *Toilet Goods* case . . . as cases that gave us a very strong leg up on making our general regulations have force and effect of law. And as things turned out later, that, of course, has been an important development in administration of the law.

Interview with William W. Goodrich, FDA Chief Counsel, 1959–1971, in Rockville, MD (Oct. 15, 1986).

2. *Companion Cases.* Two companion cases were decided the same day as *Abbott Laboratories.* In *Toilet Goods Ass'n v. Gardner*, 387 U.S. 158 (1967), a regulation authorizing FDA to suspend color additive certification for a cosmetic manufacturer who refused agency inspectors access to the firm's manufacturing facilities, processes, and formulae was held not ripe for review prior to implementation. In *Gardner v. Toilet Goods Ass'n*, 387 U.S. 167 (1967), however, the Court permitted preenforcement review of other regulations implementing the Color Additive Amendments of 1960.

3. *Ripeness Again.* In *Pfizer Inc. v. Shalala*, 182 F.3d 975 (D.C. Cir. 1999), Pfizer challenged FDA's acceptance for processing of an abbreviated new drug application submitted by Mylan Laboratories for a product that delivered the same active ingredient as Pfizer's "pioneer," though by a different mechanism. Prior to Mylan's submission of the ANDA, Pfizer had petitioned FDA to rule that Mylan's product was ineligible for ANDA treatment. After accepting the ANDA for processing, FDA denied Pfizer's petition. The Court of Appeals dismissed the case on the ground that Pfizer would not suffer any real harm until, and unless, FDA approved Mylan's ANDA and Pfizer faced actual competition in the marketplace. Even the discovery, at oral argument, that FDA had given tentative approval to the Mylan product did not convert Pfizer's distress into a justiciable law suit. Nor was the court moved by FDA's regulation, 21 C.F.R. 10.45(d), which states that the agency will consider the denial of any citizen petition to be "final" for purposes of judicial review. It pointed out that an agency's action—such as FDA's rejection of Pfizer's petition—may be "final" but yet still not yet ripe for judicial review.

4. *Regulatory and Warning Letters.* When FDA began using regulatory letters (later renamed warning letters) as an alternative to court enforcement, it intended that they represent the agency's definitive position and thus final action that could be the subject of a declaratory judgment action. The agency later retreated from this position, arguing that regulatory letters are only advisory. And the courts have accordingly held that they are not subject to preenforcement review. *See, e.g., Biotics Research Corp. v. Heckler*, 710 F.2d 1375 (9th Cir. 1983); *Estee Lauder, Inc. v. FDA*, 727 F. Supp. 1 (D.D.C. 1989); *IMS Ltd. v. Califano*, 453 F. Supp. 157 (C.D. Cal. 1977). The courts had previously held that other forms of FDA correspondence could not be immediately challenged in court. *See Helco Products Co. v. McNutt*, 137 F.2d 681 (D.C. Cir. 1943); *Wilmington Chemical Corp. v. Celebrezze*, 229 F. Supp.

168 (N.D. Ill. 1964). *See also Stauffer Chemical Co. v. FDA*, 670 F.2d 106 (9th Cir. 1982).

———

Later decisions read *Abbott Laboratories* as supporting FDA's authority under section 701(a) to adopt regulations implementing other requirements of the Act. An early influential opinion was *National Nutritional Foods Ass'n v. Weinberger*, 512 F.2d 688 (2d Cir. 1975), in which the Second Circuit wrote:

> Congress did not expressly spell out the authoritative effect that should be given to regulations promulgated under §§ 701(a) and 701(e). This naturally leads one to wonder, in view of the care with which Congress spelled out the elaborate § 701(e) procedure, whether it intended any limits on the apparently expansive delegation of rule-making power granted by § 701(a), and specifically whether (as appellants urge) the latter was meant merely to grant authority to issue interpretive, non-binding advisory opinions with respect to matters of lesser importance. . . .

> . . . We have come to recognize that, if the administrative process is to be practically effective, specific regulations promulgated pursuant to a general statutory delegation of authority must be treated as authoritative, whether labeled "substantive" or "interpretive", especially in areas where the agency possesses expertise not shared by the courts. In that event its views are unlikely to be disturbed by the court in an enforcement proceeding. Where once we may have demanded proof of specific delegation of legislative authority to an agency purporting to promulgate substantive rules we have learned from experience to accept a general delegation as sufficient in certain areas of expertise.

> Whatever doubts might have been entertained regarding the FDA's power under § 701(a) to promulgate binding regulations were dispelled by the Supreme Court's recent decision in *Weinberger v. Hynson, Westcott & Dunning, Inc.*, and its companion cases. . . .

> Our attention has not been directed to anything in the legislative history of §§ 701(a) and (e) that militates against these conclusions. On the contrary, over the last decade rulemaking has been increasingly substituted for adjudication as a regulatory technique, with the support and encouragement of courts, at least where the regulation involves specialized scientific knowledge. . . . Where the objective is essentially legislative, *i.e.*, to establish rules or principles by which an entire industry may be governed, the case-by-case adversary proceeding, in which the agency confronts a single alleged offender selected for suit with respect to a specific factual situation, has frequently proved to be an unsuitable method of enforcing the law, since it often resolves narrow issues of importance only to the immediate adversaries rather than broad questions of interest to the industry or the public. The rule-

making proceeding, on the other hand, provides the agency with an opportunity first to receive a wide spectrum of views proffered by all segments affected by the proposed rule (*e.g.*, manufacturers, vendors, doctors, consumers) and then in a legislative fashion to consider and choose from several alternatives or options rather than limit its decisions to narrow issues controlling a particular case. Furthermore, once binding regulations are promulgated, the industry and public are put on notice and may be guided accordingly rather than speculate as to the outcome of a seizure or enforcement suit....

The Supreme Court's ruling in *Abbott Laboratories* that section 701(a) regulations could be challenged in a preenforcement suit led logically to the conclusion that review should be based on the rulemaking record compiled by the agency. The posture of a preenforcement suit makes it difficult for a court to visualize a regulation's impact in the various contexts to which it might apply. The question presented, essentially, is whether the regulation is authorized by law and supported by the facts relied on by the agency. So framed, it is difficult for a reviewing court to conclude that the regulation is invalid unless the agency committed some procedural error or made an obvious error in judgment. The regulation is thus likely to be upheld, and thereby given "substantive" effect, even though it might later be applied in some contexts where a court—were it any longer free to do so—might consider it "arbitrary." *See* Richard A. Merrill, *FDA and the Effects of Substantive Rules*, 35 FOOD DRUG COSM. L.J. 270 (1980).

National Association of Pharmaceutical Manufacturers v. Food and Drug Administration

637 F.2d 877 (2d Cir. 1981).

■ FRIENDLY, CIRCUIT JUDGE:

In 1962 Congress enacted various amendments to the Federal Food, Drug, and Cosmetic Act of 1938 (the Act) to "strengthen and broaden existing laws in the drug field so as to bring about better, safer medicine and to establish a more effective system of enforcement of the drug laws." Among the amendments was a section by which a drug is deemed adulterated if its packaging, processing, holding or manufacturing fail to conform to "current good manufacturing practice ((CGMP)) to assure that such drug meets the requirements of this chapter as to safety and has the identity and strength, and meets the quality and purity characteristics, which it purports or is represented to possess". § 501(a)(2)(B).

The Food and Drug Administration (FDA) issued its first regulations under this section in 1963. In February, 1976, FDA announced a proposal to revise and update the then current CGMP regulations. This proposal, which provided for the notice and comment procedures contemplated by 5 U.S.C. 553, announced:

The Commissioner intends for CGMP regulations to become binding specific requirements that must be complied with; failure to do so shall render a drug product adulterated under section

501(a)(2)(B) of the (Act) ... Binding regulations will ... serve to inform courts of FDA's expert judgments regarding current good manufacturing practice for drugs in the United States; this will expedite and assist enforcement proceedings to assure compliance with section 501(a)(2)(B) of the act.

The FDA received numerous comments both upon the substance of its requirements and upon its proposal that the new CGMP regulations should have the force of law.[1] In an extensive preamble to the new regulations it set forth a legal analysis supporting its view that it had power to issue binding regulations, and the reasons why it believed binding rather than merely interpretive regulations would be in the public interest.[2] The regulations ... were published on September 29, 1978, to be effective March 28, 1979, 43 F.R. 45014. They cover a broad spectrum of affairs, including requirements for personnel practices, record keeping, building design, and procedures for the control of drug production, packaging and labeling.

In this action ... the National Association of Pharmaceutical Manufacturers and the National Pharmaceutical Alliance, both trade associations, sought a declaration that FDA's attempt to give binding effect to the new CGMP Regulations was beyond its authority....

Two different subsections of § 701 confer rulemaking authority upon the FDA. Section 701(a) provides:

The authority to promulgate regulations for the efficient enforcement of this chapter, except as otherwise provided in this section, is vested in the Secretary (of Health and Human Services).

The effect of § 4 of the Administrative Procedure Act of 1946 (APA), now 5 U.S.C. 553, is to require that rulemaking under § 701(a), with certain exceptions, including "interpretative rules", follow an informal notice and comment procedure, which was done here. Section 701(e) provides that "(any) action for the issuance, amendment, or repeal of any regulation" under various sections of the Act of which § 501(a)(2)(B) is not one, shall follow a complex procedure which has been read to include a trial-type hearing; § 701(f) provides that review of any order resulting from

1. A concise formulation of the distinction between "binding" and "interpretive" rules is supplied by the Final Report of the Attorney General's Committee on Administrative Procedure 100 (1941):

Administrative rule-making ... includes the formulation of both legally binding regulations and interpretative regulations. The former receive statutory force upon going into effect. The latter do not receive statutory force and their validity is subject to challenge in any court proceeding in which their application may be in question. The statutes themselves and not the regulations remain in theory the sole criterion of what the law authorizes or compels and what it forbids.

2. The most significant justification for having the regulations binding is to minimize the burden on the government and on the courts in a case where a violation does occur. When the regulations are merely interpretive, the agency must provide expert testimony in each trial to demonstrate what the current good manufacturing practice in the industry is, notwithstanding the regulation. The cost of locating and preparing such expert witnesses and bringing them to the trial, as well as the judicial time taken in hearing these witnesses, would be eliminated by having binding regulations.

such rulemaking lies in a court of appeals. Admittedly § 701(e) procedures were not followed here and the FDA's authority to give binding effect to the CGMP regulations at issue must rest on § 701(a).

Reading the language of that subsection, which comes from the Act of 1938, with the eyes of 1980, one would have little difficulty in concluding that the words suffice to empower the Commissioner of the FDA, to whom the Secretary has delegated his powers, 21 C.F.R. 5.1(a)(1) (1980), to issue regulations, substantive as well as procedural, having the force of law. The comprehensive opinion of Judge J. Skelly Wright in *National Petroleum Refiners Ass'n v. FTC*, 482 F.2d 672 (D.C. Cir.1973), catalogued the many instances in which general statutory provisions not differing essentially from § 701(a) have been held to endow agencies with power to issue binding rules and regulations. In the interest of historical accuracy, it should be noted that at one time it was widely understood that generalized grants of rulemaking authority conferred power only to make rules of a procedural or an interpretative nature, and not binding substantive regulations, for which a specific delegation was thought necessary.

As documented by Judge Wright in *National Petroleum Refiners*, this generous construction of agency rulemaking authority has become firmly entrenched. Beyond this there is formidable authority to the effect that § 701(a) itself is a grant of power to issue binding regulations. The first is the statement in *Abbott Laboratories* [*supra* p. 1535] adverting to certain drug labeling regulations issued pursuant to § 701(a):

> These regulations are not meant to advise the Attorney General, but purport to be directly authorized by the statute. Thus, if within the Commissioner's authority, they have the status of law and violations of them carry heavy criminal and civil sanctions.

The Court also spoke of the regulations as "self-operative" rules "that must be followed by an entire industry". It can be argued that the Court could not really have meant to decide whether the regulations there at issue had the "status of law" since the Government had urged throughout the case that they were merely interpretive, the court of appeals had so held, and the petitioner had not seriously challenged this, and also because in *Toilet Goods Ass'n v. Gardner*, 360 F.2d 677, heard and decided in the Supreme Court, together with *Abbott Laboratories*, we had said that we saw "little profit in debating the point, much discussed by the parties, whether the Regulations are 'interpretative' or 'legislative'," since "the interpretative character of a regulation does not necessarily make it unripe for review". However, the Court's remarks are at least impressive dicta operating in the Government's favor here.

Next came the quartet of cases decided by the Supreme Court in 1973: *Weinberger v. Hynson, Westcott & Dunning, Inc.*, 412 U.S. 609; *CIBA Corp. v. Weinberger*, 412 U.S. 640; *Weinberger v. Bentex Pharmaceuticals, Inc.*, 412 U.S. 645 and *USV Pharmaceutical Corp. v. Weinberger*, 412 U.S. 655. Although Professor Kenneth Culp Davis cites these, along with the passage just quoted from Abbott Laboratories, for the proposition that "(rules) issued under § 701(a) are legislative rules and not merely interpretive", 1 Administrative Law Treatise § 6:8 at 478 (2d ed. 1978), plaintiffs emphasize his remark that "the four cases are weak authority because the regulation rested only in part on § 701(a) and because the Court did not address itself to the question whether § 701(a) was sufficient support for the rules." Examination of the briefs confirms that discussion of § 701(a) and the legislative-interpretive distinction was meager, the only instance being in the briefs in the *Bentex* case. . . .

In any event this court, in *National Nutritional Foods Ass'n v. Weinberger*, 512 F.2d 688 (1975), characterized the 1973 quartet of Supreme Court decisions as having dispelled "(whatever) doubts might have been entertained regarding the FDA's power under § 701(a) to promulgate binding regulations". The court said: "(our) attention has not been directed to anything in the legislative history of §§ 701(a) and (e) that militates against these conclusions", and correctly stated that "over the last decade rule-making has been increasingly substituted for adjudication as a regulatory technique, with the support and encouragement of the courts, at least where the regulation involves specialized scientific knowledge", citing, among other cases, Judge Wright's opinion in *National Petroleum Refiners Ass'n v. FTC*. The decision in *National Nutritional Foods*, supra, thus reinforced our earlier reliance on *Abbott Laboratories* as supporting the Commissioner's power to issue § 701(a) regulations that are binding. In *United States v. Nova Scotia Food Products Corp.*, 568 F.2d 240 (1977), we again read the 1938 Act as authorizing the issuance of binding substantive regulations under § 701(a). . . .

Appellants' claim is that, whether or not the FDA may generally issue binding substantive regulations under § 701(a), although they obviously think it may not, it cannot do so with respect to the CGMP Regulations. In support of this position they rely on the legislative history of the portion of the 1962 amendments that added § 501(a)(2)(B). . . .

Little need be said with respect to one argument made on the basis of the legislative history. This is that President Kennedy proposed to the Senate a trade whereby the CGMP regulations would have binding rather than prima facie effect but only if they were adopted through the "formal" § 701(e) procedures, and that the Senate cannot be thought to have given him more than he sought to wit, binding effect but without § 701(e) procedures. We perceive no basis for the latter conclusion. The Senate was free to accept the President's criticism of the prima facie language without conditioning the striking of this on adherence to the complicated § 701(e) procedure. The Senate Report shows that this was what it did. The record in the House is even clearer. There the Interstate and Foreign Commerce Committee had adopted the President's proposal but, on hearing Representative Schenck's objection and Chairman Harris' endorsement of it, struck the requirement for § 701(e) procedures.

Indeed, so far as concerns the precise issue here before us, plaintiffs' resort to the legislative history of the 1962 Amendments works against rather than for them. It is clear the 1962 Congress intended to do something in response to President Kennedy's request and also that the something was not compulsory resort to the procedure required by § 701(e). Yet there is no substantial difference between the "prima facie" evidence standard in the original Senate bill and the "interpretive" limitation urged by plaintiffs.

Plaintiffs' other argument is more impressive, although not sufficiently so. This is that when the 1962 Congress decided to rely on the Secretary's rulemaking authority under § 701(a), it was to that authority as then understood; that the pre-1962 case law established that any substantive regulations issued under § 701(a) could be interpretive only; that the legislative history of the 1938 Act strongly corroborates this; and that the Supreme Court's statements in *Abbott Laboratories* in 1967 and the *Hynson* quartet in 1973 and our own still later decisions are thus not dispositive of the problem in hand. Added support for this argument is sought in the final sentences of the excerpt from the report of the Senate Committee, and in the remarks of Senator Eastland and Representative Schenck, all set out above.

We do not find the pre-1962 decisions with respect to the extent of the Secretary's power under § 701(a) to be so conclusive as plaintiffs assert. . . .

An indication of the intent of the 1962 Congress with respect to the scope of the regulatory power conferred by § 701(a) far more persuasive than this inconclusive smattering of cases under § 701(a) itself is furnished by well-known pre-1962 Supreme Court decisions which had held that rulemaking provisions similar to § 701(a) empowered [other agencies] to issue binding rules.

On the other hand plaintiffs seem on solid ground when they contend that if the 1962 Congress had made the detailed examination of the legislative history and contemporary understanding of the 1938 Act, which plaintiffs' counsel have now made at long last, it might well have concluded that § 701(a) in fact very likely was not intended to confer power to issue binding substantive rules. . . .

. . . Plaintiffs supplement this history with references to instances, not necessary here to recount, wherein the FDA at various times had represented that § 701(a) did not empower it to issue binding substantive regulations, and with citations to secondary sources supporting that view.

A principal difficulty with plaintiffs' argument is that there is no evidence that these arcana concerning the legislative history of the 1938 Act were known to the 1962 Congress. Much water had flowed under the bridge since 1938. The principal consideration in 1938 against permitting the FDA to issue binding substantive rules except by following the complex procedures of § 701(e), namely the absence of any statutorily prescribed procedures under § 701(a), was radically changed when Congress enacted the APA in 1946. Pursuant to § 4 of that Act, now 5 U.S.C. 553, the FDA, as previously indicated, cannot issue a binding substantive rule under § 701(a) without complying with notice and comment procedures that give affected parties an adequate opportunity to be heard. While the Federal Food, Drug, and Cosmetic Act has not been completely reenacted since 1946, it has been repeatedly amended to give the Secretary new powers. Many of these provisions have expressly authorized him to make implementing regulations. When it has provided for regulations but has not required this or, as in the case of the current good manufacturing practice provisions, it has said nothing about regulations, it is more reasonable to believe that Congress meant the FDA to have the same power to issue binding substantive regulations as the Supreme Court had recognized for other agencies.

Plaintiffs' argument also goes astray in asking that we disregard subsequent decisions on the effect of § 701(a) regulations for the purpose of determining the intent of the 1962 Congress. It is true, of course, that decisions dating from 1967 to the present concerning the meaning of the 1938 Act afford no key to what Congress was thinking in 1962. But since there is no evidence that the 1962 Congress was familiar with the legislative history of the 1938 Act, plaintiffs' argument is really nothing more than an invitation to reconsider the question of the power originally conferred by § 701(a) in 1938. We decline to do so. Even if it were necessary for adjudication of this case to decide what Congress meant in 1938, the evidence mustered by plaintiffs, although persuasive, is not so conclusive as to show beyond doubt that the prior cases misconstrued § 701(a). Indeed, what the plaintiffs have demonstrated convincingly is that while the 1938 Congress clearly intended § 701(e) regulations to have binding authority, it never decided just what effect § 701(a) regulations would have. A broad construction of a statute, consistent with the words enacted, and maintained for thirteen years by the Supreme Court and this court, need not be rejected simply because of a discovery that sponsors seemingly favored a narrower one more than forty years ago. This is particularly so when the basis for the attitude of the sponsors has disappeared as a result of later enactments, here 5 U.S.C. 553, and the narrower construction would place the statute apart from other regulatory acts using similar language with respect to rulemaking. Moreover, the FDA, since the decision in *Abbott Laboratories*, has issued a substantial number of binding substantive regulations under § 701(a). A decision at this late date denying such power to it would thus create turmoil throughout numerous areas subject to regulation by the FDA. . . .

3. The Debate Reopened

Thomas W. Merrill & Kathryn Tongue Watts, *Agency Rules With the Force of Law: The Original Convention*
116 Harvard Law Review 467 (2002).

. . . Statutes typically give agencies the power "to make, amend, and rescind such rules and regulations as may be necessary to carry out the provisions of this title," or "to make such rules and regulations . . . as may be necessary in the administration of this Act." The phrase "rules and regulations" in these statutes could refer to legislative rules—that is, rules that have legally binding effect on the general public—or it could refer to interpretive rules that do not have such binding effect. . . .

Although the language of most rulemaking grants is facially ambiguous, we argue in this Article that these grants were not ambiguous during the formative years of the modern administrative state—up to and beyond the enactment of the Administrative Procedure Act (APA) in 1946. Throughout the Progressive and New Deal eras, Congress followed a drafting convention that signaled to agencies whether particular rulemaking grants conferred authority to make rules with the force of law as opposed to mere housekeeping rules. That convention was simple and easy to apply in most cases: If Congress specified in the statute that a violation of agency rules would subject the offending party to some sanction—for example, a civil or criminal penalty; loss of a permit, license, or benefits; or other adverse legal consequences—then the grant conferred power to make rules with the force of law. Conversely, if Congress made no provision for sanctions for rule violations, the grant authorized only procedural or interpretive rules. . . .

. . . In the 1960s, courts and commentators began to urge an expanded use of rulemaking by agencies and a reduced emphasis on adjudication. Eventually, two influential federal appellate judges who strongly favored greater use of rulemaking—Judges J. Skelly Wright of the D.C. Circuit and Henry Friendly of the Second Circuit—authored important opinions construing facially ambiguous rulemaking grants to the FTC and FDA as authorizing legislative rulemaking. These holdings were inconsistent with what Congress had intended, as measured by the convention. . . .

. . . Section 701(a) granted general rulemaking power to the Secretary, stating that the Secretary could "promulgate regulations for the efficient enforcement of this Act." Then sections 701(e), (f), and (g) set forth detailed procedures, including procedures for public hearings and judicial review of regulations, that the Secretary was required to follow when promulgating regulations under certain enumerated, specific rulemaking grants. Notably, section 701(e) does not refer to section 701(a), and therefore rules promulgated under section 701(a) are not subject to section 701(e)'s procedural safeguards.

Under the convention, the specific rulemaking provisions that were subject to the procedural safeguards of sections 701(e), (f) and (g) conferred legislative rulemaking authority. For example, section 401 gave the Secretary the power to promulgate regulations fixing standards of identity for food. Those regulations are given legislative effect by various sections that expressly make violations of section 401 regulations unlawful and subject to criminal penalties.

In contrast to the regulations subjected to the procedural safeguards of section 701(e), nothing in the Act indicated that a regulation issued under the authority of section 701(a) would subject the violator to any sanction, penalty, or other legal consequence. This silence suggests Congress's intent to withhold legislative rulemaking powers under that section.

. . . The FDA's "belated discovery" of general rulemaking powers in section 701(a) stemmed largely from the entrepreneurial efforts of Peter Barton Hutt during his tenure as the FDA's chief counsel. In a paper presented to the Food and Drug Law Institute in 1972, Hutt expounded the theory that the FDCA should be viewed as a "constitution" that gave the FDA broad authority to implement "a set of fundamental objectives." Specifically, he argued that the Act gave the FDA power to do anything not excepted or withheld by the Act, and he cited the general rulemaking clause in section 701(a) to support his conclusion that the Act "provide[d] ample legal authority" for the FDA to adopt procedures for the enforcement of FDCA requirements. . . .

... Hutt contended that the Hyson Quartet invited the FDA to promulgate legislative rules under section 701(a)....

Hutt's prediction [that FDA would prevail on this point in court] came true in *National Nutritional Foods Ass'n v. Weinberger* [512 F.2d 688 (2d Cir. 1975)]....

One factor that did not significantly influence the Second Circuit's holding in *Nutritional Foods* was the legislative history of the FDCA, which ... provides strong evidence that Congress intended to grant legislative rulemaking authority to the FDA only pursuant to specific rulemaking grants. Judge Mansfield made just one brief reference to the legislative history in his opinion, observing that the court's attention had not been directed to anything in the legislative history of sections 701(a) or (e) that militated against the court's decision....

E.   RULEMAKING PROCEDURES

As we have learned, the FD&C Act provides for rulemaking in two circumstances: (1) informal rulemaking under section 701(a), which requires compliance with the notice-and-comment procedures of the APA, and (2) formal rulemaking under section 701(e), which requires an evidentiary hearing. Section 403(j) exemplifies the latter. It declares a food marketed for special dietary use to be misbranded unless its label provides the information about its dietary properties that FDA has, by regulation, prescribed. The procedure that FDA must follow to promulgate the regulations authorized by section 403(j) is described in section 701(e), which mandates an opportunity for a formal evidentiary hearing. Nine other provisions of the 1938 Act expressly authorized FDA to adopt implementing regulations and, directly or by cross-reference, mandated adherence to section 701(e)'s procedures.

The procedure prescribed by section 701(e), commonly known as formal rulemaking, has proved so burdensome, for FDA and for private parties, that the agency has either abandoned the authorities to which section 701(e) applies or persuaded Congress to amend the law to permit a simpler procedure.

The other ostensible source of FDA's rulemaking authority, section 701(a), differs from the ten specific grants subject to 701(e) in three important respects. One contrast is reflected in the debate over whether rules based on 701(a) have the force of law. Second, unlike each of the explicit grants of rulemaking authority, section 701(a) is not confined by text or context to specific products or addressed to specific regulatory goals. Any regulation that will facilitate implementation of any part of the Act is presumably within the agency's authority to adopt.

Third, the FD&C Act—including section 701(a) itself—says nothing at all about the procedure FDA must follow in exercising power it confers. One must look elsewhere for Congress's directions. It is universally understood that this requires reference to the Administrative Procedure Act, 5 U.S.C. 551 et seq. Section 553 describes what can be termed the default procedure for the exercise of rulemaking authority conferred by any statute that does not itself prescribe a particular procedure for adopting rules. This default—informal rulemaking—governs almost all rulemaking in which FDA engages, and so we explore its requirements here.

The procedure that the APA mandates seems straightforward on its face. Section 553 imposes only three requirements: (1) An agency must first publish in the Federal Register the rule it proposes to adopt, which can be conveyed in formal law-like text or described in more colloquial terms. (2) The agency must invite, and allow reasonable time for, the submission of data, views, or arguments—"comments" in administrative law vernacular—from persons or organizations interested in the subject. (3) Then, after considering the comments, the agency—if it is still determined to issue a rule—must publish the text of the rule it is adopting along with a "concise general statement" of its reasons. The APA text would seem to permit a reasonably informal and expeditious process, but it has been read as demanding a fair degree of formality, substantial factual support, and rigorous analysis of both supporting and opposing comments. Moreover, it is accepted that section 553's procedures are minimum procedures. An agency can do more than the APA requires to collect and analyze evidence in favor of its proposal, it can take account of issues and objections in addition to those raised by comments, and it can provide multiple opportunities for critics to question its proposal.

1. HHS AND OMB OVERSIGHT OF FDA RULEMAKING

The authority conferred by the FD&C Act is expressly lodged in the Secretary of HHS. Indeed, prior to 1988, the Act did not mention either FDA or the office of Commissioner of Food and Drugs.

Prior to 1981, Secretaries of HHS formally delegated authority to implement the FD&C Act to the Commissioner. This delegation implicitly included the authority to propose and promulgate all regulations without specific HHS approval. Commissioners generally kept Secretaries and their staffs informed about important FDA actions, including regulations, but no formal process for HHS review existed. The degree of HHS influence largely depended on the desires of the incumbent Secretary.

In 46 Fed. Reg. 26052 (May 11, 1981), HHS Secretary Richard Schweiker promulgated a regulation, codified in 21 C.F.R. 5.11, stating that "the Secretary reserves the authority to approve regulations of the Food and Drug Administration" which establish general rules applicable to a class of products or present highly significant public issues. Regulations promulgated under section 701(e) were excluded from this reservation of authority. In 47 Fed. Reg. 16010 (Apr. 14, 1982), the regulation was modified to permit, but not require, the Secretary to approve regulations promulgated through formal rulemaking as well. Accordingly, since 1981, all significant FDA regulations have been reviewed and formally or tacitly approved at the departmental level.

During the same period, successive Presidents, through the Office of Management and Budget (OMB), created an elaborate system for close supervision of most executive agency rulemaking. Executive Order 11821, 39 Fed. Reg. 41501 (Nov. 29, 1974), required that every Federal agency proposing a "major" regulation must prepare an inflation impact statement (IIS). The Office of the Federal Register required that the inflation impact analysis be referenced in the preamble to every proposed or final regulation. 40 Fed. Reg. 26312 (June 23, 1975); 40 Fed. Reg. 48979 (Oct. 20, 1975); 41 Fed. Reg. 43476 (Oct. 1, 1976).

President Carter, whose election platform promised regulatory reform, issued Executive Order 12044, 43 Fed. Reg. 12661 (Mar. 24, 1978), requiring an economic analysis of significant regulations and a review of existing regulations, and Executive Order 12174, 44 Fed. Reg. 69609 (Dec. 4, 1979), requiring a reduction in the paperwork burden imposed by the Federal government. Based upon these two executive orders, Congress enacted (1) the Regulatory Flexibility Act, 94 Stat. 1164 (1980), requiring each agency to publish a semiannual regulatory agenda, to perform regulatory flexibility analysis for each proposed and final regulation, and to conduct periodic reviews of regulations; and (2) the Paperwork Reduction Act of 1980, 94 Stat. 2812, which created the OMB Office of Information and Regulatory Affairs (OIRA) with authority to reduce the Federal paperwork burden.

President Ronald Reagan took these initiatives several steps further. He issued Executive Order 12291, 46 Fed. Reg. 13193 (Feb. 19, 1981) and Executive Order 12498, 50 Fed. Reg. 1036 (Jan. 8, 1985), requiring a regulatory impact analysis for each major proposed and final regulation, a yearly regulatory program from each agency, and OMB review of these documents. Operating under these executive orders, OMB has had a major impact on FDA regulations. *See, e.g.,* "Office of Management and Budget Influence on Agency Regulations," Senate Comm. on Environment and Public Works, 99th Cong., 2nd Sess. S. Comm. Print. 99–156 (1986); "FDA's Continuing Failure to Regulate Health Claims for Foods," Hearings Before the Human Resources and Intergovernmental Relations Subcomm. of the House Comm. on Gov't Operations, 101st Cong., 1st Sess. (1989). An attempt under the Freedom of Information Act to obtain records that would reveal the status of FDA regulations under review in OMB was denied in *Wolfe v. Department of HHS,* 839 F.2d 768 (D.C. Cir. 1988) (en banc). *See also* GAO, REGULATORY REVIEW: INFORMATION ON OMB'S REVIEW PROCESS, No. GGD–89–101FS (July 1989).

OMB promulgated regulations to implement the Paperwork Reduction Act. 45 Fed. Reg. 2586 (Jan. 11, 1980); 47 Fed. Reg. 39515 (Sept. 8, 1982); 48 Fed. Reg. 13666 (Mar. 31, 1983), 52 Fed. Reg. 27768 (July 23, 1987); 53 Fed. Reg. 16618 (May 10, 1988); codified in 5 C.F.R. Part 1320. *See* GAO, IMPLEMENTING THE PAPERWORK REDUCTION ACT: SOME PROGRESS, BUT MANY PROBLEMS REMAIN, No. GGD–83–35 (Apr. 20, 1983). In a decision that has obvious implications for FDA, the Supreme Court held in *Dole v. United Steelworkers of America,* 494 U.S. 26 (1990), that the Paperwork Reduction Act does not grant OIRA authority to review and disapprove agencies' regulations mandating disclosures by private enterprises directly to their employees or to the public.

2. INFORMAL RULEMAKING PROCEDURES

The Administrative Procedure Act, 5 U.S.C. 553(b), describes the minimum procedures for rulemaking of the type authorized by section

701(a): (1) publication of a notice of proposed rulemaking; (2) provision of an opportunity for interested persons to comment, either orally or in writing; and (3), after consideration of comments, publication of final rule accompanied by a description of its basis and purpose. Beginning in 1971, FDA adopted the practice of explaining and justifying its regulations in lengthy and detailed preambles. This practice was later incorporated in the agency's procedural regulations. Reviewing courts subsequently interpreted the spare requirements of the APA as imposing the approach pioneered by FDA, of exposing factual assumptions and observing other safeguards previously associated with more formal proceedings.

United States v. Nova Scotia Food Products Corp.

568 F.2d 240 (2d Cir. 1977).

■ GURFEIN, CIRCUIT JUDGE:

This appeal involving a regulation of the Food and Drug Administration is not here upon a direct review of agency action. It is an appeal from a judgment of the District Court for the Eastern District of New York ... enjoining the appellants, after a hearing, from processing hot smoked whitefish except in accordance with time-temperature-salinity (T–T–S) regulations contained in 21 C.F.R. Part 122 (1977)....

The regulations cited above require that hot-process smoked fish be heated by a controlled heat process that provides a monitoring system positioned in as many strategic locations in the oven as necessary to assure a continuous temperature through each fish of not less than 180 F° for a minimum of 30 minutes for fish which have been brined to contain 3.5% water phase salt or at 150 F° for a minimum of 30 minutes if the salinity was at 5% water phase. Since *each* fish must meet these requirements, it is necessary to heat an entire batch of fish to even higher temperatures so that the lowest temperature for *any* fish will meet the minimum requirements....

[The public health rationale for the regulations and FDA's authority to issue binding regulations to implement section 402(a)(4) are discussed in portions of the opinion reproduced at p. 344, *supra*. EDS.]

The Commissioner ... issued the final regulations in which he adopted certain suggestions made in the comments, including a suggestion by the National Fisheries Institute, Inc.... the intervenor herein. The original proposal provided that the fish would have to be cooked to a temperature of 180 F° for at least 30 minutes, if the fish have been brined to contain 3.5% water phase salt, with no alternative. In the final regulation, an alternative suggested by the intervenor "that the parameter of 150 F° for 30 minutes and 5% salt in the water phase be established as an alternate procedure to that stated in the proposed regulation for an interim period until specific parameters can be established" was accepted, but as a permanent part of the regulation rather than for an interim period....

The Commissioner did not answer the suggestion by the Bureau of Fisheries that nitrite and salt as additives could safely lower the high temperature otherwise required, a solution which the FDA had accepted in the case of chub. Nor did the Commissioner respond to the claim of Nova Scotia through its trade association. . . . that "[t]he proposed process requirements suggested by the FDA for hot processed smoked fish are neither commercially feasible nor based on sound scientific evidence obtained with the variety of smoked fish products to be included under this regulation."

Nova Scotia, in its own comment, wrote to the Commissioner that "the heating of certain types of fish to high temperatures will completely destroy the product." . . .

When, after several inspections and warnings, Nova Scotia failed to comply with the regulation, an action by the United States Attorney for injunctive relief was filed on April 7, 1976, six years later, and resulted in the judgment here on appeal. . . .

Appellants contend that there is an inadequate administrative record upon which to predicate judicial review, and that the failure to disclose to interested persons the factual material upon which the agency was relying vitiates the element of fairness which is essential to any kind of administrative action. Moreover, they argue that the "concise general statement of . . . basis and purpose" by the Commissioner was inadequate.

. . . The extent of the administrative record required for judicial review of informal rulemaking is largely a function of the scope of judicial review. Even when the standard of review is whether the promulgation of the rule was "arbitrary, capricious, an abuse of discretion, or otherwise not in accordance with law," as specified in 5 U.S.C. 706(2)(A), judicial review must, nevertheless, be based on the "whole record." . . .

No contemporaneous record was made or certified. When, during the enforcement action, the basis for the regulation was sought through pretrial discovery, the record was created by searching the files of the FDA and the memories of those who participated in the process of rulemaking. This resulted in what became Exhibit D at the trial of the injunction action. Exhibit D consists of (1) Tab A containing the comments received from outside parties during the administrative "notice and comment" proceedings and (2) Tabs B through L consisting of scientific data and the like upon which the Commissioner now says he relied but which were not made known to the interested parties.

Appellants object to the exclusion of evidence in the District Court "aimed directly at showing that the scientific evidence relied upon by the FDA was inaccurate and not based upon a realistic appraisal of the true facts. Appellants attempted to introduce scientific evidence to demonstrate that in fixing the processing parameters FDA relied upon tests in which ground fish were injected with many millions of botulism [sic] spores and then tested for outgrowth at various processing levels whereas the spore levels in nature are far less and outgrowth would have been prevented by far less stringent processing parameters." The District Court properly excluded the evidence.

In an enforcement action, we must rely exclusively on the record made before the agency to determine the validity of the regulation. The exception to the exclusivity of that record is that "there may be independent judicial fact-finding when issues that are not before the agency are raised in a proceeding to *enforce* non-adjudicatory agency action."

Though this is an enforcement proceeding and the question is close, we think that the "issues" *were* fairly before the agency and hence that *de novo* evidence was properly excluded by Judge Dooling. Our concern is, rather, with the manner in which the agency treated the issues tendered.

The keys issues were (1) whether, in the light of the rather scant history of botulism in whitefish, that species should have been considered separately rather than included in a general regulation which failed to distinguish species from species; (2) whether the application of the proposed T–T–S requirements for smoked whitefish made the whitefish commercially unsaleable; and (3) whether the agency recognized that prospect, but nevertheless decided that the public health needs should prevail even if that meant commercial death for the whitefish industry. The procedural issues were whether, in the light of these key questions, the agency procedure was inadequate because (i) it failed to disclose to interested parties the scientific data and the methodology upon which it relied; and (ii) because it failed utterly to address itself to the pertinent question of commercial feasibility....

Interested parties were not informed [by FDA's notice of proposed rulemaking] of the scientific data, or at least of a selection of such data deemed important by the agency, so that comments could be addressed to the data. Appellants argue that unless the scientific data relied upon by the agency are spread upon the public records, criticism of the methodology used or the meaning to be inferred from the data is rendered impossible....

We think that the scientific data should have been disclosed to focus on the proper interpretation of "insanitary conditions." When the basis for a proposed rule is a scientific decision, the scientific material which is believed to support the rule should be exposed to the view of interested parties for their comment. One cannot ask for comment on a scientific paper without allowing the participants to read the paper. Scientific research is sometimes rejected for diverse inadequacies of methodology; and statistical results are sometimes rebutted because of a lack of adequate gathering technique or of supportable extrapolation. Such is the stuff of scientific debate. To suppress meaningful comment by failure to disclose the basic data relied upon is akin to rejecting comment altogether....

Appellants additionally attack the "concise general statement" required by [the] APA as inadequate. We think that, in the circumstances, it was less than adequate. It is not in keeping with the rational process to leave vital questions, raised by comments which are of cogent materiality, completely unanswered. The agencies certainly have a good deal of discretion in expressing the basis of a rule, but the agencies do not have quite the prerogative of obscurantism reserved to legislatures....

The Secretary was squarely faced with the question whether it was necessary to formulate a rule with specific parameters that applied to all species of fish, and particularly whether lower temperatures with the addition of nitrite and salt would not be sufficient. Though this alternative was suggested by an agency of the federal government, its suggestion, though acknowledged, was never answered.

Moreover, the comment that to apply the proposed T–T–S requirements to whitefish would destroy the commercial product was neither discussed nor answered. We think that to sanction silence in the face of such vital questions would be to make the statutory requirement of a "concise general statement" less than an adequate safeguard against arbitrary decision-making. . . .

One may recognize that even commercial infeasibility cannot stand in the way of an overwhelming public interest. Yet the administrative process should disclose, at least, whether the proposed regulation is considered to be commercially feasible, or whether other considerations prevail even if commercial unfeasibility is acknowledged. This kind of forthright disclosure and basic statement was lacking in the formulation of the T–T–S standard made applicable to whitefish. . . .

We cannot, on this appeal, remand to the agency to allow further comments by interested parties, addressed to the scientific data now disclosed at the trial below. We hold in this enforcement proceeding, therefore, that the regulation, as it affects non-vacuum-packed hot-smoked whitefish, was promulgated in an arbitrary manner and is invalid. . . .

NOTES

1. *Legal Antecedents.* Even before this decision, FDA's own regulations, 21 C.F.R. 10.40(b)(1), required essentially the procedures that the Second Circuit held were mandated by the APA. But in the late 1960s, the practice of many agencies, including FDA, did not meet this standard. Professor (now Justice) Antonin Scalia offered the following explanation for the insistence of reviewing courts that agencies engaged in informal rulemaking provide procedural safeguards beyond the minimum prescribed by the bare language of section 553:

1. Not until 1956 was it established that an agency charged with issuing and denying licenses in adjudicatory hearings could establish generic disqualifying factors in informal rulemaking, thereby avoiding adversarial procedures on those issues. . . .

2. Another post-APA development of monumental importance was the establishment in 1967 [*Abbott Laboratories*] of the principle that rules could be challenged in court directly rather than merely in the context of an adjudicatory enforcement proceeding against a particular individual, combined with the doctrine (clearly enunciated in 1973) that "the focal point for judicial review should be the administrative record already in existence, not some new record made initially in the reviewing court." By reason of these holdings—and of a large number of new statutes which explicitly provided for direct court-of-appeals review of rulemaking—the validity of rules was increasingly decided on briefs in a court of appeals, or before a district court which could take no new evidence.

The cumulative effect of these developments was that by the mid-1970s vast numbers of issues of the sort which in 1946 would have been resolved in a formal adjudicatory context before the agency, or even in an adjudicatory judicial proceeding, were being resolved in informal rulemaking and informal adjudication; that the courts were expected to provide, in the words of one of the Supreme Court's more expansive descriptions (which it probably now regrets), "a thorough, probing, in-depth review" of that agency action, but taking the agency record as it was and without conducting any additional evidentiary proceedings....

Antonin Scalia, *Vermont Yankee: The APA, The D.C. Circuit, and the Supreme Court*, 1978 SUP. CT. REV. 345 (1979).

2. *Adequate Notice.* When an agency contemplates major changes in a proposed regulation, it may be obligated to provide an additional opportunity for public comment. *Compare Chocolate Mfrs Ass'n of the United States v. Block*, 755 F.2d 1098 (4th Cir. 1985), *and Animal Health Inst. v. FDA*, Food Drug Cosm. L. Rep. (CCH) ¶ 38,154 (D.D.C. 1978), *with Pharmaceutical Mfrs. Ass'n v. Gardner*, 381 F.2d 271 (D.C. Cir. 1967).

3. *Effective Date.* Since 1973, FDA has established a uniform effective date for all food labeling regulations adopted within a specified time period to avoid repeated costly labeling changes. *See, e.g.*, 43 Fed. Reg. 44830 (Sept. 29, 1978), 55 Fed. Reg. 276 (Jan. 4, 1990). FDA's choice of wording in specifying the effective date can be critical to firms which must comply. A regulation may make a new requirement effective for all products that are "manufactured," or that are "introduced into interstate commerce" or that are "initially introduced into interstate commerce," or that are "labeled" after the specified date. Each of these formulations has a different impact on product inventories, and the choice among them usually reflects a calculated policy judgment by FDA. In *Public Citizen v. Schmidt*, Food Drug Cosm. L. Rep. (CCH) ¶ 38,075 (D.D.C. 1976), the court upheld a delayed effective date for a ban of a carcinogen, chloroform, on the ground that "a precipitous ban on chloroform was both impractical and unenforceable."

4. *Effect of Regulations.* FDA regulations may alter the conditions of a product approval, even though the FD&C Act ostensibly requires an opportunity for a formal hearing before the agency may revoke or amend product approvals. In *Upjohn Co. v. FDA*, 811 F.2d 1583 (D.C. Cir. 1987), the Court of Appeals upheld an FDA regulation revoking all medicated feed application exemptions for a class of new animal drugs.

5. *Record for Judicial Review.* In *Nova Scotia*, FDA successfully argued that review of its smoked fish regulations should be confined to the record of its original rulemaking, a position also reflected in the agency's regulations. 21 C.F.R. 10.45(f). *See also Heterochemical Corp. v. FDA*, Food Drug Cosm. L. Rep. (CCH) ¶ 38,074 (E.D.N.Y. 1987). When an agency's reasoning on a critical issue is not apparent from the rulemaking record, a reviewing court ordinarily will remand the matter to the agency for further elaboration or reopening of the record. On rare occasions, a district court may allow the submission of additional testimony or accept affidavits to clarify the agency's position. *See National Nutritional Foods Ass'n v. Mathews*, 557 F.2d 325 (2d Cir. 1977). *Cf.* Almay, Inc. v. Califano, 569 F.2d 674 (D.C. Cir. 1977).

6. *Standard for Review.* Section 701(a) regulations are subject to the standards established in 5 U.S.C. 706(2)(A), *i.e.*, they will be upheld unless the court determines they are "arbitrary, capricious, an abuse of discretion, or otherwise not in accordance with law." But see *National Nutritional Foods Ass'n v. Weinberger*, 512 F.2d 688 (2d Cir. 1975), where Judge Lumbard suggested that an agency abuses its discretion in informal rulemaking "if its actions are not supported by substantial evidence." Where the intent of Congress is not clear, the courts will uphold the FDA's "permissible" or "reasonable" construction of the Act. *See, e.g., Young v. Community Nutrition Institute*, 476 U.S. 974 (1986) (relying upon *Chevron U.S.A., Inc. v. Natural Resources Defense Council, Inc.*, 467 U.S. 837 (1984)).

7. *Exhaustion of Remedies.* In *Bradley v. Weinberger*, 483 F.2d 410 (1st Cir. 1973), the Court of Appeals vacated an injunction against FDA on the ground that the plaintiffs had failed to exhaust their administrative remedies, and it remanded the matter to the agency. In court, the plaintiffs had advanced arguments that they had not brought to FDA's attention during the administrative process. *See also Public Citizen Health Research Group v. Commissioner*, 740 F.2d 21 (D.C. Cir. 1984); *National Nutritional Foods Ass'n v. Califano*, 603 F.2d 327 (2d Cir. 1979); *Public Citizen v. Goyan*, 496 F. Supp. 364 (D.D.C. 1980).

3. WHAT CONSTITUTES A "RULE"?

Not infrequently, FDA will announce what it believes to be the meaning of a provision of a statute for whose administration it is responsible. If it has not previously signaled its position or otherwise afforded members of the public an opportunity to comment, it may be accused of violating the notice and comment provisions of the Administrative Procedure Act. A court must then determine whether the agency's pronouncement constitutes a rule to which the APA applies or represents only the agency's interpretation of established law.

Syncor International Corp. v. Shalala
127 F.3d 90 (D.C. Cir. 1997).

[The opinion is reproduced in Chapter IV, *supra*, at p. 715.]

NOTES

1. *Action Levels for Contaminants.* The majority in *Syncor* relied on the Court of Appeals' own earlier ruling in *Community Nutrition Institute v. Young*, 818 F.2d 943 (D.C. Cir. 1987), which followed the Supreme Court's remand of the plaintiff's challenge to FDA's failure to establish tolerances limiting levels of aflatoxin on corn and other affected crops. The Supreme Court had ruled that the agency had discretion to determine whether formal binding tolerances were necessary to regulate such contaminants under section 406 but then remanded the case to the court of appeals to determine whether FDA's informal action levels constituted rules subject to the rulemaking requirements of the APA. The Court of Appeals concluded that FDA's action levels—which it had issued without notice or opportunity for comment—functioned as rules because, though they did not formally bind growers or sellers of corn, they effectively constrained the agency's enforcement discretion. The action levels thus required compliance with section 553 of the APA. Judge Starr dissented. He thought the Court's ruling, by requiring compliance with the APA's increasingly burdensome requirements for rulemaking, would discourage the agency from sharing with the public its assessment of the levels at which aflatoxin posed a health threat that could warrant regulatory action. Following this decision, FDA acquiesced and promulgated regulations stating that action levels constitute only guidance and not binding requirements. 53 Fed. Reg. 5043 (Feb. 19, 1988).

2. *Supporting Authority.* The courts have sometimes invalidated, or refused to enforce, FDA guidelines that have not been subjected to notice and comment. *See, e.g., Caribbean Produce Exchange, Inc. v. Secretary of HHS*, Food Drug Cosm. L. Rep. (CCH) ¶¶ 38,100, 38,110 (D.P.R. 1988), *rev'd and remanded*, 893 F.2d 3 (1st. Cir. 1989); *Bellarno International Ltd. v. FDA*, 678 F. Supp. 410 (E.D.N.Y. 1988); *United States v. Bioclinical Systems, Inc.*, 666 F. Supp. 82 (D. Md. 1987); *United*

States v. Articles of Drugs Consisting of 203 Paperbags, 634 F. Supp. 435 (N.D. Ill. 1985), *vacated* 818 F.2d 569 (7th Cir. 1987).

3. *Contrasting Authority.* In *Professionals and Patients for Customized Care v. Shalala*, 56 F.3d 592 (5th Cir. 1995), the Fifth Circuit rejected a claim that language in FDA's Compliance Policy Guide describing the practices that would make a compounding pharmacist a manufacturer of drugs constituted a rule whose announcement had to comply with the APA. The Court of Appeals considered the text, form, and context of the agency's guide in arriving at the conclusion that the guide was not meant to establish a binding norm.

4. *Discretion as to Whether to Issue Rules. See, e.g., National Wildlife Federation v. Secretary of HHS*, 808 F.2d 12 (6th Cir. 1986); *Center for Science in the Public Interest v. Novitch*, Food Drug Cosm. L. Rep. (CCH) ¶ 38,275 (D.D.C. 1984). The only cases in which a court has required FDA to promulgate a regulation are *Public Citizen v. Heckler*, 602 F. Supp. 611 (D.D.C. 1985), 653 F. Supp. 1229 (D.D.C. 1986), and *Public Citizen Health Research Group v. Commissioner, FDA*, 724 F. Supp. 1013 (D.D.C. 1989).

F.   COURT REVIEW OF AGENCY IMPLEMENTATION

As prior chapters of his book make clear, FDA actions are frequently subject to challenge in court. In this respect, FDA does not stand on a footing different from other federal agencies. Like most of the laws other agencies administer, the FD&C Act expressly authorizes suits to review several dozen types of FDA decisions, including the approval of a food or color additive, the approval or revocation of approval of a human or animal drug, and the promulgation of any regulation subject to the formal rule-making requirements of section 701(e) of the Act. And for the many rules and decisions about which the Act is silent regarding reviewability, the Administrative Procedure Act, coupled with relevant language of the FD&C Act, would seem to afford nearly inexhaustible opportunities for private parties to contest the legality of FDA's actions in court. In this respect, as well, FDA's experience may be similar to those of other health and safety agencies, such as EPA and OSHA, although one has the impression that FDA has fared somewhat better in court than its counterparts. During the 1970s and early 1980s, when FDA was vigorously engaged in rulemaking, it was usually successful in fending off suits that threatened important agency policies. For example, on a single day in 1973, FDA's position was upheld, with just one dissent, in a quartet of decisions by the Supreme Court.

In recent years, however, FDA has not been as consistently successful in court. Several of its enforcement policies have been questioned by reviewing courts and a significant number have been overturned. Whatever a litigant's chances of success, few FDA decisions are immune from judicial reexamination. There is one important exception, however; under *Heckler v. Chaney*, 470 U.S. 821 (1985), *supra* p. 1211, a court generally will not interfere with the agency's decision *not* to undertake enforcement action.

NOTES

1. *Citizen Pleas for Enforcement.* Companies often importune FDA to enforce provisions of the FD&C Act or regulations against competitors. Public interest

organizations also often urge enforcement. Few such pleas to the agency succeed, and their prospects do not improve when taken to court. *See, e.g., National Wildlife Federation v. Secretary of Health and Human Services*, 808 F.2d 12 (6th Cir. 1986). But see *Heterochemical Corporation v. FDA*, 644 F. Supp. 271 (E.D.N.Y. 1986), where the District Court entertained review of an FDA decision not to challenge VKAS after accepting a citizen petition and inviting public comment. *Chaney* was distinguished on the ground that FDA had here committed resources, carried out an investigation, and published findings. *See also Public Citizen Health Research Group v. Commissioner, FDA*, 724 F. Supp. 1013 (D.D.C. 1989) (the District Court held FDA's seven-year delay in promulgating regulations specifying tampon absorbency unreasonable).

2. *Agency Explanation for Failure to Enforce.* The agency's failure adequately to explain its failure to regulate may help a petitioner's attempt to evade *Chaney*. *See Public Citizen v. Heckler*, 602 F. Supp. 611 (D.D.C. 1985) (FDA's explanation for its failure to act on petition to ban all domestic sales of raw milk "was lame at best and irresponsible at worst.").

3. *Commentary.* For in-depth treatment of *Chaney* and its progeny, see Ronald M. Levin, *Understanding Unreviewability in Administrative Law*, 74 MINN. L. REV. 689 (1990); Carol R. Miaskoff, *Judicial Review of Agency Delay and Inaction Under Section 706(1) of the Administrative Procedure Act*, 55 GEO. WASH. L. REV. 635 (1987).

COMMENT: REGULATORY DELAY

Several provisions of the FD&C Act prescribe time limits for agency action. Like many other agencies, FDA has often missed such statutory deadlines.

For example, section 409(b)(5) of the FD&C Act requires FDA to publish a notice within 30 days after the "filing" of a food additive petition, and section 409(c)(2) requires the agency to act on the petition within 90 days after the date of filing unless it extends that period for another 90 days "to investigate and study the petition." Similar statutory time limits are imposed by sections 505(c) (new drug applications), 512(c) (new drug applications), 515(d)(1)(A) (device premarket approval applications), and 706(d)(1) (color additive petitions).

For decades it has been standard practice for FDA to conduct a preliminary review of any application for approval, and then to notify the applicant that it is "incomplete" and thus not eligible for "filing." Although FDA regulations may require the agency to send an "incomplete" letter within 15 days of receipt of the application, often it is sent just before the end of the period set by statute for review of the application. FDA thereby avoids "filing" the application and, on its theory, the statutory time limit does not begin to run. The initial submission of an application is therefore only the beginning of a negotiation process between the applicant and agency reviewers leading ultimately toward official "filing" several months, or sometimes even years, later. Applicants for marketing approval have generally been unwilling to contest the legality of this process out of fear that a court challenge might precipitate a premature negative decision on the merits, further delay ultimate FDA approval, or prejudice the agency's attitude toward other pending or future applications in which the applicant is interested.

One of the few successful legal challenges to FDA's failure to meet a statutory deadline is *Southeastern Minerals, Inc. v. Califano*, (M.D. Ga. 1978). Southeastern Minerals, a manufacturer of medicated feed premixes for livestock, in 1976 began adding gentian violet to several of its products. The firm took the position that gentian violet was GRAS, and therefore did not require a food additive regulation. When the firm realized that FDA officials took a different view and were likely to initiate enforcement proceedings against its products, it grudgingly submitted a food additive petition on August 18, 1977. The agency did not publish a notice of filing within 30 days of receiving the petition, but two months after submission FDA informed Southeastern by letter that the petition was under review. Discussions between the firm and FDA eventually resulted in suspension of production, but the threat of enforcement action against existing stocks, coupled with the agency's inaction, led Southeastern, approximately 120 days after submitting its petition, to bring suit against FDA for failure to comply with the statutory deadlines. On January 30, 1978, the firm received an "incomplete" letter from FDA, but at no time did the agency formally extend the 90–day period for review of the petition.

The District Court interpreted the Act as imposing mandatory time limits for action on FDA:

> The evidence in this case shows that the Plaintiffs have done everything within their power to cooperate and work with the Defendants, going so far in these efforts as to subordinate their own good faith interpretations and contentions to the requests and demands of the Defendants. The Defendants have reciprocated with bureaucratic arrogance. . . .
>
> The Defendants in this case on the one hand have failed and refused to perform the duties cast upon them by the Federal Food, Drug and Cosmetic Act in failing to act upon the Plaintiff' petition and at the same time have used their failure against the Plaintiffs in having Plaintiffs' product detained by the states and subsequently seized all upon the theory that it is an "unapproved" feed additive. It is the opinion of this Court that such conduct both in the failure and refusal to act upon the petition while simultaneously detaining the product on the basis that it is an unapproved feed additive constitutes a clear denial of the rights of the Plaintiffs and effectively takes their property without due process. . . .

The court enjoined FDA from interfering with the firm's marketing of gentian violet until there was final action on its food additive petition, including judicial review if sought. FDA subsequently denied the petition in 44 Fed. Reg. 19035 (Mar. 30, 1979), and then rejected the petitioner's request for a hearing on the ground that no genuine issues of material fact had been raised, 45 Fed. Reg. 20559 (Mar. 28, 1980). When these actions were reviewed, the Court of Appeals dissolved the District Court injunction against FDA but agreed that the agency had demonstrated "a bureaucratic hubris that confuses abusive power with reason." The Court declared that the agency's disregard of the statutory 180–day limit "is . . . regrettable and inexcusable," *Southeastern Minerals, Inc. v. Harris*, 622 F.2d 758 (5th Cir. 1980). The court later overturned FDA's denial of a hearing on the food additive petition. *Marshall Minerals, Inc. v. FDA*, 661 F.2d 409 (5th Cir. 1981).

In 1975 FDA voluntarily established a six-month deadline for responding to citizen petitions, 21 C.F.R. 10.30(e)(2). In practice, however, this deadline is seldom met, and, when it is, the agency's initial response often states simply that a substantive determination is not yet feasible.

In the Food Additives Amendments of 1958, the Color Additive Amendments of 1960, the Drug Amendments of 1962, the Medical Device Amendments of 1976, and the Drug Price Competition and Patent Term Restoration Act of 1984, Congress prescribed deadlines within which specific regulations were to be issued or programs were to be completed. Most of these deadlines have not been met. For example:

(a) Section 6 of the Food Additives Amendment of 1958 provided for a transition period of 30 months within which all food additives were to be subject to a food additive regulation. Because FDA could not meet that deadline, the Food Additives Transitional Provisions Amendment of 1961 was enacted to extend it to June 30, 1964 and the Food Additives Transitional Provisions Amendment of 1964 further extended it to December 31, 1965. This later deadline was met only because the majority of food ingredients were exempted from the requirement of a regulation on the ground that they were GRAS or subject to a prior sanction.

(b) More than forty-five years have elapsed, and the 1960 Color Additive Amendments are not yet fully implemented. *See* p. 440 *supra*.

(c) Section 107(c)(3) of the 1962 Drug Amendments provided a two-year "grace period" before the new proof of effectiveness requirement could be applied to new drugs for which NDA's became effective during the period 1938–1962. In *American Public Health Ass'n v. Veneman*, 349 F. Supp. 1311 (D.D.C. 1972), p. 603 *supra*, the court concluded that FDA had failed to implement the Amendments as rapidly as Congress had mandated and issued a detailed order requiring staged implementation by October 10, 1976. *See* 37 Fed. Reg. 26623 (Dec. 14, 1972). FDA still has not yet completed implementation of the 1962 Amendments.

(d) Section 520(g)(2)(A), added by the 1976 Medical Device Amendments, required FDA to promulgate regulations governing investigational use of medical devices within 120 days after the date of enactment of that provision, which was May 28, 1976. The 1976 Amendments also mandated a comment period of at least 60 days on all proposed device regulations. Implementing regulations were proposed in 41 Fed. Reg. 35282 (Aug. 20, 1976), provoking critical comments from manufacturers, clinicians, and consumer groups. A tentative final order was published in 43 Fed. Reg. 20726 (May 12, 1978), on which a public hearing was held. Final investigational device regulations were promulgated in 45 Fed. Reg. 3732 (Jan. 18, 1980).

Because of its unhappy experience with statutory deadlines, FDA successfully opposed the inclusion in the 1976 Amendments of any mandatory time period within which all class II or III devices marketed prior to 1976 must be subject to a standard or an approved application. Instead, Congress required FDA to set priorities for these actions and then to work on them as resources permit. In the Safe Medical Devices Act of 1990, however, Congress did impose deadlines for beginning the process of reviewing preamendment class III devices and for finally either reclassifying these devices or subjecting them to the PMA requirement. FDA missed both of these deadlines, and some preamendment class III devices still have not been subjected to PMA calls. *See supra* p. 989.

(e) Section 105(a) of the Drug Price Competition and Patent Term Restoration Act of 1984 required that implementing regulations be promulgated within one year of the date of enactment. Proposed regulations were not published by FDA until 1989, 54 Fed. Reg. 28872 (July 10, 1989), and final regulations did not appear until 1994, 59 Fed. Reg. 50338 (Oct. 3, 1994).

(f) FDA met a statutory deadline when it adopted regulations to implement the Drug Listing Act of 1972 prior to the effective date of that statute. 37 Fed. Reg. 26431 (Dec. 12, 1972), 38 Fed. Reg. 6258 (Mar. 7, 1973). Computerization of the drug listing information received under section 510 of the Act proceeded very slowly, however, and the entire system did not become operational until the 1980s.

(g) Congress included in the Nutrition Labeling and Education Act of 1990 and the Safe Medical Devices Act of 1990 provisions which set deadlines for the publication of proposed and final regulations and specified that the proposed regulations automatically become final if the agency did not complete rulemaking by the statutory deadline.

(h) Section 505(d) of the Act specifies that the agency must act on an application to market a new drug within 180 days. This time limit had been routinely ignored by both the industry and the agency, but in 2006, the United States District Court for the District of Columbia ordered FDA to rule on a company's NDA, rejecting the agency's argument that the statutory timetable is an aspiration rather than a requirement. *Sandoz v. Leavitt*, 427 F. Supp. 2d 29 (D.D.C. 2006).

G.   Formal Rulemaking

As discussed above, section 701(e) provides that specified regulations (*e.g.*, prescribing labeling for special dietary foods, rulings on food additive and color additive petitions) may be issued only after the agency has provided affected persons an opportunity for a formal evidentiary hearing. Hearings held pursuant to these provisions must comply with the applicable provisions of the Administrative Procedure Act, 5 U.S.C. 556 and 557.

Chapter III described FDA's frustration with this process, highlighted by its decade-long effort to establish labeling requirements for dietary supplements and other foods pursuant to section 403(j) and by increasingly protracted hearings on food standards of identity proposed pursuant to section 401. Such experiences have led the agency either to abandon use of the authorities that require formal hearings or to construe hearing requests strictly.

1.   WHEN IS AN EVIDENTIARY HEARING REQUIRED?

Dyestuffs and Chemicals, Inc. v. Flemming

271 F.2d 281 (8th Cir. 1959).

■ VOGEL, CIRCUIT JUDGE.

Petitioner is a producer of food colors, including certain coal tar colors known as FD&C Yellows 3 and 4 which have been widely used in the coloring of edible fat products, principally butter and oleomargarine. FD&C Yellows 3 and 4 have been certified by the respondent and his predecessors under § 346(b) as safe for such use for approximately the past 40 years. On January 24, 1957, the Deputy Commissioner of Food and Drugs published in the Federal Register a notice of his proposal to amend the Food and Drug Administration regulations by removing FD&C Yellow Nos. 1, 2, 3 and 4 from the approved list for unrestricted use.... After receiving comments, including those of the Certified Color Industry Committee of which petitioner is a member, the Commissioner on May 4, 1957, published an order removing the colors in question from the approved list, because they "are not harmless and suitable for use within the meaning of" 21 U.S.C. 346(b).... On May 27, 1957, within the time provided by law, the Certified Color Industry Committee filed objections to the order and requested a hearing thereon in accordance with the provisions of 21 U.S.C. 371(e)(2, 3) [FD&C Act 701(e)(2, 3)]. The objections ... were mainly on the ground that the term "harmless" had long been judicially and administratively construed to mean "harmless and suitable for use in food" *under the intended conditions of their use* and that petitioner's product could so qualify *when used within certain stated tolerances....*

On February 6, 1959, the Deputy Commissioner, without a hearing as provided for in 21 U.S.C. 371(e)(2, 3), published the final order delisting the colors in question. The order explained the failure to grant a hearing as follows:

> "The Supreme Court's (*Flemming v. Florida Citrus Exchange* [p. 440, *supra*]) decision having established the proper construction of the law, the objection of the Certified Color Industry Committee to the delisting of FD&C Yellow Nos. 1, 2, 3, and 4 is without substance, and no purpose could be served by holding a public hearing. The Department has no authority to certify colors that are themselves toxic, as is the case with FD&C Yellow Nos. 1, 2, 3, and 4, and the Department has no authority to establish a tolerance for such a color, as requested by the Industry Committee."

. . . .

... Petitioner contends that [Sections 701(e)(2) and (3)] ... constitute an unconditional statutory requirement for a hearing upon the filing of objections and that they were wholly disregarded by the order deleting the colors from the harmless list, with the result that no chance was afforded petitioner and others to raise any objections that might be available or to question and refute the pharmacological evidence referred to in the Secretary's order.

Respondent counters by claiming that the grounds set forth in petitioner's objections were wholly insufficient to warrant a hearing in that they sought the promulgation of regulations that were beyond the Department's authority. Petitioner's "grounds for objection" were four in number. The first asserted that, "The colors affected by the order serve a useful and desirable purpose in coloring food and drugs," and that they had been so used for many years, principally with margarine and butter. Objection No. 2 alleged:

"The evidence of potential injury from the use of FD&C Yellow Nos. 1, 2, 3 and 4 is inadequate to justify the order...."

Objection No. 3 asserted that:

"The reasonably anticipated uses of the four yellow colors do not justify any fear of injury from their use...."

Objection No. 4:

"... urges that the Commissioner take action to prohibit such excessive concentrations, rather than to bar the proper and harmless use now being made of the colors."

It seems to us obvious, as it did to the respondent, that under the holding of the Supreme Court in *Flemming v. Florida Citrus Exchange*, each of the objections set forth by the petitioner must be held inadequate to prevent the removal of the coal tar colors in question from the "harmless" list. Objection No. 1 merely asserts usefulness and desirability. While No. 2 alleges that the evidence of potential injury is inadequate to justify the order, it is based upon the contention that "the 'no-harm' level thus shown (500–1,000 ppm) is so far in excess of the level of actual use in the human diet that those results do not afford any basis for the order." No. 3 asserts that the reasonably anticipated uses do not justify fear of injury; and No. 4 suggests that the Commissioner do what the Supreme Court held he had no authority to do in *Flemming v. Florida Citrus Exchange....* We thus conclude that the four grounds set forth in the petitioner's objections to the order were legally insufficient and turn next to the question of whether a hearing must be held even though the prerequisite objections fail to state valid or legal grounds for the requested action.

It will be noted that 21 U.S.C. 371(e)(2) provides that objections may be filed "... stating the grounds therefor, and requesting a public hearing upon such objections ..." and (3) "... the Secretary, after due notice, *shall hold such a public hearing for the purpose of receiving evidence relevant and material to the issues raised by such objections*." (Emphasis supplied.) It is only after filing objections and "... stating the grounds therefor, and requesting a public hearing upon such objections ..." that an interested party is entitled to a hearing. The hearing is solely for the purpose of receiving evidence "relevant and material to the issues raised by such objections." Certainly, then, the objections, in order to be effective and necessitate the hearing requested, must be legally adequate so that, if true, the order complained of could not prevail. The objections must raise "issues." The issues must be material to the question involved; that is, the legality of the order attacked. They may not be frivolous or inconsequential. Where the objections stated and the issues raised thereby are, even if true, legally insufficient, their effect is a nullity and no objections have been stated. Congress did not intend the governmental agencies created by it to perform useless or unfruitful tasks. If it is perfectly clear that petitioner's appeal for a hearing contains nothing material and the objections stated do not abrogate the legality of the order attacked, no hearing is required by law. . . .

NOTES

1. *Entitlement to a Formal Hearing under Sections 505 and 512.* Sections 505(d) and (e) of the FD&C Act require FDA to provide an NDA applicant or holder an opportunity for an evidentiary hearing when the agency declines to approve, or proposes to revoke, an NDA. Parallel provisions require the agency to provide an opportunity for an evidentiary hearing upon denial or withdrawal of approval of a New Animal Drug Application. FD&C Act 512(d), (e). In *Weinberger v. Hynson, Westcott & Dunning,* 412 U.S. 609 (1973), discussed in Chapter IV, the Supreme Court upheld the agency's authority to deny a hearing and enter summary judgment when the party seeking a hearing fails to demonstrate that material factual issues are in dispute. *See* p. 745 *supra.*

2. *FDA Regulations.* 21 C.F.R. 12.24(b), sets forth criteria that must be satisfied to warrant a hearing on objections to regulations that are subject to section 701(e):

> (1) There is a genuine and substantial issue of fact for resolution at a hearing. A hearing will not be granted on issues of policy or law.
>
> . . . .
>
> (3) The data and information submitted, if established at a hearing, would be adequate to justify resolution of the factual issue in the way sought by the person. . . .
>
> (4) Resolution of the factual issue in the way sought by the person is adequate to justify the action requested. . . .

3. *Hearing Denials.* In *Community Nutrition Institute v. Young,* 773 F.2d 1356 (D.C. Cir. 1985), the Court of Appeals upheld FDA's approval of beverage uses of aspartame and denial of a formal hearing. *See also Pineapple Growers Ass'n of Hawaii v. FDA,* 673 F.2d 1083 (9th Cir. 1982). In *Cook Chocolate Co. v. Miller,* 72 F. Supp. 573 (D.D.C. 1947), 1938–1964 FDLI Jud. Rec. 985 (D.D.C. 1949), a food processor petitioned to amend a food standard and, when FDA declined to hold an evidentiary hearing, brought suit contending that he had demonstrated the statutorily required "reasonable grounds." The District Court concluded, after a trial, that the evidence failed to show that FDA had abused its discretion. *But see Marshall Minerals, Inc. v. FDA,* 661 F.2d 409 (5th Cir. 1981), overturning FDA's denial of a request for a public hearing on a food additive petition.

4. *Contrary Authority. Pactra Industries, Inc. v. Consumer Product Safety Com'n,* 555 F.2d 677 (9th Cir. 1977), overturned a ban on the use of vinyl chloride as a propellant in consumer products issued by the CPSC under the Hazardous Substances Act, which incorporates the formal rulemaking requirements of the FD&C Act. The Commission had declined to hold a hearing on objections to its "final" rule, concluding in substance that there were no facts the objectors could prove which would alter its judgment. The court of appeals rejected this reasoning:

We hold that section 371(e) leaves the agency no discretion to rule on the quality and validity of the objections prior to the formal hearing, so long as they are made in good faith and draw in question in a material way the underpinnings of the regulation at issue. It is inconsistent with the statutory scheme to require the objecting party to allege anything more.

The Commission's summary procedure may be justified where, as was the case in *Dyestuffs*, the issues raised by the objecting party have been authoritatively determined to be legally irrelevant. But a different case is presented where, merely because the agency has concluded that the scientific evidence is adequate to support its order, a hearing is denied on the assumption that it would serve no purpose. . . .

5. *Standing to Demand a Hearing or Seek Judicial Review.* Because an NDA is a private license, section 505 permits only the applicant or holder to request a hearing on an adverse agency action. Thus, FDA has declared that "a physician has no legal right to a hearing to contest withdrawal of approval of a new drug." 40 Fed. Reg. 22950, 22967 (May 27, 1975). *See also Rutherford v. American Medical Ass'n*, 379 F.2d 641 (7th Cir. 1967); *Tutoki v. Celebrezze*, 375 F.2d 105 (7th Cir. 1967) (cancer patients have no standing to contest FDA's prohibition of Krebiozen except by filing their own new drug application and appealing its denial).

6. *Adversely Affected by a Food Standard.* The issue of *who* can be "adversely affected" under sections 701(e) and (f), and thus be entitled to demand a hearing and later seek court review, arose soon after FDA first began to promulgate food standards. *See Reade v. Ewing*, 205 F.2d 630 (2d Cir. 1953) (consumer of food may be adversely affected by a food standard); *United States Cane Sugar Refiners' Ass'n v. McNutt*, 138 F.2d 116 (2d Cir. 1943) (ingredient supplier is not adversely affected by a food standard that excludes an ingredient it markets); *Land O'Lakes Creameries, Inc. v. McNutt*, 132 F.2d 653 (8th Cir. 1943) (producer of a competitive product has standing to seek review of a food standard); *A.E. Staley Mfg. Co. v. Secretary of Agriculture*, 120 F.2d 258 (7th Cir. 1941) (food processor is adversely affected by a food standard that excludes an ingredient he uses).

7. *Barriers to Judicial Review.* Under section 409(f)(1) & (g)(1), failure to file an objection to a final food additive regulation with FDA will bar judicial review. *Nader v. EPA*, 859 F.2d 747 (9th Cir. 1988). Jurisdiction to review the agency's action lies only in a court of appeals. *Community Nutrition Institute v. Young*, 773 F.2d 1356 (D.C. Cir. 1985). In *Scott v. Califano*, Food Drug Cosm. L. Rep. (CCH) ¶ 38,135 (D.D.C. 1977), the District Court dismissed an action to require publication of a proposed regulation under section 701(e) because the petitioner had sought court review before the expiration of the 180 days provided by FDA in 21 C.F.R. 10.30(e)(2) for a reply to petitions.

2. FORMAL HEARING PROCEDURES

Many formal hearings conducted by FDA have been protracted, some famously so. Several have been cited as evidence of the need to reform or dispense with formal rulemaking. President Jimmy Carter once stated that "It should not have taken 12 years and a hearing record of over 100,000 pages for the FDA to decide what percentage of peanuts there ought to be in peanut butter. . . . I would have used that example even if I had grown soybeans and wheat, by the way." 15 WEEKLY COMP. PRES. DOC. 482, 484 (Mar. 25, 1979). The most cogent criticisms of the FDA experience include Ben G. Fisher, *Procedural Techniques in Food and Drug Administration Proceedings*, 17 FOOD DRUG COSM. L.J. 724 (1962); Robert Hamilton, *Rule-*

making on a Record by the Food and Drug Administration, 50 TEX. L. REV. 1132 (1972); Note, *FDA Rulemaking Hearings: A Way Out of the Peanut Butter Quagmire*, 40 GEO. WASH. L. REV. 726 (1972). *See also* Administrative Conference of the United States, Recommendation No. 71–7, 2 RECOMMENDATIONS AND REPORTS OF THE ADMINISTRATIVE CONFERENCE OF THE UNITED STATES 42 (1973); H. Thomas Austern, *Is Government by Exhortation Desirable?*, 22 FOOD DRUG COSM. L.J. 647 (1967); William W. Goodrich, *A Reply to Professor Hamilton's Comments and Recommendations for Procedural Reform*, 26 FOOD DRUG COSM. L.J. 639 (1971); Robert Hamilton, *Procedures for the Adoption of Rules of General Applicability: The Need for Procedural Innovation in Administrative Rulemaking*, 60 CAL. L. REV. 1276 (1972); Joel Hoffman, *Some Suggestions for Improvements in the Hearing and Rulemaking Procedures of the Food and Drug Administration*, 23 FOOD DRUG COSM. L.J. 465 (1968); Selma Levine, *Separation of Functions in FDA Administrative Proceedings*, 23 FOOD DRUG COSM. L.J. 132 (1968); William Pendergast, *The Nature of Section 701 Hearings and Suggestions for Improving the Procedures for the Conduct of Such Hearings*, 24 FOOD DRUG COSM. L.J. 527 (1969); *FDA Procedures*, 25 FOOD DRUG COSM. L.J. 191 (1970).

On the premise that repetitive cross examination had been a major cause of delay at hearings, FDA has attempted to limit cross examination to the extent permitted by the Administrative Procedure Act. *See* 40 Fed. Reg. 40682 (Sept. 3, 1975), 41 Fed. Reg. 51706 (Nov. 23, 1976), 21 C.F.R. 12.87, 12.94.

3. ALTERNATIVES TO TRIAL–TYPE HEARINGS

On the premise that formal adversary hearings are not well-suited to resolving the types of scientific issues that the agency regularly confronts, FDA has experimented with the use of a process based on scientific peer review.

Administrative Practices and Procedures

40 Fed. Reg. 40682 (September 3, 1975).

... Proposed § 2.117 [now 21 C.F.R. 12.32] would provide that a person who had a right to an opportunity for a formal evidentiary hearing could waive that opportunity and, in lieu thereof, request a public hearing before a Public Board of Inquiry ..., a public hearing before a public advisory committee ..., or a public hearing before the Commissioner....

... [T]he proposed regulations would establish ... an informal public hearing before a Public Board of Inquiry that would be conducted in the form of a scientific inquiry rather than as a legal trial.... Proposed § 2.202 [now 21 C.F.R. 13.10] would require that the members of a Board have medical, technical, scientific, or other qualifications relevant to the issues to be considered at the hearing. The members would be [designated] special government employees and thus subject to the conflict of interest rules applicable to such employees....

Within 30 days after the notice of the hearing before the Board was published in the FEDERAL REGISTER, each of the parties to the proceeding and any person whose petition was the subject of the hearing would submit a list of five nominees for members of the Board. Such persons could agree upon a single list of nominees. Following receipt of such lists, such persons could submit comments on the other lists submitted. The Commissioner would then review the lists and comments and select one member of the Board from the lists submitted by the director of the agency bureau involved and any person whose petition was the subject of the hearing, one member from the lists submitted by the other parties, and one member of his own choosing from any source whatever who would serve as the Chairman of the Board....

Proposed § 2.206(a) [now 21 C.F.R. 13.30] would make it clear that the purpose of a Board is to review complex technical issues in a reasonably short time by using the informal approach of a scientific inquiry rather than the formal procedures of a legal trial. Accordingly, it is anticipated that there will be little, if any, need for participation by attorneys....

The Chairman of the Board would determine the order in which the parties and participants make their presentations. Such order of presentation could well be the subject of a prior agreement. Each participant could then proceed with his presentation, which would be made without interruptions and without objection or other legalistic procedures. At the conclusion of a participant's presentation, each of the other participants could briefly state questions or criticism and suggest further questioning with respect to specific matters. The members of the Board could interrupt a participant at any time to ask questions, and could conduct further questioning at the conclusion of the participant's full presentation either on their own initiative or at the suggestion of the other participants.

In addition to hearing the views of the participants, the Board could independently consult with any other person who it concluded may have useful information. All such consultation would have to be at an announced hearing of the Board unless all participants agreed that it could be done in writing. Moreover, any participant in the proceeding could submit to the Board a request that it consult with specific persons who could have useful information.

The administrative record of the public hearing would constitute the exclusive record for decision on the matter....

———

FDA has established a Public Board of Inquiry in two cases. *See* 44 Fed. Reg. 31716 (June 1, 1979) (aspartame); 44 Fed. Reg. 44274 (July 27, 1979) (Depo Provera). Professor Sidney Shapiro offered the following assessment of these experiments:

The FDA's experiences with the PBOI confirm the value of the "science court" idea for resolving issues of scientific judgment. Its scientific seminar format is conducive to scientific analysis and debate. As a practical matter, however, the costs of merging the PBOI and the regulatory process will limit the use of these boards. Although the two PBOIs that have been convened did engage in the type of scientific inquiry that the FDA anticipated at the hearing stage, delays and other problems in the pre-and post-hearing stages revealed the need to integrate the PBOI into the normal regulatory process. Many of these problems can be alleviated, but PBOIs will continue to be expensive. As a result, they will be cost-effective only in cases involving issues that for sophisticated scientific judgment and stimulate great public interest. In those cases, the benefits of the PBOI—enhanced accuracy and legitimacy—are likely to outweigh the costs of the process.

Even if the use of the PBOI is limited, the process offers the FDA a unique option with several important advantages over the agency's advisory committee system. One key difference is that the PBOI convenes after the agency has decided whether to license a new drug or food additive. Because the PBOI can focus on the key issues in the agency's decision, it can serve as an independent check on the validity of that decision. Another key difference is that the PBOI emphasizes data analysis and is more accountable than other processes for its conclusions. As a result, the PBOI process enhances the accuracy and legitimacy of an agency's decision making.

In an analysis of whether a "scientific" or "adversarial" process better resolves issues of scientific judgment, the results are mixed. The FDA's experience does indicate that the PBOI can be the more effective process, but at a higher price than the conventional approach. Thus, the PBOI is unlikely to be cost-effective except when it is used to resolve significant issues of scientific judgment.

Scientific Issues and the Function of Hearing Procedures: Evaluating the FDA's Public Board of Inquiry, 1986 DUKE L.J. 288.

H.   PRIMARY JURISDICTION

1.   THE PRINCIPLE

The 1938 Act consisted of definitions of adulteration and misbranding applicable to food, drugs, devices, or cosmetics, coupled with a trio of remedies the government could pursue in U.S. district court. For three decades, FDA saw its role as that of a specialized police force, responsible for discovering violations and assembling the evidence needed to prevail in court. In such cases the agency performed the role of advocate; whether the conduct charged constituted a violation of the Act was for the courts to decide.

In later amendments to the Act, exemplified by the 1962 Drug Amendments, Congress gave FDA new responsibilities that required the agency to determine how the law applied to particular facts. Was the product a "new drug" for which the law required proof of effectiveness? Did the evidence demonstrate that the drug was effective? As FDA's responsibilities expanded, the agency increasingly sought judicial endorsement for its role as the primary interpreter of the statute's requirements.

The Supreme Court acknowledged such a role in four 1973 decisions upholding FDA's implementation of the 1962 Amendments' effectiveness standard. The key opinion was *Weinberger v. Bentex Pharmaceuticals*, Inc., 412 U.S. 645 (1973). FDA had announced that it regarded generic copies of a pioneer drug for which it had approved of an NDA as "new drugs" whose legal status depended on the status of the pioneer. Manufacturers of generic versions of the drug, pentylenetrazol, insisted that only a court could determine a product's "new drug" status. The Supreme Court rejected this claim:

> [I]n holding that FDA has no jurisdiction to determine the "new drug" status of a drug [the Court of Appeals], stated that the question of "new drug" status is never presented when an application for approval is filed.... The line sought to be drawn by the Court of Appeals is FDA action on NDA's pursuant to § 505(d) and § 505(e) on the one hand and the question of "new drug" determination on the other. We can discern no such jurisdictional line under the Act.... Whether a particular drug is a "new drug" depends in part on the expert knowledge and experience of scientists based on controlled clinical experimentation and backed by substantial support in scientific literature. One function is not peculiar to judicial expertise, the other to administrative expertise. The two types of cases overlap and strongly suggest that Congress desired that the administrative agency make both kinds of determination....
>
> We think that it is implicit in the regulatory scheme, not spelled out in *haec verba*, that FDA has jurisdiction to decide with administrative finality, subject to the types of judicial review provided, the "new drug" status of individual drugs or classes of drugs....

Peter Barton Hutt, FDA's chief counsel at the time, considered the Court's ruling in *Bentex* the most significant of its four opinions. In affirming FDA's primary jurisdiction to determine how the Act applied to particular products, the Court implicitly endorsed a host of regulatory initiatives, including the OTC Drug Review, FDA's nutrition labeling requirements for food the Biologics Review, and the regulation of in vitro diagnostic products. *See FDA Court Actions and Recent Developments*, 39 Q. BULL. ASS'N OF FOOD & DRUG OFFICIALS 11 (1975).

2. THE PRINCIPLE IN OPERATION

United States v. Alcon Labs

636 F.2d 876 (1st Cir. 1981).

■ LEVIN H. CAMPBELL, CIRCUIT JUDGE....

Alcon manufactures and markets in suppository dosage a prescription antiemetic drug called "WANS." The drug contains pyrilamine maleate (an antihistamine) and pentobarbital sodium (a barbituate) and comes in three dosage strengths, WANS No. 1, WANS No. 2 and WANS Children. WANS has been used under medical supervision for approximately 25 years, and did not become an object of FDA concern until 1978. . . .

On March 17, 1978, the FDA sent Alcon a regulatory letter informing it of a report received from the agency's Neurological Drugs Advisory Committee "that children aged 6 months to seven years who were treated for nausea and vomiting with drugs containing pyrilamine maleate and pentobarbital, experienced severe and sometimes fatal reactions." The Committee had concluded, the letter went on, "that there is no evidence of safety and efficacy for drugs containing pyrilamine maleate with or without a barbiturate in the treatment of nausea and vomiting." Based on the Committee's report, "and because [the FDA was] unaware of substantial scientific evidence which demonstrates that a combination of these ingredients is generally recognized as safe and effective for the treatment of nausea and vomiting," the FDA advised Alcon that it considered Alcon's marketing of WANS to be in violation of the "new drug" provision of the Federal Food, Drug, and Cosmetic Act, 21 U.S.C. 355. The letter stated that under FDA regulatory policy as formulated in Compliance Policy Guide 7132c.08, WANS had become subject to immediate regulatory action outside the agency's ordinary enforcement priorities "because of new information concerning the safety and efficacy of these drugs." Alcon was told to reply within ten days, and was warned that failure to discontinue marketing WANS would expose the company to seizure and injunction actions. . . .

Alcon continued to manufacture WANS and on September 21, 1978 the FDA instituted a seizure action in federal district court alleging that the drug was a "new drug" being marketed in violation of Section 505 of the Act, 21 U.S.C. 355. . . . Alcon moved the district court to remand to the FDA. . . .

No further action was taken in the case until January 28, 1980. On that date the FDA instituted a second seizure against WANS. Large quantities of the drug were again confiscated. A month later, on February 27, 1980, the district court consolidated the latest seizure action with the pending actions, and ordered the entire case to be,

> "remanded to the Food and Drug Administration (FDA) with instructions to defer regulatory action against the WANS preparations involved in this matter or against defendants based upon the alleged 'new drug' status of WANS until FDA holds a hearing pursuant to 5 U.S.C. 554 and thereafter makes an administrative determination of the new drug status of WANS in conformity with the enforcement priorities enunciated in FDA's Compliance Policy Guide 7132c.08. . . ."

The district court premised its decision to remand to the FDA on interrelated procedural and substantive grounds. The court was troubled by the agency's failure to conduct "a formal administrative determination of the 'new drug' status of WANS" before instituting suit against Alcon. In the absence of such a determination, the court felt that an FDA internal regulation—Compliance Policy Guide 7132c.08—precluded enforcement action against WANS unless the agency possessed "significant new information which questions the safety of the drug." However, the court characterized itself as ill-suited to decide the "new drug" status of WANS or to determine whether "significant new information" existed that questioned WANS' safety. Citing lack of jurisdiction, the doctrine of primary agency jurisdiction and prudential considerations, the court decided that these questions were better left to "the Agency entrusted by Congress with the necessary expertise to make a responsible determination." Accordingly, it ordered the action "remanded to the Food and Drug Administration to hold a formal administrative hearing pursuant to 5 U.S.C. 554 on the issue as to whether WANS is a 'new drug' in conformity with the enforcement priorities enunciated in FDA's Compliance Policy Guide 7132c.08."

The court's concern over summary institution of enforcement proceedings is shared by some in the drug industry, but the imposition of a pre-enforcement hearing requirement (coupled with preliminary relief, as, to be meaningful, it would have to be) is at odds with the language and intent of the Act.... The district court's concern that the FDA might be proceeding in violation of its own internal regulatory guidelines was also in error....

Finally, we turn to the district court's belief that it lacked, or should not have exercised, jurisdiction over the "new drug" and "grandfather clause" questions in this case. The court's declaration that "[i]t is not within the jurisdiction of this Court to determine whether the drug in issue is or is not a new drug" is plainly incorrect. Jurisdiction over the new drug issue is shared by the FDA and the federal district courts.

Further, the district court's invocation of the doctrine of "primary jurisdiction" to justify its refusal to exercise its own jurisdiction is not persuasive. As we have elsewhere stated, deference to an agency's primary jurisdiction makes little sense in the context of an enforcement proceeding initiated by the agency. This is especially true where, as here, a party remains subject to the agency's regulatory efforts despite the remand. We have held above that a district court lacks the power to require the FDA to defer seizures *pendente lite* or to order release of seized drugs prior to a determination of the merits of the agency's claims. The effect of a remand to the agency thus would hardly be beneficial to the product's manufacturer. Without the relief afforded by the other aspects of the district court's order, Alcon would be deprived of a judicial remedy in return for an administrative procedure of uncertain duration before an unsympathetic agency. We would be surprised if either Alcon or the district court would be content with a remand under such circumstances. With this consideration in mind, and in view of the fact that the FDA's current position on the "new drug" status of WANS is already clear; that the FDA carried the burden of proving its position at trial; and that the agency has no duty to hold a pre-enforcement hearing or to justify its action under its Compliance Policy Guide, we do not see what would be gained in this case by a remand. At least it can be said that two fundamental purposes of deference to agency jurisdiction—"coordinating administrative and judicial machinery" and assuring uniformity of regulation—would not be served by the district court's order.

... In *Bentex Pharmaceuticals*, the Supreme Court upheld the power of a district court to refer to the FDA "new drug" and "grandfather clause" issues initially presented to the court in a declaratory judgment action instituted by drug manufacturers. The Court went on to note that a court could stay its hand "[e]ven where no ... administrative determination has been made and the issue arises in a district court in enforcement proceedings...." This observation, however, should be understood in relation to the situation in *Bentex*, where some 21 drug manufacturers had requested declaratory relief. There the court was in essence being asked to issue, without benefit of prior administrative proceedings, a decision upon whether a substantial portion of an industry was complying with the Act. Here the district court is being asked only to decide whether a single drug manufactured by a single company is being marketed illegally. The agency's view of the question is clear and will have to be substantiated for the agency to prevail in court. We therefore conclude that under *Bentex* this is not an appropriate case for a remand.

As the district court recognized, a third purpose of the doctrine of primary jurisdiction—taking advantage "of agencies' special expertise," weighs in favor of a remand, but not, we think, decisively. The Supreme Court has described the "new drug" and "grandfather clause" issues as "the kinds of issues peculiarly suited to initial determination by the FDA." Nevertheless, contrary to the Court's suggestion it has not been "commonplace" for courts to await an appropriate administrative declaration in enforcement proceedings, lower courts continue to hear and decide the "new drug" status of drugs challenged by the FDA in seizure and injunction actions. The government asserts, and we have found nothing to the contrary, that of the hundreds of enforcement actions brought by the FDA under section 505 since 1938, none save the present has been remanded to the agency. Returning issues in an enforcement action to the FDA imposes an administrative burden for which the Act makes no provision, and insofar as the procedure delays adjudication of the regulatory status of a drug, may work to the disadvantage not only of the agency and public, but also of the manufacturer. In such circumstances the power to remand must be used sparingly. Had the trial set for May 1979 been held, WANS' status would long since have been laid to rest. In deciding the case, the FDA's expertise would have been available to the court, in that to sustain its burden the agency would have had to present expert evidence establishing its claims regarding WANS. We therefore conclude that the district court erred in remanding the case to the FDA.

NOTES

1. *Supporting Authority. Carolina Brown, Inc. v. Weinberger*, 365 F. Supp. 310 (D.S.C. 1973), and *National Ethical Pharmaceutical Ass'n v. Weinberger*, 365 F. Supp. 735 (D.S.C. 1973), *aff'd per curiam*, 503 F.2d 1051 (4th Cir. 1974), dismissed suits seeking a judicial declaration of a product's new drug status on the ground that this issue lay within FDA's primary jurisdiction and that judicial review should be available only after the agency ruled. *See United States v. Western Serum Co., Inc.*, 666 F.2d 335 (9th Cir. 1982); *Premo Pharmaceutical Laboratories, Inc. v. United States*, 629 F.2d 795 (2d Cir. 1980); *United States v. An Article of Drug* ...

"Tutag Pharmaceuticals ... X–Otag Plus Tablets," *602 F.2d 1387 (10th Cir. 1979);* United States v. Mosinee Research Corp., *583 F.2d 930 (7th Cir. 1978);* United States v. 118/100 Tablet Bottles, *662 F. Supp. 511 (W.D. La. 1987);* United States v. 1,834/100 Capsule Bottles ... "New Formula Hauck G–2 Capsules," *Food Drug Cosm. L. Rep. (CCH)* ¶ *38,058 (N.D. Ga. 1987);* United States v. The Upjohn Co., *Food Drug Cosm. L. Rep. (CCH)* ¶ *38,302 (W.D. Mich. 1985);* United States v. Articles of Hazardous Substance, *588 F.2d 39 (4th Cir. 1978);* United States v. An Article of Drug ... "Beuthanasia–D Regular," *Food Drug Cosm. L. Rep. (CCH)* ¶ *38,265 (D. Neb. 1979).*

2. *Court–Mandated Primary Jurisdiction.* In *Rutherford v. United States,* 542 F.2d 1137 (10th Cir. 1976), the Court of Appeals instructed FDA to hold an administrative hearing to document its announced position that Laetrile is a new drug that requires formal agency approval. The plaintiff was a cancer patient who sought a judicial ruling that the agency's position was inconsistent with the statute and violated the Constitutional rights of cancer patients. The District Court had ruled in the plaintiff's favor, enjoining FDA from interfering with his right to obtain Laetrile for his personal use. The Court of Appeals refused to set aside the injunction pending FDA's completion of the judicially mandated hearing.

> ... Nothing in the record suggests that the FDA has dealt with Laetrile in a rule-making proceeding under Section 701 of the Act. Hence, if this is true the appropriate procedure for the district court is to remand the case back to the FDA for proceedings adequate to develop a record supportive of the agency's determination; the proceedings should give Laetrile proponents an opportunity to express their views....

After holding the mandated hearing, the FDA Commissioner ruled that Laetrile may not lawfully be marketed as a food or as a drug. 42 Fed. Reg. 39768 (Aug. 5, 1977). That decision was ultimately upheld by the Supreme Court in *United States v. Rutherford,* 442 U.S. 544 (1979). For an additional chapter in this long-running saga, see 806 F.2d 1455 (10th Cir. 1986).

3. *Spontaneous Primary Jurisdiction.* FDA has occasionally sought to resolve an enforcement action by asserting its primary jurisdiction. In March 1983, FDA brought a seizure action against a new generic animal drug that had been marketed without an approved NADA. After the seizure went by default, the generic manufacturer filed a declaratory judgment action seeking a court determination that the drug was not a new animal drug and therefore that a NADA was not required. FDA and the generic manufacturer then entered into a stipulation of voluntary dismissal, under which the generic manufacturer agreed to file a citizen petition with FDA seeking an administrative determination that the drug was not a new animal drug, and FDA agreed not to initiate any enforcement litigation until 18 months after the filing of the petition, or 30 days after any denial of the petition, whichever was later. The pioneer manufacturer, which had an approved NADA, sought unsuccessfully to overturn this settlement in *Schering Corp. v. Heckler,* 779 F.2d 683 (D.C. Cir. 1985). Following FDA's denial of its citizen petition, the generic manufacturer unsuccessfully renewed its suit for declaratory judgment. *Tri–Bio Laboratories, Inc. v. United States,* 836 F.2d 135 (3d Cir. 1987).

4. *Primary Jurisdiction in Private Litigation.* Suits between private parties can raise issues that fall within FDA's special competence. In *Purdue Frederick Co. v. Acme United Corp.,* Civ. No. N–74–115 (D. Conn. 1975), the plaintiff alleged violation of the false advertising provision of the Lanham Act and unfair competition. It claimed that the defendant's antiseptic drug, formulated in a novel fashion, should not be marketed under the same generic name as its own product. It suggested that FDA be asked for its views on a series of questions, most of which revolved around the issue of whether the defendant's drug was lawfully marketed

under the FD&C Act. The trial court declined to refer the matter to FDA because it appeared clear that the agency's OTC Drug Review had several years to run, but it invited the agency to submit answers to specific questions respecting the bioequivalence of the defendant's formulation. The agency answered those questions. The matter was subsequently settled out of court.

5. *FDA Regulation.* Following the *Purdue Fredrick* experience, FDA adopted a regulation providing that it will institute an administrative proceeding whenever a court holds in abeyance or refers to the agency any matter on which an administrative determination "is feasible in light of agency priorities and resources." 40 Fed. Reg. 40682 (Sept. 3, 1975), 42 Fed. Reg. 4680 (Jan. 25, 1977), at 21 C.F.R. 10.25(c). Reference of issues in private litigation to FDA can be important in product liability suits, where the status of a product or ingredient under the FD&C Act is often in dispute. *See, e.g., Hoffman v. Sterling Drug, Inc.*, 485 F.2d 132 (3d Cir. 1973).

I. FDA's Search for Expert Advice
1. FDA's Reliance on Advisory Committees

Institute of Medicine, Food and Drug Administration Advisory Committees (1992)

The FDA uses technical advisory committees of outside scientific experts to advise it on the approvability of specific products and on the scientific and clinical policy issues it confronts regarding product development and evaluation. The agency also uses these committees to legitimate the soundness of its analysis of a given product, as a public forum for discussion of controversial issues, and, on occasion, as an "appeals court" for disputed agency decisions.

. . . .

The FDA's use of agency-chartered advisory committees for drug evaluation has evolved over the three decades since the 1962 drug amendments to the Food, Drug, and Cosmetic Act. Those amendments required FDA to assess all new drugs for effectiveness, in addition to safety (as required by the 1938 amendments), and to reassess for effectiveness nearly 4,000 prescription drugs that had been introduced to the market between 1938 and 1962—before proof of effectiveness was required.

The FDA responded by seeking external advice from the National Academy of Sciences–National Research Council (NAS–NRC) on previously marketed prescription drugs, establishing its own review committees for over-the-counter drugs, and extending such committees to new prescription drugs....

Over-the-Counter Drugs

... In 1972, the FDA faced the mammoth problem of reviewing all of the OTC drugs that had been marketed between 1938 and the enactment of the 1962 Drug Amendments. Its solution was to establish an OTC review system.... The regulatory product of this process was a series of monographs consisting of approved active ingredients, labeling, and other general requirements.

. . . .

This system ... articulated some general principles of FDA advisory committees. Such committees should include nonvoting industry and consumer representatives, for example, to increase the likelihood that the results of the review would be accepted in both quarters. The participation of the former helped to avoid surprising the industry, to maintain contact with it, to detect problems early, and to minimize opposition.

Prescription Drug Review

In the early 1970s ... an advisory committee system evolved for prescription drugs. Its purpose was to secure expert advice on the evaluation and approval of new therapeutic products....

The FDA used internal memoranda to create these prescription drug advisory committees administratively. Subsequently, the agency promulgated general regulations governing the formation and operation of advisory committees, which are now codified in (21 CFR 14)....

The FDA created a system of standing, rather than ad hoc, committees so that committee members would see the fruits of their labor. Terms for advisory committee members were four years but were often shortened by such factors as slow appointments and early departures. Committee members were primarily academic physicians, although it soon became clear that other expertise was also needed.

Biologics

. . . .

During the years in which the biologics regulatory program was a component of the NIH, ad hoc advisory committees were sometimes formed to deal with matters of high public visibility, such as a major new product that was being considered for approval or an important problem that occurred with an existing marketed product. The membership of these committees generally included experts from government as well as the academic community....

The transfer [to FDA in 1972] was followed by a number of management changes in the biologics organization and a decision to reexamine the efficacy of all existing licensed biological products. At that time, there were no standing committees for biologics regulatory decisions, and the ad hoc committees that were involved had a narrow focus. To carry out its regulatory functions, the [Bureau of Biologics] created a process similar to the comprehensive OTC drug review and formed six standing committees to review the principal categories of biological products: major vaccines, bacterial vaccines, blood products, and products for which the science base was substantially less, such as allergenic extracts.

The scale and scope of the review were substantial in both administrative and logistical terms. As the committees began their work, it became apparent that these same experts could be helpful to the agency in other ways: giving ongoing advice about new products (assuming the role of earlier ad hoc committees in this regard); advising on general problems that occurred with both marketed and experimental products; and reviewing intramural research similarly to the function of the NIH DBS Board of Scientific Counselors. As the agency completed its one-time comprehensive reviews of existing products, it reduced the number of these original committees and rechartered them to provide continuing advice on all of the organization's regulatory and research programs.

. . . .

Medical Devices

The use of advisory committees by the Center for Devices and Radiological Health (CDRH) differs from that of the CDER and CBER in one critical aspect: it is required by statute. . . .

The Medical Device Amendments . . . required the creation of advisory panels or committees for two purposes. The first was the classification of medical devices. Following adoption of the amendments, the FDA revisited the classification process in accordance with the act. The new classification advisory panels had the benefit of prior efforts, which were a useful point of departure.

The second purpose was the evaluation of medical devices regulated by risk tier. . . .

For product evaluation, the amendments called for establishment of permanent advisory committees. To these advisory committees the FDA was to appoint "persons qualified in the subject matter to be referred to the committee and of appropriately diversified professional backgrounds"; the agency was also mandated to appoint a chairman and provide necessary clerical support. The performance standards section called for the appointment of nonvoting consumer and industry members; this provision was omitted from the premarketing approval section, but the practice was adopted for the product review committees nevertheless and is the basis for current policy.

Although the Safe Medical Devices Act of 1990 modified the original 1976 legislation in certain respects giving the agency greater discretion in the use of advisory committees—it did not change the basic mandate to use such committees. . . .

In 1990, the CDRH recharged its advisory committees into a single Medical Device Advisory Committee with a number of panels. Concurrently, the agency implemented the combination products requirements of the Safe Medical Devices Act by issuing regulations on product jurisdiction (which encompassed combination products) and negotiating three intercenter agreements on this subject. The CDRH rechartering of its device advisory committees converged with these product jurisdiction efforts and led to a rechartering of CDER and CBER advisory committees as well. . . .

NOTES

1. *Uses of Advisory Committees.* FDA relies heavily on technical advisory committees for advice on such issues as the approval of new drugs or the adequacy of clinical test designs. 21 C.F.R. 14.160 *et seq.* The agency has also used advisory committees to hold public hearings on a wide variety of issues, including proposed

approvals, or denials of approval, of new products. Committees have also reviewed proposed approval or denial of new uses for existing products, or new warnings, or even revocation of prior approvals. *E.g.*, 46 Fed. Reg. 14355 (Feb. 27, 1981) (announcing an advisory committee hearing on the proposed revocation of erythromycin estolate, which FDA had approved more than 20 years earlier). *See* M.S. Brown & B.W. Richard, *Advisory Committees and the Drug Approval Process*, 2 J. Clin. Res. & Drug Dev. 15 (1988). *See also* Thomas Burack, *Of Reliable Science: Scientific Peer Review, Federal Regulatory Agencies and the Courts*, 7 Va. J. of Nat. Res. Law 27 (1987).

2. *Authority to Create Advisory Committees.* Most of FDA's advisory committees have been established by the Secretary of HHS. However, section 903(c) of the FD&C Act, as added by the Food and Drug Administration Act of 1988, 102 Stat. 3048, 3120, and amended by the Food and Drug Administration Revitalization Act, 104 Stat. 4583 (1990), explicitly empowers the FDA Commissioner to "establish such technical and scientific review groups as are needed to carry out the functions" of FDA. A minority of FDA advisory committees are statutorily mandated. These include the Technical Electronic Product Radiation Safety Standards Committee, 42 U.S.C. 263t(f)(1)(A); the color additive advisory committees, 21 U.S.C. 376(b)(5)(C)(D); the Device Good Manufacturing Practice Advisory Committee, 21 U.S.C. 360j(f)(3); and the advisory review panels for medical devices, 21 U.S.C. 360c(b).

3. *Commentary.* For differing views on FDA's use of advisory committees, see David Hickman, *Advisory Committees at FDA: A Legal Perspective*, 29 Food Drug Cosm. L.J. 395 (1974); Joseph L. Kanig, *Advisory Committees: An Expanding Concept in the Field of Drug Regulation: The Perspective of a Liaison Representative*, 29 Food Drug Cosm. L.J. 353 (1974); Philip G. Walters, *Use of FDA Advisory Committees: Present and Future*, 29 Food Drug Cosm. L.J. 348 (1974).

2. Statutory Requirements for Advisory Committees

Questions about the Federal Advisory Committee Act's applicability have generated as much controversy as its particular procedural requirements. *Food Chemical News, Inc. v. Davis*, 378 F. Supp. 1048 (D.D.C. 1974), held FACA applicable to a series of meetings that the Director of the Bureau of Alcohol, Tobacco and Firearms had scheduled separately with consumer and industry groups to discuss proposals for alcoholic beverage labeling. The aim of the plaintiff, a weekly trade journal, was to force BATF to open the meetings to the public. A similar objective inspired the plaintiff in the following case.

Consumers Union of United States, Inc. v. Department of HEW

409 F. Supp. 473 (D.D.C. 1976) *aff'd*, 551 F.2d 466 (D.C. Cir. 1977).

■ John Lewis Smith, Jr. District Judge.

This case involves a relatively narrow legal question: Were the meetings held on April 9 and September 17, 1975 between Food and Drug Administration (FDA) officials and representatives of the Cosmetic, Toiletry and Fragrance Association, Inc. (CTFA, Intervenor) advisory committee meetings within the meaning of the Federal Advisory Committee Act? If so, they were invalidly held since under FACA the meetings should have been open to the public and the "advising" group authorized through administrative approval and chartering....

The FDA has considered the desirability of labeling and of testing cosmetic ingredients since 1960. The initiative in these areas has moved back and forth from agency to industry, with industry representatives (acting at times to forestall pending legislation) proposing certain voluntary programs and FDA calling for refinements and clarifications in procedures. There now exist procedures for voluntary registration of cosmetic product establishments, for voluntary filing of cosmetic product ingredients, and for voluntary filing of cosmetic product experiences....

In the area of testing cosmetic ingredients, FDA–CTFA efforts have increased in the past two years. Speaking at CTFA's annual meeting on February 27, 1974, FDA Commissioner Schmidt discussed the need for establishment of an ingredient review program. Another FDA official, Dr. Mark Novitch, stated: "Certainly, this kind of approach [*i.e.*, cosmetic ingredient safety substantiation paralleling the drug review process] is something you should consider and we *will* consider in our common effort to increase our mutual assurance and the public's confidence in the safety of our cosmetic products." (Emphasis in original.) CTFA had been developing a safety review program since 1972, and planning and consultation moved forward rapidly. After three exploratory meetings between FDA and CTFA representatives in 1974 and two briefing meetings in early 1975, CTFA requested a meeting with FDA to discuss CTFA's draft proposal. This meeting was held on April 9, 1975, and detailed minutes were kept for the session. Plaintiff's counsel subsequently requested permission to attend or participate in future FDA–CTFA meetings on the ingredient review proposal, invoking the Federal Advisory Committee Act. Commissioner Schmidt denied the request on grounds that these were private, CTFA-initiated meetings. Following the filing of this lawsuit, a second meeting was held on September 17, 1975 to discuss CTFA's revised proposal. Minutes were also kept for this meeting.

Resolution of the issues in this case requires a careful examination of FACA and its administrative and judicial construction. The Federal Advisory Committee Act was aimed at eliminating useless advisory committees, strengthening the independence of remaining advisory committees, and preventing advisory groups from becoming self-serving. The Act defines advisory committee in a general, open-ended fashion. For purposes of this action, the term includes "any committee, board, commission, council, conference, panel, task force, or other similar group ... which is ... established or utilized by one or more agencies, in the interest of obtaining advice or recommendations for ... [such] agencies...."

Several recent cases have interpreted FACA and afford some guidance to the Court in determining what constitutes an advisory committee under the Act. In *Nader v. Baroody*, 396 F. Supp. 1231 (D.D.C. 1975), the court held that certain bi-weekly meetings with various constituent and interest groups at the White House did not come within FACA's reach. The meetings were found to be of a random nature, without formally organized groups, without presidential request for policy recommendations, and without any continuity or follow-up. Further, to have applied the Act so as to impinge upon the effective discharge of the President's business might have raised serious constitutional questions.

In *Food Chemical News, Inc. v. Davis*, 378 F. Supp. 1048 (D.D.C. 1974), the court held as subject to FACA an agency's informal meetings with consumer and distilled spirits industry representatives relative to drafting proposed ingredient labeling regulations. . . .

The matter before the Court involves a factual situation different from the above-mentioned cases. The meetings complained of here were not ad hoc, amorphous or casual group meetings as in *Nader v. Baroody*. The FDA–CTFA conferences were the culmination of many months of planning, consulting, and revising. On the other hand—and unlike *Food Chemical News*—the two meetings were not called to consider proposals dealing with impending agency action. They were essentially consultations concerning the group's own proposal. This is a crucial factor for determining the group's status under the Act. . . .

Based on the record, the Court finds that CTFA was not advising the FDA about the cosmetic ingredient testing program. CTFA was presenting a voluntary, industry-sponsored proposal and seeking the FDA's comments and advice. . . . Granting that FDA had frequently expressed its concern for cosmetic ingredient testing, the Court finds that planning had evolved beyond agency control. CTFA in its own discretion was ultimately to decide whether or not to initiate a testing program. Such a relationship of agency and group does not rise to the level of a FACA "advisory" relationship. . . .

————

Later, in 21 CFR 14.1; 43 Fed. Reg. 51966 (Nov. 7, 1978), 44 Fed. Reg. 22318 (Apr. 13, 1979), FDA summarized its interpretation of the FACA's coverage:

(b) In determining whether a group is a "public advisory committee" . . . the following guidelines will be used:

(1) An advisory committee may be a standing advisory committee or an ad hoc advisory committee. . . .

. . . .

(3) An advisory committee includes any of its subgroups when the subgroup is working on behalf of the committee. . . .

(4) A committee composed entirely of full-time Federal Government employees is not an advisory committee.

(5) An advisory committee ordinarily has a fixed membership, a defined purpose of providing advice to the agency on a particular subject, regular or periodic meetings, and an organizational structure, for example, a chairman and staff, and serves as a source of independent expertise and advice rather than as a representative of or advocate for any particular interest. The following groups are not advisory committees:

(i) A group of persons convened on an ad hoc basis to discuss a matter of current interest to FDA, but which has no continuing function or organization and does not involve substantial special preparation.

(ii) A group of two or more FDA consultants meeting with the agency on an ad hoc basis.

(iii) A group of experts who are employed by a private company or a trade association which has been requested by FDA to provide its views on a regulatory matter pending before FDA.

(iv) A consulting firm hired by FDA to provide advice regarding a matter.

(6) An advisory committee that is utilized by FDA is subject to this subpart even though it was not established by FDA. In general, a committee is "utilized" when FDA requests advice or recommendations from the committee on a specific matter in order to obtain an independent review and consideration of the matter, and not when FDA is merely seeking the comments of all interested persons or of persons who have a specific interest in the matter.

National Nutritional Foods Ass'n v. Califano

603 F.2d 327 (2d Cir. 1979).

■ FRIENDLY, CIRCUIT JUDGE.

This is an appeal from an order of the District Court for the Southern District of New York, 457 F. Supp. 275 (1978), in an action by two trade associations whose members manufacture and sell protein supplements.... The action concerns FDA rulemaking designed to require warnings for protein supplements and other preparations that may be used as the sole or primary source of calories in order to lose weight....

Liquid protein products have been available for direct retail sale to the consuming public for at least 12 years. Within the last five years new medical research has suggested the usefulness of a modified fasting diet, supplemented by protein, vitamins and minerals, in alleviating obesity. Prominent in this "Protein Sparing Modified Fast" (PSMF) research was Dr. George L. Blackburn of the Harvard University Medical School, who is Director of the Center for Nutritional Research in Boston....

The controversy was heated by the publication in late 1976 of "The Last Chance Diet" by Robert Linn, a doctor of osteopathy, which popularized the use of liquid protein products for diet control. The ASBP [American Society of Bariatric Physicians] attacked the new widespread and uncontrolled use of PSMF programs and urged its members to help with the problem, through such means as writing letters to newspapers....

Primary responsibility in the FDA for products such as those manufactured and sold by plaintiffs lay in Dr. Allan Forbes, Acting Associate Director for Nutrition and Consumer Sciences in the Bureau of Foods. In the spring of 1977 he and Dr. Blackburn had various conversations about Dr. Linn's book and the consequent popularity of liquid food protein products, including Dr. Blackburn's attempts to dissuade Dr. Linn from publishing. In a letter to Dr. Forbes dated May 25, 1977, Dr. Blackburn suggested that the Bureau of Foods might become involved. During the summer of 1977, the FDA received a report of a death believed to be associated with the use of liquid protein products in dieting; a second death was reported in September. At a conference of FDA officials held on or before October 3, 1977, it was decided, among other things, "to obtain the advice of experts in the field of obesity research among whom are Dr. George L. Blackburn, Dr. Theodore B. Van Itallie, and Dr. Sanford A. Miller." ...

Later in October, Dr. Forbes learned that a conference on obesity was scheduled to take place on October 20–22, 1977, at the National Institutes of Health in Bethesda, Md., near the FDA's headquarters. Between October 18 and 22 he communicated with five clinicians who were attending the conference and arranged for them to meet with him and six other FDA officials.... The memorandum recites that the "ultimate purpose for the meeting" was to assist the FDA in selecting the best course of action "for regulating the production and promotion of [protein products used for weight reduction] and/or informing the public of their hazard potential." It described the five physicians as an "ad hoc advisory group." ... The memorandum concluded by saying:

> The members of the ad hoc advisory group have graciously agreed
> to provide further assistance to FDA as the need may arise.

On November 9, 1977 the Commissioner of Food and Drugs held a press conference and issued a press release on the subject of protein supplements used to fight obesity. He declared the FDA was aware of 16 reported deaths and a number of severe illnesses possibly associated with the use of such products and expressed special concern about the "liquid protein diets now so popular," which were being promoted in the new media and in books such as Dr. Linn's. He said that his statements reflected not only the views of the FDA but also "the information provided by the Center for Disease Control and advice given us by leading experts in obesity and obesity control," two of whom, Drs. Blackburn and Van Itallie, were present and could answer questions.

As should have been expected, this publicity resulted in a drastic decline in the sale of protein products for use in weight reduction. On December 2, 1977, the FDA gave notice of a proposed rule, 42 F.R. 61285, whereby protein supplements intended for use in weight reduction or maintenance programs would be required to bear the following warning:

> *Warning.* Very low calorie protein diets may cause serious illness
> or death. DO NOT USE FOR WEIGHT REDUCTION OR MAIN-
> TENANCE WITHOUT MEDICAL SUPERVISION. Do not use for
> any purpose without medical advice if you are taking medication.
> Not for use by infants, children, or pregnant or nursing women.

The notice relied heavily on the October 20 meeting with the ad hoc advisory group, which was described in detail, and the memorandum of the meeting was placed on file with the Hearing Clerk....

Appellants contend that the meeting of October 20, 1977, was of an advisory committee as defined in FACA and did not comply with the Act and the FDA's regulations thereunder, 21 C.F.R. 14.1 *et seq.*, in several respects. The FDA gave no notice of the meeting as required by 21 C.F.R.

14.20 and § 10(a)(2) of the Act. No advisory committee charter was filed as required by § 9(c). The meeting was not open to the public, nor were interested persons given any opportunity to appear before the committee or file statements with it, as required by § 10(a)(1) and (3). Most important, appellants claim that appointment of a group composed solely of physicians, understandably leaning in favor of medical supervision of the use of protein supplements to conquer obesity, did not comply with § 5(b)(2) and (3), made applicable to agencies by § 5(c), which require that membership of an advisory committee "be fairly balanced in terms of the points of view represented and the functions to be performed" and that suitable provision be made to assure that advice and recommendations "will not be inappropriately influenced ... by any special interest." The FDA's principal answer is that the group convened on October 20 was not an advisory committee within the meaning of FACA....

In the long run the Government's argument that the October 20 meeting was not within FACA rests mainly on what it conceives to be common sense. An agency dealing with technical matters ought to be able to get the advice of highly qualified technicians in the private sector before it even initiates proceedings or takes other action, and to get this speedily and informally. Yet the OMB guidelines require that before creating a new advisory committee, an agency must first consult with the OMB secretariat and, if the OMB concurs, a process that may be time consuming, must publish in the Federal Register a certification of need and a description of the nature and purpose of the committee at least 15 days (unless that period is shortened by the OMB secretariat) before the filing of the committee's charter, which under § 9(c) of the Act, is a precondition to the committee's meeting. Congress, the Government argues, could not have intended to place such obstacles in the way of what proved to be a one-time meeting, even though there may have been an intention to hold more....

The two most relevant reported decisions are *Food Chemical News, Inc. v. Davis* ... and *Nader v. Baroody* ... [W]e find *Food Chemical News* to be more nearly in point. One factor weighing heavily with us is that the Commissioner leaned so strongly on the advisory group in his press release and, even more so, in his proposed regulation. If an agency wishes to rely publicly on the backing of an advisory committee it must do what the statute commands. Such a situation directly implicates the concern Congress addressed in § 5(c)(2) and (3) of the Act, that agency action might be dominated by one particular viewpoint. Some two months elapsed between the initial plan for the meeting and the publication of the proposal, in which the advisory group was mentioned on four occasions. Even if the calling of the meeting without reference to FACA was a pardonable inadvertence, there was ample time for compliance before December 7. All things considered, we believe this to be a situation wherein Congress meant FACA to apply. If the straitjacket is too tight, Congress is free to loosen it.

The question of remedy remains. So far as we are aware, no court has held that a violation of FACA would invalidate a regulation adopted under otherwise appropriate procedures, simply because it stemmed from the advisory committee's recommendations, or even that pending rulemaking must be aborted and a fresh start made. We perceive no sound basis for doing so. Applicable rulemaking procedures afford ample opportunity to correct infirmities resulting from improper advisory committee action prior to the proposal. . . . We likewise cannot fault the district judge for concluding that, in light of the Government's agreement not to reconvene this particular group, there was no need for an injunction. Whether it was proper to deny declaratory relief is a closer question. . . . In any event this opinion gives appellants substantially the same relief as a declaratory order. . . .

NOTES

1. *Second Judicial Thoughts.* Reflecting on this ruling, Judge Friendly later wrote:

> No one seems even to have considered that in seeking to cure one trouble by imposing procedural requirements, the statute would create others. Just what is an advisory committee? In a recent opinion, where the FDA had consulted with a number of physicians who were attending a meeting of the nearby National Institute of Health, I regretfully found it impossible to accept the Government's position that simply by keeping things informal an agency can escape from a statute whose very purpose is to require formality.

> Against this a judge would scarcely wish to say that if on the night of Three Mile Island the NRC wanted to telephone a few eminent atomic scientists, it could not legally have done so. Assuming that a talk with one scientist would not have been subject to FACA, what about a conference call with five? What about a couple of meetings in Harrisburg during the next few days? Beyond this the statute necessitates additional staff in each agency and in the Office of Management and Budget. Would we not have been better off with a bit more trust and less law?

Should We Be Turning Back the Law Flood?, LEGAL TIMES OF WASHINGTON, Oct. 8, 1979, at 7.

2. *Application to Nongovernmental Bodies.* FACA has been held not to apply to committees formed by independent scientific bodies on whose conclusions the government may later rely to formulate Federal policy. *Food Chemical News v. Young*, 900 F.2d 328 (D.C. Cir. 1990) (decided on the authority of *Public Citizen v. United States Department of Justice*, 491 U.S. 440 (1989)); *Lombardo v. Handler*, 397 F. Supp. 792 (D.D.C. 1975), *aff'd without opinion* 546 F.2d 1043 (D.C. Cir. 1976).

3. *Open Committee Meetings.* During their first three years of operation, the OTC Drug Review panels began each meeting with an open session but conducted deliberations in closed session. Transcripts of closed meetings were made but were not released to the public. *See* 40 Fed. Reg. 40682 (Sept. 3, 1975). FDA's policy of withholding meeting transcripts was initially upheld in *Smart v. FDA*, Civ. No. C–73–118–RHS (N.D. Cal. 1974), but it was later held to contravene the Freedom of Information Act in *Wolfe v. Weinberger*, 403 F. Supp. 238 (D.D.C. 1975). In 1976 FDA reversed its policy and opened the deliberative portions of all advisory committee meetings. On September 13, 1976, Congress enacted the Government in the Sunshine Act, 90 Stat. 1241, which amended FACA to narrow the circumstances under which an advisory committee may be closed. FDA's final advisory committee regulations, 41 Fed. Reg. 52148 (Nov. 26, 1976), 21 C.F.R. 14.25 & 14.27, provide that all advisory committee meetings are to be open to the public except during

consideration of trade secrets, investigatory files, sensitive internal documents, or matters involving personal privacy.

4. *Committee Drafts.* In *Bristol Meyers Co. v. Kennedy*, Food Drug Cosm. L. Rep. (CCH) ¶ 38,224 (D.D.C. 1979), plaintiff sought the transcripts of the 1972–1976 closed sessions of an OTC drug panel and all drafts of the proposed monograph, and argued that the closed sessions violated the FACA and thus invalidated the panel's report. FDA provided the requested transcripts but not the panel drafts. The District Court held that the drafts as a whole reflected the deliberative process of the panel and thus were exempt from public disclosure. The court also ruled that any FACA violation was mooted by the release of the transcripts of the closed sessions and would in any event not be ripe for judicial review until a final regulation was promulgated.

5. *GSA Guidelines.* The General Services Administration has promulgated guidelines for federal agencies to follow in order to comply with FACA in 41 C.F.R. Part 101–6.

6. *Application to the National Academy of Sciences.* Congress has relaxed the open meeting requirements of FACA for study committees established by the National Academy of Sciences. 5 U.S.C. App. 2 § 15.

On occasion an FDA advisory committee has been challenged on the ground that its membership is not, as FACA requires, "fairly balanced."

Public Citizen v. National Advisory Committee

886 F.2d 419 (D.C. Cir. 1989).

■ Opinion, concurring in the [per curiam] judgment [of affirmance], filed by CIRCUIT JUDGE FRIEDMAN.

In November 1987, the United States Department of Agriculture (Department) announced plans to establish a National Advisory Committee on Microbiological Criteria for Foods (Committee). The purpose of the Committee was to provide advice and recommendations to the Secretaries of Agriculture and Health and Human Services (HHS) on the development of microbiological criteria by which the safety and wholesomeness of food could be assessed.

The Committee's mandate was primarily technical and scientific. Developing microbiological criteria for foods requires an understanding of the complex science in the area and an appropriate background and training. . . .

The Committee membership . . . consisted of two university professors, one state agriculture department official, one state department of agriculture and consumer services official, two persons employed by food research firms, six persons employed by federal agencies, and six persons employed by private food companies. . . .

The Committee held its first meeting on April 5, 1988. By letter dated May 12, 1988, the appellants requested the Secretary of Agriculture to "take immediate action to appoint consumer representatives with public health expertise to membership" on the Committee, and, further, offered to "recommend ... individuals with appropriate credentials in public health and consumer concerns."... . The Assistant Secretary replied:

> Although the Committee is composed of scientific experts, the consumer perspective is also brought to the Committee by its membership. In particular, Dr. Martha Rhodes, Assistant Commissioner of the Florida Department of Agriculture and Consumer Services, was selected for the Committee because of her expertise in microbiology, public health, and consumer affairs, as well as her involvement with State governmental matters. If you would like to recommend others for membership on the Committee, we will be happy to review their qualifications and consider them when there is a vacancy

. . . .

The appellants then filed the present action in the district court seeking declaratory and injunctive relief against the government's alleged violation of the Federal Advisory Committee Act... .

The appellants originally contended that because the Committee's recommendations will directly affect the interest of consumers, the Act requires that the Committee contain representatives of consumers, and that the Committee lacks such representation because "not a single member of the Committee works for, or is associated with, a consumer or public health organization, despite the fact that there are such individuals who have expertise and backgrounds in the very issues to be scrutinized by the Committee."

. . . .

The appropriate inquiry in determining whether the Committee's membership satisfies the "fairly balanced" standard in section 5(b)(2) is whether the Committee's members "represent a fair balance of viewpoints given the functions to be performed." Since the Committee's function in this case involves highly technical and scientific studies and recommendations, a "fair balance" of viewpoints can be achieved even though the Committee does not have any members who are consumer advocates or proponents of consumer interests.

The statutory directive that membership of the Committee be "fairly balanced" does not mean that such balance can be provided only by individuals who work for, or are associated with, a consumer or public health organization... .

The determination of how the "fairly balanced" membership of an advisory committee ... is to be achieved, necessarily lies largely within the discretion of the official who appoints the committee. In my view, the membership of the Committee that the Secretary of Agriculture appointed did not violate the "fairly balanced" requirement of the Act, and the secretary did not abuse his discretion by failing to include on the Committee direct representatives of consumer organizations... .

The appellants have not shown that the original Committee was dominated or "inappropriately influenced" by food industry representatives. Only six of the 18 members were employed by the food industry. The appellants' contention that four other members of the Committee—the two employees of independent food research firms and the two university professors—represent food industry interests is unconvincing. The mere fact that the individuals employed by independent food research firms have food company clients or that the professors have performed some consulting work for food companies in the past, does not demonstrate that they are a part of "special interest groups [that] may use their membership on [advisory committees] to promote their private concerns,". . . .

■ Opinion, concurring in the judgment, filed by CIRCUIT JUDGE SILBERMAN.

. . . For any claim under section 5(b)(2) of the FACA to be justiciable under the APA, we must first conclude that Congress provided "a meaningful standard against which to judge the agency's exercise of discretion." Where no such meaningful standard exists, "the statute ('law') can be taken to have 'committed' the decision making to the agency's judgment absolutely," thereby precluding judicial review under 5 U.S.C. 701(a)(2). I cannot discern any meaningful standard that is susceptible of judicial application in the formulation "fairly balanced in terms of the points of view represented and the functions to be performed." Therefore, I believe that judicial review is unavailable. . . .

■ EDWARDS, CIRCUIT JUDGE, concurring in part and dissenting in part. . . .

The Committee at issue in this case is charged with recommending regulations for a broad range of food products. These decisions have health and safety implications that directly affect consumers. Recommendations regarding these regulations involve complex policy choices, not merely—or even primarily—technical determinations. For these reasons, especially in light of the legislative history of section 5, I disagree with Judge Friedman's opinion that the Committee's mandate in this instance was "primarily technical and scientific," and I conclude that a fair balance of viewpoints cannot be achieved without representation of consumer interests. . . .

The Government argues that consumers are represented by Dr. Martha Rhodes, the Assistant Commissioner of Agriculture for the Florida Department of Agriculture and Consumer Affairs, and by Dr. Mitchell Cohen of the Centers for Disease Control. Both of these persons, however, are government employees with a variety of regulatory responsibilities. One of the dangers that Congress specifically identified in adopting FACA was the risk that governmental officials would be unduly influenced by industry leaders. That is, it is precisely the lack of representatives of the public interest independent of *both* government *and* industry that prompted Congress to enact the "fairly balanced" provision. The fact that Dr. Rhodes and Dr. Cohen are state rather than federal government officials does not demonstrate that they will be less amenable to influence by industry representatives. This is not to impugn the integrity of either individual. Rather, it is to say that it is unnecessary for the court to assess the individual viewpoints of Dr. Rhodes and Dr. Cohen in order to find that their presence does not mitigate the lack of consumer representation. . . .

FDA often has difficulty recruiting members for its drug and device advisory committees because many of the best regarded experts have served as consultants to manufacturers of regulated products.

Robert Steinbrook, M.D., *Financial Conflicts of Interest and the Food and Drug Administration's Advisory Committees*

353 NEW ENGLAND JOURNAL OF MEDICINE 126 (2005).

The FDA's management of conflicts of interest for its advisory committees is based on the Ethics Reform Act of 1989 and implementing regulations that were issued in 1996 by the Office of Government Ethics. Voting members of FDA advisory committees are considered "Special government employees." Before each meeting in which they may participate, these experts complete a detailed confidential financial disclosure report. The agency determines whether any of the reported relationships pose a potential conflict of interest, and some people are disqualified on this basis.

The FDA, like other federal agencies, is permitted to balance its needs for scientific expertise against the potential for a conflict and to grant a waiver when "the need for the individual's services outweighs the potential for a conflict of interest." If the FDA determines that only general topics are being discussed . . . it takes a different approach from that used when it determines that approval of a specific product is being considered.

     . . . .

After granting a waiver, the FDA balances the public's right to the information against the privacy of its advisory committee members. According to the agency, "information to be disclosed will adequately enable a reasonable person to understand the nature of the conflict and the degree to which it could be expected to influence the recommendations the [special government employee] will make."

The disclosure is read into the record at the beginning of the meeting. The FDA usually does not provide specifics when it grants a general waiver. When it grants a specific waiver, it usually discloses the type of interest (such as stock, consulting, or contracts and grants) as well as the magnitude, which is expressed in terms of dollar ranges rather than as a specific amount. The disclosure notes whether the financial interest is related to the product under discussion or a competing product (without naming the competitor). The actual waiver statements are not released; they can be obtained only through a written request under the Freedom of Information Act.

In February, the FDA convened a joint meeting of the Arthritis Advisory Committee and the Drug Safety and Risk Management Advisory Committee to discuss the safety of cyclooxygenase–2 (COX–2) inhibitors. At the beginning of the meeting, an agency official read a conflict-of-interest statement indicating that in the FDA's judgment the topics were "issues of broad applicability and there [were] no products being approved." Although the FDA acknowledged the possibility of conflicts of interests on the part of committee members, it declared that "because of the general nature of the discussions before the committee, these potential conflicts are mitigated." The agency issued general waivers to the members who required them in order to participate; no specific information was provided.

After the meeting, it was disclosed that 10 of the 32 voting panel members had financial associations with the manufacturers of COX–2 inhibitors, such as the receipt of speaking or consulting fees or research support. Of the 30 votes cast by these 10 members on whether rofecoxib, celecoxib, and valdecoxib should continue to be marketed, 28 favored marketing the drugs. Of the 66 votes of the other 22 members, only 37 favored marketing the drugs. If the 10 panel members with the financial associations had not participated, the committee would have voted 12 to 8 that valdecoxib should be withdrawn and 14 to 8 that rofecoxib should not return to the market. With their votes included, the tally was 17 to 13 for keeping valdecoxib on the market and 17 to 15 for the return of rofecoxib. . . .

According to Dr. Alastair J.J. Wood of Vanderbilt University Medical School, the chair of the joint meeting, the FDA made a "judgment error" when it decided to issue a general waiver and not to disclose specific information about the potential conflicts of members of the committees. In an interview, Wood said: "Of all the FDA advisory committee meetings I have attended, there has never been more money on the table. Some potential panel members had already been excluded because of conflicts. The people who were chosen had disclosed their financial interests to the FDA, although it played out as though they had something to hide."

Concern about potential conflicts of interest arose again in April, when the General and Plastic Surgery Devices Panel of the Medical Devices Advisory Committee met to consider the safety of silicone gel-filled breast implants made by Inamed and Mentor, both of Santa Barbara, California. Before the meeting, the FDA told a plastic surgeon from George Washington University School of Medicine and Health Sciences that the $50,000 to $100,000 in stock he owned in a company that is seeking to purchase Inamed did not disqualify him, and he was designated as one of 10 voting members of the panel. Days later, the agency said that he could participate but not vote; he declined a nonvoting seat. The remaining plastic surgeon on the panel had a major role in the development of an educational CD–ROM about breast-reconstruction surgery, a project that had received funding from Inamed. At the beginning of the meeting, an FDA official said that the surgeon "reported his institution's past and current involvement with firms at issue." In the absence of personal financial interests, the Agency has determined that he may participate fully in the Panel's deliberations. . . .

. . . [T]he cases raise the specific concern that the agency's disclosure statements are opaque and lack detail. They also raise the general concern that waivers for potential conflicts are common and that the agency has paid insufficient attention to its—and the public's—interest in selecting scientific advisers who are independent of industry.

. . . .

Some changes to the FDA's approach to financial conflicts of interest could probably be implemented by the agency or the Department of Health and Human Services. One possible approach would be for the FDA to publish the names and background information of proposed committee members in the *Federal Register* and on its Web site and to give the public several weeks to comment. The agency could then consider these comments before the roster of participants in an advisory meeting was made final. Such procedures for public comment are used by the National Academies and the Environmental Protection Agency. The FDA could also make public more complete financial disclosures for its outside advisers. A possible criticism of such a move is that potential advisers would be less willing to serve under these conditions. However, in recent years, detailed public disclosures have become widely accepted—for example, in articles in medical journals and in materials associated with continuing medical education activities.

NOTE

On July 24, 2006, FDA announced that it was taking several steps to enhance the integrity of its advisory committee processes. "This effort includes the development of guidances to provide greater clarity and transparency in the disclosure of waivers of relationships that could present the appearance of conflicts of interest, as well as additional efforts to implement more streamlined approaches that will improve the transparency in the appointment of members to the agency's advisory committees." FDA News, P06–102. Press coverage of this announcement focused on the dilemma posed by the following circumstance: Expert A holds an appointment in the Department of Surgery at university X. A department colleague, B, is the recipient of research funding from drug company M. Should A be viewed as having a conflict if her committee is asked to evaluate a product sponsored by M? And even if this arrangement does create the appearance of a conflict, should FDA have authority to waive the conflict—with appropriate disclosure? This paradigmatic situation may embody several variations. Suppose that B is the Chair of Surgery—and A's supervisor? Suppose the product A will review is not made by M, but instead is a clear competitor of a product for which M. already has approval? And should it matter how much funding M is providing B—or the Department of Surgery?

This account reveals that FDA confronts two sorts of issues when it applies the federal conflict of interest laws to members of its advisory committees: (1) What sorts of affiliations should be viewed as posing a possible conflict that might require disqualification? (2) Under what circumstances and for what reasons may FDA decide to waive a potential conflict? And if a waiver is to be granted, how much personal information about A should be disclosed to the public? With several hundred advisory committee members to screen, the agency faces a large challenge. *See* Gardner Harris, *F.D.A. Rules Will Regulate Experts' Ties to Drug Makers*, N.Y. Times, July 24, 2006.

J.   Public Information

1.   Overview of FOIA

The Freedom of Information Act (FOIA) is codified in 5 U.S.C. 552 as part of the expanded statutory guarantees of access to records maintained or compiled by federal agencies. FOIA significantly influences FDA's relationships with outside organizations and individuals—makers of regulated products, public advocacy organizations, professional associations, and the private bar. FDA is the recipient, and thus the custodian, of vast amounts of information from industry. For this reason it is the target of more FOIA requests than any other agency except the FBI and the Department of Defense, and a non-trivial slice of its budget is dedicated to processing responses to these requests

Briefly summarized, FOIA requires an agency to disclose to any requester—who need not disclose or justify his interest—any responsive records that it possesses, subject to a series of ten exceptions. These exceptions permit records to be withheld, inter alia, if they are related to ongoing law enforcement, if they are officially classified as secret, if they would invade personal privacy, or if they consist of or contain confidential commercial or trade secret information. FOIA's broad mandate, coupled with its express exceptions, give rise to numerous disputes, many of which have required judicial resolution. Exemption 4—for confidential commercial information or trade secrets—has been the main battleground between those who seek FDA documents and the firms that provide most of the materials that are requested.

The following prescient excerpt, authored by the then-Chief Counsel of the agency, anticipates FOIA's impact on access to information in FDA files.

Peter Barton Hutt, *Public Information and Public Participation in the Food and Drug Administration*

36 Quarterly Bulletin of the Ass'n of Food and Drug Officials 212 (1972).

... The Food and Drug Administration is the largest repository of private scientific research in the world. [It] receive[s] mountains of important data and information on the safety, effectiveness, and functionality of foods and drugs, and undoubtedly will soon be receiving the same type of information for devices and cosmetics, that is available nowhere else. Since 1938, virtually none of it has been divulged. It is now proposed [by FDA] ... that most of it will become available for public disclosure upon request.

The proposal takes precautions to protect the confidentiality of information that genuinely can be regarded as a trade secret, in that its disclosure would destroy the competitive advantage of the person who has submitted it. The safety and effectiveness data for a new drug or a new animal drug would not be released, for example, because to do so would destroy the competitive advantage obtained from that data by the holders of the NDA or the NADA. Once those products become subject to abbreviated applications or become old drugs, however, that competitive advantage no longer exists, and it is therefore proposed that the data would promptly be released to the public upon request. Similarly, since food additives, color additives, and antibiotics are subject to public regulations rather than private licenses, and thus permit any person to engage in the their manufacture, it is proposed that the scientific data underlying those regulations would promptly be released to the public upon request the moment that the regulation is promulgated.

In an area ... involving inspectional and other regulatory efforts, equally important changes in policy are proposed.... [A]n FDA inspector provides a Form 483 to an establishment upon completion of an inspection, to inform them of significant violations. The inspector then prepares an Establishment Inspection Report (EIR), which is retained for our own files, and in many instances writes a top official in the company to bring to his personal attention any violations of the law. Samples may be taken, and later analyzed, and other evidence may be accumulated....

... [FDA] propose[s] to make available to the public, upon request, the Form 483 and any correspondence with the company or the individual involved. These documents are in the nature of an informal warning, rather than an investigatory file for law enforcement purposes, and thus would not be exempt from disclosure. The remaining information, such as the EIR, sample analyses, and so forth would be retained as confidential until the file is closed or a decision is made not to pursue legal action....

A third area of interest is the Agency's general correspondence with the outside world. The [FDA] proposal adopts the position that all such documents would be released unless they fall within a specific exemption. Thus, correspondence with members of Congress, complaints from consumers, minutes of meetings with trade associations, summaries of scientific conferences, and similar documents would be available upon request....

NOTES

1. *FDA's FOIA Regulations.* FDA's public information regulations were proposed in 37 Fed. Reg. 9128 (May 5, 1972) and made effective immediately. The final regulations, which also took account of the Freedom of Information Act Amendments of 1974, 88 Stat. 1561, were promulgated in 39 Fed. Reg. 44602 (Dec. 24, 1974). Further amendments were adopted in 41 Fed. Reg. 9317 (Mar. 4, 1976) and 42 Fed. Reg. 3094 (Jan. 14, 1977). FDA's current FOI regulations are codified in 21 C.F.R. Part 20.

2. *Processing Fees.* Pursuant to the Freedom of Information Reform Act of 1986, 100 Stat. 3207, OMB has promulgated regulations in 5 C.F.R. Part 1303 setting a uniform schedule of fees applicable to all Federal agencies. Section 731 of the FD&C Act authorizes FDA to retain fees paid for searching and copying to help fund the agency's FOI activities.

3. *What Documents Are "Agency Records?"* FOIA applies only to documents actually in the possession of FDA, and does not include material to which the agency has the right of access but of which it does not have custody. This proposition was established in a case brought to challenge FDA's refusal to provide access to the raw data from a long-term multi-center clinical study of drugs approved for the treatment of diabetes, p. 496 *supra*. The study had been funded by NIH, which had a right to review or obtain custody of the data but had never done so. On the basis of the study findings that one of the drugs increased users' risk of heart attack, FDA proposed to require new label warnings. A group of physicians who questioned the study findings demanded access to the underlying patient records, claiming that even though neither agency had possession, they were "agency records" under FOIA. The Supreme Court affirmed a D.C. Circuit decision

rejecting their claim. *Forsham v. Harris*, 445 U.S. 169 (1980). The lower court observed in passing, however, that FDA might have to arrange for access if the physicians' opportunity to comment on its proposed relabeling would otherwise be undermined. *Forsham v. Califano*, 587 F.2d 1128 (D.C. Cir. 1978).

2.   CONFIDENTIALITY OF TRADE SECRETS

The most controversial issues raised by FDA's FOIA policy revolve around the definition of, and scope of protection accorded to, confidential commercial information and trade secrets. Particular attention has been focused on the status of safety and effectiveness data submitted to the agency in new drug applications and other requests for marketing approval. Prior to 1972, FDA took the position that under both section 301(j) of the FDCA Act and the so-called Trade Secrets Act, 18 U.S.C. 1905, all such data constituted trade secret information that could not be released to the public. In 37 Fed. Reg. 9128 (May 5, 1972), the agency refined its position to state that data needed to obtain a private license for a product (*e.g.*, a new drug) would be kept confidential, but that data relating to a product which did not need a private license (*e.g.*, an "old" drug) or relating to a public regulation under which any firm could market its own product (*e.g.*, a food or color additive) provided no competitive advantage and thus could not be regarded as trade secret information. Relying on the Restatement of Torts (Second), FDA arrived at and still adheres to the following definitions, codified at 21 C.F.R. 20.61:

§ 20.61   Trade secrets and commercial or financial information which is privileged or confidential.

(a) A trade secret may consist of any formula, pattern, device, or compilation of information which is used in one's business and which gives him an opportunity to obtain an advantage over competitors who do not know or use it.

(b) Commercial or financial information that is privileged or confidential means valuable data or information which is used in one's business and is of a type customarily held in strict confidence or regarded as privileged and not disclosed to any member of the public by the person to whom it belongs.

(c) Data and information submitted or divulged to the Food and Drug Administration which fall within the definitions of a trade secret or confidential commercial or financial information are not available for public disclosure.

In *Public Citizen Health Research Group v. FDA*, 704 F.2d 1280 (D.C. Cir. 1983), the court of appeals offered its own definitions. It defined a trade secret as "a secret, commercially valuable plan, formula, process, or device that is used for the making, preparing, compounding, or processing of trade commodities and that can be said to be the end product of either innovation or substantial effort." It held that commercial information could be accorded confidentiality if its disclosure would either "(1) . . . impair the Government's ability to obtain necessary information in the future; or (2) . . . cause substantial harm to the competitive position of the person from whom the information was obtained." This formulation did not prompt FDA to amend its regulation.

NOTES

1. *Confidentiality of NDA Data.* In *Tri–Bio Laboratories, Inc. v. United States*, 836 F.2d 135 (3d Cir. 1987), the Court of Appeals held that the manufacturer of a generic new animal drug could not rely upon the safety and effectiveness data submitted by the manufacturer of the pioneer drug, upholding FDA's position that unpublished safety and effectiveness data may not be disclosed until the agency determines that they are no longer needed to support FDA approval of the product. *See also Webb v. Department of HHS*, 696 F.2d 101 (D.C. Cir. 1982).

2. *Confidentiality of Device Data.* The same issue arose during Congress' consideration of the Medical Device Amendments of 1976. Section 520(c) prohibits FDA from disclosing trade secret information or using trade secret information to approve or reclassify a class III device. This provision was modified by the Safe Medical Devices Act of 1990, 104 Stat. 4511.

3. *Access by Makers of Generic Drugs.* During consideration of the Drug Price Competition and Patent Term Act of 1984, p. 760 *supra*, debate focused on the continuing trade secret status of data submitted for a pioneer drug after ANDAs for generic versions could be submitted. FDA Commissioner Frank Young submitted a letter declaring that safety and effectiveness data would be made public following approval of generic versions of a pioneer drug unless "extraordinary circumstances" were shown. Young explained this standard would require a demonstration that the data continued to represent trade secret or confidential commercial or financial information. 130 Cong. Rec. 24977–78 (Sept. 12, 1984). This position is now reflected in 21 C.F.R. 314.430(f).

4. *Adverse Reaction Reports.* The issue in *Public Citizen Health Research Group v. FDA*, 704 F.2d 1280 (D.C. Cir. 1983), involved disclosure of reports of adverse reactions to intraocular lenses. On remand, the District Court ruled that company-specific adverse reaction rates could be withheld but averaged adverse reaction data had to be disclosed. *See also Kennedy v. FDA*, 1985–1986 FDLI Jud. Rec. 471 (N.D. Ohio 1986), upholding FDA's refusal to disclose company-specific adverse reaction reports on intraocular lenses to a plaintiff suing the company. In 2001 FDA suggested that it was prepared to relax its protection for reports of adverse reactions from clinical trials involving two promising but controversial technologies—gene therapy and xenotransplants. 66 Fed. Reg. 4688 (Jan. 18, 2001). The agency acknowledged that such a shift would represent a retreat from its long-standing policy but argued that public acceptance of these technologies would depend on assurance that all safety issues had been thoroughly explored. FDA has taken no further action on this proposal.

5. *What Constitutes a "Trade Secret"?* For examples of the difficulties involved in determining whether information constitutes a "trade secret," see *Zotos International, Inc. v. Kennedy*, 460 F. Supp. 268 (D.D.C. 1978); *Zotos International, Inc. v. Young*, 830 F.2d 350 (D.C. Cir. 1987).

Pharmaceutical Manufacturers Association v. Weinberger

401 F. Supp. 444 (D.D.C. 1975).

■ SIRICA, DISTRICT JUDGE.

This action was instituted by the plaintiff, an association of drug companies, on May 7, 1975, when a complaint seeking declaratory and injunctive relief was filed. The motion for a preliminary injunction was filed the same day seeking to prohibit the defendants, the Secretary of the Department of H.E.W. and the Commissioner of Food and Drugs, from applying and enforcing certain regulations published by the Commissioner.... Specifically, plaintiff seeks to require the F.D.A. to provide notice to an affected drug company of any proposed release of information pursuant to Freedom of Information Act (hereinafter F.O.I.A.) requests, in order to provide an opportunity for the affected company to consult with the F.D.A. concerning the propriety of the release of said information, and to provide an opportunity for judicial review of the F.D.A.'s decision.

. . . .

The plaintiff argues that the notice provision of the new regulations does not satisfy due process or the confidentiality requirement of the nondisclosure statutes and exemption four ... [T]he principal thrust of the motion for a preliminary injunction is that the F.D.A. must provide for some notice to affected drug companies before it releases any material from its files....

The Court first notes that the regulations here disputed do provide for prior notice of the possible release of exempt material and judicial review of the same:

> § 4.45 [now 21 C.F.R. 20.47]. In situations where the confidentiality of data or information is uncertain and there is a request for public disclosure, the Food and Drug Administration will consult with the person who has submitted or divulged the data or information or who would be affected by disclosure before determining whether or not such data or information is available for public disclosure.

> § 4.46 [now 21 C.F.R. 20.46]. Where the Food and Drug Administration consults with a person who will be affected by a proposed disclosure of data or information contained in Food and Drug Administration records pursuant to § 4.45 and rejects the person's request that part or all of the records not be made available for public disclosure, the decision constitutes final agency action that is subject to judicial review pursuant to 5 U.S.C. chapter 7. The person affected will be permitted 5 days after receipt of notification of such decision within which to institute suit in a United States District Court to enjoin release of the records involved. If suit is brought, the Food and Drug Administration will not disclose the records involved until the matter and all related appeals have been concluded.

However, what plaintiff claims is constitutionally and legally required is that the F.D.A. must notify the drug companies of the proposed release of any and all information which they submitted or which concerns them before it is actually released. Plaintiff argues that the F.D.A. will not always know when the confidentiality of information is uncertain. Two or three incidents are noted in which allegedly confidential, nondisclosable,

F.O.I.A.-exempt information was inadvertently released by the F.D.A. pursuant to F.O.I.A. requests. In those cases the affected drug companies were not notified, consulted, or given the opportunity for judicial review before the information was disclosed. . . .

The existence of such statutes as the one involved in *American Sumatra* [*v. SEC*, 93 F.2d 236 (D.C. Cir. 1937)] implies that general constitutional principles do not provide for the relief that the plaintiff here seeks, and that legislative action is needed if such procedures are to be assured. When Congress is persuaded that such measures are necessary in light of the disclosure provisions of the F.O.I.A., it has specifically acted to insure that sensitive information is not disclosed under F.O.I.A. requests. Indeed, counsel for the defendants has notified the court that there is presently pending before Congress legislation that would, in certain cases involving the F.D.A., create a right to prior notice and judicial review comparable to that which the plaintiff seeks to obtain by injunction here.

Recent cases have implied that individuals do not have a right under the F.O.I.A. to block disclosure of information that falls within the exemptions to the F.O.I.A. because those exemptions permit, rather than require, nondisclosure. If there is no right to nondisclosure under the F.O.I.A., the Court does not perceive how there could be a right, under the F.O.I.A., to notice before a decision regarding nondisclosure is made. . . .

Furthermore, it appears that the regulations here disputed were properly promulgated, with public notice, opportunity for public comment, etc. Thus, to the extent that it could be said that the plaintiff is deprived of property rights by operation of the regulations, at least it has been afforded due process by the considered and proper manner in which the regulations have been promulgated.

Moreover, if the regulations do not provide for the absolute right to notice before the disclosure of F.D.A. information, they do provide for substantial notice and opportunity for judicial review. Indeed, those provisions can be interpreted as providing for notice and opportunity for judicial review any time the issue of confidentiality reasonably arises under a request for F.O.I.A. information. The regulation provides that the notice provisions will be applied whenever the confidentiality of information is "uncertain." The Commissioner implies that only when the material is "clearly disclosable under law" will notice not be given. The Court may assume, absent a contrary showing, that those regulations will be generously and liberally interpreted.

The plaintiff here is not seeking to prevent the disclosure of specific information which has been requested under F.O.I.A. provisions. Rather, what it seeks to prevent is some type of speculative future harm—the possibility of accidental disclosure in the future of unidentified confidential information. The threat of harm alleged, then, is not specific or certain, rather it is conjectural and speculative. Nor is it certain that the injury, if it did occur, would be irreparable injury. . . .

NOTES

1. *Reverse FOIA Suits.* As the principal case suggests, organizations that provide information to the government frequently have a strong interest in having

their confidentiality protected and may not be confident that the agency will perform this role vigorously—or at all. In *Chrysler Corp. v. Brown*, 441 U.S. 281 (1979), the Supreme Court ruled that an owner of information submitted to the government could bring suit to review the agency's decision to release records that the owner claimed were exempt from disclosure. The Court rejected Chrysler's claim that the FOIA itself implicitly recognized a right of action to enforce any of the Act's exemptions, and it likewise refused to recognize a private right to sue under the Trade Secrets Act. But it acknowledged that an agency's final decision to release information could be challenged under the Administrative Procedure Act. However, this could be an empty remedy if the owner of the information had no knowledge that the agency had received and was prepared to comply with a request for disclosure.

In 1987 President Reagan issued Executive Order No. 12,600, which required all agencies subject to FOIA "to the extent permitted by law" to "establish procedures to notify submitters of records containing [arguably] commercial information ... when those records are requested" if the agency "determines that it may be required to disclose those records." *See generally* Note, *Protecting Confidential Business Information from Federal Agency Disclosure After* Chrysler v. Brown, 80 COLUM. L. REV. 109 (1980).

2. *Cost of Implementing FOIA.* In its annual report for 1979 on FOI activities, FDA estimated that it was devoting a total of 95.68 staff-years on the program, and went on to add these details.

> The FOI operation, which is now in FDA's Office of Public Affairs, is being beefed up to wipe out the backlog of requests. Some staffers have been added to the program, and FDA-ers say the average processing time for an FOI request is now 15 days, with 95% of them processed within 11 days. The agency is starting processing of FOI requests the day they are received, so there is expected to be no backlog.

> Of 32,852 FOI requests received by FDA during 1978, there were 577 denials. . . .

In 1988, the FDA's cost of processing FOIA requests reached $5.6 million, for which $451,000 was received in fees. The work consumed 125 staff years. "Agriculture, Rural Development, and Related Agencies Appropriations for Fiscal Year 1990," Hearings before a Subcomm. of the Senate Comm. on Appropriations, 101st Cong., 1st Sess. 429 (1989).

3. *Defending Nondisclosure.* When a request for commercial information is made to FDA, the company that submitted the information usually steps forward to defend its confidentiality. If FDA refuses disclosure and is sued, the submitting company typically intervenes as a party or participates as amicus curiae. *See, e.g., Washington Post v. Department of Justice*, 863 F.2d 96 (D.C. Cir. 1988); *Greenberg v. FDA*, 803 F.2d 1213 (D.C. Cir. 1986); *Public Citizen Health Research Group v. FDA*, 704 F.2d 1280 (D.C. Cir. 1983); *Webb v. Department of HHS*, 696 F.2d 101 (D.C. Cir. 1982); *Campbell v. Department of HHS*, 682 F.2d 256 (D.C. Cir. 1982); *Lederle Laboratories v. Department of HHS*, Food Drug Cosm. L. Rep. (CCH) ¶ 38,088 (D.D.C. 1988); *Johnson v. Department of HEW*, 462 F. Supp. 336 (D.D.C. 1978).

4. *Disclosure to Other Agencies.* Section 301(j) of the FD&C Act prohibits disclosure of trade secret information to any person outside the Department of HHS. Because this appeared to bar FDA from sharing such information with contractors engaged to assist FDA (*e.g.*, to review an NDA), the Medical Device Amendments of 1976 added section 708 to permit such disclosures, with respect to all categories of FDA-regulated products, under appropriate safeguards. In 1978, the

Attorney General determined that section 301(j) prohibited FDA from disclosing trade secret information to committees of Congress. "Federal Food, Drug and Cosmetic Act—Prohibition on Disclosure of Trade Secret Information to a Congressional Committee," 43 Op. Atty. Gen., No. 21 (Sept. 8, 1978). Section 301(j) was ultimately amended in the Omnibus Budget Reconciliation Act of 1990, 104 Stat. 1388, 1388–210 to permit disclosure to Congress.

5.   *FOIA as a Vehicle for Discovery.* FOIA has become an important method of discovery in FDA enforcement actions. *See, e.g., Parke, Davis & Co. v. Califano*, 623 F.2d 1 (6th Cir. 1980); *Grand Laboratories, Inc. v. Department of HHS*, Food Drug Cosm. L. Rep. (CCH) ¶ 38,171 (D.D.C. 1982); *Sterling Drug, Inc. v. Harris*, 488 F. Supp. 1019 (S.D.N.Y. 1980); *California Canners & Growers Ass'n v. United States*, FDLI 1978–1980 Jud. Rec. 990 (Ct. Cl. 1980); *Church of Scientology v. Califano*, FDLI 1978–1980 Jud. Rec. 922 (D.D.C. 1978); *Morton–Norwich Products, Inc. v. Mathews*, 415 F. Supp. 78 (D.D.C. 1976).

6.   *FDA Confidentiality Policy Criticized.* For a critical assessment of FDA's aggressive protection of drug sponsor clinical research data, see Mitchell Oates, *Facilitating Informed Medical Treatment Through Production and Disclosure of Research into Off–Label User of Pharmaceuticals*, 80 N.Y.U. L. REV. 272 (2005).

Public Citizen Health Research Group v. Food & Drug Administration

185 F.3d 898 (D.C. Cir. 1999).

■ GINSBURG, CIRCUIT JUDGE:

Pursuant to the Freedom of Information Act, the Public Citizen Health Research Group asked the Food and Drug Administration for documents relating to drug applications that had been abandoned for health or safety reasons. The FDA denied this request and Public Citizen sued the agency in district court, where Schering Corporation, which had submitted five investigational new drug applications (INDs) of the sort requested by Public Citizen, intervened as a defendant. The FDA and Schering claimed that certain of the documents in those five INDs contained confidential commercial information and therefore could be withheld under Exemption 4 of the FOIA, 5 U.S.C. 552(b)(4). Public Citizen argued that the documents could not be withheld under that exemption and that in any event disclosure was required under 21 U.S.C. 355(l), which it asserted sets a standard for nondisclosure higher than that in Exemption 4 of the FOIA.

. . . .

The FDA and Schering argue that the agency may under § 355(l) withhold any data pertaining to the safety and effectiveness of an abandoned drug that it may withhold under Exemption 4 of the FOIA—in other words, that the standards in the two statutes are the same. Public Citizen contends that § 355(l) imposes a more stringent standard for nondisclosure than that in Exemption 4. We need not resolve this dispute over the relationship between the two statutes, however, because we hold that § 355(l) does not apply to INDs. Viewing the documents solely through the lens of Exemption 4, we conclude that the FDA has justified withholding at least some information in four of the five INDs.

A. Section 355(l)

Section 355(l) requires the FDA, upon request, to disclose "safety and effectiveness data and information which has been submitted in an application under subsection (b) [of § 355] for a drug" that subsequently was abandoned by its sponsor, "unless extraordinary circumstances are shown." 21 U.S.C. 355 (l)(1). No one disputes that an "application under subsection (b)" is an NDA. Schering argues that § 355(l), therefore, simply does not apply to information in an IND, which is submitted under subsection (i), not subsection (b). That is indeed the plain meaning of the provision, and we cannot understand how "submitted in an application under subsection (b)" could include anything other than information submitted in an NDA. Public Citizen's arguments to the contrary are not convincing.

First, Public Citizen contends that the agency applies § 355(l) to the disclosure of material submitted in an IND and that we should accord "substantial weight" to the FDA's view of its regulatory structure. As Schering notes, however, the FDA has never promulgated a regulation—nor are we apprised of any FDA decision or other document—so interpreting § 355(l). More important, it is apparent that the Congress has spoken to "the precise question at issue" here, *Chevron U.S.A. Inc. v. NRDC*, 467 U.S. 837 (1984): § 355(l) by its terms applies only to "safety and effectiveness data and information" submitted in an NDA. . . .

. . . Public Citizen contends that a plain meaning approach to § 355(l) leads to an illogical result: data and information submitted in an IND which later, rather than being resubmitted in an NDA, are incorporated by reference into the NDA would not be "submitted in an application under subsection (b)," that is, an NDA. The FDA and Schering offer a more sensible view, however: to incorporate IND materials by reference into an NDA is indeed to submit those materials as part of the NDA. By the same token, once those materials are incorporated by reference into an NDA, their disclosure is subject to the standard in § 355(l) even if the FDA keeps them in an IND file.

Finally, Public Citizen argues that "it makes no sense to assume Congress enacted a statute mandating disclosure of safety and effectiveness data only when the sponsor had filed an NDA . . . but not when the sponsor had abandoned the drug earlier in the process." In this regard Public Citizen points out that the FDA accords the same treatment to such data regardless whether they were submitted in an NDA or an IND. Specifically, the FDA by regulation (21 C.F.R. 312.130(b)) provides that disclosure of information in an IND "will be handled in accordance with" the regulation governing disclosure of information in an NDA (21 C.F.R. 314.430(f)).

Nonetheless, when the Congress enacted § 355(l) it did not mandate disclosure of information in an IND. Moreover, Schering offers a perfectly sensible explanation why the Congress did not do so. The Drug Price Competition and Patent Term Restoration Act of 1984, of which § 355(l) was a part, established an abbreviated process through which a company could obtain approval to market the generic equivalent of a drug that the FDA had previously approved on the basis of an NDA. The statute,

Schering continues, does "not deal with INDs at all, and Congress had no reason in this legislative context to extend [§ 355(l)] to them." . . .

In view of the above analysis, we hold that § 355(l) does not apply to data and information submitted solely in an IND; such information may be withheld if the agency carries its burden under Exemption 4 of the FOIA. Schering did not file an NDA for four of the five INDs at issue in this case, but concedes that it filed two NDAs relating to the drug at issue in IND No. 18113. We need not determine the import of Schering's concession, however, for we conclude that documents in that IND cannot be withheld under the allegedly more lenient standard in Exemption 4.

B.   Exemption 4

Exemption 4 of the FOIA permits an agency to withhold "commercial or financial information [that was] obtained from a person [and is] privileged or confidential." 5 U.S.C. 552(b)(4). Information that a person is required to submit to the Government is considered confidential only if its disclosure is likely either "(1) to impair the Government's ability to obtain necessary information in the future; or (2) to cause substantial harm to the competitive position of the person from whom the information was obtained." *National Parks I*, 498 F.2d at 770. In the present case the FDA and Schering invoke only the latter standard. Meanwhile, Public Citizen claims disclosure would prevent other drug companies "from repeating Schering's mistakes, thereby avoiding risk to human health," and relies upon dicta in several district court opinions in arguing that under Exemption 4 the court should gauge whether the competitive harm done to the sponsor of an IND by the public disclosure of confidential information "is outweighed by the strong public interest in safeguarding the health of human trial participants." . . .

We reject Public Citizen's proposal because a consequentialist approach to the public interest in disclosure is inconsistent with the "balance of private and public interests" the Congress struck in Exemption 4. . . . That balance is accurately reflected in the test of confidentiality set forth in *National Parks I*, which was "known to and acquiesced in by Congress" when it enacted 5 U.S.C. 552b(c)(4), an exemption to the Government in the Sunshine Act that is identical to Exemption 4 of the FOIA.

In other words, the Congress has already determined the relevant public interest: if through disclosure "the public would learn something directly about the workings of the *Government*," then the information should be disclosed unless it comes within a specific exemption. . . . It is not open to Public Citizen, however, to bolster the case for disclosure by claiming an additional public benefit in that, if the information is disclosed, then other drug companies will not conduct risky clinical trials of the drugs that Schering has abandoned. That is not related to "what the[] government is up to" and the Court has clearly stated that "whether disclosure of a . . . document . . . is warranted must turn on the nature of the requested document and its relationship to the basic purpose of the Freedom of Information Act to open agency action to the light of public scrutiny . . . rather than on the particular purpose for which the document is being requested." In other words, the public interest side of the balance is not a function of the identity of the requester, or of any potential negative consequences disclosure may have for the public, nor likewise of any collateral benefits of disclosure.

. . . .

With respect to the first three INDs, Public Citizen contends that releasing health and safety information would only "save Schering's competitors the time Schering spent developing and testing a dangerous drug, and thus save human trial participants from being exposed to a dangerous drug." . . .

. . . According to the affidavit of its Dr. George H. Miller, the Company "has just commenced clinical testing on a successor [drug] which was designed based on information learned during development of [the drugs described in those INDs]." Further, Dr. Miller states that "Schering's basic research revealed that the particular type of fungal infection for which this product was designed was not one that was relatively well-controlled by existing products." He also states that "the development and marketing of new antifungal products is . . . being actively engaged in by a number of other drug companies," which could make use of the information in the INDs in order to eliminate much of the time and effort that would otherwise be required to bring to market a product competitive with the product for which Schering filed its most recent IND. This is clearly the type of competitive harm envisioned in Exemption 4, as our case law makes clear.

The fourth IND listed above concerned a drug "designed to suppress allergic inflammations and subsequent symptoms of asthma." Public Citizen concedes that Schering is now testing compounds related to the abandoned drug. Nonetheless, Public Citizen complains that the Company does not "explain with any specificity how the pre-clinical and clinical studies on the old compound would lead its competitors to the new compounds that Schering has subsequently identified."

In the affidavit Schering filed to support withholding the documents in this IND, Dr. Francis Cuss recounts that the Company initially believed the drug was a "leukotrine inhibitor," but that its "scientists observed certain unanticipated effects during toxicity and clinical testing . . . suggesting that the drug may have achieved its anti-inflammatory effects through a [different] mechanism." Therefore, states the affiant, the "toxicity and clinical data together could direct a competitor of Schering . . . to pursue the same avenues of research and development" that Schering has pursued since abandoning this IND. We think this explanation sufficiently specific to support Schering's argument that disclosure of information in this IND would cause it substantial competitive harm.

. . . .

■ GARLAND, CIRCUIT JUDGE, concurring in the result:

My colleagues hold that in determining whether a document comes within Exemption 4, the court may not "gauge whether the competitive harm" disclosure would cause to the company that submitted the document "is outweighed by the public interest in safeguarding" human health. This means that even if disclosure were the only way to prevent the loss of human life, that would count for nothing as against a showing by the company that disclosure would cause substantial harm to its competitive position. This is an important issue, and the kind that should be decided only after full briefing and argument.

. . . [A]lthough no party cited the relevant precedent on this point, we have twice held that Exemption 4 requires a balancing of the interest in nondisclosure "against the public interest in disclosure." *See Washington Post Co. v. HHS*, 690 F.2d 252 (D.C. Cir. 1982) (*Washington Post I*); *Washington Post Co. v. HHS*, 865 F.2d 320, 326–27 (D.C. Cir. 1989) (*Washington Post II*).

Judicial Watch, Inc. v. Food & Drug Administration

449 F.3d 141 (D.C. Cir. 2006).

■ SENTELLE, CIRCUIT JUDGE.

Judicial Watch filed an action in the District Court for the District of Columbia, seeking enforcement of its Freedom of Information Act ("FOIA") request for all documents related to the Food and Drug Administration's ("FDA") approval of the drug mifepristone. It now appeals from the District Court's grant of summary judgment in favor of the FDA. Although we affirm the District Court's decision in a number of respects, because the FDA produced an inadequately detailed *Vaughn* index, we remand for further explanation of some of the index's entries.

I. Background

In September 2000, the FDA approved the drug mifepristone, better known as RU–486, for "medical abortion" during the first 49 days of pregnancy. Shortly thereafter, Judicial Watch submitted a FOIA request seeking all mifepristone-related documents in the FDA's possession. A few months later, having not received any documents, Judicial Watch sought to enforce its request in the District Court. The FDA requested a stay, which the District Court granted. The District Court ordered the FDA to produce all responsive documents by October 15, 2001.

After searching about 250,000 pages of information, the FDA disclosed over 9,000 relevant pages to Judicial Watch on a compact disc. It withheld over 4,000 other relevant documents in their entirety and parts of almost 2,000 more. The FDA compiled and produced a 1,500–page *Vaughn* index to summarize the withholdings. See *Vaughn v. Rosen*, 484 F.2d 820 (D.C. Cir. 1973). In addition to its *Vaughn* index, the FDA filed a supporting declaration by Andrea Masciale, who supervised the FDA's search and review of documents for Judicial Watch's FOIA request. The Masciale declaration described the types of withheld information and defended the application of FOIA Exemptions 3, 4, 5, and 6 to that information. Danco Laboratories and Population Council—mifepristone's creator and manufacturer, respectively—intervened in the suit and filed two additional affidavits. The intervenors' affidavits supported the FDA's reasons for using Exemptions 4 and 6 to withhold information submitted to it during mifepristone's approval.

. . . .

II.   Adequacy of the *Vaughn* Index

Judicial Watch primarily argues that the FDA has produced an inadequately detailed *Vaughn* index. In this section, we consider—and reject—the challenge in its broadest sense, as a facial attack on the structure of the *Vaughn* index. Although we find nothing structurally wrong with the FDA's submission, we find merit in the narrower part of Judicial Watch's adequacy argument, specifically that the FDA has vaguely described some individual documents. We defer discussion of the vagueness inquiries until Section III and its subsections dealing with each individual FOIA exemption at issue.

. . . .

A.   Functions of the *Vaughn* Index Requirement

Because of its unique evidentiary configuration, the typical FOIA case "distorts the traditional adversary nature of our legal system's form of dispute resolution." When a party submits a FOIA request, it faces an "asymmetrical distribution of knowledge" where the agency alone possesses, reviews, discloses, and withholds the subject matter of the request. The agency would therefore have a nearly impregnable defensive position save for the fact that the statute places the burden "on the agency to sustain its action."

Possessing both the burden of proof and all the evidence, the agency has the difficult obligation to justify its actions without compromising its original withholdings by disclosing too much information. The *Vaughn* index provides a way for the defending agency to do just that. By allowing the agency to provide descriptions of withheld documents, the index gives the court and the challenging party a measure of access without exposing the withheld information. The *Vaughn* index thereby also serves three important functions that help restore a healthy adversarial process:

> [I]t forces the government to analyze carefully any material withheld, it enables the trial court to fulfill its duty of ruling on the applicability of the exemption, and it enables the adversary system to operate by giving the requester as much information as possible, on the basis of which he can present his case to the trial court.

Keys v. U.S. Dep't of Justice, 830 F.2d 337, 349 (D.C. Cir. 1987) (internal quotation marks and citation omitted).

As past cases demonstrate, we focus on the functions of the *Vaughn* index, not the length of the document descriptions, as the touchstone of our analysis. Indeed, an agency may even submit other measures in combination with or in lieu of the index itself. Among other things, the agency may submit supporting affidavits or seek in camera review of some or all of the documents "so long as they give the reviewing court a reasonable basis to evaluate the claim of privilege." Any measure will adequately aid a court if it "provide[s] a relatively detailed justification, specifically identif[ies] the reasons why a particular exemption is relevant and correlat[es] those claims with the particular part of a withheld document to which they apply."

B. The Structure of the FDA's Index

In this case, the FDA took a combined approach. In response to Judicial Watch's FOIA request, it produced a 1,500–page *Vaughn* index and supplemented the index with the supporting declaration of Andrea Masciale. The index itself includes eleven categories, consisting of the following: (1) an index identification number; (2) the document's subject; (3) its date; (4) the author; (5) the recipient; (6) the total number of pages; (7) a category entitled "Attach Page"; (8) the disposition (that is, whether entirely or partially withheld); (9) the reason for being withheld; (10) the statutory authority for the withholding; and (11) the number of pages containing withheld information. Whereas the index takes a document-specific approach, the Masciale declaration steps through the claimed exemptions. It avoids discussion of individual documents, instead describing the kinds of information withheld and how they relate to the exemptions. The intervenors filed two additional affidavits. Each covers issues specific to the documents submitted to the FDA during mifepristone's approval process, including matters ranging from competition in the abortion market to confidentiality issues.

Judicial Watch argues that the FDA's index/affidavit combination fails because it does not treat each document individually. Context dictates our approach to the particularity required of agencies. An agency may not claim exemptions too broadly, thereby sweeping unprotected information within the statute's reach. Broad, sweeping claims of privilege without reference to the withheld documents would impede judicial review and undermine the functions served by the *Vaughn* index requirement. The agency must therefore explain why the exemption applies to the document or type of document withheld and may not ignore the contents of the withheld documents.

On the other hand, abstraction can aid court review when drawing from specific examples. We have never required repetitive, detailed explanations for each piece of withheld information—that is, codes and categories may be sufficiently particularized to carry the agency's burden of proof. Especially where the agency has disclosed and withheld a large number of documents, categorization and repetition provide efficient vehicles by which a court can review withholdings that implicate the same exemption for similar reasons. In such cases, particularity may actually impede court review and undermine the functions served by a *Vaughn* index.

Seizing on the distinction between these two approaches, Judicial Watch asserts that the FDA claimed exemptions only in sweeping and conclusory generalities. We disagree. The FDA explained itself through commonalities, not generalities. Unsurprisingly, among thousands of withheld documents, certain topics and exemptions arose on multiple occasions. The index tied each individual document to one or more exemptions, and the Masciale declaration linked the substance of each exemption to the documents' common elements. No rule of law precludes the FDA from treating common documents commonly

And we do not fault the FDA for using the language of the statute as part of its explanation for withholding documents. As long as it links the statutory language to the withheld documents, the agency may even "parrot [ ]" the language of the statute. There are only so many ways the FDA could have claimed Exemptions 4, 5, and 6 for the thousands of documents generated during mifepristone's approval. . . . The FDA's decision to tie each document to one or more claimed exemptions in its index and then summarize the commonalities of the documents in a supporting affidavit is a legitimate way of serving those functions.

III.   The Claimed Exemptions: Vagueness and Merits Challenges

Our holding that the FDA produced a structurally sound *Vaughn* index does not address the entirety of Judicial Watch's challenge to the adequacy of the index. . . .

A.   Exemption 4

Exemption 4 allows agencies to withhold documents containing matters that are "trade secrets and commercial or financial information obtained from a person and privileged or confidential." Unlike many other types of information subject to an agency's control, materials implicating Exemption 4 are generally not developed within the agency. Instead, it must procure commercial information from third parties, either by requirement or by request. The agency thus has an incentive to be a good steward of that information: Disclosure could result in competitive disadvantages to the submitting entity, discouraging them from giving quality information in the future. The agency may therefore withhold involuntarily submitted information as confidential if disclosure would (1) impair the agency's ability to get information in the future or (2) cause substantial competitive harm to the entity that submitted the information.

The same incentive applies to the FDA approval process. The FDA requires applying companies to submit volumes of information related to a drug's development, composition, safety, and manufacture. A company must submit this information in an Investigational New Drug application ("IND") even prior to conducting clinical trials of a drug. All the information from the IND also goes into the company's New Drug Application ("NDA"), the formal application for sale and marketing approval from the FDA. Each stage of the FDA's administrative processes therefore depends directly on submissions from outside the agency.

The submission-dependent nature of the approval process means Exemption 4 extends to at least some information contained in INDs and NDAs. If it did not, other companies "could make use of the information in the INDs in order to eliminate much of the time and effort that would otherwise be required to bring to market a product competitive with the product for which" the submitting company filed the IND. . . .

Exemption 4 does not categorically exempt all information in INDs and NDAs, however, and the FOIA requester must have adequate descriptions in order to distinguish between protected and unprotected information. Judicial Watch argues that the index contains many entries—such as document 3021 ("study 88/739/cn") and document 3023 ("study f/85/486/40")—with descriptions too vague to allow it to mount a merits challenge to the FDA's Exemption 4 claims

The FDA argues that each index entry must be considered in relation to surrounding entries and to the additional information listed in the index. Specifically, the FDA contends that the index clearly relates Document 3331 ("references 89/11450gn") with Document 3325 ("preclinical expert evaluation of ru38 486—cover pages—89/11450gn") and several other nearby documents, including Document 3326 ("table of contents 89/11450gn"). We agree that Document 3325 gives enough description to explain the contents—that is, a preclinical expert evaluation—of all 89/11450gn-related documents.

Other entries defy the FDA's claim of definition by association, though. For example, Documents 1787 and 1788 ("table—main lab temp") appear to be freestanding documents. In its brief, the FDA asserts that the description makes "apparent that these records were collected during an FDA inspection of a drug manufacturing facility." We disagree. In no way do these subject headings, or any other index information, connect these documents to an FDA inspection or to any particular manufacturing facility. Neither does the Masciale declaration. Although it lists "information relating to the manufacturing process" as one type of information redacted under Exemption 4, it never explains that these documents fall into that category.

The same problems infect additional entries. . . .

Documents 1902 through 1924 ("subject records") also raise questions. At oral argument, the FDA's counsel suggested that these entries may describe personal records of test subjects, which would explain the agency's reliance on Exemption 6 and personal privacy in addition to Exemption 4. Outside of counsel's post hoc explanation, though, the entries remain sufficiently ambiguous to warrant further inquiry. . . .

The FDA asserts that its affidavit, along with those of the intervenors, makes up for any deficiency in its document descriptions. We agree that the three affidavits do a number of positive things. They show that the documents containing information from INDs or NDAs likely include either trade secrets or commercial information that would be valuable to competitors. They provide evidence, sufficient to satisfy the requirements of Exemption 4, of competitive harm in the medical abortion market that would result from the release of information in the IND. Finally, they also provide sufficient evidence to satisfy Exemption 4 of actual competition in markets for nonapproved uses of mifepristone, including cancer treatment. However persuasive, though, each of these points goes to the merits and does little to flesh out the vague document descriptions. . . .

It is no surprise that the FDA labeled many index entries with scientific codes, lab jargon, or other identifications specific to the agency. But the FDA may not create its own cryptolect, unknown to the challenger and the court. Without a glossary or technical dictionary, any lay person would be hard pressed to understand the series of numbers and letters given as descriptions in this index. Although the FDA's brief gives additional explanation for the examples raised by Judicial Watch, countless others in the 1,500-page index remain impenetrable for persons outside the FDA.

By using this shorthand, the FDA missed sight of the *Vaughn* index's purpose—to enable the court and the opposing party to understand the withheld information in order to address the merits of the claimed exemptions. Scientific lingo and administrative slang, when unfamiliar, often baffle the brightest among us. To prevent confusion and aid resolution of this case, the FDA should have endeavored to make its technical world appear a little less foreign—and its shorthand a little less short—to Judicial Watch and the court. This is not to say that the FDA could not demonstrate that it properly claimed Exemption 4 as to these documents. Rather, the FDA "has failed to supply us with even the minimal information necessary to make a determination." We accordingly remand the case for further explanation of these technical descriptions.

. . . .

B.   Exemption 5

Exemption 5 permits agencies to withhold "inter-agency or intra-agency memorandums or letters which would not be available by law to a party other than an agency in litigation with the agency." Such "memorandums or letters" include those protected by the attorney-client privilege and the deliberative process privilege. The FDA relied on both privileges but has since released all documents initially withheld under the attorney-client privilege. Accordingly, we only address the question of deliberative process privilege, which Judicial Watch challenges on both adequacy grounds and the merits.

The deliberative process privilege protects agency documents that are both predecisional and deliberative. We deem a document predecisional if "it was generated before the adoption of an agency policy" and deliberative if "it reflects the give-and-take of the consultative process." Judicial Watch contends that the FDA has not demonstrated the predecisional nature of documents without dates or with dates coming after the agency approved mifepristone. The entries without dates, it argues, can never prove that a document came before the agency's decision at issue. The entries with later dates, it contends, are by definition postdecisional.

Because we have previously approved the application of the deliberative process privilege for an "undated note," we cannot adopt Judicial Watch's proposed categorical rule on undated entries. Dates are but one way to illustrate a chronology, and the FDA may have other ways to prove that the undated documents were indeed predecisional. As an example, the FDA asserts that Documents 1645 and 1646, though undated, are predecisional because they concern mifepristone's IND, filed far in advance of the NDA and the FDA's subsequent approval of the NDA. Other undated documents in the index do not have the benefit of the FDA's explanation, though. We therefore remand so that the FDA may provide more information, including dates for documents that lack them or explanations where dates cannot be found.

Likewise, documents dated after mifepristone's approval for abortion may still be predecisional and deliberative with respect to other, nonfinal agency policies, including uses of the drug that the agency has not approved. A contrary rule would undermine the privilege's purpose to encourage "honest and frank communication within the agency" without fear of public disclosure. . . . The intervenors' affidavits affirm that the companies continue to pursue other avenues of medical uses for the drug and may later seek FDA approval, which would require further final action by the agency.

The FDA admits, though, that some of the postdated documents have nothing to do with unapproved uses but instead relate to other administrative decisions, including replies to correspondence. The FDA's failure to provide an adequate explanation prevents us from determining whether every piece of correspondence after a policy is decided constitutes a new final agency action of its own. It may be that reflections on an already-decided policy are neither predecisional nor indicative of the deliberative process of the government. After all, "Exemption five is intended to protect the deliberative process of government and not just deliberative material." *Mead Data Cent.*, 566 F.2d at 256 (citation omitted). On remand, the FDA must provide additional information regarding these postdated documents and the agency policies they predate and deliberate over.

Judicial Watch also challenges many Exemption 5 entries as vague, including the FDA's use of otherwise commonly understood words and phrases that it claims shed no light on the documents. For example, Judicial Watch highlights such nontechnical entries as Document 662 ("draft internal q & a"), Document 2377 ("fda form w/attach"), and Document 3222 ("fax re: listing w/attach"). The FDA counters that anyone can understand these descriptions, including "q & a," the common short-hand for "questions and answers." Furthermore, the agency argues that many entries labeled "draft" that were transmitted between FDA employees clearly implicate the "deliberative process privilege" by their very nature.

We conclude, however, that these entries suffer from vagueness defects different in kind than those discussed in the section on Exemption 4. These descriptions pose no problems of technical knowledge, but neither do they describe the withheld information. The word "fax," though commonly understood, tells the court little about the deliberative nature of the information contained in the document in question. Likewise, the term "q & a" says nothing about the information conveyed in the questions and answers.

Certainly, the label "draft" goes to the merits of Exemption 5's predecisional and deliberative elements, and the court may take notice that a document passed between two FDA employees and had a date prior to the FDA's approval of mifepristone. The FDA did not label all Exemption 5 entries as drafts, however, and we must bear in mind "the strong policy of the FOIA that the public is entitled to know what its government is doing and why." Terms like "fax" and "q & a" standing alone give the court no way to determine whether the withheld information is of a deliberative nature. Accordingly, on remand the FDA must provide more informative descriptions of these commonly understood documents in addition to the less understood coding of many Exemption 4 entries.

. . . .

IV.   Conclusion

The FDA argues that it could have short-circuited many of Judicial Watch's claims by producing a summary index or taking a categorical approach instead of producing a full index. But the fact that the agency might have gone down a different route does not mean it can produce an inadequate submission of another variety. On remand, though, we do not expect the FDA to engage in a full reappraisal of its index. As we held above, the defects in the index are specific to the descriptions and not structural. The FDA can clarify many vague document descriptions by producing a technical lexicon for the benefit of Judicial Watch and the District Court. As always, the goal should be to allow the court to under-stand the withheld information to the extent necessary to address the merits. With these considerations in mind, we remand for further explana-tion of the entries in the *Vaughn* index for documents withheld, in their entirety, under Exemptions 4 and 5. . . .

3.   OTHER INFORMATION STATUTES

While FOIA provides the basic framework for resolving claims to access and assertions of an agency's right or duty to withhold information, it has recently been joined by two other laws that can affect how regulatory agencies, like FDA, handle information generated by private parties.

1.   *The Shelby Amendment.* In appropriations legislation for fiscal year 1999, Congress included a provision addressing public access to data produced by federal grant recipients. 112 Stat. 2681 (1998). Termed the Shelby Amendment after its Senate sponsor, the two-sentence provision did not amend the FOIA. Instead, it directed the Office of Management and Budget to amend OMB Circular A–110 to require awarding agencies to ensure that data produced under a federal grant will be made available to the public through the procedures established under the FOIA.

OMB published a final revision to Circular A–110 in October of 1999, 64 Fed. Reg. 54926 (Oct. 8, 1999). In pertinent part, the revised Circular states:

> [I]n response to a Freedom of Information Act (FOIA) request for research data relating to published research findings produced under an award that were used by the Federal Government in developing an agency action that has the force and effect of law, the Federal awarding agency shall request, and the recipient shall provide, within a reasonable time, the research data so that they can be made available to the public through the procedures estab-lished under the FOIA.

By its terms, the revised Circular applies only to data relied on by a federal agency to support action that has the force and effect of law. Moreover, the Circular applies only to data first produced under new or competing continuing funding grants after April 17, 2000, the effective date of the regulation that codified the revised Circular. In issuing the revised Circu-lar, OMB explained that it took an approach that balanced the public interest in obtaining information needed to validate federally-funded research with the need to minimize interference with the traditional scientific process.

2. *The Information Quality Act.* One aim of the Paperwork Reduction Act, 44 U.S.C. 3501 *et. seq.*, is to "ensure the greatest possible benefit from and maximize the utility of information created, collected, maintained, used, shared and disseminated by or for the Federal Government." The statute vests OMB with authority to oversee the implementation of policies, principles, standards, and guidelines to apply to federal agency dissemination of public information.

To that end, Congress included in appropriations legislation for fiscal year 2001 a provision known as the Information Quality Act, which directed OMB to issue "guidelines" that provide "policy and procedural guidance to Federal agencies for ensuring and maximizing the quality, objectivity, utility and integrity of information (including statistical information) disseminated by Federal agencies[.]" 114 Stat. 2763, (2000) (codified as a note following 44 U.S.C. 3516).

OMB published final guidelines in 67 Fed. Reg. 8452 (Feb. 22, 2002). The guidelines set out four general responsibilities for the covered agencies: (1) to "adopt specific standards of quality that are appropriate for the various categories of information they disseminate"; (2) to "develop a process for reviewing the quality (including the objectivity, utility, and integrity) of information before it is disseminated"; (3) to "establish administrative mechanisms allowing affected persons to seek and obtain, where appropriate, timely correction of information maintained and disseminated by the agency that does not comply with OMB or agency guidelines"; and (4) to report annually to OMB "on the number and nature of complaints received by the agency regarding agency compliance with these OMB guidelines and how such complaints were resolved." OMB Guidelines § III (1)–(4).

Proponents of the Information Quality Act did not disguise their hope that the Act would be interpreted to create a new right, independent of any under the APA, to challenge the accuracy and balance of information disseminated by government agencies. The first, and so far only, judicial application of the Act, therefore, must have been disappointing. In *Salt Institute v. Leavitt*, 440 F.3d 156 (4th Cir. 2006), the plaintiffs—an association of salt producers and the U.S. Chamber of Commerce—sought an injunction ordering the National Heart, Lung, and Blood Institute to correct or rescind materials it had released describing the health risks of dietary sodium. In a puzzling opinion, Judge Luttig, for a unanimous court, ruled that the plaintiffs had failed to establish their standing and in the process implied that the requirements of the Act might not be judicially enforceable.

K. ENVIRONMENTAL ASSESSMENT

The National Environmental Policy Act (NEPA), 83 Stat. 852 (1969), requires all federal agencies to consider the environmental impact of any major action they initiate that may significantly affect the quality of the environment. FDA adopted regulations to implement this requirement. 37 Fed. Reg. 13636 (July 12, 1972), 38 Fed. Reg. 7001 (Mar. 15, 1973), 21 C.F.R. Part 25. Initially, the agency took the position that NEPA required it to consider the environmental impact of every important action including, for example, the approval of a new drug or a food additive. Later, impressed with the impracticality of this policy, FDA announced, 40 Fed. Reg. 16662 (Apr. 14, 1975), that it had no legal authority to approve or disapprove a new drug or food additive on any ground other than those specified in the FD&C Act itself. The agency hoped thereby to precipitate a judicial challenge that would clarify its obligations under NEPA.

Environmental Defense Fund, Inc. v. Mathews

410 F. Supp. 336 (D.D.C. 1976).

■ Pratt, District Judge

... NEPA does not supersede other statutory duties, but, to the extent that it is reconcilable with those duties, it supplements them. Full compliance with its requirements cannot be avoided unless such compliance directly conflicts with other existing statutory duties.

... In April, 1975, FDA promulgated an amendment ... which is the subject of this action. Said amendment reads:

> A determination of adverse environmental impact has no legal or regulatory effect and does not authorize the Commissioner to take or refrain from taking any action under the laws he administers. The Commissioner may take or refrain from taking action on the basis of a determination of an adverse environmental impact only to the extent that such action is independently authorized by the laws he administers.

In effect, the amending regulation limits the grounds on which the Commissioner of FDA can base any action to those expressly provided for in the Food, Drug and Cosmetic Act or in other statutes which FDA administers. He is prohibited from acting solely on the basis of environmental considerations not identified in those statutes. This limitation of the agency's discretion to act in accordance with environmental considerations directly contravenes the mandate of NEPA to all Federal agencies to consider the environmental effects of their actions "to the fullest extent possible."

Defendants contend that FDA's statutes, particularly the FDCA, dictate that it act only in accordance with specifically expressed criteria, and that to the extent that NEPA demands consideration of additional criteria, it is in direct conflict with those statutes. Accordingly, they maintain that such a direct statutory conflict exempts FDA from full compliance with NEPA.

It appears clear to us that, contrary to defendants' contention, FDA's existing statutory duties under the FDCA and its other statutes are not in direct conflict with its duties under NEPA. The FDCA does not state that the listed considerations are the only ones which the Commissioner may take into account in reaching a decision. Nor does it explicitly require that product applications be granted if the specified grounds are met. It merely lists criteria which the Commissioner must consider in reaching his decision. In the absence of a clear statutory provision excluding consideration of environmental factors, and in light of NEPA's broad mandate that all environmental considerations be taken into account, we find that NEPA provides FDA with supplementary authority to base its substantive decisions on all environmental considerations including those not expressly identified in the FDCA and FDA's other statutes. This conclusion finds support in the legislative history, the precise statutory language, the holdings of the courts, and the construction adopted by other Federal agencies.

This is not to say that NEPA requires FDA's substantive decisions to favor environment protection over other relevant factors. Rather, it means that NEPA requires FDA to *consider* environmental factors in its decision-making process and supplements its existing authority to permit it to act on those considerations. It permits FDA to base a decision upon environmental factors, when balanced with other relevant considerations. Since the contested regulation prohibits FDA from acting on the basis of such environmental considerations, it is directly contrary to the letter and spirit of NEPA. . . .

NOTES

1. *FDA Response.* Following this decision FDA revoked the contested regulation, 41 Fed. Reg. 21768 (Mary 28, 1976). However, the agency has not since taken an action in which it has identified any environmental effects not involving risks to health as an influential consideration. When FDA denied a food additive petition on the ground that the environmental impact analysis report was insufficient, the court in *Marshall Minerals, Inc. v. FDA*, 661 F.2d 409 (5th Cir. 1981), reversed, holding that this raised no issue beyond the human safety questions previously considered, that Marshall Minerals had complied with all environmental analysis requirements, and that no separate environmental concerns prevented approval of the petition. Later FDA announced its intention to prepare an environmental impact statement on the use of polyvinyl chloride and other chlorinated polymers, 53 Fed. Reg. 47264 (Nov. 22, 1988), and published its tentative responses to environmental concerns about raising the permitted level of selenium in animal feed, 54 Fed. Reg. 29019 (July 11, 1989).

2. *CEQ Regulations.* To comply with guidelines issued by the Council on Environmental Quality (CEQ), FDA promulgated changes in its regulations, 39 Fed. Reg. 13742 (Apr. 16, 1974), 42 Fed. Reg. 19986 (Apr. 15, 1977), 44 Fed. Reg. 71742 (Dec. 11, 1979), 50 Fed. Reg. 16636 (Apr. 26, 1985). FDA announced the availability of a technical handbook providing guidance in preparing environmental assessments in 52 Fed. Reg. 37372 (Oct. 6, 1987).

3. *Challenges to FDA's Failure to Conduct an Environmental Assessment.* NEPA has occasionally been invoked by parties opposing FDA action. See, e.g., *Calorie Control Council, Inc. v. Department of HEW*, Food Drug Cosm. L. Rep. (CCH) ¶ 38,124 (D.D.C. 1977), in which the District Court refused to enjoin FDA's proposed ban of saccharin on the ground that the agency had failed to file an environmental impact statement. The Court ultimately dismissed the action in *Calorie Control Council, Inc. v. Department of HEW*, Food Drug Cosm. L. Rep. (CCH) ¶ 38,218 (D.D.C. 1978). Other cases rejecting NEPA-based objections to FDA action include *Rhone–Poulenc, Inc. v. FDA*, 636 F.2d 750 (D.C. Cir. 1980); *National Pork Producers Council v. Bergland*, 631 F.2d 1353 (8th Cir. 1980); *American Meat*

Institute v. Bergland, 459 F. Supp. 1308 (D.D.C. 1978). FDA's approval of recombinant bovine growth hormone (rBST) was unsuccessfully challenged on several grounds, including the agency's failure to prepare an environmental impact statement and its reliance on the environmental assessment prepared by the drug's sponsor, Monsanto. *Stauber v. Shalala*, 895 F. Supp. 1178 (W.D. Wis. 1995). In *Stauber*, the court also rejected claims that the agency should have weighed, as environmental effects, the potential economic impact of rBST's use on dairy producers. When FDA announced that it would presume, subject to evidence to the contrary, that genetically altered foods were GRAS (*see* the discussion in Chapter III), its statement of policy was challenged on several grounds, including failure to provide notice and invite comment and failure to prepare an environmental impact statement. These and other challenges were rejected in *Alliance for Bio–Integrity v. Shalala*, 116 F. Supp. 2d 166 (D.D.C. 2000). The court interpreted FDA's pronouncement as essentially an affirmation of the status quo, not an action that might trigger an obligation to undertake an environmental assessment.

4. *Plastic Bottles.* FDA initiated an inquiry into the environmental impact of food additive regulations for plastic beverage containers in 38 Fed. Reg. 24391 (Sept. 7, 1973). A draft environmental impact statement (EIS) was later made available, 40 Fed. Reg. 16708 (Apr. 14, 1975), and a final EIS was issued, 41 Fed. Reg. 43944 (Oct. 5, 1976). In 42 Fed. Reg. 9227 (Feb. 15, 1977), the agency stated that, in acting on food additive petitions, environmental considerations "carry no greater weight than the factors required to be considered in section 409 of the act." It concluded that "the adverse environmental effects of the action, to some extent offset by the potential beneficial effects, are not of sufficient magnitude to justify limitation or revocation of food additive regulations permitting plastic bottles for carbonated beverages and beer."

5. *Transgenic Fish.* Recent advances in the area of genetic engineering are requiring FDA directly to confront environmental issues to an unprecedented degree. Consider, for example, the following excerpts from a 2003 speech delivered to the American Enterprise Institute by Lester Crawford, the Deputy Commissioner (later Acting Commissioner) of the FDA.

> The FDA has ... ample experience, as well as legislated authority and guidance, for ensuring the safety and effectiveness of drugs, biological medications, and medical devices, and it would use all of these resources in evaluating such products manufactured with the help of transgenic animals. But what about other concerns, including the critical question whether, and to what extent, the safety of the environment would be put at risk by genetically altered animals? And what about risks that may be posed to the genetic animals themselves?

> The FDA is yet to answer these questions by approving or disapproving the application for marketing of any transgenic animal, and I am not in a position to discus specific decisions and policies that may be currently under consideration. But I can address this issue in general terms on the basis of existing laws and practices. I can also examine the provisions that would protect the public health and environment from harm that could result from the commercialization of one transgenic product that has repeatedly prompted media comments, as well as concerns among environmental and consumer groups. That product is an Atlantic salmon genetically engineered to contain additional fish hormone gene to make it grow faster and use feed more efficiently.

> One variety of this salmon has been reported to reach the market weight of 7–9 pounds in about 18 months, as against 24–30 months for non-transgenic salmon. As you will hear from Mr. McGonigle, the Vice

President of Aqua Bounty Farms, his firm has been preparing for more than a decade to put a hybrid salmon on the market. To avoid environmental damage, Aqua Bounty plans to raise brood stocks of this transgenic fish in conventional inland hatcheries, and treat them to produce 100 percent genetically female eggs. The eggs in turn would be treated to cause reproductive sterility. The reproductively sterile, all-female offsprings would be grown initially in hatcheries, and then would be transferred to ocean net pens, to mature and be harvested for food.

What are the hazards associated with this sort of enterprise? Although current methods provide high ensurance of reproductive sterility, they are not 100 percent effective. This raises the possibility that fish that would almost inevitably escape from the net pens would include some females capable of reproduction. This in turn could lead to interbreeding with wild Atlantic salmon, hybridization with the closely related brown trout, and disturbance of habitat as a consequence of competition for resources, predation, or mis-mating.

There are several federal and state agencies that would take measures to minimize the involved environmental hazards. They include the National Marine Fisheries Service, Fish and Wildlife Service, Army Corps of Engineers, and Environmental Protection Agency, all of which probably would be involved in regulating various aspects of this enterprise, such as the location and security of the ocean pens. In addition, the FDA is authorized to exercise oversight of transgenic animals under the Federal Food, Drug and Cosmetic Act, which makes our agency responsible for the safety of drugs, and defines drugs as "articles ... intended to affect the structure or any function of the body of man or other animals."

Because the genetic modification affects the structure and function of the salmon, and because it may produce a protein that is not generally recognized as safe for human consumption, the biotech salmon is, in the eyes of the law, a "new animal drug," and as such is subject to the FDA's science-based review and approval before it can be marketed. As part of this review, the FDA routinely considers evidence of a new animal drug's effect on, among other factors, animal health; diseases susceptibility; zoonotic potential; animal welfare; impact on domestic and wildlife populations; and the environment.

I am skipping a lot detail, but I want to emphasize that the FDA takes environmental issues seriously, and takes action when appropriate.

Lester M. Crawford, Deputy FDA Commissioner, FDA, at the American Enterprise Institute (June 12, 2003).

L. REFORMING FDA REGULATION

Calls for "regulatory reform" are almost as old as the pressures to create regulatory agencies. Proposals for reform have taken a variety of forms, ranging from suggestions to abandon government intervention in some areas to recommendations for improvements in agency procedure. As the size and power of administrative agencies have grown, more fundamental problems have been identified. Health and safety regulatory programs have not escaped this thrust of reform and pressures to weigh the costs of regulation and seek the lowest-cost safeguards continue.

During the 1970s and 1980s, FDA took steps to reform its approach to regulation in two principal ways. First, the agency adopted policies designed to reduce restrictions on regulated firms. Examples include the adoption of "common or usual names" for some foods rather than standards of identity; the revision of "recipe" food standards to permit any safe and suitable ingredients; and the use of class monographs for OTC drugs instead of requiring NDAs for each individual product. Second, FDA fashioned alternative procedures for resolving disputed technical issues with the objective of strengthening the scientific basis and reducing the time required for decision. Examples include its increased reliance on expert advisory committees. There are, however, limitations on the extent to which any optional reforms can speed up the administrative process, make it fairer, or reduce the economic impact of regulation in the absence of basic changes in the FD&C Act.

Peter Barton Hutt, *Safety Regulation in the Real World*
28 Food Drug Cosmetic Law Journal 460 (1973).

The Food and Drug Administration's decision-making process on safety issues, and the public perception of it, are hampered by five basic obstacles. No one of these obstacles is critical, but their combined impact can at times be severe. . . .

First, the scientific data base is seldom adequate to make a definitive safety judgment on any food or drug. . . .

Second, even when substantial safety data are available on a particular substance, there is seldom scientific agreement on the meaning or significance of that information. . . .

Third, even assuming that an adequate scientific data base were available, together with scientific agreement on the meaning and significance of the data, there appears to be no public or scientific consensus today on the risk or uncertainty acceptable to justify the marketing of any substance as a food or drug.

To some, who favor a return to more simple days, no risk or uncertainty whatever is justified for any addition of a chemical to food. They would, indeed, require a showing of some greater benefit to society before any ingredient is permitted. To others, who see enormous progress in food technology and nutrition from the use of food additives, the usual risks associated with technological innovation are regarded as entirely reasonable. . . . We must recognize that this type of issue presents fundamental differences in philosophical principles, not simply a narrow dispute on technical details. It raises the most basic questions of personal beliefs and human values—the degree of risk or uncertainty that any individual is willing to accept in his daily life. Attempts to resolve it on the basis of rigorous scientific testing or analytical discourse, therefore, simply miss the point. . . .

Fourth, there is enormous and continuing public pressure for the Food and Drug Administration to resolve whatever may be the latest current safety issue promptly and decisively.

Delay and indecision weaken public confidence and intensify fear and concern. Industrial representatives, faced with potential harm to their economic interests, demand reassurance that the public need fear no danger. Consumer activists, sensing a further victory in their war against unsafe products, intensify the public campaign to discredit the suspect product. Congress, reacting to the legitimate concern of their constituencies, demand[s] a prompt resolution. The media, recognizing a story of interest to the entire public, does not fail to give it ample prominence. Thus, regardless of the uncertainties and imponderables, a decision must frequently be reached immediately, on the basis of whatever meager information may exist....

Fifth, regardless of the outcome of the decision, those who disagree with it will continue to pursue the matter through all available channels, while those who agree with it will inevitably remain silent, preparing themselves for the next issue....

INDEX

References are to pages.

†